CurrentLaw

STATUTES

1995

VOLUME TWO

AUSTRALIA
The Law Book Company
Brisbane • Sydney • Melbourne • Perth

CANADA
Carswell
Ottawa • Toronto • Calgary • Montreal • Vancouver

Agents:
Steimatzky's Agency Ltd., Tel Aviv;
N. M. Tripathi (Private) Ltd., Bombay;
Eastern Law House (Private) Ltd., Calcutta;
M.P.P. House, Bangalore;
Universal Book Traders, Delhi;
Aditya Books, Delhi;
MacMillan Shuppan KK, Tokyo;
Pakistan Law House, Karachi

Current Law

STATUTES

1995

VOLUME TWO

SWEET & MAXWELL EDITORIAL TEAM
SARAH ANDREWS
MELANIE BHAGAT
ALA KUZMICKI
SOPHIE LOWE
CERI PICKERING

W. GREEN EDITORIAL TEAM
CHARLOTTE HALL
PETER NICHOLSON

LONDON

SWEET & MAXWELL

EDINBURGH

W. GREEN

1996

Published by
SWEET & MAXWELL LIMITED
of 100 Avenue Road, London,
and W. GREEN LIMITED
of Alva Street, Edinburgh,
Typeset by MFK Information Services Ltd., Hitchin, Herts.
and printed in Great Britain
by The Bath Press,
Somerset

ISBN This Volume only : 0 421 54770 7
As a set : 0 421 54800 2

CONTENTS

CHRONOLOGICAL TABLE

VOLUME TWO

Annotators' names are in italic

VOLUME TWO

ALPHABETICAL INDEX OF SHORT TITLES

STATUTES 1995

(References are to chapter numbers of 1995)

MERCHANT SHIPPING ACT 1995*

(1995 c. 21)

---

* Annotations by Nicholas Gaskell, Barrister, Professor of Maritime and Commercial Law, Institute of Maritime Law, University of Southampton.

Special provisions for Scots law

312. Special provisions for Scots law.

Final provisions

313. Definitions.
314. Repeals, consequential amendments and transitional provisions.
315. Extent and application.
316. Short title and commencement.

[A Table showing the derivation of the provisions of this consolidation Act will be found at the end of the Act, after Schedule 14. The Table has no official status.]

An Act to consolidate the Merchant Shipping Acts 1894 to 1994 and other enactments relating to merchant shipping.   [19th July 1995]

PARLIAMENTARY DEBATES
    Hansard: H.L. Vol. 351, cols. 1250, 1266, 1535; Vol. 352, cols. 293–301, 760; Vol. 489, cols. 642, 1292; Vol. 490, cols. 540, 744; Vol. 491, cols. 437, 925; Vol. 496, col. 327; Vol. 563, col. 582; Vol. 564, col. 1542; Vol. 565, col. 410; H.C. Standing Committee E, January 17, 22, 24, 1974; Vol. 126, col. 506; Vol. 130, col. 1164; Standing Committee C, April 4, 1988; Vol. 263, col. 467; Joint Committee on Consolidation Bills, April 20, 1995.

INTRODUCTION AND GENERAL NOTE

Merchant Shipping Acts 1894–1994
    The Merchant Shipping Act 1995 results from the work of the Law Commission and the Scottish Law Commission. It is a long overdue consolidating measure which brings together some 30 Acts or sections of Acts, dating back to the Merchant Shipping Act 1894 (c. 60). The 1894 Act was enacted at a time when many other continental (civil law) states were producing their own maritime codes. The 1894 Act mostly regulated the public law aspects of shipping, such as ship registration, manning and safety generally. It also lay down the functions of administrative officials such as registrars of shipping and receivers of wreck. The continental maritime codes also dealt with private law, such as the carriage of goods by sea. Although the 1894 Act touched on matters affecting private rights, such as the priority of registered mortgages and the rights of owners of wreck, in general it ignored most of the areas of private maritime law, which were largely the domain of the common law. Many more areas of private law were included in later Merchant Shipping Acts, but mostly in order to enact in U.K. law the provisions of international

conventions. Examples of international conventions which have regulated private law are those dealing with the marine pollution (see now Pt. VI of this Act) and the carriage of passengers (see now Pt. VII of this Act). Such international conventions, and the detailed rules made under them, have frequently been agreed at the International Maritime Organisation (IMO), the body established by treaty in 1946 to be the focus of the United Nations' moves to unify and develop the technical aspects of shipping. Most of IMO's work has concerned safety and, whereas in 1894 the rules set out in the 1894 Act would have been the product largely of national expertise, a comparison with the 1995 Act will show that most rules regulating safety have international origins (see, *e.g.* the regulations made under s.85 of this Act).

Drafting techniques used in the Merchant Shipping Acts

The 1894 Act had been amended, and added to, many times. Nearly all the succeeding Merchant Shipping Acts contained a provision, such as s.10 of the Merchant Shipping (Salvage and Pollution) Act 1994 (c. 28), which allowed the succeeding Act to be cited together with its predecessors. Unfortunately, the relationship between the various Acts was often difficult to fathom because of the nature and form of the methods of drafting used (see the comments by the writer on the Merchant Shipping Act 1988 (c. 12), in *Current Law Statutes Annotated 1988*, p. 12–4). The drafting technique which was generally used with the Merchant Shipping Acts was to have a provision stating that a particular Act was "to be construed as one" with the 1894 and other Merchant Shipping Acts (see, *e.g.* s.12(2) of the Merchant Shipping (Liability of Shipowners and Others) Act 1958 (c. 62), s.57(1) of the 1988 Act, and s.10(2) of the Merchant Shipping (Salvage and Pollution) Act 1994). It had also been the practice to provide that the Acts may be cited together as the Merchant Shipping Acts (as was also done in s.12(3) of the 1958 Act, s.58(1) of the 1988 Act and s.10(1) of the 1994 Act). When the construing provision was first introduced in this context, in the Merchant Shipping (Mercantile Marine Fund) Act 1898 (c. 44), s.9(2), it may have been anticipated that the Acts could easily be read together. By 1994, the accumulation of some 30 Merchant Shipping Acts meant that it was not always easy or possible to see how they were to be construed together. The difficulty of the consolidator's task is shown by the handful of provisions which made it clear that such references in the previous Acts included the last one of the accumulating series (see, *e.g.* the Merchant Shipping (Load Lines) Act 1967 (c. 27), s.34(2), the Merchant Shipping Act 1974 (c. 43), s.23(1), the Merchant Shipping Act 1979 (c. 39), s.37(5), the Safety at Sea Act 1986 (c. 23), s.5(3)). Some tidying up was done by the Merchant Shipping (Registration, etc.) Act 1993 (c. 22), Sched. 4, para. 3, which generalised the drafting proposition in order to avoid any implication that the same did not hold true for other Acts which had not used the formula.

Merchant Shipping Act 1995 consolidation

The eventual consolidation of the Merchant Shipping Acts was achieved with cross-party support and the use of the speedy procedure for the consolidation of Acts. This necessarily meant that there was no further room for amendments to the law. The 1995 Act contains a mere 316 sections, by comparison with the 748 sections of the 1894 Act. Much of the reduction is accounted for by the removal of detailed technical provisions from the Act to delegated legislation (as described below), and by the use in the 1995 Act of some 14 Schedules (of about 90 pages), as opposed to 22 Schedules (of only 33 pages) in the 1894 Act.

Increasing use of delegated legislation

A further comparison between the Merchant Shipping Acts 1894 and 1995 would reveal the changing format of merchant shipping legislation. The 1894 Act contained a great amount of detail (particularly concerning technical safety matters). That sort of detail is today found in statutory instruments issued under the primary legislation. The Merchant Shipping Act 1979 was a particular example of this process. It repealed many 1894 provisions and replaced them with enabling powers, of which s.85 of the 1995 Act is a successor. Any lawyer wishing, for instance, to discover the detailed rules on maritime safety will need to consult hundreds of pages of statutory instruments. The use of delegated legislation is clearly of importance to the Department of Transport, as it can avoid the bottlenecks associated with obtaining parliamentary approval through primary legislation. Whether adequate parliamentary control can be exercised is another matter. There are proposals to deregulate technical merchant shipping matters even more during the course of 1996, when the Department of Transport plans to allow technical matters to be set out in Merchant Shipping Notices (see, *e.g.* the Merchant Shipping (Delegation of Type Approval) Regulations 1996 (S.I. 1996 No. 147)). Such proposals may speed up the legislative process and make many rules more accessible to mariners, although lawyers may question the constitutional propriety or wisdom of such extensive delegatory mechanisms.

Drafting techniques: incorporating international conventions

A particular failing in British legislative drafting in the maritime area has been the method by which international maritime conventions are incorporated into U.K. law (see generally,

N. Gaskell, "The Interpretation of Maritime Conventions at Common Law", in J. P. Gardner (ed.), *United Kingdom Law in the 1990s* (British Institute of International and Comparative Law, 1990), pp. 218–40). The problem is that some of the Merchant Shipping Acts have rewritten the conventions into "legal English" (see, *e.g.* Pt. VI, Chaps. III and IV of the 1995 Act), and sometimes in a manner which may have failed fully to implement its words or intent (see, *e.g.* s.187 of the 1995 Act). The more recent, and preferable, trend has been to incorporate the convention in a Schedule where its full original text is reproduced in one Part, along with a separate Part setting out particular changes that need to be made in U.K. law to make the convention operate satisfactorily (see, *e.g.* Sched. 1 of the Merchant Shipping (Salvage and Pollution) Act 1994). The latter method allows the judges to see the exact words agreed internationally, often after significant argument and compromise, and is to be welcomed as being more transparent. The 1995 Act, as a consolidating measure, has largely reproduced the mechanisms adopted by the Acts which it consolidates. This means that there is still a variety of methods of enacting the international conventions. It is rather unfortunate that it was not possible to adopt a uniform drafting technique which used the actual text of conventions, especially for such internationally significant areas as marine pollution which, in Pt. VI of the 1995 Act, is still enacted by the "redrafting" into legal English technique. It might have been thought that, as national enactment of a Convention agreed internationally is presumed to give full effect to that Convention, there were no Parliamentary obstacles associated with the consolidation procedure which would have prevented the redrafting of legislation such as the Merchant Shipping (Oil Pollution) Act 1971 (c. 59) and the Merchant Shipping Act 1974 (c. 43) (which used the redrafting technique in respect of oil pollution liability). However, it is likely that there was not sufficient time to effect such changes at the time of consolidation. But it is to be hoped that in any future amendments to this Act the more modern drafting techniques will be used and that the opportunity will be taken to redraft those parts of the Act which still use the older technique. It is also hoped that any amendments will be accompanied by a single revised version of the Act (or relevant parts of it) so that future readers do not have to endure the same agonies, which others have undergone until the 1995 consolidation, of trying to piece together a consolidated text.

Pre-consolidation amendments

The writer had expressed the hope in an earlier annotation, to the Merchant Shipping Act 1988 (in *Current Law Statutes Annotated 1988*), that by 1994 it would have been possible to have a consolidation of the Merchant Shipping Acts in time for the centenary of the principal Act, the 1894 Act. The Department of Transport had been able to pave the way for a 1994 consolidation, by tidying up the existing legislation in the Merchant Shipping (Registration, etc.) Act 1993. This 1993 Act was a necessary precursor, as the consolidating Bill could not introduce substantive changes in the law. In the event, there was no parliamentary time to introduce the consolidating Bill in time for the centenary of the 1894 Act, despite support for it from all sides in Parliament.

The 1993 pre-consolidation Act was a feat of parliamentary drafting in itself, as it had to marshal and co-ordinate changes to a hundred years of differing drafting techniques. A typical example of the modernisation which had to take place right across the 1894 Act was the need to update and unify the description of the necessary *mens rea* for offences created by the Act, as a variety of different expressions had been used over the years. Thus, the Merchant Shipping (Registration, etc.) Act 1993, Sched. 4, para. 74 effected a general change from the use of the word "wilfully" to "intentionally" and from "suffering" or "allowing" a thing to be done, to "permitting" it to be done. Antiquated language was also updated. Thus, there were many references, dating from the days of sail, to a ship's "apparel" (see, *e.g.* s.512(1) of the 1894 Act). The word "equipment" was effectively substituted for such references by the Merchant Shipping (Registration, etc.) Act 1993, Sched. 4, para. 2(4). Similarly, references to means of conveyance such as "carriages, wagons and carts" (*e.g.* s.512(1)(c)) were also updated by the use of the expression "vehicles" (see the Merchant Shipping (Registration, etc.) Act 1993, Sched. 4, para. 2(5)). Some venerable provisions were repealed, the most remarkable, perhaps, being s.514 of the 1894 Act (re-enacting an 1854 provision) which gave the receiver of wreck power to "suppress plunder". Schedule 4 of the Merchant Shipping (Registration, etc.) Act 1993 contained a host of amendments to the Merchant Shipping Acts, some of which were quite significant. In the absence, at that time, of a single consolidated version of the Acts, many of these changes have gone unnoticed. There will probably be many practitioners who will be surprised by the 1995 Act, as they search for familiar provisions which had been repealed by the Merchant Shipping (Registration, etc.) Act 1993. Indeed, the work of the parliamentary counsel who drafted the 1993 Act (and the 1995 consolidation) must have been so complicated that some further tidying up had to be done in a rather unusual way. Under the 1894 Act, ss.492–501, there were a number of statutory provisions relating to the delivery of goods which enabled a carrier to deal with cargo which has not been collected. However, these provisions were repealed, virtually unnoticed in the shipping community, by the Statute Law (Repeals) Act 1993 (c. 50) and, accordingly, there are no equivalent provisions in the 1995 Act. Further, the Merchant Shipping Act 1970 contained a number of provisions which had never been brought into effect and there was a flurry of last minute Commencement Orders, so that consolidation could take place. Some of these measures were themselves quite controversial. See, *e.g.* the Merchant Shipping Act 1970 (Commencement No. 11) Order 1995 (S.I. 1995 No. 965), which entered into force on May 1, 1995, bringing into force s.51 of the 1970 Act concerning the power to make regulations about the employment of young persons on ships. See also, the Merchant Shipping Act 1970 (Commencement No. 12) Order 1995 (S.I. 1995 No. 1426) which entered into force on August 1, 1995. Note also the repeals effected by the Merchant Shipping (Survey and Certification) Regulations 1995 (S.I. 1995 No. 1210) (see the General Note to s.124, below).

Merchant Shipping Act 1995: consolidation not codification
The Merchant Shipping Act 1995 is the nearest that the U.K. has to a Maritime Law Code, although as noted above, it is not comprehensive, especially in the area of private law. But even viewed as a Code of Public Maritime Law, the 1995 Act is by no means comprehensive. The expression "merchant shipping" has traditionally been given a somewhat narrow meaning, probably dictated by the artificial distinctions between the functions of Whitehall Departments and the responsibilities assigned to what is now the Department of Transport (in 1894, the Board of Trade). As a result, there are inconsistencies in the areas covered by the 1995 Act. Although the 1995 Act contains some provisions on docks and harbours (see, *e.g.* s.252), there are many other Acts which regulate this area, such as the Harbours Act 1964 (c. 40) and the Ports Act 1991 (c. 52). Lighthouse authorities are regulated by Pt. VII of the 1995 Act, but pilotage is dealt with in the Pilotage Act 1987 (c. 21). The 1995 Act deals with ships, but not hovercraft (see the Hovercraft Act 1968 (c. 59)) or offshore oil rigs (see the Mineral Workings (Offshore Installations) Act 1971 (c. 61) and the Offshore Safety Act 1992 (c. 15)). Chapter II of Pt. IX of the 1995 Act contains 17 sections on wreck, but historic and military wreck continue to be regulated by the Protection of Wrecks Act 1973 (c. 33) and the Protection of Military Remains Act 1986 (c. 35). (It is probable that the 1973 Act is viewed as the future responsibility of the Department of National Heritage and the 1986 Act as the responsibility of the Ministry of Defence.) The 1995 Act contains many provisions creating criminal offences, but the hijacking of ships falls under the Aviation and Maritime Security Act 1990 (c. 31). Part VII of the 1995 Act sets out the liabilities of a carrier under a contract for the carriage of passengers, but the contractual liabilities of the carrier of cargo will be regulated by the Carriage of Goods by Sea Act 1971 (c. 19).

This Act is a very welcome consolidation, and it took a significant amount of effort and time to produce, but it is arguable that it does not consolidate enough. Indeed, on the same day that Parliament approved the Act, it also passed the Shipping and Trading Interests (Protection) Act 1995 (c. 22) (see the annotations by Gaskell and Marsh in *Current Law Statutes Annotated 1995*). This consolidated a number of provisions designed to protect trading interests, but it expressly removed from the Merchant Shipping Acts statutory protection given to merchant shipping against action by foreign governments. While there may be good reason to have a general Act on protectionism, and to deal separately with specific problems, the enactment of the Shipping and Trading Interests (Protection) Act 1995 shows that there is still a tendency to take a narrow approach to matters which can properly be included in a Merchant Shipping Act. At a time when London is fighting to maintain its ascendancy as a centre for the resolution of maritime disputes, it can only help the image of English law, in particular, to point to a modern and coherent set of maritime laws—especially when wooing potential clients who are being offered the more systematic codes of continental maritime law. The writer would prefer to see a more comprehensive consolidation (*cf.* the Australian Navigation Act) at the next available opportunity. More controversially, perhaps, he would favour a full codification of maritime law, to bring into a single Act certain areas of common law (especially in the carriage of goods by sea), which builds upon the traditions of Sir Mackenzie Chalmers' Marine Insurance Act 1906. For that radical change, we may need to wait until well into the 21st Century.

Scope of annotations: derivations and destinations
In order to assist readers, Tables of Derivations and Destinations will be found at the end of the Act, after Sched. 14. These Tables are reproduced from the HMSO publication of the Act, but have no official status. In addition, for convenience, further references to derivations are made in the General Notes to each section. These references are not meant to be definitive, *i.e.* tracing every amendment which might have been made over the years to a particular provision, but seek mainly to indicate the changes which have taken place in more recent times (especially

since the Merchant Shipping Act 1970). For the precise dates of entry into force of particular sections of the repealed Merchant Shipping Acts, readers should consult the relevant Commencement Orders (*e.g.* the Merchant Shipping Act 1970 (Commencement No. 12) Order 1995 (S.I. 1995 No. 1426)). The writer has not sought to include references to every statutory instrument which has been made under a particular section, but where appropriate has given some references by way of example. In an Act of this size and complexity it is impractical to provide the same level of detailed coverage for every provision, in particular those provisions appearing in Schedules. The writer has concentrated upon those provisions which have been more recently produced and has incorporated and updated annotations of some of the consolidated provisions (such as the Merchant Shipping (Salvage and Pollution) Act 1994).

COMMENCEMENT

This Act received Royal Assent on July 19, 1995 and under s.316 entered into force on January 1, 1996. Note the transitional provisions in s.314 and Sched. 14. Schedule 4 also contains transitional provisions, relating to the regime of oil pollution liability, which will apply before the international entry into force of two Protocols in 1996 (see further the General Notes to Pt. VI, Chaps. III and IV).

ABBREVIATIONS

1894 Act	: Merchant Shipping Act 1894
1910 Salvage Convention	: Convention for the Unification of Certain Rules of Law relating to Assistance and Salvage at Sea 1910
1969 Liability Convention	: International Convention on Civil Liability for Oil Pollution Damage 1969
1970 Act	: Merchant Shipping Act 1970
1971 Act	: Merchant Shipping (Oil Pollution) Act 1971
1971 Fund Convention	: International Convention on the Establishment of an International Fund for Compensation for Oil Pollution Damage 1971
1973 Act	: Protection of Wrecks Act 1973
1974 Act	: Merchant Shipping Act 1974
1979 Act	: Merchant Shipping Act 1979
1981 Consultative Document	: *Review of Parts I and IV of the Merchant Shipping Act 1894: the Registration of Ships*, Department of Transport Consultative Document, October 1991
1981 CMI Draft Convention	: the Draft International Convention on Salvage 1981
1984 Consultative Document	: *Proposals for Legislation on ship registration and other matters*, Department of Transport Consultative Document, March 1984
1984 Protocols	: Protocols to the International Convention on Civil Liability for Oil Pollution Damage 1969 and the International Convention on the Establishment of an International Fund for Compensation for Oil Pollution Damage 1971
1986 Act	: Protection of Military Remains Act 1986
1987 White Paper	: *Merchant Shipping: Legislative Proposals*, White Paper, presented to Parliament by the Secretary of State for Transport, October 1987, Cm. 239, HMSO
1988 Act	: Merchant Shipping Act 1988
1989 Salvage Convention	: The International Convention on Salvage 1989
1992 Protocols	: Protocols to the International Convention on Civil Liability for Oil Pollution Damage 1969 and the International Convention on the Establishment of an International Fund for Compensation for Oil Pollution Damage 1971

1993 Registration Regulations	: Merchant Shipping (Registration of Ships) Regulations 1993 (S.I. 1993 No. 3138), as amended by the Merchant Shipping (Registration of Ships) (Amendment) Regulations 1994 (S.I. 1994 No. 541)
1994 Act	: Merchant Shipping (Salvage and Pollution) Act 1994
1995 Act	: Merchant Shipping Act 1995
BIMCO	: Baltic and International Maritime Council
Brice	: G. Brice, Maritime Law of Salvage (2nd ed. 1993)
Chorley and Giles Shipping Law	: Chorley and Giles Shipping Law by N. Gaskell, C. Debattista and R. Swatton (8th ed. 1987)
CMI	: Comite Maritime International
CMI Report 1984	: Comite Maritime International Report to the IMO on the draft Convention on Salvage, prepared by Bent Nielsen, April 6, 1984 (IMO LEG 52/4, July 3, 1994 Annex 2)
DOT	: Department of Transport
DOT/GCBS 1990 Report	: British Shipping: Challenges and Opportunities (HMSO, 1990)
Donaldson Report	: Safer Ships, Cleaner Seas, Lord Donaldson of Lymington (HMSO, 1994)
Gaskell, "Policy Issues"	: N. Gaskell, "The Enactment of the 1989 Salvage Convention in English Law: Policy Issues" [1990] LMCLQ 352
Gaskell, "Interpretation of Maritime Conventions"	: N. Gaskell, "The Interpretation of Maritime Conventions at Common Law", in J. P. Gardner (ed.), United Kingdom Law in the 1990s (1990)
Gaskell, "The 1989 Salvage Convention"	: N. Gaskell, "The 1989 Salvage Convention and the Lloyd's Open Form (LOF) Salvage Agreement", [1991] 16 Tulane Maritime Law Journal, 1
GCBS	: General Council Of British Shipping
GLA	: General Lighthouse Authority
Kennedy	: D. Steel, F. Rose, Kennedy's Law of Salvage (5th ed. 1985)
IMO	: International Maritime Organisation
LLA	: Local Lighthouse Authority
LOF	: Lloyd's Open Form Standard Salvage Agreement
LOS Convention 1982	: UN Convention on the Law of the Sea 1982
MARPOL	: the International Convention on the Prevention of Pollution from Ships
MODU	: Mobile offshore drilling unit
OPRC Convention	: the International Convention on Oil Pollution Preparedness Response and Co-operation 1990
Sheen Report	: *Merchant Shipping Act 1894: mv Herald of Free Enterprise. Report of Court No. 8074 Formal Investigation*, Department of Transport, 1987, HMSO
SOLAS	: the Safety of Life at Sea Convention
Temperley	: M. Thomas, D. Steel, *Temperley: Merchant Shipping Acts* (7th ed., 1976)
Vincenzini	: E.Vincenzini, International Salvage Law (1992)
Wildeboer	: I. Wildeboer, The Brussels Salvage Convention (Sythoff, 1965)

PART I

BRITISH SHIPS

GENERAL NOTE
This Part brings together a number of provisions relating to the national character and flag of ships. They were originally consolidated in Sched. 3 of the Merchant Shipping (Registration, etc.) Act 1993, mainly from the Merchant Shipping Acts 1894 and 1988.

British ships and United Kingdom ships

1.—(1) A ship is a British ship if—
(a) the ship is registered in the United Kingdom under Part II; or
(b) the ship is, as a Government ship, registered in the United Kingdom in pursuance of an Order in Council under section 308; or
(c) the ship is registered under the law of a relevant British possession; or
(d) the ship is a small ship other than a fishing vessel and—
       (i) is not registered under Part II, but
       (ii) is wholly owned by qualified owners, and
       (iii) is not registered under the law of a country outside the United Kingdom.
(2) For the purposes of subsection (1)(d) above—
    "qualified owners" means persons of such description qualified to own British ships as is prescribed by regulations made by the Secretary of State for the purposes of that paragraph; and
    "small ship" means a ship less than 24 metres in length ("length" having the same meaning as in the tonnage regulations).
(3) A ship is a "United Kingdom ship" for the purposes of this Act (except section 85 and 144(3)) if the ship is registered in the United Kingdom under Part II (and in Part V "United Kingdom fishing vessel" has a corresponding meaning).

DEFINITIONS
    "Act, this": s.316(1).
    "British ship": subs. (1) and s.313(1).
    "fishing vessel": s.313(1) and (3).
    "Government ship": ss.308(4) and 313(1).
    "length": subs. (2).
    "person": Interpretation Act 1978, Sched. 1.
    "qualified owners": subs. (2).
    "registered": ss.23(1) and 313(1).
    "relevant British possession": s.313(1).
    "Secretary of State": Interpretation Act 1978, Sched. 1.
    "ship": s.313(1).
    "small ship": subs. (2).
    "tonnage regulations": ss.19(1) and 313(1).
    "United Kingdom": Interpretation Act 1978, Sched. 1.
    "United Kingdom fishing vessel": subs. (3).
    "United Kingdom ship": subs. (3) and s.313(1).

GENERAL NOTE
    [Derivation: Merchant Shipping (Registration, etc.) Act 1993, Sched. 3, para. 1, Sched. 4, para. 1(1).]

British and United Kingdom ships
    The definition of "British ships" in subs. (1) is wider than that of "United Kingdom ship" within subs. (3) (note the relevance of these definitions throughout the Act by virtue of s.313), as it could include ships registered in colonies (see s.1(1)(c)), as well as small unregistered ships. There are examples of provisions scattered around the Act which include references to British ships (see, *e.g.* s.2 and s.13), although they are fewer now than in the 1894 Act. The Merchant

Shipping (Registration, etc.) Act 1993, Sched. 4, para. 6, in particular, changed a number of existing references in the 1894 Act from "British" to "United Kingdom", to make it clear when powers were really to be exercised over U.K. registered ships and not over every ship registered in a colony (see, *e.g.* s.257), or when privileges were only to be available to U.K. registered ships (see, *e.g.* s.186). It is not always immediately apparent why a section applies to a "United Kingdom" and not a "British" ship, save where it is intended not to exercise control over ships registered in British possessions. The use of the expression "United Kingdom" is perhaps misleading (in comparison with subs. (1)), in that it carries notions of nationality, whereas it is clear from the definition in subs. (3) that it is merely a synonym for "U.K. registered". In any event, the distinction between registered and unregistered ships may be relatively insignificant from the point of view of state control, given the wide powers to extend the operation of the Act to unregistered ships by virtue of s.307, below.

British ships

Section 1(1) substantially re-enacts s.2 of the Merchant Shipping Act 1988. It defines a British ship, mainly in terms of whether it is registered under the Act in the U.K., or in a "relevant possession" (defined in s.313 as being the Channel Islands, the Isle of Man and any colony—such as Gibraltar). In the Merchant Shipping Act 1988, the possessions were described as Crown Dependencies or Dependent Territories. In all cases, except sub-para. 1(d), a British ship will be registered in the U.K. (or the U.K. possession). Small ships whose owners may wish to exercise the entitlement not to register, can still be considered British if they satisfy the three criteria mentioned in sub-para. 1(d). Clearly, there may be ships which are unregistered, but owned by persons who would be entitled to register them under s.9, as British ships. An example would be ships over 24 metres in length. For the treatment of unregistered ships, see the General Note to s.307, below.

Under Art. 91 of the UN Convention on the Law of the Sea 1982, every state shall fix the conditions for the grant of nationality to ships, for the registration of ships in its territory and the right to fly its flag. Ships in international law have the nationality of the state whose flag they are entitled to fly. There must exist a genuine link between the state and the ship. The U.K. is expected to ratify the Convention, perhaps in 1996, although it is arguable that many of its provisions already represent customary international law. See also the General Note to s.129, below.

Once a ship has been categorised as British a number of important consequences flow. In particular it may be crucial in deciding the ability of the British Government to exercise jurisdiction over it for a wide variety of purposes, including the enforcement of safety and other regulatory matters. Article 94 of the LOS Convention 1982 sets out the duties of flag states. The internationally accepted way of enforcing maritime regulatory standards is for each state to control the ships flying its own flag wherever in the world they may be operating, although there is an increasing recognition of the need for "port state control", *i.e.* for the state of the port in which a ship happens to be, to exercise some responsibility over it (and see Art. 21 of the LOS Convention). This approach is seen later in s.85(1), below. One of the main international purposes for the registration of a ship is to identify its nationality. This raises the whole question of "flag of convenience" ships which operate from "open" registries, *i.e.* in those countries whose Governments' financial policy is to have the register open to as many ships as possible. The "genuine link" (see the General Note to s.9, below) is often provided by having a shell company incorporated in the flag state although all the operations are controlled by the parent company from elsewhere. The most well known of the flags of convenience are Panama and Liberia, although there are many others. The incentive for the shipowner is to reduce costs, either by the employment of cheaper crews than available in traditional Western economies or (less scrupulously) by taking advantage of what are perceived to be lower safety standards.

Section 1 now makes clear the distinction between British ships and United Kingdom ships, but for all practical purposes under the 1894 Act, the terms "British ship" and "registered British ship" were synonymous. A ship which had not been registered may not have been entitled to be treated as a British ship for all purposes (see s.72 of the 1894 Act as amended by Sched. 1, para. 44 of the Merchant Shipping Act 1988), although it was unlikely to avoid control thereby (see now the General Note to s.307, below, concerning unregistered ships). Curiously, the 1894 Act nowhere defined British ship. Section 1 of the 1894 Act simply defined who may own a British ship and s.2 said that every British ship had to be registered. This seems to suggest that the expression was almost a non-technical description of ships *owned* by persons qualified under s.1. But, a ship could only be registered if British owned (within s.1 of the 1894 Act) so the link between registration and the right to fly the British flag was very close.

Although nationality (and the right to fly the British flag under s.2) is linked to the question of registration, they are separate, as ss.1 and 2 now clearly provide. Nationality is a status giving rise to rights and obligations. A ship flying the British flag (under s.2) may be entitled to protection from the state in some circumstances, as is shown by the escorting services which were provided by the Armilla patrol to British merchant ships in the Persian Gulf during the Iran-Iraq war in the 1980's. Registration is essentially a procedure which provides evidence, in the form of a record, of matters which relate to rights in the vessel. It is used as a means of recording information about the ship and its owner, *e.g.* as to evidence of title and the existence and priority of mortgages. Registration therefore has advantages, in the commercial context. Suggestions in the 1981 Consultative Document that it was not really necessary to maintain details of title and mortgages did not receive support and were rightly dropped.

"Ship"

There has been considerable doubt over the years as to exactly which craft are covered by the expression "ship" and accordingly may be registered. This definitional problem arises for many purposes and in many different contexts under the 1995 Act and has never been satisfactorily resolved. The difficulty is caused by the inclusive wording of s.313 (formerly the 1894 Act, s.742) which was perfectly adequate for most of the craft envisaged in the 19th Century (*cf. The Gas Float Whitton (No.2)* [1897] A.C. 337), but it is unclear as to whether the wide variety of craft now used in the off-shore industry, such as jack-up oil rigs, fall within it. Section 313 now states that ship "includes every description of vessel used in navigation". Note that s.311 (formerly the Merchant Shipping Act 1979. s.41) gives the Secretary of State power to provide that certain structures designed or adapted for use at sea are to be treated as ships.

Subs. (1)

To be a British ship for the purposes of this Act, it must be:

(a) registered in the U.K. under Pt. II of the Act, or

(b) registered as a Government ship, or

(c) registered in one of the British possessions, or

(d) a non-fishing vessel under 24 metres long, which is owned by those qualified to own British ships, but unregistered in the U.K. or abroad.

Sub-para. (a). Under what is now Pt. II of the 1995 Act, the Merchant Shipping (Registration of Ships) Regulations 1993 (S.I. 1993 No. 3138) have established a register which is divided into four Parts. Part I is for ordinary ships (equivalent to the old Pt. I of the 1894 Act). Part II is for fishing vessels (equivalent to the old Pt. II of the 1894 Act). Part III is for small ships (*cf.* the small ships register, set up by the Merchant Shipping Act 1983, s.5 and the Merchant Shipping (Small Ships Register) Regulations 1983 (S.I. 1983 No. 1470) and mainly designed for pleasure craft). Part IV is for bareboat chartered ships (see s.17, below, replacing s.7 of the Merchant Shipping (Registration, etc.) Act 1993).

Sub-para. (b). See the note to s.309, below. Government ships were previously registered under s.80 of the Merchant Shipping Act 1906.

Sub-para. (c). Ships registered in the British possessions such as the Channel Islands, the Isle of Man and colonies such as Gibraltar are British ships (and see s.313). Ships registered in Hong Kong will continue to be classed as British ships until July 1, 1997, when the colony reverts to China.

Sub-para. (d). This paragraph covers those small British owned (non-fishing) vessels which are not registered under Pt. II of the 1995 Act (*i.e.* in one of the Parts of the register established by the Merchant Shipping (Registration of Ships) Regulations 1993 (S.I. 1993 No. 3138)), or under the law of any other state. Compare s.3 of the 1894 Act which exempted from registration certain small ships of up to 15 or 30 net tons, depending on their type. When the International Convention on Tonnage Measurement of Ships 1969 came into force on July 18, 1982 (see the Merchant Shipping (Tonnage) Regulations 1982 (S.I. 1982 No. 841)) it only required tonnage measurement of vessels of 24 metres and above—corresponding roughly to a ship of 100–150 tons. The 1981 Consultative Document had suggested that it might be appropriate to use "Convention size" as a parameter for registration and the 24 metre figure was apparently selected to be consistent with this. It is also the figure used for the small ships register under Pt. III of the Merchant Shipping (Registration of Ships) Regulations 1993 (S.I. 1993 No. 3138).

The obvious category of vessel which is *not* British within the paragraph is an unregistered vessel which is 24 metres or *over* in length. As the shipowner has the option of registering under the regime introduced in what is now s.9 of the 1995 Act (by the Merchant Shipping Act 1988, s.4) there may be large categories of vessels which will not be British for the purposes of the 1995 Act. However, reference to s.307 (formerly the 1894 Act, s.7, as amended by the 1988 Act, Sched. 1, para. 44) and regulations made thereunder shows that the shipowners will have imposed on them most of the burdens of British nationality without being able to claim some of the advantages. Note also subs. (2) below.

Subs. (2)

For the powers of the Secretary of State to make regulations, see s.306, below. Regulation 89 of the Merchant Shipping (Registration of Ships) Regulations 1993 (S.I. 1993 No. 3138) sets out which persons are qualified to be the owners of small ships under Pt. III of the register. The main distinction between qualification under Pt. I and Pt. III of the register is that bodies corporate are not qualified to own a small ship under Pt. III. Note that the definition of small ship, as such, is made by reference to length and to the tonnage regulations made under s.19. The definition in s.1(2) is referred to elsewhere in the 1995 Act (see, *e.g.* s.5(2)).

Subs. (3)

Section 85 is the main rule-making power given to the Secretary of State in respect of health and safety. Section 144(3) relates to powers of detention of a harbour master.

British flag

2.—(1) The flag which every British ship is entitled to fly is the red ensign (without any defacement or modification) and, subject to subsections (2) and (3) below, no other colours.

(2) Subsection (1) above does not apply to Government ships.

(3) The following are also proper national colours, that is to say—

(a) any colours allowed to be worn in pursuance of a warrant from Her Majesty or from the Secretary of State;

(b) in the case of British ships registered in a relevant British possession, any colours consisting of the red ensign defaced or modified whose adoption for ships registered in that possession is authorised or confirmed by Her Majesty by Order in Council.

(4) Any Order under subsection (3)(b) above shall be laid before Parliament after being made.

DEFINITIONS

"British ship": ss.1(1) and 313(1).
"Government ship": ss.308(4) and 313(1).
"registered": ss.23(1) and 313(1).
"relevant British possession": s.313(1).
"Secretary of State": Interpretation Act 1978, Sched. 1.
"ship": s.313(1).

GENERAL NOTE

[Derivation: Merchant Shipping Act 1894, s.73(1); Merchant Shipping (Registration, etc.) Act 1993, Sched. 3, para. 2, Sched. 5; Merchant Shipping Act 1894, s.738(2).]

This section describes the red ensign which British ships are entitled to fly and substantially re-enacts s.73(1) of the 1894 Act.

For the powers of the Secretary of State to make delegated legislation, such as regulations, see s.306, below.

Offences relating to British character of ship

3.—(1) If the master or owner of a ship which is not a British ship does anything, or permits anything to be done, for the purpose of causing the ship to appear to be a British ship then, except as provided by subsections (2) and (3) below, the ship shall be liable to forfeiture and the master, the owner and any charterer shall each be guilty of an offence.

(2) No liability arises under subsection (1) above where the assumption of British nationality has been made for the purpose of escaping capture by an enemy or by a foreign ship of war in the exercise of some belligerent right.

(3) Where the registration of any ship has terminated by virtue of any provision of registration regulations, any marks prescribed by registration regulations displayed on the ship within the period of 14 days beginning with the date of termination of that registration shall be disregarded for the purposes of subsection (1) above.

(4) If the master or owner of a British ship does anything, or permits anything to be done, for the purpose of concealing the nationality of the ship, the

ship shall be liable to forfeiture and the master, the owner and any charterer of the ship shall each be guilty of an offence.

(5) Without prejudice to the generality of subsections (1) and (4) above, those subsections apply in particular to acts or deliberate omissions as respects—

(a) the flying of a national flag;

(b) the carrying or production of certificates of registration or other documents relating to the nationality of the ship; and

(c) the display of marks required by the law of any country.

(6) Any person guilty of an offence under this section shall be liable—

(a) on summary conviction, to a fine not exceeding £50,000;

(b) on conviction on indictment, to imprisonment for a term not exceeding two years or a fine, or both.

(7) This section applies to things done outside, as well as to things done within, the United Kingdom.

DEFINITIONS

"British ship": ss.1(1) and 313(1).

"foreign": s.313(1).

"master": s.313(1).

"person": Interpretation Act 1978, Sched. 1.

"registration regulations": ss.10 and 313(1).

"ship": s.313(1).

"United Kingdom": Interpretation Act 1978, Sched. 1.

GENERAL NOTE

[Derivation: Merchant Shipping Act 1894, ss.69 and 70; Merchant Shipping (Registration, etc.) Act 1993, Sched. 3, para. 5, Sched. 5.]

This section restates parts of various enactments (see ss.69(1) and 70 of the 1894 Act, as amended), involving the false attribution of nationality. It creates offences where non-British ships are made to appear as British and the penalty can include forfeiture. It also creates an offence where there is concealment of the British nationality of a ship. *Cf.* s.14, below. See also s.15(3), below, in respect of fishing vessels (restating s.22(8) of the Merchant Shipping Act 1988).

Subs. (1)

Masters or owners who conceal the nationality of their ships can commit offences. The expression "master or owner" on its own would have raised the question of whether both, or either, could have been convicted (*cf. Federal Steam Navigation Co. v. Department of Trade and Industry (sub. nom. The Huntingdon)* [1974] 1 W.L.R. 505 and the General Note to s.131, below), but the concluding words of the subsection make it clear that each can be guilty of an offence. Note that the conduct of the owner or master could result in a charterer being guilty. The rationale is that it is unlikely that any action to disguise the nature of the ship could be done without the knowledge or connivance of the charterer, as it will be the charterer who dictates the actual commercial usage of the ship. The parties may wish to assume British nationality in order to claim the protection of the Royal Navy or, more likely, to mislead other commercial parties in order to avoid trade embargoes or union blacklisting. There is no definition of charterer in the Act, nor at common law (see *The Heidberg* [1994] 2 Lloyd's Rep. 287, 311–312), and so it would appear that there is no restriction on the type of charterer which may be covered by the provision. Accordingly, a demise charterer, time charterer or voyage charterer could be liable to prosecution. It is less clear whether some of the more modern type of "charterer", such as a "slot charterer" on a container ship would be included. On balance, it is submitted that a broad definition be taken so as to include such persons who have contractual rights to use all or part of a ship, as opposed to those who merely have a contract for the carriage of goods covered by a bill of lading. (See further, the discussion in Pt. VI and Pt. VII)

Subs. (2)

There is a defence where subterfuge was used to evade capture in wartime.

Subs. (3)

On the termination of registration (*e.g.* under Reg. 56 of the Merchant Shipping (Registration of Ships) Regulations 1993 (S.I. 1993 No. 3138)), 14 days are allowed in which to remove British markings.

Subs. (4)

This subsection creates the mirror offence to that in subs. (1), namely where the master or owner of a British ship (as defined in s.1(1)) conceal its nationality. There may be commercial reasons why this would be done, *e.g.* to avoid trade embargoes, and for that reason the charterer could also be guilty.

Subs. (5)

Particular examples of offences under subss. (1) and (4) are set out, in particular the flying of a flag to which the ship is not entitled and the carrying of false registration documentation.

Subs. (7)

Note that offences under the section could be committed on the high seas, outside territorial waters. However, it would appear from s.281 that such an offence outside the U.K. must have been committed either by a British citizen (whether on a foreign registered ship or not), or by a foreign citizen but only on a U.K. registered ship. It would seem from s.282 that there would be no jurisdiction over a foreigner who, on a foreign ship on the high seas, committed the actions proscribed by subs. (1).

Penalty for carrying improper colours

4.—(1) If any of the following colours, namely—
(a) any distinctive national colours except—
(i) the red ensign,
(ii) the Union flag (commonly known as the Union Jack) with a white border, or
(iii) any colours authorised or confirmed under section 2(3)(b); or
(b) any colours usually worn by Her Majesty's ships or resembling those of Her Majesty, or
(c) the pendant usually carried by Her Majesty's ships or any pendant resembling that pendant,
are hoisted on board any British ship without warrant from Her Majesty or from the Secretary of State, the master of the ship, or the owner of the ship (if on board), and every other person hoisting them shall be guilty of an offence.

(2) A person guilty of an offence under subsection (1) above shall be liable—
(a) on summary conviction, to a fine not exceeding the statutory maximum;
(b) on conviction on indictment, to a fine.

(3) If any colours are hoisted on board a ship in contravention of subsection (1) above, any of the following, namely—
(a) any commissioned naval or military officer,
(b) any officer of customs and excise, and
(c) any British consular officer,
may board the ship and seize and take away the colours.

(4) Any colours seized under subsection (3) above shall be forfeited to Her Majesty.

(5) In this section "colours" includes any pendant.

DEFINITIONS
"British ship": ss.1(1) and 313(1).
"colours": subs. (5).
"commissioned military officer": s.313(1).
"commissioned naval officer": s.313(1).
"consular officer": s.313(1).
"contravention": s.313(1).
"master": s.313(1).

"person": Interpretation Act 1978, Sched. 1.
"Secretary of State": Interpretation Act 1978, Sched. 1.
"ship": s.313(1).
"statutory maximum": Criminal Justice Act 1982, s.74.

GENERAL NOTE
    [Derivation: Merchant Shipping Act 1894, s.73(2); Merchant Shipping (Registration, etc.) Act 1993, Sched. 3, para. 3, Sched. 5.]
    This section restates s.73(2) of the Merchant Shipping Act 1894. Subsection (1) sets out the offence of flying the wrong colours and subs. (2) specifies the appropriate penalty. Note the somewhat ambiguous use of the expression "master ... or ... owner" (and see the General Note to s.3, above). The wording derives from the 1894 Act and has not been reworded to avoid the problems indicated in *Federal Steam Navigation Co. v. Department of Trade and Industry (sub. nom. The Huntingdon)* [1974] 1 W.L.R. 505. It would seem from the context (*e.g.* the reference to the owner being on board) that a disjunctive was intended so that if the owner is on board then the master cannot also be guilty of an offence. This would also follow from the fact that any person actually hoisting the colours can be guilty. The subsection therefore creates an offence by the actual wrongdoer and one person who had authority over the ship at the time, either the master or the owner (if on board). Powers originally given by s.73(3) of the 1894 Act to remove colours are restated in subs. (3).

Duty to show British flag

    5.—(1) Subject to subsection (2) below, a British ship, other than a fishing vessel, shall hoist the red ensign or other proper national colours—
    (a) on a signal being made to the ship by one of Her Majesty's ships (including any ship under the command of a commissioned naval officer); and
    (b) on entering or leaving any foreign port; and
    (c) in the case of ships of 50 or more tons gross tonnage, on entering or leaving any British port.
    (2) Subsection (1)(c) above does not apply to a small ship (as defined in section 1(2)) registered under Part II.

DEFINITIONS
    "British ship": ss.1(1) and 313(1).
    "commissioned naval officer": s.313(1).
    "fishing vessel": s.313(1) and (3).
    "port": s.313(1).
    "ship": s.313(1).
    "small ship": s.1(2).

GENERAL NOTE
    [Derivation: Merchant Shipping Act 1894, s.74; Merchant Shipping (Registration, etc.) Act 1993, Sched. 3, para. 4, Sched. 5.]
    This section restates s.74 of the Merchant Shipping Act 1894 and sets out duties to display the ensign at stated times. The requirement to hoist the ensign on entering or leaving a British port does not apply to small ships (see s.1(2)).

Duty to declare national character of ship

    6.—(1) An officer of customs and excise shall not grant a clearance or transire for any ship until the master of such ship has declared to that officer the name of the nation to which he claims that the ship belongs, and that officer shall thereupon enter that name on the clearance or transire.
    (2) If a ship attempts to proceed to sea without such clearance or transire, the ship may be detained until the declaration is made.

DEFINITIONS
   "master": s.313(1).
   "ship": s.313(1).

GENERAL NOTE
   [Derivation: Merchant Shipping Act 1894, s.68; Merchant Shipping (Registration, etc.) Act 1993, Sched. 3, para. 6, Sched. 5.]
   This paragraph restates s.68 of the Merchant Shipping Act 1894, and imposes duties to declare the nationality of a ship. For the enforcement of powers of detention, see s.284.

Proceedings on forfeiture of a ship

7.—(1) Where any ship has either wholly or as to any share in it become liable to forfeiture under this Part—

   (a) any commissioned naval or military officer, or

   (b) any person appointed by the Secretary of State for the purposes of this section;

may seize and detain the ship and bring the ship for adjudication before the court.

   (2) Where a ship is subject to adjudication under this section the court may—

   (a) adjudge the ship and her equipment to be forfeited to Her Majesty; and

   (b) make such order in the case as seems just.

   (3) No officer or person bringing proceedings under this section shall be liable in damages in respect of the seizure or detention of the ship, notwithstanding that the ship has not been proceeded against or, if proceeded against, adjudicated not liable to forfeiture, if the court is satisfied that there were reasonable grounds for the seizure or detention.

   (4) If the court is not so satisfied the court may award costs (or in Scotland expenses) and damages to the party aggrieved and make such other order as the court thinks just.

   (5) In this section "the court" means the High Court or, in Scotland, the Court of Session.

DEFINITIONS
   "commissioned military officer": s.313(1).
   "commissioned naval officer": s.313(1).
   "court": subs. (5).
   "High Court": Interpretation Act 1978, Sched. 1.
   "person": Interpretation Act 1978, Sched. 1.
   "Secretary of State": Interpretation Act 1978, Sched. 1.
   "ship": s.313(1).

GENERAL NOTE
   [Derivation: Merchant Shipping Act 1894, s.76; Merchant Shipping Act 1988, Sched. 1, para. 47; Merchant Shipping (Registration, etc.) Act 1993, Sched. 4, para. 2(4), Sched. 5.]
   Section 7 replaces s.76 of the Merchant Shipping Act 1894 and deals with the appropriate procedure for forfeiture of a ship under the Merchant Shipping Act 1995. An example of a forfeiture power would be s.3(1) of the 1995 Act.
   Note that the Merchant Shipping (Registration, etc.) Act 1993, Sched. 4, para. 70 amended what is now subs. (2) by removing the power to award detaining officers' expenses out of the proceeds of sale. It also amended what is now subs. (3) by removing a specific reference to officers being responsible "civilly *or criminally*" (emphasis added to show deletion), so as to make it clear that officers can be criminally liable for their actions, where appropriate. They will not be *civilly* liable for seizing or detaining a ship if they can prove that there were reasonable grounds for the seizure or detention. Presumably, the relevant time is that at which the seizure or detention took place. It may be that there were reasonable grounds for an initial seizure, but not its subsequent maintenance. The defence would therefore only apply to damages resulting from the continuance of the detention. It would not be unreasonable merely to await the adjudication of the court on a doubtful point. Where there is an unreasonable seizure or detention, the court may award costs (or expenses, in Scotland) and compensation and make other orders, *e.g.* for the

release of the ship. The civil liability would, of course, normally fall ultimately on the Department of Transport (or Ministry of Defence), as employer.

For the enforcement of powers of detention generally, see s.284.

PART II

REGISTRATION

General

GENERAL NOTE

Background to the registration system

Parts I and IV of the Merchant Shipping Act 1894 established an imperial system for the registration of ships. In the period after World War II, many former dominions and colonies became independent and technological changes in communications rendered the framework of the 1894 Act anachronistic. In its 1981 and 1984 Consultative Documents, the Department of Transport highlighted many difficulties with the registration system of the 1894 Act and registrars sometimes had to adopt ad hoc solutions to problems not dealt with by that Act.

At one time, over 80 per cent of the vessels on the register were pleasure craft and these did not need the full registration procedure. Following the 1981 Consultative Document, the Merchant Shipping Act 1983 introduced a simplified procedure for the registration of small ships, but there was insufficient legislative time to introduce more fundamental registration reforms until the Merchant Shipping Act 1988. Apart from the creation of a new U.K. register, the most significant feature was the move towards a voluntary system of registration (see now s.9(1)).

One proposal which was rejected after consultations in 1988 was to centralise registry functions and procedures at the office of the Registrar-General of Shipping and Seamen at Cardiff. The proposal was made mainly to make administrative savings and the 1984 Consultative Document identified a great deal of duplication of effort between the local ports and the General Register already maintained in Cardiff, which was based on manuscript returns from the ports. The proposal threatened to remove the familiar markings on the sterns of vessels showing their ports of registration. The 1987 White Paper signalled the Government's intention "at this stage" not to proceed with centralisation. The new fishing vessel register was centralised. However, since then there has been further rationalisation and the Merchant Shipping (Registration, etc.) Act 1993 finally introduced the centralised registry now in s.8 of this Act. The Merchant Shipping (Registration of Ships) Regulations 1993 (S.I. 1993 No. 3138) now prescribe the extent to which applicants can choose a port to which a ship belongs, although the ships will not be registered in these ports as such.

Promoting the British registry

A major theme in debates on the transport industry in the last 15–20 years has been the dramatic decline in the British merchant fleet. The Labour Opposition has accused the Government of failing to provide enough support to the industry, particularly in the form of financial incentives to encourage shipowners to operate under the British flag with British seafarers. Consistent with its non-interventionist approach, the Government has been more concerned to remove obstacles facing British shipowners. A number of minor measures were introduced in the Merchant Shipping Act 1988, ss.38–40 to counter unfair competition and these have now been included in the consolidating Shipping and Trading Interests (Protection) Act 1995. However, during the Gulf War in 1990, concerns were again voiced about the declining level of investment in the British fleet. In 1990 a joint working party into the future of British shipping was chaired by the then Secretary of State for Transport, Cecil Parkinson, and the President of the General Council of British Shipping, Sir Jeffrey Sterling. The trade unions were deliberately excluded from the discussions. Later that year, the DOT and the GCBS produced a joint report, *British Shipping: Challenges and Opportunities* (HMSO, 1990). The report was concerned only with economic, and not defence, considerations and focused largely on a number of regulatory policy options that could assist investment. In particular it recommended change or action to:

1. press ahead with moves in the E.C. to secure the liberalisation of cabotage;
2. speed up and simplify technical procedures and regulations governing the DOT's registration requirements;
3. allow demise-chartered vessels to be registered in the U.K. and vice versa;
4. introduce more flexibility into the rules governing the nationality of officers on British ships;
5. raise the profile of marine training.

Recommendation 1 was given effect on December 7, 1992 when the E.C. Council agreed Regulation (EEC) No. 3577/92 (OJ L 364/7) applying the principle of freedom to provide services to maritime transport within Member States (maritime cabotage). This agreement on cabotage (coastal trade between the ports of individual Member States) may open up some markets in the Mediterranean to British shipowners, but there are lengthy phasing-in periods designed to protect the existing activities of the national fleets of those states bordering the Mediterranean.

Recommendation 2 is reflected in the changes that were introduced by the Merchant Shipping (Registration, etc.) Act 1993, ss.1–6 and Sched. 1, now ss.8–16 and Sched. 1 of the 1995 Act.

Recommendation 3 is given partial effect in s.17.

Recommendations 4 and 5 were not the subject of legislative changes in the 1988 or 1993 Acts, but note the effect of the Merchant Shipping Act 1970 (c. 36) (Commencement No. 12) Order 1995 (S.I. 1995 No. 1426) which entered into force on August 1, 1995. This Order commenced the repeal of s.5 of the Aliens Restriction (Amendment) Act 1919 (c. 92), made by the Merchant Shipping Act 1970, which stated that masters, chief engineers and skippers of British vessels have to be British subjects. See further the General Note to s.47, below. The Government has introduced the Merchant Shipping (Officer Nationality) Regulations 1995 (S.I. 1995 No. 1427), which entered into force on August 1, 1995, in order to deal with ships which have a "strategic function", *e.g.* cruise ships. A further easing of restrictions on maritime employment based on nationality is found in the Fishing Vessels (Certification of Deck Officers and Engineer Officers) (Amendment) Regulations 1995 (S.I. 1995 No. 1428), which entered into force on August 1, 1995 and provide for the recognition of equivalent foreign certificates. Similarly, the Merchant Shipping (Certification of Deck and Marine Engineer Officers) (Amendment) Regulations 1995 (S.I. 1995 No. 1429) which entered into force on August 1, 1995, deal with deck officers and marine engineer officers. They essentially replicate for these officers the provisions as laid out by S.I. 1995 No. 1428 in relation to officers on fishing vessels.

A number of other states offer inducements to foreign shipowners to register under their flags, *e.g.* by creating parallel international registers in addition to financial incentives, such as exemption from seafarers' income tax (DOT/GCBS 1990 Report, para. 3.7). In fact, British shipowners have access to offshore registries in the overseas possessions, such as the Isle of Man, Bermuda and the Cayman Islands (and see the General Note to s.18). The Baltic Exchange has argued for the creation of a new "British Open Register", available to overseas owners which would have, *inter alia*, freedom from U.K. taxation on international earnings of owners registered under the new flag and a relaxation of requirements concerning the nationality of officers (see *The Baltic*, April 1993, p.12). The scheme enacted in s.17 does not create such a new register and it is doubtful whether such a register could be introduced by regulations under s.10, without the need for the full political scrutiny that primary legislation would entail. The European Court has ruled that the German International Ship Register is compatible with the Treaty of Rome (*Firma Sloman Neptun Schiffahrts A.G. v. Seebetriebsrat Bodo Ziesemer* [1993] E.C.R. I-887, noted in Greaves, [1993] L.M.C.L.Q. 471, 473).

Central register of British ships

8.—(1) There shall continue to be a register of British ships for all registrations of ships in the United Kingdom.

(2) The register shall be maintained by the Registrar General of Shipping and Seamen as registrar.

(3) The Secretary of State may designate any person to discharge, on behalf of the registrar, all his functions or such of them as the Secretary of State may direct.

(4) The Secretary of State may give to the registrar directions of a general nature as to the discharge of any of his functions.

(5) The register shall be so constituted as to distinguish, in a separate part, registrations of fishing vessels and may be otherwise divided into parts so as to distinguish between classes or descriptions of ships.

(6) The register shall be maintained in accordance with registration regulations and the private law provisions for registered ships and any directions given by the Secretary of State under subsection (4) above.

(7) The register shall be available for public inspection.

DEFINITIONS
    "British ship": ss.1(1) and 313(1).
    "directions": subs. (4).
    "fishing vessel": s.313(1) and (3)
    "private law provisions for registered ships": ss.16 and 23(1).
    "register": ss.23(1) and 313(1).

"registrar": ss.23(1) and 313(1).
"registration regulations": s.313(1).
"Secretary of State": Interpretation Act 1978, Sched. 1.
"ship": s.313(1).
"United Kingdom": Interpretation Act 1978, Sched. 1.

GENERAL NOTE
[Derivation: Merchant Shipping (Registration, etc.) Act 1993, s.1(1)–(5).]

The register up until the 1993 Act

As a result of a century of developments, there existed by 1993 the three shipping registers referred to in s.1(7) of the Merchant Shipping (Registration, etc.) Act 1993. (1) The old register under Pt. I of the 1894 Act was administered by H.M. Customs and Excise at individual ports all around the country. Most ordinary British merchant ships were registered under Pt. I of the 1894 Act. As a result of the amendments introduced by the Merchant Shipping Act 1988, there continued to be 112 traditional ports of registry, but the number of ports at which business was transacted was reduced from 86 to 14. (2) The register of small ships under the Merchant Shipping Act 1983 was set up in order to remove many pleasure craft from the full register which, at one time, was comprised of 80 per cent of such craft. The full Pt. I registry functions were only needed for title purposes, *e.g.* in respect of craft for which it was necessary to register a mortgage. The small ships register (SSR) was administered by the RYA under regulations (Merchant Shipping (Small Ships Register) Regulations 1983 (S.I. 1983 No. 1470)). (3) A new centralised register of British fishing vessels was introduced as a result of amendments made by the 1988 Act, Pt. II, and it replaced the old fishing boat register under Pt. IV of the 1894 Act.

Subss. (1)–(4): the register after the 1993 Act

Section 1 of the Merchant Shipping (Registration, etc.) Act 1993 finally established a single central register of British ships. That register is continued by s.1 of the 1995 Act. Under s.8(2) the register is maintained in Cardiff by the Registrar General of Shipping and Seamen (for whom, see s.295). The register is now computerised. The Registrar, and any lawfully designated delegate, is effectively under the administrative control of the Secretary of State who may give "directions" under s.8(4). It is probable that this power was used when decisions were made as to the format of the new register now contained in the Merchant Shipping (Registration of Ships) Regulations 1993 (S.I. 1993 No. 3138). Presumably the powers under s.8(4) have been drafted sufficiently widely so as to allow privatisation of the service, a possibility that gave rise to some Opposition fears during debates on the 1993 Bill (see also s.10(6)(b), below). The new register came into operation on March 21, 1994, on which day all existing registrations under the 1894, 1983 and 1988 Acts were automatically transferred to the new register (under s.1(7) of the Merchant Shipping (Registration, etc.) Act 1993). Regulation 31 of the 1993 Registration Regulations (issued under the authority of what is now s.10) allows applicants to select a port listed in Sched. 2 of the Regulations as its port of choice, *i.e.* the port to which the ship belongs. Accordingly, the traditional ports of registry have only survived in the sense that a ship may be marked with the port of choice (see s.10(2)(f), s.10(9)). Under Sched. 14, para. 2, references in any other Act to ship registration will have to be construed as referring to the system established under Pt. II of the 1995 Act.

Subs. (5)

Subsection (5) provides that there will continue to be a separately recorded Part of the register for fishing vessels (currently Pt. II of the 1993 Registration Regulations). There is also provision to allow for sub-dividing the register into other parts, *e.g.* so as to maintain a separate register for small ships (currently Pt. III of the 1993 Registration Regulations), and for ships bareboat chartered-in (currently Pt. IV of the 1993 Registration Regulations: and see s.17). There is also Pt. I, in which other ships can be registered, provided that their owners pass the qualification test in Reg. 7 of the 1993 Registration Regulations.

Subs. (6)

The key change, apart from centralisation, brought about by the Merchant Shipping (Registration, etc.) Act 1993 was achieved by what is now subs. (6). This follows the approach adopted in the 1983 and 1988 Merchant Shipping Acts by transferring all the detailed provisions relating to merchant ship registration from the primary statute to regulations (now governed by s.10, below). This has enabled the DOT (and the Registrar-General) a much greater flexibility and the ability to introduce technical changes to a register which had hitherto been enshrined (or ossified) in the 1894 Act.

The register has to be operated to take account, not only of the registration regulations and any directions given by the Secretary of State, but also of the "private law provisions for registered ships". Essentially, these are the provisions dealing with matters such as title and mortgages (see s.16 and Sched. 1).

Subs. (7)

The original Merchant Shipping (Registration, etc.) Bill did not have the requirement that the register "shall be available for public inspection". Some concern was expressed that there would be difficulties for members of the public in checking on the ownership and histories of ships (such as the ill-fated bulk carrier *Derbyshire*). The Opposition tabled an amendment that would have enabled "public inspection" and for it to be "free of charge". The proposer of the Bill (in effect the DOT) was not prepared to accept any reduction in income. At that time, personal inspections for 1894 Pt. I ships cost £10 an entry and £25 a transcript (£5 and £10, respectively, for fishing vessels), although exceptions were sometimes made for genuine scholars. In Committee it was agreed that the first part of the amendment should be accepted and the second part withdrawn.

Registration of ships: basic provisions

9.—(1) A ship is entitled to be registered if—
(a) it is owned, to the prescribed extent, by persons qualified to own British ships; and
(b) such other conditions are satisfied as are prescribed under subsection (2)(b) below;
(and any application for registration is duly made).
(2) It shall be for registration regulations—
(a) to determine the persons who are qualified to be owners of British ships, or British ships of any class or description, and to prescribe the extent of the ownership required for compliance with subsection (1)(a) above;
(b) to prescribe other requirements designed to secure that, taken in conjunction with the requisite ownership, only ships having a British connection are registered.
(3) The registrar may, nevertheless, if registration regulations so provide, refuse to register or terminate the registration of a ship if, having regard to any relevant requirements of this Act, he considers it would be inappropriate for the ship to be or, as the case may be, to remain registered.
(4) The registrar may, if registration regulations so provide, register a fishing vessel notwithstanding that the requirement of subsection (1)(a) above is not satisfied in relation to a particular owner of a share in the vessel if the vessel otherwise has a British connection.
(5) Where a ship becomes registered at a time when it is already registered under the law of a country other than the United Kingdom, the owner of the ship shall take all reasonable steps to secure the termination of the ship's registration under the law of that country.
(6) Subsection (5) above does not apply to a ship which becomes registered on a transfer of registration to the register from a relevant British possession.
(7) Any person who contravenes subsection (5) above shall be liable on summary conviction to a fine not exceeding level 3 on the standard scale.
(8) In this section "the relevant requirements of this Act" means the requirements of this Act (including requirements falling to be complied with after registration) relating to—
(a) the condition of ships or their equipment so far as relevant to their safety or any risk of pollution; and
(b) the safety, health and welfare of persons employed or engaged in them.
(9) In this Part references to a ship's having a British connection are references to compliance with the conditions of entitlement imposed by subsection (1)(a) and (b) above and "declaration of British connection" is to be construed accordingly.

DEFINITIONS
    "Act, this": s.316(1).
    "British connection": subs. (9) and s.313(1).
    "British ship": ss.1(1) and 313(1).
    "contravenes": s.313(1).
    "declaration of British connection": subs. (9).
    "fishing vessel": s.313(1) and (3).
    "person": Interpretation Act 1978, Sched. 1.
    "qualified owners": s.1(2).
    "qualified to be owners of British ships": subs. (2)(a).
    "register": ss.23(1) and 313(1).
    "registered": ss.23(1) and 313(1).
    "registrar": ss.23(1) and 313(1).
    "registration regulations": s.313(1).
    "relevant British possession": s.313(1).
    "relevant requirements of this Act": subs. (8).
    "ship": s.313(1).
    "standard scale": Criminal Justice Act 1982, s.37.

GENERAL NOTE
    [Derivation: Merchant Shipping (Registration, etc.) Act 1993, s.2; Merchant Shipping Act 1988, ss.2, 3, 6, 7, 9, 10 and 14.]

Entitlement to register
    As the marginal heading indicates, s.9 sets out the basic criteria for entitlement to be registered on the new British register. In fact, the section says very little about the substance of those criteria. This contrasts with, *e.g.* s.3 of the Merchant Shipping Act 1988, which laid down extensive and detailed rules about those persons entitled to be owners of British ships. The reason for the generality of s.9 is that the detailed criteria are prescribed by the 1993 Registration Regulations issued under s.10 (see *e.g.* Regs. 7–9).

Voluntary or compulsory registration
    The Department of Transport Consultative Document 1981 considered the two questions of (i) whether there should be compulsory registration and, if so, (ii) whether the shipowners should have the choice of registry, *i.e.* in the U.K. or abroad. Broadly speaking the 1981 Consultative Document favoured the maintenance of compulsory registration for most vessels (with the exception of small vessels) and all fishing vessels. The 1984 Consultative Document proposed no changes to the Merchant Shipping Act 1894, s.2, whereby every British ship had to be registered. The 1987 White Paper and the 1988 Act, however, departed from the Consultative Documents by making registration optional. Section 9(1) of this Act now expressly records that a ship shall be "entitled" to be registered. The Merchant Shipping Act 1988 gave a shipowner the power to terminate an existing registration by giving notice to the registrar (under s.21 of the 1894 Act, as amended by the 1988 Act, Sched. 1, para. 12(c)). However, Reg. 56 of the 1993 Registration Regulations has now given the registrar a discretion to terminate the registration. In reality the 1894 Act did not present a problem to shipowners wishing to register abroad, as they could have sold one share to a person not qualified to own a British ship under the 1894 Act, s.1 and the registration would then have been closed under the 1894 Act, s.21.
    An owner which is entitled to register its ship in the U.K. under s.9 will have the choice whether: (i) to register abroad, or (ii) to register in the U.K., or (iii) not to register the ship at all or to terminate a present registration. Section 9 allows a British company based in the U.K. to operate a ship owned directly by it from the U.K., but without the obligation to register in the U.K. Whether the ship can be registered abroad will depend on the circumstances in which the foreign country allows registration. Although at first sight the option to register abroad might appear to encourage British shipowners to "flag-out", it might also persuade foreign shipowners to base their operations in the U.K. (*e.g.* to take advantage of the maritime service industries based here, such as Lloyd's or the financial institutions). The foreign operators would know that they could maintain maximum flexibility and, by incorporating in the U.K., they would not be obliged to incur the extra costs associated with the British flag. The option of not registering the vessel at all would probably not be exercised by shipowners trading internationally as most foreign ports require a registration certificate (and see further, the note to s.307, below). And, unless the vessel was under 24 metres in length, she would not be considered as a British ship (see the General Note to s.1(1), above).

One consequence of the 1988 change was to remove the power, under s.2(3) of the 1894 Act, to detain a vessel which should have been registered under s.2(1) of that Act, (see the Merchant Shipping Act 1988, ss.1, 9, Sched. 1, para. 1).

A voluntary system presents a real obstacle to maintaining an up-to-date, accurate record of British vessels. This is important for many reasons. The use of vessels by terrorists for gun-running or piracy has increased and it might be vital for the Government to obtain some information about ownership of the vessel. Likewise, fraudulently operated ships could be more easily traced. The E.U. Council Directive 95/64/EC of December 8, 1995 (No. L 320/25) has imposed an obligation on member states to collect statistics on the carriage of goods and passengers by seagoing vessels. The obligation must be complied with by January 1, 1997 and requires collection of data about vessels. Although the Directive is worded in a way which will allow for flexibility in the collection of the data, the existence of a voluntary register does not make any easier the task of collating such information. It is submitted that maritime safety, the preservation of the environment and the prevention of drug and arms trafficking all demand an accurate and up-to-date record of all ships having the nationality of a particular state such as the U.K. It is unfortunate that these particular interests may have been subordinated to a general political dogma requiring the removal of state regulation.

"Genuine link"

It is generally accepted in international law that there should be a "genuine link" between the ship and the state of registry (see *e.g.* Art. 5 of the 1958 Geneva Convention on the High Seas and Art. 92 of the UN Convention on the Law of the Sea 1982). Sections 3–5 and 14 of the Merchant Shipping Act 1988 set out requirements which related to the identity of the shipowner (*e.g.* whether it was a British or Hong Kong company) and the nature of its presence in the U.K. (if a U.K. citizen was qualified, but non-resident there would be the necessity to appoint a representative person in the U.K.). The 1993 Registration Regulations have reaffirmed the 1988 provisions in substantially the same terms (see, *e.g.* Regs. 7–9). It is generally accepted that such provisions satisfy the international requirement of the "genuine link". A "British ship" is defined in s.1(1), above.

British Connection

Subsections (1) and (2) focus on two requirements before a ship can be registered, both designed to ensure that a ship has a British connection. First, ships must be owned only by persons qualified to own British ships and, secondly, other conditions may be included in regulations to ensure that qualified owners have a sufficient connection with Britain. The 1993 Registration Regulations deal with issues such whether a ship may be registered if a minority of shares in it are held by non-qualified persons (see Reg. 8).

The exact nature of the connection that ought to exist between shipowners and Britain is one of some political and commercial sensitivity. The 1988 Act restricted somewhat the category of persons who were qualified to own British ships, mainly by removing or redefining the rights of persons who formerly had rights from the days of empire. A state which enquires too much into the beneficial ownership of corporations themselves registered in that state will not succeed in encouraging such companies to register ships under its flag.

Part II of the 1988 Act was particularly restrictive in respect of fishing vessels. It attempted in s.14 to impose British nationality requirements in order to deter the perceived practice of "quota-hopping", allegedly committed by many Spanish fishing vessels which were re-registered under the British flag in order to take advantage of British fishing quotas allocated under the Common Fishing Policy of the E.C. (and see the General Notes to the Merchant Shipping Act 1988, Pt. II, in *Current Law Statutes Annotated 1988*). In the *Factortame* litigation, the European Court ruled that the relevant parts of the 1988 Act could contravene E.C. law on discrimination against the nationals of other member states and the House of Lords was eventually obliged to declare that E.C. law could give interim relief to override the 1988 Act (see *R. v. Secretary of State for Transport, ex p. Factortame (No. 2)* (C–213/89) [1991] 1 A.C. 603; see also *R. v. Secretary of State for Transport, ex p. Factortame* [1990] 2 A.C. 85). A regulation had to be passed, in the meantime, to give effect to the order of the European Court (see the Merchant Shipping Act 1988 (Amendment) Order 1989 (S.I. 1989 No. 2006)). In *R. v. Secretary of State for Transport, ex p. Factortame (No. 4)*, *The Times*, March 7, 1996, the European Court ultimately held that the U.K. could be liable in damages for its action. The result of the litigation was to leave the nationality provisions of the 1988 Act, Pt. II in some disarray, although the Minister for Transport in London (Mr. Steven Norris) indicated at the Committee stage of the Merchant Shipping (Registration, etc.) Bill 1993 that the judgment of the Court was "currently being administratively implemented in respect of all three registers" (Standing Committee D, March 17, 1993, col. 28). At that stage, the Opposition were concerned to learn the exact approach that the DOT would take in dealing with *Factortame* and the extent to which fishermen would be protected. The promoter of the 1993 Bill played down the quota-hopping problem by stating that there were 64 Spanish vessels registered under Pt. II of the 1988 Act, a total of 0.6 per cent of the fishing fleet and 28 vessels of other E.C. states, with a total of about 0.3 per cent of the fleet. The decision of the European Court in *R. v. Secretary of State for Transport, ex p. Factortame (No. 3)* [1992] 1 Q.B. 680 did not specifically outlaw other provisions in s.14(1) of the 1988 Act requiring, *e.g.* the fishing vessel to be managed, and its operations directed and controlled, from within the U.K. It is still possible, therefore, for the DOT to insist on these and other genuine links with the U.K. Thus, the substance of s.14(1)(b) and (c) have been re-enacted in Reg. 14 of the 1993 Registration Regulations. It is for that reason that the requirement as to "British connection" has been framed widely in subs. (9), so that it may be applied to vessels of all types, whether they are fishing vessels, tankers, or pleasure craft, and to British citizens who may be resident abroad. For that reason, an Opposition amendment in 1993 which would have required an "economic connection" was recognised as being too narrow and was withdrawn.

Qualification to own a ship on the U.K. register: background
Up until the Merchant Shipping Act 1988, the definition of who was qualified to own a ship under s.1 of the 1894 Act had become difficult to operate and was outdated. One of the complications had arisen because of the changing criteria and definitions used in general nationality law as the empire came to an end. The general nationality law, now contained in the British Nationality Act 1981 (c. 61), had itself become very complex as it is used in order to control immigration. At one time it made sense to have a common system of registration throughout the Commonwealth. Thus, the 1894 Act, s.53 enabled ships registered in one "British" port to be transferred easily to another, *e.g.* from Australia to the U.K. The Commonwealth Shipping Agreement 1931 was designed to ensure that registration provisions should be broadly similar throughout the Commonwealth, but it was terminated in 1977. The ability of, *e.g.* Indian or Australian nationals to register ships in the U.K. had long been recognised as an anachronism. Indeed, most major maritime Commonwealth countries operated their own independent registries which did not use the nationality requirement of the 1894 Act, s.1 and often forbade their owners from registering elsewhere. Some Commonwealth countries (*e.g.* Cyprus) operated what were effectively open registers which allowed ships to register whether British or not. There had been criticisms that there was sometimes a lack of effective control by such flag of convenience states over shipping operations run by companies incorporated in them. The U.K. Government had even less ability to control such qualified companies if they wanted to register ships in the U.K. The 1988 Act made two major changes to the 1894 empire system. First, it removed the absolute ability of "Commonwealth" citizens (and corporations) to register ships in the U.K. Secondly, it reformed the arrangements relating to registration in the Crown Dependencies (the Isle of Man and the Channel Islands) and the Dependent Territories with shipping registers (Anguilla, Bermuda, British Virgin Islands, Cayman Islands, Falkland Islands, Gibraltar, Hong Kong, Montserrat, St Helena and Turks and Caicos). The latter, referred to in the 1995 Act as "relevant British possessions", are now regulated by s.18 of the 1995 Act (formerly s.11 of the 1988 Act).

Under s.9(2) of the 1995 Act, qualification is now determined by the 1993 Registration Regulations, which set out nine categories of eligible persons in Reg. 7. In brief, these are: (a) British citizens (see the British Nationality Act 1981, Pt. I), or E.U. citizens established in the U.K. (see Art. 52 of the E.C. Treaty); (b) British Dependent Territories citizens (see the British Nationality Act 1981, Pt. II); (c) British Overseas citizens (see the British Nationality Act 1981, Pt. III); (d) British subjects (see the British Nationality Act 1981, Pt. IV); (e) British National (Overseas) (see the Hong Kong (British Nationality) Order 1986 (S.I. 1986 No. 948)); (f) Bodies corporate, incorporated in an E.U. member state; (g) Bodies corporate, incorporated in a relevant British possession (see s.313(1)) which have their principal place of business in the U.K. (and see the heading *Corporate ownership*, below); (h) European Economic Interest Groupings formed under Council Regulation (EEC) No. 2137/85 and registered in the U.K.

Since the 1988 reforms, therefore, Commonwealth citizens are only precluded from registering *directly* on the general U.K. register if they do not fit in any of the categories listed above. The Government was anxious not to preclude foreign investment in British shipping. Apart from the ability of E.U. corporations to register ships in the U.K., any foreign company (including Commonwealth companies) could incorporate a subsidiary in the U.K. *or* relevant British possession and obtain eligibility in the U.K. In some cases where the applicant for registration is resident abroad, there may be a requirement to appoint a representative person under Pt. V of the 1993 Registration Regulations (and see below). It should also be noted that the original Merchant Shipping Bill 1988 required a ship to be *wholly* owned by qualified persons. Following representations made during the passage of that Bill, ss.3 and 4 of the 1988 Act were altered to allow unqualified persons (including Commonwealth citizens and companies) to have minority interests. That position is now continued in Reg. 8 of the 1993 Registration Regulations. Commonwealth citizens are entitled to register ships on the Small Ships Register (see Reg. 89 of the 1993 Registration Regulations).

Majority ownership
Under the 1894 Act, ss.1 and 21, the sale of only one of the 64 shares in a ship to a foreigner would disqualify a vessel from British registration. This was unfair, as a minority shareholder could dispose of his share to a foreigner and thus determine the eligibility of the vessel to be registered in Britain. On balance the 1981 Consultative Document considered that the advantages of clarity under the old system outweighed any possible advantages. This view was endorsed in the 1984 Consultative Document and was reproduced in the Merchant Shipping Bill 1988, as introduced in the House of Lords, which required that the ship should be *wholly* owned by qualified persons. In the Committee Stage in the Lords the relevant provisions were amended so that a ship could be registered as British if a *majority* interest in the ship was owned by a qualified person who was resident. Regulation 7(2) of the 1993 Registration Regulations now makes it clear that a person can still be the owner of a U.K. registered ship (although not personally qualified) if he has a minority interest in the ship where the majority owners are qualified, as defined in Reg. 8.

Individual ownership and residence
Under the 1894 Act, a British subject was entitled to register a ship as British wherever he lived, even if he was permanently resident or domiciled overseas. In its Consultative Document in 1981 the Department of Transport concluded that, although this presented theoretical enforcement difficulties, it was not a real problem because of the fact that very few individuals owned merchant ships. As it did not want to encourage non-resident British nationals to use open registers it proposed to continue to offer registration facilities to British nationals wherever they resided. Section 4 of the 1988 Act introduced the important concept of "representative person", which was an important new principle which aimed to ensure that there was someone in the country who could represent the owner. The concept has been retained in the scheme now applicable under the 1995 Act, but the detail is to be found in Pt. V of the 1993 Registration Regulations (and in Regs. 8 and 14). So if a British citizen had a majority interest in a ship, and a U.S. citizen a minority interest, the ship could still be registered in the U.K., although for larger ships the British citizen would have to be a U.K. resident or appoint a representative person (see Reg. 8).

Corporate Ownership
Corporations within Reg. 7(1)(f)–(h) of the 1993 Registration Regulations are entitled to own British ships, but the policy question when prescribing eligibility for registration was whether the beneficial interests in a corporation should be owned (wholly or substantially) by British citizens (or other persons qualified within what is now Reg. 7). The 1894 Act, s.1 had two simple requirements: that the body corporate was "established under and subject to the laws of some part of H.M. dominions" and that it had its "principal place of business in those dominions". This meant that multi-nationals (such as oil majors like Esso and Shell) and other well established companies could operate from U.K. subsidiaries and own British ships. At the Committee stage of the Merchant Shipping Bill 1988 in the House of Lords, the Government resisted an amendment which would have introduced a requirement of "genuine and substantial connection with the U.K." similar to that which appeared as s.14(3) of the 1988 Act (now Reg. 14(1) of the 1993 Registration Regulations) in relation to fishing vessels.
Residence is relevant to the question of whether a representative person must be appointed under what are now Regs. 8 and 14 of the 1993 Registration Regulations (formerly s.5 of the 1988 Act). Under Reg. 9(b) of the 1993 Registration Regulations a body corporate is treated as *resident* in the U.K. if it is incorporated in a member state and has a principal place of business in the U.K. Section 4(7)(b) of the 1988 Act had a narrower definition of residence which related to U.K. corporations having their principal place of business in the U.K., but this definition was predicated upon the (pre-*Factortame*) qualifications for ownership set out in s.3(1) of the 1988 Act, which did not allow for E.C. corporations to own British ships. The only companies incorporated overseas which were qualified under the 1988 Act, s.3(1)(f) were those in Crown Dependencies or Dependent Territories ("relevant British possessions", in the language of the 1995 Act). Regulation 7(1)(g) of the 1993 Registration Regulations still requires that such corporations have their "principal place of business in the U.K. or in any such possession". The 1981 Consultative Document had assumed that this requirement was meant to deal with situations where the real operations and direction of a business were located overseas in a state which had no connection with the U.K. (and see *The Polzeath* [1916] P. 241). It recognised that the phrase was imprecise, but was unable to suggest a formula that would not deter foreign investors. It floated, without any great enthusiasm, the possibility of listing some relevant criteria to assist in interpretation, *e.g.* where the management decisions were taken as to day to day decisions on

commercial and operational matters, or whether the company paid U.K. tax. Neither of these suggestions were taken up in the 1988 Act or the 1993 Registration Regulations.

Refusal and termination of registration

Under ss.6, 7, 15 and 16 of the Merchant Shipping Act 1988 the Secretary of State was given the power to refuse to register a ship, or to direct its removal from the register. Subsection (3) reproduces similar powers, which are filled out by Regs. 36 and 56 of the 1993 Registration Regulations issued under s.10. The registrar is given a discretion, but the cases in which it will be exercised are fairly well known and are indicated by the reference to the "relevant requirements of the Act", as defined in subs. (8). These relate to safety and pollution requirements, *e.g.* that the ship does not have the relevant certification under international Conventions such as MARPOL 1973/78 (as amended) or SOLAS 1974 (as amended) which indicate that it has been regularly surveyed and poses no hazard to human safety or to the environment. However, the DOT (through the promoter of the 1993 Bill) resisted any attempt to add "passengers" to the list of persons mentioned in subs. (8)(b), apparently because the provision was merely meant to replicate s.6(3) of the Merchant Shipping Act 1988 (with which it is broadly comparable): see also the General Note to s.17(9), below. Further powers to allow deregistration are provided for in s.10(2)(j), but it is not clear if these are subject to an implied limitation in s.9(3) (arising from the matters specifically listed in subs. (8)). It does seem curious that a registrar could refuse to register a ship that had unsafe working conditions for the crew, but not a ship which was unsafe for passengers (such as the ferry *Celtic Pride* whose defective sewerage system allegedly caused the death of two children in August 1992). Subsection (8) is specific in its reference to the 1995 Act requirements, so *other* legislation applying to ships (*e.g.* relating to taxation of seafarers) need not be complied with before an application can be made to register (*cf.* s.17(6)(b) and (c), below). Registration may also be terminated under subs. (3) where a ship ceases to be owned by a qualified person, *e.g.* where it is sold to a company seated abroad.

Subsection (4) repeats a discretion granted by s.14(4) of the 1988 Act whereby the Secretary of State was entitled to grant a dispensation for a fishing vessel to be registered even where its owners did not pass the relevant eligibility tests. Regulation 15 of the 1993 Registration Regulations provides the conditions under which such a dispensation may be granted. An example of a case where such discretion might be exercised would be where a non-E.C. citizen had been resident and fishing in the U.K. for some time and it would cause hardship to refuse registration. Apparently, only 13 such dispensations had been given between 1988–1993.

Subsection (5) deals with a related matter, namely that of the practical problems occurring when a ship transfers from a foreign registry to the British register. In practice, it may not always be technically possible to make deregistration abroad a pre-condition of entry onto the U.K. register, as there may be delays in communications with foreign administrations. The 1988 Act, s.9 accordingly introduced a duty on the shipowner to take all reasonable measures to secure deregistration abroad and subs. (5) is to similar effect. Section 17(5) now makes specific provision, in one particular instance, for the possibility of simultaneous registration in the registries of two states, namely where a ship is allowed to be entered in the U.K. register by a bareboat charterer. The requirement of subs. (5) does not apply where the ship is transferred from one of the British possessions, such as Jersey or Hong Kong (see subs. (6)).

Subsection (7) sets out the appropriate fine for failing to comply with subs. (5), according to the standard scale set out in s.37 of the Criminal Justice Act 1982 (c. 48) (as amended), currently £500.

For the powers of the Secretary of State to make delegated legislation, such as regulations, see s.306, below.

Registration regulations

10.—(1) The Secretary of State shall by regulations (to be known as registration regulations) make provision for and in connection with the registration of ships as British ships.

(2) Without prejudice to the generality of subsection (1) above, registration regulations may, in particular, make provision with respect to any of the following matters—

(a) the persons by whom and the manner in which applications in connection with registration are to be made;

(b) the information and evidence (including declarations of British connection) to be provided in connection with such applications and such supplementary information or evidence as may be required by any specified authority;

(c) the shares in the property in, and the numbers of owners (including joint owners) of, a ship permitted for the purposes of registration and the persons required or permitted to be registered in respect of a ship or to be so registered in specified circumstances;

(d) the issue of certificates (including provisional certificates) of registration, their production and surrender;

(e) restricting and regulating the names of ships registered or to be registered;

(f) the marking of ships registered or to be registered, including marks for identifying the port to which a ship is to be treated as belonging;

(g) the period for which registration is to remain effective without renewal;

(h) the production to the registrar of declarations of British connection or other information relating thereto, as respects registered ships, at specified intervals or at his request;

(i) the survey and inspection of ships registered or to be registered and the recording of their tonnage as ascertained (or re-ascertained) under the tonnage regulations;

(j) the refusal, suspension and termination of registration in specified circumstances;

(k) matters arising out of the expiration, suspension or termination of registration (including the removal of marks and the cancellation of certificates);

(l) the charging of fees in connection with registration or registered ships;

(m) the transfer of the registration of ships to and from the register from and to registers or corresponding records in countries other than the United Kingdom;

(n) inspection of the register;

(o) any other matter which is authorised or required by this Part to be prescribed in registration regulations;

but no provision determining, or providing for determining, the fees to be charged or prescribing any arrangements for their determination by other persons; shall be made without the approval of the Treasury.

(3) Registration regulations may—

(a) make different provision for different classes or descriptions of ships and for different circumstances;

(b) without prejudice to paragraph (a) above, make provision for the granting of exemptions or dispensations by the Secretary of State from specified requirements of the regulations, subject to such conditions (if any) as he thinks fit to impose; and

(c) make such transitional, incidental or supplementary provision as appears to the Secretary of State to be necessary or expedient, including provision authorising investigations and conferring powers of inspection for verifying the British connection of a ship.

(4) Registration regulations—

(a) may make provision for the registration of any class or description of ships to be such as to exclude the application of the private law provisions for registered ships and, if they do, may regulate the transfer, transmission or mortgaging of ships of the class or description so excluded;

(b) may make provision for any matter which is authorised or required by those provisions to be prescribed by registration regulations; and

(c) shall make provision precluding notice of any trust being entered in the register or being receivable by the registrar except as respects specified classes or descriptions of ships or in specified circumstances.

(5) Registration regulations may create offences subject to the limitation that no offence shall be punishable with imprisonment or punishable on summary conviction with a fine exceeding level 5 on the standard scale.

(6) Registration regulations may provide for—

(a) the approval of forms by the Secretary of State; and

(b) the discharge of specified functions by specified authorities or persons.

(7) Registration regulations may provide for any of their provisions to extend to places outside the United Kingdom.

(8) Any document purporting to be a copy of any information contained in an entry in the register and to be certified as a true copy by the registrar shall be evidence (and, in Scotland, sufficient evidence) of the matters stated in the document.

(9) Registration regulations may provide that any reference in any other Act or in any instrument made under any other Act to the port of registry or the port to which a ship belongs shall be construed as a reference to the port identified by the marks required for the purpose by registration regulations.

DEFINITIONS

"British connection": ss.9(9) and 313(1).
"British ship": ss.1(1) and 313(1).
"declaration of British connection": s.9(9).
"person": Interpretation Act 1978, Sched. 1.
"port": s.313(1).
"private law provisions for registered ships": ss.16 and 23(1).
"register": ss.23(1) and 313(1).
"registered": ss.23(1) and 313(1).
"registrar": ss.23(1) and 313(1).
"registration regulations": ss.10 and 313(1).
"Secretary of State": Interpretation Act 1978, Sched. 1.
"ship": s.313(1).
"standard scale": Criminal Justice Act 1982, s.37.
"tonnage regulations": ss.19(1) and 313(1).
"Treasury, the": Interpretation Act 1978, Sched. 1.
"United Kingdom": Interpretation Act 1978, Sched. 1.

GENERAL NOTE

[Derivation: Merchant Shipping (Registration, etc.) Act 1993, s.3(1)–(7), (9).]

The DOT/GCBS 1990 Report, para. 3.12, noted that changes to registration requirements always required amendment of the Merchant Shipping Acts. By contrast, aircraft registration requirements have been promulgated through delegated legislation, namely Air Navigation Orders made under the Civil Aviation Act 1982. It was said that "this is a more flexible arrangement which allows technical changes to be made quickly in response to modern developments and practice" (*ibid.*). Admittedly, it is inconvenient to the DOT to have to fight for Parliamentary time for technical changes. However, some changes to registration law have been politically sensitive, *e.g.* where centralisation has been seen to affect local fishing interests, and registration rules are often related to issues such as manning and labour costs. It might be thought that a movement towards the use of delegated legislation also removes possibilities for political opposition to market oriented policies favoured by shipowners. On balance, though, the lack of Parliamentary time for merchant shipping matters, and the relatively technical nature of the subject matter, of registration probably justify the approach taken by s.10, which gives effect to the DOT/GCBS recommendations.

Part II of the Merchant Shipping Act 1988 had already removed most of the detailed requirements for fishing vessels from the body of that Act to Sched. 2. The process simply moved a stage further in the 1993 Act and s.10 of the 1995 Act removes from the 1995 Act itself altogether the detailed registration requirements for all ships and puts them into the 1993 Registration Regulations.

Subss. (2), (6), (7)

Subsection (2) outlines the general scope of the Registration Regulations, without in any way limiting the general rule-making power (subject, perhaps to the comments made in relation to s.9(4), above). Most of the matters listed were already established features of the ship registration system (*cf.* Sched. 2, para. 2 of the 1988 Act) and do not call for separate comment. In

1993, the DOT indicated, however, that innovations were contemplated, *e.g.* by the introduction (under s.10(2)(g)) of a finite five year registration period for all vessels (see now Reg. 39 of the 1993 Registration Regulations). As already noted, the practice under the 1894 Act allowed for there to be a large number of "ports of registry", *e.g.* Southampton, London *etc.*, in which all the records for a ship were kept. Ships traditionally bore the name of this port on their sterns and there was a certain sentimental attachment to the practice. The centralisation of the registry, and its computerisation, meant that there ceased to be separate registries, as such. However, s.10(2) (f) envisaged that registration regulations would allow applicants to choose a port to which the ship belongs. Regulation 31 of the 1993 Registration Regulations now allows an applicant to indicate, and the registrar to allocate, the port of choice. The "belonging" would seem to have no other legal significance for registration purposes than the fact that the ship must be marked according to the choice (see Sched. 3 of the 1993 Registration Regulations). According to subs. (9), the registration regulations may provide that references in other legislation to the traditional port of registry, or the port to which a ship belongs, are to be construed as referring to the port indicated by the marking on the ship. Subsection (6)(a) allows for the approval by the Secretary of State of standard forms, *e.g.* mortgages and bills of sale (see Sched. 1, paras. 2 and 7). Subsection (6)(b) seems to overlap with s.8(3), above, in that it allows for the delegation of functions. It seems that regulations may provide for the privatisation of certain parts of the registrar's work, such as inspections or the maintenance of computerised records. Subsection (7) allows regulations to extend to places outside the U.K. to deal with circumstances where, *e.g.* provisional certificates are granted at ports outside the U.K.

Subs. (3)

Subsection (3) contains ancillary provisions which preserve the general flexibility of the powers granted by subs. (1). As the register, established under the 1993 Registration Regulations, is divided into separate Parts, the subsection permits different requirements for each Part. Exemptions may also be granted. Powers of inspection are granted by para. (c) in order to check whether a shipowner has the necessary British connection required by s.9. Presumably, an inspector may be empowered to check whether a fishing vessel is effectively controlled and managed from the U.K., as required by Reg. 14(1) of the 1993 Registration Regulations. It is clear that the work of surveying and inspecting under subs. (2)(i) may be sub-contracted to the private sector and much work is already delegated to classification societies such as Lloyd's Register of Shipping. As noted, from April 1, 1994 the Surveyor-General's Department has become the Maritime Safety Agency.

Subs. (4)

Subsection (4) is an important provision for those interested in the private law aspects of shipping registration. The small ships register under the Merchant Shipping Act 1983 was not a "title" register: that is, it did not contain any proof of title and did not allow for mortgages to be registered. Owners of pleasure craft, and lenders to such owners, were obliged to seek an entry on the full 1894 Act, Pt. I register if they wanted recognition of such private law rights. Full registration may impose too many burdens for the comparatively small sums involved and the subsection allows for the register to exclude the "private law provisions for registered ships", as defined in ss.23 and 16, below. In fact, Reg. 91 of the 1993 Registration Regulations does exclude the operation of Sched. 1 of the 1995 Act to small ships, thus preserving the previous position. Note that para. (a) does allow the regulations specifically to deal with the transfer or transmission of such ships (*e.g.* by sale or inheritance) or for their mortgaging (*cf.* ss.31–38, 1894 Act), although it does not appear that any such provision has been made in the 1993 Registration Regulations. Paragraph (c) enables a provision to re-enact substantially s.56 of the 1894 Act, although that section contains an absolute prohibition on trusts being entered in the register, while the new provision retains the flexibility of allowing such entries in circumstances to be defined. Regulation 6 of the 1993 Registration Regulations currently provides that no trust, express or implied or constructive may be registered.

Subs. (5)

Subsection (5) allows for the creation of offences and the current level of fine under the Criminal Justice Act 1982 is £5000.

Subs. (9)

Subsection (9) deals with the abolition of individual ports of registry (see the General Notes to s.8 and subs. (2), above).

For the powers of the Secretary of State to make delegated legislation, such as regulations, see s.306, below.

Tonnage ascertained for registration to be tonnage of ship

11. When the tonnage of any ship has been ascertained and registered in accordance with the tonnage regulations that tonnage shall be treated as the tonnage of the ship except so far as registration regulations provide, in specified circumstances, for the ship to be re-measured and the register amended accordingly.

DEFINITIONS
    "register": ss.23(1) and 313(1).
    "registered": ss.23(1) and 313(1).
    "registration regulations": ss.10 and 313(1).
    "ship": s.313(1).
    "tonnage regulations": ss.19(1) and 313(1).

GENERAL NOTE
    [Derivation: Merchant Shipping Act 1894, s.82; Merchant Shipping (Registration, etc.) Act 1993, Sched. 2, para. 2(a).]
    This section replaces s.82 of the 1894 Act, as amended by the Merchant Shipping (Registration, etc.) Act 1993, Sched. 2, para. 2. For the tonnage regulations, see s.19, below. The relevant regulations are the Merchant Shipping (Tonnage) Regulations 1982 (S.I. 1982 No. 841), as amended and the Merchant Shipping (Fishing Vessels—Tonnage) Regulations 1988 (S.I. 1988 No. 1909). Regulation 34 of the 1993 Registration Regulations entitles the registrar to have the tonnage measurement of a ship verified.

Tonnage of ships of foreign countries adopting tonnage regulations

12.—(1) Her Majesty may by Order in Council make such provision in relation to the ships of a foreign country as is authorised by this section where it appears to Her that the tonnage regulations have been adopted by the foreign country and are in force there.

(2) An Order under this section may order that the ships of the foreign country shall, without being re-measured in the United Kingdom, be treated as being of the tonnage denoted by their certificates of registration or other national papers, to the same extent, and for the same purposes as the tonnage denoted in the certificate of registration of a United Kingdom ship is treated as being the tonnage of that ship.

(3) Where an Order under this section is in force in relation to the ships of any country any space shown in the ship's certificate of registration or other national papers as deducted from the tonnage shall, if a similar deduction in the case of a United Kingdom ship depends on compliance with any conditions or on the compliance being evidenced in any manner, be treated as complying with those conditions and as being so evidenced, unless a surveyor of ships certifies to the Secretary of State that the construction and equipment of the ship as respects that space do not come up to the standard which would be required if the ship were a United Kingdom ship.

(4) Any such Order may—
    (a) operate for a limited time; and
    (b) be subject to such conditions and qualifications (if any) as Her Majesty may consider expedient.

(5) If it appears to Her Majesty that the tonnage of any foreign ship, as measured by the rules of the country to which the ship belongs, materially differs from what it would be under the tonnage regulations, Her Majesty

may by Order in Council order that, notwithstanding any Order in Council in force under this section, any of the ships of that country may, for all or any of the purposes of this Act, be re-measured in accordance with the tonnage regulations.

DEFINITIONS
　　"Act, this": s.316(1).
　　"foreign": s.313(1).
　　"Secretary of State": Interpretation Act 1978, Sched. 1.
　　"ship": s.313(1).
　　"surveyor of ships": ss.256(9) and 313(1).
　　"tonnage regulations": s.313(1).
　　"United Kingdom": Interpretation Act 1978, Sched. 1.
　　"United Kingdom ship": ss.1(3) and 313(1).

GENERAL NOTE
　　[Derivation: Merchant Shipping Act 1894, s.84(1), (2), (3); Merchant Shipping Act 1988, Sched. 1, para. 48; Merchant Shipping Act 1965, Sched. 1, ss.4–5.]
　　This section re-enacts s.84 of the 1894 Act, as amended. It enables recognition to be given in the U.K. of tonnage certificates issued by foreign states, *e.g.* under the Tonnage Convention 1969.
　　For the powers of the Secretary of State to make delegated legislation, such as regulations, see s.306, below.

Status of certificate of registration

13. The certificate of registration of a British ship shall be used only for the lawful navigation of the ship, and shall not be subject to detention to secure any private right or claim.

DEFINITIONS
　　"British ship": ss.1(1) and 313(1).

GENERAL NOTE
　　[Derivation: Merchant Shipping Act 1894, s.15(1); Merchant Shipping Act 1993, Sched. 3, para. 7.]
　　This section restates s.15(1) of the 1894 Act, but uses the language of "private right or claim" (*cf.* Sched. 1) in substitution for "title, lien, charge, or interest whatever claimed by any owner, mortgagee, or other person to, or on, the ship". It is not considered that there is any change of substance, at least to narrow the definition. The section prevents a private claimant from trying to use the registration certificate as security for a civil claim, *e.g.* by obtaining the certificate and refusing to release it until a cargo claim is satisfied by the shipowner. The section would seem to prevent the certificate being detained as part of an action *in rem* under the Supreme Court Act 1981 (c. 54), although if the ship was arrested there could, by definition, be no "lawful navigation". The most usual circumstance where the certificate might be withheld would be where there was a dispute between co-owners, or mortgagees, or where a ship repairer with possession of the ship sought to retain the certificate as part of a dispute with the shipowner about the price of the repairs (*cf. The Celtic King* [1894] P. 175).

Offences relating to a ship's British connection

14.—(1) Any person who, in relation to any matter relevant to the British connection of a ship—
　　(a)　makes to the registrar a statement which he knows to be false or recklessly makes a statement which is false; or
　　(b)　furnishes to the registrar information which is false,
shall be guilty of an offence.
　　(2) If at any time there occurs, in relation to a registered ship, any change affecting the British connection of the ship the owner of the ship shall, as soon as practicable after the change occurs, notify the registrar of that change; and if he fails to do so he shall be guilty of an offence.
　　(3) Any person who intentionally alters, suppresses, conceals or destroys a document which contains information relating to the British connection of a

ship and which he has been required to produce to the registrar in pursuance of registration regulations shall be guilty of an offence.

(4) A person guilty of an offence under this section shall be liable—

(a) on summary conviction, to a fine not exceeding the statutory maximum;

(b) on conviction on indictment, to imprisonment for a term not exceeding two years or a fine, or both.

(5) This section applies to things done outside, as well as to things done within, the United Kingdom.

DEFINITIONS

"British connection": ss.9(9) and 313(1).
"fails": s.313(1).
"person": Interpretation Act 1978, Sched. 1.
"registered": ss.23(1) and 313(1).
"registrar": ss.23(1) and 313(1).
"registration regulations": ss.10 and 313(1).
"ship": s.313(1).
"statutory maximum": Criminal Justice Act 1982, s.74.
"United Kingdom": Interpretation Act 1978, Sched. 1.

GENERAL NOTE

[Derivation: Merchant Shipping (Registration, etc.) Act 1993, s.4; Merchant Shipping Act 1894, s.67; Merchant Shipping Act 1988, s.8; Merchant Shipping Act 1988, Sched. 2, para. 5; Merchant Shipping Act 1894, s.30(3); Merchant Shipping Act 1894, s.70.]

This section re-enacts s.4 of the Merchant Shipping (Registration, etc.) Act 1993 which itself largely reproduced s.8 of the Merchant Shipping Act 1988 (and the equivalent in respect of fishing vessels, the Merchant Shipping Act 1988, Sched. 2, para. 5). Thus, under subs. (1) offences are created if any person knowingly or recklessly makes a false statement to the registrar or provides false information (as to recklessness, see, *e.g. R v. Lawrence* [1982] A.C. 510). An example might be where an agent handling the registration declares that a ship has already been de-registered elsewhere when he knows that an application to de-register is still pending. In a number of respects the present provision goes beyond its 1988 and 1894 forbears. Under subs. (1), para. (b) there appears to be no requirement that the information should be knowingly or recklessly furnished, by contrast with para. (a) and the 1988 provision. Mr. Page, the promoter of the Merchant Shipping (Registration, etc.) Bill 1993, sought to justify the distinction on the basis that para. (b) was designed to deal with the person who arranges for an agent to provide false information, *e.g.* forgeries, to the registrar. The explanation was not entirely convincing and there does appear to be the possibility of a strict liability offence, as Terry Davis M.P. warned at Committee Stage (Standing Committee D, March 31, 1993, col. 74). Subsection (2) creates an offence if the shipowner fails to notify the registrar of a change that affects the British character of the ship, *e.g.* where after a reasonable period of time the shipowner deliberately fails to tell the registrar that the ship has been sold to a foreign citizen or company. A further offence is created by subs. (3) and is designed to prevent the deliberate concealment, suppression, alteration or destruction of a document that might affect the British connection of a ship, *e.g.* where an executive destroys a document which indicates that a fishing vessel is being controlled from abroad. The penalties created by subs. (4) have been increased on indictment, from those in the Merchant Shipping Act 1988, from an unlimited fine to imprisonment for two years. Subsection (5) extends offences to that which is done outside, as well as within, the U.K. (and see s.279, below).

Supplementary provisions as respects fishing vessels

15.—(1) Subject to subsection (2) below, if a fishing vessel which—

(a) is either—

    (i) entitled to be registered, or

    (ii) wholly owned by persons qualified to be owners of British ships, but

(b) is registered neither under this Act in the part of the register relating to fishing vessels nor under the law of any country outside the United Kingdom, fishes for profit the vessel shall be liable to forfeiture and the skipper, the owner and the charterer of the vessel shall each be guilty of an offence.

(2) Subsection (1) above does not apply to fishing vessels of such classes or descriptions or in such circumstances as may be specified in regulations made by the Secretary of State.

(3) If the skipper or owner of a fishing vessel which is not registered in the United Kingdom does anything, or permits anything to be done, for the purpose of causing the vessel to appear to be a vessel registered in the United Kingdom, then, subject to subsection (4) below, the vessel shall be liable to forfeiture and the skipper, the owner and any charterer of the vessel shall each be guilty of an offence.

(4) Where the registration of a fishing vessel has terminated by virtue of any provision of registration regulations, any marks prescribed by registration regulations displayed on the fishing vessel within the period of 14 days beginning with the date of termination of that registration shall be disregarded for the purposes of subsection (3) above.

(5) Any person guilty of an offence under this section shall be liable—
(a) on summary conviction, to a fine not exceeding £50,000;
(b) on conviction on indictment, to imprisonment for a term not exceeding two years or a fine, or both.

(6) Proceedings for an offence under this section shall not be instituted—
(a) in England and Wales, except by or with the consent of the Attorney General, the Secretary of State or the Minister; or
(b) in Northern Ireland, except by or with the consent of the Attorney General for Northern Ireland, the Secretary of State or the Minister.

(7) In subsection (6) above "the Minister"—
(a) in relation to England and Wales, means the Minister of Agriculture, Fisheries and Food; and
(b) in relation to Northern Ireland, means the Secretary of State concerned with sea fishing in Northern Ireland.

(8) This section applies to things done outside, as well as to things done within, the United Kingdom.

(9) Sections 8 and 9 of the Sea Fisheries Act 1968 (general powers of British sea-fishery officers and powers of sea-fishery officers to enforce conventions) shall apply in relation to any provision of this section or of registration regulations in their application to fishing vessels or fishing vessels of any class or description as they apply in relation to any order mentioned in section 8 of that Act and in relation to any convention mentioned in section 9 of that Act respectively; and sections 10 to 12 and 14 of that Act (offences and supplemental proceedings as to legal proceedings) shall apply accordingly.

DEFINITIONS
　"Act, this": s.316(1).
　"British ship": ss.1(1) and 313(1).
　"England and Wales": Interpretation Act 1978, Sched. 1.
　"fishing vessel": s.313(1) and (3).
　"Minister": subs. (7).
　"person": Interpretation Act 1978, Sched. 1.
　"qualified owners": s.1(2).
　"qualified to be owners of British ships": s.9(2)(a).
　"register": ss.23(1) and 313(1).
　"registered": ss.23(1) and 313(1).
　"registration regulations": ss.10 and 313(1).
　"Secretary of State": Interpretation Act 1978, Sched. 1.
　"United Kingdom": Interpretation Act 1978, Sched. 1.

GENERAL NOTE
　[Derivation: Merchant Shipping Act 1988, ss.22–24; Merchant Shipping (Registration, etc.) Act 1993, s.5.]

Section 15 reiterates s.22 of the Merchant Shipping Act 1988. Although the 1988 Act introduced a system of voluntary registration for non-fishing vessels, s.22 of that Act, and s.15 of the 1995 Act, impose drastic penalties in respect of vessels fishing for profit which are not registered in the U.K. or overseas. Not only may the skipper, owner and charterer be guilty but the fishing vessel is liable to forfeiture. Subsection (2) repeats the possibility, raised by the Merchant Shipping Act 1988, s.22(2), of exemption for certain types of unregistered fishing vessels. Regulation 17 of the 1993 Registration Regulations exempts salmon cobles and vessels under 10 metres in overall length (if they are not propelled by engine, or are used to fish for eels).

Subsection (3) effectively repeats s.22(5) of the 1988 Act and imposes sanctions on those who cheat by trying to make it appear that the fishing vessel is registered in the U.K., *e.g.* by painting on a false name and port of registry. Again, in addition to the personal penalties set out in subs. (5), the vessel may be forfeited. Subsection (4) is to a similar effect as s.22(8) of the 1988 Act and allows a 14 day period of grace after the termination of registration (*e.g.* where the vessel has been sold to a foreign corporation for registration abroad) within which there is no offence committed under subs. (3). The period may be necessary where the registrar orders deregistration while the vessel is at sea.

Subsections (5)–(7) repeat the substantial penalties set out originally in s.24 of the 1988 Act. Like s.14(5) of the 1995 Act, offences under s.15 can be committed outside the U.K., *e.g.* on the high seas (see subs. (8)).

Subsection (9) repeats s.24(3) of the 1988 Act and continues the extension of the powers of sea-fishery officers under the Sea Fisheries Act 1968 (c. 77).

Private law provisions for registered ships and liability as owner

16.—(1) Schedule 1 (which makes provision relating to the title to, and the registration of mortgages over, ships) shall have effect.

(2) Schedule 1 does not apply in relation to ships which are excluded from its application by registration regulations under section 10(4)(a).

(3) Where any person is beneficially interested, otherwise than as mortgagee, in any ship or share in a ship registered in the name of some other person as owner, the person so interested shall, as well as the registered owner, be liable to any pecuniary penalties imposed by or under this Act or any other Act on the owners of registered ships.

(4) Where the registration of any ship terminates by virtue of any provision of registration regulations, the termination of that registration shall not affect any entry made in the register so far as relating to any undischarged registered mortgage of that ship or of any share in it.

(5) In subsection (4) above "registered mortgage" has the same meaning as in that Schedule.

(6) In this Part "the private law provisions for registered ships" means the provisions of Schedule 1 and registration regulations made for the purposes of that Schedule or the provisions of registration regulations made under section 10(4)(a).

DEFINITIONS
"person": Interpretation Act 1978, Sched. 1.
"private law provisions for registered ships": subs. (6) and s.23(1).
"register": ss.23(1) and 313(1).
"registered": ss.23(1) and 313(1).
"registered mortgage": subs. (5) and Sched. 1, para. 14.
"registration regulations": ss.10 and 313(1).
"ship": s.313(1).
"this Act": s.316(1).

GENERAL NOTE
[Derivation: Merchant Shipping (Registration, etc.) Act 1993, s.6.]
Section 16 is very important, as it provides for particular private law provisions to apply to registered ships. Until the Merchant Shipping (Registration, etc.) Act 1993, ss. 24–30 of the 1894 Act laid down the procedures for the transfer of, and transmission of property in, a ship; ss. 31–38 set out the rather antiquated provisions relating to ship mortgages; ss. 56–60 set out some equally venerable provisions relating to title, beneficial interests and liabilities of owners. Sections 19–21 and Sched. 3 of the Merchant Shipping Act 1988 contained the equivalent transfer, transmission and mortgage provisions for fishing vessels (and see also the Merchant Shipping (Registration of Fishing Vessels) Regulations 1988 (S.I. 1988 No. 1926)). Schedule 5 of the 1993 Act repealed

these provisions and s.16 and Sched. 1 of the 1995 Act now contain the necessary replacements and re-enactments. The private law provisions of Sched. 1 are not, however, designed to be applied to ships which are included on a part of the register from which, under s.10(4)(a), the Secretary of State has decided to exclude them (see subs. (2)). One such category consists of small ships such as pleasure craft which, under the small ship register established by the Merchant Shipping Act 1983, were not registered for title. Part XI of the 1993 Registration Regulations now sets out a Small Ships Register and Reg. 91 excludes the operation of Sched. 1 of the Act.

The general intention of the new provisions is, for the most part, to re-enact the earlier provisions, although note the changes introduced to the mortgagee's power of sale in Sched. 1, para. 9, below. Some of the more archaic language of the 1894 Act no longer survives. Thus, subs. (3) re-enacts s.58 of the 1894 Act, dealing with the liability of beneficial owners. It provides that a person with beneficial interests in a registered ship can be jointly liable with the registered shipowner for any pecuniary penalties imposed under the 1995 Act (or other legislation) on a registered shipowner. The subsection omits the final phrase of the original s.58 of the 1894 Act which spelt out, rather unnecessarily, that joint proceedings could be taken. Those familiar with the 1894 provisions will have to learn to navigate around the new Act to find equivalent provisions (see *e.g.* the old s.56 of the 1894 Act and Sched. 1, paras. 1(1), 1(3) of the 1995 Act, below, and the old s.57 and Sched. 1, para. 1(2), below).

Similarly, subs. (4) is a modernised version of s.21(1) of the 1894 Act (as amended by the Merchant Shipping Act 1906 (c. 48), s.52(1)). The general effect of the provision is to preserve the rights of the registered mortgagee when the registration is terminated, *e.g.* when the ship is sold abroad and re-registered. A registered mortgage is one entered on the register in accordance with Sched. 1, para. 7 (see subs. (5)). On ship mortgages generally, see A. Clarke, "Ship Mortgages", Chap. 3 of N. Palmer, E. McKendrick (eds.), *Interests in Goods* (1993); N. Gaskell, C. Debattista, R. Swatton, Chap. 6 of *Chorley and Giles Shipping Law* (8th ed., 1987); M. Thomas, D. Steel, *Temperley: Merchant Shipping Acts* (7th ed., 1976), pp. 24–40, 45–47.

Ships on bareboat charter

Ships bareboat chartered-in by British charterers

17.—(1) This section applies to any ship which—
(a) is registered under the law of a country other than the United Kingdom ("the country of original registration"),
(b) is chartered on bareboat charter terms to a charterer who is a person qualified to own British ships, and
(c) is so chartered in circumstances where the conditions of entitlement to registration prescribed under section 9(2)(b), read with the requisite modifications, are satisfied as respects the charterer and the ship.

(2) The "requisite modifications" of those conditions are the substitution for any requirement to be satisfied by or as respects the owner of a ship of a corresponding requirement to be satisfied by or as respects the charterer of the ship.

(3) A ship to which this section applies is entitled to be registered if an application for registration is duly made, but section 9(3) applies also in relation to registration by virtue of this section.

(4) The registration of a ship registered by virtue of this section shall remain in force (unless terminated earlier by virtue of registration regulations and subject to any suspension thereunder) until the end of the charter period and shall then terminate by virtue of this subsection.

(5) Section 9(5) does not apply to a ship registered by virtue of this section but registration regulations shall include provision for securing that the authority responsible for the registration of ships in the country of original registration is notified of the registration of the ship and of the termination of its registration whether by virtue of subsection (4) above or registration regulations.

(6) Accordingly, throughout the period for which a ship is registered by virtue of this section—
(a) the ship shall, as a British ship, be entitled to fly the British flag;

(b) this Act shall, subject to subsections (7) and (8) below, apply to the ship as a British ship or as a registered ship as it applies to other British ships and to registered ships; and

(c) any other enactment applicable to British ships or ships registered under this Act shall, subject to subsection (8) below, apply to the ship as a British ship or as a registered ship.

(7) The private law provisions for registered ships shall not apply to a ship registered by virtue of this section and any matters or questions corresponding to those for which the private law provisions for registered ships make provision shall be determined by reference to the law of the country of original registration.

(8) Her Majesty may, subject to subsection (9) below, by Order in Council, provide that any enactment falling within subsection (6)(b) or (c) above—

(a) shall not have effect in accordance with that subsection in relation to a ship registered by virtue of this section, or

(b) shall so have effect subject to such modifications (if any) as may be specified in the Order.

(9) No provision shall be made by an Order in Council under subsection (8) above which would have the effect of relaxing the relevant requirements of this Act (as defined in section 9(8)) in their application to a ship to which this section applies.

(10) An Order in Council under subsection (8) above may make such transitional, incidental or supplementary provision as appears to Her Majesty to be necessary or expedient (including provision divesting or providing for the divestment of ownership in the ship).

(11) In this section—

"bareboat charter terms", in relation to a ship, means the hiring of the ship for a stipulated period on terms which give the charterer possession and control of the ship, including the right to appoint the master and crew; and

"the charter period" means the period during which the ship is chartered on bareboat charter terms.

DEFINITIONS

"Act, this": s.316(1).
"bareboat charter terms": subs. (11).
"British ship": ss.1(1) and 313(1).
"charter period": subs. (11).
"country of original registration": subs. (1).
"master": s.313(1).
"person": Interpretation Act 1978, Sched. 1.
"private law provisions for registered ships": ss.16(6) and 23(1).
"qualified owners": s.1(2).
"qualified to own British ships": s.9(2)(a).
"registered": ss.23(1) and 313(1).
"registration regulations": ss.10 and 313(1).
"requisite modifications": subs. (2).
"ship": s.313(1).
"United Kingdom": Interpretation Act 1978, Sched. 1.

GENERAL NOTE

[Derivation: Merchant Shipping (Registration, etc.) Act 1993, s.7.]

The general aim of this section is to allow a ship registered abroad, but *e.g.* bareboat chartered to a British company, to be registered in the U.K. The legal effect of such registration will be that British public law regulatory rules will apply to the ship, whereas certain private law rules of the state of original registry will continue to be applied. For example, U.K. law will govern matters such as the safe maintenance and operation of the vessel (*e.g.* ss.94–100 of the 1995 Act) and the foreign law will govern issues such as the title to the ship and the existence and priority of mortgages made in respect of it. Thus, the section makes a distinction between the law of the state of registration and the law of the flag.

Bareboat chartering

A bareboat or demise charter is a contract of hire, similar to a lease, which differs from a time charter in that the bareboat charterer is given the right of possession and control of the ship, appointing its master and crew (and see subs. (11)). Thus, in the Barecon A Standard Bareboat Charter, cl. 8, the vessel is stated to be "in the full possession and at the absolute disposal for all purposes of the Charterers and under their complete control in every respect". It follows that, in law, it is the bareboat charterer which is treated as the owner of the ship *pro hac vice* and is, *e.g.* vicariously responsible for the faults of the master and crew in navigating and operating the vessel. By contrast, a time charterer merely has the right to give orders to the master (employed by the shipowner) in respect of the employment of the vessel (see, *e.g.* cl. 8 of the NYPE 1993 charterparty).

The DOT/GCBS 1990 Report, para. 6.4, recognised that "demise-chartering (with temporary re-registration) has been allowed both "in" and "out" for aircraft by U.K. law for a number of years". The report also noted that;

"U.K. law does not allow a vessel owned in a foreign country but chartered to a U.K. company who acts as the owner (bareboat or demise chartering) to be registered in the U.K. This means that when ownership of the ship must remain in a foreign country to secure or retain the most advantageous fiscal benefits U.K. companies cannot take advantage of the flexibility provided by demise chartering-in to obtain the right to fly the British flag. Nor does U.K. law allow for demise chartering outwards on a similar basis. This would enable a ship owned in the U.K. to be registered temporarily in a foreign country in order to secure cost savings, as an alternative to leaving the U.K. register altogether. The Working Party was of the view that registration law should be amended to allow demise chartering-in or out with temporary change of flag, so long as there were adequate safeguards regarding safety and availability in time of war for ships demise-chartered out." (*ibid.* para. 3.11)

It was partly as a result of this recommendation that the Merchant Shipping (Registration, etc.) Bill 1993, as introduced in the Commons, contained two provisions, cll. 7 and 8, which dealt with chartering in *and* out. The final version of the Bill contained only s.7 (now s.17 of the 1995 Act).

Legal problems with bareboat charter registers

There are theoretical legal problems involved in the whole question of temporary bareboat charter registers, concerning both public and private law (and see N. Ready, *Ship Registration* (1991), Chap. 3). One public law issue concerns the precise responsibilities of the original state of registry and that of the temporary registry. In general terms, it is the flag state which has traditionally exercised control over its ships wherever they are in the world and over ships of all nations when they are in its territorial waters. The existence of dual registration raises the possibility of confusion over which state has the obligation to see that international safety standards are maintained and to ensure that correct operational procedures are followed in order to reduce accidents and pollution. Moreover, one of the criticisms of the practice of flagging-out is that it is merely a device for shipowners to cut costs by avoiding the more stringent safety requirements of states such as the U.K. by obtaining registration in a "flag of convenience" state which has little or no control over the ships which fly its flag.

The UN Convention on Conditions for Registration of Ships 1986

The UN Convention on Conditions for Registration of Ships 1986 (to which the U.K. is not a party) requires in Art. 11.5 that in the case of a ship bareboat chartered-in, a State should assure itself that the right to fly the flag of the former flag state is suspended. It does not say in terms that the former flag state must be notified of the bareboat registration, but this must surely be implied. Under Art. 12.5, the former flag state also has to be notified of any termination of registration: see subs. (5), below. Article 12.4 provides that the state should ensure that a ship bareboat chartered-in and flying its flag will be subject to its full jurisdiction and control: see subsection (6), below.

There are also theoretical problems of private law where bareboat registries are used. The owner of the ship will still usually be a national of the original state of registry and there will normally be loans secured by way of mortgage and registered in the port of registry. Article 12.3 and 12.6 of the UN Convention on Conditions for Registration of Ships 1986 make it clear that the bareboat registration does not affect the existing ownership and other rights set out in the charter contract: see subs. (7), below, on the private law issue.

Bareboat Chartering-out

Of course, where there is an application for the registration of a ship, on the register of one state, to be suspended for a period of time while it is bareboat chartered-out and registered elsewhere, there must be a provision in the law of the original state allowing the suspension.

Otherwise there is a real potential for conflict between the respective national administrations as to which is to exercise supervisory control. Clause 8 of the Merchant Shipping (Registration, etc.) Bill 1993, as originally introduced into the Commons, provided for ships registered in the U.K. to be bareboat chartered outwards, as recommended in the DOT/GCBS 1990 Report. The commercial attraction of chartering-out was that a ship owned in the U.K. might be temporarily registered overseas, in circumstances where cost savings were required, as an alternative to leaving the register altogether (*ibid.* para. 3.11, above). The provision would have allowed for such vessels to remain on the U.K. register for the purposes of private law (*e.g.* mortgages), but for the state of temporary bareboat registry to apply its public law provisions. However, this provision, the reverse of the present s.17, was withdrawn by the promoter at Committee stage in the Commons, following strong representations from the Opposition. The concern was that ships bareboat chartered-out could then be subject to lower safety and other standards. Many so-called flag of convenience states allow for bareboat chartering-in and out, as well as more traditional shipowning states such as Italy and Australia. It is from the registers of such states that ships may come to be bareboat chartered-in to the U.K. under s.17. The original draft of the 1993 Bill worked on the supposition that a state could hardly provide for chartering-in without allowing a mirror facility for chartering-out. However, it was pointed out by the Opposition that there were even flag of convenience states, such as Cyprus, which allowed for chartering-in, but not chartering-out. On that basis, the Promoter was able to withdraw cl.8, without affecting what is now s.17, as he conceded that the shipping companies had not claimed that the clause was vital.

It follows that there are no provisions which would allow the registration of a British registered ship to be suspended so that it could temporarily be flagged out to another register. The DOT would thus continue to exercise full regulatory control over the vessel.

Subss. (1)–(5): Entitlement to registration

Subsection (1) defines the ships which may be included on the register under s.17 by reference to three criteria. First, they must already be registered in another country (*e.g.* Greece). Normally, ships cannot be registered in the U.K. if they are already registered elsewhere (see, *e.g.* the offence in, and General Note to, s.9(5), above). Section 17 creates a special exemption to this general principle (see subs. (5)).

Secondly, the ship has to be "chartered on bareboat terms" to a person qualified to own British ships. Bareboat charter terms are defined in subs. (11) in a way which would include the standard bareboat charters in use worldwide (such as Barecon A, described above). The definition in subs. (11) does not depend for its application on how the contract in question is described, but on what is its effect. Some arrangements may well be described as a lease, or long-term charter agreement, but the crucial issue concerns possession and control of the ship. In modern shipping practice, great use is made of firms of professional ship managers, whose functions may or may not include the hiring of a crew (or the use of a crewing agency to do this). Ship owners and operators are not always keen to make it clear to the outside world where the exact control of a ship lies, partly in order to avoid private law litigation. Although a ship management agreement (such as BIMCO's Shipman Contract) between owner and manager would usually be considered as an agency agreement, some care may be needed to ensure that this is the true legal effect of the contract and that the "ship manager" has not, in effect, employed the crew in its own name and taken possession and control of the ship. The qualification to own a British ship, referred to in subs. (1)(b), will be determined by the registration regulations made under s.10(2), above. The 1993 Registration Regulations, Pt. X have created a new Pt. IV of the register for bareboat charter ships. Regulation 73 of the 1993 Registration Regulations adopts the same broad approach as to qualification under Pts. I and II of the register (see the General Note to s.9, above). For "British ships", see s.8(2) and Sched. 3.

Thirdly, in addition to being chartered to a qualified person, the ship will have had to be chartered in circumstances where it has a prescribed British connection (see ss.9(9) and 9(2)(b), above). The type of circumstances envisaged were those enacted in Reg. 74, where there is a requirement that fishing vessels have to be managed, controlled and directed from the U.K. (as in Pt. II of the register). A further requirement is that in Reg. 75 where a charterer, resident abroad, is required to appoint a "representative person" in the U.K. on whom legal documents could be served. Section 17(1)(c) refers to the requirements being subject to "requisite modifications". This technical reservation means no more than that the requirements would have to be read as referring, in the case of a s.17 application, to the bareboat charterer, as opposed to the shipowner (see subs. (2)). The Opposition failed in an attempted amendment in 1993, involving a more substantial "modification", to insert in subs. (2) a requirement for the use of U.K.-domiciled seafarers. The prevailing view (in effect of the Government) was that this would be a disincentive to shipowners to bareboat charter-in (see also the General Note to Pt. II, above).

Assuming that the ship falls within subs. (1) it may be registered, as of right, on an application being made, subject only to the overriding discretion of the registrar under s.9(3), above (see subs. (3)). There is no requirement to register the fact that a ship has been bareboat chartered to a British company, although a failure to do so would mean that the ship was not entitled to fly the British flag (and see ss.2–5).

The registration of a ship will normally continue indefinitely unless, *e.g.* regulations specify a time limit (see s.10(2)(g)), or there is any suspension (see s.10(2)(j)). In fact, Reg. 83 of the 1993 Registration Regulations provides a five year period. However, under subs. (4) a bareboat registration will terminate automatically at the end of the "charter period". Subsection (11) defines the period simply as one during which the ship is actually chartered on bareboat terms. There could be any length of time laid down in the original agreement, although it would usually be a period of years. The section does not concentrate on this figure as, presumably, the period could include any expressly agreed extension, or any implied extension, *e.g.* where the ship continues after the prescribed period in the actual control and possession of a charterer continuing to pay hire on the basis of the agreement. The definition is sufficiently wide to cover the case where the parties agree to terminate the charter before the full agreed period. The registration will terminate in such a case at the earlier time. More difficult is the case where the contract is frustrated, or where one of the parties elects to treat it as having been repudiated. Where the termination of a charter is disputed, *e.g.* where the charterer denies it has been in fundamental breach or declines to accept a repudiation by the shipowner (*cf. Attica Sea Carriers Corp. v. Ferrostaal Poseidon Bulk Reederei GmbH, The Puerto Buitrago* [1976] 1 Lloyd's Rep. 250), it may be uncertain for some time whether the ship is still chartered on bareboat terms. Ultimately an arbitration award or court decision may resolve the rights of the parties, but there may be a period during which it is not clear whether the bareboat charter has terminated—and registration along with it. It seems that the vessel will remain on the register until a court decides otherwise, or the charterer requests closure. The matter is not without significance, as it ought not to be left undecided whether the U.K. or the state of original registration should be exercising regulatory control. Note that Reg. 83 of the 1993 Registration Regulations provides that the registration will expire on whichever is the *earlier* of the charter period or five years.

The question may arise as to whether the bareboat charterer who fails to inform the registrar of any such dispute can be guilty of any offence. Section 9(5), above, does not really address this issue and in any event is expressly disapplied by subs. (5), but there may be an offence under s.10(2), above if the charterer does not give notification of a change to the British connection of a ship. The problem is that a charterer might argue that there *had* been no change (on its interpretation of the contractual dispute). The "change" would be the alleged termination and it could be argued that it *might* affect the British connection, but may not definitely do so. Section 10(2)(h) does require the production to the registrar of information of certain information "at specified intervals or at his request" and the furnishing of positively wrong information is an offence under s.14(1). Section 10(2)(h) does not seem to have in mind the voluntary provision of information by a charterer arising out of changes between any "specified intervals". Although no doubt an *ultra vires* argument might be raised over the creation of any offence on the part of the charterer, it would be sensible to adopt a wide interpretation of s.14(2) so as to put a continuing obligation on a bareboat charterer to keep the registrar informed of disputes which might reasonably be considered to have terminate the charterparty. In fact, R.S.C., reg. 84 of the 1993 Registration Regulations has clarified the matter by requiring notification of any change affecting eligibility.

Subsection (5) is in accordance with Arts. 11.5 and 12.5 of the UN Convention on Conditions for Registration of Ships 1986 which require that in the case of a ship bareboat chartered-in, a State should ensure that the former flag state is notified of the bareboat registration and its eventual termination. Regulation 86 of the 1993 Registration Regulations achieves the purpose of subs. (5).

Subss. (6), (8), (9), (10): Extent of British control

Subsection (6) sets out the consequences, in public law, of bareboat registration under the section. First, the ship will be considered as a British ship and be entitled to fly the British flag (for detailed provisions on that right, see ss.2–5). Also, presumably, the bareboat charterer will be able to call on the protection of the Royal Navy, in time of conflict, in the same way as with other British ships. Secondly, the whole regulatory force of the 1995 Act, applying to British ships or U.K. ships, will be applied in the same manner to the bareboat chartered ship. The Merchant Shipping Act 1995 and, more importantly, the delegated legislation issued under it, covers safety issues (such as crewing, health and safety, ship operation and maintenance), pollution prevention (*e.g.* through restrictions on operational discharges of oil and on dumping), as well as matters such as casualty prevention and investigation. Thirdly, there is a host of general enactments and delegated legislation which have been extended to ships. This legislation includes general social security, taxation and employment law and security (*e.g.* in relation to terrorism). Such enactments shall also apply to the bareboat chartered ship.

It is apparent that not all of the various enactments included in subs. (6)(b) and (c) may be appropriate to the situation of a bareboat chartered ship. In their application to such ships subs. (8) allows an Order in Council to be made which will either (a) exclude totally the effect of a particular enactment, or (b) make modifications to the enactment. There may be rare occasions where the enactment is totally excluded. The example was given of what is now s.153 which imposes strict liability for oil pollution damage on a shipowner. The section was designed to give effect to the International Convention on Civil Liability for Oil Pollution Damage 1969 which deliberately chose to channel liability to the registered shipowner only, requiring the shipowner to obtain liability insurance, and in exchange it was provided that any pollution claimant would not be able to sue third parties under the Convention or at common law: see Art. III(4) and s.156 of the Convention and Act respectively. It may have been advisable to exclude the application of that section to make it clear that "registered owner" does not include a bareboat charterer, and it is arguable that this effect is achieved by s.170, although it is submitted that this is probably clear from the context. An obvious example of a modification under subs. (8)(b) would be the substitution of the word "bareboat charterer" for "shipowner" in any regulations made under s.117 of the Social Security Contributions and Benefits Act 1992 (c. 4).

One of the key questions in the 1993 debates was whether subs. (8) might be used by the DOT to provide *lower* standards for ships which were chartered-in than for ships which were on the register in the ordinary way. The promoter of the Bill accepted that exactly the same requirements would be imposed on a ship bareboat chartered-in as to any other ship which it is sought to register in the U.K. A certificate of survey must be produced and the ship will be inspected. However, to meet legitimate concerns about lowering of standards, the promoter (in effect, the DOT) introduced what is now subs. (9) at Committee stage in the Commons. Subsection (9) imposes a specific limitation on the Order-making power in subs. (8) by forbidding any relaxation of the "requirements of the Act" within s.9(8), above. It is clear that this is meant to stop the bareboat chartered ships having lower standards than other British ships of condition or equipment, pollution control, or health and safety of those employed or engaged in them (see the definition in s.9(8)). However, the specific reference to "this Act" makes it clear that there can be discrimination in favour of the bareboat chartered-in ships in respect of other legislation normally applicable to British ships, *e.g.* relating to the taxation of seafarers (see the comments on s.17(6)(c), above). It has already been noted in relation to s.9(8)(b), above, that an attempt to add "passengers" to the list of persons mentioned in s.9(8)(b) was successfully resisted. It seems highly unlikely that the DOT intended that lower safety standards were envisaged for passengers, although the restrictive reference in para. (b) is still slightly puzzling. The better view might be that passenger safety is covered generally in para. (a).

Subsection (10), although phrased as an ancillary provision to subs. (8), contains what appears to be a very wide rule-making power in para. (a), namely that the Order can include provision for the divestment of ownership in the ship. The apparent width of the provision might seem to suggest that the DOT could be given unlimited powers of confiscation. However, it is clear that the power must be read in the context of the section as a whole and subs. (8) in particular, which is aimed at modifying existing provisions applying to ships (ordinarily owned and registered) to those now to be bareboat chartered-in. An example given by the DOT was where existing legislation allowed for forfeiture, or for a power of sale to be exercised. The latter can be demonstrated by s.146 of the Prevention of Oil Pollution Act 1971 (c. 60) which allows a vessel to be sold where there is non-payment of a fine for illegal oil pollution. The divestment reference was included out of an abundance of caution, so as to allow such a sale even where the offence is committed by the bareboat charterer who, by definition, is not the owner. In theory, the rights of the owner are protected by an indemnity under the charterparty and, presumably, by its claim to any monies left in court after the order for sale is exercised. The British owner of a U.K. registered ship, subject to a bareboat charter, would already be faced by this risk. Any Order is subject to the negative resolution procedure.

Subs. (7): Application of U.K. private law

Subsection (7) is particularly important to the question of the application of U.K. private law to a bareboat chartered ship registered in the U.K. It must be directly contrasted with the previous subsection, as it provides that U.K. "private law provisions for registered ships" are not to be extended to a ship bareboat chartered-in. At first sight this would appear to suggest that, although public law matters are to be dealt with by U.K. public law (see subs. (6)), all private law question will fall to be dealt with according to the law of the country of original registration. It is not as simple as that for, as is shown by the reference, above, to the application of s.156, U.K. law on private liabilities may continue to be applied to the bareboat chartered ship. The "private law provisions" referred to in the subsection are those defined in s.23(1), s.16 and Sched. 1 to the Act. As can be seen from Sched. 1, it deals with issues concerning title, *e.g.* the rights of the registered owner, the existence of beneficial interests, the creation and priority of mortgages and the transfer of rights of ownership and mortgages. All these issues, which in most legal systems relate directly to the process of registration, will be dealt with by the law of the country of original registration. Matters not strictly falling within the definition of "private law provisions" could be covered by U.K. private law rules. However, there is nothing surprising in this as, under the usual principles of the conflict of laws, the U.K. courts may already have to apply the law of the appropriate part of the U.K. to the ship, *e.g.* where the Commercial Court decides on substantive disputes arising out of the bareboat charter as a result of an English choice of law clause, or where the Admiralty Court applies English salvage or collision law following a casualty on the high seas. U.K. courts are not forbidden from deciding questions of title to a foreign registered ship to which the foreign law applies provided, of course, that there is jurisdiction to do so— again according to ordinary conflicts' principles. It appears to be intended that, for a ship bareboat chartered-in, the existence of the foreign mortgage may be recorded on the U.K. register, albeit that this will be for information only. It must be emphasised that all questions relating to such registered mortgages, *e.g.* as to their priority, will be governed by the foreign law.

For the powers of the Secretary of State to make delegated legislation, such as regulations, see s.306, below.

Supplemental

Regulation of registration in British possessions by reference to categories of registries

18.—(1) Her Majesty may by Order in Council make provision for regulating the registration in relevant British possessions of ships other than small ships and fishing vessels by reference to categories of registries established by the Order.

(2) Any such Order may—

(a) establish different categories of registries to which different restrictions on the registrations of ships in such possessions apply, being restrictions framed by reference to—

    (i) ships' tonnages, or

    (ii) types of ships, or

    (iii) any other specified matter, or

    (iv) any combination of matters falling within one or more of the preceding sub-paragraphs,

as well as a category of registries to which no such restriction applies;

(b) assign any relevant British possession to such one of the categories so established as appears to Her Majesty to be appropriate;

(c) provide that, where a relevant British possession has been assigned to a category to which any such restriction on registration as is mentioned in paragraph (a) applies, no ship covered by that restriction shall be registered under the law of that possession;

(d) specify circumstances in which ships may be exempted from any provision made by virtue of paragraph (c) above.

(3) Any provision made by virtue of subsection (2)(c) above shall be expressed to be without prejudice to the operation of any provision for the time being in force under the law of any such possession as is mentioned in subsection (2)(c) above by virtue of which the registration of ships in that possession is, or may be, further restricted.

(4) An Order in Council under this section may make such transitional, incidental or supplementary provision as appears to Her Majesty to be necessary or expedient.

(5) In this section "small ship" has the meaning given by section 1(2).

DEFINITIONS
"fishing vessel": s.313(1) and (3).
"registered": ss.23(1) and 313(1).

"relevant British possession": s.313(1).
"ship": s.313(1).
"small ship": s.1(2).

GENERAL NOTE

[Derivation: Merchant Shipping Act 1988, s.11; Merchant Shipping (Registration, etc.) Act 1993, Sched. 2, para. 15(2).]

The section re-enacts s.11 of the Merchant Shipping Act 1988 (as amended by the Merchant Shipping (Registration, etc.) Act 1993, Sched. 2, para. 15) and provides the Government with power to deal with registration in the British possessions (formerly referred to as the Crown Dependencies and Dependent Territories) and, in particular, allows for registries in such overseas territories to be sorted into different categories.

Subs. (1)

Until the 1988 Act, persons qualified to own British ships under s.1 of the 1894 Act had the choice of registering in the U.K. or the Crown Dependencies (the Isle of Man and the Channel Islands) and the Dependent Territories with shipping registers (Anguilla, Bermuda, British Virgin Islands, Cayman Islands, Falkland Islands, Gibraltar, Hong Kong, Montserrat, St Helena and Turks and Caicos). One of the main reasons for choosing to register in the Crown Dependencies or Dependent Territories ("relevant British possessions" in the language of the 1995 Act, see s.313(1)), was to save on crewing costs. A further and less acceptable reason was that certain of these overseas territories were perceived to have lower safety standards than applied to ships on the U.K. register and as a result sub-standard ships might have been flying the British flag.

The reason for this state of affairs was that modern international obligations imposed through IMO-produced Conventions require a flag state to support a considerable technical and administrative staff. Examples of such IMO Conventions include the Safety of Life at Sea Convention (SOLAS), the International Convention on the Prevention of Pollution from Ships (MARPOL) 197/78 and the International Convention on Standards of Training Certification and Watchkeeping for Seafarers (STCW) 1978. Skilled surveyors are needed to inspect and certify that ships comply with the international standards. It is unrealistic for some of the smaller territories to support such staffs, especially where the number of ships on the register is comparatively small. In practice, until the 1988 Act, the U.K. Government had left the territories free to maintain a register, but had not extended all the provisions of certain Conventions to the territories. Thus, while the SOLAS and MARPOL requirements applied to Hong Kong and the Isle of Man, they had not been extended to the Cayman Islands, Gibraltar or Jersey. Gibraltar was one of the Dependent Territories which had given rise for concern since, as late as 1987, it had no inspectors despite having around 150 ships registered. At the time of passage of the 1988 Act there were only two.

The 1981 and 1984 Consultative Documents indicated that the Government would be guided by four considerations:

(1) Ships, whether registered in the U.K. or Crown Dependencies or Dependent Territories, should be regarded as British and entitled to fly the British flag.

(2) The criteria and requirements for registering a vessel in the Dependent Territories or Crown Dependencies should be similar to those in force in the U.K.

(3) Appropriate nationality requirements should be made.

(4) Every ship entitled to fly the British flag should meet all the applicable requirements of the international Conventions currently in force along with other requirements applicable to U.K. ships, such as manning. The ships should also undergo all the survey and inspection procedures to which a U.K. registered ship would be subject.

The 1987 White Paper and the 1988 Act broadly followed these principles, although that Act did differ in some details from the 1984 proposals. The first consideration was embodied in what is now s.1 of the 1995 Act. The third consideration is now met by s.1 and the qualification requirements now set out in the 1993 Registration Regulations (see the General Note to s.10, above). The second and fourth considerations were accepted by the Government, although s.18 gives a very wide power to the Secretary of State to make Orders in Council which may establish different categories of registry.

Subs. (2)

Under s.18, the Secretary of State can create restrictions in relation to certain categories for particular registries. The restrictions adopted by the Secretary of State under s.18 will depend on the ability and willingness of the possession concerned to make the necessary administrative arrangements. The 1984 Consultative Document indicated that the assignment of categories would be done in consultation with the Governments of the territories concerned and would take into account the needs of the individual territory, the extent of local shipping legislation and the arrangements for maintaining a marine administration. Consultations in 1988 with the Dependent Territories demonstrated that their Governments were sensitive to international criticisms of the existing system. Many Conventions apply detailed rules only to certain sizes of ships (*e.g.* those over 500 gross tons) or types of ship (such as oil tankers or passenger vessels) and it is possible for certain possessions to restrict their registers to the types of shipping which they can effectively and efficiently control. Thus, in a small territory, small coastal craft could be registered, but not large complex liquid petroleum gas carriers which need much highly technical safety equipment. The 1984 Consultative Document had suggested that the Crown Dependencies (Guernsey, Jersey and the Isle of Man) should effectively lose their separately administered registries and that there would be a "British Islands Registry", instead of one limited to the U.K. But the 1987 White Paper announced that they would be dealt with under the same categorisation arrangements to be introduced for the Dependent Territories.

The Merchant Shipping (Categorisation of Registries of Overseas Territories) Order 1992 (S.I. 1992 No. 1736) established two different categories of registry as set out in a Schedule to the Order. The first category (containing Bermuda, the Cayman Islands and the Isle of Man) contains no restrictions on registry and is for ships of unlimited tonnage and type. The second category (containing Anguilla, the British Virgin Islands, the Falkland Islands, Guernsey, Jersey, Montserrat, St. Helena and the Turks and Caicos Islands) does contain restrictions as to tonnage and type. Ships of more than 150 tons or passenger ships used on international voyages cannot be registered in category 2 registries. Subsection (2)(d) allows exceptions to be made to para. (c) and the Order excepts fishing vessels and local passenger ships, although even in these cases the Order requires satisfactory arrangements to have been made with the Secretary of State in respect of surveying and inspection. There may be exceptional cases where a vessel owned in a British possession with a category 2 register might be given permission to register there. This flexibility has the advantage of enabling a possession to opt for category 2, to save cost, but to have the facility for Convention certificates to be issued for certain of its ships, *e.g.* a single ship which provides the regular deliveries of oil to an island territory. The Order now allows registration of a "ship of such importance in the special local circumstances" that the Secretary of State is satisfied should not be registered elsewhere. The changes to the pre-existing registers required local legislative and administrative arrangements to be made in many of the territories and, *e.g.* Gibraltar, Jersey and Guernsey took powers to refuse registration. Hong Kong has been treated rather differently to give effect to the agreements with China over its future. The categorisation arrangements do not apply to Hong Kong. This is unlikely to be significant as it already has standards as high as the U.K. After 1997 Hong Kong will have a modified shipping register and will continue to be an associate member of IMO.

Where local conditions or requirements change, the upgrading of ports to a higher category could be achieved by Orders in Council. It is possible that the categories of registries could be changed, as the 1984 Consultative Document suggested a third category of ports of registry, *e.g.* all ships under 500 tons (as opposed to the 150 ton restriction for category 2). The significance of the tonnage figures is that the SOLAS Convention does not apply to vessels below 500 tons and the Loadline Convention does not apply to existing vessels below 150 tons. Neither of these Conventions applies to fishing vessels, although MARPOL does.

Although the suggestion that there be a British Islands Registry was dropped it would be possible for field surveys to be carried out on behalf of the local administrations by DOT surveyors on a repayment basis. The Isle of Man has been authorised to do most of its own surveying, except for passenger vessels and gas tankers. Some work could also be sub-contracted to named surveyors employed by the five leading classification societies (*e.g.* Lloyd's Register of Shipping).

Subs. (3)

Subsection (3) is a saving for local legislation which may restrict further, but not increase, the possibilities of registration.

Subs. (4)

For the powers of the Secretary of State to make delegated legislation, see s.306, below.

Tonnage regulations

19.—(1) The tonnage of any ship to be registered under this Part shall be ascertained in accordance with regulations made by the Secretary of State ("tonnage regulations").

(2) Tonnage regulations—

(a) may make different provisions for different descriptions of ships or for the same description of ships in different circumstances;

(b) may make any regulation dependent on compliance with such conditions, to be evidenced in such manner, as may be specified in the regulations;

(c) may prohibit or restrict the carriage of goods or stores in spaces not included in the registered tonnage and may provide for making the master and the owner each liable to a fine not exceeding level 3 on the standard scale where such a prohibition or restriction is contravened.

(3) Tonnage regulations may make provision—

(a) for assigning to a ship, either instead of or as an alternative to the tonnage ascertained in accordance with the other provisions of the regulations, a lower tonnage applicable where the ship is not loaded to the full depth to which it can safely be loaded;

(b) for indicating on the ship, by such mark as may be specified in the regulations, that such a lower tonnage has been assigned to it; and

(c) where the lower tonnage has been assigned to it as an alternative, for indicating on the ship the depth to which the ship may be loaded for the lower tonnage to be applicable.

(4) Tonnage regulations may provide for the measurement and survey of ships to be undertaken, in such circumstances as may be specified in the regulations by persons appointed by such organisations as may be authorised for the purpose by the Secretary of State.

(5) Tonnage regulations may provide for the issue, by the Secretary of State or by persons appointed by such organisations as may be authorised for the purpose by the Secretary of State, of certificates of the registered tonnage of any ship or of the tonnage which is to be taken for any purpose specified in the regulations as the tonnage of a ship not registered in the United Kingdom, and for the cancellation and delivery up of such certificates in such circumstances as may be prescribed by the regulations.

(6) Regulations requiring the delivery up of any certificate may make a failure to comply with the requirement an offence punishable on summary conviction with a fine not exceeding level 3 on the standard scale.

DEFINITIONS

"contravened": s.313(1).

"master": s.313(1).

"person": Interpretation Act 1978, Sched. 1.

"registered": ss.23(1) and 313(1).

"Secretary of State": Interpretation Act 1978, Sched. 1.

"ship": s.313(1).

"standard scale": Criminal Justice Act 1982, s.37.

"tonnage regulations": subs. (1) and s.313(1).

GENERAL NOTE

[Derivation: Merchant Shipping Act 1965, ss.1(1)–(4), (6), 6(A); Merchant Shipping Act 1970, s.91; Merchant Shipping Act 1979, Sched. 6, Pt. VI, para. 6.]

This section re-enacts s.1 of the Merchant Shipping Act 1965, as amended by s.91 of the Merchant Shipping Act 1970. It allows the Secretary of State to issue tonnage regulations for the measurement of ships. The U.K. is a party to the International Convention on the Tonnage Measurement of Ships 1969, which entered into force in 1982, but which provided for a 12 year phasing-in period for existing ships so that it became fully in force in 1994. The relevant regulations for measurement and certification are the Merchant Shipping (Tonnage) Regulations 1982 (S.I. 1982 No. 841), as amended and the Merchant Shipping (Fishing Vessels—Tonnage) Regulations 1988 (S.I. 1988 No. 1909). Tonnage is used as a parameter for a variety of commercial and regulatory purposes, including the calculation of harbour, canal and light dues, and the application of international Conventions and national legislation. It is used particularly to assign differing safety and crewing standards to different sizes of vessel under the 1995 Act and statutory instruments issued under it. There are many different types of "tonnage" which can be measured. In outline, deadweight tonnage (DWT) effectively represents the weight of cargo (and stores) which a ship can carry up to its Plimsoll line, as it refers to displacement. Lightweight tonnage (LWT) refers to the weight of a ship, calculated by displacement, without cargo or stores. However, the Tonnage Convention 1969 uses the more normal measurements of net and gross tonnage, which are measurements of *volume* not weight. In very broad terms, gross tonnage (GT) refers to the total volume of space enclosed by the vessel, while net tonnage (NT) refers to the amount of space available for cargo (or passenger) carrying, *e.g.* its "earning" space after deducting the space used by the engines. In legislation it is the GT and NT figures which are most usually used for measuring ships.

For the powers of the Secretary of State to make delegated legislation, such as regulations, see s.306, below.

Proceedings on forfeiture of ship

20. Section 7 applies in relation to ships or shares in ships which become liable to forfeiture under this Part as it applies in relation to ships or shares in ships which become liable to forfeiture under Part 1.

DEFINITIONS
"ship": s.313(1).

GENERAL NOTE
[Derivation: Merchant Shipping Act 1894, s.76; Merchant Shipping (Registration, etc.) Act 1993, Sched. 5.]

This section applies the same forfeiture rules to Pt. II of the 1995 Act (dealing with registration) as s.7 applies to Pt. I (dealing with British ships). See the General Note to s.7, above.

Disclosure of information relating to registration by other government departments

21.—(1) No obligation as to secrecy or other restriction on the disclosure of information (whether imposed by statute or otherwise) shall preclude any of the persons mentioned in subsection (2) below from disclosing—

    (a) to the Secretary of State, or

    (b) to the registrar, or

    (c) to an authorised officer of the Secretary of State,

information for the purpose of assisting the Secretary of State in the performance of his functions under this Part.

(2) The persons referred to in subsection (1) above are—

    (a) the Minister of Agriculture, Fisheries and Food,

    (b) the Secretaries of State respectively concerned with sea fishing in Scotland, Wales and Northern Ireland,

    (c) the Department of Agriculture for Northern Ireland,

    (d) the Commissioners of Customs and Excise, and

    (e) an authorised officer of any of the persons falling within paragraphs (a) to (d) above.

(3) Information obtained by any person in pursuance of subsection (1) above shall not be disclosed by him to any other person except where the disclosure is made—

    (a) to a person to whom the information could have been disclosed by any of the persons mentioned in subsection (2) above in accordance with subsection (1) above, or

    (b) for the purposes of any legal proceedings arising out of this Part.

DEFINITIONS
"person": Interpretation Act 1978, Sched. 1.
"registrar": ss.23(1) and 313(1).
"Secretary of State": Interpretation Act 1978, Sched. 1.
"Wales": Interpretation Act 1978, Sched. 1.

GENERAL NOTE
[Derivation: Merchant Shipping Act 1988, s.52; Merchant Shipping (Registration, etc.) Act 1993, Sched. 2, para. 15(4).]

This section allows for the interchange of information between various Government Departments. Note also s.315(5) dealing with overseas territories.

Forgery of documents: Scotland

22.—(1) In Scotland, if any person forges or fraudulently alters—

(a) any entry or endorsement in the register; or

(b) subject to subsection (2) below, any other document as respects which provision is made by, under or by virtue of this Part (or any entry or endorsement in or on such other document and as respects which provision is so made),

he shall be liable—

(i) on summary conviction, to a fine not exceeding the statutory maximum or to imprisonment for a term not exceeding six months or to both; or

(ii) on conviction on indictment, to a fine or to imprisonment or to both.

(2) Subsection (1)(b) does not apply in respect of actings which constitute an offence under section 288(6) or 300(8).

DEFINITIONS

"person": Interpretation Act 1978, Sched. 1.
"register": ss.23(1) and 313(1).
"statutory maximum": Criminal Justice Act 1982, s.74.

GENERAL NOTE

[Derivation: Merchant Shipping Act 1894, s.66; Merchant Shipping (Registration, etc.) Act 1993, Sched. 4, para. 71.]

The Forgery and Counterfeiting Act 1981 (c. 45) repealed, as respects England and Wales, a number of provisions in the 1894 Act dealing with forgery (e.g. ss.66, 695 and 722(1)). The Merchant Shipping (Registration, etc.) Act 1993, Sched. 4, paras. 71–73 replaced the 1894 provisions with the more appropriate language for Scotland now found in s.22 of the 1995 Act.

Interpretation

23.—(1) In this Part—

"British connection" and "declaration of British connection" have the meaning given in section 9(9);

"the private law provisions for registered ships" has the meaning given in section 16;

"the register" means the register of British ships maintained for the United Kingdom under section 8 and "registered" (except with reference to the law of another country) is to be construed accordingly; and

"the registrar" means the Registrar General of Shipping and Seamen in his capacity as registrar or, as respects functions of his being discharged by another authority or person, that authority or person.

(2) Where, for the purposes of any enactment the question arises whether a ship is owned by persons qualified to own British ships, the question shall be determined by reference to registration regulations made under section 9(2)(a).

DEFINITIONS

"British connection": ss.9(9) and 313(1).
"British ship": ss.1(1) and 313(1).
"declaration of British connection": s.9(9).
"person": Interpretation Act 1978, Sched. 1.
"private law provisions for registered ships": s.16(6).
"qualified to own British ships": s.9(2)(a).
"register": subs. (1).
"registered": subs. (1).

"registrar": subs. (1).
"registration regulations": ss.10 and 313(1).
"ship": s.313(1).
"United Kingdom": Interpretation Act 1978, Sched. 1.

GENERAL NOTE
[Derivation: Merchant Shipping (Registration, etc.) Act 1993, s.9(2), (3).]
Section 23 contains a set of definitions for Pt. II, in addition to those found in s.313. Subsection
(2) is designed to ensure that references in other legislation to whether a person is qualified to
own a ship are consistent with the principles on qualification now set out in the 1993 Registration
Regulations (see the General Note to s.10, above).

PART III

MASTERS AND SEAMEN

GENERAL NOTE
This Part deals with maritime employment issues and is largely derived from the Merchant
Shipping Act 1970, which effected major reforms following the seamen's strike of 1966 and the
Pearson Report on Certain Matters Concerning the Shipping Industry 1966–1967 (Cmnd. 3025,
Final Report Cmnd. 3211). The 1970 Act was subject to a number of amendments over the years
which reflected changes to political attitudes towards industrial relations generally. Some of its
provisions were only brought into force prior to the entry into force of the consolidating 1995
Act. See, *e.g.* the Merchant Shipping Act 1970 (Commencement No.11) Order 1995 (S.I. 1995
No. 965), which entered into force on May 1, 1995 and the Merchant Shipping Act 1970 (Commencement No. 12) Order 1995 (S.I. 1995 No. 1426) which entered into force on August 1, 1995.
The Merchant Shipping (Registration, etc.) Act 1993 repealed a number of provisions (*e.g.*
ss.6, 19, 87) where there was an overlap with existing legislation. Many of the provisions of this
Part create merely the framework for detailed legislation which is to be found in delegated
legislation.
The provisions generally apply to employment on U.K. ships. There has been a major decline
in the U.K. fleet over the years, partly because of the costs of employing U.K. crews. Hence the
provisions of this Part will apply to a declining number of seafarers. Note that the definition of
"seamen" in s.313(2) does not include masters, and references to seamen in the following sections should be interpreted accordingly. It was thought that masters did not normally need the
same protection as seamen, except in certain circumstances (see, *e.g.* s.38(4)).

Application of Part

Application of this Part
   24.—(1) With the exceptions specified in subsection (2) below, this Part
applies only to ships which are sea-going ships and masters and seamen
employed in sea-going ships.
   (2) Those exceptions are sections 43, 46 to 52, 54, 55, 58, 61 to 68 and 69.
   (3) This Part, in its application to fishing vessels and persons serving in
them, has effect subject to the modifications made by Part V and in particular
sections 110 and 112 apply to the exclusion of sections 30 and 31.

DEFINITIONS
"fishing vessel": s.313(1) and (3).
"master": s.313(1).
"person": Interpretation Act 1978, Sched. 1.
"seaman": s.313(1).
"ship": s.313(1).

GENERAL NOTE
[Derivation: Merchant Shipping Act 1970, s.95(1)(b) and s.96(1); Merchant Shipping Act
1988, Sched. 5.]
This section sets out the ships and persons to which Pt. III applies. Note that s.84(2) extends
the definition of going to sea.
Note that Pt. V of the 1995 Act sets out separate rules for fishing vessels.

Engagement and discharge of crews

Crew agreements
   25.—(1) Except as provided under subsection (5) below, an agreement in

writing shall be made between each person employed as a seaman in a United Kingdom ship and the persons employing him and shall be signed both by him and by or on behalf of them.

(2) The agreements made under this section with the several persons employed in a ship shall be contained in one document (in this Part referred to as a crew agreement) except that in such cases as the Secretary of State may approve—

(a) the agreements to be made under this section with the persons employed in a ship may be contained in more than one crew agreement; and

(b) one crew agreement may relate to more than one ship.

(3) The provisions and form of a crew agreement must be of a kind approved by the Secretary of State; and different provisions and forms may be so approved for different circumstances.

(4) Subject to the following provisions of this section, a crew agreement shall be carried in the ship to which it relates whenever the ship goes to sea.

(5) The Secretary of State may make regulations providing for exemptions from the requirements of this section—

(a) with respect to such descriptions of ship as may be specified in the regulations or with respect to voyages in such areas or such description of voyages as may be so specified; or

(b) with respect to such descriptions of seamen as may be specified in the regulations;

and the Secretary of State may grant other exemptions from those requirements (whether with respect to particular seamen or with respect to seamen employed by a specified person or in a specified ship or in the ships of a specified person) in cases where the Secretary of State is satisfied that the seamen to be employed otherwise than under a crew agreement will be adequately protected.

(6) Where, but for an exemption granted by the Secretary of State, a crew agreement would be required to be carried in a ship or a crew agreement carried in the ship would be required to contain an agreement with a person employed in a ship, the ship shall carry such document evidencing the exemption as the Secretary of State may direct.

(7) Regulations under this section may enable ships required under this section to carry a crew agreement to comply with the requirement by carrying a copy thereof, certified in such manner as may be provided by the regulations.

(8) If a ship goes to sea or attempts to go to sea in contravention of the requirements of this section the master or the person employing the crew shall be liable on summary conviction to a fine not exceeding level 4 on the standard scale and the ship, if in the United Kingdom, may be detained.

DEFINITIONS

"contravention": s.313(1).
"crew agreement": subs. (2) and s.84(1).
"going to sea": s.84(2).
"master": s.313(1).
"person": Interpretation Act 1978, Sched. 1.
"seaman": s.313(1).
"Secretary of State": Interpretation Act 1978, Sched. 1.
"ship": s.313(1).
"standard scale": Criminal Justice Act 1982, s.37.
"United Kingdom": Interpretation Act 1978, Sched. 1.
"United Kingdom ship": ss.1(3) and 313(1).

GENERAL NOTE

[Derivation: Merchant Shipping Act 1970, s.1; Merchant Shipping Act 1979, Sched. 6, Pt. III.]

Seafarers in a U.K. ship will have a written crew agreement (which replaced the old ships' articles), unless the Secretary of State provides otherwise by regulations. For the powers of the Secretary of State to make delegated legislation, such as regulations, see s.306, below. Note that s.84(5) allows any exemptions to be subject to conditions. For discharge, see s.84(3) and (4).

Regulations relating to crew agreements

26.—(1) The Secretary of State may make regulations—

(a) requiring such notice as may be specified in the regulations to be given to a superintendent or proper officer, except in such circumstances as may be so specified, before a crew agreement is made or an agreement with any person is added to those contained in a crew agreement;

(b) providing for the delivery to a superintendent or proper officer or the Registrar General of Shipping and Seamen of crew agreements and agreements added to those contained in a crew agreement and of copies of crew agreements and of agreements so added;

(c) requiring the posting in ships of copies of or extracts from crew agreements;

(d) requiring copies of or extracts from crew agreements to be supplied to members of the crew demanding them and requiring copies of or extracts from documents referred to in crew agreements to be made available, in such circumstances as may be specified in the regulations, for inspection by members of the crew; and

(e) requiring any documents carried in a ship in pursuance of section 25 to be produced on demand to an officer of customs and excise.

(2) Regulations under this section may make a contravention of any provision thereof an offence punishable, on summary conviction, with a fine not exceeding level 3 on the standard scale or such less amount as may be specified in the regulations.

DEFINITIONS
"contravention": s.313(1).
"crew agreement": ss.25(2) and 84(1).
"person": Interpretation Act 1978, Sched. 1.
"proper officer": s.313(1).
"Secretary of State": Interpretation Act 1978, Sched. 1.
"ship": s.313(1).
"standard scale": Criminal Justice Act 1982, s.37.
"superintendent": s.313(1).

GENERAL NOTE
[Derivation: Merchant Shipping Act 1970, s.2; Merchant Shipping Act 1979, Sched. 6, Pt. VI, para. 8.]
The Secretary of State is given wide power to make Crew Agreement Regulations. For the powers of the Secretary of State to make delegated legislation, such as regulations, see s.306, below.

Discharge of seamen

27.—(1) The Secretary of State may make regulations prescribing the procedure to be followed in connection with the discharge of seamen from United Kingdom ships.

(2) Without prejudice to the generality of subsection (1) above, regulations under this section may make provision—

(a) requiring notice of such a discharge to be given at such time as may be specified in the regulations to the superintendent or proper officer at a place specified in or determined under the regulations;

(b) requiring such a discharge to be recorded, whether by entries in the crew agreement and discharge book or otherwise, and requiring copies of any such entry to be given to a superintendent or proper officer or the Registrar General of Shipping and Seamen.

(3) Regulations under this section may provide that in such cases as may be specified in the regulations, or except in such cases as may be specified in or determined under the regulations, a seaman shall not be discharged outside the United Kingdom from a United Kingdom ship without the consent of the proper officer.

(4) Regulations under this section may make a contravention of any provision thereof an offence punishable, on summary conviction, with a fine not exceeding level 3 on the standard scale or such less amount as may be specified in the regulations.

DEFINITIONS
"contravention": s.313(1).
"crew agreement": ss.25(2) and 84(1).
"discharge from the ship": s.84(3).
"discharge outside the United Kingdom from a United Kingdom ship": s.84(4).
"proper officer": s.313(1).
"seaman": s.313(1).
"Secretary of State": Interpretation Act 1978, Sched. 1.
"ship": s.313(1).
"standard scale": Criminal Justice Act 1982, s.37.
"superintendent": s.313(1).
"United Kingdom": Interpretation Act 1978, Sched. 1.
"United Kingdom ship": ss.1(3) and 313(1).

GENERAL NOTE
[Derivation: Merchant Shipping Act 1970, s.3; Merchant Shipping Act 1979, Sched. 6, Pt. VI, para. 8.]
The Secretary of State is given wide power to make regulations concerning the discharge of seafarers. For discharge, see s.84(3) and (4). See also s.80, concerning discharge books. For the powers of the Secretary of State to make delegated legislation, such as regulations, see s.306, below.

Seamen left behind abroad otherwise than on discharge

28. Regulations made under section 27 may apply any provision thereof, with such modifications as appear to the Secretary of State to be appropriate, to cases where a seaman employed in a United Kingdom ship is left behind outside the United Kingdom otherwise than on being discharged from the ship.

DEFINITIONS
"discharge from the ship": s.84(3).
"seaman": s.313(1).
"Secretary of State": Interpretation Act 1978, Sched. 1.
"ship": s.313(1).
"United Kingdom": Interpretation Act 1978, Sched. 1.
"United Kingdom ship": ss.1(3) and 313(1).

GENERAL NOTE
[Derivation: Merchant Shipping Act 1970, s.4.]
The discharge regulations under s.27 may extend to circumstances where the seafarer is simply left overseas without being discharged. For discharge, see s.84(3) and (4).

Discharge of seamen when ship ceases to be registered in United Kingdom

29. Where a United Kingdom ship ceases to be registered, any seaman employed in the ship shall be discharged from the ship unless he consents in writing to continue his employment in the ship; and sections 30 to 33 shall apply in relation to his wages as if the ship had remained a United Kingdom ship.

DEFINITIONS
"discharge from the ship": s.84(3).
"registered": ss.23(1) and 313(1).
"seaman": s.313(1).
"ship": s.313(1).
"United Kingdom ship": ss.1(3) and 313(1).
"wages": s.313(1).

[Derivation: Merchant Shipping Act 1970, s.5.]

Where a ship is sold and ceases to be registered in the U.K., the seafarer is automatically discharged unless he consents to remain employed on the ship. However, the protection given in respect of wages by ss.30–33 continues to apply after the ship ceases to be U.K. registered. For discharge, see s.84(3) and (4).

Wages etc.

Payment of seamen's wages

30.—(1) Where a seaman employed under a crew agreement relating to a United Kingdom ship leaves the ship on being discharged from it, then, except as provided by or under this Part or any other enactment, the wages due to the seaman under the agreement shall either—

    (a) be paid to him in full at the time when he so leaves the ship (in this section and in section 31 referred to as the time of discharge), or

    (b) be paid to him in accordance with subsections (4) and (5) below.

    (2) If the amount shown in the account delivered to a seaman under section 31(1) as being the amount payable to him under subsection (1)(a) above is replaced by an increased amount shown in a further account delivered to him under section 31(3), the balance shall be paid to him within seven days of the time of discharge; and if the amount so shown in the account delivered to him under section 31(1) exceeds £50 and it is not practicable to pay the whole of it at the time of discharge, not less than £50 nor less than one-quarter of the amount so shown shall be paid to him at that time and the balance within seven days of that time.

    (3) If any amount which, under subsection (1)(a) or (2) above, is payable to a seaman is not paid at the time at which it is so payable the seaman shall be entitled to wages at the rate last payable under the crew agreement for every day on which it remains unpaid during the period of 56 days following the time of discharge; and if any such amount or any amount payable by virtue of this subsection remains unpaid after the end of that period it shall carry interest at the rate of 20 per cent. per annum.

    (4) Where the crew agreement referred to in subsection (1) above provides for the seaman's basic wages to be payable up-to-date at specified intervals not exceeding one month, and for any additional amounts of wages to be payable within the pay cycle following that to which they relate, any amount of wages due to the seaman under the agreement shall (subject to subsection (5) below) be paid to him not later than the date on which the next payment of his basic wages following the time of discharge would have fallen due if his employment under the agreement had continued.

    (5) If it is not practicable, in the case of any amount due to the seaman by way of wages additional to his basic wages, to pay that amount by the date mentioned in subsection (4) above, that amount shall be paid to him not later than what would have been the last day of the pay cycle immediately following that date if his employment under the crew agreement had continued.

    (6) If any amount which, under subsection (4) or (5) above, is payable to a seaman is not paid at the time at which it is so payable, it shall carry interest at the rate of 20 per cent. per annum.

    (7) The provisions of subsection (3) or (6) above shall not apply if the failure to pay was due to—

    (a) a mistake,

    (b) a reasonable dispute as to liability,

    (c) the act or default of the seaman, or

    (d) any other cause, not being the wrongful act or default of the persons liable to pay his wages or of their servants or agents;

and so much of those provisions as relates to interest on the amount due shall not apply if a court in proceedings for its recovery so directs.

(8) Where a seaman is employed under a crew agreement relating to more than one ship the preceding provisions of this section shall have effect, in relation to wages due to him under the agreement, as if for any reference to the time of discharge there were substituted a reference to the termination of his employment under the crew agreement.

(9) Where a seaman, in pursuance of section 29, is discharged from a ship outside the United Kingdom but returns to the United Kingdom under arrangements made by the persons who employed him, the preceding provisions of this section shall have effect, in relation to the wages due to him under a crew agreement relating to the ship, as if for the references in subsections (1) to (4) above to the time of discharge there were substituted references to the time of his return to the United Kingdom, and subsection (8) above were omitted.

(10) For the purposes of this section any amount of wages shall, if not paid to him in cash, be taken to have been paid to a seaman—

(a) on the date when a cheque, or a money or postal order issued by the Post Office, for that amount was despatched by the recorded delivery service to the seaman's last known address, or

(b) on the date when any account kept by the seaman with a bank or other institution was credited with that amount.

DEFINITIONS
"crew agreement": ss.25(2) and 84(1).
"discharge from the ship": s.84(3).
"paid": subs. (10).
"person": Interpretation Act 1978, Sched. 1.
"seaman": s.313(1).
"ship": s.313(1).
"United Kingdom": Interpretation Act 1978, Sched. 1.
"United Kingdom ship": ss.1(3) and 313(1).
"wages": s.313(1).

GENERAL NOTE
[Derivation: Merchant Shipping Act 1970, s.7; Merchant Shipping Act 1988, s.46.]

Seamen have long been given beneficial treatment and protection in the Merchant Shipping Acts in respect of the payment of their wages (see ss.30–41). Reforms in other areas have often treated seamen as a special case, see *e.g.* the Wages Act 1986 (c. 48), s.30. At one time, wages depended upon the ship earning freight, but such rules have long since ceased to apply. Traditionally seamen were paid per voyage and received cash on discharge from the ship. This method of paying wages was out of date in an age when many workers operated bank accounts and the GCBS Memorandum to the Transport Committee in 1986 recommended the amendment or repeal of ss.7, 10 and 12 of the 1970 Act so that seamen should be treated in broadly the same way as shore workers. Many crew agreements already provided for the payment of wages monthly. The pressure for change came largely from the employers and has to be viewed in the context of the general and continuing representations made to the Government about the need to reduce shipping costs in order to keep the fleet competitive. The rights of seamen were also reduced by Sched. 5 of the 1988 Act, which repealed s.42(2) of the 1970 Act (see the General Note to s.59, below). Repeals of other provisions of the 1970 Act (*e.g.* ss.23, 65, 66) by the 1988 Act, Scheds. 5 and 7 evidenced the wish of the Government to withdraw from large parts of its traditional regulatory functions over the employment of seamen. Nevertheless, the special structure of wage rules laid down by s.7 of the 1970 Act has not been destroyed by any means. In particular, the high interest rates for late payment are preserved (see subs. (6)).

Section 30 is designed to provide a legal basis for the regular payment of wages. It was therefore necessary to deal with payments of wages and, *e.g.* overtime, on discharge. It is now necessary at the outset to consult the crew agreement (see s.25). If the seaman is to be paid on discharge then all arrears must be paid then—described as the "time of discharge". If the crew agreement provides for monthly payment of basic wages they may be paid on discharge or must be paid by the next payment date falling after the discharge (see subs. (4)). For discharge, see s.84(3) and (4).

Where there are "additional amounts", *e.g.* overtime, the crew agreement must again be consulted. If the amounts have to be paid at the end of the same pay cycle to which they relate, it seems that on discharge they must be paid then. For obvious administrative reasons it may be much more likely that the crew agreement provides that overtime is to be paid at the end of the subsequent pay cycle. Subsection (4) states that even here the seaman is entitled to receive his overtime payment at the same time as the wages. However, there is a proviso set out in subs. (5). If it is not practical in such a case to make the payment at that time, the "additional amounts" must be paid no later than the end of the next pay cycle. There could easily be disputes as to what is "practicable", but the amount of time available will presumably be crucial. It was said in 1988 that most crew agreements allow seafarers to give 48 hours notice and that this might not be enough time to enable calculations to be made.

Under subs. (6), late payments shall carry interest at 20 per cent, unless there has been a mistake, a reasonable dispute as to liability or faults of the seaman.

Subsection (10) defines the amount of wages very widely. The shipowner is entitled to pay in cash, but now also by two alternative methods—by cheques/postal orders or directly into the seaman's bank account. See also s.31, below.

The changes made in 1988 may all appear minor, but might have great tactical significance in any action brought by the seaman for unpaid wages. The seaman's ultimate remedy for unpaid wages is to exercise his maritime lien and arrest the vessel. Strictly, the lien cannot arise until the wages are payable. As the wages on discharge may not now be due until some time later, it would be possible for the ship to be removed from the jurisdiction in order to defeat the claims of a discharged crew. Presumably, monthly wages which were wrongly in arrears before the date of discharge would already have given rise to a cause of action. Subsections (4)–(6) are not clear on this point as it could be said that the reference in subs. (4) to "any amount of wages due" is meant to set a date for the payment of all arrears due at the time of discharge and not simply those relating to the last month. In a sense, this is certainly what is intended. All s.30 is trying to do is to set a final date for the payment of arrears after a discharge, with punitive interest rates on the whole of any unpaid balance. What it is not intended to do, surely, is to postpone causes of action for arrears until discharge. If this view is correct, the enforcement problem may only relate to the final periodic payment. It might also be said that British shipowners would be more amenable to the ordinary *in personam* remedies.

Account of seaman's wages

31.—(1) Subject to subsections (4) and (5) below and to regulations made under section 32 or 73, the master of every United Kingdom ship shall deliver to every seaman employed in the ship under a crew agreement an account of the wages due to him under that crew agreement and of the deductions subject to which the wages are payable.

(2) The account shall indicate that the amounts stated therein are subject to any later adjustment that may be found necessary and shall be delivered not later than 24 hours before the time of discharge or, if the seaman is discharged without notice or at less than 24 hours' notice, at the time of discharge.

(3) If the amounts stated in the account require adjustment the persons who employed the seaman shall deliver to him a further account stating the adjusted amounts; and that account shall be delivered not later than the time at which the balance of his wages is payable to the seaman.

(4) Where section 30(4) or (5) applies to the payment of any amount of wages due to a seaman under a crew agreement—

(a) the persons who employed the seaman shall deliver to him an account of the wages payable to him under that subsection and of the deductions subject to which the wages are payable; and

(b) any such account shall be so delivered at the time when the wages are paid to him; and

(c) subsections (1) to (3) above shall not apply;

and section 30(10) shall apply for the purposes of this subsection as it applies for the purposes of that section.

(5) Where a seaman is employed under a crew agreement relating to more than one ship any account which under the preceding provisions of this section would be required to be delivered to him by the master shall instead be delivered to him by the persons employing him and shall be so delivered on or before the termination of his employment under the crew agreement.

(6) If a person fails without reasonable excuse to comply with the preceding provisions of this section he shall be liable, on summary conviction, to a fine not exceeding level 2 on the standard scale.

DEFINITIONS
"crew agreement": ss.25(2) and 84(1).
"discharge from the ship": s.84(3).
"fails": s.313(1).
"master": s.313(1).
"person": Interpretation Act 1978, Sched. 1.
"seaman": s.313(1).
"ship": s.313(1).
"standard scale": Criminal Justice Act 1982, s.37.
"United Kingdom ship": ss.1(3) and 313(1).
"wages": s.313(1).

GENERAL NOTE
[Derivation: Merchant Shipping Act 1970, s.8; Merchant Shipping Act 1988, s.46(a); Merchant Shipping Act 1979, Sched. 6, Part 1.]
Subsections (1)–(3) oblige the shipowner to provide, before or at the time of discharge, a formal account of wages due and of any deductions made. Where there is a payment to which s.30(4) or (5) applies, the account has to be delivered at the later time of when the wages are paid, as defined in s.30.

Regulations relating to wages and accounts

32. The Secretary of State may make regulations—

(a) authorising deductions to be made from the wages due to a seaman under a crew agreement (in addition to any authorised by any provision of this Part or of any other enactment for the time being in force) in cases where a breach of his obligations under the agreement is alleged against him and such conditions, if any, as may be specified in the regulations are complied with, or in such other cases as may be specified in the regulations;

(b) regulating the manner in which any amounts deducted under the regulations are to be dealt with;

(c) prescribing the manner in which wages due to a seaman under a crew agreement are to be or may be paid;

(d) regulating the manner in which such wages are to be dealt with and accounted for in circumstances where a seaman leaves his ship in the United Kingdom otherwise than on being discharged therefrom;

(e) prescribing the form and manner in which any account required to be delivered by section 31 is to be prepared and the particulars to be contained therein (which may include estimated amounts).

DEFINITIONS
"crew agreement": ss.25(2) and 84(1).
"discharge from the ship": s.84(3).
"seaman": s.313(1).
"Secretary of State": Interpretation Act 1978, Sched. 1.
"ship": s.313(1).
"United Kingdom": Interpretation Act 1978, Sched. 1.
"wages": s.313(1).

GENERAL NOTE
[Derivation: Merchant Shipping Act 1970, s.9.]
The Secretary of State is entitled to make regulations authorising deductions from wages, *e.g.* where there has been misconduct by a seafarer. For the powers of the Secretary of State to make delegated legislation, such as regulations, see s.306, below. Note the operation of s.111 in respect of fishing vessels.

Power of superintendent or proper officer to decide disputes about wages

33.—(1) Any dispute relating to the amount payable to a seaman employed under a crew agreement may be submitted by the parties to a superintendent or proper officer for decision; but the superintendent or proper officer shall not be bound to accept the submission or, if he has accepted it, to decide the dispute, if he is of the opinion that the dispute, whether by reason of the amount involved or for any other reason, ought not to be decided by him.

(2) The decision of a superintendent or proper officer on a dispute submitted to him under this section shall be final.

DEFINITIONS
   "crew agreement": ss.25(2) and 84(1).
   "proper officer": s.313(1).
   "seaman": s.313(1).
   "superintendent": s.313(1).

GENERAL NOTE
   [Derivation: Merchant Shipping Act 1970, s.10.]
   Disputes about wages may be submitted to a superintendent for decisions.

Restriction on assignment of and charge upon wages

34.—(1) As respects the wages due or accruing to a seaman employed in a United Kingdom ship—
   (a) the wages shall not be subject to attachment;
   (b) the wages shall not, in Scotland, be subject to any diligence other than those provided for in section 46(1) of the Debtors (Scotland) Act 1987;
   (c) an assignment thereof before they have accrued shall not bind the seaman and the payment of the wages to the seaman shall be valid notwithstanding any previous assignment or charge; and
   (d) a power of attorney or authority for the receipt of the wages shall not be irrevocable.
   (2) Nothing in this section shall affect the provisions of this Part with respect to allotment notes.
   (3) Nothing in this section applies to any disposition relating to the application of wages—
   (a) in the payment of contributions to a fund declared by regulations made by the Secretary of State to be a fund to which this section applies; or
   (b) in the payment of contributions in respect of the membership of a body declared by regulations made by the Secretary of State to be a body to which this section applies;
or to anything done or to be done for giving effect to such a disposition.
   (4) Subsection (1)(a) above is subject, in relation to England and Wales, to the Attachment of Earnings Act 1971.
   (5) Subsection (1)(a) above is subject to any provision made by or under—
   (a) section 31 or 33 of the Child Support Act 1991 (deductions from earnings orders); or
   (b) Article 31 or 32 of the Child Support (Northern Ireland) Order 1991 (deductions from earnings orders).

DEFINITIONS
   "England and Wales": Interpretation Act 1978, Sched. 1.
   "seaman": s.313(1).
   "Secretary of State": Interpretation Act 1978, Sched. 1.
   "United Kingdom ship": ss.1(3) and 313(1).
   "wages": s.313(1).

GENERAL NOTE
   [Derivation: Merchant Shipping Act 1970, s.11(1), (2), (3); Merchant Shipping Act 1979, s.39(2), (3); Merchant Shipping (Registration, etc.) Act 1993, Sched. 4, para. 9.]
   The section is designed to protect seafarers from attempts by the shipowner to abate the wages in some form, *e.g.* by the taking of assignments. However, general provisions relating to the Attachment of Earnings Act 1971 (c. 32) and to the Child Support Act 1991 (c. 48), will continue to apply as to any worker. See s.36 for the rather antiquated exception relating to allotment notes.
   Subsection (1)(b) was inserted by the Merchant Shipping (Registration, etc.) Act 1993, Sched. 4, para. 9 to correct an error in the Debtors (Scotland) Act 1987 (c. 18) where the diligence of

arrestment and furthcoming remained available against seamen, but not fishers, because of the way "earning " was defined.

Note the operation of s.113 in respect of fishing vessels.

Power of court to award interest on wages due otherwise than under crew agreement

35. In any proceedings by the master of a ship or a person employed in a ship otherwise than under a crew agreement for the recovery of any sum due to him as wages the court, unless it appears to it that the delay in paying the sum was due to—

  (a) a mistake,

  (b) a reasonable dispute as to liability,

  (c) the act or default of the person claiming the amount, or

  (d) any other cause, not being the wrongful act or default of the persons liable to make the payment or their servants or agents,

may order them to pay, in addition to the sum due, interest on it at the rate of 20 per cent. per annum or such lower rate as the court may specify, for the period beginning seven days after the sum became due and ending when the sum is paid.

DEFINITIONS

  "crew agreement": ss.25(2) and 84(1).

  "master": s.313(1).

  "person": Interpretation Act 1978, Sched. 1.

  "ship": s.313(1).

  "wages": s.313(1).

GENERAL NOTE

  [Derivation: Merchant Shipping Act 1970, s.12.]

  Where a seafarer is employed other than under a crew agreement (as set out in s.25), there is power to award interest for the late payment of wages.

Allotment notes

36.—(1) Subject to the following provisions of this section, a seaman may, by means of an allotment note issued in accordance with regulations made by the Secretary of State, allot to any person or persons part of the wages to which he will become entitled in the course of his employment in a United Kingdom ship or ships.

  (2) A seaman's right to make an allotment under this section shall be subject to such limitations as may, by virtue of the following provisions of this section, be imposed by regulations made by the Secretary of State.

  (3) Regulations made by the Secretary of State for the purposes of this section may prescribe the form of allotment notes and—

  (a) may limit the circumstances in which allotments may be made;

  (b) may limit (whether by reference to an amount or by reference to a proportion) the part of the wages that may be allotted and the number of persons to whom it may be allotted and may prescribe the method by which that part is to be calculated;

  (c) may limit the persons to whom allotments may be made by a seaman to persons of such descriptions or persons standing to him in such relationships as may be prescribed by the regulations;

  (d) may prescribe the times and the intervals at which payments under allotment notes are to be made.

  (4) Regulations under this section may make different provision in relation to different descriptions of seamen and different circumstances.

DEFINITIONS

  "person": Interpretation Act 1978, Sched. 1.

  "seaman": s.313(1).

"Secretary of State": Interpretation Act 1978, Sched. 1.
"ship": s.313(1).
"United Kingdom ship": ss.1(3) and 313(1).
"wages": s.313(1).

GENERAL NOTE
[Derivation: Merchant Shipping Act 1970, s.13.]
   Section 36 is a rather antiquated exception to the principle that the shipowner cannot make deductions from wages. The section allows allotment notes to transfer part of the wages to dependants. It dates from days when few working people had bank accounts and were unlikely to be able easily to transfer money internationally, or to arrange for transfer to be made from U.K. banks while they were at sea. The section allows the Secretary of State to issue regulations. For the powers of the Secretary of State to make delegated legislation, such as regulations, see s.306, below.

Right of person named in allotment to sue in own name

   37.—(1) A person to whom any part of a seaman's wages has been allotted by an allotment note issued in accordance with regulations made under section 36 shall have the right to recover that part in his own name and for that purpose shall have the same remedies as the seaman has for the recovery of his wages.
   (2) In any proceedings brought by a person named in such an allotment note as the person to whom any part of a seaman's wages has been allotted it shall be presumed, unless the contrary is shown, that the seaman is entitled to the wages specified in the note and that the allotment has not been varied or cancelled.

DEFINITIONS
"person": Interpretation Act 1978, Sched. 1.
"seaman": s.313(1).
"wages": s.313(1).

GENERAL NOTE
[Derivation: Merchant Shipping Act 1970, s.14.]
   See s.36 above. Section 37 overcomes any problem of privity.

Right, or loss of right, to wages in certain circumstances

   38.—(1) Where a United Kingdom ship is wrecked or lost a seaman whose employment in the ship is thereby terminated before the date, contemplated in the agreement under which he is so employed shall, subject to the following provisions of this section, be entitled to wages at the rate payable under the agreement at the date of the wreck or loss for every day on which he is unemployed in the two months following that date.
   (2) Where a United Kingdom ship is sold while outside the United Kingdom or ceases to be a United Kingdom ship and a seaman's employment in the ship is thereby terminated before the date contemplated in the agreement under which he is so employed, then, unless it is otherwise provided in the agreement, he shall, subject to the following provisions of this section, be entitled to wages at the rate payable under the agreement at the date on which his employment is terminated for every day on which he is unemployed in the two months following that date.
   (3) A seaman shall not be entitled to wages by virtue of subsection (1) or (2) above for a day on which he was unemployed, if it is shown—
      (a) that the unemployment was not due to the wreck or loss of the ship or, as the case may be, the termination of his employment on the sale of the ship or its ceasing to be a United Kingdom ship; or
      (b) that the seaman was able to obtain suitable employment for that day but unreasonably refused or failed to take it.
   (4) This section shall apply to a master as it does to a seaman.

DEFINITIONS
"agreement under which he is so employed": ss.25(2) and 84(1).
"failed": s.313(1).
"master": s.313(1).
"seaman": s.313(1).
"ship": s.313(1).
"United Kingdom": Interpretation Act 1978, Sched. 1.
"United Kingdom ship": ss.1(3) and 313(1).
"wages": s.313(1).

GENERAL NOTE
[Derivation: Merchant Shipping Act 1970, s.15, partially replaced (s.4) by s.37(1) of the Merchant Shipping Act 1979.]
The section gives some financial protection to the seafarer whose ship is wrecked or sold before the agreed termination date of the crew agreement. Note the operation of s.114 in respect of fishing vessels.

Protection of certain rights and remedies

39.—(1) A seaman's lien, his remedies for the recovery of his wages, his right to wages in case of the wreck or loss of his ship, and any right he may have or obtain in the nature of salvage shall not be capable of being renounced by any agreement.

(2) Subsection (1) above does not affect such of the terms of any agreement made with the seamen belonging to a ship which, in accordance with the agreement, is to be employed on salvage service, as provide for the remuneration to be paid to them for salvage services rendered by that ship.

DEFINITIONS
"seaman": s.313(1).
"ship": s.313(1).
"wages": s.313(1).

GENERAL NOTE
[Derivation: Merchant Shipping Act 1970, s.16.]
This section contains an important protection given to seafarers, who have a maritime lien for their wages which gives then a very high priority in the event of the shipowner becoming insolvent. The section prevents the shipowner or anyone else trying to persuade the seafarer to give up that lien. Similarly, a contract of employment could not provide that the seafarer will not claim salvage against the shipowner (see *Temperley*, para. 1368). Such an agreement would be possible, however, where the seafarer was employed on a salvage tug, as by definition the ordinary wages should cover salvage services. However, in practice most salvage crews would expect contractually to receive a percentage of any salvage reward earned by their tug. Note that the section does not apply to a master (see s.313(2)), although the master is given separate rights by s.41.

Claims against seaman's wages for maintenance, etc. of dependants

40.—(1) Where, during a seaman's employment in a ship, expenses are incurred by a responsible authority for the benefit of any dependant of his and the expenses are of a kind specified in regulations under this section 5 and such further conditions, if any, as may be so specified are satisfied, the authority may by notice in writing complying with the regulations require the persons employing the seaman—
  (a) to retain for a period specified in the notice such proportion of his net wages as may be so specified; and
  (b) to give to the responsible authority as soon as may be notice in writing of the seaman's discharge from the ship;
and the persons employing the seaman shall comply with the notice (subject to subsection (3) below) and give notice in writing of its contents to the seaman.

(2) For the purposes of this section—
  (a) the following persons, and no others, shall be taken to be a seaman's dependants, that is to say, his spouse and any person under the age of

19 whom he is liable, for the purposes of any enactment in any part of the United Kingdom, to maintain or in respect of whom he is liable under any such enactment to make contributions to a local authority; and

(b) expenses incurred for the benefit of any person include (in addition to any payments made to him or on his behalf) expenses incurred for providing him with accommodation or care or for exercising supervision over him;

but no expenses shall be specified in regulations under this section unless they are such that a magistrates' court has power under any enactment in force in any part of the United Kingdom to order the making of payments in respect thereof.

(3) Not more than the following proportion of a seaman's net wages shall be retained under subsection (1) above (whether in pursuance of one or more notices)—

(a) one-half if the notice or notices relate to one dependant only;

(b) two-thirds if the notice or notices relate to two or more dependants.

(4) Where a responsible authority have served a notice under this section on the persons employing a seaman a magistrates' court may, on the application of the authority, make an order for the payment to the authority of such sum, not exceeding the proportion of the seaman's wages which those persons were required by virtue of this section to retain, as the court, having regard to the expenses incurred by the authority and the seaman's means, thinks fit.

(5) Any sums paid out of a seaman's wages in pursuance of an order under this section shall be deemed to be paid to him in respect of his wages; and the service, on the persons who employed the seaman, of such an order or of an order dismissing an application for such an order shall terminate the period for which they were required to retain the wages.

(6) An application for an order under this section for the payment of any sum by the persons who employed a seaman shall be deemed, for the purposes of any proceedings, to be an application for an order against the seaman; but the order, when served on those persons, shall have effect as an order against them and may be enforced accordingly.

(7) Parts I and III of the Maintenance Orders Act 1950 shall have effect as if an order under this section were included among those referred to in sections 4(1) and (2), 9(1) and (2), and 12(1) and (2) of that Act; and any sum payable by any persons under an order made under this section in any part of the United Kingdom may, in any other part of the United Kingdom, be recovered from them as a debt due to the authority on whose application the order was made.

(8) Any notice or order under this section may be served by registered post or recorded delivery service.

(9) The Secretary of State may make regulations specifying—

(a) the expenses in respect of which a notice may be served by a responsible authority under subsection (1) above;

(b) any conditions that must be satisfied if such a notice is to be served;

(c) the period that may be specified in such a notice (being a period beginning with the service of the notice and ending a specified number of days after the seaman's discharge from his ship);

(d) the form of such a notice and the information to be contained therein; and

(e) the amounts to be deducted from a seaman's wages in computing his net wages for the purposes of this section;

and the amounts specified under paragraph (e) above may include amounts allotted by allotment notes issued under section 36.

(10) In this section "responsible authority" means the Secretary of State, the Department of Health and Social Services for Northern Ireland, a Health

and Social Services Board acting on behalf of that Department, or (except in Northern Ireland) any local authority.

(11) In the application of subsection (2)(a) above to Northern Ireland, for the reference to a local authority there shall be substituted a reference to a Health and Social Services Board and in subsection (10) above and this subsection "Health and Social Services Board" means such a Board established under the Health and Personal Social Services (Northern Ireland) Order 1972.

(12) In this section "magistrates' court"—

(a) in relation to Scotland, means the sheriff court, and

(b) in relation to Northern Ireland, means a court of summary jurisdiction.

DEFINITIONS

"dependants": subs. (2)(a).
"expenses": subs. (2)(b).
"magistrates' court": subs. (12) and Interpretation Act 1978, Sched. 1.
"person": Interpretation Act 1978, Sched. 1.
"responsible authority": subss. (10) and (11).
"seaman": s.313(1).
"Secretary of State": Interpretation Act 1978, Sched. 1.
"ship": s.313(1).
"United Kingdom": Interpretation Act 1978, Sched. 1.
"wages": s.313(1).

GENERAL NOTE

[Derivation: Merchant Shipping Act 1970, s.17.]

Under s.40, regulations may prescribe the extent to which a seafarer may have deductions made by public authorities from wages in order to benefit dependants. For the powers of the Secretary of State to make delegated legislation, such as regulations, see s.306, below.

Remedies of master for remuneration disbursements and liabilities

41. The master of a ship shall have the same lien for his remuneration, and all disbursements or liabilities properly made or incurred by him on account of the ship, as a seaman has for his wages.

DEFINITIONS

"master": s.313(1).
"seaman": s.313(1).
"ship": s.313(1).
"wages": s.313(1).

GENERAL NOTE

[Derivation: Merchant Shipping Act 1970, s.18.]

Under s.41, a master is granted the same lien for wages as a seafarer (see s.39, above). In Admiralty law, the master had no separate lien for wages. It may have been presumed that he needed no protection, *e.g.* where he was a part owner. In the Nineteenth Century a lien was given by statute for both wages and disbursements (see *Temperley*, paras. 1374–1377 for the full history of the provision). Disbursements are those expenses which the master would necessarily incur, usually overseas, on the shipowner's behalf in order to operate the ship. Classic examples would include fuel and stores (*ibid.* para. 1377).

Safety, health and welfare

Obligation of shipowners as to seaworthiness

42.—(1) In every contract of employment between the owner of a United Kingdom ship and the master of or any seaman employed in the ship there shall be implied an obligation on the owner of the ship that—

(a) the owner of the ship,

(b) the master of the ship, and

(c) every agent charged with—
　　　　(i) the loading of the ship,
　　　　(ii) the preparing of the ship for sea, or
　　　　(iii) the sending of the ship to sea,
shall use all reasonable means to ensure the seaworthiness of the ship for the voyage at the time when the voyage commences and to keep the ship in a seaworthy condition for the voyage during the voyage.

(2) The obligation imposed by subsection (1) above applies notwithstanding any agreement to the contrary.

(3) No liability on the owner of a ship arises under subsection (1) above in respect of the ship being sent to sea in an unseaworthy state where, owing to special circumstances, the sending of the ship to sea in such a state was reasonable and justifiable.

DEFINITIONS
　　"master": s.313(1).
　　"seaman": s.313(1).
　　"sent to sea": s.84(2).
　　"ship": s.313(1).
　　"United Kingdom ship": ss.1(3) and 313(1).
　　"wages": s.313(1).

GENERAL NOTE
　　[Derivation: Merchant Shipping Act 1894, s.458; Merchant Shipping (Registration, etc.) Act 1993, Sched. 4, paras. 6(1), 7, Sched. 5.]
　　Section 42 re-enacts s.458 of the 1894 Act, as amended. The latter implied in the seafarer's employment contract an obligation on the shipowner to use reasonable means to ensure the seaworthiness of the ship. The outdated terminology "contract of service" was superseded by that of "contract of employment" in the Merchant Shipping Act 1970, which introduced the concept of written crew agreements (see s.25, above). The Merchant Shipping (Registration, etc.) Act 1993, Sched. 4, para. 7 acknowledged this change (which may have been overlooked in 1970) and also removed a sub-paragraph from what is now subs. (3), which extended the section to all British possessions. Note that the section pre-supposes that there is a contract between the *shipowner* and the crew, which may not necessarily be the case today where all manner of crewing arrangements may be contemplated. The purpose of the section is to give the seafarer the right to damages if there has been a breach of the term causing injury. The section dates from a time when seafarers might have been faced by defences such as that of common employment and has long been regarded as a remedial provision where other remedies (for example in negligence) against the employer are for some reason ineffective (see *Temperley*, para. 353).

Crew accommodation

43.—(1) The Secretary of State may make regulations with respect to the crew accommodation to be provided in United Kingdom ships.

(2) Without prejudice to the generality of subsection (1) above, regulations made under this section may, in particular—

(a) prescribe the minimum space per man which must be provided by way of sleeping accommodation for seamen and the maximum number of persons by whom a specified part of such sleeping accommodation may be used;

(b) regulate the position in the ship in which the crew accommodation or any part thereof may be located and the standards to be observed in the construction, equipment and furnishing of any such accommodation;

(c) require the submission to a surveyor of ships of plans and specifications of any works proposed to be carried out for the purpose of the provision or alteration of any such accommodation and authorise the surveyor to inspect any such works; and

(d) provide for the maintenance and repair of any such accommodation and prohibit or restrict the use of any such accommodation for purposes other than those for which it is designed.

(3) Regulations under this section may make different provision with respect to different descriptions of ship or with respect to ships which were registered in the United Kingdom at different dates or the construction of which was begun at different dates and with respect to crew accommodation provided for seamen of different descriptions.

(4) Regulations under this section may exempt ships of any description from any requirements of the regulations and the Secretary of State may grant other exemptions from any such requirement with respect to any ship.

(5) Regulations under this section may require the master of a ship or any officer authorised by him for the purpose to carry out such inspections of the crew accommodation as may be prescribed by the regulations.

(6) If the provisions of any regulations under this section are contravened in the case of a ship the owner or master shall be liable, on summary conviction, to a fine not exceeding level 5 on the standard scale and the ship, if in the United Kingdom, may be detained.

(7) In this section "crew accommodation" includes sleeping rooms, mess rooms, sanitary accommodation, hospital accommodation, recreation accommodation, store rooms and catering accommodation provided for the use of seamen but does not include any accommodation which is also used by or provided for the use of passengers.

DEFINITIONS
    "crew accommodation": subs. (7).
    "master": s.313(1).
    "registered": ss.23(1) and 313(1).
    "seaman": s.313(1).
    "Secretary of State": Interpretation Act 1978, Sched. 1.
    "ship": s.313(1).
    "standard scale": Criminal Justice Act 1982, s.37.
    "surveyor of ships": ss.256(9) and 313(1).
    "United Kingdom": Interpretation Act 1978, Sched. 1.
    "United Kingdom ship": ss.1(3) and 313(1).

GENERAL NOTE
    [Derivation: Merchant Shipping Act 1970, s.20; Merchant Shipping Act 1979, Sched. 6, Pt. IV.]
    The Secretary of State is given power to make regulations concerning crew accommodation, *e.g.* as to the amount of space available to crew members. Note the extension of s.43 to non-sea-going ships by s.24(2), above.
    For the powers of the Secretary of State to make delegated legislation, such as regulations, see s.306, below.

Complaints about provisions or water

44.—(1) If three or more seamen employed in a United Kingdom ship consider that the provisions or water provided for the seamen employed in that ship are not in accordance with safety regulations containing requirements as to the provisions and water to be provided on ships (whether because of bad quality, unfitness for use or deficiency in quantity) they may complain to the master, who shall investigate the complaint.

(2) If the seamen are dissatisfied with the action taken by the master as a result of his investigation or by his failure to take any action they may state their dissatisfaction to him and may claim to complain to a superintendent or proper officer; and thereupon the master shall make adequate arrangements to enable the seamen to do so as soon as the service of the ship permits.

(3) The superintendent or proper officer to whom a complaint has been made under this section shall investigate the complaint and may examine the provisions or water or cause them to be examined.

(4) If the master fails without reasonable excuse to comply with the provisions of subsection (2) above he shall be liable on summary conviction to a fine not exceeding level 3 on the standard scale and if he has been notified in

writing by the person making an examination under subsection (3) above that any provisions or water are found to be unfit for use or not of the quality required by the regulations, then—

    (a) if they are not replaced within a reasonable time the master or owner shall be liable on summary conviction to a fine not exceeding level 4 on the standard scale unless he proves that the failure to replace them was not due to his neglect or default; or

    (b) if the master, without reasonable excuse, permits them to be used he shall be liable on summary conviction to a fine not exceeding level 4 on the standard scale.

DEFINITIONS
    "fails": s.313(1).
    "master": s.313(1).
    "person": Interpretation Act 1978, Sched. 1.
    "proper officer": s.313(1).
    "safety regulations": ss.85 and 313(1).
    "seaman": s.313(1).
    "ship": s.313(1).
    "standard scale": Criminal Justice Act 1982, s.37.
    "superintendent": s.313(1).
    "United Kingdom ship": ss.1(3) and 313(1).

GENERAL NOTE
    [Derivation: Merchant Shipping Act 1970, s.22; Merchant Shipping Act 1979, Sched. 6, Pts. II and III.]
    Safety Regulations are made under s.85 of the Act and s.85(1)(b) allows regulations to be made to give effect to international conventions. The ILO's Merchant Shipping (Minimum Standards) Convention 1976 sets out obligations in respect of matters such as the provisions and water available on board ship. The Merchant Shipping (Provisions And Water) Regulations 1989 (S.I. 1989 No. 100) gave effect to this Convention and at the same time repealed s.21 of the Merchant Shipping Act 1970 (under what is now s.86(2)) which formerly gave the power to make regulations on the matter. Section 44 of the Merchant Shipping Act 1995 was formerly s.22 of the Merchant Shipping Act 1970 and it allows seamen on U.K. ships to make formal complaints if the provisions and water do not meet the standards in the Safety Regulations. A master may commit an offence if he fails to make arrangements to allow the seamen to appeal against his decision to a superintendent, or if he fails to remedy any default.
    Note that s.23 of the 1970 Act was repealed by Sched. 5 of the Merchant Shipping Act 1988. Section 23 provided for complaints about the master, other seamen or conditions on the ship to be referred to a proper officer (*e.g.* British Consular Officer) when the ship was outside the U.K. The omission of this section, as well as ss.65 and 66, was foreshadowed in the 1984 Consultative Document.

Expenses of medical and other treatment during voyage

    45.—(1) If a person, while employed in a United Kingdom ship, receives outside the United Kingdom any surgical or medical treatment or such dental or optical treatment (including the repair or replacement of any appliance) as cannot be postponed without impairing efficiency, the reasonable expenses thereof shall be borne by the persons employing him.

    (2) If a person dies while employed in a United Kingdom ship and is buried or cremated outside the United Kingdom, the expenses of his burial or cremation shall also be borne by those persons.

    (3) The reference in subsection (2) above to dying in a ship includes a reference to dying in a ship's boat.

DEFINITIONS
    "person": Interpretation Act 1978, Sched. 1.
    "ship": s.313(1).

"ship's boat": s.84(1).
"United Kingdom": Interpretation Act 1978, Sched. 1.
"United Kingdom ship": ss.1(3) and 313(1).

GENERAL NOTE
[Derivation: Merchant Shipping Act 1970, ss.26, 97(5).]
Section 45 imposes an obligation on the employer of a seaman to bear the reasonable medical expenses of a seafarer, *e.g.* incurred away from the ship, during the course of employment contract. Thus, a seafarer who is incapacitated at sea (and perhaps in a road accident while on shore leave) will be entitled to have his medical costs paid, provided that the treatment cannot be postponed. Burial or cremation expenses abroad will also be borne by the employer. See, also, s.53, below.

Manning, qualifications, training and uniform

Application of sections 47 to 51

46. Sections 47 to 51 apply to every United Kingdom ship and also to any ship registered under the law of a country outside the United Kingdom which carries passengers—
(a) between places in the United Kingdom or between the United Kingdom and the Isle of Man or any of the Channel Islands; or
(b) on a voyage which begins and ends at the same place in the United Kingdom and on which the ship calls at no place outside the United Kingdom.

DEFINITIONS
"passenger": Sched. 6, Art. 1(4).
"registered": ss.23(1) and 313(1).
"ship": s.313(1).
"United Kingdom": Interpretation Act 1978, Sched. 1.
"United Kingdom ship": ss.1(3) and 313(1).

GENERAL NOTE
[Derivation: Merchant Shipping Act 1970, s.49.]
Sections 46–57 deal with manning and qualification issues. This section states that ss.47–51, dealing with manning, apply to U.K. ships (*i.e.* those registered in the U.K.) and to foreign registered ships carrying passengers within the U.K. and on excursions outside U.K. waters which start and end in the U.K., but do not call anywhere else. In effect, the section makes it clear that foreign passenger ships which serve the U.K. domestic trade may be subject to U.K. manning requirements. Note the extension of s.46 to non-sea-going ships by s.24(2), above.

Manning

47.—(1) Subject to subsection (2) below, the Secretary of State may make regulations—
(a) requiring ships to which this section applies to carry such number of qualified officers of any description, qualified doctors and qualified cooks and such number of other seamen or qualified seamen of any description as may be specified in the regulations; and
(b) prescribing or enabling the Secretary of State to specify standards of competence to be attained and other conditions to be satisfied (subject to any exceptions allowed by or under the regulations) by officers and other seamen of any description in order to be qualified for the purposes of this section.
(2) The Secretary of State shall not exercise his power to make regulations requiring ships to carry seamen other than doctors and cooks except to the extent that it appears to him necessary or expedient in the interests of safety.
(3) Regulations under this section may make different provision for different descriptions of ship or for ships of the same description in different circumstances.
(4) Without prejudice to the generality of subsection (1)(b) above, the conditions prescribed or specified under that paragraph may include con-

ditions as to nationality, and regulations made for the purposes of that paragraph may make provision, or enable the Secretary of State to make provision, for—

(a) the manner in which the attainment of any standard or the satisfaction of any other condition is to be evidenced;

(b) the conduct of any examinations, the conditions for admission to them and the appointment and remuneration of examiners; and

(c) the issue, form and recording of certificates and other documents;

and different provisions may be so made or enabled to be made for different circumstances.

(5) If a person makes a statement which he knows to be false or recklessly makes a statement which is false in a material particular for the purpose of obtaining for himself or another person a certificate or other document which may be issued under this section he shall be liable on summary conviction to a fine not exceeding level 5 on the standard scale.

DEFINITIONS

"seaman": s.313(1).
"Secretary of State": Interpretation Act 1978, Sched. 1.
"ship": s.313(1).
"standard scale": Criminal Justice Act 1982, s.37.

GENERAL NOTE

[Derivation: Merchant Shipping Act 1970, s.43; Merchant Shipping Act 1979, Sched. 6, Pt. IV.]

Section 47 gives the Secretary of State the power to make regulations concerning the number of officers and crew carried on board ships within s.46, and as to their standards of competence. In particular the Secretary of State may set conditions as to nationality (note also s.51 on knowledge of English).

The nationality provisions have always been very sensitive, especially to the seafarers' trade union, the RMT. The union has always opposed easing restrictions on the employment of foreign officers, although British ships have traditionally sailed with seamen from the Commonwealth (*e.g.* India). Note now, the Merchant Shipping Act 1970 (Commencement No. 12) Order 1995 (S.I. 1995 No. 1426) which entered into force on August 1, 1995. This Order commenced the repeal of s.5 of the Aliens Restriction (Amendment) Act 1919 (as allowed by the Merchant Shipping Act 1970, Sched. 5) which stated that masters, chief engineers and skippers of British vessels have to be British subjects. Members of Parliament (especially in the Government) have expressed concerns about the difficulties of being able to mount another Falklands style armada if all the crews on British ships are foreign. As part of a package to forestall such concerns, the Government introduced the Merchant Shipping (Officer Nationality) Regulations 1995 (S.I. 1995 No. 1427), which entered into force on August 1, 1995. These Regulations require ships of 500 tons or more and fishing vessels of 24 metres or more in length which serve a "strategic function", that is cruise ships, fishing vessels, product tankers and ro-ro ships, to have citizens or nationals of either Commonwealth, EEA or NATO countries as masters. There will be no restriction on the nationality of other members of such a ship's personnel. A further easing of restrictions on maritime employment based on nationality is found in the Fishing Vessels (Certification of Deck Officers and Engineer Officers) (Amendment) Regulations 1995 (S.I. 1995 No. 1428), which entered into force on August 1, 1995. These Regulations amend the Fishing Vessels (Certification of Deck Officers and Engineer Officers) Regulations 1984 and give effect to Council Directive 92/51/EEC and provide for the recognition of equivalent foreign certificates for Fishing Vessel Class I, II, and III Officers issued abroad. They also include provisions to enable such individuals to serve as qualified officers on U.K. fishing vessels in their own capacity. Certificates of equivalent competency are not required until August 1, 1997 by certain holders of certificates issued before then, by countries where certificates were recognised as being equivalent before August 1, 1995. Similarly, the Merchant Shipping (Certification of Deck and Marine Engineer Officers) (Amendment) Regulations 1995 (S.I. 1995 No. 1429) entered into force on August 1, 1995. These Regulations amend the Merchant Shipping (Certification of Deck Officers) Regulations 1985 and the Merchant Shipping (Certification of Marine Engineer Officers and Licensing of Marine Engine Operators) Regulations and give effect to Council Directive 89/48/EEC with regard to Class I Deck Officers and Marine Engineer Officers. They essentially replicate for these officers the provisions as laid out by S.I. 1995 No. 1428 in relation to officers on fishing vessels.

For the offence of going to sea without being qualified under s.47, see s.52, below. Note the extension of this section to non-sea-going ships by s.24(2), above.

Note that s.48 allows exemptions to be made for particular ships or descriptions of ships.

For the powers of the Secretary of State to make delegated legislation, such as regulations, see s.306, below.

Power to exempt from manning requirements

48.—(1) The Secretary of State may exempt any ship or description of ship from any requirements of regulations made under section 47.

(2) An exemption given under this section may be confined to a particular period or to one or more particular voyages.

DEFINITIONS
"Secretary of State": Interpretation Act 1978, Sched. 1.
"ship": s.313(1).

GENERAL NOTE
[Derivation: Merchant Shipping Act 1970, s.44.]
See ss.46 and 47, above. Note that this section allows exemptions to be made for particular ships or descriptions of ships, *e.g.* supply ships. Section 84(5) allows any exemptions to be subject to conditions. Note the extension of s.48 to non-sea-going ships by s.24(2), above.

Prohibition of going to sea undermanned

49.—(1) Subject to section 48, if a ship to which this section applies goes to sea or attempts to go to sea without carrying such officers and other seamen as it is required to carry under section 47, the owner or master shall be liable—

    (a) on summary conviction, to a fine not exceeding the statutory maximum;

    (b) on conviction on indictment, to a fine;

and the ship, if in the United Kingdom, may be detained.

(2) This section shall, in its application to ships which are not sea-going ships, have effect as if for the words "goes to sea or attempts to go to sea" there were substituted the words "goes on a voyage or excursion or attempts to do so" and the words "if in the United Kingdom" were omitted.

DEFINITIONS
"goes to sea": subs. (2) and s.84(2).
"master": s.313(1).
"seaman": s.313(1).
"ship": s.313(1).
"statutory maximum": Criminal Justice Act 1982, s.74.
"United Kingdom": Interpretation Act 1978, Sched. 1.

GENERAL NOTE
[Derivation: Merchant Shipping Act 1970, s.45; Merchant Shipping Act 1979, Sched. 6, Pt. IV and Criminal Justice Act 1982, s.49(1); Merchant Shipping Act 1970, s.96(2), Merchant Shipping Act 1988, Sched. 5.]
Section 49 re-enacts s.45 of the Merchant Shipping Act 1970 and creates offences where a ship goes to sea while undermanned (according to the standards set out in s.47). Note the extension of s.49 to non-sea-going ships by s.24(2), above (and see also ss.46 and 85(2)). The section can apply to ships going on excursions in harbours and estuaries as well as to those which set sail for the oceans.

Production of certificates and other documents of qualification

50.—(1) Any person serving or engaged to serve in any ship to which this section applies and holding any certificate or other document which is evidence that he is qualified for the purposes of section 47 shall on demand produce it to any superintendent, surveyor of ships or proper officer and (if he is not himself the master) to the master of the ship.

(2) If, without reasonable excuse, a person fails to comply with subsection (1) above he shall be liable on summary conviction to a fine not exceeding level 3 on the standard scale.

DEFINITIONS
    "fails": s.313(1).
    "master": s.313(1).
    "person": Interpretation Act 1978, Sched. 1.
    "proper officer": s.313(1).
    "ship": s.313(1).
    "standard scale": Criminal Justice Act 1982, s.37.
    "superintendent": s.313(1).
    "surveyor of ships": ss.256(9) and 313(1).

GENERAL NOTE
    [Derivation: Merchant Shipping Act 1970, s.47; Merchant Shipping Act 1979, Sched. 6, Pt. II.]
    Persons claiming to be qualified under s.47 may be obliged to produce their certificates and other documents as proof of that qualification. Failure to do so without reasonable excuse is an offence. Note s.46 and the extension of s.50 to non-sea-going ships by s.24(2), above.

Crew's knowledge of English

51.—(1) Where in the opinion of a superintendent or proper officer the crew of a ship to which this section applies consists of or includes persons who may not understand orders given to them in the course of their duty because of their insufficient knowledge of English and the absence of adequate arrangements for transmitting the orders in a language of which they have sufficient knowledge, then—

    (a) if the superintendent or proper officer has informed the master of that opinion, the ship shall not go to sea; and

    (b) if the ship is in the United Kingdom, it may be detained.

(2) If a ship goes to sea or attempts to go to sea in contravention of this section the owner or master shall be liable on summary conviction to a fine not exceeding level 5 on the standard scale.

DEFINITIONS
    "contravention": s.313(1).
    "fails": s.313(1).
    "going to sea": s.84(2).
    "master": s.313(1).
    "person": Interpretation Act 1978, Sched. 1.
    "proper officer": s.313(1).
    "ship": s.313(1).
    "standard scale": Criminal Justice Act 1982, s.37.
    "superintendent": s.313(1).
    "United Kingdom": Interpretation Act 1978, Sched. 1.

GENERAL NOTE
    [Derivation: Merchant Shipping Act 1970, s.48; Merchant Shipping Act 1979, Sched. 6, Pt. IV.]
    Officials may detain a ship if its crew does not understand English and there are no arrangements by which orders can be adequately translated (*e.g.* by an officer who speaks their native tongue). It is an offence for the ship to go to sea once the master has been informed of the inad-

equacy. Note s.46 and the extension of this section to non-sea-going ships by s.24(2), above (and see also s.85(2)).

Unqualified persons going to sea as qualified officers or seamen

52.—(1) If a person goes to sea as a qualified officer or seaman of any description without being such a qualified officer or seaman he shall be liable—

(a) on summary conviction, to a fine not exceeding the statutory maximum,

(b) on conviction on indictment, to a fine.

(2) In this section "qualified" means qualified for the purposes of section 47.

DEFINITIONS
"goes to sea": s.84(2).
"person": Interpretation Act 1978, Sched. 1.
"qualified": subs. (2).
"seaman": s.313(1).
"statutory maximum": Criminal Justice Act 1982, s.74.

GENERAL NOTE
[Derivation: Merchant Shipping Act 1970, s.46; Merchant Shipping Act 1979, Sched. 6, Pt. V; Criminal Justice Act 1982, s.49(1).]

It is an offence to go to sea without being qualified under s.47. Note the extension of s.52 to non-sea-going ships by s.24(2), above.

Medical treatment on board ship

53. Where a United Kingdom ship does not carry a doctor among the seamen employed in it the master shall make arrangements for securing that any medical attention on board the ship is given either by him or under his supervision by a person appointed by him for the purpose.

DEFINITIONS
"master": s.313(1).
"person": Interpretation Act 1978, Sched. 1.
"seaman": s.313(1).
"ship": s.313(1).
"United Kingdom ship": ss.1(3) and 313(1).

GENERAL NOTE
[Derivation: Merchant Shipping Act 1970, s.25.]

Where no doctor is carried on board the ship, s.53 imposes obligations on a master either to provide medical attention himself or to appoint someone else to provide the attention under his supervision. See also s.45, above.

Special certificates of competence

54.—(1) The Secretary of State may issue and record documents certifying the attainment of any standard of competence relating to ships or their operation, notwithstanding that the standard is not among those prescribed or specified under section 47(1)(b); and may, in relation thereto, make regulations for purposes corresponding to those mentioned in section 47(4).

(2) If a person makes a statement which he knows to be false or recklessly makes a statement which is false in a material particular for the purpose of obtaining for himself or another person a document which may be issued under this section he shall be liable on summary conviction to a fine not exceeding level 5 on the standard scale.

DEFINITIONS
"person": Interpretation Act 1978, Sched. 1.
"Secretary of State": Interpretation Act 1978, Sched. 1.

"ship": s.313(1).
"standard scale": Criminal Justice Act 1982, s.37.

GENERAL NOTE
[Derivation: Merchant Shipping Act 1970, s.50; Merchant Shipping Act 1979, Sched. 6, Pt. IV.]

Section 54 allows the Secretary of State to issue certificates of competence for those who have not obtained the qualifications under s.47. Note the extension of s.54 to non-sea-going ships by s.24(2), above.

See the General Note to s.47 on the recognition of equivalent foreign certificates. For the powers of the Secretary of State to make delegated legislation, such as regulations, see s.306, below.

Young persons

55.—(1) A person under school-leaving age shall not be employed in any United Kingdom ship except as permitted by regulations under this section.

(2) The Secretary of State may make regulations—

(a) prescribing circumstances in which and conditions subject to which persons under school-leaving age who have attained such age as may be specified in the regulations may be employed in a ship in such capacities as may be so specified;

(b) prescribing circumstances and capacities in which persons over school leaving-age but under the age of 18 or under such lower age as may be specified in the regulations must not be employed in a United Kingdom ship or may be so employed only subject to such conditions as may be specified in the regulations.

(3) Regulations made for the purposes of this section may make different provision for different employments and different descriptions of ship and any other different circumstances.

(4) If any person is employed in a ship in contravention of this section or if any condition subject to which a person may be employed under regulations made for the purposes of this section is not complied with, the owner or master shall be liable on summary conviction to a fine not exceeding level 3 on the standard scale.

(5) For the purposes of this section a person employed in a ship shall be deemed to be over school-leaving age if he has, and under school-leaving age if he has not, attained the age which is the upper limit of compulsory school age (in Scotland school age) under the enactments relating to education in the part of the United Kingdom in which he entered into the agreement under which he is so employed or, if he entered into that agreement outside the United Kingdom or is employed otherwise than under an agreement, under the enactments relating to education in England and Wales; and if he is treated for the purposes of those enactments as not having attained that age he shall be so treated also for the purposes of this section.

DEFINITIONS
"contravention": s.313(1).
"England and Wales": Interpretation Act 1978, Sched. 1.
"master": s.313(1).
"person": Interpretation Act 1978, Sched. 1.
"school-leaving age": subs. (5).
"Secretary of State": Interpretation Act 1978, Sched. 1.
"ship": s.313(1).
"standard scale": Criminal Justice Act 1982, s.37.
"United Kingdom": Interpretation Act 1978, Sched. 1.
"United Kingdom ship": ss.1(3) and 313(1).

GENERAL NOTE
[Derivation: Merchant Shipping Act 1970, s.51; Merchant Shipping Act 1979, Sched. 6, Pt. II.]

The Merchant Shipping Act 1970 (Commencement No. 11) Order 1995 (S.I. 1995 No. 965), entered into force on May 1, 1995, bringing into force s.51 of the Merchant Shipping Act 1970, as amended. This section re-enacts s.51 and gives the power to make regulations about the employment of young persons on ships. The Merchant Shipping (Employment of Young Persons) Regulations 1995 (S.I. 1995 No. 972) were issued as a result of the activating of s.51 of the 1970 Act and entered into force on May 1, 1995. These Regulations complement the provisions of S.I. 1995 No. 965 and prescribe the only circumstances in which children and young persons may be employed in a ship. They also prohibit the employment of young persons as trimmers or stokers. Section 55 creates offences for those who employ young persons in contravention of the rules set out. Note the extension of s.55 to non-sea-going ships by s.24(2), above.

For the powers of the Secretary of State to make delegated legislation, such as regulations, see s.306, below.

Financial assistance for training

56.—(1) The Secretary of State may, with the consent of the Treasury, give any person or body of persons of any description determined by him for the purposes of this section financial assistance in respect of expenses incurred or to be incurred by any such person or body in connection with the training (whether in the United Kingdom or elsewhere) of officers and ratings for service in merchant ships, including expenses incurred or to be incurred by any such person in connection with his undergoing any such training.

(2) Assistance under this section may be given by way of a grant or a loan or otherwise; and in giving any such assistance the Secretary of State may impose such conditions as he thinks fit, including conditions requiring a grant to be repaid in specified circumstances.

(3) This section is without prejudice to any other power of the Secretary of State to give financial assistance in connection with any such training as is mentioned in subsection (1) above.

DEFINITIONS
"person": Interpretation Act 1978, Sched. 1.
"Secretary of State": Interpretation Act 1978, Sched. 1.
"Treasury, the": Interpretation Act 1978, Sched. 1.
"United Kingdom": Interpretation Act 1978, Sched. 1.

GENERAL NOTE
[Derivation: Merchant Shipping Act 1988, s.26.]
Sections 56 and 76, below, were part of the response by the Government in 1988 to the pleas for assistance by the shipping industry with a view to arresting the decline of the British merchant fleet (see General Note to Pt. II, above). See the General Note on s.82, below, on the relationship between this provision and Britain's wartime needs.

In the GCBS memorandum to the Transport Committee in 1986 it was stated that it cost a shipping company £25,000 to train a junior officer over 3–4 years. In many countries some or all of the training costs are met by the Government. This on-cost has led many British companies to employ foreign officers trained for free by their Governments. Until the changes outlined in the General Note to s.47, above, the main officers on U.K. ships had to be British, so the only way to employ foreign officers was to flag-out. All this has led to a small number of officer cadets currently being trained. The intake of officer cadets in the federated sector declined from 1274 in 1980 to just 102 in 1986.

Section 56 enables the Secretary of State to provide financial assistance for the training of merchant navy officers and ratings (who wish to qualify as officers). The cost of this assistance in the initial years 1988–1990 was estimated at between £2.5 million to £3.5 million.

The assistance can be given to a wide body of persons. It is designed mainly for those companies which directly employ and sponsor trainees, but it was not the Government's intention to make the Merchant Navy Training Board a major recipient. It was accepted that the assistance would mostly take place on U.K. registered ships, but that in some cases training could take place on other ships. Attempts to restrict the assistance further, *e.g.* to British citizens, were rejected by the Government. It would be possible to assist Irish and Commonwealth citizens who are eligible for U.K. certificates and who have traditionally served in the U.K. fleet. Subsection (2) allows the Secretary of State to give assistance on "such conditions as he thinks fit" and for proper supervision, the training is designed to be carried out on ships manned by senior officers holding U.K. certificates of competency. Although the training of cadets was the primary aim, the assistance might also be made available to officers training for higher grade certificates of competency.

It was apparent that the Government was keen to continue to channel funds for new 16–17 year old entrants through the Youth Training Scheme on which about £1 million p.a. was then being spent, although there was a general resistance to the scheme by the trade unions. For ex-YTS trainees there was to be an additional two-year training to become officers and four years for others. The intention of the Government was said to include making funds available in respect of officer cadets who fell outside the age eligibility rules for the YTS. See also subs. (3), below. The sums paid to a company were likely to be slightly more than those paid under the YTS. The financial assistance would therefore only cover part of the total cost of training.

See s.127, below for fishing vessels.

Subs. (2)
Concern was expressed in the Lords that the subsection mentions loans as well as grants.

Subs. (3)
This would allow the continuance of existing forms of training funding, *e.g.* through the YTS.

Uniform

57.—(1) Subject to subsection (3) below, if any person, not being entitled to wear the merchant navy uniform, wears that uniform or any part thereof, or any dress having the appearance or bearing any of the distinctive marks of that uniform, he shall be guilty of an offence.

(2) A person guilty of an offence under subsection (1) above shall be liable, on summary conviction,—

    (a) except in a case falling within paragraph (b) below, to a fine not exceeding level 1 on the standard scale;

    (b) if he wears it in such a manner or under such circumstances as to be likely to bring contempt on the uniform, to a fine not exceeding level 1 on the standard scale or to imprisonment for a term not exceeding one month.

(3) Subsection (1) above shall not prevent any person from wearing any uniform or dress in the course or for the purposes of a stage play or representation, or a music-hall or circus performance if the uniform is not worn in such a manner or under such circumstances as to bring it into contempt.

(4) If any person entitled to wear the merchant navy uniform when aboard a ship in port or on shore appears dressed partly in uniform and partly not in uniform under such circumstances as to be likely to bring contempt on the uniform, or, being entitled to wear the uniform appropriate to a particular rank or position, wears the uniform appropriate to some higher rank or position, he shall be liable on summary conviction to a fine not exceeding level 1 on the standard scale.

DEFINITIONS
"person": Interpretation Act 1978, Sched. 1.
"port": s.313(1).
"ship": s.313(1).
"standard scale": Criminal Justice Act 1982, s.37.

GENERAL NOTE
[Derivation: Mercantile Marine Uniform Act 1919, s.1.]
The section creates an offence of wearing a merchant navy uniform without being so entitled.

Offences by seamen, etc.

Conduct endangering ships, structures or individuals

58.—(1) This section applies—

    (a) to the master of, or any seaman employed in, a United Kingdom ship; and

    (b) to the master of, or any seaman employed in, a ship which—

(i) is registered under the law of any country outside the United Kingdom; and

(ii) is in a port in the United Kingdom or within United Kingdom waters while proceeding to or from any such port.

(2) If a person to whom this section applies, while on board his ship or in its immediate vicinity—

(a) does any act which causes or is likely to cause—

(i) the loss or destruction of or serious damage to his ship or its machinery, navigational equipment or safety equipment, or

(ii) the loss or destruction of or serious damage to any other ship or any structure, or

(iii) the death of or serious injury to any person, or

(b) omits to do anything required—

(i) to preserve his ship or its machinery, navigational equipment or safety equipment from being lost, destroyed or seriously damaged, or

(ii) to preserve any person on board his ship from death or serious injury, or

(iii) to prevent his ship from causing the loss or destruction of or serious damage to any other ship or any structure, or the death of or serious injury to any person not on board his ship,

and either of the conditions specified in subsection (3) below is satisfied with respect to that act or omission, he shall (subject to subsections (6) and (7) below) be guilty of an offence.

(3) Those conditions are—

(a) that the act or omission was deliberate or amounted to a breach or neglect of duty;

(b) that the master or seaman in question was under the influence of drink or a drug at the time of the act or omission.

(4) If a person to whom this section applies—

(a) discharges any of his duties, or performs any other function in relation to the operation of his ship or its machinery or equipment, in such a manner as to cause, or to be likely to cause, any such loss, destruction, death or injury as is mentioned in subsection (2)(a) above, or

(b) fails to discharge any of his duties, or to perform any such function, properly to such an extent as to cause, or to be likely to cause, any of those things,

he shall (subject to subsections (6) and (7) below) be guilty of an offence.

(5) A person guilty of an offence under this section shall be liable—

(a) on summary conviction, to a fine not exceeding the statutory maximum;

(b) on conviction on indictment, to imprisonment for a term not exceeding two years or a fine, or both.

(6) In proceedings for an offence under this section it shall be a defence to prove—

(a) in the case of an offence under subsection (2) above where the act or omission alleged against the accused constituted a breach or neglect of duty, that the accused took all reasonable steps to discharge that duty;

(b) in the case of an offence under subsection (2) above, that at the time of the act or omission alleged against the accused he was under the influence of a drug taken by him for medical purposes and either that he took it on medical advice and complied with any directions given as part of that advice or that he had no reason to believe that the drug might have the influence it had;

(c) in the case of an offence under subsection (4) above, that the accused took all reasonable precautions and exercised all due diligence to avoid committing the offence; or

(d) in the case of an offence under either of those subsections—

(i) that he could have avoided committing the offence only by disobeying a lawful command, or

(ii) that in all the circumstances the loss, destruction, damage, death or injury in question, or (as the case may be) the likelihood of its being caused, either could not reasonably have been foreseen by the accused or could not reasonably have been avoided by him.

(7) In the application of this section to any person falling within subsection (1)(b) above, subsections (2) and (4) above shall have effect as if subsection (2)(a)(i) and (b)(i) above were omitted; and no proceedings for any offence under this section shall be instituted against any such person—

(a) in England and Wales, except by or with the consent of the Secretary of State or the Director of Public Prosecutions;

(b) in Northern Ireland, except by or with the consent of the Secretary of State or the Director of Public Prosecutions for Northern Ireland.

(8) In this section—

"breach or neglect of duty", except in relation to a master, includes any disobedience to a lawful command;

"duty"—

(a) in relation to a master or seaman, means any duty falling to be discharged by him in his capacity as such; and

(b) in relation to a master, includes his duty with respect to the good management of his ship and his duty with respect to the safety of operation of his ship, its machinery and equipment; and

"structure" means any fixed or movable structure (of whatever description) other than a ship.

DEFINITIONS

"breach or neglect of duty": subs. (8).
"duty": subs. (8).
"England and Wales": Interpretation Act 1978, Sched. 1.
"fails": s.313(1).
"master": s.313(1).
"person": Interpretation Act 1978, Sched. 1.
"port": s.313(1).
"seaman": s.313(1).
"Secretary of State": Interpretation Act 1978, Sched. 1.
"ship": s.313(1).
"statutory maximum": Criminal Justice Act 1982, s.74.
"structure": subs. (8).
"United Kingdom": Interpretation Act 1978, Sched. 1.
"United Kingdom ship": ss.1(3) and 313(1).
"United Kingdom waters": s.313(2)(a).

GENERAL NOTE

[Derivation: Merchant Shipping Act 1970, ss.27, 33; Merchant Shipping Act 1988, s.32.]

For general provisions in the Merchant Shipping Act 1995 on safety, see Pt. IV, below.

Section 58 re-enacts s.27 of the Merchant Shipping Act 1970, as revised and replaced by the Merchant Shipping Act 1988, s.32. It creates an offence where masters or seamen endanger the safety of their ship. The 1970 provision was itself extended by the Merchant Shipping Act 1979 to include cases where the ship's machinery, navigational equipment or safety equipment were damaged. The Merchant Shipping Act 1988 extended the provision to foreign ships in British ports and to acts causing damage to other ships. It also created a separate offence where a master or seaman breaches his duties, and set out specifically that the master's duties include overall responsibility for the safe running of the ship. The 1988 Act added a separate subsection setting out defences (see subs. (6)). The section used to be fairly simple, but is now rather convoluted in structure and there appears to be an overlap between subss. (2) and (4). The amendments follow upon the *Herald of Free Enterprise* disaster where no prosecutions were brought and the Sheen Report concluded that no offences had been committed. Sir Barry Sheen was there concentrating more on shipowners and masters. It is arguable that the type of conduct of individual seamen criticised in the Sheen Report could have been covered by s.27 of the Merchant Shipping Act 1970, before the 1988 amendments. It might have been more difficult to prosecute a master under the old section for a ship-management type of fault, such as operating a negative, as opposed to a positive, system of reporting acts such as the closing of bow doors. This is because the wording "omits to do anything required to preserve the ship" within the meaning of "breach or neglect of duty" might have suggested a more direct fault. The definition of a master's duties, now in subs. (8), might penalise such conduct. It should be noted that, in general, discipline on board ships will be regulated by a code of conduct approved by the Secretary of State under s.60, below.

Note the extension of s.58 to non-sea-going ships by s.24(2), above (and see s.106(2), below).

Subs. (1)

The section applies both to masters and seamen. The word "seaman" (as defined in s.313(1)) replaced "member of the crew" in 1979. Under s.313(1) "seaman" includes every person (except masters and pilots) employed or engaged in any capacity on board any ship. It would therefore include bar and shop staff on ferries, but would exclude those on board casually, such as visitors. It is not clear if it would apply to stevedores. Stowaways, however, are treated for the purposes of s.58 as if they were seamen (see s.106, but note the restriction in s.106(3)). Note that a separate offence for pilots is created by s.21 of the Pilotage Act 1987.

This section applies to U.K. ships (see s.1(3)) wherever they are. For unregistered ships see s.307, below. The section will now also apply to masters and seamen aboard foreign ships in British ports in most circumstances. The Government accepted an amendment in 1988 that removed a defence where the foreign vessel was driven into a U.K. port by stress of weather. This contrasts with the position under ss.98(4)(b) and 100(2)(b) (see the General Notes thereto, below). Note, however, the restrictions in para. (7), below.

Subs. (2)

Subsection (2) sets out, in respect of the persons defined in subs. (1), the conduct which will give rise to an offence. Paragraph (a) refers to acts and (b) to omissions. The conduct does not actually need to cause damage: it is enough if there is a threat which is sufficiently probable as to be "likely". The previous versions of s.58 did not state whether an offence could be committed by acts or omissions ashore. Under this section it is clear that conduct in the "immediate vicinity" of "his" ship may make a master or seaman guilty. This could presumably include reckless handling of explosive cargo on the quayside. It is meant to exclude conduct in the vicinity of another ship which endangers the latter only, but which is committed away from a person's own ship, *i.e.* the one on which the person is employed. This is because the section is primarily concerned with duties which arise by implication out of the contract of employment. Similarly excluded is conduct committed some way from the employing vessel, such as a vital crewman failing to come into work, or a master being party to a shore-side meeting which produced a set of defective standing orders. But a master can be guilty, apparently, for ship management type faults occurring on board, such as those within subs. (8)(b). This wide definition places a master at great risk of prosecution whenever a disaster occurs for, by definition, matters occurring on board are under his overall control. He may have to rely on the defences under subs. (6).

Paragraph (a). The act must cause some sort of serious consequence, *e.g.* total loss of the ship or serious damage to engines. Slight damage, or the threat of it, is not enough. The specific reference to navigational and safety equipment (such as radar and lifeboats) seems to suggest that there is some other equipment not included and cargo winches come to mind. These might be classed as "machinery", although the section is generally aimed at the type of damage that could lead to a major or minor disaster. Damaged cargo machinery is unlikely to lead to the sinking of a ship, although death or serious injury of a stevedore could result. In that case the conduct would probably be covered by sub-para. (iii). Sub-paragraph (ii) was introduced in 1988 and follows the recommendations of the 1984 Consultative Document. It would cover acts which were likely to threaten neighbouring ships. The definition in subs. (8) shows that it would also cover fixed shoreside facilities such as wharves, jetties, silos, warehouses, oil storage tanks and pumping equipment as well as moveable structures such as mobile cranes. It is doubtful, even given the width of the definition, whether the word "structures" would include conveyances such as railway rolling stock or trucks. Sub-paragraph (iii) is broadly as it was in 1979, with the minor addition of the word "any", in place of "a" person. The section covers actions on board which threaten those ashore, such as stevedores, or those on board other ships. Again, the threat or harm must not be slight. A crewman skylarking with a hosepipe would be unlikely to cause serious injury.

Paragraph (b). This paragraph is broadly as under the old s.27 with similar 1988 additions to those in para. (a) above. The omissions have to be "required" and reference should be made to subss. (3) and (8). Subsection (2)(b) of the 1988 Bill unintentionally placed a duty on masters and seamen to preserve *other* ships from loss and to rescue persons from *other* ships. While property salvage has never been compulsory, assistance which is needed to save life is already regulated by ss. 92 and 93 (formerly the Merchant Shipping Act 1894, s.422, the Maritime Conventions Act 1911, s.6 and the Merchant Shipping (Safety Conventions) Act 1949, s.22). The present subsection now relates only to omissions in respect of the ship on which the master or seaman is employed (*cf.* para. (a), where there is an offence if *acts* affect other ships).

Subs. (3)

This subsection includes the mental element necessary for the offence. Deliberately dangerous conduct and conduct under the influence of drink or drugs could be penalised. Negligent conduct can also be an offence, provided that it is in breach or neglect of a duty. The concept of a duty is now elaborated upon in subs. (8). An attempt in the Lords to make the offence depend upon "gross" neglect of duty was successfully resisted by the Government.

Subs. (4)

This subsection creates a completely separate offence which seems to overlap with that under subs. (2). A discharge of "duties" in a manner to cause loss under subs. (4)(a) could as easily be an act causing loss under subs. (2)(a). A failure under subs. (4)(b) could as easily be an omission under subs. (2)(b). Subsection (4) does not require the master or seaman to be on the ship or in its vicinity but, otherwise, it is difficult to think of cases not within subs. (2).

It appears that the provision may be designed to deal with a person who performs existing duties, but in such a way that danger is created. There was a suggestion in debates in 1988 that the courts have tended to regard s.58 as (i) dealing with offences of a disciplinary nature, such as malicious damage, and (ii) allowing prosecutions for acts and omissions that constitute breaches of regulations. These matters may have nothing to do with general duties. The paragraph was definitely a response to the Zeebrugge Disaster and it is noticeable that the penalty on summary conviction is the same as that under the Health and Safety at Work etc. Act 1974 (c. 37). But note the possibility of conviction on indictment.

See also subs. (6)(b) and note the definition of a master's duties in subs. (8).

Subs. (5)

For the statutory maximum see the Criminal Justice Act 1982, s.74.

Subs. (6)

Defences are set out in subs. (6). There is no defence under subs. (6)(a) to a subs. (2) charge where the act or omission was deliberate. For breaches or neglect of duty there is a defence of reasonableness. For some reason the defence in para. (c) to the subs. (4) charge phrases its defence of reasonableness in a different way. What difference this makes is unclear to say the least. All that can be said is that as the latter contains two criteria it may be stricter, but the reality is that there is no difference at all.

Paragraph (b) was inserted in the consolidated provisions to give effect to the defence provided by s.33 of the Merchant Shipping Act 1970 (preserved for offences under s.27(2) of the 1970 Act by the Merchant Shipping Act 1988, Sched. 6). It gives a defence where drugs are taken under medical advice. Paragraphs (c) and (d) were the old paras. (b) and (c) of the pre-1995 legislation.

Paragraph (d) also seems to add little, in that "reasonable steps" or "reasonable precautions" under the previous paragraphs would already seem to involve the foresight of consequences by the defendant. The lawful command defence was not in the original 1988 Bill. Its absence would have placed seamen at risk as they are obliged to obey lawful commands. It would be wrong for a seaman to be prosecuted if he had informed the master that a piece of equipment, such as a cable, was unsafe and the master had then ordered that repairs be delayed and the cable be used. Lawfulness is not defined in the Act. Actual disobedience of a lawful command is caught by subs. (8), below.

There is nothing to prevent an employer bringing disciplinary proceedings, even in the event of an acquittal under this section. Any unfairness would be considered at an industrial tribunal.

Subs. (7)

This subsection makes all proceedings against masters and seamen of foreign flagged vessels subject to executive approval. It will be recalled that subs. (1) was extended in 1988 to cover foreign ships. There is no offence by a foreign mariner of damaging the ship itself (or its equipment) as this will normally be regulated by the flag state: the offences that can be committed relate to loss of, or damage to, other ships or structures and to causing death or personal injury.

Subs. (8)

This subsection defines three phrases in the section. The definition of breach or neglect of duty is derived directly from the Merchant Shipping Act 1979, s.27(2).

The definition of duty was new in 1988. It seems that it will apply both to the offence under subs. (2) as well as that under subs. (4). For, although the words duty or duties do not appear in subs. (2) they must be read into it by virtue of subs. (3). Paragraph (a) presumably intends to draw the distinction between what might be considered as moral duties owed by any citizen and the contractual duties attaching to the position occupied by a master, officer or seaman. Paragraph (b) states explicitly that the master has an overall duty to manage the ship. Although this might have been implicit, the inclusion is clearly meant to deal with failures by masters to devise and operate safe systems on board ship—the type of criticism raised in the Sheen Report. The natural limitations on a master's management functions can be raised as a defence under subs. (6). Paragraph (c) defines structure for the purposes of subs. (2)(a)(ii) and (b)(iii), above (see further s.101(1), below).

Concerted disobedience and neglect of duty

59.—(1) If a seaman employed in a United Kingdom ship combines with other seamen employed in that ship—

(a) to disobey lawful commands which are required to be obeyed at a time while the ship is at sea;

(b) to neglect any duty which is required to be discharged at such a time; or

(c) to impede, at such a time, the progress of a voyage or the navigation of the ship,

he shall be liable—

(i) on summary conviction, to a fine not exceeding the statutory maximum;

(ii) on conviction on indictment, to imprisonment for a term not exceeding two years or a fine or both.

(2) For the purposes of this section a ship shall be treated as being at sea at any time when it is not securely moored in a safe berth.

DEFINITIONS
"at sea": subs. (2).
"seaman": s.313(1).
"ship": s.313(1).
"statutory maximum": Criminal Justice Act 1982, s.74.
"United Kingdom ship": ss.1(3) and 313(1).

GENERAL NOTE
[Derivation: Merchant Shipping Act 1970, s.30(c); Merchant Shipping Act 1974, s.19(4); Merchant Shipping Act 1979, Sched. 6, Pt. VII, para. 21; Criminal Justice Act 1982, s.49(1).]

The Merchant Shipping Act 1970, s.30 was designed to deal with (i) the persistently neglectful or disobedient seaman and (ii) those mutinous seamen who combine together to disobey commands, neglect their duties or impede the progress of the vessel while she is at sea. Strikes while safely in port ceased to be a criminal offence when s.30 was amended by the Merchant Shipping Act 1974, s.19. The Merchant Shipping Act 1988, Sched. 5 removed the offence caused under situation (i) (namely paras. (a) and (b) of s.30 of the Merchant Shipping Act 1970) and was designed to implement a Council of Europe recommendation that neglect of duty or disobedience alone should not be a criminal offence. Reference should also be made to s.58, above, which may make a seaman guilty for neglect or disobedience which causes or is likely to cause hazards to safety (see s.58(2)(a)).

The present s.59 retains the offence described in situation (ii) above (formerly s.30(c) of the Merchant Shipping Act 1970, as substituted by s.19 of the Merchant Shipping Act 1974). Stowaways are treated for the purposes of this section as if they were seamen (see s.106, but note the restriction in s.106(3)). Note the operation of s.119 in respect of fishing vessels.

In relation to the civil consequences of combinations, note also the repeal of the Merchant Shipping Act 1970, s.42 by the Merchant Shipping Act 1988, Sched. 5. Section 42 of the 1970 Act allowed a seaman on a U.K. registered ship to strike, provided that 48 hours notice was given and the ship was safely in a U.K. port. During the notice period the seaman could not be compelled to sail, which effectively prevented the ship from leaving. The seaman was not actually on strike, but was serving his notice. Previously, industrial action might have been considered a criminal offence and the provision was included in the 1970 Act as a result of the Pearson Inquiry in 1967. The right to strike in port was first given to seamen by the Merchant Shipping Act 1974. The repeal of s.42 was urged by the GCBS in 1986 in order to bring the law into line with that on land, but was eventually achieved at Report Stage of the Merchant Shipping Act 1988 in the House of

Lords. The major criticism of s.42 was that it enabled the unions to organise a strike by giving s.42 notice, but without organising a ballot as required by the Trade Union Act 1984. An injunction would not have been possible because there was no inducement to *break* the employment contract as the notice was deemed to be within the contract. The shipowners' case was not so much that there was regular abuse, but that they should be in the same position as other employers. A number of alleged abuses were cited from 1981, 1984 and 1985. Apparently, the provisions were often used by seamen on ferries and it was said that between 1982–1986 there were 38 short ferry stoppages. If different members of the crew staggered their notice the ship could be effectively immobilised. The Opposition, briefed by the National Union of Seamen, asserted that there was no problem, as the type of action to which the notice referred was that within the meaning of the Trade Union Act 1984. In any event the latter Act was not designed to deal with conduct short of a strike, such as that under s.42 which is merely the giving of proper contractual notice about future action. However, the passage of the 1988 Bill coincided with industrial action by the NUS, partly against the offshore supply industry, but mainly against the P&O company which planned changes in employment practices in their ferry fleet. One consequence of the repeal is that a seaman who takes action in breach of his contract of employment may be civilly liable to the shipowner under s.60 of the Merchant Shipping Act 1995. The Government view in 1988 was that an undue burden was not being placed on seafarers, as employees in other industries would be similarly liable, but without the benefit of the £100 limit on special damages granted by s.70(3).

Disciplinary offences

Breaches by seamen of codes of conduct

60.—(1) The Secretary of State may make regulations under the following provisions of this section for the purpose of maintaining discipline on board United Kingdom ships; and in this section "disciplinary body" means a body established or approved by the Secretary of State under subsection (6) below.

(2) Regulations may provide for the hearing on shore in the United Kingdom, by a disciplinary body, of a complaint by the master or owner of a United Kingdom ship, other than a fishing vessel, against a seaman alleging that during his employment on board the ship the seaman contravened a provision of a code of conduct approved by the Secretary of State for the purposes of this section.

The alleged contravention may be one on or off the ship and in the United Kingdom or elsewhere.

(3) Regulations may enable a disciplinary body—

(a) to dismiss the complaint if it finds the allegation not proved;

(b) if it finds the allegation proved—

(i) to warn the seaman;

(ii) to reprimand the seaman; or

(iii) to recommend to the Secretary of State that the seaman shall, either for a period specified in the recommendation or permanently, cease to be entitled to a discharge book in pursuance of section 80 and shall be required to surrender any such book which has been issued to him.

(4) Regulations may—

(a) enable the seaman to appeal against such a recommendation to another disciplinary body (an "appellate body");

(b) enable an appellate body—

(i) to confirm the recommendation;

(ii) to cancel the recommendation; or

(iii) in the case of a recommendation that the seaman shall cease to be entitled to a discharge book permanently or for a particular period, to substitute for it a recommendation that he shall cease to be so entitled, instead of permanently, for a period specified in the substituted recommendation or, instead of for the particular period, for a shorter period so specified.

(5) Regulations may make provision for securing that a recommendation that the seaman shall permanently cease to be entitled to a discharge book is not submitted to the Secretary of State unless it has been confirmed, either on appeal or otherwise, by an appellate body.

(6) Regulations may make provision for the establishment or approval for the purposes of this section of such number of bodies as the Secretary of State thinks fit and with respect to the composition, jurisdiction and procedure of any such body.

(7) Regulations may make provision for the payment, out of money provided by Parliament, of such remuneration and allowances as the Secretary of State may, with the consent of the Treasury, determine to any member of such a body.

(8) Regulations may make different provision for different circumstances and may contain such incidental and supplemental provisions as the Secretary of State considers appropriate.

(9) Without prejudice to the generality of the preceding provisions, regulations may include provision for any proceedings to take place notwithstanding the absence of the seaman to whom they relate.

(10) Nothing in the regulations or done in pursuance of the regulations shall be construed as affecting any power to institute, prosecute, entertain or determine proceedings (including criminal proceedings) under any other enactment or at common law.

DEFINITIONS
"appellate body": subs. (4).
"contravention": s.313(1).
"disciplinary body": subs. (1).
"fishing vessel": s.313(1) and (3).
"master": s.313(1).
"seaman": s.313(1).
"Secretary of State": Interpretation Act 1978, Sched. 1.
"ship": s.313(1).
"Treasury, the": Interpretation Act 1978, Sched. 1.
"United Kingdom": Interpretation Act 1978, Sched. 1.
"United Kingdom ship": ss.1(3) and 313(1).

GENERAL NOTE
[Derivation: Merchant Shipping Act 1979, s.23.]
Sections 34–38 of the Merchant Shipping Act 1970 set up a system for maintaining discipline on board ships (replacing that in the Merchant Shipping Act 1894, ss.220–234). Section 34 allowed the Secretary of State to make regulations which could specify disciplinary "offences", breach of which by the seaman could result in the imposition of a "fine" by the master which could be deducted from wages. The Merchant Shipping (Disciplinary Offences) Regulations 1972 (S.I. 1972 No. 1294), as amended, created offences such as disobeying lawful commands, being asleep on duty and possessing offensive weapons. It became clear that this rather authoritarian method of imposing discipline was out of keeping with modern concepts of industrial relations and reform was recommended by the Working Group on Disciplinary Needs for Seagoing Employment in the Merchant Navy (November 1975) (see R. Thomas, *Current Law Statutes Annotated 1979*). In place of the master's right to fine, s.23 of the Merchant Shipping Act 1970 set out a new system which came into operation in 1986.
Section 60 of the Merchant Shipping Act 1995 re-enacts s.23 of the Merchant Shipping Act 1970 and provides that the conduct of seamen will be regulated by a Code of Conduct approved by the Secretary of State. Instead of the power to fine, the master or shipowner can complain to a shore-based disciplinary body set up by regulations. The disciplinary body can have the power to warn, reprimand or recommend the withdrawal of the seaman's discharge book (see s.80), thus preventing the offender from working as a seaman. In 1978 the National Maritime Board published a Code of Conduct for the Merchant Navy which distinguishes between misconduct which is so severe as to justify instant dismissal and misconduct which is of a less serious nature and justifies a mere warning or reprimand (see also *Chorley and Giles Shipping Law*, pp. 149–151). Under subs. (10), it is made clear that the section and regulations made under it will leave unaf-

fected criminal sanctions created elsewhere, *e.g.* the criminal disciplinary offences under ss.117–119. Section 60(4) allows regulations to create an appeal body.

For the powers of the Secretary of State to make delegated legislation, such as regulations, see s.306, below.

Note the operation of ss.111, 119 in respect of fishing vessels.

Disqualification of seamen and inquiries

GENERAL NOTE

Section 60, above, sets out a system for complaints by employers against their seafarer employees, where the remedies are essentially contractual. Sections 61–69 deal with cases where the complaint is made by an official on behalf of the Secretary of State and where the possible penalty may extend to employment of the seafarer generally, *e.g.* where a certificate is suspended or withdrawn.

Inquiry into fitness or conduct of officer

61.—(1) If it appears to the Secretary of State that an officer—

   (a) is unfit to discharge his duties, whether by reason of incompetence or misconduct or for any other reason; or

   (b) has been seriously negligent in the discharge of his duties; or

   (c) has failed to comply with the provisions of section 92;

the Secretary of State may cause an inquiry to be held by one or more persons appointed by him and, if he does so, may, if he thinks fit, suspend, pending the outcome of the inquiry, any certificate issued to the officer in pursuance of section 47 and require the officer to deliver it to him.

(2) Where a certificate issued to an officer has been suspended under subsection (1) above the suspension may, on the application of the officer, be terminated by the High Court or, if the inquiry is held in Scotland, by the Court of Session, and the decision of the court on such an application shall be final.

(3) An inquiry under this section shall be conducted in accordance with rules made under section 65(1) and those rules shall require the persons holding the inquiry to hold it with the assistance of one or more assessors.

(4) The persons holding an inquiry under this section into the fitness or conduct of an officer—

   (a) may, if satisfied of any of the matters mentioned in paragraphs (a) to (c) of subsection (1) above, cancel or suspend any certificate issued to him under section 47 or censure him;

   (b) may make such order with regard to the costs (or in Scotland expenses) of the inquiry as they think just; and

   (c) shall make a report on the case to the Secretary of State;

and if the certificate is cancelled or suspended the officer (unless he has delivered it to the Secretary of State in pursuance of subsection (1) above) shall deliver it forthwith to the persons holding the inquiry or to the Secretary of State.

(5) Any costs (or in Scotland expenses) which a person is ordered to pay under subsection (4)(b) above may be recovered from him by the Secretary of State.

DEFINITIONS

   "court": subs. (2).
   "fails": s.313(1).
   "High Court": Interpretation Act 1978, Sched. 1.
   "person": Interpretation Act 1978, Sched. 1.
   "Secretary of State": Interpretation Act 1978, Sched. 1.

GENERAL NOTE

   [Derivation: Merchant Shipping Act 1970, s.52; Merchant Shipping Act 1988, Sched. 7.]

   Section 61 re-enacts s.52 of the Merchant Shipping Act 1970, as amended, and allows an inquiry into the fitness or conduct of an "officer". "Officer" is not defined in the Act, although categories of seamen can be identified in the regulations issued under s.47. The category of "officer" would normally include deck and engineer officers. Seamen are separately dealt with in s.63. An officer's s.47 certificate may be suspended pending the outcome of an inquiry. For the rules as to inquiries, see s.65. The result of the inquiry may be to cancel or suspend the officer's s.47 certificate. There is power to award costs. Note the powers given under ss.257–260.

Note the extension of s.61 to non-sea-going ships by s.24(2), above.

Disqualification of holder of certificate other than officer's

62.—(1) Where it appears to the Secretary of State that a person who is the holder of a certificate to which this section applies is unfit to be the holder of such a certificate, whether by reason of incompetence or misconduct or for any other reason, the Secretary of State may give him notice in writing that he is considering the suspension or cancellation of the certificate.

(2) The notice must state the reasons why it appears to the Secretary of State that that person is unfit to be the holder of such a certificate and must state that within a period specified in the notice, or such longer period as the Secretary of State may allow, he may make written representations to the Secretary of State or claim to make oral representations to the Secretary of State.

(3) After considering any representations made in pursuance of subsection (2) above the Secretary of State shall decide whether or not to suspend or cancel the certificate and shall give the holder of it written notice of his decision.

(4) Where the decision is to suspend or cancel the certificate the notice shall state the date from which the cancellation is to take effect, or the date from which and the period for which the suspension is to take effect, and shall require the holder to deliver the certificate to the Secretary of State not later than the date so specified unless before that date the holder has required the case to be dealt with by an inquiry under section 63.

(5) Where, before the date specified in the notice, he requires the case to be dealt with by such an inquiry, then, unless he withdraws the requirement, the suspension or cancellation shall not take effect except as ordered in pursuance of the inquiry.

(6) The Secretary of State may make regulations prescribing the procedure to be followed with respect to the making and consideration of representations in pursuance of this section, the form of any notice to be given under this section and the period to be specified in any such notice as the period within which any steps are to be taken.

(7) This section applies to every certificate issued under section 54 and to any certificate issued under section 47 other than one certifying that a person is qualified as an officer.

DEFINITIONS

"person": Interpretation Act 1978, Sched. 1.

"Secretary of State": Interpretation Act 1978, Sched. 1.

GENERAL NOTE

[Derivation: Merchant Shipping Act 1970, s.53.]

Section 62 re-enacts s.53 of the Merchant Shipping Act 1970, as amended, and sets out a summary procedure for making decisions about the fitness or conduct of a person other than an "officer". "Officers" are separately dealt with in s.61. Section 62 can therefore apply to seamen (see s.313(1)) with s.47 certificates and to those holding certificates of competency under s.54 (see subs. (7)). The section allows the Secretary of State to serve a notice stating that the person is unfit and allow representations to be made. The Secretary of State may then cancel or suspend the certificate from a given date. The recipient of the notice must then decide whether to elect for an inquiry under s.63.

Regulations may prescribe appropriate procedures. For the powers of the Secretary of State to make delegated legislation, such as regulations, see s.306, below. Note the powers given under ss.257–260.

Note the extension of s.62 to non-sea-going ships by s.24(2), above.

Inquiry into fitness or conduct of seaman other than officer

63.—(1) Where a person has, before the date mentioned in section 62(4), required his case to be dealt with by an inquiry under this section the Secretary of State shall cause an inquiry to be held by one or more persons appointed by him.

(2) An inquiry under this section shall be conducted in accordance with rules made under section 65(1) and those rules shall require the persons holding the inquiry to hold it with the assistance of one or more assessors.

(3) The persons holding an inquiry under this section—

(a) may confirm the decision of the Secretary of State and cancel or suspend the certificate accordingly;

(b) may, where the decision was to cancel the certificate, suspend it instead;

(c) may, where the decision was to suspend the certificate, suspend it for a different period;

(d) may, instead of confirming the decision of the Secretary of State, censure the holder of the certificate or take no further action;

(e) may make such order with regard to the costs of the inquiry as they think just; and

(f) shall make a report on the case to the Secretary of State;

and if the certificate is cancelled or suspended it shall be delivered forthwith to the persons holding the inquiry or to the Secretary of State.

(4) Any costs (or in Scotland expenses) which a person is ordered to pay under subsection (3)(e) above may be recovered from him by the Secretary of State.

DEFINITIONS
"person": Interpretation Act 1978, Sched. 1.
"Secretary of State": Interpretation Act 1978, Sched. 1.

GENERAL NOTE
[Derivation: Merchant Shipping Act 1970, s.54; Merchant Shipping Act 1988, Sched. 7.]
See the General Note to s.62, above. Where a seaman has elected under s.62 for there to be an inquiry, the Secretary of State is bound to set up an inquiry subject to the rules set out under s.65. In effect, the inquiry will operate as a sort of appeal body from the decisions of the Secretary of State under s.62. There is power to award costs and this might operate to deter applications.
Note the extension of s.63 to non-sea-going ships by s.24(2), above.

Re-hearing of and appeal from inquiries

64.—(1) Where an inquiry has been held under section 61 or 63 the Secretary of State may order the whole or part of the case to be reheard, and shall do so—

(a) if new and important evidence which could not be produced at the inquiry has been discovered; or

(b) if there appear to the Secretary of State to be other grounds for suspecting that a miscarriage of justice may have occurred.

(2) An order under subsection (1) above may provide for the re-hearing to be as follows,—

(a) if the inquiry was held in England, Wales or Northern Ireland, by the persons who held it, by a wreck commissioner or by the High Court;

(b) if it was held in Scotland, by the persons who held it, by the sheriff or by the Court of Session.

(3) Any re-hearing under this section which is not held by the High Court or the Court of Session shall be conducted in accordance with rules made under section 65(1).

(4) Where the persons holding the inquiry have decided to cancel or suspend the certificate of any person or have found any person at fault, then, if

no application for an order under subsection (1) above has been made or such an application has been refused, that person or any other person who, having an interest in the inquiry, has appeared at the hearing and is affected by the decision or finding, may appeal—

(a) to the High Court if the inquiry was held in England, Wales or Northern Ireland;

(b) to the Court of Session if it was held in Scotland.

DEFINITIONS
"England and Wales": Interpretation Act 1978, Sched. 1.
"High Court": Interpretation Act 1978, Sched. 1.
"person": Interpretation Act 1978, Sched. 1.
"Secretary of State": Interpretation Act 1978, Sched. 1.

GENERAL NOTE
[Derivation: Merchant Shipping Act 1970, s.57.]
Section 64 re-enacts s.57 of the Merchant Shipping Act 1970 and allows for a re-hearing of s.61 or s.63 inquiries.
Note the extension of s.64 to non-sea-going ships by s.24(2), above.

Rules as to inquiries and appeals

65.—(1) The Secretary of State may make rules for the conduct of inquiries under sections 61 and 63 and for the conduct of any re-hearing under section 64 which is not held by the High Court or the Court of Session.

(2) Without prejudice to the generality of subsection (1) above, rules under this section may provide for the appointment and summoning of assessors, the manner in which any facts may be proved, the persons allowed to appear, and the notices to be given to persons affected.

(3) Rules of court made for the purpose of re-hearings under section 64 which are held by the High Court, or of appeals to the High Court, may require the court, subject to such exceptions, if any, as may be allowed by the rules, to hold such a re-hearing or hear such an appeal with the assistance of one or more assessors.

DEFINITIONS
"High Court": Interpretation Act 1978, Sched. 1.
"Secretary of State": Interpretation Act 1978, Sched. 1.

GENERAL NOTE
[Derivation: Merchant Shipping Act 1970, s.58; Merchant Shipping Act 1988, Sched. 6, para. 3.]
Section 65 re-enacts s.58 of the Merchant Shipping Act 1970 and allows for the Secretary of State to make rules as to inquiries. See the Merchant Shipping (Section 52 Inquiries) Rules 1982 (S.I. 1982 No. 1752), as amended, which require at least 30 days notice to be given of an inquiry.
Note the powers given under ss.257–260.
Note the extension of s.65 to non-sea-going ships by s.24(2), above.

Failure to deliver cancelled or suspended certificate

66. If a person fails to deliver a certificate as required under section 61, 62 or 63 he shall be liable on summary conviction to a fine not exceeding level 3 on the standard scale.

DEFINITIONS
"fails": s.313(1).
"person": Interpretation Act 1978, Sched. 1.
"standard scale": Criminal Justice Act 1982, s.37.

GENERAL NOTE
[Derivation: Merchant Shipping Act 1970, s.59; Merchant Shipping Act 1979, Sched. 6, Pt. II.]

Failure to deliver up a certificate as required is an offence.
Note the extension of s.66 to non-sea-going ships by s.24(2), above.

Power to restore certificate

67. Where a certificate has been cancelled or suspended under section 61, 62, 63 or 64, the Secretary of State, if of the opinion that the justice of the case requires it, may re-issue the certificate or, as the case may be, reduce the period of suspension and return the certificate, or may grant a new certificate of the same or a lower grade in place of the cancelled or suspended certificate.

DEFINITIONS
"Secretary of State": Interpretation Act 1978, Sched. 1.

GENERAL NOTE
[Derivation: Merchant Shipping Act 1970, s.60.]
Despite the finding of an inquiry that a certificate should be suspended or withdrawn, the Secretary of State has a residual power to re-issue it.
Note the extension of s.67 to non-sea-going ships by s.24(2), above.

Power to summon witness to inquiry into fitness of conduct of officer or other seaman

68.—(1) The persons holding an inquiry under section 61 or 63 may—
(a) by summons require any person to attend, at a time and place stated in the summons, to give evidence or to produce any documents in his custody or under his control which relate to any matter in question at the inquiry; and
(b) take evidence on oath (and for that purpose administer oaths) or, instead of administering an oath, require the person examined to make a solemn affirmation.
(2) If on the failure of a person to attend such an inquiry in answer to a summons under this section—
(a) the persons holding the inquiry are satisfied by evidence on oath—
(i) that the person in question is likely to be able to give material evidence or produce any document which relates to any matter in question at the inquiry,
(ii) that he has been duly served with the summons, and
(iii) that a reasonable sum has been paid or tendered to him for costs and expenses, and
(b) it appears to them that there is no just excuse for the failure,
they may issue a warrant to arrest him and bring him before the inquiry at a time and place specified in the warrant.
(3) If any person attending or brought before such an inquiry refuses without just excuse to be sworn or give evidence, or to produce any document, the persons holding the inquiry may—
(a) commit him to custody until the end of such period not exceeding one month as may be specified in the warrant or until he gives evidence or produces the document (whichever occurs first), or
(b) impose on him a fine not exceeding £1,000,
or both.
(4) A fine imposed under subsection (3)(b) above shall be treated for the purposes of its collection, enforcement and remission as having been imposed by the magistrates' court for the area in which the inquiry in ques-

tion was held, and the persons holding the inquiry shall, as soon as practicable after imposing the fine, give particulars of it to the clerk of that court.

(5) This section does not apply to Scotland.

DEFINITIONS
"fails": s.313(1).
"magistrates' court": Interpretation Act 1978, Sched. 1.
"oath": Interpretation Act 1978, Sched. 1.
"person": Interpretation Act 1978, Sched. 1.

GENERAL NOTE
[Derivation: Merchant Shipping Act 1988, s.44.]
Under ss.257–260 persons holding an inquiry into the fitness or conduct of an officer or seaman have all the powers of an inspector appointed under the Act. These powers (given originally by s.27 of the Merchant Shipping Act 1979) were more designed to investigate faults in ships rather than persons and, although s.259(2)(i) may be used to require witnesses to answer questions, there were apparently difficulties in practice. The 1984 Consultative Document recommended that the powers should be similar to those granted to a magistrate. Accordingly, s.44 of the Merchant Shipping Act 1988 enabled the holders of inquiries under ss.61 or 63 to issue summons to witnesses to give evidence or for the production of documents. Evidence may be given under oath. Warrants of arrest can be issued to compel attendance. Failure to take the oath, give evidence, or produce documents without just excuse is an offence. Section 68 re-enacts s.44 of the Merchant Shipping Act 1988.
Note the extension of s.68 to non-sea-going ships by s.24(2), above.

Procedure where inquiry into fitness or conduct of officer or other seaman is held by sheriff

69. Where an inquiry under section 61 or 63 is held in Scotland by a sheriff—
  (a) he shall (subject to rules made under section 65(1)) dispose of the inquiry as a summary application; and
  (b) (subject to section 64) his decision on the inquiry shall be final.

DEFINITIONS
"sheriff": Interpretation Act 1978, Sched. 1.

GENERAL NOTE
[Derivation: Merchant Shipping Act 1988, s.45.]
This section regulates the procedure for inquiries into the fitness or conduct of an officer or seaman where they are conducted before a Sheriff in Scotland. Generally, the procedure is to be that for summary applications, except insofar as rules made under s.65 may provide otherwise (*cf.* the Merchant Shipping (Section 52 Inquiries) Rules 1982 (S.I. 1982 No. 1752)).
Note the extension of s.69 to non-sea-going ships by s.24(2), above.

Civil liability of seamen for offences

Civil liability for absence without leave

70.—(1) The following provisions of this section shall apply with respect to the liability of a seaman employed in a United Kingdom ship, to damages for being absent from his ship at a time when he is required, under his contract of employment to be on board.

(2) If he proves that his absence was due to an accident or mistake or some other cause beyond his control and that he took all reasonable precautions to avoid being absent his absence shall not be treated as a breach of contract.

(3) Where subsection (2) above does not apply, then—
  (a) if no special damages are claimed his liability shall be £10;
  (b) if special damages are claimed his liability shall not be more than £100.

(4) In the application of this section to Scotland for the references to special damages there shall be substituted references to damage in respect of specific expense incurred or loss sustained.

DEFINITIONS
    "seaman": s.313(1).
    "ship": s.313(1).
    "United Kingdom ship": ss.1(3) and 313(1).

GENERAL NOTE
    [Derivation: Merchant Shipping Act 1970, s.39.]
    Section 70 re-enacts s.39 of the Merchant Shipping Act 1970 and allows the employer to claim damages if the seaman (see s.313(1)) is absent without leave, contrary to the contract of employment. At one time, absence without leave was an offence under s.31 of the Merchant Shipping Act 1970, but that provision was repealed by the Merchant Shipping Act 1974, s.19. However, the liability is limited to the low figures extant in 1970. See also s.72, below.
    See also the General Note to s.60, above.

Civil liability for smuggling

71. If a seaman employed in a United Kingdom ship is found in civil proceedings before a court in the United Kingdom to have committed an act of smuggling, whether within or outside the United Kingdom, he shall be liable to make good any loss or expense that the act has caused to any other person.

DEFINITIONS
    "seaman": s.313(1).
    "United Kingdom": Interpretation Act 1978, Sched. 1.
    "United Kingdom ship": ss.1(3) and 313(1).

GENERAL NOTE
    [Derivation: Merchant Shipping Act 1970, s.40.]
    Section 71 re-enacts s.40 of the Merchant Shipping Act 1970 and creates a civil liability for smuggling. The liability can arise in respect of "any person", thus including a shipowner or charterer whose ship has been delayed. Note that smuggling may in some circumstances result in a fine or the forfeiture of a ship under the Customs and Excise Management Act 1979 (c. 2), ss.88–90. It seems highly unlikely that a seaman (as narrowly defined in s.313(1)) would have the resources to make any recourse worthwhile. The limit in s.70 does not apply.

Civil liability for fines imposed under immigration laws

72.—(1) The following provisions of this section shall apply where, at a time when a United Kingdom ship is in the national or territorial waters of any country outside the United Kingdom, a seaman employed in the ship is absent without leave and present in that country in contravention of that country's laws.
    (2) If, by reason of the contravention, a penalty is incurred under those laws by the persons employing the seaman the penalty shall be treated as being attributable to his absence without leave and may, subject to the provisions of section 70, be recovered from him as special damages for breach of contract (or, in Scotland, as damages in respect of specific expense incurred or loss sustained).
    (3) If, by reason of the contravention, a penalty is incurred under those laws by any other person the amount thereof, or, if that amount exceeds £100, £100, may be recovered by him from the seaman.

DEFINITIONS
    "contravention": s.313(1).
    "seaman": s.313(1).
    "ship": s.313(1).
    "United Kingdom": Interpretation Act 1978, Sched. 1.
    "United Kingdom ship": ss.1(3) and 313(1).

GENERAL NOTE
    [Derivation: Merchant Shipping Act 1970, s.41.]
    Section 72 re-enacts s.41 of the Merchant Shipping Act 1970 and creates a civil liability where a seaman (as narrowly defined in s.313(1)) is absent from the ship without leave and thereby the

employer (*e.g.* the shipowner) incurs a penalty under a state's immigration laws. Note that there is a limit of liability under s.70(3).

Relief and repatriation and relief costs

Relief and return of seamen etc. left behind and shipwrecked

73.—(1) Where—

(a) a person employed as a seaman in a United Kingdom ship is left behind in any country outside the United Kingdom or is taken to such a country on being shipwrecked; or

(b) a person who became so employed under an agreement entered into outside the United Kingdom is left behind in the United Kingdom or is taken to the United Kingdom on being shipwrecked;

the persons who last employed him as a seaman shall make such provision for his return and for his relief and maintenance until his return and such other provisions as may be required by regulations made by the Secretary of State.

(2) The provisions to be so made may include the repayment of expenses incurred in bringing a shipwrecked seaman ashore and maintaining him until he is brought ashore and the payment of the expenses of the burial or cremation of a seaman who dies before he can be returned.

(3) The Secretary of State may also make regulations providing for the manner in which any wages due to any person left behind or taken to any country as mentioned in subsection (1) above, and any property of his left on board ship, are to be dealt with.

(4) The Secretary of State may make regulations requiring a superintendent or proper officer—

(a) to make such provision as may be prescribed by the regulations with respect to any matter for which provision may be required to be made by regulations under the preceding provisions of this section; and

(b) to make the like provision with respect to persons who are British citizens, British Dependent Territories citizens or British overseas citizens and are found in distress in any country outside the United Kingdom after being employed in ships registered in, or belonging to the government of, such a country.

(5) Without prejudice to the generality of the preceding provisions, regulations made under this section may make provision—

(a) for determining the place to which a person is to be returned;

(b) for requiring the master of any United Kingdom ship to convey a person to a place determined in accordance with the regulations and for enabling a superintendent or proper officer to give the master directions for that purpose;

(c) for the making of payments in respect of the conveyance of a person in accordance with the regulations; and

(d) for the keeping of records and the rendering of accounts.

(6) Regulations under this section may make a contravention of any provision thereof an offence punishable on summary conviction with a fine not exceeding level 3 on the standard scale or such less amount as may be specified in the regulations.

(7) This section applies to a person left behind on being discharged in pursuance of section 29, whether or not at the time he is left behind the ship is still a United Kingdom ship.

(8) This section applies to the master of a ship as it applies to a seaman and sections 74 and 75 shall have effect accordingly.

DEFINITIONS

"British citizen": s.313(1).
"British Dependent Territories citizen": s.313(1).
"British Overseas citizen": s.313(1).
"contravention": s.313(1).

"left behind": s.84(4).
"master": s.313(1).
"person": Interpretation Act 1978, Sched. 1.
"proper officer": s.313(1).
"relief and maintenance": s.84(1).
"registered": ss.23(1) and 313(1).
"seaman": s.313(1).
"Secretary of State": Interpretation Act 1978, Sched. 1.
"ship": s.313(1).
"standard scale": Criminal Justice Act 1982, s.37.
"superintendent": s.313(1).
"United Kingdom": Interpretation Act 1978, Sched. 1.
"United Kingdom ship": ss.1(3) and 313(1).
"wages": s.313(1).

GENERAL NOTE
[Derivation: Merchant Shipping Act 1970, ss.62, 67; Merchant Shipping Act 1979, Sched. 6, Pt. VI, para. 8; British Nationality Act 1981, s.51(3).]

Section 73 re-enacts ss.62 and 67 of the Merchant Shipping Act 1970, as amended, and allows for the making of regulations so that seamen on U.K. ships who are left behind or shipwrecked overseas must be repatriated and, pending repatriation, maintained by the employer. See the Merchant Shipping (Repatriation) Regulations 1979 (S.I. 1979 No. 97). Note that under subs. (8) this is a specific protection which is extended to the master, as a master would not otherwise fall in the definition of seaman (see s.313(1)). Note the limit of liability imposed in s.74, below.

For the powers of the Secretary of State to make delegated legislation, such as regulations, see s.306, below.

Limit of employer's liability under section 73

74. Where a person left behind in or taken to any country as mentioned, in section 73(1) remains there after the end of a period of three months, the persons who last employed him as a seaman shall not be liable under that section to make provision for his return or for any matter arising after the end of that period, unless they have before the end of that period been under an obligation imposed on them by regulations under that section to make provision with respect to him.

DEFINITIONS
"left behind": s.84(4).
"person": Interpretation Act 1978, Sched. 1.
"seaman": s.313(1).

GENERAL NOTE
[Derivation: Merchant Shipping Act 1970, s.63.]

Section 74 re-enacts s.63 of the Merchant Shipping Act 1970 and imposes a limit on the employer's liability to maintain or repatriate a seafarer under s.73, above.

Recovery of expenses incurred for relief and return, etc.

75.—(1) Where any expenses are incurred in respect of any matter for which the employers of a seaman are required to make provision under section 73, then—
  (a) if the expenses are incurred by the Secretary of State, or are incurred by the government of any country outside the United Kingdom and repaid to them on behalf of the Crown, the Secretary of State may recover them from the employers;
  (b) if the expenses are incurred by the seaman he may recover them from the employers unless they prove either that under the terms of his employment they were to be borne by him or that he would not have been left behind but for his own wrongful act or neglect.

(2) Where, in the case of any seaman, expenses are incurred by the Secretary of State or are incurred by the government of any country outside the United Kingdom and repaid to them on behalf of the Crown—

(a) in respect of any matter for which, but for section 74, the seaman's last employers would have been required to make provision under section 73; or

(b) in respect of any matter for which provision is required to be made under section 73(4)(b);

the Secretary of State may recover them from the seaman (or, if he has died, from his personal representatives).

DEFINITIONS
"left behind": s.84(4).
"seaman": s.313(1).
"Secretary of State": Interpretation Act 1978, Sched. 1.
"United Kingdom": Interpretation Act 1978, Sched. 1.

GENERAL NOTE
[Derivation: Merchant Shipping Act 1970, s.64.]
Section 75 re-enacts s.64 of the Merchant Shipping Act 1970 and allows for the recovery from an employer of expenses which should have been incurred by the employer under s.73 (*e.g.* the maintenance costs of a seaman left behind overseas). Subsection (1)(b) allows an employer to insert a clause in the contract of employment which throws the burden of such costs on the seafarer.

Financial assistance of crew relief costs

76.—(1) The Secretary of State may, with the consent of the Treasury, give financial assistance to—

(a) the owner of a ship registered in the British Islands, or

(b) any manager of a ship so registered, being either an individual ordinarily resident in the British Islands or a body corporate which is incorporated in the British Islands and has its principal place of business there,

in respect of travel and other costs incurred by the owner or manager in connection with members of the ship's crew joining or leaving the ship outside the limited European trading area.

(2) If the Secretary of State so determines, eligibility for assistance under this section shall be conditional on the fulfilment of such conditions with respect to all or any of the following matters as are specified in his determination—

(a) the nationality of any person in relation to whom any such costs as are mentioned in subsection (1) above are incurred;

(b) the ordinary residence of any such person;

(c) the place (outside the limited European trading area) where any such person joins or leaves his ship.

(3) Assistance under this section may be given by way of a grant or loan or otherwise; and in giving any such assistance the Secretary of State may impose such conditions as he thinks fit.

(4) For the purposes of this section—

(a) the crew of a ship shall be taken to include the master and other officers of the ship; and

(b) "the limited European trading area" has the same meaning as it has for the purposes of any regulations made under section 47.

DEFINITIONS
"British Islands": Interpretation Act 1978, s.5 and Sched. 1.
"crew": subs. (4)(a).
"limited European trading area": subs. (4)(b).

"registered": ss.23(1) and 313(1).
"Secretary of State": Interpretation Act 1978, Sched. 1.
"ship": s.313(1).
"Treasury, the": Interpretation Act 1978, Sched. 1.

GENERAL NOTE
[Derivation: Merchant Shipping Act 1988, s.27.]
See the General Note to s.56, above.

Shipowners have an obligation under s.73 to pay the repatriation costs of seamen shipwrecked or left behind in foreign ports. In 1988, the GCBS wanted the obligations under s.73 to be limited further than under s.74. It also wanted help with the costs of repatriation of British seamen for leave purposes. Denmark, Finland and Norway apparently provided contributions towards the repatriation costs of mariners away for a minimum period of duty.

Section 75 allows the Secretary of State to give financial assistance towards the travel and other costs when the crew joins or leaves a ship in distant waters. The place from which repatriation takes place has to be outside the "Limited European Trading Area". This "Area" is roughly the trading area from Bergen to Cadiz. The expression "crew" for these purposes is given a wider than normal meaning and includes the master, officers and ratings. The assistance is mainly designed for leave purposes, although the words "costs ... in connection with ... leaving the ship ..." may be sufficiently wide to allow assistance to be given in respect of repatriation under s.73.

The cost of the financial assistance for crew relief was estimated to be about £5 million in the year 1989–90. The GCBS estimated in 1988 that the annual cost to the industry was £13 million, but that figure included ships registered in the Dependent Territories whereas the scheme will be restricted to ships registered in the U.K. and Crown Dependencies.

The payments are not made to the seamen themselves, but are in the form of reimbursement to the shipowners. Subsection (1) states that the assistance can *only* be given to two categories of persons, (i) owners of ships registered in the British Islands, or (ii) ship managers ordinarily resident, or incorporated, in the British Islands. The latter provision was necessary because many shipowners employ firms of professional ship management to run the day-to-day operations of the ships and it may be the managers who incur the direct obligations involved in employing the crew. For registration, see Pt. II of the Merchant Shipping Act 1995 above. There was some confusion in the 1988 debates over the meaning of the phrase "British Islands", but this is defined by the Interpretation Act 1978 as "The United Kingdom, the Channel Islands and the Isle of Man".

The payments are discretionary and may be subject to any conditions that the Secretary of State thinks fit (subs. (3)). In particular, eligibility may be subject to a number of conditions as set out in subs. (2). These relate to (i) the nationality of the crew, (ii) where the crew members are ordinarily resident, (iii) the place where the crew joins the ship. It was broadly intended that the assistance is to be given in respect of the costs of repatriating British mariners (*e.g.* those who were ordinarily resident in the British Isles and therefore paying tax there), although the Act does not require this. The Under Secretary of State stated in the House of Lords in 1988 that the payments would not be restricted to British citizens and would be made available in respect of others, such as Irish seamen. In the light of the *Factortame* litigation (see the General Note to s.9, above) there would be difficulties if the U.K. was seen to be discriminating against E.U. citizens. The subsidy was designed to assist British shipowners rather than British seamen. Nevertheless, the shipowners were disappointed that the aid was not extended to British subjects serving on U.K.-owned British ships registered in the British possessions (and see the General Note to s.18, above).

As with s.56, above, concern was expressed that the payments could take the form of loans, but the Government refused in 1988 to vary either provision. It remains to be seen whether the assistance is more apparent than real, as the expenditure figures do not make it clear whether they include loan repayments.

See the General Note to s.82, below, concerning the relationship between this provision and Britain's wartime needs.

Documentation

Official log books

77.—(1) Except as provided by regulations under this section an official log book in a form approved by the Secretary of State shall be kept in every United Kingdom ship.

(2) The Secretary of State may make regulations prescribing the particulars to be entered in official log books, the persons by whom such entries are to be made, signed or witnessed, and the procedure to be followed in the making of such entries and in their amendment or cancellation.

(3) The regulations may require the production or delivery of official log books to such persons, in such circumstances and within such times as may be specified therein.

(4) Regulations under this section may exempt ships of any description from any requirements thereof, either generally or in such circumstances as may be specified in the regulations.

(5) Regulations under this section may make a contravention of any provision thereof an offence punishable on summary conviction with a fine not exceeding level 2 on the standard scale or not exceeding a lesser amount.

(6) If a person intentionally destroys or mutilates or renders illegible any entry in an official log book he shall be liable on summary conviction to a fine not exceeding level 4 on the standard scale.

DEFINITIONS
    "contravention": s.313(1).
    "person": Interpretation Act 1978, Sched. 1.
    "Secretary of State": Interpretation Act 1978, Sched. 1.
    "ship": s.313(1).
    "standard scale": Criminal Justice Act 1982, s.37.
    "United Kingdom ship": ss.1(3) and 313(1).

GENERAL NOTE
    [Derivation: Merchant Shipping Act 1970, s.68; Merchant Shipping Act 1979, Sched. 6, Pt. III, Pt. IV, para. 4; Criminal Justice Act 1982, s.46(2).]
    Section 77 re-enacts s.68 of the Merchant Shipping Act 1970 which required the keeping of an official log book to record what happens on board the ship during a voyage. The Secretary of State is given the power to prescribe the detailed contents of a log book in regulations (see, *e.g.* the Merchant Shipping (Official Log Books) Regulations 1981 (S.I. 1981 No. 569), as amended, and the Merchant Shipping (Official Log Books) (Fishing Vessels) Regulations 1981 (S.I. 1981 No. 570)). For the powers of the Secretary of State to make delegated legislation, such as regulations, see s.306, below.

Lists of crew

78.—(1) Except as provided by regulations made under this section, the master of every United Kingdom ship shall make and maintain a list of the crew containing such particulars as may be required by the regulations.

(2) The Secretary of State may make regulations—
(a) specifying the particulars to be entered in a list of the crew;
(b) limiting the time for which a list of the crew may remain in force;
(c) providing for the maintenance by such persons and either in such place as may be specified in the regulations or, if it is so specified, in the ship, of a copy or copies of each list of a crew, and for the notification to such persons of any changes therein;
(d) for the production of a list of the crew to such persons, in such circumstances and within such time as may be specified in the regulations; and
(e) for the delivery to a superintendent or proper officer or the Registrar General of Shipping and Seamen, in such circumstances as may be specified in the regulations, of a list of the crew or a copy thereof maintained under the regulations and for the notification to him of any changes in such a list.

(3) Regulations under this section may enable a list of the crew to be contained in the same document as a crew agreement and may treat any particu-

lars entered in the crew agreement as forming part of the particulars entered in the list.

(4) Regulations under this section may exempt from the requirements thereof such descriptions of ship as may be specified in the regulations and may make different provisions for different circumstances.

(5) Regulations under this section may make a contravention of any provision thereof an offence punishable on summary conviction with a fine not exceeding level 2 on the standard scale or not exceeding a lesser amount.

DEFINITIONS
  "contravention": s.313(1).
  "crew agreement": ss.25(2) and 84(1).
  "master": s.313(1).
  "person": Interpretation Act 1978, Sched. 1.
  "proper officer": s.313(1).
  "Secretary of State": Interpretation Act 1978, Sched. 1.
  "ship": s.313(1).
  "standard scale": Criminal Justice Act 1982, s.37.
  "superintendent": s.313(1).
  "United Kingdom ship": ss.1(3) and 313(1).

GENERAL NOTE
  [Derivation: Merchant Shipping Act 1970, s.69; Merchant Shipping Act 1979, Sched. 6, Pt. VI, para. 4; Criminal Justice Act 1982, s.46(2).]
  Section 78 re-enacts s.69 of the Merchant Shipping Act 1970 and obliges a master to maintain a crew list, in accordance with regulations. For the powers of the Secretary of State to make delegated legislation, such as regulations, see s.306, below.

British seamen's cards

79.—(1) The Secretary of State may make regulations providing—
  (a) for the issue to British seamen of cards (in this section referred to as "British seamen's cards") in such form and containing such particulars with respect to the holders thereof and such other particulars (if any) as may be prescribed by the regulations, and for requiring British seamen to apply for such cards;
  (b) for requiring the holders of British seamen's cards to produce them to such persons and in such circumstances as may be prescribed by the regulations;
  (c) for the surrender of British seamen's cards in such circumstances as may be prescribed by the regulations;
  (d) for any incidental or supplementary matters for which the Secretary of State thinks it expedient for the purposes of the regulations to provide;
and any provision of the regulations having effect by virtue of paragraph (a) above may be so framed as to apply to all British seamen or any description of them and as to have effect subject to any exemptions for which provision may be made by the regulations.

(2) Regulations under this section may make a contravention of any provision thereof an offence punishable on summary conviction with a fine not exceeding level 2 on the standard scale or not exceeding a lesser amount.

(3) In this section "British seamen" means persons who are not aliens within the meaning of the British Nationality Act 1981 and are employed, or ordinarily employed, as masters or seamen.

(4) If a person makes a statement which he knows to be false or recklessly makes a statement which is false in a material particular for the purpose of obtaining for himself or another person a British seaman's card he shall be liable on summary conviction to a fine not exceeding level 4 on the standard scale.

DEFINITIONS
"British seamen": subs. (3).
"contravention": s.313(1).
"master": s.313(1).
"person": Interpretation Act 1978, Sched. 1.
"seaman": s.313(1).
"Secretary of State": Interpretation Act 1978, Sched. 1.
"standard scale": Criminal Justice Act 1982, s.37.

GENERAL NOTE
[Derivation: Merchant Shipping Act 1970, s.70; Merchant Shipping Act 1979, Sched. 6, Pts. III, VI, para. 4; British Nationality Act 1981, Sched. 7.]

Section 79 re-enacts s.70 of the Merchant Shipping Act 1970, as amended. It provides for the issue of British seamen's cards. These cards can be issued to masters or seamen (as defined in s.313(1)) and their content is set out in regulations. For the powers of the Secretary of State to make delegated legislation, such as regulations, see s.306, below. The Merchant Shipping (Seamen's Documents) Regulations 1987 (S.I. 1987 No. 408) set out the form and content of the cards. The main purpose of the cards seems to be that of identification.

Discharge books

80.—(1) The Secretary of State may make regulations providing—
(a) for the issue to persons who are or have been employed in United Kingdom ships of discharge books in such form and containing such particulars with respect to the holders thereof and such other particulars (if any) as may be prescribed by the regulations and for requiring such persons to apply for such discharge books;
(b) for requiring the holders of discharge books to produce them to such persons and in such circumstances as may be prescribed by the regulations;
(c) for the surrender of discharge books in such circumstances as may be prescribed by the regulations;
(d) for any incidental or supplementary matters for which the Secretary of State thinks it expedient for the purposes of the regulations to provide;
and any provision of the regulations having effect by virtue of paragraph (a) above may be so framed as to apply to all such persons as are mentioned in that paragraph or any description of such persons and as to have effect subject to any exemptions for which provision may be made by the regulations.
(2) Regulations under this section may—
(a) provide for a person to cease to be entitled to a discharge book in consequence of a recommendation made by a disciplinary body by virtue of regulations made under section 60(3) or (4); and
(b) provide for the re-issue of discharge books which have been surrendered in consequence of such a recommendation.
(3) Regulations under this section may make a contravention of any provision thereof an offence punishable on summary conviction with a fine not exceeding level 2 on the standard scale or not exceeding a lesser amount.
(4) A person who, in the United Kingdom or elsewhere—
(a) obtains employment as a seaman on board a United Kingdom ship and does so when he is disentitled to a discharge book by virtue of regulations made under subsection (2)(a) above; or
(b) employs as such a seaman a person who he knows or has reason to suspect is disentitled as aforesaid,
shall be liable on summary conviction to a fine not exceeding the statutory maximum or, on conviction on indictment, to imprisonment for a term not exceeding two years or a fine or both.

DEFINITIONS
"contravention": s.313(1).
"person": Interpretation Act 1978, Sched. 1.
"seaman": s.313(1).

"Secretary of State": Interpretation Act 1978, Sched. 1.
"standard scale": Criminal Justice Act 1982, s.37.
"statutory maximum": Criminal Justice Act 1982, s.74.
"United Kingdom": Interpretation Act 1978, Sched. 1.
"United Kingdom ship": ss.1(3) and 313(1).

GENERAL NOTE
　[Derivation: Merchant Shipping Act 1970, s.71; Merchant Shipping Act 1979, ss.23(5) and (6), 52(2) and Sched. 6, Pt. VI, para. 4 and s.46(2) and s.49(1) of Criminal Justice Act 1982.]
　Section 80 re-enacts s.71 of the Merchant Shipping Act 1970, as amended. It provides for the issue of "discharge books". The detailed contents of the discharge books is set out in regulations. For the powers of the Secretary of State to make delegated legislation, such as regulations, see s.306, below. The Merchant Shipping (Seamen's Documents) Regulations 1987 (S.I. 1987 No. 408) set out the form and content of the discharge books. These books replaced the old "continuous certificate of discharge" required under the 1894 Act, ss.128–130, but the general purpose is broadly the same. The main purpose is to provide a record of employment, *e.g.* by showing details of voyages, ships, training courses, vaccinations and medical certificates.

Handing over of documents by master

81.—(1) If a person ceases to be the master of a United Kingdom ship during a voyage of the ship he shall deliver to his successor the documents relating to the ship or its crew which are in his custody.
　(2) If, without reasonable excuse, the master of such a ship fails to comply with subsection (1) above, he shall be liable on summary conviction to a fine not exceeding level 3 on the standard scale.

DEFINITIONS
　"fails": s.313(1).
　"master": s.313(1).
　"person": Interpretation Act 1978, Sched. 1.
　"ship": s.313(1).
　"standard scale": Criminal Justice Act 1982, s.37.
　"United Kingdom ship": ss.1(3) and 313(1).

GENERAL NOTE
　[Derivation: Merchant Shipping Act 1970, s.74; Merchant Shipping Act 1979, Sched. 6, Pt. II.]
　Section 81 re-enacts s.74 of the Merchant Shipping Act 1970, as amended. It obliges a master to deliver to a successor all documents relating to the ship or crew. A master who decided to withhold documents, as part of an employment dispute with a shipowner, would be guilty of an offence.

Merchant Navy Reserve

Maintenance of Merchant Navy Reserve

82.—(1) The Secretary of State may maintain the body of persons known as the Merchant Navy Reserve whose members may, in such circumstances and for such periods as the Secretary of State may determine, be required by him to serve in ships belonging to or employed in the service of Her Majesty.
　(2) The Merchant Navy Reserve shall consist of such number of persons as the Secretary of State may determine who voluntarily undertake to become members of the Reserve and are accepted as members of it.
　(3) The Secretary of State may determine the procedure by which, and the conditions under which, persons may become, or (subject to any regulations made by him under this section) may cease to be, members of the Merchant Navy Reserve.
　(4) The Secretary of State may make regulations with respect to the calling into, and discharge from, service of members of the Merchant Navy Reserve and with respect to other matters relating to the service of members of the Reserve.
　(5) Any such regulations may, in particular, make provision—

(a) for call-out notices to be served on members of the Reserve;
(b) for the requirements to be complied with by persons on whom such notices have been served;
(c) as to the uniform and equipment with which members of the Reserve are to be provided;
(d) for regulating the conduct and discipline of members of the Reserve who have entered into service, and for securing their attendance at their places of duty;
(e) for the imposition of fines, or the forfeiture of pay or other amounts, for misconduct or breaches of discipline or for contravention of provisions of the regulations.

(6) Without prejudice to the operation of subsection (5)(e) above, regulations under this section may provide that a contravention of the regulations shall be an offence punishable on summary conviction by a fine not exceeding level 3 on the standard scale or such lower amount as is prescribed by the regulations.

(7) Regulations under this section may make different provision for different circumstances.

DEFINITIONS
   "contravention": s.313(1).
   "person": Interpretation Act 1978, Sched. 1.
   "Secretary of State": Interpretation Act 1978, Sched. 1.
   "ship": s.313(1).
   "standard scale": Criminal Justice Act 1982, s.37.

GENERAL NOTE
   [Derivation: Merchant Shipping Act 1988, ss.28 and 53(2)(a).]

Wartime needs
   The military strategic needs of the nation could be seriously affected by the decline in the merchant fleet. In the 1988 discussions about that decline, the Government had to meet the anxieties of its own supporters about defence as well as the general commercial concerns of the industry and opposition. In the speech by the Rt Hon. John Moore M.P. (the then Secretary of State for Transport) to the GCBS on December 10, 1986 (see Annex A to the 1987 White Paper) he noted three strategic needs for shipping, (i) direct support of the Royal Navy and the Army, (ii) civil supply to the U.K., (iii) the U.K. contribution to the rapid reinforcement of Europe.
   Direct support has been affected by the decline in the merchant fleet, *e.g.* by the reduction in the number of deep-sea trawlers since the Cod Wars with Iceland. The need for auxiliary minesweepers has been partially met by the modification of off-shore support vessels used in the North Sea oil industry. The Royal Navy has also been prepared to refuel at sea from larger tankers, some of which are registered in overseas British possessions. It was suggested in 1988 that the Falkland Islands operations in 1982 might not still be possible, given the dramatic decline in tonnage even since 1982 (which on the basis of dead weight tonnage had declined to a quarter of the 1982 level by 1988). In 1982, 50 merchant ships, 5 per cent of the then fleet, were needed and the industry was severely stretched to provide certain of the specialist vessel, such as troop carriers and repair ships. Similar concerns have been voiced since the Gulf War of 1990, when the U.K. Government was obliged to charter-in a great deal of tonnage, much of it with no British connection.
   For civil supply and reinforcement in times of tension and war, the Government would seek to ensure access to shipping by a combination of requisitioning, chartering, purchase and capture, although the latter two options would be less significant. Requisitioning is performed under prerogative powers, but can only be exercised in relation to British ships. There were plans, in 1988, for a NATO pool of merchant ships under the control of a Defence Shipping Authority (DSA) and covering all ocean-going ships over 1600 gt registered in NATO countries.
   It is evident that there are a number of other sources of ships which depend heavily on commercial and political factors. The financial question underlies all the discussions: is it cheaper to subsidise British ships and have the security of knowing that their availability is assured, or is it sounder to rely on the combination of methods described above?

Many ships which are flagged out will use non-Nato crews and the question of their reliability in emergencies has been questioned. One suggestion was to retain U.K. crews, but to employ them on offshore terms, with the ship registered in an overseas possession (*e.g.* Isle of Man or Gibraltar). This solution has more attractions to the nation than having foreign crews on British registered ships (involving a loss of British seafaring expertise), or of having U.K. ships sold completely to foreign interests (where the ship as well as the crew are lost as a resource). But some of the vessels operated under the British flag in overseas possessions have been manned by crews from countries such as Poland, Yugoslavia and China, whose loyalty the Royal Navy might doubt. It was reported in 1988 that Polish sailors operating on British flagged ships between Cork and Wales received operational papers for a British military exercise, Purple Warrior (*The Independent*, March 29, 1988). The Government has responded to some concerns by the introduction of the Merchant Shipping (Officer Nationality) Regulations 1995 (S.I. 1995 No. 1427), which entered into force on August 1, 1995, in order to deal with the crewing of ships which have a "strategic function", *e.g.* cruise ships (see the General Notes to Pt. II and to s.47, above).

In 1986 the Secretary of State asked two questions (i) Could the U.K. find those with experience quickly enough in an emergency? (ii) Would sufficient officers and ratings be trained in future to man ships not on the U.K. registry? It is in this context that the provisions now in ss.82 and 83 were announced.

Merchant Navy Reserve

Sections 82 and 83 provide for the maintenance of a Merchant Navy Reserve, which consists of experienced volunteer mariners who can crew merchant vessels in time of tension or war. The Merchant Navy Reserve is not designed to be open to mariners *currently* serving on British registered ships as it is said that their suitability and whereabouts can be otherwise established (presumably from British shipowners). Recruitment is designed to come from the pool of former seafarers who have taken shore-side employment, although an upper age limit of 55 was proposed. The provision would be useful, *e.g.* for replacing foreign crews on British registered vessels. It was stated by the Minister at Committee Stage of the Merchant Shipping Act 1988 in the Commons, that there was nothing to prevent a fisherman with a merchant navy qualification from signing on the Reserve and continuing to act as a fisherman.

The details of the scheme are set out in the Merchant Shipping (Merchant Navy Reserve) Regulations 1989 (S.I. 1989 No. 662). It should be noted that subs. (5)(b) provides that the various requirements may be made compulsory. The intention was that there would be a legal obligation to obey a call-up in an emergency, although at other times members could resign without notice.

See also s.83, below, for payment.

Supplementary provisions as respects the Reserve

83.—(1) Subject to such conditions as the Secretary of State may determine, there shall be payable to members of the Merchant Navy Reserve such pay, bounties and allowances as he may determine.

(2) The Secretary of State may make such payments as he thinks fit in connection with the training and certification of members of the Merchant Navy Reserve (including payments to persons undergoing such training and payments in connection with the re-validation of certificates).

(3) The Secretary of State shall not make any determination under subsection (1) above, or any payment under subsection (2) above, except with the consent of the Treasury.

(4) Where any person is called into service by virtue of regulations under section 82—

    (a) the provisions of the Reserve Forces (Safeguard of Employment) Act 1985 shall apply to that person as if any service rendered by him in pursuance of the call-out were whole-time service within the meaning of that Act; and

    (b) any service so rendered shall be relevant service within the meaning of the Reserve and Auxiliary Forces (Protection of Civil Interests) Act 1951.

DEFINITIONS

"Secretary of State": Interpretation Act 1978, Sched. 1.

"Treasury, the": Interpretation Act 1978, Sched. 1.

GENERAL NOTE

[Derivation: Merchant Shipping Act 1988, s.29.]

Members of the Merchant Navy Reserve maintained under s. 82, above, will be remunerated and the costs of the Reserve will depend on the number of volunteers coming forward, but were estimated in 1988 to be about £1 million per year. A bounty of £200 p.a. was mentioned in the 1988 debates, where a figure of several thousand officers and ratings was also given. Although subs. (2) allows for training there was no intention to instigate a programme at the outset, despite Opposition criticism. In essence, the Reserve is simply a list of people who have given an address and a declaration of willingness to serve in exchange for an annual bounty. Subsection (4) preserves certain civil rights during service, *e.g.* concerning employment.

Interpretation

Interpretation

84.—(1) In this Part—

"crew agreement" has the meaning given to it by section 25(2);

"relief and maintenance" includes the provision of surgical or medical treatment and such dental and optical treatment (including the repair or replacement of any appliance) as cannot be postponed without impairing efficiency; and

"ship's boat" includes a life-raft.

(2) References in this Part to going to sea include references to going to sea from any country outside the United Kingdom.

(3) For the purposes of this Part a seaman is discharged from a ship when his employment in that ship is terminated.

(4) For the purposes of this Part a seaman discharged from a ship in any country and left there shall be deemed to be left behind in that country notwithstanding that the ship also remains there.

(5) Any power conferred by this Part to provide for or grant an exemption includes power to provide for or grant the exemption subject to conditions.

DEFINITIONS

"crew agreement": subs. (1) and s.25(2).

"discharged from a ship": subs. (3).

"discharged from a ship in any country and left there": subs. (4).

"going to sea": subs. (2).

"relief and maintenance": subs. (1).

"ship's boat": subs. (1).

"United Kingdom": Interpretation Act 1978, Sched. 1.

GENERAL NOTE

[Derivation: Merchant Shipping Act 1970, s.97(1)–(4), (6).]

PART IV

SAFETY

Safety and Health on Ships

GENERAL NOTE

Part V of the Merchant Shipping Act 1894, ss.418–463, dealt with safety matters, although significant provisions could also be found in Pt. IV, dealing with passenger and emigrant ships. Many subsequent Merchant Shipping Acts also legislated for safety and there was an increasing move to place the detailed safety requirements into regulations. Part IV of the Merchant Shipping Act 1995 now brings together in a more coherent form all the relevant provisions concerning the safe construction and operation of ships (although crewing matters are governed by Pt. III, above). Some provisions were introduced or amended by the Merchant Shipping Act 1988 when the Government announced its intention to strengthen the law as a result of the Sheen Report into the *Herald of Free Enterprise* disaster. It was in this context that the Government introduced ss.30–32 of the Merchant Shipping Act 1988 (now ss.98, 100, 58 of this Act).

Safety and health on ships

85.—(1) The Secretary of State may by regulations (in this Act referred to as "safety regulations") make such provision as he considers appropriate for all or any of the following purposes—
  (a) for securing the safety of United Kingdom ships and persons on them, and for protecting the health of persons on United Kingdom ships;
  (b) for giving effect to any provisions of an international agreement ratified by the United Kingdom so far as the agreement relates to the safety of other ships or persons on them or to the protection of the health of persons on other ships;
  (c) for securing the safety of other ships and persons on them while they are within United Kingdom national waters;
and the power conferred by paragraph (b) to make provision for giving effect to an agreement includes power to provide for the provision to come into force although the agreement has not yet come into force.
  (2) In subsection (1) above "United Kingdom ship" means a ship which—
  (a) is registered in the United Kingdom; or
  (b) is not registered under the law of any country but is wholly owned by persons each of whom is—
    (i) a British citizen, a British Dependent Territories citizen or a British Overseas citizen, or
    (ii) a body corporate which is established under the law of a part of the United Kingdom and has its principal place of business in the United Kingdom.
  (3) Regulations in pursuance of subsection (1)(a) or (b) above may make provision with respect to any of the following matters, and regulations in pursuance of subsection (1)(c) above may make provision with respect to any of the following matters so far as relates to safety, that is to say—
  (a) the design, construction, maintenance, repair, alteration, inspection, surveying and marking of ships and their machinery and equipment;
  (b) the packaging, marking, loading, placing, moving, inspection, testing and measuring of cargo and anything on a ship which is not cargo, machinery or equipment;
  (c) the carrying out of any operation involving a ship;
  (d) the use of the machinery and equipment of a ship and of anything on a ship which is not cargo, machinery or equipment;
  (e) the manning of ships, including the employment on ships of persons qualified to attend to the health and safety of persons on the ships;
  (f) the arrangements for ensuring communication between persons in different parts of a ship and between persons in the ship and other persons;
  (g) the access to, presence in and egress from a ship, and different parts of it, of persons of any description;
  (h) the ventilation, temperature and lighting of different parts of a ship;
  (i) the steps to be taken to prevent or control noise, vibration and radiation in and from a ship and the emission in or from a ship of smoke, gas and dust;
  (j) the steps to be taken to prevent, detect and deal with outbreaks of fire on a ship;

(k) the steps to be taken to prevent any collision involving a ship and in consequence of any collision involving a ship;

(l) the steps to be taken, in a case where a ship is in distress or stranded or wrecked, for the purpose of saving the ship and its machinery, equipment and cargo and the lives of persons on or from the ship, including the steps to be taken by other persons for giving assistance in such a case;

(m) the removal, by jettisoning or otherwise, of its equipment and of other things from a ship for the purpose of avoiding, removing or reducing danger to persons or property;

(n) the steps to be taken, in a case where danger of any kind occurs or is suspected on a ship, for removing or reducing the danger and for warning persons who are not on the ship of the danger or suspected danger;

(o) the making of records and the keeping of documents relating to ships and the keeping and use on a ship of information to facilitate the navigation of the ship;

(p) the keeping of registers and the issue of certificates in cases for which registration or a certificate is required by virtue of the regulations; and

(q) the furnishing of information;

but the mention of specific matters in this subsection shall not be construed as restricting the generality of the power conferred by paragraphs (a), (b) or (c) of subsection (1) above.

(4) The power to make regulations conferred by subsection (1)(a) above shall extend also to the making of regulations for the prevention of collisions between seaplanes on the surface of water and between ships and seaplanes and subsection (3)(k) above and (5) to (7) below and section 86(1) shall have effect accordingly.

(5) Safety regulations—

(a) may make provision in terms of approvals given by the Secretary of State or another person and in terms of any document which the Secretary of State or another person considers relevant from time to time;

(b) may provide for the cancellation of an approval given in pursuance of the regulations and for the alteration of the terms of such an approval; and

(c) must provide for any approval in pursuance of the regulations to be given in writing and to specify the date on which it takes effect and the conditions (if any) on which it is given.

(6) Without prejudice to section 86(1)(b), safety regulations may provide—

(a) for the granting by the Secretary of State or another person, on such terms (if any) as the Secretary of State or other person may specify, of exemptions from specified provisions of the regulations for classes of cases or individual cases; and

(b) for the alteration or cancellation of exemptions granted in pursuance of the regulations.

(7) Safety regulations may provide—

(a) that in such cases as are prescribed by the regulations a ship shall be liable to be detained and that section 284 shall have effect, with such modifications (if any) as are prescribed by the regulations, in relation to the ship;

(b) that a contravention of the regulations shall be an offence punishable on summary conviction by a fine not exceeding the statutory maximum and on conviction on indictment by imprisonment for a term not exceeding two years and a fine;

(c) that any such contravention shall be an offence punishable only on summary conviction by a maximum fine of an amount not exceeding level 5 on the standard scale, or such less amount as is prescribed by the regulations;

(d) that, in such cases as are prescribed by the regulations, such persons as are so prescribed shall each be guilty of an offence created by virtue of paragraphs (b) or (c) above;

(e) that, notwithstanding anything in paragraphs (b) or (c) above, a person convicted summarily of an offence under the regulations of a kind which is stated by the regulations to correspond to an offence which is triable either summarily or on indictment under an enactment specified in the regulations which authorises or authorised a fine on summary conviction of a maximum amount exceeding the statutory maximum shall be liable to a fine not exceeding that maximum amount.

DEFINITIONS

"Act, this": Interpretation Act 1978, Sched. 1.
"British citizen": s.313(1).
"British Dependent Territories citizen": s.313(1).
"British Overseas citizen": s.313(1).
"contravention": s.313(1).
"national waters": s.313(2)(b).
"offence triable either way": Interpretation Act 1978, Sched. 1.
"person": Interpretation Act 1978, Sched. 1.
"register": ss.23(1) and 313(1).
"registered": ss.23(1) and 313(1).
"safety regulations": subs. (1) and s.313(1).
"Secretary of State": Interpretation Act 1978, Sched. 1.
"ship": s.313(1).
"standard scale": Criminal Justice Act 1982, s.37.
"statutory maximum": Criminal Justice Act 1982, s.74.
"United Kingdom": Interpretation Act 1978, Sched. 1.
"United Kingdom ship": subs. (2).
"writing": Interpretation Act 1978, Sched. 1.

GENERAL NOTE

[Derivation: Merchant Shipping Act 1979, s.21; Safety at Sea Act 1986, s.11(1)(2)(4); Merchant Shipping (Registration, etc.) Act 1993, Sched. 4, paras. 6, 13, Sched. 5; British Nationality Act 1981, s.51(3); Criminal Justice Act 1982, s.49(3).]

The Merchant Shipping Act 1979, s.21 effected a significant change in legislative approach by giving very wide enabling powers so that most detailed safety matters would be dealt with in regulations issued under it, as opposed to being set out in detail in the primary legislation, as was the case with the Merchant Shipping Act 1894. The pre-consolidating Merchant Shipping (Registration, etc.) Act 1993 continued the policy of repealing redundant rules contained in the primary Acts (and see subs. (4), below). As noted by DR Thomas (in the General Note to the Merchant Shipping Act 1979, s.21 *Current Law Statutes Annotated 1979*), the section is analogous to the scheme under the Health and Safety at Work, etc. Act 1974 and represented a policy of bringing the regulation of health and safety on ships into line with those relating to persons on land.

Section 85 re-enacts s.21 of the Merchant Shipping Act 1979, as it has been amended (*e.g.* by the Safety at Sea Act 1986), and must be read together with s.86. The two sections provide a safety framework, but the detail is to be found in the mass of regulations issued under them.

Subs. (1)

This subsection sets out the purposes for which safety regulations may be issued and reflects the limits of national jurisdiction. Under Art. 21 of the UN Convention on the Law of the Sea 1982, a coastal state may regulate the right of innocent passage through territorial waters in respect of safety and, under Art. 94, it is the duty of the flag state to ensure the safety of its ships at sea. Paragraphs (a) and (c) relate to securing safety on U.K. ships wherever they are and to other ships wherever registered when they are in U.K. waters. Note how the Merchant Shipping (Registration, etc.) Act 1993, Sched. 4, para. 6(4) extended the power to make health and safety regulations under s.85(1)(c) (formerly s.21(1)(c) of the Merchant Shipping Act 1979, as amended by the Safety at Sea Act 1986, s.11), from port limits to U.K. national waters. Paragraph (b) allows the Secretary of State to make regulations to give effect to international Conventions on health and safety matters relating to ships which have been ratified by the U.K. Such Conventions would include SOLAS and the International Convention on Standards of Training, Certification and Watchkeeping for Seafarers 1978 (the STCW Convention), both of which were revised in 1995. Section 85(1)(b) would be used to incorporate those revisions in U.K. law. It is particularly important to note that the concluding words of the subsection allow the Secretary of State to incorporate the substance of such a Convention ratified by the U.K. in advance of its international entry into force. That possibility is particularly important, as it may take many years for the international instrument to enter into force, but the U.K. may consider that there is an urgent need for it to act immediately so as to protect seafarers or the public. Note the considerable change in approach heralded by the Merchant Shipping (Delegation of Type Approval) Regulations 1996 (S.I. 1996 No. 147), which allow approval of equipment in regulations to be delegated by the use of Merchant Shipping Notices, as opposed to regulations themselves.

Subs. (2)

Note how a wider definition of U.K. ship is used in this subsection, than in s.1(3), above.

Subs. (3)

The regulations which may be issued under subs. (1) may cover any of the matters listed in subs. (2), which are extremely varied and broad in their wording. Even so, the matters listed are not definitive but only indicative of the powers conferred by subs. (1).

Subs. (4)

The Merchant Shipping (Registration, etc.) Act 1993, Sched. 4, para. 13 repealed the remaining parts of the Merchant Shipping Act 1894, ss.418–419 and 421, dealing with the minor topic of collision regulations for seaplanes. Specific action was needed by the 1993 Act because of the extension to the rule-making power which was made by what is now s.85(4). Note the repeal, by the Merchant Shipping (Registration, etc.) Act 1993, Sched. 5, of a saving power for local navigation rules in the 1894 Act, s.421. This was presumably needed because the international collision regulations, applied by the latest statutory instruments (S.I. 1989 Nos. 1798, 2400; S.I. 1991 No. 638), themselves contain in Rule 1(b) a saving for local rules.

Subs. (5)

The Safety Regulations may allow for the approval by the Secretary of State of specific documents, *e.g.* certificates, but the approval must be given in writing and contain details of its conditions and date of operation. This requirement is presumably because inspectors may need to be able easily to check on compliance with the Safety Regulations.

Subss. (6) and (7)

There are powers to grant exemptions for particular cases.

Subs. (7)

The Safety Regulations may, and usually do, contain the enforcement provisions listed in subs. (7), including powers of detention (see s.284) and specific offences. The offences created by the Safety Regulations have a maximum penalty as set out in paras. (b) and (c). On indictment, the maximum penalty is two years imprisonment or an unlimited fine. Note that para. (d) allows Safety Regulations to provide for convictions of persons such as the owner and master and charterer, and not simply one of them (see the General Note to s.131, below).

Provisions supplementary to section 85: general

86.—Safety regulations may—

(a) make different provision for different circumstances and, in particular, make provision for an individual case;

(b) be made so as to apply only in such circumstances as are prescribed by the regulations;

(c) be made so as to extend outside the United Kingdom;

(d) contain such incidental, supplemental and transitional provisions as the Secretary of State considers appropriate;

(e) make provision for compensation to be paid, where a signal is used or displayed otherwise than in accordance with the regulations, for any expense or loss caused in consequence of the signal's being taken for a signal of distress;

and any compensation falling to be paid by virtue of regulations under paragraph (e) above may, without prejudice to any other remedy, be recovered in the same manner as salvage.

(2) The Secretary of State may by regulations—

(a) make such repeals or other modifications of provisions of the Merchant Shipping Acts 1894 to 1977 re-enacted in this Act, and of any instruments made under those Acts as he considers appropriate in consequence or in anticipation of the making of safety regulations;

(b) make such repeals or other modifications of provisions of any enactment passed and any instrument made before 4th April 1979 as he considers appropriate in connection with any modification made or to be made in pursuance of paragraph (a);

(c) provide for anything done under a provision repealed or otherwise modified by virtue of either of the preceding paragraphs to have effect as if done under safety regulations and make such other transitional provision and such incidental and supplemental provision as he considers appropriate in connection with any modification made by virtue of either of those paragraphs.

(3) Nothing in section 85(3) to (6) or subsection (1) above shall be construed as prejudicing the generality of section 85(1).

(4) Where the Secretary of State proposes to make safety regulations or he or another person proposes to give an approval in pursuance of safety regulations it shall be the duty of the Secretary of State or other person, before he gives effect to the proposal, to consult such persons in the United Kingdom (if any) as he considers will be affected by the proposal.

(5) Except where subsections (6) below applies, a statutory instrument containing regulations under section 85 of the following descriptions shall be subject to annulment in pursuance of a resolution of either House of Parliament—

(a) regulations under subsection (1)(a) of that section;

(b) regulations under subsection (1)(b) of that section which—

     (i) relate to an international agreement laid before Parliament before 4th April 1979, or

     (ii) relate to safety matters and give effect to amendments in force to an international agreement already implemented under that paragraph; and

(c) regulations under subsection (1)(c) of that section which contain a statement that they are made only for the purpose of applying to certain other ships the provisions of an international agreement implemented under subsection (1)(b) of that section;

and regulations of any other description under section 85 shall not be made unless a draft of the regulations has been approved by resolution of each House of Parliament.

(6) Regulations falling within paragraphs (a) to (c) of subsection (5) above, if contained in the same instrument as any regulations required to be approved in draft by virtue of that subsection, shall also require to be so approved.

DEFINITIONS
     "Act, this": Interpretation Act 1978, Sched. 1
     "person": Interpretation Act 1978, Sched. 1.
     "safety regulations": ss.85(1) and 313(1).
     "Secretary of State": Interpretation Act 1978, Sched. 1.
     "ship": s.313(1).
     "United Kingdom": Interpretation Act 1978, Sched. 1.

GENERAL NOTE
     [Derivation: Merchant Shipping Act 1979, ss.22, 49(4A), (4B); Safety at Sea Act 1986, s.11(3); Merchant Shipping (Registration, etc.) Act 1993, Sched. 4, para. 13(3).]
     This section has to be read together with s.85, above. It widens the power to issue Safety Regulations in the circumstances listed, mainly in order to meet any potential *ultra vires* allegations. In particular the Safety Regulations may extend outside the U.K. (and *cf.* s.279, below).
     An extension to the supplementary provisions section was made by the Merchant Shipping (Registration, etc.) Act 1993, Sched. 13, which created what is now s.86(1)(e), in order to

allow regulations to provide for compensation for reliance by a master on misleading distress signals given by another ship. Those powers had been contained in s.21(2) of the Merchant Shipping (Safety Conventions) Act 1949 (c. 43), which was repealed by the Merchant Shipping (Registration, etc.) Act 1993, Sched. 5. The expenses may be recovered "in the same manner" as salvage (see s.224 and Sched. 11, below), although it is not clear if this is intended to grant a maritime lien to the master. It is assumed that such a lien would be granted, but note that the expenses could not be claimed where signals were properly displayed, although the services were not in fact needed (and see *Temperley*, p. 484, note 7).

Subs. (2)

Section 22(3) of the 1979 Act gave wide powers to the Secretary of State to repeal or modify the Merchant Shipping Acts by regulations. This was done, for instance, in respect of the redundant powers to make collision regulations given by ss.418–419 of the Merchant Shipping Act 1894, which were repealed by the Merchant Shipping (Distress Signals and Prevention of Collision) Regulations 1983 (S.I. 1983 No. 708). Subsection (2) repeats the essence of the earlier provision, although paras. (a) and (b) are modified to allow the regulations only to refer to the Merchant Shipping Acts 1894–1977 provisions. Note that the Merchant Shipping Act 1979 received Royal Assent on April 4, 1979 and so would not fall within subs. (2). The restriction in the language of the subsection may make it necessary to embark upon a rather tortuous tracing exercise through the Merchant Shipping Acts. This is unfortunate, given the purpose of the Merchant Shipping Act 1995 to sweep away the old law, and may well have been a minor omission in the pre-consolidation process.

Subs. (5)

Certain statutory instruments may need a positive resolution of Parliament. For the general powers of the Secretary of State to make delegated legislation, such as regulations, see s.306, below.

Provisions supplementary to section 85: dangerous goods

87.—(1) Where any dangerous goods have been sent or carried, or attempted to be sent or carried, on board any ship, whether or not a United Kingdom ship—

(a) without being marked as required by safety regulations,

(b) without such notice having been given as is required by safety regulations,

(c) under a false description, or

(d) with a false description of their sender or carrier,

any court having Admiralty jurisdiction may declare the goods, and any package or receptacle in which they are contained, to be forfeited.

(2) On a declaration of forfeiture being made, the goods shall be forfeited and they shall be disposed of as the court directs.

(3) The powers conferred on the court by subsections (1) and (2) above are exercisable notwithstanding that the owner of the goods—

(a) has not committed any offence under safety regulations relating to dangerous goods;

(b) is not before the court; and

(c) has no notice of the proceedings;

and notwithstanding that there is no evidence to show to whom the goods belong.

(4) Nevertheless, the court may, in their discretion, require such notice as they may direct to be given to the owner or shipper of the goods before they are forfeited.

(5) In this section "dangerous goods" means goods designated as dangerous goods by safety regulations.

DEFINITIONS

"court": subs. (1).

"dangerous goods": subs. (5).

"safety regulations": ss.85(1) and 313(1).
"United Kingdom ship": ss.1(3) and 313(1).

GENERAL NOTE
[Derivation: Merchant Shipping Act 1894, s.449; Merchant Shipping (Registration, etc.) Act 1993, Sched. 4, para. 11(2).]
Dangerous goods are now regulated by the Merchant Shipping (Dangerous Goods) Regulations 1981 (S.I. 1981 No. 1747), as amended, issued under s.85 (formerly s.21 of the Merchant Shipping Act 1979). In effect these Regulations made ss.446–448 of the Merchant Shipping Act 1894 redundant and the provisions were repealed by the Merchant Shipping (Registration, etc.) Act 1993, Sched. 4, para. 11(1). Section 449 of the 1894 Act allowed for forfeiture of dangerous goods carried without being marked or under a false description. This provision was adapted by the Merchant Shipping (Registration, etc.) Act 1993 to reflect the fact that the obligations are set out in the regulations and not under s.446 (see, *e.g.* the reference to Safety Regulations in sub-para. 1(a)).

Safety of submersible and supporting apparatus

88.—(1) This section applies to any submersible or supporting apparatus—
  (a) operated within United Kingdom waters, or
  (b) launched or operated from, or comprising, a United Kingdom ship.
  (2) The Secretary of State may make regulations—
  (a) for the safety of submersible and supporting apparatus;
  (b) for the prevention of accidents in or near submersible or supporting apparatus;
  (c) for the safety, health and welfare of persons on or in submersible and supporting apparatus;
  (d) for prohibiting or otherwise restricting the operation of any submersible apparatus except in accordance with the conditions of a licence granted under the regulations; and
  (e) for the registration of submersible apparatus.
  (3) Schedule 2 shall have effect for supplementing the provisions of this section.
  (4) In this section—
  "apparatus" includes any vessel, vehicle or hovercraft, any structure, any diving plant or equipment and any other form of equipment;
  "specified" means specified in regulations made by the Secretary of State for the purposes of this section;
  "submersible apparatus" means any apparatus used, or designed for use, in supporting human life on or under the bed of any waters or elsewhere under the surface of any waters; and
  "supporting apparatus" means any apparatus used, or designed for use, in connection with the operation of any submersible apparatus.

DEFINITIONS
"apparatus": subs. (4).
"person": Interpretation Act 1978, Sched. 1.
"regulations": Sched. 2, para. 1(1).
"Secretary of State": Interpretation Act 1978, Sched. 1.
"specified": subs. (4).
"submersible apparatus": subs. (4).
"supporting apparatus": subs. (4).
"United Kingdom ship": ss.1(3) and 313(1).
"United Kingdom waters": s.313(2)(a).

GENERAL NOTE
[Derivation: Merchant Shipping Act 1974, ss.16 and 17; Merchant Shipping (Registration, etc.) Act 1993, Sched. 4, para. 6(3).]
This section re-enacts ss.16 and 17 of the Merchant Shipping Act 1974, as amended. That Act was passed after an incident involving a midget submarine which failed to.surface in 1973, trapping its crew for three days. Section 88 allows Regulations to be made relating to the safety of

submersibles and supporting apparatus. In essence, the Regulations may deal with the many types of miniature submarine often used in marine exploration or, more particularly, in the offshore and cable-laying industries. These machines now take many forms, including remotely operated vehicles and trenching equipment for digging pipes and cables. The apparatus could also include ordinary diving suits. See the Merchant Shipping (Registration of Submersible Craft) Regulations 1976 (S.I. 1976 No. 940), as amended; the Merchant Shipping (Submersible Craft Construction and Survey) Regulations 1981 (S.I. 1981 No. 1098), as amended; and the Merchant Shipping (Submersible Craft Operations) Regulations 1987 (S.I. 1987 No. 311).

Special provisions

Load lines

89. Schedule 3 (which makes provision as to load lines) shall have effect.

DEFINITIONS
    "load lines": Sched. 3, para. 2(6).

GENERAL NOTE
    [Derivation: Merchant Shipping (Load Lines) Act 1967 (c. 27).]
    The section gives effect to Sched. 3, which re-enacts the Merchant Shipping (Load Lines) Act 1967, as amended. The 1967 Act gave effect to the International Convention on Load Lines 1966. Regulations issued under what is now Sched. 3, para. 2 are the Merchant Shipping (Load Lines) Rules 1968 (S.I. 1968 No. 1053), as amended.

Charts and other information

90.—(1) The Secretary of State may make rules specifying such charts, directions or information as appear to him necessary or expedient for the safe operation of ships.

(2) Rules under this section may require United Kingdom ships, or such descriptions of United Kingdom ships as may be specified in the rules, to carry (either at all times or on such voyages as may be specified in the rules) copies of the charts, directions or information so specified.

(3) If a ship goes to sea or attempts to go to sea without carrying copies of the charts, directions or information which it is required to carry by rules under this section the master or owner shall be liable on summary conviction to a fine not exceeding level 4 on the standard scale.

DEFINITIONS
    "master": s.313(1).
    "Secretary of State": Interpretation Act 1978, Sched. 1.
    "ship": s.313(1).
    "standard scale": Criminal Justice Act 1982, s.37.
    "United Kingdom ship": subs. (2) and ss.1(3) and 313(1).

GENERAL NOTE
    [Derivation: Merchant Shipping Act 1970, s.86; Merchant Shipping Act 1979, Sched. 6, Pt. III.]
    Section 90 re-enacts s.86 of the Merchant Shipping Act 1970, as amended. It allows the Secretary of State to create obligations concerning the carrying of charts and similar safety information (*e.g.* Merchant Shipping Notices). A ship which fails to carry the appropriate charts may render its "master or owner" liable to a fine. Both may be convicted (see *Federal Steam Navigation Co. v. Department of Trade and Industry; Huntingdon, The* [1974] 1 W.L.R. 505 and the General Note to s.131, below).

Report of dangers to navigation

91.—The master of any United Kingdom ship, on meeting with any of the dangers to navigation specified in subsection (2) below, shall send information accordingly, by all means of communication at his disposal and in accordance with rules to be made for the purposes of this section, to ships in the vicinity and to such authorities on shore as may be prescribed by those rules.

(2) The dangers to navigation referred to in subsection (1) above are—

(a) dangerous ice;

(b) a dangerous derelict;

(c) a tropical storm;

(d) air temperatures below freezing point associated with gale force winds causing severe ice accretion on the superstructure of ships;

(e) winds of force 10 or above on the Beaufort Scale for which no storm warning has been received; or

(f) any other direct danger to navigation.

(3) Rules for the purposes of this section shall be made by the Secretary of State.

(4) If the master of a ship fails to comply with the provisions of this section, he shall be liable to a fine not exceeding level 4 on the standard scale.

(5) Every person in charge of a controlled station for wireless telegraphy shall, on receiving the signal prescribed by the said rules for indicating that a message is about to be sent under this section, refrain from sending messages for a time sufficient to allow other stations to receive the message, and, if so required by the Secretary of State, shall transmit the message in such manner as may be required by the Secretary of State.

(6) Compliance with subsection (5) above shall be deemed to be a condition of every wireless telegraphy licence.

(7) In this section—

"controlled station for wireless telegraphy" means such a station controlled by the Secretary of State; and "controlled" includes controlled by means of a licence granted by him;

"tropical storm" means a hurricane, typhoon, cyclone, or other storm of a similar nature;

"wireless telegraphy licence" and "station for wireless telegraphy" have the same meaning as in the Wireless Telegraphy Act 1949,

and the master of a ship shall be deemed to have met with a tropical storm if he has reason to believe that there is such a storm in his vicinity.

DEFINITIONS

"controlled": subs. (7).

"controlled station for wireless telegraphy": subs. (7).

"dangers to navigation": subs. (2).

"master": s.313(1).

"met with a tropical storm": subs. (7).

"Secretary of State": Interpretation Act 1978, Sched. 1.

"ship": s.313(1).

"standard scale": Criminal Justice Act 1982, s.37.

"station for wireless telegraphy": subs. (7).

"tropical storm": subs. (7).

"United Kingdom ship": ss.1(3) and 313(1).

"wireless telegraphy licence": subs. (7).

GENERAL NOTE

[Derivation: Merchant Shipping (Safety and Load Line Conventions) Act 1932 (c. 9), s.24; Merchant Shipping Act 1964, s.16; Merchant Shipping Act 1979, Sched. 6, Pt. III.]

This section re-enacts s.24 Merchant Shipping (Safety and Load Line Conventions) Act 1932 as amended and derives from concern caused by such disasters as the *Titanic*, where it was appreciated that early warning of dangerous marine conditions could be given by masters of merchant ships to each other. Although modern meteorology aided by satellites has greatly improved the navigational information available to mariners, the provision of localised information about hazards can still be of use. The section requires information to be sent by a master, in accordance with statutory rules, both to ships in the vicinity and to prescribed authorities. The information which must be sent is contained in subs. (2) and paras. (d) and (e) which were added by s.16 of the Merchant Shipping Act 1964. Warnings about ice on superstructures is particularly important for fishing vessels, which might be at risk of capsizing. Note that para. (f) could include dangers which are not caused by the weather, *e.g.* where a ship has gone aground in a main channel. Subsection (5) also provides echoes of the *Titanic*, in that it places obligations on those at shore stations to refrain from sending messages, *e.g.* about commercial or social matters, which might prevent the safety warning being heard by others. There were suggestions that the radio waves at the time of the Titanic's last voyage were too full of messages being sent to passengers, so that safety warnings might not have been heard.

Assistance at sea

Duty of ship to assist the other in case of collision

92.—In every case of collision between two ships, it shall be the duty of the master of each ship, if and so far as he can do so without danger to his own ship, crew and passengers (if any)—

(a) to render to the other ship, its master, crew and passengers (if any) such assistance as may be practicable, and may be necessary to save them from any danger caused by the collision, and to stay by the other ship until he has ascertained that it has no need of further assistance; and

(b) to give to the master of the other ship the name of his own ship and also the names of the ports from which it comes and to which it is bound.

(2) The duties imposed on the master of a ship by subsection (1) above apply to the masters of United Kingdom ships and to the masters of foreign ships when in United Kingdom waters.

(3) The failure of the master of a ship to comply with the provisions of this section shall not raise any presumption of law that the collision was caused by his wrongful act, neglect, or default.

(4) If the master fails without reasonable excuse to comply with this section, he shall—

(a) in the case of a failure to comply with subsection (1)(a) above, be liable—

(i) on summary conviction, to a fine not exceeding £50,000 or imprisonment for a term not exceeding six months or both;

(ii) on conviction on indictment, to a fine or imprisonment for a term not exceeding two years or both; and

(b) in the case of a failure to comply with subsection (1)(b) above, be liable—

(i) on summary conviction, to a fine not exceeding the statutory maximum;

(ii) on conviction on indictment, to a fine;

and in either case if he is a certified officer, an inquiry into his conduct may be held, and his certificate cancelled or suspended.

DEFINITIONS
"fails": s.313(1).
"foreign": s.313(1).
"master": s.313(1).
"passenger": Sched. 6, Art.1(4).
"port": s.313(1).
"ship": s.313(1).
"statutory maximum": Criminal Justice Act 1982, s.74.
"United Kingdom ship": ss.1(3) and 313(1).
"United Kingdom waters": s.313(2)(a).

GENERAL NOTE
[Derivation: Merchant Shipping Act 1894, s.422; Merchant Shipping Act 1979, Sched. 6, Pt. VII, para. 6; Merchant Shipping (Registration, etc.) Act 1993, Sched. 4, para. 6(2); Maritime Conventions Act 1911, s.4(2).]

This section derives from s.422 of the Merchant Shipping Act 1894, as amended, and gives effect to obligations agreed in the Collision Convention 1910, Art. 8. It imposes a duty to render assistance after a collision and should be read together with s.93, below and Sched. 11, Pt. II, para. 3, below. There have been instances of ships sailing away after a collision, sometimes in the belief that there had only been a minor impact. The section requires what is both practical and necessary, but cannot impose an absolute obligation on those on one ship to risk their lives to assist others. At the very minimum, there is an obligation to stand by until it is clear that help is no longer required. The stand-by ship could then operate as a haven should the other ship sink. Subsection (1)(b) places an obligation on the ships to exchange names and ports. The information about port of destination may be of use where one of the ships later sinks and it is desired to check her course, but the information about identity may be of significance to the legal advisers who wish later to bring a civil claim for collision damage. Note that there is no presumption of fault caused by the fact of a collision being in breach of the Collision Regulations or of the duties under this section. Subsection (3) was added as a result of the Collision Convention 1910, which abolished the presumption of fault (see the Maritime Conventions Act 1911, s.4(2)). Rather paradoxically, the section might not apply where there has been a "near-miss" which involved one or more ships going aground, but without actually colliding with each other, albeit that such facts would be sufficient to found a cause of action in negligence. It would seem that the existence of the duty to assist does not *absolutely* bar the assister from being considered as a salvor in respect of the services rendered, although Art. 18 of the 1989 Salvage Convention (see Sched. 11, below) may result in any reward being reduced or extinguished (*cf. Temperley*, p.115 and the General Note to s.93, below).

Subsection (2) was added by the Merchant Shipping (Registration, etc.) Act 1993, Sched. 4, para. 6 and makes it clear that the duties apply to U.K. ships (as defined in s.1(3)) and not British ships. Section 424 of the Merchant Shipping Act 1894 originally allowed for the duties to be extended to foreign vessels by Order, but that section has now been repealed (see S.I. 1983 No. 708) and subsumed into the general power to issue Safety Regulations under s.85(3). Consistent with international practice, foreign ships are subject to the s.92 duties when in U.K. waters (see subs. (2)).

Duty to assist ships, etc. in distress

93.—(1) The master of a ship, on receiving at sea a signal of distress or information from any source that a ship or aircraft is in distress, shall proceed with all speed to the assistance of the persons in distress (informing them if possible that he is doing so) unless he is unable, or in the special circumstances of the case considers it unreasonable or unnecessary, to do so, or unless he is released from this duty under subsection (4) or (5) below.

(2) Where the master of any ship in distress has requisitioned any ship that has answered his call, it shall be the duty of the master of the requisitioned ship to comply with the requisition by continuing to proceed with all speed to the assistance of the persons in distress.

(3) The duties imposed on the master of a ship by subsections (1) and (2) above apply to the masters of United Kingdom ships and to the masters of foreign ships when in United Kingdom waters.

(4) A master shall be released from the duty imposed by subsection (1) above as soon as he is informed of the requisition of one or more ships other than his own and that the requisition is being complied with by the ship or ships requisitioned.

(5) A master shall be released from the duty imposed by subsection (1) above, and, if his ship has been requisitioned, from the duty imposed by subsection (2) above, if he is informed by the persons in distress, or by the master of any ship that has reached the persons in distress, that assistance is no longer required.

(6) If a master fails to comply with the preceding provisions of this section he shall be liable—

    (a) on summary conviction, to imprisonment for a term not exceeding six
        months or to a fine not exceeding the statutory maximum, or both;

    (b) on conviction on indictment, to imprisonment for a term not exceed-
        ing two years or to a fine, or both.

(7) Compliance by the master of a ship with the provisions of this section shall not affect his right, or the right of any other person, to salvage.

DEFINITIONS
   "fails": s.313(1).
   "foreign": s.313(1).

"master": s.313(1).
"person": Interpretation Act 1978, Sched. 1.
"ship": s.313(1).
"statutory maximum": Criminal Justice Act 1982, s.74.
"United Kingdom ship": ss.1(3) and 313(1).
"United Kingdom waters": s.313(2)(a).

GENERAL NOTE

[Derivation: Merchant Shipping (Safety Conventions) Act 1949, s.22; Merchant Shipping (Registration, etc.) Act 1993, Sched. 4, para. 6(2).]

This section re-enacts s.22 of the Merchant Shipping (Safety Conventions) Act 1949 (c. 43), as amended, which itself replaced an earlier provision of 1932. Article 11 of the Salvage Convention 1910 created an obligation on a master to render assistance to those in danger at sea. Article 11 was enacted in s.6 of the Maritime Conventions Act 1911, which was repealed and replaced by Art. 10 of the 1989 Salvage Convention (see Sched. 11, below). There is some overlap in that Sched. 11, Pt. I, para. 3, below also creates an offence for failing to assist, albeit that the penalties are similar. It would seem that the marginal note to the section is a little misleading, in that the section is mainly concerned with ensuring that a master responds to a signal by changing course and taking his vessel to the location of the one which has sent a distress signal. The section does not seem to create an obligation to assist, as such, despite the wording "proceed . . . to the assistance". The duty is directed to the speed of response to a distress signal, and that which ought to be done on arrival should probably be considered under the Sched. 11, Pt. I, para. 3 offence. Like s.92, above, the section does not impose absolute duties. Note that the duty is specifically placed on the master and not the owner (and see Art. 10.3 of the 1989 Salvage Convention, Sched. 11, below), although it may be that owners could put pressure on masters not to disturb tight sailing schedules. Note that reciprocal duties are placed on the master of a ship in distress to release those ships which have been summoned by the distress call from their statutory duties to respond. Subsection (7) confirms the position in Admiralty law (and arising impliedly under Art. 11 of the 1910 Salvage Convention and now under Art. 10 of the 1989 Salvage Convention) that compliance with the statutory duty does not affect any right to salvage by reason of the putative salvor not having been a "volunteer" (see the General Note to Art. 17 of the 1989 Salvage Convention, Sched. 11, Pt. I, below).

It is to be noted that the duty is imposed on the master, who is defined by s.313 of the Merchant Shipping Act 1995 as including "every person (except a pilot) having command or charge of any ship . . .". This definition would therefore include the officer of the watch who had the conduct of the vessel for the time being.

The reference in the 1949 Act to a British ship was changed to a U.K. ship by the Merchant Shipping (Registration, etc.) Act 1993, Sched. 4, para. 6 (and see the General Note to s.92(2), above).

Unsafe ships

Meaning of "dangerously unsafe ship"

94.—(1) For the purposes of sections 95, 96, 97 and 98 a ship is "dangerously unsafe" if, having regard to the nature of the service for which it is intended, the ship is, by reason of the matters mentioned in subsection (2) below, unfit to go to sea without serious danger to human life.

(2) Those matters are—
  (a) the condition, or the unsuitability for its purpose, of—
          (i) the ship or its machinery or equipment, or
          (ii) any part of the ship or its machinery or equipment;
  (b) undermanning;
  (c) overloading or unsafe or improper loading;
  (d) any other matter relevant to the safety of the ship;
and are referred to in those sections, in relation to any ship, as "the matters relevant to its safety".

(3) Any reference in those sections to "going to sea" shall, in a case where the service for which the ship is intended consists of going on voyages or

excursions that do not involve going to sea, be construed as a reference to going on such a voyage or excursion.

DEFINITIONS
"dangerously unsafe": subs. (1).
"going to sea": subs. (3).
"ship": s.313(1).
"the matters relevant to its safety": subs. (2).

GENERAL NOTE
[Derivation: Merchant Shipping Act 1988, s.30(1), (3), (9); Merchant Shipping (Registration, etc.) Act 1993, s.30A(5), Sched. 4, para. 12.]

Sections 94–100 group together a series of provisions dealing with unsafe ships.

Section 94 provides common definitions of "dangerously unsafe ship" and "going to sea" for the purposes of the detention of dangerously unsafe ships and the criminal liability of shipowners and masters in respect of them. Subsection (2) provides a common explanation for the phrase "the matters relevant to its safety" which appears, *e.g.* in s.98(2). That definition is largely derived from the 1894 Act, s.457, as amended by the Merchant Shipping Act 1979, s.44 and the Merchant Shipping Act 1988, s.30. Subsection (2) is materially identical to s.30(3) of the Merchant Shipping Act 1988, but in s.94 of the Merchant Shipping Act 1995 is made available to the other sections indicated. For offences to which the "matters" relate, see ss.95–98, below.

Subs. (2)
In order for the commission of the various offences to which subs. (2) applies (*e.g.* under s.98), the ship must be unfit only by reason of one of the matters mentioned in it. Those relating to the condition of the ship (and its machinery) repeat the provisions in the Merchant Shipping Act 1979, s.44, as do those on undermanning and overloading. It is not quite clear whether "the ship or its ... equipment" includes equipment put on board by a charterer. At what stage can it be said that such equipment becomes "its" machinery or equipment? Machinery essential to the commercial operation of a ship, such as a pump, could be classified as part of the ship. But portable generators used for some ancillary purpose might not be so classified.

A minor addition to the definition as it appeared in the Merchant Shipping Act 1979, s.44 was made by the Merchant Shipping Act 1988, s.30 by the addition of "unsafe" loading in para. (c), which seems to add little to "improper". Two major additions were those relating to "unsuitability" for the purpose in para. (a) and the whole of para. (d).

The stated object of the "unsuitability" provision was to cover equipment which was in good condition, but below the specification necessary for its intended purpose, *e.g.* pumps of inadequate capacity. There may be cases where the shipowner deliberately purchases inadequate equipment and the added provisions were necessary to cover this, as it could otherwise be said that there was nothing wrong with the *condition* of the equipment which worked perfectly within its own design limitations. But the *unsuitability* of the ship or its equipment could be matters wholly outside the knowledge or control of the shipowner or, more particularly, the master, as they could include design defects.

Paragraph (d) is so widely phrased that virtually anything which could cause a danger to human life would be covered by it and in Parliamentary debates on the Merchant Shipping Act 1988 it was strongly opposed by speakers from all sides of the shipping industry. Although it appears simply to be an addition to a list of examples of unfitness, it is really capable of encompassing paras. (a)–(c). In effect it means that if the ship is in fact a danger, then there may be an offence under a relevant section, subject only to the defences in those sections (see, *e.g.* ss.98(5) and 98(6)). This would be perfectly satisfactory were it not for the limited nature of those defences. Not surprisingly, the Government had some difficulty in thinking of a specific example to show how the para. (d) might operate. One example given was of a ship not adequately equipped for a particularly hazardous cargo. Another was of dangerous cargoes that needed to be segregated, stowed and carried according to strict requirements of the Merchant Shipping (Dangerous Goods) Regulations 1981 (S.I. 1981 No. 1747). A narrow construction of para. (a) might not call such activities "improper loading". Likewise, the inability to use safety equipment because of unsatisfactory stowage of cargo on a Ro-Ro ship might not be considered "unsafe loading".

Subs. (3)
The reference to "going to sea" is derived from a technical amendment to s.30(9) of the Merchant Shipping Act 1988 made during the Third Reading in the Commons. Its purpose was to cover inshore navigation generally, as large numbers of passengers could be carried there, *e.g.* across the Solent. It would also seem to include those vessels which might make only harbour,

river or dock trips, as opposed to deep water voyages. This means that many pleasure craft may be subject to the section, even if they operate in dock or river systems, provided that they are "ships used in navigation" within s.313(2).

Power to detain dangerously unsafe ship

95.—(1) Where a ship in a port in the United Kingdom appears to a relevant inspector to be a dangerously unsafe ship the ship may be detained.

(2) The power of detention conferred by subsection (1) above is exercisable in relation to foreign ships as well as United Kingdom ships.

(3) The officer detaining the ship shall serve on the master of the ship a detention notice which shall—

(a) state that the relevant inspector is of the opinion that the ship is a dangerously unsafe ship;

(b) specify the matters which, in the relevant inspector's opinion, make the ship a dangerously unsafe ship; and

(c) prohibit the ship from going to sea until it is released by a competent authority.

(4) In the case of a ship which is not a British ship the officer detaining the ship shall cause a copy of the detention notice to be sent as soon as practicable to the nearest consular officer for the country to which the ship belongs.

(5) In this section—

"competent authority" means any officer mentioned in section 284(1); and

"relevant inspector" means any person mentioned in paragraph (a), (b) or (c) of section 258(1).

DEFINITIONS

"British ship": ss.1(1) and 313(1).
"competent authority": subs. (5) and s.284(1).
"consular officer": s.313(1).
"dangerously unsafe": s.94(1).
"foreign": s.313(1).
"going to sea": s.94(3).
"master": s.313(1).
"port": s.313(1).
"relevant inspector": subs. (5) and s.258(1).
"ship": s.313(1).
"United Kingdom": Interpretation Act 1978, Sched. 1.
"United Kingdom ship": ss.1(3) and 313(1).

GENERAL NOTE

[Derivation: Merchant Shipping Act 1988, s.30A; Merchant Shipping (Registration, etc.) Act 1993, Sched. 4, para. 12(2).]

Sections 459–461 of the Merchant Shipping Act 1894 established a rigorous system (for its day) for the detention of British and foreign ships which were found to be unsafe in a British port. Gradually, these powers were superseded by more specific provisions laid down in later Acts (see, e.g. the Merchant Shipping Act 1988, ss.30–33 dealing with maritime safety as a result of the Zeebrugge disaster) and in individual Regulations. Some procedural provisions, such as provisional and final detention (s.459(4)) and courts of survey (s.459(7)), did not reflect modern practice and were repealed by the Merchant Shipping (Registration, etc.) Act 1993.

Section 95(2) is a modern replacement, enacted by the Merchant Shipping (Registration, etc.) Act 1993, Sched. 4, para. 12, which enables an inspector to serve a "detention notice" on a master. The structure of the new provision is based upon the equivalent concept of a prohibition notice, set out in s.262 (formerly the Merchant Shipping Act 1984, s.2). Section 95 is now integrated into the series of sections dealing with dangerously unsafe ships.

References of detention notices to arbitration

96.—(1) Any question as to whether any of the matters specified in relation to a ship in a detention notice in pursuance of section 95(3)(b) in connection with any opinion formed by the relevant inspector constituted a valid basis for that opinion shall, if the master or owner of the ship so requires by a notice given to the relevant inspector within 21 days from the service of the detention notice, be referred to a single arbitrator appointed by agreement between the parties for that question to be decided by him.

(2) Where a notice is given by the master or owner of the ship in accordance with subsection (1) above, the giving of the notice shall not suspend the operation of the detention notice unless, on the application of the person requiring the reference, the arbitrator so directs.

(3) The arbitrator shall have regard, in coming to his decision, to any other matters not specified in the detention notice which appear to him to be relevant to whether the ship was or was not a dangerously unsafe ship.

(4) Where on a reference under this section the arbitrator decides as respects any matter to which the reference relates, that in all the circumstances the matter did not constitute a valid basis for the inspector's opinion he shall either cancel the detention notice or affirm it with such modifications as he may in the circumstances think fit; and in any other case the arbitrator shall affirm the notice in its original form.

(5) The arbitrator shall include in his decision a finding whether there was or was not a valid basis for the detention of the ship as a dangerously unsafe ship.

(6) A person shall not be qualified for appointment as an arbitrator under this section unless he is—

    (a) a person holding a certificate of competency as a master mariner or as a marine engineer officer class 1, or a person holding a certificate equivalent to any such certificate;

    (b) a naval architect;

    (c) a person falling within subsection (7); or

    (d) a person with special experience of shipping matters, of the fishing industry, or of activities carried on in ports.

(7) For the purposes of subsection (6)(c) a person falls within this subsection if—

    (a) he has a 10 year general qualification (within the meaning of section 71 of the Courts and Legal Services Act 1990);

    (b) he is an advocate or solicitor in Scotland of at least 10 years' standing; or

    (c) he is a member of the bar of Northern Ireland or solicitor of the Supreme Court of Northern Ireland of at least 10 years' standing.

(8) In connection with his functions under this section an arbitrator shall have the powers conferred on an inspector by section 259.

(9) In the application of this section to Scotland any reference to an arbitrator shall be construed as a reference to an arbiter and the reference in subsection (1) above to a single arbitrator appointed by agreement between the parties shall be construed as a reference to a single arbiter so appointed or, in default of agreement, appointed by the sheriff.

(10) The Arbitration Act (Northern Ireland) 1937 shall apply in relation to an arbitration in pursuance of this section as if this section related to a matter in respect of which the Parliament of Northern Ireland had power to make laws.

(11) In this section "relevant inspector" has the same meaning as in section 95.

<small>DEFINITIONS</small>
    "dangerously unsafe": s.94(1).
    "master": s.313(1).
    "person": Interpretation Act 1978, Sched. 1.
    "port": s.313(1).
    "qualified arbitrator": subss. (6) and (7).
    "relevant inspector": ss.95(5) and 258(1).
    "sheriff": Interpretation Act 1978, Sched. 1.

"ship": s.313(1).
"Supreme Court": Interpretation Act 1978, Sched. 1.

GENERAL NOTE
[Derivation: Merchant Shipping Act 1984, s.4; Courts and Legal Services Act 1990, Sched. 10, para. 55; Merchant Shipping (Registration, etc.) Act 1993, Sched. 4, para. 12(3) and (4).]
    Section 96 provides for the reference of questions concerning detention notices (issued under s.95) to arbitration. Sections 96 and 97 use the model of the arbitration and compensation system in ss.264–265 (as established in ss.4 and 5 of the Merchant Shipping Act 1984) which apply to disputes about the validity of prohibition notices (see ss.262–263, below). That model was subject to necessary modifications effected by the Merchant Shipping (Registration, etc.) Act 1993, Sched. 4, para. 12 which now appear in ss.95 and 96. Thus, under subs. (1) the right to refer a question to the arbitrator is available to the shipowner irrespective of whether the master also exercises that right. Under subs. (2) the reference to the arbitrator cannot suspend the operation of the detention notice. Under subs. (3) the arbitrator is entitled to take into account matters not specified in the detention notice. The arbitrator is also obliged to provide a finding as to whether there was a valid basis for the detention. Failure to have such a basis may render the Secretary of State liable to pay compensation under s.97. Subsections (6) and (7) set out the qualifications of an arbitrator, and subs. (8) gives the arbitrator the extensive powers of inspection and sampling provided by s.259.

Compensation in connection with invalid detention of ship

97.—(1) If on a reference under section 96 relating to a detention notice in relation to a ship—
   (a) the arbitrator decides that any matter did not constitute a valid basis for the relevant inspector's opinion, and
   (b) it appears to him that there were no reasonable grounds for the inspector to form that opinion,
the arbitrator may award the owner of the ship such compensation in respect of any loss suffered by him in consequence of the detention of the ship as the arbitrator thinks fit.
   (2) Any compensation awarded under this section shall be payable by the Secretary of State.
   (3) In the application of this section to Scotland any reference to an arbitrator shall be construed as a reference to an arbiter.
   (4) In this section "relevant inspector" has the same meaning as in section 95.

DEFINITIONS
    "arbitrator": s.96(6) and (7).
    "relevant inspector": ss.95(5) and 258(1).
    "Secretary of State": Interpretation Act 1978, Sched. 1.
    "ship": s.313(1).

GENERAL NOTE
[Derivation: Merchant Shipping Act 1984, s.5; Merchant Shipping (Registration, etc.) Act 1993, Sched. 4, para. 12(3), (4).]
    See the General Note to s.96, above, and *cf.* s.265, below. Section 97 gives a discretionary power to the arbitrator to award compensation. An example of compensation claimed could be the extra expenses of keeping the vessel in port or, possibly, the lost revenue (at contract or market rates) which the shipowner suffered while the ship was detained. Under a time charter the vessel might be off-hire and the shipowner would then lose the daily rate set out in the contract. Note that it is only the shipowner which can claim compensation and not a charterer which under the charterparty was obliged to pay the hire during such a detention. The power to award compensation must presumably be exercised on rational grounds and any finding would be subject to review where it was not so made. An arbitrator might consider that it would not be "fit" to award detention rates which were based on contract prices which were considerably higher than market rates. More difficult would be whether the arbitrator would be entitled, *e.g.* to award token sums or to take into account the general conduct of the shipowner and how much the detention was brought on itself. It would appear that there is no right to have full compen-

sation, but that there must be some rational reason for depriving a shipowner of it where there was no valid basis for the detention.

Owner and master liable in respect of dangerously unsafe ship

98.—(1) If a ship which—

(a) is in a port in the United Kingdom, or

(b) is a United Kingdom ship and is in any other port,

is dangerously unsafe, then, subject to subsections (4) and (5) below, the master and the owner of the ship shall each be guilty of an offence.

(2) Where, at the time when a ship is dangerously unsafe, any responsibilities of the owner with respect to the matters relevant to its safety have been assumed (whether wholly or in part) by any person or persons other than the owner, and have been so assumed by that person or (as the case may be) by each of those persons either—

(a) directly, under the terms of a charter-party or management agreement made with the owner, or

(b) indirectly, under the terms of a series of charter-parties or management agreements,

the reference to the owner in subsection (1) above shall be construed as a reference to that other person or (as the case may be) to each of those other persons.

(3) A person guilty of an offence under this section shall be liable—

(a) on summary conviction, to a fine not exceeding £50,000;

(b) on conviction on indictment, to imprisonment for a term not exceeding two years or a fine, or both.

(4) It shall be a defence in proceedings for an offence under this section to prove that at the time of the alleged offence—

(a) arrangements had been made which were appropriate to ensure that before the ship went to sea it was made fit to do so without serious danger to human life by reason of the matters relevant to its safety which are specified in the charge (or, in Scotland, which are libelled in the complaint, petition or indictment); or

(b) it was reasonable for such arrangements not to have been made.

(5) It shall also be a defence in proceedings for an offence under this section to prove—

(a) that, under the terms of one or more charter-parties or management agreements entered into by the accused, the relevant responsibilities, namely—

(i) where the accused is the owner, his responsibilities with respect to the matters relevant to the ship's safety, or

(ii) where the accused is liable to proceedings under this section by virtue of subsection (2) above, so much of those responsibilities as had been assumed by him as mentioned in that subsection,

had at the time of the alleged offence been wholly assumed by some other person or persons party thereto; and

(b) that in all the circumstances of the case the accused had taken such steps as it was reasonable for him to take, and exercised such diligence as it was reasonable for him to exercise, to secure the proper discharge of the relevant responsibilities during the period during which they had been assumed by some other person or persons as mentioned in paragraph (a) above;

and, in determining whether the accused had done so, regard shall be had in particular to the matters mentioned in subsection (6) below.

(6) Those matters are—

(a) whether prior to the time of the alleged offence the accused was, or in all the circumstances ought reasonably to have been, aware of any deficiency in the discharge of the relevant responsibilities; and

(b) the extent to which the accused was or was not able, under the terms of any such charter-party or management agreement as is mentioned in subsection (5)(a) above—
    (i) to terminate it, or
    (ii) to intervene in the management of the ship,
in the event of any such deficiency, and whether it was reasonable for the accused to place himself in that position.

(7) No proceedings for an offence under this section shall be instituted—

(a) in England and Wales, except by or with the consent of the Secretary of State or the Director of Public Prosecutions;

(b) in Northern Ireland, except by or with the consent of the Secretary of State or the Director of Public Prosecutions for Northern Ireland.

(8) In this section—

"management agreement", in relation to a ship, means any agreement (other than a charter-party or a contract of employment) under which the ship is managed, either wholly or in part, by a person other than the owner (whether on behalf of the owner or on behalf of some other person); and

"relevant responsibilities" shall be construed in accordance with subsection (5) above.

(9) References in this section to responsibilities being assumed by a person under the terms of a charter-party or management agreement are references to their being so assumed by him whether or not he has entered into a further charter-party or management agreement providing for them to be assumed by some other person.

DEFINITIONS
"dangerously unsafe": s.94(1).
"England and Wales": Interpretation Act 1978, Sched. 1.
"management agreement": subs. (8).
"master": s.313(1).
"person": Interpretation Act 1978, Sched. 1.
"port": s.313(1).
"relevant responsibilities": subs. (8).
"responsibilities being assumed": subs. (9).
"Secretary of State": Interpretation Act 1978, Sched. 1.
"ship": s.313(1).
"United Kingdom": Interpretation Act 1978, Sched. 1.
"United Kingdom ship": ss.1(3) and 313(1).
"went to sea": s.94(3).

GENERAL NOTE
[Derivation: Merchant Shipping Act 1988, s.30(1), (2), (4)–(10).]

This section re-enacts s.30 of the Merchant Shipping Act 1988 which superseded the Merchant Shipping Act 1979, s.44 (which in its turn replaced the Merchant Shipping Act 1894, s.457). Section 457 of the Merchant Shipping Act 1894 provided for an offence of sending an unseaworthy British ship to sea. The 1979 Act was more specific about unfitness, and introduced the criterion of "serious danger to human life" which is retained in s.94(1) of the Merchant Shipping Act 1995. The 1988 provision extended both the range of the previous offence and the persons who may be prosecuted. In particular, charterers and ship managers could face punishment (see subs. (2)).

The section was the subject of much discussion and amendment during its passage through Parliament in 1988. There is a basic conflict between the desire to create a broad general offence to discourage the grossly culpable conduct involved in sending dangerous ships to sea, and the concern not to draft the provision so widely that it catches those with a lesser degree of involvement or blameworthiness (particularly masters). As a result the section is hedged around with qualifications and defences which make its exact scope somewhat uncertain. The impression was given that the DOT wanted to create an offence so wide that, if there is an accident involving a ship or its equipment, a prosecution could always be brought. This may solve the political problem of being seen to act after a tragedy such as that involving the disaster to the *Herald of Free*

Enterprise in 1987, but it raises basic questions of justice, particularly so far as masters are concerned. While it is understandable that there is a feeling after a disaster that *somebody* must be punished, care must be taken to see that seafarers are not treated more harshly than, *e.g.* truck or train drivers or airline pilots. Where there is gross negligence a prosecution for manslaughter can be brought, but this section can make a master liable to imprisonment for what might be small errors of judgment. The section draws no distinction between the responsibilities of the master and owner and it must be left to the courts to do so.

The section leaves untouched s.99, below, relating to unsafe lighters, barges and like vessels. Note also the powers of the registrar under s.9(3) of the Merchant Shipping Act 1995 to refuse to register a ship which does not meet safety standards.

Subs. (1)

The offence created by this subsection does not involve *sending* the ship to sea, as such, but in having it in port in an unfit state. The old offence under s.457 of the Merchant Shipping Act 1894 did require a sending to sea (or attempted sending). This was thought to be defective because unfitness was only discoverable after an inspection and although detention was possible, no offence would then have been committed. Once the ship sails, it may be difficult to enforce obligations. Presumably, it was difficult to prove an attempt to send an unseaworthy ship to sea. Hence a change was made in the 1979 Act (followed here) to make the offence depend upon the state of the vessel in port. That is an objective test although the offence is obviously designed for vessels which it is intended to take to sea. In 1988, the Government resisted an attempt in the Lords to make the offence depend on proof of an intent to go to sea. It is apparent that this was done after much deliberation as to whether the subsection could be improved. In the end the Government accepted, in the words of the Under Secretary of State, Lord Brabazon of Tara, that this "clearly puts a certain burden on the courts to ensure that natural justice is achieved, but there is nothing unusual in that."

The basic offence depends upon the ship being "dangerously unsafe". That expression cannot be considered on its own as it is defined in s.94(1). It consists of two main elements: unfitness (as defined exclusively in s.94(2)) and serious danger to human life. The latter element is not defined, but the introduction of the word "serious" in 1979 presumably indicated that the risk was to be more than slight. It is not quite clear whether the seriousness refers to the likelihood of the danger occurring, or to the degree of harm to be suffered by human beings—or to both. But, given the heavy penalties which can be imposed under subs. (3), a court will probably take a broad view and require proof of a strong risk of some life threatening event. Defences are set out in subss. (4) and (5). It is necessary to take into account the type of service which the vessel is expected to face. She may be perfectly fit for a short coastal voyage in sheltered waters, but not for an ocean journey. Under subs. (1) it is the intended service that is relevant. Section 94(1) refers to the ship being "unfit to go to sea", but this must be read subject to s.94(3). It is clear from s.307 (replacing in part s.50 of the Merchant Shipping Act 1988) that unregistered pleasure craft could be covered by s.98 if regulations under s.307 so provide.

The section applies to ships of any nationality in British ports, but extends to U.K. ships even when in foreign ports. The Merchant Shipping Act 1894, s.457 only applied to British ships. For unregistered ships see s.307, below.

The wording "the master and the owner" is a deliberate formulation used to overcome problems raised by the expression "owner or master" (see, *e.g. Federal Steam Navigation Co. v. Department of Trade and Industry; The Huntingdon* [1974] 1 W.L.R. 505). Under s.98 both master *and* owner are guilty of an offence and charges may be brought against both simultaneously. The rationale for this is to punish the master for neglect while recognising that owners could turn a blind eye to conduct that could save them money. A prosecution against the master alone might not be a deterrent for the owner, as the punishment for the individual would tend to be lower than that for the corporation. However, a heavy fine on a master is often the only way to enforce a penalty against a foreign-based company. Attempts during the progress of the Merchant Shipping Act 1988 through Parliament to restrict the responsibility of masters, as opposed to owners, were resisted by the Government. The reason was that it was said to be impossible to separate their responsibilities. The Government was content to make them "jointly responsible and allow the courts to choose which one has committed the offence". Shore staff, as such, would not be guilty, but where the owner is a company, reference must be made to ss.277 and 278 to discover which individuals in the corporate structure may be prosecuted. The supplier of unsuitable equipment is not guilty of an offence under the section, although the shipowner will be, subject to the defence in subs. (5) that appropriate arrangements were made. Note that there may be a duplication of offences, in that detailed specifications are often laid down in the Safety Regulations made under s.85, but note that the penalties may differ.

For complementary powers of detention, see s.95.

Subs. (2)

This subsection was originally introduced at the Committee Stage of the Merchant Shipping Act 1988 in the Lords, but needed considerable rewording before the present version was finally added at Committee Stage in the Commons. It extends the categories of persons who can commit the offence to include those who may have assumed some of the obligations of maintaining or operating the ship as are listed in s.94(2). This will particularly affect demise (or bareboat) charterers who normally assume contractual rights to control the ship as if she were owned by them. Time or voyage charterers would not normally assume any direct responsibilities concerning the manner of operation of the vessel which remains under the control of a master employed by the owners. However, such charterers might conceivably be responsible under the contract for certain cargo-related equipment (such as specialised pumps) and these may fall within s.94(2). Owners may commonly employ firms of professional ship managers to operate their ships. These managers would assume all the usual functions of owners, such as hiring the crew and arranging for maintenance and supplies. Such managers could also be guilty of an offence under subs. (1) in respect of functions assumed by them.

In the case of both charterers and managers, the responsibilities could be assumed directly by contract with the registered shipowners. They would fall within para. (a). It is very common to find a series of sub-contracts concerning ships, and it might be that the person with the actual responsibility was a sub-contractor with no direct contractual relationship with the shipowner. Paragraph (b) ensures that this person is also liable to prosecution under subs. (1).

The introduction of this provision necessarily raised the position of the owner (or other person) who no longer had effective control of the ship, but who could still be liable under subs. (1). This had to be dealt with in what is now subs. (5).

Subs. (3)

The Merchant Shipping Act 1988 increased the penalty on conviction on indictment to allow for imprisonment for up to two years as well as an unlimited fine. The purpose was presumably to scare owners and masters into being ultra careful, but it must be doubted whether such an increase can really have that effect. Masters and owners can already commit a huge number of technical offences under the Merchant Shipping Act and regulations issued under it. It might seem hard to allow imprisonment for an offence that does not necessarily involve deliberate harm or grossly negligent conduct. Although a fine may be the more usual punishment, one should not discount the stress caused by the threat of a prison sentence on a master awaiting trial after a disaster. At Committee Stage of the Merchant Shipping Act 1988 in the Lords, the Government defended the £50,000 fine on the master by explaining that this enables proceedings to be taken against the master of a foreign ship in circumstances where it would not be possible to proceed against the overseas company. Once the fine has been paid and the ship made fit, the ship is allowed to sail. It was accepted that it might be rather draconian to imprison a master in many circumstances, but the punishment might be appropriate where the master had been personally responsible for overloading the vessel.

Subs. (4)

Subsections (4)–(6) contain defences. This section does not require proof of an *intent* to send an unfit ship to sea or that there be any wilful disregard of human life. It would appear to be no defence that the master had properly delegated responsibilities to shore staff (*e.g.* in relation to loading).

This subsection contains a general defence that appropriate arrangements had already been made, or that it was reasonable to have postponed making arrangements. It is quite common for ships to be in port waiting for repairs, or for equipment to be fitted, or for crews to arrive. Although then technically unfit, by the time of sailing all problems would be rectified. It is possible that a ship may arrive in an unfit state (due to a storm) but that no positive arrangements had been made to rectify the damage before a safety inspection occurred. It should not be difficult to show that it was reasonable not to have made arrangements in all these examples. The difficulties will occur where repairs are delayed for a considerable period. The owner may plead financial difficulties and that there was no immediate intention to send the ship to sea. The prosecuting authorities would then have to decide in practice whether there was a likelihood of the ship sailing before repairs were effected.

Paragraph (b) is a deliberate rewording of what was s.44(2)(b) of the Merchant Shipping Act 1979. The latter, and the original Merchant Shipping Bill 1988, framed the defence in terms of whether "it was reasonable not to have made such arrangements". This could have been interpreted as allowing a master, owner or manager to shift responsibility by saying it was not his job to correct something before the ship sailed. The present paragraph is designed to prevent this by emphasising the arrangements that *somebody* should have made, rather than focusing on that which the particular defendant could have arranged. This might seem hard on a master who had reported defects to the owners, but who had been ignored. The change in wording is very slight and it would have been clearer if the paragraph had indicated expressly who was expected to act, *e.g.* by adding at the end "by any person".

Where a ship was dangerously unsafe because of unsuitable equipment it might not be a defence to say that reasonable steps had been taken to check in the technical literature that a particular piece of equipment was suitable. This is because para. (a) refers to "appropriate" and not "reasonable" arrangements. This suggests an objective test of whether the arrangements were (or would have been) effective and not whether the shipowner or master had taken care. It is noticeable as a comparison that the Merchant Shipping (Health and Safety: General Duties) Regulations 1984 (S.I. 1984 No. 408), as amended, create duties on shipowners to ensure safety on board, but provide a defence where all reasonable precautions and all due diligence are exercised. This defence is available in relation to an offence which only has a fine as a punishment, and not imprisonment, as here. Moreover the defence available under subs. (5) for companies does make reference to reasonable diligence.

Paragraph (b) would also seem to cover the position of ships driven into British ports by stress of weather, at least until there had been time to make arrangements.

A partial answer to criticisms that technical offences may be committed is that executive discretion not to prosecute may be exercised under subs. (7).

Subss. (5)–(6)

Subsection (2) makes charterers and managers guilty in some circumstances. Concern was expressed during debates that shipowners might be reluctant to use firms of professional ship managers where there was the possibility of the shipowners *also* being criminally responsible for the actions of the charterers or managers. In some financing arrangements the shipowner might be a bank which would normally and reasonably entrust management to charterers or managers.

Where an owner (or charterer or manager) has *wholly* divested himself of responsibilities by arranging for someone else to perform them, there will be a defence of reasonableness. The shipowner would have to show (i) that he has no joint control over the particular matter and (ii) that reasonable steps had been taken to select the other person and (iii) that reasonable steps had been taken to supervise the performance of the operations by that person. The intention is to leave the burden of proof with the shipowner so that, for instance, a court cannot be frustrated by the obscure corporate arrangements undertaken by foreign-based companies.

Subsection (6) requires attention to be paid to the actual knowledge of the defendant and the extent to which contracts would give the right to control the conduct of the other person, *e.g.* by positively intervening or by terminating the contract. There might be more power to intervene in *management* in the case of a management contract than under a demise charterparty. Most demise charterparties, however, contain clauses allowing the shipowners to inspect the vessel to ascertain that she is being properly maintained and repaired, see, *e.g.* the Barecon A Standard Bareboat Charter, cl. 6. Clause 8 of Barecon A gives the owner the right to withdraw the vessel if repairs are not done within a reasonable time. A decision to terminate under this clause must now take into account the possibility of being held criminally liable for the dangerous condition of the vessel if the right to terminate is not exercised.

In the case of both subss. (5) and (6) it must also now be considered whether a corporation can be guilty of the offence where the acts or omissions giving rise to the dangerous unsafeness have been committed by any employee in the hierarchy, or whether a personal offence is created which, in the case of a corporation, can only be committed by higher management (see *Seaboard Offshore v. Secretary of State for Transport* [1994] 1 W.L.R. 541 and the General Note to s.100, below). Note that s.100 has an objective standard in the offence itself ("reasonable steps"), whereas there is no such qualification in the offence-creating subsection in s.98. There is a reasonableness qualification, however, in the defences in subss. (5) and (6) and the defence in subs. (5) is phrased as a personal one ("reasonable for *him*") in terms which persuaded the House of Lords in the *Seaboard Offshore* case that attention had to be focused on the senior management. It is tentatively submitted that a corporation could be guilty of an offence under s.98 even where the ship was dangerously unsafe by reason of the actions of junior personnel, albeit that there might be a defence if the senior management had exercised reasonable diligence within subs. (5)(b). Even if that view is wrong, and there must be some failing of the senior management under subs. (1), the matters mentioned in s.94(2) are so broad or fundamental that it may not be too difficult to point to personal faults in the senior management in respect of the management system in operation (and see the reference to the ISM Code in the General Note to s.100, below).

Subs. (7)
No reference is made to Scotland because private prosecutions are not allowed there.

Subs. (8)
See generally the notes to subss. (2), (5) and (6).

Subs. (9)
Once a person has assumed a responsibility he may be caught by the section, even though he later contracts the duties to another. Thus, a demise charterer who never had the intention of running the vessel, but sub-demise chartered immediately, would still have to rely on the defence in para. (5). Thus, banks and other financial institutions might unwittingly find themselves subject to a criminal charge.

Use of unsafe lighters, etc.

99.—(1) If any person uses or causes or permits to be used in navigation any lighter, barge or like vessel when, because of—
  (a) the defective condition of its hull or equipment,
  (b) overloading or improper loading, or
  (c) undermanning,
it is so unsafe that human life is thereby endangered, he shall be liable—
  (i) on summary conviction, to a fine not exceeding the statutory maximum;
  (ii) on conviction on indictment, to a fine.
(2) Proceedings for an offence under this section shall not be instituted—
  (a) in England and Wales, except by or with the consent of the Secretary of State; or
  (b) in Northern Ireland, except by or with the consent of the Secretary of State.
(3) This section does not affect the liability of the owners of any lighter, barge or like vessel in respect of loss of life or personal injury caused to any person carried in the vessel.

DEFINITIONS
"England and Wales": Interpretation Act 1978, Sched. 1.
"person": Interpretation Act 1978, Sched. 1.
"Secretary of State": Interpretation Act 1978, Sched. 1.
"statutory maximum": Criminal Justice Act 1982, s.74.

GENERAL NOTE
[Derivation: Merchant Shipping Act 1921, ss.2 and 3; Merchant Shipping Act 1979, Sched. 6, Pt. VII, para. 15.]
This section derives from the Merchant Shipping Act 1921, s.2 and was left untouched by developments to what is now s.98, above. It creates separate offences relating to unsafe lighters, barges and like vessels. It was necessary in 1921 because of the narrow and overly technical definition of "ship" for the purposes of s.742 of the Merchant Shipping Act 1894 (see *Temperley* pp. 276–278). The definition of ship in what is now s.313(2) covers every description of vessel. It is not quite clear why s.99 was left on the statute book, when a charge could have been brought under s.98 if suitably amended. No reference is made to Scotland in subs. (2) because private prosecutions are not allowed there.

Owner liable for unsafe operation of ship

100.—(1) It shall be the duty of the owner of a ship to which this section applies to take all reasonable steps to secure that the ship is operated in a safe manner.
(2) This section applies to—
  (a) any United Kingdom ship; and
  (b) any ship which—
        (i) is registered under the law of any country outside the United Kingdom, and
        (ii) is within United Kingdom waters while proceeding to or from a port in the United Kingdom,

unless the ship would not be so proceeding but for weather conditions or any other unavoidable circumstances.

(3) If the owner of a ship to which this section applies fails to discharge the duty imposed on him by subsection (1) above, he shall be liable—

(a) on summary conviction, to a fine not exceeding £50,000;

(b) on conviction on indictment, to imprisonment for a term not exceeding two years or a fine, or both.

(4) Where any such ship—

(a) is chartered by demise, or

(b) is managed, either wholly or in part, by a person other than the owner under the terms of a management agreement within the meaning of section 98,

any reference to the owner of the ship in subsection (1) or (3) above shall be construed as including a reference—

(i) to the charterer under the charter by demise, or

(ii) to any such manager as is referred to in paragraph (b) above, or

(iii) (if the ship is both chartered and managed as mentioned above) to both the charterer and any such manager,

and accordingly the reference in subsection (1) above to the taking of all reasonable steps shall, in relation to the owner, the charterer or any such manager, be construed as a reference to the taking of all such steps as it is reasonable for him to take in the circumstances of the case.

(5) No proceedings for an offence under this section shall be instituted—

(a) in England and Wales, except by or with the consent of the Secretary of State or the Director of Public Prosecutions;

(b) in Northern Ireland, except by or with the consent of the Secretary of State or the Director of Public Prosecutions for Northern Ireland.

Definitions

"all reasonable steps": subs. (4).

"England and Wales": Interpretation Act 1978, Sched. 1.

"fails": s.313(1).

"management agreement": s.98(8).

"owner": subs. (4)(b).

"port": s.313(1).

"registered": ss.23(1) and 313(1).

"Secretary of State": Interpretation Act 1978, Sched. 1.

"ship": s.313(1).

"taking of all reasonable steps": subs. (4)(b).

"United Kingdom": Interpretation Act 1978, Sched. 1.

"United Kingdom ship": ss.1(3) and 313(1).

"United Kingdom waters": s.313(2)(a).

General Note

[Derivation: Merchant Shipping Act 1988, s.31.]

This section was created by the Merchant Shipping Act 1988, s.31 and places a statutory duty on shipowners to take all reasonable steps to ensure that their ships are *operated* in a safe manner. Whereas s.98 relates essentially to the condition of the ship, s.100 concentrates on how it is being used. The conduct which could be caught is very wide ranging. It could cover the owner who encourages his master to proceed as quickly as possible in all weather conditions—including fog; or who fails to have a supervisory staff ashore to check on faults of the master; or who fails to respond to repeated requests from masters for new safety equipment; or who employs seafarers who have the necessary certificates, but whom he knows are incompetent; or who fails to provide standing orders for his ships, or provides orders which are unclear or inadequate; or who condones practices by his staff which cut corners to the detriment of safety, *e.g.* overloading.

As with s.98, the degree of culpability will vary widely from case to case and the punishment will no doubt reflect this. It is possible that some of the actions of management criticised in the Sheen Report into the Zeebrugge disaster would now fall foul of this section, although see *Seaboard Offshore v. Secretary of State for Transport* [1994] 1 W.L.R. 541, below.

Note also the powers of the registrar in respect of unsafe ships under s.9(3).

Subs. (1)
Subsection (1) creates the offence of failing to take reasonable steps to secure that the ship is operated safely. See ss.277–278 for offences by the officers of a corporation.

Subs. (2)
The section applies to U.K. registered ships and foreign registered vessels within U.K. waters (extending to 12 miles under the Territorial Sea Act 1987 (c. 49)). Subsection (2) provides that the foreign vessel must be intentionally proceeding to or from a U.K. port. The section does not apply to such vessels where they have been driven in to a U.K. port by storms. It is presumed that "unavoidable circumstances" is to be interpreted *ejuisdem generis* with "weather conditions" so that it would cover, *e.g.* war, but not perhaps strikes.

Note that s.307 gives the Secretary of State a power to extend, by regulation, the provisions of the section in respect of unregistered ships.

Subs. (3)
Although the only appropriate penalty for a company is a fine (which may be unlimited if a prosecution is brought in the Crown Court), it should be noted that the officers of the company may face imprisonment, see ss.277–278, below.

Subs. (4)
See generally the note to s.98(2), above. Demise charterers and ship managers can also be guilty of the offence under this section along with the shipowners. Paragraph (a) makes specific reference to demise charterers, which is in contrast to s.98(2) which refers to all types of charterers. The reason for this is apparent from the note to s.98(2), above, as a time or voyage charterer might have responsibilities for certain equipment, but would normally have no control over the manner of operation of a ship.

It is possible for shipowners, demise charterers and ship managers all to be convicted, although an owner who has employed a reasonable firm of ship-managers would have taken "reasonable steps" within subs. (1) unless he had reason to believe that they were performing their task improperly. He would thus be protected if the managers unexpectedly fail to perform satisfactorily. His power to intervene in the operation of a demise charterparty is likely to be more limited for the very reason that the purpose of the charter is to allow the demise charterer to run the ship almost as if it were his own. If the ship is damaged, the charterer must repair it before redelivery, see, *e.g.* the Barecon A Standard Bareboat Charter, cl. 13. See generally the General Note to s.98(5) and (6), above.

In *Seaboard Offshore v. Secretary of State for Transport* [1994] 1 W.L.R. 541 a prosecution was brought against a firm of ship managers after the chief engineer had been responsible for an engine breakdown on a ship which had sailed, after he had joined her only about three hours previously. It was held that for a conviction under s.100, the prosecution must prove beyond reasonable doubt that the accused owner, charterer or manager of a ship had himself failed to take all reasonable steps to secure that the ship was operated in a safe manner and that the section did not make the managers vicariously liable for a breach of duty arising from any act or omission of any of the managers' servants or agents. Particular emphasis was placed on the words "reasonable for *him* to take" in subs. (4), as it was said that these showed that the section was concentrating on those involved with the *actual* operation of the ship and that in the case of a company the natural persons who would be considered as being the corporation would be those at a senior level (see *Tesco Supermarkets v. Nattrass* [1972] A.C. 153 and now also *Meridian Global Funds Management Asia v. Securities Commission* [1995] 3 All E.R. 918). The House of Lords apparently considered that Parliament could not have intended a company to be liable for any act or omission of an employee which resulted in unsafe operation of the ship "ranging from a failure by the managing director to arrange repairs to a failure by the bosun or cabin steward to close portholes". Given the climate of opinion following the *Zeebrugge* disaster, when the Merchant Shipping Act 1988 was enacted, it is entirely conceivable that Parliament would have voted for quite stringent measures involving safety, even if that resulted in the creation of strict liability offences. Some protection was offered by the existence of subs. (5) and the variety of sentences which could be imposed. Senior officers could be punished for their connivance under ss.277–278. The House of Lords did not consider it useful to try to categorise the offence as one of strict liability, as the section merely required a failure to take steps which by an objective standard are held to be reasonable steps to take in the safe operation of a ship, and the duty which it places is a personal one. Accordingly, the owner, charterer or manager is criminally liable if he fails personally in the duty, but is not criminally liable for the acts and omissions of his subordinate employees if he himself has taken all such reasonable steps.

The House of Lords did leave open the possibility that a charge could be brought against the manager personally by showing that it had failed to operate a safe *system* for securing that the engineer had an opportunity to familiarise himself with the ship before it set to sea. In the *Seaboard Offshore* case the Secretary of State had not presented the case in that way at the trial and had not proved that the failure of any system was the responsibility of a *senior* manager within the *Tesco* ruling. It would seem that such a charge could now be brought, using as evidence the requirements of the International Management Code for the Safe Operation of Ships and for Pollution Prevention (ISM Code) adopted by the IMO on November 4, 1993. Paragraph 6.3 requires that new personnel and personnel transferred to new assignments are given proper familiarisation with their duties. The E.U. has already extended the ISM Code to Ro-Ro ferries (see Council Regulation (E.C.) No. 3051/95 and IMO has incorporated the ISM Code in SOLAS for such ferries as from 1998. In the meantime the ISM Code should be a guide and the House of Lords referred to the ICS/ISF Code of Good Management Practice in Safe Ship Operation.

The *Seaboard Offshore* case indicated the continued reluctance of the courts to impose criminal liability on a company where there is no personal fault of higher management. However, the application of the *Tesco* ruling will vary according to each particular statutory provision and care should be taken when considering the application of the *Seaboard Offshore* case to other sections of this Act. It may be distinguished on the two grounds indicated above. First, that there was a particular reference in s.100(4) to a personal element in the offence ("reasonable for *him*") and, secondly, the option was left open of proving a defective system of management which was the responsibility of senior managers whose acts would be considered as those of the corporation.

Subs. (5)

As with s.98, a safeguard against a vindictive or unreasonable prosecution is the requirement that the appropriate Secretary of State or official should consent.

Control of, and returns as to, persons on ships

Offences in connection with passenger ships

101.—(1) A person commits an offence if, in relation to a ship to which this section applies, he does any of the following things, that is to say—

    (a) if, being drunk or disorderly, he has been on that account refused admission to the ship by the owner or any person in his employment, and, after having the amount of his fare (if he has paid it) returned or tendered to him, nevertheless persists in attempting to enter the ship;

    (b) if, being drunk or disorderly on board the ship, he is requested by the owner or any person in his employment to leave the ship at any place in the United Kingdom at which he can conveniently do so, and, after having the amount of his fare (if he has paid it) returned or tendered to him, does not comply with the request;

    (c) if, on board the ship, after warning by the master or other officer thereof, he molests or continues to molest any passenger;

    (d) if, after having been refused admission to the ship by the owner or any person in his employment on account of the ship being full, and having had the amount of his fare (if he has paid it) returned or tendered to him, he nevertheless persists in attempting to enter the ship;

    (e) if, having gone on board the ship at any place, and being requested, on account of the ship being full, by the owner or any person in his employment to leave the ship before it has left that place, and having had the amount of his fare (if he has paid it) returned or tendered to him, he does not comply with that request;

    (f) if, on arriving in the ship at a point to which he has paid his fare, he knowingly and intentionally refuses or neglects to leave the ship; and

    (g) if, on board the ship he fails, when requested by the master or other officer thereof, either to pay his fare or show such ticket or other receipt, if any, showing the payment of his fare, as is usually given to persons travelling by and paying their fare for the ship;

but his liability in respect of any such offence shall not prejudice the recovery of any fare payable by him.

(2) A person commits an offence if, on board any ship to which this section applies he intentionally does or causes to be done anything in such a manner as to—
  (a) obstruct or damage any part of the machinery or equipment of the ship, or
  (b) obstruct, impede or molest the crew, or any of them, in the navigation or management of the ship, or otherwise in the execution of their duty on or about the ship.

(3) The master or other officer of any ship to which this section applies, and all persons called by him to his assistance, may, without any warrant, detain any person who commits any offence against subsection (1) or (2) above and whose name and address are unknown to the master or officer, and deliver that person to a constable.

(4) A person guilty of an offence against subsection (1) or (2) above shall be liable, on summary conviction, to a fine not exceeding level 2 on the standard scale.

(5) If any person commits an offence against subsection (1) or (2) above and on the application of the master of the ship, or any other person in the employment of the owner thereof, refuses to give his name and address, or gives a false name or address, that person shall be liable, on summary conviction, to a fine not exceeding level 2 on the standard scale.

(6) This section applies to a ship for which there is in force a Passenger Ship Safety Certificate or Passenger Certificate, as the case may be, issued under or recognised by safety regulations.

DEFINITIONS
  "commits an offence": subss. (1) and (2).
  "fails": s.313(1).
  "master": s.313(1).
  "passenger": Sched. 6, Art. 1(4).
  "person": Interpretation Act 1978, Sched. 1.
  "safety regulations": ss.85 and 313(1).
  "ship": subs. (6).
  "standard scale": Criminal Justice Act 1982, s.37.
  "United Kingdom": Interpretation Act 1978, Sched. 1.

GENERAL NOTE
  [Derivation: Merchant Shipping Act 1894, s.287; Merchant Shipping (Registration, etc.) Act 1993, Sched. 4, para. 14, Sched. 5; Merchant Shipping (Survey and Certification) Regulations 1995 (S.I. 1995 No. 1210), reg. 1(5); Merchant Shipping Act 1979, Sched. 6, Pt. I.]
  Section 101 is derived from s.287 of the Merchant Shipping Act 1894, whose title "offences in connection with passenger steamers", betrayed its ancestry which dated from the time of emigrant ships. The Merchant Shipping (Registration, etc.) Act 1993, Sched. 4, para. 14 modernised it by: removing fare-dodging provisions (now covered by the Theft Act 1968 (c. 60)); using the word "damage" instead of "injury" in relation to the ship and its equipment; removing a requirement that offenders be delivered to a justice of the peace.
  The original Merchant Shipping (Registration, etc.) Bill included provisions to update other references in s.287 of the 1894 Act so that there would be an offence not only for being "drunk", but also "under the influence of drink or drugs", and so that "molests" would include *annoyance* of other passengers (and *cf.* s.102, below). The drink and drugs provision seemed unremarkable (and *cf.* s.58(3)(b), derived from s.27(3)(b) of the Merchant Shipping Act 1970, as amended by the Merchant Shipping Act 1988, s.32), but in 1993 one M.P. objected at Committee Stage that the suggested provisions were too vague. Perhaps in order to speed the passage of the 1993 Bill without opposition the promoter, Mr. Page, agreed to their deletion. It is submitted that the objection was unfounded and unfortunate. For powers to deal with annoying drunks, see s.102, below.

Power to exclude drunken passengers from certain passenger ships

102.—(1) The master of any ship to which this section applies may refuse to receive on board any person who by reason of drunkenness or otherwise is in such a state, or misconducts himself in such a manner, as to cause annoyance or injury to passengers on board, and if any such person is on board, may put him on shore at any convenient place.

(2) A person so refused admittance or put on shore shall not be entitled to the return of any fare he has paid.

(3) This section applies to a ship (whether or not a United Kingdom ship) carrying more than 12 passengers and employed in carrying passengers between places in the limited European trading area as for the time being defined in regulations made under section 47 by the Secretary of State.

DEFINITIONS

"limited European trading area": s.76(4)(b).
"master": s.313(1).
"passenger": Sched. 6, Art. 1(4).
"person": Interpretation Act 1978, Sched. 1.
"Secretary of State": Interpretation Act 1978, Sched. 1.
"ship": subs. (3) and s.313(1).
"United Kingdom ship": ss.1(3) and 313(1).

GENERAL NOTE

[Derivation: Merchant Shipping Act 1894, s.288; Merchant Shipping (Registration, etc.) Act 1993, Sched. 4, para. 2(1)(g); Merchant Shipping (Survey and Certification) Regulations 1995 (S.I. 1995 No. 1210), reg. 1(6).]

This section gives the master power to deal with drunks by refusing to let them board or by actually forcing them to leave the ship at a place convenient to the ship and not to the drunk. Note that this power does not necessarily mean that the drunk commits a criminal offence. An offence can arise under s.101, above.

Stowaways

103.—(1) If a person, without the consent of the master or of any other person authorised to give it, goes to sea or attempts to go to sea in a United Kingdom ship, he shall be liable on summary conviction to a fine not exceeding level 3 on the standard scale.

(2) Nothing in section 281 shall be taken to limit the jurisdiction of any court in the United Kingdom to deal with an offence under this section which has been committed in a country outside the United Kingdom by a person who is not a British citizen.

DEFINITIONS

"British citizen": s.313(1).
"master": s.313(1).
"person": Interpretation Act 1978, Sched. 1.
"ship": s.313(1).
"standard scale": Criminal Justice Act 1982, s.37.
"United Kingdom": Interpretation Act 1978, Sched. 1.
"United Kingdom ship": ss.1(3) and 313(1).

GENERAL NOTE

[Derivation: Merchant Shipping Act 1970, s.77; Merchant Shipping Act 1979, Sched. 6, Pt. VI, para. 9.]

The section derives from s.77 of the Merchant Shipping Act 1970, as amended, and creates an offence if a person stows away on a U.K. ship. The offence can be committed by a non-British citizen on board a ship on the high seas (see the General Note to s.281 and *Temperley*, para. 1453). For unregistered ships see s.307. For offences on board committed by stowaways, see s.106, below.

Unauthorised presence on board ship

104. Where a United Kingdom ship or a ship registered in any other country is in a port in the United Kingdom and a person who is neither in Her Majesty's service nor authorised by law to do so—

(a) goes on board the ship without the consent of the master or of any other persons authorised to give it; or

(b) remains on board the ship after being requested to leave by the master, a constable, an officer authorised by the Secretary of State or an officer of customs and excise,

he shall be liable on summary conviction to a fine not exceeding level 5 on the standard scale.

DEFINITIONS
  "master": s.313(1).
  "person": Interpretation Act 1978, Sched. 1.
  "port": s.313(1).
  "registered": ss.23(1) and 313(1).
  "Secretary of State": Interpretation Act 1978, Sched. 1.
  "ship": s.313(1).
  "standard scale": Criminal Justice Act 1982, s.37.
  "United Kingdom": Interpretation Act 1978, Sched. 1.
  "United Kingdom ship": ss.1(3) and 313(1).

GENERAL NOTE
  [Derivation: Merchant Shipping Act 1970, s.78; Aviation and Maritime Security Act 1990, Sched. 3, para. 2.]
  The section creates a summary offence if a person boards a ship in a U.K. port without authority. Note also the Aviation and Maritime Security Act 1990 (c. 31), Pts. II and III for more serious offences against ships and harbour areas (see N. Gaskell, Aviation and Maritime Security Act 1990 in *Current Law Statutes Annotated 1990*).

Master's power of arrest

105. The master of any United Kingdom ship may cause any person on board the ship to be put under restraint if and for so long as it appears to him necessary or expedient in the interest of safety or for the preservation of good order or discipline on board the ship.

DEFINITIONS
  "master": s.313(1).
  "person": Interpretation Act 1978, Sched. 1.
  "ship": s.313(1).
  "United Kingdom ship": ss.1(3) and 313(1).

GENERAL NOTE
  [Derivation: Merchant Shipping Act 1970, s.79.]
  This section re-enacts s.79 of Merchant Shipping Act 1970 and gives the master a very wide power of arrest aboard ship. Note the wide definition of master in s.313(2).

Unauthorised persons: offences relating to safety

106.—(1) Where a person goes to sea in a ship without the consent of the master or of any other person authorised to give it or is conveyed in a ship in pursuance of section 73(5)(b), sections 58 and 59 shall apply as if he were a seaman employed in the ship.

(2) Subsection (1) above shall, in its application to section 58 so far as that section applies to ships which are not sea-going ships have effect—
  (a) with the omission of the words "goes to sea in a ship"; and
  (b) with the insertion, after the words "to give it", of the words "is on board a ship while it is on a voyage or excursion".

(3) This section does not apply to fishing vessels.

DEFINITIONS
  "fishing vessel": s.313(1) and (3).
  "master": s.313(1).
  "person": Interpretation Act 1978, Sched. 1.
  "seaman": s.313(1).
  "ship": s.313(1).

GENERAL NOTE
  [Derivation: Merchant Shipping Act 1970, ss.32, 95(1)(a) and 96(2); Merchant Shipping Act 1974, s.19(6)(a); Merchant Shipping Act 1988, Sched. 5.]

This section re-enacts provisions in the Merchant Shipping Act 1970 so as to treat stowaways as if they were seamen, except on fishing vessels. Sections 58 and 59 create offences which may be committed by seamen. See also ss.103–104 on stowaways.

Return to be furnished by masters of ships as to passengers

107.—(1) The master of every ship, whether or not a United Kingdom ship, which carries any passenger to a place in the United Kingdom from any place out of the United Kingdom, or from any place in the United Kingdom to any place out of the United Kingdom, shall furnish to such person and in such manner as the Secretary of State directs a return giving the total number of any passengers so carried, distinguishing, if so directed by the Secretary of State, the total number of any class of passengers so carried, and giving, if the Secretary of State so directs, such particulars with respect to passengers as may be for the time being required by the Secretary of State.

(2) Any passenger shall furnish the master of the ship with any information required by him for the purpose of the return.

(3) If—

(a) the master of a ship fails to make a return as required by this section, or makes a false return,

(b) any passenger refuses to give any information required by the master of the ship for the purpose of the return required by this section, or, for that purpose, gives to the master information which he knows to be false or recklessly gives to him information which is false,

the master or (as the case may be) passenger shall be liable on summary conviction to a fine not exceeding level 2 on the standard scale in the case of a failure or refusal and level 3 on the standard scale in the case of a false return or false information.

DEFINITIONS
   "fails": s.313(1).
   "master": s.313(1).
   "passenger": Sched. 6, Art. 1(4).
   "person": Interpretation Act 1978, Sched. 1.
   "Secretary of State": Interpretation Act 1978, Sched. 1.
   "ship": s.313(1).
   "standard scale": Criminal Justice Act 1982, s.37.
   "United Kingdom": Interpretation Act 1978, Sched. 1.
   "United Kingdom ship": ss.1(3) and 313(1).

GENERAL NOTE
   [Derivation: Merchant Shipping Act 1906, s.76; Merchant Shipping (Registration, etc.) Act 1993, Sched. 4, para. 15; Merchant Shipping Act 1979, Sched. 6, Pt. VI, para. 13.]
   This section re-enacts s.76(3) of the Merchant Shipping Act 1906 (c. 48) which created an offence where a master provided a false return as to the number of passengers carried. The Merchant Shipping (Registration, etc.) Act 1993 imposed a more modern mental element for the offence in subs. (3)(b) by referring specifically to knowledge and recklessness.

Returns of births and deaths in ships, etc.

108.—(1) The Secretary of State may make regulations under the following provisions of this section in relation to births and deaths in the circumstances specified in those provisions.

(2) Regulations under this section may require the master of any United Kingdom ship to make a return to a superintendent or proper officer of—

(a) the birth or death of any person occurring in the ship; and

(b) the death of any person employed in the ship, wherever occurring outside the United Kingdom;

and to notify any such death to such person (if any) as the deceased may have named to him as his next of kin.

(3) Regulations under this section may require the master of any ship not registered in the United Kingdom which calls at a port in the United Kingdom in the course of or at the end of a voyage to make a return to a superintendent of any birth or death of a British citizen, a British Dependent Territories citizen or a British Overseas citizen which has occurred in the ship during the voyage.

(4) The returns referred to in subsections (2) and (3) above shall be for transmission to the Registrar General of Shipping and Seamen.

(5) Regulations under this section may require the Registrar General of Shipping and Seamen to record such information as may be specified in the regulations about such a death as is referred to in subsection (2) above in a case where—

(a) it appears to him that the master of the ship cannot perform his duty under that subsection because he has himself died or is incapacitated or missing; and

(b) any of the circumstances specified in subsection (6) below exist.

(6) Those circumstances are that—

(a) the death in question has been the subject of—

(i) an inquest held by a coroner,

(ii) an inquiry held in pursuance of section 271, or

(iii) an inquiry held in pursuance of the Fatal Accidents and Sudden Deaths Inquiry (Scotland) Act 1976;

and the findings of the inquest or inquiry include a finding that the death occurred;

(b) the deceased's body has been the subject of—

(i) a post-mortem examination in England and Wales, or

(ii) a preliminary investigation in Northern Ireland;

and in consequence the coroner is satisfied that an inquest is unnecessary; or

(c) in Scotland, it does not appear to the Lord Advocate, under section 1(1)(b) of the Fatal Accidents and Sudden Deaths Inquiry (Scotland) Act 1976, to be expedient in the public interest that an inquiry under that Act should be held.

(7) Regulations under this section may require the Registrar General of Shipping and Seamen to send a certified copy of any return or record made thereunder to the Registrar General for England and Wales, the Registrar General of Births, Deaths and Marriages for Scotland or the Registrar General for Northern Ireland, as the case may require.

(8) The Registrar General to whom any such certified copies are sent—

(a) shall record the information contained therein in the marine register; and

(b) may record in the marine register such additional information as appears to him desirable for the purpose of ensuring the completeness and correctness of the register;

and the enactments relating to the registration of births and deaths in England, Scotland and Northern Ireland shall have effect as if the marine register were a register of births (other than stillbirths) or deaths or certified copies of entries in such a register had been transmitted to the Registrar General in accordance with those enactments.

(9) Regulations under this section may make a contravention of any provision thereof an offence punishable on summary conviction with a fine not exceeding level 2 on the standard scale or not exceeding a lesser amount.

(10) Regulations under this section may contain provisions authorising the registration of the following births and deaths occurring outside the United

Kingdom in circumstances where no return is required to be made under the preceding provisions of this section—
  (a) any birth or death of a British citizen, a British Dependent Territories citizen or a British Overseas citizen which occurs in a ship not registered in the United Kingdom;
  (b) any death of any such citizen who has been employed in a ship not registered in the United Kingdom which occurs elsewhere than in the ship; and
  (c) any death of a person who has been employed in a United Kingdom ship which occurs elsewhere than in the ship.
  (11) References in this section to deaths occurring in a ship include references to deaths occurring in a ship's boat.

DEFINITIONS
  "British citizen": s.313(1).
  "British Dependent Territories citizen": s.313(1).
  "British Overseas citizen": s.313(1).
  "contravention": s.313(1).
  "deaths occurring in a ship": subs. (11).
  "England and Wales": Interpretation Act 1978, Sched. 1.
  "master": s.313(1).
  "person": Interpretation Act 1978, Sched. 1.
  "port": s.313(1).
  "proper officer": s.313(1).
  "registered": ss.23(1) and 313(1).
  "Secretary of State": Interpretation Act 1978, Sched. 1.
  "ship": s.313(1).
  "ship's boat": s.84(1).
  "standard scale": Criminal Justice Act 1982, s.37.
  "superintendent": s.313(1).
  "United Kingdom": Interpretation Act 1978, Sched. 1.
  "United Kingdom ship": ss.1(3) and 313(1).

GENERAL NOTE
  [Derivation: Merchant Shipping Act 1970, s.72; Merchant Shipping Act 1979, s.30(1); British Nationality Act 1981, s.51(3); Merchant Shipping Act 1979, Sched. 6, Pt. VI, para. 4; Criminal Justice Act 1982, s.46(3).]
  Section 108 allows the Secretary of State to make Regulations concerning records of births and deaths aboard ships. For the powers of the Secretary of State to make delegated legislation, such as regulations, see s.306, below.

PART V

FISHING VESSELS

GENERAL NOTE
  Part V deals with employment and safety matters concerning fishing vessels. Many provisions in this Part reflect equivalent provisions in Pt. III (concerning merchant ships generally). According to s.24(3), Pt. III can be applied to fishing vessels, but with the modifications set out specifically in Pt. V. Note in particular that ss.110 and 112 apply special rules about wages to the exclusion of the general rules in ss.30 and 31. Part V recognises the fact that there are many particular problems concerning fishing vessels, especially their safety. The Merchant Shipping Act 1894 had a separate Pt. IV to reflect the special position of fishing vessels and the Merchant Shipping Act 1970, s.95 and Sched. 2 made a thorough reform of the statutory framework.
  For registration of fishing vessels note s.15, above.

CHAPTER I

SKIPPER AND SEAMEN

Engagement and discharge of crews

Regulations relating to crew agreements

109.—(1) The Secretary of State may make regulations prescribing the procedure to be followed in connection with the making of crew agreements between persons employed in United Kingdom fishing vessels and persons employing them and prescribing the places where such crew agreements are to be made or where an agreement with any person may be added to those contained in such a crew agreement.

(2) Regulations under this section may make a contravention of any provision thereof an offence punishable on summary conviction with a fine not exceeding level 3 on the standard scale or such less amount as may be specified in the regulations.

DEFINITIONS
"contravention": s.313(1).
"crew agreement": ss.25(2) and 84(1).
"fishing vessel": s.313(1) and (3).
"person": Interpretation Act 1978, Sched. 1.
"Secretary of State": Interpretation Act 1978, Sched. 1.
"standard scale": Criminal Justice Act 1982, s.37.
"United Kingdom": Interpretation Act 1978, Sched. 1.
"United Kingdom fishing vessel": ss.1(3) and 313(1).

GENERAL NOTE
[Derivation: Merchant Shipping Act 1970, s.95(1), Sched. 2, Pt. I, para. 1; Criminal Justice Act 1982, s.38(8).]
Section 109 allows the Secretary of State to make regulations concerning crew agreements. *Cf.* s.26 for non-fishing vessels. For the powers of the Secretary of State to make delegated legislation, such as regulations, see s.306, below.

Wages

Payments of seamen's wages

110. Except as provided by or under Part III or any other enactment, the wages due to a seaman under a crew agreement relating to a United Kingdom fishing vessel shall be paid to him in full.

DEFINITIONS
"crew agreement": ss.25(2) and 84(1).
"fishing vessel": s.313(1) and (3).
"seaman": s.313(1).
"United Kingdom fishing vessel": ss.1(3) and 313(1).
"wages": s.313(1).

GENERAL NOTE
[Derivation: Merchant Shipping Act 1970, ss.7, 95(1)(b), Sched. 2, Pt. II.]
Cf. s.30 for non-fishing vessels.

Regulations relating to wages: deductions

111. The power to make regulations conferred by section 32 shall include power to provide that the amount of a deduction of a description specified in the regulations from wages in respect of employment in a fishing vessel is to be determined by a body established or approved by the Secretary of State in pursuance of regulations made under section 60.

DEFINITIONS
   "fishing vessel": s.313(1) and (3).
   "Secretary of State": Interpretation Act 1978, Sched. 1.
   "wages": s.313(1).

GENERAL NOTE
   [Derivation: Merchant Shipping Act 1979, s.24.]
   Section 32 deals with the power of the Secretary of State to make regulations dealing with wages in respect of non-fishing vessels. Section 111 allows for the Secretary of State to establish a separate disciplinary body to deal with deductions from wages as a result of the breach by a seaman of the Code of Conduct described in s.60.

Accounts of wages and catch

112.—(1) Subject to regulations made under section 32 or 73, the persons employing any seaman under a crew agreement relating to a United Kingdom fishing vessel shall deliver to him at a time prescribed by regulations under this section an account of the wages due to him under that crew agreement and of the deductions subject to which the wages are payable.

(2) Where the wages of any person employed in a United Kingdom fishing vessel are in any manner related to the catch the persons employing him shall at a time prescribed by regulations under this section deliver to the master an account (or, if the master is the person employing him, make out an account) showing how those wages (or any part thereof related to the catch) are arrived at and shall make the account available to the crew in such manner as may be prescribed by the regulations.

(3) Where there is a partnership between the master and any members of the crew of a United Kingdom fishing vessel the owner of the vessel shall at a time prescribed by regulations under this section make out an account showing the sums due to each partner in respect of his share and shall make the account available to the partners.

(4) The Secretary of State may make regulations prescribing the time at which any account required by this section is to be delivered or made out and the manner in which the account required by subsections (2) and (3) above is to be made available.

(5) If a person fails without reasonable excuse to comply with the preceding provisions of this section he shall be liable on summary conviction to a fine not exceeding level 2 on the standard scale.

DEFINITIONS
   "crew agreement": ss.25(2) and 84(1).
   "fails": s.313(1).
   "fishing vessel": s.313(1) and (3).
   "master": s.313(1).
   "person": Interpretation Act 1978, Sched. 1.
   "seaman": s.313(1).
   "Secretary of State": Interpretation Act 1978, Sched. 1.
   "standard scale": Criminal Justice Act 1982, s.37.
   "United Kingdom fishing vessel": ss.1(3) and 313(1).
   "wages": s.313(1).

GENERAL NOTE
   [Derivation: Merchant Shipping Act 1970, ss.8, 95(1)(b), Sched. 2, Pt. II.]
   Sections 31 and 32 deal with accounts of wages generally. Section 112 reflects the fact that wages on fishing vessels may be calculated differently, *e.g.* on the size of the particular catch. Nevertheless, an account is still required. Subsection (3) deals with the situation where payment is based on a partnership, or sharing, model. For the powers of the Secretary of State to make delegated legislation, such as regulations, see s.306, below.

Restriction on assignment of and charge upon wages

113.—(1) Nothing in section 34 shall affect the operation of—

(a) the Attachment of Earnings Act 1971, or

(b) without prejudice to Article 97(2) of the Judgments Enforcement (Northern Ireland) Order 1981, Articles 73 to 79 and 97 to 105 of that Order,

in relation to wages due to a person employed in a fishing vessel.

(2) The provisions of the Magistrates' Courts (Northern Ireland) Order 1981 and the Judgments Enforcement (Northern Ireland) Order 1981 relating to the attachment of wages shall apply in relation to wages due to a person employed in a fishing vessel as they apply in relation to other wages.

DEFINITIONS
 "fishing vessel": s.313(1) and (3).
 "person": Interpretation Act 1978, Sched. 1.
 "wages": s.313(1).

GENERAL NOTE
 [Derivation: Merchant Shipping Act 1970, s.95(4).]
 Section 34 deals with attachment of wages generally and s.113 contains a saving for particular enactments.

Right, or loss of right, to wages in certain circumstances

114. Section 38 does not apply to so much of the wages of a seaman employed in a fishing vessel as is in any manner related to the catch.

DEFINITIONS
 "fishing vessel": s.313(1) and (3).
 "seaman": s.313(1).
 "wages": s.313(1).

GENERAL NOTE
 [Derivation: Merchant Shipping Act 1970, s.95(2).]
 Section 38 allows for wages to be paid for a period after a shipwreck. Section 114 re-enacts s.95(2) of the Merchant Shipping Act 1970 and exercises a reservation in respect of fishing vessels where the wages might depend upon the catch.

Safety, health and welfare

Hours of work

115.—(1) The Secretary of State may make regulations prescribing maximum periods of duty and minimum periods of rest for seamen employed in United Kingdom fishing vessels, and such regulations may make different provision for different descriptions of fishing vessels or seamen employed in them or for fishing vessels and seamen of the same description in different circumstances.

(2) If any provision of regulations made under this section is contravened in the case of any seaman employed in a fishing vessel the persons employing him and the master shall each be liable on summary conviction to a fine not exceeding level 4 on the standard scale.

DEFINITIONS
 "contravened": s.313(1).
 "fishing vessel": s.313(1) and (3).
 "master": s.313(1).
 "person": Interpretation Act 1978, Sched. 1.
 "seaman": s.313(1).
 "Secretary of State": Interpretation Act 1978, Sched. 1.

"standard scale": Criminal Justice Act 1982, s.37.
"United Kingdom fishing vessel": ss.1(3) and 313(1).

GENERAL NOTE
[Derivation: Merchant Shipping Act 1970, s.95(1)(a), Sched. 2, para. 4; Merchant Shipping Act 1979, Sched. 6, Pt. III.]

Section 115 allows the Secretary of State to make regulations specifying hours of work on board fishing vessels, as tiredness has been shown to be a particular cause of accidents. For the powers of the Secretary of State to make delegated legislation, such as regulations, see s.306, below.

Manning and qualifications

Production of crew certificates and other documents of qualification

116.—(1) Any person serving or engaged to serve in a United Kingdom fishing vessel and holding any certificate or other document which is evidence that he is qualified for the purposes of section 47 shall on demand produce it to any person who is a British sea-fishery officer for the purposes of the Sea Fisheries Acts.

(2) If a person fails without reasonable excuse to produce on demand any such certificate or other document he shall be liable on summary conviction to a fine not exceeding level 3 on the standard scale.

(3) In this section the "Sea Fisheries Acts" means any enactment for the time being in force relating to sea fishing, including any enactment relating to fishing for shellfish, salmon or migratory trout.

DEFINITIONS
"fails": s.313(1).
"person": Interpretation Act 1978, Sched. 1.
"Sea Fisheries Acts": subs. (3).
"standard scale": Criminal Justice Act 1982, s.37.
"United Kingdom fishing vessel": ss.1(3) and 313(1).

GENERAL NOTE
[Derivation: Merchant Shipping Act 1970, s.95(1)(a), Sched. 2, para. 3; Merchant Shipping Act 1979, Sched. 6, Pt. II and Criminal Justice Act 1982, s.38(8).]

Section 116 places an obligation on persons to produce the necessary documentation under s.47, above, which will show their competence.

Cf. s.50 in respect of non-fishing vessels.

Offences by seamen

Drunkenness on duty

117.—If the skipper of or a seaman employed or engaged in a United Kingdom fishing vessel is, while on board the vessel, under the influence of drink or a drug to such an extent that his capacity to fulfil his responsibility for the vessel or, as the case may be, carry out the duties of his employment or engagement is impaired, he shall (subject to subsection (2) below) be liable—

    (a) on summary conviction, to a fine not exceeding the statutory maximum;

    (b) on conviction on indictment, to imprisonment for a term not exceeding two years or a fine or both.

(2) In proceedings for an offence under this section it shall be a defence to prove that at the time of the act or omission alleged against the accused he was under the influence of a drug taken by him for medical purposes and either that he took it on medical advice and complied with any directions given as part of that advice or that he had no reason to believe that the drug might have the influence it had.

DEFINITIONS

"seaman": s.313(1).
"skipper": s.313(1).
"statutory maximum": Criminal Justice Act 1982, s.74.
"United Kingdom fishing vessel": ss.1(3) and 313(1).

GENERAL NOTE

[Derivation: Merchant Shipping Act 1970, ss.28 and 33; Merchant Shipping Act 1979, s.45(2), Sched. 6, Pt. VII, para. 20; Safety at Sea Act 1986, s.10.]

Section 28 of the Merchant Shipping Act 1970 created a general offence of drunkenness, but this was restricted by the Merchant Shipping Act 1979, s.45(2) and the Safety at Sea Act 1986, s.10 to seamen employed on fishing vessels. Note, however, the offence in s.58 (and see especially s.58(3)(b)). In view of the persistent problem of alcohol on fishing vessels, s.117 is retained as a specific offence for circumstances where seamen on fishing vessels have their work capacities impaired. See also s.118, below.

Unauthorised liquor

118.—(1) A person who, in the United Kingdom or elsewhere—

(a) takes any unauthorised liquor on board a United Kingdom fishing vessel;

(b) has any unauthorised liquor in his possession on board such a vessel;

(c) permits another person to take on board such a vessel, or to have in his possession on board such a vessel, any unauthorised liquor; or

(d) intentionally obstructs another person in the exercise of powers conferred on the other person by subsection (5) below,

shall, subject to subsection (3) and (4) below, be guilty of an offence.

(2) A person guilty of an offence under subsection (1) above shall be liable—

(a) on summary conviction, to a fine not exceeding the statutory maximum;

(b) on conviction on indictment, to imprisonment for a term not exceeding two years or a fine or both.

(3) It shall be a defence in proceedings for an offence under subsection (1)(a) or (b) above to prove—

(a) that the accused believed that the liquor in question was not unauthorised liquor in relation to the vessel in question and that he had reasonable grounds for the belief; or

(b) that the accused did not know that the liquor in question was in his possession.

(4) It shall be a defence in proceedings for an offence under subsection (1)(c) above to prove that the accused believed that the liquor in question was not unauthorised liquor in relation to the vessel in question and that he had reasonable grounds for the belief.

(5) If an authorised person has reason to believe that an offence under subsection (1)(a) or (b) above has been committed by another person in connection with a fishing vessel, the authorised person—

(a) may go on board the vessel and search it and any property on it and may, if the other person is on board the vessel, search him there in an authorised manner; and

(b) may take possession of any liquor which he finds on the vessel and has reason to believe is unauthorised liquor and may detain the liquor for the period needed to ensure that the liquor is available as evidence in proceedings for the offence.

(6) In this section—

"an authorised manner" means a manner authorised by regulations made by the Secretary of State;

"authorised person", in relation to a vessel, means—

(a) a superintendent;
(b) a proper officer;
(c) a person appointed in pursuance of section 258(1)(c);
(d) the master of the vessel in question;
(e) the owner of the vessel in question;
(f) any person instructed by the master or owner to prevent the commission of offences under subsection (1) above in relation to the vessel;

"liquor" means spirits, wine, beer, cider, perry and any other fermented, distilled or spirituous liquor; and

"unauthorised liquor" means, in relation to a vessel, liquor as to which permission to take it on board the vessel has been given neither by the master nor the owner of the vessel nor by a person authorised by the owner of the vessel to give such permission.

(7) Any reference in subsection (6) above to the owner of a vessel shall be construed—

(a) as excluding any member of the crew of the vessel; and
(b) subject to that, as a reference to the person or all the persons who, in the certificate of registration of the vessel, is or are stated to be the registered owner or owners of the vessel.

DEFINITIONS

"authorised manner, an": subs. (6).
"authorised person": subs. (6).
"fishing vessel": s.313(1) and (3).
"liquor": subs. (6).
"master": s.313(1).
"owner": subs. (7).
"person": Interpretation Act 1978, Sched. 1.
"proper officer": s.313(1).
"registered": ss.23(1) and 313(1).
"statutory maximum": Criminal Justice Act 1982, s.74.
"superintendent": s.313(1).
"unauthorised liquor": subs. (6).
"United Kingdom": Interpretation Act 1978, Sched. 1.
"United Kingdom fishing vessel": ss.1(3) and 313(1).

GENERAL NOTE

[Derivation: Merchant Shipping Act 1979, s.25.]

Section 118 re-enacts s.25 of the Merchant Shipping Act 1979, which was introduced to try to cut down on the incidence of alcohol on board fishing vessels. The problem had been highlighted by a number of formal inquiries and by the Working Group on the Disciplinary Needs for Sea-going Employment in the Fishing Industry 1975 (see R. Thomas, *Current Law Statutes Annotated 1979*). See also s.117, above. It may be noted that the section could result in the conviction of the owner or master who allows liquor to be taken on board, as well as the person who actually brings or possesses it.

Disciplinary offences

119.—(1) Section 59(1)(a) and (b) shall not apply to fishing vessels and persons serving in them.

(2) In relation to United Kingdom fishing vessels, section 60 shall have effect with the substitution for subsection (2) of the following—

(2) Regulations may provide for the hearing on shore in the United Kingdom, by a disciplinary body, of a complaint by the master or owner of such a fishing vessel against a seaman alleging that during his employment in the vessel, the seaman contravened a local industrial agreement relating to his employment on the vessel and for requiring the disciplinary body to have regard to the agreement in determining whether the allegation is proved.

The alleged contravention may be one on or off the ship and in the United Kingdom or elsewhere.

(3) Regulations under section 60 may include provision authorising persons to determine, for the purposes of that section in its application to United Kingdom fishing vessels what agreements are or were local industrial agreements and which local industrial agreement relates or related to a person's employment in a particular vessel.

DEFINITIONS
"contravention": s.313(1).
"fishing vessel": s.313(1) and (3).
"master": s.313(1).
"person": Interpretation Act 1978, Sched. 1.
"seaman": s.313(1).
"ship": s.313(1).
"United Kingdom": Interpretation Act 1978, Sched. 1.
"United Kingdom fishing vessel": ss.1(3) and 313(1).

GENERAL NOTE
[Derivation: Merchant Shipping Act 1970, s.95(1)(a); Merchant Shipping Act 1979, s.23(2) and s.45(3).]

Section 119 restricts the extent to which a seaman on a fishing vessel can be guilty of an offence under s.59 when in combination with other seamen on board. It also allows for special regulations to be made under s.60 in respect of disciplinary hearings concerning breaches of local industrial agreements concerning fishing vessels. For the powers of the Secretary of State to make delegated legislation, such as regulations, see s.306, below.

Exemptions

Power to grant exemptions from this Chapter

120. The Secretary of State may grant exemptions from any requirements of Part III or this Chapter or of any regulations made thereunder—
   (a) with respect to any fishing vessel or to a fishing vessel of any description; or
   (b) with respect to any person or a person of any description serving in a fishing vessel or in a fishing vessel of any description;
and nothing in any other provision of Part III or this Chapter conferring a power to provide for or grant exemptions shall be taken to restrict the power conferred by this section.

DEFINITIONS
"fishing vessel": s.313(1) and (3).
"person": Interpretation Act 1978, Sched. 1.
"Secretary of State": Interpretation Act 1978, Sched. 1.

GENERAL NOTE
[Derivation: Merchant Shipping Act 1970, s.95(5).]
Section 120 re-enacts s.95(5) of the Merchant Shipping Act 1970 and gives the Secretary of

State wide powers to grant exemptions in respect of fishing vessels. For the powers of the Secretary of State to make delegated legislation, such as regulations, see s.306, below.

CHAPTER II

SAFETY

GENERAL NOTE

While the Merchant Shipping Act 1970 contained detailed provisions on shipping and seamen, the contemporaneous Fishing Vessels (Safety Provisions) Act 1970 (c. 27) set out a framework for regulation of safety on board fishing vessels. By contrast to merchant shipping generally (see s.85), there has been less international agreement on the subject of fishing vessel safety and construction rules. The Torremolinos International Convention for the Safety of Fishing Vessels 1977 never entered into force, partly because of treaty difficulties, but a Protocol was agreed in 1993. The Protocol is designed to update the 1977 Convention but will require the ratification of states with about 50 per cent of the world fishing fleet before it enters into force. Note also that a new International Convention on Standards of Training, Certification and Watchkeeping for Fishing Vessel Personnel 1978 (the STCW-F Convention) was agreed in 1995. This Convention recognises that it was very difficult to apply the STCW Convention 1978 (itself revised in 1995) to fishing vessels. In the event of the U.K. ratifying or acceding to any of these instruments, it is likely that Orders can be made under ss.85 and 86.

Fishing vessel construction rules

121.—(1) The Secretary of State may make rules (in this Chapter referred to as "fishing vessel construction rules") prescribing requirements for the hull, equipment and machinery of United Kingdom fishing vessels of any description (including any description framed by reference to the areas in which the vessels operate or the dates on which they were first registered in the United Kingdom or on which their construction was begun).

(2) The Secretary of State may exempt any fishing vessel or description of fishing vessel from any requirement of the fishing vessel construction rules.

(3) He may do so generally or for a specified time or with respect to a specified voyage or to voyages in a specified area, and may do so subject to any specified conditions.

(4) A surveyor of ships may inspect any fishing vessel for the purpose of seeing that it complies with the fishing vessel construction rules.

(5) If—

(a) the fishing vessel construction rules are contravened with respect to any vessel; or

(b) a vessel is, under subsection (2) above, exempted from any requirement subject to a condition and the condition is not complied with;

the owner or master of the vessel shall be liable—

(i) on summary conviction, to a fine not exceeding the statutory maximum;

(ii) on conviction on indictment, to a fine.

DEFINITIONS

"contravened": s.313(1).

"fishing vessel": s.313(1) and (3).

"fishing vessel construction rules": subs. (1).

"master": s.313(1).

"registered": ss.23(1) and 313(1).

"Secretary of State": Interpretation Act 1978, Sched. 1.

"statutory maximum": Criminal Justice Act 1982, s.74.

"surveyor of ships": ss.256(9) and 313(1).

"United Kingdom": Interpretation Act 1978, Sched. 1.

"United Kingdom fishing vessel": ss.1(3) and 313(1).

GENERAL NOTE

[Derivation: Fishing Vessels (Safety Provisions) Act 1970, s.1; Merchant Shipping Act 1979, Sched. 6, Pt. V.]

Wide powers are given to the Secretary of State to make special "fishing vessel construction rules" for the construction of fishing vessels. *Cf.* the general powers under s.85. For the powers of the Secretary of State to make delegated legislation, such as regulations, see s.306, below.

Fishing vessel survey rules

122.—(1) The Secretary of State may make rules (in this Chapter referred to as "fishing vessel survey rules") for the surveying and periodical inspection of United Kingdom fishing vessels or any description of such fishing vessels, for the purpose of ensuring their compliance with the requirements of the fishing vessel construction and equipment provisions.

(2) In this Chapter "the fishing vessel construction and equipment provisions" means fishing vessel construction rules and rules or safety regulations relating to life-saving, radio and navigational equipment for fishing vessels.

DEFINITIONS
"fishing vessel": s.313(1) and (3).
"fishing vessel construction and equipment provisions": subs. (2).
"fishing vessel survey rules": subs. (1).
"Secretary of State": Interpretation Act 1978, Sched. 1.
"United Kingdom fishing vessel": ss.1(3) and 313(1).

GENERAL NOTE
[Derivation: Fishing Vessels (Safety Provisions) Act 1970, s.2(1); Safety at Sea Act 1986, s.5(1).]
Wide powers are given to the Secretary of State to make special "fishing vessel survey rules" for the surveying and inspection of fishing vessels. *Cf.* the general powers under s.85.

Fishing vessel certificates

123.—(1) If the Secretary of State or any person authorised by him for the purpose is satisfied, on receipt of a declaration of survey in respect of a fishing vessel surveyed under the fishing vessel survey rules, that the vessel complies with such of the requirements of the fishing vessel construction and equipment provisions as are or will be applicable to the vessel, then, subject to subsection (2) below, the Secretary of State or person shall, on the application of the owner, issue a certificate (in this and the following sections referred to as a "fishing vessel certificate") showing that the vessel complies with those requirements; and for this purpose any requirement from which the vessel has been exempted under section 121(2) or any other provision of this Act shall be deemed not to be applicable to it.

(2) Fishing vessel survey rules may require, in the case of such fishing vessel certificate as may be specified in the rules, that the Secretary of State or person authorised to issue it shall not issue the certificate unless satisfied that the vessel in respect of which it is to be issued is provided with the lights, shapes and means of making fog signals required by safety regulations for the prevention of collisions.

(3) A fishing vessel certificate shall be in such form as may be prescribed by the fishing vessel survey rules; and those rules may make provision for the duration, extension or cancellation of any such certificate and for the endorsement on it of information relating to the inspection, in accordance with the rules, of the vessel to which it relates and of any extension of the period for which the certificate was issued.

DEFINITIONS
"Act, this": s.316(1).
"fishing vessel": s.313(1) and (3).
"fishing vessel certificate": subs. (1).
"fishing vessel construction and equipment provisions": s.122(2).
"fishing vessel survey rules": s.122(1).
"person": Interpretation Act 1978, Sched. 1.
"Secretary of State": Interpretation Act 1978, Sched. 1.

GENERAL NOTE
[Derivation: Fishing Vessels (Safety Provisions) Act 1970, ss.3(1)–(3) and 9(1).]

Wide powers are given to the Secretary of State to issue special "fishing vessel certificates" to fishing vessels which have complied with the requirements of ss.121 and 122. For the powers of the Secretary of State to make delegated legislation, such as regulations, see s.306, below.

Provisions supplementary to section 123

124.—(1) The Secretary of State may require a fishing vessel certificate which has expired or been cancelled, to be delivered up as he directs.

(2) If the owner or skipper of the fishing vessel fails without reasonable excuse to comply with a requirement made under subsection (1) above, he shall be liable on summary conviction to a fine not exceeding level 2 on the standard scale.

(3) The owner or skipper of a fishing vessel to whom a fishing vessel certificate is issued shall forthwith, on the receipt of the certificate by him (or his agent), cause a copy of it to be put up in some conspicuous place on board the vessel, so as to be legible to all persons on board, and to be kept so put up and legible while the certificate remains in force and the vessel is in use.

(4) If the owner or skipper of a fishing vessel fails without reasonable excuse to comply with subsection (3) above, he shall be liable, on summary conviction, to a fine not exceeding level 2 on the standard scale.

(5) If any person intentionally makes, or assists in making, or procures to be made, a false or fraudulent fishing vessel certificate he shall be liable—

    (a) on summary conviction, to a fine not exceeding the statutory maximum or to imprisonment for a term not exceeding six months or both;

    (b) on conviction on indictment, to imprisonment for a term not exceeding two years or a fine or both.

(6) In Scotland, if any person—

    (a) forges, assists in forging or procures to be forged,

    (b) fraudulently alters, assists in fraudulently altering or procures to be fraudulently altered,

any fishing vessel certificate he shall be liable—

    (i) on summary conviction, to a fine not exceeding the statutory maximum or to imprisonment for a term not exceeding six months or to both; or

    (ii) on conviction on indictment, to a fine or to imprisonment or to both.

(7) A fishing vessel certificate shall be admissible in evidence.

DEFINITIONS
"fails": s.313(1).
"fishing vessel": s.313(1) and (3).
"fishing vessel certificate": s.123(1).
"person": Interpretation Act 1978, Sched. 1.
"Secretary of State": Interpretation Act 1978, Sched. 1.
"skipper": s.313(1).
"standard scale": Criminal Justice Act 1982, s.37.
"statutory maximum": Criminal Justice Act 1982, s.74.

GENERAL NOTE
[Derivation: Merchant Shipping Act 1894, ss.280–282 and 680(1); Fishing Vessels (Safety Provisions) Act 1970, s.3(4)(5); Merchant Shipping (Registration, etc.) Act 1993, Sched. 4, para. 16.]

The fishing vessels (Safety Provisions) Act 1970, s.3(4) applied to fishing vessels certain enforcement provisions of the Merchant Shipping Act 1894 relating to the display and delivery up of "passenger steamer certificates". Those requirements were no longer entirely appropriate and were amended by the Merchant Shipping (Registration, etc.) Act 1993, Sched. 4, para. 16.

The 1894 provisions were themselves repealed by the Merchant Shipping (Survey and Certification) Regulations 1995 (S.I. 1995 No. 1210), but s.124 re-enacts those parts relevant to fishing vessels. Under s.124, the Secretary of State can demand the return of a fishing vessel certificate issued under s.123, above.

Prohibition on going to sea without appropriate certificate

125.—(1) No fishing vessel required to be surveyed under the fishing vessel survey rules shall go to sea unless there are in force fishing vessel certificates showing that the vessel complies with such of the requirements of the fishing vessel construction and equipment provisions as are applicable to the vessel.

(2) If a fishing vessel goes to sea in contravention of subsection (1) above the owner or skipper of the vessel shall be liable—

(a) on summary conviction, to a fine not exceeding the statutory maximum;

(b) on conviction on indictment, to a fine.

(3) The skipper of any United Kingdom fishing vessel shall on demand produce to any officer of customs and excise or of the Secretary of State any certificate required by this Chapter; and the fishing vessel may be detained until the certificate is so produced.

DEFINITIONS
"contravention": s.313(1).
"fishing vessel": s.313(1) and (3).
"fishing vessel certificate": s.123(1).
"fishing vessel construction and equipment provisions": s.122(2).
"fishing vessel survey rules": s.122(1).
"Secretary of State": Interpretation Act 1978, Sched. 1.
"skipper": s.313(1).
"statutory maximum": Criminal Justice Act 1982, s.74.
"United Kingdom fishing vessel": ss.1(3) and 313(1).

GENERAL NOTE
[Derivation: Fishing Vessels (Safety Provisions) Act 1970, s.4(1)–(3); Merchant Shipping Act 1979, Sched. 6, Pt. V; Merchant Shipping (Registration, etc.) Act 1993, Sched. 5.]
Section 125 imposes a prohibition on fishing vessels going to sea without the appropriate fishing vessel certificate.

Notice of alterations

126.—(1) Where a fishing vessel certificate is in force in respect of a fishing vessel and—

(a) the certificate shows compliance with requirements of the fishing vessel construction rules and an alteration is made in the vessel's hull, equipment or machinery which affects the efficiency thereof or the seaworthiness of the vessel; or

(b) the certificate shows compliance with requirements of the fishing vessel equipment provisions and an alteration is made affecting the efficiency or completeness of the appliances or equipment which the vessel is required to carry by the fishing vessel equipment provisions;

the owner or skipper shall, as soon as possible after the alteration is made, give written notice containing full particulars of it to the Secretary of State or, if the certificate was issued by another person, to that person.

(2) If the notice required by subsection (1) above is not given as required by that subsection the owner or skipper shall be liable on summary conviction to a fine not exceeding level 3 on the standard scale.

(3) In this section—
"alteration" in relation to anything includes the renewal of any part of it and
"the fishing vessel equipment provisions" means the provisions of the fishing vessel construction and equipment provisions other than the fishing vessel construction rules.

DEFINITIONS
"alteration": subs. (3).
"fishing vessel": s.313(1) and (3).
"fishing vessel certificate": s.123(1).
"fishing vessel construction and equipment provisions": s.122(2).
"fishing vessel construction rules": s.121(1).
"fishing vessel equipment provisions": subs. (3).
"person": Interpretation Act 1978, Sched. 1.
"Secretary of State": Interpretation Act 1978, Sched. 1.
"skipper": s.313(1).
"standard scale": Criminal Justice Act 1982, s.37.
"writing": Interpretation Act 1978, Sched. 1.

GENERAL NOTE
[Derivation: Fishing Vessels (Safety Provisions) Act 1970, s.5; Criminal Justice Act 1982, s.38(8).]

Section 126 requires notice to be given to the Secretary of State of any alterations to fishing vessels so that certificates may be reissued after appropriate surveys.

Training

Training in safety matters

127.—(1) The Secretary of State may make regulations for securing that the skipper of and every seaman employed or engaged in a United Kingdom fishing vessel is trained in safety matters.

(2) The regulations may provide that if a person goes to sea on a fishing vessel in contravention of a requirement of the regulations—

(a) he commits an offence and is liable on summary conviction to a fine not exceeding level 2, or if he is the skipper or an owner of the vessel level 5, on the standard scale; and

(b) the skipper and each owner of the vessel is (except in respect of a contravention by himself) liable on summary conviction to a fine not exceeding level 5 on the standard scale.

(3) Regulations under this section may make different provision for different cases, or descriptions of case, including different provisions for different descriptions of vessel or according to the circumstances of operation of a vessel.

DEFINITIONS
"contravention": s.313(1).
"fishing vessel": s.313(1) and (3).
"seaman": s.313(1).
"Secretary of State": Interpretation Act 1978, Sched. 1.
"skipper": s.313(1).
"standard scale": Criminal Justice Act 1982, s.37.
"United Kingdom fishing vessel": ss.1(3) and 313(1).

GENERAL NOTE
[Derivation: Safety at Sea Act 1986, ss.7, 9(1).]

See the General Note to Chap. II on the STCW-F Convention, above at p.21–142.

Section 127 re-enacts provisions of the Safety at Sea Act 1986 and allows the Secretary of State to make regulations concerning the training of seafarers engaged on fishing vessels. For the powers of the Secretary of State to make delegated legislation, such as regulations, see s.306, below.

See s.56, above, for financial assistance available for the training of seamen generally. That support was designed for the merchant navy and not the fishing industry where there was apparently no shortage of trained seamen. During Committee Stage of the 1988 Bill in the Commons, an attempt was made to allow subsidies for the training of fishermen. It was estimated then that the additional cost to the industry of carrying out the mandatory safety training required by the Safety at Sea Act 1986 (now s.127) would be £250,000. But the Government view was that as the 1986 Act was a Private Member's Bill there should be no charge on public funds and the fishing industry should meet the costs before any regulations were introduced. The Sea Fish Industry

Authority spent at that time some £800,000 p.a. on training, although the Government contribution of £250,000 to this ended in 1989. The Government view was that it was open to industry to continue to fund training through the Authority's levy and through any sums available through the Manpower Services Commission and the European Social Fund.

PART VI

PREVENTION OF POLLUTION

GENERAL NOTE
    Part VI brings together a number of enactments concerning both the civil and criminal aspects of marine pollution law (see generally, *Chorley and Giles Shipping Law*, Chap. 22 and J. Bates, C. Benson, *Marine Environment Law* (1993)). There are public law provisions, enforced through the criminal law, which seek to regulate marine pollution by ships. Chapter II is particularly concerned with operational pollution. Note that construction rules which might help to prevent accidental spillages will generally be issued under s.128 or ss.85 and 86 in order to comply with international conventions. The occurrence of marine pollution disasters, such as those involving the *Torrey Canyon* (1967), the *Amoco Cadiz* (1978), the *Exxon Valdez* (1989), and the *Braer* (1993), has always prompted a reaction from the international community and developments in marine pollution law can nearly always be traced to a particular casualty. There have been a number of instruments which have dealt with the private law aspects of pollution, in particular the civil liability for damage caused by oil pollution. These issues are dealt with in Chaps. III and IV, although it should be noted that Scheds. 4 and 5 contain transitional provisions to deal with the fact that two major Conventions will be brought into force in 1996. It is those Conventions whose texts appear in a rather unsatisfactory "translation" in Chaps. III and IV (see the comments on incorporating international Conventions in the Introductory and General Note to this Act).
    In April 1996 a diplomatic conference will take place to agree a *Convention on Liability and Compensation for Damage Resulting from the Carriage of Hazardous and Noxious Substances* (the HNS Convention). If that diplomatic conference is successful, it is likely that the U.K. will incorporate the Convention into Pt. VI of the Merchant Shipping Act 1995. The draft HNS Convention highlights the fact that there is a glaring omission in the laws regulating marine pollution, in that there are liability Conventions dealing only with *oil* pollution and not pollution from substances other than oil. That is because there have not yet been any major disasters involving liquid natural gas or poisonous chemicals.
    It is noticeable that the approach of the U.K. legislation is to separate issues of control of pollution casualties from compensation. There is no express obligation on the shipowner to undertake preventive or clean-up operations itself. The "polluter pays" principle is adopted more directly in the USA and Canada where very clear burdens are placed on ship operators to have in hand contractual arrangements for the removal of pollution after an incident. In the U.K. the initial burden of decision and action seems to fall on the local or national authorities, with claims for compensation being left until later. It might be thought that local authorities, in particular, will have increasing difficulties in financing and organising clean-up operations and that there may be a case for requiring greater activity from shipowners whose ships are involved in environmental incidents.

CHAPTER I

POLLUTION GENERALLY

Prevention of pollution from ships etc.

    128.—(1) Her Majesty may by Order in Council make such provision as She considers appropriate for the purpose of giving effect to any provision of any of the following which have been ratified by the United Kingdom—
    (a) the International Convention for the Prevention of Pollution from Ships (including its protocols, annexes and appendices) which constitutes attachment 1 to the final act of the International Conference on Marine Pollution signed in London on 2nd November 1973;
    (b) the Protocol relating to Intervention on the High Seas in Cases of Marine Pollution by Substances other than Oil which constitutes attachment 2 to the final act aforesaid;
    (c) the Protocol relating to the said Convention which constitutes attachment 2 to the final act of the International Conference on Tanker

Safety and Pollution Prevention signed in London on 17th February 1978;

(d) the International Convention on Oil Pollution Preparedness, Response and Co-operation, 1990 (including the Final Act of the Conference and the attached resolutions) signed in London on 30th November 1990;

(e) any international agreement not mentioned in paragraphs (a) to (d) above which relates to the prevention, reduction or control of pollution of the sea or other waters by matter from ships;

and in paragraph (e) above the reference to an agreement includes an agreement which provides for the modification of another agreement, including the modification of an agreement mentioned in paragraphs (a) to (c) above.

(2) The powers conferred by subsection (1) above to make provision for the purpose of giving effect to an agreement include power to provide for the provision to come into force although the agreement has not come into force.

(3) Without prejudice to the generality of subsection (1) above, an Order under that subsection may in particular include provision—

(a) for applying for the purpose mentioned in that subsection any enactment or instrument relating to the pollution of the sea or other waters and also any of sections 87, 268, 269 and 270;

(b) with respect to the carrying out of surveys and inspections for the purpose aforesaid and the issue, duration and recognition of certificates for that purpose;

(c) for repealing the provisions of any enactment or instrument so far as it appears to Her Majesty that those provisions are not required having regard to any provision made or proposed to be made by virtue of this section;

(d) with respect to the application of the Order to the Crown and the extra-territorial operation of any provision made by or under the Order;

(e) for the extension of any provisions of the Order, with or without modifications, to any relevant British possession;

(f) that a contravention of a provision made by or under the Order shall be an offence punishable on summary conviction by a fine not exceeding the statutory maximum and on conviction on indictment by imprisonment for a term not exceeding two years and a fine;

(g) that any such contravention shall be an offence punishable only on summary conviction by a maximum fine of an amount not exceeding level 5 on the standard scale or such less amount as is prescribed by the Order;

(h) in connection with offences created by or under the Order, corresponding to that made in connection with offences under section 131 by section 143(6), 144 and 146 (whether by applying, or making provision for the application of, any of those sections, subject to such modifications as may be specified by or under the Order, or otherwise);

(i) for detaining any ship in respect of which such a contravention is suspected to have occurred and, in relation to such a ship, for applying section 284 with such modifications, if any, as are prescribed by the Order;

and nothing in any of the preceding provisions of this subsection shall be construed as prejudicing the generality of any other of those provisions and in particular neither paragraph (f) nor (g) above shall prejudice paragraph (a) above.

(4) An Order under subsection (1) above may—

(a) make different provision for different circumstances;

(b) make provision in terms of any document which the Secretary of State or any person considers relevant from time to time;

(c) provide for exemptions from any provisions of the Order;

(d) provide for the delegation of functions exercisable by virtue of the Order;

(e) include such incidental, supplemental and transitional provisions as appear to Her Majesty to be expedient for the purposes of the Order;

(f) authorise the making of regulations and other instruments for any of the purposes of this section (except the purposes of subsection (3)(a) and (c) above) and apply the Statutory Instruments Act 1946 to instruments made under the Order; and

(g) provide that any enactment or instrument applied by the Order shall have effect as so applied subject to such modifications as may be specified in the Order.

(5) Where an Order in Council under subsection (1) above authorises the making of regulations for the purpose of giving effect to an agreement mentioned in paragraphs (a) to (d) or falling within paragraph (e) of that subsection the Order also authorises the making of regulations for the purpose of giving effect to an agreement which provides for the modification of such an agreement.

This subsection applies in relation to Orders in Council and international agreements whenever made.

(6) Regulations made by virtue of paragraph (f) of subsection (4) above may make provision corresponding to the provision authorised for an Order by paragraphs (a) to (e) of subsection (4) above.

(7) An Order in Council in pursuance of subsection (1)(b) or (e) above may apply to areas of land or sea or other United Kingdom waters notwithstanding that the agreement in question does not relate to those areas.

(8) A draft of an Order in Council proposed to be made by virtue of subsection (1) above shall not be submitted to Her Majesty in Council unless—

(a) the draft has been approved by a resolution of each House of Parliament;

(b) the Order is to contain a statement that it is made only for any of the purposes specified in subsection (9) below; or

(c) the Order extends only to a possession mentioned in subsection (3)(e) above.

(9) The purposes referred to in subsection (8)(b) above are—

(a) giving effect to an agreement mentioned in subsection (1)(a) to (d) above;

(b) providing as authorised by subsection (2) above in relation to such an agreement and the purposes of subsection (5) above;

and a statutory instrument containing an Order which contains a statement that it is made only for any of those purposes shall be subject to annulment in pursuance of a resolution of either House of Parliament.

DEFINITIONS

"agreement": subs. (1).
"contravention": s.313(1).
"person": Interpretation Act 1978, Sched. 1.
"relevant British possession": s.313(1).
"Secretary of State": Interpretation Act 1978, Sched. 1.
"ship": s.313(1).
"standard scale": Criminal Justice Act 1982, s.37.
"statutory maximum": Criminal Justice Act 1982, s.74.
"United Kingdom": Interpretation Act 1978, Sched. 1.
"United Kingdom waters": s.313(2)(a).

GENERAL NOTE

[Derivation: Merchant Shipping Act 1979, s.20; Merchant Shipping Act 1988, Sched. 6, para. 1; Criminal Justice Act 1982, s.49(2); Environmental Protection Act 1990, s.148(2); Merchant Shipping (Salvage and Pollution) Act 1994, ss.2, 3.]

Subss. (1) and (2)

Section 128 re-enacts s.20 of the Merchant Shipping Act 1979, as amended. The section gives the Secretary of State wide powers to give effect to international pollution Conventions by Order (*cf.* ss.85, 86). Section 20 of the Merchant Shipping Act 1979 was enacted to enable the U.K. to respond quickly to changes in international marine pollution law. Section 20(1) allowed an Order in Council to be made which would give effect to three specified IMO conventions, the International Convention for the Prevention of Pollution from Ships 1973 (MARPOL), its 1978 Protocol and the Protocol relating to Intervention on the High Seas in Cases of Marine Pollution by Substances other than Oil 1973, as well as to modifications of these instruments. The Merchant Shipping (Salvage and Pollution) Act 1994, s.2, added to the list the International Convention on Oil Pollution Preparedness, Response and Co-operation 1990 (the OPRC Convention), which is now s.128(1)(d). The aim of the section was to allow the U.K. to ratify the Conventions internationally, but to bring them into force in national law if it appeared that the international entry into force would be delayed (see D.R. Thomas' annotations to the 1979 Act in *Current Law Statutes Annotated 1979*). It takes many years for Conventions to achieve the necessary number of ratifications, but the matters dealt with by them might be so urgent as to require immediate action. The powers extend, in what is now s.128(1)(e) (formerly sub-para. (d)), to "any international agreement", not mentioned above, which relates to "the prevention, reduction or control of pollution of the sea", whether such agreement is in force or not. This apparently wide provision gives the Government very great powers to by-pass the normal Parliamentary process, although the affirmative resolution procedure is required. See s.141 below, for an example of an Order issued under s.128.

MARPOL and its Protocols. These have been given effect through the Merchant Shipping (Prevention of Pollution) Order 1983 (S.I. 1983 No. 1106) and detailed regulations have been issued to deal with technical matters, *e.g.* the Merchant Shipping (Prevention of Oil Pollution) Regulations 1983 (S.I. 1983 No. 1398).

The OPRC Convention. The International Convention on Oil Pollution Preparedness, Response and Co-operation 1990 (the OPRC Convention), which entered into force in May 1995, is designed to increase international co-operation in the event of threats to the marine environment from oil pollution, incidents involving ships, offshore units (*e.g.* oil platforms), sea ports and oil handling facilities. It obliges states to ensure that oil pollution emergency plans are in existence, *e.g.* on ships flying its flag, and that these plans are co-ordinated with national and regional systems for responding promptly to oil pollution incidents. The Convention sets out oil pollution reporting procedures, *e.g.* for ships which discharge oil, and the action which must be taken by a State on receiving such a pollution report. As between contracting states there are obligations of co-operation, *e.g.* to facilitate the movement of pollution prevention equipment, which include obligations to provide technical assistance and to co-operate in research and development.

It might have been thought that the 1990 OPRC Convention already fell within s.20(1)(d) of the Merchant Shipping Act 1979 (now s.128(1)(e) of the Merchant Shipping Act 1995), given that it covers pollution from ships. However, the Convention also covers oil platforms and terminals, which would not fall within the definition. Accordingly, s.2 of the 1994 Act added the 1990 OPRC Convention to the list of specific instruments in s.128(1).

Note that the method of giving national effect to the 1990 Convention is not to incorporate it in total in a Schedule to the Act (as s.224 does with the 1989 Salvage Convention), but merely to allow the Government to give effect to its provisions by way of delegated legislation. The reason for the different treatment probably lies in the nature of the different Conventions. The OPRC Convention sets out general duties on states which must be translated into national law, whereas the 1989 Salvage Convention is effectively a code which can be enacted as it stands.

Subs. (3)

This subsection contains an extensive list of matters which may be dealt with in any Order under subs. (1). Paragraph (a) contains a list of specific enactments which may be applied to implement the various international instruments listed in s.128(1). Section 3(2) of the Merchant Shipping (Salvage and Pollution) Act 1994 added s.33 of the Merchant Shipping Act 1988 to the list in s.20(3)(a) of the 1979 Act, but it does not appear that the consolidated provision, s.128(3)(a) has included the equivalent reference in the Merchant Shipping Act 1995, namely s.267. Section 33 of the Merchant Shipping Act 1988 was enacted in response to the *Herald of Free Enterprise* disaster and allowed for the setting up of an independent Marine Accidents Investigation Branch (MAIB) to investigate shipping casualties to U.K. ships and foreign ships in U.K. waters (see now s.267). Section 267(8) now allows an inspector to have the powers of investigators under s.259. Section 3(2) of the 1994 Act adds s.33 of the 1988 Act to the list in s.128

so that, *e.g.* an investigator would be able to inquire into accidents involving breaches of requirements set out in IMO Conventions as they are amended from time to time. It is not clear if this power has been lost in the consolidation.

Subs. (4)

Subsection (4) enables an Order made under subs. (1) to provide for various matters. A new para. (b) was added by the Merchant Shipping (Salvage and Pollution) Act 1994 which allows provision to be made for relevant documents and is similar to para. (a). Thus an Order could refer to technical details in one of the DOT Merchant Shipping Notices and it would be possible to alter the Notice without amending the Order. The intention is that small technical changes would not need to be subject to Parliamentary scrutiny. See now the Merchant Shipping (Delegation of Type Approval) Regulations 1996 (S.I. 1996 No. 147).

Subss. (5) and (6)

It has long since been impractical to include detailed technical provisions relating to ship safety and marine pollution in the primary legislation, and the 1979 Act marked a major shift to the practice of including such technical provisions in subordinate legislation. Sections 128 and 85 contain complicated rule-making powers designed, in part, to safeguard the supervisory power of Parliament over the executive. The detailed procedures necessary or appropriate for the passing of such subordinate legislation will be a matter of interest mainly for students of Parliamentary procedures and the DOT officials responsible for drafting. The Merchant Shipping (Salvage and Pollution) Act 1994, s.3 made some technical amendments so that the primary powers should be phrased sufficiently widely to allow speedy amendment in response to international changes (*e.g.* to SOLAS and MARPOL under their tacit amendment procedures).

An Order under subs. (1) to implement one of the international instruments or agreements referred to in that subsection will allow for detailed regulations to be made under it, so as to give effect to the substance of the instrument or agreement. If the agreement was not one of those specifically listed in subs. (1)(a)–(c), *e.g.* it was a post-1978 amendment of MARPOL which fell within what is now para. (e), any Order had to be made under the affirmative resolution procedure (see s.20(6) of the 1979 Act, before it was amended by the Merchant Shipping (Salvage and Pollution) Act 1994, s.3).

Detailed regulations on the safe construction of ships will be made under s.85, often deriving from the International Convention on the Safety of Life at Sea 1974 (SOLAS). In a similar manner to s.128, s.85 gives the Secretary of State the power to make regulations dealing with health and safety on ships. It is not always easy to distinguish between technical changes to ship construction and operation which are designed for pollution prevention, as opposed to safety purposes, and the IMO is increasingly making simultaneous amendments to MARPOL and SOLAS. As a result, IMO has tried to ensure that SOLAS and MARPOL remain up-to-date by introducing modifications and amendments under "tacit amendment procedures" which do not require the convening of a full-blown diplomatic conference. It clearly proved irksome for the DOT to obtain affirmative approval of an Order where technical amendments were concerned. Accordingly, subs. (5) (as inserted by the Merchant Shipping (Salvage and Pollution) Act 1994, s.3) allows for the original Order, made under subs. (1), to authorise the making of regulations to give effect to amendments of the relevant conventions. Moreover, this authorisation was made to apply to *existing* Orders in Council and mirrors the change made to s.21 of the Merchant Shipping Act 1979 (now s.85) by the Safety at Sea Act 1986, s.11.

Subsection (6) offers some enhancement of Parliamentary control, in exchange for the removal of the need for an Order in Council, by providing that any regulations issued are to be subject to annulment. Previously, such regulations were merely required to be laid. Subsection (6) was amended by the Merchant Shipping (Salvage and Pollution) Act 1994 merely to ensure that the 1990 OPRC Convention is not subject to the affirmative resolution procedure which would apply to subs. (1)(e) agreements. The draft Order must, however, contain a statement that it is for the purpose of subs. (1)(a)–(e), and in such a case will be subject to the negative resolution procedure.

The overall effect of subss. (5) and (6) is that linked SOLAS and MARPOL amendments can be contained in a single set of regulations made under the authority of ss.20 and 21 of the 1979 Act and subject to the same Parliamentary procedure.

Further provision for prevention of pollution from ships

129.—(1) Her Majesty may by Order in Council make such provision as She considers appropriate for the purpose of giving effect to any provision of the United Nations Convention on the Law of the Sea 1982 (Cmnd 8941) for the protection and preservation of the marine environment from pollution by matter from ships.

(2) Without prejudice to the generality of subsection (1) above, an Order under that subsection may in particular include provision—

(a) corresponding to any provision that is authorised for the purposes of section 128 by subsections (3) and (4) of that section; and

(b) specifying areas of sea above any of the areas for the time being designated under section 1(7) of the Continental Shelf Act 1964 as waters within which the jurisdiction and rights of the United Kingdom are exercisable in accordance with Part XII of that Convention for the protection and preservation of the marine environment;

and provision authorising the making of regulations authorises the amendment or revocation of regulations made by virtue of paragraph (f) of the said subsection (4).

(3) A draft of an Order in Council proposed to be made by virtue of subsection (1) above shall not be submitted to Her Majesty in Council unless the draft has been approved by resolution of each House of Parliament.

DEFINITIONS

"ship": s.313(1).
"United Kingdom": Interpretation Act 1978, Sched. 1.

GENERAL NOTE

[Derivation: Merchant Shipping Act 1979, s.20(A); Merchant Shipping (Salvage and Pollution) Act 1994, s.4.]

The UN Convention on the Law of the Sea 1982 was the culmination of much work to up-date the international law of the sea, many of whose principles had been contained in four 1958 Conventions. The LOS Convention 1982 contained much that was relatively uncontroversial and many of its provisions are mere codifications of existing law and international practice. But its entry into force was significantly delayed as a result of disputes between the developing world and certain industrialised countries (including the USA and the U.K.) over the provisions in Pt. XI relating to deep seabed mining (for the U.K. objections, see the statement of Malcolm Rifkind in the House of Commons on December 2, 1982). The Convention, nevertheless, entered into force on November 16, 1994 following a compromise over the mining issue (see, *e.g.* E. Brown, *"Neither necessary nor prudent at this stage: The regime of seabed mining and its impact on the universality of the UN Convention on the Law of the Sea"* (1993) 17 Marine Policy 81; G. Mangone, *"Negotiations on the 1982 LOSC given extra urgency by the 60th ratification"* (1994) 9 IJMCL 57; D. Freestone, G. Mangone, *"The Law of the Sea Convention: Unfinished Agendas and Future Challenges"* (1995) 10 IJMCL ix). Of particular relevance is Pt. V of the Convention which recognises the establishment of a 200 mile exclusive economic zone (EEZ) within which coastal states can exercise rights, *e.g.* to explore and exploit, *conserve and manage* natural resources such as oil and fisheries (see Art. 56).

The North Sea is obviously an area in which many European states have an interest. Three International Conferences on the Protection of the North Sea have been held, in 1984, 1987 and 1990. At the 1990 Conference at the Hague a declaration was made concerning the co-ordination of action to increase State jurisdiction over the North Sea. This was followed, in 1992, by the "Paris Declaration", signed by Belgium, Denmark, France, Germany, the Netherlands, Norway, Sweden and the U.K. (see T. IJlstra, *"North Sea Pollution: vessel source pollution, environmental management and the establishment of EEZs"* (1993) 17 Marine Policy 130). The Declaration on Co-ordinated Extension of Jurisdiction in the North Sea 1992 concluded that "coastal State jurisdiction should be increased to the full extent permitted by the rules of international law in order to prevent, reduce and control pollution of the marine environment" (*ibid.* p. 134). This increase would be both geographical (*e.g.* up to 200 miles) and in terms of the powers available. In 1993 at an Intermediate Ministerial Meeting in Copenhagen, para. 9.6 of the Statement of Conclusions recorded that "aspects of enforceability and the relevant rules of international law, as set out in the UN Convention on the Law of the Sea, in particular Arts. 218 and 220, are fully taken into account" (cited in T. IJlstra, *"The 1993 Copenhagen Intermediate Ministerial Meeting: North Sea Cooperation at a turning point?"* (1994) 9 IJMCL 173, 183). Articles 218 and 220 deal with enforcement of applicable international rules and standards by port and coastal states.

The concepts of Pt. V of the LOS Convention 1982 are used as the jurisdictional limit agreed in the 1992 Paris Declaration. Moreover, the signatories to that 1992 Declaration, including the U.K., undertook to initiate the process of implementing in their national legislation the accepted international rules and standards which are of particular importance to the protection and preservation of the marine environment of the North Sea. These include the relevant provisions of the LOS Convention 1982 (including Arts. 218 and 220) which allow enforcement against vessels violating MARPOL. In February 1996, the U.K. issued three Orders which will enable it to accede to the LOS Convention 1982 (see below).

The purpose of s.129 is to allow an Order in Council to give effect to particular provisions of the LOS Convention 1982 which relate to the "protection and preservation of the marine environment from pollution by matter from ships". This action will enable the U.K. to fulfil its undertakings under the 1992 Paris Declaration, without requiring ratification of the whole of the LOS Convention 1982 (although it is expected that such ratification will now take place). In effect it "will allow the U.K.'s jurisdiction for counter-pollution measures to be extended beyond the territorial sea" (*per* Lord Donaldson, *Hansard*, H.L. Vol. 555, col. 687). Lord Mackay of Ardbrecknish (the Parliamentary Under-Secretary of State, Department of Transport) stated at the Second Reading of the Merchant Shipping (Salvage and Pollution) Bill 1994 in the House of Lords that the U.K. prevention of pollution regulations would be extended to cover discharge by all ships out to the 200 mile limit. The Merchant Shipping (Prevention of Pollution) (Law of the Sea Convention) Order 1996 (S.I. 1996 No. 282), entered into force on February 28, 1996 and enables the Secretary of State to issue regulations to give effect to the relevant parts of the LOS Convention 1982. (Note also, generally, the International Sea-Bed Authority (Immunities and Privileges) Order 1996 (S.I. 1996 No. 270), and the International Tribunal for the Law of the Sea (Immunities and Privileges) Order 1996 (S.I. 1996 No. 272).)

Section 129(2)(a) allows a very wide flexibility in rule-making power, *e.g.* in applying existing U.K. merchant shipping legislation (see s.128(3)(a)). Also, the reference to the corresponding provisions in s.128(3) will allow for any Order in Council under the new s.129 to be extended to the coasts off U.K. colonies, *e.g.* the Channel Islands, the Isle of Man and the Falkland Islands. Orders under s.129 will be subject to the affirmative resolution procedure. Section 129 would appear to allow jurisdiction to be extended up to 200 nautical miles but, without prejudice to that, the new s.129(2)(b) allows for jurisdiction to be extended to the waters over the U.K. continental shelf, as specified in s.1(7) of the Continental Shelf Act 1964 (c. 29) (and as presently permitted under the Convention on the Continental Shelf 1958).

The principal provisions of the LOS Convention 1982 which will be covered, are those contained in "Part XII. Protection and Preservation of the Marine Environment", but excluding those which do not relate to pollution by matter from ships (*e.g.* Art. 207 dealing with pollution from land-based sources). In addition to the enforcement articles (218 and 220), mentioned above, the 1996 LOS Order (S.I. 1996 No. 282) will cover quite significant areas of maritime activity undertaken by foreign vessels visiting U.K. ports or offshore terminals (see, *e.g.* Art. 211). Although innocent rights of passage cannot be restricted, laws and regulations can be applied to foreign vessels in territorial waters (Art. 211(4)). One of the difficulties with which the DOT will have to grapple is the extent to which enforcement powers can be extended to vessels outside territorial waters, but within the EEZ. This is a topical problem in the light of numerous incidents to "*Klondikers*" referred to in Chap. 17 of the Donaldson Report. These are the large fish factory ships (mostly from former Soviet Bloc states) operating outside U.K. territorial waters off the Shetland Islands, in respect of which there are many allegations of unseaworthiness. Under Art. 220(3) enforcement powers over offences committed in the EEZ are severely limited (*e.g.* the power to require the vessel to identify itself and its itinerary), although detention powers may be applied by coastal states in respect of pollution in the territorial sea (see Art. 220(2)). Under Art. 220(1) proceedings may be taken against offenders voluntarily within ports or offshore terminals and one of the recommendations of the Donaldson Report was that the U.K. needed to widen its definition of "port" so as to deal with vessels which are outside the narrow confines of a harbour (see para. 17.42). The new s.129 will clearly not enable Orders to be made which go beyond that permitted by the LOS Convention 1982, although the precise extent of that Convention on particular matters will always be open to debate (*cf.* Art. 211(5) and Art. 220(3)).

Regulation of transfers between ships in territorial waters

130.—(1) The Secretary of State may by regulations make, in relation F to the transfer of cargo, stores, bunker fuel or ballast between ships while within United Kingdom waters, such provision as he considers appropriate for preventing pollution, danger to health or to navigation, or hazards to the environment or to natural resources.

(2) Regulations under this section may, in particular, do any of the following things—

(a) prohibit transfers of any specified description or prohibit transfers if, or unless, carried out in specified areas, circumstances or ways;

(b) make provision about—

(i) the design of, and standards to be met by, ships and equipment,

(ii) the manning of ships, including the qualifications and experience to be possessed by persons of any specified description employed on board, and

(iii) the qualifications and experience to be possessed by persons (whether masters or not) controlling the carrying out of transfers or operations ancillary thereto;

(c) provide for proposed transfers to be notified to and approved by persons appointed by the Secretary of State or another person, and for the supervision of transfers, and the inspection of ships and equipment, by persons so appointed;

(d) provide—

(i) for the procedure to be followed in relation to the approval of transfers to be such as may be prescribed by any document specified in the regulations, and

(ii) for references in the regulations to any document so specified to operate as references to that document as revised or re-issued from time to time;

(e) provide for the making and keeping of records about ships and equipment, the issuing of certificates, and the furnishing of information;

(f) provide for the granting by the Secretary of State or another person of exemptions from specified provisions of the regulations, on such terms (if any) as the Secretary of State or that other person may specify, and for altering or cancelling exemptions;

(g) limit any provision of the regulations to specified cases or kinds of case.

(3) Regulations under this section may provide—

(a) that a contravention of the regulations shall be an offence punishable on summary conviction by a fine not exceeding £25,000 and on conviction on indictment by imprisonment for a term not exceeding two years or a fine or both;

(b) that any such contravention shall be an offence punishable only on summary conviction by a fine not exceeding £25,000 or such lower amount as is prescribed by the regulations;

(c) that, in such cases as are prescribed by the regulations, such persons as are so prescribed shall each be guilty of an offence created by virtue of paragraph (a) or (b) above.

(4) Regulations under this section may—

(a) make different provision for different classes or descriptions of ships and for different circumstances; and

(b) make such transitional, incidental or supplementary provision as appears to the Secretary of State to be necessary or expedient.

DEFINITIONS

"contravention": s.313(1).

"master": s.313(1).

"person": Interpretation Act 1978, Sched. 1.

"Secretary of State": Interpretation Act 1978, Sched. 1.

"ship": s.313(1).

"United Kingdom": Interpretation Act 1978, Sched. 1.

"United Kingdom waters": s.313(2)(a).

GENERAL NOTE

[Derivation: Merchant Shipping Act 1988, ss.35 and 53(2).]

Section 130 re-enacts s.35 of the Merchant Shipping Act 1988. It is quite common for large tankers to perform lightening operations off the British coast in which cargoes are discharged into smaller vessels. These operations may be undertaken for a number of reasons, *e.g.* in order to allow the tanker to get into a small port, to enable the tanker to proceed on a main voyage without delay, or because there are no free discharging berths available at the time. Although the transfer of bulk oil or chemical cargoes is probably most common, other commodities may be transferred—some of which may be hazardous. The Royal Commission on Environmental Pollution recognised that there were risks involved and the 1984 Consultative Document recommended that powers be created to regulate such activities.

Accordingly, this section gives the Secretary of State wide powers to make regulations concerning transfers between ships at sea. The transfers covered are not only of cargo, but also stores (*e.g.* tank cleaning chemicals), bunker fuel and ballast. The latter would normally consist only of water, but this could often be contaminated, *e.g.* if it had been in dirty cargo tanks. The discharging of oily mixtures could be an offence already under the Merchant Shipping (Prevention of Oil Pollution) Regulations 1983 (S.I. 1983 No. 1398), but the section could stop transfers in sensitive coastal areas when there is the possibility of leakage. It was never the intention to apply the powers to transfers of fish between trawlers and factory ships, or to naval replenishment operations.

The regulations under this section can only be made to prevent threats to safety or the environment: the powers could not be exercised for commercial reasons, *e.g.* to encourage the greater use of facilities in a different port. The regulations can apply only to ships "within the seaward limits of the territorial sea" of the U.K. The territorial waters of the U.K. are now 12 miles (see the Territorial Sea Act 1987). There is less of a need to introduce legislation in ports because of the existence of harbour bylaws, the Dangerous Vessels Act 1985 (c. 22) and the Dangerous Substances in Harbour Areas Regulations 1987 (S.I. 1987 No. 37). The latter already restrict the transfer of explosives in British territorial waters.

Subsection (2) lists particular matters that may be regulated. It is noticeable that certain transfers may be completely prohibited or designated for certain safe or controllable areas. The types of ship and personnel can also be specified and prior notification can be required. The latter is particularly important as it enables inspections of ships that might appear to be ill-equipped.

The Secretary of State is entitled to grant exemptions, and concern was expressed that blanket exemptions would be made. The Government gave an assurance in 1988 that the power was intended for very exceptional circumstances, such as emergencies where a cargo was leaking. This is an important matter for salvors who may need to arrange transhipment in a great hurry. In the case of a tanker casualty the salvors will be trying to prevent loss of cargo from the sinking ship, as well as seeking to keep the ship itself afloat.

Subsection (3) lays down fairly stiff penalties, which on indictment may include two years' imprisonment and an unlimited fine. The persons who may be guilty will be prescribed by the regulations, but will probably include the owner and master—even of a foreign ship.

For the powers of the Secretary of State to make delegated legislation, such as regulations, see s.306, below.

CHAPTER II

OIL POLLUTION

General provisions for preventing pollution

Discharge of oil from ships into certain United Kingdom waters

131.—(1) If any oil or mixture containing oil is discharged as mentioned in the following paragraphs into United Kingdom national waters which are navigable by sea-going ships, then, subject to the following provisions of this Chapter, the following shall be guilty of an offence, that is to say—
  (a) if the discharge is from a ship, the owner or master of the ship, unless he proves that the discharge took place and was caused as mentioned in paragraph (b) below;
  (b) if the discharge is from a ship but takes place in the course of a transfer of oil to or from another ship or a place on land and is caused by the act or omission of any person in charge of any apparatus in that other ship or that place, the owner or master of that other ship or, as the case may be, the occupier of that place.
(2) Subsection (1) above does not apply to any discharge which—
  (a) is made into the sea; and
  (b) is of a kind or is made in circumstances for the time being prescribed by regulations made by the Secretary of State.
(3) A person guilty of an offence under this section shall be liable—

(a) on summary conviction, to a fine not exceeding £50,000;

(b) on conviction on indictment, to a fine.

(4) In this section "sea" includes any estuary or arm of the sea.

(5) In this section "place on land" includes anything resting on the bed or shore of the sea, or of any other waters included in United Kingdom national waters, and also includes anything afloat (other than a ship) if it is anchored or attached to the bed or shore of the sea or any such waters.

(6) In this section "occupier", in relation to any such thing as is mentioned in subsection (5) above, if it has no occupier, means the owner thereof.

DEFINITIONS
"discharge": s.151(4).
"master": s.313(1).
"mixture containing oil": s.151(3).
"occupier": subs. (6).
"oil": s.151(1).
"place on land": subs. (5) and s.151(1).
"sea": subs. (4).
"Secretary of State": Interpretation Act 1978, Sched. 1.
"ship": ss.151(5) and 313(1).
"transfer": s.151(1).
"United Kingdom national waters": s.313(2).

GENERAL NOTE
[Derivation: Prevention of Oil Pollution Act 1971, ss.2(2A), (2B), (3), (4); Prevention of Oil Pollution Act 1971, s.29(1); Prevention of Oil Pollution Act 1986, s.1(1).]

The Prevention of Oil Pollution Act 1971 consolidated the Oil in Navigable Waters Acts 1955–1971 and s.5 of the Continental Shelf Act 1964. It gave effect to the International Convention for the Prevention of Pollution of the Sea by Oil 1954 (the Oilpol Convention), as amended in 1962 and 1970. That Convention has now generally been superseded by MARPOL in its detailed requirements, but the enforcement system found in the Prevention of Oil Pollution Act 1971 has largely been retained in the Merchant Shipping Act 1995. The Prevention of Oil Pollution Act 1971 also gave effect to the International Convention relating to Intervention on the High Seas in Cases of Oil Pollution Casualties 1969 (see s.137, below) and part of the Convention on the High Seas 1958.

Section 131 re-enacts s.2 of the Prevention of Oil Pollution Act 1971, as amended, and creates an offence where oil is discharged into U.K. waters in circumstances which may be prescribed by the Secretary of State (*e.g.* as to quantities or concentrations of oil). For the powers of the Secretary of State to make delegated legislation, such as regulations, see s.306, below.

In *Federal Steam Navigation v. Department of Trade and Industry (sub. nom. The Hunting- don)* [1974] 1 W.L.R. 505 the House of Lords had to consider the expression "owner or master" in order to decide whether *both* could be guilty of an offence. The House considered the mischief of the section and, despite the apparent disjunctive, found that prosecutions could indeed be brought against both. Provisions of the Merchant Shipping Act 1995 with a more modern history tend to have been drafted more clearly to indicate that "each" may be guilty of an offence (see for example s.3(1), above).

See s.144, below, for powers of detention. Note also the extensions possible under s.129, above.

Defences of owner or master charged with offence under section 131

132.—(1) Where a person is charged with an offence under section 131 as the owner or master of a ship, it shall be a defence to prove that the oil or mixture was discharged for the purpose of—

(a) securing the safety of any ship;

(b) preventing damage to any ship or cargo, or

(c) saving life,

unless the court is satisfied that the discharge of the oil or mixture was not necessary for that purpose or was not a reasonable step to take in the circumstances.

(2) Where a person is charged with an offence under section 131 as the owner or master of a ship, it shall also be a defence to prove—

(a) that the oil or mixture escaped in consequence of damage to the ship, and that as soon as practicable after the damage occurred all reasonable steps were taken for preventing, or (if it could not be prevented) for stopping or reducing, the escape of the oil or mixture; or

(b) that the oil or mixture escaped by reason of leakage, that neither the leakage nor any delay in discovering it was due to any want of reasonable care, and that as soon as practicable after the escape was discovered all reasonable steps were taken for stopping or reducing it.

DEFINITIONS
"discharge of the oil": s.151(4).
"master": s.313(1).
"mixture": s.151(3).
"oil": s.151(1).
"person": Interpretation Act 1978, Sched. 1.
"ship": ss.151(5) and 313(1).

GENERAL NOTE
[Derivation: Prevention of Oil Pollution Act 1971, s.5.]
Section 132 re-enacts s.5 of the Prevention of Oil Pollution Act 1971 and sets out the defences to an offence under s.131 which are available to a shipowner and a master.

Defences of occupier charged with offence under section 131

133. Where a person is charged, in respect of the escape of any oil or mixture containing oil, with an offence under section 131 as the occupier of a place on land, it shall be a defence to prove that neither the escape nor any delay in discovering it was due to any want of reasonable care and that as soon as practicable after it was discovered all reasonable steps were taken for stopping or reducing it.

DEFINITIONS
"mixture containing oil": s.151(3).
"occupier": s.131(6).
"oil": s.151(1).
"person": Interpretation Act 1978, Sched. 1.
"place on land": ss.131(5) and 151(1).

GENERAL NOTE
[Derivation: Prevention of Oil Pollution Act 1971, s.6(1).]
Section 133 re-enacts parts of s.6 of the Prevention of Oil Pollution Act 1971, with the exception of s.6(1)(b) and (c), and sets out further defences to a s.131 offence, but where the person is charged as an occupier of land.

Protection for acts done in exercise of certain powers of harbour authorities, etc.

134.—(1) Where any oil, or mixture containing oil, is discharged in consequence of—

(a) the exercise of any power conferred by section 252 or 253; or

(b) the exercise, for the purpose of preventing obstruction or danger to navigation, of any power to dispose of sunk, stranded or abandoned ships which is exercisable by a harbour authority under any local enactment;

and apart from this subsection the authority exercising the power, or a person employed by or acting on behalf of the authority, would be guilty of an offence under section 131 in respect of that discharge, the authority or person shall not be convicted unless it is shown that they or he failed to take such steps (if any) as were reasonable in the circumstances for preventing, stopping or reducing the discharge.

(2) Subsection (1) above shall apply to the exercise of any power conferred by section 13 of the Dockyard Ports Regulation Act 1865 (removal of obstructions to dockyard ports) as it applies to the exercise of the powers under sections 252 and 253, and shall, as so applying, have effect as if references to the authority exercising the power were references to the Queen's harbour master for the port in question.

DEFINITIONS
    "discharge": s.151(4).
    "fails": s.313(1).
    "harbour authority": s.151(1).
    "harbour master": s.151(1).
    "local enactment": s.151(1).
    "mixture containing oil": s.151(3).
    "oil": s.151(1).
    "person": Interpretation Act 1978, Sched. 1.
    "port": s.313(1).
    "ship": ss.151(5) and 313(1).

GENERAL NOTE
[Derivation: Prevention of Oil Pollution Act 1971, s.7.]
Section 134 re-enacts s.7 of the Prevention of Oil Pollution Act 1971 and provides defences to a s.131 charge in respect of the exercise of powers by harbour or conservancy authorities.

Restrictions on transfer of oil at night

135.—(1) No oil shall be transferred between sunset and sunrise to or from a ship in any harbour in the United Kingdom unless the requisite notice has been given in accordance with this section or the transfer is for the purposes of a fire brigade.

(2) A general notice may be given to the harbour master of a harbour that transfers of oil between sunset and sunrise will be frequently carried out at a place in the harbour within such period, not ending later than twelve months after the date on which the notice is given, as is specified in the notice; and if such a notice is given it shall be the requisite notice for the purposes of this section as regards transfers of oil at that place within the period specified in the notice.

(3) Subject to subsection (2) above, the requisite notice for the purposes of this section shall be a notice given to the harbour master not less than three hours nor more than 96 hours before the transfer of oil begins.

(4) In the case of a harbour which has no harbour master, references in this section to the harbour master shall be construed as references to the harbour authority.

(5) If any oil is transferred to or from a ship in contravention of this section, the master of the ship, and, if the oil is transferred from or to a place on land, the occupier of that place, shall be liable on summary conviction to a fine not exceeding level 3 on the standard scale.

DEFINITIONS
    "contravention": s.313(1).
    "harbour": s.313(1).
    "harbour in the United Kingdom": s.151(1).
    "harbour authority": s.151(1).
    "harbour master": s.151(1).
    "master": s.313(1).
    "month": Interpretation Act 1978, Sched. 1.
    "occupier": s.131(6).
    "oil": s.151(1).
    "place on land": ss.131(5) and 151(1).
    "requisite notice": subs. (3).
    "ship": s.313(1).
    "standard scale": Criminal Justice Act 1982, s.37.

"transfer": s.151(1).
"United Kingdom": Interpretation Act 1978, Sched. 1.

General Note
[Derivation: Prevention of Oil Pollution Act 1971, s.10; Merchant Shipping Act 1979, Sched. 6, Pt. II.]
Section 135 re-enacts s.10 of the Prevention of Oil Pollution Act 1971 as amended and places restrictions on night-time transfers of oil, cf. s.130.

Duty to report discharge of oil into waters of harbours

136.—(1) If any oil or mixture containing oil—
(a) is discharged from a ship into the waters of a harbour in the United Kingdom; or
(b) is found to be escaping or to have escaped from a ship into any such waters;
the owner or master of the ship shall forthwith report the occurrence to the harbour master, or, if the harbour has no harbour master, to the harbour authority.

(2) A report made under subsection (1) above shall state whether the occurrence falls within subsection (1)(a) or (b) above.

(3) If a person fails to make a report as required by this section he shall be liable on summary conviction to a fine not exceeding level 5 on the standard scale.

Definitions
"discharged": s.151(4).
"fails": s.313(1).
"harbour": s.313(1).
"harbour in the United Kingdom": s.151(1).
"harbour authority": s.151(1).
"harbour master": s.151(1).
"master": s.313(1).
"mixture containing oil": s.151(3).
"oil": s.151(1).
"person": Interpretation Act 1978, Sched. 1.
"ship": ss.151(5) and 313(1).
"standard scale": Criminal Justice Act 1982, s.37.
"United Kingdom": Interpretation Act 1978, Sched. 1.

General Note
[Derivation: Prevention of Oil Pollution Act 1971, ss.11 and 29(1); Merchant Shipping Act 1979, Sched. 6, Pt. IV.]
Section 136 re-enacts s.11 of the Prevention of Oil Pollution Act 1971 (with the exception of s.11(1)(c) relating to discharges from land) and imposes a duty to report any discharge to the harbour master.

Shipping casualties

Shipping casualties

137.—(1) The powers conferred by this section shall be exercisable where—
(a) an accident has occurred to or in a ship; and
(b) in the opinion of the Secretary of State oil from the ship will or may cause pollution on a large scale in the United Kingdom or in United Kingdom waters; and
(c) in the opinion of the Secretary of State the use of the powers conferred by this section is urgently needed;
but those powers are subject to the limitations contained in subsections (6) and (7) below.

(2) For the purpose of preventing or reducing oil pollution, or the risk of oil

pollution, the Secretary of State may give directions as respects the ship or its cargo—

  (a) to the owner of the ship, or to any person in possession of the ship; or

  (b) to the master of the ship; or

  (c) to any salvor in possession of the ship, or to any person who is the servant or agent of any salvor in possession of the ship, and who is in charge of the salvage operation.

(3) Directions under subsection (2) above may require the person to whom they are given to take, or refrain from taking, any action of any kind whatsoever, and without prejudice to the generality of the preceding provisions of this subsection the directions may require—

  (a) that the ship is to be, or is not to be, moved, or is to be moved to a specified place, or is to be removed from a specified area or locality; or

  (b) that the ship is not to be moved to a specified place or area, or over a specified route; or

  (c) that any oil or other cargo is to be, or is not to be, unloaded or discharged; or

  (d) that specified salvage measures are to be, or are not to be, taken.

(4) If in the opinion of the Secretary of State the powers conferred by subsection (2) above are, or have proved to be, inadequate for the purpose, the Secretary of State may, for the purpose of preventing or reducing oil pollution, or the risk of oil pollution, take, as respects the ship or its cargo, any action of any kind whatsoever, and without prejudice to the generality of the preceding provisions of this subsection the Secretary of State may—

  (a) take any such action as he has power to require to be taken by a direction under this section;

  (b) undertake operations for the sinking or destruction of the ship, or any part of it, of a kind which is not within the means of any person to whom he can give directions;

  (c) undertake operations which involve the taking over of control of the ship.

(5) The powers of the Secretary of State under subsection (4) above shall also be exercisable by such persons as may be authorised for the purpose by the Secretary of State.

(6) Every person concerned with compliance with directions given, or with action taken, under this section shall use his best endeavours to avoid any risk to human life.

(7) The provisions of this section and of section 141 are without prejudice to any rights or powers of Her Majesty's Government in the United Kingdom exercisable apart from those sections whether under international law or otherwise.

(8) It is hereby declared that any action taken as respects a ship which is under arrest or as respects the cargo of such a ship, being action duly taken in pursuance of a direction given under this section, or being any action taken under subsection (4) or (5) above—

  (a) does not constitute contempt of court; and

  (b) does not in any circumstances make the Admiralty Marshal liable in any civil proceedings.

(9) In this section, unless the context otherwise requires—

  "accident" includes the loss, stranding, abandonment of or damage to a ship;

  "owner", in relation to the ship to or in which an accident has occurred, includes its owner at the time of the accident; and

  "specified" in relation to a direction under this section, means specified by the direction;

and the reference in subsection (8) above to the Admiralty Marshal includes a reference to the Admiralty Marshal of the Supreme Court of Northern Ireland.

DEFINITIONS

"accident": subs. (9).
"discharged": s.151(4).
"master": s.313(1).
"oil": s.151(1).
"owner": subs. (9).
"person": Interpretation Act 1978, Sched. 1.
"Secretary of State": Interpretation Act 1978, Sched. 1.
"ship": ss.151(5) and 313(1).
"specified": subs. (9).
"Supreme Court": Interpretation Act 1978, Sched. 1.
"United Kingdom": Interpretation Act 1978, Sched. 1.
"United Kingdom waters": s.313(2)(a).

GENERAL NOTE

[Derivation: Prevention of Oil Pollution Act 1971, s.12; Merchant Shipping (Salvage and Pollution) Act 1994, s.8(6).]

Section 137 re-enacts s.12 of the Prevention of Oil Pollution Act 1971, as amended (see *Chorley and Giles, Shipping Law*, p.488). The section gives powers to intervene in a pollution incident in the circumstances indicated in subs. (1). It is based on the rights of a coastal state to protect its marine environment (see Arts. 21, 211, 221 of the LOS Convention 1982).

In respect of all U.K. ships, and foreign ships in U.K. waters, the powers in subss. (2) and (4) may be exercised where an accident has occurred to a ship and the Secretary of State thinks that substances from the ship could cause pollution on a large scale in the U.K. or its waters and in his opinion he needs to exercise his powers urgently. Under subs. (2) there is a wide power to give directions to owners, masters and salvors in possession of the vessel. Note that the Merchant Shipping (Salvage and Pollution) Act 1994, s.8(6) added the definition of "owner" now in subs. (9). This definition ensures that control may be exercised over the person who was the owner at the time of the incident and prevents any abandonment by the shipowner, or attempts to circumvent Government control by selling the ship before any directions under subs. (2) are given (and see the General Note to s.253, below). The owner, master and salvor may be told to move (or not move) the vessel, to take a particular route or go to a specified place, or to unload (or not unload) the cargo. If these powers seem inadequate the Secretary of State may under subs. (4) take any action of any kind whatsoever as respects the ship and cargo. In particular, he may take over control of the ship or, indeed sink or destroy it. The Secretary of State has delegated powers to the Marine Pollution Control Unit (MPCU), as confirmed by s.293(2)(d), below.

For offences in relation to this section, see s.139, below. For the exercise of intervention powers *outside* territorial waters, see s.141, below.

Right to recover in respect of unreasonable loss or damage

138.—(1) If any action duly taken by a person in pursuance of a direction given to him under section 137, or any action taken under section 137(4) or (5)—

(a) was not reasonably necessary to prevent or reduce oil pollution, or risk of oil pollution; or

(b) was such that the good it did or was likely to do was disproportionately less than the expense incurred, or damage suffered, as a result of the action,

a person incurring expense or suffering damage as a result of, or by himself taking, the action shall be entitled to recover compensation from the Secretary of State.

(2) In considering whether subsection (1) above applies, account shall be taken of—

(a) the extent and risk of oil pollution if the action had not been taken;

(b) the likelihood of the action being effective; and

(c) the extent of the damage which has been caused by the action.

(3) Any reference in this section to the taking of any action includes a reference to a compliance with a direction not to take some specified action.

(4) The Admiralty jurisdiction of the High Court and of the Court of Session shall include jurisdiction to hear and determine any claim arising under this section.

DEFINITIONS
  "High Court": Interpretation Act 1978, Sched. 1.
  "oil": s.151(1).
  "person": Interpretation Act 1978, Sched. 1.
  "Secretary of State": Interpretation Act 1978, Sched. 1.
  "taking of any action": subs. (3).

GENERAL NOTE
  [Derivation: Prevention of Oil Pollution Act 1971, s.13.]
  There is no general right to compensation from the Government for damage or loss caused by the ordinary exercise of the intervention powers, *unless* the action taken was not reasonably necessary to prevent oil pollution or was disproportionate (*cf.* the Dangerous Vessels Act 1985, s.2). Most shipowners would be insured against the risk of intervention damage, *e.g.* under the Institute Time Clauses (Hulls) 1983, cl. 7.

Offences in relation to section 137

139.—(1) If the person to whom a direction is duly given under section 137 contravenes, or fails to comply with, any requirement of the direction, he shall be guilty of an offence.

(2) If a person intentionally obstructs any person who is—

(a) acting on behalf of the Secretary of State in connection with the giving or service of a direction under section 137;

(b) acting in compliance with a direction under that section; or

(c) acting under section 137(4) or (5);

he shall be guilty of an offence.

(3) In proceedings for an offence under subsection (1) above, it shall be a defence for the accused to prove that he has used all due diligence to ensure compliance with the direction, or that he had reasonable cause for believing that compliance with the direction would have involved a serious risk to human life.

(4) A person guilty of an offence under this section shall be liable—

(a) on summary conviction, to a fine not exceeding £50,000;

(b) on conviction on indictment, to a fine.

DEFINITIONS
  "contravenes": s.313(1).
  "fails": s.313(1).
  "person": Interpretation Act 1978, Sched. 1.
  "Secretary of State": Interpretation Act 1978, Sched. 1.

GENERAL NOTE
  [Derivation: Prevention of Oil Pollution Act 1971, s.14.]
  Failure to obey directions given under s.137, or wilfully obstructing a person serving them, is an offence. It is a defence under subs. (3) to show all due diligence had been used or that compliance might have involved a serious risk to human life.

Service of directions under section 137

140.—(1) If the Secretary of State is satisfied that a company or other body is not one to whom section 695 or section 725 of the Companies Act 1985 (service of notices) applies so as to authorise the service of a direction on that body under either of those sections, he may give a direction under section 137 of this Act—

(a) to that body, as the owner of, or the person in possession of, a ship, by serving the direction on the master of the ship; or

(b) to that body, as a salvor, by serving the direction on the person in charge of the salvage operations.

(2) For the purpose of giving or serving a direction under section 137 to or on any person on a ship, a person acting on behalf of the Secretary of State shall have the right to go on board the ship.

(3) In the application of subsection (1) above to Northern Ireland, for references to sections 695 and 725 of the Companies Act 1985 there shall be substituted references to Articles 645 and 673 of the Companies (Northern Ireland) Order 1986.

DEFINITIONS
"Act, this": s.316(1).
"master": s.313(1).
"person": Interpretation Act 1978, Sched. 1.
"Secretary of State": Interpretation Act 1978, Sched. 1.
"ship": s.313(1).

GENERAL NOTE
[Derivation: Prevention of Oil Pollution Act 1971, s.15.]
This section re-enacts s.15 of the Prevention of Oil Pollution Act 1971 and gives the Secretary of State flexibility in relation to the serving of s.137 directions on a corporation which may not be incorporated under the Companies Act 1985. In appropriate cases the Secretary of State could serve the directions on the person in possession of the ship and this would constitute good service on the company.

Application of sections 137 to 140 to certain foreign and other ships

141.—(1) Her Majesty may by Order in Council provide that sections 137 to 140, together with any other provisions of this Chapter, shall apply to a ship—
(a) which is not a United Kingdom ship; and
(b) which is for the time being outside United Kingdom waters;
in such cases and circumstances as may be specified in the Order, and subject to such exceptions, adaptations and modifications, if any, as may be so specified.

(2) An Order in Council under subsection (1) above may contain such transitional and other consequential provisions as appear to Her Majesty to be expedient.

(3) Except as provided by an Order in Council under subsection (1) above, no direction under section 137 shall apply to a ship which is not a United Kingdom ship and which is for the time being outside United Kingdom waters, and no action shall be taken under section 137(4) or (5) as respects any such ship.

(4) No direction under section 137 shall apply to any ship of Her Majesty's navy or to any Government ship and no action shall be taken under section 137(4) or (5) as respects any such ship.

DEFINITIONS
"Government ship": ss.308(4) and 313(1).
"ship": s.313(1).
"United Kingdom ship": ss.1(3) and 313(1).
"United Kingdom waters": s.313(2)(a).

GENERAL NOTE
[Derivation: Prevention of Oil Pollution Act 1971, s.16.]
When the *Torrey Canyon* went aground in 1967, there was uncertainty as to the extent to which, after a casualty, Governments could intervene and control operations, particularly where foreign ships on the high seas were concerned. The *Torrey Canyon* was eventually destroyed. Many states, including the U.K., asserted that there was a customary right to take measures beyond their territorial waters (now 12 miles in the U.K.) to protect those waters from actual or threatened damage (and see Art. 221 of the LOS Convention 1982). For the U.K. rights in territorial waters, see s.137, above.

To provide some clarity, the IMO produced the International Convention Relating to Intervention on the High Seas in Cases of Oil Pollution Casualties 1969 (the 1969 Intervention Convention). This enabled states to take measures on the high seas to prevent, mitigate or eliminate "grave and imminent danger" to coastlines or related interests from oil pollution resulting from a marine casualty: provided that major harmful consequences could reasonably be expected. The power to intervene was extended by a Protocol in 1973 to a long list of dangerous or noxious chemicals other than oil. Note also Art. 11 of the 1989 Salvage Convention (Sched. 11, Pt. I, below).

Section 141 gives the Government the power to extend the operation of ss.137–140 outside territorial waters. In fact, the Merchant Shipping (Prevention of Pollution) (Intervention) Order 1980 (S.I. 1980 No. 1093), was made under s.128. This Order has given effect to the 1969 Intervention Convention and its 1973 Protocol. Intervention action may thus be taken against foreign registered vessels. Under s.141(3) and Art. 7 of the Order, directions to foreign ships beyond territorial waters can only be served on a U.K. citizen or company. Note, however that the limitation in subs. (3) in respect of the powers under s.137(4) and (5) does not apply where the 1969 Intervention Convention operates through the Order.

Enforcement

Oil records

142.—(1) The Secretary of State may make regulations requiring oil record books to be carried in United Kingdom ships and requiring the master of any such ship to record in the oil record book carried by it—

   (a) the carrying out, on board or in connection with the ship, of such of the following operations as may be prescribed relating to—

      (i) the loading of oil cargo,

      (ii) the transfer of oil cargo during a voyage,

      (iii) the discharge of oil cargo,

      (iv) the ballasting of oil tanks (whether cargo or bunker fuel tanks) and the discharge of ballast from, and cleaning of, such tanks,

      (v) the separation of oil from water, or from other substances, in any mixture containing oil,

      (vi) the disposal of any oil or water, or any other substance, arising from operations relating to any of the matters specified in (i) to (v) above, or

      (vii) the disposal of any other oil residues;

   (b) any occasion on which oil or a mixture containing oil is discharged from the ship for the purpose of securing the safety of any ship, or of preventing damage to any ship or cargo, or of saving life;

   (c) any occasion on which oil or a mixture containing oil is found to be escaping, or to have escaped, from the ship in consequence of damage to the ship, or by reason of leakage.

(2) The Secretary of State may make regulations requiring the keeping of records relating to the transfer of oil to and from ships while they are within United Kingdom waters; and the requirements of any regulations made under this subsection shall be in addition to the requirements of any regulations made under subsection (1) above.

(3) Any records required to be kept by regulations made under subsection (2) above shall, unless the ship is a barge, be kept by the master of the ship, and shall, if the ship is a barge, be kept, in so far as they relate to the transfer of oil to the barge, by the person supplying the oil and, in so far as they relate to the transfer of oil from the barge, by the person to whom the oil is delivered.

(4) Regulations under this section requiring the carrying of oil record books or the keeping of records may—

(a) prescribe the form of the oil record books or records and the nature of the entries to be made in them;

(b) require the person providing or keeping the books or records to retain them for a prescribed period;

(c) require that person, at the end of the prescribed period, to transmit the books or records to a place or person determined by or under the regulations;

(d) provide for the custody or disposal of the books or records after their transmission to such a place or person.

(5) Regulations under this section may—

(a) be made with respect to all or with respect to any one or more of the classes of ship or other matters to which this section relates;

(b) make different provision for different classes of ship or otherwise for different classes of case or different circumstances.

(6) If any ship fails to carry such an oil record book as it is required to carry under this section the owner or master shall be liable on summary conviction to a fine not exceeding level 5 on the standard scale.

(7) If any person fails to comply with any requirements imposed on him by or under this section, he shall be liable on summary conviction to a fine not exceeding level 5 on the standard scale.

(8) If any person makes an entry in any oil record book carried or record kept under this section which is to his knowledge false or misleading in any material particular, he shall be liable—

(a) on summary conviction, to a fine not exceeding the statutory maximum, or imprisonment for a term not exceeding six months, or both;

(b) on conviction on indictment, to a fine or to imprisonment for a term not exceeding two years, or both.

(9) In any proceedings under this Chapter—

(a) any oil record book carried or record kept in pursuance of regulations made under this section shall be admissible as evidence, and in Scotland shall be sufficient evidence, of the facts stated in it;

(b) any copy of an entry in such an oil record book or record which is certified by the master of the ship in which the book is carried or by the person by whom the record is required to be kept to be a true copy of the entry shall be admissible as evidence, and in Scotland shall be sufficient evidence, of the facts stated in the entry;

(c) any document purporting to be an oil record book carried or record kept in pursuance of regulations made under this section, or purporting to be such a certified copy as is mentioned in paragraph (b) above, shall, unless the contrary is proved, be presumed to be such a book, record or copy, as the case may be.

(10) In this section "barge" includes a lighter and any similar vessel.

DEFINITIONS

"barge": subs. (10).
"discharge of oil": s.151(4).
"fails": s.313(1).
"master": s.313(1).
"mixture containing oil": s.151(3).
"oil": s.151(1).
"oil residues": s.151(1).
"person": Interpretation Act 1978, Sched. 1.
"Secretary of State": Interpretation Act 1978, Sched. 1.
"ship": ss.151(5) and 313(1).
"standard scale": Criminal Justice Act 1982, s.37.
"statutory maximum": Criminal Justice Act 1982, s.74.
"transfer": s.151(1).

"United Kingdom ship": ss.1(3) and 313(1).
"United Kingdom waters": s.313(2)(a).

GENERAL NOTE
[Derivation: Prevention of Oil Pollution Act 1971, s.17; Merchant Shipping Act 1979, ss.27(4), 29(1), Sched. 6, Pt. VI, para. 17.]
Section 142 re-enacts s.17 of the Prevention of Oil Pollution Act 1971 and allows the Secretary of State to make regulations requiring ships to carry oil record books, so that officials can check whether any oil has been lost. For the powers of the Secretary of State to make delegated legislation, such as regulations, see s.306, below.

Prosecutions and enforcement of fines

143.—(1) Proceedings for an offence under this Chapter may, in England and Wales be brought only—
 (a) by or with the consent of the Attorney General, or
 (b) if the offence is one to which subsection (4) below applies, by the harbour authority, or
 (c) unless the offence is one mentioned in subsection (4)(b) or (c) below, by the Secretary of State or a person authorised by any general or special direction of the Secretary of State.
 (2) Subject to subsection (3) below, proceedings for an offence under this Chapter may, in Northern Ireland, be brought only—
 (a) by or with the consent of the Attorney General for Northern Ireland,
 (b) if the offence is one to which subsection (4) below applies, by a harbour authority, or
 (c) unless the offence is one mentioned in subsection (4)(b) or (c) below, by the Secretary of State or a person authorised by any general or special direction of the Secretary of State.
 (3) Subsection (2) above shall have effect in relation to proceedings for an offence under section 131 relating to the discharge of oil or a mixture containing oil from a ship in a harbour in Northern Ireland as if the references in paragraph (c) to the Secretary of State were references to the Secretary of State or the Department of the Environment for Northern Ireland.
 (4) This subsection applies to the following offences—
 (a) any offence under section 131 which is alleged to have been committed by the discharge of oil, or a mixture containing oil, into the waters of a harbour in the United Kingdom;
 (b) any offence in relation to a harbour in the United Kingdom under section 135 or 136; and
 (c) any offence under section 142 relating to the keeping of records of the transfer of oil within such a harbour.
 (5) The preceding provisions of this section shall apply in relation to any part of a dockyard port within the meaning of the Dockyard Ports Regulation Act 1865 as follows—
 (a) if that part is comprised in a harbour in the United Kingdom, the reference to the harbour authority shall be construed as including a reference to the Queen's harbour master for the port;
 (b) if that part is not comprised in a harbour in the United Kingdom, the references to such a harbour shall be construed as references to such a dockyard port and the reference to the harbour authority as a reference to the Queen's harbour master for the port.
 (6) Any document required or authorised, by virtue of any statutory provision, to be served on a foreign company for the purposes of the institution of, or otherwise in connection with, proceedings for an offence under section 131 alleged to have been committed by the company as the owner of the ship shall be treated as duly served on that company if the document is served on the master of the ship.

In this subsection "foreign company" means a company or body which is not one to which any of sections 695 and 725 of the Companies Act 1985 and Articles 645 and 673 of the Companies (Northern Ireland) Order 1986 applies so as to authorise the service of the document in question, under any of those provisions.

(7) Any person authorised to serve any document for the purposes of the institution of, or otherwise in connection with, proceedings for an offence under this Chapter shall, for that purpose, have the right to go on board the ship in question.

DEFINITIONS
 "discharge of oil": s.151(4).
 "England and Wales": Interpretation Act 1978, Sched. 1.
 "foreign company": subs. (6).
 "harbour": s.313(1).
 "harbour authority": s.151(1).
 "harbour in the United Kingdom": s.151(1).
 "harbour master": s.151(1).
 "master": s.313(1).
 "mixture containing oil": s.151(3).
 "oil": s.151(1).
 "person": Interpretation Act 1978, Sched. 1.
 "port": s.313(1).
 "Secretary of State": Interpretation Act 1978, Sched. 1.
 "ship": ss.151(5) and 313(1).
 "United Kingdom": Interpretation Act 1978, Sched. 1.

GENERAL NOTE
 [Derivation: Prevention of Oil Pollution Act 1971, ss.19, 30(4); Environmental Protection Act 1990, Sched. 4, para. 2.]
 Section 143 sets out various enforcement provisions, *e.g.* relating to who may bring a prosecution.

Power to detain ships for section 131 offences

144.—(1) Where a harbour master has reason to believe that the master or owner of a ship has committed an offence under section 131 by the discharge from the ship of oil, or a mixture containing oil, into the waters of the harbour, the harbour master may detain the ship.

(2) Section 284, in its application to the detention of a ship under this section, shall have effect with the omission of subsections (1), (6) and (7) and as if—

(a) in subsection (2), the reference to competent authority were a reference to the harbour authority; and

(b) in subsection (4), the persons in relation to whom that subsection applies were the harbour master or any person acting on his behalf.

(3) Where a harbour master detains a ship other than a United Kingdom ship under this section he shall immediately notify the Secretary of State, who shall then inform the consul or diplomatic representative of the State whose flag the ship is entitled to fly or the appropriate maritime authorities of that State.

In this subsection "United Kingdom ship" has the same meaning as in section 85.

(4) A harbour master who detains a ship under this section shall immediately release the ship—

(a) if no proceedings for the offence are instituted within the period of seven days beginning with the day on which the ship is detained;

(b) if proceedings for the offence, having been instituted within that period, are concluded without the master or owner being convicted;

  (c) if either—
         (i) the sum of £55,000 is paid to the harbour authority by way of security, or
         (ii) security which, in the opinion of the harbour authority, is satisfactory and is for an amount not less than £55,000 is given to the harbour authority,
     by or on behalf of the master or owner; or
  (d) where the master or owner is convicted of the offence, if any costs or expenses ordered to be paid by him, and any fine imposed on him, have been paid.

  (5) The harbour authority shall repay any sum paid in pursuance of subsection (4)(c) above or release any security so given—
  (a) if no proceedings for the offence are instituted within the period of seven days beginning with the day on which the sum is paid; or
  (b) if proceedings for the offence, having been instituted within that period, are concluded without the master or owner being convicted.

  (6) Where a sum has been paid, or security has been given, by any person in pursuance of subsection (4)(c) above and the master or owner is convicted of the offence, the sum so paid or the amount made available under the security shall be applied as follows—
  (a) first in payment of any costs or expenses ordered by the court to be paid by the master or owner; and
  (b) next in payment of any fine imposed by the court;
and any balance shall be repaid to the first-mentioned person.

  (7) Any reference in this section to a harbour master or a harbour authority shall, where the harbour in question consists of or includes the whole or any part of a dockyard port within the meaning of the Dockyard Ports Regulation Act 1865, be construed as including a reference to the Queen's harbour master for the port.

  (8) This section does not apply in relation to a ship of Her Majesty's navy or any Government ship.

DEFINITIONS
  "discharge": s.151(4)
  "Government ship": ss.308(4) and 313(1).
  "harbour": s.313(1).
  "harbour authority": subs. (7) and s.151(1).
  "harbour master": subs. (7) and s.151(1).
  "master": s.313(1).
  "mixture containing oil": s.151(3).
  "oil": s.151(1).
  "port": s.313(1).
  "Secretary of State": Interpretation Act 1978, Sched. 1.
  "ship": ss.151(5) and 313(1).
  "United Kingdom ship": subs. (3) and s.85(2).

GENERAL NOTE
  [Derivation: Prevention of Oil Pollution Act 1971, s.19A; Environmental Protection Act 1990, s.148(1) and (3), Sched. 14, paras. 1 and 3.]
  Section 143 re-enacts s.19A of the Prevention of Oil Pollution Act 1971 which was added by the Environmental Protection Act 1990, Sched. 14. It allows for a harbour master to detain a ship suspected of committing an offence under s.131. Section 284 which deals with detention generally, is amended accordingly. See also s.145, below.

Interpretation of section 144

  145.—(1) This section has effect for the interpretation of the references in section 144 to the institution of proceedings or their conclusion without the master or owner of a ship being convicted of an offence under section 131.

(2) For the purposes of section 144 in its application to England and Wales—

(a) proceedings for an offence under section 131 are instituted—

(i) when a justice of the peace issues a summons or warrant under section 1 of the Magistrates' Courts Act 1980 in respect of the offence;

(ii) when a person is charged with the offence after being taken into custody without a warrant;

(iii) when a bill of indictment is preferred under section 2(2)(b) of the Administration of Justice (Miscellaneous Provisions) Act 1933; and

(b) proceedings for the offence are concluded without the master or owner being convicted on the occurrence of one of the following events—

(i) the discontinuance of the proceedings;

(ii) the acquittal of the master or owner;

(iii) the quashing of the master's or owner's conviction of the offence;

(iv) the grant of Her Majesty's pardon in respect of the master's or owner's conviction of the offence.

(3) For the purposes of section 144 in its application to Northern Ireland—

(a) proceedings for an offence under section 131 are instituted—

(i) when a justice of the peace issues a summons or warrant under Article 20 of the Magistrates' Courts (Northern Ireland) Order 1981;

(ii) when a person is charged with the offence after being taken into custody without a warrant;

(iii) when an indictment is presented under section 2(2)(c), (e) or (f) of the Grand Jury (Abolition) Act (Northern Ireland) 1969; and

(b) proceedings for an offence under section 131 are concluded without the master or owner being convicted on the occurrence of one of the following events—

(i) the discontinuance of the proceedings;

(ii) the acquittal of the master or owner;

(iii) the quashing of the master's or owner's conviction of the offence;

(iv) the grant of Her Majesty's pardon in respect of the master's or owner's conviction of the offence.

(4) Where the application of subsection (2)(a) or (3)(a) above would result in there being more than one time for the institution of proceedings, they shall be taken to have been instituted at the earliest of those times.

(5) For the purposes of section 144 in its application to Scotland—

(a) proceedings for an offence under section 131 are instituted—

(i) on the granting by the sheriff of a warrant in respect of the offence on presentation of a petition under section 12 of the Criminal Procedure (Scotland) Act 1975;

(ii) when, in the absence of a warrant or citation, the master or owner is first brought before a court competent to deal with the case;

(iii) when, in a case where he is liberated upon a written undertaking in terms of section 18(2)(a), 294(2)(a) or 295(1)(a) of the Criminal Procedure (Scotland) Act 1975, the master or owner appears at the specified time;

(iv) when, in a case mentioned in (iii) above where the master or owner fails to appear at the specified court at the specified time, the court grants warrant for his apprehension;

(v) when summary proceedings are commenced in terms of section 331(3) of the Criminal Procedure (Scotland) Act 1975;

(b) proceedings for an offence under section 131 are concluded without the master or owner being convicted on the occurrence of one of the following events—

(i) the court makes a finding of not guilty or not proven against the master or owner in respect of the offence;

(ii) the proceedings are expressly abandoned (other than *pro loco et tempore*) by the prosecutor or are deserted simpliciter;

(iii) the conviction is quashed;

(iv) the accused receives Her Majesty's pardon in respect of the conviction.

DEFINITIONS
"England and Wales": Interpretation Act 1978, Sched. 1.
"fails": s.313(1).
"master": s.313(1).
"person": Interpretation Act 1978, Sched. 1.
"sheriff": Interpretation Act 1978, Sched. 1.
"ship": s.313(1).
"written": Interpretation Act 1978, Sched. 1.

GENERAL NOTE
[Derivation: Prevention of Oil Pollution Act 1971, s.19A; Environmental Protection Act 1990, s.148(1) and (3), Sched. 14, paras. 1 and 3.]
Section 145 provides the interpretations of expressions used in s.144, above.

Enforcement and application of fines

146.—(1) Where a fine imposed by a court in proceedings against the owner or master of a ship for an offence under this Chapter is not paid, or any costs or expenses ordered to be paid by him are not paid, at the time ordered by the court, the court shall, in addition to any other powers of enforcing payment, have power—

(a) except in Scotland, to direct the amount remaining unpaid to be levied by distress,

(b) in Scotland, to grant warrant authorising the arrestment and sale, of the ship and its equipment.

(2) Where a person is convicted of an offence under section 131, and the court imposes a fine in respect of the offence, then, if it appears to the court that any person has incurred, or will incur, expenses in removing any pollution, or making good any damage, which is attributable to the offence, the court may order the whole or part of the fine to be paid to that person for or towards defraying those expenses.

DEFINITIONS
"master": s.313(1).
"person": Interpretation Act 1978, Sched. 1.
"ship": s.313(1).

GENERAL NOTE
[Derivation: Prevention of Oil Pollution Act 1971, s.20; Environmental Protection Act 1990, Sched. 14, para. 4; Merchant Shipping (Registration, etc.) Act 1993, Sched. 4, para. 66.]
Section 146 provides for the enforcement of fines.

Enforcement of Conventions relating to oil pollution

147.—(1) Her Majesty may by Order in Council empower such persons as may be designated by or under the Order to go on board any Convention ship while the ship is within a harbour in the United Kingdom, and to require production of any oil record book required to be carried in accordance with the Convention.

(2) An Order in Council under this section may, for the purposes of the Order, and with any necessary modifications, apply any of the provisions of

this Chapter relating to the production and inspection of oil record books and the taking of copies of entries therein, and to the admissibility in evidence of such oil record books and copies, including any penal provisions of this Chapter in so far as they relate to those matters, and may also apply section 259.

(3) Her Majesty, if satisfied that the government of any country has accepted, or denounced, the Convention, or that the Convention extends, or has ceased to extend, to any territory, may by Order in Council make a declaration to that effect.

(4) In this section—

"the Convention" means any Convention accepted by Her Majesty's Government in the United Kingdom in so far as it relates to the prevention of pollution of the sea by oil; and

"Convention ship" means a ship registered in—

(a) a country the government of which has been declared by an Order in Council under subsection (3) above to have accepted the Convention, and has not been so declared to have denounced it; or

(b) a territory to which it has been so declared that the Convention extends, not being a territory to which it has been so declared that the Convention has ceased to extend.

DEFINITIONS
"Convention, the": subs. (4).
"Convention ship": subs. (4).
"harbour": s.313(1).
"harbour in the United Kingdom": s.151(1).
"oil": s.151(1).
"person": Interpretation Act 1978, Sched. 1.
"registered": ss.23(1) and 313(1).
"ship": s.313(1).
"United Kingdom": Interpretation Act 1978, Sched. 1.

GENERAL NOTE
[Derivation: Prevention of Oil Pollution Act 1971, s.21.]
  Section 147 re-enacts s.21 of the Prevention of Oil Pollution Act 1971 and enables persons designated in an Order to obtain the production of oil record books required under MARPOL.

Miscellaneous and supplementary

Power of Secretary of State to grant exemptions

148. The Secretary of State may exempt from any of the provisions of this Chapter or of any regulations made thereunder, either absolutely or subject to such conditions as he thinks fit—

(a) any ship or classes of ships;

(b) any discharge of, or of a mixture containing, oil.

DEFINITIONS
"discharge": s.151(4).
"mixture containing oil": s.151(3).
"oil": s.151(1).
"ship": ss.151(5) and 313(1).
"Secretary of State": Interpretation Act 1978, Sched. 1.

GENERAL NOTE
[Derivation: Prevention of Oil Pollution Act 1971, s.23; Petroleum and Submarine Pipelines Act 1975, s.45(2); Merchant Shipping Act 1979, s.37(8).]

Application to Government ships

149.—(1) This Chapter does not apply to ships of Her Majesty's navy, nor to Government ships in the service of the Secretary of State while employed for the purposes of Her Majesty's navy.

(2) Subject to subsection (1) above and to section 141(4) and section 144(8)—

(a) provisions of this Chapter which are expressed to apply only to United Kingdom ships apply to Government ships registered in the United Kingdom and also to Government ships not so registered but held for the purposes of Her Majesty's Government in the United Kingdom;

(b) provisions of this Chapter which are expressed to apply to ships generally apply to Government ships.

DEFINITIONS
"Government ship": ss.308(4) and 313(1).
"registered": ss.23(1) and 313(1).
"ship": s.313(1).
"Secretary of State": Interpretation Act 1978, Sched. 1.
"United Kingdom": Interpretation Act 1978, Sched. 1.
"United Kingdom ship": ss.1(3) and 313(1).

GENERAL NOTE
[Derivation: Prevention of Oil Pollution Act 1971, s.24; Environmental Protection Act 1990, Sched. 14, para. 5.]
Section 149 re-enacts s.24 of the Prevention of Oil Pollution Act 1971, as amended, and excludes certain state ships from the scope of this Chapter of the Act.

Annual Report

150.—(1) The Secretary of State shall, as soon as possible after the end of each calendar year, make a report on the exercise and performance of his functions under this Chapter during that year.

(2) Every such report shall include such observations as he may think fit to make on the operation during that year of this Chapter and of any Convention accepted by Her Majesty's Government in the United Kingdom in so far as it relates to the prevention of pollution of the sea by oil.

(3) The Secretary of State shall lay a copy of every such report before each House of Parliament.

DEFINITIONS
"oil": s.151(1).
"Secretary of State": Interpretation Act 1978, Sched. 1.
"United Kingdom": Interpretation Act 1978, Sched. 1.

GENERAL NOTE
[Derivation: Prevention of Oil Pollution Act 1971, s.26; Merchant Shipping (Registration, etc.) Act 1993, Sched. 4, para. 17.]

Interpretation

151.—(1) In this Chapter—
"harbour authority" means a person or body of persons empowered by an enactment to make charges in respect of ships entering a harbour in the United Kingdom or using facilities therein;

"harbour in the United Kingdom" means a port, estuary, haven, dock or other place the waters of which are within United Kingdom national waters and in respect of entry into or the use of which by ships a person or body of persons is empowered by an enactment (including a local enactment) to make any charges other than charges in respect of navigational aids or pilotage;

"harbour master" includes a dock master or pier master and any person specially appointed by a harbour authority for the purpose of enforcing the provisions of this Chapter in relation to the harbour;

"local enactment" means a local or private Act, or an order confirmed by Parliament or brought into operation in accordance with special Parliamentary procedure;

"oil" means oil of any description and includes spirit produced from oil of any description, and also includes coal tar;

"oil residues" means any waste consisting of, or arising from, oil or a mixture containing oil;

"place on land" has the meaning given in section 131;

"transfer", in relation to oil, means transfer in bulk.

(2) For the purposes of the definition of "harbour in the United Kingdom" "charges in respect of navigational aids" means general light dues, local light dues and any other charges payable in respect of lighthouses, buoys or beacons.

(3) Any reference in any provision of this Chapter to a mixture containing oil shall be construed as a reference to any mixture of oil (or, as the case may be, of oil of a description referred to in that provision) with water or with any other substance.

(4) Any reference in this Chapter, other than in section 136, to the discharge of oil or a mixture containing oil, or to its being discharged, from a ship, place or thing, except where the reference is to its being discharged for a specific purpose, includes a reference to the escape of oil or mixture, or (as the case may be) to its escaping, from that ship, place or thing.

(5) For the purposes of any provision of this Chapter relating to the discharge of oil or a mixture containing oil from a ship, any floating craft (other than a ship) which is attached to a ship shall be treated as part of the ship.

(6) Any power conferred by section 259 in its application to this Chapter to test any equipment on board a ship shall be construed as including a power to require persons on board the ship to carry out such work as may be requisite for the purpose of testing the equipment; and any provision of that section as to submitting equipment for testing shall be construed accordingly.

(7) Subject to section 18 of the Interpretation Act 1978 (offence under two or more laws) nothing in this Chapter shall—

(a) affect any restriction imposed by or under any other enactment, whether contained in a public general Act or a local or private Act; or

(b) derogate from any right of action or other remedy (whether civil or criminal) in proceedings instituted otherwise than under this Chapter.

DEFINITIONS

"buoys and beacons": s.223(1), (2) and (3).
"charges in respect of navigational aids": subs. (2).
"discharge of oil, or mixture containing oil": subs. (4).
"general light dues": ss.205(1) and 223(1).
"harbour": s.313(1).
"harbour authority": subs. (1).
"harbour in the United Kingdom": subs. (1).
"harbour master": subs. (1).
"lighthouse": s.223(1) and (2).
"local enactment": subs. (1).
"local light dues": s.210(1).
"mixture containing oil": subs. (3).

"oil": subs. (1).
"oil residues": subs. (1).
"person": Interpretation Act 1978, Sched. 1.
"port": s.313(1).
"power to test any equipment on board": subs. (6).
"place on land": subs. (1) and s.131(5).
"ship": subs. (5) and s.313(1).
"transfer": subs. (1).
"United Kingdom": Interpretation Act 1978, Sched. 1.
"United Kingdom national waters": s.313(2).

GENERAL NOTE
[Derivation: Prevention of Oil Pollution Act 1971, ss.8(2), 29 and 32; Merchant Shipping (Registration, etc.) Act 1993, Sched. 4, para. 17(c).]

CHAPTER III

LIABILITY FOR OIL POLLUTION

GENERAL NOTE
Compensation for oil pollution damage caused by ships is regulated internationally by the International Convention on Civil Liability for Oil Pollution Damage 1969 (the 1969 Liability Convention) and the International Convention on the Establishment of a Fund for Compensation for Oil Pollution Damage 1971 (the 1971 Fund Convention). The U.K. is a party to both Conventions (and their 1976 Protocols) and enacted them respectively in the Merchant Shipping (Oil Pollution) Act 1971 and the Merchant Shipping Act 1974 (see generally, *Chorley and Giles, Shipping Law*, Chapter 25.2.2). In 1984, the IMO agreed two Protocols to the 1969 Liability Convention and the 1971 Fund Convention. Two further Protocols were agreed in 1992.

The 1969 Liability Convention and 1971 Fund Convention
The 1969 Liability Convention and 1971 Fund Convention were the international community's response to the *Torrey Canyon* disaster in 1967 which caused extensive pollution off the coasts of Britain and France. The two conventions were a compromise solution, which was thought adequate to deal with the problems caused by the new generation of large tankers. The 1969 Liability Convention established a regime of strict liability for pollution resulting from oil escaping from tankers. Shipowners were allowed a number of restricted defences and given the right to limit liability according to the size of the tanker. The maximum limit is currently about £12.5 million, but could be considerably less for smaller vessels. Shipowners were to carry compulsory insurance for this new liability (something not generally required in maritime law), and insurers could be sued directly. There was a procedure to ensure that claims from a single disaster affecting a number of Convention countries could be brought in just one action. "Channelling" provisions were introduced to prevent claimants proceeding under the general law in circumstances where the Convention applied.
The 1971 Fund Convention recognised the creation of a Fund, administered in London, and contributed to by oil cargo importers. The purpose of the Fund was to provide a supplement to the 1969 Liability Convention and to give recognition to the fact that oil pollution may be as much the responsibility of the cargo interests as the carrier. The Fund limits were originally about £24 million and from December 1, 1987 were raised to about £47 million. Minor changes to the method of calculating the limits of liability under the 1969 and 1971 Conventions were made by Protocols in 1976. Only the 1976 Protocol to the 1969 Liability Convention was in force at the date of the pre-consolidation 1993 Act (and see s.4 of the Merchant Shipping (Oil Pollution) Act 1971, as amended by the Merchant Shipping Act 1979, s.38). The fact that the 1976 Protocol to the 1971 Fund Convention was not yet in force gave rise to considerable problems in respect of the *Haven* disaster in Italy in 1991. On August 24, 1994 Japan deposited its instrument of ratification and the 1976 Protocol to the 1971 Fund Convention entered into force on November 22, 1994. However, the limits of liability of both the 1969 and 1971 Conventions already appeared to be unrealistic, particularly after the *Amoco Cadiz* sank off Brittany in 1978. Eventually, the IMO managed, at a diplomatic conference in London in May 1984, to produce amendments to both the 1969 and 1971 Conventions in the form of two Protocols. The 1984 Protocols were incorporated in s.34 and Sched. 4 of the Merchant Shipping Act 1988.

The 1984 Protocols
These 1984 Protocols have not entered into force internationally. This is mainly because of the failure of the USA to ratify them, following the *Exxon Valdez* disaster in 1989 and the resulting enactment of its own Oil Pollution Act 1990. So s.34 and Sched. 4 of the Merchant Shipping Act

1988 were never brought into force. The fact that the 1984 Protocols would never enter into force was recognised in the pre-consolidating measure, the Merchant Shipping (Registration, etc.) Act 1993, Sched. 4 para. 18, which stated that the 1988 amendments "shall not have effect". In 1993 it was anticipated that the expected consolidation of the Merchant Shipping Acts (now the 1995 Act) would take place before any further international developments required legislation. However, an international compromise had produced two more Protocols in 1992.

The 1992 Protocols

The U.K. played a leading part in the agreement of the 1992 Protocols, whose main effect was to change the entry-into-force requirements in the 1984 Protocols solution with a view to ensuring ratification of the up-dated instruments by Japan (see N. Gaskell, "Compensation for Oil Pollution: 1992 Protocols to the Civil Liability Convention and the Fund Convention" (1993) 8 IJMCL 286–290). There was widespread agreement among European states, at least, that the Protocols should be ratified as soon as possible (see the recommendations in the Donaldson Report, para. 23.116). In fact, on September 29, 1994 the U.K. deposited its instrument of ratification to the 1992 Protocols. Other ratifying states include Denmark, France, Germany, Japan, Liberia, Sweden and Greece, while more states expect to ratify in 1996. The Protocols will enter into force on May 30, 1996.

Differences between 1984 and 1992 Protocols

It is important to note that the 1992 Protocols do *not* make any significant changes to the overall scheme produced by the 1984 Protocols, other than those concerning entry into force and a minor temporary change to contribution levels to the Fund (effectively providing a safeguard against excessive Japanese contributions). Thus, for instance, there are no increases in the limits of liability to reflect inflationary changes between 1984–1992. This means that the U.K., in order to ratify, needed to make comparatively minor changes to its domestic legislation.

U.K. legislative changes to enact the 1992 Protocols

Section 5 of the Merchant Shipping (Salvage and Pollution) Act 1994 enabled the U.K. to ratify the 1992 Protocols, by giving effect to them as enacted in the 1988 Act. The main textual changes effected by s.5(1) and (2) were to substitute the appropriate 1992 definitions in place of those 1984 definitions which had appeared in the 1988 Act. In particular, the 1992 Protocols referred to the amended Conventions by their 1992 (rather than their 1984) dates. Hence the amended 1969 Act referred to the International Convention on Civil Liability for Oil Pollution Damage 1992 (the 1992 Liability Convention) and the 1971 Act referred to the International Convention on the Establishment of a Fund for Compensation for Oil Pollution Damage 1992 (the 1992 Fund Convention). The pre-consolidation repeal, contained in Sched. 4, para. 18 of the Merchant Shipping (Registration, etc.) Act 1993 (explained above), was itself repealed. Section 5(3) of the 1994 Act enabled the appropriate transitional provisions to be made by Order in Council to give effect to Art. XII *bis* of the 1992 Liability Protocol and Art. 36 *bis* of the 1992 Fund Protocol. It was anticipated that there could be particular problems where some states are party to the 1992 Conventions and others only to the 1969 and 1971 Conventions. Section 5(3) of the Merchant Shipping (Salvage and Pollution) Act 1994 allowed the respective provisions of the unamended 1971 and 1974 Acts to be in force at the same time as those for the amended 1971 and 1974 Acts.

Drafting techniques

The 1971 and 1974 Acts adopted the unfortunate drafting technique of rewriting the 1969 and 1971 Conventions into "legal English". This was largely unnecessary and has produced text which is often difficult to read and which differs in some respects from the international originals. It is unfortunate that Parliamentary time was not available in 1994 to repeal the 1971 and 1974 Acts and to enact the provisions of the 1992 Protocols by including them in a Schedule (in the same manner as is adopted in respect of the 1989 Salvage Convention, by s.224, and the 1974 Athens Convention and 1976 Limitation Convention, by ss.183 and 185, respectively). The result is that the 1995 Act gives effect to a number of significant private law maritime conventions, but by the use of differing techniques. This is to be regretted.

Merchant Shipping Act 1995 transitional provisions

Having traced the somewhat confusing history of the Conventions and Acts, it is now necessary to explain how to navigate around the consolidated provisions in the 1995 Act. Until the 1992 Protocols enter into force on May 30, 1996, the U.K. is bound to give effect to the regimes in the 1969 Liability Convention and the 1971 Fund Convention. For this reason, it was necessary for the drafter of the 1995 Act to include some transitional provisions, namely ss.171 and 182. They provide that the transitory provisions set out in Sched. 4 (*i.e.* the old law) shall have effect until the Secretary of State orders that the provisions in ss.152–182 (*i.e.* the new law) shall have effect.

A draft Merchant Shipping Act 1995 (Appointed Day No. 1) Order 1996 has been laid which appoints May 30, 1996 as the relevant day for the purposes of ss.171 and 182.

As both the old and the new provisions have the same numbering, care should be taken to ensure that reference is made to the appropriate sections. Sections 171 and 182 both allow the Secretary of State to issue transitional Orders to smooth the entry into force of the new law. It should be understood that for a period both schemes will be operating side by side, as there will continue to be claims which fall to be decided on the basis of the old law prior to May 30, 1996. A draft Merchant Shipping (Liability and Compensation for Oil Pollution Damage) (Transitional Provisions) Order 1996 has been laid which deals with the complicated question of when and how the U.K.'s denunciation of the old regime will take effect. The DOT has taken the entirely commendable step of incorporating in the Order the verbatim text of the transitional provisions of the 1992 Protocols themselves (namely Art. XII *bis* of the 1992 Liability Convention and Art. 36 *bis* of the 1992 Fund Convention). The transitional period ends 18 months after the date on which the total reported receipts during the preceding calendar year of contributing oil in the states which have agreed to be bound by the 1992 Conventions exceed 750 million tonnes. It is expected that this figure will be reached fairly soon. If an incident occurs during the transitional period compensation may be available under both the old and the new law. If the claim cannot be met from the 1969 Liability Convention and the 1971 Fund Convention (up to 60 million SDR (special drawing rights)), the shipowner will be liable for the balance under the 1992 Liability Convention (up to the appropriate 1992 Liability Convention limits in aggregate). The 1992 IOPC Fund would only pay additional sums if the shipowner had met its 1992 Liability Convention obligations and the 1971 IOPC Fund had similarly met its obligations.

Bunker liability

One further point should be noted. The Merchant Shipping (Salvage and Pollution) Act 1994, s.6 introduced a new liability for shipowners where pollution was caused by bunkers. Bunkers were not covered under the Conventions. Nevertheless, the bunker liability provisions have been integrated into the general framework provided by the 1992 Liability Convention (see s.154), or as the case may be, the 1969 Liability Convention (see Sched. 4, s.154).

Annotations to Chapters III and IV

In the light of the impending entry into force of the new law as contained in Chaps. III and IV, it is proposed to concentrate on the changes brought about by the 1992 Protocols.

Preliminary

Meaning of "the Liability Convention" and related expressions

152.—(1) In this Chapter—

"the Liability Convention" means the International Convention on Civil Liability for Oil Pollution Damage 1992;

"Liability Convention country" means a country in respect of which the Liability Convention is in force; and

"Liability Convention State" means a State which is a party to the Convention.

(2) If Her Majesty by Order in Council declares that any State specified in the Order is a party to the Liability Convention in respect of any country so specified the Order shall, while in force, be conclusive evidence that that State is a party to the Liability Convention in respect of that country.

DEFINITIONS

"Liability Convention, the": subs. (1).
"Liability Convention country": subs. (1).
"Liability Convention state": subs. (1).
"oil": s.170(1).

GENERAL NOTE

[Derivation: Merchant Shipping (Oil Pollution) Act 1971, s.19; Merchant Shipping Act 1988, Sched. 4, Pt. I, para. 13; Merchant Shipping (Salvage and Pollution) Act 1994, s.5(1) and (4).]

The 1969 Liability Convention and 1971 Fund Convention were the international community's response to the *Torrey Canyon* disaster in 1967, which caused extensive pollution off the coasts of Britain and France. The legal solutions were a compromise, but were thought to be adequate to deal with the problems caused by the new generation of large tankers. The Convention limits soon appeared unrealistic, particularly after the *Amoco Cadiz* sinking off Brittany in 1978. Moves were made at IMO to produce amendments and Protocols were eventually approved by a diplomatic conference in May 1984 in London. (See the General Note to Chapter III, above.)

It should also be noted that minor changes to the method of calculating the limits of liability under the 1969 and 1971 Conventions were made by Protocols in 1976.

Liability

Liability for oil pollution in case of tankers

153.—(1) Where, as a result of any occurrence, any oil is discharged or escapes from a ship to which this section applies, then (except as otherwise provided by this Chapter) the owner of the ship shall be liable—

  (a) for any damage caused outside the ship in the territory of the United Kingdom by contamination resulting from the discharge or escape; and

  (b) for the cost of any measures reasonably taken after the discharge or escape for the purpose of preventing or minimising any damage so caused in the territory of the United Kingdom by contamination resulting from the discharge or escape; and

  (c) for any damage caused in the territory of the United Kingdom by any measures so taken.

(2) Where, as a result of any occurrence, there arises a grave and imminent threat of damage being caused outside a ship to which this section applies by the contamination that might result if there were a discharge or escape of oil from the ship, then (except as otherwise provided by this Chapter) the owner of the ship shall be liable—

  (a) for the cost of any measures reasonably taken for the purpose of preventing or minimising any such damage in the territory of the United Kingdom; and

  (b) for any damage caused outside the ship in the territory of the United Kingdom by any measures so taken;

and in this Chapter any such threat is referred to as a relevant threat of contamination.

(3) Subject to subsection (4) below, this section applies to any ship constructed or adapted for carrying oil in bulk as cargo.

(4) Where any ship so constructed or adapted is capable of carrying other cargoes besides oil, this section shall apply to any such ship—

  (a) while it is carrying oil in bulk as cargo; and

  (b) unless it is proved that no residues from the carriage of any such oil remain in the ship, while it is on any voyage following the carriage of any such oil,

but not otherwise.

(5) Where a person incurs a liability under subsection (1) or (2) above he shall also be liable for any damage or cost for which he would be liable under that subsection if the references in it to the territory of the United Kingdom included the territory of any other Liability Convention country.

(6) Where—

  (a) as a result of any occurrence, a liability is incurred under this section by the owner of each of two or more ships, but

  (b) the damage or cost for which each of the owners would be liable cannot reasonably be separated from that for which the other or others would be liable,

each of the owners shall be liable, jointly with the other or others, for the whole of the damage or cost for which the owners together would be liable under this section.

(7) For the purposes of this Chapter—

(a) references to a discharge or escape of oil from a ship are references to such a discharge or escape wherever it may occur, and whether it is of oil carried in a cargo tank or of oil carried in a bunker fuel tank;

(b) where more than one discharge or escape results from the same occurrence or from a series of occurrences having the same origin, they shall be treated as one, but any measures taken after the first of them shall be deemed to have been taken after the discharge or escape; and

(c) where a relevant threat of contamination results from a series of occurrences having the same origin, they shall be treated as a single occurrence.

(8) The Law Reform (Contributory Negligence) Act 1945 and, in Northern Ireland, the Law Reform (Miscellaneous Provisions) Act (Northern Ireland) 1948 shall apply in relation to any damage or cost for which a person is liable under this section, but which is not due to his fault, as if it were due to his fault.

DEFINITIONS
"damage": s.170(1).
"discharge or escape": subs. (7).
"Liability Convention country": s.152(1).
"oil": s.170(1).
"owner": s.170(2).
"person": Interpretation Act 1978, Sched. 1.
"relevant threat of contamination": subs. (2) and s.170(1).
"residues": s.151(1).
"ship": s.170(1).
"territory": s.170(4).
"United Kingdom": Interpretation Act 1978, Sched. 1.

GENERAL NOTE
[Derivation: Merchant Shipping (Oil Pollution) Act 1971, s.1; Merchant Shipping Act 1988, Sched. 4, Pt. I, para. 1; Merchant Shipping (Salvage and Pollution) Act 1994, Sched. 3, Pt. II, para. 1.]
Section 153 sets out the basic rule of strict liability, with limited defences, of the registered shipowner for pollution damage defined in subs. (2).

Liability. The basic strict liability imposed on the shipowner is unchanged by the 1992 Liability Convention, but an anomaly has been removed whereby threat removal costs could not be claimed. The wording of the 1969 Convention and the 1971 Act only allowed clean-up expenses to be recovered *after* the first drop of oil had been discharged. The 1992 Protocol altered the definition of "incident" to allow recompense for such costs and subs. (2) of this section now contains the relevant U.K. provision. Costs incurred in taking reasonable measures to reduce a threat of oil pollution will be recoverable provided that there is a "grave and imminent threat of damage". Note also s.156(3), below.

Ships. See subs. (1) for part of the definition of "ship" contained in Art. I(1) of the 1992 Liability Convention and subss. (3) and (4) for the remainder. There are two principal changes introduced by the 1992 Liability Convention. First, the Act is to apply to tankers which are in ballast, but whose bunkers cause pollution (and see subs. (7)(a)). Secondly, the Convention is expressly extended to combination bulk carriers, such as OBOs (oil, bulk, ore carriers), but only in relation to the carriage of oil. The rules will apply not only when such carriers are carrying bulk oil cargoes, but also when they are on an immediately following voyage during which they have oil residues on board.

Liability for oil pollution in case of other ships

154.—(1) Where, as a result of any occurrence, any oil is discharged or escapes from a ship other than a ship to which section 153 applies, then (except as otherwise provided by this Chapter) the owner of the ship shall be liable—

(a) for any damage caused outside the ship in the territory of the United Kingdom by contamination resulting from the discharge or escape; and

(b) for the cost of any measures reasonably taken after the discharge or escape for the purpose of preventing or minimising any damage so caused in the territory of the United Kingdom by contamination resulting from the discharge or escape; and

(c) for any damage so caused in the territory of the United Kingdom by any measures so taken.

(2) Where, as a result of any occurrence, there arises a grave and imminent threat of damage being caused outside a ship other than a ship to which section 153 applies by the contamination which might result if there were a discharge or escape of oil from the ship, then (except as otherwise provided by this Chapter) the owner of the ship shall be liable—

(a) for the cost of any measures reasonably taken for the purpose of preventing or minimising any such damage in the territory of the United Kingdom; and

(b) for any damage caused outside the ship in the territory of the United Kingdom by any measures so taken;

and in the subsequent provisions of this Chapter any such threat is referred to as a relevant threat of contamination.

(3) Where—

(a) as a result of any occurrence, a liability is incurred under this section by the owner of each of two or more ships, but

(b) the damage or cost for which each of the owners would be liable cannot reasonably be separated from that for which the other or others would be liable,

each of the owners shall be liable, jointly with the other or others, for the whole of the damage or cost for which the owners together would be liable under this section.

(4) The Law Reform (Contributory Negligence) Act 1945 and, in Northern Ireland, the Law Reform (Miscellaneous Provisions) Act (Northern Ireland) 1948 shall apply in relation to any damage or cost for which a person is liable under this section, but which is not due to his fault, as if it were due to his fault.

(5) In this section "ship" includes a vessel which is not seagoing.

DEFINITIONS

"damage": s.170(1).
"discharge or escape": s.153(7).
"oil": s.170(1).
"owner": s.170(2).
"person": Interpretation Act 1978, Sched. 1.
"relevant threat of contamination": subs. (2) and s.170(1).
"ship": subs. (5) and s.170(1).
"territory": s.170(4).
"United Kingdom": Interpretation Act 1978, Sched. 1.

GENERAL NOTE

[Derivation: Merchant Shipping (Oil Pollution) Act 1971, s.1A; Merchant Shipping (Salvage and Pollution) Act 1994, Sched. 3, Pt. II, para. 2.]

When the 1969 Liability Convention was agreed, there was for the first time a regime of strict liability for damage caused by oil pollution from ships. However, the regime of liability only applied to oil being carried in bulk as cargo (see the Merchant Shipping (Oil Pollution) Act 1971, s.1(1), which enacted the 1969 Convention in the U.K.). That is, it applied to the cargo carried in oil tankers but, as originally enacted, it did not even apply to the tanker's bunkers. Bunker oil is the marine term for the fuel being carried by a ship to power its own engines. The oil industry voluntarily agreed to extend protection to the victims of bunker oil from tankers in the TOVA-

LOP scheme. The 1992 Protocols to both the 1969 Liability Convention and the 1971 Fund Convention have now extended the Convention scheme to cover bunker oil from tankers. There was still a gap in the legislation, however, as even the 1992 Protocols only applied to oil tankers and not to the great mass of bulk carriers, general cargo vessels and passenger vessels. It might be thought that a ship's own fuel could not constitute much of a hazard, but the bunkers on board a large bulk carrier could amount to several thousand tons and the nature of the oil could mean that it was a serious pollution risk. When the *Freija Svea* went aground off the Yorkshire coast in February 1993 she was carrying 1500 tonnes of heavy fuel oil. Salvage operations were ultimately successful, but the small amount of oil which did come ashore clearly required expenditure to remove it and greater damage was possible. In November 1993 two fish processing vessels went aground in the Shetlands carrying large quantities of fuel oil. In respect of the Russian ship *Boorodinskoye Polye* the DOT removed 600 tonnes of fuel oil at a cost of some £650,000. At the Third Reading of the Merchant Shipping (Salvage and Pollution) Act 1994 in the Commons, the Government indicated that there were some 20–30 incidents a year of bunker spills.

At the international level, the only vehicle for extending protection against pollution from bunkers was through the draft Convention on Liability and Compensation for Damage Resulting from the Carriage of Hazardous and Noxious Substances which is currently being negotiated by the IMO Legal Committee with a view to the holding of a diplomatic conference in 1996. The Donaldson Report (see para. 19.44) recommended that any HNS Convention (whether international or regional) should cover spills of bunker oil, but the negotiations in the IMO indicate that there is resistance to introducing such a scheme internationally within the scope of the present draft HNS Convention. The reason is that those who would contribute to the second tier "Scheme" under the draft (similar to the IOPC Fund) are mainly those involved in the chemical industry and they do not see why they should fund clean-up operations caused by the ship's own fuel, which is not carried as cargo.

Given the likely international impasse, the U.K. Government indicated that it would take steps to impose strict liability for spills of bunker oil in U.K. waters and this approach was supported in the Donaldson Report (see para. 19.44). Strict liability already exists in Scandinavia and the USA. The present section was added at the Third Reading of the Merchant Shipping (Salvage and Pollution) Act 1994 in the Commons and creates a special U.K. regime of liability for bunker oil from ships.

The effect of s.154 (deriving from Sched. 3, Pt. II of the Merchant Shipping (Salvage and Pollution) Act 1994) is to introduce a strict liability regime for oil pollution caused by the bunkers of ships generally, and not simply pollution from oil tankers (see the General Note to this Chapter). Section 154 produces a bunker liability regime equivalent to the international tanker liability regime governed by s.153. The new provisions mirror those for oil tankers. It should be emphasised that the reference to "ships" in subs. (1) is deliberate and replaced an earlier version of the clause which had referred to "non-tankers". The new provisions can apply in some circumstances to oil tankers where liability is not already regulated by the 1969 Liability Convention and the Merchant Shipping (Oil Pollution) Act 1971.

Note that Sched. 4, s.154, below contains a regime similar to that for the Merchant Shipping (Oil Pollution) Act 1971 as it was originally enacted to give effect to the 1969 Liability Convention (*i.e.* without the amendments which were to be inserted by the Merchant Shipping Act 1988). Schedule 4, s.154 will be appropriate for that period before the 1992 Protocols come into force (see the General Note to this Chapter, above). This section was originally brought into force on October 1, 1994, in time to apply to the *Pionersk*, a so-called Klondiker fish factory ship. She went aground in the Shetlands in October 1994, causing oil pollution from her bunkers. A sister ship was arrested under the Supreme Court Act 1981, s.21 by the DOT in order to enforce its claim for investigation and clean-up expenses, for which there could be liability under Sched. 4, s.154. When the 1992 Protocols are in force the U.K. will apply s.154 as it appears here in order that the national strict liability regime for bunker oil pollution mirrors that for tanker cargo pollution.

Section 154 would allow a claim for damages by the victims of pollution from a ships' bunkers and also by the DOT in respect of threat removal or clean-up costs. The original 1969 Liability Convention, relating to oil tankers, only allowed for removal costs to be recovered *once* there had been a discharge of oil. Threat removal costs incurred before any oil was discharged were not covered by the 1969 Convention or the 1971 Act (although they were covered under TOVALOP). Subsection (2) now clearly allows for threat removal costs to be recovered where there is a "grave and imminent threat of damage" to the environment. This is the expression which was used in the Intervention Convention 1969 to allow intervention on the high seas (see the General Note to s.137, above). The lacuna in the original Convention will be removed once s.153 is in force. In the meantime, there is better legislative protection against the threat of bunker spills than for oil tanker spills.

Oil tankers carrying oil in bulk fall within the 1969 Liability Convention and an owner whose tanker spills oil cargo and bunkers oil would be strictly liable under s.153 for any damage caused. However, there was not strict liability for bunker spills from oil tankers which were not actually carrying oil at the time of the incident, *e.g.* where they were on a ballast run, even though there might be residues of oil in the cargo tanks. The 1992 Protocols will only exempt a tanker where its tanks are clean, but will apply the strict liability rule to tanker bunkers irrespective of the contents of its cargo tanks. Section 154 will apply the bunker liability rule to tankers before the 1992 Protocols are in force, as it will apply to any ship, other than one to which s.153 would apply. In its unamended (Sched. 4) form s.153 does not yet apply to empty tankers and so s.154 would apply to them for the time being.

For limitation of liability see s.168, below.

A further distinction between the liability of a tanker owner under s.153 and that of a shipowner under s.154, is that the former is required to have compulsory insurance when carrying more than 2,000 tonnes of oil in bulk. There is no other general requirement on shipowners to carry liability insurance and there will be none in respect of s.154 liabilities. In practice, virtually all vessels will carry P & I insurance cover for such risks. There are moves, perhaps long overdue, whereby such cover will be compulsory, *e.g.* for passenger claims, but there is resistance from the insurance industry which is hostile to any notion of direct actions against insurers (despite the existence of the Third Party (Rights Against Insurers) Act 1930).

The proposer of the Merchant Shipping (Salvage and Pollution) Act 1994, Mr. Harris, indicated at the Third Reading in the Commons that the provisions "will not affect small ships" (*Hansard*, H.C. Vol. 241, col. 541). There is no exemption for small ships and it appears that he meant that there would be no real commercial risks for fishing vessels and the like because they "use light diesel fuel which poses little environmental threat because it disperses quickly". There would be a liability under the new provision, but it is not likely to be great.

Exceptions from liability under sections 153 and 154

155. No liability shall be incurred by the owner of a ship under section 153 or 154 by reason of any discharge or escape of oil from the ship, or by reason of any relevant threat of contamination, if he proves that the discharge or escape, or (as the case may be) the threat of contamination—

  (a) resulted from an act of war, hostilities, civil war, insurrection or an exceptional, inevitable and irresistible natural phenomenon; or
  (b) was due wholly to anything done or omitted to be done by another person, not being a servant or agent of the owner, with intent to do damage; or
  (c) was due wholly to the negligence or wrongful act of a government or other authority in exercising its function of maintaining lights or other navigational aids for the maintenance of which it was responsible.

DEFINITIONS
  "damage": s.170(1).
  "discharge or escape": s.153(7).
  "oil": s.170(1).
  "owner": s.170(1).
  "person": Interpretation Act 1978, Sched. 1.
  "relevant threat of contamination": ss.153(2), 154(2) and 170(1).
  "ship": s.170(1).

GENERAL NOTE
  [Derivation: Merchant Shipping (Oil Pollution) Act 1971, s.2; Merchant Shipping Act 1988, Sched. 4, Pt. I, para. 2; Merchant Shipping Act 1994, Sched. 3, Pt. II, para. 3.]

Section 155 sets out exceptions from liability which are very limited in scope, given the basic concept of strict liability.

Restriction of liability for oil pollution

156.—(1) Where, as a result of any occurrence—

  (a) any oil is discharged or escapes from a ship (whether one to which section 153 or one to which section 154 applies), or
  (b) there arises a relevant threat of contamination,
then, whether or not the owner of the ship in question incurs a liability under section 153 or 154—

(i) he shall not be liable otherwise than under that section for any such damage or cost as is mentioned in it, and

(ii) no person to whom this paragraph applies shall be liable for any such damage or cost unless it resulted from anything done or omitted to be done by him either with intent to cause any such damage or cost or recklessly and in the knowledge that any such damage or cost would probably result.

(2) Subsection (1)(ii) above applies to—

(a) any servant or agent of the owner of the ship;

(b) any person not falling within paragraph (a) above but employed or engaged in any capacity on board the ship or to perform any service for the ship;

(c) any charterer of the ship (however described and including a bareboat charterer), and any manager or operator of the ship;

(d) any person performing salvage operations with the consent of the owner of the ship or on the instructions of a competent public authority;

(e) any person taking any such measures as are mentioned in subsection (1)(b) or (2)(a) of section 153 or 154;

(f) any servant or agent of a person falling within paragraph (c), (d) or (e) above.

(3) The liability of the owner of a ship under section 153 or 154 for any impairment of the environment shall be taken to be a liability only in respect of—

(a) any resulting loss of profits, and

(b) the cost of any reasonable measures of reinstatement actually taken or to be taken.

DEFINITIONS

"damage": s.170(1).

"discharge or escape": s.153(7).

"oil": s.170(1).

"owner": s.170(2).

"person": Interpretation Act 1978, Sched. 1.

"relevant threat of contamination": ss.153(2), 154(2) and 170(1).

"ship": s.170(1).

GENERAL NOTE

[Derivation: Merchant Shipping (Oil Pollution) Act 1971, s.3; Merchant Shipping Act 1988, Sched. 4, Pt. I, para. 3; Merchant Shipping (Salvage and Pollution) Act 1994, Sched. 3, Pt. II, para. 4.]

Channelling of Liability

The basic scheme of the 1969 Liability Convention was to make the registered shipowners liable, and to prevent any action being taken against them outside of the Convention, *e.g.* in a common law negligence action. Section 156(1)(i) provides that where ss.153 and 154 apply, a claimant cannot bring suit at common law, *e.g.* for negligence.

The Convention was designed so that liability was to be "channelled" to the registered shipowners *only*. Under Art. III(4) suits were not to be brought against others, *e.g.* employees, and claimants were protected as the registered shipowners were obliged to carry insurance. But the provision was slightly ambiguous as it referred to "servants or agents" and it was not clear how this was to apply to independent contractors, or managers.

The 1992 Protocol has both clarified and extended the previous law under the 1969 Liability Convention. Section 156(1)(ii), in consequence, is a more detailed version of what used to be s.156(b). Section 156(1)(ii) prevents a claim being made against those listed in subs. (2), *e.g.* where a claimant wanted to sue them in negligence in order to gain procedural or limitation-of-liability advantages. It extends the categories of persons who are immune from suit where the Convention applies, but opens up the possibility of them being made liable where they are guilty of the grossest misconduct. Although pilots are specifically mentioned in the 1992 Protocol there is no such reference to them in the U.K. provision. However, they would fall within s.156(2)(b) as would surveyors or service engineers.

Salvors are listed in s.156(2)(d), but they are not completely protected because the paragraph does not exclude them unless they have the advance permission of the shipowners or are acting under public orders. Under s.156(2)(f) the individual employees of, for example, charterers, managers, operators and authorities would also be immune from suit.

Pollution damage

One of the biggest areas of disagreement in pollution cases (and at the 1984 Diplomatic Conference) was the type of loss or damage that should be compensated and, in particular, to what extent economic loss should be recoverable. Art. I(6) of the 1969 Liability Convention (as enacted in s.153(1) of Sched. 4) referred only to "damage caused ... by contamination", "preventive measures" and damage caused by the latter. This produced many different interpretations as to whether hoteliers could claim for lost profits, say, or fishermen for reduced catches. Even more difficult are cases of environmental damage, as some states have enacted laws which entitle the state to claim sums for non-economic loss (sometimes according to an arbitrary mathematical scale).

The 1992 Liability Convention Art. I(6) provides an extended definition. The normal types of damage are listed in s.153(1), as before, but s.156(3) states when damages for "impairment of the environment" are allowed. These can only be recovered where there is some direct *financial* consequence—which would have to be proved by the claimant. Thus, loss of profits of hoteliers or fishermen could be claimed, provided that they could establish the necessary causal link. Where there is a claim for general environmental harm, *e.g.* to wildlife or to habitat, a government will have to point to the *actual* (rather than notional) costs it has incurred. Moreover, the measures must be reasonable, so that the claim does not become the occasion for a state to obtain a subsidy to upgrade its coastlines generally. However, some states may not have the resources to perform the reinstatement *before* being compensated. They are entitled to the expected costs in advance, but it is clear that there must be the intention to carry out the work: the state does not have the common law option of making an "unrepaired damage" claim, electing to keep the money while bearing the loss. Subsection (3) imposes a restriction on very wide environmental damage claims.

Limitation of liability

Limitation of liability under section 153

157.—(1) Where, as a result of any occurrence, the owner of a ship incurs liability under section 153 by reason of a discharge or escape or by reason of any relevant threat of contamination, then (subject to subsection (3) below)—

(a) he may limit that liability in accordance with the provisions of this Chapter, and

(b) if he does so, his liability (being the aggregate of his liabilities under section 153 resulting from the occurrence) shall not exceed the relevant amount.

(2) In subsection (1) above, "the relevant amount" means—

(a) in relation to a ship not exceeding 5,000 tons, three million special drawing rights;

(b) in relation to a ship exceeding 5,000 tons, three million special drawing rights together with an additional 420 special drawing rights for each ton of its tonnage in excess of 5,000 tons up to a maximum amount of 59.7 million special drawing rights;

but the Secretary of State may by order make such amendments of paragraphs (a) and (b) above as appear to him to be appropriate for the purpose of giving effect to the entry into force of any amendment of the limits of liability laid down in paragraph 1 of Article V of the Liability Convention.

(3) Subsection (1) above shall not apply in a case where it is proved that the discharge or escape, or (as the case may be) the relevant threat of contamination, resulted from anything done or omitted to be done by the owner either with intent to cause any such damage or cost as is mentioned in section 153 or recklessly and in the knowledge that any such damage or cost would probably result.

(4) For the purposes of this section a ship's tonnage shall be its gross tonnage calculated in such manner as may be prescribed by an order made by the Secretary of State.

(5) Any such order shall, so far as it appears to the Secretary of State to be practicable, give effect to the regulations in Annex 1 of the International Convention on Tonnage Measurement of Ships 1969.

DEFINITIONS
"damage": s.170(1).
"discharge or escape": s.153(7).
"Liability Convention, the": s.152(1).
"owner": s.170(2).
"relevant amount, the": subs. (2).
"relevant threat of contamination": ss.153(2), 154(2) and 170(1).
"Secretary of State": Interpretation Act 1978, Sched. 1.
"ship": s.170(1).
"ship's tonnage": subs. (4).

GENERAL NOTE
[Derivation: Merchant Shipping (Oil Pollution) Act 1971, s.4; Merchant Shipping Act 1988, Sched. 4, Pt. I, para. 4.]

Limitation of Liability

(a) The amounts. Although it was recognised that the limits under the 1969 Liability Convention were too low, there were disagreements during the negotiations for the Protocols as to (a) the maximum and minimum levels to be set in the new Protocols, and (b) the balance to be struck between the shipowner limits (under the Liability Convention) and the cargo limits (under the Fund Convention).

A compromise solution is found in s.157 and is expressed in special drawing rights (SDR) of the IMF, per ton of the ship (as defined in s.157(4) and (5)). For the first time there is a minimum limitation figure for ships up to 5,000 tons of 3 million SDR—about £2.7 million (the amounts will vary daily according to currency movements). For ships in excess of 5,000 tons there is an additional limit that increases at the rate of 420 SDR (about £410) per ton, but the shipowner will have a maximum liability of 59.7 million SDR, about £53.7 million. This is reached when the ship is 140,000 tons. For the 1992 Fund limits, see s.176 below.

(b) Tonnage. The tonnage measure to be used for limitation purposes is now to be the gross tonnage measured under the 1969 Tonnage Convention, see subs. (4). The U.K. is a party to this Convention and the relevant regulations are the Merchant Shipping (Tonnage) Regulations 1982 (S.I. 1982 No. 841). The Convention has been in force since 1982 and all ships had to be remeasured under it by 1994.

(c) Breaking limitation. Most limitation regimes contain a formula by which the person claiming the right to limit is deprived of the privilege. The test for breaking limitation used in the 1969 Liability Convention (and in s.157(1) of Sched. 4) was the "actual fault or privity" test, which was used internationally in the 1957 Convention relating to the Limitation of the Liability of Owners of Sea-Going Ships. The expression was itself derived from the British limitation statutes, particularly the Merchant Shipping Act 1894, s.503. There has been nearly a century of litigation on the meaning of the expression in British law and cases such as *Grand Champion Tankers v. Norpipe A/S* (*The Marion*) [1984] A.C. 563 showed that it was very difficult in practice for a shipowner successfully to claim limitation. Interpretations in other countries differed. The other main test for breaking limits in international transport Conventions was that used in the War-saw-Hague air Convention. It is that test which has been substantially adopted in the maritime context, first in the Hague-Visby Rules 1968, Art. IV, r. 5 (see the Schedule to the Carriage of Goods by Sea Act 1971) and then in Art. 4 of the 1976 Limitation Convention (see Sched. 7, Pt. I). The 1992 Liability Convention Art. V(2) largely repeated the version in the 1976 Limitation Convention.

Astonishingly, s.157(3) chooses to redraft the 1992 Liability Convention provision in a way that does not add to clarity at all and in at least two respects makes changes to Art. V(2) of the Convention which might be significant. First, the Convention refers to the "personal" act or omission of the owner, but the section leaves out the word "personal". Secondly, the section refers to "*any* such damage", but the Convention refers simply to "such damage". These changes are particularly unfortunate, because it might mean that differing interpretations might be given to two British statutory provisions (s.157(3) and Sched. 7, Pt. I, Art. 4) which were meant to give international effect to Convention provisions which are in material respects identical. Such "tidying up" of carefully thought out international provisions should really be avoided as it does little to promote uniformity of law.

The detailed effects of the change from the old test have been described elsewhere (see, R. Grime, "The loss of the right to limit" Ch. IV of N. Gaskell (ed.), *Limitation of Shipowners' Liability: The New Law*, (1986, Sweet & Maxwell)), but the salient points will be noted here.

The burden under the s.157(3) test is upon the pollution victim to prove the necessary intention or recklessness. Previously the owners could lose the limit if *fault* could be traced to them. Now a higher evidential burden will be required of the victim who must show more than mere negligence. Intentional harm will be unlikely and it will not be enough to show, in the alternative that there has been recklessness. There must be acts or omissions of the owner done recklessly "*and* in the knowledge that any such damage or cost would *probably* result". It is clear that a subjective test is imposed (see *Goldman v. Thai Airways International* [1983] 3 All E.R. 693) and that a mere possibility that the damage could occur will not be enough to deprive the owner of the right to limit (see further, N. Gaskell (1987) N.L.J. 322). The introduction of the word "any" in s.157(3) might be said to alter the Convention test in favour of the victims, by reducing the extent of knowledge of the shipowner that must be proved. It may be that an owner has knowledge that a small oil spill is possible as a result of his conduct, but no idea at all that catastrophic loss is probable. The Convention test would seem to require proof of knowledge that the *particular* damage incurred was probable—not *some* damage. The section would seem to indicate that the test is satisfied provided "any" damage is contemplated as probable, *e.g.* a very small leak. Of course, it is arguable that this is only what is intended by the Convention, but in the writer's opinion there are very strong arguments against this—not the least being the general purpose of having generally unbreakable limits.

Assuming that the necessary conduct is proved the victim must show that the acts or omissions were those of the "owner". It is vital to separate the issue of vicarious liability of the owner for the acts of persons such as masters, from that of identifying the person(s) whose conduct will *deprive* the owner of the right to limit. In maritime law it is necessary to find "breakable" conduct of the owner himself. This may be straightforward if the owner is a natural person, but there are more problems if the owner is a company. There has been much case law on where in the corporate structure the relevant conduct must be identified, for example, *Lennards Carrying Co. v. Asiatic Petroleum* [1915] A.C. 705, *The Lady Gwendolen* [1965] 2 All E.R. 283, *Grand Champion Tankers v. Norpipe A/S (The Marion)* [1984] A.C. 563. Most of these cases should still be relevant, although care should be taken to note that they were decided on the basis that the conduct necessary to break limitation was fault and not the higher intention/recklessness requirement described above. What they show is that breakable conduct at main board level will suffice, while that at deck level will probably not. The position of intermediate managers, *e.g.* marine superintendents, is rather unclear following *The Lady Gwendolen*, but the better view is probably that the breakable conduct should be of persons at the highest level. As a result of the strictures of the House of Lords in *Tesco Supermarkets v. Nattrass* [1972] A.C. 153 and now also *Meridian Global Funds Management Asia Ltd v. Securities Commission* [1995] 3 All E.R. 918 (see the General Note to s.100) it is misleading, though tempting, to seek an *alter ego* of the company. Even though an individual who is the directing mind and will of the company can be identified, that should not stop the search for others at main board level who may also be guilty of the relevant breakable conduct (see *Société Anonyme des Minerais v. Grant Trading (The Ert Stephanie)* [1987] 2 Lloyd's Rep. 371). The *Meridian Global* case may also require one to ask whether the acts or omissions in question are ones which should be attributed to the corporate shipowner and may have indicated that delegated responsibilities could more easily give rise to the breaking of limits than might have been thought before.

As already noted, the Convention required there to be a "personal" act or omission of the shipowner, while s.157(3) has omitted that word (and *cf.* s.156(1)(ii)) from the Act. The terminology was taken from the 1976 Limitation Convention and was clearly intended to restrict the category of person whose conduct could result in the shipowner losing the limits. It is arguable that the word added little to British law. It is also possible that the word was intended to remove arguments that would enable the owner to lose the right to limit when functions had been delegated, *e.g.* to a ship-management company (*cf. The Marion*, above). The latter argument, of great practical significance given the number of ships managed worldwide, would have been particularly strong in the case of the 1992 Liability Convention as "owner" is defined restrictively as being the registered owner (see s.170(1)) and not, for example, a disponent owner. The omission of the word "personal" must throw open the question, under the British statute, of whose conduct is considered as the owner's. It might be argued that the omission was a deliberate attempt to alter the clear provisions of a Convention, particularly as an almost identical international formula was reproduced exactly in the Merchant Shipping Act 1979 (see Sched. 4, Pt. I, Art. 4). The result is unsatisfactory, because there is no international reason whatsoever to interpret differently the provisions of the 1976 Limitation Convention and the 1984 Liability Convention.

(d) Up-rating. Inflation has been one of the main worries in fixing limits in international Conventions, given the amount of time it takes to bring Conventions into force. Article 15 of the 1992 Protocol allows for a (comparatively) rapid amendment procedure for the limits laid down in Art. V(1) of the 1992 Liability Convention and described above. In the U.K., the Secretary of State will give effect to the changes, by statutory instrument, under s.157(2).

Limitation actions

158.—(1) Where the owner of a ship has or is alleged to have incurred a liability under section 153 he may apply to the court for the limitation of that liability to an amount determined in accordance with section 157.

(2) If on such an application the court finds that the applicant has incurred such a liability and is entitled to limit it, the court shall, after determining the limit of the liability and directing payment into court of the amount of that limit—

(a) determine the amounts that would, apart from the limit, be due in respect of the liability to the several persons making claims in the proceedings; and

(b) direct the distribution of the amount paid into court (or, as the case may be, so much of it as does not exceed the liability) among those persons in proportion to their claims, subject to the following provisions of this section.

(3) A payment into court of the amount of a limit determined in pursuance of this section shall be made in sterling; and

(a) for the purpose of converting such an amount from special drawing rights into sterling one special drawing right shall be treated as equal to such a sum in sterling as the International Monetary Fund have fixed as being the equivalent of one special drawing right for—
(i) the day on which the determination is made; or
(ii) if no sum has been so fixed for that day, the last day before that day for which a sum has been so fixed;

(b) a certificate given by or on behalf of the Treasury stating—
(i) that a particular sum in sterling has been so fixed for the day on which the determination was made, or
(ii) that no sum has been so fixed for that day and that a particular sum in sterling has been so fixed for a day which is the last day for which a sum has been so fixed before the day on which the determination was made,
shall be conclusive evidence of those matters for the purposes of this Chapter;

(c) a document purporting to be such a certificate shall, in any proceedings, be received in evidence and, unless the contrary is proved, be deemed to be such a certificate.

(4) No claim shall be admitted in proceedings under this section unless it is made within such time as the court may direct or such further time as the court may allow.

(5) Where any sum has been paid in or towards satisfaction of any claim in respect of the damage or cost to which the liability extends—

(a) by the owner or the persons referred to in section 165 as "the insurer"; or

(b) by a person who has or is alleged to have incurred a liability, otherwise than under section 153, for the damage or cost and who is entitled to limit his liability in connection with the ship by virtue of section 185 or 186;

the person who paid the sum shall, to the extent of that sum, be in the same position with respect to any distribution made in proceedings under this section as the person to whom it was paid would have been.

(6) Where the person who incurred the liability has voluntarily made any reasonable sacrifice or taken any other reasonable measures to prevent or reduce damage to which the liability extends or might have extended he shall be in the same position with respect to any distribution made in proceedings under this section as if he had a claim in respect of the liability equal to the cost of the sacrifice or other measures.

(7) The court may, if it thinks fit, postpone the distribution of such part of the amount to be distributed as it deems appropriate having regard to any claims that may later be established before a court of any country outside the United Kingdom.

(8) No lien or other right in respect of any ship or other property shall affect the proportions in which any amount is distributed in accordance with subsection (2)(b) above.

DEFINITIONS
    "court": s.170(1).
    "damage": s.170(1).
    "insurer, the": s.165(1).
    "owner": s.170(2).
    "person": Interpretation Act 1978, Sched. 1.
    "ship": s.170(1).
    "Treasury, the": Interpretation Act 1978, Sched. 1.
    "United Kingdom": Interpretation Act 1978, Sched. 1.

GENERAL NOTE
    [Derivation: Merchant Shipping (Oil Pollution) Act 1971, s.5; Merchant Shipping Act 1979, s.38(2), Sched. 5, para. 6(1); Merchant Shipping Act 1988, Sched. 4, Pt. I, para. 5.]
    Section 158 sets out the appropriate procedure in a limitation action and the method by which the special drawing right is to be translated into sterling figures. Subsection (8) was inserted to correct an omission in the original 1971 Act and is a familiar provision in limitation statutes (see Sched. 7, Pt. II, para. 9). It ensures that payments are unaffected by existing maritime or other liens. Where the claims exceed the statutory limits they will be paid out proportionately.

Restriction on enforcement after establishment of limitation fund

159.—(1) Where the court has found that a person who has incurred a liability under section 153 is entitled to limit that liability to any amount and he has paid into court a sum not less than that amount—

    (a) the court shall order the release of any ship or other property arrested in connection with a claim in respect of that liability or any security given to prevent or obtain release from such an arrest; and

    (b) no judgment or decree for any such claim shall be enforced, except so far as it is for costs (or, in Scotland, expenses);

if the sum paid into court, or such part thereof as corresponds to the claim, will be actually available to the claimant or would have been available to him if the proper steps in the proceedings under section 158 had been taken.

(2) In the application of this section to Scotland, any reference (however expressed) to release from arrest shall be construed as a reference to the recall of an arrestment.

DEFINITIONS
    "court": s.170(1).
    "person": Interpretation Act 1978, Sched. 1.

"release from arrest": subs. (2).
"ship": s.170(1).

GENERAL NOTE
[Derivation: Merchant Shipping (Oil Pollution) Act 1971, s.6.]
Section 159 imposes restrictions on the extent to which a claimant may try to obtain judgment or security for sums in excess of the applicable limits under s.157.

Concurrent liabilities of owners and others

160. Where, as a result of any discharge or escape of oil from a ship or as a result of any relevant threat of contamination, the owner of the ship incurs a liability under section 153 and any other person incurs a liability, otherwise than under that section, for any such damage or cost as is mentioned in subsection (1) or (2) of that section then, if—

(a) the owner has been found, in proceedings under section 158 to be entitled to limit his liability to any amount and has paid into court a sum not less than that amount; and

(b) the other person is entitled to limit his liability in connection with the ship by virtue of section 185 or 186;

no proceedings shall be taken against the other person in respect of his liability, and if any such proceedings were commenced before the owner paid the sum into court, no further steps shall be taken in the proceedings except in relation to costs.

DEFINITIONS
"court": s.170(1).
"damage": s.170(1).
"discharge or escape": s.153(7).
"oil": s.170(1).
"owner": s.170(2).
"person": Interpretation Act 1978, Sched. 1.
"relevant threat of contamination": ss.153(2), 154(2) and 170(1).
"ship": s.170(1).

GENERAL NOTE
[Derivation: Merchant Shipping (Oil Pollution) Act 1971, s.7; Merchant Shipping Act 1988, Sched. 4, Pt. I, para. 6.]

Establishment of limitation fund outside United Kingdom

161. Where the events resulting in the liability of any person under 1 section 153 also resulted in a corresponding liability under the law of another Liability Convention country sections 159 and 160 shall apply as if the references to sections 153 and 158 included references to the corresponding provisions of that law and the references to sums paid into court included references to any sums secured under those provisions in respect of the liability.

DEFINITIONS
"court": s.170(1).
"Liability Convention country": s.152(1).
"person": Interpretation Act 1978, Sched. 1.

GENERAL NOTE
[Derivation: Merchant Shipping (Oil Pollution) Act 1971, s.8.]

Extinguishment of claims

162. No action to enforce a claim in respect of a liability incurred under section 153 or 154 shall be entertained by any court in the United Kingdom unless the action is commenced not later than three years after the claim arose nor later than six years after the occurrence or first of the occurrences resulting in the discharge or escape, or (as the case may be) in the relevant threat of contamination, by reason of which the liability was incurred.

GENERAL NOTE
[Derivation: Merchant Shipping (Oil Pollution) Act 1971, s.9; Merchant Shipping Act 1988, Sched. 4, Pt. I, para. 7; Merchant Shipping (Salvage and Pollution) Act 1994, Sched. 3, Pt. II, para. 5.]
Section 162 sets out the dual time bar under the 1992 Liability Convention. The distinction is important because a ship may sink, but oil may not leak out until many years later. There is an absolute bar of six years from the date of the "occurrence", *e.g.* a collision.

Compulsory insurance

Compulsory insurance against liability for pollution

163.—(1) Subject to the provisions of this Chapter relating to Government ships, subsection (2) below shall apply to any ship carrying in bulk a cargo of more than 2,000 tons of oil of a description specified in regulations made by the Secretary of State.

(2) The ship shall not enter or leave a port in the United Kingdom or arrive at or leave a terminal in the territorial sea of the United Kingdom nor, if the ship is a United Kingdom ship, a port in any other country or a terminal in the territorial sea of any other country, unless there is in force a certificate complying with the provisions of subsection (3) below and showing that there is in force in respect of the ship a contract of insurance or other security satisfying the requirements of Article VII of the Liability Convention (cover for owner's liability).

(3) The certificate must be—

(a) if the ship is a United Kingdom ship, a certificate issued by the Secretary of State;

(b) if the ship is registered in a Liability Convention country other than the United Kingdom, a certificate issued by or under the authority of the government of the other Liability Convention country; and

(c) if the ship is registered in a country which is not a Liability Convention country, a certificate issued by the Secretary of State or by or under the authority of the government of any Liability Convention country other than the United Kingdom.

(4) Any certificate required by this section to be in force in respect of a ship shall be carried in the ship and shall, on demand, be produced by the master to any officer of customs and excise or of the Secretary of State and, if the ship is a United Kingdom ship, to any proper officer.

(5) If a ship enters or leaves, or attempts to enter or leave, a port or arrives at or leaves, or attempts to arrive at or leave, a terminal in contravention of subsection (2) above, the master or owner shall be liable on conviction on indictment to a fine, or on summary conviction to a fine not exceeding £50,000.

(6) If a ship fails to carry, or the master of a ship fails to produce, a certificate as required by subsection (4) above, the master shall be liable on summary conviction to a fine not exceeding level 4 on the standard scale.

(7) If a ship attempts to leave a port in the United Kingdom in contravention of this section the ship may be detained.

"Government ship": ss.308(4) and 313(1).
"Liability Convention, the": s.152(1).
"Liability Convention country": s.152(1).
"master": s.313(1).
"oil": s.151(1).
"owner": s.170(2).
"port": s.313(1).
"proper officer": s.313(1).
"registered": ss.23(1) and 313(1).
"Secretary of State": Interpretation Act 1978, Sched. 1.
"ship": s.170(1).
"standard scale": Criminal Justice Act 1982, s.37.
"United Kingdom": Interpretation Act 1978, Sched. 1.
"United Kingdom ship": ss.1(3) and 313(1).

GENERAL NOTE
[Derivation: Merchant Shipping (Oil Pollution) Act 1971, s.10; Merchant Shipping Act 1979, Sched. 6, Pt. III; Merchant Shipping Act 1988, Sched. 4, Pt. I, para. 8(6), Sched. 5.]
The existence of compulsory insurance was an important factor behind the scheme of protection given to claimants.

Issue of certificate by Secretary of State

164.—(1) Subject to subsection (2) below, if the Secretary of State is satisfied, on the application for such a certificate as is mentioned in section 163 in respect of a United Kingdom ship or a ship registered in any country which is not a Liability Convention country, that there will be in force in respect of the ship, throughout the period for which the certificate is to be issued, a contract of insurance or other security satisfying the requirements of Article VII of the Liability Convention, the Secretary of State shall issue such a certificate to the owner.

(2) If the Secretary of State is of opinion that there is a doubt whether the person providing the insurance or other security will be able to meet his obligations thereunder, or whether the insurance or other security will cover the owner's liability under section 153 in all circumstances, he may refuse the certificate.

(3) The Secretary of State may make regulations providing for the cancellation and delivery up of a certificate under this section in such circumstances as may be prescribed by the regulations.

(4) If a person required by regulations under subsection (3) above to deliver up a certificate fails to do so he shall be liable on summary conviction to a fine not exceeding level 4 on the standard scale.

(5) The Secretary of State shall send a copy of any certificate issued by him under this section in respect of a United Kingdom ship to the Registrar General of Shipping and Seamen, and the Registrar shall make the copy available for public inspection.

DEFINITIONS
"certificate": s.163(3).
"fails": s.313(1).
"Liability Convention, the": s.152(1).
"Liability Convention country": s.152(1).
"person": Interpretation Act 1978, Sched. 1.
"owner": s.170(2).
"registered": ss.23(1) and 313(1).
"Secretary of State": Interpretation Act 1978, Sched. 1.
"ship": s.170(1).
"standard scale": Criminal Justice Act 1982, s.37.
"United Kingdom ship": ss.1(3) and 313(1).

GENERAL NOTE
[Derivation: Merchant Shipping (Oil Pollution) Act 1971, s.11; Criminal Justice Act 1982, s.46; Merchant Shipping (Registration, etc.) Act 1993, Sched. 5.]
Compulsory insurance can be verified by the issue of a certificate under s.164.

Rights of third parties against insurers

165.—(1) Where it is alleged that the owner of a ship has incurred a liability under section 153 as a result of any discharge or escape of oil occurring, or as a result of any relevant threat of contamination arising, while there was in force a contract of insurance or other security to which such a certificate as is mentioned in section 163 related, proceedings to enforce a claim in respect of the liability may be brought against the person who provided the insurance or other security (in the following provisions of this section referred to as "the insurer").

(2) In any proceedings brought against the insurer by virtue of this section it shall be a defence (in addition to any defence affecting the owner's liability) to prove that the discharge or escape, or (as the case may be) the threat of contamination, was due to the wilful misconduct of the owner himself.

(3) The insurer may limit his liability in respect of claims made against him by virtue of this section in like manner and to the same extent as the owner may limit his liability but the insurer may do so whether or not the discharge or escape, or (as the case may be) the threat of contamination, resulted from anything done or omitted to be done by the owner as mentioned in section 157(3).

(4) Where the owner and the insurer each apply to the court for the limitation of his liability any sum paid into court in pursuance of either application shall be treated as paid also in pursuance of the other.

(5) The Third Parties (Rights against Insurers) Act 1930 and the Third Parties (Rights against Insurers) Act (Northern Ireland) 1930 shall not apply in relation to any contract of insurance to which such a certificate as is mentioned in section 163 relates.

DEFINITIONS
   "certificate": s.163(3).
   "court": s.170(1).
   "discharge or escape": s.153(7).
   "insurer, the": subs. (1).
   "owner": s.170(2).
   "oil": s.170(1).
   "person": Interpretation Act 1978, Sched. 1.
   "relevant threat of contamination": ss.153(2), 154(2) and 170(1).
   "ship": s.170(1).

GENERAL NOTE
   [Derivation: Merchant Shipping (Oil Pollution) Act 1971, s.12; Merchant Shipping Act 1988, Sched. 4, Pt. I, para. 9.]
   Compulsory insurance is combined with a direct right of action against an insurer (usually the shipowner's P & I Club).

Supplementary

Jurisdiction of United Kingdom courts and registration of foreign judgments

166.—(1) Paragraph 1(1)(d) of Schedule 1 to the Administration of Justice Act 1956 (Admiralty jurisdiction in claims for damage done by ships) shall be construed as extending to any claim in respect of a liability incurred under this Chapter, and the Admiralty jurisdiction of the Court of Session shall extend to any case arising out of any such claim.

(2) Where—

(a) any oil is discharged or escapes from a ship but does not result in any damage caused by contamination in the territory of the United Kingdom and no measures are reasonably taken to prevent or minimise such damage in that territory, or

(b) any relevant threat of contamination arises but no measures are reasonably taken to prevent or minimise such damage in the territory of the United Kingdom,

no court in the United Kingdom shall entertain any action (whether in rem or in personam) to enforce a claim arising from any relevant damage or cost—

   (i) against the owner of the ship, or

  (ii) against any person to whom section 156(1)(ii) applies, unless any such damage or cost resulted from anything done or omitted to be done as mentioned in that provision.

(3) In subsection (2) above, "relevant damage or cost" means—

(a) in relation to any such discharge or escape as is mentioned in paragraph (a) of that subsection, any damage caused in the territory of another Liability Convention country by contamination resulting from the discharge or escape, or any cost incurred in taking measures to prevent or minimise such damage in the territory of another Liability Convention country,

(b) in relation to any such threat of contamination as is mentioned in paragraph (b) of that subsection, any cost incurred in taking measures to prevent or minimise such damage in the territory of another Liability Convention country; or

(c) any damage caused by any measures taken as mentioned in paragraph (a) or (b) above;

and section 156(2)(e) shall have effect for the purposes of subsection (2)(ii) above as if it referred to any person taking any such measures as are mentioned in paragraph (a) or (b) above.

(4) Part I of the Foreign Judgments (Reciprocal Enforcement) Act 1933 shall apply, whether or not it would so apply apart from this section, to any judgment given by a court in a Liability Convention country to enforce a claim in respect of a liability incurred under any provision corresponding to section 153; and in its application to such a judgment that Part shall have effect with the omission of sections 4(2) and (3) of that Act.

DEFINITIONS
   "court": s.170(1).
   "damage": s.170(1).
   "discharge or escape": s.153(7).
   "Liability Convention country": s.152(1).
   "owner": s.170(1).
   "oil": s.170(1).
   "person": Interpretation Act 1978, Sched. 1.
   "relevant damage or cost": subs. (3).
   "relevant threat of contamination": ss.153(2), 154(2) and 170(1).
   "ship": s.170(1).
   "territory": s.170(4).
   "United Kingdom": Interpretation Act 1978, Sched. 1.

GENERAL NOTE
   [Derivation: Merchant Shipping (Oil Pollution) Act 1971, s.13; Supreme Court Act 1981, Sched. 5; Merchant Shipping Act 1988, Sched. 4, Pt. I, para. 10; Merchant Shipping (Salvage and Pollution) Act 1994, Sched. 3, Pt. II, para. 6.]
   Section 166 deals with jurisdiction and registration of foreign judgments. Section 13 of the Merchant Shipping (Oil Pollution) Act 1971 (as amended by the Supreme Court Act 1981) gave jurisdiction to the Admiralty Court. The 1969 Convention was designed to ensure that there should not be a multiplicity of suits following one incident and that actions could only be brought in the courts of contracting states in whose territory damage had occurred. This was dealt with by Sched. 4, s.166(2) which is now replaced by s.166(2) and (3) as found in Pt. VI, Chap. III. The changes are mainly to take account of the wider definitions already discussed, *e.g.* of liability and pollution damage. But, in essence, no U.K. court will have jurisdiction if there is Convention damage in another contracting state: the action should be brought in such a country.

The U.K. court will have jurisdiction to hear a claim against one of the categories of persons listed in s.156(2), but only if that person was himself guilty of the "breakable conduct" defined in s.156(1)(ii) and described above.

Government ships

167.—(1) Nothing in the preceding provisions of this Chapter applies in relation to any warship or any ship for the time being used by the government of any State for other than commercial purposes.

(2) In relation to a ship owned by a State and for the time being used for commercial purposes it shall be a sufficient compliance with section 163(2) if there is in force a certificate issued by the government of that State and showing that the ship is owned by that State and that any liability for pollution damage as defined in Article I of the Liability Convention will be met up to the limit prescribed by Article V of the Convention.

(3) Every Liability Convention State shall, for the purposes of any proceedings brought in a court in the United Kingdom to enforce a claim in respect of a liability incurred under section 153, be deemed to have submitted to the jurisdiction of that court, and accordingly rules of court may provide for the manner in which such proceedings are to be commenced and carried on; but nothing in this subsection shall authorise the issue of execution, or in Scotland the execution of diligence, against the property of any State.

DEFINITIONS
  "certificate": s.163(3).
  "court": s.170(1).
  "damage": s.170(1).
  "Government ship": ss.308(4) and 313(1).
  "Liability Convention, the": s.152(1).
  "Liability Convention State": s.152(1).
  "ship": s.170(1).
  "United Kingdom": Interpretation Act 1978, Sched. 1.

GENERAL NOTE
  [Derivation: Merchant Shipping (Oil Pollution) Act 1971, s.14; Merchant Shipping Act 1979, s.38(3); Merchant Shipping Act 1988, Sched. 4, Pt. I, para. 11.]
  Section 167 contains the usual exception for warships and Government ships which are not trading (*e.g.* fleet auxiliaries).

Limitation of liability under section 154

168. For the purposes of section 185 any liability incurred under section 154 shall be deemed to be a liability to damages in respect of such damage to property as is mentioned in paragraph 1(a) of Article 2 of the Convention in Part I of Schedule 7.

DEFINITIONS
  "damage": s.170(1).

GENERAL NOTE
  [Derivation: Merchant Shipping Act 1971, s.15(2); Merchant Shipping Act 1979, Sched. 5, para. 6(2); Merchant Shipping (Salvage and Pollution) Act 1994, Sched. 3, Pt. II, para. 7.]
  Limitation of liability is generally allowed to tanker owners under s.157. Other maritime liabilities are subject to limitation of liability under the 1976 Limitation Convention (as enacted in Sched. 7) which, in general, provides for lower limits of liability and whereby many claimants will have to share in the limitation fund established after a disaster. The limits in the 1976 Limitation Convention will almost certainly be increased at a diplomatic conference in 1996. Where the 1992 Liability Convention applies, that Convention will govern liability and limitation. Where a shipowner is liable under s.154, the liabilities will continue to be subject to limitation under the 1976 Limitation Convention. That right to limit could arise under Sched. 7, Pt. I, Art. 2.1(a), (c), (e) or (f), although by virtue of s.168 the liability under s.154 is deemed conclusively to fall under para. 1(a).
  Until the 1992 Protocols enter into force, the owner of a tanker in ballast whose bunkers cause pollution will be liable only under Sched. 4, s.154 and will be entitled to limit according to the

1976 Limitation Convention. When the 1992 Protocols enter into force, there will be liability and limitation in such circumstances under the 1992 Liability Convention (see s.157).

See, further, the General Notes to ss.154, 157, above.

Saving for recourse actions

169. Nothing in this Chapter shall prejudice any claim, or the enforcement of any claim, a person incurring any liability under this Chapter may have against another person in respect of that liability.

DEFINITIONS

"person": Interpretation Act 1978, Sched. 1.

GENERAL NOTE

[Derivation: Merchant Shipping (Oil Pollution) Act 1971, s.16.]

A right of recourse might arise against the shipowner of a colliding ship who was solely at fault. There would still be liability under s.153 because of the strict liability rule. The owner of the colliding ship would have to limit under the 1976 Limitation Convention and not the 1992 Liability Convention.

Interpretation

170.—(1) In this Chapter—
"the court" means the High Court or, in Scotland, the Court of Session;
"damage" includes loss;
"oil" means persistent hydrocarbon mineral oil;
"owner" means the person or persons registered as the owner of the ship or, in the absence of registration, the person or persons owning the ship, except that, in relation to a ship owned by a State which is operated by a person registered as the ship's operator, it means the person registered as its operator;
"relevant threat of contamination" shall be construed in accordance with section 153(2) or 154(2); and
"ship" (subject to section 154(5)) means any sea-going vessel or sea-borne craft of any type whatsoever.

(2) In relation to any damage or cost resulting from the discharge or escape of any oil from a ship, or from a relevant threat of contamination, references in this Chapter to the owner of the ship are references to the owner at the time of the occurrence or first of the occurrences resulting in the discharge or escape or (as the case may be) in the threat of contamination.

(3) References in this Chapter in its application to Scotland—

(a) to payment into court, shall be construed as references to the payment to the Accountant of Court for Consignation (within the meaning of the Court of Session Consignations (Scotland) Act 1895; and

(b) to costs, shall be construed as references to expenses.

(4) References in this Chapter to the territory of any country include the territorial sea of that country and—

(a) in the case of the United Kingdom, any area within the British fishery limits set by or under the Fishery Limits Act 1976; and

(b) in the case of any other Liability Convention country, the exclusive economic zone of that country established in accordance with international law, or, if such a zone has not been established, such area adjacent to the territorial sea of that country and extending not more that 200 nautical miles from the baselines from which the breadth of that sea is measured as may have been determined by that State in question in accordance with international law.

DEFINITIONS

"court, the": subs. (1).

"damage": subs. (1).

"discharge or escape": s.153(7).

"High Court": Interpretation Act 1978, Sched. 1.
"Liability Convention country": s.152(1).
"oil": subs. (1).
"owner": subss. (1) and (2).
"person": Interpretation Act 1978, Sched. 1.
"registered": ss.23(1) and 313(1).
"relevant threat of contamination": subs. (1).
"ship": subs. (1).
"territory": subs. (4).
"United Kingdom": Interpretation Act 1978, Sched. 1.

GENERAL NOTE
[Derivation: Merchant Shipping (Oil Pollution) Act 1971, s.20; Merchant Shipping Act 1988, Sched. 4, Pt. II, para. 8.]

Oil. Section 170(1) redefines oil in terms of hydrocarbon mineral oil (excluding the previous references to examples, such as fuel oil). Whale oil has now been omitted from the 1992 Liability Convention.

Geographical scope. Liability under the 1969 Liability Convention could arise even where the discharge occurred in the area of another contracting state. Section 153(2) of Sched. 4 merely repeats the old law. The 1992 Protocol produced a new Art. II to the Liability Convention which significantly widened the scope of application of the Convention. It applies not only to pollution damage in territorial waters but also in the Exclusive Economic Zone. This is a concept recognised by Art. 57 of the UN Convention on the Law of the Sea 1982 and is fixed at no more than 200 nautical miles. The new provision is to be found in subs. (3), which must be read with s.153(5). Whether a state is a Convention country will continue to be determined by an Order in Council issued under s.152.

Transitory text of this Chapter and power to make transitional provisions

171.—(1) Until such day as the Secretary of State may by order appoint, the provisions set out in Schedule 4 as Chapter III shall have effect instead of the foregoing provisions of this Chapter; and references in that Schedule to a section whose number is included in that Schedule is a reference to the section so included.

(2) Notwithstanding subsection (1) above, Her Majesty may by Order in Council make such provision as appears to Her Majesty to be appropriate in connection with the implementation of any transitional provisions contained in the 1992 Protocol or the Conventions which they amend; and any such Order may in particular provide, in relation to occurrences of any description specified in the Order—

(a) for specified provisions of this Chapter, whether as contained in this Chapter or in the Chapter III set out in Schedule 4, to have effect;

(b) for any such provisions to have effect subject to specified modifications.

(3) In subsection (2) above—

"the 1992 Protocol" means the Protocol of 1992 to amend the International Convention for Oil Pollution Damage 1969 signed in London on 27th November 1992; and

"specified" means specified in the Order.

DEFINITIONS
"1992 Protocols, the": subs. (3).
"Secretary of State": Interpretation Act 1978, Sched. 1.
"specified": subs. (3).

GENERAL NOTE
[Derivation: Merchant Shipping (Salvage and Pollution) Act 1994, ss.5(1), (3), (4) and 10(3).]
For an explanation of the transitional provisions, see the General Note to this Chapter of the Act, above.

CHAPTER IV

INTERNATIONAL OIL POLLUTION COMPENSATION FUND

GENERAL NOTE
For the background to the oil pollution compensation system, see the General Note to Chapter III of this Part of the Act, above. The International Oil Pollution Compensation Fund (IOPC Fund) was established by the 1971 Fund Convention and has been operating since 1978. The IOPC Fund has its headquarters in London and, under Art. 2, it "shall in each Contracting State be recognised as a legal person capable under the laws of that State of assuming rights and obligations and of being a party in legal proceedings before the Courts of that State ...". But the important role of the IOPC Fund is that it provides a second tier of liability to which an oil pollution victim can have access in the event that a claim against the shipowner (originally under the 1969 Liability Convention and the Merchant Shipping (Oil Pollution) Act 1971) is unsuccessful or only partially successful. The Fund's 1994 Annual Report shows that it has dealt with some 73 cases since it entered into force in 1978. In the U.K., the 1971 Fund Convention was given effect by the Merchant Shipping Act 1974 and the amendments contained in the Merchant Shipping Act 1988 were triggered with minor amendments to give effect to the 1992 Fund Convention by the Merchant Shipping (Salvage and Pollution) Act 1994.
The 1992 amendments to the 1971 Fund Convention largely mirror those to the 1969 Liability Convention. They are contained in Chapter IV, while the old law under the 1971 Fund Convention is to be found in Sched. 4, Chapter IV.

Preliminary

Meaning of the "Liability Convention", "the Fund Convention" and related expressions

172.—(1) In this Chapter—
(a) "the Liability Convention" has the same meaning as in Chapter III of this Part;
(b) "the Fund Convention" means the International Convention on the Establishment of an International Fund for Compensation for Oil Pollution Damage 1992;
(c) "the Fund" means the International Fund established by the Fund Convention; and
(d) "Fund Convention country" means a country in respect of which the Fund Convention is in force.

(2) If Her Majesty by Order in Council declares that any State specified in the Order is a party to the Fund Convention in respect of any country so specified, the Order shall, while in force, be conclusive evidence that that State is a party to that Convention in respect of that country.

DEFINITIONS
"Fund, the": subs. (1)(c).
"Fund Convention, the": subs. (1)(b).
"Fund Convention country": subs. (1)(d).
"Liability Convention, the": subs. (1)(a) and s.152(1).
"pollution damage": s.181(1).

GENERAL NOTE
[Derivation: Merchant Shipping Act 1974, s.1(1) and (2); Merchant Shipping Act 1988, Sched. 4, Pt. II, para. 15; Merchant Shipping (Salvage and Pollution) Act 1994, s.5(1) and (4).]

Contributions to Fund

Contributions by importers of oil and others

173.—(1) Contributions shall be payable to the Fund in respect of oil carried by sea to ports or terminal installations in the United Kingdom otherwise than on a voyage only within its national waters.

(2) Subsection (1) above applies whether or not the oil is being imported, and applies even if contributions are payable in respect of carriage of the same oil on a previous voyage.

(3) Contributions shall also be payable to the Fund in respect of oil when first received in any installation in the United Kingdom after having been carried by sea and discharged in a port or terminal installation in a country which is not a Fund Convention country.

(4) The person liable to pay contributions is—

(a) in the case of oil which is being imported into the United Kingdom, the importer, and

(b) otherwise, the person by whom the oil is received.

(5) A person shall not be liable to make contributions in respect of the oil imported or received by him in any year if the oil so imported or received in the year does not exceed 150,000 tonnes.

(6) For the purpose of subsection (5) above—

(a) all the members of a group of companies shall be treated as a single person, and

(b) any two or more companies which have been amalgamated into a single company shall be treated as the same person as that single company.

(7) The contributions payable by a person for any year shall—

(a) be of such amount as may be determined by the Director of the Fund under Article 12 of the Fund Convention and notified to that person by the Fund;

(b) be payable in such instalments, becoming due at such times, as may be so notified to him;

and if any amount due from him remains unpaid after the date on which it became due, it shall from then on bear interest, at a rate determined from time to time by the Assembly of the Fund, until it is paid.

(8) The Secretary of State may by regulations impose on persons who are or may be liable to pay contributions under this section obligations to give security for payment to the Secretary of State, or the Fund.

(9) Regulations under subsubsection (8) above—

(a) may contain such supplemental or incidental provisions as appear to the Secretary of State expedient, and

(b) may impose penalties for contravention of the regulations punishable on summary conviction by a fine not exceeding level 5 on the standard scale, or such lower limit as may be specified in the regulations.

(10) In this section and in section 174, unless the context otherwise requires—

"company" means a body incorporated under the law of the United Kingdom, or of any other country;

"group" in relation to companies, means a holding company and its subsidiaries as defined by section 736 of the Companies Act 1985 (or for companies in Northern Ireland Article 4 of the Companies (Northern Ireland) Order 1986), subject, in the case of a company incorporated outside the United Kingdom, to any necessary modifications of those definitions;

"importer" means the person by whom or on whose behalf the oil in question is entered for customs or excise purposes on importation, and "import" shall be construed accordingly;

"oil" means crude oil and fuel oil, and

(a) "crude oil" means any liquid hydrocarbon mixture occurring naturally in the earth whether or not treated to render it suitable for transportation, and includes—

(i) crude oils from which distillate fractions have been removed, and

(ii) crude oils to which distillate fractions have been added,

(b) "fuel oil" means heavy distillates or residues from crude oil or blends of such materials intended for use as a fuel for the production of heat or power of a quality equivalent to the "American Society for Testing and Materials' Specification for Number Four Fuel Oil (Designation D396-69)", or heavier,

"terminal installation" means any site for the storage of oil in bulk which is capable of receiving oil from waterborne transportation, including any facility situated offshore and linked to any such site.

DEFINITIONS

"company": subs. (10).
"contravention": s.313(1).
"crude oil": subs. (10)(a).
"fuel oil": subs. (10)(b).
"Fund, the": s.172(1)(c).
"Fund Convention, the": s.172(1)(b).
"Fund Convention country": s.172(1)(d).
"group": subs. (10).
"import": subs. (10).
"importer": subs. (10).
"national waters": s.313(2)(b).
"oil": subs. (10).
"person": subs. (6).
"port": s.313(1).
"Secretary of State": Interpretation Act 1978, Sched. 1.
"standard scale": Criminal Justice Act 1982, s.37.
"terminal installation": subs. (10).
"United Kingdom": Interpretation Act 1978, Sched. 1.

GENERAL NOTE

[Derivation: Merchant Shipping Act 1974, s.2; Merchant Shipping Act 1979, Sched. 4, para. 16; Customs and Excise Management Act 1979, Sched. 4; Criminal Justice Act 1982, s.46; Companies Consolidation (Consequential Provisions) Act 1985, Sched. 2; Merchant Shipping Act 1988, Sched. 4, Pt. II, para. 16.]

The 1992 International Oil Pollution Compensation Fund is not an insurance based organisation. It charges levies on importers of oil, if the importer receives more than 150,000 tonnes of oil per year. The Fund operates a post-event collection system, so that levies are only assessed and charged after a pollution incident has arisen.

Power to obtain information

174.—(1) For the purpose of transmitting to the Fund the names and addresses of the persons who under section 173 are liable to make contributions to the Fund for any year, and the quantity of oil in respect of which they are so liable, the Secretary of State may by notice require any person engaged in producing, treating, distributing or transporting oil to furnish such information as may be specified in the notice.

(2) A notice under this section may require a company to give such information as may be required to ascertain whether its liability is affected by section 173(6).

(3) A notice under this section may specify the way in which, and the time within which, it is to be complied with.

(4) In proceedings by the Fund against any person to recover any amount due under section 173, particulars contained in any list transmitted by the Secretary of State to the Fund shall, so far as those particulars are based on information obtained under this section, be admissible as evidence of the facts stated in the list; and so far as particulars which are so admissible are based on information given by the person against whom the proceedings are brought, those particulars shall be presumed to be accurate until the contrary is proved.

(5) If a person discloses any information which has been furnished to or obtained by him under this section, or in connection with the execution of this section, then, unless the disclosure is made—

(a) with the consent of the person from whom the information was obtained, or

(b) in connection with the execution of this section, or

(c) for the purposes of any legal proceedings arising out of this section or of any report of such proceedings,

he shall be liable on summary conviction to a fine not exceeding level 5 on the standard scale.

(6) A person who—

(a) refuses or wilfully neglects to comply with a notice under this section, or

(b) in furnishing any information in compliance with a notice under this section makes any statement which he knows to be false in a material particular, or recklessly makes any statement which is false in a material particular,

shall be liable—

(i) on summary conviction, to a fine not exceeding level 4 on the standard scale in the case of an offence under paragraph (a) above and not exceeding the statutory maximum in the case of an offence under paragraph (b) above, and

(ii) on conviction on indictment, to a fine, or to imprisonment for a term not exceeding twelve months, or to both.

DEFINITIONS
"company": s.173(10).
"Fund, the": s.172(1)(c).
"month": Interpretation Act 1978, Sched. 1.
"oil": s.173(10).
"person": s.173(6) and Interpretation Act 1978, Sched. 1.
"Secretary of State": Interpretation Act 1978, Sched. 1.
"standard scale": Criminal Justice Act 1982, s.37.
"statutory maximum": Criminal Justice Act 1982, s.74.

GENERAL NOTE
[Derivation: Merchant Shipping Act 1974, s.3; Merchant Shipping Act 1979, Sched. 6, Pt. IV, Pt. VI, para. 18.]

The system of contribution can only work if the Fund can receive details of contributors and the 1992 Fund Convention puts obligations on contracting states to supply information.

Compensation for persons suffering pollution damage

Liability of the Fund

175.—(1) The Fund shall be liable for pollution damage in the territory of the United Kingdom if the person suffering the damage has been unable to obtain full compensation under section 153—

(a) because the discharge or escape, or the relevant threat of contamination, by reason of which the damage was caused—

(i) resulted from an exceptional, inevitable and irresistible phenomenon, or

(ii) was due wholly to anything done or omitted to be done by another person (not being a servant or agent of the owner) with intent to do damage, or

(iii) was due wholly to the negligence or wrongful act of a government or other authority in exercising its function of maintaining lights or other navigational aids for the maintenance of which it was responsible,

(and because liability is accordingly wholly displaced by section 155), or

    (b) because the owner or guarantor liable for the damage cannot meet his obligations in full, or

    (c) because the damage exceeds the liability under section 153 as limited by section 157.

(2) Subsection (1) above shall apply with the substitution for the words "United Kingdom" of the words "a Fund Convention country" where—

    (a) the headquarters of the Fund is for the time being in the United Kingdom, and proceedings under the Liability Convention for compensation for the pollution damage have been brought in a country which is not a Fund Convention country, or

    (b) the incident has caused pollution damage in the territory of the United Kingdom and of another Fund Convention country, and proceedings under the Liability Convention for compensation for the pollution damage have been brought in a country which is not a Fund Convention country or in the United Kingdom.

(3) Where the incident has caused pollution damage in the territory of the United Kingdom and of another country in respect of which the Liability Convention is in force, references in this section to the provisions of Chapter III of this Part shall include references to the corresponding provisions of the law of any country giving effect to the Liability Convention.

(4) Where proceedings under the Liability Convention for compensation for pollution damage have been brought in a country which is not a Fund Convention country and the Fund is liable for that pollution damage by virtue of subsection (2)(a) above, references in this section to the provisions of Chapter III of this Part shall be treated as references to the corresponding provisions of the law of the country in which those proceedings were brought.

(5) For the purposes of this section an owner or guarantor is to be treated as incapable of meeting his obligations if the obligations have not been met after all reasonable steps to pursue the legal remedies available have been taken.

(6) Expenses reasonably incurred, and sacrifices reasonably made, by the owner voluntarily to prevent or minimise pollution damage shall be treated as pollution damage for the purposes of this section, and accordingly he shall be in the same position with respect to claims against the Fund under this section as if he had a claim in respect of liability under section 153.

(7) The Fund shall incur no obligation under this section if—

    (a) it proves that the pollution damage—

        (i) resulted from an act of war, hostilities, civil war or insurrection, or

        (ii) was caused by oil which has escaped or been discharged from a warship or other ship owned or operated by a State and used, at the time of the occurrence, only on Government non-commercial service, or

    (b) the claimant cannot prove that the damage resulted from an occurrence involving a ship identified by him, or involving two or more ships one of which is identified by him.

(8) If the Fund proves that the pollution damage resulted wholly or partly—

    (a) from anything done or omitted to be done with intent to cause damage by the person who suffered the damage, or

    (b) from the negligence of that person,

the Fund may (subject to subsection (10) below) be exonerated wholly or partly from its obligations to pay compensation to that person.

(9) Where the liability under section 153 in respect of the pollution damage is limited to any extent by subsection (8) of that section, the Fund shall (subject to subsection (10) below) be exonerated to the same extent.

(10) Subsections (8) and (9) above shall not apply where the pollution damage consists of the costs of preventive measures or any damage caused by such measures.

<small>DEFINITIONS</small>
"commercial": State Immunity Act 1978, s.17(1).
"damage": s.181(1).
"discharge or escape": s.181(1) and (2).
"Fund, the": s.172(1)(c).
"Fund Convention country": s.172(1)(d).
"guarantor": s.181(1).
"incapable of meeting his obligations": subs. (5)
"incident": s.181(1).
"Liability Convention, the": ss.172(1)(a) and 152(1).
"oil": s.181(1).
"owner": s.181(1).
"person": Interpretation Act 1978, Sched. 1.
"pollution damage": subs. (6) and s.181(1).
"preventive measures": s.181(1).
"relevant threat of contamination": s.181(1).
"ship": ss.153(3) and (4) and 181(1).
"territory": ss.170(4) and 181(3).
"United Kingdom": Interpretation Act 1978, Sched. 1.

<small>GENERAL NOTE</small>
[Derivation: Merchant Shipping Act 1974, s.4; Merchant Shipping Act 1979, Sched. 7, Pt. I; Merchant Shipping Act 1988, Sched. 4, Pt. II, para. 17(2), (3), Sched. 7.]

Section 175 sets out the liability of the 1992 International Oil Pollution Compensation Fund (IOPC Fund) to claimants. As already noted, the Fund operates to "top-up" claims which have not been satisfied under Chapter III for the reasons specified in subs. (1). Under subs. (7) the Fund has limited defences, of which those in para. (a) are similar to those available to a ship-owner under Chapter III. In particular, under Art. 4.1 (as enacted in s.175(1)) the 1992 IOPC Fund is liable to a victim (a) where the shipowner is exempted from liability under the 1992 Liability Convention, (b) where a shipowner or its insurer is incapable of meeting its primary obligations under the 1992 Liability Convention, or (c) where the limits of liability under the 1992 Liability Convention are exceeded. One purpose of the Fund is to cover the cases where a shipowner might be insolvent or has a s.155(b) or (c) defence, and so the defences under the two Chapters are not identical. The most difficult defence for claimants to meet is that in subs. (7)(b) where they cannot prove that pollution came from a ship (as opposed to land-based sources).

The so-called "roll-back" relief in s.176A of Sched. 4 has been abolished for Chapter IV where the 1992 Fund Convention applies.

The contributory negligence defence remains open to the Fund in all cases of damage or loss except where the damage consists of preventive measures (see subss. (8)–(10)).

Limitation of Fund's liability under section 175

176.—(1) The Fund's liability under section 175 shall be subject to the limits imposed by paragraphs 4 and 5 of Article 4 of the Fund Convention (which impose an overall limit on the liabilities of the Fund and the text of which is set out in Part I of Schedule 5), and in those provisions references to the Liability Convention are references to the Liability Convention within the meaning of this Chapter.

(2) A certificate given by the Director of the Fund stating that sub-paragraph (c) of paragraph 4 of Article 4 of the Fund Convention is applicable to any claim under section 175 shall be conclusive evidence for the purposes of this Chapter that it is so applicable.

(3) For the purpose of giving effect to paragraphs 4 and 5 of Article 4 of the Fund Convention a court giving judgment against the Fund in proceedings under section 175 shall notify the Fund, and—

  (a) no steps shall be taken to enforce the judgment unless and until the court gives leave to enforce it,
  (b) that leave shall not be given unless and until the Fund notifies the court either that the amount of the claim is not to be reduced under those paragraphs, or that it is to be reduced to a specified amount, and

(c) in the latter case the judgment shall be enforceable only for the reduced amount.

(4) Any steps taken to obtain payment of an amount or a reduced amount in pursuance of such a judgment as is mentioned in subsection (3) above shall be steps to obtain payment in sterling; and—

(a) for the purpose of converting such an amount from special drawing rights into sterling one special drawing right shall be treated as equal to such a sum in sterling as the International Monetary Fund have fixed as being the equivalent of one special drawing right for—

(i) the relevant day, namely the day on which the Assembly of the Fund decide the date for the first payment of compensation in respect of the incident, or

(ii) if no sum has been so fixed for the relevant day, the last day before that day for which a sum has been so fixed; and

(b) a certificate given by or on behalf of the Treasury stating—

(i) that a particular sum in sterling has been so fixed for the relevant day, or

(ii) that no sum has been so fixed for the relevant day and that a particular sum in sterling has been so fixed for a day which is the last day for which a sum has been so fixed before the relevant day,

shall be conclusive evidence of those matters for the purposes of this Chapter.

(5) The Secretary of State may by order make such amendments of this section and Part I of Schedule 5 as appear to him to be appropriate for the purpose of giving effect to the entry into force of any amendment of the provisions set out in that Schedule.

(6) Any document purporting to be such a certificate as is mentioned in subsection (2) or (4)(b) above shall, in any legal proceedings, be received in evidence and, unless the contrary is proved, be deemed to be such a certificate.

DEFINITIONS

"Fund, the": s.172(1)(c).
"Fund Convention, the": s.172(1)(b).
"Liability Convention, the": ss.172(1)(a) and 152(1).
"relevant day, the": subs. (4)(a)(i).
"Secretary of State": Interpretation Act 1978, Sched. 1.
"Treasury, the": Interpretation Act 1978, Sched. 1.

GENERAL NOTE

[Derivation: Merchant Shipping Act 1974, s.4A; Merchant Shipping Act 1988, Sched. 4, Pt. II, para. 17(5).]

Section 176 deals with the limitation of liability of the 1992 International Oil Pollution Compensation Fund (IOPC Fund) and represents a major change to the limits of liability available under Sched. 4, s.176 (*i.e.* those under the 1971 Fund Convention). Section 176 sets out a new Sched. 5, Pt. I which contains the text of the 1992 Fund Convention, Art. 4. The amount of compensation payable by the 1992 IOPC Fund is increased so that, in aggregate with liability under the 1992 Liability Convention, it is not to exceed 135 million special drawing rights (SDR) (about £121.5 million) which is approximately twice the current limit. There is also provision for the limit to be 200 million SDR (about £180 million) once three states become party which make a large contribution to the Fund. At present, Japan is by far the largest contributor to the 1971 IOPC Fund, but Japan's contributions are pegged for the first few years of the 1992 IOPC Fund. Interest which has accrued on a fund constituted under the 1992 Liability Convention is not included in the 1992 IOPC Fund's limit. Under Art. 4(e) (in Sched. 5, Pt. I) the date of conversion of the SDR into sterling shall be on the day that the Fund's Assembly resolves to be the first date of compensation. If the IMF had not fixed an exchange rate for that particular day a court will look to the last day on which a rate was fixed. A Treasury certificate as to the rate will be conclusive (see subs. (4)(b)). There is also power under subs. (5) for the Secretary of State to increase the limits in Sched. 5 where the 1992 Fund Convention is amended. Like the 1992 Liability Protocol, Art. 15 (see s.157(2), above) the 1992 Fund Protocol, Art. 35 allows the tacit amendment of the limitation amounts.

Supplemental

Jurisdiction and effect of judgments

177.—(1) Paragraph 1(1)(d) of Schedule 1 to the Administration of Justice Act 1956 (Admiralty jurisdiction in claims for damage done by ships) shall be construed as extending to any claim in respect of a liability falling on the Fund under this Chapter; and the Admiralty jurisdiction of the Court of Session shall extend to any case arising out of any such claim.

(2) Where in accordance with rules of court made for the purposes of this subsection the Fund has been given notice of proceedings brought against an owner or guarantor in respect of liability under section 153, any judgment given in the proceedings shall, after it has become final and enforceable, become binding upon the Fund in the sense that the facts and evidence in the judgment may not be disputed by the Fund even if the Fund has not intervened in the proceedings.

(3) Where a person incurs a liability under the law of a Fund Convention country corresponding to Chapter III of this Part for damage which is partly in the territory of the United Kingdom, subsection (2) above shall, for the purpose of proceedings under this Chapter, apply with any necessary modifications to a judgment in proceedings under that law of the said country.

(4) Subject to subsection (5) below, Part I of the Foreign Judgments (Reciprocal Enforcement) Act 1933 shall apply, whether or not it would so apply apart from this subsection, to any judgment given by a court in a Fund Convention country to enforce a claim in respect of liability incurred under any provision corresponding to section 175; and in its application to such a judgment the said Part I shall have effect with the omission of sections 4(2) and (3).

(5) No steps shall be taken to enforce such a judgment unless and until the court in which it is registered under Part I of the Act of 1933 gives leave to enforce it; and—

(a) that leave shall not be given unless and until the Fund notifies the court either that the amount of the claim is not to be reduced under paragraph 4 of Article 4 of the Fund Convention (as set out in Part I of Schedule 5 to this Act) or that it is to be reduced to a specified amount; and

(b) in the latter case, the judgment shall be enforceable only for the reduced amount.

DEFINITIONS
   "Act, this": s.316(1).
   "damage": s.181(1).
   "Fund, the": s.172(1)(c).
   "Fund Convention, the": s.172(1)(b).
   "Fund Convention country": s.172(1)(d).
   "guarantor": s.181(1).
   "owner": s.181(1).
   "person": s.173(6).
   "rules of court": Interpretation Act 1978, Sched. 1.
   "territory": ss.170(4) and 181(3).
   "United Kingdom": Interpretation Act 1978, Sched. 1.

GENERAL NOTE
   [Derivation: Merchant Shipping Act 1974, s.6; Supreme Court Act 1981, Sched. 5.]
   Cf. s.166, above.

Extinguishment of claims

178.—(1) No action to enforce a claim against the Fund under this Chapter shall be entertained by a court in the United Kingdom unless—
    (a) the action is commenced, or
    (b) a third party notice of an action to enforce a claim against the owner or his guarantor in respect of the same damage is given to the Fund,
not later than three years after the claim against the Fund arose.

In this subsection "third party notice" means a notice of the kind described in section 177(2) and (3).

(2) No action to enforce a claim against the Fund under this Chapter shall be entertained by a court in the United Kingdom unless the action is commenced not later than six years after the occurrence, or first of the occurrences, resulting in the discharge or escape, or (as the case may be) in the relevant threat of contamination, by reason of which the claim against the Fund arose.

DEFINITIONS
    "discharge or escape": s.181(1) and (2).
    "Fund, the": s.172(1)(c).
    "guarantor": s.181(1).
    "owner": s.181(1).
    "relevant threat of contamination": s.181(1).
    "third party notice": subs. (1).
    "United Kingdom": Interpretation Act 1978, Sched. 1.

GENERAL NOTE
    [Derivation: Merchant Shipping Act 1974, s.7(1) and (2); Merchant Shipping Act 1988, Sched. 4, Pt. II, para. 20(a).]
    Section 178 sets out the International Oil Pollution Compensation Fund's three year time bar. It is to be noticed that this period operates in a similar way to that in s.162, but the claim will be extinguished unless the claimant takes the action in subs. (1). In the aftermath of a number of cases under the 1971 Fund Convention, *e.g. The Haven* (1991) and *The Braer* (1993), there were complicated negotiations involving claimants, shipowners, P & I Clubs and the IOPC Fund. In a number of instances, claims had been presented and discussed, but quantum had not been settled. In such cases the claimants believed that they did not have to face the time bar but the Fund took the view that it was not liable. In *The Haven*, claimants may have been deceived by the fact that there were limitation of liability proceedings brought by the shipowner (not the Fund). In *The Aegean Sea* (1992) the Fund had established a local claims office and some claimants assumed that as they had told the office of the claims that the Fund had notice. The Fund took the view that it was obliged to operate the Convention provisions, which appear to operate to extinguish the claim and not simply to bar it. As the 1992 Fund Convention (and the 1971 Fund Convention) only operates through national law, there is still room to argue that the time-limit may have been waived by the Fund or that the Fund is estopped from relying on it. It is submitted that a court should be extremely reluctant to tamper in this way with an internationally agreed regime, where it is absolutely vital that the Fund should know when it has received all claims. The existence of the limitation of liability means that in a case such as *The Braer* where the claims may exceed the limits of liability, the Fund would have to pro rate claimants on a speculative basis if it were not able to rely on the time bar. It might also be noted that the Fund has produced two booklets in 1995, one giving general information and the other being a Claims Manual.

Subrogation

179.—(1) In respect of any sum paid by the Fund as compensation for pollution damage the Fund shall acquire by subrogation any rights in respect of the damage which the recipient has (or but for the payment would have) against any other person.

(2) In respect of any sum paid by a public authority in the United Kingdom as compensation for pollution damage, that authority shall acquire by subrogation any rights which the recipient has against the Fund under this Chapter.

DEFINITIONS
"damage": s.181(1).
"Fund, the": s.172(1)(c).
"person": Interpretation Act 1978, Sched. 1.
"pollution damage": s.181(1).
"United Kingdom": Interpretation Act 1978, Sched. 1.

GENERAL NOTE
[Derivation: Merchant Shipping Act 1974, s.8; Merchant Shipping (Salvage and Pollution) Act 1994, s.7(1).]

Under Art. 9 of the 1971 Convention (Sched. 4, s.179) the International Oil Pollution Compensation Fund (IOPC Fund) has rights of subrogation against the defaulting shipowner or its insurer. It also has subrogation rights against other persons, *e.g.* those rights of the shipowner against a third party ship which caused or contributed to a collision which resulted in the pollution damage.

It became apparent by 1994 that the scheme of settling oil pollution claims set out in the 1969 and 1971 Conventions had not worked in practice in the way the drafters may strictly have imagined when producing a two-tier system of liability. The formal scheme envisaged a claimant suing a shipowner under the 1969 Liability Convention and then suing the IOPC Fund under the 1971 Fund Convention. It assumed that the interests of the shipowner and the Fund would conflict. In practice, the shipowners' liability insurers, the P & I Clubs, and the Secretariat of the Fund have worked very closely together in handling claims. They have recognised that there may be many common interests and that much time and expense can be saved if they co-ordinate their responses to claimants. This fact is recognised in the IOPC Fund's *Claims Manual* (4th ed., 1995), p.9, which states that the "IOPC Fund co-operates closely with the P & I Clubs in the settlement of claims. The P & I Club concerned and the IOPC Fund usually jointly investigate the incident and assess the damage." In the event of a major casualty, such as that to the *Braer* in 1993, it will quickly become apparent that there will be liability falling on both the P & I Club and the IOPC Fund. Both will endeavour to settle claims out of court. In many cases the IOPC Fund is able to start paying claims very quickly indeed. In the case of the *Braer* some payments were being made within days of the casualty. Whatever criticisms may be made of the system, it has many advantages over the alternative of suing in tort—which is what some of the victims of the 1978 *Amoco Cadiz* disaster attempted in the USA. Some of the claims are still being litigated. It should be noted that where the 1992 Liability Convention applies, the separate right to sue in tort is removed (see s.156, above).

The problem which arose in 1994 was that the Merchant Shipping (Oil Pollution) Act 1971, s.8 did not give a right of recourse where the Fund paid a claim *before* the shipowner had been found liable and had limited its liability. This was because of the wording of s.8(3) which only gave the right against third parties where the shipowner had "paid" the appropriate sum. It might be added that this problem arose entirely out of the drafting of the 1971 Act and not from the words of Art. 9 of the Convention. It provides a further example of why it was poor practice to attempt to rewrite the Convention into "legal English" (see the General Note to Chapter III of this Part of the Act, above). In this case, the broad language of the Convention was reduced to the over-technical language of some U.K. statutes. While it is fair to say that the drafter would not have been instructed to consider the particular problem, and that the Convention does not deal with the point explicitly, the message must be that it is better to leave the international instrument as it was negotiated. After the *Braer* incident, salmon farmers and others were compensated quickly by the IOPC Fund, although it was under no obligation to do so, but its rights of recourse were questioned.

Accordingly, s.8 of the Merchant Shipping (Oil Pollution) Act 1971 (now Sched. 4, s.179) was amended by the repeal of the offending subs. (3) and by rewording subs. (1) so as to allow the Fund to acquire by subrogation rights which the recipient (*e.g.* the pollution victim) has, for example, against a wrongdoing shipowner. Under s.179 of Chapter III, if the IOPC Fund settles the whole of the victim's claim, including those parts for which the shipowner would be liable under the Liability Convention, it is entitled now to recoup that first tier of liability from the shipowner by subrogation. The right of subrogation can now be "exercised irrespective of when payment was made" (Ms. J Whalley, moving the new section at Third Reading in the Commons, *Hansard*, H.C. Vol. 241, col. 571).

Supplementary provisions as to proceedings involving the Fund

180.—(1) Any proceedings by or against the Fund may either be instituted by or against the Fund in its own name or be instituted by or against the Director of the Fund as the Fund's representative.

(2) Evidence of any instrument issued by any organ of the Fund or of any document in the custody of the Fund, or any entry in or extract from such a document, may be given in any legal proceedings by production of a copy certified as a true copy by an official of the Fund; and any document purporting to be such a copy shall, in any such proceedings, be received in evidence without proof of the official position or handwriting of the person signing the certificate.

<small>DEFINITIONS</small>
"Fund, the": s.172(1)(c).
"person": Interpretation Act 1978, Sched. 1.

<small>GENERAL NOTE</small>
[Derivation: Merchant Shipping Act 1974, s.8A; Merchant Shipping Act 1988, Sched. 4, Pt. II, para. 22.]
Section 180 re-enacts s.8A of the Merchant Shipping Act 1974 and gives locus standi to the Fund or its Director and allows for officials of the Fund to certify documents for evidentiary purposes.

Interpretation

181.—(1) In this Chapter, unless the context otherwise requires—
"damage" includes loss;
"discharge or escape", in relation to pollution damage, means the discharge or escape of oil from the ship;
"guarantor" means any person providing insurance or other financial security to cover the owner's liability of the kind described in section 163;
"incident" means any occurrence, or series of occurrences having the same origin, resulting in a discharge or escape of oil from a ship or in a relevant threat of contamination;
"oil", except in sections 173 and 174, means persistent hydrocarbon mineral oil;
"owner" means the person or persons registered as the owner of the ship or, in the absence of registration, the person or persons owning the ship, except that, in relation to a ship owned by a State which is operated by a person registered as the ship's operator, it means the person registered as its operator;
"pollution damage" means—
    (a) damage caused outside a ship by contamination resulting from a discharge or escape of oil from the ship,
    (b) the cost of preventive measures, and
    (c) further damage caused by preventive measures,
but does not include any damage attributable to any impairment of the environment except to the extent that any such damage consists of—
    (i) any loss of profits, or
    (ii) the cost of any reasonable measures of reinstatement actually taken or to be taken;
"preventive measures" means any reasonable measures taken by any person to prevent or minimise pollution damage, being measures taken—
    (a) after an incident has occurred, or
    (b) in the case of an incident consisting of a series of occurrences, after the first of those occurrences;
"relevant threat of contamination" means a grave and imminent threat of damage being caused outside a ship by contamination resulting from a discharge or escape of oil from the ship; and
"ship" means any ship (within the meaning of Chapter III of this Part) to which section 153 applies.

(2) For the purposes of this Chapter—

(a) references to a discharge or escape of oil from a ship are references to such a discharge or escape wherever it may occur, and whether it is of oil carried in a cargo tank or of oil carried in a bunker fuel tank; and

(b) where more than one discharge or escape results from the same occurrence or from a series of occurrences having the same origin, they shall be treated as one.

(3) References in this Chapter to the territory of any country shall be construed in accordance with section 170(4) reading the reference to a Liability Convention country as a reference to a Fund Convention country.

DEFINITIONS

"damage": subs. (1).
"discharge or escape": subss. (1) and (2).
"Fund Convention country": s.172(1)(d).
"guarantor": subs. (1).
"incident": subs. (1).
"Liability Convention country": s.152(1).
"oil": subs. (1) and ss.173 and 174.
"owner": subs. (1).
"person": Interpretation Act 1978, Sched. 1.
"pollution damage": subs. (1).
"preventive measures": subs. (1).
"registered": ss.23(1) and 313(1).
"relevant threat of contamination": subs. (1).
"ship": subs. (1) and s.153.
"territory": subs. (3) and s.170(4).

GENERAL NOTE

[Derivation: Merchant Shipping Act 1974, s.1(3), (4), (5) and (6); Merchant Shipping Act 1988, Sched. 4, Pt. II, para. 15; Merchant Shipping Act 1971, s.20(3); Merchant Shipping Act 1988, Sched. 4, Pt. II, para. 14.]

Section 181 contains the definitions for Chapter IV. The 1992 Fund Convention provisions have meant that there are new definitions, in s.181, of oil, pollution damage, preventive measures, relevant threat of contamination, and ship.

Transitory text of this Chapter and power to make transitional provisions

182.—(1) Until such day as the Secretary of State may by order appoint the provisions set out in Schedule 4 as Chapter IV shall have effect instead of the foregoing provisions of this Chapter; and references in that Schedule to a section whose number is included in that Schedule is a reference to the section so included.

(2) Notwithstanding subsection (1) above, Her Majesty may by Order in Council make such provision as appears to Her Majesty to be appropriate in connection with the implementation of any transitional provisions contained in the 1992 Protocol or the Conventions which they amend; and any such Order may in particular provide, in relation to occurrences of any description specified in the Order—

(a) for specified provisions of this Chapter, whether as contained in this Chapter or in the Chapter IV set out in Schedule 4, to have effect;

(b) for any such provisions to have effect subject to specified modifications.

(3) In subsection (2) above—

"the 1992 Protocol" means the Protocol of 1992 to amend the International Convention on the Establishment of an International Fund for Compensation for Oil Pollution Damage 1971 signed in London on 27th November 1992; and

"specified" means specified in the Order.

DEFINITIONS
"1992 Protocol, the": subs. (3).
"Secretary of State": Interpretation Act 1978, Sched. 1.
"specified": subs. (3).

GENERAL NOTE
[Derivation: Merchant Shipping Act 1994, ss.5(1), (3), (4) and 10(3).]
See the General Note to Chapter III of this Part of the Act, above, for an explanation of the transitional provisions in ss.171 and 182.

PART VII

LIABILITY OF SHIPOWNERS AND OTHERS

Carriage of passengers and luggage by sea

Scheduled convention to have force of law

183.—(1) The provisions of the Convention relating to the Carriage of Passengers and their Luggage by Sea as set out in Part I of Schedule 6 (hereafter in this section and in Part II of that Schedule referred to as "the Convention") shall have the force of law in the United Kingdom.

(2) The provisions of Part II of that Schedule shall have effect in connection with the Convention and subsection (1) above shall have effect subject to the provisions of that Part.

(3) If it appears to Her Majesty in Council that there is a conflict between the provisions of this section or of Part I or II of Schedule 6 and any provisions relating to the carriage of passengers or luggage for reward by land, sea or air in—

(a) any convention which has been signed or ratified by or on behalf of the government of the United Kingdom before 4th April 1979 (excluding the Convention); or

(b) any enactment of the Parliament of the United Kingdom giving effect to such a convention,

She may by Order in Council make such modifications of this section or that Schedule or any such enactment as She considers appropriate for resolving the conflict.

(4) If it appears to Her Majesty in Council that the government of the United Kingdom has agreed to any revision of the Convention She may by Order in Council make such modification of Parts I and II of Schedule 6 as She considers appropriate in consequence of the revision.

(5) Nothing in subsection (1) or (2) above or in any modification made by virtue of subsection (3) or (4) above shall affect any rights or liabilities arising out of an occurrence which took place before the day on which the said subsection (1) or (2) above, or as the case may be, the modification, comes into force.

(6) This section shall bind the Crown, and any Order in Council made by virtue of this section may provide that the Order or specified provisions of it shall bind the Crown.

(7) A draft of an Order in Council proposed to be made under subsection (3) or (4) above shall not be submitted to Her Majesty in Council unless the draft has been approved by a resolution of each House of Parliament.

DEFINITIONS
"carriage": Sched. 6, Art. 1(8).
"Convention, the": subs. (1).
"luggage": Sched. 6, Art. 1(5).
"passenger": Sched. 6, Art. 1(4).
"United Kingdom": Interpretation Act 1978, Sched. 1.

GENERAL NOTE
[Derivation: Merchant Shipping Act 1979, ss.14(1), (2), (4)–(7) and 15(2).]

Section 183 (formerly the Merchant Shipping Act 1979, s.14) gives the force of law to the Athens Convention Relating to the Carriage of Passengers and their Luggage by Sea 1974 (the Athens Convention 1974). The Convention entered into force internationally in 1987, but the U.K. gave it interim national effect under s.16 of the Merchant Shipping Act 1979. The Athens Convention 1974 operates in a similar manner to other international transport Conventions, such as the Warsaw Convention governing air transport. It does not lay down all the rights and obligations which might arise under the contract of carriage. It is principally concerned with death and injury to passengers and the loss of their luggage. Disputes about the facilities offered in a cruise holiday, or the promises made in a travel brochure are outside the Convention (and *cf.* the E.C. Directive on Package Holidays 1990/314, as enacted in the Package Travel, Package Holidays and Package Tours Regulations 1992 (S.I. 1992 No. 3288)). Its main object, from the standpoint of U.K. law, was to outlaw certain standard clauses which carriers commonly inserted in their tickets, such as exclusions for death or injury and onerous jurisdiction clauses. It also provided a system of liability whereby the carrier had to disprove negligence in defined circumstances such as shipwrecks. The Athens Convention 1974 has been overtaken somewhat by developments elsewhere in the law. For instance, the Unfair Contract Terms Act 1977, s.2 outlawed some of the more extreme exclusions clauses (and see also the EC Directive on Unfair Terms in Consumer Contracts 1993 and the Unfair Terms in Consumer Contracts Regulations 1994 (S.I. 1994 No. 3159)). The continued application of the Convention in the U.K. may now be somewhat controversial as a number of well-publicised disasters have indicated that it may work seriously to the disadvantage of consumers. The most serious drawback of the Convention is its granting to the carrier of a right to limit liability to a very low figure, per passenger claimant. After the *Zeebrugge* disaster in 1987, it became apparent that the limits of liability were far too low and a 1990 Protocol was agreed which would have increased the limits, albeit to figures which were well below the likely losses from a fatality to a person with dependants.

In the pre-consolidation enactments (such as the Merchant Shipping (Salvage and Pollution) Act 1994) the opportunity was not taken to ratify the 1990 Protocol to the Athens Convention 1974. However, there are moves to revise global passenger limits through amendments to the 1976 Limitation Convention (see s.185 and Sched. 7, below), scheduled for debate at a Diplomatic Conference in April 1996. It may be that the Government is waiting on such developments at the IMO, but it is to be regretted that it was not possible to provide for ratification of the 1990 Protocol in the meantime. There are now strong grounds for considering whether the U.K. ought to denounce the Convention because of the way it may operate against consumers.

The detailed provisions of the Convention are set out in Sched. 6. Schedule 6, Pt. I contains the relevant articles of the Convention and Pt. II contains the necessary modifications to make the Convention operate in U.K. law. The two parts of the Schedule must be read together (see generally *Chorley and Giles, Shipping Law*, at pp.329–335).

Application of Schedule 6 to carriage within British Islands

184.—(1) Her Majesty may by Order in Council provide that Part I of Schedule 6—

(a) shall have the force of law in the United Kingdom, with such modifications as are specified in the Order, in relation to, and to matters connected with, a contract of carriage where the places of departure and destination under the contract are within the British Islands and under the contract there is no intermediate port of call outside those Islands; and

(b) shall, as modified in pursuance of paragraph (a) above, have effect in relation to, and to matters connected with, any such contract subject to the provisions of Part II of that Schedule or to those provisions with such modifications as are specified in the Order.

(2) An Order in Council made by virtue of subsection (1) above may contain such provisions, including provisions modifying section 28 of the Unfair Contract Terms Act 1977 (which relates to certain contracts as respects which the Convention mentioned in section 183(1) does not have the force of law in the United Kingdom), as the Secretary of State considers appropriate for the purpose of dealing with matters arising in connection with any contract to which the said section 28 applies before the Order is made.

(3) An Order in Council made by virtue of subsection (1) above may provide that the Order or specified provisions of it shall bind the Crown.

(4) A draft of an Order in Council proposed to be made by virtue of subsection (1) above shall not be submitted to Her Majesty in Council unless the draft of the Order in Council has been approved by a resolution of each House of Parliament.

(5) In subsection (1) above expressions to which meanings are assigned by article 1 of the Convention set out in Part I of Schedule 6 have those meanings but any reference to a contract of carriage excludes such a contract which is not for reward.

DEFINITIONS
"British Islands": Interpretation Act 1978, Sched. 1.
"contract of carriage": subs. (5).
"Convention, the": s.183(1).
"United Kingdom": Interpretation Act 1978, Sched. 1.

GENERAL NOTE
[Derivation: Merchant Shipping Act 1979, s.16.]
Section 184 re-enacts s.16 of the Merchant Shipping Act 1979, with the exception of what was subs. (1) of s.16 (which became redundant when the Convention entered into force internationally). The present s.184 allows an Order to be made extending the operation of the Athens Convention 1974 to U.K. domestic traffic. The Carriage of Passengers and their Luggage by Sea (Domestic Carriage) Order 1987 (S.I. 1987 No. 670) did extend the operation of the Convention, with some modifications, to journeys within the U.K., *e.g.* from England to the Channel Islands.

Limitation of liability of shipowners, etc. and salvors for maritime claims

Limitation of liability for maritime claims

185.—(1) The provisions of the Convention on Limitation of Liability for Maritime Claims 1976 as set out in Part I of Schedule 7 (in this section and Part II of that Schedule referred to as "the Convention") shall have the force of law in the United Kingdom.

(2) The provisions of Part II of that Schedule shall have effect in connection with the Convention, and subsection (1) above shall have effect subject to the provisions of that Part.

(3) The provisions having the force of law under this section shall apply in relation to Her Majesty's ships as they apply in relation to other ships.

(4) The provisions having the force of law under this section shall not apply to any liability in respect of loss of life or personal injury caused to, or loss of or damage to any property of, a person who is on board the ship in question or employed in connection with that ship or with the salvage operations in question if—

    (a) he is so on board or employed under a contract of service governed by the law of any part of the United Kingdom; and

    (b) the liability arises from an occurrence which took place after the commencement of this Act.

In this subsection, "ship" and "salvage operations" have the same meaning as in the Convention.

DEFINITIONS
"Act, this": s.316(1).
"commencement": Interpretation Act 1978, Sched. 1.
"Convention, the": subs. (1).
"person": Interpretation Act 1978, Sched. 1.
"salvage operations": Sched. 7, Art. 1(3).
"ship": Sched. 7, Part II, para. 12.
"United Kingdom": Interpretation Act 1978, Sched. 1.

GENERAL NOTE
[Derivation: Merchant Shipping Act 1979, ss.17, 35(2); Sched. 5, para 3.]
Section 185 re-enacts s.17 of the Merchant Shipping Act 1979 and gives the force of law to the

Convention on Limitation of Liability for Maritime Claims 1976 (the 1976 Limitation Convention) as set out in Sched. 7, below. Limitation of liability is a concept long known to maritime law (see *Chorley and Giles, Shipping Law*, Chapter 22, N. Gaskell (ed.), *Limitation of Shipowners Liability: The New Law*, (1986)). At various times it has been justified on the basis that it encourages trade and enterprise and that it is necessary in order to be able to obtain realistic and effective liability insurance cover. It is the last justification which has most credence today. The limitation under consideration here is sometimes referred to as "global" because it is designed to deal with disasters where the owner faces claims from a variety of different sources and seeks to create one overall maximum limit in relation to them. This type of limitation of liability provision contrasts with those which might apply in individual contracts, *e.g.* with passengers (see the Athens Convention 1974 and s.183, above) and cargo owners (see the Hague-Visby Rules, as enacted in the Carriage of Goods by Sea Act 1971). The limits under the 1976 Limitation Convention are not really global in that there may be separate limits for special regimes, *e.g.* for oil pollution (see for example s.157, above).

The earliest limitation of liability statutes were based on the value of the vessel. The justification was that a shipowner would know that its maximum liability was the value of its investment in the risk-creating vessel. In the last century, the U.K. Merchant Shipping Acts (culminating in the 1894 Act, s.503) based the limits on the size, rather than the value, of a ship. There have been a number of attempts to achieve international uniformity, with Conventions in 1924 and 1957. The 1976 Limitation Convention, which entered into force in 1986, is the most recent, although it is expected that its limitation levels will be increased by a Protocol to be discussed at a diplomatic conference in April 1996. There is also the Strasbourg Convention on Limitation of Liability in Internal Navigation 1988, which is similar in form to the 1976 Limitation Convention, but the U.K. is not a party to it.

As with the Athens Convention 1974, dealt with by s.183 above, the detailed provisions of the 1976 Limitation Convention are set out in a Schedule. Schedule 7, Pt. I contains the relevant articles of the Convention and Pt. II contains the necessary modifications to make the Convention operate in U.K. law. The two parts of the Schedule must be read together.

Subsection (4) re-enacts s.35 of the Merchant Shipping Act 1979 and effectively exercises the option given by Art. 3(e) of the 1976 Limitation Convention (see Sched. 7, Pt. I), by providing that there shall be no limitation of liability for employment claims, *e.g.* by a crew member against his shipowner employer, but the contract of service must be governed by U.K. law. In the much more likely event that the employment contract is governed by some other law (*e.g.* that of Korea) it will be necessary to see if there is an equivalent provision in that legal system. In its absence the shipowner will be entitled to limit for crew claims.

For the limitation of liability of harbour and dock owners, see s.191, below.

For the application of ss.185–190 to the Crown, see s.192, below.

Exclusion of liability

186.—(1) Subject to subsection (3) below, the owner of a United Kingdom ship shall not be liable for any loss or damage in the following cases, namely—

(a) where any property on board the ship is lost or damaged by reason of fire on board the ship; or

(b) where any gold, silver, watches, jewels or precious stones on board the ship are lost or damaged by reason of theft, robbery or other dishonest conduct and their nature and value were not at the time of shipment declared by their owner or shipper to the owner or master of the ship in the bill of lading or otherwise in writing.

(2) Subject to subsection (3) below, where the loss or damage arises from anything done or omitted by any person in his capacity of master or member of the crew or (otherwise than in that capacity) in the course of his employment as a servant of the owner of the ship, subsection (1) above shall also exclude the liability of—

(a) the master, member of the crew or servant; and

(b) in a case where the master or member of the crew is the servant of a person whose liability would not be excluded by that subsection apart from this paragraph, the person whose servant he is.

(3) This section does not exclude the liability of any person for any loss or damage resulting from any such personal act or omission of his as is mentioned in Article 4 of the Convention set out in Part I of Schedule 7.

(4) This section shall apply in relation to Her Majesty's ships as it applies in relation to other ships.

(5) In this section "owner", in relation to a ship, includes any part owner and any charterer, manager or operator of the ship.

DEFINITIONS
  "Convention, the": s.185(1).
  "master": s.313(1).
  "owner": subs. (5).
  "person": Interpretation Act 1978, Sched. 1.
  "ship": s.185(4) and Sched. 7, Pt. II, para. 12.
  "United Kingdom ship": ss.1(3) and 313(1).
  "writing": Interpretation Act 1978, Sched. 1.

GENERAL NOTE
  [Derivation: Merchant Shipping Act 1979, s.18; Merchant Shipping (Registration, etc.) Act 1993, Sched. 4, para. 6(1).]
  Section 186 re-enacts s.18 of the Merchant Shipping Act 1979 and can trace its immediate lineage back to the Merchant Shipping Act 1894, s.502. The section provides a special defence to owners of U.K. ships, by exempting them from liability for fire damage (*e.g.* to cargo) or for the loss of valuable items such as jewellery, which have not been declared by their owner. The rationale for the section is that it would be unfair to make the shipowner liable for highly expensive cargo when there is no opportunity to charge extra freight. There are broadly equivalent provisions in the Hague and Hague-Visby Rules, although the respective provisions differ in their scope and application.
  One significant change brought about when the Merchant Shipping Act 1979, s.18 was enacted was that the test for breaking the right of exclusion was taken from Art. 4 of the 1976 Limitation Convention in place of the old "actual fault or privity" test which existed in the 1894 Act, s.502. The difference in the tests has been touched on in the General Note to s.157, above.
  Note that the benefit of s.186 can extend beyond the registered shipowner and can include charterers and managers (see subs. (5) and *cf.* Art. 1 of the 1976 Limitation Convention in Sched. 7, below).
  For the application of ss.185–190 to the Crown, see s.192, below.

Multiple fault; apportionment, liability and contribution

Damage or loss: apportionment of liability

187.—(1) Where, by the fault of two or more ships, damage or loss is caused to one or more of those ships, to their cargoes or freight, or to any property on board, the liability to make good the damage or loss shall be in proportion to the degree in which each ship was in fault.

(2) If, in any such case, having regard to all the circumstances, it is not possible to establish different degrees of fault, the liability shall be apportioned equally.

(3) This section applies to persons other than the owners of a ship who are responsible for the fault of the ships, as well as to the owners of a ship and where, by virtue of any charter or demise, or for any other reason, the owners are not responsible for the navigation and management of the ship, this section applies to the charterers or other persons for the time being so responsible instead of the owners.

(4) Nothing in this section shall operate so as to render any ship liable for any loss or damage to which the fault of the ship has not contributed.

(5) Nothing in this section shall affect the liability of any person under a contract of carriage or any contract, or shall be construed as imposing any liability upon any person from which he is exempted by any contract or by any provision of law, or as affecting the right of any person to limit his liability in the manner provided by law.

(6) In this section "freight" includes passage money and hire.

(7) In this section references to damage or loss caused by the fault of a ship include references to any salvage or other expenses, consequent upon that fault, recoverable at law by way of damages.

DEFINITIONS
    "contract of carriage": s.184(5).
    "damage or loss caused by the fault of a ship": subs. (7).
    "freight": subs. (6).
    "owner": subs. (3).
    "person": Interpretation Act 1978, Sched. 1.
    "salvage": s.255(1).
    "ship": s.313(1).

GENERAL NOTE
    [Derivation: Maritime Conventions Act 1911, ss.1 and 9(4).]
    The Collision Convention 1910 was enacted in the Maritime Conventions Act 1911 and ss.188–190 re-enact the substantial provisions of that Act. Prior to the 1910 Convention, the Admiralty Court applied a rule of divided damages in collision cases, whereby respective liabilities for fault were not distinguished and where liability was apportioned equally whatever the degree of fault of each vessel. The Convention abolished that rule and substituted the rule of proportionate fault which is now found in s.187 (formerly s.1 of the Maritime Conventions Act 1911).
    Under s.187, the proportionate fault rule will be applied to the ships at fault in a collision and to the cargoes on board those ships, no matter how "innocent" one might consider the cargo (*The Milan* (1861) Lush 388). As to the meaning of fault and the situation when more than one ship is at fault, see *Miraflores v. Livanos (George) (Owners)* [1967] 1 A.C. 826, *Eglantine, Credo & Inez, The* [1990] 2 Lloyd's Rep. 390. For recent examples of apportionment, see *The Mancunium* [1987] 2 Lloyd's Rep. 627, *The Iran Torab* [1988] 2 Lloyd's Rep. 38, *Christian Salvesen and Christian Salvesen (Shipping) v. Cory Lighterage and Wm. Cory; General VII, The* [1990] 2 Lloyd's Rep. 1. Where a wholly innocent ship is damaged by the fault of two others, the section does not apply and so the ordinary rules of joint tortfeasorship would allow the innocent ship to recover all of its damages against either or both wrongdoers. This curious result is certainly contrary to the Convention and it has never been clear whether the difference was deliberate. It arises out of the use of the words "fault of two or more ships … caused to one or more of *those* ships" (emphasis added) and it is interesting that the Australian enactment of an equivalent provision misses out the last seven words so as to give full effect to the Convention. This may be another example of the defects of redrafting Conventions into legal English.
    The section does not create liabilities or raise any presumptions of fault: a plaintiff would have to prove negligence and causation in the ordinary way. See generally *Chorley and Giles, Shipping Law*, at pp. 382–386; H Brandon, "Apportionment in British Courts", (1977) Tul. L. Rev. 1025; K. McGuffie (ed.), *Marsden: Collisions at Sea*, Chapter 5.
    For the application of ss.185–190 to the Crown, see s.192, below.

Loss of life or personal injuries: joint and several liability

188.—(1) Where loss of life or personal injuries are suffered by any person on board a ship owing to the fault of that ship and of any other ship or ships, the liability of the owners of the ships shall be joint and several.

(2) Subsection (3) of section 187 applies also to this section.

(3) Nothing in this section shall be construed as depriving any person of any right of defence on which, apart from this section, he might have relied in an action brought against him by the person injured, or any person or persons entitled to sue in respect of such loss of life, or shall affect the right of any person to limit his liability in the manner provided by law.

(4) Subsection (7) of section 187 applies also for the interpretation of this section.

DEFINITIONS
    "owner": s.187(3).
    "person": Interpretation Act 1978, Sched. 1.
    "ship": s.313(1).

GENERAL NOTE
[Derivation: Maritime Conventions Act 1911, ss.1(2), 2 and 9(4).
The proportionate fault rule in s.187 is not applied in the case of loss of life or personal injury claims, where the joint and several liability principle prevails to the advantage of the victim.
For the application of ss.185–190 to the Crown, see s.192, below.

Loss of life or personal injuries: right of contribution

189.—(1) Where loss of life or personal injuries are suffered by any person on board a ship owing to the fault of that ship and any other ship or ships, and a proportion of the damages is recovered against the owners of one of the ships which exceeds the proportion in which the ship was in fault, they may recover by way of contribution the amount of the excess from the owners of the other ship or ships to the extent to which those ships were respectively in fault.

(2) Subsection (3) of section 187 applies also to this section.

(3) Nothing in this section authorises the recovery of any amount which could not, by reason of any statutory or contractual limitation of, or exemption from, liability, or which could not for any other reason, have been recovered in the first instance as damages by the persons entitled to sue therefor.

(4) In addition to any other remedy provided by law, the persons entitled to any contribution recoverable under this section shall, for the purposes of recovering it, have the same rights and powers as the persons entitled to sue for damages in the first instance.

DEFINITIONS
"owner": s.187(3).
"person": Interpretation Act 1978, Sched. 1.
"ship": s.313(1).

GENERAL NOTE
[Derivation: Maritime Conventions Act 1911, ss.3 and 9(4).]
This section allows for there to be contribution between the joint tortfeasors held liable under s.188.
For the application of ss.185–190 to the Crown, see s.192, below.

Time limit for proceedings against owners or ship

Time limit for proceedings against owners or ship

190.—(1) This section applies to any proceedings to enforce any claim or lien against a ship or her owners—
  (a) in respect of damage or loss caused by the fault of that ship to another ship, its cargo or freight or any property on board it; or
  (b) for damages for loss of life or personal injury caused by the fault of that ship to any person on board another ship.

(2) The extent of the fault is immaterial for the purposes of this section.

(3) Subject to subsections (5) and (6) below, no proceedings to which this section applies shall be brought after the period of two years from the date when—
  (a) the damage or loss was caused; or
  (b) the loss of life or injury was suffered.

(4) Subject to subsections (5) and (6) below, no proceedings under any of sections 187 to 189 to enforce any contribution in respect of any overpaid proportion of any damages for loss of life or personal injury shall be brought after the period of one year from the date of payment.

(5) Any court having jurisdiction in such proceedings may, in accordance with rules of court, extend the period allowed for bringing proceedings to such extent and on such conditions as it thinks fit.

(6) Any such court, if satisfied that there has not been during any period allowed for bringing proceedings any reasonable opportunity of arresting the defendant ship within—
(a) the jurisdiction of the court, or
(b) the territorial sea of the country to which the plaintiff's ship belongs or in which the plaintiff resides or has his principal place of business,
shall extend the period allowed for bringing proceedings to an extent sufficient to give a reasonable opportunity of so arresting the ship.

DEFINITIONS
"freight": s.187(6).
"owner": s.187(3).
"person": Interpretation Act 1978, Sched. 1.
"rules of court": Interpretation Act 1978, Sched. 1.
"ship": s.313(1).

GENERAL NOTE
[Derivation: Maritime Conventions Act 1911, s.8; Crown Proceedings Act 1947, ss.30 and 38(2).]
Section 190 re-enacts s.8 of the Maritime Conventions Act 1911 and gives effect to the time-bar laid down in the Collision Convention 1910. Note that the Merchant Shipping (Salvage and Pollution) Act 1994 removed the references in the section to the salvage time-bar as that is now dealt with in Art. 23 of the 1989 Salvage Convention (see Sched. 11, Pt. I, below).
The time-bar in collision cases is two years. Note that the section applies to collisions between vessels. A collision between a vessel and a pier would not be covered by s.190 and the court would apply the ordinary six year period under the Limitation Act 1980. Note also that subs. (1)(b) refers to the time-bar applying to personal claims caused by the fault of that ship "to any person on board *another* ship". It follows that a crew claim against its own shipowner-employer does not fall within the section and the normal Limitation Act 1980 three year period would apply (see *The Niceto de Larringa* [1965] 2 All E.R. 930).
Those with little experience of maritime law may be caught out into thinking that the normal three year Limitation Act 1980 period would apply to all injury and death claims even if caused by a collision, but under s.190 the time-bar for injury and death is two years. This difference has led the courts to apply the proviso to s.190 (now subs. (5) and (6)), or to strain the rules of interpretation so as not to apply the section. See, *e.g. Curtis v. Wild* [1991] 4 All E.R. 172, *Steedman v. Scofield* [1992] 2 Lloyd's Rep. 163.
For the application of ss.185–190 to the Crown, see s.192, below.

Limitation of liability of harbour, conservancy, dock and canal authorities

Limitation of liability

191.—(1) This section applies in relation to the following authorities and persons, that is to say, a harbour authority, a conservancy authority and the owners of any dock or canal.
(2) The liability of any authority or person to which this section applies for any loss or damage caused to any ship, or to any goods, merchandise or other things whatsoever on board any ship shall be limited in accordance with subsection (5) below by reference to the tonnage of the largest United Kingdom ship which, at the time of the loss or damage is, or within the preceding five years has been, within the area over which the authority or person discharges any functions.
(3) The limitation of liability under this section relates to the whole of any losses and damages which may arise on any one distinct occasion, although such losses and damages may be sustained by more than one person, and shall apply whether the liability arises at common law or under any general or local or private Act, and notwithstanding anything contained in such an Act.

(4) This section does not exclude the liability of an authority or person to which it applies for any loss or damage resulting from any such personal act or omission of the authority or person as is mentioned in Article 4 of the Convention set out in Part I of Schedule 7.

(5) The limit of liability shall be ascertained by applying to the ship by reference to which the liability is to be determined the method of calculation specified in paragraph 1(b) of Article 6 of the Convention set out in Part I of Schedule 7 read with paragraph 5(1) and (2) of Part II of that Schedule.

(6) Articles 11 and 12 of that Convention and paragraphs 8 and 9 of Part II of that Schedule shall apply for the purposes of this section.

(7) For the purposes of subsection (2) above a ship shall not be treated as having been within the area over which a harbour authority or conservancy authority discharges any functions by reason only that it has been built or fitted out within the area, or that it has taken shelter within or passed through the area on a voyage between two places both situated outside that area, or that it has loaded or unloaded mails or passengers within the area.

(8) Nothing in this section imposes any liability for any loss or damage where no liability exists apart from this section.

(9) In this section—

"dock" includes wet docks and basins, tidal docks and basins, locks, cuts, entrances, dry docks, graving docks, gridirons, slips, quays, wharves, piers, stages, landing places and jetties; and

"owners of any dock or canal" includes any authority or person having the control and management of any dock or canal, as the case may be.

DEFINITIONS

"conservancy authority": s.313(1).
"dock": subs. (9).
"harbour authority": s.313(1).
"owners of any dock or canal": subs. (9).
"passenger": Sched. 6, Art.1(4).
"person": Interpretation Act 1978, Sched. 1.
"ship": s.185(4) and Sched. 7, Part II, para. 12.
"United Kingdom ship": ss.1(3) and 313(1).
"within the area": subs. (7).

GENERAL NOTE

[Derivation: Merchant Shipping (Liability of Shipowners and Others) Act 1900, s.2; Merchant Shipping Act 1979, Sched. 5, para. 1(1)–(3), s.50(4), Sched. 7, Pt. I and s.3.]

Section 191 re-enacts the somewhat curious s.2 of the Merchant Shipping (Liability of Ship-owners and Others) Act 1900, as amended by the Merchant Shipping Act 1979. This section exists independently of any Convention (see *Chorley and Giles, Shipping Law*, at pp. 407–8, 415). It enables the owners of docks, harbours and landing places (such as jetties, see subs. (9)) to limit their liabilities for property damage caused to vessels. It will be of use to ship repairers who damage the ship under repair. The method of calculating the limit is bizarre and certainly out-dated, given the fact that there may not be records of the U.K. ships which have visited in the last five years, as required by subs. (2). Subsections (4)–(6) otherwise align key provisions with those in the 1976 Limitation Convention. The section is not effective to protect employees of the dock company if the individual is sued directly (see *Mason v. Uxbridge Boat Centre and Wright* [1980] 2 Lloyd's Rep. 593). *Cf.* Art. 1.4 of the 1976 Limitation Convention (Sched. 7, Pt. 1, below).

Note also that pilots and pilotage authorities are entitled to limit their liabilities under the Pilotage Act 1987, s.22.

Application to Crown and its ships

Application to Crown and its ships

192.—(1) Sections 185, 186, 187, 188, 189 and 190 (except subsection (6)) apply in the case of Her Majesty's ships as they apply in relation to other ships and section 191 applies to the Crown in its capacity as an authority or person specified in subsection (1).

(2) In this section "Her Majesty's ships" means—
(a) ships of which the beneficial interest is vested in Her Majesty;
(b) ships which are registered as Government ships;
(c) ships which are for the time being demised or sub-demised to or in the exclusive possession of the Crown;
except that it does not include any ship in which Her Majesty is interested otherwise than in right of Her Government in the United Kingdom unless that ship is for the time being demised or sub-demised to Her Majesty in right of Her Government in the United Kingdom or in the exclusive possession of Her Majesty in that right.

(3) In the application of subsection (2) above to Northern Ireland, any reference to Her Majesty's Government in the United Kingdom includes a reference to Her Government in Northern Ireland.

DEFINITIONS
"Government ship": ss.308(4) and 313(1).
"Her Majesty's ships": subs. (2).
"person": Interpretation Act 1978, Sched. 1.
"registered": ss.23(1) and 313(1).
"ship": s.313(1).
"United Kingdom": Interpretation Act 1978, Sched. 1.

GENERAL NOTE
[Derivation: Crown Proceedings Act 1947, ss.5, 6, 7 and 30(1); Merchant Shipping Act 1979, Sched. 5, para. 3 and s.38(2); Crown Proceedings Order 1981 (S.I. 1981 No. 233).]
Section 192 deals with the application of ss.185–190 to the Crown.

PART VIII

LIGHTHOUSES

GENERAL NOTE
Provisions relating to lighthouses were originally contained in Pt. XI of the 1894 Act, and a number of amendments were made by the Merchant Shipping Act 1988 and the Merchant Shipping (Registration, etc.) Act 1993 in order to reflect changes to the organisation of lighthouse authorities and the funding of the lighthouse service through light dues.
Note also Scheds. 8 and 9, below.

Lighthouse authorities

General and local lighthouse authorities

193.—(1) For the purposes of this Part—
(a) the Trinity House, as respects England and Wales and the adjacent seas and islands,
(b) the Commissioners of Northern Lighthouses, as respects Scotland and the adjacent seas and islands, and
(c) the Commissioners of Irish Lights, as respects Northern Ireland and the adjacent seas and islands,
are the general lighthouse authority.
(2) For the purposes of this Part—
(a) each harbour authority, as respects their area, and
(b) any other existing local lighthouse authority, as respects their area,
are the local lighthouse authority.

(3) Schedule 8 shall have effect as respects the Commissioners of Northern Lighthouses.

(4) In this Part "area" means—

(a) in relation to a general lighthouse authority specified in subsection (1)(a), (b) or (c) above, the area specified in that paragraph as the area of that authority;

(b) in relation to a harbour authority, the area or areas inside the limits within which the authority's statutory powers and duties as a harbour authority are exercisable; and

(c) in relation to any other existing local lighthouse authority, the existing area over which their authority extends in relation to lighthouses, buoys and beacons;

and for the purposes of subsection (2)(b) above and paragraph (c) above "existing" means existing for the purposes of the 1894 Act immediately before the repeal of that Act by this Act.

(5) Subject to paragraph 9(1) of Schedule 14, the Trinity House are also the general lighthouse authority as respects Gibraltar and, subject to sub-paragraph (2) of that paragraph, the Channel Islands; and the Commissioners of Northern Lights are also the general lighthouse authority as respects the Isle of Man, and the seas adjacent to those territories.

DEFINITIONS

"1894 Act, the": s.223(1).
"Act, this": s.316(1).
"area": subs. (4).
"buoys and beacons": s.223(1) and (2) and (3).
"Commissioners of Irish Lights": s.223(1).
"Commissioners of Northern Lighthouses": Sched. 8, para.. 1(2).
"England and Wales": Interpretation Act 1978, Sched. 1.
"existing": subs. (4).
"general lighthouse authority": subs. (1).
"harbour authority": s.313(1).
"lighthouse": s.223(1) and (2).
"local lighthouse authority": subs. (2).
"Trinity House": s.223(1).

GENERAL NOTE

[Derivation: Merchant Shipping Act 1894, ss.634(1) and 668; Ports Act 1991, ss.31(3) and 34(3).]

Section 193 defines the general lighthouse authorities (GLAs) and the Local Lighthouse Authority (LLA).

Part III of the Ports Act 1991 rationalised the responsibility for lighthouses in ports. The GLAs responsible for lighthouses are Trinity House (in England and Wales), the Commissioners of Northern Lighthouses (in Scotland) and the Commissioners of Irish Lights (in Northern Ireland). Difficulties arose over whether it should be the GLAs, such as Trinity House, who should have powers to place lighthouses, buoys and beacons in harbours, or whether it should be the harbour authorities. Part III took away the powers of the GLAs and enabled local harbour authorities to exercise the lighthouse functions under the 1894 Act. It also set out the administrative arrangements for the transfer of local lights by the GLAs to the harbour authorities. It would appear that about 150 navigational aids were likely to be affected by the Ports Act 1991. The Government declined the Opposition's suggestion to make the general funding of lighthouses from central sources. It seems that the GLAs will continue, under their statutory powers, to incur the costs of inspecting local aids.

Subsection (2) re-enacts s.31(3) of the Ports Act 1991 and provides that harbour authorities are to be regarded as local lighthouse authorities.

Subsection (3) incorporates Sched. 8 which sets out the structure of the Commissioners of Northern Lighthouses.

The Merchant Shipping (Registration, etc.) Act 1993 repealed a number of provisions which applied to colonies, such as the Channel Islands, Gibraltar and the Isle of Man (see, for example, s.669 of the Merchant Shipping Act 1894). The definitions of England and Wales in the

Interpretation Act 1978 would clearly exclude these possessions from the references in s.193(1). See also the repeal of s.655 of the 1894 Act, which was necessary because the Harbours Act 1964, s.29 (which abolished the fixing of light dues by Order) did not extend to Northern Ireland.

Information to Secretary of State

Returns and information to Secretary of State

194. Every general lighthouse authority and their officers shall give to the Secretary of State all such returns, explanations or information in relation to the lighthouses, buoys or beacons within their area and their management as the Secretary of State requires.

DEFINITIONS
"area": s.193(4).
"buoys and beacons": s.223(1) and (2) and (3).
"general lighthouse authority": s.193(1).
"lighthouse": s.223(1) and (2).
"Secretary of State": Interpretation Act 1978, Sched. 1.

GENERAL NOTE
[Derivation: Merchant Shipping Act 1894, s.635.]
Section 194 requires a general lighthouse authority to provide returns to the Secretary of State.

Functions of general lighthouse authorities

General function of management of lighthouses, etc.

195.—(1) Subject to the following provisions of this Part and to the powers and rights of any local lighthouse authority, the general lighthouse authorities shall have the superintendence and management of all lighthouses, buoys and beacons within their respective areas.

(2) Subject to the following provisions of this Part, the general lighthouse authorities shall continue to hold and maintain all property vested in them at the commencement of this Act in the same manner and for the same purposes as before.

DEFINITIONS
"Act, this": s.316(1).
"area": s.193(4).
"buoys and beacons": s.223(1) and (2) and (3).
"general lighthouse authorities": s.193(1).
"lighthouse": s.223(1) and (2).
"local lighthouse authority": s.193(2).

GENERAL NOTE
[Derivation: Merchant Shipping Act 1894, s.634.]
Section 195 sets out the functions of a general lighthouse authority.

Joint discharge of functions

196.—(1) Two or more general lighthouse authorities may discharge any of their functions jointly, and for that purpose—
   (a) those authorities may share any part of their respective establishments; and
   (b) any of them may, in the area of another and on that other's behalf, execute any works or do any other thing which the authority have power to execute or do in their own area;
and any enactment relating to the functions in question or to the authorities by whom or the areas in which those functions are to be discharged shall be construed accordingly.

(2) Any expenses incurred by any of the general lighthouse authorities in pursuance of this section shall be apportioned between that authority and the other authority or authorities concerned in such manner as may be agreed between them or (in default of agreement) determined by the Secretary of State.

DEFINITIONS
"area": s.193(4).
"general lighthouse authorities": s.193(1).
"Secretary of State": Interpretation Act 1978, Sched. 1.

GENERAL NOTE
[Derivation: Merchant Shipping Act 1894, s.634A; Merchant Shipping Act 1988, s.41.]
Section 196 was designed to remove any legal obstacles to the three general lighthouse authorities operating jointly, *e.g.* by sharing staff and assets. In practice this will mean that it is easier to arrange redundancies and allow for natural wastage. This may be necessary because of the increasing automation of lighthouses and the closure of sound fog signals. Concern was expressed in the Commons debates in 1988 on the effects that redundancies would have on small communities, particularly in the Highlands of Scotland, but no special redundancy provisions were enacted (*cf.* the Pilotage Act 1987).

General powers of general lighthouse authority

197.—(1) Subject to subsection (2) below, a general lighthouse authority shall, within their area, have power—
  (a) to erect or place any lighthouse, with all requisite works, roads and appurtenances;
  (b) to add to, alter, or remove any lighthouse;
  (c) to erect or place any buoy or beacon, or alter or remove any buoy or beacon;
  (d) to vary the character of any lighthouse or the mode of exhibiting lights therein.
(2) A general lighthouse authority shall not in the area of a harbour authority—
  (a) erect or place any lighthouse, works, roads or appurtenances under subsection (1)(a) above, or
  (b) erect or place any buoy or beacon under subsection (1)(c) above,
except in pursuance of a direction given by the Secretary of State.
(3) The Secretary of State may give such a direction to a general lighthouse authority if he considers it appropriate to do so in the interests of general navigation.
(4) Where any improved light or beacon, or any siren or any description of fog signal has been added to an existing lighthouse, the light or beacon, siren or signal may, for the purposes of this Part, be treated as if it were a separate lighthouse.
(5) A general lighthouse authority may acquire any land which may be necessary for—
  (a) the exercise of their powers under subsection (1) above;
  (b) the maintenance of their works; or
  (c) the residence of the light keepers.
(6) For the purposes of the acquisition of land by a general lighthouse authority under subsection (5) above the following provisions shall apply—
  (a) if the land is in England and Wales, the provisions of Part I of the Compulsory Purchase Act 1965 (so far as applicable) except sections 4 to 8, 27 and 31;
  (b) if the land is in Scotland, the provisions of the Lands Clauses Acts (so far as applicable) except sections 120 to 125, 127, 142 and 143 of the Lands Clauses Consolidation (Scotland) Act 1845;

(c) if the land is in Northern Ireland, the provisions of the Lands Clauses Acts (so far as applicable) except sections 16 to 20, 92 to 94, 123, 127 to 132, 150 and 151 of the Lands Clauses Consolidation Act 1845.

(7) A general lighthouse authority may sell any land belonging to them.

DEFINITIONS
"area": s.193(4).
"buoys and beacons": s.223(1) and (2) and (3).
"England and Wales": Interpretation Act 1978, Sched. 1.
"general lighthouse authority": s.193(1).
"harbour authority": s.313(1).
"lighthouse": s.223(1) and (2).
"Secretary of State": Interpretation Act 1978, Sched. 1 and 642.

GENERAL NOTE
[Derivation: Merchant Shipping Act 1894, ss.638, 639 and 642; Merchant Shipping (Registration, etc.) Act 1993, Sched. 4, paras. 37, 38 and 39; Ports Act 1991, s.31(4)(5).]
Appurtenances. See s.223(2).
Beacon. There are many modern appliances, often unstaffed, that now do the work of lighthouses and lightships. Subsection (4) (added by the Merchant Shipping (Registration, etc.) Act 1993, Sched. 4) makes it clear that additions to lighthouses under s.642 include radio beacons and racons.

Subsections (2) and (3) re-enact the Ports Act 1991, s.31(4) and (5). They remove any powers of a general lighthouse authority to install lighthouses, buoys, or beacons within the harbour authority's area—unless directed to do so by the Secretary of State. The latter's power might be used where it appears that the local harbour authority is not fulfilling its duties.

Subsection (6) was added to the Merchant Shipping Act 1894 provision (s.639) by the Merchant Shipping (Registration, etc.) Act 1993, Sched. 4, para. 38 in order to modernise the land acquisition references to take account of the current practices under the Compulsory Purchase Act 1965.

Inspection of local lighthouses

198.—(1) It shall be the duty of the general lighthouse authority for any area, or of any person authorised by that authority for the purpose, to—
   (a) inspect all lighthouses, buoys and beacons situated within their area but belonging to or under the management of any local lighthouse authority; and
   (b) make such inquiries about them and their management as they think fit.

(2) All officers and others having the care, or concerned in the management, of any such local lighthouses, buoys or beacons shall furnish all such information and explanations concerning them as the general lighthouse authority require.

(3) All local lighthouse authorities and their officers shall give to the general lighthouse authority all such returns, explanations or information concerning the lighthouses, buoys and beacons under their management and the management of them as the general lighthouse authority may require.

(4) The general lighthouse authority shall—
   (a) communicate to each local lighthouse authority the results of their inspection of their lighthouses, buoys and beacons; and
   (b) make to the Secretary of State general reports of the results of the inspection of local lighthouses, buoys and beacons.

DEFINITIONS
"area": s.193(4).
"buoys and beacons": s.223(1) and (2) and (3).
"general lighthouse authority": s.193(1).
"lighthouse": s.223(1) and (2).
"local lighthouse authority": s.193(2).
"person": Interpretation Act 1978, Sched. 1.
"Secretary of State": Interpretation Act 1978, Sched. 1.

GENERAL NOTE

[Derivation: Merchant Shipping Act 1894, s.652; Merchant Shipping Act 1988, Sched. 5, para. 6.]

Section 198 requires a general lighthouse authority to inspect lighthouses under local lighthouse authority management.

Control of local lighthouse authorities

199.—(1) A general lighthouse authority may, within their area, with the consent of the Secretary of State, direct a local lighthouse authority to—

(a) lay down buoys;

(b) remove or discontinue any lighthouse, buoy or beacon; or

(c) make any variation in the character of any lighthouse, buoy or beacon or in the mode of exhibiting lights in any lighthouse, buoy or beacon;

but the authority shall not give a direction without first giving due notice of their intention to do so.

(2) A local lighthouse authority shall not, without the consent of the general lighthouse authority,—

(a) erect or place any lighthouse, buoy or beacon;

(b) remove or discontinue any lighthouse, buoy or beacon;

(c) vary the character of any lighthouse, buoy or beacon or the mode of exhibiting lights in any lighthouse, buoy or beacon.

(3) A direction under subsection (1) above shall be given in writing; and it shall be the duty of a local lighthouse authority to whom such a direction is given to comply with it.

(4) Nothing in this section shall apply to local buoys and beacons placed or erected for temporary purposes.

DEFINITIONS

"area": s.193(4).

"buoys and beacons": s.223(1), (2) and (3).

"general lighthouse authority": s.193(1).

"lighthouse": s.223(1) and (2).

"local lighthouse authority": s.193(2).

"Secretary of State": Interpretation Act 1978, Sched. 1.

"writing": Interpretation Act 1978, Sched. 1.

GENERAL NOTE

[Derivation: Merchant Shipping Act 1894, s.653; Ports Act 1991, s.31(6).]

Section 199 sets out the extent of the control which a general lighthouse authority (GLA) can exercise over a local lighthouse authority (LLA). Note that subs. (3) was inserted by the Ports Act 1991, s.31(6) to change the law in respect of the circumstances where a LLA fails to comply with a direction from a GLA. Under the Merchant Shipping Act 1894, s.653(3) the powers of the LLA were then transferred to the GLA—which would have defeated the purpose as it would also transfer the cost to the GLA. Subsection (3) was inserted to impose a duty to comply with the direction.

Inspections by Secretary of State

Powers of inspection by Secretary of State

200.—(1) The Secretary of State may, on complaint that any lighthouse, buoy or beacon under the management of a general lighthouse authority, or any work connected with it, is—

(a) inefficient,

(b) improperly managed, or

(c) unnecessary,

authorise any persons appointed by him to inspect the lighthouse, buoy or beacon or any connected work.

(2) A person so authorised may—

(a) inspect the lighthouse, buoy or beacon; and

(b) make any inquiries which he thinks fit as to the lighthouse, buoy or beacon and its management.

(3) All officers and others having the care, or concerned in the management, of any lighthouse, buoy or beacon in relation to which powers under this section are being exercised shall furnish any information and explanations in relation to it and its management which the person inspecting it requires.

DEFINITIONS

"buoys and beacons": s.223(1), (2) and (3).
"general lighthouse authority": s.193(1).
"lighthouse": s.223(1) and (2).
"person": Interpretation Act 1978, Sched. 1.
"Secretary of State": Interpretation Act 1978, Sched. 1.

GENERAL NOTE

[Derivation: Merchant Shipping Act 1894, s.636.]

Section 200 enables the Secretary of State to inspect facilities under the control of a general lighthouse authority.

Powers of harbour authorities as local lighthouse authorities

Powers of harbour authorities

201.—(1) Every harbour authority shall have power to carry out harbour operations to which subsection (2) below applies either within the authority's area or on harbour land.

(2) This subsection applies to harbour operations consisting of the marking or lighting of a harbour or any part of a harbour.

(3) In this section "harbour land" and "harbour operations" have the same meanings as in the Harbours Act 1964 or, as respects Northern Ireland, as in the Harbours Act (Northern Ireland) 1970.

DEFINITIONS

"area": s.193(4).
"harbour": s.313(1).
"harbour authority": s.313(1).
"harbour land": subs. (3) and Harbours Act 1964, s.57(1).
"harbour operations": subs. (3) and Harbours Act 1964, s.57(1).

GENERAL NOTE

[Derivation: Ports Act 1991, s.31(1), (2) and (7).]

Transfers between general and local lighthouse authorities

General transfer of local lighthouses from general lighthouse authorities to harbour authorities

202. Schedule 9 (which requires general lighthouse authorities to transfer certain local lighthouses held by them to harbour authorities) shall have effect.

DEFINITIONS
"general lighthouse authorities": s.193(1).
"harbour authorities": s.313(1).
"lighthouse": s.223(1) and (2).

GENERAL NOTE
[Derivation: Ports Act 1991, s.32.]
Section 202 re-enacts s.32 of the Ports Act 1991, but places the detail in Sched. 9. The general lighthouse authorities (GLAs) are obliged to present written proposals to the Secretary of State for the transfer of local lights (*i.e.* lighthouses, buoys and beacons for a particular harbour) to the relevant harbour authority (*i.e.* the one where the lights are situated). Para. (1)(b) of what is now Sched. 9 had the words "or mainly" added to deal with difficult questions of judgment as to whether a navigational aid was used partly for the benefit of ships passing generally at sea—as opposed to ships within the harbour. The idea is only to transfer those aids which are used essentially for local navigation. The theory is that the costs of local lights should be borne by those using the port and not by commercial shipping and the fishing industry in general through light dues. The costs transferred might be quite substantial for a small port: a figure of £30,000 was mentioned in debates on the Ports Act 1991 in relation to the port of Inverness.
The GLA is obliged to consult the harbour authority. The Secretary of State can approve the proposals, with or without modifications, and will then specify a transfer date.

Individual transfers of local lighthouses to harbour authorities

203. A general lighthouse authority may, at any time, with the consent of the Secretary of State, transfer to a harbour authority any lighthouse, buoy or beacon held by the general lighthouse authority which—

  (a) is situated in the area of that harbour authority or on land adjacent to that area or any part of it; and

  (b) appears to the general lighthouse authority to be of benefit solely or mainly to ships within, or entering or leaving, that harbour authority's area.

DEFINITIONS
"area": s.193(4).
"buoys and beacons": s.223(1), (2) and (3).
"general lighthouse authority": s.193(1).
"harbour authority": s.313(1).
"lighthouse": s.223(1) and (2).
"Secretary of State": Interpretation Act 1978, Sched. 1.
"ship": s.313(1).

GENERAL NOTE
[Derivation: Ports Act 1991, ss.33(1), 34(2).]
This section allows for the transfer by the general lighthouse authorities of individual local lights to harbour authorities.

Surrender of local lighthouses

204.—(1) A local lighthouse authority may, if they think fit, surrender or sell any lighthouse, buoy or beacon held by them to the general lighthouse authority within whose area it is situated, and that general lighthouse may, with the consent of the Secretary of State, accept or purchase it.

(2) The Secretary of State shall not give his consent for the purposes of subsection (1) above in any case where the local lighthouse authority concerned are a harbour authority unless he considers that the maintenance of the lighthouse, buoy or beacon in question is in the interests of general navigation.

DEFINITIONS
"area": s.193(4).
"buoys and beacons": s.223(1), (2) and (3).
"general lighthouse authority": s.193(1).
"harbour authority": s.313(1).

"lighthouse": s.223(1) and (2).
"local lighthouse authority": s.193(2).
"Secretary of State": Interpretation Act 1978, Sched. 1.

GENERAL NOTE

[Derivation: Merchant Shipping Act 1894, s.654(1), as partially substituted by the Ports Act 1991, ss.33(3) and 34(2).]

Section 204 re-enacts s.654 of the Merchant Shipping Act 1894, as amended. It also restricts the extent to which local lighthouse authorities can transfer local lights to a general lighthouse authority.

General light dues

Light dues leviable by general lighthouse authorities

205.—(1) This section applies to dues leviable by a general lighthouse authority in respect of lighthouses, buoys or beacons under their management (in this Part called "general light dues").

(2) A general lighthouse authority may demand, take and recover general light dues in accordance with this section and for that purpose appoint persons to collect them.

(3) General light dues shall be levied only by reference to the voyages made by ships or by way of periodical payments.

(4) General light dues shall be payable in respect of all ships whatever, except—

(a) ships belonging to Her Majesty, and

(b) ships exempted from payment in pursuance of subsection (5) below.

(5) The Secretary of State may make regulations with respect to the amounts and the levying of general light dues (including the cases in which the dues are not to be levied) and the regulations may make different provision for different circumstances.

(6) A copy of the regulations in force under subsection (5) above in respect of general light dues shall be kept at—

(a) the principal office of the general lighthouse authority, and

(b) the office of the appointed collector at every port where such dues are collected;

and shall be open for inspection there during reasonable hours by any person without charge.

(7) Every person appointed by a general lighthouse authority to collect general light dues shall collect all such dues payable at the port at which he is so appointed or (as the case may be) such of those dues as he is appointed to collect, whether they are collected on account of that authority or on account of one of the other general lighthouse authorities.

(8) Any person appointed by a general lighthouse authority to collect general light dues shall pay over to that authority, or as that authority directs, the whole of the general light dues received by him.

(9) A general lighthouse authority receiving dues (whether themselves or from a collector) shall keep accounts of the dues and shall cause the dues to be remitted to Her Majesty's Paymaster-General in such manner as the Secretary of State directs.

DEFINITIONS

"buoys and beacons": s.223(1) and (2) and (3).
"general light dues": subs. (1) and s.223(1).
"general lighthouse authority": s.193(1).
"lighthouse": s.223(1) and (2).

"person": Interpretation Act 1978, Sched. 1.
"port": s.313(1).
"Secretary of State": Interpretation Act 1978, Sched. 1.
"ship": s.313(1).

GENERAL NOTE

[Derivation: Merchant Shipping Act 1894, ss.643, 647, 648(2) and (3) (see the Merchant Shipping (Registration, etc.) Act 1993, Sched. 4, paras. 40, 42 and 43 respectively); Merchant Shipping (Mercantile Marine Fund) Act 1898, s.5(1) and (2) (as partially substituted by Merchant Shipping Act 1979, Sched. 7, Pt. II).]

The general lighthouse fund (GLF) is financed by light dues collected by the general lighthouse authorities (see ss.205–210). The Harbours Act 1964 s.29(2) gave local lighthouse authorities the power to levy light dues on ships to help defray the costs of running the service, but the power of a general lighthouse authority (GLA) under the 1894 Act arose only by implication. For the consolidation it was thought necessary to include express powers and this was done by the Merchant Shipping (Registration, etc.) Act 1993, Sched. 4, para. 40. Section 205(2) now allows a GLA to recover "general light dues".

As noted in relation to wreck (s.238, below), the practice of posting information at customs houses no longer operates as a reliable source of shipping knowledge. Subsection (6) (inserted into s.647 of the Merchant Shipping Act 1894 by the Merchant Shipping (Registration, etc.) Act 1993, Sched. 4, para. 42) now requires the display of light dues tables at the GLA's central office and at the offices of the local collector of dues. For the charging procedure for local lighthouse authorities which are not harbour authorities, see the Harbours Act 1964, s.30(2), as amended by the Merchant Shipping (Registration, etc.) Act 1993, Sched. 4, para. 55.

The payment of light dues has always been enforced through customs officers requiring the production of a receipt before giving clearance to the ship and allowing it to sail. The assumption in s.651 (and s.648) of the 1894 Act (now ss.209 and 205, respectively) had been that the receipt would be given by the local collector, who in turn paid the GLA. It appears that, in practice, payment is often made directly to the GLA and subs. (9) and s.209(1) (inserted in the Merchant Shipping Act 1894 by the Merchant Shipping (Registration, etc.) Act 1993, Sched. 4, paras. 43 and 46) recognised this fact by obliging the GLA to keep accounts of sums received and to give a receipt.

Information to determine light dues

206.—(1) A general lighthouse authority may, for the purpose of determining whether any and, if so, what general light dues are payable in respect of any ship, require any relevant authority or any person who is liable to pay general light dues in respect of the ship, to furnish to the general lighthouse authority such information in that authority's or person's possession or control relating to the arrival or departure of the ship at or from any port within their area as they may reasonably require for that purpose.

(2) A general lighthouse authority may require any relevant authority to furnish to them such information in the relevant authority's possession or control relating to the movements within the relevant authoritys' area of ships or ships of any class or description for the purpose of determining whether any and, if so, what general light dues are payable in respect of the ships.

(3) The powers conferred on a general lighthouse authority by subsections (1) and (2) above shall also be available to the person appointed by them to collect dues at a port.

(4) It shall be the duty of a relevant authority or person of whom a requirement for information is made under subsection (1), (2) or (3) above to furnish information as soon as is reasonably practicable.

(5) In this section "relevant authority" means—
(a) a harbour authority;
(b) the Commissioners of Customs and Excise; and
(c) a conservancy authority.

DEFINITIONS

"area": s.193(4).
"conservancy authority": s.313(1).

"general light dues": ss.205(1) and 223(1).
"general lighthouse authority": s.193(1).
"harbour authority": s.313(1).
"person": Interpretation Act 1978, Sched. 1.
"port": s.313(1).
"relevant authority": subs. (5).
"ship": s.313(1).

GENERAL NOTE

[Derivation: Merchant Shipping Act 1894, s.643A; Merchant Shipping (Registration, etc.) Act 1993, Sched. 4, para. 41.]

Section 206 (derived from the Merchant Shipping (Registration, etc.) Act 1993, Sched. 4, para. 41) allows the general lighthouse authority to require the provision of information to it so that it can calculate the dues payable. These powers did not exist under the 1894 Act. Effectively, it is the harbour authority which will be the likely source of the information, but the shipowner may also be required to give it.

Recovery of general light dues

207.—(1) The following persons shall be liable to pay general light dues in respect of any ship in respect of which such dues are payable, namely—

(a) the owner or master; or

(b) such consignees or agents of the owner or master as have paid, or made themselves liable to pay, any other charge on account of the ship in the port of her arrival or discharge.

(2) General light dues so payable in respect of any ship may, in England and Wales and Northern Ireland, be recovered summarily as a civil debt.

(3) In Scotland general light dues shall, for the purposes of their recovery, be regarded as a debt due to the general lighthouse authority.

(4) Any consignee or agent (not being the owner or master of the ship) who is, by this section, made liable for the payment of general light dues in respect of any ship may, out of any money received by him on account of the ship or belonging to its owner, retain the amount of all general light dues paid by him, together with any reasonable expenses he may have incurred by reason of the payment of the dues or his liability to pay them.

DEFINITIONS

"England and Wales": Interpretation Act 1978, Sched. 1.
"general light dues": ss.205(1) and 223(1).
"general lighthouse authority": s.193(1).
"master": s.313(1).
"person": Interpretation Act 1978, Sched. 1.
"port": s.313(1).
"ship": s.313(1).

GENERAL NOTE

[Derivation: Merchant Shipping Act 1894, s.649(1), (1A) and (2), 681; Merchant Shipping (Registration, etc.) Act 1993, Sched. 4, paras. 44 and 58.

Section 207 (formerly the Merchant Shipping Act 1894, s.649(1)) deals with the mode of recovering light dues throughout the U.K. General light dues are payable by the master or, in some circumstances, agents.

Distress on ship for general light dues

208.—(1) If the owner or master of any ship fails, on demand of the appointed collector, to pay the general light dues due in respect of the ship, the collector may enter the ship and distrain the goods or any equipment or other thing belonging to, or on board, the ship and detain that distress until those dues are paid.

(2) If payment of the dues so demanded is not made within the period of five days following the distress, the collector may, at any time during the continuance of the non-payment, cause the distress to be independently appraised and thereupon sold by public auction.

(3) The collector shall apply the proceeds of the sale in payment of—

(a) the general light dues due; and

(b) all reasonable expenses incurred by him under this section;

and shall pay the surplus (if any), on demand, to the owner or master of the ship.

(4) The remedy conferred by this section is in addition to any other remedy available to the collector or the general lighthouse authority by whom he was appointed.

(5) This section does not apply to Scotland.

DEFINITIONS

"fails": s.313(1).

"general light dues": ss.205(1) and 223(1).

"general lighthouse authority": s.193(1).

"master": s.313(1).

"ship": s.313(1).

GENERAL NOTE

[Derivation: Merchant Shipping Act 1894, s.650; Merchant Shipping (Registration, etc.) Act 1993, Sched. 4, para. 45, Sched. 5.]

Section 208 (formerly the Merchant Shipping Act 1894, s.650) gives the collector of dues the power to levy distress in respect of moveables on the ship. A number of changes were made by the Merchant Shipping (Registration, etc.) Act 1993, Sched. 4, para. 45 to the procedures envisaged. Guns cannot now be distrained. The period of non-payment after which distraint can be exercised was increased from three to five days. Valuation is no longer to be by a process of "appraisal", but by independent valuation and sale at auction.

Receipt for general light dues and its production

209.—(1) A receipt for general light dues shall be given to the person paying them by the authority or person receiving them from him.

(2) A ship may be detained at any port until the receipt for any general light dues due in respect of the ship is produced to the proper officer of customs and excise or the person appointed to collect general light dues at the port.

DEFINITIONS

"general light dues": ss.205(1) and 223(1).

"person": Interpretation Act 1978, Sched. 1.

"port": s.313(1).

"proper officer": s.313(1).

"ship": s.313(1).

GENERAL NOTE

[Derivation: Merchant Shipping Act 1894, s.651; Merchant Shipping (Registration, etc.) Act 1993, Sched. 4, para. 46.]

Payment is often made directly to the general lighthouse authority (GLA) and subs. (1) and s.205(9) (inserted in the Merchant Shipping Act 1894 by the Merchant Shipping (Registration, etc.) Act 1993, Sched. 4 paras. 43 and 46) recognise this fact by obliging the GLA to keep accounts of sums received and to give a receipt.

Local light dues

Light dues leviable by local lighthouse authorities

210.—(1) This section applies to charges leviable by a local lighthouse authority who are not a harbour authority in respect of lighthouses, buoys or beacons over which they have authority (in this section referred to as "local light dues").

(2) A local lighthouse authority (who are not a harbour authority) may demand, take and recover in respect of every ship which—

(a) enters or leaves the port, harbour or estuary in which is situated any lighthouse, buoy or beacon over which they have authority; and

(b) passes the lighthouse, buoy or beacon and derives benefit from it, such charges as they think fit.

(3) The same persons shall be liable to pay local light dues as are liable to pay general light dues under section 207.

(4) Local light dues may be recovered in the same manner as general light dues may be recovered under sections 207 and 208.

(5) A list showing the local light dues leviable by a local lighthouse authority shall be kept at the authority's office and shall be open there during reasonable hours for inspection by any person without charge, and copies of the list shall be kept for sale there at such reasonable price (if any) as the authority determine.

(6) No local light due shall be levied by a local lighthouse authority if, at the time at which it is leviable,—

(a) the authority are in default in compliance with subsection (5) above as respects the keeping of the list of dues; or

(b) the light due is not shown in the list kept there at that time.

(7) A copy of the list kept by a local lighthouse authority in pursuance of subsection (5) above shall be supplied by them to the Secretary of State without charge.

(8) Section 31 of the Harbours Act 1964 (right of objection to ship, passenger and goods dues) shall apply in relation to local light dues subject, however, to the modifications specified in Schedule 10 to this Act.

(9) All local light dues shall be applied by the authority by whom they are levied for the purpose of the construction, placing, maintenance and improvement of the lighthouses, buoys or beacons in respect of which the dues are levied, and for no other purpose.

(10) The local lighthouse authority to whom any local light dues are paid shall keep a separate account of the receipt and expenditure of those dues.

(11) This section does not apply to Northern Ireland.

DEFINITIONS
"Act, this": s.316(1).
"buoys and beacons": s.223(1), (2) and (3).
"general light dues": ss.205(1) and 223(1).
"harbour": s.313(1).
"harbour authority": s.313(1).
"lighthouse": s.223(1) and (2).
"local light dues": subs. (1).
"local lighthouse authority": s.193(2).
"passenger": Harbours Act 1964, s.57(1).
"person": Interpretation Act 1978, Sched. 1.
"port": s.313(1).
"Secretary of State": Interpretation Act 1978, Sched. 1.
"ship": s.313(1).

GENERAL NOTE
[Derivation: Merchant Shipping Act 1894, s.655(2) (see the Harbours Act 1964, Sched. 6 and the Merchant Shipping (Registration, etc.) Act 1993, Scheds. 4, 5); Merchant Shipping Act 1894, s.656 (see the Merchant Shipping (Registration, etc.) Act 1993, Sched. 4, para. 48); Harbours Act 1964. ss.29(2), (3) and 30(2), (3) and (4) (see the Merchant Shipping (Registration, etc.) Act 1993, Sched. 4, para. 55).]

Section 210 allows a local lighthouse authority (LLA) to levy "Local light dues". The LLAs need no longer send accounts to the DOT as required by s.656(2) of the Merchant Shipping Act 1894 (see the Merchant Shipping (Registration, etc.) Act 1993, Sched. 4, para. 48), although see s.218, below.

Financial and administrative provisions

General Lighthouse Fund: expenses and receipts

211.—(1) There shall continue to be a fund called the General Lighthouse Fund administered by the Secretary of State.

(2) The following shall be paid out of that Fund—

(a) any expenses incurred by general lighthouse authorities in connection with the discharge of their functions under this Part and, in the case of the Commissioners of Irish Lights as respects their functions in the Republic of Ireland, under the corresponding Part of the 1894 Act, subject, however, to section 213;

(b) any expenses (whether of a capital nature or not) incurred by the Secretary of State in pursuance of any international agreement relating to the provision of an electronic position-fixing system intended as an aid to the navigation of ships or incurred by him preliminary to his entering into such an agreement;

(c) such sums as the Secretary of State may determine as sums appearing to him to represent the amount or estimated amount of any expenses incurred or likely to be incurred by him in connection with the administration of the Fund;

(d) any expenses incurred by the Secretary of State in maintaining the Sombrero lighthouse in the Leeward Islands;

(e) any other sums made payable out of the Fund by any other provision of this Part or Part IX.

(3) The following shall be paid into that Fund—

(a) all general light dues and other sums received by or accruing to any of the general lighthouse authorities by virtue of, or in connection with the discharge of their functions under, this Part and, in the case of the Commissioners of Irish Lights as respects their functions in the Republic of Ireland, under the corresponding Part of the 1894 Act;

(b) any sums received by the Secretary of State in pursuance of any such agreement as is mentioned in subsection (2)(b) above in respect of—

    (i) expenses incurred by him in pursuance of the agreement, or

    (ii) expenses incurred by any of the general lighthouse authorities which, by virtue of subsection (2) above, are payable out of the Fund;

(c) any other sums made payable into the Fund by any other provision of this Part or Part IX.

(4) The accounts of the Fund for each year shall be examined by the Comptroller and Auditor General who shall send a copy of the accounts certified by him to the Secretary of State.

(5) The Secretary of State shall lay copies of the accounts before each House of Parliament.

DEFINITIONS

"1894 Act, the": s.223(1).
"Commissioners of Irish Lights": s.223(1).
"general lighthouse authorities": s.193(1).
"general light dues": ss.205(1) and 223(1).
"lighthouse": s.223(1) and (2).
"Secretary of State": Interpretation Act 1978, Sched. 1.
"ship": s.313(1).

GENERAL NOTE

[Derivation: Merchant Shipping Act 1894, s.658 (see the Merchant Shipping Act 1988, Sched. 5, para. 7); Merchant Shipping Act 1894, s.679 (see the Merchant Shipping (Registration, etc.) Act 1993, Sched. 4, para. 53); Merchant Shipping (Mercantile Marine Fund) Act 1898, s.1(1), (2), (3) and 2A(1), (2), 2B, (3), (7) (see the Merchant Shipping Act 1988, Sched. 5, s.43).]

The Merchant Shipping (Mercantile Marine Fund) Act 1898, s.1 created a General Lighthouse Fund (GLF) to pay for the expenses relating to lighthouses, buoys and beacons which were then maintained around the coasts of the empire. Section 211 of the 1995 Act continues the GLF. The expense of maintaining the colonial Sombrero lighthouse (near Anguilla) which remains from the days of empire, continues to fall on the GLF by virtue of s.211(2)(d). The GLF is financed by light dues collected by the general lighthouse authorities (GLAs) (see ss.205–210). Shortfalls have been met from reserves accumulated in previous years.

Section 215 was amended by the Merchant Shipping Act 1988, s.43 and was designed to reimburse the Secretary of State, from the GLF, for two types of expenditure. The first, set out in the new subs. (2)(b) and subs. (3)(b) relates to the costs involved in a possible international agreement to develop the LORAN C as a civil electronic aid to navigation in North-West Europe. LORAN C is a long range navigation system allowing the exact positions of vessels to be established. The second type of expense which the Secretary of State can claim from the GLF, relates to the general administrative expenses incurred in operating the GLF. This power is in subs. (2)(c) and proved to be controversial in its passage through Parliament in 1988. The complaint was that the industry should not be made to pay for matters which were properly a national expense. The Government purpose was to remove specific burdens on the taxpayer. It was then costing about £150,000 a year to manage the accounts and investments of the GLF. An assurance was given that general administrative costs (including the Minister's gin and tonics!) would not be a charge.

Light dues are in effect a tax collected from all ships entering U.K. ports and can be very expensive. The GCBS evidence to the House of Commons Transport Committee (published in its "Interim report" in 1987) noted that a container ship could pay up to £13,000 for each voyage which included a British port of call. The GCBS criticised this tax which it claimed operated unfairly against British ships and ports. At that time, most North West European trading competitors funded the navigational aids from general taxation. Most fishermen, yachtsmen and the Royal Navy pay nothing and are subsidised by merchant shipping. There was also an indirect subsidy to the Irish Republic. An attempt to charge the full amount to the Irish Republic failed at Committee Stage in the Commons. In 1988, the Government took the view that the GLF should be looked at as a whole and that individual areas were not expected to balance high expenses against income.

The Government was under pressure to give full relief to shipowners, but this was resisted throughout the passage of the 1988 Bill. Although s.215 gives greater financial flexibility to the GLAs, the underlying purpose of the 1988 revisions seems to have been to reduce public expenditure and to free capital sums held in the GLF.

Subsections (4) and (5) were added to the Merchant Shipping Act 1894, s.679 by the Merchant Shipping (Registration, etc.) Act 1993, Sched. 4, para. 53 so as to reform the auditing requirements of s.679 to accord with contemporary practice.

Establishments of general lighthouse authorities

212.—(1) The Secretary of State may determine—

(a) the establishments to be maintained by each of the general lighthouse authorities on account of the services of lighthouses, buoys and beacons;

(b) the annual or other sums to be paid out of the General Lighthouse Fund in respect of those establishments or to members of the general lighthouse authority for England and Wales.

(2) If it appears that any part of the establishments of the general lighthouse authorities is maintained for other purposes as well as for the purposes of their duties as general lighthouse authorities, the Secretary of State may determine the portion of the expenses of those establishments to be paid out of the General Lighthouse Fund.

(3) An increase in any establishment or part of an establishment determined under this section shall not be made without the consent of the Secretary of State.

DEFINITIONS
"buoys and beacons": s.223(1), (2) and (3).
"England and Wales": Interpretation Act 1978, Sched. 1.
"general lighthouse authorities": s.193(1).
"lighthouse": s.223(1) and (2).
"Secretary of State": Interpretation Act 1978, Sched. 1.

GENERAL NOTE
[Derivation: Merchant Shipping Act 1894, s.659; Merchant Shipping (Amendment) Act 1920, s.1; Merchant Shipping Act 1988, Sched. 5, para. 8.]

Estimates or accounts of expenses to Secretary of State

213.—(1) An expense of a general lighthouse authority in respect of the services of lighthouses, buoys and beacons shall not be paid out of the General Lighthouse Fund, or allowed in account, unless—

(a) it has been allowed as part of the establishment expenses under section 212; or

(b) an estimate or account of it has been approved by the Secretary of State.

(2) For the purpose of approval by the Secretary of State, each of the general lighthouse authorities shall, except as provided by subsection (3) below, submit to him an estimate of all expenses to be incurred by them in respect of lighthouses, buoys and beacons, other than expenses allowed under section 212 on account of their establishments.

(3) In a case where it is necessary for a general lighthouse authority, in providing for any sudden emergency, to incur any such expense as is mentioned in subsection (2) above without waiting for the approval of the Secretary of State under that subsection, the authority shall as soon as possible submit to him a full account of the expense incurred.

(4) The Secretary of State shall consider any estimates and accounts submitted to him under this section and may approve them either with or without modification.

DEFINITIONS
"buoys and beacons": s.223(1), (2) and (3).
"general lighthouse authority": s.193(1).
"lighthouse": s.223(1) and (2).
"Secretary of State": Interpretation Act 1978, Sched. 1.

GENERAL NOTE
[Derivation: Merchant Shipping Act 1894, s.660; Merchant Shipping (Mercantile Marine Fund) Act 1898, s.1(1)(c).]

Pension rights of certain employees

214. There shall be payable to or in respect of persons whose salaries are paid out of the General Lighthouse Fund such pensions, allowances and gratuities as may be determined in accordance with—

(a) in the case of such of those persons as are employed by the Secretary of State, arrangements made by him, and

(b) in the case of other such persons, arrangements made by a general lighthouse authority and approved by the Secretary of State;

and those benefits shall be charged on and payable out of that Fund.

DEFINITIONS
"general lighthouse authority": s.193(1).
"person": Interpretation Act 1978, Sched. 1.
"Secretary of State": Interpretation Act 1978, Sched. 1.

GENERAL NOTE
[Derivation: Merchant Shipping (Mercantile Marine Fund) Act 1898, s.1A(1); Superannuation Act 1972, s.17(1).]

Borrowing powers of general lighthouse authorities

215.—(1) A general lighthouse authority may, with the consent of the Secretary of State and the Treasury, borrow money for the purpose of defraying any expenses incurred or to be incurred by the authority in connection with the discharge of their functions under this Part or Part IX.

(2) A general lighthouse authority may, in connection with any advance to them under this section, mortgage any land or other property belonging to them.

(3) Any sums payable by a general lighthouse authority under the terms of an advance under this section by way of principal, interest or otherwise shall be paid out of the General Lighthouse Fund.

DEFINITIONS
"general lighthouse authority": s.193(1).
"Secretary of State": Interpretation Act 1978, Sched. 1.
"Treasury, the": Interpretation Act 1978, Sched. 1.

GENERAL NOTE
[Derivation: Merchant Shipping Act 1894, s.662; Merchant Shipping Act 1988, s.42(1).]
Sections 215–217 were designed to clarify the borrowing powers of the general lighthouse authorities (GLAs), which were rather uncertain under ss.662–663 of the 1894 Act. The latter section was repealed by s.55 (and s.42(2)) of the Merchant Shipping Act 1988 and the former was replaced by s.215.
The underlying purpose of the revisions seems to have been to reduce the substantial liquid funds which had been retained in the General Lighthouse Fund (GLF) to guard against contingencies (such as storm damage). The 1987 White Paper stated that the new powers would enable the Secretary of State to review, with the Lights Finance Committee, the appropriate level of funds to maintain in the GLF. In 1988, the Government dropped a clause designed to update s.215 by allowing the Secretary of State to mortgage the GLF to defray capital expenses. The present s.215 of the Merchant Shipping Act 1894 allows a GLA to borrow money (up to the limits in s.216, below) and to create mortgages. Guarantees may be given by the Secretary of State under s.217.

Limit on borrowings under section 215

216.—(1) The aggregate amount outstanding in respect of the principal of any sums borrowed under section 215 shall not at any time exceed £100 million.

(2) The Secretary of State may, by order, with the approval of the Treasury, increase or further increase that limit, but not by more than £33 million at a time.

(3) An order shall not be made under subsection (2) above unless a draft of the order has been laid before and approved by a resolution of the House of Commons.

DEFINITIONS
"Secretary of State": Interpretation Act 1978, Sched. 1.
"Treasury, the": Interpretation Act 1978, Sched. 1.

GENERAL NOTE
[Derivation: Merchant Shipping Act 1894, s.662A; Merchant Shipping Act 1988, s.42(1).]
See the General Note to s.215, above.

Guarantees by Secretary of State

217.—(1) The Secretary of State with the consent of the Treasury may guarantee, in such manner and on such conditions as he thinks fit, the repayment of the principal of, the payment of interest on, and the discharge of any other financial obligation in connection with, any sums borrowed by a general lighthouse authority under section 215.

(2) Immediately after a guarantee is given under this section, the Secretary of State shall lay a statement of the guarantee before each House of Parliament, and where any sum is issued for fulfilling a guarantee so given the Secretary of State shall, as soon as possible after the end of each financial year beginning with that in which the sum is issued and ending with that in which all liability in respect of the principal of the sum and in respect of interest thereon is finally discharged, lay before each House of Parliament a statement relating to that sum.

(3) Any sums required by the Secretary of State for fulfilling any guarantee under this section shall be paid out of money provided by Parliament.

(4) If any sums are issued in fulfilment of any guarantee given under this section there shall be made to the Secretary of State out of the General Lighthouse Fund, at such times and in such manner as the Secretary of State may determine with the consent of the Treasury, payments of such amounts as the Secretary of State may so determine in or towards repayment of the sums so issued, and payments of interest on what is outstanding for the time being in respect of sums so issued at such rate as the Secretary of State may so determine.

(5) The Secretary of State, with the consent of the Treasury, may vary or revoke any determination made by him under subsection (4) above.

(6) Any sums received by the Secretary of State under subsection (4) above shall be paid into the Consolidated Fund.

DEFINITIONS
"general lighthouse authority": s.193(1).
"Secretary of State": Interpretation Act 1978, Sched. 1.
"Treasury, the": Interpretation Act 1978, Sched. 1.

GENERAL NOTE
[Derivation: Merchant Shipping Act 1894, s.662B; Merchant Shipping Act 1988, s.42(1).]
See the General Note to s.215, above.

Accounts of general lighthouse authorities

218.—(1) Each of the general lighthouse authorities shall account to the Secretary of State for the general light dues and other sums received by or accruing to them by virtue of, or in connection with, the discharge of their functions under this Part or Part IX and for their expenditure in respect of expenses paid out of the General Lighthouse Fund in such form, at such times, and with such details, explanations and vouchers as the Secretary of State requires.

(2) Each of the general lighthouse authorities shall, when required by the Secretary of State, permit all accounting records kept by or under their respective direction to be inspected and examined by such persons as the Secretary of State appoints for the purpose.

DEFINITIONS
"general lighthouse authorities": s.193(1).
"general light dues": ss.205(1) and 223(1).
"Secretary of State": Interpretation Act 1978, Sched. 1.

GENERAL NOTE
[Derivation: Merchant Shipping Act 1894, s.664; Merchant Shipping (Registration, etc.) Act 1993, Sched. 4, para. 49.]
General lighthouse authorities are obliged to account to the DOT for other sources of income, *e.g.* property.

Offences in connection with lighthouses, buoys, beacons, etc.

Damage etc. to lighthouses etc.

219.—(1) A person who, without lawful authority—
(a) intentionally or recklessly damages—
      (i) any lighthouse or the lights exhibited in it, or
      (ii) any lightship, buoy or beacon;
(b) removes, casts adrift or sinks any lightship, buoy or beacon; or
(c) conceals or obscures any lighthouse, buoy or beacon;
commits an offence.

(2) A person who, without reasonable excuse,—
(a) rides by,
(b) makes fast to, or

(c) runs foul of,

any lightship, buoy or beacon commits an offence.

(3) A person who is guilty of an offence under this section shall, in addition to being liable for the expenses of making good any damage so occasioned, be liable, on summary conviction, to a fine not exceeding level 4 on the standard scale.

DEFINITIONS
"buoys and beacons": s.223(1), (2) and (3).
"general lighthouse authority": s.193(1).
"lighthouse": s.223(1) and (2).
"person": Interpretation Act 1978, Sched. 1.
"standard scale": Criminal Justice Act 1982, s.37.

GENERAL NOTE
[Derivation: Merchant Shipping Act 1894, s.666; Merchant Shipping (Registration, etc.) Act 1993, Sched. 4, para. 50; Merchant Shipping Act 1979, Sched. 6, Part III.]

The Merchant Shipping (Registration, etc.) Act 1993, Sched. 4 modernised the offence in s.666 of the 1894 Act of damaging lighthouses, lightships, buoys or the automatic beacons that are widely used at sea. The modern language of intention and recklessness now in s.219, replaced the more dated expressions "wilfully or negligently". The 1993 Act also repealed superfluous provisions in the Malicious Damage Act 1861 relating to false signals and the damage, removal, or concealment of buoys or other sea marks.

Prevention of false lights

220.—(1) Whenever any light is exhibited at such place or in such manner as to be liable to be mistaken for a light proceeding from a lighthouse, the general lighthouse authority within whose area the place is situated, may serve a notice ("a prevention notice") upon the owner of the place where the light is exhibited or upon the person having the charge of the light.

(2) A prevention notice is a notice directing the person to whom it is addressed to take, within a reasonable time specified in the notice, effectual means for extinguishing or effectually screening the light and for preventing for the future any similar light.

(3) A prevention notice may, in addition to any other mode of service authorised by this Act, be served by affixing the notice in some conspicuous spot near to the light to which it relates.

(4) If a person on whom a prevention notice is served fails, without reasonable excuse, to comply with the directions contained in the notice, he shall be liable, on summary conviction, to a fine not exceeding level 5 on the standard scale.

(5) If a person on whom a prevention notice is served neglects for a period of seven days to extinguish or effectually screen the light mentioned in the notice, the general lighthouse authority may enter the place where the light is and forthwith extinguish it, doing no unnecessary damage.

(6) Where a general lighthouse authority incur any expenses in exercising their powers under subsection (5) above they may recover the expenses from the person on whom the prevention notice was served.

(7) Any such expenses may, in England and Wales and Northern Ireland, be recovered summarily as a civil debt.

(8) In Scotland any such expenses shall, for the purposes of their recovery, be regarded as a debt due by the person on whom the notice has been served to the general lighthouse authority.

DEFINITIONS
"Act, the": s.316(1).
"area": s.193(4).
"England and Wales": Interpretation Act 1978, Sched. 1.

"fails": s.313(1).
"general lighthouse authority": s.193(1).
"lighthouse": s.223(1) and (2).
"person": Interpretation Act 1978, Sched. 1.
"prevention notice": subs. (2).
"standard scale": Criminal Justice Act 1982, s.37.

GENERAL NOTE
[Derivation: Merchant Shipping Act 1894, s.667; Merchant Shipping Act 1979, Sched. 6, Part VII, para. (9); Merchant Shipping (Registration, etc.) Act 1993, Sched. 4, para. 51, Sched. 5; Merchant Shipping Act 1894, s.681(2).]
Section 220 (formerly s.667 of the 1894 Act) deals with the powers of a general lighthouse authority to prevent misleading lights being used in the vicinity of a lighthouse. The Merchant Shipping (Registration, etc.) Act 1993, Sched. 4, para. 51 removed the mischief of burning fires from the section, so that now it only refers to the exhibiting of lights.

Exemptions from taxes, duties, etc.

Exemption from taxes, duties, rates etc.

221.—(1) The following, that is to say—
(a) all lighthouses, buoys and beacons,
(b) all general light dues and other rates, fees or payments accruing to or forming part of the General Lighthouse Fund, and
(c) all premises or property belonging to or occupied by any of the general lighthouse authorities,
which are used or applied for the purposes of any of the services for which those dues, rates, fees and payments are received shall be exempt from all public or local taxes, duties or rates.

(2) All instruments used by or under the direction of any general lighthouse authority in carrying on those services shall be exempt from stamp duty.

(3) Stamp duty shall not be chargeable on any proposals under Schedule 9.

(4) All instruments used by or under the direction of the Secretary of State in carrying this Part into effect shall be exempt from stamp duty.

(5) All instruments which are required by any provision of this Part to be in a form approved by the Secretary of State, if made in that form, shall be exempt from stamp duty.

DEFINITIONS
"buoys and beacons": s.223(1), (2) and (3).
"general light dues": ss.205(1) and 223(1).
"general lighthouse authorities": s.193(1).
"lighthouse": s.223(1) and (2).
"Secretary of State": Interpretation Act 1978, Sched. 1.

GENERAL NOTE
[Derivation: Merchant Shipping Act 1894, ss.721 and 731; Merchant Shipping Act 1988, Sched. 5; Ports Act 1991, s.36(2)(c).]

Exemption from harbour dues

222. All ships belonging to or used by any of the general lighthouse authorities or the Secretary of State shall be entitled to enter, resort to, and use any harbours, ports, docks or piers in the United Kingdom without any payment of tolls, dues or rates of any kind.

DEFINITIONS
"general lighthouse authorities": s.193(1).
"harbour": s.313(1).

"port": s.313(1).
"Secretary of State": Interpretation Act 1978, Sched. 1.
"ship": s.313(1).
"United Kingdom": Interpretation Act 1978, Sched. 1.

GENERAL NOTE
[Derivation: Merchant Shipping Act 1894, s.732.]

Supplemental

Interpretation, etc.

223.—(1) In this Part—
"buoys and beacons" includes all other marks and signs of the sea;
"the Commissioners of Irish Lights" means the body incorporated by
that name under the local Act of the session held in the 30th and
31st years of the reign of Queen Victoria intituled "An Act to alter
the constitution of the Corporation for preserving and improving
the port of Dublin and for other purposes connected with that body
and with the Port of Dublin Corporation";
"general light dues" has the meaning given in section 205(1);
"lighthouse" includes any floating and other light exhibited for the guidance of ships, and also any sirens and any other description of fog
signals, and also any addition to a lighthouse of any improved light,
or any siren, or any description of fog signal;
"the Trinity House" means the master, wardens and assistants of the
guild, fraternity or brotherhood of the most glorious and undivided
Trinity and of St Clement in the parish of Deptford Strond in the
county of Kent, commonly called the corporation of the Trinity
House of Deptford Strond;
"the 1894 Act" means the Merchant Shipping Act 1894.
(2) Any reference in this Part to a lighthouse, buoy or beacon includes its
appurtenances.
(3) The Secretary of State may by order provide that references or a particular reference to a buoy or beacon in this Part shall be construed as including, in such circumstances as are specified in the order, equipment of a kind so
specified which is intended as an aid in the navigation of ships.
(4) No order shall be made under subsection (3) above unless a draft of the
order has been laid before and approved by resolution of each House of
Parliament.

DEFINITIONS
"1894 Act, the": subs. (1).
"buoys and beacons": subss. (1) and (2) and (3).
"Commissioners of Irish Lights": subs. (1).
"general light dues": subs. (1) and s.205(1).
"lighthouse": subss. (1) and (2).
"port": s.313(1).
"Secretary of State": Interpretation Act 1978, Sched. 1.
"ship": s.313(1).
"Trinity House": subs. (1).

GENERAL NOTE
[Derivation: Merchant Shipping Act 1894, s.742, Merchant Shipping (Registration, etc.) Act
1993, Sched. 2, para. 2; Merchant Shipping Act 1894, s.638; Merchant Shipping (Registration,
etc.) Act 1993, Sched. 4, para. 37; Merchant Shipping Act 1979, s.49(3); Safety at Sea Act 1986,
s.11(3), (4)(c)(d); Merchant Shipping Act 1979, s.34(3).]

Subs. (2)
Section 638(1) of the 1894 Act (now s.197) gave a lighthouse authority power to construct a
lighthouse with all requisite roads and "appurtenances". Under s.654(3) the appurtenances

would pass on sale to the acquirer (and see s.33 of the Ports Act 1991). Section 223(2) (formerly s.638(1) of the 1894 Act, as amended by the Merchant Shipping (Registration, etc.) Act 1993, Sched. 4, para. 37) makes the references to appurtenances general throughout Pt. VIII, as opposed to the expression only being directly referred to in s.638 of the Merchant Shipping Act 1894 (now s.197).

PART IX

SALVAGE AND WRECK

CHAPTER I

SALVAGE

Salvage Convention 1989 to have force of law

224.—(1) The provisions of the International Convention on Salvage, 1989 as set out in Part I of Schedule 11 (in this Chapter referred to as "the Salvage Convention") shall have the force of law in the United Kingdom.

(2) The provisions of Part II of that Schedule shall have effect in connection with the Salvage Convention, and subsection (1) above shall have effect subject to the provisions of that Part.

(3) If it appears to Her Majesty in Council that the Government of the United Kingdom has agreed to any revision of the Salvage Convention She may by Order in Council make such modifications of Parts I and II of Schedule 11 as She considers appropriate in consequence of the revision.

(4) Nothing in subsection (1) or (2) above shall affect any rights or liabilities arising out of any salvage operations started or other acts done before 1st January 1995.

(5) Nothing in any modification made by virtue of subsection (3) above shall affect any rights or liabilities arising out of any salvage operations started or other acts done before the day on which the modification comes into force.

(6) As respects any period before the entry into force of the Salvage Convention any reference in the Salvage Convention to a State Party to the Convention shall be read as a reference to the United Kingdom.

(7) A draft of an Order in Council proposed to be made by virtue of subsection (3) above shall not be submitted to Her Majesty in Council unless the draft has been approved by a resolution of each House of Parliament.

DEFINITIONS
    "Salvage Convention, the": subs. (1) and s.255(1).
    "salvage operation": Sched. 11, Art. 1(a).
    "State Party": Sched. 11, para. (7).
    "United Kingdom": Interpretation Act 1978, Sched. 1.

GENERAL NOTE
    [Derivation: Merchant Shipping (Salvage and Pollution) Act 1994, s.1.]

Introduction
    The main purpose of s.224 is to give the force of law to the 1989 Salvage Convention. An Opposition private member's Bill to allow such ratification had been introduced on February 2, 1993, but failed for lack of time. At the Committee stage of the Merchant Shipping (Registration, etc.) Act 1993 the Minister of Transport in London, Mr. Norris, had given an undertaking that the Government would take an early legislative opportunity to incorporate the Convention, and the Donaldson Report in May 1994 had encouraged what became the Merchant Shipping (Salvage and Pollution) Act 1994.
    On September 29, 1994 the U.K. deposited its instrument of ratification to the 1989 Salvage Convention. At that time there was no denunciation of the 1910 Salvage Convention. Although it is arguable that the 1989 Convention impliedly supersedes the 1910 Convention (as stated by Mr. Norris when replying to the debate on the Lords' amendments, *Hansard*, H.C. Vol. 246, col. 1290), the absence of any express statement to this effect leads to the better view that a denunci-

ation is necessary. Where a State, such as the U.K., intends to give interim national effect to the 1989 Salvage Convention it could be in breach of its obligations to existing 1910 states. The U.K. denounced the 1910 Convention before January 1, 1995, the date when the 1989 Salvage Convention was given effect in the U.K. Under Art. 19 of the 1910 Convention a denunciation shall not take effect until a year from when notice was given to the depository.

Background to the 1989 Convention

See generally, Gaskell, "The 1989 Salvage Convention" at pp. 5–7. The 1910 Salvage Convention had been produced under the auspices of the International Maritime Committee (CMI) and had received a wide measure of international acceptance. In recent years it has become apparent that it is not fully suited to conditions in the latter part of the century. This is in part due to its dated form and language, but is mainly caused by changes in the shipping and salvage industries. Ships have become fewer in number, but larger in size and more technically sophisticated. Cargoes of all kinds (and particularly those with the potential to cause pollution) are being carried in greater quantities. The effect of the loss of such quantities of toxic cargo on the environment is much more readily appreciated, especially after the strandings of the oil tankers *Torrey Canyon* (in 1967), *Amoco Cadiz* (in 1978) and *Exxon Valdez* (in March 1989) and, more recently, the *Braer* (in January 1993). At the same time, the task of the potential salvor has increased enormously. Salvage operations are increasingly difficult and expensive to mount, not only because of the size and sophistication of vessels in distress, but also because of the cost of building and operating the large salvage craft necessary to save them. In some cases salvors have spent large sums of money in saving a ship only to have on their hands an 'international leper' which national authorities refuse to allow into port. The ship may even be destroyed under State intervention powers. The traditional principle of 'no cure, no pay' would leave the salvor unrewarded. In other cases the salvors have been sued for damage to vessels or for causing pollution in trying to save them.

Salvors complained that they were not being rewarded enough for the salvage operations that they undertook. Although there are suggestions that the salvage industry had been 'crying wolf', the insolvency of some of the world's leading salvage companies forced a realisation that there may no longer be an industry voluntarily supplying tugs on station at crucial parts of the world. This was recognised as being in the interests of nobody, as the costs to national governments of maintaining such services would be considerable (a fact recognised in the Donaldson Report in 1994).

The first major reform step was achieved not by Convention, but by the amendment in 1980 of the Lloyd's Open Form (LOF). The LOF 1980 introduced a number of novel features of benefit to the salvor. These included an enhanced award, a safety net, and new obligations on the salvee concerning co-operation, redelivery and security. The changes were achieved after a compromise between certain insurance interests who would have to bear the financial consequences of salvage operations (successful or not). It must be noted that the LOF 1980 revisions, and the insurance compromise, played an important part in the drafting of the 1989 Convention. For the salvors pressed for these and other changes to be incorporated in legislation, rather than a contractual document.

The CMI had produced the 1910 Convention and an international sub-committee of CMI undertook a great deal of preparatory work on its revision after 1978. At its 1981 Conference in Montreal, the CMI approved a draft Convention (the 1981 CMI Draft Convention). This document, by agreement with the International Maritime Organisation (IMO), formed the basis of the subsequent discussions in the IMO Legal Committee. It went beyond the LOF 1980, which had addressed itself to oil tanker casualties, and introduced the concept of rewarding services which prevented damage to the environment by substances other than oil. Crucial to the adoption of the 1981 CMI Draft Convention was the so-called 'Montreal Compromise'. This was an agreement, largely reached behind the scenes, between those arguing for salvors and those who were likely to have to meet any increases in payments to them. Under the Montreal Compromise the salvors agreed to give up some of their more radical proposals (including the concept of liability salvage). In exchange, representatives of insurers, shipowners and cargo owners agreed to certain provisions which would increase their liabilities (see further the General Note to Arts. 14.1, 14.4, below). Those involved in the Montreal Compromise regarded the core compensation provisions in the 1981 CMI Draft Convention as a package. In particular, there was to be a balance in the responsibility for paying for pollution prevention between ship and cargo interests. As with most compromises, nobody was happy with everything, but the need to reach agreement was regarded as paramount. Later, at the 1989 diplomatic conference, there was much discussion as to who had actually been represented when this Montreal Compromise was agreed. A number of countries were unhappy at being presented, at a diplomatic conference of sovereign governments, with a fait accompli produced essentially by commercial interests. Nevertheless, the substance of the Montreal Compromise was eventually incorporated in the

1989 Convention. The 1981 CMI Draft Convention was, by agreement, handed on to the IMO Legal Committee. Discussions took place between the 50th Session of the Legal Committee in 1983 and the 58th Session in 1987. Substantial changes of detail were made—although the drafts always retained the essentials of the Montreal Compromise. By 1988 the Committee had produced a final draft Convention for consideration by the 1989 Diplomatic Conference.

The 1989 Diplomatic Conference lasted for two weeks, beginning on April 17, 1989. The most protracted discussions concerned Art. 14 and its relationship with Art. 13. Who would have to pay for environmental protection and at what level? The crucial turning points were the reaching of a Common Understanding on Arts. 13 and 14 (see now Sched. 11, Pt. I, para. 4, below) on April 24, and the agreement on 'special compensation' (the safety net) on April 26, which led to the acceptance of the whole compensation package on April 27 (see the General Note to Art. 14.4, below). The Convention was produced in a single version in five languages which are equally authentic.

Subss. (1) and (2)

Subsection (1) gives the "force of law" to the 1989 Salvage Convention as set out in Sched. 11. Schedule 11 is in two parts. Part I sets out the Convention articles verbatim, with the exception of international law provisions which are redundant in a national enacting statute (*e.g.* Arts. 1(f) and (g) defining the International Maritime Organisation and its Secretary-General and Arts. 28–34 which contain the Final Clauses of the Convention). Subsection (2) gives effect to Sched. 11, Pt. II, which contains "Provisions having effect with the Convention" *i.e.* those provisions which are necessary to make the Convention articles work in U.K. law. In particular, Pt. II reflects a number of the reservations which an enacting State is entitled to make under Art. 30 (see Sched. 11, Pt. II, para. 2) and also the so-called 'Common Understanding', which was Attachment 1 to the Final Act of the 1989 Diplomatic Conference (see Sched. 11, Pt. II, para. 4). In all cases, Pt. I must be read subject to Pt. II, reflecting the U.K. view of international law that a Convention only has effect in national law to the extent that Parliament has provided expressly.

The expression "shall have the force of law" was considered in *Hollandia, the (sub. nom. Morviken, the)* [1983] 1 A.C. 565, a carriage of goods case under the Hague-Visby Rules, where it was held that these Convention provisions must be treated as if they were part of directly enacted statute law, rather than as a set of implied terms in a carriage contract. The distinction, which was important in the context of a choice of law clause, may have less significance in the context of the 1989 Salvage Convention, as Art. 6 specifically allows for the parties to exclude the application of the Convention in any salvage contract (subject to a number of important exceptions set out in Art. 6.3). The important point is that, unless the contract provides otherwise, the 1989 Convention will operate as positive statutory law, in contradistinction to the 1910 Salvage Convention, which it replaces. The U.K. was a party to the 1910 Salvage Convention, but the Maritime Conventions Act 1911 enacted only parts of the Convention into U.K. law. One difficult matter which needs to be resolved is the extent to which pre-existing U.K. salvage law and practice continue to apply (see the General Note to subs. (6), below).

The method of incorporating the Convention is that used in other modern maritime Conventions, see, *e.g.* the Athens Convention 1974 and the 1976 Limitation Convention (Scheds. 3 and 4, respectively, of the Merchant Shipping Act 1979) and is greatly to be preferred to the alternative technique of rewriting the Convention into "legal English" (see Gaskell, "Policy Issues"). The latter approach runs the risk of the drafter altering the meaning of Convention provision which are often the detailed product of a laboriously negotiated set of compromises (see further Gaskell, "Interpretation of Maritime Conventions", at pp. 218–40).

In view of the fact that the 1989 Salvage Convention enters into force internationally on July 14, 1996, detailed consideration of the individual articles of the Convention will be given in the General Note to Sched. 11, below. The most obvious change to English law and practice is that the effective codification of the substantive law of salvage (see point 3 of the General Note to subs. (6), below) will require maritime lawyers to start with the Convention when any salvage question arises (see point 6 of the General Note to subs. (6), below). Some of the substantive changes were already familiar through the LOF 1990, which incorporated parts of the 1989 Salvage Convention. A few of the more significant features for English practitioners may be outlined here (and see also Gaskell, "Policy Issues", at pp. 352–353).

1. Definition of salved property widened (see Art. 1)
2. Geographical limits of salvage widened (see Art. 1, Sched. 1, Pt. II, para. 2)
3. Increased authority of ship's master to bind cargo (see Art. 6)
4. Enhanced reward for environmental protection (see Art. 13)
5. Exception to 'no cure, no pay' principle in environmental incidents (see Art. 14)
6. Life salvage by rescue agencies facilitated (Art. 16.2, 14)
7. Life salvage claims to be directed at salvors (Art. 16.2)
8. Sister ship salvage possible (see Art. 12.3)

9. Obligations of salvor stated (see Art. 8)
10. Obligations of salvee stated (see Art. 8)
11. Security obligations stated (see Art. 21)
12. Jurisdiction and rights *in rem* widened (see Merchant Shipping (Salvage and Pollution) Act 1994, Sched. 2, para. 6)
13. Restrictions imposed on arrest (see Arts. 25, 26)
14. Abolition of time-bar extension (see Art. 23, Merchant Shipping (Salvage and Pollution) Act 1994, Sched. 2, para. 2)
15. 1976 Limitation Convention "clarified" (see Sched. 7, Pt. II, para. 4)

Subss. (3) and (7)
The Act contains a number of provisions designed so that speedy action may be taken to give effect to amendments to international Conventions (see, *e.g.* the General Note to s.86, above). Subsection (3) allows effect to be given by Order in Council to any future amendment of the 1989 Salvage Convention, thus doing away with any requirement to pass primary legislation. At the Committee Stage of the Merchant Shipping (Salvage and Pollution) Act 1994 in the House of Lords, Lord Donaldson introduced subs. (7) which makes any Order under subs. (3) subject to Parliamentary control.

Subss. (4) and (5)
The 1989 Salvage Convention applies to salvage operations (see Art. 1(a)), which may take place over a period of time. Subsection (4) deals with the situation when the operations may span the entry into force of the Convention (or any later modification of it under subs. (3)) and provides that it will be the law in force when the salvage operations *start* which will determine rights and liabilities. As the Convention was given interim effect from January 1, 1995 the provisions of Sched. 11 will be applied to operations which start on that date. A salvage operation which started on or before December 31, 1994 would be governed by the pre-existing salvage law, even if those operations continued on into 1995, or if court or arbitration proceedings took place in 1995. There are circumstances where a dispute might occur as to whether operations by a salvor to mobilise equipment, or to set out in response to a distress call, were the start of any salvage operations. Ultimately this would be a question of fact which would not trouble an experienced tribunal. The alternative formula might have been to take the relevant date as that of 'termination' of services. This is a more usual expression for practitioners, although it would have raised the prospect of a salvage operation being governed by 'floating' legal rules, in the sense that a salvor could prolong operations, or a salvee could terminate them early, in order to take advantage of, or avoid, various provisions in the Convention. The formula used in the present subsection is the better solution.

Subs. (6)
Under Art. 29 the Convention will enter into force internationally one year after the date on which 15 states have expressed their consent to be bound by it, in fact July 15, 1996. Section 1(5) of the Merchant Shipping (Salvage and Pollution) Act 1994 allowed the 1989 Salvage Convention to be brought into force nationally for the interim period before it entered into force internationally. A similar solution was adopted in respect of the Athens Convention 1974 (see now Sched. 6). During the interim operation of the Convention, it will be necessary to read references in the Convention to "State party" as a reference to the U.K. (see subs. (6)). The reason is that there will not be any State parties until the Convention comes into force internationally. References to "State party" appear in Arts. 2, 10.2, 11, 13.2 and 27.
Schedule 2 of the Merchant Shipping (Salvage and Pollution) Act 1994 contained amendments consequential and related to the enactment of the 1989 Salvage Convention. Like subs. (4), above, rights and liabilities arising in respect of salvage operations *started* before the date on which the amendments in the Schedule come into force will continue to be governed by pre-existing law (*e.g.* the Supreme Court Act 1981, s.20 as it was before amendment). That Schedule contained a number of changes to the law which are significant. Detailed comments will be found in the annotations by N. Gaskell in *Current Law Statutes Annotated 1994* to the Merchant Shipping (Salvage and Pollution) Act 1994, Sched. 2, but note particularly the removal of the time-bar extension in s.8 of the Maritime Conventions Act 1911 and the inclusion of the words "in the nature of salvage" in the English jurisdictional provisions, the Supreme Court Act 1981, s.20 and the County Courts Act 1984, s.27 (but not the Scottish equivalent, the Administration of Justice Act 1956, s.47). The English provisions are potentially controversial, for they pose problems as to how far (pre-1995) principles of English salvage law have been retained, despite the apparent comprehensiveness of the Convention. This issue is of such significance that it is addressed here.

1. Interpretation of the 1989 Convention.

When interpreting an international Convention it is not appropriate to adopt the narrow approach often used in the interpretation of contracts and the courts have emphasised that a broad and liberal construction should be given (see, *e.g. Samick Lines Co. v. Autonis P Lemos (Owners)*; *Antonis P Lemos, the* [1985] A.C. 711, at p.725 *et seq.*). A court will note the international origins of any statute and the fact that a convention will have been created for many different legal systems which may not require the same degree of detail that is common in England. It is not so much a question of having formal rules of international law to interpret a Convention, as being aware of its international character. To defeat unduly literalistic interpretations, conventions should be interpreted "unconstrained by technical rules of English law, or by English legal precedent, but on broad principles of general acceptance" (per Lord Wilberforce in *Buchanan (James) & Co. v. Babco Forwarding and Shipping (U.K.)* [1978] A.C. 141, at p. 152).

When interpreting statutes which implement a maritime convention the courts will construe ambiguities so that the U.K. legislation gives effect to its international obligations and is in conformity with the Convention (see *Norwhale, The* [1975] Q.B. 589, at pp. 592, 598, citing *Salomon v. Customs and Excise Commissioners* [1967] 2 Q.B. 116). It is rare for a court to have the job of interpreting maritime conventions without there being some pre-existing national law. The court is then faced with the dilemma of whether to ignore this law or not. Existing rules of law may be expressly removed by the statute enacting the Convention (see, *e.g.* the Carriage of Goods by Sea Acts 1924 and 1971, ss.2 and 3). More often the court has to assess the extent to which Parliament has intended the existing law to continue (see *Gatoil International Inc. v. Arkwright-Boston Manufacturers Mutual Insurance Co. (The Sandrina)* [1985] A.C. 255 and *River Rima, The* [1988] 1 W.L.R. 758). There has been a reluctance to assume that long established principles are no longer to be applied. For instance, the earliest cases on the Hague Rules assumed that its meaning could be devined from existing precedents. There were soon to be found more liberal judicial statements about the proper interpretative techniques to be applied to the Hague Rules. The most widely cited statement of the liberal approach is to be found in the speech of Lord Macmillan in *Stag Line v. Foscolo Mango* [1932] AC 328, at p.350. "It is important to remember that the Act of 1924 was the outcome of an International Conference and that the rules in the Schedule have an international currency. As these rules must come under the consideration of foreign courts it is desirable in the interests of uniformity that their interpretation should not be rigidly controlled by domestic precedents of antecedent date, but rather that the language of the rules should be considered on broad principles of general acceptance." Although the principle that the courts should not have any predilection for the former law is often quoted, it is clear that they reserve the right to decide that English words that have already received a judicial interpretation will be presumed to be used in that sense (*ibid.*, per Lord Atkin at p. 343). In *The Norman* [1960] 1, Lloyd's Rep. 1 a particular expression, "actual fault or privity", had appeared in, and largely been taken from, the unamended Merchant Shipping Act 1894. The lawyers in the case were all familiar with the expression and there was not even the suggestion that this could be other than a straightforward question of domestic law. Such an insular approach should be less common today when there is a greater familiarity with E.C. law (*e.g.* the E.C. Jurisdiction and Judgments Convention 1968) and ought not to be adopted with the 1989 Salvage Convention.

2. Sources for interpreting the 1989 Salvage Convention.

Since *Pepper (Inspector of Taxes) v. Hart* [1993] A.C. 593 the courts may have access to the proceedings in Hansard. With a few exceptions (see point 6(c) of the General Note to subs. (6), below) the debates on the 1994 Act are not particularly revealing about the meaning of the 1989 Convention, partly because of the comparatively brief attention given to a private member's bill. Lord Donaldson, when introducing the Bill at Second Reading in the House of Lords, simply reiterated the desire to encourage salvors to become involved in environmentally threatening disasters. It is now permissible to refer to the travaux preparatoires of Conventions, although the House of Lords has indicated two conditions that would be necessary. The travaux preparatoires must be "public, accessible, and, secondly, . . . [must] clearly and indisputably point to a definite legislative intention" (*Fothergill v. Monarch Airlines* [1981] A.C. 251, at p. 278).

The travaux preparatoires for the 1989 Salvage Convention consist of four categories of material, in descending order of importance: (i) the proceedings of the 1989 diplomatic conference, (ii) the proceedings of the IMO Legal Committee 1983–1988, (iii) the proceedings of the CMI from 1978–1981, (iv) the travaux preparatoires relating to the 1910 Convention.

The proceedings in IMO are not yet in "public, accessible" form (although the Institute of Maritime Law, University of Southampton, is editing the travaux preparatoires in conjunction with the IMO). The travaux preparatoires relating to the 1910 Convention will be particularly relevant where the 1989 Convention has borrowed heavily from its predecessor (see, *e.g.* Arts. 16, 23 and Wildeboer).

It is probably legitimate to refer to the CMI proceedings, even though that is a body consisting of private, non-governmental representatives, because the CMI drafted the original 1910 Convention and undertook to prepare a draft Convention for the IMO. In April 1984 Bent Neilsen prepared a report on behalf of the CMI which was submitted to the IMO Legal Committee at its 52nd session in 1984 (see LEG 52/4, July 3, 1994, Annex 2). The report was considered by the Legal Committee, and used as a basis for initial discussions, although its influence as a source document during later proceedings declined as State representatives became more familiar with the draft Convention and prepared their own working documents. Care should be exercised not to attach too much significance to decisions taken within the CMI, especially at its 1981 Montreal Conference. There may be a tendency for practitioners to point to the understandings reached before, and at, Montreal (many of which were admittedly continued through to the agreement of the 1989 Convention) as a major source for the interpretation of the Convention. What may have been of significance to private practitioners in 1981 may not have been of such importance to governmental negotiators later at the more important meetings at the IMO. It may be unrealistic or dangerous to transfer all the assumptions of those who produced the original 1981 CMI draft to those who produced the 1989 Convention. With that caveat, the 1984 CMI Report can be a useful source of information, particularly on matters which were little discussed at the IMO Legal Committee (see, *e.g.* the discussion on Art. 16, below).

3. The 1989 Salvage Convention as a codification.

The second recital to the 1989 Salvage Convention noted that "substantial developments, in particular the increased concern for the protection of the environment, have demonstrated the need to review the international rules presently contained in the Convention for the Unification of Certain Rules of Law relating to Assistance and Salvage at Sea, done at Brussels, September 23, 1910". There is nothing in the 1989 Salvage Convention which otherwise indicates that it is to supersede the 1910 Convention, although that was clearly its intended purpose and effect. Following the agreement of the 1989 Salvage Convention there was some international discussion as to whether it was necessary to denounce the 1910 Convention. As indicated, the better view is that it was. At the Committee stage in the Commons, Richard Ottaway M.P. (who happened to be a maritime lawyer in practice) described the 1989 Convention as "essentially a recodification of the law of salvage" (cols. 9–10) and this was echoed by Lord Mackay of Ardbrecknish (the Parliamentary Under-Secretary of State, Department of Transport) who stated that the Convention was "intended to codify the law of salvage" (*Hansard*, H.L. Vol. 555, col. 695). Many of the principles of the 1989 Salvage Convention are to be found in the 1910 Convention (*e.g.* Arts. 16–19). Although the 1910 Convention was never formally incorporated into U.K. law, it was always recognised that it reflected many principles of English Admiralty law. Thus, the 1910 Convention adopted the English definition of salvage and rejected the distinction maintained by French law between "assistance" and "salvage".

4. Use of existing salvage law to interpret 1989 Salvage Convention.

The enactment of the 1994 Act raised directly the question of the relationship between the 1989 Salvage Convention as enacted, and existing salvage law. It is submitted that there are two separate issues. First, how far does the 1989 Salvage Convention itself allow reference to existing concepts and practice. Secondly, how far does the last minute retention (in Sched. 2, para. 6, of the Merchant Shipping (Salvage and Pollution) Act 1994) of the words "in the nature of salvage" in the Supreme Court Act 1981, s.20(2)(j) mean that, irrespective of the intention of the drafters of the international instrument, a U.K. court *must* (i) pay regard to pre-existing salvage law, and/or (ii) give priority to that pre-existing law and practice?

A contrast may be seen when the Hague Rules (in the Carriage of Goods by Sea Act 1924) were replaced by the Hague-Visby Rules 1968 (in the Carriage of Goods by Sea Act 1971). The Hague and Hague-Visby Rules were essentially similar, with the 1968 Protocol merely making a number of changes to the established structure of the Hague Rules 1924. In that context, there was no need for the courts to make radical changes to their approach towards basic concepts. Existing case law on the 1924 Act would still be good law, unless specifically changed by the 1971 Act. The 1989 Salvage Convention, with the exception of Art. 14, does retain the same basic principles of the 1910 Convention (*e.g.* in Arts 12 and 13), although it has enlarged objectives, contains much more detail and adopts language which in its modernity offers a different drafting approach. There are two reasons why matters of interpretation are not so straightforward for a

U.K. lawyer with the 1994 Act as they were when the Hague-Visby Rules were introduced. First, the 1989 Salvage Convention probably makes proportionately greater changes of style and content to the 1910 Act than did the Hague-Visby Rules to the Hague Rules. Secondly, the U.K. salvage lawyer cannot simply compare judicial decisions and practices on two international instruments, for U.K. salvage practice has not hitherto taken much account (if any) of the 1910 Convention itself. It is necessary to make the rather more indirect connection between a modern enacting Convention and a previous law and practice which was presumed to reflect the provisions of the earlier Convention. By way of parenthesis it could, of course, be put the other way round: namely that the 1910 Convention itself was recognised to build on English salvage law and practice, so that pre-1995 English salvage law and the 1910 Convention were effectively the same. The difficulty here is that there were differences in substance between the 1910 Convention and English salvage law, and that post-1910 salvage case law was effectively made without reference to the 1910 Convention. Either way, there is the question of how far it would be legitimate to refer to pre-existing law and practice in interpreting the 1989 Salvage Convention. (This point is logically separate from that concerning jurisdiction made in point 6, "in the nature of salvage", below).

It is submitted that it would be right and proper for the U.K. courts to refer to the general principles of English salvage law, but only in order to aid the interpretation and application of the Convention. Leaving aside the natural inclination of lawyers to continue existing practices, and the pre-eminence of London as a centre of salvage law expertise, it will be necessary to refer to existing law for many purposes. A number of examples may be given. The criteria in Art. 13(a) and (c) to (j) represent, in broad terms, the criteria which are presently applied. Even para. (b) is familiar from the LOF 1980 and 1990. Although Art. 12.1 does not use the traditional language of 'no cure, no pay', or 'success', its concept of "useful result" does not differ markedly in effect, nor was it intended to. Danger is not separately defined in Art. 1(a) of the 1989 Salvage Convention, nor was it in Art. of the 1910 Convention. The existing English case law on danger will be fully applicable. Indeed, it was anticipated at the 1989 diplomatic conference that states would apply their own notions to questions of whether sunken vessels and cargoes are in danger (see *Sunken vessels and cargoes*, in the General Note to Art. 1(c) in Sched. 11, Pt. I, below).

5. Approach to 1989 Salvage Convention.

The important change in approach must be that it will be necessary to start with the Convention and relate existing English law and practice to that rather than the other way round. This change must also apply to the LOF 1990 and 1995, as it is no longer satisfactory to state that the rights and obligations of the parties are governed by the terms, express and implied, of the LOF contract and that the general maritime law of salvage applies only in so far as it is expressly or impliedly incorporated into it (*The Unique Mariner (No. 2)* [1979] 1 Lloyd's Rep. 37, at pp. 50–51). Art. 6.1 of the 1989 Salvage Convention puts the matter the other way round in that the "Convention shall apply to any salvage operations save to the extent that a contract otherwise provides expressly or by implication".

The House of Lords has been prepared to extend a search for the meaning of maritime Conventions back into U.K. national antecedents (see, *e.g. Gatoil International Inc. v. Arkwright-Boston Manufacturers Mutual Insurance Co. Sandrina, The* [1985] A.C. 255, *River Rima, The* [1988] 1 W.L.R. 758), but this may be a somewhat questionable process (see, generally, Gaskell, "Interpretation of Maritime Conventions"). It would require very clear indications in the *travaux preparatoires* that an international conference intended to adopt the law and practices of one particular State. The 1989 Salvage Convention borrowed a number of *ideas* from LOF practice, but that is a different matter.

6. Schedule 2, para. 6: "In the nature of salvage".

(a) Supreme Court Act 1981, s. 20(2)(j). Section 20(2) of the Supreme Court Act 1981 lists the cases where the English Admiralty Court has jurisdiction. The original (pre-1994) version of s.20(2)(j) gave jurisdiction "in the nature of salvage". The expression is used in other contexts, *e.g.* in the York-Antwerp Rules 1994, R.XI, although the precise meaning and extent of these words has been the subject of some dispute. Professor Thomas has asked whether the wording "embraces the totality of questions and claims which may arise within the province of salvage or whether it has a more limited connotation" (D. Thomas, *Maritime Liens*, 1980, para. 252). He concluded that it had a restricted meaning and was confined to a salvage reward arising from a beneficial service (*ibid.*). The point is whether other issues which are connected to salvage are within the phrase, *e.g.* the power of a court to make a declaration as to salved value, apportion a reward, reduce or extinguish a reward or condemn a salvor in costs for misconduct. Thomas argued that all these matters would be within the jurisdiction in any event under the general

jurisdictional "sweeping-up" clause (now s.20(1)(c) of the Supreme Court Act 1981 and see Jackson, p. 12–14 and *The Tubantia* [1924] P. 78). As the Law Reform Commission of Australia noted in its Report No. 33, *Civil Admiralty Jurisdiction* (1986), p. 117, "it is undesirable to rely on a "sweeping-up" clause to pick up matters which presently fall within the admiralty jurisdiction under the rubric of 'salvage'" (such as declarations of salved value). With respect to Thomas, it might have been thought more appropriate if the matters listed were interpreted as being "in the nature of salvage" (see also Jackson, p. 48). The rights of a dismissed salvor have been held to give rise to a claim which is treated as if it is salvage (see the General Note to Art. 19 of Sched. 11, below). Similarly, the ancillary matters, listed above, relate directly to the establishment of a salvage reward. The difficulty is over the wording: what does "in the nature of" mean? In *The Tesaba* [1982] 1 Lloyd's Rep. 397, Sheen J. held that a claim for breach of the LOF 1980, clause 5 (see now Art. 21.2 of the 1989 Salvage Convention) was not "in the nature of salvage" as (i) it was a claim for damages and not for a reward, and (ii) the breach occurred after the performance of the salvage services. The actual decision would now be different, because of the effect of Art. 21.2 of the 1989 Convention and Sched. 2, para. 6 of the 1994 Act, but it indicates that there may be doubts about how far claims ancillary to salvage operations fall within the Admiralty jurisdiction (and see also *McAllister Towing and Salvage v. General Security Insurance Co of Canada* [1982] 2 F.C. 34 where a post-operation security dispute was not considered to be a salvage dispute). In principle the decision in *The Tesaba* is unduly narrow, as it clearly makes sense for a specialist court to hear disputes relating to that specialism. The complications arise not in the jurisdictional allocation of cases, but as a result of the procedural advantages of the right *in rem* which follow under s.21.

The Law Reform Commission of Australia preferred the broader language of the Navigation Act 1912 (Aust. Cth) which referred to "all claims whatsoever relating to salvage", and it is a pity that this wording was not adopted in the 1994 Act, given the difficulty with *The Tesaba*. The 1985 CMI Draft Arrest Convention (as adopted as a draft text by the joint UNCTAD/IMO Group of Experts at a meeting in December 1994) refers more broadly to claims concerning or arising out of salvage operations or any salvage agreement.

(b) 1994 Act Schedule 2: the amended Supreme Court Act 1981, s.20(2)(j). Schedule 2, para. 6 of the Merchant Shipping (Salvage and Pollution) Act 1994 added new sub-paragraphs (i) and (ii) to the Supreme Court Act 1981, s.20(2)(j) to refer to claims under the 1989 Salvage Convention and under salvage contracts such as the LOF. It might have been thought that these sub-paragraphs were sufficient in order to provide a satisfactory jurisdictional base for the new salvage law introduced by the 1989 Salvage Convention. This is clearly what the drafter thought as the original version of the Bill contained only the two sub-paragraphs referred to above. A new sub-paragraph (iii), containing the words "in the nature of salvage", was inserted after representations were made by, amongst others, the Admiralty Solicitors Group and professional salvors. The DOT bowed to pressure to reintroduce the traditional wording, partly in order to avoid any possible delays to the Bill. Note that the same amendment appears in the amended County Courts Act 1984, so as to apply the equivalent law when a County Court with admiralty jurisdiction hears a salvage dispute (see Sched. 2, para. 7, of the 1994 Act).

The question which arises is what was the intention and effect of this sub-paragraph? It is submitted that there is room for considerable doubt as to both matters and there is the risk that, in the words used in the office of Parliamentary Counsel, "unnecessary words in a Bill may go septic". Drafters do not like to use words unless their effect is clear and there is a reluctance to use general catch-all sweeping up provisions which may cause uncertainty.

The difficulty lies at the heart of the English predilection for running together, perhaps even confusing, questions of jurisdiction and substantive law. The decision in *The Goring* [1988] A.C. 831, on whether salvage could take place in non-tidal waters, might be thought to have raised a question of substance, but the House of Lords essentially decided the question on whether or not the Admiralty Court traditionally had jurisdiction to deal with such matters. By retaining jurisdiction over claims "in the nature of salvage", did the 1994 Act merely restate that salvage-type disputes should continue to be heard in the Admiralty Court (a narrow jurisdictional effect) or has it retained aspects of the pre-existing substantive salvage law and, if so, which?

(c) Debates in Parliament on Supreme Court Act 1981, s.20(2)(j)(iii). At the Second Reading in the House of Lords of the Merchant Shipping (Salvage and Pollution) Act 1994 Lord Byron expressed concerns that the jurisdiction of the Admiralty Court might be ousted in a number of cases if the Bill did not include the reference to "in the nature of salvage" (now in the Supreme Court Act 1981, s.20(2)(j)(iii)). These cases included 'engaged services' or 'services at request'; claims relating solely to determination of whether a casualty has a salved value; and claims contesting agency of necessity in respect of engaged services or services at request (*Hansard*, H.L. Vol. 555, col. 688). In purely jurisdictional terms these cases may now be covered by sub-paragraph (iii), although whether the principle of 'engaged services' is contrary to the

Convention is another matter (see below and Art. 12.2). In any event, an application for a declaration as to salved value would almost certainly be "under the Convention", given the requirements of Art. 13.1(a).

At the Committee Stage in the House of Lords, a number of statements were made which are of great relevance. Lord Donaldson moved the amendment that resulted in the new subparagraph (iii) (see *Hansard*, H.L. Vol. 555, col. 1663) and reiterated that this "in no way represents a derogation from the salvage convention. When there is a conflict between the convention and the common law the convention, if its terms apply, will take precedence. The amendments merely ensure that the competent court will be able to rule on any dispute" (*ibid.*). Lord Byron then thanked Lord Donaldson for bringing the amendment and stated that "it is an important amendment retaining the historic jurisdiction of the Admiralty Court in relation to claims in the nature of salvage" (*ibid.*). Lord Mackay of Ardbrecknish (the Parliamentary Under-Secretary of State, Department of Transport) concluded the debate, noting his own lack of knowledge of the area, by stating,

"Our main concern regarding the use in the Bill of references to claims in the nature of salvage has been that such wording might be understood as sanctioning the continuance of some types of claim which might otherwise be inconsistent with the Convention as given the force of law in the U.K. by the Bill. The sanctioning of such claims by the Bill would mean derogating from the Convention. As I stated at Second Reading, we cannot do that. I accept, however, that [the amendments], properly understood, relate only to jurisdiction and do not affect the substantive law. Therefore, if, for instance, the giving of a salvage reward for so-called engaged services is inconsistent with the terms of the Convention, then the amendments that we are considering now will not have the effect of derogating from the Convention or of enabling a court or arbiter to make a salvage award inconsistent with the provisions of the Convention. Clause 1(1) of the Bill [s.224(1) of the Act] provides that the Convention as set out in Schedule [11] is to have the force of law in the U.K. It follows that no rule of law relating to salvage can continue in force if that rule is inconsistent with the Convention. The law in the Convention will supersede any existing rule of salvage law where there is any inconsistency. That principle is not diminished by the jurisdictional provisions contained in [the amendments.] On that basis I welcome the amendments and support them" (*Hansard*, H.L. Vol. 555, cols. 1663–1664).

The amendments to the Supreme Court Act 1981 and the County Courts Act 1984 were then agreed.

How far is it legitimate to refer to these debates? In *Pepper (Inspector of Taxes) v. Hart* [1993] A.C. 593 the House of Lords set out three criteria on which it would be permissible to refer to the debates, (a) that the legislation was ambiguous or obscure or the literal meaning led to an absurdity, (b) the material relied on consisted of statements made by a minister or other promoter of the Bill, (c) the statements relied on were clear (see the speech of Lord Browne-Wilkinson at p. 21 with which the majority of the Law Lords agreed). All the Law Lords were keen to emphasise that resort to Hansard should be rare. On the threshold condition (a) there is no question of any absurdity as the Convention provisions can work perfectly satisfactorily on their own (see above). However, the writer is of the opinion that sub-paragraph (iii) is ambiguous or obscure. It is not self-explanatory and needs considerable analysis, such as that given above, to discern its purpose and effect. The second condition is satisfied, both because Lord Donaldson moved the relevant amendments and because Lord Mackay of Ardbrecknish (the Parliamentary Under-Secretary of State, Department of Transport) was effectively the Government proposer of the Bill in all but name. It is finally submitted that the statements at Committee Stage were clear (within condition (c)) to the following extent. Both Lords Donaldson and Mackay emphasised that there was no question of derogating from the Convention and that the measure was essentially jurisdictional in the narrow sense to "ensure that the competent court will be able to rule on any dispute" in the words of Lord Donaldson. (For another legitimate use of *Pepper (Inspector of Taxes) v. Hart* see the General Note to Sched. 11, Pt. II, para. 2, below, on maritime cultural property.)

It would follow that it is necessary to identify areas where existing law and practice differ from the Convention. It may be that (i) there is a direct conflict, (ii) the Convention is wider than pre-existing law, or (iii) pre-existing law is wider than the Convention. "Wider" needs some explaining as there may be cases where the Convention is merely silent on a particular point, or where it may have an apparent rule which does conflict. It is to be presumed, as a matter of interpretation that the U.K. will not enact any provision which would conflict with the Convention as ratified (see above) and, it is submitted, the Admiralty Court should hesitate long before allowing encrustations on a Convention which was debated exhaustively and which for most purposes provides a coherent, self-sufficient regime. One purpose of such Conventions is to achieve international uniformity and this would not be assisted by the preservation, or creation, of doctrines which, if not directly inconsistent with Convention provisions, are nevertheless unnecessary to give effect to the aims and scheme of that Convention. Thus, pre-existing doctrines should be made to fit within the Convention structure, rather than somehow standing outside it, and sub-paragraph (iii) should be interpreted restrictively so as not to undermine the conceptual unity of that Convention.

(d) Existing salvage principles possibly preserved by the words "in the nature of salvage". The supporters of sub-paragraph (iii) were clearly reluctant to see several centuries of case law and practice be rendered irrelevant by the new Act. To a large extent, this fear was misfounded for, as stated above, the Convention builds on existing practices and much of the case law, *e.g.* on danger, would naturally still be relevant under the Convention. The sub-paragraph was not necessary to ensure that most pre-existing principles could continue. The supporters specifically had in mind a number of English law principles which were not directly mentioned in the Convention but which, it is submitted, ordinary rules of interpretation would have preserved. An example is *The Tojo Maru* [1972] A.C. 242 principle that a salvor may be held liable in damages for negligence in excess of any salvage reward which has been earned. As submitted in (iv), below, this principle is impliedly recognised by the Convention. But what other substantive rules may have been preserved and how far are they consistent with the Convention? It may be helpful to consider the following issues or "principles" by way of example: (i) 'engaged services', (ii) 'common law salvage' and 'restitution for salvage', (iii) "superseded salvors", (iv) *The Tojo Maru*, (v) offshore platforms and other subjects of salvage, (vi) passage money. It was the principle of engaged services which was probably the most significant factor in the pressure to retain the old wording.

(i) Engaged services. English salvage law has a principle of 'engaged services' (which is dealt with under Art. 12.2 of Sched. 11, below). Entitlement depends on the making of a request for services, even though they have not been of any use. It might be said that the principle sets out an exception to another principle, namely that services must have contributed to success, or have "had a useful result" (Art. 12.1). The problem is that a right currently exists in English salvage law, but the 1989 Salvage Convention does not specifically deal with the matter. It is submitted that the existence of a separate doctrine of engaged services in the 1994 Act may be contrary to the intention of the Convention (see the General Note to Art. 12.2, below).

However, against this view, which derives from the wording of the Convention and the statute, must be set the context in which sub-paragraph (iii) was introduced in Parliament. The practitioners voiced their views through the British Maritime Law Association Salvage Sub-Committee and representations were apparently made by the International Salvage Union (representing professional salvors). The concerns were first expressed by Lord Byron at the Second Reading in the House of Lords (*Hansard*, H.L. Vol. 555, col. 688). He referred to a number of cases where the jurisdiction of the Admiralty Court might be ousted if the Bill did not include sub-paragraph (iii) (for an analysis of these cases, see the General Note to the Merchant Shipping (Salvage and Pollution) Act 1994, Sched. 2, para. 6, in *Current Law Statutes Annotated 1994*). In respect of engaged services, he noted that it "would be a pity if this important additional area of present salvage jurisdiction were to be lost as a result of this Bill coming into effect" (*ibid.*, col. 689). Lord Byron recognised that it was not open to Parliament to redraft the Convention and therefore did not press for an amendment to another article of the Convention with which concerns had been expressed, namely Art. 16 dealing with life salvage (see the General Note to Art. 16, below). In relation to the jurisdiction point he stated that "I am not sure that this difficulty arises" (*ibid.*). With respect, the difficulty of conflict with the Convention can arise in the sense that the principle of engaged services was always considered as an integral part of salvage law, the very subject which the Convention codifies. Lord Donaldson, in reply, lamented that the original Bill would abolish the jurisdiction in respect of claims "in the nature of salvage" and added firmly that para. 6 "is jurisdictional; it neither adds to nor subtracts from the Salvage Convention or anything else" (*Hansard*, H.L. Vol. 555, col. 697). If the matter were simply one of extending the jurisdiction of the Admiralty Court, in the sense of enlarging the category of cases it was entitled to hear, there would be no problem. The point is that the enlargement of jurisdiction (or preservation of it in this case) *may* be held to carry with it the substantive law to which that jurisdiction relates (*cf.* the sensible approach taken in the dissenting judgment of Lord Donaldson in *The Goring* [1987] Q.B. 687, which was not upheld in the House of Lords [1988] 1 A.C. 831).

However, it is clear from the statements of Lords Donaldson and Mackay of Ardbrecknish made later at the Committee Stage in the House of Lords (point 6(c), above) that a court would not be entitled to apply the principle of engaged services if it was inconsistent with the Convention. Lord Byron may have assumed that there was no inconsistency, but Lord Mackay obviously had misgivings. Lord Donaldson was merely leaving the matter to the Admiralty judge to decide whether there was a conflict. It has already been submitted that there is a possible conflict and that, therefore, sub-paragraph (iii) ought not to be used to introduce or retain a separate doctrine of engaged services in English law.

(ii) 'Common law salvage', 'restitution for salvage'. There has been some discussion of whether there does, or ever did, exist a separate notion of 'common law salvage' (see the discussion in Kennedy, p. 60). The question is whether there is a distinction between it and the normal principles of salvage law developed by the Court of Admiralty at the time of conflicts between the King's courts (and see *The Goring* [1988] A.C. 831). Care must be taken not to be confused over terminology as the expression 'common law salvage' is sometimes used to refer to 'pure' admiralty salvage where rights arise irrespective of contract (it is in this sense that Lord Donaldson used the term in the passage from Hansard, cited above). There is also the possibility that general developments in the law of restitution mean that rescuers can claim a restitutionary award (see F.D. Rose, "Restitution for the Rescuer", (1989) 9 OJLS 167 for a persuasive argument that there is a framework for such claims). If the law develops on these lines the strict distinction between the saving of property on water and on land may reduce in significance. Given that that the U.K. has exercised the reservation in Art. 30 in respect of inland navigation (see Sched. 11, Pt. II, para. 2, below) it will not be possible to have salvage rewards under the Convention for services performed between inland vessels, but restitutionary claims, restricted to an indemnity for liabilities and a reimbursement for expenses, may still be arguable. In Scottish law there is apparently the possibility that a claim may be based on *negotiorum gestio* which is outside of the Convention (see A. Forte, "Salvage operations, salvage contracts and *negotiorum gestio*" [1993] J.R. 247).

Has the insertion of the sweeping-up provision of sub-paragraph (iii) made it clear that the Admiralty Court is to hear such 'non-Convention' claims? This approach would treat sub-paragraph (iii) as dealing with 'narrow jurisdictional' grounds which will have little or no substantive effects. Section 20 of the Supreme Court Act 1981 is concerned with the jurisdiction of the Admiralty Court to hear cases. Other parts of that Act assign matters to other courts, *e.g.* the Commercial Court. It would clearly make sense for the Admiralty Court, with its expertise, to hear all cases which might relate to salvage. Absent a clear statement that the Admiralty Court was to deal with a salvage-related dispute, the matter would be heard elsewhere in the High Court, *e.g.* in the Queen's Bench Division. The problem is that these "non-Convention" claims may not have fallen within the pre-existing salvage jurisdiction of the Admiralty Court as they might not be claims "in the nature of salvage" (see *The Tesaba* [1982] 1 Lloyd's Rep. 397, dealt with above). Unless the approach in *The Tesaba* is held to be wrong, it would appear to be consistent with principle to interpret the sweeping-up para. (iii) narrowly. Otherwise, it would have been perfectly sensible to interpret it widely as a simple jurisdictional sweeping-up of other claims similar to salvage, although noting that the Australian Admiralty Act 1988 deliberately chose a wider form of words. The words "any contract for or *in relation* to salvage services" in sub-paragraph (ii) might be interpreted more widely. But, this sub-paragraph could only apply where there was a *contract*, and the word "salvage" may again be interpreted narrowly. It is submitted that a wide meaning should be given to the words "in the nature of salvage" and that *The Tesaba* type restrictions should be overruled. Alternatively, it may be necessary to use s.20(1)(c) of the Supreme Court Act 1981.

Even assuming that the Admiralty Court would have jurisdiction in the narrow sense over common law salvage, and restitutionary, claims, how far can such claims be considered to exist after the enactment of the 1989 Salvage Convention? Is there a conflict, or can they stand with the international codification? It is submitted that there is no need to develop any notion of 'common law salvage' (as distinct from the principles of salvage developed by the Admiralty Court), and that the express enactment of the 1989 Convention by Parliament indicates that it has legislated decisively on the matter. Similarly, the existence of restitutionary claims must also be doubtful, at least in a case where the parties agreed a 'salvage' contract or where the services are performed by a professional salvor aware of the 'no cure, no pay' principle. It is debatable whether a non-professional salvor, unaware of salvage law, should be able to assert a restitutionary claim outside of the salvage regime (and perhaps in the Commercial Court). At the very least it would seem incongruous for such a claim to be allowed in circumstances where the salvage regime applied.

(iii) Superseded salvors. Under the (pre-1995) salvage law of England a salvor who was superseded may have been entitled to some reward or compensation. This reward or compensation would vary, depending on whether the salvor was performing 'pure' non-contractual services or engaged on a contract such as the LOF (see the General Note to Article 19, below). Article 19 of the 1989 Salvage Convention gives the power to prohibit salvage services and dismissal is specifically addressed in Art. 8.1(c) and (d). Where the Convention deals expressly with a matter such as this, it is doubtful how far it is open to national law to provide an *extra* remedy. In the context of sub-paragraph (iii) this is a case where there is no direct conflict between the pre-existing salvage law and the Convention, but where a reasonable interpretation of the Convention would mean that it would be inappropriate for the existing remedy in a pure salvage situation to overlay

a remedy, and criterion, expressly set out by the Convention. It is submitted in the General Note to Art. 19 that the Admiralty Court could interpret the 1989 Salvage Convention as impliedly removing any other remedy deriving from salvage law.

(iv) The Tojo Maru. It was held in *The Tojo Maru* [1972] A.C. 242 that a negligent salvor could be subject to a counter-claim for damages which could exceed any salvage reward payable. It is submitted that an action for damages is available where the salvor has failed to exercise due care to carry out the salvage operations (see the General Note to Art. 8.1(a), below). Article 18 of the 1989 Salvage Convention allows the reduction, or complete deprivation, of rewards where there has been misconduct of the salvor (and *cf.* Art. 14.5), but does not deal with the counter-claims.

What is the effect of sub-paragraph (iii) on the rule in *The Tojo Maru*? It might be said that as the Convention does not expressly deal with counter-claims, this could be interpreted to mean that the remedies supplied in the Convention (*e.g.* deprivation of the reward) are definitive (and see the discussion on engaged services, above). However, it is argued below (in the General Note to Art. 8.1(a)) that, as a matter of interpretation of the Convention, the salvor could be held liable for a counter-claim. On analysis, the rule in *The Tojo Maru* survives through the Convention itself and the need for a residual sweeping up through sub-paragraph (iii) is unnecessary.

(v) Offshore platforms and other subjects of salvage. Under (pre-1995) English salvage law it would almost certainly not have been possible to salve oil platforms as they would not be considered as subjects of salvage (see *Wells v. Gas Float Whitton No. 2* [1897] A.C. 337 and the discussion of salvable property under the Convention in the General Note to Sched. 11, below). To this extent the 1989 Salvage Convention will widen the category of property which may be salved. However, in Art. 3 of the Convention there is a complete exclusion from the Convention of offshore platforms when on location. As a matter of interpretation, it would be sensible to apply the Act as a codification of salvage law which has removed any possibility of making salvage claims, under any pre-existing law, in respect of platforms in Art. 3. As it happens, such claims would not fall within the sweeping up sub-paragraph (iii) as they never were "in the nature of salvage" if that phrase is interpreted narrowly (see, point 6(a), above).

It is theoretically possible to agree a *contract* that salvage services be provided to such platforms, although any rights and obligations would arise outside of the Convention (see Art. 6.1 and Gaskell, "the 1989 Salvage Convention", pp. 23–24). It may be difficult to fit such a contractual claim within the jurisdiction of the Admiralty Court under any part of the Supreme Court Act 1981, s.20. The same reasoning would apply to other subjects of salvage which fall outside the scope of the Convention (as enacted in the U.K. with the reservations made under Art. 30 and stated in Sched. 11, Pt. II, para. 2).

(vi) Passage money. One very minor area where the pre-1995 salvage law is possibly *wider* than the Convention concerns the issue of whether passage money (*e.g.* passenger fares payable on the vessel reaching its destination) is a subject of salvage within Art. 1(c) of the 1989 Salvage Convention. It is submitted later that passage money is a subject of salvage (see the General Note to Art. 1(c), below), but once again this would not be because it is swept up by sub-paragraph (iii), but because the proper interpretation of the Convention would allow such payments to be treated as property.

Valuation of property by receiver

225.—(1) Where any dispute as to salvage arises, the receiver may, on the application of either party, appoint a valuer to value the property.

(2) When the valuation has been made the receiver shall give copies of it to both parties.

(3) A copy of the valuation purporting to be signed by the valuer, and to be certified as a true copy by the receiver, shall be admissible as evidence in any subsequent proceedings.

(4) There shall be paid in respect of the valuation by the person applying for it such fee as the Secretary of State may direct.

DEFINITIONS
"property": Sched. 11, Art.1(c).
"receiver": s.255(1).
"salvage": s.255(1).
"Secretary of State": Interpretation Act 1978, Sched. 1.

GENERAL NOTE
[Derivation: Merchant Shipping Act 1894, s.551; Merchant Shipping (Registration, etc.) Act 1993, Sched. 4, para. 33, Sched. 5.]

Section 225 gives the receiver power to value salved property. See the General Note to Chapter II of this Part of the Act, below, on receivers.

Detention of property liable for salvage by receiver

226.—(1) Where salvage is due to any person under this Chapter, the receiver shall—
(a) if the salvage is due in respect of services rendered—
(i) in assisting a vessel, or
(ii) in saving life from a vessel, or
(iii) in saving the cargo and equipment of a vessel,
detain the vessel and cargo or equipment; and
(b) if the salvage is due in respect of the saving of any wreck, and the wreck is not sold as unclaimed under this Chapter, detain the wreck.
(2) Subject to subsection (3) below, the receiver shall detain the vessel and the cargo and equipment, or the wreck, as the case may be, until payment is made for salvage, or process is issued for the arrest or detention of the property by the court.
(3) The receiver may release any property detained under subsection (2) above if security is given—
(a) to his satisfaction, or
(b) where—
(i) the claim for salvage exceeds £5,000, and
(ii) any question is raised as to the sufficiency of the security,
to the satisfaction of the court.
(4) Any security given for salvage under this section to an amount exceeding £5,000 may be enforced by the court in the same manner as if bail had been given in that court.
(5) In this section "the court" means the High Court or, in Scotland, the Court of Session.
(6) As respects Scotland the reference in subsection (2) to process being issued for arrest shall be construed as a reference to warrant for arrestment being granted.

DEFINITIONS
"High Court": Interpretation Act 1978, Sched. 1.
"payment": Sched. 11, Art.1(e).
"person": Interpretation Act 1978, Sched. 1.
"the court": subs. (5).
"receiver": s.255(1).
"salvage": s.255(1).
"vessel": s.255(1).
"wreck": s.255(1) and (2).

GENERAL NOTE
[Derivation: Merchant Shipping Act 1894, s.552; Merchant Shipping (Registration, etc.) Act 1993, Sched. 4, para. 30, Sched. 5; Merchant Shipping (Salvage and Pollution) Act 1994, Sched. 2, para. 1(3).]
Section 226 gives the receiver power to detain salved property.

Sale of detained property by receiver

227.—(1) The receiver may sell any detained property if the persons liable to pay the salvage in respect of which the property is detained are aware of the detention, in the following cases.
(2) Those cases are—
(a) where the amount is not disputed, and payment of the amount due is not made within twenty days after the amount is due;

(b) where the amount is disputed, but no appeal lies from the first court to which the dispute is referred, and payment is not made within twenty days after the decision of the first court;

(c) where the amount is disputed and an appeal lies from the decision of the first court to some other court, and within twenty days of the decision of the first court neither payment of the sum due is made nor proceedings are commenced for an appeal.

(3) The proceeds of sale of detained property shall, after payment of the expenses of the sale, be applied by the receiver in payment of the expenses, fees and salvage and any excess shall be paid to the owners of the property or any other persons entitled to it.

(4) In this section "detained property" means property detained by the receiver under section 226(2).

DEFINITIONS
"detained property": subs. (4) and s.226(2).
"payment": Sched. 11, Art.1(e).
"person": Interpretation Act 1978, Sched. 1.
"property": Sched. 11, Art.1(c).
"receiver": s.255(1).
"salvage": s.255(1).

GENERAL NOTE
[Derivation: Merchant Shipping Act 1894, s.553.]
Section 227 gives the receiver power to sell salved property which has been detained.

Apportionment of salvage under £5,000 by the receiver

228.—(1) Where—
(a) the aggregate amount of salvage payable in respect of salvage services rendered in United Kingdom waters has been finally determined and does not exceed £5,000; but
(b) a dispute arises as to the apportionment of the amount among several claimants,

the person liable to pay the amount may apply to the receiver for leave to pay it to him.

(2) The receiver shall, if he thinks fit, receive the amount and, if he does, he shall give the person paying it a certificate stating the amount paid and the services in respect of which it is paid.

(3) A certificate under subsection (2) above shall be a full discharge and indemnity to the person by whom it was paid, and to his vessel, cargo, equipment and effects against the claims of all persons in respect of the services mentioned in the certificate.

(4) The receiver shall with all convenient speed distribute any amount received by him under this section among the persons entitled to it, on such evidence, and in such shares and proportions, as he thinks fit.

(5) Any decision by the receiver under subsection (4) above shall be made on the basis of the criteria contained in Article 13 of the Salvage Convention.

(6) The receiver may retain any money which appears to him to be payable to any person who is absent.

(7) A distribution made by a receiver under this section shall be final and conclusive as against all persons claiming to be entitled to any part of the amount distributed.

DEFINITIONS
"person": Interpretation Act 1978, Sched. 1.
"receiver": s.255(1).
"salvage": s.255(1).
"Salvage Convention, the": ss.224(1) and 255(1).
"United Kingdom": Interpretation Act 1978, Sched. 1.
"United Kingdom waters": s.313(2)(a).
"vessel": s.255(1).

GENERAL NOTE
[Derivation: Merchant Shipping Act 1894, s.555; Merchant Shipping (Registration, etc.) Act 1993, Sched. 4, para. 30; Merchant Shipping (Salvage and Pollution) Act 1994, Sched. 2, para. 1(4).]

Sections 555 and 556 of the Merchant Shipping Act 1894 dealt with apportionment of salvage awards amongst claimants by the receiver of wreck (where salvage rewards were, originally, under £200) and the Admiralty Court. The amount was increased to £5,000 by Sched. 2 of the Merchant Shipping (Salvage and Pollution) Act 1994. That Act also inserted what is now subs. (5) to make it clear that the apportionment is to be made on the basis of the criteria listed in Art. 13 of the 1989 Salvage Convention. Although it may be useful to have a summary procedure to deal with wreck (ss. 226–228), it might have been thought that there was no need for any residual national rules on apportionment once the Convention was given effect. Article 15.2 of the Convention leaves apportionment to the law of the flag of the vessel or to the contract between the salvor and its employees. Neither the 1894 nor the 1995 provisions directly address the conflicts issue. As Art. 15 has the force of law, the receiver or court must inquire into foreign apportionment rules where the article so directs. Note the repeal of the Maritime Conventions Act 1911, s.7, by the Merchant Shipping (Salvage and Pollution) Act 1994, Sched. 2, para. 2.

Apportionment of salvage by the court

229.—(1) Where—

(a) the aggregate amount of salvage payable in respect of salvage services rendered in United Kingdom waters has been finally determined and exceeds £5,000; or

(b) the aggregate amount of salvage payable in respect of salvage services rendered outside United Kingdom waters (of whatever amount) has been finally determined; but

(c) in either case, any delay or dispute arises as to the apportionment of the amount,

the court may cause the amount of salvage to be apportioned among the persons entitled to it in such manner as it thinks just.

(2) Any decision of the court under this section shall be made on the basis of the criteria contained in Article 13 of the Salvage Convention.

(3) For the purpose of making that apportionment, the court may—

(a) appoint any person to carry that apportionment into effect;

(b) compel any person in whose hands or under whose control the amount may be to distribute it or to pay it into court to be dealt with as the court directs; and

(c) issue such process as it thinks fit.

(4) In this section "the court" means the High Court or, in Scotland, the Court of Session or a sheriff.

DEFINITIONS
"court, the": subs. (4).
"High Court": Interpretation Act 1978, Sched. 1.
"person": Interpretation Act 1978, Sched. 1.
"salvage": s.255(1).
"Salvage Convention, the": ss.224(1) and 255(1).
"United Kingdom": Interpretation Act 1978, Sched. 1.
"United Kingdom waters": s.313(2)(a).

GENERAL NOTE
[Derivation: Merchant Shipping Act 1894, s.556; Merchant Shipping (Registration, etc.) Act 1993, Sched. 4, para. 30; Merchant Shipping (Salvage and Pollution) Act 1994, Sched. 2, para. 1(5).]

See the General Note to s.228, above.

Salvage claims against the Crown and Crown rights of salvage and regulation thereof

230.—(1) Subject to section 29 of the Crown Proceedings Act 1947 (exclusion of proceedings in rem against the Crown) (so far as consistent with the Salvage Convention) the law relating to civil salvage, whether of life or property, except sections 225, 226 and 227, shall apply in relation to salvage services in assisting any of Her Majesty's ships, or in saving life therefrom, or in saving any cargo or equipment belonging to Her Majesty in right of Her Government in the United Kingdom, in the same manner as if the ship, cargo or equipment belonged to a private person.

(2) Where salvage services are rendered by or on behalf of Her Majesty, whether in right of Her Government in the United Kingdom or otherwise, Her Majesty shall be entitled to claim salvage in respect of those services to the same extent as any other salvor, and shall have the same rights and remedies in respect of those services as any other salvor.

(3) No claim for salvage services by the commander or crew, or part of the crew, of any of Her Majesty's ships shall be finally adjudicated upon without the consent of the Secretary of State to the prosecution of the claim.

(4) Any document purporting to give the consent of the Secretary of State for the purposes of subsection (3) above and to be signed by an officer of the Ministry of Defence shall be evidence of that consent.

(5) If a claim is prosecuted without the consent required by subsection (3) above the claim shall be dismissed with costs.

(6) The reference in subsection (5) above to dismissal with costs shall in Scotland be construed as a reference to dismissal with the defender being found entitled to expenses.

(7) "Her Majesty's ships" has the same meaning in this section as in section 192.

(8) In the application of this section to Northern Ireland, any reference to Her Majesty's Government in the United Kingdom includes a reference to Her Government in Northern Ireland.

DEFINITIONS
   "Her Majesty's ships": subs. (7) and s.192(2).
   "person": Interpretation Act 1978, Sched. 1.
   "property": Sched. 11, Art. 1(c).
   "salvage": s.255(1).
   "Salvage Convention": ss.224(1) and 255(1).
   "salvor": s.255(1).
   "Secretary of State": Interpretation Act 1978, Sched. 1.
   "ship": s.313(1).
   "United Kingdom": Interpretation Act 1978, Sched. 1.

GENERAL NOTE
   [Derivation: Merchant Shipping Act 1894, s.557 (Defence (Transfer of Functions) Act 1964, ss.1(2), 3(2)) and Crown Proceedings Act 1947, s.8 (Merchant Shipping (Salvage and Pollution) Act 1994, Sched. 2, para. 3) and s.38(2), and Crown Proceedings Order 1981 (S.I. 1981 No. 233), Art. 30(1).]
   In general, salvage claims may be brought against and by the Crown. See Sched. 11, Pt. I, Art. 25, below.

CHAPTER II

WRECK

GENERAL NOTE
   Part IX, Chapter II of the Merchant Shipping Act 1995 is derived from Pt. IX of the Merchant Shipping Act 1894. It is unfortunate that the Protection of Wrecks Act 1973, and the Protection of Military Remains Act 1986, have not been included in the consolidation.

Reform of wreck law
   Many of the provisions of Pt. IX of the 1894 Act dealing with wreck and salvage were totally inappropriate to deal with modern conditions (see generally, S. Dromgoole, N. Gaskell, "Interests in Wreck", Chapter 13, in N. Palmer, E. McKendrick, *Interests in Goods* (1993)). The Merchant Shipping (Registration, etc.) Act 1993, Sched. 4, paras. 19–34 attempted to remove some absurdities in the old law and to modernise it where appropriate, but these amendments were

largely cosmetic. In particular, the 1894 scheme was designed to deal with commercial wrecks, *i.e.* with ordinary merchant ships which have recently sunk. That scheme, perpetuated in the Merchant Shipping Act 1995, is no longer appropriate for dealing with historic or cultural artefacts, which on land are dealt with in legislation such as the Ancient Monuments Act 1979. One fundamental principle which has been retained by the Merchant Shipping Act 1995 is that the law of salvage can continue to apply to all wrecks (and see the General Note to s.224 and Sched. 11).

Internationally, the International Law Association produced in 1994 a draft Convention on the Protection of the Underwater Cultural Heritage which is being considered by UNESCO for adoption by an international conference in 1999. The IMO is also working on a draft Convention on Wreck Removal, of which the U.K. is one of the main sponsors. It will probably take until at least 1999 before this Convention could be considered at a diplomatic conference. It seems as though the thorough reform of wreck law that is required must await another day.

Minor revisions to wreck law

"Wreck" is still defined in s.255 in the same terms as in s.510 of the 1894 Act, but a number of anachronistic references in the 1894 Act were removed by the Merchant Shipping (Registration, etc.) Act 1993, including, s.514 of the Merchant Shipping Act 1894, which gave the receiver of wreck the right to suppress plunder! Wreck law is more concerned today about the environment and underwater archaeology than it is with deliberate plunder (although *cf.* s.235(1)). A number of other changes in the 1993 Act increased figures in the 1894 Act which had become hopelessly outdated: see, *e.g.* s.522(a) (now s.240(1)(a)); s.537(2) (now s.247(3)); s.552(3) (now s.226); s.555(1) (now s.228); and s.556 (now s.229). The wording of s.524 (now s.242) was changed by the 1993 Act to remove specific references to Lords of the Manor and the like, but did not effect a change of substance.

Receivers of wreck

The Merchant Shipping Act 1894 continued a system whereby control over wrecks was exercised by local officials described as receivers of wreck. Such officials were appointed by the Secretary of State, and could have been any person, although they were usually customs, coastguard or Inland Revenue officials (see s.566 of the Merchant Shipping 1894). Their original functions seem mainly to have been to prevent plunder and the activities of "wreckers". In practice the receiver of wreck service declined in importance (Dromgoole, N. Gaskell, op. cit., pp. 352–354). The powers of a receiver have been exercised this century by H.M. Customs and the hierarchy of officials mentioned in s.516 of the Merchant Shipping Act 1894 did not operate. The Merchant Shipping (Registration, etc.) Act 1993, Sched. 4, para. 31 amended s.566 of the Merchant Shipping Act 1894 on the appointment of receivers so as to allow for there to be a single central receiver, if desired (see s.248(2), below).

Repealed wreck provisions

The Merchant Shipping (Registration, etc.) Act 1993 removed altogether a number of wreck provisions from the Merchant Shipping Act 1894. Thus, s.528 of the Merchant Shipping Act 1894 used to allow the Secretary of State to purchase rights to wreck. It is not clear if this power was ever used as a compulsory purchase provision, but the state no longer exercises the power. It is not clear, either, exactly why the provision was repealed. If there is no restriction on the extent to which the state could contract to buy wrecks in the ordinary way, the provision was surplussage. If specific power was needed, there may well be occasions in the future when it is in the national interest to purchase historic wrecks but where no power will exist. Section 529 used to deal with the powers of those exercising Admiralty jurisdiction, such as an "admiral or vice-admiral", but had no modern significance. Section 543 used to deal with the marking of anchors, a subject later dealt with by the Anchors and Chain Cables Act 1967 and which are now dealt with by regulations (on the repeal of the 1967 Act by the Merchant Shipping (Registration, etc.) Act 1993, Sched. 5). Sections 558–564 used to deal with salvage by naval vessels, particularly overseas. The decline in size of the navy and the existence of specialist salvors means that there is little call for such work, at least for that which would involve special procedures. Section 230 now regulates salvage claims by or against Crown vessels and there is nothing to prevent the Crown making use of standard contracts such as the Lloyd's Open Form Salvage Agreement 1995.

Vessels in distress

Application of, and discharge of functions under, sections 232, 233, 234 and 235

231.—(1) Sections 232, 233, 234 and 235 apply in circumstances where a United Kingdom or foreign vessel is wrecked, stranded, or in distress at any place on or near the coasts of the United Kingdom or any tidal water within United Kingdom waters.

(2) Where any function is conferred on the receiver by any of those sections that function may be discharged by any officer of customs and excise or any principal officer of the coastguard.

(3) An officer discharging any such functions of the receiver shall, with respect to any goods or articles belonging to a vessel the delivery of which to the receiver is required by any provision of this Chapter, be treated as the agent of the receiver.

(4) However, an officer discharging such functions shall not—

(a) be entitled to any fees payable to receivers, or

(b) be deprived of any right to salvage to which he would otherwise be entitled.

(5) In any of those sections "shipwrecked persons", in relation to a vessel, means persons belonging to the vessel.

DEFINITIONS
"foreign": s.313(1).
"person": Interpretation Act 1978, Sched. 1.
"receiver": s.255(1).
"salvage": s.255(1).
"shipwrecked persons": subs. (5).
"tidal water": s.255(1).
"United Kingdom": Interpretation Act 1978, Sched. 1.
"United Kingdom waters": s.313(2)(a).
"vessel": s.255(1).

GENERAL NOTE
[Derivation: Merchant Shipping Act 1894, ss.511, 512, 513, 515 and 516; Merchant Shipping (Registration, etc.) Act 1993, Sched. 4, paras. 20 and 21.]

Duty of receiver where vessel in distress

232.—(1) In circumstances in which this section applies by virtue of section 231 in relation to any vessel the receiver shall, on being informed of the circumstances, discharge the following functions.

(2) Subject to subsection (4) below, the receiver shall—

(a) forthwith proceed to the place where the vessel is;

(b) take command of all persons present; and

(c) assign such duties and give such directions to each person as he thinks fit for the preservation of the vessel and of the lives of the shipwrecked persons.

(3) The receiver shall not interfere between the master and crew of the vessel in reference to the management of the vessel unless he is requested to do so by the master.

(4) Subject to subsection (3) above, if any person intentionally disobeys the direction of the receiver he shall be liable, on summary conviction, to a fine not exceeding level 3 on the standard scale.

DEFINITIONS
"master": s.313(1).
"person": Interpretation Act 1978, Sched. 1.
"receiver": s.255(1).
"shipwrecked persons": s.231(5).
"standard scale": Criminal Justice Act 1982, s.37.
"vessel": s.255(1).

GENERAL NOTE
[Derivation: Merchant Shipping Act 1894, ss.511 and 680(1)(b); Criminal Justice Act 1982, Sched. 14, para. 2(1); Merchant Shipping Act 1979, Sched. 6, Pt. VII, para. 9.]

Section 232 sets out the duties of the receiver. For the applications and discharge of the receiver's functions, see s.231, above.

Powers of receiver in case of vessel in distress

233.—(1) In circumstances where this section applies by virtue of section 231 in relation to any vessel the receiver may, for the purpose of the preservation of shipwrecked persons or of the vessel, cargo and equipment—

(a) require such persons as he thinks necessary to assist him;

(b) require the master, or other person having the charge, of any vessel near at hand to give such assistance with his men, or vessel, as may be in his power; and

(c) require the use of any vehicle that may be near at hand.

(2) If any person refuses, without reasonable excuse, to comply with any requirement made under subsection (1) above he shall be liable, on summary conviction, to a fine not exceeding level 3 on the standard scale.

DEFINITIONS
"master": s.313(1).
"person": Interpretation Act 1978, Sched. 1.
"receiver": s.255(1).
"shipwrecked persons": s.231(5).
"standard scale": Criminal Justice Act 1982, s.37.
"vessel": s.255(1).

GENERAL NOTE
[Derivation: Merchant Shipping Act 1894, ss.512 and 680(1)(b); Criminal Justice Act 1982, Sched. 14, para. 2(1); Merchant Shipping Act 1979, Sched. 6, Pt. VII, para. 9; Merchant Shipping (Registration, etc.) Act 1993, Sched. 4, para. 2(5).]
Section 233 sets out the powers of the receiver to preserve shipwrecks. For the applications and discharge of the receiver's functions, see s.231, above.

Power to pass over adjoining land

234.—(1) In circumstances where this section applies by virtue of section 231 in relation to any vessel, all persons may, subject to subsections (3) and (4) below, for the purpose of—

(a) rendering assistance to the vessel,

(b) saving the lives of shipwrecked persons, or

(c) saving the cargo or equipment of the vessel,

pass and repass over any adjoining land without being subject to interruption by the owner or occupier and deposit on the land any cargo or other article recovered from the vessel.

(2) The right of passage conferred by subsection (1) above is a right of passage with or without vehicles.

(3) No right of passage is conferred by subsection (1) above where there is some public road equally convenient.

(4) The rights conferred by subsection (1) above shall be so exercised as to do as little damage as possible.

(5) Any damage sustained by an owner or occupier of land in consequence of the exercise of the rights conferred by this section shall be a charge on the vessel, cargo or articles in respect of or by which the damage is caused.

(6) Any amount payable in respect of such damage shall, in case of dispute, be determined and shall, in default of payment, be recoverable in the same manner as the amount of salvage is determined and recoverable under this Part.

(7) If the owner or occupier of any land—

(a) impedes or hinders any person in the exercise of the rights conferred by this section;

(b) impedes or hinders the deposit on the land of any cargo or other article recovered from the vessel; or

(c) prevents or attempts to prevent any cargo or other article recovered from the vessel from remaining deposited on the land for a reasonable time until it can be removed to a safe place of public deposit;

he shall be liable, on summary conviction, to a fine not exceeding level 3 on the standard scale.

DEFINITIONS

"person": Interpretation Act 1978, Sched. 1.
"right of passage": subss. (2) and (3).
"salvage": s.255(1).
"shipwrecked persons": s.231(5).
"standard scale": Criminal Justice Act 1982, s.37.
"vessel": s.255(1).

GENERAL NOTE

[Derivation: Merchant Shipping Act 1894, s.513; Criminal Justice Act 1982, s.38(8).]

Section 234 sets out the powers of the receiver to cross private land in order to reach a wreck. Any damage caused becomes a charge on salved property. For the applications and discharge of the receiver's functions, see s.231, above.

Liability for damage in case of plundered vessel

235.—(1) Where, in circumstances in which this section applies by virtue of section 231 in relation to any vessel, the vessel or any part of its cargo and equipment is plundered, damaged or destroyed by persons in circumstances in which those persons commit the offence of riot or, in Scotland, of mobbing and rioting, compensation shall be made to the owner of the vessel, cargo or equipment in accordance with the following provisions of this section.

(2) Compensation under subsection (1) above in England and Wales shall be made by the compensation authority in the manner provided by the Riot (Damages) Act 1886 with respect to claims for compensation under that Act.

(3) Where the vessel, cargo or equipment is not within a police area, the plundering, damage or destruction shall be treated for the purposes of subsection (2) above as taking place within the nearest police area.

(4) Compensation under subsection (1) above in Scotland shall, as if entitlement to it arose under section 10 of the Riotous Assemblies (Scotland) Act 1822, be made by the council constituted under section 2 of the Local Government etc. (Scotland) Act 1994 within whose area, or nearest to whose area, the plundering, damage or destruction took place.

(5) Compensation under subsection (1) above in Northern Ireland shall be made in pursuance of an application under the Criminal Injuries to Property (Compensation) Act (Northern Ireland) 1971 as modified for the purposes of this section by the Transfer of Functions (Criminal Injuries to Vessels) (Northern Ireland) Order 1973.

DEFINITIONS

"England and Wales": Interpretation Act 1978, Sched. 1.
"person": Interpretation Act 1978, Sched. 1.
"vessel": s.255(1).

GENERAL NOTE

[Derivation: Merchant Shipping Act 1894, s.515; Transfer of Functions (Criminal Injuries to Vessels) (Northern Ireland) Order 1973, Art. 3(1); Local Government (Scotland) Act 1973, Sched. 27, Pt. II, para. 21; Public Order Act 1986, s.10; Merchant Shipping (Registration, etc.) Act 1993, Sched. 4, para. 20, Sched. 5.]

Section 235 allows compensation to be paid where a wreck is destroyed in circumstances which appertain to a riot. For riots, see now the Public Order Act 1986. An anachronistic reference to persons riotously and *"tumultuously"* assembled to plunder was removed from s.235(1) by the Merchant Shipping (Registration, etc.) Act 1993, Sched. 4, para. 20. For the applications and discharge of the receiver's functions, see s.231, above.

Dealing with wreck

Duties of finder etc. of wreck

236.—(1) If any person finds or takes possession of any wreck in United Kingdom waters or finds or takes possession of any wreck outside United Kingdom waters and brings it within those waters he shall—
  (a) if he is the owner of it, give notice to the receiver stating that he has found or taken possession of it and describing the marks by which it may be recognised;
  (b) if he is not the owner of it, give notice to the receiver that he has found or taken possession of it and, as directed by the receiver, either hold it to the receiver's order or deliver it to the receiver.

(2) If any person fails, without reasonable excuse, to comply with subsection (1) above he shall be liable, on summary conviction, to a fine not exceeding level 4 on the standard scale and if he is not the owner of the wreck he shall also—
  (a) forfeit any claim to salvage; and
  (b) be liable to pay twice the value of the wreck—
      (i) if it is claimed, to the owner of it; or
      (ii) if it is unclaimed, to the person entitled to the wreck.

(3) Any sum payable under subsection (2)(b) above to the owner of the wreck or to the persons entitled to the wreck may, in England and Wales and Northern Ireland, be recovered summarily as a civil debt.

(4) In Scotland any sum payable under subsection (2)(b) above to the owner of the wreck or to the persons entitled to the wreck shall, for the purposes of the sum's recovery, be regarded as a debt due to the owner or, as the case may be, to those persons.

DEFINITIONS
  "England and Wales": Interpretation Act 1978, Sched. 1.
  "fails": s.313(1).
  "person": Interpretation Act 1978, Sched. 1.
  "receiver": s.255(1).
  "salvage": s.255(1).
  "standard scale": Criminal Justice Act 1982, s.37.
  "United Kingdom waters": s.313(2)(a).
  "wreck": s.255(1) and (2).

GENERAL NOTE
  [Derivation: Merchant Shipping Act 1894, s.518; Merchant Shipping Act 1906, s.72; Merchant Shipping Act 1979, Sched. 6, Pt. III, Merchant Shipping (Registration, etc.) Act 1993, Sched. 4, para. 22; Merchant Shipping Act 1894, s.681(2).]
  Section 518 of the 1894 Act imposed an obligation on a finder of wreck brought within the U.K. (see the Merchant Shipping Act 1906, s.72 and *Pierce v. Bemis (The Lusitania)* [1986] Q.B. 384) both to report the find *and* to "deliver the same to the receiver". In practice there are very few reports made (Dromgoole and Gaskell, *op. cit.*, p.353) and the Customs service has no real mechanism for the receiving and conservation of finds which may have some historical importance. Still less does it desire to receive artefacts. The assumption of the 1894 Act was that it was in the public good for wreck to be brought ashore, but the Act was designed to deal with commercial property issues, where removal, sale and disposal was the sensible alternative. These days there may well be heritage considerations in relation to ancient wreck. Archaeologists may prefer for the wreck not to be moved from its situation, *e.g.* on the seabed, where it may constitute a time capsule with each artefact having a significance in relation to the others. More destruction to the archaeological integrity of the site may occur by attempts to remove the wreck and, ironically, to comply with s.518. The Merchant Shipping (Registration, etc.) Act 1993, Sched. 4,

para. 22 was a welcome and significant change in the law, as it removed the obligation of a finder always to deliver a wreck to the receiver. Instead, a person who finds or takes possession of the wreck must still report that fact (under what is now s.236(a)), but must obey any instruction then given by the receiver. That instruction might be to hold the wreck (or artefacts), or actually to deliver it as before.

Section 236 still leaves many problems of interpretation. First, what are the relative meanings of the expressions "finds" or "takes possession" as utilised in the section? In particular, does a person "find" a wreck by discovering it, or is finding in this context a synonym for taking possession? The distinction is of some significance, because a failure to report or deliver is a criminal offence. If a diver spots a hulk on the seabed, must this be reported? If a stroller on a beach comes across some flotsam, must that be reported? Reporting is an important feature for the establishing of any archaeological record, but that is not what Pt. IX was originally designed to achieve (although see now s.238, below). It is difficult to see how s.236(1) (formerly s.72 of the Merchant Shipping Act 1906) can refer to wreck found outside the U.K. and brought within it unless the finding is the equivalent of taking possession. It is submitted that the context shows that there must be more than mere discovery for s.236 to operate and that in most contexts "finding" must involve the taking into possession of the wreck (and see *The Tubantia* [1924] P. 78, Dromgoole and Gaskell, "Interests in Wreck", *op. cit.*, pp.386–398), or the exercising of some control over it. In the nineteenth century there must have been little prospect of deep sea recovery and most finding will have occurred on the sea shore. If the shore was privately owned, the landowner who discovered it might also be said to have found it, in that he may have been able to exercise control over it without physically reducing it into possession. It may well be that this was the type of finding that the section had in mind. More likely is that the provision was either loosely drafted or used a general colloquial expression followed by a more specific legal concept (justifying a kind of *ejuisdem generis* approach).

Secondly, what powers does the receiver have under s.236(1)(b)? The finder may be obliged to hold the wreck to the "receiver's order". Can any conditions be attached to this direction? Does the direction relate merely to the exercise of the two options given, or can the receiver require the finder to hold the wreck and conserve it, or keep it in a particular place, or make it available to members of the public or researchers? Who is to bear any costs involved? Presumably, if the finder is directed to hold the wreck to the receiver's order the latter ought to bear any costs involved, *e.g.* in storage or conservation. It may be unlikely that this was what the Government intended, yet it would be unjust if a specific request as to storage made by the receiver was complied with but no remuneration was provided. Note that under s.249 the receiver is entitled to claim expenses "properly incurred" by him, although the provision does not say from whom the expenses are claimable. The assumption is that the receiver has a lien on the find (see s.249(3) which assimilates the receiver's claim to that of a salvor who would also have an action *in personam* against the owner of the find, but preserves "other rights" for the recovery of expenses). It would seem that there is little in the section to allow for precise, onerous conditions to be attached to any direction without there being a concomitant obligation for the receiver to pay for them. This conclusion would also follow from s.240, which allows the receiver to sell a wreck if its value would not justify the costs of "storage". In practice, it seems unlikely that the receiver would give such directions, except where it is generally convenient for remains to be left where they are. Although it may not be possible for a receiver to impose onerous conditions, other than that the finder shall retain possession to the order of the receiver, it may well be in the interests of the finder *voluntarily* to incur expenditure to preserve the wreck in order to be able to maintain or reinforce a salvage claim under ss.239 or 243.

Subss. (3), (4)

Section 236(3) makes the amount recoverable summarily in a magistrate's court in England and Wales as a civil debt. Section 236(4) contains a specific provision to deal with the recovery of sums under the section in Scottish law. For Scotland it is apparently unnecessary for any special procedure to be mentioned and it is sufficient for s.236 and diligence that the sum be treated as a debt. Note also s.312 on Scots law.

Provisions as respects cargo, etc.

237.—(1) Where a vessel is wrecked, stranded, or in distress at any place on or near the coasts of the United Kingdom or any tidal water within United Kingdom waters, any cargo or other articles belonging to or separated from the vessel which are washed on shore or otherwise lost or taken from the vessel shall be delivered to the receiver.

(2) If any person (whether the owner or not)—

(a) conceals or keeps possession of any such cargo or article, or

(b) refuses to deliver any such cargo or article to the receiver or to any person authorised by the receiver to require delivery,

he shall be liable, on summary conviction, to a fine not exceeding level 4 on the standard scale.

(3) The receiver or any person authorised by him may take any such cargo or article (if necessary by force) from any person who refuses to deliver it.

DEFINITIONS

"person": Interpretation Act 1978, Sched. 1.
"receiver": s.255(1).
"standard scale": Criminal Justice Act 1982, s.37.
"tidal water": s.255(1).
"United Kingdom": Interpretation Act 1978, Sched. 1.
"United Kingdom waters": s.313(2)(a).
"vessel": s.255(1).
"wreck": s.255(1) and (2).

GENERAL NOTE

[Derivation: Merchant Shipping Act 1894, s.519; Merchant Shipping Act 1979, Sched. 6, Pt. VI.]

Section 237 puts an obligation on finders of cargo or articles from a wreck to deliver the same to the receiver. *Cf.* s.236.

Receiver to give notice of wreck

238.—(1) Where the receiver takes possession of any wreck he shall, within 48 hours—
   (a) make a record describing the wreck and any marks by which it is distinguished; and
   (b) if in his opinion the value of the wreck exceeds £5,000, also transmit a similar description to the chief executive officer of Lloyd's in London.

(2) The record made by the receiver under subsection (1)(a) above shall be kept by him available for inspection by any person during reasonable hours without charge.

(3) The notice sent under subsection (1)(b) above to the chief executive officer of Lloyd's shall be posted by him in some conspicuous position for inspection.

DEFINITIONS

"person": Interpretation Act 1978, Sched. 1.
"receiver": s.255(1).
"wreck": s.255(1) and (2).

GENERAL NOTE

[Derivation: Merchant Shipping Act 1894, s.520; Merchant Shipping (Registration, etc.) Act 1993, Sched. 4, para. 23.]

The Merchant Shipping (Registration, etc.) Act 1993, Sched. 4, para. 23 updated s.520 of the 1894 Act in relation to the action which has to be taken by receivers to publicise the taking possession of a wreck by them. Section 520(1) originally required the receiver to post a description of the wreck and any marks in the nearest customs house to where the wreck was found or seized. This was designed to allow the owners to find out about their lost property, but probably has little significance today. Section 238(1)(a) merely requires the receiver to make a "record" and this may well be kept centrally (and *cf.* s.225). It will probably be as useful to archaeologists as owners, particularly as inspection is to be free of charge. Section 238(1)(b) reflects the fact that the person with most interest in modern commercial wreck is likely to be the insurer of it (see Dromgoole and Gaskell, "Interests in Wreck", *op. cit.*, pp. 366–375). The 1894 provision required notice to be given to Lloyd's when the value of the wreck exceeded £20: that figure is now £5000. Of course, there may be plenty of underwriters who are not based at Lloyd's, although it would be quite common for insurance companies in the London market to have a line on a Lloyd's slip.

Claims of owners to wreck

239.—(1) The owner of any wreck in the possession of the receiver who establishes his claim to the wreck to the satisfaction of the receiver within one year from the time when the wreck came into the receiver's possession shall, on paying the salvage, fees and expenses due, be entitled to have the wreck delivered or the proceeds of sale paid to him.

(2) Where—

(a) a foreign ship has been wrecked on or near the coasts of the United Kingdom, or

(b) any articles belonging to or forming part of or of the cargo of a foreign ship which has been wrecked on or near the coasts of the United Kingdom are found on or near the coast or are brought into any port,

the appropriate consular officer shall, in the absence of the owner and of the master or other agent of the owner, be treated as the agent of the owner for the purposes of the custody and disposal of the wreck and such articles.

(3) In subsection (2) above "the appropriate consular officer", in relation to a foreign ship, means the consul general of the country to which the ship or, as the case may be, the owners of the cargo may have belonged or any consular officer of that country authorised for the purpose by any treaty or arrangement with that country.

DEFINITIONS
"appropriate consular officer, the": subs. (3).
"foreign": s.313(1).
"master": s.313(1).
"port": s.313(1).
"receiver": s.255(1).
"salvage": s.255(1).
"ship": s.313(1).
"United Kingdom": Interpretation Act 1978, Sched. 1.
"wreck": s.255(1) and (2).

GENERAL NOTE
[Derivation: Merchant Shipping Act 1894, s.521; Consular Conventions Act 1949, s.5(2).]
Section 239 preserves the rights of an owner of wreck to claim the wreck back on the payment of salvage and any fees.

Immediate sale of wreck in certain cases

240.—(1) The receiver may at any time sell any wreck in his possession if, in his opinion—

(a) it is under the value of £5,000;

(b) it is so much damaged or of so perishable a nature that it cannot with advantage be kept; or

(c) it is not of sufficient value to pay for storage.

(2) The proceeds of sale shall, after defraying the expenses of the sale, be held by the receiver for the same purposes and subject to the same claims, rights and liabilities as if the wreck had remained unsold.

DEFINITIONS
"receiver": s.255(1).
"wreck": s.255(1) and (2).

GENERAL NOTE
[Derivation: Merchant Shipping Act 1894, s.522; Merchant Shipping (Registration, etc.) Act 1993, Sched. 4, para. 24.]
Section 240 allows the receiver to sell damaged or perishable wreck, but any proceeds will be held in the usual way, *e.g.* on behalf of the owner who may claim under s.239.

Unclaimed wreck

Right of Crown to unclaimed wreck

241. Her Majesty and Her Royal successors are entitled to all unclaimed wreck found in the United Kingdom or in United Kingdom waters except in places where Her Majesty or any of Her Royal predecessors has granted the right to any other person.

DEFINITIONS
"person": Interpretation Act 1978, Sched. 1.
"United Kingdom": Interpretation Act 1978, Sched. 1.
"United Kingdom waters": s.313(2)(a).
"wreck": s.255(1) and (2).

GENERAL NOTE
[Derivation: Merchant Shipping Act 1894, s.523.]
In *Pierce v. Bemis (The Lusitania)* [1986] Q.B. 384 it was held that the Crown has no rights to unclaimed wreck outside territorial waters.

Notice of unclaimed wreck to be given to persons entitled

242.—(1) Any person who is entitled to unclaimed wreck found at any place in the United Kingdom or in United Kingdom waters shall give the receiver a statement containing the particulars of his entitlement and specifying an address to which notices may be sent.

(2) Where a statement has been given to the receiver under subsection (1) above and the entitlement is proved to the satisfaction of the receiver, the receiver shall, on taking possession of any wreck found at a place to which the statement refers, within 48 hours, send to the specified address a description of the wreck and of any marks distinguishing it.

DEFINITIONS
"person": Interpretation Act 1978, Sched. 1.
"receiver": s.255(1).
"United Kingdom": Interpretation Act 1978, Sched. 1.
"United Kingdom waters": s.313(2)(a).
"wreck": s.255(1) and (2).

GENERAL NOTE
[Derivation: Merchant Shipping Act 1894, s.524; Merchant Shipping (Registration, etc.) Act 1993, Sched. 4, para. 25.]
Section 242 deals with claims and notices by purported owners of wreck. The wording of s.242 (formerly s.524 of the Merchant Shipping Act 1894) was changed by the Merchant Shipping (Registration, etc.) Act 1993, Sched. 4, para. 25 to remove specific references to Lords of the Manor, but there was no change of substance.

Disposal of unclaimed wreck

243.—(1) Where, as respects any wreck found in the United Kingdom or in United Kingdom waters and in the possession of the receiver, no owner establishes a claim to it within one year after it came into the receiver's possession, the wreck shall be dealt with as follows.

(2) If the wreck is claimed by any person who has delivered the statement required by section 242 and has proved to the satisfaction of the receiver his entitlement to receive unclaimed wreck found at the place where the wreck was found, the wreck shall, on payment of all expenses, costs, fees and salvage due in respect of it, be delivered to that person.

(3) If the wreck is not claimed by any person in accordance with section 242, the receiver shall sell the wreck and pay the proceeds as directed by subsection (6) below, after making the deductions required by subsection (4) below and paying to the salvors the amount of salvage determined under subsection (5) below.

(4) The amounts to be deducted by the receiver are—
(a) the expenses of the sale;
(b) any other expenses incurred by him; and
(c) his fees.

(5) The amount of salvage to be paid by the receiver to the salvors shall be such amount as the Secretary of State directs generally or in the particular case.

(6) The proceeds of sale (after making those deductions and salvage payments) shall be paid by the receiver for the benefit of Her Majesty—
(a) if the wreck is claimed in right of the Duchy of Lancaster, to the receiver-general of the duchy or his deputies as part of its revenues;
(b) if the wreck is claimed in right of the Duchy of Cornwall, to the receiver-general of the duchy or his deputies as part of its revenues; and
(c) in any other case, into the Consolidated Fund.

DEFINITIONS
"person": Interpretation Act 1978, Sched. 1.
"receiver": s.255(1).
"salvage": s.255(1).
"salvor": s.255(1).
"Secretary of State": Interpretation Act 1978, Sched. 1.
"United Kingdom": Interpretation Act 1978, Sched. 1.
"United Kingdom waters": s.313(2)(a).
"wreck": s.255(1) and (2).

GENERAL NOTE
[Derivation: Merchant Shipping Act 1894, s.525; Merchant Shipping Act 1898, s.1(1)(a).]

Effect of delivery of wreck etc. under this Part

244.—(1) Delivery of wreck or payment of the proceeds of sale of wreck by the receiver under this Chapter shall discharge the receiver from all liability in respect of the delivery or payment.

(2) Delivery of wreck by the receiver under this Chapter shall not, however, prejudice or affect any question which may be raised by third parties concerning the right or title to the wreck or concerning the title to the soil of the place at which the wreck was found.

DEFINITIONS
"receiver": s.255(1).
"wreck": s.255(1) and (2).

GENERAL NOTE
[Derivation: Merchant Shipping Act 1894, s.527.]

Offences in respect of wreck

Taking wreck to foreign port

245.—(1) A person commits an offence if he takes into any foreign port and sells—
(a) any vessel stranded, derelict or otherwise in distress found on or near the coasts of the United Kingdom or any tidal water within United Kingdom waters;
(b) any part of the cargo or equipment of, or anything belonging to, such a vessel; or
(c) any wreck found within those waters.

(2) A person who is guilty of an offence under this section shall be liable, on conviction on indictment, to imprisonment for a term not exceeding five years.

DEFINITIONS
"foreign": s.313(1).
"person": Interpretation Act 1978, Sched. 1.
"port": s.313(1).
"tidal water": s.255(1).
"United Kingdom": Interpretation Act 1978, Sched. 1.
"United Kingdom waters": s.313(2)(a).
"vessel": s.255(1).

GENERAL NOTE
[Derivation: Merchant Shipping Act 1894, s.535; Criminal Justice Act 1948, s.1; Merchant Shipping (Registration, etc.) Act 1993, Sched. 4, para. 2(5).]

Interfering with wrecked vessel or wreck

246.—(1) Subject to subsection (2) below, a person commits an offence if, without the permission of the master, he boards or attempts to board any vessel which is wrecked, stranded or in distress.

(2) No offence is committed under subsection (1) above if the person is the receiver or a person lawfully acting as the receiver or if he acts by command of the receiver or a person so acting.

(3) A person commits an offence if—

(a) he impedes or hinders or attempts to impede or hinder the saving of—
  (i) any vessel stranded or in danger of being stranded, or otherwise in distress, on or near any coast or tidal water; or
  (ii) any part of the cargo or equipment of any such vessel; or
  (iii) any wreck;
(b) he conceals any wreck;
(c) he defaces or obliterates any mark on a vessel; or
(d) he wrongfully carries away or removes—
  (i) any part of any vessel stranded or in danger of being stranded, or otherwise in distress, on or near any coast or tidal water;
  (ii) any part of the cargo or equipment of any such vessel; or
  (iii) any wreck.

(4) The master of a vessel may forcibly repel any person committing or attempting to commit an offence under subsection (1) above.

(5) A person who is guilty of an offence under this section shall be liable, on summary conviction—

(a) in the case of an offence under subsection (1) above, to a fine not exceeding level 3 on the standard scale;
(b) in the case of an offence under subsection (3) above, to a fine not exceeding level 4 on the standard scale.

DEFINITIONS
"master": s.313(1).
"person": Interpretation Act 1978, Sched. 1.
"receiver": s.255(1).
"standard scale": Criminal Justice Act 1982, s.37.
"tidal water": s.255(1).
"vessel": s.255(1).
"wreck": s.255(1) and (2).

GENERAL NOTE
[Derivation: Merchant Shipping Act 1894, s.536; Merchant Shipping Act 1979, Sched. 6, Pt. II.]

Powers of entry etc.

247.—(1) Where the receiver has reason to believe that—

(a) any wreck is being concealed by or is in the possession of some person who is not the owner of it; or
(b) any wreck is being otherwise improperly dealt with,

he may apply to a justice of the peace for a search warrant.

(2) Where a search warrant is granted under subsection (1) above to the receiver, the receiver may, by virtue of the warrant—

(a) enter any house, or other place (wherever situated) or any vessel; and

(b) search for, seize and detain any wreck found there.

(3) If any seizure of wreck is made under this section in consequence of information given by any person to the receiver, the person giving the information shall be entitled, by way of salvage, to such sum, not exceeding £100, as the receiver may allow.

DEFINITIONS
"person": Interpretation Act 1978, Sched. 1.
"receiver": s.255(1).
"salvage": s.255(1).
"vessel": s.255(1).
"wreck": s.255(1) and (2).

GENERAL NOTE
[Derivation: Merchant Shipping Act 1894, s.537; Merchant Shipping (Registration, etc.) Act 1993, Sched. 4, para. 28, Sched. 5.]

CHAPTER III

SUPPLEMENTAL

GENERAL NOTE
Chapter III deals with administrative matters concerning wreck and the remuneration due to officials other than the receiver, such as the coastguard.

Administration

Functions of Secretary of State as to wreck

248.—(1) The Secretary of State shall have the general superintendence throughout the United Kingdom of all matters relating to wreck.

(2) The Secretary of State may, with the consent of the Treasury, appoint one or more persons to be receiver of wreck for the purposes of this Part and a receiver so appointed shall discharge such functions as are assigned to him by the Secretary of State.

(3) Such public notice of appointments to the office of receiver shall be given as appears to the Secretary of State to be appropriate.

DEFINITIONS
"person": Interpretation Act 1978, Sched. 1.
"receiver": s.255(1).
"Secretary of State": Interpretation Act 1978, Sched. 1.
"Treasury, the": Interpretation Act 1978, Sched. 1.
"United Kingdom": Interpretation Act 1978, Sched. 1.
"wreck": s.255(1) and (2).

GENERAL NOTE
[Derivation: Merchant Shipping Act 1894, s.566; Merchant Shipping (Registration, etc.) Act 1993, Sched. 4, para. 31.]
As to the general system of receivers of wreck, see the General Note to Chapter II of this part of the Act, above. As noted there, the Merchant Shipping Act 1894, was amended to allow for there to be a single central receiver, if desired. This indicates the decline in the office.

Expenses and fees of receivers

249.—(1) There shall be paid to the receiver the expenses properly incurred by him in the discharge of his functions and also, in respect of such matters as may be prescribed by regulations made by the Secretary of State, such fees as may be so prescribed.

(2) The receiver shall not be entitled to any other remuneration.

(3) The receiver shall, in addition to all other rights and remedies for the recovery of those expenses and fees, have the same rights and remedies in respect of those expenses and fees as a salvor has in respect of salvage due to him.

(4) Whenever any dispute arises as to the amount payable to the receiver in respect of expenses or fees, that dispute shall be determined by the Secretary of State whose decision shall be final.

DEFINITIONS
"person": Interpretation Act 1978, Sched. 1.
"receiver": s.255(1).
"salvage": s.255(1).
"salvor": s.255(1).
"Secretary of State": Interpretation Act 1978, Sched. 1.

GENERAL NOTE
[Derivation: Merchant Shipping Act 1894, s.567(1)–(3); Merchant Shipping (Registration, etc.) Act 1993, Sched. 4, para. 32.]

Receivers' fees are set out in statutory instruments. One of the difficulties in allowing charges to be made is that discoverers of wreck may be reluctant to declare it if they will be liable to any fee. For the powers of the Secretary of State to make delegated legislation, such as regulations, see s.306, below.

Coastguard services

Remuneration for services of coastguard

250.—(1) Subject to subsection (2) below, where services are rendered by any officers or men of the coastguard service in watching or protecting ship-wrecked property the owner of the property shall pay in respect of those services remuneration according to a scale fixed by the Secretary of State.

(2) No liability in respect of those services arises under subsection (1) above where—

(a) the services have been declined by the owner of the property or his agent at the time they were tendered; or

(b) salvage has been claimed and awarded for the services.

(3) Remuneration under this section shall—

(a) be recoverable by the same means,

(b) be paid to the same persons, and

(c) be accounted for and applied in the same manner,

as fees received by the receiver under section 249.

(4) The scale fixed by the Secretary of State shall not exceed the scale by which remuneration to officers and men of the coastguard for extra duties in the ordinary service of the Commissioners of Customs and Excise is for the time being regulated.

DEFINITIONS
"property": Sched. 11, Art. 1(c).
"receiver": s.255(1).
"salvage": s.255(1).
"Secretary of State": Interpretation Act 1978, Sched. 1.

GENERAL NOTE
[Derivation: Merchant Shipping Act 1894, s.568.]

Release from customs and excise control

Release of goods from customs and excise control

251.—(1) The Commissioners of Customs and Excise shall, subject to taking security for the protection of the revenue in respect of the goods, permit all goods saved from any ship stranded or wrecked on its homeward voyage to be forwarded to the port of its original destination.

(2) The Commissioners of Customs and Excise shall, subject to taking such security, permit all goods saved from any ship stranded or wrecked on her outward voyage to be returned to the port at which they were shipped.

(3) In this section "goods" includes wares and merchandise.

DEFINITIONS
"goods": subs. (3).
"port": s.313(1).
"ship": s.313(1).
"wreck": s.255(1) and (2).

GENERAL NOTE
[Derivation: Merchant Shipping Act 1894, s.569(2).]

Removal of wrecks

Powers of harbour and conservancy authorities in relation to wrecks

252.—(1) Where any vessel is sunk, stranded or abandoned in, or in or near any approach to, any harbour or tidal water under the control of a harbour authority or conservancy authority in such a manner as, in the opinion of the authority, to be, or be likely to become, an obstruction or danger to navigation or to lifeboats engaged in lifeboat service in that harbour or water or approach thereto, that authority may exercise any of the following powers.

(2) Those powers are—

(a) to take possession of, and raise, remove or destroy the whole or any part of the vessel and any other property to which the power extends;

(b) to light or buoy the vessel or part of the vessel and any such other property until it is raised, removed or destroyed; and

(c) subject to subsections (5) and (6) below, to sell, in such manner as the authority think fit, the vessel or part of the vessel so raised or removed and any other property recovered in the exercise of the powers conferred by paragraph (a) or (b) above;

(d) to reimburse themselves, out of the proceeds of the sale, for the expenses incurred by them in relation to the sale.

(3) The other property to which the powers conferred by subsection (2) above extend is every article or thing or collection of things being or forming part of the equipment, cargo, stores or ballast of the vessel.

(4) Any surplus of the proceeds of a sale under subsection (2)(c) above shall be held by the authority on trust for the persons entitled thereto.

(5) Except in the case of property which is of a perishable nature or which would deteriorate in value by delay, no sale shall be made under subsection (2)(c) above until at least seven days notice of the intended sale has been given by advertisement in a local newspaper circulating in or near the area over which the authority have control.

(6) At any time before any property is sold under subsection (2)(c) above, the owner of the property shall be entitled to have it delivered to him on payment of its fair market value.

(7) The market value of property for the purposes of subsection (6) above shall be that agreed on between the authority and the owner or, failing agreement, that determined by a person appointed for the purpose by the Secretary of State.

(8) The sum paid to the authority in respect of any property under subsection (6) above shall, for the purposes of this section, be treated as the proceeds of sale of the property.

(9) Any proceeds of sale arising under subsection (2)(c) above from the sale of a vessel and any other property recovered from the vessel shall be treated as a common fund.

(10) This section is without prejudice to any other powers of a harbour authority or conservancy authority.

DEFINITIONS
"conservancy authority": s.313(1).
"harbour" s.313(1).
"harbour authority": s.313(1).
"market value": subs. (7).
"other property": subs. (3).
"person": Interpretation Act 1978, Sched. 1.
"Secretary of State": Interpretation Act 1978, Sched. 1.
"tidal water": s.255(1).
"vessel": s.255(1).

GENERAL NOTE
[Derivation: Merchant Shipping Act 1894, ss.530, 532 and 534.]
Section 252 gives power to a harbour authority to remove a wreck which is "an obstruction to navigation". The powers under subs. (2) are quite extensive, but as noted in the General Note to s.253, below, the provision is defective because it does not give the authority the right to charge the shipowner for the expenses of any operation. The sunken vessel is likely to have little value and the costs of wreck raising are notoriously high. The section does not require any proof of fault before the powers can be exercised. Where a vessel is wrecked and an eyesore, but is not an obstruction then there is probably no power to intervene under the section. In practice, the harbour authority will probably rely on the powers granted in the local private legislation.
For the powers of a general lighthouse authority and harbour authorities under private Acts, see s.253, below. *Cf.* the powers available to a harbour master under the Dangerous Vessels Act 1985. For limitation of liability, see Sched. 7, Pt. II, para. 3, below.

Powers of lighthouse authorities in relation to wrecks

253.—(1) Where—
(a) any vessel is sunk, stranded or abandoned in any fairway or on the seashore or on or near any rock, shoal or bank in the United Kingdom or any of the adjacent seas or islands; and
(b) there is no harbour authority or conservancy authority having power to raise, remove or destroy the vessel;
the general lighthouse authority for the place in or near which the vessel is situated shall, if in the authority's opinion the vessel is, or is likely to become, an obstruction or danger to navigation or to lifeboats engaged in lifeboat service, have the same powers in relation thereto as are conferred by section 252.
(2) Where a general lighthouse authority have incurred expenses in the exercise of their powers under this section in relation to any vessel, then—
(a) if the proceeds of any sale made under section 252 in connection with the exercise of those powers in relation to the vessel are insufficient to reimburse the authority for the full amount of those expenses, the authority may recover the amount of the deficiency from the relevant person, or
(b) if there is no such sale, the authority may recover the full amount of those expenses from the relevant person.
(3) Any expenses so incurred which are not recovered by the authority either out of the proceeds of any such sale or in accordance with subsection (2) above shall be paid out of the General Lighthouse Fund, but section 213 shall apply to those expenses as if they were expenses of the authority falling within subsection (1) of that section other than establishment expenses.
(4) In this section "the relevant person", in relation to any vessel, means the owner of the vessel at the time of the sinking, stranding or abandonment of the vessel.

DEFINITIONS
"conservancy authority": s.313(1).
"general lighthouse authority": s.193(1).

"harbour authority": s.313(1).
"person": Interpretation Act 1978, Sched. 1.
"relevant person, the": subs. (4).
"United Kingdom": Interpretation Act 1978, Sched. 1.
"vessel": s.255(1).

GENERAL NOTE
[Derivation: Merchant Shipping Act 1894, s.531; Merchant Shipping Act 1988, Sched. 5, para. 2.]
Section 253 re-enacts s.531 of the Merchant Shipping Act 1894, and is designed to allow a general lighthouse authority (GLA) to raise wrecks where there is no harbour or conservancy authority with that power. Subsection (1) gives the GLA the same power to claim the expenses of the wreck-raising out of the proceeds of sale of the wreck as were available to the harbour or conservancy authorities under s.252 of the Merchant Shipping Act 1995 (formerly s.530 of the Merchant Shipping Act 1894). One difficulty is that it has long been recognised that s.252 is of little use where the wreck is valueless (as it invariably is). For s.252 gives no personal cause of action against the owner to recover the expenses and s.252(2) merely gives rights against the thing which has been raised. Most harbour authorities will have powers under other legislation, such as s.56 of the Harbour Docks and Piers Clauses Act 1847, or by-laws made under local Acts of Parliament. Such Acts will often give wider powers to recover expenses than the 1894 Act. Accordingly, the Merchant Shipping Act 1988, Sched. 5 inserted the new subss. (2)–(4). Subsection (2)(b) gives a direct cause of action to the GLA against the shipowner.
Three points may be noted: (i) the wreck raising claim will not be subject to limitation of liability (see Sched. 7, Pt. I, Art. 2.1(d), Pt. II, para. 3); (ii) the person liable, "the relevant person", is defined in subs. (4) as being the owner *at the time of sinking*. This removes a defence provided by *The Crystal* [1894] A.C. 508 (a case under s.56 of the Harbour Docks and Piers Clauses Act 1847). That case held that the expenses could only be claimed from the person who was the owner at the time when the sum was demanded and that an owner who had earlier claimed to abandon the ship was not liable. As a matter of principle the case should be doubted and it is significant that much local legislation contains provisions similar to subs. (4); (iii) the GLAs now have wider rights of recovery because of the direct personal action under s.253(2)(b) than harbour or conservancy authorities under s.252. But, as noted above, much recent *local* legislation would give the same wide powers to harbour or conservancy authorities.

Referral of questions as to powers between authorities

254.—(1) If any question arises between a harbour authority or conservancy authority and a general lighthouse authority as to their respective powers under sections 252 and 253 in relation to any place in or near an approach to a harbour or tidal water, that question shall, on the application of either authority, be referred to the Secretary of State for his decision.

(2) Any decision of the Secretary of State under this section shall be final.

DEFINITIONS
"conservancy authority": s.313(1).
"general lighthouse authority": s.193(1).
"harbour" s.313(1).
"harbour authority": s.313(1).
"Secretary of State": Interpretation Act 1978, Sched. 1.
"tidal water": s.255(1).

GENERAL NOTE
[Derivation: Merchant Shipping Act 1894, s.533.]

Interpretation

Interpretation

255.—(1) In this Part—
"receiver" means a receiver of wreck appointed under section 248;
"salvage" includes, subject to the Salvage Convention, all expenses properly incurred by the salvor in the performance of the salvage services;
"the Salvage Convention" has the meaning given by section 224(1);

"salvor" means, in the case of salvage services rendered by the officers or crew or part of the crew of any ship belonging to Her Majesty, the person in command of the ship;

"tidal water" means any part of the sea and any part of a river within the ebb and flow of the tide at ordinary spring tides, and not being a harbour;

"vessel" includes any ship or boat, or any other description of vessel used in navigation; and

"wreck" includes jetsam, flotsam, lagan and derelict found in or on the shores of the sea or any tidal water.

(2) Fishing boats or fishing gear lost or abandoned at sea and either—

(a) found or taken possession of within United Kingdom waters; or

(b) found or taken possession of beyond those waters and brought within those waters;

shall be treated as wreck for the purposes of this Part.

(3) In the application of this Part in relation to Scotland, any reference to a justice of the peace includes a reference to a sheriff.

DEFINITIONS
"harbour" s.313(1).
"person": Interpretation Act 1978, Sched. 1.
"receiver": subs. (1).
"salvage": subs. (1).
"Salvage Convention, the": subs. (1) and s.224(1).
"salvor": subs. (1).
"sheriff": Interpretation Act 1978, Sched. 1.
"ship": s.313(1).
"tidal water": subs. (1).
"United Kingdom waters": s.313(2)(a).
"vessel": subs. (1).
"wreck": subss. (1) and (2).

GENERAL NOTE
[Derivation: Merchant Shipping Act 1894, s.510 (Fisheries Act 1968, s.17); Merchant Shipping Act 1894, ss.570 and 742, (Merchant Shipping (Registration, etc.) Act 1993, Sched. 2, para. 2).]

PART X

ENFORCEMENT OFFICERS AND POWERS

GENERAL NOTE
This Part brings together in a coherent form the powers granted to officials to enforce the provisions of the Merchant Shipping Act 1995.

Enforcement Officers

Appointment of inspectors and surveyors

256.—(1) The Secretary of State may, if he thinks fit, appoint any person as an inspector to report to him—

(a) upon the nature and causes of any accident or damage which any ship has or is alleged to have sustained or caused;

(b) whether any requirements, restrictions or prohibitions imposed by or under this Act have been complied with or (as the case may be) contravened;

(c) whether the hull and machinery of a ship are sufficient and in good condition;

(d) what measures have been taken to prevent the escape of oil or mixtures containing oil.

(2) The Secretary of State may, at such ports as he thinks fit, appoint persons to be surveyors of ships for the purposes of this Act and may remove any person so appointed.

(3) A surveyor of ships may be appointed either as a ship surveyor or as an engineer surveyor or as both.

(4) Surveyor of ships may be appointed either generally or for any particular case or purpose.

(5) The Secretary of State may also appoint a surveyor general of ships for the United Kingdom and such other officers in connection with the survey of ships and other matters incidental thereto as he thinks fit.

(6) The Secretary of State may appoint persons to be inspectors for the purposes of sections 261 to 266.

(7) Every inspector appointed under section (1) above shall be treated as appointed under subsection (6) above.

(8) Every surveyor of ships shall be treated as a person appointed generally under subsection (1) above to report to the Secretary of State in every kind of case falling within paragraphs (b) and (d) of that subsection in relation to Chapter II of Part VI.

(9) In this Act—

(a) "Departmental inspector" means an inspector appointed under subsection (1) above;

(b) "surveyor of ships" means a surveyor appointed under subsection (2) above;

(c) "Departmental officer" means any officer of the Secretary of State discharging functions of his for the purposes of this Act;

and the reference to requirements, restrictions or prohibitions under this Act includes any such requirements, restrictions or prohibitions constituting the terms of any approval, licence, consent or exemption given in any document issued under this Act.

DEFINITIONS
"Act, this": s.316(1).
"contravened": s.313(1).
"Departmental inspector": subs. (9)(a).
"Departmental officer": subs. (9)(c).
"escape": s.151(4).
"mixture containing oil": s.151(3).
"oil": s.151(1).
"person": Interpretation Act 1978, Sched. 1.
"port": s.313(1).
"Secretary of State": Interpretation Act 1978, Sched. 1.
"surveyor of ships": subs. (9)(b) and s.313(1).
"ship": s.313(1).
"United Kingdom": Interpretation Act 1978, Sched. 1.

GENERAL NOTE
[Derivation: Merchant Shipping Act 1894, s.728; Prevention of Oil Pollution Act 1971, s.18(1)(a) and (b); Merchant Shipping (Registration, etc.) Act 1993, Sched. 4, paras. 17, 56; Merchant Shipping Act 1894, s.724; Merchant Shipping Act 1906, s.75; Merchant Shipping Act 1984, s.7(1) and (2); Prevention of Oil Pollution Act 1971, s.18(2); Merchant Shipping (Registration, etc.) Act 1993, Sched. 4, para. 17(a).]

Section 256(1) replaces the Merchant Shipping Act 1894, s.728, which gave powers to the Secretary of State to appoint inspectors to report on (a) accidents, (b) whether the Act was being complied with and (c) as to the seaworthiness of ships. Some pre-consolidation harmonisation was achieved by the Merchant Shipping (Registration, etc.) Act 1993, Sched. 4. The Merchant Shipping Act 1988, Sched. 7 had prospectively repealed the power of inspectors to make reports on accidents at sea under s.728(a) of the 1894 Act. The reason appears to have been related to the delicate issue of how far DOT inspectors could independently report on matters where there might be criticism of the DOT itself (see further the General Note to s.267, below). That repeal was prevented from coming into force by the Merchant Shipping (Registration, etc.) Act 1993,

Sched. 4, para. 56. Accordingly, DOT inspectors are still fully enabled to make reports on marine casualties, without prejudice to the powers of the Marine Accident Inspectorate under s.276, below. Section 256(1), paras. (a)–(c) are in substantially the same form as the Merchant Shipping Act 1894, s.728, although para. (b) now makes specific reference to "requirements, restrictions or prohibitions" imposed by the Act (to reflect the more modern powers to inquire into compliance with the Merchant Shipping Act). Subsection (9) gives a wide definition of "requirements, restrictions or prohibitions" so as to include not only the more formal procedures, such as the use of enforcement notices now in s.262, but also less formal documentation such as consents or exemptions given under the authority of the Act. The section has been carefully worded so as to avoid any possibility of challenge to the authority of an inspector. Section 256 distinguishes between the Departmental inspector who is appointed to report under subs. (1) and surveyors appointed actually to inspect ships. Section 724 of the Merchant Shipping Act 1894, contained detailed powers to enable regulations to be made concerning the activities of surveyors. It was no longer thought necessary or desirable to set out such powers for the employment of surveyors, and the Merchant Shipping (Registration, etc.) Act 1993, Sched. 4, para. 78 amended the section accordingly. However, the power to remove surveyors was preserved in what is now subs. (2).

Note that the Secretary of State is given powers under other provisions of this Act to appoint persons to represent him other than inspectors or surveyors (see, *e.g.* s.7(1) and, generally, Pt. XIII).

Under subs. (5), the Secretary of State is entitled to appoint a Surveyor-General. On April 1, 1994, the Secretary of State established the existing Surveyor-General's Organisation as the Marine Safety Agency. Under that framework, the Secretary of State devolved responsibility for day-to-day management to the Chief Executive of the Agency (see *Marine Safety Agency: Framework Document*, (1994)).

The Prevention of Oil Pollution Act 1971 was an example of a piece of legislation relating to merchant shipping that was not integrated with the Merchant Shipping Acts. For the 1995 consolidation it was necessary to harmonise the various inspection powers given by s.18 of the Prevention of Oil Pollution Act 1971 with those in the Merchant Shipping Acts. The Merchant Shipping (Registration, etc.) Act 1993, Sched. 4, para. 17 effectively provided that the general merchant shipping powers, then in s.27 of the Merchant Shipping Act 1979, were to prevail. Subsection (1)(d) is one example of the harmonisation, as it allows DOT inspectors to report on oil pollution prevention measures on a ship. It seems rather curious to have omitted a reference to measures to prevent the escape of polluting substances other than oil, although it should be noted that under para. (b) there would be power for inspectors to report on breaches of the many regulations relating to pollution.

The powers of inspectors once contained in s.729 of the Merchant Shipping Act 1894, were replaced by those in the Merchant Shipping Act 1979, s.27 and are now consolidated in s.259. Note also ss.257–258.

Inspection etc. powers

Powers to require production of ships documents

257.—(1) The powers conferred by this section are conferred in relation to United Kingdom ships and are available to any of the following officers, namely—

(a) any Departmental officer,
(b) any commissioned naval officer,
(c) any British consular officer,
(d) the Registrar General of Shipping and Seamen or any person discharging his functions,
(e) any chief officer of customs and excise,
(f) any superintendent,

whenever the officer has reason to suspect that this Act or any law for the time being in force relating to merchant seamen or navigation is not complied with.

(2) Those powers are—

(a) to require the owner, master, or any of the crew to produce any official log-books or other documents relating to the crew or any member of the crew in their possession or control;

(b) to require the master to produce a list of all persons on board his ship, and take copies of or extracts from the official log-books or other such documents;

(c) to muster the crew; and

(d) to require the master to appear and give any explanation concerning the ship or her crew or the official log-books or documents produced or required to be produced.

(3) If any person, on being duly required by an officer under this section to produce a log-book or any document, fails without reasonable excuse to produce the log-book or document, he shall be liable on summary conviction to a fine not exceeding level 3 on the standard scale.

(4) If any person, on being duly required by any officer under this section—

(a) to produce a log-book or document, refuses to allow the log-book or document to be inspected or copied;

(b) to muster the crew, impedes the muster; or

(c) to give any explanation, refuses or neglects to give the explanation or knowingly misleads or deceives the officer;

he shall be liable on summary conviction to a fine not exceeding level 5 on the standard scale.

DEFINITIONS
    "Act, this": s.316(1).
    "commissioned naval officer": s.313(1).
    "Departmental officer": s.256(9)(c).
    "fails": s.313(1).
    "master": s.313(1).
    "person": Interpretation Act 1978, Sched. 1.
    "seaman": s.313(1).
    "ship": s.313(1).
    "standard scale": Criminal Justice Act 1982, s.37.
    "superintendent": s.313(1).
    "United Kingdom ship": ss.1(3) and 313(1).

GENERAL NOTE
    [Derivation: Merchant Shipping Act 1894, s.723, Merchant Shipping Act 1979, Sched. 6, Pts. I, VI, para. 11(a), Merchant Shipping (Registration, etc.) Act 1993, Sched. 4, para. 6(1).]

Powers to inspect ships and their equipment, etc.

258.—(1) For the purpose of seeing that the provisions of this Act other than Chapter II of Part VI and of regulations and rules made under this Act (other than that Chapter) or that the terms of any approval, licence, consent, direction or exemption given by virtue of such regulations are duly complied with, the following persons, namely—

(a) a surveyor of ships,

(b) a superintendent,

(c) any person appointed by the Secretary of State, either generally or in a particular case, to exercise powers under this section,

may at all reasonable times go on board a ship and inspect the ship and its equipment or any part thereof, any articles on board and any document carried in the ship in pursuance of this Act other than Chapter II of Part VI or in pursuance of regulations or rules under this Act (other than that Chapter).

(2) The powers conferred by subsection (1) above are, if the ship is a United Kingdom ship, also exercisable outside the United Kingdom and may be so exercised by a proper officer as well as the persons mentioned in that subsection.

(3) A person exercising powers under this section shall not unnecessarily detain or delay a ship but may, if he considers it necessary in consequence of an accident or for any other reason, require a ship to be taken into dock for a survey of its hull or machinery.

(4) Where any such person as is mentioned in subsection (1) above has reasonable grounds for believing that there are on any premises provisions or water intended for supply to a United Kingdom ship which, if provided on the ship, would not be in accordance with safety regulations containing requirements as to provisions and water to be provided on ships he may enter the premises and inspect the provisions or water for the purpose of ascertaining whether they would be in accordance with the regulations.

(5) If any person obstructs a person in the exercise of his powers under this section, or fails to comply with a requirement made under subsection (3) above, he shall be liable, on summary conviction, to a fine not exceeding level 5 on the standard scale.

DEFINITIONS
"Act, this": s.316(1).
"fails": s.313(1).
"person": Interpretation Act 1978, Sched. 1.
"proper officer": s.313(1).
"Secretary of State": Interpretation Act 1978, Sched. 1.
"ship": s.313(1).
"standard scale": Criminal Justice Act 1982, s.37.
"superintendent": s.313(1).
"surveyor of ships": ss.256(9)(b) and 313(1).
"United Kingdom": Interpretation Act 1978, Sched. 1.
"United Kingdom ship": ss.1(3) and 313(1).

GENERAL NOTE
[Derivation: Merchant Shipping Act 1970, s.76, Merchant Shipping Act 1979, s.37(5), Sched. 6, Pt. IV; Criminal Justice Act 1982, s.46; Merchant Shipping (Provisions and Water) Regulations 1989, reg. 1(3)(b).]

Powers of inspectors in relation to premises and ships

259.—(1) The powers conferred by this section are conferred in relation to—

(a) any premises in the United Kingdom; or

(b) any United Kingdom ship wherever it may be and any other ship which is present in the United Kingdom or in United Kingdom waters;

and are available to any Departmental inspector, or any inspector appointed under section 256(6), for the purpose of performing his functions.

(2) Such an inspector—

(a) may at any reasonable time (or, in a situation which in his opinion is or may be dangerous, at any time)—

(i) enter any premises, or

(ii) board any ship,

if he has reason to believe that it is necessary for him to do so;

(b) may, on entering any premises by virtue of paragraph (a) above or on boarding a ship by virtue of that paragraph, take with him any other person authorised for the purpose by the Secretary of State and any equipment or materials he requires;

(c) may make such examination and investigation as he considers necessary;

(d) may give a direction requiring that the premises or ship or any part of the premises or ship or any thing in the premises or ship or such a part shall be left undisturbed (whether generally or in particular respects) for so long as is reasonably necessary for the purposes of any examination or investigation under paragraph (c) above;

(e) may take such measurements and photographs and make such recordings as he considers necessary for the purpose of any examination or investigation under paragraph (c) above;

(f) may take samples of any articles or substances found in the premises or ship and of the atmosphere in or in the vicinity of the premises or ship;

(g) may, in the case of any article or substance which he finds in the premises or ship and which appears to him to have caused or to be likely to cause danger to health or safety, cause it to be dismantled or subjected to any process or test (but not so as to damage or destroy it unless that is in the circumstances necessary);

(h) may, in the case of any such article or substance as is mentioned in paragraph (g) above, take possession of it and detain it for so long as is necessary for all or any of the following purposes, namely—

(i) to examine it and do to it anything which he has power to do under that paragraph,

(ii) to ensure that it is not tampered with before his examination of it is completed,

(iii) to ensure that it is available for use as evidence in any proceedings for an offence under this Act or any instrument made under it;

(i) may require any person who he has reasonable cause to believe is able to give any information relevant to any examination or investigation under paragraph (c) above—

(i) to attend at a place and time specified by the inspector, and

(ii) to answer (in the absence of persons other than any persons whom the inspector may allow to be present and a person nominated to be present by the person on whom the requirement is imposed) such questions as the inspector thinks fit to ask, and

(iii) to sign a declaration of the truth of his answers;

(j) may require the production of, and inspect and take copies of or of any entry in,—

(i) any books or documents which by virtue of any provision of this Act are required to be kept; and

(ii) any other books or documents which he considers it necessary for him to see for the purposes of any examination or investigation under paragraph (c) above;

(k) may require any person to afford him such facilities and assistance with respect to any matters or things within that person's control or in relation to which that person has responsibilities as the inspector considers are necessary to enable him to exercise any of the powers conferred on him by this subsection.

(3) The powers conferred by subsection (2) above to require the production of any document and copy it include, in relation to oil record books required to be carried under section 142, power to require the master to certify the copy as a true copy.

(4) The powers conferred by subsection (2) above to inspect premises shall also be exercisable, for the purpose of Chapter II of Part VI, in relation to any apparatus used for transferring oil.

(5) The powers of entry and inspection of premises conferred by subsections (2) and (4) above for the purposes of Chapter II of Part VI shall not be exercisable by Departmental inspectors (or surveyors of ships in their capacity as Departmental inspectors) in relation to places on land in Northern Ireland and apparatus located in Northern Ireland otherwise than on board ships; but persons appointed by the Department of the Environment for Northern Ireland shall have the like powers; and those subsections shall have effect accordingly in relation to persons so appointed.

(6) The powers conferred by subsection (2)(a), (c) and (j) above shall also be exercisable, in relation to a ship in a harbour in the United Kingdom, by the harbour master or other persons appointed by the Secretary of State for the purpose, for the purpose of ascertaining the circumstances relating to an

alleged discharge of oil or a mixture containing oil from the ship into the harbour.

(7) It is hereby declared that nothing in the preceding provisions of this section authorises a person unnecessarily to prevent a ship from proceeding on a voyage.

(8) The Secretary of State may by regulations make provision as to the procedure to be followed in connection with the taking of samples under subsection (2)(f) above and subsection (11) below and provision as to the way in which samples that have been so taken are to be dealt with.

(9) Where an inspector proposes to exercise the power conferred by subsection (2)(g) above in the case of an article or substance found in any premises or ship, he shall, if so requested by a person who at the time is present in and has responsibilities in relation to the premises or ship, cause anything which is to be done by virtue of that power to be done in the presence of that person unless the inspector considers that its being done in that person's presence would be prejudicial to the safety of that person.

(10) Before exercising the power conferred by subsection (2)(g) above, an inspector shall consult such persons as appear to him appropriate for the purpose of ascertaining what dangers, if any, there may be in doing anything which he proposes to do under that power.

(11) Where under the power conferred by subsection (2)(h) above an inspector takes possession of any article or substance found in any premises or ship, he shall leave there, either with a responsible person or, if that is impracticable, fixed in a conspicuous position, a notice giving particulars of that article or substance sufficient to identify it and stating that he has taken possession of it under that power; and before taking possession of any such substance under that power an inspector shall, if it is practicable for him to do so, take a sample of the substance and give to a responsible person at the premises or on board the ship a portion of the sample marked in a manner sufficient to identify it.

(12) No answer given by a person in pursuance of a requirement imposed under subsection (2)(i) above shall be admissible in evidence against that person or the husband or wife of that person in any proceedings except proceedings in pursuance of subsection (1)(c) of section 260 in respect of a statement in or a declaration relating to the answer; and a person nominated as mentioned in the said subsection (2)(i) shall be entitled, on the occasion on which the questions there mentioned are asked, to make representations to the inspector on behalf of the person who nominated him.

DEFINITIONS
    "Act, this": s.316(1).
    "Departmental inspector": s.256(9)(a).
    "Departmental officer": s.256(9)(c).
    "discharge": s.151(4).
    "harbour": s.313(1).
    "harbour master": s.151(1).
    "master": s.313(1).
    "mixture containing oil": s.151(3).
    "oil": s.151(1).
    "person": Interpretation Act 1978, Sched. 1.
    "Secretary of State": Interpretation Act 1978, Sched. 1.
    "ship": s.313(1).
    "surveyor of ships": ss.256(9)(b) and 313(1).
    "United Kingdom": Interpretation Act 1978, Sched. 1.
    "United Kingdom ship": ss.1(3) and 313(1).
    "United Kingdom waters": s.313(2)(a).

GENERAL NOTE
 [Derivation: Merchant Shipping Act 1979, s.27(1); Prevention of Oil Pollution Act 1971, s.18(3); Merchant Shipping Act 1984, s.7(3); Merchant Shipping (Registration, etc.) Act 1993, Sched. 4, para. 57; Prevention of Oil Pollution Act 1971, s.18(3)(b); Merchant Shipping Act 1979, s.28(7)(c); Prevention of Oil Pollution Act 1971, s.18(5), (6); Merchant Shipping (Registration, etc.) Act 1993, Sched. 4, para. 17(b); Prevention of Oil Pollution Act 1971, s.18(7); Merchant Shipping Act 1979, s.27(2); Prevention of Oil Pollution Act 1971, s.30(3); Merchant Shipping (Registration, etc.) Act 1993, Sched. 4, para. 17(a) and (d); Merchant Shipping Act 1979. s.27(3)–(7).]

Provisions supplementary to section 259

260.—(1) A person who—
 (a) intentionally obstructs an inspector in the exercise of any power available to him under section 259; or
 (b) without reasonable excuse, does not comply with a requirement imposed in pursuance of section 259 or prevents another person from complying with such a requirement; or
 (c) without prejudice to the generality of paragraph (b) above, makes a statement or signs a declaration which he knows is false, or recklessly makes a statement or signs a declaration which is false, in purported compliance with a requirement made in pursuance of subsection (2)(i) of section 259,
shall be liable—
 (i) on summary conviction, to a fine not exceeding the statutory maximum;
 (ii) on conviction on indictment, to imprisonment for a term not exceeding two years, or a fine or both.

 (2) Nothing in section 259 shall be taken to compel the production by any person of a document of which he would on grounds of legal professional privilege be entitled to withhold production on an order for discovery in an action in the High Court or, as the case may be, on an order for the production of documents in an action in the Court of Session.

 (3) A person who complies with a requirement imposed on him in pursuance of paragraph (i)(i) or (k) of subsection (2) of section 259 shall be entitled to recover from the person who imposed the requirement such sums in respect of the expenses incurred in complying with the requirement as are prescribed by regulations made by the Secretary of State.

 (4) Regulations under subsection (3) above may make different provision for different circumstances.

 (5) Any payments under subsection (3) above shall be made out of money provided by Parliament.

DEFINITIONS
 "High Court": Interpretation Act 1978, Sched. 1.
 "person": Interpretation Act 1978, Sched. 1.
 "Secretary of State": Interpretation Act 1978, Sched. 1.
 "statutory maximum": Criminal Justice Act 1982, s.74.

GENERAL NOTE
 [Derivation: Merchant Shipping Act 1974, s.28(1)–(4).]

Improvement notices and prohibition notices

Improvement notices

261.—(1) If an inspector appointed under section 256(6) is of the opinion that a person—
 (a) is contravening one or more of the relevant statutory provisions, or

(b) has contravened one or more of those provisions in circumstances that make it likely that the contravention will continue or be repeated,

he may serve on that person a notice under this section, (referred to in the following sections of this Part as an improvement notice).

(2) An improvement notice shall—

(a) state that the inspector is of the said opinion, specify the provision or provisions as to which he is of that opinion, and give particulars of the reasons why he is of that opinion, and

(b) require the person on whom the notice is served to remedy the contravention in question or (as the case may be) the matters occasioning it within such period as may be specified in the notice.

(3) The period specified in pursuance of subsection (2)(b) above shall not expire before the end of the period within which a notice can be given under section 264 requiring questions relating to the improvement notice to be referred to arbitration.

(4) In this and the following sections of this Part "the relevant statutory provisions" means—

(a) sections 43, 44, 46 to 55, 85, 86, 88 (and Schedule 2), 89 (and Schedule 3), 90, 99, 109, 115, 116, 121 to 126, 128, 129, 130, 131 to 151 and 272; and

(b) the provisions of any instrument of a legislative character having effect under any of those provisions.

DEFINITIONS
"contravention": s.313(1).
"improvement notice": subs. (1).
"person": Interpretation Act 1978, Sched. 1.
"relevant statutory provisions, the": subs. (4).

GENERAL NOTE
[Derivation: Merchant Shipping Act 1984, ss.1, 11, Sched. 1.]

Sections 261–266 provide inspectors appointed under s.256 with a variety of powers in their armoury to ensure compliance with the various statutory requirements laid down in the Act.

Under s.261 they can issue an "improvement notice" to ensure compliance with the various statutory requirements laid down in the provisions of the Act listed in subs. (4) and relating to such matters as crewing, safety and pollution. Contravention of the notice is an offence under s.266.

Prohibition notices

262.—(1) If, as regards any relevant activities which are being or are likely to be carried on on board any ship by or under the control of any person, an inspector appointed under section 256(6) is of the opinion that, as so carried on or as likely to be so carried on, the activities involve or (as the case may be) will involve the risk of—

(a) serious personal injury to any person (whether on board the ship or not), or

(b) serious pollution of any navigable waters,

the inspector may serve on the first-mentioned person a notice under this section (referred to in the following sections of this Part as a "prohibition notice").

(2) In subsection (1) above "relevant activities" means activities to or in relation to which any of the relevant statutory provisions apply or will, if the activities are carried on as mentioned in that subsection, apply.

(3) A prohibition notice shall—

(a) state that the inspector is of the said opinion;

(b) specify the matters which in his opinion give or (as the case may be) will give rise to the said risk;

(c) where in his opinion any of those matters involve or (as the case may be) will involve a contravention of any of the relevant statutory provisions state that he is of that opinion, specify the provision or provisions as to which he is of that opinion, and give particulars of the reasons why he is of that opinion; and

(d) direct—

(i) that the activities to which the notice relates shall not be carried on by or under the control of the person on whom the notice is served, or

(ii) that the ship shall not go to sea,

(or both of those things) unless the matters specified in the notice in pursuance of paragraph (b) above, and any associated contraventions of any provision so specified in pursuance of paragraph (c) above, have been remedied.

(4) A direction contained in a prohibition notice in pursuance of subsection (3)(d) above shall take effect—

(a) at the end of a period specified in the notice, or

(b) if the direction is given in pursuance of subsection (3)(d)(ii) above or the notice so declares, immediately.

DEFINITIONS

"contravention": s.313(1).
"person": Interpretation Act 1978, Sched. 1.
"prohibition notice": subs. (1).
"relevant activities": subs. (2).
"relevant statutory provisions, the": s.261(4).
"ship": s.313(1).

GENERAL NOTE

[Derivation: Merchant Shipping Act 1984, s.2, Merchant Shipping Act 1988, Sched. 5.]

Sections 261–266 provide inspectors appointed under s.256 with a variety of powers in their armoury to ensure compliance with the various statutory requirements laid down in the Act. Under s.262 they can issue a "prohibition notice" to prevent injury or pollution and to ensure compliance with the various statutory requirements laid down in the provisions of the Act listed in s.261(4) and relating to such matters as crewing, safety and pollution. Contravention of the notice is an offence under s.266.

The Merchant Shipping Act 1984, s.2 allowed inspectors to issue prohibition notices in respect of activities which were, or were "about" to be, "carried on on board" any ship and which involved a risk of serious injury or pollution. The Merchant Shipping Act 1988, Sched. 5 substituted the word "likely" for "about", thus removing any need to show the immediate nature of the activities, although some degree of probability is still required.

Provisions supplementary to sections 261 and 262

263.—(1) An improvement notice or a prohibition notice may (but need not) include directions as to the measures to be taken to remedy any contravention or matter to which the notice relates; and any such directions may be framed so as to afford the person on whom the notice is served a choice between different ways of remedying the contravention or matter.

(2) An improvement notice or a prohibition notice shall not direct any measures to be taken to remedy the contravention of any of the relevant statutory provisions that are more onerous than those necessary to secure compliance with that provision.

(3) Where an improvement notice or a prohibition notice that is not to take immediate effect has been served—

(a) the notice may be withdrawn by an inspector at any time before the end of the period specified in it in pursuance of section 261(2)(b) or (as the case may be) section 262(4); and

(b) the period so specified may be extended or further extended by an inspector at any time when a reference to arbitration in respect of the notice is not pending under section 264.

DEFINITIONS
   "contravention": s.313(1).
   "improvement notice": s.261(1).
   "person": Interpretation Act 1978, Sched. 1.
   "prohibition notice": s.262(1).
   "relevant statutory provisions, the": s.261(4).

GENERAL NOTE
   [Derivation: Merchant Shipping Act 1984, s.3.]
   Improvement or prohibition notices may give directions as to the ways in which they can be complied with, but must be proportionate to the level of compliance necessary.

References of notices to arbitration

   264.—(1) Any question—
   (a) as to whether any of the reasons or matters specified in an improve-
       ment notice or a prohibition notice in pursuance of section 261(2)(a)
       or 262(3)(b) or (c) in connection with any opinion formed by the
       inspector constituted a valid basis for that opinion, or
   (b) as to whether any directions included in the notice in pursuance of
       section 263(1) were reasonable,
   shall, if the person on whom the notice was served so requires by a notice
   given to the inspector within 21 days from the service of the notice, be
   referred to a single arbitrator appointed by agreement between the parties
   for that question to be decided by him.
   (2) Where a notice is given by a person in accordance with subsection (1)
   above, then—
   (a) in the case of an improvement notice, the giving of the notice shall
       have the effect of suspending the operation of the improvement notice
       until the decision of the arbitrator is published to the parties or the
       reference is abandoned by that person;
   (b) in the case of a prohibition notice, the giving of the notice shall have
       the effect of so suspending the operation of the prohibition notice if,
       but only if, on the application of that person the arbitrator so directs
       (and then only from the giving of the direction).
   (3) Where on a reference under this section the arbitrator decides as
   respects any reason, matter or direction to which the reference relates, that in
   all the circumstances—
   (a) the reason or matter did not constitute a valid basis for the inspector's
       opinion, or
   (b) the direction was unreasonable,
   he shall either cancel the notice or affirm it with such modifications as he may
   in the circumstances think fit; and in any other case the arbitrator shall affirm
   the notice in its original form.
   (4) Where any reference under this section involves the consideration by
   the arbitrator of the effects of any particular activities or state of affairs on
   the health or safety of any persons, he shall not on that reference make any
   decision such as is mentioned in subsection (3)(a) or (b) above except after—
   (a) in the case of an improvement notice, affording an opportunity of
       making oral representations to him with respect to those effects to a
       member of any such panel of representatives of maritime trade unions
       as may be appointed by the Secretary of State for the purposes of this
       subsection; or
   (b) in the case of a prohibition notice, affording an opportunity of making
       such representations to him to either—
           (i) a representative of a trade union representing persons whose
       interests it appears to him that the notice was designed to safe-
       guard, or
           (ii) a member of any such panel as is referred to in paragraph (a)
       above,

as he thinks appropriate; and
(c) (in either case) considering any representations made to him in pursuance of paragraph (a) or (b) above.

(5) A person shall not be qualified for appointment as an arbitrator under this section unless he is—
(a) a person holding a certificate of competency as a master mariner or as a marine engineer officer class 1, or a person holding a certificate equivalent to any such certificate;
(b) a naval architect;
(c) a person falling with subsection (6); or
(d) a person with special experience of shipping matters, of the fishing industry, or of activities carried on in ports.

(6) For the purposes of subsection (5)(c) a person falls within this subsection if—
(a) he has a 10 year general qualification (within the meaning of section 71 of the Courts and Legal Services Act 1990);
(b) he is an advocate or solicitor in Scotland of at least 10 years' standing; or
(c) he is a member of the bar of Northern Ireland or solicitor of the Supreme Court of Northern Ireland of at least 10 years' standing.

(7) In connection with his functions under this section an arbitrator shall have the powers conferred on an inspector by section 259 other than subsections (3), (4) and (6).

(8) In the application of this section to Scotland any reference to an arbitrator shall be construed as a reference to an arbiter and the reference in subsection (1) above to a single arbitrator appointed by agreement between the parties shall be construed as a reference to a single arbiter so appointed or, in default of agreement, appointed by the sheriff.

(9) The Arbitration Act (Northern Ireland) 1937 shall apply in relation to an arbitration in pursuance of this section as if this section related to a matter in respect of which the Parliament of Northern Ireland had power to make laws.

DEFINITIONS
"arbitrator": subss. (5) and (6).
"improvement notice": s.261(1).
"person": Interpretation Act 1978, Sched. 1.
"port": s.313(1).
"prohibition notice": s.262(1).
"Secretary of State": Interpretation Act 1978, Sched. 1.

GENERAL NOTE
[Derivation: Merchant Shipping Act 1984, s.4; Courts and Legal Services Act 1990, Sched. 10, para. 55.]
Questions as to the basis or extent of improvement or prohibition notices may be referred to an arbitrator.

Compensation in connection with invalid prohibition notices

265.—(1) If on a reference under section 264 relating to a prohibition notice—
(a) the arbitrator decides that any reason or matter did not constitute a valid basis for the inspector's opinion, and
(b) it appears to him that there were no reasonable grounds for the inspector to form that opinion,
the arbitrator may, subject to subsection (3) below, award the person on whom the notice was served such compensation in respect of any loss suf-

fered by him in consequence of the service of the notice as the arbitrator thinks fit.

(2) If on any such reference the arbitrator decides that any direction included in the notice was unreasonable, the arbitrator may, subject to subsection (3) below, award the person on whom the notice was served such compensation in respect of any loss suffered by him in consequence of the direction as the arbitrator thinks fit.

(3) An arbitrator shall not award any compensation under subsection (1) or (2) above in the case of any prohibition notice unless—

(a) it appears to him that the direction given in pursuance of section 262(3)(d) contained any such requirement as is mentioned in subparagraph (ii) of that provision; or

(b) it appears to him that—

(i) the inspector was of the opinion that there would be such a risk of injury or pollution as is referred to in the notice if the ship went to sea, and

(ii) the effect of the direction given in pursuance of section 262(3) (d) was to prohibit the departure of the ship unless the matters, or (as the case may be) the matters and contraventions, referred to in the direction were remedied.

(4) Any compensation awarded under this section shall be payable by the Secretary of State.

(5) In the application of this section to Scotland any reference to an arbitrator shall be construed as a reference to an arbiter.

DEFINITIONS
  "arbitrator": s.264(5) and (6).
  "contraventions": s.313(1).
  "person": Interpretation Act 1978, Sched. 1.
  "prohibition notice": s.262(1).
  "ship": s.313(1).
  "Secretary of State": Interpretation Act 1978, Sched. 1.

GENERAL NOTE
  [Derivation: Merchant Shipping Act 1984, s.5; Merchant Shipping (Registration, etc.) Act 1993, Sched. 4, para. 12.]
  If the arbitrator, to whom a question about a prohibition notice has been referred under s.264, decides against the inspector's opinion, he is allowed to award compensation under s.265. Subsection (3) imposes restrictions on the exercise of that power, for example, by requiring that the ship must effectively have been prevented from going to sea.

Offences

266.—(1) Any person who contravenes any requirement imposed by an improvement notice shall be liable—

(a) on summary conviction, to a fine not exceeding the statutory maximum;

(b) on conviction on indictment, to a fine.

(2) Any person who contravenes any prohibition imposed by a prohibition notice shall be liable—

(a) on summary conviction, to a fine not exceeding the statutory maximum;

(b) on conviction on indictment, to imprisonment for a term not exceeding two years or a fine or both.

(3) It shall be a defence for a person charged with an offence under this section to prove that he exercised all due diligence to avoid a contravention of the requirement or prohibition in question.

(4) In this section any reference to an improvement notice or a prohibition notice includes a reference to any such notice as modified under section 264(3).

"contravenes": s.313(1).
"improvement notice": s.261(1).
"person": Interpretation Act 1978, Sched. 1.
"prohibition notice": s.262(1).
"statutory maximum": Criminal Justice Act 1982, s.74.

GENERAL NOTE
[Derivation: Merchant Shipping Act 1984, s.6.]
For improvement or prohibition notices, see ss.261–262.

PART XI

ACCIDENT INVESTIGATIONS AND INQUIRIES

Marine accident investigations

Investigation of marine accidents

267.—(1) The Secretary of State shall, for the purpose of the investigation of any such accidents as are mentioned in subsection (2) below, appoint such number of persons as he may determine to be inspectors of marine accidents, and he shall appoint one of those persons to be Chief Inspector of Marine Accidents.

(2) The accidents referred to in subsection (1) above are—
(a) any accident involving a ship or ship's boat where, at the time of the accident—
   (i) the ship is a United Kingdom ship, or
   (ii) the ship, or (in the case of an accident involving a ship's boat) that boat, is within United Kingdom waters, and
(b) such other accidents involving ships or ships' boats as the Secretary of State may determine.

(3) The Secretary of State may by regulations make such provision as he considers appropriate with respect to the investigation of any such accidents as are mentioned in subsection (2) above.

(4) Any such regulations may, in particular, make provision—
(a) with respect to the definition of "accident" for the purposes of this section and the regulations;
(b) imposing requirements as to the reporting of accidents;
(c) prohibiting, pending investigation, access to or interference with any ship or ship's boat involved in an accident;
(d) authorising any person, so far as may be necessary for the purpose of determining whether an investigation should be carried out, to have access to, examine, remove, test, take measures for the preservation of, or otherwise deal with, any such ship or boat or any other ship or ship's boat;
(e) specifying, with respect to the investigation of accidents, the functions of the Chief Inspector of Marine Accidents (which may include the function of determining whether, and if so by whom, particular accidents should be investigated), the functions of other inspectors of marine accidents, and the manner in which any such functions are to be discharged;
(f) for the appointment by the Chief Inspector of Marine Accidents, in such circumstances as may be specified in the regulations, of persons

to carry out investigations under this section who are not inspectors of marine accidents;

(g) for the appointment by any Minister of the Crown of persons to review any findings or conclusions of a person carrying out an investigation under this section;

(h) for the procedure to be followed in connection with investigations or reviews under this section;

(i) for conferring on persons discharging functions under the regulations who are not inspectors of marine accidents all or any of the powers conferred on an inspector by section 259;

(j) for the submission to the Secretary of State, and the publication by him, of reports of investigations or reviews under this section;

(k) for the publication by the Chief Inspector of Marine Accidents of reports and other information relating to accidents.

(5) Regulations under this section may provide for any provisions of the regulations to apply to any specified class or description of incidents or situations which involve, or occur on board, ships or ships' boats but are not accidents for the purposes of the regulations, being a class or description framed by reference to any of the following, namely—

(a) the loss or destruction of or serious damage to any ship or structure,

(b) the death of or serious injury to any person, or

(c) environmental damage,

whether actually occurring or not, and (subject to such modifications as may be specified in the regulations) for those provisions to apply in relation to any such incidents or situations as they apply in relation to accidents.

(6) Regulations under this section may provide that a contravention of the regulations shall be an offence punishable on summary conviction by a fine not exceeding the statutory maximum and on conviction on indictment by a fine.

(7) The Chief Inspector of Marine Accidents, or (as the case may be) inspectors of marine accidents generally, shall discharge such functions in addition to those conferred by or under the preceding provisions of this section as the Secretary of State may determine.

(8) Any inspector of marine accidents shall, for the purpose of discharging any functions conferred on him by or under this section, have the powers conferred on an inspector by section 259.

(9) Nothing in this section shall limit the powers of any authority under sections 252, 253 and 254.

(10) In this section—

(a) references to an accident involving a ship or ship's boat include references to an accident occurring on board a ship or ship's boat (and any reference to a ship or ship's boat involved in an accident shall be construed accordingly); and

(b) "ship's boat" includes a life-raft.

Definitions

"accidents": subs. (2).
"accidents involving a ship or ship's boat": subs. (10)(a).
"contravention": s.313(1).
"person": Interpretation Act 1978, Sched. 1.
"Secretary of State": Interpretation Act 1978, Sched. 1.
"ship": s.313(1).
"ship's boat": subs. (10)(b).
"statutory maximum": Criminal Justice Act 1982, s.74.
"United Kingdom ship": ss.1(3) and 313(1).
"United Kingdom waters": s.313(2)(a).

GENERAL NOTE

[Derivation: Merchant Shipping Act 1988, s.33.]

The *Herald of Free Enterprise* disaster highlighted the difficult position of the DOT, whose Marine Directorate was charged with the responsibility of co-ordinating the investigation *and* any formal investigation under s.268. Accidents at sea were generally investigated by inspectors appointed by the DOT under powers granted by s.256 (formerly the Merchant Shipping Act 1894, s.728, as amended by the Merchant Shipping Act 1979, s.27). There was a problem when the Department itself was criticised, usually by a shipowner, for failing to make regulations on certain aspects of safety. One of the responses to the criticisms of the shipowners after the *Herald of Free Enterprise* disaster was that they had a ship that conformed precisely to all the DOT requirements and that it was the DOT's job to decide whether Ro-Ro ferries were inherently unsafe and whether bridge indicator lights should be fitted to show whether the bow doors were closed. The Secretary of State had stated that any conflict of interest could be met by appointing separate counsel to represent the Secretary of State and the Marine Directorate of the DOT. But, as Sheen J. noted, this laid the Department open to charges of being involved in a cover-up, especially as both counsel would receive instructions from the same source. Also, inspectors' reports were not published.

The DOT had proposed in 1986 to establish an internal Inspector of Marine Casualties who would publish the more important reports. But the criticisms of the Sheen Report (echoing misgivings expressed by the same judge in his 1984 Report after the collision involving the *European Gateway*) merely emphasised that these proposals would hardly meet public concern. The 1987 White paper recognised the difficulty and the Government agreed to establish a Marine Accident Investigation Branch, under a Chief Inspector of Marine Accidents, which would not be part of the Marine Directorate. The Chief Inspector reports directly to the Secretary of State for Transport and those reports on the more important or significant accidents are now published. The arrangement is deliberately modelled on that operating in the aviation field, where there is a separate accident investigation branch based at Farnborough (see generally s.75 of the Civil Aviation Act 1982).

Nothing in the provision meets the specific criticism of Sheen J., that in a Formal Investigation under s.268 there ought to be a separate counsel appointed to assist the tribunal. Specific legislative action is probably not required for this and at the Second Reading debate on the Merchant Shipping Act 1988 in the Commons, the Secretary of State for Transport, Paul Channon, announced that responsibility for instructing counsel assisting the Court will rest with the Attorney-General and not the Secretary of State.

This section applies to accidents involving U.K. ships or any ships (including foreign ones) within U.K. territorial waters: see subs. (2). The section will also apply to ship's boats, including life-rafts: see subs. (10).

Subsection (4) lists the matters which Regulations may cover. The section gives wide rule-making powers to the Secretary of State, *e.g.* as to the type of accident to be investigated. One matter raised by the Sheen Report into the *Herald of Free Enterprise* disaster was whether there should be a broader requirement to report accidents. The Merchant Shipping (Safety Officials and Reporting of Accidents) Regulations 1982 (S.I. 1982 No. 876) as amended, did not require potentially hazardous occurrences to be reported. The Department of Transport Consultative Document No. 6 in 1987 proposed completely new regulations covering the reporting of potentially hazardous occurrences, with a voluntary system to be introduced in the interim. The 1987 White Paper declared that it was the intention to include the full range of accidents, including occupational accidents and hazardous incidents (and see subs. (5)). The accident does not have to involve another ship or boat and may occur solely on board one ship. At the Third Reading in the Lords, there was discussion of whether there was a need for the type of "near-miss" reporting that takes place in the aviation field. It was recognised that there might be room for a system involving both public and confidential reporting. The latter is particularly useful to encourage reporting of incidents by those who might otherwise be frightened of disciplinary proceedings. The idea of voluntary reporting was supported on all sides and it seems likely that the regulations will incorporate such a system.

Although subs. (4)(j) allows for the publication of reports, the Government resisted an attempt to force the Secretary of State to make a detailed annual report to Parliament on ship safety. But an undertaking was given at the Third Reading in the Commons that the Inspectorate of marine accidents would produce an annual report to be laid before the House. A similar undertaking was given at Committee stage that an individual report would be published for serious accidents.

Under subs. (8), the inspectors in the MAIB will have all the extensive powers currently available to inspectors under s.259. These include powers to enter ships or premises, take recordings or samples and compel the attendance of witnesses to answer questions.

Subsection (9) echoes s.75(6) of the Civil Aviation Act 1982 and makes it clear that the investigation is not to restrict the powers of harbour authorities under ss.252–254 to remove wrecks which are creating an obstruction or danger to navigation. Otherwise s.259(2)(d) might give the inspector the power to order that the ship be left undisturbed.

Note that an investigation under this section may be followed by a formal investigation under s.268.

Formal investigation into marine accidents

268.—(1) Where any accident has occurred, the Secretary of State may (whether or not an investigation into it has been carried out under section 267) cause a formal investigation into the accident to be held—

(a) if in England, Wales or Northern Ireland, by a wreck commissioner, and

(b) if in Scotland, by the sheriff;

and in this section "accident" means any accident to which regulations under that section apply or any incident or situation to which any such regulations apply by virtue of subsection (5) of that section.

(2) A wreck commissioner or sheriff holding a formal investigation shall conduct it in accordance with rules under section 270(1); and those rules shall require the assistance of one or more assessors and, if any question as to the cancellation or suspension of an officer's certificate is likely, the assistance of not less than two assessors.

(3) Subsections (1), (3) and (4) of section 97 of the Magistrates' Courts Act 1980 (which provide for the attendance of witnesses and the production of evidence) shall apply in relation to a formal investigation held by a wreck commissioner as if the wreck commissioner were a magistrates' court and the investigation a complaint; and the wreck commissioner shall have power to administer oaths for the purposes of the investigation.

(4) Where a formal investigation is held in Scotland the sheriff shall, subject to any rules made under section 270(1), dispose of it as a summary application, and, subject to section 269, his decision on the investigation shall be final.

(5) If as a result of the investigation the wreck commissioner or sheriff is satisfied, with respect to any officer, of any of the matters mentioned in paragraphs (a) to (c) of section 61(1) and, if it is a matter mentioned in paragraph (a) or (b) of that section, is further satisfied that it caused or contributed to the accident, he may cancel or suspend any certificate issued to the officer under section 47 or censure him; and if he cancels or suspends the certificate the officer shall deliver it forthwith to him or to the Secretary of State.

(6) If a person fails to deliver a certificate as required under subsection (5) above he shall be liable on summary conviction to a fine not exceeding level 3 on the standard scale.

(7) Where a certificate has been cancelled or suspended under this section, the Secretary of State, if of the opinion that the justice of the case requires it, may re-issue the certificate or, as the case may be, reduce the period of suspension and return the certificate, or may grant a new certificate of the same or a lower grade in place of the cancelled or suspended certificate.

(8) The wreck commissioner or sheriff may make such awards as he thinks just with regard to the costs (or, as the case may be, expenses) of the investigation and of any parties at the investigation, and with regard to the parties by whom those costs or expenses are to be paid; and any such award of the wreck commissioner may, on the application of any party named in it, be made an order of the High Court.

(9) Any costs or expenses directed by an award to be paid shall be taxable—

(a) in the High Court, or

(b) where the investigation was held in Scotland, by the auditor of the sheriff court in which it was held and in accordance with the table of fees regulating the taxation of solicitors' accounts.

(10) The wreck commissioner or sheriff shall make a report on the investigation to the Secretary of State.

(11) In its application to Northern Ireland this section shall have effect as if in subsection (3) above for the references to subsections (1), (3) and (4) of section 97 of the Magistrates' Courts Act 1980 there were substituted references to paragraphs (1) and (3) of Article 118 and paragraph (1) of Article 120 of the Magistrates' Courts (Northern Ireland) Order 1981.

DEFINITIONS

"accident": subs. (1).
"England and Wales": Interpretation Act 1978, Sched. 1.
"fails": s.313(1).
"High Court": Interpretation Act 1978, Sched. 1.
"oath": Interpretation Act 1978, Sched. 1.
"person": Interpretation Act 1978, Sched. 1.
"Secretary of State": Interpretation Act 1978, Sched. 1.
"sheriff": Interpretation Act 1978, Sched. 1.
"standard scale": Criminal Justice Act 1982, s.37.

GENERAL NOTE

[Derivation: Merchant Shipping Act 1970, s.56, Merchant Shipping Act 1988, Sched. 6, para. 2 and Sched. 5 para. 4; Merchant Shipping Act 1970, s.59, Merchant Shipping Act 1979, Sched. 6, Pt. II; Merchant Shipping Act 1970, s.60.]

The scheme established by the Merchant Shipping Act 1970 for the inquiries and investigations into shipping casualties was to start with a preliminary inquiry into a casualty under the Merchant Shipping Act 1970, s.55, before any Formal Investigation under s.56 (now s.268 of the Merchant Shipping Act 1995). The creation of an Inspectorate of Marine Accidents by s.33 of the Merchant Shipping Act 1988 (see now s.267 above) meant that there was no need for a separate provision dealing with the initial investigation. Accordingly, the Merchant Shipping Act 1970, s.55 was repealed by the Merchant Shipping Act 1988, Sched. 7.

Section 278 now sets out the circumstances in which there may be a Formal Investigation. Note that the bracketed words were introduced by the Merchant Shipping Act 1988, Sched. 5 to make it clear that there can still be a Formal Investigation, despite the fact there has been a s.267 investigation. Subsection (1) also uses the expression "accident" in place of the rather vague words "casualty or incident" as appeared in the Merchant Shipping Act 1970, s.56 (before it was amended by the Merchant Shipping Act 1988, Sched. 5). Although this expression itself may seem equally vague, it is arguably broader and has the advantage that it can be expanded by regulations issued under s.267(4)(a).

Subss. (8)–(10)

Subsection (8) allows a wreck commissioner or Sheriff to make orders for costs and was added by the Merchant Shipping Act 1988, Sched. 5. Under subs. (9), the actual work of assessing the costs and expenses may be referred to a taxing master (or in Scotland, an auditor of the sheriff court). The practice of producing a detailed assessment of costs incurred and justifying it in a Supplementary Report on costs, as occurred in Sheen J.'s Report into the *Herald of Free Enterprise* disaster, is now established in subs. (10). Sheen J. noted that the wording of the Merchant Shipping (Formal Investigation) Rules 1985 (S.I. 1985 No. 1001) suggested that the normal rule was for the Secretary of State to bear the costs of the investigation, but that it was accepted practice that an order for costs could be made to penalise parties. The shipowners of the *Herald of Free Enterprise* were ordered to pay £350,000 costs.

Re-hearing of and appeal from investigations

269.—(1) Where a formal investigation has been held under section 268 the Secretary of State may order the whole or part of the case to be re-heard, and shall do so—

(a) if new and important evidence which could not be produced at the investigation has been discovered; or
(b) if there appear to the Secretary of State to be other grounds for suspecting that a miscarriage of justice may have occurred.

(2) An order under subsection (1) above may provide for the re-hearing to be as follows—

    (a) if the investigation was held in England, Wales or Northern Ireland, by a wreck commissioner or by the High Court;

    (b) if it was held in Scotland, by the sheriff or by the Court of Session.

(3) Any re-hearing under this section which is not held by the High Court or the Court of Session shall be conducted in accordance with rules made under section 270(1); and section 268 shall apply in relation to a re-hearing of an investigation by a wreck commissioner or sheriff as it applies in relation to the holding of an investigation.

(4) Where the wreck commissioner or sheriff holding the investigation has decided to cancel or suspend the certificate of any person or has found any person at fault, then, if no application for an order under subsection (1) above has been made or such an application has been refused, that person or any other person who, having an interest in the investigation, has appeared at the hearing and is affected by the decision or finding, may appeal—

    (a) to the High Court if the investigation was held in England, Wales or Northern Ireland;

    (b) to the Court of Session if it was held in Scotland.

(5) Section 268(7) applies for the purposes of this section as it applies for the purposes of that section.

DEFINITIONS

    "England and Wales": Interpretation Act 1978, Sched. 1.
    "High Court": Interpretation Act 1978, Sched. 1.
    "person": Interpretation Act 1978, Sched. 1.
    "Secretary of State": Interpretation Act 1978, Sched. 1.
    "sheriff": Interpretation Act 1978, Sched. 1.

GENERAL NOTE

    [Derivation: Merchant Shipping Act 1970, s.57 and s.60.]
    Section 269 provides for a rehearing of a formal investigation held under s.268.

Rules as to investigations and appeals

270.—(1) The Secretary of State may make rules for the conduct of formal investigations under section 268 and for the conduct of any re-hearing under section 269 which is not held by the High Court or the Court of Session.

(2) Without prejudice to the generality of subsection (1) above, rules under this section may provide for the appointment and summoning of assessors, the manner in which any facts may be proved, the persons allowed to appear, and the notices to be given to persons affected.

(3) Rules of court made for the purpose of re-hearings under section 269 which are held by the High Court, or of appeals to the High Court, may require the court, subject to such exceptions, if any, as may be allowed by the rules, to hold such a re-hearing or hear such an appeal with the assistance of one or more assessors.

DEFINITIONS

    "High Court": Interpretation Act 1978, Sched. 1.
    "person": Interpretation Act 1978, Sched. 1.
    "Rules of Court": Interpretation Act 1978, Sched. 1.
    "Secretary of State": Interpretation Act 1978, Sched. 1.

GENERAL NOTE

    [Derivation: Merchant Shipping Act 1970, s.58, Merchant Shipping Act 1988, Sched. 6.]
    For the powers of the Secretary of State to make delegated legislation, such as regulations, see s.306, below.

Inquiries into and reports on deaths and injuries

Inquiries into deaths of crew members and others

271.—(1) Subject to subsection (6) below, where—
  (a) any person dies in a United Kingdom ship or in a boat or life-raft from such a ship, or
  (b) the master of or a seaman employed in such a ship dies in a country outside the United Kingdom,
an inquiry into the cause of the death shall be held by a superintendent or proper officer at the next port where the ship calls after the death and where there is a superintendent or proper officer, or at such other place as the Secretary of State may direct.

(2) Subject to subsection (6) below, where it appears to the Secretary of State that—
  (a) in consequence of an injury sustained or a disease contracted by a person when he was the master of or a seaman employed in a United Kingdom ship, he ceased to be employed in the ship and subsequently died, and
  (b) the death occurred in a country outside the United Kingdom during the period of one year beginning with the day on which he so ceased,
the Secretary of State may arrange for an inquiry into the cause of the death to be held by a superintendent or proper officer.

(3) Subject to subsection (6) below, where it appears to the Secretary of State that a person may—
  (a) have died in a United Kingdom ship or in a boat or life-raft from such a ship, or
  (b) have been lost from such a ship, boat or life-raft and have died in consequence of being so lost,
the Secretary of State may arrange for an inquiry to be held by a superintendent or proper officer into whether the person died as mentioned above and, if the superintendent or officer finds that he did, into the cause of the death.

(4) The superintendent or proper officer holding the inquiry shall for the purpose of the inquiry have the powers conferred on an inspector by section 259.

(5) The person holding the inquiry shall make a report of his findings to the Secretary of State who shall make the report available—
  (a) if the person to whom the report relates was employed in the ship and a person was named as his next of kin in the crew agreement or list of the crew in which the name of the person to whom the report relates last appeared, to the person so named;
  (b) in any case, to any person requesting it who appears to the Secretary of State to be interested.

(6) No inquiry shall be held under this section where, in England, Wales or Northern Ireland, a coroner's inquest is to be held or, in Scotland, an inquiry is to be held under the Fatal Accidents and Sudden Deaths Inquiry (Scotland) Act 1976.

DEFINITIONS
  "crew agreement": s.25(2).
  "England and Wales": Interpretation Act 1978, Sched. 1.
  "master": s.313(1).
  "person": Interpretation Act 1978, Sched. 1.
  "port": s.313(1).
  "proper officer": s.313(1).
  "seaman": s.313(1).
  "Secretary of State": Interpretation Act 1978, Sched. 1.
  "ship": s.313(1).
  "superintendent": s.313(1).
  "United Kingdom": Interpretation Act 1978, Sched. 1.
  "United Kingdom ship": ss.1(3) and 313(1).

GENERAL NOTE
[Derivation: Merchant Shipping Act 1970, s.61, Merchant Shipping Act 1979, ss.28, 29.]
An inquiry must be held where any person dies on a U.K. ship, or where mariners employed on such a ship die abroad. For injuries to seafarers on fishing vessels, see s.272. See also s.273.

Reports of and inquiries into injuries

272.—(1) Where the master or a member of the crew of a United Kingdom fishing vessel is injured during a voyage, an inquiry into the cause and nature of the injury may be held by a superintendent or proper officer.

(2) The superintendent or proper officer holding an inquiry under this section shall, for the purposes of the inquiry, have the powers conferred on a Departmental inspector by section 259 and shall make a report of his findings to the Secretary of State.

DEFINITIONS
"Departmental inspector": s.256(9).
"master": s.313(1).
"proper officer": s.313(1).
"Secretary of State": Interpretation Act 1978, Sched. 1.
"superintendent": s.313(1).
"United Kingdom fishing vessel": ss.1(3) and 313(1).

GENERAL NOTE
[Derivation: Merchant Shipping Act 1970, s.95(1), Sched. 2, Pt. I, para. 5, Merchant Shipping Act 1979, s.28(7)(b).]
An inquiry may be held in situations where seafarers are injured on U.K. fishing vessels. For deaths to seafarers, see s.271, above.

Transmission of particulars of certain deaths on ships

273. Where—
(a) an inquest is held into a death or a post mortem examination, or a preliminary investigation in Northern Ireland, is made of a dead body as a result of which the coroner is satisfied that an inquest is unnecessary; and
(b) it appears to the coroner that the death in question is such as is mentioned in section 108(2) or in that subsection as extended (with or without amendments) by virtue of section 307,

it shall be the duty of the coroner to send to the Registrar General of Shipping and Seamen particulars in respect of the deceased of a kind prescribed by regulations made by the Secretary of State.

DEFINITIONS
"Secretary of State": Interpretation Act 1978, Sched. 1.

GENERAL NOTE
[Derivation: Merchant Shipping Act 1979, s.30(2).]
Where a coroner conducts an inquest into, or investigates, a death and it appears that it has occurred on a U.K. ship, he is obliged to send details as may be required by regulations to the Registrar-General. For the powers of the Secretary of State to make delegated legislation, such as regulations, see s.306, below.

PART XII

LEGAL PROCEEDINGS

GENERAL NOTE
Part XII deals with a variety of matters concerning legal proceedings, most of which relate to criminal proceedings and evidence.

Prosecution of offences

Time limit for summary offences

274.—(1) Subject to subsections (2) and (3) below, no person shall be convicted of an offence under this Act in summary proceedings unless—

(a) the proceedings were commenced within six months beginning with the date on which the offence was committed; or

(b) in a case where the accused happens during that period to be out of the United Kingdom, the proceedings were commenced within two months after he first happens to arrive within the United Kingdom and before the expiration of three years beginning with the date on which the offence was committed.

(2) Nothing in subsection (1) above shall apply in relation to any indictable offence.

(3) Subsection (1) above shall not prevent a conviction for an offence in summary proceedings begun before the expiration of three years beginning with the date on which the offence was committed and before—

(a) the expiration of the period of six months beginning with the day when evidence which the Secretary of State considers is sufficient to justify a prosecution for the offence came to his knowledge; or

(b) the expiration of two months beginning with the day when the accused was first present in the United Kingdom after the expiration of the period mentioned in paragraph (a) above if throughout that period the accused was absent from the United Kingdom.

(4) For the purpose of subsection (3) above—

(a) a certificate of the Secretary of State stating that evidence came to his knowledge on a particular day shall be conclusive evidence of that fact; and

(b) a document purporting to be a certificate of the Secretary of State and to be signed on his behalf shall be presumed to be such a certificate unless the contrary is proved.

(5) In the application of this section to Scotland—

(a) in subsection (3)(a) above, for the words from "Secretary" to "knowledge" there shall be substituted the words "Lord Advocate considers is sufficient to justify a prosecution for the offence came to his knowledge, or, where such evidence is reported to him by the Secretary of State, the expiration of the period of six months beginning with the day when it came to the knowledge of the Secretary of State";

(b) in subsection (4)(a) and (b) above, for the words "Secretary of State" there shall be substituted the words "Lord Advocate or the Secretary of State, as the case may be,".

DEFINITIONS

"Act, this": s.316(1).
"indictable offence": Interpretation Act 1978, Sched. 1.
"month": Interpretation Act 1978, Sched. 1.
"person": Interpretation Act 1978, Sched. 1.
"Secretary of State": Interpretation Act 1978, Sched. 1.
"summary offence": Interpretation Act 1978, Sched. 1.

GENERAL NOTE

[Derivation: Merchant Shipping Act 1894, s.683(1), Prevention of Pollution Act 1971, s.19, Merchant Shipping Act 1979, s.42(1), Merchant Shipping (Registration, etc.) Act 1993, Sched 4, para. 59.]

Time limit for summary orders

275. No order for the payment of money shall be made under this Act in proceedings before a magistrates' court unless—

(a) the proceedings were commenced within six months beginning with the date on which the matter of complaint arose; or

(b) in a case where both or either of the parties to the proceedings happen during that period to be out of the United Kingdom, the proceedings were commenced within six months after they both first happen to arrive, or to be at one time, within the United Kingdom.

DEFINITIONS
"Act, this": s.316(1).
"magistrates' court": Interpretation Act 1978, Sched. 1.
"month": Interpretation Act 1978, Sched. 1.
"United Kingdom": Interpretation Act 1978, Sched. 1.

GENERAL NOTE
[Derivation: Merchant Shipping Act 1894, s.683(2), Merchant Shipping (Registration, etc.) Act 1993, Sched. 4, para. 59.]
The short time limit for summary proceedings may be quite crucial in cases where a person has been out of the U.K. on a ship for a considerable period after the offence, hence the extra time allowed by subs. (1)(b).

Summary offences: Scotland

276. In Scotland all prosecutions in respect of offences under this Act in respect of which the maximum penalty which may be imposed does not exceed imprisonment for a period of three months or a fine of level 4 on the standard scale or both may be tried in a summary manner before the district court.

DEFINITIONS
"Act, this": s.316(1).
"month": Interpretation Act 1978, Sched. 1.
"standard scale": Criminal Justice Act 1978, s.37.
"summary": Interpretation Act 1978, Sched. 1.

GENERAL NOTE
[Derivation: Merchant Shipping Act 1894, s.703(b), Merchant Shipping Act 1979 , Sched. 6, Pt. VII, para. 14.]
The present section, inserted by the Merchant Shipping Act 1979, Sched. 6, Pt. VII, para. 14, sets out which offences under the Merchant Shipping Act 1995 may be tried summarily in Scotland. A number of procedural rules concerning summary proceedings in Scotland were contained in the Merchant Shipping Act 1894, ss.704–709, *e.g.* relating to warrants. As their utility had always been open to doubt they were repealed by the Merchant Shipping (Registration, etc.) Act 1993, Sched. 4, para. 75. See also the General Note to s.312(1), below.

Offences by officers of bodies corporate

277.—(1) Where a body corporate is guilty of an offence under this Act or any instrument made under it, and that offence is proved to have been committed with the consent or connivance of, or to be attributable to any neglect on the part of, a director, manager, secretary or other similar officer of the body corporate or any person who was purporting to act in such a capacity, he as well as the body corporate shall be guilty of that offence and shall be liable to be proceeded against and punished accordingly.
(2) Where the affairs of a body corporate are managed by its members, subsection (1) above shall apply in relation to the acts and defaults of a member in connection with his functions of management as if he were a director of the body corporate.

DEFINITIONS
"Act, this": s.316(1).

GENERAL NOTE
[Derivation: Merchant Shipping Act 1894, s.687A, Merchant Shipping (Registration, etc.) Act 1993, Sched. 4, para. 63.]
Merchant shipping legislation normally makes express provision for offences which may be committed by companies, *e.g.* where the shipowner is liable for having a dangerously unsafe ship

under s.98 (formerly the Merchant Shipping Act 1988, s.30). There is not much of a deterrent if the only criminal liability, *e.g.* under s.98, is of an individual such as the master and upon the company as a corporate entity. It is recognised that there is not much point in fining a company if the senior management cannot also be convicted for their consent to, or connivance in, the company's breaches. Accordingly, merchant shipping legislation has contained provisions creating offences by the officers of bodies corporate (see, *e.g.* s.46 of the Merchant Shipping Act 1979, and s.51 of the Merchant Shipping Act 1988). For the question of whether the *company* can be guilty for the acts or omissions of its more junior staff, see the discussion in the General Note to s.131, above).

Section 277 (derived from the Merchant Shipping (Registration, etc.) Act 1993, Sched. 4, para. 63) unifies the provisions for the Merchant Shipping Act 1995. Section 278, below, similarly unifies the provisions for Scotland in respect of partnerships. The section enables prosecutions to be brought against individual managers where they consented to or connived at the offence, *or* where it is attributable to their neglect. Thus, a manager who knows that the master habitually overloads a ferry, or who fails to check the loading records, could be guilty of an offence under s.100. It is not every member of the shoreside team that can be *personally* guilty (as opposed to creating a criminal liability for the company itself). The person concerned must be fairly high up the corporate ladder, such as a director or company secretary. The difficulty is in defining the word "manager", because that could include some quite junior employees. The legislative purpose is obviously to ensure that senior managers are called to account. Like the reference to "other similar officer purporting to act in any such capacity", to which the *ejuisdem generis* rule would apply, the word "manager" must be read in the context of directors and [company] secretaries. Nevertheless, the word is unqualified and could include junior managers. Hardship could be avoided in offences such as those in ss.98 and 100, by the DPP withholding consent to the prosecution. Members of a company may also be prosecuted under the Act where they are involved in its management.

The Merchant Shipping Act 1988, Sched. 5 contained an important extension to the law by applying the rule to *regulations* made under the Merchant Shipping Act 1979. Subsection (1) repeats this provision for delegated legislation made under the 1995 Act.

Note that the wording of this section presupposes that for the officers to be guilty, the body corporate must itself have been guilty of an offence. The officers could not be convicted if, for some reason, no charge was successfully brought and proved against the body corporate. This matter may be of relevance where prosecutions are not properly co-ordinated, or where there are joinder problems.

Offences by partners, etc. in Scotland

278. Where, in Scotland, a partnership or unincorporated association (other than a partnership) is guilty of an offence under this Act or any instrument made under it, and that offence is proved to have been committed with the consent or connivance of, or to be attributable to any neglect on the part of, a partner in the partnership or, as the case may be, a person concerned in the management or control of the association, he as well as the partnership or association shall be guilty of that offence and shall be liable to be proceeded against and punished accordingly.

DEFINITIONS
   "Act, this": s.316(1).

GENERAL NOTE
   [Derivation: Merchant Shipping Act 1894, s.687B, Merchant Shipping (Registration, etc.) Act 1993, Sched. 4, para. 63.]
   This section unifies for Scotland the provisions creating offences under the Merchant Shipping Act 1995, and delegated legislation made under it, by the officers of partnerships or unincorporated associations. See the General Note to s.277, above for the background.

Jurisdiction

Jurisdiction in relation to offences

279.—(1) For the purpose of conferring jurisdiction, any offence under this Act shall be deemed to have been committed in any place in the United Kingdom where the offender may for the time being be.

(2) For the same purpose, any matter of complaint under this Act shall be deemed to have arisen in any place in the United Kingdom where the person complained against may for the time being be.

(3) The jurisdiction under subsections (1) and (2) above shall be in addition to and not in derogation of any jurisdiction or power of a court under any other enactment.

DEFINITIONS
"Act, this": s.316(1).
"person": Interpretation Act 1978, Sched. 1.
"United Kingdom": Interpretation Act 1978, Sched. 1.

GENERAL NOTE
[Derivation: Merchant Shipping Act 1894, s.684, Prevention of Oil Pollution Act 1971, s.19(5), Merchant Shipping (Registration, etc.) Act 1993, Sched. 4, para. 60.]
This section gives personal criminal jurisdiction in the place where the offender happens to be. See also ss.280–281 for offences on board ship.

Jurisdiction over ships lying off coasts

280.—(1) Where the area within which a court in any part of the United Kingdom has jurisdiction is situated on the coast of any sea or abuts on or projects into any bay, channel, lake, river or other navigable water the court shall have jurisdiction as respects offences under this Act over any vessel being on, or lying or passing off, that coast or being in or near that bay, channel, lake, river or navigable water and over all persons on board that vessel or for the time being belonging to it.

(2) The jurisdiction under subsection (1) above shall be in addition to and not in derogation of any jurisdiction or power of a court under the Magistrates' Courts Act 1980 or the Magistrates' Courts (Northern Ireland) Order 1981.

DEFINITIONS
"Act, this": s.316(1).
"magistrates' court": Interpretation Act 1978, Sched. 1.
"United Kingdom": Interpretation Act 1978, Sched. 1.

GENERAL NOTE
[Derivation: Merchant Shipping Act 1894, s.685.]
Note that on the U.K.'s accession, perhaps in 1996, to the UN Convention on the Law of the Sea 1982, the criminal jurisdiction of the U.K. as a coastal state over foreign ships in U.K. waters, or on the high seas, will be governed by that Convention (see, *e.g.* Arts. 27, 97). See also Art. 94 on the duties of the U.K. as a flag state. See the General Note to s.129, above.

Jurisdiction in case of offences on board ship

281. Where any person is charged with having committed any offence under this Act then—
  (a) if he is a British citizen and is charged with having committed it—
                (i) on board any United Kingdom ship on the high seas,
               (ii) in any foreign port or harbour, or
              (iii) on board any foreign ship to which he does not belong; or
  (b) if he is not a British citizen and is charged with having committed it on board any United Kingdom ship on the high seas;
and he is found within the jurisdiction of any court in any part of the United Kingdom which would have had jurisdiction in relation to the offence if it had been committed on board a United Kingdom ship within the limits of its ordinary jurisdiction to try the offence that court shall have jurisdiction to try the offence as if it had been so committed.

DEFINITIONS
"Act, this": s.316(1).
"British citizen": s.313(1).

"foreign": s.313(1).
"harbour" s.313(1).
"person": Interpretation Act 1978, Sched. 1.
"port": s.313(1).
"ship": s.313(1).
"United Kingdom": Interpretation Act 1978, Sched. 1.
"United Kingdom ship": ss.1(3) and 313(1).

GENERAL NOTE

[Derivation: Merchant Shipping Act 1894, s.686, Merchant Shipping (Registration, etc.) Act 1993, Sched. 4, para. 61, Sched. 5.]

Section 281 deals with criminal jurisdiction in respect of offences on board ship and replaces s.686 of the Merchant Shipping Act 1894. Section 686 of the 1894 Act allowed "British subjects" to be prosecuted for offences on ships almost anywhere in the world, *e.g.* on British ships on the high seas, in foreign ports, or on foreign ships to which they did not "belong" (*cf. R. v. Keyn; Franconia, The* (1876) 46 L.J.M.C. 17). Foreigners could also be prosecuted for offences on board British ships on the high seas. The Merchant Shipping (Registration, etc.) Act 1993, Sched. 4, para. 61 reduced what had been described as an extraordinary jurisdiction in two ways. First, it restricted the criminal jurisdiction in subs. (a) to "British citizens" as defined in the British Nationality Act 1981, Pt. I. This means that the personal jurisdiction is founded on having a link with the U.K. closer than that envisaged in the days of empire when British subject included a variety of persons with allegiance to the Crown, *e.g.* commonwealth citizens (see *Temperley*, p.4, note 1 and the General Note to s.3(1) of the Merchant Shipping Act 1988, in *Current Law Statutes Annotated 1988*). Secondly, the criminal jurisdiction was restricted to offences on "U.K. ships" (*i.e.* U.K. registered ships, see s.1(3), above) and not, as previously, to "British ships" which was a wider expression (see s.1(1), above, and *Temperley*, p.4, note 1).

In summary then, under para. (a), a British citizen will be subject to the criminal jurisdiction of the U.K. courts for offences committed under the 1995 Act in a wide variety of locations, including, *e.g.* on a foreign cruise liner while on a holiday in the Caribbean (*cf.* s.101(6)). Under para. (b), a foreigner can be subject to the criminal jurisdiction of the U.K. courts if the allegation relates to offences on U.K. ships on the high seas. In both cases, the defendant must be found within the jurisdiction of a U.K. court having jurisdiction over offences committed on a U.K. ship within the limits of that court's ordinary jurisdiction. It will always be necessary, therefore, to consider the ordinary jurisdiction of the appropriate court. Note also that Sched. 13, paras. 55, 59(4) and 63 of the Merchant Shipping Act 1995 make amendments to the Magistrates' Courts Act 1980, s.3, the Supreme Court Act 1981, s.46 and the Magistrates' Courts (Northern Ireland) Order 1981 (respectively), by applying ss.280–282 of the Merchant Shipping Act 1995 to other offences under the law of England and Wales and Northern Ireland as they apply in relation to the 1995 Act or instruments made under it.

There is some ambiguity concerning jurisdiction under s.281 over offences committed on unregistered ships. An unregistered ship is not a "United Kingdom ship" within s.1(3) (see s.313). Presumably, the section must be read subject to the power granted by s.307 to extend the operation of the Act to "non-United Kingdom ships", including unregistered ships.

Note the exception in s.103.

Note also that on the U.K.'s accession (perhaps in 1996) to the UN Convention on the Law of the Sea 1982, the criminal jurisdiction of the U.K. as a coastal state over foreign ships in U.K. waters, or on the high seas, will be governed by that Convention (see, *e.g.* Arts. 27, 97). See also Art. 94 on the duties of the U.K. as a flag state. See also the General Note to s.129, above.

Offences committed by British seamen

282.—(1) Any act in relation to property or person done in or at any place (ashore or afloat) outside the United Kingdom by any master or seaman who at the time is employed in a United Kingdom ship, which, if done in any part of the United Kingdom, would be an offence under the law of any part of the United Kingdom, shall—

(a) be an offence under that law, and

(b) be treated for the purposes of jurisdiction and trial, as if it had been done within the jurisdiction of the Admiralty of England.

(2) Subsection (1) above also applies in relation to a person who had been so employed within the period of three months expiring with the time when the act was done.

(3) Subsections (1) and (2) above apply to omissions as they apply to acts.

DEFINITIONS
"master": s.313(1).
"month": Interpretation Act 1978, Sched. 1.
"person": Interpretation Act 1978, Sched. 1.
"seaman": s.313(1).
"United Kingdom": Interpretation Act 1978, Sched. 1.
"United Kingdom ship": ss.1(3) and 313(1).

GENERAL NOTE
[Derivation: Merchant Shipping Act 1894, s.687, Merchant Shipping (Registration, etc.) Act 1993, Sched. 4, para. 62.]

It seems that nineteenth century legislation did not draw the same distinctions which modern legislation does between conferring (i) local criminal jurisdiction over offences committed outside the U.K. and (ii) making acts done outside the U.K. offences against U.K. law. The assumption seems to have been that doing the former implied the latter. Thus, s.687 of the Merchant Shipping Act 1894 made seamen employed on British ships liable for offences committed afloat or ashore outside the U.K. Apparently, the section was treated in practice as an offence-making provision. The Merchant Shipping (Registration, etc.) Act 1993, Sched. 4, para. 62 restated the section as it is now, in the modern form used in, *e.g.* the Civil Aviation Act 1982, s.92 and the Oil and Gas Enterprise Act 1982, s.22. Note also that Art. 94 of the LOS Convention 1982, to which the U.K. may accede in 1996, gives the U.K., as a flag state, duties to exercise control over ships flying its flag.

Return of offenders

Return of offenders

283.—(1) The powers conferred on a British consular officer by subsection (2) below are exercisable in the event of any complaint being made to him—
  (a) that any offence against property or persons has been committed at any place (ashore or afloat) outside the United Kingdom by any master or seaman who at the time when the offence was committed, or within three months before that time, was employed in a United Kingdom ship; or
  (b) that any offence on the high seas has been committed by any master or seaman belonging to any United Kingdom ship.
(2) Those powers are—
  (a) to inquire into the case upon oath, and
  (b) if the case so requires, to take any steps in his power for the purpose of placing the offender under the necessary restraint and sending him by United Kingdom ship as soon as practicable in safe custody to the United Kingdom for proceedings to be taken against him.
(3) The consular officer may, subject to subsections (4) and (5) below, order the master of any United Kingdom ship bound for the United Kingdom to receive and carry the offender and the witnesses to the United Kingdom; and the officer shall endorse upon the agreement of the ship such particulars with respect to them as the Secretary of State requires.
(4) A consular officer shall not exercise the power conferred by subsection (3) above unless no more convenient means of transport is available or it is available only at disproportionate expense.
(5) No master of a ship may be required under subsection (3) above to receive more than one offender for every 100 tons of his ship's registered tonnage, or more than one witness for every 50 tons of his ship's registered tonnage.
(6) The master of any ship to whose charge an offender has been committed under subsection (3) above shall, on his ship's arrival in the United Kingdom, give the offender into the custody of some police officer or constable.
(7) If any master of a ship, when required under subsection (3) above to receive and carry any offender or witness in his ship—

(a) fails to do so; or

(b) in the case of an offender, fails to deliver him as required by subsection (6) above;

he shall be liable on summary conviction to a fine not exceeding level 5 on the standard scale.

(8) The expense of imprisoning any such offender and of carrying him and witnesses to the United Kingdom otherwise than in the ship to which they respectively belong shall be paid out of money provided by Parliament.

(9) References in this section to carrying a person in a ship include affording him subsistence during the voyage.

DEFINITIONS

"carrying a person": subs. (9).
"fails": s.313(1).
"master": s.313(1).
"month": Interpretation Act 1978, Sched. 1.
"oath": Interpretation Act 1978, Sched. 1.
"person": Interpretation Act 1978, Sched. 1.
"registered": ss.23(1) and 313(1).
"seaman": s.313(1).
"Secretary of State": Interpretation Act 1978, Sched. 1.
"ship": s.313(1).
"standard scale": Criminal Justice Act 1978, s.37.
"United Kingdom": Interpretation Act 1978, Sched. 1.
"United Kingdom ship": ss.1(3) and 313(1).

GENERAL NOTE

[Derivation: Merchant Shipping Act 1894, s.689, Merchant Shipping Act 1970, Sched. 3, para. 2, Merchant Shipping Act 1979, Sched. 6, Pt. IV, Merchant Shipping (Registration, etc.) Act 1993, Sched. 4, para. 64, Sched. 5.]

Section 689 of the Merchant Shipping Act 1894 gave power, which was occasionally used, to British consular officers to order a master to allow an offender to be transported back to the U.K. for trial. Section 283(4) (inserted by the Merchant Shipping (Registration, etc.) Act 1993, Sched. 4, para. 64) qualifies the requirement so that a discretion is given where there are more convenient or less expensive means of transport (*e.g.* air).

Detention of ship and distress on ship

Enforcing detention of ship

284.—(1) Where under this Act a ship is to be or may be detained any of the following officers may detain the ship—

(a) any commissioned naval or military officer,

(b) any Departmental officer,

(c) any officer of customs and excise, and

(d) any British consular officer.

(2) If a ship which has been detained or as respects which notice of detention or an order for detention has been served on the master proceeds to sea before it is released by competent authority the master of the ship shall be liable—

(a) on summary conviction, to a fine not exceeding £50,000;

(b) on conviction on indictment, to a fine.

(3) The owner of a ship, and any person who sends to sea a ship, as respects which an offence is committed under subsection (2) above shall, if party or privy to the offence, also be guilty of an offence under that subsection and liable accordingly.

(4) Where a ship proceeding to sea in contravention of subsection (2) above takes to sea any of the following who is on board the ship in the execution of his duty, namely—

(a) any officer authorised by subsection (1) above to detain the ship, or

(b) any surveyor of ships,

the owner and master of the ship shall each—

   (i) be liable to pay all expenses of and incidental to the officer or surveyor being so taken to sea; and

   (ii) be guilty of an offence.

(5) A person guilty of an offence under subsection (4) above shall be liable—

   (a) on summary conviction, to a fine not exceeding the statutory maximum;

   (b) on conviction on indictment, to a fine.

(6) Where under this Act a ship is to be detained an officer of customs and excise shall, and where under this Act a ship may be detained an officer of customs and excise may, refuse to clear the ship outwards or grant a transire to the ship.

(7) When any provision of this Act provides that a ship may be detained until any document is produced to the proper officer of customs and excise the officer able to grant a clearance or transire of the ship is (unless the context otherwise requires) that officer.

(8) Any reference in this section to proceeding to sea includes a reference to going on a voyage or excursion that does not involve going to sea, and references to sending or taking to sea shall be construed accordingly.

DEFINITIONS
   "Act, this": s.316(1).
   "commissioned military officer": s.313(1).
   "commissioned naval officer": s.313(1).
   "contravention": s.313(1).
   "Departmental officer": ss.256(9)(c) and 313(1).
   "master": s.313(1).
   "person": Interpretation Act 1978, Sched. 1.
   "proceeding to sea": subs. (8).
   "proper officer": s.313(1).
   "sends to sea": subs. (9).
   "ship": s.313(1).
   "statutory maximum": Criminal Justice Act 1982, s.74.
   "surveyor of ships": ss.256(9)(b) and 313(1).
   "takes to sea": subs. (9).

GENERAL NOTE
   [Derivation: Merchant Shipping Act 1894, s.692; Merchant Shipping Act 1979, Sched. 6, Pt. VII, paras. 10 and 11, Merchant Shipping Act 1988, Sched. 6.]
   This section sets out who may detain a ship under powers granted by the Act (see, *e.g.* s.144). An offence is created if a detention notice is disobeyed.

Sums ordered to be paid leviable by distress on the ship

   285.—(1) Where any court has power to make an order directing payment to be made of any seaman's wages, fines or other sums of money, then, if the person directed to pay is the master or owner of the ship and the money directed to be paid is not paid in accordance with the order, the court who made the order may—

   (a) except in Scotland, direct the amount remaining unpaid to be levied by distress,

   (b) in Scotland, grant warrant authorising the arrestment and sale,

of the ship and its equipment.

(2) The remedy made available by this section is in addition to any other powers for compelling the payment of money ordered to be paid.

DEFINITIONS
   "master": s.313(1).
   "person": Interpretation Act 1978, Sched. 1.
   "seaman": s.313(1).

"ship": s.313(1).
"wages": s.313(1).

GENERAL NOTE
[Derivation: Merchant Shipping Act 1894, s.693; Merchant Shipping (Registration, etc.) Act 1993, Sched. 4, para. 65.]
Section 285 allows for fines and unpaid wages to be levied against the ship by distress (in addition to any other rights which might exist, *e.g.* an action *in rem* to enforce a maritime lien for unpaid wages). It re-enacts earlier provisions such as s.693 of the Merchant Shipping Act 1894. That section, and s.20 of the Prevention of Oil Pollution Act 1971, allowed for certain sums to be levied against a ship by distress but, as this system was not known in Scottish law, separate provision was made by the Merchant Shipping (Registration, etc.) Act 1993, Sched. 4, paras. 65 and 66. Section 285 now provides that in Scotland there must be a grant warrant authorising the arrestment and sale.

Special evidential provisions

GENERAL NOTE
Sections 286–290 set out particular evidential requirements for the Act, *e.g.* as to the taking of depositions and admissibility of documents. Note the application of s.290 to defences under the Act.

Depositions of persons abroad admissible

286.—(1) If the evidence of any person is required in the course of any legal proceeding before a judge or magistrate in relation to the subject matter of the proceeding and it is proved that that person cannot be found in the United Kingdom, any deposition that he may have previously made at a place outside the United Kingdom in relation to the same subject matter shall, subject to subsection (2) below, be admissible in evidence in those proceedings.

(2) For a deposition to be admissible under subsection (1) above in any proceedings, the deposition—

(a) must have been taken on oath;

(b) must have been taken before a justice or magistrate in any colony or a British consular officer in any other place;

(c) must be authenticated by the signature of the justice, magistrate or officer taking it; and

(d) must, if the proceedings are criminal proceedings, have been taken in the presence of the accused;

and, in a case falling within paragraph (d) above, the deposition shall be certified by the justice, magistrate or officer taking it to have been taken in the presence of the accused.

(3) No proof need be given of the signature or official character of the person appearing to have signed any such deposition and, in any criminal proceedings, a certificate stating that the deposition was taken in the presence of the accused shall, unless the contrary is proved, be evidence (and in Scotland sufficient evidence) of that fact.

(4) This section also applies to proceedings before any person authorised by law or consent of the parties to receive evidence.

(5) Nothing in this section affects the admissibility in evidence of depositions under any other enactment or the practice of any court.

DEFINITIONS
"colony": Interpretation Act 1978, Sched. 1.
"oath": Interpretation Act 1978, Sched. 1.

"person": Interpretation Act 1978, Sched. 1.
"United Kingdom": Interpretation Act 1978, Sched. 1.

GENERAL NOTE
[Derivation: Merchant Shipping Act 1894, s.691.]

Admissibility in evidence and inspection of certain documents

287.—(1) The following documents shall be admissible in evidence and, when in the custody of the Registrar General of Shipping and Seamen, shall be open to public inspection—
   (a) documents purporting to be submissions to or decisions by superintendents or proper officers under section 33;
   (b) the official log book of any ship kept under section 77 and, without prejudice to section 288(2), any document purporting to be a copy of an entry therein and to be certified as a true copy by the master of the ship;
   (c) crew agreements, lists of crews made under section 78 and notices given under Part III of additions to or changes in crew agreements and lists of crews;
   (d) returns or reports under section 108;
   (e) documents transmitted to the Registrar General of Shipping and Seamen under section 298.

(2) A certificate issued under section 47 shall be admissible in evidence.

DEFINITIONS
"crew agreement": ss.25(2) and 84(1).
"master": s.313(1).
"proper officer": s.313(1).
"ship": s.313(1).
"superintendent": s.313(1).

GENERAL NOTE
[Derivation: Merchant Shipping Act 1894, s.256(1); Merchant Shipping Act 1970, s.75; Merchant Shipping Act 1988, Sched. 7.]

Admissibility of documents in evidence

288.—(1) Where a document is by this Act declared to be admissible in evidence the document shall, on its production from proper custody—
   (a) be admissible in evidence in any court or before any person having by law or consent of parties authority to receive evidence; and
   (b) subject to all just exceptions, be evidence (or in Scotland sufficient evidence) of the matters stated in the document.

(2) A copy of, or extract from, any document so made admissible in evidence shall, subject to subsection (3) below, also be admissible in evidence and evidence (and in Scotland sufficient evidence) of the matters stated in the document.

(3) A copy of, or extract from, a document shall not be admissible by virtue of subsection (2) above unless—
   (a) it is proved to be an examined copy or extract; or
   (b) it purports to be signed and certified as a true copy or extract by the officer to whose custody the original document was entrusted;
and that officer shall furnish the certified copy or extract to any person who applies for it at a reasonable time and pays such reasonable price as the Secretary of State determines.

(4) A person shall, on payment of such reasonable price as the Secretary of State determines, be entitled to have a certified copy of any declaration or document a copy of which is made evidence by this Act.

(5) If any officer having duties of certification under subsection (3) above in relation to any document intentionally certifies any document as being a

true copy or extract knowing that the copy or extract is not a true copy or extract he shall be liable—

(a) on summary conviction, to imprisonment for a term not exceeding six months or a fine not exceeding the statutory maximum;

(b) on conviction on indictment, to imprisonment for a term not exceeding two years or a fine or both.

(6) Subject to subsection (7) below, in Scotland, if any person forges the seal, stamp or signature of any document (or copy document) declared by this Act to be admissible in evidence or tenders in evidence any such document (or copy document) with, and knowing it to have, a false or counterfeit seal, stamp or signature he shall be liable—

(a) on summary conviction, to a fine not exceeding the statutory maximum or to imprisonment for a term not exceeding six months or to both; or

(b) on conviction on indictment, to a fine or to imprisonment for a term not exceeding seven years or to both.

(7) Subsection (6) above does not apply in respect of actings which constitute an offence under section 300(8).

(8) Without prejudice to section 6(1) of the Civil Evidence (Scotland) Act 1988 (production of copy documents) subsections (2) and (3) above shall not apply, for the purposes of civil proceedings in Scotland, as respects the admissibility of a copy document; but subsection (5) above shall apply to a person purporting to authenticate any such document and to authentication as it applies to an officer purporting to certify any such document and to certification.

DEFINITIONS

"Act, this": s.316(1).
"person": Interpretation Act 1978, Sched. 1.
"Secretary of State": Interpretation Act 1978, Sched. 1.
"statutory maximum": Criminal Justice Act 1982, s.74.

GENERAL NOTE

[Derivation: Merchant Shipping Act 1894, s.695; Merchant Shipping Act 1970, Sched. 3, para. 3; Merchant Shipping (Safety Convention) Act 1949, s.33(2); Merchant Shipping Act 1988, Sched. 7; Merchant Shipping (Registration, etc.) Act 1993, Sched. 4, paras. 67, 72; Merchant Shipping Act 1894, s.680(1).]

Section 288 re-enacts s.695 of the Merchant Shipping Act 1894. The Merchant Shipping (Registration, etc.) Act 1993, Sched. 4, para. 67 made three small changes to the evidentiary requirements now set out in s.288: first, by allowing the Secretary of State to determine a reasonable price under subs. (3); second, by increasing the maximum sentence in subs. (5) from 18 months to two years; and third, by inserting what is now subs. (8).

Inspection and admissibility in evidence of copies of certain documents

289.—(1) Where under any enactment a document is open to public inspection when in the custody of the Registrar General of Shipping and Seamen—

(a) there may be supplied for public inspection a copy or other reproduction of the document instead of the original; but

(b) the original shall nevertheless be made available for public inspection if the copy or other reproduction is illegible.

(2) Where the Registrar General of Shipping and Seamen destroys any document which has been sent to him under or by virtue of any enactment, and keeps a copy or other reproduction of that document, then—

(a) any enactment providing for that document to be admissible in evidence or open to public inspection, and

(b) in the case of a document falling within subsection (1) above, that subsection,

shall apply to the copy or other reproduction as if it were the original.

(3) For the purposes of this section, and of section 288(2) in its application to documents in the custody of the Registrar General of Shipping and Seamen, a copy is to be taken to be the copy of a document notwithstanding that it is taken from a copy or other reproduction of the original.

DEFINITIONS
"copy": subs. (3).

GENERAL NOTE
[Derivation: Merchant Shipping Act, 1970, s.75A; Merchant Shipping Act 1988, Sched. 5, para. 6.]
This section allows for the use of photocopies and other modern methods of reproduction, such as microfiches, of various documents held by the Registrar General of Shipping and Seamen.

Proof, etc. of exemptions

290.—(1) Where any exception, exemption, excuse or qualification applies in relation to an offence under this Act—
(a) it may be proved by the defendant, but
(b) need not be specified or negatived in any information or complaint;
and, if so specified or negatived, shall not require to be proved by the informant or complainant.
(2) This section applies in relation to an offence whether or not the exception, exemption, excuse or qualification is contained in the section creating the offence.
(3) This section does not apply to Scotland.

DEFINITIONS
"Act, this": s.316(1).

GENERAL NOTE
[Derivation: Merchant Shipping Act 1894, s.697; Merchant Shipping (Registration, etc.) Act 1993, Sched. 4, para. 69.]
This section replaces the Merchant Shipping Act 1894, s.697. Separate provision is already made for Scotland in ss.66 and 312(v) of the Criminal Procedure (Scotland) Act 1975 and so the Merchant Shipping (Registration, etc.) Act 1993, Sched. 4, para. 69 inserted what is now subs. (3), disapplying s.290 of the Merchant Shipping Act 1995 to Scotland.

Service of documents

Service of documents

291.—(1) Any document authorised or required to be served on any person may be served on that person—
(a) by delivering it to him;
(b) by leaving it at his proper address; or
(c) by sending it by post to him at his proper address.
(2) Any such document required to be served on the master of a ship may be served—
(a) where there is a master, by leaving it for him on board the ship with the person appearing to be in command or charge of the ship;
(b) where there is no master, on—

  (i) the managing owner of the ship; or

  (ii) if there is no managing owner, on any agent of the owner; or

  (iii) where no such agent is known or can be found, by leaving a copy of the document fixed to the mast of the ship.

(3) Any document authorised or required to be served on any person may—

 (a) in the case of a body corporate, be served on the secretary or clerk of that body;

 (b) in the case of a partnership, be served on a partner or a person having the control or management of the partnership business or, in Scotland, on the firm.

(4) Any notice authorised or required by or under Part II to be served on the Secretary of State may be served by post.

(5) Any notice authorised by section 261, 262, 263 or 264 to be given to an inspector may be given by delivering it to him or by leaving it at, or sending it by post to, his office.

(6) Any document authorised or required by or under any enactment to be served on the registered owner of a United Kingdom ship shall be treated as duly served on him if served on such persons, in such circumstances and by such method, as may be specified in registration regulations.

(7) For the purposes of this section and of section 7 of the Interpretation Act 1978 (service of documents by post) in its application to this section, the proper address of any person on whom any document is to be served shall be his last known address, except that—

 (a) in the case of a body corporate or their secretary or clerk it shall be the address of the registered or principal office of that body;

 (b) in the case of a partnership or a person having the control or management of the partnership business, it shall be the principal office of the partnership;

and for the purposes of this subsection the principal office of a company registered outside the United Kingdom or of a partnership carrying on business outside the United Kingdom shall be their principal office in the United Kingdom.

(8) If the person to be served with any notice has (whether in pursuance of registration regulations or otherwise) specified an address in the United Kingdom other than his proper address within the meaning of subsection (7) above as the one at which he or someone on his behalf will accept notices of the same description as that notice, that address shall also be treated for the purposes of this section and section 7 of the Interpretation Act 1978 as his proper address.

(9) For the purposes of the said section 7 a letter containing—

 (a) a notice to be served on any person in pursuance of subsection (6) above, or

 (b) a notice authorised or required to be served under registration regulations on a representative person (within the meaning of those regulations),

shall be deemed to be properly addressed if it is addressed to that person at the address for the time being recorded in relation to him in the register; and a letter containing any other notice under registration regulations shall be deemed to be properly addressed if it is addressed to the last known address of the person to be served (whether of his residence or of a place where he carries on business).

Definitions

 "master": s.313(1).

 "person": Interpretation Act 1978, Sched. 1.

 "proper address": subss. (7) and (8).

 "properly addressed": subs. (9).

"register": ss.23(1) and 313(1).
"registered": ss.23(1) and 313(1).
"registration regulations": s.313(1).
"Secretary of State": Interpretation Act 1978, Sched. 1.
"ship": s.313(1).
"United Kingdom": Interpretation Act 1978, Sched. 1.
"United Kingdom ship": ss.1(3) and 313(1).

GENERAL NOTE
[Derivation: Merchant Shipping Act 1894, s.696; Merchant Shipping (Registration, etc.) Act 1993, Sched. 4, para. 68.]
A number of provisions in the Merchant Shipping Act 1894 dealt with the service of documents. The Merchant Shipping (Registration, etc.) Act 1993, Sched. 4, para. 68 replaced s.696 with the modern uniform provision, now s.291 of the Merchant Shipping Act 1995.

PART XIII

SUPPLEMENTAL

GENERAL NOTE
Part XIII deals with a number of general matters applying across the Merchant Shipping Act 1995, such as the administration of the Act, expenses caused by its operation, the making of delegated legislation and its application and interpretation. Sections 307–311 are particularly important.

Administration

GENERAL NOTE
Sections 290–297 and 301 deal with the personnel who are to administer merchant shipping. Sections 298–300 deal with forms and other documents.

General functions of Secretary of State

292.—(1) The Secretary of State shall continue to have the general superintendence of all matters relating to merchant shipping and seamen and is authorised to carry into execution the provisions of this Act and of all Acts relating to merchant shipping and seaman for the time being in force, except where otherwise provided or so far as relating to revenue.

(2) The Secretary of State may take any legal proceedings under this Act in the name of any of his officers.

DEFINITIONS
"Act, this": s.316(1).
"seaman": s.313(1).
"Secretary of State": Interpretation Act 1978, Sched. 1.

GENERAL NOTE
[Derivation: Merchant Shipping Act 1894, ss.713 and 717.]

Functions of Secretary of State in relation to marine pollution

293.—(1) The Secretary of State shall continue to have the functions of taking, or co-ordinating, measures to prevent, reduce and minimise the effects of, marine pollution.

(2) Without prejudice to the generality of subsection (1) above, the functions of the Secretary of State under that subsection include—
  (a) the acquisition, maintenance, use and disposal of ships, aircraft, equipment and other property;
  (b) the provision of services, including research, training and advice;
  (c) the giving of assistance to any other State or international institution under any international agreement relating to the prevention, reduction or control of marine pollution; and

(d) any other functions exercisable on his behalf on 1st October 1994 by the Marine Pollution Control Unit.

(3) Assistance under subsection (2)(c) above shall be given on such terms as will secure reimbursement of the cost of giving the assistance if and to the extent that reimbursement will be practicable in the circumstances.

(4) The Secretary of State may make reasonable charges for the supply of goods or services.

(5) In this section—

"marine pollution" means pollution caused by ships, offshore installations or submarine pipelines affecting or likely to affect the United Kingdom or United Kingdom waters or controlled waters;

"offshore installation" means any installation which is maintained for underwater exploitation or exploration to which the Mineral Working (Offshore Installations) Act 1971 applies;

"pipeline" has the same meaning as in Part III of the Petroleum and Submarine Pipelines Act 1975 and "submarine" means in, under or over United Kingdom waters or controlled waters;

"United Kingdom controlled waters" means any part of the sea within the limits of an area designated under section 1(7) of the Continental Shelf Act 1964;

but no restriction as to the seas to which functions under this section extend is implied as regards the functions mentioned in subsection (2)(c) above.

DEFINITIONS

"marine pollution": subs. (5).
"offshore installation": subs. (5).
"pipeline": subs. (5) and Petroleum and Submarine Pipelines Act 1975, Pt. III.
"Secretary of State": Interpretation Act 1978, Sched. 1.
"ship": s.313(1).
"submarine": subs. (5).
"United Kingdom": Interpretation Act 1978, Sched. 1.
"United Kingdom controlled waters": subs. (5) and Continental Shelf Act 1964, s.1(7).
"United Kingdom waters": s.313(2)(a).

GENERAL NOTE

[Derivation: Merchant Shipping (Salvage and Pollution) Act 1994, s.8.]

The Secretary of State for Transport in practice has the ministerial responsibility for dealing with marine pollution, but this was never spelt out clearly in the primary legislation (see, *e.g.* Pt. XIV of the Merchant Shipping Act 1894). The functions have been exercised as a result of powers given, or inferred from, various Merchant Shipping Acts. Accordingly, the present s.292 was originally enacted by the Merchant Shipping (Salvage and Pollution) Act 1994, s.8. Subsection (1) is emphatic that the Secretary of State shall "continue" to have the functions generally described. Subsection (2) sets out some of the particular functions which may be exercised. These functions include the purchase of anti-pollution equipment, such as oil booms, and the operation of aircraft to spray dispersants, as well as the running of courses (see subss. (2)(a) and (b)).

Subsection (2)(c) enables the Secretary of State to provide the assistance which may be requested by other states under the provisions of the OPRC Convention (to which effect may be given by s.128(d)), or regional Conventions, such as the Bonn Agreement for Co-operation in dealing with Pollution of the North Sea by Oil Pollution and other Harmful Substances 1983. The latter entered into force in 1989 and is administered by the same Secretariat which administers the Convention for the Prevention of Marine Pollution by Dumping from Ships and Aircraft 1972 (the Oslo Convention) and the Convention for the Prevention of Marine Pollution from Land-Based Sources 1974 (the Paris Convention) (see generally, P. Ehlers, "The History of the International North Sea Conferences" (1990) 5 IJECL 3, 4). Note that there is no restriction as to the seas in which the subs. (2)(c) functions may be exercised and assistance may be provided both in U.K. territorial waters and elsewhere (see subs. (5)). However, the assistance given under subs. (2)(c) will not be free of charge, for subs. (3) requires the Secretary of State to seek reimbursement of costs, where practicable. Such reimbursement will no doubt be possible in the case of assistance to most European states, although assistance to less developed states might better be regarded as aid as they will often not be in a position to pay for any help. Even in such cases, the coastal State which is a victim of marine pollution might have a claim against a shipowner (*e.g.* under the International Convention on Civil Liability for Oil Pollution Damage

1992, see the General Note to Pt. VI, Ch. III, above) and this could cover preventive costs which it was obliged to pay to a third party such as the U.K. Subsection (4) allows reasonable charges to be made for any of the functions.

The Marine Pollution Control Unit (MPCU) was set up in 1978 within the DOT to provide expert advice to the Secretary of State and to co-ordinate responses to disasters. The MPCU is now part of the Coastguard Agency. Under s.12 of the Prevention of Oil Pollution Act 1971 (now s.137 of the 1995 Act) the Secretary of State was given wide powers to intervene in a pollution casualty, even in cases where the casualty occurred on the high seas (as allowed by the International Convention relating to Intervention on the High Seas in Cases of Oil Pollution Casualties 1969). In particular, s.12(5) of the Prevention of Oil Pollution Act 1971 gave the Secretary of State power to delegate the intervention functions and, in practice, these were delegated to the MPCU (although the Unit was not mentioned specifically in that Act). When the 1994 Bill was introduced, the MPCU was a part of the Department of Transport Marine Directorate, but in April 1994 became an executive agency of the DOT. Subsection (2)(d) confirms that the Secretary of State has the functions which are carried out by the MPCU (see, *e.g.* s.137, above). It seems a rather curious reversal of the normal position to give a principal power to exercise functions which his delegate is exercising. By definition, the delegate's powers must be derived from those given to the principal. Presumably, the purpose of the reference is to describe an identifiable category of activities which the DOT in fact performs. However, the provision was inserted in order to "remove any threat of a legal challenge to the unit's operations" (Lord Donaldson, *Hansard*, H.L. Vol. 555, col. 686).

The Government resisted an amendment tabled at the Third Reading of the 1994 Act in the Commons which would have created a "marine incident pollution control officer", on the grounds that this would have duplicated the functions of the MPCU. The MPCU has the responsibility for planning contingency arrangements and has a national contingency plan (and see the General Note to s.128(1)(d), above). It owns eight aircraft and has a stockpile of dispersants, cargo transfer equipment, vessels, breathing apparatus and other equipment. About half of the stockpile is for oil pollution cases and the remainder for chemical pollution. The equipment is operated and maintained by a private sector contract. The chief executive of the Coastguard Agency has overall responsibility, but otherwise responsibility is exercised by the Director of the MPCU. The activities of the MPCU would be reported on in documents produced by the Coastguard Agency, although the Government was not prepared to commit itself to an annual report by the MPCU. The Government resisted a further amendment which would have enabled the Secretary of State to give directions to local authorities as this "would go further than is considered necessary" (*Hansard*, H.C. Vol. 241, col. 565). At present the power to give directions is limited to those listed in s.137(2), which mainly concerns shipowners, masters and salvors. The Government evidently preferred that there should be co-operation rather than coercion in its relations with local authorities.

The Opposition pressed in 1994 for the inclusion of an additional paragraph in subs. (2) which would have added to the functions of the Secretary of State the approval of the reimbursement of the costs of registered charities which carry out preventive or supervisory activities in relation to environmental damage. The intention was to benefit bodies such as Care for the Wild, the RSPB and the RSPCA. The Government resisted such an amendment, mainly on financial grounds, but partly because it has been the practice under the 1969 Liability Convention and the 1971 Fund Convention for payments to be made, in appropriate circumstances, to charities which have carried out preventative work. This occurred in relation to the *Braer* (see the General Note to Pt. VI, Ch. III, above).

General power to dispense

294.—(1) The Secretary of State may, if he thinks fit, and upon such conditions (if any) as he thinks fit to impose, exempt any ship from any specified requirement of, or prescribed under, this Act other than Chapter II of Part VI, or dispense with the observance of any such requirement in the case of any ship, if he is satisfied, as respects that requirement, of the matters specified in subsection (2) below.

(2) Those matters are—

  (a) that the requirement has been substantially complied with in the case of that ship or that compliance with it is unnecessary in the circumstances; and

  (b) that the action taken or provision made as respects the subject-matter of the requirement in the case of the ship is as effective as, or more effective than, actual compliance with the requirement.

(3) The Secretary of State shall annually lay before both Houses of Parliament a special report stating—

(a) the cases in which he has exercised his powers under this section during the preceding year; and

(b) the grounds upon which he has acted in each case.

DEFINITIONS
  "Act, this": s.316(1).
  "Secretary of State": Interpretation Act 1978, Sched. 1.
  "ship": s.313(1).

GENERAL NOTE
  [Derivation: Merchant Shipping Act 1906, s.78.]

Registrar General of Shipping and Seamen

295.—(1) There shall continue to be an officer known as the Registrar General of Shipping and Seamen.

(2) The Registrar General of Shipping and Seamen shall be appointed, and may be removed, by the Secretary of State.

(3) The Registrar General of Shipping and Seamen shall exercise such functions as are conferred on him by this Act and keep such records and perform such other duties as the Secretary of State may direct.

(4) The Secretary of State may appoint and remove persons to perform on behalf of the Registrar General of Shipping and Seamae such of his functions as the Secretary of State or the Registrar General of Shipping and Seamen may direct.

(5) Subsection (4) above does not apply in relation to the functions of the Registrar General of Shipping and Seaman as registrar under Part II.

DEFINITIONS
  "Act, this": s.316(1).
  "person": Interpretation Act 1978, Sched. 1.
  "Secretary of State": Interpretation Act 1978, Sched. 1.

GENERAL NOTE
  [Derivation: Merchant Shipping Act 1970, s.80 and Merchant Shipping (Registration, etc.) Act 1993, s.1(3).]

Mercantile marine superintendents

296.—(1) There shall continue to be officers known as mercantile marine superintendents.

(2) Mercantile marine superintendents shall be appointed, and may be removed, by the Secretary of State.

(3) Mercantile marine superintendents shall exercise the functions conferred on superintendents by this Act.

DEFINITIONS
  "Act, this": s.316(1).
  "Secretary of State": Interpretation Act 1978, Sched. 1.
  "superintendent": s.313(1).

GENERAL NOTE
  [Derivation: Merchant Shipping Act 1970, s.81.]

Wreck commissioners, etc.

297.—(1) The Lord Chancellor may appoint such number of persons as he thinks fit to be wreck commissioners and may remove any wreck commissioners appointed by him.

(2) A wreck commissioner shall vacate his office on the day on which he attains the age of seventy years; but this subsection is subject to section 26(4)

to (6) of the Judicial Pensions and Retirement Act 1993 (power to authorise continuance in office up to the age of seventy-five years).

(3) Before appointing a person to act as wreck commissioner in Northern Ireland the Lord Chancellor shall consult the Chief Justice of Northern Ireland.

(4) There shall be paid to any wreck commissioner such remuneration, out of money provided by Parliament, as the Lord Chancellor may with the consent of the Treasury determine.

(5) There shall be paid to any assessor appointed under this Act such remuneration, out of money provided by Parliament, as the Lord Chancellor may with the consent of the Treasury determine.

DEFINITIONS
   "Act, this": s.316(1).
   "Lord Chancellor": Interpretation Act 1978, Sched. 1.
   "person": Interpretation Act 1978, Sched. 1.
   "Treasury": Interpretation Act 1978, Sched. 1.

GENERAL NOTE
   [Derivation: Merchant Shipping Act 1970, ss.82 and 83; Judicial Pensions and Retirement Act 1993, Sched. 6, para. 59.

Transmission of documents to Registrar General

298.—(1) The following duties are imposed on all superintendents and all officers of customs and excise as respects all documents which are delivered or transmitted to or retained by them in pursuance of this Act.

(2) They shall take charge of the documents and keep them for such time (if any) as may be necessary for the purpose of settling any business arising at the place where the documents come into their hands, or for any other proper purpose.

(3) They shall, if required, produce them for any of those purposes, and shall then transmit them to the Registrar General of Shipping and Seamen.

(4) The Registrar General of Shipping and Seamen shall record and preserve all documents transmitted to him in pursuance of the foregoing provisions of this section.

DEFINITIONS
   "Act, this": s.316(1).
   "fails": s.313(1).
   "master": s.313(1).
   "seaman": s.313(1).
   "ship": s.313(1).
   "superintendent": s.313(1).
   "surveyor of ships": ss.256(9)(b) and 313(1).

GENERAL NOTE
   [Derivation: Merchant Shipping Act 1894, s.256(1).]

Returns, etc. to Secretary of State

299.—(1) All superintendents shall make and send to the Secretary of State such returns or reports on any matter relating to British merchant shipping or seamen as he may require.

(2) All consular officers abroad and all officers of customs and excise abroad shall make and send to the Secretary of State such returns or reports on any matter relating to British merchant shipping or seamen as he may require.

(3) All superintendents shall, when required by the Secretary of State, produce to him or to his officers all official log-books and other documents which are delivered to them under this Act.

(4) All surveyors of ships shall make such returns to the Secretary of State as he may require with respect to—

(a) the build, dimensions, draught, burden, speed and room for fuel of ships surveyed by them; and

(b) the nature and particulars of machinery and equipment of such ships.

(5) The owner, master and engineer of any ship being surveyed shall, when required to do so, give to the surveyors all such information and assistance within his power as the surveyors require for the purpose of returns under subsection (4) above.

(6) If the owner, master or engineer, on being required under subsection (5) above to give any information or assistance, fails, without reasonable excuse, to give the information or assistance he shall be liable on summary conviction to a fine not exceeding level 3 on the standard scale.

DEFINITIONS

"Act, this": s.316(1).
"Secretary of State": Interpretation Act 1978, Sched. 1.
"standard scale": Criminal Justice Act 1982, s.37.

GENERAL NOTE

[Derivation: Merchant Shipping Act 1894, ss.714, 715 and 726 (Merchant Shipping Act 1979, Sched. 6, Pt. II).]

Forms

300.—(1) The Secretary of State may prepare and approve forms for any book, instrument or paper required under this Act, and may alter such forms as he thinks fit.

(2) The Secretary of State shall cause every such form to be marked with the distinguishing mark of his Department and, before finally issuing any form or making any alteration in a form, shall cause public notice thereof to be given in such manner as he thinks requisite in order to avoid inconvenience.

(3) The Secretary of State shall cause such forms to be supplied at offices of customs and excise and Department of Transport Marine Offices, free of charge or at such reasonable prices as the Secretary of State may fix, or he may licence any persons to print and sell the forms.

(4) Every such book, instrument or paper shall be made in the form (if any) approved by the Secretary of State, or as near as circumstances permit; and unless so made shall not be admissible in evidence in any civil proceedings on the part of the owner or master of any ship.

(5) Every such book, instrument or paper if made in a form purporting to be the proper form and to be marked in accordance with subsection (2) above shall be deemed to be in the form required by this Act, unless the contrary is proved.

(6) The foregoing provisions do not apply where special provision is made by this Act.

(7) If any person prints, sells or uses any document purporting to be a form approved by the Secretary of State knowing that the document is not the form approved for the time being or that the document has not been prepared or issued by the Secretary of State that person shall be liable, on summary conviction, to a fine not exceeding level 2 on the standard scale.

(8) In Scotland, if any person forges any distinguishing mark on any form issued under this Act or fraudulently alters any such form he shall be liable—

(a) on summary conviction, to a fine not exceeding the statutory maximum or to imprisonment for a term not exceeding six months or to both; or

(b) on conviction on indictment, to a fine or to imprisonment or to both.

DEFINITIONS
"Act, this": s.316(1).
"master": s.313(1).
"person": Interpretation Act 1978, Sched. 1.
"Secretary of State": Interpretation Act 1978, Sched. 1.
"ship": s.313(1).
"standard scale": Criminal Justice Act 1982, s.37.
"statutory maximum": Criminal Justice Act 1982, s.74.

GENERAL NOTE
[Derivation: Merchant Shipping Act 1894, ss.720 and 722(1); Merchant Shipping (Registration, etc.) Act 1993, Sched. 4, para. 73. Merchant Shipping Act 1894, s.722(2)(b); Merchant Shipping Act 1979, Sched. 6, Pt. I.]

Advisory committees

301.—(1) The Secretary of State may, if he thinks fit, appoint committees for the purpose of advising him when considering the making or alteration of any regulations, rules or scales for the purpose of this Act other than Chapter II of Part VI.

(2) A committee appointed under this section shall consist of persons representing the interests principally affected or having special knowledge of the subject matter.

(3) The Secretary of State shall pay to the members of any committee under this section such travelling and other allowances as the Secretary of State determines with the consent of the Treasury.

(4) Committees may be appointed under this section to advise the Secretary of State specially as regards any special regulations, rules or scales or generally as regards any class or classes of regulations, rules or scales which the Secretary of State may assign to them.

DEFINITIONS
"Act, this": s.316(1).
"person": Interpretation Act 1978, Sched. 1.
"Secretary of State": Interpretation Act 1978, Sched. 1.
"Treasury": Interpretation Act 1978, Sched. 1.

GENERAL NOTE
[Derivation: Merchant Shipping Act 1906, s.79.]

Financial Provisions

Fees

302.—(1) The Secretary of State may, with the consent of the Treasury, make regulations prescribing fees to be charged in respect of—

(a) the issue or recording in pursuance of this Act of any certificate, licence or other document; or

(b) the doing of any thing in pursuance of this Act.

(2) In the case of fees for the measurement of a ship's tonnage the fees may be prescribed as maximum fees.

(3) All fees received by the Secretary of State under this Act shall be paid into the Consolidated Fund.

DEFINITIONS
"Act, this": s.316(1).
"Secretary of State": Interpretation Act 1978, Sched. 1.
"ship": s.313(1).
"Treasury": Interpretation Act 1978, Sched. 1.

GENERAL NOTE
[Derivation: Merchant Shipping (Registration, etc.) Act 1993, Sched. 4, para. 79; Merchant Shipping (Safety Convention) Act 1949, s.33(2); Merchant Shipping (Registration, etc.) Act 1993, Sched. 5.]
It has been common for merchant shipping legislation to provide for the payment of fees (see, e.g. the Merchant Shipping Act 1979, s.51(2)) and fees regulations have been issued regularly (see, e.g. the Merchant Shipping (Fees) Regulations 1991 (S.I. 1991 No. 784).
Section 302 (inserted by the Merchant Shipping (Registration, etc.) Act 1993, Sched. 4, para. 79) provides for a uniform general fee prescribing power which will apply in all cases (for ship registration, see the General Note to s.10(2)(1), above).

Expenses of Commissioners of Customs and Excise

303.—(1) All expenses incurred by the Commissioners of Customs and Excise in the conduct of proceedings or otherwise in carrying into effect the provisions of this Act shall be treated as expenses relating to the revenue of customs and excise and shall be paid accordingly.

(2) The Secretary of State may, however, with the consent of the Treasury, repay all or any part of such of the expenses paid in accordance with subsection (1) above as are chargeable under this Act on money provided by Parliament.

DEFINITIONS
"Act, this": s.316(1).
"Secretary of State": Interpretation Act 1978, Sched. 1.
"Treasury": Interpretation Act 1978, Sched. 1.

GENERAL NOTE
[Derivation: Merchant Shipping Act 1894, s.718; Merchant Shipping Act 1898, s.1(1)(b).]

Expenses charged on money provided by Parliament

304.—(1) The following expenses and other amounts shall be payable out of money provided by Parliament—
  (a) the expenses incurred by the Secretary of State under this Act;
  (b) the salaries, pensions, gratuities and allowances of surveyors of ships, Departmental inspectors and superintendents;
  (c) the sums required for the contribution from the United Kingdom towards maintaining, in accordance with the Safety Convention, a service in the North Atlantic for the study and observation of ice and for the ice patrol;
  (d) the expenses of obtaining depositions, reports and returns respecting wrecks and casualties;
  (e) such sums as the Secretary of State may, in his discretion, think fit to pay in respect of claims on account of the proceeds of wreck;
  (f) the expenses incurred in respect of receivers of wrecks and the performance of their duties;
  (g) such expenses as the Secretary of State directs for—
        (i) establishing and maintaining on the coasts of the United Kingdom proper lifeboats with the necessary crews and equipment;
        (ii) affording assistance towards the preservation of life and property in cases of shipwreck and distress at sea; or
        (iii) rewarding the preservation of life in such cases;

(h) any other amounts which are by virtue of any provision of this Act payable out of money provided by Parliament.

(2) In subsection (1)(c) above "the Safety Convention" means the International Convention for the Safety of Life at Sea signed in London on 1st November 1974.

DEFINITIONS
"Act, this": s.316(1).
"Departmental inspector": s.256(9)(a).
"property": Sched. 11, Art. 1(c).
"receiver": s.255(1).
"Safety Convention": subs. (2).
"Secretary of State": Interpretation Act 1978, Sched. 1.
"superintendent": s.313(1).
"surveyor of ships": ss.256(9)(b) and 313(1).
"United Kingdom": Interpretation Act 1978, Sched. 1.
"wreck": s.255(1).

GENERAL NOTE
[Derivation: Merchant Shipping Act 1894, s.662B; Merchant Shipping Act 1988, s.42(1); Merchant Shipping Act 1970, s.98(1); Fishing Vessels (Safety Provisions) Act 1970, s.10; Prevention of Oil Pollution Act 1971, s.28(1); Merchant Shipping Act 1979, ss.23(1)(f), 51(1); Merchant Shipping Act 1984, s.10; Merchant Shipping Act 1988, s.55(1); Merchant Shipping Act 1894, s.677; Merchant Shipping Act 1988, Sched. 5; Merchant Shipping (Safety Convention) Act 1949, s.25; Merchant Shipping (Safety Convention) Act 1977, s.1(2)(a).]

Payments to be made into Consolidated Fund

305.—(1) The following sums shall be paid into the Consolidated Fund—
(a) all fees, charges and expenses payable in respect of the survey and measurement of ships;
(b) any fees received by receivers of wrecks;
(c) any sums received by the Secretary of State under this Act or which are, by any provision of it, required to be paid into the Consolidated Fund.

(2) All fees mentioned in this section shall be paid at such time and in such manner as the Secretary of State directs.

DEFINITIONS
"Act, this": s.316(1).
"receiver": s.255(1).
"Secretary of State": Interpretation Act 1978, Sched. 1.
"ship": s.313(1).

GENERAL NOTE
[Derivation: Merchant Shipping Act 1894, s.676; Merchant Shipping Act 1988, Sched. 5; Merchant Shipping (Registration, etc.) Act 1993, Sched. 5.]

Subordinate Legislation

Regulations, rules and orders, etc.

306.—(1) Any power of the Secretary of State to make regulations, orders or rules under this Act shall be exercisable by statutory instrument but this does not apply to rules under section 91.

(2) Any statutory instrument containing regulations, orders or rules under this Act shall be subject to annulment in pursuance of a resolution of either House of Parliament but this subsection does not apply to commencement orders, transitory provision orders or orders under section 216(2), 223(3), or paragraph 8 of Part II of Schedule 7 or paragraph 5 of Schedule 9 or regulations under section 85, 259(8), or 260(4).

In this subsection "transitory provision order" means an order under any provision of Schedule 14.

(3) Any statutory instrument containing an Order in Council under this Act shall be subject to annulment in pursuance of a resolution of either House of Parliament but this subsection does not apply to Orders under section 2(4), 128, 129, 152(2), 172(2), 183, 184, 224, 308 or 315(2) or under paragraph 29 of Schedule 3, paragraph 10 of Part II of Schedule 6 or paragraph 13 of Part II of Schedule 7.

(4) Before making the following regulations, rules or orders, namely—

(a) regulations under Part III or under section 108;

(b) rules under Chapter II of Part V;

(c) an order under section 311,

the Secretary of State shall consult with organisations in the United Kingdom appearing to him representative of persons who will be affected by the regulations, rules or orders.

(5) Any direction, notice, order or authorisation under this Act given or made by the Secretary of State shall be in writing.

(6) Any power to give a direction includes power to vary or revoke the direction by a subsequent direction.

DEFINITIONS

"Act, this": s.316(1).

"person": Interpretation Act 1978, Sched. 1.

"Secretary of State": Interpretation Act 1978, Sched. 1.

"transitory provision order": subs. (2).

"United Kingdom": Interpretation Act 1978, Sched. 1.

"writing": Interpretation Act 1978, Sched. 1.

GENERAL NOTE

[Derivation: Merchant Shipping Act 1894, s.739(1); Merchant Shipping (Load Lines) Act 1967, s.30(3); Merchant Shipping Act 1970, s.99; Prevention of Oil Pollution Act 1971, s.27; Merchant Shipping Act 1974, s.17(2); Merchant Shipping Act 1979, ss.23(4), 41(2), 49; Fishing Vessels (Safety Provisions) Act 1970, s.7(2); Safety at Sea Act 1986, s.9(2), (3); Merchant Shipping Act 1988, s.53(1); Merchant Shipping (Registration, etc.) Act 1993, Sched. 4, para. 1(2).]

Note that subordinate legislation issued under any of the consolidated Acts will be preserved in force by the Interpretation Act 1978 (c. 30), s.17(2)(b).

Application of Act to certain descriptions of ships, etc.

Application of Act to non-United Kingdom ships

307.—(1) The Secretary of State may make regulations specifying any description of non-United Kingdom ships and directing that such of the provisions of this Act and of instruments under this Act as may be specified in the regulations—

(a) shall extend to non-United Kingdom ships of that description and to masters and seamen employed in them, or

(b) shall so extend in such circumstances as may be so specified, with such modifications (if any) as may be so specified.

(2) Regulations under this section may contain such transitional, supplementary and consequential provisions as appear to the Secretary of State to be expedient.

(3) In this section "non-United Kingdom ships" means ships which are not registered in the United Kingdom.

DEFINITIONS

"Act, this": s.316(1).

"master": s.313(1).

"non-United Kingdom ships": subs. (3).

"registered": ss.23(1) and 313(1).
"seaman": s.313(1).
"Secretary of State": Interpretation Act 1978, Sched. 1.
"United Kingdom": Interpretation Act 1978, Sched. 1.

GENERAL NOTE

[Derivation: Merchant Shipping (Registration, etc.) Act 1993, Sched. 4, para. 5.]

Much merchant shipping legislation applies to U.K. ships, *i.e.* ships registered in the U.K. It might be questioned whether an unscrupulous shipowner could avoid responsibilities by failing to register a ship. Before the consolidation a number of Acts dealt with particular problems by extending their operation (especially on regulatory matters) to unregistered ships. Thus, the Merchant Shipping Act 1894, s.72 (as amended by the Merchant Shipping Act 1988, Sched. 1, para. 44) provided for the liabilities of unregistered ships. In particular, ships which were not registered elsewhere but could have been registered in the U.K. were treated as British ships in respect of dues, fines, forfeiture and "the punishment of offences committed on board the ship, or by any persons belonging to the ship" (and *cf.* the Merchant Shipping Act 1894, s.734; the Merchant Shipping (Load Lines) Act 1967, s.29; the Merchant Shipping Act 1970, s.92; the Prevention of Oil Pollution Act 1971, s.22; and the Merchant Shipping Act 1988, s.50). Section 72 and the other provisions listed were repealed by Sched. 5 of the 1993 Act. The 1993 Act also created the present s.307 (see Sched. 4, para. 5 of the 1993 Act, modelled on the Merchant Shipping Act 1988, s.50).

This section was introduced mainly to deal with what were termed (somewhat misleadingly) in debates on the 1993 Act as "unregistered U.K. ships" when outside U.K. ports and territorial waters. Most unregistered ships are pleasure boats which have no need to register—unless the buyer of such a craft wants to finance the purchase using a mortgage. Pirate radio ships are often unregistered and there are sometimes vessels between registers. The need for legislation to cover unregistered ships was particularly evident once registration became theoretically optional in the Merchant Shipping Act 1988 (see now s.9 of the 1995 Act). Section 307 will enable much of the sort of statutory material referred to above to be replaced by regulations. There will thus be little point in failing to register in order to avoid the regulatory effects of the Merchant Shipping Act. Note that this section does extend to foreign ships and ships which would otherwise be British ships within s.1 if they had been registered. The expression "non -United Kingdom ships" in subsection (1)(a) must be read in accordance with subsection (3) and does not exclude ships, *e.g.*, which were based in the U.K. but unregistered.

For regulations which have previously been issued, see the Merchant Shipping Act 1970 (Unregistered Fishing Vessels) Regulations 1991 (S.I. 1991 No. 1365); the Merchant Shipping Act 1970 (Unregistered Ships) Regulations 1991 (S.I. 1991 No. 1366); and the Merchant Shipping Act 1988 (Unregistered Ships) Regulations 1991 (S.I. 1991 No. 1367). These Regulations contain lists of sections of the relevant Act which are extended to unregistered ships. Thus, the Regulations extended the application of what are now ss.58 and 94 to such ships.

Application of Act to government ships

308.—(1) Subject to any other provision of it, this Act shall not apply to ships belonging to Her Majesty.

(2) Her Majesty may by Order in Council make regulations with respect to the manner in which Government ships may be registered as British ships under Part II; and this Act, subject to any exceptions and modifications which may be made by Order in Council, either generally or as respects any special class of Government ships, shall apply to government ships registered in accordance with the Order as if they were registered in accordance with Part II.

(3) Any Order in Council under subsection (2) above shall be laid before Parliament after being made.

(4) In this section "Government ships" means ships not forming part of Her Majesty's Navy which belong to Her Majesty, or are held by any person on behalf of or for the benefit of the Crown (and for that reason cannot be registered under Part II).

DEFINITIONS

"Act, this": s.316(1).
"British ship": ss.1(1) and 313(1).
"Government ship": ss.308(4) and 313(1).

"person": Interpretation Act 1978, Sched. 1.
"registered": ss.23(1) and 313(1).
"ship": s.313(1).

GENERAL NOTE
[Derivation: Merchant Shipping Act 1894, ss.738(2) and 741; Merchant Shipping Act 1906, s.80; Merchant Shipping (Registration, etc.) Act 1993, Sched. 2, para. 3.]
Section 308 re-enacts two main separate provisions of the previous law. "Ships belonging to Her Majesty" are generally exempted from the provisions of the Merchant Shipping Act 1995 by s.308(1), re-enacting s.741 of the Merchant Shipping Act 1894. It follows that they cannot therefore be registered. The Merchant Shipping Act 1906, s.80, allowed Government ships (*i.e.* those not forming part of the Navy) to be registered under Orders in Council (*e.g.* S.I. 1911 No. 338). Section 308(2) re-enacts this provision with appropriate modifications. Royal Fleet Auxiliaries are normally registered in this way and most of the provisions of the Merchant Shipping Act 1995 will apply to them. See also s.309, below, for demise chartered ships.

Application of Act to ships chartered by demise to the Crown

309.—(1) This section applies to a ship if for the time being—
(a) the ship is—
    (i) registered in the United Kingdom, and
    (ii) in the service of a government department (including a Northern Ireland department) ("the relevant department") by reason of a charter by demise to the Crown; and
(b) there is in force under section 308(2) an Order in Council of providing for the registration of Government ships in the service of the relevant department.

(2) Where this section applies to any ship, the following statutory provisions, namely—
(a) the provisions of the Order in Council referred to in subsection (1)(b) above (excluding those relating to registration under the Order), and
(b) the provisions of this Act (as they apply by virtue of section 308(2) and that Order in Council),
shall (subject to subsections (3) and (4) below) have the same effect in relation to that ship as they have in relation to a Government ship in the service of the relevant department (whether referred to as such or as such a ship registered in pursuance of that Order in Council).

(3) Subject to subsection (4) below, Part II shall have effect in relation to a ship to which this section applies in like manner as if it were not, for the purposes of this Act, a ship belonging to Her Majesty.

(4) Her Majesty may by Order in Council provide that any statutory provision falling within subsection (2) or (3) above and specified in the Order—
(a) shall not have effect in accordance with that subsection in relation to a ship to which this section applies, or
(b) shall so have effect in relation to such a ship, but subject to such modifications as are specified in the Order.

(5) In the application of any provision of this Act (other than a provision of Part II) in relation to a ship to which this section applies, any reference to the owner of the ship shall be construed as a reference to the relevant department.

(6) An Order in Council under this section may make such transitional, incidental or supplementary provision as appears to Her Majesty to be necessary or expedient.

DEFINITIONS
"Act, this": s.316(1).
"Government ship": ss.308(4) and 313(1).
"registered": ss.23(1) and 313(1).
"ship": s.313(1).
"relevant department": subs. (1)(a).
"United Kingdom": Interpretation Act 1978, Sched. 1.

GENERAL NOTE
[Derivation: Merchant Shipping Act 1988, s.47; Merchant Shipping (Registration, etc.) Act 1993, Sched. 2, para. 15(3), Sched. 5.]
Section 309 re-enacts s.47 of the Merchant Shipping Act 1988, as amended from March 21, 1994 by the Merchant Shipping (Registration, etc.) Act 1993. As noted in the General Note to s.308, above, "ships belonging to Her Majesty" are generally exempted from the provisions of the Merchant Shipping Act 1995 by s.308(1), and so cannot be registered. Section 308(2) deals with certain Government owned ships and allows for registration. The position of ships demise chartered to the Crown for the service of Government Departments was unclear for a long time. A demise, or bareboat, charter would be used where the Government wanted complete control of a vessel and to install its own crew, *e.g.* on prolonged NATO exercises, or for campaigns such as that in the Falkland Islands, or the Gulf. Foreign registered vessels presumably retain their national characteristics and remain subject to the law of the flag for regulatory purposes. It could be said that U.K. registered vessels under demise charter to the Crown should be similarly treated as ordinary registered U.K. ships. But such ships are treated as H.M. ships for liability purposes (see s.182, above) and it could be said that they are, in effect, ships belonging to Her Majesty.

Section 309 was introduced in 1988 to clarify matters. In effect, the section treats such demise chartered ships as if they were Government ships registered under s.308(2). The ordinary provisions of the Merchant Shipping Act 1995 will apply, but only to the extent that s.308(2) and Orders made under it allow. Under subs. (4) the ordinary registration requirements will apply normally but, for other Merchant Shipping Act 1995 provisions, subs. (4) allows an Order to be made modifying the application of the enactment in a given case.

In accordance with ordinary commercial practice the demise charterer is for most purposes treated as a "disponent" owner. Sections 98 and 100, above, also now recognise this fact. Subsection (5) makes it clear that for Merchant Shipping Act 1995 purposes references to the owner are to be considered as references to the relevant Government Department. Presumably, this provision will exonerate the registered owner from most criminal liability under the Merchant Shipping Act 1995. In particular, the registered owner could not be prosecuted for the offences described in ss.98 and 100 above. The registered owner is still to be considered as the owner for registration purposes.

Application of Act to hovercraft

310. The enactments and instruments with respect to which provision may be made by Order in Council under section 1(1)(h) of the Hovercraft Act 1968 shall include this Act (except Parts I and II) and any instrument made thereunder.

DEFINITIONS
"Act, this": s.316(1).

GENERAL NOTE
[Derivation: Merchant Shipping Act 1970, Sched. 3, para. 13; Merchant Shipping Act 1971, s.17; Prevention of Oil Pollution Act 1971, s.31; Merchant Shipping Act 1979, s.48; Merchant Shipping Act 1984, s.9; Merchant Shipping Act 1988, s.49.]
The Hovercraft Act 1968 lays down separate rules for the regulation, and liabilities, of hovercraft. In general the regulatory rules applying to ships are adapted for hovercraft by Orders in Council made under s.1 of the 1968 Act. Section 310 adds the Merchant Shipping Act (and statutory instruments made under it) to the enactments mentioned in ss.1(1)(h) and 4(1) of the 1968 Act. The exceptions are Pts. I and II of the Merchant Shipping Act 1995 which are dealt with separately in the 1968 Act.

Application of Act to certain structures, etc.

311.—(1) The Secretary of State may by order provide that a thing designed or adapted for use at sea and described in the order is or is not to be treated as a ship for the purposes of any specified provision of this Act or of an instrument made thereunder.

(2) An order under this section may—
(a) make different provision in relation to different occasions;
(b) if it provides that a thing is to be treated as a ship for the purposes of a specified provision, provide that the provision shall have effect in relation to the thing with such modifications as are specified.

(3) In this section "specified" means specified in the order.

DEFINITIONS
"Secretary of State": Interpretation Act 1978, Sched. 1.
"ship": s.313(1).
"specified": subs. (3).

GENERAL NOTE
[Derivation: Merchant Shipping Act 1979, s.41(1).]
In the last twenty years there has been a great increase in the number and type of craft oper-
ating offshore, such as mobile offshore drilling units (MODUs). The IMO has produced a
MODU Code (see the General Note to Art. 3 of the 1989 Salvage Convention, Sched. 11,
below). The IMO Legal Committee has had referred to it from the CMI a draft Convention on
Offshore Mobile Craft and work is proceeding within the CMI to see how such a Convention
might apply existing Conventions to offshore craft (as opposed to fixed production platforms).
Section 311 re-enacts s.41 of the Merchant Shipping Act 1979 which recognised the potential
problems by giving the Secretary of State power to provide that certain structures designed or
adapted for use at sea are to be treated as ships. The Secretary of State could thus declare that
certain structures such as oil rigs were or were not ships for one or more purposes of the Act.
The Merchant Shipping Act 1995, s.313(1) definition of "ship" has traditionally been very
narrow and has not perhaps been appropriate for all the different purposes for which a definition
is required (see the General Note to s.313(1), below). Thus, judges have taken a restrictive
approach to the definition when it would mean excluding some provisions of the Act which
would work to the disadvantage of victims. See the General Note to s.190, for example. There
are similar problems in relation to limitation of liability under the 1976 Limitation Convention
(see s.185 and Sched. 7, Pt. II, paras. 2 and 12). Yet in other contexts, such as salvage, it might be
more appropriate to have a wider definition so that potential salvors can be encouraged to go to
the assistance of unusual craft which are in danger (see the General Notes to Arts. 1(b) and (c)
and 3 of the 1989 Salvage Convention in Sched. 11, below). In other contexts, such as ship registration and safety, different considerations may apply.
In 1981, in the context of ship registration, a DOT Consultative Document indicated that the
DOT would, after consultation, seek greater precision in the application of the law to offshore
craft but, unfortunately, the powers under s.311 have not been exercised.

Special provisions for Scots law

Special provisions for Scots law

312.—(1) Nothing in this Act shall be held in any way to annul or restrict
the common law of Scotland with regard to the prosecution or punishment of
offences at the instance or on the authority or with the concurrence of the
Lord Advocate, or on the authority of the High Court or to any punishment
consequent on such prosecution or the rights of owners or creditors in regard
to enforcing a judicial sale of any ship and equipment, or to give to the High
Court in England and Wales any jurisdiction in respect of salvage in Scotland
which it did not have or exercise before 25 August 1894.

(2) Any enactment which confers on any court in Scotland Admiralty jurisdiction in respect of damage shall have effect as if references to damage
included reference to damages for loss of life or personal injury, and accordingly proceedings in respect of such damages may be brought in rem or in
personam.

DEFINITIONS
"Act, this": s.316(1).
"England and Wales": Interpretation Act 1978, Sched. 1.
"High Court": Interpretation Act 1978, Sched. 1.
"salvage": s.255(1).
"ship": s.313(1).

GENERAL NOTE
[Derivation: Merchant Shipping Act 1894, s.710; Merchant Shipping (Registration, etc.) Act
1993, Sched. 4, para. 76; Maritime Conventions Act 1911, s.5.]
Section 312 re-enacts s.710 of the Merchant Shipping Act 1894 and preserves certain rules of
Scottish law and procedure. It appears that offences never were punishable at the instance "or

direction" [emphasis added] of the Lord Advocate, as suggested in s.710 of the Merchant Shipping Act 1894. That provision was amended by the Merchant Shipping (Registration, etc.) Act 1993, Sched. 4, para. 76 to reflect Scots law more accurately. Section 312 now refers to the "authority or concurrence" of the Lord Advocate and the "authority" of the High Court.

A number of sections of the Merchant Shipping Act 1995 contain specific provisions to deal with the recovery of sums under the section in Scottish law (see, *e.g.*, s.236(4)). For Scotland it is apparently unnecessary for any special procedure to be mentioned and it is sufficient for s.236 and diligence that the sum be treated as a debt.

The pre-consolidation work also involved correcting other infelicities of expression, from a Scottish viewpoint, which were contained in the Merchant Shipping Acts. See for example, the Merchant Shipping (Registration, etc.) Act 1993, Sched. 4, para. 77 which amended what is now the Merchant Shipping Act 1995, Sched. 2, para. 5(c) (formerly the Merchant Shipping Act 1974, Sched. 5, para. 5) to use appropriate Scottish evidentiary terms.

Final provisions

Definitions

313.—(1) In this Act, unless the context otherwise requires—
"British connection" has the meaning given in section 9(9);
"British citizen", "British Dependent Territories citizen", "British Overseas citizen" and "Commonwealth citizen" have the same meaning as in the British Nationality Act 1981;
"British ship" has the meaning given in section 1(1);
"commissioned military officer" means a commissioned officer in Her Majesty's land forces on full pay;
"commissioned naval officer" means a commissioned officer of Her Majesty's Navy on full pay;
"conservancy authority" includes all persons entrusted with the function of conserving, maintaining or improving the navigation of a tidal water (as defined in section 255);
"consular officer", in relation to a foreign country, means the officer recognised by Her Majesty as a consular officer of that foreign country;
"contravention" includes failure to comply (and "failure" includes refusal);
"Departmental inspector" and "Departmental officer" have the meanings given in section 256(9);
"fishing vessel" means a vessel for the time being used (or, in the context of an application for registration, intended to be used) for, or in connection with fishing for sea fish other than a vessel used (or intended to be used) for fishing otherwise than for profit; and for the purposes of this definition "sea fish" includes shellfish, salmon and migratory trout (as defined by section 44 of the Fisheries Act 1981);
"foreign", in relation to a ship, means that it is neither a United Kingdom ship nor a small ship (as defined in section 1(2)) which is a British ship;
"Government ship" has the meaning given in section 308;
"harbour" includes estuaries, navigable rivers, piers, jetties and other works in or at which ships can obtain shelter or ship and unship goods or passengers;
"harbour authority" includes all persons entrusted with the function of constructing, improving, managing, regulating, maintaining or lighting a harbour;
"master" includes every person (except a pilot) having command or charge of a ship and, in relation to a fishing vessel, means the skipper;

"port" includes place;
"proper officer" means a consular officer appointed by Her Majesty's
   Government in the United Kingdom and, in relation to a port in a
   country outside the United Kingdom which is not a foreign country,
   also any officer exercising in that port functions similar to those of a
   superintendent;
"the register" and "registered" have the meaning given in section 23(1);
"the registrar", in relation to the registration of ships, has the meaning
   given in section 8;
"registration regulations" means regulations under section 10;
"relevant British possession" means—
        (a) the Isle of Man;
        (b) any of the Channel Islands; and
        (c) any colony;
"safety regulations" means regulations under section 85;
"seaman" includes every person (except masters and pilots) employed
   or engaged in any capacity on board any ship;
"ship" includes every description of vessel used in navigation;
"superintendent" means a mercantile marine superintendent appointed
   under section 296;
"surveyor of ships" has the meaning given in section 256(9);
"the tonnage regulations" means regulations under section 19;
"United Kingdom ship" (and in Part V "United Kingdom fishing vessel") has the meaning given in section 1(3) except in the contexts
   there mentioned; and
"wages" includes emoluments.
(2) In this Act—
(a) "United Kingdom waters" means the sea or other waters within the
   seaward limits of the territorial sea of the United Kingdom; and
(b) "national waters", in relation to the United Kingdom, means United
   Kingdom waters landward of the baselines for measuring the breadth
   of its territorial sea.
(3) A vessel for the time being used (or intended to be used) wholly for the
purpose of conveying persons wishing to fish for pleasure is not a fishing
vessel.

DEFINITIONS
   "Act, this": s.316(1).
   "colony": Interpretation Act 1978, Sched. 1.
   "passenger": Sched. 6, Art. 1(4).
   "person": Interpretation Act 1978, Sched. 1.
   "small ship": s.1(2).
   "tidal water": s.255(1).
   "United Kingdom": Interpretation Act 1978, Sched. 1.

GENERAL NOTE
   [Derivation: Merchant Shipping Act 1894, s.742; Merchant Shipping (Registration, etc.) Act
1993, Sched. 4, para. 2.]
   This section is of central importance in the consolidated Act as it contains definitions. It is not
possible here to give an exhaustive interpretation of the expressions, which replace those in s.742
of the Merchant Shipping Act 1894 (see generally *Temperley*, pp. 274–282). Note that a number
of definitional changes were made by the Merchant Shipping (Registration, etc.) Act 1993,
Sched. 4 and that individual Parts of the Merchant Shipping Act 1995 may have their own special
set of definitions which will apply to that Part. See particularly, ss.23, 84, 181, 223, 255. Other
provisions will have special definitions applying to a Chapter within a Part (see, *e.g.*, s.152).

Subsection (1)
   "*Fishing vessel*". The definition of fishing vessel is that used originally in the Merchant Ship-
ping Act 1988, s.12(1) and later in the Merchant Shipping (Salvage and Pollution) Act 1994,
Sched. 4, para. 2. It is intended to apply to commercial fishing operations (*cf.* the definition in the
Merchant Shipping Act 1894, s.370, as amended by the Merchant Shipping Act 1970, s.100(3),

Sched. V). According to subs. (3), it would not include the fishing boat operated by an individual for the sport of fishing nor, apparently, the fishing boat used by a company as a courtesy leisure craft for clients. Nor would it extend to the type of fishing boat found in holiday resorts which, for payment, offer to take private fishermen for a day's recreational fishing (see subs. (3)), taken from s.12(2) of the Merchant Shipping Act 1988). But in this latter case the fishing boat must be used *wholly* for that purpose: if its owner was a part-time commercial fisherman, who took pleasure fishers along on his trips, it would fall within the definition of a fishing vessel. The definition of fishing vessel relates to its usage for the time being (as did s.370 of the 1894 Act), a recognition of the fact that boats are used for a variety of purposes.

"*Ship*". It might be thought that defining "ship" was the simplest of tasks. Unfortunately, there has been a mass of litigation on whether a particular structure was a ship, under s.742 of the Merchant Shipping Act 1894, for a variety of purposes, from marine salvage to the application of safety regulations and time bars (see *Temperley*, pp. 276–277). Suffice it to say that the courts have generally taken a rather restrictive view of what is a ship and have laid particular emphasis on the expression "used in navigation" (see, *e.g.*, *The Gas Float Whitton (No. 2)* [1897] A.C. 337). Sometimes that emphasis has been artificial and seemingly only designed to protect personal injury claimants where the operation of a maritime rule would disadvantage them. Thus, in an unconvincing judgment, Sheen J. declared that a jet ski was not a ship, partly because it was not used in "navigation" in a traditional sense (see *Steedman v. Scofield* [1992] 2 Lloyd's Rep. 163). Similarly, Henry J. held that a sailing dinghy used on a reservoir was not used in navigation, as the users were merely "messing about in boats" (*Curtis v. Wild* [1991] 4 All E.R. 172).

Whatever the merits of the individual cases, the reasoning is not always consistent. The real question is not so much whether particular craft fall within a simple definition of ship, but the more complex one of whether substantive maritime rules of many different types and on many different subjects (*e.g.* on safety, salvage, limits of liability, time bars, registration) can and should be applied to craft of vastly differing size and construction and designed for a multiplicity of purposes. Thus, one may quite rationally want to apply strict regulatory safety requirements on pleasure craft operating on a reservoir, but might think it quite inappropriate or unfair to apply limits of liability or time bars, designed for merchant ships, which will provide radically different remedies to those injured in a bus crash. Similarly, at sea, there is great uncertainty how the definition of ship is to be applied to whole categories of modern offshore craft, such as semi-submersible platforms and jack-up oil rigs (see M. Summerskill, *Oil Rigs: Law and Insurance* (1979), where the author wrestles for the best part of Ch. 2 in an attempt to define oil rigs).

The definition of "ship" does use the word "includes", so that there is the possibility of recognising new craft as ships. Note that s.311, above, gives the Secretary of State power to provide that certain structures designed or adapted for use at sea are to be treated as ships but this useful power has not been exercised. The CMI (Comite Maritime International) produced in 1977 a draft Convention on Offshore Mobile Craft. In 1991 the 64th Session of the IMO Legal Committee recorded sufficient interest in an up-dated study of the earlier draft that the subject was placed on the work programme of the Legal Committee. At the 74th Session of the Legal Committee in October 1995, the matter was given a low priority and referred back to the CMI for further consideration.

The 1995 Act does not solve any of the modern problems, although one anachronism was removed from the definition of ship (in what was then s.742 of the 1894 Act) by the Merchant Shipping (Salvage and Pollution) Act 1994, Sched. 4, para. 2. Section 742 stated that "ship" included every description of vessel used in navigation "not propelled by oars". The present definition has removed the quoted phrase, so that a rowing boat can be a "ship". This seemed to be the only distinction between ship and "vessel" in s.742. "Vessel" can thus be absorbed into "ship" except in relation to wreck (see s.255(1)), midget submarines and submersibles (see s.88, above) and fishing vessels which are separately defined elsewhere in subs. (1). However, if judges wish to exclude the application of rules such as those relating to limitation of liability (which under Sched. 7, Pt. II, para. 2 do not depend on a vessel being sea-going) to rowing boats they will have to continue in a strained interpretation of "used in navigation". It would be better if, after consolidation, a detailed look was taken at each part of the consolidated Act and a principled decision was taken on how far the relevant provisions should extend to particular maritime craft. To some extent, this is the approach that has always been taken for fishing vessels, for wrecks and for submarines.

Subsection (2)

Subsection 2 provides consistent expressions for use when it is necessary to refer to territorial or national waters, *e.g.*, s.58 (formerly s.27 of the Merchant Shipping Act 1970, as amended by s.32 of the Merchant Shipping Act 1988) which creates an offence where seafarers endanger ships in waters now within the definition in subs. (2). See also Sched. 11, Pt. II, para. 5 (formerly s.544 of the Merchant Shipping Act 1894) which sets out the circumstances when life salvage is payable for services performed in "United Kingdom waters", an expression that is now to be read as the territorial sea (and see the Territorial Sea Act 1987 (c. 49)).

Subsection (3)
    See the notes on fishing vessels under subs. (1), above.

Repeals, consequential amendments and transitional provisions

314.—(1) The enactments specified in Schedule 12 (which include enactments which are spent) are, subject to subsection (3) below and to any Note at the end of the Schedule, repealed to the extent specified in the third column of that Schedule.

(2) The enactments specified in Schedule 13 shall have effect subject to the amendments specified in that Schedule.

(3) The saving and transitional provisions in Schedule 14 shall have effect.

(4) The Secretary of State may, by order, make such amendments of any local Act or instrument so far as it provides for the registration of ships in local registers as appear to him to be appropriate in view of the provisions made for the register mentioned in section 8.

DEFINITIONS
    "register": ss.23(1) and 313(1).
    "Secretary of State": Interpretation Act 1978, Sched. 1.
    "ship": s.313(1).

GENERAL NOTE
    [Derivation: Merchant Shipping (Registration, etc.) Act 1993, s.10(6).]
    Schedule 12 contains repeals. Schedule 13 contains consequential amendments, *e.g.* so that other Acts refer to the 1995 Act rather than the pre-consolidation provisions. Schedule 14 contains a number of transitory, saving or transitional provisions (*e.g.* preserving the jurisdiction of the cinque ports).
    Subsection (4) deals with the possibility that there may be local legislation dealing with the registration of ships. There are probably hundreds of local Acts that may apply and the Secretary of State is given the power to amend them by statutory instrument where necessary.

Extent and application

315.—(1) Except for sections 18 and 193(5), this Act extends to England and Wales, Scotland and Northern Ireland.

(2) Her Majesty may by Order in Council direct that any provision of this Act and instruments made under this Act shall, with such exceptions, adaptations and modifications (if any) as may be specified in the Order, extend to any relevant British possession.

(3) Her Majesty may, in relation to any relevant British possession, by Order in Council direct that, with such exceptions, adaptations and modifications (if any) as may be specified in the Order, any of the provisions of this Act shall have effect as if references in them to the United Kingdom included a reference to that possession.

(4) An Order in Council under subsection (2) above may make such transitional, incidental or supplementary provision as appears to Her Majesty to be necessary or expedient.

(5) Without prejudice to the generality of subsection (4) above, an Order in Council under this section may, in its application to any relevant British possession, provide for such authority in that possession as is specified in the Order to furnish the Secretary of State or the registrar with such information with respect to the registration of ships in that possession under its law as is specified in the Order or as the Secretary of State may from time to time require, and for any such information to be so furnished at such time or times and in such manner as is or are so specified or (as the case may be) as the Secretary of State may so require.

DEFINITIONS
"Act, this": s.316(1).
"England and Wales": Interpretation Act 1978, Sched. 1.
"registrar": ss.23(1) and 313(1).
"relevant British possession": s.313(1).
"Secretary of State": Interpretation Act 1978, Sched. 1.
"ship": s.313(1).
"United Kingdom": Interpretation Act 1978, Sched. 1.

GENERAL NOTE
[Derivation: Merchant Shipping (Registration, etc.) Act 1993, Sched. 4, para. 4(1)–(5).]
There were some 15 Merchant Shipping Acts which allowed their provisions to be extended overseas by Order in Council (see, *e.g.*, the Merchant Shipping Act 1988, s.56). The existence of the empire and an empire register meant that many merchant shipping provisions were applied to the colonies. Early references were to dominions and territories (*e.g.* the Maritime Conventions Act 1911, s.9(1)), but later references had to take account of mandates and trust territories and all the other confusing array of states over which the U.K. has exercised some form of control. The Merchant Shipping Act 1988, s.57(2) used the expression "relevant overseas territory" to refer to Crown Dependencies and Dependent Territories. Section 315 now sets out uniform provisions for applying merchant shipping legislation to the possessions now listed in s.313(1). For an example of an order see, *e.g.*, the Merchant Shipping Act 1988 (Cayman Islands) Order 1988 (S.I. 1988 No. 1841), which extended many of the provisions of the Merchant Shipping Act 1988 to the Cayman Islands.

Short title and commencement

316.—(1) This Act may be cited as the Merchant Shipping Act 1995.
(2) This Act shall come into force on 1st January 1996.

DEFINITIONS
"Act, this": subs. (1).

GENERAL NOTE
Note that existing subordinate legislation made under the consolidated Acts will continue to have effect (see the Interpretation Act 1978, s.17(2)(b)).

SCHEDULES

Section 16   SCHEDULE 1

PRIVATE LAW PROVISIONS FOR REGISTERED SHIPS

DEFINITIONS
"British connection": s.313(1).
"mortgage": para. 14.
"person": Interpretation Act 1978, Sched. 1.
"prescribed": para. 14.
"registered": s.313(1).
"registered mortgage": para. 14.
"registrar": s.313(1).

GENERAL NOTE
Schedule 1 re-enacts Sched. 1 of the Merchant Shipping (Registration, etc.) Act 1993.
This Schedule sets out certain private law provisions which (i) are to apply to U.K. registered ships according to ss.8(6) and 16, or (ii) may be excluded in their application to certain kinds of registered ships under s.10(4), or (iii) shall not be applied to ships bareboat chartered-in to the U.K. register under s.17. As mentioned in the General Note to s.16(3), above, the provisions are essentially those from the Merchant Shipping Act 1894 in a more up-dated form. They deal with matters such as rights of ownership, transfer and mortgages. In general, the existing provisions have been modernised by the removal of arcane or unnecessary language and the breaking up of large complex sections into more manageable sub-paragraphs. Where appropriate the origin of the provision will be given.

General

1.—(1) Subject to any rights and powers appearing from the register to be vested in any other person, the registered owner of a ship or of a share in a ship shall have power absolutely to dispose of it provided the disposal is made in accordance with this Schedule and registration regulations.

(2) Sub-paragraph (1) above does not imply that interests arising under contract or other equitable interests cannot subsist in relation to a ship or a share in a ship; and such interests may be enforced by or against owners and mortgagees of ships in respect of their interest in the ship or share in the same manner as in respect of any other personal property.

(3) The registered owner of a ship or of a share in a ship shall have power to give effectual receipts for any money paid or advanced by way of consideration on any disposal of the ship or share.

GENERAL NOTE

Sub-paragraph (1) is derived from the Merchant Shipping Act 1894, s.56. It gives the registered shipowner the absolute right to sell the ship in accordance with Sched. 1 and the Merchant Shipping (Registration of Ships) Regulations 1993 (S.I. 1993 No. 3138). References here and elsewhere to "shares" in a ship refer to the traditional division of the ship into 64 shares effected by s.5 of the Merchant Shipping Act 1894. Section 5 of the 1894 Act was repealed by Sched. 5 of the 1993 Act, but the 1993 Registration Regulations preserve the existing position (see reg. 2). The shares referred to must not be confused with the shares which might exist in a company which itself had an interest in the ship (*e.g.* by holding all 64 shares under reg. 2 of the 1993 Registration Regulations).

Examples of rights and powers which might exist in another person would be the priority accorded by para. 8 to a mortgagee whose mortgage was registered under para. 7 and the power of sale given to a mortgagee under para. 9. The final part of the old s.56 is now in sub-paragraph (3), (see *Barclay v. Poole* [1907] 2 Ch. 284, *Temperley,* p. 46).

The original s.57 of the Merchant Shipping Act 1894 contained a definition of "beneficial interests" for the purpose, *inter alia,* of s.58 (itself now re-enacted in s.16(3)). It will now be found, in a slightly different form, in sub-para. (2), but with the omission of three rather distracting "without prejudice to..." references which appeared in the middle of the old s.57 (relating to ss.35, 56 and 1 of the 1894 Act). The effect of the sub-para. is to make it clear that there may be contractual or other equitable rights (*e.g.* an equitable mortgage) in a ship which are not recorded on the register. These may be enforced against the shipowner or mortgagee, but in the event of insolvency they may not enjoy the same priority as that accorded to a registered mortgage. The section was originally passed to reverse the effect of *Liverpool Borough Bank v. Turner* (1860) 29 L.J. Ch. 827, 30 L.J. Ch. 379 (see *Temperley,* p. 46 and Clarke, "Ship Mortgages", Chap. 3 of N. Palmer, E. McKendrick (eds.), *Interests in Goods* (1993), at p. 79). The provision would not seem to cover the position of a legal mortgage of an unregistered ship and it could not be implied from the 1894 Act that an unregistered mortgage of an unregistered ship had to be treated as an equitable mortgage (see *The Shizelle* [1992] 2 Lloyd's Rep. 445, but *cf.* Clarke, *op. cit.,* pp. 85, 88). The effect of *The Shizelle* was that *bona fide* purchasers for value without notice of an unregistered yacht were held bound by an unregistered and undiscoverable mortgage. Unfortunately, the opportunity has not been taken to fill in what the judge in that case described as a statutory lacuna, although it is conceivable that the matter might be dealt with in future by registration regulations (but note s.10(4)(a)). It is submitted that it should still be considered open for the higher courts to overrule *The Shizelle* and hold that the implication of the old s.31 (now para. 7, below) was that all unregistered mortgages must be equitable.

Transfers etc. of registered ships

GENERAL NOTE

Paragraphs 2–6 deal with the transfer of registered ships and restate ss.24–30 of the Merchant Shipping Act 1894 (dealing with ships generally) and ss.19–20 of the Merchant Shipping Act 1988 (dealing with fishing vessels).

2.—(1) Any transfer of a registered ship, or a share in such a ship, shall be effected by a bill of sale satisfying the prescribed requirements, unless the transfer will result in the ship ceasing to have a British connection.

(2) Where any such ship or share has been transferred in accordance with sub-paragraph (1) above, the transferee shall not be registered as owner of the ship or share unless—

(a) he has made the prescribed application to the registrar; and
(b) the registrar is satisfied that the ship retains a British connection and that he would not refuse to register the ship.

(3) If an application under sub-paragraph (2) above is granted by the registrar, the registrar shall register the bill of sale in the prescribed manner.

(4) Bills of sale shall be registered in the order in which they are produced to the registrar for the purposes of registration.

GENERAL NOTE

Under sub-para. (1) transfers of ships, or any of the 64 shares in them, have to be made by a bill of sale (see s.24 of the 1894 Act). At one time the format of the bill of sale was set out in s.24(2) of the 1894 Act. The 1995 Act now allows the whole question of approved forms to be dealt with by registration regulations (see s.10(6), above). Under s.24(1) of the Merchant Shipping Act 1894, as substituted by the Merchant Shipping Act 1988, Sched. 1, para. 15, there was a reference to the bill of sale requirement not applying where a *majority* interest in the ship is sold to a non-qualified person (*cf.* s.19(1) of the 1988 Act). The present version is an example of the greater flexibility brought about originally by the 1993 Act, as it leaves the precise British connection requirements to registration regulations. The bill of sale requirement will not apply, *e.g.*, if the ship is sold to a foreign company not entitled to own a U.K. ship under s.2.

Sub-paragraph (2) deals with the circumstances when the transferee can be registered as owner (*cf.* s.25 of the 1894 Act, as amended by Sched. 1, para. 16 of the 1988 Act, and s.19(3) of the 1988 Act).

Under sub-para. (3), once the application is granted the registrar will register the bill of sale (*cf.* s.26 of the 1894 Act and s.19(4) of the 1988 Act).

Under sub-para. (4), the bills of sale are registered in the order of their production (*cf.* s.26(2) of the 1894 Act and s.19(5) of the 1988 Act).

3.—(1) Where a registered ship, or a share in a registered ship, is transmitted to any person by any lawful means other than a transfer under paragraph 2 above and the ship continues to have a British connection, that person shall not be registered as owner of the ship or share unless—
 (a) he has made the prescribed application to the registrar; and
 (b) the registrar is satisfied that the ship retains a British connection and that he would not refuse to register the ship.
(2) If an application under sub-paragraph (1) is granted by the registrar, the registrar shall cause the applicant's name to be registered as owner of the ship or share.

GENERAL NOTE

This para. replaces s.27 of the Merchant Shipping Act 1894 and s.20(1) of the Merchant Shipping Act 1988. The old s.27 dealt with the transfer of a ship by means such as death, bankruptcy, marriage *etc.*, but was amended by Sched. 1, para. 16 of the 1988 Act to refer, like s.20(1), to transfers generally other than by way of bill of sale (see now para. 2 of this Schedule, above). Paragraph 3 is to the same effect, but has the added flexibility given by the ability to produce registration regulations (as explained in relation to para. 2(1), above). The paragraph is designed for those types of transfers which operate automatically as a matter of law. Thus on the death of a registered owner, an heir would be entitled to be registered as owner, provided he could satisfy the registrar as to his British connection as required in s.9, *e.g.* that he was a British citizen and, if resident abroad, that he had appointed a representative person in the U.K.

4.—(1) Where the property in a registered ship or share in a registered ship is transmitted to any person by any lawful means other than a transfer under paragraph 2 above, but as a result the ship no longer has a British connection, the High Court or in Scotland the Court of Session may, on application by or on behalf of that person, order a sale of the property so transmitted and direct that the proceeds of sale, after deducting the expenses of the sale, shall be paid to that person or otherwise as the court direct.
(2) The court may require any evidence in support of the application they think requisite, and may make the order on any terms and conditions they think just, or may refuse to make the order, and generally may act in the case as the justice of the case requires.
(3) Every such application must be made within the period of 28 days beginning with the date of the occurrence of the event on which the transmission has taken place, or within such further time (not exceeding one year) as the court may allow.
(4) If—
 (a) such an application is not made within the time allowed by or under sub-paragraph (3) above; or
 (b) the court refuse an order for sale,
the ship or share transmitted shall be liable to forfeiture.

GENERAL NOTE

If property is automatically transmitted by operation of law (*e.g.* on bankruptcy) to a transmittee who could not demonstrate the necessary British connection required by s.9, the court may order a sale of the ship, as previously provided for by s.28 of the Merchant Shipping Act 1894, as amended by Sched. 1, para. 16 of the Merchant Shipping Act 1988 (*cf.* s.20(4) of the 1988 Act). The penalty for failing to apply for any order within the strict time-limits is severe, namely the potential forfeiture of the vessel. Although sub-para. (4) uses the word "shall", the words "be liable to", which follow, indicate that there is a court discretion. It would seem unlikely that the court would order forfeiture in the type of case where administrative delays and communication difficulties arose as a result of death or insolvency (see ss.7, 20 of the Merchant Shipping

Act 1995 on forfeiture). The attitude might differ where there was some evidence of the unqualified transmittee deliberately trying to run the ship under the British flag, knowing that there was not the necessary British connection. Presumably, the transmittee might wish to continue its ownership of the ship. To maintain the U.K. registration it would be necessary for the ship to be transferred to some associated person, *e.g.* a U.K. company, which could satisfy the criteria in s.9(2).

5.—(1) Where any court (whether under paragraph 4 above or otherwise) order the sale of any registered ship or share in a registered ship, the order of the court shall contain a declaration vesting in some named person the right to transfer the ship or share.

(2) The person so named shall be entitled to transfer the ship or share in the same manner and to the same extent as if he were the registered owner of the ship or share.

(3) The registrar shall deal with any application relating to the transfer of the ship or share made by the person so named as if that person were the registered owner.

GENERAL NOTE

Where a court does order the sale of a ship, *e.g.* under para. 4, the buyer will want to deal with someone who has the same status as the registered owner and who can give effective receipts under para. 1(3), above. Paragraph 5 re-enacts s.29 of the Merchant Shipping Act 1894 by allowing the court to declare that a particular person has the right to transfer the ship. There appears to be no legal reason why that person cannot be the transmittee. The power of a court to order a sale of a ship might arise in circumstances other than those envisaged by para. 4, *e.g.* where mortgagees have arrested the ship for non-payment and have obtained a judgment *in rem* which they seek to enforce by an order of sale. It is a general principle that sale by court order gives the purchaser a title free of all liens and encumbrances (*The Cerro Colorado* [1993] 1 Lloyd's Rep. 58, *The Acrux* [1962] 1 Lloyd's Rep. 405 and *cf. The Blitz* [1992] 2 Lloyd's Rep. 441).

6.—(1) The High Court or in Scotland the Court of Session may, if they think fit (without prejudice to the exercise of any other power), on the application of any interested person, make an order prohibiting for a specified time any dealing with a registered ship or share in a registered ship.

(2) The court may make the order on any terms or conditions they think just, or may refuse to make the order, or may discharge the order when made (with or without costs or, in Scotland, expenses) and generally may act in the case as the justice of the case requires.

(3) The order, when a copy is served on the registrar, shall be binding on him whether or not he was made a party to the proceedings.

GENERAL NOTE

This paragraph re-enacts s.30 of the Merchant Shipping Act 1894 and allows an interested person to apply for an order delaying dealing in a ship. In effect, there is a form of interim injunction and the order might be used where a mortgagee suspected fraudulent dealings, or where it appeared that a purchaser would not pay the purchase money. In *Richard Hughes v. Vail Blyth Clewly (The Siben)* [1994] 2 Lloyd's Rep. 420 (Jersey C.A.) a dispute arose about the transfer of a yacht in a part-exchange arrangement. The plaintiff yacht seller applied for an order under s.30 of the Merchant Shipping Act 1894 prohibiting dealings in the yacht by the transferee for a year, and also brought separate proceedings to rescind the contract for misrepresentation. It was held that mere creditors were not "interested persons" within what is now para. 6(1), but that the plaintiff did have an interest in this property of the defendant more than in any other of the defendant's assets. Moreover, the effect of rescission would be for the yacht to be returned to the plaintiff's ownership. The power was discretionary, but the court decided to exercise it in the plaintiff's favour as the defendant was trying to mortgage the yacht and had provided no answer to the misrepresentation charge.

Mortgages of registered ships

GENERAL NOTE

Paragraphs 7–13 deal with mortgages and restate ss.31–43 of the Merchant Shipping Act 1894 (in relation to ships generally) and s.21 and Sched. 3 of the Merchant Shipping Act 1988 (in relation to fishing vessels).

7.—(1) A registered ship, or share in a registered ship, may be made a security for the repayment of a loan or the discharge of any other obligation.

(2) The instrument creating any such security (referred to in the following provisions of this Schedule as a "mortgage") shall be in the form prescribed by or approved under registration regulations.

(3) Where a mortgage executed in accordance with sub-paragraph (2) above is produced to the registrar, he shall register the mortgage in the prescribed manner.

(4) Mortgages shall be registered in the order in which they are produced to the registrar for the purposes of registration.

GENERAL NOTE

The wording used in this paragraph is taken from s.31 of the Merchant Shipping Act 1894, as it was amended by the Merchant Shipping Act 1988, Sched. 1, para. 21, and is substantially similar to that introduced in Sched. 3 of the Merchant Shipping Act 1988 for fishing vessels. The mortgage is simply the instrument containing the security and its precise form will be set out in the registration regulations. Mortgages are registered in the order in which they are produced to the registrar, although there is no longer the requirement in s.31(2) of the Merchant Shipping Act 1894 that the registrar include a hand-written memorandum of the date and hour.

The statute does not deal with mortgage obligations, which are generally dealt with by contract (see Clarke, *op. cit.*, p. 75). There is still some dispute about whether the registered ship mortgage is a *sui generis* "statutory security perfectible by registration" or whether it is a "chattel mortgage whose attributes have been modified by statute" (*ibid.*, p. 74). Neither the original s.31 *et seq.*, nor the present provisions, give any clear answer to this rather fundamental point. The traditional view (and the recent rather unsatisfactory decision in *The Shizelle* [1992] 2 Lloyd's Rep. 445) support the latter view, although there are persuasive arguments to the contrary in 0favour of the former (see Clarke, *op. cit.*, generally). The provisions unfortunately do not make clear what is the nature of unregistered mortgages, particularly in respect of unregistered ships (see further *The Shizelle*).

Priority of registered mortgages

8.—(1) Where two or more mortgages are registered in respect of the same ship or share, the priority of the mortgagees between themselves shall, subject to sub-paragraph (2) below, be determined by the order in which the mortgages were registered (and not by reference to any other matter).

(2) Registration regulations may provide for the giving to the registrar by intending mortgagees of "priority notices" in a form prescribed by or approved under the regulations which, when recorded in the register, determine the priority of the interest to which the notice relates.

GENERAL NOTE

The priority of registered mortgages between themselves is determined by the order in which they are registered under para. 7 and not the date of their creation (restating s.33 of the Merchant Shipping Act 1894 and Sched. 3, para. 3 of the Merchant Shipping Act 1988). The priority of registered mortgages against other forms of security, such as unregistered mortgages, or maritime liens, will be determined by general maritime law principles. Thus, for instance, a registered mortgage will take priority over a subsequent statutory lien for repairs, but not over a maritime lien (see *Bankers Trust International v. Todd Shipyards Corp.; Halcyon Isle, The* [1981] A.C. 221 and also *Chorley and Giles Shipping Law* (8th ed., 1987), pp. 78–81).

Schedule 3, para. 3 of the Merchant Shipping Act 1988 introduced a new and useful provision whereby the interests of *intending* mortgagees could be recorded on the register. The facility was only available under that Act for fishing vessels, but para. 8(2) of Sched. 1 of the Merchant Shipping Act 1995 allows the registration regulations to produce a similar system for all ships. Note that the 1993 Registration Regulations (S.I. 1993 No. 3138), Pt. VII, now deal with the registration and priority of mortgages. Paragraph 8(2) of Sched. 1 of the Merchant Shipping Act 1995 allows intending mortgagees to give notices, in prescribed form, which "determine" priority when recorded on the register. The provision does not fully define priority notices, or exactly how they will determine priority, but that is dealt with in reg. 59 of the 1993 Registration Regulations. The system used is similar to that in Sched. 3, para. 4(3) of the Merchant Shipping Act 1988. Under reg. 59, once notice of an intended mortgage is given and recorded the mortgage will, if later executed and registered, take priority over another registered mortgage—even where the latter was the first to be actually registered in the ordinary way. To this extent, para. 8(2) derogates from the general priority principle under para. 8(1). The provision is sensible and helpful, because there may be a gap in time between the execution of the mortgage and its registration, during which the owner might persuade others to execute a mortgage. Clearly, an intending mortgagee cannot be expected to have a provisional priority recorded for an indefinite period of time. Regulation 59 allows an initial, renewable, period of 30 days.

Registered mortgagee's power of sale

9.—(1) Subject to sub-paragraph (2) below, every registered mortgagee shall have power, if the mortgage money or any part of it is due, to sell the ship or share in respect of which he is registered, and to give effectual receipts for the purchase money.

(2) Where two or more mortgagees are registered in respect of the same ship or share, a subsequent mortgagee shall not, except under an order of a court of competent jurisdiction, sell the ship or share without the concurrence of every prior mortgagee.

GENERAL NOTE

Mortgagees have a variety of remedies available to them in the event that they are unhappy about the security provided by the mortgage. Many of these remedies arise expressly from the mortgage contract, or derive from the common law (see *Temperley*, pp. 28–34, Clarke, *op. cit.*, pp. 91–99, *Chorley and Giles Shipping Law*, pp. 63–65). Section 35 of the Merchant Shipping Act 1894 gave a statutory power of sale to the mortgagee which could be exercised without leave of the court. There were doubts as to whether any implied limitation could have been placed on the apparently wide power of the mortgagee under s.35, *e.g.* so as to require that the security of the mortgage be threatened in some way (see Clarke, *op. cit.*, p. 93). Section 34 (now para. 10, below) contained a limitation on the extent to which the mortgagee can be treated as owner (*e.g.* where it can take over control), namely where it may be necessary to make the ship "available" as security for the mortgage debt. It might be strange to have this limitation, yet grant an unfettered right of sale.

Paragraph 9 restates the mortgagee's statutory power of sale given by s.35 of the 1894 Act, but reproduces it in the modernised version first introduced in respect of fishing vessels by the Merchant Shipping Act 1988, Sched. 3, para. 5. Section 35 of the 1894 Act was repealed by Sched. 5 of the Merchant Shipping (Registration, etc.) Act 1993, but there are two differences in wording between s.35 and the present provision which may be of some significance. First, s.35 referred to the registered mortgagee having the power "absolutely" to dispose of the ship and there were no express limitations on the right (for the doubts about implied limitations, see above). Secondly, para. 9(1) now makes the power exercisable "if the mortgage money or any part of it is due" (the wording used for fishing vessels in Sched. 3, para. 5 of the 1988 Act).

Has the removal of the word "absolutely", either alone or together with the newly added words, imposed restrictions on the power of sale? The answer must be in the affirmative. It is not entirely clear if the changes have been made by inadvertence. Clearly, the mortgagee can now only exercise the power of sale under the Act in the circumstance specified, namely "if the mortgage money or any part of it is due". "Mortgage money" is not defined (although para. 7(1) refers to a loan) and could refer to the capital sum, or repayments, and interest due under it (or possibly both). It is submitted that any change in the law has been made partly as a result of a reliance on the law relating to land mortgages set out in s.101(1) of the Law of Property Act 1925 (see generally J. Farrand, *Wolstenholme and Cherry's Conveyancing Statutes* (13th ed., 1972) p. 206 *et seq.*). Section 101(1)(i) sets out the mortgagee's power "when the mortgage money has become due, to sell ...". Section 205(xvi) of the 1925 Act defines "mortgage money" to be "money or money's worth secured by a mortgage". On this basis the money would be "due" once the legal date for redemption of the loan had passed. If it was repayable by instalments of capital, the power could apparently be exercised not only when the whole sum was in arrears, but when any instalment was in arrears (*Payne v. Cardiff Rural District Council* [1932] 1 K.B. 241). In the *Payne* case, instalments of capital and interest upon them were due and the mortgagee was held entitled to exercise its rights under the Act to sell, but *only* in respect of that instalment that had fallen due and not future instalments. In fact the only claim in that case was for the instalments in arrear (and the case did not concern a normal loan, but a statutory charge under public works legislation).

The drafter of the present provisions must have had the *Payne* decision in mind, as para. 9(1) expressly refers to "part" of the money becoming due. The 1925 Act refers to money which "has become due", while the 1993 Act talks of money which "is due", although it is submitted that there is no material difference. However, the 1925 Act contains, in s.103, express limitations on the power of the mortgagee to *exercise* the power of sale, *e.g.* (i) a requirement that a notice to pay has been served and thereafter there has been a default for three months, or (ii) that interest is two months overdue, or (iii) that there has been a breach of some other provision in the mortgage deed. No equivalent provisions exist in the 1995 Act and it is extremely unlikely that they can now be implied. If this view is right, the extreme view that s.35 of the 1894 Act imposed no restrictions whatsoever has been narrowed, so that some money must at least be due. If the correct view of the 1894 Act was that it was subject to an implied limitation by virtue of s.34, or one requiring the type of defaults listed in s.103 of the 1894 Act, then the scope of the power of sale has been widened. Either way, it is arguable that the result is not particularly coherent in the context of ship mortgages (see also A. Clarke, N. Gaskell, "Sailing Towards Consolidation" [1994] LMCLQ 146, 150).

Whether any new limitation will have a great effect in practice may, perhaps, be doubted. As noted by Clarke (*op cit.*, p. 76) sale by court order following a mortgagee's action *in rem* may be preferable in many circumstances to the extra-judicial power of sale under s.35 (now para. 9(1)), in that the former will involve a sale free of encumbrances (see further *The Cerro Colorado* [1993] 1 Lloyd's Rep. 58, para. 5, above). Moreover, there is no reason why the mortgage contract could not also provide for a power of sale, which may not require any notice to be given (see, *e.g.* N. Meeson, *Ship and Aircraft Mortgages* (1989), p. 73). In practice, the mortgage covenant will also provide a large number of circumstances of default when the outstanding indebtedness will become due, including failure to pay any sum, failure to observe specific covenants (*e.g.* illegal trading), or conduct which imperils the security (*ibid.*, p. 72).

Paragraph 9(2) re-enacts the second part of s.35 of the 1894 Act and Sched. 3, para. 5(2) of the 1988 Act and provides that a registered mortgagee cannot sell the ship without the agreement of prior (registered) mortgagees. It follows that the mortgagee can sell without the agreement of subsequent registered mortgagees and mortgagees whose mortgages are unregistered.

Protection of registered mortgagees

10. Where a ship or share is subject to a registered mortgage then—
(a) except so far as may be necessary for making the ship or share available as a security for the mortgage debt, the mortgagee shall not by reason of the mortgage be treated as owner of the ship or share; and
(b) the mortgagor shall be treated as not having ceased to be owner of the ship or share.

GENERAL NOTE
The paragraph re-enacts s.34 of the Merchant Shipping Act 1894, referred to in the General Note to para. 9(1), above. The mortgagee has a number of remedies at common law, including the right to take possession of the ship in certain circumstances. Rights may be, and in practice are, granted by the mortgage covenant (and see Meeson, *op. cit.*). The extent of the general rights and the effect that this has on the status of the mortgagee has been the subject of much litigation and discussion (see *Temperley*, pp. 28–44; Clarke, *op. cit.*, pp. 91–99). It might have been helpful if the Merchant Shipping Act 1995 could have codified and clarified some of the issues under discussion. However, the general effect of the paragraph is simply stated, namely that the mortgagor does not cease to be treated as a shipowner where there is a registered mortgage and the mortgagee is not treated as the shipowner, except where it has taken possession and control in order to protect its security (*cf.* s.6(3)).

Transfer of registered mortgage

11.—(1) A registered mortgage may be transferred by an instrument made in the form prescribed by or approved under registration regulations.
(2) Where any such instrument is produced to the registrar, the registrar shall register the transferee in the prescribed manner.

GENERAL NOTE
This paragraph repeats in substance s.37 of the 1894 Act (as amended by Sched. 1, para. 23 of the 1988 Act and its more modern counterpart for fishing vessels, Sched. 3, para. 6 of the 1988 Act). A mortgagee is allowed to transfer a mortgage in accordance with registration regulations under s.10 and the registrar will register the name of the transferee accordingly.

Transmission of registered mortgage by operation of law

12. Where the interest of a mortgagee in a registered mortgage is transmitted to any person by any lawful means other than by a transfer under paragraph 11 above, the registrar shall, on production of the prescribed evidence, cause the name of that person to be entered in the register as mortgagee of the ship or share in question.

GENERAL NOTE
This paragraph repeats in substance s.38 of the 1894 Act and its more modern counterpart for fishing vessels, Sched. 3, para. 7 of the 1988 Act. It allows transmission of a mortgage, *e.g.* by inheritance or insolvency, and the name of the transferee is recorded accordingly. *Cf.* para. 3, above.

Discharge of registered mortgage

13. Where a registered mortgage has been discharged, the registrar shall, on production of the mortgage deed and such evidence of the discharge of the mortgage as may be prescribed, cause an entry to be made in the register to the effect that the mortgage has been discharged.

GENERAL NOTE
This paragraph repeats in substance s.38 of the 1894 Act and its more modern counterpart for fishing vessels, Sched. 3, para. 8 of the 1988 Act. It allows for the discharge of the mortgage on

production to the registrar of such information as is required by the registration regulations under s.10. Note also s.16(3), above.

Definitions

14. In this Schedule—

"mortgage" shall be construed in accordance with paragraph 7(2) above;

"prescribed" means prescribed in registration regulations; and

"registered mortgage" means a mortgage registered under paragraph 7(3) above.

Section 88 SCHEDULE 2

REGULATIONS RELATING TO SUBMERSIBLE AND SUPPORTING APPARATUS

1.—(1) In this Schedule "regulations" means regulations made under section 88 and "prescribed" means prescribed by regulations.

(2) Nothing in this Schedule shall be taken to prejudice the generality of section 88.

Registration of submersible apparatus

2. Regulations made by virtue of section 88(2)(e) of this Act may make provision—

(a) for all matters relevant to the maintenance of a register of submersible apparatus,

(b) without prejudice to sub-paragraph (a) above, for the period for which any registration or exemption is to remain effective without renewal, the alteration or cancellation in any prescribed circumstances of registration or exemption or of any conditions attached thereto, the person by whom and manner in which applications in connection with any registration or exemption are to be made, and information and evidence to be furnished in connection with any such application,

(c) for the marking or other means of identification of any submersible apparatus,

(d) for the issue of certificates of registration or exemption, and the custody, surrender, production or display of the certificates or copies of them,

(e) for matters arising out of the termination of any registration or exemption, or any conditions attached thereto.

Offences

3.—(1) Subject to sub-paragraph (2) below, regulations—

(a) may provide for the creation of offences and for their punishment on summary conviction or on conviction on indictment, and

(b) may afford, in respect of any description of offence created by the regulations, such defence (if any) as may be prescribed.

(2) The punishment for an offence created by regulations shall be—

(a) on summary conviction, a fine not exceeding the statutory maximum,

(b) on conviction on indictment, imprisonment for a term not exceeding two years, or a fine, or both,

but without prejudice to any further restriction contained in the regulations on the punishments which can be awarded and without prejudice to the exclusion by the regulations of proceedings on indictment.

Exemptions from regulations

4.—(1) The operation of any regulations may be excluded in whole or in part in relation to any class or description of submersible or supporting apparatus by regulations, or in relation to any particular apparatus by the direction of the Secretary of State given in such manner as he thinks appropriate.

(2) Any exemption or exclusion by regulations or by directions of the Secretary of State under this paragraph may be made subject to the imposition of conditions specified by the regulations or directions.

(3) Where, in pursuance of this paragraph, a person is exempted or excluded from the requirements of the provisions of regulations but subject to a condition, and the condition is not observed, the exemption or exclusion shall not have effect, and accordingly proceedings may be brought in respect of any offence created by the regulations.

General

5. Regulations—

(a) may provide for their operation anywhere outside the United Kingdom and for their application to persons, whether or not Commonwealth citizens, and to companies, whether or not incorporated under the law of any part of the United Kingdom;

(b) may provide that in any proceedings for an offence under the regulations (other than proceedings to which sub-paragraph (c) below applies) an averment in any process of the fact that anything was done or situated within United Kingdom waters shall, until the contrary is proved, be sufficient evidence of that fact as stated in the averment;

(c) may provide that in any proceedings in Scotland for an offence under the regulations a statement in any complaint or indictment of any such fact as is mentioned in sub-paragraph (b) above shall, until the contrary is proved, be sufficient evidence of the fact as so stated;

(d) may provide that proceedings for an offence under the regulations may be taken, and the offence be treated for all incidental purposes as having been committed, in any place in the United Kingdom;

(e) may provide for any provisions of Part XI relating to inquiries and investigations into marine accidents to apply (with such modifications as may be specified) in relation to accidents involving any submersible apparatus which is not a ship as they apply to ships;

(f) may provide that specified provisions of any enactment (other than section 88 and this Schedule) shall, in such circumstances as may be prescribed, not have effect in relation to such class or description of, or to such particular, submersible or supporting apparatus as may be prescribed;

(g) may make different provision for different classes or descriptions of submersible or supporting apparatus and for different circumstances;

(h) may contain such supplemental and incidental provisions as appear to the Secretary of State to be expedient.

Section 89SCHEDULE 3

LOAD LINES

GENERAL PROVISIONS

Ships to which Schedule applies

1. This Schedule applies to all ships except—
(a) ships of war;
(b) ships solely engaged in fishing; and
(c) pleasure yachts.

Load Line rules

2.—(1) The Secretary of State shall make rules in accordance with the following provisions of this Schedule (referred to as "the load line rules"); and in making those rules the Secretary of State shall have regard in particular to the Convention of 1966.

(2) The load line rules shall make provision—

(a) for the surveying and periodical inspection of ships to which this Schedule applies;

(b) for determining freeboards to be assigned from time to time to such ships;

(c) for determining, in relation to any such ship, the deck which is to be taken to be the freeboard deck of the ship, and for requiring the position of that deck to be indicated on each side of the ship by a mark of a description prescribed by the rules; and

(d) for determining, by reference to that mark and the freeboards for the time being assigned to any such ship, the positions in which each side of the ship is to be marked with lines of a description prescribed by the rules, indicating the various maximum depths to which the ship may be loaded in circumstances prescribed by the rules.

(3) The load line rules shall include the following provisions—

(a) provisions specifying such requirements in respect of the hulls, superstructures, fittings and appliances of ships to which this Schedule applies as appear to the Secretary of State to be relevant to the assignment of freeboards to such ships;

(b) provisions whereby, at the time when freeboards are assigned to a ship in accordance with the load line rules, such particulars relating to those requirements as may be determined in accordance with the rules are to be recorded in such manner as may be so determined; and

(c) provisions for determining by reference to those requirements and that record whether, at any time after freeboards have been so assigned to a ship and while they continue to be so assigned, the ship is for the purposes of this Schedule to be taken to comply, or not to comply, with the conditions of assignment;

and those provisions shall be set out separately in the load line rules under the title of "rules as to conditions of assignment".

(4) The load line rules shall also include provisions requiring such information relating to the stability of any ship to which freeboards are assigned thereunder, and such information relating to the loading and ballasting of any such ship, as may be determined in accordance with the rules to be provided for the guidance of the master of the ship in such manner as may be so determined.

(5) In relation to any matter authorised or required by this Schedule to be prescribed by the load line rules, those rules may make different provision by reference to (or to any combination of) any of the following, that is to say, different descriptions of ships, different areas, different seasons of the year and any other different circumstances.

(6) Except in so far as the context otherwise requires, in this Schedule "deck-line" means such a mark as is referred to in sub-paragraph (2)(c) above, and "load lines" means such lines as are referred to in sub-paragraph (2)(d) above.

UNITED KINGDOM SHIPS

Compliance with load line rules

3.—(1) Subject to any exemption conferred by or under this Schedule, no United Kingdom ship to which this Schedule applies shall proceed or attempt to proceed to sea unless—
   (a) the ship has been surveyed in accordance with the load line rules;
   (b) the ship is marked with a deck-line and with load lines in accordance with those rules;
   (c) the ship complies with the conditions of assignment; and
   (d) the information required by those rules to be provided as mentioned in paragraph 2(4) of this Schedule is provided for the guidance of the master of the ship in the manner determined in accordance with the rules.

(2) If any ship proceeds or attempts to proceed to sea in contravention of sub-paragraph (1) above, the owner or master of the ship shall be liable—
   (a) on summary conviction, to a fine not exceeding the statutory maximum;
   (b) on conviction on indictment, to a fine.

(3) Any ship which in contravention of sub-paragraph (1) above attempts to proceed to sea without being surveyed and marked as mentioned in sub-paragraph (1)(a) and (b) above may be detained until it has been so surveyed and marked.

(4) Any such ship as is mentioned in sub-paragraph (1) above which does not comply with the conditions of assignment shall be deemed to be dangerously unsafe for the purposes of sections 95, 96 and 97.

Submersion of load lines

4.—(1) Where a United Kingdom ship to which this Schedule applies is marked with load lines, the ship shall not be so loaded that—
   (a) if the ship is in salt water and has no list, the appropriate load line on each side of the ship is submerged, or
   (b) in any other case, the appropriate load line on each side of the ship would be submerged if the ship were in salt water and had no list.

(2) If any ship is loaded in contravention of sub-paragraph (1) above, the owner or master of the ship shall (subject to sub-paragraph (5) below) be liable—
   (a) on summary conviction, to a fine not exceeding the statutory maximum and to such additional fine, not exceeding an amount calculated in accordance with sub-paragraph (3) below, as the court thinks fit to impose, having regard to the extent to which the earning capacity of the ship was increased by reason of the contravention;
   (b) on conviction on indictment, to a fine.

(3) Any additional fine imposed under sub-paragraph (2)(a) above shall not exceed £1,000 for each complete centimetre by which—
   (a) in a case falling within sub-paragraph (1)(a) above, the appropriate load line on each side of the ship was submerged, or
   (b) in a case falling within sub-paragraph (1)(b) above, the appropriate load line on each side of the ship would have been submerged as therein mentioned.

(4) If the master of a ship takes the ship to sea when it is loaded in contravention of sub-paragraph (1) above, or if any other person, having reason to believe that the ship is so loaded, sends or is party to sending the ship to sea when it is loaded in contravention of that sub-paragraph, then (without prejudice to any fine to which he may be liable in respect of an offence under sub-paragraph (2) above) he shall be liable—
   (a) on summary conviction, to a fine not exceeding the statutory maximum;

(b) on conviction on indictment, to a fine.

(5) Where a person is charged with an offence under sub-paragraph (2) above, it shall be a defence to prove that the contravention was due solely to deviation or delay and that the deviation or delay was caused solely by stress of weather or other circumstances which neither the master nor the owner nor the charterer (if any) could have prevented or forestalled.

(6) Without prejudice to any proceedings under the preceding provisions of this paragraph, any ship which is loaded in contravention of sub-paragraph (1) above may be detained until it ceases to be so loaded.

(7) For the purposes of the application of this paragraph to a ship in any circumstances prescribed by the load line rules in accordance with paragraph 2(2)(d) of this Schedule, "the appropriate load line" means the load line which, in accordance with those rules, indicates the maximum depth to which the ship may be loaded in salt water in those circumstances.

Miscellaneous offences in relation to marks

5. Where a United Kingdom ship to which this Schedule applies is marked in accordance with any requirements as to marking imposed by or under this Schedule, then if—
 (a) the owner or master of the ship fails without reasonable excuse to keep the ship so marked, or
 (b) any person conceals, removes, alters, defaces or obliterates, or causes or permits any person under his control to conceal, remove, alter, deface or obliterate, any mark with which the ship is so marked, except where he does so under the authority of a person empowered under the load line rules to authorise him for that purpose,
he shall be liable on summary conviction to a fine not exceeding level 5 on the standard scale.

Issue of load line certificates

6.—(1) Where a United Kingdom ship to which this Schedule applies has been surveyed and marked in accordance with the load line rules, the appropriate certificate shall be issued to the owner of the ship on his application.

(2) For the purposes of this paragraph the appropriate certificate—
 (a) in the case of a pre-1966 Convention ship of not less than 150 tons gross tonnage, and in the case of a post-1966 Convention ship of not less than 24 metres in length, is a certificate which shall continue to be called an "International Load Line Certificate (1966)", and
 (b) in the case of any other ship, is a certificate which shall continue to be called a "United Kingdom load line certificate".

(3) Subject to sub-paragraph (4) below, any certificate required by sub-paragraph (1) above to be issued—
 (a) shall be issued by the Secretary of State or by a person authorised for that purpose by the Secretary of State, and
 (b) shall be in such form, and shall be issued in such manner, as may be prescribed by the load line rules.

(4) The Secretary of State may request a Contracting Government, other than Her Majesty's Government in the United Kingdom, to issue an International Load Line Certificate (1966) in respect of any ship to which this Schedule applies which is a United Kingdom ship falling within sub-paragraph (2)(a) above; and the following provisions of this Schedule shall have effect in relation to such a certificate so issued, which contains a statement that it has been issued at the request of Her Majesty's Government in the United Kingdom, as they have effect in relation to an International Load Line Certificate (1966) issued by the Secretary of State.

Effect of load line certificate

7. Where a certificate, issued in pursuance of paragraph 6 and for the time being in force, is produced in respect of the ship to which the certificate relates—
 (a) the ship shall be deemed to have been surveyed in accordance with the load line rules, and
 (b) if lines are marked on the ship corresponding in number and description to the deck-line and load lines as required by the load line rules, and the positions of those lines so marked correspond to the positions of the deck-line and load lines so specified in the certificate, the ship shall be deemed to be marked as required by those rules.

Duration, endorsement and cancellation of load line certificates

8.—(1) The load line rules shall make provision for determining the period during which any certificate issued under paragraph 6 of this Schedule is to remain in force, including—
 (a) provision enabling the period for which any such certificate is originally issued to be extended within such limits and in such circumstances as may be prescribed by the rules, and

(b) provision for cancelling any such certificate in such circumstances as may be so prescribed.

(2) While any such certificate is in force in respect of a ship, there shall be endorsed on the certificate such information relating to—

(a) periodical inspections of the ship in accordance with the load line rules, and

(b) any extension of the period for which the certificate was issued,

as may be prescribed by the rules.

Ships not to proceed to sea without load line certificate

9.—(1) Subject to any exemption conferred by or under this Schedule, no United Kingdom ship to which this Schedule applies shall proceed or attempt to proceed to sea unless the appropriate certificate is in force in respect of the ship.

(2) Before any such ship proceeds to sea, the master of the ship shall produce the appropriate certificate to the officer of customs and excise from whom a clearance for the ship is demanded; and a clearance shall not be granted, and the ship may be detained, until the appropriate certificate is so produced.

(3) If any ship proceeds or attempts to proceed to sea in contravention of this paragraph, the master of the ship shall be liable—

(a) on summary conviction, to a fine not exceeding the statutory maximum;

(b) on conviction on indictment, to a fine.

(4) In this paragraph "the appropriate certificate" means the certificate which is the appropriate certificate for the purposes of paragraph 6 of this Schedule.

Publication of load line certificate and entry of particulars in official log book

10.—(1) Where a certificate is issued in respect of a ship under paragraph 6 of this Schedule the owner of the ship shall forthwith on receipt of the certificate cause it to be framed and posted up in some conspicuous place on board the ship, and shall cause it to be kept so framed and posted up and legible so long as the certificate remains in force and the ship is in use.

(2) Before any United Kingdom ship to which this Schedule applies leaves any dock, wharf, harbour or other place for the purpose of proceeding to sea, the master of the ship, subject to sub-paragraph (4) below, shall cause a notice to be posted up in some conspicuous place on board the ship, which shall be in such form and containing such particulars relating to the depth to which the ship is for the time being loaded as may be specified in regulations made by the Secretary of State under this Schedule.

(3) Where a notice required by sub-paragraph (2) above has been posted up, the master of the ship shall cause it to be kept posted up and legible as required by that sub-paragraph until the ship arrives at some other dock, wharf, harbour or place.

(4) The regulations may exempt ships employed in trading or going between places in the limited European trading area, or any class of such ships specified in the regulations, from the requirements as to notices contained in sub-paragraph (2) above.

(5) If the owner or master of a ship fails to comply with any requirement imposed on him by the preceding provisions of this paragraph, he shall be liable on summary conviction to a fine not exceeding level 3 on the standard scale.

(6) In this paragraph "the limited European trading area" has the same meaning as in regulations under section 47.

Inspection of ships

11. A ship surveyor or engineer surveyor may inspect any United Kingdom ship to which this Schedule applies for the purpose of seeing that the provisions of this Schedule have been complied with in respect of the ship.

NON-UNITED KINGDOM SHIPS

Valid Convention certificates

12.—(1) This paragraph applies to any non-United Kingdom ship to which this Schedule applies which—

(a) is registered in a Convention country or, not being registered in any such country or elsewhere, flies the flag of a Convention country, and

(b) is either a pre-1966 Convention ship of not less than 150 tons gross tonnage or a post-1966 Convention ship of not less than 24 metres in length.

(2) The Secretary of State may, at the request of the Government of the parent country of a ship to which this paragraph applies, issue in respect of the ship a certificate in such form as may

be prescribed by the load line rules, if the Secretary of State is satisfied that he could properly issue a certificate in respect of the ship under paragraph 6(1) of this Schedule if the ship were a United Kingdom ship.

(3) The load line rules shall make such provision as appears to the Secretary of State to be appropriate for securing that certificates which are issued as International Load Line Certificates (1966) in respect of ships to which this paragraph applies, and are so issued by Governments other than Her Majesty's Government in the United Kingdom, shall be recognised for the purposes of this Schedule in such circumstances as may be prescribed by the rules.

(4) Certificates issued as mentioned in sub-paragraph (2) or (3) above shall be included among the certificates called "International Load Line Certificates (1966)".

(5) In this Schedule "valid Convention certificate" means a certificate which either—

(a) has been issued under sub-paragraph (2) above and is for the time being in force, or

(b) having been issued as mentioned in sub-paragraph (3) above, is produced in circumstances in which it is required by the load line rules to be recognised for the purposes of this Schedule.

Compliance with load line rules

13.—(1) Subject to sub-paragraph (2) below, and to any exemption conferred by or under this Schedule, no non-United Kingdom ship to which this Schedule applies shall proceed or attempt to proceed to sea from any port in the United Kingdom unless—

(a) the ship has been surveyed in accordance with the load line rules;

(b) the ship is marked with a deck-line and with load lines in accordance with those rules;

(c) the ship complies with the conditions of assignment; and

(d) the information required by those rules to be provided as mentioned in paragraph 2(4) of this Schedule is provided for the guidance of the master of the ship in the manner determined in accordance with the rules.

(2) Sub-paragraph (1) above does not apply to a ship in respect of which a valid Convention certificate is produced.

(3) If any ship proceeds or attempts to proceed to sea in contravention of the preceding provisions of this paragraph, the owner or master of the ship shall be liable—

(a) on summary conviction, to a fine not exceeding the statutory maximum;

(b) on conviction on indictment, to a fine.

(4) Any ship which in contravention of this paragraph attempts to proceed to sea without being surveyed and marked as mentioned in sub-paragraphs (1)(a) and (b) above may be detained until it has been so surveyed and marked.

(5) If any such ship as is mentioned in sub-paragraph (1) above, not being a ship in respect of which a valid Convention certificate is produced, does not comply with the conditions of assignment it shall be deemed to be dangerously unsafe for the purposes of sections 95, 96 and 97.

Submersion of load lines

14.—(1) Where a non-United Kingdom ship to which this Schedule applies is within any port in the United Kingdom, and is marked with load lines, the ship shall not be so loaded that—

(a) if the ship is in salt water and has no list, the appropriate load line on each side of the ship is submerged, or

(b) in any other case, the appropriate load line on each side of the ship would be submerged if the ship were in salt water and had no list.

(2) Sub-paragraphs (2), (3), (5) and (6) of paragraph 4 of this Schedule shall have effect for the purposes of this paragraph as if any reference in those sub-paragraphs to sub-paragraph (1) of that paragraph, or to sub-paragraph (1)(a) or (b) of that paragraph, were a reference to sub-paragraph (1), or (as the case may be) to the corresponding provision of sub-paragraph (1) of this paragraph, subject, however, to sub-paragraph (3) below.

(3) In the case of a ship to which paragraph 12 of this Schedule applies, the ship shall not be detained, and no proceedings shall be brought by virtue of sub-paragraph (2) above, unless the ship has been inspected by a ship surveyor or engineer surveyor in pursuance of paragraph 17 of this Schedule.

(4) In relation to a ship in respect of which a valid Convention certificate is produced, "load line" in sub-paragraph (1) above means a line marked on the ship in the position of a load line specified in that certificate; and for the purposes of the application of the relevant provisions to such a ship in any circumstances for which a particular load line is specified in the certificate, the "appropriate load line" means the load line which, in accordance with the certificate, indicates the maximum depth to which the ship may be loaded in salt water in those circumstances.

(5) Where a valid Convention certificate is not produced in respect of a ship, then, for the purposes of the application of the relevant provisions to that ship in any circumstances prescribed by the load line rules in accordance with paragraph 2(2)(d) of this Schedule, "the appropriate load line" means the load line which, in accordance with those rules, indicates the maximum depth to which the ship may be loaded in salt water in those circumstances.

(6) In sub-paragraphs (4) and (5) above "the relevant provisions" means the provisions of sub-paragraph (1) above and any provisions of paragraph 4 of this Schedule as applied by sub-paragraph (2) above.

United Kingdom load line certificates

15.—(1) Where a non-United Kingdom ship to which this Schedule applies has been surveyed and marked in accordance with the load line rules, then on the application of the owner of the ship a United Kingdom load line certificate shall be issued to him by the Secretary of State or by a person authorised for the purpose by the Secretary of State.

(2) Subject to sub-paragraph (3) below, paragraphs 7 and 8 of this Schedule shall have effect in relation to a certificate issued under sub-paragraph (1) above as they have effect in relation to a certificate issued under paragraph 6 of this Schedule.

(3) Any certificate issued under sub-paragraph (1) above in respect of a ship to which paragraph 12 of this Schedule applies shall be valid only so long as the ship is not plying on international voyages, and shall be cancelled by the Secretary of State if he has reason to believe that the ship is plying on international voyages.

Production of certificate to customs and excise officer

16.—(1) Subject to any exemption conferred by or under this Schedule, before a non-United Kingdom ship to which this Schedule applies proceeds to sea from any port in the United Kingdom, the master of the ship shall produce the appropriate certificate to the officer of customs and excise from whom a clearance for the ship is demanded, and a clearance shall not be granted, and the ship may be detained, until the appropriate certificate is so produced.

(2) For the purposes of this paragraph the appropriate certificate—

(a) in the case of a ship to which paragraph 12 of this Schedule applies, where a clearance for the ship is demanded in respect of an international voyage, is a valid Convention certificate;

(b) in the case of any such ship, where a clearance for the ship is demanded in respect of any other voyage, is either a valid Convention certificate or a United Kingdom load line certificate for the time being in force in respect of the ship; and

(c) in any other case, is a United Kingdom load line certificate for the time being in force in respect of the ship.

Provisions as to inspection

17.—(1) Subject to the following provisions of this paragraph, a ship surveyor or engineer surveyor may inspect any non-United Kingdom ship to which this Schedule applies while the ship is within any port in the United Kingdom.

(2) Any such surveyor may go on board any ship to which paragraph 12 of this Schedule applies, while the ship is within any port in the United Kingdom, for the purpose of demanding production of any International Load Line Certificate (1966) or United Kingdom load line certificate for the time being in force in respect of the ship.

(3) If on any such demand a valid Convention certificate is produced to the surveyor in respect of the ship, the powers of the surveyor under sub-paragraph (1) above shall be limited to seeing—

(a) that the ship is not loaded beyond the limits allowed by the certificate;

(b) that lines are marked on the ship in the positions of the load lines specified in the certificate;

(c) that no material alterations have taken place in the hull or superstructures of the ship which affect the position in which any of those lines ought to be marked; and

(d) that the fittings and appliances for the protection of openings, the guard rails, the freeing ports and the means of access to the crew's quarters have been maintained on the ship in as effective a condition as they were in when the certificate was issued.

(4) If on an inspection of a ship under this paragraph the ship is found to have been so materially altered in respect of the matters referred to in sub-paragraph (3)(c) or (d) above that the ship

is manifestly unfit to proceed to sea without danger to human life, it shall be deemed to be dangerously unsafe for the purposes of sections 95, 96 and 97.

(5) Where a ship is detained under the provisions of this Act as applied by sub-paragraph (4) above, the Secretary of State shall order the ship to be released as soon as he is satisfied that the ship is fit to proceed to sea without danger to human life.

EXEMPTIONS

Power to make exemption orders

18.—(1) If in the opinion of the Secretary of State the sheltered nature and conditions of international voyages—

(a) between near neighbouring ports in the United Kingdom and in another Convention country, or

(b) between near neighbouring ports in any two or more countries or territories outside the United Kingdom,

make it unreasonable or impracticable to apply the provisions of this Schedule to ships plying on such voyages, and the Secretary of State is satisfied that the Government of the other country or territory (or, as the case may be, of each of the other countries or territories) concurs in that opinion, the Secretary of State may by order specifying those ports direct that ships plying on international voyages between those ports, or any class of such ships specified in the order, shall be exempt from the provisions of this Schedule.

(2) The Secretary of State may by order direct that ships under 80 tons register engaged solely in the coasting trade, or any class of such ships specified in the order, shall be exempt from the provisions of this Schedule while not carrying cargo, or (if the order so provides) shall be exempt from the provisions of this Schedule whether carrying cargo or not.

(3) Any order under this paragraph may be made subject to such conditions as the Secretary of State thinks fit; and, where any such order is made subject to conditions, the exemption conferred by that order shall not have effect in relation to a ship unless the ship complies with those conditions.

Further powers to exempt ships

19.—(1) In this paragraph any reference to exempting a ship is a reference to exempting the ship either—

(a) from all the provisions of this Schedule and of the load line rules, or

(b) from such of those provisions as are specified in the instrument conferring the exemption.

(2) On the application of the owner of a United Kingdom ship to which this Schedule applies which is either a pre-1966 Convention ship of not less than 150 tons gross tonnage or a post-1966 Convention ship of not less than 24 metres in length, the Secretary of State may exempt the ship if in his opinion the ship embodies features of a novel kind such that, if the ship had to comply with all the requirements of this Schedule and of the load line rules, the development of those features and their incorporation in ships engaged on international voyages might be seriously impeded.

(3) On the application of the owner of a United Kingdom ship to which this Schedule applies which is either—

(a) a pre-1966 Convention ship of less than 150 tons gross tonnage or a post-1966 Convention ship of less than 24 metres in length, or

(b) a ship (not falling within (a) above) which does not ply on international voyages,

the Secretary of State may exempt the ship.

(4) Without prejudice to sub-paragraph (3) above, where a United Kingdom ship to which this Schedule applies which is either a pre-1966 Convention ship of not less than 150 tons gross tonnage or a post-1966 Convention ship of not less than 24 metres in length, does not normally ply on international voyages but is, in exceptional circumstances, required to undertake a single international voyage, the Secretary of State, on the application of the owner of the ship, specifying the international voyage in question, may exempt the ship while engaged on that voyage.

(5) Any exemption conferred under this paragraph may be conferred subject to such conditions as the Secretary of State thinks fit; and, where any such exemption is conferred subject to conditions, the exemption shall not have effect unless those conditions are complied with.

Issue of exemption certificates

20.—(1) Where the Secretary of State exempts a ship under paragraph 19 of this Schedule, the Secretary of State shall issue the appropriate certificate to the owner of the ship.

(2) For the purposes of this paragraph the appropriate certificate—

(a) where the exemption is conferred under sub-paragraph (2) or sub-paragraph (4) of paragraph 19 of this Schedule, is an "International Load Line Exemption Certificate", and

(b) where the certificate is conferred under sub-paragraph (3) of that paragraph, is a "United Kingdom load line exemption certificate".

(3) Any certificate issued under this paragraph shall be in such form, and shall be issued in such manner, as may be prescribed by the load line rules.

Duration and termination of exemptions, and duration, endorsement and cancellation of exemption certificates

21.—(1) The load line rules shall make provision for determining the period during which any exemption conferred under paragraph 19 of this Schedule, or any certificate issued under paragraph 20 of this Schedule, is to remain in force, including—

(a) provision enabling the period for which any exemption or certificate is originally conferred or issued to be extended within such limits and in such circumstances as may be prescribed by the rules, and

(b) provision for terminating any such exemption, and for cancelling any such certificate, in such circumstances as may be so prescribed.

(2) While any such certificate is in force in respect of a ship, there shall be endorsed on the certificate such information relating to—

(a) periodical inspections of the ship in accordance with the load line rules, and

(b) any extension of the period for which the certificate was issued,

as may be prescribed by the rules.

International Load Line Exemption Certificates

22.—(1) The load line rules shall make such provision as appears to the Secretary of State to be appropriate for securing that exemption certificates which, in accordance with the Convention of 1966, are issued in respect of ships to which paragraph 12 of this Schedule applies, and are so issued by Governments other than Her Majesty's Government in the United Kingdom, shall in such circumstances as may be prescribed by the rules have the like effect for the purposes of this Schedule as if they were valid Convention certificates.

(2) Certificates issued as mentioned in sub-paragraph (1) above shall be included among "International Load Line Exemption Certificates".

SUBDIVISION LOAD LINES AND DECK CARGO

Subdivision load lines

23.—(1) Where in pursuance of safety regulations a United Kingdom passenger ship to which this Schedule applies is marked with subdivision load lines, and the lowest of those lines is lower than the line which, apart from this sub-paragraph, would be the appropriate load line for the purposes of paragraph 4 of this Schedule, the said paragraph 4 shall have effect as if that subdivision load line were the appropriate load line for the purposes of that paragraph.

(2) Where in pursuance of safety regulations a non-United Kingdom passenger ship to which this Schedule applies is marked with subdivision load lines, and the lowest of those load lines is lower than the line which, apart from this sub-paragraph, would be the appropriate load line for the purposes of paragraph 14 of this Schedule, that paragraph shall have effect as if that subdivision load line were the appropriate load line for the purposes of that paragraph.

Deck cargo

24.—(1) The Secretary of State shall make regulations (in this paragraph referred to as "the deck cargo regulations") prescribing requirements to be complied with where cargo is carried in any uncovered space on the deck of a ship to which this Schedule applies; and different requirements may be so prescribed in relation to different descriptions of ships, different descriptions of cargo, different voyages or classes of voyages, different seasons of the year or any other different circumstances.

(2) If the load line rules provide (either generally or in particular cases or classes of cases) for assigning special freeboards to ships which are to have effect only where a cargo of timber is so carried, then (without prejudice to the generality of sub-paragraph (1) above) the deck cargo regulations may prescribe special requirements to be complied with in circumstances where any such special freeboard has effect.

(3) In prescribing any such special requirements as are mentioned in sub-paragraph (2) above, the Secretary of State shall have regard in particular to the provisions of Chapter IV of the Convention of 1966.

(4) If any provisions of the deck cargo regulations are contravened—

(a) in the case of a United Kingdom ship, or

(b) in the case of any other ship while the ship is within any port in the United Kingdom,

the master of the ship shall (subject to sub-paragraph (5) below) be liable—

   (i) on summary conviction, to a fine not exceeding the statutory maximum;

   (ii) on conviction on indictment, to a fine.

(5) Where a person is charged with an offence under sub-paragraph (4) above, it shall be a defence to prove that the contravention was due solely to deviation or delay and that the deviation or delay was caused solely by stress of weather or other circumstances which neither the master nor the owner nor the charterer (if any) could have prevented or forestalled.

(6) For the purpose of securing compliance with the deck cargo regulations, any person authorised for the purpose by the Secretary of State may inspect any ship to which this Schedule applies which is carrying cargo in any uncovered space on its deck.

MISCELLANEOUS PROVISIONS

Notice to consular officer of proceedings against foreign ships

25.—(1) Where any non-United Kingdom ship is detained under this Schedule, and where any proceedings are taken under this Schedule against the master or owner of any such ship, notice shall forthwith be served on the consular officer for the country to which the ship belongs at or nearest to the port where the ship is for the time being.

(2) A notice under this paragraph shall specify the grounds on which the ship has been detained or the proceedings have been taken.

Delivery up of certificates

26.—(1) The Secretary of State may require any certificate which can be issued under this Schedule, which has expired or been cancelled, to be delivered up as he directs.

(2) If any owner or master of a ship fails without reasonable excuse to comply with such a requirement he shall be liable, on summary conviction, to a fine not exceeding level 2 on the standard scale.

Penalty for false statements etc.

27.—(1) If any person intentionally makes, or assists in making, or procures to be made, a false or fraudulent certificate which can be issued under this Schedule he shall be liable—

(a) on summary conviction, to a fine not exceeding the statutory maximum or to imprisonment for a term not exceeding six months or both;

(b) on conviction on indictment, to imprisonment for a term not exceeding two years or a fine.

(2) In Scotland, if any person—

(a) forges, assists in forging or procures to be forged,

(b) fraudulently alters, assists in fraudulently altering or procures to be fraudulently altered,

any certificate which can be issued under this Schedule he shall be liable—

   (i) on summary conviction, to a fine not exceeding the statutory maximum or to imprisonment for a term not exceeding six months or both; or

   (ii) on conviction on indictment, to a fine or to imprisonment or to both.

Admissibility of certificates in evidence

28. Any certificate issued under this Schedule shall be admissible in evidence.

Convention countries

29.—(1) Her Majesty, if satisfied—

(a) that the Government of a country has accepted or acceded to, or has denounced, the Convention of 1966, or

(b) that the Convention of 1966 extends, or has ceased to extend, to a particular territory, may by Order in Council make a declaration to that effect.

(2) In this Schedule "Convention country" means a country or territory which is either—

(a) a country the Government of which has been declared under this paragraph to have accepted or acceded to the Convention of 1966, and has not been so declared to have denounced that Convention, or

(b) a territory to which it has been so declared that the Convention of 1966 extends, not being a territory to which it has been so declared that that Convention has ceased to extend, and "Contracting Government" means any such Government as is referred to in (a) above.

Orders, rules and regulations

30. Any Order in Council, order, rules or regulations made under this Schedule may contain such transitional or other incidental and supplementary provisions as may appear to Her Majesty in Council, or (as the case may be) to the Secretary of State, to be appropriate.

Interpretation

31.—(1) In this Schedule, except in so far as the context otherwise requires—

"alteration" includes deterioration;

"clearance" includes transire;

"the Convention of 1966" means the International Convention on Load Lines which was signed in London on 5th April 1966;

"Convention country" and "Contracting Government" have the meanings given to them by paragraph 29(2) of this Schedule;

"non-United Kingdom ship" means a ship which is not registered in the United Kingdom;

"post-1966 Convention ship" means a ship whose keel is laid, or which is at a similar stage of construction, on or after the material date; and "pre-1966 Convention ship" means a ship which is not a post-1966 Convention ship;

"parent country", in relation to a ship, means the country or territory in which the ship is registered, or, if the ship is not registered anywhere, means the country or territory whose flag the ship flies;

"valid Convention certificate" has the meaning given to it by paragraph 12(5) of this Schedule.

(2) For the purposes of the definitions of pre-1966 and post-1966 Convention ship the material date—

(a) in relation to a ship whose parent country is a Convention country other than the United Kingdom, is the date as from which it is declared under paragraph 29 of this Schedule either that the Government of that country has accepted or acceded to the Convention of 1966 or that it is a territory to which that Convention extends, and

(b) in relation to any other ship, is 21st July 1968.

(3) In this Schedule, subject to sub-paragraph (4) below, "international voyage" means a voyage between—

(a) a port in the United Kingdom and a port outside the United Kingdom, or

(b) a port in a Convention country (other than the United Kingdom) and a port in any other country or territory (whether a Convention country or not) which is outside the United Kingdom.

(4) In determining, for the purposes of sub-paragraph (3) above, what are the ports between which a voyage is made, no account shall be taken of any deviation by a ship from its intended voyage which is due solely to stress of weather or any other circumstance which neither the master nor the owner nor the charterer (if any) of the ship could have prevented or forestalled; and for the purposes of that sub-paragraph any colony, protectorate or other dependency, and any territory for whose international relations a Government is separately responsible shall be taken to be a separate territory.

(5) Any reference in this Schedule to the gross tonnage of a ship shall be construed as a reference to the tonnage of the ship as ascertained in accordance with the tonnage regulations, and, where in accordance with those regulations alternative tonnages are assigned to a ship, the gross tonnage of the ship shall, for the purposes of this Schedule, be taken to be the larger of those tonnages.

(6) For the purposes of this Schedule the length of a ship shall be ascertained in accordance with regulations made by the Secretary of State under this Schedule.

(7) Any reference in this Schedule to any provision of the Convention of 1966 shall, in relation to any time after that provision has been amended in pursuance of Article 29 of that Convention, be construed as a reference to that provision as so amended.

PREVENTION OF OIL POLLUTION: TRANSITORY PROVISIONS

GENERAL NOTE

Schedule 4 contains the law relating to liability for oil pollution damage as it now applies under the 1969 Liability Convention and the 1971 Fund Convention: see the General Notes to Pt. VI, Ch. III and s.152, above. A brief overview will be given of the provisions in Sched. 4, as derived from the Merchant Shipping (Oil Pollution) Act 1971 and the Merchant Shipping Act 1974.

Schedule 4, Ch. III is derived from the 1971 Act (designed to implement the 1969 Liability Convention) which established a regime of strict liability for oil pollution resulting from escapes from tankers. Shipowners were allowed a number of restricted defences and given the right to limit liability according to the size of the tanker. The maximum limit is about £12.5 million, but could be considerably less for smaller vessels. Shipowners were to carry compulsory insurance for this new liability (something not generally required in maritime law), and insurers could be sued directly. There was a procedure to ensure that claims from a single disaster affecting a number of Convention countries could be brought in just one action. "Channelling" provisions were introduced to prevent claimants proceeding under the general law in circumstances where the Convention applied. Schedule 4, s.154 produces a bunker liability regime equivalent to the law under the existing international tanker liability regime governed by the 1969 Liability Convention as enacted in the Merchant Shipping (Oil Pollution) Act 1971.

Schedule 4, Ch. IV is derived from the 1974 Act (designed to implement the 1971 Fund Convention) which recognised the creation of a Fund, administered in London, and contributed to by oil cargo importers. The purpose of the Fund was to provide a supplement to the 1969 Liability Convention and to give recognition to the fact that oil pollution may be as much the responsibility of the cargo owner as the carrier. The Fund limits were originally about £24 million and from December 1, 1987 were raised to about £55 million.

CHAPTER III

LIABILITY FOR OIL POLLUTION

Meaning of "the Liability Convention" and related expressions

152.—(1) In this Chapter—

"the Liability Convention" means the International Convention on Civil Liability for Oil Pollution Damage signed in Brussels in 1969;

"Liability Convention country" means a country in respect of which the Liability Convention is in force; and

"Liability Convention State" means a State which is a party to the Convention.

(2) If Her Majesty by Order in Council declares that any State specified in the Order is a party to the Liability Convention in respect of any country so specified the Order shall, while in force, be conclusive evidence that that State is a party to the Liability Convention in respect of that country.

Liability

Liability for oil pollution in case of tankers

153.—(1) Where, as a result of any occurrence taking place while a ship is carrying a cargo of persistent oil in bulk, any persistent oil carried by the ship (whether as part of the cargo or otherwise) is discharged or escapes from the ship, the owner of the ship shall be liable, (except as otherwise provided by this Chapter),—

(a) for any damage caused in the territory of the United Kingdom by contamination resulting from the discharge or escape; and

(b) for the cost of any measures reasonably taken after the discharge or escape for the purpose of preventing or reducing any such damage in the territory of the United Kingdom; and

(c) for any damage caused in the territory of the United Kingdom by any measures so taken.

(2) Where a person incurs a liability under subsection (1) above he shall also be liable for any damage or cost for which he would be liable under that subsection if the references therein to the territory of the United Kingdom included the territory of any other Liability Convention country.

(3) Where persistent oil is discharged or escapes from two or more ships and—

(a) a liability is incurred under this section by the owner of each of them; but

(b) the damage or cost for which each of the owners would be liable cannot reasonably be separated from that for which the other or others would be liable;

each of the owners shall be liable, jointly with the other or others, for the whole of the damage or cost for which the owners together would be liable under this section.

(4) For the purposes of this Chapter, where more than one discharge or escape results from the same occurrence or from a series of occurrences having the same origin, they shall be treated as one; but any measures taken after the first of them shall be deemed to have been taken after the discharge or escape.

(5) The Law Reform (Contributory Negligence) Act 1945 and, in Northern Ireland, the Law Reform (Miscellaneous Provisions) Act (Northern Ireland) 1948 shall apply in relation to any damage or cost for which a person is liable under this section, but which is not due to his fault, as if it were due to his fault.

Liability for oil pollution in case of other ships

154.—(1) Where, as a result of any occurrence, any persistent oil is discharged or escapes from a ship other than a ship to which section 153 applies, then (except as otherwise provided by this Chapter) the owner of the ship shall be liable—

(a) for any damage caused outside the ship in the territory of the United Kingdom by contamination resulting from the discharge or escape; and

(b) for the cost of any measures reasonably taken after the discharge or escape for the purpose of preventing or minimising any damage so caused in the territory of the United Kingdom by contamination resulting from the discharge or escape; and

(c) for any damage so caused in the territory of the United Kingdom by any measures so taken.

(2) Where, as a result of any occurrence, there arises a grave and imminent threat of damage being caused outside a ship other than a ship to which section 153 applies by the contamination which might result if there were a discharge or escape of persistent oil from the ship, then (except as otherwise provided by this Chapter) the owner of the ship shall be liable—

(a) for the cost of any measures reasonably taken for the purpose of preventing or minimising any such damage in the territory of the United Kingdom; and

(b) for any damage caused outside the ship in the territory of the United Kingdom by any measures so taken;

and in the subsequent provisions of this Chapter any such threat is referred to as a relevant threat of contamination.

(3) Where—

(a) as a result of any occurrence, a liability is incurred under this section by the owner of each of two or more ships, but

(b) the damage or cost for which each of the owners would be liable cannot reasonably be separated from that for which the other or others would be liable,

each of the owners shall be liable, jointly with the other or others, for the whole of the damage or cost for which the owners together would be liable under this section.

(4) The Law Reform (Contributory Negligence) Act 1945 and, in Northern Ireland, the Law Reform (Miscellaneous Provisions) Act (Northern Ireland) 1948 shall apply in relation to any damage or cost for which a person is liable under this section, but which is not due to his fault, as if it were due to his fault.

(5) In this section "ship" includes a vessel which is not seagoing.

Exceptions from liability under section 153

155. The owner of a ship from which persistent oil has been discharged or has escaped shall not incur any liability under section 153 if he proves that the discharge or escape—

(a) resulted from an act of war, hostilities, civil war, insurrection or an exceptional, inevitable and irresistible natural phenomenon; or

(b) was due wholly to anything done or left undone by another person, not being a servant or agent of the owner, with intent to do damage; or

(c) was due wholly to the negligence or wrongful act of a government or other authority in exercising its function of maintaining lights or other navigational aids for the maintenance of which it was responsible.

Exceptions from liability under section 154

155A. No liability shall be incurred by the owner of a ship under section 154 by reason of any discharge or escape of persistent oil from the ship, or by reason of any relevant threat of contamination, if he proves that the discharge or escape, or (as the case may be) the threat of contamination—

(a) resulted from an act of war, hostilities, civil war, insurrection or an exceptional, inevitable and irresistible natural phenomenon; or

(b) was due wholly to anything done or omitted to be done by another person, not being a servant or agent of the owner, with intent to do damage; or

(c) was due wholly to the negligence or wrongful act of a government or other authority in exercising its function of maintaining lights or other navigational aids for the maintenance of which it was responsible.

Restriction of liability for oil pollution

156. Where, as a result of any occurrence taking place while a ship is carrying a cargo of persistent oil in bulk, any persistent oil carried by the ship is discharged or escapes then, whether or not the owner incurs a liability under section 153—
  (a) he shall not be liable otherwise than under that section for any such damage or cost as is mentioned therein; and
  (b) no servant or agent of the owner nor any person performing salvage operations with the agreement of the owner shall be liable for any such damage or cost.

Restriction of liability for oil pollution from ship within section 154

156A.—(1) Where, as a result of any occurrence—
  (a) any persistent oil is discharged or escapes from a ship to which section 154 applies, or
  (b) there arises a relevant threat of contamination,
then, whether or not the owner of the ship in question incurs a liability under section 154—
  (i) he shall not be liable otherwise than under that section for any such damage or cost as is mentioned in it, and
  (ii) no person to whom this paragraph applies shall be liable for any such damage or cost unless it resulted from anything done or omitted to be done by him either with intent by him to cause any such damage or cost or recklessly and in the knowledge that any such damage or cost would probably result.
(2) Subsection (1)(ii) of this section applies to—
  (a) any servant or agent of the owner of the ship;
  (b) any person not falling within paragraph (a) above but employed or engaged in any capacity on board the ship or to perform any service for the ship;
  (c) any charterer of the ship (however described and including a bareboat charterer), and any manager or operator of the ship;
  (d) any person performing salvage operations with the consent of the owner of the ship or on the instructions of a competent public authority;
  (e) any person taking any such measures as are mentioned in subsection (1)(b) or (2)(a) of section 154;
  (f) any servant or agent of a person falling within paragraph (c), (d) or (e) above.
(3) The liability of the owner of a ship under section 154 for any impairment of the environment shall be taken to be a liability only in respect of—
  (a) any resulting loss of profits, and
  (b) the cost of any reasonable measures of reinstatement actually taken or to be taken.

Limitation of liability

Limitation of liability under section 153

157.—(1) Where the owner of a ship incurs liability under section 153 by reason of a discharge or escape which has occurred without his actual fault or privity then—
  (a) he may limit that liability in accordance with the provisions of this Chapter, and
  (b) if he does so, his liability (that is to say, the aggregate of his liabilities under section 153 resulting from the discharge or escape) shall not exceed 133 special drawing rights for each ton of the ship's tonnage nor (where that tonnage would result in a greater amount) 14 million special drawing rights.
(2) For the purposes of this section the tonnage of a ship shall be ascertained as follows—
  (a) where the registered tonnage of the ship has been or can be ascertained in accordance with the tonnage regulations, the ship's tonnage shall be the registered tonnage of the ship as so ascertained but without making any deduction required by those regulations of any tonnage allowance for propelling machinery space;
  (b) where the ship is of a description with respect to which no provision is for the time being made by the tonnage regulations, the tonnage of the ship shall be taken to be 40 per cent of the weight (expressed in tons of 2,240 lbs) of oil which the ship is capable of carrying;
  (c) where the tonnage of the ship cannot be ascertained in accordance with either paragraph (a) or paragraph (b) above, a surveyor of ships shall, if so directed by the court, certify what, on the evidence specified in the direction, would in his opinion be the tonnage of the ship as ascertained in accordance with paragraph (a), or (as the case may be) paragraph (b), above if the ship could be duly measured for the purpose; and the tonnage stated in his certificate shall be taken to be the tonnage of the ship.

Limitation actions

158.—(1) Where the owner of a ship has or is alleged to have incurred a liability under section 153 he may apply to the court for the limitation of that liability to an amount determined in accordance with section 157.

(2) If on such an application the court finds that the applicant has incurred such a liability and is entitled to limit it, the court shall, after determining the limit of the liability and directing payment into the court of the amount of that limit,—

(a) determine the amounts that would, apart from the limit, be due in respect of the liability to the several persons making claims in the proceedings; and

(b) direct the distribution of the amount paid into court (or, as the case may be, so much of it as does not exceed the liability) among those persons in proportion to their claims, subject to subsections (7) to (10) below.

(3) A payment into court of the amount of a limit determined in pursuance of this section shall be made in sterling in accordance with subsection (4) below.

(4) For the purpose of converting such an amount from special drawing rights into sterling one special drawing right shall be treated as equal to such a sum in sterling as the International Monetary Fund have fixed as being the equivalent of one special drawing right for—

(a) the day on which the determination is made, or

(b) if no sum has been so fixed for that day, the last day before that day for which a sum has been so fixed.

(5) A certificate given by or on behalf of the Treasury stating—

(a) that a particular sum in sterling has been fixed by the International Monetary Fund for the day on which the determination was made; or

(b) that no sum has been so fixed for that day and that a particular sum in sterling has been so fixed for a day which is the last day for which a sum has been so fixed before the day on which the determination was made,

shall be conclusive evidence of those matters for the purposes of this Chapter.

(6) A document purporting to be such a certificate shall, in any proceedings, be received in evidence and, unless the contrary is proved, be deemed to be such a certificate.

(7) No claim shall be admitted in proceedings under this section unless it is made within such time as the court may direct or such further time as the court may allow.

(8) Where any sum has been paid in or towards satisfaction of any claim in respect of the damage or cost to which the liability extends,—

(a) by the owner or the person referred to in section 165 as "the insurer"; or

(b) by a person who has or is alleged to have incurred a liability, otherwise than under section 153, for the damage or cost and who is entitled to limit his liability in connection with the ship by virtue of section 185 or 186;

the person who paid the sum shall, to the extent of that sum, be in the same position with respect to any distribution made in proceedings under this section as the person to whom it was paid would have been.

(9) Where the person who incurred the liability has voluntarily made any reasonable sacrifice or taken any other reasonable measures to prevent or reduce damage to which the liability extends or might have extended he shall be in the same position with respect to any distribution made in proceedings under this section as if he had a claim in respect of the liability equal to the cost of the sacrifice or other measures.

(10) The court may, if it thinks fit, postpone the distribution of such part of the amount to be distributed as it deems appropriate having regard to any claims that may later be established before a court of any country outside the United Kingdom.

Restriction on enforcement after establishment of limitation fund

159.—(1) Where the court has found that a person who has incurred a liability under section 153 is entitled to limit that liability to any amount and he has paid into court a sum not less than that amount—

(a) the court shall order the release of any ship or other property arrested in connection with a claim in respect of that liability or any security given to prevent or obtain release from such an arrest; and

(b) no judgment or decree for any such claim shall be enforced, except so far as it is for costs (or, in Scotland, expenses);

if the sum paid into court, or such part thereof as corresponds to the claim, will be actually available to the claimant or would have been available to him if the proper steps in the proceedings under section 158 had been taken.

(2) In the application of this section to Scotland, any reference (however expressed) to release from arrest shall be construed as a reference to the recall of an arrestment.

Concurrent liabilities of owners and others

160. Where, as a result of any discharge or escape of persistent oil from a ship, the owner of the ship incurs a liability under section 153 and any other person incurs a liability, otherwise than under that section, for any such damage or cost as is mentioned in subsection (1) of that section then, if—

(a) the owner has been found, in proceedings under section 158 to be entitled to limit his liability to any amount and has paid into court a sum not less than that amount; and

(b) the other person is entitled to limit his liability in connection with the ship by virtue of section 185 or 186;

no proceedings shall be taken against the other person in respect of his liability, and if any such proceedings were commenced before the owner paid the sum into court, no further steps shall be taken in the proceedings except in relation to costs.

Establishment of limitation fund outside United Kingdom

161. Where the events resulting in the liability of any person under section 153 also resulted in a corresponding liability under the law of another Liability Convention country sections 159 and 160 shall apply as if the references to sections 153 and 158 included references to the corresponding provisions of that law and the references to sums paid into court included references to any sums secured under those provisions in respect of the liability.

Extinguishment of claims

162. No action to enforce a claim in respect of a liability incurred under section 153 or 154 shall be entertained by any court in the United Kingdom unless the action is commenced not later than three years after the claim arose nor later than six years after the occurrence or first of the occurrences resulting in the discharge or escape by reason of which the liability was incurred.

Compulsory insurance

Compulsory insurance against liability for pollution

163.—(1) Subject to the provisions of this Chapter relating to Government ships, subsection (2) below shall apply to any ship carrying in bulk a cargo of more than 2,000 tons of persistent oil of a description specified in regulations made by the Secretary of State.

(2) The ship shall not enter or leave a port in the United Kingdom or arrive at or leave a terminal in the territorial sea of the United Kingdom nor, if the ship is a United Kingdom ship, a port in any other country or a terminal in the territorial sea of any other country, unless there is in force a certificate complying with the provisions of subsection (3) below and showing that there is in force in respect of the ship a contract of insurance or other security satisfying the requirements of Article VII of the Liability Convention (cover for owner's liability).

For the purposes of this subsection the reference in Article VII to Article V of the Liability Convention shall be construed as a reference to Article V as amended by Article II of the protocol dated 19th November 1976 to the Liability Convention.

(3) The certificate must be—

(a) if the ship is a United Kingdom ship, a certificate issued by the Secretary of State;

(b) if the ship is registered in a Liability Convention country other than the United Kingdom, a certificate issued by or under the authority of the government of the other Liability Convention country; and

(c) if the ship is registered in a country which is not a Liability Convention country, a certificate issued by the Secretary of State or a certificate recognised for the purposes of this paragraph by regulations made under this section.

(4) The Secretary of State may by regulations provide that certificates in respect of ships registered in any, or any specified, country which is not a Liability Convention country shall, in such circumstances as may be specified in the regulations, be recognised for the purposes of subsection (3)(c) above if issued by or under the authority of the government of the country designated in the regulations for that purpose; and the country that may be so designated may be either or both of the following, that is to say—

(a) the country in which the ship is registered; and

(b) any country specified in the regulations for the purposes of this paragraph.

(5) Any certificate required by this section to be in force in respect of a ship shall be carried in the ship and shall, on demand, be produced by the master to any officer of customs and excise or of the Secretary of State and, if the ship is a United Kingdom ship, to any proper officer.

(6) If a ship enters or leaves, or attempts to enter or leave, a port or arrives at or leaves, or attempts to arrive at or leave, a terminal in contravention of subsection (2) above, the master or owner shall be liable—

(a) on summary conviction, to a fine not exceeding £50,000;

(b) on conviction on indictment, to a fine.

(7) If a ship fails to carry, or the master of a ship fails to produce, a certificate as required by subsection (5) above, the master shall be liable on summary conviction to a fine not exceeding level 4 on the standard scale.

(8) If a ship attempts to leave a port in the United Kingdom in contravention of this section the ship may be detained.

Issue of certificate by Secretary of State

164.—(1) Subject to subsection (2) below, if the Secretary of State is satisfied, on an application for such a certificate as is mentioned in section 163 in respect of a United Kingdom ship or a ship registered in any country which is not a Liability Convention country, that there will be in force in respect of the ship, throughout the period for which the certificate is to be issued, a contract of insurance or other security satisfying the requirements of Article VII of the Liability Convention, the Secretary of State shall issue such a certificate to the owner.

For the purposes of this subsection the reference in Article VII to Article V of the Liability Convention shall be construed as a reference to Article V as amended by Article II of the protocol dated 19th November 1976 to the Liability Convention.

(2) If the Secretary of State is of opinion that there is a doubt whether the person providing the insurance or other security will be able to meet his obligations thereunder, or whether the insurance or other security will cover the owner's liability under section 153 in all circumstances, he may refuse the certificates.

(3) The Secretary of State may make regulations providing for the cancellation and delivery up of a certificate under this section in such circumstances as may be prescribed by the regulations.

(4) If a person required by regulations under subsection (3) above to deliver up a certificate fails to do so he shall be liable on summary conviction to a fine not exceeding level 4 on the standard scale.

(5) The Secretary of State shall send a copy of any certificate issued by him under this section in respect of a United Kingdom ship to the Registrar General of Shipping and Seamen, and the Registrar shall make the copy available for public inspection.

Rights of third parties against insurers

165.—(1) Where it is alleged that the owner of a ship has incurred a liability under section 153 as a result of any discharge or escape of oil occurring while there was in force a contract of insurance or other security to which such a certificate as is mentioned in section 163 related, proceedings to enforce a claim in respect of the liability may be brought against the person who provided the insurance or other security (in the following provisions of this section referred to as "the insurer").

(2) In any proceedings brought against the insurer by virtue of this section it shall be a defence (in addition to any defence affecting the owner's liability) to prove that the discharge or escape was due to the wilful misconduct of the owner himself.

(3) The insurer may limit his liability in respect of claims made against him by virtue of this section in like manner and to the same extent as the owner may limit his liability but the insurer may do so whether or not the discharge or escape occurred without the owner's fault or privity.

(4) Where the owner and the insurer each apply to the court for the limitation of his liability any sum paid into court in pursuance of either application shall be treated as paid also in pursuance of the other.

(5) The Third Parties (Rights against Insurers) Act 1930 and the Third Parties (Rights against Insurers) Act (Northern Ireland) 1930 shall not apply in relation to any contract of insurance to which such a certificate as is mentioned in section 163 relates.

Supplementary

Jurisdiction of United Kingdom courts and registration of foreign judgments

166.—(1) Paragraph 1(1)(d) of Schedule 1 to the Administration of Justice Act 1956 (Admiralty jurisdiction in claims for damage done by ships) shall be construed as extending to any claim in respect of a liability incurred under this Chapter, and the Admiralty jurisdiction of the Court of Session shall extend to any case arising out of any such claim.

(2) Where any persistent oil is discharged or escapes from a ship but does not result in any damage caused by contamination in the territory of the United Kingdom and no measures are reasonably taken to prevent or reduce such damage in that territory, no court in the United Kingdom shall entertain an action (whether in rem or in personam) to enforce a claim arising from—

(a) any damage caused in the territory of another Liability Convention country by contamination resulting from the discharge or escape;

(b) any cost incurred in taking measures to prevent or reduce such damage in the territory of another Liability Convention country; or

(c) any damage caused by any measures so taken.

(3) Part I of the Foreign Judgments (Reciprocal Enforcement) Act 1933 shall apply, whether or not it would so apply apart from this section, to any judgment given by a court in a Liability Convention country to enforce a claim in respect of a liability incurred under any provision corresponding to section 153; and in its application to such a judgment that Part shall have effect with the omission of section 4(2) and (3) of that Act.

Government ships

167.—(1) Nothing in the preceding provisions of this Chapter applies in relation to any warship or any ship for the time being used by the government of any State for other than commercial purposes.

(2) In relation to a ship owned by a State and for the time being used for commercial purposes it shall be a sufficient compliance with section 163(2) if there is in force a certificate issued by the government of that State and showing that the ship is owned by that State and that any liability for pollution damage as defined in Article 1 of the Liability Convention will be met up to the limit prescribed by Article V of the Liability Convention as amended by Article II of the protocol dated 19th November 1976 to the Liability Convention.

(3) Every Liability Convention State shall, for the purposes of any proceedings brought in a court in the United Kingdom to enforce a claim in respect of a liability incurred under section 153, be deemed to have submitted to the jurisdiction of that court, and accordingly rules of court may provide for the manner in which such proceedings are to be commenced and carried on; but nothing in this subsection shall authorise the issue of execution, or in Scotland the execution of diligence, against the property of any State.

Limitation of liability under section 154

168. For the purposes of section 185 any liability incurred under section 154 shall be deemed to be a liability to damages in respect of such damage to property as is mentioned in paragraph 1(a) of Article 2 of the Liability Convention in Part I of Schedule 7.

Saving for recourse actions

169. Nothing in this Chapter shall prejudice any claim, or the enforcement of any claim, a person incurring any liability under this Chapter may have against another person in respect of that liability.

Interpretation

170.—(1) In this Chapter—

"the court" means the High Court or the Court of Session;

"damage" includes loss;

"owner", in relation to a registered ship, means the person registered as its owner, except that in relation to a ship owned by a State which is operated by a person registered as the ship's operator, it means the person registered as its operator; and

"relevant threat of contamination" shall be construed in accordance with section 154(2).

(2) In relation to any damage or cost resulting from the discharge or escape of any oil carried in a ship, or from a relevant threat of contamination, references in this Chapter to the owner of the ship are references to the owner at the time of the occurrence or first of the occurrences resulting in the discharge or escape or (as the case may be) in the threat of contamination.

(3) References in this Chapter in its application to Scotland—

(a) to payment into court, shall be construed as references to payment to the Accountant of Court for Consignation (within the meaning of the Court of Session Consignations (Scotland) Act 1895); and

(b) to costs, shall be construed as references to expenses.

(4) References in this Chapter to the territory of any country include the territorial sea of that country.

Preliminary

Meaning of the "Liability Convention", "the Fund Convention" and related expressions

172.—(1) In this Chapter—

(a) "the Liability Convention" has the same meaning as in Chapter III of this Part;

(b) "the Fund Convention" means the International Convention on the Establishment of an International Fund for Compensation for Oil Pollution Damage opened for signature in Brussels on 18th December 1971;

(c) "the Fund" means the International Fund established by the Fund Convention; and

(d) "Fund Convention country" means a country in respect of which the Fund Convention is in force.

(2) If Her Majesty by Order in Council declares that any State specified in the Order is a party to the Fund Convention in respect of any country so specified, the Order shall, while in force, be conclusive evidence that that State is a party to that Convention in respect of that country.

Contributions to Fund

Contributions by importers of oil and others

173.—(1) Contributions shall be payable to the Fund in respect of oil carried by sea to ports or terminal installations in the United Kingdom otherwise than on a voyage only within its national waters.

(2) Subsection (1) above applies whether or not the oil is being imported, and applies even if contributions are payable in respect of carriage of the same oil on a previous voyage.

(3) Contributions shall also be payable to the Fund in respect of oil when first received in any installation in the United Kingdom after having been carried by sea and discharged in a port or terminal installation in a country which is not a Fund Convention country.

(4) The person liable to pay contributions is—

(a) in the case of oil which is being imported into the United Kingdom, the importer, and

(b) otherwise, the person by whom the oil is received.

(5) A person shall not be liable to make contributions in respect of the oil imported or received by him in any year if the oil so imported or received in the year does not exceed 150,000 tonnes.

(6) For the purpose of subsection (5) above—

(a) all the members of a group of companies shall be treated as a single person, and

(b) any two or more companies which have been amalgamated into a single company shall be treated as the same person as that single company.

(7) The contributions payable by a person for any year shall—

(a) be of such amount as may be determined by the Assembly of the Fund under articles 11 and 12 of the Fund Convention (as amended by article III of the protocol dated 19th November 1976 to that Convention) and notified to that person by the Fund;

(b) be payable in such instalments, becoming due at such times, as may be so notified to him; and if any amount due from him remains unpaid after the date on which it became due, it shall from then on bear interest, at a rate determined from time to time by the Assembly of the Fund, until it is paid.

(8) The Secretary of State may by regulations impose on persons who are or may be liable to pay contributions under this section obligations to give security for payment to the Secretary of State, or the Fund.

(9) Regulations under subsection (8) above—

(a) may contain such supplemental or incidental provisions as appear to the Secretary of State expedient, and

(b) may impose penalties for contravention of the regulations punishable on summary conviction by a fine not exceeding level 5 on the standard scale, or such lower limit as may be specified in the regulations.

(10) In this section and in section 174, unless the context otherwise requires—

"company" means a body incorporated under the law of the United Kingdom, or of any other country;

"group" in relation to companies, means a holding company and its subsidiaries as defined by section 736 of the Companies Act 1985 (or for companies in Northern Ireland Article 4 of the Companies (Northern Ireland) Order 1986), subject, in the case of a company incorporated outside the United Kingdom, to any necessary modifications of those definitions;

"importer" means the person by whom or on whose behalf the oil in question is entered for customs or excise purposes on importation, and "import" shall be construed accordingly;

"oil" means crude oil and fuel oil, and—

(a) "crude oil" means any liquid hydrocarbon mixture occurring naturally in the earth whether or not treated to render it suitable for transportation, and includes—

(i) crude oils from which distillate fractions have been removed, and

(ii) crude oils to which distillate fractions have been added,

(b) "fuel oil" means heavy distillates or residues from crude oil or blends of such materials intended for use as a fuel for the production of heat or power of a quality equivalent to the "American Society for Testing and Materials' Specification for Number Four Fuel Oil (Designation D396–69)", or heavier,

"terminal installation" means any site for the storage of oil in bulk which is capable of receiving oil from waterborne transportation, including any facility situated offshore and linked to any such site.

Power to obtain information

174.—(1) For the purpose of transmitting to the Fund the names and addresses of the persons who under section 173 are liable to make contributions to the Fund for any year, and the quantity of oil in respect of which they are so liable, the Secretary of State may by notice require any person engaged in producing, treating, distributing or transporting oil to furnish such information as may be specified in the notice.

(2) A notice under this section may require a company to give such information as may be required to ascertain whether its liability is affected by section 173(6).

(3) A notice under this section may specify the way in which, and the time within which, it is to be complied with.

(4) In proceedings by the Fund against any person to recover any amount due under section 173, particulars contained in any list transmitted by the Secretary of State to the Fund shall, so far as those particulars are based on information obtained under this section, be admissible as evidence of the facts stated in the list; and so far as particulars which are so admissible are based on information given by the person against whom the proceedings are brought, those particulars shall be presumed to be accurate until the contrary is proved.

(5) If a person discloses any information which has been furnished to or obtained by him under this section, or in connection with the execution of this section, then, unless the disclosure is made—

(a) with the consent of the person from whom the information was obtained, or

(b) in connection with the execution of this section, or

(c) for the purposes of any legal proceedings arising out of this section or of any report of such proceedings,

he shall be liable on summary conviction to a fine not exceeding level 5 on the standard scale.

(6) A person who—

(a) refuses or intentionally neglects to comply with a notice under this section, or

(b) in furnishing any information in compliance with a notice under this section makes any statement which he knows to be false in a material particular, or recklessly makes any statement which is false in a material particular,

shall be liable—

(i) on summary conviction, to a fine not exceeding level 4 on the standard scale in the case of an offence under paragraph (a) above and not exceeding the statutory maximum in the case of an offence under paragraph (b) above, and

(ii) on conviction on indictment, to a fine, or to imprisonment for a term not exceeding twelve months, or to both.

Compensation for persons suffering pollution damage

Liability of the Fund

175.—(1) The Fund shall be liable for pollution damage in the territory of the United Kingdom if the person suffering the damage has been unable to obtain full compensation under section 153—

(a) because the discharge or escape causing the damage—

    (i) resulted from an exceptional, inevitable and irresistible phenomenon, or

    (ii) was due wholly to anything done or left undone by another person (not being a servant or agent of the owner) with intent to do damage, or

    (iii) was due wholly to the negligence or wrongful act of a government or other authority in exercising its function of maintaining lights or other navigational aids for the maintenance of which it was responsible,

(and because liability is accordingly wholly displaced by section 155), or

(b) because the owner or guarantor liable for the damage cannot meet his obligations in full, or

(c) because the damage exceeds the liability under section 153 as limited by section 157.

(2) Subsection (1) above shall apply with the substitution for the words "United Kingdom" of the words "a Fund Convention country" where—

(a) the headquarters of the Fund is for the time being in the United Kingdom, and proceedings under the Liability Convention for compensation for the pollution damage have been brought in a country which is not a Fund Convention country, or

(b) the incident has caused pollution damage in the territory of the United Kingdom and of another Fund Convention country, and proceedings under the Liability Convention for compensation for the pollution damage have been brought in a country which is not a Fund Convention country or in the United Kingdom.

(3) Where the incident has caused pollution damage in the territory of the United Kingdom and of another country in respect of which the Liability Convention is in force, references in this section to the provisions of Chapter III of this Part shall include references to the corresponding provisions of the law of any country giving effect to the Liability Convention.

(4) Where proceedings under the Liability Convention for compensation for pollution damage have been brought in a country which is not a Fund Convention country and the Fund is liable for that pollution damage by virtue of subsection (2)(a) above, references in this section to the provisions of Chapter III of this Part shall be treated as references to the corresponding provisions of the law of the country in which those proceedings were brought.

(5) For the purposes of this section an owner or guarantor is to be treated as incapable of meeting his obligations if the obligations have not been met after all reasonable steps to pursue the legal remedies available have been taken.

(6) Expenses reasonably incurred, and sacrifices reasonably made, by the owner voluntarily to prevent or minimise pollution damage shall be treated as pollution damage for the purposes of this section, and accordingly he shall be in the same position with respect to claims against the Fund under this section as if he had a claim in respect of liability under section 153.

(7) The Fund shall incur no obligation under this section if—

(a) it proves that the pollution damage—

    (i) resulted from an act of war, hostilities, civil war or insurrection, or

    (ii) was caused by oil which has escaped or been discharged from a warship or other ship owned or operated by a State and used, at the time of the occurrence, only on Government non-commercial service, or

(b) the claimant cannot prove that the damage resulted from an occurrence involving a ship identified by him, or involving two or more ships one of which is identified by him.

(8) Subject to subsection (9) below, if the Fund proves that the pollution damage resulted wholly or partly—

(a) from an act or omission done with intent to cause damage by the person who suffered the damage, or

(b) from the negligence of that person,

the Fund may be exonerated wholly or partly from its obligation to pay compensation to that person.

(9) Subsection (8) above does not apply to a claim in respect of expenses or sacrifices made voluntarily to prevent or minimise pollution damage.

(10) Where the liability under section 153 is limited to any extent by subsection (5) of that section, the Fund shall be exonerated to the same extent.

Limitation of Fund's liability under section 175

176.—(1) The Fund's liability under section 175 shall be subject to the limits imposed by paragraphs 4, 5 and 6 of article 4 of the Fund Convention (as amended by Article III of the protocol dated 19th November 1976 to that Convention) which impose an overall limit on the liabilities of the owner and of the Fund, and the text of which is set out in Part II of Schedule 5.

(2) Evidence of any instrument issued by any organ of the Fund or of any document in the custody of the Fund, or any entry in or extract from such a document, may be given in any legal

proceedings by production of a copy certified as a true copy by an official of the Fund; and any document purporting to be such a copy shall be received in evidence without proof of the official position or handwriting of the person signing the certificate.

(3) For the purpose of giving effect to paragraphs 4, 5 and 6 of Article 4 of the Fund Convention a court giving judgment against the Fund in proceedings under section 175 shall notify the Fund, and—

(a) no steps shall be taken to enforce the judgment unless and until the court gives leave to enforce it,

(b) that leave shall not be given unless and until the Fund notifies the court either that the amount of the claim is not to be reduced under those paragraphs, or that it is to be reduced to a specified amount, and

(c) in the latter case the judgment shall be enforceable only for the reduced amount.

(4) Any steps taken to obtain payment of an amount or a reduced amount in pursuance of such a judgment as is mentioned in subsection (3) above shall be steps to obtain payment in sterling; and for the purpose of converting such an amount from special drawing rights into sterling one special drawing right shall be treated as equal to such a sum in sterling as the International Monetary Fund have fixed as being the equivalent of one special drawing right for—

(a) the day on which the judgment is given; or

(b) if no sum has been fixed for that day, the last day before that day for which a sum has been so fixed.

(5) A certificate given by or on behalf of the Treasury stating—

(a) that a particular sum in sterling has been so fixed for the day on which the judgment was given; or

(b) that no sum has been fixed for that day and that a particular sum in sterling has been so fixed for a day which is the last day for which a sum has been so fixed before the day on which the judgment was given,

shall be conclusive evidence of those matters for the purposes of this Chapter.

(6) A document purporting to be such a certificate shall, in any proceedings, be received in evidence and, unless the contrary is proved, be deemed to be such a certificate.

Indemnification of shipowners

Indemnification where damage is caused by ship registered in Fund Convention country

176A.—(1) Where a liability is incurred under section 153 in respect of a ship registered in a Fund Convention country the Fund shall indemnify the owner and his guarantor for that portion of the aggregate amount of the liability which—

(a) is in excess of an amount equivalent to 100 special drawing rights for each ton of the ship's tonnage or of an amount of 8,333,000 special drawing rights, whichever is the less, and

(b) is not in excess of an amount equivalent to 133 special drawing rights for each ton of the said tonnage or an amount of 14 million special drawing rights, whichever is the less.

(2) Where proceedings under the Liability Convention for compensation for pollution damage have been brought in a country which is not a Fund Convention country (but is a country in respect of which the Liability Convention is in force), and either—

(a) the incident has caused pollution damage in the territory of the United Kingdom (as well as in the territory of that other country); or

(b) the headquarters of the Fund is for the time being in the United Kingdom,

subsection (1) above shall apply with the omission of the words "under section 153".

(3) The Fund shall not incur an obligation under this section where the pollution damage resulted from the wilful misconduct of the owner.

(4) In proceedings to enforce the Fund's obligation under this section the court may exonerate the Fund wholly or partly if it is proved that, as a result of the actual fault or privity of the owner—

(a) the ship did not comply with such requirements as the Secretary of State may by order prescribe for the purposes of this section, and

(b) the occurrence or damage was caused wholly or partly by that non-compliance.

(5) The requirements referred to in subsection (4) above are such requirements as appear to the Secretary of State appropriate to implement the provisions of—

(a) Article 5(3) of the Fund Convention (marine safety conventions), and

(b) Article 5(4) of the Fund Convention (which enables the Assembly of the Fund to substitute new conventions).

(6) An order made under subsection (4) above may contain such transitional and other supplemental provisions as appear to the Secretary of State to be expedient.

(7) Expenses reasonably incurred, and sacrifices reasonably made, by the owner voluntarily to prevent or minimise the pollution damage shall be treated as included in the owner's liability for the purposes of this section.

(8) For the purpose of converting into sterling the amount in special drawing rights adjudged to be payable by the Fund by way of indemnity in such proceedings as are mentioned in subsection (4) above, subsections (4) to (6) of section 176 shall have effect—

(a) if the liability in question has been limited in pursuance of section 158, as if—

(i) for the reference in the said subsection (4) to the amount there mentioned there were substituted a reference to the amount adjudged as aforesaid, and

(ii) for any reference to the day on which the judgment is or was given there were substituted a reference to the day on which the determination of the limit was made in pursuance of the said section 158; and

(b) if the liability in question has not been so limited, with the modification made by paragraph (a)(i) of this subsection and as if for any reference to the day on which the judgment is or was given there were substituted a reference to the day on which the said amount was so adjudged.

Supplemental

Jurisdiction and effect of judgments

177.—(1) Paragraph 1(1)(d) of Schedule 1 to the Administration of Justice Act 1956 (Admiralty jurisdiction in claims for damage done by ships) shall be construed as extending to any claim in respect of a liability falling on the Fund under this Chapter; and the Admiralty jurisdiction of the Court of Session shall extend to any case arising out of any such claim.

(2) Where in accordance with rules of court made for the purposes of this subsection the Fund has been given notice of proceedings brought against an owner or guarantor in respect of liability under section 153, any judgment given in the proceedings shall, after it has become final and enforceable, become binding upon the Fund in the sense that the facts and evidence in the judgment may not be disputed by the Fund even if the Fund has not intervened in the proceedings.

(3) Where a person incurs a liability under the law of a Fund Convention Country corresponding to Chapter III of this Part for damage which is partly in the territory of the United Kingdom, subsection (2) above shall, for the purpose of proceedings under this Chapter, apply with any necessary modifications to a judgment in proceedings under that law of the said country.

(4) Subject to subsection (5) below, Part I of the Foreign Judgments (Reciprocal Enforcement) Act 1933 shall apply, whether or not it would so apply apart from this subsection, to any judgment given by a court in a Fund Convention country to enforce a claim in respect of liability incurred under any provision corresponding to section 175 or 176A; and in its application to such a judgment the said Part I shall have effect with the omission of sections 4(2) and (3) of the Act of 1933.

(5) No steps shall be taken to enforce such a judgment unless and until the court in which it is registered under Part I of the Act of 1933 gives leave to enforce it; and—

(a) that leave shall not be given unless and until the Fund notifies the court either that the amount of the claim is not to be reduced under paragraph 4 of article 4 of the Fund Convention (as set out in Part II of Schedule 5) or that it is to be reduced to a specified amount; and

(b) in the latter case, the judgment shall be enforceable only for the reduced amount.

Extinguishment of claims

178.—(1) No action to enforce a claim against the Fund under this Chapter shall be entertained by a court in the United Kingdom unless—

(a) the action is commenced, or

(b) a third party notice of an action to enforce a claim against the owner or his guarantor in respect of the same damage is given to the Fund,

not later than three years after the claim against the Fund arose.

In this subsection "third party notice" means a notice of the kind described in section 177(2) and (3).

(2) No action to enforce a claim against the Fund under this Chapter shall be entertained by a court in the United Kingdom unless the action is commenced not later than six years after the occurrence, or first of the occurrences, resulting in the discharge or escape by reason of which the claim against the Fund arose.

(3) Notwithstanding the preceding provisions of this section, a person's right to bring an action under the section 176A shall not be extinguished before six months from the date when that person first acquired knowledge of the bringing of an action against him under Chapter III of this Part, or under the corresponding provisions of the law of any country outside the United Kingdom giving effect to the Liability Convention.

Subrogation

179.—(1) In respect of any sum paid by the Fund as compensation for pollution damage the Fund shall acquire by subrogation any rights in respect of the damage which the recipient has (or but for the payment would have) against any other person.

(2) The right of the Fund under subsection (1) above is subject to any obligation of the Fund under section 176A above to indemnify the owner or guarantor for any part of the liability on which he has defaulted.

(3) In respect of any sum paid by a public authority in the United Kingdom as compensation for pollution damage, that authority shall acquire by subrogation any rights which the recipient has against the Fund under this Chapter.

Interpretation

181.—(1) In this Chapter, unless the context otherwise requires—
"damage" includes loss;
"discharge or escape", in relation to pollution damage, means the discharge or escape of oil carried by the ship;
"guarantor" means any person providing insurance or other financial security to cover the owner's liability of the kind described in section 163;
"oil", except in sections 173 and 174, means persistent hydrocarbon mineral oil;
"owner" means the person or persons registered as the owner of the ship or, in the absence of registration, the person or persons owning the ship, except that, in relation to a ship owned by a State which is operated by a person registered as the ship's operator, it means the person registered as its operator;
"pollution damage" means damage caused outside the ship carrying oil by contamination resulting from the escape or discharge of oil from the ship, wherever the escape or discharge may occur, and includes the cost of preventive measures and further damage caused by preventive measures;
"preventive measures" means any reasonable measures taken by any person after the occurrence to prevent or minimise pollution damage; and
"ship" means any sea-going ship and any seaborne craft of any type whatsoever carrying oil in bulk as cargo.

(2) References in this Chapter to the territory of any country include the territorial sea of that country, and references to pollution damage in the United Kingdom shall be construed accordingly.

(3) For the purposes of this Chapter a ship's tonnage shall be the net tonnage of the ship with the addition of the amount deducted from the gross tonnage on account of engine room space for the purpose of ascertaining the net tonnage.

If the ship cannot be measured in accordance with the normal rules, its tonnage shall be deemed to be 40 per cent of the weight in tons (of 2,240 lbs) of oil which the ship is capable of carrying.

(4) For the purposes of this Chapter, where more than one discharge or escape results from the same occurrence or from a series of occurrences having the same origin, they shall be treated as one.

OVERALL LIMIT ON LIABILITY OF FUND

PART I

PERMANENT PROVISION

Article 4—paragraphs 4 and 5

4. (a) Except as otherwise provided in sub-paragraphs (b) and (c) of this paragraph, the aggregate amount of compensation payable by the Fund under this Article shall in respect of any one incident be limited, so that the total sum of that amount and the amount of compensation actually paid under the Liability Convention for pollution damage within the scope of application of this Convention as defined in Article 3 shall not exceed 135 million units of account.

(b) Except as otherwise provided in sub-paragraph (c), the aggregate amount of compensation payable by the Fund under this Article for pollution damage resulting from a natural phenomenon of an exceptional, inevitable and irresistible character shall not exceed 135 million units of account.

(c) The maximum amount of compensation referred to in sub-paragraphs (a) and (c) shall be 200 million units of account with respect to any incident occurring during any period when there are three Parties to this Convention in respect of which the combined relevant quantity of contributing oil received by persons in the territories of such Parties, during the preceding calendar year, equalled or exceeded 600 million tons.

(d) Interest accrued on a fund constituted in accordance with Article V, paragraph 3, of the Liability Convention, if any, shall not be taken into account for the computation of the maximum compensation payable by the Fund under this Article.

(e) The amounts mentioned in this Article shall be converted into national currency on the basis of the value of that currency by reference to the Special Drawing Right on the date of the decision of the Assembly of the Fund as to the first date of payment of compensation.

5. Where the amount of established claims against the Fund exceeds the aggregate amount of compensation payable under paragraph 4, the amount available shall be distributed in such a manner that the proportion between any established claim and the amount of compensation actually recovered by the claimant under this Convention shall be the same for all claimants.

PART II

TRANSITORY PROVISION

Article 4—paragraphs 4, 5 and 6

4. (a) Except as otherwise provided in sub-paragraph (b) of this paragraph, the aggregate amount of compensation payable by the Fund under this Article shall in respect of any one incident be limited, so that the total sum of that amount and the amount of compensation actually paid under the Liability Convention for pollution damage caused in the territory of the Contracting States, including any sums in respect of which the Fund is under an obligation to indemnify the owner pursuant to Article 5, paragraph 1, of this Convention, shall not exceed 30 million special drawing rights,

(b) The aggregate amount of compensation payable by the Fund under this Article for pollution damage resulting from a natural phenomenon of an exceptional, inevitable and irresistible character shall not exceed 30 million special drawing rights.

5. Where the amount of established claims against the Fund exceeds the aggregate amount of compensation payable under paragraph 4, the amount available shall be distributed in such manner that the proportion between any established claim and the amount of compensation actually recovered by the claimant under the Liability Convention and this Convention shall be the same for all claimants.

6. The Assembly of the Fund (hereinafter referred to as "the Assembly") may, having regard to the experience of incidents which have occurred and in particular the amount of damage resulting therefrom and to changes in the monetary values, decide that the amount of 30 million special drawing rights referred to in paragraph 4, subparagraph (a) and (b), shall be changed; provided, however, that this amount shall in no case exceed 60 million special drawing rights or be lower than 30 million special drawing rights. The changed amount shall apply to incidents which occur after the date of the decision effecting the change.

GENERAL NOTE

Schedule 5 contains the law relating to the limitation of liability of the 1992 IOPC Fund (see the General Notes to Pt. VI, Ch. IV, above). It is significant that the drafter of the Merchant Shipping Act 1995 could find no better way of explaining the meaning of the 1992 Fund Convention than by reproducing its provisions. It is to be hoped that this method will be adopted in any future amendment of the Act.

Section 183   SCHEDULE 6

CONVENTION RELATING TO THE CARRIAGE OF PASSENGERS AND THEIR LUGGAGE BY SEA

PART I

TEXT OF CONVENTION

ARTICLE I

Definitions

In this Convention the following expressions have the meaning hereby assigned to them:
1. (a) "carrier" means a person by or on behalf of whom a contract of carriage has been concluded, whether the carriage is actually performed by him or by a performing carrier;
    (b) "performing carrier" means a person other than the carrier, being the owner, charterer or operator of a ship, who actually performs the whole or a part of the carriage;
2. "contract of carriage" means a contract made by or on behalf of a carrier for the carriage by sea of a passenger or of a passenger and his luggage, as the case may be;
3. "ship" means only a seagoing vessel, excluding an air-cushion vehicle;
4. "passenger" means any person carried in a ship,
(a) under a contract of carriage, or
(b) who, with the consent of the carrier, is accompanying a vehicle or live animals which are covered by a contract for the carriage of goods not governed by this Convention,
5. "luggage" means any article or vehicle carried by the carrier under a contract of carriage, excluding:
    (a) articles and vehicles carried under a charter party, bill of lading or other contract primarily concerned with the carriage of goods, and
    (b) live animals;
6. "cabin luggage" means luggage which the passenger has in his cabin or is otherwise in his possession, custody or control. Except for the application of paragraph 8 of this Article and Article 8, cabin luggage includes luggage which the passenger has in or on his vehicle.
7. "loss of or damage to luggage" includes pecuniary loss resulting from the luggage not having been re-delivered to the passenger within a reasonable time after the arrival of the ship on which the luggage has been or should have been carried, but does not include delays resulting from labour disputes;
8. "carriage" covers the following periods:
    (a) with regard to the passenger and his cabin luggage, the period during which the passenger and/or his cabin luggage are on board the ship or in the course of embarkation or disembarkation, and the period during which the passenger and his cabin luggage are transported by water from land to the ship or vice versa, if the cost of such transport is included in the fare or if the vessel used for the purpose of auxiliary transport has been put at the disposal of the passenger by the carrier. However, with regard to the passenger, carriage does not include the period during which he is in a marine terminal or station or on a quay or in or on any other port installation;
    (b) with regard to cabin luggage, also the period during which the passenger is in a marine terminal or station or on a quay or in or on any other port installation if that luggage has been taken over by the carrier or his servant or agent and has not been re-delivered to the passenger;

(c) with regard to other luggage which is not cabin luggage, the period from the time of its taking over by the carrier or his servant or agent onshore or on board until the time of its re-delivery by the carrier or his servant or agent;

9. "international carriage" means any carriage in which, according to the contract of carriage, the place of departure and the place of destination are situated in two different States, or in a single State if, according to the contract of carriage or the scheduled itinerary, there is an intermediate port of call in another State.

ARTICLE 2

Application

1. This Convention shall apply to any international carriage if:
(a) the ship is flying the flag of or is registered in a State Party to this Convention, or
(b) the contract of carriage has been made in a State Party to this Convention, or
(c) the place of departure or destination, according to the contract of carriage, is in a State Party to this Convention.

2. Notwithstanding paragraph 1 of this Article, this Convention shall not apply when the carriage is subject, under any other international convention concerning the carriage of passengers or luggage by another mode of transport, to a civil liability regime under the provisions of such convention, in so far as those provisions have mandatory application to carriage by sea.

ARTICLE 3

Liability of the carrier

1. The carrier shall be liable for the damage suffered as a result of the death of or personal injury to a passenger and the loss of or damage to luggage if the incident which caused the damage so suffered occurred in the course of the carriage and was due to the fault or neglect of the carrier or of his servants or agents acting within the scope of their employment.

2. The burden of proving that the incident which caused the loss or damage occurred in the course of the carriage, and the extent of the loss or damage, shall lie with the claimant.

3. Fault or neglect of the carrier or of his servants or agents acting within the scope of their employment shall be presumed, unless the contrary is proved, if the death of or personal injury to the passenger or the loss of or damage to cabin luggage arose from or in connection with the shipwreck, collision, stranding, explosion or fire, or defect in the ship. In respect of loss of or damage to other luggage, such fault or neglect shall be presumed, unless the contrary is proved, irrespective of the nature of the incident which caused the loss or damage. In all other cases the burden of proving fault or neglect shall lie with the claimant.

ARTICLE 4

Performing carrier

1. If the performance of the carriage or part thereof has been entrusted to a performing carrier, the carrier shall nevertheless remain liable for the entire carriage according to the provisions of this Convention. In addition, the performing carrier shall be subject and entitled to the provisions of this Convention for the part of the carriage performed by him.

2. The carrier shall, in relation to the carriage performed by the performing carrier, be liable for the acts and omissions of the performing carrier and of his servants and agents acting within the scope of their employment.

3. Any special agreement under which the carrier assumes obligations not imposed by this Convention or any waiver of rights conferred by this Convention shall affect the performing carrier only if agreed by him expressly and in writing.

4. Where and to the extent that both the carrier and the performing carrier are liable, their liability shall be joint and several.

5. Nothing in this Article shall prejudice any right of recourse as between the carrier and the performing carrier.

ARTICLE 5

Valuables

The carrier shall not be liable for the loss of or damage to monies, negotiable securities, gold, silverware, jewellery, ornaments, works of art, or other valuables, except where such valuables have been deposited with the carrier for the agreed purpose of safe-keeping in which case the carrier shall be liable up to the limit provided for in paragraph 3 of Article 8 unless a higher limit is agreed upon in accordance with paragraph 1 of Article 10.

ARTICLE 6

Contributory fault

If the carrier proves that the death of or personal injury to a passenger or the loss of or damage to his luggage was caused or contributed to by the fault or neglect of the passenger, the court seized of the case may exonerate the carrier wholly or partly from his liability in accordance with the provisions of the law of that court.

ARTICLE 7

Limit of liability for personal injury

1. The liability of the carrier for the death of or personal injury to a passenger shall in no case exceed 46,666 units of account per carriage. Where in accordance with the law of the court seized of the case damages are awarded in the form of periodical income payments, the equivalent capital value of those payments shall not exceed the said limit.

2. Notwithstanding paragraph 1 of this Article, the national law of any State Party to this Convention may fix, as far as carriers who are nationals of such State are concerned, a higher *per capita* limit of liability.

ARTICLE 8

Limit of liability for loss of or damage to luggage

1. The liability of the carrier for the loss of or damage to cabin luggage shall in no case exceed 833 units of account per passenger, per carriage.

2. The liability of the carrier for the loss of or damage to vehicles including all luggage carried in or on the vehicle shall in no case exceed 3,333 units of account per vehicle, per carriage.

3. The liability of the carrier for the loss of or damage to luggage other than that mentioned in paragraphs 1 and 2 of this Article shall in no case exceed 1,200 units of account per passenger, per carriage.

4. The carrier and the passenger may agree that the liability of the carrier shall be subject to a deduction not exceeding 117 units of account in the case of damage to a vehicle and not exceeding 13 units of account per passenger in the case of loss of or damage to other luggage, such sum to be deducted from the loss or damage.

ARTICLE 9

Unit of account and conversion

The Unit of Account mentioned in this Convention is the special drawing right as defined by the International Monetary Fund. The amounts mentioned in Articles 7 and 8 shall be converted into the national currency of the State of the court seized of the case on the basis of the value of that currency on the date of the judgment or the date agreed upon by the Parties.

ARTICLE 10

Supplementary provisions on limits of liability

1. The carrier and the passenger may agree, expressly and in writing, to higher limits of liability than those prescribed in Articles 7 and 8.

2. Interest on damages and legal costs shall not be included in the limits of liability prescribed in Articles 7 and 8.

ARTICLE 11

Defences and limits for carriers' servants

If an action is brought against a servant or agent of the carrier or of the performing carrier arising out of damage covered by this Convention, such servant or agent, if he proves that he acted within the scope of his employment, shall be entitled to avail himself of the defences and limits of liability which the carrier or the performing carrier is entitled to invoke under this Convention.

ARTICLE 12

Aggregation of claims

1. Where the limits of liability prescribed in Articles 7 and 8 take effect, they shall apply to the aggregate of the amounts recoverable in all claims arising out of the death of or personal injury to any one passenger or the loss of or damage to his luggage.

2. In relation to the carriage performed by a performing carrier, the aggregate of the amounts recoverable from the carrier and the performing carrier and from their servants and agents acting within the scope of their employment shall not exceed the highest amount which could be awarded against either the carrier or the performing carrier under this Convention, but none of the persons mentioned shall be liable for a sum in excess of the limit applicable to him.

3. In any case where a servant or agent of the carrier or of the performing carrier is entitled under Article 11 of this Convention to avail himself of the limits of liability prescribed in Articles 7 and 8, the aggregate of the amounts recoverable from the carrier, or the performing carrier as the case may be, and from that servant or agent, shall not exceed those limits.

ARTICLE 13

Loss of right to limit liability

1. The carrier shall not be entitled to the benefit of the limits of liability prescribed in Articles 7 and 8 and paragraph 1 of Article 10, if it is proved that the damage resulted from an act or omission of the carrier done with the intent to cause such damage, or recklessly and with knowledge that such damage would probably result.

2. The servant or agent of the carrier or of the performing carrier shall not be entitled to the benefit of those limits if it is proved that the damage resulted from an act or omission of that servant or agent done with the intent to cause such damage, or recklessly and with knowledge that such damage would probably result.

ARTICLE 14

Basis for claims

No action for damages for the death of or personal injury to a passenger, or for the loss of or damage to luggage, shall be brought against a carrier or performing carrier otherwise than in accordance with this Convention.

ARTICLE 15

Notice of loss or damage to luggage

1. The passenger shall give written notice to the carrier or his agent:
(a) in the case of apparent damage to luggage:
    (i) for cabin luggage, before or at the time of disembarkation of the passenger;
    (ii) for all other luggage, before or at the time of its re-delivery;
(b) in the case of damage to luggage which is not apparent, or loss of luggage, within 15 days from the date of disembarkation or re-delivery or from the time when such re-delivery should have taken place.

2. If the passenger fails to comply with this Article, he shall be presumed, unless the contrary is proved, to have received the luggage undamaged.

3. The notice in writing need not be given if the condition of the luggage has at the time of its receipt been the subject of joint survey or inspection.

ARTICLE 16

Time-bar for actions

1. Any action for damages arising out of the death of or personal injury to a passenger or for the loss of or damage to luggage shall be time-barred after a period of two years.

2. The limitation period shall be calculated as follows:
(a) in the case of personal injury, from the date of disembarkation of the passenger;
(b) in the case of death occurring during carriage, from the date when the passenger should have disembarked, and in the case of personal injury occurring during carriage and resulting in the death of the passenger after disembarkation, from the date of death, provided that this period shall not exceed three years from the date of disembarkation;

(c) in the case of loss of or damage to luggage, from the date of disembarkation or from the date when disembarkation should have taken place, whichever is later.

3. The law of the court seized of the case shall govern the grounds of suspension and interruption of limitation periods, but in no case shall an action under this Convention be brought after the expiration of a period of three years from the date of disembarkation of the passenger or from the date when disembarkation should have taken place, whichever is later.

4. Notwithstanding paragraphs 1, 2 and 3 of this Article, the period of limitation may be extended by a declaration of the carrier or by agreement of the parties after the cause of action has arisen. The declaration or agreement shall be in writing.

ARTICLE 17

Competent jurisdiction

1. An action arising under this Convention shall, at the option of the claimant, be brought before one of the courts listed below, provided that the court is located in a State Party to this Convention:

(a) the court of the place of permanent residence or principal place of business of the defendant, or

(b) the court of the place of departure or that of the destination according to the contract of carriage, or

(c) a court of the State of the domicile or permanent residence of the claimant, if the defendant has a place of business and is subject to jurisdiction in that State, or

(d) a court of the State where the contract of carriage was made, if the defendant has a place of business and is subject to jurisdiction in that State.

2. After the occurrence of the incident which has caused the damage, the parties may agree that the claim for damages shall be submitted to any jurisdiction or to arbitration.

ARTICLE 18

Invalidity of contractual provisions

Any contractual provision concluded before the occurrence of the incident which has caused the death of or personal injury to a passenger or the loss of or damage to his luggage, purporting to relieve the carrier of his liability towards the passenger or to prescribe a lower limit of liability than that fixed in this Convention except as provided in paragraph 4 of Article 8, and any such provision purporting to shift the burden of proof which rests on the carrier, or having the effect of restricting the option specified in paragraph 1 of Article 17, shall be null and void, but the nullity of that provision shall not render void the contract of carriage which shall remain subject to the provisions of this Convention.

ARTICLE 19

Other conventions on limitation of liability

This Convention shall not modify the rights or duties of the carrier, the performing carrier, and their servants or agents provided for in international conventions relating to the limitation of liability of owners of seagoing ships.

ARTICLE 20

Nuclear damage

No liability shall arise under this Convention for damage caused by a nuclear incident:

(a) if the operator of a nuclear installation is liable to such damage under either the Paris Convention of 29 July 1960 on Third Party Liability in the Field of Nuclear Energy as amended by its Additional Protocol of 28 January 1964, or the Vienna Convention of 21 May 1963 on Civil Liability for Nuclear Damage, or

(b) if the operator of a nuclear installation is liable for such damage by virtue of a national law governing the liability for such damage, provided that such law is in all respects as favourable to persons who may suffer damage as either the Paris or the Vienna Conventions.

ARTICLE 21

Commercial carriage by public authorities

This Convention shall apply to commercial carriage undertaken by States or Public Authorities under contracts of carriage within the meaning of Article 1.

PART II

PROVISIONS HAVING EFFECT IN CONNECTION WITH CONVENTION

Interpretation

1. In this Part of this Schedule any reference to a numbered article is a reference to the article of the Convention which is so numbered and any expression to which a meaning is assigned by article 1 of the Convention has that meaning.

Provisions adapting or supplementing specified articles of the Convention

2. For the purposes of paragraph 2 of article 2, provisions of such an international convention as is mentioned in that paragraph which apart from this paragraph do not have mandatory application to carriage by sea shall be treated as having mandatory application to carriage by sea if it is stated in the contract of carriage for the carriage in question that those provisions are to apply in connection with the carriage.

3. The reference to the law of the court in article 6 shall be construed as a reference to the Law Reform (Contributory Negligence) Act 1945 except that in relation to Northern Ireland it shall be construed as a reference to section 2 of the Law Reform (Miscellaneous Provisions) Act (Northern Ireland) 1948.

4. The Secretary of State may by order provide that, in relation to a carrier whose principal place of business is in the United Kingdom, paragraph 1 of article 7 shall have effect with the substitution for the limit for the time being specified in that paragraph of a different limit specified in the order (which shall not be lower than 46,666 units of account).

5.—(1) For the purpose of converting from special drawing rights into sterling the amounts mentioned in articles 7 and 8 of the Convention in respect of which a judgment is given, one special drawing right shall be treated as equal to such a sum in sterling as the International Monetary Fund have fixed as being the equivalent of one special drawing right for—

(a) the day on which the judgment is given; or

(b) if no sum has been so fixed for that day, the last day before that day for which a sum has been so fixed.

(2) A certificate given by or on behalf of the Treasury stating—

(a) that a particular sum in sterling has been fixed as mentioned in sub-paragraph (1) above for a particular day; or

(b) that no sum has been so fixed for that day and a particular sum in sterling has been so fixed for a day which is the last day for which a sum has been so fixed before the particular day,

shall be conclusive evidence of those matters for the purposes of articles 7 to 9 of the Convention; and a document purporting to be such a certificate shall, in any proceedings, be received in evidence and, unless the contrary is proved, be deemed to be such a certificate.

6. It is hereby declared that by virtue of article 12 the limitations on liability there mentioned in respect of a passenger or his luggage apply to the aggregate liabilities of the persons in question in all proceedings for enforcing the liabilities or any of them which may be brought whether in the United Kingdom or elsewhere.

7. Article 16 shall apply to an arbitration as it applies to an action, and section 34(3) and (4) of the Limitation Act 1980 and Article 73(2) and (4) of the Limitation (Northern Ireland) Order 1989 (which determine when an arbitration is deemed to commence) shall apply for the purposes of article 16 as they apply for the purposes of that Act and Order.

8. The court before which proceedings are brought in pursuance of article 17 to enforce a liability which is limited by virtue of article 12 may at any stage of the proceedings make such orders as appear to the court to be just and equitable in view of the provisions of article 12 and of any other proceedings which have been or are likely to be begun in the United Kingdom or elsewhere to enforce the liability in whole or in part; and without prejudice to the generality of the preceding provisions of this paragraph such a court shall, where the liability is or may be partly enforceable in other proceedings in the United Kingdom or elsewhere, have jurisdiction to award an amount less than the court would have awarded if the limitation applied solely to the proceedings before the court or to make any part of its award conditional on the results of any other proceedings.

Other provisions adapting or supplementing the Convention

9. Any reference in the Convention to a contract of carriage excludes a contract of carriage which is not for reward.

10. If Her Majesty by Order in Council declares that any State specified in the Order is a party to the Convention in respect of a particular country the Order shall, subject to the provisions of any subsequent Order made by virtue of this paragraph, be conclusive evidence that the State is a party to the Convention in respect of that country.

11. The Secretary of State may by order make provision—

(a) for requiring a person who is the carrier in relation to a passenger to give to the passenger, in a manner specified in the order, notice of such of the provisions of Part I of this Schedule as are so specified;

(b) for a person who fails to comply with a requirement imposed on him by the order to be guilty of an offence and liable on summary conviction to a fine of an amount not exceeding level 4 on the standard scale or not exceeding a lesser amount.

Application of ss.185 and 186 of this Act

12. It is hereby declared that nothing in the Convention affects the operation of section 185 of this Act (which limits a shipowner's liability in certain cases of loss of life, injury or damage).

13. Nothing is section 186 of this Act (which among other things limits a shipowner's liability for the loss or damage of goods in certain cases) shall relieve a person of any liability imposed on him by the Convention.

GENERAL NOTE

Schedule 6 contains the text of the Athens Convention 1974. Schedule 6, Pt. I contains the relevant articles of the Convention and Pt. II contains the necessary modifications to make the Convention operate in U.K. law. See further the General Note to s.183, above. Also *Chorley and Giles Shipping Law*, pp. 327–341; N.Gaskell "The Zeebrugge Disaster: Application of the Athens Convention 1974" (1987) 137 NLJ 285–288; "The Athens Convention 1974 and Limitation of Liability" (1987) 137 NLJ 322–323; "Athens Convention 1974: the Concept of Limitation" (1987) 137 NLJ 383–386.

The Athens Convention 1974 provides a special regime for sea passengers, but it is no longer clear why they should be treated differently by comparison with bus or train passengers. It is strongly arguable that the Convention operates in such an unfair way to passengers that the U.K. ought to denounce it.

The international background to the Convention was that there were separate Conventions dealing with passengers and their luggage, namely the Carriage of Passengers Convention 1961 and the Passenger Luggage Convention 1967. There have been two Protocols to the Athens Convention 1974, in 1976 and 1990. Only the 1976 Protocol is in force. The 1990 Protocol aims to increase the limits of liability as a result of the Zeebrugge Disaster in 1987. The U.K. gave the Athens Convention 1974 interim effect from 1981. Note that the Athens Convention 1974 does not cover every liability to passengers and that it is also necessary to consider the general law of contract and tort for matters not within the Convention (*cf.* the Athens Convention 1974, Art. 14). Ordinary contractual terms on a ticket might therefore be relevant to some claims (see *Dillon v. Baltic Shipping Co.; Mikhail Lermontov, The* [1990] 1 Lloyd's Rep. 579) and the Supply of Goods and Services Act 1982, Pt. II might also apply.

The most difficult question is in deciding when the Athens Convention 1974 should apply and to whom.

Voyages. The Athens Convention 1974, Art. 2 applies to international carriage in the circumstances listed in Art. 2(1). It would cover the following examples: (1) a German passenger who booked a cruise on a U.K. ship (the U.K. is a party to the Convention); (2) a British passenger who booked a holiday in the U.K. for a trip down the Nile; (3) a foreign passenger who boarded a foreign flagged ship in the U.K. for a trip to a country which was a non-party to the Convention. See Sched. 6, Pt. II, para. 10 for "Convention" states.

Note that the Carriage of Passengers and their Luggage by Sea (Domestic Carriage) Order 1987 (S.I. 1987 No. 670), made under s.184, extended the operation of the Convention, with some modifications, to journeys within the U.K., *e.g.* from England to the Isle of Man.

Ships. The Athens Convention 1974, Art. 1(3) applies to sea-going ships, but excludes hovercraft (which are dealt with in the Hovercraft Act 1968 and Hovercraft (Civil Liability) Order 1986 (S.I. 1986 No. 1305), as amended. For discussion of sea-going ships, see the General Note to Sched. 11, Pt. II, para. 2. The *Marchioness* disaster in 1989 raised the initial question of whether the pleasure craft was a ship (and see *The Goring* [1988] A.C. 831, and General Note to Sched. 11, Pt. I, Art. 1). As the vessel operated wholly in the river Thames, it was probably not within the Athens Convention 1974. This meant that ordinary tort rules of liability applied, but note that Art. 7 of the 1976 Limitation Convention would have applied an overall limit of liability.

Contracts of carriage. Article 1.1 applies to contracts of carriage. The Convention does not apply to gratuitous carriage, *e.g.* on a friend's boat. Schedule 6, Pt, II, para. 9 excludes a contract not for reward (which is probably a contradiction in terms). See also the Domestic Carriage

Order 1987, Art. 2. Where passengers obtain free tickets in a promotion it may be that their suppliers (*e.g.* newspapers) act as agents. Where parties are booked on a boat, with passengers as guests (*cf.* the *Marchioness*), the organiser might be liable as agent or as contracting carrier.

Carrier. Article 1(1) distinguishes between a performing (actual) carrier and the person who made the contract (the contracting carrier). Under Arts. 3 and 4 both can be liable.

Passengers and Luggage. Article 1(4) defines passengers so that they may include vets accompanying animals or the "crew" of a truck whose only contract is one for the transport of the truck itself.

Article 1(5), (6), (7) define the luggage covered. Different limits apply to different categories of luggage.

Period of responsibility. Article 1(8) governs the period of responsibility in which the Convention applies. Essentially, the Athens Convention 1974 applies to passengers on board ship and boarding the ship's gangplank (see *Alder v. Dickson; The Himalaya* [1955] 1 Q.B. 158). While they are on the quayside or in a terminal the Convention does not apply. Where they are injured as a result of the collapse of a shore-based linkspan (functionally separate from the ship) it would seem that the Convention would not apply. If the ship uses tenders to transport passengers, the Convention will only apply if the fare covers such transport. If a payment is made to the tender operator, *e.g.* in a port of call, the Convention will not apply and the passengers will have to sue the operator of what may be a small craft (often with very low limits of liability under Sched. 7, below). If the payment is made to the carrier as an extra payment, it will be important to see if the carrier was acting as principal or agent.

Persons liable. Under Art. 3 the contracting carrier is liable. Under Art. 4 the performing carrier is also liable despite the existence of any *Himalaya* clause in the ticket (see Art. 18). Under the Athens Convention 1974, Art. 11, a servant or agent is entitled to defences and limits in any event, but that article does not apply to the carriers themselves.

Liability regime. Article 3 essentially provides a fault-based regime, with the burden of proof being initially on the claimant to show negligence (see Art. 3(2)). This might be relevant where the passenger claimed injury as a result of a slippy deck. However, where there are disasters such as shipwrecks, Art. 3(3) reverses the burden of proof.

The extent of liability is set out in Art. 3(1) and is for death or injury or loss of luggage. Economic loss, or disappointment, is now covered by the Convention. Luggage claims require notice of loss to be given (see Art. 15). There is an exclusion for valuables (Art. 5) unless they are deposited with the carrier (and see s.186 and Sched. 6, Pt. II, para. 13). Contributory negligence is a defence (Art. 6 and Sched. 6, Pt. II, para. 3).

Liability may be increased (Art. 10, but *cf.* Art. 4(3)), but not reduced (see Art. 18). It is not therefore possible to contract out of the Athens Convention 1974. In particular, the choice of jurisdiction given by Art. 17 cannot be removed.

Time bar. Article 16 provides a two year time bar (*cf.* s.190), which is shorter than the Limitation Act 1980, ss.11, 12 three year limit.

Limitation of liability. See Gaskell, "The Athens Convention 1974 and Limitation of Liability" (1987) 137 NLJ 322–323, N. Gaskell (ed.) *Limitation of Shipowners Liability: The New Law*, (1986), pp. 53–57.

The Athens Convention 1974, Arts. 7 and 8 apply limits of liability in respect of *each* claim by a passenger. If one passenger is injured then the limit applies to that passenger. If 15 are injured each would have a separate limit applying to them. By contrast, the limits under the 1976 Limitation convention, Art. 7 (Sched. 7, below) apply to the totality of claims. The 1976 Limitation Convention, Art. 7 limit will apply even if there is only one claimant (*i.e.* it is reserved for disasters). The Athens Convention 1974 limits will apply in every single case and can cause hardship.

The limit under Art. 7 of the Athens Convention 1974 is about £42,000 per passenger, a ridiculously low figure. The Athens Convention 1974 allows states to increase the limits for their own carriers (see Sched. 6, Pt. II, para. 4). The Carriage of Passengers and their Luggage by Sea (United Kingdom Carriers) Order 1987 (S.I. 1987 No. 855), amended in 1989 (S.I. 1989 No. 1880), increases the limit for carriers whose principal place of business is in the U.K. to 100,000 special drawing rights (SDR) (about £90,000). The 1990 Protocol to the Athens Convention 1974 will increase the limit to 175,000 SDR (about £158,000), as well as increasing the luggage limits.

The luggage limits under Art. 8 of the Athens Convention 1974 are also very low. The limit for a car is about £3,000. There is greater justification for property limits as passengers are more likely to carry insurance.

Article 19 makes it clear that the Athens Convention 1974 limits are subject to those in the 1976 Limitation Convention (Sched. 7, below). Schedule 6, Pt. II, para. 12 confirms this principle.

Breaking limits. See the General Notes to s.57, above, and to Art. 4 of the 1976 Limitation Convention (Sched. 7, Pt. I, below). It will be difficult to break limits under the Athens Convention 1974 as Art. 13 of that Convention is similar to that in Art. 4 of the 1976 Limitation Convention, and is unlike the Warsaw Convention for air transport, in that the limits cannot be broken by finding misconduct on the part of the master crew (see *R.G. Mayor (t/a Granville Coaches) v. P. & O Ferries; Lion, The* [1990] 2 Lloyd's Rep. 144 and *cf. Goldman v. Thai Airways International* [1983] 3 All E.R. 693).

Schedule 6, Pt. II, para. 11 allows the Secretary of State to make an Order concerning the information to be given to a passenger. The Carriage of Passengers and their Luggage by Sea (Notice) Order 1987 (S.I. 1987 No. 703) requires a carrier to give passengers notice of limits, but failure to do so is a criminal offence and does not deprive the carrier of limits.

Section 185   SCHEDULE 7

CONVENTION ON LIMITATION OF LIABILITY FOR MARITIME CLAIMS 1976

GENERAL NOTE

See the General Note to s.185, above. Also N. Gaskell (ed.) *Limitation of Shipowners Liability: The New Law*, 1986).

Schedule 7 contains the text of the 1976 Limitation Convention. Schedule 7, Pt. I contains the relevant articles of the Convention and Pt. II contains the necessary modifications to make the Convention operate in U.K. law.

The 1976 Limitation Convention came into force on December 1, 1986. A draft Protocol has been submitted to a diplomatic conference to be held in 1996.

PART I

TEXT OF CONVENTION

CHAPTER I. THE RIGHT OF LIMITATION

ARTICLE 1

Persons entitled to limit liability

1. Shipowners and salvors, as hereinafter defined, may limit their liability in accordance with the rules of this Convention for claims set out in Article 2.

2. The term "shipowner" shall mean the owner, charterer, manager or operator of a seagoing ship.

3. Salvor shall mean any person rendering services in direct connection with salvage operations. Salvage operations shall also include operations referred to in Article 2, paragraph 1(d), (e) and (f).

4. If any claims set out in Article 2 are made against any person for whose act, neglect or default the shipowner or salvor is responsible, such person shall be entitled to avail himself of the limitation of liability provided for in this Convention.

5. In this Convention the liability of a shipowner shall include liability in an action brought against the vessel herself.

6. An insurer of liability for claims subject to limitation in accordance with the rules of this Convention shall be entitled to the benefits of this Convention to the same extent as the assured himself.

7. The act of invoking limitation of liability shall not constitute an admission of liability.

GENERAL NOTE

The 1976 Limitation Convention, Art. 1 sets out which persons are entitled to claim the benefit of limitation. Note that the definition of shipowner in Art. 1.1 includes operators, charterers and parent companies (*cf. The Amoco Cadiz* [1984] 2 Lloyd's Rep. 304, 336–7). Article 1.5 allows the shipowner to limit even if the claimant brings an action *in rem* which might be considered otherwise as an action against the vessel not the shipowner. Article 1.6 also gives some protection to liability insurers who may be sued directly under long arm statutes. Salvors are entitled to limit and the decision in *Owners of the Motor Vessel Tojo Maru v. N.V. Bureau Wijsmuller; Tojo Maru, The* [1972] A.C. 242 is effectively reversed (see Art. 1.3). Article 1.4 allows persons such as the master and crew members to limit if sued individually.

Note that dock owners and repairers may be entitled to limit under s.191, above. Pilots may be entitled to limit under the Pilotage Act 1987, s.22.

ARTICLE 2

Claims subject to limitation

1. Subject to Articles 3 and 4 the following claims, whatever the basis of liability may be, shall be subject to limitation of liability:

(a) claims in respect of loss of life or personal injury or loss of or damage to property (including damage to harbour works, basins and waterways and aids to navigation), occurring on board or in direct connection with the operation of the ship or with salvage operations, and consequential loss resulting therefrom;

(b) claims in respect of loss resulting from delay in the carriage by sea of cargo, passengers or their luggage;

(c) claims in respect of other loss resulting from infringement of rights other than contractual rights, occurring in direct connection with the operation of the ship or salvage operations;

(d) claims in respect of the raising, removal, destruction or the rendering harmless of a ship which is sunk, wrecked, stranded or abandoned, including anything that is or has been on board such ship;

(e) claims in respect of the removal, destruction or the rendering harmless of the cargo of the ship;

(f) claims of a person other than the person liable in respect of measures taken in order to avert or minimise loss for which the person liable may limit his liability in accordance with this Convention, and further loss caused by such measures.

2. Claims set out in paragraph 1 shall be subject to limitation of liability even if brought by way of recourse or for indemnity under a contract or otherwise. However, claims set out under paragraph 1(d), (e) and (f) shall not be subject to limitation of liability to the extent that they relate to remuneration under a contract with the person liable.

GENERAL NOTE

Article 2 lists the claims which are subject to limitation, whether the claims arise in contract, tort or through any other cause of action.

Under Art. 2.1(a), death and injury claims are subject to the limits, *e.g.* where the crew or passengers on one ship claim damages from a colliding ship. Property claims are also covered, including harbour damage claims (*e.g.* where there is strict liability under local harbour legislation, such as the Harbours, Docks & Piers Clauses Act 1847, s.74).

Article 2.1(d) allows limitation of liability for wreck raising (*e.g.* under the Harbours, Docks & Piers Clauses Act 1847, s.56, or s.201 of the Merchant Shipping Act 1995). However, Art. 18 of the 1976 Limitation Convention allows reservations to be made by states and the U.K. has made such a reservation. Schedule 7, Pt. II, para. 3 negates Art. 2.1(d). Where the wreck raising claim is included in a recourse action by the sunken ship against a colliding vessel, it is unclear whether the full amount of the claim can be included or whether the colliding ship can rely on its limits (*cf. The Stonedale No. 1 (Owners) v. Manchester Ship Canal Co.* [1956] A.C. 1, *Barameda Enterprises v. O'Connor and K.F.V. Fisheries; Tiruna and Pelorus, The* [1987] 2 Lloyd's Rep. 666). The better view is that the recourse action is not a claim for "wreck raising" and can therefore be subject to limitation. There is limitation of liability for cargo raising (see Art. 2.1(e)).

Under Art. 2.2 contractual indemnities may also be subject to limitation of liability (*cf. Alsey Steam Fishing Co. v. Hillman (Owners); The Kirknes* [1957] P. 51.

ARTICLE 3

Claims excepted from limitation

The rules of this Convention shall not apply to:

(a) claims for salvage or contribution in general average;

(b) claims for oil pollution damage within the meaning of the International Convention on Civil Liability for Oil Pollution Damage dated 29th November 1969 or of any amendment or Protocol thereto which is in force;

(c) claims subject to any international convention or national legislation governing or prohibiting limitation of liability for nuclear damage;

(d) claims against the shipowner of a nuclear ship for nuclear damage;

(e) claims by servants of the shipowner or salvor whose duties are connected with the ship or the salvage operations, including claims of their heirs, dependants or other persons entitled to make such claims, if under the law governing the contract of service between the shipowner or salvor and such servants the shipowner or salvor is not entitled to limit his liability in respect of such claims, or if he is by such law only permitted to limit his liability to an amount greater than that provided for in Article 6.

GENERAL NOTE

Article 3 sets out claims which are excepted from limitation of liability, in respect of which liability will be unlimited.

Article 3(a) of the 1976 Limitation Convention excludes claims for salvage from limitation of liability (although *cf. The Breydon Merchant* [1992] 1 Lloyd's Rep. 373). Accordingly, it will not be possible for a shipowner to limit liability for claims under Art. 13 of the 1989 Salvage Convention (Sched. 11, below). Under Art. 14.1 special compensation is payable by the shipowner and not the cargo owners (see the General Note to Art. 14.1, Sched. 11, Pt. I, below). See Sched. 7, Pt. II, para. 4, below.

For the interpretation of paras. (b) and (c) see Sched. 7, Pt. II, para. 4, below.

Under Art. 3(e) master and crew claims against employers may be subject to limitation of liability, depending on the application of the law governing the contract of employment; see s.185(4) above.

ARTICLE 4

Conduct barring limitation

A person liable shall not be entitled to limit his liability if it is proved that the loss resulted from his personal act or omission, committed with the intent to cause such loss, or recklessly and with knowledge that such loss would probably result.

GENERAL NOTE

Most limitation provisions have rules defining when the right to limit is lost. The old rules under the 1894 Act and the 1957 Limitation Convention depended on a test which meant that it was comparatively easy to break the limits in the U.K. The 1976 Limitation Convention uses a test largely borrowed from air law. It should mean that limitation will only be denied where the damage has been inflicted intentionally or by conduct that is virtually equivalent to such deliberate action. Mere negligence will give rise to liability, but the limits should still be available—unless the judges weaken.

Limitation of liability is a sensitive and sometimes emotive topic, but it is absolutely vital to separate two questions, (i) is limitation of liability socially justifiable, and (ii) is limitation breakable according to the test in Art. 4? The first is a question of policy and the second is a question of law. It would be foolish to suppose that questions of policy and law can be rigidly separated and it will always be the function of the judge to achieve a "just" result. It is well-known that judges have been hostile to limitation, particularly when the carriers have sought to rely on limits which appear absurdly low in relation to the loss. Limits in property, and not personal injury/death, cases are useful in assisting claims settlement and fixing liability insurance risks. However, there is a danger in approaching the interpretation of limitation provisions by asking "should there really be a system of limitation of liability" instead of "what is the rule that the diplomatic conference and legislature have enacted".

A final difficult question will be to identify the person(s) in a corporate structure whose acts or omissions will deprive a company of the limits. Again, faults of a master will give rise to liability through principles of vicarious liability, but the right of an owner to limit will only be lost if there is the requisite conduct of someone more senior, *e.g.* a managing director.

There are two "streams" of legal principles which have converged to produce the "breaking" test now in Art. 4 and the difficulty is in tracing accurately which principles have survived in that provision. See also the General Note to s.157, above.

The old test was that of "actual fault or privity" as set out in the Merchant Shipping Act 1894, s.503 (and the 1957 Limitation Convention, Art. 1(1)). Essentially it depended on fault. The new test in Art. 4 requires a much higher level of misconduct (*cf. Goldman v. Thai Airways International* [1983] 3 All E.R. 693). The burden of proof under s.503 of the Merchant Shipping Act 1894 was on the shipowner (*Northern Fishing Co. (Hull) v. Eddam; Norman, The* [1960] 1 Lloyd's Rep. 1). Under Art. 4 the burden is now on the claimant, *i.e.* the victim, (see *The Capitan San Luis* [1993] 2 Lloyd's Rep. 573).

Where there is a shipowning company, the misconduct of mere servants or agents should not deprive the shipowner of the limitation of liability (*cf. R.G. Mayor (t/a Granville Coaches) v. P & O. Ferries; Lion, The* [1990] 2 Lloyd's Rep. 144). It may be necessary to examine the corporate structure very closely. Who was the directing mind and will of the company? Whose acts are the acts of the company itself? A management company employed by the shipowner will be such a directing mind and will (see *Lennards Carrying Co v. Asiatic Petroleum* [1915] A.C. 705, *Grand Champion Tankers v. Norpipe A/S; Marion, The* [1984] A.C. 563). It is misleading to look for a single alter ego. Misconduct by directors of the main board may suffice, even if there is also an alter ego figure (see *Société Anonyme des Minerals v. Grant Trading Inc.*, *Ert Stephanie, The* [1989] 1 Lloyd's Rep. 349). In *Meridian Global Funds Management Asia v. Securities Commission* [1995] 3 All E.R. 918, the House of Lords has emphasised that there may be circumstances where those below board level might deprive the company of limits, depending on the functions of the individual concerned (see the General Notes to ss.100 and 157, and *The Lady Gwendolen* [1965] P. 294, *The Garden City* [1982] 2 Lloyd's Rep. 382). A major question arising from the decision in *The Lady Gwendolen* is how far one can look to any person to whom powers are delegated. If so, how far down the corporate ladder does one look? Note that in *The Marion* the management company to whom powers were delegated was the "shipowner", but the House of Lords looked to the conduct of the board of directors of the management company, rather than the conduct of that company's marine superintendent (*cf. Meridian Global*).

ARTICLE 5

Counterclaims

Where a person entitled to limitation of liability under the rules of this Convention has a claim against the claimant arising out of the same occurrence, their respective claims shall be set off against each other and the provisions of this Convention shall only apply to the balance, if any.

GENERAL NOTE
Limitation of liability is applied after the respective claims of two ships have been set off. The 1976 Limitation Convention limits are applied to the balance.

CHAPTER II. LIMITS OF LIABILITY

GENERAL NOTE

Articles 6–9
Limitation Unit. The limitation unit under the 1976 Limitation Convention is the special drawing right (SDR) of the IMF. It is based on the daily value of a basket of currencies (see Art. 8 and Sched. 7, Pt. II, para. 7).
Extent of Limit. The limit is calculated on a sliding scale depending on the size of the vessel involved, with minimum limits for small vessels. Personal claims are treated preferentially in comparison to other claims by having part of the overall limit reserved solely for them. Individual claims are scaled down in proportion to their size. See the tables and examples in N. Gaskell (ed.), *Limitation of Shipowners Liability: The New Law* (1986), p. 67 *eq seq.*
There are minimum limits for small ships, see *e.g.* Art. 6.1(b)(i), but *cf.* Sched. 7, Pt. II, para. 5. The total limits for a small ship in the United Kingdom are at half the Convention levels, *i.e.* at 250,000 SDR (about £225,000). This is allowed by Art. 15.2 of the Convention.
Where there are mixed personal and other claims, the personal claimants have reserved for them the top two thirds of the limits available, see the 1976 Limitation Convention, Art. 6.1(a). They also share in the figures in Art. 6.1(b).
The 1976 Limitation Convention, Art. 7 provides a separate set of limits for passengers. This operates as an overall maximum. Individual claims may also be subject to limits under the Athens Convention 1974. Note also Sched. 7, Pt. II, para. 6. It seems as though the limits of liability under the Athens Convention 1974 and its 1976 Protocol (see Sched. 6, above) will be applied first before the court will consider the limits under Art. 7.
Where there are tugs with a number of tows, there is a question as to whether limitation of liability is based on the flotilla or that of individual ships. It appears as though the court will look to see whether a cause of action arises in respect of a vessel before applying limits to that vessel (*cf. The Bramley Moore* [1964] P. 200; *The Smjeli* [1982] 2 Lloyd's Rep. 74).
There is a special limit for salvors under Art. 6.4 where they are not operating from a vessel, *e.g.* where they are airlifted on to a ship in distress (*cf. The Tojo Maru* [1972] A.C. 242).
For pilots, see the Pilotage Act 1987, s.22.
Under Art. 9, the limits apply to each "distinct occasion", *i.e.* a ship involved in two separate incidents in a voyage will generate two limits.

ARTICLE 6

The general limits

1. The limits of liability for claims other than those mentioned in Article 7, arising on any distinct occasion, shall be calculated as follows:
(a) in respect of claims for loss of life or personal injury,

(i) 333,000 Units of Account for a ship with a tonnage not exceeding 500 tons,

(ii) for a ship with a tonnage in excess thereof, the following amount in addition to that mentioned in (i):

for each ton from 501 to 3,000 tons, 500 Units of Account;

for each ton from 3,001 to 30,000 tons, 333 Units of Account;

for each ton from 30,001 to 70,000 tons, 250 Units of Account, and

for each ton in excess of 70,000 tons, 167 Units of Account,

(b) in respect of any other claims,

(i) 167,000 Units of Account for a ship with a tonnage not exceeding 500 tons,

(ii) for a ship with a tonnage in excess thereof the following amount in addition to that mentioned in (i):

for each ton from 501 to 30,000 tons, 167 Units of Account;

for each ton from 30,001 to 70,000 tons, 125 Units of Account; and

for each ton in excess of 70,000 tons, 83 Units of Account.

2. Where the amount calculated in accordance with paragraph 1(a) is insufficient to pay the claims mentioned therein in full, the amount calculated in accordance with paragraph 1(b) shall be available for payment of the unpaid balance of claims under paragraph 1(a) and such unpaid balance shall rank rateably with claims mentioned under paragraph 1(b).

4. The limits of liability for any salvor not operating from any ship or for any salvor operating solely on the ship to, or in respect of which he is rendering salvage services, shall be calculated according to a tonnage of 1,500 tons.

ARTICLE 7

The limit for passenger claims

1. In respect of claims arising on any distinct occasion for loss of life or personal injury to passengers of a ship, the limit of liability of the shipowner thereof shall be an amount of 46,666 Units of Account multiplied by the number of passengers which the ship is authorised to carry according to the ship's certificate, but not exceeding 25 million Units of Account.

2. For the purpose of this Article "claims for loss of life or personal injury to passengers of a ship" shall mean any such claims brought by or on behalf of any person carried in that ship:

(a) under a contract of passenger carriage, or

(b) who, with the consent of the carrier, is accompanying a vehicle or live animals which are covered by a contract for the carriage of goods.

ARTICLE 8

Unit of Account

The Unit of Account referred to in Articles 6 and 7 is the special drawing right as defined by the International Monetary Fund. The amounts mentioned in Articles 6 and 7 shall be converted into the national currency of the State in which limitation is sought, according to the value of that currency at the date the limitation fund shall have been constituted, payment is made, or security is given which under the law of that State is equivalent to such payment.

ARTICLE 9

Aggregation of claims

1. The limits of liability determined in accordance with Article 6 shall apply to the aggregate of all claims which arise on any distinct occasion:

(a) against the person or persons mentioned in paragraph 2 of Article 1 and any person for whose act, neglect or default he or they are responsible; or

(b) against the shipowner of a ship rendering salvage services from that ship and the salvor or salvors operating from such ship and any person for whose act, neglect or default he or they are responsible; or

(c) against the salvor or salvors who are not operating from a ship or who are operating solely on the ship to, or in respect of which, the salvage services are rendered and any person for whose act, neglect or default he or they are responsible.

2. The limits of liability determined in accordance with Article 7 shall apply to the aggregate of all claims subject thereto which may arise on any distinct occasion against the person or persons mentioned in paragraph 2 of Article 1 in respect of the ship referred to in Article 7 and any person for whose act, neglect or default he or they are responsible.

ARTICLE 10

Limitation of liability without constitution of a limitation fund

1. Limitation of liability may be invoked notwithstanding that a limitation fund as mentioned in Article 11 has not been constituted.

2. If limitation of liability is invoked without the constitution of a limitation fund, the provisions of Article 12 shall apply correspondingly.

3. Questions of procedure arising under the rules of this Article shall be decided in accordance with the national law of the State Party in which action is brought.

GENERAL NOTE
Limitation of liability can be pleaded as a defence. For the detailed rules, see R.S.C., Ord. 75.

CHAPTER III. THE LIMITATION FUND

GENERAL NOTE

Articles 11–14
The establishment of the limitation fund and its administration is dealt with in Arts. 11–14. The scheme of the 1976 Limitation Convention is to have all claims brought before one jurisdiction so that rateably reduced claims can be paid accordingly. Article 13 prevents claims being brought in other Convention states.

ARTICLE 11

Constitution of the Fund

1. Any person alleged to be liable may constitute a fund with the Court or other competent authority in any State Party in which legal proceedings are instituted in respect of claims subject to limitation. The fund shall be constituted in the sum of such of the amounts set out in Articles 6 and 7 as are applicable to claims for which that person may be liable, together with interest thereon from the date of the occurrence giving rise to the liability until the date of the constitution of the fund. Any fund thus constituted shall be available only for the payment of claims in respect of which limitation of liability can be invoked.

2. A fund may be constituted, either by depositing the sum, or by producing a guarantee acceptable under the legislation of the State Party where the fund is constituted and considered to be adequate by the Court or other competent authority.

3. A fund constituted by one of the persons mentioned in paragraph 1(a), (b) or (c) or paragraph 2 of Article 9 or his insurer shall be deemed constituted by all persons mentioned in paragraph 1(a), (b) or (c) or paragraph 2, respectively.

ARTICLE 12

Distribution of the fund

1. Subject to the provisions of paragraphs 1 and 2 of Article 6 and of Article 7, the fund shall be distributed among the claimants in proportion to their established claims against the fund.

2. If, before the fund is distributed, the person liable, or his insurer, has settled a claim against the fund such person shall, up to the amount he has paid, acquire by subrogation the rights which the person so compensated would have enjoyed under this Convention.

3. The right of subrogation provided for in paragraph 2 may also be exercised by persons other than those therein mentioned in respect of any amount of compensation which they may have paid, but only to the extent that such subrogation is permitted under the applicable national law.

4. Where the person liable or any other person establishes that he may be compelled to pay, at a later date, in whole or in part any such amount of compensation with regard to which such person would have enjoyed a right of subrogation pursuant to paragraphs 2 and 3 had the compensation been paid before the fund was distributed, the Court or other competent authority of the State where the fund has been constituted may order that a sufficient sum shall be provisionally set aside to enable such person at such later date to enforce his claim against the fund.

ARTICLE 13

Bar to other actions

1. Where a limitation fund has been constituted in accordance with Article 11, any person having made a claim against the fund shall be barred from exercising any right in respect of such a claim against any other assets of a person by or on behalf of whom the fund has been constituted.

2. After a limitation fund has been constituted in accordance with Article 11, any ship or other property, belonging to a person on behalf of whom the fund has been constituted, which has been arrested or attached within the jurisdiction of a State Party for a claim which may be raised against the fund, or any security given, may be released by order of the Court or other competent authority of such State. However, such release shall always be ordered if the limitation fund has been constituted:

    (a) at the port where the occurrence took place, or, if it took place out of port, at the first port of call thereafter; or

    (b) at the port of disembarkation in respect of claims for loss of life or personal injury; or

    (c) at the port of discharge in respect of damage to cargo; or

    (d) in the State where the arrest is made.

3. The rules of paragraphs 1 and 2 shall apply only if the claimant may bring a claim against the limitation fund before the Court administering that fund and the fund is actually available and freely transferable in respect of that claim.

ARTICLE 14

Governing law

Subject to the provisions of this Chapter the rules relating to the constitution and distribution of a limitation fund, and all rules of procedure in connection therewith, shall be governed by the law of the State Party in which the fund is constituted.

CHAPTER IV. SCOPE OF APPLICATION

ARTICLE 15

This Convention shall apply whenever any person referred to in Article 1 seeks to limit his liability before the Court of a State Party or seeks to procure the release of a ship or other property or the discharge of any security given within the jurisdiction of any such State.

GENERAL NOTE

The version of Art. 15 reproduced here is a partial version of the full text. The 1976 Limitation Convention sets out a set of principles for the application of the Convention to craft such as off-shore mobile units.

PART II

PROVISIONS HAVING EFFECT IN CONNECTION WITH CONVENTION

GENERAL NOTE

See the General Notes to Pt. I, for corresponding provisions.

Interpretation

1. In this Part of this Schedule any reference to a numbered article is a reference to the article of the Convention which is so numbered.

Right to limit liability

2. The right to limit liability under the Convention shall apply in relation to any ship whether seagoing or not, and the definition of "shipowner" in paragraph 2 of article 1 shall be construed accordingly.

GENERAL NOTE

For the craft for which limitation is available, see Art. 15 of the 1976 Limitation Convention (not in the Act) and para. 12. The Act applies limits to all ships (but see s.313(1)). See also s.311, above, and the General Note to s.313(1). For hovercraft, see the Hovercraft Act 1968, Hovercraft (Civil Liability) Order 1986 (S.I. 1986 No. 1305), as amended (S.I. 1987 No. 1835).

Claims subject to limitation

3.—(1) Paragraph 1(d) of article 2 shall not apply unless provision has been made by an order of the Secretary of State for the setting up and management of a fund to be used for the making to harbour or conservancy authorities of payments needed to compensate them for the reduction, in consequence of the said paragraph 1(d), of amounts recoverable by them in claims of the kind there mentioned, and to be maintained by contributions from such authorities raised and collected by them in respect of vessels in like manner as other sums so raised by them.

(2) Any order under sub-paragraph (1) above may contain such incidental and supplemental provisions as appear to the Secretary of State to be necessary or expedient.

GENERAL NOTE

See the General Note to Art. 2 in Pt. I, above.

Claims excluded from limitation

4.—(1) The claims excluded from the Convention by paragraph (a) of article 3 include claims under article 14 of the International Convention on Salvage, 1989 as set out in Part I of Schedule 11 and corresponding claims under a contract.

(2) The claims excluded from the Convention by paragraph (b) of article 3 are claims in respect of any liability incurred under section 153 of this Act.

(3) The claims excluded from the Convention by paragraph (c) of article 3 are claims made by virtue of any of sections 7 to 11 of the Nuclear Installations Act 1965.

GENERAL NOTE

See the General Note to Art. 3, above.

One difficult question that was not addressed in the 1989 Salvage Convention was the extent to which a shipowner could claim to limit liability for Art. 14 claims. It was doubtful if Art. 14 claims could be considered as "salvage", even though they derive from a Salvage Convention. They are simply special payments made under it. If this analysis is correct (and it would probably have surprised many delegates as the 1989 diplomatic conference) it would have to be seen whether or not the claims would fall within Art. 2 of the 1976 Limitation Convention. It is arguable that the claims would fit squarely into Art. 2.1(d) and/or (e). Although the limits might only be relevant in the most rare cases, it was surely the intention of those producing the 1989 Convention that Art. 14 claims be unlimited. An amendment to the 1976 Limitation Convention will be proposed when a Protocol to that Convention is discussed within the IMO in 1996.

The U.K. has made it clear by an amendment (inserted by the Merchant Shipping (Salvage and Pollution) Act 1994) now in Sched. 7, Pt. II, para. 4(1) that claims for special compensation under Art. 14 are not to be subject to limitation (and *cf.* Rule VI(b) of the York-Antwerp Rules 1994 which has provided that Art. 14 claims cannot be recovered from cargo in general average). Other claims which derive from the Convention may be subject to limitation of liability under the 1976 Limitation Convention in the ordinary way, *e.g.* where a claim is brought under Art. 8 for negligent damage caused to the salved property, or to the salvor's tug.

The general limits

5.—(1) In the application of article 6 to a ship with a tonnage less than 300 tons that article shall have effect as if—

(a) paragraph 1(a)(i) referred to 166,667 Units of Account; and
(b) paragraph 1(b)(i) referred to 83,333 Units of Account.

(2) For the purposes of article 6 and this paragraph a ship's tonnage shall be its gross tonnage calculated in such manner as may be prescribed by an order made by the Secretary of State.

(3) Any order under this paragraph shall, so far as appears to the Secretary of State to be practicable, give effect to the regulations in Annex I of the International Convention on Tonnage Measurement of Ships 1969.

GENERAL NOTE

See the General Note to Art. 6, above.

The tonnage is calculated according to the 1969 Tonnage Convention, see the 1976 Limitation Convention, Art. 6.5 (not included in the Merchant Shipping Act 1995 because of para. 5). Under para. 5 the calculation is made according to the Merchant Shipping (Liability of Shipowners and Others) (Calculation of Tonnage) Order 1986 (S.I. 1986 No. 1040).

Limit for passenger claims

6.—(1) In the case of a ship for which there is in force a Passenger Ship Safety Certificate or Passenger Certificate, as the case may be, issued under or recognised by safety regulations, the ship's certificate mentioned in paragraph 1 of article 7 shall be that certificate.

(2) In paragraph 2 of article 7 the reference to claims brought on behalf of a person includes a reference to any claim in respect of the death of a person under the Fatal Accidents Act 1976, the Fatal Accidents (Northern Ireland) Order 1977 or the Damages (Scotland) Act 1976.

GENERAL NOTE
See the General Note to Art. 7, above.

Units of Account

7.—(1) For the purpose of converting the amounts mentioned in articles 6 and 7 from special drawing rights into sterling one special drawing right shall be treated as equal to such a sum in sterling as the International Monetary Fund have fixed as being the equivalent of one special drawing right for—
(a) the relevant date under paragraph 1 of article 8; or
(b) if no sum has been so fixed for that date, the last preceding date for which a sum has been so fixed.

(2) A certificate given by or on behalf of the Treasury stating—
(a) that a particular sum in sterling has been fixed as mentioned in sub-paragraph (1) above for a particular date; or
(b) that no sum has been so fixed for that date and that a particular sum in sterling has been so fixed for a date which is the last preceding date for which a sum has been so fixed,
shall be conclusive evidence of those matters for the purposes of those articles; and a document purporting to be such a certificate shall, in any proceedings, be received in evidence and, unless the contrary is proved, be deemed to be such a certificate.

GENERAL NOTE
See the General Note to Art. 8, above.

Constitution of fund

8.—(1) The Secretary of State may, with the concurrence of the Treasury, by order prescribe the rate of interest to be applied for the purposes of paragraph 1 of article 11.

(2) Any statutory instrument containing an order under sub-paragraph (1) above shall be laid before Parliament after being made.

(3) Where a fund is constituted with the court in accordance with article 11 for the payment of claims arising out of any occurrence, the court may stay any proceedings relating to any claim arising out of that occurrence which are pending against the person by whom the fund has been constituted.

GENERAL NOTE
See the General Note to Art. 11, above.

Distribution of fund

9. No lien or other right in respect of any ship or property shall affect the proportions in which under article 12 the fund is distributed among several claimants.

GENERAL NOTE
See the General Note to Art. 12, above. Liens do not affect limitation of liability.

Bar to other actions

10. Where the release of a ship or other property is ordered under paragraph 2 of article 13 the person on whose application it is ordered to be released shall be deemed to have submitted to (or, in Scotland, prorogated) the jurisdiction of the court to adjudicate on the claim for which the ship or property was arrested or attached.

Meaning of "court"

11. References in the Convention and the preceding provisions of this Part of this Schedule to the court are references to the High Court or, in relation to Scotland, the Court of Session.

Meaning of "ship"

12. References in the Convention and in the preceding provisions of this Part of this Schedule to a ship include references to any structure (whether completed or in course of completion) launched and intended for use in navigation as a ship or part of a ship.

GENERAL NOTE
See the General Note to para. 2, above.

Meaning of "State Party"

13. An Order in Council made for the purposes of this paragraph and declaring that any State specified in the Order is a party to the Convention shall, subject to the provisions of any subsequent Order made for those purposes, be conclusive evidence that the State is a party to the Convention.

Section 193   SCHEDULE 8

COMMISSIONERS OF NORTHERN LIGHTHOUSES

1.—(1) The Commissioners of Northern Lighthouses shall continue to exist under that name as a body corporate constituted as follows.

(2) The following persons holding the following offices constitute the Commissioners of Northern Lighthouses, that is to say—

(a) the Lord Advocate and the Solicitor-General for Scotland;
(b) the lords provosts of Edinburgh, Glasgow and Aberdeen, and the conveners of the councils for Highland and Argyll and Bute;
(c) the sheriffs principal of all the sheriffdoms in Scotland;
(d) a person nominated by the Lieutenant Governor of the Isle of Man and appointed by the Secretary of State;
(e) any person elected under paragraph 2 below.

2.—(1) The Commissioners may elect, as members of their body, the convener of any council whose area includes any part of the coasts of Scotland.

(2) The Commissioners may elect, as members of their body, not more than five other persons; but a person shall not be elected in pursuance of this sub-paragraph unless either he appears to the Commissioners to have special knowledge and experience of nautical matters or three persons who so appear are members of that body.

3. A person appointed by the Secretary of State under paragraph 1(2)(d) above, or a person appointed by the Commissioners under paragraph 2(2) above, shall hold office for three years, but shall be eligible for re-appointment.

4.—(1) Any five of the Commissioners shall constitute a quorum.

(2) The Commissioners constituting a quorum shall have power to do all such matters and things as might be done by the whole body.

5. In this Schedule "council" means a council constituted under section 2 of the Local Government etc. (Scotland) Act 1994.

Section 202   SCHEDULE 9

GENERAL TRANSFER OF LOCAL LIGHTHOUSES TO HARBOUR AUTHORITIES

1.—(1) Before such date as may be specified in a direction given by the Secretary of State to each of the general lighthouse authorities, each of those authorities shall submit to the Secretary of State proposals in writing for the transfer under this Schedule to the appropriate harbour authorities of such of the lighthouses, buoys and beacons held by the general lighthouse authority concerned as—

(a) are situated in the area of any harbour authority or on land adjacent to the area, or any part of the area, of such an authority; and

(b) appear to the general lighthouse authority concerned to be of benefit solely or mainly to ships within, or entering or leaving, that harbour authority's area.

(2) For the purposes of this Schedule, a harbour authority are the appropriate harbour authority in relation to any such lighthouse, buoy or beacon if the lighthouse, buoy or beacon is situated in that authority's area or on land adjacent to that area or any part of it.

2.—(1) The proposals submitted by each general lighthouse authority shall—

(a) specify the lighthouses, buoys and beacons which the authority consider are required by paragraph 1 above to be covered by the proposals;

(b) specify in relation to each lighthouse, buoy or beacon specified in the proposals the harbour authority who are the appropriate harbour authority in relation to it; and

(c) specify in relation to each harbour authority so specified any property of the general lighthouse authority which has been used up to the date of the proposals exclusively in connection with the exercise by that authority of their functions in relation to lighthouses, buoys or beacons so specified which are situated in that harbour authority's area or on land adjacent to that area or any part of it.

(2) The proposals may specify in relation to any harbour authority so specified any property of the general lighthouse authority—

(a) which has been used up to the date of the proposals substantially but not exclusively as mentioned in sub-paragraph (1)(c) above; and

(b) which the general lighthouse authority consider it would be appropriate to transfer to that harbour authority.

3. Before submitting any proposals under paragraph 1 above a general lighthouse authority shall consult each harbour authority specified in the proposals.

4.—(1) The Secretary of State may make such modifications of any proposals submitted to him in accordance with the foregoing provisions of this Schedule as he thinks fit after consulting the general lighthouse authority who submitted the proposals; and if he does so, references in paragraph 5 below to any proposals under this Schedule are references to the proposals as modified.

(2) Before deciding whether to make any such modifications—

(a) affecting any harbour authority specified in the proposals; or

(b) by virtue of which provision would be included in the proposals for the transfer to a harbour authority under this Schedule of any lighthouse, buoy or beacon;

the Secretary of State shall consult the harbour authority concerned.

5. On such day as the Secretary of State may by order appoint as the transfer date for the purposes of this Schedule—

(a) all lighthouses, buoys and beacons specified in any proposals under this Schedule; and

(b) any other property of a general lighthouse authority so specified;

shall be transferred and vest in accordance with the proposals.

Section 210   SCHEDULE 10

LOCAL LIGHT DUES: OBJECTIONS

The modifications to which section 31 of the Harbours Act 1964 is subject in its application in relation to local light dues by virtue of section 210 are as follows—

(a) references to charges shall be construed as references to local light dues;

(b) subsection (1) shall be omitted;

(c) in subsection (2), for the words from "a charge" to "maintaining or managing" there shall be substituted the words "a local light due imposed under section 210 of the Merchant Shipping Act 1995 by a local lighthouse authority", and the words "passengers or goods" (in both places) shall be omitted;

(d) in subsection (6)(b), the reference to subsection (2) shall be construed as referring to that subsection as modified by paragraph (c) above;

(e) in subsection (8), for the reference to a harbour authority there shall be substituted a reference to a local lighthouse authority;

(f) in subsection (9), for the reference to the harbour authority concerned there shall be substituted a reference to the local lighthouse authority concerned;

(g) in subsection (10), for the words "a charge imposed at a harbour" there shall be substituted the words "a local light due imposed by a local lighthouse authority"; and

(h) subsection (13) shall be omitted.

INTERNATIONAL CONVENTION ON SALVAGE 1989

GENERAL NOTE

See the General Note to s.224, above. This General Note draws upon material in Gaskell, "The 1989 Salvage Convention", Gaskell, "The International Convention on Salvage 1989" (1989) 4 IJECL 268 and Gaskell, "Policy Issues", to which reference may be made. See also, on the 1989 Salvage Convention, the following: G. Brice, *Maritime Law of Salvage* (2nd ed., 1993); E. Vincenzini, *International Salvage Law* (1992); G. Brice, "New Salvage Convention: green seas and grey areas" [1990] LMCLQ 32; D. Watkins, "Salvage Convention 1989, new perspectives" [1989] LMCLQ 416; E. Gold, "Marine salvage—Towards a new regime" (1989) 20 JMLC 487; J. Wooder, "New Salvage Convention: A Shipowners' perspective" (1990) 21 JMLC 81; D. Kerr, "The 1989 Salvage Convention: expediency or equity?" (1989) 20 JMLC 505. See also N. Gaskell, "LOF 1990" [1991] LMCLQ 104.

Part I of Sched. 11 contains the provisions of the 1989 Salvage Convention which are given the force of law. Note that the Act reproduces the exact text of the Convention, but with certain parts omitted where they are not relevant to U.K. law. For the full text of the Convention see [1990] LMCLQ 54). In particular, Arts. 28–34 (Chapter V Final Clauses) are not reproduced. Of these, Art. 30 is still relevant because it contains the reservations which a State is entitled to make when ratifying the Convention. For the U.K. reservations, see the General Note to Sched. 11, Pt. II, para. 2, below. Under Art. 29 the Convention will enter into force internationally on July 14, 1996, following its ratification by 15 states. The U.K. gave interim national effect to the Convention from January 1, 1995 by virtue of s.1(5) of the Merchant Shipping (Salvage and Pollution) Act 1994.

Part II of Sched. 11 contains provisions of U.K. law which must be read together with the Convention as set out in Part I.

For the background to the 1989 Salvage Convention see the General Note to s.224, above.

PART I

TEXT OF CONVENTION

CHAPTER I—GENERAL PROVISIONS

ARTICLE 1

Definitions

For the purpose of this Convention—

(a) Salvage operation means any act or activity undertaken to assist a vessel or any other property in danger in navigable waters or in any other waters whatsoever.

(b) Vessel means any ship or craft, or any structure capable of navigation.

(c) Property means any property not permanently and intentionally attached to the shoreline and includes freight at risk.

(d) Damage to the environment means substantial physical damage to human health or to marine life or resources in coastal or inland waters or areas adjacent thereto, caused by pollution, contamination, fire, explosion or similar major incidents.

(e) Payment means any reward, remuneration or compensation due under this Convention.

(f) Organisation means the International Maritime Organisation.

(g) Secretary-General means the Secretary-General of the Organisation.

GENERAL NOTE

It should be recalled that Art. 1, containing the definitions, formed part of a package and must be read together with other articles, particularly Art. 30 dealing with reservations. A number of States had quite strong views on what salvage was, or ought to be. Throughout the negotiations for the Convention there were many amendments suggested, or made, concerning the definitions. Phrases were included in draft articles, then removed only to resurface in later discussions, depending on whether a wide or narrow definition of salvage was desired. The solution to the seemingly interminable desire of lawyers to debate definitions involved making a choice between complete exclusion of certain topics from the scope of the Convention and allowing States with strong objections to make an individual reservation under Art. 30. This approach was designed to remove the risk of States being unwilling to ratify the Convention, although it may have had the effect of creating differences in salvage law around the world. In view of the many advances made by the Convention, and the comparatively minor nature of the reservations allowed, this was a small price to pay.

(a) Salvage Operations

Danger. Article 1(a) defines salvage operations very widely to be any form of assistance to vessels or other property in danger. The traditional requirement of danger to salved property is preserved and it will be left to the courts to decide exactly what this entails (and see the discussion of *Sunken vessels,* below). It will be a question of fact, and existing case law can continue to provide guidance. If the salved vessel or property is not in danger then there cannot be a salvage operation. This point should be borne in mind when considering the extent to which, under Art. 6.2, a cargo owner is bound by a salvage contract signed by the master on its behalf. If the cargo owner wishes to allege that it is not bound by the contract, it cannot any longer dispute the authority of the master. But in a case where the cargo owner alleges that there was never any necessity for the service (*i.e.* that there was no danger and it could have been performed by an ordinary tug at towage rates), it could still assert that the master only had authority under Art. 6.2 "to conclude contracts for salvage operations" and that as there was no salvage operation (within Art. 1(a)) neither could there be any authority.

Salvor. One surprising feature of the Convention is that there is no separate definition in Art. 1 of "salvor". A salvor is simply a person who performs the operations under Art. 1(a) and who is not precluded from claiming a reward under the voluntariness rules now in Art. 17. Therefore the Convention can apply to any category of person performing the operations, including non-professional salvors, such as fishermen. Such persons will have all the duties specified in the Convention relating to the preservation of the environment. There is no requirement that the assistance has to be given by any class of person, such as a professional salvor, nor does the service even have to be performed by a mariner from a vessel. A radio operator, or a pilot, can assist others in providing salvage services (for apportionment, see Art. 15). In *The Sava Star* [1995] 2 Lloyd's Rep. 134, it was held that there was no reason why a salvage claim should not be brought by a cargo owner which provided assistance to the ship in distress. It will be for the courts to decide, as now, whether the service performed any useful result within Art. 13(1). The duties are all qualified by the need to exercise due care under Art. 8, which will obviously be judged according to the skills and knowledge of the salvor concerned.

It will be for national law to decide whether persons with possessory or other interests will be entitled to claim. The standard demise charter, the Barecon 89, provides in cl. 17 that all salvage earned by a vessel under that charter will ultimately be for the demise charterer's account, and this is logical as the charterer provides the crew who perform the service. Such a charterer should have title to sue in English law, but the position of others, such as time charterers, is doubtful (see Brice, p. 60). In practice, modern time charters (such as Baltime, cl. 19 and NYPE 93, cl. 24) assume that the shipowner will make the claim, but that the net proceeds will be shared between the shipowner and charterer.

Geographical Extent. The rules of the 1910 Convention applied "in whatever waters the services have been rendered" and required that at least one of the vessels performing or receiving salvage services be a seagoing vessel (see Art. 1). The 1981 CMI Draft Convention simply repeated the "whatever waters" formula. The present wording of Art. 1(a) was inserted by the IMO Legal Committee and remained unamended despite a vigorous attempt by the U.K. (and, later, Saudi Arabia and France) to return to the 1910 formula.

Article 1(a) accepts that salvage can take place within a very wide geographical limit. There can be salvage, provided the property in danger is in "navigable waters or in any other waters whatsoever". Salvage is not restricted to seas or oceans. Accordingly, under Art. 1(a) as it stands, there can be salvage in the following locations: in any river whether it is tidal or not, or whether it is separated from the sea by locks; in any canal; or in any inland lake (apparently whether it is natural or man-made). In English law, this would be a major extension of the geographical limits of the law of salvage, as the House of Lords in *The Goring* [1988] A.C. 831 reaffirmed the existence of the anachronistic "tidal waters" test in English law. However, the wide definition has to be read subject to the restrictions in relation to "inland waters" imposed by Sched. 11, Pt. II, para. 2, below. The difference in U.K. law will be that the old reliance on tidal waters, as such, will no longer be possible although the actual result in a case such as *The Goring* would probably be the same. There will always be a somewhat arbitrary dividing line between admiralty and common law, if only because rewards for unrequested services were never recognised by the latter (*cf. Falke v. Scottish Imperial Insurance Co.* (1886) 34 Ch. D 234, 248).

(b) Vessel

Salvage can only be claimed for saving certain types of property. Traditionally these included a vessel, her equipment, cargo and freight. The extent to which other things are included varies between legal systems. The U.K. allowed for the salvage of wrecks and aircraft, but not certain types of buoy (*The Gas Float Whitton No. 2* [1897] A.C. 337). This unduly narrow view of what can be salved causes uncertainty with respect to modern structures operating offshore, was anachronistic and out of line with the law in other countries. See the General Notes to ss.312 and 313(1), above.

In respect of oil rigs and other offshore craft, the position in English law was unclear, although there is every reason in practice for such creatures to be subject to the salvage regime: apart from the fact that they are often very valuable, many of them have persons on board. The general spirit behind the 1989 Convention was to make its scope as broad as possible. Hence the definitions of vessel and property in Art. 1(b) and (c) are very wide and only restricted by Arts. 3 and 4 and Sched. 11, Pt. II, para. 2, below.

The definition of vessel is reasonably clear and would cover ships, barges and hovercraft. The word "any" was added to make it clear that the word navigation was not meant to qualify "ship" or "craft". The addition of the word "structures" is helpful, as it would cover floating cranes, floating dry docks and semi-submersible heavy lift barges, provided that a court would accept that these structures were "capable of navigation" (*cf. The Gas Float Whitton No. 2*). It no longer matters if a narrow view is taken of the phrase, as the structures would still fall within the definition of property in Art. 1(c), below. The same reasoning would have applied to oil and gas rigs, were it not for the exclusion in Art. 3, below. Article 4 restricts the application of the Convention in respect of State-owned vessels.

(c) Property

This sub-paragraph is mainly designed to ensure that virtually all property on board a ship, such as cargo, equipment, stores and personal belongings, can be a subject of salvage. It is deliberately wide. Even if a particular category of craft did not fit into Art. 1(b), it would almost certainly fall under Art. 1(c). Under the Civil Aviation Act 1982, s.87(1) aircraft may be salved in, on or over the sea.

Offshore platforms which are not excluded by Art. 3. Article 3, below, completely excludes from the Convention certain platform and drilling units, but there may be circumstances where even these could be salved. The exclusion in Art. 3 only applies when the units are (i) on location and (ii) engaged in exploration, exploitation or production. While in *transit* to the place of operation, such rigs would fall within the general definition of vessel or property. Further, it was never intended that the exclusion would cover vessels involved in the transportation of seabed resources. The expression "on location" in Art. 3 was used instead of "directly", which appeared in the original U.S. proposal. There may be difficult temporal questions. Presumably, if a mobile oil drilling unit drifts away accidentally from its drilling site it can be salved. Yet it would seem odd that a salvor would have to wait until after anchor lines had broken before being able to commence salvage.

Further, a platform or unit may be engaged in exploration without at the particular moment of distress having any form of physical attachment to the seabed. Although the drafters clearly had in mind drilling structures, Art. 3 does not say "engaged in drilling". If the excluded activities can consist of work other than drilling, it may be very difficult to tell whether the structure is "engaged" in a particular activity or not. In particular, it is not clear whether a fixed accommodation platform is "engaged" in transportation, or whether it is servicing the main drilling unit "engaged" in exploitation. It would seem preferable to exclude all these ancillary platforms. This conclusion will be of particular concern to a salvor, who will not want to perform some expensive and risky service only to be told that the rig was excluded at the relevant time and that the service had been performed gratuitously.

In many circumstances, a potential salvor may be best advised to arrange a contract, *e.g.* on LOF terms, in order to ensure that there is a binding obligation as to payment. This would be allowed by Art. 6.1, below. The LOF 1990 pointedly did not incorporate Art. 3 by reference, and the effect of this must be that its general arbitration and payment structure can apply to services provided to platforms. There is then either a waiver of the right to exclude salvage by the rig owner in signing the agreement, or an implied undertaking to put the salvor in the same position as he would have been in if there had been a salvage service. There might not then be a maritime lien or some of the other incidents (such as special time bars) that distinguish salvage claims from ordinary contractual work and labour contracts.

Other offshore structures. Article 3 does not exclude certain other structures found offshore which could not be described as platforms, but are even less like traditional maritime property. In the North Sea there are oil storage modules, usually made from concrete and of huge size and value, such as the *Brent Spar* platform (which aroused environmental concerns when Shell proposed to dump it in deep water in 1995). Likewise, there are the pipelines connecting platforms. The skilful actions of a salvage diver could preserve a very valuable facility. It may be very difficult to describe all such structures as "platforms"—although it seems that the word is used very widely in the industry. It would seem illogical not to exclude such structures and equipment.

Even if pipelines are not platforms (within Art. 3) they would only be capable of salvage if they fall within the definition of "property" in Art. 1(c). The question is whether they are permanently and intentionally attached to the shoreline. They are certainly attached to the seabed and indirectly by pipes to the shoreline somewhere (except in the case of those facilities that operate as mini-ports with single-buoy moorings). But the reference to the shoreline seems more to contemplate piers and jetties that depend on the shore for support. In an intervention at the diplomatic conference, the U.K. suggested adding "seabed" as it was considered that shoreline was not sufficient, but unfortunately no formal amendment was brought. There is some support for the view that such facilities are subject to salvage, as the IMO Legal Committee draft Art. 24(1)(c) had placed oil rigs and their like as an optional reservation. This referred specifically to property attached to the seabed for "production, storage and transportation". The U.S. amendment designed to replace this made no reference to storage and indeed, specifically disclaimed an intention to exclude vessels such as tankers involved in transportation of seabed resources. It is conceivable that the U.S. then had only in mind oil storage vessels, as opposed to fixed facilities. But it is understood that there was apparently no support in the informal negotiations for retaining storage or transportation as a reservation. The result, rather anomalously, is that these facilities may be subject to salvage under the Convention.

Sunken vessels and cargoes. The salvage of valuable wrecks must be distinguished from the raising of valueless wrecks in order to remove a blockage or a pollution risk (and see the General Note to Art. 5.2, below). Throughout the negotiations there was misunderstanding or disagreement (sometimes both) as to the conceptual nature of services performed to valuable sunken vessels and their cargoes (for the position of historic wrecks, see the General Note to Sched. 11, Pt. II, para. 2, below). The final version of Art. 1(c) makes no reference to such property and the question must be asked whether the Convention applies to it. According to some States it was not possible to salve property at the bottom of the ocean: others, mainly in the common law world, saw no reason why it could not be salvaged.

The salvors did not seem particularly interested in the controversy. This is probably because the International Salvage Union (ISU) represents professional salvors operating on floating or stranded casualties. They tend to steer clear of wrecks as they are likely to involve them in great expense for little reward and much aggravation from local authorities. The salvors would be much more likely to accept contractual daily rate or lump sum non-salvage agreements for wreck raising (such as Wreckcon 1993).

The 1981 CMI Draft Convention draft Art. 1–1(2) included in the definition of vessel one "which is stranded left by its crew or sunk" (but ignored the question of sunken cargo). It also excluded wreck raising in Art. 2 (*ibid.*). After discussion in the IMO Legal Committee all such references were removed.

For the 1989 diplomatic conference the Federal Republic of Germany argued that the Convention ought to deal with the matter one way or the other and proposed an amendment to para. (b) that would have specifically applied the Convention to sunken ships, except so far as wreck removal was concerned. For some countries, especially the Spanish-speaking ones, any form of raising was considered as a 'recovery' or an 'extraction' and could not be considered as salvage— even, apparently, where the wreck was valuable and not a danger or obstruction. Argentina submitted a more radical alternative than the German one that would have excluded wreck salvage except where it was performed immediately after the accident and was designed to prevent damage to the environment. Spain suggested adding sunken vessels and property to the list of reservations now in Art. 30. This would have enabled a State to apply its own concepts, at least to its own internal waters.

Discussions were then complicated by disagreement over whether wrecks were already covered by the general definition of property in Art. 1(c) of the IMO Legal Committee Draft. The German delegation had noted that it seemed unusual for a vessel to be considered as within Art. 1(b) and a sunken vessel within Art. 1(c), but that it did not really matter so long as there was a common understanding that they could be salved. Spain proposed a clarifying amendment which would have meant that vessels capable of navigation were considered under para. (b) and those incapable of navigation under para. (c). It would then have been left to the courts to decide under which category an object fell (the result presumably being the same in each case). This view received some South American support. As the final versions of paras. (b) and (c) do not contain any specific reference to sunken property, the crucial question is whether there was some common understanding that they could be salved. A number of delegations (including the U.K.) expressly accepted in interventions that sunken property could be salved under Art. 1.

The feeling of many who did not speak may well have been that expressed by Canada which stated that there had been much discussion in the IMO Legal Committee on the definitions in Art. 1 and that the 1989 Diplomatic Conference should be wary of redrafting at such a late stage. The German amendment was withdrawn after this view had been noted, with the observation that the time was not right to solve the matter, if it was solvable. That there was a lack of clarity was emphasised when Spain later pressed its proposal for a reservation in what became Art. 30. However, when the U.K. delegation then added its view that sunken vessels were included in "property" within Art. 1(c) and that this was assumed to be the general consensus, Prof. Dr. Trotz intervened to say that there had to be danger, but that the fear of certain countries was that sunken vessels were included, hence the need for the power to make the reservation for internal waters and the territorial sea. At this point the Spanish delegation intervened to say it agreed. It follows from the Spanish amendment that, although there were doubts, Spain assumed the Convention would apply to sunken vessels, as that is why she pressed so strongly throughout the 1989 diplomatic conference for the reservation. Her proposal was eventually lost on the indicative and formal votes.

It is submitted that, although there are doubts about the meaning of the paragraphs, the natural meaning of the English wording, and the understanding of the 1989 diplomatic conference, was that sunken property could be salved. It would be a matter for national courts to decide whether the property would be in danger, but this is generally assumed in the English cases (*cf. The Tubantia* [1924] P. 78 and see S. Dromgoole, N. Gaskell, "Interests in Wreck", Ch. 13 of N. Palmer, E. McKendrick, *Interests in Goods* (1993)). Although danger is largely a question of fact, there are decisions which raise questions of law, *e.g.* whether gold at the bottom of the sea is in danger (*The Egypt* (1932) 44 Ll. L. Rep. 21) or whether danger can include the threat from thieves (*cf. The Cythera* [1965] 2 Lloyd's Rep. 454 (S.C. NSW)). States such as Spain would be free to hold that sunken property was not in danger (but they could not decide that there was no "property"). In *King and Chapman v. The Owners and all Persons claiming an Interest in the Sailing Vessels La Lavia, Juliana and Santa Maria de la Vision* (High Court of Ireland, unreported, July 26, 1994), the court ruled that Spanish Armada wrecks had passed from the realm of maritime salvage law into the domain of archaeological law. That might be another way of saying that there was no danger. See also the General Notes to Sched. 11, Pt. II, para. 2, below, on the consequences of such a decision, and the General Note to Art. 14.1 (under the heading *Wreck and cargo recovery*) for a view that there may be no danger to *valueless* property.

Historic wrecks. Amongst all the disagreements on the salvage of sunken wrecks, a French proposal was considered which would have excluded cultural or historic wrecks from the definition of property in Art. 1(c)—and hence also the Convention. This was not received very enthusiastically and was withdrawn, but it reappeared in the form of a reservation in what became Art. 30(1)(d). As such it was accepted with very little discussion. The result is that a State can make its own rules for the preservation of such property and can control, at least in territorial waters, salvage attempts by treasure seekers. The reservation extends to ships and their cargo but, for instance, could include certain artefacts that were once in a coastal village that has since been overrun by the sea. The provision does nothing about substantive rights in historic wrecks, which is a matter left to national law. For the U.K. position, see the General Note to Sched. 11, Pt. II, para. 2, below.

Freight. Article 1(c) has retained the concept of freight being a subject of salvage. It seems at first sight rather strange to be able to salve something intangible such as a sum of money which is due. But the law is that it is only freight at risk that can be salved. What must usually happen is for the ship to be brought to her contractual destination in order to earn freight payable on delivery (which would otherwise be lost). If freight is payable in advance, and is not dependent on delivery, then it is not at risk and cannot be saved. It was not intended that hire be included in the concept of property "unless in the particular case the provision on the freight for the actual carriage of the goods is contained in the charterparty" (see the 1984 CMI Report, p. 10).

Passage money. Article 1(c) defines the "property" capable of being salved as "any property ... and *includes* freight at risk" (emphasis added). Passage money would not fall within the expression "freight" as the latter is only applied to sums payable for the carriage of *cargo*. There may be few occasions these days where passage money in the old sense (*e.g.* passenger fares payable on the vessel reaching its destination) is payable. It is submitted that existing English salvage law which includes passage money as a subject of salvage (*e.g. The Medina* (1877) 2 P.D. 5) could still apply. This would not be because it is swept up by s.20(2)(j)(iii) of the Supreme Court Act 1981 (see the General Note to s.224(6), point 6(d)(vi) and to the Merchant Shipping (Salvage and Pollution) Act 1994, Sched. 2, para. 6, in *Current Law Statutes Annotated 1994*), but because the inclusionary wording of the Convention would allow such payments to be treated as property. There is no indication in the travaux preparatoires that such money was to be excluded (*cf.* the treatment of hire, above).

(d) Damage to the environment

Salvage has traditionally been designed to protect life and property at sea. But as the preamble to the Convention states, salvage can also help protect the environment if the services are timely and efficient. Throughout the Convention there are references to the environment (see, *e.g.* Arts. 6.3, 8.1(b), 8.2(b), 11, 13.2, 14.2, 14.5 and 16), and these are particularly relevant in the articles dealing with payment (itself defined in Art. 1(e)) and the duties of the salvor and salvee. Article 1(d) defines "damage to the environment". The relevance of the expression is more easily seen in the context of the particular articles listed above. However, the extent of the new duties and payments will be measured by reference to Article 1(d), which is also very important to the understanding of the LOF 1990, into which it is incorporated. The LOF 1995 has removed references to particular articles of the Convention and simply refers to English law, "including the English law of salvage". Article 1(d) was designed to go further than cl. 1(a) of the LOF 1980, which only covered the risks of oil pollution from tankers. The article originally appeared in the 1981 CMI Draft Convention and thereafter was changed in only one trivial respect. The insurance interests were concerned about a woolly concept of environmental damage and a definition was adopted as part of the overall "Montreal Compromise" (see the General Note to s.224, above and to Art. 14, below) which was restrictive in a number of respects.

The damage must be substantial. Two environmental organisations opposed this requirement but without support. The damage must also be physical. The threat only of economic loss, or some intangible loss of amenity, would not be enough. The 'victims' of the damage have to be human health, marine life or marine resources. Thus, there would be damage if fish were killed or seaweed beds were destroyed. The place where the harm has to occur is in coastal or inland waters, or "areas adjacent thereto". As was noted by ACOPS, this geographical limit excludes the high seas where there could be serious environmental damage. It is also a pity that it does not use the same language as the CLC Protocol 1984, which refers to the exclusive economic zone (*i.e.* up to 200 miles). This particular restriction will cause problems where there are high seas salvages (see the General Note to Art. 14.4, below).

Finally, the damage has to fall within one of the major causes listed. These include most of the serious effects to be imagined following a serious casualty to a ship carrying hazardous or noxious substances. But the emphasis on "major" indicates that there will not be environmental damage by small scale pollution. In many ways the word "major" is more restrictive than "substantial". There could be "substantial" damage to a penguin if it is killed by oil, even though only a small amount has been discharged. But the linkage of "substantial" and "major" seems to indicate that the damage must be more widespread and general than merely to one installation or individual (and see the 1984 CMI Report, pp. 10–11). Overall, the type of circumstance that is envisaged is very similar to that which will justify a State in using its powers under the Intervention Convention 1969 (see s.137, above). If that is right, Art. 1(d) may be too restrictive. There is no reason why the threat of small scale environmental damage should be excluded as a factor in fixing a salvage payment. A small threat would result in a small payment for preventing it. It may be that there was a need to fix a fairly high standard for the purposes of the duties in Art. 8 as it would not be desirable for a salvor to weigh unduly the risk of a very small amount of bunker loss against the chance of saving life or, perhaps, a very valuable cargo. The restrictive definition ought to make the calculation of payments under Arts. 13 and 14 much easier. Perhaps certainty will be of more advantage to a salvor than the chance of some small extra reward.

There has been one significant decision of the Lloyd's Appeal Arbitrator on the meaning of "substantial" in Art. 1(d) where there was a threat to a SSSI (see Lloyd's Appeal Arbitration 4/11/1994 and the General Note to Art. 14.1, below).

(e) Payment

The expression "payment" is used as a noun in Arts. 7(b), 6.2, 12.2, 17, 18, 21.1, 22.2, 23.1, and 24. The purpose is generally to make sure that references are not limited to Art. 13 rewards, but may include Art. 14 special compensation, *e.g.* when interim payments are considered under Art. 22 (see the 1984 CMI Report, p. 11).

One question of construction is whether "remuneration or compensation" can include damages payable for breach of Convention obligations, *e.g.* under Art. 8 or Art. 21.2. Under Art. 8.2 the salvor may want to claim for damage to the tug and may ask for security under Art. 21.1, below. Under Art. 21.2, a salvor may want to bring a damages claim against a shipowner which had not taken best endeavours to ensure that a cargo owner had provided security. Would the two year time bar for payment under Art. 23 apply to such a claim?

The definition under Art. 1(e) is clearly aimed at other types of payments (see, *e.g.*, the use in Art. 12.2), but it may be inappropriate for there to be different security obligations or different time-limits to apply for various obligations arising out of the same Convention. Wildeboer considered that the use of the expression "remuneration" in the French text of the 1910 Convention was to cover remuneration for salvage (*e.g.* under Art. 13 of the 1989 Salvage Convention) and indemnification of expenses and damage suffered by the salvor, so that claims in relation to salvage services which are brought with a purpose other than the obtaining of salvage would not have fallen within the time bar article in the 1910 Convention (see Wildeboer, pp. 95–97, 359).

The issue is neither clear nor easy to resolve. It is tentatively submitted that Art. 1(e) could result in there being a different interpretation under the 1989 Salvage Convention and that uniformity of salvage law would best be served by interpreting Art. 1(e) widely so as to include all monetary claims which may arise under the Convention. However, there would be no great problem of principle if a narrower view were taken.

ARTICLE 2

Application of the Convention

This Convention shall apply whenever judicial or arbitral proceedings relating to matters dealt with in this Convention are brought in a State Party.

GENERAL NOTE

Applicable law
   Section 224 of the 1995 Act gives the Convention the force of law, but it will always be necess-ary to decide exactly when and to which judicial or arbitral proceedings the 1989 Convention applies. Article 2 states simply that it applies to proceedings brought in a State Party. Other articles define issues such as what may be salved and where salvage may take place. Most of the scope of application questions are resolved by the definitions in Art. 1. Unless a claim can be fitted within these definitions then the various rights and duties will not apply. The position of the parties may then depend on provisions of national law (and see the General Note to s.224(6), above). The Convention will apply unless a salvage contract provides otherwise (see Art. 6.1). The underlying law of the 1989 Convention could therefore apply to some obligations, but not to those where the contract clearly indicates otherwise.
   Relatively little attention has been paid to questions of the proper law of salvage (see, *e.g.* the lack of discussion in Brice and Kennedy). The reason for this may have been because of the extensive use of the LOF or other salvage contracts with an express choice of law clause, and also the very wide acceptance of the unifying 1910 Convention. L. Collins, (ed.) *Dicey and Morris, The Conflict of Laws* (12th ed., 1993) has barely a paragraph on the subject (at p. 1478), which quotes with approval from an article by Gutteridge and Lipstein in (1939) 7 Camb. L.J. 80, 92. They state that maritime law has found its own solutions to the question of conflict and that "no useful purpose is served by the introduction of rules of conflict into questions which are so essen-tially international in character that conflicts are best solved by the process of unification of law". There have been comparatively few differences between legal systems applying the 1910 Con-vention, but the acceptance of the 1989 Salvage Convention by some countries and not others may undermine uniformity, particularly in cases where it is sought to apply, or avoid, Art. 14. A court might then be asked to apply the 1989 Salvage Convention, even in circumstances which indicated that there might arguably be a different proper law (*e.g.* where the salvor, ship and cargo were all from a non-party State and the salvage operations took place in that State). The giving of the force of law to the Convention, and the plain terms of Art. 2, would seem to leave little room for an English court to apply any other system of law (*cf. The Hollandia (sub. nom. The Morviken)* [1983] 1 A.C. 565 and the heading *Jurisdiction*, below). The only exception would seem to be Art. 15.2, which specifically refers one issue to the law of the flag (and *cf.* Art. 5.3). Historically the English courts have not required a close connection between the oper-ations and the U.K. and the scope of the jurisdiction of the Admiralty Court has not been nar-rowed by the Merchant Shipping (Salvage and Pollution) Act 1994, Sched. 2, para. 6.
   One clear consequence of signing an LOF 1990 or an LOF 1995 is that cl. 1(g) will make the arbitration subject to the "law of England, including the English law of salvage". That will nat-urally include the 1989 Salvage Convention as enacted in the 1995 Act. Where there is a dispute about the extent of the master's authority to bind cargo to a salvage contract, Art. 6.2 will be applied in an English court. It seems that it will be of no use to the cargo owner to claim that under the proper law of the bill of lading the master had no authority to bind it to an LOF salvage contract, as it may be held in any event that the proper law, when considering the cargo owner's liability to the salvor, is the proper law of the salvage contract which, in the case of the LOF, is English law (see R. Olsen, "Sacking a Salvor" Tug and Salvage Convention Proceedings, South-ampton, October 1994, p. 11, citing from the decision of a Lloyd's arbitrator).

Jurisdiction
   The IMO Legal Committee draft Art. 21 contained an elaborate jurisdictional provision, giv-ing wide options to the salvor. The 1989 diplomatic conference agreed with a Liberian amend-ment to delete it as being unnecessary. The result of the deletion is that salvors will therefore have to rely either on a forum clause in a contract, or on the jurisdictional rules of the State in which they choose to bring proceedings. In a case where the Convention was thought to work

against salvors (*e.g.* Arts. 26 or 8.1(d)) there is nothing to stop them obtaining jurisdiction in a non-party State by ordinary means, *e.g.* by exercising a maritime lien. In a case where a salvage contract chose a non-party forum, but the salvor brought suit in a State Party, the court would presumably have to apply its own jurisdictional rules to determine whether to respect the forum clause. An English court would be bound to recognise the clause as Art. 6.1 allows derogations from the Convention. Thus, there could be no question of the Convention somehow striking down the clause on the basis that it would inevitably lead to the foreign court applying a less favourable law of salvage (*cf. The Hollandia* [1983] 1 A.C. 565, where Art. III, r. 8 of the Hague-Visby Rules expressly declared void any clause which derogated from the Rules).

ARTICLE 3

Platforms and drilling units

This Convention shall not apply to fixed or floating platforms or to mobile offshore drilling units when such platforms or units are on location engaged in the exploration, exploitation or production of sea-bed mineral resources.

GENERAL NOTE
    It has already been noted that the definition of "vessel" in Art. 1(b) might be wide enough to cover offshore mobile platforms and that the definition of "property" in Art. 1(c) would have been sufficiently wide to cover many other fixed platforms. In the negotiations a vital question was whether to include offshore structures in the Convention, to allow a reservation in respect of them, or to exclude them altogether. The 1981 CMI Draft Convention took the first course. The IMO Legal Committee chose the second. The third method was proposed in a U.S. amendment at the 1989 diplomatic conference. An informal Working Group of interested delegations was established to consider the proposals and it produced a redraft of the U.S. proposal which was eventually adopted as Art. 3.
    The Art. 3 exclusion applies to the three main types of structure now being used, be they platforms permanently installed on the sea-bed; or semi-submersibles which can raise or lower legs to or from the seabed; or mobile oil drilling units (MODUs). These are defined in the IMO MODU Code, adopted by Res. A.414(XI), 15, but may be described as drilling ships. The effect of Art. 3 is that it will not be possible to salve most of the offshore structures now working in places such as the Gulf of Mexico or the North Sea. The rationale was partly that such structures often have detailed safety and response plans which could be interfered with by a salvor having experience of ships rather than oil rigs. In view of the potential for explosions it is probably better that there is an exclusion. There is nothing to stop the salvor offering services under contract, *e.g.* under the LOF 1995.
    Note that the exclusion does not apply to structures within Art. 3 when they are in transit. For an analysis of this issue and of the type of platforms which do not fall within Art. 3, see the General Note to Art. 1(c), above.

ARTICLE 4

State-owned vessels

1. Without prejudice to article 5, this Convention shall not apply to warships or other non-commercial vessels owned or operated by a State and entitled, at the time of salvage operations, to sovereign immunity under generally recognised principles of international law unless that State decides otherwise.
2. Where a State Party decides to apply the Convention to its warships or other vessels described in paragraph 1, it shall notify the Secretary-General thereof specifying the terms and conditions of such application.

GENERAL NOTE
    The extent to which the provisions of a private law Convention should apply to State-owned property is always a thorny one, particularly as the fleets of many countries are government-owned, but run on normal commercial lines. Warships could clearly be subject to sovereign immunity under the International Convention for the Unification of Certain Rules Concerning the Immunity of State-Owned Ships 1926 (and see the State Immunity Act 1978). The 1910 Convention did not apply to ships of war or to Government ships (see Art. 13), although a 1967 Protocol was agreed to extend the Convention to such ships. Although ratified by the U.K., the Protocol was not widely accepted and the 1989 Convention, Art. 4.1 adopts a compromise by referring the issue of warships and other non-commercial ships to the generally recognised principles of international law, but allowing a State to decide otherwise for its own ships. There is

then an obligation under Art. 4.2 to inform the IMO of any terms or conditions of such application of salvage rules to its ships. The normal position will be for the Convention to apply to State-owned commercial ships. The Crown Proceedings Act 1947, s. 29 states that nothing in that Act shall authorise proceedings *in rem* in respect of the arrest of any Crown ships. Otherwise, s.230 allows salvage claims to be made against and by the Crown, without distinction as to the character of the ships concerned.

Note also, Art. 25, dealing with State-owned non-commercial cargoes, and Art. 26, concerning humanitarian cargoes.

ARTICLE 5

Salvage operations controlled by public authorities

1. This Convention shall not affect any provisions of national law or any international convention relating to salvage operations by or under the control of public authorities.

2. Nevertheless, salvors carrying out such salvage operations shall be entitled to avail themselves of the rights and remedies provided for in this Convention in respect of salvage operations.

3. The extent to which a public authority under a duty to perform salvage operations may avail itself of the rights and remedies provided for in this Convention shall be determined by the law of the State where such authority is situated.

GENERAL NOTE

Article 5.1

Article 5 deals with the relationship between the Convention and salvage operations carried out or controlled by public authorities. Article 13 of the 1910 Convention was more limited in its wording, in that it preserved national laws regarding the "organisation" of salvage services by or under the control of public authorities. It seems that this provision was designed not to restrict the public law functions of bodies such as the receiver of wreck although, as noted by Wildeboer (Wildeboer, p. 32), it is difficult to see how the 1910 Convention could have restricted these. Wildeboer considered that the 1910 provision was unclear but that, like the equivalent of Art. 4 of the 1989 Salvage Convention, it was designed to prevent the Convention from trespassing in the sphere of public law, *e.g.* the remuneration of salvage services by public bodies (*op. cit.*, pp. 32–33).

It is sensible to read Art. 5.1 as similarly designed not to restrict the public law functions of public authorities, not only in relation to wrecks, but also possibly in relation to the control of pollution. Here there is a potential overlap with Art. 9 which preserves the rights of coastal states. This latter provision was added at a later stage in the drafting of the Convention to deal with the particular concerns of states such as Australia and was very much a political provision. That is, it adds very little but was necessary to achieve international agreement. Existing provisions governing the public control of salvage operations (*e.g.* s.137) may also be restricted by Art. 11.

Does Art. 5.1 go beyond public law issues and "not affect" national law on the recovery of salvage remuneration by a public authority? Strictly, that is a matter dealt with by Arts. 5.2 and 5.3, below, and the only question of remuneration to which Art. 5.1 might apply is the extent to which a private salvor might have a claim for payment from a public authority. That would be a matter of national law (and see the 1984 CMI Report, p. 13). If it were held that Art. 5.1 could cover the recovery of salvage remuneration by a public authority, it might be stretching the language somewhat to read the word "provisions" as applying to the admiralty law of salvage, as it would normally refer to legislative provisions (*cf.* the more general use of "law" in Art. 5.3, below).

Article 5.2

Article 5 was virtually unchanged from the 1981 CMI Draft Convention Arts. 1–3 and the 1984 CMI Report (p. 14) confirms that Article 5.2 would entitle the private salvor which was carrying out operations under the control of a public authority to the various rights given by the 1989 Convention as against the salved interests under Art. 13 or the shipowner under Art. 14 (*cf.* the voluntariness issue discussed under Art. 17, below). The 1984 CMI Report noted that any claim against an authority for wreck removal payments would be a matter for national law. The 1981 CMI Draft Convention excluded wreck removal from its scope of application, although this provision was later deleted as being unnecessary. More difficult is the case of the authority which itself carries out such work. Literally, such an authority could be a salvor entitled to claim salvage under Art. 5.2, as the paragraph refers to "such salvage operations", *i.e.* those in Art. 5.1 which may be carried out "by ... public authorities". Article 5.2 must, however, be read subject to Art. 5.3, which imposes restrictions on the rights and remedies which an authority would otherwise have.

Article 5.3

The 1984 CMI Report recorded that the law varied between states as to whether, for instance, the Coast Guard or Fire Service could recover in salvage and it was intended that Art. 5.3 would preserve this position. Accordingly, the rights of foreign public authorities to claim salvage in the U.K. will be governed by the law of their State, *e.g.* where a French authority provides assistance in the Channel and a claim for salvage is later brought in the Admiralty Court. The rights of English public authorities would be governed by English law including, in this case, the law laid down by the Admiralty Court. It might be said that the previous law concerning salvage by public authorities was regarded as an application of the principle of voluntariness (see *e.g.* Kennedy, Ch. 6) and that, as the 1989 Salvage Convention deals with most voluntariness issues in Art. 17 without mentioning public duties, there is no longer any objection to such a claim on the grounds that the services are not voluntary. Such an approach would ignore the clear purpose and intent of Art. 5.3, which will helpfully force English lawyers to focus separately on the two main issues within the general concept of voluntariness, namely existing contractual rights (Art. 17) and public duties (Art. 5).

A preliminary point concerns the "public authorities" to which reference is being made. They could be local or national. The Coast Guard or fire services would clearly fall within the definition, but what of port authorities? Since the privatisation of most ports (see, *e.g.* the Ports Act 1991, *Current Law Statutes Annotated 1991*), it is a little difficult to say that a company like Associated British Ports, which owns and runs the port of Southampton, is a "public authority", as such. It is a private company which may also have public functions, such as operating as a port authority, given by local or public and general legislation. Halsbury's Laws of England, Vol. 1(1) (paras. 6–8) notes that the mere fact that a person exercises functions of a public nature does not mean that it is a "public authority". There is some legal authority that a private corporation exercising statutory powers as a port authority is not a "public authority". The decision in *Att. Gen. v. Company of Proprietors of Margate Pier and Harbour* [1900] 1 Ch. 749, is an ex tempore one of Kekewich J. (not perhaps the highest authority), relying on dicta in *The Ydun* [1899] P. 236, 239 and was for the purposes of the Public Authorities Protection Act 1893 (since repealed). It was held in *The Ydun* that a local authority was a "public authority" under the 1893 Act if it operated as a port authority, but did not deal with the situation of a private company exercising similar powers. It is submitted that although a private port authority exercising public regulatory or conservatory functions under statutory powers may more accurately be described as a statutory undertaker in English law, it is a public authority for the purposes of Art. 5 of the Convention which ought not to be interpreted restrictively. However, it must still be considered what English law actually is in respect of services performed by these public authorities.

The extent to which public authorities may charge for the performance of services will often depend upon whether there is a duty, usually statutory, to perform the service. In the absence of some clear statutory provision, it may be a question of seeing whether there is an absolute duty to provide a service, or a mere power for which a charge may be made (*cf. Glasbrook v. Glamorgan C.C.* [1925] A.C. 279, *China Navigation Co. v. Att. Gen.* [1932] 2 K.B. 197, *Harris v. Sheffield United F.C.* [1988] Q.B. 77). If there is a public duty arising from an office, the authority cannot claim money in the form of a tax without the sanction of Parliament (*cf. Att. Gen. v. Wilts United Dairies* 91 L.J. (K.B.) 897). If there is no requirement to perform the particular service, then a charge may be made (and see the pre-Crown Proceedings Act 1947 salvage cases cited in *China Navigation Co. v. Att. Gen.* [1932] 2 K.B. 197, at pp. 217, 231, 241).

It follows that the mere fact that a service is provided by a public authority does not mean that it must be provided gratuitously (*cf. The Lustre* 3 Hagg. Adm. 154, 155) and it is important to examine carefully any specific statutory provisions which govern the particular service. Section 250 of the Merchant Shipping Act 1995, for instance, allows for payments to be made to the DOT by shipowners when the coastguards watch or protect property (like a receiver of wreck), unless salvage has been claimed for such services. This assumes that a salvage claim can in appropriate circumstances be made, but not perhaps where a radio co-ordinating role is being played (*cf.* Brice, p. 68 *et seq.*, Kennedy, p. 253 *et seq.*). It may be that a cost-conscious Treasury will seek to make greater use of such a provision, which has not been much invoked. A further example concerns the air sea rescue service provided by the Royal Navy and the RAF. In the absence of a specific statutory duty to perform such services, the Treasury may seek to make use of Arts. 16.2 and 14 in order to recoup some of the considerable costs involved in providing the service (and see s.230 and the General Note to Art. 4, above).

Under the Fire Services Act 1947, s.3(4), fire authorities may not generally charge for services rendered by them unless that Act expressly provides. Certain fire authorities are able to make statutory charges, *e.g.* on insurers in London (see Halsbury's Laws of England, Vol. 18, paras. 408, 469). It is not clear if the Fire Services Act 1947 intends to forbid all charges, in all circumstances. Fire authorities often have arrangements with local salvors to provide assistance in fire fighting. In many cases, the salvors will have an informal arrangement under which they will pay the expenses of the fire authority, *e.g.* in sending personnel on a tug out to deal with a fire on a vessel. Such fire authorities will rarely claim a salvage reward, although it is believed that some (*e.g.* in the Channel area) may do so. The question which would then arise is whether the Fire Services Act 1947 would always prevent a claim.

It will always be relevant to ask whether particular public authorities have exceeded their duties. A fire authority may be obliged to provide local services in a port, but not on the high seas. In those circumstances, it is arguable that, notwithstanding the Fire Services Act 1947, it would be entitled to claim salvage. Some statutory powers do not forbid the making of financial claims, but may specifically mention that certain costs may be claimed. Thus, wreck-raising powers given to a harbour or lighthouse authority (*e.g.* under ss.252–253) usually give the right to recover expenses from the shipowner. This might indicate that no other charging method may be used (*The Citos* (1925) Ll.L.Reports 275, *The Mars* (1948) 81 Ll.L.Reports 452). A port authority may be obliged to remove a ship obstructing a passage (see *Bostonian (Owners, Master and Crew) v. Gregerso (Owners); Gregerso, The* [1973] L1 Q.B. 274), but not then to provide further services to save its cargo, or to effect temporary repairs. In *The Gregerso* the services provided could not be distinguished from the public duty and there could therefore be no claim for salvage on the basis of public duties being exceeded.

Whether it is advisable for public authorities to become involved in salvage operations is one issue, but the assumption in some of the case law seems to have been that it is wrong for port authorities to claim salvage. Most of the rules on voluntariness (see Art. 17) were designed to exclude certain claimants because of a conflict of motives. In the latter part of the 20th Century, it may not seem so strange for public bodies to act in a private commercial way. Indeed they may be encouraged to do so, both for fiscal reasons and in order to protect lives, the environment and property. It might be thought that, while accepting general rules of public law, the courts do not need to strive to find that a particular statutory power excludes any possibility of claiming payment under the 1989 Salvage Convention, unless there is some clear possibility of abuse, *e.g.* such as extortion. In English law, the effect of the wide definition of "salvage operations" in Art. 1(a), above, means that there may be many cases where public authorities could not sue for salvage under Art. 13. Nor could they claim under Art. 14 where they have incurred clean-up costs as part of their public duties. They would, however, have a strict liability claim in respect of oil pollution damage under s.153, above), but not where there was chemical pollution. In such circumstances, a common law negligence claim would be necessary against the shipowner.

ARTICLE 6

Salvage contracts

1. This Convention shall apply to any salvage operations save to the extent that a contract otherwise provides expressly or by implication.

2. The master shall have the authority to conclude contracts for salvage operations on behalf of the owner of the vessel. The master or the owner of the vessel shall have the authority to conclude such contracts on behalf of the owner of the property on board the vessel.

3. Nothing in this article shall affect the application of article 7 nor duties to prevent or minimise damage to the environment.

GENERAL NOTE

The use of salvage contracts

Although it is of fundamental importance to recognise that the right to a salvage reward under Art. 13 does *not* depend on contract, but arises as a *sui generis* incident of maritime law, most professional salvors will seek to offer salvage operations on the basis of standard form salvage contracts. International Salvage Union (ISU) statistics indicate that in 2,400 cases over a 15 year period, relating to salvage carried out all over the world, 74 per cent were carried out under a Lloyd's Open Form contract ([1993] ISU Bulletin). In 1993, there were 156 LOF cases, involving property worth £202.3 million, resulting in salvage awards of some £18.1 million. It might be noted that this was lower than in previous years and that in 1992 the figures were respectively £527.1 million and £33.6 million (source: Lloyd's Salvage and Arbitration Branch, 1994). There are other forms in use, *e.g.* the French Form of Maritime Salvage Agreement (Edition JV 1990), the Standard Form of the Maritime Arbitration Commission of the China Council for the Promotion of International Trade, the Salvage Agreement of the Documentary Committee of the Japan Shipping Exchange (1991), the USSR Salvage Contract of the Maritime Arbitration Commission at the Chamber of Commerce, Moscow, the Conditions of the German Court of Maritime Arbitration, Hamburg and the Turkish Maritime Organisation Salvage and Assistance Agreement.

The terms of the various contracts vary, but one reason for the popularity of the LOF amongst salvors is the fact that it provides arbitration before experienced arbitrators backed by a tried and reasonably quick method of obtaining security and payment. Implicit in the salvors' preference for contracts is the ability to choose a jurisdiction in the contract (London in the case of the LOF). This allows all claims to be brought in one court, but also prevents salvors having to litigate in the courts of countries without great experience of salvage cases. The risk is that the level of normal salvage awards would appear enormous to a bench used to a "work and labour" system of reward and which did not fully appreciate that a salvor may have to wait months for a 'no cure, no pay' job.

Article 6.1: Contracting out of the Convention

One of the preliminary questions during all the negotiations for the 1989 Salvage Convention was the extent to which it should be mandatory in nature. The IMO Legal Committee had followed the 1981 CMI Draft Convention in allowing parties to a salvage service to contract out of the Convention. A number of countries objected to this, partly because it would affect the uniformity of salvage law. There was a concern over the dominant practical influence of the Committee of Lloyd's in its role of drafting the LOF. Lloyd's is an industry, rather than a governmental, body and was seen by some overseas lawyers as a somewhat cosy English club, heavily influenced by English insurers and the large professional salvors. Yet those salvors were happy with the draft text and the underlying mood of the 1989 Diplomatic Conference was to assist them. It cannot be over-emphasised that the purpose of the Conference was to encourage salvors. Accordingly Art. 6.1, allowing the parties to contract out of the Convention, was eventually agreed at the diplomatic conference without difficulty. Accordingly, the continued existence of industry salvage contracts such as the LOF is assured—at least so long as the salvors continue to want to use them.

It has already been noted (see the General Note to s.224(6), point *5, Approach to the 1989 Salvage Convention*, above) that the effect of Art. 6.1 is to reverse the previous view of the relationship between salvage and contract law, which was that the general maritime law of salvage applied only in so far as it was expressly or impliedly incorporated into it. Article 6.1 of the 1989 Salvage Convention puts the matter the other way round in that the "Convention shall apply to any salvage operations save to the extent that a contract otherwise provides expressly or by implication".

The freedom to contract out of the Convention is expressly limited by Art. 6.3, below.

Article 6.2: Authority

The salvor wants to ensure that all salved interests are bound by any contract which is signed, in order to avoid having to bring proceedings all over the world in respect of a single operation. The master of a vessel in distress will normally have had authority to bind his owners to a reasonable salvage contract (see, *e.g. The Unique Mariner* [1978] 1 Lloyd's Rep. 438). Under Art. 6.2, the master is now given express authority to bind the "owners of the vessel" to a salvage contract. In the case of a demise charterparty, it appears that the master will have authority under the Convention to bind the shipowners and not the demise charterer who is his employer. To this extent it may be necessary to rely on indemnities in the demise charter if the shipowners are not to find themselves in court for contractual obligations undertaken by the charterer. The diplomatic conference was mindful of the consequence of using the expression "owner" as it rejected a French amendment to replace the word with "operator", perhaps because of the enforcement consequences. Article 6.2 does not state that it is only the shipowner which can have authority and the master employed by the demise charterer would be able to bind his employer as a matter of general law.

The Convention does not state whether "master" can include the first officer or other person who takes over the ship in the absence or death of the master. This will presumably be a matter for national law, but it is submitted that the expression be interpreted broadly so as to include the person who has the effective control of the ship at the relevant time (*cf.* the reference to master elsewhere, *e.g.* in Art. 19). Now that the Convention is enacted in the Merchant Shipping Act 1995 the court is presumably entitled to refer to the wide definition in s.313(1).

Under cl. 14 of the LOF 1990, "the master or other person signing this agreement on behalf of the property to be salved enters into this agreement as agent for the vessel her cargo freight bunkers stores and any other property thereon and the respective owners thereof and binds each (but not the one for the other or himself personally) to the due performance thereof". The master of the vessel in distress thus promises that his signature is effected with the authority of the other interests. If there is no such authority, the vessel's owners could be liable to the salvor for breach of the warranty of authority. How far are the other interests bound, especially where a master does not have the time to obtain express authority from them all? In *The Choko Star* [1990] 1 Lloyd's Rep. 516 it was held that the authority of the master to act as an agent to bind a cargo owner to a salvage contract only arises where the master acts as agent of necessity and does not arise as a matter of implied actual authority from the carriage of goods contract. There would be necessity where the master has no reasonable means of communicating with cargo interests, *e.g.* where a container ship is involved in a collision and there are thousands of bill of lading holders. By contrast, there might be no agency of necessity if a bulk carrier went aground with cargo belonging to a single owner, in circumstances where refloating operations were expected to take a week and there was time to communicate with the cargo owner. Cargo owners some-times suspect that they are victims of collusion between the shipowners and the salvors. A suc-cessful challenge to the validity of an LOF does not mean that cargo owners will escape liability for salvage: it is simply that they are not bound by the contract, including its arbitration provisions.

Article 6.2 of the 1989 Convention reverses the effect of *The Choko Star*, partly because of the desire to avoid delays at the scene of a casualty while authority is sought. The master of the vessel in distress will have full authority to bind cargo owners, or other owners of property (as defined in Art. 1(c) to include freight) on board. Article 6.2 goes further than this by also granting auth-ority to the "owner" of the vessel in distress to make salvage contracts. It might be doubted whether this extension of the rules of authority was needed, although it may obviously facilitate the settling of salvage contracts. A salvor could expect that the decision of the master taken at the scene of a casualty on nautical grounds should bind all interests, but the same considerations do not apply to decisions taken by an owner in its head office thousands of miles away on com-mercial grounds. Ships' masters should be encouraged by their owners to make decisions about salvage, but this discretion may be undermined by giving owners express authority. Delay might be caused while owners haggle over salvage terms with the salvage brokers who are increasingly being used. The distinction may be more apparent than real where owners can communicate with their masters by satellite communications. Article 6.2 may obviously have a great impact on the extent to which salvors will be able to force cargo interests to participate in the arbitration procedures of contracts such as the LOF 1990. Cargo owners may find themselves bound, by a contract of which they were unaware, to arbitrate in London. The advantage for the salvors is that they can avoid complications caused by having to arrange different proceedings against each interest, perhaps according to different rules in different jurisdictions.

The new provision contains no restriction on the power of the master, for instance by requir-ing the contract agreed to be reasonable. A Polish attempt to tie the authority to terms that were based on the Convention was not supported. There will be authority and the contract will, *prima facie*, be binding. The cargo owners will be able to come into court to apply for annulment under Art. 7, below, but it could not be argued that they were never bound in the first place. This may be significant for the validity of jurisdictional clauses.

The Convention gives the master full authority to conclude a salvage contract, but does not say whether this authority can stand in the face of any express prohibition, *e.g.* in the carriage contract. It appears that a number of charterers shipping their own oil cargoes have insisted upon express terms in the charter which withdraw the authority of masters to bind them to a salvage contract (*cf. The M. Vatan* [1990] 1 Lloyd's Rep. 336). The matter does not appear to have arisen in the negotiations for the 1989 Salvage Convention and the use of the imperative could suggest that the authority is conclusively given. Alternatively, it could be argued that Art. 6.2 only supplies authority in the case where actual authority was lacking rather than where it was expressly reserved. The provision was designed to assist salvors and where a salvor has no notice of the limitation on the master's authority it could cause great inconvenience to the salvor if the cargo owners were allowed to suggest at a later time that whatever authority the Conven-tion gave the express contract took away. It might be difficult to draw a distinction (on the wording of the Convention) between that situation and one where the salvors had actual notice of the restriction. In the latter case, it would not be possible for a salvor to insist that the cargo owner would be bound by the master's contract. Article 6.2 does not say that the property inter-est will be "bound" by any contract made by the master. It merely uses an existing principle of agency law to grant permission to contract where none had been given. Article 6.1 does allow the Convention to be excluded from salvage operations if "a contract" otherwise provides. It does not say, in terms, that the contract has to be that between the salvor and the salvee, although that is what is implied. If that is the correct view, it would only be a salvage contract which could restrict the application of the Convention. There is some logic in this argument, in that Art. 6.1 was proposed very much by the salvors who wished to retain the scope to choose the LOF. Section 39 of the Merchant Shipping Act 1995 prevents a seaman from renouncing rights to salvage in an employment contract, which indicates that in the absence of such a provision an agreement would have been effective to restrict salvage rights (*cf.* the where towage contracts contain a "no-salvage" clause, *Kennedy*, pp. 225–226).

However, the tenor of Art. 6.1 is that the Convention is not laying down a mandatory code and Art. 6.2 can be interpreted in this light. It is submitted that the Convention does not prevent the authority of the master being expressly withdrawn in the carriage contract and that a salvor will not be able to insist that a charterer or cargo owner will be bound by a salvage contract signed contrary to the express prohibition.

This conclusion may present a salvor with great practical problems if it discovers after the salvage that a number of cargo owners had, in the carriage contract, expressly removed the authority of the master. It would seem contrary to the spirit of the Convention (and Art. 6.1 specifically) for the salvor to be placed in such a dilemma after the event where it had no *knowledge* of the lack of authority. If there is no actual authority, and if the Convention allows the authority given by it to be withdrawn, then the salvor might be driven to arguing that there was still apparent or implied authority. That apparent or implied authority could derive either from the existence of the Convention itself, or because there was an agency of necessity. It is submitted that it would be justifiable to adopt either of these approaches. The latter argument would entail overruling the decision of the Court of Appeal in *The Choko Star* [1990] 1 Lloyd's Rep. 516 and restoring the sensible decision of Sheen J. at first instance ([1989] 2 Lloyd's Rep. 42).

In any event, if there is no authority, the salvor may be protected against losses in that it will be able to sue the shipowner for breach of the warranty of authority in a case where cl. 14 of the LOF applies.

Note that a cargo owner might still be able to evade the authority of a master or owner where it was able to establish that a contract had been agreed in circumstances where there was no danger (see the General Note to Art. 1(a), above).

It might also be noted that if the principle of engaged services survives the incorporation of the Convention into English law (but see the General Note to Art. 12.2, below), but is treated merely as an aspect of a useful salvage operation within Art. 12 of the Convention, then Art. 6.2 will apply generally.

Article 6.3

Although Art. 6.1 allows the parties to a salvage contract to exclude the Convention, they cannot avoid its mandatory effects in two circumstances. These are Art. 7, below, dealing with the powers of a court to annul unfair contracts, and Art. 8.1(b) and 8.2(b), below, putting environmental obligations on the salvor or salvee. The Art. 7 reference appeared in the 1981 CMI Draft Convention: the Art. 8 reference was added by the IMO Legal Committee.

ARTICLE 7

Annulment and modification of contracts

A contract or any terms thereof may be annulled or modified if—
(a) the contract has been entered into under undue influence or the influence of danger and its terms are inequitable; or
(b) the payment under the contract is in an excessive degree too large or too small for the services actually rendered.

GENERAL NOTE

As noted above, Art. 6.3 provides that parties may not contract out of Art. 7 of the Convention. Article 7 broadly reflects the inherent jurisdiction of the Admiralty Court in salvage cases (see *The Unique Mariner* [1978] 1 Lloyd's Rep. 438). It re-enacts Art. 7 of the 1910 Convention in more modern language (see Wildeboer, Chap. 11). The 1984 CMI Report states that it was not intended to prevent national rules on the invalidity of contracts or terms (see pp. 16–17). The Unfair Contract Terms Act 1977, Sched. 11, para. 2 excludes the operation of the Act from most salvage contracts, except where the salvee is a consumer (and see also the E.C. Directive on Unfair Terms in Consumer Contracts 1993), *e.g.* where there is salvage of a private yacht. Other remedies of national law may also apply, especially those relating to misrepresentation (*e.g.*

under the Misrepresentation Act 1967) or mistake (*cf. The Unique Mariner* [1978] 1 Lloyd's Rep. 438). The 1910 Convention, Art. 7 specifically mentioned fraud and concealment. Their omission in the 1989 Salvage Convention is not intended to remove any remedy and it may be that they are included within Art. 7(a).

Article 7(a)

Article 7(a) gives a court a wide jurisdiction to interfere with contracts entered into under undue influence or the influence of danger. "Undue influence" cannot be given a narrow technical meaning, *e.g.* as it has in the English contract cases. A broad approach should be taken, which may include cases involving fraud or misrepresentation within "undue influence" (and see also the question of employment contracts, below). In one sense all salvage operations must require danger (see Art. 1(a)), but the provision is aimed at the master in a position of peril and not the shipowner who agrees a contract from its head office (*cf.* Art. 6.2, above, and Wildeboer, p. 176). The applicant must prove a causative link between the undue influence or danger and the entering into of the contract and it must also show that the terms are inequitable. It would be consistent with the powers given to courts generally in contract cases (*e.g.* s.11 of the Unfair Contract Terms Act 1977) if the requirement of inequitability had to be judged at the time of the contract and not later (and see Wildeboer, p.177). The undue influence or the influence of danger requirements go to the formation of the contract: the inequitability criterion goes to the substance of the terms agreed.

The court is given two powers: it can annul the contract completely (or parts of it), or it can modify all or any of its terms. The latter power is far wider than any normally referred to in salvage cases (which have mostly related to the amount of any salvage reward), as it can be exercised in relation to any clause and it could enable the court almost to rewrite the contract. A court is extremely unlikely to do so, except where it may be appropriate to do something more than applying the blue pencil rule, or in the type of case dealt with under Art. 7(b). The salvor would not necessarily be denied a remedy altogether if a court exercised its jurisdiction under Art. 7, as the result of the court's order would be that the case would be decided under the general provisions of the Convention. The court would be entitled in an appropriate case to make use of Art. 18, below.

With detailed modern salvage contracts there may be more scope for disputing individual clauses. While the LOF might be thought of as no more than a glorified arbitration clause, it has over the years developed into something more sophisticated. It imposes obligations on salvor and salvee, breach of which could give rise to damages—as with any contract. Apart from the London forum/choice of law clause, the clauses which impose obligations on the salvee (and might be questioned as "inequitable") are those such as cl. 3 (co-operation), or cl. 4(c) (security). It is submitted that it is extremely unlikely that a court would find that the LOF, as a whole or in part, was inequitable. The terms of the LOF have always been negotiated by a Committee representing underwriting interests and it is not a contract dictated by salvors. However, it is not impossible to imagine a small uninsured owner in an 1989 Salvage Convention State claiming in its courts that it would be inequitable for it to be forced to incur the cost of appearing at an arbitration in London. The salvor's answer would be that the LOF was internationally recognised, that the practice of arbitration in shipping is normal and that the law of salvage ought to have, as a major concern, the interests and convenience of the salvor (at least to the extent that salvors need to be encouraged).

In view of the sort of practical problems thrown up by the Convention, the salvors may try to amend a standard form, such as the LOF, by obtaining agreement to riders or amendments. They may propose that the ship and cargo are to have a minimum salved value; or that the expenses of the salvor for the purposes of Art. 14.3 are agreed at a certain rate; or that it is agreed that there is a threat of "substantial" damage to the environment within Art. 1(d); or that waters 50 miles from a coast line are "coastal waters" within Art. 1(d). These claims would have to be fitted in Art. 7(a), as Art. 7(b) would not appear to apply. It may be that some of these terms are inequitable for one party, *e.g.* the cargo, but not for the others. An agreement that the cargo shall have a disproportionately high salved value to that of the ship would be inequitable because this would not reflect the respective liabilities under Art. 13.2. The difficulty here would be to find the element of undue influence on the cargo, given that the master may have authority to bind cargo. It is submitted that a court ought to find that the salvor has exercised an undue influence over cargo interests through the agency of the master. Alternatively, if there is no jurisdiction under Art. 7, a court could find that there was fraud under ordinary principles of English law. The inequitability of these special terms cannot be easily assessed. The salvors see a particular risk and are not prepared to take that risk, *e.g.* where they may incur enormous expenses to protect the environment, only to be told that these cannot be claimed because the salvage took place on the high seas away from coasts. It may be that a master asked to sign an amended LOF does not appreciate the significance of the changes proposed, and the salvor may not have been forthcoming in explaining how a standard LOF, for instance, has been altered. This absence of good faith may be relevant, but that only establishes the undue influence in Art. 7(a) and does not relate to the inherent inequitability of the term. In the absence of some clear abuse, it is difficult to see that the rider terms outlined are inherently inequitable. To some extent the remedy for the salvee in such circumstances is to argue that the salvage reward, or Art. 14.2 uplift, should take into account the special agreement.

Article 7(b)

Article 7(b) deals with the situation where a fixed price salvage contract is agreed. An excessive price can be reduced to a reasonable amount. This is declaratory of existing English salvage law. In all cases, the court can intervene only if the payment agreed is "excessively" large or small. The mere fact that the payment is higher than a court would have awarded is not sufficient. Although Art. 7(b) is generally concerned with cases where there is an element of abuse of position, a court could intervene where the parties genuinely fixed a figure which was either far too high or low on the facts known to them at the time. The court has a complete discretion in the matter, however, and although it could increase the reward where the operation is much more difficult than both parties had anticipated, it would seem unlikely that a court would raise the figure demanded by a salvor in the absence of some misleading conduct on the part of the salvee. Salvors must be presumed to know their business sufficiently well to be able to fix a price. The position might be different in the case of a non-professional salvor.

Although Art. 7 does not say so expressly, the contracts referred to would seem to be the salvage contracts referred to in Art. 6 (*cf.* Art. 7 of the 1910 Convention which was clearer), *i.e.* those between the salvor and the owner of the property to be salved. To what extent can the article apply to contracts related to salvage in a wider sense? It is possible that a towage contract may contain a term which relates to the possibility of salvage, *e.g.* in the event of supervening circumstances. To the extent that the contract would seek to regulate payment under the Convention it ought to be covered by Art. 7(b) (and see Wildeboer, p. 168), although it is difficult to see how Art. 7(a) could apply. Salvors may engage sub-contractors to perform the services. These may be on the basis of a salvage contract, such as the ISU Sub-contract (Award Sharing) 1994, to which Art. 7 would apply (and see Art. 15.1, below). The sub-contract might also be on the basis of an ordinary daily rate work and labour basis. Although this would, expressly or impliedly, not be a salvage contract as such, the salvor may have exerted "undue influence" in the form of economic duress on the sub-contractor to accept a daily rate or nothing. It seems that the article is open on whether such third party contracts are covered (*cf.* Wildeboer, p. 168, note 12). The quick settlement of salvage claims might be held up if, after the event, every sub-contractor tried to argue that the contract should be set aside (*e.g.* so that they could then claim as joint salvors). The Convention does not seek to regulate contracts which do not provide for payment, as defined in Art. 1(e), above, and it is submitted that the validity and effect of a "no-salvage" sub-contract is best dealt with by national contract law. In any event, Art. 7(b) could not apply as there would not be a "payment" under the Convention and it is difficult to see many circumstances where Art. 7(a) might be applied.

More difficult is the case of an agreement between the salvor and its employees as to the apportionment of a reward. Under Art. 15.2, the apportionment will be governed by the law of the flag, although it might follow from Art. 6.1 that a contract could vary the applicable law (if the contract was covered by Art. 6). If a wide view is taken of "contract" within Art. 6.1, then it would also follow that Art. 7 should apply (and see Wildeboer, p. 168), even though employment contracts may be regulated by the law of the flag. What if the contract of employment did not provide for apportionment, but for a "no-salvage" agreement by the crew? It may be difficult to draw a distinction between the salvor's crew and the salvage sub-contractor (see above). Section 16 of the Merchant Shipping Act 1970 would protect the seafarers whose employment contract was governed by English law, but would the Admiralty Court be unable to interfere in an unfair bargain forced on the crew of a flag of convenience ship where the law of the flag was silent? Historically, the courts have tried to protect seafarers and the only possible distinction between them and sub-contractors is that they are often in a weak position as a class and more susceptible to undue influence in a broad sense. Although a wide interpretation of "contract" to include an employment contract which contains a "no-salvage term" would seem to overlap with the specific protection of s.39, it is submitted that it would be entirely consistent with the general purpose to give jurisdiction under the Convention in such a case. There would not necessarily be a conflict with the employment law of the flag State (any more than there would be a conflict with the proper law of the towage contract, in the example above) as the court exercising jurisdiction under Art. 7 would only be doing it in relation to that part of the employment contract as relates to salvage. Even so, the crew would still have to show undue influence (in addition to inequitability) and they could easily fail on this criterion.

In all the cases discussed in the previous two paragraphs, difficult questions arise because of the need to decide to which contracts Art. 7 (and, to some extent, Art. 6) relates. The problems recede if it is held that the Convention is only dealing with contracts of salvage between salvor and salvee and that all other contractual matters will be left to the law of the particular contract.

Article 7 does not state whether the powers to annul or modify are to be exercised by a court or arbitrator. As the Convention is given the force of law, there is no reason why arbitrators chosen to hear a salvage dispute should not decide upon questions of annulment as they would upon other general questions of law. An exception might be where a challenge was made to a jurisdiction clause. The question of the applicable time bar will be dealt with in Art. 23.1, below.

CHAPTER II—PERFORMANCE OF SALVAGE OPERATIONS

ARTICLE 8

Duties of the salvor and of the owner and master

1. The salvor shall owe a duty to the owner of the vessel or other property in danger—
   (a) to carry out the salvage operations with due care;
   (b) in performing the duty specified in subparagraph (a), to exercise due care to prevent or minimise damage to the environment;
   (c) whenever circumstances reasonably require, to seek assistance from other salvors; and
   (d) to accept the intervention of other salvors when reasonably requested to do so by the owner or master of the vessel or other property in danger; provided however that the amount of his reward shall not be prejudiced should it be found that such a request was unreasonable.
2. The owner and master of the vessel or the owner of other property in danger shall owe a duty to the salvor—
   (a) to co-operate fully with him during the course of the salvage operations;
   (b) in so doing, to exercise due care to prevent or minimise damage to the environment; and
   (c) when the vessel or other property has been brought to a place of safety, to accept redelivery when reasonably requested by the salvor to do so.

GENERAL NOTE

Sanctions

Article 8 sets out a variety of duties on the salvor and salvee. These duties under the Convention are owed to the other parties to the adventure, rather than the public at large (see Gaskell, "The 1989 Salvage Convention", p. 18). This is an important distinction which was not always made clear in the 1981 CMI Draft Convention (and see the 1984 CMI Report, p. 16). There was remarkably little discussion within the IMO of what the sanction was for breach of the various Art. 8 duties: none is stated in the Convention. Where the duties appear in a contract such as the LOF 1990, the remedies would clearly be for breach of contract, for instance damages or an injunction (and see Gaskell, "Policy Issues", p. 359). Salvage under the Convention does not depend on any contract or agreement, but upon services being performed. Yet there are many similarities with a contractual service. It could almost be said that Art. 8 operates as if it were implying terms into a contract—although manifestly it does not do so. Breach of the Convention duties does carry with it at least one sanction within the Convention. A salvor may have a payment reduced or withheld altogether for misconduct under Art. 18, but that would not deal with the situation where the salvor's breach caused actual loss of or damage to the vessel in excess of any salvage reward (*cf.* Vincenzini, p. 184). Moreover, the failure by the salvee to co-operate may mean that no property is salved at all. In such a case, involving no environmental risks, the salvor would obtain no reward. Accordingly, unless the various duties are not to have equivalent rights, there must be a remedy of damages for breach of the various obligations.

If there is a right to damages, on what basis are they to be calculated, *e.g.* on a contractual or tortious basis? The answer may make a considerable difference. There seems little doubt that the breach by salvor or salvee of any of the obligations under Art. 8, as it appears in the LOF 1990, will sound in contractual damages. But, where the question as to the meaning of Art. 8 arises under the 1995 Act, giving the force of law to the Convention, it could be argued that the statute would normally compensate for reliance, rather than expectation. It might seem odd to have different results from breach of essentially the same provision, but the better answer is to decide that the Convention does not fix which type of damages should be awarded. The matter would be left to the judges in every case. Given the public policy element behind salvage, it may be acceptable in an appropriate case to award expectation damages. A salvor might also expect to limit liability in appropriate cases (under the 1976 Limitation Convention as enacted in Sched. 7).

Standard of Care

A general issue concerns the standard of care set out in Art. 8.1(a) and (b) and Art. 8.2(b) (and see N. Gaskell, "LOF 1990", [1991] LMCLQ 104, 112 *et seq.*). The LOF 1980 and the 1981 CMI Draft Convention had used a familiar expression in the salvage industry, that of "best endeavours" (repeated in the LOF 1995). The IMO Legal Committee changed this to "due care". Although the change may, in part, have been to ease translation, it is nevertheless recognised as being one of substance. If anything, it is a reduction in the standard required. The requirement of due care is an objective one based on reasonableness, taking account of the general standards in the salvage and marine industries. The emphasis on "best" endeavours might indicate a more subjective test, looking to the actual capabilities of the salvor in question. A particular professional salvor could, in fact, do more than an average salvor. This difference may be small, but there may be another. Clause 1(a)(i) of the LOF 1995 requires best endeavours "to" salve. Article 8.1(b) of the Convention requires the salvor to exercise due care "during" the salvage. The LOF obligation relates not just to the operations actually undertaken, but also to those services selected in the first place. The Convention simply requires that what a salvor actually does must be done with due care. It is arguable that the Convention does not impose any obligation on the salvor to continue with an uneconomic salvage operation, while under the LOF 1995 the salvors have promised to do their best actually to save the property in danger. The difference could be relevant in the type of case where a salvor is engaged on salving cargo from a ship and decides, on commercial grounds, that it may not be worthwhile removing the remaining cargo at the bottom of the hold. Arguably, this could be a breach of the best endeavours obligation if the cargo was physically capable of removal (and assuming, perhaps, that it had some value). If there is a distinction, it may reflect the different obligations undertaken by one who promises contractually to salve and one who is a volunteer in the full sense.

The Convention specifically preserved the "best endeavours" formula in Art. 21(2), relating to the duty of the shipowner to ensure that cargo on his ship provides security to the salvor. The only explanation for this, apart from oversight, is that a different standard was intended in Arts. 8 and 21. Security is vital to the salvor and it is entirely consistent with the overall purposes of the Convention for a higher duty to have been placed on the salvee than that of due, or ordinary, care.

Article 8.1: Duties of Salvor

Article 8.1(a). Article 8.1 sets out four duties of the salvor. The first obligation is to exercise due care in carrying out the salvage operations (as defined in Art. 1(a), above) in respect of the vessel and its cargo (or other property). The standard of care has been discussed above, but examples of breach would be where the salvor unnecessarily damages the ship or cargo, or is so careless that the operations take longer than is reasonable. In such circumstances the salvor's reward might be reduced.

The first line (the chapeau) of Art. 8.1 uses the word "or", but it seems that this is an example of the word being used to mean "and", rather than being disjunctive (*cf. Federal Steam Navigation v. Department of Trade and Industry (sub. nom. The Huntingdon)* [1974] 1 W.L.R. 505 and the General Note to s.131, above). It would be peculiar for there to be a duty of care to the ship but not simultaneously to the cargo. The duties are thus owed not only to the owner of the vessel in distress, but also to each cargo owner. It is not clear if this gives an individual owner, *e.g.* of cargo, the right to demand that the salvor save his particular piece of cargo, whatever the expense. Nowhere in the article is there an obligation to carry out salvage operations: it is only that such operations as are undertaken by the salvor must be done carefully. It is here that the distinction between "due care" and "best endeavours" is most apparent. If a salvor has to use best endeavours to salve, then it has an obligation to continue with the service. The obligations would only be the same if the obligation was to use best endeavours "in" salving. If this analysis is correct, the salvor is perfectly entitled to leave a salvage job when it has become too difficult or expensive. The salvor should certainly be liable for damages for failing to exercise due care if it left the ship in a perilous position. But, otherwise, there seems to be no concept that it is compulsory to continue a salvage service once started. To his extent the Convention preserves the true voluntary nature of salvage (*cf.* the position under the LOF, N. Gaskell, "The Lloyd's Open Form and Contractual Remedies" [1986] LMCLQ 306).

It was held in *Owners of the Motor Vessel Tojo Maru v. N.V. Bureau Wijsmuller; Tojo Maru, The* [1972] A.C. 242 that a salvor could be held liable in damages to a salvee for negligent performance of an ultimately successful salvage operation. Although entitled to a salvage reward for what was done, this may be met by a counterclaim for damages which could exceed the reward payable. The counterclaim would now be subject to limitation of liability under the 1976 Limitation Convention.

The Tojo Maru was, strictly speaking, a case on contractual salvage under the LOF, but the judgments do not appear to suggest that a different rule would apply in a non-contractual salvage situation. It is theoretically possible that there may be a different calculation of the damages, depending upon whether a contractual or tortious measure is adopted (see the heading *Sanctions* above), but in most cases the measure will be the same, namely the cost of making good the damage caused. It might be said that there is no place for the rule, as the Convention does not expressly deal with the matter and the absence of such treatment could be interpreted to mean that the remedies supplied in the Convention (*e.g.* deprivation of reward under Art. 18, below) are definitive. This approach would be favoured by salvors, who have always considered that *The Tojo Maru* decision was unjust or inappropriate. However, it is submitted that this would be an incorrect approach for, as argued above, the Convention does itself contemplate that a salvor can be held liable in damages for breach of the Art. 8.1 duties to use due care. There is no inconsistency in reading this together with Art. 18, which can deal with circumstances where the damages caused by the conduct do not exceed the Art. 13 reward or Art. 14 special compensation. In the case of a contractual salvage, the same arguments would hold, as Art. 8 of the 1989 Salvage Convention would apply to the LOF. There was no express provision to the contrary in the LOF 1990 and none in the LOF 1995. Indeed, *The Tojo Maru* was based upon an analysis of the best endeavours obligation in cl. 1 of the LOF. On this reading of the Convention, the rule in *The Tojo Maru* survives through the Convention itself and, it might be added, there is no need for a sweeping up of the pre-1994 salvage law through sub-para. (iii) of s.20(2)(j) of the Supreme Court Act 1981 (see the General Notes to s.224(6), above, and to the Merchant Shipping (Salvage and Pollution) Act 1994, Sched. 2, para. 6, in *Current Law Statutes Annotated 1994*).

Article 8.1(b). The second obligation of the salvor is to exercise due care to prevent or minimise damage to the environment (as defined in Art. 1(e)). This is an important addition to the LOF 1980 obligation which, under cl. 1, was limited to preventing the escape of oil. But it must be emphasised that this is a duty owed only to the salved interests, despite attempts to provide wider public duties. An incentive is provided by the prospect of a higher than usual salvage award under Art. 13, or a safety net payment under Art. 14 if the property salvage fails to succeed. There is no other public or private duty under the Convention, or any sanction, as such, for failing to exercise due care to prevent or minimise damage to the environment. Third party rights may already exist outside of the Convention, *e.g.* in negligence or under s.153 in the case of oil pollution (see the General Note to s.163, above). The shipowner who is held liable under the latter may seek to bring a recourse action against the salvor for breach of Art. 8.1(b), but that claim would almost certainly be subject to limitation of liability under the 1976 Limitation Convention (as enacted in the Merchant Shipping Act 1979).

Article 8.1(c). The third obligation is to seek assistance from other salvors. The idea of sharing a reward with a competitor is not something that is likely to appeal to salvors. The duty is suitably hedged by the use of the qualifier "whenever circumstances reasonably require". An example of this might be where the first salvor's tug is not sufficiently powerful, or where the second salvor has better equipment or more experienced personnel. The sanction if the operations fail or are unduly delayed is a reduced reward under Art. 13, or a possible damages action by the salved interests.

Article 8.1(d). The fourth obligation on the salvor is similar to the third and suggests that the latter is really designed more for those situations where the vessel in distress is unmanned. Article 8.1(d) was added by the IMO Legal Committee and requires the salvor to accept help from other salvors when requested to do so by the (i) the owner or master of the vessel in danger, or (ii) the owner of other property in danger, such as the cargo. The latter proposition is not entirely clear because of the peculiar phrasing "owner *or master* of the vessel or other property in danger" (emphasis added). The words italicised do not make much sense where the other property is cargo. It is submitted that a sensible reading would be to add "*or owner of* other property in danger". This is similar to the chapeau of Art. 8.2.

The master of a ship normally has the final say over operations concerning it. The concept that the ultimate control of salvage operations lies with the master of the vessel in distress seems to be accepted by the Convention in this article and also in Art. 19, below. Art. 8.1(d) gives an express power to the master to insist that a second salvor join the operation. It is submitted that it follows from the word "intervention" that the power extends to allow the salvee's master completely to supersede the first salvor and not merely to allow the second salvor to assist (as in Art. 8.1(d)). The request must be reasonable. This requirement may not be easy to assess where the salvor receives conflicting orders from the master of the ship and from cargo owners, particularly where the request relates to commercial rather than nautical matters. A shipowner may instruct its master to allow the intervention of a sister ship, in order that the latter may become a salvor. Cargo owners may require a local tug to be used whose owner is of the same nationality as them. It is submitted that reasonableness ought to be judged on nautical grounds and that an intervention should only be allowed if it was necessary to protect the whole adventure. Again, there is some ambiguity in the phrase "owner or master". Is this meant to be conjunctive (as in the chapeau) or disjunctive? It might make sense for the "or" to be read disjunctively, as a salvor would not then have to resolve conflicts between the master and shipowner. However, it is submitted that a conjunctive approach makes more sense as the overall criterion will still be reasonableness.

Article 8.1(d) provides that if the first salvor accepts an unreasonable order to let a second salvor become involved, the first salvor's reward is not to be prejudiced. It is assumed that the first salvor will have a right to salvage under Art. 13 for those services already performed. Where the first salvor is superseded completely, the proviso could mean (i) that the first salvor will have a personal action for breach against the owner of the ship (or other property) who made the unreasonable request, or (ii) that the "accrued" salvage reward for the first salvor's prior services is to be protected (in the sense that it must be taken into account in the final reckoning as a useful contribution), or (iii) that the "accrued" salvage reward for the first salvor's prior services is to be protected (in the sense that it must be taken to exist even in the case of a later total loss), or (iv) that the salvage reward for the first salvor's prior services is to be enhanced (in the event of success by the second salvor) to include a notional amount for the contributions which would have been made if there had been no intervention. Where the first salvor is obliged to share the performance of the salvage services, the alternatives are similar, although the main question which would arise is whether the first salvor is entitled to a larger share of the joint salvage reward than that to which it would have been entitled if one simply assessed what each salvor had done (alternative (v)). The salved fund may not be sufficient and so it could be said that the first salvor has been "prejudiced", in that its position is worse than if there had been no unreasonable intervention. Could there be a personal claim against the owner of the ship (or other property) for the difference? If the claim is in the nature of salvage, there would be a maritime lien and other property owners would have to contribute. If there is a personal claim only, there would not be a maritime lien and the salvor may have enforcement problems (*cf. The Tesaba* [1982] 1 Lloyd's Rep. 397, and the General Note to s.224(6), point 6(d)(ii), above).

The reference to "reward" should make it clear that the provision is referring to salvage rewards under Art. 13. "Reward" must be distinguished from "payment", which is a wider expression (see the General Note to Art. 1(e), above). A first salvor who has been unreasonably forced to accept an intervention which resulted in the sinking of the ship in distress might have a claim to recover its expenses under Art. 14, provided that there was a threat to the environment. In the absence of such a threat, there would be no recovery under Arts. 13 or 14. In this context it will be necessary to decide if there can be a separate action for breach of Art. 8.1(d), as in alternative (i) above, or whether the proviso can be interpreted in the manner indicated in alternative (iii), above.

The reference to "prejudiced" would suggest that alternative (ii) is the minimum interpretation which can be accepted. It is doubtful if this result needed to be stated and to that extent the proviso exists for the avoidance of doubt. Alternative (iii) is not workable without a separate right to damages, as there is no salved fund. The specific reference to an Art. 13 "reward" might seem to preclude a separate action for damages, on the basis that the two concepts are inconsistent. If this is right, the main relevance of the reasonableness of the order would be to confirm alternative (ii) and to give the salvor a choice to refuse to accept an intervention.

Article 8.1(d) does not say what the position is if an unreasonable order is given which the first salvor declines to accept. The example envisages that the master of the ship remains in possession of her, although a salvor might have a maritime lien entitling it to arrest the vessel. The mere fact that a salvor is working on a ship under the authority of the master does not give that salvor the right to take over complete possession of the ship and override decisions taken by the master (*cf.* Brice, p. 189 *et seq.*). A salvor which resisted an unreasonable order to allow the intervention of another and went on to salve the ship would be entitled to make an Art. 13 claim, subject to the application of Art. 19. It seems unlikely that Art. 19 would apply as it is hard to see that there could be a reasonable prohibition under that article where there had been an unreasonable request to accept intervention. If the salvor did not succeed in saving the vessel, it might be liable to the salvee for beach of one of the other obligations in Art. 8, but not, it seems, for breach of paragraph (d).

An able and willing salvor who is unreasonably superseded is entitled to some recompense under existing English law (see *The Unique Mariner* (*No. 2*) [1979] 1 Lloyd's Rep. 37, *The Hassel*

[1959] 2 Lloyd's Rep. 82, N. Gaskell, "The Lloyd's Open Form and Contractual Remedies", [1986] LMCLQ 306 and the General Note to Art. 19, below) and the better approach would be to allow a judge to take into account the lost opportunity to salve by giving an enhanced salvage reward where the second salvor succeeded, *i.e.* alternative (iv), above. The same result ought to follow where the first salvor has been forced to share the salvage operations (*i.e.*, alternative (v), above). There would be an enhanced liability on all saved interests here, even though it may only have been the master who gave the unreasonable order: the other interests might be able to claim an indemnity under the carriage contract. If there is no saved fund available, it is submitted that the salvor should be able to bring a personal action against the owner of the ship (or other property) for breach of the Convention. All this is conjecture, as the Convention is unclear except, perhaps, in respect of alternative (ii), above. The intention of the provision is not to penalise the salvor, but to ensure that it is not to be adversely affected by the power of the master to select salvors.

In the context of the supersession of salvors, it may be convenient to note here that cl. 18 of the LOF 1990 gives the option to the owners of the salved ship to terminate the salvage services where there "is no longer any reasonable prospect of a useful result leading to a salvage award under Art. 13". "Useful result" is the expression used in Art. 12 of the 1989 Convention and is broadly equivalent to the principle of "success". The LOF provision was very much an afterthought, particularly by the P & I Clubs, and its aim is to prevent salvors continuing with the service merely to run up costs (particularly in order to increase the increment under Art. 14). The option is only available to the owners of the salved ship, not to cargo interests, and the LOF 1990 is silent on the question of termination by the salvor. Article 19, below, would provide some sort of remedy where the salvor was unreasonably incurring expenses for wreck raising (a matter which was excluded from the Convention under the original 1981 CMI Draft).

Article 8.2: Duties of Salvee
Article 8.2 lays down three specific obligations on the salvees (although it was argued above that Article 8.1(d) may have created a fourth, namely the obligation not unreasonably to request a salvor to allow the intervention of another). Paragraphs (a) and (c) derive from the LOF 1980: para. (b) was introduced in the 1981 CMI Draft Convention. The duties are owed to the salvor by the owner and master of the vessel on the one hand, and on the other, by each owner of property saved. It has already been noted that the chapeau to Art. 8.1 and Art. 8.1(d) makes rather confusing use of the word "or". The chapeau to Art. 8.2 provides another variant. Again it is submitted that the drafting is poor, but that the duties are not owed *either* by the ship *or* the other property. It is submitted that there may be actions for breach of Art. 8.2 (see the heading *Sanctions*, in the General Note to Art. 8.1, above), although no wider public duties are created (see the General Note to Art. 8.1, above).
Article 8.2(a). Article 8.2(a) requires the full co-operation of the salvee with the salvor during the salvage operations, but apparently not before or after (although see Art. 21.2, below). The LOF 1990, cl. 3 goes into more detail about the extent of the salvor's rights to use equipment and machinery on board the salved vessel. It is often necessary to use ship's pumps or engines in circumstances where strain might be caused. Sometimes holes have to be cut in decks or lifting points have to be welded to the hull. The ship's master may be reluctant to allow this. Although the Convention does not go into such detail, it seems that the salvor would be entitled to request that such actions be carried out. As usual, the test might be that which a reasonably prudent master of a vessel in danger would accept. Article 8.2(a), imposes a duty of co-operation on persons other than shipowners. This may mean that cargo owners have an obligation to assist, for instance by providing information, or sending technical experts to assist with hazardous cargo.
One form of co-operation mentioned in the LOF 1995, cl. 3 is that needed to obtain consent from a coastal State to take a "maritime leper" into a port of refuge. This may be easier to arrange where ship and cargo owners are residents of that State. Although Art. 8.2 makes no specific reference to this form of co-operation, it is submitted that it is covered by the general duty under Art. 8.2(a).
Failure to co-operate may be taken into account by the tribunal assessing the reward under Art. 13. If the failure results in the loss of the vessel and cargo, the salvor may be entitled to its expenses under Art. 14 where there was a threat to the environment. In other cases, not involving such a threat, the salvor may have an action for breach of the Convention (see the heading *Sanctions*, in the General Note to Art. 8.1, above).
Article 8.2(b). The second obligation, in Art. 8.2(b), is a limited one to exercise due care to prevent damage to the environment. This is not expressed as a general duty, as it is primarily the salvor that is performing the salvage operations. It is only in relation to the duty to co-operate with the salvor that the salvee has to take care. It is difficult to see what the sanction is for breach

of this duty by the salvee—which is owed *only* to the salvor. Failure to supply local information might result in pollution which would otherwise have been prevented. This would reduce the salvage payment under Arts. 13 or 14 and might lead to Government intervention resulting in the loss of an Art. 13 award. The salvor might have a claim for this lost income, if not otherwise covered under Art. 14, but there seems little other incentive under the Convention for the salvee to exercise care to prevent damage to the environment. The greater incentive might be the prospect of liability to third parties under other Conventions, *e.g.* the 1992 Liability Convention (see the General Note to s.153, above). This is an unfortunate, but inevitable, consequence of the decision to concentrate on the private law aspects of salvage. The salvee, as well as the salvor, is in a particularly good position to be able to reduce the environmental effects of a casualty. There is no direct obligation on a ship's master to request salvage services (although *cf.* Art. 19) and there could be great delay after the ship was first in trouble before the master finally decided he could not cope without help. The environmental duty in Art. 8.2(d) applies only during the performance of the salvage operations, but not before. The 1981 CMI Draft Convention Art. 2–1(1) imposed a duty on the owner and master of a vessel in distress to "take timely and reasonable action to arrange for salvage operations". This could only have any real effect as a public law duty and was removed by the IMO Legal Committee from its draft Convention. Some disquiet at this was expressed by at least two Governments, and amendments were proposed which would have reintroduced the CMI obligation. An environmental organisation proposed a similar amendment to the effect that a duty to prevent damage to the environment should exist from the moment the danger had arisen. The proposals were withdrawn through lack of support.

Article 8.2(c). The third obligation, in Art. 8.2(c), is to accept redelivery of the vessel following a reasonable request by salvors who have brought the vessel to a place of safety. "Redelivery" is the term used in salvage practice, but it is a misnomer in many cases where the owner of ship or cargo has never been out of possession of the ship or cargo. In the ordinary case of services provided to a ship under the control of its master, the salvor may never have taken possession and so cannot redeliver anything. In such cases, the expression is better understood as a synonym for "completion", *i.e.* an express recognition that the salvage operations governed by the Convention have come to an end. This moment of time may have some significance in terms of the Art. 8 duties, the time bar under Art. 23 and the extent to which subsequent services are to be treated as salvage under Art. 13. Salvors who incur expenses after the completion of the salvage services may be entitled to a restitutionary payment (see *China-Pacific S.A. v. Food Corp. of India; The Winson* [1982] A.C. 939 and Art. 12, below).

In many cases it will be in the interests of a salvor to argue that the salvage operations continued for as long as possible, in order that the reward will be increased accordingly (see Art. 13.1(f)). The Art. 8.2(c) provision was first introduced into the LOF 1980 to meet the particular problem of shipowners who refuse to accept that the salvage services had been completed. A stranded vessel may have been patched sufficiently for her to enter a port of refuge, but the shipowners may want more substantial temporary repairs to be done, *e.g.* to enable her to travel to a port where final repairs can be effected more cheaply. Under Art. 8.2(c) the shipowners would have to accept redelivery at the port of refuge, and arrange local repairs, or accept towage to a second port on a contract basis. What exactly is a place of safety will vary enormously from vessel to vessel, but merely being in a position of immediate physical safety is not likely to be decisive (*cf. Troilus (Cargo Owners) v. Glenogle (Owners, Master and Crew); The Troilus* [1951] A.C. 820 and Brice, p. 50 *et seq.*). Account will have to be taken of the interests of all parties to the adventure. A vessel may no longer be in danger of sinking, but lack of power might mean that a refrigerated cargo is in danger of perishing in a port with no suitable storage facilities. It follows from the wording of the paragraph that there might be circumstances where the vessel or other property is in a place of safety, but that there may still be an unreasonable request by the salvor to accept redelivery. It is difficult to think of an example, but the requirement of reasonableness might be of most use to rebut an argument that a vessel was in a place of safety when taken to a perfect natural haven in a deserted island in the middle of the Indian Ocean (*cf. The Troilus*, above).

An attempt at the 1989 diplomatic conference to restrict the obligation in Art. 8.2(c) to contractual salvages was not supported and was withdrawn. The obligation can clearly arise in a non-contractual salvage. Where the shipowner or cargo owner fails to accept redelivery the salvor may be faced with difficult practical questions as to what to do with the salved property. There may have been restitutionary rights in respect of post-salvage services (see *The Winson*, above), but the Convention could be interpreted to come to the same result. If the owner acted in breach of Art. 8.2(c) the salvor ought to be entitled to damages representing its loss. That loss could include reasonable expenses of looking after the cargo. It may be that the salvage operations under the Convention have ceased at the place of safety because of the absence of danger, even though there has been no redelivery. In those circumstances the salvor may well have continuing duties as a bailee (see *The Winson*, above).

ARTICLE 9

Rights of coastal States

Nothing in this Convention shall affect the right of the coastal State concerned to take measures in accordance with generally recognised principles of international law to protect its coastline or related interests from pollution or the threat of pollution following upon a maritime casualty or acts relating to such a casualty which may reasonably be expected to result in major harmful consequences, including the right of a coastal State to give directions in relation to salvage operations.

GENERAL NOTE

It might have been thought that Art. 5.1 was sufficient to preserve the rights of coastal states, but there was concern in the IMO Legal Committee that if the Convention was not to give increased powers to coastal states it should not prejudice those powers which already existed. A number of states wanted to include wide public powers, *e.g.* which would have allowed states effectively to commandeer passing foreign salvage vessels in the vicinity of an incident. Such a proposal could have undermined the exercise of innocent rights of passage. For the 1989 diplomatic conference, Australia proposed an amendment specifically requiring salvors to comply with directions from the coastal State (*e.g.* as to the method of salvage). After discussion in an Informal Working Group, it was agreed that the 1989 Salvage Convention was not the proper place for such new public law measures and the present Art. 9 was agreed. In effect, this is a re-wording of the Australian proposal, but in the form of a statement preserving existing coastal State rights to intervene according to recognised present, or future, principles of international law.

The main powers to intervene internationally are given by the International Convention relating to Intervention on the High Seas in Cases of Oil Pollution Casualties 1969 and its 1973 Protocol, as enacted under s.139. Under s.137(7) the U.K.'s powers to intervene are without prejudice to rights or powers which arise under international law or otherwise and similarly, to the extent that there are wider powers than allowed under the Intervention Convention 1969, there is nothing in the 1995 Act which limits them. Article 9 does not put any obligation on a State to intervene and grants no new powers to the Crown (as recognised by the Minister of Transport in London, Mr. Steven Norris, at the Committee Stage of the 1994 Act in the Commons (Standing Committee C, February 9, 1994, col. 13)).

The Minister indicated that "directions" to foreigners could not be given outside the 12 mile limit because of lack of jurisdiction. The reference to "directions" in Art. 9 must be read in the light of the present jurisdictional limitation in s.141, *i.e.* that the Secretary of State could give directions to a British registered ship, but not to those of other nations except so far as an Order in Council so provides. The Merchant Shipping (Prevention of Pollution) (Intervention) Order 1980 (S.I. 1980 No. 1093), Art. 7, restricts the power of the Secretary of State to give directions, in respect of ships *outside* territorial waters, to U.K. citizens or bodies corporate established under U.K. law. It follows that directions can be given to foreign ships and citizens in U.K. waters. This presumably represents the U.K. view of the extent of its powers under international law on the high seas. Some states considered that the Intervention Convention 1969 and its 1973 Protocol did not reflect the current state of customary international law, or were not sufficiently specific in their terms, and they pressed for the inclusion of Art. 9 of the 1989 Salvage Convention. It may be that the Intervention Convention 1969 was not sufficiently specific. By contrast, s.137 goes into much more detail. Under Art. 1 of the Intervention Convention 1969 a State can take "such measures as may be necessary" and it is arguable that these measures could include directions, providing that they were proportionate within Art. 5 of the Intervention Convention 1969. Although the Intervention Convention 1969 is couched in terms of the measures which a State can take, *e.g.* destroying an abandoned oil tanker, it will often be impossible to take measures in respect of a manned ship without some sort of instruction being given to those on board. Under Art. III of the Intervention Convention 1969 there is an obligation to repatriate ships' crews. This may imply a right to force them to leave a stricken ship (provided that risks to life are avoided within Art. III (e)). Thus, although there are present restrictions in U.K. law on the extent to which directions may be given to foreign citizens on the high seas, Art. 9 of the 1989 Salvage Convention will not prevent the U.K. from extending its powers in the future. It may even be arguable that there is already international power to extend the 1980 Order. Although the 1989 Convention does not seek to define those rights, the fact that it made specific reference to the right of the coastal State to give directions in relation to salvage operations might indicate that such a right is now generally recognised. Australia agreed to withdraw a further amendment that would have inserted a new Art. 15 *bis* in the IMO Legal Committee draft Convention. The new provision was aimed at trying to protect the salvor who did obey a State's directions by leaving payment unaffected by the action taken. In fact, this situation, in which there would be "no cure, no pay", was exactly the purpose for which the special compensation in Art. 14 was required.

ARTICLE 10

Duty to render assistance

1. Every master is bound, so far as he can do so without serious danger to his vessel and persons thereon, to render assistance to any person in danger of being lost at sea.
2. The States Parties shall adopt the measures necessary to enforce the duty set out in paragraph 1.
3. The owner of the vessel shall incur no liability for a breach of the duty of the master under paragraph 1.

GENERAL NOTE

Article 10 reproduces provisions first found in Art. 11 of the 1910 Salvage Convention, with minor drafting changes. The 1910 Convention provision was enacted in s.6 of the Maritime Conventions Act 1911, which is now repealed (see Sched. 12, below) and replaced by the new Art. 10 (and Sched. 11, Pt. II; para. 3, below). The article is one of the few public law references which remain in an essentially private law Convention. It is aimed at making sure that a master is bound to render such assistance as is possible to others in distress. It is to be noted that the duty is imposed on the master, who is defined by s.313(1) as including "every person (except a pilot) having command or charge of any ship". This definition would therefore include the officer of the watch who had the conduct of the vessel for the time being. Article 10.3 specifically excludes the shipowner from the Art. 10.1 obligation, which is viewed as personal to the mariner concerned. The obligation applies except where "*serious* danger" would result to the master or his vessel. It may not be safe to moor alongside to take off survivors from a ship in distress, but the master might be expected to stand by. There is no obligation to salve, as such, and it is not quite clear how far the assistance must go beyond the mere saving of life, as opposed to property. The context and history indicates that the provision is designed for the saving of life.

The original provision of the 1910 Convention expressly stated that the obligation to assist also applied to an enemy. Although this wording has not been reproduced, it is submitted that it is now covered by the wide reference to "*any* person" in Art. 10.1.

For the U.K. provisions to give effect to the obligation in Art. 10.2, see Sched. 11, Pt. II, para. 3, below.

ARTICLE 11

Co-operation

A State Party shall, whenever regulating or deciding upon matters relating to salvage operations such as admittance to ports of vessels in distress or the provision of facilities to salvors, take into account the need for co-operation between salvors, other interested parties and public authorities in order to ensure the efficient and successful performance of salvage operations for the purpose of saving life or property in danger as well as preventing damage to the environment in general.

GENERAL NOTE

Salvors have found that while States are loud in their support for introducing legal rules to protect the environment, not all are sufficiently active when it comes to casualties in their own waters. Many states have legislation prohibiting foreign salvors operating in their waters, yet delay caused by sending a local contractor could be disastrous—even assuming it had the necessary expertise. States are also reluctant to take into their ports the "international leper", the damaged oil tanker under tow. For obligations of the salvee to assist the salvor in such circumstances, see the General Note to Art. 8.2, above.

Article 11 was derived from the 1981 CMI Draft Convention and it is apparent from the 1984 CMI Report, p. 19, that the drafting of provisions to deal with the problems outlined "was a most delicate matter". The resulting article is a rather empty exhortation, at an international level, for states parties to "take into account" the need for co-operation when exercising powers relating to salvage operations. At the 1989 diplomatic conference an unlikely combination of environmental organisations and shipowners (ACOPS, International Chamber of Shipping and Intertanko) wanted this provision strengthened in order to put an obligation on states to admit vessels in distress into their ports. There was no support for such a proposal and it was withdrawn. This is a matter that would best be dealt with in a general public law Convention dealing with rights and obligations arising out of casualties threatening the environment, perhaps in a revision of the Intervention Convention 1969 (and see the General Note to Art. 9, above).

What is the effect of including this article, dealing with the obligations of State parties, in a Schedule which is given the force of law? It might have been thought that the inclusion of the article was merely a reflection of the legislative procedure, recommended elsewhere by this writer, of including the whole Convention in a Schedule and that some parts of the Convention would necessarily be redundant. It should be noted that the Final Clauses (Arts. 28–33) are excluded from the Schedule because they are irrelevant in national law and that other public law obligations on states have deliberately been included (see, *e.g.* Art. 27, below). It follows that Art. 11 is intended to have some effect in U.K. law and there are two possible legal consequences, one public, the other private. First, there is a public law duty imposed on the U.K. to take into account the listed matters when exercising statutory powers under, *e.g.* s.293, or s.137 (implementing the Intervention Convention 1969, see the General Note to Art. 9, above). Thus, the power of the Secretary of State, under s.137, to give directions to a salvor not to enter a particular Channel port with a sinking vessel must now be exercised only after specific consideration has been given to the need for co-operation between public authorities in the U.K. and France. Failure to take Art. 11 into account could result in a judicial review, although the prospect of an emergency hearing, while a vessel is sinking, cannot hold much attraction to a salvor who may have to show that the particular decision was irrational or one which no reasonable Secretary of State could reach.

A further question is whether Art. 11 is intended to deal with powers exercised by public authorities generally, or simply to the exercise of State powers by central government. The object of Art. 11 is to ensure that co-operation takes place in salvage operations where there is an element of public control and States are likely to delegate many functions to port and other local authorities. However, there is no reference to "public authorities", as in Art. 5, above, and this would suggest that the obligation is only effectively placed on the Crown in the person of the Secretary of State for Transport. In those circumstances, it is difficult to see that the obligation also extends to local authorities, as distinct from the Crown when collaborating with them.

The second possible legal consequence concerns the private law rights of the salvor or salvee in circumstances where the vessel is totally lost as a result of the failure, *e.g.* by the Secretary of State, adequately to take into account Art. 11. Assuming that a causative link could be established, could the salvor (who has lost the possibility of obtaining an Art. 13 reward) or the salvee (whose vessel and cargo have sunk) claim damages against the Secretary of State for breach of statutory duty? Any claimant would have to establish that the 1995 Act intended to allow the State to be sued for breach of statutory duty, even where, as here, there were no corresponding obligations placed on individuals (*cf.* ss.2(2), 40(2)(f) of the Crown Proceedings Act 1947). It would be difficult to prove such an intention, given the public law consequence referred to in the previous paragraph. A deliberate misuse of statutory powers could be actionable (see, *e.g. Micosta S.A. v. Shetland Islands Council; The Mihalis* [1984] 2 Lloyd's Rep. 525), but proving misfeasance in a public office is difficult and it is hard to see how Art. 11 could greatly assist such a claim, unless the public authority concerned refused to consider the Art. 11 criteria. The salvor would have an alternative remedy through Art. 14, and so might not have suffered any loss, but the salvee might be able to show that if the vessel had been allowed into port it (or its cargo) could have been saved and that this was obviously the best method to prevent pollution. Section 138 gives a remedy where the powers under that Act have been exercised unreasonably and it is difficult to conceive of circumstances where this would not be an adequate remedy. But powers under local Acts may be invoked to keep out vessels and the Dangerous Vessels Act 1985 gives general exclusionary powers to harbour masters, *e.g.* in respect of ships at risk of exploding. It may be that the harbour master declines to take into account the wider picture and the Secretary of State does not intervene to override the harbour master under s.137 (as permitted by s.4(1) of the Dangerous Vessels Act 1985). Here there might be a possible claim against the Crown for failure to consider its duties under Art. 11, even though there may be no liability under the

Convention of the local harbour authority (which would in any event be entitled to limit its liability under s.191). Overall, it is difficult to see that Art. 11 will be of much assistance to private interests claiming against the Crown.

CHAPTER III—RIGHTS OF SALVORS

ARTICLE 12

Conditions for reward

1. Salvage operations which have had a useful result give right to a reward.

2. Except as otherwise provided, no payment is due under this Convention if the salvage operations have had no useful result.

3. This chapter shall apply, notwithstanding that the salved vessel and the vessel undertaking the salvage operations belong to the same owner.

GENERAL NOTE

Article 12.1

Articles 12 and 13 set out the basic rules for the payment of a salvage reward. They are largely as appeared in the IMO Legal Committee Draft Convention (which itself largely followed the 1981 CMI Draft Convention), but with drafting amendments. The ancient principle of "no cure, no pay" is described by the less colourful language of Art. 12.1 (and Art. 12.2) which requires a "useful result" for an Art. 13 reward. The interpretation of the phrase will be a matter for national courts, as it was under the 1910 Convention. In the U.K. there will be little difficulty in applying the case law on "no cure, no pay" and it was clear that this is what was intended (see the 1984 CMI Report, p. 20). Essentially, there is a useful result if property of value is saved. A small, but well recognised, exception concerns the salvors of life who are present at the salvage operations, but who do not themselves save any property. Under Art. 16.2 they are entitled to share in the property salvage reward. The final element of the traditional success principle is found in Art. 13.3, below, in that the maximum award (excluding interest and costs) can never exceed the value of that which is saved. It is arguable, perhaps, that persons who perform "engaged services" (see the General Notes to Art. 12.2, below, and s.224, point 6(d)) may be providing a useful result.

Article 12.2

In Art. 12.2, "payment" has to be interpreted according to Art. 1(e), above, but in this context refers to salvage reward payable to the salvor. See Art. 13.1(f), below, on when expenses are included in the reward (*e.g.* damage to the tug).

Article 12.2 is the mirror image of Art. 12.1. There can be no payment *unless* the salvage operations have had a useful result. Exceptions to the "useful result" principle have to be express. Article 14 is an example of a case where it is "otherwise provided" that payment is due even if there is no useful result (see the 1984 CMI Report, p. 20). This is because Art. 14 is specifically designed as an exception to the "no cure, no pay" principle. See also the General Note to Art. 14.1, below, on cargo removal claims.

English salvage law does have a principle of "engaged services", which derives from the case of *The Undaunted* (1860) Lush. 90 (see Kennedy, pp. 272, 279 *et seq.*). In essence, it sets out an exception to the principle that services must have contributed to ultimate success. Entitlement "depends on the making of a request for services, a determination of the nature of the services requested and a finding that the claimant has performed his engagement as far as he was able to do so" (Kennedy, p. 280). The classic example is where a person is requested by the salvee to obtain some equipment, but who for some reason is unable to do so despite the exercise of best efforts (*e.g.* when prevented by bad weather). A reward may be given on a salvage, and not a *quantum meruit* basis, provided that there has ultimately been some property saved. The precise basis for such a reward may be open to doubt, although salvage practitioners have asserted that the doctrine does have some use in encouraging assistance. It would be possible in some circumstances to imply a contractual undertaking, but the difficulty is that the "salvor" would presumably like to take the chance of a normal "cure" with its prospect of a large salvage reward under Art. 13. In other circumstances it would be possible to argue that there was assistance in the form of comfort to the salvee, on the same basis that a vessel which stands by may be held to have contributed to success.

The definition of "salvage operations" in Art. 1(d) would clearly cover engaged services, as there would be an "act or activity taken to assist a vessel . . . in danger" (and see Brice, p.111). The main question is whether the salvage operations have had a "useful result" within Art. 12.1 (see the General Note to Art. 12.1, above). If the operations have not had a useful result then there cannot be a claim under Art. 12, or an apportionment amongst salvors under Art. 15 of the overall reward assessed under Art. 13. If a putative "salvor" is requested to do something which contributes *in no way* to the ultimate success of the operation, it is difficult to see what the useful result is. The 1989 Salvage Convention has dealt specifically with the case of a salvor who has performed services which have failed, through no fault of its own, by creating in Art. 14 a special and *limited* exception to the success principle. That exception operates only in the case of threats of damage to the environment. No other exception was canvassed and it would seem contrary to Art. 12.2 for another to be created. Admittedly, Art. 14 deals with the situation where there is no ultimate success because no property has been saved and the engaged services principle deals with contributions to an admitted success, but the identical question has to be asked under Art. 13, namely whether there has been a useful result. It may be significant that there was a British proposal that the 1981 CMI Draft Convention should remunerate "particular services which have been specially and expressly ordered" (see Vincenzini, p. 63, fn. 161). The engaged services issue never surfaced again in the IMO Legal Committee. The issue was raised in the context of the 1910 Convention and Wildeboer concludes that the principle cannot stand, in the majority of cases, with what is now Art. 12.2 (see Wildeboer, pp. 115–124). Vincenzini, by contrast, considers that such services can qualify as a "useful result" if they are useful in any way (Vincenzini, p. 63). While it is right that a modest contribution is "useful" and that any act of assistance is a "salvage operation", it must be doubted how far the giving of comfort by providing useless services should be treated as salvage.

It is submitted that there is no room for a *separate* doctrine of engaged services in the 1995 Act, notwithstanding sub-para. (iii) of s.20(2)(j) of the Supreme Court Act 1981 (see the General Note to s.224(6), above). For it is contrary to the Convention to allow a salvage claim in most of the circumstances in which the principle has been used. In an appropriate case the court could (i) consider contributions in a broad manner (as with standing-by services), or (ii) declare there to have been a contractual undertaking, or (iii) give the "salvor" its expenses in circumstances where there was a threat to the environment but where it is held that there was no contribution to a useful result. In relation to the latter, it is submitted that there is nothing in Art. 14.1 which precludes the special compensation being payable provided that there are "salvage operations" within Art. 1(d). That definition would clearly encompass the engaged services, as indicated above. Article 14.1 does not specify *why* the "salvor" has failed to earn a reward under Art. 13 and, although it envisages the circumstance where the vessel has sunk, there is no reason why it should not also cover the case where the expenses were incurred in circumstances where they were not in fact useful. Indeed, it is submitted below (see the General Note to Art. 14.1) that Art. 14.1 is designed to cover circumstances where there is an apparent threat to the environment, although one did not actually exist (*e.g.* where expenses are incurred to raise a container which it is reasonably believed to contain poison but which, unknown to the salvor, is empty). On the basis that Art. 14.1 is available to the provider of services there is no need to preserve any separate doctrine of engaged services. That is not to say that a tribunal should take an unduly restrictive view of the services undertaken in a particular case: it is to indicate that it may be unhelpful to continue to think of a separate category of cases.

Article 12.3

Under Art. 12.3 salvage can be claimed even where the service is provided by a sister ship. This is the same as under Art. 5 of the 1910 Convention, but in one respect this may represent a change in English law. It was accepted in English salvage law that where ship and cargo are salved by a vessel in the same ownership, the master and crew of the salving ship are entitled to a reward from the owners of the salved ship and cargo (see *The Sava Star* [1995] 2 Lloyd's Rep. 134, 139). In such a case the shipowners may be entitled to claim salvage from the cargo on the salved ship, save to the extent that the cargo could claim that there was an actionable breach of the carriage contract by the carrying ship (*ibid.*). The fact that the ships are in common ownership may be relevant to quantum (*ibid.*, and see Art. 13 and note Art. 18). Before the 1989 Salvage Convention it was also accepted that a shipowner was not entitled to claim salvage against itself (see *The Caroline* (1861) Lush. 334, 167 E.R. 149; *The Goring* [1988] A.C. 831, *The Sava Star* [1995] 2 Lloyd's Rep. 134, 139). Although there would seem to be little logic in shipowners claiming from themselves, two points must be noted. First, as salvage charges will normally be covered by insurance, the claims may ultimately be paid by the hull and cargo insurers. Sister-ship salvage claims are covered under the normal hull and cargo policies (see the Institute Time Clauses (Hulls), cll. 9, 11, Institute Cargo Clauses (B), cl. 2). Secondly, as salvage is paid by all salved interests it has always been accepted, as noted above, that a contribution from cargo owners can be claimed. One concern has been that the shipowner will manufacture a salvage situation, or, by asserting danger, convert the ordinary contractual towage of a disabled ship (for which it alone would pay) into salvage (in respect of which payment would be shared and insured). This concern no doubt lay behind the case of *Troilus (Cargo Owners) v. Glenogle*

(Owners, Master and Crew; The Troilus; [1951] A.C. 820 (and see the General Notes to Art. 1(a) and Art. 8.2(c), above). In *The Sava Star* [1995] 2 Lloyd's Rep. 134, Clarke J. noted that it was the policy of the court to encourage sister-ship salvage and he left open the question as to whether the Art. 12.3 of the 1989 Salvage Convention had altered the existing salvage principle, described above, that a shipowner could not claim salvage from itself. It is submitted that there has been a change and that such a claim could now be brought.

ARTICLE 13

Criteria for fixing the reward

1. The reward shall be fixed with a view to encouraging salvage operations, taking into account the following criteria without regard to the order in which they are presented below—
    (a) the salved value of the vessel and other property;
    (b) the skill and efforts of the salvors in preventing or minimising damage to the environment;
    (c) the measure of success obtained by the salvor;
    (d) the nature and degree of the danger;
    (e) the skill and efforts of the salvors in salving the vessel, other property and life;
    (f) the time used and expenses and losses incurred by the salvors;
    (g) the risk of liability and other risks run by the salvors or their equipment;
    (h) the promptness of the services rendered;
    (i) the availability and use of vessels or other equipment intended for salvage operations;
    (j) the state of readiness and efficiency of the salvor's equipment and the value thereof.
2. Payment of a reward fixed according to paragraph 1 shall be made by all of the vessel and other property interests in proportion to their respective salved values. However, a State Party may in its national law provide that the payment of a reward has to be made by one of these interests, subject to a right of recourse of this interest against the other interests for their respective shares. Nothing in this article shall prevent any right of defence.
3. The rewards, exclusive of any interest and recoverable legal costs that may be payable thereon, shall not exceed the salved value of the vessel and other property.

GENERAL NOTE

Article 13.1
    Article 13.1 lists the criteria that have to be taken into account when the tribunal determines the appropriate salvage reward. There is an overriding criterion, not specifically mentioned in the 1910 Convention, that the reward has to be "fixed with a view to encouraging salvage operations". This criterion is well recognised in English salvage law (see, *e.g. The Rilland* [1979] 1 Lloyd's Rep. 455, 458) and is the key to understanding why salvage services are viewed by the law as different to an ordinary contract for work and services, *e.g.* towage. The general absence of national or international agencies to save lives or property meant that it was vital to encourage seafarers to go to each other's assistance. Although there is increasingly pressure on states to provide salvage services (see, *e.g.* the Donaldson Report), the international community still depends on a thriving professional salvage industry. Environmental concerns have increased the need for such salvors. In reaching a conclusion as to the appropriate reward, the tribunal is in an unusual position. It is not simply rewarding the actual efforts of the particular salvor. It is also trying to send a message to other potential salvors about why it would be worth their while to take part in future salvage operations.
    Article 13.1, paras. (a) to (e) list a number of criteria which the tribunal must take into account. It is not obliged to give particular preference to any of them and they are not put in any specific order. The range of factors indicates how wide the judicial discretion can be. The criteria listed repeat many of those from the 1910 Convention (represented by established English case law), although there are a number of significant additions. Attention is specifically drawn to para. (b), which is central to the 1989 Salvage Convention. Reference can be made to the 1984 CMI Report, although with the reservations already expressed (see the General Note to s.224(6), point 2, above).
    Paragraph (a). Although the reward must not exceed the salved value (see Art. 13.3, below), a tribunal will have that value very much in mind when considering the level of payment. While it is too simplistic to suggest that judges and arbitrators think only in terms of percentages of salved value when fixing payments, that percentage will be one of the first measures to which salvage lawyers will look when considering settlements. Lloyd's Salvage and Arbitration Branch publishes annually a table of statistics on LOF cases which includes a column indicating the percentage of awards to values. Between 1983–1993 those percentages were, respectively, 5.9, 5.7, 9.7, 5.5, 8.8, 8.0, 4.8, 4.9, 5.5, 6.4, and 8.9 (an average of 6.7 per cent). In the same period, the overall amount awarded to salvors has declined. This itself is one of the factors which led them to promote the new Convention. It is natural that the higher the salved value, the higher the reward. Where there is a very low salved value, the courts may be inclined to give a comparatively high

percentage of salved value as a reward in order to make sure that the salvor has received sufficient remuneration (see, *e.g. The Lyrma (No. 1)* [1978] 2 Lloyd's Rep. 27 for a 40 per cent reward). It is a mistake to take the average award at Lloyd's and use it as a starting point, as the services may merit a much higher percentage, taking into account the other factors in Art. 13. The difficulty for the observer is in obtaining objective evidence upon which to make a calculation. Few salvage cases reach the courts and the decisions of Lloyd's arbitrators are private (but see Art. 27, below).

Paragraph (b), Enhanced rewards. The major change to the list of criteria in the 1910 Convention (and to those applied in the English case law) is para. (b). It forms the basis for what has been called the "enhanced reward". It entitles a tribunal to take into account the skill of the salvors in preventing or minimising "damage to the environment", as that phrase is defined in Art. 1(d), above. The other criteria are relevant to the saving of the property of the persons who will pay the reward. The LOF 1980, cl. 1 had, for the first time, created an obligation on salvors to prevent oil escaping from tankers (*cf.* Art. 8(1)(b)). Although it did not say so anywhere in the contract, it was understood that the purpose of the clause was to allow arbitrators to give salvors a higher award than usual to reflect the extent of pollution prevention efforts. Such efforts do not directly benefit property and the hull and cargo underwriters could have declined to pay the extra amount (if it had been separately quantified). The underwriters on the London market agreed to pay the "enhanced award" in exchange for the agreement by the P & I Clubs to pay for the "safety net" (now Art. 14, below, and see A. Bessemer-Clark, "The Role of the LOF 1980" [1980] LMCLQ 297).

The concept of the enhanced award was taken up by the CMI in the 1981 Draft Convention, but with the important extension, through the definition in Art. 1(d), to cover environmental damage generally, as opposed to mere oil pollution damage, as covered in the LOF 1980. The paragraph is unchanged from the 1981 CMI Draft Convention and the 1984 CMI Report noted that enhancement is already the practice in many states and that "it was felt very important in the new Convention to draw attention specifically to this consideration and to leave it to future practice to decide the particular weight to be given to it" (p. 23).

Thus, a judge or arbitrator is entitled to increase the reward which might otherwise have been given for "property success" because of the environmental factor. This major change in the direction of the law of salvage is somewhat buried in Art. 13.1(b). It is correct that the paragraph is given no special priority by Art. 13, because this might have affected the very sensitive issues of balance which were the foundation for the Montreal Compromise introduced in the General Note to s.224 (and referred to in more detail in the General Note to Art. 14.4, below). Nevertheless, the paragraph will inevitably be in the forefront of arguments by salvors in the future and it will be a factor over which there could be more arguments than any other of the Art. 13 criteria. The salved value in para. (a) can sometimes be difficult to work out, but practitioners are familiar with the problems. Paragraph (b) is a relative novelty. Although the judge will not be required to put a financial estimate on the pollution liability that has been avoided by a salvor's skill (see the General Note to para. (g), below), the extent of the catastrophe that has been averted will be relevant. No doubt a greater enhancement will be appropriate for efforts which prevent, as opposed to minimise, damage to the environment. The reward could also be decreased if the salvor has behaved irresponsibly towards the environment: this is a necessary corollary of creating the obligation to use due care to prevent damage to the environment within Art. 8.1(b) (and see Art. 18, below). There may be fine questions of judgment of when it may be necessary to risk pollution in order to save the vessel, or when it may be necessary to risk the vessel in order to prevent pollution. A classic example is where the vessel is aground and it could be refloated by discharging oil cargo, bunkers or oily wastes from slop tanks. It would be in the salvor's interests to try to preserve oil cargo and bunkers, to whose owners a duty of care is owed by Art. 8.1. That duty theoretically exists in relation to the owner of the slops, but they are unlikely to have a value and in the past there may have been the temptation to discharge them into the sea. Now, the salvor who ensures that the slops are discharged into a barge or portable tanks will be entitled to point to the prevention of damage to the environment. The tribunal will be entitled to take into account the fact that these efforts may have resulted in a lower salved fund being preserved, because the efforts to protect the environment may have caused further damage to the vessel. It seems that an enhancement will not be appropriate where, in fact, there has been no prevention or minimisation of damage to the environment. This interpretation follows from the use of the words "in preventing" and not "to prevent", and is consistent with the distinction between Art. 14.1 and 14.2, below. What Art. 13 is rewarding is success, not simply effort: para. (b) is merely widening the notion of what might be considered as success.

Enhancement will be entirely a matter of discretion and it is also unlikely that courts or arbitrators will indicate the extent of any enhancement, so that the precise effect of Art. 13.1(b) will be difficult to gauge. It is correct to say that at the diplomatic conference nobody expected huge enhancements. It must be recalled that Art. 13.3 provides that the reward in total can never exceed the salved value. In practice it is very rare for normal rewards to reach more than 50 per cent of the salved value, except where that value is very low.

There have been a number of Lloyd's arbitrations involving enhancements, but the first case before the Lloyd's Appeal Arbitrator was decided on October 20, 1994. That case was taken on appeal to the Admiralty Court (see *Semco Salvage & Marine Pte v. Lancer Navigation Co.; The Nagasaki Spirit* [1995] 2 Lloyd's Rep. 44) and an appeal to the Court of Appeal was dismissed by a majority on December 21, 1995 (unreported). *The Nagasaki Spirit* is currently on appeal to the House of Lords and a hearing is expected in 1996. The case was mainly about Art. 14 and its relationship with Art. 13, and will be referred to in more detail in the General Note to Art. 14.2, 14.3 and 14.4, below. There was also an important issue concerning Art. 13. Professional salvors provided successful services to an oil tanker, damaged in a collision, where the potential for environmental damage was high and no alternative salvors were available. Extremely high expenses were incurred and it was apparent that although there was to be an Art. 13 reward, there might also need to be Art. 14 special compensation. The salved values were over £6 million and the original arbitrator agreed that an Art. 13 award of 61 per cent of salved values was appropriate. The Appeal Arbitrator made specific reference to the Donaldson Report's recommendation that arbitrators "should take greater account of the cost of maintaining standby facilities" when fixing salvage rewards and that there was evidence that the salvors were under pressure from their parent company to justify the high overheads and fixed operating costs in a year when salvage income did not exceed these figures. He considered that virtually all of the criteria in Art. 13 applied. The risk was high, with an almost inevitable danger of stranding, with a high risk of stranding on a rock and a distinct possibility of the vessel being supported in one area only. The vessel was already weakened after the collision and the probability was that a strand on a rock would result in loss of cargo and consequent pollution. There was a possibility of fire and/or explosion leading to further loss of oil. There would have been clean up and pollution compensation claims as the potential environmental damage was high. The Appeal Arbitrator accordingly awarded as Art. 13 salvage some £4.6 million (69 per cent of the salved fund). It may be noted that the salvors' expenses were assessed by the Appeal Arbitrator at £3.7 million, although they had claimed much more (and had originally been awarded £5.5 million). However, on appeal in *The Nagasaki Spirit* [1995] 2 Lloyd's Rep. 44, Clarke J. held that the Appeal Arbitrator had erred by increasing the Art. 13 award because of the amount of special compensation he had assessed under Art. 14 and that the comparison was irrelevant as the assessment under Art. 14.2 was independent of the assessment under Art. 13 and vice versa. He held that each should be assessed separately and special compensation only considered if it was more than the salvage remuneration. It is submitted that such an approach is somewhat unrealistic and the existence of the Common Understanding (see Sched. 11, Pt. II, para. 4, below) shows that the drafters of the Convention were acutely aware of the need to consider the balance between Arts. 13 and 14. Indeed the judge recanted somewhat (see p. 61, col. 1) when he recognised that it would be permissible and understandable for an arbitrator to make a "cross-check" in his mind to the sum assessed under Art. 14, provided that it was recognised that the two assessments were independent. It may be that the Art. 13 award produced a somewhat uneven balance between Arts. 13 and 14, given the relatively high salved value (and see the General Note to Art. 14.4, below). Without knowing what the reward would have been before Art. 13.1(b), it is difficult to assess the generosity of the award. Nevertheless, Clarke J. referred the Art. 13 assessment back to the Appeal Arbitrator, not because a cross-check had been made, but because the Appeal Arbitrator had made the cross-check on the basis of the wrong calculation of the Art. 14 special compensation. It is the latter issue which has been the subject of the appeals to the Court of Appeal and House of Lords and will be discussed in the General Note to Art. 14, below. Leave to appeal to the Court of Appeal was not given in respect of the decision of Clarke J. on Art. 13 and that ruling now stands. It is submitted that the ability to make a cross-check will give the arbitrators flexibility to balance Art. 13 and Art. 14 decisions, whether or not they refer expressly to the way in which they have achieved the balance.

Liability to pay the salvage reward, including any enhancement, is decided by Art. 13.2, below, but there were concerns that the hull and cargo underwriters would not meet claims which contained an enhancement. The 1984 CMI Report noted (p. 24) that there was an understanding between most of the world's marine insurers that the underwriters would fund the total reward for property salvage including any enhancement, in exchange for the ship's liability insurers funding what was then the safety net under the LOF 1980 (for more on this compromise, see the General Note to Art. 14.4, below). That understanding has been maintained after 1989, but there have not been express changes to the cover provided in the standard ILU clauses. A further concern was how far the shipowner could continue to make a general average claim where it paid all the salvage claim, including an enhancement, to the salvor and sought reimbursement from cargo interests. The 1984 CMI Report noted that the average adjusters had discussed a common approach in 1983. Under Rule VI(a) of the York-Antwerp Rules 1974, as amended in 1990, a salvage claim including an environmental enhancement was to be allowable in general average. This solution is repeated in the York-Antwerp Rules 1994 Rule VI(a), which is recommended to apply to adjustments after December 31, 1994 (see also the General Note to Art. 14.6, below).

Paragraph (c). A salvor may expend great time and effort, but achieve little success in terms of the amount of property salved. The reward looks to success, perhaps more so than to effort. It is interesting that the Convention uses the expression "success" here, rather than the "usefulness of the result" (*cf.* Art. 12, above). This confirms that existing case law on the measure of success is still good law.

Paragraph (d). Danger is a prerequisite to salvage (see Art. 1(a), above). There may be great danger to the salvee, but little to the salvor (*e.g.* where a powerful salvage tug is engaged to pull a grounded ship off a sandbank in a falling tide but in good weather). Alternatively, there may be great danger to both vessels, *e.g.* where the salvage tug has to take a line in difficult seas on a lee shore, or particular danger to individuals, *e.g.* the fire fighters on board the vessel in distress.

Paragraph (e). This paragraph looks to the work undertaken by the salvor and the manner in which it was done. The 1910 Convention merely referred only to the "efforts" of the salvors and this formula was repeated in the 1981 CMI Draft Convention, although the latter specifically referred to the "skill and efforts" of the salvor in para. (b). There was no intention for there to be any terminological distinction between the two paragraphs and the present text was inserted by the IMO. The theoretical distinction between the two paragraphs lies in the fact that para. (e) is looking simply at the efforts to save property (*e.g.* ship and cargo), while para. (b) concerns itself with the protection of the environment. A professional salvor will emphasise para. (e) (along with para. (i) and (j)).

Paragraph (f). This paragraph refers to the "expenses and losses incurred by the salvors" as a criterion to be taken into account. The English practice is normally to include such expenses within the overall Art. 13 reward, although separate allowances are sometimes made (see Kennedy, p. 472 *et seq.* and *cf.* Brice, p. 165 *et seq.*). It would be better practice to make one overall assessment (including the reward and any losses) rather than to separate them, at least when the salved fund is much greater than any losses suffered. The salvor may have a separate claim for losses suffered as a result of a breach by the salvee of Art. 8.2, above. These could be included in the overall assessment of the reward within para. (e), but there may be cases where the losses exceed the salved value or any salvage reward. In such a case, there is no reason why a separate claim cannot be brought, although it will be necessary to see how far allowance was given in any salvage reward so that there is not double recovery. A salvor may be best advised to indicate to an arbitrator that a separate claim is likely to be brought, so that it is not met by any claim of *res judicata*, although the arbitrator ought then to discount any alleged losses when fixing the reward. Double recovery can also be raised where the salvor is insured for losses (and see Wildeboer, p. 95 *et seq.*). It seems that the English practice is not to inquire into the salvor's insurance position, although any recovery for losses would no doubt affect any insurance claim (see Brice, p. 171).

The time used would nearly always be relevant to expenses, but will also be particularly important for a non-professional salvor which suffers commercial losses as a result of the delay caused by the salvage operations.

There may be circumstances where the salvor has a separate claim in bailment for expenses incurred after the termination of the services, but that would not be a matter regulated by the Convention (see, *e.g. China-Pacific S.A. v. Food Corp. of India; The Winson* [1982] A.C. 939 and the General Note to Art. 8.2(c), above).

One of the factors which justifies a high reward to salvors is the risk that they might incur great expenditure which is wasted if there is no property salved. Article 14 now provides a safety net in cases where there is a threat to the environment. To what extent is it proper under para. (f) (and para. (g), below) to take into account that the salvor does in fact have this safety net, so that it would be appropriate to fix the salvage reward at a lower level, at least in an "environmental" case? The 1984 CMI Report is explicit on this point (p. 25). "It is, however, not the intention that the introduction of the rules of Art. [13.1(f)] shall have such an effect. This must be kept in mind when fixing the general level of salvage rewards and in particular when considering the effect of sub-paragraph (b) relating to prevention of damage to the environment". Care must be taken with this statement, which cannot be accepted as decisive of the issue simply because the wording of paras. (f) and (g) were substantially unchanged. The precise relationship between Arts. 13 and 14 was a matter of detailed discussion within the IMO Legal Committee and at the 1989 diplomatic conference (as witnessed by the "Common Understanding", see the General Note to Art. 14 and Sched. 11, Pt. II, para. 4, below). Nevertheless, it was never the intention of those having responsibility for drafting the Convention from 1978–1989 that the changes to the Convention designed to protect the environment should have the effect of *reducing* payments to the salvor, certainly where there was only an Art. 13, and not an Art. 14, payment. It may well be that where there is a low salved value in a case to which Art. 14 might apply, an arbitrator would be justified in giving a lower reward under Art. 13 than would be the case if there was no possibility of recovering expenses under Art. 14. The balance between Arts. 13 and 14 should be entirely a matter for the tribunal (and see the General Note to Art. 14, below). In *The Nagasaki Spirit* [1995] 2 Lloyd's Rep. 44, the fact that there were high salvage expenses clearly influenced the Appeal Arbitrator to give a high salvage reward (some 69 per cent of salved value), but Clarke J. on appeal thought that such a comparison was "strictly irrelevant". However, it is submitted that the reference to "strictly" indicates that the judge recognised that it was not possible to take an overly technical approach (see the General Note to para. (b), above) and that an arbitrator will in practice be able to exercise some flexibility in maintaining the balance between Arts. 13 and 14.

Paragraph (g). At one stage, before the 1981 Montreal CMI conference, salvors tried to argue that the risk of liability to the *salvee* was a relevant criterion. This concept of "liability salvage" implied that it might be possible notionally to take into account any salved value to the salvee liability which might be saved to the salvee. It would have been difficult practically to calculate such a figure and the concept was rejected by the CMI, never to re-emerge. The present paragraph looks to the liabilities, actual or potential, run by the *salvor*. The salvor would run the risks of liability to the other parties to the service (*e.g.* under Art. 8.1, above), or to other persons. There could be tort liabilities to assisting ships or, more seriously, the threat of claims for pollution caused by negligence in the salvage (see, *e.g. The Jade* [1976] 1 W.L.R. 430 and *cf. The Amoco Cadiz* [1984] 2 Lloyd's Rep. 304). There might also be contractual liabilities to subcontractors who have provided expensive equipment on an indemnity basis. The "other" risks might include commercial or political risks, *e.g.* where delay causes the risk of loss of business already fixed, or where by entering the waters of a coastal State the salvor rendered itself liable to fines or arrest for not having the necessary paper approvals. See the General Note to para. (f), above, on the relevance of Art. 14.

On the wording of the paragraph it is a little difficult to see how there is a "risk of liability and other risks run *by* ... their equipment". It is probable that the wording (derived from the 1981 CMI Draft Convention) should be read as if it meant "... by the salvors or to, or in respect of, their equipment". Thus, the tribunal could take account of the fact that all the salvor's equipment on board the vessel in distress was at risk of total loss, even though there was no loss in the events which happened. A further problem of interpretation is apparent from the fact that this paragraph talks about "equipment", whereas para. (i) draws a distinction between "vessels or other equipment". How far can the salvage tug be included in the expression equipment? On an ordinary interpretation there might be difficulties (although *Coltman v. Bibby Tankers; The Derbyshire* [1988] A.C. 276 would now allow a wide view to be taken), but the use of the word "other" in para. (i) indicates that in Art. 13 a vessel is considered to be equipment.

Paragraph (h). A salvage service which takes a long time may give grounds for a substantial reward, but time (in para. (f), above) is not the only relevant factor. An efficient professional salvor with expensive powerful equipment may be able to succeed very quickly where a less skilled or well-equipped salvor would have struggled. This paragraph recognises that efficiency can be rewarded and that there is no need for a salvor to drag out the services in order to enhance its reward (and see the General Note to Art. 8.2(c), above). Like paras. (i) and (j) this paragraph is also relevant to Art. 14.3, below.

Paragraph (i). This paragraph recognises that professional salvors may deserve extra rewards because they commit expensive equipment to await an emergency. However, the wording does not require reference to their status as professional salvors, as such. The shipping market has forced some quite large salvors to commit tugs to ordinary towage work and these tugs would not be available for use or ready within paras. (i) and (j). In salvage arbitrations it is the practice for salvors to include documentation for the arbitrator listing their tugs and other equipment, their cost and the work they do. The arbitrators are well able to distinguish between the following: the harbour tug operator which does salvage work as circumstances arise; the "yellow pages salvor" which has no equipment of its own but simply hires in sub-contractors to work with its salvage superintendent; and the full professional salvor which maintains specially equipped salvage vessels, pumps and other equipment at a state of readiness which allows for quick reaction to disasters. It is this latter category of salvor which will receive the most encouragement through a generous salvage reward, as this salvor maintains vessels and equipment "*intended* for salvage operations" and not simply for other purposes. The tribunal is specifically directed to look not only at the range of equipment which this salvor could call upon, but also how much was in fact used. Like paras. (h) and (j) this paragraph is also relevant to Art. 14.3, below. Where it is necessary to consider this paragraph in the context of threats to the environment (either under

Art. 13.1(b) or Art. 14.3), it will also be relevant to inquire how far the vessels and equipment were purchased and intended for use to meet the environmental duties placed on the salvor in Art. 8.1, above.

Paragraph (j). Like paras. (h) and (i) this paragraph is of particular relevance to a professional salvor and is also relevant to Art. 14.3, below. A salvor may have plenty of equipment, but it may not be available for the particular salvage operations in question. The salvor may have an old set of pumps and fenders, or it may be able to demonstrate a long term investment programme in new or replacement salvage equipment. The latter type of salvor is entitled to more encouragement than the former, as it is in the interests of the maritime community that salvors should have the latest equipment available. Where it is necessary to consider this paragraph in the context of threats to the environment (either under Art. 13.1(b) or Art. 14.3), it will also be relevant to inquire how far the equipment was purchased and intended for use to meet the environmental duties placed on the salvor in Art. 8.1, above. Again, all these matters would be dealt with in the documentation supplied to an arbitrator. Like para. (g), the paragraph specifically refers to equipment and not to vessels, which is in contrast to para. (i), above. Although the "availability" of vessels in the latter is equivalent to the "readiness" in this paragraph, it would be strange if the efficiency and value of the salvor's vessels were irrelevant considerations. As with para. (i), above, it is submitted that "equipment" includes "vessel" and a tribunal should certainly be entitled to take into account the fact that the salvor had an old fleet of tugs or that it had acquired high value salvage tugs.

Article 13.2

The first sentence of Art. 13.2 sets out who is liable to pay the salvage reward under Art. 13.1. It preserves the basic rule of English law that payment is to be made by each salved interest according to the proportion that its salved value bears to the total. Thus, if a ship and cargo are each worth £1 million, they will each pay half of any salvage reward. The individual cargo owners will also pay proportionately. In recent years, the relative values of cargoes have increased greatly in comparison with the value of the carrying ship, so that, *e.g.*, cargo could bear 90 per cent of an award and the ship 10 per cent. This fact has certainly increased the vigilance of cargo underwriters in cases where they suspect collusion between salvor and shipowner. It also explains some of the concern expressed at the diplomatic conference on behalf of US underwriters as to the correct balance to be struck between Arts. 13 and 14 (and see further the General Note to Art. 14.4, below). The general principle of proportionate liability also has an effect on salvage security (see Art. 21, below).

Although each interest has a liability only for its proportion of the salvage reward, it is not unknown for some shipowners (particularly those in the liner trade) to undertake the whole primary liability themselves. They will then seek to claim cargo's proportion in general average (see further the General Note to Art. 13.1(b), above). The practice whereby the shipowner is liable to the salvor for the whole of the salvage reward represents the law in a number of states, of which the Netherlands is the most notable example. At the diplomatic conference the Netherlands successfully proposed what is now the second sentence of Art. 13.2, which allows states to apply this rule of salvage liability. However, cargo owners may well wish to resist a general average claim on a number of grounds, such as the non-seaworthiness of the carrier's ship. The final sentence of Art. 13.2 preserves such rights of defence.

The second sentence of Art. 13.2 has been retained in the 1995 Act, despite the fact that the U.K. has not expressly exercised the choice allowed by that sentence. It might have been more usual for this sentence to be omitted from the text of the Convention as reproduced in the Schedule to an incorporating Act. There is no rule-making power in the Act to allow the Secretary of State to exercise the option in that sentence, as s.224(3) only applies where there are revisions to the basic Convention itself (*e.g.* by Protocol). It might be argued that it was retained for some specific purpose, *e.g.* to allow reference to be made to some foreign law on liability. It is submitted that this would be a misreading which would undermine the application of Art. 2 in U.K. courts. The inclusion of the sentence was a matter of convenience only, so that the full text of the Convention could be incorporated and so that practitioners might not be misled when other states applied a different rule. It has no direct significance in U.K. law, except perhaps to indicate that it would not be contrary to U.K. law to recognise a foreign judgment based on the liability rules of the second sentence.

Article 13.2 does not define which of the "interests" will be obliged to contribute where there are legal *and* possessory interests involved. This matter will be determined by national law. In England the interests might include those in possession, such as a demise charterer (*cf. Five Steel Barges* (1890) 25 P.D. 142, Kennedy, p. 492 *et seq.* and Brice, p. 234 *et seq.*). Under Art. 13 there may be a maritime lien enforced by an action *in rem* against the vessel (and thus indirectly against the registered shipowner), but an action *in personam* against the person in possession. Under standard demise charters, such as the Barecon 89, there is non-lien cl. 15 which obliges a demise charterer to indemnify the registered shipowner against any consequences of a lien being asserted against the vessel and to put up security for an arrest. *Cf.* Art. 14.1, below.

Article 13.3

The rewards payable to all the salvors must not exceed the salved value of the ship, its cargo and other property saved (and see Art. 1(c), above). The concept that the salved value is the maximum that can be awarded is fundamental to salvage law and is at the heart of the 'no cure, no pay' principle. It is the existence of this principle which has made necessary the safety net exception in Art. 14 and the special treatment of life salvage (in Sched. 11, Pt. II, para. 5 of the 1995 Act, below). By contrast with Art. 2 of the 1910 Convention, legal costs and interest are not included in the salved value, and it is important that the salvor obtains sufficient security for them from the salved interests (see Art. 21.1, below).

Note that there is no limitation of liability for salvage claims under the 1976 Limitation Convention, Art. 3, as enacted in Sched. 7, above (although *cf. The Breydon Merchant* [1992] 1 Lloyd's Rep. 373).

ARTICLE 14

Special compensation

1. If the salvor has carried out salvage operations in respect of a vessel which by itself or its cargo threatened damage to the environment and has failed to earn a reward under article 13 at least equivalent to the special compensation assessable in accordance with this article, he shall be entitled to special compensation from the owner of that vessel equivalent to his expenses as herein defined.

2. If, in the circumstances set out in paragraph 1, the salvor by his salvage operations has prevented or minimised damage to the environment, the special compensation payable by the owner to the salvor under paragraph 1 may be increased up to a maximum of 30 per cent of the expenses incurred by the salvor. However, the tribunal, if it deems it fair and just to do so and bearing in mind the relevant criteria set out in article 13, paragraph 1, may increase such special compensation further, but in no event shall the total increase be more than 100 per cent of the expenses incurred by the salvor.

3. Salvor's expenses for the purpose of paragraphs 1 and 2 means the out-of-pocket expenses reasonably incurred by the salvor in the salvage operation and a fair rate for equipment and personnel actually and reasonably used in the salvage operation, taking into consideration the criteria set out in article 13, paragraph 1(h), (i) and (j).

4. The total special compensation under this article shall be paid only if and to the extent that such compensation is greater than any reward recoverable by the salvor under article 13.

5. If the salvor has been negligent and has thereby failed to prevent or minimise damage to the environment, he may be deprived of the whole or part of any special compensation due under this article.

6. Nothing in this article shall affect any right of recourse on the part of the owner of the vessel.

GENERAL NOTE

Article 14 deals with special compensation and is probably the most important new provision in the whole Convention. It introduces an exception to the principle of 'no cure, no pay' which is sometimes called the "safety net", although the expression is not a term of art and does not appear in either the 1989 Convention or the LOF. In order to understand the meaning of Art. 14 it is necessary to refer to its background.

The Montreal Compromise

The Montreal Compromise (see *Background to the 1989 Salvage Convention*, in the General Note to s.224, above) was designed to provide better rewards for salvors when they undertook environmentally sensitive services which carried with them the risk that the salvor might expend much money but receive little or no salvage reward. Salvors were to be encouraged to protect the environment by the knowledge that (i) if they did save maritime property their reward would be higher than normal (under Art. 13), (ii) if no maritime property was saved, they would be protected by a "safety net" consisting (under Art. 14) of a guaranteed refund of their expenses and an uplift of up to 100 per cent of those expenses, (iii) if there was only a small amount of maritime property recovered they would receive whatever reward this would bear, topped up by the safety net. Cargo and hull interests (through their insurers) would pay for the ordinary reward element under Art. 13, but the special compensation under Art. 14 would be met as a ship's liability only (through the shipowner's liability insurers). See generally the 1984 CMI Report,

p. 24. Although there is no formal record of the parties to the Montreal Compromise, there is no doubt that the effective agreement was between the same parties as to the compromise reached during the production of the LOF 1980, which was mirrored in Montreal. These included, in particular, the London underwriters on the one hand, and the P & I Clubs on the other.

1989 Diplomatic Conference
By the time of the 1989 Diplomatic Conference the basic concepts of enhanced award (Art. 13.1(b)) and special compensation (Art. 14) were acceptable to most States, but three groups were concerned about the draft text of the IMO Legal Committee. Some South American States were unhappy with the extent to which the safety net expenses could be increased by up to 100 per cent and suggested a figure of 15 per cent (as in the LOF 1980). Their worry, that developing world shipping costs would be greatly increased, was supported, for slightly different reasons, by shipowner organisations. The shipowners were anxious about their own costs and perhaps a little suspicious that the Montreal Compromise was a cosy agreement between insurers which would raise premiums or calls to the shipping industry.
The USA was more concerned that the cargo owners (and their insurers) would have to pay too much in comparison with the ship's interests. The particular concern of the USA was to establish a clear and fair balance where some property was saved and there was to be a shared payment under both Arts. 13 and 14. The undeniable fact was that the insurers with the most to gain from environmental protection were the P & I Clubs who would normally end up paying for pollution liabilities of shipowners (and see the General Note to Pt. VI, Chap. III, above). Why should the cargo underwriters have to make large payments to reduce the liabilities of their traditional opponents? It was uncertain how often the P & I Clubs would be called on to make Art. 14 payments. With high value ships and cargoes, the Clubs might only have to meet an occasional special compensation claim. There was already, however, a precedent for cargo to share in the general costs of pollution prevention in the form of the 1969 Liability Convention and the Fund Convention 1971 (see the General Note to Pt. VI, Chs. III and IV, above). The 1981 CMI Draft Convention and the final version of the IMO Legal Committee Draft Convention had left unresolved the issues of balance, preferring to trust to the discretion of judges and arbitrators. The USA was determined to have a clearer statement of intent. One major problem with the Montreal Compromise was that it was not transparent in the draft Convention.
The USA put forward two alternatives for amending the Arts. 13/14 package. The first assumed a significant, but moderate increase in Art. 13 salvage awards generally. Some states might have had in mind a figure such as the increment of 15 per cent in the LOF 1980. In such a case, the court should be required to decide the ordinary Art. 13 award first and then assess the environmental enhancement as a separate item, but up to a maximum percentage to be agreed by the 1989 diplomatic conference. This enhancement would be a matter for hull and cargo interests to pay. When the total sum was insufficient to meet the salvor's expenses, the shipowner's guarantee in Art. 14 would come into play. The second alternative was proposed on the basis that the 1989 diplomatic conference wanted significant increases in the basic Art. 13 rewards, such as 50 per cent or 100 per cent. In that case, where the enhancement exceeded a given percentage (such as the 15 per cent figure, above) the excess would automatically be borne by the shipowners (and their P & I Clubs). The result would be the same—a clear limit on cargo (and hull) contributions.
In order that the shipowners should not be able to recoup the special compensation from cargo owners in a round about way, the US alternatives included a provision that would have prevented special compensation being subject to general average. That point has now been taken care of by the 1990 amendments to the York-Antwerp Rules 1974, as repeated in the York-Antwerp Rules 1994 (see Art. 14.6, below).

Article 14.1
Article 14.1 sets out the safety net for salvors who fail to earn a salvage reward sufficient to cover their expenses. They are entitled to special compensation when (i) they have carried out salvage operations in respect of a vessel, and (ii) the vessel or its cargo threatened damage to the environment (as defined in Art. 1(d), above), and (iii) they have not managed to earn under Art. 13 a sum equivalent to their expenses (as defined in Art. 14.3, below). Theoretically, there is no discretion involved as to the *amount* of the special compensation. The salvor "shall" be entitled to its expenses if it has satisfied the above criteria, although there is some flexibility when a tribunal assesses expenses for the purposes of Art. 14.3, below.
Person liable. The special compensation is payable by the shipowner alone, not by the cargo or other interests. The Convention is quite specific in its reference to "owner", although it does not say "registered shipowner". It may be necessary to consult the other language versions of the Convention to see if Art. 14 can be said to apply to persons other than registered shipowner, such

as "operators", but it would seem that there could be no personal liability of a demise charterer. This is in contrast to Art. 13.2, above, which simply refers to all "interests" and might include those in possession, such as a demise charterer (see the General Note to Art. 13.2, above). Although there would be no maritime lien for an Art. 14 liability (*e.g.* where there was some salved property against which to exercise such a lien), there will be an action *in rem* available in English law (see the General Note to the Merchant Shipping (Salvage and Pollution) Act 1994, Sched. 2, para. 6(2) in *Current Law Statutes Annotated 1994*). Under a standard demise charter, such as the Barecon 89, there is a non-lien cl. 15 which obliges a demise charterer to indemnify the registered shipowner against any consequences of a lien being asserted against the vessel and to put up security for an arrest. In practice, therefore, it may be the demise charterer which arranges Art. 14 security through its P & I Club on behalf of the vessel.

When payable. It is not necessary that the salvors have actually prevented damage to the environment in order to gain the special compensation. It is enough that there is a *threat* of such damage. Actual prevention of such damage is dealt with in Art. 14.2. It follows that the salvor will still be entitled to the Art. 14.1 special compensation where the salvor reasonably supposes that there is the possibility of damage to the environment, but it later turns out that, unknown to the salvor, there was in fact no possibility of such damage. Thus, a salvor may have information from the ship's manifest, or from oral communications with the crew, that there are dangerous chemicals aboard a ship. It later turns out that these were not shipped or that they are harmless. There would be a "threat" within Art. 14.1, as threats by their nature involve those perceiving them making estimates as to whether they will occur (and see the example cited in Brice, p. 290, of threats being made by a gun which may or may not be loaded). The aim is that the salvors should have some assurance that they will at least be able to recoup their expenses if they accept a difficult, environmentally sensitive, task. If they also succeed in saving property then they know that they *may* obtain a more generous salvage reward. In *The Nagasaki Spirit* [1995] 2 Lloyd's Rep. 44, Clarke J., obiter at p. 57, rightly considered that there would also be a threat where there was initially a threat, but it had gone by the time the services started. The point is that the salvor is to be encouraged to attend at the scene of threats, whether they materialise or not. The same conclusion would apply where the salvor responds and is immediately able to remove the threat by quite simple action, *e.g.* by turning off a valve.

The application of the Art. 14.1 was considered in the second case to come before the Lloyd's Appeal Arbitrator under the LOF 1990 on November 4, 1994, in an award which will be referred to as Lloyd's Appeal Arbitration 4/11/1994. A small vessel went aground on a Scottish island while estimated to be carrying about 30 tonnes of bunkers in addition to lubricating and other oils. There was no threat of substantial damage to the mainland from the bunkers (of gas oil) which would have been carried out to the Pentland Firth by the tide and dispersed in the turbulent conditions, but there was some threat to the west coast of the island where there were seals and birds. 500 metres north of the vessel was a National Heritage site of special scientific interest (SSSI), designated under the Wildlife and Countryside Act 1981. The salvors expended over £150,000 in trying to salve the vessel and in removing some 20 tonnes of the oil, but the vessel became a total loss. Two questions arose on the interpretation of Art. 14.1, namely (i) the nature of the threat which was necessary and, (ii) whether there was a threat of damage to the environment (within Art. 1(d)).

The Appeal Arbitrator found it difficult to believe that the Art. 8.1(a) obligation would not arise when there was a reasonable apprehension of damage (whether or not it would have occurred). He also noted the distinction between the use of "danger" in Art. 13 and "threat" in Art. 14. He concluded, rightly it is submitted, that a reasonable apprehension of damage to the environment was a threat.

The crucial question was whether there was a threat of "substantial" damage within Art. 1(d). The Appeal Arbitrator asked the question "Was the threatened damage to human health or to marine life or resources *something worthy of consideration*", adopting the italicised words from *R. v. Monopolies and Mergers Commission, ex parte South Yorkshire Transport Authority* [1993] 1 W.L.R. 23, 29. It is entirely right to adopt a purposive construction of the Convention, although it must be doubted how far it is necessary to put a gloss on the Convention's wording on the basis of an interpretation of a domestic statute. The Appeal Arbitrator concluded that pollution and other incidents in Art. 1(d) are to be regarded as "major". On the facts he found that seal casualties were generally small and mortalities were unlikely, so that this threat on its own was not substantial. However, a count taken four months after the operations showed that within 2 km of the casualty there were 14,000 auks and other birds in the SSSI, including large quantities of guillemots at particular risk from surface oil. The SSSI described the bird colonies as of national importance and the Appeal Arbitrator held that "mortalities of any significant number of these birds must be regarded as substantial physical damage within the meaning of Art. 1(d)" and "clearly worthy of consideration for the purposes of the Convention". It is submitted that this decision was correct, even though there was a small quantity of oil aboard and there was no certainty that the oil would cause damage to the birds. The salvors, acting on the information available at the time, knew that there was an SSSI and that the MPCU (see the General Note to s.293(1)(d), above) had expressed particular concern about the fuel. In these circumstances, there was a clear threat, but it must be doubted whether the salvors would have succeeded but for the crucial designation of the relevant site as a SSSI. This factor appeared crucial for them in a case where the risks were difficult to establish. Indeed, the Appeal Arbitrator made a significant distinction between the burden of proof required of a salvor under Art. 14.1 and Art. 14.2, below. The evidence showed that the oil was in a double bottom tank and the likelihood was that breach of the tank would occur at high water and 20 tonnes of oil (all that remained in the vessel) would be carried towards the SSSI and this constituted a risk of substantial damage. The result in the case is just, as to find otherwise would mean that the shipowners (and their P & I Club) would have received the benefit of cargo removal services without having to pay for them. As it was, the salvors were no doubt dissatisfied with the overall result as they failed to achieve an increment under Art. 14.2, below.

Crew claim. The salvor's expenses may indirectly include sums paid to the crew, but there is no crew claim for a share of Art. 14 payments made to a salvage company, as the intention was simply to reimburse the salvor's expenses. This fact is recognised by the limited apportionment rules in Art. 15, below, which relate only to Art. 13. The position would be different if the individual crew members had themselves incurred expenses, as they could then be treated as salvors who would have a direct right to recover those expenses from the shipowner.

Wreck and cargo recovery. Although the salvor can obtain special compensation for preventing cargo or bunker pollution, it must have been carrying out salvage operations "in respect of a vessel". This almost certainly means that operations to recover a container of dangerous chemicals which has simply been washed overboard cannot fall within Art. 14.1. It would be different if, *e.g.*, a ship which was itself in danger after a collision had deliberately jettisoned cargo, or if the cargo had been lost overboard during the post-collision emergency. But it would appear that straight-forward cargo recovery work, unconnected with vessel salvage, is not covered. There is no point in salvors committing expenditure for looking for such cargo, as they will have no guarantee of recovering their expenses and the value of a single container may be very low. In one sense, this is unfortunate, because quick action to recover dangerous cargoes lost overboard could avert major environmental damage. Nevertheless, it is a logical exclusion because the Art. 14 payment is made by shipowners. It appears that under existing law shipowners may be under no obligation to recover cargo lost overboard on the high seas and their liability for damage caused by such loss would probably be dependent on fault in most legal systems (see N. Gaskell, "Lessons of the Mont Louis" [1986] IJECL 269). A draft Wreck Removal Convention has been presented to IMO, at its 63rd and 70th Sessions (in 1990 and 1994), although it is unlikely to be considered for some time. It would impose removal obligations on shipowners whose ships sink on the high seas where there are hazards from the ship or its cargo, including environmental hazards. In the absence of an international regime, or national laws in territorial waters, services might better be performed under standard form work and labour contracts, such as the Wreckcon 1993 contract for wreck removal and marine services.

Yet there may be cases where some services have been performed by salvors to the vessel, but she has sunk. What is to stop the salvors mounting a major operation to raise the cargo of dangerous chemicals? Assuming that sunken cargo can be in danger (see the General Note to Art. 1(b) and (c), above), the salvors have formed the link necessary under Art. 14.1 as they have carried out operations in respect of a vessel. The cargo owners might be happy for operations to continue as their liability to pay for the services could only be limited to the value of the cargo raised—which might not be much. There would then be a question as to whether the shipowner could issue a prohibition under Art. 19, below, and whether it would be reasonable to do so. It might be reasonable from the cost point of view, but how is this to be balanced against the threat to the environment? It must be recalled that no special compensation can be claimed unless the damage to the environment is substantial or major as required by Art. 1(e). As that provision is so restrictive, it may be that it is difficult to claim the special compensation for removing small parcels of dangerous or hazardous cargo, unless the damage they are likely to cause is on a large scale. In such a case, shipowners might find themselves in receipt of a claim for large cargo removal expenses even though there was no legal obligation to remove such cargo.

Whether this possibility was fully comprehended by the P & I Clubs in 1989 is not clear, but cl. 18 of the LOF 1990 (now cl. 4 of LOF 1995) was specifically introduced to give shipowners the right to terminate services when the cargo is worthless. It gives to the owners of the salved ship (not the other salved parties) the option to terminate the salvage services (by notice in writing to the salvor) if there "is no longer any reasonable prospect of a useful result leading to a salvage award under Art. 13". "Useful result" is the expression in Art. 12 of the 1989 Salvage Convention. The idea seems to be to prevent salvors continuing with the service merely to run up costs, particularly in order to increase the increment under Art. 14, *e.g.* where there is no real prospect of any more cargo being salved from a vessel, or where it is likely to be of negligible value. It should be noted that the option of termination is here given only to the owner of the ship being salved, and not to the salvor.

Wreck removal was excluded from the 1981 CMI Draft Convention Art. 1–2.2(d) (see the 1984 CMI Report, pp. 9, 13) and it does not seem that there was later any intention to change the substance of this provision in the sort of case under discussion. The better view is probably that the 1989 Salvage Convention was not meant to provide a regime for unrestricted wreck removal. It would be better to interpret Art. 19 widely so as to allow the shipowner to prohibit such activities, or to hold that there can be no salvage operations within Art. 1(a) to sunken property which is effectively valueless as that property cannot be in danger. This latter possibility was adverted to in Lloyd's Appeal Arbitration Award 20/10/1994. Alternatively, Art. 12.2 states that no "payment" is due under the Convention if the salvage operations have had no useful result. "Payment" includes special compensation under Art. 14.1 (see Art. 1(e)) and it might be argued that there could be no useful result, in terms of successful property salvage, to sunken, valueless property. The fundamental difficulty is that Art. 14 is within the caveat "except as otherwise provided" in Art. 12.2. It might conceivably be said that it was nowhere *expressly* provided in Art. 14 that unrestricted claims for cargo-raising could be made, but this argument is rather unconvincing.

Article 14.2

Under Art. 14.2 the tribunal is given a discretion to uplift the special compensation under Art. 14.1 (*i.e.* expenses) where the salvor has *actually* prevented or minimised damage to the environment. This uplift, or increment, was up to 15 per cent under the LOF 1980, a figure that was raised to 100 per cent in the 1981 CMI Draft Convention. Following the discussions in the IMO Legal Committee the amount in the Draft Convention was left open (in square brackets), but the CMI figure was footnoted. The initial discussions at the 1989 Diplomatic Conference confirmed the existing division of opinions and, although there was a recognition that the 100 per cent figure was a maximum, states were concerned that the reference to 100 per cent would lead tribunals to make awards near that level. Many South American States indicated that they thought a fair compromise figure would be somewhere in between the 100 per cent and the 15 per cent in the LOF 1980. Ecuador suggested 30 per cent, but states which supported the Montreal Compromise felt that this could undermine the whole balance of the Convention. With deadlock looming, it was agreed to set up a formal working group of some 20 States to discuss the matter. A compromise was finally hammered out with two days of the diplomatic conference remaining and the product was the present version of Art. 14.2.

Article 14.2 provides a two-tier safety net. Where the salvor has *actually* prevented or minimised damage to the environment, a tribunal will award the salvor his expenses under Art. 14.1 and *may* (not must) award an additional uplift of *up to* 30 per cent of those expenses. The 30 per cent is expressed as a maximum uplift, but Art. 14.2 continues by saying the court may increase this uplift to 100 per cent of the expenses if it "deems it fair and just to do so". This solution apparently satisfied the South American States, although it does not alter the substance of the original CMI proposal. It may have the desired psychological effect, however, of concentrating the mind of the tribunal on the first stage figure as a matter of normal practice, while reserving the second stage for more exceptional cases. It is important to record that there is no obligation to raise the special compensation to any particular figure, or at all—it is entirely a matter for the tribunal. At the Committee stage in the Commons (*Hansard*, col. 10), Richard Ottaway MP noted an "ambiguity of drafting" in the provision and that "practitioners have already interpreted it to mean that the ceiling will be 100 per cent, so that the 30 per cent ceiling has fallen by the wayside.

The application of the Art. 14.2 has been considered in Lloyd's Appeal Arbitration 4/11/1994, the facts of which were outlined in the General Note to Art. 14.1, above. Having found that there had been a threat of damage to the environment at the start of the services, the Appeal Arbitrator then examined very closely the events which happened afterwards to see if the salvor could establish that it had actually prevented or minimised the damage to the environment. It appeared that although nearly 20 tonnes of oil had been pumped ashore, between 11–15 tonnes had escaped during the night without being detected. No damage from pollution was caused by the leakage. The original arbitrator had simply decided that as the salvors had removed the threat, they were entitled to the increment. This was strictly incorrect as there is no *entitlement* to an increment. The matter is one within the discretion of the arbitrator. But the Appeal Arbitrator also drew attention to the fact that the arbitrator had not considered the matter of causation and proof. There was a distinction between "threat" in Art. 14.1 and "prevented" in Art. 14.2. The tribunal could not ignore the fact that oil had escaped, without any pollution being caused. If there had been no intervention to discharge the 20 tonnes, the escape would probably have continued. Even if all the oil had escaped at one time, the heavy sea conditions necessary to cause such a leak would have dispersed the oil. In the circumstances the salvors had failed to prove that they had prevented damage to the environment and Art. 14.2 could not apply. The decision is significant, because it shows that salvors may have considerable difficulties in providing what would have happened, on a balance of probabilities, if they had not intervened. It may be extremely difficult in retrospect to establish a causative link whereby it is shown that oil would have leaked, that it would have been carried in certain quantities, in a certain direction and that particular birds would have been in the sea at the relevant time. It is submitted that the decision is justified on the facts, which should be regarded as somewhat exceptional. The Appeal Arbitrator recognised this when he stated that it was an unusual case in its combination of circumstances. It is right that there should be a careful examination of the facts. Arbitrators should be careful not to demand too high a degree of proof in circumstances where the threat is obvious, but the exact mechanism by which it may be realised is difficult to predict.

A second issue concerning Art. 14.2 which arose was the appropriate percentage increment to apply if there had been a prevention of damage to the environment. The arbitrator had decided that there must be some special reason to exceed the 30 per cent figure and that, possibly, the most important consideration was the benefit conferred. He found that it was a case with a realistic possibility of damage to the environment, but that the order of possible damage was limited. It was a low benefit case. Taking into account the fact that there were professional salvors, he awarded a 30 per cent increment. The Appeal Arbitrator indicated that, if he had considered that Art. 14.2 applied, he would not have awarded as high an increment because the benefit would at best have been so marginal. It is submitted that this was a valid observation and that the increment should be directly related to the actual benefit.

In *Semco Salvage & Marine Pte v. Lancer Navigation Co.; The Nagasaki Spirit* [1995] 2 Lloyd's Rep. 44, (C.A., December 21, 1995, unreported, appeal to H.L. pending) there had been a particularly meritorious service by professional salvors (see the facts described in the General Note to Art. 13.1(b), above) and the arbitrator had awarded an increment of 65 per cent (half way between the 30 per cent and 100 per cent figures). The Appeal Arbitrator stated that the 30 per cent maximum increment must be regarded as the normal maximum and that it was impossible to lay down a definitive guide to where justice would demand a higher increment. This is surely right, but the Appeal Arbitrator helpfully set out a range of possible cases where it would be appropriate (and there was no appeal against this part of his decision). These cases included the following (i) the avoidance of a major disaster to the environment, (ii) dealing with a particularly toxic or dangerous substance, (iii) the incurring of high risk for the salvor's personnel and vessels, (iv) the necessity to assemble a large number of vessels or other resources, (v) the brevity of the operation, (vi) the requirement of skills or qualifications, (vii) frustration or the difficulties arising from the intervention of authorities, (viii) lack of co-operation or the inability to assist of those in charge of the casualty. He added that the degree to which such factors are present will also determine how far up the scale the increment should go. It is submitted that these criteria are helpful and that particular significance should be attached to the presence of the first two. On the facts of the case, there was a real possibility of a serious spill affecting an environmentally sensitive area, although not to such an extent as with the *Amoco Cadiz* or *Exxon Valdez*. There was a major salvage operation which required to be undertaken by skilled and highly equipped professional salvors, to whom no alternative was available. The Appeal Arbitrator concluded that 65 per cent was an appropriate increment (although only on the basis of the lower expenses allowed by him under Art. 14.3, below) and it is hard to see that a lower figure would have been just.

Article 14.3

The special compensation payable to the salvors under Art. 14.1 is to be equivalent to their expenses as defined in Art. 14.3. These are (i) their out of pocket expenses incurred in the salvage operation and (ii) a fair rate for the equipment and personnel that are actually used in the operation. The expenses might include the hiring in of booms and the purchase of chemical dispersants. The equipment and personnel component is to make an allowance for the salvor's own staff and resources which are actually used. It will not be possible for the salvors to inflate their expenses by including their general administrative overheads not referable to the operation. This does not mean that headquarters expenses are totally excluded, as shore based communications equipment and personnel may be used to co-ordinate operations. In all cases of expenditure, the salvor must satisfy the tribunal as to reasonableness. Again, the expenses cannot be inflated by hiring in unnecessary equipment (perhaps from a "friendly" or associated company), or by sending a huge team out for a small job. Nevertheless, an experienced tribunal will recognise that it is always better for salvor to overreact to an emergency, rather than to find itself short-handed and under-equipped at a crucial moment. The tribunal is specifically requested by Art. 14.3 to take into consideration the promptness of the services rendered, the availability of vessels and equipment and its state of readiness and value (as set out in Art. 13.1(h)–(j), above). It is clear that their deliberate inclusion was to ensure that "due account shall be taken of the salvor's standing costs, overheads, etc. when determining what is a fair rate" (1984 CMI Report, p. 27). These criteria will also be relevant when judging reasonableness, although they can hardly be taken into account when deciding *which* expenses were actually incurred.

Period. Article 14.3 covers the whole of the expenses incurred in the salvage operation and not simply those which arise in preventing or minimising damage to the environment. So, in Lloyd's Appeal Arbitration 4/11/1994 (the facts of which are described in the General Note to Art. 14.1, above) the arbitrator had allowed for the expenses of a sub-contracted tug, even though it did not participate in the removal of the bunkers from the casualty. It also follows that the expenses can relate to the whole of the period of the salvage operations. In *The Nagasaki Spirit* [1995] 2 Lloyd's Rep. 44 (C.A., December 21, 1995, unreported, appeal to H.L. pending) it was alleged by the shipowners that the threat to the environment ended well before the conclusion of the salvage services and that it would not be possible to include in an Art. 14 claim those expenses incurred after that date. It was held by the Appeal Arbitrator that this fact would be irrelevant where the salvors went out initially to a ship which threatened the environment and that the expenses for the whole of the subsequent salvage operation should be counted. The key moment in time upon which to focus is that moment when the salvor has to make the decision to become involved and it is not possible thereafter to start dividing up a long service into periods when there might, or might not, have been a threat. Of course, it would be right to recognise that the threat to the environment diminished when deciding whether to award an increment under Art. 14.2 and, if so, how great it should be. This was the view properly taken by the Appeal Arbitrator in *The Nagasaki Spirit*. The decision on this "period point" was upheld by Clarke J. and unanimously by the Court of Appeal and it is submitted that they were right to do so. The same conclusions would apply in a case such as *The Troilus* [1951] A.C. 820, where the salvage service was held to have continued for some 5,350 miles from the Indian Ocean to the U.K. However, as Clarke J. noted ([1995] 2 Lloyd's Rep. 44, 57), that was a most unusual case on its facts.

By contrast, a threat to the environment might only arise late in the provision of the services, *e.g.* where a tanker was taken in tow in the middle of the Atlantic, when it was not threatening coastal waters within Art. 1(d), and a dangerous storm arose when the vessels were off the U.K. coast. The Appeal Arbitrator in *The Nagasaki Spirit* doubted whether it was possible to include the expenses of the whole operation as this would involve implying the words "at any time" after "threatened damage to the environment". There is force in this argument, although the services described would be one indivisible salvage operation and the salvor going to the assistance of a tanker in such a position must anticipate that it would be necessary to reach a port of refuge within coastal waters. Unfortunately, it is not possible to redraft Art. 1(d) so as to widen the definition of damage to the environment. Clarke J., obiter, in *The Nagasaki Spirit* [1995] 2 Lloyd's Rep. 44, 57, was firmly of the view that the 1989 Salvage Convention only extended to salvage services rendered after a threat to the environment had arisen. Salvors have already indicated that they may be reluctant to undertake salvage services to vessels in such a position, if it can be argued that there is no threat to the environment. Some have even indicated that they might prefer to offer salvage services on the basis of the LOF 1980, in which there was no such geographical restriction.

Fair Rate. In practice, one of the biggest difficulties which has emerged in the application of Art. 14 under the LOF 1990 is in deciding what is a "fair rate" for salvage tugs and equipment. Should the arbitrator approach the issue as an accounting exercise, merely assessing the costs of running the tugs in question, or would it be appropriate to take a market rate for the tugs? In the latter case, it might be said that there was a profit element being built in to Art. 14.3, whereas one of the objects of Art. 14.2 was to allow an increment to reflect some profit. The issue is of particular importance in a case where only Art. 14.1 applies, as the salvor would not then be able to ask for any increment. It appears that the practice grew amongst Lloyd's arbitrators of using Art. 14.3 as a means of providing remuneration which was seen to be encouraging.

In *The Nagasaki Spirit* the Appeal Arbitrator disagreed with this general approach, as did Clarke J. and the majority of the Court of Appeal. It is submitted that they were right and that Art. 14.3 should be a mere mechanism for operating Art. 14.1 and Art. 14.2. It deals with costs or expenses and not encouragement, as such. The encouragement is provided by the fact that for the first time the salvors may have a guarantee that expenses may be met, or indeed supplemented, in environmental cases. That is not to say that it would be right to take a narrow accounting approach and simply isolate an artificial "costs only" element. That would only encourage a salvor to hire in a sub-contractor to provide a tug at a market rate which would necessarily include a profit element. The Appeal Arbitrator found that it would be too narrow to take a costs only approach, as this would not pay sufficient regard to Art. 13.1(h)–(j). "A fair rate will not be the same as but higher than the bare cost of operating the tug in the particular service. The salvor will not be limited to the actual cost of the tug in the salvage operation as if it were a true out-of-pocket expense." When Art. 14.3 refers to a "fair rate", it must to some extent pre-suppose that there is a market by reference to which a rate is to be judged. The Appeal Arbitrator gave some guidance as to how far it was appropriate to consider market rates and concluded that in a straight-forward case, which was comparable with ordinary commercial work, it was of use to consider the market rate. An example would be where mere towage of a disabled ship was involved. He rightly recognised that in many types of salvage operation there would be no market rate, as salvors would normally only offer 'no cure, no pay' terms. The market rate could not be applied to a non-professional salvor which offered its ship. In the actual case the parties had agreed a basic daily cost for tugs, averaged over a full year (including over-heads), at 50 per cent utilisation of the vessels. The rates took account of idle time, but that alone did not reflect the criteria in Art. 13.1(h)–(j). A fair rate had to be higher than these figures. It should take account of actual bunker usage, crew overtime and any salvage commission paid to a salvage broker (*e.g.* 10 per cent of any payments). There was a prompt service by specially equipped tugs and it was relevant to note that there was a salvage (not towage) service, although there was some standing by. The Appeal Arbitrator accordingly found daily rate figures which were significantly below those of the arbitrator, but much greater than the basic daily cost. In general, the fair rate was about twice the agreed daily rate per tug. There was an overall reduction of about 32 per cent in the allowable expenses as found by the arbitrator.

The Appeal Arbitrator's decision on fair rate was rejected by Clarke J. and by a majority of the Court of Appeal. Clarke J. considered that the Appeal Arbitrator's figures had been plucked out of the air and that it was not possible to include an element of profit in the rate. He decided that there must be an assessment of the overall costs of the operation, including a fair figure for the indirect costs (*e.g.* those involved in having vessels and equipment on stand by) and in addition to out of pocket expenses there should be included bunkers, crew overtime and the costs of paying a salvage agent a percentage of the overall reward. Clarke J. accepted that the exercise was one for an accountant and was unimpressed by the argument that such an approach would involve major accountancy exercises for each case. He rejected market rates as evidence, except in so far as it might assist to test evidence about fair rates. The majority in the Court of Appeal broadly upheld the decisions of Clarke J.; Staughton L.J., with whom Swinton-Thomas L.J. agreed, rightly rejected the notion that Art. 14.3 was itself meant to be an encouragement. It is submitted that it is highly unlikely that those at the diplomatic conference would have agreed with such a proposition; there is no support for it in the travaux preparatoires and the express limitation to Art. 13.1(h)–(j) in Art. 14.3 as matters to be taken into consideration indicates that it was not intended to allow reference to the opening words of Art. 13.1. Staughton L.J. preferred to take a less precise approach than Clarke J. He considered that fair rate "means a rate of expense, which is to be comprehensive of indirect or overhead expenses and take into account the additional cost of having resources instantly available ... Beyond that what is a fair rate is a matter for the tribunal(s) of fact. It is not necessarily the result of any exact calculation". Evans L.J. dissented on this point and considered that it was unrealistic to disregard loss of profit and that the rate should be established by reference to the commercial value of those services. If there was no market comparison possible, then the salvors' costs should be taken into account along with any lost profits suffered from being unable to use the vessels.

It is submitted that the issue has become clouded by the emphasis which the salvors have put on the "encouragement" point. Once this has been dismissed, attention should concentrate upon the task which must be undertaken by the judge or arbitrator. It seems highly unlikely that the drafters of the convention would have required the type of clinical mathematical exercise contemplated by Clarke J. The assessment of salvage rewards (under Art. 13) has traditionally involved great flexibility and a large measure of common sense and any interpretation of Art. 14.3 should leave as much discretion to experienced arbitrators as possible. Staughton L.J. seemed to recognise this fact in the conclusion of his judgment. It seems difficult not to include some market comparisons when deciding what the daily rate is for a salvage tug and it would be invidious if a salvor could recover a daily rate expense payable to a sub-contractor yet would receive a lesser figure in respect of its own tugs. An arbitrator would no doubt be cautious in trying to assess the market rate for services, as a professional salvor would not normally offer its vessels for such daily rate services if it thought that there was the possibility of a 'no cure, no pay' operation. To this extent, the conclusions of Evans L.J. have some force. It is submitted that the approach of the Appeal Arbitrator was right in principle. He did not use Art. 14.3 as a means of providing an indirect increment (which could apply in Art. 14.1 cases), but he appeared to have taken a generous view of what the fair rate was for the use of the tugs. Although the salvors would have preferred the approach of the original arbitrator, it is submitted that the Appeal Arbitrator struck the right balance and provided a rough, but workable, solution.

This result in the Admiralty Court was no doubt a blow to salvors, but it is considered that the decision of the Appeal Arbitrator was sufficiently encouraging (in a broad sense) so as not to undermine the purposes of the 1989 Salvage Convention. If upheld by the House of Lords, the decision of the Court of Appeal will require a change in the approach of arbitrators. Thus, in the original arbitration which was the subject of Lloyd's Appeal Arbitration Award 4/11/1994, the arbitrator found that the 1988 market rate for the tugs working outside a harbour was £5,500 a day, but that by 1993 it would be appropriate to increase this by 20 per cent to allow for inflation. This seems questionable where the actual market rate may have been unchanged, but it would be appropriate to add a figure to represent the fact that the market rate may be for an ordinary open water service and not for a service involving serious maritime risks. The question must be what the fair rate should be for a tug performing the type of service which was actually undertaken or anticipated, and not simply for a daily rate towage service. The arbitrator in that case took into account the need to "remain encouraging" and awarded a daily rate of £9,000 per day. In so far as this figure reflected the need to encourage, rather than a fair market rate, the award would now be wrong. Still, tribunals must be careful not to allow so restrictive an approach to expenses that shipowners (and their P & I Clubs) are able to obtain wreck removal services on the cheap.

Article 14.4

A French proposal at the diplomatic conference would have given the special compensation to the salvor, irrespective of whether it also recovered a reward under Art. 13. This proposal, which could have allowed for double recovery when expenses would be taken into account under Art. 13, was not supported. Art. 14.4 makes it clear that the special compensation is payable only to the extent that it is greater than any Art. 13 award. What Art. 14.4 does not decide, however, is how a tribunal faced with a low salved value is to decide what the Art. 13 reward is to be, knowing that it may also have to make an Art. 14 award. It is that question of balance which was addressed by US amendments proposed at the diplomatic conference (see the heading *1989 Diplomatic Conference* in the General Note to Art. 14, above).

An informal consultation group was established, with the U.K. as contact delegation, to discuss the US concerns about the relationship between Arts. 13 and 14. After a week of difficult meetings, the U.K. delegation was able to report agreement on three matters: (i) that the tribunal had wide discretion, subject to the upper limits set in Arts. 13 and 14 and the provisions of Art. 14.4, (ii) that exhaustion of the salved fund was not necessary under Art. 13 before the tribunal could consider special compensation under Art. 14, and (iii) that any guidance offered should be neutral, pointing both at Art. 13 and 14, and that the wording should be consistent with the wording of the [draft] Convention. The text of the agreement was read out by the U.K. delegation and later distributed informally without an official number, but it is a key part of the travaux preparatoires. The consultation group proposed a Rule of Interpretation similar to those in the Athens Convention 1974 and the Hamburg Rules 1978. After discussion it was agreed that a more appropriate heading would refer to a "Common Understanding" and that it would be Attachment 2 to the Final Act. See generally, document LEG/Conf.7/CW/WP.28, April 24, 1989 which was adopted by consensus of the conference, despite some misgivings. The Attachment states that it is the common understanding of the conference that a tribunal is under no obligation to fix a reward under Art. 13 up to the maximum salved value of the vessel and other property before assessing the special compensation to be paid under Art. 14. Although this probably follows from the wording of the Convention itself, it met a particular US worry that the argument might be raised. Nor was there an intention that, when considering awards under Arts. 13 and 14, a tribunal had to give special compensation under Art. 14. There seems little doubt that the Common Understanding was a compromise to avoid dealing with the contentious issues of quantum which might have divided the diplomatic conference. The Common Understanding has rightly been included expressly in the 1995 Act, in Sched. 11, Pt. II, para. 4, below. This paragraph would now have to be referred to by a judge or Lloyd's arbitrator.

In *The Nagasaki Spirit* [1995] 2 Lloyd's Rep. 44 (C.A., December 21, 1995, unreported, appeal to H.L. pending) the salved values were over £6 million and the original arbitrator agreed that an award of 61 per cent of salved values was appropriate (about £4.1 million). He also considered that a sum of nearly £5.5 million constituted the expenses under Art. 14.3 and that this would be appropriate as special compensation under Art. 14. It appears that he then deducted the salved value from the total allowable expenses and awarded the salvors the *balance* as special compensation, as the latter was only to be paid to the extent that it was greater than the Art. 13 reward (see Art. 14.4). While strictly speaking this follows Art. 14.4, it fails to take account of the fact that Art. 14.4 sets out a *maximum* which can be awarded under Art. 14. It does not state that this is automatically the amount to be awarded. Of course, the tribunal is not obliged to balance Art. 13 and Art. 14 in any particular way and the original arbitrator would have been entitled to exercise his discretion to reach the result that he did. It is arguable that there would be an error of law, however, if the arbitrator merely applied Art. 14.4 automatically, in the belief that it was necessary separately to establish the two figures (for salvage and special compensation) and then mechanically subtract one from the other. For there would have been no balancing of the two interests, as implied by the Common Understanding and the very compromises underlying the Convention. On appeal, the parties apparently agreed that there ought to be two separate calculations and the Appeal Arbitrator stated that "it is primarily the salvage reward which is intended to be encouraging to salvors" and that the special compensation was very much a safety net. It followed that in any case where the services are substantial the salvage reward ought ordinarily to be more, and where possible significantly more, than what would be awarded by way of special compensation, unless the amount which can be awarded for salvage is constrained by the value of the salved fund. On this basis the Appeal Arbitrator awarded as Art. 13 salvage some £4.6 million (69 per cent of the salved fund). As he assessed the Art. 14 expenses at £3.7 million, there was no special compensation payable as the expenses were not greater than the salvage payable under Art. 13. It is submitted, with respect, that it is questionable whether it is a correct, or necessary, interpretation of the Convention to give *primacy* to Art. 13 over Art. 14. The whole tenor of the negotiations was to avoid making such judgments. It is doubtful if the Convention could have been agreed if this interpretation had been expressly reproduced in Art. 14. It all depends on the nature of the services and the amount of the salved fund. The point of the Common Understanding is that there should be a total discretion, unfettered in any way. It has already been noted that Clarke J. considered that the approach of the Appeal Arbitrator was erroneous (see the General Note to Art. 13.1(b), above). It may be unfair to criticise the Appeal Arbitrator for being open about his priorities, but it is submitted that his decision *on the facts* may be entirely justified, particularly given his restrictive approach to expenses in Art. 14.3, above. This is not a case where the salvage reward in any way came near to exhausting the salved fund.

For general average and Art. 14, see the General Note to Art. 14.6, below.

Note that there is no limitation of liability under the 1976 Limitation Convention available to a shipowner for salvage claims made against it, but that the 1989 Salvage Convention did not expressly make clear whether an Art. 14 claim was a salvage claim for these purposes. To overcome any problems the U.K. has stretched the limits of convention interpretation by amending Sched. 7, Pt. II, para. 4 so that Art. 14 claims are not subject to limitation.

Article 14.5

The tribunal may reduce the special compensation or award none at all where the salvor has been negligent and this has effected the success of the environmental part of the salvage operations. The salvor might face a counterclaim for negligence from the salvee for breach of Art. 8.1(b), above. Article 14.5 overlaps slightly with the more general misconduct provisions in Art. 18, below.

Article 14.6

This paragraph formed part of the 1981 CMI Draft Convention. The 1984 CMI Report, p. 29, explained that although the shipowner had the primary duty to pay the salvor under Art. 14 "he is allowed to seek any recovery from other parties as appropriate, in particular cargo owners or charterers".

The most obvious right of recourse in salvage cases is against third parties in tort, *e.g.* those who have negligently caused a collision with the ship which made salvage services necessary. The 1989 Salvage Convention does not generally deal with this issue, which is matter for the ordinary law of collision and limitation of liability (*cf. The Breydon Merchant* [1992] 1 Lloyd's Rep. 373). It would only be appropriate to have a right of recourse against contracting parties either under a contract, or by implication of law.

As already noted, there may be an express right of recourse by a shipowner against a demise charterer under cl. 15 of the Barecon 89 charterparty (see the General Note to Art. 14.1, above) in respect of liens or encumbrances on the vessel, or in respect of claims arising from the operation of the vessel by the charterer. Although there would be no maritime lien under the Convention, there could be a statutory lien under the Supreme Court Act 1981 (see the General Note to Sched. 2, para. 6 of the Merchant Shipping (Salvage and Pollution) Act 1994 in *Current Law Statutes Annotated 1994*) and an Art. 14 claim would almost certainly arise from the operation of the vessel by the charterer. It would be necessary to study closely the terms of the standard form time and voyage charters to find an equivalent provision. It might be said that a time charterer could be liable to indemnify the shipowner under the standard employment and indemnity clause, but otherwise the shipowner may have to rely on express indemnities in bills and charters, or point to some breach by the charterer or bill of lading holder which made the salvage services necessary. A shipper which supplied dangerous cargo in breach of the contract of carriage could face a claim for indemnification against salvage costs, including those under Art. 14. It would be difficult to say that such claims were too remote once the Act was in force.

One direct way in which there may be recourse is through the principles of general average. It is apparent from elsewhere in the 1984 CMI Report (see p. 24) that Art. 14.6 was not intended to deal with general average, which it was expected would be dealt with separately. The informal consultation group which considered the relationship between Art. 13 and Art. 14, above, also agreed that special compensation under Art. 14 was not to be subject to general average. The only question was how to deal with this in a Convention on salvage. It was agreed that a resolution of the 1989 Diplomatic Conference be made requesting the CMI to achieve the above result by a speedy amendment of the York-Antwerp Rules 1974. The CMI produced the York-Antwerp Rules 1974, as amended in 1990, Rule VI(b) of which made it clear that Art. 14 special compensation is not allowable in general average. That amendment has been repeated in the York-Antwerp Rules 1994, Rule VI(b), which the CMI has recommended should apply to adjustments after December 31, 1994 (and see the General Note to Art. 13.1(b), above, on general average and enhancement).

ARTICLE 15

Apportionment between salvors

1. The apportionment of a reward under article 13 between salvors shall be made on the basis of the criteria contained in that article.
2. The apportionment between the owner, master and other persons in the service of each salving vessel shall be determined by the law of the flag of that vessel. If the salvage has not been carried out from a vessel, the apportionment shall be determined by the law governing the contract between the salvor and his servants.

GENERAL NOTE

Article 15 deals with the division of any Art. 13 salvage remuneration between the various claimants. These claimants fall into two categories, dealt with in Art. 15.1 and Art. 15.2, respectively.

Where a number of salvors have contributed to the services, *e.g.* where salvage teams from a number of independent salvage tugs are involved, Art. 15.1 provides for the tribunal to divide up the award in accordance with the criteria in Art. 13.1, above.

As between the owner, master and crew of each salving vessel, Art. 15.2 repeats Art. 6.3 of the 1910 Convention by providing that the law of the flag will govern apportionment (see also the repeal of s.7 of the Maritime Conventions Act 1911 by Sched. 12). Where the salvor does not use a vessel, *e.g.* where a salvage team are landed on a casualty by helicopter, the law of the contract of employment will govern the division of any remuneration between themselves. Where the law of the flag is U.K. law, apportionment will be governed by ss.228–229 for services rendered in the U.K. Note also the protection given by s.39, which regulates the extent to which mariners' salvage rights may be regulated by contract.

ARTICLE 16

Salvage of persons

1. No remuneration is due from persons whose lives are saved, but nothing in this article shall affect the provisions of national law on this subject.
2. A salvor of human life, who has taken part in the services rendered on the occasion of the accident giving rise to salvage, is entitled to a fair share of the payment awarded to the salvor for salving the vessel or other property or preventing or minimising damage to the environment.

GENERAL NOTE

Article 16 of the Convention re-enacts (with some significant additions) Art. 9 of the 1910 Salvage Convention which was never specifically enacted into U.K. law. Some changes in practice will be necessary as a result.

Article 16.1 is uncontroversial in that it makes clear that a salvor cannot claim anything from human beings who are saved. The provision has to be read in the light of the duty in Art. 10, above. There are no provisions in U.K. national law which differ from this principle. Some states apparently require contributions from the shipowner.

In Art. 16.2 the 1910 law was restated, but with the addition of the words "or other property", to reflect the modern definition of salvable property set out in Art. 1(c). Also, "payment" was inserted for "remuneration" (in the 1910 version) and the words "or preventing or minimising damage to the environment" were added. The effect of these latter changes was to make it clear that the life salvor was entitled to share in any Art. 14 special compensation payment, in addition to any Art. 13 reward. This view is confirmed by the CMI Report 1984 (p. 30) which stated that "it follows from [Art. 14.1] that the life salvor, who has taken part in salvage operations, shall have his reasonable expenses paid".

Article 16.2 recognises that it has long been accepted that a life salvor is entitled to something *if* there has also been property salvage. English salvage law allowed a life salvor who also saved property to be awarded a higher amount of salvage, and that factor is fully recognised by Art. 13.1(e) of the Convention. It appears that there was, however, no *independent* claim for salvage if that salvor had not also saved property (see the cases discussed in *Kennedy*, p. 100 *et seq.*). This did not matter much in practice, because statutory provisions covered life salvage from 1846. The Merchant Shipping Act 1894, s.544(1) provided that the owner of salved property had a liability to pay a reasonable amount of salvage to a life salvor in certain circumstances (*e.g.* where lives were saved in British waters or from a British ship). Section 544(2) gave a life salvor priority against other salvage claimants when life salvage was due from a shipowner. Section 544 was repealed by the Merchant Shipping (Salvage and Pollution) Act 1994, Sched. 2, para. 1, which means that the life salvor's rights must be determined solely according to Art. 16.

The concern that has arisen since the Convention was agreed is that under Art. 16.2 the life salvor has to direct its claim to the property salvor rather than to the property salved itself. This interpretation arises from the words "entitled to a fair share of the payment awarded to the *salvor . . .*" (emphasis added). An alternative interpretation is that all Art. 16.2 says is that, when considering the appropriate Art. 13 or Art. 14 payment, a court should award a fair share of the appropriate figure to the life salvor. The reference to the "salvor" may, it would then be argued, indicate simply that the salvee under Art. 13 (or shipowner under Art. 14) does not have a dual liability as such. The assumption here would be that the tribunal would be hearing all claims at one time. The difficulty with this latter interpretation is that it hardly fits with the words used.

The crucial question, therefore, is the nature of the right that is given by Art. 16.2. In particular, has it declared (i) that the life salvor has no independent right to any payment under the Convention, but only a claim dependent upon the claim of the property salvor (a "parasitic" view), or (ii) that, without prejudice to any other rights to obtain remuneration under the Convention, the life salvor is given a summary method of being paid, *i.e.* through the salvor (a "wide view")?

The problem posed for professional salvors is that they might have to wait for the expiry of the two year time-limit under Art. 23 in case a potential life salvor comes forward or, alternatively, actively to promote claims by the life salvor in order to ensure that they are taken into account when assessing any reward under Art. 13. The ensuing delay would not assist the very salvors whom the Convention was designed to assist. It does not appear that this concern was ever expressed during the negotiations, partly because those representing the salvors' interests may have assumed that there was no change to existing law and practice. This was the case for those states which had properly implemented the 1910 Convention, but not for the U.K. In debates, these concerns were voiced by Lord Byron (at *Hansard*, H.L. Vol. 555, col. 689), who recognised that it was not open to Parliament to redraft the Convention. No relevant amendments were made to the draft Bill and the repeal of s.544 of the Merchant Shipping Act 1894 went ahead, presumably because it was assumed that it was inconsistent with Art. 16, and for two reasons. First, s.544(1) made the owner of property liable for life salvage, not the salvor. Secondly, s.544(2) gave priority over other claims, while the Convention did not sanction such an approach. It cannot be argued that the problem was overlooked in Parliament, so what is the position under Art. 16? It will be helpful to consider both the travaux preparatoires of the 1989 Salvage Convention Art. 16 and its predecessor in the 1910 Convention, Art. 9.

The draft Convention which was submitted to the CMI Conference in 1981 (see CMI Documentation 1981, Vol. 1, p. 60) provided expressly for a salvor to have a right to special compensation (similar to, but separate from, that now in Art. 14.1) if "at the request of any party concerned or a public authority" it had "salved or undertaken to salve any person from a vessel in danger". There was to have been the equivalent of Art. 14.2 of the 1989 Salvage Convention allowing the special life salvage compensation to be increased by up to 100 per cent. Like Art. 14 it was only to be paid by the shipowner, or "the State in which that vessel was registered . . .", and only to the extent that there was no recovery under the equivalent of Art. 13. The CMI Report 1984 (p. 31) records that the Montreal Conference of the CMI did not adopt this proposal. "It was felt that the commercial aspects in the proposal were too strongly emphasised. It was feared that the proposed rules could lead to new problems, and, on the other hand, it was felt that the present system, under which salvage at sea of human lives is often not compensated, was generally functioning satisfactorily". It can been seen that what was dropped was the "commercial" idea of the uplift (*cf.* Art. 14.2), along with the possibility of State liability. The rejected text does not help in deciding whether there was an independent right to life salvage or, to put it another way, to whom the life salvor can turn in order to claim some payment. It does, however, indicate that one method of giving an independent claim *against the shipowner* was discarded and this may suggest that it was also intended that there be no other similar independent claim. Further, it seems to have been accepted that life salvors may not be "not compensated" in some circumstances, perhaps if the property salvor did not make a claim.

A leading analysis of the 1910 Salvage Convention and its travaux preparatoires is by Wildeboer. She states, in respect of the equivalent of Art. 16.2, that "it is apparent from the reports [that] the states remained free to grant a larger or smaller amount of rights to the life salvors in their national laws, for instance, to give them a right of remuneration independent of the salvage services rendered to vessel and cargo" (p. 244). In effect, this view would read Art. 16.2 as regulating what happens to a life salvor within a salvage regime, but does not preclude a State from providing for a *separate* way in which to remunerate life salvors. She adds (at p. 246) that "there was no unanimity among the delegates about the ratio of the provision [*i.e.* Art. 16.2]". There was evidently a disagreement of principle between the English and French points of view, in that the latter wanted a text which made the property salvor liable to pay the life salvor, while the former wanted the payment to be made by the salved interests (*i.e.* an independent right). At the last minute there were obviously English doubts about whether the final version of the text achieved their aims, as an unsuccessful attempt was made to change it. Wildeboer concludes (at p. 247) that the relevant text "contains the elements of the French point of view. The salvors of human life have been given a right to a fair share of the remuneration which is awarded to the salvors of ship and cargo. If nothing or only a reduced compensation is awarded to them, the life salvors receive nothing or a smaller amount".

The only way in which the writer can see an independent right of the life salvor being preserved is through a rather liberal interpretation of "salvage operation" in Art. 1(a). It might be possible to say that as salvage operation means "*any* activity to assist a vessel in danger", it could include the assistance of saving life. If such a view is adopted, there would be an independent right for a life salvor to claim under Art. 14 (even where it was not really involved in measures to save property or the environment) as it had carried out salvage operations. There would even be a "useful result" within Art. 12.1, which is a view consistent with current practice which would recognise life salvage claims in the event of property being salved. In order for this interpretation to be maintained it would be necessary to assume that Art. 16.2 was only providing for one way in which the life salvor could be rewarded (*i.e.* a "wide" view). While such an approach has attractions, it must be said that it strains the language of the Conventions and it would be unlikely to succeed.

With some reluctance it is submitted that, although the text of Art. 16 is (just) capable of either the "wide" or "parasitic" meanings, the better view on the wording used is that there is no independent right of the life salvor against the salved interests and that the only claim is one against the successful property/environmental salvors. Even if the 1910 Convention or the 1989 Conventions allowed states to produce separate (non-salvage) provisions to remunerate those who save life at sea, the inescapable consequence of incorporating the Convention provision in U.K. law (without any separate regime) is, unfortunately, that the "parasitic" view of life salvage has prevailed. This appears to have been the assumption of Parliament in repealing s.544(2) of the Merchant Shipping Act 1894 (see the Merchant Shipping (Salvage and Pollution) Act 1994, Sched. 2, para. 1).

On the basis that the only rights of a saver of life are to be derived from the successful salvor under Arts. 13 or 14, it is probably a misnomer to continue to speak of a "life salvor", rather than of a "life saver" (although the traditional terminology is preserved in Art. 16 itself and Sched. 11, Pt. II, para. 5, below). For the life saver under Art. 16.2 cannot have a maritime lien on the salved property as these interests have no liability towards it. With the repeal of s.544(2) of the Merchant Shipping Act 1894 there would be no separate priority over other salvage claims. A life saver may be well advised to make sure that it has saved some property itself, if it wants to assert an independent claim against the ship and cargo and not against the salvor. It follows that the life saver may be affected by the following factors: the insolvency of the property/environmental salvor (after a Convention payment has been made to it); the misconduct of the property/environmental salvor under Art. 18; the negligence of the property/environmental salvor under Art. 14.5; a prohibition issued to the property/environmental salvor under Art. 19; because the property/environmental salvor is not a volunteer under Art. 17; or because the ship escaped her dangerous position without assistance after some crew members had been taken off (*cf. The Cargo ex Schiller* (1877) 2 P.D. 1435, 160, Wildeboer, p. 248, 250).

However, there is nothing in the wording of Art. 16.2 which requires, for instance in a misconduct case, that the tribunal must decide what the life saver's remuneration ought to be and then reduce it pro rata with any reduction in the claim of the property/environmental salvor. It would be perfectly possible for the life saver to be awarded its full fair share, even if that meant that the property/environmental salvor received considerably less. Moreover, there is no definition of fair share and the tribunal would be entitled, though not bound, to treat this as the life saver's expenses. It should be noted that it is assumed in the passage cited above from the CMI Report 1984 (p. 30) that the reasonable expenses of the life saver and a "fair share of the payment awarded to the salvor" would be the same. One 1910 French view of the meaning of what is now Art. 16.2, for which there is no clear support in the wording, was that the tribunal which decided on the appropriate remuneration for the property salvor was *not* entitled to take into account the fact that there had been a life salvage (Wildeboer, p. 248). As already noted, the tribunal is directed to consider the saving of life in Art. 13.1(e) and it would seem inconsistent and contrary to principle for a tribunal to ignore the fact that the property/environmental salvor may have to pay a life saver.

Where a property/environmental salvor has been awarded special compensation under Art. 14, it would seem that the tribunal cannot take into account the life saver's expenses in assessing the "salvor's" expenses under Art. 14.3. Article 14.1 allows the salvor to claim "his expenses" and it may be stretching the language of Art. 14.3 rather far to suggest that the expenses incurred by the life saver were somehow the expenses of the property/environmental salvor (although as noted, there is no separate definition of salvor). There may be circumstances where the property/environmental salvor specifically requests or contracts for the life saver to perform services of saving life. Here, any payment expressly or impliedly due to the life saver would count as expenses of the property/environmental salvor, but the costs of a life saver who operates independently could not be included, even if the property/environmental salvor has subsequently to share its remuneration with that person. This unsatisfactory and impractical state of affairs is only alleviated by the fact that the tribunal *would* be entitled to take into account the existence of a parasitic life salvage claim in deciding whether to exercise its discretion to award an uplift under Art. 14.2. In some cases it will not be necessary for the life saver to make a parasitic claim as it may have been involved in Art. 14 operations itself.

The correct treatment of life savers may have to be reconsidered some day. As a matter of practice the "parasitic" claim has many disadvantages for professional salvors. Wildeboer stated in 1965 that the 1910 formula is open to much criticism and it "is almost universally agreed that the saving of life should be remunerated and that this reward should not be paid by the salvors" (*op. cit.*, p. 256). As a matter of policy, it may be that it is the shipowners who ought to pay for the saving of crew or passengers—a solution rejected by the CMI in 1981. In the U.K., the life saver who is paid nothing might be able to claim a discretionary payment from the Secretary of State (see Sched. 11, Pt. II, para. 5, below).

ARTICLE 17

Services rendered under existing contracts

No payment is due under the provisions of this Convention unless the services rendered exceed what can be reasonably considered as due performance of a contract entered into before the danger arose.

GENERAL NOTE

This article "forms part of the important principle under which a salvage service must be voluntary to give right to the remedies under the Convention" (1984 CMI Report, p. 31). Article 4 of the 1910 Convention was more restricted in that it only applied to towage contracts. The principle of voluntariness is fundamental to salvage law (see, *e.g. Kennedy*, Chap. 6, Brice, p. 62 *et seq.*), but it is something of a misnomer. It is meant to indicate that only those who act without pre-existing duty can be salvors. Most of the case law is concerned not with those who can claim, but with those who cannot or ought not to be entitled to claim. Underlying much of the law is the fear that if certain categories of persons are allowed to be claimants they may abuse their position so as to manufacture a claim. The most obvious examples concern members of the crew of a ship who are not normally entitled to claim because of the concern that they may deliberately put their own ship in peril in order to claim salvage for saving it. They are said not to be "volunteers", as they are under an existing contract of employment to work the ship. In *The Sava Star* [1995] 2 Lloyd's Rep. 134, it was held that cargo owners could claim salvage for services provided to the ship. Such a case may not be as rare as might be thought, especially where a large chemical manufacturer has consigned a bulk cargo with handling characteristics of which it alone has experience. However, care should be taken to investigate the bill of lading or charterparty to ensure that the cargo owner is not contractually obliged to provide assistance.

The Convention does not talk about voluntariness, as such, but states that there shall be no entitlement to salvage unless the services rendered exceed pre-existing *contractual* duties.

Article 17 is not appropriate to regulate that category of case which concerns pre-existing public duties which has traditionally, if misleadingly, been categorised in English law under the same voluntariness principles as the contract cases. Such public law cases, *e.g.* concerning harbour authorities (see *Bostonian (Owners, Master and Crew) v. Gregerson (Owners); Gregerso, The* [1973] 1 Q.B. 274), will now fall to be dealt with under Art. 5, above.

Article 17 restates existing English law principles concerning contractual voluntariness, *e.g.* applying to ships' crews and tugs under contracts of towage (see, *e.g. The Homewood* (1928) 31 Ll. L. Rep. 336, *The Aldora* [1975] Q.B. 748, [1975] 1 Lloyd's Rep. 617). There is a two stage process which is reminiscent of that used in some of the consideration cases in contract. First, it is necessary to establish the exact duties of the parties under the contract in question. Secondly, the services actually rendered must go beyond the agreed contractual duties. If they did, the provider of the service is a volunteer and is not debarred from claiming salvage. The classic case is of a tug, *already* engaged under a towage contract, which meets with supervening circumstances, *e.g.* a collision, requiring services far in excess of a mere expedition of the tow's progress. Fire fighting and extensive refloating operations would not have been part of the existing contractual duties. These duties will vary in extent along with the contractual payments. An ocean tug will probably expect to have more problems in a long ocean towage than a harbour tug engaged in berthing a ship. The standard daily-rate ocean towage contract, Towhire 1985, expressly provides that the tug has a duty to reconnect the towline if it parts, without claiming for salvage. This probably states expressly what would be implied, but there would be a difference where the reconnection required dangerous navigation into rocky waters in a gale. Similarly, harbour tugs would not normally be able to claim salvage where the tow went briefly aground. The position would be different where extensive and strenuous operations were required to effect a refloating.

One difficulty with Art. 17 is that it does not state in respect of whom the contractual duty must arise before the article operates as a bar. The main category of voluntariness was designed to deal with pre-existing contractual duties owed by the putative salvor to the salvee (see, *e.g. The Sarpen* [1916] P. 306, 315). The question is how far Art. 17 can operate where the contractual duties are owed to some *third* party. In a case such as *The Gregerso* [1973] Q.B. 274 (see the General Note to Art. 5.2, above) if the harbour authority itself could not claim salvage for operations performed in order to comply with statutory duties, is there any reason why the same rule should not apply to tugs which it has contracted-in to perform the service? Recommendation 85 of the Donaldson Report invited the U.K. Government to ensure that salvage tugs with adequate capacity should be available at key points around U.K. shores, albeit that they should be owned, operated and managed by commercial operators. Tenders have already been prepared for trials of such services and the contractors will want to know if they will lose their salvage rights.

It is submitted that these questions should be decided on the basis of first principles. Is there any public policy reason why a useful service should not be treated as salvage? It is unlikely that there could be any public policy reason why such salvors should not be able to claim salvage from private shipping interests, particularly as any income would necessarily reduce the strain on the public purse of subsidising such operations (and see the General Note to Art. 5.3, above). The existence of a subsidy would naturally be relevant in deciding the quantum of a salvage reward according to the criteria listed in Art. 13.1, above. A salvor which received cross-subsidisation from public funds could be viewed in the same way as a salvor which subsidised its salvage operations from commercial towage. There would not need to be a complete bar on claiming salvage (which is the effect of applying Art. 17), but a tribunal might be less generous in an Art. 13 reward than it would if there was no subsidisation. There is no need for the tribunal to feel that the ordinary salvage reward should be reduced drastically. The treatment should vary, depending on whether there is a mere subsidy to keep vessels operating in a particular area, or whether the tugs are effectively hired on a basis which appropriates them solely to the particular service.

The same principles should apply where a tug is hired in by the harbour authority to remove a wreck. By contrast, where the contractor is hired by, or on behalf of, the owners of the property concerned specifically to raise a wreck, there would be a direct contract which would fall foul of Art. 17 (*cf. The Solway Firth* [1893] P. 120), even assuming that there was property of any value to be salved. There may also be an express or implied provision in the contract indicating that there would be no salvage claim or, like the Wreckcon International Wreck Removal and Marine Services Agreement 1993, the contractual obligations may be set out in such detail that it would be difficult to imagine them being exceeded.

Particular problems are caused by the use of sub-contractors to perform salvage operations. Salvors may hire in barges for the lightening of a ship, or sub-contract tugs from other salvors in order to perform the salvage operations. The sub-contractors may prefer to be paid on a lump sum or daily rate basis, irrespective of "success". In effect they might specifically agree a "no salvage" contract. Alternatively, they may prefer to become joint salvors. The ordinary barge owner might prefer the former basis, while the professional salvor might prefer to be treated as a salvor (*e.g.* by signing the ISU Sub-contract (Award Sharing) 1994). In either case there would be a commercial weighing of risks. The certainty of payment (probably at a high contractual rate) would be off-set against the chance of sharing in a large salvage reward, but which was on the highly risky 'no cure, no pay' basis. In neither case is there a contractual relationship with the salvee so as to raise the normal problem of voluntariness, but there are authorities which indicate that the sub-contractor may be barred from claiming (see, *e.g. The Texaco Southampton* [1983] 1 Lloyd's Rep. 94 (C.A. NSW)).

The cases cited by Brice (at pp. 78–80) are not wholly consistent and there is a danger that a decision to bar a claim by a sub-contractor (unless it exceeded its duties) may unfairly affect the employees of the sub-contractor. In the ordinary case, the courts and Parliament have been anxious to see that the crews of salving ships are not deprived of their claim for salvage by a "no salvage" contract signed by their employers (see, *e.g. The Leon Blum* [1915] P. 290, s.39). In the absence of misrepresentation, it may be possible to imply a term in the sub-contract that there would be no direct claim by the sub-contractor against the salved property for salvage and in such circumstances the main contractor might be able to obtain an injunction to block the suit. Alternatively, the tribunal should be entitled to refuse to treat the sub-contractor's services as giving rise to any salvage claim when it had a clear commercial choice as to the basis on which it ought to be remunerated, and it chose not to accept the risk of a 'no cure, no pay' contract. In such a case, the court must be careful not to treat the employees of the sub-contractor unfairly. In *The Texaco Southampton* a sub-contracted tug performed services which, had they been provided to a "stranger", would certainly have merited a salvage reward for the crew. The sub-contractor had, however, agreed to provide the services on a towage contract basis only, and it was held that the crew were not volunteers because they had not exceeded their contractual duties. While it may be right that the sub-contractor itself should not be allowed to claim, it is not entirely clear that the same approach should have been taken with the crew. It may be that the courts are anxious to discourage such claims by the employees of sub-contractors because of the complications which might be caused in the settlement of the main claim.

ARTICLE 18

The effect of salvor's misconduct

A salvor may be deprived of the whole or part of the payment due under this Convention to the extent that the salvage operations have become necessary or more difficult because of fault or neglect on his part or if the salvor has been guilty of fraud or other dishonest conduct.

GENERAL NOTE

Article 18 follows the pattern of Art. 8 of the 1910 Convention, by allowing the tribunal to reduce payments to the salvor, or disallow claims completely, where there has been misconduct of the salvor (for discussion of the 1910 Convention position, see Vincenzini, p. 214 *et seq.* and Wildeboer, p. 84 *et seq.*). The word "misconduct" only appears in the title and not in the text of the article. The powers may be exercised when the salvage was made necessary in the first place by the fault of the salvor, *e.g.* where one ship brings about a collision and then salved the other, or where the actual operations of salvage have become more difficult as a result of incompetence. Fraud or dishonest conduct are separate grounds for penalising the salvor. What Art. 18 does not say is that salvors can be subject to counter-claims for damage done by them which exceeds any salvage reward payable under Art. 13 (as in *The Tojo Maru* [1972] A.C. 242). It has already been submitted that damages actions would follow from breach of Art. 8.1 (see the heading *Sanctions* in the General Note to Art. 8, and *cf.* Vincenzini, p. 283 *et seq.*) and it is submitted that Art. 18 is only relevant to the question of reducing rewards and does not preclude a claim under Art. 8. To that extent, *The Tojo Maru* is still good law. For limitation of liability, see the General Note to Sched. 7, Pt. II, para. 4, above).

It has already been noted that, under Art. 14.5, salvors can be deprived of the whole or part of the special compensation under that article if they have been negligent and thereby failed to prevent damage to the environment. This is the incentive to exercise due care under Art. 8.1(b). Article 14.5 may well be superfluous in view of the wide definition of payment in Art. 1(e), which covers both salvage rewards and special compensation, but it does emphasise the environmental objectives.

Note also Art. 19, below.

ARTICLE 19

Prohibition of salvage operations

Services rendered notwithstanding the express and reasonable prohibition of the owner or master of the vessel or the owner of any other property in danger which is not and has not been on board the vessel shall not give rise to payment under this Convention.

GENERAL NOTE

Article 3 of the 1910 Convention provided expressly that a salvor would not be entitled to any remuneration where it had taken part in salvage services despite the "express and reasonable" prohibition of the vessel in distress. This provision is repeated and expanded upon in Art. 19. The original 1981 CMI Draft Convention referred only to the prohibition issued by the owner and master of the ship in distress (see the 1984 CMI Report, p. 32). In Art. 2–1.1 of the 1981 CMI Draft Convention there was also an obligation on such persons to take timely and reasonable action to arrange for salvage operations. The final version of the Convention allows prohibitions to be made by the owners of certain other property in danger. This property does not include cargo which has been carried on board the ship in distress. Thus, the final decision concerning services is left to the master of the vessel in distress, but subject to prohibitions issued by other property owners. The wording of the provision is not entirely clear, but an example might be the owners of cargo aboard another vessel with which the first vessel was in collision (and whose master or owners have not issued a prohibition), or the owners of a floating platform which might not fit within the definition of vessel in Art. 1(b). Freight, although "property" is intangible and cannot have been "on board", although it is not clear why it should be treated differently from the cargo in respect of which it is paid. This possibility of conflicting orders should be avoided (and see also the General Note to Art. 8.1(d), above). The overall criterion is reasonableness, but in considering Art. 19 the court must take into account the variety of duties owed by the salvor under Art. 8.1.

Under the (pre-1995) salvage law of England a salvor who was superseded may be entitled to some reward or compensation which will vary, depending on whether the salvor is performing 'pure' non-contractual services on or engaged on a contract such as the LOF (see N. Gaskell, "The Lloyd's Open Form and Contractual Remedies", [1986] LMCLQ 306, Kennedy, p. 285, Brice, p. 193 *et seq.*). A 'pure' salvor who was dismissed may be entitled to some reward 'in the nature of salvage' both for services already performed before dismissal (this would be an ordinary contribution to success) and for the lost opportunity of participating in a successful service (see *The Unique Mariner (No. 2)* [1979] 1 Lloyd's Rep. 37, reviewing the earlier cases such as *The Hassel* [1959] 2 Lloyd's Rep. 82). An LOF contract has been held to contain an implied term that a salvor who is willing and able to perform the engaged service will not be dismissed by the salvee (*The Unique Mariner (No. 2)* [1979] 1 Lloyd's Rep. 37) and any wrongful dismissal would be treated as a repudiatory breach of contract entitling the salvor to damages for breach, and not a reward for salvage, as in the case of a "pure" salvor.

Article 3 of the 1910 Convention did not directly address the question of a contracted salvor but, in any event, the provision was never specifically enacted in English law and formed no part of the reasoning in *The Unique Mariner* litigation. The matter of dismissal is specifically addressed in the 1989 Salvage Convention Art. 8.1(c) and (d). Article 8.1(d) obliges the salvor to accept the intervention of other salvors "when reasonably requested" by the salvee, provided that the amount of its reward "shall not be prejudiced should it be found that such a request was reasonable". Like the 1910 Convention, the 1989 Salvage Convention provision bases the rights of a dismissed salvor on the reasonableness of the request. This criterion was not the basis for the approach of the English courts, referred to above, although it no doubt underlies it. It has already been doubted how far it is open to national law to provide an *extra* remedy where the Convention deals expressly with the same or a similar matter (see the General Note to s.224(6)). This is a case where there is no contradiction between the pre-existing salvage law and the Convention, but where a reasonable interpretation of the Convention as enacted would mean that it would be inappropriate for the existing remedy in a pure salvage situation to overlay a remedy, and criterion, expressly set out by the Convention. If this view is correct, the rights of the superseded salvor should be wholly governed by the Convention provision and *The Hassel* and *The Unique Mariner* line of cases on this 'pure' salvage point should not be followed. Such cases may have been unnecessary, in any event, if the U.K. had fully enacted the 1910 Convention as it was internationally agreed. It follows from Art. 6.1 of the 1989 Salvage Convention that any salvage *contract* would only override Art. 8 if it was express, and not implied as in *The Unique Mariner (No. 2)*. It cannot be said that it is any longer *necessary* to imply a term where the Convention provides a remedy and, to this extent, it is submitted that the decision in *The Unique Mariner*

(No. 2) has been reversed. See, however, discussion of the effect of the enactment of sub-para. (iii) of s.20(2)(j) of the Supreme Court Act 1981 which causes unnecessary doubt (within the General Note to s.224(6), above), for it is arguable that *The Hassel* has clearly held that the payment to a superseded pure salvor is a claim "in the nature of salvage". It is submitted that, nevertheless, the Admiralty Court ought to interpret the 1989 Salvage Convention, which has the force of law, as impliedly removing any other remedy deriving from salvage law.

CHAPTER IV—CLAIMS AND ACTIONS

ARTICLE 20

Maritime lien

1. Nothing in this Convention shall affect the salvor's maritime lien under any international convention or national law.

2. The salvor may not enforce his maritime lien when satisfactory security for his claim, including interest and costs, has been duly tendered or provided.

GENERAL NOTE

In English law salvors have been entitled to a maritime lien for their services. This has two advantages. First, it gives them provisional security in the right to retain the salved property until they have been paid, or until adequate security has been given to meet a future award. Secondly, in the event of insolvency of the salvee, the salvor also has a secured interest with a high degree of priority. Article 20 preserves existing national and international law on the salvor's maritime lien. This was partly because the concept is fairly well understood in practice, but also because discussions were taking place at UNCTAD for the revision of the 1926 Convention on Liens and Mortgages. The International Convention on Maritime Liens and Mortgages 1993 provides in Art. 4.1(c) that there is a maritime lien in respect of claims for reward for the salvage of a vessel (effectively repeating Art. 2(3) of the 1926 Convention). Although there may be doubts whether the U.K. will ever ratify the 1993 Convention, which is not yet in force, the salvage maritime lien is recognised internationally. It would seem unlikely that a court would deny a maritime lien for claims falling within Art. 13, even though they might contain an environmental element. To do so would require the apportionment of a claim between the property and environmental elements—something that is practically impossible until after the award is made. It is submitted that all Art. 13 rewards give rise to maritime liens. It seems that this is what was intended in the negotiation for the 1993 Convention.

The 1989 Convention leaves open the question of whether certain of the other new obligations created by it will give rise to maritime liens. The salvage lien has only existed in respect of payment for saving the property in distress. But what of the new environmental payments that may be made under Art. 14, or the compensation that might be claimed for breach of the various obligations under Art. 8? As the Convention specifically leaves national law unaffected on this point, the issue will therefore be one for national courts to decide. The Maritime Liens and Mortgages Convention 1993 was worded deliberately so as to exclude the Art. 14 payment. This fact has been recognised in the negotiations taking place for the revision of the Arrest Convention 1952. It has been provisionally decided at a joint UNCTAD/IMO meeting in Geneva in December 1994 that, although there should be no maritime lien in the 1993 Convention for Art. 14 claims, there should be a right of arrest in the amended 1952 Convention (and see the General Note to the Merchant Shipping (Salvage and Pollution) Act 1994, Sched. 2, para. 6, in *Current Law Statutes Annotated 1994*). The same approach is likely to be taken in respect of claims under Art. 8, except in cases where the salvor's failure to exercise due care gives rise to an existing lien, *e.g.* as a result of a collision.

It may be relevant to consider the extent to which a right is given by Art. 21 of the 1989 Salvage Convention to demand security for potential claims under the Convention. The existence of a wide right to security for all Convention claims might be said to support the view that there is a corresponding maritime lien. The better view is that Art. 21 should be considered on its own, although it may be argued that Art. 21.3 creates some new form of possessory lien in respect of certain Convention claims. The 1989 Salvage Convention, Art. 20.2 merely puts a restriction on salvors exercising the lien once provision has been made for satisfactory security in respect of the claim, interest and costs.

ARTICLE 21

Duty to provide security

1. Upon the request of the salvor a person liable for a payment due under this Convention shall provide satisfactory security for the claim, including interest and costs of the salvor.

2. Without prejudice to paragraph 1, the owner of the salved vessel shall use his best endeavours to ensure that the owners of the cargo provide satisfactory security for the claims against them including interest and costs before the cargo is released.

3. The salved vessel and other property shall not, without the consent of the salvor, be removed from the port or place at which they first arrive after the completion of the salvage operations until satisfactory security has been put up for the salvor's claim against the relevant vessel or property.

GENERAL NOTE

Article 21.1
Practical needs of salvors. The obtaining of security for a claim is one of the first tasks a salvor will undertake once the salvage is complete. In practice, the salvor exercises a maritime lien over ship and cargo, where possible, and arrangements are made to contact the various owners of both ship and cargo and their respective underwriters. As the latter will often pay the bulk of any salvage claim, it is customary for them to provide some security to the salvor in the form of an undertaking to pay any future award or judgment. On provision of the security the ship and cargo are released to their owners.

The 1910 Convention did not deal at all with security. Article 21.1 of the 1989 Convention requires persons liable for Convention payments to provide satisfactory security on the request of the salvor. It is to the advantage of all that valuable ships and cargoes are not held up in ports of refuge, incurring costs and suffering deterioration, while the salvor is persuaded to give up his only effective means of enforcement. Once parcels of cargo are released without security it is often impractical for the salvor to pursue each individual owner in the courts of many countries in order to enforce a personal claim.

Request. A request under Art. 21.1 must be made before the obligation arises to put up security. Normally this will automatically follow the arrest or exercise of the maritime lien. There may be cases where the salvor is forced to release the ship or cargo, for instance under the orders of a local harbour master. As Art. 21.1 does not impose a time-limit within which the request must be made, a salvor will be able to demand security even when the salved property is out of his possession. Failure to provide the security is then, presumably, a breach of a Convention obligation which might give rise to a damages action by the salvor (*cf.* the General Note to Art. 8, above). As the loss is likely to be the failure to pay the underlying salvage claim, it is difficult to see the need to bring such a separate action. There may be cases, however, where the salvage claim is admitted, or ultimately paid, but the salvor incurs extra expenditure in trying to enforce it.

Clause 4 of the LOF 1990 requires a salvor to notify Lloyd's immediately after the termination of the service of the amount of security it requires. Doubts have been raised as to how far it is possible to attempt to increase the security at a later stage when it becomes apparent that the claim may be greater than originally anticipated. Under Art. 21.1 there is no restriction on the number of requests for security, provided they are reasonable.

Payment. The obligation to give security arises in respect of a "payment" due under the Convention. The definition of payment in Art. 1(e) includes sums payable under Arts. 13 and 14, whether or not there is a maritime lien in respect of them. "Compensation" in Art. 1(e) was obviously meant as a shorthand for the special compensation in Art. 14. Thus, shipowners and P & I Clubs must give security for Art. 14 special compensation claims, even where the vessel is totally lost. The problem will then be in assessing "satisfactory" security.

Does the word "compensation" in Art. 1(e) cover those forms of compensation that might be claimed by the salvor for breach of the Convention obligations, *e.g.* under Art. 8, or Art. 21.2? The simple fact is that the negotiators of the 1989 Salvage Convention were focused on Art. 13 and Art. 14 claims only and that the definition must be made to work for a number of different objectives. While the matter cannot be free from doubt, there is some logic in having a uniform treatment of the salvor's Convention claims. It is submitted that Art. 21 does apply to wider Convention obligations. It seems clear, however, that Art. 21.1 is designed for security to be given for the *salvor's* claim, so that a life salvor's claim under Art. 16.2 for life salvage would not be entitled to security, nor would a salvee's claim for breach of Art. 8.

Satisfactory. The security under Art. 21.1 has to be "satisfactory". This relates both to the amount for which the security is to be established and to the quality of the undertaking given (or the person giving it). Clause 4 of the LOF 1980 allowed salvors to notify Lloyd's of the amount required for security, but it has been implied that this does not entitle a salvor to name any sum, for instance the entire salved value (*The Tribels* [1985] 1 Lloyd's Rep. 128). Security has to be sufficient to pay the salvor's highest reasonable claim (plus interest and legal costs) and the LOF 1990, cl. 4(c) provided that the amount of security has to be reasonable in the light of the knowledge available to the salvor at the time the demand is made. It is likely that the word "satisfactory" will be given a similarly objective interpretation. As security must be given for Art. 14

special compensation there will be some difficult questions as to the level at which to set it. Experienced lawyers can have a rough idea as to a normal range of salvage awards, but the special compensation "safety net" is still a new concept. There is the added difficulty that security for Art. 13 awards will normally be given on behalf of the ship by hull underwriters, but the liability for Art. 14 awards will be on the liability insurers, such as P & I Clubs and they will have to give salvage undertakings. The ISU has produced a Guarantee Form (ISU 3) for the giving of Art. 14 security. Again, it may be difficult to set a figure for security where there is the prospect of rewards under both Arts. 13 and 14 (and see the General Note to Art. 14.4, above). Note that where interim payments are made under Art. 22.1, the security is to be reduced accordingly (see Art. 22.2).

There are always difficulties where a ship is salved containing cargoes belonging to many owners of different nationalities. How can the salvor ensure that all claims are to be heard in one forum and which is it to be? This type of problem can be overcome at the security stage if consent to a jurisdiction is given. As the word "satisfactory" in Art. 21.1 relates to financial matters, it would not seem possible for a salvor to claim that it would not be satisfied unless there was a jurisdictional agreement attached to the security. The 1989 Convention does not compel the salvee to accept jurisdictional (or other non-financial) conditions to be attached to the security, although there is nothing to prevent the salvor asking for them. A typical form of security will be a guarantee of payment upon the final adjudication of a court of competent jurisdiction. It might not say which court that will be.

The type of security is not specified, but the present practice of the courts will provide a guide. Undertakings or guarantees from first class banks and insurers would be acceptable, but personal undertakings by the salved interests would not. In the case of doubt, a court should err in favour of the salvor.

Article 21.2

Article 21.2 was taken directly from the LOF 1980, cl. 5 (later the LOF 1990, cl. 4(d), LOF 1995, cl. 5(d)). It derives from the principle that each interest is only liable for its proportion of the salvage reward. Article 21.2 is designed to deal with the particular problem of the shipowner who only has the obligation to put up security for its part of the reward and who, through indifference or collusion, allows the cargo owners to remove their cargo without them first having provided security to the salvor. It is because of this problem that strong arguments were made in favour of the Dutch system whereby the shipowner is liable for the whole reward (see the General Note to Art. 13.2, above). There, the shipowner would put up security for all the claims and claim contributions in general average from the cargo owners. This system has much to commend it, for it is the shipowner rather than the salvor who has detailed knowledge of the identity of all the cargo owners through the bills of lading in the manifest and office records. A single liability is also in keeping with the concept of the single maritime adventure. Art. 21.2 puts a direct obligation on the shipowner to use "best endeavours" to ensure the cargo owners put up security. It is significant that "best endeavours" was used rather than the less rigorous "due care" (see under the heading *Standard of Care* in the General Note to Art. 8, above). In practice the shipowner may not always be in a position to prevent cargo removal, *e.g.* where the port authority orders it. Even so, there will always be the possibility of warning the salvor what is happening.

The salvor has a valid claim against the cargo owner but it may be worthless without security, so the loss likely to result will be that proportion of the salvage award payable by the cargo owner. It is assumed that the salvor will have the right to bring a damages claim against the shipowner.

Article 21.3

Article 21.3 forbids the removal of the salved property from the port of refuge without security having been provided, unless the salvor consents. This covers the case where the salvor does not have possession of the vessel and its cargo. In a sense there is an overlap with Art. 21.1 and Art. 21.2 as the sanction for the removal of salved property without consent must be a claim by a salvor for the type of amounts which would arise for breach of them. But Art. 21.3 deals with the situation where no formal request for security has yet been made. This may be because the salvor has been unable to identify the correct owners, or has made a request to the wrong owners—*e.g.* where goods have been sold in transit. The salvor would also be able to obtain injunctive relief to prevent removal.

ARTICLE 22

Interim payment

1. The tribunal having jurisdiction over the claim of the salvor may, by interim decision, order that the salvor shall be paid on account such amount as seems fair and just, and on such terms

including terms as to security where appropriate, as may be fair and just according to the circumstances of the case.

2. In the event of an interim payment under this article the security provided under article 21 shall be reduced accordingly.

GENERAL NOTE

Salvors' finances are often desperately affected by cash flow. They may incur huge expenses to perform the service, but may have to wait a long time before receiving payment. Some help was provided by the LOF 1980, cl. 10 which allowed the Lloyd's arbitrator to make an interim award. This concept has been reproduced in Art. 22.1 (and in the LOF 1995, cl. 10(a)(iv)). A wide discretion is given to the tribunal to pay the salvor a fair and just sum on account. The practice of Lloyd's arbitrators is to make particular use of this provision for out-of-pocket expenses. While this is certainly a good yardstick, there is no reason why in an appropriate case a salvor could not be awarded something more, especially in a case where there are low expenses but a high value salved fund. There may be cases where salvage is admitted and the only question is whether the award should be greater than £1 million. In such a case an interim award of up to that figure would not be inappropriate.

For security issues, see the General Note to Art. 21, above.

ARTICLE 23

Limitation of actions

1. Any action relating to payment under this Convention shall be time-barred if judicial or arbitral proceedings have not been instituted within a period of two years. The limitation period commences on the day on which the salvage operations are terminated.

2. The person against whom a claim is made may at any time during the running of the limitation period extend that period by a declaration to the claimant. This period may in the like manner be further extended.

3. An action for indemnity by a person liable may be instituted even after the expiration of the limitation period provided for in the preceding paragraphs, if brought within the time allowed by the law of the State where proceedings are instituted.

GENERAL NOTE

Article 23.1

The 1910 Convention provided that a "salvage action" must be brought within two years of the termination of the services. The French text referred to "l'action en payment de la remuneration" (see Wildeboer, pp. 258–259). This limit has been repeated in Art. 23.1 in relation to "payment under this Convention". Clearly, the limit will apply to Art. 13 and Art. 14 claims (see Art. 1(e), above). It would cover both any amount of salvage and any separate awarding of indemnification for a salvor's expenses and damages, if the tribunal decides to award these separately, as opposed to including them in the overall Art. 13 reward (*cf.* Wildeboer, pp. 95–97). It is submitted that it would also apply to a life saver's claim under Art. 16.2, above. The Art. 23 limit could be read as covering damages claims for breach of the obligations in Arts. 8 or 21, if a wide definition is given to "payment" in Art. 1(e) (see the General Note to that article, above). The issue is not easy because the drafters of Art. 23 were almost certainly only considering Art. 13 and Art. 14 claims. It would not be wholly inconsistent for there to be damages actions made on the law governed by national time bars, but it is submitted that it would be acceptable to take a wide definition of payment in order to provide uniformity (*cf.* Gaskell, "the 1989 Salvage Convention", p. 74). If Art. 23 only applied to Art. 13 and Art. 14 claims, it would be necessary to look to national law, which may provide differing periods, *e.g.* for a tort claim for negligence.

Difficulties may arise when a claim is being made under a salvage *contract*. Is there an action relating to payment under the Convention? In English law, any salvage contract would be subject to the Convention unless the Convention was specifically excluded (see Art. 6.1) and it is difficult to imagine any contract excluding the salvor's rights under Arts. 13 and 14. However, it is doubtful if the limit would apply to an Art. 14 claim under the LOF 1990 before the Convention itself became part of the general U.K. law on January 1, 1995. The existing two year salvage limit derives from the 1910 Convention, where the concept of "special compensation" was unknown, and the Art. 14 claim under the LOF would probably be treated as a straight-forward contract claim to which a six year limit would apply. After January 1, 1995, the LOF 1995 simply refers to the English law of salvage and so the claim under Art. 14 will be one which does arise under the Convention, although it will be decided upon at arbitration. There may be other breaches of obligations contained in the salvage contract. Clause 5(d) of the LOF 1995 mirrors Art. 21.2 of the Convention. If a salvor brought an action for breach, would it arise under the contract (where a normal six year time-limit would apply) or would it be a claim for payment under the Convention (when the Art. 23 two year limit may apply, see above)? The better view is that there would be two causes of action, one to which the Convention applied and one arising under the contract: the salvor could choose either. The same analysis would apply if there was an action against the salvor for negligence (under Art. 8, above), or for breach of the best endeavours obligation under cl. 1(a) of the LOF. In such a *Tojo Maru* claim, there would again be a choice, ignoring for the moment any distinction between the "best endeavours" and "due care" (see the General Note to Art. 8, above).

A similar problem arises where a party seeks to set aside a contract under Art. 7, above. If a salvee claims that the salvage payment was too large, under Art. 7(b), it will presumably be asking for a proper amount to be substituted under Art. 13. The same would apply to a salvor which had been misled into agreeing a contract at too low a level. It is difficult to say that there was not an "action relating to payment" which was covered by the two year time bar. More problematic is the case where it is sought to set aside a contract under Art. 7(a). Here, the applicant may claim that because of misrepresentation there was never any danger giving rise to a reward. The action would still relate to payment. It is arguable that the 1910 Convention time bar would not have applied to an application to annul or modify the contract (see Wildeboer, p. 174), but it is difficult to imagine a case where the action did not now "relate to" payment, an expression which did not appear in 1910. To this extent, it is submitted that an action under Art. 7 would, in most circumstances, relate to payment under the Convention.

The law of the forum will presumably decide when proceedings have been instituted (*cf. Dresser U.K. v. Falcongate Freight Management; The Duke of Yare* [1992] Q.B. 502).

Section 8 of the Maritime Conventions Act 1911 (repealed by Sched. 12) provided that proceedings had to commence "within two years from the date when the salvage services were "rendered". This was an unnecessary change to the 1910 Convention which used the same terminology as the 1989 Salvage Convention, *i.e.* "terminated". Although there may not be much difference in practice, there may have been disputes as to the meaning of "rendered". The wording is now clearer, but there still be problems, *e.g.* where different parts of the cargo are saved at different times by one salvor, or where different salvors are involved. Wildeboer considered (at p. 260) that the equivalent provision in the 1910 Convention meant that if services are rendered by various sets of salvors consecutively the service of each set terminates at a different moment and the limitation period of the various actions would then commence at different times. Where a number of salvors contribute, whether successively or not, to the saving of a ship in circumstances where a court is likely to give a reward based on the single salved value, it would seem inappropriate to regard each of the services separately. In essence there has been one salvage service performed by a number of salvors and in respect of which Art. 15 would apply to regulate apportionment. It would be better to regard the service as a whole, so that there would be a termination when the last salvor had enabled the vessel to reach a place of safety. This approach would be beneficial to salvors and would enable the first salvor to let the salvage claim be coordinated by the final salvor. In effect, the whole service would be treated as a "distinct occasion", a principle adopted in limitation of liability. The result ought to be different when a ship is subject to a number of *independent* salvages during the course of a single voyage. "Salvage operation" is defined widely, however, in Art. 1(a) to mean "any act or activity undertaken to assist a vessel". On that basis it could be said that time commences when *any* activity terminates. This approach would support the Wildeboer view of many different commencement times. Article 23.1 does, though, refer to the day on which "*the* salvage *operations*" are terminated and this seems to support the view that the operations must be viewed as a whole. On that basis, there would only be one time bar operating for the whole series of services.

Article 23.2

The 1910 Convention contained an express provision allowing State Parties to decide the extent to which there may be interruptions to, or suspensions of, the time bar, *e.g.* where a ship could not be arrested. No such reference is made in Art. 23, although para. 2 allows the salvee to extend the period by a declaration to the salvor (presumably this can be made orally or in writing). For that reason it was necessary to repeal the relevant part of s.8 of the Maritime Conventions Act 1911 (see Merchant Shipping (Salvage and Pollution) Act 1994, Sched. 2, para. 2, Sched. 12 of the 1995 Act), which contained a proviso giving the Admiralty Court a discretion to extend the two year time bar and imposed a duty to do so when there had been no reasonable opportunity to arrest the defendant ship in the jurisdiction. The proviso had been used by the

Admiralty Court to correct minor delays (see, *e.g. The Albany* [1983] 2 Lloyd's Rep. 195, *The Salviscount and the Oltet* [1984] 1 Lloyd's Rep. 164). No such extensions may be granted under the 1989 Salvage Convention, Art. 23 and the proviso has had to be removed for salvage cases. It might be thought that this is a matter of regret, although it does achieve a more uniform application of the Convention.

Article 23.3

Under Art. 23.3 actions for indemnities are to be brought according to the law of the forum. Part of the reason for allowing extra time is that it is not easy to claim an indemnity until the primary liability has been established. It is not quite clear which "indemnities" are contemplated, but the 1984 CMI Report, at p. 35 seemed to have in mind the kind of contractual indemnities which arise under the Hague-Visby Rules, Art. III, r. 6 *bis* (see the Schedule to the Carriage of Goods by Sea Act 1971). Cargo owners may claim an indemnity in respect of salvage paid as a result of breaches of the contract of carriage (*e.g.* unseaworthiness). Shipowners may claim an indemnity from demise charterers who have allowed a maritime lien to be created in respect of the vessel. On the wording, Art. 23.3 could cover those tort claims by shipowners for damages against a colliding ship whose negligence made the salvage necessary. There might also be claims by a shipowner under Art. 14.6, but they are described there as a right of "recourse". The difference in terminology may simply reflect the antecedents of Art. 23.3. There could be the right of recourse under Art. 13.2 (second sentence) which a shipowner under Dutch law might have against cargo if the shipowner had paid the whole of the salvage award. It is arguable that the limit could refer to the type of damages claim (*e.g.*, for breach of Arts. 8 or 21) already discussed in the General Note to Art. 23.1 (*cf.* Wildeboer, p. 259). In any event, if they are not within Art. 23.1 they would be subject to national limits.

So far as English law is concerned, it would be necessary to see how far the Limitation Act 1980, s.5 applied, with its six year time bars for contract or tort actions. It would seem that the cargo owner claim, given above, would not be subject to the Hague-Visby Rules and the six year time-limit would apply (*cf. China Ocean Shipping Co. (Owners of Xingcheng) v. Andros (Owners)* [1987] 1 W.L.R. 1213). The shipowner's collision tort action might, however, be governed by the two year time bar of s.190 of the 1995 Act.

ARTICLE 24

Interest

The right of the salvor to interest on any payment due under this Convention shall be determined according to the law of the State in which the tribunal seized of the case is situated.

GENERAL NOTE

Art. 24 refers the question of interest on salvage rewards to the law of the State seized of the case. The U.K. practice has been to allow interest on salvage rewards (see *The Aldora* [1975] Q.B. 748). The time for commencing the calculation of interest has varied greatly, *e.g.* from (at the earliest) the date of termination of services, to (at the latest) a period of six months following the completion of the services (see, *e.g. The Pergo* [1987] 1 Lloyd's Rep. 582). When the LOF 1990 was being drafted, salvors complained that the six month practice (often used with the LOF) led to salvees delaying all settlements until the elapse of the period. The LOF 1990, cl. 10 (now LOF 1995, cl. 11) gave the arbitrator a complete discretion to fix interest rates but, in general, made it payable as from the date of termination of the services. The Admiralty Court has recently been persuaded to adopt the same practice (see *The Yolaine* [1995] 2 Lloyd's Rep. 7).

ARTICLE 25

State-owned cargoes

Unless the State owner consents, no provision of this Convention shall be used as a basis for the seizure, arrest or detention by any legal process of, nor for any proceedings in rem against, non-commercial cargoes owned by a State and entitled, at the time of the salvage operations, to sovereign immunity under generally recognised principles of international law.

GENERAL NOTE

A new and useful provision is found in Art. 25, dealing with State-owned non-commercial cargoes (such as military supplies) carried on board ordinary commercial ships. Article 25 differs from Art. 4, above, in that it presupposes that such cargoes *can* be the subject of the salvage rules of the Convention, but removes any right of the salvors to arrest the cargo. Thus, where a ship is under arrest to enforce the salvors' claim they could not prevent the removal of the non-commercial State cargo from the arrested ship. In practice this may have the same effect as a complete exclusion of the cargo from the Convention, as the salvor may have difficulties in bringing *in personam* actions against many states.

The article is in accordance with the Crown Proceedings Act 1947, s.29, which states that nothing in that Act shall authorise proceedings *in rem* respect of the arrest of any Crown ships "or of any cargo or other property belonging to the Crown". Otherwise, s.230 of the 1995 Act allows salvage claims to be made against and by the Crown.

Cf. Article 26, below.

ARTICLE 26

Humanitarian cargoes

No provision of this Convention shall be used as a basis for the seizure, arrest or detention of humanitarian cargoes donated by a State, if such State has agreed to pay for salvage services rendered in respect of such humanitarian cargoes.

GENERAL NOTE

Article 26 was a US proposal which was passed rather hurriedly at the end of the diplomatic conference, without a great deal of consideration, while a spirit of compromise prevailed. Few were prepared to argue against any proposal which contained the word "humanitarian". Hundreds of millions of tons of food and other aid is carried by sea. It makes sense not to have grain rotting in a hold while a salvage dispute occurs. Like Art. 25, Art. 26 prevents the arrest of such cargoes, but only when a State has agreed to pay for salvage services in respect of them. What is not entirely clear is when the State is supposed to agree. The past tense is used in the article, but no mechanism is provided whereby the State can notify the Secretary-General of IMO. Moreover, there may be considerable uncertainty in some cases as to who exactly does own the cargo, particulary where it is a part-cargo in a general ship, or where all the papers have been lost in a casualty. States may even purchase ordinary commercial cargoes already afloat. Is a seizure in good faith to be held unlawful when it is later discovered that the cargo falls within Art. 26? It must be implicit that the salvor has notice of the state's interest. If it does not have such notice, the State must make an application to the court where the cargo has been arrested and apply to have it released.

See also the General Note to Art. 4, above.

ARTICLE 27

Publication of arbitral awards

States Parties shall encourage, as far as possible and with the consent of the parties, the publication of arbitral awards made in salvage cases.

GENERAL NOTE

Article 27 survived from the 1981 CMI Draft Convention. It encourages a State Party to publish arbitral awards. It is aimed at Lloyd's arbitrations, the details of which are confidential. Knowledge of the general level of awards, and the extent to which arbitrators take into account particular factors, are the stock in trade of London salvage lawyers. There is an international benefit in having a wider dissemination of expertise, particularly as concerns the approach taken to applying the environmental factors under Arts. 13 and 14 of the 1989 Convention. Article 27 was deliberately left in the Schedule to the 1995 Act, presumably so that the DOT could encourage Lloyd's to try, in turn, to encourage parties to its arbitrations to publish suitably anonymous reports of major decisions of principle (as has been done in this annotation).

Articles 28–34

Note that the Final Articles of the Convention (Articles 28–34) are not reproduced in the Act as they deal with matters such as adherence, reservations, denunciation, revision, and amendment, the depository and the original languages of the Convention. They do not need to be given the force of law as they relate to the international functions of the Convention. Attention should be paid to Art. 30, however, as it sets out four reservations which a State may make (and see the General Notes to Art. 1 and Sched. 11, Pt. II, para. 2).

PART II

PROVISIONS HAVING EFFECT IN CONNECTION WITH CONVENTION

GENERAL NOTE
The purpose of Part II of the Schedule is similar to that in other merchant shipping statutes which have incorporated an international convention. It comprises specified provisions necessary to make the Convention work in domestic law, *e.g.* by interpreting, adapting or supplementing the text of the Convention as reproduced in Sched. 11, Pt. I.

Interpretation

1. In this Part of this Schedule "the Convention" means the Convention as set out in Part I of this Schedule and any reference to a numbered article is a reference to the article of the Convention which is so numbered.

Claims excluded from Convention

2.—(1) The provisions of the Convention do not apply—
  (a) to a salvage operation which takes place in inland waters of the United Kingdom and in which all the vessels involved are of inland navigation; and
  (b) to a salvage operation which takes place in inland waters of the United Kingdom and in which no vessel is involved.
(2) In this paragraph "inland waters" does not include any waters within the ebb and flow of the tide at ordinary spring tides or the waters of any dock which is directly or (by means of one or more other docks) indirectly, connected with such waters.

GENERAL NOTE
This paragraph contains two of the four reservations which a State is entitled, under Art. 30, to make to the 1989 Salvage Convention. The U.K. decided not to exercise the option to make a reservation in respect of cases where all the nationals are U.K. nationals (Art. 30.1(c)). The other three reservations were exercised when the U.K. deposited its instrument of ratification with the IMO. Only two appear in the final version of the Act: the position of the third, relating to maritime cultural property is explained below.
Inland waters. Article 1(a) applies a very wide definition of the areas within which there can be salvage services under the Convention (see the General Note to Art. 1(a), above). There are certain practical and theoretical arguments against applying salvage to inland waters, *e.g.* because most claims are likely to be so small that it is hardly worth applying the complicated liability and enforcement regime of the maritime law of salvage. In all cases there will be difficulties with dividing lines between the maritime and non-maritime rules, *e.g.* where a person simultaneously puts out fires on board a ship and in a neighbouring warehouse. One claim will give rise to salvage, the other not. In view of the likely differences on the matter the IMO Legal Committee allowed, in its draft Art. 24(1)(a), for a reservation to be made by States. Following the defeat of the proposals to exclude inland navigation totally from Art. 1(a), the U.K. put forward an amendment with two alternative reservations, the second of which was actually agreed by the Committee of the Whole. The version that appeared from the Drafting Committee split the reservation into two parts, Art. 30(1)(a) and (b). It is these reservations that have been enacted in Sched. 11, Pt. II, para. 2.
  Under sub-para. (a) the U.K. has excluded the operation of the Convention from "inland waters", but only where all vessels are "of inland navigation". Neither phrase is defined, although there was one suggestion at the diplomatic conference that reference should be made to the LOS Convention 1982, Art. 8 of which defines "internal waters", but for the purpose of describing territorial waters. "Inland" seems more a geographical or physical definition than a legal one (such as territorial sea). The Administration of Justice Act 1956, s.45(4), which applies in Scotland, defines "inland waters" for the purpose of collision jurisdiction and states that it "includes any part of the sea adjacent to the coast of the U.K. certified by the Secretary of State to be waters falling by international law to be treated as within the territorial sovereignty of Her Majesty apart from the operation of that law in relation to territorial waters". It is submitted that such a definition, provided in a domestic statute for one purpose, will be of little use in interpreting a provision of international origin designed for another purpose. What is clear is that it

will not be possible to make a simple equation between "tidal waters" and inland waters, as the former is a narrow technical usage of English law. After *The Goring* [1988] A.C. 831, s.546 of the Merchant Shipping Act 1894 was amended (by Sched. 5 of the Merchant Shipping Act 1988) to make it clear that there could be salvage in places such as enclosed docks and tidal harbours (*cf. The Powstaniec Wielkopolski* [1989] 1 Lloyd's Rep. 58 where Sheen J. held that a ship could be salved in Gravesend Reach although that might have appeared to be a "harbour" which was excluded from the definition of "tidal waters" in the Merchant Shipping Act 1894, s.742). Paragraph 2(2) re-uses the earlier clarification, but it should be noted that the paragraph does not reintroduce the old tidal waters test. What it does is to state that the exclusion of salvage law from inland waters does not affect services provided in *tidal* waters or in *certain* dock systems. It would seem that dock systems at the end of a canal such as Manchester or Gloucester docks would not fall within sub-para. (2) as they are not connected with tidal waters *directly*. Whether such systems are part of "inland waters" would then be a matter of interpretation of sub-para. (1).

It might have been possible to say that a vessel of inland navigation excludes a "sea-going" vessel. Even here, problems have been caused in practice in knowing which test to apply, *e.g.* in relation to pleasure craft such as the *Marchioness* (in the Thames disaster) and the *Goring* (which was reputed to have gone to Dunkirk in 1940 although not designed for the open sea). Does one ask (i) is the craft legally capable of going to sea, or (ii) is it reasonably physically capable of going to sea, or (iii) does it in practice, or in fact, operate at sea? *The Salt Union* [1893] 1 Q.B. 370, considered the words "sea-going" in s.109 of the Merchant Shipping Act 1854. It is a rather inconclusive authority because of the nature of the facts (despite Lord Coleridge C.J.'s requirement of a simple clear test), but seemed to favour the third approach. Moreover, it seems as if the Mersey was not considered as part of the "sea" although it would now be tidal water to which the Convention applied. The absence of any attempted definition means that the matter was deliberately left for the courts. A "vessel of inland navigation" refers mainly to the physical or legal incapacity of the vessel to go to sea, rather than the purpose for which it is presently being used, because the reference is not to a vessel which happens to be engaged "in inland navigation". The difficulty of defining an inland vessel will arise not with the large sea-going vessel that occasionally ventures inland, but with the reverse situation of the vessel which is mainly used inland but which in theory could also go to sea. It is submitted that a vessel should not be categorised as inland for these purposes if it is fully capable, physically and legally, of going to sea but has not in fact done so. How the vessel was regarded in practice (*i.e.* a combination of (ii) and (iii)) may be relevant, but in this context it is difficult to accept that a vessel legally incapable of going to see could escape the appellation "inland".

Note that both limbs of sub-para. (a) must be satisfied for the Convention to be *excluded*. The Convention would apply if one of the "salving" vessels or the vessels in distress were sea-going, or if the salvage operation partly took place in inland waters and partly not. Thus where a sinking inland pleasure cruiser is towed from inland waters to a place of safety in a tidal harbour it would seem that the Convention would apply to the whole of the services (and not simply to that part of the service which took place in the harbour). The court would be wary of an obvious attempt to convert a non-salvage service into a salvage operation merely by towing the craft in distress into waters where salvage can take place if the purpose of the manoeuvre was not to achieve a useful result under Art. 12. The court could hold that the putative salvage service had ceased at a place of safety in the inland waters and there never was any salvage service in the harbour.

A sea-going tug which provided services to a vessel (whether of inland navigation or not) in the Manchester Ship Canal would now certainly be able to claim salvage, even though the canal was not within the old definition of tidal waters as provided by the Merchant Shipping Act, s.546 as amended. If the same tug was transferred by road to Lake Windermere, there might then be a difficult question as to whether it was a vessel of inland navigation or had become one. Although there may be strong policy grounds for encouraging salvage services in such waters, it is difficult not to draw the conclusion that Parliament must have intended a restrictive approach. During the hearing of *The Goring* [1988] A.C. 831 one of the Law Lords inquired rhetorically whether there could be salvage of a vessel in the man-made indoor arena artificially created at the London Boat Show. The question is not so far fetched as it may seem, as there may be significant fire risks. It is submitted that such an arena must be inland, but the "vessels involved" almost certainly would be capable of going to sea and not even designed for inland navigation. There must be something of an arbitrary line drawn, but it is difficult to believe that a State which excluded inland lakes would include, in some circumstances, inland man-made lakes. It may be that the proper interpretation of "waters" in Art. 1(a) and this paragraph is that it is not intended to include man-made enclosed lakes (although man-made docks could be covered). Nor, it might be added, would it include rowing boats or motor launches used on a boating lake.

Sub-paragraph (b) was designed to deal with examples, raised during debates at the diplomatic conference in 1989 by the U.K. delegation, of absurd situations where there might be salvage if no exclusion or reservation was allowed. One example was of diamond rings being found in lakes: another of cars falling into rivers and being hauled out by other vehicles or a crane operating from land. Such examples would not justify a salvage claim under the Convention.

Maritime cultural property. The original version of the 1994 Bill contained a third sub-paragraph (c) which corresponded to the 1989 Salvage Convention, Art. 30.1(d). This reservation to the Convention arose "when the property involved is maritime cultural property of prehistoric, archaeological or historic interest and is situated on the sea-bed". The U.K. always intended to exercise this reservation when ratifying the Convention and that is why it appeared in the Bill. However, it was pointed out that this might have had unintended consequences in respect of the treatment of the very subject matter to which it related.

Under pre-existing salvage law it is perfectly possible to salvage wrecks at the bottom of the sea. To some extent this is regarded with disfavour by archaeologists as it serves as an encouragement to treasure hunters who may have little or no regard for the time capsule that the wreck may represent. But the administrative provisions of Part IX do provide some procedural framework for the protection of wrecks (in addition to that provided by the Protection of Wrecks Act 1973 and the Protection of Military Remains Act 1986). In particular, s.236 obliges a finder of wreck to report that fact to the receiver of wreck (see further S. Dromgoole, N. Gaskell, "Interests in Wreck", Chapter 13 of N. Palmer, E. McKendrick, *Interests in Goods* (1993) and the General Note to s.239, above). The archaeological interests, especially in the House of Lords, were accordingly very sensitive about how far the maritime law of salvage should apply to wrecks and, if it did not, what would apply in its place. To have included the reservation expressly in the 1994 Bill would have meant that the maritime law of salvage under the Convention would not apply, when taken in conjunction with the repeal of s.546 of the Merchant Shipping Act 1894 by the Merchant Shipping (Salvage and Pollution) Act 1994, Sched. 2, para. 1. This would have created a potential vacuum in which the precise legal framework for the treatment of wrecks was unclear. There might then have been great difficulties about whether some residual law of salvage outside the Convention could apply to such wrecks. At the stage when the matter was first aired in the House of Lords the controversial amendment to include a new sub-para. (iii) in s.20(2)(j) of the Supreme Court Act 1981 had not yet been resolved by the inclusion of the words "in the nature of salvage": see the General Note to s.224(6), above. The effect of that phrase might have ensured in any event that the pre-existing rules on salvage of wrecks were preserved.

The removal of the reference to the reservation was intended by the Government as "technical amendments intended purely to retain the status quo" (Lord Mackay of Ardbrecknish, the Parliamentary Under-Secretary of State, Department of Transport, *Hansard*, H.L. Vol. 555, col. 696), as regards "the right to make a reward for salvage from an historic wreck, and to make clear that it is to be treated on the same statutory basis as all other salvage" (Baroness Trumpington moving the amendment on behalf of the Department of National Heritage at the Committee Stage in the House of Lords, *Hansard*, H.L. Vol. 555, col. 1661). By taking out of the Bill the express reservation, the amendment "restores the full statutory right to salvage rewards in respect of any finds from historic wrecks on the same basis as all other salvage" (*ibid.*, col. 1662). It is submitted that this statement, from the Government proposer of an amendment which was accepted, can be properly referred to when interpreting the Act (and see the comments on *Pepper (Inspector of Taxes) v. Hart* [1993] A.C. 593 in the General Note to s.224(6), above).

The position now is that, as there is no specific reservation in the 1995 Act in respect of wrecks, the general provisions of the 1989 Salvage Convention will apply to such wrecks, *to the extent* that the Convention itself is intended to allow salvage of such property. It might have been thought that the inclusion of a specific reservation as to maritime cultural property (including wrecks) meant that it must follow otherwise that the Convention would apply to them. But there was considerable discussion at the 1989 diplomatic conference and before as to whether it was theoretically advisable, or legally possible, to salve a ship which had sunk (see further Gaskell, "The 1989 Salvage Convention", p. 34 *et seq.*). In essence the argument was whether (i) a sunken vessel was a "vessel" or "property" within Art. 1, and (ii) such a sunken vessel could still be in danger within Art. 1(a) once it had sunk. The writer has submitted in the General Note to Art. 1(a), above, that the effect of the discussions was clearly that a sunken vessel and its cargo were subject of salvage within Art. 1 (*ibid.*) and it would be a question of fact for a national court to decide whether property was in danger. In the U.K. it seems that the courts would continue to find that such property was in danger so as to apply salvage rules. It should perhaps be noted that in a recent case in the High Court of Ireland, *King and Chapman v. The Owners of all Persons claiming an Interest in the Sailing Vessels "La Lavia", "Juliana" and "Santa Maria de la Vision"* (unreported, July 26, 1994) the court held that the wrecks of three Spanish Armada vessels lost in 1588 "should be regarded as having passed from the commercial realm of maritime salvage law into the domain of archaeological law". One conclusion of this was that it may then be appropriate to apply the law of finds, following US law. Such an approach may be even worse from an archaeological point of view and the law of finding has been criticised elsewhere (see S. Dromgoole, N. Gaskell, "Interests in Wreck", in N. Palmer, E. McKendrick, *Interests in Goods* (1993), p. 393 *et seq.*). The International Law Association produced in 1994 a draft Convention on the Protection of the Underwater Cultural Heritage. In 1995 this draft was placed on the work programme of UNESCO, with a view to a Convention being concluded in 1999, or 2001. The Convention has a number of good, and some controversial, features. The latter mainly concern the creation of cultural heritage zones, which would cut across those agreed in the LOS Convention 1982. The draft Convention also deems underwater cultural heritage to have been abandoned in two circumstances: (i) 10 years after the discovery of technology which would allow recovery, provided that at least 50 years have elapsed since the sinking, or (ii) 50 years have elapsed since the last recorded assertion of interest by the owner. These are rather arbitrary tests, although any test is likely to draw some arbitrary line. The draft Convention also declares that underwater cultural heritage shall not be subject to the law of salvage. This latter provision is anathema to the commercial treasure seekers.

    The Government has exercised the right to reserve its position internationally by making the reservation allowed by the Convention, although this has not been reproduced in the Act. This will enable it to bring forward at a later date comprehensive legislation, perhaps dealing with both marine and non-marine artefacts, without being in breach of its international obligations.

Assistance to persons in danger at sea

3.—(1) The master of a vessel who fails to comply with the duty imposed on him by article 10, paragraph 1 commits an offence and shall be liable—
    (a) on summary conviction, to imprisonment for a term not exceeding six months or a fine not exceeding the statutory maximum or both;
    (b) on conviction on indictment, to imprisonment for a term not exceeding two years or a fine, or both.

    (2) Compliance by the master of a vessel with that duty shall not affect his right or the right of any other person to a payment under the Convention or under any contract.

General Note

    Article 10, above, set out the obligation of masters to provide assistance to those in danger of being lost at sea. Article 10.2 puts the obligation on State parties to create the appropriate duty and para. 3 gives effect to that obligation, while re-enacting provisions originally found in the Maritime Conventions Act 1911, s.6. Failure to comply with the duty is an offence only by the master (as widely defined in s.313(1) of the Merchant Shipping Act 1995). This contrasts with most maritime regulatory offences, where the master *and* shipowner are usually liable (*e.g.* for a breach of the collision regulations by the master). The penalties vary according to whether there is a summary conviction or a conviction on indictment. For the "statutory maximum" fine on summary conviction see the Criminal Justice Act 1982, s.46. A number of other statutory offences may be committed by failure to respond to a casualty. Section 422 of the Merchant Shipping Act (now s.92 of the 1995 Act) always required assistance to be given after a collision and, to avoid a repeat of the *Titanic* disaster, masters must respond to distress signals by proceeding to the ship in danger (see s.93).

    Sub-paragraph (2) re-enacts s.6(2) of the Maritime Conventions Act 1911, which made it clear that any public duty to save life would not affect any claims for salvage. Otherwise, it might have been said that the salvor was not a "volunteer" in English law (see the General Note to Art. 5, above). The reference to "payment under the Convention" now clearly covers claims under both Arts. 13 and 14 of the 1989 Salvage Convention.

The reward and special compensation: the common understanding

4. In fixing a reward under article 13 and assessing special compensation under article 14 the court or arbitrator (or, in Scotland, arbiter) is under no duty to fix a reward under article 13 up to the maximum salved value of the vessel and other property before assessing the special compensation to be paid under article 14.

General Note

    This paragraph contains the so-called "Common Understanding", which was Attachment 1 to the Final Act of the 1989 Diplomatic Conference, but with the specific reference to arbiters in Scotland. The effect of the Understanding is to remove the argument that a tribunal *must* exhaust the salved fund under Art. 13 before considering special compensation under Art. 14. The Understanding merely preserves the total discretion of the tribunal. The potential problem will only arise in a case where there is a very low salved fund in relation to the expenses of the salvor in preventing damage to the environment. See further, the General Note to Art. 14.4, above.

Recourse for life salvage payment

5.—(1) This paragraph applies where—
(a) services are rendered wholly or in part in United Kingdom waters in saving life from a
    vessel of any nationality or elsewhere in saving life from any United Kingdom ship; and
(b) either—
    (i) the vessel and other property are destroyed, or
    (ii) the sum to which the salvor is entitled under article 16, paragraph 2 is less than a
    reasonable amount for the services rendered in saving life.
(2) Where this paragraph applies, the Secretary of State may, if he thinks fit, pay to the salvor
such sum or, as the case may be, such additional sum as he thinks fit in respect of the services
rendered in saving life.

GENERAL NOTE
    This paragraph is a back-stop provision to allow the Secretary of State to make a reward to life
savers who have not been able to obtain a reward in any other manner and repeats the provisions
in s.544(3) of the Merchant Shipping Act 1894 (which was repealed by the Merchant Shipping
(Salvage and Pollution) Act 1994, Sched. 2, para. 1(2)). The power has been used very sparingly
and the most recent instances recorded were in 1939 and 1951 and for very modest sums (see
Lord Mackay of Ardbrecknish (the Parliamentary Under-Secretary of State, Department of
Transport), *Hansard*, H.L. Vol. 555, col. 695). The 1951 payment was apparently for £250. The
provision was retained at the suggestion of practitioners and others as a useful final recourse for
those who have not been able to obtain life salvage under Art. 16.2, above.
    The life salvage services must have a U.K. connection, *e.g.* where the services are rendered in
U.K. waters or to a U.K. ship anywhere. For these purposes a U.K. ship is one registered in the
U.K. (see Pt. II of the Merchant Shipping Act 1995). The life salvor may be unrewarded either
because there is no salved fund to pay for the services (*e.g.* where the crew is taken off, but the
ship sinks) or where there is such a low salved value that the life salvor has obtained less than a
"reasonable amount" for its services. The provision, unsurprisingly, does not define "reasonable", nor does it make reference to the life salvor's "expenses" (as in Art. 14). Note that the
effect of Arts. 16.2 and 14 is that a life salvor may now be entitled to "a fair share of the payment
awarded to the salvor for … preventing or minimising damage to the environment". The difficulties of that provision are referred to in the General Note to Art. 16, above, but the "fair share"
might be less than the life salvor's actual expenses. It would not be stretching the language to
assume that a "reasonable amount" could cover the difference between the actual expenses and
the amount recovered under Arts. 13 and 14, provided that those expenses had not themselves
been incurred unreasonably. Although s.544(3) of the Merchant Shipping Act 1894 may not
have been much used, the principles of judicial review have developed considerably since then,
and it would be open to shipowners and operators to claim quite large expenses from the DOT.
It is for this reason that sub-para. (2) is deliberately worded to give the widest possible discretion
to the Secretary of State to pay such sum as he "thinks fit". It was never intended that the provision should be an open-ended invitation for mariners to make claims, but was to be reserved
for the sort of case where a non-professional impecunious life salvor has incurred great expenses
which it cannot afford and where some payment might alleviate hardship and encourage others.

Meaning of "judicial proceedings"

6. References in the Convention to judicial proceedings are references to proceedings—
(a) in England and Wales, in the High Court or the county court;
(b) in Scotland, in the Court of Session or in the sheriff court;
(c) in Northern Ireland, in the High Court;
and any reference to the tribunal having jurisdiction (so far as it refers to judicial proceedings)
shall be construed accordingly.

GENERAL NOTE
    The Convention is designed to be applied in court and in arbitration hearings, but the refer-
ence to "judicial proceedings" (*e.g.* in Arts. 2, 23) or "tribunal having jurisdiction" (*e.g.* in Art.
22) means the appropriate U.K. court.

Meaning of "State Party"

7.—(1) An Order in Council made for the purposes of this paragraph and declaring that any
State specified in the Order is a party to the Convention in respect of a specified country shall,
subject to the provisions of any subsequent Order made for those purposes, be conclusive evidence that the State is a party to the Convention in respect of that country.
    (2) In this paragraph "country" includes "territory".

The Convention makes a number of references to a State Party and para. 7 is a standard provision which provides that State Parties will be identified by Order in Council. See also the General Note to s.224(6), above.

Section 314　　　　　　　SCHEDULE 12

REPEALS

Chapter or number	Short title	Extent of repeal
17 & 18 Vict. c.120.	Merchant Shipping Repeal Act 1854.	Section 7.
34 & 35 Vict. c.xxi.	Lloyd's Act 1871.	Section 33.
57 & 58 Vict. c.60.	Merchant Shipping Act 1894.	Section 66.
		Section 76.
		Section 82.
		Section 84.
		Sections 287 and 288.
		Section 422.
		Section 449.
		Section 458.
		Sections 510 to 513.
		Sections 515 and 516.
		Sections 518 to 525.
		Section 527.
		Sections 530 to 537.
		Sections 551 to 553.
		Sections 555 to 557.
		Sections 566 to 568.
		Section 569(2).
		Section 570.
		Section 571.
		Sections 634 to 636.
		Sections 638 and 639.
		Sections 642 to 643A.
		Sections 647 to 656.
		Section 657 so far as relating to Northern Ireland.
		Sections 658 to 660.
		Sections 662 to 662B.
		Section 664.
		Sections 666 to 669.
		Sections 676 and 677.
		Sections 679 to 681.
		Sections 683 to 687B.
		Section 688 so far as relating to Scotland.
		Section 689.
		Sections 691 to 693.
		Sections 695 to 697.
		Sections 702 and 703.
		Sections 710 to 715.
		Sections 717 and 718.
		Sections 720 to 724.
		Sections 726 to 728.
		Sections 731 and 732.
		Sections 735 and 736.
		Section 738(1) and (2).
		Section 739.
		Sections 741 to 743.
		Sections 745 to 747.
		Schedule 17.
		Schedule 19.

Chapter or number	Short title	Extent of repeal
60 & 61 Vict. c.21.	Mersey Channels Act 1897.	The whole Act.
60 & 61 Vict. c.59.	Merchant Shipping Act 1897.	The whole Act.
61 & 62 Vict. c.44.	Merchant Shipping (Mercantile Marine Fund) Act 1898.	Sections 1 and 1A. Section 2(3) so far as relating to the Sombrero lighthouse in the Leeward Islands. Sections 2A and 2B. Section 5(1)(2). Section 9. In Schedule 3, the entry for the Sombrero lighthouse in the Leeward Islands.
63 & 64 Vict. c.32.	Merchant Shipping (Liability of Shipowners and Others) Act 1900.	Sections 2 to 5.
6 Edw. 7 c.48.	Merchant Shipping Act 1906.	Section 72. Sections 75 and 76. Sections 78 to 80. Sections 84 and 86.
1 & 2 Geo. 5 c.57.	Maritime Conventions Act 1911.	Sections 1 to 3 and 4(2). Sections 5 to 10.
9 & 10 Geo. 5 c.62.	British Mercantile Marine Uniform Act 1919.	The whole Act.
9 & 10 Geo. 5 c.92.	Aliens Restriction (Amendment) Act 1919.	Section 5.
10 & 11 Geo. 5 c.2.	Merchant Shipping (Amendment) Act 1920.	The whole Act.
10 & 11 Geo. 5 c.39.	Merchant Shipping (Scottish Fishing Boats) Act 1920.	The whole Act.
11 & 12 Geo. 5 c.28.	Merchant Shipping Act 1921.	Sections 2 to 4.
22 & 23 Geo. 5 c.4.	Statute of Westminster 1931.	Section 5.
22 & 23 Geo. 5 c.9.	Merchant Shipping (Safety and Load Line Conventions) Act 1932.	Section 5(2) and (3). Section 8. Section 24. Section 62(1) and (3). Section 69. Sections 73 and 74. Schedule 1.
2 & 3 Geo. 6 c.83.	Pensions (Navy, Army, Air Force and Mercantile Marine) Act 1939.	Section 6(3).
11 & 12 Geo. 6 c.7.	Ceylon Independence Act 1947.	In Schedule 1, paragraph 3.
11 & 12 Geo. 6 c.44.	Crown Proceedings Act 1947.	Sections 5 to 8. Section 30.
11 & 12 Geo. 6 c.44.	Merchant Shipping Act 1948.	Section 5.
12, 13 & 14 Geo. 6 c.29.	Consular Conventions Act 1949.	Section 5(2).
12, 13 & 14 Geo. 6 c.43.	Merchant Shipping (Safety Conventions) Act 1949.	Section 22. Section 25. Section 32. Section 34. Section 35(1). Sections 36 (so far as unrepealed) and 37. In Schedule 1, paragraph 1.

Chapter or number	Short title	Extent of repeal
14 Geo. 6 c.9.	Merchant Shipping Act 1950.	Sections 7 and 8.
14 Geo. 6 c.27.	Arbitration Act 1950.	In section 29, subsection (1) and in subsection (2) the words preceding "an arbitration".
4 & 5 Eliz. 2 c.46.	Administration of Justice Act 1956.	In section 47(2)(n) the words from "(including" to "way of wages)". Section 49(1). In Part I of Schedule 1, in paragraph 1(1)(j), from the beginning to "cases" and, in paragraph 1(3), the words "sections five hundred and forty-four to five hundred and forty-six of the Merchant Shipping Act, 1894, or".
5 & 6 Eliz. 2 c.6.	Ghana Independence Act 1957.	In Schedule 1, paragraph 4. In Schedule 2, paragraphs 7 and 8.
5 & 6 Eliz. 2 c.60.	Federation of Malaya Independence Act 1957.	In Schedule 1, paragraphs 9 and 10.
8 & 9 Eliz. 2 c.52.	Cyprus Act 1960.	In the Schedule, paragraph 10.
8 & 9 Eliz. 2 c.55.	Nigeria Independence Act 1960.	In Schedule 1, paragraph 4. In Schedule 2, paragraphs 7 and 8.
9 & 10 Eliz. 2 c.1.	Tanganyika Independence Act 1961.	In Schedule 1, paragraph 4. In Schedule 2, paragraphs 7 and 8.
9 & 10 Eliz. 2 c.16.	Sierra Leone Independence Act 1961.	In Schedule 2, paragraph 4. In Schedule 3, paragraphs 8 and 9.
10 & 11 Eliz. 2 c.23.	South Africa Act 1962.	In Schedule 3, paragraph 6.
10 & 11 Eliz. 2 c.30.	Northern Ireland Act 1962.	Section 25(1)(a).
10 & 11 Eliz. 2 c.40.	Jamaica Independence Act 1962.	In Schedule 1, paragraph 4. In Schedule 2, paragraphs 7 and 8.
10 & 11 Eliz. 2 c.54.	Trinidad and Tobago Independence Act 1962.	In Schedule 1, paragraph 4. In Schedule 3, paragraphs 7 and 8.
10 & 11 Eliz. 2 c.57.	Uganda Independence Act 1962.	In Schedule 1, paragraph 4. In Schedule 2, paragraphs 7 and 8.
1963 c.54.	Kenya Independence Act 1963.	In Schedule 1, paragraph 4. In Schedule 2, paragraphs 7 and 8.
1963 c.55.	Zanzibar Act 1963.	In Schedule 1, paragraph 8.
1964 c.26.	Licensing Act 1964.	Section 158.
1964 c.40.	Harbours Act 1964.	Section 29(2) and (3). Section 30(2). In section 30(3) the words from "and no charge" to the end. Section 35.
1964 c.46.	Malawi Independence Act 1964.	In Schedule 1, paragraph 4(a). In Schedule 2, paragraphs 7 and 8.
1964 c.47.	Merchant Shipping Act 1964.	Section 9 so far as unrepealed. Section 11. Section 16. Sections 19 and 20.
1964 c.86.	Malta Independence Act 1964.	In Schedule 1, paragraph 4(a). In Schedule 2, paragraphs 7 and 8.
1964 c.93.	Gambia Independence Act 1964 c.93.	In Schedule 1, paragraph 4(a). In Schedule 2, paragraphs 7 and 8.

Chapter or number	Short title	Extent of repeal
1965 c.32.	Administration of Estates (Small Payments) Act 1965.	Section 6(1)(c).
1965 c.47.	Merchant Shipping Act 1965.	The whole Act so far as unrepealed.
1966 c.14.	Guyana Independence Act 1966.	In Schedule 1, paragraph 4(a). In Schedule 2, paragraphs 7 and 8.
1966 c.29.	Singapore Act 1966.	In the Schedule, paragraphs 10 and 11.
1966 c.37.	Barbados Independence Act 1966.	In Schedule 1, paragraph 4(a). In Schedule 2, paragraphs 7 and 8.
1967 c.27.	Merchant Shipping (Load Lines) Act 1967.	Sections 1 to 25. Section 27(1), (3) and (5). Sections 30 to 34. Schedules 1 and 2.
1968 c.8.	Mauritius Independence Act 1968.	In Schedule 1, paragraph 4(a). In Schedule 2, paragraphs 7 and 8.
1969 c.48.	Post Office Act 1969.	In section 3, in subsection (1) the words from "and the first reference" to "to navigation)" and, in subsection (6) the words from "and section 36" to the end.
1970 c.27.	Fishing Vessels (Safety Provisions) Act 1970.	Section 1. Section 2(1). Sections 3 to 5. Section 7. Sections 9 to 11.
1970 c.36.	Merchant Shipping Act 1970.	Sections 1 to 5. Sections 7 to 18. Section 20. Section 22. Sections 25 to 28. Section 30. Sections 32 and 33. Sections 39 to 41. Sections 43 to 54. Sections 56 to 64. Sections 67 to 72. Sections 74 to 83. Section 85. Section 86. Section 88. Section 91. Sections 95 to 101. Schedules 1 to 5.
1970 c.50.	Fiji Independence Act 1970.	In Schedule 1, paragraph 4(a). In Schedule 2, paragraph 6.
1971 c.59.	Merchant Shipping (Oil Pollution) Act 1971.	The whole Act.
1971 c.60.	Prevention of Oil Pollution Act 1971.	Section 2(2A) and (2B). Section 5. Section 6(1)(a). Section 7. Section 8(2). Section 10. In section 11, in subsection (1), paragraphs (a) and (b) and the words "the owner or master of the vessel, or" and ", as the case may be," and subsection (2). Sections 12 to 17. Section 18(4). Section 19(2)(b) and (c).

Chapter or number	Short title	Extent of repeal
		Section 19A.
		Section 20.
		Section 21.
		Section 23 so far as it relates to vessels.
		Section 24.
		Section 25(2) and (3).
		Section 27(4).
		In section 29(1) the definitions of—
		"barge"; and
		"outside the territorial waters of the United Kingdom";
		and subsections (2), (4), (5) and (6).
		Section 30(1) and (2).
1972 c.5 (N.I.).	Water Act (Northern Ireland) 1972.	Section 32(3).
1972 c.11.	Superannuation Act 1972.	Section 17.
1973 c.27.	Bahamas Independence Act 1973.	In Schedule 1, paragraph 4(a). In Schedule 2, paragraph 5.
1973 c.49.	Bangladesh Act 1973.	In the Schedule, paragraph 6.
1974 c.43.	Merchant Shipping Act 1974.	Sections 1 to 8A. Sections 16 to 18. Section 19(1) and (3) to (6). Section 21. Sections 23 and 24. Schedules 1 and 5.
1976 c.19.	Seychelles Act 1976.	In the Schedule, paragraph 6.
1978 c.15.	Solomon Islands Act 1978.	In the Schedule, paragraph 4.
1978 c.20.	Tuvalu Act 1978.	In Schedule 1, paragraph 4(a). In Schedule 2, paragraph 4.
1979 c.27.	Kiribati Act 1979.	In the Schedule, paragraph 5.
1979 c.39.	Merchant Shipping Act 1979.	Sections 14 to 39. Sections 41 to 43. Section 45. Sections 48 to 52. Schedules 3 to 7.
1980 c.2.	Papua New Guinea, Western Samoa and Nauru (Miscellaneous Provisions) Act 1980.	In the Schedule, paragraphs 4 and 5.
1980 c.16.	New Hebrides Act 1980.	In Schedule 1, paragraph 5.
1981 c.10.	Merchant Shipping Act 1981.	The whole Act.
1981 c.52.	Belize Act 1981.	In Schedule 1, paragraph 4(a). In Schedule 2, paragraph 4.
1981 c.54.	Supreme Court Act 1981.	In section 153(4)(d), the words from "section 13(1)" to "1974". In Schedule 5, the entries relating to the Merchant Shipping (Oil Pollution) Act 1971 and the Merchant Shipping Act 1974.
S.I. 1981/226 (NI 6).	Judgments Enforcement (Northern Ireland) Order 1981.	In Schedule 2, paragraph 17.
S.I. 1981/1675 (NI 26).	Magistrates' Courts (Northern Ireland) Order 1981.	In Part I of Schedule 6, paragraphs 18 and 19.
1982 c.16.	Civil Aviation Act 1982.	Section 97(1).
1982 c.27.	Civil Jurisdiction and Judgments Act 1982.	In section 32(4)(a) the words "section 13(3) of the Merchant Shipping (Oil Pollution) Act 1971".

Chapter or number	Short title	Extent of repeal
1982 c.48.	Criminal Justice Act 1982.	Section 49. Section 81(13). In Schedule 7, paragraph 1. In Schedule 14, paragraph 2. In Schedule 15, paragraphs 3 to 5.
1984 c.5.	Merchant Shipping Act 1984.	Sections 1 to 12. Section 14. Schedule 1. Schedule 2.
1984 c.28.	County Courts Act 1984.	Section 27(11).
1985 c.3.	Brunei and Maldives Act 1985.	In the Schedule, paragraph 1.
1985 c.22.	Dangerous Vessels Act 1985.	Section 4.
1986 c.2.	Australia Act 1986.	Section 4.
1986 c.6.	Prevention of Oil Pollution Act 1986.	The whole Act.
1986 c.23.	Safety at Sea Act 1986.	Sections 7 to 13. Section 15.
1986 c.64.	Public Order Act 1986.	In section 10(1), the words "and in section 515 of the Merchant Shipping Act 1894".
S.I. 1986/1035 (NI 9).	Companies Consolidation (Consequential Provisions) (Northern Ireland) Order 1986.	In Part II of Schedule 1, the entries relating to the Prevention of Oil Pollution Act 1971 and the Merchant Shipping Act 1974.
1988 c.12.	Merchant Shipping Act 1988.	Section 11. Sections 26 to 35. Sections 41 to 49. Section 52. Sections 53 and 55 except for purposes of section 37. Section 57(1) and (3) to (5). In Schedule 1, paragraph 48. Schedule 4. Schedules 5 to 8.
S.I. 1989/1339 (NI 11).	Limitation (Northern Ireland) Order 1989.	In Schedule 3, paragraph 11.
1990 c.31.	Aviation and Maritime Security Act 1990.	In section 51(2), the words "section 94 of the Merchant Shipping Act 1970". In Schedule 3, paragraph 2.
1990 c.41.	Courts and Legal Services Act 1990.	In Schedule 10, paragraph 55.
1990 c.43.	Environmental Protection Act 1990.	Section 148. Schedule 14 except so far as the amendments relate to offences under section 2(1) of the Prevention of Oil Pollution Act 1971.
1991 c.52.	Ports Act 1991.	Sections 31 to 34. Section "36(2)(c)". In section 41, in subsection (1) the words "31 to" and "36(2)(c)" and subsection (2). Section 42(2).
S.I. 1991/1219 (NI 10).	Dangerous Vessels (Northern Ireland) Order 1991.	Article 6.
1993 c.8.	Judicial Pensions and Retirement Act 1993.	In Schedule 6, paragraph 59.
1993 c.22.	Merchant Shipping (Registration, etc.) Act 1993.	The whole Act.
1994 c.28.	Merchant Shipping (Salvage and Pollution) Act 1994.	The whole Act.

Chapter or number	Short title	Extent of repeal
1994 c.39.	The Local Government etc. (Scotland) Act 1994.	In Schedule 13, paragraph 7.

Notes. The repeals of sections 5 to 7, 29(2) and 30(1) of the Prevention of Oil Pollution Act 1971 do not apply so far as those provisions relate to sections 2(1) and (3) of that Act.

The repeals in the Crown Proceedings Act 1947 apply in relation to Her Majesty's Government in Northern Ireland as they apply in relation to Her Majesty's Government in the United Kingdom.

Section 314   SCHEDULE 13

CONSEQUENTIAL AMENDMENTS

General Pier and Harbour Act 1861 Amendment Act 1862 (c. 19)

1. In section 21 of the General Pier and Harbour Act 1861 Amendment Act 1862, for "Merchant Shipping Act 1854" substitute "Merchant Shipping Act 1995".

Sea Fisheries Act 1868 (c. 45)

2. For section 26 of the Sea Fisheries Act 1868 substitute—

"Registered fishing boats and foreign fishing boats within British waters to have official papers
26.—(1) The master of every sea-fishing boat which is registered under Part II of the Merchant Shipping Act 1995 shall (whether his boat is within British waters or not) have on board the certificate of registration issued in pursuance of registration regulations.

(2) The master of every sea-fishing boat within British waters shall have on board official papers evidencing its nationality.

(3) If any person, without reasonable excuse (the proof of which lies on him), contravenes subsection (1) or (2) of this section, he shall be liable on summary conviction to a fine not exceeding level 2 on the standard scale; and where a fine is imposed under this subsection on the master of a foreign sea-fishing boat the court may order the boat to be detained for a period not exceeding three months from the date of the conviction or until the fine is paid (whichever period is the shorter).

(4) Section 8(4) of the Sea Fisheries Act 1968 (power of British sea-fishery officer to take fishing boat to nearest port and detain it there) shall apply in relation to a contravention of subsection (1) or (2) of this section as it applies in relation to such a contravention as is mentioned in that provision.

(5) In this section—
    "British waters" means waters within the seaward limits of the territorial sea adjacent to the United Kingdom, the Channel Islands and the Isle of Man;
    "foreign sea-fishing boat" means a sea-fishing boat which—
        (a) is not registered in the United Kingdom, the Channel Islands or the Isle of Man, and
        (b) is not wholly owned by persons qualified to own British ships for the purposes of Part II of the Merchant Shipping Act 1995; and
    "master" includes, in relation to any sea-fishing boat, a person for the time being in command or charge of the boat."

Lloyd's Act 1871 (c. xxi)

3. In section 41 of the Lloyd's Act 1871, for "Merchant Shipping Act 1854", in both places where it occurs, substitute "Merchant Shipping Act 1995".

Slave Trade Act 1873 (c. 88)

4. In section 26 of the Slave Trade Act 1873, for "section two hundred and sixty-eight of the Merchant Shipping Act 1854" substitute "section 283 of the Merchant Shipping Act 1995".

Explosives Act 1875 (c. 17)

5. In the Explosives Act 1875—
(a) in section 58(b), for "Merchant Shipping Act 1854, or the Acts amending the same" substitute "Merchant Shipping Act 1995";

(b) in section 98(2), for "Merchant Shipping Act 1854" substitute "Merchant Shipping Act 1995"; and

(c) in section 101, for "Merchant Shipping Act 1854 and the Acts amending the same, or any order or regulation made under any of those Acts" substitute "Merchant Shipping Act 1995 or any order or regulation made under that Act".

Explosive Substances Act 1883 (c. 3)

6. In section 8(2) of the Explosive Substances Act 1883, for "Merchant Shipping Act 1873" substitute "safety regulations under section 85 of the Merchant Shipping Act 1995".

Submarine Telegraph Act 1885 (c. 49)

7. In the Submarine Telegraph Act 1885—

(a) in section 5(1), for the words from the beginning to "collisions" substitute "Safety regulations under section 85 of the Merchant Shipping Act 1995"; and

(b) in section 7, for "Part X of the Merchant Shipping Act 1854 (which relates to legal procedure), and the enactments amending the same, so far as unrepealed," substitute "Part XII of the Merchant Shipping Act 1995 (legal proceedings)".

Foreign Jurisdiction Act 1890 (c. 37)

8. In Schedule 1 to the Foreign Jurisdiction Act 1890, at the end insert—

"1995 c.00.   Merchant Shipping Act   Chapter II of Part VI."
               1995.

Fisheries Act 1891 (c. 37)

9. In section 2(1) of the Fisheries Act 1891, for "in pursuance of section fourteen of the Merchant Shipping Act 1854" substitute "under section 256 of the Merchant Shipping Act 1995", and for "sections fifteen and sixteen of that Act" substitute "Part X of that Act".

Commissioners for Oaths Act 1891 (c. 50)

10. In section 1 of the Commissioners for Oaths Act 1891, for "Merchant Shipping Acts 1854 to 1889" substitute "Merchant Shipping Act 1995".

Seal Fisheries (North Pacific) Act 1895 (c.21)

11. In the Seal Fisheries (North Pacific) Act 1895—

(a) in section 1(3) for the words from "a misdemeanor" to "1894" substitute "an offence and shall be liable—

   (a) on summary conviction, to a fine not exceeding the statutory maximum or to imprisonment for a term not exceeding six months or to both; or

   (b) on conviction on indictment, to a fine or to imprisonment for a period not exceeding two years or to both,";

(b) in section 2(3), for "Merchant Shipping Act 1894" substitute "Merchant Shipping Act 1995"; and

(c) in section 3—

   (i) in subsection (1) for "Merchant ShippingAct 1894" substitute "Merchant Shipping Act 1995"; and

   (ii) in subsection (2), for "section seventy-six of the Merchant Shipping Act 1894" substitute "section seven of the Merchant Shipping Act 1995".

Seal Fisheries (North Pacific) Act 1912 (c. 10)

12. In section 3 of the Seal Fisheries (North Pacific) Act 1912—

(a) in subsection (1), for the words from "liable" to "1894" substitute "liable—

   (a) on summary conviction, to a fine not exceeding the statutory maximum or to imprisonment for a term not exceeding six months or to both; or

   (b) on conviction on indictment, to a fine or to imprisonment for a term not exceeding two years or to both"; and

(b) in subsection (2), for "Merchant Shipping Acts 1894 to 1907" substitute "Merchant Shipping Act 1995".

Trustee Act 1925 (c. 19)

13. In section 51(6) of the Trustee Act 1925, for "Acts relating to merchant shipping" substitute "Merchant Shipping Act 1995".

Whaling Industry (Regulations) Act 1934 (c. 49)

14. In section 17(1) of the Whaling Industry (Regulations) Act 1934, in the definition of "ship", for "Merchant Shipping Act 1894" substitute "Merchant Shipping Act 1995".

Public Health Act 1936 (c. 49)

15. In section 343(1) of the Public Health Act 1936, in the definition of "vessel", for "in the Merchant Shipping Act 1894" substitute " "ship" in the Merchant Shipping Act 1995".

Public Health (Drainage of Trade Premises) Act 1937 (c. 40)

16. In section 14 of the Public Health (Drainage of Trade Premises) Act 1937, for "section seven hundred and forty-two of the Merchant Shipping Act 1894" substitute "the Merchant Shipping Act 1995".

Superannuation (Various Services) Act 1938 (c. 13)

17. In Part I of the Schedule to the Superannuation (Various Services) Act 1938, for "Merchant Shipping (Mercantile Marine Fund) Act 1898, section 1A, as inserted by section 17 of the Superannuation Act 1972" substitute "Merchant Shipping Act 1995, section 214".

Compensation (Defence) Act 1939 (c. 75)

18. In section 17(1) of the Compensation (Defence) Act 1939, in the definitions of "ship" and "vessel", for "have respectively the same meaning as in the Merchant Shipping Act 1894" substitute "have the same meaning as "ship" in the Merchant Shipping Act 1995".

Pensions (Navy, Army, Air Force and Mercantile Marine) Act 1939 (c. 83)

19. In the Pensions (Navy, Army, Air Force and Mercantile Marine) Act 1939—
(a) in section 4(4), in the definition of "lightship", for "Merchant Shipping Act 1894" substitute "Merchant Shipping Act 1995"; and
(b) in section 10, in the definition of "ship", for "Merchant Shipping Act 1894" substitute "Merchant Shipping Act 1995".

Public Health (Scotland) Act 1945 (c. 15)

20. In section 1(8) of the Public Health (Scotland) Act 1945, in the definition of "vessel", for "in the Merchant Shipping Act 1894" substitute " "ship" in the Merchant Shipping Act 1995".

Crown Proceedings Act 1947 (c. 44)

21. In section 38(2) of the Crown Proceedings Act 1947—
(a) in the definition of "His Majesty's ships", for "Merchant Shipping Acts 1894 to 1940" substitute "Merchant Shipping Act 1995"; and
(b) in the definition of "ship", for "meaning assigned to it by section seven hundred and forty-two of the Merchant Shipping Act 1894" substitute "the same meaning as in the Merchant Shipping Act 1995".

British Nationality Act 1948 (c. 56)

22. In section 3(1) of the British Nationality Act 1948, for "Merchant Shipping Acts 1894 to 1948" substitute "Merchant Shipping Act 1995".

Law Reform (Miscellaneous Provisions) Act (Northern Ireland) 1948 (c. 23 (N.I.))

23. In section 4(2) of the Law Reform (Miscellaneous Provisions) Act (Northern Ireland) 1948, for "section one of the Maritime Conventions Act, 1911," substitute "section 187 of the Merchant Shipping Act 1995".

Wireless Telegraphy Act 1949 (c. 54)

24. In section 19(7) of the Wireless Telegraphy Act 1949, for "meanings respectively assigned to them by section seven hundred and forty-two of the Merchant Shipping Act 1894" substitute "same meaning as "ship" in the Merchant Shipping Act 1995".

Coast Protection Act 1949 (c. 74)

25. In section 49(1) of the Coast Protection Act 1949, in the definitions of "conservancy authority" and "harbour authority", for "Merchant Shipping Act 1894" substitute "Merchant Shipping Act 1995".

Registered Designs Act 1949 (c. 88)

26. In section 8(6), at the end insert "and, in the case of the right of the Secretary of State in any design forming part of the British mercantile marine uniform registered under this Act, to that right's subsisting so long as the design remains on the register."

Rivers (Prevention of Pollution) (Scotland) Act 1951 (c. 66)

27. In section 29(4) of the Rivers (Prevention of Pollution) (Scotland) Act 1951 for "Merchant Shipping Act 1894" substitute "Merchant Shipping Act 1995".

Post Office Act 1953 (c. 36)

28. In section 29(1) of the Post Office Act 1953—
(a) for the words from "or which" to "1894" substitute "or within the limited European trading area"; and
(b) at the end insert—
"In this subsection 'the limited European trading area' means the same as in regulations under section 47 of the Merchant Shipping Act 1995".

Administration of Justice Act 1956 (c. 46)

29.—(1) The Administration of the Justice Act 1956 shall be amended as follows.
(2) In section 47—
(a) in subsection (2)(n), the words from "(including" to "way of wages)" shall cease to have effect; and
(b) in subsection (8)(a) for "section 1 of the Merchant Shipping Salvage and Pollution Act 1994" substitute "section 224 of the Merchant Shipping Act 1995".
(3) In section 48(f)—
(a) in the definition of "collision regulations", for the words from "regulations" to the end substitute "safety regulations under section 85 of the Merchant Shipping Act 1995"; and
(b) in the definition of "master", for "Merchant Shipping Act 1894" substitute "Merchant Shipping Act 1995".
(4) In Part I of Schedule 1—
(a) in paragraph 1—
    (i) in sub-paragraph (1)(o), for "Merchant Shipping Acts 1894 to 1954" substitute "Merchant Shipping Act 1995"; and
    (ii) in sub-paragraph (4), for "Merchant Shipping Acts 1894 to 1954" substitute "Merchant Shipping Act 1995".
(b) in paragraph 7(1), for "five hundred and fifty-two of the Merchant Shipping Act 1894" substitute "226 of the Merchant Shipping Act 1995"; and
(c) in paragraph 8(1)—
    (i) in the definition of "collision regulations", for the words from "section 21" to the end substitute "section 85 of the Merchant Shipping Act 1995"; and
    (ii) in the definition of "master", for "Merchant Shipping Act 1894" substitute "Merchant Shipping Act 1995".

Trustee Act (Northern Ireland) 1958 (c. 23 (N.I.))

30. In section 51(7) of the Trustee Act (Northern Ireland) 1958, for "Acts relating to merchant shipping" substitute "Merchant Shipping Act 1995".

Factories Act 1961 (c. 34)

31. In section 176(1) of the Factories Act 1961, for the definitions of "ship", "vessel" and "harbour" substitute " "ship" and "vessel" have the same meaning as "ship" in the Merchant Shipping Act 1995, and "harbour" has the same meaning as in the Merchant Shipping Act 1995;".

Pipe-Lines Act 1962 (c. 58)

32. In section 39(4) of the Pipe-Lines Act 1962, for "section 8 of the Prevention of Oil Pollution Act 1971" substitute "section 151 of the Merchant Shipping Act 1995".

Harbours Act 1964 (c. 40)

33. In section 57(1) of the Harbours Act 1964—
(a) in the definition of "harbour", for "meaning assigned to it by section 742 of the Merchant Shipping Act 1894" substitute "same meaning as in the Merchant Shipping Act 1995"; and

(b) in the definition of "lighthouse", for "meaning assigned to it by section 742 of the Merchant Shipping Act 1894" substitute "same meaning as in the Merchant Shipping Act 1995".

Contracts of Employment and Redundancy Payments Act (Northern Ireland) 1965 (c. 19 (N.I.))

34. In section 6(1)(c) of the Contracts of Employment and Redundancy Payments Act (Northern Ireland) (excluded categories of employees), for "Merchant Shipping (Registration, etc.) Act 1993" substitute "Part II of the Merchant Shipping Act 1995".

Factories Act (Northern Ireland) 1965 (c. 20 (N.I.))

35. In section 176(1) of the Factories Act (Northern Ireland) 1965, for the definitions of "ship", "vessel" and "harbour" substitute "ship" and "vessel" have the same meaning as "ship" in the Merchant Shipping Act 1995, and "harbour" has the same meaning as in the Merchant Shipping Act 1995;".

Fisheries Act (Northern Ireland) 1966 (c. 17 (N.I.))

36. In the Fisheries Act (Northern Ireland) 1966—
(a) in section 163(3), for "Merchant Shipping (Registration, etc.) Act 1993" substitute "Part II of the Merchant Shipping Act 1995"; and
(b) in section 174(4), for "Merchant Shipping (Registration, etc.) Act 1993" substitute "Part II of the Merchant Shipping Act 1995".

Finance Act 1966 (c. 18)

37. In section 2(5)(a) of the Finance Act 1966, for "Merchant Shipping Acts 1894 to 1965" substitute "Merchant Shipping Act 1995", and for "those Acts" substitute "that Act".

Sea Fish (Conservation) Act 1967 (c. 84)

38. In the Sea Fish (Conservation) Act 1967—
(a) for section 1(9), substitute—
"(9) In this section—
"British fishing boat" means a fishing boat which either is registered in the United Kingdom under Part II of the Merchant Shipping Act 1995 or is owned wholly by persons qualified to own British ships for the purposes of that Part of that Act; and
"foreign fishing boat" means any fishing boat other than a British fishing boat.";
(b) in section 5(8)(b), for "Merchant Shipping (Registration, etc.) Act 1993" substitute "Merchant Shipping Act 1995"; and
(c) in section 22(1), for the definition of "British-owned" substitute—
" "British-owned", in relation to a fishing boat, means owned by a person who is for the purposes of Part II of the Merchant Shipping Act 1995 a person qualified to own a British ship, or owned by two or more persons any one of whom is for those purposes a person so qualified;".

Public Health Act (Northern Ireland) 1967 (c. 36 (N.I.))

39. In section 32 of the Public Health Act (Northern Ireland) 1967, in the definition of "vessel", for "in the Merchant Shipping Act 1894" substitute " "ship" in the Merchant Shipping Act 1995".

Consular Relations Act 1968 (c. 18)

40. In the Consular Relations Act 1968—
(a) in section 13(3), in paragraph (b), for "Merchant Shipping Acts 1894 to 1967" substitute "Merchant Shipping Act 1995"; and
(b) in section 15, for "685 or section 686 of the Merchant Shipping Act 1894" substitute "280 or section 281 of the Merchant Shipping Act 1995".

Countryside Act 1968 (c. 41)

41. In section 13(6)(a) of the Countryside Act 1968, for "Merchant Shipping Act 1894" substitute "Merchant Shipping Act 1995".

Hovercraft Act 1968 (c. 59)

42. In section 1(1)(i) of the Hovercraft Act 1968—
(a) in sub-paragraph (ii), for the words after "1924" substitute "sections 185 and 186 of the

Merchant Shipping Act 1995 so far as those sections relate to property on board a ship"; and

(b) in sub-paragraph (iii), for the words after "hovercraft" (where it occurs last) substitute "sections 185 and 186 of the Merchant Shipping Act 1995".

Sea Fisheries Act 1968 (c. 77)

43. In the Sea Fisheries Act 1968—

(a) in section 8(6)—

(i) for "418 of the Merchant Shipping Act 1894" substitute "85 of the Merchant Shipping Act 1995";

(ii) for "723(1) of that Act (enforcement)" substitute "257 of the Merchant Shipping Act 1995 (powers to require production of ships documents)";

(iii) for "subsection" substitute "section"; and

(iv) for "723(2)" substitute "257".

(b) in section 17, for "72 of the Merchant Shipping Act 1906 (wreck brought within the limits of the United Kingdom)" substitute "236(1) of the Merchant Shipping Act 1995 (delivery of wreck to receiver)", and for "Merchant Shipping Act 1894" substitute "Merchant Shipping Act 1995"; and

(c) in section 19(1)—

(i) for the definitions of "British fishing boat" and "foreign fishing boat" substitute—

" "British fishing boat" means a fishing boat which either is registered in the United Kingdom under Part II of the Merchant Shipping Act 1995 or is wholly British-owned;" and

(ii) in the appropriate places insert—

" "foreign fishing boat" means any fishing boat other than a British fishing boat;" and

" "wholly British-owned" means wholly owned by persons qualified to own British ships for the purposes of Part II of the Merchant Shipping Act 1995;".

Harbours Act (Northern Ireland) 1970 (c. 1 (N.I.))

44. In Part II of Schedule 1 to the Harbours Act (Northern Ireland) 1970, in paragraph 7, for "section 2 of the Merchant Shipping (Liability of Shipowners and Others) Act 1900" substitute "section 191 of the Merchant Shipping Act 1995".

Carriage of Goods by Sea Act 1971 (c. 19)

45.—(1) The Carriage of Goods by Sea Act 1971 shall be amended as follows ("the Rules" meaning the Rules set out in the Schedule to that Act).

(2) Section 1 shall continue to have effect with the addition, after "1968", of "and by the Protocol signed at Brussels on 21st December 1979".

(3) After section 1 insert the following section—

"**Conversion of special drawing rights into sterling**

1A.—(1) For the purposes of Article IV of the Rules the value on a particular day of one special drawing right shall be treated as equal to such a sum in sterling as the International Monetary Fund have fixed as being the equivalent of one special drawing right—

(a) for that day; or

(b) if no sum has been so fixed for that day, for the last day before that day for which a sum has been so fixed.

(2) A certificate given by or on behalf of the Treasury stating—

(a) that a particular sum in sterling has been fixed as aforesaid for a particular day; or

(b) that no sum has been so fixed for a particular day and that a particular sum in sterling has been so fixed for a day which is the last day for which a sum has been so fixed before the particular day,

shall be conclusive evidence of those matters for the purposes of subsection (1) above; and a document purporting to be such a certificate shall in any proceedings be received in evidence and, unless the contrary is proved, be deemed to be such a certificate.

(3) The Treasury may charge a reasonable fee for any certificate given in pursuance of subsection (2) above, and any fee received by the Treasury by virtue of this subsection shall be paid into the Consolidated Fund."

(4) For section 6(4) substitute—

"(4) It is hereby declared that for the purposes of Article VIII of the Rules section 186 of the Merchant Shipping Act 1995 (which entirely exempts shipowners and others in certain circumstances for loss of, or damage to, goods) is a provision relating to limitation of liability."

(5) Article IV of the Rules shall continue to have effect with the following amendments—

(a) for "the equivalent of 10,000 francs" substitute "666.67 units of account";

(b) for "30 francs per kilo" substitute "2 units of account per kilogramme"; and

(c) for paragraph 5(d) substitute—

"(d) The unit of account mentioned in this Article is the special drawing right as defined by the International Monetary Fund. The amounts mentioned in sub-paragraph (a) of this paragraph shall be converted into national currency on the basis of the value of that currency on a date to be determined by the law of the Court seized of the case."

(6) Article 4, paragraph 5(d) of the Rules shall continue to have effect as if the date there mentioned were the date of the judgment in question.

(7) Article X of the Rules shall continue to have effect as if references to a Contracting State included references to a State that is a contracting State in respect of the Rules without the amendments made by the Protocol signed at Brussels on 21st December 1979 as well as to one that is a contracting State in respect of the Rules as so amended, and section 2 shall have effect accordingly.

Attachment of Earnings Act 1971 (c. 32)

46. In section 24(3) of the Attachment of Earnings Act 1971, for the words following "above" substitute—

" "fishing boat" means a vessel of whatever size, and in whatever way propelled, which is for the time being employed in sea fishing or in the sea-fishing service;

"seaman" includes every person (except masters and pilots) employed or engaged in any capacity on board any ship; and

"wages" includes emoluments."

Industry Act 1972 (c. 63)

47. In section 12(2)(a) of the Industry Act 1972, for "1 of the Merchant Shipping Act 1965" substitute "19 of the Merchant Shipping Act 1995".

Education (Work Experience) Act 1973 (c. 23)

48. In section 1(2)(b) of the Education (Work Experience) Act 1973, for "(when it comes into force) section 51(1) of the Merchant Shipping Act 1970" substitute "section 55(1) of the Merchant Shipping Act 1995".

Fishery Limits Act 1976 (c. 86)

49. In section 8 of the Fishery Limits Act 1976—

(a) for the definition of "foreign fishing boat" substitute—

" "foreign fishing boat" means a fishing boat which is not—

(a) registered in the United Kingdom, the Channel Islands or the Isle of Man; or

(b) wholly British-owned;" and

(b) in the appropriate place insert—

" "wholly British-owned" means wholly owned by persons qualified to own British fishing boats for the purposes of Part II of the Merchant Shipping Act 1995;".

Aircraft and Shipbuilding Industry Act 1977 (c. 3)

50. In paragraph 5(1)(a) of Schedule 2 to the Aircraft and Shipbuilding Industry Act 1977 for "Merchant Shipping Act 1894" substitute "Merchant Shipping Act 1995".

Rates (Northern Ireland) Order 1977 (S.I. 1977/2157 (N.I. 28))

51. In the Rates (Northern Ireland) Order 1977—

(a) in Schedule 4, in the definition of "vessel", for "meaning assigned to it by section 742 of the Merchant Shipping Act 1894" substitute "same meaning as "ship" in the Merchant Shipping Act 1995"; and

(b) in Schedule 11, in paragraph 6, for "section 731 of the Merchant Shipping Act 1894" substitute "section 221(1) of the Merchant Shipping Act 1995".

Judicature (Northern Ireland) Act 1978 (c. 23)

52. In section 46 of the Judicature (Northern Ireland) Act 1978, after subsection (3) insert the following subsection—

"(3A) Sections 280, 281 and 282 of the Merchant Shipping Act 1995 (offences on ships and abroad by British citizens and others) apply in relation to other offences under the law of Northern Ireland as they apply in relation to offences under that Act or instruments under that Act."

Customs and Excise Management Act 1979 (c. 2)

53.—(1) The Customs and Excise Management Act 1979 shall be amended as follows.

(2) In section 1(1)—

(a) in the definition of "British ship", for the words from "Merchant Shipping Act 1894" to the end substitute "Merchant Shipping Act 1995";

(b) in the definition of "tons register", for "Merchant Shipping Act 1894" substitute "Merchant Shipping Act 1995".

(3) In section 81(7), for "not being a fishing vessel registered under the Merchant Shipping (Registration, etc.) Act 1993" substitute "not being a fishing vessel registered under Part II of the Merchant Shipping Act 1995".

Hydrocarbon Oil Duties Act 1979 (c. 5)

54. In section 19(1)(a) of the Hydrocarbon Oil Duties Act 1979, for "fishing boat register under the Merchant Shipping Act 1894" substitute "register of British ships under the Merchant Shipping Act 1995".

Magistrates' Courts Act 1980 (c. 43)

55. After section 3 of the Magistrates' Courts Act 1980 insert the following section—

"Offences committed on ships and abroad

3A. Sections 280, 281 and 282 of the Merchant Shipping Act 1995 (offences on ships and abroad by British citizens and others) apply in relation to other offences under the law of England and Wales as they apply in relation to offences under that Act or instruments under that Act."

Education (Scotland) Act 1980 (c. 44)

56. In section 123(2)(b) of the Education (Scotland) Act 1980, for "(when it comes into force) section 51(1) of the Merchant Shipping Act 1970" substitute "section 55(1) of the Merchant Shipping Act 1995".

Private Streets (Northern Ireland) Order 1980 (S.I. 1980/1086 (NI 12))

57. In Article 2(2) of the Private Streets (Northern Ireland) Order 1980, in the definition of "industrial undertaking", for "vessel as defined in section 742 of the Merchant Shipping Act 1894" substitute "ship as defined in the Merchant Shipping Act 1995".

Animal Health Act 1981 (c. 22)

58. In the Animal Health Act 1981—

(a) in section 49(4), for paragraph (a) substitute—

"(a) "master", "owner" and "port" have the same meanings as in the Merchant Shipping Act 1995, and "vessel" has the same meaning as "ship" in the Merchant Shipping Act 1995; and"; and

(b) in section 65—

(i) in subsection (3), for "692 of the Merchant Shipping Act 1894" substitute "284 of the Merchant Shipping Act 1995"; and

(ii) in subsection (4)(a), for "1894 Act" substitute "1995 Act".

Supreme Court Act 1981 (c. 54)

59.—(1) The Supreme Court Act 1981 shall be amended as follows.

(2) In section 20—

(a) in subsection (3)—

(i) in paragraph (a), for the words after "under" substitute "the Merchant Shipping Act 1995";

(ii) in paragraph (c), for "Merchant Shipping Acts 1894 to 1979" substitute "Merchant Shipping Act 1995";

(b) in subsection (5)—

(i) in paragraph (a), for "the Merchant Shipping (Oil Pollution) Act 1971" substitute "Chapter III of Part VI of the Merchant Shipping Act 1995";

(ii) in paragraph (b), for the words following "falling on the" substitute "International Oil Pollution Compensation Fund, or on the International Oil Compensation Fund 1984, under Chapter IV of Part VI of the Merchant Shipping Act 1995.";

(c) in subsection (6)(a), for "section 1 of the Merchant Shipping Salvage and Pollution Act 1994" substitute "section 224 of the Merchant Shipping Act 1995";

(d) in subsection (7), for "Merchant Shipping Acts 1894 to 1979" substitute "Merchant Shipping Act 1995".

(3) In section 24—

(a) in subsection (1)—

(i) in the definition of "collision regulations", for the words after "means" substitute "safety regulations under section 85 of the Merchant Shipping Act 1995"; and

(ii) in the definition of "master", for "Merchant Shipping Act 1894" substitute "Merchant Shipping Act 1995";

(b) in subsection (2), in paragraph (b), for "552 of the Merchant Shipping Act 1894" substitute "226 of the Merchant Shipping Act 1995".

(4) After section 46 insert the following section—

"**Offences committed on ships and abroad**

46A.—(1) Sections 280, 281 and 282 of the Merchant Shipping Act 1995 (offences on ships and abroad by British citizens and others) apply in relation to other offences under the law of England and Wales as they apply in relation to offences under that Act or instruments under that Act."

Judgments Enforcement (Northern Ireland) Order 1981 (S.I. 1981/226 (N.I. 16))

60. In the Judgments Enforcement (Northern Ireland) Order 1981—

(a) in Article 3(5)(f), for "section 11(1) of the Merchant Shipping Act 1970" substitute "section 34(1) of the Merchant Shipping Act 1995";

(b) in Article 3(6), for "Merchant Shipping Act 1894" substitute "Merchant Shipping Act 1995";

(c) in Article 97(2), for "section 11(1) of the Merchant Shipping Act 1970" substitute "section 34(1)(a) of the Merchant Shipping Act 1995".

Clean Air (Northern Ireland) Order 1981 (S.I. 1981/158 (N.I. 14))

61. In Article 29(6) of the Clean Air (Northern Ireland) Order 1981, in the definition of "Government ship", for "section 80 of the Merchant Shipping Act 1906" substitute "the Merchant Shipping Act 1995".

Diseases of Animals (Northern Ireland) Order 1981 (S.I. 1981/1115 (N.I. 22))

62. In Article 48(3) of the Diseases of Animals (Northern Ireland) Order 1981, for "section 692 of the Merchant Shipping Act 1894" substitute "section 284 of the Merchant Shipping Act 1995".

Magistrates' Courts (Northern Ireland) Order 1981 (S.I. 1981/1675 (N.I. 26))

63. After Article 17 of the Magistrates' Courts Order 1981 insert the following Article—

"**Offences committed on ships and abroad**

17A. Sections 280, 281 and 282 of the Merchant Shipping Act 1995 (offences on ships and abroad by British citizens and others) apply in relation to other offences under the law of Northern Ireland as they apply in relation to offences under that Act or instruments under that Act."

Civil Aviation Act 1982 (c. 16)

64. In the Civil Aviation Act 1982—

(a) in section 75(6), for "530 to 537 of the Merchant Shipping Act 1894 or any enactment amending those sections" substitute "245 to 247 and sections 252 to 254 of the Merchant Shipping Act 1995";

(b) in section 86(2), for "Merchant Shipping Act 1894" substitute "Merchant Shipping Act 1995"; and

(c) in section 97(6), in the definition of "conservancy authority" and "harbour authority", for "meanings assigned to them by section 742 of the Merchant Shipping Act 1894" substitute "the same meaning as in the Merchant Shipping Act 1995".

Oil and Gas (Enterprise) Act 1982 (c. 23)

65. In the Oil and Gas (Enterprise) Act 1982—

(a) in section 27(2), for paragraphs (a) and (b) substitute—

"(a) the Merchant Shipping Act 1995;
(b) the Pilotage Act 1987;"
(b) in section 28(1), in the definition of "submersible apparatus", for "16(2) of the Merchant Shipping Act 1974" substitute "88 of the Merchant Shipping Act 1995".

Civil Jurisdiction and Judgments Act 1982 (c. 27)

66. In the Civil Jurisdiction and Judgments Act 1982—
(a) in section 31(3), for "13(3) of the Merchant Shipping (Oil Pollution) Act 1971" substitute "166(4) of the Merchant Shipping Act 1995"; and
(b) in section 32(4)(a)—
(i) omit "section 13(3) of the Merchant Shipping (Oil Pollution) Act 1971,";
(ii) for "section 6(4) of the Merchant Shipping Act 1974" substitute "section 177(4) of the Merchant Shipping Act 1995".

Civic Government (Scotland) Act 1982 (c. 45)

67. In section 38(4)(a) of the Civic Government (Scotland) Act 1982, for "Merchant Shipping Acts 1894 to 1981" substitute "Merchant Shipping Act 1995".

British Fishing Boats Act 1983 (c. 8)

68. In section 9 of the British Fishing Boats Act 1983—
(a) for the definition of "British fishing boat" substitute—
" "British fishing boat" means a fishing vessel which either is registered in the United Kingdom under Part II of the Merchant Shipping Act 1995 or is wholly British-owned"; and
(b) in the appropriate place insert—
" "wholly British-owned" means wholly owned by persons qualified to own British ships for the purposes of Part II of the Merchant Shipping Act 1995;".

Public Health (Control of Disease) Act 1984 (c. 22)

69. In the Public Health (Control of Disease) Act 1984—
(a) in section 53(a) of the definition of "canal boat", for "Merchant Shipping Acts 1894 to 1983" substitute "Merchant Shipping Act 1995"; and
(b) in section 74, in the definition of "vessel", for "in the Merchant Shipping Act 1894" substitute " "ship" in the Merchant Shipping Act 1995".

Inshore Fishing (Scotland) Act 1984 (c. 26)

70. In section 9(1) of the Inshore Fishing (Scotland) Act 1984—
(a) for the definition of "British fishing boat" substitute—
" "British fishing boat" means a fishing boat which either is registered under Part II of the Merchant Shipping Act 1995 or is wholly British-owned"; and
(b) in the appropriate place insert—
" "wholly British-owned" means wholly owned by persons qualified to own British ships for the purposes of Part II of the Merchant Shipping Act 1995;".

Road Traffic Regulation Act 1984 (c. 27)

71. In section 133(1) of the Road Traffic Regulation Act 1984, for "Part IV of the Merchant Shipping Act 1894" substitute "Part IX of the Merchant Shipping Act 1995".

County Courts Act 1984 (c. 28)

72.—(1) The County Courts Act 1984 shall be amended as follows.
(2) In section 27—
(a) in subsection (3)(a), for "section 1 of the Merchant Shipping (Salvage and Pollution) Act 1994" substitute "section 224 of the Merchant Shipping Act 1995"; and
(b) in subsection (5), for "Merchant Shipping Acts 1894 to 1983" substitute "Merchant Shipping Act 1995".
(3) In section 30(1)(c), for the words after "ships" substitute "with safety regulations under section 85 of the Merchant Shipping Act 1995".
(4) In section 31—
(a) in subsection (1), in the definition of "master", for "Merchant Shipping Act 1894" substitute "Merchant Shipping Act 1995";

(b) in subsection (2)(b), for "552 of the Merchant Shipping Act 1894" substitute "226 of the Merchant Shipping Act 1995".

Repatriation of Prisoners Act 1984 (c. 47)

73. In section 5(6) of the Repatriation of Prisoners Act 1984, in the definition of "British ship", for "Merchant Shipping Act 1894" substitute "Merchant Shipping Act 1995".

Dangerous Vessels Act 1985 (c. 22)

74. In section 2(b) of the Dangerous Vessels Act 1985, for "Merchant Shipping (Liability of Shipowners and Others) Act 1900" substitute "section 191 of the Merchant Shipping Act 1995 (which limits the liability of harbour, conservancy, dock and canal authorities)".

Food and Environment Protection Act 1985 (c. 48)

75. In section 24(1) of the Food and Environment Protection Act 1985—
(a) in the definition of "British vessel", for "Merchant Shipping Act 1894" substitute "Merchant Shipping Act 1995";
(b) in the definition of "vessel", for "it by section 742 of the Merchant Shipping Act 1894", substitute "ship" by the Merchant Shipping Act 1995".

Protection of Military Remains Act 1986 (c. 35)

76. In section 9 of the Protection of Military Remains Act 1986, in the definition of "British-controlled ship", for "Merchant Shipping Act 1894" substitute "Merchant Shipping Act 1995".

Wages Act 1986 (c. 48)

77. In section 30(3) of the Wages Act 1986, for "Merchant Shipping Act 1970" substitute "Part III of the Merchant Shipping Act 1995".

Petroleum Act 1987 (c. 12)

78. In section 23(8) of the Petroleum Act 1987, for "16(2) of the Merchant Shipping Act 1974" substitute "88(4) of the Merchant Shipping Act 1995".

Debtors (Scotland) Act 1987 (c. 18)

79. In section 73(4) of the Debtors (Scotland) Act 1987—
(a) in paragraph (a), for "section 742 of the Merchant Shipping Act 1894" substitute "section 313 of the Merchant Shipping Act 1995"; and
(b) in paragraph (b), for the words from "has" to the end substitute "means any ship which is for the time being employed in sea fishing or in the sea fishing service, and includes any ship which is both—
(i) engaged in whale fisheries off the coast of Scotland; and
(ii) registered under the Merchant Shipping Act 1995".

Pilotage Act 1987 (c. 21)

80. In the Pilotage Act 1987—
(a) in section 22—
(i) in subsection (3), for "Schedule 4 to the Merchant Shipping Act 1979" substitute "Schedule 7 to the Merchant Shipping Act 1995";
(ii) in subsection (7), for "17 or is excluded under section 18 of the Merchant Shipping Act 1979" substitute " 185 or is excluded under section 186 of the Merchant Shipping Act 1995"; and
(b) in section 31(1)—
(i) in the definition of "master", for "Merchant Shipping Act 1894" substitute "Merchant Shipping Act 1995";
(ii) in the definition of "pilot", for "has the same meaning as in the Merchant Shipping Act 1894" substitute "means any person not belonging to a ship who has the conduct thereof".

Channel Tunnel Act 1987 (c. 53)

81. In Part III of Schedule 7 to the Channel Tunnel Act 1987, in paragraph 1(2), in the definition of "the Trinity House", for "742 of the Merchant Shipping Act 1894" substitute " 223 of the Merchant Shipping Act 1995".

Norfolk and Suffolk Broads Act 1988 (c. 4)

82. In section 25(1) of the Norfolk and Suffolk Broads Act 1988, in subsection (1), in the definition of "Trinity House", for "742 of the Merchant Shipping Act 1894" substitute "223 of the Merchant Shipping Act 1995".

Local Government Finance Act 1988 (c. 41)

83. In Schedule 5 to the Local Government Finance Act 1988, in paragraph 12(2), for "731 of the Merchant Shipping Act 1894" substitute " 221(1) of the Merchant Shipping Act 1995".

Copyright, Designs and Patents Act 1988 (c. 48)

84. In the Copyright, Designs and Patents Act 1988—
(a) in section 162(2), in the definition of "British ship", for "Merchant Shipping Acts (see section 2 of the Merchant Shipping Act 1988)" substitute "Merchant Shipping Act 1995"; and
(b) in section 210(2), in the definition of "British ship", for "Merchant Shipping Acts (see section 2 of the Merchant Shipping Act 1988)" substitute "Merchant Shipping Act 1995".

Road Traffic Act 1988 (c. 52)

85. In section 144(2)(c) of the Road Traffic Act 1988, for "Merchant Shipping Act 1894" substitute "Merchant Shipping Act 1995".

Wages (Northern Ireland) Order 1988 (S.I. 1988/796 (N.I. 7))

86. In Article 26(3) of the Wages (Northern Ireland) Order 1988, for "the Merchant Shipping Act 1970" substitute "Part III of the Merchant Shipping Act 1995".

Criminal Justice (International Co-operation) Act 1990 (c. 5)

87. In section 5(7) of the Criminal Justice (International Co-operation) Act 1990, in the definition of "British ship", for "Merchant Shipping Acts 1894 to 1988" substitute "Merchant Shipping Act 1995".

Aviation and Maritime Security Act 1990 (c. 31)

88.—(1) The Aviation and Maritime Security Act 1990 shall be amended as follows.
(2) In section 14(3), for "686 or 687 of the Merchant Shipping Act 1894" substitute " 281 or 282 of the Merchant Shipping Act 1995".
(3) In section 15(8), in the definition of "master", for "Merchant Shipping Act 1894" substitute "Merchant Shipping Act 1995".
(4) In section 35(4), for "692 of the Merchant Shipping Act 1894" substitute "284 of the Merchant Shipping Act 1995".
(5) In section 45—
(a) in subsection (7)(a), for "section 59(1) of the Merchant Shipping Act 1894" substitute "registration regulations"; and
(b) in subsection (10), for the words following "provisions" substitute "mean Part II of the Merchant Shipping Act 1995, or any Order in Council under section 1 of the Hovercraft Act 1968.".
(6) In section 46(1)—
(a) in the definition of "British ship"—
(i) in paragraph (a), for "Part I of the Merchant Shipping Act 1894, section 5 of the Merchant Shipping Act 1983, Part II of the Merchant Shipping Act 1988" substitute "Part II of the Merchant Shipping Act 1995";
(ii) in paragraph (b), for "Part I of the Merchant Shipping Act 1894" substitute "Part II of the Merchant Shipping Act 1995"; and
(b) in the definition of "master", for "Merchant Shipping Act 1894" substitute "Merchant Shipping Act 1995".

Water Industry Act 1991 (c. 56)

89. In the Water Industry Act 1991—
(a) in section 121(6), for "Merchant Shipping Act 1894" substitute "Merchant Shipping Act 1995"; and
(b) in section 219(1), in the definition of "harbour authority", for "the Prevention of Oil Pollution Act 1971" substitute "Chapter II of Part VI of the Merchant Shipping Act 1995".

Water Resources Act 1991 (c. 57)

90. In section 221(1) of the Water Resources Act 1991—
(a) in the definition of "harbour", for "the Merchant Shipping Act 1894" substitute "section 313 of the Merchant Shipping Act 1995"; and
(b) in the definition of "harbour authority", for "the Merchant Shipping Act 1894" substitute "section 313 of the Merchant Shipping Act 1995", and for "within the meaning of the Prevention of Oil Pollution Act 1971" substitute "as defined in section 151 for the purposes of Chapter II of Part VI of that Act".

Land Drainage Act 1991 (c. 59)

91. In the Land Drainage Act 1991—
(a) in section 12(7), for "the Prevention of Oil Pollution Act 1971" substitute "Chapter II of Part VI of the Merchant Shipping Act 1995";
(b) in section 72(1)—
    (i) in the definition of "conservancy authority", for "the Prevention of Oil Pollution Act 1971" substitute "Chapter II of Part VI of the Merchant Shipping Act 1995"; and
    (ii) in the definitions of "harbour" and "harbour authority", for "Merchant Shipping Act 1894" substitute "Merchant Shipping Act 1995".

Dangerous Vessels (Northern Ireland) Order 1991 (S.I. 1991/1219 (NI 10))

92. In Article 4(b) of the Dangerous Vessels (Northern Ireland) Order 1991, for "Merchant Shipping (Liability of Shipowners and Others) Act 1900" substitute "section 191 of the Merchant Shipping Act 1995 (which limits the liability of harbour, conservancy, dock and canal authorities)".

Judicial Pensions and Retirement Act 1993 (c. 8)

93. In the Judicial Pensions and Retirement Act 1993—
(a) in section 26(8)(c), for "52 of the Merchant Shipping Act 1970" substitute " 61 of the Merchant Shipping Act 1995";
(b) in Schedule 5, in the entry for a "Wreck commissioner", for "82 of the Merchant Shipping Act 1970" substitute " 297(1) of the Merchant Shipping Act 1995"; and
(c) in Schedule 7, in paragraph 5(5)(xxxiii), for "82 of the Merchant Shipping Act 1970" substitute " 297(1) of the Merchant Shipping Act 1995".

Clean Air Act 1993 (c. 11)

94. In the Clean Air Act 1993—
(a) in section 46(6), in the definition of "Government ship", for "section 80 of the Merchant Shipping Act 1906" substitute "the Merchant Shipping Act 1995"; and
(b) in section 64(1), in the definition of "vessel", for "in the Merchant Shipping Act 1894" substitute "ship" in the Merchant Shipping Act 1995".

Value Added Tax Act 1994 (c. 23)

95. In section 33(3)(h), for "Part XI of the Merchant Shipping Act 1894" substitute "Part VIII of the Merchant Shipping Act 1995".

Section 314   SCHEDULE 14

TRANSITORY, SAVING AND TRANSITIONAL PROVISIONS

Extra-territorial provisions

1.—(1) Without prejudice to section 315(1), the repeals made by this Act shall not affect the law in force in any country or territory which is outside the United Kingdom.

(2) In particular, the repeal of section 735 of the Merchant Shipping Act 1894 shall not affect the power of Her Majesty in Council to confirm any legislation made by the legislature of a British possession under that section as it extends to that possession.

(3) The provisions of this Act (including the repeal of any power by Order in Council to extend any enactment to a relevant British possession) or of any enactment which has been so extended, do not extend to any such possession except in so far as they are extended to that possession by an Order in Council under section 315(2) of this Act.

References to registration in other legislation

2. Any reference in an enactment in any other Act (not amended by Schedule 13), or in any instrument made under any other Act to the registration of a ship (or fishing vessel) under—
   (a) Part I of the Merchant Shipping Act 1894,
   (b) section 5 of the Merchant Shipping Act 1983,
   (c) section 13 of the Merchant Shipping Act 1988, or
   (d) section 1 of the Merchant Shipping (Registration, etc.) Act 1993,
shall be construed, unless the context otherwise requires, as, or as including, a reference to registration under Part II of this Act; and connected phrases shall be construed accordingly.

Qualifications: certificates of A.B.

3.—(1) A seaman engaged in any United Kingdom ship shall not be rated as A.B. unless he is the holder of a certificate of competency granted in pursuance of regulations under this paragraph.

(2) The Secretary of State may make regulations providing for the grant of certificates of competency as A.B. for the purposes of this paragraph.

(3) The regulations shall direct that no certificate shall be granted to any person unless—
   (a) he has reached such minimum age as may be prescribed;
   (b) he has performed such qualifying service at sea as may be prescribed; and
   (c) he has passed such examination as may be prescribed.

(4) The regulations may make such consequential provisions as appear to the Secretary of State to be necessary or expedient, including provision—
   (a) for the payment of prescribed fees in respect of any application for the grant or replacement of a certificate;
   (b) for applying section 104 of the Merchant Shipping Act 1894 (offences) to certificates, subject to such adaptations and modifications as may be prescribed.

(5) Where provision is made by the law of any Commonwealth country for the grant of certificates of competency as A.B. and the Secretary of State is satisfied that the conditions under which such a certificate is granted require standards of competency not lower than those required for the grant of a certificate under the regulations, Her Majesty may by Order in Council direct that certificates granted in that country shall have the same effect for the purposes of this paragraph as if they had been granted under the regulations; and any such Order may apply to any such certificate any of the provisions of the regulations.

(6) Any Order in Council under sub-paragraph (5) above shall be laid before Parliament after being made.

(7) Any superintendent or other officer before whom a seaman is engaged in any United Kingdom ship shall refuse to enter the man as A.B. on the crew agreement unless the seaman produces a certificate or such other proof that he is the holder of such a certificate as may appear to the superintendent or other officer to be satisfactory.

(8) In this paragraph—
   "certificate" means a certificate of competency under the regulations;
   "prescribed" means prescribed by the regulations; and
   "the regulations" means regulations under this paragraph.

Manning: certificates existing in 1979

4.—(1) The power to make regulations under section 47 includes power to make regulations providing that pre-1979 certificates shall, except in such cases as are specified in the regulations, be deemed for the purposes of such of the provisions of Part III as are so specified to be issued in pursuance of that section and to confer on the persons to whom they were issued such qualifications for the purposes of that section as are so specified.

(2) In this paragraph "pre-1979 certificate" means a certificate granted under section 93, 99 or 414 of the Merchant Shipping Act 1894, a certificate referred to in an Order in Council made under section 102 of that Act, a certificate granted under section 27(2) of the Merchant Shipping Act 1906 or by an institution approved in pursuance of that subsection and a certificate granted under section 5 of the Merchant Shipping Act 1948.

Masters and seamen: postponed commencements

5.—(1) No provision to which this paragraph applies shall have effect until the Secretary of State by order appoints a day for that provision to come into force.

(2) This paragraph applies to sections 60, 80(2) and (4), 111, 115, 116, 118, 119(2) and (3), 127, 314(1) so far as it relates to the repeal in the Aliens Restriction (Amendment) Act 1919 or in the Local Government etc. (Scotland) Act 1994.

Masters and seamen and documents: transitory provisions

6.—(1) A provision to which this paragraph applies shall cease to have effect on such day as the Secretary of State by order appoints.

(2) This paragraph applies to sections 57, 287(1)(a) and 298, paragraph 26 of Schedule 3 and paragraph 3 of this Schedule.

Safety provisions: saving of instruments, etc.

7.—(1) Notwithstanding the repeal by the Merchant Shipping (Registration, etc.) Act 1993 of the following provisions, instruments in force before the repeal under the provisions specified in the left-hand column shall continue in force until superseded by safety regulations and the related provisions specified in the right-hand column shall continue in force for the purposes of those instruments:

Empowering provisions			*Related provisions*
1894 Act:	section 427	—	Section 430.
1949 Act:	section 3	—	Sections 3(5) and (6) and 28.
	section 21	—	Section 21(3).
1964 Act:	section 2	—	—
1967 Act (c.64):	section 1	—	Section 1(2) and (3).
1977 Act:	section 2	—	—

(2) The Secretary of State may exempt any ships or classes of ships from any requirements of the rules for life-saving appliances or the radio rules, either absolutely or subject to such conditions as he thinks fit.

In this sub-paragraph—

"the rules for life-saving appliances" means rules under section 427 of the 1894 Act saved by sub-paragraph (1) above; and

"the radio rules" means rules under section 3 of the 1949 Act saved by that sub-paragraph.

Oil pollution: saving for certain transitional provisions

8. Notwithstanding the repeal of section 38 of the Merchant Shipping Act 1979 any transitional provisions included by virtue of subsection (6) of that section in a commencement order under section 52(2) of that Act shall continue to have effect.

Lighthouses: dependencies

9.—(1) Section 193(5) shall cease to have effect on such day or days as the Secretary of State by order appoints.

(2) Until that day, the powers of the Trinity House under Part VIII with respect to lighthouses, buoys and beacons in the islands of Guernsey or Jersey other than their powers under sections 204 and 220 shall not be exercised without the consent of Her Majesty in Council.

(3) Until that day, no dues for any lighthouse, buoy or beacon erected or placed in or near the islands of Guernsey, Jersey, Sark or Alderney shall be levied in the islands of Guernsey or Jersey without the consent of the States of those Islands respectively.

(4) Any Order in Council under sub-paragraph (2) above shall be laid before Parliament.

(5) There shall continue to be paid out of the General Lighthouse Fund under section 211 any expenditure incurred by the Government of the United Kingdom in pursuance of the arrangement made with the Government of Sri Lanka on 27th February 1976 for the transfer of certain lighthouses off the coast of that country.

Lighthouses: Scotland

10. Prior to the commencement of paragraph 7 of Schedule 13 to the Local Government etc. (Scotland) Act 1994, Schedule 8 shall have effect as if—

(a) in paragraph 1(2), in head (a), for the words from "conveners" to "Bute" there were substituted "chairmen of the Inverness and Argyll district councils";

(b) in paragraph 2(1), for the words "convener of any" there were substituted "chairmen of any district"; and

(c) paragraph 5 were omitted.

Wreck and salvage: Cinque ports

11. Nothing in Part IX shall prejudice or affect any jurisdiction or powers of the Lord Warden or any officers of the Cinque ports or of any court of those ports or of any court having concurrent jurisdiction within the boundaries of those ports; and disputes as to salvage arising without those boundaries shall, subject to the Salvage Convention as set out in Schedule 11, be determined in the manner in which they have been hitherto determined.

Wreck: Liability for damage in case of plundered vessel in Scotland

12. Prior to the commencement of paragraph (1) of Schedule 13 to the Local Government etc. (Scotland) Act 1994, section 235(4) shall have effect as if for the words "constituted under section 2 of the Local Government etc. (Scotland) Act 1994" there were substituted "of the regional or islands area".

Behring Sea Award

13. Nothing in this Act shall affect the Behring Sea Award Act 1894.

Table of Derivations

Notes

1. This Table shows the derivations of the provisions of the Bill.
2. The following abbreviations are used in the Table:—

Acts of Parliament

1894	=	Merchant Shipping Act 1894 (c.60)
1900	=	Merchant Shipping (Liability of Shipowners and others) Act 1900 (c.32)
1906	=	Merchant Shipping Act 1906 (c.48)
1911 MC	=	Maritime Conventions Act 1911 (c.57)
1970 FV	=	Fishing Vessels (Safety Provisions) Act 1970 (c.27)
1970	=	Merchant Shipping Act 1970 (c.36)
1971	=	Merchant Shipping (Oil Pollution) Act 1971 (c.59)
1971 POP	=	Prevention of Oil Pollution Act 1971 (c.60)
1974	=	Merchant Shipping Act 1974 (c.43)
1979	=	Merchant Shipping Act 1979 (c.39)
1981	=	Merchant Shipping Act 1981 (c.10)
1982 CJ	=	Criminal Justice Act 1982 (c.48)
1984	=	Merchant Shipping Act 1984 (c.5)
1988	=	Merchant Shipping Act 1988 (c.12)
1993	=	Merchant Shipping (Registration etc.) Act 1993 (c.22)
1994	=	Merchant Shipping (Salvage and Pollution) Act 1994 (c.28)

Subordinate Legislation

1995 SC	=	Merchant Shipping (Survey and Certification) Regulations 1995 (S.I. 1995/1210)

3. By the Transfer of Functions (Trade and Industry) Order 1983, S.I.1983/1127, the functions of the Secretary of State for Trade (who succeeded to the functions of the Board of Trade under previous Orders) relating to shipping were transferred to the Secretary of State for Transport. This effect on the numerous references to the Board of Trade is not noted in the Table.

4. By Schedule 1, paragraph (1) to the Customs and Excise Management Act 1979 (c. 2) references to the Commissioners of Customs or to officers of customs in pre-1.4.1909 (when the respective Commissioners and their officers were assimilated) enactments became references to the Commissioners of Customs and Excise and officers of customs and excise respectively. This effect is not noted in the Table.

5. Schedule 4, paragraph 2 of the 1993 Act effected general changes in the terminology used in the Merchant Shipping Acts. These included—

(a) assimilating "ship" and "vessel" so that generally only "ship" is used;

(b) enabling use to be made in the many contexts where the provision has one or other of these meanings of the expressions "United Kingdom waters" and "national waters"; and

(c) substituting its "equipment" for the tackle, equipments, furniture or apparel of a ship. These changes in terminology are not noted against the numerous provisions affected.

6. The general conversion of then-existing fines in terms of amounts of money into levels on the standard scale effected by section 46 of the Criminal Justice Act 1982 (c. 48) is not noted in the Table against the numerous provisions affected by the conversion; nor is the general increase in summary penalties effected in pre-1949 enactments by section 31(6) of the Criminal Law Act 1977 (c. 45). But specific alterations are noted.

7. As regards offences, paragraph 74 of Schedule 4 to the 1993 Act made three changes. These were—

(a) the substitution of "intentionally" for "wilfully";
(b) the substitution of "permitting" for "suffering" or "allowing" a thing to be done; and
(c) the substitution of "excuse" for "cause" in the expression "reasonable cause".

These are not noted against the provisions affected.

8. Section 1(1)(c) of the Merchant Shipping (Mercantile Marine Fund) Act 1898 (c. 44) translated all references to that Fund into references to the General Lighthouse Fund constituted by that section. These are not noted in the Table against the numerous provisions affected.

Provision	Derivation
1(1), (2)	1993 Sch. 3 para. 1(1), (2); Sch. 4 para. 1(1).
(3)	Drafting.
2(1) to (3)	1993 Sch. 3 para. 2.
(4)	1894 s.738(2)
3	1993 Sch. 3 para. 5.
4	1993 Sch. 3 para. 3.
5	1993 Sch. 3 para. 4.
6	1993 Sch. 3 para. 6.
7(1), (2)	1894 s.76(1); 1988 Sch. 1 para. 47; 1993 Sch. 4 para. 2(4)
(3), (4)	1894 s.76(2); 1988 Sch. 1 para. 47.
(5)	1894 s.76(1).
8	1993 s.1(1) to (5)
9	1993 s.2.
10	1993 s.3(1) to (7), (9).
11	1894 s.82; 1993 Sch. 2 para. 2(a).
12(1), (2)	1894 s.84(1); 1988 Sch. 1 para. 48.
(3)	Merchant Shipping Act 1965 (c.47) Schedule 1.
(4), (5)	1894 s.84(2), (3).
13	1993 Sch. 3 para. 7.
14	1993 s.4.
15	1993 s.5.
16	1993 s.6.
17	1993 s.7.
18	1988 s.11; 1993 Sch. 2 para. 15(2).
19	1965 s.1(1) to (4), (6), (6A); 1970 s.91; 1979 Sch. 6 Pt. VI para. 6.
20	1894 s.76.
21	1988 s.52; 1993 Sch. 2 para. 15(4).
22	1894 s.66; 1993 Sch. 4 para. 71.
23	1993 s.9(2), (3).
24(1), (2)	1970 s.96(1); 1988 Sch. 5.
(3)	1970 s.95(1).
25	1970 s.1; 1979 Sch. 6 Pt. III.
26	1970 s.2; 1979 Sch. 6 Pt. VI para. 8.
27	1970 s.3; 1979 Sch. 6 Pt. VI para. 8.
28	1970 s.4.
29	1970 s.5.
30(1)	1970 s.7(1); 1988 s.46(2).
(2)	1970 s.7(2); 1988 s.46(3).
(3)	1970 s.7(3); 1988 s.46(4).
(4) to (6)	1970 s.7(3A) to (3C); 1988 s.46(5).
(7)	1970 s.7(4); 1988 s.46(6).
(8), (9)	1970 s.7(5), (6); 1988 s.46(7).
(10)	1970 s.7(7); 1988 s.46(8).
31(1) to (3)	1970 s.8(1) to (3); 1988 s.46(9).
(4)	1970 s.8(3A); 1988 s.46(9)

Provision	Derivation
31(5), (6)	1970 s.8(4), (5); 1979 Sch. 6 Pt. I.
32	1970 s.9.
33	1970 s.10.
34(1)	1970 s.11(1); 1993 Sch. 4 para. 9.
(2), (3)	1970 s.11(2), (3).
(4)	1979 s.39(3).
(5)	Child Support Act 1991 (Consequential Amendments) Order 1993 (S.I. 1993/785) art. 5; Child Support (Northern Ireland) Order 1991 (Consequential Amendments) Order (Northern Ireland) 1993 (S.R. (NI) 1993 No. 157) art. 5.
(6)	1979 s.39(2).
35	1970 s.12.
36	1970 s.13.
37	1970 s.14.
38(1) to (3)	1970 s.15(1) to (3).
(4)	1979 s.37(1).
39	1970 s.16.
40(1) to (9)	1970 s.17(1) to (9).
(10), (11)	1970 s.17(10), (11); Transfer of Functions (Local Government etc.) (Northern Ireland) Order 1973 (1973 SR&O (NI) 1973/256) Sch. 1; Sch. 2 Social Security Act 1989 (c.24) s.5(5); 1993 Sch. 4 para. 10; S.I.
41	1970 s.18.
42(1), (2)	1894 s.458(1); 1993 Sch. 4 paras. 6(1), 7.
(3)	1894 s.458(2)(a).
43	1970 s.20; 1979 Sch. 6 Pt. IV.
44(1)	1970 s.22(1); S.I. 1989/102 reg. 1(3)(b).
(2), (3)	1970 s.22(2), (3).
(4)	1970 s.22(4); 1979 Sch. 6 Pts. II, III.
45	1970 ss.26, 97(5).
46	1970 s.49.
47	1970 s.43; 1979 Sch. 6 Pt. IV.
48	1970 s.44.
49(1)	1970 s.45; 1979 Sch. 6 Pt. IV; 1982 CJ s.49(1).
(2)	1970 s.96(2); 1988 Sch. 5.
50	1970 s.47; 1979 Sch. 6 Pt. II.
51	1970 s.48; 1979 Sch. 6 Pt. IV.
52	1970 s.46; 1979 s.43(2) Sch. 6 Pt. V; 1982 CJ s.49(1).
53	1970 s.25.
54	1970 s.50; 1979 Sch. 6 Pt. IV.
55	1970 s.51; 1979 Sch. 6 Pt. II.
56	1988 s.26.
57	Mercantile Marine Uniform Act 1919 (c.62) s.1.
58(1) to (5)	1970 s.27(1) to (5); 1988 s.32.
(6)	1970 ss.27(6), 33.
(7), (8)	1970 s.27(7), (8); 1988 s.32.
59	1970 s.30(c); 1974 s.19(4); 1979 Sch. 6 Pt. VII para. 21; 1982 CJ s.49(1).
60(1)	1979 s.23(1)
(2)	1979 s.23(1)(a).
(3)	1979 s.23(1)(b).
(4)	1979 s.23(1)(c).
(5)	1979 s.23(1)(d).
(6)	1979 s.23(1)(e).
(7)	1979 s.23(1)(f).
(8)	1979 s.23(1) full out.
(9), (10)	1979 s.23(3).
61	1970 s.52.
62	1970 s.53.
63	1970 s.54.

Provision	Derivation
64	1970 s.57.
65	1970 s.58; 1988 Sch. 6.
66	1970 s.59; 1979 Sch. 6 Pt. II.
67	1970 s.60.
68	1988 s.44.
69	1988 s.45.
70	1970 s.39.
71	1970 s.40.
72	1970 s.41.
73(1) to (3)	1970 s.62(1) to (3).
(4)	1970 s.62(4); British Nationality Act 1981 (c.61) s.51(3).
(5)	1970 s.62(5).
(6)	1970 s.62(6); 1979 Sch. 6 Pt. VI para. 8.
(7)	1970 s.62(7).
(8)	1970 s.67.
74	1970 s.63.
75	1970 s.64.
76	1988 s.27.
77	1970 s.68; 1979 Sch. 6 Pt. III, Pt. IV para. 4; 1982 CJ s.46(2).
78	1970 s.69; 1979 Sch. 6 Pt. VI para. 4; 1982 CJ s.46(2).
79(1)	1970 s.70(1).
(2)	1970 s.70(2); 1979 Sch. 6 Pt. VI para. 4; 1982 s.46(2).
(3)	1970 s.70(3); British Nationality Act 1981 (c.61) Sch. 7.
(4)	1970 s.70(4); 1979 Sch. 6 Pt. III.
80(1)	1970 s.71(1)
(2)	1979 s.23(5).
(3)	1970 s.71(2); 1979 Sch. 6 Pt. VI para. 4; 1982 CJ s.46(2).
(4)	1979 s.23(6); 1982 CJ s.49(1).
81	1970 s.74; 1979 Sch. 6 Pt. II.
82	1988 ss.28, 53(2)(a).
83	1988 s.29.
84	1970 s.97(1) to (4), (6).
85(1)	1979 s.21(1); Safety at Sea Act 1986 (c.23) s.11(1), (4); 1993 Sch. 4 para. 6(4).
(2)	1979 s.21(2); British Nationality Act 1981 (c.61) s.51(3).
(3)	1979 s.21(3); Safety at Sea Act 1986 (c.23) s.11(2), (4).
(4)	1979 s.21(3A); 1993 Sch. 4 para. 13(3).
(5), (6)	1979 s.21(4), (5).
(7)	1979 s.21(6); 1982 CJ s.49(3).
86(1)	1979 s.22(1); 1993 Sch. 4 para. 13.
(2)	1979 s.22(3).
(3)	1979 s.22(4)
(4)	1979 s.22(2).
(5), (6)	1979 s.49(4A), (4B); Safety at Sea Act 1986 (c.23) s.11(3); 1988 Sch. 5.
87(1), (2)	1894 s.449(1); 1993 Sch. 4 para. 11(2)(a).
(3), (4)	1894 s.449(2); 1993 Sch. 4 para. 11(2)(b).
(5)	1894 s.449(3); 1993 Sch. 4 para. 11(2)(c).
88(1)	1974 s.16(1); 1993 Sch. 4. para. 6(3).
(2)	1974 s.17(1); 1993 Sch. 4 para. 6(3).
(3)	1974 s.17(3).
(4)	1974 s.16(2).
89	Drafting.
90	1970 s.86.
91(1)	Merchant Shipping (Safety and Load Line Conventions) Act 1932 (c.9) s.24(1).
(2)	1932 (c.9) s.24(1); Merchant Shipping Act 1964 (c.47) s.16.
(3)	1932 (c.9) s.24(2).
(4)	1932 (c.9) s.24(3); 1979 Sch. 6 Pt. III.
(5), (6)	1932 (c.9) s.24(4); Post Office Act 1969 (c.48) s.3(1)(i).
(7)	1932 (c.9) s.24(4), (5).

Provision	Derivation
92(1)	1894 s.422(1).
(2)	1993 Sch. 4 para. 6(2).
(3)	1911 MC s.4(2).
(4)	1894 s.422(3); 1979 Sch. 6 Pt. VII para. 6.
93(1), (2)	Merchant Shipping (Safety Convention) Act 1949 (c.43) s.22(1), (2).
(3)	1993 Sch. 4 para. 6(2).
(4), (5)	1949 (c.43) s.22(3), (4).
(6)	1949 (c.43) ss.22(5), 37(3) incorporating 1894 s.680(1)(a).
(7)	1949 (c.43) s.22(8).
94(1), (2)	1988 ss.30(1), (3), 30A(5).
(3)	1988 s.30(9).
95	1988 s.30A; 1993 Sch. 4 para. 12(2).
96(1)	1984 s.4(1); 1993 Sch. 4 para. 12(3), (4).
(2)	1984 s.4(2); 1993 Sch. 4 para. 12(4)(c).
(3)	1993 Sch. 4 para. 12(4)(d).
(4)	1984 s.4(3).
(5)	1993 Sch. 4 para. 12(4)(e).
(6), (7)	1984 s.4(5); Courts and Legal Services Act 1990 (c.41) Sch. 10 para. 55.
(8), (9)	1984 s.4(6), (7).
(10)	1993 Sch. 4 para. 12(4)(a).
97(1)	1984 s.5(1); 1993 Sch. 4 para. 12(3), (4).
(2)	1984 s.5(4).
(3)	1984 s.5(5).
(4)	1993 Sch. 4 para. 12(4)(a).
98	1988 s.30(1), (2), (4) to (10).
99	Merchant Shipping Act 1921 (c.28) ss.2, 3.
100	1988 s.31.
101(1)	1894 s.287(1); 1995 SC reg.1(5).
(2)	1894 s.287(2); 1993 Sch. 4 para. 14.
(3)	1894 s.287(3); 1993 Sch. 4 para. 14.
(4)	1894 s.287(1), (2); 1979 Sch. 6 Pt. I.
(5)	1894 s.287(4).
(6)	1995 SC reg. 1(5).
102	1894 s.288; 1993 Sch. 4 para. 2(1)(g); 1995 SC reg. 1(6).
103	1970 s.77; 1979 Sch. 6 Pt. VI para. 9.
104	1970 s.78; Aviation and Maritime Security Act 1990 (c.31) Sch. 3.
105	1970 s.79.
106(1)	1970 s.32.
(2)	1970 s.96(2); 1988 Sch. 5.
(3)	1970 s.95(1)(a).
107	1906 s.76; 1979 Sch. 6 Pt. VI para. 13; 1993 Sch. 4 para. 15.
108(1)	1970 s.72(1).
(2), (4)	1970 s.72(1)(a).
(3), (4)	1970 s.72(1)(b); British Nationality Act 1981 (c.61) s.51(3).
(5), (6)	1979 s.30(1).
(7)	1970 s.72(2); 1979 s.30(1).
(8)	1970 s.72(3).
(9)	1970 s.72(4); 1979 Sch. 6 Pt. VI para. 4; 1982 CJ s.46(3).
(10)	1970 s.72(5).
(11)	1970 s.97(5).
109	1970 s.95(1), Sch. 2 Pt. I para. 1; 1982 CJ s.38(8).
110	1970 ss.7, 95(1)(b), Sch. 2 Pt. II.
111	1979 s.24.
112	1970 ss.8, 95(1)(b), Sch. 2 Pt. II.
113	1970 s.95(4); Attachment of Earnings Act 1971 (c.32) s.27(3); Judgments Enforcement (Northern Ireland) Order (S.I. 1981/226 Sch. 2 para. 17).
114	1970 s.95(2).
115	1970 s.95(1)(a), Sch. 2 para. 4; 1979 Sch. 6 Pt. III.

Provision	Derivation
116	1970 s.95(1)(a), Sch. 2 para. 3; 1979 Sch. 6 Pt. II; 1982 CJ s.38(8).
117	1970 ss.28, 33; 1979 s.45(2) Sch. 6 Pt. VII para. 20; Safety at Sea Act 1986 (c.23) s.10.
118	1979 s.25.
119(1)	1970 s.95(1)(a); 1979 s.45(3).
(2), (3)	1979 s.23(2).
120	1970 s.95(5).
121	1970 FV s.1; 1979 Sch. 6 Pt. V.
122(1)	1970 FV s.2(1); 1986 s.5(1).
(2)	Drafting.
123	1970 FV s.3(1) to (3), 9(1).
124(1) to (4)	1970 FV s.3(4); 1894 ss.280, 281(1), (2); 1993 Sch. 4. para. 16.
(5), (6)	1970 FV s.3(4); 1894 ss.282, 680(1).
(7)	1970 FV s.3(5).
125	1970 FV s.4(1) to (3); 1979 s.43(2), Sch. 6 Pt. V.
126	1970 FV s.5; 1982 CJ s.38(8).
127	Safety at Sea Act 1986 (c.23) ss.7, 9(1).
128(1)	1979 s.20(1); 1994 s.2(1).
(2)	1979 s.20(2).
(3)	1979 s.20(3); Environmental Protection Act 1990 (c.43) s.148(2); 1988 Sch. 6; 1994 s.3(2).
(4)	1979 s.20(4); 1994 s.3(3).
(5), (6)	1979 s.20(4A), (4B); 1994 s.3(4).
(7)	1979 s.20(5).
(8), (9)	1979 s.20(6); 1994 s.2(2).
129	1979 s.20A; 1994 s.4.
130(1) to (3)	1988 s.35.
(4)	1988 s.53(2).
131(1), (2)	1971 POP s.2(2A), (2B); Prevention of Oil Pollution Act 1986 (c.6) s.1(1).
(3)	1971 POP s.2(4).
(4)	1971 POP s.29(1).
(5), (6)	1971 POP s.2(3).
132	1971 POP s.5.
133	1971 POP s.6(1) except (b) and (c).
134	1971 POP s.7.
135	1971 POP s.10; 1979 Sch. 6 Pt. II.
136	1971 POP ss.11 except (c), 29(1); 1979 Sch. 6 Pt. IV.
137	1971 POP s.12; 1994 s.8(6).
138	1971 POP s.13.
139	1971 POP s.14.
140(1)	1971 POP s.15(1); Companies Consolidation (Consequential Provisions) Act (c.9) 1985 Sch. 2.
(2)	1971 POP s.15(2).
(3)	1971 POP s.15(3); S.I. 1986/1032 (NI 6) Sch. 1 Pt. II.
141	1971 POP s.16.
142(1) to (4)	1971 POP s.17(1) to (4).
(5)	1971 POP s.27(4).
(6) to (8)	1971 POP s.17(5); 1979 Sch. 6 Pt. VI para. 17.
(9)	1971 POP s.17(6).
(10)	1971 POP s.29(1).
143(1)	1971 POP s.19(1).
(2), (3)	1971 POP ss.19(1), 30(4).
(4)	1971 POP s.19(2).
(5)	1971 POP s.19(3).
(6), (7)	1971 POP s.19(4A); Environmental Protection Act 1990 (c.43) Sch. 14 para. 2.
144(1) to (7), (10)	1971 POP s.19A; Environmental Protection Act 1990 s.148(1), (3), Sch. 14 paras. 1, 3.

Provision	Derivation
145	1971 POP s.19A(8), (9); Environmental Protection Act 1990 s.148(1), (3), Sch. 14 paras. 1, 3.
146	1971 POP s.20; Debtors (Scotland) Act 1987 (c.18) Sch. 6 para. 14; Environmental Protection Act 1990 (c.43) Sch. 14 para. 4; 1993 Sch. 4 para. 66.
147	1971 POP s.21.
148	1971 POP s.23; Petroleum and Submarine Pipelines Act 1975 (c.74) s.45(2); 1979 s.37(8).
149	1971 POP s.24.
150	1971 POP s.26.
151(1), (2)	1971 POP ss.8(2), 29(1).
(3) to (5)	1971 POP s.29(2) to (4).
(6)	1971 POP s.29(5); 1993 Sch. 4 para. 17(c).
(7)	1971 POP s.32.
152	1971 s.19; 1988 Sch. 4 Pt. I para. 13; 1994 s.5(1), (4).
153	1971 s.1; 1988 Sch. 4 Pt. I para. 1; 1994 Sch. 3 Pt. II para. 1.
154	1971 s.1A; 1994 Sch. 3 Pt. II para. 2.
155	1971 s.2; 1988 Sch. 4 Pt. I para. 2; 1994 Sch. 3 Pt. II para. 3.
156	1971 s.3; 1988 Sch. 4 Pt. I para. 3; 1994 Sch. 3 Pt. II para. 4.
157	1971 s.4; 1988 Sch. 4 Pt. I para. 4.
158(1), (2)	1971 s.5(1), (2).
(3)	1971 s.5(2A); 1979 s.38(2).
(4)	1971 s.5(3).
(5)	1971 s.5(4); 1979 Sch. 5 para. 6(1).
(6), (7)	1971 s.5(5), (6).
(8)	1988 Sch. 4 Pt. I para. 5.
159	1971 s.6.
160	1971 s.7; 1988 Sch. 4 Pt. I para. 6.
161	1971 s.8.
162	1971 s.9; 1994 Sch. 3 Pt. I para. 5.
163(1)	1971 s.10(1).
(2)	1971 s.10(2).
(3)	1971 s.10(3); 1988 Sch. 4 Pt. I para. 8(b).
(4)	1971 s.10(5).
(5)	1971 s.10(6); 1988 Sch. 5.
(6)	1971 s.10(7); 1979 Sch. 6 Pt. III.
(7)	1971 s.10(8).
164	1971 s.11.
165	1971 s.12; 1988 Sch. 4 Pt. I para. 9.
166(1)	1971 s.13(1); Supreme Court Act 1981 (c.54) Sch. 5.
(2), (3)	1971 s.13(2), (2A); 1988 Sch. 4 Pt. I para. 10.
(4)	1971 s.13(3).
167	1971 s.14; 1988 Sch. 4 Pt. I para. 11.
168	1971 s.15(2); 1979 Sch. 5 para. 6(2); 1994 Sch. 3 Pt. II para. 7.
169	1971 s.16.
170	1971 s.20; 1988 Sch. 4 Pt. II para. 8.
171(1)	1994 ss.5(1), 10(3).
(2), (3)	1994 s.5(3), (4).
172	1974 s.1(1), (2); 1988 Sch. 4 Pt. II para. 15; 1994 s.5(1), (4).
173(1)	1974 s.2(1), (10).
(2) to (6)	1974 s.2(2) to (6).
(7)	1974 s.2(7); 1988 Sch. 4 Pt. II para. 16.
(8) to (10)	1974 s.2(8), (9); 1982 CJ s.38(9); Companies Consolidation (Consequential Provisions) Act 1985 (c.9) Sch. 2.
174(1) to (4)	1974 s.3(1) to (4).
(5)	1974 s.3(5); 1979 Sch. 6 Pt. IV.
(6)	1974 s.3(6); 1979 Sch. 6 Pt. VI para. 18.
175(1) to (7)	1974 s.4(1) to (7); 1988 Sch. 4 Pt. II para. 17(2).
(8) to (10)	1974 s.4(8), (9), (9A); 1988 Sch. 4 Pt. II para. 17(3).

Provision	Derivation
176	1974 s.4A; 1988 Sch. 4 Pt. II para. 17(5).
177	1974 s.6; Supreme Court Act 1981 (c.54) Sch. 5.
178	1974 s.7(1), (2); 1988 Sch. 4 Pt. II para. 20(a).
179(1)	1974 s.8(1); 1994 s.7(1).
(2)	1974 s.8(4).
180	1974 s.8A; 1988 Sch. 4 Pt. II para. 22.
181(1), (2)	1974 s.1(3) to (6); 1988 Sch. 4 Pt. II para. 15.
(3)	1971 s.20(3); 1988 Sch. 4 Pt. I para. 14.
182(1)	1994 ss.5(1), 10(3).
(2), (3)	1994 s.5(3), (4).
183	1979 ss.14(1), (2), (4) to (7), 15(2).
184	1979 s.16(2), (3), (5), (6).
185(1), (2)	1979 s.17.
(3)	1979 Sch. 5 para. 3.
(4)	1979 s.35(2).
186	1979 s.18; 1993 Sch. 4 para. 6(1).
187(1)	1911 MC s.1(1).
(2)	1911 MC s.1(1) proviso (a).
(3)	1911 MC s.9(4).
(4)	1911 MC s.1(1) proviso (b)
(5)	1911 MC s.1(1) proviso (c).
(6), (7)	1911 MC s.1(2).
188(1)	1911 MC s.2.
(2)	1911 MC s.9(4).
(3)	1911 MC s.2 proviso.
(4)	1911 MC s.1(2).
189(1)	1911 MC s.3(1).
(2)	1911 MC s.9(4).
(3)	1911 MC s.3(1) proviso.
(4)	1911 MC s.3(2).
190(1) to (4)	1911 MC s.8.
(5), (6)	1911 MC s.8 proviso.
191(1), (2)	Merchant Shipping (Liability of Shipowners and others) 1900 (c.32) s.2(1).
(3)	Ibid. s.3.
(4)	1979 Sch. 5 para. 1(1).
(5)	1979 Sch. 5 para. 1(2).
(6)	1979 Sch. 5 para. 1(3).
(7)	1900 (c.32) s.2(1).
(8)	1900 (c.32) s.2(6).
(9)	Ibid. s.2(4), (5).
192(1)	Crown Proceedings Act 1947 (c.44) ss.5,6,7,30(1); 1979 Sch. 5 para. 3.
(2)	Ibid. s.38(2).
(3)	Crown Proceedings Order 1981 (SI 1981/233) art. 30(1).
193(1)	1894 s.634(1).
(2)	1894 s.634(1); Ports Act 1991 (c.52) s.31(3).
(3)	1894 s.668.
(4)	1894 s.634(1); Ports Act 1991 (c.52) s.34(3).
(5)	1894 s.634(1)(a), (b).
194	1894 s.635.
195(1)	1894 s.634(1).
(2)	1894 s.634(2).
196	1894 s.634A; 1988 s.41.
197(1)	1894 s.638.
(2), (3)	Ports Act 1991 (c.52) s.31(4), (5).
(4)	1894 s.642; 1993 Sch. 4 para. 39.
(5)	1894 s.639(1).
(6)	1894 s.639(1A); 1993 Sch. 4 para. 38.
(7)	1894 s.639(2).

Provision	Derivation
198	1894 s.652.
199(1)	1894 s.653(1).
(2)	1894 s.653(2).
(3)	1894 s.653(3); Ports Act 1991 (c.52) s.31(6).
(4)	1894 s.653(5).
200	1894 s.636.
201	Ports Act 1991 (c.52) s.31(1), (2), (7).
202	Ports Act 1991 (c.52) s.32.
203	Ports Act 1991 (c.52) ss.33(1), 34(2).
204(1)	1894 s.654(1).
(2)	Ports Act 1991 (c.52) ss.33(3), 34(2).
205(1), (2)	1894 s.643; 1993 Sch. 4 para. 40.
(3)	Merchant Shipping (Mercantile Marine Fund) Act 1898 (c.44) s.5(1).
(4)	1894 s.643.
(5)	Merchant Shipping (Mercantile Marine Fund) Act 1898 (c.44) s.5(2); 1979 s.36(2).
(6)	1894 s.647; 1993 Sch. 4 para. 42.
(7) to (9)	1894 s.648(2), (3); 1993 Sch. 4 para. 43.
206	1894 s.643A; 1993 Sch. 4 para 41.
207(1)	1894 s.649(1).
(2)	1894 ss.649(1), 681(2).
(3)	1894 s.649(1A); 1993 Sch. 4 para. 44.
(4)	1894 s.649(2).
208	1894 s.650; 1993 Sch. 4 para. 45.
209	1894 s.651; 1993 Sch. 4 para. 46.
210(1)	Harbours Act 1964 (c.40) s.29(2), (3).
(2)	1964 (c.40) s.29(2).
(3), (4)	1894 s.655(2).
(5)	1964 (c.40) s.30(2); 1993 Sch. 4 para. 55.
(6)	1964 (c.40) s.30(3).
(7)	1964 (c.40) s.30(4).
(8)	1964 (c.40) s.35.
(9), (10)	1894 s.656.
(11)	1993 Sch. 4 para. 47.
211(1)	Merchant Shipping (Mercantile Marine Fund) Act 1894 (c.44) s.1(1); 1988 Sch. 5.
(2)(a)	1894 s.658; 1988 Sch. 5.
(b)	1898 ibid. s.2A(1); 1988 s.43.
(c)	1898 ibid. s.2B; 1988 s.43.
(d)	1898 ibid. s.2(3), (7), Sch. 3.
(e)	Drafting.
(3)(a)	1898 ibid. s.1(2); 1988 Sch. 5.
(b)	1898 ibid. s.2A(2); 1988 s.43.
(c)	Drafting.
(4), (5)	1894 s.679; 1993 Sch. 4 para. 53.
212	1894 s.659; Merchant Shipping (Amendment) Act 1920 (c.2) s.1; 1988 Sch. 5.
213	1894 s.660.
214	1898 s.1A(1); Superannuation Act 1972 (c.11) s.17(1).
215	1894 s.662; 1988 s.42.
216	1894 s.662A; 1988 s.42.
217	1894 s.662B; 1988 s.42.
218	1894 s.664; 1993, Sch. 4 para. 49.
219(1), (2)	1894 s.666(1), (1A); 1993, Sch. 4 para. 50.
(3)	1894 s.666(2); 1979 s.43(1), Sch. 6 Pt. III.
220(1), (2)	1894 s.667(1).
(3)	1894 s.667(2).
(4)	1894 s.667(3); 1979 Sch. 6 Pt. VIII para. 9.
(5), (6), (7)	1894 ss.667(4), 681(2); 1993 Sch. 4 para. 51.

Provision	Derivation
220(8)	1894 s.667(4A); 1993 Sch. 4 para. 51.
221(1), (2)	1894 s.731; 1988 Sch. 5.
(3)	Ports Act 1991 (c.52) s.36(2)(c).
(4), (5)	1894 s.721(b), (c).
222	1894 s.732.
223(1)	1894 s.742.
(2)	1894 s.638; 1993 Sch. 4 para. 37.
(3), (4)	1979 ss.34(3), 49(3).
224	1994 s.1.
225	1894 s.551.
226(1), (2)	1894 s.552(1), (2).
(3), (4)	1894 s.552(3), (4); 1993 Sch. 4 para. 30; 1994 Sch. 2 para. 1(3).
(5)	Drafting.
(6)	Drafting.
227	1894 s.553.
228(1) to (3)	1894 s.555(1); 1993 Sch. 4 para. 30.
(4)	1894 s.555(2).
(5)	1894 s.555(2A); 1994 Sch. 2 para. 1(4).
(6)	1894 s.555(2).
(7)	1894 s.555(3).
229(1)	1894 s.556; 1993 Sch. 4 para. 30.
(2)	1894 s.556; 1994 Sch. 2 para. 1(5).
(3)	1894 s.556.
(4)	Drafting.
230(1), (2)	Crown Proceedings Act 1947 (c.44) s.8; 1994 Sch. 2 para. 3.
(3) to (5)	1894 s.557; Defence (Transfer of Functions) Act 1964 (c.15) ss.1(2), 3(2).
(6)	Drafting.
(7)	Crown Proceedings Act 1947 s.38(2).
(8)	Crown Proceedings Order 1981 (SI 1981/233) art. 30(1).
231(1)	1894 ss.511, 512, 513, 515.
(2)	1894 s.516(1); 1993 Sch. 4 para. 21.
(3), (4)	1894 s.516(2).
(5)	1894 s.511(1).
232	1894 ss.511, 680(1)(b).
233	1894 ss.512, 680(1)(b); 1993 Sch. 4 para. 2(5).
234(1) to (4)	1894 s.513(1).
(5), (6)	1894 s.513(2).
(7)	1894 s.513(3); 1982 CJ s.38(8).
235(1)	1894 s.515; Public Order Act 1986 (c.64) s.10(1).
(2), (3)	1894 s.515, first paragraph.
(4)	1894 s.515, second paragraph; Local Government (Scotland) Act 1973 (c.65) Sch. 27 Pt. II para. 24; 1993 Sch. 4 para. 20.
(5)	1894 s.515, third paragraph; Transfer of Functions (Criminal Injuries to Vessels) (Northern Ireland) Order 1973, SR&O (NI) 1973/56 art. 3(1).
236(1) to (3)	1894 ss.518, 681(2); 1906 s.72, 1979 Sch. 6 Pt. III; 1993 Sch. 4 para. 22.
(4)	1894 s.518(2); 1993 Sch. 4 para. 22(e).
237	1894 s.519; 1979 Sch. 6 Pt. VI.
238	1894 s.520; 1993 Sch. 4 para. 23.
239(1)	1894 s. 521(1).
(2), (3)	1894 s.521(2); Consular Conventions Act 1949 (c.29) s.5(2).
240	1894 s.522; 1993 Sch. 4 para. 24.
241	1894 s.523.
242	1894 s.524; 1993 Sch. 4 para. 25.
243	1894 s.525; 1898 s.1(1)(a).
244	1894 s.527.
245	1894 s.535; Criminal Justice Act 1948 (c.58) s.1; 1993 Sch. 4 para. 2(5).
246(1), (2)	1894 s.536(1).

Provision	Derivation
246(3)	1894 s.536(2).
(4)	1894 s.536(1).
(5)	1894 s.536(1), (2); 1979 Sch. 6 Pt. II.
247	1894 s.537; 1993 Sch. 4 para. 28.
248	1894 s.566; 1993 Sch. 4 para. 31.
249	1894 s.567(1) to (3); 1993 Sch. 4 para. 32.
250	1894 s.568.
251	1894 s.569(2).
252(1), (2)	1894 s.530.
(3)	1894 s.532.
(4)	1894 s.530(c).
(5)	1894 s.530, proviso (1).
(6), (7), (8)	1894 s.530, proviso (2).
(9)	1894 s.532.
(10)	1894 s.534.
253(1)	1894 s.531(1).
(2) to (4)	1894 s.531(2) to (4); 1988 Sch. 5.
254	1894 s.533.
255(1)	1894 ss.510, 742.
(2)	Sea Fisheries Act 1968 (c.77) s.17.
(3)	1894 s.570.
256(1)	1894 ss.728; 1971 POP s.18(1)(a), (b); 1993 Sch. 4 paras. 17(a), final limb, 56.
(2), (3), (4)	1894 ss.724(1); 1906 s.75(1).
(5)	1894 s.724(2); 1906 s.75(4).
(6), (7)	1984 s.7(1), (2).
(8)	1971 POP s.18(2); 1993 Sch. 4 para. 17(a).
(9)	1894 s.724(1); 1979 s.28(5); 1993 Sch. 4 para. 56(c).
257	1894 s.723; 1979 Sch. 6 Pts. I, VI; 1993 Sch. 4 para. 6(1).
258(1), (2)	1970 s.76(1); 1979 s.37(5).
(3)	1970 s.76(2).
(4)	1970 s.76(3); S.I. 1989/102 reg. 1(3)(b).
(5)	1970 s.76(4); 1979 Sch. 6 Pt. IV.
259(1)	1979 s.27(1); 1971 POP s.18(3); 1984 s.7(3).
(2)	1979 s.27(1); 1971 POP s.18(3); 1993 Sch. 4 para. 57.
(3)	1971 POP s.18(5).
(4)	1971 POP s.18(3)(b); 1979 s.28(7)(c).
(5)	1971 POP s.30(3); 1993 Sch. 4 para. 17(a), (d).
(6)	1971 POP s.18(6); 1993 Sch. 4 para. 17(b).
(7)	1971 POP s.18(7); 1979 s.27(2).
(8) to (12)	1979 s.27(3) to (7).
260	1979 s.28(1) to (4).
261	1984 ss.1, 11, Sch. 1.
262	1984 s.2; 1988 Sch. 5.
263	1984 s.3.
264	1984 s.4; Courts and Legal Services Act 1990 (c.41) Sch. 10 para. 55.
265	1984 s.5.
266	1984 s.6.
267	1988 s.33.
268(1), (2)	1970 ss.56(1), (1A); 1988 Sch. 6.
(3)	1970 s.56(2); Magistrates' Courts Act 1980 (c.43) Sch. 7 para. 90.
(4), (5)	1970 s.56(3), (4).
(6)	1970 s.59; 1979 s.43(1) Sch. 6 Pt. II.
(7)	1970 s.60.
(8), (9), (10)	1970 s.56(5), (6), (6A); 1988 s.48, Sch. 5.
(11)	1970 s.56(7); Magistrates' Courts Act 1980 (c.43) Sch. 7 para 90; Magistrates' Courts (Northern Ireland) Order 1981 (SI 1981/1675, Sch. 6 Pt. I para. 18).
269(1) to (4)	1970 s.57.
(5)	1970 s.60.

Provision	Derivation
270	1970 s.58; 1988 Sch. 6.
271(1)	1970 s.61(1).
(2), (3)	1970 s.61(1A), (1B); 1979 s.29(1).
(4)	1970 s.61(2); 1979 s.28(7)(b).
(5)	1970 s.61(3); 1979 s.29(2).
(6)	1970 s.61(4); Fatal Accidents and Sudden Deaths Inquiry (Scotland) Act 1976 (c.14) Sch. 1 para. 1.
272	1970 s.95(1), Sch. 2, Pt. I para. 5; 1979 s.28(7)(b).
273	1979 s.30(2).
274(1), (2)	1894 s.683(1); 1971 POP s.19(4); 1979 s.42(1), 1993 Sch. 4 para. 59.
(3), (4)	1979 s.42(2), (3).
(5)	1979 s.42(5).
275	1894 s.683(2); 1993 Sch. 4 para. 59.
276	1894 s.703(b); 1979 Sch. 6 Pt. VII para. 14.
277	1894 s.687A; 1993 Sch. 4 para. 63.
278	1894 s.687B; 1993 Sch. 4 para. 63.
279	1894 s.684; 1971 POP s.19(5); 1993 Sch. 4 para. 60.
280	1894 s.685.
281	1894 s.686(1); 1993 Sch. 4 para. 61.
282	1894 s.687; 1993 Sch. 4 para. 62.
283(1), (2)	1894 s.689(1); 1970 Sch. 3 para. 2.
(3) to (5)	1894 s.689(2); 1993 Sch. 4 para. 64.
(6)	1894 s.689(3).
(7)	1894 s.689(4); 1979 Sch. 6 Pt. IV.
(8)	1894 s.689(5).
(9)	1894 s.689(2), (4).
284(1) to (3)	1894 s.692(1); 1979, Sch. 6 Pt. VII para. 10.
(4), (5)	1894 s.692(2); 1979, Sch. 6 Pt. VII para. 11.
(6), (7)	1894 s.692(3), (4).
(8)	1894 s.692(5); 1988 Sch. 6.
285	1894 s.693; 1993 Sch. 4 para. 65.
286(1), (2)	1894 s.691(1), (2).
(3)	1894 s.691(3).
(4)	1894 s.691(1).
(5)	1894 s.691(4) part.
287	1894 s.256(1); 1970 s.75.
288(1)	1894 s.695(1) 1970 Sch. 3 para. 3.
(2), (3)	1894 s.695(2); 1970 Sch. 3 para. 3; Merchant Shipping Act (Safety Conventions) 1949 (c.43) s.33(2), Sch. 2; 1993 Sch. 4 para. 67(a).
(4)	1894 s.695(2)(b); 1949 ibid, 1993 Sch. 4 para. 67(a).
(5)	1894 ss.695(3), 680(1)(a); 1993 Sch. 4 para. 67(b).
(6), (7)	1894 s.695(4), (5); 1993 Sch. 4 para. 72.
(8)	1894 s.695(3A); 1993 Sch. 4 para. 67(c).
289	1970 s.75A; 1988 Sch. 5.
290(1), (2)	1894 s.697.
(3)	1894 s.697(2); 1993 Sch. 4 para. 69.
291	1894 s.696; 1993 s.9(3), Sch. 4 para. 68.
292(1)	1894 s.713.
(2)	1894 s.717.
293	1994 s.8.
294	1906 s.78.
295(1) to (3)	1970 s.80(1).
(4)	1970 s.80(2).
(5)	1993 s.1(3).
296	1970 s.81.
297(1)	1970 s.82(1).
(2)	1970 s.82(1A); Judicial Pensions and Retirement Act 1993 (c.8) Sch. 6 para. 59.
(3)	1970 s.82(2).

Provision	*Derivation*
297(4), (5)	1970 s.83.
298	1894 s.256(1).
299(1), (2)	1894 s.714.
(3)	1894 s.715.
(4) to (6)	1894 s.726; 1979 Sch. 6 Pt. II.
300(1) to (6)	1894 s.720.
(7)	1894 s.722(2)(b); 1979 Sch. 6 Pt. I.
(8)	1894 s.722(1); 1993 Sch. 4 para. 73.
301	1906 s.79.
302(1), (3)	1993 Sch. 4 para. 79.
(2)	Merchant Shipping (Safety Convention) Act 1949 (c.43) s.33(2), Sch.2 (1894 s.83).
303	1894 s.718; 1898 s.1(1)(b).
304(1)(a)	1894 s.662B; 1970 s.98(1); 1970 FV s.10; 1971 POP s.28(1); 1979 ss.23(1)(f), 51(1); 1984 s.10; 1988 s.55(1).
(b)	1894 s.677(1)(b), (d); 1988 Sch. 5.
(c)	Merchant Shipping (Safety Conventions) Act 1949 (c.43) s.25.
(d)	1894 s.677(1)(g).
(e)	1894 s.677(1)(f).
(f)	1894 s.677(1)(h).
(g)	1894 s.677(1)(l); Merchant Shipping Repeal Act 1854 (c.120) s.7.
(h)	1894 s.677(1)(o); 1988 Sch. 5.
(2)	1949 ibid; Merchant Shipping (Safety Convention) Act 1977 (c.24) s.1(2).
305(1)(a)	1894 s.676(1)(a); 1988 Sch. 5.
(b)	1894 s.676(1)(h).
(c)	1894 s.676(1)(l); 1988 Sch. 5.
(2)	1894 s.676(2).
306	1894 s.739(1); Merchant Shipping (Load Lines) Act 1967 (c.27) s.30(3); 1970 s.99; 1970 FV s.7; 1971 POP s.27; 1974 s.17(2); 1979 ss.23(4), 41(2), 49; Safety at Sea Act 1986 (c.23) s.9(2), (3); 1988 s.53(1); 1993 Sch. 4 para. 1(2).
307	1993 Sch. 4 para. 5.
308	1894 s.738(2), s.741; 1906 s.80; 1993 Sch. 2 para. 3.
309	1988 s.47; 1993 Sch. 2 para. 15(3).
310	1970 Sch. 3 para. 13; 1971 s.17; 1971 POP s.31; 1979 s.48; 1984 s.9; 1988 s.49.
311	1979 s.41(1).
312(1)	1894 s.710; 1993 Sch. 4 para. 76.
(2)	1911 MC s.5.
313	1894 s.742; 1993 Sch. 4 para. 2(1), (2).
314(1) to (3)	—
(4)	1993 s.10(6).
315(2) to (5)	1993 s.9(3), Sch. 4 para. 4(1) to (5).
316	—
Sch. 1	1993 s.6(1), Sch. 1.
Sch. 2	1974 s.17(3), Sch. 5; 1979 Sch. 6 Pt. VI para. 20.
Sch. 3	Merchant Shipping (Load Lines) Act 1967 (c.27).
paras. 1, 2	ss. 1, 2.
3	s.3; 1979 Sch. 6 Pt. V, 1993 Sch. 4 para. 12(6).
4	s.4; 1979 Sch. 6 Pt. V, Pt. VII para. 7.
5	s.5; 1979 Sch. 6 Pt. IV.
6 to 9	ss.6 to 9.
10	s.10; 1970 Sch. 3 para. 12.
11	s.11(1).
12	s.12.
13	s.13; 1979 Sch. 6 Pt. V, 1993 Sch. 4 para. 12(6).
14 to 16	ss.14 to 16.
17	s.17; 1993 Sch. 4 para. 12(6).

Provision	Derivation
paras. 18 to 22	ss.18 to 22.
23	s.23; 1995 SC reg. 1(7).
24	s.24; 1979 Sch. 6 Pt. IV.
25	s.27(1).
26	s.27(3); 1894 s.280(1), (2).
27	s.27(3); 1894 s.282.
28	s.27(5).
29	s.31.
30	s.30(1).
31	s.32(1) to (7).
Sch. 4	
Chap. III	
152	1971 s.19.
153	1971 s.1.
154	1971 s.1A; 1994 Sch. 3 Pt. I para. 1.
155	1971 s.2.
155A	1971 s.2A; 1994 Sch. 3 Pt. I para. 2.
156	1971 s.3.
156A	1971 s.3A; 1994 Sch. 3 Pt. I para. 3.
157	1971 s.4; 1979 s.38(1)(a), (b); 1984 s.12(2).
158	1971 s.5; 1979 s.38(2); 1979 Sch. 5 para. 6(1).
159	1971 s.6.
160	1971 s.7; 1979 Sch. 5 para. 6(1).
161	1971 s.8.
162	1971 s.9; 1994 Sch. 3 Pt. I para. 4.
163	1971 s.10; 1979 s.38(3).
164	1971 s.11; 1979 s.38(3).
165	1971 s.12.
166	1971 s.13; Supreme Court Act 1981 (c.54) Sch. 5.
167	1971 s.14; 1979 s.38(3).
168	1971 s.15(2); 1979 Sch. 5 para. 6(2); 1994 Sch. 3 Pt. I para. 5.
169	1971 s.16.
170	1971 s.20; 1994 Sch. 3 Pt. I para. 6.
Chap. IV	
172	1974 s.1(1), (2).
173	1974 s.2; 1979 s.38(4)(b); 1982 CJ s.38(9), Companies Consolidation (Consequential Provisions) Act 1985 (c.9) Sch. 2, Companies Consolidation (Consequential Provisions) Order 1986 (SI 1986/1035 (N.I. 9)), Sch. 1 Pt. II.
174	1974 s.3; 1979 Sch. 6 Pt. IV; 1979 Sch. 6 Pt. VI para. 18.
175	1974 s.4(4) to (9).
176	1974 s.4(10) to (13); 1979 s.38(4)(b), (c).
176A	1974 s.5; 1979 s.38(4)(d), (e).
177	1974 s.6; 1979 s.38(4)(b); Supreme Court Act 1981 (c.54) Sch. 5.
178	1974 s.7.
179	1974 s.8; 1994 s.7(1).
181	1974 ss.1(3), (4), (5), 23(2).
Sch. 5	
Part I	1974 Sch. 1; 1988 Sch. 4 Pt. II para. 24; 1994 s.5(2)(a).
Part II	1974 Sch. 1; 1979 s.38(4)(g).
Sch. 6	
Part I	1979 Sch. 3 Pts. I, III.
Part II	1979 Sch. 3 Pts. II, III.
Sch. 7	
Part I	1979 Sch. 4, Pt. I.
Part II	1979 s.49(5), Sch. 4, Pt. II; 1995 SC reg. 1(8).
Sch. 8	1894 s.668; 1974 s.18, 1979 s.33(2), Local Government (Scotland) Act 1994 (c.39) Sch. 13 para. 7.
Sch. 9	Ports Act 1991 (c.52) s.32.

Provision	Derivation
Sch. 10	Harbours Act 1964 (c.40) s.35.
Sch. 11	
Part I	1994 Sch. 1, Pt. I.
Part II	1994 Sch. 1, Pt. II.
Sch. 12	—
Sch. 13	—
Sch. 14	
para. 2	1993 s.9(4).
3	Merchant Shipping Act 1948 (c.44) s.5.
4	1979 s.37(2), (3).
7	1993 Sch. 5; saving.
8	1979 s.38(6).
9	1894 s.669; 1979 s.36(3).
10	1894 s.571.
11	1894 s.745(1)(f).

TABLE OF DESTINATIONS

TABLE OF DESTINATIONS

MERCHANT SHIPPING (LIABILITY OF SHIP OWNER AND OTHERS) ACT 1900
(C. 32)

1900	1995
s.2(1)........	s.191(7)
(4)........	191(9)
(5)........	191(9)
(6)........	191(8)

MERCHANT SHIPPING ACT 1906
(C. 48)

1906	1995
s.72	s.236(1)–(3)
75(1).......	256(2)–(4)
(4).......	256(5)
76	107
78	294
79	301
80	308

MARITIME CONVENTIONS ACT 1911
(C. 57)

1911	1995
s.1(1)........	s.187(1), (6), (7)
(1) proviso (a)	187(2)
(b)	187(4)
(c)	187(5)
s.1 (2)	187(6), (7), 188(4)
2	188(1)
proviso......	188(3)
3(1)........	189(1)
(1) proviso .	189(3)
(2)........	189(4)
4(2)........	92(3)
5	312(2)
8	190(1)–(4)
proviso	190(5), (6)
9(4)........	187(3), 188(2), 189(2)

FISHING VESSELS (SAFETY PROVISIONS) ACT 1970
(C. 27)

1970	1995
s.1	s.121
2(1)........	122
3(1)........	123
(2)........	123
(3)........	123
(4).......	124(1)–(6)
(5).......	124(7)
4(1)........	125
(2)........	125
(3)........	125
5	126
7	306
9(1)........	123
10	304(1)(a)

MERCHANT SHIPPING ACT 1970
(c. 36)

TABLE OF DESTINATIONS

MERCHANT SHIPPING (OIL POLLUTION) ACT 1971
(c. 59)

1971	1995	1971	1995	1971	1995
s.1	s.153	s.6	s.159	s.12	s.165
	Sched. 4, Chap.		Sched. 4, Chap.		Sched. 4, Chap.
	III, para. 153		III, para. 159		III, para. 165
1A	154	7	160	13(1)	166(1)
	Sched. 4, Chap.		Sched. 4, Chap.	(2)	166(2), (3)
	III, para. 154		III, para. 160	(2A)	166(2), (3)
2	155	8	161	(3)	166(4)
	Sched. 4, Chap.		Sched. 4, Chap.	13	Sched. 4, Chap.
	III, para. 155		III, para. 161		III, para. 166
3	156	9	162	s.14	167
	Sched. 4, Chap.		Sched. 4, Chap.		Sched. 4, Chap.
	III, para. 156		III, para. 162		III, para. 167
4	157	10(1)	163(1)	15(2)	168
	Sched. 4, Chap.	(2)	163(2)		Sched. 4, Chap.
	III, para. 157	(3)	163(3)		III, para. 168
5(1)	158(1), (2)	(5)	163(4)	16	169
(2)	158(1), (2)	(6)	163(5)		Sched. 4, Chap.
(2A)	158(3)	(7)	163(6)		III, para. 169
(3)	158(4)	(8)	163(7)	17	310
(4)	158(5)	10	Sched. 4, Chap.	19	152
(5)	158(6)		III, para. 163		Sched. 4, Chap.
(6)	158(6)	11	164		III, para. 152
5	Sched. 4, Chap.		Sched. 4, Chap.	20	170
	III, para. 158		III, para. 164	(3)	181(3)
					Sched. 4, Chap.
					III, para. 170

PREVENTION OF OIL POLLUTION ACT 1971
(c. 60)

1971	1995	1971	1995	1971	1995
s.2(2A)	s.131(1), (2)	s.17(1)	s.142(1)–(4)	s.20	s.146
(2B)	131(1), (2)	(2)	142(1)–(4)	21	147
(3)	131(5), (6)	(3)	142(1)–(4)	23	148
(4)	131(3)	(4)	142(1)–(4)	24	149
5	132	(5)	142(6)–(8)	26	150
6(1) except		(6)	142(9)	27	306
(b), (c)	133	18(1)(a)	156(1)	(4)	142(5)
7	134	(b)	156(1)	28(1)	304(1)(a)
8(2)	151(1), (2)	(3)	259(1), (2)	29(1)	131(4), 136,
10	135	19(1)	143(1)–(3)		142(10), 151(1),
11 except (c)	136	(2)	143(4)		(2)
12	137	(3)	143(5)	(2)	151(3)–(5)
13	138	(4)	274(1), (2)	(3)	151(3)–(5)
14	139	(4A)	143(6), (7)	(4)	151(3)–(5)
15(1)	140(1)	(5)	279	(5)	151(6)
(2)	140(2)	19A	144(1)–(7),	30(4)	143(2), (3)
(3)	140(3)		(10)	31	310
16	141	(8)	145	32	151(7)
		(9)	145		

MERCHANT SHIPPING ACT 1974
(c. 43)

1974	1995	1974	1995	1974	1995
s.1(1)	s.172	s.1(4)	Sched. 4,	s.2(2)	s.173(1)
(2)	172		Chap. IV, 179	(3)	173(1)
(3)	181(1), (2)	(5)	Sched. 4,	(4)	173(1)
(4)	181(1), (2)		Chap. IV, 179	(5)	173(1)
(5)	181(1), (2)	1(1)	Sched. 4,	(6)	173(1)
(6)	181(1), (2)		Chap. IV, 172	(7)	173(1)
1(1)	Sched. 4,	(2)	Sched. 4,	(8)	173(1)
	Chap. IV, 179		Chap. IV, 172	(9)	173(1)
(3)	Sched. 4,	2(1)	173(1)	(10)	173(1)
	Chap. IV, 179			(2)	173(2)–(6)

MERCHANT SHIPPING ACT 1979
(c. 39)

CRIMINAL JUSTICE ACT 1982
(C. 48)

MERCHANT SHIPPING ACT 1984
(C. 5)

TABLE OF DESTINATIONS

TABLE OF DESTINATIONS

INDEX

SHIPPING AND TRADING INTERESTS (PROTECTION) ACT 1995*

(1995 c. 22)

An Act to consolidate certain enactments for the protection of shipping and trading interests. [19th July 1995]

PARLIAMENTARY DEBATES
Hansard, H.L. Vol. 351, cols. 1250, 1266, 1535; Vol. 352, cols. 293–301, 760; Vol. 489, cols. 642, 1292; Vol. 490, cols. 540, 744; Vol. 491, cols. 437, 925; Vol. 496, col. 327; Vol. 563, col. 583; Vol. 564, col 1543; Vol. 565, col. 410; H.C. Standing Committee E, January 17, 22, 24, 1974; Vol. 126, col. 506; Vol. 130, col. 1164; Standing Committee C, April 4, 1988; Vol. 263, col. 468; Joint Committee on Consolidation Bills, April 20, 1995.

INTRODUCTION AND GENERAL NOTE
The Shipping and Trading Interests (Protection) Act 1995 is a pure consolidation measure. It derives from the work of the Law Commissions and was enacted at the same time as the more significant Merchant Shipping Act 1995, which consolidated all the merchant shipping legislation dating back to 1894. During the debate on the Shipping and Trading Interests (Protection) Bill in the Joint Committee on Consolidation Bills, it was stated that its provisions would not be given new statutory form in the Merchant Shipping Act 1995. Instead, they were to be considered separately from that Act for perceived drafting and technical reasons. Part of the rationale for enacting the Merchant Shipping Act 1995 was that it would "tidy-up" a large number of disparate Acts and it is perhaps unfortunate that the drafters could not have integrated the two Acts. The Merchant Shipping Act 1995 does include some provisions designed to encourage the British fleet (see for example s.17), but it is probably fair to say that the Shipping and Trading Interests (Protection) Act 1995 is rooted more in the law relating to international commercial competition and its relationship to shipping is largely incidental.
The Shipping and Trading Interests (Protection) Act 1995 can be analysed in two main parts. The first part encompasses ss.14 and 15 of the Merchant Shipping Act 1974, as subsequently amended by s.38 of the Merchant Shipping Act 1988. The provisions concerned the retaliatory measures open to the Secretary of State to be taken against foreign discriminatory action against U.K. shipping or trading interests. The second part of the Act is dedicated to what were formerly s.39 and s.40 of the Merchant Shipping Act 1988. These provisions empowered the Secretary of State to prohibit shipping services not permanently based in Britain from costal shipping in U.K. waters.
Although the two main parts of the Shipping and Trading Interests (Protection) Act 1995

---

* Annotations by Nicholas Gaskell, Barrister, Professor of Maritime and Commercial Law, Institute of Maritime Law, University of Southampton and Anthony Marsh LLB, University of Southampton.

concern different matters there is a single, underlying theme to the whole Act. In the lengthy Parliamentary debates which preceded both the 1974 and 1988 Merchant Shipping Acts it was continually asserted by the relevant Secretaries of State that they considered the provisions before them as a necessary response and deterrent to unfair competition abroad. It is also understood that the provisions are unlikely ever to be used: they exist so that the deterrent has some force.

1. Protection of shipping and trading interests from foreign action.

Sections 14 and 15 of the Merchant Shipping Act 1974 (now ss.1–4 of the Shipping and Trading Interests (Protection) Act 1995) were originally considered as a response to the increase in unilateral regulation which was adversely affecting British shipping. Those countries which were highlighted in 1974 as being particularly culpable were the USA, Venezuela, New Zealand, Sri Lanka, Canada and Australia. It was felt that their measures, such as fixing freight rates, were undermining the proper workings of the Liner Conference organisations at the expense of British shipping. The concept of "flag discrimination" was a particular concern of the 1960's and 1970's, although such practices existed in the mercantilist doctrines exemplified by the Navigation Acts which existed from 1660 until 1850 and restricted commerce by sea to English ships (see L. Harper, *The English Navigation Laws* (1939)). The repeal of such measures in 1850 (17 & 18 Vict., c.5) heralded a free trade policy which has largely continued. In the Rochdale Report (1970) the Government's policy towards shipping was confirmed as being one of freedom from regulation, except in matters of safety (see F. Cadwallader, "Free Shipping—a British Preference", in Transport Law Association, conference papers from *Flag Preference: Discrimination or Peaceful Co-Existence*", June 27 1990). The Shipping Contracts and Commercial Documents Act 1964 had already been passed to give protection against demands from foreign courts for production and discovery of documents. This legislation was aimed at protecting British shipping companies, particularly those operating in Liner Conferences, from the extra-territorial effects of U.S. anti-trust legislation. The 1964 Act was itself repealed by, and subsumed in, the Protection of Trading Interests Act 1980. That Act was designed to give wider protection generally, to U.K. trading interests from principally U.S. laws (see P. Roth, "*Protection of Trading Interests Act 1980*", Current Law Statutes Annotated (1980)).

The 1970s saw a growth in the movement for many less developed countries to participate in world shipping. The United Nations Conference on Trade and Development (UNCTAD) produced, in 1974, the Convention on a Code of Conduct for Liner Conferences. "Liner Conferences" are groups of shipowners who come together to provide a regular cargo service in which there are uniform freight rates and shared sailings (see for example A. Herman, *Shipping Conferences* (1983)). The UNCTAD Liner Code sought to share the right to carry cargo between countries, thereby affecting the so-called "cross-traders" (including many British shipping companies). Moves towards an international solution to flag preference can also be seen in the EEC's attitude towards the Code, as illustrated in its 1979 compromise Council Regulation ((EEC) No. 954/7), which encouraged EEC member states to ratify the Code, but subject to a number of reservations to ensure that there was no discrimination between the shipping lines of EEC member states and certain other OECD countries (see Herman *op. cit.*, pp.188–192). The U.K. passed the Merchant Shipping (Liner Conferences) Act 1982 in order to implement the Code's provisions, subject to the EEC reservations. The Code entered force on October 6, 1983 and the Act was brought into force on March 14, 1985 (see the Merchant Shipping (Liner Conferences) Act 1982 (Commencement) Order 1985 (S.I. 1985 No. 182), the Merchant Shipping (Liner Conferences) (Mandatory Provisions) Regulations 1985 (S.I. 1985 No. 406), the Merchant Shipping (Liner Conferences) (Conditions for Recognition) Regulations 1985 (S.I. 1985 No. 405).

However, in 1974, the existence of various flag preference provisions in many states highlighted the precarious and complex relationship between shippers, the U.K. government, foreign governments and the Liner Conference system. With diplomatic routes to solving such problems of flag discrimination having been viewed as fairly ineffective, the enactment of ss.14 and 15 of the Merchant Shipping Act 1974 was described as "regrettable but necessary" to protect British shipping interests against unfair flag discrimination (see C. MacDonald, "*Merchant Shipping Act 1974*", Current Law Statutes Annoted (1974)).

The powers contained in ss.1–4 are extensive (see Cadwallader, *op. cit.*). Indeed, the Secretary of State may take retaliatory action against a foreign country not formally recognised as a state merely to protect an informal agreement with a third state. Orders can be made to obtain information, regulate the provision of shipping services, refuse admittance of ships to U.K. ports, approve or disapprove agreements relating to the carriage of goods by sea and levy taxes and duties on any person (including therefore shipowners *or* cargo owners). It is an offence intentionally to contravene or to fail to comply with any part of an Order made under s.1 or s.2. Moreover, it is also an offence to disclose to unauthorised persons information obtained under this part of the Act and to supply false information to the Secretary of State.

2. Protection of coastal shipping services.

The Merchant Shipping Act 1988 ss.39–40 (now ss.5–6 of the Shipping and Trading Interests (Protection) Act 1995) heralded the assumption of powers not provided for on the statute books since the 19th century (see generally, N. Gaskell, "*Merchant Shipping Act 1988*", Current Law Statutes Annotated 1988). The rationale for this legislation was to try to open up the coastal waters of other, mainly European, countries. Despite the Secretary of State's assertion in 1988 that the "primary objective on cabotage remains liberalisation throughout the E.C.", there is still perceived to be a need for such legislation. Considering the supposed "threshold" of the open E.C. market in 1992, it is significant to note the continued existence of similar "protectionist" legislation in other E.C. states. In 1992, the E.C. Council produced Regulation 3577/92 applying the principle of freedom to provide services to maritime transport within Member States (cabotage). This Regulation suspends operation of the liberalisation until December 31, 1996 to take account of the interests of Mediterranean states, such as Greece, which want to protect their island trade. The European Commission is obliged under the Regulation to undertake an in-depth examination of the economic and social impact of the liberalisation of island cabotage and must submit a report by January 1, 1997. In the meantime, it should be noted that the powers open to the Secretary of State are not restricted to operators from E.C. countries alone.

The possible restrictions on coastal shipping services can cover all shipping activities. These include the carriage of goods and passengers and the provison of offshore services. It is an offence to engage in services covered by s.5 unless there is the necessary British connection (s.6). Masters and owners can commit the offence, as can demise charterers and ship managers in some circumstances.

COMMENCEMENT

The Act received Royal Assent on July 19, 1995 and will come into force on January 1, 1996.

Protection of shipping etc interests from foreign action

Power to regulate provision of shipping services, etc in event of foreign action

1.—(1) The Secretary of State may exercise the powers conferred by this section if he is satisfied that—

(a) a foreign government, or

(b) persons purporting to exercise governing authority over any territory outside the United Kingdom, or

(c) any agency or authority of a foreign government or of such persons,

have adopted, or propose to adopt, measures or practices concerning or affecting any shipping services which—

(i) are damaging or threaten to damage the shipping or trading interests of the United Kingdom, or

(ii) are damaging or threaten to damage the shipping or trading interests of another State,

and, in the latter case, the Secretary of State is satisfied that action under this section would be in fulfilment of the obligations of the United Kingdom to that other State or would be appropriate in view of any arrangements made between Her Majesty's Government and the government of that other State.

(2) The Secretary of State may by order make provision for requiring persons in the United Kingdom carrying on any trade or business to provide the Secretary of State with all such information as he may require for the purpose of enabling him—

(a) to determine what further action to take under this section, and

(b) to ensure compliance with any orders or directions made or given under this section.

(3) The Secretary of State may by order (a "protective order") provide for—

(a) regulating the provision of any shipping services and the rates, fares or other amounts which may or must be charged for providing those services;

(b) regulating—

      (i) the admission and departure of ships to and from United Kingdom ports,

      (ii) the nature of the shipping services they may be used to provide (whether by reference to the cargoes or passengers they may carry or otherwise), and

      (iii) the loading or unloading of cargoes, the embarkation or disembarkation of passengers, or the doing of other things in connection with the provision of any shipping services;

  (c) regulating the making and implementation of agreements (including charter-parties) whose subject matter relates directly or indirectly to the provision of any shipping services, and requiring such agreements to be subject to the Secretary of State's approval in such cases as he may specify;

  (d) imposing charges in respect of ships which enter United Kingdom ports in connection with the provision of any shipping services;

  (e) imposing, in pursuance of any Community obligation, such tax or duty payable by such persons and in such circumstances as the Secretary of State may specify;

and in this subsection "regulating", except in relation to the rates, fares or other amounts which may or must be charged as mentioned in paragraph (a) above, includes imposing a prohibition.

    (4) In a case falling within subsection (1)(i) above, a protective order shall specify the measures or practices which in the opinion of the Secretary of State are damaging or threaten to damage shipping or trading interests of the United Kingdom.

    (5) An order under this section may authorise the Secretary of State to give directions to any person for the purposes of the order.

    (6) Any order or direction made or given under this section—

  (a) may be either general or special, and may be subject to such conditions or exceptions as the Secretary of State specifies (including conditions and exceptions operating by reference to the giving or withholding of his approval for any course of action);

  (b) may be in terms that require compliance either generally or only in specified cases.

    (7) The power to make an order under this section shall be exercisable by statutory instrument.

    (8) Before the Secretary of State makes an order under this section he shall consult such representatives of the shipping or trading interests of the United Kingdom, and such other persons, as appear to him appropriate.

    (9) In this section—

  (a) "foreign government" means the government of any State other than the United Kingdom;

  (b) references to an agency or authority of a foreign government or of such persons as are mentioned in subsection (1)(b) above include references to any undertaking appearing to the Secretary of State to be, or to be acting on behalf of, an undertaking which is in effect owned or controlled (directly or indirectly) by a State other than, or by a territory outside, the United Kingdom;

  (c) "port" includes an offshore terminal, and references to entering or leaving a port include references to using or ceasing to use an offshore terminal;

  (d) "shipping services" means services provided by means of ships, and includes the carriage of goods or passengers by sea, cable laying, dredging, and services provided by offshore support vessels; and

  (e) references to ships are to ships of any registration.

    (10) A recital in an order under this section that the persons who have adopted, or propose to adopt, the measures or practices in question are—

  (a) a foreign government, or

   (b) such persons as are mentioned in subsection (1)(b) above, or
   (c) an agency or authority of a foreign government or of such persons,
shall be conclusive.

DEFINITIONS
   "agency or authority of a foreign government": s.1(9).
   "community obligation": European Communities Act 1972, Sched. 1.
   "foreign government": subs. (9).
   "port": subs. (9).
   "protective order": subs. (3) and s.9(2).
   "regulating": subs. (3).
   "Secretary of State": the Interpretation Act 1978, Sched. 1.
   "shipping services": subs. (9).
   "ships": subs. (9) and the Merchant Shipping Act 1995, s.313.
   "United Kingdom": the Interpretation Act 1978, Sched. 1.

GENERAL NOTE
   [Derivation: Merchant Shipping Act 1974, s.14, as amended by the Merchant Shipping Act 1988, s.38.]
   As previously noted, this section provides the basis on which retaliatory measures can be taken by the Secretary of State against foreign shipping in order to protect the U.K.'s own shipping and trading interests or those of another state. The original powers under the Merchant Shipping Act 1974, s.14 were significantly extended by the provisions of s.38 of the Merchant Shipping Act 1988. These changes were made in order to implement the recommendations of the 1984 Consultative Document, Council Regulation (EEC) No. 4058/86 and arguably, Art. 6(3) of Council Regulation (EEC) No. 4055/86. The consolidated provisions could cover a particularly wide range of circumstances where the Secretary of State may consider it in the national interest to intervene, although it was always stressed that the powers were to be used as a last resort where normal commercial and diplomatic approaches have failed to solve a particular problem (see MacDonald, *op. cit.*). For the background to the changes introduced in 1988 see the 1987 White paper, *Merchant Shipping: Legislative Proposals* (Cm. 239), as explained in Gaskell (*op. cit.*).

Subs. (1)
   This subsection provides the criteria which the Secretary of State must use when deciding to exercise his discretion to take retaliatory action. Neither the proposed nor adopted action in the first instance has to be attributed to a country formally recognised as a state. Moreover, the action proposed or adopted does not necessarily have to be directed towards shipping or trading interests of the U.K. Thus, the Secretary of State may well be satisfied to intervene where a foreign power discriminates against the interests of a third country. The original s.14(1)(b) of the Merchant Shipping Act 1974 referred specifically to an "international obligation" of H.M. Government towards third states, but that was amended by the Merchant Shipping Act 1988 so as to cover the fulfilment of an informal agreement with that third country. Subsection (1)(c) was added by the Merchant Shipping Act 1988 so as to cover bodies such as the state trading authorities of states with centrally planned economies. The decision by the Secretary of State that a government or other person intends to take action, shall, under subs. (10), be conclusive that such persons have adopted, or proposed adopting, the damaging measures in question. It is to be noted that measures or practices adopted or proposed by foreign shipowners, foreign traders or harbour authorities, are not covered (except in so far as they are in obedience to the actions of the foreign government or agency: see Cadwallader, *op. cit.*).

Subs. (2)
   This subsection empowers the Secretary of State to demand information from any person in reach of the U.K. courts. This provision was considered to be of importance in the debates leading up to the Merchant Shipping Act 1974. It was suggested that an intelligent application of the measures could not be achieved without having the power to gain commercial information from the perceived secretive operations of the Liner Conference system. The power has been described as an "information order" (see Cadwallader, *op. cit.*), although that is not the specific wording of the Act. It has been suggested that the power to make an information order can only be exercised when an order has been made under subs. (3) (see Cadwallader, *op. cit.*), although the better view is probably that the orders under subss. (2) and (3) are separate.

Subs. (3)

This subsection provides the range of measures that the Secretary of State may consider appropriate in the circumstances. The phrase "protective order" is new to the 1995 Act but represents nothing more than a statutory classification of the Secretray of State's powers under the subsection (*cf.* Cadwallader, *op. cit.*). Section 14(3) of the Merchant Shipping Act 1974 enabled the powers to be directed towards the carriage of goods and the admission and departure of ships from ports. Note that the definition of "port" in subs. (9) covers offshore terminals. In respect of the carriage of goods, the Secretary of State would appear to be able to regulate the form and manner of carriage, as well as the nature and type of cargoes which could be carried (see Cadwallader, *op. cit.*). The power to "regulate the making and implementation of agreements" in subs. (3)(c) has been described as the most "lethal of the incidents which may be regulated" (see Cadwallader, *op. cit.*). The powers could be exercised in respect of charter-parties, which are expressly mentioned, but also bills of lading in a general ship and to contracts of sale, for example c.i.f. or f.o.b. contracts. At the very least, these sale contracts could relate "indirectly" to shipping services. In a DoT Consultative Document, *Proposals for Legislation on Ship Registration and other matters* (March 1984), it was recommended that the powers needed to be extended so as to cover the carriage of passengers. During the passage of the Merchant Shipping Act 1988, a further extension was added so that "any shipping services" were to be covered. This could cover cable laying operations, dredging services, offshore support services and salvage: see subs. (9)(d). Subsection (9)(d) is so worded that the shipping services must be provided by ships, thus excluding the work of marine insurers, classification societies and surveyors. The ships in question do not have to be registered in the U.K. Subsection 3(e) was added by the Merchant Shipping Act 1988 so that retaliatory taxes and duties could be imposed, in addition to the "charges" mentioned in para. (d). These taxes and duties could be levied on any person specified, not only shipowners and operators, so that cargo owners would be covered.

Subs. (4)

A "protective order" has to set out the specific measures or practices which made the order necessary.

Subss. (5)–(6)

The Secretary of State is empowered to direct an order at a particular individual as well as a corporation. The power to issue directions is commonly given in other statutes (see N. Gaskell, "*Aviation and Maritime Security Act 1990*" in Current Law Statutes Annotated 1990). Thus, an order could be given to a manager forbidding him from supplying information to a foreign court and it could be general or relate to quite specific matters, e.g. as to whether a particular undertaking should be given to a foreign regulatory authority.

Subs. (8)

This subsection imposes on the Secretary of State an obligation to consult, *e.g.* with the General Council of British Shipping, as the commercial interests may consider that any action in a particular case would be detrimental to British trading interests overall.

Special provision for orders under section 1 imposing taxation etc

2.—(1) This section applies in relation to protective orders made under subsection (3)(d) or (e) of section 1 (such an order being referred to below as a "charging order").

(2) No charging order shall authorise the Secretary of State to give directions to any person for the purpose of recovering any charge, tax or duty.

(3) Without prejudice to subsection (6) of that section, a charging order—

(a) may apply to ships of any description specified in the order, and may apply in particular to ships registered in a specified country, or to ships carrying goods or cargoes of a specified description or providing any other specified shipping services;

(b) may contain such provisions as appear to the Secretary of State expedient to enable the Commissioners of Customs and Excise to collect any charge, tax or duty imposed by the order; and

(c) may apply, subject to any modifications or exceptions specified in the order, any of the enactments for the time being in force relating to duties (whether of customs or excise) chargeable on goods imported into the United Kingdom.

(4) Any charge, tax or duty imposed by a charging order—

(a) may be a fixed amount, or an amount depending on the tonnage of the ship;

(b) shall be payable to the Secretary of State.

(5) A charging order shall not be made except with the consent of the Treasury.

(6) Any sum received by the Secretary of State shall be paid into the Consolidated Fund.

DEFINITIONS

"charging order": s.2(3)–(5).
"Secretary of State": the Interpretation Act 1978, Sched. 1.
"ships": s.1(9) and the Merchant Shipping Act 1995, s.313.

GENERAL NOTE

[Derivation: Merchant Shipping Act 1974, s.14, as amended by the Merchant Shipping Act 1988, s.38.]

This section puts in the main body of the Act provisions which were originally contained in Sched. 4 of the Merchant Shipping Act 1974, as amended. This section also introduces a new phrase to the consolidated legislation. When the Secretary of State wishes to make a protective order of a fiscal rather than a regulatory nature, this "charging order" must receive the approval of the Treasury.

Enforcement of section 1

3.—(1) An order made under section 1 with the consent of the Commissioners of Customs and Excise may provide for the enforcement and execution of any order or direction under that section by officers of customs and excise.

(2) Officers of customs and excise acting under any provision made under subsection (1) above shall have power to enter any premises or ship.

(3) Section 65 of the Customs and Excise Management Act 1979 (power to refuse or cancel clearance of ship or aircraft) shall apply as if sections 1 and 2 and this section were contained in that Act.

(4) If a person discloses any information which has been furnished to or obtained by him under section 1 or 2, or in connection with the execution of section 1 or 2, he shall, unless the disclosure is made—

(a) with the consent of the person from whom the information was obtained, or

(b) in connection with the execution of section 1 or 2, or

(c) for the purposes of any legal proceedings arising out of this section or of any report of such proceedings, or

(d) in pursuance of a Community obligation to a Community institution, be liable, on summary conviction, to a fine not exceeding level 5 on the standard scale.

(5) A person who—

(a) refuses or intentionally neglects to furnish any information which he is required to furnish under section 1 or 2, or

(b) in furnishing any such information makes any statement which he knows to be false in a material particular, or recklessly makes any statement which is false in a material particular,

shall be liable, on summary conviction, to a fine not exceeding level 4 on the standard scale in the case of an offence under paragraph (a) above and not exceeding level 5 on the standard scale in the case of an offence under paragraph (b) above.

(6) A person who intentionally contravenes or fails to comply with any provision of an order or direction made or given pursuant to section 1 or 2, other than a provision requiring him to give any information, shall be liable—

(a) on summary conviction, to a fine of not more than £5,000;

(b) on conviction on indictment, to a fine;

and where the order or direction requires anything to be done, or not to be done, by, to or on a ship, and the requirement is not complied with, the owner and master of the ship are each to be regarded as intentionally failing to comply, without prejudice to the liability of anyone else.

(7) A person shall not be guilty of an offence against any provision contained in or having effect under section 1 or 2 by reason only of something done by that person wholly outside the territory of the United Kingdom unless that person is a Commonwealth citizen under the British Nationality Act 1981 or a company incorporated under the law of any part of the United Kingdom.

DEFINITIONS

"Commissioner of Customs and Excise": the Customs and Excise Management Act 1979, s.1.

"community obligation": the European Communities Act 1972, Sched. 1.

"master": the Merchant Shipping Act 1995, s.313.

"ship": s.1(9) and the Merchant Shipping Act 1995, s.313.

"standard scale": the Criminal Justice Act 1982, s.37.

"commonwealth citizen": the British Nationality Act 1981, Sched. 3.

GENERAL NOTE

[Derivation: Merchant Shipping Act 1974, s.14, as amended by the Merchant Shipping Act 1988, s.38.]

See the General Note to s.1 and s.2, above. This section again puts in the main body of the Act provisions which were originally contained in Schedule 4 of the Merchant Shipping Act 1974, as amended.

Non-compliance with or contravention of the provisions in a protective order creates the possibility of four separate offences. Subs. (6) first makes it an offence for any party intentionally to fail to comply with or to contravene any part of an order made under ss.1 and 2. Secondly, where the order concerns a ship, the owner and master are necessarily considered as having committed an offence where any non-compliance or contravention of the order is evident. Neither "owner" nor "master" are defined in the Act. However, s.7 applies Part XII of the Merchant Shipping Act 1995 for the purposes of the Shipping and Trading Interests (Protection) Act 1995. Part XII of the Merchant Shipping Act 1995 sets out rules and procedures for the bringing of legal proceedings, including prosecutions. Accordingly, it would appear to be legitimate to refer to the definition of "master" in s.313 of the Merchant Shipping Act 1995 in interpreting s.3(6) of the Shipping and Trading Interests (Protection) Act 1995. That definition includes persons having control of the ship, for example an officer of the watch. "Owner" is not separately defined in the Merchant Shipping Act 1988, but presumably it would include a registered shipowner (although note that the scheme of Part I of the Merchant Shipping Act 1995 does not make registration compulsory). However, s.277 of the Merchant Shipping Act 1995 contains provisions dealing with offences committed by a corporate body. In particular, directors and senior officers of a corporation can be guilty of offences where they have been involved in the commission of an offence by the corporation. This provision would also apply to offences under the Shipping and Trading Interests (Protection) Act 1995, as it is clear that this provision merely replicates s.51 of the Merchant Shipping Act 1988 (which itself applied to the Merchant Shipping Act 1974 provisions which were amended by the Merchant Shipping Act 1988).

Under subs. (5) it would also be an offence either to refuse to supply or, recklessly to supply false, information which is demanded by the Secretary of State under his powers in s.1(2). Subsection (4) creates the fourth offence possible under s.3. This is concerned with the unauthorised disclosure of information. Subject to the four exceptions provided for in this subsection this disclosure is punishable by a fine. The imposition of such an offence was seen as necessary to ensuring the sensitive and confidential nature of the commercial information sought by the Secretary of State.

Parliamentary control of orders under section 1

4.—(1) Subject to subsection (3) below, no protective order shall be made unless—

(a) a draft has been approved by resolution of each House of Parliament, or

(b) it is declared in the order that it appears to the Secretary of State that by reason of urgency it is necessary to make the order without a draft having been so approved.

(2) Subject to subsection (3) below, a protective order made without a draft having been approved by resolution of each House of Parliament shall cease to have effect at the expiration of a period of 28 days beginning with the date on which it was made unless before the expiration of that period it has been approved by resolution of each House of Parliament, but without prejudice to anything previously done, or to the making of a new order.

In reckoning for the purposes of this subsection any period of 28 days, no account shall be taken of any period during which Parliament is dissolved or prorogued or during which both Houses are adjourned for more than four days.

(3) Subsections (1) and (2) above do not apply to a protective order which is made for the purpose only of implementing any Community obligation.

(4) An order under section 1 which is not a protective order shall be subject to annulment in pursuance of a resolution of either House of Parliament.

(5) If an order under that section recites that it is made as mentioned in subsection (3) above, or that it is not a protective order, the recital shall be conclusive.

DEFINITIONS
   "community obligation": see the European Communities Act 1972, Sched. 1.

GENERAL NOTE
   [Derivation: Merchant Shipping Act 1974, s.15, as amended by the Merchant Shipping Act 1988, s.38.]
   Orders made under s.1 and s.2 of this Act are made by statutory instrument, see s.1(7), above and are therefore subject to strict parliamentary control. Subsection (3) was added to the Merchant Shipping Act 1974 by the Merchant Shipping Act 1988, as orders to implement Community obligations are already subject to Parliamentary Scrutiny Committee procedures.

Protection of coastal shipping services

Power to prohibit provision of coastal shipping services which are not British-based

5.—(1) The Secretary of State may by order provide for the provision of shipping services to which this section applies to be prohibited except where such services are provided from one or more permanent places of business maintained in the British Islands.

(2) This section applies to the following shipping services—

(a) the carriage of goods or passengers by sea—
   (i) between ports in the United Kingdom, or
   (ii) between a port in the United Kingdom and an offshore installation in United Kingdom controlled waters, or
   (iii) between offshore installations in United Kingdom controlled waters;

(b) the carriage of passengers by sea on voyages or excursions beginning and ending at the same port in the United Kingdom, other than voyages or excursions which involve calling at any port or ports outside the British Islands (whether passengers disembark there or not); and

(c) shipping services (other than the carriage of goods or passengers by sea) which are—

     (i) provided by means of ships operating out of ports in the United Kingdom (whether so provided within United Kingdom controlled waters or not), or

     (ii) provided within United Kingdom controlled waters by means of ships operating out of ports outside the United Kingdom.

(3) An order under this section may make provision—

(a) with respect to the circumstances in which shipping services are to be regarded for the purposes of the order as being provided from one or more permanent places of business maintained in the British Islands;

(b) authorising the Secretary of State to issue licences sanctioning the provision of shipping services to which this section applies, notwithstanding that they are not provided as mentioned in paragraph (a) above, in cases where he is satisfied that there is no-one willing and able to provide the services in question as mentioned in that paragraph;

(c) requiring the payment, in connection with applications for such licences, of fees determined with the approval of the Treasury;

(d) exempting any prescribed class or description of shipping services from any prohibition imposed by virtue of subsection (1) above;

(e) authorising the Secretary of State, or a person appointed by him for the purpose, to serve notices requiring the production or furnishing of documents or information appearing to the Secretary of State or any such person to be necessary to enable him to determine such matters as may be prescribed;

(f) with respect to the manner of service of notices in pursuance of paragraph (e) above.

(4) An order under this section may—

(a) make different provision for different circumstances;

(b) make such transitional, incidental or supplementary provision as appears to the Secretary of State to be necessary or expedient.

(5) The provisions of an order under this section shall not discriminate between shipping services provided by different persons on the basis of the place of registration of the ships by means of which the services are provided.

(6) Section 256(1) of the Merchant Shipping Act 1995 (appointment of inspectors) shall have effect in relation to—

(a) any order under this section, or

(b) any licence issued by virtue of subsection (3)(b) above,

as it has effect in relation to any such regulations or licence as is referred to in subsection (1)(b) and (9) of that section; but section 259 of that Act shall have effect in relation to any inspector appointed by virtue of this subsection with the omission of paragraphs (f) to (h) of subsection (2) of that section.

(7) The power to make an order under this section shall be exercisable by statutory instrument, but no such order shall be made unless a draft of it has been laid before and approved by resolution of each House of Parliament.

(8) In this section—

    "offshore installation" has the same meaning as in the Mineral Workings (Offshore Installations) Act 1971;

    "prescribed" means prescribed by an order under this section;

    "shipping services" means—

      (a) the carriage of goods or passengers by sea;

      (b) services provided by offshore support vessels, and

      (c) such other services provided by means of ships as the Secretary of State may specify in an order under this section;

    "United Kingdom controlled waters" means waters within the seaward limits of the territorial sea of the United Kingdom and waters in any area designated under section 1(7) of the Continental Shelf Act 1964.

DEFINITIONS
"British Islands": Interpretation Act 1978, Sched. 1.
"offshore installation": s.5(8).
"port": s.1(9).
"prescribed": subs. (8).
"Secretary of State": the Interpretation Act 1978, Sched. 1.
"shipping services": subs. (8).
"territorial sea": the Territorial Waters Act 1987.
"United Kingdom": the Interpretation Act 1978, Sched. 1.
"United Kingdom controlled waters": subs. (8).

GENERAL NOTE
[Derivation: Merchant Shipping Act 1988, s.39.]
The purpose of this section is to give the Secretary of State enabling powers to restrict cabotage where foreign operators are concerned. Cabotage concerns coastal shipping from one port
to another, where there is no intermediate port of call in another country. Many states have
traditionally imposed restrictions on cabotage in order to protect their own shipping interests.
There are presently no restrictions on foreign flag operators wishing to enter the U.K. coastal
trade, although this was not always the case. As noted above (see the Introduction and General
Note to the Act), discriminatory provisions in the Navigation Acts were repealed in the 19th
century. It is interesting to note that the repeal of the Navigation Acts (12 & 13 Vict. c.29)
reserved the right to retaliate if other countries discriminated and that the coasting trade was not
opened until 1854 (17 & 18 Vict. c.5). Unlike s.1 and s.2 of the Shipping and Trading Interests
(Protection) Act 1995, s.5 provides for a measure of protectionism that, theoretically, could be
established without reference to the overt discriminatory actions of a foreign state. The provision was introduced at the behest of the General Council of British Shipping so that the U.K.
could demonstrate the will to take prompt action as a bargaining counter against the protectionism of other states, particularly within the E.C. At the time of the enactment of the Merchant
Shipping Act 1988, the U.K. was trying to force the E.C. to take action to liberalise the cabotage
trade within the E.C., particularly in the Mediterranean. In particular, Greece had long reserved
its inter-island trade to its own ships, thus preventing access by passing British cruise liners.

Subs. (1)
This subsection gives the power to make orders to prohibit shipping services not permanently
based in Britain. It is noticeable that the provision does not require that the ship is British registered. But if the other countries at which the provision is aimed have similar registration laws it
will not be possible for their companies to be based in Britain and still maintain the foreign flag.
So, in reality, British registration must be an important factor.

Subs. (2)
This subsection sets out the shipping services to which the section applies (see also the definition in subs. (8)). These would include ferry services for passengers and cargo to the Isle of
Man as well as to the carriage of people and materials to offshore oil rigs in U.K. waters. It may
be noted that this section uses the expression "United Kingdom controlled waters", as defined in
s.5(8). The original provision, s.39 of the Merchant Shipping Act 1988 simply referred to "U.K.
waters". The expression in s.5(8) is the more accurate, because it distinguishes between territorial waters as defined in the Territorial Sea Act 1987 and waters over the continental shelf,
over which the U.K. may exercise control under the Continental Shelf Act 1964.

Subs. (3)
This subsection specifies the type of order which can be made. Para. (a) should remove the
worries about foreign companies evading the controls by having a brass plate presence, as it
gives the Secretary of State power to define when the services are to be regarded as being provided from a permanent U.K. base. There are provisions for licensing services and for providing
exemptions (although see subs. (5) below). Where there are doubts as to the true nature of the
service concerned it may be possible for the Secretary of State to require the production of
documentation (subs. (3)(e)).

Subs. (5)
There must be no discrimination between ships registered under different flags, *e.g.* in the
issuing of licences or exemptions.

Subs. (6)
This subsection enables inspectors to be appointed under the Merchant Shipping Act 1995,
s.256 (which replaces s.728 of the Merchant Shipping Act 1894 and s.27 of the Merchant Ship-

ping Act 1988). It follows that they should have the powers given by s.259 of that same Act, with the exception of those under subs. 2, paras. (f) to (h) of s.259, which relate to the taking of samples, articles and substances from vessels. The Merchant Shipping Act 1995, s.260, creates offences for obstructing inspectors, failing to comply with requirements or signing false declarations.

Enforcement of section 5

6.—(1) Where—

(a) any ship is used in the course of the provision of any shipping services to which section 5 applies, or

(b) anything is done on board a ship with a view to its being used to provide such services,

and the provision of those services is prohibited by virtue of subsection (1) of that section and is not sanctioned by any licence issued by virtue of subsection (3)(b) of that section, then (subject to subsections (6) and (7) below), the master and the owner of the ship shall each be guilty of an offence.

(2) Where the ship—

(a) is chartered by demise, or

(b) is managed, either wholly or in part, by a person other than the owner under the terms of a management agreement,

the reference in subsection (1) above to the owner of the ship shall be construed as including a reference—

(i) to the charterer under the charter by demise, or

(ii) to any such manager as is referred to in paragraph (b) above, or

(iii) (if the ship is both chartered and managed as mentioned above) to both the charterer and any such manager.

(3) Any person who—

(a) in connection with an application for such a licence as is mentioned in section 5(3)(b), or

(b) in purported compliance with the requirements of any notice served on him by virtue of section 5(3)(e),

knowingly or recklessly furnishes information which is false in a material particular shall be guilty of an offence.

(4) Any person who—

(a) without reasonable excuse (the proof of which lies on him) fails to comply with the requirements of any such notice, or

(b) intentionally alters, suppresses, conceals or destroys a document which he has been required to produce in pursuance of section 5(3)(e),

shall be guilty of an offence.

(5) Any person guilty of an offence under this section shall be liable—

(a) on summary conviction, to a fine not exceeding £50,000;

(b) on conviction on indictment, to imprisonment for a term not exceeding two years or a fine, or both.

(6) It shall be a defence in proceedings under subsection (1) above against the master of a ship to prove—

(a) that he did not know and had no reason to suspect that, in the circumstances of the case, the provision of the shipping services referred to in paragraph (a) or (as the case may be) paragraph (b) of that subsection was prohibited by virtue of section 5(1), or

(b) that he had reasonable grounds for believing that the provision of those services was sanctioned by a licence issued by virtue of section 5(3)(b).

(7) It shall be a defence in proceedings brought under subsection (1) above against a person other than the master of a ship to prove that, under the terms of one or more charter-parties or management agreements entered into by the defendant, the right to determine the purpose for which the ship in question was being used at the time of the alleged offence was wholly vested in some other person or persons party thereto (whether or not any such other

person or persons had entered into a further charter-party or management agreement providing for that right to be vested in some other person).

(8) Subsections (1), (3) and (4) above apply to offences falling within those subsections wherever committed.

(9) In this section "management agreement", in relation to a ship, means any agreement (other than a charter-party or a contract of employment) under which the ship is managed, either wholly or in part, by a person other than the owner (whether on behalf of the owner or on behalf of some other person).

DEFINITIONS
"licence": s.6(3).
"management agreement": subs. (9).
"owner": sub. (2).
"ship": s.1(9) and the Merchant Shipping Act 1995, s.313.
"shipping services": s.1(9).

GENERAL NOTE
[Derivation: Merchant Shipping Act 1988, s.40.] See the note to s.5, above.

This section makes it an offence for a master and owner to use the ship for any of the services prohibited under s.5. For the treatment of "owner" and "master", see the General Note to s.3, above. Subsection (1)(b) may also penalise certain preparatory acts on board vessels, *e.g.* the loading, as opposed to the carriage, of goods. Under subs. (2), a bareboat charterer or professional firm of ship managers could also be guilty. The wording of the subsection does not make it clear whether a sub-demise charterer can commit an offence. The reference in para. (i) to "the charterer" would appear to indicate that only one demise charterer could be guilty. On ordinary shipping principles, a sub-demise charterer would have effective control and possession of the vessel and would appoint the master. In such circumstances, it is submitted that this demise charterer is the one referred to in the subsection. See also the remarks on subs. (7) below. Where the vessel is subject to a demise charter or is also being managed by a professional firm of ship managers, these persons could be guilty along with the shipowner. As in s.3, above, neither "owner" nor "master" are defined in this section. However, s.7 applies Part XII of the Merchant Shipping Act 1995 for the purposes of the Shipping and Trading Interests (Protection) Act 1995 and the Merchant Shipping Act 1995 contains a definition of "master" (see the General Note to s.3, above). There are also offences of supplying false information, failing to comply with a notice and suppressing, concealing or destroying a document (see subs. (3) and (4)).

Subs. (6) gives defences to masters who had no knowledge or reason to suspect a prohibition existed, or who believed a licence was in force. In subs. (7), there is a defence for those, such as owners or charterers, who may have had no contractual right to determine the use of the vessel. This subsection appears to have repeated an ambiguity, or gap in the legislation (from s.40 of the Merchant Shipping Act 1988), because a shipowner might arrange a voyage, or more particularly, a time charter under which "at the time of the alleged offence" the *charterer* had the right to decide which voyages were undertaken and which cargoes were carried. The shipowner might have been able to impose restrictions on trading at the time of *negotiating* the charter, but this would not appear to undermine its defence under subs. (7). The subsection does speak of the right to determine the purpose for which the ship was being used as being "*wholly* vested" in some other person. Under normal contractual arrangements, the shipowner which agrees a time or voyage charter does have some practical rights to determine voyages to be undertaken, as its master will be in possession of the ship and the master would not be bound to obey any order which was illegal. If a shipowner was given a notice that a certain service was to be prohibited then it would seem that the master ought to be instructed to disregard the instructions of the time or voyage charterer. It would then follow that such a shipowner would not have the defence under subs. (7). The wording of the subsection is more apt to describe the position where a demise charter is agreed. In those circumstances the rights are "wholly vested" in the demise charterer and the shipowner would have the defence. Moreover, subs. (2) does not create offences in respect of sub-charterers except, perhaps, if they are sub-demise charterers (see the General Note to s.6(2), above). Although coastal shipping may be less subject to the string of charters associated with bulk and liner shipping, there may be occasions where an intermediate disponent owner (*e.g.* a middle charterer in a string of time charters) has little or no knowledge of, or control over, the operations of the vessel. What s.6 is aiming at is to ensure that those who do have effective control are subject to the criminal sanction.

Supplementary

7.—(1) Part XII of the Merchant Shipping Act 1995 (which makes provision in relation to legal proceedings and related matters) shall apply for the purposes of this Act as it applies for the purposes of that Act.

(2) Proceedings for an offence under section 6 shall not be instituted—

(a) in England and Wales, except by or with the consent of the Attorney General or the Secretary of State; or

(b) in Northern Ireland, except by or with the consent of the Attorney General for Northern Ireland or the Secretary of State.

(3) Without prejudice to section 291 of the Merchant Shipping Act 1995 in its application to this Act, any document required or authorised by or under any enactment to be served for the purpose of the institution of, or otherwise in connection with, proceedings for an offence under section 6(1) shall, where it is to be served on a person who was, at the time of the alleged offence—

(a) the owner of the ship in question, or

(b) such a charterer by demise or manager of that ship as is mentioned in subsection (2) of that section,

be treated as duly served on that person if—

(i) sent to him by post at his last-known address (whether of his residence or of a place where he carries on business), or

(ii) left for him at that address,

or if the document is served on the master of the ship in question.

DEFINITIONS

"master": the Merchant Shipping Act 1995, s.313.
"Secretary of State": the Interpretation Act 1978, Sched. 1.
"ship": s.1(9) and the Merchant Shipping Act 1995, s.313.

GENERAL NOTE

Subsection (2) requires official consent for a prosecution. Subsection (3) provides for the service of documents. As in s.3, above, neither "owner" nor "master" are defined in this section. However, s.7 applies Part XII of the Merchant Shipping Act 1995 (effectively a uniform code for legal proceedings) for the purposes of the Shipping and Trading Interests (Protection) Act 1995 and the Merchant Shipping Act 1995 contains a definition of "master" (see the General Note to s.3, above).

Repeals

8. The enactments mentioned in the Schedule to this Act are hereby repealed to the extent specified in the third column of that Schedule.

Short title, interpretation, citation, commencement and extent

9.—(1) This Act may be cited as the Shipping and Trading Interests (Protection) Act 1995.

(2) In this Act "protective order" has the meaning given by section 1(3) and, subject to this Act, other expressions used in this Act and in the Merchant Shipping Act 1995 shall have the same meaning in this Act as in that Act.

(3) Any power to give directions conferred by this Act includes power to vary or revoke directions so given.

(4) This Act shall come into force on 1st January 1996.
(5) This Act extends to Northern Ireland.

DEFINITIONS
"protective order": subs. (2) and s.1(3).

Section 8   SCHEDULE

REPEALS

Chapter	Short title	Extent of repeal
1974 c. 43.	Merchant Shipping Act 1974.	Sections 14 and 15. Schedule 4.
1979 c. 39.	Merchant Shipping Act 1979.	Section 40(1)(b).
1988 c. 12.	Merchant Shipping Act 1988.	Sections 38, 39 and 40.

TABLE OF DERIVATIONS

Notes

1. This Table shows the derivations of the provisions of the Bill.
2. The following abbreviations are used in this Table:—

1974	=	Merchant Shipping Act 1974 (c. 43)
1979	=	Merchant Shipping Act 1979 (c. 39)
1982 CJ	=	Criminal Justice Act 1982 (c. 48)
1988	=	Merchant Shipping Act 1988 (c. 12)
1993	=	Merchant Shipping (Registration, etc) Act 1993 (c. 22)

Provision	Derivation
1(1)	1974 s.14(1); 1988 s.38(2).
(2)	1974 s.14(2).
(3)	1974 s.14(3); 1988 s.38(3).
(4)	1974 s.14(4); 1988 s.38(4).
(5)	1974 s.14(5).
(6), (7)	1974 s.14(6).
(8)	1974 s.14(7).
(9)	1974 s.14(11), Sch. 4 para. 4; 1988 s.38(6).
(10)	1974 s.14(11A); 1988 s.38(6).
2(1), (2)	1974 s.14(5) proviso; 1988 s.38(5).
(3)	1974 Sch. 4 para. 2(1), (5); 1988 s.38(8).
(4)	1974 Sch. 4 para. 2(2), (3).
(5)	1974 Sch. 4 para. 2(4).
(6)	1974 s.21.
3(1) to (3)	1974 Sch. 4 para. 1.
(4)	1974 s.14(8); 1979 ss.40(1)(b), 43(1) Sch. 6 Pt. IV; 1982 CJ s.46.
(5)	1974 s.14(9); 1979 s.43(3), Sch. 6 Pt. VI para. 19; 1982 CJ s.46; 1993 s.8 Sch. 4 para. 74(a).
(6)	1974 s.14(10); 1993 s.8 Sch. 4 para. 74(a).
(7)	1974 Sch. 4 para. 3; British Nationality Act 1981 (c. 61) s.51(1)(b).
4(1), (2)	1974 s.15(1), (2); 1988 s.38(7)(a).
(3)	1974 s.15(2A); 1988 s.38(7)(b).
(4)	1974 s.15(3).
(5)	1974 s.15(4); 1988 s.38(7)(c).
5	1988 s.39.
6(1) to (8)	1988 s.40(1) to (8).

Provision	Derivation
(9)	1988 s.40(12).
7(1)	1974 s.23(1); 1988 s.57(1).
(2), (3)	1988 s.40(10), (11).
8	—
9(1)	—
(2)	1974 s.23(1); 1988 s.57(1).
(3)	1974 s.23(3).
(4)	—
(5)	1974 s.24(5); 1988 s.58(5).

TABLE OF DESTINATIONS

TABLE OF DESTINATIONS

INDEX

References are to sections and Schedule

GOODS VEHICLES (LICENSING OF OPERATORS) ACT 1995*

(1995 c. 23)

ARRANGEMENT OF SECTIONS

---

*Annotations by Barry A. Prior, Partner, Wedlake Saint, Solicitors.

Supplementary provisions

An Act to consolidate Part V of the Transport Act 1968 and related provisions concerning the licensing of operators of certain goods vehicles.
[19th July 1995]

PARLIAMENTARY DEBATES
    Hansard, H.L. Vol. 564, cols. 297, 1543, Vol. 565, col. 410. H.C. Vol. 263, col. 467.

INTRODUCTION AND GENERAL NOTE

This is an Act to consolidate Pt. V of the Transport Act 1968 (c. 73) as amended by the Road Traffic Act 1974 (c. 50), the Transport Act 1982 (c. 49), the Road Traffic (Consequential Provisions) Act 1988 (c. 54) and the Deregulation and Contracting Out Act 1994 (c. 40) and the various Regulations which have been introduced most particularly since the Transport Act 1982. In particular, it incorporates the environmental requirements to which operators' licences were made subject in the Transport Act 1982 and the Goods Vehicles (Operators' Licences, Qualifications and Fees) Regulations 1984 (S.I. 1984 No. 176) and Chap. 3 of the Deregulation and Contracting Out Act 1994 and substitutes continuous licensing for the previous regime of five yearly licences.

In respect of licences in force before January 1, 1996, "old style licences", ss.5, 6, 11, 15–18, 26, 30–32 and 45 are subject to the provisions of the Schedule to the Goods Vehicles (Licensing of Operators) Act 1995 (Commencement and Transitional Provisions) Order 1995 (S.I. 1995 No. 2181 (c. 44)).

COMMENCEMENT

The commencement date of the Act will be January 1, 1996, except for s.50 and Sched. 5 (S.I. 1995, No. 2181).

ABBREVIATIONS
    1968 Act   : Transport Act 1968.
    1982 Act   : Transport Act 1982.
    1994 Act   : Deregulation and Contracting Out Act 1994.
    RTA 1960   : Road Traffic Act 1960.
    RT(CP)A 1988   : Road Traffic (Consequential Provisions) Act 1988.
    S.I. 1984 No. 176 : Goods Vehicle (Operators' Licences, Qualifications and Fees) Regulations 1984.
    S.I. 1995 No. 2181 : Goods Vehicles (Licensing of Operators) Act 1995 (Commencement and Transitional Provisions) Order 1995.

Functions of traffic commissioners

Functions of traffic commissioners

1.—(1) The traffic commissioner for any traffic area constituted for the purposes of the Public Passenger Vehicles Act 1981 shall exercise the functions conferred on him by this Act.

(2) In the exercise of his functions under this Act a traffic commissioner shall act under the general directions of the Secretary of State.

Definitions
"traffic area": Public Passenger Vehicles Act 1981, s.3(1).
"traffic commissioner": Public Passenger Vehicles Act 1981, s.3.

General Note
The 1968 Act designated the Chairman of the Traffic Commissioners for the relevant Traffic Area to be known as the Licensing Authority. Originally, the Public Passenger Vehicles Act 1981 (c. 14) provided for the appointment of three Traffic Commissioners for each Traffic Area, however the number was reduced to one. Section 1 of this Act abolishes the two separate titles and the person appointed by the Secretary of State will now bear the common title of Traffic Commissioner when dealing with operators' licences for both goods vehicles and public passenger vehicles.
See also s.3(4) of the Transport Act 1985 (c. 67).

Operators' licences

Obligation to hold operator's licence

2.—(1) Subject to subsection (2) and section 4, no person shall use a goods vehicle on a road for the carriage of goods—
(a) for hire or reward, or
(b) for or in connection with any trade or business carried on by him,
except under a licence issued under this Act; and in this Act such a licence is referred to as an "operator's licence".
(2) Subsection (1) does not apply to—
(a) the use of a small goods vehicle within the meaning given in Schedule 1;
(b) the use of a goods vehicle for international carriage by a haulier established in a member State other than the United Kingdom and not established in the United Kingdom;
(c) the use of a goods vehicle for international carriage by a haulier established in Northern Ireland and not established in Great Britain; or
(d) the use of a vehicle of any class specified in regulations.
(3) In subsection (2)(b) and (c) "established", "haulier" and "international carriage" have the same meaning as in Community Council Regulation (EEC) No. 881/92 dated 26 March 1992 concerning access to the market in the carriage of goods by road within the Community to or from the territory of a member State or passing across the territory of one or more member States.
(4) It is hereby declared that, for the purposes of this Act, the performance by a local or public authority of their functions constitutes the carrying on of a business.
(5) A person who uses a vehicle in contravention of this section is guilty of an offence and liable on summary conviction to a fine not exceeding level 4 on the standard scale.

Definitions
"carriage of goods": s.58(1).
"contravention": s.58(1).
"goods vehicle": s.58(1).
"operator's licence": subs. (1).
"road": s.58(1).
"small goods vehicle": Sched. 1, paras. 2–4.

General Note
This section derives from s.60 of the 1968 Act. The concept of "using the vehicle" on the road is dealt with in s.58(2) of this Act. It should be noted that the necessity to obtain an "operator's licence" applies to local and public authorities when carrying out their functions which shall be regarded as the carrying on of a business. The penalty for failing to obtain an operator's licence is set out in subs. (5).

An operator's licence is not required for a goods vehicle being used for international carriage by a haulier established in the member state as well as the U.K. or Northern Ireland provided that the operator is not also established in the U.K.: see Community Council Regulation (EEC) 881/92.

"Standard" and "restricted" licences

3.—(1) An operator's licence may be either a standard licence or a restricted licence.

(2) A standard licence is an operator's licence under which a goods vehicle may be used on a road for the carriage of goods—

(a) for hire or reward, or

(b) for or in connection with any trade or business carried on by the holder of the licence.

(3) A restricted licence is an operator's licence under which a goods vehicle may be used on a road for the carriage of goods for or in connection with any trade or business carried on by the holder of the licence, other than that of carrying goods for hire or reward.

(4) Notwithstanding subsections (2) and (3), a company may use a goods vehicle on a road for the carriage of goods for hire or reward under a restricted licence instead of a standard licence if (but only if) the goods concerned are the property of a company which is—

(a) a subsidiary of the first company,

(b) a holding company for the first company, or

(c) a subsidiary of a company which is a holding company both for that subsidiary and for the first company.

(5) A standard licence may authorise a goods vehicle to be used for the carriage of goods—

(a) on both national and international transport operations; or

(b) on national transport operations only.

(6) Except as provided in subsection (4) and subject to section 4, a person who uses a goods vehicle under a restricted licence for carrying goods for hire or reward is guilty of an offence and liable on summary conviction to a fine not exceeding £500.

(7) A person who uses a goods vehicle for carrying goods for hire or reward on international transport operations under a standard licence which covers the carriage of goods on national transport operations only is guilty of an offence and liable on summary conviction to a fine not exceeding £500.

DEFINITIONS
"company": Companies Act 1985, s.736.
"holding": Companies Act 1985, s.736.
"restricted licence": subs. (3).
"standard licence": subs. (2).
"subsidiary": Companies Act 1985, s.736.

GENERAL NOTE
This section derives from reg. 4 of S.I. 1984 No. 176 which implemented the provisions of the Community Council Directive 74/561/EEC. The section provides for the issue of two categories of operator's licence; one a "standard" licence for operators of vehicles carrying goods for hire and reward or in connection with a trade or business, and a "restricted" licence for operators of vehicles which are used for carriage of goods only in connection with the trade or business carried on by the holder and in which there is no hire and reward element. A standard licence may authorise the use of the vehicles for both national and international transport operations or for national operations only: subs. (5).

The penalty for using vehicles covered by a restricted licence for carriage of goods for hire and reward is set out in subs. (6).

The penalty for using goods vehicles for carrying goods on international transport operations under a standard licence is set out in subs. (7).

Temporary exemptions

4.—(1) A traffic commissioner may, for the purpose of—
(a) enabling an emergency to be dealt with, or
(b) enabling some other special need to be met,
by notice in writing grant to any person falling within subsection (2) a temporary exemption from any requirement to hold a standard licence which would otherwise be imposed on him by sections 2 and 3 in respect of any vehicle specified in the notice or any vehicle of a class so specified.

(2) A person falls within this subsection if he is engaged exclusively in national transport operations which have only a minor impact on the transport market because of the nature of the goods carried or the short distances over which goods are carried.

(3) A temporary exemption granted under subsection (1) permits the person to whom it is granted to use the specified vehicle or (as the case may be) any vehicle of the specified class for the carriage of goods for hire or reward for the purposes of transport operations of his such as are referred to in subsection (2) (and, accordingly, sections 2(1) and 3(6) shall not to that extent apply to that person's use of goods vehicles).

(4) A temporary exemption has effect until consultations with the European Commission for the purposes of Article 2(2) of the 1974 Council Directive are completed.

DEFINITIONS
"traffic commissioner": s.1.

GENERAL NOTE
This section enacts reg. 34A of S.I. 1984 No. 176 and empowers the traffic commissioner to grant temporary exemptions from a requirement for a standard licence for the use of vehicles for hire and reward on national transport operations in the circumstances set out in this section.

Vehicles authorised to be used under a licence

Vehicles authorised to be used under operator's licence

5.—(1) Subject to the following provisions of this section, the vehicles authorised to be used under an operator's licence are—
(a) any motor vehicle in the lawful possession of the licence-holder (whether that motor vehicle is specified in the licence or not); and
(b) any trailer in the lawful possession of the licence-holder.
(2) An operator's licence may provide—
(a) that no motor vehicle, or no trailer, whose relevant weight exceeds a weight specified in the licence is authorised to be used under it;
(b) that no trailers are authorised to be used under the licence; or
(c) that no motor vehicle that is not specified in the licence is authorised to be used under it.
(3) In subsection (2) "relevant weight", in relation to a motor vehicle or trailer of any prescribed class, means a weight of the description specified in relation to motor vehicles or trailers of that class by regulations.
(4) An operator's licence shall not authorise the use of any vehicle unless the place which is for the time being its operating centre—
(a) is in the area of the traffic commissioner by whom the licence was issued; or
(b) is outside that area but has not been the operating centre of that vehicle for a period of more than three months.
(5) For the purposes of subsection (4)(b), two or more successive periods which are not separated from each other by an interval of at least three months shall be treated as a single period having a duration equal to the total duration of those periods.

(6) A motor vehicle which is not specified in an operator's licence is not authorised to be used under that licence by virtue of subsection (1) after the period of one month beginning with—

(a) the day on which the vehicle was first in the lawful possession of the licence-holder, or

(b) (if later) the day on which the licence came into force,

unless, during that period, the licence-holder has given to the traffic commissioner by whom the licence was issued a notice in such form and containing such information about the vehicle as the commissioner may require, and has paid to him a prescribed fee.

(7) Where notice of a vehicle has been duly given and the prescribed fee has been duly paid under subsection (6), the traffic commissioner shall vary the licence by directing that the vehicle be specified in it.

(8) A motor vehicle specified in an operator's licence shall not, while it remains so specified, be capable of being effectively specified in any other operator's licence.

(9) Where it comes to the knowledge of the traffic commissioner by whom an operator's licence ("the first licence") was issued that a vehicle specified in that licence—

(a) has ceased to be used under the licence (otherwise than because of a fluctuation in business or because it is undergoing repair or maintenance), or

(b) is specified in another operator's licence,

he may vary the first licence by directing that the vehicle be removed from it.

DEFINITIONS

"area of the traffic commissioner": Public Passenger Vehicles Act 1981, s.3.

"operating centre": s.7(3).

"operator's licence": s.2(b).

"prescribed": s.58.

"relevant weight": subs. (3).

GENERAL NOTE

This section derives from s.42(1) of the 1994 Act. It contains a number of modifications from the original wording in s.42. The original categorisation of vehicles which would be authorised has been simplified to embrace vehicles in the "lawful possession" of the licence holder. Similarly, the list of trailers is redefined.

The section provides that motor vehicles in the lawful possession of the licence holder are potentially authorised vehicles, however, the licence when issued may specify a maximum weight of vehicles and trailers to be authorised and may provide that vehicles must also be specified upon the licence. Subsection (6) re-enacts in a simplified form, subs. (3) of s.61 of the 1968 Act and operators continue to have the facility to use an authorised vehicle, that is a vehicle in their lawful possession, for up to a month without the vehicle being specified on the licence, provided that within that month notice is given to the traffic commissioner, together with such information as the traffic commissioner may require, and the prescribed fee paid.

The section provides that the licence shall not authorise the use of any vehicle which has an operating centre outside the area of the traffic commissioner granting the licence, or, if outside the area, has not been used for more than three months or multiples of three months where they are not separated by more than three months.

Provision is also made for traffic commissioners to remove from the licence as specified vehicles any vehicles which have ceased to be used under the licence or have been specified on a licence granted in another area.

In respect of "old style licences" this section should be read subject to para. 5 of the Schedule to S.I. 1995 No. 2181.

Maximum numbers of vehicles

6.—(1) An operator's licence—

(a) shall specify a maximum number for motor vehicles, and

(b) may specify a maximum number for motor vehicles whose relevant weight exceeds a weight specified in the licence.

(2) An operator's licence that does not contain a provision such as is mentioned in section 5(2)(b)—

(a) shall specify a maximum number for trailers, and

(b) may specify a maximum number for trailers whose relevant weight exceeds a weight specified in the licence.

(3) The number of motor vehicles which at any one time are being used under an operator's licence while not specified in that licence may not exceed the maximum number specified in the licence under subsection (1)(a) less however many motor vehicles are specified in the licence.

(4) Where, under subsection (1)(b), an operator's licence specifies a maximum number for motor vehicles whose relevant weight exceeds a specified weight—

(a) the number of such motor vehicles which at any one time are being used under the licence while not specified in it may not exceed that maximum number less however many motor vehicles whose relevant weight exceeds the specified weight are specified in the licence, and

(b) the number of such motor vehicles that are specified in the licence and are being used under it at any one time may not exceed that maximum number.

(5) The number of trailers being used under an operator's licence at any one time may not exceed the maximum number specified in the licence under subsection (2)(a).

(6) Where, under subsection (2)(b), an operator's licence specifies a maximum number for trailers whose relevant weight exceeds a specified weight, the number of such trailers being used under the licence at any one time may not exceed that maximum number.

(7) The definition of "relevant weight" in section 5(3) applies for the purposes of this section as it applies for the purposes of section 5(2).

(8) If subsection (3), (4)(a) or (b), (5) or (6) is contravened, the licence-holder is guilty of an offence and liable on summary conviction to a fine not exceeding level 4 on the standard scale.

DEFINITIONS
"operator's licence": s.2.
"relevant weight": s.5(3).

GENERAL NOTE
This section derives from s.42(3) of the 1994 Act and distinguishes between what are authorised vehicles as set out in s.5 and vehicles which are specified on the licence. It maintains the concept of a "margin" on the licence, being the difference between the total number of authorised vehicles and the number of vehicles specified. It gives to the traffic commissioner the power not only to specify the vehicles by number, but also by weight. It also makes clear that any authorised vehicles being use, but not yet specified on the licence, should not exceed the difference between the total number of vehicles specified and the total number of vehicles authorised.

Where trailers have not been expressly excluded as provided for under s.5(2)(b), similar provisions apply in respect of trailers, both as to number and weight.

In respect of "old style licences", this section should be read subject to para. 5(6) of the Schedule to S.I. 1995 No. 2181.

Operating centres

Operating centres to be specified in operators' licences

7.—(1) A person may not use a place in the area of any traffic commissioner as an operating centre for vehicles authorised to be used under any operator's licence issued to him by that commissioner unless that place is specified as an operating centre of his in that licence.

(2) Any person who contravenes subsection (1) is guilty of an offence and liable on summary conviction to a fine not exceeding level 4 on the standard scale.

(3) In this Act "operating centre", in relation to any vehicle, means the base or centre at which the vehicle is normally kept, and references to an

operating centre of the holder of an operator's licence are references to any place which is an operating centre for vehicles used under that licence.

DEFINITIONS
  "operating centre": s.7(3).
  "operator's licence": s.2.
  "traffic commissioner": s.1, Public Passenger Vehicles Act 1981 s.1.

GENERAL NOTE
  The importance and significance of the individual operating centre was introduced by the 1982 Act and subsequently amended in Sched. 13 to the 1994 Act.

  Not only must an operator obtain an operator's licence in respect of the number and type of vehicles to be used, but the place where those vehicles are normally to be kept must also have been approved by the traffic commissioner and specified on the operator's licence. Subsection (3) defines the operating centre as being where the vehicle is normally kept. Difficulties can arise in relation to trailers which are frequently regarded as being itinerate.

  For a traffic commissioner to be satisfied that an operating centre can be specified on an operator's licence, it must meet the criteria set out in the following sections.

Applications for licences

Applications for operator's licences

8.—(1) An application for an operator's licence shall be made to the traffic commissioner for each area in which, if the licence is issued, the applicant will have an operating centre or operating centres.

(2) Accordingly, a person may hold separate operator's licences in respect of different areas; but he shall not at any time hold more than one such licence in respect of the same area.

(3) A person applying for an operator's licence shall give to the traffic commissioner a statement—

(a) containing such particulars as the commissioner may require of the motor vehicles proposed to be used under the licence and stating the number and type of any trailers proposed to be used under the licence; and

(b) containing such particulars as the commissioner may require of each place in the area of the commissioner which will be an operating centre of the applicant if the licence is issued.

(4) A person applying for an operator's licence shall also give to the traffic commissioner any further information which the commissioner may reasonably require for the discharge of his duties in relation to the application, and in particular shall, if required by the commissioner to do so, give to him any of the information specified in paragraph 1 of Schedule 2.

(5) Without prejudice to subsection (4), a person applying for an operator's licence shall also, if required by the traffic commissioner to do so, give to him such particulars as he may require with respect to the use which the applicant proposes to make, for vehicles used under the licence, of any place referred to in the statement under subsection (3)(b).

(6) Any statement, information or particulars to be given to a traffic commissioner under this section shall be given in such form as the commissioner may require.

DEFINITIONS
  "operating centre": s.7(3).
  "traffic commissioner": s.1, Public Passenger Vehicles Act 1981 s.1.

GENERAL NOTE
  If an operator wishes to have an operating centre which lies within the geographical area of a particular traffic area, then the operator must make an application for an operator's licence to the traffic commissioner for that area specifying the operating centre. Although an operator can have operator's licences in more than one traffic area, it cannot have more than one licence

in any one area. The section provides for the information which an applying operator should provide to the traffic commissioner in respect of both number and type of vehicles and location of the operating centre. The information which a traffic commissioner may require is set out in greater detail in Sched. 2.

Subsection (5) suggests that a traffic commissioner may require particulars of the use to which the operator would put the vehicle. At the moment, the present request for information (GV79E) is essentially limited to hours of operation of the vehicles and of any workshop activity in relation to the vehicles.

Convictions etc. subsequent to the making of an application

9.—(1) A person who has made an application for an operator's licence shall forthwith notify the traffic commissioner to whom it was made if, in the interval between the making of the application and the date on which it is disposed of, there occurs a notifiable conviction within the meaning given in paragraph 4 of Schedule 2.

(2) A person who—

(a) has made an application for a standard licence, and

(b) has included in that application particulars of a transport manager,

shall forthwith notify the traffic commissioner to whom the application was made if, in the interval between the making of the application and the date on which it is disposed of, there occurs any event affecting any information about the transport manager given to the commissioner under section 8.

(3) A person is guilty of an offence if he—

(a) knowingly fails to comply with subsection (1), or

(b) knowingly fails to comply with subsection (2) in a case where the event which occurs as mentioned in that subsection is the conviction of the transport manager of an offence such as is mentioned in paragraph 5 of Schedule 2;

and a person who is guilty of an offence under paragraph (a) or (b) is liable on summary conviction to a fine not exceeding level 4 on the standard scale.

(4) For the purposes of this section an application shall be taken to be disposed of—

(a) in a case where the traffic commissioner is required, by virtue of regulations under section 57(2)(a), to cause a statement containing his decision on the application to be issued, on the date on which that statement is issued, and

(b) in any other case, on the date on which the applicant receives notice from the traffic commissioner of his decision on the application.

GENERAL NOTE

When making an application for an operator's licence, an operator is required to disclose notifiable convictions which are set out in full in paras. 4 and 5 of Sched. 2. This section provides that if any notifiable conviction of the operator or any transport manager named in the application occurs between the lodging of the application and the issue of the licence, then these should be notified to the Licensing Authority. A failure to notify such a conviction or offence may not only constitute an offence attracting a fine not exceeding level 4, but the failure to notify any conviction will be taken into account when reviewing a licence.

It is of interest to note that the time for notifying such conviction differs in the case where the traffic commissioner has caused a statement containing his decision to be made; in this case the time for notification ceases on the date that the statement is made, irrespective of when the statement is received by the applicant whereas in other circumstances, the time for notification expires when the notice of the decision is received by the applicant.

Publication by traffic commissioner of notice of application for licence

10.—(1) A traffic commissioner shall publish in the prescribed manner notice of any application for an operator's licence made to him.

(2) The notice shall state—
(a) the time within which, and
(b) the manner in which,
any objection to, or representations against, the grant of the application is or are to be made under section 12 (that is to say, the time and manner prescribed under subsection (6) or, as the case may be, (7) of that section).

DEFINITIONS
"objection": s.12(1).
"prescribed": s.58.
"representation": s.12(4).

GENERAL NOTE
Upon receipt of an application, a traffic commissioner is obliged to publish the fact that an application has been made to him. Such applications will be published in the publication "Applications and Decisions" published by each Traffic Office.

Publication in locality affected of notice of application for licence

11.—(1) Subject to subsection (3), the traffic commissioner to whom an application for an operator's licence is made shall refuse the application without considering the merits unless he is satisfied that subsection (2) has been complied with in respect of each locality affected by the application.

(2) This subsection has been complied with in respect of a locality affected by an application if, within the period beginning 21 days before the date on which the application is made and ending 21 days after that date, notice of the application in such form and containing such information as may be prescribed has been published in one or more local newspapers circulating in the locality.

(3) The traffic commissioner is not required by this section to refuse an application if—
(a) he is satisfied as mentioned in subsection (1), save only that the form or contents of the notice of application as published in any newspaper did not comply with the prescribed requirements, and
(b) he is satisfied that no person's interests are likely to have been prejudiced by the failure to comply with those requirements.

(4) For the purposes of this section a locality is affected by an application for an operator's licence if it contains any place in the area of the traffic commissioner that will be an operating centre of the licence-holder if the application is granted.

DEFINITIONS
"locality": s.11(4).

GENERAL NOTE
The 1982 Act granted to certain members of the public the right to make representation against the grant of operators' licences. To enable such potential representors to be aware of the submission of applications for operators' licences, s.11 provides that an applicant should advertise the fact that the application has been submitted in one or more local newspapers circulating in the locality of the operating centre. The advertisement may be inserted at any time within the period of 21 days before and 21 days after the date on which the application is made. If such an advertisement is not placed, then the traffic commissioner must refuse the application.

Subsection (3) introduces some flexibility to enable minor errors in the form of the advertisement to be disregarded where the traffic commissioner is satisfied that no prejudice has occurred. This is a welcome discretion given to the traffic commissioners as an over rigid form of advertisement has in the past resulted in the refusal of applications and unnecessary expense both to applicants and to representors.

Objections to, and representations against, issue of operators' licences

12.—(1) Any of the persons mentioned in subsection (2) may make an objection to the grant of an application for an operator's licence on the ground—

(a) that any of the requirements of section 13 are not satisfied in the case of the application; or

(b) that any place in the traffic commissioner's area which, if the licence is issued, will be an operating centre of the holder of the licence will be unsuitable on environmental grounds for use as such.

(2) The persons who may make such an objection are—

(a) a prescribed trade union or association;

(b) a chief officer of police;

(c) a local authority; and

(d) a planning authority.

(3) The trade unions and associations which may be prescribed for the purposes of subsection (2)(a) are trade unions or associations whose membership consists of or includes—

(a) persons holding operators' licences, or

(b) employees of any such persons.

(4) Where an application for an operator's licence is made, any person who is the owner or occupier of land in the vicinity of any place in the traffic commissioner's area which, if the licence is issued, will be an operating centre of the holder of the licence may make representations against the grant of the application on the ground that that place will be unsuitable on environmental grounds for use as such.

(5) A person may not make representations under subsection (4) unless any adverse effects on environmental conditions arising from the use of the place in question as an operating centre of the holder of the licence would be capable of prejudicially affecting the use or enjoyment of the land mentioned in that subsection.

(6) Any objection under subsection (1)(a) shall be made—

(a) within the prescribed time; and

(b) in the prescribed manner.

(7) Any objection under subsection (1)(b) or representations under subsection (4) shall be made—

(a) within the prescribed time after the making of the application to which they relate; and

(b) in the prescribed manner.

(8) Where the traffic commissioner considers there to be exceptional circumstances that justify his doing so, he may direct that an objection or representations be treated for the purposes of this Act as duly made under this section, notwithstanding that the objection was not, or the representations were not, made within the prescribed time or in the prescribed manner.

(9) Any objection under subsection (1) shall contain—

(a) in the case of an objection under paragraph (a), particulars of the ground on which it is made, and

(b) in the case of an objection under paragraph (b), particulars of any matters alleged by the person making the objection to be relevant to the issue to which it relates.

(10) Any representations under subsection (4) shall contain particulars of any matters alleged by the person making the representations to be relevant to the issue to which they relate.

(11) In subsection (1) the reference to "the requirements of section 13" is a reference—

(a) in the case of an application for a standard licence, to the requirements of subsections (3), (5) and (6) of that section; and

(b) in the case of an application for a restricted licence, to the requirements of subsections (4), (5) and (6) of that section.

(12) In this section—

"local authority" means—

(a) as respects England, the council of a county, district or London borough and the Common Council of the City of London;

(b) as respects Wales, the council of a county or county borough; and

(c) as respects Scotland, a council constituted under section 2 of the Local Government etc. (Scotland) Act 1994;

"planning authority" means any body other than a local authority which by virtue of any statutory provision for the time being in force is—

(a) in England and Wales, the local planning authority for any area for the purpose of determining applications for planning permission under Part III of the Town and Country Planning Act 1990 (general planning control); and

(b) in Scotland, the planning authority for any area for the purpose of determining applications for planning permission under Part III of the Town and Country Planning (Scotland) Act 1972 (general planning control); and

"trade union" has the same meaning as in the Trade Union and Labour Relations (Consolidation) Act 1992;

and, in relation to any application for an operator's licence, references to the traffic commissioner are references to the traffic commissioner to whom the application has been made.

DEFINITIONS

"Chief Officer of Police": Police Act 1964 and Police (Scotland) Act 1967.
"local authority": subs. (12) and Sched. 6.
"owner": s.58.
"planning authority": subs. (12).
"prescribed": s.58.
"prescribed trade union or association": subs. (3).
"representation": s.12(4).
"trade union": s.12(12).

GENERAL NOTE

Subsections (1)–(3) set out those bodies which are entitled to make objections (as opposed to representations) against the grant of a licence and, by reference to s.13, set out the grounds upon which they can base those objections, that is either by bringing to the traffic commissioner's attention any of the matters set out in s.13 or, alternatively, by establishing that the proposed operating centre will be unsuitable on environmental grounds. Subsections (4) and (5) grant to the owner or occupier of land in the vicinity of the proposed operating centre a right to make representations against the grant if the use of the operating centre would have an adverse effect on the environmental conditions capable of prejudicially affecting the use of enjoyment of the actual land.

"Vicinity" remains undefined.

Subsections (6)–(10) embody the procedural matters introduced by Pt. IV of S.I. 1984 No. 126. Subsection (7) does, however, introduce a potential problem in respect of representations. Section 11(2) provides that any advertisement inserted in a newspaper may be made up to 21 days before the application is submitted or within 21 days of it having been submitted. Regulation 19(2) of S.I. 1984 No. 176 provided that a representation shall be made so as to be received by the Licensing Authority within 21 days "from the date on which notice of the application is published as required by Regulation 13(2)". Thus, an operator could advertise a proposed application before making the application and could, shortly after lodging that application, know whether or not valid representations had been made. Subsection (7) states that a representation shall now be made "within the prescribed time *after the making of the application*". This would suggest that in fact the calculation of time for the lodging of the representation will start to run not from the appearance of the advertisement, but from the making of the application. Unless the present format of the advertisement is changed to indicate when the application is made, then representors will not know of that date and from an applicant's point of view little will be served by advertising the application in advance of its submission.

Subsection (8) gives to the traffic commissioner a discretion to accept late objections or representations in "exceptional circumstances". The traffic commissioners are likely to continue their practice of expecting a higher appreciation of the Act and its requirements from objectors than from representors.

Subsection (11) identifies the relevant parts of s.13 which relate to applications for standard licences and those which apply to applications for restricted licences, the requirements not being identical.

Determination of applications

Determination of applications for operators' licences

13.—(1) Subject to sections 11 and 45(2), on an application for a standard licence a traffic commissioner shall consider—

(a) whether the requirements of subsections (3) and (5) are satisfied, and

(b) if he thinks fit, whether the requirements of subsection (6) are satisfied.

(2) Subject to sections 11 and 45(2), on an application for a restricted licence a traffic commissioner shall consider—

(a) whether the requirements of subsections (4) and (5) are satisfied, and

(b) if he thinks fit, whether the requirements of subsection (6) are satisfied.

(3) For the requirements of this subsection to be satisfied the traffic commissioner must be satisfied that the applicant fulfils the following requirements, namely—

(a) that he is of good repute,

(b) that he is of the appropriate financial standing, and

(c) that he is professionally competent;

and the traffic commissioner shall determine whether or not that is the case in accordance with Schedule 3.

(4) For the requirements of this subsection to be satisfied the applicant must not be unfit to hold an operator's licence by reason of—

(a) any activities or convictions of which particulars may be required to be given under section 8(4) by virtue of paragraph 1(e) or (f) of Schedule 2, or

(b) any conviction required to be notified in accordance with section 9(1).

(5) For the requirements of this subsection to be satisfied it must be possible (taking into account the traffic commissioner's powers under section 15(3) to issue a licence in terms that differ from those applied for) to issue a licence on the application in relation to which paragraphs (a) to (e) will apply—

(a) there are satisfactory arrangements for securing that—

(i) Part VI of the Transport Act 1968 (drivers' hours), and

(ii) the applicable Community rules, within the meaning of that Part,

are complied with in the case of the vehicles used under the licence;

(b) there are satisfactory arrangements for securing that the vehicles used under the licence are not overloaded;

(c) there are satisfactory facilities and arrangements for maintaining the vehicles used under the licence in a fit and serviceable condition;

(d) at least one place in the traffic commissioner's area is specified in the licence as an operating centre of the licence-holder, and each place so specified is available and suitable for use as such an operating centre (disregarding any respect in which it may be unsuitable on environmental grounds);

(e) the capacity of the place so specified (if there is only one) or of both or all the places so specified taken together (if there are more than one) is sufficient to provide an operating centre for all the vehicles used under the licence.

(6) For the requirements of this subsection to be satisfied the provision of such facilities and arrangements as are mentioned in subsection (5)(c) must not be prejudiced by reason of the applicant's having insufficient financial resources for that purpose.

(7) In considering whether any of the requirements of subsections (3) to (6) are satisfied, the traffic commissioner shall have regard to any objection duly made under section 12(1)(a) in respect of the application.

(8) In considering whether the requirements of subsection (5) are satisfied, the traffic commissioner may take into account any undertakings given by the applicant (or procured by him to be given) for the purposes of the application, and may assume that those undertakings will be fulfilled.

(9) In considering whether subsection (5)(d) will apply in relation to a licence, the traffic commissioner may take into account any conditions that could be attached to the licence under section 21, and may assume that any conditions so attached will not be contravened.

(10) In considering whether subsection (5)(d) or (e) will apply in relation to a licence, the traffic commissioner may take into account (if that is the case) that any proposed operating centre of the applicant would be used—

(a) as an operating centre of the holders of other operators' licences as well as of the applicant; or

(b) by the applicant or by other persons for purposes other than keeping vehicles used under the licence.

(11) If the traffic commissioner determines that any of the requirements that he has taken into consideration in accordance with subsection (1) or (2) are not satisfied he shall refuse the application, but in any other case he shall, subject to sections 14 and 45(2), grant the application.

DEFINITIONS
"activities": Sched. 2, para. 3.
"conviction required to be notified": Sched. 2, para. 4.
"operating centre": s.7(3).
"restricted licence": s.3(3).
"standard licence": s.3(2).
"traffic commissioner": s.1.

GENERAL NOTE
This section sets out what might be regarded as the basic necessary requirements which an applicant must meet if he is to obtain an operator's licence. If he fails to meet the requirements, subs. (11) provides that the traffic commissioner "shall refuse the application". The requirements specifically exclude environmental considerations which are dealt with under s.14. The requirements vary depending whether the application is for a standard licence or for a restricted licence. The requirements in respect of an application for a restricted licence are found at subss. (4), (5) and (6) and are less onerous than those required for a standard licence, be it national or international. In respect of an application for a standard licence, subs. (3) sets out the three main requirements which are then expanded upon in Sched. 3.

Subsections (3) and (4) might be considered to deal with the eligibility of the operator whereas subs. (5) deals with the technical suitability of the system to be operated by the operator at the operating centre imposing upon the operator the responsibility for compliance with the laws relating to drivers' hours and mechanical condition of the vehicles and the physical capability of the site to accommodate the number of vehicles sought. Whereas the requirement to be of appropriate financial standing relates only to an application for a standard licence, subs. (6) gives to the traffic commissioner power to investigate an applicant's financial position, be it for a standard or a restricted licence insofar as there should be sufficient financial resources for maintaining the vehicles.

Subsection (8) permits a traffic commissioner to invite and receive undertakings by an applicant which may satisfy him should he have reservations as to whether the requirements of subs. (5) are satisfied.

Section 21 does enable a traffic commissioner to consider whether a potential shortcoming in the suitability of the operating centre can be rectified by the imposition of conditions relating to road safety.

Determinations where objections etc are made on environmental grounds

14.—(1) This section applies to any application for an operator's licence in respect of which—

(a) any objection is duly made under section 12(1)(b), or

(b) any representations are duly made under section 12(4).

(2) A traffic commissioner may refuse an application to which this section applies on the ground that, as respects any place in his area which, if the licence were issued, would be an operating centre of the holder of the licence—

   (a) the parking of vehicles used under the licence at or in the vicinity of the place in question would cause adverse effects on environmental conditions in the vicinity of that place; or

   (b) the place in question would be unsuitable for use as an operating centre of the holder of the licence on other environmental grounds.

(3) The traffic commissioner may not refuse an application for an operator's licence on the ground that any place would be unsuitable as mentioned in subsection (2)(b) if—

   (a) on the date the application was made, that place was already specified in an operator's licence issued by the commissioner as an operating centre of the holder of that licence, or

   (b) the applicant has produced to the commissioner a certificate in force in respect of that place under—

      (i) section 191 or 192 of the Town and Country Planning Act 1990, or

      (ii) section 90 or 90A of the Town and Country Planning (Scotland) Act 1972,

   stating that its use as an operating centre for vehicles used under any operator's licence is or would be lawful.

(4) Subsection (3) does not apply in relation to any place that, at the time the application is determined by the traffic commissioner, is specified in an operator's licence as an operating centre of the holder of that licence.

(5) A place is not to be regarded for the purposes of paragraph (a) of subsection (3) as being specified in an operator's licence by reason only that it forms part of a place so specified; and a place that was, on the date mentioned in that paragraph, a place specified in an operator's licence as mentioned in that paragraph shall be disregarded for the purposes of that paragraph if, on that date—

   (a) the operator's licence in which that place was specified was an interim licence issued under section 24; or

   (b) that place was so specified by virtue of an interim direction such as is mentioned in section 25; or

   (c) such conditions relating to—

      (i) the exercise of the right of any person to appeal against a place being specified in an operator's licence, or

      (ii) the review under section 36 of any decision so to specify a place,

   as may be prescribed were not satisfied in relation to that place.

(6) Where in the case of any application for an operator's licence—

   (a) the traffic commissioner has power to refuse the application under subsection (2), and

   (b) any place other than a place that will be unsuitable for use as an operating centre is mentioned in the statement given by the applicant under section 8(3) as a proposed operating centre of his,

the commissioner may, instead of refusing the application, issue the licence but specify in it only such place or such places mentioned in that statement as will not be unsuitable for use as an operating centre.

(7) For the purposes of subsection (6), a place will be unsuitable for use as an operating centre if the traffic commissioner has power to refuse the application under subsection (2) in consequence of the proposed use of that place as an operating centre.

DEFINITIONS
"operator's licence": s.2.

GENERAL NOTE

This section sets out the circumstances in which the traffic commissioner may refuse an application on environmental grounds. Prior to the commencement of this Act, licences would have been granted for a five-year period and, at the expiration of that period, an application for a new licence was necessary. It was provided that where the application for a new licence mirrored the existing licence as to location of an operating centre, the number of vehicles and the use of the operating centre, then the traffic commissioner was precluded from refusing to grant the new licence; there being "no material change".

The advent of continuous licences makes such a test no longer appropriate. Subsections (3)–(5) introduce a different test. Subsection (3) provides that a traffic commissioner may not refuse an application on grounds of unsuitability if the place was already an operating centre at the date the application was made or if planning permissions exist authorising the use of the place as an operating centre for goods vehicles. It might appear difficult to reconcile subs. (4) and subs. (3)(a); a possible explanation is that subs. (4) relates to a situation existing at the date of the determination of the application as opposed to the date upon which the application is made and therefore could envisage a change of circumstances occurring during that interval which would remove the protection given at subs. (3)(a).

Subsection (5) enables a traffic commissioner to look at specific parts of a place and to judge the suitability of specific areas, and provides that his power to refuse an application exists irrespective of whether an interim licence has already been granted.

As an extension of subs. (5), subs. (6) does appear to allow a traffic commissioner to isolate specific unsuitable areas within a proposed operating centre rather than to reject the whole site.

Issue of operators' licences

15.—(1) Subject to subsection (2) and to sections 14(6), 21, 22, 23 and 45(2), on granting an application for an operator's licence a traffic commissioner shall issue that licence in the terms applied for.

(2) If a traffic commissioner has determined that any of the requirements of subsection (5) or (6) of section 13 that he has taken into consideration in accordance with subsection (1) or (as the case may be) (2) of that section would not be satisfied unless he were to exercise any of his powers under subsection (3) below, he shall exercise those powers accordingly.

(3) A traffic commissioner may issue the licence in terms that differ from the terms applied for in any of the following respects—

 (a) more or fewer motor vehicles are specified in the licence;
 (b) different motor vehicles are specified in it;
 (c) it includes a provision such as is mentioned in section 5(2);
 (d) it includes a provision such as is mentioned in section 6(1)(b) or (2)(b);
 (e) higher or lower maximum numbers are specified in it under section 6;
 (f) fewer places are specified in it as operating centres of the licence-holder.

(4) Any undertakings taken into account by the traffic commissioner under section 13(8) that he considers to be material to the granting of the application shall be recorded in the licence issued.

(5) A statement shall appear on the face of every operator's licence indicating whether it is a standard licence or a restricted licence.

(6) A statement shall appear on the face of every standard licence indicating whether it covers both national and international transport operations or national transport operations only.

DEFINITIONS
"International Transport Operation": S.I. 1984 No. 176, reg. 3.
"motor vehicle": Road Traffic Act 1960, s.253.
"National Transport Operation": S.I. 1984 No. 176, reg. 3.
"operator's licence": s.2.
"restricted licence": s.3(3).
"standard licence": s.3(2).
"traffic commissioner": s.1.

GENERAL NOTE
This section sets out the powers of the traffic commissioner to grant a licence in a form differ-ent to that applied for example by imposing restrictions on the number or type of vehicle, geo-graphical limitations dictated by environmental consideration or accepting undertakings to meet the requirements of s.13 or to impose conditions relating to road safety under s.21.

Duration of operators' licences

16.—(1) The date on which an operator's licence is to come into force shall be specified in the licence.

(2) Subject to its revocation or other termination under any provision of this Act or any other statutory provision, an operator's licence (other than an interim licence issued under section 24) shall continue in force indefinitely.

(3) If the holder of an operator's licence requests the traffic commissioner by whom it was issued to terminate it at any time, the commissioner shall, subject to subsection (4), comply with the request.

(4) The traffic commissioner may refuse to comply with the request if he is considering giving a direction in respect of the licence under section 26 or 27.

(5) An operator's licence held by an individual terminates if he dies, if he becomes a patient within the meaning of Part VII of the Mental Health Act 1983, or if (in Scotland) a curator bonis is appointed in respect of him on the ground that he is incapable, by reason of mental disorder, of adequately man-aging and administering his property and affairs.

DEFINITIONS
"interim licence": s.24.
"operator's licence": s.2.
"revocation": s.26.

GENERAL NOTE
This section introduces the concept of continuous licensing so replacing the earlier concept of five-year licences.

Although the section permits the surrender of a licence, subs. (4) provides that a traffic com-missioner may refuse to accept a request to terminate a licence if he is considering taking any punitive action against the licence under ss.26 or 27. Although s.28 is not referred to, that section does indicate that where revocation is being considered, disqualification of the holder, be it a corporate body or individual, can also be ordered and hence the necessity for the traffic com-missioner to have the power to refuse to accept a request to terminate a licence.

Subsection (2) is subject to paras. 2 and 3 of the Schedule to S.I. 1995 No. 2181.

Variation of licences

Variation of operators' licences

17.—(1) Subject to section 18, on the application of the holder of an oper-ator's licence, the traffic commissioner by whom the licence was issued may vary the licence by directing—

(a) that additional motor vehicles be specified in the licence or that any maximum number specified in it under section 6 be increased;

(b) that any vehicle cease to be specified in the licence or that any maxi-mum number specified in it under section 6 be reduced;

(c) that any provision in the licence such as is mentioned in section 5(2) cease to have effect;

(d) that a provision such as is mentioned in section 5(2) be included in the licence;

(e) that any provision in the licence such as is mentioned in section 6(1)(b) or (2)(b) cease to have effect;

(f) that a provision such as is mentioned in section 6(1)(b) or (2)(b) be included in the licence;

(g) that a new place in the traffic commissioner's area be specified in the licence as an operating centre of the licence-holder, or that any place cease to be so specified;

(h) that any undertaking recorded in the licence be varied or removed;

(i) that any condition attached to the licence be varied or removed;

(j) in the case of a restricted licence, that it be converted into a standard licence or, in the case of a standard licence, that it be converted into a restricted licence;

(k) in the case of a standard licence, that it cover both international and national transport operations instead of national transport operations only, or vice versa.

(2) A person applying for the variation of an operator's licence under this section shall give to the traffic commissioner, in such form as he may require, such information as he may reasonably require for disposing of the application.

(3) Except in the cases mentioned in subsection (4), the traffic commissioner shall publish notice of any application for the variation under this section of an operator's licence, and shall do so in the manner prescribed for the publication of notices under section 10(1).

(4) The excepted cases are—

(a) where the application is for a direction under subsection (1)(a) that additional motor vehicles be specified in the licence;

(b) where the application is for a direction under subsection (1)(b), (d) or (f);

(c) where the application is for a direction under subsection (1)(g) that a place cease to be specified in a licence as an operating centre of the licence-holder;

(d) where the application is for a direction under subsection (1)(j) that a standard licence be converted into a restricted licence;

(e) where the application is for a direction under subsection (1)(k) that a licence cover national transport operations only, instead of both national and international transport operations;

(f) where the traffic commissioner is satisfied that the application is of so trivial a nature that it is not necessary that an opportunity should be given for objecting to it or making representations against it.

(5) Where notice of an application is published under subsection (3), the following provisions, namely—

(a) section 10(2),

(b) section 12(1)(a), (6), (8) and (9)(a),

(c) section 13, and

(d) section 15,

shall, with any necessary modifications and subject to section 19, apply in relation to that application as they apply in relation to an application for an operator's licence of which notice is published under section 10(1).

Definitions

"International Transport Operations": S.I. 1984 No. 176, reg. 3.

"motor vehicle": Road Traffic Act 1960, s.253.

"National Transport Operations": S.I. 1984 No. 176, reg. 3.

"operating centre": s.7.

"operator's licence": s.2.

"prescribed": s.58.

"restricted licence": s.3(3).

"standard licence": s.3(2).

"traffic commissioner": s.1.

General Note

It is anticipated that from time to time, an operator will wish to apply to vary any licence issued and subs. (1) lists the variations which can be directed by the traffic commissioner. It further provides at subs. (3) that any application to vary shall be published in the same way as applications for a licence are published in the official publications of the Traffic Areas. Subsection (4) lists the nine variations which can be granted without publication.

Subsection (5) indicates that all requirements which relate to the publication of an application for a licence shall apply to the application to vary.

In respect of "old style licences", this section should be read subject to para. 6 of the Schedule to S.I. 1995 No. 2181.

Publication of notice of applications for variation in any locality affected

18.—(1) Subject to subsection (4), the traffic commissioner to whom an application for any of the directions mentioned in subsection (2) is made shall refuse the application without considering the merits unless he is satisfied that subsection (3) has been complied with in respect of each locality affected by the application.

(2) The directions referred to in subsection (1) are—

(a) any direction under section 17(1)(a) that a maximum number specified in a licence under section 6 be increased;

(b) any direction under section 17(1)(c) or (e);

(c) any direction under section 17(1)(g) that a new place be specified in a licence as an operating centre of the licence-holder; and

(d) any direction under section 17(1)(h) or (i) which might result in a material change in the use of any operating centre of the licence-holder in the traffic commissioner's area.

(3) This subsection has been complied with in respect of a locality affected by an application if, within the period beginning 21 days before the date on which the application is made and ending 21 days after that date, notice of the application in such form and containing such information as may be prescribed has been published in one or more local newspapers circulating in the locality.

(4) The traffic commissioner is not required by this section to refuse an application if—

(a) he is satisfied as mentioned in subsection (1), save only that the form or contents of the notice of application as published in any newspaper did not comply with the prescribed requirements; and

(b) he is satisfied that no person's interests are likely to have been prejudiced by the failure to comply with those requirements.

(5) For the purposes of this section a locality is affected by an application for the variation of an operator's licence if—

(a) it contains any place in the area of the traffic commissioner that will be an operating centre of the licence-holder if the application is granted; or

(b) it contains an existing operating centre of the licence-holder in the area of the commissioner and—

(i) the granting of the application would or could result in an increase in the number of vehicles, or the number of vehicles above a certain weight, that have that centre as their operating centre; or

(ii) any undertaking recorded in, or condition attached to, the licence that the application seeks to have varied or removed relates to that centre.

DEFINITIONS
"locality": s.11(4).
"traffic commissioner": s.1.

GENERAL NOTE
This section mirrors s.14 in that it provides that a traffic commissioner shall refuse an application to vary a licence where it has not been advertised in one or more local newspapers circulating in the locality of the operating centre within the same overall 42 day period as provided for in s.11. Again, the refusal is not mandatory if the traffic commissioner is satisfied that minor errors have occurred in the advertisement and that no persons interested have been prejudiced.

Applications for the variation of a licence made before January 1, 1996 are subject to paras. 8 and 9 of the Schedule to S.I. 1995 No. 2181.

Objection to, and refusal of, applications to vary operators' licences on environmental grounds

19.—(1) This section applies where notice of an application for the variation of an operator's licence has been published under section 17(3).

(2) Where the application relates to an existing operating centre of the licence-holder in the traffic commissioner's area—

(a) any of the persons mentioned in section 12(2) may object to the grant of the application on the ground that the use of that operating centre in any manner which would be permitted if the application were granted would cause adverse effects on environmental conditions in the vicinity of that centre;

(b) subject to subsection (5), any person who is the owner or occupier of any land in the vicinity of that operating centre may make representations against the grant of the application on the ground mentioned in paragraph (a); and

(c) whether or not anyone objects or makes representations under paragraph (a) or (b), the commissioner may refuse the application on the ground mentioned in paragraph (a).

(3) For the purposes of subsection (2), an application shall be taken to relate to an operating centre if—

(a) granting it would or could result in an increase in the number of vehicles, or the number of vehicles above a certain weight, that have that centre as their operating centre; or

(b) any undertaking recorded in, or condition attached to, the licence that the application seeks to have varied or removed relates to that centre.

(4) Where the application is for a place in the traffic commissioner's area to be specified in the licence as an operating centre of the licence-holder—

(a) any of the persons mentioned in section 12(2) may object to the grant of the application on the ground that that place will be unsuitable on environmental grounds for use as an operating centre of the licence-holder; and

(b) subject to subsection (5), any person who is the owner or occupier of any land in the vicinity of that place may make representations against the grant of the application on that ground.

(5) A person may not make representations under subsection (2)(b) or (4)(b) unless any adverse effects on environmental conditions arising from the use of the operating centre or place in question would be capable of prejudicially affecting the use or enjoyment of the land there mentioned.

(6) If any person duly objects or makes representations under subsection (4) against an application for a place in the traffic commissioner's area to be specified in the licence as an operating centre of the licence-holder, the commissioner may refuse the application—

(a) on the ground that the parking of vehicles used under the licence at or in the vicinity of that place would cause adverse effects on environmental conditions in the vicinity of that place; or

(b) subject to subsection (7), on the ground that that place would be unsuitable on environmental grounds other than the ground mentioned in paragraph (a) above for use as an operating centre of the licence-holder.

(7) The traffic commissioner may not refuse the application on the ground mentioned in subsection (6)(b) if—

(a) on the date the application was made, the place in question was already specified in an operator's licence issued by the commissioner as an operating centre of the holder of that licence, or

(b) the applicant has produced to the commissioner a certificate in force in respect of that place under—

(i) section 191 or 192 of the Town and Country Planning Act 1990, or

(ii) section 90 or 90A of the Town and Country Planning (Scotland) Act 1972,

stating that its use as an operating centre for vehicles used under any operator's licence is or would be lawful.

(8) Subsection (7) does not apply in relation to any place that, at the time the application is determined by the traffic commissioner, is specified in an operator's licence as an operating centre of the holder of that licence.

(9) A place is not to be regarded for the purposes of paragraph (a) of subsection (7) as being specified in an operator's licence by reason only that it forms part of a place so specified; and a place that was, on the date mentioned in that paragraph, a place specified in an operator's licence as mentioned in that paragraph shall be disregarded for the purposes of that paragraph if, on that date—

(a) the operator's licence in which that place was specified was an interim licence issued under section 24; or

(b) that place was so specified by virtue of an interim direction such as is mentioned in section 25; or

(c) such conditions relating to—

(i) the exercise of the right of any person to appeal against a place being specified in an operator's licence, or

(ii) the review under section 36 of any decision so to specify a place,

as may be prescribed were not satisfied in relation to that place.

(10) Any objection or representations under this section—

(a) shall contain particulars of any matters alleged by the person making the objection or representations to be relevant to the issue to which the objection relates or the representations relate; and

(b) shall be made in the prescribed manner and within the prescribed time after the making of the application to which the objection relates or the representations relate.

(11) Where the traffic commissioner considers there to be exceptional circumstances that justify his doing so, he may direct that an objection or representations be treated for the purposes of this Act as duly made under this section, notwithstanding that the objection was not, or the representations were not, made within the prescribed time or in the prescribed manner.

DEFINITIONS
"interim direction": s.25.
"interim licence": s.24.
"may object": s.12(1) and (2).
"operators' licence": s.2.
"owners": s.58.
"prescribed": s.58.
"representations": s.12(4).

GENERAL NOTE
This section mirrors, in respect of applications to vary, s.14 of the Act in that those who are entitled to raise objections upon environmental grounds against the grant of an operator's licence can similarly object to applications to vary, and owners or occupiers of land within the vicinity of an operating centre can make representations against such grant.

It should be noted that subs. (2)(c) gives to the traffic commissioner the power to refuse an application on environmental grounds even where no objection or representation has been made. One assumes in such circumstances the traffic commissioner will heed information given to him by his staff or representatives of the Vehicle Inspectorate.

Subsection (3) illustrates the manner in which a variation may impinge upon a particular operating centre. A variation may include an application to add a new operating centre and subs.

(4) repeats the power to make objections and representations. Subsections (7) and (8) mirror subss. (3) and (4) of s.14 in relation to the traffic commissioner's power to refuse to grant such variation and again, as was seen in s.14, the traffic commissioner has the power to look at specific parts of an operating site.

Subsection (10)(b) again states that the time for making a representation is the prescribed time "after the making of the application". Again, this provision may well cause confusion when compared with earlier legislation.

Variation of licences: further provisions

20.—(1) Where the holder of a restricted licence makes an application under section 17 to the traffic commissioner by whom the licence was issued to vary it by directing that it be converted into a standard licence—

(a) section 9(2) and (3)(b) and (without prejudice to the generality of section 17(5)) section 13(1) shall apply in relation to that application as they apply in relation to an application for a standard licence; and

(b) if the application is granted, section 22(2) shall apply to the giving of the direction to vary the restricted licence as it applies to the issuing of a standard licence.

(2) Where the holder of a standard licence which covers only national transport operations makes an application under section 17 to the traffic commissioner by whom the licence was issued for a direction that the licence be varied to cover both national and international transport operations—

(a) the applicant shall include in his application particulars about the professional competence on which he intends to rely; and

(b) the traffic commissioner shall refuse to direct the variation applied for unless he is satisfied that the professional competence on which the applicant proposes to rely is sufficient for the purposes of international transport operations.

<small>DEFINITIONS</small>
    "international transport operations": S.I. 1984 No. 176, reg. 3.
    "national transport operations": S.I. 1984 No. 176, reg. 3.
    "professional competence": s.13 and Sched. 3.
    "restricted licence": s.3(3).
    "standard licence": s.3(2).

<small>GENERAL NOTE</small>
    This section provides that where the nature of an application to vary the licence is to change a restricted licence into a standard licence or a standard national into a standard international licence then the applicant must fulfil the criteria relevant to that type of application and the holder of a restricted licence will need to meet the requirements of a standard licence holder whilst the holder of a standard licence who wishes to vary it to permit international operation will need to show that its professional competence extends to international operation rather than simply national operations. For details, see Sched. 3.

Conditions attached to licences

Conditions for securing road safety

21.—(1) On issuing an operator's licence, or on varying such a licence under section 17, a traffic commissioner may attach to the licence such conditions as he thinks fit for preventing vehicles that are authorised to be used under it from causing danger to the public—

(a) at any point where vehicles first join a public road on their way from an operating centre of the licence-holder (or last leave a public road on their way to such an operating centre); and

(b) on any road (other than a public road) along which vehicles are driven between such a point and the operating centre.

(2) On varying an operator's licence under section 17 a traffic commissioner may vary or remove any condition attached to the licence under this section.

(3) The traffic commissioner shall not—

(a) attach to an operator's licence any condition such as is mentioned in this section, or

(b) vary in such manner as imposes new or further restrictions or requirements any condition attached to an operator's licence under this section,

without first giving the applicant for the licence or (as the case may be) the licence-holder an opportunity to make representations to the commissioner with respect to the effect on his business of the proposed condition or variation.

(4) The traffic commissioner shall give special consideration to any representations made under subsection (3) in determining whether to attach the proposed condition or make the proposed variation.

(5) In this section "public road"—

(a) in relation to England and Wales, means a highway maintainable at the public expense for the purposes of the Highways Act 1980; and

(b) in relation to Scotland, has the same meaning as in the Roads (Scotland) Act 1984.

(6) Any person who contravenes any condition attached under this section to a licence of which he is the holder is guilty of an offence and liable on summary conviction to a fine not exceeding level 4 on the standard scale.

DEFINITIONS

"operators' licence": s.2.
"public road": subs. (5).
"traffic commissioner": s.1.

GENERAL NOTE

On issuing an operator's licence or varying an existing licence, the traffic commissioner is empowered to impose conditions designed to improve road safety at the point where vehicles join or leave the public highway or any other road between the public highway and the operating centre.

Where the changes are as a result of an application to vary, the traffic commissioner can vary or remove any existing conditions. Subsection (3) provides that he shall not, however, have the power to impose new conditions or renew restrictions without first giving the operator the opportunity of making representations with respect to the effect on his business of any proposed conditions. This subsection reflects the earlier position where a traffic commissioner would have been precluded from refusing a licence upon environmental grounds where there had been no material change but could impose conditions but only after giving to the operator the opportunity of contesting those conditions. The traffic commissioner remains under a duty to give special consideration to any such representations. The contravention of any condition attached to a licence may incur a penalty of a fine not exceeding level 4.

Conditions as to matters required to be notified to traffic commissioner

22.—(1) On issuing an operator's licence, a traffic commissioner may attach to the licence such conditions as he thinks fit for requiring the holder to inform him—

(a) of any change of a kind specified in the conditions in the organisation, management or ownership of the trade or business in the course of which vehicles are used under the licence or, if the licence is at any time suspended under section 26 or 28, were used under the licence immediately before its suspension;

(b) where the licence-holder is a company, of any change, or of any change of a kind specified in the conditions, in the persons holding shares in the company; or

(c) of any other event of a kind specified in the conditions which affects the licence-holder and which is relevant to the exercise of any powers of the traffic commissioner in relation to the licence.

(2) On issuing a standard licence, a traffic commissioner shall attach to it the following conditions, namely—

(a) a condition requiring the licence-holder to inform the commissioner of any event which could affect the fulfilment by the licence-holder of any of the requirements of section 13(3), and to do so within 28 days of the event; and

(b) a condition requiring the licence-holder to inform the commissioner of any event which could affect the fulfilment by a relevant transport manager of the requirements mentioned in section 13(3)(a) or (c), and to do so within 28 days of the event coming to the licence-holder's knowledge.

(3) In subsection (2)(b) the reference to a "relevant transport manager" is a reference to any transport manager employed by the licence-holder who is relied on by the licence-holder to fulfil the requirements of section 13(3)(c).

(4) In a case where the licence-holder is a company, no condition attached under subsection (2) shall be taken to require the company to inform the traffic commissioner of any change in the identity of the persons holding shares in the company unless the change is such as to cause a change in the control of the company.

(5) For the purposes of subsection (4), a change in the control of a company occurs when the beneficial ownership of more than half its equity share capital (as defined in section 744 of the Companies Act 1985) passes from one person to another person or from one group of persons to a wholly or substantially different group of persons.

(6) Any person who contravenes any condition attached under this section to a licence of which he is the holder is guilty of an offence and liable on summary conviction to a fine not exceeding level 4 on the standard scale.

DEFINITIONS
    "operator's licence": s.2.
    "standard licence": s.3(2).
    "traffic commissioner": s.1.
    "transport manager": s.58.

GENERAL NOTE
It remains discretionary as to whether a traffic commissioner attaches a condition to the licence requiring an operator to inform him of changes in the ownership and management of the business, be it a company or partnership.

In respect of standard licences, a traffic commissioner shall attach conditions to the effect that he should be informed within 28 days of any event which could affect compliance with the requirements set out in s.13(3) and by reference, Sched. 3, and similarly in respect of any transport manager, if that transport manager is relied upon as providing "professional competence". Subsections (4) and (5) limit and define ownership and changes in ownership. A contravention of any of the conditions imposed under s.22 makes an operator liable on summary conviction to a fine not exceeding level 4.

Conditions as to use of operating centres

23.—(1) On issuing an operator's licence, or on varying such a licence on an application of which notice has been published under section 17(3), a traffic commissioner may attach to the licence such conditions as he thinks fit for preventing or minimising any adverse effects on environmental conditions arising from the use of a place in his area as an operating centre of the licence-holder.

(2) The conditions which may be attached to a licence under this section shall be of such description as may be prescribed; and, without prejudice to the generality of the preceding provision, the descriptions which may be prescribed include conditions regulating—

(a) the number, type and size of motor vehicles or trailers which may at any one time be at any operating centre of the licence-holder in the area of the traffic commissioner for any prescribed purpose;

(b) the parking arrangements to be provided at or in the vicinity of any such centre; and

(c) the hours at which operations of any prescribed description may be carried on at any such centre.

(3) On varying an operator's licence on an application of which notice has been published under section 17(3), a traffic commissioner may vary or remove any condition attached to the licence under this section.

(4) The traffic commissioner shall not—

(a) attach any condition such as is mentioned in this section to an operator's licence, or

(b) vary in such manner as imposes new or further restrictions or requirements any condition attached to an operator's licence under this section,

without first giving the applicant for the licence or (as the case may be) the licence-holder an opportunity to make representations to the commissioner with respect to the effect on his business of the proposed condition or variation.

(5) The traffic commissioner shall give special consideration to any representations made under subsection (4) in determining whether to attach the proposed condition or make the proposed variation.

(6) Any person who contravenes any condition attached under this section to a licence of which he is the holder is guilty of an offence and liable on summary conviction to a fine not exceeding level 4 on the standard scale.

DEFINITIONS
"motor vehicles": s.58.
"operating centre": s.7.
"operators' licence": s.2.
"prescribed": s.58.
"traffic commissioner": s.1.
"trailers": s.58.

GENERAL NOTE
This section gives to the Licensing Authority power to impose environmental conditions and subs. (2) repeats by way of illustration examples of the conditions which can be imposed as introduced into the 1968 Act by Sched. 4 to the 1982 Act. The section incorporates the power to impose such conditions when granting a variation of the licence. Subsection (4) provides that a traffic commissioner shall not impose new conditions or vary existing conditions so as to create greater restrictions without giving to the operator the opportunity of making representations against the conditions and those representations should be given special consideration.

Interim licences and interim variations

Interim operators' licences

24.—(1) On an application for an operator's licence (a "full" licence), a traffic commissioner may, if the applicant so requests, issue to him an interim licence.

(2) An interim licence is an operator's licence that (subject to its revocation or other termination under any provision of this Act or any other statutory provision) will continue in force until it terminates under subsection (4), (5) or (6).

(3) The traffic commissioner may issue an interim licence in the same terms as those applied for in relation to the full licence or in terms that differ from those terms in any of the respects mentioned in section 15(3).

(4) If the traffic commissioner grants the application and issues to the applicant a full licence that—

(a) is in the terms applied for, or

(b) is in those terms subject only to the attachment under section 21, 22 or 23 of any conditions that are also attached to the interim licence, the interim licence shall terminate on the date on which the full licence comes into force.

(5) If, on an appeal under section 37 arising out of the application, the Transport Tribunal orders the traffic commissioner to issue a full licence to the applicant, the interim licence shall terminate—

   (a) on the date on which the full licence issued in pursuance of the order comes into force, or

   (b) at the time at which the application is withdrawn or treated as withdrawn by virtue of section 45(3).

(6) If neither subsection (4) nor subsection (5) applies, the interim licence shall terminate on the date on which the application is finally disposed of or such earlier date as the applicant may specify in a written request to the traffic commissioner.

(7) Where, in a case within subsection (6), the application is granted, the full licence issued to the applicant shall be of no effect before the interim licence terminates (notwithstanding any statement in it to the contrary).

(8) A request for the issuing of an interim licence—

   (a) shall not be treated as an application for an operator's licence for the purposes of section 10, 11, 12, 13, 14, 15(1) to (4), 36 or 37 or Schedule 4, but

   (b) shall be treated as such an application for the purposes of any other provision of this Act.

(9) In this section and section 25 references to the date on which an application is finally disposed of are references—

   (a) subject to paragraph (b), to the earliest date by which the application and any appeal to the Transport Tribunal arising out of the application have been determined and any time for bringing such an appeal has expired, or

   (b) if the application is withdrawn or any such appeal is abandoned, to the date of the withdrawal or abandonment.

DEFINITIONS

"finally disposed of": subs. (9).
"operators' licence": s.2.
"revocation": s.26.
"traffic commissioner": s.1.

GENERAL NOTE

The Traffic Area Offices recommend that at least nine weeks should be allowed between the making of an application and its grant. If objections or representations are made against the grant, this period can frequently be extended. This section gives to the traffic commissioner the power to issue an interim licence pending the determination of an application if requested by the applicant. An interim licence may be granted in the same terms as that applied for in the full licence or upon different terms. If subsequently a full licence is granted in the terms applied for but subject to conditions provided for under ss.21, 22 or 23, then the interim licence terminates on the date when the full licence comes into force. If an applicant appeals to the Transport Tribunal from a decision of the traffic commissioner, then the interim licence will terminate from the date where a full licence is issued in accordance with an order made by the Transport Tribunal or if the application is withdrawn at any intermediate time, from the date of the withdrawal. In all other circumstances, the interim licence terminates at the date when the application is disposed of. Subsection (9) defines when an application is "finally disposed of".

Interim variations

25.—(1) On an application for the variation under section 17 of an operator's licence, if the applicant so requests the traffic commissioner may, before he has determined the application, vary the licence by giving an interim direction in respect of it.

(2) An interim direction is a direction under section 17(1) that is expressed to continue in force until it ceases to have effect under subsection (3) or (4) below.

(3) If on determining the application the traffic commissioner varies the licence by giving a direction in the terms applied for and does not also under section 21(1) or (2) or 23(1) or (3) attach or vary any conditions, the interim direction shall cease to have effect on the date on which the direction given on the application comes into force.

(4) If subsection (3) does not apply, the interim direction shall cease to have effect on the date on which the application is finally disposed of or such earlier date as the applicant may specify in a written request to the traffic commissioner.

(5) Where, in a case within subsection (4), on determining the application the traffic commissioner gives a direction varying the licence, that direction shall be of no effect before the interim direction ceases to have effect.

(6) A request for an interim direction to be given—
(a) shall not be treated as an application for the variation of an operator's licence for the purposes of section 17(3) or 37 or Schedule 4, but
(b) shall be treated as such an application for the purposes of any other provision of this Act.

(7) The reference in subsection (4) to the date on which an application is finally disposed of is to be construed in accordance with section 24(9).

DEFINITIONS
"finally disposed of": s.24(9).
"operator's licence": s.2.
"traffic commissioner": s.1.

GENERAL NOTE
As with an application for a new licence, an application to vary the licence can be accompanied by a request for the giving of an interim direction. If the variation is granted as requested, the interim direction will cease to have effect on the date when it is directed that the direction comes into force. If the variation is not granted as sought, the interim direction will cease to have effect when the application is finally disposed of unless an earlier date has been specified by the operator. The request for an interim direction is not treated as an application to vary and is not, therefore, subject to ss.13(3), 37 or Sched. 4 in that it is not required to be published, not subject to the rights of appeal or to the regulation relating to transfers of operating centres.

Revocation etc. of operators' licences

Revocation, suspension and curtailment of operators' licences

26.—(1) Subject to the following provisions of this section and the provisions of section 29, the traffic commissioner by whom an operator's licence was issued may direct that it be revoked, suspended or curtailed (within the meaning given in subsection (11)) on any of the following grounds—
(a) that a place in the commissioner's area has, at a time when it was not specified in the licence as an operating centre of the licence-holder, been used as an operating centre for vehicles authorised to be used under the licence;
(b) that the licence-holder has contravened any condition attached to the licence;
(c) that during the five years ending with the date on which the direction is given there has been—
(i) a conviction of the licence-holder of an offence such as is mentioned in any of sub-paragraphs (a) to (i) of paragraph 5 of Schedule 2;
(ii) a conviction of a servant or agent of the licence-holder of any such offence, other than an offence such as is mentioned in sub-paragraph (c), (e) or (h) of that paragraph; or
(iii) a prohibition under section 69 or 70 of the Road Traffic Act 1988 (power to prohibit driving of unfit or overloaded vehicles) of

the driving of a vehicle of which the licence-holder was the owner when the prohibition was imposed;

(d) that during those five years, on occasions appearing to the commissioner to be sufficiently numerous to justify the giving of a direction under this subsection, there has been a conviction of the licence-holder or a servant or agent of his of an offence such as is mentioned in paragraph 5(j) of Schedule 2;

(e) that the licence-holder made, or procured to be made, for the purposes of—

(i) his application for the licence,

(ii) an application for the variation of the licence, or

(iii) a request for a direction under paragraph 1 or 3 of Schedule 4,

a statement of fact that, whether to his knowledge or not, was false, or a statement of expectation that has not been fulfilled;

(f) that any undertaking recorded in the licence has not been fulfilled;

(g) that the licence-holder, being an individual, has been adjudged bankrupt or, being a company, has gone into liquidation, other than voluntary liquidation for the purpose of reconstruction;

(h) that since the licence was issued or varied there has been a material change in any of the circumstances of the licence-holder that were relevant to the issue or variation of the licence;

(i) that the licence is liable to revocation, suspension or curtailment by virtue of a direction under section 28(4).

(2) Where the traffic commissioner has power to give a direction in respect of a licence under subsection (1), the commissioner also has power to direct that a condition, or additional condition, such as is mentioned in section 22(1) be attached to the licence.

(3) In this Act any reference, in relation to an operator's licence, to a condition attached to the licence under section 22(1) includes any condition attached to the licence under subsection (2) above.

(4) Where the existence of any of the grounds mentioned in subsection (1) is brought to the notice of the traffic commissioner in the case of the holder of any licence issued by him, the commissioner shall consider whether or not to give a direction under this section in respect of that licence.

(5) Where, in a case falling within subsection (1)(c)(i)—

(a) the conviction in question is a conviction of the licence-holder of an offence under section 3(6) or of the corresponding offence under regulation 33(2) of the Goods Vehicles (Operators' Licences, Qualifications and Fees) Regulations 1984, and

(b) there has been, within the 5 years preceding that conviction, a previous conviction of the licence-holder of an offence under either of those provisions,

the traffic commissioner shall give a direction under subsection (1) to revoke the licence.

(6) Where the traffic commissioner directs that an operator's licence be suspended or curtailed, the commissioner may order—

(a) in the case of a suspension, that any motor vehicle specified in the licence may not be used under any other operator's licence (notwithstanding anything in section 5(1)(a)), or

(b) in the case of a curtailment having the effect of removing any motor vehicle from the licence, that the motor vehicle may not be used as mentioned in paragraph (a) and shall not be capable of being effectively specified in any other operator's licence.

(7) An order made under subsection (6) shall cease to have effect—

(a) on such date, not being more than 6 months after the order is made, as may be specified in the order, or

(b) if, before that date, the licence which is directed to be suspended or curtailed ceases to be in force, on the date on which it ceases to be in force.

(8) The traffic commissioner by whom any direction suspending or curtailing a licence under subsection (1) was given may at any time—

   (a) cancel the direction together with any order under subsection (6) that was made when the direction was given;

   (b) cancel any such order; or

   (c) with the consent of the licence-holder, vary the direction or any such order (or both the direction and any such order).

(9) Where an operator's licence is suspended under this section, the licence remains in force during the time of its suspension subject to the limitation that no vehicles are authorised to be used under it.

(10) In subsection (1)(g) the reference to an individual having been adjudged bankrupt shall, as respects Scotland, be construed as a reference to an award of sequestration having been made of his estate.

(11) In this Act references to directing that an operator's licence be curtailed are references to directing (with effect for the remainder of the duration of the licence or for any shorter period) all or any of the following, that is to say—

   (a) that one or more of the vehicles specified in the licence be removed from it;

   (b) that a provision such as is mentioned in section 5(2) or 6(1)(b) or (2)(b) be included in the licence;

   (c) that any maximum number specified in the licence under section 6 be reduced;

   (d) that any one or more of the places specified in the licence as operating centres be removed from it.

DEFINITIONS
"contravened": s.58.
"operating centre": s.7.
"operators' licence": s.2.
"traffic commissioner": s.1.

GENERAL NOTE
This section clarifies and combines existing provisions for the revocation, suspension or curtailment of licences and inserts new grounds for doing so. It also enables suspensions, curtailments and other disciplinary decisions to be varied or cancelled by the Licensing Authority. In particular, subs. (1)(d) introduces a degree of discretion on the part of the traffic commissioner to consider whether the convictions of the licence holder have been "sufficiently numerous" to justify disciplinary action. With the exception of subs. (5), the directions are discretionary, however, in respect of subs. (5) it is mandatory if the conviction is for using a vehicle subject to a restricted licence for hire or reward and the licence holder has been convicted of a similar offence during the previous five years. Reflecting the fact that licences will be held continuously, subs. (7) provides that any suspension or curtailment shall cease not more than six months after the order is made.

The section introduces a new meaning of curtailment. In the past, curtailment of the licence has equated with early termination of the licence. Subsection (11) applies curtailment to specific situations.

In respect of "old style licences", this section should be read subject to para. 11 of the Schedule to S.I. 1995 No. 2181.

Revocation of standard licences

27.—(1) The traffic commissioner by whom a standard licence was issued shall direct that it be revoked if at any time it appears to him that the licence-holder is no longer—

   (a) of good repute,

   (b) of the appropriate financial standing, or

   (c) professionally competent;

and the traffic commissioner shall determine whether or not that is the case in accordance with Schedule 3.

(2) Before giving a direction under subsection (1) in respect of a licence, the traffic commissioner shall give to its holder notice in writing that he is considering giving such a direction.

(3) A notice under subsection (2) shall state the grounds on which the traffic commissioner is considering giving a direction under subsection (1) and shall also state—

(a) that written representations with respect to those grounds may be made to the commissioner by the licence-holder, and

(b) that any such representations must be received by the commissioner within 21 days of the date of the notice;

and the traffic commissioner shall consider any representations duly made under this subsection.

(4) This section has effect subject to section 29 (and, in particular, nothing in subsection (3) above shall be taken to affect a person's right under section 29(1) to require the holding of an inquiry).

DEFINITIONS
"standard licence": s.3(2).
"traffic commissioner": s.1.

GENERAL NOTE
This section sets out the circumstances in which a traffic commissioner shall revoke a standard licence. Subsection (2) provides, however, that such a direction can only be given after the traffic commissioner has given to the holder notice that he is considering giving such a direction. The traffic commissioner is then required to consider representations. The right of an operator to require the holding of a public inquiry remains.

Disqualification

28.—(1) Where, under section 26(1) or 27(1), a traffic commissioner directs that an operator's licence be revoked, the commissioner may order the person who was the holder of the licence to be disqualified (either indefinitely or for such period as the commissioner thinks fit) from holding or obtaining an operator's licence; and so long as the disqualification is in force—

(a) any operator's licence held by him at the date of the making of the order (other than the licence revoked) shall be suspended, and

(b) notwithstanding anything in section 13 or 24, no operator's licence may be issued to him.

(2) If a person applies for or obtains an operator's licence while he is disqualified under subsection (1)—

(a) he is guilty of an offence and liable on summary conviction to a fine not exceeding level 4 on the standard scale, and

(b) any operator's licence issued to him on the application, or (as the case may be) the operator's licence obtained by him, shall be void.

(3) An order under subsection (1) may be limited so as to apply only to the holding or obtaining of an operator's licence in respect of one or more specified traffic areas and, if the order is so limited—

(a) paragraphs (a) and (b) of that subsection and subsection (2) shall apply only to any operator's licence to which the order applies, but

(b) notwithstanding section 5(4)(b), no other operator's licence held by the person in question shall authorise the use by him of any vehicle at a time when its operating centre is in a traffic area in respect of which he is disqualified by virtue of the order.

(4) Where the traffic commissioner makes an order under subsection (1) in respect of any person, the commissioner may direct that if that person, at any time or during such period as the commissioner may specify—

(a) is a director of, or holds a controlling interest in—

(i) a company which holds a licence of the kind to which the order in question applies, or

          (ii) a company of which such a company is a subsidiary, or
  (b) operates any goods vehicles in partnership with a person who holds
     such a licence,
that licence of that company or, as the case may be, of that person, shall be liable to revocation, suspension or curtailment under section 26.

(5) The powers conferred by subsections (1) and (4) in relation to the person who was the holder of a licence shall be exercisable also—
  (a) where that person was a company, in relation to any director of that
     company, and
  (b) where that person operated vehicles under the licence in partnership
     with other persons, in relation to any of those other persons;
and any reference in this section or in section 26 or 29 to subsection (1) or (4) above includes a reference to that subsection as it applies by virtue of this subsection.

(6) The traffic commissioner by whom any order disqualifying a person was made under subsection (1) may at any time—
  (a) cancel that order together with any direction that was given under sub-
     section (4) when the order was made;
  (b) cancel any such direction; or
  (c) with the consent of the person disqualified, vary the order or any such
     direction (or both the order and any such direction).

(7) Where an operator's licence is suspended under this section, the licence remains in force during the time of its suspension subject to the limitation that no vehicles are authorised to be used under it.

(8) For the purposes of this section a person holds a controlling interest in a company if he is the beneficial owner of more than half its equity share capital (as defined in section 744 of the Companies Act 1985).

DEFINITIONS
    "company controlling interest": Companies Act 1985, s.744.
    "operator's licence": s.2.
    "traffic commissioner": s.1.

GENERAL NOTE
    This section gives power to the traffic commissioner when revoking a licence to disqualify the holder from holding an operator's licence in his own Traffic Area or any other Traffic Area and, where the holder is a company, disqualifying other directors from that company from holding a licence. It is an offence for a person to apply for an operator's licence whilst disqualified, the penalty upon conviction being a fine not exceeding level 4.
    Where the licence holder holds licences other than the one revoked, those licences will be suspended during the period of disqualification.

Revocation and disqualification etc: supplementary provisions

  29.—(1) A traffic commissioner shall not—
  (a) give a direction under section 26(1) or (2) or 27(1) in respect of any
     licence,
  (b) make an order under section 26(6) in respect of any vehicle, or
  (c) make an order or give a direction under section 28(1) or (4) in respect
     of any person,
without first holding an inquiry if the holder of the licence or (as the case may be) the person concerned requests him to do so.

(2) The traffic commissioner may direct that any direction or order given or made by him under—
  (a) section 26(1), (2) or (6),
  (b) section 27(1), or
  (c) section 28(1) or (4),
shall not take effect until the expiry of the time within which an appeal may be made to the Transport Tribunal against the direction or order and, if such an appeal is made, until the appeal has been disposed of.

(3) If the traffic commissioner refuses to give a direction under subsection (2) the holder of the licence or, as the case may be, the person in respect of whom the direction or order was given or made may apply to the Tribunal for such a direction.

(4) The Tribunal shall give its decision on any application under subsection (3) within 14 days.

DEFINITIONS
"operating centre": s.7(3).
"operator's licence": s.2.
"regulations": s.58.
"traffic commissioner": s.1.

GENERAL NOTE
This section provides that the traffic commissioner shall not make an order revoking, suspending or curtailing a licence or a disqualification order without first holding an inquiry if the holder of the licence requests him to do so. The traffic commissioner is given a discretion to order a stay of any direction or order pending an appeal to the Transport Tribunal. Should he refuse to do so, the operator retains the right to apply to the Transport Tribunal for a stay and the Tribunal is required to give its decision within 14 days.

This section and ss.31 and 32 embody the provision of the 1994 Act consequent on the introduction of the continuous licensing system. The sections provide for operating centres to be reviewed at five-yearly intervals. Before doing so, notice should be given by the traffic commissioner to the licence holder in accordance with Regulations to be introduced.

Review of operating centres

Periods of review for operating centres

30.—(1) Within such time after any period of review as may be prescribed, the traffic commissioner by whom an operator's licence was issued may serve a notice on the licence-holder stating that the commissioner is considering whether to exercise any of his powers under sections 31 and 32 in relation to a place specified in the licence as an operating centre of the licence-holder.

(2) The periods of review in relation to an operator's licence are—
(a) the period of five years beginning with the date specified in the licence as the date on which it came into force; and
(b) each consecutive period of five years.

(3) Regulations may amend subsection (2) by substituting a higher or lower number (but not a number lower than five) for the number of years for the time being specified in paragraphs (a) and (b).

(4) Regulations may make provision as to the manner in which notices under this section are to be or may be served, including provision as to the circumstances in which, and the time at which, any such notice is to be treated as having been duly served (whether or not it has in fact been served).

GENERAL NOTE
This section should be read subject to paras. 2, 3 and 12 of the Schedule to S.I. 1995 No. 2181.

Power to remove operating centres on review

31.—(1) If, having served notice under section 30 in respect of a place specified in an operator's licence, the traffic commissioner determines that the place is unsuitable—
(a) on grounds other than environmental grounds, or
(b) on the ground mentioned in subsection (2),
for use as an operating centre of the licence-holder, he may (subject to subsection (3)) direct that it cease to be specified in the licence.

(2) The ground referred to in subsection (1)(b) is that the parking of vehicles used under the licence at or in the vicinity of the place causes adverse effects on environmental conditions in that vicinity.

(3) Where the only ground for giving a direction under subsection (1) is the ground mentioned in subsection (2), the traffic commissioner may not give

such a direction unless during the period of review in question representations were made to him—
(a) by such a person as is mentioned in section 12(2), or
(b) by a person who is the owner or occupier of any land in the vicinity of
the place in question,
as to the unsuitability of the place on environmental grounds for continued
use as an operating centre for vehicles used under any operator's licence.

(4) Representations made by a person such as is mentioned in paragraph
(b) of subsection (3) shall be disregarded for the purposes of this section if,
when they were made, any adverse effects on environmental conditions arising from the continued use of the place in question would not have been
capable of prejudicially affecting the use or enjoyment of the land mentioned
in that paragraph.

(5) Any representations under this section—
(a) shall be made in the prescribed manner; and
(b) shall contain particulars of any matters alleged by the person making
the representations to be relevant to the issue to which they relate;
but where the traffic commissioner considers there to be exceptional circumstances that justify his doing so, he may direct that representations be treated
for the purposes of this Act as duly made under this section notwithstanding
that they were not made in the prescribed manner or within the period of
review in question.

DEFINITIONS
"operating centre": s.7(3).
"operator's licence": s.2.
"owner": s.58.
"prescribed": s.58.
"representations": s.12(4).
"traffic commissioner": s.1.

GENERAL NOTE
This section gives to the traffic commissioner the power to remove operating centres upon
review where he has received complaints as to suitability or upon environmental grounds during
the review period.
This section should be read subject to paras. 2, 3 and 12 of the Schedule to S.I. 1995 No. 2181.

Power to attach conditions on review

32.—(1) If, having served notice under section 30 in respect of a place
specified in an operator's licence, the traffic commissioner does not give a
direction in respect of the place under section 31, he may direct—
(a) that conditions (or additional conditions) such as are mentioned in
section 21, 22(1)(c) or 23 be attached to the licence;
(b) that any conditions already attached to the licence under section 21,
22(1)(c) or 23 be varied.

(2) Any conditions attached to the licence under subsection (1)(a) shall
relate or, in the case of conditions such as are mentioned in section 22(1)(c),
shall only require the traffic commissioner to be informed of events that
relate—
(a) only to the place referred to in subsection (1), or
(b) only to that place and any other places in respect of which the commissioner has power to attach conditions under that subsection.

(3) Any variation under subsection (1)(b) shall be such as imposes new or
further restrictions or requirements—
(a) only in relation to the place referred to in subsection (1), or
(b) only in relation to that place and any other places in respect of which
the commissioner has power to attach conditions under that
subsection.

(4) Where the traffic commissioner gives a direction in respect of an operator's licence under section 31 or subsection (1)(a) above, he may also vary
the licence by directing—

(a) that any vehicle cease to be specified in the licence;
(b) that any maximum number specified in the licence under section 6 be reduced;
(c) that a provision such as is mentioned in section 5(2) be included in the licence;
(d) that a provision such as is mentioned in section 6(1)(b) or (2)(b) be included in the licence.

(5) In this Act any reference, in relation to an operator's licence, to a condition attached to the licence under section 21, 22 or 23 includes a reference to any condition such as is mentioned in section 21, 22 or (as the case may be) 23 attached to the licence under subsection (1)(a) above.

DEFINITIONS
   "operator's licence": s.2.
   "traffic commissioner": s.1.

GENERAL NOTE
   As an alternative to the removal of an operating centre upon review, this section empowers the traffic commissioner to impose or vary conditions.
   This section should be read subject to paras. 2, 3, and 12 of the Schedule to S.I. 1995 No. 2181.

Transfer of operating centres

Transfer of operating centres

33. Schedule 4 (which makes provision in relation to certain applications for, or for the variation of, operators' licences where the proposed operating centres of the applicant are already specified in an operator's licence) shall have effect.

DEFINITIONS
   "operating centre": s.7(3).
   "operator's licence": s.2.

GENERAL NOTE
   This section introduces by reference to Sched. 4 a simplified procedure for applications where an operating centre to be included on the licence is already specified on another licence.

Environmental matters

Determinations as to environmental matters

34.—(1) In making any determination of a description mentioned in subsection (2), a traffic commissioner shall have regard to such considerations as may be prescribed as relevant to determinations of that description.

(2) The determinations referred to are—
(a) any determination with respect to the suitability of any place on environmental grounds for use as an operating centre of the holder of an operator's licence;
(b) any determination with respect to attaching to an operator's licence any condition such as is mentioned in section 23 or varying or removing any such condition attached to an operator's licence; and
(c) any determination with respect to the effect on environmental conditions in any locality of the use in any particular manner of any operating centre of the holder of an operator's licence.

(3) In making any such determination for the purposes of exercising—
(a) any of his functions in relation to an application for, or for the variation of, an operator's licence, or
(b) any of his functions under sections 30 to 32,
a traffic commissioner may take into account any undertakings given by the applicant or licence-holder (or procured by him to be given) for the purposes of the application or the review under sections 30 to 32, and may assume that those undertakings will be fulfilled.

(4) In making for those purposes a determination of a description mentioned in subsection (2)(a) or (c), a traffic commissioner may take into account any conditions such as are mentioned in section 23 that could be attached to the licence in question, and may assume that any conditions so attached will not be contravened.

(5) Where a traffic commissioner—

(a) grants an application for, or for the variation of, an operator's licence, or

(b) having served notice under section 30 in respect of any place specified in such a licence, exercises or determines not to exercise any of his powers under sections 31 and 32 in relation to that place,

any undertakings taken into account by the commissioner under subsection (3) that he considers to be material to the application or (as the case may be) to his decision under sections 31 and 32 shall be recorded in the licence in question.

DEFINITIONS
   "locality": s.11(4).
   "operating centre": s.7(3).
   "operator's licence": s.2.
   "traffic commissioner": s.1.

GENERAL NOTE
   This states that, when making any determination upon environmental matters, a traffic commissioner shall have regard to conditions as may be prescribed.
   At the moment, the conditions which might be relevant are those set out in reg. 22 of S.I. 1984 No. 176; however, these are themselves being redrafted.

Inquiries

Power of traffic commissioners to hold inquiries

35.—(1) A traffic commissioner may hold such inquiries as he thinks necessary for the proper exercise of his functions under this Act.

(2) Where, as respects the proposed exercise on any occasion of any of his powers under section 26, 27 or 28, a traffic commissioner receives a request for an inquiry (made pursuant to section 29(1)) from two or more persons, he may hold a single inquiry in response to both or all of those requests.

(3) Subject to any provision made by regulations, any inquiry held by a traffic commissioner for the purposes of this Act shall be held in public.

(4) Information with respect to any particular trade or business which is given at any such inquiry while admission to the inquiry is restricted in accordance with regulations shall not, so long as that trade or business continues to be carried on, be disclosed except—

(a) with the consent of the person for the time being carrying on that trade or business;

(b) for the purpose of the discharge by any person of his functions under this Act; or

(c) with a view to the institution of, or otherwise for the purposes of, any legal proceedings pursuant to or arising out of this Act, including proceedings before the Transport Tribunal.

(5) Any person who discloses any information in contravention of subsection (4) is guilty of an offence and liable on summary conviction to a fine not exceeding level 4 on the standard scale.

DEFINITIONS
   "contravention": s.58.
   "traffic commissioner": s.1.

GENERAL NOTE
This section enacts the relevant regulations of S.I. 1984 No. 176 in relation to the powers of the traffic commissioners to hold public inquiries and to take certain evidence in private. Such evidence is not to be disclosed. Contravention can attract a fine not exceeding level 4.

Review of decisions and appeals

Review of decisions

36.—(1) Subject to subsection (2), a traffic commissioner may review and, if he thinks fit, vary or revoke any decision of his to grant or refuse—

(a) an application for an operator's licence, or

(b) an application for the variation of such a licence in a case where section 17(3) required notice of the application to be published,

if he is satisfied that a procedural requirement imposed by or under any enactment has not been complied with in relation to the decision.

(2) The traffic commissioner may under subsection (1) review a decision only—

(a) if, within such period after taking the decision as may be prescribed, he has given notice to the applicant or (as the case may be) the licence-holder that he intends to review the decision;

(b) if, within that period, a person who appears to him to have an interest in the decision has requested him to review it; or

(c) (where neither paragraph (a) nor paragraph (b) applies), if he considers there to be exceptional circumstances that justify the review.

(3) Regulations may make provision as to the manner in which notices under subsection (2)(a) are to be or may be served, including provision as to the circumstances in which, and the time at which, any such notice is to be treated as having been duly served (whether or not it has in fact been served).

(4) The variation or revocation under this section of any decision shall not make unlawful anything done in reliance on the decision before the variation or revocation takes effect.

DEFINITIONS
"operator's licence": s.2.
"regulations": s.58.
"traffic commissioner": s.1.

GENERAL NOTE
This section empowers a traffic commissioner to review decisions where there has been a procedural irregularity and to correct errors in documents.

Rights of appeal in connection with operators' licences

37.—(1) An applicant for, or for the variation of, an operator's licence may appeal to the Transport Tribunal against the refusal of the application or (as the case may be) against the terms of the licence or of the variation.

(2) The holder of an operator's licence may appeal to the Tribunal against any direction given under section 5(9), 26(1) or (2), 27(1), 31 or 32 in respect of the licence.

(3) The holder of an operator's licence may appeal to the Tribunal against any order made under section 26(6) on the suspension or curtailment of the licence.

(4) A person in respect of whom an order has been made under section 28(1) (including section 28(1) as it applies by virtue of section 28(5)) may appeal to the Tribunal against that order and against any direction given under section 28(4) (including section 28(4) as it so applies) when the order was made.

(5) A person who has duly made an objection to an application for, or for a variation of, an operator's licence may appeal to the Tribunal against the grant of the application.

(6) A person who—
(a) within the prescribed period has made an application for a review under section 36, and
(b) has been certified by the traffic commissioner as a person such as is mentioned in subsection (2)(b) of that section,
may appeal to the Tribunal against the refusal of the application.

(7) In subsections (1) and (2) "operator's licence" does not include an interim licence issued under section 24.

DEFINITIONS
"operator's licence": s.2.
"prescribed": s.58.

GENERAL NOTE
This section restates and extends the right of appeal from the traffic commissioners to the Transport Tribunal. It is of interest that the right of appeal has not been extended to representors despite the fact that it is common for the Transport Tribunal to invite representors to attend appeal hearings which involve environmental issues.

Forgery, false statements, etc.

Forgery of documents, etc.

38.—(1) A person is guilty of an offence if, with intent to deceive, he—
(a) forges, alters or uses a document or other thing to which this section applies;
(b) lends to, or allows to be used by, any other person a document or other thing to which this section applies; or
(c) makes or has in his possession any document or other thing so closely resembling a document or other thing to which this section applies as to be calculated to deceive.

(2) This section applies to the following documents and other things, namely—
(a) any operator's licence;
(b) any document, plate, mark or other thing by which, in pursuance of regulations, a vehicle is to be identified as being authorised to be used, or as being used, under an operator's licence;
(c) any document evidencing the authorisation of any person for the purposes of sections 40 and 41;
(d) any certificate of qualification under section 49; and
(e) any certificate or diploma such as is mentioned in paragraph 13(1) of Schedule 3.

(3) A person guilty of an offence under subsection (1) is liable—
(a) on summary conviction, to a fine not exceeding the statutory maximum;
(b) on conviction on indictment, to imprisonment for a term not exceeding two years or to a fine or to both.

(4) In the application of subsection (1) to England and Wales, "forges" means makes a false document or other thing in order that it may be used as genuine.

DEFINITIONS
"false": Forgery and Counterfeiting Act 1981, s.9.
"operator's licence": s.2.

GENERAL NOTE
This section restates s.233 of the RTA 1960 and creates either/or offences in respect of forgery and fraudulent use of operators' licences and ancillary documents.

False statements

39.—(1) A person is guilty of an offence if he knowingly makes a false statement for the purpose of—

(a) obtaining the issue to himself or any other person of an operator's licence;

(b) obtaining the variation of any such licence;

(c) preventing the issue or variation of any such licence;

(d) procuring the imposition of a condition or limitation in relation to any such licence; or

(e) obtaining the issue to himself or any other person of a certificate of qualification under section 49 or a certificate or diploma such as is mentioned in paragraph 13(1) of Schedule 3.

(2) A person guilty of an offence under subsection (1) is liable on summary conviction to a fine not exceeding level 4 on the standard scale.

DEFINITIONS

"false": Forgery and Counterfeiting Act 1981, s.9.

"operator's licence": s.2.

GENERAL NOTE

This section restates s.235 of the RTA 1960 and creates a summary offence in respect of the making of false statements in relation to the obtaining or varying of operators' licences.

Enforcement etc.

Inspection of maintenance facilities

40.—(1) An officer may, at any time which is reasonable having regard to the circumstances of the case, enter any premises of an applicant for an operator's licence or of the holder of such a licence and inspect any facilities on those premises for maintaining the vehicles used under the licence in a fit and serviceable condition.

(2) Any person who obstructs an officer in the exercise of his powers under subsection (1) is guilty of an offence and liable on summary conviction to a fine not exceeding level 3 on the standard scale.

DEFINITIONS

"officer": s.41(1).

GENERAL NOTE

This section gives power to authorise officers of the Vehicle Inspectorate to enter premises to inspect maintenance facilities. The penalty for obstructing an officer is a fine not exceeding level 3.

Power to seize documents etc.

41.—(1) If an officer has reason to believe that—

(a) a document or article carried on or by the driver of a vehicle, or

(b) a document produced to him in pursuance of this Act,

is a document or article in relation to which an offence has been committed under section 38 or 39, he may seize that document or article.

(2) Where—

(a) a document or article is seized under subsection (1),

(b) no person has, within six months of the date on which the document or article was seized, been charged since that date with an offence in relation to it under section 38 or 39, and

(c) the document or article is still detained,

then any of the persons mentioned in subsection (3) may make an application to a magistrates' court or (in the case of an application made in Scotland) the sheriff.

(3) The persons who may make an application under subsection (2) are—

(a) an officer;

(b) the driver or owner of the vehicle;

(c) the person from whom the document was seized.

(4) On an application under subsection (2), the magistrates' court or the sheriff shall—

(a) make such order respecting the disposal of the document or article, and

(b) award such costs or (in Scotland) expenses,

as the justice of the case may require.

(5) Any application made under subsection (2) to the sheriff shall be made by way of summary application.

DEFINITIONS
"driver": s.58.
"officer": s.42(1).

GENERAL NOTE
This section re-enacts the power of Examiners or other persons appointed by the traffic commissioners to seize documents they believe to be false. If documents have not been returned or charges made within six months of seizure, application can be made to a magistrate for their return.

Meaning of "officer" and powers of police constables

42.—(1) In sections 40 and 41 "officer" means—

(a) an examiner appointed under section 66A of the Road Traffic Act 1988, or

(b) any person authorised for the purposes of sections 40 and 41 by the traffic commissioner for any area.

(2) The powers conferred by sections 40 and 41 on an officer shall be exercisable also by a police constable.

GENERAL NOTE
This section defines an officer for the purposes of ss.40 and 41 and provides that evidence relating to forgery or falsification of documents can be given by traffic commissioners by certificate rather than by personal attendance.

Evidence by certificate

43.—(1) In any proceedings for an offence under this Act a certificate such as is mentioned in subsection (2) shall be evidence, and in Scotland sufficient evidence, of the facts stated in it.

(2) The certificate referred to in subsection (1) is a certificate signed by or on behalf of a traffic commissioner which states—

(a) that, on any date, a person was or was not the holder of an operator's licence issued by the commissioner;

(b) that, by virtue of a direction given by the commissioner under regulations made under section 48(2)(b) or (3), a person is to be treated as having been the holder of an operator's licence on any date;

(c) the date of the coming into force of any operator's licence issued by the commissioner;

(d) the date on which any operator's licence issued by the commissioner ceased to be in force;

(e) the terms and conditions of any operator's licence issued by the commissioner;

(f) that a person is by virtue of an order of the commissioner disqualified from holding or obtaining an operator's licence, either indefinitely or for a specified period;

(g) that a direction, having effect indefinitely or for a specified period, has been given by the commissioner under section 28(4) in relation to any person;

(h) that an operator's licence was on any date or during any specified period suspended by virtue of a direction given by the commissioner under section 26(1); or

(i) that, by virtue of a direction given by the commissioner under regulations made under section 48(2)(a), an operator's licence is to be treated as having been suspended on any date or during any specified period.

(3) Any such certificate which purports to be signed by or on behalf of a traffic commissioner shall be taken to be so signed unless the contrary is proved.

Miscellaneous

Assessors

44.—(1) In considering any financial question which appears to him to arise in relation to the exercise of his functions under this Act, the traffic commissioner may be assisted by an assessor drawn from a panel of persons appointed for the purpose by the Secretary of State.

(2) The Secretary of State shall pay to any such assessor in respect of his services such remuneration as may be determined by the Secretary of State with the consent of the Treasury.

DEFINITIONS

"traffic commissioner": s.1.

GENERAL NOTE

This section empowers a traffic commissioner to appoint a financial assessor to assist him in considering financial questions.

Fees

45.—(1) Such fees, payable at such times, and whether in one sum or by instalments, as may be prescribed shall be charged by a traffic commissioner in respect of—

(a) applications for, or for the variation of, operators' licences;
(b) the issue or variation of operators' licences;
(c) the continuation in force of operators' licences;
(d) any arrangements made with the holder of an operator's licence to treat the licence for certain administrative purposes as if it were two or more licences.

(2) A traffic commissioner may decline to proceed with—

(a) any application for, or for the variation of, an operator's licence, or
(b) the issue or variation of any operator's licence,

until any fee or instalment of a fee in respect of the application, issue or variation (as the case may be) is duly paid.

(3) If, in the case of any application for, or for the variation of, an operator's licence, any fee or instalment of a fee in respect of the application or the issue or variation of the licence is not duly paid by the prescribed time—

(a) the application shall be treated as withdrawn at that time, and

(b) any decision made or direction given on the application, and any licence issued or variation effected in pursuance of such a direction, ceases to have effect or terminates at that time.

(4) If any fee or instalment of a fee in respect of the continuation in force of an operator's licence is not duly paid by the prescribed time, the licence terminates at that time.

(5) The traffic commissioner may, if he considers there to be exceptional circumstances that justify his doing so in any case where subsection (3) or (4) has applied, direct that as from the time mentioned in that subsection its effect in that case be disregarded.

(6) Where, by virtue of such a direction, the effect of subsection (3)(a) is to be disregarded in any case, any termination—

(a) of an interim licence under section 24(5)(b) or (6), or

(b) of an interim direction under section 25(4),

by virtue of the operation of subsection (3)(a) in that case before the direction was given shall be cancelled with effect from the same time.

(7) Where such a direction is given in respect of an operator's licence—

(a) any condition attached to the licence under section 22 shall be treated as having been of no effect during the period beginning with the time when the licence terminated by virtue of subsection (3) or (4) above and ending with the time when the direction comes into force, and

(b) subject to paragraph (a), the traffic commissioner may vary any such condition as it applies in relation to events occurring before the direction comes into force.

(8) All fees payable under this Act, other than those payable under section 49, shall be paid into the Consolidated Fund in such manner as the Treasury may direct.

DEFINITIONS
"traffic commissioner": s.1.

GENERAL NOTE
This section provides for a revised fee system consequent upon the introduction of continuous licences. In particular, it introduces a charge for processing applications and a charge for continuation in force of licences. It grants to the traffic commissioner the power to refuse to proceed with any application if a fee is not paid and for a continuous licence to lapse if a fee is not paid.

Holding companies and subsidiaries

46.—(1) The Secretary of State may by regulations make provision for the purpose of enabling any company or other body corporate which has one or more subsidiaries to hold an operator's licence under which the vehicles authorised to be used consist of or include vehicles belonging to or in the possession of any of its subsidiaries.

(2) Regulations under this section may—

(a) modify or supplement any of the provisions of this Act, other than the excepted provisions, so far as appears to the Secretary of State to be necessary or expedient for or in connection with the purpose mentioned in subsection (1), and

(b) may contain such other supplementary and incidental provisions as appear to the Secretary of State to be requisite.

(3) In this Act "the excepted provisions" means the following provisions (which are provisions that reproduce the effect of provisions of the Goods Vehicles (Operators' Licences, Qualifications and Fees) Regulations 1984), namely—

(a) sections 3, 4, 9(2) and (3)(b), 13(3), 15(5) and (6), 20, 22(2) to (5), 27 and 49;

(b) in section 58, in subsection (1), the definitions of "international transport operations", "national transport operations", "road transport undertaking" and "transport manager", and subsection (4); and

(c) Schedule 3.

DEFINITIONS
"holding company": Sched. 6, para. 7.
"operator's licence": s.2.
"regulations": s.58.
"subsidiary": Sched. 6, para. 7.

GENERAL NOTE
This section deals with the relationship between holding and subsidiary companies and empowers the Secretary of State to introduce regulations permitting the holding of an operator's licence by a holding company in respect of vehicles operated or belonging to subsidiaries.

Partnerships

47. Regulations may provide for this Act to apply in relation to partnerships with such modifications as may be specified in the regulations; but nothing in any such regulations may make modifications in any of the excepted provisions (within the meaning given in section 46(3)).

DEFINITIONS
"regulations": s.58.

GENERAL NOTE
This section makes provision for operator's licence provisions to be modified where the holder is a partnership.

Operators' licences not to be transferable etc.

48.—(1) Subject to any regulations under section 46, an operator's licence is neither transferable nor assignable.

(2) Regulations may make provision enabling a traffic commissioner, where the holder of an operator's licence issued by him has died or become a patient within the meaning of Part VII of the Mental Health Act 1983, to direct that the licence be treated—

(a) as not having terminated at the time when the licence-holder died or became a patient but as having been suspended (that is, as having remained in force but subject to the limitation that no vehicles were authorised to be used under it) from that time until the time when the direction comes into force; and

(b) as having effect from the time when the direction comes into force for a specified period and as being held during that period (for such purposes and to such extent as may be specified) not by the person to whom it was issued but by such other person carrying on that person's business, or part of that person's business, as may be specified.

(3) Regulations may make provision enabling a traffic commissioner in prescribed circumstances to direct that any operator's licence issued by him is to be treated (for such purposes, for such period and to such extent as may be specified) as held not by the person to whom it was issued but by such other person carrying on that person's business, or part of that person's business, as may be specified.

(4) Regulations may make provision enabling a traffic commissioner to direct, for the purpose of giving effect to or supplementing a direction given by him by virtue of subsection (2) or (3), that this Act is to apply with specified modifications in relation to the person who is to be treated under the

direction as the holder of an operator's licence; but nothing in any such regulations shall permit the commissioner to modify the operation of any of the excepted provisions (within the meaning given in section 46(3)).

(5) In subsection (2) references to a person becoming a patient within the meaning of Part VII of the Mental Health Act 1983 include references to a curator bonis being appointed in respect of him in Scotland on the ground that he is incapable, by reason of mental disorder, of adequately managing and administering his property and affairs.

(6) In this section "specified", in relation to a direction, means specified—
(a) in the regulations under which the direction was given; or
(b) in the direction in accordance with those regulations.

DEFINITIONS
"operator's licence": s.2.
"prescribed": s.58.
"regulations": s.58.
"traffic commissioner": s.1.

GENERAL NOTE
Until the new regulations are introduced, it remains the case that an operator's licence is neither transferable nor assignable. The section does make provision for regulations to be introduced to allow persons to operate vehicles under a licence that would otherwise be terminated on death or mental incapacity subject to a direction being given by the traffic commissioner.

Certificates of qualification

49.—(1) On an application made to him by a person wishing to engage in a road transport undertaking in a member State other than the United Kingdom, the appropriate person shall issue to the applicant a certificate (a "certificate of qualification") as to such matters relating to—
(a) the applicant's repute,
(b) his professional competence, or
(c) (where relevant) his financial standing,
as the appropriate person is satisfied he may properly certify and as appear to him to be of assistance to the applicant in satisfying any requirements imposed by the law of the other member State as regards the repute, professional competence and financial standing of persons engaged in road transport undertakings in that member State.

(2) A certificate of qualification shall—
(a) be in such form as the Secretary of State for Transport may specify; and
(b) have effect for the purposes of Article 3, 4 or (as the case may be) 5 of the 1977 Council Directive.

(3) No certificate of qualification shall be issued before a fee of £20 has been paid.

(4) The applicant shall give to the appropriate person such information as that person may reasonably require for the discharge of his duties in relation to the application.

(5) In this section "the appropriate person"—
(a) in relation to an applicant who holds only one operator's licence, means the traffic commissioner who issued that licence;
(b) in relation to an applicant who holds more than one such licence, means the traffic commissioner who issued any one of those licences; and
(c) in relation to an applicant who holds no such licence, means the Secretary of State;
and in subsection (1) references to repute, professional competence or financial standing are to be construed in accordance with the 1974 Council Directive.

(6) All fees payable under this section shall be paid into the Consolidated Fund.

DEFINITIONS
   "financial standing": Sched. 3.
   "professional competence": Sched. 3.
   "repute": Sched. 3.
   "road transport undertaking": s.58.
   "traffic commissioner": s.1.

GENERAL NOTE
   This section empowers a traffic commissioner to issue a certificate of qualification to operators who wish to operate outside the U.K. confirming that the operator has satisfied the test as to repute, professional competence and financial standing in the U.K. The certificate can be given by a traffic commissioner in relation to a single licence held in his area or in respect of licences held in his own area and others.

Large goods vehicles

Large goods vehicles

   50.—(1) Schedule 5 (which requires certain documents to be carried by the drivers of large goods vehicles and makes other provision in connection with such vehicles) shall have effect.
   (2) This section and Schedule 5 shall come into force on such day as the Secretary of State may by order appoint; and different days may be appointed for different purposes and different provisions.

DEFINITIONS
   "drivers": s.58.
   "large goods vehicles": Sched. 5, paras. 1–6.

GENERAL NOTE
   This section will come into effect upon days to be appointed. The section requires consignment notes as described in Sched. 5 to be carried by the drivers of large goods vehicles as defined in the Schedule.
   This section is expressly excluded from S.I. 1995 No. 2181.

General provisions

Time for bringing proceedings

   51. Section 6 of the Road Traffic Offenders Act 1988 (time for bringing summary proceedings for certain offences) shall apply to an offence under section 9(3)(a) or (b), 38 or 39.

GENERAL NOTE
   This section provides that the time-limit for bringing summary proceedings under ss.9(3)(a) or (b), 38 or 39 will be subject to the time-limits set out under s.6 of the Act referred to.

Destination of fines: Scotland

   52. There shall be paid into the Consolidated Fund all fines imposed in respect of offences committed in Scotland under the provisions of this Act or regulations made under it.

GENERAL NOTE
   Fines in respect of offences committed in Scotland will be paid into the Consolidated Fund.

Method of calculating weight of motor vehicles

   53. For the purposes of this Act the weight unladen of a vehicle shall be taken to be the weight of the vehicle inclusive of the body and all parts (the heavier being taken where alternative bodies or parts are used) which are necessary to or ordinarily used with the vehicle when working on a road, but exclusive of the weight of water, fuel or accumulators used for the purpose of the supply of power for the propulsion of the vehicle, and of loose tools and loose equipment.

This section sets out the manner of arriving at the unladen weight of the vehicle.

Saving for law of nuisance

54. Nothing in this Act shall authorise a person to use on a road a vehicle so constructed or used as to cause a public or private nuisance, or in Scotland a nuisance, or affect the liability, whether under statute or common law, of the driver or owner so using such a vehicle.

This section repeats s.269 of the RTA 1960 in that the authorising of the use of a vehicle on the road will not excuse an operator from being liable for causing a public or private nuisance.

Protection of public interests

55. It is hereby declared that nothing in this Act is to be treated as conferring on the holder of an operator's licence any right to the continuance of any benefits arising from this Act or from any such licence or from any conditions attached to any such licence.

This section provides that the granting of a licence does not create absolute benefits.

Secretary of State's power to hold inquiries

56. In sections 248 and 249 of the Road Traffic Act 1960 (which give the Secretary of State power to hold inquiries for the purposes of that Act, and make general provision as to such inquiries) any reference to that Act shall be taken to include a reference to this Act, except that such a reference shall not be taken to include a reference to any of the excepted provisions (within the meaning given in section 46(3) above).

This section extends the power of the Secretary of State as previously set out in the RTA 1960 to hold enquiries.

Regulations and orders

Regulations and orders

57.—(1) The Secretary of State may make regulations for any purpose for which regulations may be made under this Act, and for prescribing anything which may be prescribed under this Act, and generally for carrying this Act into effect.

(2) In particular, but without prejudice to the generality of subsection (1), the Secretary of State may make regulations with respect to the following matters—

  (a) the procedure on applications for, and the determination of questions in connection with, the issuing and variation of operators' licences and the procedure under, and the determination of questions for the purposes of, sections 26 to 32 and 36;

  (b) the issue of operators' licences and the issue on payment of the prescribed fee of copies of such licences in the case of licences lost or defaced;

  (c) the forms which operators' licences are to take in order to show a distinction—

    (i) between a standard licence and a restricted licence; and

    (ii) between a licence covering both international and national transport operations and a licence covering national transport operations only;

(d) the means by which vehicles may be identified, whether by plates, marks or otherwise, as being used or authorised to be used under an operator's licence;

(e) the custody, production, return and cancellation of operators' licences and of documents, plates and any other means of identification prescribed under paragraph (d);

(f) the payment of a prescribed fee in respect of any document, plate or other means of identification so prescribed that has been lost, defaced or broken;

(g) the notification to a traffic commissioner of vehicles which have ceased to be used under an operator's licence;

(h) the repayment (or partial repayment) in the prescribed circumstances of fees paid under this Act;

(i) the circumstances in which goods are to be treated for the purposes of this Act as carried for hire or reward and the circumstances in which goods are to be treated for those purposes as carried by any person for or in connection with a trade or business carried on by him.

(3) The power under subsection (2)(a) shall include power to require a person applying for an operator's licence to state in his application—

(a) whether his application is for a standard licence or a restricted licence, and

(b) (if his application is for a standard licence) whether his application is for a licence to cover both international and national transport operations or for one to cover national transport operations only.

(4) The power under subsection (2)(d) shall include power to require that any means of identification prescribed for a vehicle shall be carried notwithstanding that for the time being the vehicle is not being used for a purpose for which an operator's licence is required.

(5) The power under subsection (2)(d) shall also include power to make provision with respect to the means by which—

(a) any vehicle may be identified as being used under a standard licence or, as the case may be, a restricted licence; and

(b) any vehicle which is being used under a standard licence may be identified as being used under a licence that permits it to be used—

(i) for both international and national transport operations, or

(ii) for national transport operations only.

(6) The Secretary of State may make regulations for providing that any provision of this Act shall, in relation to vehicles brought temporarily into Great Britain, have effect subject to such modifications as may be prescribed.

(7) Any regulations under this Act may make—

(a) different provision for different cases or classes of case and different circumstances, and

(b) transitional provision,

and regulations made by virtue of subsection (2)(d) may make different provision for different traffic areas.

(8) A definition or description of a class of vehicles for the purposes of any regulation under this Act may be framed by reference to any characteristic of the vehicles or to any other circumstances whatever.

(9) Any person who contravenes a provision of regulations under this section, a contravention of which is declared by the regulations to be an offence, is guilty of an offence and liable on summary conviction to a fine not exceeding level 1 on the standard scale.

(10) No regulations shall be made under section 30(3) unless a draft of them has been laid before, and approved by a resolution of, each House of Parliament.

(11) Any regulations made by the Secretary of State under this Act, other than regulations under section 30(3), shall be subject to annulment in pursuance of a resolution of either House of Parliament.

(12) Before making any regulations under this Act the Secretary of State shall consult with such representative organisations as he thinks fit.

(13) Any power to make orders or regulations conferred on the Secretary of State by any provision of this Act shall be exercisable by statutory instrument.

GENERAL NOTE

This section brings together the powers granted to the Secretary of State to make regulations under the various Acts which are consolidated. Subsection (2) lists a number of circumstances in which regulations may be made, but such circumstances are not exhaustive.

The powers extend to requiring an applicant to state the type of licence which he requires and the form of identification which should be carried out in vehicles to indicate that they are being used in accordance with the particular type of licence granted.

Interpretation

General interpretation

58.—(1) In this Act, unless the context otherwise requires—

"area", in relation to a traffic commissioner, means the traffic area for which he is the traffic commissioner;

"articulated combination" means a combination made up of—

(a) a motor vehicle which is so constructed that a trailer may by partial superimposition be attached to the vehicle in such a manner as to cause a substantial part of the weight of the trailer to be borne by the vehicle, and

(b) a trailer attached to it as described in paragraph (a);

"carriage of goods" includes haulage of goods;

"contravention", in relation to any condition or provision, includes a failure to comply with the condition or provision, and "contravenes" shall be construed accordingly;

"the 1974 Council Directive" means Community Council Directive No. 74/561/EEC dated 12 November 1974 on admission to the occupation of road haulage operator in national and international transport operations, as amended by Community Council Directive No. 89/438/EEC dated 21 June 1989;

"the 1977 Council Directive" means Community Council Directive No. 77/796/EEC dated 12 December 1977 concerning the mutual recognition of diplomas, certificates and other evidence of formal qualifications for goods haulage operators and road passenger transport operators, including measures to encourage such operators effectively to exercise their right of freedom of establishment, as amended by Community Council Directive No. 89/438/EEC dated 21 June 1989;

"driver"—

(a) where a separate person acts as steersman of a motor vehicle, includes that person as well as any other person engaged in the driving of the vehicle; and

(b) in relation to a trailer, means the driver of the vehicle by which the trailer is drawn;

and "drive" shall be construed accordingly;

"functions" includes powers, duties and obligations;

"goods" includes goods or burden of any description;

"goods vehicle" means a motor vehicle constructed or adapted for use for the carriage of goods, or a trailer so constructed or adapted, but does not include a tramcar or trolley vehicle within the meaning of the Road Traffic Act 1988;

"holding company" and "subsidiary" have the meaning given by section 736 of the Companies Act 1985;

"international transport operations" and "national transport operations" have the same meaning as in the 1974 Council Directive;

"modification" includes addition, omission and alteration, and related expressions shall be construed accordingly;

"motor vehicle" and "trailer" have the same meaning as in section 253 of the Road Traffic Act 1960;

"operating centre" has the meaning given in section 7(3);

"operator's licence" has the meaning given in section 2(1);

"owner", in relation to any land in England and Wales, means a person, other than a mortgagee not in possession, who, whether in his own right or as trustee for any other person, is entitled to receive the rack rent of the land or, where the land is not let at a rack rent, would be so entitled if it were so let;

"plated weight", in relation to a vehicle, means a weight required to be marked on it by means of a plate in pursuance of regulations made by virtue of section 41 of the Road Traffic Act 1988 or required to be so marked by section 57 or 58 of that Act;

"prescribed" means prescribed by regulations;

"regulations" means regulations made by the Secretary of State under this Act;

"restricted licence" has the meaning given in section 3(3);

"road"—

        (a) in relation to England and Wales, means any highway and any other road to which the public has access, and includes bridges over which a road passes; and

        (b) in relation to Scotland, has the same meaning as in the Roads (Scotland) Act 1984;

"road transport undertaking" means an undertaking which involves the use of goods vehicles—

        (a) under an operator's licence, or

        (b) in accordance with the law of Northern Ireland or the law of any member State other than the United Kingdom;

"standard licence" has the meaning given in section 3(2);

"statutory provision" means a provision contained in an Act or in subordinate legislation within the meaning of the Interpretation Act 1978;

"traffic area" means a traffic area constituted for the purposes of the Public Passenger Vehicles Act 1981;

"transport manager", in relation to a business, means an individual who is in, or who is engaged to enter into, the employment of the holder of a standard licence and who, either alone or jointly with one or more other persons, has continuous and effective responsibility for the management of the transport operations of the business in so far as they relate to the carriage of goods;

"vehicle combination" means a combination of goods vehicles made up of one or more motor vehicles and one or more trailers all of which are linked together when travelling.

(2) For the purposes of this Act, the driver of a vehicle, if it belongs to him or is in his possession under an agreement for hire, hire-purchase or loan, and in any other case the person whose servant or agent the driver is, shall be deemed to be the person using the vehicle; and references to using a vehicle shall be construed accordingly.

(3) In this Act references to vehicles being authorised to be used under an operator's licence are to be read in accordance with section 5.

(4) For the purposes of this Act, a person who is an applicant for, or a holder of, a standard licence, or who is a transport manager, shall be regarded as being engaged in a road transport undertaking if—

  (a) in a case where that person is an individual, he is either—

(i) the holder, or one of the joint holders, of an operator's licence, or

(ii) in the employment of a person who carries on a road transport undertaking and that undertaking gives him responsibility for the operation of goods vehicles used under an operator's licence; or

(b) in a case where that person is a company, either—

(i) the company is the holder of an operator's licence, or

(ii) the company is a subsidiary of the holder of an operator's licence and goods vehicles used under that licence belong to the company or are in its possession.

(5) Anything required or authorised by this Act to be done by or to a traffic commissioner by whom a licence was issued may be done by or to any person for the time being acting as traffic commissioner for the area for which the first-mentioned commissioner was acting at the time of the issuing of the licence.

Supplementary provisions

Transitional provision etc.

59.—(1) The transitional provisions and transitory modifications of this Act contained in Schedule 6 shall have effect.

(2) Without prejudice to the generality of paragraphs 2 to 4 of that Schedule, an existing licence shall continue in force as if it had been issued under this Act, and in this Act or any other enactment, instrument or document, any reference to, or including a reference to, an operator's licence issued under this Act shall, so far as the nature of the reference permits, be construed as including a reference to an existing licence.

(3) In subsection (2) "existing licence" means any operator's licence within the meaning of Part V of the Transport Act 1968 which was in force immediately before the commencement of this Act.

Consequential amendments and repeals

60.—(1) The enactments mentioned in Schedule 7 shall have effect subject to the amendments there specified (being amendments consequential upon the provisions of this Act).

(2) The enactments and instruments specified in Schedule 8 are repealed or revoked to the extent specified in the third column of that Schedule.

GENERAL NOTE

This section gives effect to the amendments specified in Sched. 7 and the repeal and revocation of the enactments and statutory instruments set out in Sched. 8.

Commencement

61.—(1) Subject to section 50(2) (which makes provision in relation to the commencement of section 50 and Schedule 5) this Act shall come into force on such day as the Secretary of State may by order appoint.

(2) An order under subsection (1) may contain such transitional provisions and savings as appear to the Secretary of State to be necessary or expedient in connection with the coming into force of any provision of this Act which reproduces the effect of any provision of the Deregulation and Contracting Out Act 1994 which was not brought into force before the appointed day.

(3) Where any provision of the Deregulation and Contracting Out Act 1994 was brought into force before the appointed day by an order containing transitional provisions or savings in connection with the coming into force of that provision, an order under subsection (1) may contain corresponding transitional provisions or savings in connection with the coming into force of any provision of this Act which reproduces the effect of that provision of that Act.

(4) In subsections (2) and (3) "the appointed day" means the day appointed under subsection (1).

General Note
The day appointed for the coming into force of this Act is January 1, 1996 (S.I. 1995 No. 2181).

Short title and extent

62.—(1) This Act may be cited as the Goods Vehicles (Licensing of Operators) Act 1995.

(2) The amendments specified in Schedule 7 and the repeals and revocations specified in Schedule 8 have the same extent as the enactments and instruments to which they relate.

(3) Subject to subsection (2), this Act does not extend to Northern Ireland.

SCHEDULES

Section 2   SCHEDULE 1

MEANING OF "SMALL GOODS VEHICLE"

1. For the purposes of section 2 a small goods vehicle is a goods vehicle falling within any of paragraphs 2 to 4.

2. A goods vehicle falls within this paragraph if it does not form part of a vehicle combination and—
   (a) has a relevant plated weight not exceeding 3.5 tonnes, or
   (b) if it does not have a relevant plated weight, has an unladen weight not exceeding 1525 kilograms.

3.—(1) A goods vehicle falls within this paragraph if it forms part of a vehicle combination, other than an articulated combination, and the combination is such that—
   (a) in a case where all the vehicles comprised in it, or all of those vehicles except any small trailer, have relevant plated weights, the aggregate of the relevant plated weights of those vehicles, exclusive of any such trailer, does not exceed 3.5 tonnes, or
   (b) in any other case, the aggregate of the unladen weights of the vehicles comprised in the combination, exclusive of any small trailer, does not exceed 1525 kilograms.

(2) In this paragraph "small trailer" means a trailer having an unladen weight not exceeding 1020 kilograms.

4. A goods vehicle falls within this paragraph if it forms part of an articulated combination which is such that—
   (a) in a case where the trailer comprised in the combination has a relevant plated weight, the aggregate of—
      (i) the unladen weight of the motor vehicle comprised in the combination, and
      (ii) the relevant plated weight of that trailer,
   does not exceed 3.5 tonnes, or
   (b) in any other case, the aggregate of the unladen weights of the motor vehicle and the trailer comprised in the combination does not exceed 1525 kilograms.

5. In any provision of paragraphs 2 to 4 "relevant plated weight" means a plated weight of the description specified in relation to that provision by regulations.

DEFINITIONS
"articulated combination": s.58.
"goods vehicles": s.58.
"plated weight": s.58.
"regulations": s.58.
"trailer": s.58.

"unladen weight": s.53.
"vehicle combination": s.58.

General Note

This Schedule sets out the definition of a "small goods vehicle" as is referred to in s.2. All weights are now metric.

Sections 8, 9 and 26   SCHEDULE 2

Information about, and convictions of, applicants for and holders of operators' licences

Information to be given under section 8

1. The information referred to in section 8(4) is the following—
(a) such particulars as the traffic commissioner may require with respect to the purposes for which the vehicles referred to in the statement under section 8(3) are proposed to be used;
(b) particulars of the arrangements for securing that—
(i) Part VI of the Transport Act 1968 (drivers' hours), and
(ii) the applicable Community rules, within the meaning of that Part,
will be complied with in the case of those vehicles;
(c) particulars of the arrangements for securing that those vehicles will not be overloaded;
(d) particulars of the facilities and arrangements for securing that those vehicles will be maintained in a fit and serviceable condition;
(e) particulars of any relevant activities carried on, at any time before the making of the application, by any relevant person;
(f) particulars of any notifiable convictions which have occurred during the five years preceding the making of the application;
(g) particulars of the financial resources which are or are likely to be available to the applicant;
(h) where the applicant is a company, the names of the directors and officers of—
(i) the company, and
(ii) any company of which that company is a subsidiary;
(i) where the vehicles referred to in the statement under section 8(3) are proposed to be operated by the applicant in partnership with other persons, the names of those other persons.

"Relevant person"

2. In this Schedule "relevant person" means any of the following persons, namely—
(a) the applicant;
(b) any company of which the applicant is or has been a director;
(c) where the applicant is a company, any person who is a director of the company;
(d) where the applicant proposes to operate the vehicles referred to in the statement under section 8(3) in partnership with other persons, any of those other persons;
(e) any company of which any such person as is mentioned in sub-paragraph (c) or (d) is or has been a director; or
(f) where the applicant is a company, any company of which the applicant is a subsidiary.

"Relevant activities"

3. In paragraph 1(e) "relevant activities" means any of the following—
(a) activities in carrying on any trade or business in the course of which vehicles of any description are operated;
(b) activities as a person employed for the purposes of any such trade or business; or
(c) activities as a director of a company carrying on any such trade or business.

"Notifiable convictions"

4. The following are "notifiable convictions", namely—
(a) any conviction of a relevant person of an offence such as is mentioned in paragraph 5, and
(b) any conviction of a servant or agent of a relevant person of an offence such as is mentioned in sub-paragraph (a), (b), (d), (f), (g), (i) or (j) of that paragraph.

Offences

5. The offences are—
(a) an offence under section 53 of the Road Traffic Act 1988 (plating certificates and goods vehicle test certificates);

(b) an offence committed in relation to a goods vehicle consisting in the contravention of any provision (however expressed) contained in or having effect under any enactment (including any enactment passed after this Act) relating to—
    (i) the maintenance of vehicles in a fit and serviceable condition;
    (ii) limits of speed and weight laden and unladen, and the loading of goods vehicles; or
    (iii) the licensing of drivers;
(c) an offence under—
    (i) this Act;
    (ii) Part V of the Transport Act 1968 or section 233 or 235 of the Road Traffic Act 1960 so far as applicable (by virtue of Schedule 10 to the 1968 Act) to licences or means of identification under that Part;
    (iii) regulation 33(2) or (3) of the Goods Vehicles (Operators' Licences, Qualifications and Fees) Regulations 1984; or
    (iv) any regulation made under this Act or the Transport Act 1968 which is prescribed for the purposes of this paragraph;
(d) an offence under, or of conspiracy to contravene, Part VI of the Transport Act 1968 (drivers' hours) committed in relation to a goods vehicle;
(e) an offence under, or of conspiracy to contravene, section 13 of the Hydrocarbon Oil Duties Act 1979 (unlawful use of rebated fuel oil) committed in relation to a goods vehicle;
(f) an offence under section 173 or 174 of the Road Traffic Act 1988 (forgery, false statements and withholding of information) committed in relation to an international road haulage permit within the meaning of that Act;
(g) an offence under section 2 of the International Road Haulage Permits Act 1975 (removing, or causing or permitting the removal of, a goods vehicle or trailer from the United Kingdom in contravention of a prohibition imposed under that section);
(h) an offence under section 74 of the Road Traffic Act 1988 (operator's duty to inspect, and keep records of inspection of, goods vehicles);
(i) an offence under—
    (i) section 3 of the Control of Pollution Act 1974;
    (ii) section 2 of the Refuse Disposal (Amenity) Act 1978;
    (iii) section 1 of the Control of Pollution (Amendment) Act 1989; or
    (iv) section 33 of the Environmental Protection Act 1990;
(j) an offence committed in relation to a goods vehicle consisting in the contravention of—
    (i) any provision (however expressed) prohibiting or restricting the waiting of vehicles which is contained in an order made under section 1, 6, 9 or 12 of the Road Traffic Regulation Act 1984, including any such order made by virtue of paragraph 3 of Schedule 9 to that Act (local authority powers to be exercisable also by Secretary of State); or
    (ii) any provision which is contained in a traffic regulation order, within the meaning of section 1 of that Act, by virtue of section 2(4) of that Act (lorry routes).

Repealed enactments

6.—(1) In paragraph 5 any reference to an offence under a provision of the Road Traffic Act 1988 includes a reference to an offence under any corresponding provision of the Road Traffic Act 1972 repealed by the Road Traffic (Consequential Provisions) Act 1988.
(2) In paragraph 5(j)—
(a) the reference to a provision contained in an order made under section 1, 6, 9 or 12 of the Road Traffic Regulation Act 1984 includes a reference to a provision contained in an order made under any enactment repealed by the 1984 Act and re-enacted by any of those sections, including any such order made by virtue of section 84A(2) of the Road Traffic Regulation Act 1967; and
(b) the reference to a provision contained in a traffic regulation order by virtue of section 2(4) of the 1984 Act includes a reference to a provision included in such an order by virtue of section 1(3AA) of the 1967 Act.

DEFINITIONS
  "contravention": s.58.
  "notifiable convictions": Sched. 2, para. 4.
  "relevant person": para. 2.

"traffic commissioner": s.1.

GENERAL NOTE

This Schedule sets out in detail the information which may be required by the traffic commissioner under s.8 and defines "relevant person" as referred to in that section and "relevant activities". It further defines the notifiable convictions and offences which will be taken into account by a traffic commissioner when considering an application and the offences which will be considered under s.26 when the traffic commissioner considers revocation, suspension or curtailment of a licence.

Sections 13 and 27   SCHEDULE 3

QUALIFICATIONS FOR STANDARD LICENCE

Good repute

1.—(1) In determining whether an individual is of good repute, a traffic commissioner may have regard to any matter but shall, in particular, have regard to—
(a) any relevant convictions of the individual or of his servants or agents; and
(b) any other information in his possession which appears to him to relate to the individual's fitness to hold a licence.

(2) In determining whether a company is of good repute, a traffic commissioner shall have regard to all the material evidence including, in particular—
(a) any relevant convictions of the company or of any of its officers, servants or agents; and
(b) any other information in his possession as to the previous conduct of—
    (i) any of the company's officers, servants or agents, or
    (ii) any of its directors, in whatever capacity,
if that conduct appears to him to relate to the company's fitness to hold a licence.

(3) For the purposes of this paragraph, the relevant convictions of any person are—
(a) any conviction of that person of an offence such as is mentioned in paragraph 5 of Schedule 2;
(b) any conviction of that person of an offence under the law of Northern Ireland or of the law of any country or territory outside the United Kingdom corresponding to an offence such as is mentioned in that paragraph;
(c) any conviction of that person of a serious offence within the meaning given in paragraph 3; and
(d) any conviction of that person of a road transport offence within the meaning given in paragraph 4.

2. Without prejudice to the generality of a traffic commissioner's power under paragraph 1 to determine that a person is not of good repute, a commissioner shall determine that an individual is not of good repute if that individual—
(a) has more than one conviction of a serious offence; or
(b) has repeatedly been convicted of road transport offences.

3.—(1) A person has a conviction of a "serious offence" if—
(a) he has been convicted of any offence under the law of any part of the United Kingdom or under the law of a country or territory outside the United Kingdom, and
(b) on such conviction there was imposed on him for that offence a punishment falling within sub-paragraph (2).

(2) The punishments are—
(a) a sentence of imprisonment for a term exceeding three months;
(b) a fine exceeding level 4 on the standard scale;
(c) a community service order requiring him to perform work for more than 60 hours; and
(d) in the case of an offence committed under the law of a country or territory outside the United Kingdom, any punishment corresponding to those mentioned in paragraphs (a) to (c).

(3) In sub-paragraph (2)—
(a) the reference to a sentence of imprisonment includes a reference to any form of custodial sentence or order, other than one imposed under the enactments relating to mental health; and
(b) "community service order" means an order under section 14 of the Powers of Criminal Courts Act 1973 or under the Community Service by Offenders (Scotland) Act 1978.

4. "Road transport offence" means—
(a) an offence under the law of any part of the United Kingdom relating to road transport including, in particular, offences relating to—
    (i) drivers' hours of work and rest periods;

(ii) the weights and dimensions of commercial vehicles; and

(iii) road and vehicle safety; or

(b) any corresponding offence under the law of a country or territory outside the United Kingdom.

5.—(1) Any reference in paragraphs 1 to 4 to an offence under the law of any part of the United Kingdom includes a reference to a civil offence (wherever committed) within the meaning of the Army Act 1955, the Air Force Act 1955 or (as the case may be) the Naval Discipline Act 1957.

(2) For the purposes of paragraphs 1 to 4—

(a) convictions which are spent for the purposes of the Rehabilitation of Offenders Act 1974 shall be disregarded; and

(b) a traffic commissioner may also disregard an offence if such time as he thinks appropriate has elapsed since the date of the conviction.

Appropriate financial standing

6.—(1) An applicant for, or the holder of, a standard licence is of the appropriate financial standing if he has available to him sufficient financial resources to ensure the establishment and proper administration of the road transport undertaking carried on, or proposed to be carried on, under the licence.

(2) An applicant for, or the holder of, a standard licence authorising the use of vehicles for international transport operations shall not be considered to be of the appropriate financial standing unless he has available to him capital and reserves of an amount equal to or exceeding whichever of the following amounts is, in his case, the lesser—

(a) 3000 European Currency Units multiplied by the number of vehicles which are, or are to be, used under the licence, or

(b) 150 European Currency Units multiplied by the number of tonnes of the aggregate of the relevant maximum weights of those vehicles.

(3) In sub-paragraph (2) "relevant maximum weight" has the meaning given in section 108(1) of the Road Traffic Act 1988.

(4) Sub-paragraph (2) does not apply in relation to—

(a) any licence issued before 11 October 1990, or

(b) any licence issued on or after that date to a person who has continuously held a licence since before that date and up to the time when the new licence is issued.

Professional competence

7. In this Schedule references to "the requirement of professional competence" are references to any requirement imposed by a provision of this Act that a person be (or continue to be) professionally competent.

8.—(1) The requirement of professional competence falls to be satisfied by an individual.

(2) Accordingly, where a company is required to satisfy that requirement, it does so if and so long as—

(a) it has in respect of its road transport undertaking a transport manager or managers, and such number of them as the traffic commissioner concerned may require; and

(b) that transport manager, or (as the case may be) each such manager, is—

(i) of good repute, and

(ii) professionally competent.

9. Where an individual is not himself professionally competent, he shall be regarded as satisfying the requirement of professional competence if and so long as he has as the transport manager of the transport undertaking which he carries on an individual who is—

(a) of good repute, and

(b) professionally competent.

10. Where the holder of a standard licence relies on a single transport manager to satisfy the requirement of professional competence and that manager—

(a) dies,

(b) ceases, by reason of physical disability or mental disorder, to be capable of discharging his duties as transport manager,

(c) ceases to work for the business, or

(d) ceases to be of good repute,

the holder of the licence shall not be treated as failing to satisfy the requirement of professional competence until the expiry of such period (not exceeding 18 months) as, in the opinion of the traffic commissioner by whom the licence was issued, is reasonably required for the appointment of a new transport manager.

11. Where—

(a) the holder of a standard licence is a company which has two or more transport managers, and

(b) any of those managers ceases to be of good repute,

the company shall not be treated as failing to satisfy the requirement of professional competence until the expiry of such period as, in the opinion of the traffic commissioner by whom the licence was issued, is reasonably required for that manager's removal or the appointment of another transport manager in his place.

12. Paragraphs 1 to 5 shall have effect for the purposes of any provision of paragraphs 8 to 11 by virtue of which it falls to be determined whether or not a transport manager is of good repute as they have effect for the purpose of determining for the purposes of any other provision of this Act whether or not any other individual is of good repute, but disregarding the reference in paragraph 1(1)(a) to the servants or agents of an individual.

13.—(1) An individual shall be regarded as professionally competent if, and only if—

(a) he has demonstrated that he possesses the requisite skills by passing a written examination organised by an approved body and is the holder of a certificate to that effect issued by that body; or

(b) he is the holder of any other certificate of competence, diploma or other qualification recognised for the purposes of this sub-paragraph by the Secretary of State.

(2) The written examination mentioned in sub-paragraph (1)(a) may take the form of a multiple-choice examination.

(3) In sub-paragraph (1)—

"approved body" means—

(a) a body approved by the Secretary of State for the purposes of that sub-paragraph;

(b) a body approved by the Department of the Environment for Northern Ireland for the purposes of section 46A(5)(c) of the Transport Act (Northern Ireland) 1967; or

(c) a body or authority designated for the purposes of Article 3.4 of the 1974 Council Directive by a member State other than the United Kingdom; and

"the requisite skills" means skills in the subjects listed in Part A and, in the case of a licence to cover international operations, Part B, of the Annex to the 1974 Council Directive.

14. In relation to a certificate of professional competence which was issued before 4 February 1991, or which was issued on or after that date to a person who before that date passed the whole or any part of the examination leading to the issue of that certificate, paragraph 13 has effect with the following modifications—

(a) for sub-paragraph (1)(a) there shall be substituted—

"(a) he is the holder of a certificate issued by an approved body to the effect that he possesses the requisite skills; or";

(b) sub-paragraph (2) shall be omitted; and

(c) references in sub-paragraph (3) to the 1974 Council Directive shall be construed as references to that Directive as it had effect immediately before it was amended by Community Council Directive No. 89/438/EEC dated 21 June 1989.

Transport manager to be notified of proceedings

15.—(1) A traffic commissioner shall not in any proceedings under this Act make a finding that a transport manager is not of good repute or is not professionally competent unless the commissioner is satisfied that the transport manager has been served with a notice—

(a) stating that the question whether he is of good repute or (as the case may be) professionally competent is an issue in the proceedings;

(b) setting out the nature of the allegations against him; and

(c) stating that he is entitled to make representations under this paragraph within 28 days beginning with the date on which the notice is served on him.

(2) Where a transport manager makes representations under this paragraph, the traffic commissioner shall consider the representations—

(a) in considering whether or not to hold an inquiry as provided in section 35; and

(b) in determining whether the transport manager is of good repute or (as the case may be) professionally competent.

(3) A notice shall be deemed for the purposes of sub-paragraph (1) to have been served on a transport manager on the date on which it would have been delivered in the ordinary course of post if it was sent by post addressed to him at his last known address, notwithstanding that the notice was returned as undelivered or was for any other reason not received by him.

GENERAL NOTE
  This Schedule sets out the qualifications for a standard licence as previously set out in S.I. 1984 No. 176 subject to the amendments introduced by S.I. 1990 No. 2640 and S.I. 1991 No. 2239.

Section 33   SCHEDULE 4

TRANSFER OF OPERATING CENTRES

Transfers in connection with new licences

1.—(1) Where in the case of any application for an operator's licence—
  (a) the requirements of sub-paragraphs (2) to (5) are satisfied at the time when the application is made, and
  (b) the applicant so requests,
the traffic commissioner may direct that paragraph 2 is to apply in relation to the application.

  (2) Each place referred to in the statement under section 8(3) as a proposed operating centre of the applicant must already be specified in an operator's licence as an operating centre of its holder.

  (3) That licence must be the same in the case of each such place, and no such place may be specified in more than the one operator's licence.

  (4) Where any conditions under section 21 or 23 relating to any such place are attached to that licence, the applicant must have consented to conditions in the same terms being attached to the licence he is applying for.

  (5) Where any undertakings relating to any such place are recorded in that licence, undertakings in the same terms must have been given by the applicant (or have been procured by him to be given) for the purposes of the application.

  (6) In determining whether to give a direction under this paragraph, the traffic commissioner shall take account of whether any new adverse effects on environmental conditions are likely to arise from the use as an operating centre of the applicant of any such place, and may take account of any other matters he considers relevant.

  (7) A place is not to be regarded for the purposes of sub-paragraph (2) as being specified in an operator's licence by reason only that it forms part of a place so specified; and a place that was, at the time mentioned in sub-paragraph (1)(a), a place specified in an operator's licence as mentioned in sub-paragraph (2) shall be disregarded for the purposes of sub-paragraph (2) if, at that time—
  (a) that place was so specified by virtue of an interim direction such as is mentioned in section 25; or
  (b) such conditions relating to—
      (i) the exercise of the right of any person to appeal against a place being specified in an operator's licence, or
      (ii) the review under section 36 of any decision so to specify a place,
    as may be prescribed were not satisfied in relation to that place.

  (8) In this paragraph "operator's licence" does not include an interim licence issued under section 24.

  2.—(1) The provisions of this paragraph have effect in relation to any application for an operator's licence in respect of which a direction has been given under paragraph 1.

  (2) The notice published under section 10(1) shall state that the direction has been given.

  (3) The following provisions of this Act shall not apply—
      section 11;
      section 12(1)(b) and (4);
      section 13(5)(d) so far as relating to the suitability of any place specified in the licence for use as an operating centre of the licence-holder;
      section 14; and

section 15(3)(f).

(4) Notwithstanding anything in section 13(11) the traffic commissioner may refuse the application if—

(a) any statement of fact made by the applicant (or procured by him to be made) for the purposes of the request for the direction under paragraph 1 was false, whether to his knowledge or not; or

(b) any undertaking given or statement of expectation made by the applicant (or procured by him to be given or made) for those purposes has not been fulfilled.

(5) If the application is granted, the traffic commissioner—

(a) shall attach to the licence issued to the applicant any conditions in respect of which the applicant has consented under paragraph 1(4); and

(b) shall not attach any other conditions to the licence under section 21 or 23.

(6) If the application is granted, the traffic commissioner shall record in the licence—

(a) any undertakings given or procured to be given under paragraph 1(5); and

(b) any other undertakings given by the applicant (or procured by him to be given), whether for the purposes of the application or for the purposes of the request for the direction under paragraph 1, that the traffic commissioner considers to be material to his decision to give the direction (and that would not otherwise be required by section 15(4) to be recorded in the licence).

Transfers in connection with the variation of licences

3.—(1) Where in the case of an application for the variation of an operator's licence under section 17—

(a) the only direction applied for is one under subsection (1)(g) of that section that one or more new places be specified in the licence as an operating centre of the licence-holder,

(b) the requirements of sub-paragraphs (2) to (5) are satisfied at the time when the application is made, and

(c) the applicant so requests,

the traffic commissioner may direct that paragraph 4 is to apply in relation to the application.

(2) Each new place that is proposed to be specified in the licence must already be specified in another operator's licence as an operating centre of its holder.

(3) That other licence must be the same in the case of each such place, and no such place may be specified in more than the one other operator's licence.

(4) Where any conditions under section 21 or 23 relating to any such place are attached to that other licence, the applicant must have consented to conditions in the same terms being attached to the licence he is applying to have varied.

(5) Where any undertakings relating to any such place are recorded in that other licence, undertakings in the same terms must have been given by the applicant (or have been procured by him to be given) for the purposes of the application.

(6) In determining whether to give a direction under this paragraph, the traffic commissioner shall take account of whether any new adverse effects on environmental conditions are likely to arise from the use as an operating centre of the applicant of any such place, and may take account of any other matters he considers relevant.

(7) A place is not to be regarded for the purposes of sub-paragraph (2) as being specified in an operator's licence by reason only that it forms part of a place so specified; and a place that was, at the time mentioned in sub-paragraph (1)(b), a place specified in an operator's licence as mentioned in sub-paragraph (2) shall be disregarded for the purposes of sub-paragraph (2) if, at that time—

(a) that place was so specified by virtue of an interim direction such as is mentioned in section 25; or

(b) such conditions relating to—

(i) the exercise of the right of any person to appeal against a place being specified in an operator's licence, or

(ii) the review under section 36 of any decision so to specify a place,

as may be prescribed were not satisfied in relation to that place.

(8) In this paragraph "operator's licence" does not include an interim licence issued under section 24.

4.—(1) The provisions of this paragraph have effect in relation to any application for the variation of an operator's licence in respect of which a direction has been given under paragraph 3.

(2) Sections 17(3) and 18 shall not apply.

(3) If the application is granted, the traffic commissioner—

(a) shall attach to the licence as varied any conditions in respect of which the applicant has consented under paragraph 3(4); and

(b) shall not attach any other conditions to the licence under section 21 or 23.

(4) If the application is granted, the traffic commissioner shall record in the licence as varied—

(a) any undertakings given or procured to be given under paragraph 3(5); and

(b) any other undertakings given by the applicant (or procured by him to be given), whether for the purposes of the application or for the purposes of the request for the direction under paragraph 3, that the traffic commissioner considers to be material to his decision to give the direction.

DEFINITIONS
"operating centre": s.7(3).
"operator's licence": s.2.
"traffic commissioner": s.1.

GENERAL NOTE
This Schedule provides a simplified procedure for the transfer of operating centres from one licence to another in circumstances where there is no change other than that of the identity of the user. This Schedule defines large goods vehicles for the purposes of s.50 and the documents (consignment notes) to be carried by drivers of those vehicles and sets out the power of officers to enter vehicles and require production of such documents. The creation of such false documents or the alteration of such a document with intent to deceive creates an either/or offence.

Section 50   SCHEDULE 5

LARGE GOODS VEHICLES

Meaning of "large goods vehicle"

1.—(1) For the purposes of this Schedule, a large goods vehicle is a goods vehicle, other than a hauling vehicle, falling within any of sub-paragraphs (2) to (4).

(2) A goods vehicle falls within this sub-paragraph if—

(a) it has a relevant plated weight exceeding 16260 kilograms, or

(b) in the case of a vehicle which does not have a relevant plated weight, it has an unladen weight exceeding 5080 kilograms.

(3) A goods vehicle falls within this sub-paragraph if it forms part of a vehicle combination, other than an articulated combination, and the combination is such that—

(a) in a case where all the vehicles comprised in the combination, or all of those vehicles except any small trailer, have relevant plated weights, the aggregate of the relevant plated weights of the vehicles comprised in the combination, exclusive of any such trailer, exceeds 16260 kilograms, or

(b) in any other case, the aggregate of the unladen weights of the vehicles comprised in it, exclusive of any small trailer, exceeds 5080 kilograms;

and in this sub-paragraph "small trailer" means a trailer having an unladen weight not exceeding 1020 kilograms.

(4) A goods vehicle falls within this sub-paragraph if it forms part of an articulated combination which is such that—

(a) in a case where the trailer comprised in the combination has a relevant plated weight, the aggregate of—

(i) the unladen weight of the motor vehicle comprised in the combination, and

(ii) the relevant plated weight of that trailer,

exceeds 16260 kilograms, or

(b) in any other case, the aggregate of the unladen weights of the motor vehicle and the trailer comprised in the combination exceeds 5080 kilograms.

(5) In any provision of sub-paragraphs (2) to (4) "relevant plated weight" means a plated weight of the description specified in relation to that provision by regulations.

(6) In sub-paragraph (1) "hauling vehicle" means a motor tractor, a light locomotive, a heavy locomotive or the motor vehicle comprised in an articulated combination; and in this sub-paragraph "motor tractor", "light locomotive" and "heavy locomotive" have the same meaning as in the Road Traffic Act 1960.

Consignment notes

2.—(1) Subject to sub-paragraph (2), no goods shall be carried on a large goods vehicle unless a document (a "consignment note") in the prescribed form and containing the prescribed particulars has been completed and signed in the prescribed manner and is carried by the driver of the vehicle.

(2) Sub-paragraph (1) shall not apply—

(a) to the carriage of goods on any journey or on a vehicle of any class exempted from that sub-paragraph by regulations; or

(b) to any carriage of goods which is lawful without the authority of an operator's licence.

(3) Subject to the provisions of regulations, a traffic commissioner may dispense with the observance, as respects the carriage of goods under an operator's licence issued by him, of any requirement of sub-paragraph (1), where he is satisfied that it is not reasonably practicable for that requirement to be observed.

(4) Such a dispensation may be granted—

(a) generally;

(b) as respects a particular vehicle; or

(c) as respects the use of vehicles for a particular purpose.

(5) The consignment note relating to the goods carried on a vehicle on any journey shall, at the conclusion of that journey, be preserved for the prescribed period by the person who used the vehicle for carrying the goods on that journey.

(6) Any person who—

(a) uses or drives a vehicle in contravention of sub-paragraph (1), or

(b) fails to comply with sub-paragraph (5),

is guilty of an offence and liable on summary conviction to a fine not exceeding level 4 on the standard scale.

Powers of entry and inspection

3.—(1) An officer may require any person to produce and permit him to inspect and copy—

(a) any document which is required by or under paragraph 2 to be carried by that person as driver of a vehicle; or

(b) any document which that person is required by or under that paragraph to preserve;

and that document shall, if the officer so requires by notice in writing served on that person, be produced at the office of the traffic commissioner specified in the notice within such time (not being less than 10 days) from the service of the notice as may be so specified.

(2) An officer may at any time enter any large goods vehicle and inspect that vehicle and any goods carried on it.

(3) Where an officer has reason to believe—

(a) that a large goods vehicle is being kept on any premises, or

(b) that any such documents as are mentioned in sub-paragraph (1) are to be found on any premises,

he may, at any time which is reasonable having regard to the circumstances of the case, enter those premises and inspect any such vehicle, and inspect and copy any such document, which he finds there.

(4) For the purpose of exercising his powers under sub-paragraph (1)(a) or (2), an officer may detain the vehicle in question during such time as is required for the exercise of that power.

(5) The powers conferred by sub-paragraphs (1) to (4) are exercisable on production by the officer, if so required, of his authority.

(6) Any person who—

(a) fails to comply with any requirement under sub-paragraph (1), or

(b) obstructs any officer in the exercise of his powers under sub-paragraph (2), (3) or (4),

is guilty of an offence and liable on summary conviction to a fine not exceeding level 3 on the standard scale.

(7) In this paragraph "officer" has meaning given in section 42(1) (as amended by paragraph 5 below).

(8) The powers conferred by this paragraph on an officer shall be exercisable also by a police constable who shall not, if wearing uniform, be required to produce any authority.

Falsification of consignment notes and records

4.—(1) Any person who—

(a) makes, or causes to be made, any document required to be made under paragraph 2 which he knows to be false, or

(b) with intent to deceive, alters or causes to be altered any document required to be made under that paragraph,

is guilty of an offence.

(2) A person guilty of an offence under sub-paragraph (1) is liable—

(a) on summary conviction, to a fine not exceeding the statutory maximum;

(b) on conviction on indictment, to imprisonment for a term not exceeding two years or to a fine or to both.

Amendment of sections 38, 41 and 42 of this Act

5.—(1) The following amendments shall take effect on the day appointed for the coming into force of paragraph 3, namely, in sections 38(2)(c) and 42(1)(b), after the words "sections 40 and 41" there shall be inserted the words "and paragraph 3 of Schedule 5".

(2) The following amendments shall take effect on the day appointed for the coming into force of paragraph 4, namely, in section 41(1) and (2)(b), after the words "section 38 or 39" there shall be inserted the words "or paragraph 4(1) of Schedule 5".

GENERAL NOTE
This Schedule is expressly excluded from commencement on January 1, 1996 by S.I. 1995 No. 2181.

Section 59   SCHEDULE 6

TRANSITIONAL PROVISIONS, TRANSITORY MODIFICATIONS AND SAVINGS

General transitional provisions

1. The substitution of this Act for the provisions repealed and revoked by it shall not affect the continuity of the law.

2. In so far as any thing done (including any subordinate legislation made or other instrument issued) under a provision repealed or revoked by this Act could have been done under the corresponding provision of this Act, it shall have effect as if done under that corresponding provision.

3. Any reference (express or implied) in this Act or any other enactment, instrument or document to—
(a) any provision of this Act, or
(b) things done or falling to be done under or for the purposes of any provision of this Act,
shall, so far as the nature of the reference permits, be construed as including, in relation to the times, circumstances or purposes in relation to which the corresponding provision repealed or revoked by this Act had effect, a reference to that corresponding provision or (as the case may be) to things done or falling to be done under or for the purposes of that corresponding provision.

4. Any reference (express or implied) in any enactment, instrument or document to—
(a) a provision repealed or revoked by this Act, or
(b) things done or falling to be done under or for the purposes of such a provision,
shall, so far as the nature of the reference permits, be construed as including, in relation to the times, circumstances or purposes in relation to which the corresponding provision of this Act has effect, a reference to that corresponding provision or (as the case may be) to things done or falling to be done under or for the purposes of that corresponding provision.

5. Paragraphs 1 to 4 have effect, in relation to the substitution of this Act for the provisions repealed and revoked by it, in place of section 17(2) of the Interpretation Act 1978 (but without prejudice to any other provision of that Act).

Meaning of "local authority" in relation to Scotland or Wales

6. In section 12(12), in the definition of the expression "local authority"—
(a) in paragraph (b), until 1st April 1996, for the words from "the council" onwards there shall be substituted the words "the council of a county or district"; and
(b) in paragraph (c), until 1st April 1996, for the words from "a council" onwards, there shall be substituted the words "a regional, islands or district council".

Meaning of "holding company" and "subsidiary"

7. For the purposes of this Act as it applies in relation to licences granted before 11 November 1990 (the date on which section 144(1) of the Companies Act 1989 came into force) the expressions "holding company" and "subsidiary" have the meaning given by section 736 of the Companies Act 1985 as originally enacted.

GENERAL NOTE
This Schedule sets out the general transitory provisions and, for the purposes of s.12(12), extends the definition of "local authority" to reflect the changes anticipated on April 1, 1996.

Section 60(1)   SCHEDULE 7

CONSEQUENTIAL AMENDMENTS

The Road Traffic Act 1960 (c. 16)

1. In section 232 of the Road Traffic Act 1960 (duty to give information as to identity of driver), for subsection (1)(b) there shall be substituted—

"(b) to any offence under section 2 of the Goods Vehicles (Licensing of Operators) Act 1995;".

2. In section 244 of that Act (time for bringing summary proceedings), the words from "under section 233" to the second occurrence of the words "or an offence" shall be omitted.

The Transport Act 1968 (c. 73)

3. In section 51 of the Transport Act 1968 (subsidiaries and joint subsidiaries), in subsection (5), for the words "Parts V and VI" there shall be substituted the words "Part VI".

4. In section 158 of that Act (inquiries), in subsection (1), the words "other than Part V" shall be omitted.

Road Traffic (Foreign Vehicles) Act 1972 (c. 27)

5.—(1) In section 4 of the Road Traffic (Foreign Vehicles) Act 1972 (duty to produce certain documents), in subsection (1)—
(a) in paragraph (a), for the words "section 91(4) of the Transport Act 1968" there shall be substituted the words "section 57(6) of the Goods Vehicles (Licensing of Operators) Act 1995"; and
(b) in paragraph (b), for the words "section 60(1)" there shall be substituted the words "section 2(1)".

6. In Schedule 2 to that Act (provisions relating to vehicles and their drivers), in the first column—
(a) for the words "Section 60 of the Transport Act 1968" there shall be substituted the words "Section 2 of the Goods Vehicles (Licensing of Operators) Act 1995"; and
(b) for the words "section 91(1)(c) of the Transport Act 1968" there shall be substituted the words "section 57(2)(d) of the Goods Vehicles (Licensing of Operators) Act 1995".

International Road Haulage Permits Act 1975 (c. 46)

7. In section 1 of the International Road Haulage Permits Act 1975 (duty to carry and produce international road haulage permits), in subsection (8), for the words "Part V of the Transport Act 1968" there shall be substituted the words "the Goods Vehicles (Licensing of Operators) Act 1995".

Transport Act 1982 (c. 49)

8. In section.8 of the Transport Act 1982 (private-sector vehicle testing), in subsection (2)(a), after "1968" there shall be inserted the words "or the Goods Vehicles (Licensing of Operators) Act 1995".

London Regional Transport Act 1984 (c. 32)

9. In section 62 of the London Regional Transport Act 1984 (joint subsidiaries), in subsection (3)(a), for the words "Parts V and VI" there shall be substituted the words "Part VI".

Transport Act 1985 (c. 67)

10. In Schedule 4 to the Transport Act 1985 (constitution, powers and proceedings of the Transport Tribunal), in paragraph 9(1), the words "Part V of the 1968 Act," shall be omitted and after the words "the 1981 Act" there shall be inserted the words ", the Goods Vehicles (Licensing of Operators) Act 1995".

Road Traffic Act 1988 (c. 52)

11. In section 66A of the Road Traffic Act 1988 (appointment of examiners), in subsection (1), after the words "this Part of this Act," there shall be inserted the words "the Goods Vehicles (Licensing of Operators) Act 1995,".

12.—(1) In section 73 of that Act (provisions supplementary to sections 69 to 72), in subsection (1)—
(a) for the words "an authorised vehicle" there shall be substituted the words ", by virtue of section 5 of the Goods Vehicles (Licensing of Operators) Act 1995, authorised to be used under an operator's licence,"; and
(b) in paragraph (a), for the words "the operator's licence was granted for the vehicle" there shall be substituted the words "the licence was issued".

(2) In that section, after subsection (1), there shall be inserted—
"(1ZA) Where in a case within subsection (1) above it appears to the person giving the notice that the vehicle is authorised to be used under two or more operators' licences—

(a) if those licences were issued by different traffic commissioners, his duty under paragraph (a) of that subsection may be discharged by taking steps to bring the contents of the notice to the attention of any one of those commissioners,

(b) if those licences are held by different persons and none of those persons is in charge of the vehicle at the time when the notice is given, his duty under paragraph (b) of that subsection may be discharged by taking steps to bring the contents of the notice to the attention of any one of those persons, and

(c) if those licences are held by different persons and any of those persons is in charge of the vehicle at the time when the notice is given, no steps need be taken under that subsection to bring the contents of the notice to the attention of the others.".

(3) In subsection (4) of that section, for the words from "and section 72" to "Transport Act 1968" there shall be substituted the words " "operator's licence" has the same meaning as in the Goods Vehicles (Licensing of Operators) Act 1995".

13. In section 85 of that Act (interpretation of Part II), the definition of "licensing authority" (which is no longer needed) shall be omitted.

14. In section 86 of that Act (index of defined expressions), the entry relating to the expression "licensing authority" shall be omitted.

Section 60(2)   SCHEDULE 8

REPEALS AND REVOCATIONS

PART I

ENACTMENTS REPEALED

Chapter	*Short Title*	*Extent of repeal*
8 & 9 Eliz. 2 c.16.	The Road Traffic Act 1960.	Section 233. Section 235. In section 244, the words from "under section 233" to the second occurrence of the words "or an offence". Section 263. Section 265.
1968 c.73.	The Transport Act 1968.	Part V. In section 158(1), the words "other than Part V". Schedule 8A. Schedule 10.
1973 c.65.	The Local Government (Scotland) Act 1973.	In Schedule 18, paragraph 18.
1974 c.50.	The Road Traffic Act 1974.	Section 16. Schedule 4.
1975 c.46.	The International Road Haulage Permits Act 1975.	Section 3.
1976 c.3.	The Road Traffic (Drivers' Ages and Hours of Work) Act 1976.	Section 2(2).
1979 c.5.	The Hydrocarbon Oil Duties Act 1979.	In Schedule 6, paragraph 2.
1980 c.34.	The Transport Act 1980.	Section 66(2). In Schedule 4, the entry relating to section 235 of the Road Traffic Act 1960.
1981 c.14.	The Public Passenger Vehicles Act 1981.	In Schedule 7, paragraph 9.
1981 c.45.	The Forgery and Counterfeiting Act 1981.	In section 12, the words "section 233(2) of the Road Traffic Act 1960, and".
1982 c.49.	The Transport Act 1982.	Section 52. Section 76(5). Schedule 4. In Schedule 5, paragraph 6.
1984 c.27.	The Road Traffic Regulation Act 1984.	In Schedule 13, paragraph 6.

Chapter	Short Title	Extent of repeal
1985 c.9.	The Companies Consolidation (Consequential Provisions) Act 1985.	In Schedule 2, the entries relating to sections 69(11) and 92(1) of the Transport Act 1968.
1985 c.65.	The Insolvency Act 1985.	In Schedule 8, paragraph 16.
1985 c.67.	The Transport Act 1985.	Section 3(4). In Schedule 4, in paragraph 9(1), the words "Part V of the 1968 Act".
1988 c.52.	The Road Traffic Act 1988.	In section 85, the definition of "licensing authority". In section 86, the entry relating to the expression "licensing authority".
1988 c.54.	The Road Traffic (Consequential Provisions) Act 1988.	In Schedule 3, paragraphs 2(1) and 6(1), (2) and (4).
1989 c.40.	The Companies Act 1989.	In Schedule 18, paragraph 7.
1990 c.11.	The Planning (Consequential Provisions) Act 1990.	In Schedule 2, paragraph 22(1).
1990 c.43.	The Environmental Protection Act 1990.	In Schedule 15, paragraph 10(2).
1991 c.40.	The Road Traffic Act 1991.	In Schedule 4, paragraph 1.
1992 c.52.	The Trade Union and Labour Relations (Consolidation) Act 1992.	In Schedule 2, paragraph 2.
1994 c.39.	The Local Government etc. (Scotland) Act 1994.	In Schedule 13, paragraph 80(8).
1994 c.40.	The Deregulation and Contracting Out Act 1994.	Chapter III of Part I. Schedule 12. Schedule 13.

PART II

SUBORDINATE LEGISLATION REVOKED

Year and number	Title	Extent of Revocation
S.I. 1981/1373.	The Road Traffic Acts 1960 and 1972, Road Traffic Regulation Act 1967, and Transport Act 1968 (Metrication) Regulations 1981.	Regulation 4(1) and in the Schedule, Part IIIA.
S.I. 1984/176.	The Goods Vehicles (Operators' Licences, Qualifications and Fees) Regulations 1984.	Regulations 4 to 9. Regulation 23A. Regulation 33(2) and (3). Regulation 34A. Regulation 36. Schedule 6.
S.I. 1984/177.	The Road Traffic Acts 1960 and 1972, Road Traffic Regulation Act 1967, and Transport Act 1968 (Metrication) (Amendment) Regulations 1984.	Both Regulations.
S.I. 1986/666.	The Goods Vehicles (Operators' Licences, Qualifications and Fees) (Amendment) Regulations 1986.	Regulations 3, 8 and 10.

Year and number	Title	Extent of Revocation
S.I. 1987/841.	The Goods Vehicles (Operators' Licences, Qualifications and Fees) (Amendment) Regulations 1987.	Regulation 5.
S.I. 1990/1849.	The Goods Vehicles (Operators' Licences, Qualifications and Fees) (Amendment) Regulations 1990.	Regulations 2(3), 4, 6 and 7.
S.I. 1990/2640.	The Goods Vehicles (Operators' Licences, Qualifications and Fees) (Amendment) (No. 2) Regulations 1990.	Regulation 4.
S.I. 1991/2239.	The Goods Vehicles (Operators' Licences, Qualifications and Fees) (Amendment) (No. 2) Regulations 1991.	Regulations 4 and 7.
S.I. 1992/2319.	The Goods Vehicles (Operators' Licences, Qualifications and Fees) (Amendment) Regulations 1992.	Regulation 4.
S.I. 1992/3077.	The Goods Vehicles (Community Authorisations) Regulations 1992.	Regulation 14.

TABLE OF DERIVATIONS

Notes

1. This Table shows the derivation of the provisions of the Act.

2. The following abbreviations are used in the Table:—

Acts of Parliament

1960	=	The Road Traffic Act 1960 (c.16)
1968	=	The Transport Act 1968 (c.73)
1974	=	The Transport Act 1974 (c.50)
1982	=	The Transport Act 1982 (c.49)
1988	=	The Road Traffic (Consequential Provisions) Act 1988 (c.54)
1994	=	The Deregulation and Contracting Out Act 1994 (c.40)

Subordinate legislation

S.I. 1981/1373	=	The Road Traffic Acts 1960 and 1972, Road Traffic Regulation Act 1967, and Transport Act 1968 (Metrication) Regulations 1981.
S.I. 1984/176	=	The Goods Vehicles (Operators' Licences, Qualifications and Fees) Regulations 1984
S.I. 1984/177	=	The Road Traffic Acts 1960 and 1972, Road Traffic Regulation Act 1967, and Transport Act 1968 (Metrication) (Amendment) Regulations 1984.
S.I. 1986/666	=	The Goods Vehicles (Operators' Licences, Qualifications and Fees) (Amendment) Regulations 1986.
S.I. 1986/1391	=	The Goods Vehicles (Operators' Licences, Qualifications and Fees) (Amendment) (No. 2) Regulations 1986.
S.I. 1987/841	=	The Goods Vehicles (Operators' Licences, Qualifications and Fees) (Amendment) Regulations 1987.
S.I. 1990/1849	=	The Goods Vehicles (Operators' Licences, Qualifications and Fees) (Amendment) Regulations 1990.

S.I. 1990/2640   =   The Goods Vehicles (Operators' Licences, Qualifications and Fees) (Amendment) (No. 2) Regulations 1990.
S.I. 1991/2239   =   The Goods Vehicles (Operators' Licences, Qualifications and Fees) (Amendment) (No. 2) Regulations 1991.
S.I. 1992/3077   =   The Goods Vehicles (Community Authorisations) Regulations 1992.

3. The Table does not separately acknowledge the provisions in the Magistrates' Courts Act 1980 (c.43), the Criminal Justice Act 1982 (c.48) and the Criminal Procedure (Scotland) Act 1975 (c.21) by virtue of which the fines which may be imposed on conviction of the offences consolidated were increased and references to the amount of the maximum fines to which persons are liable in respect of the offences were translated into levels on the standard scale.

4. The functions originally vested in the Minister of Transport by the Transport Act 1968 have become vested in the Secretary of State by virtue of the following transfer of functions orders: the Secretary of State for the Environment Order 1970 (S.I. 1970/1681), the Secretary of State for Transport Order 1976 (S.I. 1976/1775), the Minister of Transport Order 1979 (S.I. 1979/571) and the Transfer of Functions (Transport) Order 1981 (S.I. 1981/238). The Table does not separately acknowledge the effect of those Orders.

Provision	Derivation
1(1)	1968 s.59(1); Transport Act 1985 (c.67) s.3(4).
(2)	1968 s.59(2).
2(1)	1968 s.60(1).
(2)	1968 s.60(2); S.I. 1992/3077 reg. 14(2).
(3)	1968 s.60(4A); S.I. 1992/3077 reg. 14(3).
(4)	1968 s.60(3).
(5)	1968 s.60(5).
3(1)	S.I. 1984/176 reg. 4(1).
(2)	S.I. 1984/176 reg. 3(2) "standard licence".
(3)	S.I. 1984/176 reg. 3(2) "restricted licence".
(4)	S.I. 1984/176 reg. 4(2); S.I. 1986/666 reg. 3.
(5)	S.I. 1984/176 reg. 4(3).
(6)	S.I. 1984/176 reg. 33(2).
(7)	S.I. 1984/176 reg. 33(3).
4	S.I. 1984/176 reg. 34A; S.I. 1990/1849 reg. 6.
5(1) to (3)	1968 s.61(1) to (1B); 1994 s.42(1).
(4), (5)	1968 s.61(2).
(6), (7)	1968 s.61(3), (4); 1994 s.42(2).
(8), (9)	1968 s.61(5), (6).
6	1968 s.61A; 1994 s.42(3).
7(1)	1968 s.69A(1); 1982 Sch. 4 Pt. I; 1994 Sch. 13 para. 5(1).
(2)	1968 s.69A(4); 1982 Sch. 4 Pt. I.
(3)	1968 s.92(1) "operating centre"; 1982 s.52(1); 1994 Sch. 13 para. 15(1) (c).
8(1), (2)	1968 s.62(1).
(3)	1968 ss.62(2), 69A(2); 1982 Sch. 4 Pt. I.
(4)	1968 s.62(4) (part).
(5)	1968 s.69A(3); 1982 Sch. 4 Pt. I; 1994 Sch. 13 para. 5(2).
(6)	1968 ss.62(5), 69A(3A); 1994 Sch. 13 para. 5(3).
9(1)	1968 s.62(4A) (part); 1974 Sch. 4 para. 1.
(2)	1968 s.62(4A) (part); 1974 Sch. 4 para. 1; S.I. 1984/176 reg. 5(5) (part).
(3)	1968 s.62(4B) (part); 1974 Sch. 4 para. 1; S.I. 1984/176 reg. 5(5) (part).
(4)	1968 s.62(4A) (part); 1974 Sch. 4 para. 1.
10(1)	1968 s.63(1).
(2)	1968 ss.63(4) (part), 69G(3) (part); 1994 Sch. 13 para. 9.
11	1968 s.69E(1) (part), (3) (part), (4) (part), (5) (part); 1994 s.49.
12(1)	1968 ss.63(3) (part), 69B(1); 1982 Sch. 4 Pt. I, Pt. II para. 1(c); 1994 Sch. 13 paras. 2(1), 6(1).
(2)	1968 s.63(3) (part); 1982 Sch. 4 Pt. II para. 8(a).
(3)	1968 s.63(3) (part).

Provision	Derivation
(4), (5)	1968 s.69B(2); 1982 Sch. 4 Pt. I; 1994 Sch. 13 para. 6(1).
(6)	1968 s.63(4) (part).
(7)	1968 s.69G(2) (part); 1994 Sch. 13 para. 9.
(8)	1968 ss.63(4A), 69G(4) (part); 1994 s.43, Sch. 13 para. 9.
(9)	1968 s.63(4) (part), 69G(1) (part); 1994 Sch. 13 para. 9.
(10)	1968 s.69G(1) (part); 1994 Sch. 13 para. 9.
(11)	Drafting.
(12)	1968 ss.63(6), 159(3)(a), (b); Local Government Act 1972 (c.70) s.179 (3); 1982 Sch. 4 Pt. II para. 8(b); Planning (Consequential Provisions) Act 1990 (c.11) Sch. 2 para. 22(1); Trade Union and Labour Relations (Consolidation) Act 1992 (c.52) Sch. 2 para. 2; Local Government (Wales) Act 1994 (c.19) Sch. 7 para. 35; Local Government etc. (Scotland) Act 1994 (c.39) Sch. 13 para. 80(8).
13(1)	1968 s.64(1) (part); Interpretation Act 1978 (c.30) s.17(2); 1994 s.44(1); S.I. 1984/176 regs. 5(1) (part), 36(7) (part).
(2)	1968 s.64(1) (part); 1994 s.44(1).
(3)	S.I. 1984/176 reg. 5(1) (part), (2).
(4)	1968 s.64(2); 1994 s.44(1).
(5)	1968 s.64(3); Road Traffic (Drivers' Ages and Hours of Work) Act 1976 (c.3) s.2(2) (part); 1994 s.44(1), Sch. 13 para. 17.
(6) to (11)	1968 s.64(4) to (9); 1994 s.44(1).
14(1)	Drafting.
(2)	1968 s.69B(3), (4); 1982 Sch. 4 Pt. I; 1994 Sch. 13 para. 6(2), (3).
(3) to (5)	1968 s.69B(5), (5A), (5B); 1994 s.44(2).
(6), (7)	1968 s.69B(6), (6A); 1994 Sch. 13 para. 6(4).
15(1) to (4)	1968 s.64A; 1994 s.44(1).
(5), (6)	S.I. 1984/176 reg. 4(4).
16(1) to (3)	1968 s.67(1) to (4); 1994 s.46.
(4)	1968 s.67(4); 1994 s.46; S.I. 1984/176 reg. 9(4) (part); S.I. 1987/841 reg. 5.
(5)	1968 ss.67(5), 92(4A) (part); 1994 s.46, Sch. 13 para. 15(4).
17	1968 s.68(1) and (3) to (6); 1994 s.47(1).
18	1968 s.69E(1) (part), (2), (3) (part), (4) (part), (5) (part); 1994 s.49.
19	1968 s.69D; 1994 s.47(2).
20	S.I. 1984/176 reg. 8.
21(1) to (4)	1968 s.64B(1) to (4); 1994 s.45.
(5)	1968 ss.64B(5), 159(1) "public road"; Roads (Scotland) Act 1984 (c.54) Sch. 9 para. 66(10)(d); 1994 s.45.
(6)	1968 s.64B(6); 1994 s.45.
22(1)	1968 s.66(1); 1994 Sch. 13 para. 3.
(2), (3)	S.I. 1984/176 reg. 7(1).
(4), (5)	S.I. 1984/176 reg. 7(3), (4).
(6)	1968 s.66(2); S.I. 1984/176 reg. 7(2) (part).
23(1)	1968 s.69C(1); 1994 Sch. 13 para. 7(1).
(2)	1968 s.69C(2); 1982 Sch. 4 Pt. I.
(3)	1968 s.69C(3); 1994 Sch. 13 para. 7(2).
(4), (5)	1968 s.69C(5), (5A); 1994 Sch. 13 para. 7(3).
(6)	1968 s.69C(6); 1982 Sch. 4 Pt. I.
24(1), (2)	1968 s.67A(1), (2); 1994 s.46.
(3)	1968 s.67A(8); 1994 s.46.
(4) to (8)	1968 s.67(3) to (7); 1994 s.46.
(9)	1968 s.92(2B) (part); 1994 Sch. 13 para. 15(2).
25(1) to (6)	1968 s.68A; 1994 s.47(1).
(7)	1968 s.92(2B) (part); 1994 Sch. 13 para. 15(2).
26(1)	1968 s.69(1), (4) (part); 1988 Sch. 3 para. 6(2)(d); 1994 s.48(2).
(2), (3)	1968 s.69(2), (2A); 1994 s.48(2).
(4)	1968 s.69(3).
(5)	1968 s.69(3A), (4) (part); S.I. 1984/176 reg. 36(3)(b), (c).
(6), (7)	1968 s.69(7A); 1974 Sch. 4 para. 4(4); 1994 Sch. 13 para. 4(4).
(8)	1968 s.69(8); 1994 s.48(5).

Provision	Derivation
(9)	1968 s.69(10A) (part); 1994 Sch. 13 para. 4(7).
(10)	1968 s.92(4).
(11)	1968 s.92(3); 1982 Sch. 4 Pt. II para. 7(b); 1994 Sch. 13 para. 15(3).
27(1)	S.I. 1984/176 reg. 9(1).
(2), (3)	S.I. 1984/176 reg. 9(2).
(4)	S.I. 1984/176 reg. 9(4) (part); S.I. 1987/841 reg. 5.
28(1)	1968 s.69(5); 1994 s.48(3); S.I. 1984/176 reg. 9(4) (part); S.I. 1987/841 reg. 5.
(2), (3)	1968 s.69(5A), (5B); 1994 s.48(3).
(4)	1968 s.69(6).
(5)	1968 s.69(7); 1994 s.48(4), Sch. 13 para. 4(3).
(6)	1968 s.69(8A); 1994 s.48(5).
(7)	1968 s.69(10A) (part); 1994 Sch. 13 para. 4(7).
(8)	1968 s.69(11); Companies Consolidation (Consequential Provisions) Act 1985 (c.9) Sch. 2.
29(1)	1968 s.69(9); 1974 Sch. 4 para. 4(6); 1994 Sch. 13 para. 4(5); S.I. 1984/176 reg. 9(4) (part); S.I. 1987/841 reg. 5.
(2)	1968 s.69(10) (part); 1994 Sch. 13 para. 4(6); S.I. 1984/176 reg. 9(4) (part); S.I. 1987/841 reg. 5.
(3), (4)	1968 s.69(10) (part).
30	1968 s.69EA; 1994 s.50(1).
31(1) to (4)	1968 s.69EB; 1994 s.50(1).
(5)	1968 s.69G(1) (part), (2) (part), (4) (part); 1994 Sch. 13 para. 9.
32	1968 ss.69EC; 1994 s.50(1).
33	1968 ss.69ED; 1994 s.50(1).
34	1968 s.69H; 1994 Sch. 13 para. 9.
35(1)	1968 s.87(1); S.I. 1984/176 reg. 36(4) (part).
(2)	1968 s.87(3); S.I. 1984/176 regs. 9(4) (part), 36(4) (part); S.I. 1987/841 reg. 5.
(3)	1968 s.87(4); S.I. 1984/176 reg. 36(4) (part).
(4)	1968 s.87(5).
36	1968 s.69J; 1994 s.52.
37(1)	1968 s.70(1) (part), (2); 1994 s.53.
(2)	1968 s.70(1) (part), (3); Interpretation Act 1978 (c.30) s.17(2); 1994 s.53; S.I. 1984/176 reg. 9(3).
(3) to (7)	1968 s.70(1) (part), (4) to (8); 1994 s.53.
38(1)	1960 s.233(2) (part).
(2)	1960 s.233(1); 1968 Sch. 10 Pts. I, II; 1994 Sch. 13 para. 16; S.I. 1984/176 reg. 36(9) (part).
(3)	1960 s.233(3); Powers of Criminal Courts Act 1973 (c.62) s.30; 1988 Sch. 3 para. 2(1).
(4)	1960 s.233(2) (part); Forgery and Counterfeiting Act 1981 (c.45) s.12.
39(1)	1960 s.235(1); 1968 Sch. 10 Pt. I; S.I. 1984/176 reg. 36(9) (part).
(2)	1960 s.235(3); 1974 Sch. 5 Pt. I; Transport Act 1980 (c.34) Sch. 4.
40(1)	1968 s.82(4); 1994 Sch. 13 para. 10.
(2)	1968 s.82(5) (part).
41	1968 s.82(6) (part).
(2)	1968 s.82(6) (part), (7) (part).
(3)	1968 s.82(6) (part).
(4)	1968 s.82(6) (part), (7) (part).
(5)	1968 s.82(7) (part).
42(1)	1968 s.82(8); Road Traffic Act 1991 (c.40) Sch. 4 para. 1.
(2)	1968 s.82(9) (part).
43(1)	1968 s.84 (part); S.I. 1984/176 reg. 36(4) (part).
(2)	1968 s.84 (part); 1994 Sch. 13 para. 11.
(3)	1968 s.84 (part).
44	1968 s.69I; 1994 s.51.
45	1968 s.89; 1994 s.56.
46(1)	1968 s.85(1); 1994 Sch. 13 para. 12.

Provision	Derivation
(2)	1968 s.85(2); Transport Act 1982 (c.49) Sch. 5 para. 6.
(3)	Drafting.
47	1968 s.85A; 1994 s.54.
48(1) to (4)	1968 s.86(1) to (4); 1994 s.55.
(5)	1968 s.92(4A) (part); 1994 Sch. 13 para. 15(4).
(6)	1968 s.86(5); 1994 s.55.
49(1)	S.I. 1984/176 reg. 6(1) and (2) to (4).
(5)	S.I. 1984/176 reg. 6(1A); S.I. 1991/2239 reg. 4(3).
(6)	European Communities Act 1972 (c.68) s.2(3)(b).
50(1)	Drafting.
(2)	1968 s.166(2) (part).
51	1960 s.244 (part); 1968 s.62(4B) (part); Driver and Vehicle Licensing Act 1969 (c.27) Sch. 2 para. 11; 1974 Sch. 4 para. 1; 1988 Sch. 3 para. 6(1).
52	1960 s.247(2) (part); 1968 Sch. 10 Pt. I; 1988 Sch. 3 para. 2(3).
53	1960 s.255 (part); 1968 Sch. 10 Pt. I.
54	1960 s.269 (part); 1968 Sch. 10 Pt. I.
55	1960 s.263; 1968 Sch. 10 Pt. II.
56	1968 Sch. 10 Pt. I.
57(1)	1968 s.91(1) (part); S.I. 1984/176 reg. 36(6) (part).
(2)	1968 s.91(1) (part); 1982 Sch. 4 Pt. II para. 6(a); 1994 Sch. 13 para. 14(1) (a) to (d); S.I. 1984/176 regs. 9(4) (part), 36(4) (part), (5) (part); S.I. 1987/841 reg. 5.
(3)	S.I. 1984/176 reg. 36(5) (part).
(4)	1968 s.91(2); 1994 Sch. 13 para. 14(2); S.I. 1984/176 reg. 36(4) (part).
(5)	S.I. 1984/176 reg. 36(5) (part).
(6)	1968 s.91(4); S.I. 1984/176 reg. 36(4) (part).
(7)	1968 s.91(4A); 1994 Sch. 13 para. 14(4).
(8), (9)	1968 s.91(5), (6).
(10)	1968 s.91(6A); 1994 Sch. 13 para. 14(5).
(11)	1968 s.91(7); 1994 Sch. 13 para. 14(6).
(12)	1968 s.91(8).
(13)	1968 s.157 (part).
58(1)	"area": drafting;
	"articulated combination": 1968 s.92(1) "articulated combination";
	"carriage of goods": 1968 s.92(1) "carriage of goods";
	"contravention": 1968 s.92(1) "contravention";
	"the 1974 Council Directive": S.I. 1984/176 reg. 3(2) "the 1974 Council Directive"; S.I. 1990/1849 reg. 3(b); S.I. 1990/2640 reg. 3;
	"the 1977 Council Directive": S.I. 1984/176 reg. 3(2) "the 1977 Council Directive"; S.I. 1990/1849 reg. 3(c);
	"driver": 1960 s.257(1) "driver"; 1968 s.92(1) "driver";
	"functions": 1968 s.159(1) "functions";
	"goods": 1968 s.92(1) "goods";
	"goods vehicle": 1968 s.92(1) "goods vehicle", (5); 1994 Sch. 13 para. 15(5);
	"holding company" and "subsidiary": S.I. 1984/176 reg. 3(2) "holding company" and "subsidiary"; S.I. 1987/841 reg. 4(1)(a);
	"international transport operations" and "national transport operations": S.I. 1984/176 reg. 3(2) "international transport operations" and "national transport operations"; S.I. 1986/1391 reg. 3(a);
	"modification": 1968 s.92(1) "modification"; 1994 Sch. 13 para. 15(1)(b);
	"motor vehicle" and "trailer": 1968 s.92(1) (part);
	"operating centre": drafting;
	"operator's licence": drafting;
	"owner": 1968 s.92(1) "owner"; 1982 Sch. 4 Pt. II para. 7(a);
	"plated weight": 1968 s.159(1) "plated weight"; 1988 sch. 3 para. 6(8);
	"prescribed": 1968 s.92(1) "prescribed";
	"regulations": 1968 s.92(1) "regulations";

Provision	Derivation
	"restricted licence": drafting;
	"road": 1960 s.257(1) "road"; 1968 s.159(1) "road"; Roads (Scotland) Act 1984 (c.54) Sch. 9 para. 66(10)(e);
	"road transport undertaking": S.I. 1984/176 reg. 3(2) "road transport undertaking";
	"standard licence": drafting;
	"statutory provision": 1968 s.92(1) "statutory provision"; 1994 Sch. 13 para. 15(1)(d);
	"traffic area": drafting;
	"transport manager": S.I. 1984/176 "transport manager";
	"vehicle combination": 1968 s.92(1) "vehicle combination".
(2)	1968 s.92(2).
(3)	1968 s.92(2A); 1994 Sch. 13 para. 15(2).
(4)	S.I. 1984/176 reg. 3(3).
(5)	1968 s.92(6).
59 to 62	—
Sch. 1	
para. 1	1968 s.60(4) (part).
para. 2	1968 s.60(4)(a); S.I. 1981/1373 Sch. Pt. IIIA; S.I. 1984/177 reg. 2.
para. 3(1)	1968 s.60(4)(b); S.I. 1981/1373 Sch. Pt. IIIA; S.I. 1984/177 reg. 2.
para. 3(2)	1968 s.60(4) (part); S.I. 1981/1373 Sch. Pt. IIIA.
para. 4	1968 s.60(4)(c); S.I. 1981/1373 Sch. Pt. IIIA; S.I. 1984/177 reg. 2.
para. 5	1968 s.60(4) (part).
Sch. 2	
para. 1	1968 s.62(4) (part); Road Traffic (Drivers' Ages and Hours of Work) Act 1976 (c.3) s.2(2) (part); 1994 Sch. 13 para. 1(2).
para. 2	1968 s.62(4)(d) (part).
para. 3	1968 s.62(4)(d) (part).
para. 4	1968 s.62(4)(e) (part).
paras. 5, 6	1968 s.69(4) (part); Road Traffic Act 1972 (c.20) Sch. 7; 1974 Sch. 4 para. 4(2); International Road Haulage Permits Act 1975 (c.46) s.3(1); Hydrocarbon Oil Duties Act 1979 (c.5) Sch. 6 para. 2; Road Traffic Regulation Act 1984 (c.27) Sch. 13 para. 6(a), (b); 1988 Sch. 3 para. 6(2)(a), (b), (c); Environmental Protection Act 1990 (c.43) Sch. 15 para. 10(2)(b); 1994 Sch. 13 para. 4(1); S.I. 1984/176 reg. 36(3)(c).
Sch. 3	
para. 1(1), (2)	S.I. 1984/176 Sch. 6 para. 1(1), (2).
para. 1(3)	S.I. 1984/176 reg. 3(2) "relevant conviction" (part); S.I. 1990/1849 reg. 3(a).
para. 2	S.I. 1984/176 Sch. 6 para. 1(3), (9) (part); S.I. 1990/1849 reg. 7(a).
para. 3(1), (2)	S.I. 1984/176 Sch. 6 para. 1(4); S.I. 1990/1849 reg. 7(a).
para. 3(3)	S.I. 1984/176 Sch. 6 para. 1(6); S.I. 1990/1849 reg. 7(a).
para. 4	S.I. 1984/176 Sch. 6 para. 1(5); S.I. 1990/1849 reg. 7(a).
para. 5(1)	S.I. 1984/176 Sch. 6 para. 1(7); S.I. 1990/1849 reg. 7(a).
para. 5(2)	S.I. 1984/176 reg. 3(2) "relevant conviction" (part), Sch. 6 para. 1(8); S.I. 1990/1849 regs. 3(a), 7(a).
para. 6(1)	S.I. 1984/176 Sch. 6 para. 2(1).
para. 6(2), (3)	S.I. 1984/176 Sch. 6 paras. 2(2), (3); S.I. 1990/1849 reg. 7(b).
para. 6(4)	S.I. 1990/1849 reg. 2(3).
para. 7	Drafting.
para. 8(1)	S.I. 1984/176 Sch. 6 para. 3; S.I. 1986/666 reg. 10.
para. 8(2)	S.I. 1984/176 Sch. 6 para. 3A; S.I. 1986/666 reg. 10; S.I. 1990/1849 reg. 7(c).
para. 9	S.I. 1984/176 Sch. 6 para. 4.
para. 10	S.I. 1984/176 Sch. 6 para. 5(1); S.I. 1990/1849 reg. 7(d).
para. 11	S.I. 1984/176 Sch. 6 para. 5(2); S.I. 1990/1849 reg. 7(e).
para. 12	S.I. 1984/176 Sch. 6 para. 1(10); S.I. 1990/1849 reg. 7(a).
para. 13(1), (2)	S.I. 1984/176 Sch. 6 para. 6; S.I. 1990/2640 reg. 4.
para. 13(3)	S.I. 1984/176 Sch. 6 para. 7.

Provision	Derivation
para. 14	S.I. 1990/2640 regs. 1 (part), 2(2).
para. 15	S.I. 1984/176 reg. 23A; S.I. 1991/2239 reg. 7.
Sch. 4	1968 Sch. 8A; 1994 Sch. 12.
Sch. 5	
para. 1(1)	1968 s.71(6) (part).
para. 1(2) to (4)	1968 s.71(6) (part); S.I. 1981/1373 Sch. Pt. IIIA.
para. 1(5)	1968 s.71(6) (part).
para. 1(6)	1968 ss.71(8), 92(1) (part).
para. 2	1968 s.81.
para. 3(1)	1968 s.82(1).
para. 3(2), (3)	1968 s.82(2).
para. 3(4)	1968 s.82(3).
para. 3(5)	1968 s.82(1) (part), (2) (part).
para. 3(6)	1968 s.82(5) (part).
para. 3(7)	1968 s.82(8) (part); Road Traffic Act 1991 (c.40) Sch. 4 para. 1.
para. 3(8)	1968 s.82(9) (part).
para. 4(1)	1968 s.83 (part).
para. 4(2)	1968 s.83 (part); Powers of Criminal Courts Act 1973 (c.62) s.30.
para. 5	Drafting.
Schs. 6 to 8	—

TABLE OF DESTINATIONS

Road Traffic Act 1960
(c.16)

Transport Act 1968
(c.73)

TRANSPORT ACT 1974
(c.50)

TRANSPORT ACT 1982
(c.49)

ROAD TRAFFIC (CONSEQUENTIAL PROVISIONS) ACT 1988
(c.54)

DEREGULATION AND CONTRACTING OUT ACT 1994
(c.40)

ROAD TRAFFIC ACTS 1960 AND 1972,
ROAD TRAFFIC REGULATION ACT 1967, AND
TRANSPORT ACT 1968 (METRICATION) REGULATIONS 1981
(S.I. 1981 No. 1373)

GOODS VEHICLES (OPERATORS' LICENCES, QUALIFICATION AND FEES)
REGULATIONS 1984 (S.I. 1984 No. 176)

23–75

TABLE OF DESTINATIONS

GOODS VEHICLES (OPERATORS' LICENCES, QUALIFICATIONS AND FEES)
(AMENDMENT) (NO. 2) REGULATIONS 1990
(S.I. 1990 No. 2640)

S.I. 1990 No. 2640	1995
regs.1 (part), 2(2)	Sched. 3, para. 14
reg.3	s.58(1)
reg.4	Sched. 3, para. 13(1), (2)

GOODS VEHICLES (OPERATORS' LICENCES, QUALIFICATIONS AND FEES)
(AMENDMENT) (NO. 2) REGULATIONS 1991
(S.I. 1991 No. 2239)

S.I. 1990 No. 2239	1995
reg.4(3)	s.49(5)
reg.7	Sched. 3, para. 15

GOODS VEHICLES (COMMUNITY AUTHORISATIONS) REGULATIONS 1992
(S.I. 1992 No. 3077)

S.I. 1992 No. 3077	1995
reg.14(2)	s.2(2)
(3)	2(3)

INDEX

References are to sections and Schedules

CROWN AGENTS ACT 1995*

(1995 c. 24)

An Act to provide for the vesting of the property, rights and liabilities of the Crown Agents in a company nominated by the Secretary of State and for the subsequent dissolution of the Crown Agents; and for connected purposes.   [19th July 1995]

PARLIAMENTARY DEBATES
Hansard, H.L. Vol. 561, cols. 1409, 1428; Vol. 562, col. 1322; Vol. 563, cols. 762, 1521; Vol. 565, col. 1569. H.C. Vol. 261, col. 35; Vol. 262, col. 501.

INTRODUCTION AND GENERAL NOTE
   The Crown Agents Act 1995 provides for the privatisation of the body whose full title is Crown Agents for Oversea Governments and Administration. In line with current practice the Act is little more than a bare enabling skeleton provision. Section 1 provides for the vesting of all the property rights and liabilities of the Crown Agents in a company formed and registered under the Companies Act 1985 (c. 6), wholly owned by the Crown. Section 3 allows the Secretary of State, with the consent of the Treasury, to dispose of the shares in the newly established company. An unusual feature of this privatisation, however, is that the Government gave repeated assurances in both Houses that the Secretary of State would not sell the company on the open market in the ordinary way, but would ensure its transfer to an independent foundation, established as a company limited by guarantee. The memorandum and articles of the foundation would reflect the social, ethical and development principles on which Crown Agents' business is based. Despite its firm commitment to this plan Government ministers in both Houses rejected attempts to write any reference to the proposed foundation into the Bill. While any retreat from this position would entail political difficulties it is difficult to see how it could be

---

* Annotations by Professor Paul Jackson, University of Reading.

argued that the Secretary of State could be prevented from a sale on the open market. The wording of s.3 can hardly be thought to fall within the principle enunciated in *Pepper (Inspector of Taxes) v. Hart* [1993] AC 593. The wording is not ambiguous or obscure. Ministers gave no assurances about the *meaning* of the section. It was precisely because of its unlimited meaning that opponents of the legislation sought unsuccessfully to introduce an amendment. The remaining provisions of the Act are consequential on the creation of the new company.

The Crown Agents were established by Royal Prerogative in 1833 to procure goods and services for colonial administrations. In 1863 the official title became Crown Agents for Colonies. In 1954, to reflect changing circumstances, this, in turn, was altered to Crown Agents for Oversea Governments and Administrations. Statutory regulation was effected for the first time by the Crown Agents Act 1979 (c. 43) which constituted the Crown Agents a body corporate and created the Crown Agents Holding and Realisation Board as a separate entity to manage and wind up the assets and liabilities of the unincorporated Crown Agents' own account business which had incurred substantial losses following the collapse of the property market in the mid-seventies. The purpose of the 1979 Act was to establish strict limits on the activities of the Agents in order to avoid the risk of future losses arising from ill advised business activities on their own behalf in the future. The purpose of the 1995 Act is to remove the Crown Agents from the public sector and free them from ministerial controls which, in the view of the Government, are inconsistent with the effective carrying out of their functions. From supplying goods and services to the colonies the Crown Agents have moved to a position where over 70 per cent of their work is undertaken on behalf of non-UK principals—including Japan, the Netherlands, the World Bank, the European Union and the United Nations.

Commencement
The provisions of the Act become effective on the "appointed day", that is such day as the Secretary of State may by order appoint: s.1(1). Such power to make an order is exercisable by statutory instrument: s.12(2).

Vesting of property, &c. of Crown Agents in a successor company

Vesting of property, &c. of Crown Agents in a successor company

1.—(1) On such day as the Secretary of State may by order appoint all property, rights and liabilities to which the Crown Agents for Oversea Governments and Administrations (referred to in this Act as "the Crown Agents") were entitled or subject immediately before that day shall become by virtue of this section property, rights and liabilities of a company nominated for the purposes of this section by the Secretary of State.

References in this Act to the appointed day and to the successor company are to the day so appointed and the company so nominated.

(2) The Secretary of State may, after consulting the Crown Agents, by order nominate for the purposes of this section any company formed and registered under the Companies Act 1985; but on the appointed day the company in question must be a company limited by shares which is wholly owned by the Crown.

(3) References in this Act to property, rights and liabilities of the Crown Agents shall be construed as follows—

   (a) the references are to all property, rights and liabilities of the Crown Agents, whether or not capable of being transferred or assigned by them;

   (b) references to property are to property of the Crown Agents whether situated in the United Kingdom or elsewhere; and

   (c) references to rights or liabilities of the Crown Agents are to rights or liabilities under the law of the United Kingdom or of any part of the United Kingdom or under the law of any country or territory outside the United Kingdom.

(4) An order appointing a day under subsection (1) or nominating a company for the purposes of this section may be varied or revoked by a sub-

sequent order at any time before any property, rights or liabilities of the Crown Agents vest in a company by virtue of this section.

(5) Schedule 1 has effect for the purpose of supplementing the provisions of this section.

DEFINITIONS
"appointed day": subs. (1), s.14.
"Crown Agents" : subs. (1), s.14.
"successor company": s.14.

GENERAL NOTE
This section confers on the Secretary of State the power to transfer the property, rights and liabilities of the Crown Agents to a company nominated by him. Various attempts to restrict his powers were made in both Houses, to no avail. An amendment to provide that the successor company and any company to which that company was subsequently transferred should be a company limited by guarantee, in the form of a foundation committed to social and developmental objectives, was withdrawn in the House of Lords: *Hansard*, H.L. Vol. 563, cols. 762–767.

Subs. (2)
After consulting the Crown Agents. A statutory duty to consult requires a genuine consultation and a reasonable opportunity for comment: see H.W.R. Wade and C.F. Forsyth, *Administrative Law* (7th ed.) pp. 255 and 897.

Subs. (5)
Schedule 1 supplements the provisions of s.1. In particular it protects the position of the staff of the Crown Agents with regard to employment rights and the application of the Transfer of Undertakings (Protection of Employment) Regulations 1981 (S.I. 1981 No. 1794): see para. 3. The Government resisted an attempt to insert an explicit reference to the right of staff to belong to a trade union of their choice: *Hansard*, H.L. Vol. 263, col. 777.

Provisions with respect to capital structure

2.—(1) The commencing capital debt assumed by the Crown Agents under section 17 of the Crown Agents Act 1979 shall be repaid; and the Secretary of State may give directions as to the time and manner of repayment.

(2) If the Secretary of State so directs before the appointed day, the Crown Agents shall be deemed to assume a debt to the Secretary of State of such amount as may be specified in the direction.

The terms of the debt, including the terms as to the payment of interest and repayment, shall be such as the Secretary of State may from time to time determine.

(3) Any sums received by the Secretary of State by virtue of subsection (1) shall be paid into the National Loans Fund; and any sums received by him by way of interest on or repayment of a debt assumed by virtue of subsection (2) shall be paid into the Consolidated Fund.

(4) The approval of the Treasury is required for any exercise by the Secretary of State of the powers conferred by this section.

GENERAL NOTE
Under the Crown Agents Act 1979, s.17, the newly incorporated body assumed a debt (the commencing capital debt) in respect of the property and rights transferred to it by s.2 of the 1979 Act.

This section provides machinery for the repayment to the National Loans Fund of the outstanding balance of that debt. The National Loans Fund was established by the National Loans Act 1968 (c. 13) and may be used under the Government Trading Funds Act 1973 (c. 63) and the Government Trading Act 1990 (c. 30) for funding the operations of government departments. The statutory provisions would not, however, extend to the Crown Agents after it had joined the private sector.

Subsection (2), however, provides for the possibility of the Secretary of State making other arrangements (with the consent of the Treasury: subs. (4)) for the creation of a new debt on such terms as he may determine.

Initial Government holding in the successor company

3.—(1) As a consequence of the vesting in the successor company by virtue of section 1 of property, rights and liabilities of the Crown Agents, the successor company shall issue to the Secretary of State such securities of the company as he may from time to time direct.

(2) The Secretary of State shall not give a direction under subsection (1) after the successor company has ceased to be wholly owned by the Crown.

(3) Securities to be issued in pursuance of this section shall be issued at such time or times, and on such terms, as the Secretary of State may direct.

(4) Any shares issued in pursuance of this section shall be of such nominal value as the Secretary of State may direct.

(5) The Secretary of State may not exercise any power conferred on him by this section or dispose of, for consideration or otherwise, any securities issued to him in pursuance of this section, without the consent of the Treasury.

(6) Any dividends or other sums received by the Secretary of State in right of, or on the disposal of, any securities acquired by virtue of this section shall be paid into the Consolidated Fund.

DEFINITIONS
"securities": s.14.
"successor company": s.14.

GENERAL NOTE
Government ministers in both Houses gave unequivocal assurances that shares in the successor company would not be offered on the open market but transferred to a specially established, independent foundation. The Government resisted any attempt to write any reference to the proposed foundation into the Act but, in response to constant pressure produced, as evidence of its good faith, drafts of the memorandum and articles of association of the new body before the meeting of the House of Commons, Standing Committee F, on June 15, 1995.

Government investment in securities of the successor company

4.—(1) The Secretary of State may, with the consent of the Treasury, at any time when the successor company is wholly owned by the Crown, acquire—
(a) securities of the successor company, or
(b) rights to subscribe for any such securities.

(2) The Secretary of State may not dispose of, for consideration or otherwise, any securities or rights acquired by him by virtue of this section without the consent of the Treasury.

(3) Any expenses incurred by the Secretary of State in consequence of the provisions of this section shall be paid out of money provided by Parliament.

(4) Any dividends or other sums received by the Secretary of State in right of, or on the disposal of, any securities or rights acquired by virtue of this section shall be paid into the Consolidated Fund.

DEFINITIONS
"securities": s.14.
"successor company": s.14.

Provisions as to statutory accounts of successor company

5.—(1) For the purposes of any statutory accounts of the successor company—
(a) all the property, rights and liabilities to which the Crown Agents were entitled or subject immediately before the end of their last financial year ending before the appointed day shall be taken to have vested in the successor company by virtue of section 1, and to have so vested immediately after the end of that year; and

(b) the value or amount (as at the time of vesting) of any asset or liability of the Crown Agents taken to have vested in the successor company by virtue of paragraph (a) shall be taken to be the value or (as the case may be) the amount assigned to that asset·or liability for the purposes of the corresponding statement of accounts prepared by the Crown Agents in respect of the financial year referred to in paragraph (a).

(2) For the purposes of any statutory accounts of the successor company the amount to be included in respect of any item shall be determined as if anything done by the Crown Agents (whether by way of acquiring, revaluing or disposing of any asset or incurring, revaluing or discharging any liability, or by carrying any amount to any provision or reserve, or otherwise) had been done by the successor company.

(3) Accordingly, but without prejudice to the generality of the preceding provision—

(a) the amount to be included from time to time in any reserves of the successor company as representing its accumulated realised profits shall be determined as if any profits realised and retained by the Crown Agents had been realised and retained by the company; and

(b) the amount to be included in any such accounts as representing the accumulated realised losses of the successor company shall be determined as if any losses realised by the Crown Agents had been realised by the company.

(4) References in this section to the statutory accounts of the successor company are to any accounts prepared by the successor company for the purposes of any provision of the Companies Act 1985 (including group accounts).

DEFINITIONS
"Crown Agents": ss.1(1), 14.
"successor company": s.14.

Use of "Crown Agents" as part of company name

6. The words "Crown Agents" may, notwithstanding anything in section 26(2)(a) of the Companies Act 1985 (prohibition of name giving impression of connection with Her Majesty's Government), be used as part of the name of—

(a) the successor company,
(b) any company of which the successor company is a wholly-owned subsidiary, or,
(c) any subsidiary of the successor company or any such company;
and the power conferred by section 32 of that Act (power to require company to abandon misleading name) shall not apply in relation to the use of those words as part of the name of any such company.

GENERAL NOTE
The name "Crown Agents" was recognised in the debates as a valuable business asset. Continued use of the name by any body created under the 1995 Act was regarded as important commercially as indicating a continuance of the traditional virtues of probity, impartiality and integrity associated with the former Crown Agents.
Fears that such use might lead to a mistaken belief that any new private sector body was connected with the Crown were regarded as unfounded and unjustified. The name itself, according to a minister, no more implies a connection with the Government or the Crown than "having a nightly tipple at the Rose and Crown" means that it has anything to do with someone called Rose or the Crown: *Hansard*, H.L. Vol. 562, col. 1344.

Corporation tax

7.—(1) The successor company shall be treated for all purposes of corporation tax as if it were the same person as the Crown Agents.

(2) The existence or exercise of the powers of the Secretary of State under section 1 shall not be regarded as constituting or creating arrangements within the meaning of section 410 of the Income and Corporation Taxes Act 1988 (arrangements for the transfer of a company to another group or consortium) or as constituting or creating option arrangements for the purposes of paragraph 5B of Schedule 18 to that Act.

(3) Any debt assumed under section 2 shall be treated for the purposes of the Corporation Tax Acts as if it had been assumed—

(a) wholly in consideration of a loan made to the Crown Agents of an amount equal to the principal sum payable under the debt, and

(b) wholly and exclusively for the purposes of the trade carried on by them.

If the terms of any such debt include provision for the payment of a sum expressed as interest in respect of a period which falls wholly or partly before the debt was assumed, any payment made in pursuance of that provision in respect of that period shall be treated for the purposes of the Corporation Tax Acts as if the debt had been assumed at the commencement of that period and, accordingly, as interest on the principal sum payable under the debt.

(4) Any security (other than a share) issued by the successor company in pursuance of section 3 shall be treated for the purposes of the Corporation Tax Acts as if it had been issued—

(a) wholly in consideration of a loan made to the company of an amount equal to the principal sum payable under the security, and

(b) wholly and exclusively for the purposes of the trade carried on by that company.

If the terms of any such security include provision for the payment of a sum expressed as interest in respect of a period which falls wholly or partly before the security was issued, any payment made in pursuance of that provision in respect of that period shall be treated for the purposes of the Corporation Tax Acts as if the security had been issued at the commencement of that period and, accordingly, as interest on the principal sum payable under the security.

(5) Any share issued by the successor company in pursuance of section 3 shall be treated for the purposes of the Corporation Tax Acts as if it had been issued wholly in consideration of a subscription paid to the company of an amount equal to the nominal value of the share.

DEFINITIONS
"Crown Agents": ss.1(1), 14.
"successor company": s.14.

Dissolution of Crown Agents

Residual functions and dissolution of Crown Agents

8.—(1) The Crown Agents shall continue in existence after the appointed day for the purpose of performing the functions conferred on them by sections 9 and 10 (vesting of foreign property, &c. and final reports and accounts).

The period of their continued existence after the appointed day is referred to below as "the transitional period".

(2) During the transitional period—

(a) section 1(3) of the Crown Agents Act 1979 (constitution of the Crown Agents: number of members) shall have effect as if for "not less than six" there were substituted "not less than two";

(b) at any time when there are only two members of the Crown Agents it shall not be incumbent upon the Secretary of State to appoint one of those members as deputy chairman; and

(c) no remuneration shall be payable to any member of the Crown Agents.

(3) Any expenses incurred by the Crown Agents during the transitional period shall be met by the successor company.

(4) Once the Secretary of State is satisfied that the functions of the Crown Agents under sections 9 and 10 below are substantially discharged, he may, after consulting the Crown Agents and the successor company, by order dissolve the Crown Agents on a day specified in the order.

DEFINITIONS

"appointed day": ss.1(1), 14.

"Crown Agents": ss.1(1), 14.

"transitional period": subs. (1), s.14.

GENERAL NOTE

Section 8 provides for the continued existence of the Crown Agents as established by the Crown Agents Act 1979 after the appointed day until the Secretary of State is satisfied that their functions under ss.9 and 10 are substantially discharged when he may, after consulting the Crown Agents and the successor company, dissolve the Crown Agents by order.

Subs. 4

Satisfied. The power conferred on the Secretary of State is framed in a subjective form that does not necessarily exclude the possibility of judicial review: see *Secretary of State for Education and Science v. Tameside Metropolitan Borough Council* [1971] A.C. 1014.

Substantially. This is a word which accommodates a wide range of meanings, from "not trifling" to "nearly complete"; see *R v. Monopolies and Mergers Commission, ex p. South Yorkshire Transport and South Yorkshire Transport Authority* [1993] 1 W.L.R. 23, at p.29 *per* Lord Mustill. The context here, it is submitted, suggests a meaning closer to nearly complete than to not trifling.

Consulting. See General Note to s.1(2), above.

Functions with respect to vesting of foreign property, &c. in successor company

9.—(1) It shall be the duty of the Crown Agents and of the successor company to take, as and when during the transitional period the successor company considers appropriate, all such steps as may be requisite to secure that the vesting in the successor company by virtue of this Act of any foreign property, right or liability is effective under the relevant foreign law.

(2) Until the vesting in the successor company by virtue of this Act of any foreign property, right or liability is effective under the relevant foreign law, it shall be the duty of the Crown Agents during the transitional period to hold that property or right for the benefit of, or to discharge that liability on behalf of, the successor company.

(3) Nothing in subsections (1) and (2) shall be taken as prejudicing the effect under the law of the United Kingdom, or of any part of the United Kingdom, of the vesting in the successor company by virtue of this Act of any foreign property, right or liability.

(4) The Crown Agents shall have all such powers as may be requisite for the performance of their duties under this section; but—

(a) it shall be the duty of the successor company during the transitional period to act on behalf of the Crown Agents (so far as possible) in performing the duties imposed on the Crown Agents by this section, and

(b) any foreign property, rights and liabilities acquired or incurred by the Crown Agents during that period shall immediately become property, rights and liabilities of the successor company.

(5) References in this section to any foreign property, right or liability are to any property, right or liability as respects which any issue arising in any

proceedings would have been determined (in accordance with the rules of private international law) by reference to the law of a country or territory outside the United Kingdom.

GENERAL NOTE
Section 9 provides for the vesting of the property of the Crown Agents wherever situated, in the successor company.

Final reports and accounts of Crown Agents

10.—(1) Notwithstanding the repeal of section 11 of the Crown Agents Act 1979 (annual reports to the Secretary of State)—
  (a) it shall continue to be the duty of the Crown Agents to make a report to the Secretary of State in accordance with that section in respect of each accounting year of the Crown Agents ending before the appointed day; and
  (b) the Secretary of State shall lay a copy of any such report before each House of Parliament.

(2) Notwithstanding the repeal of section 22 of the Crown Agents Act 1979 (accounts of the Crown Agents and audit)—
  (a) it shall continue to be the duty of the Crown Agents to prepare such statements of accounts as are mentioned in subsection (1) of that section in respect of each accounting year of the Crown Agents ending before the appointed day; and
  (b) that section shall continue to apply during the transitional period in relation to those accounts and in relation also to the auditing of accounts kept in accordance with subsection (1) of that section in respect of each such accounting year.

DEFINITIONS
"appointed day": ss.1(1), 14.
"Crown Agents": ss.1(1), 14.
"transitional period": ss.8(1), 14.

GENERAL NOTE
This section provides for the continued obligation of the Crown Agents to provide annual reports and statements of accounts for each accounting year ending before the appointed day notwithstanding the repeal of the relevant sections (ss.11 and 22) in the Crown Agents Act 1979.

Crown Agents Holding and Realisation Board

Constitution, &c. of the Board after the appointed day

11.—(1) The following provisions have effect in relation to the Crown Agents Holding and Realisation Board as from the appointed day.

(2) In section 25 of the Crown Agents Act 1979, for subsection (2) substitute—

  "(2) The Board shall consist of not less than two nor more than ten members appointed by the Secretary of State; and the Secretary of State shall appoint one member to be the chairman, and another member to be the deputy chairman, of the Board.".

(3) For paragraph 1 of Schedule 5 to the Crown Agents Act 1979 substitute—

"Appointment and tenure of members

1. Paragraphs 1 to 6 of Schedule 1 shall apply to the Board as they apply to the Crown Agents.".

(4) For paragraph 2 of Schedule 5 to the Crown Agents Act 1979 substitute—

"*Remuneration, &c.*

2.—(1) The Board shall pay to each of their members such remuneration and such reasonable allowances in respect of expenses as the Secretary of State may determine.

(2) If the Secretary of State so determines in the case of a person who is or has been a member of the Board, the Board shall pay or make arrangements for the payment of such pension to or in respect of that person as the Secretary of State may determine.

(3) Where a person ceases to be a member of the Board otherwise than on the expiry of his term of office and it appears to the Secretary of State that there are special circumstances which make it right for that person to receive compensation, the Secretary of State may direct the Board to make to that person a payment of such amount as the Secretary of State may determine.".

(5) For paragraph 4 of Schedule 5 to the Crown Agents Act 1979 substitute—

"*Performance of functions*

4. The Board may authorise any person to perform on behalf of the Board any of the Board's functions, other than a function in respect of which the Secretary of State has instructed the Board that no such authorisation is to be given.".

(6) In paragraph 7(4)(b) of Schedule 5 to the Crown Agents Act 1979 for "the officer of the Crown Agents acting for the Board who so corresponds" substitute "the Chairman of the Board".

(7) In paragraph 8 of Schedule 5 to the Crown Agents Act 1979, in sub-paragraph (3) (ancillary powers exercisable with consent of Secretary of State), after paragraph (g) insert—

"(h) to employ staff;
(i) to incur expenses in respect of office accommodation, office equipment or other office facilities;
(j) to engage the services of any person as consultant or adviser to the Board.";

and omit sub-paragraphs (4) and (5).

(8) The repeal by this Act of any provision of the Crown Agents Act 1979 relating to the Crown Agents which is applied by any provision of that Act in relation to the Crown Agents Holding and Realisation Board does not affect its continued operation as so applied.

DEFINITIONS
"appointed day": ss.1(1), 14.

GENERAL NOTE
The Crown Agents Holding and Realisation Board was established by the Crown Agents Act 1979, s.25, to manage and wind up the assets and liabilities of the unincorporated Crown Agents' own account business which had incurred losses as a consequence of the collapse of the property market.

The Board will remain in the public sector until it has tied up the few loose ends still surviving from the pre-1979 activities of the unincorporated Crown Agents. It will then be wound up by the Secretary of State under Sched. 5, para. 23, to the 1979 Act.

Supplementary provisions

Orders

12.—(1) An order under this Act may contain such supplementary, incidental or transitional provisions as appear to the Secretary of State to be expedient.

(2) Any power to make an order under this Act is exercisable by statutory instrument.

GENERAL NOTE

The specific provisions conferring power to make Orders are to be found in s.1(1) which deals with the vesting of the property of the Crown Agents in a nominated company, s.1(2) which provides for the nomination of the successor company and s.8(4) which governs the dissolution of the Crown Agents.

Subsection (1) ensures that orders made under those sections may include supplementary, incidental or transitional provisions where those appear to the Secretary of State to be expedient. The scope of the Secretary of State's discretion, although subjectively worded, is subject to judicial review, for example on the ground of *Wednesbury* unreasonableness.

Consequential amendments and repeals

13.—(1) As from the appointed day the House of Commons Disqualification Act 1975 is amended as follows—

(a) in Part III of Schedule 1 (other disqualifying offices) insert at the appropriate place—

"Director of the successor company (within the meaning of the Crown Agents Act 1995) being a director nominated or appointed by a Minister of the Crown or by a person acting on behalf of the Crown"; and

(b) in Part II of that Schedule (bodies of which all members are disqualified) insert at the appropriate place—

"The Crown Agents Holding and Realisation Board".

Corresponding amendments shall be made in Schedule 1 to the Northern Ireland Assembly Disqualification Act 1975.

(2) The enactments specified in Schedule 2 are repealed to the extent specified.

The repeals in Part I of that Schedule come into force on the appointed day; and the repeals in Part II of that Schedule come into force on the dissolution of the Crown Agents.

(3) The Secretary of State may by order make such consequential amendments or revocations of subordinate legislation within the meaning of the Interpretation Act 1978 as appear to him necessary or expedient in consequence of this Act.

Any order under this subsection shall be subject to annulment in pursuance of a resolution of either House of Parliament.

DEFINITIONS

"appointed day": ss.1(1), 14.
"subordinate legislation": Interpretation Act 1978, s.21(1).
"Successor Company": s.14.

GENERAL NOTE

Subsection (1) amends the House of Commons Disqualification Act 1975 (c. 24) and the Northern Ireland Assembly Disqualification Act 1975 (c. 25) to exclude from membership directors of the successor company to the Crown Agents nominated or appointed by a Minister of the Crown or by a person acting on behalf of the Crown and all members of the Crown Agents Holding and Realisation Board.

Subsection (2) provides for the repeal of statutory provisions specified in Schedule 2.

Subsection (3) confers power on the Secretary of State to amend or revoke subordinate legislation as appears to him necessary or expedient in consequence of the Crown Agents Act.

Orders made under the subsection are statutory instruments by virtue of s.12(2) and are subject to annulment by resolution of either House of Parliament.

As appear to him necessary or expedient. Although subjectively worded this phrase is not sufficient to exclude judicial review for example on the ground of *Wednesbury* unreasonableness.

Interpretation

14. In this Act—

"the appointed day" means the day appointed under section 1(1);

"the Crown Agents" means the body corporate established by section 1 of the Crown Agents Act 1979 by the name of the Crown Agents for Oversea Governments and Administrations;

"securities", in relation to the successor company, includes shares, debentures, bonds and other securities of the company, whether or not constituting a charge on the assets of the company;

"subsidiary" and "wholly-owned subsidiary" shall be construed in accordance with section 736 of the Companies Act 1985;

"the successor company" means the company nominated for the purposes of section 1; and

"the transitional period", in relation to the Crown Agents, has the meaning given by section 8(1).

Citation and extent

15.—(1) This Act may be cited as the Crown Agents Act 1995.

(2) This Act extends to Northern Ireland.

SCHEDULES

Section 1(5)   SCHEDULE 1

SUPPLEMENTARY PROVISIONS AS TO VESTING OF PROPERTY, ETC.

1.—(1) Any agreement made, transaction effected or other thing done by, to or in relation to the Crown Agents which is in force or effective immediately before the appointed day shall have effect as from that day as if made, effected or done by, to or in relation to the successor company, in all respects as if the successor company were the same person, in law, as the Crown Agents.

(2) Accordingly, references to the Crown Agents—

(a) in any agreement (whether or not in writing) and in any deed, bond or instrument,

(b) in any process or other document issued, prepared or employed for the purpose of any proceeding before any court or other tribunal or authority, and

(c) in any other document whatever (other than an enactment) relating to or affecting any property, right or liability of the Crown Agents which vests by virtue of section 1 in the successor company,

shall be taken as from the appointed day as referring to the successor company.

2. Where immediately before the appointed day there is in force an agreement which—

(a) confers or imposes on the Crown Agents any rights or liabilities which vest in the successor company by virtue of section 1, and

(b) refers (in whatever terms and whether expressly or by implication) to a member or officer of the Crown Agents,

the agreement shall have effect, in relation to anything falling to be done on or after that day, as if for that reference there were substituted a reference to such person as that company may appoint or, in default of appointment, to the officer of that company who corresponds as nearly as may be to the member or officer of the Crown Agents in question.

3.—(1) The effect of section 1 in relation to any contract of employment with the Crown Agents in force immediately before the appointed day is merely to modify the contract (as from that day) by substituting the successor company as the employer (and not to terminate the contract or vary it in any other way).

(2) Nothing in this Act affects the operation of the Transfer of Undertakings (Protection of Employment) Regulations 1981 in relation to the transfer of the undertaking of the Crown Agents to the successor company by virtue of section 1; and the Secretary of State shall before appointing a day under section 1(1) give to the Crown Agents such notice of his proposals as he considers appropriate for enabling any provisions of those regulations applicable to the transfer to be complied with.

4.—(1) Section 1 is effective to vest the rights and liabilities of the Crown Agents under any agreement or arrangement for the payment of pensions, allowances or gratuities in the successor company along with all other rights and liabilities of the Crown Agents.

(2) Accordingly, for the purposes of any such agreement or arrangement as it has effect as from the appointed day—

    (a) any period of employment with the Crown Agents or with a subsidiary of the Crown Agents, and

    (b) any period of employment which would, immediately before that day, have been treated as such employment for the purposes of any such agreement or arrangement,

shall count as employment with the successor company or (as the case may be) with a subsidiary of that company.

GENERAL NOTE

Schedule 1 supplements the provisions of s.1. Please see the General Note to that section.

Section 13(2)   SCHEDULE 2

REPEALS

PART I

REPEALS COMING INTO FORCE ON THE APPOINTED DAY

Chapter	Short title	Extent of repeal
1975 c. 24.	House of Commons Disqualification Act 1975.	In Schedule 1, in Part III, the entry relating to the Chairman, Deputy Chairman or Managing Director of the Crown Agents.
1975 c. 25.	Northern Ireland Assembly Disqualification Act 1975.	In Schedule 1, in Part II, the entry relating to the Crown Agents for Oversea Governments and Administrations.

1979 c. 43.	Crown Agents Act 1979.	Section 1(7).
		Sections 2 to 24.
		Section 27(2).
		In section 27(3), the words "the Crown Agents or".
		Section 28.
		In section 30(3)(a), the words "or 31(2)".
		In section 31(1)—
		   (a) in the definition of "accounting year", the words from "subject to subsection (2)" to "Crown Agents";
		   (b) the definitions of "commencing capital debt", "financial year" and "scheduled authority or body".
		Section 31(2) and (3).
		In Schedule 1—
		   (a) in paragraph 7, the words "such remuneration and" and "with the approval of the Minister for the Civil Service";
		   (b) paragraphs 8, 9, 11 and 13 to 15.
		Schedules 2 to 4.
		In Schedule 5—
		   (a) paragraph 8(4) and (5);
		   (b) in paragraph 23(2)(a), the words "or to the Crown Agents".
		In Schedule 6, Part II.

Chapter	Short title	Extent of repeal
1982 c. 39.	Finance Act 1982.	Section 153(4).
1982 c. 46.	Employment Act 1982.	In Schedule 3, paragraph 31.
1985 c. 9.	Companies Consolidation (Consequential Provisions) Act 1985.	In Schedule 2, the entry relating to section 22(6) of the Crown Agents Act 1979.
1986 c. 43.	Crown Agents (Amendment) Act 1986.	The whole Act.
1987 c. 22.	Banking Act 1987.	In Schedule 2, paragraphs 14 and 14A. In Schedule 6, paragraph 8.
1989 c. 40.	Companies Act 1989.	In Schedule 10, paragraph 29.
1992 c. 52.	Trade Union and Labour Relations (Consolidation) Act 1992.	In Schedule 2, paragraph 26.

PART II

REPEALS COMING INTO FORCE ON DISSOLUTION OF CROWN AGENTS

Chapter	Short title	Extent of repeal
1979 c. 43.	Crown Agents Act 1979.	Section 1, so far as unrepealed. In section 30(3)(a), the words "section 1(1) or". Schedule 1, so far as unrepealed.

INDEX

References are to sections and Schedules

ENVIRONMENT ACT 1995*

(1995 c. 25)

---

* Annotations by Stephen Tromans, MA, FRSA, MCIWEM, Solicitor, Partner and Head of Environmental Law Department, Simmons & Simmons, Michael Nash, Solicitor, Environmental Law Department, Simmons & Simmons and Mark Poustie, MA, LLB, Solicitor, Lecturer in Law, University of Strathclyde.

An Act to provide for the establishment of a body corporate to be known as the Environment Agency and a body corporate to be known as the Scottish Environment Protection Agency; to provide for the transfer of functions, property, rights and liabilities to those bodies and for the conferring of other functions on them; to make provision with respect to contaminated land and abandoned mines; to make further provision in relation to National Parks; to make further provision for the control of pollution, the conservation of natural resources and the conservation or enhancement of the environment; to make provision for imposing obligations on certain persons in respect of certain products or materials; to make provision in relation to fisheries; to make provision for certain enactments to bind the Crown; to make provision with respect to the application of certain enactments in relation to the Isles of Scilly; and for connected purposes.

[19th July 1995]

PARLIAMENTARY DEBATES
Hansard, H.L. Vol. 559, cols. 1375, 1480, Vol. 560, cols. 537, 621, 758, 817, 1184, 1337, 1414, 1591, 1655, Vol. 561, cols. 311, 391, 595, 1308, 1586, 1645, Vol. 562, cols. 120, 205, 400, 478, 1016, 1096, Vol. 565, cols. 1472, 1570. H.C. Vol. 258, col. 35, Vol. 262, cols. 711, 913.

The Bill was discussed in Standing Committee B between April 27 and June 15, 1995.

INTRODUCTION AND GENERAL NOTE

During the passage of the Environmental Protection Act 1990, the Government indicated that the 1990 Act could not be regarded as its "last word" on the environment: see *Hansard*, H.C. Vol. 165, col. 33. How true that was. The Environment Act 1995 is the product of a further five years' evolution of Government policy, including some notable changes of direction. In the five years between the Environmental Protection Act 1990 and the 1995 Act, environmental law and policy have been the subject of continuous, and in some cases concentrated, attention. At the most general level, the Government's environmental policy document, *This Common Inheritance* (Cm. 1200, September 1990) has been kept under review by regular reports monitoring progress in implementation and adding further objectives. In January 1994 the Government published four key strategy documents (Cm. 2426–2429) relating to obligations under the UNCED (Rio) Conference dealing with sustainable development, climate change, biodiversity, and sustainable forestry. At the same time the Government appointed an advisory panel on sustainable development, which was also the subject of an important report by the House of Lords Committee on the subject: Session 1994–1995, H.L. Paper 72, Vols. I and II, June 21, 1995.

More specifically, considerable problems have been encountered in the implementation of Pt. II of the 1990 Act dealing with waste, and in particular the consistency of that legislation with EC law in terms of scope and general objectives. The result of such deliberations can be seen in various changes made by the 1995 Act. In these and other respects, thinking has moved on considerably since 1990. Such changes are referred to in the relevant context in the 1995 Act and its modifications to the 1990 Act.

Like the Environmental Protection Act 1990, the 1995 Act is heterogeneous in content, opportunity having been taken to include various new provisions or refinements of existing law which had for some time been under consideration. However, the heart, and origin, of the Act lies in Pt. I which establishes two new bodies, the Environment Agency and the Scottish Environment Protection Agency. These bodies will assume key functions of environmental protection and resource management from existing authorities, and will be under a variety of general and specific duties; some of which have aroused considerable interest and controversy. Whilst the 1995 Act is still far from the goal of complete and effective integration of the environment with other areas of policy and regulation—or even full integration within the field of environmental protection—it represents a significant step in that direction. It includes, at s.4(3), the first statutory mention of the concept and objective of sustainable development (see above), although it should be noted that since 1991 Scottish Natural Heritage has been under a duty in regard to "sustainability" which is in some respects comparable: see the General Note to s.31.

Part II of the 1995 Act deals with what has proven for the Government to be an extremely thorny topic, that of contaminated land. The proposal contained in s.143 of the Environmental Protection Act 1990, for registers of land subject to past or present contaminative uses, proved to be unacceptable and has been replaced by a scheme for identifying and securing the remediation of actually contaminated land. The new provisions are modelled—though with numerous refinements and complexities—on the traditional scheme for abating statutory nuisances. Not surprisingly, the creation of law which might potentially have both strict and retrospective effect, as well as applying to the detriment of current landowners and lenders, aroused much concern. The result was that the provisions of Pt. II were heavily amended in both Houses, allaying at least partially the concerns of the relevant interests. Part II also contains provisions to deal with what has, over the years since 1990, been a recurrent concern: that of water pollution emanating from abandoned mines.

Parts III and IV of the 1995 Act deal with the diverse but important issues of national parks and air quality. Part III amends existing legislation on national parks (in particular the National Parks and Access to the Countryside Act 1949) to provide for the creation of new National Park Authorities which will become the local planning authorities for the parks. The 1995 Act also modifies the statutory purposes of national parks—an issue which aroused strong feelings and much debate in the House of Lords. Problems with air quality in the UK's towns and cities have become increasingly high-profile and acute since 1990, and Part IV of the Act attempts to address what may be a very intractable problem by way of creating a national air quality strategy and imposing new duties on local authorities.

Part V (Miscellaneous, General and Supplemental Provisions) is indeed miscellaneous in content. It contains provisions on waste, the review of mineral planning permissions, protection of hedgerows, drainage, fisheries, water pollution and statutory nuisance.

As with the 1990 Act, to appreciate fully the new provisions, it is helpful to be aware of the underlying evolution of policy. Reference is accordingly made in the notes and annotations to the relevant consultation papers, ministerial statements and similar material. Some of the provisions also relate to current or proposed EC measures, particularly in the field of packaging waste recovery.

In conclusion, what is not in the 1995 Act is perhaps equally important as what is contained. The Secretary of State for the Environment, in moving the Second Reading of the Bill in the Commons, saw the Bill as the latest in a long line of Bills to protect the UK environment, but also to be seen in the context of ". . . a new century and a new millennium, in which sustainable development will be the watchword of well-being for all our people. The Bill puts in place a key instrument for preserving and enhancing the quality of life for the British people as we enter a new era" (*Hansard*, H.C. Vol. 258, col. 48).

In giving the Labour Party's response, Mr Frank Dobson, MP acknowledged that many of the Bill's proposals were in line with Labour Party policy and were welcomed as such. However, he went on to criticise what he saw as missed opportunities:

"The Bill could have placed on all Government Departments and public bodies a general duty to further the protection and enhancement of the environment; it does not. It could have enshrined in law the precautionary principle that could be applied to new materials and processes; it does not . . . The Bill proposes no action to tackle noise pollution. The Government have not taken the opportunity provided by the establishment of the new Agencies to end the present confusion over responsibility, which is holding back an integrated effort to reduce marine pollution, especially in the North and Irish seas. In short, the Bill is welcome in general, but it falls short of what is needed if the environment is to be given proper priority as we approach the 21st century" (*Hansard*, H.C. Vol. 258, cols. 49–50).

The Act is ambitious in what it sets out to achieve, and its success or failure may ultimately depend on the resources made available to those charged with duties and functions under it. In many respects, however, the success or failure of environmental policy will depend on the willingness of an often misleadingly educated public to modify its behaviour. It is perhaps therefore to be regretted that Mr Matthew Taylor, MP (Truro) did not succeed in his objective of inserting a provision on environmental claims into the Bill. He pointed out that too many misleading, meaningless and unsubstantiated environmental claims are made for products. In particular, he gave the example of a make of sock promoted as "ozone friendly", with a label bearing the following rubric:

"Helps prevent foot odour which is probably a major cause of the destruction of the ozone layer" (*Hansard*, H.C. Vol. 258, col. 66).

EC AND INTERNATIONAL LAW

The underlying international and EC law was vital to the understanding of the 1990 Act and its operation in practice. If anything, the importance of such law has increased over the intervening five years. Implementation of the 1992 UN Convention on Climate Change has been a major preoccupation both within the UK and European Community, and likewise the 1987 Montreal Protocol on Substances that Deplete the Ozone Layer and the 1989 Basel Convention on the Transboundary Movement of Hazardous Wastes and their Disposal.

Similarly, many aspects of EC environmental policy have generated activity, some of which is reflected in the UK legislation, and some of which may in due course necessitate further legislative changes. Of particular relevance to the Environment Act 1995 are the various directives dealing with air quality (Pt. IV), the waste framework directives 75/442/EEC and 91/156/EEC, the packaging waste directive 94/62/EC and the proposed landfill directive (COM(93)275 final; political agreement June 1994) (Pt. V). The proposed directive on integrated pollution prevention and control (COM(93)423 final; amended COM(95)88 final; political agreement June 1995) may result in changes of approach under Pt. I of the 1990 Act.

The importance of EC law is shown by the various provisions in the 1990 and 1995 Acts which make provision for its implementation. Examples in the 1990 Act include s.7(2)(b) relating to the conditions of authorisation for prescribed processes, and s.156, giving a general power to make regulations. Similarly under the 1995 Act, reference may be made to ss.80(2) and 87(1) referring to the national air quality strategy, ss.44A(10) and 44B(9) of the 1990 Act (as inserted by s.92 of the 1995 Act) dealing with the national waste strategy, and ss.93(2) and 94(2) dealing with producer responsibility for re-use, recovery and recycling.

As well as such overt references to EC measures, the doctrine of indirect effect or sympathetic interpretation will ensure that the legislation receives a purposive construction so as to ensure compliance with the relevant EC legislation: see the Occasional Paper in the Sweet & Maxwell *Environmental Law Bulletin* No. 8 (September/October 1994).

PARLIAMENTARY PROCEEDINGS: *Pepper v. Hart*

In the annotations of a number of sections of the Act, reference is made to statements made in Parliament on behalf of the Government during the passage of the Bill. Such statements may be interesting in their own right as background information and may aid understanding of the section under consideration. However, by virtue of what has become known as the rule in *Pepper (Inspector of Taxes) v. Hart* [1992] 3 WLR 1032, in some cases they may also be admissible in court to determine the meaning which the court should attribute to the section.

In *Pepper v. Hart*, the House of Lords went beyond the existing "mischief" rule whereby official sources such as Law Commission Reports could be used in court to provide a purposive account of the mischief a piece of legislation was intended to remedy. Their Lordships ruled that it was appropriate in that case to depart from its previous authority which forbade reference to Parliamentary material in construing statutory provisions in primary legislation. In so doing, Lord Browne-Wilkinson, in delivering the leading judgment in the case, identified circumstances in which, as in that case, explanations of a specific statutory provision, put forward by the promoter of the bill containing it, may be admissible in court and used to identify not merely the mischief but the means by which that provision was to remedy it.

In Lord Browne-Wilkinson's words, those circumstances are where such reference will serve "as an aid to the construction of legislation which is ambiguous or obscure or the literal meaning of which leads to obscurity" (p. 1056). What is meant by the terms ambiguity, obscurity and absurdity in this context is examined in the light of subsequent case law by T St. J N Bates in [1995] CLJ pp. 127–152.

It was clearly Lord Browne-Wilkinson's view that, notwithstanding the judgment in *Pepper v. Hart*,

"the function of the Court [is] to construe the actual words enacted by Parliament so that in no circumstances could the Court attach to words a meaning that they were incapable of bearing [and that] the Court should only attach importance to clear statements showing the intention of the promoter of the Bill, whether a minister or private member; there [can] be no dredging through conflicting statements of intention with a view to discovering the true intention of Parliament in using the statutory words" (p. 1053).

It is also important to note that the potential interpretative usefulness of a statement could depend not only on its context but also upon whether the provision under consideration at that time was subsequently debated again or amended in any way.

The statutory provision under consideration in *Pepper v. Hart* may serve as an illustration of the application of the rule developed in that case. The provision was considered to involve an ambiguity in the phrase "any expense incurred in or in connection with" provision of a benefit. One party argued that this was properly construed as the marginal cost of its provision to one recipient. The other party argued that on the proper construction such cost should be considered as a proportion of the cost of provision of the benefit in question to all of its recipients.

A number of implications of the rule in *Pepper v. Hart* are perhaps worthy of note:

1) Some provisions of the Environment Act 1995 may be argued to be ambiguous, obscure or to lead to absurdity if taken literally; if it appears to the editors that this may be the case, it will be indicated.

2) It has been suggested (V Tunkel, [1993] *Tax.* 394) that for legal practitioners, where a statutory provision fulfils one or more limbs of the *Pepper v. Hart* test of ambiguity, obscurity or absurdity, to seek to discover a relevant explanatory ministerial statement is "not optional but compulsory". It may be that this is the case even where there is case law interpreting the provision, if such case law did not itself consider such ministerial statements.

3) Although discussions of *Pepper v. Hart*, and the case itself, often refer to "Hansard", the ministerial explanation employed as an aid to construction in that case was taken from the officially published report of a sitting of a Commons Standing Committee.

4) Statements made in such proceedings would thus appear capable of being used in this way even though, as in the case of the Environment Bill, such reports (although HMSO Publications) are not published in Hansard.

5) Reference is made in *Pepper v. Hart* (at pp. 1052–1053) to the previous case of *Pickstone v. Freemans* [1989] A.C. 66, in which the House of Lords, in construing a statutory instrument, had regard to a relevant ministerial statement made in the debate on that instrument. Whilst most statutory instruments are not debated in Parliament, there are instances where either the 1990 or 1995 Act makes provision for regulations which may prove sufficiently significant that a debate might ensue. Statements made in such a debate may be relevant in construing that statutory instrument, though not in construing the Act itself.

6) There is also the possibility that the unusual status and procedural provisions granted in s.57 of the Act to guidance made in relation to contaminated land might lead to such guidance being debated in Parliament. It is an interesting question whether and in what circumstances ministerial statements made in any such debate could be employed in construing the provisions of the guidance (although as before, not in construing any provisions in the Act itself). One aspect of this question is whether the threefold *Pepper v. Hart* test (absurdity, obscurity, ambiguity) is applicable. It could be argued that it need not be, since the guidance, like a statutory

instrument, is either accepted or rejected by Parliament and cannot be amended following the making of any ministerial statement in its regard. Thus the previous case of *Pickstone v. Freemans*, referred to above, would appear likely to be the relevant authority.

COMMENCEMENT

The following provisions of the Environment Act 1995 have been brought into force by commencement orders up to and including S.I. 1995 No. 2765 or by s.125(2) and (3) of the Act.

Provision	Date of Commencement	S.I. No.
Section 1	28.7.1995	1995/1983
Section 3(2) to (8)	28.7.1995	
Section 4	28.7.1995	
Section 7	28.7.1995	
Section 9	28.7.1995	
Section 12	28.7.1995	
Section 20	12.10.1995	1995/2649
Section 21	12.10.1995	
Section 22	12.10.1995	
Section 23	12.10.1995	
Section 30	12.10.1995	
Section 31	12.10.1995	
Section 32	12.10.1995	
Section 36	12.10.1995	
Section 37(1), (2) and (9)	28.7.1995	1995/1983
Sections 38 to 40	28.7.1995	
Section 41 (partially)	21.9.1995	
Section 42	21.9.1995	
Sections 43 to 52	28.7.1995	
Section 56	28.7.1995	
Section 57 (partially)	21.9.1995	
Section 58 (partially)	21.9.1995	
Section 59 (partially)	12.10.1995	1995/2649
Section 61	19.9.1995	s.125(2)
Section 62	19.9.1995	s.125(2)
Section 63 and all but paragraph 7(2) of Schedule 7	19.9.1995	s.125(2)
Section 64	19.9.1995	s.125(2)
Section 65	19.9.1995	s.125(2)
Section 66	19.9.1995	s.125(2)
Section 67	19.9.1995	s.125(2)
Section 68	19.9.1995	s.125(2)
Section 69	19.9.1995	s.125(2)
Section 70	19.9.1995	s.125(2)
Section 71	19.9.1995	s.125(2)
Section 72	19.9.1995	s.125(2)
Section 73	19.9.1995	s.125(2)
Section 74	19.7.1995	s.125(3)
Section 75	19.9.1995	s.125(2)
Section 76	19.9.1995	s.125(2)
Section 77	19.9.1995	s.125(2)
Section 79	19.9.1995	s.125(2)
Sections 93 to 95	21.9.1995	1995/1983
Section 96(1) and 96(4) to (6) (partially)	1.11.1995	1995/2765
Section 96(2)	1.11.1995	1995/2765
Sections 97 to 103	21.9.1995	
Section 105 (partially) and paragraphs 25 and 26(1) of Schedule 15	21.9.1995	

Section 105 (partially) and paragraphs 13, 14(1) and (4), 17, 20 and 26(2) of Schedule 15	1.1.1999	
Section 116 (partially) and paragraphs 2(1) to (3) of Schedule 21	21.9.1995	
Section 120(1) (partially) and paragraphs 4, 31, 42, 213(1), (2)(b) and (3) and 223(1)(c) of Schedule 22	28.7.1995	
Section 120(1) (partially) and paragraphs 15, 29(1) and (22) (partially), 51(1) to (3) and (5) and 53	12.10.1995	1995/2649
Section 120(1) (partially) and paragraphs 37(1) and (4), 38, 39, 76(1) and (3), 80(1) and (2), 82(1) and (5) (partially), 133(1), 137 to 139, 147, 153, 162 (partially), 182, 187(1) and 192 of Schedule 22	21.9.1995	1995/1983
Section 120(2) (partially) and paragraphs 14(5), (6) and (8) (partially) of Schedule 23	1.1.1999	
Section 120(3) (partially) and the repeals in Schedule 24 in relation to sections 68, 69(5), 126(6) and 129(4) of the Water Resources Act 1991	21.9.1995	
Section 120(3) (partially) and the repeals in Schedule 24 in relation to sections 30 and 41(1) of the Salmon and Freshwater Fisheries Act 1975	1.1.1999	
Section 120(3) (partially) and the repeal in Schedule 24 in relation to section 105 of the Town and Country Planning Act 1990	1.11.1995	1995/2765
Section 120(4) to (6)	28.7.1995	
Sections 121 to 124	28.7.1995	

ABBREVIATIONS
ACBE: Advisory Committee on Business and the Environment
Agency, the: the Environment Agency
BATNEEC: Best Available Techniques Not Entailing Excessive Cost
BPEO: Best Practicable Environmental Option
CPRE: Council for the Protection of Rural England
DOE: Department of the Environment
DWI: Drinking Water Inspectorate
Edwards Report: Report of the National Parks Review Committee, 1990, Fit for the Future
EAAC: Environment Agency Advisory Committee
EPAC: Environment Protection Advisory Committee
HMIP: Her Majesty's Inspectorate of Pollution
HMIPI: Her Majesty's Industrial Pollution Inspectorate
IPC: Integrated pollution control
LAPC: Local Air Pollution Control
MAFF: Ministry of Agriculture, Fisheries and Food
NRA: National Rivers Authority
RPA: River Purification Authority
RPB: River Purification Board
SEPA: Scottish Environment Protection Agency
WRA: Waste Regulation Authority
WWF: Worldwide Fund for Nature
1906 Act: Alkali etc., Works Regulation Act 1906
1949 Act: National Parks and Access to the Countryside Act 1949
1974 Act: Control of Pollution Act 1974
1981 Act: Wildlife and Countryside Act 1981
1990 Act: Environmental Protection Act 1990
1991 Act: Water Resources Act 1991
1992 Regulations: Environmental Information Regulations 1992 (S.I. 1992 No. 3240)
1994 Regulations: Waste Management Licensing Regulations 1994 (S.I. 1994 No. 1056)

PART I

THE ENVIRONMENT AGENCY AND THE SCOTTISH ENVIRONMENT PROTECTION
AGENCY

GENERAL NOTE

Part I of the Act fulfils a longstanding Government commitment to create a unified environmental regulatory body for England and Wales, and an equivalent for Scotland.

As will no doubt be appreciated, such a major reorganisation does not come about overnight
nor without decisions being taken on a large number of significant and often hotly disputed
issues. This introduction looks first at the policy background to, and the evolution of the proposals, from the first announcement of a Government commitment to establish such agencies to
the publication of the first full Environment Bill in December 1994. It then examines briefly
some of the key issues: the functions transferred to the Environment Agency and Scottish
Environment Protection Agency ("the Agency" and "SEPA"), those functions which were not
transferred, new functions given to them, their statutory functions, aims and objectives, the
question of the agencies' regional and managerial structure, and finally the implications of the
agencies for public access to environmental information.

Policy background: environmental integration and a "One-Stop Shop"?

The establishment of unified environmental agencies had for some time been advocated by
both business interests and environmentalists as well as by distinguished bodies such as the
House of Commons Environment Committee, and this is considered more fully below in the
separate contexts north and south of the border.

A business might previously have had to deal on environmental matters (to take the example
of England) with: HM Inspectorate of Pollution (HMIP); The National Rivers Authority
(NRA); the county council as waste regulation authority and mineral planning authority; the
district council for air pollution control and statutory nuisance, as local planning authority and in
relation to hazardous substance control; the Health and Safety Executive in relation to major
accident hazards, genetically modified organisms, the carriage of dangerous goods and general
health and safety (and possibly also the HSE's Inspectorates such as its Nuclear Installations
Inspectorate); the Ministry of Agriculture, Fisheries and Food in relation to disposal at sea; and
the local statutory water and sewerage undertaker in relation to discharges to sewer. A Scottish
business might also have been required to deal with a similar range of environmental regulators,
albeit different ones.

Although numerous provisions seek to define the relationships between these various
regimes, not all overlap is avoided and these provisions themselves can be complex. The number
of bodies with which a business may have to deal on environmental matters is reduced by the
establishment of the agencies, although there may still be several because of the range of functions not transferred to the agencies (see below, at p. 25–18), and there is no change in the
number of consents, authorisations and licences which a business may require.

However, the Government has indicated that the "Establishment of the Agency [and by
implication, one would assume, SEPA] offers an advance towards single permitting... In the
medium term the Government would review in the light of experience whether the legislation
might be amended to achieve greater integration": Advisory Committee on Business and the
Environment (ACBE) Fifth Progress Report to and Response From the President of the Board
of Trade and the Secretary of State for the Environment (July 1995).

Environmentalists saw the creation of unified agencies as a key step, not only in the direction
of the effective integration of different strands of environmental policy, but also towards the
integration of environmental concerns into general Government policy, which was perceived as
a pre-condition for the attainment of sustainable development. The extent to which the Agencies, as established by the Act, are viewed as likely to fulfil the aspirations of industry and
environmentalists is considered below in the discussion of the evolution of the Environment Bill
in the course of its passage through Parliament and in the discussion of the functions which were
not transferred.

The bringing together of staff from various disciplines in a single organisation offers the
potential for more effective integration of a range of pollution control (and, especially in the
case of the Agency, non-pollution control) functions. This might occur through the combining of
staff with expertise in different areas into multi-disciplinary teams replacing the previous network of formal and informal consultation processes. Indeed, given the range of matters to which
the Agency and SEPA are to have regard in carrying out their functions, the alternative would
presumably be daunting in the extreme to ordinary Agency/SEPA officers.

Policy Background: England and Wales

The Earl of Cranbrook's attempt in 1990 to introduce an integrated system of environmental regulation is noted in the Introduction to the 1990 Act. This attempt failed in the face of Government opposition, yet in July 1991 the Prime Minister John Major announced a firm Government intention to do just that. As the House of Commons Environment Select Committee noted at the time: "In just two years, the government's policy had shifted from outright rejection of the notion of such an agency to enthusiastic acceptance": First Report, Session 1991/92 (H.C. Paper 55). For an analysis of the political issues and choices which the Government sought to address in developing its plans for the Environment Agency, see N. Carter and P. Lowe, *Environmental Politics and Administrative Reform, Political Quarterly*, 1994, pp. 263–274, which cites this Select Committee remark.

The following table lists many of the announcements and publications which chart the development of Government policy on the Agency since the first indication that it was under active consideration.

Statement or document	Issue
This Common Inheritance ((HMSO) 1990, Cm.1200)	Government considering possible "umbrella" organisation to oversee the pollution control work of the NRA and Her Majesty's Inspectorate of Pollution (HMIP).
Speech by Prime Minister John Major, July 8, 1991	"I can announce today that we plan to set up an Environment Agency. This will bring together HMIP, and related functions of the NRA, to create a new agency for environmental protection and enhancement".
Improving Environmental Quality: the Government Proposals for a new, independent Environment Agency (DoE, Ministry of Agriculture, Fisheries and Food Welsh Office, October 1991, DoE News Release 589, October 3, 1991)	Set out four options: 1. Agency to take over waste regulation and HMIP's non-water functions; HMIP's water functions to be taken over by NRA; 2. Agency to be an "umbrella body" to co-ordinate NRA and HMIP; 3. Agency to take over waste regulation, NRA, HMIP; or 4. Agency to take over waste regulation, NRA (water pollution only), HMIP. NB: Government "minded" also to transfer the Drinking Water Inspectorate (DWI).
Statement by Environment Secretary Michael Heseltine (*Independent*, October 4, 1991)	Agency to be a "one-stop shop" for environmental regulation.
H.C. Written Answer *Hansard*, H.C. July 8, 1992)	Government decided to transfer NRA, HMIP and Waste Regulation, but not the DWI, to the Agency.
H.C. Written Answers *Hansard*, H.C. July 15, 1992, C857-8W and February 23, 1993, c519W	Government states that legislation to establish the Agency to be introduced at the earliest opportunity.
Queen's Speech, November 18, 1993	"Paving Bill" to enable preparatory work for establishment of the Agency/SEPA to be introduced into Parliament in 1993/1994 session: "[A Bill] will be introduced to take forward Environmental Agency planning".
Statement to Parliament by Parliamentary Under Secretary of State for Wales, (*Hansard* H.C. cols. 1195–1196, November 30, 1994)	"The Government propose that the Environment Agency should be established as an England and Wales organisation": no separate Welsh Agency.
Options for the Geographical and Managerial Structure of the proposed Environment Agency (Touche Ross report to DoE, June 1994, deposited paper ns 348)	Five options proposed: Options A–E. Model D is closest to what has ultimately been decided: see below at p. 25–20 for outline of the options.

Statement or document	Issue
DoE News Release 440, July 20, 1994	Paving Bill cancelled as no longer necessary in view of progress already made towards establishing the Agency/SEPA. Intention to produce main Bill in draft by October 1994, establish Agency during 1995 and transferfunction at beginning of 1996/1997 financial year indicated. Intention to establish Environment Agency Advisory Committee (EAAC) indicated. Touche Ross report published.
Draft Environment Agencies Bill (Deposited Paper 486) published, October 13, 1994 (DoE News Release 576)	A draft of the part of the Bill dealing with establishing the Agency published together with a draft Management Statement for the Agency (appended to the News Release).
DoE News Release 650, November 18, 1994	Amendments to clause 7 published (appended to News Release), in response to concern over absence of duty to "further" conservation; EAAC (the "shadow Board" of the Agency) established and its membership announced.
Environment Bill (H.L. Bill to 1994/1995), December 1, 1994 (subsequent versions of the Bill not listed here)	Bill published and enters House of Lords.
Draft Guidance to Agency: January 17, 1995, DoE News Release 010	"Draft outline showing the scope of guidance Ministers intend to give to the Environment Agency on its Contribution to sustainable development" under Clause 4 of the Bills published (appended to News Release).
Draft Guidance to Agency: April 21, 1995, DoE News Release 202	Full draft of the guidance under clause 4 issued by DoE, MAFF and Welsh Office
Environment Agency Update No. 5 (September 1995)	Regional structure of the Agency announced: See below at p. 25–21.

One influential body which has commented on the issue of a unified environmental regulator a number of times is the House of Commons Environment Select Committee. In February 1989 it recommended the establishment of an Environmental Protection Agency or Commission, to which much of the Department of the Environment's work, at least in the area of waste management policy, would be transferred: Second Report, Session 1988–1989, *Toxic Waste*, 22I, p. xvi. The Committee scrutinised the Government's proposals for an agency in its First Report of House of Commons Session 1991–1992, *The Government's Proposals for an Environment Agency* (55I–III) (to which the Government responded in November 1992: the Committee's First Special Report of Session 1992–1993 (256)). More recently, the Committee took evidence on the first draft of what became Pt. I of the 1995 Act: Session 1994–1995, *Environment Bill: Hearings on the Draft Environment Agencies Bill* (40 I–iii), from which no report has been forthcoming.

Policy background: Scotland
   Until the establishment of SEPA by virtue of this Act, environmental protection in Scotland was the responsibility of several bodies. Water pollution control functions were performed by the river purification authorities (consisting of the seven river purification boards and three islands councils); integrated pollution control functions were performed by Her Majesty's Industrial Pollution Inspectorate (HMIPI) and river purification authorities in their respective capacities; radioactive substances control functions were performed by HMIPI; while district and islands councils performed waste regulation functions in their capacity as waste regulation authorities and air pollution control functions in their capacity as enforcing authorities for Pt. B processes by virtue of Pt. I of the Environmental Protection Act 1990 and the Environmental Protection (Prescribed Processes and Substances) Regulations 1991 (S.I. 1991 No. 472 (as amended)). It should be noted that in Scotland the 1990 Act did not provide, as in England and Wales, for the separation of local authority waste regulation and disposal functions; hence the potential for conflict remained.

Although a more integrated approach to pollution control was seen as desirable, for example, in the Government White Paper, *This Common Inheritance* (Cm.1200, 1990), the fragmented nature of the existing Scottish regulatory system posed problems for developing such an approach and also posed problems for business given the lack of a one-door approach to environmental licensing. It was against this background that proposals for a Scottish Environment Protection Agency were developed. The following table lists many of the announcements and publications which chart the development of Government policy on SEPA since the first indication that it was under active consideration.

Statement or document	Issue
Statement by Secretary of State for Scotland (September 23, 1991)	Annnouncement that a Scottish Environment Protection Agency was to be established.
H.C. Written Answer *Hansard*, H.C. Vol. 196, col. 405w	Government confirms proposal to establish SEPA, that primary legislation would be needed for this and indicates that consultation paper on SEPA's functions will be issued.
Improving Scotland's Environment The Way Forward (Scottish Office, January 1992)	Scottish Office presents case for SEPA: (a) present fragmented system of pollution control lacks benefit of integrated approach which a single agency could offer; (b) industry would benefit from a one-door approach to environmental regulation. Three key principles should underpin proposals for reform: 1. need to remove potential for overlap and conflict between different regulatory agencies; 2. operational and regulatory responsibilities should be separated; and 3. effective pollution control requires centralised expertise which a unified agency could offer. Accordingly proposed that SEPA should take over all the functions of HMIPI; the Hazardous Waste Inspectorate; the river purification authorities; and the functions of local authorities as waste regulation authorities and air pollution control enforcing authorities under Part I of the 1990 Act.
H.C. Written Answer, *Hansard*, H.C. Vol. 219, cols. 713–4w, February 25, 1993	Government announces: major proposals in *Improving Scotland's Environment* would not be altered, but that in the light of consultation there may be scope for delegating responsibility to regional committees and that further work would be commissioned on SEPA's regional structure; and that legislation to establish SEPA would be established at the earliest opportunity.
Scottish Environment Protection Agency Consultancy Report (KPMG Management Consultancy, March 1993)	Four options for SEPA's regional structure proposed. Option 3 proposing three or four regional boards exercising limited executive boards is recommended.
Queen's Speech, November 18, 1993	Announcement of "Paving Bill" to enable preparatory work for establishment of the Agency/SEPA to be introduced into Parliament in 1993/1994 session.
DoE News Release 440, July 20, 1994	Paving Bill cancelled as no longer necessary in view of progress already made towards establishing the Agency/SEPA. Intention to produce main Bill in draft by October 1994, establish the Agency/SEPA during 1995 and to transfer functions to the Agency/SEPA at beginning of financial year 1996/97.
Draft Environment Agencies Bill (Deposited Paper 486) published, October 13, 1994	A draft of the part of the Bill dealing with establishing the Agency/SEPA published together with a draft Management Statement for SEPA.

Statement or document	Issue
Environment Bill (H.L. Bill to 1994/1995), December 1, 1994 (subsequent versions of the Bill not listed here)	Bill published and enters House of Lords.
H.C. Written Answer *Hansard,* H.C. Vol. 258, col. 218w, April 19, 1995.	Secretary of State announces that he intends to appoint Professor William Turmeau as Chairman of SEPA.
Draft Guidance to SEPA (Scottish Office Environment Department, May 1995)	"Draft Guidance to the Scottish Environment Protection Agency under Clause 29 of the Environment Bill". Guidance on SEPA's aims and objectives, contribution to sustainable development and costs and benefits.
SEPA Newsletter No. 4, August 1995	Appointment of SEPA's Chief Executive announced.
Scottish Office Press Release (October 5, 1995)	Secretary of State announces appointment of remaining SEPA board members.
Scottish Office Environment Department Circular 19/1995 (October 12, 1995)	"Environment Act 1995: Transfer of Property, Rights and Liabilities from District and Islands Councils to the Scottish Environment Protection Agency". Guidance for local authorities.
Scottish Office Press Release (October 27, 1995)	Announcement of SEPA's headquarters and that three Regional Boards are being established.
Revised Draft Guidance to SEPA (Scottish Office Environment Department, November 1995)	"The Scottish Environment Protection Agency and Sustainable Development" including Statutory Guidance under s.31 of the Environment Act on SEPA's aims and objectives and its contribution towards achieving sustainable development.

It should also be noted that the transfer of local authority functions to SEPA is proceeding against the background of local government reorganisation in Scotland. Briefly, the Local Government etc. (Scotland) Act 1994 (c. 39) provides for the replacement of the existing two-tier structure of local government in Scotland, consisting of regional and district councils, together with the three islands councils by a system of 32 unitary authorities. The Government indicated in Parliament that having local government reorganisation and the establishment of SEPA proceeding in tandem was deliberate and that:

"There is a great advantage in transferring local authority functions to SEPA at the same time as local government is to be reorganised. The transfer can be taken into account by the new unitary authorities and they can be given a fresh start with their full new range of responsibilities" (*per* Earl of Lindsay *Hansard,* H.L. Vol. 560, col. 1423).

The functions of the new agencies

The discussion which follows examines first the existing functions which the Act transfers to the Agency/SEPA, both the common features and the notable differences, then the new functions bestowed upon the two agencies, and finally the other functions which might have been transferred to the Agency/SEPA, as in some cases the Government was urged to do, but which were not.

Functions transferred: common features

The main functions transferred to the agencies relate to water pollution and management (although the discussion below should be noted in relation to water management), integrated pollution control, radioactive substances control and waste regulation (see the General Notes to ss. 2 and 21 at pp. 25–30 and 25–72 below).

It should be noted that the staff and resources of the existing bodies are transferred along with the relevant functions (see General Notes to ss.3 and 22 at pp. 25–34 and 25–77, below). It should also be noted that even where the Agencies take over existing functions, the legislative position will have changed following the transfer, for three reasons.

1. The Act makes a number of amendments to existing legislation, such as the introduction by paras. 29(22) and 162 of Sched. 22 of "works notices" in relation to water pollution;

2. The Agencies have aims, objectives and duties, such as the Environment Agency's principal aim of contributing to the achievement of sustainable development (s.4), which differ from those of the bodies previously responsible for exercising those functions; and

3. The powers of entry, *etc.*, granted to the bodies whose functions have been taken over by the Agencies varied from body to body.

In relation to given legislative provisions, therefore, the powers of the relevant Agency (see ss.108 and 9) may differ from those which were previously applicable.

Functions transferred and differences between the Agencies

There are two principal differences between the Agency and SEPA in terms of functions transferred. First, the functions of local authorities in their capacity as enforcing authorities for air pollution control for Pt. B processes under Pt. I of the 1990 Act are transferred to SEPA in Scotland but not to the Agency, and there was never any likelihood of such a transfer being effected in England and Wales. This gave rise to considerable concern in Parliament both on the grounds that it might lead to an inconsistent approach to air pollution control as between England and Wales on the one hand and Scotland on the other, and because of the perceived removal of this function from local accountable control which it was argued was more appropriate. This issue is considered in more detail in relation to SEPA in the General Note to s.21 at p. 25–73 below: for debate on a proposed amendment which would have required the Agency to "work together with local authorities", see H.C. Standing Committee B, Third sitting, May 2, 1995, cols. 8–24. It should also be noted that the transfer of local authority waste regulation functions also gave rise to similar concerns and opposition both north and south of the border: see, for example, a discussion paper *Protecting the Future—the Environment Agency and its relationship with local government in England and Wales—a new approach* published by the Association of County Councils, Association of District Councils and Association of Metropolitan Authorities; see also *Hansard*, H.L. Vol. 562, cols. 1016–1018; H.C. Standing Committee B, Third sitting, May 2, 1995, cols. 80–89 (in which both English and Scottish concerns were raised, and the fear of a loss of integration at a local level between regulatory and planning controls over waste activities was expressed). The Government response, and reasons for effecting the transfer in the face of such opposition could, said the then Minister for the Environment and Countryside, Mr Robert Atkins, be summed up "in three words: integration, consistency and expertise": H.C. Standing Committee B, Second sitting, May 2, 1995, col. 76.

The second principal difference is that the functions of river purification authorities (RPAs) have never been as broad as those of the National Rivers Authority (NRA), and hence SEPA's functions are not as broad as those of the Agency. For example, RPAs had very limited powers to control water abstraction for irrigation purposes under Pt. II of the Natural Heritage (Scotland) Act 1991 (c. 28), they had no flood defence powers nor had they catchment management powers, all of which were enjoyed by the NRA, and indeed which constituted the workload of the majority of NRA staff. This is primarily the reason why SEPA is essentially a pollution control body in contrast to the Agency, which has integrated environmental management functions relating, for example, to water resources management and flood defence in addition to its pollution control functions.

Proposals were made in Parliament for giving SEPA (1) the Scottish local authorities' flood defence powers (see *e.g.* Lord Ewing of Kirkford, *Hansard*, H.L. Vol. 560, cols. 553–554; Lord Carmichael of Kelvingrove, *Hansard*, H.L. Vol. 560, col. 1185; (2) a new integrated catchment management function for river systems in Scotland (Lord Carmichael of Kelvingrove, *Hansard*, H.L. Vol. 560, col. 1209; see also Sam Galbraith, Standing Committee B, May 16, 1995, col. 249); and (3) a new comprehensive water abstraction control function (*per* Lord Carmichael of Kelvingrove, *Hansard*, H.L. Vol. 560, cols. 1217–1219, Archie Kirkwood, *Hansard* H.C. Vol. 262, cols. 920–921).

These proposals were all rejected by the Government on the basis (1) that river purification authorities had never exercised flood defence powers (see also the General Note on functions not transferred at p. 25–18 below); and (2) that the pressures on the water environment were not the same as those in England and Wales and did not therefore justify giving these powers to SEPA:

"Scotland's geography is very different from that south of the Border. Its rivers are relatively short and fast flowing with nothing comparable to the long meandering rivers such as the Thames, the Severn, the Ouse and Bristol Avon. In addition, 95 per cent of Scotland's public water supplies come from upland sources whereas that is true for only one-third of water supplies in England. The other two-thirds in England come from abstraction lower down the river or from groundwater sources.

These factors, combined with Scotland's relatively lower density of population and comparative lack of heavy industry, mean that the scale of potential pollution is less. As Scotland's river flow is greater, the result is that the effects of any pollution incidents are mitigated. Against this background there is less of a need for comprehensive controls of the kind which have been adopted in England and Wales." (*per* the Earl of Lindsay, *Hansard*, H.L. Vol. 560, col. 1210; see also Viscount Ullswater, Minister of State, Department of the Environment, *Hansard*, H.L. Vol. 560, col. 558 and Sir Hector Monro, the then Parliamentary Under-Secretary of State for Scotland, Standing Committee B, May 16, 1995 cols. 250–252).

However, the Government accepted that in specific locations and at specific times there were temporary pressures, and that there was accordingly a need for selective abstraction controls in Scotland, and re-affirmed the Secretary of State's announcement made on November 1, 1994 that they intended to introduce such controls in separate legislation in the light of the European Commission's action programme on groundwater, on which proposals were due by mid-1995. The timing of the European action programme meant that it was not practical to include such provisions in the Act. Furthermore, the Government indicated that it envisaged further public consultation on the proposed charging arrangements before any scheme was introduced (*per* Earl of Lindsay, *Hansard*, H.L. Vol. 560, cols. 1220–1221; Sir Hector Monro, Parliamentary Under-Secretary of State for the Environment, Standing Committee B, May 16, 1995, col. 251; Mr Robert Atkins, Minister for the Environment and Countryside, *Hansard*, H.C. Vol. 262, col. 922).

The Government also acknowledged that the existing arrangements relating to catchment management in Scotland could be improved. This would be achieved by the integration of pollution control functions in SEPA and by the establishment of memoranda of understanding between SEPA and other public bodies which impinged on its work, for example, the Health and Safety Executive or Scottish Natural Heritage (*per* the Earl of Lindsay *Hansard*, H.L. Vol. 560, cols. 1210–1211).

Although there were no concerted campaigns during the passage of the Bill to exclude the NRA's non–pollution control functions from transfer to the Agency, concern was expressed about the transfer specifically of its navigation authority functions (see H.C. Standing Committee B, Third sitting, May 2, 1995, cols. 103–105; *Hansard*, H.L. Vol. 560, cols. 630–633 and Vol. 561, cols. 1610–1612, *per* Lord McNair). These concerns were twofold: that such transfer would perpetuate an arbitrary division of responsibilities whereby the NRA (now the Agency) has responsibility for navigation on one-third of the inland waterways in England and Wales, whilst the British Waterways Board has responsibility for navigation on the remainder: that navigation had a low priority within the NRA and was likely to have even lower priority within the Agency, and that the transfer would make meaningless the recent Government consultation on a number of options for restructuring the allocation of navigation responsibilities: Sir Paul Beresford, Parliamentary Under-Secretary of State for the Environment, assured the Commons Standing Committee that "no decisions will be taken until the consultation is completed" (*ibid.* col. 104).

New functions

A number of functions to be exercised by the Agencies are new. Some of these are considered in the annotations to the relevant sections in Pt. I of the Act. Some new functions, however, are created not by Pt. I but as a part of new legislation in the Act. These include the following:

Contaminated Land (s.57). Powers to give guidance to local authorities as enforcing authorities, and a role as enforcing authorities themselves in relation to the so-called "special sites". These are sites designated as such in accordance with the procedures inserted by s.57 into the 1990 Act as new ss.78C and 78D. Land is required to be so designated if it meets a description to be prescribed by regulations to be made under those provisions.

Air quality (Pt. IV). The role of statutory consultee when the Secretary of State: (i) prepares a national air quality strategy for Great Britain; and (ii) makes regulations in relation to the implementation of the air quality strategy and international obligations regarding air quality, and generally in relation to the assessment and management of air quality. In Scotland SEPA also has reserve powers, which in England and Wales are held by the Secretary of State, to assess whether and in what areas air quality standards or objectives are not being met and, in certain circumstances, to give directions to local authorities.

Waste strategy (s.92). As with the air quality strategy, the Environment Agency is a statutory consultee for the Secretary of State's National Waste Strategy for England and Wales. The Agency is to carry out a national survey of waste arisings, on which the strategy will be based. In Scotland SEPA itself is charged with preparing the waste strategy.

Producer responsibility (ss.93 and 94). A significant role for the Agencies is anticipated by the Act in connection with producer responsibility for waste and for other materials which may be used, recovered or recycled. The Act provides for regulations to be made imposing producer responsibility obligations. Agency and SEPA duties of compliance monitoring, enforcement and guidance in relation to such obligations appear to be envisaged, and certainly form the basis on which consultation has been conducted on the introduction of producer responsibility for packaging waste.

Nuclear installations (paras. 7 to 9 of Sched. 22). The Agency or SEPA must be consulted by the Health and Safety Executive before it grants or revokes a nuclear site licence and also before it places a condition on or varies such a licence where such condition or variation relates to or affects the creation, accumulation or disposal of radioactive waste.

Functions not transferred: features common to the Agency and SEPA

Air pollution control, unlike in Scotland, is retained by local authorities in England and Wales, and this is considered more fully in the General Note to s.21 at p. 25–74, below.

A number of other functions which were not transferred to the agencies were mooted for transfer in various quarters, both within and outside Parliament. Some of these functions and notable advocates of their transfer are noted here.

1. A monitoring and co-ordinating role for marine pollution, marine disposal of wastes and radionuclide monitoring (currently the responsibility of the Ministry of Agriculture, Fisheries and Food (MAFF) in England and Wales and the Scottish Office in Scotland; this was advocated for transfer by the WWF in its Memorandum to the House of Commons Select Committee's Hearings on the draft Environment Agencies Bill (H.C. Paper 40 I–iii; App. 8)).

2. Pesticide registration and enforcement (currently dealt with by the Pesticide Safety Directorate and Welsh Office/MAFF in England and Wales and the Scottish Office in Scotland; transfer advocated by the Labour Party: for this and the references below to Labour Party policy, see its policy document *In Trust for Tomorrow*, and *the Surveyor*, December 8, 1994, p. 14).

3. Policy on coastal protection (currently the responsibility of the Welsh Office/MAFF/Scottish Office; transfer was advocated by the Labour Party: see also H.C. Standing Committee B, Third sitting, May 2, 1995, cols. 94–99. In relation to this, *Hansard*, H.C., Vol. 258, cols. 77–78 may be noted, where Mr Gareth Wardell urges that the Crown Estates' function of licensing aggregate dredging, which can affect Agency coastal protection/flood defence schemes, be transferred).

4. Drinking water standards regulation (currently dealt with by the Drinking Water Inspectorate in England and Wales and the Secretary of State in Scotland; transfer advocated by the Labour Party; see also H.C. Standing Committee B, Third sitting, May 2, 1995, cols. 89–94).

5. The authorisation and regulation of nuclear installation operation, bringing this together with radioactive substance control (currently the responsibility of the Nuclear Installations Inspectorate both south and north of the border: transfer advocated by the Labour Party).

6. The role of consenting and regulatory authority in relation to the contained use and deliberate release of genetically modified organisms (GMOs, currently the responsibility of the Secretary of State; transfer advocated by Mrs Anne Campbell, whose speech in support of a proposed amendment to this effect, citing GMO research on agricultural crops, prompted the Chairman of the Commons Standing Committee, Mrs Gwyneth Dunwoody, to remark that "the Hon. Lady . . . has put me off tomatoes for life" : H.C. Standing Committee B, Third sitting, May 2, 1995, cols. 99–103. During that debate the then Parliamentary Under-Secretary of State for the Environment, Sir Paul Beresford, commented that "we think that once the divisions of responsibility between the Department and the agency for work on genetically modified organisms can be clearly identified, clause 36 [s.38 of the Act] . . . could be used to transfer at least some of the Secretary of State's functions in this regard to the agency" (col. 102)).

7. A supervisory and guidance role on the effective implementation of environmental impact assessment procedures for those operations regulated by it (currently DoE responsibility in England and Wales and Scottish Office responsibility in Scotland; transfer was advocated by the WWF).

8. In the House of Lords, amendments proposed the transfer to a separate Welsh Environment Agency of the functions of the Countryside Commission for Wales: *Hansard*, H.L. Vol. 560, col. 587.

Functions not transferred: Scotland

Many environmental protection functions are not transferred to SEPA by the Act which raises doubts about the extent to which the administration of environmental protection has truly become integrated.

Local authority functions. District and islands councils retain their functions by virtue of the Clean Air Act 1993 (c. 11) and their functions in relation to statutory nuisance by virtue of the Public Health (Scotland) Act 1897 (c. 38) which are replaced by the extension of Pt. III of the 1990 Act to Scotland by virtue of s.107 of and Sched. 17 to this Act. These functions will be transferred to the new unitary local authorities by virtue of the Local Government etc. (Scotland) Act 1994.

Regional and islands councils also retain their flood defence powers under the Flood Prevention (Scotland) Act 1961 (c. 41) and their coast protection powers under the Coast Protection Act 1949 (c. 74) although these functions will be transferred to the new unitary local authorities by virtue of the Local Government etc. (Scotland) Act 1994.

Although regional and islands councils are losing their functions in relation to water supply and provision of sewerage, which they exercise by virtue of the Water (Scotland) Act 1980 (c. 45), these functions are being transferred not to SEPA nor to the new unitary local authorities but to three new public non-departmental water authorities by virtue of Pt. II of the Local Government etc. (Scotland) Act 1994, namely the North, East and West of Scotland Water Authorities.

Functions, aims and objectives

The Agency and SEPA both operate within a complex web of aims, objectives, purposes, powers, duties and other functions. Some of these are to be found in the 1995 Act, of which some are transferred from other legislation and extended to cover regulatory regimes to which they had not previously applied (for the Agency, notably the Water Resources Act 1991: see ss.6 to 8), and others are new or extended in scope (notably ss.4, 5, 31, 33 and 39: see also the General Note on p. 25–17 on new functions established by the Act). Of course, separate legislation (such as the 1990 Act) contains the main regulatory regimes for which the agencies are responsible, and that legislation may contain its own purposes and objectives. Of the new functions, those which prompted the most debate in Parliament were the agencies' objectives (which debate led to the introduction of a "principal aim" for the Agency, but not for SEPA: see ss.4 and 31), and the duty imposed on them to have regard to costs and benefits in certain cases (see s.39).

The range of duties on the Agency and SEPA is so wide that, if they were all couched in absolute terms there would be a real possibility of their being incompatible in particular circumstances: accordingly some are couched in terms such as "to have regard to" specified matters (see ss.7 and 32; the term is considered further at the end of this discussion of aims and objectives) or "to such extent as it considers desirable, to promote…"(*e.g.* s.6, s.34(2)). Similarly, some duties are expressed to be subject to others (s.7(2) is subject to s.7(1), of which subs. (1)(a) is in turn subject to s.4). Wide discretion is thus granted to the Agency and to SEPA as to the weight to be given to such matters, and in practice, therefore, only if they ignore the matters in question in a given instance is this likely to enable a decision to be successfully challenged in the courts. However, to ensure and be able to show that all the relevant matters are considered, requires effective management systems not previously required to anything like the same extent, and in all probability increased paperwork.

"Functions" includes powers and duties (s.124(1)). Generally, one discharges one's duties through the exercise of one's powers, although powers may be exercised where there is no duty to act. It may be that particular functions are to be exercised for a particular purpose (see ss.5 and 33) or so as to obtain a specific objective or set of objectives. The imposition of statutory objectives in the context of specific functions is increasingly prevalent in U.K. environmental law, primarily through the requirement to implement EC legislation containing such objectives. A good example is the Waste Framework Directive (as amended by Directive 91/156/EEC), which led to the Waste Management Licensing Regulations 1994 (S.I. 1994 No. 1056), Sched. 4, imposing "relevant objectives" on a range of bodies including the waste regulation authorities whose functions are to be taken on by the Agency and SEPA. The same objectives appear again in relation to the waste strategies (s.92) in the production of which the Agency and SEPA will play major parts. Such objectives also feature, for example, in EC water pollution legislation, and the statutory requirement that they be attained significantly limits the discretion available to the Agency and SEPA in the exercise of their powers.

Overlaid on to these functions are the general aims and objectives of the agencies themselves, provided by ss.4 and 31. The context of these is to be provided by guidance to which the agencies must have regard (although the General Note to s.4 suggests that, as regards the Agency's principal aim, the role of the guidance is more significant than this, and accordingly that aim is qualified by being "subject to and in accordance with" other provisions with which it might otherwise have conflicted; see p. 25–37 below). Once again, whilst the agencies cannot disregard such guidance, they have discretion as to how much weight to accord it in given circumstances: the term "have regard to" is considered further below.

Finally, there is the duty to have regard to costs and benefits, so far as is reasonable, in the exercise, non-exercise and manner of exercise of the agencies' powers (s.39; again, this duty is heavily qualified: see especially s.39(2)). It will be noted that this duty applies only to the exercise of the agencies' powers, not to the fulfilment of their duties. This, and the way in which it is qualified, restricts the significance of the s.39 duty, and an example of it as applicable only in the exercise of discretionary powers in fulfilment of a duty (in that case the setting of discharge consent conditions) was given by the Government in Parliament: see the General Note to s.39 at p. 25–105. A particularly limiting factor will, it is submitted, prove to be the (frequently EC-driven) statutory objectives to be attained, noted above. Where one must exercise one's duties so as to *ensure* that waste is disposed of "without risk to water, air, soil, plants and animals [and] without adversely affecting the countryside or places of special interest" (these are two of the

Waste Framework Directive objectives), then the scope for taking into account costs and benefits, and (as in the case of the Agency) for pursuing one's principal aim are significantly constrained.

The s.39 duty remains important, however: where, for example, the Agency or SEPA is considering the service of a works notice for water pollution (introduced by Sched. 22: see General Note to s.120 at p. 25–302), it is submitted that it will in most cases have to take into account costs and benefits in determining whether or not to serve the notice and what requirements to impose. As this is a pollution control function, the s.5/s.33 duty will be relevant (prevention or minimisation of pollution); but in determining what, in the circumstances, constitutes the "minimising" of pollution, costs and benefits will be a consideration.

"... have regard to ...". As the above comments illustrate, the Agency and SEPA must "have regard to" certain goals in the exercise of their functions. Case law on the term is therefore worth consideration, since the meaning given to the term by the courts will play a large part in determining the scope for challenging the actions of the Agency/SEPA where such duties are relevant. Planning and housing law are both fruitful areas for such judicial decisions. For example, a legal requirement to have regard to a Code of Guidance issued by the Secretary of State is imposed on housing authorities when dealing with the homeless. In that area of law it is clear that ignoring the guidance will result in a decision being unlawful as, for example, occurred in *Kelly v. Monklands District Council* 1986 S.L.T. 169 where a housing authority ignored provisions in the Scottish Code in relation to their assessment that a 17-year-old girl was not vulnerable. However, it is also clear from case law that as long as regard is had to the guidance it is possible to depart from it as, for example, in *Mazzaccherini v. Argyll and Bute District Council* 1987 S.C.L.R. 475 where Lord Jauncey held that while a housing authority had to have regard to the Code of Guidance it could depart from it and added, "if a housing authority considers that in a particular case the circumstances do not merit the rigid application of a part of the Code I do not consider they could be faulted at law or said to have acted unreasonably" (see also *De Falco v. Crawley Borough Council; Silvestri v. Crawley Borough Council* [1980] Q.B. 460). However, in the planning case *Pye (J.A.) (Oxford) Estates v. Wychavon District Council and the Secretary of State for the Environment* [1982] J.P.L. 575 it was held that a body departing from guidance provided by a ministerial circular must justify such a departure by giving sound and clear reasons. Where there is a conflict between the wording of the Act and the guidance, it is the terms of the Act which must be followed (see also: *Tower Hamlets London Borough Council v. Secretary of State for the Environment* (1993) 25 H.L.R. 524 (C.A.)). Once final guidance is issued regard must be had to the current edition of such guidance; see *e.g. R. v. Slough Borough Council, ex p. Casey* May 28, 1993, unreported, in which the decision of a housing authority was quashed after regard was had to an old edition of the Code of Guidance produced for housing authorities in relation to the legislation dealing with the homeless.

Regional and managerial structure: England and Wales
In July 1994, the Government published a report it had commissioned from Touche Ross: *Options for the Geographical and Managerial Structure of the Proposed Environment Agency*. The report set out five Models, A to E, for consultation: unsurprisingly, it will be noted that each of the NRA, HMIP and the waste regulation authorities (WRA) were proponents of the options that significantly reflected their own existing structures.

Model A. Initially proposed by the WRAs. The NRA, HMIP and waste organisations would continue to run in parallel but there would be a new regional and national structure for waste. Integration would be achieved through joint input in planning and policy at national level and sub-regional co-operation.

Model B. Initially proposed by HMIP. Operation and regulation would be separated. One large HQ would have three "field" directorates (Regulation, Flood Defence and River Basin Management) and an Environmental Quality Directorate for policy and planning. Multi-media regulatory teams would work to regional managers with support centres of excellence. Seven regions would be based on local authority boundaries, even for water management.

Model C. The NRA model; based on river catchment boundaries. A small head office would have one policy-making directorate and a single field/operations directorate. Co-located staff at regional level would work in multi-media teams and multi-disciplinary managers, with shared support services.

Model D. Separation of regulation and operations; regulation based on local authority boundaries and operation on river catchment areas. HMIP, NRA and waste staff would be co-located at regional level but would work in separate teams, with a more integrated approach being aimed at long-term.

Model E. Separate operation and regulation but brought together at Head Office level. Multi-skilled industry-facing (not media-facing) teams supported by technical specialists. River catchment boundaries.

HMIP at the time had seven regions, the NRA had eight, and the nine voluntary waste regulation committees in England represented the closest waste regulation came to formal regional structures. Neither the number of regions, nor their boundaries, corresponded with the NRA boundaries based on river catchment areas and waste regulation boundaries on local authority (primarily County Council) boundaries.

The issues of principle at stake were primarily the following:

1. The difference of opinion between the NRA and HMIP over the desirability of separating operational (*e.g.* water management) and regulatory functions: the NRA saw the two as mutually supportive in terms of shared knowledge and expertise, and also as a cost effective way of structuring the Agency, and their division as inappropriate. The NRA itself had no such structural divide. HMIP saw the issue as the avoidance of conflicts of interest which might arise when an organisation is "self-policing". See further Viscount Mills, *Hansard*, H.L. Vol. 559, col. 1451.

2. The NRA's desire to retain boundaries based on environmental rather than political considerations, to further integrate river catchment management.

3. The local accountability and public access argument that the public and business are familiar with and already have to deal with local authority boundaries.

4. The "business facing Agency/one-stop shop" argument that to operate one set of boundaries for water management and another for pollution control would mean that some members of the public and businesses would, where boundaries differed, find themselves having to deal with different Agency regions on different matters.

In the event, the third of those arguments lost out as a compromise solution has been adopted to reconcile as far as possible the first two positions: *Environment Agency Update No. 5*, September 1995. Water management boundaries are to remain based on the NRA's river catchment areas, but pollution (including water pollution) control functions are to be organised on the basis of political (*i.e.* local authority) boundaries. These will principally be county council boundaries, but district council boundaries will be used in places where that gives a better "'match" with the water management boundaries.

Regional and managerial structure: Scotland

Improving Scotland's Environment sought views on local participation (paras. 20–22) and envisaged that "'SEPA might set up a regional advisory committee structure in order to provide for local involvement and participation" (para. 20). The consultation paper appeared to envisage that these committees would be purely advisory and that they would not exercise any delegated executive functions (para. 21). However, as a result of misgivings expressed about this approach in the consultation exercise, the Secretary of State announced that he believed that there was scope for delegating responsibilities to regional staff without prejudicing SEPA's overall control and that he intended to commission further work on this issue (*Hansard*, H.C. Vol. 219, cols. 713–4w). Subsequently management consultants KPMG were commissioned to produce a report on possible regional structures for SEPA. Their report, *Scottish Environment Protection Agency: Consultancy Report*, (March 1993) considered four options:

1. *Minimum change.* SEPA itself would continue to operate along the lines of existing bodies. The regional structure would involve seven local boards based on the existing river purification board structure. There would be strong local authority representation on these boards which would exercise major executive powers.

2. *Reduced number of regional boards with full executive powers.* This option envisaged a clearer break from present arrangements with SEPA having a regional structure of three or four boards although these would retain full executive powers.

3. *Reduced number of regional boards with delegated authority.* This would involve the same number of regional boards as in option 2 above but their executive powers would be more limited and would be delegated by the main SEPA board.

4. *Regional advisory committees.* This option involved regional committees with a consultative role only and no executive powers which would be exercised by the main SEPA board. This was in line with the Government's original proposals in *Improving Scotland's Environment: The Way Forward*, paras. 20–21.

These four options were evaluated on the basis of the following criteria developed by KPMG Management Consulting: ability to plan and set policy centrally and deliver services locally; organisational effectiveness; independence and professionalism; and sensitivity to local needs. KPMG argued that the first option would fail to change the status quo and that there would still be the potential for regional inconsistencies and it would hinder SEPA's development as a cohesive agency committed to an integrated approach to pollution control. In relation to the second option they considered that having regional boards with full executive powers could not be reconciled with the concept of a unified agency. They also rejected the fourth option on the basis that an agency with such a structure would be too centralised, remote and unresponsive to local sensitivities.

Their preferred option was the third option:
> "It gives the main board of the agency the authority to ensure that policy is applied consistently and rigorously throughout the agency, but it allows for the delegation of some decisions to a local level, where appropriate. It therefore strikes a balance between the need for an effective, unified organisation, and the requirement for an agency which is responsive to local needs." (Executive Summary)

In relation to the remote rural areas, in particular the Orkney Islands, Shetland Islands and Western Isles, KPMG also recommended that the main SEPA board should be empowered "to enter into contractual arrangements with third parties for the delivery of services, where this does not involve a conflict between regulatory and operational responsibilities" (*ibid.*)

KPMG's recommended option has been adopted as the appropriate model in the 1995 Act which provides that SEPA must establish Regional Boards with the approval of the Secretary of State who is also to issue guidance to assist SEPA in appointing members to such Boards (Sched. 6, para. 16). Each Board is to be chaired by a member of the main SEPA Board and is to have executive functions delegated to it by the main Board with the approval of the Secretary of State (Sched. 6, para. 16). It should be noted that in contrast in England and Wales, the Agency's Regional Advisory Committees will not have executive functions delegated to them. The 1995 Act does not, however, specify the number of Boards to be established and the Government stressed that this was a matter for SEPA (*per* Sir Hector Monro, Standing Committee B, May 16, 1995, col. 235). On October 27, 1995 it was announced that SEPA was establishing three Regional Boards for the North, East and West of Scotland (Scottish Office Press Release October 27, 1995). These Boards will be based in Dingwall, Riccarton near Edinburgh and East Kilbride respectively (*ibid.*) and are based upon river purification board catchment areas, with the North Regional Board incorporating the Highland and North East RPB areas, the East Regional Board the Forth, Tay and Tweed RPB areas and the West Regional Board the Clyde and Solway RPB areas. It was also announced that SEPA's headquarters is to be at Stirling (*ibid.*). The issues of accountability raised by these provisions are discussed in the General Note to s.20 and Sched. 6 at p. 25–68.

The Agencies and Access to Information
An increasingly important function of environmental regulatory bodies is the provision of information to the public by means of statutory registers or under the Environmental Information Regulations 1992 (S.I. 1992 No. 3240) (the 1992 Regulations). The Agency and SEPA are to hold the statutory registers previously held by a variety of regulatory bodies in relation to functions transferred to the agencies. The statutory registers transferred to the Agency, and the regulatory bodies which dealt with them, are described in the following table.

Information on register	*Statute and regulator*
Integrated Pollution Control Part A processes	Environmental Protection Act 1990, s.20; HMIP
Prescribed Works	Alkali etc. Works Regulation Act 1906, s.9; Control of Industrial Air Pollution (Registration of Works) Regulations 1989 (S.I. 1989 No. 318); HMIP
Radioactive substances registrations and authorisations	Radioactive Substances Act 1993, s.39; HMIP
Registration of activities exempt from waste management licensing	Waste Management Licensing Regulations 1994 (S.I. 1994 No. 1056), reg. 18; WRA
Registration of brokers of controlled waste	1994 Regulations, reg. 20 and Sched. 5; WRA
Registration of waste carriers	Control of Pollution (Amendment) Act 1989, s.2; Controlled Waste (Registration of Carriers and Seizure of Vehicles) Regulations 1991, reg. 3 (S.I. 1991 No. 1624); WRA
Water abstraction and impounding licences	Water Resources Act 1991, s.189; NRA
Water Quality Objectives, discharge consents to controlled waters and sampling results	1991 Act, s.190; Control of Pollution (Registers) Regulations 1989 (S.I. 1989 No. 1160); NRA
Waste management licenses	1990 Act, s.64, WRA

The statutory registers which will be transferred to SEPA are as follows:

Information on register	Statute and regulator
Air Pollution Control Part B processes	Environmental Protection Act 1990, s.20; district and islands councils
Integrated Pollution Control Part A processes	1990 Act, s.20; HMIPI and RPAs
Prescribed works	Alkali etc. Works Regulation Act 1906, s.9; Control of Industrial Air Pollution (Registration of Works) Regulations 1989 (S.I. 1989 No. 318); HMIPI
Radioactive substances registrations and authorisations	Radioactive Substances Act 1993, s.39; HMIPI
Registration of activities exempt from waste management licensing	Waste Management Licensing Regulations 1994 (S.I. 1994 No. 1056), reg. 18; WRA
Registration of brokers of controlled waste	1994 Regulations, reg. 20, Sched. 5; WRA
Registration of waste carriers	Control of Pollution (Amendment) Act 1989, s.2; Controlled Waste (Registration of Carriers and Seizure of Vehicles) Regulations 1991, reg. 3 (S.I. 1991 No. 1624); WRA
Waste management licenses	1990 Act, s.64; WRA
Water Quality Objectives, discharge consents to controlled waters and sampling results	Control of Pollution Act 1974, s.41; Control of Pollution (Registers) (Scotland) Regulations 1993 (S.I. 1993 No. 1155); RPAs

Both agencies also inherit responsibility for the non-statutory Chemical Releases Inventory.

Aside from their statutory duties in relation to registers, the Agency and SEPA are also clearly subject to the 1992 Regulations (see *e.g.* Viscount Ullswater, Minister of State, *Hansard*, H.L. Vol. 560, col. 792 and the Earl of Lindsay *Hansard*, H.L. Vol. 560, cols. 1198–1199) and the Directive on Freedom of Access to Information on the Environment (90/313/EEC) which those regulations implement. Although the 1992 Regulations provide a general right of access to environmental information, there are several grounds on which refusal to supply information is legitimate (regs. 3(3) and 4). This explains why in s.30, which relates to record keeping by SEPA, and s.37(5), which empowers the Agency/SEPA to carry out research, the two agencies are given a discretion to provide access to records or the results of research to the public. They may withhold information where one of the grounds for refusal to disclose information under the 1992 Regulations applies but, it is submitted, they cannot do so in any other circumstances.

As to the rejection by the Government of the suggestion that the Agency/SEPA should be obliged to make their meetings public, see the General Note to s.1 and Sched. 1 at p. 25–26.

The Government appear committed to a culture of openness in the agencies:

"The Government are keen to ensure maximum openness in the affairs of SEPA, without compromising its ability to discharge its functions effectively" (*per* the Earl of Lindsay *Hansard*, H.L. Vol. 560 col. 1198). The draft Agency Management Statement (December 1995) states that "the Agency should meet the standards of openness and transparency expected of public bodies. It should publish its own Code on openness. The Code should be drawn up in consultation with the Department, and should reflect the principles of the Government's Code of Practice on Access to Government Information" (para. 6.1).

The Government have indicated in relation to SEPA at least that "minutes of its meetings will be available to the public through the Environmental Information Regulations 1992." (*ibid.*; see also Sir Hector Monro, the then Parliamentary Under-Secretary of State for Scotland, Standing Committee B, May 16, 1995, col. 248). This commitment may also be seen in the agencies' respective draft management statements which each contain a section on public access to information.

Certain advantages may accrue to members of the public from this concentration of registers and information. First, administrative practices and photocopying charges should be standardised:

"One of the potential benefits of SEPA is consistency of procedures and I would hope for a standard photocopying charge, not fluctuations depending on which local office is involved" (*per* the Earl of Lindsay, *Hansard*, H.L. Vol. 561, col. 1698).

This will clearly benefit the public since previous administrative practices and charging regimes varied significantly between the various bodies responsible for keeping statutory registers. For examples of diverse administrative practices in respect of integrated pollution control registers, see *Integrated Pollution Control: The First Three Years* (ENDS, 1994, para. 13.1) and in respect of LAAPC registers in Scotland, see *Come Clean! Public Access to Information about Local Authority Air Pollution Control* (Scottish Consumer Council & Friends of the Earth Scotland, 1993). Concerns have, however, been expressed about the Agencies' powers to charge for providing copies or extracts and, in certain instances (*e.g.* s.30), to charge for the provision of inspection facilities. The fear is that the agencies will seek to maximise their income and hence in effect deny access to information to many members of the public.

Second, the Government argued that the accessibility of the registers would also improve:

"One immediate and tangible benefit of the establishment of SEPA will be in relation to the greater ease of access to its public registers. For the first time, those registers will be available for inspection at single points of contact, greatly improving the existing arrangements where the registers are dispersed across a number of authorities" (the Earl of Lindsay *Hansard*, H.L. Vol. 560, col. 1198).

This statement, however, overlooks the fact that having registers at single points of contact may actually be disadvantageous to the public as the point of contact concerned may be much less accessible than a local authority based register. It is not yet clear how far a person will have to travel to inspect the registers after the Agencies are established or what information will actually be held by regional offices. To an extent the 1992 Regulations will assist in overcoming problems of accessibility as they may be used to request information by letter or telephone. *Integrated Pollution Control: The First Three Years* (ENDS, 1994) identified the accessibility of HMIP registers held by the then three regional headquarters as somewhat problematic (paras. 13.1–13.2). These registers were subsequently devolved to seven new regional sites. Furthermore it is not clear that the lack of a central register, which would benefit those with a legitimate interest in the wider national impact of integrated pollution control, which was identified as a serious problem by that study, will be rectified with the advent of the agencies.

In cases where a person wished to challenge the refusal of one of the agencies to disclose information or the level of its charge for inspection facilities or copies, it should be noted that the only remedies available would be judicial review or recourse to the Parliamentary Ombudsman. Formerly in relation to information held by local authorities, recourse could have been had to the Local Government Ombudsman. With the transfer to the agencies of various local authority function and the information associated therewith, this remedy will no longer be available to aggrieved persons who will require to seek redress from the Parliamentary Ombudsman. However, the Government indicated in their White Paper, *Open Government* (Cm. 2290, July 1993) that they would consider establishing a tribunal to hear disputes relating to access to health and safety and environmental information (para. 6.16). Subsequently, a commitment has been made to legislate for such a tribunal: see [1995] 243 ENDS Report at p. 32.

CHAPTER I

THE ENVIRONMENT AGENCY

Establishment of the Agency

The Environment Agency

1.—(1) There shall be a body corporate to be known as the Environment Agency or, in Welsh, Asiantaeth yr Amgylchedd (in this Act referred to as "the Agency"), for the purpose of carrying out the functions transferred or assigned to it by or under this Act.

(2) The Agency shall consist of not less than eight nor more than fifteen members of whom—

(a) three shall be appointed by the Minister; and

(b) the others shall be appointed by the Secretary of State.

(3) The Secretary of State shall designate—

(a) one of the members as the chairman of the Agency, and

(b) another of them as the deputy chairman of the Agency.

(4) In appointing a person to be a member of the Agency, the Secretary of State or, as the case may be, the Minister shall have regard to the desirability of appointing a person who has experience of, and has shown capacity in, some matter relevant to the functions of the Agency.

(5) Subject to the provisions of section 38 below, the Agency shall not be regarded—

(a) as the servant or agent of the Crown, or as enjoying any status, immunity or privilege of the Crown; or

(b) by virtue of any connection with the Crown, as exempt from any tax, duty, rate, levy or other charge whatsoever, whether general or local;

and the Agency's property shall not be regarded as property of, or property held on behalf of, the Crown.

(6) The provisions of Schedule 1 to this Act shall have effect with respect to the Agency.

DEFINITIONS
  "Agency, the": s.124(1).
  "functions": s.124(1).
  "Minister, the": s.56(1).

COMMENCEMENT
  July 28, 1995 (S.I. 1995 No. 1983).

GENERAL NOTE
  This section provides for the establishment of the Environment Agency (the Agency) and gives effect to Sched. 1 which deals with the constitution of the Agency. The constituent elements of the Agency and the background to its establishment are discussed in the General Note to this Part of the Act, and the functions transferred to it are considered in the General Note to s.2 below. It should be noted that if the Agency were to carry out other functions it would be acting *ultra vires*, and that as non-departmental public body, the Agency is accountable to Parliament through the Secretary of State for the Environment.

Subs. (1): body corporate
  By subs. (1), the Agency is a body corporate. This has implications in relation to officers' liability. Were the Agency itself to commit any one of a range of offences (including, in the environmental sphere, any offence under the Environmental Protection Act 1990 and the Water Resources Act 1991), then individual criminal liability for its officers might follow.
  Typical wording can be found in s.157 of the 1990 Act. By virtue of such provisions liability can accrue not only to officers, but also to members where the affairs of the body corporate are managed by its members. In a limited liability company, the shareholders are the members of the company, but it will be noted from subs.(2) below that the members of the Agency are the members of its Board. Whilst it is not possible for the Agency as enforcing authority to prosecute itself, and unlikely that the Agency would prosecute one of its officers or members under such provisions, most environmental legislation does not rule out the possibility of private prosecution. It is therefore possible in principle for the Agency to be prosecuted for offences for which it is the statutory enforcing authority, and the liability of its officers under such provisions could in principle follow.

Subs. (2): Appointments
  Subs. (2) provides for the appointment of the members of the Agency, who are effectively its Board, and of whom there are to be between 8 and 15. At least three are to be appointed by the Minister of Agriculture, Fisheries and Food; the remainder by the Secretary of State, who also designates the chairman and deputy chairman (subs. (3)). On August 8, 1995, the Secretary of State appointed the following as members: Lord De Ramsey as Chairman (a Cambridgeshire farmer and former President of the Country Landowners Association, President of the Association of Drainage Authorities and former Chairman of the Cambridge Water Company); Peter Burnham (previously associated with Coopers & Lybrand, the HMIP Advisory Committee and English Heritage); Imtiaz Farookhi (Leicester City Council); Nigel Haigh (Institute of European Environment Policy and the Green Alliance); Christopher Hampson (Yorkshire Electricity, HMIP Advisory Committee, former Chairman of CBI Environment Committee); John Harman (Kirklees Council, Association of Metropolitan Authorities); Karen Morgan (NRA,

University of West England, formerly ICI); Joan Wykes (NRA, London Borough of Bromley, formerly London Waste Regulation Committee, GLC and Thames Water Authority); Ed Gallagher (Chief Executive of Agency and formerly of NRA, formerly Amersham International and Black & Decker); Professor Ronald Edwards (appointee of Secretary of State for Wales; formerly NRA and its Welsh Regional Advisory Committee, formerly Welsh Water, Natural Environment Research Council and National Parks Review Panel). The Minister of Agriculture Fisheries and Food made three appointments: Sir Richard George (Weetabix, Food and Drink Federation, Institute of Food Research); John Norris (NRA, Essex farmer, Country Landowners Association, Crown Estate Commissioner, involvement in flood defence and land drainage); Dr. Anne Powell (NRA fisheries, WWF, Agenda 21 Steering Group for Oxfordshire, Inland Waterways Amenity Advisory Council). Of these, Lord de Ramsey (as chairman,) Peter Burnham, Imtiaz Farookhi, Nigel Haigh, Christopher Hampson, John Harman and John Norris had previously been members of the Environment Agency Advisory Committee appointed on November 18, 1994 (DoE News Release 650) and charged with setting up the Agency. It was anticipated by the Government that the Environment Agency Advisory Committee, which advised the Government on the establishment of the Agency and was chaired by Lord de Ramsey, would form the nucleus of the Agency's Board, and so it proved.

Subs. (4) indicates that the desirability of an appointee having experience relevant to the Agency's functions is something to which the Secretary of State and minister must have regard in making appointments. Given the wide range of functions to be exercised by the Agency, and indeed of its aims and objectives in discharging those functions, it appears likely that it would be extremely difficult in practice to challenge an appointment on this basis.

Other appointments

A number of members of Agency staff were appointed between June and September 1995 including the Chief Executive Ed Gallagher, six Directors of Environmental Strategy, Water Management, Finance, Pollution Prevention and Control, Operations and Personnel (three, like Mr Gallagher, from the NRA: one from HMIP), and eight Regional General Managers (seven of whom are from the NRA, the other from HMIP). The regions are Anglian, Midlands, North East, North West, Southern, South West, Thames and Welsh.

Crown Immunity

Subsection (5) provides that the Agency does not have Crown privilege, immunity or exemption from taxation. Section 38 qualifies this position. Under that section, the Agency and any Minister of the Crown may enter into an agreement authorising the Agency or any of its employees to exercise a ministerial function. In such a case, by s.38(5), where the Agency's acts or omissions are in, or in connection with, the exercise or purported exercise by the Agency of a ministerial function pursuant to such an agreement, those acts and omissions are to be treated as the acts or omissions of the Minister of the Crown in question. It should be noted that, even in such circumstances, the immunity provided by s.38 is not total and in particular does not extend to criminal proceedings in respect of such act or omission (see s.38(6)).

Schedule 1—Constitution of the Agency

Subsection (6) gives effect to Sched. 1, which contains a number of provisions relating to the constitution of the Environment Agency. These provisions fall under the following headings: Membership; chairman and deputy chairman; remuneration, pensions etc.; staff; proceedings of the Agency; delegation of powers; members' interests; vacancies and defective appointments; minutes; application of seal and proof of instruments; documents served etc. by or on the Agency; and interpretation. Certain of these provisions are outlined below.

Membership, chairman and deputy chairman. Paragraphs 1 and 2 of Sched. 1 provide for the resignation or removal from office, and reappointment, of members appointed to the Agency under subs. (2) above, and of the chairman and deputy chairman designated under subs. (3) above. By para. 1(3) and the definition of "appropriate Minister" in para. 12 (which, should be noted, differs from the definition of that term provided by s.56(1) for the purposes of Pt. I of the Act), a member of the Agency may only be removed from office by the person who appointed him—that is, the Secretary of State, or the Minister of Agriculture, Fisheries and Food, as appropriate. Ceasing to be a member of the Agency automatically terminates an individual's office as chairman or deputy chairman.

Staff, remuneration and pensions. By para. 4, the Agency has absolute discretion in the appointment of officers and employees, save that the Secretary of State's consent is required to the appointment of the chief executive. Remuneration and pension arrangements for each member are determined by the person who appointed that member: para. 3. For other officers and employees, the Agency may determine its provisions for their pensions, allowances and gratuities (this does not appear to cover remuneration, but does include compensation for loss of employment or diminution of emoluments), subject to the approval of the Secretary of State to the setting of those pensions, allowances and gratuities: para. 4. The Agency's discretion is presumably also restricted by the provisions in para. 3 regarding the transfer to the Agency of rights or liabilities under existing contracts of employment.

Proceedings. Subject to the subsequent provisions of Sched. 1, and to the obligation in s.106 of the Water Resources Act 1991 (c.57) to carry out its flood defence functions through committees, para. 5 allows the Agency to regulate its own procedure, including quorum. Sections 14 to 19 of, and Scheds. 4 and 5 to, this Act modify the 1991 Act's provisions in relation to flood defence committees.

During debates on SEPA's proceedings, concern was expressed that its meetings would not be open to the public, unlike local authority meetings (see, for example, Sam Galbraith, Standing Committee B, May 2, 1995, col. 59). However, the Government's view was that it was not appropriate to compel SEPA or the Agency to have meetings in public since it is a national body and opening its meetings "would inhibit the informal development of its strategic thinking ahead of wider exposure to the public. Unlike local authorities, for whom such access is part of their accountability to local electorates, the agencies will be responsible to Ministers who are accountable to Parliament" (*per* Sir Paul Beresford, Parliamentary Under-Secretary of State for the Environment, Standing Committee B, May 2, 1995, cols. 62–63).

Delegation of powers. Paragraph 6 (again subject to s.106 of the 1991 Act) provides that anything authorised or required to be done by the Agency may be done by the member, officer, employee, committee or sub-committee authorised (whether generally or specially) by the Agency to do so. This administrative provision is distinct from those in ss.108 and 109 of this Act which provide that the Agency (*i.e.* any employee, etc., authorised to do so pursuant to this paragraph) may also authorise any suitable person (not necessarily an employee, etc.) to exercise a range of powers including entry and seizure, contained in those sections.

Members' interests. Paragraph 7 provides, subject to relieving provisions where para. 7 would impede the transaction of business, that a member of the Agency who is "in any way directly or indirectly interested" in any matter brought up for consideration of a meeting of the Agency, or any of its committees or sub-committees must disclose that interest and not take part in any deliberation or decision taken with respect to that matter. What would constitute sufficient disclosure is outlined. This applies whether or not the interested member attends the meeting and, by subpara. (3), the interest may be declared by way of a written notice read and considered at the meeting. It would appear that the provision applies even where the member is not a member of the committee or sub-committee considering the matter.

Documents served etc. by or on the Agency. Notices required or authorised to be served by or on the Agency must be in writing. Any notice or other document may be signed on behalf of the Agency by any member, officer or employee who is authorised (generally or specially) by the Agency to do so. Documents purporting to be made, issued, executed or signed on its behalf by the Agency, or by a duly authorised person on its behalf, shall be received in evidence as being so made, issued, executed or signed unless the contrary is shown. This evidential provision may be of importance in cases where a party seeks to challenge the authority of someone who has acted purportedly with the authority of the Agency.

As to the service of documents generally, see s.123, below, at p. 25–306.

Transfer of functions, property etc. to the Agency

Transfer of functions to the Agency

2.—(1) On the transfer date there shall by virtue of this section be transferred to the Agency—

(a) the functions of the National Rivers Authority, that is to say—

(i) its functions under or by virtue of Part II (water resources management) of the Water Resources Act 1991 (in this Part referred to as "the 1991 Act");

(ii) its functions under or by virtue of Part III of that Act (control of pollution of water resources);

(iii) its functions under or by virtue of Part IV of that Act (flood defence) and the Land Drainage Act 1991 and the functions transferred to the Authority by virtue of section 136(8) of the Water Act 1989 and paragraph 1(3) of Schedule 15 to that Act (transfer of land drainage functions under local statutory provisions and subordinate legislation);

(iv) its functions under or by virtue of Part VII of the 1991 Act (land and works powers);

(v) its functions under or by virtue of the Diseases of Fish Act 1937, the Sea Fisheries Regulation Act 1966, the Salmon and Freshwater Fisheries Act 1975, Part V of the 1991 Act or any other enactment relating to fisheries;

(vi) the functions as a navigation authority, harbour authority or conservancy authority which were transferred to the Authority by virtue of Chapter V of Part III of the Water Act 1989 or paragraph 23(3) of Schedule 13 to that Act or which have been transferred to the Authority by any order or agreement under Schedule 2 to the 1991 Act;

(vii) its functions under Schedule 2 to the 1991 Act;

(viii) the functions assigned to the Authority by or under any other enactment, apart from this Act;

(b) the functions of waste regulation authorities, that is to say, the functions conferred or imposed on them by or under—

(i) the Control of Pollution (Amendment) Act 1989, or

(ii) Part II of the Environmental Protection Act 1990 (in this Part referred to as "the 1990 Act"),

or assigned to them by or under any other enactment, apart from this Act;

(c) the functions of disposal authorities under or by virtue of the waste regulation provisions of the Control of Pollution Act 1974;

(d) the functions of the chief inspector for England and Wales constituted under section 16(3) of the 1990 Act, that is to say, the functions conferred or imposed on him by or under Part I of that Act or assigned to him by or under any other enactment, apart from this Act;

(e) the functions of the chief inspector for England and Wales appointed under section 4(2)(a) of the Radioactive Substances Act 1993, that is to say, the functions conferred or imposed on him by or under that Act or assigned to him by or under any other enactment, apart from this Act;

(f) the functions conferred or imposed by or under the Alkali, &c, Works Regulation Act 1906 (in this section referred to as "the 1906 Act") on the chief, or any other, inspector (within the meaning of that Act), so far as exercisable in relation to England and Wales;

(g) so far as exercisable in relation to England and Wales, the functions in relation to improvement notices and prohibition notices under Part I of the Health and Safety at Work etc. Act 1974 (in this section referred to as "the 1974 Act") of inspectors appointed under section 19 of that Act by the Secretary of State in his capacity as the enforcing authority responsible in relation to England and Wales for the enforcement of the 1906 Act and section 5 of the 1974 Act; and

(h) the functions of the Secretary of State specified in subsection (2) below.

(2) The functions of the Secretary of State mentioned in subsection (1)(h) above are the following, that is to say—

(a) so far as exercisable in relation to England and Wales, his functions under section 30(1) of the Radioactive Substances Act 1993 (power to dispose of radioactive waste);

(b) his functions under Chapter III of Part IV of the Water Industry Act 1991 in relation to special category effluent, within the meaning of that Chapter, other than any function of making regulations or of making orders under section 139 of that Act;

(c) so far as exercisable in relation to England and Wales, the functions conferred or imposed on him by virtue of his being, for the purposes of Part I of the 1974 Act, the authority which is by any of the relevant statutory provisions made responsible for the enforcement of the 1906 Act and section 5 of the 1974 Act;

(d) so far as exercisable in relation to England and Wales, his functions under, or under regulations made by virtue of, section 9 of the 1906 Act (registration of works), other than any functions of his as an appellate authority or any function of making regulations;

(e) so far as exercisable in relation to England and Wales, his functions under regulations 7(1) and 8(2) of, and paragraph 2(2)(c) of Schedule 2 to, the Sludge (Use in Agriculture) Regulations 1989 (which relate to the provision of information and the testing of soil).

(3) The National Rivers Authority and the London Waste Regulation Authority are hereby abolished.

DEFINITIONS

"1906 Act, the": subs. (1)(f).
"1974 Act, the": subs. (1)(g).
"1990 Act, the": s.56(1).
"1991 Act, the": s.56(1).
"Agency, the": s.124(1).
"conservancy authority": s.56(1).
"disposal authority": s.56(1).
"functions": s.124(1).
"harbour authority": s.56(1).
"navigation authority": s.56(1).
"transfer date": s.56(1).
"waste regulation authority": s.56(1).

COMMENCEMENT

April 1, 1996 (S.I. 1996 No. 186).

GENERAL NOTE

This section transfers from existing persons or bodies to the Agency established by s.1, a range of functions (summarised below) previously exercised by those persons or bodies (subss. (1) and (2)). Schedule 22 to the Act makes a large number of consequential amendments to other enactments, introducing references to the Agency in the place of references to the persons or bodies replaced by the Agency, and para. 223 of that Schedule has the same effect in relation to subordinate and local legislation.

National Rivers Authority and Waste Regulation Authorities. Two of these bodies (the National Rivers Authority and the London Waste Regulation Authority) are consequently abolished by subs. (3), since all of their functions have been transferred. By s.30(1) of the 1990 Act the waste regulation authorities outside London were the Greater Manchester Waste Disposal Authority, Merseyside Waste Disposal Authority and elsewhere in England the county or metropolitan district councils; in Wales they are district councils. All of these bodies of course, retain other functions and are not, therefore, abolished. Reference in s.2(1)(c) to disposal authorities is to the Greater Manchester and Merseyside Waste Disposal Authorities in their waste regulation capacities.

HM Inspectorate of Pollution and the Secretary of State. Although HMIP could easily be thought of as a body similar in kind to the NRA, it is not. In fact, its functions are the functions of the chief inspector or other inspectors as individuals, or delegated functions of the Secretary of State: this is reflected in the wording of subs. 2(1)(d)–(g) and subs. 2(2). It should be noted that the Secretary of State's power to make regulations under the Water Industry Act 1991 and the Alkali, etc., Works Regulation Act 1906, and his appellate function under the latter Act, are excluded from the transfer of his functions under those two Acts: subs. 2(2)(b) and (d).

Functions transferred

The main functions transferred to the Agency, which are those transferred from the NRA and HMIP, are summarised here in simplified form. Reference should be made to the statutes in question for the detail of the duties, and for consequential and administrative duties. It should be noted that powers are usually exercisable only in certain circumstances and/or for the carrying out of certain functions.

Subs. (1)(a)—NRA functions

All of the NRA's functions are transferred, as follows. These functions fall under the headings of general water resource management; control of pollution of water resources; flood defence; land and works powers; fisheries; various functions of navigation, harbour or conservancy authorities; and other miscellaneous functions.

Water resources management. By virtue of subs. (1)(a)(i) the Agency takes over the NRA's functions in relation to the management of water resources, which arose under Pt. II of the Water Resources Act 1991. The general water resource management duty (s.19 of the 1991 Act) is now found in s.6(2) of this Act. The duty so far as reasonably practicable to enter into arrangements with water undertakers for securing the proper management or operation of such waters, etc., as the Agency considers appropriate for the undertakers to carry out their functions (s.20 of the 1991 Act) is also transferred. The Agency also receives the power (duty where directed by Secretary of State) to submit to him a draft statement containing provisions determining the minimum acceptable flow, level or volume of specified inland waters (ss.21–23 of the 1991 Act).

The Agency also obtains the NRA's functions as licensing and enforcement authority for water abstraction and for water impoundment (*i.e.* dams, weirs, etc.) (ss.24–25 of the 1991 Act). Note that para. 20 of Sched. 23 to the 1995 Act makes transitional provision regarding such licences. These functions include the emergency power to restrict quantities of water used for irrigation spraying under abstraction licence (s. 57 of the 1991 Act); the duty in some cases to pay compensation where a licence is varied or revoked (although there is a possible indemnity from Secretary of State); the potential liability to an action for breach of statutory duty against NRA (now Agency) by person with a protected right (s.60 of the 1991 Act); and the right to challenge certain decisions of the Secretary of State (s.69 of the 1991 Act).

The Agency also obtains NRA functions in relation to drought orders. These include the power to apply to the Secretary of State for ordinary or emergency drought orders (s.73 of the 1991 Act) and to exercise powers granted thereby; the duty to pay compensation for certain acts carried out under drought orders (s.79 of the 1991 Act); and the power to prosecute for breach of drought order provision (s.80 of the 1991 Act). Note that paras. 139–141 of Sched. 22 to the 1995 Act modify these provisions.

Control of pollution of water resources. The Agency takes over the functions of the NRA conferred by Pt. III of the Water Resources Act 1991, in relation to the control of pollution of water resources, see subs. (1)(a)(ii). Note that the Secretary of State has the power to modify the water pollution provisions of the 1991 Act so as to give effect to European Community or international obligations (s.102). See also s.40 of the Environment Act 1995.

In relation to water quality objectives, the Agency assumes the duty to exercise its powers in relation to water pollution, so as to ensure, so far as practicable, that water quality objectives established by Secretary of State are achieved at all times (s.84 of the 1991 Act); the duty to monitor water pollution and to consult with Scottish counterparts, for the purposes of carrying out its water pollution functions (s.84); and the power to request review of any such water quality objectives (s.83).

With regard to the enforcement of water pollution law, the Agency obtains the power to prosecute for causing or knowingly permitting water pollution (s.85); the power to prohibit by notice certain discharges to water (s.86) and to prosecute for breach of such prohibition (s.85); the role of consenting authority in relation to applications for consent to discharge to controlled waters (s.88). (Note that para. 21 of Sched. 23 to the 1995 Act makes transitional provision regarding such consents); and the power to consent, subject to conditions, to the removal of deposits from inland freshwaters, or the cutting or uprooting of vegetation in or near such waters, and the power to prosecute such actions where carried out without, or in breach of such consent (s.90).

The Agency takes over various functions in relation to the control and prevention of water pollution, including the power (where provided for in regulations) to require any person who has custody or control of poisonous, noxious or polluting matter, to carry out works, or take precautions or other steps, to prevent or control entry of that matter into controlled waters (s.92); the role (where provided for in regulations) of consenting and enforcing authority in relation to *water protection zones* (s.93); and the role of enforcing authority for *nitrate sensitive areas* (s.94).

Flood Defence. By subs. (1)(a)(iii), various functions in relation to flood defence which arose under the Water Resources Act 1991, Pt. IV, the Land Drainage Act 1991 and the Water Act 1989 are transferred to the Agency, although note that the general flood defence supervision duty is now found in s.6(4) of the 1995 Act. This includes the duty to have due regard to the interests of sea and other fisheries in exercising its flood defence powers (s.105(3)); the duty to carry out surveys of the areas in which it has flood defence functions (s.105(2)); the duty to carry out its flood defence functions under the Water Resources Act 1991 and the Land Drainage Act 1991 through regional flood defence committees (s.106). The flood defence committees continued or established under the Water Resources Act 1991 are replaced by committees established under ss.14–19 of the 1995 Act, but s.15(2) provides for transitional continuity of membership of the old and new committees; in relation to main rivers, the functions of drainage boards in relation to other watercourses (s.107), including the functions of the NRA (now the Agency) which under the Land Drainage Act 1991 are exercisable by it concurrently with an internal drainage board, any rights, powers, duties, obligations and liabilities of any drainage body transferred to it by a transfer scheme under s.108 Water Resources Act 1991, the power to give or withhold consent to the erection of certain structures in, under, over or designed to contain or divert a main river (s.109), the power to alter or pull down such works and recover costs (s.109), the power to make arrangements with a navigation or conservancy authority for the transfer of functions and property to the NRA (now the Agency) or for the carrying out of works by it (s.111), and functions as a drainage board (Land Drainage Act 1991). The amendments to drainage legislation made by ss.100 and 101 of the 1995 Act should be noted.

Land and works powers. By subs. (1)(a)(iv) functions arising under Pt. VII of the Water Resources Act 1991 relating to land and works powers are transferred. This includes the power to (compulsorily or otherwise) purchase or lease land or interests in land (ss.154–6, 168). The power to carry out or arrange for works, lay and maintain pipes, drains etc. (ss.156, 158–161), to recover costs (s.161) and to prosecute for or consent to interference with such works (s.176). The power to serve a works notice requiring anti-pollution works to be carried out and to prosecute for failure to do so (ss.161–161D, of which ss.161A-D have been inserted by the 1995 Act). The power to enter premises or authorise entry for enforcement purposes, carry out tests, take away samples, carry out experimental borings or other works and install monitoring apparatus (ss.169–172): but once the Agency's powers exercisable under s.108 of the 1995 Act in relation to its pollution control functions come into force, the s.169 powers are to be exercisable only for the purposes of its other functions: 1995 Act, Sched. 22, para. 165. The 1995 Act, Sched. 22, para. 166 restricts s.172 powers to exercise for the purpose of non-pollution control functions only.

Fisheries. Various functions in relation to fisheries are transferred to the Agency. Note that both the Secretary of State and the Minister of Agriculture, Fisheries and Food have the power to modify the NRA's (now the Agency) fisheries functions under any enactment so as to give effect to EU or international obligations (s.116 of the 1991 Act). See also s.40 of the 1995 Act. The general fisheries duty of the NRA (s.114 of the 1991 Act) is now found in s.6(6) of the 1995 Act. The role of consultee in relation to the making of ministerial fisheries orders (s.115 of the 1991 Act) is transferred.

Under the Sea Fisheries Regulation Act 1966 the powers, pursuant to order, of a local fisheries committee (s.18), the power to appoint a representative to such a committee (s.2), and fisheries byelaws enforcement where appointed (s.19), are all transferred.

The Agency receives functions in relation to infected waters originating under the Diseases of Fish Act 1937. Under the Salmon and Freshwater Fisheries Act 1975, various functions are transferred, including a bye-law making function (Sched. 3); and an enforcement function under the 1975 Act or for the protection of fisheries in any area (Sched. 3). The enforcement function (s.32) originating under the Salmon Act 1986 is transferred.

The amendments to fisheries legislation made by ss.102–105 of and Sched. 15 to the 1995 Act should be noted.

Navigation, harbour or conservancy authority functions. Under both subs. (1)(a)(vi) and subs. (1)(a)(vii) the Agency is able to take over the functions of navigation, harbour or conservancy authorities, whether directly from the authority or through the NRA. The NRA inherited under the Water Act 1989 the functions that water authorities exercised under a variety of local Acts, and these functions are transferred to the Agency (see subs. (1)(a)(vi)): their nature varies according to the local Act in question.

The Agency obtains their power to apply for an order transferring to it functions or property of a navigation, harbour or conservancy authority (see s.221(1) of the Water Resources Act 1991 for definitions of those authorities), or, with ministerial consent, to agree such transfer with the authority in question (para. 1) (see subs. (1)(a)(vii)).

Miscellaneous NRA functions. The Agency takes over various other NRA functions. The following are of particular note. The role as statutory consultee under a range of legislation, including the planning process. The NRA's *Policy and Practice for the Protection of Groundwater* (1992) contains at p. 13 a useful list of its functions as consultee in relation especially to groundwater protection. The power (or duty if so directed) to agree exemption from charges due from abstraction licence holder in certain circumstances (ss.127–130 of the 1991 Act). The surviving information functions in Pt. VIII of the Water Resources Act 1991, in relation to registers, maps and the obtainment and provision of information (ss.188–208 of the 1991 Act). The power to make and enforce byelaws, and the duty to pay compensation in respect of certain fisheries byelaws (ss.210–212 of the 1991 Act).

Subs. (1)(b)—waste regulation

The following waste regulation functions are transferred to the Agency: the licensing of waste management activities, including inspections, compliance monitoring and enforcement (Part II, the 1990 Act). The assessment of site completion, power to accept the transfer and surrender of site licences and the issue of completion certificates (the 1990 Act, ss.39 and 40). The registration of licensing exemptions (Waste Management Licensing Regulations 1994, reg. 18). The inspection of sites used for the recovery of scrap metal etc. which are registered as exempt from waste management licensing (1994 Regulations, regs. 17 and 18; Waste Management Licensing (Amendment etc.) Regulations 1995 (S.I. 1995 No. 288). The registration and regulation of waste carriers and brokers (Control of Pollution (Amendment) Act 1989, s.2; Controlled Waste (Registration of Carriers and Seizure of Vehicles) Regulations 1991; 1994 Regulations, reg. 20). Functions in connection with the duty of care for waste (1990 Act, s.34). The regulation of the transfrontier shipment of waste including enforcement (Transfrontier Shipment of Waste Regulations 1994 (S.I. 1994 No. 1137)). Enforcement action against unlicensed waste management (1990 Act, s.33), and collecting fees and charges in respect of waste management licensing, the registration of carriers and brokers and the transfrontier shipment of waste. The provision of waste management advice and information, including the maintenance of public registers (1990 Act, Part II; Waste Management Licensing Regulations 1994 (S.I. 1994 No. 1056); Control of Pollution (Amendment) Act 1989; the production of the Waste Disposal Plan (1990 Act, s.50; superseded by the waste strategy provisions of the 1995 Act, s.92: see the General Note to that section): Role as statutory consultees in relation to proposals for development adjacent to landfill sites and former landfill sites.

Subs. (1)(c): waste regulation: residual COPA functions

By s.30(1) of the Control of Pollution Act 1974, waste regulation functions for the purposes of that Act are as follows:

1. functions relating to disposal licences (ss.3–11);
2. the removal of waste deposited in breach of licensing provisions (s.16);
3. the giving of directions in relation to special waste, where provided for by regulations under s.17 (s.17(1)(a)); and
4. the supervision of activities authorised by such special waste regulations, recovery of cost and expenses and functions in relation to appeals against disposal authority decisions under those regulations (s.17(2)(b)–(d)).

This subsection transfers to the Agency all functions undertaken by local authorities in the capacity of waste disposal authorities under Pt. I of the 1974 Act. They include the old waste disposal licensing provisions which were only replaced when the new waste management licensing regime under Pt. II of the 1990 Act was brought into force on May 1, 1994. These functions have been transferred to the Agency as there may still be actions pending under the old legislation. Therefore, the importance of these transferred functions will become progressively less important with the passage of time and will become redundant when the last action under the 1974 Act is dealt with. However, the special waste controls in the 1974 Act, and the Control of Pollution (Special Waste) Regulations 1980 (S.I. 1980 No. 1709) which were made under it, are far from being residual functions and run alongside the 1990 Act provisions. However, it is anticipated that by the time waste regulation is transferred, the 1980 Regulations will have been replaced by new regulations implementing the EC Hazardous Waste Directive 91/689/EEC.

Subss. 1(d)–(g): the Chief Inspector's functions

All of the functions of HMIP are transferred to the Agency in the following manner:

Subs. (1)(d): IPC. This subsection transfers to the Agency all HMIP functions as enforcing authority for processes prescribed under Pt. A of Sched. 1 to the Environmental Protection (Prescribed Processes and Substances) Regulations 1991 (S.I. 1991 No. 472 (as amended)) for integrated pollution control (IPC) by virtue of Pt. I of the 1990 Act.

Subs. (1)(e): radioactive substances. This subsection transfers to the Agency all HMIP functions under the Radioactive Substances Act 1993, namely the registration of the keeping and use of radioactive material on premises and the registration of mobile radioactive apparatus (1993 Act, ss.7 and 10); the authorisation of the disposal or accumulation of radioactive waste (1993 Act, s.16); the enforcement of controls over radioactive substances (1993 Act, ss.6, 9, 13–14, 17, 21–22, and 32); and the maintenance of registers of registrations and authorisations (1993 Act, s.39).

Subss. (1)(f) and (g): pre-1990 Act controls. These subsections transfer to the Agency all functions conferred on or delegated to HMIP by virtue of the Alkali etc. Works Regulation Act 1906 and Pt. I of the Health and Safety at Work, etc. Act 1974. The significance of these transferred functions will cease when the last process registered under the 1906 Act is authorised under Pt. I of the 1990 Act (see subs. (1)(d) above) and when the last action under the old legislation has been concluded. The functions transferred are the registration of prescribed works (Alkali etc. Works Regulation Act 1906, s.9; Control of Industrial Air Pollution (Registration of Works) Regulations 1989 (S.I. 1989 No 318)); the enforcement of 1906 Act controls by means of prohibition and improvement notices (Health and Safety at Work etc. Act 1974); and the maintenance of a register of prescribed works registrations (1906 Act, s.9; 1989 Regulations).

Subss. (1)(h) and (2)—the Secretary of State's functions
    The following functions of the Secretary of State are transferred to the Agency:

Subs. (2)(a): radioactive substances. The Secretary of State's power in England and Wales to dispose of radioactive waste where he is satisfied that it is likely for any reason that it will be unlawfully disposed of (Radioactive Substances Act 1993, s.30(1)).

Subs. (2)(b): special category effluent. The Secretary of State's supervisory and enforcement roles under the Water Industry Act 1991 in relation to the discharge of "special category effluent" to sewers. This includes the referral of questions relating to such effluent by sewerage undertakers prior to their giving consent to such discharges to sewer (s.120); the review of agreements and consents for such discharges (ss.127, 130–131); the determination of appeals in relation to applications for consent to make such discharges (s.123); and the power to prosecute for breach of the legislation relating to special category effluent.

Subs. (2)(c) and (d): miscellaneous 1906 Act functions. The Secretary of State's enforcement role under the 1906 Act and s.5 of the Health and Safety at Work, etc., Act 1974. This role, although not his appellate function which is not transferred, was in practice delegated to HMIP.

Subs. (2)(e): Sludge (Use in Agriculture) Regulations 1989 (S.I. 1989 No. 1263) functions. The functions of the Secretary of State which are transferred include the inspection of a sludge producer's register; the receipt of certain information which sludge producers are required to supply; requesting sludge producers to check the soil of agricultural land; and acting as enforcing authority for breach of the regulations (see further the General Note to s.37(1)(a), at p. 25–99, in which Viscount Ullswater's comments in Parliament in this connection are cited).

Transfer of property, rights and liabilities to the Agency

3.—(1) On the transfer date—
    (a) the property, rights and liabilities—
                (i) of the National Rivers Authority, and
                (ii) of the London Waste Regulation Authority,
        shall, by virtue of this paragraph, be transferred to and vested in the Agency;
    (b) any property, rights or liabilities which are the subject of—
                (i) a scheme made under the following provisions of this section by the Secretary of State, or
                (ii) a scheme made under those provisions by a body which is a waste regulation authority and approved (with or without modifications) under those provisions by the Secretary of State,
        shall be transferred to and vested in the Agency by and in accordance with the scheme.
    (2) The Secretary of State may, before the transfer date, make a scheme for the transfer to the Agency of such of—
    (a) his property, rights and liabilities, or

(b) the property, rights and liabilities of any of the inspectors or chief inspectors mentioned in subsection (1) of section 2 above,

as appear to the Secretary of State appropriate to be so transferred in consequence of the transfer of any functions to the Agency by virtue of any of paragraphs (d) to (h) of that subsection.

(3) It shall be the duty of every body which is a waste regulation authority, other than the London Waste Regulation Authority—

(a) to make a scheme, after consultation with the Agency, for the transfer to the Agency of such of the body's property, rights and liabilities as appear to the body appropriate to be so transferred in consequence of the transfer of any functions to the Agency by virtue of section 2(1)(b) or (c) above; and

(b) to submit that scheme to the Secretary of State for his approval before such date as he may direct.

(4) Any body preparing a scheme in pursuance of subsection (3) above shall take into account any guidance given by the Secretary of State as to the provisions which he regards as appropriate for inclusion in the scheme.

(5) Where a scheme under subsection (3) above is submitted to the Secretary of State, he may—

(a) approve the scheme;

(b) approve the scheme subject to such modifications as he considers appropriate; or

(c) reject the scheme;

but the power conferred on the Secretary of State by paragraph (b) above shall only be exercisable after consultation with the body which submitted the scheme to him and with the Agency.

(6) The Secretary of State may, in the case of any body which is required to make a scheme under subsection (3) above, himself make a scheme for the transfer to the Agency of such of the body's property, rights or liabilities as appear to him appropriate to be so transferred in consequence of the transfer of any functions to the Agency by virtue of section 2(1)(b) or (c) above, if—

(a) the body fails to submit a scheme under subsection (3) above to him for approval before the due date; or

(b) the Secretary of State rejects a scheme under that subsection submitted to him by that body;

but nothing in this subsection shall prevent the Secretary of State from approving any scheme which may be submitted to him after the due date.

(7) The Secretary of State may, at any time before the transfer date, modify any scheme made or approved by him under this section but only after consultation with the Agency and, in the case of a scheme which was approved by him (with or without modifications), after consultation with the body which submitted the scheme to him for approval.

(8) Schedule 2 to this Act shall have effect in relation to transfers by or under this section.

DEFINITIONS
"Agency, the": s.124(1).
"functions": s.124(1).
"transfer date": s.56(1).
"waste regulation authority": s.56(1).

COMMENCEMENT
Subsections 3(2)–(8) came into force on July 28, 1995 (S.I. 1995 No. 1983).
Subsection 3(1) came into force on April 1, 1996 (S.I. 1996 No. 186).

GENERAL NOTE
This section, and Sched. 2 to which it gives effect (see subs. (8)), deal with the transfer of property, rights and liabilities to the Agency. Department of the Environment Circular 15/95 *Transfer of Property, Rights and Liabilities from Waste Regulation Authorities to the Environment Agency* (August 29, 1995) gives guidance to waste regulation authorities in England: separate guidance is to be given by the Welsh Office to Welsh waste regulation authorities.

Property, rights and liabilities. These terms are not defined, but details of what they include are given in paras. 2 and 3 of Sched. 3. These paragraphs are summarised below in the discussion of Sched. 3, but of particular importance is the transfer to the Agency of the employers' rights and liabilities under certain contracts of employment: para. 3.

The transfer date. The key date, on which all transfers to the Agency of property, rights and liabilities take effect, is "the transfer date". The Secretary of State, by order under s.56(1), set April 1, 1996 as the transfer date: S.I. 1996 No. 234. On the transfer date, by subs. (1), all property, rights and liabilities of the NRA and London Waste Regulation Authority (which bodies, when s.2(3) comes into force are abolished) are transferred to and vested in the Agency, as are such other property, rights and liabilities as are subject to a scheme made under this section.

Schemes of transfer. Two kinds of scheme of transfer are provided for by s.3. First, s.2(1)(d)–(h) transfer the various functions of the Secretary of State and of inspectors and chief inspectors to the Agency. Before the transfer date the Secretary of State may make a scheme for the transfer to the Agency of such of his and their property, rights and liabilities as appears to him to be appropriate in consequence of the transfer of those functions: subs. (2).

Secondly s.2(1)(b) and (c) transfer waste regulation functions of waste regulation authorities (including the Greater Manchester Waste Regulation Authority and Merseyside Waste Regulation Authority, which are disposal authorities with waste regulation functions) to the Agency. Each of these bodies is placed under a duty to make a scheme for the transfer to the Agency of such of its property, rights and liabilities as appear to it (after consultation with the Agency, and (subs. (4)) taking into account any guidance from the Secretary of State , including Circular 15/95) to be appropriate to be transferred in consequence of the transfer to the Agency of those functions: subs. (3). (It will be noted that these bodies are under a duty to make a scheme, whereas the Secretary of State is merely empowered to do so by subs. (2)). Circular 15/95 includes, at Annex B, a Model Transfer Scheme which is divided into Supporting Information and the Scheme itself which in turn divides into:

1. rights and liabilities in respect of contracts of employment;
2. property and rights and liability in respect of property;
3. rights and liabilities under contracts for services to be provided to or by the authority;
4. interests, rights and liabilities to be created between the authority and the Agency; and
5. a provision that all other (unspecified) minor items of property which the authority was accustomed to use in discharging its waste regulation functions shall transfer to the Agency.

It is interesting that Circular 15/95 contains speculation as to the descriptions of "special site" which are to be designated by the Secretary of State for the purposes of the contaminated land provisions inserted in the Environmental Protection Act 1990 by s.57 of the 1995 Act:

"at this stage the Department considers the following types of former landfill sites might be prescribed as "special sites": sites which are designated as active gas-producing sites; sites which are generating leachate containing red list substances; and sites which were formerly licensed for the deposit of special wastes" (para. A.15).

The significance of this in the present context is that responsibility for special sites rests with the Agency by reason of its relevant expertise. It is therefore suggested in the Model Transfer Scheme that the names of employees "who have been spending a significant proportion of their time carrying out functions on behalf of a district with respect to sites of [the] type described" or advising districts in this regard, be included where the authority considers that it would be appropriate for their contracts of employment to transfer to the Agency (Model Transfer Scheme, para. I.5).

Each body's scheme must be submitted to the Secretary of State by such date as he may direct, although he may nonetheless approve a scheme received after that date: subss. (3) and (6). Circular 15/95 indicated that for waste regulation authorities in England "the Secretary of State is directing [them] to submit their transfer schemes for approval no later than Friday December 1, 1995" (para. 3).

The Secretary of State may approve or reject the scheme, or (following consultation with the body in question and with the Agency) may approve it with modifications: subs. (5). Where he rejects it, or it is received after the date directed, he may himself make a scheme in relation to the transfer of that body's property, rights and liabilities: subs (6). Even once he has made or approved a scheme, he may modify it prior to the transfer date provided that he has consulted the Agency and (if the scheme had been approved rather than made by him) with the body in question: subs. (7).

Schedule 2. Subsection (8) gives effect to Sched. 2, which deals with transfers of property, rights and liabilities to the Agency. The Schedule falls into three parts, covering property and contracts of employment, the content of transfer schemes, and general provisions relating to transfers (whether or not pursuant to transfer schemes).

Schedule 2, Pt. I—Property, etc. and contracts of employment. By para. 2, property, rights and liabilities transferred include those which would not otherwise be capable of being so transferred; any (if specified in the relevant scheme of transfer) which are required between the making of the scheme and the transfer date; property wherever in the world it is situated; and rights and liabilities under enactments or the law of any country or territory (including the UK and any part of it).

By para. 3, employers' rights and liabilities under the contracts of employment of "qualifying employees" are transferred to the Agency. Criteria are set out which must be met in order for a person to be a qualifying employee. The person must be employed (either by the Civil Service or by a waste regulation authority) for the purposes of, or in connection with, functions which are being transferred to the Agency. In addition, that person's transfer into the employment of the Agency must be considered necessary or expedient by the Secretary of State (in the case of a civil servant) or (in the case of a waste regulation authority employee) by the waste regulation authority in question. Paragraph 3 goes on to make transitional provisions for the transfer of such contracts of employment, and for the termination of the employment of any qualifying employee who objects to becoming employed by the Agency.

In Parliament, Mr Robert Atkins, Minister for the Environment and Countryside, confirmed that,

"the Agency will, through secondary legislation, be designated as an administering authority for the local government pension scheme. That will allow all eligible employees to join the scheme, but we do not need the Bill to so designate the Agency. The usual procedure of an amendment to the relevant statutory instrument, which will be subject to consultation with relevant parties, will be sufficient" (*Hansard*, H.C., Vol. 262, col. 1027).

He went on to indicate that,

"the Agency will inherit a wide variety of terms and conditions of employment. It will undoubtedly wish to draw up systems of pay, grading, terms and conditions which are more consistent than those it inherits, but the legislation should not prevent the Agency from adopting variations to take account of factors such as the job market" (*ibid.*).

Schedule 2, Pt. II—Transfer schemes. Transfer schemes may describe the property, etc., being transferred either inclusively or specifically or partly in one way and partly in the other: para. 4. Where appropriate, the property need not be transferred outright: an interest in or right over it may be created in favour of the Agency, or it could be transferred subject to the creation of such right or interest in favour of the transferor. Equally, new rights and liabilities between the two parties may be created: para. 5.

Incidental, supplemental and consequential provisions may be made in transfer schemes, including provision for arbitration in the event of subsequent dispute between the parties as to the effect of the scheme in question: para. 6.

After a transfer scheme has come into force, the Secretary of State may make an order modifying it, having first consulted with the Agency and, where the transferor under the scheme is a waste regulation authority, with that authority: para. 7. The order may make consequential, supplemental or transitional provisions. The statutory instrument may be annulled by a resolution of either House of Parliament.

Since the exercise by the Agency and the Secretary of State of their functions in relation to transfer schemes is to a significant degree dependent on information from HMIP and waste regulation authorities, it is the duty of the Chief Inspector and the waste regulation authorities to provide such information and assistance as they reasonably require: para. 8.

Schedule 2, Pt. III—General provisions regarding transfers: consideration, continuity, remedies and foreign property. Consideration may be provided by the Agency under a transfer scheme in relation to new rights, liabilities or interests created by the scheme, but no consideration may be provided in relation to the transfer (whether or not under a transfer scheme) of existing rights, liabilities or interests: para. 9.

To ensure that all relevant rights, liabilities and property are transferred (by a transfer scheme or otherwise), para. 10 provides that subject to contrary provision in a transfer scheme, all references to the transferor in agreements (written or otherwise) or documents are from the transfer date to be references to the Agency, and all agreements or transactions made by or affecting the transferor are to be treated as made by or affecting the Agency. Thus in particular all rights, powers and remedies existing in relation to the rights and liabilities in question are transferred to the Agency: para. 11.

Where legal proceedings in relation to any rights, liabilities and property which are being transferred would be subject to foreign law, both the transferor and the Agency are to ensure that their vesting in the Agency is effective under that foreign law. Until that point, such right and property, are to be held for the benefit of the Agency and such liabilities discharged by the transferor on behalf of the Agency: para. 12.

Principal aim and objectives of the Agency

4.—(1) It shall be the principal aim of the Agency (subject to and in accordance with the provisions of this Act or any other enactment and taking into account any likely costs) in discharging its functions so to protect or enhance the environment, taken as a whole, as to make the contribution towards attaining the objective of achieving sustainable development mentioned in subsection (3) below.

(2) The Ministers shall from time to time give guidance to the Agency with respect to objectives which they consider it appropriate for the Agency to pursue in the discharge of its functions.

(3) The guidance given under subsection (2) above must include guidance with respect to the contribution which, having regard to the Agency's responsibilities and resources, the Ministers consider it appropriate for the Agency to make, by the discharge of its functions, towards attaining the objective of achieving sustainable development.

(4) In discharging its functions, the Agency shall have regard to guidance given under this section.

(5) The power to give guidance to the Agency under this section shall only be exercisable after consultation with the Agency and such other bodies or persons as the Ministers consider it appropriate to consult in relation to the guidance in question.

(6) A draft of any guidance proposed to be given under this section shall be laid before each House of Parliament and the guidance shall not be given until after the period of 40 days beginning with the day on which the draft was so laid or, if the draft is laid on different days, the later of the two days.

(7) If, within the period mentioned in subsection (6) above, either House resolves that the guidance, the draft of which was laid before it, should not be given, the Ministers shall not give that guidance.

(8) In reckoning any period of 40 days for the purposes of subsection (6) or (7) above, no account shall be taken of any time during which Parliament is dissolved or prorogued or during which both Houses are adjourned for more than four days.

(9) The Ministers shall arrange for any guidance given under this section to be published in such manner as they consider appropriate.

DEFINITIONS
"Agency, the": s.124(1).
"costs": s.56(1).
"environment": s.56(1).
"functions": s.124(1).
"Ministers, the": s.56(1).

COMMENCEMENT
July 28, 1995 (S.I. 1995 No. 1983).

GENERAL NOTE

Background
    This section started life, in the draft Environment Agencies Bill published by the Department of the Environment in October 1994, containing only provision for the Secretary of State and Minister of Agriculture, Fisheries and Food to give guidance to the Agency as to the appropriate objectives for it to pursue in carrying out its functions: such guidance would have to include guidance as to the appropriate contribution for the Agency to make towards the attainment of sustainable development, and the Agency would have to have regard to such guidance. At the Bill's Second Reading in the Lords, Viscount Ullswater, Minister of State for the Environment, described this as "the inclusion for the first time in English law of a duty in relation to sustainable development" (*Hansard*, H.L. Vol. 559, col. 1462).
    These provisions raised significant concern (expressed, for instance, in the House of Lords by Lord Crickhowell and Viscount Mills (*Hansard*, H.L. Vol. 560, col. 1776 and Vol. 559, col. 1450)) at the scope of discretion left to the Government to determine the Agency's objectives and thus

its approach to its functions, following enactment of the Act. The Government therefore introduced, at the Lords Report Stage, amendments (equivalent to what are now subss. (1), (5) and (9)) introducing the Agency's principal aim and the obligation on the Government to consult before issuing such guidance and publish it once issued.

By the time the Bill entered the House of Commons on March 21, 1995, the Government had added further amendments (now subss. (6) to (8)). These provide the further safeguards, typically afforded in relation to statutory instruments, of Parliamentary scrutiny and an opportunity for either House to resolve within 40 days that the guidance should not be given.

The principal aim: subs. (1)

The principal aim relates to the Agency's contribution to the attainment of the objective of sustainable development. In moving the amendment to introduce the principal aim, Viscount Ullswater, Minister of State for the Environment, said that it:

"seeks to meet the desire expressed by a number of noble Lords in Committee for a strategic purpose for the Agency to be included on the face of the Bill. It incorporates within Clause 4 a new principal aim [which] is not to overrule the specific purpose of the various enactments under which the agency operates" (*Hansard*, H.L. Vol. 561, cols. 1620–1621).

What is meant by sustainable development, and the contribution considered appropriate for the Agency to make to its attainment, are discussed below in the note to subs. (3). However, several points should be noted in relation to the principal aim.

Status of the principal aim. The principal aim only applies "subject to and in accordance with the provisions of this Act or any other enactment". It can thus be seen as applicable only where the Agency has discretion in the exercise of its statutory duties, powers and other functions. The principal aim would appear for the same reason to be subject to any statutory purpose or objective specified for a given function. Thus, the principal aim may only be pursued in relation, for example, to the Agency's pollution control duties within the context of the statutory purpose for which powers are required by s.5 to be exercised.

Such discretion clearly exists where the duty in question is to "have regard to" or "take account of" a consideration (see, for example, s.7(1)(c) and, in relation to the national air quality strategy, s.81(1)). See the General Introduction to this Part of the Act at p. 25–20 for a discussion of the term "have regard to". One can have regard to a consideration and in appropriate circumstances can properly act contrary to that consideration. It is likely, moreover, that even where the duty in question is "to further" a consideration, there will in practice be scope for discretion in the manner of exercise of one's powers in order to comply with that duty. In the exercise of discretion by the Agency its principal aim (and indeed its other objectives where relevant) would be applicable.

The significance of the word "principal" would, then, appear to be confined to the situation where the Agency is deciding whether to act so as to further its principal aim or another objective, but in the circumstances cannot act so as to further both. In that situation, the principal aim ought to prevail. Even this, however, could be disputed since the principal aim is subject to other provisions of the Act and its duty to have regard to guidance on its other objectives are other such provisions. It is submitted that to suggest that the principal aim is subject (by implication) to its subsidiary objectives leads to absurdity. The choice of the term "principal aim" is perhaps curious, however, in that the Agency has no other "aims" characterised as such: the others are "objectives".

It should be noted that, in contrast to the Agency, SEPA lacks a principal aim. For a discussion of SEPA's aims and objectives see the General Note to s.31, at p. 25–87.

Importance of guidance. The principal aim is entirely dependent on guidance: if none were in force, the Agency's principal aim would be devoid of content. The role of such guidance is considered further below.

Nature of Agency's contribution. The principal aim is not simply "so to discharge its functions as to make" the appropriate contribution to such development. Rather, the Agency must make that contribution through the protection and enhancement of the environment.

"*Any likely costs*". However, the Agency must take into account "any likely costs": this includes the likely costs to any person and to the environment (s.56(1)). It will be noted that, unless the principal aim is considered not itself to be a form of objective, the controversial "costs and benefits" duty imposed on both agencies by s.39 would appear not to apply to the Agency's pursuit of its principal aim, as that duty is expressed not to affect the pursuit of any statutory Agency objectives (s.39(2)). Thus, without the costs provision in this section, the Agency would not have had an explicit duty on the face of the Act to take account of costs in pursuing its principal aim. As Viscount Ullswater, Minister of State for the Environment, put it, in the absence of a statutory definition or judicial interpretation of "sustainable development", "the inclusion of the reference to costs is therefore intended to ensure that the principal aim includes explicit recognition of both sides of the equation to reduce the risk of challenge in the courts from anyone who might seek to argue that sustainable development is to be interpreted exclusively in environmental terms" (*Hansard*, H.L. Vol. 561, col. 1628). The relationship between the principal aim and the s.39 duty is considered further in the note to subs. (3).

"*Environment*". The definition of the environment as "all or any of the following media: land, water and the air" (taken from s.29(2) of the 1990 Act) does not include man or any other organisms which are or might be dependent on the environment. As regards the aquatic environment, the principal aim will, together with other Agency objectives, determine what (under s.6(1)(b)) the Agency considers desirable in terms of the conservation of flora and fauna which are dependent on that environment. As regards flora and fauna which are dependent on the non-aquatic (*i.e.* air and land) environment, the Agency's explicit concern in relation to the exercise of its functions generally appears to be restricted to those which are of special interest or natural beauty (see s.7(1)(a)–(c)), excluded as they are from the principal aim. Nevertheless, it is submitted that the notions of a cost to an environmental medium and the protection and enhancement of the environment can ultimately only be understood in terms of harm and benefit to organisms or ecosystems in or dependent on that medium.

"*Taken as a whole*". The principal aim relates to the conservation and enhancement of the environment "taken as a whole". In Parliament Viscount Ullswater, Minister of State for the Environment, explained this term as follows:

"we mean by that an integrated analysis of all the environmental media of air, land and water and the judgments should be taken in the round and be based on overall factors and should not be preoccupied by the minutiae of the detail" (*Hansard*, H.L. Vol. 561, col. 1630).

Were this phrase ever to be considered by a court to be ambiguous or obscure, then this Parliamentary explanation may be admissible in court to clarify the meaning of the term, under the principles considered in the General Introduction (*Parliamentary Proceedings*) at p. 25–7, which discusses *Pepper v. Hart* [1993] A.C. 593 and related cases.

Role of guidance on the principal aim. By subs. (4), the Agency need only "have regard to" guidance given to it under subs. (3). That is, the considerations in the guidance must influence its decision-making processes but it can, where other considerations are of sufficient importance, act contrary to the guidance : see further the General Introduction to this Part at p. 25–20. The implications of this for the Agency's principal aim are unclear. The principal aim is worded in such a way that its content is actually to be found in the relevant parts of the guidance (some of which relate not to the principal aim but to the Agency's other objectives). Yet if this is so, and subs. (4) is taken to indicate the status of the guidance in relation to the Agency, it follows that the Agency may by virtue of subs. (4) in appropriate circumstances act contrary to its own principal aim. The principal aim is, as is noted above, already subject to the other statutory provisions affecting the Agency.

This difficulty may be resolved by taking the view that, insofar as such guidance is expressed to relate to the Agency's contribution to sustainable development, the Agency is obliged (subject to the qualifications in the language of the principal aim which are considered above) to act in accordance with that guidance rather than merely to have regard to it, since it is the Agency's principal aim to do so.

Guidance on objectives and principal aim: subss. (2) and (3)

On October 13, 1994 (revised December 1995), the Government published a draft *Management Statement* for the Agency. This non-statutory document contained a number of proposed main objectives for the Agency. Similar main objectives appeared in s.2 of the draft *Outline of Scope of Guidance to the Environment Agency under Clause 4 of the Environment Bill*, which was published on January 17, 1995 (DoE News Release 010) in order to assist the House of Lords in its consideration of clause 4—a number of their Lordships had requested sight of such a draft. On April 21, 1995 the Government issued a full draft of the proposed guidance (revised December 1995 as *The Environment Agency and Sustainable Development, including at Appx. 1 draft statutory guidance under s.4 of the Environment Act 1995 with respect to the objectives of the Environment Agency and its contribution towards achieving sustainable development*). This contained at Appx. 1, para. 9, a revised set of proposed objectives:

(a) to adopt, across all its functions, an integrated approach to environment protection and enhancement which considers impacts of substances and activities on all environmental media and on natural resources;

(b) to work with all relevant sectors of society, including regulated organisations, to develop approaches which deliver environmental requirements and goals without imposing excessive costs (in relation to the benefits gained) on regulated organisations or society as a whole;

(c) to adopt clear and effective procedures for serving its customers, including by developing single points of contact through which regulated organisations can deal with the Agency;

(d) to operate to high professional standards, based on sound science, information and analysis of the environment and of processes which affect it;

(e) to organize its activities in ways which reflect good environmental practice and provide value for money for those who pay its charges and taxpayers as a whole;

(f) to provide clear and readily available advice and information on its work; and,

(g) to develop a close and responsive relationship with the public, local communities and regulated organizations.

The key parts of the draft guidance are Chapters 3, 4 and 5, setting out the principles of sustainable development, the contribution which the Environment Agency is to make towards achieving sustainable development, and issues of costs and benefits (the draft guidance on costs and benefits is set out in full in the note to s.39). Although these are non-statutory, the principles are reflected in the more condensed draft statutory guidance at Appx. 1. The guidance stresses that sustainable development does not mean having less economic development: "on the contrary, a healthy economy is better able to generate the resources to meet people's needs, and new investment and environmental improvement often go hand in hand. Nor does it mean that every aspect of the present environment should be preserved at all costs. What it requires is that decisions throughout society are taken with proper regard to environmental impact" (para. 3.3). Paragraph 3.8 of the draft contains one of the first explicit comments on the importance of natural environmental capital to be found in Government policy. The guidance points out that natural capital consists of both renewable and non-renewable resources and that the challenge of sustainable development is to find ways of enhancing total wealth while using common natural resources prudently, so that renewable resources can be conserved and non-renewable used at a rate which considers the needs of future generations. In this, the guidance points out that it is especially important to consider whether there is a risk of irreversible environmental effects and, if so, how significant they may be.

The guidance points out that the Government must take the broadest view of the action the UK needs to achieve sustainable development, domestically and globally, and that the Agency cannot itself achieve sustainable development but will have a crucial role to play in operating a regulatory framework so as to ensure that the development which it regulates is sustainable. The draft statutory guidance in Appx. 1, para. 11, indicates that it would be "appropriate" for the Agency to act (in summary) as follows: (a) take a holistic approach to the protection and enhancement of the environment; (b) take a long-term perspective in considering sustainable development, seeking to take properly into account longer term implications and effects, particularly those which appear likely to be irreversible or reversible only at high cost over a long time scale, or which would raise issues of intergenerational equity; (c) maintaining bio-diversity as an essential element of sustainable development, paying particular attention to its statutory obligations with respect to conservation; (d) recognising, within the areas for which the Agency is responsible, the great scope for reconciling the needs of the environment to the needs of development by the adoption of improved technologies and management techniques by regulated organisations, discharging its functions where possible in partnership with business, including the encouragement of adoption of plans and management techniques such as BS7750 and the EU eco-management and audit regulation, and promoting environmental initiatives, high standards and high levels of understanding and knowledge of the best pollution prevention and minimisation techniques; (e) recognising that the achievement of sustainable development will involve contributions from many different organisations and individuals and the desirability of maximising the value of the Agency's contribution to those wider developments, striving to develop close and responsible relationships with the public, local communities, regulated organisations, non-governmental organisations and local government; and (f) recognising the importance of the availability of high quality information and advice on the environment, striving within the areas of its responsibility to become a recognised centre of knowledge and expertise and to provide and promulgate clear and readily available advice and information on its work and on best environmental practice.

On the issue of costs and benefits, the guidance suggests that the Agency should concern itself primarily with the costs and benefits of its actions for society as a whole, the effects on welfare of people and business, changes in the use of resources and impacts on the environment. The Agency should take into account the views of the Government's chief medical officer, impacts on individual companies and industry sectors and the distribution of costs and benefits across the economy. The Agency should develop practical procedures to ensure it meets the requirements of the duty to have regard to costs and benefits. Such procedures should include advice to staff on relevant techniques for assessing costs and benefits; on those cases where the Agency's discretion is limited by obligations arising from other duties, requirements or objectives; and on identification of circumstances in which detailed consideration of costs and benefits might be unreasonable.

In developing practical procedures, the Agency should ensure consistency with principles to be set out in new Government guidance on risk assessment and existing guidance on economic and policy appraisal. The way in which the Agency reaches its judgment should involve due rigour in all cases, but be proportionate to the implications in the circumstances of the particular case. Costs and benefits which are unquantifiable or which cannot readily be given monetary values should also be considered.

Status of guidance: subs. (4)
The Agency is required to have regard to guidance given under subs. (2). This is the usual requirement in relation to guidance, and allows the Agency in appropriate circumstances to act contrary to the guidance, having had due regard to it: see p. 25–20. See the final paragraph of the note to subs. (1) above, however, as to the status of such of the guidance as relates to the Agency's principal aim. Unusually and by contrast, it will be noted that the enforcing authorities, including the Agency, for the contaminated land provisions in s.57, are required to "act in accordance with" some of the guidance provided for in that section.

Consultation: subs. (5)
It is submitted that the duties on the Ministers and the Agency under s.7 in relation to the formulation and consideration of proposals in relation to the Agency's functions can be argued to apply to the process of consultation required in relation to guidance issued under subs. (2). Both Houses of Parliament will have the power to prevent any proposed guidance under subs. (2) from being issued, but as with statutory instruments they may not amend the proposed guidance.

Publication: subs. (9)
The draft Guidance states that "the final text of this document will be published".

General functions with respect to pollution control

5.—(1) The Agency's pollution control powers shall be exercisable for the purpose of preventing or minimising, or remedying or mitigating the effects of, pollution of the environment.
(2) The Agency shall, for the purpose—
(a) of facilitating the carrying out of its pollution control functions, or
(b) of enabling it to form an opinion of the general state of pollution of the environment,
compile information relating to such pollution (whether the information is acquired by the Agency carrying out observations or is obtained in any other way).
(3) If required by either of the Ministers to do so, the Agency shall—
(a) carry out assessments (whether generally or for such particular purpose as may be specified in the requirement) of the effect, or likely effect, on the environment of existing or potential levels of pollution of the environment and report its findings to that Minister; or
(b) prepare and send to that Minister a report identifying—
(i) the options which the Agency considers to be available for preventing or minimising, or remedying or mitigating the effects of, pollution of the environment, whether generally or in cases or circumstances specified in the requirement; and
(ii) the costs and benefits of such options as are identified by the Agency pursuant to sub-paragraph (i) above.
(4) The Agency shall follow developments in technology and techniques for preventing or minimising, or remedying or mitigating the effects of, pollution of the environment.
(5) In this section, "pollution control powers" and "pollution control functions", in relation to the Agency, mean respectively its powers or its functions under or by virtue of the following enactments, that is to say—
(a) the Alkali, &c, Works Regulation Act 1906;
(b) Part I of the Health and Safety at Work etc. Act 1974;
(c) Part I of the Control of Pollution Act 1974;
(d) the Control of Pollution (Amendment) Act 1989;

(e) Parts I, II and IIA of the 1990 Act (integrated pollution control etc, waste on land and contaminated land);
(f) Chapter III of Part IV of the Water Industry Act 1991 (special category effluent);
(g) Part III and sections 161 to 161D of the 1991 Act (control of pollution of water resources);
(h) the Radioactive Substances Act 1993;
(j) regulations made by virtue of section 2(2) of the European Communities Act 1972, to the extent that the regulations relate to pollution.

DEFINITIONS
"Agency, the": s.124(1).
"costs": s.56(1).
"environment": s.56(1).
"Ministers, the": s.56(1).
"pollution control functions": subs. (5).
"pollution control powers": subs. (5).

COMMENCEMENT
Subss. (2) and (5) came into force on February 1, 1996, and the remainder on April 1, 1996 (S.I. 1996 No. 186).

GENERAL NOTE
This section introduces a distinction between the Agency's pollution control and non-pollution powers and functions, and makes general provision in relation to its pollution control functions. The same distinction is also employed in s.7 and, in relation to the national air quality strategy, in s.81(1). It is discussed further in the General Note to s.7. Pollution control powers and functions are defined here and in those sections by reference to a list of Agency functions: see subs. (5).

Purpose: subs. (1)
By subs. (1) the Agency's pollution control powers are exercisable for the purpose of preventing or minimising pollution of the environment or remedying or mitigating its effects. The key term "pollution of the environment" is undefined: however, the term is defined in the 1990 Act for the purposes of both Pt. I and Pt. II of that Act (in ss.1(3) and 29(3) respectively), and it is submitted that for the application of this subsection for the purposes of the Agency's pollution control functions under both of those Parts (IPC and waste regulation respectively), those definitions should apply. Each defines the term by reference to harm to human health or the health of living organisms.

IPC. The Agency inherits (by virtue of para. 46 of Sched. 22 to the 1995 Act) the similar duty imposed by s.4(2) of the Environmental Protection Act 1990 on HMIP in relation to its functions under Pt. I of that Act. The position is thus that the Agency's IPC pollution control functions are all exercisable for the purpose of preventing or minimising pollution of the environment, and such of those functions as are powers (rather than, for instance, duties) are additionally exercisable for the purpose of remedying or mitigating the effects of such pollution.

Waste regulation. Authorities under both Pts. I and II of the 1990 Act (IPC and waste regulation, as far as the Agency is concerned) must discharge their functions under those Parts so as to fulfil the "relevant objectives" as defined in Sched. 4, paras. 2 and 4 to the Waste Management Licensing Regulations 1994 (S.I. 1994 No. 1056). Waste regulation authorities had no duty under Pt. II of the 1990 Act comparable to that imposed on HMIP under Pt. I. As noted above, Pt. II of the 1990 Act contains a definition of "pollution of the environment".

Water pollution. The NRA had no comparable duty in relation to its pollution control functions, although it has a power to serve works notices requiring, *inter alia*, the remedying or mitigation of any water pollution and to carry out such works itself: ss.161–161D Water Resources Act 1991. Nowhere in the legislation containing those functions is a definition of pollution of the environment to be found. Courts may look to the definitions in Parts I and II of the 1990 Act for guidance as to the interpretation of the term, although there is also case law on this matter (see, for instance, *R. v. Dovermoss* [1995] Env. L.R. 258 (C.A.), *NRA v. Eggar U.K. Ltd.*, Newcastle-upon-Tyne Crown Court, June 15–17, 1992 (unreported) in the water pollution context as to the meaning of "polluting matter" in s.85(1) of the Water Resources Act 1991).

Radioactive Substances Control. There is no comparable duty on the regulator under the Radioactive Substances Act 1993 (c. 12) and no reference to pollution of the environment. Authorisations under that Act may be granted simply subject to such conditions or limitations as HMIP or the Minister "think fit".

Research and information: subss. (2)–(4)

An integrated approach to environmental protection requires accurate information on the often complex relationship between impacts on the different environmental media. Accordingly, the Agency has specific research and information duties in relation to environmental pollution (a) to compile information on it (subs. (2)); (b) to carry out assessments (where required to do so) on its effect on the environment (subs. (3)(a)); (c) to report (where required to do so) on the available options for tackling it and its effects (subs. (3)(b)); and, (d) to follow developments in technology and techniques for tackling it and its effects (subs. (4)). A similar duty had previously been placed on HMIP and local authorities in relation to developments in technology and techniques for preventing or reducing pollution from prescribed processes under Pt. I of the 1990 Act (s.4(9)). Now of course, a significantly wider range of technologies and techniques is required to be followed. The word "techniques", as contrasted with technology, is worthy of note: matters such as operator training and management systems are included as with the term in its "BATNEEC" context (Pt. I of the 1990 Act). The Government's draft Guidance to the Agency under s.4, discussed in the General Note to subss. 4(2) and (3) at p. 25–39, states that it should "encourage knowledge and understanding, particularly in regulated organisations, of best available techniques not entailing excessive costs for the prevention and minimisation of pollution, including the efficient use of resources, such as energy, and the minimisation of waste" (para. 11(iv)(e)), adding that the Agency should "strive within its area of responsibility to become a recognised centre of knowledge and expertise, and to provide and promulgate clear and readily accessible advice and information on its work and on best environmental practice" (para. 11(vi)).

It will be noted that the subs. (2) duty is not only to facilitate the exercise of the Agency's pollution control functions, but also to enable the Agency to form an opinion on the general state of environment pollution: it is in part on the basis of this opinion that the Agency's consultative role, in particular on policy matters such as the national air quality and waste strategies, is likely to be exercised.

General provisions with respect to water

6.—(1) It shall be the duty of the Agency, to such extent as it considers desirable, generally to promote—
   (a) the conservation and enhancement of the natural beauty and amenity of inland and coastal waters and of land associated with such waters;
   (b) the conservation of flora and fauna which are dependent on an aquatic environment; and
   (c) the use of such waters and land for recreational purposes;
and it shall be the duty of the Agency, in determining what steps to take in performance of the duty imposed by virtue of paragraph (c) above, to take into account the needs of persons who are chronically sick or disabled.

This subsection is without prejudice to the duties of the Agency under section 7 below.

(2) It shall be the duty of the Agency to take all such action as it may from time to time consider, in accordance with any directions given under section 40 below, to be necessary or expedient for the purpose—
   (a) of conserving, redistributing or otherwise augmenting water resources in England and Wales; and
   (b) of securing the proper use of water resources in England and Wales;
but nothing in this subsection shall be construed as relieving any water undertaker of the obligation to develop water resources for the purpose of performing any duty imposed on it by virtue of section 37 of the Water Industry Act 1991 (general duty to maintain water supply system).

(3) The provisions of the 1991 Act relating to the functions of the Agency under Chapter II of Part II of that Act and the related water resources provisions so far as they relate to other functions of the Agency shall not apply to so much of any inland waters as—
   (a) are part of the River Tweed;
   (b) are part of the River Esk or River Sark at a point where either of the banks of the river is in Scotland; or
   (c) are part of any tributary stream of the River Esk or the River Sark at a point where either of the banks of the tributary stream is in Scotland.

(4) Subject to section 106 of the 1991 Act (obligation to carry out flood defence functions through committees), the Agency shall in relation to England and Wales exercise a general supervision over all matters relating to flood defence.

(5) The Agency's flood defence functions shall extend to the territorial sea adjacent to England and Wales in so far as—

(a) the area of any regional flood defence committee includes any area of that territorial sea; or

(b) section 165(2) or (3) of the 1991 Act (drainage works for the purpose of defence against sea water or tidal water, and works etc. to secure an adequate outfall for a main river) provides for the exercise of any power in the territorial sea.

(6) It shall be the duty of the Agency to maintain, improve and develop salmon fisheries, trout fisheries, freshwater fisheries and eel fisheries.

(7) The area in respect of which the Agency shall carry out its functions relating to fisheries shall be the whole of England and Wales, together with—

(a) such part of the territorial sea adjacent to England and Wales as extends for six miles from the baselines from which the breadth of that sea is measured,

(b) in the case of—

(i) the Diseases of Fish Act 1937,

(ii) the Salmon and Freshwater Fisheries Act 1975,

(iii) Part V of the 1991 Act (general control of fisheries), and

(iv) subsection (6) above,

so much of the River Esk, with its banks and tributary streams up to their source, as is situated in Scotland, and

(c) in the case of sections 31 to 34 and 36(2) of the Salmon and Freshwater Fisheries Act 1975 as applied by section 39(1B) of that Act, so much of the catchment area of the River Esk as is situated in Scotland,

but, in the case of the enactments specified in paragraph (b) above, excluding the River Tweed.

(8) In this section—

"miles" means international nautical miles of 1,852 metres;

"the related water resources provisions" has the same meaning as it has in the 1991 Act;

"the River Tweed" means "the river" within the meaning of the Tweed Fisheries Amendment Act 1859 as amended by byelaws.

DEFINITIONS

"the 1991 Act": s.56(1).

"the Agency": s.124(1).

"functions": s.124(1).

"miles": subs. (8).

"the related water resources provisions": subs. (8).

"the River Tweed": subs. (8).

COMMENCEMENT

April 1, 1996 (S.I. 1996 No. 186).

GENERAL NOTE

This section imposes on the Agency a range of duties in relation to its water functions, and defines the geographical extent of certain of those functions. The duties are all modelled on duties imposed on the NRA by provisions in the Water Resources Act 1991, and which this section replaces, as follows: subs. (1) replaces s.2(2) of the 1991 Act (environmental and recreational); subs. (2) replaces s.19 of the 1991 Act (water resource management); subs. (4) replaces s.105(1) of the 1991 Act (flood defence); and subs. (6) replaces s.114 of the 1991 Act (fisheries). The other subsections, (3), (5) and (7) relate to the geographical extent of the Agency's functions in relation respectively to water resource management, flood defence and fisheries. They replace subss. (4), (5) and (6) respectively of s.2 of the 1991 Act.

Environmental and recreational duties: subs. (1)

These duties, as under the 1991 Act, are without prejudice to the Agency's other duties under what is now s.7 of the 1995 Act. The duties require action from the Agency only to such extent as it considers desirable. In exercising such discretion, the Agency's objectives and principal aim under s.4 will apply. So will the relevant duties under s.7 insofar as its exercise involves the formulation or consideration of proposals for the promotion of the matters specified in this subsection. The subs. (1)(c) duty, relating to the recreational use of inland and coastal waters, should be read in conjunction with the duty in s.7(4) which relates to the recreational use of water or associated land over which the Agency has rights of use.

The term "chronically sick or disabled" is not defined in the Act. One source of definition which might be of some use in construing the term is the Chronically Sick and Disabled Persons Act 1970 (c. 44), which provides for the welfare of such persons. Section 28 of the Act provides for the terms (*inter alia*) "chronically sick" and "disabled" to be defined by statutory instrument, but the Secretary of State has not exercised that power. The Agency has a duty (which s.7(5) also imposes in relation to its duty under s.7(4)) to take account of the needs of persons who fit that description in determining the steps it should take in the performance of its duty generally to promote, to the extent which it considers desirable, the use of water for recreational purposes. Two aspects of the draft guidance to the Agency on its aims and objectives (revised December 1995: see the note to s.4) would appear particularly relevant to this duty. First, the Agency's objective of developing a close and responsive relationship with the public and local communities (Appx. 1, para. 9(vii)). And second, the non-statutory guidance that the Agency should take into account the distribution as well as the absolute level of costs and benefits: "some options open to the Agency may impose particularly heavy costs on particular groups of people or companies or on certain parts of the environment" (para. 5.6(d)). Taken together, these suggest that the Agency should seek to learn from sick and disabled people themselves, and from people working with them, what their needs are in terms of access and facilities and what costs would be imposed on them by the different options available to the Agency, before the Agency reaches its view on the desirable extent to which it should promote such recreational use.

It will be noted that the subs. (1)(b) duty relates only to the aquatic environment. There is no comparable duty elsewhere in relation to flora and fauna dependent on other environments: the duties in s.7(1)–(3) below relate only to the formulation and consideration of proposals.

Subs. (2): Water resources management

Subsection (2) imposes a general water management duty on the Agency, subject to the strategic responsibility which still rests with the duty on the water undertakers under the Water Industry Act 1991 (c. 56), s.37, to maintain the water supply system by developing an efficient and economical system of water supply for premises in their area. The subsection gives the Agency considerable discretion, subject only to the requirement to act in accordance with directions of the Secretary of State, in relation to the wide-ranging subject matter of its duty to conserve, redistribute or otherwise augment water resources (subs. (2)(a)) and secure their proper use (subs. (2)(b)). As a transitional arrangement, para. 2 of Sched. 23 to the 1995 Act provides that any directions given to the NRA for the purposes of s.19 of the Water Resources Act 1991 (which this subsection replaces) have effect after the transfer date (April 1, 1996) as directions given to the Agency by this subsection.

Subss. (4) and (5): Flood defence

The NRA's flood defence functions are transferred to the Agency by s.2(1)(iii) and are summarised in the General Note to that section. Subsection (5) specifies the geographical extent of the Agency's flood defence functions, and subs. (4) places the Agency under a general supervisory duty in relation to all matters relating to flood defence. This duty is in addition to its other, more specific flood defence functions, and by the Water Resources Act 1991, s.106, it and all of those other functions are to be carried out through regional flood defence committees. Such committees are now provided for by ss.14 to 19 of, and Sched. 5 to, this Act.

The amendments to land drainage legislation made by ss.100 and 101 of this Act should be noted.

Subss. (6) and (7): Fisheries

The NRA's fisheries functions under a number of Acts are transferred to the Agency by s.2(1)(v) and are summarised in the General Note to that section at p. 25–31. Subsection (7) defines the geographical extent of those functions and subs. (6) adds the transfer to the Agency of the NRA's duty to maintain, improve and develop a range of fisheries. The amendments to fisheries legislation made by ss.102–105 of and Sched. 15 to this Act will be noted, although not all of them relate directly to Agency functions.

It should be noted that, by s.105(3) of the Water Resources Act 1991, the Agency has a duty, in the exercise of its flood defence functions (see the General Note to subs. (4)), to have due regard to the interests of fisheries, including sea fisheries.

Subsection (7)(c) was introduced as a Government amendment during the Bill's Third Reading in the Commons. Sir Hector Monro, the then Parliamentary Under-Secretary of State for Scotland, in moving the amendment, said that:

"[The] mouth of the Tweed is in England, and most of the river is in Scotland, but the Tweed Commissioners look after the whole river. With the Border Esk, however, which runs into the Solway, the mouth is in England and the rest of the river is in Scotland, but there has been a difficulty.

The bailiffs who are the responsibility of the National Rivers Authority and are managing the river have not been able to take all the action they have wanted to take when operating in Scotland. When Scottish poachers are running, the bailiffs have had to stop once they have left the river. If we pass the amendment, the bailiffs could follow them up the banks to their motor cars and take appropriate action.

This will be a helpful opportunity to improve the policing of the river ..." (*Hansard*, H.C. Vol. 262, col. 940. See also *Hansard*, H.L. Vol. 565, col. 1476 *per* the Earl of Lindsay).

The provisions of para. 19 of Sched. 15 to this Act should be noted in this regard.

General environmental and recreational duties

7.—(1) It shall be the duty of each of the Ministers and of the Agency, in formulating or considering—

(a) any proposals relating to any functions of the Agency other than its pollution control functions, so far as may be consistent—

    (i) with the purposes of any enactment relating to the functions of the Agency,

    (ii) in the case of each of the Ministers, with the objective of achieving sustainable development,

    (iii) in the case of the Agency, with any guidance under section 4 above,

    (iv) in the case of the Secretary of State, with his duties under section 2 of the Water Industry Act 1991,

so to exercise any power conferred on him or it with respect to the proposals as to further the conservation and enhancement of natural beauty and the conservation of flora, fauna and geological or physiographical features of special interest;

(b) any proposals relating to pollution control functions of the Agency, to have regard to the desirability of conserving and enhancing natural beauty and of conserving flora, fauna and geological or physiographical features of special interest;

(c) any proposal relating to any functions of the Agency—

    (i) to have regard to the desirability of protecting and conserving buildings, sites and objects of archaeological, architectural, engineering or historic interest;

    (ii) to take into account any effect which the proposals would have on the beauty or amenity of any rural or urban area or on any such flora, fauna, features, buildings, sites or objects; and

    (iii) to have regard to any effect which the proposals would have on the economic and social well-being of local communities in rural areas.

(2) Subject to subsection (1) above, it shall be the duty of each of the Ministers and of the Agency, in formulating or considering any proposals relating to any functions of the Agency—

(a) to have regard to the desirability of preserving for the public any freedom of access to areas of woodland, mountains, moor, heath, down, cliff or foreshore and other places of natural beauty;

(b) to have regard to the desirability of maintaining the availability to the public of any facility for visiting or inspecting any building, site or object of archaeological, architectural, engineering or historic interest; and

(c) to take into account any effect which the proposals would have on any such freedom of access or on the availability of any such facility.

(3) Subsections (1) and (2) above shall apply so as to impose duties on the Agency in relation to—

(a) any proposals relating to the functions of a water undertaker or sewerage undertaker,

(b) any proposals relating to the management, by the company holding an appointment as such an undertaker, of any land for the time being held by that company for any purpose whatever (whether or not connected with the carrying out of the functions of a water undertaker or sewerage undertaker), and

(c) any proposal which by virtue of section 156(7) of the Water Industry Act 1991 (disposals of protected land) falls to be treated for the purposes of section 3 of that Act as a proposal relating to the functions of a water undertaker or sewerage undertaker,

as they apply in relation to proposals relating to the Agency's own functions, other than its pollution control functions.

(4) Subject to obtaining the consent of any navigation authority, harbour authority or conservancy authority before doing anything which causes obstruction of, or other interference with, navigation which is subject to the control of that authority, it shall be the duty of the Agency to take such steps as are—

(a) reasonably practicable, and

(b) consistent with the purposes of the enactments relating to the functions of the Agency,

for securing, so long as the Agency has rights to the use of water or land associated with water, that those rights are exercised so as to ensure that the water or land is made available for recreational purposes and is so made available in the best manner.

(5) It shall be the duty of the Agency, in determining what steps to take in performance of any duty imposed by virtue of subsection (4) above, to take into account the needs of persons who are chronically sick or disabled.

(6) Nothing in this section, the following provisions of this Act or the 1991 Act shall require recreational facilities made available by the Agency to be made available free of charge.

(7) In this section—

"building" includes structure;

"pollution control functions", in relation to the Agency, has the same meaning as in section 5 above.

DEFINITIONS

"Agency, the": s.124(1).
"building": subs. (7).
"conservancy authority": s.56(1).
"functions": s.124(1).
"harbour authority": s.56(1).
"Ministers, the": s.56(1).
"navigation authority": s.56(1).
"pollution control functions": subs. (7) and s.5(5).

COMMENCEMENT

July 28, 1995 (S.I. 1995 No. 1983).

GENERAL NOTE

This section falls into two halves. Subsections (1)–(3) impose duties on the Agency and the Ministers concerned in relation to certain policy functions, and subss. (4)–(6) impose a duty on the Agency in relation to public recreational access to water.

Subss. (1)–(3): Consideration of proposals

These subsections impose on the Agency, the Secretary of State and the Minister of Agriculture, Fisheries and Food duties in relation specifically to their functions of formulating or considering proposals relating to the functions of the Agency.

Background. The duties in this section are closely aligned to the duties which sewerage undertakers have by virtue of s.3 of the Water Industry Act 1991, and are modelled, in modified form, on the duties imposed on the NRA and the same Ministers by s.16 of the Water Resources Act 1991 (c. 57) (which these provisions replace). Those s.16 duties were in turn modelled on those previously imposed on water authorities by the Water Act 1973 (c. 37) and the Wildlife and Countryside Act 1981. It should be noted, however, that the duties do not apply solely to the Agency's water functions but to all of its functions which meet the description of formulating or considering proposals.

There are four main differences between this section and its Water Resources Act 1991 predecessor, other than the fact that references to the Agency replace references to the NRA. The first arises under subss. (1)(a) and (b). The former subs. 16(1)(a) of the 1991 Act imposed a duty on the Ministers and the NRA (subject to consistency with other enactments relating to NRA functions and, in the case of the Secretary of State, his duties under s.2 of the Water Industry Act 1991), to exercise any power conferred on them with respect to the proposals so as to further the conservation and enhancement of natural beauty and the conservation of flora, fauna and geological or physiographical features of special interest. This duty now exists only where the proposals concern the Agency's non-pollution control functions: see subs. (1)(a). Where the proposals concern the Agency's pollution control functions, the weaker duty to "have regard to the desirability of" such conservation and enhancement applies: see subs. (1)(b).

The original draft Environment Agencies Bill (October 1994) contained the weaker, subs. (1)(b) duty for all Agency functions. The *Financial Times* commented, on November 19, 1994, that environmental groups were "universal in their condemnation" of what they saw as a weakening of the Agency's duty compared to the NRA's duty. In November 1994, the Secretary of State announced that the Bill had been amended to apply the stronger duty in relation to the Agency's non-pollution control functions: DoE News Release 650. The fact that the weaker duty applies in relation to its pollution control functions apparently reflects the Government's view that it is conceptually flawed for a regulatory body on the one hand to have duties in relation to the licensing or authorisation of polluting activities (as the Agency does, in relation both to IPC and discharge to controlled waters), which will inevitably in some cases adversely affect environmental and recreational conservation and enhancement which, on the other hand, it has a duty to further. See, for example, H.C. Standing Committee B, Sixth Sitting, May 11, 1995, cols. 196–198 *per* Mr Robert Atkins, Minister for the Environment and Countryside; *Hansard*, H.L. Vol. 560, cols. 805–806, *per* Viscount Ullswater, Minister of State, Department of the Environment. It might with some justification be argued, however, that the qualifications applied by subs. (1)(a)(i) and (iii) would be adequate to reconcile this perceived conflict. To provide further comfort to those who remained concerned about the new formulation, the Government assured the Commons Standing Committee considering the Bill that "if the Agency failed against reasonable expectations to do what was right and reasonable to further conservation, we would not hesitate to use our powers to ensure that it did more": H.C. Standing Committee B, Ninth Sitting, May 18, 1995, col. 285 *per* Mr Robert Atkins, Minister for the Environment and Countryside. These powers would include in particular the power to give directions to the Agency/SEPA under s.40 of the Act.

It will be noted that s.5 employs a distinction between pollution control and non-pollution control powers (as opposed to the broader term "functions" used here).

The second difference between this section and its Water Resources Act 1991 predecessor arises under subs. (1)(a). Whilst this subsection, as indicated above, contains a duty couched in similar terms to its s.16 predecessor, the duty is subject to two new qualifications: see subss. (1)(a)(ii) and (iii). These introduce a ministerial objective of achieving sustainable development, and make the Agency's duty subject to the guidance it receives under s.4 relating to its objectives and its principal aim of making an appropriate contribution to the attainment of sustainable development. Sustainable development is defined nowhere in the Act (or indeed in English law) but its meaning is considered in the draft of the s.4 guidance which is discussed in the note to s.4. Interestingly, the Scottish Office's draft guidance to SEPA does contain a definition of the term: see the General Note to s.31 at p. 25–87.

The third difference between this section and its predecessor arises in connection with the duty provided for by subs. (1)(c)(i). This duty equates to that in s.16(1)(b) of the Water Resources Act 1991, save that the word "engineering" has been inserted (see the note to s.32(1)(b) at p. 25–91 as regards the introduction of this term in relation to SEPA's equivalent duty), creating a duty to have regard, in formulating or considering proposals relating to any Agency functions, to the desirability of protecting and conserving buildings, sites and objects of engineering interest.

Subsection (1)(c)(iii) provides the fourth difference between this section and its predecessor. This creates a new duty to have regard, in relation to any such proposals, to any effect which they would have on the economic and social well-being of local communities in rural areas. This duty is significantly different from the equivalent duty imposed by s.32(1)(d) on SEPA and the Secretary of State in relation to Scotland (see note on p. 25–91).

It should be noted that in s.7(1)(c)(ii) and (iii) and in s.7(2)(c) the phrase "effect which the proposal would have" (as opposed to "might have") is used. This suggests that a degree of certainty that the effect would follow is necessary in order for any duty to have regard to it or take it into account to exist.

Examples of functions in relation to the formulation or consideration of proposals are provided by the functions of the Agency, Secretary of State and Minister arising under s.2 of the Water Resources Act 1991 in relation to the proposals for the revocation or variation of water abstraction or impoundment licences. Another example is provided by their s.82(4) of the Water Resources Act 1991 functions in relation to the proposals for the establishment of statutory water quality objectives.

However, the key term "proposals" is undefined both in the 1995 Act and the 1991 Act. Thus, insofar as the Agency's role as statutory consultee, for example in relation to "special site" designation (s.78C(3) Environmental Protection Act 1990, inserted by s.57 of the 1995 Act), the national air quality strategy (s.80(6)(a) of the 1995 Act) or national waste strategy (s.92(1), inserting s.44A(5)(a) into the 1990 Act), can be construed as involving the consideration of proposals, then the duties in this section would appear to apply to such deliberations.

Similarly, the Secretary of State's role in formulating those proposals, or indeed in preparing consultation papers, and the Agency's role in considering licence applications, could be argued to fall within this section. Indeed, that a wide reading of the term "proposals" was intended by the Government might be inferred from the remarks at the Bill's Second Reading in the Commons by the Minister for the Environment and Countryside, Mr Robert Atkins: "Clause 7 [s.7] provides a specific duty on the agency to take account of conservation in exercising its function under integrated pollution control, for example, and waste management licensing for the first time. ... Although the conservation considerations are.... relevant to the issue of water discharge consents, they do not override all other considerations": *Hansard*, H.C. Vol. 258, col. 117.

The duties in subs. (1) are expressed by subs. (2) to take priority over the duties in subs. (2). The latter duties are worded identically to those imposed on the Ministers and the NRA by s.16(2) of the 1991 Act.

Subss. (4)–(6): Recreational access to water

These subsections impose a duty on the Agency which is qualified by requirements of reasonable practicability and consistency with certain other enactments, and is subject to obtaining the consent of the appropriate authority where navigation will be interfered with or obstructed. The duty (which closely parallels that imposed on water and sewerage undertakers by s.3(5) of the Water Industry Act 1991) is to ensure that water, or land associated with water, over which the Agency has rights of use, are made available in the best manner for recreational purposes (subs. (4)), taking into account the needs of chronically sick or disabled people (subs. (5)), but not necessarily free of charge (subs. (6)). The word "best" is potentially a very strong requirement, but it is qualified by the notion of reasonable practicability. As regards the term "chronically sick or disabled", note the related duty in relation to the recreational use of inland and coastal waters imposed by s.6(1), and for a discussion of the implications of its parallel provision regarding chronically sick and disabled people, see the General Note to s.6 at p. 25–45.

In formulating or considering proposals relating to Agency functions, the Ministers and the Agency must (subject to certain qualifications) act so as to further, or have regard to the desirability of, or take account of any effect on, specified environmental or recreational matters.

Environmental duties with respect to sites of special interest

8.—(1) Where the Nature Conservancy Council for England or the Countryside Council for Wales is of the opinion that any area of land in England or, as the case may be, in Wales—

    (a) is of special interest by reason of its flora, fauna or geological or physiographical features, and

    (b) may at any time be affected by schemes, works, operations or activities of the Agency or by an authorisation given by the Agency,

that Council shall notify the fact that the land is of special interest for that reason to the Agency.

(2) Where a National Park authority or the Broads Authority is of the opinion that any area of land in a National Park or in the Broads—

(a) is land in relation to which the matters for the purposes of which sections 6(1) and 7 above (other than section 7(1)(c)(iii) above) have effect are of particular importance, and

(b) may at any time be affected by schemes, works, operations or activities of the Agency or by an authorisation given by the Agency,

the National Park authority or Broads Authority shall notify the Agency of the fact that the land is such land, and of the reasons why those matters are of particular importance in relation to the land.

(3) Where the Agency has received a notification under subsection (1) or (2) above with respect to any land, it shall consult the notifying body before carrying out or authorising any works, operations or activities which appear to the Agency to be likely—

(a) to destroy or damage any of the flora, fauna, or geological or physiographical features by reason of which the land is of special interest; or

(b) significantly to prejudice anything the importance of which is one of the reasons why the matters mentioned in subsection (2) above are of particular importance in relation to that land.

(4) Subsection (3) above shall not apply in relation to anything done in an emergency where particulars of what is done and of the emergency are notified to the Nature Conservancy Council for England, the Countryside Council for Wales, the National Park authority in question or, as the case may be, the Broads Authority as soon as practicable after that thing is done.

(5) In this section—

"authorisation" includes any consent or licence;

"the Broads" has the same meaning as in the Norfolk and Suffolk, Broads Act 1988; and

"National Park authority", subject to subsection (6) below, means a National Park authority established under section 63 below which has become the local planning authority for the National Park in question.

(6) As respects any period before a National Park authority established under section 63 below in relation to a National Park becomes the local planning authority for that National Park, any reference in subsections (1) to (4) above to a National Park authority shall be taken as a reference to the National Park Committee or joint or special planning board for that National Park.

DEFINITIONS

"Agency, the": s.124(1).
"authorisation": subs. (5).
"Broads, the": subs. (5).
"National Park authority": subss. (5) and (6) and s.63(1).

COMMENCEMENT

April 1, 1996 (S.I. 1996 No. 186).

GENERAL NOTE

This section confers on the Agency duties modelled on those originally conferred upon the NRA by s.17 of the Water Resources Act 1991, which it replaces. It adds to the general environmental and recreational duties imposed on the Agency by ss.6(1) and 7 the extra requirement, where land falls into the categories identified in subss. (1)(a) and (2)(a), to consult with specified bodies (except in emergency: see subs. (4)) before undertaking or authorising potentially damaging operations and works: see subs. (3). As to the Government's view of what might constitute an "emergency", the commentary at p. 25–95 on the equivalent provision for Scotland (s.35), should be noted.

However, s.7(1)(c)(iii), unlike the rest of ss.6(1) and 7, is an entirely new Agency duty, not transferred to it in identical or modified form from the NRA. It relates to economic and social well-being rather than to environmental or recreational matters. It is thus expressly excluded from the scope of s.8(2)(a).

Transitional provision is made by subs. (6) for the period prior to the establishment of a National Park authority: until then the relevant, predecessing local planning authority is the notifier and consultee in its stead.

Codes of practice with respect to environmental and recreational duties

9.—(1) Each of the Ministers shall have power by order to approve any code of practice issued (whether by him or by another person) for the purpose of—

(a) giving practical guidance to the Agency with respect to any of the matters for the purposes of which sections 6(1), 7 and 8 above have effect, and

(b) promoting what appear to him to be desirable practices by the Agency with respect to those matters,

and may at any time by such an order approve a modification of such a code or withdraw his approval of such a code or modification.

(2) In discharging its duties under section 6(1), 7 or 8 above, the Agency shall have regard to any code of practice, and any modifications of a code of practice, for the time being approved under this section.

(3) Neither of the Ministers shall make an order under this section unless he has first consulted—

(a) the Agency;

(b) the Countryside Commission, the Nature Conservancy Council for England and the Countryside Council for Wales;

(c) the Historic Buildings and Monuments Commission for England;

(d) the Sports Council and the Sports Council for Wales; and

(e) such other persons as he considers it appropriate to consult.

(4) The power of each of the Ministers to make an order under this section shall be exercisable by statutory instrument; and any statutory instrument containing such an order shall be subject to annulment in pursuance of a resolution of either House of Parliament.

DEFINITIONS
"Agency, the": s.124(1).
"Ministers, the": s.56(1).
"modification": s.124(1).

COMMENCEMENT
July 28, 1995 (S.I. 1995 No. 1983).

GENERAL NOTE
This section parallels s.18 of the Water Resources Act 1991, which it replaces. It gives to each of the Secretary of State and the Minister of Agriculture, Fisheries and Food the power to give and withdraw, by statutory instrument (subs. (4)), statutory approval of any code of practice which promotes desirable Agency practices in relation to specified environmental or recreational functions: see subs. (1). Codes of practice which are approved under this section provide a mechanism for translating the Agency's general environmental and recreational duties into more specific requirements. Under its predecessor section of the 1991 Act, only one code of practice was approved, by the Water and Sewerage (Conservation, Access and Recreation) (Code of Practice) Order 1989 (S.I. 1989 No. 1152). Since the NRA's functions have been transferred to the Agency, this Code is applicable to the Agency's exercise of the relevant functions.

The Code states that the functions of the NRA and internal drainage boards and their management of their resources can affect in many ways the conservation of the environment, the preservation of public access to the countryside, and the provision of facilities for sport and other forms of recreation. In the process there are bound to be conflicting environmental, operational and recreational considerations which can rarely be reconciled by decisions taken solely in relation to individual projects. Consistent, cost-effective reconciliation is likely to be achieved through the preparation of land use and management plans, particularly for sites which are likely to be subject to competing uses and pressures. In carrying out these functions the NRA should ensure that channels for liaison and consultation with appropriate organisations and individuals are established and open at all times so that action can proceed speedily in appropriate cases. In relation to the NRA's functions of issuing abstraction and discharge licences, the Code advises that where it proposes granting licences for abstraction which would affect a site of special scientific interest, a scheduled ancient monument or a site of importance for conservation, it should consult the appropriate conservation bodies. Similarly, the NRA should be alert to circumstances in which steps to upgrade standards of effluent quality are required to avoid impact on sites of scientific interest, or other sites of importance to conservation. In particular where an SSSI is sustaining damage as a consequence of nutrient enrichment, to which sewage disposal is making a significant contribution, it should consider suitable remedial action.

Subs. (2): Status of approved codes
The requirement in subs. (2) is new. Section 18 of the 1991 Act expressly provided that breach of a code which was approved under it did not of itself constitute a contravention of any of the conservation duties now found, as regards the Agency, in ss.6(1), 7 and 8. The new position is that, in carrying out those duties, the Agency must "have regard to" such an approved code (see the General Introduction to this Part of the Act for a discussion of this term, at p. 25–20). The 1991 Act provisions also stated that breach of such a code would not have given rise to any civil or criminal liability on the part of the NRA, but this protection has been removed, and no comparable provision appears in relation to the Agency anywhere in the Act. In principle, therefore, an action for breach of statutory duty could, if the general criteria for such an action were met, be brought against the Agency as a result of a failure on its part to have regard to the code, although a breach of the code would not of itself amount to a breach of statutory duty.

Subs. (3): Consultation
The Ministers must consult a number of bodies, including the Agency, before making an order under this section. In what is now subs. (3)(e), specific reference to consultation of sewerage and water undertakers has been removed. This latter change does not appear to be significant in practice: such undertakers may still, of course, be considered appropriate to consult and could before have been considered inappropriate to consult notwithstanding the specific reference to them.

Incidental functions of the Agency

10.—(1) This section has effect—
(a) for the purposes of section 37(1) below, as it applies in relation to the Agency; and
(b) for the construction of any other enactment which, by reference to the functions of the Agency, confers any power on or in relation to the Agency;
and any reference in this section to "the relevant purposes" is a reference to the purposes described in paragraphs (a) and (b) above.
(2) For the relevant purposes, the functions of the Agency shall be taken to include the protection against pollution of—
(a) any waters, whether on the surface or underground, which belong to the Agency or any water undertaker or from which the Agency or any water undertaker is authorised to take water;
(b) without prejudice to paragraph (a) above, any reservoir which belongs to or is operated by the Agency or any water undertaker or which the Agency or any water undertaker is proposing to acquire or construct for the purpose of being so operated; and
(c) any underground strata from which the Agency or any water undertaker is for the time being authorised to abstract water in pursuance of a licence under Chapter II of Part II of the 1991 Act (abstraction and impounding).
(3) For the relevant purposes, the functions of the Agency shall be taken to include joining with or acting on behalf of one or more relevant undertakers for the purpose of carrying out any works or acquiring any land which at least one of the undertakers with which it joins, or on whose behalf it acts, is authorised to carry out or acquire for the purposes of—
(a) any function of that undertaker under any enactment; or

(b) any function which is taken to be a function of that undertaker for the purposes to which section 217 of the Water Industry Act 1991 applies.

(4) For the relevant purposes, the functions of the Agency shall be taken to include the provision of supplies of water in bulk, whether or not such supplies are provided for the purposes of, or in connection with, the carrying out of any other function of the Agency.

(5) For the relevant purposes, the functions of the Agency shall be taken to include the provision of houses and other buildings for the use of persons employed by the Agency and the provision of recreation grounds for persons so employed.

(6) In this section—

"relevant undertaker" means a water undertaker or sewerage undertaker; and

"supply of water in bulk" means a supply of water for distribution by a water undertaker taking the supply.

DEFINITIONS
"1991 Act, the": s.56(1).
"Agency, the": s.124(1).
"functions": s.124(1).
"relevant purposes": subs. (1).
"relevant undertaker": subs. (6).
"supply of water in bulk": subs. (6).

COMMENCEMENT
April 1, 1996 (S.I. 1996 No. 186).

GENERAL NOTE
This section confers upon the Agency incidental functions which are modelled on those conferred on the National Rivers Authority by s.3 of the Water Resources Act 1991, which it replaces. The Agency's functions, conferred on it by statute, include powers and duties to act in certain ways. A number of statutory provisions confer additional powers to facilitate the Agency's carrying out of these functions. As a residual provision, s.37(1) of the Act confers on the Agency very widely worded incidental general powers, including the power to do anything which in its opinion will facilitate the carrying out of its functions.

This section extends the range of functions for the purposes of which the Agency may exercise those powers, to include the functions listed in subss. (2)–(5). Because of their origin in the 1991 Act, the functions primarily relate to water: they are the protection against pollution of certain waters, reservoirs and underground strata, (subs. (2)), the carrying out of works with or on behalf of water or sewerage undertakers (subs. (3)), the provision of supplies of water in bulk (subs. (4)), and the provision of housing and recreation grounds for Agency employees (subs. (5)). These functions correspond to those in subss. (2), (4), (5) and (6) respectively of s.3 of the 1991 Act. Section 3(3) of the 1991 Act, which conferred the function of furthering research into matters relating to the functions of the NRA or of water or sewerage undertakers, will not apply to the Agency as it does not appear in this section.

As an example of the effect of this section, subs. (5) provides that the functions of the Agency shall be taken to include the provision of housing for Agency employees: this allows the s.37(1)(b) power to acquire land to be exercised for that purpose.

Advisory committees

Advisory committee for Wales

11.—(1) The Secretary of State shall establish and maintain a committee for advising him with respect to matters affecting, or otherwise connected with, the carrying out in Wales of the Agency's functions.

(2) The committee shall consist of such persons as may from time to time be appointed by the Secretary of State.

(3) The committee shall meet at least once a year.

(4) The Secretary of State may pay to the members of the committee such sums by way of reimbursement (whether in whole or in part) for loss of remuneration, for travelling expenses and for other out-of-pocket expenses as he may determine.

DEFINITIONS
"Agency, the": s.124(1).
"functions": s.124(1).

COMMENCEMENT
April 1, 1996 (S.I. 1996 No. 186).

GENERAL NOTE
This section provides for an advisory committee to meet at least once a year (subs. (3)) and advise the Secretary of State on the carrying out in Wales of the Agency's functions. Reference in this section to the Secretary of State is to the Secretary of State for Wales. This Committee should be distinguished from the Environmental Protection Advisory Committee for Wales, established under s.12, which advises the Agency rather than the Secretary of State.

Background
The committee established by this section is to carry out a similar role to that previously carried out in relation to the NRA's functions in Wales by a committee under s.6 of the 1991 Act, which this section replaces. As the Environment Bill passed through Parliament, the argument that there should be a separate Agency for Wales, as there is for Scotland, was raised on more than one occasion. In the debate in the House of Lords on an amendment to this effect tabled by Lord Prys-Davies (*Hansard*, H.L. Vol. 560, cols. 585–605), two former Secretaries of State for Wales, Lord Cledwyn of Penthos and Lord Crickhowell, disagreed on the question. The former argued that a separate Welsh Agency could be combined sensibly with the Countryside Council for Wales and that environmental protection in Wales is "the duty and privilege of the Welsh people and, therefore, of a Welsh agency."

Lord Crickhowell opposed the amendment primarily on two grounds. First, that "the rivers of Wales do not, as they do on the whole rather conveniently in the Scottish context, flow along and apart from the national boundary. They happen to cross the boundary" (*Hansard*, H.L. Vol. 560, col. 592). Therefore integrated management, in his view, required one Agency. Secondly, to duplicate the specialist skill and expertise developed by the NRA and other constituent elements of the Agency "would be a shocking waste of resources" (*ibid.*, col. 593).

In the same debate, Viscount Ullswater, Minister of State, Department of the Environment, set the committee envisaged by this section into the context of other provisions. He indicated that the Secretary of State for Wales

"... will be responsible for setting the policy framework within which the Environment Agency will discharge its functions in Wales and the Agency will report to him on its operations in Wales. There will also be arrangements for Welsh Office Ministers to have an input into the policy and the corporate planning processes of the agency, and these will be defined in a memorandum of understanding between the agency and the Welsh Office. My noble friend will be responsible also for the appointment of one member to the agency board [the first appointee was Professor Ronald Edwards: see the General Note to s.1 at p. 25–25] and the Welsh interests will be further protected by the existence of the Advisory Committee for Wales. [*i.e.* the Committee established by this section.] That committee will advise my right honourable friend on the issues relating to the agency's activities in the principality and inform his input into the agency's corporate planning process.

There will be an environment protection advisory committee for the Welsh region [see s.12(6) below] which will advise the agency itself on the specific needs of Wales and matters of particular relevance to its operations in Wales. The chairman of that committee will be appointed by my right honourable friend the Secretary of State for Wales, he will also approve the membership scheme prepared by the agency for its Welsh region and in doing so will ensure that its composition reflects a representative balance of interests [see s.12(2)]. The NRA was set up on an England and Wales basis and the arrangements for the authority to take the needs of Wales fully into account have been very successful" (*ibid.*, col. 603).

Viscount Ullswater could have added that by s.13(5) there is to be a regional fisheries advisory committee for a region consisting wholly or mainly of, or of most of, Wales.

Environment protection advisory committees

12.—(1) It shall be the duty of the Agency—

(a) to establish and maintain advisory committees, to be known as Environment Protection Advisory Committees, for the different regions of England and Wales;

(b) to consult the advisory committee for any region as to any proposals of the Agency relating generally to the manner in which the Agency carries out its functions in that region; and

(c) to consider any representations made to it by the advisory committee for any region (whether in response to consultation under paragraph (b) above or otherwise) as to the manner in which the Agency carries out its functions in that region.

(2) The advisory committee for any region shall consist of—

(a) a chairman appointed by the Secretary of State; and

(b) such other members as the Agency may appoint in accordance with the provisions of the approved membership scheme for that region.

(3) In appointing the chairman of any advisory committee, the Secretary of State shall have regard to the desirability of appointing a person who has experience of, and has shown capacity in, some matter relevant to the functions of the committee.

(4) The members of advisory committees appointed by virtue of subsection (2)(b) above—

(a) must not be members of the Agency; but

(b) must be persons who appear to the Agency to have a significant interest in matters likely to be affected by the manner in which the Agency carries out any of its functions in the region of the advisory committee in question.

(5) The duty imposed by subsection (1)(a) above to establish and maintain advisory committees is a duty to establish and maintain an advisory committee for each area which the Agency considers it appropriate for the time being to regard as a region of England and Wales for the purposes of this section.

(6) It shall be the duty of the Agency, in determining the regions for which advisory committees are established and maintained under this section, to ensure that one of those regions consists wholly or mainly of, or of most of, Wales.

(7) For the purposes of this section, functions of the Agency which are carried out in any area of Scotland, or of the territorial sea, which is adjacent to any region for which an advisory committee is maintained, shall be regarded as carried out in that region.

(8) Schedule 3 to this Act shall have effect with respect to advisory committees.

(9) In this section—

"advisory committee" means an advisory committee under this section;

"approved membership scheme" means a scheme, as in force for the time being, prepared by the Agency and approved (with or without modification) by the Secretary of State under Schedule 3 to this Act which makes provision with respect to the membership of the advisory committee for a region.

DEFINITIONS

"advisory committee": subs. (9).

"Agency, the": s.124(1).

"approved membership scheme": subs. (9).
"functions": s.124(1).

COMMENCEMENT
July 28, 1995 (S.I. 1995 No. 1983).

GENERAL NOTE
This section provides for the establishment of regional Environment Protection Advisory Committees (EPACs) to advise the Agency on the exercise of its functions, and gives effect to Sched. 3 which makes provision in relation to such EPACs. It is closely modelled on existing provisions in s.7 of the Water Resources Act 1991 (which this section replaces) for regional rivers advisory committees to advise the NRA on the exercise of its functions in the various regions, but the EPACs will advise in relation to all Agency functions. Waste regulation authorities, which prior to the advent of the Agency have been local authorities, were advised by non-statutory regional advisory bodies such as the South East Waste Regulation Advisory Committee. There has been no such arrangement on a regional basis, statutory or otherwise, in relation to the exercise by HMIP of its functions.

Subss. (1)–(2): EPACs
EPACs are to be established and consulted by the Agency, and any representations made to the Agency by an EPAC in relation to the exercise of the Agency's functions in the region in question must be considered by the Agency (subs. (1)). However, unlike the previous provisions in s.7 of the 1991 Act, under which the NRA had sole discretion over the appointment of a committee's members and chairman, the Secretary of State appoints the chairman in accordance with subs. (3), and the Agency's scheme for appointing the other members requires the Secretary of State's approval. It may be noted that the proposals put to EPACs by the Agency would appear to be proposals to which the duties in s.7 apply.

Subss. (3) and (4): Committee Members
No member of the Agency may also be a member of an EPAC. Members must appear to the Agency to have a significant interest in the relevant matters (in s.7 of the 1991 Act the element of significance was absent), and the Secretary of State must have regard, in appointing the chairman, to the desirability of his having experience and capacity in such matters.

Subss. (5) and (6): Regions
The Agency must appoint an EPAC for each area which it considers to be a region, and one such region must consist wholly or mainly of Wales, or be most of Wales. Viscount Ullswater's description in Parliament of the specific provisions for Wales, such as subs. (6), is quoted in the General Note to s.11. In particular, for the Wales EPAC, references in subss. (2) and (3) to the Secretary of State are references to the Secretary of State for Wales.

Schedule 3
Paragraph 2 of Sched. 3 makes it the duty of the Agency to prepare a Membership Scheme for each region and submit it to the Secretary of State for approval: each such scheme must identify bodies and persons with a significant interest in the Agency's functions and activities in the region in question, and must provide for the EPAC to reflect those interests. The Government has indicated that "experience of business will be an important contribution for the Agency to take into account" (Advisory Committee on Business and the Environment (ACBE), Fifth Progress Report (July 1995)).
Paragraph 3 requires the Agency to publish its proposed scheme when it is submitted to the Secretary of State for approval, so that people may make representations to the Secretary of State. The Agency must also submit a statement of the Agency's justification of the scheme and supporting evidence; however, it need not publish these. The Secretary of State may approve the scheme, reject it or approve it in modified form: para. 3(4). When the scheme is approved, the Agency must publicise it to the interested parties: para. 3(5). The Agency may (and, if so directed, must) vary the scheme in accordance with the same procedures as apply to the original preparation of a scheme: para. 4. Before actually appointing a member, the Agency must consult at least the bodies and persons identified in the scheme under para. 2(2) as having a significant interest: para. 5. Provision is made for EPAC proceedings to be valid notwithstanding a number

of specified problems (para. 6), and for remuneration of various kinds to the chairman and members of an EPAC (para. 7).

Regional and local fisheries advisory committees

13.—(1) It shall be the duty of the Agency—

(a) to establish and maintain advisory committees of persons who are not members of the Agency but appear to it to be interested in salmon fisheries, trout fisheries, freshwater fisheries or eel fisheries in the different parts of the controlled area; and

(b) to consult those committees as to the manner in which the Agency is to perform its duty under section 6(6) above.

(2) If the Agency, with the consent of the Ministers, so determines, it shall also be under a duty to consult those committees, or such of them as may be specified or described in the determination, as to—

(a) the manner in which it is to perform its duties under or by virtue of such of the enactments relating to recreation, conservation or navigation as may be the subject of the determination, or

(b) such matters relating to recreation, conservation or navigation as may be the subject of the determination.

(3) Where, by virtue of subsection (2) above, the Agency is under a duty to consult those committees or any of them, there may be included among the members of the committees in question persons who are not members of the Agency but who appear to it to be interested in matters—

(a) likely to be affected by the manner in which it performs the duties to which the determination in question relates, or

(b) which are the subject of the determination,

if the Ministers consent to the inclusion of persons of that description.

(4) The duty to establish and maintain advisory committees imposed by subsection (1) above is a duty to establish and maintain—

(a) a regional advisory committee for each such region of the controlled area as the Agency considers it appropriate for the time being to regard as a region of that area for the purposes of this section; and

(b) such local advisory committees as the Agency considers necessary to represent—

(i) the interests referred to in subsection (1)(a) above, and

(ii) where persons may be appointed members of those committees by virtue of subsection (3) above by reference to any such interests as are mentioned in that subsection, the interests in question,

in the different parts of each such region.

(5) It shall be the duty of the Agency in determining the regions for which regional advisory committees are established and maintained under this section to ensure that one of those regions consists (apart from territorial waters) wholly or mainly of, or of most of, Wales.

(6) In addition to any members appointed under the foregoing provisions of this section, there shall, in the case of each regional advisory committee established and maintained under this section, also be a chairman appointed—

(a) by the Secretary of State, in the case of the committee established and maintained for the region described in subsection (5) above; or

(b) by the Minister, in any other case.

(7) There shall be paid by the Agency—

(a) to the chairman of any regional or local advisory committee established and maintained under this section such remuneration and such travelling and other allowances; and

(b) to any other members of that committee such sums by way of reimbursement (whether in whole or in part) for loss of remuneration, for travelling expenses or for any other out-of-pocket expenses, as may be determined by one of the Ministers.

(8) In this section "the controlled area" means the area specified in section 6(7) above in respect of which the Agency carries out functions under section 6(6) above and Part V of the 1991 Act.

DEFINITIONS
"Agency, the": s.124(1).
"controlled area": subs. (8).
"Minister, the": s.56(1).
"Ministers, the": s.56(1).

COMMENCEMENT
April 1, 1996 (S.I. 1996 No. 186).

GENERAL NOTE
This section requires the Agency to establish and consult regional (and where considered necessary, local, see subs. (4)(b)) fisheries advisory committees. The section is modelled on s.8 of the Water Resources Act 1991 which established such committees for the NRA, but modifies those provisions in three ways. First, the duty is to consult regional and local (*i.e.* sub-regional) committees not only (as previously) in relation to the Agency's fisheries duties (subs. (1)(b)) but also, if it so determines and if the Ministers consent, in relation to the exercise of its recreation, conservation or navigation functions (subs. (2)). Secondly, the chairman of the Welsh committee is required by subs. (5) to be appointed by the Secretary of State for Wales, and the Minister of Agriculture, Fisheries and Food appoints the chairman of the other committees including, it would seem, local committees established in Wales (subs. (6)). Previously the chairman for every committee, like the members, had been an NRA appointee. And thirdly, remuneration of chairmen and members of the Committees, whilst still determined by the Ministers, no longer requires Treasury consent (s.7).

The functions of these committees, other than as consultees under subss. (1) and (2), are not precisely spelt out. In practice the predecessor committees established under s.8 of the 1991 Act often exercised considerable delegated powers, such as setting fishing licence charges and promoting bye-laws. Whether this will continue, and even (as a result of subs. (2)) be extended beyond fisheries matters to recreation, conservation or navigation matters, remains to be seen.

Subss. (2) and (3): Matters other than fisheries
The formal nature of the process by which the Agency may consult the committees on matters other than its exercise of its fisheries duties should be noted. The Agency must make a formal determination to consult, which the Ministers must both approve (subs. (2)). Although the Agency is under no duty to make a determination, once a determination is made, the Agency has a duty to consult in accordance with it. The determination must specify which of the committees which have been established are to be consulted, and on what (subs. (2)). Consultation with different committees on different matters does not appear to be ruled out, nor does the making of more than one concurrent determination relating to different committees or matters. The subject-matter of the determination, and therefore of the consultation, is not limited to the performance of the Agency's duties, but may include other matters (subs. (2)(b)). This appears to create the curious situation whereby the Agency may consult with fisheries committees more widely in relation to navigation, recreation or conservation than it can (under subs. (1)(b)) in relation to fisheries. The membership of committees which, by virtue of a determination, the Agency must consult on non-fisheries matters, may (but need not) include persons who are interested in those matters (subs. (3)). This contrasts with the requirement, in subs. (1)(a), that the committees must comprise persons interested in fisheries.

Subs. (5): Wales
The Agency's discretion to determine the areas which, for the purposes of this section, it considers appropriate for the time being to consider as a region (subs. (4)(a)) is constrained by subs. (5): one such region must consist (apart from territorial waters) wholly or mainly of, or of most of, Wales.

Flood defence committees

Regional flood defence committees

14.—(1) There shall be committees, known as regional flood defence committees, for the purpose of carrying out the functions which fall to be carried out by such committees by virtue of this Act and the 1991 Act.

(2) Subject to Schedule 4 to this Act (which makes provision for the alteration of the boundaries of and the amalgamation of the areas of regional flood defence committees)—

(a) there shall be a regional flood defence committee for each of the areas for which there was an old committee immediately before the transfer date; but

(b) where under section 165(2) or (3) of the 1991 Act any function of the Agency falls to be carried out at a place beyond the seaward boundaries of the area of any regional flood defence committee, that place shall be assumed for the purposes of this Act and the 1991 Act to be within the area of the regional flood defence committee to whose area the area of sea where that place is situated is adjacent.

(3) The Agency shall maintain a principal office for the area of each regional flood defence committee.

(4) In this section "old committee" means a regional flood defence committee for the purposes of section 9 of the 1991 Act.

DEFINITIONS
    "1991 Act, the": s.56(1).
    "Agency, the": s.124(1).
    "function": s.124(1).
    "old committee": subs. (9).
    "regional flood defence committee": subs. (1).

COMMENCEMENT
    April 1, 1996 (S.I. 1996 No. 186).

GENERAL NOTE

Flood defence and regional flood defence committees (ss.14–19)
    Sections 14 to 19, and Sched. 5, of this Act all deal with flood defence committees. Section 14 establishes regional flood defence committees, s.15 determines their composition and s.16 provides a mechanism for changing their composition. Section 14 also gives effect to Sched. 4, which makes provisions in relation to the boundaries of regional flood defence committees. Section 17 allows a regional flood defence committee to prepare and submit to the Agency a local flood defence scheme for any district within its region, establishing and determining the functions of a local flood defence committee for that district. Section 18 determines the composition of such local committees. Section 19 gives effect to Sched. 5, which makes provisions in relation to the membership and proceedings of both regional and local flood defence committees.
    The NRA's flood defence functions and its general supervision duty in relation to all matters relating to flood defence are all transferred to the Agency by this Act (by ss. 2(1)(iii) and 6(4)— see s.6(5) for the geographical extent of these functions and the General Note to s.2(1)(iii) for a summary of them). Section 106 of the Water Resources Act 1991 requires the Agency to arrange for all of its functions relating to flood defence under that Act and the Land Drainage Act 1991 to be carried out by regional flood defence committees. These committees have semi-autonomous powers and quasi-independent status from the Agency, but at the same time essentially act as its agent in carrying out its flood defence functions subject to its general supervision. The Agency may only go beyond its general supervisory relationship with such committees, and give them directions as to the carrying out of their functions, where their manner of operation appears to the Agency likely materially to affect its management of water for non-flood defence purposes (s.106(3) of the Water Resources Act 1991). A committee must comply with such a direction. Regional and local flood defence committees are thus very different from the various advisory committees provided for by ss.11–13 above, in that they are executive bodies. The provisions of ss.14–19 reflect this. In particular they give a significant role to local authorities, both in the determination of the composition of regional and local flood defence committees (ss.15(3)(b), 16(7), 18(4)(c) and 18(5)) and as consultees in the preparation of local flood defence schemes which create local flood defence committees (s.17(4)(a)). Also, Sched. 4 contains tight procedural safeguards on the amalgamation of regions.

Section 14: Regional flood defence committees
    The Water Resources Act 1991 provided (s.9(1)) that there would continue to be the regional flood defence committees which were established under previous legislation. This section takes a different approach: on the transfer date which the Secretary of State will determine by order,

new regional flood defence committees are to replace the existing ones (subs. (2)). Although Sched. 4 provides a procedure for the amalgamation of regions and the alteration of their boundaries, which is summarised in the General Note to s.19, below at p. 25–67, without such procedures being undertaken regions and boundaries are to be the same as was previously the case.

As before (s.9(2) of the 1991 Act), the area of a regional flood defence committee includes any place which is adjacent to it but is beyond its seaward boundaries, if the Agency has to exercise its functions under s.165(2) or (3) of the 1991 Act in that place. Section 165(2) and (3) of the 1991 Act give the Agency power to carry out drainage works for defence against sea or tidal water and to carry out works to secure an adequate outfall for a main river.

The requirement that the Agency shall maintain a principal office for each committee region is carried over from s.9(3) of the 1991 Act (subs. (3)).

Composition of regional flood defence committees

15.—(1) Subject to subsection (2) below, a regional flood defence committee shall consist of the following, none of whom shall be a member of the Agency, that is to say—

(a) a chairman and a number of other members appointed by the relevant Minister;

(b) two members appointed by the Agency;

(c) a number of members appointed by or on behalf of the constituent councils.

(2) Any person who immediately before the transfer date is, by virtue of his appointment—

(a) by a Minister of the Crown,

(b) by or on behalf of any council, or

(c) by the National Rivers Authority,

the chairman or a member of an old committee which, by virtue of section 14 above, is replaced by a new committee shall be treated, on and after that date, for the remainder of the period for which he would, under the terms of his appointment, have held office in relation to the old committee, as if he had been appointed as the chairman or, as the case may be, a member of the new committee, and on the same terms, by that Minister or, as the case may be, by or on behalf of that council or, in the case of a person appointed by the National Rivers Authority, by the Agency.

(3) Subject to section 16 below and to any order under Schedule 4 to this Act amalgamating the areas of any two or more regional flood defence committees—

(a) the total number of members of a new committee for any area shall be the same as the total number of members of the old committee for that area immediately before the transfer date;

(b) the number of members to be appointed to a new committee for any area by or on behalf of each of the constituent councils or, as the case may be, jointly by or on behalf of more than one of them shall be the same as the number of members of the old committee for that area which fell to be so appointed immediately before the transfer date.

(4) In any case where—

(a) the appointment of one or more members of a regional flood defence committee is (by virtue of subsection (3) above or an order under section 16(5) below), to be made jointly by more than one constituent council, and

(b) the councils by whom that appointment is to be made are unable to agree on an appointment,

the member or members in question shall be appointed by the relevant Minister on behalf of those councils.

(5) In appointing a person to be the chairman or a member of a regional flood defence committee under subsection (1)(a) or (c) or (4) above the rel-

evant Minister or, as the case may be, a constituent council shall have regard to the desirability of appointing a person who has experience of, and has shown capacity in, some matter relevant to the functions of the committee.

(6) The councils of every county, county borough, metropolitan district or London borough any part of which is in the area of a regional flood defence committee shall be the constituent councils for the regional flood defence committee for that area, and the Common Council of the City of London shall be a constituent council for the regional flood defence committee for any area which comprises any part of the City.

(7) In this section—

"old committee" has the same meaning as in section 14 above;

"new committee" means a regional flood defence committee established under section 14 above;

"the relevant Minister"—

(a) in relation to the regional flood defence committee for an area the whole or the greater part of which is in Wales, means the Secretary of State; and

(b) in relation to any other regional flood defence committee, means the Minister.

DEFINITIONS

"Agency, the": s.124(1).
"constitutional council": subs. (6).
"functions": s.124(1).
"Minister, the": s.56(1).
"new committee": subs. (7).
"old committee": subs. (7) and s.14(4).
"regional flood defence committee": s.14(1).
"relevant Minister": subs. (7).
"transfer date": s.56(1).

COMMENCEMENT

April 1, 1996 (S.I. 1996 No. 186).

GENERAL NOTE

This section determines the membership of the regional flood defence committees established under s.14. As a transitional arrangement, the members and chairman of each old committee are to be treated as being the members and chairman of its replacement committee, on the same terms, and as appointees of the same body or person, as before (subs. (2)). Subject to these transitional provisions, the Agency appoints two members (subs. (1)(b)). Each local authority in the region (see subs. (6)) appoints the same number of members (in some cases jointly with other local authorities) as it did before (subss. (1)(c) and (3)(b)). The Minister of Agriculture, Fisheries and Food (or in Wales, the Secretary of State) appoints the chairman, the balance of the members and any member whose appointment could not be agreed on by local authorities who were to have jointly appointed him (subss. (1)(a) and (4)). However, s.16 and Sched. 4 provide procedures, respectively, for altering the number of members of a committee and amalgamating two or more regions (with a possible consequent effect on the membership of the committee for the resulting region).

The Minister or Secretary of State, as the case may be, and the local authorities, must have regard, in making their appointments, to the desirability of appointing persons with relevant capacity and experience. The discretion (subs. (5)) which this allows them is considerable and identical to that granted by s.1(4) in relation to the appointment of members of the Agency itself. (See the General Note to that section at p. 25–25). Notably, subs. (5) does not place the Agency under the same duty with regard to its appointments to the committees.

Schedule 4

Section 14 gives effect to Sched. 4, which allows the Minister of Agriculture, Fisheries and Food (or in Wales, the Secretary of State) by order to alter the boundaries of any regional flood defence committee's area or to amalgamate two or more such areas. Where such a change is made, the order making it may (but need not) make supplemental, consequential and transitional provisions (para. 1(3)). Where the change is the amalgamation of regions, provision may (but again, need not) be made regarding the number of members of the committee for the amalgamated region and their appointors (para.1(4)). Such provisions are subject to the s.16(7) and (8) provisions that the number of local council appointees must exceed by one the number of other appointees but that individual local councils may have their right to appoint, or to solely appoint, members withdrawn. It appears that where no express provision is made regarding membership of the flood defence committee for an amalgamated region, the committees for the predecessor regions are themselves simply amalgamated.

Before making the order. Alteration or amalgamation must be by order made by the Minister (or, in Wales, the Secretary of State) by statutory instrument (para. 1(1)), after carrying out a process of consultation. The Minister must consult persons he considers it appropriate to consult (para. 2(1)); publish a notice stating his intention and its general effect (para. 2(2)); make a draft of the proposed order available both generally (para. 2(2)) and to every person considered to have relevant statutory functions (para. 2(3)); consider objections made within the time specified in the published notice and, if he thinks fit, holding a public inquiry (para. 3(1)); and modify the order, if he thinks fit, in the light of such objections and inquiry (para. 3(2)—note the restriction on modification in para. 3(3)).

Making the order. When the order is made, he must serve notice of that fact on any person who was entitled to receive notice of the original draft order, has duly objected to the draft order and has not withdrawn that objection (para. 4(1)). Any such person then has 28 days within which to object by notice to the order (para. 4(3)), and, if even one such objection is made and not withdrawn, then the order is subject to special Parliamentary procedure (para. 4(4)). If there is no such person, or if there is such a person and they do not object to the order in its final form, it has effect at the end of the 28 days (para. 4(2)).

Once the order is made. If an order is made without the special Parliamentary procedure being triggered then it can be annulled by a resolution of either House of Parliament (para. 4(4)). Notice that once the order has been made it must be published, after the 28-day period if such is necessary under para. 4(2), and must state if it is to be subject to special Parliamentary procedure (para. (5)). The validity of a Sched. 4 order may not be questioned in legal proceedings (para. 6(4)) unless it is questioned (by application to the High Court) within six weeks of such notice being published (para. 6(1)); on such application the order may be quashed either generally or in so far as it affects the applicant (para. 6(2)).

Change of composition of regional flood defence committee

16.—(1) The Agency may, in accordance with the following provisions of this section, from time to time make a determination varying the total number of members of a regional flood defence committee.

(2) The Agency shall submit any determination under subsection (1) above to the relevant Minister.

(3) For the purposes of this section—

  (a) the total number of members of a regional flood defence committee shall not be less than eleven; and

  (b) any determination by the Agency under subsection (1) above that a regional flood defence committee should consist of more than seventeen members shall be provisional and shall take effect only if the relevant Minister makes an order under subsection (4) below.

(4) If the Agency submits a provisional determination to the relevant Minister with respect to any regional flood defence committee and he considers that the committee should consist of more than seventeen members, he may by order made by statutory instrument—

  (a) confirm it; or

  (b) substitute for the number of members determined by the Agency some other number not less than seventeen.

(5) Subject to the following provisions of this section, whenever—

  (a) the total number of members of a regional flood defence committee is varied under this section, or

  (b) the relevant Minister considers it necessary or expedient to make an order under this subsection,

the relevant Minister shall by order made by statutory instrument specify the number of members to be appointed to the committee by each of the constituent councils.

(6) An order under subsection (5) above shall relate—

(a) where paragraph (a) of that subsection applies, to times after the coming into force of the variation; and

(b) where paragraph (b) of that subsection applies, to such times as are specified in the order.

(7) An order under subsection (5) above shall be so framed that the total number of members appointed under section 15(1)(a) and (b) above is one less than the number of those appointed by or on behalf of constituent councils.

(8) For the purpose of determining for the purposes of subsection (5) above the number of persons to be appointed to a regional flood defence committee by or on behalf of each constituent council, the relevant Minister—

(a) if he considers it to be inappropriate that that council should appoint a member of the committee, or

(b) if he considers that one or more members should be appointed jointly by that council and one or more other constituent councils,

may include provision to that effect in the order.

(9) In this section—

"member", in relation to a regional flood defence committee, includes the chairman of the committee;

"the relevant Minister" has the same meaning as in section 15 above.

DEFINITIONS
"Agency, the": s.124(1).
"constituent council": s.15(6).
"member": subs. (9).
"regional flood defence committee": s.14(1).
"relevant Minister": subs. (9) and s.15(7).

COMMENCEMENT
April 1, 1996 (S.I. 1996 No. 186).

GENERAL NOTE
This section, which is in all key respects identical to s.11 of the Water Resources Act 1991 which it replaces, provides first, a procedure for the Agency to vary the number of members of a regional flood defence committee; and second, a procedure for the relevant Minister (the Minister of Agriculture, Fisheries and Food or, in Wales, the Secretary of State), whether or not as a result of such a variation in the number of members, to vary the composition of such a committee.

The Agency may vary the number of members by making a determination to this effect and submitting it to the relevant minister (subss. (1) and (2)). The number of members must always be at least 11, and, if the determination would make the number of members more than 17, then it is provisional until the relevant Minister confirms or varies it by order made by statutory instrument (subss. (3) and (4)).

Since all members are appointed by someone, a change in the number of members requires provision to be made deciding the composition of the committee in terms of who is whose appointee. In such circumstances, or (in the absence of such a determination by the Agency) where the relevant Minister considers it necessary or expedient, the relevant Minister must make such provision by order made by statutory instrument (subs. (5)). In so doing, he may if appropriate remove an individual local authority's right to appoint, or to solely (as opposed to jointly) appoint, a committee member (subs. (8)), and he must ensure that local authority appointees outnumber by one the other members of the committee: (subs. (7)).

Local flood defence schemes and local flood defence committees

17.—(1) A scheme, known as a local flood defence scheme, may be made by the Agency, in accordance with the following provisions of this section—

(a) for the creation in the area of a regional flood defence committee of one or more districts, to be known as local flood defence districts; and

(b) for the constitution, membership, functions and procedure of a committee for each such district, to be known as the local flood defence committee for that district.

(2) Any local flood defence scheme which was made under the 1991 Act or continued in force by virtue of paragraph 14(1) of Schedule 2 to the Water Consolidation (Consequential Provisions) Act 1991 and which, immediately before the transfer date, is in force in relation to the area of a regional flood defence committee, shall on and after that date have effect, and may be amended or revoked, as if it were a local flood defence scheme made under this section in relation to that area; and, accordingly, subject to any such amendment or revocation—

(a) any local flood defence district created by that scheme and in being immediately before that date shall be treated, on and after that date, as a local flood defence district created by a scheme under this section in relation to the area of that regional flood defence committee; and

(b) any local flood defence committee created by that scheme for any such district and in being immediately before that date shall be treated, on and after that date, as the local flood defence committee for that district.

(3) A regional flood defence committee may at any time submit to the Agency—

(a) a local flood defence scheme for any part of their area for which there is then no such scheme in force; or

(b) a scheme varying a local flood defence scheme or revoking such a scheme and, if the committee think fit, replacing it with another such scheme;

and references in the following provisions of this section and in section 18 below to local flood defence schemes are references to schemes under either of paragraphs (a) and (b) above.

(4) Before submitting a scheme to the Agency under subsection (3) above, a regional flood defence committee shall consult—

(a) every local authority any part of whose area will fall within the area to which the scheme is proposed to relate; and

(b) such organisations representative of persons interested in flood defence (within the meaning of Part IV of the 1991 Act) or agriculture as the regional flood defence committee consider to be appropriate.

(5) It shall be the duty of the Agency to send any scheme submitted to it under subsection (3) above to one of the Ministers.

(6) A local flood defence scheme may define a local flood defence district—

(a) by reference to the districts which were local land drainage districts immediately before 1st September 1989;

(b) by reference to the area of the regional flood defence committee in which that district is situated;

(c) by reference to a map;

or partly by one of those means and partly by another or others.

(7) A local flood defence scheme may contain incidental, consequential and supplementary provisions.

(8) Either of the Ministers may approve a local flood defence scheme with or without modifications; and any scheme approved under this subsection shall come into force on a date fixed by the Minister approving it.

DEFINITIONS
  "1991 Act, the": s.56(1).
  "Agency, the": s.124(1).
  "local authority": s.56(1).

"local flood defence committee": subs. (1).
"local flood defence district": subs. (1).
"local flood defence scheme": subs. (1).
"Ministers, the": s.56(1).
"regional flood defence committee": s.14(1).
"transfer date": s.56(1).

COMMENCEMENT
April 1, 1996 (S.I. 1996 No. 186).

GENERAL NOTE
This section, which is closely modelled on s.12 of the Water Resources Act 1991 which it
replaces, provides for local flood defence committees for areas within regions, which are in
addition to the regional flood defence committees established under s.14 of this Act. The procedure is triggered by a regional flood defence committee submitting to the Agency under subs.
(3) a local flood defence scheme (or a proposed variation or revocation or replacement of such a
scheme) which (a) defines as a district an area within its region, by reference to one or more of
the criteria set out in subs. (6) (but apparently not otherwise); (b) establishes a local flood
defence committee for that district (subs. (1)(a)); and (c) establishes functions, constitution,
membership and procedure for that local flood defence committee (regarding which, the provisions of Sched. 5 in relation to membership and proceedings apply).

The regional flood defence committee must, before submitting such a scheme, consult local
authorities for the district in question and such organisations representing interested persons as
it considers appropriate (subs. (4)). On receiving the scheme, the Agency must send it to "one of
the Ministers" (subs. (5)) for approval and the fixing of a date for entry into force under subs. (8).
The term "one of the Ministers", used instead of the term "the relevant Minister" which is
employed elsewhere in ss.14–19, appears to give the Agency the option in England to send such a
scheme to the Secretary of State rather than to the Minister of Agriculture, Fisheries and Food
since "the Ministers" is a defined term including the Secretary of State.

Subsection (2) makes transitional provision under which any local flood defence district and
committee existing prior to the transfer date (April 1, 1996) is treated as a local flood defence
district and committee under this section.

Composition of local flood defence committees

18.—(1) Subject to subsections (2) and (3) below, a local flood defence
scheme shall provide that any local flood defence committee to which it
relates shall consist of not less than eleven and not more than fifteen
members.

(2) A regional flood defence committee may include in a local flood
defence scheme which they submit to the Agency a recommendation that a
committee to which the scheme relates should consist of a number of members greater than fifteen; and a scheme so submitted shall be taken to provide
for the number of members of a committee if it contains a recommendation
under this subsection relating to that committee.

(3) The power conferred on each of the Ministers by section 17(8) above
shall include power to direct that a committee to which a recommendation
under subsection (2) above relates shall consist either of the recommended
number of members or of some other number of members greater than
fifteen.

(4) A local flood defence committee shall consist of—

(a) a chairman appointed from among their own members by the regional
    flood defence committee;

(b) other members appointed by that committee; and

(c) members appointed, in accordance with and subject to the terms of the
    local flood defence scheme, by or on behalf of constituent councils.

(5) The number of members appointed to a local flood defence committee
by or on behalf of constituent councils shall be one more than the total number of members appointed by the regional flood defence committee.

(6) In appointing a person to be a member of a local flood defence committee, the regional flood defence committee shall have regard to the desirability of appointing a person who has experience of, and has shown capacity

in, some matter relevant to the functions of the committee to which he is appointed.

(7) Any person who, immediately before the transfer date is, by virtue of an appointment by an old regional committee or by or on behalf of any council, the chairman or a member of a local flood defence committee which is continued in force by virtue of section 17(2) above shall be treated, on and after that date, for the remainder of the period for which he would, under the terms of his appointment, have held office in relation to the local flood defence committee—

    (a) as if he had been appointed as such under this section by the regional flood defence committee or, as the case may be, by or on behalf of that council; and

    (b) in the case of the chairman, as if he were a member of the regional flood defence committee.

(8) The councils of every county, county borough, metropolitan district or London borough any part of which is in a local flood defence district shall be the constituent councils for the local flood defence committee for that district, and the Common Council of the City of London shall be a constituent council for the local flood defence committee of any local flood defence district which comprises any part of the City.

(9) In this section "old regional committee" means a regional flood defence committee for the purposes of section 9 of the 1991 Act.

DEFINITIONS
    "1991 Act, the": s.56(1).
    "Agency, the": s.124(1).
    "constituent councils": subs. (8).
    "functions": s.124(1).
    "local flood defence committee": s.17(1).
    "local flood defence scheme": s.17(1).
    "Ministers, the": s.56(1).
    "old regional committee": subs. (9).
    "regional flood defence committee": s.14(1).
    "transfer date": s.56(1).

COMMENCEMENT
    April 1, 1996 (S.I. 1996 No. 186).

GENERAL NOTE
    This section, which is closely modelled on s.13 of the Water Resources Act 1991 which it replaces, provides for the determination of the compensation of the local flood defence committees established by s.17. In a transitional provision set out in s.17(2), the chairman and members of any local flood defence committee existing at the transfer date (April 1, 1996) are to be treated for the remainder of their appointment as if appointed under this section, by whoever originally appointed them. Subject to those provisions, there are to be between 11 and 15 members of such a local committee (subs. (1)), unless a Minister directs otherwise on the basis of a recommendation in the scheme submitted by the regional flood defence committee that there should be more than 15 members (subs. (3)).

    Members are appointed either by the regional flood defence committee (including the chairman, who must be a member of that regional committee), or, in accordance with the scheme, by the local authorities for the district in question (subs. (4)). Local authority appointees must outnumber by one the regional committee appointees (subs. (5)). The regional flood defence committee must, in appointing members of a local committee, have regard to the desirability of the appointees having relevant experience and capacity (subs. (6)). This provision mirrors that in s.15(5) in relation to appointments to regional flood defence committees, and as there, the implication is that wide discretion may be exercised in making appointments. However, in contrast to s.15(5), local authorities are not also under this duty in making their appointments.

Membership and proceedings of flood defence committees

19. Schedule 5 to this Act shall have effect in relation to regional flood defence committees and local flood defence committees.

DEFINITIONS
"local flood defence committee": s.17(1).
"regional flood defence committee": s.14(1).

COMMENCEMENT
April 1, 1996 (S.I. 1996 No. 186).

GENERAL NOTE

This section gives effect to Sched. 5, which makes provision in relation to the membership and proceedings of both regional and local flood defence committees.

Membership of flood defence committees—Sched. 5, Pt. I

Members hold office according to their terms of appointment and, in most cases, do so for four years from the start of June after their appointment (para. 1). A member may also be a member of the local authority which appoints him to the committee (para. 2), just as there is nothing in s.18 barring a regional flood defence committee from appointing its own members to a local committee. However, he may not be a paid Agency officer (see para. 3, which also details other grounds for disqualification including bankruptcy and certain criminal convictions). Extended absence from committee meetings without approved cause is one of the disqualifying events listed in para. 4 which result in a member's office becoming vacant.

Paragraph 7 provides for casual vacancies to be filled, and para. 9 allows local authorities to nominate deputies to attend and vote at committee meetings in place of their appointees. Paragraph 10 provides for the payment, as determined by the relevant Minister, of remuneration, allowances, pension and compensation in appropriate circumstances, to any present or past chairman and of allowances to other members.

Proceedings of flood defence committees—Sched. 5, Pt. II

A flood defence committee, or two or more jointly, may appoint sub-committees and determine the number, terms of appointment and identity of the members of such sub-committees, save that anyone disqualified from committee membership cannot be a sub-committee member (para. 11).

A flood defence committee or sub-committee may delegate the carrying out of its functions to one or more other committees or sub-committees, acting jointly or alone, or to an Agency officer. It may also carry out its functions jointly with another committee (para. 12). However, s.106 of the Water Resources Act 1991, which requires the Agency to delegate the carrying out of its functions to regional committees, restricts the scope of delegation back to the Agency (para. 12(1)). Having delegated functions under s.17 to a local committee, a regional committee may not then arrange under para. 12 for the carrying out by itself or anyone else of those functions (para. 12(6)) but in contrast may do so in relation to functions it has delegated under para. 12.

A flood defence committee may, with the approval of the relevant Minister, make rules regulating its own proceedings, and the Agency may not regulate committee proceedings (para. 13). However, as regards declarations of interest, committee members are bound by ss.94–98 of the Local Government Act 1972, as modified to suit committee circumstances by para. 14. Provision is also made for the authentication of documents given, made or issued by such a committee and for the proof and validity of its proceedings (paras. 15 and 16). In particular, an Agency official whom a committee has authorised by resolution to sign on its behalf may do so.

CHAPTER II

THE SCOTTISH ENVIRONMENT PROTECTION AGENCY

Establishment of SEPA

The Scottish Environment Protection Agency

20.—(1) There shall be a body to be known as the Scottish Environment Protection Agency (in this Act referred to as "SEPA"), for the purpose of carrying out the functions transferred or assigned to it by or under this Act.

(2) Schedule 6 to this Act shall have effect with respect to SEPA.

DEFINITIONS
"functions": s.124(1).
"SEPA": s.124(1).

COMMENCEMENT
October 12, 1995 (S.I. 1995 No. 2649 (S.199)).

GENERAL NOTE
This section provides for the establishment of SEPA and gives effect to Sched. 6 which deals in detail with the constitution and proceedings of SEPA. It should be noted that references to the Secretary of State throughout Chapter II and Sched. 6 are references to the Secretary of State for Scotland. SEPA exists for the purpose of carrying out the functions transferred or assigned to it by the Act (subs. (1)). If SEPA were to carry out any other functions, it would be acting *ultra vires*. Subsection (2) gives effect to Sched. 6 which makes detailed provision regarding the composition, constitution and proceedings of SEPA. These are considered below.

Status
SEPA is given the status of a body corporate. The implications of this are similar to those outlined in the equivalent General Note on s.1(1) in relation to the Agency on p. 25–25. However, although a private prosecution of SEPA or its officers is a possibility in Scotland as in England and Wales, it is submitted that such a private prosecution is extremely unlikely to occur in practice given that the consent of the Lord Advocate is required for initiating a private prosecution in Scotland (Renton & Brown *Criminal Procedure* (5th ed., 1983) at p. 4–04; *Robertson v. H.M.A.* (1892) 3 White 230). Such consent is unlikely to be forthcoming and while the refusal of the Lord Advocate to give consent is reviewable (*J & P Coats v. Brown* (1909) 6 Adam 19; *X v. Sweeney* 1982 J.C. 70), such a review is, it is submitted, unlikely to succeed. It should also be noted that as a non-departmental public body, SEPA is accountable to Parliament through the Secretary of State for Scotland. Paragraph 2 provides that SEPA does not have Crown privilege, immunity or exemption from taxation. See also the General Note to s.1(5) on p. 25–26.

Membership, chairman and deputy-chairman
There was considerable debate in Parliament relating to the composition of SEPA (see *e.g. Hansard*, H.L. Vol. 560, cols. 1188–1192). Fears that there would be a loss of accountability by having all of SEPA's members appointed by the Secretary of State led to amendments being proposed which would require all its members to be local councillors appointed by the Convention of Scottish Local Authorities (*per* Lord Carmichael of Kelvingrove, *Hansard*, H.L. Vol. 560, col. 1188). This amendment was rejected by the Government which argued that members "would be appointed for their personal qualities and, most important, those appointments would not be made simply because their status is that of a councillor" and that "It would be very difficult for this non-departmental public body to be accountable to the Secretary of State and through him to Parliament, if he was not responsible for appointing the members of that body" (*per* the Earl of Lindsay, *Hansard*, H.L. Vol. 560, cols. 1191–1192). In fact, no fewer than four councillors have been appointed to the 11 strong board (see below).

Schedule 6, paras. 3–8 make provision in relation to the membership, chairman and deputy-chairman of SEPA. Paragraph 3 provides for the appointment of members of SEPA of whom there are to be between 8 and 12. The Secretary of State is responsible for all the appointments and also has the power to alter the maximum/minimum membership of SEPA by statutory instrument using the negative resolution procedure (para. 6). The Secretary of State is also required to appoint a chairman and deputy chairman of SEPA from amongst the members who have been appointed under para. 3 (para. 8). On April 19, 1995 it was announced by the Secretary of State that Professor William Turmeau, recently retired Principal and Vice-Chancellor of Napier University, would be appointed as the first Chairman of SEPA (*Hansard*, H.C. Vol. 258, col. 218w). In addition the Secretary of State appointed the following Board members on October 5, 1995: Councillor Basil Baird (Councillor for Eastwood District Council and the new East Renfrewshire Council; Member of Clyde River Purification Board; farmer); Alexander Buchan (Vice-Chairman, North East River Purification Board; farmer and Vice-Chairman, NFU Area executive; former President of the Royal Northern Agricultural Society); Brian Fitzgerald (Vice-Chairman of CBI Scotland and Chairman CBI Scotland Environment Committee; civil engineer; formerly director John Laing Construction Ltd); Graeme Gordon OBE (Vice-Chairman, Solway River Purification Board; Convenor of the Scottish Landowners Federation; Managing Director/Owner, Kenmure Fisheries; member, Advisory Committee, Institute of Agriculture, University of Stirling); David Hughes Hallett FRICS (Director of the Scottish Wildlife Trust; chartered surveyor; former Chairman of the Royal Institute of Chartered Surveyors in Scotland; former Director of the Scottish Landowners Federation); Professor Cliff Johnston (Head of Heriot-Watt University's Institute of Offshore Engineering Group); Councillor Cormick McChord (Vice-Convenor and Leader, Central Regional Council and Leader of the new Stirling Council; represents, Convention of Scottish Local Authorities ("COSLA") on the UK Central Local Government Environment Forum and the Local Agenda 21 Steering

Committee); Cameron McLatchie (Chairman & Chief Executive, British Polythene Industries; non-executive director, Motherwell Bridge Holdings Ltd; member, Advisory Group on Sustainable Development; formerly member, UK Advisory Committee on Business and the Environment); Councillor Alison Magee (Convenor, Sutherland District Council, and the new Highland Council; Vice-Chairman, non-aligned group, COSLA); Councillor Jennifer Shaw JP (Moray District Council, and the new Moray Council; Member, North-East River Purification Board). Alasdair Paton, who has been appointed as SEPA's Chief Executive, is also a Board member, bringing the total number of Board members to 12.

In appointing members the Secretary of State for Scotland is required to have regard to the desirability of appointing persons with knowledge or experience in a matter relevant to SEPA's functions (para. 4). It should be noted that this provision differs from the equivalent English provision (s.1(4)) which requires an appointee to have some experience of, and to have shown some capacity in, a matter relevant to the functions of the Agency. In contrast, Scottish appointees need not have shown any capacity in a matter relevant to SEPA's functions. It would appear, therefore, that the requisite standard for appointment to the Agency in England is slightly higher than the standard applicable in Scotland. Furthermore, it is most unlikely that an appointment could be challenged given the breadth of SEPA's functions. See also the General Note to s.1(4) on p. 25–25. It should also be noted that the Scottish Office has indicated on the membership application form that before appointing a person as a member of SEPA, the Secretary of State must be satisfied that the person has no interests likely to be prejudicial to performance as a member.

Paragraph 5 provides for the tenure of office, resignation and reappointment of the members of SEPA appointed under para. 3. The initial term of appointment has been fixed at four years (Scottish Office Press Release, October 5, 1995). Furthermore, the membership application form also indicates that members are not normally to be more than 67 years old at the date of their appointment. Ceasing to be a member of SEPA automatically terminates an individual's office as chairman or deputy chairman (para. 8(3)). The Secretary of State may remove a member from office on the grounds (a) of being absent from SEPA's meetings for more than three months without permission; (b) that he has been adjudged bankrupt etc.; or (c) that he is unable or unfit to carry out his functions (para. 7).

Remuneration, pensions and staff
Remuneration and pension arrangements for members of SEPA are determined by the Secretary of State (para. 9). He announced on April 19, 1995 that the Chairman's salary would initially be £36,000 *per annum* (*Hansard*, H.C. Vol. 258, col. 218) and subsequently he has determined that members are to be paid £5,000 per year plus expenses (Scottish Office Press Release, October 5, 1995). In relation to its staff SEPA must determine their remuneration and pension arrangements subject to the approval of the Secretary of State (para. 12(1)). Like the Agency, SEPA has absolute discretion in the appointment of staff (para. 11) except in the case of its first chief officer who is to be appointed by the Secretary of State following consultation with the person appointed as Chairman (para. 10(2)). Subsequent chief officers are to be appointed by SEPA with the approval of the Secretary of State (*ibid.*). On August 17, 1995 the Earl of Lindsay, Minister for the Environment at the Scottish Office, appointed Alasdair Paton (Director and Chief Engineer of the Engineering, Water and Waste Directorate, Scottish Office Environment Department) as SEPA's Chief Executive. A number of other SEPA staff have since been appointed including a Director of Corporate Services, a Director of Environmental Strategy and three Regional Directors (SEPA Bulletin, Issue 10, November 7, 1995).

Proceedings
SEPA may regulate its own procedure, including quorum for its meetings and meetings of its committees (para. 13). None of these meetings will be open to the public: see p. 25–70 and the General Note to s.1 at p. 25–26.

Committees
SEPA may establish committees and appoint persons who are not members to these committees subject to the proviso that at least one member of each committee must be a member of SEPA (para. 14(1)). The Secretary of State is to determine what remuneration is to be paid by SEPA to any such persons appointed (para. 14(2)).

Delegation of powers
SEPA may by para. 15 delegate anything which it is authorised or required to do to any committee, member or employee who is authorised by SEPA for that purpose.

Regional Boards

The question of SEPA's accountability at local level occupied much time in Parliament as several of the functions being transferred to it were previously subject to local accountable control. These functions were those previously performed by local authorities (air pollution control under Pt. I of the 1990 Act and waste regulation) and those performed by river purification authorities (RPAs). In contrast to the NRA in England and Wales, RPAs were accountable at a local level as they comprised the three islands councils and the RPBs whose boards consisted of one-half Secretary of State appointees and one-half local authority appointees (by virtue of s.135A of the Local Government (Scotland) Act 1973, added by s.27 and Sched. 10, para. 6 of the Natural Heritage (Scotland) Act 1991). The Government acknowledged this concern in its consultation paper on SEPA, *Improving Scotland's Environment: The Way Forward* where it was stated that "[T]he Government therefore envisage that SEPA might set up a regional advisory committee structure in order to provide for local involvement and participation" (para. 20). In the light of misgivings expressed by respondents in the consultation process, the Government indicated that rather than simply having regional advisory committees there might be scope for delegating certain executive responsibility to regional bodies (*Hansard*, H.C. Vol. 219, cols. 713–714). This resulted in KPMG Management Consulting being commissioned to report on this issue. In their *Scottish Environment Protection Agency Consultancy Report* (March, 1993) they argued for the creation of three or four regional boards with delegated executive functions. In Parliament, various attempts were made to force the Government to reserve places on regional boards for elected councillors (*e.g. per* Lord Ewing of Kirkford, *Hansard*, H.L. Vol. 560, col. 581). Although the Government rejected such moves, they explained that they would be "keen to secure the services of effective board members from all sources. We certainly envisage elected councillors playing a full part on the regional boards" (*per* Viscount Ullswater, Minister of State, Department of the Environment, *Hansard*, H.L. Vol. 560, col. 583; see also the Earl of Lindsay, *Hansard*, H.L. Vol. 560, col. 1192 and Sir Hector Monro, Parliamentary Under-Secretary of State for Scotland, Standing Committee B, col. 235, May 16, 1995).

The Government accepted KPMG's recommendations. Accordingly, the 1995 Act provides that SEPA must establish regional boards although the number of boards to be established is not specified (para. 16(1)). Subject to the approval of the Secretary of State, SEPA is to determine the functions which the regional boards are to discharge and the areas which they are to cover (para. 16(1)). SEPA will appoint the chairman of each regional board from amongst its own members (para. 16(2)). SEPA must comply with guidance issued by the Secretary of State in relation to such issues as the number of members regional boards are to have, their qualifications and experience (para. 16(3)). SEPA's regional boards are notable in that they are not simply advisory bodies but will exercise such powers as may be delegated by SEPA's Board. In this respect they differ significantly from the Regional Advisory Committees which are to be established in Wales and the English regions by the Agency. It is for this reason that, in contrast to the position in respect of Regional Advisory Committees in England and Wales, the Government is

> "not minded to require SEPA to provide for open access to meetings at regional level, as the regional boards will exercise delegated powers on behalf of the main SEPA board, so the same considerations will apply to the regional boards as to the main board" (Sir Paul Beresford, Standing Committee B, col. 68, May 2, 1995).

The regional boards may delegate their powers either to a member of the board in question or to an employee of SEPA authorised for that purpose.

On October 27, 1995 it was announced that SEPA was establishing three Regional Boards for the North, East and West of Scotland (see also the Introduction and General Note on p. 25–21). These Boards are based upon river purification board catchment areas with the North Regional Board incorporating the Highland and North East RPB areas, the East Regional Board the Forth, Tay and Tweed RPB areas and the West Regional Board the Clyde and Solway RPB areas.

Members' interests

Paragraph 17 makes provision in relation to members' interests. See also the General Note to s.1 and Sched. 1, para. 7 at p. 25–27.

Minutes

Paragraph 18 makes provision in relation to minutes. The Government has indicated that it hopes that SEPA will make its minutes available to any member of the public who requests them under the Environmental Information Regulations 1992 (*e.g.* the Earl of Lindsay, *Hansard*, H.L. Vol. 560, col. 1198). See also the Introduction and General Note to Pt. I at p. 25–23 above.

Transfer of functions to SEPA

21.—(1) On the transfer date there shall by virtue of this section be transferred to SEPA—

(a) the functions of river purification authorities, that is to say—

    (i) their functions with respect to water resources under or by virtue of Part III of the Rivers (Prevention of Pollution) (Scotland) Act 1951 (in this Part referred to as "the 1951 Act") and Part II of the Natural Heritage (Scotland) Act 1991;

    (ii) their functions with respect to water pollution under or by virtue of Part III of the 1951 Act, the Rivers (Prevention of Pollution) (Scotland) Act 1965 and Part II of the Control of Pollution Act 1974;

    (iii) their functions as enforcing authority, in relation to releases of substances into the environment, under or by virtue of Part I of the 1990 Act;

    (iv) their functions with respect to flood warning systems under or by virtue of Part VI of the Agriculture Act 1970; and

    (v) the functions assigned to them by or under any other enactment apart from this Act;

(b) the functions of waste regulation authorities, that is to say, the functions conferred or imposed on them by or under—

    (i) the Control of Pollution (Amendment) Act 1989; or

    (ii) Part II of the 1990 Act,

or assigned to them by or under any other enactment apart from this Act;

(c) the functions of disposal authorities under or by virtue of sections 3 to 10, 16, 17(1)(a) and 17(2)(b) to (d) of the Control of Pollution Act 1974;

(d) the functions of the chief inspector for Scotland constituted under section 16(3) of the 1990 Act, that is to say, the functions conferred or imposed on him by or under Part I of that Act or assigned to him by or under any other enactment apart from this Act;

(e) the functions of the chief inspector for Scotland appointed under section 4(2)(b) of the Radioactive Substances Act 1993, that is to say, the functions conferred or imposed on him by or under that Act or assigned to him by or under any other enactment apart from this Act;

(f) the functions conferred or imposed by or under the Alkali, &c, Works Regulation Act 1906 (in this section referred to as "the 1906 Act") on the chief, or any other, inspector (within the meaning of that Act), so far as exercisable in relation to Scotland;

(g) so far as exercisable in relation to Scotland, the functions in relation to improvement notices and prohibition notices under Part I of the Health and Safety at Work etc. Act 1974 (in this section referred to as "the 1974 Act") of inspectors appointed under section 19 of that Act by the Secretary of State in his capacity as enforcing authority responsible in relation to Scotland for the enforcement of the 1906 Act and section 5 of the 1974 Act;

(h) the functions of local authorities as enforcing authority, in relation to releases of substances into the air, under or by virtue of Part I of the 1990 Act; and

(i) the functions of the Secretary of State specified in subsection (2) below.

(2) The functions of the Secretary of State mentioned in subsection (1)(i) above are, so far as exercisable in relation to Scotland—

(a) the functions conferred or imposed on him by virtue of his being, for the purposes of Part I of the 1974 Act, the authority which is by any of the relevant statutory provisions made responsible for the enforcement of the 1906 Act and section 5 of the 1974 Act;

(b) his functions under, or under regulations made by virtue of, section 9 of the 1906 Act (registration of works), other than any functions of his as an appellate authority or any function of making regulations;

(c) his functions under section 19 of the Clean Air Act 1993 with respect to the creation of smoke control areas by local authorities; and

(d) his functions under section 30(1) of the Radioactive Substances Act 1993 (power to dispose of radioactive waste).

(3) River purification boards shall be dissolved on the transfer date.

DEFINITIONS

"disposal authority": s.56(1); s.30(2) of the 1974 Act.
"the environment": s.56(1); s.1(2) of the 1990 Act.
"functions": s.124(1).
"local authority": s.56(1)–(2).
"river purification authority": s.56(1); s.17(2) of the Rivers (Prevention of Pollution) (Scotland) Act 1951.
"river purification board": s.56(1); s.135 of the Local Government (Scotland) Act 1973.
"SEPA": s.124(1).
"transfer date": s.56(1).
"waste regulation authority": s.56(1); s.30(1)(g) of the 1990 Act.

COMMENCEMENT

October 12, 1995 (S.I. 1995 No. 2649 (S.199)).

GENERAL NOTE

This section provides for the transfer of various functions from existing Scottish environmental regulatory bodies to SEPA which is established by s.20. River purification boards are consequently dissolved by subs. (3) since all of their functions are transferred by subs. (1). The functions of Her Majesty's Industrial Pollution Inspectorate (HMIPI) are also transferred. Although HMIPI could be thought of as a body similar to a river purification board, it is not. Its functions are the functions of the chief inspector or other inspectors as individuals, or delegated functions of the Secretary of State: this is reflected in the wording of s.21(1)(d)–(g) and subs. (2). It should be noted that the Secretary of State's power to make regulations under the Alkali etc. Works Regulation Act 1906 and his appellate function thereunder are excluded from the transfer of his functions under that Act: subs. (2)(b).

Functions transferred

All the functions of river purification authorities and HMIPI together with the functions of local authorities in their capacities as waste regulation authorities and enforcing authorities for air pollution control for Part B processes under Part I of the 1990 Act and certain functions of the Secretary of State are transferred by subss. (1) and (2). The functions transferred are identified in the section by reference to the statutes in which they are set out. The main functions transferred to SEPA are summarised below in simplified form. Reference should be made to the statutes in question for the detail of the functions transferred.

River Purification Authority functions

Subs. (1)(a)(i)

This subsection transfers to SEPA all RPA water resources management functions including: the promotion of the cleanliness of rivers, other inland waters or tidal waters and the conservation of water resources (s.17, Rivers (Prevention of Pollution) (Scotland) Act 1951); powers to survey, gauge and keep records of flow or volume of water bodies and rainfall (s.18, Rivers (Prevention of Pollution) (Scotland) Act 1951); and the power to take samples of water or of effluent (s.19, Rivers (Prevention of Pollution) (Scotland) Act 1951); and the power to control water abstraction for irrigation purposes (Part II (ss.15–19) and Sched. 5 to the Natural Heritage (Scotland) Act 1991).

The functions transferred to SEPA in this respect are less broad than those transferred to the Agency, and this reflects the fact that RPAs enjoyed a less extensive role than the NRA. For example, in contrast to the NRA, RPAs have very limited powers in relation to water abstraction. Attempts in Parliament to secure for SEPA broader powers in this regard are discussed above in the Introduction and General Note to Pt. I at p. 25–16.

Subs. (1)(a)(ii)

This subsection transfers to SEPA all general RPA water pollution functions (excluding IPC functions which are transferred by subs. (1)(a)(iii)) including: the duty to ensure that specified water quality objectives are achieved (Control of Pollution Act 1974, s.30D(1)); the duty to consent discharges of trade and sewage effluent (s.34 of the 1974 Act) and to keep consents under review (the 1974 Act, s.37); the duty to monitor pollution in controlled waters (s.30D(2) of the 1974 Act); the duty to maintain registers of consents for public inspection (s.41 of the 1974 Act; the Control of Pollution (Registers) (Scotland) Regulations 1993 (S.I. 1993 No. 1155)); the power to enforce water pollution controls (ss.31–32; s.37 of the 1974 Act); the power to carry out preventive or remedial anti-pollution works and operations (s.46 of the 1974 Act).

It should be noted that the provisions contained in Pt. II of the 1974 Act (as amended by Sched. 23 to the Water Act 1989) which govern water pollution controls in Scotland are substantially amended by s.106, Sched. 16 and Sched. 22 to this Act. These amendments include the replacement of the general water pollution offence sections (ss.31–32) by a new s.30F (see the note to s.30F in Sched. 16 at p. 25–380); the introduction of a new s.30G providing for a system of prohibitions in relation to certain discharges (see the note to s.30G in Sched. 16 at p. 25–382); the introduction of new ss.49A–B providing for enforcement notices in relation to contraventions of consent conditions (see the General Note to s.120 at p. 25–302); and the introduction of new ss.46A–D providing for works notices which may require persons to carry out preventive or remedial anti-pollution works or operations (see the General Note to s.120 at p. 25–302).

Subs. (1)(a)(iii)

This subsection transfers to SEPA all RPA integrated pollution control (IPC) functions as enforcing authorities for processes prescribed under Pt. A of Sched. 1 to the Environmental Protection (Prescribed Processes and Substances) Regulations 1991 (S.I. 1991 No. 472 (as amended)) by virtue of Pt. I of the 1990 Act. In Scotland it should be noted that RPAs are the enforcing authority for IPC in cases where there are emissions to water only or to water and land only by virtue of s.5 of the 1990 Act and the Environmental Protection (Determination of Enforcing Authority etc.) (Scotland) Regulations 1992 (S.I. 1992 No. 530). HMIPI are the enforcing authority in all other instances.

Subs. (1)(a)(iv)

This subsection transfers to SEPA all RPA flood warning functions under Pt. VI of the Agriculture Act 1970 (c. 40) (as amended). Despite attempts in Parliament to extend SEPA's role in this respect, flood defence functions in Scotland which are governed by the Flood Prevention (Scotland) Act 1961 (c. 41) are not being transferred to SEPA and will remain with local authorities. See the Introduction and General Note to Pt. I at pp. 25–16 and 25–18.

Subs. (1)(a)(v)

These functions include the role of RPAs as consultees in certain cases under the planning legislation: Town and Country Planning (General Development Procedure) (Scotland) Order 1992 (S.I. 1992 No. 224 (as amended)), art. 15(1)(h).

Local authority functions: subs. (1)(b), (c) and (h).

Subs. (1)(b)—waste regulation

This subsection transfers to SEPA all functions exercised by local authorities in their capacity as waste regulation authorities under the Control of Pollution (Amendment) Act 1989 and Pt. II of the 1990 Act, including: the registration of carriers of controlled waste (Control of Pollution (Amendment) Act 1989, s.2; Controlled Waste (Registration of Carriers and Seizure of Vehicles) Regulations 1991 (S.I. 1991 No. 1624); the licensing of sites and plant for the disposal, treatment and storage of controlled waste (1990 Act, ss.35–36; Waste Management Licensing Regulations 1994 (S.I. 1994 No. 1056)); the registration of sites and plant exempt from waste management licensing requirements (1994 Regulations, reg. 18); the inspection of sites used for the recovery of scrap metal etc., which are registered as exempt from waste management licensing (1994 Regulations, regs. 17 and 18; Waste Management Licensing (Amendment etc.) Regulations 1995 (S.I. 1995 No. 288)); the supervision and enforcement of waste law including the suspension and revocation of licences and the prosecution of offenders of waste facilities (1990 Act, ss.33; 37–38; and 42); functions in connection with the duty of care for waste (1990 Act, s.34; Environmental Protection (Duty of Care) Regulations 1991 (S.I. 1991 No. 2839)); the regulation of the transfrontier shipment of waste including enforcement (Transfrontier Shipment of Waste Regulations 1994 (S.I. 1994 No. 1137)); the registration of waste brokers (the 1994 Regulations, reg. 20, Sched. 5); the power to accept the transfer and surrender of waste management licences (1990 Act, ss.39–40); and the maintenance of registers of waste carrier registration, waste management licences, exemption from waste management licensing registration and waste broker registration (1990 Act, s.64; 1994 Regulations). Other functions transferred include the production of the waste disposal plan (1990 Act, s.50; superseded by the waste strategy provisions of the 1995 Act, s.92: see the General Note to that section at p. 25–250); and acting as statutory consultees in relation to proposals for development adjacent to landfill sites and former landfill sites (Town and Country Planning (General Development Procedure) (Scotland) Order 1992 (S.I. 1992 No. 224 (as amended)), art. 15(1)(l).

Whereas in England and Wales, Pt. II of the 1990 Act brought about the division of waste regulatory and operational functions by requiring local authorities to set up arm's length local authority waste disposal companies or engage private waste contractors, similar changes were not introduced in Scotland where both regulatory and operational functions remained with district and islands councils. The potential for conflict which this arrangement might cause was identified in the Government's consultation paper on SEPA, *Improving Scotland's Environment: The Way Forward* (para. 13), and was one of the key principles underlying the proposal to reform existing regulatory arrangements. However, there was considerable criticism of the transfer of waste regulation functions to SEPA in Parliament on the grounds first, that waste was essentially a local problem and, secondly, that there presently existed perfectly satisfactory local accountable control over these functions (*per* Lord Carmichael of Kelvingrove *Hansard*, H.L. Vol. 560, col. 1188; see also Sam Galbraith—Standing Committee B, May 2, 1995, cols. 83–84). The Government reiterated that the removal of the potential for conflict arising from the dual responsibility of district and islands councils for waste regulation and waste disposal was a key benefit which the transfer of WRA functions to SEPA would bring about along with the wider benefits which integration of these functions with other pollution control functions would secure (*per* Earl of Lindsay, *Hansard* H.L. Vol. 560, col. 1192; see also Sir Hector Monro, the then Parliamentary Under-Secretary of State for Scotland, H.C. Standing Committee B, May 2, 1995, cols. 84–85).

Subs. (1)(c): waste regulation: residual functions under the 1974 Act
By s.30(1) of the Control of Pollution Act 1974, waste regulation functions for the purposes of that Act are as follows: functions relating to disposal licences (ss.3–11); the removal of waste deposited in breach of licensing provisions (s.16); the giving of directions in relation to special waste, where provided for by regulations under s.17 (s.17(1)(a)); and the supervision of activities authorised by such special waste regulations, recovery of cost and expenses and functions in relation to appeals against disposal authority decisions under such regulations (s.17(2)(b)–(d)).

This subsection transfers to SEPA all local authority functions exercised in the capacity of waste disposal authorities under Pt. I of the 1974 Act. They include the old waste disposal licensing functions which were only replaced when the new waste management licensing regime under Pt. II of the 1990 Act was brought into force on May 1, 1994. These functions have been transferred to SEPA as there may still be actions pending under the old legislation. Therefore, the importance of these transferred functions will become progressively less important with the passage of time and will become redundant when the last action under the 1974 Act is dealt with. However, the special waste controls in the 1974 Act, and the Control of Pollution (Special Waste) Regulations 1980 which were made under it, are far from being residual functions and run alongside the 1990 Act provisions. However, it is anticipated that soon after waste regulation is transferred the 1980 Regulations will have been supplanted by new regulations implementing the EC Hazardous Waste Directive 91/689/EEC draft Special Waste Regulations 1995, to be made under s.62 of the 1990 Act.

Subs. (1)(h): Air Pollution Control
This subsection transfers to SEPA all local authority functions exercised in the capacity of enforcing authorities for processes prescribed under Pt. B of Sched. 1 to the Environmental Protection (Prescribed Processes and Substances) Regulations 1991 for air pollution control by virtue of Pt. I of the 1990 Act. In England and Wales this function has not been transferred to the Agency and remains with local authorities (see also the Introduction and General Note to Pt. I at p.25–16).

The transfer of these functions to SEPA provoked considerable debate in Parliament. It was argued that it appeared inconsistent as this function was not being transferred to the Agency in England and Wales and might therefore lead to differing approaches to air pollution control within Great Britain (see, for example, Lord Williams of Elvel, *Hansard*, H.L. Vol. 560, cols. 1194–1195). It was also argued that this function was being transferred from local accountable control which could respond quickly to an incident to a centralised, less accountable and less responsive control (see, for example, Archie Kirkwood, *Hansard*, H.C. Vol. 262, cols. 936–937). However, the Government explained that the reasons for transferring this function to SEPA in Scotland were first, that there were comparatively few Pt. B processes in Scotland in contrast to

England and Wales and, of those, most were located in a very small number of local authority areas in the central belt with many local authorities having little or no experience of Pt. B processes at all even after taking into account local government reorganisation; and secondly, that given that SEPA was being established with all the facilities and back-up which that entailed it made little sense to leave the 25–30 local authority staff who worked on air pollution dispersed throughout the country as the pooling of resources would bring real benefits (see, for example, the Earl of Lindsay, *Hansard*, H.L. Vol. 560, col. 1193 and Sir Hector Monro, Standing Committee B, May 16, 1995, col. 240).

Subs. (1)(d)–(g): HMIPI Functions
All of the functions of HMIPI are transferred to SEPA, as detailed below.

Subs. (1)(d): Integrated Pollution Control
This subsection transfers to SEPA all HMIPI functions as enforcing authority for processes prescribed under Pt. A of Sched. 1 to the Environmental Protection (Prescribed Processes and Substances) Regulations 1991 for integrated pollution control (IPC) by virtue of Pt. I of the 1990 Act. In Scotland it should be noted that HMIPI is the enforcing authority for IPC in all cases except where there are emissions to water only or to water and land only in which case the relevant RPA is the enforcing authority by virtue of s.5 of the 1990 Act and the Environmental Protection (Determination of Enforcing Authority etc.) (Scotland) Regulations 1992 (S.I. 1992 No. 530)

Subs. (1)(e): Radioactive Substances
This subsection transfers to SEPA all HMIPI functions under the Radioactive Substances Act 1993 including: the registration of the keeping and use of radioactive material on premises and the registration of mobile radioactive apparatus (1993 Act, ss.7 and 10); the authorisation of the disposal or accumulation of radioactive waste (1993 Act, s.16); the enforcement of controls over radioactive substances (1993 Act, ss.6, 9, 13–14, 17, 21–22, and 32); the maintenance of registers of registrations and authorisations (1993 Act, s.39).

Subs. (1)(f)–(g): pre-1990 Act controls
These subsections transfer to SEPA all functions conferred on or delegated to HMIPI by virtue of the Alkali etc. Works Regulation Act 1906 and Pt. I of the Health and Safety at Work etc. Act 1974 including: the registration of prescribed works (Alkali etc. Works Regulation Act 1906, s.9; Control of Industrial Air Pollution (Registration of Works) Regulations 1989 (S.I. 1989 No. 318)); the enforcement of 1906 Act controls by means of prohibition and improvement notices (Health and Safety at Work etc. Act 1974); and the maintenance of a register of prescribed works registrations (1906 Act, s.9; 1989 Regulations). The functions in subss. (1)(f)–(g) have been transferred to SEPA since they continue to apply to certain existing industrial processes which are not yet subject to Pt. I of the 1990 Act. For example, applications for chapter 6 processes must be made by January 31, 1996 (Sched. 3, para. 18 to the Environmental Protection (Prescribed Processes and Substances) Regulations 1991 (S.I. 1991 No. 472 (as amended)). There may also still be actions pending under the old legislation. However, the significance of these transferred functions will progressively diminish with the passage of time and will cease when the last process registered under the 1906 Act is authorised under Pt. I of the 1990 Act and when the last action under the old legislation has been concluded.

Subs. (1)(i) and subs. (2): Functions of the Secretary of State
The miscellaneous functions specified in subs. (2) which have been exercised by the Secretary of State are transferred to SEPA by subs. (1)(i). These functions include his powers to enforce controls under the Alkali etc. Works Regulation Act 1906 and s.5 of the Health and Safety at Work etc. Act 1974 (Health and Safety at Work etc. Act 1974, s.33). It should be noted that this role has been delegated to HMIPI. Note that certain other miscellaneous functions are also transferred: (a) in relation to the registration of works under the 1906 Act, although these do not include his appellate function; (b) the power to require local authorities to declare smoke control areas (Clean Air Act 1993, s.19); and (c) the power to dispose of radioactive waste on any premises where he is satisfied that it is unlikely for any reason that it will be lawfully disposed of (Radioactive Substances Act 1993, s.30).

Transfer of property, rights and liabilities to SEPA

22.—(1) On the transfer date—
(a) the property, rights and liabilities of every river purification board shall, by virtue of this paragraph, be transferred to and vested in SEPA;

(b) any property, rights and liabilities which are the subject of a scheme under this section—
    (i) made by the Secretary of State; or
    (ii) made by a local authority and approved by the Secretary of State,
shall be transferred to and vested in SEPA by and in accordance with the scheme.

(2) The Secretary of State may, before the transfer date, make a scheme for the transfer to SEPA of such of—
(a) his property, rights and liabilities; or
(b) the property, rights and liabilities of any of the inspectors or chief inspectors mentioned in subsection (1) of section 21 above,
as appear to the Secretary of State appropriate to be so transferred in consequence of the transfer of any functions to SEPA by virtue of that subsection.

(3) It shall be the duty of every local authority to make a scheme, after consultation with SEPA, for the transfer to SEPA of—
(a) such of the authority's property and rights as are held by it for the purposes of its functions as—
    (i) a waste regulation authority;
    (ii) a disposal authority under or by virtue of the provisions mentioned in section 21(1)(c) above;
    (iii) enforcing authority, in relation to releases of substances into the air, by virtue of Part I of the 1990 Act; and
    (iv) in the case of an islands council, a river purification authority; and
(b) such of its liabilities as are liabilities to which it is subject by virtue of its being an authority mentioned in paragraph (a)(i) to (iv) above,
and to submit that scheme to the Secretary of State for his approval before such date as he may direct.

(4) Any local authority preparing a scheme in pursuance of subsection (3) above shall take into account any guidance given by the Secretary of State as to the provisions which he regards as appropriate for inclusion in the scheme.

(5) Where a scheme under subsection (3) above is submitted to the Secretary of State, he may—
(a) approve the scheme;
(b) approve the scheme subject to such modifications as he considers appropriate; or
(c) reject the scheme;
but the power conferred on the Secretary of State by paragraph (b) above shall be exercisable only after consultation with the local authority which submitted the scheme to him and with SEPA.

(6) The Secretary of State may, in the case of any local authority which is required to make a scheme under subsection (3) above, himself make a scheme for the transfer to SEPA of such of the body's property, rights or liabilities as are mentioned in paragraph (a) or (b) of that subsection, if—
(a) the authority fails to submit a scheme under that subsection to him for his approval before the due date; or
(b) the Secretary of State rejects a scheme under that subsection submitted to him by the authority;
but nothing in this subsection shall prevent the Secretary of State from approving any scheme which may be submitted to him after the due date.

(7) Where the Secretary of State makes a transfer scheme under subsection (6) above, he may recover his reasonable expenses in doing so, or such proportion of those expenses as he thinks fit, from the local authority in question by such means as appear to him to be appropriate including, without prejudice to that generality, setting off the expenses payable by the local authority against revenue support grant or non-domestic rate income payable by the Secretary of State to the local authority under paragraph 3 of Schedule 12 to the Local Government Finance Act 1992.

(8) The Secretary of State may, at any time before the transfer date, modify any scheme made or approved by him under this section but only after consultation with SEPA and, in the case of a scheme which was approved by him (with or without modifications), after consultation with the local authority which submitted the scheme to him for approval.

(9) Schedule 2 to this Act shall have effect in relation to transfers by or under this section.

DEFINITIONS
"disposal authority": s.56(1); s.30(2) of the 1974 Act.
"enforcing authority": s.1(8) of the 1990 Act.
"functions": s.124(1).
"local authority": s.56(1)–(2).
"modifications": s.124(1).
"river purification authority": s.56(1); s.17(2) of the Rivers (Prevention of Pollution) (Scotland) Act 1951.
"river purification board": s.56(1); s.135 of the Local Government (Scotland) Act 1973.
"transfer date": s.56(1).
"SEPA": s.124(1).
"waste regulation authority": s.56(1).

COMMENCEMENT
October 12, 1995 (S.I. 1995 No. 2649 (S.199)).

GENERAL NOTE
This section and Schedule 2 to which it gives effect (subs. (9)), deal with the transfer of property, rights and liabilities from existing bodies to SEPA. The provisions mirror those in relation to the Agency. See also the General Note to s.3 on p. 25–35. Scottish Office Environment Department Circular 19/95, *Transfer of Property, Rights and Liabilities from District and Islands Councils to the Scottish Environment Protection Agency* (October 12, 1995) provides guidance to local authorities on their duties under this section in respect of these transfers. Circular 19/95 was produced following consultation with COSLA, UNISON and the Local Government Staff Commission on draft guidance.

Property, rights and liabilities. These terms are not further defined but details of what they include are given in paras. 2 and 3 of Sched. 2.

The transfer date. The date on which all transfers of property, rights and liabilities from existing bodies to SEPA take effect is the "transfer date". This date will be appointed by the Secretary of State by statutory instrument (s.56(1)). Circular 19/95 indicates that the Secretary of State intends appointing April 1, 1996 as the transfer date. This is the same date as the Secretary of State for the Environment intends to appoint in England and Wales (see the General Note to s.3 on p. 25–35).

On the transfer date, by subs. (1) all the property, rights and liabilities of every river purification board (which bodies, when s.21(3) comes into force are dissolved) are transferred to and vested in SEPA, as are such other property, rights and liabilities as are subject to a scheme made under this section by the Secretary of State or by a local authority and approved by the Secretary of State. See also the note to s.3 on p. 25–35.

Schemes of Transfer. Two kinds of transfer schemes are provided for by s.22. First, s.21(1)(d)–(g) and (i) transfer functions of the inspectors, the chief inspector (HMIPI) and the Secretary of State to SEPA. Subs. (2) provides that before the transfer date the Secretary of State may make a scheme of such of his and their property, rights and liabilities as appear to him appropriate in consequence of the transfer of those functions. Secondly, s.21(1)(b)–(c) and (h) transfer the local authority functions as waste regulation authorities, disposal authorities and as enforcing authorities in relation to air pollution control by virtue of Pt. I of the 1990 Act and, in the case of islands councils, as river purification authorities to SEPA.

Subs. (3) provides that every local authority is placed under a duty to make a scheme for the transfer to SEPA of such of its property, rights and liabilities as are held by it or, to which it is subject, in relation to its transferred functions. This must be done after consultation with SEPA and taking into account any guidance issued by the Secretary of State under subs. (4), including Circular 19/95. Circular 19/95 includes, at Annex B, a Model Transfer Scheme which is divided into two sections: I—Supporting Information; and II—Scheme. The Scheme is further divided into rights and liabilities under the following heads: contracts of employment; property (including land and buildings, vehicles, equipment, intellectual property and records); rights and liabilities under contracts for the provision of services to or by the council; and interests, rights and liabilities to be created between the council and SEPA. The Circular also indicates that the Scheme should include all other minor items of property which the council is accustomed to use in the discharge of any of its functions which are to be transferred to SEPA and are not specified fully elsewhere in the Scheme.

Circular 19/95 indicates that where waste regulation authority staff within a council have been working on the monitoring or control of closed landfill sites which will not come under the control of SEPA they should not be included in a transfer scheme (para. A19). However, where they have been engaged in spending a significant proportion of their working in performing an advisory role in relation to contaminated land and closed landfills, the Circular indicates that councils may consider it appropriate for them to transfer to SEPA since their advisory role may be seen as analogous to the advisory, guidance giving role which SEPA will have in relation to contaminated land (paras. A20–A21). Each local authority must submit its scheme to the Secretary of State for his approval by such date as he may direct, although he may nonetheless approve a scheme received after that date: subs. (3) and (6). Circular 19/95 indicates that the Secretary of State is directing all district and islands councils to submit their transfer schemes for approval no later than Friday, December 15, 1995 (para. 3).

Subs. (5)

The Secretary of State has considerable discretion on receipt of a scheme. He may approve it (with or without modifications) or reject it. However, the Secretary of State may only exercise the power to approve the scheme subject to modifications after consultation with the local authority which submitted the scheme and with SEPA.

Subs. (6)

This subsection provides the Secretary of State with default powers enabling him to make a scheme which he may exercise (a) where no scheme is submitted by a local authority by the due date or (b) where he has rejected a scheme which has been submitted. However, he may also approve a scheme submitted after the due date.

Subs. (7)

This subsection applies where the Secretary of State has exercised his default powers under subs. (6) to make a scheme and enables him to recover his reasonable expenses or such proportion of those expenses as he thinks fit from the local authority in question. The method of recovery may include setting off his expenses against revenue support grant or non-domestic rate income payable by the Secretary of State to the local authority.

Functions of staff commission

23. The functions of the staff commission established under section 12 of the Local Government etc. (Scotland) Act 1994 shall include—

    (a) considering and keeping under review the arrangements for the transfer to SEPA, in consequence of this Act or of any scheme made under it, of staff employed by local authorities;

    (b) considering such staffing problems arising out of, consequential on or connected with any provision of, or scheme made under, this Act as may be referred to them by the Secretary of State or by any local authority;

    (c) advising the Secretary of State as to the steps necessary to safeguard the interests of the staff referred to in paragraph (a) above.

DEFINITIONS

"local authority": s.56(1)–(2).

"SEPA": s.124(1).

COMMENCEMENT

October 12, 1995 (S.I. 1995 No. 2649 (S.199)).

GENERAL NOTE

The remit of the staff commission provided for by s.12 of the Local Government etc. (Scotland) Act 1994 in connection with local government reorganisation in Scotland (see Introduction and General Note to Pt. I on p. 25–15) is extended by this section to cover issues arising out of the transfer of staff to SEPA (s.23(a)–(b)) and advising the Secretary of State on steps necessary to safeguard the interests of staff being transferred to SEPA (s.23(c)). This is due to the fact that local government reorganisation is proceeding in tandem with the establishment of SEPA and because not only WRA functions but also local air pollution control functions are being transferred to SEPA. The Government have assured Parliament that "... staff who transfer to SEPA will have protection under TUPE or equivalent provisions..." (Viscount Ullswater, Minister of State, Department of the Environment, *Hansard*, H.L. Vol. 560, col. 624. See also Circular 19/95, *Transfer of Property, Rights and Liabilities from District and Islands Councils to the Scottish Environment Protection Agency* (October 12, 1995, para. 7)).

It should be noted that the staff commission was established by order on November 25, 1994 (see the Local Government Staff Commission (Scotland) Order 1994 (S.I. 1994 No. 2958)).

Other functions etc. of SEPA

Consultation with respect to drainage works

24.—(1) Subject to subsection (2) below, any person proposing to carry out drainage works shall—

    (a) before commencing such works, consult SEPA as to precautions to be taken to prevent pollution to controlled waters as a result of the works; and

    (b) in carrying out such works, take account of SEPA's views.

(2) The Secretary of State may, by regulations made by statutory instrument subject to annulment in pursuance of a resolution of either House of Parliament, prescribe types of drainage works in relation to which subsection (1) above shall not apply.

(3) In this section, "drainage works" has the same meaning as in the Land Drainage (Scotland) Act 1958 and "controlled waters" has the same meaning as in the Control of Pollution Act 1974.

DEFINITIONS

"controlled waters": subs. (3); s.30A of COPA 1974.
"drainage works": subs. (3); s.18(1) of the Land Drainage (Scotland) Act 1958.
"SEPA": s.124.

COMMENCEMENT

This section comes into force on a day to be appointed (s.125(3)).

GENERAL NOTE

This section provides SEPA with one of its new functions. It requires persons proposing to undertake drainage works to consult with SEPA except in certain cases which are to be prescribed in regulations which the Secretary of State is empowered to make (subs. (2)). The Government explained that their intention was "to place on a statutory footing the consultation which is currently required as a condition of the payment of grant for drainage works from the Forestry Commission and the Scottish Office, and to extend the consultation requirement to other significant drainage works" (*per* the Earl of Lindsay, *Hansard*, H.L. Vol. 560, col. 1216).

Concern was expressed that there is no criminal penalty attached to this section for failure to consult with SEPA before undertaking drainage works (see *e.g.* Sam Galbraith, Standing Committee B, May 16, 1995, col. 241). However, interdict may be available to SEPA in the absence of a prescribed statutory remedy (see also the note to s.37 at p. 25–100) and, if the works in question resulted in pollution of controlled waters, a charge of causing or knowingly permitting pollution of controlled waters could be brought under the new s.30F (which replaces s.31 of the 1974 Act) of the 1974 Act introduced by this Act.

Subs. (1)

Consultation is restricted to precautions to be taken to prevent pollution of controlled waters. The rather limited scope of consultation appears, for example, to exclude precautions to prevent any environmental damage and flooding. Concern was expressed about this at Report Stage in the House of Lords (*per* Lord Carmichael of Kelvingrove, *Hansard*, H.L. Vol. 560, col. 1692). However, the Government stated that they considered that any amendment which would widen the range of precautions to be included in the consultation would considerably extend SEPA's interest beyond its normal span of responsibilities, *i.e.* pollution prevention and control:

"There is one very clear reason why it would make sense for SEPA to be consulted as to the precautions to prevent pollution resulting from drainage works. If pollution was to result from the carrying on of such works, SEPA might have to prepare a case for the procurator fiscal. The agency would have no corresponding role if the drainage works were alleged to have caused other environmental damage" (*per* the Earl of Lindsay, *Hansard*, H.L. Vol. 560, cols. 1692–1693).

Subs. (2)

The Secretary of State is empowered to prescribe exceptions to the duty to consult by means of regulations using the negative resolution procedure which gives Parliament some degree of oversight in that it may reject the proposed regulations although it cannot amend them. The Government envisaged that regulations made under this subsection would prescribe minor drainage works such as tile drains and repairs to existing drains where the risk of pollution was so low as to make the need to consult unwarranted and promised wide consultation among interested parties (see, for example, the Earl of Lindsay, *Hansard*, H.L. Vol. 560, col. 1216; see also Sir Hector Monro, the then Parliamentary Under-Secretary of State for Scotland, Standing Committee B, May 16, 1995, col. 242).

Assessing flood risk

25.—(1) Without prejudice to section 92 of the Agriculture Act 1970 (provision of flood warning systems), SEPA shall have the function of assessing, as far as it considers it appropriate, the risk of flooding in any area of Scotland.

(2) If requested by a planning authority to do so, SEPA shall, on the basis of such information as it holds with respect to the risk of flooding in any part of the authority's area, provide the authority with advice as to such risk.

DEFINITIONS

"planning authority": s.172(1) of the Local Government (Scotland) Act 1973.
"SEPA": s.124(1).

COMMENCEMENT

April 1, 1996 (S.I. 1996 No. 186).

GENERAL NOTE

This section provides SEPA with another new function. Recent flooding in various parts of Scotland gave rise to considerable parliamentary debate regarding SEPA's role in relation to flood prevention and defence (see also Introduction and General Note to Part I at p. 25–16). Responsibility for functions in relation to flooding has in the past been split between river purification authorities (RPAs) and local authorities. Part VI of the Agriculture Act 1970 empowered RPAs to provide and operate flood warning systems within their areas. However, responsibility for flood defence works under the Flood Prevention (Scotland) Act 1961 lay with regional and islands councils. Although the 1995 Act transfers RPA responsibility for flood warning systems to SEPA by s.21(1)(a)(iv) and Sched. 22, para. 14 which makes the necessary consequential amendments, flood defence powers will remain with local authorities although they will be transferred to the new unitary authorities established by the Local Government etc. (Scotland) Act 1994 in April 1996. The Government did not consider that it was appropriate to transfer flood prevention and defence powers to SEPA as:

"We believe that the lead in all planning matters must be unambiguous. Local authorities already have all the powers they need to tackle flooding and to take any precautionary measures against the threat of flooding. Local authorities must retain unambiguously that responsibility to prevent flooding. Similarly, with its undoubted role in planning, we believe that it is much better that an elected council makes the final decision as to where development can or cannot take place, having taken all factors into account" (*per* the Earl of Lindsay, *Hansard*, H.L. Vol. 565, col. 1482).

This section is intended to complement those existing provisions by imposing on SEPA a new duty to assess the risk of flooding in any area of Scotland. A planning authority will also be able to request SEPA to provide it with advice on the risk of flooding anywhere within its area. This provision was introduced to "ensure that councils can take well-informed decisions on flooding matters which will reflect local concerns and the general public interest" (*per* the Earl of Lindsay, *Hansard*, H.L. Vol. 565, col. 1481).

Subs. (1)

SEPA's duty to assess flood risk in any area of Scotland is limited to the extent that any assessment it makes is only to the extent that it considers appropriate.

Subs. (2)

SEPA is placed under a duty to advise any planning authority which requests advice as to flood risk within any part of the authority's area. The Government explained that:

"Local authorities must give flood prevention a high priority if SEPA's advice is that flooding is a serious risk. ... SEPA will give advice to the planning authority before it gives approval. It is important to realise that, if SEPA's advice is that the area in question is dangerous, and if the planning authority still wants to go ahead, the application must go to the Secretary of State, and, if necessary, he will call it in." (Sir Hector Monro, the then Parliamentary Under-Secretary of State for Scotland, *Hansard,* H.C. Vol. 262, cols. 948–949).

It should also be noted that the Government have produced a National Planning Policy Guideline, *NPPG 7 Planning and Flooding* (Scottish Office Environment Department, September 1995) which provides that the susceptibility of land to flooding is a material consideration in determining a planning application even if flooding is not mentioned in the current development plan (para. 60). It is in the context of preparing development plans and determining planning applications that planning authorities should request SEPA to provide advice on the risk of flooding (paras. 13 and 60).

Power of SEPA to purchase land compulsorily

26.—(1) The Secretary of State may authorise SEPA, for the purpose of any of its functions, to purchase land compulsorily.

(2) The Acquisition of Land (Authorisation Procedure) (Scotland) Act 1947 shall apply in relation to the compulsory purchase of land under this section as if this section had been in force immediately before the commencement of that Act and, in relation to such purchase of land, SEPA shall be treated as if it were a local authority within the meaning of that Act.

DEFINITIONS
"functions": s.124(1).
"SEPA": s.124(1).

COMMENCEMENT
April 1, 1996 (S.I. 1996 No. 186).

GENERAL NOTE

This section re-enacts the existing power of the Secretary of State to authorise compulsory purchase by river purification authorities under s.9 of the Rivers (Prevention of Pollution) (Scotland) Act 1951. Despite this considerable concern was expressed in Parliament regarding the potential for misuse of these powers and amendments were proposed to provide additional safeguards for landowners on their use (*Hansard,* H.L. Vol. 560, cols. 1221–1222; Vol. 561, cols. 1694–1697; Vol. 562, cols. 1029–1031). In particular, it was pointed out that additional safeguards involving the use of a special parliamentary procedure (provided in the Statutory Orders (Special Procedure) Acts 1945 and 1965) had been placed on similar powers in s.5(4) of the Natural Heritage (Scotland) Act 1991 in relation to Scottish Natural Heritage (SNH). However, the Government argued that greater safeguards were necessary in the case of SNH as the power to purchase land compulsorily was potentially a powerful tool in the hands of a nature conservation body whereas the purchase of land was not a normal means of preventing or controlling pollution (*per* the Earl of Lindsay, *Hansard,* H.L. Vol. 561, col. 1696 and Vol. 562, col. 1031). Accordingly, the Government argued that additional safeguards were unnecessary and that the Secretary of State's role would provide "a safety net against any unreasonable use of such powers" (*per* the Earl of Lindsay, *Hansard,* H.L. Vol. 560, col. 1223). Moreover, it was pointed out that the compulsory purchase powers in the 1951 Act had never in fact been used (*per* the Earl of Lindsay, *Hansard,* H.L. Vol. 561, col. 1696). Use of the powers would be authorised by the Secretary of State as a last resort "in relation to specific land required by the agency to discharge its functions effectively only in circumstances where other locations were unsuitable and where it was not possible for a reasonable agreement between SEPA and the landowner to be reached". (*per* the Earl of Lindsay, *Hansard,* H.L. Vol. 561, col. 1696). The powers are further limited by being exercisable only for the purpose of any of SEPA's functions (subs. (1)).

Land. Since there is no definition of land in the Act, it would appear that the definition of land in the Interpretation Act 1978 is applicable. Therefore, land includes, for example, a right over land and also land covered by water.

Power of SEPA to obtain information about land

27.—(1) Where, with a view to performing a function conferred on it by any enactment, SEPA considers that it ought to have information connected with any land, it may serve on one or more of the persons mentioned in subsection (2) below a notice—
    (a) specifying the land, the function and the enactment; and
    (b) requiring the recipient of the notice to furnish to SEPA, within such period of not less than 14 days from the date of service of the notice as is specified in the notice—
          (i) the nature of his interest in the land; and
          (ii) the name and address of each person whom he believes is, as respects the land, a person mentioned in subsection (2) below.
  (2) The persons referred to in subsection (1) above are—
    (a) the occupier of the land;
    (b) any person—
          (i) who has an interest in the land as owner, creditor in a heritable security or lessee; or
          (ii) who directly or indirectly receives rent for the land; and
    (c) any person who, in pursuance of an agreement between himself and a person interested in the land, is authorised to manage the land or to arrange for the letting of it.
  (3) A person who—
    (a) fails to comply with the requirements of a notice served on him in pursuance of subsection (1) above; or
    (b) in furnishing any information in compliance with such a notice makes a statement which he knows to be false in a material particular or recklessly makes a statement which is false in a material particular,
shall be guilty of an offence and liable on summary conviction to a fine not exceeding level 5 on the standard scale.

DEFINITIONS
   "functions": s.124(1).
   "notice": s.124(1).
   "SEPA": s.124(1).

COMMENCEMENT
   April 1, 1996 (S.I. 1996 No. 186).

GENERAL NOTE
   This section empowers SEPA to obtain information regarding the persons who have an interest in a particular piece of land. The Government explained that "The power is needed by the agencies in order to enable them to carry out their pollution control and prevention functions" (*per* the Earl of Lindsay, *Hansard*, H.L. Vol. 565, col. 1484), which can hardly be said to shed much light on the need for this power. However, the need for the power was clearly illustrated in *R. v. Dovermoss* [1995] Env. L.R. 258 (C.A.), a prosecution under s.85 of the Water Resources Act 1991 in Wales, in which the appellants succeeded on appeal in having their conviction quashed as they established that the prosecution had not proved that they owned or occupied the farm at which the pollution had occurred or that they carried on the farming enterprise there. It should be noted that similar provision is made for England and Wales in Sched. 22, para. 33 to the 1995 Act which amends the Local Government (Miscellaneous Provisions) Act 1976 to enable the Agency to exercise similar powers.

Subs. (1)
   The notice must comply with the procedural requirements in subs. (1)(a) and may only be served on a person specified in subs. (2). The information which may be sought is also limited to that detailed in subs. (1)(b).

Subs. (3)

Failure to comply with the requirements of a notice, or to knowingly or recklessly make a statement which is false in a material particular, is made a criminal offence with a maximum penalty not exceeding level 5, presently £5,000.

Power of SEPA to promote or oppose private legislation

28.—(1) SEPA may, where it is satisfied that it is expedient to do so—

(a) with the consent of the Secretary of State, petition for the issue of a provisional order under the Private Legislation Procedure (Scotland) Act 1936; or

(b) oppose any private legislation in Parliament.

(2) An application for the consent mentioned in paragraph (a) of subsection (1) above shall be accompanied by a concise summary of the purposes of the order petitioned for.

(3) In paragraph (b) of subsection (1) above, "private legislation in Parliament" includes—

(a) a provisional order and a Confirmation Bill relating to such an order; and

(b) any local or personal Bill.

DEFINITIONS

"private legislation in Parliament": subs. (3).
"SEPA": s.124(1).

COMMENCEMENT

This section comes into force on a day to be appointed (s.125(3)).

GENERAL NOTE

SEPA is empowered by this section to promote private legislation with the consent of the Secretary of State under the Private Legislation Procedure (Scotland) Act 1936 or to oppose such legislation.

Procedure relating to making of byelaws

29. The following provisions of the Local Government (Scotland) Act 1973—

(a) section 202 (procedure etc. for byelaws);

(b) section 202C (revocation of byelaws);

(c) section 204 (evidence of byelaws),

shall apply in relation to SEPA as they apply in relation to a local authority, provided that in the application of the said section 202 to SEPA for subsection (13) there shall be substituted—

"(13) The Scottish Environment Protection Agency shall send a copy of any byelaws made by it to the proper officer of the local authority for any area to the whole or any part of which the byelaws will apply.".

DEFINITIONS

"local authority": s.56(1)–(2).
"SEPA": s.124(1).

COMMENCEMENT

April 1, 1996 (S.I. 1996 No. 186).

GENERAL NOTE

Certain provisions of the Local Government (Scotland) Act 1973 relating to byelaws are extended by this section to include SEPA, which is empowered thereunder to make byelaws as though it were a local authority.

Records held by SEPA

30.—(1) Subject to subsection (3) below—

(a) this section applies to all records (in whatever form or medium)—

    (i) transferred to and vested in SEPA by or under section 22 above;

    (ii) created or acquired by it in the exercise of any of its functions; or

    (iii) otherwise in its keeping;

(b) SEPA shall ensure that the records, other than such as are mentioned in paragraph (c) below, are preserved and managed in accordance with such arrangements as it, after consulting the Keeper of the Records of Scotland, shall put into effect;

(c) records which in SEPA's opinion are not worthy of preservation may be disposed of by it;

(d) SEPA may from time to time revise the arrangements mentioned in paragraph (b) above but before making any material change to those arrangements shall consult the Keeper; and

(e) SEPA—

    (i) shall secure that the Keeper has, at all reasonable hours, unrestricted access to the records preserved by it;

    (ii) may afford members of the public, free of charge or on payment of reasonable charges, facilities for inspecting and for obtaining copies or extracts from those records.

(2) Nothing in subsection (1)(e)(ii) above permits infringement of copyright or contravention of conditions subject to which records are in SEPA's keeping.

(3) Insofar as any provision of any enactment, being a provision which relates to records of a specific kind, is (but for this subsection) inconsistent with subsection (1) above, that subsection is subject to the provision in question.

DEFINITIONS
  "functions": s.124(1).
  "records": s.124(1).
  "SEPA": s.124(1).

COMMENCEMENT
  October 12, 1995 (S.I. 1995 No. 2649 (S.199)).

GENERAL NOTE
  This section provides for record keeping and disposal by SEPA and makes provision for access to records held by SEPA. It should be noted that these provisions are distinct from statutory requirements to keep registers in relation to SEPA's various pollution control functions.
  The provisions relating to public access to records held by SEPA proved to be highly controversial in Parliament. This is because subs. (1)(e)(ii) gives SEPA discretion in deciding whether to allow members of the public access to its records and whether to provide inspection facilities and copies free of charge or on payment of a reasonable sum. First, it was argued in Parliament that SEPA should be placed under a duty to provide access to its records rather than merely having a power to provide such access (*e.g. per* Lord Carmichael of Kelvingrove, *Hansard*, H.L. Vol. 561, col. 1697). However, the Government pointed out that SEPA's discretion in this respect was limited as it was subject to the Environmental Information Regulations 1992 (S.I. 1992 No. 3240) (*per* the Earl of Lindsay, *Hansard*, H.L. Vol. 560, cols. 1198–1199), and that refusal to afford access would only be possible on the basis of exemptions provided for in those Regulations (*per* the Earl of Lindsay, *Hansard*, H.L. Vol. 561, col. 1697). Secondly, concern was also expressed about the power given to SEPA to set "reasonable" charges for inspection facilities or for obtaining copies of records. The Government justification for this discretion was that "[I]f the inconvenience and staff time involved appears disproportionate to the value of the data on the record, then it is surely right that SEPA should have some discretion" (*per* the Earl of Lindsay, *Hansard*, H.L. Vol. 561, col. 1698). As to the interpretation of "reasonable", the Earl of Lindsay explained:

"I recognise the concern that can arise about the interpretation which may be placed on the 'reasonableness' of photocopying charges. The establishment of a single, national agency should assist in this respect. I also believe that it is right in principle that SEPA should be able to set reasonable charges which recover the costs it incurs in providing copies of documents. But I agree that it should not seek to debar access through inflated charges" (*Hansard*, H.L. Vol. 560, col. 1198).

It should be noted that in the past photocopying charges imposed by local authorities for copies from the statutory air pollution control register under Part I of the Environmental Protection Act 1990 have in some cases been as high as £5 per page which may be sufficient to debar access (see: *Come Clean! Public access to information about local authority air pollution control* (Scottish Consumer Council and Friends of the Earth Scotland, 1993)). Reference should also be made to the Introduction and General Note to Pt. I at p. 25–22.

Subs. (1)

SEPA must consult the Keeper of the Records of Scotland prior to making arrangements for preserving and managing records (subs. (1)(b)) except in the case of records which, in SEPA's opinion, are not worthy of preservation and which may accordingly be disposed of (subs. (1)(c)). Although record keeping arrangements may be revised, SEPA must consult with the Keeper before any material change is made (subs. (1)(d)). A material change would clearly not include minor changes but nonetheless what constituted a *material change* is likely to be very largely a matter of fact and degree as planning law illustrates: *East Barnet U.D.C. v. British Transport Commission* [1963] 1 W.L.R. 247; and *Braddon v. Secretary of State for the Environment* [1977] J.P.L. 450. Although SEPA has a discretion as regards public access to records (subs. (1)(e)(ii)), it is under a duty to ensure that the Keeper has unrestricted access to its records at all reasonable hours (subs. (1)(e)(i)).

Subs. (3)

Where any provision in any other enactment is inconsistent with subs. (1), the provision in question is to prevail over subs. (1). This is of considerable significance in the context of the relationship between subs. (1)(c) and the Environmental Information Regulations 1992 (S.I. 1992 No. 3240). There appears to be potential for conflict between subs. (1)(c) and those Regulations as SEPA has discretion in determining which records are worthy of preservation. It may be that in exercising that discretion SEPA disposes of records which contain information relating to the environment in terms of the Regulations and which are not subject to any of the exemptions set out in the Regulations. The disposal of such records may be unlawful, although clearly no legal action could recover them. If a person were aware that such records had existed, it presumably would be possible to raise an action of proving the tenor in the Court of Session to attempt to ascertain details of the contents of the records disposed of.

General powers and duties

Guidance on sustainable development and other aims and objectives

31.—(1) The Secretary of State shall from time to time give guidance to SEPA with respect to aims and objectives which he considers it appropriate for SEPA to pursue in the performance of its functions.

(2) The guidance given under subsection (1) above must include guidance with respect to the contribution which, having regard to SEPA's responsibilities and resources, the Secretary of State considers it appropriate for SEPA to make, by the performance of its functions, towards attaining the objective of achieving sustainable development.

(3) In performing its functions, SEPA shall have regard to guidance given under this section.

(4) The power to give guidance to SEPA under this section shall be exercisable only after consultation with SEPA and such other bodies or persons as the Secretary of State considers it appropriate to consult in relation to the guidance in question.

(5) A draft of any guidance proposed to be given under this section shall be laid before each House of Parliament and the guidance shall not be given until after the period of 40 days beginning with the day on which the draft was so laid or, if the draft is laid on different days, the later of the two days.

(6) If, within the period mentioned in subsection (5) above, either House resolves that the guidance, the draft of which was laid before it, should not be given, the Secretary of State shall not give that guidance.

(7) In reckoning any period of 40 days for the purposes of subsection (5) or (6) above, no account shall be taken of any time during which Parliament is dissolved or prorogued or during which both Houses are adjourned for more than four days.

(8) The Secretary of State shall arrange for any guidance given under this section to be published in such manner as he considers appropriate.

DEFINITIONS
"functions": s.124(1).
"SEPA": s.124(1).

COMMENCEMENT
October 12, 1995 (S.I. 1995 No. 2649 (S.199)).

GENERAL NOTE
Unlike the Agency, SEPA has no principal aim. The Secretary of State is under a duty to give SEPA guidance on the aims and objectives he considers it appropriate for SEPA to pursue (subs. (1)). However, this guidance must include guidance on the contribution SEPA is to make to the objective of achieving sustainable development (subs. (2)). In the original Environment Bill, wording identical to s.31(1)–(3) was used in relation to the Agency in what was then cl. 4. Concerns were expressed in Parliament that the Agencies had no specified statutory aims and objectives particularly in relation to sustainable development (see, for example, *Hansard*, H.L. Vol. 559, col. 1450; Vol. 560, col. 1776). However, the Government argued that specifying a statutory purpose for the Agencies related to sustainable development was not appropriate, first, as it was "dangerous to seek to overspecify on the face of the Bill the full contents of the guidance. A long list might appear exhaustive but not cover all issues on which, in future, the Ministers might need to give guidance to the Agency to SEPA". Thus specification in detail might lead to the wrong emphasis being given to certain aspects of sustainable development (*per* Viscount Ullswater, Minister of State, Department of the Environment, *Hansard*, H.L. Vol. 560, cols. 574–575). Secondly, they argued that the Agencies could not on their own achieve sustainable development (*per* Viscount Ullswater, *Hansard*, H.L. Vol. 560, col. 575).

Although a principal aim was subsequently introduced for the Agency in s.4, no similar provision was made for SEPA. The Government's reasons for refusing to introduce a parallel principal aim for SEPA were essentially the same as those given by Viscount Ullswater above (see, for example, Robert Atkins, M.P., Minister for the Environment and Countryside, Standing Committee B, April 27, 1995, col. 32) although they also explained:

"Given the fact that SEPA would already have a more defined focus on the prevention and control of pollution than the Environment Agency for England and Wales, which would have wider functions, the Government are not convinced that it is necessary for SEPA to have a principal aim set out in legislation" (*per* the Earl of Lindsay, *Hansard*, H.L. Vol. 561, col. 1689).

SEPA's narrower focus essentially arises from the fact that the functions transferred to it from the RPAs do not include the wide ranging functions in relation to water resources management and flood defence which the NRA enjoyed in England and Wales (see also the Introduction and General Note to Part I on p. 25–16 and the note to s.21 on p. 25–73). It is, however, noteworthy that SEPA's sister agency, Scottish Natural Heritage, which deals, *inter alia*, with nature conservation matters, is required to have regard to the desirability of ensuring that anything which it does in relation to natural heritage "is undertaken in a manner which is sustainable" (Natural Heritage (Scotland) Act 1991, s.1(1)).

There was also debate on whether SEPA should be given a statutory aim to protect or enhance the environment in discharging its functions along lines similar to the aim given to the Agency in s.4 (*e.g. per* Lord Carmichael of Kelvingrove, *Hansard*, H.L. Vol. 560, col. 1687). The Government again rejected such suggestions and explained:

"In practice, an aim of this type in a management statement or guidance can sit more comfortably alongside any duties of the agency which could in other circumstances have led to conflict with the aim. However, if that non-statutory duty were to be enshrined in the Bill as a duty ... there would be no obvious way of establishing a hierarchy of action" (*per* the Earl of Lindsay, *Hansard*, H.L. Vol. 560, col. 1689).

This explanation leaves something to be desired since the Government were prepared to give such a principal aim to the Agency: the implications of that aim are considered in the General Note to s.4 at p. 25–38.

Guidance on aims and objectives

On October 13, 1994, the Government published a draft *Management Statement* for SEPA. This non-statutory document contained a number of proposed main objectives for SEPA. On May 3, 1995 the Government issued a preliminary draft of the proposed guidance: *Draft Guidance to the Scottish Environment Protection Agency under Clause 29 of the Environment Bill.*

Revised draft guidance, *The Scottish Environment Protection Agency and Sustainable Development* (November 1995), was issued for consultation on December 12, 1995. It is divided into statutory and non-statutory sections. The statutory guidance on SEPA's aims and objectives and its contribution towards achieving sustainable development to which SEPA must have regard by virtue of subs. (3) is contained in Appendix I while the remainder of the guidance on the principles of sustainable development and costs and benefits is non-statutory. Although SEPA is not obliged to have regard to non-statutory guidance such guidance will still be of considerable significance in, for example, appeals to the Secretary of State where all relevant matters whether statutory or not would be considered. However, it is not always apparent why certain provisions have been omitted from the statutory section of the guidance as, for example, in the case of the guidance on SEPA's contribution to sustainable development (see further below).

The revised draft guidance indicates that the Government's main purpose in creating SEPA was:

"to enable existing functions to be exercised in such a way as to bring greater benefit both to the environment and to those who are being regulated" (App. I, para. 4).

SEPA's principal aim is to be:

"to deliver well-managed integrated environmental protection, not only as an end in itself but as a contribution to the Government's goal of sustainable development" (App. I, para. 6).

SEPA's principal aim is subject to the provisions of the Environment Act 1995, any other enactment under which SEPA will operate and the requirement to take into account costs (App. I, para. 7) and is therefore only applicable where SEPA has some discretion in the exercise of its functions and even then SEPA must only have regard to it. See also the note to s.4 on p. 25–38. As regards objectives, the guidance provides that SEPA should:

"(i) adopt, across all its functions, an integrated approach to environmental protection and enhancement which considers impacts of substances and activities on all environmental media and on natural resources:

(ii) work with all relevant sectors of society, including regulated organisations, to develop approaches which deliver environmental requirements and goals without imposing excessive costs (in relation to benefits gained) on regulated organisations or society as a whole;

(iii) adopt clear and effective procedures for serving its customers, including by developing single points of contact through which regulated organisations can deal with the Agency [*sic*];

(iv) operate to high professional standards, based on sound science, information and analysis of the environment and of processes which affect it;

(v) organise its activities in ways which reflect good environmental and management practice and provide value for money for those who pay its charges and taxpayers as a whole;

(vi) provide clear and readily available advice and information on its work; and

(vii) develop a close and responsive relationship with the public, local authorities and other representatives of local communities and regulated organisations" (App. I, para. 8).

Principles of sustainable development. The non-statutory part of the revised draft guidance outlines the principles of sustainable development and provides the definition of sustainable development adopted by the World Commission on Environment and Development in 1987:

"Development that meets the needs of the present without compromising the ability of future generations to meet their own needs" (para. 2.2).

However, it does not attempt to define the phrase further. What it does do is to refer to the *UK Strategy on Sustainable Development* (Cm. 2426, 1994) which emphasises both the need for economic development and the importance of caring for the environment (para. 2.1). The specific principles which the guidance indicates are of especial relevance to SEPA are the following: using the best scientific information available; the precautionary principle on which action should be based when damage to the environment is both uncertain and significant; the "polluter pays" principle which "requires that, when production processes threaten or cause damage to the environment, the cost of necessary environmental measures should be borne by the producer, and not by society at large, giving incentives to reduce the pollution"; the wise use of natural environmental capital which involves finding ways of enhancing total wealth while using common natural resources in prudent ways which consider the interests of future generations and whether there is a risk of irreversible environmental effects and, if so, how significant they may be; the carrying capacity of habitats and ecosystems which involves the consideration of the ability of a habitat to support a particular species or the capacity of the environmental to absorb pollution or waste; and the interests of future generations, which should be allowed for when judgements are being made about whether environmental costs have to be accepted as the price of economic development or not (paras. 2.3–2.9).

SEPA's contribution. The statutory section of the guidance (App. I, para. 9) indicates that SEPA should (i) take a holistic approach to the protection and enhancement of the environment and accordingly carry out its functions so as to take account of the cross media impacts of pollutants; (ii) take a long term perspective taking into account longer term implications and effects; (iii) pay particular attention to its statutory conservation obligations since maintaining biodiversity is an essential element of sustainable development; (iv) where possible discharge its regulatory functions in partnership with business in ways which maximise the scope for cost-effective investment in improved technologies and management techniques and, in general, SEPA should seek "(a) to establish clear and stable policy parameters, so that regulated organisations can plan for the future; (b) to encourage regulated organisations to adopt plans and management techniques—such as those envisaged in BS7750 and the EU Eco-Management and Audit Scheme—to enable them to meet the policy parameters at (a) above and to seek innovative ways of meeting environmental objectives. In doing so it should bear in mind that different approaches may be appropriate for large and small businesses; (c) to encourage regulated organisations fully to exploit the potential for environmental initiatives to result in cost savings, thus enhancing their own and the UK's competitive position; (d) to encourage regulated organisations to adopt high environmental standards where cost-effective, for example, by co-operating with business organisations such as the Advisory Committee on Business and the Environment and the CBI to promote voluntary initiatives; and (e) to encourage knowledge and understanding, particularly in regulated organisations, of best available techniques not entailing excessive costs for the prevention and minimisation of pollution, including the efficient use of resources, such as energy, and the minimisation of waste"; (v) since achieving sustainable development will involve contributions from many different groups in society, SEPA should strive to develop close and responsive relationships with the different groups and to work in partnership with them; (vi) SEPA should strive to become a recognised centre of knowledge and expertise and to provide clear and readily accessible advice and information on its work and on best environmental practice since high quality information and advice is an important element in advancing sustainable development strategies.

The non-statutory section of the revised draft guidance points out that SEPA cannot by itself achieve sustainable development but that it is expected to make "a significant contribution" to it in relation to its functions which are designed to ensure environmental protection (para. 3.1). SEPA is encouraged (in paras. 3.1 and 3.3) to seek to integrate environmental requirements with the need for economic and social development to allow improvements in the overall quality of life; to consider the distinct characteristics of Scotland's environment and economy in performing its functions which may mean that national standards need to be tempered by sensitivity to local circumstances given Scotland's diverse natural environment, its remote rural communities and extremes of population density except where significant global effects would suggest otherwise. It is unclear why this latter provision has not been included in the statutory guidance, as it would seem to be of considerable importance.

Costs and benefits. The non-statutory section of the revised draft guidance also discusses the issue of costs and benefits which SEPA must take into account in certain circumstances under s.39 (see also the General Note to s.39 at p. 25–105). The guidance explains the purpose of this duty as follows:

"The Secretary of State considers that as SEPA is a body with powers to make decisions with significant impacts on individuals, organisations and the environment, it should take account of all types of costs and benefits when making such decisions. This will not only ensure that financial and other considerations are taken into account, but also that environmental considerations are given the central role that is necessary for sustainable development" (para. 4.2).

The restrictions on the scope of the duty are noted whereby it does not apply where it would be unreasonable and that it does not affect SEPA's mandatory obligations to discharge specific duties, comply with requirements or pursue objectives (paras. 4.1 and 4.2). It is made clear that the duty is to apply where SEPA is exercising discretion either in considering whether or not to take action and the manner in which action should be taken (para. 4.4). While all costs and benefits should be taken into account, there is no need for precise quantification especially where such quantification is inherently difficult as, for example, in relation to likely environmental costs and benefits such as the value of a forest (para. 4.5). In assessing costs and benefits the guidance suggests that SEPA may consider it appropriate to consider principles, procedures and techniques, particularly risk assessment and economic and policy appraisal, the precautionary principle, reliance on sound science, the likely impact on the carrying capacity of the environment and on natural environmental capital and longer term implications and effects (para. 4.6). It is stressed that such analyses should take proper account of long-term environmental benefits as well as immediate financial costs (*ibid.*).

SEPA should concern itself with the costs and benefits of its actions for society as a whole, the effects on the welfare of people and business, changes in the use of resources and impacts on the environment (para. 4.6(vi)). SEPA should take into account the views of the chief medical officer, impacts on individual companies and industry sectors and the distribution of costs and benefits across the economy (*ibid.*). The guidance urges SEPA to develop practical procedures to ensure that it meets the requirements of the duty to take into account costs and benefits where appropriate. Such procedures should include advice to staff on relevant techniques for assessing costs and benefits; circumstances where SEPA's discretion is limited by obligations arising from other duties, requirements and objectives; and on the extent to which consideration of costs and benefits might be unreasonable (para. 4.7). It would appear to be sensible to ensure that such procedures are similar to those developed by the Agency so that there is consistency throughout Great Britain in the application of this duty.

Subs. (3)
Shall have regard to. SEPA is required to have regard to the guidance given under subs. (1). The phrase "have regard to" is considered in the Introduction and General Note to Part I of the Act at p. 25–20. It is submitted that it may not be easy to establish as an evidential point that SEPA has failed to have regard to the guidance issued under s.31(1). Also the fact that the final guidance is likely to be couched in very general terms will also not assist those who wish to challenge SEPA on the basis that it did not have regard to the guidance.

Subss. (4)–(7)
The original Environment Bill contained no provisions for consultation or Parliamentary scrutiny of the guidance issued by the Secretary of State. There was considerable criticism of this omission in Parliament especially regarding the degree of control over SEPA which the original provisions gave to the Secretary of State (see, for example, the Earl of Kintore, *Hansard*, H.L. Vol. 560, col. 1687). To allay such criticism the Government introduced provisions requiring the Secretary of State to consult with SEPA itself and such other bodies as he considered appropriate before issuing guidance. Furthermore some degree of Parliamentary scrutiny has also been provided for as the guidance is to be laid before Parliament under the negative resolution procedure, which enables either House of Parliament to reject the guidance although it may not be amended.

Subs. (8)
No provision was originally made for publication of the guidance issued by the Secretary of State. This subsection is designed to rectify that.

General environmental and recreational duties

32.—(1) It shall be the duty of the Secretary of State and of SEPA, in formulating or considering any proposals relating to any functions of SEPA—
  (a) to have regard to the desirability of conserving and enhancing the natural heritage of Scotland;
  (b) to have regard to the desirability of protecting and conserving buildings, sites and objects of archaeological, architectural, engineering or historic interest;
  (c) to take into account any effect which the proposals would have on the natural heritage of Scotland or on any such buildings, sites or objects; and
  (d) to have regard to the social and economic needs of any area or description of area of Scotland and, in particular, to such needs of rural areas.
  (2) Subject to subsection (1) above, it shall be the duty of the Secretary of State and of SEPA, in formulating or considering any proposals relating to any functions of SEPA—

(a) to have regard to the desirability of preserving for the public any free-dom of access (including access for recreational purposes) to areas of forest, woodland, mountains, moor, bog, cliff, foreshore, loch or reservoir and other places of natural beauty;

(b) to have regard to the desirability of maintaining the availability to the public of any facility for visiting or inspecting any building, site or object of archaeological, architectural, engineering or historic interest; and

(c) to take into account any effect which the proposals would have on any such freedom of access or on the availability of any such facility.

(3) In this section—

"building" includes structure; and

"the natural heritage of Scotland" has the same meaning as in section 1(3) of the Natural Heritage (Scotland) Act 1991.

DEFINITIONS

"building": subs. (3).

"functions": s.124(1).

"natural heritage": subs. (3); s.1(3) of the Natural Heritage (Scotland) Act 1991.

"SEPA": s.124(1).

COMMENCEMENT

October 12, 1995 (S.I. 1995 No. 2649 (S.199)).

GENERAL NOTE

This section imposes on the Secretary of State and SEPA a duty either to have regard to or take account of certain environmental and recreational matters. It should be noted that the duty only applies where the Secretary of State or SEPA is formulating or considering proposals in relation to any of SEPA's functions. However, the term "proposals" is not defined. (See the General Note to s.7 at p. 25–49.) It arguably includes any proposal by the Secretary of State to issue guidance under s.31(1).

The duties imposed in subs. (2) are subject to those in subs. (1) which means that those in subs. (1) must be given priority. It is left to the discretion of the Secretary of State and SEPA to determine how much weight such considerations should be given in the case of a particular proposal, which means that it is only if SEPA completely ignores a relevant issue that its decision could be challenged in the courts. In exercising its discretion, SEPA must have regard to the guidance issued under s.31(1). In legal terms the duties, which may prompt the development of appropriate memoranda of understanding, do serve a useful purpose in ensuring that the matters listed are always going to be relevant considerations, which must at least be addressed by the Secretary of State and SEPA in formulating or considering any proposals, and in giving some standing to bodies representing the listed interests to make representations both to the Secretary of State and to SEPA and, ultimately, to the courts. The statutory requirement to have regard to such matters will also influence the policy-making of SEPA.

No distinction is drawn in the section between pollution control and non-pollution control functions as is the case in s.7, the equivalent provision for England and Wales. This is because SEPA's functions are largely pollution control functions and it has a much narrower focus than the Agency with regard, for example, to conserving water resources.

The lack of a stronger duty to promote or further the conservation and enhancement of the natural heritage of Scotland was severely criticised both in Parliamentary debates and outside Parliament. In England and Wales, a stronger duty does apply in s.7(1) but only in relation to the Agency's non-pollution control functions. The Government's rationale for not imposing the stronger duty on SEPA was as follows:

"The Bill recognises that matters such as nature conservation are important, and SEPA should, where appropriate, take account of them. However, a duty to further nature conservation could distort the exercise of SEPA's pollution control functions, and its pollution prevention and control functions lie at the heart of its very existence. Few pollution control licences could be issued if SEPA were required to ensure that the levels of pollution they permitted furthered nature conservation.

"Unlike the provisions for the Environment Agency for England and Wales, there is no need to make a distinction in the Scottish provisions between SEPA's pollution control and other functions. The more limited scope of the Scottish agency means that it will not have functions for which a duty to "further" would be appropriate" (*per* the Earl of Lindsay, *Hansard*, H.L. Vol. 560, col. 1220).

This is certainly a logical approach in the light of SEPA's focus on pollution control functions. Furthermore, Scottish Natural Heritage, is much better placed than SEPA to further the conservation and enhancement of Scotland's natural heritage as it is given the aim of securing the conservation and enhancement of, and fostering the understanding and enjoyment of, the natural heritage of Scotland (Natural Heritage (Scotland) Act 1991, s.1(1)).

Subss. (1)–(2)

No equivalent duties were imposed on the bodies whose functions are transferred by the Act to SEPA. However, duties similar to subss. (1)(b), (2)(a) and (b) are imposed on the Secretary of State and the new Scottish water authorities by virtue of s.65 of the Local Government etc. (Scotland) Act 1994, which substitutes a new s.1 for the existing s.1 of the Water (Scotland) Act 1980. The new water authorities are, however, under a stronger duty to further conservation by virtue of s.1(2)(b) of the amended Water (Scotland) Act 1980. SEPA should have regard to the guidance issued under s.31(1) in the discharge of these duties which involve considerable discretion.

Subss. (1)(b)

The word "engineering" did not appear in the original provision in the Environment Bill and was included after it was pointed out in Parliament (by, for example, Lord Howie of Troon, *Hansard*, H.L. Vol. 560, cols. 1224–1225) that the existing wording would not cover buildings, objects or sites such as the Forth Railway Bridge or the Glenfinnan Viaduct on the West Highland railway line which could not properly be said to be of architectural or historic interest but were of engineering interest.

Subss. (1)(d)

The wording of this subsection is significantly different from s.7(1)(c)(iii), its approximate equivalent in the legislation for England and Wales which provides that it shall be the duty of the Ministers and the Agency "to have regard to any effect which the proposals would have on the economic and social well-being of local communities in rural areas". However, the scope of the Scottish provision is considerably wider in that the duty extends to having regard to social and economic effects in any area of Scotland not just in rural areas, although regard should be had to their needs in particular.

Subs. (3)

The definition of building includes structure in order for it to include, for example, viaducts, bridges and tunnels, none of which could otherwise be said to be "buildings".

General duties with respect to pollution control

33.—(1) SEPA's pollution control powers shall be exercisable for the purpose of preventing or minimising, or remedying or mitigating the effects of, pollution of the environment.

(2) SEPA shall, for the purpose—

(a) of facilitating the carrying out of its pollution control functions; or

(b) of enabling it to form an opinion of the general state of pollution of the environment,

compile information relating to such pollution (whether the information is acquired by SEPA carrying out observations or is obtained in any other way).

(3) If required by the Secretary of State to do so, SEPA shall—

(a) carry out assessments (whether generally or for such particular purpose as may be specified in the requirement) of the effect, or likely effect, on the environment of existing or potential levels of pollution of the environment and report its findings to the Secretary of State; or

(b) prepare and send to the Secretary of State a report identifying—

(i) the options which SEPA considers to be available for preventing or minimising, or remedying or mitigating the effects of, pollution of the environment, whether generally or in cases or circumstances specified in the requirement; and

(ii) the costs and benefits of such options as are identified by SEPA pursuant to sub-paragraph (i) above.

(4) SEPA shall follow developments in technology and techniques for preventing or minimising, or remedying or mitigating the effects of, pollution of the environment.

(5) In this section, "pollution control powers" and "pollution control functions" in relation to SEPA, mean respectively its powers or its functions under or by virtue of—

(a) the Alkali, &c. Works Regulation Act 1906;
(b) Part III of the 1951 Act, the Rivers (Prevention of Pollution) (Scotland) Act 1965 and Parts I, IA and II of the Control of Pollution Act 1974;
(c) Part I of the Health and Safety at Work etc. Act 1974;
(d) the Control of Pollution (Amendment) Act 1989;
(e) Parts I, II and IIA of the 1990 Act;
(f) section 19 of the Clean Air Act 1993;
(g) the Radioactive Substances Act 1993; and
(h) regulations made by virtue of section 2(2) of the European Communities Act 1972, to the extent that the regulations relate to pollution.

DEFINITIONS
"costs": s.56(1).
"environment": s.56(1); s.1(2) of the 1990 Act.
"pollution control powers": subs. (5).
"pollution control functions": subs. (5).
"SEPA": s.124(1).

COMMENCEMENT
April 1, 1996 (S.I. 1996 No. 186).

GENERAL NOTE
This section provides a single statutory purpose for all SEPA's pollution control functions which are listed by the statutes in which they are contained in subs. (5). Of the pollution control functions transferred to SEPA, only those functions in relation to integrated pollution control and air pollution were exercisable for a similar purpose under s.4(2)–(3) of the 1990 Act. For example, s.4(2) indicated that "[t]hose functions ... shall be exercisable for the purpose of preventing or minimising pollution of the environment due to the release of substances into any environmental medium". Neither waste regulation functions nor radioactive substances control functions nor general water pollution control functions were exercisable for a similar purpose although it should be noted that the Waste Management Licensing Regulations 1994 provide that waste regulation authorities must discharge their functions under both Parts I and II of the 1990 Act so as to fulfil the "relevant objectives": Sched. 4, paras. 2 and 4, 1994 Regulations and that RPAs may exercise their powers to carry out preventive or remedial works under s.46 for a similar purpose.

The key term "pollution of the environment" is not defined in subs. (1). However, definitions may be found in s.1(3) and s.29(3) of the 1990 Act. The former definition applies in the case of IPC and LAPC functions and the latter in the case of waste regulation functions and it is submitted that those definitions would apply in relation to those particular functions of SEPA. There may, however, be an argument that since the wording of s.33(1) is drawn from Pt. I of the 1990 Act which deals with IPC and LAPC, and since SEPA will be integrating pollution control functions to a greater degree at least in administrative terms, the definition in s.1(3) is to be preferred for wider application across all of SEPA's pollution control functions. Certainly, there is no definition of "pollution of the environment" which could be drawn from Scots water pollution legislation under the 1974 Act. There is, however, some case law on the definition of "polluting matter" as discussed in the General Note to s.5 at p. 25–42.

The circumstances in which a legal challenge for breach of this statutory duty might be issued against SEPA are probably fairly limited and might include, for example, malicious use of pollution control powers against a company; although it is hard to envisage such a situation occurring in practice.

Subss. (2)–(3)
The revised draft guidance to SEPA notes that the Government is currently undertaking work on sustainable development indicators (para. 5). The duties to compile information and carry out specified assessments for the Secretary of State prescribed by subss. (2) and (3), which are new functions, should have an important role in that context. These duties will also be of

importance in relation (i) to SEPA's duty to prepare a national waste strategy for Scotland (see the General Note to s.92 at p. 25–250); (ii) to its consultative role in relation to the new national air quality strategy under s.80(6); and (iii) to the duty of Member States under Art. 7 of Directive 90/313/EEC on the freedom of access to information on the environment to provide general information to the public on the state of the environment by such means as the periodic publication of descriptive reports. It should also be noted that an integrated approach to environmental protection requires accurate information on the often complex relationship between impacts on the different environmental media. See also the General Note to s.5(2)–(4) at p. 25–43.

Subs. (4)

A similar duty was imposed on HMIPI and RPAs in relation to integrated pollution control and on local authorities in relation to air pollution control under the 1990 Act:

> "It shall be the duty of the chief inspector or, in Scotland, of the chief inspector and river purification authorities to follow developments in technology and techniques for preventing or reducing pollution of the environment due to releases of substances from prescribed processes; and the local enforcing authorities shall follow such of those development as concern releases into the air of substances from prescribed processes designated for local control" (s.4(9)).

This duty is now applied across the whole field of pollution control functions, so that it would also now apply, for example, to developments in landfill technology or waste disposal techniques in relation to radioactive substances. The duty is very important in relation to the concept of best available techniques not entailing excessive cost.

General duties with respect to water

34.—(1) It shall be the duty of SEPA—

  (a) to promote the cleanliness of—

        (i) rivers, other inland waters and ground waters in Scotland; and

        (ii) the tidal waters of Scotland; and

  (b) to conserve so far as practicable the water resources of Scotland.

(2) Without prejudice to section 32 above, it shall be the duty of SEPA, to such extent as it considers desirable, generally to promote—

  (a) the conservation and enhancement of the natural beauty and amenity of inland and coastal waters and of land associated with such waters; and

  (b) the conservation of flora and fauna which are dependent on an aquatic environment.

(3) Subsection (1) above is without prejudice to section 1 of the Water (Scotland) Act 1980 (general duties of Secretary of State and water authorities as respects water resources and supplies).

(4) In subsection (1) above, "tidal waters" means any part of the sea or the tidal part of any river, watercourse or inland water (whether natural or artificial) and includes the waters of any enclosed dock which adjoins tidal waters.

DEFINITIONS

  "tidal waters": subs. (4).

  "SEPA": s.124(1).

COMMENCEMENT

  April 1, 1996 (S.I. 1996 No. 186).

GENERAL NOTE

  This section includes a re-enactment of the duties imposed on river purification authorities (RPAs) by s.17 of the Rivers (Prevention of Pollution) (Scotland) Act 1951 as amended and, significantly, extends that duty to ground waters. Cleanliness is not defined. Given the limited functions SEPA will have in relation to the conservation of water resources in Scotland, particularly as it lacks powers to control abstraction except in the case of abstraction for irrigation purposes by virtue of Pt. II of the Natural Heritage (Scotland) Act, it is unlikely that SEPA will be able in discharging the duty in subs. (1)(b) to make a significant contribution to conserving water resources in Scotland on its own. The Secretary of State and the new Scottish water authorities established by the Local Government etc. (Scotland) Act 1994 have a conservation duty in relation to water resources in Scotland by virtue of s.1 of the Water (Scotland) Act 1980 (as substituted by s.65 of the Local Government etc. (Scotland) Act 1994) and will have a much more significant contribution to make in this regard than SEPA given their much more extensive role in this context. Their duties are unaffected by the duty imposed on SEPA (subs. (3)). Consultation, and perhaps even memoranda of understanding, between SEPA and the new water authorities may be required in order for SEPA effectively to discharge its duties under subs. (1).

The Environment Bill as originally drafted provided that the duty now contained in s.34(1) was to be "in accordance with any directions under section 38 [now s.40] below", *i.e.* in accordance with any directions made by the Secretary of State. However, this latter part of the provision was removed by the Government in recognition of their intention to leave day-to-day operational matters with SEPA (*per* the Earl of Lindsay, *Hansard*, H.L. Vol. 562, cols. 1032–1033) following concerns expressed in the House of Lords regarding meddling by the Secretary of State in SEPA's day-to-day operations (see, for example, the Earl of Dundonald, *Hansard*, H.L. Vol. 562, col. 1033).

Subs. (2)
The extent to which SEPA discharges this duty to promote conservation of specified waters is left to its discretion although in discharging this duty it should have regard to guidance issued under s.31(1). The effective discharge of SEPA's duty may require a memorandum of understanding with Scottish Natural Heritage.

Environmental duties as respects Natural Heritage Areas and sites of special interest

35.—(1) Where an area of land—

(a) has been designated, under section 6(2) of the Natural Heritage (Scotland) Act 1991 (in this section referred to as "the 1991 Act") as a Natural Heritage Area; or

(b) is, in the opinion of Scottish Natural Heritage (in this section referred to as "SNH"), of special interest by reason of its flora, fauna or geological or physiographical features,

and SNH consider that it may at any time be affected by schemes, works, operations or activities of SEPA or by an authorisation given by SEPA, SNH shall give notice to SEPA in accordance with subsection (2) below.

(2) A notice under subsection (1) above shall specify—

(a) in the case of an area of land mentioned in paragraph (a) of that subsection, SNH's reasons for considering that the area is of outstanding value to the natural heritage of Scotland; and

(b) in the case of an area of land mentioned in paragraph (b) of that subsection, SNH's reasons for holding the opinion there mentioned.

(3) Where SNH has given notice under subsection (1) above in respect of an area of land and—

(a) in the case of an area of land mentioned in paragraph (a) of that subsection, the designation is cancelled or varied under section 6(7) of the 1991 Act; or

(b) in the case of an area of land mentioned in paragraph (b) of that subsection, SNH ceases to be of the opinion there mentioned,

SNH shall forthwith notify SEPA of that fact.

(4) Where SEPA has received notice under subsection (1) above with respect to any area of land, it shall (unless SNH has given notice under subsection (3) above with respect to the land) consult SNH before carrying out or authorising any schemes, works, operations or activities which appear to SEPA to be likely—

(a) in the case of an area of land mentioned in subsection (1)(a), significantly to prejudice the value of the land, or any part of it, as a Natural Heritage Area; and

(b) in the case of an area of land mentioned in subsection (1)(b), to destroy or damage any of the flora or fauna or features by reason of which SNH formed the opinion there mentioned.

(5) Subsection (4) above shall not apply in relation to anything done in an emergency if particulars of what is done and of the emergency are notified by SEPA to SNH as soon as practicable after the thing is done.

(6) In this section, "authorisation" includes any consent, licence or permission.

(7) Any expression used in this section and in Part I of the 1991 Act and not defined in this Act shall be construed in accordance with that Part.

DEFINITIONS

"authorisation": subs. (6).
"land": s.22(1) of the Natural Heritage (Scotland) Act 1991.
"natural heritage": s.1(3) of the Natural Heritage (Scotland) Act 1991.
"Natural Heritage Area": s.6 of the Natural Heritage (Scotland) Act 1991.
"notice": s.124(1).
"SEPA": s.124(1).

COMMENCEMENT

April 1, 1996 (S.I. 1996 No. 186).

GENERAL NOTE

The Natural Heritage (Scotland) Act 1991 merged the Countryside Commission for Scotland and the Nature Conservancy Council for Scotland into a single body called Scottish Natural Heritage (SNH). SNH performs all the functions of its predecessors as well as having powers to provide for access in the countryside. The Natural Heritage (Scotland) Act 1991 also gives SNH the power to designate land as a Natural Heritage Area, in order to assist in the care of natural heritage which is defined by s.1(3) thereof as including "the flora and fauna of Scotland, its geological and physiographical features, its natural beauty and amenity". Natural heritage is a concept designed to draw together the areas of responsibility of SNH's predecessors and reflects the integrated approach which SNH was intended to take. This section requires SNH to notify (subs. (2)) SEPA of Natural Heritage Areas (subs. (1)(a)) and sites of special interest (subs. (1)(b)) which SNH considers may be affected by schemes, works, operations or activities of SEPA or by authorisations granted by SEPA and must give its reasons for holding this opinion (subs. (2)). The Government explained why they had introduced the requirement that SNH should provide reasons for its opinion:

"I believe that it is appropriate for SNH to be additionally obliged to make the reasons for its considerations known to SEPA. SEPA must, except in an emergency, consult SNH where it appears likely to SEPA that its actions may affect such land. Knowing why SNH thought that the land might be so affected in the first place would, I suggest, help SEPA meet that obligation" (*per* the Earl of Lindsay, *Hansard*, H.L. Vol. 560, col. 1229).

Where SEPA has been so notified by SNH it must consult SNH before carrying out or authorising any schemes, works, operations or activities or granting any authorisations which appear likely to give rise to the circumstances specified in subs. (4)(a) and (b). There is an exception to this requirement in the case of an emergency. A proposal to restrict definition of emergency to "danger to life or health" was opposed by the Government on the grounds that it would fetter SEPA's discretion to an unreasonable extent:

"For example, it does not seem to cover an emergency which may cause serious environmental harm. Much would depend on how "life" was interpreted. Contamination of soil may not directly threaten life but it could well constitute an emergency. We should be prepared to trust SEPA to discharge its statutory functions to protect the environment when it believes it is imperative to do so urgently" (*per* the Earl of Lindsay, *Hansard*, H.L. Vol. 560, col. 1229).

Codes of practice with respect to environmental and recreational duties

36.—(1) The Secretary of State shall have power by order to approve any code of practice issued (whether by him or by another person) for the purpose of—

(a) giving practical guidance to SEPA with respect to any of the matters for the purposes of which sections 32, 34(2) and 35 above have effect; and

(b) promoting what appear to him to be desirable practices by SEPA with respect to those matters, and may at any time by such an order approve a modification of such a code or withdraw his approval of such a code or modification.

(2) In discharging its duties under section 32, 34(2) or 35 above, SEPA shall have regard to any code of practice, and any modifications of a code of practice, for the time being approved under this section.

(3) The Secretary of State shall not make an order under this section unless he has first consulted—
  (a) SEPA;
  (b) Scottish Natural Heritage;
  (c) Scottish Enterprise;
  (d) Highlands and Islands Enterprise;
  (e) the East of Scotland Water Authority;
  (f) the West of Scotland Water Authority;
  (g) the North of Scotland Water Authority; and
  (h) such other persons as he considers it appropriate to consult.

(4) The power of the Secretary of State to make an order under this section shall be exercisable by statutory instrument; and any statutory instrument containing such an order shall be subject to annulment in pursuance of a resolution of either House of Parliament.

DEFINITIONS
  "modifications": s.124(1).
  "SEPA": s.124(1).

COMMENCEMENT
  October 12, 1995 (S.I. 1995 No. 2649 (S.199)).

GENERAL NOTE
  This section is modelled to an extent upon s.51 of the 1974 Act (as amended by Sched. 23 to the Water Act 1989) which makes provision for the Secretary of State to approve codes of practice giving practical guidance to persons engaged in agriculture with respect to activities that might affect controlled waters and promoting desirable practices by such persons for avoiding or minimising water pollution. However, this section applies to codes of practice issued to SEPA giving guidance on the discharge of its environmental and recreational duties under ss.32, 34(2) and 35. The Codes of Practice will provide SEPA with more detailed guidance on how they should discharge these duties. Interestingly, s.51(2) of the 1974 Act provides that a contravention of a Code of Practice would not of itself give rise to any criminal or civil liability, but that is not the case here, see further the General Note to s.9(2) on p. 25–52.

Subs. (2)
Shall have regard to. SEPA is not bound by the codes of practice, and may depart from them. However, they must be considered and a failure to do so would render any action by SEPA in the discharge of its duties under ss.32, 34(2) or 35 unlawful. See also the discussion of this phrase in the Introduction and General Note to this Part of the Act at p. 25–20. SEPA must only have regard to any Codes of Practice which are for the time being approved under s.36. This means that it need not have regard to any draft code issued for consultation but not yet approved under this section.

Subs. (3)
  Concern was expressed in Parliament that all the consultees specified were quangos, and it was argued that if there was to be any accountability the list of consultees should include democratically elected councillors (*per* Lord Carmichael of Kelvingrove, *Hansard*, H.L. Vol. 560, cols. 1233–1234). Although the Government declined to extend the list to include councillors (*per* the Earl of Lindsay, *Hansard*, H.L. Vol. 560, col. 1234) it is difficult to envisage a situation in which the Secretary of State would not consult the appropriate councils in relation to any proposed Code of Practice under s.36(3)(h).
  It should be noted that the list of statutory consultees is more extensive than that appearing in the equivalent provision for England and Wales, namely s.9, from which references to sewerage and water undertakers were removed during the passage of the Bill through Parliament. However, in Scotland, the three new water authorities are listed as statutory consultees and Scottish Enterprise and Highlands and Islands Enterprise also appear on the list. Interestingly, however, although the Historic Buildings and Monuments Commission, the Sports Council and the Sports

Council for Wales are included in the list of statutory consultees in s.9, neither Historic Scotland nor the Scottish Sports Council are listed as consultees in s.36. The omission of these bodies from the list of consultees was explained for the Government by the Earl of Lindsay:

"I agree … that it is important that the views of Historic Scotland are fed into the process of approving a code of practice. But as that body is an executive agency of the Scottish Office, a requirement on the Secretary of State to consult Historic Scotland is tantamount to a requirement to consult himself.

As SEPA will not have the range of responsibilities of the Environment Agency, I do not believe the Scottish Sports Council has a strong enough interest in the activities of SEPA to justify its specific and automatic inclusion" (*Hansard*, H.L. Vol. 560, col. 1234).

CHAPTER III

MISCELLANEOUS, GENERAL AND SUPPLEMENTAL PROVISIONS RELATING TO THE NEW AGENCIES

Additional general powers and duties

Incidental general functions

37.—(1) Each new Agency (that is to say, in this Part, the Agency or SEPA)—

(a) may do anything which, in its opinion, is calculated to facilitate, or is conducive or incidental to, the carrying out of its functions; and

(b) without prejudice to the generality of that power, may, for the purposes of, or in connection with, the carrying out of those functions, acquire and dispose of land and other property and carry out such engineering or building operations as it considers appropriate;

and the Agency may institute criminal proceedings in England and Wales.

(2) It shall be the duty of each new Agency to provide the Secretary of State or the Minister with such advice and assistance as he may request.

(3) Subject to subsection (4) below, each new Agency may provide for any person, whether in or outside the United Kingdom, advice or assistance, including training facilities, as respects any matter in which that new Agency has skill or experience.

(4) Without prejudice to any power of either new Agency apart from subsection (3) above to provide advice or assistance of the kind mentioned in that subsection, the power conferred by that subsection shall not be exercised in a case where the person for whom the advice or assistance is provided is outside the United Kingdom, except with the consent in writing of the appropriate Minister which consent may be given subject to such conditions as the Minister giving it thinks fit.

(5) Each new Agency—

(a) shall make arrangements for the carrying out of research and related activities (whether by itself or by others) in respect of matters to which its functions relate; and

(b) may make the results of any such research or related activities available to any person in return for payment of such fee as it considers appropriate.

(6) Subsection (5) above shall not be taken as preventing a new Agency from making the results of any research available to the public free of charge whenever it considers it appropriate to do so.

(7) Each new Agency may by agreement with any person charge that person a fee in respect of work done, or services or facilities provided, as a result of a request made by him for advice or assistance, whether of a general or specific character, in connection with any matter involving or relating to environmental licences.

(8) Subsection (7) above—

(a) is without prejudice to the generality of the powers of either new Agency to make charges; but

(b) is subject to any such express provision with respect to charging by the new Agency in question as is contained in the other provisions of this Part or in any other enactment.

(9) In this section "engineering or building operations", without prejudice to the generality of that expression, includes—

(a) the construction, alteration, improvement, maintenance or demolition of any building or structure or of any reservoir, watercourse, dam, weir, well, borehole or other works; and

(b) the installation, modification or removal of any machinery or apparatus.

DEFINITIONS

"Agency, the": s.124(1).
"appropriate Minister": s.56(1).
"engineering or building operations": subs. (9).
"environmental licence": s.56(1).
"functions": s.124(1).
"Minister, the": s.56(1).
"new Agency": s.56(1).
"SEPA": s.124(1).

COMMENCEMENT

Subsections (1), (2) and (9) came into force on July 28, 1995 (S.I. 1995 No. 1983). The remainder of this section came into force on April 1, 1996 (S.I. 1996 No. 186).

GENERAL NOTE

This section provides, for each of the Agency and SEPA additional powers (under subss. (1), (3), (5)(b), (6) and (7)) and additional duties (by virtue of subs. (2) and (5)(a)) which are considered incidental to the carrying out of its functions. In relation to the Agency it should be noted that its "functions" referred to in subss. (1)(a) and (b) are expressed by s.10 to include the functions set out in that section. See the General Note to that section on p. 25–53.

Subs. (1): General incidental powers

This subsection is modelled on the provisions of s.4(1) of the Water Resources Act 1991 in relation to the NRA. Each Agency is given extremely wide incidental powers to do anything which, in its opinion will facilitate or is conducive or incidental to the carrying out of its functions (subs. (1)(a)). The opinion of the Agency in question is the test: thus it would be extremely difficult for any action which could reasonably (in the wide *Wednesbury* sense of reasonableness employed in judicial review cases) be said to so relate to its functions to be challenged. This avoids the need for a lengthy list of incidental powers, although for the avoidance of doubt the power to carry out the activities most likely to involve large commitments of an Agency's resources are expressly included by subss. (1)(b) and (9). Subsection (7) gives the Agency/SEPA the power to charge for the provision of services or facilities in connection with advice or assistance on any matter relating to environmental licences. Subsection (1) would in any event appear wide enough to allow such charging for services not covered by subs. (7), provided that in the opinion of the agency in question those services relate to its functions in the way required by the subsection. It will also be noted that the power provided by s.43 to charge for services and facilities provided in the course of carrying out its functions is expressly without prejudice to the generality of the Agency/SEPA's powers by virtue of this subsection.

Criminal proceedings: the Agency

The Agency may institute criminal proceedings in England and Wales, as could its predecessor bodies. Section 54 provides additionally that anyone authorised by the Agency to prosecute on its behalf before a magistrates' court may do so even though they are not a solicitor or barrister: see the General Note to that section at p. 25–126.

Criminal proceedings: SEPA

Although the Agency may institute criminal proceedings, SEPA may not do so. In Scotland, environmental regulatory bodies have not in the past been able to bring their own prosecutions. They must report incidents to the Procurator Fiscal who will decide whether or not to institute criminal proceedings. Thus, whereas in England and Wales, there is only one level of discretion operating in the decision whether or not to prosecute, in Scotland there are two levels. The regulator must decide whether or not the matter is serious enough to be reported to the Procurator Fiscal and the Procurator Fiscal will then decide whether or not to prosecute. This system has recently been subject to considerable criticism from various quarters (see, for example, Scottish River Purification Boards' Association, Annual Report 1994–95; Friends of the Earth Scotland, *Watered Down—Why the Law is Failing to Protect Scotland's Water*, 1994). It is alleged that Procurators Fiscal are not specialists in environmental law and are unfamiliar with it; that they do not take environmental crime as seriously as "traditional" crime, and that this is adversely affecting the enforcement of environmental law. Criticism has also been levelled at environmental regulators for not preparing cases adequately. However, the 1995 Act does not enable SEPA to bring its own prosecutions. It should, however, be noted that SEPA is apparently to have its own legal staff to prepare cases for the Procurator Fiscal (*Improving Scotland's Environment, The Way Forward*, 1992, para. 17) and that the Crown Office is presently improving its liaison with the existing environmental regulators and is instituting training for Procurators Fiscal and is issuing guidance to them on the prosecution of environmental offences (*Herald*, October 6, 1995; Crown Office Environmental Criminal Law Handbook). The establishment of SEPA should certainly bring benefits with respect to the prosecution of environmental offences as the Crown Office and the Procurator Fiscal service will now have to deal with one organisation only rather than a whole range of RPAs and local authorities together with HMIPI. Standardised reporting procedures and a more consistent enforcement policy should become possible across Scotland.

Subs. (1): The Agency: Injunctions

The NRA supported an amendment to subs. (1) to the effect that the Agency "may institute and appear in any legal proceedings in England and Wales": NRA Media Briefing "Environment Bill—Lords Committee Stage, 17 January 1995". Its argument was that the Agency needs "a clear specific power to institute and appear in not only criminal but also civil proceedings". The prime significance of such a power is that it enables a regulator to apply for an injunction to prevent action which criminal sanctions are failing or likely to fail to deter. An injunction can be a particularly powerful remedy because it is backed by the threat of imprisonment or sequestration of assets for contempt of court, but with two exceptions the Attorney General's leave is required to bring an injunction for the purpose of restraining a criminal action, where the legislation under consideration contains no express provision allowing the authority to take civil proceedings. One exception is where one's own interest in property is affected by the act in question and one is a member of a specific class of persons whom the legislation in question was intended to protect. The Agency is not likely to be in this situation. The second exception is provided by s.222 of the Local Government Act 1972 for local authorities, provided that they consider it "expedient for the promotion or protection of the interests of the inhabitants of their area."

The Agency's waste regulation authority predecessors, benefiting from the Local Government Act provision, have in some cases succeeded in obtaining injunctions which have led to imprisonment for contempt of court through the continued breach of waste legislation. A good example is provided by *Lancashire County Council and Blackpool Borough Council v. Owen Baguley* (unreported). In that case, the waste regulation authority and planning authority are understood to have obtained High Court orders for imprisonment of the defendant, first (on December 15, 1992) for three months, and subsequently (on November 11, 1994) for seven periods totalling five years and seven months but running concurrently (the seven periods included five of 12 months each).

It is submitted, however, that notwithstanding the lack of the specific provision sought by the NRA, it is probable that the Agency does have the ability, by virtue of subs. (1)(a), to seek and obtain injunctions in appropriate cases to secure compliance. This certainly appears to be the Government's understanding of the provision. Arguing that an amendment which would simply have inserted the words "and civil" after "criminal" in subs. (1)(a), and was thus similar in effect to that supported by the NRA was unnecessary, Viscount Ullswater, Minister of State, Department of the Environment, for the Government, suggested in Parliament that "so far as civil proceedings are concerned the agency will be able to take any civil proceedings which in its opinion are calculated to facilitate or are conducive or incidental to the carrying out of its functions by virtue of Clause 35 [now s.37(1)(a)]" (*Hansard*, H.L., Vol. 562, col. 1035). He contrasted this situation with that for criminal proceedings ("it is necessary to give the agency express power to take criminal proceedings since it is to be a prosecuting authority under the legislation in respect of which it has functions") and gave the example of the agency's functions under the Sludge (Use in Agriculture) Regulations 1989:

"The agency's functions under these regulations are limited, for example, to inspecting the sludge producer's register and being provided with information, but it is wished that the agency be the prosecuting authority for any breach in the regulations. It could not be said in this case that prosecuting would facilitate or be conducive or incidental to the specific functions given to the agency by the regulations and thus fall within [what became s.37(1)(a)]; therefore an express provision is required on the face of the Bill" (*ibid.*, col. 1035).

Since subs. (1)(a) and s.4(1) of the Water Resources Act 1991 are worded identically for present purposes, and the NRA's understanding of that provision appears to be that it may not have served to authorise the seeking of an injunction for these purposes without the Attorney General's consent, this explanation is particularly valuable. It may, in appropriate circumstances, be admissible in court to inform the interpretation of subs. (1)(a) (see the Introduction and General Note: *Parliamentary Proceedings* at p. 25–7).

Subs. (1): SEPA: Interdicts
The position with regard to the ability of regulatory agencies in Scotland to obtain interdicts to restrain criminal action is less clear than in England and Wales. In *Buckhaven and Methil Magistrates v. Wemyss Coal Company Limited* 1932 S.C. 201, a case involving an attempt to obtain an interdict to prevent the dumping of colliery waste on the foreshore in circumstances in which the burgh had a statutory duty to prevent the deposit of rubbish under the Burgh Police (Scotland) Act 1892 which was reinforced with criminal sanctions against offending waste tippers, the then Lord President held:

"It has long been settled in Scotland that a statutory body which is set up to enforce a system of statutory regulations, or to establish and enforce a system of bye-laws of its own, has no power to resort to the common law process of interdict for the purpose of enforcing such regulations or bye-laws, when the statute provides penalties for their breach and authorises recovery of such penalties" (*ibid.*, at p. 211. See also *Kelso Magistrates v. Alexander* 1939 S.C. 78).

Although this would appear to settle matters, nonetheless there are conflicting authorities, *e.g. Watney v. Menzies* (1898) 6 S.L.T. 189; and *National Dock Labour Board v. Sheppard Group* 1989 S.L.T. 661. Furthermore, the principle in *Buckhaven and Methil Magistrates* has been modified in relation to local authorities in subsequent legislation, which provides that local authorities may institute legal proceedings where they "consider it expedient for the promotion or protection of the interests of the inhabitants of their area" (Local Government (Scotland) Act 1973, s.189). However, this provision did not apply to river purification boards. Nonetheless, it should also be noted that in practice river purification boards have obtained interdict or interim interdict against persons who have been committing ongoing water pollution offences: *e.g. Forth River Purification Board v. Adam Robertson, The Scotsman*, December 7, 1990. In that case the defender had been previously convicted for water pollution offences under the 1974 Act and despite subsequent warnings had continued to pollute a river. An interim interdict was granted, apparently on the basis of nuisance rather than to prevent an ongoing breach of the criminal law under the 1974 Act (see Scott-Robinson, *The Law of Interdict* (2nd ed., Butterworths, 1994, at pp. 50 and 222).

However, in the light of *Buckhaven and Methil Magistrates* it remains unclear whether, in the absence of express statutory language, the wording of s.37(1)(a) is sufficient to give SEPA the power to seek an interdict in circumstances where a statutory interdict is not otherwise expressly available despite the views of Viscount Ullswater discussed above which, it should be noted, referred expressly to the Agency alone. It is possible that where the offence constituted a nuisance as in the *Adam Robertson* case (above) an interdict or at least an interim interdict may be available.

Availability of statutory injunctions or interdicts
To some extent the question of whether or not this general provision allows the Agency to obtain an injunction in England and Wales, and SEPA an interdict in Scotland, is becoming of less importance as the tendency appears increasingly to be to make provision for such a power expressly in the context of various statutory regimes. The 1995 Act itself amends existing legislation to include further such express provisions. Such express provisions generally relate to circumstances of non-compliance with an extant licence, consent or notice although there are Agency licensing regimes which do not contain such provisions (*e.g.* water abstraction licensing), and the circumstance where a person is operating without the benefit of a licence at all, to which such express provisions do in general apply, may be of particular concern to a regulator. Given the view expressed by Viscount Ullswater, quoted above, as to the effect of s.37(1)(a), this may seem unnecessary, and it is conceivable that the existence of such express provisions in such cases may be taken by a court to cast doubt on whether s.37(1)(a) is indeed capable of being construed so as to permit civil proceedings where they are absent. For the regimes for which the Agency/SEPA are to be regulatory authorities, the position is set out below.

IPC (and, for SEPA, LAPC). The Agency/SEPA have an express power to apply to the High Court or, in Scotland, any court of competent jurisdiction for the purpose of securing compliance with a prohibition or enforcement notice where it is of the opinion that criminal proceedings for a breach of such a notice would afford an ineffectual remedy (s.24 of the 1990 Act). This effectively gives the Agency/SEPA standing to apply for an injunction (or, in Scotland, an interdict), but is of course no guarantee that they will succeed in obtaining one. However, where the criminal act is the operation of a prescribed process without any authorisation at all, neither prohibition nor enforcement notices may be served, so s.24 does not assist the enforcing authority in that situation.

Waste regulation. The 1990 Act (as amended by the 1995 Act: see paras. 72(2) and 76(7) of Sched. 22) provides an equivalent power in the context of waste regulation, where (a) the breach is a failure to comply with requirements imposed under s.38(9) of the 1990 Act in the context of the suspension of a waste management licence, and the Agency/SEPA considers that proceedings under subss. 38(10) or (11) would be ineffectual (s.38(13)); or (b) the breach is a failure to comply with requirements imposed under s.42(5)(a) of the 1990 Act in the context of breach of licence condition, and the Agency/SEPA considers that suspension or revocation of the licence would be ineffectual (s.42(6A)).

Prior to the transfer to the Agency/SEPA of waste regulation, the power to take civil proceedings was available by virtue of s.222 of the Local Government Act 1972 or, in Scotland, s.189 of the Local Government (Scotland) Act 1973. It will be noted that provisions equivalent to ss.38(13) and 42(6A) have not been inserted in relation to other waste offences, such as breach of s.33(1)(c). For these, it would appear that the Agency/SEPA will have to rely on the general subs. (1)(a) power.

Contaminated land. In relation to "special sites", the Agency/SEPA are enforcing authorities under Part IIA of the 1990 Act, as inserted by the 1995 Act. They may take civil proceedings where they are of the opinion that proceedings under s.78M for non-compliance with a remediation notice would be an ineffectual remedy (s.78M(5)).

Water pollution. This Act inserts new ss.90A and 90B into the Water Resources Act 1991, and ss.49A and 49B into the Control of Pollution Act 1974, providing for the service by the Agency/SEPA of enforcement notices for contravention of conditions of consents to discharge to controlled waters (see paras. 29(26) and 142 of Sched. 22). Section 90B(4) permits the Agency to take civil proceedings where proceedings under s.90B(3) for breach of an enforcement notice would in the opinion of the Agency afford an ineffectual remedy for such breach. Section 49B(4) is of identical effect for SEPA.

Where a consent has not been applied for, however, or where it is another licence such as a drought permit or abstraction or impoundment licence whose conditions are being breached, it appears that the Agencies will have to rely on the general subs. (1)(a) power. Schedule 22 also introduces works notices for the remediation of actual or likely water pollution (ss.161A–D of the 1991 Act and ss.46A–D of the 1974 Act), and similar provision for civil action is made where such notices are not complied with: paras. 29(22) and 162 of Sched. 22.

Radioactive Substances Act 1993. Where a person fails to comply with a prohibition or enforcement notice served in relation to a registration or authorisation under the 1993 Act, the 1995 Act inserts a provision for the Agency/SEPA to take civil proceedings where it considers that criminal proceedings would be ineffectual to remedy the breach (see s.32(3), inserted by para. 219 of Sched. 22).

Subss. (3) and (4): advice and assistance

The Agency/SEPA are given a range of powers in relation to research and advice. The benefits which the Agency/SEPA should bring in terms of the pooling, sharing and development of knowledge and expertise which staff in their constituent bodies already possessed in a range of fields have been widely emphasised. This anticipated role is reflected in their duties to compile information on pollution, assess and report on its effects and follow developments in technologies and techniques for its abatement (ss.5(2)–(4) and 33(2)–(4)). It can also be seen in their roles in relation to contaminated land "special sites" (s.57), the national air quality strategies (ss.80(6)(a) and 87(7)(a)) and the national waste strategies (ss.44A(5)(a) and (6) and 44B of the Environmental Protection Act 1990, as inserted into that Act by s.92(1) of this Act). Note also SEPA's lead role (held by the Secretary of State in England and Wales) in relation to air quality review and assessment in Scotland, and in particular its power to give directions to local authorities where it considers that developments in science and technology have rendered their actions inappropriate (s.85(2) and (3)(d)). Each of the Agency and SEPA is placed under a specific duty to provide the Secretary of State or the Minister of Agriculture, Fisheries and Food with such advice and assistance as he may request (subs. (2)). These Ministers can thus call on such advice and assistance without resort to directions under s.40.

In addition to these statutory roles, each Agency may provide any person with advice, assistance or training: subs. (3). In this regard, it is notable that the Government's draft Guidance to the Agency on its objectives (April 1995, discussed in the General Note to s.4(2) and (3)) indicates that the Agency "should strive within the areas of its responsibility to become a recognised centre of knowledge and expertise and to provide and promulgate clear and readily available advice and information on its work and on best environmental practice" (para. 5.7). The revised draft guidance to SEPA contains an almost identical provision (App. 1, para. 9(vi)). The equivalent provision relating to the NRA, which this subsection replaces (s.4(2) of the Water Resources Act 1991), referred only to persons outside the United Kingdom; that the Agency/SEPA may provide such advice to persons within the United Kingdom is made clear.

It would appear possible for the Agency/SEPA to find itself in the potentially embarrassing position of serving a notice such as a contaminated land remediation notice (in relation to a "special site") or a water pollution works notice, and then charging for advice as to how best the remediation might be carried out so as to comply with the notice. This will become more likely the more the Agency/SEPA succeeds in establishing itself as a recognised centre of expertise on the remediation techniques involved, since it will already have at least a threefold commercial advantage over its "competitors". First, the Agency/SEPA is in the best position to decide whether it is satisfied that the notice has been complied with, where there is any scope for differing interpretations of its terms; secondly the Agency/SEPA is already familiar with the site, having investigated it sufficiently to allow the requirements in the notice to be determined; and thirdly the Agency/SEPA is "on the spot" and already in contact with the recipient of the notice: indeed, where the notice is a remediation notice or (depending on the content of the regulations to be made under s.161A(5)(a) of the 1991 Act or, in Scotland, s.46A(5)(a) of the 1974 Act) a works notice, the Agency/SEPA has already consulted with the recipient over what might be done by way of remediation. Indeed, depending on the point at which "consultation" becomes "advice", it may be that the potential conflict between the Agency/SEPA's roles of enforcing authority and commercial supplier of technical advice could emerge even prior to the service of the notice.

A further potential conflict would manifest itself if the awkward situation arose where commercially-given Agency/SEPA advice proved to be less than adequate. If remediation was carried out in accordance with that advice, then the Agency/SEPA would have a commercial interest in nevertheless declining to serve a further notice or otherwise pursue the matter, since to do so would be to expose itself to possible legal action for negligence or breach of contract.

It should be noted that subs. (3) makes no reference to charging for the advice or assistance to which it refers, and the Agency/SEPA are not under any obligation to charge for it, merely empowered to do so (for example, by subs. (1)(a)). However, it may be that budgetary constraints will encourage them to charge for such services and even to compete actively to supply them. It is in the latter circumstance, should it arise, that the potential for conflict—or at least, for perceived conflict—would be greatest.

Subsection (4) places a restriction on the agencies' ability to provide such advice, etc. Written ministerial consent is required where the advice etc. is being provided to any person outside the United Kingdom, and such consent may be subject to conditions. Four points may be noted in relation to this provision. First, the same restriction previously existed in relation to advice etc. to persons outside the United Kingdom by the NRA (s.4(3) of the Water Resources Act 1991), but an additional restriction imposed by that section of the 1991 Act in such a case (that Treasury approval be required where capital expenditure of the guaranteeing of a liability by the NRA was involved) is not imposed on the Agency. Secondly the restriction is, as it is seen by Nigel Haigh, an Agency board member, intended to ensure that the Agency (and presumably SEPA) concentrates on issues affecting the U.K. (*The Guardian*, September 6, 1995, Society Section p. 5). However, it has been criticised as "an intolerable restriction [which] needs to be challenged if British environmental expertise is to play its full role in the development of European policy" (P. Lowe, H. Talbot and S. Ward in *Ecos*, [September, 1995]). Thirdly, the consent requirement would appear to apply to advice, etc. provided to U.K. citizens and residents who happen to be abroad, whilst not applying to advice, etc., given in relation to non-U.K. environmental matters to any person who happens to be within the U.K. at the time. Finally the consent requirement applies only where advice, etc., is given under the subs. (3) power, and is without prejudice to other Agency or SEPA powers. It could be argued, therefore, that advice, etc. may be given to persons outside the U.K. by virtue of the wide power contained in subs. (1)(a), provided that in the opinion of the agency the provision of such advice, etc. will facilitate, or is conducive or incidental to the carrying out of its functions.

Subss. (5) and (6): research

The Agency and SEPA must each carry out or commission relevant research and related activities (subs. (5)(a)). This duty supports the s.5(4) duty to follow developments in pollution control technology and techniques. To whom the results are made available, and at what price, is left to their discretion (subs. (5)(b)), and they may make such results publicly available free of charge (subs. (6)). It is submitted that the discretion granted in these provisions is subject to the Environmental Information Regulations 1992 and the EU directive on Freedom of Access to Environmental Information (90/313/EEC) which it implements. Therefore any decision by the Agency/SEPA to refuse access to documents relating to such research must be supported by reference to an exemption provided by that legislation.

Subss. (7) and (8): charging for services in connection with environmental licences

The Agency/SEPA may by agreement charge for advice and assistance provided on request in connection with the range of consents, licences and authorisations which are granted and administered by them. Such charges are separate from charging schemes in relation to such environmental licences as are provided for by ss.41 and 42 and are discussed in the General Note to s.41 at p. 25–113. However, the Agency/SEPA's constituent bodies have often provided such advice and assistance free of charge, for example, in the course of discussions prior to an application being made. Since environmental licence charging schemes have typically been based on fixed fees, this situation is capable of being seen as violating the "polluter pays" principle, since less time-consuming businesses, paying the same fee as equivalent but more time-consuming ones, are effectively subsidising them, even assuming that the charging scheme recovers overall regulatory costs. Charges levied under subs. (7), and outside the charging scheme, may therefore be seen as a step towards remedying this situation. For further discussion of this issue, see the General Notes to ss.41 and 42 at pp. 25–113 and 25–116 respectively.

By subs. (8), subs. (7) does not restrict any other charging powers of the Agency/SEPA (under ss.41–43 and s.37(1)), and any statutory provision made in relation to Agency/SEPA charges (for example, a charging scheme under s.41) takes precedence over subs. (7) so the Agency/SEPA may not charge separately or on a different basis for any services or facilities expressly covered by another charging provision.

Delegation of functions by Ministers etc. to the new Agencies

38.—(1) Agreements may be made between—

(a) any Minister of the Crown, and

(b) a new Agency,

authorising the new Agency (or any of its employees) to exercise on behalf of that Minister, with or without payment, any eligible function of his.

(2) An agreement under subsection (1) above shall not authorise the new Agency (or any of its employees) to exercise on behalf of a Minister of the Crown any function which consists of a power to make regulations or other instruments of a legislative character or a power to fix fees or charges.

(3) An agreement under this section may provide for any eligible function to which it relates to be exercisable by the new Agency in question (or any of its employees)—

(a) either wholly or to such extent as may be specified in the agreement;

(b) either generally or in such cases or areas as may be so specified; or

(c) either unconditionally or subject to the fulfilment of such conditions as may be so specified.

(4) Subsection (5) below applies where, by virtue of an agreement under this section, a new Agency (or any of its employees) is authorised to exercise any function of a Minister of the Crown.

(5) Subject to subsection (6) below, anything done or omitted to be done by the new Agency (or an employee of the new Agency) in, or in connection with, the exercise or purported exercise of the function shall be treated for all purposes as done or omitted to be done by that Minister in his capacity as such.

(6) Subsection (5) above shall not apply—

(a) for the purposes of so much of any agreement made between that Minister and the new Agency as relates to the exercise of the function; or

(b) for the purposes of any criminal proceedings brought in respect of anything done or omitted to be done as mentioned in that subsection.

(7) An agreement under this section shall not prevent a Minister of the Crown exercising any function to which the agreement relates.

(8) Where a Minister of the Crown has power to include, in any arrangements which he makes in relation to the performance by him of an eligible function, provision for the making of payments to him—

(a) by other parties to the arrangements, or

(b) by persons who use any facilities or services provided by him pursuant to the arrangements or in relation to whom the function is otherwise exercisable,

he may include in any such arrangements provision for the making of such payments to him or a new Agency in cases where the new Agency (or any of its employees) acts on his behalf by virtue of an agreement under this section.

(9) The power conferred on a Minister of the Crown by subsection (1) above is in addition to any other power by virtue of which functions of his may be exercised by other persons on his behalf.

(10) In this section—

"eligible function" means any function of a Minister of the Crown which the Secretary of State, having regard to the functions conferred or imposed upon the new Agency in question under or by virtue of this Act or any other enactment, considers can appropriately be exercised by that new Agency (or any of its employees) on behalf of that Minister;

"Minister of the Crown" has the same meaning as in the Ministers of the Crown Act 1975.

DEFINITIONS
"eligible function": subs. (10).
"functions": s.124(1).
"Minister of the Crown": subs. (10).
"new Agency": s.56(1).

COMMENCEMENT
July 28, 1995 (S.I. 1995 No. 1983).

GENERAL NOTE
This section provides considerable scope for the Government to delegate ministerial functions to either agency by agreement with that agency. When this section, then clause 36, was introduced into the Bill, one commentator suggested that "early candidates for transfer from the DoE are aspects of chemicals control and the provision of technical guidance on waste and contaminated land. The Ministry of Agriculture, Fisheries and Food's (or, in Scotland, the Scottish Office's) responsibilities in relation to the dumping of waste at sea, effluent pipelines and radioactive discharges are also understood to be candidates for transfer": *ENDS Report* 238, November 1994, pp. 20–21. In Commons Standing Committee, the then Parliamentary Under-Secretary of State for the Environment, Sir Paul Beresford, indicated that "at least some of the Secretary of State's functions" under Pt. VI of the 1990 Act in relation to genetically modified organisms could be transferred to the Environment Agency under this section": H.C. Standing Committee B, Third Sitting, May 2, 1995, col. 102.

Such an agreement may be made between any Minister of the Crown and either of the Agency/SEPA (subs. (1)) and may provide for payment to the Agency/SEPA by that Minister (subs. (1)) or by any other person who would otherwise be required to make payment to that Minister in connection with the delegated function: subs. (3). It may transfer all or only part of a function, conditionally or unconditionally: subs. (3).

However, there are two important restrictions on a Minister's right to enter into such an agreement: (a) only a function which the Secretary of State considers can appropriately be exercised by the agency in question, given that agency's existing functions, may be delegated under this section: subss. (1) and (10); and (b) no legislative power or power to fix fees or charges may be delegated under this section: subs. (2).

Further, the Minister in question retains the power to exercise the delegated function himself: subs. (7). Sir Paul Beresford indicated on behalf of the Government in Committee that:

"Except in the case of consequential criminal proceedings [see below], the Minister has responsibility for ultimately ensuring that the function is exercised or performed satisfactorily and is, of course, therefore accountable to Parliament. [Subsection] (7) ensures that the Minister will have sufficient power to exercise those delegated functions should it be exceptionally necessary" (H.C. Standing Committee B, Eighth Sitting, col. 256, May 16, 1995).

Ministers of the Crown have, as a rule, Crown immunity from criminal or civil liability in respect of actions or omissions in their ministerial capacity. Neither of the agencies has such Crown immunity (s.1(5)(a) and Sched. 6, para. 2), but subs. (5) provides that any act or omission by the Agency/SEPA or its employee in connection with the exercise or, (importantly) the purported exercise of a function delegated under this section, is deemed to be the act or omission of the delegating Minister. This effectively confers Crown immunity in relation to such acts or omissions, but it is qualified by subs. (6)(b) so that the Agency/SEPA have no such immunity from criminal liability.

Subsection (5) alone would also, without subs. (6)(a), have the unpalatable effect of removing any Agency/SEPA responsibility to the delegating Minister for failing to carry out the delegated functions, by providing that the Agency/SEPA's failure to do so was in fact an omission by that Minister. Subsection (6)(a) therefore qualifies subs. (5) so that it does not apply for the purposes of the agreement between the parties.

General duty of the new Agencies to have regard to costs and benefits in exercising powers

39.—(1) Each new Agency—

(a) in considering whether or not to exercise any power conferred upon it by or under any enactment, or

(b) in deciding the manner in which to exercise any such power,

shall, unless and to the extent that it is unreasonable for it to do so in view of the nature or purpose of the power or in the circumstances of the particular case, take into account the likely costs and benefits of the exercise or non-exercise of the power or its exercise in the manner in question.

(2) The duty imposed upon a new Agency by subsection (1) above does not affect its obligation, nevertheless, to discharge any duties, comply with any requirements, or pursue any objectives, imposed upon or given to it otherwise than under this section.

DEFINITIONS
"costs": s.56(1).
"new Agency": s.56(1).

COMMENCEMENT
July 28, 1995 (S.I. 1995 No. 1983).

GENERAL NOTE

This section places both the Agency and SEPA, in certain circumstances, under a duty to take into account the likely costs and benefits of their exercise and non-exercise of their statutory powers. Of all the provisions in the Act, this section has been among the most controversial. None of the Agency/SEPA's predecessors, and (whilst it was welcomed by many in industry and elsewhere, notably the Director General of Water Services: see OFWAT News Release 27/94, December 12, 1994) no other U.K. environmental regulators, had been placed under a duty couched in these terms, and on its publication it was reported to have alarmed environmentalists, who feared that it would leave "any aggrieved industry open to challenge the agency in the courts if benefits could not be shown to outweigh costs—an almost impossible task": *Guardian*, p. 10, "Lobbyists attack environment agency plans," October 14, 1994.

The provision also provoked concern in Parliament that the potential for such challenges might lead to excessive bureaucracy within the agencies and might conflict with or undermine its conservation and pollution prevention functions, (see generally the eighth and ninth sittings of H.C. Standing Committee B (May 16 and 18, 1995) when the clause was discussed), which prompted the then Minister for the Environment and Countryside, Robert Atkins, to give the following example of its application in relation to discharge consents:

"My hon. Friend ... asked about the relationship of clause 37 [s.39] to the conservation duties in clause 7 [s.7]. The two clauses do not conflict. The requirement to consider costs and benefits does not override obligations to conservation. However, it rightly requires that in deciding how far to pursue discretionary programmes the agency should take costs and benefits into account. My hon. Friend mentioned Bassenthwaite Lake. If, in pursuing conservation there, the agency wanted to impose discharge requirements beyond those necessary to reach water quality targets, it would need to consider the costs and benefits. ... However, it would not be prevented from pursuing conservation programmes simply because it could not demonstrate that benefits exceeded costs" (H.C. Standing Committee B, Ninth Sitting, May 18, 1995, cols. 284–285).

Mr Atkins went on to indicate that "on the strength of our legal advice, [legal opinions obtained by the CPRE and Greenpeace] gravely overstate the danger that new agencies will become bogged down in judicial review as a result of clause 37 [s.39]" (col. 285). The relationship between this duty and the agencies' other functions is considered further in the General Note to this Part of the Act, at p.25–19.

The Government's draft Guidance to the Agency on its contribution to sustainable development (April 1995, revised December 1995) considers this section in Chapter 5. Chapter 4 of the Scottish Office draft Guidance to SEPA on its objectives is essentially identical. Chapter 5 is, it should be noted, non-statutory, but it is worth quoting in full:

"Chapter V

Costs and Benefits

Scope of the duty

5.1 Section 4 of the Environment Act requires the Agency to take into account any likely costs in achieving its principal aim (set out at paragraph 2.4 above). Section 39 places the Agency under a duty when it considers whether or how to exercise any power to take into account the likely costs and benefits of its action or inaction. Costs are defined in section 56(1) as including costs to any person (which also means organizations) and to the environment. This duty:

(i) does not apply if it would be unreasonable in the circumstances of a particular case. Or there might be cases where it would be unreasonable for the duty to apply to the full extent.

(ii) does not affect the Agency's mandatory obligations to discharge specific duties, comply with requirements or pursue objectives. Legal requirements (such as water quality objectives) remain unaffected by the duty; they must still be observed. But the general duty with regard to costs and benefits will apply whenever there is more than one way of achieving the legal requirements, and if the Agency retains discretion as to how they should be achieved.

Purpose of the duty

5.2 These provisions recognise that sustainable development involves reconciling the need for economic development with that for protecting and enhancing the environment. Ministers consider that as the Agency is a body with powers to make decisions with significant impacts on individuals, organizations and the environment, it should take account of all types of costs and benefits when making such decisions. This will not only ensure that financial and other considerations are taken into account, but also that environmental considerations are given the central role that is necessary for sustainable development. But the duty does not apply in cases where it would be unreasonable nor can it be used to override other statutory requirements.

Principle of application

5.3 The principle behind section 39 is that generally in appropriate circumstances—whether in individual cases or in guiding the Agency's policy-making and executive functions—the Agency should take account of all types of likely costs and benefits, including the environmental impact of a project and the compliance and any other economic costs and benefits. Sometimes this may involve environmental assessment. This is already a statutory requirement in many cases and may also be appropriate in others. While it cannot of itself make decisions, environmental appraisal can when properly applied highlight new options such as remediation. It can also reduce the extent of uncertainty confronting decision makers and improve the quality of the decision making process and inform public debate.

Selection of options

5.4 In discharging its duty, the Agency will need to decide what are the relevant options to consider, for example:

(i) whether or not to take actions, and

(ii) the various options, including the appropriate levels of any controls, for achieving a given environmental outcome.

Quantification

5.5 Whilst the Agency should take into account all likely costs and benefits, Ministers consider that it does not follow that all need to be precisely quantified. For example:

(i) where the Agency has no discretion about the outcome it may only be the differences in likely costs and benefits between the particular options that are relevant

(ii) the Agency may be able to take account of clear and appropriate precedent, for example for the granting of individual fishing licences or certain types of discharge consents

(iii) many likely costs and benefits, particularly in relation to the environment, are inherently difficult to quantify, especially in monetary terms: for example, the possible health effects of exposure to very low levels of pollutants, the value of a forest, the visual impacts of development or global warming. Judgments will therefore sometimes need to be made.

Methodologies and procedures

5.6 When assessing likely costs and benefits in the circumstances of the case, the Agency may consider it appropriate to consider the following:

(i) principles, procedures and techniques—in particular, risk assessment, and economic and policy appraisal[8]—for giving proper consideration to non-market impacts including those on the environment

(ii) the precautionary principle

(iii) reliance on sound science

(iv) the likely impact on the carrying capacity of the environment, and on natural environmental capital

(v) the likely longer-term implications and effects, having particular regard to those which appear likely to be irreversible or reversible only at high cost and over a long time-scale. In the Ministers' view, such analyses should take proper account of long-term environmental benefits as well as immediate financial costs.

(vi) the likely costs and benefits of its actions for society as a whole, including the effects on the welfare of people and business, impacts on the environment and changes in the use of resources (labour, capital and natural resources). In so doing the Agency may be guided where appropriate by:

(a) the views of the Government's Chief Medical Officers, the Health and Safety Executive and Commission and other interested bodies as to the effects on human health

(b) evidence within the UK and internationally about proven and likely impacts on the environment

(c) the impacts on the economy and on all affected business sectors and individual companies, and

(d) the distribution of costs and benefits across the economy. For example, some options open to the Agency may impose particularly heavy costs on particular groups of people or companies or on certain parts of the environment.

Internal guidance

5.7 The Agency should develop and make available practical procedures to ensure that it meets the requirements of the duty having regard to this guidance. Such procedures should be set out in a document which provides internal advice for staff and is made available to others so as to promote public understanding of the principles it adopts. It should include advice to staff on:

(i) relevant techniques for assessing costs and benefits

(ii) where the Agency's discretion is limited by obligations arising from other duties, requirements and objectives, and

(iii) the extent to which detailed consideration of costs and benefits might be unreasonable in particular circumstances."

The question of where the duty in this section fits into the array of duties, powers, aims, objectives and purposes to which the two agencies are subject is discussed in the General Note to Pt. I of the Act (see p. 25–19, below) but a number of points may be noted.

Comparison with cost-benefit analysis. The duty, where it applies, is only to take into account likely costs and benefits: it is neither a requirement for a cost-benefit analysis of a kind which would demonstrate costs outweighing benefits or vice versa (and once again, the statement by Mr Atkins quoted above may be admissible were a court to consider that the provision might have this effect and is ambiguous or obscure), nor a requirement to act in accordance with the conclusions yielded by a consideration of likely costs and benefits. Paragraph 5.5 of the revised draft Guidance to the Agency, quoted above, confirms this.

Circumstances where the duty applies. The duty only applies "unless and to the extent that it is unreasonable for it to do so in view of the nature or purpose of the power or in the circumstances of the particular case" (subs. (1)).

---

[8] useful guidance is contained in
A Guide to Risk Assessment and Risk Management for Environmental Protection HMSO 1995
Economic Appraisal in Central Government: A Technical Guide for Departments, HM Treasury 1991
Policy Appraisal and the Environment: A Guide for Government Departments, Department of the Environment HMSO 1991
Environmental Appraisal in Government Departments, Department of the Environment HMSO 1994
Checking the Cost to Business: A Guide to Compliance Cost Assessment, Department of Trade and Industry 1992
Policy Appraisal and Health, Department of Health (in preparation)

Duty subject to other duties, requirements and objectives. The duty is subject to the agencies' respective obligations to discharge their duties, comply with requirements and pursue objectives imposed on them. It thus operates only where the agencies' duties and objectives may be fulfilled equally well in different ways and there thus remains a discretion as to how to do so. The relationship of the duty with these other matters is considered in the Introduction to this Part of the Act, under the heading *"Functions, Aims and Objectives"* (see p. 25–19).

"Costs and benefits". "Costs" are defined by s.56(1) to include costs to the environment as well as to any person. "Benefits" is not a defined term but it appears beyond doubt, particularly in view of paras. 5.3 and 5.5(iii) of the draft Guidance, that the Government expects the Agency to treat the term as including benefits to the environment as well as to any person.

Geographical extent of costs and benefits. It would appear that costs and benefits to the environment outside the U.K. are to be taken into account under s.39 but the position is less clear regarding costs and benefits to persons outside the U.K. The definition of "the environment" at s.56(1) does not geographically restrict the scope of the term to the U.K. environment. Equally, the Government's draft Guidance referred to above indicates that, "In the present age, [environmental] concerns have broadened beyond people's immediate environment to global issues, such as the protection of the stratospheric ozone layer and the world's climate" (para. 3.4), and that the Agency's judgements "should make a proper allowance for the interests of *future generations* and for the pressures that society places upon the *global environment*" (para. 3.9—emphasis in the original text). It may also be noted that a number of EU and international U.K. obligations are to be implemented by the agencies, which contain references to the "environment" in contexts which clearly envisage the term having international scope. The proposed Directive on Integrated Pollution Prevention and Control, on which political agreement was reached by the Council of Environment Ministers in June 1995, is an example (see Art. 8.1).

Equally important is the question whether costs and benefits to any person includes persons outside the U.K. The answer to this question would determine whether the agencies are allowed (or indeed required) by s.39, where it applies, to give any weight to the U.K.'s competitive advantage. No geographical limitation to the term is set by the Act, and in the draft of its Guidance to the Agency under s.4 the Government indicates that it "has to take the broadest view of the action the U.K. needs to take to achieve sustainable development, domestically and globally": para. 4.1. Thus it would appear that references in the draft Guidance's discussion of costs and benefits to "impacts on the economy and on all affected business sectors and individual companies" (para. 5.6(c)) are to companies and sectors wherever located, and no ground is provided on which to justify giving a greater weight to impacts on U.K. persons and businesses than to those on persons and businesses elsewhere. However, it should be noted that there is reference in the statutory part of the draft Guidance to the Agency encouraging regulated organisations to enhance "their own and the UK's competitive position" (App. 1, para. 11(iv)(c)).

Challenges under section 39. It is noted above that there has been concern in some quarters that the Agency/SEPA may face numerous challenges under this section. The duty is sufficiently hedged in with qualifications that it may prove difficult for a judicial review application to succeed in practice. In addition, where the relevant statute provides an appeal mechanism in relation to the action or omission complained of, then the appropriate means of challenge is an appeal under those provisions.

Ministerial directions to the new Agencies

40.—(1) The appropriate Minister may give a new Agency directions of a general or specific character with respect to the carrying out of any of its functions.

(2) The appropriate Minister may give a new Agency such directions of a general or specific character as he considers appropriate for the implementation of—

(a) any obligations of the United Kingdom under the Community Treaties, or

(b) any international agreement to which the United Kingdom is for the time being a party.

(3) Any direction under subsection (2) above shall be published in such manner as the Minister giving it considers appropriate for the purpose of bringing the matters to which it relates to the attention of persons likely to be affected by them; and—

(a) copies of the direction shall be made available to the public; and

(b) notice shall be given—
    (i) in the case of a direction given to the Agency, in the London Gazette, or
    (ii) in the case of a direction given to SEPA, in the Edinburgh Gazette,
of the giving of the direction and of where a copy of the direction may be obtained.

(4) The provisions of subsection (3) above shall have effect in relation to any direction given to a new Agency under an enactment other than subsection (2) above for the implementation of—

(a) any obligations of the United Kingdom under the Community Treaties, or

(b) any international agreement to which the United Kingdom is for the time being a party,

as those provisions have effect in relation to a direction given under subsection (2) above.

(5) In determining—

(a) any appeal against, or reference or review of, a decision of a new Agency, or

(b) any application transmitted from a new Agency,

the body or person making the determination shall be bound by any direction given under this section or any other enactment by a Minister of the Crown to the new Agency to the same extent as the new Agency.

(6) Any power to give a direction under this section shall be exercisable, except in an emergency, only after consultation with the new Agency concerned.

(7) Any power of the appropriate Minister to give directions to a new Agency otherwise than by virtue of this section shall be without prejudice to any power to give directions conferred by this section.

(8) It is the duty of a new Agency to comply with any direction which is given to that new Agency by a Minister of the Crown under this section or any other enactment.

DEFINITIONS
    "appropriate Minister": s.56(1).
    "functions": s.124(1).
    "new Agency": s.56(1).
    "notice": s.124(1).

COMMENCEMENT
    July 28, 1995 (S.I. 1995 No. 1983).

GENERAL NOTE
    This section (which should be read together with s.122) allows the Secretary of State (and additionally, in the case of the Agency, the Minister of Agriculture, Fisheries and Food) to exercise considerable control over any activity of the agencies by giving them directions as to the carrying out of their functions (subs. (1)), with which the agency concerned must comply (subs. (8)). Subsection (8) also requires the agencies to comply with any directions given to them by other Ministers of the Crown by virtue of other legislation.

Directions under other legislation
    A range of other legislation provides for directions to be given to the Agency/SEPA: see, for instance, the Environmental Protection Act 1990 where directions may require specified conditions to be included or not included in IPC authorisations (s.7(3)) and waste management licences (s.35(7)), or may govern enforcement measures under IPC (ss.12(5), 13(3) and 14(4)) and waste management licensing (ss.37(3), 38(7) and 42(8)). Sections 44A(6) and 44B of the 1990 Act, as inserted by s.92 of this Act, also provide for directions to be given to the Agency and SEPA in relation to their respective national waste strategies, see also s.207 of the Water Resources Act 1991, which allows for directions to be given to the Agency on grounds of civil emergency or national security. Such other powers to give directions to the agencies do not restrict the power to give directions which is established under this section: subs. (7). The draft Guidance issued to the Agency under s.4 contains at Annex B a list of directions issued to HMIP and the NRA, which are as follows:

Date of issue	Direction	Purpose
1/4/91	Large Combustion Plant (New Plant) Directions 1991	To give effect to EC Directive 88/609/EEC
1/11/91	Municipal Waste-Incineration Directions 1991	To give effect to EC Directive 89/369/EEC and 89/429/EEC
28/3/94	Environmental Protection (Titanium Dioxide) Direction 1994	To give effect to EC Direction 92/112/EEC
10/10/89	Security Measures (National Rivers Authority) Direction 1989	To give effect to s.170(1) of the Water Act 1989 (superseded by s.207(1) of the Water Resources Act 1991) on directions in the interests of national security
5/5/92	National Rivers Authority (Bathing Water) Directions 1992	To give effect to Council Directive 76/160/EEC concerning the quality of bathing water and to S.I. 1991 No. 1597, Bathing Waters (Classification) Regulations 1991
27/1/92	National Rivers Authority (Nitrate Pollution) (Council Directive 91/676/EEC) Directions 1992	To give effect to Council Directive 91/676/EEC concerning the protection of waters against pollution caused by nitrates from agricultural sources
13/7/92	Directions to the National Rivers Authority under s.5 of the Water Resources Act 1991 and relating to Council Directive 80/68/EEC on the protection of groundwater	To give effect to Council Directive 80/68/EEC on the protection of groundwater against pollution caused by certain dangerous substances

It may be noted that the draft Guidance to SEPA does not contain such a list.

This list is not to be included in the final form of that Guidance. Since then, there has been one set of directions issued: on June 23, 1995, the Large Combustion Plant (New Plant) Directions 1995 were issued to HMIP to replace the 1991 Directions of the same name listed in the table, and to give effect to amendments to the 1988 Directive by Directive 94/66/EC.

Procedure
It is important in practice which provision is relied upon in giving a direction, where it may be that several alternative provisions could have been relied upon, because different procedures may be involved. Directions given under this section may be made only after consultation with the agency concerned, unless in emergency (subs. (6)), and directions given so as to implement EC or international obligations whether or not they are given under this section, must be published: subss. (3) and (4).

Appeals and transmissions
The role of directions in appeals against Agency/SEPA decisions or called-in applications is notable: subs. (5). Whoever hears an appeal—generally an inspector (or, in Scotland, a reporter) appointed by the Secretary of State—is bound by any relevant direction to the Agency/SEPA concerned just as that agency is. Since directions are often given in order to implement EC or international obligations, this provision affords the Government a degree of control which can ensure that such obligations are complied with.

Previous directions

Directions given to the NRA for the purposes of s.19 of the Water Resources Act 1991 have effect after the transfer date as directions to the Agency under s.6(2) of this Act (Sched. 23, para. 2). More generally, any direction given to a predecessor of either the Agency/SEPA, in relation to a function which has been transferred to one of them, has effect after the transfer date as if given to the Agency/SEPA: s.55(4)(d).

This section should be read in conjunction with s.122 which makes general provision in relation to directions given to any person or body under this Act and makes specific provision for the circumstance where a direction given to either of the agencies to give effect to EC obligations is varied or revoked by virtue of that section. The Agency/SEPA's annual reports must set out any directions given to them under this section (s.52(2)). This provision is important as directions which do not implement EC or international obligations are not covered by subss. (3) and (4) and therefore need not be published at the time they are given, although there is nothing in the legislation which bars the Agency/SEPA from publishing the direction at the time.

Charging schemes

Power to make schemes imposing charges

41.—(1) Subject to the following provisions of this section and section 42 below—

(a) in the case of any particular licence under Chapter II of Part II of the 1991 Act (abstraction and impounding), the Agency may require the payment to it of such charges as may from time to time be prescribed;

(b) in relation to other environmental licences, there shall be charged by and paid to a new Agency such charges as may from time to time be prescribed; and

(c) as a means of recovering costs incurred by it in performing functions conferred by regulations under section 62 of the 1990 Act (dangerous or intractable waste) each of the new Agencies may require the payment to it of such charges as may from time to time be prescribed;

and in this section "prescribed" means specified in, or determined under, a scheme (in this section referred to as a "charging scheme") made under this section by the new Agency in question.

(2) As respects environmental licences, charges may be prescribed in respect of—

(a) the grant or variation of an environmental licence, or any application for, or for a variation of, such a licence;

(b) the subsistence of an environmental licence;

(c) the transfer (where permitted) of an environmental licence to another person, or any application for such a transfer;

(d) the renewal (where permitted) of an environmental licence, or any application for such a renewal;

(e) the surrender (where permitted) of an environmental licence, or any application for such a surrender; or

(f) any application for the revocation (where permitted) of an environmental licence.

(3) A charging scheme may, for the purposes of subsection (2)(b) above, impose—

(a) a single charge in respect of the whole of any relevant licensed period;

(b) separate charges in respect of different parts of any such period; or

(c) both such a single charge and such separate charges;

and in this subsection "relevant licensed period" means the period during which an environmental licence is in force or such part of that period as may be prescribed.

(4) Without prejudice to subsection (7)(a) below, a charging scheme may, as respects environmental licences, provide for different charges to be payable according to—

(a) the description of environmental licence in question;

(b) the description of authorised activity in question;

(c) the scale on which the authorised activity in question is carried on;

(d) the description or amount of the substance to which the authorised activity in question relates;

(e) the number of different authorised activities carried on by the same person.

(5) A charging scheme—

(a) shall specify, in relation to any charge prescribed by the scheme, the description of person who is liable to pay the charge; and

(b) may provide that it shall be a condition of an environmental licence of any particular description that any charge prescribed by a charging scheme in relation to an environmental licence of that description is paid in accordance with the scheme.

(6) Without prejudice to subsection (5)(b) above, if it appears to a new Agency that any charges due and payable to it in respect of the subsistence of an environmental licence have not been paid, it may, in accordance with the appropriate procedure, suspend or revoke the environmental licence to the extent that it authorises the carrying on of an authorised activity.

(7) A charging scheme may—

(a) make different provision for different cases, including different provision in relation to different persons, circumstances or localities;

(b) provide for the times at which, and the manner in which, the charges prescribed by the scheme are to be paid;

(c) revoke or amend any previous charging scheme;

(d) contain supplemental, incidental, consequential or transitional provision for the purposes of the scheme.

(8) If and to the extent that a charging scheme relates to licences under Chapter II of Part II of the 1991 Act (abstraction and impounding), the scheme shall have effect subject to any provision made by or under sections 125 to 130 of that Act (exemption from charges, imposition of special charges for spray irrigation, and charges in respect of abstraction from waters of the British Waterways Board).

(9) A new Agency shall not make a charging scheme unless the provisions of the scheme have been approved by the Secretary of State under section 42 below.

(10) In this section—

"the appropriate procedure" means such procedure as may be specified or described in regulations made for the purpose by the Secretary of State;

"authorised activity" means any activity to which an environmental licence relates.

(11) Any power to make regulations under this section shall be exercisable by statutory instrument; and a statutory instrument containing any such regulations shall be subject to annulment pursuant to a resolution of either House of Parliament.

DEFINITIONS

"1990 Act": s.56(1).

"1991 Act": s.56(1).

"Agency": s.124(1).

"appropriate procedure": subs. (10).

"authorised activity": subs. (10).

"charging scheme": subs. (1).

"environmental licence": s.56(1).

"new Agency": s.56(1).

"prescribed": subs. (1).

"relevant licensed period": subs. (3).

COMMENCEMENT
February 1, 1996 insofar as this section confers power on the Secretary of State to make regulations and makes provision in relation to the exercise of that power; the remainder came into force on April 1, 1996: S.I. 1996 No. 186.

GENERAL NOTE
This section provides for each of the Agency/SEPA to make charging schemes for its range of licensing activities (subs. (1)(a) and (b)) and for the recovery of costs incurred by them under regulations made under s.62 of the Environmental Protection Act 1990: subs. (1)(c). The range of environmental licences, as they are termed in this Act, to which this section applies is listed in s.56(1). The most recent of them is the registration of exempt scrap metal recovery and motor vehicle dismantling activities which have been added to Sched. 3 to the Waste Management Licensing Regulations 1994 by S.I. 1995 No. 288, for which, unlike the other Sched. 3 exemptions, a registration fee is payable.
The particular regulations in the legislators' minds in respect of s.62 of the 1990 Act are presumably the draft Special Waste Regulations on which the 1995 consultation had closed by the time this Act received Royal Assent. The consultation draft of these regulations introduced, among other things, charges for the waste regulators' involvement in the consignment note procedure for special waste, and in part for this reason, para. 80(1) and (2) of Sched. 22 to the Act, which have the same commencement date as this subsection, amend s.62 of the 1990 Act to extend the range of supervisory activities for which costs may be recovered in relation to special waste.

Procedure for making charging schemes
The fact that charging schemes are made by the agencies themselves rather than by the Secretary of State is a departure from the previous position for both Pts. I and II of the 1990 Act (IPC and waste regulation) and for Radioactive Substances Act 1993 registration and licensing, although charging schemes for the other principal licensing regimes in England and Wales—abstraction licensing and discharge consenting—have until the advent of the Agency been exercised by the NRA under ss.123 and 131 of the Water Resources Act 1991. In Scotland, charging schemes in relation to discharge consents have been made by the river purification authorities under s.53 of the Control of Pollution Act 1974.
Just as with the NRA under the 1991 Act, there are significant procedural checks on the agencies' freedom in relation to the making of charging schemes: a draft must be published (s.42(1)); the proposed scheme must be approved, and may be modified, by the Secretary of State (subs. (9)); such approval in turn requires the consent of the Treasury (s.42(7)); the additional consent of the Minister of Agriculture, Fisheries and Food is required by the Agency where the scheme relates to authorisations for the disposal of radioactive waste (s.42(7)); and the charging scheme must be made by statutory instrument which may be annulled by a resolution of either House of Parliament (subs. (11)).

Content of charging schemes
The agencies enjoy a wide discretion as to the focus and charging structure of a charging scheme, although this is subject to the procedural checks listed above, and in particular: water abstraction and impoundment licence charges are subject to the British Waterways Board's statutory exemptions (subs. (8)); and in approving a scheme, the Secretary of State must have regard to a cost recovery criterion (s. 42(2) and (3)), the policy background to which is discussed in the General Note to that section.
The flexibility in this regard which is provided by subss. (4) and (7)(a) reflects a significant point of principle.
Charging structures based on a fixed fee will inevitably approximate only crudely to the widely differing burdens placed on a regulator by different applications, even of the same description—an application for a waste management licence to operate a landfill site, for example, can involve lengthy and complex negotiations on the question of adequate financial provision for the purposes of s.74(3)(c) of the Environmental Protection Act 1990, whereas an application for a waste management licence for a waste transfer station is unlikely to do so. Similarly, IPC fees and charges have been levied at fixed rates on the grant or variation of an authorisation and there is a fixed annual subsistence charge. These fees and charges only crudely reflect the amount of regulators' time taken by the kind of activity concerned (to take the example of IPC again, the annual subsistence charge is levied per component of the process authorised, which reflects only to a degree the complexity of the process). HMIP and HMIPI in particular can spend a great deal of time discussing and advising on particular authorisation applications, even before the application is made.

It has been suggested that this situation fails to accord with the "polluter pays" principle: see for example the Interim Report by Her Majesty's Inspectorate of Pollution Advisory Committee (February 13, 1995, available from Department of Environment), which recommends that "HMIP develop a method of classifying customers which will both apportion costs more fairly and reward those firms which by their own actions, reduce the work required by HMIP" (para. 12). HMIP's consultation paper on its 1995/1996 charging scheme for IPC (January 1995 also raised this issue, with the comment that "HMIP encourages operators to discuss their approach to making an application before it falls due, and this has proved a valuable process. It does, however, involve a substantial cost to HMIP [and] Ministers may conclude that it should more properly be borne by the polluter than by the tax-payer". This approach was not in fact pursued in the 1995/1996 charging scheme for IPC. It may be noted that the "polluter pays" principle was itself questioned in the House of Lords: Baroness Hamwee commented that "we shall have a body that will be vulnerable to control by the polluters themselves. In other words, they will become the paymasters in a sense": *Hansard*, H.L. Vol 559, col. 1454.

Subsection (7)(a), and the provisions of subs. (4) which can be seen as examples of the kind of provision allowed by subs. (7)(a), allow the Agency/SEPA to tackle this issue. So too does s.37(7), which operates outside the charging scheme system.

The Agency/SEPA may charge for unsuccessful or withdrawn, as well as for successful, applications for the grant, variation, transfer, renewal, surrender or revocation of an environmental licence (subs. (2)). They may charge a subsistence fee, and this may be a one-off charge for the whole period of the licence combined with, or in place of a periodic (for example, annual) fee (subss. (2)(b) and (3)).

Subss. (5) and (6): payment under charging schemes

The only statutory requirement as regards the content of a charging scheme is that it must specify who is liable to pay the charges it imposes (subs. (5)(a)). It may in addition make payment of charges prescribed by it a condition of any licence to which those charges relate (subs. (5)(b)), and both agencies have the power to revoke or suspend any licence where such a payment condition, relating to a subsistence fee, is breached (subs. (6)). This revocation or suspension power is, however, subject to such procedures as may be prescribed in regulations (subss. (6) and (10)).

Previous charging schemes and transitional arrangements

The Agency/SEPA take over existing charging schemes in relation to transferred functions from their predecessors as from the transfer date. Fees and charges paid to a predecessor of one of the agencies have effect as if paid to that agency: s.55(3) and (4)(g). Such a charging scheme takes effect as if made under this section: Sched. 23, para. 4. Circular 15/95, discussed in the General Note to s.3 (or, in relation to Scotland, Circular 19/95, discussed in the General Note to s.22), gives guidance that "the general approach to payments and receipts is that there should be a clean cut-off at April 1, 1996, with [waste regulation] authorities responsible for payments and receipts arising before that date and the Agency for those after" (para. 19). It goes on to give an example of the application of these principles to payments and receipts in respect of waste regulation fees and charges: para. 20(a).

The main relevant charging schemes at the time of writing are as follows:

1. *The HMIP Integrated Pollution Control Fees and Charges Scheme (England and Wales) Revised 1995* and the *Integrated Pollution Control Fees and Charges (Scotland) Scheme 1995* (which were made under s.8(2) of the 1990 Act and came into operation on April 1, 1995).

2. *The Radioactive Substances Authorisations and Registrations Fees and Charges Scheme (England and Wales) Revised 1995* and the *Radioactive Substances Act 1993 Fees and Charges (Scotland) Scheme 1995* (which were made under s.43 of the Radioactive Substances Act 1993 and came into force on April 1, 1995).

3. *The Waste Management Licensing (Fees and Charges) Scheme 1995* (which was made under s.41 of the 1990 Act, came into force on September 1, 1995 and applies throughout England, Wales and Scotland).

4. *The National Rivers Authority Applications and Discharges Charges Scheme* (which was made under s.131 of the Water Resources Act 1991 and has effect from April 1, 1994 to March 31, 1999, with the figures specified revised for each subsequent year from April 1) and *Schemes for Charges for Applications for Consent to Discharge* made under s.53 of the Control of Pollution Act 1974 by each of the river purification authorities in Scotland and which came into force on January 1, 1992.

5. *The National Rivers Authority Scheme of Abstraction Charges* (which was made under s.123 of the Water Resources Act 1991 and came into force on April 1, 1993, with the figures specified revised for each subsequent year beginning April 1, and relates to applications and licences for the abstraction and impoundment of water in England and Wales).

6. *The Local Authority Air Pollution Control Fees and Charges (Scotland) Scheme 1995* (as revised) (which was made under s.8(2) of the 1990 Act, came into force on April 1, 1995 and is included here as a result of the transfer of LAPC functions to SEPA in Scotland but not to the Agency in England and Wales).

Approval of charging schemes

42.—(1) Before submitting a proposed charging scheme to the Secretary of State for his approval, a new Agency shall, in such manner as it considers appropriate for bringing it to the attention of persons likely to be affected by the scheme, publish a notice—
  (a) setting out its proposals; and
  (b) specifying the period within which representations or objections with respect to the proposals may be made to the Secretary of State.
(2) Where any proposed charging scheme has been submitted to the Secretary of State for his approval, he shall, in determining whether or not to approve the scheme or to approve it subject to modifications,—
  (a) consider any representations or objections duly made to him and not withdrawn; and
  (b) have regard to the matter specified in subsection (3) below.
(3) The matter mentioned in subsection (2)(b) above is the desirability of ensuring that, in the case of each of the descriptions of environmental licence specified in the paragraphs of the definition of that expression in section 56 below, the amounts recovered by the new Agency in question by way of charges prescribed by charging schemes are the amounts which, taking one year with another, need to be recovered by that new Agency to meet such of the costs and expenses (whether of a revenue or capital nature)—
  (a) which it incurs in carrying out its functions,
  (b) in the case of environmental licences which are authorisations under section 13(1) of the Radioactive Substances Act 1993—
      (i) which the Minister incurs in carrying out his functions under or in consequence of that Act, and
      (ii) which the Secretary of State incurs under that Act in carrying out in relation to Scotland or Wales such of his functions under or in consequence of that Act as are exercised by the Minister in relation to England,
as the Secretary of State may consider it appropriate to attribute to the carrying out of those functions in relation to activities to which environmental licences of the description in question relate.
(4) Without prejudice to the generality of the expression "costs and expenses", in determining for the purposes of subsection (3) above the amounts of the costs and expenses which the Secretary of State considers it appropriate to attribute to the carrying out of a new Agency's or the Minister's or the Secretary of State's functions in relation to the activities to which environmental licences of any particular description relate, the Secretary of State—
  (a) shall take into account any determination of the new Agency's financial duties under section 44 below; and
  (b) may include amounts in respect of the depreciation of, and the provision of a return on, such assets as are held by the new Agency, the Minister or the Secretary of State, as the case may be, for purposes connected with the carrying out of the functions in question.
(5) If and to the extent that a charging scheme relates to any licence under Chapter II of Part II of the 1991 Act (abstraction and impounding), the Secretary of State may consider it appropriate to attribute to the carrying out of the Agency's functions in relation to activities to which such a licence relates any costs and expenses incurred by the Agency in carrying out any of its functions under Part II of that Act or under section 6(2) above.

(6) Subsection (5) above is without prejudice to what costs and expenses the Secretary of State may consider it appropriate to attribute to the carrying out of any functions of a new Agency, the Minister or the Secretary of State in relation to activities to which environmental licences of any particular description relate.

(7) The consent of the Treasury shall be required for the giving of approval to a charging scheme and, if and to the extent that the scheme relates to authorisations by the Agency under section 13 of the Radioactive Substances Act 1993 (disposal of radioactive waste), the consent of the Minister shall also be required.

(8) It shall be the duty of a new Agency to take such steps as it considers appropriate for bringing the provisions of any charging scheme made by it which is for the time being in force to the attention of persons likely to be affected by them.

(9) If and to the extent that any sums recovered by a new Agency by way of charges prescribed by charging schemes may fairly be regarded as so recovered for the purpose of recovering the amount required to meet (whether in whole or in part)—

    (a) such of the costs and expenses incurred by the Secretary of State as fall within subsection (3) above, or

    (b) such of the costs and expenses incurred by the Minister as fall within that subsection,

those sums shall be paid by that new Agency to the Secretary of State or, as the case may be, to the Minister.

(10) For the purposes of subsection (9) above, any question as to the extent to which any sums may fairly be regarded as recovered for the purpose of recovering the amount required to meet the costs and expenses falling within paragraph (a) or paragraph (b) of that subsection shall be determined—

    (a) in the case of costs and expenses falling within paragraph (a) of that subsection, by the Secretary of State; and

    (b) in the case of costs and expenses falling within paragraph (b) of that subsection, by the Secretary of State and the Minister.

(11) In this section "charging scheme" has the same meaning as in section 41 above.

DEFINITIONS
  "1991 Act": s.56(1).
  "Agency": s.124(1).
  "charging scheme": s.41(1).
  "environmental licence": s.56(1).
  "functions": s.124(1).
  "Minister": s.56(1).
  "modifications": s.124(1).
  "new Agency": s.56(1).
  "notice": s.124(1).

COMMENCEMENT
  September 21, 1995 (S.I. 1995 No. 1983).

GENERAL NOTE
  This section makes further provisions in relation to the charging schemes provided for by s.41. The procedural constraints on the making of such schemes are noted in the General Note to that section at p. 25–113.

Secretary of State's approval of schemes
  The requirement (s.41(9)) for the Secretary of State to approve a s.41 charging scheme does not give him complete discretion in deciding whether to give or withhold such approval. He must first consider any representations or objections made to him within the required period following the publication by the agency in question of the proposed scheme: subs. (2)(a).

Cost recovery

In addition, the Secretary of State must have regard to the desirability of ensuring that the regulatory costs and expenses associated with the particular licensing regime under consideration will be recovered by the scheme: subs. (3). The statutory position in relation to cost recovery varied between the different regimes now covered by this provision: in relation to IPC, for example, the Secretary of State was under a duty "so far as practicable [to] secure" that costs were recovered: s.8(6) of the Environmental Protection Act 1990. At the other extreme, waste management licensing charging schemes had no legislative link with cost recovery (s.41 of the 1990 Act), although the Government's intention that regulatory costs should be covered was made clear by the Earl of Arran on behalf of the Government during Parliamentary debate on what was to become the 1990 Act (*Hansard*, H.L. Vol. 522, col. 335). Notwithstanding this, there has been criticism of the level of fees and charges set by the 1995/1996 fees and charges scheme for waste management licensing: it has been suggested by the National Association of Waste Regulation officers that the levels set will not permit full cost recovery (*ENDS Report* 247, August 1995, p. 32). The same article also suggests that waste regulation authorities have not attributed the full overheads of waste regulation work to the function, thus concealing overheads which the Agency/SEPA will have to bear. If true, this can be expected to exacerbate any shortfall. This provision aims to minimise the amount of cross-subsidisation between different functions within an agency and must inevitably involve the apportionment between different functions of the costs of shared facilities and assets. This exercise may include the imputation of depreciation of or return on assets (subs. (4)(b)) so that as far as possible the real value of an asset is reflected in this consideration by the Secretary of State.

In the special case of water abstraction or impoundment licences, a charging scheme may, if the Secretary of State considers it appropriate, treat the Agency's water resource management costs and expenses generally as attributable to its licensing activities: subs. (5).

Overall cost recovery is only one aspect of the application of the "polluter pays" principle. Others are the equitable apportionment of overall cost recovery among different businesses, which is considered in the General Note to s.41 above, and the issue of charging for advice and assistance, in particular at the pre-application stage, which is considered there and in the General Note to s.37 at p. 25–102. The cost recovery provisions limit the scope for other charging options, such as incentive charging (on which Agency Chief Executive Ed Gallagher is reported to be keen: *ENDS Report* [1995] 249, p. 6).

Incidental power to impose charges

Incidental power of the new Agencies to impose charges

43. Without prejudice to the generality of its powers by virtue of section 37(1)(a) above and subject to any such express provision with respect to charging by a new Agency as is contained in the preceding provisions of this Chapter or any other enactment, each new Agency shall have power to fix and recover charges for services and facilities provided in the course of carrying out its functions.

DEFINITIONS
"functions": s.124(1).
"new Agency": s.56(1).

COMMENCEMENT
July 28, 1995 (S.I. 1995 No. 1983).

GENERAL NOTE

This section permits the Agency/SEPA to charge for services and facilities provided in the course of carrying out their functions. It is expressed not to be taken as limiting in any way the agencies' general incidental power to do whatever they consider conducive to the exercise of their functions: s.37(1)(a). This section contains none of the procedural constraints imposed by ss.41 and 42 on the setting of charging schemes, and it is therefore expressed to be subject to the express provision for such schemes in those sections and any other enactment. Otherwise the agencies could have used this section to bypass those constraints.

It would appear that where the services and facilities are provided in connection with environmental licences, this section is also subject to s.37(7). The implication of this would appear to be that even where charges have been fixed under this section, different charges may in the context of an environmental licence be agreed and charged for services and facilities.

General financial provisions

General financial duties

44.—(1) The appropriate Ministers may—

(a) after consultation with a new Agency, and

(b) with the approval of the Treasury,

determine the financial duties of that new Agency; and different determinations may be made for different functions and activities of the new Agency.

(2) The appropriate Ministers shall give a new Agency notice of every determination of its financial duties under this section, and such a determination may—

(a) relate to a period beginning before, on, or after, the date on which it is made;

(b) contain supplemental provisions; and

(c) be varied by a subsequent determination.

(3) The appropriate Minister may, after consultation with the Treasury and a new Agency, give a direction to that new Agency requiring it to pay to him an amount equal to the whole or such part as may be specified in the direction of any sum, or any sum of a description, so specified which is or has been received by that new Agency.

(4) Where it appears to the appropriate Minister that a new Agency has a surplus, whether on capital or revenue account, he may, after consultation with the Treasury and the new Agency, direct the new Agency to pay to him such amount not exceeding the amount of that surplus as may be specified in the direction.

(5) In the case of the Agency—

(a) subsection (1) above is subject to section 118 of the 1991 Act (special duties with respect to flood defence revenue);

(b) subsection (3) above is subject to sections 118(1)(a) and 119(1) of the 1991 Act (special duties with respect to flood defence revenue and funds raised for fishery purposes under local enactments); and

(c) subsection (4) above is subject to sections 118(1)(b) and 119(2) of the 1991 Act (which provide for flood defence revenue and certain funds raised under local enactments to be disregarded in determining whether there is a surplus).

DEFINITIONS

"1991 Act": s.56(1).

"appropriate Minister": s.56(1).

"appropriate Ministers": s.56(1).

"functions": s.124(1).

"new Agency": s.56(1).

COMMENCEMENT

July 28, 1995 (S.I. 1995 No. 1983).

GENERAL NOTE

This section is closely modelled on s.117 of the Water Resources Act 1991 which imposed financial duties on the NRA. A general purpose of the section is to enable the Government to ensure that the agencies do not accumulate surplus payments or funds without them being claimed from the agency in question for central funds. Both agencies have the power to buy and sell property, for example, which could lead to capital gains, and it is possible that charging schemes may in a given year more than cover regulatory costs. The Agency in particular, with its water management functions in relation especially to flood defence might find itself in receipt of such payments or surpluses. The section essentially contains two mechanisms, the first relating to financial duties and the second to surpluses held or received by the Agency/SEPA.

Financial duties

Subsections (1) and (2) provide a procedure for the Secretary of State (acting jointly, as regards the Agency, with the Minister of Agriculture, Fisheries and Food) to determine and notify to the agencies their respective financial duties. Such a determination must be taken into account by the Secretary of State when seeking to ensure that the Agency/SEPA's charging schemes are set so as to recover costs: s.42(2).

Surpluses
  The section also contains an extremely widely phrased power for the Secretary of State to direct the Agency/SEPA to pay to him an amount equal to or less than the amount of a payment which it has received (subs. (3)) or a surplus it possesses (subs. (4)). In relation to the Agency, the Minister of Agriculture, Fisheries and Food also has this power. In introducing subs. (3) as an amendment, the then Parliamentary Under-Secretary of State for the Environment, Sir Paul Beresford, explained that it "will enable the return to the Consolidated Fund of receipts, other than surpluses [see subs. (4)], which, in line with the normal rules of Government accounting, ought to be returned to the Exchequer" H.C. Standing Committee B, Ninth Sitting, May 18, 1995, col. 296.
  Much of the Agency's funding for the exercise of its flood defence functions will, as was the case for the NRA before it, be raised through levies on local authorities and for specific local flood defence purposes, and the effect of subs. (5) is to prevent such funds becoming subject to the provisions of this section.

Accounts and records

45.—(1) Each new Agency shall—
(a) keep proper accounts and proper accounting records; and
(b) prepare in respect of each accounting year a statement of accounts giving a true and fair view of the state of affairs and the income and expenditure of the new Agency.

(2) Every statement of accounts prepared by a new Agency in accordance with this section shall comply with any requirement which the appropriate Ministers have, with the consent of the Treasury, notified in writing to the new Agency and which relates to any of the following matters, namely—
(a) the information to be contained in the statement;
(b) the manner in which that information is to be presented;
(c) the methods and principles according to which the statement is to be prepared.

(3) In this section—
  "accounting records", in the case of a new Agency, includes all books, papers and other records of the new Agency relating to, or to matters dealt with in, the accounts required to be kept by virtue of this section;
  "accounting year", subject to subsection (4) below, means, in relation to a new Agency, a financial year.

(4) If the Secretary of State so directs in relation to any accounting year of either new Agency, that accounting year shall end with such date other than the next 31st March as may be specified in the direction; and, where the Secretary of State has given such a direction, the following accounting year shall begin with the day after the date so specified and, subject to any further direction under this subsection, shall end with the next 31st March.

<small>DEFINITIONS</small>
  "accounting records": subs. (3).
  "accounting year": subs. (3).
  "appropriate Ministers": s.56(1).
  "financial year": s.124(1).
  "new Agency": s.56(1).

<small>COMMENCEMENT</small>
  July 28, 1995 (S.I. 1995 No. 1983).

<small>GENERAL NOTE</small>
  This section, which is closely modelled on s.121 of the Water Resources Act 1991 in relation to the NRA, requires each of the Agency/SEPA to keep proper accounts and accounting records giving a true and fair view of its income and expenditure (subs. (1)), and to do so in accordance with such requirements as are notified to it under subs. (2) and for such financial year as it is directed under subs. (4) to use.
  Neither HMIP, HMIPI nor waste regulation authorities were previously under such a duty, although waste regulation authorities were all under a duty to publish an annual report containing some very limited financial information (s.67 of the Environmental Protection Act 1990; see s.52 of the 1995 Act). The NRA's latest Annual Report and Accounts is its sixth, covering the financial year ending March 31, 1995 (ISBN 1 873160 25 9).

Audit

46.—(1) The accounts of each new Agency shall be audited by an auditor appointed for each accounting year by the Secretary of State.

(2) A person shall not be qualified for appointment under subsection (1) above unless—

(a) he is eligible for appointment as a company auditor under Part II of the Companies Act 1989; and

(b) he would not be ineligible for appointment as company auditor of the new Agency in question by virtue of section 27 of that Act (ineligibility on ground of lack of independence), if that new Agency were a body to which section 384 of the Companies Act 1985 (duty to appoint auditor) applies.

(3) A copy of—

(a) any accounts of a new Agency which are audited under subsection (1) above, and

(b) the report made on those accounts by the auditor,

shall be sent to each of the appropriate Ministers as soon as reasonably practicable after the report is received by the new Agency; and the Secretary of State shall lay before each House of Parliament a copy of those accounts and that report.

(4) The Comptroller and Auditor General—

(a) shall be entitled to inspect the contents of all accounts and accounting records of a new Agency; and

(b) may report to the House of Commons the results of any inspection carried out by him under paragraph (a) above;

and section 6 of the National Audit Act 1983 (examinations of economy, efficiency and effectiveness) accordingly applies to each new Agency.

(5) In this section—

"accounting records" has the same meaning as in section 45 above;

"accounting year" has the same meaning as in section 45 above;

"accounts", in relation to the Agency, includes any statement under section 45 above.

DEFINITIONS
"accounting records": subs. (5).
"accounting year": subs. (5).
"accounts": subs. (5).
"appropriate Ministers": s.56(1).
"new Agency": s.56(1).

COMMENCEMENT
July 28, 1995 (S.I. 1995 No. 1983).

GENERAL NOTE
This section, which is modelled on s.122 of the Water Resources Act 1991 in relation to the NRA, regulates the auditing of the accounts required to be prepared under s.45.

Grants to the new Agencies

47. The appropriate Minister may, with the approval of the Treasury, make to a new Agency grants of such amounts, and on such terms, as he thinks fit.

DEFINITIONS
"appropriate Minister": s.56(1).
"new Agency": s.56(1).

COMMENCEMENT
July 28, 1995 (S.I. 1995 No. 1983).

GENERAL NOTE
Sections 41 to 43 deal with the Agency/SEPA's specific powers to raise funds through charging schemes which are generally intended to recover from regulated businesses the costs of regulating them.

Sections 47 to 50 make provision for other ways in which the agencies may raise funds: through grants or loans from the Government (ss.47 and 49 respectively) and by borrowing (s.48), with or without the backing of Government guarantees (s.50). Grants under this section require Treasury approval.

Borrowing powers

48.—(1) Each new Agency shall be entitled to borrow in accordance with the following provisions of this section, but not otherwise.

(2) Subject to subsection (5) below, each new Agency may—
(a) with the consent of the appropriate Minister, and
(b) with the approval of the Treasury,
borrow temporarily in sterling, by way of overdraft or otherwise, from persons other than the appropriate Ministers, such sums as it may require for meeting its obligations and carrying out its functions.

(3) Subject to subsection (5) below, each new Agency may borrow from the appropriate Minister, by way of temporary loan or otherwise, such sums in sterling as it may require for meeting its obligations and carrying out its functions.

(4) Any consent under subsection (2)(a) above may be granted subject to conditions.

(5) The aggregate amount outstanding in respect of the principal of sums borrowed under this section by a new Agency shall not at any time exceed—
(a) in the case of the Agency, £100 million or such greater sum, not exceeding £160 million, as the Ministers may by order specify; or
(b) in the case of SEPA, £5 million or such greater sum, not exceeding £10 million, as the Secretary of State may by order specify.

(6) The power to make an order under subsection (5) above shall be exercisable by statutory instrument; but no order shall be made under that subsection unless a draft of the order has been laid before, and approved by a resolution of, the House of Commons.

DEFINITIONS
"Agency": s.124(1).
"appropriate Minister": s.56(1).
"appropriate Ministers": s.56(1).
"functions": s.124(1).
"new Agency": s.56(1).
"SEPA": s.124(1).

COMMENCEMENT
July 28, 1995 (S.I. 1995 No. 1983).

GENERAL NOTE
In addition to charging schemes (ss.41 to 43) and Government grants (s.47), the Agency/SEPA have the power under this section to borrow sums which borrowing may in some circumstances be backed by a Government guarantee: s.50.

The power is circumscribed in a number of ways: borrowing may only be for the purposes of meeting the obligations of the agency in question and carrying out its functions: subss. (2) and (3); where borrowing is from Ministers, Treasury approval is required (s.49(1)) and the terms of the loan are governed by s.49; where borrowing is from someone other than the appropriate Ministers, Ministerial consent and Treasury approval is required (subs. (2)) and such consent may be conditional (subs. (4)); and the aggregate sum borrowed at any one time is restricted to £100 million for the Agency and £5 million for SEPA, unless a Ministerial order made by statutory instrument and expressly approved by the House of Commons raises those sums to not more than £160 million and £10 million respectively (subss. (5) and (6)).

The Environment Bill as originally drafted fixed SEPA's borrowing limits as between £2 and £5 million. These were amended in Standing Committee to between £5 and £10 million (*per* Sir Hector Monro, the then Parliamentary Under-Secretary of State for Scotland, Standing

Committee B, May 18, 1995, col. 297). The reason for SEPA's significantly smaller borrowing limits is related to the fact that since SEPA lacks flood defence powers in contrast to the Agency it is unlikely to be undertaking any major capital works (see *e.g.* Earl of Lindsay, *Hansard*, H.L. Vol. 560, col. 1414).

The insertion in respect of England and Wales of ss.161A to 161D into the Water Resources Act 1991, and the equivalent provisions for Scotland into the 1974 Act as ss.46A–46D, are notable in this context. They provide for the Agency/SEPA to serve "works notices" requiring remedial works to be carried out where pollution of controlled waters has occurred or is likely to occur. Previously, the regulators only had at their disposal in such circumstances a power to carry out such works themselves and then seek to recover its costs from the polluter, always an uncertain exercise. It is understood that this constrained their ability to secure remediation in such circumstances, in part because of the limits on their ability to raise funds for the carrying out of such works. The new provisions, by reducing one source of possible pressure on Agency/SEPA funding, may make the borrowing limits in this section less problematic than they might otherwise have been.

Government loans to the new Agencies

49.—(1) The appropriate Minister may, with the approval of the Treasury, lend to a new Agency any sums which it has power to borrow under section 48(3) above.

(2) Any loan made under this section by one of the appropriate Ministers shall be repaid to him at such times and by such methods, and interest on the loan shall be paid to him at such rates and at such times, as that Minister may with the approval of the Treasury from time to time determine.

(3) If in any financial year any of the appropriate Ministers lends any sums to a new Agency under this section, he shall—

(a) prepare in respect of that financial year an account of the sums so lent by him; and

(b) send that account to the Comptroller and Auditor General before the end of September in the following financial year;

and the form of the account and the manner of preparing it shall be such as the Treasury may direct.

(4) The Comptroller and Auditor General shall examine, certify and report on each account sent to him under this section and shall lay copies of it and of his report before each House of Parliament.

(5) The Treasury may issue to any of the appropriate Ministers—

(a) out of the National Loans Fund, or

(b) out of money provided by Parliament,

such sums as are necessary to enable him to make loans to a new Agency under this section; and any sums received by a Minister of the Crown in pursuance of subsection (2) above shall be paid into the National Loans Fund or, as the case may be, the Consolidated Fund.

DEFINITIONS

"appropriate Minister": s.56(1).

"appropriate Ministers": s.56(1).

"financial year": s.124(1).

"new Agency": s.56(1).

COMMENCEMENT

July 28, 1995 (S.I. 1995 No. 1983).

GENERAL NOTE

Where sums authorised to be borrowed by the Agency/SEPA under s.48 are borrowed from the Government, Treasury approval is required both for the loan (subs. (1)) and for its terms (subs. (2)). The action of the Minister concerned in making the loan is subject to reporting and Parliamentary scrutiny requirements (subss. (3) and (4)). Subsection (5) allows for the origin of the funds to be the Treasury, as will often be the case.

Government guarantees of a new Agency's borrowing

50.—(1) The appropriate Minister may, with the consent of the Treasury, guarantee, in such manner and on such conditions as he may think fit, the repayment of the principal of, the payment of interest on, and the discharge of any other financial obligation in connection with, any sum which a new Agency borrows from any person.

(2) A Minister who gives a guarantee under this section shall forthwith lay a statement of the guarantee before each House of Parliament.

(3) Where any sum is paid out for fulfilling a guarantee under this section, the Minister who gave the guarantee shall, as soon as reasonably practicable after the end of each financial year (beginning with that in which the sum is paid out and ending with that in which all liability in respect of the principal of the sum and in respect of interest on it is finally discharged), lay before each House of Parliament a statement relating to that sum.

(4) If any sums are paid out in fulfilment of a guarantee under this section, the new Agency which borrowed the sum by reference to which the guarantee was given shall make to the Minister who gave the guarantee, at such times and in such manner as he may from time to time direct,—

(a) payments of such amounts as he may so direct in or towards repayment of the sums so paid out; and

(b) payments of interest, at such rate as he may so direct, on what is outstanding for the time being in respect of sums so paid out;

and the consent of the Treasury shall be required for the giving of a direction under this subsection.

DEFINITIONS
"appropriate Minister": s.56(1).
"financial year": s.124(1).
"new Agency": s.56(1).

COMMENCEMENT
July 28, 1995 (S.I. 1995 No. 1983).

GENERAL NOTE

Section 48 allows the Agency/SEPA to borrow, and s.49 provides for the case where that borrowing is from the Government. An alternative where private sector funds might otherwise be unforthcoming is provided by this section: a Government guarantee of the financial obligations of the Agency/SEPA in question under the loans (subs. (1)).

A statement of the guarantee must be laid before each House of Parliament (subs. (2)) and, where the guarantee is called upon so that the Minister concerned has to pay out any sum, he must lay a statement about this sum before each House of Parliament (subs. (3)), and the agency in question must repay him on such terms as, with the consent of the Treasury, he may direct (subs. (4)).

Information

Provision of information by the new Agencies

51.—(1) A new Agency shall furnish the appropriate Minister with all such information as he may reasonably require relating to—

(a) the new Agency's property;

(b) the carrying out and proposed carrying out of its functions; and

(c) its responsibilities generally.

(2) Information required under this section shall be furnished in such form and manner, and be accompanied or supplemented by such explanations, as the appropriate Minister may reasonably require.

(3) The information which a new Agency may be required to furnish to the appropriate Minister under this section shall include information which, although it is not in the possession of the new Agency or would not otherwise come into the possession of the new Agency, is information which it is reasonable to require the new Agency to obtain.

(4) A requirement for the purposes of this section shall be contained in a direction which—

(a) may describe the information to be furnished in such manner as the Minister giving the direction considers appropriate; and

(b) may require the information to be furnished on a particular occasion, in particular circumstances or from time to time.

(5) For the purposes of this section a new Agency shall—

(a) permit any person authorised for the purpose by the appropriate Minister to inspect and make copies of the contents of any accounts or other records of the new Agency; and

(b) give such explanation of them as that person or the appropriate Minister may reasonably require.

DEFINITIONS
"appropriate Minister": s.56(1).
"functions": s.124(1).
"new Agency": s.56(1).
"records": s.124(1).

COMMENCEMENT
July 28, 1995 (S.I. 1995 No. 1983).

GENERAL NOTE
Section 45 provides for each agency to publish accounts and s.52 requires them each to publish an annual report; this section can be seen as plugging the gaps in such information by providing that the Secretary of State (or, additionally, in the case of the Agency the Minister of Agriculture, Fisheries and Food) may direct the agencies to furnish him with information on its property, activities and responsibilities (subs. (1)). Such information need not be in the possession of the agency in question (subs. (3)). The section also allows these Ministers to authorise a person to inspect and copy agency records and have them explained to that person (subs. (5)).

Annual report

52.—(1) As soon as reasonably practicable after the end of each financial year, each new Agency shall prepare a report on its activities during that year and shall send a copy of that report to each of the appropriate Ministers.

(2) Every such report shall set out any directions under section 40 above which have been given to the new Agency in question during the year to which the report relates, other than directions given under subsection (1) of that section which are identified to that new Agency in writing by the appropriate Minister as being directions the disclosure of which would, in his opinion, be contrary to the interests of national security.

(3) The Secretary of State shall lay a copy of every such report before each House of Parliament and shall arrange for copies of every such report to be published in such manner as he considers appropriate.

(4) A new Agency's annual report shall be in such form and contain such information as may be specified in any direction given to the new Agency by the appropriate Ministers.

DEFINITIONS
"appropriate Ministers": s.56(1).
"financial year": s.124(1).
"new Agency": s.56(1).

GENERAL NOTE
This section requires the Agency/SEPA to prepare an annual report and submit it to the Secretary of State (and also, in the case of the Agency, to the Minister of Agriculture, Fisheries and Food): subs. (1). There is a separate obligation on each of them to prepare and publish accounts: s.45.

The form and content of such annual reports may be specified in a direction given to the agency in question (subs. (4)), and also (except in the case of certain directions which may be excluded by the appropriate Minister on national security grounds). The report must list directions received during the period of the report: subs. (2). Otherwise there are no restrictions on the form or content of the annual report. It is the responsibility of the Secretary of State to publish the report and place it before Parliament: subs. (3).

Previous provisions: England and Wales
   This section is similar to s.187 of the Water Resources Act 1991 which placed a duty on the NRA to produce an annual report, but is less prescriptive than the equivalent provision for waste regulation authorities (s.67 of the Environmental Protection Act 1990) which it supersedes. It remains to be seen whether directions under subs. (4) will replicate the list of matters to be included in an annual report under s.67(2) of the 1990 Act: (a) modifications, grants, revocations etc. of waste management licences; (b) exercise of certain powers; (c) implementation of its own waste recycling plan; (d) number and description of prosecutions brought; and (e) costs incurred and sums received in the course of waste regulation.

Previous provisions: Scotland
   Prior to the advent of SEPA, under s.16 of the Rivers (Prevention of Pollution) (Scotland) Act 1951 (c. 66), river purification boards were under a duty to produce annual reports for the Secretary of State, which were also published. In contrast, there were no reporting duties laid on HMIPI. Nevertheless, HMIPI produced two reports, the first covering the period 1987–1988 which was published in 1990 and the second, covering the period April 1988 and March 1992, was published in 1994. Given the time lag between the publication of these reports and the period they cover, they cannot be said to be particularly useful. For example, HMIPI have not yet published a report on the implementation of IPC in Scotland. The duty on SEPA to produce an annual report is therefore welcome and will assist in making its operations more accessible to the public. In relation to reporting requirements in Scotland, the Government explained in Parliament that:
   "The situation in Scotland is somewhat different. The Scottish Office does not compile and publish environmental information on this scale. Because of that, the Government intends SEPA to publish an annual report on the state of the environment. My right honourable friend the Secretary of State for Scotland will use his powers under Clause 49(4) [s.52(4)] to require SEPA to publish as an annexe to its annual report a state of the environment report. That will be based on SEPA's duty to compile such information under Clause 31(2) [s.33(2)]" (*per* Viscount Ullswater, Minister of State, Department of the Environment, *Hansard*, H.L. Vol. 560, col. 1418).

Transitional arrangements
   The first report of one of the agencies may include a report on the activities of one or more of its predecessor bodies, and SEPA must, as soon as reasonably practicable after the transfer date, prepare a report on the activities of river purification boards and waste regulation authorities (para. 5 of Sched. 23 to the 1995 Act).

Supplemental provisions

Inquiries and other hearings

53.—(1) Without prejudice to any other provision of this Act or any other enactment by virtue of which an inquiry or other hearing is authorised or required to be held, the appropriate Minister may cause an inquiry or other hearing to be held if it appears to him expedient to do so—
   (a) in connection with any of the functions of a new Agency; or
   (b) in connection with any of his functions in relation to a new Agency.
   (2) Subsections (2) to (5) of section 250 of the Local Government Act 1972 (which contain supplementary provisions with respect to local inquiries held in pursuance of that section) shall apply to inquiries or other hearings under this section or any other enactment—
   (a) in connection with any of the functions of the Agency, or
   (b) in connection with any functions of the Secretary of State or the Minister in relation to the Agency,
as they apply to inquiries under that section, but taking the reference in subsection (4) of that section to a local authority as including a reference to the Agency.
   (3) The provisions of subsections (2) to (8) of section 210 of the Local Government (Scotland) Act 1973 (which relate to the holding of local inquiries) shall apply to inquiries or other hearings held under this section or any other enactment—
   (a) in connection with any of the functions of SEPA, or
   (b) in connection with any functions of the Secretary of State in relation to SEPA,
as they apply to inquiries held under that section.

DEFINITIONS
　"Agency": s.124(1).
　"appropriate Minister": s.56(1).
　"functions": s.124(1).
　"Minister": s.56(1).
　"new Agency": s.56(1).
　"SEPA": s.124(1).

COMMENCEMENT
　April 1, 1996 (S.I. 1996 No. 186).

GENERAL NOTE
　This section gives the Secretary of State (and additionally in respect of the Agency, the Minister of Agriculture, Fisheries and Food) a wide power to cause a public inquiry or other hearing to be held, in connection with any Agency/SEPA function or any function of his own in relation to either of them. This power is expressed to be without prejudice to other provisions which may allow for such inquiries or hearings: these will generally relate to appeals against Agency/SEPA acts or omissions. Thus, for example, it does not override the appeals procedure in relation to IPC which is found in s.15 of the Environmental Protection Act 1990.
　This section is not the only provision in the 1995 Act with a bearing on the conduct of inquiries: s.114 gives the Secretary of State the power in specified circumstances to delegate his appellate function or refer matters involved in appeals, and Sched. 22 contains amendments to certain provisions in relation to appeals and inquiries.

Subs. (3)
　This subsection applies the provisions of s.210(2) to (8) of the Local Government (Scotland) Act 1973 (c. 65) to the holding of inquiries or other hearings in connection with any functions of SEPA and the Secretary of State in relation to SEPA.

Appearance in legal proceedings

54. In England and Wales, a person who is authorised by the Agency to prosecute on its behalf in proceedings before a magistrates' court shall be entitled to prosecute in any such proceedings although not of counsel or a solicitor.

DEFINITIONS
　"Agency": s.124(1).

COMMENCEMENT
　April 1, 1996 (S.I. 1996 No. 186).

GENERAL NOTE
　This important section, which builds upon the provision in s.37(1) that the Agency may institute legal proceedings, and which accordingly applies only to the Agency, allows its enforcing officers to prosecute cases which they have worked on, even if they are not legally qualified, thus avoiding duplication of time spent familiarising a legally qualified advocate with the matter. It will be noted that the right does not extend beyond the level of the magistrates' court, however, it is in such a court that almost all Agency enforcement actions will commence.
　It should be noted also that this section does not provide a "blanket" right of audience for authorised Agency personnel before a magistrates' court. It applies only to prosecutions and not, therefore, to other matters such as appeals before magistrates' courts against remediation notices under the contaminated land provisions inserted into the 1990 Act by s.57 of this Act.

Scotland
　Since SEPA cannot institute criminal proceedings, this section does not apply to Scotland. See also the General Note to s.37 at p. 25–98.

Continuity of exercise of functions: the new Agencies

55.—(1) The abolition of—
　(a) the National Rivers Authority,
　(b) the London Waste Regulation Authority, or
　(c) a river purification board,
shall not affect the validity of anything done by that Authority or board before the transfer date.

(2) Anything which, at the transfer date, is in the process of being done by or in relation to a transferor in the exercise of, or in connection with, any of the transferred functions may be continued by or in relation to the transferee.

(3) Anything done by or in relation to a transferor before the transfer date in the exercise of, or otherwise in connection with, any of the transferred functions, shall, so far as is required for continuing its effect on and after that date, have effect as if done by or in relation to the transferee.

(4) Subsection (3) above applies in particular to—

(a) any decision, determination, declaration, designation, agreement or instrument made by a transferor;

(b) any regulations or byelaws made by a transferor;

(c) any licence, permission, consent, approval, authorisation, exemption, dispensation or relaxation granted by or to a transferor;

(d) any notice, direction or certificate given by or to a transferor;

(e) any application, request, proposal or objection made by or to a transferor;

(f) any condition or requirement imposed by or on a transferor;

(g) any fee or charge paid by or to a transferor;

(h) any appeal allowed by or in favour of or against a transferor;

(j) any proceedings instituted by or against a transferor.

(5) Any reference in the foregoing provisions of this section to anything done by or in relation to a transferor includes a reference to anything which, by virtue of any enactment, is treated as having been done by or in relation to that transferor.

(6) Any reference to a transferor in any document constituting or relating to anything to which the foregoing provisions of this section apply shall, so far as is required for giving effect to those provisions, be construed as a reference to the transferee.

(7) The foregoing provisions of this section—

(a) are without prejudice to any provision made by this Act in relation to any particular functions; and

(b) shall not be construed as continuing in force any contract of employment made by a transferor;

and the Secretary of State may, in relation to any particular functions, by order exclude, modify or supplement any of the foregoing provisions of this section or make such other transitional provisions as he thinks necessary or expedient.

(8) Where, by virtue of any provision of Schedule 15 to this Act, the Minister is the transferor in the case of any functions, he shall have the same powers under subsection (7) above in relation to those functions as the Secretary of State.

(9) The power to make an order under subsection (7) above shall be exercisable by statutory instrument; and any statutory instrument containing such an order shall be subject to annulment pursuant to a resolution of either House of Parliament.

(10) In this section—

"the transferee", in the case of any transferred functions, means the new Agency whose functions they become by virtue of any provision made by or under this Act;

"transferred functions" means any functions which, by virtue of any provision made by or under this Act, become functions of a new Agency; and

"transferor" means any body or person any or all of whose functions become, by virtue of any provision made by or under this Act, functions of a new Agency.

Definitions
"functions": s.124(1).

"Minister": s.56(1).
"modify": s.124(1).
"new Agency": s.56(1).
"transfer date": s.56(1).
"transferee": subs. (10).
"transferor": subs. (10).
"transferred functions": subs. (10).

COMMENCEMENT
    Subss. (7)–(10) came into force on February 1, 1996; the remainder came into force on April 1, 1996 (S.I. 1996 No. 186).

GENERAL NOTE
    This section provides for continuity between the Agency/SEPA and their predecessors on the transfer from those bodies or persons to the Agency/SEPA of some or all of their functions. In particular licences, conditions and legal proceedings granted, imposed or commenced by a transferor take effect following the transfer date as if done by the relevant agency: subs. (4). It should be noted that the list at subs. (4) is an inclusive one.
    The Secretary of State may modify the extent of this section's otherwise very comprehensive continuity provisions: subs. (7). Schedule 15 transfers to the Agency a number of fisheries functions. Mostly these are transferred from the NRA but several functions of the Minister of Agriculture, Fisheries and Food under the Salmon and Freshwater Fisheries Act 1975 (c. 51) are also transferred. Where this is the case, that Minister rather than the Secretary of State, may modify the continuity provision in this section: subs. (8).
    To an extent this section duplicates provisions such as those made under s.3 or, in Scotland, under s.22 in relation to transfers and schemes of transfer of property, rights and liabilities, and it is expressed by subs. (7) to be without prejudice to such other provisions.

Interpretation of Part I

    56.—(1) In this Part of this Act, except where the context otherwise requires—
        "the 1951 Act" means the Rivers (Prevention of Pollution) (Scotland) Act 1951;
        "the 1990 Act" means the Environmental Protection Act 1990;
        "the 1991 Act" means the Water Resources Act 1991;
        "the appropriate Minister"—
            (a) in the case of the Agency, means the Secretary of State or the Minister; and
            (b) in the case of SEPA, means the Secretary of State;
        "the appropriate Ministers"—
            (a) in the case of the Agency, means the Secretary of State and the Minister; and
            (b) in the case of SEPA, means the Secretary of State;
        "conservancy authority" has the meaning given by section 221(1) of the 1991 Act;
        "costs" includes—
            (a) costs to any person; and
            (b) costs to the environment;
        "disposal authority"—
            (a) in the application of this Part in relation to the Agency, has the same meaning as it has in Part I of the Control of Pollution Act 1974 by virtue of section 30(1) of that Act; and
            (b) in the application of this Part in relation to SEPA, has the meaning assigned to it by section 30(2) of that Act;
        "the environment" has the same meaning as in Part I of the 1990 Act;
        "environmental licence", in the application of this Part in relation to the Agency, means any of the following—
            (a) registration of a person as a carrier of controlled waste under section 2 of the Control of Pollution (Amendment) Act 1989,

(b) an authorisation under Part I of the 1990 Act, other than any such authorisation granted by a local enforcing authority,

(c) a waste management licence under Part II of that Act,

(d) a licence under Chapter II of Part II of the 1991 Act,

(e) a consent for the purposes of section 88(1)(a), 89(4)(a) or 90 of that Act,

(f) registration under the Radioactive Substances Act 1993,

(g) an authorisation under that Act,

(h) registration of a person as a broker of controlled waste under the Waste Management Licensing Regulations 1994,

(j) registration in respect of an activity falling within paragraph 45(1) or (2) of Schedule 3 to those Regulations,

so far as having effect in relation to England and Wales;

"environmental licence", in the application of this Part in relation to SEPA, means any of the following—

(a) a consent under Part II of the Control of Pollution Act 1974,

(b) registration of a person as a carrier of controlled waste under section 2 of the Control of Pollution (Amendment) Act 1989,

(c) an authorisation under Part I of the 1990 Act,

(d) a waste management licence under Part II of that Act,

(e) a licence under section 17 of the Natural Heritage (Scotland) Act 1991,

(f) registration under the Radioactive Substances Act 1993,

(g) an authorisation under that Act,

(h) registration of a person as a broker of controlled waste under the Waste Management Licensing Regulations 1994,

(j) registration in respect of an activity falling within paragraph 45(1) or (2) of Schedule 3 to those Regulations,

so far as having effect in relation to Scotland;

"flood defence functions", in relation to the Agency, has the same meaning as in the 1991 Act;

"harbour authority" has the meaning given by section 221(1) of the 1991 Act;

"local authority", in the application of this Part in relation to SEPA, means a district or islands council in Scotland;

"the Minister" means the Minister of Agriculture, Fisheries and Food;

"the Ministers" means the Secretary of State and the Minister;

"navigation authority, has the meaning given by section 221(1) of the 1991 Act;

"new Agency" means the Agency or SEPA;

"river purification authority" means a river purification authority within the meaning of the 1951 Act;

"river purification board" means a river purification board established by virtue of section 135 of the Local Government (Scotland) Act 1973;

"the transfer date" means such date as the Secretary of State may by order made by statutory instrument appoint as the transfer date for the purposes of this Part; and different dates may be appointed for the purposes of this Part—

(i) as it applies for or in connection with transfers under or by virtue of Chapter I above, and

(ii) as it applies for or in connection with transfers under or by virtue of Chapter II above;

"waste regulation authority"—

(a) in the application of this Part in relation to the Agency, means any authority in England or Wales which, by virtue of section 30(1) of the 1990 Act, is a waste regulation authority for the purposes of Part II of that Act; and

(b) in the application of this Part in relation to SEPA, means any council which, by virtue of section 30(1)(g) of the 1990 Act, is a waste regulation authority for the purposes of Part II of that Act.

(2) In relation to any time on or after 1st April 1996—

(a) subsection (1) above shall have effect as if, in the definition of "local authority", for the words "district or islands council in Scotland" there were substituted the words "council constituted under section 2 of the Local Government etc. (Scotland) Act 1994"; and

(b) in section 22(3)(a)(iv) above the reference to an islands council shall be construed as a reference to a council mentioned in section 3(1) of the Local Government etc. (Scotland) Act 1994.

(3) Where by virtue of any provision of this Part any function of a Minister of the Crown is exercisable concurrently by different Ministers, that function shall also be exercisable jointly by any two or more of those Ministers.

DEFINITIONS
"Agency": s.124(1).
"functions": s.124(1).
"SEPA": s.124(1).

COMMENCEMENT
July 28, 1995 (S.I. 1995 No. 1983).

GENERAL NOTE
"the appropriate Minister". Note the distinction between this term and the one immediately following, and the provision in relation to this term that any function exercisable concurrently by Ministers is also exercisable jointly: subs. (3).

Although it is a constitutional principle that the office of Secretary of State is indivisible, nevertheless in practice, as regards Scotland, the Secretary of State will be the Secretary of State for Scotland.

"conservancy authority". Section 22(1) of the Water Resources Act 1991 defines this term to mean "any person who has a duty or power under any enactment to conserve, maintain or improve the navigation of a tidal water and is not a navigation authority or harbour authority". For the meaning of these last two kinds of authority, see below.

"costs". For a consideration of the geographical extent of this term and the undefined "benefits", see the General Note to s.39 at p. 25–108.

"disposal authority". By ss.2(1)(c) and 21(1)(c) of the 1995 Act only the functions of waste disposal authorities under or by virtue of the *waste regulation* provisions of the Control of Pollution Act 1974 are transferred to the Agency.

England and Wales
Section 30(1) of the 1974 Act defines disposal authorities for the purposes of those waste regulation functions as: the London Waste Regulation Authority; the Greater Manchester Waste Disposal Authority; in all other local authority areas in England, the council of the county or metropolitan district; and in Wales, the council of the district.

Scotland
"Disposal authority" means a district or islands council. However, from April 1, 1996 when local government reorganisation under the Local Government etc. (Scotland) Act 1994 takes effect, "disposal authority" will mean a council established under the 1994 Act.

"the environment". This term is defined for the purposes of Pt. I of the Environmental Protection Act 1990 by s.1(2) of that Act as consisting of "all, or any, of the following media, namely, the air, water and land; and the medium of air includes the air within buildings and the air within other natural or man-made structures above or below ground". For a consideration of the geographical extent of this term in the context of costs and benefits to the environment, see the General Note to s.39 at p. 25–108.

The term "pollution of the environment" is not defined. For a consideration of the meaning of that term, see the General Note to s.5 at p. 25–42.

"environmental licence". This term is defined for each of the two agencies by reference to a specific range of registrations, consents, licences and authorisations, which exist under regimes

the regulation of which has been transferred to the agency in question. It should be noted that in the case of the Agency there are consent functions which are not on this list. An example is its function of consenting, subject to conditions, to the erection of structures in, over or under main rivers (s.109 of the Water Resources Act 1991).

The Government has indicated that it is its medium-term aim to move towards a system whereby each agency issues a single environmental licence to any business which at present needs a number of environmental licences from it in respect of its activities on one site. See further the Introduction and General Note to Pt. I of this Act at p. 25–11.

It may not be immediately clear what activities are governed by certain of the environmental licences listed here. In relation to the Agency, para. (b) refers to IPC authorisation; para. (d) to water abstraction and impoundment; para. (e) to discharging to controlled waters; paras. (f) and (g) to registration as a person holding a radioactive substance and authorisation to do so; and para. (j) to scrap metal activities and the dismantling of motor vehicles, the registration requirements for which are more onerous than for other activities exempted from waste management licensing by Sched. 3 to the 1994 Regulations. In relation to SEPA, para. (a) refers to discharging to controlled waters; para. (c) to IPC and LAPC authorisation; para. (e) to water abstraction for irrigation purposes; para. (f) to registration as a person holding a radioactive substance; and para. (j) to scrap metal activities and the dismantling of motor vehicles as in para. (j) in relation to the Agency.

"*Flood defence functions*". The definition of this term in the 1991 Act is substituted by para. 175(7) of Sched. 22 to the 1995 Act.

"*harbour authority*". Section 221(1) of the Water Resources Act defines this term in two different ways: in relation to the flood defence provisions of that Act (that is, those provisions cited above in the definition of "flood defence provisions"), it is defined by reference to the Merchant Shipping Act 1894 (c. 60), which is now consolidated into the Merchant Shipping Act 1995 (c. 21), and defines it as "includ[ing] all persons entrusted with the function of constructing, improving, managing, regulating, maintaining or lighting a harbour": s.313(1); otherwise, it is defined as a person who is a harbour authority within the meaning of the Prevention of Oil Pollution Act 1971 but who is not a navigation authority (see below). The 1971 Act definition reads: "a person or body or persons empowered by an enactment to make charges in respect of vessels entering a harbour in the United Kingdom or using facilities therein": s.8(2).

"*Local authority*". This definition applies to Scotland only. Prior to April 1, 1996 this means a district or islands council. However, from that date when local government reorganisation takes effect in Scotland, the meaning will change to a council constituted under the Local Government etc. (Scotland) Act 1994: s.56(2).

"*navigation authority*". This term is defined by s.221(1) of the Water Resources Act 1991 to mean "any person who has a duty or power under any enactment to work, maintain, conserve, improve or control any canal or other inland navigation, navigable river, estuary, harbour or dock".

"*river purification authority*". Section 17(2) of the Rivers (Prevention of Pollution) (Scotland) Act 1951 (c.66), as substituted by Sched. 16, para. 5 of the Local Government (Scotland) Act 1973, provides that RPAs are "river purification boards established under section 135 of the Local Government (Scotland) Act 1973 and islands councils".

"*River purification board*". River Purification Boards were originally established under the Rivers (Prevention of Pollution) (Scotland) Act 1951. However, the presently constituted boards were established under s.135 of the Local Government (Scotland) Act 1973. Under this provision, each board could have a membership of up to three times the number of local authority districts wholly or partly within its area. Section 135 also provided for one-third of the board to be appointed by regional councils within its area, one-third by district councils within its area and one-third by the Secretary of State to represent interests such as agriculture, fisheries and industry. However, s.135A of the 1973 Act which was inserted by s.27 and Sched. 10, para. 6 of the Natural Heritage (Scotland) Act 1991, gave the Secretary of State the power to vary the size of the boards and to appoint up to half the members with regional and district councils being restricted to one-quarter each. There are presently seven RPBs: Tweed, Solway, Clyde, Forth, Tay, North-East and Highland.

"*Waste regulation authority*". By s.30(1) of the 1990 Act, prior to the transfer date waste regulation authorities in England and Wales were: county councils for English non-metropolitan counties; district councils, the Greater Manchester Waste Disposal Authority or the Merseyside Waste Disposal Authority as appropriate for English metropolitan counties; the London Waste Regulation Authority for Greater London; and district councils in Wales. Waste regulation authorities in Scotland are islands or district councils. However, from the transfer date these functions are transferred to the Agency/SEPA.

Subs. (2): "Local authority"
The new definition which takes effect from April 1, 1996 reflects reorganisation of local government in Scotland under the Local Government etc. (Scotland) Act 1994 whereby unitary authorities are set up in place of existing regional and district councils.

PART II

CONTAMINATED LAND AND ABANDONED MINES

INTRODUCTION AND GENERAL NOTE
This Part of the Act comprises s.57 (contaminated land), to which this General Note is an introduction, and ss.58–60 (abandoned mines) to which there is a separate introductory note (see below at p. 25–190). Section 57 represents the Government's attempt to formulate a new regime for dealing with the problems arising from contaminated land. While existing provisions such as those on statutory nuisance (Pt. III of the Environmental Protection Act 1990), the removal of unlawfully deposited waste (s.59 of the 1990 Act) and works to prevent or remedy water pollution (s.161 of the Water Resources Act 1991 or, in Scotland, s.46 of the Control of Pollution Act 1974) were capable of application to contaminated land situations, they were in some respects inadequate and did not provide a comprehensive framework for the identification, assessment and remediation of the wide variety of contaminated sites in Great Britain.

Policy background
Concern was focused on contaminated land by two reports of the House of Commons Select Committee on the Environment dealing with toxic waste and contaminated land: House of Commons Session 1988–1989; Second Report, *Toxic Waste* (22 I–III); Session 1989–1990, First Report, *Contaminated Land* (170 I–III). See also S.R. Tromans and R.T.F. Turrall-Clarke, *Contaminated Land* (Sweet & Maxwell, 1994), in particular Chap 1. In the second of these Reports, the Select Committee recognised the difficult policy issues raised by any statutory scheme of liability but suggested that nonetheless action was needed:
> "... urgent attention [must] be given to the question of creating statutory liability for damage caused by contamination to land—particularly where this causes damage to neighbouring property or the environment. We recognise that this will raise complex questions as to retrospection, insurance cover and limitation periods in particular, but we believe that the present lack of clarity in relation to civil liability hampers the development of appropriate policies on the issue of contaminated land".

The initial response of the Government was not to address the issue of statutory liability directly, but to introduce a provision (s.143 of the Environmental Protection Act 1990) for public registers of land which had been subject to a "contaminative use": a use which might cause land to be contaminated with noxious substances. This approach was intended, with "minimal demands" on local authority resources (*Hansard*, H.L. Vol. 520, col. 2269), to provide a means of alerting interested parties to the possible existence of contamination without "extending planning blight in those areas of the country with a legacy of industrial land use" (DoE News Release 279, April 30, 1990). This proved to be a somewhat optimistic assumption. Section 143 of the 1990 Act was intended to be implemented late in 1991. However, following an initial consultation exercise as to the range of uses to be prescribed as "contaminative", the Government announced on March 10, 1992 that it was postponing the introduction of the registers in view of the concerns that had been expressed over them relating to the likelihood of serious blight in an already depressed property market.

A second consultation process ensued, with a markedly reduced list of contaminative uses, and with a proposed timetable leading to the opening of the registers to public inspection in about April 1994. This exercise enabled the Government to identify three serious grounds for criticism of the proposed registers. Being based on current or former use of land rather than actual contamination, they would include a number of sites which were not actually contaminated, whilst excluding others which were. Furthermore, the logical consequence of a register based on historical fact as to land use would have been the inability to have land removed from the register following completion of clean-up. Finally, the system would have left it unclear what action should be taken and by whom, *i.e.* whether the land should be cleaned up and, if so, who should pay and how much. These misgivings led the Government to withdraw the proposal for registers, a decision announced by the then Secretary of State for the Environment, Michael Howard, on March 24, 1993. Mr Howard announced the institution of a "wide-ranging review" of the legal powers of public bodies to control and tackle contaminated land, to be conducted by an inter-departmental group under the chairmanship of the Department of Environment. Following similar consultation exercises in Scotland, the Secretary of State for Scotland announced an equivalent review on the same date.

As part of this review process, the Government's first step was to issue the consultation paper, *Paying for Our Past: the Arrangements for Controlling Contaminated Land and Meeting the Cost of Remedying Damage to the Environment* (March 1994). In Scotland, a similar though not identical consultation paper entitled *Contaminated Land Clean-up and Control* (March 1994) was issued by the Scottish Office Environment Department. Its conclusions did not differ in any material respect from those of the consultation paper issued in England and Wales. Neither Paper presented any firm proposals but rather set out a number of "preliminary conclusions" and posed a series of questions for respondents, grouped under seven issues:

A. What should the objectives be within policy?

B. How should the statutory framework meet the objectives?

C. What relationship should the statutory framework have with the common law?

D. Should there be any extension of strict liability?

E. Who should pay for putting right environmental damage?

F. How should markets be provided with information?

G. What other roles should public sector bodies have?

These Papers, inconclusive even by consultation paper standards, instituted another phase of the debate, which culminated on November 24, 1994 with the publication of the outcome of the review, *Framework for Contaminated Land* (and in Scotland, *Contaminated Land Clean-up and Control: Outcome of Review*), and the subsequent passage of the Environment Act 1995, s.57 of which introduced into the Environmental Protection Act 1990 a new Pt. IIA dealing with contaminated land. The central planks of the *Framework*, which were substantially mirrored by those of its Scottish counterpart, were said to be the following.

1. The maintenance of the "suitable for use" approach, requiring remedial action only where the contamination poses unacceptable actual or potential risks to health or the environment, and where there are "appropriate and cost-effective means to do so, taking into account the actual or intended use of the site".

2. To deal with "urgent and real problems, but in an orderly and controlled fashion with which the economy at large and individual businesses and land-owners can cope".

3. The creation of greater clarity and certainty than the law currently provides, so as to assist in the development of an efficient market in land which is contaminated and in land which has been subject to remedial works.

4. The replacement of the existing statutory nuisance powers, which "have provided an essentially sound basis for dealing with contaminated land", with a modern, specific contaminated land power. Here the position in Scotland differs, and the *Outcome of Review* indicated that the introduction of the contaminated land regime was to coincide with the extension to Scotland of the statutory nuisance provisions already existing in England and Wales, replacing existing provisions. This is achieved by s.107 of, and Sched. 17 to, the 1995 Act.

Time will no doubt tell to what extent the actual drafting of the relevant provisions achieves those objectives. Substantial amendments were made to the provisions during the Parliamentary process, in response to concerns expressed by the industrial, financial, land-owning and legal communities. Taken together, these amendments have had the effect of mitigating somewhat the harshness of the proposed liability regime and of making its provisions more palatable. Nonetheless the fact remains that the new sections constitute a regime of strict and retroactive liability for historic contamination, and that liability can extend in certain circumstances not only to the original polluter, but also to an "innocent" landowner or occupier. As mentioned below, much reliance is placed on Government guidance as a means of mitigating the potentially harsher operations of the legislation, for example, what degree of contamination or risk is sufficient to justify action, and how liability is to be apportioned between a number of potentially liable parties. At the time of the passage of the Act, none of this guidance was in final form, and much had not emerged even in draft form.

The scheme of the provisions

The new provisions follow through a sequence from the identification of contaminated land to securing its remediation. Primary responsibility for this process rests with district councils and unitary authorities, though both the Secretary of State and the Environment Agency/SEPA also have very important roles to play, as explained below.

1. *Identifying Contaminated Land.* "Contaminated Land" is defined at s.78A(2) of the 1990 Act (as inserted by s.57 of the 1995 Act) by reference to the subjective opinion of the local authority in whose area it is situated as to whether it is in such a condition by reason of substances in, on or under it, that significant harm is being caused or there is a significant possibility of such harm being caused, *or* that pollution of controlled waters is being or is likely to be caused. The local authority is under a statutory duty to cause its area to be inspected from time to time for the purpose of identifying such land (s.78B(1)). In making the determination as to whether the land is contaminated or not, the local authority is required to act in accordance with guidance from the Secretary of State as to the manner in which the determination is to be made (s.78A(2)).

2. *Notification.* Upon identifying contaminated land, the local authority is required to give notice of that fact to: (a) the Agency or SEPA; (b) the owner of the land; (c) any person who appears to be the owner or occupier of all or part of the land; and (d) the person who appears to be the "appropriate person", *i.e.* who caused or knowingly permitted the contamination, and as such may be served with a remediation notice.

3. *Special Sites.* As well as identifying contaminated land, the local authority must decide whether such land is required to be designated as a "special site": ss.78B(1)(b) and 78C(1). The significance of this distinction is that in the case of special sites the Agency/SEPA is the enforcing authority rather than the local authority (s.78A(9)). Before making this decision, the local authority must request the advice of the Agency/SEPA and have regard to the advice received (s.78C(3)). Land is, however, only required to be designated as a special site if it falls within a description prescribed for this purpose by the Secretary of State (s.78C(8)). The Agency/SEPA may itself consider that contaminated land falls within such a description, and may give notice of that fact to the local authority (s.78C(4)). Disagreements between the Agency/SEPA and the local authority are resolved by referral to the Secretary of State (s.78D).

4. *Duty to require remediation.* Where land has been identified as contaminated or has been designated as a special site, then the relevant enforcing authority falls under a duty to serve on the "appropriate person" a remediation notice, specifying what is to be done by way of remediation and within what period (s.78E(1)). In this context remediation can mean either works to assess the situation, or actual remedial or mitigating measures, or subsequent inspections (s.78A(10)). This duty is, however, qualified in four important respects: (a) the requirement of prior consultation under s.78H (see below); (b) restrictions on service of a notice under s.78H; (c) the requirement that remediation may only comprise those things the authority considers reasonable, having regard to the cost likely to be involved and the seriousness of the harm in question (s.78E(4)); and (d) the requirement to have regard to guidance issued by the Secretary of State (s.78E(5)).

5. *Determination of the "appropriate person".* Section 78F deals with the vital issue of who is the appropriate person or persons to bear responsibility to comply with the remediation notice. As might be expected, the section was extremely controversial at the Parliamentary stage, and has been heavily amended. Responsibility rests primarily with the person or persons who caused or knowingly permitted the contaminating substances to be in, on or under the land: s.78F(2). However, the current owner or occupier may also be liable where, after reasonable inquiry, no such person can be found: s.78F(4) and (5). Specific provision is made with regard to those acting in the context of insolvency (*e.g.* receivers): s.78X(3). No special provision is, however, made for lenders, other than the definition of "owner", which makes it clear that a mortgagee or, in Scotland, a creditor in a heritable security not in possession, is not within the definition: s.78A(9). One very difficult issue is that of joint and several liability. The starting point is that where a number of persons have contributed the same, or different, contaminating substances, liability may be joint and several: s.78F(2). However, this potential liability is mitigated in two respects: first, by the requirement that the remedial action required to be taken by any appropriate person be "referable" to the substances he contributed (s.78F(3)) and, secondly, by the obligation of the enforcing authority, in determining who is the appropriate person, to act in accordance with guidance issued by the Secretary of State: s.78F(6) and (7). Special provision is also made for the situation where substances migrate from their original source, so as to cause other land to become contaminated: s.78K.

6. *Consultation.* One of the numerous amendments to the original provisions is the requirement for the enforcing authority to use reasonable endeavours to consult with the person who appears to be the responsible person, and with the owner and the occupier of the relevant land: s.78H(1). The consultation must relate to what is to be done by way of remediation and no remediation notice may be served during a three-month period from the original notification (see 2. above): s.78H(3). Certain circumstances are specified where no remediation notice may be served at all, for example where the authority is satisfied that there is nothing that could reasonably be required, having balanced cost considerations against the seriousness of the contamination, or where the authority is satisfied that appropriate steps are being or will be taken by way of remediation voluntarily, without the need for service of a remediation notice: s.78H(5). In such cases, the outcome will be the preparation and publication of either a remediation declaration (by the authority) or a remediation statement (by the responsible person): s.78H(6) and (7).

7. *Appeals against remediation notices.* Where a remediation notice is served, the recipient has a right of appeal: s.78L. Notices served by local authorities are appealed to the magistrates' court or, in Scotland, to the sheriff by way of summary application. Appeals against notices served by the Agency/SEPA are determined by the Secretary of State.

8. *Offences.* Failure, without reasonable excuse, to comply with any of the requirements of a remediation notice is an offence: s.78M(1). The offence is punishable, on summary conviction only, by a maximum fine of £5,000 and a further fine of £500 per day for which failure continues after conviction. Where the contaminated land in question is "industrial, trade or business premises", the respective figures are £20,000 and £2,000.

9. *Default powers.* As well as instigating a prosecution, an enforcing authority may itself carry out remediation works in a number of cases, for example where works are urgently required to prevent serious harm of which there is imminent danger, or where the responsible person has entered into a written agreement for the authority to carry out the works, or where the recipient

of a remediation notice fails to comply with it: s.78N. In a number of these cases, the authority is entitled to recover its reasonable costs, subject to considerations of hardship and guidance issued by the Secretary of State: s.78P. Additionally, in England and Wales (but not in Scotland) the authority may serve a charging notice, the effect of which is that the sums expended carry interest and that the cost and accrued interest form a charge on the premises.

In England and Wales, the enforcing authorities may bring their own prosecutions, whereas in Scotland, enforcing authorities have no prosecution powers: they must report any alleged offences to the Procurator Fiscal who may bring a prosecution (see the General Note to s.37 at p. 25–98, above).

10. *Registers.* Section 143 of the 1990 Act is repealed by Sched. 24 to the 1995 Act. Whilst the registers envisaged by s.143 have thus come to nothing, the new provisions include the maintenance of public registers of remediation notices and other matters (such as appeals and convictions): s.78R. Provisions deal with the exclusion of information from the register on grounds of national security and commercial confidentiality: ss.78S and 78T.

The role of statutory guidance

A number of the provisions on contaminated land require the exercise of discretion in making difficult decisions: Is land contaminated? What should be required by way of remediation? On whom should the remediation notice be served? Such issues are not susceptible to ready answers being given in the primary legislation, yet consistency and equity could be said to require something more than non-statutory guidance. The Government's solution has been to create a strong form of statutory guidance which the enforcing authority is required to follow, and which is itself subject to a negative resolution type of Parliamentary procedure: s.78YA. In other cases, the guidance is not subject to this special procedure and does not have prescriptive effect.

The types of guidance for which provision is made are as follows:—

Type of Guidance	Provision	Effect of Guidance
Whether land is "contaminated"	s.78A(2) and 78A(8)	Local authority required to act in accordance with it
Inspection of area to identify contaminated land	s.78B(2)	Local authority required to act in accordance with it
What is to be done by way of remediation; standard of remediation in terms of cost	s.78E(5)	Enforcing authority to have regard to it. (*NB:* guidance not issued under s.78YA)
Which of two or more persons who may be "appropriate" is to be treated as not being appropriate	s.78F(6)	Enforcing authority to make determination in accordance with it
Where two or more persons are "appropriate" in what proportions they are to bear the cost of remediation	s.78F(7)	Enforcing authority to make determination in accordance with it
Whether to recover all or part of remediation costs incurred by enforcing authority from the appropriate person	s.78P(2)	Enforcing authority to have regard to guidance (*NB:* guidance not issued under s.78YA)
Inspection and review of special sites and termination of designation as special sites	s.78Q(6)	Agency/SEPA to act in accordance with it
Site specific guidance by Agency/SEPA with regard to exercise or performance of local authority's functions in relation to any particular contaminated land	s.78V(1) and (2)	Local authority to have regard to it except insofar as it is inconsistent with any guidance issued by the Secretary of State
Guidance to Agency/SEPA with respect to the exercise or performance of its powers or duties	s.78W(1)	Agency/SEPA to have regard to it

Regulations, orders and directions

Quite apart from the wealth of guidance provided for by the new Pt. IIA of the 1990 Act, there is also bestowed on the Secretary of State in a number of places the power to make regulations or orders or to give directions, and for ease of reference these are listed below.

Type of Regulations	Provision
Designating descriptions of land required to be designated as a special site	s.78C(8)
Prescribing procedure for service of a remediation notice	s.78E(1)
Prescribing procedure for application for compensation, and determining the amount of such compensation, where rights granted enabling compliance with a remediation notice	s.78G(5)
Prescribing manner of consultation prior to service of a remediation notice	s.78H(2)
Making provision in respect of appeals against a remediation notice	s.78L(4)
Making provision in respect of appeals against a charging notice	s.78P(10)
Prescribing the offences and other additional matters to be included on registers of contaminated land	s.78R(1)
Prescribing the form in which certain notifications may be included on such registers	s.78R(2)
Prescribing the places at which such registers are to be made available to the public	s.78R(8)
Applying Pt. IIA provisions (modified as appropriate) to apply to radioactive contamination, and modifying Radioactive Substances Act 1993	s.78YC
NB. s.78X(5) provides that regulations may make different provision for different cases or circumstances	

Type of Order	Provision
Order increasing maximum fine for s.78M(1) offence in relation to industrial, trade or business premises	s.78M(4)
Order extending provisions (modified as appropriate) to the Isles of Scilly	s.78Y(2)

Type of direction	Provision
Direction to exclude information from the registers, or refer it to Secretary of State for determination, on grounds of national security	s.78S(2)
Direction to include commercially confidential information on the registers, on grounds of public interest	s.78T(7)

Relationship of Pt. IIA and previous law

The Government has been anxious to stress on a number of occasions that the provisions on contaminated land are not intended to create new categories of liability, and simply reflect the pattern of powers and duties under previous law, most notably statutory nuisance. See for example, *Hansard*, H.L. Vol. 560, col. 1461 and H.L. Vol. 562, col. 1054. Certainly the scheme of liability bears many striking similarities to statutory nuisance, with the primary responsibility resting with the originator of the contamination and residual liability with the current owner or occupier.

Specifically, steps have been taken to restrict liability where the harm or risk presented by the contaminated land takes the form of water pollution: s.78J. Here, liability does not extend to the owner or occupier purely in their capacity as owner or occupier, thereby according broadly with the position under s.161 of the Water Resources Act 1991 (or, in Scotland, under s.46 of the Control of Pollution Act 1974) which refers to those causing or knowingly permitting pollution, but not to the owner or occupier. See H.C. Standing Committee B, Eleventh sitting, col. 354, May 23, 1995. Similarly, restrictions apply in relation to remediation in respect of water from abandoned mines, so as to reflect the position under the Water Resources Act 1991 (or, in Scotland, under the Control of Pollution Act 1974), as modified by the 1995 Act. Indeed, the Government can with some justice point out that there are safeguards such as the requirements for consultation before service of a notice, the role of Government guidance and the provisions on financial hardship, which make Pt. IIA preferable to statutory nuisance from the perspective of anyone facing potential liability. See *Hansard*, H.L. Vol. 562, col. 1055. There is also no provision in Pt. IIA corresponding to that in s.82 of the 1990 Act which permits any person aggrieved by the existence of a statutory nuisance to make a complaint direct to a magistrates' court.

Despite these similarities and safeguards, Pt. IIA cannot with total credibility be presented as nothing more than incremental change to previous law. The provisions on liability exist within an overarching framework of statutory duties to seek out, identify, prioritise and remediate contaminated land as such. If those duties are not performed, or are perceived by a non-governmental environmental organisation as being performed inadequately, they may well provide the basis for actual or threatened judicial review proceedings. Overall, it seems unlikely simply to be "business as usual" so far as contaminated land is concerned. See, for example, the views of Baroness Hilton of Eggardon at *Hansard*, H.L. Vol. 565, col. 1499:

> "For the first time local authorities will have an explicit duty to inspect their areas in order to identify contaminated land. The existing provisions, which are much more vague and tenuous, require only that they identify nuisances".

One measure of the significance of this new explicit duty is the extent to which local authorities had active programmes to identify contaminated land prior to the introduction of the regime. A survey of local authorities in England and Wales by the Chartered Institute of Environmental Health (CIEH), to which 303 out of a total of 405 responded, indicated that only 64 out of the 303 respondents had such a programme in 1993/1994: CIEH *Report on Environmental Health 1993/94.*

Relationship with other relevant areas of law

Provision is made as to the relationship between the provisions on contaminated land and other potentially relevant areas of law, so as to avoid duplication or conflict of regulation.

1. *1990 Act, Pt. I.* Where it appears that clean up powers exist under s.27 of the 1990 Act in respect of contamination caused by breach of IPC or LAPC provisions, a remediation notice may not be served: s.78YB(1).

2. *1990 Act, Pt. II.* Where a waste site licence is in force in relation to land, Pt. IIA is inapplicable, except to the extent that the relevant harm or pollution is attributable to causes other than breach of the site licence, or the carrying on of any activity authorised by the licence and in accordance with its conditions: s.78YB(2). Contamination which results from carrying on the licensed activities, or from breach of the licence conditions, is therefore outside the scope of Pt. IIA.

3. *Clean up powers under the 1990 Act, s.59.* A remediation notice may not be served where the contamination results from the deposit of controlled waste and powers exist under s.59 to secure the removal of unlawfully deposited controlled waste: s.78YB(3).

4. *Consented discharges to water.* A remediation notice may not require a person to do anything which would impede the making of a discharge to controlled waters pursuant to a consent under Chap. II of Pt. III of the Water Resources Act 1991 (or, in Scotland, Pt. II of the Control of Pollution Act 1974): s.78YB(4).

5. *Radioactive substances.* The provisions on contaminated land do not apply in relation to harm or pollution of controlled waters, so far as attributable to radioactivity: s.78YC. However, regulations may apply the provisions of Pt. IIA to such radioactivity, with such modifications as the Secretary of State considers appropriate.

6. *Statutory nuisance.* No matter shall constitute a statutory nuisance to the extent that it consists of, or is caused by, any land being in a contaminated state: 1990 Act, s.79(1A) and (1B), as inserted by the 1995 Act, Sched. 22, para. 89(3). Statutory nuisance powers are thus disapplied in relation to contaminated land situations. It should be noted, however, that for this purpose the test of land being in a "contaminated state" is simply that of harm or risk of harm, not significant harm or significant risk. The practical effect of this is to avoid the prospect of land which presented a risk of harm but fell short of the significant harm test being subject to liability under statutory nuisance, which would have circumvented the policy decision to confine clean-up to cases of significant harm. If contaminated land is presenting a statutory nuisance in some way unrelated to the contamination (*e.g.* by noise from operations carried out on the land) then of course statutory nuisance provisions remain applicable. The independent overhaul of statutory nuisance in Scotland is discussed in the General Note to s.107 at p. 25–280, below.

7. *Water pollution clean-up powers.* Powers exercisable by the NRA in relation to anti-pollution measures under s.161 of the Water Resources Act 1991 (or, in Scotland, by river purification authorities under s.46 of the Control of Pollution Act 1974) were generally regarded as inadequate to deal with complex and contentious problems such as those presented by contaminated land. Those provisions have now been supplemented by the more powerful means of works notices requiring clean-up under s.161A (inserted by Sched. 22, para. 162, to the 1995 Act) (or, in Scotland, under s.46A of the Control of Pollution Act 1974 (inserted by Sched. 22, para. 29(22), to the 1995 Act)). There appears to be nothing to prevent s.161A, (or, in Scotland, s.46A) being used in relation to contaminated land, thus presenting the possibility of dual enforcement. See further the General Note to s.78YB at p. 25–188, below.

Contaminated land

57. After section 78 of the Environmental Protection Act 1990 there shall be inserted—

"PART IIA

CONTAMINATED LAND

Preliminary

78A.—(1) The following provisions have effect for the interpretation of this Part.

(2) "Contaminated land" is any land which appears to the local authority in whose area it is situated to be in such a condition, by reason of substances in, on or under the land, that—

(a) significant harm is being caused or there is a significant possibility of such harm being caused; or

(b) pollution of controlled waters is being, or is likely to be, caused; and, in determining whether any land appears to be such land, a local authority shall, subject to subsection (5) below, act in accordance with guidance issued by the Secretary of State in accordance with section 78YA below with respect to the manner in which that determination is to be made.

(3) A "special site" is any contaminated land—

(a) which has been designated as such a site by virtue of section 78C(7) or 78D(6) below; and

(b) whose designation as such has not been terminated by the appropriate Agency under section 78Q(4) below.

(4) "Harm" means harm to the health of living organisms or other interference with the ecological systems of which they form part and, in the case of man, includes harm to his property.

(5) The questions—

(a) what harm is to be regarded as "significant",

(b) whether the possibility of significant harm being caused is "significant",

(c) whether pollution of controlled waters is being, or is likely to be caused, shall be determined in accordance with guidance issued for the purpose by the Secretary of State in accordance with section 78YA below.

(6) Without prejudice to the guidance that may be issued under subsection (5) above, guidance under paragraph (a) of that subsection may make provision for different degrees of importance to be assigned to, or for the disregard of,—

(a) different descriptions of living organisms or ecological systems;

(b) different descriptions of places; or

(c) different descriptions of harm to health or property, or other interference;

and guidance under paragraph (b) of that subsection may make provision for different degrees of possibility to be regarded as "significant" (or as not being "significant') in relation to different descriptions of significant harm.

(7) "Remediation" means—

(a) the doing of anything for the purpose of assessing the condition of—

(i) the contaminated land in question;

(ii) any controlled waters affected by that land; or

(iii) any land adjoining or adjacent to that land;

(b) the doing of any works, the carrying out of any operations or the taking of any steps in relation to any such land or waters for the purpose—

(i) of preventing or minimising, or remedying or mitigating the effects of, any significant harm, or any pollution of controlled waters, by reason of which the contaminated land is such land; or

(ii) of restoring the land or waters to their former state; or

(c) the making of subsequent inspections from time to time for the purpose of keeping under review the condition of the land or waters;

and cognate expressions shall be construed accordingly.

(8) Controlled waters are "affected by" contaminated land if (and only if) it appears to the enforcing authority that the contaminated land in question is, for the purposes of subsection (2) above, in such a condition, by reason of substances in, on or under the land, that pollution of those waters is being, or is likely to be caused.

(9) The following expressions have the meaning respectively assigned to them—

"the appropriate Agency" means—

(a) in relation to England and Wales, the Environment Agency;

(b) in relation to Scotland, the Scottish Environment Protection Agency;

"appropriate person" means any person who is an appropriate person, determined in accordance with section 78F below, to bear responsibility for any thing which is to be done by way of remediation in any particular case;

"charging notice" has the meaning given by section 78P(3)(b) below;

"controlled waters"—

(a) in relation to England and Wales, has the same meaning as in Part III of the Water Resources Act 1991; and

(b) in relation to Scotland, has the same meaning as in section 30A of the Control of Pollution Act 1974;

"creditor" has the same meaning as in the Conveyancing and Feudal Reform (Scotland) Act 1970;

"enforcing authority" means—

    (a) in relation to a special site, the appropriate Agency;

    (b) in relation to contaminated land other than a special site, the local authority in whose area the land is situated;

"heritable security" has the same meaning as in the Conveyancing and Feudal Reform (Scotland) Act 1970;

"local authority" in relation to England and Wales means—

    (a) any unitary authority;

    (b) any district council, so far as it is not a unitary authority;

    (c) the Common Council of the City of London and, as respects the Temples, the Sub-Treasurer of the Inner Temple and the Under-Treasurer of the Middle Temple respectively;

and in relation to Scotland means a council for an area constituted under section 2 of the Local Government etc. (Scotland) Act 1994;

"notice" means notice in writing;

"notification" means notification in writing;

"owner", in relation to any land in England and Wales, means a person (other than a mortgagee not in possession) who, whether in his own right or as trustee for any other person, is entitled to receive the rack rent of the land, or, where the land is not let at a rack rent, would be so entitled if it were so let;

"owner", in relation to any land in Scotland, means a person (other than a creditor in a heritable security not in possession of the security subjects) for the time being entitled to receive or who would, if the land were let, be entitled to receive, the rents of the land in connection with which the word is used and includes a trustee, factor, guardian or curator and in the case of public or municipal land includes the persons to whom the management of the land is entrusted;

"pollution of controlled waters" means the entry into controlled waters of any poisonous, noxious or polluting matter or any solid waste matter;

"prescribed" means prescribed by regulations;

"regulations" means regulations made by the Secretary of State;

"remediation declaration" has the meaning given by section 78H(6) below;

"remediation notice" has the meaning given by section 78E(1) below;

"remediation statement" has the meaning given by section 78H(7) below;

"required to be designated as a special site" shall be construed in accordance with section 78C(8) below;

"substance" means any natural or artificial substance, whether in solid or liquid form or in the form of a gas or vapour;

"unitary authority" means—

    (a) the council of a county, so far as it is the council of an area for which there are no district councils;

    (b) the council of any district comprised in an area for which there is no county council;

    (c) the council of a London borough;

    (d) the council of a county borough in Wales.

COMMENCEMENT

September 21, 1995 insofar as this section confers power on the Secretary of State to issue guidance or makes provision with respect to the exercise of such power (S.I. 1995 No. 1983).

The remainder will be brought into force by a commencement order made under s.125(3) of the 1995 Act.

GENERAL NOTE
This section contains the various definitions relating to the new Part IIA of the 1990 Act.

Contaminated land
The starting point of the definition is whether land appears to the local authority, in whose area it is situated, to be in a certain condition. The words "appears to the local authority" are subjective in effect, though the appearance of subjectivity is deceptive. In determining whether land appears to it to be contaminated, the local authority must act in accordance with the Secretary of State's guidance: s.78(2).
The definition of contaminated land must be read together with the supplementary provisions in s.78X, which allow the effects of two or more sites to be considered together, and deal with the situation where land adjoining or adjacent to the local authority's area causes the relevant problems within its area.

Substances in, on or under the land
The adverse environmental condition of the land must result from "substances in, on or under the land". The definition of "substance" is wide and includes both natural and artificial substances, as well as gases: s.78B(9). There is nothing in the legislation which expressly confines it to substances the presence of which results from human activity, as opposed to substances naturally present: however, the draftsman clearly had it in mind, in s.78F(2), that someone would have caused or knowingly permitted them to be present. The substances may be within the land, or on its surface. In most cases, the substances will be present in the subsurface or underlying strata. However, since "land" itself is not defined for the purpose of the provisions, its definition in Sched. 1 to the Interpretation Act 1978 is applicable: " 'Land' includes buildings and other structures, land covered with water, and any estate, interest, easement, servitude or right in or over land".
Thus the words of the definition are also wide enough to catch substances which are present in underground or surface structures or containers, if the relevant conditions of harm or risk of harm are fulfilled: for example, chemicals stored in corroded drums, or friable asbestos in a building. There is in principle no restriction on where in the building in question the substances which render the land contaminated are located. The words would also cover substances present in groundwater beneath land, or present in the soil beneath inland waters (for example, contaminated sediments under a river bed; see also "controlled waters" below).
One issue which arose in debate was that of deep contamination, for example in underground mine workings. Lord Northbourne posed the question: "Is a landowner to be made responsible for whatever goes on under his land, however deep down?" (*Hansard*, H.L. Vol. 560, col. 1424). In answering, Viscount Ullswater indicated that the Government's intention in including the word "under" in the definition was to ensure that there were no undesirable omissions and that substrata and contaminated silts under streams or ponds were covered: *Hansard*, H.L. Vol. 560, col. 1425. In relation to mineral workings, Viscount Ullswater referred to the Interpretation Act 1978 definition noted above, whereby land includes any estate, interest, easement, servitude or right in or over land. The Government's intention was that in general, the owner of the mine or mineral rights, not the surface owner, would be liable:
"The primary responsibility for remediation of any mines identified as contaminated land would obviously fall on anyone who caused or knowingly permitted the contaminating substances to be there. But any residual responsibility passing to the "owner" of the land would, as a result of the definition of land in the Interpretation Act [1978] fall to the owner of the mine or mineral rights, and not to the owner of the surface land where he is a different person": *Hansard*, H.L. Vol. 562, col. 1038; See also *Hansard*, H.L. Vol. 562, cols. 165–166.

Harm
One limb of the test relates to significant harm or the significant possibility of significant harm. Originally, the term "harm" had not been qualified in any way. At Lords Committee Stage the test of "serious" harm was proposed by Lord Northbourne: this was however rejected by the Government as too narrow and restrictive: *Hansard*, H.L. Vol. 560, cols. 1427–1428.
"Harm" is defined by s.78A(7). Unlike other definitions of harm contained in the 1990 Act, it does not include offence to man's senses. This was a deliberate decision as the Government did not wish land to be regarded as contaminated, for example, on the basis of odours which were not harmful to health, and in respect of which statutory nuisance powers would be available. See *Hansard*, H.L. Vol. 560, col. 1440. The word "significant" was introduced at the Lords Report Stage and is used in two separate contexts, relating both to the harm itself and to the possibility

of the harm. "Significant" is clearly a word which may have various shades of meaning, and the precise meaning to be placed upon it in this context is determined by the guidance to be issued by the Secretary of State (s.78A(2), as to which, see below).

Pollution of controlled waters

Pollution of ground or surface water is one of the most serious problems presented by contaminated land and provides a second limb of the test. "Controlled waters" are given the same meaning as in the Water Resources Act 1991 in England and Wales and the Control of Pollution Act 1974 in Scotland (see below at p. 25–143). "Pollution" is defined to mean the entry of poisonous, noxious or polluting matter, or any waste matter. This does not mean that harm must be shown to have resulted from that entry: see *R.* v. *Dovermoss* [1995] Env. L.R. 258 (C.A.), where it was held that the likelihood or capability of causing harm was sufficient.

By s.78A(8) controlled waters are only to be treated as affected by contaminated land if the condition of the land is such that pollution of the waters is being, or is likely to be, caused. As with the "harm" limb of the test, under s.78A(2) guidance by the Secretary of State is crucial to what is regarded as pollution or the likelihood of pollution (see below).

Guidance on determining whether land is contaminated

Subsections (2) and (8) of s.78A make reference to guidance by the Secretary of State on the manner in which the determination is to be made and on the question of whether harm or the possibility of harm are to be regarded as significant. The relevant determinations are to be made in accordance with that guidance. The Government took the view that it would not be possible to prescribe for all possible circumstances what answers should be given on the detailed technical judgements required for each individual site: *Hansard*, H.L. Vol. 562, col. 138. Guidance for England and Wales was published in draft form on May 5, 1995, for information during passage of the Environment Bill. Draft guidance had, at the time of writing, yet to be issued for Scotland although it is likely to be very similar to the draft guidance for England and Wales. The draft is to be developed further for consultation, before being laid before Parliament under the procedure set out in s.78YA. The guidance may therefore change in the course of being finalised, but the first draft indicates the following approach.

1. The local authority should disregard harm or interference other than certain types, *i.e.* harm to human users or occupiers of the land in its current use, or to the health of current human users or occupiers of other land, harm to or interference with ecosystems protected under the Wildlife and Countryside Act 1981 or the EC Directives on wild birds (79/409/EEC) and habitats (92/43/EEC), or harm to property in relation to the present use of the land or other land. In relation to wildlife protection, the Government indicated in debate that its intention was not to introduce new requirements for the protection of habitats and ecological systems over and above those already in place under existing legislation: *Hansard*, H.L. Vol. 562, col. 138.

2. The authority should disregard any harm or interference other than certain types, *i.e.* death, serious injury or clinical toxicity in the case of harm to human health, a significant change in the functioning of ecosystems in protected areas or physical damage to property which cannot be rectified without substantial works and which, in the case of livestock and crops, causes loss in value.

3. The authority should disregard harm to living organisms or interference with ecosystems where the harm or interference is an intended and legal result of the addition of substances to the land, *e.g.* the controlled use of pesticides.

4. The approach to the determination should be based on the fundamental principles of risk assessment which will usually involve identification of a source-pathway-target relationship, with risk estimation as a final stage.

5. The same approach is applicable to the question of whether pollution of controlled waters is being or is likely to be caused, though the sensitivity of the relevant controlled waters and the effectiveness of any possible preventive measures will also be relevant.

6. The guidance deals in tabular form with the significance to be attached to the various combinations of possibility and degree of harm (covering "severe, moderate, mild and minimal harm", and "high, medium, low and very low" degrees of possibility).

Remediation

Subsection (7) defines remediation, *i.e.* those actions which may be required by a remediation notice. It covers three types of activity.

1. Assessment of the condition of the contaminated land, any controlled waters "affected by" the land (see subs. (8)), and any land adjoining or adjacent to the contaminated land. This will cover, for example, the taking and analysis of soil or water samples, on-site or off-site.

2. Works, operations or steps in relation to such land or waters (*i.e.* the contaminated land itself, controlled waters affected by it, and adjoining or adjacent land). Those works may be for the purpose of preventing, minimising, mitigating or remedying the relevant harm or pollution, or for restoring the land or waters to their former state. "Former state" must presumably refer to the condition of the land or water prior to the introduction of the relevant harmful substances or pollutants, though precisely what that condition was may be difficult to establish.

3. Subsequent inspections from time to time for the purpose of keeping under review the condition of the land or waters. "Inspection" in this context must presumably mean more than visual inspection and would cover works required to review the condition of soil or water; in many cases this will mean a continued regime of sampling.

As will be appreciated, the definition of remediation is a comprehensive one, which makes it important to note the restrictions, contained elsewhere, on what may be required by way of remediation, particularly subss. 78E(4) and (5).

Controlled waters

The definition is by reference to the Water Resources Act 1991 for England and Wales (s.104) and to the Control of Pollution Act 1974 for Scotland (s.30A as inserted by Sched. 23 to the Water Act 1989). Both definitions cover essentially: (a) territorial waters, *i.e.* those extending seaward for three miles from the relevant baseline (and areas of territorial sea beyond that limit up to a maximum of 12 miles fixed by the Territorial Sea Act 1987 if added by order of the Secretary of State); (b) coastal waters, *i.e.* those inland from that baseline as far as the highest tide or freshwater limit; (c) inland waters, *i.e.* relevant lochs, lakes and ponds, and relevant rivers and watercourses above the fresh water limit; and (d) groundwaters, *i.e.* any waters contained in underground strata.

However, the definitions differ in certain details, which may or may not be significant. The definition applying to Scotland includes within the definition of groundwater, water in wells, boreholes and other excavations. The definition applying to England and Wales states that references to waters of lakes, ponds or watercourses include reference to the bottom, channel or bed which is for the time being dry: s.104(2).

Creditor

Section 9(8)(c) of the Conveyancing and Feudal Reform (Scotland) Act 1970 reads as follows:
" 'debt' means any obligation due, or which will or may become due, to repay or pay money, including any such obligation arising from a transaction or part of a transaction in the course of any trade, business or profession, and any obligation to pay an annuity or *ad factum praestandum*, but does not include an obligation to pay any feuduty, ground annual, rent or other periodical sum payable in respect of land, and 'creditor' and 'debtor', in relation to a standard security, shall be construed accordingly".

The Government's intention was that the definition of owner in terms of lenders should be of similar effect in Scotland as in England and Wales: see *Hansard*, H.L. Vol. 562, col. 1040.

Heritable security

Section 9(8)(a) of the Conveyancing and Feudal Reform (Scotland) Act 1970 reads as follows:
" 'heritable security' ... means any security capable of being constituted over any interest in land by disposition or assignation of that interest in security of any debt and of being recorded in the Register of Sasines".

Identification of contaminated land

78B.—(1) Every local authority shall cause its area to be inspected from time to time for the purpose—

(a) of identifying contaminated land; and

(b) of enabling the authority to decide whether any such land is land which is required to be designated as a special site.

(2) In performing its functions under subsection (1) above a local authority shall act in accordance with any guidance issued for the purpose by the Secretary of State in accordance with section 78YA below.

(3) If a local authority identifies any contaminated land in its area, it shall give notice of that fact to—

(a) the appropriate Agency;

(b) the owner of the land;

(c) any person who appears to the authority to be in occupation of the whole or any part of the land; and

(d) each person who appears to the authority to be an appropriate person;

and any notice given under this subsection shall state by virtue of which of paragraphs (a) to (d) above it is given.

(4) If, at any time after a local authority has given any person a notice pursuant to subsection (3)(d) above in respect of any land, it appears to the enforcing authority that another person is an appropriate person, the enforcing authority shall give notice to that other person—

(a) of the fact that the local authority has identified the land in question as contaminated land; and

(b) that he appears to the enforcing authority to be an appropriate person.

DEFINITIONS

"appropriate Agency": s.78A(9) of the 1990 Act.
"appropriate person": s.78A(9) of the 1990 Act.
"contaminated land": s.78A(9) of the 1990 Act.
"enforcing authority": s.78A(9) of the 1990 Act.
"local authority": s.78A(9) of the 1990 Act.
"notice": s.78A(9) of the 1990 Act.
"owner": s.78A(9) of the 1990 Act.
"required to be designated as a special site": s.78C(8) of the 1990 Act.
"special site": s.78A(3) of the 1990 Act.

COMMENCEMENT

September 21, 1995 insofar as this section confers power on the Secretary of State to issue guidance or makes provision with respect to the exercise of such power (S.I. 1995 No. 1983). The remainder will be brought into force by a commencement order made under s.125(3) of the 1995 Act.

GENERAL NOTE

This section creates a statutory duty on local authorities at district or unitary authority level to cause their area to be inspected for the purpose of identifying contaminated land and enabling a decision to be made as to whether any contaminated land identified is required to be designated as a special site.

Cause its area to be inspected

The language here is the same as that used in relation to statutory nuisance, though whereas a typical statutory nuisance is likely to be self-evident, a very different approach will be necessary to identify contaminated land, the risks and problems of which will not necessarily be apparent on visual inspection. The Government rejected an amendment imposing a requirement for quinquennial review, stating that local authorities should concentrate resources on areas where there were likely to be problems: *Hansard*, H.L. Vol. 562, col. 167. No express power is provided to cover default by local authorities in their statutory duties. An amendment proposing the inclusion of such a power was rejected on the basis that default was a matter for "local political judgments and remedies": *Hansard*, H.L. Vol. 562, col. 229.

Secretary of State's guidance

As with other issues, guidance issued by the Secretary of State is determinative of how a local authority is to exercise its function of inspection. The draft guidance issued for information in May 1995 (see General Note to s.78A at p. 25–142 above) includes guidance as to the issue of inspection. This stresses that different local authorities will inevitably face different levels of problems associated with contaminated land in their areas, resulting from different historical factors and underlying geology. The preliminary draft states that each authority should prepare an "appropriate local strategy", making effective use of resources and ensuring effort is concentrated first on the areas where the change of discovery of significant harm is greatest. This strategy should include: the use of existing information held by the authority; the identification of those areas in which vulnerable targets are present, as a first priority for inspection; and the way in which new information on the condition or circumstances of land in its area can be taken into account.

The draft guidance lists various factors which the authority should consider in preparing its strategy. These include: the extent to which information is already available; the extent to which vulnerable targets are likely to be in contact with contaminated land; history, scale and nature of former industrial use; the relative likelihood of different descriptions of harm; the extent to which action has already been taken to deal with contamination; geological and hydrogeological features; and the nature and timing of redevelopment in different parts of the area. The draft guidance also highlights the fact that some authorities will already have information about the condition of land in their area which will inform their views on the general likelihood of contaminated land being found; other authorities may be assisted by a pilot study of a representative part of their area. Some authorities may already be aware of specific sites which give cause for concern, or may become aware of such sites by reason of third party complaints or through the planning process. Other authorities may have already collated information on past uses of land in readiness for compilation of the registers under s.143 of the 1990 Act, at the time when it seemed that the section would be brought into force.

Powers of entry
The rights of entry, testing, *etc.*, available to local authorities in pursuance of their statutory duties are provided by s.108 of the 1995 Act, the provisions on contaminated land being one of the "pollution control functions" set out in that section (s.108(15)). See the General Note to s.108 for further discussion, which includes consideration of whether the power to carry out experimental borings and install, keep or maintain monitoring and other apparatus (s.108(5)) is available for the purpose of establishing whether land is contaminated.

Notification
By s.78B(4) a local authority which identifies contaminated land is required to give notice of that fact (no form of notice is specified) to various parties, including the person who appears to have caused or knowingly permitted the contaminating substances to be in, on or under the land (if such person can be found). By subs. (5), where after notice has been given to a person who appears to be the "appropriate person", it appears that some other person or persons is/are the appropriate person or persons, a fresh notice must be given to that person or persons. No provision is made for withdrawal of a notice where it no longer appears that the recipient is the appropriate person, though it presumably is possible for the authority to do this.

Identification and designation of special sites

78C.—(1) If at any time it appears to a local authority that any contaminated land in its area might be land which is required to be designated as a special site, the authority—

(a) shall decide whether or not the land is land which is required to be so designated; and

(b) if the authority decides that the land is land which is required to be so designated, shall give notice of that decision to the relevant persons.

(2) For the purposes of this section, "the relevant persons" at any time in the case of any land are the persons who at that time fall within paragraphs (a) to (d) below, that is to say—

(a) the appropriate Agency;

(b) the owner of the land;

(c) any person who appears to the local authority concerned to be in occupation of the whole or any part of the land; and

(d) each person who appears to that authority to be an appropriate person.

(3) Before making a decision under paragraph (a) of subsection (1) above in any particular case, a local authority shall request the advice of the appropriate Agency, and in making its decision shall have regard to any advice given by that Agency in response to the request.

(4) If at any time the appropriate Agency considers that any contaminated land is land which is required to be designated as a special site, that Agency may give notice of that fact to the local authority in whose area the land is situated.

(5) Where notice under subsection (4) above is given to a local authority, the authority shall decide whether the land in question—

(a) is land which is required to be designated as a special site, or

(b) is not land which is required to be so designated,
and shall give notice of that decision to the relevant persons.

(6) Where a local authority makes a decision falling within subsection (1)(b) or (5)(a) above, the decision shall, subject to section 78D below, take effect on the day after whichever of the following events first occurs, that is to say—

(a) the expiration of the period of twenty-one days beginning with the day on which the notice required by virtue of subsection (1)(b) or, as the case may be, (5)(a) above is given to the appropriate Agency; or

(b) if the appropriate Agency gives notification to the local authority in question that it agrees with the decision, the giving of that notification;

and where a decision takes effect by virtue of this subsection, the local authority shall give notice of that fact to the relevant persons.

(7) Where a decision that any land is land which is required to be designated as a special site takes effect in accordance with subsection (6) above, the notice given under subsection (1)(b) or, as the case may be, (5)(a) above shall have effect, as from the time when the decision takes effect, as the designation of that land as such a site.

(8) For the purposes of this Part, land is required to be designated as a special site if, and only if, it is land of a description prescribed for the purposes of this subsection.

(9) Regulations under subsection (8) above may make different provision for different cases or circumstances or different areas or localities and may, in particular, describe land by reference to the area or locality in which it is situated.

(10) Without prejudice to the generality of his power to prescribe any description of land for the purposes of subsection (8) above, the Secretary of State, in deciding whether to prescribe a particular description of contaminated land for those purposes, may, in particular, have regard to—

(a) whether land of the description in question appears to him to be land which is likely to be in such a condition, by reason of substances in, on or under the land that—

(i) serious harm would or might be caused, or

(ii) serious pollution of controlled waters would be, or would be likely to be, caused; or

(b) whether the appropriate Agency is likely to have expertise in dealing with the kind of significant harm, or pollution of controlled waters, by reason of which land of the description in question is contaminated land.

DEFINITIONS
"appropriate Agency": s.78A(9) of the 1990 Act.
"appropriate person": s.78A(9) of the 1990 Act.
"contaminated land": s.78A(2) of the 1990 Act.
"harm": s.78A(9) of the 1990 Act.
"local authority": s.78A(9) of the 1990 Act.
"notice": s.78A(9) of the 1990 Act.
"owner": s.78A(9) of the 1990 Act.
"regulations": s.78A(9) of the 1990 Act.
"relevant persons": subs. (2).
"required to be designated as a special site": s.78C(8) of the 1990 Act.
"significant": s.78A(5) of the 1990 Act.
"special site": s.78A(3) of the 1990 Act.

COMMENCEMENT
September 21, 1995 insofar as this section confers power on the Secretary of State to make regulations or makes provision with respect to the exercise of such power (S.I. 1995 No. 1983). The remainder will be brought into force by a commencement order made under s.125(3) of the 1995 Act.

GENERAL NOTE

This section deals with the designation of special sites. The importance of such designation is that the Agency or SEPA, rather than the local authority, is the enforcing authority (s.78A(9)). Land is only required to be designated as a special site if it is of a description prescribed by regulations (s.78C(8)). The criteria for prescribing descriptions of land for this purpose may, in particular, have regard to: (a) whether the harm or pollution that might be caused by the substances in, on or under the land is "serious" as opposed to "significant"; and (b) whether the Agency/SEPA is likely to have expertise in dealing with the type of harm or pollution in question (s.78C(10)).

As initially drafted, the Bill proposed the creation of a special category of "closed landfills" so as to give this type of site a "more tailored approach": *Hansard*, H.L. Vol. 560, col. 1432. However, the Government ultimately acceded to the arguments against such a distinction, which were compellingly put by Lord Crickhowell on the basis that it was not clear why a closed steelworks or gasworks should be seen as posing less serious problems than a closed landfill: see *Hansard*, H.L. Vol. 562, cols. 156, 158, 160.

Procedure for designation

The initial onus is with the local authority to decide, following inspection, whether land is required to be designated as a special site: ss.78B(1)(b) and 78C(1)(a). In making its decision, the local authority must request the advice of the Agency/SEPA and have regard to any advice given: s.78C(3). If the local authority decides that the land is required to be designated as a special site, then notice of that fact must be given to the persons specified at s.78C(2); it appears that this notification may be combined with that required by s.78B(3) (that the land has been identified as contaminated land) or may be given separately.

The Agency/SEPA may itself form the view that land is required to be designated as a special site, in which case it may give notice of that fact to the local authority, which must then decide whether or not this is the case: ss.78C(4) and (5). The outcome of that decision must be notified to the relevant persons including the Agency/SEPA: s.78C(5). A decision that land is required to be designated as a special site takes effect, under s.78C(6), 21 days from the date of notification to the Agency/SEPA (subject to the referral procedure under s.78D) or upon notification by the Agency/SEPA of agreement with the decision. The notice given of the decision to the relevant persons then takes effect as the designation (s.78C(7)) and notice that the decision has taken effect must be given by the authority to the relevant persons: s.78C(6).

It should be noted that a site can be designated as a special site even after service of a remediation notice by the local authority. Provisions covering this eventuality are to be found in s.78Q.

Referral of special site decisions to the Secretary of State

78D.—(1) In any case where—

(a) a local authority gives notice of a decision to the appropriate Agency pursuant to subsection (1)(b) or (5)(b) of section 78C above, but

(b) before the expiration of the period of twenty-one days beginning with the day on which that notice is so given, that Agency gives the local authority notice that it disagrees with the decision, together with a statement of its reasons for disagreeing,

the authority shall refer the decision to the Secretary of State and shall send to him a statement of its reasons for reaching the decision.

(2) Where the appropriate Agency gives notice to a local authority under paragraph (b) of subsection (1) above, it shall also send to the Secretary of State a copy of the notice and of the statement given under that paragraph.

(3) Where a local authority refers a decision to the Secretary of State under subsection (1) above, it shall give notice of that fact to the relevant persons.

(4) Where a decision of a local authority is referred to the Secretary of State under subsection (1) above, he—

(a) may confirm or reverse the decision with respect to the whole or any part of the land to which it relates; and

(b) shall give notice of his decision on the referral—

(i) to the relevant persons; and

(ii) to the local authority.

(5) Where a decision of a local authority is referred to the Secretary of State under subsection (1) above, the decision shall not take effect until the day after that on which the Secretary of State gives the notice required by subsection (4) above to the persons there mentioned and shall then take effect as confirmed or reversed by him.

(6) Where a decision which takes effect in accordance with subsection (5) above is to the effect that at least some land is land which is required to be designated as a special site, the notice given under subsection (4)(b) above shall have effect, as from the time when the decision takes effect, as the designation of that land as such a site.

(7) In this section "the relevant persons" has the same meaning as in section 78C above.

DEFINITIONS

"appropriate Agency": s.78A(9) of the 1990 Act.
"local authority": s.78A(9) of the 1990 Act.
"notice": s.78A(9) of the 1990 Act.
"relevant persons": subs. (7); s.78C(2) of the 1990 Act.
"required to be designated as a special site": s.78C(8) of the 1990 Act.

COMMENCEMENT

These provisions will be brought into force by a commencement order made under s.125(3) of the 1995 Act.

GENERAL NOTE

This section provides a mechanism for resolving disagreement between the local authority and the Agency/SEPA as to whether land is required to be designated as a special site. The disagreement may arise either where the authority makes the initial decision under s.78C(1), or where the Agency/SEPA has notified the authority of its view that the land is required to be designated, but the authority decides under s.78C(5) that it does not. In either case the Agency/SEPA has a 21-day period from being notified of the decision to give notice to the authority that it disagrees with the decision, together with a statement of its reasons for disagreeing (s.78D(1)(b)). The authority must then refer the decision to the Secretary of State.

The relevant persons (referred to in s.78C as including the owner, occupier and appropriate person) must be notified of the referral to the Secretary of State and must also be notified of the final decision: ss.78D(3) and 78D(4)(b). There is no statutory right for them to make representations to the Secretary of State, though there is nothing to prevent them doing so. The Secretary of State has a wide discretion in making his determination and may decide, for example, that part only of the relevant land is to be designated as a special site: ss.78D(4)(a) and 78D(6).

Duty of enforcing authority to require remediation of contaminated land etc.

78E.—(1) In any case where—

(a) any land has been designated as a special site by virtue of section 78C(7) or 78D(6) above, or

(b) a local authority has identified any contaminated land (other than a special site) in its area,

the enforcing authority shall, in accordance with such procedure as may be prescribed and subject to the following provisions of this Part, serve on each person who is an appropriate person a notice (in this Part referred to as a "remediation notice") specifying what that person is to do by way of remediation and the periods within which he is required to do each of the things so specified.

(2) Different remediation notices requiring the doing of different things by way of remediation may be served on different persons in consequence of the presence of different substances in, on or under any land or waters.

(3) Where two or more persons are appropriate persons in relation to any particular thing which is to be done by way of remediation, the remediation notice served on each of them shall state the proportion, determined under section 78F(7) below, of the cost of doing that thing which each of them respectively is liable to bear.

(4) The only things by way of remediation which the enforcing authority may do, or require to be done, under or by virtue of this Part are things which it considers reasonable, having regard to—

(a) the cost which is likely to be involved; and

(b) the seriousness of the harm, or pollution of controlled waters, in question.

(5) In determining for any purpose of this Part—

(a) what is to be done (whether by an appropriate person, the enforcing authority or any other person) by way of remediation in any particular case,

(b) the standard to which any land is, or waters are, to be remediated pursuant to the notice, or

(c) what is, or is not, to be regarded as reasonable for the purposes of subsection (4) above,

the enforcing authority shall have regard to any guidance issued for the purpose by the Secretary of State.

(6) Regulations may make provision for or in connection with—

(a) the form or content of remediation notices; or

(b) any steps of a procedural nature which are to be taken in connection with, or in consequence of, the service of a remediation notice.

DEFINITIONS

"appropriate person": s.78A(9) of the 1990 Act.
"contaminated land": 78A(2) of the 1990 Act.
"enforcing authority": s.78A(9) of the 1990 Act.
"harm": s.78A(4) of the 1990 Act.
"local authority": s.78A(9) of the 1990 Act.
"notice": s.78A(9) of the 1990 Act.
"pollution of controlled waters": s.78A(9) of the 1990 Act.
"regulations": s.78A(9) of the 1990 Act.
"remediation notice": subs. (1).
"special site": s.78A(3) of the 1990 Act.
"substance": s.78A(9) of the 1990 Act.

COMMENCEMENT

September 21, 1995 insofar as this section confers power on the Secretary of State to issue guidance or make regulations or makes provision with respect to the exercise of such power (S.I. 1995 No. 1983). The remainder will be brought into force by a commencement order made under s.125(3) of the 1995 Act.

GENERAL NOTE

This section imposes a duty on the relevant enforcing authority, when contaminated land has been identified or a special site has been designated, to serve a remediation notice on each person who is an appropriate person, as determined under s.78F.

Suspicion not a ground for serving notice

During debate the question arose as to whether an enforcing authority might form the view that land was likely to be contaminated by virtue of its past use, and then serve a notice requiring detailed investigation. This is clearly not the Government's intention, as Viscount Ullswater indicated that the Government believed that the enforcing authority:

"... should have to be able to demonstrate that actual contamination existed on any site, and that there was sufficient contamination for the site to qualify as contaminated land, before it could require any remediation work, including further assessment" (*Hansard,* H.L. Vol. 562, col. 175: see also H.C. Standing Committee B, Eleventh Sitting, Pt. I, col. 341, May 23, 1995).

Form of notice

No form is prescribed in the section for a remediation notice, though form and content and procedures for service may be prescribed by regulations: s.78E(1) and (6). The notice must specify: (a) what is to be done by way of remediation by the person on whom it is served; and (b) the periods within which he is to do each of the things so specified.

"Remediation" is widely defined (see General Note to s.78A above) and can include a variety of actions. Difficult questions may arise as to the degree of exactitude with which the remedial actions required by the notice must be specified, and the risk is that a notice which does not give sufficient detail may be held void for uncertainty. The wording of s.78E(1) itself, referring to "each of the things so specified" is indicative that some precision is required. Case law also suggests that a notice which may have penal consequences if not complied with should tell the recipient what works are to be carried out so that he can be clear that he has complied with the notice: see *Network Housing Association v. Westminster City Council, The Times*, November 8, 1994 (noise nuisance); *Berridge Incinerators v. Nottinghamshire County Council* (Nottingham Crown Court, June 12, 1992, unreported—notice under s.59 of the 1990 Act); *R. v. Fenny Stratford Justices, ex p. Watney Mann Midlands* [1976] 1 W.L.R. 1101 (noise nuisance); *R. v. East Northamptonshire District Council, ex p. Brian Fossett* [1994] Env. L.R. 388. For a Scottish case on the clarity required in a notice, see *McNaughton v. Peter McIntyre (Clyde)* 1981 SPLP 15 in which a planning enforcement notice requiring removal of stone from the foreshore was invalid because it was impossible to tell from the notice which stone was to be removed. However, the Government gave an indication in debate that they intended that remediation notices "should generally be phrased in terms of objectives to be achieved rather than specific works which have to be undertaken" (*Hansard*, H.L. Vol. 562, col. 1047, Viscount Ullswater).

Multiple notices

The section contemplates two separate situations where multiple notices may be served in relation to the same land. The first is where there is more than one person who is the appropriate person in relation to the remedial action required, and in this respect the section needs to be read in conjunction with s.78F. In this situation, a remediation notice must be served on each appropriate person (s.78E(1)) but each notice must state the proportion, determined under s.78F(7), of the cost which each of them respectively is liable to bear in doing the thing for which they are the appropriate person: s.78E(3). The second situation is where different contaminating substances are present and require the doing of different things by way of remediation. In this case, different remediation notices may be served on different persons: s.78E(2).

Consecutive notices

The remediation of contaminated land may require a phased approach, involving sampling, trials and feasibility studies prior to remedial action, which in turn may be followed by post-operational monitoring. If land continues to fall within the definition of "contaminated land" after one notice has been served and complied with, there would be nothing to prevent a subsequent notice being served. For example, the enforcing authority may know that land is contaminated but may not be able to specify what should be done to clean it up until further monitoring has been completed. There seems no reason why a first notice should not be served requiring such monitoring, followed by a second notice containing the clean up requirements, since the land will still be contaminated after the monitoring has been completed. Indeed, if those clean up requirements proved to be inadequate to the extent that after their completion the land still fell within the definition of contaminated land, the authority would be obliged to determine whether service of a further notice was required.

There is no provision for a civil remedy against the authority if the cost of remediation in such a case proves to be greater than it would have been had the initial clean up requirements been worded so as to secure adequate remediation without the service of a further notice. Although the possibility remains of an action against the authority on common law principles of negligence, the practical likelihood of success for such an action is limited both by the hurdles which are required to be overcome in establishing the liability of a public authority for the negligent exercise of its statutory functions and by the opportunity which the appropriate person had to influence the content of the remediation notice during the three-month period before its service. Clearly, this latter factor will not weigh against the plaintiff where by virtue of s.78H(4) the consultation period was not observed in a case of imminent danger of serious harm or where the plaintiff's (in Scotland, the pursuer's) views were ignored by the local authority in its formulation of the notice requirements.

Subs. (4): Restriction on content of remediation notice

This subsection represents an overriding restriction on what may be required by way of remediation. The test is subjective, referring to what is reasonable in the opinion of the authority, which must have regard to the likely cost involved and the seriousness of the harm. The authority will presumably already have formed a view on the second issue (*i.e.* seriousness of harm) in the course of determining whether the land is contaminated. The first consideration will, however, involve the authority in taking steps to inform itself of the likely cost of what it proposes to require: failure to take adequate steps to do so may result in the notice being challenged.

It should be noted that the factors expressly referred to relate simply to the objective cost and seriousness of harm, and not to more specific issues such as the value of the land or financial hardship to the appropriate person (compare in the latter respect, s.78P(2)(a)). However, it could be argued that the two matters expressly referred to at (a) and (b) are not exclusive and do not preclude the authority having regard to other considerations in determining what is reasonable. This may be clarified in the guidance referred to in s.78E(5) (see below).

Subs. (5): Secretary of State's guidance

In determining the three issues referred to in this subsection, the authority must have regard to any guidance issued by the Secretary of State. This guidance is not required to be issued under the special Parliamentary procedure of s.78YA(2)–(4) and is therefore subject simply to the consultation and publication requirements of s.78YA(1) and (5). The guidance is not prescriptive but the enforcing authority must have regard to it. The guidance is relevant not only to determining what should be considered as reasonable under subs. (2) but in determining for any purpose under Pt. IIA what is to be done by way of remediation by any person, and the standard to which land or waters are to be remediated.

Remediation declarations

Where subs. (4) or (5) applies so as to preclude the inclusion of some thing within a remediation notice, the authority must serve a remediation declaration under s.78H(6).

Determination of the appropriate person to bear responsibility for remediation

78F.—(1) This section has effect for the purpose of determining who is the appropriate person to bear responsibility for any particular thing which the enforcing authority determines is to be done by way of remediation in any particular case.

(2) Subject to the following provisions of this section, any person, or any of the persons, who caused or knowingly permitted the substances, or any of the substances, by reason of which the contaminated land in question is such land to be in, on or under that land is an appropriate person.

(3) A person shall only be an appropriate person by virtue of subsection (2) above in relation to things which are to be done by way of remediation which are to any extent referable to substances which he caused or knowingly permitted to be present in, on or under the contaminated land in question.

(4) If no person has, after reasonable inquiry, been found who is by virtue of subsection (2) above an appropriate person to bear responsibility for the things which are to be done by way of remediation, the owner or occupier for the time being of the contaminated land in question is an appropriate person.

(5) If, in consequence of subsection (3) above, there are things which are to be done by way of remediation in relation to which no person has, after reasonable inquiry, been found who is an appropriate person by virtue of subsection (2) above, the owner or occupier for the time being of the contaminated land in question is an appropriate person in relation to those things.

(6) Where two or more persons would, apart from this subsection, be appropriate persons in relation to any particular thing which is to be done by way of remediation, the enforcing authority shall determine in accordance with guidance issued for the purpose by the Secretary of State whether any, and if so which, of them is to be treated as not being an appropriate person in relation to that thing.

(7) Where two or more persons are appropriate persons in relation to any particular thing which is to be done by way of remediation, they shall

be liable to bear the cost of doing that thing in proportions determined by the enforcing authority in accordance with guidance issued for the purpose by the Secretary of State.

(8) Any guidance issued for the purposes of subsection (6) or (7) above shall be issued in accordance with section 78YA below.

(9) A person who has caused or knowingly permitted any substance ("substance A") to be in, on or under any land shall also be taken for the purposes of this section to have caused or knowingly permitted there to be in, on or under that land any substance which is there as a result of a chemical reaction or biological process affecting substance A.

(10) A thing which is to be done by way of remediation may be regarded for the purposes of this Part as referable to the presence of any substance notwithstanding that the thing in question would not have to be done—

(a) in consequence only of the presence of that substance in any quantity; or

(b) in consequence only of the quantity of that substance which any particular person caused, or knowingly permitted to be present.

DEFINITIONS

"appropriate person": s.78A(9) of the 1990 Act.
"contaminated land": s.78A(2) of the 1990 Act.
"enforcing authority": s.78A(9) of the 1990 Act.
"owner": s.78A(9) of the 1990 Act.
"remediation": s.78A(7) of the 1990 Act.
"substance": s.78A(9) of the 1990 Act.
"substance A": subs. (9).

COMMENCEMENT

September 21, 1995 insofar as this section confers power on the Secretary of State to issue guidance or makes provision with respect to the exercise of such power (S.I. 1995 No. 1983). The remainder will be brought into force by a commencement order made under s.125(3) of the 1995 Act.

GENERAL NOTE

This is a vitally important section. Its purpose, as indicated by subs. (1), is the determination of who is the appropriate person to bear responsibility for remediation. It is important to note that the concept of appropriate person is referable to the particular thing which the enforcing authority determines is to be done by way of remediation: it is not simply a case of saying that there is one person responsible for everything required by way of remediation in relation to a given piece of land. The significance of guidance to be issued under subss. (6) and (7) should also be noted: this may address some of the potentially harsh consequences to which attention is drawn below.

Subs. (2): primary responsibility

Primary responsibility rests with the person, or any of the persons, who either caused or knowingly permitted all or any of the contaminating substances to be in, on or under the land in question. Where two or more persons fall within this category then the prescriptive guidance to be issued by the Secretary of State will determine which of them is responsible, and in what proportions: subss. (6) and (7). Liability is also limited by the concept of referability under subss. (3) and (10) (see below). Apart from these provisions, the starting point of subs. (2) is that of joint and several liability, as indicated by the words "any of the persons" and "any of the substances".

Subs. (2): "caused"

The question of which person or persons caused a contaminating substance to be present will generally be a question of fact. The issue is likely to be approached by the courts in a common sense way but without knowledge, fault or any other state of mind being required to be shown: see *Alphacell v. Woodward* [1972] A.C. 824 (H.L.) and (in relation to Scotland) *Lockhart v. NCB* 1981 S.L.T. 161 in the context of causing water pollution. In that context, it has been held that causation may be attributable to an operation or chain of operations which result in the water pollution: *Alphacell v. Woodward*; see also *National Rivers Authority v. Yorkshire Water Services* [1994] 3 W.L.R. 1202 (H.L.). More than one person may be held to have caused the same event, even where they executed different and separate acts: *Att.-Gen.'s Reference (No. 1 of 1994)* [1995] 2 All E.R. 1007. However, the causal link between a person and the polluting incident may in some cases be broken by intervening factors such as natural forces (although see *Southern Water Authority v. Pegrum* [1989] Crim.L.R. 442), the act of a third party or an Act of God: *Lockhart v. NCB; Impress (Worcester) v. Rees* [1971] 2 All E.R. 357 (although note Lord Wilberforce's remarks in *Alphacell* on this case: p. 834H) and *National Rivers Authority v. Wright Engineering Co.* [1994] 4 All E.R. 281.

It seems unlikely that someone will be regarded as having caused the substances to be on land where their role has been an entirely passive one: the question of a party's "passivity" may also be a factor where multiple parties are involved (subject to the judgment in *Att.-Gen.'s Reference (No. 1 of 1994)* noted above): *Price v. Cromack* [1975] 2 All E.R. 113; *Northwest Water Authority v. McTay Construction* Q.B.D. April 14, 1986, unreported and *Welsh Water Authority v. Williams Motors (Cwmdu), The Times*, December 5, 1988. However, the House of Lords in *National Rivers Authority v. Yorkshire Water Services*, whilst declining to overrule *Price v. Cromack* and *Wychavon District Council v. National Rivers Authority* [1993] 1 W.L.R. 125, indicated *obiter* that those cases are not to be read as having established any general principle that a positive act is required before causation may be established. In "passivity" cases, the issue of "knowingly permitted" will then become relevant, and this term is considered below.

Where substances have migrated from one piece of land to another, the rules under s.78K will be relevant.

Subs. (2): Consignment to landfill

Whilst landfill sites which still have a licence will not be subject to Pt. IIA, the question may arise in the case of closed sites which constitute contaminated land as to which of the myriad parties involved could be said to have caused the substances to be there. The Government expressly indicated that it did not intend the words "caused or knowingly permitted" to be construed as including persons "merely on the grounds that they had consigned materials to an authorised waste stream"; they believed that such was already the effect of the words without the need for amendment: see *Hansard*, H.L. Vol. 562, col. 182.

However, comments made in the Commons Standing Committee Stage indicate that the Government was not necessarily as sympathetic to those transporting waste to sites: "When individual lorry drivers or companies deliver material, they bear some responsibility for the quality of the material" (H.C. Standing Committee B, Eleventh Sitting, col. 341, May 23, 1995).

Subs. (2): "knowingly permitted"

The concept of "knowingly permitted" presents greater problems than the straightforward notion of causing. Case law on the phrase is limited, but it is clear that two elements are necessary. These are knowledge as to the presence of the substances, and failure to take steps to prevent or terminate their presence: *Berton v. Alliance Economic Investment Co.* [1922] 1 K.B. 742 (C.A.); *Commercial General Administration v. Thomsett* (1979) 250 E.G. 547; *Webb v. Maidstone and District Motor Services* 78 S.J. 336. See also *Carmichael v. L.A.W. Mining* [1995] Env. L.R. 258 (C.A.).

Such case law as there is on "knowingly permitting" in other contexts such as water pollution should be treated with caution, perhaps more so than with regard to "causing". There is a potentially important distinction between permitting an *event*, such as the entry of polluting matter into controlled waters, and permitting a *state of affairs*, such as the presence of substances under land. In this context the Government's rejection of a proposed amendment to the "knowingly permitting" provisions should be noted (see *"in, on or under the land,"* at p. 25–155 below).

"Permitting" may involve giving permission, leave or licence for something to be done: in this sense it might include, for example, the owner of land who knowingly allows another to carry out a contaminating activity there, aware that contaminating substances are being introduced into the land. However, it can carry another sense, that of failure to take steps within one's power, and it is in this sense that it might be construed as applying to a subsequent owner or occupier who becomes aware that contamination is present and fails to take action. If that interpretation were upheld, the consequences for future owners would be serious, in that they could be held primarily liable together with the original polluter (and not just in their capacity as a subsequent owner). Thus they would be potentially liable even if the original polluter could be found, and they would not benefit from the specific protections which apply to persons liable simply as owner or occupier. Indeed it does not appear out of the question that the notice required to be served under s.78B(3) might render an owner or occupier capable of being described as having "knowingly permitted" by the time the authority decides the appropriate persons on whom to serve remediation notices.

General principles of corporate liability will apply to determine whose state of knowledge may be attributed to a company: see, for example, *Tesco Supermarkets v. Nattrass* [1972] A.C. 153 (H.L.).

What must be known? Another issue is what knowledge needs to be shown in order to establish that a person knowingly permitted something. There is clearly a difference between knowing that a substance is present on or is being introduced into land and knowing in addition that it is a contaminative substance or is rendering the land contaminated. These two levels of knowledge correspond to what appear to be the only two possible readings of the relevant part of subs. (2) in relation to "knowingly permitting", which are described here and followed by an example which illustrates the practical significance of the issue.

(a) One possibility is that one is an appropriate person if the substances are in fact contaminative and (whether or not one knows that fact) one "knowingly permitted the substances . . . to be in, on or under the land".

(b) The alternative is that one is only an appropriate person if one permits their presence in, on or under the land knowing that they fit the description of "substances, by reason of which the contaminated land in question is such land".

There does not appear to be available a "middle" reading whereby one is only an appropriate person if one permits the substances' presence in, on or under the land knowing that the substances are, in the ordinary sense of the word, contaminative: "contaminated land" is a precisely defined term, which involves the land "appearing" in a certain way to a local authority, incorporates the equally technical definition of "harm" and depends for its application on prescriptive guidance, so ordinary senses of the term would appear irrelevant.

The difficulty with the second possible reading above also follows from this. It seems absurd to argue that Parliament can have intended subs. (2) to require that, to be an appropriate person by virtue of having "knowingly permitted" something, the relevant knowledge is knowledge both that substances are in, on or under the land and also that those substances are contaminative in the very technical sense required by the Act. Indeed, if this were the reading, then the provision would be toothless against anyone whose alleged state of knowledge relates to a time prior to the point at which the land first appeared to the authority to be contaminated. Yet if (as is submitted) the first reading is correct then the scope of subs. (2) is very wide and injustice may conceivably result, with the increased likelihood of future owners being liable as having "knowingly permitted".

The implications of the distinction between interpretations (a) (in which liability follows from mere knowledge that one is permitting substances to be present) and (b) (in which one must also know that the substances render the land contaminated within the meaning of Pt. IIA) may be illustrated by the following example. Prior to the advent of waste disposal licensing (so that s.78YB(2) or (3) does not disapply Pt. IIA), person X allows his land to be used by person Y for the disposal of waste. He does not at the time realise that the substances being disposed of have contaminative potential. Many years later, after Pt. IIA comes into force, the local authority identifies the land as having been contaminated by those substances. On reading (a) there can be little doubt that X is an appropriate person as having knowingly permitted the substances to be present. On reading (b), X's state of mind at the time when the substances were deposited does not make him an appropriate person in this capacity, since at the time he could not have had knowledge that the land "appeared" to the local authority to be in particular condition as a result of the substances: the authority had not yet formed that view.

However, having formed that view, if the authority then notifies its view to X under s.78B(3) then from that point on, X does have the requisite knowledge to be an appropriate person even under reading (b). If X still has control over the land, perhaps as owner or occupier, then he may after that time become liable for knowingly permitting the continuing presence on the land of the substances. If in the intervening years X had relinquished control over the land, however, then his subsequent knowledge does not render him an appropriate person under reading (b), although he remains an appropriate person under reading (a).

If Y deposited on X's land substances of a kind which X had prohibited or which had not been contemplated by X when agreeing to allow Y to use his land, then even on the harsher reading (a), it could not be said that X had knowingly permitted the presence on his land of those substances.

What constitutes "knowledge"? There is authority, again from water pollution law, to suggest that "constructive knowledge" will suffice: that is, that one may be held to know that which one could in the circumstances reasonably be expected to know: *Schulmans Incorporated v. National Rivers Authority* [1993] Env.L.R. D.1. In the context of knowingly permitting unlicensed entertainments, wilful blindness (closing one's eyes to the obvious or failing to make enquiries which would have confirmed one's suspicions) has been held to constitute knowledge: *Westminster City Council v. Croyalgrange* [1986] 2 All E.R. 353.

Subs. (2): creating a "target" for contamination
A somewhat clearer case for liability may arise where a subsequent owner has redeveloped the site but has failed to remove contamination or indeed by changing the use of the land has

increased the risks presented by the substances. It seems clear that the Government had the responsibilities of such a person in mind in the drafting:

"We believe that it would be reasonable for somebody who has had active control over contaminants on a site, for example when redeveloping it, to become responsible for any harm to health or the environment that may result, even if he did not originally cause or knowingly permit the site to become contaminated" (*Hansard*, H.L. Vol. 560, col. 1461, Viscount Ullswater).

In this context the risk-orientated approach to contamination required by the definition is particularly important: although development or otherwise creating or knowingly permitted contamination may not of itself constitute causing or knowingly permitting contamination, it is clear from Viscount Ullswater's comments that where such a developer could be described as having also knowingly permitted the presence or continued presence of the substances, the Government would not find the consequent attachment of liability an unpalatable result.

Subs. (2): "in, on or under the land"

A substance may be present on land before it makes its way into or under the land. An example would be chemicals which are stored in a surface installation at an industrial plant, but then are accidentally released and contaminate the subsurface: the chemicals were originally "on" the land, but are now "in" or "under" the land. The person (A) who caused or knowingly permitted the chemicals to be placed originally on the land may be a different person to the person (B) who caused or knowingly permitted them to escape and to be in or under the land. Since the chemical which was in the tank or the surface is the same substance by reason of which the land is now contaminated, a strict and literal reading of subs. (2) would indicate that A, as well as B, is an "appropriate person". Such a result could obviously be unjust to A, and might be avoided by construing the subsection so that the presence of the substance in, on or under the land is read as referable only to the point at which the land is in such a condition that harm or pollution of controlled waters (or the possibility or likelihood thereof) occur. On that basis the presence of the substances on land in a safe storage installation would not be relevant so as to fix A with liability. Such a reading is difficult to reconcile with the wording of the subsection, and in any event would not benefit A who had placed the chemical in a defective storage installation which presented the significant possibility of a harmful escape—there A would have caused the substances to be on land *and* the land thereby to come within the definition of contaminated land in s.78A.

The point was not addressed directly in debate, though at one point an amendment was proposed to replace the words "be in, on or under land" with "come into, onto or under land" as defining more accurately the polluter: *Hansard*, H.L. Vol. 562, col. 189. Such an amendment would also have limited scope for subsequent owners to be liable, and was rejected by the Government on the basis that it would ignore the responsibility of those who "... genuinely and actively permit the continued presence of contaminating substances in land" (*Hansard*, H.L. Vol. 562, col. 189, Viscount Ullswater).

One implication of the storage installation scenario is that a seller of land on which potentially contaminative substances are stored should consider emptying such installations on sale or seeking indemnities from any purchaser whose activities or failure to maintain such installations might result in the escape of substances originally brought on to the land by the seller.

Subss. (3) and (10): the referability limitation

As mentioned above, subs. (3) is intended to soften what would otherwise be the harsh consequences of joint and several liability which might otherwise arise under subs. (2). A person will only be "appropriate" if the relevant things required to be done by way of remediation are to any extent referable to substances which he caused or knowingly permitted to be in, on or under the land. It is necessary therefore to identify the substances which the person in question caused or knowingly permitted to be there, and to ask whether the specific remedial action is to any extent (however small) referable to those substances. For example, to take an extreme case, if two separate persons (A and B) have caused land to be contaminated with different substances (say, oil and asbestos), it would not be possible for the authority to impose a single remediation obligation for both substances so making A and B jointly and severally liable — unless, that is, the clean-up operations necessary for the oil could be said to be referable to the asbestos, and vice versa. However, the position may also be affected by subss. (9) (see p. 25–158) and (10).

Subsection (10) clarifies the meaning of the term "referable" under subs. (3). It should be remembered that subs. (3) requires the remedial action to be referable to the substances in question only "to any extent". Subsection (10) essentially avoids arguments by a potentially appropriate person that the type or amount of the substance they introduced would not of itself necessitate the relevant remedial action. The operation of paras. (a) and (b) of the subsection may perhaps best be illustrated by example.

(a) Persons A and B each introduce different substances into land. Each substance is individually harmless and would not of itself require remedial action. However, the combined presence of the two substances necessitates remediation. Subsection (10)(a) would prevent any argument by either A or B that the remediation was not referable to their substance. Note, however, that where a chemical reaction or biological process has occurred between the two substances, resulting in a third substance being formed, subs. (9) may also be relevant (see below).

(b) Persons A and B each introduce different quantities of the same substance into land. Neither quantity of the substance would itself require remediation, but their combined quantity makes it necessary. The effect of subs. (10)(b) is that neither A nor B can argue that the clean-up is not referable to the quantity of the substance for which they are responsible.

Subss. (4) and (5): liability of owner and occupier
Government policy is that the owner and occupier of land, even if "innocent" in relation to the presence of the contaminating substances, should bear responsibility for the condition of their land. Lord Northbourne, in debate, put extreme examples of cases where it would be unjust to regard an innocent owner as liable: for example an owner whose land was contaminated by a crashed tanker, or by migrating dust or particles (*Hansard*, H.L. Vol. 562, col. 1052). The Government's response was that it was not justifiable to relieve owners of liabilities which they might already incur under existing legislation and that it was reasonable for owners to bear responsibility for their property and its effects on others and the wider environment in cases where no original polluter can be found: *Hansard*, H.L. Vol. 562, col. 1052.

As originally drafted, there were three circumstances where the current owner or occupier would be the appropriate person to bear responsibility for remediation. Two of these circumstances were dropped in the course of the passage of the Bill: namely cases where the owner/occupier refused consent for remediation works to be carried out on their land and cases where the liability of the original "polluter" had been directly or indirectly transferred. The original provisions on transfer of liability were particularly difficult to understand, though they were basically prompted by the Government's wish to respect contractual provisions: see *Hansard*, H.L. Vol. 562, cols. 1048–1051. On looking at the matter more closely, however, the Government concluded that it would be more practical to leave the question to be dealt with through the normal contractual means of guarantees and indemnities rather than detailed statutory provisions: *Hansard*, H.L. Vol. 565, col. 1498.

Two circumstances now remain where the owner or occupier is liable under this provision; namely where after "reasonable inquiry" no person has been found who bears responsibility as an appropriate person under subs. (2) or where something to be done by way of remediation cannot be regarded as "referable" to anyone under subs. (3).

Subss. (4) and (5): "no person ... has been found"
Where the identity of the original person or company causing contamination is known but that person or company no longer exists (*i.e.* because of death or liquidation) the question is whether it can be said that no person "has been found". The Government's view is that circumstances where a polluter cannot be found would include cases where the relevant company has gone into liquidation: *Hansard*, H.L. Vol. 562, col. 209. It is submitted, however, that where a person or company is located but dies or goes into liquidation during the s.78H(3) consultation period so that a remediation notice may no longer be served on them, they have nevertheless been "found" and subs. (4) cannot operate to make the owner or occupier of the land liable as such.

Owners and occupiers may well be prompted by the attentions of the authority themselves to seek to locate others who may have caused or knowingly permitted the presence of the substances in question. If they are successful in doing so, but death or liquidation of the located person or company follows before the authority establishes contact with them, it is a moot point whether they can be described as having been "found".

Subss. (4) and (5): "owner"
The term "owner" is defined separately for England and Wales and for Scotland at s.78A(9).

Subss. (4) and (5): lenders as "owners"
The question of potential liability of lenders under the new provisions aroused considerable interest in debate. The Government did not regard it as likely that the act of lending money to a polluter would of itself constitute causing or knowingly permitting contamination: *Hansard*, H.L. Vol. 565, col. 1497.

The definition of "owner" adopted in the Act expressly excludes a mortgagee not in possession and the Scottish equivalent. The Government expressed the view that banks should not be treated as "deep pockets", that the simple act of lending should not result in liability and that the lender should retain the right to walk away from security without taking possession if the costs of remediation appeared to exceed its ultimate value: *Hansard*, H.L. Vol. 560, col. 1448. However, the banks and other institutions such as the Council of Mortgage Lenders were still concerned as to the possibilities for a lender to find itself in possession by default where the borrower abandoned the property and sent the keys to the lender: *Hansard*, H.L. Vol. 560, col. 1445; Vol. 562, col. 1040. Although it agreed to look into the issue, the Government concluded that no changes were necessary to protect lenders in this situation: they were already exposed to similar liabilities under existing legislation on public health, highways and building standards: *Hansard*, H.L. Vol. 562, col. 165. Similarly the Government were not sympathetic to the argument that special provision was needed to protect lenders who took possession to a limited extent to secure property or deal with obvious hazards: see *Hansard*, H.L. Vol. 562, cols. 1042–1043.

Subss. (4) and (5): trustees as "owners"
The possible hardship of the provisions to trustees was drawn to the attention of the Government in debate: *Hansard*, H.L. Vol. 562, col. 163. The response was that to provide an exemption for trustees would be to open up an easy route for evasion: *Hansard*, H.L. Vol. 562, col. 165; Vol. 560, col. 1448.

Subss. (4) and (5): the innocent fly-tipped owner
One problem for which the Government did have evident sympathy was that of the owner or occupier who suffers from fly-tipping on their land. Imposing liability for clean-up of such contamination on the owner or occupier on the basis that the fly-tipper could not be found would have resulted in significantly harsher liabilities than under s.59 of the 1990 Act, which deals with the removal of unlawfully deposited waste. The Government's view was that the best way of dealing with the problem was to disapply Pt. IIA in cases where s.59 could be used: *Hansard*, H.L. Vol. 562, col. 182. This was achieved by an amendment at third reading stage in the Lords. Full responsibility for dealing with unlawfully deposited waste would thereby be placed with the Agency/SEPA as the waste regulation authority and the exemption for innocent victims of fly-tipping was retained: *Hansard*, H.L. Vol. 562, col. 1045. Certainly in relation to contamination occurring after controls over waste deposits on land were introduced, the availability of s.59 as a remedy could be a significant restriction on the use of Pt. IIA powers.

Subss. (4) and (5): "occupier"
The term "occupier" is not defined in Pt. IIA and the question of whether a person is in occupation will have to be determined on the facts of each case. The test is that of the degree of control exercised over the land rather than exclusivity of rights of occupation: *Wheat v. E. Lacon & Co.* [1966] A.C. 552. A licence entitling a person to possession may make someone an "occupier": *Stevens v. Bromley London Borough Council* [1972] 1 All E.R. 712 (C.A.). Similarly it appears that a statutory tenant is an "occupier" (*Brown v. Minister of Housing and Local Government* [1953] 2 All E.R. 1385), but there is authority to suggest that a person who entered premises forcibly and unlawfully is not: *Woodcock v. South West Electricity Board* [1975] 2 All E.R. 545.

In Scotland it has been established that receivers may become occupiers: *Lord Advocate v. Aero Technologies (in receivership)* 1991 SLT 134. Thus, those receivers acting in a management capacity may conceivably find themselves regarded as occupiers for the purposes of the contaminated land provisions, although the specific protection afforded to them by s.78(3)–(4) should be noted.

Subss. (4) and (5): protection of owner and occupier
Persons liable under subs. (4) and (5) are in a better position than persons liable under subs. (2) in one respect. This relates to the situation where the contamination results or is likely to result in pollution of controlled waters: see General Note to s.78J at p. 25–165 below.

Subss. (2), (4) and (5): insolvency practitioners and similar persons
Persons acting in certain capacities in relation to insolvency enjoy specific protection: see s.78X(3)–(4).

Subss. (6) and (7): apportionment of liability

It will be appreciated that notwithstanding the Government's aversion to creating joint and several liability, there are a number of potential instances where more than one person could be held responsible for a particular remediation requirement. These include: (a) persons who at the same time or at different times have contributed the same substance to contaminated land; (b) persons who have contributed different substances that have combined or reacted together; (c) a person who has caused and a person or persons who have knowingly permitted contaminating substances to be in land (possibly the original polluter plus a subsequent owner); and (d) where no polluter can be found, the owner and the occupier (if different persons) or possibly co-owners or co-occupiers.

The existence of such potential situations of joint and several liability (and there may well be others) means that guidance issued under subss. (6) and (7) on apportionment of liability is likely to be important. Such guidance will have prescriptive and decisive effect. Under subs. (6) the authority may exempt one or more persons entirely. Where a number of persons fall into the first category of liability, it is questionable whether subs. (6) allows *all* of them to be treated as not being an appropriate person. The effect of so doing could be to make liability shift to owners and occupiers in the second category; who might however argue that persons in the first category have in fact been "found" within the meaning of subs. (4) but having been found have simply been treated as not appropriate. Under subs. (7) the authority may determine the proportions in which such persons are to bear the responsibility. Again, various questions arise here. Can someone be attributed a nil share under this provision? This could have a different effect on second tier owners and occupiers than excluding that person under subs. (6). Do the shares have to add up to 100% of the cost? And where both subss. (6) and (7) operate, in which order do they operate? It is to be hoped that guidance will address these issues.

The proportions of responsibility in such cases are to be stated in the remediation notice: s.78E(3). In that case the defence under s.78M(2) should be noted, *i.e.* that non-compliance with the notice was due solely to the refusal or inability of the others involved to comply with the requirement. The only indication given in debate as to the Government's views on apportionment was given by Viscount Ullswater at *Hansard*, H.L. Vol. 562, col. 215. He rejected any suggestion that liability should be joint and several where different persons have separately contributed to an overall problem and went on to say that where one person caused substances to be present but another in knowingly permitting them to remain brought about the circumstances in which they came to result in significant harm it may be "... entirely appropriate for the whole responsibility for remediation to rest on the person with the most recent involvement with the contamination".

Subs. (9): chemical and biological reactions and processes

The harm or risk arising from contaminated land may in some cases derive from a reaction or process affecting the substances within the land. Examples are the synergistic effect of chemicals which react together, or the biological processes resulting in the formation of poisonous or explosive gases from putrescible materials. Subsection (9) deals with this situation by providing that the person who caused or knowingly permitted the original substance to be present will also be regarded as having caused or knowingly permitted such harmful products to be present.

To take an example: A deposits substance X in land which reacts to form noxious substance Y; B then unwittingly purchases the land. A will be regarded as having *caused* substance Y to be present. B might also be liable for having *knowingly permitted* substance Y to be present, as he now has control of the land.

Grant of, and compensation for, rights of entry etc.

78G.—(1) A remediation notice may require an appropriate person to do things by way of remediation, notwithstanding that he is not entitled to do those things.

(2) Any person whose consent is required before any thing required by a remediation notice may be done shall grant, or join in granting, such rights in relation to any of the relevant land or waters as will enable the appropriate person to comply with any requirements imposed by the remediation notice.

(3) Before serving a remediation notice, the enforcing authority shall reasonably endeavour to consult every person who appears to the authority—

(a) to be the owner or occupier of any of the relevant land or waters, and

(b) to be a person who might be required by subsection (2) above to grant, or join in granting, any rights,

concerning the rights which that person may be so required to grant.

(4) Subsection (3) above shall not preclude the service of a remediation notice in any case where it appears to the enforcing authority that the contaminated land in question is in such a condition, by reason of substances in, on or under the land, that there is imminent danger of serious harm, or serious pollution of controlled waters, being caused.

(5) A person who grants, or joins in granting, any rights pursuant to subsection (2) above shall be entitled on making an application within such period as may be prescribed and in such manner as may be prescribed to such person as may be prescribed, to be paid by the appropriate person compensation of such amount as may be determined in such manner as may be prescribed.

(6) Without prejudice to the generality of the regulations that may be made by virtue of subsection (5) above, regulations by virtue of that subsection may make such provision in relation to compensation under this section as may be made by regulations by virtue of subsection (4) of section 35A above in relation to compensation under that section.

(7) In this section, "relevant land or waters" means—

(a) the contaminated land in question;

(b) any controlled waters affected by that land; or

(c) any land adjoining or adjacent to that land or those waters.

DEFINITIONS

"appropriate person": s.78A(9) of the 1990 Act.
"contaminated land": s.78A(2) of the 1990 Act.
"controlled waters": s.78A(9) of the 1990 Act.
"enforcing authority": s.78A(9) of the 1990 Act.
"harm": s.78A(4) of the 1990 Act.
"owner": s.78A(9) of the 1990 Act.
"pollution of controlled waters": s.78A(9) of the 1990 Act.
"regulations": s.78A(9) of the 1990 Act.
"relevant land or waters": subs. (7).
"remediation": s.78A(7) of the 1990 Act.
"remediation notice": s.78E(1) of the 1990 Act.

COMMENCEMENT

September 21, 1995 insofar as this section confers power on the Secretary of State to make regulations or makes provision with respect to the exercise of such power (S.I. 1995 No. 1983). The remainder will be brought into force by a commencement order made under s.125(3) of the 1995 Act.

GENERAL NOTE

This section governs the situation where the appropriate person has no right to carry out the remediation works required, *e.g.* because he is no longer in ownership or occupation of the land, or the works are off-site. This fact is not a bar to service of a remediation notice (subs. (1)) and any person whose consent is required is obliged to grant, or join in granting such rights as are necessary (subs. (2)). This may of course involve cost, disruption and inconvenience. The owner or occupier affected is protected by: (a) the requirement on the enforcing authority to use reasonable endeavours to consult before serving the remediation notice (subs. (3)), save in cases of imminent danger of serious harm (subs. (4)) and (b) the entitlement, on application, to be paid compensation by the appropriate person, to be determined in such manner as may be prescribed (subs. (5)).

No offence is created of failing to grant the necessary rights: the onus would appear to be on the appropriate person to secure that the rights are in fact granted so as to allow remediation to be carried out, through civil action if necessary.

Restrictions and prohibitions on serving remediation notices

78H.—(1) Before serving a remediation notice, the enforcing authority shall reasonably endeavour to consult—

(a) the person on whom the notice is to be served,

(b) the owner of any land to which the notice relates,

(c) any person who appears to that authority to be in occupation of the whole or any part of the land, and

(d) any person of such other description as may be prescribed, concerning what is to be done by way of remediation.

(2) Regulations may make provision for, or in connection with, steps to be taken for the purposes of subsection (1) above.

(3) No remediation notice shall be served on any person by reference to any contaminated land during any of the following periods, that is to say—

(a) the period—

(i) beginning with the identification of the contaminated land in question pursuant to section 78B(1) above, and

(ii) ending with the expiration of the period of three months beginning with the day on which the notice required by subsection (3)(d) or, as the case may be, (4) of section 78B above is given to that person in respect of that land;

(b) if a decision falling within paragraph (b) of section 78C(1) above is made in relation to the contaminated land in question, the period beginning with the making of the decision and ending with the expiration of the period of three months beginning with—

(i) in a case where the decision is not referred to the Secretary of State under section 78D above, the day on which the notice required by section 78C(6) above is given, or

(ii) in a case where the decision is referred to the Secretary of State under section 78D above, the day on which he gives the notice required by subsection (4)(b) of that section;

(c) if the appropriate Agency gives a notice under subsection (4) of section 78C above to a local authority in relation to the contaminated land in question, the period beginning with the day on which that notice is given and ending with the expiration of the period of three months beginning with—

(i) in a case where notice is given under subsection (6) of that section, the day on which that notice is given;

(ii) in a case where the authority makes a decision falling within subsection (5)(b) of that section and the appropriate Agency fails to give notice under paragraph (b) of section 78D (1) above, the day following the expiration of the period of twenty-one days mentioned in that paragraph; or

(iii) in a case where the authority makes a decision falling within section 78C(5)(b) above which is referred to the Secretary of State under section 78D above, the day on which the Secretary of State gives the notice required by subsection (4) (b) of that section.

(4) Neither subsection (1) nor subsection (3) above shall preclude the service of a remediation notice in any case where it appears to the enforcing authority that the land in question is in such a condition, by reason of substances in, on or under the land, that there is imminent danger of serious harm, or serious pollution of controlled waters, being caused.

(5) The enforcing authority shall not serve a remediation notice on a person if and so long as any one or more of the following conditions is for the time being satisfied in the particular case, that is to say—

(a) the authority is satisfied, in consequence of section 78E(4) and (5) above, that there is nothing by way of remediation which could be specified in a remediation notice served on that person;

(b) the authority is satisfied that appropriate things are being, or will be, done by way of remediation without the service of a remediation notice on that person;

(c) it appears to the authority that the person on whom the notice would be served is the authority itself; or

(d) the authority is satisfied that the powers conferred on it by section 78N below to do what is appropriate by way of remediation are exercisable.

(6) Where the enforcing authority is precluded by virtue of section 78E(4) or (5) above from specifying in a remediation notice any particular thing by way of remediation which it would otherwise have specified in such a notice, the authority shall prepare and publish a document (in this Part referred to as a "remediation declaration") which shall record—

(a) the reasons why the authority would have specified that thing; and

(b) the grounds on which the authority is satisfied that it is precluded from specifying that thing in such a notice.

(7) In any case where the enforcing authority is precluded, by virtue of paragraph (b), (c) or (d) of subsection (5) above, from serving a remediation notice, the responsible person shall prepare and publish a document (in this Part referred to as a "remediation statement") which shall record—

(a) the things which are being, have been, or are expected to be, done by way of remediation in the particular case;

(b) the name and address of the person who is doing, has done, or is expected to do, each of those things; and

(c) the periods within which each of those things is being, or is expected to be, done.

(8) For the purposes of subsection (7) above, the "responsible person" is—

(a) in a case where the condition in paragraph (b) of subsection (5) above is satisfied, the person who is doing or has done, or who the enforcing authority is satisfied will do, the things there mentioned; or

(b) in a case where the condition in paragraph (c) or (d) of that subsection is satisfied, the enforcing authority.

(9) If a person who is required by virtue of subsection (8)(a) above to prepare and publish a remediation statement fails to do so within a reasonable time after the date on which a remediation notice specifying the things there mentioned could, apart from subsection (5) above, have been served, the enforcing authority may itself prepare and publish the statement and may recover its reasonable costs of doing so from that person.

(10) Where the enforcing authority has been precluded by virtue only of subsection (5) above from serving a remediation notice on an appropriate person but—

(a) none of the conditions in that subsection is for the time being satisfied in the particular case, and

(b) the authority is not precluded by any other provision of this Part from serving a remediation notice on that appropriate person, the authority shall serve a remediation notice on that person; and any such notice may be so served without any further endeavours by the authority to consult persons pursuant to subsection (1) above, if and to the extent that that person has been consulted pursuant to that subsection concerning the things which will be specified in the notice.

DEFINITIONS
"appropriate Agency": s.78A(9) of the 1990 Act.
"appropriate person": s.78A(9) of the 1990 Act.
"contaminated land": s.78A(2) of the 1990 Act.
"enforcing authority": s.78A(9) of the 1990 Act.
"harm": s.78A(4) of the 1990 Act.
"local authority": s.78A(9) of the 1990 Act.
"notice": s.78A(9) of the 1990 Act.
"pollution of controlled waters": s.78A(9) of the 1990 Act.
"regulations": s.78A(9) of the 1990 Act.
"remediation": s.78A(7) of the 1990 Act.
"remediation declaration": subs. (6).
"remediation notice": s.78A(9) of the 1990 Act.
"responsible person": subs. (8).

COMMENCEMENT
September 21, 1995 insofar as this section confers power on the Secretary of State to make regulations or makes provision with respect to the exercise of such power (S.I. 1995 No. 1983). The remainder will be brought into force by a commencement order made under s.125(3) of the 1995 Act.

GENERAL NOTE
This section contains various restrictions and prohibitions on service of a remediation notice, designed in part to meet concerns expressed by various interested organisations during the passage of the Bill.

Subss. (1)–(4): consultation as to remediation requirements
The enforcing authority is subject to a general requirement that before serving a remediation notice it should use reasonable endeavours to consult the persons specified in subs. (1) concerning what is to be done by way of remediation. Such a requirement was initially opposed by the Government on the basis that it would impose a considerable bureaucratic burden for little benefit: *Hansard*, H.L. Vol. 562, col. 171. This obligation is coupled with an embargo on service of a remediation notice during a period running from the date of identification of the contaminated land until three months from the date of notification of identification under s.78B or notification of designation as a special site under ss.78C or 78D (subs. (3)). However, the requirement and restriction will not prevent a remediation notice being served in cases where it appears to the enforcing authority that the condition of the land presents a risk of imminent danger of serious land or serious water pollution (subs. (4)).

Subs. (5): cases where enforcing authority is restrained from serving notice
Subsection (5) gives four cases (a) to (d) where the authority may not serve a remediation notice so long as the conditions specified there are applicable. Note that the section does not create a permanent restriction on service of a notice: circumstances may change so that the restriction no longer applies. In such a case, if no other restriction applies, a remediation notice must be served, and no further consultation may be necessary if this has already taken place with the appropriate person: subs. (10). The four cases are as follows.
Paragraph (a). The authority is satisfied that nothing could reasonably be specified by way of remediation, having regard to cost, seriousness of harm and Secretary of State's guidance.
Paragraph (b). The authority is satisfied that appropriate remedial action will be undertaken voluntarily, without a remediation notice being served. Whilst the intended recipient of the notice may offer assurances that remedial action will be taken, in order to be satisfied that those things will be done (or completed if they have already been commenced), it is submitted that the authority may be prudent to require the appropriate person or persons to enter into a binding written agreement.
Paragraph (c). The authority itself is the appropriate person, *e.g.* because the site is owned by the authority, or was operated by the authority in the past as a landfill site or similar facility.
Paragraph (d). The effect of this paragraph is complex. The authority will be precluded from serving notice so long as it is satisfied that it could exercise its s.78N powers to carry out remedia-

tion. Section 78N(3) lists six cases (a) to (f) where the authority has power to act itself. Specifically these include cases where the authority considers it necessary to act to avoid the occurrence of serious harm or pollution in cases of imminent danger ((a)); where an appropriate person has entered into a written agreement for the authority to carry out the work at the cost of that person ((b)) (though presumably the authority would then anyway be satisfied under s.78H(5)(b) that the appropriate things would be done); where ss.78J or 78K operate to preclude something being included in a remediation notice ((d)); or—most importantly—where there are circumstances of hardship ((e); or where no appropriate person has been found after reasonable inquiry (f)). In all of these cases the authority will not be able to serve notice: its remedy will lie in carrying out the works itself and then seeking (if possible) to recover its expenses under the procedures contained in s.78P.

Hardship. One of the most important practical effects of subs. (5) as outlined above is that before serving notice the authority must consider the question of hardship: H.C. Standing Committee B, Eleventh Sitting, cols. 361–362, May 23, 1995; *Hansard*, H.L. Vol. 565, col. 1496. Apart from taking blanket policy decisions such as not to serve notices on residential owners, it is difficult to see how the authority could consider the issue adequately without eliciting information from the intended recipient of the notice. Yet any adoption of such a blanket policy would have to remain sufficiently flexible to avoid the threat of judicial review perhaps by another appropriate person on the basis that the enforcing authority has fettered its discretion.

Subs. (6): remediation declarations
   Where the authority is precluded by s.78E(4) or (5) from requiring some particular thing by way of remediation it must prepare and publish a remediation declaration recording the reasons why the thing would have been specified were it not for s.78E(4) and (5), and the grounds on which the authority is satisfied it is precluded from specifying the relevant thing. The declaration must be placed on the public register: s.78R(1)(c).
   For the owner of land, the remediation declaration is something of a two-edged sword: on the one hand the polluter or owner may welcome the public recognition that the authority cannot require a particular type of remediation. On the other hand the notice will make it clear that but for considerations of cost or Government guidance, such action would be required. A prospective purchaser may be understandably nervous that the circumstances which led the authority to be satisfied that the action cannot be required may change: the seriousness of the risk of harm may increase, possibly due to factors outside the owner's control; the cost of remedial techniques may fall, or cheaper techniques may become available; or Government guidance may change. Such factors, and others, may lead the authority to reconsider its decision under s.78E(4) or (5). Where an owner does not consider that the land should be the subject of a remediation declaration (*e.g.* because it is not within the definition of contaminated land at all) there is no statutory mechanism for appeal, though the declaration could no doubt be challenged by way of judicial review.

Subs. (7): remediation statements
   Where the authority is precluded from serving a remediation notice by s.78H(5)(b) to (d) (see above), an obligation falls on the "responsible person" (see subs. (8)) to prepare and publish a remediation statement recording the matters specified at subs. (7)(a) to (c). This will, where the remediation is to be carried out voluntarily, be the person who is to do the works; in all other cases, it will be the authority itself (either in its capacity as original polluter or current owner/occupier or because it is entitled to carry out the work itself under s.78N).
   As with a remediation declaration, the remediation statement must be placed on the public register: s.78R(1)(c). Where the responsible person is someone other than the authority and fails to produce a remediation statement within a reasonable time then the authority may itself prepare and publish the statement and may recover its reasonable costs of so doing: subs. (9). There is no express remedy or sanction in cases of failure to carry out the steps contained in a remediation statement when this has been prepared; nor does s.78N appear to contain any reserve power for the authority to carry out the works itself in such a case. The remedy of the authority would be to serve a remediation notice on the basis that it is no longer satisfied (under subs. (5)(b)) that the works will be carried out. There is no express sanction or default power where the authority itself is the responsible person, although the Agency/SEPA has the power under s.78V to issue site-specific guidance. Ordinary principles of judicial review would no doubt apply in the case of failure to take necessary action.

Restrictions on liability relating to the pollution of controlled waters
   78J.—(1) This section applies where any land is contaminated land by virtue of paragraph (b) of subsection (2) of section 78A above (whether or not the land is also contaminated land by virtue of paragraph (a) of that subsection).

(2) Where this section applies, no remediation notice given in consequence of the land in question being contaminated land shall require a person who is an appropriate person by virtue of section 78F(4) or (5) above to do anything by way of remediation to that or any other land, or any waters, which he could not have been required to do by such a notice had paragraph (b) of section 78A(2) above (and all other references to pollution of controlled waters) been omitted from this Part.

(3) If, in a case where this section applies, a person permits, has permitted, or might permit, water from an abandoned mine or part of a mine—

    (a) to enter any controlled waters, or

    (b) to reach a place from which it is or, as the case may be, was likely,

      in the opinion of the enforcing authority, to enter such waters,

no remediation notice shall require him in consequence to do anything by way of remediation (whether to the contaminated land in question or to any other land or waters) which he could not have been required to do by such a notice had paragraph (b) of section 78A(2) above (and all other references to pollution of controlled waters) been omitted from this Part.

(4) Subsection (3) above shall not apply to the owner or former operator of any mine or part of a mine if the mine or part in question became abandoned after 31st December 1999.

(5) In determining for the purposes of subsection (4) above whether a mine or part of a mine became abandoned before, on or after 31st December 1999 in a case where the mine or part has become abandoned on two or more occasions, of which—

    (a) at least one falls on or before that date, and

    (b) at least one falls after that date,

the mine or part shall be regarded as becoming abandoned after that date (but without prejudice to the operation of subsection (3) above in relation to that mine or part at, or in relation to, any time before the first of those occasions which falls after that date).

(6) Where, immediately before a part of a mine becomes abandoned, that part is the only part of the mine not falling to be regarded as abandoned for the time being, the abandonment of that part shall not be regarded for the purposes of subsection (4) or (5) above as constituting the abandonment of the mine, but only of that part of it.

(7) Nothing in subsection (2) or (3) above prevents the enforcing authority from doing anything by way of remediation under section 78N below which it could have done apart from that subsection, but the authority shall not be entitled under section 78P below to recover from any person any part of the cost incurred by the authority in doing by way of remediation anything which it is precluded by subsection (2) or (3) above from requiring that person to do.

(8) In this section "mine" has the same meaning as in the Mines and Quarries Act 1954.

DEFINITIONS

    "appropriate person": s.78A(9) of the 1990 Act.
    "contaminated land": s.78A(2) of the 1990 Act.
    "controlled waters": s.78A(9) of the 1990 Act.
    "enforcing authority: s.78A(9) of the 1990 Act.
    "mine": subs. (8).
    "pollution of controlled waters": s.78A(9) of the 1990 Act.
    "remediation": s.78A(7) of the 1990 Act.
    "remediation notice": s.78E(1) of the 1990 Act.

COMMENCEMENT

    These provisions will be brought into force by a commencement order made under s.125(3) of the 1995 Act.

GENERAL NOTE
This section places certain restrictions on liability under Pt. IIA which relates to pollution of controlled waters. The first is a general restriction under subs. (2), the second is a specific restriction relating to water from abandoned mines in subs. (3). Both restrictions apply where land is regarded as contaminated because pollution of controlled waters is being caused or is likely to be caused, even if the land is also regarded as contaminated on the basis of the separate 'harm' test: subs. (1).

Subs. (2): general restriction
The effect of this restriction is that a person who is regarded as an appropriate person by virtue of s.78F(4) or (5), *i.e.* as an owner or occupier where the original polluter cannot be found, shall not be required to do anything which he could not have been required to do if the water pollution limb of the definition of contaminated land did not exist. In other words, the remediation required may relate only to the general "harm" limb of the definition of contamination, *i.e.* significant harm to health of living organisms, interference with ecological systems, or harm to property. It is submitted that contamination of percolating groundwater so as to render it unfit for a purpose for which it is abstracted could constitute "harm to property", abstraction being a natural right incidental to the ownership of land.
The object of this restriction is to avoid any additional liability accruing to an owner or occupier of land, beyond that which could already attach in relation to the clean up of water pollution under s.161 of the Water Resources Act 1991 (or, in Scotland, under s.46 of the Control of Pollution Act 1974). Section 161/s.46 liability is based upon causing or knowingly permitting pollution and subs. (2) seeks to mirror this concept. The extent to which it provides protection to an owner or occupier will however depend upon the interpretation placed on the words "knowingly permitted" in s.78F(2): a current owner may find that they are liable on that basis and unable to take advantage of s.78J(2). Their only comfort in that situation is that they might well also have been liable under the law as it stood under s.161/s.46, the difference being, of course, that those sections imposed only a power, rather than a duty, to act on the enforcing authority. It should also be noted in this respect that those sections have been amended by the 1995 Act to allow a "works notice" to be served, with similar effect to a remediation notice, requiring clean up or anti-pollution operations: s.161A as inserted by Sched. 22, para. 162; and s.46A as inserted by para. 29(22) of that Schedule.

Subs. (3): abandoned mines
The issue of who is an appropriate person in relation to contamination present in underground mine workings is discussed above in relation to s.78A.
The effect of subs. (3) is to mirror the position as to liability for pollution from abandoned mines, contained in the Water Resources Act 1991 (or, in Scotland, the Control of Pollution Act 1974) as amended by the 1995 Act. The exemption is applicable to a person who permits, has permitted, or might permit, water from an abandoned mine to enter controlled waters, or to reach a place from which it is likely to do so. As with the defence/exception under the 1991 Act (or, in Scotland, the 1974 Act), it will not apply to owners or former operators of mines which become abandoned after December 31, 1999: subs. (4). As to the meaning of "mine" see subs. (8)—the definition in the 1954 Act, s.180 is as follows:
"... an excavation or system of excavations, including all such excavations to which a common system of ventilation is provided, made for the purpose of, or in connection with, the getting, wholly or substantially by means involving the employment of persons below ground, of minerals (whether in their natural state or in solution or suspension) or products of minerals".
The question of when abandonment is to be regarded as occurring is dealt with by subss. (5) and (6). See further the General Notes to ss.58 and 59 at pp. 25–195, 25–202, below.
The effect of subs. (3) is that the person who is responsible for knowingly permitting under s.78F(2) (as opposed to causing) can only be required to remediate contamination which is harmful within the first limb of the s.78A test, and not that which results or is likely to result in water pollution without causing harm in that sense: see General Note to subs. (2) above.

Liability in respect of contaminating substances which escape to other land
78K.—(1) A person who has caused or knowingly permitted any substances to be in, on or under any land shall also be taken for the purposes of this Part to have caused or, as the case may be, knowingly permitted

those substances to be in, on or under any other land to which they appear to have escaped.

(2) Subsections (3) and (4) below apply in any case where it appears that any substances are or have been in, on or under any land (in this section referred to as "land A") as a result of their escape, whether directly or indirectly, from other land in, on or under which a person caused or knowingly permitted them to be.

(3) Where this subsection applies, no remediation notice shall require a person—

(a) who is the owner or occupier of land A, and

(b) who has not caused or knowingly permitted the substances in question to be in, on or under that land,

to do anything by way of remediation to any land or waters (other than land or waters of which he is the owner or occupier) in consequence of land A appearing to be in such a condition, by reason of the presence of those substances in, on or under it, that significant harm is being caused, or there is a significant possibility of such harm being caused, or that pollution of controlled waters is being, or is likely to be caused.

(4) Where this subsection applies, no remediation notice shall require a person—

(a) who is the owner or occupier of land A, and

(b) who has not caused or knowingly permitted the substances in question to be in, on or under that land,

to do anything by way of remediation in consequence of any further land in, on or under which those substances or any of them appear to be or to have been present as a result of their escape from land A ("land B") appearing to be in such a condition, by reason of the presence of those substances in, on or under it, that significant harm is being caused, or there is a significant possibility of such harm being caused, or that pollution of controlled waters is being, or is likely to be caused, unless he is also the owner or occupier of land B.

(5) In any case where—

(a) a person ("person A") has caused or knowingly permitted any substances to be in, on, or under any land,

(b) another person ("person B") who has not caused or knowingly permitted those substances to be in, on or under that land becomes the owner or occupier of that land, and

(c) the substances, or any of the substances, mentioned in paragraph (a) above appear to have escaped to other land,

no remediation notice shall require person B to do anything by way of remediation to that other land in consequence of the apparent acts or omissions of person A, except to the extent that person B caused or knowingly permitted the escape.

(6) Nothing in subsection (3), (4) or (5) above prevents the enforcing authority from doing anything by way of remediation under section 78N below which it could have done apart from that subsection, but the authority shall not be entitled under section 78P below to recover from any person any part of the cost incurred by the authority in doing by way of remediation anything which it is precluded by subsection (3), (4) or (5) above from requiring that person to do.

(7) In this section, "appear" means appear to the enforcing authority, and cognate expressions shall be construed accordingly.

Definitions
    "enforcing authority": s.78A(9) of the 1990 Act.
    "harm": s.78A(4) of the 1990 Act.
    "land A": subs. (2).
    "land B": subs. (4).

"owner": s.78A(9) of the 1990 Act.
"person A": subs. (5)(a).
"person B": subs. (5)(b).
"pollution of controlled waters": s.78A(9) of the 1990 Act.
"remediation": s.78A(7) of the 1990 Act.
"remediation notice": s.78E(1) of the 1990 Act.
"significant": s.78A(5) of the 1990 Act.
"substance": s.78A(9) of the 1990 Act.

COMMENCEMENT
These provisions will be brought into force by a commencement order made under s.125(3) of the 1995 Act.

GENERAL NOTE
This complex section attempts to deal with the complex situations which can arise where contamination migrates from its original location to other land. So far as this commentator is aware (at least in relation to environmental legislation) it sets the precedent for a new drafting style by its references to "land A", "person B", *etc.*

Subs. (1): migrating contaminants—primary liability
The effect of this subsection is that a person who has caused or knowingly permitted substances to be in, on or under land shall also be taken to have caused or knowingly permitted them (as the case may be) to be in, on or under any other land to which they appear ("appear" in this context means appear to the enforcing authority) to have escaped: subss. (1) and (7). The result is that such a person will be an appropriate person under s.78F(2) in relation to the land to which the substances have escaped. It is possible, as discussed under s.78F, that the words "knowingly permit" could apply to a subsequent owner or occupier. The correct construction of subs. (1) appears to be that it will only apply to substances which escaped to the other land after the time by which the owner could be said to have knowingly permitted them to be on the first land: this would avoid the inconsistency which could otherwise arise with subs. (5) which envisages an "innocent" owner or occupier being liable only to the extent that they caused or knowingly permitted the escape to the other land.

Subs. (3): responsibility of owner and occupier of land to which contaminants migrate
Subsection (3) is applied by subs. (2) to any case where it appears that substances are in, on or under any land (land A) as a result of their escape directly or indirectly from other land in, on or under which a person knowingly permitted them to be. Again, "appears" is to be construed by reference to what appears to the enforcing authority: subs. (7). The subsection refers to a direct or indirect escape, which is wide enough language to cover subsurface percolation or transport by wind or flowing water; it could therefore cover, for example, the situation where land A is contaminated by the fall-out of airborne emissions from other land.
In such cases, the remediation notice may not require the owner or occupier of land A to do anything by way of remediation to any land or waters, other than the land or waters of which he is owner or occupier. The inference is that he may be required to carry out remediation of land or waters of which he is in ownership or occupation: however, by virtue of subs. (1) the person who originally caused or knowingly permitted the substances to escape on to land A will bear primary responsibility in relation to land A under s.78F(2), and the owner or occupier of land A should only be liable under s.78F(4) if that person cannot be found.
The only problem with this logical scheme lies in the words "knowingly permitted" in subs. 78K(3)(b) in relation to the owner or occupier of land A: if such a person becomes aware that their land has become contaminated by substances from other land and fails to take action which is within his power, he might be said to be knowingly permitting the substances to be there, in which case he would: (a) lose the protection of subs. (3); and (b) potentially be jointly liable with the person responsible for the escape, subject to apportionment under s.78F, and to any civil remedies available.

Subs. (4): liability in respect of onward migration
Having escaped from other land to land A, contamination may then migrate on to land B. In this situation the effect of subs. (4) is that the owner or the occupier of land A—provided he may not be said to have caused or knowingly permitted the substances to be in, on or under their land—will not be responsible for the remediation of land B unless he is also the owner or occupier of that land. In such circumstances the authority should be able to pursue either the original polluter who caused or knowingly permitted the substances to escape to land A (see s.78K(1)) or, if such person cannot be found, the owner or occupier of land B.

Subs. (5): escapes prior to acquiring land

The effect of subs. (5) is that a purchaser or new occupier of contaminated land should not be responsible for the remediation of other land in respect of contaminants which have previously escaped from his land to that land. In this way the purchaser/occupier (person B) is not responsible for the acts or omissions of their predecessor (person A) except to the extent that person B caused or knowingly permitted the escape. Person B may thus be responsible for remediation works necessary to prevent further escapes, or for remediation to clean up contamination which escapes after they acquired ownership or occupation. Remediation liability in respect of person B's own land may be based on being a knowing permitter or an owner/occupier; remediation liability in respect of other land can only arise where person B caused or knowingly permitted the escape. It is submitted that, in this respect, the specific drafting of subs. (5) should prevail over the more general principle of subs. (1), which might indicate that if person B is knowingly permitting the substances to be under his land after acquisition, he will be treated also as having knowingly permitted them to be under the land to which they appear to have escaped, even though he did not cause or knowingly permit the escape itself.

Subs. (6): remediation by authority

Subsections (3) to (5) may preclude a remediation notice being served or restrict what may be required, but they will not prevent the authority taking action itself under s.78N. The authority will, however, be restricted in the exercise of its cost recovery powers if it does take such action.

Appeals against remediation notices

78L.—(1) A person on whom a remediation notice is served may, within the period of twenty-one days beginning with the day on which the notice is served, appeal against the notice—

    (a) if it was served by a local authority, to a magistrates' court or, in Scotland, to the sheriff by way of summary application; or

    (b) if it was served by the appropriate Agency, to the Secretary of State;

and in the following provisions of this section "the appellate authority" means the magistrates' court, the sheriff or the Secretary of State, as the case may be.

    (2) On any appeal under subsection (1) above the appellate authority—

    (a) shall quash the notice, if it is satisfied that there is a material defect in the notice; but

    (b) subject to that, may confirm the remediation notice, with or without modification, or quash it.

    (3) Where an appellate authority confirms a remediation notice, with or without modification, it may extend the period specified in the notice for doing what the notice requires to be done.

    (4) Regulations may make provision with respect to—

    (a) the grounds on which appeals under subsection (1) above may be made;

    (b) the cases in which, grounds on which, court or tribunal to which, or person at whose instance, an appeal against a decision of a magistrates' court or sheriff court in pursuance of an appeal under subsection (1) above shall lie; or

    (c) the procedure on an appeal under subsection (1) above or on an appeal by virtue of paragraph (b) above.

    (5) Regulations under subsection (4) above may (among other things)—

    (a) include provisions comparable to those in section 290 of the Public Health Act 1936 (appeals against notices requiring the execution of works);

    (b) prescribe the cases in which a remediation notice is, or is not, to be suspended until the appeal is decided, or until some other stage in the proceedings;

(c) prescribe the cases in which the decision on an appeal may in some respects be less favourable to the appellant than the remediation notice against which he is appealing;

(d) prescribe the cases in which the appellant may claim that a remediation notice should have been served on some other person and prescribe the procedure to be followed in those cases;

(e) make provision as respects—

(i) the particulars to be included in the notice of appeal;

(ii) the persons on whom notice of appeal is to be served and the particulars, if any, which are to accompany the notice; and

(iii) the abandonment of an appeal;

(f) make different provision for different cases or classes of case.

(6) This section, so far as relating to appeals to the Secretary of State, is subject to section 114 of the Environment Act 1995 (delegation or reference of appeals etc).

DEFINITIONS

"appellate authority": s.78L(1) of the 1990 Act.
"appropriate Agency": s.78A(9) of the 1990 Act.
"local authority": s.78A(9) of the 1990 Act.
"notice": s.78A(9) of the 1990 Act.
"regulations" s.78A(9) of the 1990 Act.
"remediation notice": s.78(E)(1) of the 1990 Act.
"remediations": s.78A(7) of the 1990 Act.

COMMENCEMENT

September 21, 1995 insofar as this section confers power on the Secretary of State to make regulations or makes provision with respect to the exercise of such power (S.I. 1995 No. 1983). The remainder will be brought into force by a commencement order made under s.125(3) of the 1995 Act.

GENERAL NOTE

This section refers a right of appeal against a remediation notice. Appeal is to the magistrates' court (or sheriff court in Scotland: see further below) where the notice is served by a local authority, or to the Secretary of State where it is served by the Agency/SEPA. Regulations will be required as to the grounds of appeal and appeal procedure. One point of particular interest is subs. (4)(b), which allows the regulations to provide for appeals from the decision of the magistrates' or sheriff court other than on points of law.

It can be anticipated that, given the complexity of the issues involved, and the substantial sums likely to be at stake, the costs incurred in appeal proceedings in the magistrates' court may be considerable. The magistrates have a wide jurisdiction as to the award of costs under the Magistrates' Courts Act 1980 and a court is unlikely to interfere with their decision by way of judicial review unless it is perverse: see *R. v. Stipendiary Magistrate for Southend, ex p. Rochford District Council* [1995] Env. L.R. 1 (£75,000 costs awarded against authority in statutory nuisance case).

Scotland

The procedure for summary applications to the sheriff court in Scotland is currently governed by the Sheriff Court Summary Application Rules 1993 (S.I. 1993 No. 3240) which came into force on January 1, 1993. It appears that the regulations to be made under s.78L(4) with respect to appeals from the sheriff court will include a right of appeal to the Sheriff Principal and thence to the Inner House of the Court of Session (*per* Sir Hector Monro, Standing Committee B, May 23, 1995, col. 371).

Offences of not complying with a remediation notice

78M.—(1) If a person on whom an enforcing authority serves a remediation notice fails, without reasonable excuse, to comply with any of the requirements of the notice, he shall be guilty of an offence.

(2) Where the remediation notice in question is one which was required by section 78E(3) above to state, in relation to the requirement which has not been complied with, the proportion of the cost involved

which the person charged with the offence is liable to bear, it shall be a defence for that person to prove that the only reason why he has not complied with the requirement is that one or more of the other persons who are liable to bear a proportion of that cost refused, or was not able, to comply with the requirement.

(3) Except in a case falling within subsection (4) below, a person who commits an offence under subsection (1) above shall be liable, on summary conviction, to a fine not exceeding level 5 on the standard scale and to a further fine of an amount equal to one-tenth of level 5 on the standard scale for each day on which the failure continues after conviction of the offence and before the enforcing authority has begun to exercise its powers by virtue of section 78N(3)(c) below.

(4) A person who commits an offence under subsection (1) above in a case where the contaminated land to which the remediation notice relates is industrial, trade or business premises shall be liable on summary conviction to a fine not exceeding £20,000 or such greater sum as the Secretary of State may from time to time by order substitute and to a further fine of an amount equal to one-tenth of that sum for each day on which the failure continues after conviction of the offence and before the enforcing authority has begun to exercise its powers by virtue of section 78N(3)(c) below.

(5) If the enforcing authority is of the opinion that proceedings for an offence under this section would afford an ineffectual remedy against a person who has failed to comply with any of the requirements of a remediation notice which that authority has served on him, that authority may take proceedings in the High Court or, in Scotland, in any court of competent jurisdiction, for the purpose of securing compliance with the remediation notice.

(6) In this section, "industrial, trade or business premises" means premises used for any industrial, trade or business purposes or premises not so used on which matter is burnt in connection with any industrial, trade or business process, and premises are used for industrial purposes where they are used for the purposes of any treatment or process as well as where they are used for the purpose of manufacturing.

(7) No order shall be made under subsection (4) above unless a draft of the order has been laid before, and approved by a resolution of, each House of Parliament.

DEFINITIONS
"enforcing authority": s.78A(9) of the 1990 Act.
"industrial trade or business premises": subs. (6).
"remediation notice": s.78E(1) of the 1990 Act.

COMMENCEMENT
September 21, 1995 insofar as this section confers power on the Secretary of State to make orders or makes provision with respect to the exercise of such power (S.I. 1995 No. 1983). The remainder will be brought into force by a commencement order made under s.125(3) of the 1995 Act.

GENERAL NOTE
This section creates the offence of failure to comply, without reasonable excuse, with any of the requirements of a remediation notice. The main penalty is a fine, but a daily fine is also payable for each day that the offence continues between conviction and the date (if any) on which the authority begins to exercise its own default clean-up powers under s.78N. Separate penalties are prescribed for cases where the contaminated land to which the notice relates is industrial, trade or business premises (see below).

Subs. (1): "without reasonable excuse"
Lack of funds to complete the work required to comply with the notice is unlikely to constitute "reasonable excuse": see *Saddleworth U.D.C. v. Aggregate and Sand* (1990) 114 S.J. 931. The

same case leaves it unclear whether reliance on the advice of an expert can be a reasonable excuse. Where access to land for remediation purposes is required but refused, the appropriate person will presumably have to resort to legal action on the basis of s.78G(2) to secure the grant of the necessary rights: in the absence of such efforts it may be difficult for an appropriate person to argue that such refusal of access constitutes a reasonable excuse.

Subs. (2): defence of non-co-operation by other liable persons

Subsection (2) recognises that in cases where two or more persons are appropriate persons in relation to a single aspect of remediation and are liable each to pay a proportion of the cost, it may be impossible for one party alone to comply with the notice if the other does not pay their proportion. In many cases compliance with the notice will presumably involve entering into contracts with consultants, engineers or contractors. A responsible party will not wish to be committed contractually to the cost of remediation until he is satisfied that a contribution is likely to be forthcoming from the other responsible parties. The onus of making out this defence rests with the defendant, since as it is worded he has to "prove" certain matters. The standard of proof which he has to meet is that of the balance of probabilities: *Islington London Borough Council v. Panico* [1973] 3 All E.R. 485 and, in Scotland, *Neish v. Stevenson* 1969 SLT 229. It would therefore be prudent for the recipient of a remediation notice seeking to rely on the defence to demonstrate that tenders have been obtained for the works, that attempts have been made to invite the other responsible party or parties to contribute, and that the defendant is willing and able to contribute his share.

Subss. (3) and (4): penalties where land is industrial, trade or business premises

Where the contaminated land in question is industrial, trade or business premises (as defined in subs. (6)) the maximum fine and daily fine on summary conviction are both higher than those applicable to other contaminated land. The maximum fine is £20,000, and this figure may be increased by the Secretary of State. It should be noted that the court has discretion over the initial fine but no discretion over the level of the daily fine of £2,000; in principle, therefore, it would appear that a conviction could result in a fine of as little as £500 plus a daily fine of £2,000.

For other land, the maximum fine is £5,000, and accordingly the daily fine is a fixed £500.

Subs. (5): civil proceedings

The authority may enforce compliance with a remediation notice by civil proceedings where it is of the opinion that a criminal prosecution would provide an ineffectual remedy. This is a common form provision, the usual purpose of which is to allow an authority to use injunctive proceedings. Given that a remediation notice will normally impose positive requirements, the appropriate civil remedy would appear to be a mandatory injunction.

In Scotland, civil proceedings may be brought in either the sheriff court or the Court of Session for securing compliance with a remediation notice. Since a remediation notice is unlikely to impose negative requirements, the proceedings brought would usually be for specific implement or *ad factum praestandum* rather than interdict.

Powers of the enforcing authority to carry out remediation

78N.—(1) Where this section applies, the enforcing authority shall itself have power, in a case falling within paragraph (a) or (b) of section 78E(1) above, to do what is appropriate by way of remediation to the relevant land or waters.

(2) Subsection (1) above shall not confer power on the enforcing authority to do anything by way of remediation if the authority would, in the particular case, be precluded by section 78YB below from serving a remediation notice requiring that thing to be done.

(3) This section applies in each of the following cases, that is to say—

(a) where the enforcing authority considers it necessary to do anything itself by way of remediation for the purpose of preventing the occurrence of any serious harm, or serious pollution of controlled waters, of which there is imminent danger;

(b) where an appropriate person has entered into a written agreement with the enforcing authority for that authority to do, at the cost of that person, that which he would otherwise be required to do under this Part by way of remediation;

(c) where a person on whom the enforcing authority serves a remediation notice fails to comply with any of the requirements of the notice;

(d) where the enforcing authority is precluded by section 78J or 78K above from including something by way of remediation in a remediation notice;

(e) where the enforcing authority considers that, were it to do some particular thing by way of remediation, it would decide, by virtue of subsection (2) of section 78P below or any guidance issued under that subsection,—

(i) not to seek to recover under subsection (1) of that section any of the reasonable cost incurred by it in doing that thing; or

(ii) to seek so to recover only a portion of that cost;

(f) where no person has, after reasonable inquiry, been found who is an appropriate person in relation to any particular thing.

(4) Subject to section 78E(4) and (5) above, for the purposes of this section, the things which it is appropriate for the enforcing authority to do by way of remediation are—

(a) in a case falling within paragraph (a) of subsection (3) above, anything by way of remediation which the enforcing authority considers necessary for the purpose mentioned in that paragraph;

(b) in a case falling within paragraph (b) of that subsection, anything specified in, or determined under, the agreement mentioned in that paragraph;

(c) in a case falling within paragraph (c) of that subsection, anything which the person mentioned in that paragraph was required to do by virtue of the remediation notice;

(d) in a case falling within paragraph (d) of that subsection, anything by way of remediation which the enforcing authority is precluded by section 78J or 78K above from including in a remediation notice;

(e) in a case falling within paragraph (e) or (f) of that subsection, the particular thing mentioned in the paragraph in question.

(5) In this section "the relevant land or waters" means—

(a) the contaminated land in question;

(b) any controlled waters affected by that land; or

(c) any land adjoining or adjacent to that land or those waters.

DEFINITIONS

"appropriate person": s.78A(9) of the 1990 Act.
"contaminated land": s.78A(2) of the 1990 Act.
"controlled waters": s.78A(9) of the 1990 Act.
"enforcing authority": s.78A(9) of the 1990 Act.
"harm": s.78A(4) of the 1990 Act.
"notice": s.78A(9) of the 1990 Act.
"pollution of controlled waters": s.78A(9) of the 1990 Act.
"relevant land or waters": subs. (5).
"remediation": s.78A(7) of the 1990 Act.
"remediation notice": s.78E(1) of the 1990 Act.

COMMENCEMENT

These provisions will be brought into force by a commencement order made under s.125(3) of the 1995 Act.

GENERAL NOTE

This section confers upon the local authority (or Agency/SEPA, in relation to special sites) power to carry out appropriate remediation itself, provided that: (a) the land has been identified as contaminated land or designated as a special site (subs. (1)); (b) service of a remediation notice would not be precluded by s.78YB (subs. (2)); and (c) one of the cases specified in subs. (3) applies.

Subs. (3): cases where the section applies

These cases (a) to (f) are generally self-explanatory and do not require comment. Paragraph (b) provides a potentially useful method of securing voluntary remediation, though whether such agreements will be popular with responsible persons remains to be seen; enforcing authorities may themselves also be concerned at the potential liability implications of assuming responsibility for clean-up, and such an agreement may be more appropriate where the remediation action in question consists of monitoring. Paragraph (c) clearly provides an important default power, and para. (f) can be used for "orphan sites" where no appropriate person at all (including an owner) can be found. It should be noted in relation to para. (e), which deals with hardship, that the authority may itself act in cases not only where there is "total hardship" (*i.e.* the authority would not seek to recover any of its costs) but also "partial hardship" where it would seek to recover its costs in part.

Subs. (4): appropriate action

This subsection defines those things which it will be appropriate for the authority to do in each case. The precise wording is important, since this may limit the authority's power to recover its costs subsequently under s.78P. For example, if under para. (c) the authority in carrying out remediation goes beyond the requirements of the remediation notice, it may not be able to recover its costs (or at least not its full costs).

Recovery of, and security for, the cost of remediation by the enforcing authority

78P.—(1) Where, by virtue of section 78N(3)(a), (c), (e) or (f) above, the enforcing authority does any particular thing by way of remediation, it shall be entitled, subject to sections 78J(7) and 78K(6) above, to recover the reasonable cost incurred in doing it from the appropriate person or, if there are two or more appropriate persons in relation to the thing in question, from those persons in proportions determined pursuant to section 78F(7) above.

(2) In deciding whether to recover the cost, and, if so, how much of the cost, which it is entitled to recover under subsection (1) above, the enforcing authority shall have regard—

    (a) to any hardship which the recovery may cause to the person from whom the cost is recoverable; and

    (b) to any guidance issued by the Secretary of State for the purposes of this subsection.

(3) Subsection (4) below shall apply in any case where—

    (a) any cost is recoverable under subsection (1) above from a person—

        (i) who is the owner of any premises which consist of or include the contaminated land in question; and

        (ii) who caused or knowingly permitted the substances, or any of the substances, by reason of which the land is contaminated land to be in, on or under the land; and

    (b) the enforcing authority serves a notice under this subsection (in this Part referred to as a "charging notice") on that person.

(4) Where this subsection applies—

    (a) the cost shall carry interest, at such reasonable rate as the enforcing authority may determine, from the date of service of the notice until the whole amount is paid; and

    (b) subject to the following provisions of this section, the cost and accrued interest shall be a charge on the premises mentioned in subsection (3)(a)(i) above.

(5) A charging notice shall—

(a) specify the amount of the cost which the enforcing authority claims is recoverable;

(b) state the effect of subsection (4) above and the rate of interest determined by the authority under that subsection; and

(c) state the effect of subsections (7) and (8) below.

(6) On the date on which an enforcing authority serves a charging notice on a person, the authority shall also serve a copy of the notice on every other person who, to the knowledge of the authority, has an interest in the premises capable of being affected by the charge.

(7) Subject to any order under subsection (9)(b) or (c) below, the amount of any cost specified in a charging notice and the accrued interest shall be a charge on the premises—

(a) as from the end of the period of twenty-one days beginning with the service of the charging notice, or

(b) where an appeal is brought under subsection (8) below, as from the final determination or (as the case may be) the withdrawal, of the appeal,

until the cost and interest are recovered.

(8) A person served with a charging notice or a copy of a charging notice may appeal against the notice to a county court within the period of twenty-one days beginning with the date of service.

(9) On an appeal under subsection (8) above, the court may—

(a) confirm the notice without modification;

(b) order that the notice is to have effect with the substitution of a different amount for the amount originally specified in it; or

(c) order that the notice is to be of no effect.

(10) Regulations may make provision with respect to—

(a) the grounds on which appeals under this section may be made; or

(b) the procedure on any such appeal.

(11) An enforcing authority shall, for the purpose of enforcing a charge under this section, have all the same powers and remedies under the Law of Property Act 1925, and otherwise, as if it were a mortgagee by deed having powers of sale and lease, of accepting surrenders of leases and of appointing a receiver.

(12) Where any cost is a charge on premises under this section, the enforcing authority may by order declare the cost to be payable with interest by instalments within the specified period until the whole amount is paid.

(13) In subsection (12) above—

"interest" means interest at the rate determined by the enforcing authority under subsection (4) above; and

"the specified period" means such period of thirty years or less from the date of service of the charging notice as is specified in the order.

(14) Subsections (3) to (13) above do not extend to Scotland.

DEFINITIONS

"appropriate person": s.78A(9) of the 1990 Act.

"charging notice": subs. (3)(b).

"contaminated land": s.78A(2) of the 1990 Act.

"enforcing authority": s.78A(9) of the 1990 Act.

"interest": subs. (13).

"regulations": s.78A(9) of the 1990 Act.

"specified period": subs. (13).

"substance": s.78A(9) of the 1990 Act.

COMMENCEMENT

September 21, 1995 insofar as this section confers power on the Secretary of State to issue guidance or make regulations or makes provision with respect to the exercise of such power (S.I.

1995 No. 1983). The remainder will be brought into force by a commencement order made under s.125(3) of the 1995 Act.

<small>GENERAL NOTE</small>

This section provides the "teeth" in relation to s.78N, namely a power in certain cases for the enforcing authority to recover its reasonable costs of taking appropriate remedial action under that section, together with charging powers in relation to property. The provisions do not apply in all cases where action is taken under s.78N (nor would it be appropriate for them to do so). In particular they do not apply where the specific immunities in ss.78J and K are applicable or where there is a written agreement for the authority to carry out remediation (since, obviously, the authority can recover its costs under that agreement).

Limitations on costs recovery

The costs recoverable will be limited by:
(a) whether the notice was "appropriate" action under s.78N;
(b) whether the costs incurred were reasonable (subs. (1));
(c) apportionments where there are two or more appropriate persons involved (subs. (1));
(d) hardship which recovery might cause (subs. (2)(a)); and
(e) any guidance issued by the Secretary of State (subs. (2)(b)).

Charging notice

Under subs. (3) the authority may serve a charging notice in certain circumstances. These provisions do not apply to Scotland (subs. (14): see the note to that subsection). The notice may only be served on a person from whom costs are recoverable who: (a) is the owner of any premises consisting of or including the contaminated land; *and* (b) caused or knowingly permitted the contaminating substances to be in, on or under the land.

Such notice cannot therefore be served on an occupier, or on an original polluter who is no longer owner. Whether it can be served on an owner who acquires already contaminated property depends on whether they can be said to have knowingly permitted the substances to be in the land; a question discussed under s.78F at p. 25–153, above.

Effect of charging notice

A charging notice has three effects: (a) the remedial cost then carries interest (subs. (4)(a)); (b) the cost and accrued interest are a statutory charge on the premises (subss. (4)(b) and (7)); and (c) the authority may by order declare the cost to be payable by instalments (subs. (12)) over a period of up to 30 years (subs. (13)).

Procedure for charging notices

A charging notice must specify the amount of the cost which the authority claims is recoverable, together with the explanatory matters referred to in subs. (5). A copy must be served contemporaneously on every other person who, to the knowledge of the authority, has an interest in the premises capable of being affected by the charge (subs. (6)). There is no express obligation on the authority to make inquiry to discover such persons, though many such interests could presumably be discovered readily enough by a land registry or land charges search. A right of appeal against a charging notice (to the county court) is provided by subs. (8), on such grounds and under such procedures as may be provided for by regulations: subs. (10).

Effect and priority of statutory charge

A statutory charge under s.78P may be enforced by the powers and remedies of sale, lease and receivership available to a mortgagee by deed under the Law of Property Act 1925 (see subs. (11)). The statutory charge is a charge on "the premises" (subs. (6)) "consisting of or including" (subs. (3)(a)(i)) the contaminated land. This raises the question of what constitutes "the premises" where these may be greater in extent than the contaminated area—a possibility which subs. (3)(a)(i) acknowledges. Where a charging notice may be served, there appears to be nothing to prevent the enforcing authority serving a notice charging the whole of any premises in the ownership of the same person, provided that those premises include the previously contaminated land. Such premises may be far more valuable than the part of it which had been contaminated, and this is an important protection for the enforcing authority.

The second question is how the statutory charge rates in terms of priority with existing mortgages. If the wording were a charge "on the land", on the authority of *Westminster City Council v. Haymarket Publishing* [1981] 2 All E.R. 555 it could be said that the charge is on all the estates and interests in the land, including prior mortgages. The wording here is "premises", but in fact this phraseology was used in earlier statutes and was held to have the effect of charging all proprietary interests in a series of cases followed in the *Westminster City Council* case: see *Birmingham Corpn. v. Baker* (1881) 17 Ch. D. 782, *Tendring Union Guardians v. Dowton* [1891] 3 Ch. 265 and *Paddington Borough Council v. Finucane* [1928] Ch. 567. The conclusion thus seems inescapable that the statutory charge will affect, and take priority over, all existing mortgages, charges, options and other legal or equitable estates or interests in land, and this is another important protection for the enforcing authority.

Subs. (14): Scotland

Although the cost recovery provisions (subss. (1) and (2)) extend to Scotland, the charging powers in relation to property do not. However, there seems in principle no reason why subss. (3) to (13) should not have been extended to Scotland and amendments were introduced in Parliament to that effect albeit unsuccessfully: *e.g. Hansard*, H.L. Vol. 562, col. 250. Explaining its refusal to accept these amendments, the Government stated that existing mechanisms for recovering sums due under Scots law were adequate and that the amendments would require Scotland to change its system of conveyancing: *Hansard*, H.L. Vol. 562, col. 221 *per* the Earl of Lindsay; see also Standing Committee B, May 23, 1995, col. 368 *per* Sir Hector Monro, Parliamentary Under-Secretary of State for Scotland; and *Hansard*, H.C. Vol. 262, col. 959 *per* Sir Paul Beresford. This reasoning appears to be highly unsatisfactory as statutory charging orders are by no means a new concept in Scots law as was indeed pointed out in Parliament: Standing Committee B, May 23, 1995, col. 364 *per* Sam Galbraith. For example, the Building (Scotland) Act 1959, Sched. 6, the Sewerage (Scotland) Act 1968, s.47, the Water (Scotland) Act 1980, s.65, the Civic Government (Scotland) Act 1982, s.102, and the Housing (Scotland) Act 1987, Sched. 9 all make provision for charging orders. Primarily these charges may be created by local authorities in relation to works carried out as, for example, under the Building (Scotland) Act 1959 and the Housing (Scotland) Act 1987. Since their existence has not required the reform of the system of conveyancing in Scotland, it is not easy to understand the Government's refusal to give Scottish local authorities the power to make charging orders for remediation costs in relation to contaminated land. It may as a result be significantly more difficult for enforcing authorities to recover their costs in Scotland than in England and Wales although this would to a degree have been true in any event: unlike the English provisions which as noted above give the enforcing authority the same power as a mortgagee under the Law of Property Act 1925, the charging order provisions in the Scottish statutes do not put the enforcing authority in the same position as a heritable creditor under the Conveyancing and Feudal Reform (Scotland) Act 1970. They merely provide, if the charge is registered as appropriate, for the burdening of the property concerned with an annuity to pay the amount due. In the absence of provisions for charging orders in Scotland, local authorities will be required to rely on standard court procedures and methods of diligence such as inhibition and adjudication. These methods of diligence are not ideal. For example, inhibition may only be used against the owner of the property and is merely a means of preventing its sale until the debt secured is paid. Furthermore, adjudication involves a rather lengthy and complex procedure.

Special sites

78Q.—(1) If, in a case where a local authority has served a remediation notice, the contaminated land in question becomes a special site, the appropriate Agency may adopt the remediation notice and, if it does so,—

    (a) it shall give notice of its decision to adopt the remediation notice to the appropriate person and to the local authority;

    (b) the remediation notice shall have effect, as from the time at which the appropriate Agency decides to adopt it, as a remediation notice given by that Agency; and

    (c) the validity of the remediation notice shall not be affected by—

        (i) the contaminated land having become a special site;

        (ii) the adoption of the remediation notice by the appropriate Agency; or

        (iii) anything in paragraph (b) above.

(2) Where a local authority has, by virtue of section 78N above, begun to do any thing, or any series of things, by way of remediation—

    (a) the authority may continue doing that thing, or that series of things, by virtue of that section, notwithstanding that the contaminated land in question becomes a special site; and

(b) section 78P above shall apply in relation to the reasonable cost incurred by the authority in doing that thing or those things as if that authority were the enforcing authority.

(3) If and so long as any land is a special site, the appropriate Agency may from time to time inspect that land for the purpose of keeping its condition under review.

(4) If it appears to the appropriate Agency that a special site is no longer land which is required to be designated as such a site, the appropriate Agency may give notice—

(a) to the Secretary of State, and

(b) to the local authority in whose area the site is situated,

terminating the designation of the land in question as a special site as from such date as may be specified in the notice.

(5) A notice under subsection (4) above shall not prevent the land, or any of the land, to which the notice relates being designated as a special site on a subsequent occasion.

(6) In exercising its functions under subsection (3) or (4) above, the appropriate Agency shall act in accordance with any guidance given for the purpose by the Secretary of State.

DEFINITIONS
"appropriate Agency": s.78A(9) of the 1990 Act.
"appropriate person": s.78E(1) of the 1990 Act.
"contaminated land": s.78A(2) of the 1990 Act.
"local authority": s.78A(9) of the 1990 Act.
"remediation": s.78A(7) of the 1990 Act.
"remediation notice": s.78E(1) of the 1990 Act.
"required to be designated as a special site": s.78C(8) of the 1990 Act.
"special site": s.78A(3) of the 1990 Act.

COMMENCEMENT
September 21, 1995 insofar as this section confers power on the Secretary of State to issue guidance or makes provision with respect to the exercise of such power (S.I. 1995 No. 1983). The remainder will be brought into force by a commencement order made under s.125(3) of the 1995 Act.

GENERAL NOTE
This section contains provisions dealing specifically with special sites and the change in status of land as regards that designation.

Subss. (1) and (2): transition to special site
These subsections make provision for the case where land has been identified as contaminated and enforcement action has begun, either under s.78E or s.78N, and the land then becomes designated as a special site. The Agency/SEPA becomes the enforcing authority and may elect to adopt any remediation notice served (subs. (1)), but the local authority may continue to do things which have already been commenced under s.78N and recover costs under s.78P in respect of such things.

It may be a corollary of subs. (1)(c)(ii) that the validity of a remediation notice served by the local authority prior to a site's designation as a special site *is* affected by the Agency/SEPA choosing *not* to adopt the notice. Even if this is not the case, the local authority, no longer the enforcing authority, cannot enforce the notice. However, there are two ways in which a remediation notice served by the local authority prior to the site becoming a special site might continue to affect the appropriate person under the notice. First, if in fact the site becoming a special site does *not* affect the validity of the notice, then nothing in s.78M (the offences section of Pt. IIA) prevents a private individual or a local or environmental group bringing a private prosecution against an appropriate person for failure to comply with the remediation notice (in Scotland, however, the consent of the Lord Advocate would be required for such a prosecution and hence it is a very remote possibility north of the border). It may be, however, that the unusual circumstances envisaged here would have a bearing on whether the courts accepted that that person had a "reasonable excuse" (s.78M(1)) for the non-compliance.

Secondly, subs. (2), which gives the local authority the power to continue remediation it has already commenced, gives a limited scope for continued involvement by a local authority with a special site. Subsection (2) does not appear to distinguish between circumstances where the Agency/SEPA has or has not adopted any notice. Subject to the power of the Agency/SEPA to give the local authority site specific guidance under s.78V, it would appear that the local authority could press on with remediation which was already underway when the site became a special site, and then seek to recover its costs under subs. (2)(b). Such remediation work might, although it need not, have been commenced following non-compliance with the notice by the appropriate person, and the cost recovery position appears unaffected by whether or not the Agency/SEPA subsequently adopts the notice. As to how far the local authority can continue, it will be noted that it is allowed to continue any "series of things" it has begun to do: subs. (2)(a).

Subs. (3): inspection of special sites
The Agency/SEPA has the power to inspect special sites for keeping their condition under review. The power is to be exercised in accordance with guidance from the Secretary of State (subs. (6)).

Subss. (4) and (5): termination of designation as special site
These subsections provide a procedure whereby designation of land as a special site may be terminated at the instigation of the Agency/SEPA. Following termination of such designation, the land may of course continue to be contaminated land. Termination of designation will not prevent redesignation as a special site subsequently (subs. (5)). The power to terminate designation is to be exercised in accordance with the Secretary of State's guidance (subs. (6)).

Registers
78R.—(1) Every enforcing authority shall maintain a register containing prescribed particulars of or relating to—
   (a) remediation notices served by that authority;
   (b) appeals against any such remediation notices;
   (c) remediation statements or remediation declarations prepared and published under section 78H above;
   (d) in relation to an enforcing authority in England and Wales, appeals against charging notices served by that authority;
   (e) notices under subsection (1)(b) or (5)(a) of section 78C above which have effect by virtue of subsection (7) of that section as the designation of any land as a special site;
   (f) notices under subsection (4)(b) of section 78D above which have effect by virtue of subsection (6) of that section as the designation of any land as a special site;
   (g) notices given by or to the enforcing authority under section 78Q (4) above terminating the designation of any land as a special site;
   (h) notifications given to that authority by persons—
          (i) on whom a remediation notice has been served, or
          (ii) who are or were required by virtue of section 78H(8)(a) above to prepare and publish a remediation statement,
       of what they claim has been done by them by way of remediation;
   (j) notifications given to that authority by owners or occupiers of land—
          (i) in respect of which a remediation notice has been served, or
          (ii) in respect of which a remediation statement has been prepared and published,
       of what they claim has been done on the land in question by way of remediation;
   (k) convictions for such offences under section 78M above as may be prescribed;
   (l) such other matters relating to contaminated land as may be prescribed;
but that duty is subject to sections 78S and 78T below.
   (2) The form of, and the descriptions of information to be contained in, notifications for the purposes of subsection (1)(h) or (j) above may be prescribed by the Secretary of State.

(3) No entry made in a register by virtue of subsection (1)(h) or (j) above constitutes a representation by the body maintaining the register or, in a case where the entry is made by virtue of subsection (6) below, the authority which sent the copy of the particulars in question pursuant to subsection (4) or (5) below—

(a) that what is stated in the entry to have been done has in fact been done; or

(b) as to the manner in which it has been done.

(4) Where any particulars are entered on a register maintained under this section by the appropriate Agency, the appropriate Agency shall send a copy of those particulars to the local authority in whose area is situated the land to which the particulars relate.

(5) In any case where—

(a) any land is treated by virtue of section 78X(2) below as situated in the area of a local authority other than the local authority in whose area it is in fact situated, and

(b) any particulars relating to that land are entered on the register maintained under this section by the local authority in whose area the land is so treated as situated,

that authority shall send a copy of those particulars to the local authority in whose area the land is in fact situated.

(6) Where a local authority receives a copy of any particulars sent to it pursuant to subsection (4) or (5) above, it shall enter those particulars on the register maintained by it under this section.

(7) Where information of any description is excluded by virtue of section 78T below from any register maintained under this section, a statement shall be entered in the register indicating the existence of information of that description.

(8) It shall be the duty of each enforcing authority—

(a) to secure that the registers maintained by it under this section are available, at all reasonable times, for inspection by the public free of charge; and

(b) to afford to members of the public facilities for obtaining copies of entries, on payment of reasonable charges;

and, for the purposes of this subsection, places may be prescribed by the Secretary of State at which any such registers or facilities as are mentioned in paragraph (a) or (b) above are to be available or afforded to the public in pursuance of the paragraph in question.

(9) Registers under this section may be kept in any form.

DEFINITIONS
"appropriate Agency": s.78A(9) of the 1990 Act.
"charging notice": s.78P(3)(b) of the 1990 Act.
"enforcing authority": s.78A(9) of the 1990 Act.
"local authority": s.78A(9) of the 1990 Act.
"notification": s.78A(9) of the 1990 Act.
"prescribed": s.78A(9) of the 1990 Act.
"remediation": s.78A(7) of the 1990 Act.
"remediation declaration": s.78H(6) of the 1990 Act.
"remediation notice": s.78E(1) of the 1990 Act.
"remediation statement": s.78H(7) of the 1990 Act.
"special site": s.78A(3) of the 1990 Act.

COMMENCEMENT
September 21, 1995 insofar as this section confers power on the Secretary of State to make regulations or makes provision with respect to the exercise of such power (S.I. 1995 No. 1983). The remainder will be brought into force by a commencement order made under s.125(3) of the 1995 Act.

GENERAL NOTE

Registers are to be maintained by local authorities (or the Agency/SEPA in the case of special sites) containing particulars relating to the matters specified in subs. (1). Particulars relating to special sites are also to be kept on the relevant local register: subss. (4) and (6).

Details of remedial action

Most of the matters to be contained in the registers relate to notices, notifications and the like, and are self-explanatory. However, paras. (h) and (j) of subs. (1) stand on a somewhat different footing. They require the authority to place on the register notifications by appropriate persons and owners or occupiers of what they claim has been done by way of remediation.

These paragraphs were inserted by a Government amendment in response to an amendment proposed by the Law Society of England and Wales and provide a means by which an appropriate person, owner or occupier can record in a public form what has been done to comply with a remediation notice or remediation statement. In this way some of the blight which might otherwise affect the land may be alleviated. However, it is important to note subs. (3), which negatives any implied representation by the authority that what is stated on the register as having been done has in fact been done, or has been done adequately. The authority's role is therefore simply one of a "postbox", recording notification which it receives: as it was put in debate, it is not the responsibility of the enforcing authority to indicate that the land has "a clean bill of health" (*Hansard*, H.L. Vol. 562, col. 1047, Viscount Ullswater).

Exclusion from registers of information affecting national security

78S.—(1) No information shall be included in a register maintained under section 78R above if and so long as, in the opinion of the Secretary of State, the inclusion in the register of that information, or information of that description, would be contrary to the interests of national security.

(2) The Secretary of State may, for the purpose of securing the exclusion from registers of information to which subsection (1) above applies, give to enforcing authorities directions—

(a) specifying information, or descriptions of information, to be excluded from their registers; or

(b) specifying descriptions of information to be referred to the Secretary of State for his determination;

and no information referred to the Secretary of State in pursuance of paragraph (b) above shall be included in any such register until the Secretary of State determines that it should be so included.

(3) The enforcing authority shall notify the Secretary of State of any information which it excludes from the register in pursuance of directions under subsection (2) above.

(4) A person may, as respects any information which appears to him to be information to which subsection (1) above may apply, give a notice to the Secretary of State specifying the information and indicating its apparent nature; and, if he does so—

(a) he shall notify the enforcing authority that he has done so; and

(b) no information so notified to the Secretary of State shall be included in any such register until the Secretary of State has determined that it should be so included.

DEFINITIONS

"enforcing authority": s.78A(9) of the 1990 Act.
"notice": s.78A(9) of the 1990 Act.

COMMENCEMENT

September 21, 1995 insofar as this section confers power on the Secretary of State to give directions or makes provision with respect to the exercise of such power (S.I. 1995 No. 1983). The remainder will be brought into force by a commencement order made under s.125(3) of the 1995 Act.

GENERAL NOTE

This section provides a means of excluding from the public registers under s.78R information the disclosure of which would be contrary to national security.

Exclusion from registers of certain confidential information

78T.—(1) No information relating to the affairs of any individual or business shall be included in a register maintained under section 78R above, without the consent of that individual or the person for the time being carrying on that business, if and so long as the information—

(a) is, in relation to him, commercially confidential; and

(b) is not required to be included in the register in pursuance of directions under subsection (7) below;

but information is not commercially confidential for the purposes of this section unless it is determined under this section to be so by the enforcing authority or, on appeal, by the Secretary of State.

(2) Where it appears to an enforcing authority that any information which has been obtained by the authority under or by virtue of any provision of this Part might be commercially confidential, the authority shall—

(a) give to the person to whom or whose business it relates notice that that information is required to be included in the register unless excluded under this section; and

(b) give him a reasonable opportunity—

(i) of objecting to the inclusion of the information on the ground that it is commercially confidential; and

(ii) of making representations to the authority for the purpose of justifying any such objection;

and, if any representations are made, the enforcing authority shall, having taken the representations into account, determine whether the information is or is not commercially confidential.

(3) Where, under subsection (2) above, an authority determines that information is not commercially confidential—

(a) the information shall not be entered in the register until the end of the period of twenty-one days beginning with the date on which the determination is notified to the person concerned;

(b) that person may appeal to the Secretary of State against the decision;

and, where an appeal is brought in respect of any information, the information shall not be entered in the register until the end of the period of seven days following the day on which the appeal is finally determined or withdrawn.

(4) An appeal under subsection (3) above shall, if either party to the appeal so requests or the Secretary of State so decides, take or continue in the form of a hearing (which must be held in private).

(5) Subsection (10) of section 15 above shall apply in relation to an appeal under subsection (3) above as it applies in relation to an appeal under that section.

(6) Subsection (3) above is subject to section 114 of the Environment Act 1995 (delegation or reference of appeals etc.).

(7) The Secretary of State may give to the enforcing authorities directions as to specified information, or descriptions of information, which the public interest requires to be included in registers maintained under section 78R above notwithstanding that the information may be commercially confidential.

(8) Information excluded from a register shall be treated as ceasing to be commercially confidential for the purposes of this section at the expiry of the period of four years beginning with the date of the determination by virtue of which it was excluded; but the person who furnished it may apply to the authority for the information to remain excluded from the register on the ground that it is still commercially confidential and the authority shall determine whether or not that is the case.

(9) Subsections (3) to (6) above shall apply in relation to a determination under subsection (8) above as they apply in relation to a determination under subsection (2) above.

(10) Information is, for the purposes of any determination under this section, commercially confidential, in relation to any individual or person, if its being contained in the register would prejudice to an unreasonable degree the commercial interests of that individual or person.

(11) For the purposes of subsection (10) above, there shall be disregarded any prejudice to the commercial interests of any individual or person so far as relating only to the value of the contaminated land in question or otherwise to the ownership or occupation of that land.

DEFINITIONS
"contaminated land": s.78A(2) of the 1990 Act.
"enforcing authority": s.78A(9) of the 1990 Act.
"owner": s.78A(9) of the 1990 Act.

COMMENCEMENT
September 21, 1995 insofar as this section confers power on the Secretary of State to give directions or makes provision with respect to the exercise of such power (S.I. 1995 No. 1983). The remainder will be brought into force by a commencement order made under s.125(3) of the 1995 Act.

GENERAL NOTE
This section provides safeguards against disclosure on the register of information which is determined to be commercially confidential in relation to the affairs of any individual or business. Information which is excluded from the register on that basis will only be treated as confidential for a period of four years, subject to any application for it to remain excluded: subs. (8).

The meaning of commercial confidentiality
The test of what is commercially confidential is set out at subs. (10) and depends on whether entry on the register would prejudice the commercial interests of the relevant person or business to an unreasonable degree. One of the most likely ways in which such prejudice might be expected to occur is a negative effect on the value of the land or on its use or development. However, prejudice relating solely to land value or to the ownership or occupation of the land is to be disregarded (subs. (11)).

Reports by the appropriate Agency on the state of contaminated land
78U.—(1) The appropriate Agency shall—
(a) from time to time, or
(b) if the Secretary of State at any time so requests,
prepare and publish a report on the state of contaminated land in England and Wales or in Scotland, as the case may be.

(2) A local authority shall, at the written request of the appropriate Agency, furnish the appropriate Agency with such information to which this subsection applies as the appropriate Agency may require for the purpose of enabling it to perform its functions under subsection (1) above.

(3) The information to which subsection (2) above applies is such information as the local authority may have, or may reasonably be expected to obtain, with respect to the condition of contaminated land in its area, being information which the authority has acquired or may acquire in the exercise of its functions under this Part.

DEFINITIONS
"appropriate Agency": s.78A(9) of the 1990 Act.
"contaminated land": s.78A(2) of the 1990 Act.
"local authority": s.78A(9) of the 1990 Act.

COMMENCEMENT
These provisions will be brought into force by a commencement order made under s.125(3) of the 1995 Act.

GENERAL NOTE
The Agency/SEPA is given the responsibility of producing and publishing reports on the state of contaminated land on a national basis. Local authorities are required to co-operate in this by providing relevant information: subss. (2) and (3).

Site-specific guidance by the appropriate Agency concerning contaminated land

78V.—(1) The appropriate Agency may issue guidance to any local authority with respect to the exercise or performance of the authority's powers or duties under this Part in relation to any particular contaminated land; and in exercising or performing those powers or duties in relation to that land the authority shall have regard to any such guidance so issued.

(2) If and to the extent that any guidance issued under subsection (1) above to a local authority is inconsistent with any guidance issued under this Part by the Secretary of State, the local authority shall disregard the guidance under that subsection.

(3) A local authority shall, at the written request of the appropriate Agency, furnish the appropriate Agency with such information to which this subsection applies as the appropriate Agency may require for the purpose of enabling it to issue guidance for the purposes of subsection (1) above.

(4) The information to which subsection (3) above applies is such information as the local authority may have, or may reasonably be expected to obtain, with respect to any contaminated land in its area, being information which the authority has acquired, or may acquire, in the exercise of its functions under this Part.

DEFINITIONS
"appropriate Agency": s.78A(9) of the 1990 Act.
"contaminated land": s.78A(2) of the 1990 Act.
"local authority": s.78A(9) of the 1990 Act.

COMMENCEMENT
These provisions will be brought into force by a commencement order made under s.125(3) of the 1995 Act.

GENERAL NOTE
This section allows the Agency/SEPA to issue site specific guidance to local authorities with regard to the local authority's functions: such guidance is not prescriptive but the local authority must have regard to it: subs. (1). Subsection (2) makes it clear that in the event of any conflict between Agency/SEPA and the Secretary of State's guidance the latter will prevail.

The appropriate Agency to have regard to guidance given by the Secretary of State

78W.—(1) The Secretary of State may issue guidance to the appropriate Agency with respect to the exercise or performance of that Agency's powers or duties under this Part; and in exercising or performing those powers or duties the appropriate Agency shall have regard to any such guidance so issued.

(2) The duty imposed on the appropriate Agency by subsection (1) above is without prejudice to any duty imposed by any other provision of this Part on that Agency to act in accordance with guidance issued by the Secretary of State.

DEFINITIONS
"appropriate Agency": s.78A(9) of the 1990 Act.

COMMENCEMENT
September 21, 1995 insofar as this section confers power on the Secretary of State to issue guidance or makes provision with respect to the exercise of such power (S.I. 1995 No. 1983). The remainder will be brought into force by a commencement order made under s.125(3) of the 1995 Act.

GENERAL NOTE
This section provides a general reserve power to the Secretary of State to issue guidance (which may be generic or site-specific) to the Agency/SEPA.

Supplementary provisions

78X.—(1) Where it appears to a local authority that two or more different sites, when considered together, are in such a condition, by reason of substances in, on or under the land, that—

(a) significant harm is being caused or there is a significant possibility of such harm being caused, or

(b) pollution of controlled waters is being, or is likely to be, caused, this Part shall apply in relation to each of those sites, whether or not the condition of the land at any of them, when considered alone, appears to the authority to be such that significant harm is being caused, or there is a significant possibility of such harm being caused, or that pollution of controlled waters is being or is likely to be caused.

(2) Where it appears to a local authority that any land outside, but adjoining or adjacent to, its area is in such a condition, by reason of substances in, on or under the land, that significant harm is being caused, or there is a significant possibility of such harm being caused, or that pollution of controlled waters is being, or is likely to be, caused within its area—

(a) the authority may, in exercising its functions under this Part, treat that land as if it were land situated within its area; and

(b) except in this subsection, any reference—

(i) to land within the area of a local authority, or

(ii) to the local authority in whose area any land is situated, shall be construed accordingly;

but this subsection is without prejudice to the functions of the local authority in whose area the land is in fact situated.

(3) A person acting in a relevant capacity—

(a) shall not thereby be personally liable, under this Part, to bear the whole or any part of the cost of doing any thing by way of remediation, unless that thing is to any extent referable to substances whose presence in, on or under the contaminated land in question is a result of any act done or omission made by him which it was unreasonable for a person acting in that capacity to do or make; and

(b) shall not thereby be guilty of an offence under or by virtue of section 78M above unless the requirement which has not been complied with is a requirement to do some particular thing for which he is personally liable to bear the whole or any part of the cost.

(4) In subsection (3) above, "person acting in a relevant capacity" means—

    (a) a person acting as an insolvency practitioner, within the meaning of section 388 of the Insolvency Act 1986 (including that section as it applies in relation to an insolvent partnership by virtue of any order made under section 421 of that Act);

    (b) the official receiver acting in a capacity in which he would be regarded as acting as an insolvency practitioner within the meaning of section 388 of the Insolvency Act 1986 if subsection (5) of that section were disregarded;

    (c) the official receiver acting as receiver or manager;

    (d) a person acting as a special manager under section 177 or 370 of the Insolvency Act 1986;

    (e) the Accountant in Bankruptcy acting as permanent or interim trustee in a sequestration (within the meaning of the Bankruptcy (Scotland) Act 1985);

    (f) a person acting as a receiver or receiver and manager—

        (i) under or by virtue of any enactment; or

        (ii) by virtue of his appointment as such by an order of a court or by any other instrument.

(5) Regulations may make different provision for different cases or circumstances.

DEFINITIONS

    "contaminated land": s.78A(2) of the 1990 Act.
    "harm": s.78A(4) of the 1990 Act.
    "local authority": s.78A(9) of the 1990 Act.
    "pollution of controlled waters": s.78A(9) of the 1990 Act.
    "remediation": s.78A(7) of the 1990 Act.
    "significant": s.78A(5) of the 1990 Act.
    "substance": s.78A(9) of the 1990 Act.

COMMENCEMENT

    September 21, 1995 insofar as this section confers power on the Secretary of State to make regulations or makes provision with respect to the exercise of such power (S.I. 1995 No. 1983). The remainder will be brought into force by a commencement order made under s.125(3) of the 1995 Act.

GENERAL NOTE

    This section contains a number of important supplementary provisions dealing with various matters.

Subs. (1): combined effect of sites

    This subsection covers the situation where a number of sites taken together present the conditions of harm or pollution necessary for land to be regarded as contaminated, even though each site of itself would not be sufficiently significant to be regarded as contaminated. An example might be where a number of sites together contribute a significant pollution load to a watercourse flowing past them, or to groundwater resources. The subsection allows each site in its own right to be regarded as contaminated: the correct procedure is therefore to serve separate remediation notices in relation to each site.

Subs. (2): land outside local authority's area

    Contamination is no respecter of local government boundaries, and land situated outside a local authority's area may quite conceivably represent a threat of harm within the area. An example would be the migration of landfill gas across a boundary so as to affect residential property. The authority in whose area the residential property is located would be able, under this subsection, to take enforcement action against the land from which the gas emanates. A similar provision applies to statutory nuisances under s.81(2) of the 1990 Act.

    The relevant land must be "adjoining or adjacent to" the authority's area. If the use of the two terms together were not sufficient to indicate that the land can be adjacent to an authority's area without adjoining it, then case law confirms this: " 'Adjacent' is not a word to which a precise and uniform meaning is attached by ordinary usage. It is not confined to places adjoining, and it includes places close to or nearby. What degree of proximity would justify the application of the word is entirely a question of circumstance" (*Wellington v. Lower Hutt* [1904] A.C. 773, in which two New Zealand boroughs were held to be adjacent for the purpose of making statutory contributions to the cost of building a bridge, despite being nowhere closer to each other than six miles apart); see also *Stanward Corpn. v. Denison Mines*, 67 D.L.R. (2d) 743, in which a similar approach was taken but two mining claims one-and-a-quarter miles apart were held *not* to be adjacent. In Scotland it has similarly been held that the word does not require actual contact: *Anderson v. Lochgelly Iron & Coal Co.* (1904) 7 F. 187, where an accident which took place on a private railway connecting a mine to the main line some 800 yards from the mine was held (with the Lord Justice-Clerk dissenting) to be "adjacent to" the mine in terms of the statutory definition in the Coal Mines Regulation Act 1887; see also *Dunbeath Estate Ltd. v. Henderson* 1989 S.L.T. (Land Ct.) 99.

The power of an affected local authority to take action under this section is without prejudice to the functions of the local authority in whose area that land is in fact located. That authority may itself be required to take enforcement action because of harm or pollution within its own area; indeed, there seems to be nothing in the legislation to limit the consideration by the local authority to harm or pollution within its own area. Accordingly there must be the risk of an appropriate person being faced with possibly conflicting remediation requirements by two local authorities. It is suggested that to avoid this situation, any authority considering exercising its powers under s.78X(2) should as a matter of good practice consult the local authority in whose area the relevant land is located.

Subss. (3) and (4): insolvency

Subsection (3) is intended to protect persons acting in various capacities (specified in subs. (4)) in insolvency situations. The provisions cover liquidators, administrators, administrative receivers, supervisors of voluntary arrangements, trustees in bankruptcy, the official receiver, and any person acting as a receiver under an enactment (*e.g.* the Law of Property Act 1925) or appointed as such by a court, or by any instrument. The protection is twofold: (a) the person is not liable in a personal capacity for remediation costs unless the remediation requirement is referable (see s.78F(10) above at p. 25–155 for the meaning of this) to substances whose presence in, on or under the land is a result of any act done or omission made by him, which was unreasonable for a person acting in his capacity; and (b) he shall not be guilty of an offence of failing to comply with a remediation notice unless the relevant requirement relates to a thing for which he is personally responsible under (a).

This wording is potentially difficult. It seems unlikely that the presence of contamination is likely to be the result of the positive act of an insolvency practitioner or similar person, but its presence might well be said to result from an omission on his part, *i.e.* failure to remove it, or failure to take steps which would have prevented it occurring. The concept of an unreasonable omission is a difficult one, raising issues of what it is or is not reasonable to expect an insolvency practitioner to do as regards land which is or might be contaminated. It might be questioned to what extent a person should investigate for possible contamination, or expend money on remedial measures, in order to avoid being held to have acted (or failed to act) unreasonably. In this respect, the case of *John Willment (Ashford), Re* [1979] 2 All E.R. 615 may be relevant, in that it was suggested there that a receiver could not exercise his discretion in such a way as to lead the company to act unlawfully.

Application to the Isles of Scilly

78Y.—(1) Subject to the provisions of any order under this section, this Part shall not apply in relation to the Isles of Scilly.

(2) The Secretary of State may, after consultation with the Council of the Isles of Scilly, by order provide for the application of any provisions of this Part to the Isles of Scilly; and any such order may provide for the application of those provisions to those Isles with such modifications as may be specified in the order.

(3) An order under this section may—

(a) make different provision for different cases, including different provision in relation to different persons, circumstances or localities; and

(b) contain such supplemental, consequential and transitional provision as the Secretary of State considers appropriate, including provision saving provision repealed by or under any enactment.

DEFINITIONS
"modifications": s.124(1).

COMMENCEMENT
September 21, 1995 insofar as this section confers power on the Secretary of State to make orders or makes provision with respect to the exercise of such power (S.I. 1995 No. 1983). The remainder will be brought into force by a commencement order made under s.125(3) of the 1995 Act.

Supplementary provisions with respect to guidance by the Secretary of State

78YA.—(1) Any power of the Secretary of State to issue guidance under this Part shall only be exercisable after consultation with the appropriate Agency and such other bodies or persons as he may consider it appropriate to consult in relation to the guidance in question.

(2) A draft of any guidance proposed to be issued under section 78A (2) or (5), 78B(2) or 78F(6) or (7) above shall be laid before each House of Parliament and the guidance shall not be issued until after the period of 40 days beginning with the day on which the draft was so laid or, if the draft is laid on different days, the later of the two days.

(3) If, within the period mentioned in subsection (2) above, either House resolves that the guidance, the draft of which was laid before it, should not be issued, the Secretary of State shall not issue that guidance.

(4) In reckoning any period of 40 days for the purposes of subsection (2) or (3) above, no account shall be taken of any time during which Parliament is dissolved or prorogued or during which both Houses are adjourned for more than four days.

(5) The Secretary of State shall arrange for any guidance issued by him under this Part to be published in such manner as he considers appropriate.

DEFINITIONS
"appropriate Agency": s.78A(9) of the 1990 Act.

COMMENCEMENT
September 21, 1995 since this entire section makes provision with respect to the exercise by the Secretary of State of his power to issue guidance (S.I. 1995 No. 1983).

GENERAL NOTE
This section provides the special procedure (subss. (2) to (4)) by which the prescriptive guidance, with which enforcing authorities must act in accordance, is to be issued. The Parliamentary procedure is one of negative resolution (subs. (3)). Additionally, for *all* guidance, there are more general requirements of consultation (subs. (1)) and publication (subs. (5)).

Interaction of this Part with other enactments

78YB.—(1) A remediation notice shall not be served if and to the extent that it appears to the enforcing authority that the powers of the appropriate Agency under section 27 above may be exercised in relation to—

(a) the significant harm (if any), and
(b) the pollution of controlled waters (if any),

by reason of which the contaminated land in question is such land.

(2) Nothing in this Part shall apply in relation to any land in respect of which there is for the time being in force a site licence under Part II above, except to the extent that any significant harm, or pollution of controlled waters, by reason of which that land would otherwise fall to be regarded as contaminated land is attributable to causes other than—

(a) breach of the conditions of the licence; or
(b) the carrying on, in accordance with the conditions of the licence, of any activity authorised by the licence.

(3) If, in a case falling within subsection (1) or (7) of section 59 above, the land in question is contaminated land, or becomes such land by

reason of the deposit of the controlled waste in question, a remediation notice shall not be served in respect of that land by reason of that waste or any consequences of its deposit, if and to the extent that it appears to the enforcing authority that the powers of a waste regulation authority or waste collection authority under that section may be exercised in relation to that waste or the consequences of its deposit.

(4) No remediation notice shall require a person to do anything the effect of which would be to impede or prevent the making of a discharge in pursuance of a consent given under Chapter II of Part III of the Water Resources Act 1991 (pollution offences) or, in relation to Scotland, in pursuance of a consent given under Part II of the Control of Pollution Act 1974.

DEFINITIONS

"appropriate Agency": s.78A(9) of the 1990 Act.
"contaminated land": s.78A(2) of the 1990 Act.
"enforcing authority": s.78A(9) of the 1990 Act.
"harm": s.78A(4) of the 1990 Act.
"pollution of controlled waters": s.78A(9) of the 1990 Act.
"remediation notice": s.78E(1) of the 1990 Act.
"significant": s.78A(5) of the 1990 Act.

COMMENCEMENT

These provisions will be brought into force by a commencement order made under s.125(3) of the 1995 Act.

GENERAL NOTE

This important section governs the relationship between the contaminated land provisions and other forms of environmental control so as to avoid duplication or conflict. For completeness reference should also be made to Sched. 22, para. 89, which deals with the relationship with statutory nuisance provisions. The relationship with works notices for water pollution is not addressed, and this situation is commented on briefly below.

Subs. (1): IPC and LAPC

Where contamination results from the commission of an offence under Pt. I of the 1990 Act (integrated pollution control and local air pollution control) action should be taken under s.27 powers (powers of enforcing authority to remedy harm) rather than under Pt. IIA.

Subs. (2): waste site licences

The implementation of a waste management licence for the deposit of waste may inevitably involve the contamination of that land, though the risk of harm to health and the environment and to controlled waters should be managed through the imposition and enforcement of licence conditions and the strict requirements relating to surrender of licences under s.39 of the 1990 Act.

The provisions on contaminated land are generally disapplied to land in respect of which a waste site licence is in force. However, they can be used in cases where the harm or pollution is attributable to causes other than: (a) breach of licence conditions; or (b) carrying on activities authorised by the licence, in accordance with the licence conditions.

The rationale appears to be that if contamination results from breach of licence conditions, then enforcement should be under Pt. II of the 1990 Act, *i.e.* prosecution under s.33 or (see below) under the powers in s.59. Where the contamination results from the carrying on of authorised activities in accordance with conditions, then the intention is that the contaminated land provisions should not be used. So to take the example of a landfill site, if waste deposited lawfully results in contamination, a remediation notice cannot be served and the licensing authority can take whatever action is appropriate and possible under the provisions of Pt. II. Rather more problematic is the case of, say, a waste transfer station or treatment plant operating on land subject to contamination from a previous use. Remedial action may be taken under Pt. IIA in relation to the previous contamination, but not in relation to any contamination caused by operation of the treatment plant or transfer station; provided that the later contamination was caused by the lawful carrying on of authorised activities, or by breach of a licence condition.

Subs. (3): removal of unlawful waste deposits

Powers exist under s.59 of the 1990 Act to deal with controlled waste which has been fly-tipped or otherwise unlawfully deposited. In relation to such waste and contamination caused by its deposit, a contaminated land remediation notice may not be served if and to the extent it appears that s.59 powers may be exercised. The Government's intention in giving precedence to the s.59 powers is partly to preserve the effect of the defence of innocent occupiers which arises under s.59(3). See the General Note to s.78F at p. 25–157 above.

Subs. (4): consented discharges to controlled waters
By subs. (4) no remediation notice shall require a person to do anything which would impede or prevent the making of a consented discharge to controlled waters.

Water pollution: remediation notices and works notice
It will be noted that there is no express provision dealing with the relationship between the contaminated land regime and the Agency/SEPA powers in respect of water pollution.

The 1995 Act gives the Agency (and SEPA in Scotland) the power to serve a "works notice" requiring works to be carried out remediating or preventing pollution of controlled waters: Sched. 22, paras. 22 and 162, respectively inserting ss.46A to D into the Control of Pollution Act 1974 for Scotland and ss.161A to D into the Water Resources Act 1991 for England and Wales. See the General Note to s.120 and Sched. 22 to the 1995 Act at p. 25–302.

There is the possibility, without adequate co-operation between the relevant local authority and the Agency/SEPA, that someone may be served with both a remediation notice and a works notice containing different requirements, although it will be noted that: (a) the Agency/SEPA is not under a duty to serve a works notice: it merely has a power to do so; (b) in some cases where a works notice may be served, the land may also have been designated as a "special site" under s.78C, in which case the Agency/SEPA is the enforcing authority; (c) the Agency/SEPA has power under s.78V to give site specific guidance to which the local authority must have regard unless it conflicts with Secretary of State's guidance; and (d) a works notice, once served, may satisfy the local authority that appropriate things are being, or will be, done by way of remediation in which case it cannot serve a remediation notice: s.78H(5)(b).

This Part and radioactivity

78YC. Except as provided by regulations, nothing in this Part applies in relation to harm, or pollution of controlled waters, so far as attributable, to any radioactivity possessed by any substance; but regulations may—
(a) provide for prescribed provisions of this Part to have effect with such modifications as the Secretary of State considers appropriate for the purpose of dealing with harm, or pollution of controlled waters, so far as attributable to any radioactivity possessed by any substances; or
(b) make such modifications of the Radioactive Substances Act 1993 or any other Act as the Secretary of State considers appropriate."

Definitions
"harm": s.78A(4) of the 1990 Act.
"pollution of controlled waters": s.78A(5) of the 1990 Act.
"prescribed": s.78A(5) of the 1990 Act.
"regulations": s.78A(5) of the 1990 Act.
"significant": s.78A(5) of the 1990 Act.

Commencement
September 21, 1995 insofar as this section confers power on the Secretary of State to make regulations or makes provision with respect to the exercise of such power (S.I. 1995 No. 1983). The remainder will be brought into force by a commencement order made under s.125(3) of the 1995 Act.

General Note
Part IIA does not apply to harm or pollution so far as attributable to the radioactive properties of any substance, except where those provisions are applied by regulations. The fact that the substance in question is radioactive will not prevent the application of contaminated land powers in relation to other properties of the substance (*e.g.* toxicity) if these result in significant harm or pollution.

The Government in debate indicated that it saw Pt. IIA as providing a suitable basis for dealing with radioactive contamination on old industrial sites, *e.g.* old radium luminescing works. However, because of the particular scientific problems involved, some changes to the detail might be needed: H.C. Standing Committee B, Eleventh Sitting, Pt. II, col. 386, May 23, 1995.

Abandoned mines: England and Wales

<small>INTRODUCTION AND GENERAL NOTE</small>

Background

Part II, through ss.58–60, also brings about significant changes in the law relating to water pollution from abandoned mines in Great Britain, including the removal as from December 31, 1999 of an important defence against the criminal charge of having knowingly permitted water pollution, and the introduction of notification procedures on abandonment.

The problem of water pollution from abandoned mines has worsened in recent years with the demise of much of the coal and other mining industries. Some 200km of waters are affected by abandoned coal mines in England and Wales together with 400km of waters affected by abandoned metal mines (*Abandoned Mines and the Water Environment*, NRA, March 1994, p. 1). In Scotland 134km of surface waters were affected by discharges from abandoned coal mines (*per* Mr Sam Galbraith MP, Standing Committee B, May 23, 1995, col. 411). No figures appear to be available for the length of rivers polluted by abandoned metal mines in Scotland. When a mine is abandoned the cessation of pumping operations may result in the mine filling up with water which becomes contaminated by reason of its lengthy residence time underground. Commonly the water reacts with oxidised iron pyrite to form a ferruginous compound which is highly acidic. This contaminated water may then break out of old shafts or adits and cause tremendous damage to aquatic life. Notable examples include the water pollution from the Wheal Jane tin mine in Cornwall (see (1991) 195 ENDS Report 8) and from the Dalquharran Colliery in Ayrshire which resulted in the death of all fish along a 16km stretch of the Water of Girvan, an important salmon river, the threatened closure of a factory employing 500 people which abstracted water from the river and the corrosion of ships' hulls in Girvan Harbour (see (1993) 57 Mineral Planning 25). Much concern has also focused on the possible cessation of pumping operations and the likely effects thereof in the now closed Durham coalfield (see (1993) 223 ENDS Report 11; and e.g. *Hansard*, H.C. Vol. 258, cols. 57–58) although pumping operations there are presently being continued.

Under the currently applicable legislation contained in s.85 of the Water Resources Act 1991 and, in Scotland, in s.31 of the Control of Pollution Act 1974 (the 1974 Act), although it is an offence for a person to "cause or knowingly permit any poisonous, noxious or polluting matter or any solid waste matter to enter any controlled waters", there is a specific defence available to any person who *permits* water pollution from abandoned mines, contained in s.89(3) of the 1991 Act and s.31(2) of the 1974 Act. No definition of abandoned mines is given in this legislation although in the 1974 Act, the definition of "mine" is the same as in the Mines and Quarries Act 1954.

An exemption is also available for any person permitting water pollution from abandoned mines in the case of statutory cost recovery actions under s.161 of the 1991 Act and, in Scotland, s.46 of the 1974 Act for preventive or remedial works undertaken by the NRA or, in Scotland, by the relevant river purification authority (RPA). Hence, while it is possible for the NRA or, in Scotland, the relevant RPA, to carry out preventive or remedial works where a person has permitted water pollution from an abandoned mine, they may not recover the costs of doing so.

The rationale for the defence and exemption was that they are needed to protect innocent landowners or occupiers who may be aware of old mineshafts or adits on their land which are discharging polluted water or who may have polluted water from abandoned mines on another person's land crossing their land and entering controlled waters. During the Parliamentary passage of the Coal Industry Act 1994 the Government explained that:

> "The legislation [the 1991 Act and, in Scotland, the 1974 Act] is there in that form because when the Bill was introduced and the Act debated it was felt to be unreasonable to place an absolute obligation in respect of environmental damage on a landowner who may never have been responsible for mining at all and who may have bought the land without being aware that it was undermined" (*per* the Minister for Energy, *Hansard*, H.C. Vol. 240, col. 297).

Since the defence and exemption apply only to a person who permits water pollution from an abandoned mine, it is possible (1) for a person to be prosecuted for causing or for knowingly permitting water pollution from an *active* mine; (2) for a person to be prosecuted for *causing* pollution from abandoned mines; and (3) for the water pollution regulator (now the Agency/SEPA) to recover costs from a person who has caused such pollution in relation to preventive or remedial anti-pollution works which the regulator has undertaken (see generally, Poustie, *The demise of coal and causing water pollution*, [1994] 6 ELM 95). The 1995 Act introduces the further possibility (4) that the Agency/SEPA may serve a works notice, by inserting ss.46A to D into the 1974 Act (Scotland) and ss.161A to D into the 1991 Act (England and Wales). However, there are considerable difficulties in establishing that a person has *caused* water pollution from an abandoned mine. The act of switching off the pumps is not in itself regarded as the cause of the pollution but rather the whole sequence of events involving the sinking of the mine, the carrying on of pumping operations and the cessation of pumping operations is regarded as the cause. This view of causation was adopted by the High Court of Justiciary in Scotland in the only successful prosecution for an abandoned mine causing pollution: *Lockhart v. NCB* 1981 SLT 161 at p. 172 (see also NRA, *Abandoned Mines and the Water Environment*, March 1994, p. 37). This view of causation essentially appears to be concerned with creation of the latent risk of pollution. The person who created the risk of pollution will be liable for *causing* the pollution. This has major implications for the privatised coal industry. Since, in the case of existing mines, the new private operators did not create any of the pollution risks which they inherited from British Coal, they cannot be held liable for pollution on the abandonment of a mine if any of those risks subsequently result in water pollution as the Coal Industry Act 1994 did not transfer liability for such risks to them. They would only be liable for pollution resulting from such risks if liability had been transferred to them as part of the transfer of British Coal's undertaking. The only other occasions on which the new operators could be held liable for *causing* pollution is where it results from a latent risk of pollution which they themselves created, for example by sinking new mines or by driving new roads and opening up new coal faces in their existing mines.

The causal link between a person and a pollution incident may be broken by intervening factors such as natural forces, the act of a third party or an Act of God (*Lockhart v. NCB* 1981 SLT 161 at p. 171). Thus, where the real cause of the pollution was created by someone or something else (*e.g.* another mine operator or extreme weather conditions) then the alleged offender will escape conviction. This was illustrated by the case *R. v. British Coal Corp.*, Cardiff Crown Court, December 2, 1993, (1993) 227 ENDS Report 44, a private prosecution brought by the Anglers Co-operative Association. In that case British Coal were prosecuted for causing pollution by switching off the pumps at a colliery which resulted in severe water pollution of a river. However, it was established that the water became contaminated in old mine workings adjacent to the British Coal workings for which British Coal had never had any responsibility and escaped from old adits into the river. It was also established in the trial that, as a result of these old workings, the pollution would have occurred in any event regardless of British Coal's pumping operations and, in fact, but for those operations, would have occurred many years earlier. The trial judge instructed the jury to acquit British Coal since the cessation of pumping had allowed what he described as natural forces to operate again and that that was the real cause of the pollution. It would arguably have been more correct to say that the pollution was actually caused by the act of a third party, *i.e.* the pre-nationalisation mine operators who had sunk and operated the old workings in which the water actually became contaminated. Since current mine operators will often be working in seams where there are adjacent old mineworkings in many cases it will be difficult to establish that a person *caused* the water pollution.

Given these difficulties with establishing *causation* and the demise of deep mining, the pressure for reform of the law to withdraw the statutory protections in respect of *permitting* pollution has been considerable. The passage of the Coal Industry Act 1994 through Parliament saw attempts to bring about legislative amendments in relation to water pollution from abandoned mines and to impose on the new Coal Authority a duty to deal with water pollution from abandoned mines. The Government resisted these proposals although they indicated that they expected the Coal Authority to go beyond the minimum standards of environmental responsibility set by its legal duties (*per* Lord Strathclyde, *Hansard*, H.L. Vol. 554, col. 541). This "expectation", however, does not amount even to a commitment and is not enforceable or legally binding. Furthermore, it may be that this expectation cannot be met by the Coal Authority if it lacks sufficient resources.

The problem of water pollution from abandoned mines has been under consideration for some time as the Commission on Energy and the Environment report, *Coal and the Environment*, (HMSO, 1981) illustrates. However, more recently a considerable number of reports have also focused on this issue and how to deal with it, for example, *A Clear Future for Waters in the Forth Catchment* (Forth River Purification Board, 1993), *Abandoned Mines and the Water Environment*, (NRA, March 1994) which recommended, *inter alia*, clarification of the definition of abandoned mine, *Sixteenth Report: Freshwater Quality* (Royal Commission on Environmental Pollution, Cm.1966, June 1992), and the *Government Response to the Sixteenth Report of the Royal Commission on Environmental Pollution* (DoE, January 1995). The Government's consultation papers on contaminated land, *Paying for Our Past* (DoE, March 1994) and *Contaminated Land Clean-up and Control* (Scottish Office, March 1994) also acknowledged the unique exemptions under water pollution legislation from criminal liability and recommended that the justification for those special exemptions should be reassessed in the light of the emerging conclusions of the review. The results of that consultation exercise (*Framework for Contaminated Land* (DoE, November 1994); *Contaminated Land Clean-up and Control: Outcome of Review* (Scottish Office, November 1994)) indicated that proposals for legislative amendments to withdraw the defence and exemption in relation to permitting water pollution from abandoned mines and to impose a duty on mine operators to give six months' prior notice of a proposed abandonment would be introduced.

A small step forward in dealing with the problem was also made when the NRA entered into a Memorandum of Understanding with British Coal (November 18, 1993) which provided, *inter alia*, for regular meetings of the two parties and for two weeks' notice of cessation of pumping operations to be given to the NRA (see *Abandoned Mines and the Water Environment*, NRA, March 1994, Appendix 2). The NRA has subsequently entered into a similar Memorandum of Understanding with RJB Mining PLC (dated August 10, 1995). In Scotland, Forth River Purification Board has entered into an agreement (made on April 21, 1995) with the British Coal Corporation and the Coal Authority which requires British Coal to notify the Board of cessation of pumping, and British Coal and the Coal Authority to carry out a specified monitoring and pumping programme. The agreement relates to the protection of the water environment from possible long-term pollution from the connected workings of the Frances Colliery (mothballed in 1984) and the Michael Colliery (where coal production ceased in 1967 but pumping operations have continued) in Fife (*per* Sir Hector Monro, Standing Committee B, May 23, 1995, cols. 411–412). At the time of writing pumping operations had recently ceased at both collieries.

Since the law of contract in Scotland differs from that in England and Wales, in that there is no requirement for consideration and therefore unilateral obligations are enforceable, it appears to be the case that the Scottish agreement would be enforceable in the Scottish courts by way of interdict to prevent the breach of its terms or specific implement to require performance of the positive obligations contained in it, provided that the obligations contained therein are sufficiently clear and precise.

It was against this background that the provisions in Pt. II of the 1995 Act in relation to abandoned mines were introduced.

The scheme of the provisions

The new provisions contained in ss.58–60 impose a new duty on mine operators to give the appropriate Agency six months' notice of any proposed abandonment, introduce a definition of "abandonment" in respect of mines for the purposes of that notification duty and, in relation to England and Wales only, withdraw the defence and exemption contained in s.89(3) and s.161 of the Water Resources Act 1991, but only after December 31, 1999. In relation to Scotland only, the 1995 Act does withdraw the defence and exemption in relation to permitting pollution from abandoned mines, but this is done in Sched. 16, which introduces a new s.30J(3)–(6) (in relation to the defence) and in Sched. 22 which introduces a new s.46(3) and (3A) into the 1974 Act (in relation to the cost recovery exemption).

Although these changes to the law were broadly welcomed in Parliament the delayed withdrawal of the defence and exemption to the end of 1999 was severely criticised, for example, on the ground that it enabled current mine operators to abandon their mines before that date and escape liability for permitting any water pollution from them once they had closed (*e.g. Hansard*, H.L. Vol. 560, cols. 1481–1483; *Hansard*, H.C. Vol. 258, col. 52; Standing Committee B, May 23, 1995, cols. 414–415). In the Government's note on the financial effects of the original Bill (p. xiii) it was stated that:

"Since these proposals are coming forward in parallel with the privatisation of the coal industry, there could be some adverse effect on proceeds to the Government. Accordingly, the removal of the statutory protections is being timed to reduce any possible effect".

The impression given by these comments is that the delay in the changes was solely to benefit the privatisation of the industry and that they showed "a blatant disregard for the environment and the likely pollution problems caused by the abandonment of mines" (*per* Lord Mason of Barnsley, *Hansard*, H.L. Vol. 560, col. 1482). Amendments were accordingly proposed at Report stage to bring forward the date of withdrawal of the defence and the exemption to January 1, 1996 (*e.g. per* Baroness Hilton of Eggardon, *Hansard*, H.L. Vol. 560, cols. 1481–1482). However, the Government rejected such an amendment, explaining:

"Our decision to remove the defence and exemption was taken in the knowledge that that would be a step of great significance not just as a means of improving the quality of discharges from mines abandoned in the future, but with the practical and financial implications for the current owners and operators of mines.

The effect on revenue from coal privatisation was only one of a number of issues considered in deciding that the statutory protections would be lifted at the end of 1999. The Government wanted to allow all mine owners time to adapt to the change. In addition, the agency will have powers to clean up or prevent pollution if it considers that necessary under the Water Resources Act 1991.

The measures in Clause 55 [s.58], which define abandonment and require mine operators to notify the agency six months before abandoning a mine, will take effect from the transfer date. [That is, the date of the transfer of water pollution regulation to the Agency/SEPA]. They are designed to work as a precursor to the removal of the defence and exemption. However, we have taken the view that it would be right to allow those involved a period until the end of 1999 in which to adjust to the proposed changes in the existing regulatory regime because of the obvious practical and financial implications" (*per* Viscount Ullswater, *Hansard*, H.L. Vol. 560, col. 1484).

In contrast to the position in England and Wales, the defence only became available to Scottish mine operators with the coming into force of the 1974 Act in the mid-1980s, since it was not provided for in the Rivers (Prevention of Pollution) (Scotland) Act 1951. As a result, insofar as the Government's concern was to ease the transition from a long-standing statutory protection, this concern has less force in Scotland than south of the border.

It may also be of significance that the major coal supply contracts inherited by RJB and Mining (Scotland) Ltd for the supply of the principal generators, National Power plc, PowerGen plc and Scottish Power plc all expire in 1998 (see DTI, *The Energy Report: Markets in Transition*, HMSO 1994, ch. 4.24, p. 54). If these contracts are not renewed or are renewed in a much reduced form, the 1999 date might allow the private mine operators to abandon many of the remaining coal mines before the withdrawal of the defence and the exemption, although clearly they would be under an obligation in ss.58–59 to notify the appropriate Agency of a proposed abandonment.

There were also attempts to make the Coal Authority (established by the Coal Industry Act 1994) liable for pollution from abandoned mines (*per* Baroness Hilton of Eggardon, *Hansard*, H.L. Vol. 560, col. 1479 and *per* Ms Joan Ruddock MP, *Hansard*, H.C. Vol. 262, cols. 761–776). Although the Coal Authority does have responsibility for *all* abandoned mines by virtue of the operation of s.7(3) of the Coal Industry Act 1994, the Government nevertheless rejected this proposal. They argued that:

"Outright removal of the defence and exemption as proposed in the amendment would require the Coal Authority to seek discharge consents for all discharges regardless of the degree of pollution, and to comply with them. That would not be justified in many cases and would place a heavy burden on the public purse. ... We believe it would be wrong to withdraw suddenly those statutory protections which apply now to all abandoned coal mines for which the Coal Authority has responsibility. The Government have already said that they would expect the Coal Authority to go beyond the minimum standards of environmental responsibility which are set by its legal duties and to seek the best environmental result which can be secured by the use of the resources that are available to it. We must accept that the Coal Authority, like all public bodies, has limited financial resources" (*per* Viscount Ullswater, *Hansard*, H.L. Vol. 560, col. 1480; see also *Hansard*, H.L. Vol. 562, col. 226).

There remain uncertainties about the role of the Coal Authority in relation to abandoned mines. Under the Coal Industry Act 1994, the Coal Authority has a duty, so far as practicable, to ensure that mine operators "are able to finance both the proper carrying on of the coal mining operations that they are authorised to carry on and the discharge of liabilities arising from the carrying on of those operations" (s.2(1) of the Coal Industry Act 1994). In this licensing role the Coal Authority may impose such conditions as it thinks fit (s.28(1) of the 1994 Act) which clearly could include conditions relating to water pollution issues. However, in relation to mines which have already been abandoned the position is less clear. Furthermore, by virtue of s.29(1) of the 1994 Act, the Coal Authority may also impose conditions to provide for security for the performance of obligations imposed by other conditions of the licence. Such security could include a requirement for bonds for potential environmental liabilities. As the owner of already abandoned mines, the Coal Authority benefits from the statutory protections afforded by water pollution legislation until after December 31, 1999 when it will lose those protections. However, the Coal Authority itself appears unsure of the extent of its potential liabilities with respect to abandoned mines, with conflicting statements being made by senior officials. While Neville Washington, Chief Executive of the Coal Authority explained "The Coal Authority is not responsible for water that emerges from pits" (*Newcastle Evening Chronicle*, April 26, 1995), Albert Schofield, Director of Contracts, interviewed on the "Report Back" programme broadcast on BBC

Radio Nottingham indicated that the Bill was not clear in assigning responsibility for minewater pollution from abandoned mines to the Coal Authority. However, on several occasions during the passage of the 1995 Act through Parliament the Government reiterated its pledge that the Coal Authority would continue pumping where necessary (*e.g. per* Robert Atkins, *Hansard*, H.C. Vol. 262, col. 776) and would not limit itself to minimum standards of environmental responsibility (col. 774).

Concerns were also expressed by Lord Crickhowell (*Hansard*, H.L. Vol. 562, cols. 148–149) in relation to the abandonment of metalliferous mines and the applicability of Directive 76/464/EEC on pollution caused by certain dangerous substances discharged into the aquatic environment (1976 OJ L129/23) and Directive 80/68/EEC on the protection of groundwater against pollution caused by certain dangerous substances (1980 OJ L20/43). However, although the Government recognised these concerns, significantly they failed to address them to any extent at all (*Hansard*, H.L. Vol. 562, col. 152). It is clear that whereas the Coal Authority has responsibility for abandoned coal mines, no similar authority has responsibility for abandoned metalliferous mines. Furthermore, Lord Crickhowell went on to suggest that by not withdrawing the defence and exemption for permitting water pollution from abandoned mines until December 31, 1999 the UK may be in non-compliance with the provisions of Directives 76/464/EEC and 80/68/EEC (cols. 148–149).

Relationship of new abandoned mines provisions and contaminated land provisions
　　Section 78A(2) of the new Pt. IIA of the 1990 Act (see p. 25–141 above) defines contaminated land as "any land which appears to the local authority in whose area it is situated to be in such a condition, by reason of substances in, on or under the land, that ... (b) pollution of controlled waters is being, or is likely to be, caused". This would appear to encompass the issue of water pollution from abandoned mines. Furthermore, since s.91B of the Water Resources Act 1991 and, in relation to Scotland, s.30Z of the 1974 Act provide that the appropriate Agency must inform the relevant local authority of any proposed abandonment when it receives notice of the same from a mine operator where it considers that in consequence of the abandonment or proposed abandonment any land has or is likely to become contaminated land, there is a clear intention to give local authorities a role in the remediation of contamination resulting from water pollution from abandoned mines using their new contaminated land powers.

　　However, at Report Stage in the House of Lords, Lord Williams of Elvel (*Hansard*, H.L. Vol. 562, cols. 144–145) attempted to ensure that abandoned mines would be treated as contaminated land between the date of the Royal Assent and the withdrawal of the defence and exemption in water pollution legislation since the Bill as originally drafted did not restrict the application of the contaminated land provisions in the case of permitting water pollution from abandoned mines. The Government responded that:

　　"It was no part of the Government's intention that the current clause, establishing the contaminated land powers, would have the effect of removing the existing defence and exemption which apply in the circumstances. However, that appears to have been the inadvertent result of the existing provisions in the Bill and the Government will be bringing forward an amendment at a later date to rectify this" (*per* Viscount Ullswater, *Hansard*, H.L. Vol. 562, col. 151).

　　The Government duly moved swiftly to close this loophole and introduced the provision which is now s.78J(3) of the 1990 Act (see p. 25–165, above) which limits the application of the contaminated land provisions in cases where a person is permitting water pollution from abandoned mines until December 31, 1999 so that those provisions are consistent with the delay in the withdrawal of the defence/exemption in the abandoned mines provisions. However, it would still be possible for a local authority to use the contaminated land provisions where a person has caused water pollution and indeed where a person has knowingly permitted contamination in terms of the first limb of the s.78A(2) test (see also General Notes to ss.78A and 78J(3) of the 1990 Act, pp. 25–141 and 25–165, above).

　　58. After Chapter II of Part III of the Water Resources Act 1991 (pollution offences) there shall be inserted—

"Chapter IIA

Abandoned Mines

Introductory
　　91A.—(1) For the purposes of this Chapter, "abandonment", in relation to a mine,—

(a) subject to paragraph (b) below, includes—

    (i) the discontinuance of any or all of the operations for the removal of water from the mine;

    (ii) the cessation of working of any relevant seam, vein or vein-system;

    (iii) the cessation of use of any shaft or outlet of the mine;

    (iv) in the case of a mine in which activities other than mining activities are carried on (whether or not mining activities are also carried on in the mine)—

        (A) the discontinuance of some or all of those other activities in the mine; and

        (B) any substantial change in the operations for the removal of water from the mine; but

(b) does not include—

    (i) any disclaimer under section 178 or 315 of the Insolvency Act 1986 (power of liquidator, or trustee of a bankrupt's estate, to disclaim onerous property) by the official receiver acting in a compulsory capacity; or

    (ii) the abandonment of any rights, interests or liabilities by the Accountant in Bankruptcy acting as permanent or interim trustee in a sequestration (within the meaning of the Bankruptcy (Scotland) Act 1985);

and cognate expressions shall be construed accordingly.

(2) In this Chapter, except where the context otherwise requires—

"the 1954 Act" means the Mines and Quarries Act 1954;

"acting in a compulsory capacity", in the case of the official receiver, means acting as—

    (a) liquidator of a company;

    (b) receiver or manager of a bankrupt's estate, pursuant to section 287 of the Insolvency Act 1986;

    (c) trustee of a bankrupt's estate;

    (d) liquidator of an insolvent partnership;

    (e) trustee of an insolvent partnership;

    (f) trustee, or receiver or manager, of the insolvent estate of a deceased person;

"mine" has the same meaning as in the 1954 Act;

"the official receiver" has the same meaning as it has in the Insolvency Act 1986 by virtue of section 399(1) of that Act;

"prescribed" means prescribed in regulations;

"regulations" means regulations made by the Secretary of State;

"relevant seam, vein or vein-system", in the case of any mine, means any seam, vein or vein-system for the purpose of, or in connection with, whose working any excavation constituting or comprised in the mine was made.

DEFINITIONS

"1954 Act": subs. (2).

"acting in a compulsory capacity": subs. (2).

"mine": subs. (2); s.180(1) of the Mines and Quarries Act 1954.

"official receiver": subs. (2); s.399(1) of the Insolvency Act 1986.

"prescribed": subs. (2).

"regulations": subs. (2).

"relevant seam, vein or vein-system": subs. (2).

COMMENCEMENT

This section will be brought into force by a commencement order made under s.125(3) of the 1995 Act.

GENERAL NOTE

This section provides a definition of "abandonment" in relation to mines for the purposes of the new Chap. IIA of the Water Resources Act 1991 which it also introduces. This was one of the changes which the NRA wished to see brought about in its report, *Abandoned Mines and the Water Environment* (March 1994), pp. 38 and 42.

The definition of abandonment provided by subs. (1) must be read together with the definition of mine which is that appearing in s.180(1) of the Mines and Quarries Act 1954 (subs. (2)):

"... an excavation or system of excavations, including all such excavations to which a common system of ventilation is provided, made for the purpose of, or in connection with, the getting, wholly or substantially by means involving the employment of persons below ground, of minerals (whether in their natural state or in solution or suspension) or products of minerals".

This definition is elaborated upon in s.180(3):

"there shall be deemed to form part of a mine so much of the surface (including buildings, structures and works thereon) surrounding or adjacent to the shafts or outlets of the mine as is occupied together with the mine for the purpose of, or in connection with, the working of the mine, the treatment, preparation for sale, consumption or use, storage or removal from the mine of the minerals or products thereof gotten from the mine or the removal from the mine of the refuse thereof ...";

by s.182(2) which provides that:

"For the purposes of this Act mine workings having a common system of ventilation, or any part of a system of ventilation in common, shall be deemed to form part of the same mine";

and by s.183(1) which provides:

"For the purposes of this Act an excavation or system of excavations made for training purposes shall be deemed to be a mine, and the use for those purposes of any premises which are a mine as defined by subsection (1) of section one hundred and eighty of this Act ... shall be deemed, for the purposes of this Act, to constitute the working of the mine ...".

It is thus clear that the definition of a mine includes, for example, the surface buildings, a number of mineworkings which share a common system of ventilation and a mine used for training purposes.

Subs. (1)

The definition of abandonment provided is not exhaustive but is very wide. A variety of physical indicators are used to define abandonment. Importantly, it is abundantly clear that abandonment of a mine includes abandonment of part of a mine. The combination of this definition and the duty contained in the new s.91B to give six months' prior notice to the Agency of any proposed abandonment should provide the Agency with very valuable information and may enable any likely pollution problems to be dealt with at an early stage. It should be noted that the definition of abandonment does not apply beyond the boundaries of Chap. IIA of the Water Resources Act 1991. This means it is only applicable in relation to the notification duty in the new s.91B of the 1991 Act. In the original Bill this clause did apply the definition of abandonment to the whole Act. However, the definition was restricted by a Government amendment at Standing Committee stage in the House of Commons (Standing Committee B, May 23, 1995, col. 389). The defence in s.89(3) of the 1991 Act to permitting water pollution from an abandoned mine is amended to include an abandoned part of a mine by s.60. See the note on p. 25–204.

The non-exhaustive definition of abandonment in subs. (1) appears to be broken into two groupings: subs. (1)(a)(i) to (iii) which may be regarded as covering examples of mining activities and subs. (1)(a)(iv) which covers non-mining activities.

Paragraph (a)(i). This provision clearly encompasses the cessation of pumping and drainage operations in a mine. As originally drafted it did not include the words "any or all of the". However, the Government moved amendments at the Standing Committee Stage to extend the scope of the provision:

"We wanted to ensure that acts of abandonment that affected large parts of a mine would be notifiable even when the mine continued to be worked—that is possible through changes in the mine–water pumping regime. We did not want it to be necessary for operators to notify cessation of working in small parts of a mine when that would have no implication for water pollution" (Mr Robert Atkins, Standing Committee B, May 23, 1995, col. 390).

As the provision now stands it includes partial cessation of these activities in addition to total cessation. However, it is not clear that the words of the statute actually have the effect which the Government intended since they do not have the *de minimis* exception to which Mr Atkins referred. They appear to refer to the discontinuation of any pumping or drainage operations without qualification.

Paragraph (a)(ii). This would encompass the common situation where a mine has several working seams and the work on a particular seam or vein in a mine ceased presumably even if pumping operations were continued in that seam or elsewhere in the mine.

Paragraph (a)(iii). The cessation of use of any shaft or outlet of the mine will count as abandonment. Shaft means a shaft the top of which is, or is intended to be, at the surface (see s.182(1) of the Mines and Quarries Act 1954). Although outlet is not defined in the Mines and Quarries

Act 1954, it is clear, *e.g.* from s.30(2) thereof that an outlet may be one through which it is not possible to walk. Outlets may often be used for drainage or ventilation purposes.

Paragraph (a)(iv). This provision deals with situations where mining activities have ceased at a mine but non-mining activities are being carried on. Mining activities are not defined in the Act. However, in the light of the definition of mine in the Mines and Quarries Act 1954 (see above) it would appear that a mine which was being used only for ventilation or training purposes is still a mine in which mining activities are being carried on. It is further submitted that a mine which is used solely for pumping water from mineworkings which are still in use from another mine or a mine which has been "mothballed" (*i.e.* which is maintained on a care and maintenance basis only) is still a mine in which mining activities are being carried on. Further assistance on what constitutes a mining activity, in relation to coal mines at least, may be found in the Coal Industry Act 1994 which includes a definition of coal-mining operations in s.65(1). While an operation is not necessarily synonymous with an activity, the definition still provides useful guidance. Coal-mining operations include:

"(a) searching for coal and boring for it,
(b) winning, working and getting it (whether underground or in the course of opencast operations),
(c) bringing underground coal to the surface, treating coal and rendering it saleable,
(d) treating coal in the strata for the purpose of winning any product of coal and winning, working or getting any product of coal resulting from such treatment, and
(e) depositing spoil from any activities carried on in the course of any coal-mining operations and draining coal mines,

and an operation carried on in relation to minerals other than coal is a coal-mining operation in so far as it is carried on in relation to those minerals as part of, or as ancillary to, operations carried on in relation to coal".

Furthermore, although this definition applies to coal-mining operations, it is of some relevance in terms of what constitutes a mining operation or activity more generally.

It is likely that the provision in subs. (1)(a)(iv) is targetted at the following types of situation: (i) where part of or all of a mine ceases to be used for mining but remains open to facilitate salvage of equipment; (ii) where a mine has become a museum; or (iii) where a mine is being used, for example, for the disposal of waste unconnected with mining. If a mine is being used in such a way and some or all of those activities are discontinued and there is any substantial change in pumping or drainage operations then that will constitute abandonment. A substantial change is one which is considerable: *Granada Theatres v. Freehold Investment (Leytonstone)* [1958] 1 W.L.R. 845; *Palser v. Grinling*; *Property Holding Co. v. Mischeff* [1948] AC 291.

There was considerable uncertainty as to the scope of the definition in subs. (1) in Parliament (*per* Mr William O'Brien MP, Standing Committee B, May 23, 1995, cols. 390–391 and *per* Mr Tipping MP, col. 394) particularly in relation to mines where coal production and pumping had ceased but salvage works or surface activities such as coal storage, stocking and removal were still continuing. However, the Government argued:

"If activities other than mining activities are being carried on in the mine, there is no act of abandonment. If mining, pumping and storage activities have ceased, the mine is considered to be abandoned for the purposes of these provisions" (*per* Mr Robert Atkin, Standing Committee B, May 23, 1995, col. 393).

It is submitted that this explanation is not very helpful. The implication of the definition in subs. (1) is in fact that there may be several acts of abandonment at the same mine. For example, work on a particular seam could cease while work elsewhere continued; thereafter, work on all remaining seams could cease although pumping operations continued. Finally, pumping operations could cease. Each of these occurrences would in itself count as an abandonment in terms of the new statutory definition and hence require advance notification. That this is anticipated is apparent from the wording of the new s.89(3B) and (3C) of the 1991 Act. Hence Mr Atkin's statement that "If activities other than mining activities are being carried on in the mine, there is no act of abandonment" is somewhat misleading. In fact there may well have been several acts of abandonment up to that point.

Paragraph (b). This paragraph makes provision for certain exceptions in relation to the official receiver and the Accountant in Bankruptcy. These are designed to deal with the fact that abandonment sometimes accompanies the insolvency of the operator and to provide protection for the official receiver and the Accountant in Bankruptcy (see also note to s.91B(5) below).

Mine operators to give the Agency six months' notice of any proposed abandonment

91B.—(1) If, in the case of any mine, there is to be an abandonment at any time after the expiration of the initial period, it shall be the duty of the operator of the mine to give notice of the proposed abandonment to the Agency at least six months before the abandonment takes effect.

(2) A notice under subsection (1) above shall contain such information (if any) as is prescribed for the purpose, which may include information about the operator's opinion as to any consequences of the abandonment.

(3) A person who fails to give the notice required by subsection (1) above shall be guilty of an offence and liable—

(a) on summary conviction, to a fine not exceeding the statutory maximum;

(b) on conviction on indictment, to a fine.

(4) A person shall not be guilty of an offence under subsection (3) above if—

(a) the abandonment happens in an emergency in order to avoid danger to life or health; and

(b) notice of the abandonment, containing such information as may be prescribed, is given as soon as reasonably practicable after the abandonment has happened.

(5) Where the operator of a mine is—

(a) the official receiver acting in a compulsory capacity, or

(b) the Accountant in Bankruptcy acting as permanent or interim trustee in a sequestration (within the meaning of the Bankruptcy (Scotland) Act 1985),

he shall not be guilty of an offence under subsection (3) above by reason of any failure to give the notice required by subsection (1) above if, as soon as reasonably practicable (whether before or after the abandonment), he gives to the Agency notice of the abandonment or proposed abandonment, containing such information as may be prescribed.

(6) Where a person gives notice under subsection (1), (4)(b) or (5) above, he shall publish prescribed particulars of, or relating to, the notice in one or more local newspapers circulating in the locality where the mine is situated.

(7) Where the Agency—

(a) receives notice under this section or otherwise learns of an abandonment or proposed abandonment in the case of any mine, and

(b) considers that, in consequence of the abandonment or proposed abandonment taking effect, any land has or is likely to become contaminated land, within the meaning of Part IIA of the Environmental Protection Act 1990,

it shall be the duty of the Agency to inform the local authority in whose area that land is situated of the abandonment or proposed abandonment.

(8) In this section—

"the initial period" means the period of six months beginning with the day on which subsection (1) above comes into force;

"local authority" means—

(a) any unitary authority;

(b) any district council, so far as it is not a unitary authority;

(c) the Common Council of the City of London and, as respects the Temples, the Sub-Treasurer of the Inner Temple and the Under-Treasurer of the Middle Temple respectively;

"unitary authority" means—

(a) the council of a county, so far as it is the council of an area for which there are no district councils;

(b) the council of any district comprised in an area for which there is no county council;

(c) the council of a London borough;
(d) the council of a county borough in Wales."

DEFINITIONS
　　"abandonment": s.91A(1) of the Water Resources Act 1991.
　　"acting in a compulsory capacity": s.91A(2) of the Water Resources Act 1991.
　　"initial period": subs. (8).
　　"local authority": subs. (8).
　　"mine": s.91A(2) of the Water Resources Act 1991; s.180 of the 1954 Act.
　　"notice": s.221(1) of the Water Resources Act 1991.
　　"official receiver": s.91A(2) of the Water Resources Act 1991; s.399(1) of the Insolvency Act 1986.
　　"prescribed": s.91A(2) of the Water Resources Act 1991.
　　"unitary authority": subs. (8).

COMMENCEMENT
　　September 21, 1995 insofar as this section confers power on the Secretary of State to make regulations (S.I. 1995 No. 1983). The remainder will be brought into force by a commencement order made under s.125(3) of the 1995 Act.

GENERAL NOTE
　　This section imposes a new duty on mine operators to give six months' prior notice of a proposed abandonment to the Agency. Notification of abandonment of mines has been a legislative requirement since the Mines Inspection and Regulation Act 1870 although the requirement was to notify a Mines' Inspector within two months after the abandonment. However this requirement and its successors have had little, if anything, to do with the environmental consequences of the abandonment of a mine. The rationale for this new measure is simple and was explained by the Government at Committee Stage in the House of Lords:
　　　　"It is sensible that mineowners should give notice to the agency of their intention to abandon a mine so that proper steps can be taken to prevent minewater pollution in future" (*per* Viscount Ullswater, *Hansard*, H.L. Vol. 559, col. 1465).
　　Given the wide definition of "abandonment" in the new s.91A of the Water Resources Act 1991, the imposition of this duty on mine operators should provide the Agency with considerably more information than the NRA currently has access to in relation to proposed abandonments, especially abandonments of parts of mines. This should put the Agency in a better position to plan or advise on or undertake anti-pollution measures. Since the definition of abandonment in s.91A(1) also clearly encompasses several abandonments at the same mine, it may be prudent for an operator who intends to cease production and close a mine to give notification to the Agency at the same time (*i.e.* at least six months prior to the first of the proposed abandonments) that a series of abandonments are to take place, *e.g.* (1) cessation of working of seams which will be followed by salvage, *i.e.* a non-mining activity; (2) cessation of salvage activities and total cessation of pumping operations.
　　It should also be noted that these provisions for prior notification to the Agency on abandonment supplement lease conditions requiring notification to the Coal Authority, imposed by it on the operators of coal mines. (See further the Coal Authority's Model Underground Mine Lease, Sched. 7, para. 4.2.) The Government explained:
　　　　"Under those arrangements, the mine operator has to give the Coal Authority six months' notice of any proposed abandonment and a report on the consequences, except in the case of real emergency.
　　　　As regards the consequences for the water environment, the report is to be based on consultation with the appropriate regulator, the agencies or the present bodies. The operator then has to take all steps necessary to ensure that the mine can be returned to the authority in a satisfactory condition; that is, a condition which does not expose the authority to future liability. If necessary, the operator would have to make an appropriate payment to the authority for any continuing cost before he could relinquish the lease" (*per* Viscount Ullswater, *Hansard*, H.L. Vol. 562, col. 152).
　　In the case of metalliferous mines there is no similar licensing system, although it is submitted that, in relation to new metal mines at least, the planning authority could impose conditions in relation to aftercare of the site which might to a limited extent include certain anti-pollution measures insofar as they related to land use.

Subs. (1)
　　The duty on mine operators to give notice only applies in relation to an abandonment after the expiry of the initial period, *i.e.* the period of six months after the subsection comes into force. The implications of this are that mine operators are free to abandon mines within the initial period but that if they are proposing to abandon at any time after the expiry of that period they

would require to give at least six months' notice. Therefore, if a mine operator wished to abandon a mine on the day following the expiry of the initial period he would be required to give notice on the day following the start of the initial period.

Operator of the mine

This phrase is not defined in the Act. However, the person who is conducting mining operations may be regarded as the operator. In relation to coal mines, the Coal Industry Act 1994 definition of coal-mining operations is set out above in the General Note to subs. (1)(a)(iv). Thus, in relation to a coal mine, the operator of such a mine is likely to be the person carrying on such operations in the mine. In relation to other mines, the 1994 Act provides a good indication of the sorts of operations which the operator of the mine is carrying on.

In the case of coal mines, it may be possible to narrow the scope of the term "mine operator" still further as the operator will usually be the person licensed to carry on coal-mining operations, *i.e.* the licensed operator under Pt. II of the Coal Industry Act 1994 (as defined in s.65(1) of that Act). However, it should be noted that the definition of coal-mining operations given in s.65(1) is wider than the definition of coal-mining operations which require to be licensed under Pt. II (s.25) and hence the operator of the mine may not always be the licensed operator in terms of the Coal Industry Act 1994. It should also be noted that even in the case of a licensed coal mine, it may be that the operator of the mine for the purposes of Chap. IIA of the WRA is not the licensed operator at all. The reason for this is that it is possible for a licensed operator to subcontract the work at a mine to another person: Model Underground Operating Licence, clause 12. In such a situation, it may be that it should be the contractor who notifies the Agency and not necessarily the licensed operator. If the Agency wished to prosecute a person in such a situation for failing to comply with the notification requirement it might be well advised to prosecute both the licensed operator and the contractor.

Subs. (2)

The Secretary of State may make regulations prescribing the information (if any) which must be contained in a notice. No regulations have yet been made. Little guidance is given by the subsection as to the possible scope of the information which may be required except that it may include information about the operator's opinion on the consequences of any abandonment which will be of considerable importance. There may be practical limitations on the information which may be required. For example, although a mine operator may be able to indicate that mining activities involving working the seams of a mine will cease on a particular date, he may be in no position to notify the Agency of the identity of the contractors who will subsequently carry out salvage work and may not yet be in a position to indicate how long salvage operations will take.

Subs. (3)

The maximum penalty on summary conviction is presently a fine of £5,000.

Subs. (4)

No offence is committed in the limited emergency circumstances provided by this subsection.

Subs. (5)

A defence is also available to the official receiver acting in a compulsory capacity and the Accountant in Bankruptcy acting as permanent or interim trustee in a sequestration (within the meaning of the Bankruptcy (Scotland) Act 1985 if he gives notice of the abandonment or proposed abandonment as soon as reasonably practicable. This defence is designed to deal with the fact that abandonment sometimes accompanies the insolvency of the operator. While private sector insolvency practitioners may refuse to act, neither the official receiver nor the Accountant in Bankruptcy may do so. If this defence were not available, they could be compelled to continue some mining operations when there were no assets in the company to fund this, or face prosecution for the criminal offence of failure to notify. These provisions are therefore designed to provide protection to the official receiver and the Accountant in Bankruptcy so that even if the physical factors denoting abandonment apply, nevertheless no offence is committed by the official receiver or Accountant in Bankruptcy when he abandons a mine or part of a mine without giving six months' notice providing he notifies the agency as soon as possible (*per* Earl Ferrers, *Hansard*, H.L. Vol. 565, col. 1521).

Subs. (6)

This subsection lays down publicity requirements which apply in all cases where notice is given under subs. (1). Hence, even when an operator ceases working a seam, then notice will be required. The Government initially took the view that this was "an unnecessary bureaucratic burden on industry" (Mr Robert Atkins, Standing Committee B, May 23, 1995, col. 397), although having considered the matter further they brought forward their own amendment (*per* Earl Ferrers, *Hansard*, H.L. Vol. 565, cols. 1520–1521) laying down publicity requirements. No offence appears to be committed by an operator if he fails to comply with these publicity requirements.

Subs. (7)

This subsection provides a link between the abandoned mines provisions and the new contaminated land provisions. The Agency is under a duty to inform the relevant local authority where it receives a notice of abandonment or proposed abandonment and as a consequence thereof any land has or is likely to become contaminated in terms of the definition of contaminated land in Pt. IIA of the 1990 Act. Insofar as it is not prevented from doing so by s.78J(3), the local authority must then serve a remediation notice if the appropriate tests of contamination in s.78A are met.

Abandoned mines: Scotland

59. After Part I of the Control of Pollution Act 1974 (waste on land) there shall be inserted—

"PART IA

ABANDONED MINES

Introductory

30Y.—(1) For the purposes of this Part, "abandonment", in relation to a mine,—

(a) subject to paragraph (b) below, includes—

(i) the discontinuance of any or all of the operations for the removal of water from the mine;

(ii) the cessation of working of any relevant seam, vein or vein-system;

(iii) the cessation of use of any shaft or outlet of the mine;

(iv) in the case of a mine in which activities other than mining activities are carried on (whether or not mining activities are also carried on in the mine)—

(A) the discontinuance of some or all of those other activities in the mine; and

(B) any substantial change in the operations for the removal of water from the mine; but

(b) does not include—

(i) the abandonment of any rights, interests or liabilities by the Accountant in Bankruptcy acting as permanent or interim trustee in a sequestration (within the meaning of the Bankruptcy (Scotland) Act 1985); or

(ii) any disclaimer under section 178 or 315 of the Insolvency Act 1986 (power of liquidator, or trustee of bankrupt's estate, to disclaim onerous property) by the official receiver acting in a compulsory capacity;

and cognate expressions shall be construed accordingly.

(2) In this Part, except where the context otherwise requires—

"acting in a compulsory capacity", in the case of the official receiver, means acting as—

(a) liquidator of a company;

(b) receiver or manager of a bankrupt's estate, pursuant to section 287 of the Insolvency Act 1986;

(c) trustee of a bankrupt's estate;

(d) liquidator of an insolvent partnership;

(e) trustee of an insolvent partnership;

(f) trustee, or receiver or manager, of the insolvent estate of a deceased person;

"the official receiver" has the same meaning as it has in the Insolvency Act 1986 by virtue of section 399(1) of that Act;

"relevant seam, vein or vein-system", in the case of any mine, means any seam, vein or vein-system for the purpose of, or in connection with, whose working any excavation constituting or comprised in the mine was made.

(3) This Part extends only to Scotland.

DEFINITIONS

"acting in a compulsory capacity": subs. (2).
"mine": s.105(1) of the 1974 Act; s.180(1) of the 1954 Act.
"official receiver": subs. (2); s.399(1) of the Insolvency Act 1986.
"relevant seam, vein or vein-system": subs. (2).

COMMENCEMENT

This section will be brought into force by a commencement order made under s.125(3) of the 1995 Act.

GENERAL NOTE

This section makes identical provision for Scotland relating to the definition of abandonment. See the General Note to s.91A of the 1991 Act at p. 25–195 above. References to the relevant sections of the Control of Pollution Act 1974 should be substituted for references to the provisions of the 1991 Act in that note. This section and s.30Z which follows are inserted into the 1974 Act out of sequence. Section 59 of the 1995 Act inserts them as Part IA, after s.30 (the final section of Part I of the 1974 Act), and therefore before ss.30A–30J (ss.30F–30J are inserted by Sched. 16 to the 1995 Act).

Mine operators to give SEPA six months' notice of any proposed abandonment

30Z.—(1) If, in the case of any mine, there is to be an abandonment at any time after the expiration of the initial period, it shall be the duty of the operator of the mine to give notice of the proposed abandonment to SEPA at least six months before the abandonment takes effect.

(2) A notice under subsection (1) above shall contain such information (if any) as is prescribed for the purpose, which may include information about the operator's opinion as to any consequences of the abandonment.

(3) A person who fails to give the notice required by subsection (1) above shall be guilty of an offence and liable—

(a) on summary conviction, to a fine not exceeding the statutory maximum;

(b) on conviction on indictment, to a fine.

(4) A person shall not be guilty of an offence under subsection (3) above if—

(a) the abandonment happens in an emergency in order to avoid danger to life or health; and

(b) notice of the abandonment, containing such information as may be prescribed, is given as soon as reasonably practicable after the abandonment has happened.

(5) Where the operator of a mine is—

(a) the Accountant in Bankruptcy acting as permanent or interim trustee in a sequestration (within the meaning of the Bankruptcy (Scotland) Act 1985); or

(b) the official receiver acting in a compulsory capacity,

he shall not be guilty of an offence under subsection (3) above by reason of any failure to give the notice required by subsection (1) above if, as soon as is reasonably practicable (whether before or after the abandonment), he gives to SEPA notice of the abandonment or proposed abandonment, containing such information as may be prescribed.

(6) Where a person gives notice under subsection (1), (4)(b) or (5) above, he shall publish prescribed particulars of, or relating to, the notice in one or more local newspapers circulating in the locality where the mine is situated.

(7) Where SEPA—
  (a) receives notice under this section or otherwise learns of an abandonment or proposed abandonment in the case of any mine, and
  (b) considers that, in consequence of the abandonment or proposed abandonment taking effect, any land has or is likely to become contaminated land, within the meaning of Part IIA of the Environmental Protection Act 1990,
it shall be the duty of SEPA to inform the local authority in whose area that land is situated of the abandonment or proposed abandonment.

(8) In this section—
  "the initial period" means the period of six months beginning with the day on which subsection (1) above comes into force;
  "local authority" means a council constituted under section 2 of the Local Government etc. (Scotland) Act 1994."

DEFINITIONS
"abandonment": s.30Y(1) of the 1974 Act.
"acting in a compulsory capacity": s.30Y(2) of the 1974 Act.
"initial period": subs. (8).
"local authority": subs. (8).
"mine": s.105(1) of the 1974 Act; s.180(1) of the 1954 Act.
"notice": s.105(1) of the 1974 Act.
"official receiver": s.30Y(2) of the 1974 Act; s.399(1) of the Insolvency Act 1986.
"prescribed": s.105(1) of the 1974 Act.
"regulations": s.105(1) of the 1974 Act.

COMMENCEMENT
This section will be brought into force by a commencement order made under s.125(3).

GENERAL NOTE
This section is the Scottish equivalent of s.91B of the Water Resources Act. See also General Note to s.91B of the 1991 Act at p. 25–199 above.

Amendments to sections 89 and 161 of the Water Resources Act 1991

60.—(1) In section 89 of the Water Resources Act 1991 (defences) in subsection (3) (person not to be guilty of an offence under section 85 by reason only of permitting water from an abandoned mine to enter controlled waters) after the words "an abandoned mine" there shall be inserted the words "or an abandoned part of a mine".

(2) After that subsection there shall be inserted—
  "(3A) Subsection (3) above shall not apply to the owner or former operator of any mine or part of a mine if the mine or part in question became abandoned after 31st December 1999.

  (3B) In determining for the purposes of subsection (3A) above whether a mine or part of a mine became abandoned before, on or after 31st December 1999 in a case where the mine or part has become abandoned on two or more occasions, of which—
    (a) at least one falls on or before that date, and
    (b) at least one falls after that date,
  the mine or part shall be regarded as becoming abandoned after that date (but without prejudice to the operation of subsection (3) above in relation to that mine or part at, or in relation to, any time before the first of those occasions which falls after that date).

(3C) Where, immediately before a part of a mine becomes abandoned, that part is the only part of the mine not falling to be regarded as abandoned for the time being, the abandonment of that part shall not be regarded for the purposes of subsection (3A) or (3B) above as constituting the abandonment of the mine, but only of that part of it."

(3) In section 161 of that Act (anti-pollution works and operations) in subsection (1), after paragraph (b) there shall be inserted the words—

"and, in either case, the Agency shall be entitled to carry out investigations for the purpose of establishing the source of the matter and the identity of the person who has caused or knowingly permitted it to be present in controlled waters or at a place from which it was likely, in the opinion of the Agency, to enter controlled waters."

(4) In subsection (3) of that section (Agency entitled to recover expenses of works or operations from the person responsible for the pollution) for the words "or operations" there shall be substituted the words "operations or investigations".

(5) In subsection (4) of that section (exception for expenses of works or operations in respect of water from an abandoned mine)—

    (a) for the words "or operations" there shall be substituted the words "operations or investigations"; and

    (b) after the words "an abandoned mine" there shall be inserted the words "or an abandoned part of a mine".

(6) After that subsection there shall be inserted—

"(4A) Subsection (4) above shall not apply to the owner or former operator of any mine or part of a mine if the mine or part in question became abandoned after 31st December 1999.

(4B) Subsections (3B) and (3C) of section 89 above shall apply in relation to subsections (4) and (4A) above as they apply in relation to subsections (3) and (3A) of that section."

(7) In subsection (6) of that section (definitions), after the definition of "controlled waters" there shall be inserted—

""expenses" includes costs;".

DEFINITIONS

    "abandonment": s.91A(1) of the Water Resources Act 1991.
    "controlled waters": s.104 of the Water Resources Act 1991.
    "expenses": subs. (7).
    "mine": s.91A(2) of the Water Resources Act 1991; s.180 of the Mines and Quarries Act 1954.

COMMENCEMENT

    October 12, 1995 insofar as this section confers power on the Secretary of State to make regulations (S.I. 1995 No. 2649). The remainder will be brought into force by a commencement order made under s.125(3) of the 1995 Act.

GENERAL NOTE

    This section, which applies only to England and Wales, amends, by subs. (1) and (2), s.89 of the Water Resources Act 1991, removing the defence to a charge of permitting water pollution from an abandoned mine after December 31, 1999 insofar as it is available to the owner and former operator of an abandoned mine; and by subss. (3) to (6) amends s.161 of the Water Resources Act 1991 enabling the Agency to recover the costs of preventive or remedial works undertaken from the owner or former operator of an abandoned mine who permitted pollution of controlled waters or who permitted pollution to be at a place where it was likely to enter controlled waters after December 31, 1999. The equivalent Scottish legislative changes may be found in Sched. 16, para. 2 which introduces a new s.30J(3) to (6) which removes the defence after December 31, 1999 and in Sched. 22, para. 21(e) which introduces a new s.46(3A) of the 1974 Act which removes the cost recovery exemption from the same date.

Subs. (1)

    The defence in s.89(3) of the Water Resources Act 1991 is amended to include permitting water pollution from "an abandoned part of a mine". This will have the effect of widening the ambit of the defence since it is not clear at present whether the current definition of abandoned mine includes part of an abandoned mine. Although this widening of the scope of the defence is only temporary it is clearly a retrograde step as at present, where a mine is only partially abandoned, it could be argued that a prosecution for permitting water pollution from a mine might succeed on the basis that partial abandonment is not currently part of the definition of abandonment. However, it is understandable in the light of the new definition of abandonment in s.58. Although that definition does not apply in Chap. II as is made clear by the words "For the purposes of this Chapter [*i.e.* IIA of the 1991 Act], 'abandonment', in relation to a mine ... includes ...", an awkward situation might otherwise have arisen whereby under s.91A and B an operator might have to give notice that he was discontinuing some pumping operations in his mine which would constitute abandonment in terms of s.91A(1)(a)(i) but could still be prosecuted for permitting water pollution from a mine since the defence in s.89(3) did not originally refer to permitting water pollution from an abandoned part of a mine. The addition of the words "or part of an abandoned mine" to s.89(3) ensures that such a situation could not arise.

Schedule 16, para. 2 makes identical provision for Scotland inserting a new s.30J(3) and (4) into the 1974 Act.

Subs. (2)

This subsection inserts new ss.89(3A) to (3C) into the Water Resources Act 1991. Section 89(3) of the Water Resources Act 1991 provides:

"A person shall not be guilty of an offence under section 85 by reason only of his permitting water from an abandoned mine to enter controlled waters".

New s.89(3A) provides for the removal of that defence from December 31, 1999 but it should be noted that the defence will not be withdrawn from every person after that date. It is only withdrawn from the owner or former operator of the abandoned mine. Thus, landowners who never operated an abandoned mine on their property, yet are aware of water pollution issuing from it, will be liable along with the former operator after December 31, 1999.

Concerns regarding the extension of liability to innocent landowners and occupiers were expressed in Parliament (*e.g. per* Lord Stanley of Alderley, *Hansard*, H.L. Vol. 562, cols. 231–232; and cols. 1057–1058). Lord Stanley of Alderley managed to force an amendment at Third Reading in the House of Lords (Vol. 562, cols. 1057–1058) which limited the scope of persons from whom the defence is withdrawn from December 31, 1999. As originally drafted the clause had provided for the defence being withdrawn from every person. However, Lord Stanley's amendment which was subsequently accepted by the Government provides protection for an innocent landowner or occupier who is aware of polluted water from an abandoned mine located on someone else's land coming on to his land and entering controlled waters. Formerly the Government's intention had been to remove the defence from such innocent occupiers.

However, the Government were not prepared to accept an amendment preserving the defence for innocent landowners on whose land an abandoned mine was actually situated:

"An offence would be committed only if a person had caused or knowingly permitted the pollution of controlled waters. This is a strong test and there would be no liability for truly innocent landowners. To be liable a landowner would have to know about the discharge and it would have to be within his or her power to do something to prevent it. ... The knowledge of an ability to prevent the pollution occurring is required to satisfy "knowingly permitted". That would be a difficult test to meet where there was pollution of an aquifer deep underground. The owner of the surface land would be unlikely to know about it or be able to prevent such pollution" (*per* Viscount Ullswater, *Hansard*, H.L. Vol. 562, cols. 237–238).

Furthermore, given that the Government's intention is to bring into force the notification of abandonment provisions "immediately", the Agency will be aware of who the operator is and should be equipped with the appropriate information to tackle any possible pollution problems (*per* Viscount Ullswater, *Hansard*, H.L. Vol. 562, col. 1060). In the light of such assurances it seems very unlikely that the Agency would wish to proceed against an innocent landowner since it should have details of the former operator.

The provisions in s.89(3B) and (3C) are designed to ensure that mines or parts of mines abandoned before the end of 1999, and so benefiting from the existing statutory protections, will not lose those protections if another part of the mine or an adjoining mine, possibly under separate ownership, is abandoned after that date (Mr Robert Atkins, Standing Committee B, May 23, 1995, col. 412).

The new s.89(3B) provides assistance in determining whether a mine which has undergone a number of abandonments partial or otherwise was abandoned before, on or after December 31, 1999. Thus, a mine or part of a mine is considered to have been abandoned after December 31, 1999 where it has been abandoned on two or more occasions and at least one of those occasions falls on or before that date and at least one after that date. However, the wording in brackets ensures that the statutory defence continues to apply up to the first abandonment which occurs after December 31, 1999. The implication of this is that although a mine is abandoned several times and at least one of those occasions occurs before December 31, 1999 and another after that date, and although the mine will be regarded as being abandoned after that date, nonetheless the defence will be available in relation to any potential criminal liability which arose as a result of any abandonment of the mine before December 31, 1999.

The new s.89(3C) covers the type of situation where a mine has been largely abandoned and the final part of the mine is about to be abandoned. It provides that the abandonment of that final part of the mine must not be regarded for the purposes of s.3A and s.3B as the abandonment of the whole mine but only that final part which is actually abandoned. This provision is presumably designed to limit the potential liability of an operator who has abandoned most parts of a mine by December 31, 1999 and abandons the final part of the mine after that date. Although being the final abandonment of the mine, that abandonment will only be regarded as the abandonment of that part of the mine and hence liability will only arise in respect of water pollution which is permitted from that abandonment. In practice it may be extremely difficult to distinguish between water pollution which is being permitted from that final part of the abandoned mine and that being permitted from other parts of the mine which were abandoned earlier.

Schedule 16, para. 2 makes identical provision for Scotland inserting a new s.30J(5)–(6) of the 1974 Act (see also General Note to Sched. 16 at p. 25–386, below).

Subss. (3) and (4)

This subsection amends s.161(1) of the Water Resources Act 1991 in order to provide the Agency with a valuable new power to carry out investigations to ascertain the source of the polluting matter and the identity of the person who caused or knowingly permitted it to be present in controlled waters or to reach a place from which it was likely, to enter controlled waters. Since the Agency is given this power in addition to its power to undertake preventive or remedial anti-pollution works or operations, it is also given the power by subs. (4), which amends s.161(3) of the 1991 Act, to recover expenses from the person responsible for the pollution for investigations as well as the anti-pollution works or operations.

Schedule 22, para. 21(b) and (c) make equivalent provision for Scotland by inserting a new s.46(1A) into the 1974 Act and making the appropriate amendment to s.46(2) of the 1974 Act.

Subs. (5)

The exception for recovery of expenses for preventive or remedial anti-pollution works or operations in relation to permitting water pollution from abandoned mines is extended to include (a) investigations given the amendments in subss. (3) and (4) and (b) an abandoned part of a mine in addition to an abandoned mine in the light of the new definition of abandonment which includes partial abandonment (see General Note to s.91A of the 1991 Act at p. 25–196, above).

Schedule 22, para. 21(d) makes equivalent provision for Scotland by making the appropriate amendments to the 1974 Act, s.46(3)(b).

Subs. (6)

This subsection, which inserts a new s.161(4A) and (4B) to the Water Resources Act 1991 removes the expense recovery exception after December 31, 1999. It also applies the provisions in s.89(3B) and (3C) to the removal of the cost recovery exemption in s.161(4A) and (4B) in the same way as they apply to the withdrawal of the defence in s.89(3) and (3A) of the 1991 Act.

Schedule 22, para. 21(e) makes equivalent provision for Scotland by inserting new s.46(3A) and (3B) into the 1974 Act (see also the General Note to Sched. 22, para. 21).

Subs. (7)

This subsection inserts a definition of expenses into s.161(6) of the Water Resources Act 1991 to clarify that expenses includes costs.

PART III

NATIONAL PARKS

GENERAL NOTE

The purpose of Pt. III of the Act was succinctly summarised by Viscount Ullswater, the Minister of State, at the Lords Committee stage as follows:

"The Bill fulfils our central commitment to establish independent authorities for the 10 national parks in England and Wales. It also updates park purposes which will enable the new authorities to take a more integrated approach to the management of their areas. Those measures will enable the national park authorities more effectively to protect the qualities for which the national parks have been designated" (*Hansard*, H.L. Vol. 560, col. 1593).

These reforms have been under consideration for some time, since a number of them stem from the 1990 report of the National Parks Review Committee, *Fit for the Future* (often referred to as the Edwards Report) and the Government's 1992 policy statement on national parks which was published in response to that report. Some of the changes made by the Act were therefore uncontroversial. However, the changes are to be seen against a background of increasing pressures on national parks, pressures which led to much concerned debate in the House of Lords on issues such as noisy recreational activities, the problem of "honeypot" attractions to large numbers of tourists, overflying and other military training uses of national parks, the economic well-being of such areas, and public footpaths and other forms of access.

Scotland

Like the provisions contained in the National Parks and Access to the Countryside Act 1949 (c. 97) relating to national parks, Pt. III does not extend to Scotland. This was because at the time when national parks were established in England and Wales, there was no comparable pressure from urban areas in Scotland on scenic areas. However, that has now changed with great pressures on areas such as Loch Lomond and the Cairngorms. There are even fears that restrictions on certain activities in Lake Windermere will drive power boaters and jet skiers from England to Loch Lomond (*per* Sam Galbraith, Standing Committee B, May 25, 1995, col. 444). For these reasons there is now considerable pressure to designate national parks in Scotland (see *e.g.* Sam Galbraith, *Hansard*, H.C. Vol. 258, col. 74). Prior to its incorporation into Scottish Natural Heritage, the Countryside Commission for Scotland recommended in its 1990 report on Scottish mountain areas the establishment of national parks for the Cairngorms, Loch Lomond, Ben Nevis, Glencoe, the Black Mount and Wester Ross. As a result there was an attempt during the passage of the Bill through Parliament to include an amendment to extend Pts. I, II, V and VI of the National Parks and Access to the Countryside Act 1949 to Scotland (*per* Maria Fyfe, *Hansard*, H.C. Vol. 262, col. 784). The Government was not prepared to accept such an amendment, preferring to rely on the voluntary partnership scheme for the Cairngorms and similar proposals for Loch Lomond together with the byelaws which are being promoted for that loch (*per* Sir Hector Monro, Parliamentary Under-Secretary of State for Scotland, *Hansard*, H.C. Vol. 262, cols. 788–789; see also Sir Hector Monro, Standing Committee B, May 25, 1995, col. 443).

Purposes of National Parks

Purposes of National Parks

61.—(1) In section 5 of the National Parks and Access to the Countryside Act 1949 (National Parks) for subsection (1) (which provides that Part II of that Act has effect for the purpose of preserving and enhancing the natural beauty of the areas specified in subsection (2) of that section and for the purpose of promoting their enjoyment by the public) there shall be substituted—

"(1) The provisions of this Part of this Act shall have effect for the purpose—

(a) of conserving and enhancing the natural beauty, wildlife and cultural heritage of the areas specified in the next following subsection; and

(b) of promoting opportunities for the understanding and enjoyment of the special qualities of those areas by the public."

(2) The amendment made by subsection (1) above is without prejudice to the continuing validity of any designation of an area as a National Park under subsection (3) of that section.

(3) The following enactments (which refer to the purposes specified in section 5(1) of the National Parks and Access to the Countryside Act 1949), that is to say—

(a) sections 6(3) and (4)(g), 11 and 101(3) of that Act, and

(b) sections 2(5)(b) and 13(4) of the Countryside Act 1968, shall have effect in accordance with subsection (4) below.

(4) In the appliction of any provision specified in subsection (3) above, any reference to the purposes specified in subsection (1) of section 5 of the National Parks and Access to the Countryside Act 1949—

　(a) in relation to any particular National Park, shall be construed as a reference to the substituted purposes as from the time when a National Park authority becomes the local planning authority for that Park; and

　(b) in relation to National Parks generally, shall be construed as a reference—

　　(i) to the original purposes, so far as relating to National Parks in the case of which the National Park authority has not become the local planning authority since the coming into force of this section, and

　　(ii) to the substituted purposes, so far as relating to National Parks in the case of which the National Park authority has become the local planning authority since the coming into force of this section.

(5) In subsection (4) above—

"original purposes" means the purposes specified in subsection (1) of section 5 of that Act, as originally enacted;

"substituted purposes" means the purposes specified in that subsection as substituted by subsection (1) above.

COMMENCEMENT

September 19, 1995 (s.125(2)).

GENERAL NOTE

This section amends s.5(1) of the National Parks and Access to the Countryside Act 1949 to provide a redefinition of the purposes for which Pt. II of that Act (National Parks) shall have effect. The purposes as originally set out in the 1949 Act were preserving and enhancing natural beauty in National Parks, and promoting their enjoyment by the public.

The new purposes: conservation and enhancement

The conservation and enhancement aspect is widened to include wildlife and cultural heritage, as well as natural beauty. The word "conservation" used in the new provision, is therefore more apt than "preservation", as in the original purposes. The Edwards Report had suggested a purpose which would expressly include natural systems and land forms, a point drawn to the attention of the Government in debate by Lord Cranbrook (Chairman of English Nature). However, the Government regarded any such reference as unnecessary since, in their view, characteristic natural features were an integral part of natural beauty: *Hansard*, H.L. Vol. 560, col. 1592.

The new purposes: understanding and enjoyment by the public

This limb of the new statutory purposes was highly controversial in the House of Lords' debates. The issue of recreation in national parks has become a difficult one since 1949 as a result of the emergence of noisy forms of leisure such as jet-skis, off-road vehicles, microlight aircraft, and the like. It was for this reason that Lord Norrie introduced an amendment to refer to "quiet enjoyment and understanding", pointing out that when the recreational purpose was drafted in 1949 its intention was to promote quiet pursuits:

　　"At that stage no-one could envisage the growth in noisy and intrusive motorised recreation activities. No Minister imagined the emergence of the jet ski or the towed inflatable crocodile onto the waters of our parks" (*Hansard*, H.L. Vol. 560, col. 1594).

In support of his amendment, Lord Norrie was able to point to the views of the Edwards Report in 1990, and the subsequent commitment by the Government to introduce legislation referring expressly to quiet enjoyment and understanding. Lord Norrie was also at pains to stress that the provision was in the context of promoting recreational activities, and not banning any particular forms of activity. Although a number of members of the Lords expressed disquiet as to the uncertainty involved in trying to define what was "quiet" enjoyment, and the possible confusion which might arise from using a term with an established meaning in landlord and tenant law, the amendment was agreed to by a narrow majority of 129 to 121.

The Government in the Lords' debate took the view that whilst its 1992 policy statement on national parks referred to quiet enjoyment, it also recognised that national parks should provide a wide range of experiences for the visitor. Co-operation was seen as the best means of resolving such issues, but the Government did not accept as a matter of principle that any particular recreational activities should be excluded from national parks; see *Hansard*, H.L. Vol. 560, col. 1609.

At Commons Committee Stage, the insertion of the word "quiet" was opposed by various interests, including the sailing and motor-sport fraternities. The ultimate result was that the Lords' amendment was reversed. In bringing the Bill back to the Lords, Earl Ferrers indicated that after deliberation the Government had come to the conclusion that the "quiet enjoyment" terminology might be more detrimental to the future of the parks than its supporters realised. The Government intended to make it clear in guidance that conservation values should be fully respected: it was not appropriate for all forms of recreation to take place in national parks and "... Large areas of the parks will, and should, continue to be quietly enjoyed for much of the time" (*Hansard*, H.L. Vol. 565, col. 1524).

The Government's draft circular on the new provisions on national parks, issued for consultation on January 31, 1995, and in revised form on November 6, 1995, simply refers to the opportunities offered by the parks for "open-air recreation" and indicates that decisions on how best to promote understanding and enjoyment will depend on the special qualities of each individual park: "Particular emphasis should be placed on opportunities to enjoy the wide open spaces, and the wildness and tranquillity which are to be found in the parks' more remote or less heavily visited areas, without endangering those special characteristics". See also the General Note to s.62 below on reconciling conflicts in national park purposes.

Relevant provisions of Pt. II

The provisions of Pt. II of the 1949 Act in relation to which the new purposes will be relevant include s.5 (designation of new National Parks), s.6 (duties of Countryside Commission and, in Wales, the Countryside Council), s.7 (designation and variation of National Park authorities), s.11 (powers of local planning authorities), s.11A (duties of National Parks authorities), s.12 (provision of accommodation, refreshments, camping sites and parking places), s.13 (improvement of waterways for open-air recreation) and s.14 (acquisition of land by Minister).

Subs. (2)

The change to National Park purposes does not prejudice the continuing validity of existing orders designating National Parks.

Subss. (3)–(5)

A number of other provisions, mentioned at subs. (3) adopt or refer to the s.5(1) purposes. These include, for example, the management of Crown land (s.101(3) of the 1949 Act), functions of the Countryside Commission (s.2(5)(b) of the Countryside Act 1968) and byelaws for the control of boats in National Parks (s.13(4) of the 1968 Act). Subsection (4) makes it clear whether the reference is to the original purposes or to the new substituted purposes. The issue turns on whether, in relation to the National Park under consideration, the National Park authority has yet become the local planning authority: see s.63.

Ministry of Defence Activities

Large areas of National Park land have historically been owned, occupied or used by the Ministry of Defence for training and other purposes. There is an argument that this has furthered nature conservation in some areas, but concerns have also been expressed that such activities conflict with the statutory purposes of the Parks both previously and as now amended. A recent example is the concern expressed by the Council for the Protection of Rural England at the Ministry's submission of a notice of proposed development in relation to the Otterburn Training Area in the Northumberland National Park: *CPRE* Press Release 96/95, September 12, 1995. The Press Release appends an extract of a letter from the CPRE to the Park's National Park Officer objecting to the proposed development on the ground, *inter alia*, that it conflicts with the statutory purposes of the Park under this section.

A very different view of the issue was expressed at the Bill's Second Reading in the House of Commons earlier in the year by Mr Peter Atkinson, whose constituency contained the training area. Suggesting that local people "are very supportive of the military training area at Otterburn", he proposed that the power to instigate a change in the boundaries of a National Park (in this case so as to exclude the training area from the Park and thus end any debate about its compatibility with Park purposes) be transferred by the Bill from the Countryside Commission to the Secretary of State. His concern appears to have been that the Commission might be hostile in principle to reducing the size of a National Park in order to further military activities: citing the Commission's annual report for 1993–1994 ("We have always advocated that military use of land in the National Parks is inconsistent with their purposes"), he concluded that "In other words, the organisation responsible for setting the boundaries of national parks is in this case acting as judge and jury in its own court, and local people find that unacceptable" (*Hansard*, H.C. Vol. 258, cols. 88–89).

Duty of certain bodies and persons to have regard to the purposes for which National Parks are designated

62.—(1) After section 11 of the National Parks and Access to the Countryside Act 1949 (general powers of local planning authorities in relation to National Parks) there shall be inserted—

> **"Duty of certain bodies and persons to have regard to the purposes for which National Parks are designated**
>
> 11A.—(1) A National Park authority, in pursuing in relation to the National Park the purposes specified in subsection (1) of section five of this Act, shall seek to foster the economic and social well-being of local communities within the National Park, but without incurring significant expenditure in doing so, and shall for that purpose co-operate with local authorities and public bodies whose functions include the promotion of economic or social development within the area of the National Park.
>
> (2) In exercising or performing any functions in relation to, or so as to affect, land in a National Park, any relevant authority shall have regard to the purposes specified in subsection (1) of section five of this Act and, if it appears that there is a conflict between those purposes, shall attach greater weight to the purpose of conserving and enhancing the natural beauty, wildlife and cultural heritage of the area comprised in the National Park.
>
> (3) For the purposes of this section "relevant authority" means—
> (a) any Minister of the Crown,
> (b) any public body,
> (c) any statutory undertaker, or
> (d) any person holding public office.
> (4) In subsection (3) of this section—
> "public body" includes—
>> (a) any local authority, joint board or joint committee;
>> (b) any National Park authority;
> "public office" means—
>> (a) an office under Her Majesty;
>> (b) an office created or continued in existence by a public general Act of Parliament; or
>> (c) an office the remuneration in respect of which is paid out of money provided by Parliament.
> (5) In subsection (4) of this section, "joint board" and "joint committee" mean—
> (a) a joint or special planning board for a National Park reconstituted by order under paragraph 1 or 3 of Schedule 17 to the Local Government Act 1972, or a joint planning board within the meaning of section 2 of the Town and Country Planning Act 1990;
> (b) a joint committee appointed under section 102(1)(b) of the Local Government Act 1972.
> (6) In this section, "local authority'—
> (a) in relation to England, means a county council, district council or parish council;
> (b) in relation to Wales, means a county council, county borough council, district council or community council."

(2) The duty imposed by subsection (1) of the section 11A inserted by subsection (1) above shall take effect, in the case of any particular National Park, as from the time when a National Park authority becomes the local planning authority for that Park.

DEFINITIONS
"National Park authority": s.63(1).

COMMENCEMENT
September 19, 1995 (s.125(2)).

GENERAL NOTE
This section inserts into the 1949 Act a new s.11A, which imposes upon the new National Parks authorities to be created under s.63, duties to have regard to various matters. The duty takes effect from the time when the National Parks authority becomes the local planning authority for the National Park in question.

The key features of the new provision are:

(1) In pursuing the purposes specified in the new provisions of s.5(1) of the 1949 Act (see s.61 above), the authority must seek to foster the economic and social well-being of local communities within National Parks, but without incurring substantial financial expenditure in so doing (s.11A(1)). The word "foster" was chosen deliberately as reflecting a sense of responsibility whilst avoiding any implication of active financial support for local communities which it would not be appropriate for the national park authorities to take on: *Hansard*, H.L. Vol. 562, col. 1066 and the draft circular on national parks (November 6, 1995), para. 22.

(2) The authority must, for that purpose, cooperate with local authorities and public bodies which promote economic or social development within the area (for example, The Rural Development Commission, Welsh Development Agency, and Development Board for Rural Wales): see, *Hansard*, H.L. Vol. 562, col. 412.

(3) In exercising or performing functions generally in relation to a National Park, the authority must have regard to the statutory purposes set out in the new provisions of s.5(1). The Government saw the "have regard to" terminology as more appropriate than a suggested amendment to "further" in the light of the differing and conflicting pressures likely to arise in the case of national parks: *Hansard*, H.L. Vol. 562, col. 1643.

(4) In having such regard, if there is a perceived conflict between the first objective (of conserving and enhancing natural beauty, wildlife and the cultural heritage) and the second (of promoting opportunities for the understanding and enjoyment by the public of the special qualities of the Park), authorities shall attach greater weight to the first objective. This principle (the so-called "Sandford principle") has been Government policy in relation to national parks for many years. The Government indicated in debate that every opportunity should be taken for negotiation and mediation before the principle was applied: *Hansard*, H.L. Vol. 560, col. 1660. Paragraph 17 of the Government's revised draft circular on national parks (November 6, 1995) states that national park authorities and other public bodies will be expected to make every effort to reconcile conflicts between the two purposes. National parks are seen by the Government as capable of accommodating many different types of leisure activity: park authorities are especially encouraged to work closely with the relevant sports bodies in drawing up and promoting codes of practice. The Government accepts, however, that some recreational activities for which a place will be sought in the parks could cause unacceptable damage or disturbance to their natural beauty, wildlife or cultural heritage, which in turn may affect others' understanding and enjoyment of them: it is here that the Sandford principle in its legislative form will come into play.

Establishment of National Park authorities

Establishment of National Park authorities

63.—(1) The Secretary of State may—

(a) in the case of any National Park for which there is an existing authority, or

(b) in connection with the designation of any area as a new such Park,

by order establish an authority (to be known as "a National Park authority") to carry out in relation to that Park the functions conferred on such an authority by or under this Part.

(2) An order under this section may provide, in relation to any National Park for which there is an existing authority—

(a) for the existing authority to cease to have any functions in relation to that Park as from the time when a National Park authority becomes the local planning authority for that Park;

(b) for such (if any) of the functions of the existing authority as, by virtue of this Part, are not as from that time to be functions of the National

Park authority for that Park to become functions of the person on whom they would be conferred if the area in question were not in a National Park; and

(c) for the winding up of the existing authority and for that authority to cease to exist, or to be dissolved, as from such time as may be specified in the order.

(3) Subject to any order under subsection (4) below, where there is a variation of the area of a National Park for which there is or is to be a National Park authority, the Park for which that authority is or is to be the authority shall be deemed, as from the time when the variation takes effect, to be that area as varied.

(4) Where provision is made for the variation of the area of a National Park for which there is or is to be a National Park authority, the Secretary of State may by order make such transitional provision as he thinks fit with respect to—

(a) any functions which, in relation to any area that becomes part of the National Park, are by virtue of the variation to become functions of that authority; and

(b) any functions which, in relation to any area that ceases to be part of the National Park, are by virtue of the variation to become functions of a person other than that authority.

(5) Schedule 7 to this Act shall have effect with respect to National Park authorities.

DEFINITIONS
"existing authority": s.79(1).
"functions": s.124(1).
"National Park authority": subs. (1).

COMMENCEMENT
Save insofar as it gives effect to para. 7(2) of Sched. 7, this section comes into force on September 19, 1995: the remainder comes into force on a day to be appointed: s.125(2) and (3).

GENERAL NOTE
This section allows the Secretary of State to make orders establishing authorities (known as National Parks authorities) to assume the statutory functions of the existing planning authority either for National Parks where there is already such an authority, or for new National Parks. The Government's thinking behind the creation of the new authorities is that they will provide the advantages of greater clarity of vision, higher profile, freedom to manage their own affairs, and a more undivided commitment to national park objectives: *Hansard*, H.L. Vol. 560, col. 1665.

The existing planning authorities for national parks are either the joint or special planning board, or the National Park Committee: s.79(1). There are currently two planning boards, the Lake District Special Planning Board (reconstituted by S.I. 1973 No. 2001) and the Peak Park Joint Planning Board (reconstituted by S.I. 1973 No. 2061). These boards are statutorily responsible for all district and county council local planning authority functions. In the other National Parks, planning functions are vested in the county council and in general are required to be exercised through the National Park Committees established by the council or councils concerned. The functions of the new authorities are dealt with in ss.65–70. The order establishing the authority may provide for the winding up of the existing authority, and for any of its functions not transferred to the new authority to revert to the person on whom they would be conferred if the area were not a National Park: subs. (2)(b) and (c).

Constitution of new authorities
Schedule 7 deals with the status and constitution of the new authorities, which are to be bodies corporate. Their composition will be determined by the order establishing them, but must include local authority members, members appointed by the Secretary of State, and (in England) parish members: para. 1(2) and (3). In Wales, the number of local authority members is to be twice that of Secretary of State members: para. 1(4)(b). In England, the number of local authority members must be two greater than the number of Secretary of State members (including parish members): para. 1(4)(a). The parish members in turn must comprise one less than one-half of the total Secretary of State members: para. 1(5). The proposal for parish members

was put forward by the Government with a view to giving local people greater involvement in the management of parish affairs: see DoE News Releases 239 and 253 (May 22 and 26, 1995).

Local authority members are to be appointed by such of the councils as are specified in or determined under the relevant order, and must be council members: para. 2. Parish members are to be appointed by the Secretary of State and must be members of the relevant parish councils (or if there is not one for a particular parish, chairman of the parish meeting): para. 3. In relation to appointment of Secretary or State members (other than parish members) the Countryside Commission or the Countryside Council for Wales are to be consulted: para. 4. Schedule 7 also deals with chairmanship (para. 5), removal and disqualification of members (paras. 6 and 7), failure to attend meetings (para. 8), code of conduct and members' interests (paras. 9 and 10), allowances and time off (para. 11), meetings and proceedings (para. 12), committees, sub-committees and officers (paras. 13 and 14), personal liability of members and officers (para. 15), liaison with parish and community councils (para. 16), documents, notices, records and byelaws (para. 17), maladministration (para. 18) and audit (para. 19).

Relationship to local government changes
The creation of the new authorities will be influenced in its timing by changes to local government structure under Pt. II of the Local Government Act 1994 and the Local Government (Wales) Act 1994. Each park will be considered individually: *Hansard*, H.L. Vol. 560, col. 1665.

National Park authorities in Wales

64.—(1) Where a National Park planning board has been constituted for the area of any particular existing National Park in Wales, the Secretary of State may exercise his power under section 63 above to establish a National Park Authority in relation to that National Park by making an order under that section designating for the body corporate constituted as that board a date earlier than 31st March 1997 on which that body—

(a) shall cease to be a National Park planning board, and

(b) shall be constituted the National Park authority in relation to that National Park,

without affecting its corporate status (and an order made under or by virtue of that section may make provision re-naming that body accordingly).

(2) Any order under—

(a) paragraph 3A of Schedule 17 to the 1972 Act (special planning boards), or

(b) section 2(1B) of the Town and Country Planning Act 1990 (joint planning boards),

relating to the body corporate constituted as the National Park planning board in question shall have effect on and after the designated date for that body as an order under section 63 above relating to that body in its capacity as the National Park authority in relation to the National Park in question.

(3) For the purposes of any order establishing a National Park authority under section 63 above by virtue of subsection (1) above, or any order which, by virtue of subsection (2) above, has effect as an order under that section—

(a) the requirements of paragraph 2(3) of Schedule 7 to this Act with respect to consultation with councils for principal areas shall, by virtue of the establishment of the National Park planning board, be deemed to have been complied with as respects any provision of the order;

(b) in the case of any member of the National Park planning board immediately before the designated date who was holding that office by virtue of his appointment as such by the Secretary of State under and in accordance with paragraph 11 of Schedule 17 to the 1972 Act (which requires prior consultation), the appointment shall, on and after the designated date, have effect for the remainder of the period for which it was made as an appointment as a member of the National Park authority made by the Secretary of State in accordance with paragraph 4(1) of Schedule 7 to this Act;

(c) in the case of any other member of the National Park planning board immediately before the designated date who is on that date a member of a principal council for an area which includes the whole or any part of the National Park in question, his appointment as a member of that board shall, on and after the designated date, have effect for the remainder of the period for which it was made as an appointment as a local authority member of the National Park authority made in accordance with paragraph 2 of that Schedule; and

(d) any other requirement, whether statutory or otherwise, which must be complied with in connection with the establishment of a National Park authority shall be deemed to have been complied with by virtue of the establishment of the National Park planning board;

and, except as provided by paragraphs (b) and (c) above, no person who is a member of the National Park planning board immediately before the designated date shall, by virtue of the order, become a member of the National Park authority.

(4) The functions of a National Park planning board shall include the duty to take such steps as it considers necessary to enable it (that is to say, the body corporate constituted as that board) on being constituted the National Park authority in relation to the National Park in question by an order made by virtue of subsection (1) above, to perform its functions as a National Park authority on and after the designated date; and the functions conferred on such a board by this subsection—

(a) shall be exercisable before (as well as on or after) 1st April 1996; and

(b) are in addition to any other functions which are exercisable by such a board before that date by virtue of paragraph 13 of Schedule 17 to the Local Government (Wales) Act 1994.

(5) The functions of a principal council for an area which includes the whole or any part of the area of a National Park planning board shall include the duty to take such steps as it considers necessary to enable the body corporate constituted as that board, on being constituted the National Park authority in relation to the National Park in question by an order made by virtue of subsection (1) above, to perform those functions which would, apart from the order, be exercisable by a principal council but which will become functions of that body, as the National Park authority, on the designated date.

(6) Where the Secretary of State—

(a) has taken any steps with a view to, or otherwise in connection with, the establishment of a National Park planning board for the area of an existing National Park in Wales ("the proposed board"), but

(b) decides not to proceed with the establishment of the proposed board and to establish instead a National Park authority in relation to that National Park ("the proposed authority"), and

(c) the proposed authority is, or is to be, established before 31st March 1997,

the doing of anything by or in relation to the Secretary of State (other than the making by the Secretary of State of an instrument of a legislative character) with a view to, or otherwise in connection with, establishing the proposed board shall be treated, as respects the proposed authority, as the doing of any corresponding or reasonably similar thing falling to be done for the purposes of, or otherwise in connection with, the establishment of that authority.

(7) Without prejudice to the generality of subsection (6) above, in any case falling within paragraphs (a) to (c) of that subsection—

(a) any consultation with a principal council after 15th December 1994 by the Secretary of State as respects the proposed board (whether or not required by or under any enactment) shall be deemed, as respects the proposed authority, to have been carried out for the purposes of the consultation with councils for principal areas required by paragraph 2(3) of Schedule 7 to this Act;

(b) anything done by or in relation to the Secretary of State for the purposes of the consultation required by paragraph 11 of Schedule 17 to the 1972 Act (appointment of members by Secretary of State) preparatory to the appointment of a person as a member of the proposed board shall be deemed, as respects the proposed authority, to have been done for the purposes of the consultation required by paragraph 4(1) of Schedule 7 to this Act preparatory to the appointment of that person as a member of that authority;

(c) anything done by or in relation to the Secretary of State (other than the making by the Secretary of State of an instrument of a legislative character) for the purposes of, or otherwise in connection with, any other requirement, whether statutory or otherwise, of a consultative or procedural nature—

(i) which relates to a National Park planning board, and

(ii) for which there is a corresponding or reasonably similar requirement which relates to a National Park authority,

shall be treated, as respects the proposed authority, as done for the purposes of, or otherwise in connection with, that other corresponding or reasonably similar requirement.

(8) Section 54 of the Local Government (Wales) Act 1994 (powers to make incidental, consequential, transitional or supplemental provision) shall have effect as if this Part were contained in that Act, except that subsection (2)(e) of that section shall have effect as if this Part were contained in an Act passed in the same Session as that Act.

(9) In this section—

"the designated date", in the case of any body corporate constituted as a National Park planning board which becomes, or is to become, a National Park authority by virtue of this section, means the date designated by virtue of subsection (1) above in the order relating to that body;

"existing National Park" means a National Park in respect of which there was in force on 15th December 1994 an order under section 5 of the National Parks and Access to the Countryside Act 1949 (designation of areas as National Parks);

"National Park planning board" means—

(a) a special planning board constituted by order under paragraph 3A of Schedule 17 to the 1972 Act to discharge, as respects the area of a National Park in Wales, the functions to which Part I of that Schedule applies, or

(b) a joint planning board constituted by order under subsection (1B) of section 2 of the Town and Country Planning Act 1990 for a united district comprising the area of a National Park in Wales.

DEFINITIONS

"1972 Act, the": s.79(1).
"designated date, the": subs. (9).
"existing National Park": subs. (9).
"functions": s.124(1).
"National Park authority": s.63(1).
"National Park planning board": subs. (9).
"principal area" : s.79(1).
"principal council": s.79(1).
"proposed authority, the": subs. (6).
"proposed board, the": subs. (6).

COMMENCEMENT
September 19, 1995 (s.125(2)).

GENERAL NOTE

This section makes specific provision for Wales. Express provision for Wales was made in response to concerns expressed by Lord Elis-Thomas in the Lords, and in the context of the comprehensive reorganisation of Welsh local government to take place on April 1, 1996 under the Local Government (Wales) Act 1994 which contains provision for the establishment of planning boards for Welsh national parks: *Hansard*, H.L. Vol. 562, col. 421. Where a National Park planning board has been constituted for an existing National Park in Wales, the order made under s.63 may reconstitute, before March 31, 1997, the board as the National Park authority without affecting its corporate status. The body thus will remain constituted by its original order, which will have effect as an order under s.63: s.64(2). Provision may be made for renaming the body. Effectively, therefore, the existing planning board is converted to a National Park authority.

The effect of such an order is that members appointed to the planning board by the Secretary of State and local authority members will continue to be members for the remainder of their original term: subs. (3)(b) and (c). Consultation and other requirements relating to the establishment of National Park authorities are deemed to have been complied with: subs. (3)(a) and (d).

Subss. (4) and (5)

National Park planning boards which are to become National Park authorities under s.64 are under a duty to take such steps as they consider necessary to enable them to perform their new functions: subs. (4). The relevant district councils must also take such enabling steps: subs. (5).

Subss. (6) and (7)

Where the Secretary of State has taken steps to establish a National Park planning board, but decides instead to establish a National Park authority before March 31, 1997, anything done by or in relation to the Secretary of State (other than legislative measures) with regard to the establishment of such a board is to be treated as if done for corresponding or similar purposes in relation to the establishment of the authority: subs. (6). Subsection (7) particularises certain things which are to be so treated, without prejudice to the generality of subs. (6). The significance of the date of December 15, 1994 in subs. (7)(a) is that this was the date when the Environment Bill received its Second Reading in the Lords.

Functions of National Park authorities

General purposes and powers

65.—(1) This Part so far as it relates to the establishment and functions of National Park authorities shall have effect for the purposes specified in section 5(1) of the National Parks and Access to the Countryside Act 1949 (purposes of conserving and enhancing the natural beauty, wildlife and cultural heritage of National Parks and of promoting opportunities for the understanding and enjoyment of the special qualities of those Parks by the public).

(2) Sections 37 and 38 of the Countryside Act 1968 (general duties as to the protection of interests of the countryside and the avoidance of pollution) shall apply to National Park authorities as they apply to local authorities.

(3) The functions of a National Park authority in the period (if any) between the time when it is established and the time when it becomes the local planning authority for the relevant Park shall be confined to the taking of such steps as the authority, after consultation with the Secretary of State and any existing authority for that Park, considers appropriate for securing that it is able properly to carry out its functions after that time.

(4) In the application of subsection (3) above in the case of a National Park authority established in relation to a National Park in Wales, the reference to

any existing authority for that Park shall have effect as respects consultation carried out during so much of that period as falls before 1st April 1996 as including a reference to any principal council whose area is wholly or partly comprised in that Park.

(5) The powers of a National Park authority shall include power to do anything which, in the opinion of that authority, is calculated to facilitate, or is conducive or incidental to—

(a) the accomplishment of the purposes mentioned in subsection (1) above; or

(b) the carrying out of any functions conferred on it by virtue of any other enactment.

(6) The powers conferred on a National Park authority by subsection (5) above shall not include either—

(a) power to do anything in contravention of any restriction imposed by virtue of this Part in relation to any express power of the authority; or

(b) a power to raise money (whether by borrowing or otherwise) in a manner which is not authorised apart from that subsection;

but the things that may be done in exercise of those powers shall not be treated as excluding anything by reason only that it involves the expenditure, borrowing or lending of money or the acquisition or disposal of any property or rights.

(7) Schedule 8 to this Act shall have effect with respect to the supplemental and incidental powers of a National Park authority.

Definitions
"existing authority": s.79(1).
"functions": s.124(1).
"National Park authority": s.63(1).
"principal council": s.79(1).
"relevant Park, the": s.79(1).

Commencement
September 19, 1995 (s.125(2)).

General Note
This section deals with the general purposes and powers of National Park authorities.

Subs. (1)
As to the purposes specified in s.5(1) of the 1949 Act, see s.61.

Subs. (2)
The duty under s.37 of the 1968 Act is "to have due regard to the needs of agriculture and forestry and to the economic and social interests of rural areas". The duty under s.38 is "to have due regard to the protection against pollution of any water, whether on the surface or underground which belongs to the National Rivers Authority or a water undertaker or which that Authority or a water undertaker is for the time being authorised to take".

Subs. (3)
This subsection applies to limit the functions of a National Park authority during the period between its establishment and the time when it becomes the local planning authority.

Subs. (4)
In relation to Wales, see also s.64.

Subs. (7)
Schedule 8 deals with the supplemental and incidental powers of National Park authorities. These include the acquisition, disposal and compulsory purchase of land under the Local Government (Miscellaneous Provisions) Act 1976 and the Town and Country Planning Act 1990. The authority may also promote local or personal bills (though not to modify its area or constitution). Provisions relating to direct labour, competitive tendering, companies and contracting out apply to National Park authorities.

National Park Management Plans

66.—(1) Subject to subsection (2) below, every National Park authority shall, within three years after its operational date, prepare and publish a plan, to be known as a National Park Management Plan, which formulates its policy for the management of the relevant Park and for the carrying out of its functions in relation to that Park.

(2) A National Park authority for a Park wholly or mainly comprising any area which, immediately before the authority's operational date, was or was included in an area for which there was a National Park Plan prepared and published under paragraph 18 of Schedule 17 to the 1972 Act (National Park plans) shall not be required to prepare a Management Plan under subsection (1) above if, within six months of that date, it adopts the existing National Park Plan as its Management Plan and publishes notice that it has done so.

(3) Where a National Park authority is proposing to adopt a plan under subsection (2) above, it may review the plan before adopting it and shall do so if the plan would have fallen to be reviewed under paragraph 18 of Schedule 17 to the 1972 Act in the period of twelve months beginning with the authority's operational date.

(4) A National Park authority shall review its National Park Management Plan within the period of five years of its operational date and, after the first review, at intervals of not more than five years.

(5) Where a National Park authority has adopted a plan under subsection (2) above as its National Park Management Plan and has not reviewed that Plan before adopting it, the first review of that Plan under subsection (4) above shall take place no later than the time when the adopted plan would otherwise have fallen to be reviewed under paragraph 18 of Schedule 17 to the 1972 Act.

(6) Where a National Park authority reviews any plan under this section, it shall—

(a) determine on that review whether it would be expedient to amend the plan and what (if any) amendments would be appropriate;

(b) make any amendments that it considers appropriate; and

(c) publish a report on the review specifying any amendments made.

(7) A National Park authority which is proposing to publish, adopt or review any plan under this section shall—

(a) give notice of the proposal to every principal council whose area is wholly or partly comprised in the relevant Park and, according to whether that Park is in England or in Wales, to the Countryside Commission and the Nature Conservancy Council for England or to the Countryside Council for Wales;

(b) send a copy of the plan, together (where appropriate) with any proposed amendments of the plan, to every body to which notice of the proposal is required to be given by paragraph (a) above; and

(c) take into consideration any observations made by any such body.

(8) A National Park authority shall send to the Secretary of State a copy of every plan, notice or report which it is required to publish under this section.

(9) In this section "operational date", in relation to a National Park authority, means the date on which the authority becomes the local planning authority for the relevant Park.

DEFINITIONS
   "1972 Act, the": s.124(1).
   "functions": s.124(1).
   "National Park authority": s.63(1).
   "notice": s.124(1).
   "operational date": subs. (9).
   "principal council": s.79(1).

"relevant park, the": s.79(1).

COMMENCEMENT
September 19, 1995 (s.125(2)).

GENERAL NOTE

This section requires National Park authorities to prepare, and to keep under review at intervals of not more than five years, a National Park Management Plan: subss. (1) and (4). The Plan should formulate the authority's policy for the management of the relevant National Park and for the carrying out of the authority's functions in relation to it. The Plans required by s.66 have the same function as the National Park Plans which National Park Planning Boards and Committees were required to prepare under Sched. 17, para. 18 of the Local Government Act 1982. Indeed, there is a provision for existing National Park Plans to be adopted as the Management Plan under s.66: subss. (2) and (3).

National Park Plans under the 1972 Act are not part of the development plan system, but rather a means of formulating management policies, establishing a framework for coordination with other bodies, providing a basis for programming implementation of policy and for financial estimates, and informing the public. See the *Encyclopedia of Planning Law*, para. 2–012 (Sweet & Maxwell). This seems equally true of Management Plans under s.66, though of course the assumption of local planning authority functions by National Park authorities will give a new focus to the Plans.

The Government's revised draft national parks circular of November 6, 1995 states (para. 23) that in formulating policies for the administration and management of the parks, the National Park authorities must have in mind the wide range of interests which can be offered by their decisions, including those who live in, work in and visit the parks. Reference is also made, in the light of the statutory purposes for national parks, to working closely with the Countryside Commission, English Nature, English Heritage, The Sports Council and the regional Tourist Boards (para. 24) and for those organisations in turn to involve the National Park authorities in their work (para. 26). The importance of effective consultation procedures with local people, including voluntary groups, is also stressed (para. 27).

National Park authority to be local planning authority

67.—(1) After section 4 of the Town and Country Planning Act 1990 (National Parks) there shall be inserted—

"National Parks with National Park authorities

4A.—(1) Where a National Park authority has been established for any area, this section, instead of section 4(1) to (4), shall apply, as from such time as may be specified for the purposes of this section in the order establishing that authority, in relation to the Park for which it is the authority.

(2) Subject to subsections (4) and (5) below, the National Park authority for the Park shall be the sole local planning authority for the area of the Park and, accordingly—

    (a) functions conferred by or under the planning Acts on a planning authority of any description (including the functions of a mineral planning authority under those Acts and under the Planning and Compensation Act 1991) shall, in relation to the Park, be functions of the National Park authority, and not of any other authority; and

    (b) so much of the area of any other authority as is included in the Park shall be treated as excluded from any area for which that other authority is a planning authority of any description.

(3) For the purposes of subsection (2) above functions under the planning Acts which (apart from this section) are conferred—

    (a) in relation to some areas on the county or district planning authorities for those areas, and

    (b) in relation to other areas on the councils for those areas,

shall be treated, in relation to those other areas, as conferred on each of those councils as the local planning authority for their area.

(4) The functions of a local planning authority by virtue of sections 198 to 201, 206 to 209 and 211 to 215 so far as they are functions of a National Park authority by virtue of this section, shall be exercisable as respects any area which is or is included in an area for which there is a district council, concurrently with the National Park authority, by that council.

(5) For the purposes of any enactment relating to the functions of a district planning authority, the functions of a district council by virtue of subsection (4) above shall be deemed to be conferred on them as a district planning authority and as if the district were the area for which they are such an authority."

(2) The Secretary of State may by order make provision—

(a) for applying Chapter I of Part II of that Act of 1990 (unitary development plans), instead of provisions of Chapter II of that Part (structure and local plans), in relation to the area of any National Park; or

(b) for applying Chapter II of that Part in relation to the area of such a Park—

(i) as if functions under that Chapter of a planning authority of any description were functions of such public authority as may be specified in the order (and not of the National Park authority); and

(ii) as if that Part had effect with such other modifications as may be so specified in relation to the carrying out of those functions by an authority so specified.

(3) Without prejudice to any power conferred by virtue of section 75 below, the Secretary of State shall have power by order, for the purposes of any provision made by virtue of this section, to modify the provisions of Part II of that Act of 1990 (development plans) in relation to any such area of a local planning authority as, but for any exclusion by virtue of section 4A of that Act, would include the whole or any part of a National Park.

(4) References in this section to provisions of Part II of that Act of 1990 include references to any provisions for modifying those provisions which are contained in any enactment passed after this Act.

(5) Before section 148 of that Act of 1990 (interpretation of provisions relating to purchase notices) there shall be inserted—

"Application of Chapter I to National Parks

147A. This Chapter shall have effect as if—

(a) the bodies on whom a purchase notice may be served under section 137 included any National Park authority which is the local planning authority for the area in which the land is situated; and

(b) a National Park authority were a local authority for the purposes of this Act and the National Park for which it is the local planning authority were its area;

and the references in this Chapter and in section 288(10)(a) to a council and to a local authority shall be construed accordingly."

DEFINITIONS

"functions": s.124(1).
"modifications": s.124(1).
"National Park authority": s.63(1).
"public authority": s.79(1).

COMMENCEMENT

September 19, 1995 (s.125(2)).

GENERAL NOTE

This is a key section of Part III. It transfers local planning authority functions within National Parks to the National Park authorities, each of which will become the sole planning authority for the area of the Park: subs. (1), inserting s.4A(2) into the Town and Country Planning Act 1990. The only exceptions are the limited range of functions specified in new s.4A(4) of the 1990 Act which are exercisable by the district council concurrently with the National Park authority: these essentially relate to tree preservation and replacement, and to waste-land notices. The functions of the authorities will include those of mineral planning authorities under the Planning and Compensation Act 1991.

Subss. (2) and (3)

These subsections deal with development planning and allow the Secretary of State by order to do two things:

(a) apply the provisions of the 1990 Act for unitary development plans to National Parks; and

(b) apply the provisions of the 1990 Act on structure and local plans to National Parks, as if the relevant functions were those of some other body, not the National Parks Authority.

Taken together, subss. (2) and (3) provide flexibility for the Secretary of State to make appropriate adjustments to the development plan system for National Parks in response to changes which may be brought about under the Local Government Act 1992, or to continue the current development plan system for those Parks currently administered by National Park Committees.

In Wales the unitary development plan system will apply to all areas of Wales, under the Local Government (Wales) Act 1994, and consequently each of the three Welsh National Parks will become a unitary planning area.

Subs. (5)

This sub-section will allow purchase notices under the 1990 Act to be served on the National Park authorities.

Planning authority functions under National Parks legislation etc.

68.—(1) Where a National Park authority is the local planning authority for any National Park, section 184 of the 1972 Act and paragraph 37 of Schedule 17 to that Act (functions under certain legislation relating to the National Parks and the countryside) shall not apply as respects that Park in relation to any of the functions conferred by or under—

(a) the National Parks and Access to the Countryside Act 1949 ("the 1949 Act"), or

(b) the Countryside Act 1968 ("the 1968 Act"),

on a planning authority of any description.

(2) In consequence of subsection (1) above, but subject to subsections (3) to (7) below—

(a) functions which are conferred on a local planning authority by or under the 1949 Act or the 1968 Act, and the functions conferred on a county planning authority (or, in relation to Wales, a local planning authority) by section 69 of the 1949 Act (suspension of access to avoid risk of fire), shall, as respects the whole or any part of a National Park for which a National Park authority is the local planning authority, be functions of that authority and not of any other authority;

(b) references in those Acts to a local planning authority whose area consists of or includes the whole or any part of a National Park shall be construed, in relation to any National Park for which a National Park authority is the local planning authority, as references to the National Park authority; and

(c) other references in those Acts to a local planning authority and the references to a local authority in section 103 of the 1949 Act and sections 10 and 43 to 45 of the 1968 Act (which contain provision applying in relation to local authorities in their capacity as local planning authorities) shall have effect accordingly.

(3) Section 11 of the 1949 Act (which makes provision in relation to a local planning authority that corresponds to provision made by section 65 above in relation to a National Park authority) shall not apply in relation to any National Park authority.

(4) The functions conferred by or under section 12 of the 1949 Act or section 12 of the 1968 Act (facilities for National Parks) which are exercisable by virtue of this section by a National Park authority in a National Park—

  (a) shall be exercisable by that authority outside the relevant Park on any land in the neighbourhood of that Park; but

  (b) shall be so exercisable only under arrangements made with the local planning authority for the area where they are exercised.

(5) Sections 61 to 63 of the 1949 Act (survey of access requirements and action in response to the survey) shall have effect in accordance with subsection (2) above as respects the area of any National Park for which a National Park authority has become the local planning authority—

  (a) in the case of a Park designated after the commencement of this section, as if section 61(1) applied with the substitution for the reference to the commencement of that Act of a reference to the time when that authority became the local planning authority for that Park;

  (b) as if no area were required by virtue of subsection (3) of section 61 of that Act, or of any previous review under that section, to be excluded from any area to be reviewed by virtue of paragraph (a) above; and

  (c) in the case of a Park designated before the commencement of this section, as if—

      (i) the power (if any) to make a resolution for the purposes of the proviso to that subsection (3) as respects any part of the area of the Park which has not previously been reviewed under that section, and

      (ii) the functions which, where such a resolution has been so made, are conferred on the authority which made it or on any authority which has conducted a review in pursuance of the resolution,

    were a power or, as the case may be, functions of the National Park authority, and not of any other authority.

(6) The following functions, so far as exercisable by a National Park authority in relation to land or countryside in a National Park in England for which that authority is the local planning authority, that is to say—

  (a) those conferred by or under section 89 of the 1949 Act (planting of trees and treatment of derelict land), and

  (b) those conferred by section 10 of the 1968 Act (camping and picnic sites),

shall be exercisable in relation to so much of that Park as is comprised in a district for which there is a district council, concurrently with the National Park authority, by that district council.

(7) For the purposes of any enactment relating to the functions of a district planning authority, the functions of a district council by virtue of subsection (6) above shall be deemed to be conferred on them as a district planning authority and as if the district were the area for which they are such an authority.

(8) The following powers, that is to say—

  (a) those conferred on a local authority by or under section 92 of the 1949 Act (wardens), and

  (b) those conferred on a local authority by or under section 41 of the 1968 Act (byelaws),

so far as they are conferred in relation to any of the functions which by virtue of this section are functions of a National Park authority as respects the relevant Park, shall be exercisable by that authority and also in the case of those conferred by or under section 41 of the 1968 Act, by a district council in relation to that council's functions by virtue of subsection (6)(b) above, but not by any other authority.

(9) Section 104 of the 1949 Act (general provisions as to appropriation and disposal of land), except subsection (11), shall have effect as if references in

that section to a local authority included references to a National Park authority.

(10) For the purposes of any functions conferred on a National Park authority by virtue of this section references in any enactment to the area of the authority shall be construed as references to the relevant Park.

DEFINITIONS
"1949 Act": subs. (1).
"1968 Act": subs. (1).
"1972 Act": s.79(1).
"functions": s.124(1).
"National Park authority": s.63(1).
"relevant Park": s.79(1).

COMMENCEMENT
September 19, 1995 (s.125(2)).

GENERAL NOTE
The effect of this section, which complements s.67, is to confer on National Park authorities the functions of local planning authorities under the National Parks and Access to the Countryside Act 1949 and the Countryside Act 1968. Various consequential adjustments are made, for example, s.11 of the 1949 Act (general powers of local planning authorities in National Parks) is redundant in view of the powers and functions conferred on National Park authorities by the new provisions, and is accordingly disapplied: subs. (3).

Planning authority functions under the Wildlife and Countryside Act 1981

69.—(1) A National Park authority which is the local planning authority for any National Park, and not any other authority, shall have all the functions under the Wildlife and Countryside Act 1981 which are conferred as respects that Park on a planning authority of any description.

(2) Accordingly—
(a) a National Park authority shall be the relevant authority for the purposes of sections 39, 41 and 50 of that Act (management agreements and duties of agriculture Ministers in relation to the countryside) as respects any land in any National Park for which that authority is the local planning authority; and
(b) section 52(2) of that Act (construction of references to a local planning authority) shall not apply as respects any National Park for which a National Park authority is the local planning authority.

(3) Section 43 of that Act (maps of National Parks) shall have effect in accordance with the preceding provisions of this section—
(a) in the case of a National Park designated after the commencement of this section, as if the relevant date for the purposes of that section were the date on which a National Park authority becomes the local planning authority for the Park; and
(b) in any other case, as if the function of reviewing and revising any map of a part of the Park in question included a power, in pursuance of the review and revisions, to consolidate that map with other maps prepared under that section as respects other parts of that Park.

(4) In section 44 of that Act (grants and loans for purposes of National Parks), after subsection (1) there shall be inserted the following subsection—
"(1A) Subsection (1) above shall not apply in relation to any National Park for which a National Park authority is the local planning authority; but the National Park authority for such a Park may give financial assistance by way of grant or loan, or partly in one way and partly in the other, to any person in respect of expenditure incurred by him in doing anything which, in the opinion of the authority, is conducive to the attainment in the Park in question of any of the purposes mentioned in section 5(1) of the 1949 Act (purposes of conserving and enhancing the natural beauty, wildlife and cultural heritage of National Parks and of promot-

ing opportunities for the understanding and enjoyment of the special qualities of those Parks by the public)."

DEFINITIONS
    "functions": s.124(1).
    "National Park authority": s.63(1).

COMMENCEMENT
    September 19, 1995 (s.125(2)).

GENERAL NOTE
    This section confers on National Park authorities, in their capacity as local planning authority for the National Park, the functions conferred on planning authorities by the Wildlife and Countryside Act 1981.

Subs. (3)
    This subsection updates s.43 of the 1981 Act (maps of National Parks): (a) to make provision for the possibility of new National Parks being designated; and (b) to allow National Park authorities to consolidate maps of different parts of their Park.

Subs. (4)
    The new subs. (1A) to be inserted into s.44 of the 1981 Act (grants and loans for the purposes of National Parks) confers powers on National Park authorities to give financial assistance parallel to those conferred by s.44(1) on other local planning authorities. Subsection (1) will be repealed when the last National Park Planning Board or Committee is replaced by a National Park authority.

Other statutory functions

70. In addition to its functions under the enactments mentioned in sections 67 to 69 above and to such of its functions under any other enactment as are conferred by virtue of its being a local planning authority within the meaning of the Town and Country Planning Act 1990, a National Park authority shall have the further miscellaneous functions conferred on it by virtue of Schedule 9 to this Act.

DEFINITIONS
    "functions": s.124(1).
    "National Park authority": s.63(1).

COMMENCEMENT
    September 19, 1995 (s.125(2)).

GENERAL NOTE
    Schedule 9 confers other miscellaneous functions on National Park authorities. These relate to: common land, open spaces, nature reserves, caravan sites, country parks, provision of information and encouragement of visitors, derelict land, recreational facilities, refuse disposal, ancient monuments and archaeological areas, footpaths and bridleways, litter, listed and historic buildings, hazardous substances, local charities and overseas assistance.

Finances of National Park authorities

National Park authorities to be levying bodies

71.—(1) A National Park authority shall have power in respect of every financial year beginning after the establishment of that authority to issue levies to the councils by whom the local authority members of that authority fall to be appointed.

(2) Subject to the following provisions of this section, a levy issued by virtue of this section shall be issued in accordance with regulations under section 74 of the Local Government Finance Act 1988 (power to make regulations authorising a levying body to issue a levy); and, accordingly, a

National Park authority shall be deemed to be a levying body within the meaning of that section.

(3) Subject to any maximum specified in or determined in accordance with any regulations under that section 74, the amount of the levies issued by a National Park authority in respect of any financial year shall be equal to the sum by which the aggregate of the amounts specified in subsection (4) below is exceeded by the aggregate of the sums which it estimates it will require in respect of that year for the following purposes, that is to say—

(a) meeting the expenditure of the authority which will fall to be charged for that year to any revenue account;

(b) making such provision as may be appropriate for meeting contingencies the expenditure on which would fall to be so charged;

(c) securing the availability to the authority of adequate working balances on its revenue accounts; and

(d) providing the authority with the funds required for covering any deficit carried forward from a previous financial year in any revenue account.

(4) The amounts mentioned in subsection (3) above in relation to any financial year are—

(a) any amounts to be received by the authority in respect of that year by way of grant under section 72 below;

(b) the authority's estimate of the amounts which are likely for that year to be credited to any revenue account in respect of sums payable to the authority for things done in the course of, or in connection with, the carrying out of its functions; and

(c) the authority's estimate of the amounts not falling within paragraph (a) or (b) above which apart from this section are, or are likely to be, available to it for that year for the purposes mentioned in subsection (3) above.

(5) Where agreement as to the apportionment of the amount to be raised by a National Park authority in respect of any financial year by way of levies is entered into, before 1st December in the immediately preceding financial year, by all the authorities to whom the levies in respect of that year may be issued by that authority, that amount shall be apportioned between those authorities in accordance with the agreement, instead of in accordance with any provision made by virtue of that section 74.

(6) Regulations under that section 74 may include provision for requiring an authority to anticipate a levy by virtue of this section when making any calculations which fall, for the financial year following that in which any National Park authority is established, to be made (whether originally or by way of substitute) under section 32 or 43 of the Local Government Finance Act 1992 (calculation of budget requirement).

(7) A National Park authority shall not by virtue of this section be a local authority within the meaning of the Town and Country Planning Act 1990.

DEFINITIONS
"financial year": s.124(1).
"National Park authority": s.63(1).

COMMENCEMENT
September 19, 1995 (s.125(2)).

GENERAL NOTE
National Park authorities may issue annual levies to the local councils who appoint members to the authority. The section deals with the procedure for and amount of such levies. In the revised draft national parks circular of November 6, 1995, the Secretary of State expresses confidence that local authorities will be able to reach agreement on their respective contributions: if they cannot, the Act makes provision for the matter to be determined under regulations made under s.74 of the Local Government Finance Act 1988. The Secretary of State expects to provide 75 per cent of the approved expenditure, with local authorities providing the remaining 25 per

cent (para. 42). Local authorities may make representations to the Secretary of State on their contributions through the consultative panel on local government finance.

National Park grant

72.—(1) The Secretary of State may make grants to a National Park authority for such purposes, of such amounts and on such terms and conditions as he thinks fit.

(2) Before determining the amount of any grant which he proposes to make to a National Park authority under this section, or the purpose for which it is to be made, the Secretary of State shall consult, according to whether the relevant Park is in England or in Wales, either the Countryside Commission or the Countryside Council for Wales.

(3) The consent of the Treasury shall be required for the making of a grant under this section.

DEFINITIONS
"National Park authority": s.63(1).
"relevant Park": s.79(1).

COMMENCEMENT
September 19, 1995 (s.125(2)).

GENERAL NOTE
This section provides a general grant-making power in favour of National Park authorities.

Capital finances and borrowing

73. In section 39(1) of the Local Government and Housing Act 1989 (which specifies the authorities to which the provisions of Part IV of that Act relating to capital accounts and borrowing powers apply), after paragraph (i) there shall be inserted—
"(ia) a National Park authority;".

COMMENCEMENT
September 19, 1995 (s.125(2)).

GENERAL NOTE
This section has the effect of adding National Park authorities to the list of bodies to which Pt. IV of the Local Government and Housing Act 1989 applies (revenue accounts and capital finances of local authorities).

Validation of certain grants paid to local authorities in respect of expenditure relating to National Parks

74.—(1) No payment made for any year beginning on or after 1st April 1990 and ending on or before 31st March 1996 by the Secretary of State by way of grant to the council of a county or a metropolitan district in respect of the council's expenditure or estimated expenditure in connection with National Parks shall be regarded as made otherwise than under and in accordance with the relevant enactments by reason only of—
- (a) the aggregate amount of such grants for the year to such councils not having been duly prescribed;
- (b) the method of determining the proportion of such aggregate amount payable to that council not having been duly prescribed; or
- (c) payment of the grant being, or having been, made—
    - (i) otherwise than in accordance with an approved Rate Support Grant Report or such a Report as varied by an approved supplementary report for the year; or
    - (ii) without there being an approved Rate Support Grant Report for the year.

(2) Any reference in this section to a payment by way of grant made under and in accordance with the relevant enactments is a reference to a payment of grant made under section 7 of the Local Government Act 1974 (supplementary grants towards expenditure with respect to National Parks) in accordance with the provisions of that section and those of section 60 or 61 of the Local Government, Planning and Land Act 1980 (rate support grant reports and supplementary reports) as they apply in relation to grants under the said section 7.

(3) In this section—

"approved Rate Support Grant Report" means a Rate Support Grant Report which has been laid before and approved by a resolution of the House of Commons;

"approved supplementary report" means a supplementary report which has been laid before and approved by a resolution of the House of Commons;

"duly prescribed" means prescribed by a Rate Support Grant Report or a supplementary report;

"Rate Support Grant Report" means a Rate Support Grant Report made under section 60 of the Local Government, Planning and Land Act 1980;

"supplementary report" means a supplementary report made under section 61 of that Act; and

"year" means a period of 12 months beginning with 1st April.

DEFINITIONS
"approved Rate Support Grant Report": subs. (3).
"approved supplementary report": subs. (3).
"duly prescribed": subs. (3).
"Rate Support Grant Report": subs. (3).
"supplementary report": subs. (3).
"year": subs. (3).

COMMENCEMENT
July 19, 1995 (s.125(2)).

GENERAL NOTE
This section operates to validate certain grants made to county or metropolitan district councils in connection with National Parks for the financial years between April 1, 1990 and March 31, 1996.

Supplemental provisions

Powers to make orders

75.—(1) This section applies to every power of the Secretary of State under the preceding provisions of this Part to make an order.

(2) The powers to which this section applies shall, in each case, be exercisable by statutory instrument; and, except in the case of a statutory instrument made by virtue of section 64 above which only—

(a) designates a date,

(b) specifies a time for the purposes of section 4A of the Town and Country Planning Act 1990,

(c) renames a body,

(d) makes provision under paragraph 2 of Schedule 7 to this Act—

(i) for excluding a council from the councils by whom the local authority members of a National Park authority are to be appointed, or

(ii) for so increasing the number of local authority members of a National Park authority to be appointed by any council as to secure that the number of local authority members of that authority remains unchanged notwithstanding any such exclusion of a council, or

(e) makes provision under section 63(2) above,
any such statutory instrument shall be subject to annulment in pursuance of a resolution of either House of Parliament.

(3) The powers to which this section applies shall, in each case, include power to make such incidental, supplemental, consequential and transitional provision as the Secretary of State thinks necessary or expedient.

(4) A power of the Secretary of State by an order under this Part to make incidental, supplemental, consequential or transitional provision shall include power for any incidental, supplemental, consequential or, as the case may be, transitional purpose—

(a) to apply with or without modifications,
(b) to extend, exclude or modify, or
(c) to repeal or revoke with or without savings,
any enactment or any instrument made under any enactment.

(5) The provision that may be made for incidental, supplemental, consequential or transitional purposes in the case of any order under this Part which—

(a) establishes a National Park authority or winds up the existing authority for any National Park, or
(b) otherwise has the effect of transferring functions from one person to another or of providing for functions to become exercisable concurrently by two or more persons or to cease to be so exercisable,
shall include provision for the transfer of property, rights and liabilities from one person to another.

(6) A power of the Secretary of State under this Part to provide by order for the transfer of any property, rights or liabilities, or to make transitional provision in connection with any such transfer or with any order by which functions become or cease to be exercisable by any authority, shall include power to provide, in particular—

(a) for the management and custody of any transferred property (whether real or personal);
(b) for any liabilities transferred to include liabilities under any enactment;
(c) for legal proceedings commenced by or against any person to be continued by or against a person to whom property, rights or liabilities are transferred or, as the case may be, any authority by whom any functions are to become exercisable;
(d) for the transfer of staff, compensation for loss of office, pensions and other staffing matters; and
(e) for treating any person to whom a transfer of property, rights or liabilities is made or, as the case may be, by whom any functions are to become exercisable as, for some or all purposes, the same person in law as the person from whom the transfer is made or the authority by whom the functions have previously been exercisable.

(7) The powers to which this section applies shall, in each case, include power to make different provision for different cases, including different provision for different areas or localities and for different authorities.

(8) The powers to which this section applies shall be without prejudice to any powers conferred by Part II of the Local Government Act 1992 or any other enactment.

(9) In this section "enactment" includes an enactment contained in an Act passed after this Act.

DEFINITIONS
   "existing authority": s.79(1).
   "functions": s.124(1).

"liability": s.79(1).
"modifications": s.124(1).
"National Park authority": s.63(1).

COMMENCEMENT
September 19, 1995 (s.125(2)).

GENERAL NOTE
This supplementary provision deals with the Secretary of State's order-making powers under Pt. III, which are exercisable by statutory instrument and in general are subject to the negative resolution procedure: subs. (2). The orders may include incidental, supplemental, consequential or transitional provisions.

Agreements as to incidental matters

76.—(1) Any public authorities affected by an order under this Part may from time to time make agreements with respect to—
  (a) any property, income, rights, liabilities or expenses (so far as affected by the order) of the parties to the agreement; or
  (b) any financial relations between those parties.
  (2) Such an agreement may provide—
  (a) for the transfer or retention of any property, rights and liabilities, with or without conditions, and for the joint use of any property;
  (b) for the making of payments by any party to the agreement in respect of—
      (i) property, rights and liabilities transferred or retained,
      (ii) the joint use of any property, or
      (iii) remuneration or compensation payable to any person;
    and
  (c) for the making of any such payment either by way of a capital sum or of a terminable annuity.
  (3) In default of agreement as to any disputed matter, the matter shall be referred to the arbitration of a single arbitrator agreed on by the parties or, in default of agreement, appointed by the Secretary of State; and the award of the arbitrator may make any provision that might be contained in an agreement under this section.
  (4) In subsection (3) above "disputed matter" means any matter which—
  (a) might be the subject of provision contained in an agreement under this section; and
  (b) is the subject of such a dispute between two or more public authorities as is not resolved by or under provision contained in any order under this Part.

DEFINITIONS
"disputed matter": subs. (4).
"liability": s.79(1).
"public authority": s.79(1).

COMMENCEMENT
September 19, 1995 (s.125(2)).

GENERAL NOTE
This section allows all public authorities affected by an order under Pt. III to make agreements with regard to property, income, rights, liabilities or expenses, or any financial relations

between such authorities. Such agreements may deal with the transfer and retention of property, rights and liabilities. A procedure for arbitration is provided by subs. (3), but the Secretary of State has indicated his willingness to assist local authorities and the national park boards and committees in reaching agreement: draft circular, January 31, 1995, (revised draft issued November 6, 1995).

Isles of Scilly

77.—(1) This Part shall have effect in relation to the Isles of Scilly subject to any such modifications as may be provided for by the Secretary of State by order made by statutory instrument.

(2) Before making an order under this section the Secretary of State shall consult with the Council of the Isles of Scilly.

(3) The power to make an order under this section shall include power to make such incidental, supplemental, consequential or transitional provision as the Secretary of State thinks necessary or expedient.

DEFINITIONS
  "modifications": s.124(1).

COMMENCEMENT
  September 19, 1995 (s.125(2)).

Minor and consequential amendments relating to National Parks

78. The enactments mentioned in Schedule 10 to this Act shall have effect subject to the amendments contained in that Schedule (being minor amendments and consequential amendments in connection with the provisions of this Part).

COMMENCEMENT
  This section was brought into force, insofar as it relates to certain paragraphs of Sched. 10, on November 23, 1995 and insofar as it relates to certain other paragraphs of that Schedule on April 1, 1996 (in both cases subject to saving provisions): S.I. 1995 No. 2950. The remainder will come into force on a day to be appointed: s.125(2) and (3).

Interpretation of Part III

79.—(1) In this Part, except in so far as the context otherwise requires—
  "the 1972 Act" means the Local Government Act 1972;
  "existing authority", in relation to a National Park, means—
      (a) any such joint or special planning board for that Park or for any area wholly or partly comprised in that Park as was reconstituted by an order under paragraph 1 or 3 of Schedule 17 to the 1972 Act or constituted by an order under paragraph 3A of that Schedule or section 2(1B) of the Town and Country Planning Act 1990; or
      (b) any National Park Committee for that Park or for any such area;
  "liability", in relation to the transfer of liabilities from one person to another, does not include any criminal liability;
  "principal council" and "principal area" have the same meanings as in the 1972 Act;
  "public authority" means any local authority within the meaning of the 1972 Act (including any such authority in their capacity as a local planning authority), any National Park authority, any existing authority for a National Park, any joint authority or residuary body established under Part II of the Local Government Act 1992, any joint authority established under section 34 of the Local Government (Wales) Act 1994 or the Residuary Body for Wales established by section 39 of that Act;
  "the relevant Park", in relation to a National Park authority, means the area for which that authority is or is to be the National Park authority.

(2) Where—

(a) any enactment that is applied by virtue of this Part in relation to National Park authorities refers, or falls to be construed as referring, to any other enactment, and

(b) that other enactment is also one which is so applied,

the reference shall be construed (so far as it would not be so construed apart from this subsection) as including a reference to the other enactment as it is applied in relation to National Park authorities.

DEFINITIONS
   "National Park authority": s.63(1).

COMMENCEMENT
   September 19, 1995 (s.125(2)).

PART IV

AIR QUALITY

INTRODUCTION AND GENERAL NOTE
   Part IV of the Act contains new provisions aimed at addressing the seemingly intractable problems of national and local air quality. Attention has focused sharply in recent years on poor air quality in many urban areas, with the attendant loss of amenity and potentially serious health implications. By way of example, it was reported in *The Times* on June 23, 1994, that the incidence of traffic which generated winter smog in London over four days in December 1991, was estimated to have led to about 155 deaths. Nitrogen dioxide and black smoke reached particularly high levels over that period. In January 1992, it was reported that the Government was threatened with EC action in relation to sulphur dioxide and particulate levels in Sunderland, following a complaint by a local resident which led to the issue of a reasoned opinion by the European Commission: *The Surveyor*, January 23, 1992.
   Whereas the problem which prompted the Clean Air Act of 1956 (now consolidated in the Clean Air Act 1993) was that of smoke, dust and grit from domestic hearths and industrial furnaces, the most widely perceived cause of urban air quality problems in the 1990s is that of vehicle emissions, a problem recognised only in the 1970s, and then regarded as an area where expenditure on control was unlikely to be cost effective (see Eric Ashby and Mary Anderson, *The Politics of Clean Air* (Clarendon Press, Oxford, 1981, p. 143)). The most recent problem encountered is that of photochemical smog arising from processes such as the oxidation of the nitrous oxides arising from vehicle engine combustion, resulting in increases in ozone levels and the formation of potentially harmful compounds. Somewhat ironically, the cleaner air resulting from the Clean Air legislation has contributed to this problem, since sunlight provides suitable conditions for photo-oxidation processes: see Peter Brimblecombe, *The Big Smoke* (Routledge, London, 1988). It remains to be seen whether the provisions of Part IV will be as effective in improving air quality as the 1956 Act.

Policy Background
   A considerable amount of factual material on the current problems of air quality in Britain can be found in two reports of House of Commons Committees. In October 1994 the Commons Transport Committee published its report on *Transport-related Air Pollution in London* (Session 1993–94, Sixth Report, H.C. 506–I and II). The Committee was persuaded by the evidence that the quality of air in London was deteriorating and that, in relation to the possible link between air pollution and ill-health, a precautionary approach was justified. The Commons Environment Committee reported in April 1995 on *Volatile Organic Compounds* (Session 1994–5, First Report, H.C. 39–I and II). This report called for further work in monitoring volatile organic compounds (VOCs) and further research into their possible health impacts. Again, a precautionary approach was supported.
   Another extremely important review of the problems of air quality caused by vehicle emissions is provided by the Eighteenth Report of the Royal Commission on Environment Pollution, *Transport and the Environment*, published in October 1994 (Cm.2674). The Report unequivocally stated that emissions from road vehicles are the major source of outdoor exposure to air pollution and proposed two specific targets. First, to achieve full compliance by the year 2005 with World Health Organisation guidelines for transport-related pollutants; and secondly to establish in appropriate areas by 2005 local air quality standards based on the critical levels required to protect sensitive eco-systems. One of the recommendations of the Commission was

that local authorities be given new duties to assess ambient air quality, the sources of air pollution in their area, and the risk of pollutant concentrations exceeding threshold levels to be set by the Government; they should also have the duty to draw up and implement an air quality management plan, if necessary, to prevent any thresholds from being breached (para. 14.23). As will be seen, these proposals are very similar to the system created by Pt. IV of the Act. The Commission recommended that the Government should set thresholds for the major pollutants at levels enabling action to be taken to prevent air quality from deteriorating to a dangerous level. Such pollutants include carbon monoxide, nitrogen dioxide and PM10 (*i.e.* particles with a diameter of less than 10μm (10 millionths of a metre)).

The Government's progress towards legislation on air quality should be seen against this background. Significant developments include the following:

1. The publication in November 1992 of a draft "UK VOC Strategy Document", detailing the Government's proposed strategy for reducing VOC emissions by 30 per cent by 1999, so as to meet the UK's obligations under the UNECE protocol on VOC emissions signed in 1991.

2. The publication in November 1993 of proposals entitled *The Future of Air Quality Monitoring Networks in the UK*, setting out ways in which local and national monitoring can be encouraged by better harmonisation and co-ordination.

3. In January 1994 the Government published a comprehensive paper setting out its strategy for reducing emissions of VOCs and consequent formation of ground-level ozone.

4. The announcement by the Secretary of State for the Environment, on February 23, 1994, of new action for the improvement of local air quality, comprising three main elements: development of a new set of health related air quality standards, better management of air quality at local level, and a review of the scope for tightening vehicle emission limits from the year 2000.

5. This announcement was followed by a discussion paper, *Improving Air Quality*, in April 1994. This paper stressed the Government's belief that progress must be based on an effects-based approach, complemented by source-based controls, and that traditional regulation and control methods were unlikely to be sufficient in themselves. Sections III–V of the paper dealt with the issue of air quality standards and local air quality management. This contemplated a framework based on a strategic approach dealing with all sources and deploying a variety of measures in a concerted way.

6. The series of reports by the Government's independent Expert Panel on Air Quality Standards (EPAQS) recommending the establishment of air quality standards for a range of pollutants in the UK. To date there have been six EPAQS reports, on benzene (February 1994), ozone (May 1994), 1, 3-butadiene (December 1994), carbon monoxide (December 1994), sulphur dioxide (September 1995) and particles (November 1995: in the same month the Government published a combined response (entitled *Health Effects of Particles*) to the particles report and to a separate report, *Non-Biological Particles and Health*, by the Committee on the Medical Effects of Air Pollutants).

7. The announcement in January 1995 of a wide package of proposals intended to improve air quality in towns and cities: *Improving Air Quality: Meeting the Challenge*. This expanded upon the 1994 discussion paper in identifying three main areas: namely a new framework of national air quality standards and targets, local air quality management areas, and air pollution and transport.

8. New measures to reduce urban air pollution from vehicles were announced by the Department of Transport in February 1995: Press Release 53. These include the expediting of tougher MOT standards and stricter enforcement against drivers and vehicle operators.

9. During the Lords Committee Stage of the Environment Bill, the Minister, Viscount Ullswater, announced in response to an amendment proposing the insertion of a clause on air quality management, that the Government would bring forward their own proposals at the Commons stage: *Hansard*, H.L. Vol. 561, col. 318.

Overview of the Legislation

The scheme of Part IV may be summarised as follows:

1. The Secretary of State is required to prepare and publish a statement, referred to as the national air quality strategy, and containing policies with respect to the assessment or management of the quality of air (s.80).

2. The Environment Agency/SEPA must have regard to the national air quality strategy in discharging its own pollution control functions (s.81). For SEPA these functions include the role of enforcing authority under the air pollution control regime, exercised in England and Wales by local authorities, and the reserve power to establish smoke control areas under s.19 of the Clean Air Act 1993 which is held by the Secretary of State in England and Wales.

3. Wide powers to make regulations are conferred by s.87, which may include prescribing air quality standards, prescribing objectives for restricting levels of particular substances in air, conferring new powers and duties on local authorities, prohibiting or restricting activities or the access of vehicles to prescribed areas, and prescribing measures to be taken by local authorities or others in ensuring the attainment of air quality standards or objectives.

4. Every local authority (at district level) is under a duty to cause reviews to be conducted of current and likely future air quality within its area (s.82). The review should include an assessment of whether air quality standards and objectives are being or are likely to be achieved; the authority should also identify any parts of its areas where standards and objectives are not likely to be achieved within the relevant period.

5. Areas identified in this way are to be designated by the local authority as air quality management areas (s.83). Where an order designating such an area comes into force a further assessment must be made of air quality in the area and the respects in which the relevant standards or objectives are not likely to be achieved. This must be followed by a written report and action plan, with a timescale, for the exercise by the authority of any powers exercisable by it, to achieve the relevant objectives and standards (s.84). Here it should be noted that Scottish local authorities have fewer functions exercisable in this regard than their counterparts in England and Wales. This is a consequence of the transfer to SEPA by s.21(1)(h) of the Act of the role of enforcing authority in relation to the air pollution control regime, a role retained by local authorities in England and Wales.

6. Local authorities are placed under no express statutory duty to implement such an action plan. However, the Secretary of State in England and Wales and SEPA in Scotland have wide reserve powers in the event of default or non-attainment by local authorities (s.85). The Secretary of State may also issue guidance to local authorities (s.88).

7. County councils in England may make recommendations and proposals to district councils with respect to reviews, assessments and action plans, and in relation to the exercise by the county council of powers available to it (s.86). A procedure for reference to the Secretary of State is provided to resolve any disagreement between county and district as to the contents of proposed action plans (s.84(5)).

8. Schedule 11 contains various supplementary provisions relating to consultation by local authorities in carrying out their functions, joint exercise of local authority functions, exchange of information with county councils, public access to information about air quality, and the creation of fixed penalty offences by regulations made under Pt. IV.

National air quality strategy

80.—(1) The Secretary of State shall as soon as possible prepare and publish a statement (in this Part referred to as "the strategy") containing policies with respect to the assessment or management of the quality of air.

(2) The strategy may also contain policies for implementing—
    (a) obligations of the United Kingdom under the Community Treaties, or
    (b) international agreements to which the United Kingdom is for the time being a party,
so far as relating to the quality of air.

(3) The strategy shall consist of or include—
    (a) a statement which relates to the whole of Great Britain; or
    (b) two or more statements which between them relate to every part of Great Britain.

(4) The Secretary of State—
    (a) shall keep under review his policies with respect to the quality of air; and
    (b) may from time to time modify the strategy.

(5) Without prejudice to the generality of what may be included in the strategy, the strategy must include statements with respect to—
    (a) standards relating to the quality of air;
    (b) objectives for the restriction of the levels at which particular substances are present in the air; and
    (c) measures which are to be taken by local authorities and other persons for the purpose of achieving those objectives.

(6) In preparing the strategy or any modification of it, the Secretary of State shall consult—
    (a) the appropriate new Agency;
    (b) such bodies or persons appearing to him to be representative of the interests of local government as he may consider appropriate;

(c) such bodies or persons appearing to him to be representative of the interests of industry as he may consider appropriate; and

(d) such other bodies or persons as he may consider appropriate.

(7) Before publishing the strategy or any modification of it, the Secretary of State—

(a) shall publish a draft of the proposed strategy or modification, together with notice of a date before which, and an address at which, representations may be made to him concerning the draft so published; and

(b) shall take into account any such representations which are duly made and not withdrawn.

DEFINITIONS

"appropriate new Agency": s.91(1).
"modification": s.124(1).
"notice": s.124(1).
"strategy": subs. (1).

COMMENCEMENT

February 1, 1996 (S.I. 1996 No. 186).

GENERAL NOTE

This section requires the preparation of a national air quality strategy taking the form of a statement or statements of policies. There may be a single statement relating to the whole of Great Britain, or a number of statements giving such coverage (subs. (3)).

Content of strategy

As a minimum, the strategy must include statements with respect to the three matters set out at subs. (5), which equate to a number of the matters which may be dealt with by regulations made under s.87. The strategy may also contain policies for implementing obligations of the U.K. under EC law, or under international agreements. Relevant directives and agreements imposing such obligations include the following (references are to paragraph numbers in *The Encyclopedia of Environmental Law*, Sweet & Maxwell):

International Agreements

1985 Vienna Convention for Protection of the Ozone Layer (B17–001).
1987 Montreal Protocol on Substances that Deplete the Ozone Layer (B17–026).

EC Measures

1980 Directive on air quality limit values and guide values for sulphur dioxide and suspended particulates 80/779/EEC (C80/5–001).
1982 Directive on limit value for lead in air 82/884/EEC (C82/4–001).
1985 Directive on air quality standards for nitrogen dioxide 82/203/EEC (C85/1–001).
1991 Regulation on substances that deplete the ozone layer 91/594/EEC (C91/6–001).
1992 Directive on air pollution by ozone 92/72/EEC (C91/1b–001).
1994 Proposed directive on ambient air quality assessment and management COM(94)109 final, O.J. No. C216/4, August 6, 1994, on which a Common Position was reached by the Council of Environment Ministers in June 1995.
1994 Proposed Council decision establishing a reciprocal exchange of information and data from networks and individual stations measuring ambient air pollution within the Member States COM (94) 345 Final, O.J. No. C281/9, October 7, 1994, on which a Common Position was agreed by the Council of Environment Ministers in October 1995.

Implementation of Strategy

The strategy will be implemented by: (a) regulations made under s.87; (b) guidance issued by the Secretary of State under s.88; (c) the exercise of pollution control functions by the Agency/SEPA (s.81); and (d) the powers and duties conferred on local authorities by ss.82–84.

Functions of the new Agencies

81.—(1) In discharging its pollution control functions, each new Agency shall have regard to the strategy.

(2) In this section "pollution control functions", in relation to a new Agency, means—

(a) in the case of the Agency, the functions conferred on it by or under the enactments specified in section 5(5) above; or

(b) in the case of SEPA, the functions conferred on it by or under the enactments specified in section 33(5) above.

DEFINITIONS
"Agency, the": s.124(1).
"air quality objectives": s.91(1).
"air quality standards": s.91(1).
"functions": s.124(1).
"local authority": s.91(1).
"pollution control functions": subs. (2).
"relevant period": s.91(1).
"SEPA": s.124(1).

COMMENCEMENT
April 1, 1996 (S.I. 1996 No. 186).

GENERAL NOTE
This section requires the Agency and SEPA to have regard to the national air quality strategy in the exercise of their pollution control functions, which are different as between England and Wales and Scotland. Those functions have wider application than air quality, relating as they do to other environmental media and to waste disposal and recovery. The most obvious functions relating to air are those under Pt. I of the Environmental Protection Act 1990 (in relation to integrated pollution control). In relation to Scotland, those powers include the functions exercised by local authorities in relation to air pollution control under Pt. I of the 1990 Act: see the General Note to s.21 at p. 25–74.

It may also be noted that an amendment by Sched. 22, para. 36 of this Act to the Road Traffic Regulation Act 1984 requires local authorities to have regard to the national air quality strategy, so far as practicable, in exercising their functions under the 1984 Act.

Local authority reviews

82.—(1) Every local authority shall from time to time cause a review to be conducted of the quality for the time being, and the likely future quality within the relevant period, of air within the authority's area.

(2) Where a local authority causes a review under subsection (1) above to be conducted, it shall also cause an assessment to be made of whether air quality standards and objectives are being achieved, or are likely to be achieved within the relevant period, within the authority's area.

(3) If, on an assessment under subsection (2) above, it appears that any air quality standards or objectives are not being achieved, or are not likely within the relevant period to be achieved, within the local authority's area, the local authority shall identify any parts of its area in which it appears that those standards or objectives are not likely to be achieved within the relevant period.

DEFINITIONS
"air quality objectives": s.91(1).
"air quality standards": s.91(1).
"local authority": s.91(1).
"relevant period": s.91(1).

COMMENCEMENT
This section comes into force on a day to be appointed (s.125(3)).

GENERAL NOTE
This section requires local authorities to carry out reviews of the quality of air within their area, and its likely future quality within the relevant period (to be prescribed). The review should relate to any air quality standards or objectives prescribed by regulations, in that the authority should assess whether such standards or objectives are being achieved, or are likely to be achieved within the relevant period. This then leads to the identification of those areas where this is not the case (subs. (3)) which in its turn will trigger the obligation under s.83 to designate air quality management areas.

The Government's consultation paper, *Air Quality: Meeting the Challenge* suggests that the new duty to review air quality ought not to be more onerous than the appraisal required in connection with development planning under Planning Policy Guidance Note 12: nonetheless it should be carried out regularly and systematically. The Government intends to expand the national database of air quality information, and to improve the arrangements for local authority access to it. It is also the Government's intention to develop guidance on when central data should be supplemented by further work, and to develop good practice guidance.

County Councils

In England, county councils may make recommendations to their districts with respect to the review and assessment, and such recommendations must be taken into account (s.86(2)).

Procedural Issues

Schedule 11 contains a number of relevant requirements relating to air quality reviews. These include consultation (para. 1), exchange of information with county councils (para. 2), joint exercise of functions with other local authorities (para. 3), and public access to the results (para. 4).

Designation of air quality management areas

83.—(1) Where, as a result of an air quality review, it appears that any air quality standards or objectives are not being achieved, or are not likely within the relevant period to be achieved, within the area of a local authority, the local authority shall by order designate as an air quality management area (in this Part referred to as a "designated area") any part of its area in which it appears that those standards or objectives are not being achieved, or are not likely to be achieved within the relevant period.

(2) An order under this section may, as a result of a subsequent air quality review,—

(a) be varied by a subsequent order; or

(b) be revoked by such an order, if it appears on that subsequent air quality review that the air quality standards and objectives are being achieved, and are likely throughout the relevant period to be achieved, within the designated area.

DEFINITIONS

"air quality objectives": s.91(1).
"air quality review": s.91(1).
"air quality standards": s.91(1).
"designated area": subs. (1).
"local authority": s.91(1).
"relevant period": s.91(1).

COMMENCEMENT

This section comes into force on a day to be appointed (s.125(3)).

GENERAL NOTE

This section follows logically from s.82 and requires local authorities to make orders designating as "air quality management areas" those areas identified on review where air quality standards or objectives are not, and are not likely to be, complied with. The consequence of such designation is that the local authority then falls under further duties by virtue of s.84. If the problems of non-compliance are successfully addressed, then the order may be revoked under s.83(2)(b), or may be varied under s.83(2)(a).

Procedure

The section should be read in conjunction with the requirements of Sched. 11, for example as to consultation. Provision may also be made in regulations under s.87 as to designation orders under s.83, or in circumstances falling outside s.83 (s.87(2)(f)–(h)).

Smoke Control Areas

In *Improving Air Quality: Meeting the Challenge* the Government indicated that apart from Northern Ireland, where around 80 per cent of homes rely on coal for heating, there were no plans to implement any further controls on domestic fuels. Existing Smoke Control Areas under the Clean Air Act will remain in force, but the procedure for declaring any further Smoke Control Areas will be brought within the general framework of Pt. IV of the Act.

Duties of local authorities in relation to designated areas

84.—(1) Where an order under section 83 above comes into operation, the local authority which made the order shall, for the purpose of supplementing such information as it has in relation to the designated area in question, cause an assessment to be made of—

(a) the quality for the time being, and the likely future quality within the relevant period, of air within the designated area to which the order relates; and

(b) the respects (if any) in which it appears that air quality standards or objectives are not being achieved, or are not likely within the relevant period to be achieved, within that designated area.

(2) A local authority which is required by subsection (1) above to cause an assessment to be made shall also be under a duty—

(a) to prepare, before the expiration of the period of twelve months beginning with the coming into operation of the order mentioned in that subsection, a report of the results of that assessment; and

(b) to prepare, in accordance with the following provisions of this Part, a written plan (in this Part referred to as an "action plan") for the exercise by the authority, in pursuit of the achievement of air quality standards and objectives in the designated area, of any powers exercisable by the authority.

(3) An action plan shall include a statement of the time or times by or within which the local authority in question proposes to implement each of the proposed measures comprised in the plan.

(4) A local authority may from time to time revise an action plan.

(5) This subsection applies in any case where the local authority preparing an action plan or a revision of an action plan is the council of a district in England which is comprised in an area for which there is a county council; and if, in a case where this subsection applies, the county council disagrees with the authority about the contents of the proposed action plan or revision of the action plan—

(a) either of them may refer the matter to the Secretary of State;

(b) on any such reference the Secretary of State may confirm the authority's proposed action plan or revision of the action plan, with or without modifications (whether or not proposed by the county council) or reject it and, if he rejects it, he may also exercise any powers of his under section 85 below; and

(c) the authority shall not finally determine the content of the action plan, or the revision of the action plan, except in accordance with his decision on the reference or in pursuance of directions under section 85 below.

DEFINITIONS
"action plan": subs. (2).
"air quality objectives": s.91(1).
"air quality standards": s.91(1).
"designated area": s.83(1).
"local authority": s.91(1).
"modifications": s.124(1).
"relevant period": s.91(1).

COMMENCEMENT
This section comes into force on a day to be appointed (s.125(3)).

GENERAL NOTE
This section imposes various duties on local authorities in relation to air quality management areas designated by order under s.83. The requirements are essentially first, to supplement exist-

ing information by an assessment of current and likely future air quality within the area and the respects in which it appears that air quality standards or objectives are not being met (subs. (1)); second, to prepare, within 12 months of the designating order coming into effect, a report of the results of that assessment (subs. (2)(a)); and third, to prepare an action plan (subs. (2)(b)) as to which, see below.

The Government's intention is that local authorities will be able to bid for central funding to support the preparation of the assessment: see *Improving Air Quality: Meeting the Challenge*, p. 18. The system is to be phased in, following consultation with local authority associations and taking account of local government reorganisation; however, it is intended that reviews should be completed within two years.

Action Plans

The action plan must be in writing, and relates to the use of any powers exercisable by the authority in pursuit of achieving air quality standards and objectives (subs. (2)(b)). It must include a timetable by which the measures referred to in the plan are proposed to be completed (subs. (3)).

The reference is to "any" powers exercisable; the authority must therefore consider all powers available to it, in terms of the possible contribution their exercise may make to fulfilment of the plan. Such powers will include those relating to air pollution control under Pt. I of the 1990 Act (except in Scotland, where these powers are transferred to SEPA), statutory nuisance powers, (smoke control powers under the Clean Air Act 1993), land-use planning powers under the Town and Country Planning Act 1990 or, in Scotland, under the Town and Country Planning (Scotland) Act 1972, and road traffic regulation powers. The Government's strategy document, *Improving Air Quality: Meeting the Challenge*, indicates that whilst traffic is the greatest single source of many pollutants, other sources (*e.g.* domestic and industrial) should not be overlooked. Part V of that paper is devoted exclusively to an action programme for air pollution and transport.

Local authorities are placed under no statutory duty to implement action plans, although clearly they would be under considerable political pressure to do so and the reserve powers exercisable under s.85 are capable of placing them under such a duty.

County Councils

Under Sched. 11, para. 2, in England county and district councils are to cooperate in sharing relevant information. In the course of preparation of the action plan, the county council (if any) must submit to the district its proposals for the exercise of any powers exercisable by the county council, for example highway powers (s.86(3) and (4)). Such proposals must then be included in the action plan (s.86(5)). Where the county and district disagree about the content of the action plan, either may refer the issue to the Secretary of State for determination under s.85(5).

Reserve powers of the Secretary of State or SEPA

85.—(1) In this section, "the appropriate authority" means—

(a) in relation to England and Wales, the Secretary of State; and

(b) in relation to Scotland, SEPA acting with the approval of the Secretary of State.

(2) The appropriate authority may conduct or make, or cause to be conducted or made,—

(a) a review of the quality for the time being, and the likely future quality within the relevant period, of air within the area of any local authority;

(b) an assessment of whether air quality standards and objectives are being achieved, or are likely to be achieved within the relevant period, within the area of a local authority;

(c) an identification of any parts of the area of a local authority in which it appears that those standards or objectives are not likely to be achieved within the relevant period; or

(d) an assessment of the respects (if any) in which it appears that air quality standards or objectives are not being achieved, or are not likely within the relevant period to be achieved, within the area of a local authority or within a designated area.

(3) If it appears to the appropriate authority—

(a) that air quality standards or objectives are not being achieved, or are not likely within the relevant period to be achieved, within the area of a local authority,

   (b) that a local authority has failed to discharge any duty imposed on it under or by virtue of this Part,

   (c) that the actions, or proposed actions, of a local authority in purported compliance with the provisions of this Part are inappropriate in all the circumstances of the case, or

   (d) that developments in science or technology, or material changes in circumstances, have rendered inappropriate the actions or proposed actions of a local authority in pursuance of this Part,

the appropriate authority may give directions to the local authority requiring it to take such steps as may be specified in the directions.

(4) Without prejudice to the generality of subsection (3) above, directions under that subsection may, in particular, require a local authority—

   (a) to cause an air quality review to be conducted under section 82 above in accordance with the directions;

   (b) to cause an air quality review under section 82 above to be conducted afresh, whether in whole or in part, or to be so conducted with such differences as may be specified or described in the directions;

   (c) to make an order under section 83 above designating as an air quality management area an area specified in, or determined in accordance with, the directions;

   (d) to revoke, or modify in accordance with the directions, any order under that section;

   (e) to prepare in accordance with the directions an action plan for a designated area;

   (f) to modify, in accordance with the directions, any action plan prepared by the authority; or

   (g) to implement, in accordance with the directions, any measures in an action plan.

(5) The Secretary of State shall also have power to give directions to local authorities requiring them to take such steps specified in the directions as he considers appropriate for the implementation of—

   (a) any obligations of the United Kingdom under the Community Treaties, or

   (b) any international agreement to which the United Kingdom is for the time being a party,

so far as relating to the quality of air.

(6) Any direction given under this section shall be published in such manner as the body or person giving it considers appropriate for the purpose of bringing the matters to which it relates to the attention of persons likely to be affected by them; and—

   (a) copies of the direction shall be made available to the public; and

   (b) notice shall be given—

      (i) in the case of a direction given to a local authority in England and Wales, in the London Gazette, or

      (ii) in the case of a direction given to a local authority in Scotland, in the Edinburgh Gazette,

   of the giving of the direction and of where a copy of the direction may be obtained.

(7) It is the duty of a local authority to comply with any direction given to it under or by virtue of this Part.

DEFINITIONS

   "action plan": s.84(2).
   "air quality objectives": s.91(1).
   "air quality review": s.91(1).
   "air quality standards": s.91(1).
   "appropriate authority": subs. (1).
   "designated area": s.83(1).
   "local authority": s.91(1).

"modify": s.124(1).
"notice": s.124(1).
"relevant period": s.91(1).
"SEPA": s.124(1).

COMMENCEMENT
This section comes into force on a day to be appointed (s.125(3)).

GENERAL NOTE
This section contains wide reserve powers exercisable by the Secretary of State in England
and Wales or, in Scotland, by SEPA with the approval of the Secretary of State. The reserve
powers include the carrying out of reviews and assessments of air quality (subs. (2)) and the
giving of directions to local authorities (subs. (3)), in cases of default or inappropriate actions by
local authorities (subs. (3)(b) and (c)), or where changes in science or technology or in general
circumstances have rendered their actions inappropriate (subs. (3)(d)), or to comply with E.C.
or international obligations (subs. (5)). The local authority is under a duty to comply with directions (subs. (7)). Perhaps most importantly, the direction may require the local authority to
implement any measures in an action plan (subs. (4)(g)). Power to give directions to county
councils in England is contained in s.86(6)–(10).
SEPA would appear to have been given these reserve powers for the same reason as was given
for the allocation to it of responsibility to draw up the Scottish national waste strategy (see the
General Note to s.92 at pp. 25–252—25–253). The explanation there was that SEPA, unlike the
Scottish Office, has the specialist staff required to carry out the function.

Functions of county councils for areas for which there are district councils

86.—(1) This section applies in any case where a district in England for
which there is a district council is comprised in an area for which there is a
county council; and in this paragraph—
    (a) any reference to the county council is a reference to the council of that
          area; and
    (b) any reference to a district council is a reference to the council of a
          district comprised in that area.
    (2) The county council may make recommendations to a district council
with respect to the carrying out of—
    (a) any particular air quality review,
    (b) any particular assessment under section 82 or 84 above, or
    (c) the preparation of any particular action plan or revision of an action
          plan,
and the district council shall take into account any such recommendations.
    (3) Where a district council is preparing an action plan, the county council
shall, within the relevant period, submit to the district council proposals for
the exercise (so far as relating to the designated area) by the county council,
in pursuit of the achievement of air quality standards and objectives, of any
powers exercisable by the county council.
    (4) Where the county council submits proposals to a district council in pur-
suance of subsection (3) above, it shall also submit a statement of the time or
times by or within which it proposes to implement each of the proposals.
    (5) An action plan shall include a statement of—
    (a) any proposals submitted pursuant to subsection (3) above; and
    (b) any time or times set out in the statement submitted pursuant to sub-
          section (4) above.
    (6) If it appears to the Secretary of State—
    (a) that air quality standards or objectives are not being achieved, or are
          not likely within the relevant period to be achieved, within the area of
          a district council,
    (b) that the county council has failed to discharge any duty imposed on it
          under or by virtue of this Part,

(c) that the actions, or proposed actions, of the county council in purported compliance with the provisions of this Part are inappropriate in all the circumstances of the case, or

(d) that developments in science or technology, or material changes in circumstances, have rendered inappropriate the actions or proposed actions of the county council in pursuance of this Part,

the Secretary of State may give directions to the county council requiring it to take such steps as may be specified in the directions.

(7) Without prejudice to the generality of subsection (6) above, directions under that subsection may, in particular, require the county council—

(a) to submit, in accordance with the directions, proposals pursuant to subsection (3) above or a statement pursuant to subsection (4) above;

(b) to modify, in accordance with the directions, any proposals or statement submitted by the county council pursuant to subsection (3) or (4) above;

(c) to submit any proposals or statement so modified to the district council in question pursuant to subsection (3) or (4) above; or

(d) to implement, in accordance with the directions, any measures included in an action plan.

(8) The Secretary of State shall also have power to give directions to county councils for areas for which there are district councils requiring them to take such steps specified in the directions as he considers appropriate for the implementation of—

(a) any obligations of the United Kingdom under the Community Treaties, or

(b) any international agreement to which the United Kingdom is for the time being a party,

so far as relating to the quality of air.

(9) Any direction given under this section shall be published in such manner as the Secretary of State considers appropriate for the purpose of bringing the matters to which it relates to the attention of persons likely to be affected by them; and—

(a) copies of the direction shall be made available to the public; and

(b) notice of the giving of the direction, and of where a copy of the direction may be obtained, shall be given in the London Gazette.

(10) It is the duty of a county council for an area for which there are district councils to comply with any direction given to it under or by virtue of this Part.

DEFINITIONS

"action plan": s.84(2).
"air quality objectives": s.91(1).
"air quality review": s.91(1).
"air quality standards": s.91(1).
"designated area": s.83(1).
"notice": s.124(1).
"relevant period": s.91(1).

COMMENCEMENT

This section comes into force on a day to be appointed (s.125(3)).

GENERAL NOTE

This section applies in those areas of England where there are county councils. It allows counties to make recommendations to districts with regard to air quality reviews, assessments and action plans, and such recommendations are to be taken into account (subs. (2)). Subsections (3) to (5) provide a mechanism by which the proposed exercise of county council powers is to be incorporated into action plans, and subss. (6) to (10) provide a means to secure the co-operation and action of county councils by directions given by the Secretary of State.

Regulations for the purposes of Part IV

87.—(1) Regulations may make provision—

(a) for, or in connection with, implementing the strategy;

(b) for, or in connection with, implementing—

(i) obligations of the United Kingdom under the Community Treaties, or

(ii) international agreements to which the United Kingdom is for the time being a party,

so far as relating to the quality of air; or

(c) otherwise with respect to the assessment or management of the quality of air.

(2) Without prejudice to the generality of subsection (1) above, regulations under that subsection may make provision—

(a) prescribing standards relating to the quality of air;

(b) prescribing objectives for the restriction of the levels at which particular substances are present in the air;

(c) conferring powers or imposing duties on local authorities;

(d) for or in connection with—

(i) authorising local authorities (whether by agreements or otherwise) to exercise any functions of a Minister of the Crown on his behalf;

(ii) directing that functions of a Minister of the Crown shall be exercisable concurrently with local authorities; or

(iii) transferring functions of a Minister of the Crown to local authorities;

(e) prohibiting or restricting, or for or in connection with prohibiting or restricting,—

(i) the carrying on of prescribed activities, or

(ii) the access of prescribed vehicles or mobile equipment to prescribed areas,

whether generally or in prescribed circumstances;

(f) for or in connection with the designation of air quality management areas by orders made by local authorities in such cases or circumstances not falling within section 83 above as may be prescribed;

(g) for the application, with or without modifications, of any provisions of this Part in relation to areas designated by virtue of paragraph (f) above or in relation to orders made by virtue of that paragraph;

(h) with respect to—

(i) air quality reviews;

(ii) assessments under this Part;

(iii) orders designating air quality management areas; or

(iv) action plans;

(j) prescribing measures which are to be adopted by local authorities (whether in action plans or otherwise) or other persons in pursuance of the achievement of air quality standards or objectives;

(k) for or in connection with the communication to the public of information relating to quality for the time being, or likely future quality, of the air;

(l) for or in connection with the obtaining by local authorities from any person of information which is reasonably necessary for the discharge of functions conferred or imposed on them under or by virtue of this Part;

(m) for or in connection with the recovery by a local authority from prescribed persons in prescribed circumstances, and in such manner as may be prescribed, of costs incurred by the authority in discharging functions conferred or imposed on the authority under or by virtue of this Part;

(n) for a person who contravenes, or fails to comply with, any prescribed provision of the regulations to be guilty of an offence and liable on summary conviction to a fine not exceeding level 5 on the standard scale or such lower level on that scale as may be prescribed in relation to the offence;

(o) for or in connection with arrangements under which a person may discharge any liability to conviction for a prescribed offence by payment of a penalty of a prescribed amount;

(p) for or in connection with appeals against determinations or decisions made, notices given or served, or other things done under or by virtue of the regulations.

(3) Without prejudice to the generality of paragraph (h) of subsection (2) above, the provision that may be made by virtue of that paragraph includes provision for or in connection with any of the following, that is to say—

(a) the scope or form of a review or assessment;

(b) the scope, content or form of an action plan;

(c) the time at which, period within which, or manner in which a review or assessment is to be carried out or an action plan is to be prepared;

(d) the methods to be employed—
    (i) in carrying out reviews or assessments; or
    (ii) in monitoring the effectiveness of action plans;

(e) the factors to be taken into account in preparing action plans;

(f) the actions which must be taken by local authorities or other persons in consequence of reviews, assessments or action plans;

(g) requirements for consultation;

(h) the treatment of representations or objections duly made;

(j) the publication of, or the making available to the public of, or of copies of,—
    (i) the results, or reports of the results, of reviews or assessments; or
    (ii) orders or action plans;

(k) requirements for—
    (i) copies of any such reports, orders or action plans, or
    (ii) prescribed information, in such form as may be prescribed, relating to reviews or assessments,
to be sent to the Secretary of State or to the appropriate new Agency.

(4) In determining—

(a) any appeal against, or reference or review of, a decision of a local authority under or by virtue of regulations under this Part, or

(b) any application transmitted from a local authority under or by virtue of any such regulations,
the body or person making the determination shall be bound by any direction given by a Minister of the Crown or SEPA to the local authority to the same extent as the local authority.

(5) The provisions of any regulations under this Part may include—

(a) provision for anything that may be prescribed by the regulations to be determined under the regulations and for anything falling to be so determined to be determined by such persons, in accordance with such procedure and by reference to such matters, and to the opinion of such persons, as may be prescribed;

(b) different provision for different cases, including different provision in relation to different persons, circumstances, areas or localities; and

(c) such supplemental, consequential, incidental or transitional provision (including provision amending any enactment or any instrument made under any enactment) as the Secretary of State considers appropriate.

(6) Nothing in regulations under this Part shall authorise any person other than a constable in uniform to stop a vehicle on any road.

(7) Before making any regulations under this Part, the Secretary of State shall consult—

    (a) the appropriate new Agency;

    (b) such bodies or persons appearing to him to be representative of the interests of local government as he may consider appropriate;

    (c) such bodies or persons appearing to him to be representative of the interests of industry as he may consider appropriate; and

    (d) such other bodies or persons as he may consider appropriate.

(8) Any power conferred by this Part to make regulations shall be exercisable by statutory instrument; and no statutory instrument containing regulations under this Part shall be made unless a draft of the instrument has been laid before, and approved by a resolution of, each House of Parliament.

(9) If, apart from this subsection, the draft of an instrument containing regulations under this Part would be treated for the purposes of the Standing Orders of either House of Parliament as a hybrid instrument, it shall proceed in that House as if it were not such an instrument.

DEFINITIONS

    "action plan": s.84(2).
    "air quality objectives": s.91(1).
    "air quality review": s.91(1).
    "air quality standards": s.91(1).
    "appropriate new Agency": s.91(1).
    "functions": s.124(1).
    "local authority": s.91(1).
    "notice": s.124(1).
    "prescribed": s.91(1).
    "regulations": s.91(1).
    "strategy, the": s.80(1).

COMMENCEMENT

    February 1, 1996 (S.I. 1996 No. 186).

GENERAL NOTE

This section provides the power to make regulations for the general purposes specified in subs. (1), namely the implementation of the national strategy, implementation of Community obligations and international agreements, and generally with respect to the assessment and management of air quality. It should also be noted that the Act amends the Road Traffic Regulation Act 1984 so as to allow traffic regulation orders made under the 1984 Act to be made for any of these three purposes (Sched. 22, para. 36).

The specific matters which may be covered are listed at subs. (2). These matters include the prescribing of air quality standards and objectives (see below). They also include issues of manner and form as to the exercise of local authority functions under Pt. IV (subss. (2)(f)–(l) and (3)), the prohibition or restriction of prescribed activities or vehicular access (subss. (2)(e) and (6)), appeals (subss. (2)(p) and (4)) and the creation of offences, including fixed penalty offences (subs. (2)(a) and (o) and Sched. 11, para. 5).

Air Quality Standards

Air quality standards already exist for certain substances, as required by E.C. law: the Air Quality Standards Regulations 1989 (S.I. 1989 No. 317) (sulphur dioxide, suspended particulates, lead and nitrogen dioxide). Essentially these Regulations impose an obligation on the Secretary of State to take any necessary measures to ensure that the relevant E.C. limit values are not exceeded.

Part 2 of the Government's policy document, *Improving Air Quality: Meeting the Challenge*, suggests two main levels of air quality standards as "anchor points". One will be a guideline figure, essentially a long-term goal, representing a level at which the pollutant had been rendered harmless or where no significant further benefit could be obtained by reasonable expenditure. This would be achieved by measures such as cost-effective progressive introduction of new technology. The second standard would be a trigger level, denoting cases where air quality is so poor that an immediate response would be justified to prevent serious damage. In terms of the scope of standards, the Government has concluded that the following pollutants should be covered: ozone, benzene, 1,3-butadiene, sulphur dioxide, carbon monoxide, nitrogen dioxide, particles, polycyclic aromatic hydrocarbons (PAHs), and lead. Further information on each of these pollutants is given in Part 3 of *Improving Air Quality: Meeting the Challenge*. In setting the standards, the Government is advised by the independent Expert Panel on Air Quality Standards (EPAQS). As noted in the Introduction and General Note to this Part at p. 25–232, this body has already made recommendations for or has reported on benzene, ozone, 1,3-butadiene, carbon monoxide and sulphur dioxide.

Guidance for the purposes of Part IV

88.—(1) The Secretary of State may issue guidance to local authorities with respect to, or in connection with, the exercise of any of the powers conferred, or the discharge of any of the duties imposed, on those authorities by or under this Part.

(2) A local authority, in carrying out any of its functions under or by virtue of this Part, shall have regard to any guidance issued by the Secretary of State under this Part.

(3) This section shall apply in relation to county councils for areas for which there are district councils as it applies in relation to local authorities.

DEFINITIONS
 "functions": s.124(1).
 "local authorities": s.91(1).

COMMENCEMENT
 February 1, 1996 (S.I. 1996 No. 186).

GENERAL NOTE
 This section allows the Secretary of State to issue guidance to district councils (and in England, where applicable, county councils) in relation to the carrying out of duties and the exercise of functions under Pt. IV. The local authority must have regard to such guidance.

Application of Part IV to the Isles of Scilly

89.—(1) Subject to the provisions of any order under this section, this Part, other than section 80, shall not apply in relation to the Isles of Scilly.

(2) The Secretary of State may, after consultation with the Council of the Isles of Scilly, by order provide for the application of any provisions of this Part (other than section 80) to the Isles of Scilly; and any such order may provide for the application of those provisions to those Isles with such modifications as may be specified in the order.

(3) An order under this section may—
 (a) make different provision for different cases, including different provision in relation to different persons, circumstances or localities; and
 (b) contain such supplemental, consequential and transitional provision as the Secretary of State considers appropriate, including provision saving provision repealed by or under any enactment.

(4) The power of the Secretary of State to make an order under this section shall be exercisable by statutory instrument; and a statutory instrument containing such an order shall be subject to annulment in pursuance of a resolution of either House of Parliament.

DEFINITIONS
"modifications": s.124(1).

COMMENCEMENT
February 1, 1996 (S.I. 1996 No. 186).

Supplemental provisions

90. Schedule 11 to this Act shall have effect.

COMMENCEMENT
February 1, 1996, insofar as this section relates to paras. 2, 3 and 5 of Sched. 11 (S.I. 1996 No. 186); the remainder comes into force on a day to be appointed (s.125(3)).

GENERAL NOTE
Schedule 11 deals with (a) consultation by local authorities in the course of carrying out functions of review, assessment and action plan preparation (para. 1); (b) the mutual exchange of information between district and county councils in England (para. 2); (c) the joint exercise of functions by two or more local authorities under direction from the Secretary of State or SEPA (para. 3); (d) the provision to the public of copies of the various documents produced under Part IV (para. 4); and (e) express authority for the creation of fixed penalty offences by regulations under s.87 (para. 5).

Joint exercise of functions
In relation to the joint exercise of functions, Government Offices for the Regions will be expected to consider and consult on the need for joint arrangements in areas such as conurbations, metropolitan areas and estuaries: see *Improving Air Quality: Meeting the Challenge*, p. 19.

Interpretation of Part IV

91.—(1) In this Part—
"action plan" shall be construed in accordance with section 84(2)(b) above;
"air quality objectives" means objectives prescribed by virtue of section 87(2)(b) above;
"air quality review" means a review under section 82 or 85 above;
"air quality standards" means standards prescribed by virtue of section 87(2)(a) above;
"the appropriate new Agency" means—
(a) in relation to England and Wales, the Agency;
(b) in relation to Scotland, SEPA;
"designated area" has the meaning given by section 83(1) above;
"local authority", in relation to England and Wales, means—
(a) any unitary authority,
(b) any district council, so far as it is not a unitary authority,
(c) the Common Council of the City of London and, as respects the Temples, the Sub-Treasurer of the Inner Temple and the Under-Treasurer of the Middle Temple respectively,
and, in relation to Scotland, means a council for an area constituted under section 2 of the Local Government etc. (Scotland) Act 1994;
"new Agency" means the Agency or SEPA;
"prescribed" means prescribed, or of a description prescribed, by or under regulations;
"regulations" means regulations made by the Secretary of State;
"the relevant period", in the case of any provision of this Part, means such period as may be prescribed for the purposes of that provision;
"the strategy" has the meaning given by section 80(1) above;
"unitary authority" means—
(a) the council of a county, so far as it is the council of an area for which there are no district councils;
(b) the council of any district comprised in an area for which there is no county council;

(c) the council of a London borough;

(d) the council of a county borough in Wales.

(2) Any reference in this Part to it appearing that any air quality standards or objectives are not likely within the relevant period to be achieved includes a reference to it appearing that those standards or objectives are likely within that period not to be achieved.

DEFINITIONS
"Agency, the": s.124(1).
"SEPA": s.124(1).

COMMENCEMENT
February 1, 1996 (S.I. 1996 No. 186).

GENERAL NOTE

Subs. (2)
Possibly from an abundance of caution, this subsection makes it clear that references to it appearing that air quality standards or objectives are not likely to be achieved include the more pessimistic assessment that they are likely not to be achieved.

PART V

MISCELLANEOUS, GENERAL AND SUPPLEMENTAL PROVISIONS

Waste

National waste strategy

92.—(1) Before section 45 of the Environmental Protection Act 1990 there shall be inserted—

"National waste strategy: England and Wales

44A.—(1) The Secretary of State shall as soon as possible prepare a statement ("the strategy") containing his policies in relation to the recovery and disposal of waste in England and Wales.

(2) The strategy shall consist of or include—

(a) a statement which relates to the whole of England and Wales; or

(b) two or more statements which between them relate to the whole of England and Wales.

(3) The Secretary of State may from time to time modify the strategy.

(4) Without prejudice to the generality of what may be included in the strategy, the strategy must include—

(a) a statement of the Secretary of State's policies for attaining the objectives specified in Schedule 2A to this Act;

(b) provisions relating to each of the following, that is to say—

(i) the type, quantity and origin of waste to be recovered or disposed of;

(ii) general technical requirements; and

(iii) any special requirements for particular wastes.

(5) In preparing the strategy or any modification of it, the Secretary of State—

(a) shall consult the Environment Agency,

(b) shall consult—

(i) such bodies or persons appearing to him to be representative of the interests of local government, and

(ii) such bodies or persons appearing to him to be representative of the interests of industry,

as he may consider appropriate, and

(c) may consult such other bodies or persons as he considers appropriate.

(6) Without prejudice to any power to give directions conferred by section 40 of the Environment Act 1995, the Secretary of State may give directions to the Environment Agency requiring it—

(a) to advise him on the policies which are to be included in the strategy;

(b) to carry out a survey of or investigation into—

    (i) the kinds or quantities of waste which it appears to that Agency is likely to be situated in England and Wales,

    (ii) the facilities which are or appear to that Agency likely to be available or needed in England and Wales for recovering or disposing of any such waste,

    (iii) any other matter upon which the Secretary of State wishes to be informed in connection with his preparation of the strategy or any modification of it,

and to report its findings to him.

(7) A direction under subsection (6)(b) above—

(a) shall specify or describe the matters or the areas which are to be the subject of the survey or investigation; and

(b) may make provision in relation to the manner in which—

    (i) the survey or investigation is to be carried out, or

    (ii) the findings are to be reported or made available to other persons.

(8) Where a direction is given under subsection (6)(b) above, the Environment Agency shall, in accordance with any requirement of the direction,—

(a) before carrying out the survey or investigation, consult—

    (i) such bodies or persons appearing to it to be representative of local planning authorities, and

    (ii) such bodies or persons appearing to it to be representative of the interests of industry,

as it may consider appropriate; and

(b) make its findings available to those authorities.

(9) In this section—

"local planning authority" has the same meaning as in the Town and Country Planning Act 1990;

"strategy" includes the strategy as modified from time to time and "statement" shall be construed accordingly.

(10) This section makes provision for the purpose of implementing Article 7 of the directive of the Council of the European Communities, dated 15th July 1975, on waste, as amended by—

(a) the directive of that Council, dated 18th March 1991, amending directive 75/442/EEC on waste; and

(b) the directive of that Council, dated 23rd December 1991, standardising and rationalising reports on the implementation of certain Directives relating to the environment.

National waste strategy: Scotland

44B.—(1) SEPA shall as soon as possible prepare a statement ("the strategy") containing its policies in relation to the recovery and disposal of waste in Scotland.

(2) SEPA may from time to time modify the strategy.

(3) Without prejudice to the generality of what may be included in the strategy, the strategy must include—

(a) a statement of SEPA's policies for attaining the objectives specified in Schedule 2A to this Act;

(b) provisions relating to each of the following, that is to say—

    (i) the type, quantity and origin of waste to be recovered or disposed of;

(ii) general technical requirements; and

(iii) any special requirements for particular wastes.

(4) In preparing the strategy or any modification of it SEPA shall consult—

(a) such bodies or persons appearing to it to be representative of the interests of industry as it may consider appropriate;

(b) such local authorities as appear to it to be likely to be affected by the strategy or modification,

and may consult such other bodies or persons as it considers appropriate.

(5) Without prejudice to any power to give directions conferred by section 40 of the Environment Act 1995, the Secretary of State may give directions to SEPA—

(a) as to the policies which are to be included in the strategy;

(b) requiring it to carry out a survey or investigation into—

(i) the kinds or quantities of waste which it appears to it is likely to be situated in Scotland,

(ii) the facilities which are or appear to it likely to be available or needed in Scotland for recovering or disposing of any such waste,

(iii) any other matter which the Secretary of State considers appropriate in connection with its preparation of the strategy or any modifications of it.

(6) A direction under subsection (5)(b) above—

(a) shall specify or describe the matters or the areas which are to be the subject of the survey or investigation; and

(b) may make provision in relation to the manner in which—

(i) the survey or investigation is to be carried out, or

(ii) the findings are to be reported or made available to other persons.

(7) Where a direction is given under subsection (5)(b) above SEPA shall, in accordance with any requirement of the direction—

(a) before carrying out the survey or investigation, consult—

(i) such bodies or persons appearing to it to be representative of planning authorities, and

(ii) such bodies or persons appearing to it to be representative of the interests of industry,

as it may consider appropriate; and

(b) make its findings available to those authorities.

(8) In this section—

"planning authority" means an authority within the meaning of section 172 of the Local Government (Scotland) Act 1973;

"strategy" includes the strategy as modified from time to time and "statement" shall be construed accordingly.

(9) This section makes provision for the purpose of implementing Article 7 of the directive of the Council of the European Communities dated 15th July 1975 on waste, as amended by—

(a) the directive of that Council dated 18th March 1991 amending directive 75/442/EEC on waste; and

(b) the directive of that Council dated 23rd December 1991 standardising and rationalising reports on the implementation of certain Directives relating to the environment."

(2) After Schedule 2 to that Act there shall be inserted the Schedule set out in Schedule 12 to this Act.

COMMENCEMENT

April 1, 1996 (S.I. 1996 No. 186).

GENERAL NOTE

This section inserts new ss.44A and 44B and a new Sched. 2A into the Environmental Protection Act 1990. The new sections provide, for England and Wales and for Scotland respectively, for the preparation "as soon as possible" of a national waste strategy and its subsequent modification. The new Schedule, to which the sections refer, contains objectives which the strategies are to attain in order to implement EC legislation. It is anticipated that each strategy will be informed by a survey or investigation by the Environment Agency/SEPA into the circumstances of waste production and management in their respective areas. A process of consultation is required in the course of such a survey and in the course of the preparation or modification of a strategy.

The strategy for England and Wales is to be prepared by the Secretary of State, with a significant role in its preparation envisaged for the Environment Agency. The Scottish strategy, by contrast, is to be prepared by SEPA itself, overseen by the Secretary of State. This contrast is considered further below. It accounts for most of the differences in the wording of the two sections: the content of each is essentially the same, which is unsurprising since both were inserted in order to implement provisions in Article 7 of Directive 75/442/EEC (as amended, generally known as the Waste Framework Directive). Accordingly, the discussion below refers to both sections except where the contrary is indicated.

Despite the EC dimension to the provisions, the national waste strategies can be expected to be wider in scope than that dimension and these provisions would strictly require: see the discussion below of *Making Waste Work*, the non-statutory predecessor of the strategy for England and Wales.

Policy Context

Sections 44A and 44B draw together a number of interrelated dimensions of waste policy:

Waste management at national level. The national waste strategies are to replace the waste disposal plans previously drawn up at local level by waste regulation authorities under the 1990 Act, s.50, which encompassed waste recovery as well as disposal, and which the 1995 Act repeals (Sched. 24). This shift mirrors the transfer of waste regulation from local to national level by Part I of the 1995 Act. Transitional provisions (Sched. 23, paras. 16 and 17) keep s.50 plans in force until replaced by a statutory waste strategy made under s.44A or s.44B. Operational waste disposal itself, however, remains the responsibility of local waste disposal authorities. The change in emphasis from waste disposal to waste management is itself significant in the light of the "waste hierarchy" (see further below).

In November 1995 the Department of the Environment (DoE) published *Waste Management Planning: Principles and Practice* as guidance to waste regulation authorities and an initial framework of best practice for their successor, the Agency. The guidance encompasses waste management planning "in its broader sense, [which] includes, but encompasses much more than, the preparation of a waste management plan" (para. 1.1), and sees such planning as "an iterative process, requiring frequent reassessment of the position" in the light of new data (para. 1.2), which is "to govern the policies and provide a framework for the everyday decisions of the Environment Agency in relation to waste management" (para. 1.11).

Land use planning. One purpose of s.50 waste disposal plans is to identify the waste management needs of each area so that local land use planning authorities can ensure that structure and local (or unitary) development plans for each area cater for those needs. Waste disposal plans include, as well as strategy, a great deal of information on local waste arisings. This information is not to be contained in the strategies themselves, but rather in the surveys on which they will be based. The surveys will therefore be an important source of information for local planning authorities: see the notes to ss.44A(5)–(8) and 44B(4)–(7) (below) in this regard. Individual land use planning decisions are then made on the basis of the development plans, and *Making Waste Work* (see below) notes that the DoE "intends to produce a Planning Policy Guidance (PPG) Note on Waste Management Planning by the end of 1996". This is because despite the publication of PPG23 on planning and pollution control (1994), "It has become clear that further advice is needed on the planning of waste facilities" (para. 1.80). *Waste Management Planning*, referred to above, "underlines the significance and the role of waste management planning in development control planning for waste management facilities" (para. 1.3).

EC obligations. It has been noted above that ss.44A and 44B, and Sched. 2A which is inserted by s.92(2) of the 1995 Act, play a part in implementing Art. 7 of the Waste Framework Directive (see further the note to ss.44A(4) and 44B(3) below, which notes the role of local development plans in this regard). Alongside these provisions is the UK Plan for Imports and Exports of Waste, published in draft for consultation in June 1994. The UK Plan will also be a statutory waste management plan for the purposes of Art. 7, as well as implementing aspects of the 1993 EC waste shipments regulation (EEC) No. 259/93 (OJ L30/1, 6.2.93) and the 1993 Basel Convention on the Control of Transboundary Movement of Hazardous Wastes and their Disposal. As to EC waste policy, see also *Making Waste Work*, below.

Making Waste Work. In tandem with the passage of the Environment Bill, the DoE and Welsh Office were consulting on a Draft Waste Strategy for England and Wales (January 1995), which eventually became a White Paper published in December 1995 as *Making Waste Work: a strategy for sustainable waste management in England and Wales* (Cm. 3040). Although advisory and non-statutory, *Making Waste Work* "prepares the way" for the statutory strategies (para. 1.115). (Although it applies only to England and Wales, it is likely that the Secretary of State for Scotland will ensure (note s.44B(5)) that SEPA takes a policy approach which is broadly in line with that taken by the Secretary of State in *Making Waste Work*). In addition, it notes that as national policy, to which local planning authorities are required by the Town and Country Planning Act 1990 to have regard, it "will be an important source of guidance" to them (para. 1.113).

Making Waste Work indicates that its aims include setting out the Government's policy framework for waste management, identifying ways in which waste can be managed in a more sustainable way, setting targets for achieving that aim, and enabling industry, regulators and public authorities to plan ahead with a common understanding of the longer term objectives for waste management (para. 1.1). It is based on three key objectives: first, the reduction of the amount of waste that society produces (waste reduction); secondly, making the best use of the waste that is produced; and thirdly, choosing waste management practices which minimise the risks of immediate and future environmental pollution and harm to human health (para. 1.21).

This is turn leads the Government to adopt a "waste hierarchy" (which it first set out in *Sustainable Development: The UK Strategy* (January 1994)), and an overall policy aim of increasing the proportion of waste managed by the options towards the top of the hierarchy (para. 1.24). The hierarchy is, from top down, waste reduction (giving priority to reducing or eliminating production of hazardous wastes); reuse (for example, reusing bottles); recovery, which consists of, from top down, recycling (putting materials back into use), composting and energy recovery (either from incineration or through the burning of methane emitted from landfilled waste); disposal (landfill or incineration without energy recovery: no benefit obtained from materials in the waste).

Making Waste Work identifies five complementary strategies for achieving its aims (a "five point plan": para. 1.57): a regulatory strategy, a market based strategy (the centrepieces of which are the landfill tax to be introduced from October 1, 1996 by the Finance Act 1996, and the Government's producer responsibility initiatives—see further the General Note to s.93 at p.25–256), a planning (as in land-use planning) strategy, a promotion strategy (promoting both the message of the strategy and good practice by waste producers which favours options such as waste reduction) and an information strategy (to develop sound information on which the strategy itself and individual decisions can be based).

The attitude adopted towards the use of targets in policy is ambivalent: "the Government believes that it can be more useful to use targets to give a steer to the direction of policy than not to set targets" (para. 1.33), and accordingly *Making Waste Work* contains the following targets (the first two are "primary targets", along with targets for the Government's own waste, the others are "secondary"): to reduce the proportion of controlled waste going to landfill from 70 per cent to 60 per cent by 2005 (para. 1.39); to recycle 25 per cent of household waste by 2000 (para. 1.48); to recover 40 per cent of municipal waste by 2005 (para. 1.41); the provision of easily accessible recycling facilities for 80 per cent of households by 2000 (para. 1.50); to increase the use of secondary and recycled waste materials as aggregates in England from 30 million tonnes p.a. in 1995 to 55 million tonnes p.a. by 2006 (para. 1.53); and to ensure that 40 per cent of households with gardens carry out composting by 2000 (para. 1.50).

As regards the wastes to which *Making Waste Work* applies, they are principally non-radioactive solid wastes and may well be "substances which are not waste at all under the new European Union definition of waste [now in s.75(2) of the 1990 Act]" (para. 1.13). This latter point is significant since, without it, aspects of the Strategy become impossible to fulfil: in Circular 11/94 the DoE argues that in many cases reuse of an item means that it does not become waste within the EC definition; and it follows that achieving higher rates of reuse, as the Strategy seeks to do, does not achieve higher levels of the reuse of *waste* (as thus defined).

The EU policy specifically on waste, on which much EC waste legislation has subsequently been based, is contained in the 1990 Council Resolution on the subject (O.J. C122/2, May 18, 1990), although the role of the Community's Action Programmes on the Environment, of which the fifth (O.J. No C138/1, May 17, 1993) runs until the year 2000, and the Commission's Communication on a Community Strategy for Waste Management (SEC (89) 934 final) which led to the 1990 Resolution, should also be noted. The Council Resolution is currently under review, and as *Making Waste Work* suggests, "having decided on its overall objectives for waste management policy, the UK should therefore be in a position to make a positive contribution in the forthcoming discussions about a European Union waste strategy" (para. 1.105).

Sections 44A(1) and 44B(1) : Strategies to be prepared
Each strategy governing policies for the disposal and recovery of waste is to be prepared "as soon as possible". This phrase is borrowed from Article 7 of the Waste Framework Directive, which the strategies are to play a part in implementing.

As noted above, the Scottish strategy is to be prepared by SEPA rather than by the Secretary of State as in England and Wales. Rejecting a proposed amendment during the House of Lords debate on the Government Bill, which sought to require the Secretary of State to prepare the strategy in Scotland, the Government gave the explanation that "Unlike the Department of the Environment, the Scottish Office will not have the appropriate staff available to it to prepare a waste strategy for Scotland. SEPA, on the other hand, will be well placed to undertake that task, as it would be staffed in part by those expert staff who previously prepared plans for their local authorities" (*Hansard*, H.L. Vol. 561, col. 347, *per* the Earl of Lindsay). The Earl of Lindsay went on to reassure the House of Lords Committee that "the Secretary of State will ultimately remain responsible for waste management policy in Scotland", and that he envisaged "that SEPA will wish to ensure that due regard is paid to the strategy for England and Wales, so that where possible there will be a common framework across Great Britain" (*ibid.*).

Disposal and recovery
The strategies relate to the disposal and recovery of waste. As to the three kinds of recovery distinguished by the DoE in its "waste hierarchy", see the discussion of the draft Waste Strategy above. Section 29 provides an inclusive definition of "disposal" for the purposes of this Part of the Act, which definition now, by virtue of Sched. 4 to the Waste Management Licensing Regulations 1994 (S.I. 1994 No. 1056), includes reference to the operations listed in Annex II of the Waste Framework Directive.

"Recovery" is not defined. However, it is submitted that, since ss.44A(10) and 44B(9) make express reference to the provisions implementing part of the Waste Framework Directive, "recovery", as well as "disposal" and any other terms used in ss.44A and 44B which are also employed in the Directive, should where the context permits bear the meaning which they have in the Directive. "Recovery" is defined in the Directive by reference to the list of recovery operations set out in its Annex IIB. That list is also to be found at Pt. IV of Sched. 3 to the Waste Management Licensing Regulations 1994.

Section 44A(2): Strategy or strategies
The only provision in s.44A with no counterpart in s.44B is subs. (2), which provides for the possibility of separate strategies for geographical areas within England and Wales. Viscount Ullswater explained this in the House of Lords during debate on the Environment Bill as follows:
"The issues which need to be covered in a waste strategy are generally common to both Wales and England, and our approach to waste management policy in each country is the same. The Government therefore believe that a single waste strategy covering the whole of England and Wales is the most effective means of presenting their policies. However, circumstances may change, and the Bill accordingly makes provision ... for the preparation of separate statements for different areas of England and Wales. If it appeared appropriate at the time one of those could relate to the whole of Wales" (*Hansard*, H.L. Vol. 561, col. 339).

Sections 44A(3) and 44B(2): Modifications
Each of the strategies may be modified from time to time. The Government rejected a proposed amendment to the Environment Bill which would have required their annual review:
"The production of such a strategy is a major undertaking. Annual review would be inappropriate for many of the targets it will contain, which will need an implementation period of longer than one year—in some cases considerably longer. Moreover, annual review would sit uncomfortably with the timescale required for a national waste strategy" (*Hansard*, H.L. Vol. 561, col. 399, *per* Viscount Ullswater).

Sections 44A(4) and 44B(3): Content of strategies
Each of the strategies may include any policies of the kind specified in subs. (1) of both sections, but each of them must at least contain both (a) a statement of policies to attain specified objectives and (b) certain specified provisions. The objectives to be attained are set out in Sched. 2A, which the 1995 Act inserts into the Environmental Protection Act 1990. All of the objectives are reproduced from the Waste Framework Directive. Paragraph 1 deals with avoiding harm to human health or the environment, nuisance and adverse effects on conservation interests. It originated in Article 4 of the Waste Framework Directive. Paragraphs 2 and 3(a) concern the integrated, BATNEEC network of disposal installations, and EC and eventual Member State self-sufficiency in waste disposal. These objectives come from Article 5(1). Paragraph 3(b) contains the goal of ensuring environmental and health protection through the appropriate means

of waste disposal in one of the nearest appropriate installations. Article 5(2) is the source of this goal. Paragraph 4 seeks to encourage the prevention or reduction of waste production and its harmfulness. This aim comes from Article 3(1)(a). Paragraph 5 deals with encouraging waste recovery and its use as a source of energy. This originated in Article 3(1)(b). It will be noted that the para. 1 (Article 4) objectives are also the "relevant objectives" of the Agency/SEPA in its waste licensing functions, and of planning authorities in their planning functions in relation to the recovery and disposal of waste: see the Waste Management Licensing Regulations 1994, Sched. 4.

Provisions to be contained in the strategies

The provisions set out in ss.44A(4)(b)(i)–(iii) and 44B(3)(b)(i)–(iii), as required to be contained in each strategy, are essentially reproduced from Article 7(1) of the Waste Framework Directive as provisions required to be contained in waste management plans under that Article. However, Article 7(1) contains a fourth required provision (relating to suitable disposal sites or installations) which is not reproduced in ss.44A or 44B, and an amendment was moved in the House of Lords during the passage of the Environment Bill to rectify this perceived failure to fully implement the Directive. The Government's response is a useful clarification of the relationship between the waste strategies and the planning process.

"the omission...is deliberate, and reflects the existing arrangements for implementing Article 7...which will be partly superseded by [what are now ss.44A and 44B]. At present, Article 7 is implemented jointly by waste disposal plans drawn up by waste regulation authorities under Section 50 [of the 1990 Act], and by development plans drawn up by local planning authorities. The precise arrangements for implementing the directive are contained in Schedule 4 to the Waste Management Licensing regulations 1994. Paragraph 7 specifically requires the waste policies in development plans to include policies in respect of suitable disposal sites or installations. This is because the siting—and criteria for siting—new waste facilities is a matter for the planning rather than the waste regulation authority. In drawing up the waste strategy provisions we have been careful to retain this distinction..." (*Hansard*, H.L. Vol. 562, col. 455, *per* Viscount Ullswater).

Sections 44A(5)–(8) and 44B(4)–(7): Consultation, waste surveys and land use planning

Both the Agency and SEPA may be directed to carry out a waste survey or investigation (ss.44A(6)(b) and 44B(5)(b)). *Making Waste Work* goes further, indicating that "the Secretary of State will [in England and Wales] draw up the statutory strategy on the basis of advice from the Environment Agency, including the results of a national survey of waste arisings. The strategy could not be issued until 1997 at the earliest" (para. 1.116). Each of the sections contains two separate requirements for consultation, which must take place both when the strategy is being drawn up or modified, and before the Agency/SEPA carries out such a survey or investigation. The Secretary of State must consult the Agency in drawing up the strategy for England and Wales (s.44A(5)(a)).

It will be noted that, whilst the provisions for consultation on the strategy itself refer to "local" government or authorities, consultation prior to the carrying out of an investigation or survey is to be with planning authorities. Viscount Ullswater explained that:

"The reason for providing a statutory duty to consult planning authorities in relation to a survey is their requirement for data on waste to enable them to draw up their development plan policies for waste. It is essential that the survey is carried out in a way which will enable disaggregation of results to a local level for the same reason it is essential that planning authorities receive the results of a Survey" (*Hansard*, H.L. Vol. 561, col. 344).

In this regard the reference to directions to the Agency/SEPA making provision regarding the manner in which the findings are reported or made available to other persons is significant (ss.44A(7)(b)(ii) and 44B(6)(b)(ii)). It is clearly appropriate for the Agency and SEPA to have regard to the needs of planning authorities in carrying out their survey or investigation and to provide their findings to such authorities in an appropriate manner. See further *Land use planning* on p.25–250.

There was an attempt in the House of Lords to extend the s.44(B)(7)(a)(i) requirement, for consultation prior to SEPA's carrying out a waste survey or investigation, to refer to "local" rather than merely planning authorities. However the Earl of Lindsay responded that, following local government reorganisation in Scotland, all local authorities become planning authorities, and "although COSLA would be consulted in its capacity as a representative of planning authorities, there would be nothing to stop it responding for its wider interests [such as] environmental health...or its responsibilities for waste disposal" (*Hansard*, H.L. Vol. 561, col. 349).

Sections 44A(9) and 44B(8): Planning authorities

The Town and Country Planning Act 1990, s.1, defines "local planning authority" as the county and county borough councils in Wales, the metropolitan district council in metropolitan districts, the London borough council in London boroughs and the county and district councils in English non-metropolitan counties. Viscount Ullswater noted that "that includes all principal councils in England and Wales, as well as certain other authorities such as the National park authorities and urban development corporations" (*Hansard*, H.L. Vol. 561, col. 343). In Scotland, the Local Government (Scotland) Act 1973, s.172 (as amended by the Local Government etc. (Scotland) Act 1994) defines "planning authority" as a local authority, *i.e.* a council constituted under s.2 of the 1994 Act.

Sections 44A(10) and 44B(9): Waste Framework Directive
These subsections state the EC provisions which the sections make provision for implementing. It will be noted that the sections themselves do not implement the Directive: they make provision for the production of strategies which will do so. It is perhaps in anticipation of protracted periods during which strategies would be produced across the Community that Article 7, unusually, requires implementation only "as soon as possible", rather than by a specific date. Paragraphs 16 and 17 of Sched. 23 to the 1995 Act ensure continuity of implementation by providing for s.50 waste disposal plans to remain in force until replaced by a statutory national waste strategy.

    Making Waste Work notes at para. 1.114 that, whilst non-statutory and "not written for that purpose, [it] may also go some way to meeting the [Article 7] requirements". As for Northern Ireland, its waste strategy "will be drawn up by the Northern Ireland Office to complement the introduction of a new Waste Management (N.I.) Order" (para. 1.117).

Producer responsibility: general

   93.—(1) For the purpose of promoting or securing an increase in the re-use, recovery or recycling of products or materials, the Secretary of State may by regulations make provision for imposing producer responsibility obligations on such persons, and in respect of such products or materials, as may be prescribed.

   (2) The power of the Secretary of State to make regulations shall be exercisable only after consultation with bodies or persons appearing to him to be representative of bodies or persons whose interests are, or are likely to be, substantially affected by the regulations which he proposes to make.

   (3) Except in the case of regulations for the implementation of—

   (a) any obligations of the United Kingdom under the Community Treaties, or

   (b) any international agreement to which the United Kingdom is for the time being a party,

the power to make regulations shall be exercisable only where the Secretary of State, after such consultation as is required by subsection (2) above, is satisfied as to the matters specified in subsection (6) below.

   (4) The powers conferred by subsection (1) above shall also be exercisable, in a case falling within paragraph (a) or (b) of subsection (3) above, for the purpose of sustaining at least a minimum level of (rather than promoting or securing an increase in) re-use, recovery or recycling of products or materials.

   (5) In making regulations by virtue of paragraph (a) or (b) of subsection (3) above, the Secretary of State shall have regard to the matters specified in subsection (6) below; and in its application in relation to the power conferred by, virtue of subsection (4) above, subsection (6) below shall have effect as if—

   (a) any reference to an increase in the re-use, recovery or recycling of products or materials were a reference to the sustaining of at least a minimum level of re-use, recovery or recycling of the products or materials in question, and

   (b) any reference to the production of environmental or economic benefits included a reference to the sustaining of at least a minimum level of any such existing benefits,

and any reference in this section or section 94 below to securing or achieving any such benefits shall accordingly include a reference to sustaining at least a minimum level of any such existing benefits.

(6) The matters mentioned in subsections (3) and (5) above are—

(a) that the proposed exercise of the power would be likely to result in an increase in the re-use, recovery or recycling of the products or materials in question;

(b) that any such increase would produce environmental or economic benefits;

(c) that those benefits are significant as against the likely costs resulting from the imposition of the proposed producer responsibility obligation;

(d) that the burdens imposed on businesses by the regulations are the minimum necessary to secure those benefits; and

(e) that those burdens are imposed on persons most able to make a contribution to the achievement of the relevant targets—

(i) having regard to the desirability of acting fairly between persons who manufacture, process, distribute or supply products or materials; and

(ii) taking account of the need to ensure that the proposed producer responsibility obligation is so framed as to be effective in achieving the purposes for which it is to be imposed;

but nothing in sub-paragraph (i) of paragraph (e) above shall be taken to prevent regulations imposing a producer responsibility obligation on any class or description of person to the exclusion of any others.

(7) The Secretary of State shall have a duty to exercise the power to make regulations in the manner which he considers best calculated to secure that the exercise does not have the effect of restricting, distorting or preventing competition or, if it is likely to have any such effect, that the effect is no greater than is necessary for achieving the environmental or economic benefits mentioned in subsection (6) above.

(8) In this section—

"prescribed" means prescribed in regulations;

"product" and "material" include a reference to any product or material (as the case may be) at a time when it becomes, or has become, waste;

"producer responsibility obligation" means the steps which are required to be taken by relevant persons of the classes or descriptions to which the regulations in question apply in order to secure attainment of the targets specified or described in the regulations;

"recovery", in relation to products or materials, includes—

(a) composting, or any other form of transformation by biological processes, of products or materials; or

(b) the obtaining, by any means, of energy from products or materials;

"regulations" means regulations under this section;

"relevant persons", in the case of any regulations or any producer responsibility obligation, means persons of the class or description to which the producer responsibility obligation imposed by the regulations applies;

"relevant targets" means the targets specified or described in the regulations imposing the producer responsibility obligation in question;

and regulations may prescribe, in relation to prescribed products or materials, activities, or the activities, which are to be regarded for the purposes of this section and sections 94 and 95 below or any regulations as re-use, recovery or recycling of those products or materials.

(9) The power to make regulations shall be exercisable by statutory instrument.

(10) Subject to the following provisions of this section, a statutory instrument containing regulations shall not be made unless a draft of the instrument has been laid before and approved by a resolution of each House of Parliament.

(11) Subsection (10) above shall not apply to a statutory instrument by reason only that it contains regulations varying any relevant targets.

(12) A statutory instrument which, by virtue of subsection (11) above, is not subject to any requirement that a draft of the instrument be laid before and approved by a resolution of each House of Parliament shall be subject to annulment in pursuance of a resolution of either House of Parliament.

DEFINITIONS
"material": subs. (8).
"prescribed": subs. (8).
"producer responsibility obligation": subs. (8).
"product": subs. (8).
"recovery": subs. (8).
"regulations": subs. (8).
"relevant persons": subs. (8).
"relevant targets": subs. (8).

COMMENCEMENT
This section came into force on September 21, 1995 (S.I. 1995 No. 1983).

GENERAL NOTE
Sections 93 to 95 provide for regulations to be made, following consultation, imposing "producer responsibility" obligations on such persons as the regulations prescribe (ss.93 and 94), and make provision in relation to the offences of contravening requirements of the regulations (s.95).

Policy background
Even more than is often the case with framework or "enabling" legislation, the significance of many of the producer responsibility provisions is difficult to appreciate without an understanding of the policy background: namely the EC priority waste streams project and Directive on Packaging and Packaging Waste, the development of the Government's thinking on its waste strategy (see the General Note to s.92 at pp. 25–250—25–253), and the Government's "producer responsibility challenge" to industry. Much, though far from all, of this background relates to developments in connection with packaging and packaging waste.

Priority waste streams. As part of its Fourth Action Programme on the Environment (O.J. C328, December 7, 1987), in the late 1980s and early 1990s the European Commission singled out a number of "priority waste streams" for special attention, with a view to the identification of the specific problems and opportunities they present and the development of an EU policy response which might include legislation. The Commission established a Priority Waste Streams Programme which involved a number of Working Groups comprised of representatives from Member States, and each Working Group was allocated a waste stream for consideration. Included in the remit of each Working Group was the making of recommendations as to the appropriate policy response. The priority waste streams were chlorinated solvents, used tyres, healthcare waste, end of life vehicles, construction and demolition waste, and waste electrical and electronic equipment. Packaging and packaging waste was not included in the programme because plans were already underway for a directive on such waste.

The producer responsibility challenge. In part in response to this development at EC level, and in particular to the submission by the European Commission in 1992 of a proposal for a Directive on Packaging and Packaging Waste (O.J. No. C263/1, October 12, 1992), which was ultimately adopted as Directive 94/62/EC in December 1994 (O.J. No. L365/10, December 31, 1994), on July 27, 1993 the DoE and Department of Trade and Industry launched the Government's "producer responsibility challenge" to the businesses involved in the "packaging chain". The packaging chain consists of the raw material producers, the businesses which convert such materials into packaging (converters), those which place goods into the packaging (packer/fillers), those who wholesale or retail such goods and those businesses, and arguably private consumers, in whose hands the packaging becomes waste. It also includes those who import raw materials for use in packaging or import packaging or packaged goods. The challenge was to make voluntary, industry-led arrangements to meet a recovery target of 50–70 per cent recovery of packaging waste by the year 2000 (DoE News Release 519, DTI P/93/442).

Later that year, six other industrial sectors were issued with the challenge (DTI Press Releases P/93/658 and P/93/745): newspapers, automotive batteries, consumer batteries, electrical and electronic goods, tyres and end of life motor vehicles.

The "match" between priority waste streams and producer responsibility sectors is not total: batteries, like packaging waste, were dealt with by way of a directive at EC level (in the case of batteries, Directive 91/157/EEC, O.J. L78/38, March 26, 1991), and it will be noted that there are EC priority waste streams, such as "healthcare waste," for which no U.K. producer responsibility challenge has yet been issued. None of the Working Group recommendations have as yet prompted the European Commission to propose formally a directive on the waste stream concerned, although the Commission is understood to be planning a proposal for a directive on end of life motor vehicles—contrary to the recommendations of that Working Group. Whilst packaging waste leads the way, both the Priority Waste Streams Programme and the series of producer responsibility challenges might ultimately lead to producer responsibility legislation of the kind provided for in ss.93 to 95.

Free riders and the need for legislation. The initial aim behind the producer responsibility challenges was to avoid the use of legislation to achieve recycling and recovery of waste and other improvements in industry's management of its wastes and the wastes from its products. However, as the Government noted in its draft Waste Strategy for England and Wales (January 1995) "In some cases, the relevant business groups have asked for legislative underpinning to deter 'free riders' who seek to avoid involvement in a business-led scheme" (para. 2.94). This pressure culminated in the announcement in October 1994 that the Government would legislate to support industry-led schemes for packaging waste, which legislation would be "minimum required to provide an effective deterrent to free-riders" (DoE News Release 579).

Packaging and Packaging Waste
The Packaging and Packaging Waste Directive 94/62/EC was adopted in December 1994 (O.J. No. L365/10, December 31, 1994). It contains a number of requirements, including those for the establishment of packaging/packaging waste return, collection and recovery systems (Article 7), a "daughter" directive on the uniform marking of packaging (Article 8), the content of packaging (Articles 9 and 11), and the establishment of databases on packaging and packaging waste and dissemination to consumers of information on their role in its recovery and recycling (Articles 12 and 13). However, the provisions on which the producer responsibility initiative focuses are those in Article 6 which require Member States to meet the following targets by June 30, 2001: recovery of 50–65 per cent (by weight) of all packaging waste; within this target, 25–45 per cent (by weight) of all packaging waste to be recycled; within this target, 15 per cent (by weight) of each material type (*e.g.* glass, plastic) to be recycled.

Given impetus by the Packaging and Packaging Waste Directive, as noted above, the producer responsibility initiative has progressed significantly further for this waste stream than for the others, and once it was conceded that underpinning legislation for it was required (DoE News Release 579), then the inclusion of such legislation in the 1995 Act became inevitable. Packaging and packaging waste is to be the first subject of regulations under the provisions. Indeed, the form taken by the provisions in the Act was undoubtedly influenced by the ongoing debate between the Government and various business and industry bodies in the packaging chain, since this debate informed Government thinking on the kinds of industry-led scheme which are workable, enforceable and, where necessary (as in the case of packaging waste), are demonstrably capable of implementing the U.K.'s EC obligations.

One key industry organisation has been the Producer Responsibility Group (PRG), which produced a plan entitled "*Real Value From Packaging Waste*", first in consultation draft form in February 1994 and then in final form in November that year. The PRG Plan envisaged the setting up of an industry body, funded by a levy from companies in the packaging chain, to procure the collection and recycling or recovery of packaging waste on behalf of the packaging chain. It named this future body "VALPAK", and envisaged the possibility of VALPAK and perhaps other competing bodies being approved by Government or the Environment Agency/SEPA to carry out these tasks. The requirement for approval was considered necessary since the payment of a levy to VALPAK would serve to discharge a packaging chain company's statutory producer responsibility obligations under the anticipated underpinning legislation.

On the crucial question of where in the packaging chain the producer responsibility and consequent levy obligation should be placed, PRG commissioned a report by Sir Sydney Lipworth QC which, entitled "*Packaging Levy Report on Point of Funding*", was published in July 1994. The report envisaged what it called a "modified converter levy", under which the levy would be placed on those who convert raw material into packaging (converters) or who import packaging, subject to provisions for the burden of the levy to be passed on instead to "packer/fillers" of packaging and/or retailers and wholesalers of packaged goods. The final version of the PRG Plan endorsed this approach for the medium- to long-term. The PRG Plan proposed achievement of a 58 per cent recovery rate for packaging waste by the year 2000, estimated that an annual levy of £100 million would be required, and envisaged the establishment of five "Material Organisations" (for aluminium, glass, packaging paper, plastics and steel) which would be represented on the VALPAK Board to ensure co-ordination of efforts. Having produced its Plan, the PRG disbanded, to give way to a body entitled V-WRAG (VALPAK Working

Representative Advisory Group), to continue dialogue with the Government and produce a prospectus for the establishment of VALPAK.

In May 1995 the DoE, DTI, Welsh and Scottish Offices issued a consultation paper, *Producer Responsibility for Packaging Waste*, which sought views on options for the form of the legal obligations on individual businesses needed to underpin collaborative industry schemes and to ensure that recovery and recycling of packaging waste reaches national and international targets. The paper was concerned specifically with the scope and nature of the legal obligation to be placed on individual businesses, to be contained in regulations made under ss.93–95.

In the paper the Government indicated eight tests which it proposed to bear in mind in formulating its approach to legislation. These were (a) the need to be confident that the targets set by the EC Packaging Waste Directive can be met; (b) the practicality, cost effectiveness, and potential benefits as against the likely cost (taking into account environmental and economic considerations) and fairness of the available options; (c) the desirability of minimising regulatory burdens on business; (d) the desirability of business choice in the manner in which the obligation is satisfied; (e) compatibility of the available options with existing EC and domestic law, *e.g.* to ensure that they do not create a barrier to trade with other Member States; (f) the need to take account of competition policy, *e.g.* to ensure that regulations do not have the effect of distorting competition unnecessarily; (g) the desirability of business freedom and flexibility and of minimising the public sector role; and (h) the desirability of targeting as closely as possible those responsible for determining the content, nature and amount of packaging used for a particular product.

Various chapters of the paper covered the different possible schemes which had at that point been put forward. The various schemes were entitled Single-point, Omni-point, Multi-point and Equi-point. Their differences can be characterised as relating to the extent to which they spread the obligation along the packaging chain, and thus the extent to which they relied upon market forces to spread the cost burden along the chain, and to the form which the obligation would take. The Equi-point option proposed two sets of targets relating to own use packaging/packaging waste arising on the premises of any business in the chain (this being the easiest form of packaging waste to deal with) and, separately, household packaging waste. In working up the various options, some forms of "supplementary legal obligation" were proposed by supporters of various options.

In the paper the Government urged the proponents of different approaches to build a consensus behind the best option, and the paper indicated that in order to be considered at the close of the exercise any new proposal not described in whole or in part of the paper must receive a wide circulation to interested parties and trade associations, in sufficient time for them to consider the proposal fully and comment on it before the end of the consultation period.

One subsequent proposal was put forward, by V-WRAG, entitled Shared Producer Responsibility. This option appears to have excited widespread interest within the industry, and accordingly a supplementary consultation paper was issued in August 1995 by the DoE containing it as a seventh option. However, the version circulated by the DoE was acknowledged to have been "supplemented and amended by Government" to indicate how it would enable the Government to implement the Directive. One key aspect of the option as originally formulated was excluded by the DoE from the consultation paper version. This was its employment of a duty of care on businesses (modelled on that in the Environmental Protection Act 1990, s.34) in relation to packaging which becomes waste in the hands of consumers, rather than an obligation which could be related in some way to a target for the recycling or recovery of a particular quantity of packaging waste. Debate and discussion continued, culminating in the announcement on December 15, 1995, that a consensus had been reached by industry representatives on the form of obligation to be imposed (DoE News Release 639). The principles agreed involved a staged approach with legal obligations upon businesses operating outside what s.94(6) terms an "exemption scheme" allocated (having taken into account imports and exports) primarily to retailers and to packer fillers, who would be responsible for 45 per cent and 35 per cent respectively of the target imposed in respect of a given weight of material passing through their hands. Raw material producers (5½ per cent) and converters (14½ per cent) would bear the remainder of the obligation. Companies joining an exemption scheme would be charged a turnover-related annual membership fee as well as complying with the conditions of membership. The Secretary of State commented that "Government will now need to consider and decide on the best form of legal obligation, taking account of all relevant considerations", no doubt including the industry consensus which Government had been seeking, before producing draft regulations which were awaited at the time of writing.

Subss. (1)–(7): increasing or maintaining re-use, recovery or recycling levels
The elaborate provisions of subss. (1)–(7) may perhaps be best understood if a distinction is drawn at the outset between two circumstances in which regulations may be made under s.93.

The first circumstance is where the regulations are to implement EC or international obligations, and the second is where they are not, and are thus a solely domestic initiative. In the first circumstance, it may be that levels or rates of recycling and so forth, once achieved, need only to be maintained (rather than increased), or perhaps could even be allowed to fall as long as a minimum level was maintained, in order to implement the obligation. The provisions therefore allow for that possibility (subs. (4)—see Viscount Ullswater, *Hansard*, H.L. Vol. 561, col. 355). In the other circumstance, however, it is assumed that the Government (if it is legislating at all) will wish to promote an increase in such levels, so regulations may only be made for this reason (subs. (1)).

The extent to which the Secretary of State may act on considerations which the Government considers important in this context is also affected by the EC/international dimension. Thus, where the regulations are a domestic initiative, the Secretary of State must (after the consultation required by subs. (2)) be "satisfied" as to the subs. (6) list of likely benefits and burdens of the regulations (subs. (3)). By contrast, where an EC/international obligation is being implemented, he need only "have regard to" that list, which as before must in that circumstance be read to include maintaining a minimum level of recycling and so forth, or of economic or environmental benefits, as well as promoting their increase (subs. (5)).

The obligation to consult (subs. (2)) applies in either circumstance, although unusually the requirement is only to consult bodies representative of those who are, or are likely to be, "substantially affected" by the proposed regulations.

The Secretary of State's duty in relation to competition in making the regulations should be noted: subs. (7).

Subs. (6): matters to be considered

The Secretary of State must be satisfied as to (subs. (3)), or, where an EC/international obligation is being implemented, must have regard to (subs. (5)) the matters listed in subs. (6). These are that the regulations will not only (a) have the intended outcome but will (b) as a result lead to environmental or economic benefits; that the benefits are (c) significant as against the likely costs; and that the burdens imposed are (d) the minimum necessary and (e) fairly and efficiently placed. Such a concern for fairness is expressly disbarred, however, from preventing an uneven imposition of the producer responsibility burden. This is reinforced by s.94(7).

Subs. (8): "product" and "material"

These terms allow extremely wide scope for the subject-matter of producer responsibility regulations. They are defined inclusively: they include waste products and materials. It follows that they may well include products and materials which are not waste, and there is good reason for this. One purpose of the regulations might be to promote their re-use (subs. (1)), and where something is re-used it is the Government's view that in many cases it does not become "waste" as statutorily defined (s.75(2) of the 1990 Act as inserted by the 1995 Act, Sched. 22, para. 88 and interpreted by DoE/Welsh Office Circular 11/94: although that definition is not applicable to s.93, the Government would no doubt wish to avoid introducing a different definition for those purposes, and in any event this may lead to complexities where the provisions are to be used to implement EC legislation which employs the definition which s.75(2) implements). Thus there are difficulties with the notion of re-using waste, which are avoided by the provisions as drafted.

Subs. (8): "re-use", "recovery" and "recycling"

"Recovery" is also defined inclusively. This definition was introduced by the Government at the Commons Committee stage, and its wording was queried by Mr Tipping. He expressed the view that "one could have a fire and get energy from it, but it would still be waste if one did not apply the result" (H.C. Standing Committee B, 13th Sitting, June 6, 1995, col. 556). The suggestion appeared to be that any form of decomposition or burning could be brought within the definition by the wording. Whether this is the case turns in part on the meaning of "obtaining" in part (b) of the definition: one could argue that simply to release energy is not to obtain it since it is not released in usable form, in which case Mr Tipping's concern would be unfounded.

It is not clear precisely how the wording might fit with the definition of recovery in EC legislation which the provisions might be employed to implement. The wording does not map neatly onto the definitions of "recovery", "recycling", "energy recovery" and "organic recycling" in the Packaging and Packaging Waste Directive, nor onto the list of recovery operations set out at Annex II B to the Waste Framework Directive 75/442/EEC as amended by Directive 91/156/EEC (O.J. L78/32, March 26, 1991). However, this definition should be read together with the concluding clause of this subsection, which provides that regulations may stipulate what will constitute the re-use, recovery or recycling of given products or materials. Thus the appropriate EC definitions, where applicable, may be employed.

Subss. (9)–(12): Parliamentary procedures

Regulations under s.93, imposing or (by implication) modifying, removing or replacing producer responsibility obligations, must be made by statutory instrument and approved by both Houses of Parliament (the "affirmative resolution" procedure) (see subss. (9) and (10)). However, where such a statutory instrument only varies any targets by reference to which producer responsibility obligations are determined, it is subject only to the "negative resolution" procedure whereby no such approval is required but both Houses have an opportunity to annul it (subss. (11) and (12)).

An amendment to remove subss. (11) and (12) was moved at the Commons Committee stage by Mr Bennett, who argued that "if something is important enough to be done in the first instance using…the affirmative method—the same considerations should apply if it is to be altered" (H.C. Standing Committee B, 13th Sitting, June 6, 1995, col. 556). The amendment was rejected by Mr Atkins on behalf of the Government on the grounds that "we may need to make changes to targets at short notice and perhaps respond quickly to problems such as fluctuations in market prices" (*ibid.*).

Producer responsibility: supplementary provisions

94.—(1) Without prejudice to the generality of section 93 above, regulations may, in particular, make provision for or with respect to—

(a) the classes or descriptions of person to whom the producer responsibility obligation imposed by the regulations applies;

(b) the classes or descriptions of products or materials in respect of which the obligation applies;

(c) the targets which are to be achieved with respect to the proportion (whether by weight, volume or otherwise) of the products or materials in question which are to be re-used, recovered or recycled, whether generally or in any prescribed way;

(d) particulars of the obligation imposed by the regulations;

(e) the registration of persons who are subject to a producer responsibility obligation and who are not members of registered exemption schemes, the imposition of requirements in connection with such registration, the variation of such requirements, the making of applications for such registration, the period for which any such registration is to remain in force and the cancellation of any such registration;

(f) the approval, or withdrawal of approval, of exemption schemes by the Secretary of State;

(g) the imposition of requirements on persons who are not members of registered exemption schemes to furnish certificates of compliance to the appropriate Agency;

(h) the approval of persons by the appropriate Agency for the purpose of issuing certificates of compliance;

(j) the registration of exemption schemes, the imposition of conditions in connection with such registration, the variation of such conditions, the making of applications for such registration and the period for which any such registration is to remain in force;

(k) the requirements which must be fulfilled, and the criteria which must be met, before an exemption scheme may be registered;

(l) the powers of the appropriate Agency in relation to applications received by it for registration of exemption schemes;

(m) the cancellation of the registration of an exemption scheme;

(n) competition scrutiny of registered exemption schemes or of exemption schemes in whose case applications for registration have been received by the appropriate Agency;

(o) the exclusion or modification of any provision of the Restrictive Trade Practices Acts 1976 and 1977 in relation to exemption schemes or in relation to agreements where at least one of the parties is an operator of an exemption scheme;

(p) the fees, or the method of determining the fees, which are to be paid to the appropriate Agency—

(i) in respect of the approval of persons for the purpose of issuing certificates of compliance;

(ii) on the making of an application for registration of an exemption scheme;

(iii) in respect of the subsistence of the registration of that scheme;

(iv) on submission to the appropriate Agency of a certificate of compliance;

(v) on the making of an application for, or for the renewal of, registration of a person required to register under the regulations;

(vi) in respect of the renewal of the registration of that person;

(q) appeals against the refusal of registration, the imposition of conditions in connection with registration, or the cancellation of the registration, of any exemption scheme;

(r) the procedure on any such appeal;

(s) cases, or classes of case,—

(i) in which an exemption scheme is, or is not, to be treated as registered, or

(ii) in which a person is, or is not, to be treated as a member of a registered exemption scheme,

pending the determination or withdrawal of an appeal, and otherwise with respect to the position of persons and exemption schemes pending such determination or withdrawal;

(t) the imposition on the appropriate Agency of a duty to monitor compliance with any of the obligations imposed by the regulations;

(u) the imposition on prescribed persons of duties to maintain records, and furnish to the Secretary of State or to the appropriate Agency returns, in such form as may be prescribed of such information as may be prescribed for any purposes of, or for any purposes connected with, or related to, sections 93 to 95 of this Act or any regulations;

(w) the imposition on the appropriate Agency of a duty to maintain, and make available for inspection by the public, a register containing prescribed information relating to registered exemption schemes or persons required to register under the regulations;

(y) the powers of entry and inspection which are exercisable by a new Agency for the purposes of its functions under the regulations;

(ya) the conferring on prescribed persons of power to require, for the purposes of or otherwise in connection with competition scrutiny, the provision by any person of any information which he has, or which he may at any future time acquire, relating to any exemption scheme or to any acts or omissions of an operator of such a scheme or of any person dealing with such an operator.

(2) If it appears to the Secretary of State—

(a) that any action proposed to be taken by the operator of a registered exemption scheme would be incompatible with—

(i) any obligations of the United Kingdom under the Community Treaties, or

(ii) any international agreement to which the United Kingdom is for the time being a party, or

(b) that any action which the operator of such a scheme has power to take is required for the purpose of implementing any such obligations or agreement,

he may direct that operator not to take or, as the case may be, to take the action in question.

(3) Regulations may make provision as to which of the new Agencies is the appropriate Agency for the purposes of any function conferred or imposed by or under this section or section 93 above, or for the purposes of the exercise of that function in relation to the whole or a prescribed part of Great

Britain, and may make provision for things done or omitted to be done by either new Agency in relation to any part of Great Britain to be treated for prescribed purposes as done or omitted to be done by the other of them in relation to some other part of Great Britain.

(4) Persons issuing certificates of compliance shall act in accordance with guidance issued for the purpose by the appropriate Agency, which may include guidance as to matters which are, or are not, to be treated as evidence of compliance or as evidence of non-compliance.

(5) In making any provision in relation to fees, regard shall be had to the desirability of securing that the fees received by each new Agency under the regulations are sufficient to meet the costs and expenses incurred by that Agency in the performance of its functions under the regulations.

(6) In this section—

"the appropriate Agency", subject to regulations made by virtue of subsection (3) above, means—

(a) in relation to England and Wales, the Agency;

(b) in relation to Scotland, SEPA;

"certificate of compliance" means a certificate issued by a person approved for the purpose by the appropriate Agency to the effect that that person is satisfied that the person in respect of whom the certificate is issued is complying with any producer responsibility obligation to which he is subject;

"competition scrutiny", in the case of any scheme, means scrutiny of the scheme for the purpose of enabling the Secretary of State to satisfy himself—

(i) whether or not the scheme has or is likely to have the effect of restricting, distorting or preventing competition or, if it appears to him that the scheme has or is likely to have any such effect, that the effect is or is likely to be no greater than is necessary for achieving the environmental or economic benefits mentioned in section 93(6) above; or

(ii) whether or not the scheme leads or is likely to lead to an abuse of market power;

"exemption scheme" means a scheme which is (or, if it were to be registered in accordance with the regulations, would be) a scheme whose members for the time being are, by virtue of the regulations and their membership of that scheme, exempt from the requirement to comply with the producer responsibility obligation imposed by the regulations;

"new Agency" means the Agency or SEPA;

"operator", in relation to an exemption scheme, includes any person responsible for establishing, maintaining or managing the scheme;

"registered exemption scheme" means an exemption scheme which is registered pursuant to regulations;

and expressions used in this section and in section 93 above have the same meaning in this section as they have in that section.

(7) Regulations—

(a) may make different provision for different cases;

(b) without prejudice to the generality of paragraph (a) above, may impose different producer responsibility obligations in respect of different classes or descriptions of products or materials and for different classes or descriptions of person or exemption scheme;

(c) may include incidental, consequential, supplemental or transitional provision.

(8) Any direction under this section—

(a) may include such incidental, consequential, supplemental or transitional provision as the Secretary of State considers necessary or expedient; and

(b) shall, on the application of the Secretary of State, be enforceable by injunction or, in Scotland, by interdict or by an order for specific performance under section 45 of the Court of Session Act 1988.

DEFINITIONS
"appropriate Agency": subs. (6).
"certificate of compliance": subs. (6).
"competition scrutiny": subs. (6).
"exemption scheme": subs. (6).
"functions": s.124(1).
"materials": s.93(8).
"modification": s.124(1).
"new Agency": subs. (6).
"operator": subs. (6).
"prescribed": s.93(8).
"producer responsibility obligation": s.93(8).
"product": s.93(8).
"records": s.124(1).
"recovery": s.93(8).
"registered exemption scheme": subs. (6).
"regulations": s.93(8).

COMMENCEMENT
This section came into force on September 21, 1995 (S.I. 1995 No. 1983).

GENERAL NOTE
This section makes supplementary provisions in relation to the producer responsibility provisions contained in s.93. It identifies some 23 different matters which might be addressed by regulations made under s.93 (subs. (1)(a)–(ya)), although it should be noted that the list is expressed to be without prejudice to the generality of s.93. Thus it appears that Mr Clifton-Brown may have been incorrect in suggesting that "an opportunity will be lost" if the Government rejected his proposed amendment to include in the list the possibility that regulations might make provision for the imposition of a duty of care and issuing of a related Code of Practice (H.C. Standing Committee B, 13th Sitting, June 6, 1995, cols. 557–558). The amendment, which the Government rejected, was clearly related to the V-WRAG Shared Producer Responsibility proposal discussed in the General Note to s.93 at p. 25–257.

Subss. (1) and (7): Content of regulations
The extensive list of possible considerations which regulations might address is in most cases self-explanatory, although a few comments may be made. The considerable flexibility at the Government's disposal in making regulations is reinforced by subs. (7) which, for example, would expressly allow a "single point" option for packaging waste to be adopted.

Subs. (1)(a)–(d): targets, materials, obligations and classes of person
The opening items on the list are the key issues which, in relation to packaging and packaging waste, were addressed by the different options in the consultation paper discussed in the General Note to s.93 at p. 25–257.

Subs. (1)(e)–(o): individual and collective routes to compliance
One Government concern which is apparent from the consultation paper on packaging and packaging waste (see pp. 25–257 and 25–258) is that an individual route to compliance should be available. They did not consider it appropriate to force businesses to group together or join schemes, and thus regulations may provide for targets for the registration of, and a certificate of compliance for, individual businesses (paras. (e) and (g)).
At the same time, they recognised that what many businesses needed was the ability to discharge their obligations by joining, or paying a levy to, a collective scheme which would undertake (to oversimplify) to meet a business' target on its behalf. In those circumstances, it may be appropriate for the obligation to transfer to the collective scheme and the business to be exempt from its obligation. Hence use of the term "exemption scheme" (paras. (e)–(g), (j)–(q), (s)). However, the Government's view is that only suitable collective schemes may have this role, and they should be registered: hence "registered exemption scheme".
The need to ensure that collective schemes are not hampered by inappropriate competition laws whilst being prevented from acting anti-competitively is also acknowledged (paras. (n) and (o)).

Subs. (1)(g), (h), (l), (n), (p), (t)–(y) and subs. (4): the Agency/SEPA

A substantial role is envisaged for the Environment Agency and SEPA, some of which may be taking at least some of their staff into hitherto uncharted waters: aside from their role in compliance monitoring and the registration of exemption schemes, they may be approving and (subs. (4)) giving guidance to persons who are to issue certificates of compliance (effectively delegating compliance monitoring) (para. (h)) and perhaps exercising competition scrutiny (para. (n)). Extended powers of entry and inspection are catered for (para. (y)).

Subs. (1)(t)–(ya): records and compliance monitoring

One concern evidenced by the Government was that it must be able to monitor compliance and to demonstrate the same to the European Commission to show that EC obligations had been implemented, as required for example by Article 17 of the Packaging and Packaging Waste Directive (see the Earl of Lindsay's remarks in the House of Lords: *Hansard*, H.L. Vol. 562, col. 1563). Another was that any collective schemes should not operate as cartels or otherwise anti-competitively. These provisions suggest that regulations will address those concerns, although the Earl of Lindsay added that "we shall, of course, take the necessary steps to ensure that commercial confidentiality is maintained" (*ibid.*).

Subss. (2) and (8): Directions and EC and international obligations

Subsection (2) allows considerable scope for the Secretary of State to act outside the regulations so as to implement EC or international obligations, to the extent of issuing directions to private individuals (operators of collective schemes). Such directions may be enforced by way of injunction or (in Scotland) interdict or an order for specific performance in the Court of Session (subs. (8)(b)).

Subs. (3): Great Britain

It is clearly considered possible that a simple geographical divide between the spheres of activity of the Agency and SEPA may not be appropriate. One example of this might be where a given business operates both in England or Wales and in Scotland. Normally Agency/SEPA functions (such as licensing) relate to businesses on a site by site basis, so a business which operates both north and south of the border neither causes nor is caused a problem, but where compliance is an issue for the corporate entity as a whole, that may not be the case.

Producer responsibility offences

95.—(1) Regulations may make provision for a person who contravenes a prescribed requirement of the regulations to be guilty of an offence and liable—

(a) on summary conviction, to a fine not exceeding the statutory maximum;

(b) on conviction on indictment, to a fine.

(2) Where an offence under any provision of the regulations committed by a body corporate is proved to have been committed with the consent or connivance of, or to have been attributable to any neglect on the part of, any director, manager, secretary or other similar officer of the body corporate or a person who was purporting to act in any such capacity, he as well as the body corporate shall be guilty of that offence and shall be liable to be proceeded against and punished accordingly.

(3) Where the affairs of a body corporate are managed by its members, subsection (2) above shall apply in relation to the acts or defaults of a member in connection with his functions of management as if he were a director of the body corporate.

(4) Where the commission by any person of an offence under the regulations is due to the act or default of some other person, that other person may be charged with and convicted of the offence by virtue of this section whether or not proceedings for the offence are taken against the first-mentioned person.

(5) Expressions used in this section and in section 93 or 94 above have the same meaning in this section as they have in that section.

DEFINITIONS
  "functions": s.124(1).
  "prescribed": s.93(8).

"regulations": s.93(8).

COMMENCEMENT
This section came into force on September 21, 1995 (S.I. 1995 No. 1983 (C.40)).

GENERAL NOTE
With ss.93 and 94 having provided for regulations to impose producer responsibility obligations, s.95 makes provision for offences where such obligations are not complied with.

The regulations may provide for contravention to be punishable on summary conviction with the maximum fine available (presently £5,000) and, on conviction on indictment, with an unlimited fine (subs. (1)). The standard environmental legislation provisions for officers' and members' criminal liability are included (subss. (2) and (3)), as is the common provision that, where one person causes another to contravene the regulations, both or either may be convicted of the offence (subs. (4)). This last provision is potentially very significant in the light of one frequently expressed concern in the public debate over the form and content of the anticipated producer responsibility obligations for packaging and packaging waste. This was that one person's compliance may be dependent on the conduct of another, since most companies do not have the capacity themselves to recycle or otherwise recover, or indeed to collect, packaging waste. The spectre of a company holding another to "ransom" over its fear of criminal liability was also raised. This provision does not necessarily protect a company in that unfortunate position. It does, however, allow it to point out to the miscreant that it may be rendering itself criminally liable, and it gives the enforcing authority the power to prosecute the miscreant instead of the innocent company.

Mineral planning permissions

Mineral planning permissions

96.—(1) Schedules 13 and 14 to this Act shall have effect.

(2) This section, those Schedules as they apply to England and Wales, and the 1990 Act shall have effect as if this section and those Schedules (as so applying) were included in Part III of that Act.

(3) This section, those Schedules as they apply to Scotland, and the 1972 Act shall have effect as if this section and those Schedules (as so applying) were included in Part III of that Act.

(4) Section 105 of the 1990 Act and section 251A of the 1972 Act shall cease to have effect.

(5) Without prejudice to the generality of sections 59 to 61 of the 1990 Act or, as the case may be, section 21 of the 1972 Act, a development order may make, in relation to any planning permission which is granted by a development order for minerals development, provision similar to any provision made by Schedule 13 or 14 to this Act.

(6) In this section and those Schedules—
"the 1972 Act" means the Town and Country Planning (Scotland) Act 1972;
"the 1990 Act" means the Town and Country Planning Act 1990;
"the 1991 Act" means the Planning and Compensation Act 1991; and
"minerals development" means development consisting of the winning and working of minerals, or involving the depositing of mineral waste.

DEFINITIONS
"1972 Act, the": subs. (6).
"1990 Act, the": subs. (6).
"1991 Act, the": subs. (6).

COMMENCEMENT
This section will come into force on a day to be appointed (s.125(3)).

GENERAL NOTE
This section gives effect to Scheds. 13 and 14 of the Act dealing with the sensitive issue of mineral permissions, *i.e.* planning permission for the winning and working of minerals and the

deposit of mineral waste. Schedule 13 deals with the review of old mineral permissions granted between 1948 and 1982 and Sched. 14 deals with the periodic review of all mineral permissions. See the General Notes below at p. 25–365 and p. 25–373 for the effect of Scheds. 13 and 14 respectively. In both cases the intention is to ensure that the environmental controls placed upon mineral workings reflect modern standards.

Subss. (2) and (3): incorporation into Planning Acts

By virtue of subss. (2) and (3), both this section and the two Schedules are deemed to be incorporated into the Town and Country Planning Act 1990 and the Town and Country Planning (Scotland) Act 1972.

It is understood that these provisions will not be brought into force in Scotland until late 1996 at the earliest. The reason for this delayed commencement is that the reorganisation of local government which is currently underway in Scotland by virtue of the Local Government etc. (Scotland) Act 1994 will have a significant impact on the administration of planning in Scotland.

Subs. (4): repeals

Section 105 of the Town and Country Planning Act 1990, which is repealed, imposes a duty on mineral planning authorities to undertake periodic reviews of mineral extraction and mineral waste deposit sites in their area. No specific frequency of review was stipulated by this section, which was originally introduced by the Town and Country Planning (Minerals) Act 1981. Section 251A of the Town and Country Planning (Scotland) Act 1972 is to the same effect and is also repealed.

Subs. (5): development orders

Any future special or general development order, or any amendments to existing orders, may make similar provision to Scheds. 13 and 14 in relation to planning permission for minerals development which is granted by the order. This will allow such provisions to be applied to underground coal mines, which benefit from permitted development rights under the Town and Country Planning (General Permitted Development) Order 1995 (S.I. 1995 No. 418) or, in Scotland, the Town and Country Planning (General Permitted Development) (Scotland) Order 1992 (S.I. 1992 No. 223 (as amended)).

Guidance : MPG 14

In September 1995 the Department of the Environment and Welsh Office published Minerals Planning Guidance MPG 14 *Environment Act 1995: Review of Mineral Planning Permissions.* MPG 14 gives advice to mineral planning authorities and the minerals industry on the statutory procedures to be followed under Scheds. 13 and 14 and the approach to be adopted to the preparation and consideration of updated planning conditions in the initial (Sched. 13) and periodic (Sched. 14) review processes.

The annexes to MPG 14 contain statutory forms and suggested forms for the variety of notices provided for under the review processes, and of particular note is Annex M, which contains an illustrative guide to conditions to be contained in the revised permissions.

Draft guidance for Scotland is to be issued in the near future with final guidance to be issued in late 1996. Such guidance will be identical in all material respects to the guidance contained in MPG 14.

Hedgerows etc.

Hedgerows

97.—(1) The appropriate Ministers may by regulations make provision for, or in connection with, the protection of important hedgerows in England or Wales.

(2) The question whether a hedgerow is or is not "important" for the purposes of this section shall be determined in accordance with prescribed criteria.

(3) For the purpose of facilitating the protection of important hedgerows, regulations under subsection (1) above may also make provision in relation to other hedgerows in England or Wales.

(4) Without prejudice to the generality of subsections (1) to (3) above, regulations under subsection (1) above may provide for the application (with or without modifications) of, or include provision comparable to any provision contained in the planning Acts and may, in particular, make provision—

(a) prohibiting, or for prohibiting, the removal of, or the carrying out of prescribed acts in relation to, a hedgerow except in prescribed cases;

(b) for or with respect to appeals against determinations or decisions made, or notices given or served, under or by virtue of the regulations, including provision authorising or requiring any body or person to whom an appeal lies to consult prescribed persons with respect to the appeal in prescribed cases;

(c) for a person who contravenes, or fails to comply with, any prescribed provision of the regulations to be guilty of an offence;

(d) for a person guilty of an offence by virtue of paragraph (c) above which consists of the removal, in contravention of the regulations, of a hedgerow of a description prescribed for the purposes of this paragraph to be liable—

(i) on summary conviction, to a fine not exceeding the statutory maximum, or

(ii) on conviction on indictment, to a fine;

(e) for a person guilty of any other offence by virtue of paragraph (c) above to be liable on summary conviction to a fine not exceeding such level on the standard scale as may be prescribed.

(5) Regulations under this section may make different provision for different cases, including different provision in relation to different descriptions of hedgerow, different descriptions of person, different areas or localities or different circumstances.

(6) Before making any regulations under this section the appropriate Ministers shall consult—

(a) such bodies appearing to them to be representative of persons whose business interests are likely to be affected by the proposed regulations,

(b) such bodies appearing to them to be representative of the interests of owners or occupiers of land,

(c) such bodies appearing to them to be representative of the interests of local authorities,

(d) such bodies whose statutory functions include the provision to Ministers of the Crown of advice concerning matters relating to environmental conservation, and

(e) such bodies not falling within paragraphs (a) to (d) above,

as the appropriate Ministers may consider appropriate.

(7) No statutory instrument containing regulations under this section shall be made unless a draft of the instrument has been laid before, and approved by a resolution of, each House of Parliament.

(8) In this section—

"the appropriate Ministers" means—

(a) as respects England, the Secretary of State and the Minister of Agriculture, Fisheries and Food;

(b) as respects Wales, the Secretary of State;

"environmental conservation" means conservation—

(a) of the natural beauty or amenity, or flora or fauna, of England or Wales; or

(b) of features of archaeological or historic interest in England or Wales;

"hedgerow" includes any stretch of hedgerow;

"local authority" means—

(a) the council of a county, county borough, district, London borough, parish or community;

(b) the Common Council of the City of London;

(c) the Council of the Isles of Scilly;

"the planning Acts" has the same meaning as it has in the Town and Country Planning Act 1990 by virtue of section 336(1) of that Act;

"prescribed" means specified, or of a description specified, in regulations;

"regulations" means regulations made by statutory instrument;

"remove", in relation to a hedgerow, means uproot or otherwise destroy, and cognate expressions shall be construed accordingly;

"statutory functions" means functions conferred or imposed by or under any enactment.

(9) Any reference in this section to removing, or carrying out an act in relation to, a hedgerow includes a reference to causing or permitting another to remove, or (as the case may be) carry out an act in relation to, a hedgerow.

DEFINITIONS

"appropriate Ministers": subs. (8).

"environmental conservations": subs. (8).

"functions": s.124(1).

"hedgerow": subs. (8).

"important": subs. (2).

"local authority": subs. (8).

"notice": s.124(1).

"Planning Acts, the": subs. (8).

"prescribed": subs. (8).

"regulations": subs. (8).

"remove": subs. (8).

"statutory functions": subs. (8).

COMMENCEMENT

This section came into force on September 21, 1995 (S.I. 1995 No. 1983).

GENERAL NOTE

This section contains enabling provisions allowing regulations to be made for the protection of important hedgerows (subs. (1)). It lays down requirements for consultation prior to their being made (subs. (6)) and for Parliamentary approval of them (subs. (7)). However, almost all of the substance of the legislation is left to the regulations, including: the meaning of "important" (subs. (2)); the relationship with planning legislation (subs. (4)); the nature of the protection to be provided (subs. (4)(a)); the enforcement measures to be employed—whether determinations, decisions or notices—and procedures applicable to them (subs. (4)(b)); and offences and penalties (subs. (4)(c)–(e)).

The Second Reading stage in the Lords, Viscount Ullswater outlined the system envisaged by the Government as follows:

"Land managers would be required to give notice of their intention to remove hedgerows to the local planning authority who would have 28 days in which to refuse a proposal. If the land manager hears nothing within the 28 day period, the proposed work may go ahead.

We plan to limit the requirement to notify to rural hedges ... Newly planted hedges will be excluded so as not to discourage new planting. We regard it as essential that controls are focused only on the most important hedges; for example, the ancient parish boundary hedge for which no amount of replanting can substitute. We propose, therefore, that local planning authorities should be required to make their decisions in accordance with statutory criteria, prescribed in regulations. We have research in hand to develop and test workable criteria.

We propose that there should be a right of appeal against a local planning authority's refusal of a notice to the Secretary of State, in respect of England, and to the Secretary of State for Wales, in respect of Wales" (*Hansard*, H.L. Vol. 559, col. 1379).

As regards timing, Viscount Ullswater indicated in Parliament that the Government intends to have the regulations in place by July 1996 (*Hansard*, H.L. Vol. 562, col. 484).

Policy Background

The inclusion in this Act of provisions relating to the protection of hedgerows follows the failure of two Private Members' Bills which would have enacted such legislation, and thus represents a reward for considerable effort on the part of their proponents. The first Hedgerows Bill

(Bill 28, 1992/1993) was introduced by Mr Peter Ainsworth. However, it was allegedly "talked out" of Parliamentary time at its report stage by Members representing farming and landowning interests (*The Times*, August 17, 1993). The Bill would have made it an offence to destroy or reduce the quality of hedges situated on certain land in the absence of planning permission. The second Hedgerows Bill (Bill 31, 1993/94), introduced by Mr Peter Hardy, was introduced on January 11, 1994 but in the face of objection it did not reach its second reading.

Hedgerows can be seen as an example of the classic conflict between the interests of conservation and of industry, in this case agriculture. On the one hand, they "mark ancient boundaries and can be the oldest visible feature in the countryside. Hedgerows also support wildlife: birds nest and feed within them, they provide corridors for small mammals and contain a mix of shrubs, trees and flowers" (Countryside Commission, *Countryside Stewardship: Handbook and Application Form*, CCP453, 1995). On the other hand, they have been accused of harbouring pests and diseases which may affect crops (although studies of hedgerow ecology suggest otherwise: see, for example, *New Hedges for the Countryside*, Murray Maclean, 1992), and perhaps more importantly of preventing farms from having fields of the optimum size for modern farming methods. Figures cited in *The Times* article noted above suggest that in a 100-acre field a tractor need spend only one-fifth of its time manoeuvring (as opposed to performing useful work), whereas in a five-acre field this proportion rises to around two-thirds of its time.

The response of farmers to these factors, in the absence of any requirement for planning permission to remove a hedge or any equivalent of the protection for trees afforded by tree preservation orders under planning legislation, has contributed to a marked decline in hedgerows, estimated as a net decrease of 23 per cent between 1984 and 1990 (*The Countryside Survey 1990*, DoE, 1993), although a follow-up survey led Environment Minister Robert Atkins to suggest that the rate of hedgerow loss in 1990–93 had been reduced to 3,600 km per year and that this rate of loss was exceeded by the rate of replanting (*Hansard*, H.C. col. 470 W, July 21, 1994). Government concern for hedgerows was evidenced in concrete form by the launching of the Hedgerow Incentive Scheme in July 1992, which provided funding of £550,000 in 1992/93 in the form of grants to landowners to help cover the cost of maintaining hedges.

Scotland

This section does not extend to Scotland. Disquiet regarding this was expressed in Parliament (see for example Frank Dobson, *Hansard*, H.C. Vol. 258, cols. 53–54; Sam Galbraith, *Hansard*, H.C. Vol. 258, col. 74) and amendments were tabled at Standing Committee stage to extend the provisions to Scotland and to extend their scope to include "dykes", *i.e.* dry stone walls. However, the Government argued that

"the evidence of hedge loss or removal of dykes in Scotland is extremely unreliable . . . only seven per cent of Britain's hedgerows, in kilometres, are in Scotland, and that therefore the problem in practical terms is not as severe there as in England and Wales. We should not exaggerate and suggest that the situation is as serious as it was 20 or 30 years ago" (*per* Sir Hector Monro, Standing Committee B, June 8, 1995, col. 586).

Subs. (1): hedgerows

The term "hedgerow" is undefined save that it includes any stretch of hedgerow (subs. (8)). Nor does the Hedgerow Incentive Scheme, a part of the Countryside Stewardship programme which (as noted above) makes available grants for the restoration of damaged or degraded hedgerows, contain a definition of the term.

During Parliamentary debate a number of attempts to extend the scope of the provisions to include Cornish banks, ponds and dry-stone walls were rejected by the Government.

Subss. (2) and (3): "important"

The criteria employed to determine the "importance" of a hedgerow are clearly critical. The Government gave a number of clues as to its thinking on this during the passage of the Bill. Viscount Ullswater referred to "ancient parish boundary hedges" (quoted above) and in the same debate to "those of particular historic interest or that made a particularly valuable contribution to the wildlife or landscape of an area" (*Hansard*, H.L. Vol. 559, col. 1468), subsequently noting in Committee that research is "looking at the biodiversity of certain hedges" (*Hansard*, H.L. Vol. 561, col. 400). In the Commons, Environment Minister Robert Atkins noted that although the intention remained to concentrate on rural hedgerows, nevertheless "some exceptionally important [urban] hedgerows might have to be considered" (*Hansard*, H.C. Vol. 262, col. 1010).

It should be noted that some hedgerows other than important hedgerows may receive protection under the regulations, but that such other hedgerows will only receive protection where this facilitates the protection of important hedgerows (subs. (3)).

Subs. (4): Planning Acts

Subsection (4) leaves open both the possibility of extending aspects of planning legislation to the protection of hedgerows and also the alternative of borrowing enforcement measures from that legislation. The latter might include enforcement notices and stop notices (ss.171A and 183 respectively of the Town and Country Planning Act 1990), and also arrangements analogous to the tree preservation order system.

Subss. (4)(a) and (9): prohibited acts

Whilst subs. (4) expressly places no restriction on the scope of the regulations provided for by subs. (1), it is clear both from Viscount Ullswater's account of the Government's intentions, cited above, and from subs. (4)(a), that the main focus of the regulations is likely to be on the removal of hedgerows. Subsection (9) is therefore potentially very significant, in that the person who actually removes a hedgerow is likely to be an employee, and subs. (9) renders anyone (in most cases an employer and/or an owner or occupier of land) guilty of the same offence where they have caused or permitted it. In environmental legislation generally, "permissive" offences are usually couched in terms of "knowingly permitting", (for which, see for example the new s.78F of the Environmental Protection Act 1990, noted above at pp. 25–153—25–154) but the requirement of such a mental state, which has made successful prosecutions for such offences rare, is absent here.

Subs. (6): consultation

The appropriate Ministers must, before making regulations under this section, consult such bodies (including those which appear to them to represent affected business interests, owners or occupiers of land, local authorities and statutory conservation agencies) as they consider appropriate. In Parliament, Viscount Ullswater for the Government indicated that "we will of course consult the statutory agencies [apparently a reference to the Countryside Commission, English Nature and English Heritage], the National Farmers Union and the Country Landowners' Association as well as other representative organisations" (*Hansard*, H.L. Vol. 561, col. 396). He subsequently made similar references to the Councils for the Protection of Rural England and Rural Wales and the Royal Societies for Nature Conservation and for the Protection of Birds (*Hansard*, H.L. Vol. 562, cols. 492–493).

Grants for purposes conducive to conservation

98.—(1) The appropriate Minister, with the consent of the Treasury, may by regulations make provision for and in connection with the making of grants to persons who do, or who undertake to that Minister that they will do, anything which in the opinion of that Minister is conducive to—

  (a) the conservation or enhancement of the natural beauty or amenity of the countryside (including its flora and fauna and geological and physiographical features) or of any features of archaeological interest there; or

  (b) the promotion of the enjoyment of the countryside by the public.

(2) Regulations under this section may—

  (a) make different provision for different cases or classes of case or for different areas;

  (b) provide for grants to be made subject to conditions;

  (c) confer power on the appropriate Minister to modify, in any particular case, the conditions to which a grant would otherwise be subject, if he is satisfied that the making of that grant, subject to the conditions as so modified, is consistent with the purposes for which the regulations are made;

  (d) make provision for or in connection with the recovery of any sums paid by way of grant, or the withholding of any further payments of grant, in cases where the applicant for the grant—

     (i) in making the application, or in furnishing any information in connection with the application, has made a statement which was false or misleading in a material respect;

     (ii) has failed to do something which he undertook to do if the grant was made; or

     (iii) is in breach of any condition subject to which the grant was made.

(3) The power to make regulations under this section shall be exercisable by statutory instrument; and a statutory instrument containing any such regulations shall be subject to annulment pursuant to a resolution of either House of Parliament.

(4) The powers conferred by this section are in addition to any other powers of the Secretary of State or the Minister of Agriculture, Fisheries and Food.

(5) In this section "the appropriate Minister" means—

(a) as respects England, the Minister of Agriculture, Fisheries and Food;
(b) as respects Wales, the Secretary of State;
(c) as respects Scotland, the Secretary of State.

DEFINITIONS
"appropriate Minister": subs. (5).

COMMENCEMENT
This section came into force on September 21, 1995 (S.I. 1995 No. 1983).

GENERAL NOTE
This section allows the Minister of Agriculture, Fisheries and Food in England and the Secretary of State in Scotland and Wales, to make regulations providing for grants for anything they consider conducive to either the conservation of certain aspects of the countryside, or the promotion of its enjoyment by the public. The consent of the Treasury to making such regulations is required (subs. (1)). Such grants will complement existing grants, and in particular this section allows the Minister of Agriculture, Fisheries and Food to operate the Countryside Stewardship scheme following the transfer to it of that scheme at the conclusion of its pilot phase at the end of March 1996. It is perhaps worthy of note that the Hedgerow Incentive Scheme which now forms part of Countryside Stewardship complements the statutory protection to be afforded to important hedgerows under s.97.

As regards timing, Viscount Ullswater indicated in Parliament that the Government intends to have the regulations in place by July 1996 (*Hansard*, H.L. Vol. 562, col. 484).

The duties imposed on the Minister, the Secretary of State and the Agency/SEPA by ss.6–8, 32, 34 and 35, which in some cases relate to nature conservation and enhancement and access issues of the same kind as are contemplated by this section will be noted, although it is not suggested that the Agency/SEPA are likely to be recipients of grants under this section, which are intended primarily for individuals and businesses engaged in agriculture and other rural activities.

Consultation before making or modifying certain subordinate legislation for England

99.—(1) The Minister shall consult the bodies and persons specified in subsection (2) below before—

(a) making any legislation to which this section applies (other than a modification of any such legislation);
(b) modifying any such legislation in a way which changes the purpose of the legislation in question; or
(c) modifying any such legislation in a way which modifies, in a respect which he considers material, any conditions subject to which grants or other payments are payable under that legislation.

(2) The bodies and persons mentioned in subsection (1) above are—

(a) the Secretary of State;
(b) the Countryside Commission;
(c) the Nature Conservancy Council for England;
(d) the Historic Buildings and Monuments Commission for England.

(3) The legislation to which this section applies is—

(a) any order under section 18 of the Agriculture Act 1986 (orders establishing environmentally sensitive areas);
(b) any regulations under section 98 above;
(c) any statutory instrument specified in subsection (4) below;
(d) any other statutory instrument which concerns the management of land and whose primary purpose is the promotion of—

(i) the conservation or enhancement of the natural beauty or amenity of the countryside (including its flora and fauna and geological and physiographical features) or of any features of archaeological interest there; or

(ii) the enjoyment of the countryside by the public.

(4) The statutory instruments mentioned in subsection (3)(c) above are—

(a) the Farm Woodlands Premium Scheme 1992;

(b) the Habitat (Water Fringe) Regulations 1994;

(c) the Habitat (Former Set-Aside Land) Regulations 1994;

(d) the Habitat (Salt Marsh) Regulations 1994;

(e) the Organic Farming (Aid) Regulations 1994;

(f) the Nitrate Sensitive Areas Regulations 1994;

(g) the Countryside Access Regulations 1994;

(h) the Moorland (Livestock Extensification) Regulations 1995.

(5) In this section, "the Minister" means the Minister of Agriculture, Fisheries and Food.

(6) This section applies in relation to any legislation only so far as relating to land in England.

DEFINITIONS

"Minister, the": subs. (5).

"modification": s.124(1).

COMMENCEMENT

This section came into force on September 21, 1995 (S.I. 1995 No. 1983).

GENERAL NOTE

This section makes the Secretary of State and the statutory conservation bodies listed in subs. (2)(b)–(d) statutory consultees when specified subordinate legislation is made or modified in certain ways (subs. (1)). Much of the subordinate legislation in question (subss. (3) and (4)) relates to the conservation aspects of, and promotion of, environmental good practice in agriculture (described by the Government in debate as "environmental land management legislation" *per* Earl Howe, *Hansard*, H.L. Vol. 562, col. 500). The consultation requirement will no doubt promote the co-ordination of the activities of the bodies involved. All the subordinate legislation is the responsibility of the Minister of Agriculture, Fisheries and Food (subss. (1) and (5)). It will be noted that the consultation requirement only holds in so far as the subordinate legislation in question relates to land in England (subs. (6)).

In response to a probing amendment by the Baroness Hamwee as to the meaning of "changes the purpose" in subs. (1)(b), Earl Howe for the Government illustrated "the kinds of situations in which that might apply. For example, it might happen where we proposed to add a new option to an existing conservation scheme. That would change the purpose of the scheme in the sense of adding a new purpose to the existing ones. An example occurred last year when we added a new public access tier to all English environmentally sensitive areas [see subs. (3)(a)], thereby widening the objectives of the scheme" (*ibid.*).

Drainage

Meaning of "drainage" in certain enactments

100.—(1) In the definition of "drainage" in section 113(1) of the Water Resources Act 1991, after paragraph (c) there shall be added the words

"and

(d) the carrying on, for any purpose, of any other practice which involves management of the level of water in a watercourse;".

(2) For the definition of "drainage" in section 72(1) of the Land Drainage Act 1991 there shall be substituted—

"drainage" includes—

(a) defence against water (including sea water);

(b) irrigation, other than spray irrigation;

(c) warping; and

(d) the carrying on, for any purpose, of any other practice which involves management of the level of water in a watercourse;".

COMMENCEMENT
This section came into force on September 21, 1995 (S.I. 1995 No. 1983).

GENERAL NOTE
This section widens the definitions of "drainage" in Pt. IV of the Water Resources Act 1991 and in the Land Drainage Act 1991, to clarify that they include the management of watercourse water levels. These Acts (together with ss.6 and 14–19 of the 1995 Act) govern land drainage (or "flood defence", as the Water Resources Act terms it) in England and Wales. The Water Resources Act deals with the role of the Environment Agency (previously the NRA) and its flood defence committees, whilst the Land Drainage Act deals with internal drainage boards. The definitions in the two Acts remain identical with each other.

In debate at the Lords Committee stage, in rejecting an amendment which would have deleted the words "other than spray irrigation" from subs. (1)(b) of the amended Land Drainage Act definition proposed by the clause, Earl Howe provided the following explanation both of the amended definitions and of the retention in them of the spray irrigation exclusions:

"Although in the past [internal drainage boards] concentrated on drainage matters, over the years there has been a change of emphasis, and indeed the purpose of [s.100] is to clarify that drainage bodies can undertake water level management, for example for conservation purposes. I recognise that there are also arguments for changing the definition so as to include spray irrigation but, on the other hand, it would be important to ensure that any such change did not have unforeseen adverse repercussions on the water abstraction provisions in Part II of the Water Resources Act 1991, which will continue in force, in particular section 29, which deals with the right to abstract for drainage purposes. We do not think it would be appropriate to extend the exemption from restrictions on abstraction, which drainage operations enjoy, to cover spray irrigation" (*Hansard*, H.L. Vol. 561, col. 607).

Grants in connection with drainage works

101.—(1) In section 147 of the Water Resources Act 1991 (grants for drainage works) in subsection (4), after the words "expenditure properly incurred by it with a view to" there shall be inserted "(a)" and at the end of that subsection there shall be added—

"(b) enabling it to determine in any particular case whether drainage works, or drainage works of any particular description, should or should not be carried out;

(c) obtaining or organising information, including information about natural processes affecting the coastline, to enable it to formulate or develop its plans with respect to the defence against sea water of any part of the coastline; or

(d) obtaining, at any time after the carrying out of drainage works, information with respect to—

(i) the quality or effectiveness, or the effect on the environment, of those works; or

(ii) any matter of a financial nature relating to those works.

(4A) Paragraphs (b) to (d) of subsection (4) above are without prejudice to any power—

(a) to make any grant under subsection (1) or (4)(a) above, or

(b) to impose any condition under subsection (2) above,

which could be made or imposed apart from those paragraphs."

(2) In section 59 of the Land Drainage Act 1991 (grants to drainage bodies) in subsection (4), after the words "expenditure properly incurred by them with a view to" there shall be inserted "(a)" and at the end of that subsection there shall be added—

"(b) enabling them to determine in any particular case whether drainage works, or drainage works of any particular description, should or should not be carried out;

(c) obtaining or organising information, including information about natural processes affecting the coastline, to enable them to formulate or develop their plans with respect to the defence against sea water of any part of the coastline; or

(d) obtaining, at any time after the carrying out of drainage works, information with respect to—
      (i) the quality or effectiveness, or the effect on the environment, of those works; or
      (ii) any matter of a financial nature relating to those works.
  (4A) Paragraphs (b) to (d) of subsection (4) above are without prejudice to any power—
  (a) to make any grant under subsection (1) or (4)(a) above, or
  (b) to impose any condition under subsection (2) above,
which could be made or imposed apart from those paragraphs."

COMMENCEMENT
This section came into force on September 21, 1995 (S.I. 1995 No. 1983).

GENERAL NOTE
  This section, like s.100, widens the scope of the drainage provisions in the Water Resources Act 1991 (WRA) and the Land Drainage Act 1991 (LDA). The provisions in question provide for grants for drainage purposes to be made by the Minister of Agriculture, Fisheries and Food or, in Wales, the Secretary of State, to the NRA (now the Environment Agency: see s.2 of the 1995 Act) in the case of s.147 of the WRA and to internal drainage boards in the case of s.59 of the LDA. The amendments allow grants to be made not only as previously for drainage works themselves but also for research and investigation work to underpin coastal defence plans, to determine whether works are appropriate, and to assess such works following their completion.
  It will be noted that the new ss.147(4A) and 59(4A) in each case ensure that the new grounds for grants are additional to the existing grounds and are not to be read as in any way limiting their scope. Equally, however, those subsections provide that grants made on the new grounds may be subject to conditions in the same way as grants made on the previous grounds.

Fisheries

Sea fisheries

  102.—(1) The Sea Fisheries Regulation Act 1966 shall be amended in accordance with the following provisions of this section.
  (2) In section 2 (constitution of local fisheries committees) in subsection (2) (which includes provision for the members appointed by the Minister to be persons acquainted with the needs and opinions of the fishing interests of that district) after the words "of that district" there shall be added the words "or as being persons having knowledge of, or expertise in, marine environmental matters".
  (3) After that subsection there shall be inserted—
    "(2A) In addition to the members appointed as mentioned in subsection (1) above, a local fisheries committee may appoint such number of persons with knowledge of or expertise in marine environmental matters as it thinks fit as further members of the committee for those occasions on which it is considering any proposed byelaw under section 5 below by virtue of section 5A below, or any proposed amendment or revocation of such a byelaw."
  (4) At the end of that section there shall be added—
    "(7) In this section "marine environmental matters" means—
    (a) the conservation or enhancement of the natural beauty or amenity of marine or coastal areas (including their geological or physiographical features) or of any features of archaeological or historic interest in such areas; or
    (b) the conservation of flora or fauna which are dependent on, or associated with, a marine or coastal environment."

(5) After section 5 (byelaws for regulation etc of sea fisheries) there shall be inserted—

"Byelaws under section 5 for marine environmental purposes

5A.—(1) Any power to make byelaws conferred by section 5 above may be exercised for marine environmental purposes.

(2) The power to make byelaws under section 5 above by virtue of this section is in addition to, and not in derogation from, the power to make byelaws under that section otherwise than by virtue of this section.

(3) Byelaws under section 5 above by virtue of this section shall be submitted for confirmation under section 7 below—

(a) in the case of a byelaw which is to have effect in England, only after consultation with the Nature Conservancy Council for England;

(b) in the case of a byelaw which is to have effect in Wales, only after consultation with the Countryside Council for Wales.

(4) In this section "marine environmental purposes" means the purposes—

(a) of conserving or enhancing the natural beauty or amenity of marine or coastal areas (including their geological or physiographical features) or of any features of archaeological or historic interest in such areas; or

(b) of conserving flora or fauna which are dependent on, or associated with, a marine or coastal environment."

(6) In section 8 (power of Minister to revoke byelaws if it appears necessary or desirable for the maintenance or improvement of fisheries) after the words "maintenance or improvement of fisheries" there shall be inserted the words "or for marine environmental purposes, within the meaning of section 5A above,".

COMMENCEMENT

This section came into force on September 21, 1995 (S.I. 1995 No. 1983).

GENERAL NOTE

Sections 102 and 103 both introduce the notion of "marine environmental purposes" (as defined) into a range of legislation dealing with fisheries byelaws and orders. Section 102 amends the Sea Fisheries Regulation Act 1966 to add "marine environmental purposes" (defined in the new s.5A(4) of the 1966 Act) to the list of purposes for which a local sea fisheries committee for a sea fisheries district may make byelaws. The changes accord with Government proposals on which it consulted in August 1994. It will be noted that the new s.5A(3) requires the committee to consult the relevant statutory conservation body before submitting for confirmation a byelaw made for the new purposes.

Provision is made for the membership of such committees to include persons with knowledge of marine environmental matters when the proposal of such a byelaw is being considered (see the amended s.2(2) and new s.2(2A) of the 1966 Act).

Other marine or aquatic environmental conservation powers

103.—(1) After section 5 of the Sea Fish (Conservation) Act 1967 (power to restrict fishing for sea fish) there shall be inserted—

"Powers to restrict fishing for marine environmental purposes

5A.—(1) Any power to make an order under section 5 above may be exercised for marine environmental purposes.

(2) The power to make an order under section 5 above by virtue of this section is in addition to, and not in derogation from, the power to make an order under that section otherwise than by virtue of this section.

(3) In this section "marine environmental purposes" means the purposes—

    (a) of conserving or enhancing the natural beauty or amenity of marine or coastal areas (including their geological or physiographical features) or of any features of archaeological or historic interest in such areas; or

    (b) of conserving flora or fauna which are dependent on, or associated with, a marine or coastal environment."

(2) After section 2 of the Inshore Fishing (Scotland) Act 1984 there shall be inserted—

"Powers to restrict fishing, or to prohibit the carriage of specified types of net, for marine environmental purposes

2A.—(1) Any power to make an order under section 1 or 2 above may be exercised for marine environmental purposes.

(2) The power to make an order under section 1 or 2 above by virtue of this section is in addition to, and not in derogation from, the power to make an order under that section otherwise than by virtue of this section.

(3) In this section "marine environmental purposes" means the purposes—

    (a) of conserving or enhancing the natural beauty or amenity of marine or coastal areas (including their geological or physiographical features) or of any features of archaeological or historic interest in such areas; or

    (b) of conserving flora or fauna which are dependent on, or associated with, a marine or coastal environment."

(3) In Schedule 25 to the Water Resources Act 1991 (byelaw making powers) after paragraph 6 (byelaws for purposes of fisheries functions) there shall be inserted—

"*Fisheries byelaws for marine or aquatic environmental purposes*

6A.—(1) Any power to make byelaws conferred by paragraph 6 above may be exercised for marine or aquatic environmental purposes.

(2) The power to make byelaws under paragraph 6 above by virtue of this paragraph is in addition to, and not in derogation from, the power to make byelaws under that paragraph otherwise than by virtue of this paragraph.

(3) In this paragraph "marine or aquatic environmental purposes" means—

    (a) the conservation or enhancement of the natural beauty or amenity of marine or coastal, or aquatic or waterside, areas (including their geological or physiographical features) or of any features of archaeological or historic interest in such areas; or

    (b) the conservation of flora or fauna which are dependent on, or associated with, a marine or coastal, or aquatic or waterside, environment."

COMMENCEMENT

This section came into force on September 21, 1995 (S.I. 1995 No. 1983).

GENERAL NOTE

Section 103, which is parallel in some respects to s.102, amends three pieces of fisheries legislation. The first is the Sea Fish (Conservation) Act 1967. "Marine environmental purposes" (as defined in the new s.5A(3) of the 1967 Act) are added to the purposes for which an order restricting fishing in England and Wales may be made under s.5 of that Act. Parallel provision is made in relation to Scotland by an amendment of the Inshore Fishing (Scotland) Act 1984. It will be noted that the scope of the orders which can be made under the latter Act is wider then under the amended 1967 Act provision, since it encompasses restrictions on the carriage of specified types of net. The third amendment, to the Water Resources Act 1991, is broader in scope in that it adds "marine *or aquatic* environmental purposes" (as defined in the new para. 6 of Sched. 25 of the 1991 Act) to the purposes for which the Environment Agency (previously the NRA) may make fisheries byelaws.. The wider scope reflects the fact that the NRA regulates inland fresh waters as well as marine and coastal waters.

Fixed penalty system for certain fisheries offences

104.—(1) After section 37 of the Salmon and Freshwater Fisheries Act 1975 there shall be inserted—

"Fixed penalty notices for certain offences

37A.—(1) Where on any occasion a water bailiff or other officer of the Agency finds a person who he has reason to believe is committing, or has on that occasion committed, a fixed penalty offence, he may give to that person a notice (in this section referred to as a "fixed penalty notice") offering him the opportunity of discharging any liability to conviction for that offence by payment of a fixed penalty.

(2) Where a person is given a fixed penalty notice in respect of a fixed penalty offence—

    (a) no proceedings shall be instituted for that offence before the expiration of the period for paying the fixed penalty; and

    (b) he shall not be convicted of that offence if the fixed penalty is paid before the expiration of that period.

(3) The Agency may extend the period for paying the fixed penalty in any particular case if it considers it appropriate to do so in all the circumstances of the case.

(4) If, in any particular case, the Agency considers that a fixed penalty notice which has been given ought not to have been given, it may give to the person to whom the fixed penalty notice was given a notice withdrawing the fixed penalty notice; and where notice under this subsection is given—

    (a) the Agency shall repay any amount which has been paid by way of fixed penalty in pursuance of the fixed penalty notice; and

    (b) no proceedings shall be instituted or continued against that person for the offence in question.

(5) The amount by which the sums received by the Agency by way of fixed penalties exceed the sums repaid by it under subsection (4)(a) above shall be paid into the Consolidated Fund.

(6) In any proceedings, a certificate purporting to be signed by or on behalf of the Chief Executive of the Agency and stating either—

    (a) that payment of a fixed penalty was, or (as the case may be) was not, received by the Agency on or before a date specified in the certificate, or

    (b) that an envelope containing an amount sent by post in payment of a fixed penalty was marked as posted on a date specified in the certificate,

shall be received as evidence of the matters so stated and shall be treated, without further proof, as being so signed unless the contrary is shown.

(7) A fixed penalty notice shall give such reasonable particulars of the circumstances alleged to constitute the fixed penalty offence to which the notice relates as are necessary for giving reasonable information of the offence and shall state—

    (a) the monetary amount of the fixed penalty which may be paid;

    (b) the person to whom and the address at which—

        (i) the fixed penalty may be paid, and

        (ii) any correspondence relating to the fixed penalty notice may be sent;

    (c) the method or methods by which payment of the fixed penalty may be made;

(d) the period for paying the fixed penalty;

(e) the consequences of the fixed penalty not being paid before the expiration of that period.

(8) A fixed penalty notice may also contain such other information relating to or for the purpose of facilitating, the administration of the fixed penalty system as the Agency considers necessary or desirable.

(9) Regulations may—

(a) make provision with respect to the giving of fixed penalty notices, including, in particular, provision with respect to—

(i) the methods by which,

(ii) the officers, servants or agents by, to or on whom, and

(iii) the places at which,

fixed penalty notices may be given by, or served on behalf of, a water bailiff or other officer of the Agency;

(b) prescribe the method or methods by which fixed penalties may be paid;

(c) make provision for or with respect to the issue of prescribed documents to persons to whom fixed penalty notices are or have been given.

(10) In this section—

"fixed penalty" means a penalty of such amount as may be prescribed (whether by being specified in, or made calculable under, regulations);

"fixed penalty offence" means, subject to subsection (11) below, any offence—

(a) under this Act,

(b) under the Salmon Act 1986,

(c) under or by virtue of regulations or orders made under section 115, 116 or 142 of the Water Resources Act 1991, or

(d) under section 211(3) of that Act, so far as relating to byelaws made by virtue of paragraph 6 of Schedule 25 to that Act,

which is for the time being prescribed for the purpose;

"the fixed penalty system" means the system implementing this section and regulations made under it;

"the Ministers" means the Secretary of State and the Minister;

"notice" means notice in writing;

"the period for paying", in relation to any fixed penalty, means such period as may be prescribed for the purpose;

"prescribed" means prescribed by regulations;

"regulations" means regulations made under this section by the Ministers.

(11) The provision that may be made by regulations prescribing fixed penalty offences includes provision for an offence to be a fixed penalty offence—

(a) only if it is committed in such circumstances or manner as may be prescribed; or

(b) except if it is committed in such circumstances or manner as may be prescribed.

(12) Regulations may provide for any offence which is a fixed penalty offence to cease to be such an offence.

(13) An offence which, in consequence of regulations made by virtue of subsection (12) above, has ceased to be a fixed penalty offence shall be eligible to be prescribed as such an offence again.

(14) Regulations may—

(a) make different provision in relation to different cases or classes of case; or

(b) provide for such exceptions, limitations and conditions, or make such incidental, supplemental, consequential or transitional provision, as the Ministers consider necessary or expedient.

(15) Any power to make regulations under this section shall be exercisable by statutory instrument made by the Ministers; and a statutory instrument containing any such regulations shall be subject to annulment pursuant to a resolution of either House of Parliament."

(2) In section 35 of that Act (which, among other things, creates an offence of failing to state one's name and address when required to do so under that section) in subsection (1) (water bailiffs and constables), for the words from "A water bailiff" to "any constable" there shall be substituted the words "A water bailiff or other officer of the Agency, or any constable,".

(3) After that subsection there shall be inserted—

"(1A) Without prejudice to subsection (1) above, a water bailiff or other officer of the Agency who on any occasion finds a person who he has reason to believe is committing, or has on that occasion committed, a fixed penalty offence, within the meaning of section 37A below, may require that person to state his name and address."

(4) In section 41(1) of that Act (definitions), before the definition of "authorised officer" there shall be inserted—

" "the Agency" means the Environment Agency;".

COMMENCEMENT
April 1, 1996 (S.I. 1996 No. 186).

GENERAL NOTE
This section provides for regulations to designate as fixed penalty offences a range of fisheries offences under certain provisions of the Salmon and Freshwater Fisheries Act 1975, Salmon Act 1986 and Water Resources Act 1991 (see new s.37A(10) of the 1975 Act). A fixed penalty notice system for such offences is introduced and an amendment to s.35 of the 1975 Act by subs. (3) enables Environment Agency officers to obtain the name and address of a person whom they have reason to believe is committing or has committed such an offence.

Minor and consequential amendments relating to fisheries

105. Schedule 15 to this Act (which makes minor and consequential amendments relating to fisheries) shall have effect.

COMMENCEMENT
September 21, 1995 insofar as this section gives effect to paras. 25 and 26(1) of Sched. 15; January 1, 1999 insofar as it gives effect to paras. 13, 14(1) and (4), 17, 20 and 26(2) of that Schedule (S.I. 1995 No. 1983); February 1, 1996 (paras. 3 and 5(1)), and April 1, 1996 (paras. 1, 2, 4, 5(2) and (3), 6–12, 14(2) and (3), 15, 16, 18, 19 and 21–24 of that Schedule) (S.I. 1996 No. 186). The remainder of the section comes into force on a day to be appointed (s.125(3)).

GENERAL NOTE
This section gives effect to Sched. 15, which makes a number of minor and consequential amendments to fisheries legislation. The majority of these fall into one of five categories. First, the introduction of references to the Environment Agency in substitution for references to the NRA as from the date of transfer of fisheries functions to the Agency (especially para. 2). Secondly, the transfer of certain Ministerial functions under the Salmon and Freshwater Fisheries Act 1975 to the Agency and the removal of certain requirements under that Act for Ministerial consent to Agency (previously NRA) actions (paras. 7 to 16). Thirdly, provision for Ministerial Orders amending or revoking previous subordinate legislation so as to facilitate the coming into force of the provisions of the Act (paras. 3 and 5). Fourthly, the amendment of Salmon and Freshwater Fisheries Act 1975 provisions relating to the use of gratings in fish farms and else-

where, substituting provisions relating to the use of "screens", which term is defined to include gratings (paras. 13–17). And fifthly, the extension of the geographical scope of certain enforcement powers of Agency officers and water bailiffs (para. 19; see also s.6(7).

In Parliament, the Earl of Lindsay explained the fourth of these sets of amendments as follows:

"the ... amendments ... have two main purposes—to prevent salmon and migrating trout from becoming trapped in fish farm intakes and outfalls and to prevent farmed fish from escaping into the wild". Replacement of s.14 of the Act "extends the requirements to fit gratings (now referred to as 'screens') to fish farms and provides that these must be capable of preventing the ingress of wild fish and the escape of farmed fish. It also removes the requirement for ministerial approval. Instead, more general requirements similar to those enshrined in recent Scottish legislation will apply to the placing and nature of screens and will allow for the use of devices other than gratings to prevent the passage of fish" *Hansard* H.L. Vol. 565, cols. 1476 and 1477.

New provisions for Scotland

Control of pollution of water in Scotland

106. Schedule 16 to this Act (which amends the Control of Pollution Act 1974 as respects the control of pollution of rivers and coastal waters in Scotland) shall have effect.

COMMENCEMENT
April 1, 1996 (S.I. 1996 No. 186).

GENERAL NOTE
This section gives effect to Sched. 16 which makes considerable changes to Pt. II of the 1974 Act which contains the principal provisions relating to water pollution control in Scotland. The effect of these changes is to bring Scottish water pollution legislation broadly in line with the provisions of the Water Resources Act 1991, although certain differences remain. These are noted in the General Note to Sched. 16. The new ss.30F–J which Sched. 16 inserts into the 1974 Act are modelled closely on ss.85–89 of the 1991 Act. These provisions replace the main water pollution offence provisions which were contained in ss.31 and 32 of the 1974 Act (s.30F), together with the available statutory defences (ss.30H–J) and they also introduce a system for controlling certain discharges by prohibition notices (s.30G). Fuller details are provided in the General Notes to Sched. 16 itself, below at pp. 25–380 to 25–387.

It should also be noted that considerable additional amendments are made to Scottish water pollution legislation by other provisions of the 1995 Act: s.59, s.120 and Sched. 22, para. 29. Section 59 introduces a new definition of abandonment in relation to mines (see the General Notes to ss.58 and 59 on pp. 25–199 to 25–203), while Sched. 22(21) makes the necessary amendments to withdraw the cost recovery exemption in relation to water pollution from abandoned mines from after December 31, 1999 (see the General Note to s.60 on p. 25–204), Sched. 22, para. 29(22) introduces notices known as "works notices" whereby SEPA may require certain persons to undertake anti-pollution works (see the General Note to s.120 on p. 25–302) and Sched. 22, para. 29(26) which introduces notices known as "enforcement notices" whereby SEPA may require a consent holder to remedy any contravention of a consent condition (see the General Note to s.120 on p. 25–302). The scattered arrangement of these amendments is hardly satisfactory from a Scottish perspective.

Statutory nuisances: Scotland

107. Schedule 17 to this Act (which makes provision with respect to statutory nuisances in Scotland) shall have effect.

COMMENCEMENT
April 1, 1996 (S.I. 1996 No. 186).

GENERAL NOTE
Part III of the 1990 Act which established a comprehensive set of controls for statutory nuisances in England and Wales did not originally extend to Scotland where, as a result, the existing controls contained in the Public Health (Scotland) Act 1897 (the 1897 Act) and Pt. III of the 1974 Act (in relation to noise nuisances) continued to apply. However, in August 1994 the Scottish Office Environment Department issued a consultation paper: *The Extension of Part III of the Environmental Protection Act 1990 to Scotland: A Consultation Paper.*

Although this paper noted that advantages had been perceived in retaining a separate framework of statutory nuisance law in Scotland at the time of the passage of the 1990 Act through Parliament, it nevertheless pointed out that experience of the more streamlined system provided by Pt. III of the 1990 Act in England and Wales had highlighted deficiencies in the Scottish system. The paper also noted that the removal of some processes from Pt. I control under the 1990 Act by virtue of the Environmental Protection (Prescribed Processes and Substances) (Amendment) Regulations 1994 (S.I. 1994 No. 1271) necessitated an alternative form of control which Pt. III of the 1990 Act was capable of providing whereas the Scottish provisions in the 1897 Act were perceived as less robust, particularly in the light of the lower penalties available under the 1897 Act.

A further reason for seeking to overhaul the system of statutory nuisance in Scotland was that the operation of the 1897 and 1990 Acts created a potential for double jeopardy. Whereas in England and Wales, s.79(10) of the 1990 Act provides that a local authority cannot take action against a nuisance caused by the operation of a process subject to Pt. I control without the consent of the Secretary of State, the 1897 Act had no such provision. This meant that a local authority could take action against a nuisance caused by a Pt. I process under the 1897 Act even if the process operator was complying with all his authorisation conditions under Pt. I of the 1990 Act. The Government argued that the extension of Pt. III of the 1990 Act to Scotland would remove this double jeopardy altogether.

The Government also indicated that the extension of Pt. III to Scotland would replace the provisions of the Clean Air Act 1993 which provide for smoke to be treated as a nuisance, and the noise provisions of the 1974 Act. They argued that this would broaden the scope of nuisance control in Scotland.

Finally, the paper noted that the extension of Pt. III to Scotland would provide for redress by individuals which hitherto had been lacking in relation to nuisances under the 1897 Act. It should, however, be noted that, under the 1897 Act, where a local authority failed in their duty as regards nuisances, 10 council tax payers who resided in the district could give written notice to the authority of the alleged neglect of duty, and if the authority did nothing within 14 days to remedy the nuisance, they could petition the sheriff who could enforce the abatement of the nuisance at the expense of the local authority (1897 Act, s.146). Alternatively, the procurator fiscal might, with the approval of the Lord Advocate, institute proceedings to compel the authority to carry out their duty (1897 Act, s.148). In relation to noise nuisances the 1974 Act provided for individual remedies for affected occupiers. Part III of the 1990 Act, however, provides for enforcement of the statutory nuisance provisions by any aggrieved person (s.82(1)). Accordingly, the Government announced in *Contaminated Land Clean-up and Control: Outcome of Review* (November 24, 1994) that Pt. III of the 1990 Act was to be extended to Scotland, replacing the relevant provisions of the 1897 and 1974 Acts (see also *Hansard*, H.C. Vol. 250, col. 196w and *ibid.*, cols. 347–348w).

This section gives effect to Sched. 17 which extends Pt. III of the 1990 Act to Scotland. The necessary repeals of the statutory nuisance provisions in the 1897 Act and Pt. III of the 1974 Act are effected by Sched. 24. Accordingly, English and Welsh case law on statutory nuisance will become relevant for Scotland also.

Enforcement of the statutory nuisance provisions in s.82 of the 1990 Act by an aggrieved person in Scotland is to be by way of summary application to the Sheriff (s.82(1) as amended by Sched. 17, para. 6). See the Sheriff Court Summary Application Rules 1993 (S.I. 1993 No. 3240).

Powers of entry

Powers of enforcing authorities and persons authorised by them

108.—(1) A person who appears suitable to an enforcing authority may be authorised in writing by that authority to exercise, in accordance with the terms of the authorisation, any of the powers specified in subsection (4) below for the purpose—

    (a) of determining whether any provision of the pollution control enactments in the case of that authority is being, or has been, complied with;

    (b) of exercising or performing one or more of the pollution control functions of that authority; or

    (c) of determining whether and, if so, how such a function should be exercised or performed.

(2) A person who appears suitable to the Agency or SEPA may be authorised in writing by the Agency or, as the case may be, SEPA to exercise, in accordance with the terms of the authorisation, any of the powers specified in subsection (4) below for the purpose of enabling the Agency or, as the case

may be, SEPA to carry out any assessment or prepare any report which the Agency or, as the case may be, SEPA is required to carry out or prepare under section 5(3) or 33(3) above.

(3) Subsection (2) above only applies where the Minister who required the assessment to be carried out, or the report to be prepared, has, whether at the time of making the requirement or at any later time, notified the Agency or, as the case may be, SEPA that the assessment or report appears to him to relate to an incident or possible incident involving or having the potential to involve—

(a) serious pollution of the environment,

(b) serious harm to human health, or

(c) danger to life or health.

(4) The powers which a person may be authorised to exercise under sub-section (1) or (2) above are—

(a) to enter at any reasonable time (or, in an emergency, at any time and, if need be, by force) any premises which he has reason to believe it is necessary for him to enter;

(b) on entering any premises by virtue of paragraph (a) above, to take with him—

(i) any other person duly authorised by the enforcing authority and, if the authorised person has reasonable cause to apprehend any serious obstruction in the execution of his duty, a constable; and

(ii) any equipment or materials required for any purpose for which the power of entry is being exercised;

(c) to make such examination and investigation as may in any circumstances be necessary;

(d) as regards any premises which he has power to enter, to direct that those premises or any part of them, or anything in them, shall be left undisturbed (whether generally or in particular respects) for so long as is reasonably necessary for the purpose of any examination or investigation under paragraph (c) above;

(e) to take such measurements and photographs and make such recordings as he considers necessary for the purpose of any examination or investigation under paragraph (c) above;

(f) to take samples, or cause samples to be taken, of any articles or substances found in or on any premises which he has power to enter, and of the air, water or land in, on, or in the vicinity of, the premises;

(g) in the case of any article or substance found in or on any premises which he has power to enter, being an article or substance which appears to him to have caused or to be likely to cause pollution of the environment or harm to human health, to cause it to be dismantled or subjected to any process or test (but not so as to damage or destroy it, unless that is necessary);

(h) in the case of any such article or substance as is mentioned in paragraph (g) above, to take possession of it and detain it for so long as is necessary for all or any of the following purposes, namely—

(i) to examine it, or cause it to be examined, and to do, or cause to be done, to it anything which he has power to do under that paragraph;

(ii) to ensure that it is not tampered with before examination of it is completed;

(iii) to ensure that it is available for use as evidence in any proceedings for an offence under the pollution control enactments in the case of the enforcing authority under whose authorisation he acts or in any other proceedings relating to a variation notice, enforcement notice or prohibition notice under those enactments;

(j) to require any person whom he has reasonable cause to believe to be able to give any information relevant to any examination or investigation under paragraph (c) above to answer (in the absence of persons other than a person nominated by that person to be present and any persons whom the authorised person may allow to be present) such questions as the authorised person thinks fit to ask and to sign a declaration of the truth of his answers;

(k) to require the production of, or where the information is recorded in computerised form, the furnishing of extracts from, any records—
    (i) which are required to be kept under the pollution control enactments for the enforcing authority under whose authorisation he acts, or
    (ii) which it is necessary for him to see for the purposes of an examination or investigation under paragraph (c) above,
and to inspect and take copies of, or of any entry in, the records;

(l) to require any person to afford him such facilities and assistance with respect to any matters or things within that person's control or in relation to which that person has responsibilities as are necessary to enable the authorised person to exercise any of the powers conferred on him by this section;

(m) any other power for—
    (i) a purpose falling within any paragraph of subsection (1) above, or
    (ii) any such purpose as is mentioned in subsection (2) above,
which is conferred by regulations made by the Secretary of State.

(5) The powers which by virtue of subsections (1) and (4) above are conferred in relation to any premises for the purpose of enabling an enforcing authority to determine whether any provision of the pollution control enactments in the case of that authority is being, or has been, complied with shall include power, in order to obtain the information on which that determination may be made,—

(a) to carry out experimental borings or other works on those premises; and

(b) to install, keep or maintain monitoring and other apparatus there.

(6) Except in an emergency, in any case where it is proposed to enter any premises used for residential purposes, or to take heavy equipment on to any premises which are to be entered, any entry by virtue of this section shall only be effected—

(a) after the expiration of at least seven days' notice of the proposed entry given to a person who appears to the authorised person in question to be in occupation of the premises in question, and

(b) either—
    (i) with the consent of a person who is in occupation of those premises; or
    (ii) under the authority of a warrant by virtue of Schedule 18 to this Act.

(7) Except in an emergency, where an authorised person proposes to enter any premises and—

(a) entry has been refused and he apprehends on reasonable grounds that the use of force may be necessary to effect entry, or

(b) he apprehends on reasonable grounds that entry is likely to be refused and that the use of force may be necessary to effect entry,

any entry on to those premises by virtue of this section shall only be effected under the authority of a warrant by virtue of Schedule 18 to this Act.

(8) In relation to any premises belonging to or used for the purposes of the United Kingdom Atomic Energy Authority, subsections (1) to (4) above shall have effect subject to section 6(3) of the Atomic Energy Authority Act

1954 (which restricts entry to such premises where they have been declared to be prohibited places for the purposes of the Official Secrets Act 1911).

(9) The Secretary of State may by regulations make provision as to the procedure to be followed in connection with the taking of, and the dealing with, samples under subsection (4)(f) above.

(10) Where an authorised person proposes to exercise the power conferred by subsection (4)(g) above in the case of an article or substance found on any premises, he shall, if so requested by a person who at the time is present on and has responsibilities in relation to those premises, cause anything which is to be done by virtue of that power to be done in the presence of that person.

(11) Before exercising the power conferred by subsection (4)(g) above in the case of any article or substance, an authorised person shall consult—

(a) such persons having duties on the premises where the article or substance is to be dismantled or subjected to the process or test, and

(b) such other persons,

as appear to him appropriate for the purpose of ascertaining what dangers, if any, there may be in doing anything which he proposes to do or cause to be done under the power.

(12) No answer given by a person in pursuance of a requirement imposed under subsection (4)(j) above shall be admissible in evidence in England and Wales against that person in any proceedings, or in Scotland against that person in any criminal proceedings.

(13) Nothing in this section shall be taken to compel the production by any person of a document of which he would on grounds of legal professional privilege be entitled to withhold production on an order for discovery in an action in the High Court or, in relation to Scotland, on an order for the production of documents in an action in the Court of Session.

(14) Schedule 18 to this Act shall have effect with respect to the powers of entry and related powers which are conferred by this section.

(15) In this section—

"authorised person" means a person authorised under subsection (1) or (2) above;

"emergency" means a case in which it appears to the authorised person in question—

(a) that there is an immediate risk of serious pollution of the environment or serious harm to human health, or

(b) that circumstances exist which are likely to endanger life or health,

and that immediate entry to any premises is necessary to verify the existence of that risk or those circumstances or to ascertain the cause of that risk or those circumstances or to effect a remedy;

"enforcing authority" means—

(a) the Secretary of State;

(b) the Agency;

(c) SEPA; or

(d) a local enforcing authority;

"local enforcing authority" means—

(a) a local enforcing authority, within the meaning of Part I of the Environmental Protection Act 1990;

(b) a local authority, within the meaning of Part IIA of that Act, in its capacity as an enforcing authority for the purposes of that Part;

(c) a local authority for the purposes of Part IV of this Act or regulations under that Part;

"mobile plant" means plant which is designed to move or to be moved whether on roads or otherwise;

"pollution control enactments", in relation to an enforcing authority, means the enactments and instruments relating to the pollution control functions of that authority;

"pollution control functions", in relation to the Agency or SEPA, means the functions conferred or imposed on it by or under—

(a) the Alkali, &c, Works Regulation Act 1906;

(b) Part III of the Rivers (Prevention of Pollution) (Scotland) Act 1951;

(c) the Rivers (Prevention of Pollution) (Scotland) Act 1965;

(d) Part I of the Health and Safety at Work etc. Act 1974;

(e) Parts I, IA and II of the Control of Pollution Act 1974;

(f) the Control of Pollution (Amendment) Act 1989;

(g) Parts I, II and IIA of the Environmental Protection Act 1990 (integrated pollution control, waste on land and contaminated land);

(h) Chapter III of Part IV of the Water Industry Act 1991 (special category effluent);

(j) Part III and sections 161 to 161D of the Water Resources Act 1991;

(k) section 19 of the Clean Air Act 1993;

(l) the Radioactive Substances Act 1993;

(m) regulations made by virtue of section 2(2) of the European Communities Act 1972, to the extent that the regulations relate to pollution;

"pollution control functions", in relation to a local enforcing authority, means the functions conferred or imposed on, or transferred to, that authority—

(a) by or under Part I or IIA of the Environmental Protection Act 1990;

(b) by or under regulations made by virtue of Part IV of this Act; or

(c) by or under regulations made by virtue of section 2(2) of the European Communities Act 1972, to the extent that the regulations relate to pollution;

"pollution control functions", in relation to the Secretary of State, means any functions which are conferred or imposed upon him by or under any enactment or instrument and which relate to the control of pollution;

"premises" includes any land, vehicle, vessel or mobile plant.

(16) Any power to make regulations under this section shall be exercisable by statutory instrument; and a statutory instrument containing any such regulations shall be subject to annulment pursuant to a resolution of either House of Parliament.

DEFINITIONS

"Agency, the": s.124(1).

"authorised person": subs. (15).

"emergency": subs. (15).

"enforcing authority": subs. (15).

"functions": s.124(1).

"local enforcing authority": subs. (15).

"mobile plant": subs. (15).

"notice": s.124(1).

"pollution control enactments": subs. (15).

"pollution control functions": subs. (15).

"premises": subs. (15).

"records": s.124(1).

"SEPA": s.124(1).

COMMENCEMENT

April 1, 1996 (S.I. 1996 No. 186).

GENERAL NOTE

This section is of great practical importance in that it provides a comprehensive set of powers of entry and investigation which apply to all enforcing authorities exercising pollution control functions at central and local level. The authorities to which the powers apply are defined at subs. (15) and are the Secretary of State, the Agency, SEPA and local authorities. Existing statutory powers of entry (for example, those relating to Pts. I and II of the 1990 Act) cease to have effect (see Sched. 22, paras. 55, 85 and 86).

The pollution control functions of the Agency and SEPA are as listed at paras. (a)–(m) in subs. (15), and are comprehensive. The pollution control functions of local authorities are also listed at subs. (15) and cover local authority air pollution control in England and Wales under Pt. I of the 1990 Act, contaminated land functions under Pt. IIA of that Act (as inserted), regulations under Pt. IV of the 1995 Act relating to air quality, and any pollution control regulations made under s.2(2) of the European Communities Act 1972. Notably, the functions of local authorities in relation to statutory nuisance under Pt. III of the 1990 Act, noise under the Control of Pollution Act 1974, and air pollution under the Clean Air Act 1993 are not included. In the case of the Secretary of State, those functions are any conferred on him which relate to the control of pollution.

Extensions to the geographical scope of Agency officers' powers in relation to the enforcement of certain fisheries provisions in the catchment area of the River Esk should be noted: s.6(7) and Sched. 15, para. 19.

Subs. (1): authorisation to exercise powers

The enforcing authorities (see above) may under this subsection authorise in writing the exercise of the relevant powers by any suitable person, for three purposes. Those purposes are (a) determining whether pollution control law is being or has been complied with, for example compliance monitoring and investigation of possible offences; (b) exercising or performing one of the pollution control functions of the authority, for example supervision of licensed activities; and (c) determining whether and, if so, how such a function should be performed.

The terms of this subsection and of the written authorisation are important, since they will affect the validity of the exercise of the relevant powers, and may affect the admissibility of evidence gained as a result of such exercise. The enforcing authority will therefore need to be sure that each pollution control officer is authorised in writing and that when acting they do so within the terms of their authorisation. The authorisation may relate to all the pollution control powers vested in the authority, or to specified powers, for example waste regulation. If the authorisation is limited in such a way—which would seem inadvisable from the point of view of the authority—then the individual's powers will be limited, to continue the example, to waste regulatory functions.

Even when authorised, the exercise of the powers must not only be within the ambit of subs. (4), but must also be for one of the three purposes listed in subs. (1). The designated officer ought therefore to be prepared to state what his purpose was in exercising the powers. By Sched. 18, para. 3, the designated person must produce evidence of his designation and other authority before exercising the power. By para. 6(4) a designated person shall not be liable in civil or criminal proceedings for anything done in the purported exercise of a relevant power if the court is satisfied the act was done in good faith and on reasonable grounds.

Information obtained by exercise of powers

Information obtained in consequence of the exercise of the relevant powers, whether with or without consent, is admissible in evidence against any person (Sched. 18, para. 4).

Subss. (2) and (3): assessments and reports

Subsection (2) confers an additional power on the Agency/SEPA to authorise persons to exercise the powers listed at subs. (4) for the purpose of enabling the preparation of assessments and reports on the actual or likely effects of existing or potential levels of pollution, on the options available for control and clean-up, and on the respective costs and benefits. The Agency/SEPA will only be under a duty to carry out such an assessment where required to do so by the Secretary of State or Minister, and will then only have the ability to authorise the exercise of the powers where notified by the Secretary of State/Minister that the assessment relates to an incident or possible incident involving the serious consequences set out at subs. (3). The powers are not available in relation to the Agency/SEPA's general duty to follow developments in technology and techniques under ss.5(4) and 33(4).

Subs. (4): powers

This is the vital subsection which lists the powers available, and which a person may be authorised to exercise. There is no reason why a person could not be authorised to exercise merely some and not all of those powers, though to avoid complications, the authority will presumably wish to authorise the exercise of all or any of the powers. The conditions for the exercise of the powers are phrased in various terms, and close attention needs to be paid to the wording in each case. The powers are considered in the following groups.

Entry. Paragraphs (a) and (b) together provide a power of entry based upon whether the authorised officer has reason to believe that it is necessary for him to enter the premises. Whilst it is not stated expressly, it is submitted that the necessity to enter the premises must relate to the statutory purposes set out at subs. (1) (see above). Case law on wording in the field of police powers of entry suggests that the authorised officer must not only have reason to believe it necessary to enter, but must actually have that belief: *R. v. Banks* [1916] 2 K.B. 621; *R. v. Harrison* [1938] 3 All E.R. 134; *Nakkuda Ali v. Jayaratwe* [1951] A.C. 66 (P.C.); *Chapman v. DPP* (1988) 89 Cr.App.Rep. 190. It is submitted that there must be reasonable grounds on which the belief is based, such that a reasonable person could hold that belief: see *McArdle v. Egan* (1933) 150 L.T. 412; *IRC v. Rossminster* [1980] A.C. 952.

The power of entry is substantially wider in cases of emergency, where it can be exercised at any time (whether reasonable or not) and by force if necessary. "Emergency" is defined at subs. (15). The power is extended by para. (b) to other authorised persons and to necessary equipment and materials, as well as to police presence if there is a reasonable cause to apprehend serious obstruction (which may be an offence under s.110(1)). The provisions need to be read together with subss. (6)–(8). Entry is restricted by subs. (6) in the case of residential premises, or where heavy equipment is to be taken onto the premises. Unless the situation is one of emergency, entry may only be effected after seven days' notice to the apparent occupier, and then either with the occupier's consent or under a warrant.

Forcible entry may be effected where there is an emergency (subs. (1)), but in other cases by subs. (7) a warrant will be necessary if entry has been or is likely to be refused. In the case of premises belonging to or used for the purposes of the U.K. Atomic Energy Authority entry may be restricted under subs. (8). Entry to Crown Premises generally may be subject to restriction on grounds of national security under s.115(5).

Schedule 18 is also relevant to powers of entry. Paragraph 2 thereof deals with the issue of warrants in cases where entry is refused or refusal is anticipated, where the premises are unoccupied, where the occupier is temporarily absent and the case is one of urgency or where application for admission would defeat the object of the proposed entry. Paragraph 5 imposes a duty in the case of entry on unoccupied premises, or where the occupier is temporarily absent, to leave the premises secured as effectively as they were initially. Paragraph 6 provides for the payment of full compensation for loss or damage sustained by reason of entry or failure to leave the premises secure.

Examination and inspection. The power to examine and investigate is a very general one, simply related to what may in any circumstances be necessary (para. (c)). In relation to premises which have been or may be entered under para. (a), a direction may be given (not necessarily in writing) that the premises or anything in them shall be left undisturbed for so long as is reasonably necessary for examination or investigation (para. (d)).

Measurements, photographs and recordings. This useful power, contained in para. (e), is related to examination and investigation, in that the authorised person must consider it necessary for such purposes.

Samples. Under para. (f), samples may be taken of articles or substances on the premises entered, and of the air, water or land in, on or in the vicinity of premises which the authorised person has power to enter. Where samples are taken outside the premises, there may in practical terms be no need to enter, but it appears that there must still be power to do so. Regulations on sampling procedures may be made under subs. (9).

Subsection (5) is also relevant to sampling. It enables the authorised person to carry out experimental borings or other works (for example to obtain soil or groundwater samples) and to install and keep monitoring or other apparatus on the premises. This power is ancillary to the purpose of determining whether environmental legislation is being complied with (subs. (1)(a)) and is exercisable only in that context. This may give rise to difficulty in the case of investigation for contaminated land under Pt. II of the Act, which may well require "experimental borings" to be carried out. Such investigation is for the purpose of determining whether the land is contaminated, not whether environmental law is being complied with. This in turn raises the question of the relationship of subs. (5) to subs. (4)(f), and whether the soil or groundwater samples could be obtained under the latter provision. The s.108(4)(m) provision for regulations to extend the list of powers in subs. (4) may need to be called upon to resolve such difficulties.

Possession, testing and destruction of articles and substances. By paras. (g) and (h) there is power to dismantle and test articles or substances which appear to the authorised person to have caused or be likely to cause pollution (including power to damage or destroy them if necessary), or to take possession of such an article or substance and detain it for the purposes set out in para. (h). Those purposes include ensuring it is not tampered with, and use as evidence in subsequent criminal or enforcement proceedings. The article or substance must be found in or on premises which the authorised person has power to enter. By subs. (10) any person present on the premises and having responsibilities in relation to them may require that they be present during the exercise of the power under para. (g).

Before exercising the powers mentioned in para. (g), the procedure set out at subs. (11) must be followed. Thus the authorised person must consult such persons having duties on the premises, and such other persons, as seem appropriate, to ascertain the possible hazards involved in taking the proposed action. The power of detention under para. (h) applies for so long as detention is necessary for the three purposes (i)–(iii) set out in the paragraph. It is likely that the power to take possession of the article or substance may only be exercised by the authorised person and not by any person accompanying him (*R. v. Central Criminal Court and British Railways Board, ex p. A.J.D. Holdings, Royle and Stanley* [1992] Crim. L.R. 669). If possession is taken of the article or substance unlawfully or following unlawful entry, then it is doubtful whether it can lawfully be retained even if required as evidence: see *R. v. Chief Constable of Lancashire, ex p. Parker and McGrath* [1993] 2 All E.R. 56.

Information requests. Paragraph (j) allows any person who with reasonable cause is believed to have relevant information to be required to answer questions and to sign a declaration as to the truth of the answers. The authority may require the interview to be conducted in private, except for the presence of a person nominated by the person under questioning, and any other person who the authority may allow to be present.

Failure to comply with the request is an offence under s.110(1)(a), but no answer given will be admissible against the person giving it in any proceedings in England and Wales, or in criminal proceedings in Scotland (subs. (12)).

Production of records. The authorised person may, under para. (k), require the production of records. Two types of records are covered: those required to be kept under a pollution control enactment (for example monitoring data required by an authorisation condition) or those which it is necessary for the authorised person to see for the purposes of his powers of examination and investigation. Computer records and any other records kept otherwise than in a document are within the provision (s.124(1)). The term "record" may give rise to difficulties of interpretation in this context. There is some authority to suggest that the term extends only to primary sources of information: see *R. v. Tirado* (1974) 59 Cr.App.R. 50. If so, it might not cover reports, files of correspondence, memoranda or consignment notes which are secondary rather than primary sources: see *R. v. Gwilliam* [1968] 1 W.L.R. 1839 (files of correspondence). Documents which are a digest or analysis of primary or original sources of information may not constitute a record: see *R. v. Schering Chemicals Ltd.* [1983] 1 W.L.R. 143. On the other hand, notes of a meeting or a report might be said to constitute a record of that meeting or of events referred to in the report, and at least one case suggests a wider interpretation of the term: see *R. v. Jones (Benjamin)* [1978] 1 W.L.R. 195. Matters of opinion may be distinguished from records: see *Savings and Investment Bank v. Gasco Investments (Netherlands) B.V.* [1984] 1 W.L.R. 271 (report of inspector).

Documents covered by legal professional privilege cannot be required to be disclosed: see subs. (13) below. The power to require production of records does not include the power to remove them: see *Barge v. British Gas Corporation* (1983) 81 L.G.R. 53. However para. (k) does give the right to take copies. If copying facilities are not available at the premises on which the records are held, the authorised person may have difficulties in legitimately taking copies where the para. (l) power does not assist.

Other facilities and assistance. Any person may be required to afford the authorised person with facilities or assistance necessary to enable the exercise of the statutory powers, so far as those things are within their control or they have responsibility for them (para. (l)). This might include, for example, the use of equipment or office or changing facilities.

Subs. (13): privilege

Nothing in s.108 can compel the production of documents protected by legal professional privilege. This exemption would cover communications between clients and legal professional advisors, whether independent or "in-house". It would not cover communications with other professional advisors, such as engineers or chemists, nor would it cover the giving of legal advice by other professionals such as accountants in the course of their work. It is doubtful whether businesses could obtain protection for their documents simply by depositing them with their legal advisors. The matter protected by privilege must have formed part of the substance of the seeking or giving of legal advice and not have a completely independent origin: *R. v. Peterborough Justices, ex p. Hicks* [1977] 1 W.L.R. 1371; *R. v. King* [1983] 1 All E.R. 929. However, privilege would attach to documents which were fairly referable to a contemplated relationship: *Minter v. Priest* [1930] A.C. 558. Furthermore, documents "are privileged, although they may not relate to any suit pending or contemplated or apprehended": *McCowan v. Wright* (1852) 15 D. 229 *per* Lord Wood at p. 237. Attendance notes recording meetings or advice between legal advisors and clients would also be privileged (*Balabel v. Air India* [1988] Ch. 317) but not notes simply recording meetings or conversations between opposing parties or their legal advisors (*Parry v. News Group Newspapers* (1990) 140 NLJ 1791). Nor is legal professional privilege conferred simply by marking a document "without prejudice". A legal advisor's professional duty need not be confined to giving advice on matters of law or on the construction of documents. It may extend to the commercial wisdom of entering into a particular transaction in respect of which legal advice is also sought (*Nederlandse Reassurantie Group Holding N.V. v. Bacon & Woodrow* [1995] 1 All E.R. 976).

Subs. (14): Schedule 18
    Schedule 18 contains supplementary provisions dealing with the procedure for the issue of warrants required under the section. The detailed grounds for the issue of warrants are set out at para. 2. Paragraph 3 requires an authorised person to produce evidence of their authority before exercising a statutory power under s.108, and to produce evidence of their warrant if acting under one. As to the production of warrants, see *R. v. Chief Constable of Lancashire, ex p. Parker* [1993] 2 All E.R. 56, and in respect of the position in Scotland: Stoddart, *Criminal Warrants* (Butterworths, 1991), para. 3.14; and Hume, *Commentaries on the Law of Scotland Respecting Crimes* (1844 Ed. by B.R. Bell).
    By para. 4 evidence obtained in the exercise of the powers, whether with or without consent, is admissible in evidence against any person, subject to the special limitation provided by subs. (12) relating to self-incrimination.

Relevance of Police and Criminal Evidence Act Codes of Practice
    Various matters dealt with in s.108 are regulated in England and Wales by the Codes of Practice issued under ss.60 and 66 of the Police and Criminal Evidence Act 1984, namely powers of search and questioning. By s.67(9) of the 1984 Act, persons other than police officers who are charged with the duty of investigating offences or charging offenders shall in the discharge of that duty have regard to the relevant provisions of any such Code. The Codes may therefore apply to routine inspections to establish compliance with legislation, as well as to the investigation of specific infractions: *Dudley Metropolitan County Council v. Debenhams, The Times,* August 19, 1994. Since the purposes for which the statutory pollution control powers are provided include, but are not confined to, establishing compliance with legislation, it will be a question of fact as to whether the officer in question was, at the relevant time, discharging the duty of investigating offences as opposed to some other duty, for example the exercise of licensing functions.

Power to deal with cause of imminent danger of serious pollution etc.

    109.—(1) Where, in the case of any article or substance found by him on any premises which he has power to enter, an authorised person has reasonable cause to believe that, in the circumstances in which he finds it, the article or substance is a cause of imminent danger of serious pollution of the environment or serious harm to human health, he may seize it and cause it to be rendered harmless (whether by destruction or otherwise).
    (2) As soon as may be after any article or substance has been seized and rendered harmless under this section, the authorised person shall prepare and sign a written report giving particulars of the circumstances in which the article or substance was seized and so dealt with by him, and shall—
    (a) give a signed copy of the report to a responsible person at the premises where the article or substance was found by him; and
    (b) unless that person is the owner of the article or substance, also serve a signed copy of the report on the owner;
and if, where paragraph (b) above applies, the authorised person cannot after reasonable inquiry ascertain the name or address of the owner, the copy may be served on him by giving it to the person to whom a copy was given under paragraph (a) above.
    (3) In this section, "authorised person" has the same meaning as in section 108 above.

DEFINITIONS
　"authorised person": s.108(15).

COMMENCEMENT
　April 1, 1996 (S.I. 1996 No. 186).

GENERAL NOTE
　This section provides a power to seize articles or substances found on premises which there is power to enter under s.108. The authorised person must have reasonable cause to believe the article or substance to be a cause of imminent danger in the circumstances in which it is found. As to the words "reasonable cause to believe", see the General Note to s.108 at p. 25–287. Subsection (2) requires a written report of the circumstances of seizure to be prepared.
　The section must be read alongside s.108(4)(g) and (h) which also gives power to take possession of substances and articles, but for the purposes of investigation, examination, testing and evidence. The purpose of s.109 is to render harmless a source of imminent danger. It will be important for the pollution control officer who intends to remove substances or articles or to interfere with them in some other way to be clear as to which provision he is acting under, since the procedural requirements of the two sections are quite different.

Offences

　110.—(1) It is an offence for a person intentionally to obstruct an authorised person in the exercise or performance of his powers or duties.
　(2) It is an offence for a person, without reasonable excuse,—
　　(a) to fail to comply with any requirement imposed under section 108 above;
　　(b) to fail or refuse to provide facilities or assistance or any information or to permit any inspection reasonably required by an authorised person in the execution of his powers or duties under or by virtue of that section; or
　　(c) to prevent any other person from appearing before an authorised person, or answering any question to which an authorised person may require an answer, pursuant to subsection (4) of that section.
　(3) It is an offence for a person falsely to pretend to be an authorised person.
　(4) A person guilty of an offence under subsection (1) above shall be liable—
　　(a) in the case of an offence of obstructing an authorised person in the execution of his powers under section 109 above—
　　　　(i) on summary conviction, to a fine not exceeding the statutory maximum;
　　　　(ii) on conviction on indictment, to a fine or to imprisonment for a term not exceeding two years, or to both;
　　(b) in any other case, on summary conviction, to a fine not exceeding level 5 on the standard scale.
　(5) A person guilty of an offence under subsection (2) or (3) above shall be liable on summary conviction to a fine not exceeding level 5 on the standard scale.
　(6) In this section—
　　　"authorised person" means a person authorised under section 108 above and includes a person designated under paragraph 2 of Schedule 18 to this Act;
　　　"powers and duties" includes powers or duties exercisable by virtue of a warrant under Schedule 18 to this Act.

DEFINITIONS
　"authorised person": subs. (6).
　"powers and duties": subs. (6).

COMMENCEMENT
April 1, 1996 (S.I. 1996 No. 186).

GENERAL NOTE

This section creates a number of separate offences relating to the exercise of powers under ss.108 and 109. These are:

1. *The intentional obstruction of an authorised person in the exercise of his powers or duties (subs. (1))*. Obstruction need not include physical violence and may involve anything which makes the exercise of the powers more difficult: *Hinchcliffe v. Sheldon* [1955] 1 W.L.R. 1207. Giving a warning to someone may therefore constitute obstruction: *Green v. Moore* [1982] Q.B. 1044. (It should be noted that in Scotland the offence has been construed much more narrowly and it has been held that there must be a physical element to obstruction: *Curlett v. McKechnie* 1938 J.C. 176 *per* Lord Fleming at p. 179 (making false statements to the police not obstruction). This position was modified to some extent by *Skeen v. Shaw* 1979 S.L.T. (Notes) 58 where it was held that the addition of the word "hinder" to the statutory definition of the offence in s.41 of the Police (Scotland) Act 1967 reduced any necessary physical element to a minimum and hence that standing in front of officers and shouting at them constituted the offence although no physical contact had occurred. Given that the word "hinder" does not appear in s.110 of the 1995 Act, it is likely that the Scottish courts would require the presence of a physical element for there to be obstruction.)

However, in order to be an offence the obstruction must be intentional, *i.e.* done with the intention of obstructing: *Willmott v. Atack* [1977] Q.B. 498. If the act was done intentionally it will be immaterial that the person doing the act did not appreciate that it constituted obstruction at law, or that it was not aimed primarily at the person obstructed: see for example *Green v. Moore* [1982] Q.B. 1044; *Hills v. Ellis* [1983] Q.B. 680; *Lewis v. Cox* [1984] 3 All E.R. 672. However, it would appear to be necessary for the accused to know that the person he was obstructing was indeed an authorised person. *Ostler v. Elliott* [1980] Crim. L.R. 584 indicates that the requirement of wilfulness in the offence of "wilful obstruction" under s.51 the Police Act 1967 could provide a defence for a person who honestly and reasonably believed that the police officers were robbers. The position is the same in Scotland: *Annan v. Tait* 1981 S.C.C.R. 326 (accused acquitted where he did not realise that he was struggling with plain-clothes police officers). The authorised person must also be acting in the exercise or performance of his powers. Where this is not the case it would appear to be common ground both south and north of the border that obstruction would not be unlawful: *Pedro v. Diss* [1981] 2 All E.R. 59; *Twycross v. Farrell* 1973 S.L.T. (Notes) 85; *Wither v. Reid* 1979 S.L.T. 192; *Stocks v. Hamilton* 1991 S.C.C.R. 190.

2. *Failure to comply with any requirement under s.108 without reasonable excuse (subs. (2)(a))*. What is a reasonable excuse will depend on the circumstances of each case, but the standard will be objective in that the excuse must be capable of being regarded as reasonable, in the sense of being consistent with a reasonable standard of conduct: *Pascoe v. Nominal Defendant (Queensland) (No. 2)* [1964] Qd. R. 373. The fact that the defendant did not know that he was obliged to comply with the requirement may not of itself constitute a reasonable excuse: *Greenwich London Borough Council v. Millcroft Construction Ltd* [1986] 85 L.G.R. 66; 150 J.P. 645. Complete lack of comprehension of what was being required may however be an excuse: *Beck v. Sager* [1979] Crim. L.R. 257.

3. *Failure, without reasonable excuse, to provide facilities or assistance which are reasonably required (subs. (2)(b))*.

4. *Without reasonable excuse, preventing any other person from appearing before an authorised person or answering any question (subs. (2)(c))*.

5. *Impersonating an authorised person (subs. (3))*.

Penalties

Most of the offences under the section are punishable on summary conviction only. However, the obstruction of an authorised person acting under s.109 in relation to a substance or article which is a cause of imminent danger is punishable on indictment by an unlimited fine and up to two years imprisonment (subs. (4)(a)).

Evidence

Evidence in connection with certain pollution offences

111.—(1) The following provisions (which restrict the admissibility in evidence of information obtained from samples) shall cease to have effect—

(a) section 19(2) to (2B) of the Rivers (Prevention of Pollution) (Scotland) 1951;

  (b) section 49 of the Sewerage (Scotland) Act 1968;

  (c) section 171(4) and (5) of the Water Industry Act 1991; and

  (d) section 209(1), (2) and (4) of the Water Resources Act 1991.

  (2) Information provided or obtained pursuant to or by virtue of a condition of a relevant licence (including information so provided or obtained, or recorded, by means of any apparatus) shall be admissible in evidence in any proceedings, whether against the person subject to the condition or any other person.

  (3) For the purposes of subsection (2) above, apparatus shall be presumed in any proceedings to register or record accurately, unless the contrary is shown or the relevant licence otherwise provides.

  (4) Where—

  (a) by virtue of a condition of a relevant licence, an entry is required to be made in any record as to the observance of any condition of the relevant licence, and

  (b) the entry has not been made,

that fact shall be admissible in any proceedings as evidence that that condition has not been observed.

  (5) In this section—

    "apparatus" includes any meter or other device for measuring, assessing, determining, recording or enabling to be recorded, the volume, temperature, radioactivity, rate, nature, origin, composition or effect of any substance, flow, discharge, emission, deposit or abstraction;

    "condition of a relevant licence" includes any requirement to which a person is subject under, by virtue of or in consequence of a relevant licence;

    "environmental licence" has the same meaning as it has in Part I above as it applies in relation to the Agency or SEPA, as the case may be;

    "relevant licence" means—

      (a) any environmental licence;

      (b) any consent under Part II of the Sewerage (Scotland) Act 1968 to make discharges of trade effluent;

      (c) any agreement under section 37 of that Act with respect to, or to any matter connected with, the reception, treatment or disposal of such effluent;

      (d) any consent under Chapter III of Part IV of the Water Industry Act 1991 to make discharges of special category effluent; or

      (e) any agreement under section 129 of that Act with respect to, or to any matter connected with, the reception or disposal of such effluent.

  (6) In section 25 of the Environmental Protection Act, after subsection (2) (which makes similar provision to subsection (4) above) there shall be inserted—

    "(3) Subsection (2) above shall not have effect in relation to any entry required to be made in any record by virtue of a condition of a relevant licence, within the meaning of section 111 of the Environment Act 1995 (which makes corresponding provision in relation to such licences)."

<small>DEFINITIONS</small>
  "Agency, the": s.124(1).
  "apparatus": subs. (5).
  "condition of a relevant licence": subs. (5).
  "environmental licence": subs. (5).
  "SEPA": s.124(1).

<small>COMMENCEMENT</small>
  April 1, 1996 (S.I. 1996 No. 186).

This section deals with the issue of evidence in relation to pollution offences, and makes some important changes to existing law.

Subs. (1): removal of tripartite sampling requirement
This subsection removes the time-honoured requirement relating to evidence of samples in various water pollution offences, namely that the sample on being taken should be divided into three parts, one for the authority, the second to be given to the occupier of the relevant premises, and the third to be retained for future analysis. This procedure was seen as becoming increasingly inconvenient, incompatible with automated sampling methods, and had given rise to some difficult issues of interpretation. See *Attorney General's Reference (No. 2 of 1994), The Times*, August 4, 1994; *R. v. CPC (UK), The Times*, August 4, 1994. For an article on the issue, see Albert Mumma [1993] J.E.L. Vol. 5, No. 2, p. 191.
It should be noted that, in relation to Scotland, the removal of the requirement for tripartite sampling does not affect the need for corroboration of the material facts.

Subs. (2)
This subsection deals with information obtained pursuant to or by virtue of a condition of an environmental licence and makes it clear that such information is admissible if obtained by means of apparatus. Consent conditions, for example on discharge consents, may require self-monitoring and the making of returns: see for example Sched. 10, para. 2(4) of the Water Resources Act 1991. Advances in technology mean that much environmental monitoring is carried out on a continuous basis by various types of device: indeed, many environmental licences will contain conditions requiring the licensee to carry out such monitoring. Similarly, the enforcing authorities themselves make use of such devices, which will sometimes operate on a remote sensing basis to generate data elsewhere.
It should be noted that the subsection applies only to information provided or obtained pursuant to or by virtue of a licence condition. This leaves some doubt over the position of information produced by apparatus in other circumstances: for example, apparatus maintained by the enforcing authority on other land, or apparatus used by environmental groups. It is submitted that such information would be admissible in evidence, but would not benefit from the presumption contained in subs. (3), as to which see below.

Subs. (3)
Apparatus which produces information falling within subs. (2) is presumed by this subsection to have registered or recorded accurately, unless the contrary is shown, or the licence pursuant to which the information is obtained provides otherwise.

Subs. (4)
Under this subsection, which is similar in effect to s.25(2) of the 1990 Act, where a licence condition requires compliance with other conditions to be recorded, the absence of any such record is admissible as evidence that that condition has not been observed. There is, however, one problem of interpretation raised by the new provision. Under s.25(2) of the 1990 Act it was clear that the condition in question was that in respect of which observance was required to be recorded: in subs. (4) the final reference to "that condition" could be taken to refer either to the condition requiring the entry to be made, or the condition the observance of which is required to be recorded. It is submitted that the second interpretation is correct.

Subs. (5)
The definition of "apparatus" is not exhaustive, and could clearly include automatic samplers.

Offences

Amendment of certain offences relating to false or misleading statements or false entries

112. Schedule 19 to this Act shall have effect.

COMMENCEMENT
April 1, 1996 (S.I. 1996 No. 186).

GENERAL NOTE
Schedule 19 creates various offences relating to false or misleading statements made in the course of applications, or in response to requests for information made by authorities, or false records. The offences are created in relation to the existing legislation referred to in the Schedule, which hitherto have lacked such sanctions or (like s.44 of the 1990 Act) have phrased the offence in different terms. The essentials of the offences are the making of a statement which is known to be false or misleading in a material particular, or recklessly making a statement which is false or misleading in a material particular.

Information

Disclosure of information

113.—(1) Notwithstanding any prohibition or restriction imposed by or under any enactment or rule of law, information of any description may be disclosed—
    (a) by a new Agency to a Minister of the Crown, the other new Agency or a local enforcing authority,
    (b) by a Minister of the Crown to a new Agency, another Minister of the Crown or a local enforcing authority, or
    (c) by a local enforcing authority to a Minister of the Crown, a new Agency or another local enforcing authority,
for the purpose of facilitating the carrying out by either of the new Agencies of any of its functions, by any such Minister of any of his environmental functions or by any local enforcing authority of any of its relevant functions; and no person shall be subject to any civil or criminal liability in consequence of any disclosure made by virtue of this subsection.
    (2) Nothing in this section shall authorise the disclosure to a local enforcing authority by a new Agency or another local enforcing authority of information—
    (a) disclosure of which would, in the opinion of a Minister of the Crown, be contrary to the interests of national security; or
    (b) which was obtained under or by virtue of the Statistics of Trade Act 1947 and which was disclosed to a new Agency or any of its officers by the Secretary of State.
    (3) No information disclosed to any person under or by virtue of this section shall be disclosed by that person to any other person otherwise than in accordance with the provisions of this section, or any provision of any other enactment which authorises or requires the disclosure, if that information is information—
    (a) which relates to a trade secret of any person or which otherwise is or might be commercially confidential in relation to any person; or
    (b) whose disclosure otherwise than under or by virtue of this section would, in the opinion of a Minister of the Crown, be contrary to the interests of national security.
    (4) Any authorisation by or under this section of the disclosure of information by or to any person shall also be taken to authorise the disclosure of that information by or, as the case may be, to any officer of his who is authorised by him to make the disclosure or, as the case may be, to receive the information.
    (5) In this section—
    "new Agency" means the Agency or SEPA;
    "the environment" has the same meaning as in Part I of the Environmental Protection Act 1990;

"environmental functions", in relation to a Minister of the Crown, means any function of that Minister, whether conferred or imposed under or by virtue of any enactment or otherwise, relating to the environment; and

"local enforcing authority" means—

(a) any local authority within the meaning of Part IIA of the Environmental Protection Act 1990, and the "relevant functions" of such an authority are its functions under or by virtue of that Part;

(b) any local authority within the meaning of Part IV of this Act, and the "relevant functions" of such an authority are its functions under or by virtue of that Part;

(c) in relation to England, any county council for an area for which there are district councils, and the "relevant functions" of such a county council are its functions under or by virtue of Part IV of this Act; or

(d) in relation to England and Wales, any local enforcing authority within the meaning of section 1(7) of the Environmental Protection Act 1990, and the "relevant functions" of such an authority are its functions under or by virtue of Part I of that Act.

Definitions

"Agency, the": s.124(1).
"environment, the": subs. (5).
"environmental functions": subs. (5).
"functions": s.124(1).
"local enforcing authority": subs. (5).
"relevant functions": subs. (5).
"SEPA": s.124(1).

Commencement

April 1, 1996 (S.I. 1996 No. 186).

General Note

This section gives a general power of mutual disclosure of information between Ministers, the new Agencies and local authorities for the purpose of facilitating the carrying out of their relevant environmental functions. Immunity against civil or criminal liability is given in respect of such disclosure. The power is potentially important: the Agency in the course of its functions may, for example, obtain information relevant to the identification by a local enforcing authority of contaminated land. Power to disclose information extends to officers of the relevant bodies who are authorised to make the disclosure or to receive the information (subs. (4)). However, restrictions are imposed by subs. (2) in relation to the disclosure of certain information to local enforcing authorities.

Subsection (3) is important as it deals with the treatment of information disclosed under the section. The further disclosure of that information is restricted where the information relates to a trade secret, is commercially confidential in nature, or affects national security. In those cases the information may only be further disclosed in accordance with the provisions of s.113 (*i.e.* under subs. (1)) or in accordance with any other provision which authorises or requires its disclosure. Such provisions will include those relating to the placing of information on public registers and to requests for information under the Environmental Information Regulations 1992 (S.I. 1992 No. 3240). Those provisions themselves contain in-built restrictions on the disclosure of information which is commercially confidential or affects national security.

The power to disclose information contained in subs. (1) is overriding in nature, in that it applies notwithstanding any statutory prohibition or restriction, or any rule of law (for example confidentiality). The general principle is that information obtained pursuant to statutory powers can only be disclosed by the recipient to such persons and for such purposes as are envisaged by the statute conferring those powers: *Marcel v. Commissioner of Police of the Metropolis* [1992] 1 W.L.R. 50; *Hoechst U.K. v. Chemiculture Ltd* [1993] F.S.R. 270. That principle of confidentiality will be overridden in cases to which s.113 applies but, it is submitted, will continue to apply to disclosure outside the scope of the section (subject to any statutory rights of access to information).

Subs. (5): "the environment"

In Pt. I of the 1990 Act, the "environment" is defined as "consist[ing] of all, or any, of the following media, namely, the air, water and land; and the medium of air includes the air within buildings and the air within other natural or man-made structures above or below ground" (s.1(2)). Although subs. (11) of that section of the 1990 Act provides rules for the determination of whether a "release" is a release into land or water, the term "land" is not defined and therefore the definition in Sched. 1 to the Interpretation Act 1978 is applicable: "land" includes buildings and other structures, land covered with water, and any estate, interest, easement, servitude or right in or over land.

Appeals

Power of Secretary of State to delegate his functions of determining, or to refer matters involved in, appeals

114.—(1) The Secretary of State may—

  (a) appoint any person to exercise on his behalf, with or without payment, any function to which this paragraph applies; or

  (b) refer any item to which this paragraph applies to such person as the Secretary of State may appoint for the purpose, with or without payment.

(2) The functions to which paragraph (a) of subsection (1) above applies are any of the Secretary of State's functions of determining—

  (a) an appeal under—

     (i) section 31A(2)(b), 42B(5), 46C or 49B of the Control of Pollution Act 1974,

     (ii) section 4 of the Control of Pollution (Amendment) Act 1989,

     (iii) section 15, 22(5),43, 62(3)(c), 66(5), 78L or 78T of the Environmental Protection Act 1990,

     (iv) paragraph 2 or paragraph 3(3) of Schedule 6 to the Natural Heritage (Scotland) Act 1991,

     (v) section 43, 91, 92, 96, 161C or 191B(5) of the Water Resources Act 1991,

     (vi) section 26 of the Radioactive Substances Act 1993 against any decision of, or notice served by, SEPA,

     (vii) paragraph 6 of Schedule 5 to the Waste Management Licensing Regulations 1994,

  or any matter involved in such an appeal;

  (b) the questions, or any of the questions, which fall to be determined by the Secretary of State under section 39(1) or section 49(4) of the Control of Pollution Act 1974.

(3) The items to which paragraph (b) of subsection (1) above applies are—

  (a) any matter involved in an appeal falling within subsection (2)(a) above;

  (b) any of the questions which fall to be determined by the Secretary of State under section 39(1) or section 49(4) of the Control of Pollution Act 1974.

(4) Schedule 20 to this Act shall have effect with respect to appointments under subsection (1)(a) above.

DEFINITIONS

  "function": s.124(1).

COMMENCEMENT

  April 1, 1996 (S.I. 1996 No. 186).

GENERAL NOTE
This section, together with Sched. 20, provides a general power for the Secretary of State to delegate to any appointed person his appellate functions under the relevant environmental legislation. The appointed person has basically the same powers as the Secretary of State in relation to the appeal (Sched. 20, para. 3). Provision is made for hearings and the holding of local inquiries (para. 4). Either party is entitled as of right to a hearing, but a local inquiry may be held whether or not a party to the appeal requests it. No local inquiry may be held in relation to appeals on commercial confidentiality: or para. 4(3). The appointed person is bound by any direction given to the Agency/SEPA when determining any appeal from a decision of that body: s.40(5).

Crown application

Application of this Act to the Crown

115.—(1) Subject to the provisions of this section, this Act shall bind the Crown.

(2) Part III of this Act and any amendments, repeals and revocations made by other provisions of this Act (other than those made by Schedule 21, which shall bind the Crown) bind the Crown to the extent that the enactments to which they relate bind the Crown.

(3) No contravention by the Crown of any provision made by or under this Act shall make the Crown criminally liable; but the High Court or, in Scotland, the Court of Session may, on the application of the Agency or, in Scotland, SEPA, declare unlawful any act or omission of the Crown which constitutes such a contravention.

(4) Notwithstanding anything in subsection (3) above, any provision made by or under this Act shall apply to persons in the public service of the Crown as it applies to other persons.

(5) If the Secretary of State certifies that it appears to him, as respects any Crown premises and any powers of entry exercisable in relation to them specified in the certificate, that it is requisite or expedient that, in the interests of national security, the powers should not be exercisable in relation, to those premises, those powers shall not be exercisable in relation to those premises; and in this subsection "Crown premises" means premises held or used by or on behalf of the Crown.

(6) Nothing in this section shall be taken as in any way affecting Her Majesty in her private capacity; and this subsection shall be construed as if section 38(3) of the Crown Proceedings Act 1947 (interpretation of references to Her Majesty in her private capacity) were contained in this Act.

DEFINITIONS
"Agency, the": s.124(1).
"Crown premises": subs. (5).
"SEPA": s.124(1).

COMMENCEMENT
April 1, 1996 (S.I.s 1995 No. 2950 and 1996 No. 186).

GENERAL NOTE
The general principle is that the 1995 Act binds the Crown (as is the case with the 1990 Act). The main exceptions are that contravention does not render the Crown criminally liable (though its acts may be declared unlawful), and the certification procedure for exclusion of powers of entry to Crown premises on national security grounds (subss. (3) and (5)). Application for a declaration (or, in Scotland, a declarator) of unlawfulness in relation to contravention by the Crown may only be made by the Agency or SEPA.

Application of certain other enactments to the Crown

116. Schedule 21 to this Act shall have effect.

COMMENCEMENT
The date of commencement is September 21, 1995 in so far as this section gives effect to paras. 2(1)–(3) of Sched. 21 (S.I. 1995 No. 1983). The remainder comes into force on a day to be appointed (s.125(3)).

GENERAL NOTE
Schedule 21 ensures consistency on the issue of Crown application by inserting a provision in the same terms as s.115 into the Water Industry Act 1991, the Water Resources Act 1991 (with various modifications in relation to land drainage), the Sewerage (Scotland) Act 1968, the Control of Pollution Act 1974, the Water (Scotland) Act 1980, and the Local Government etc. (Scotland) Act 1994.

Isles of Scilly

Application of this Act to the Isles of Scilly

117.—(1) Subject to sections 77, 80 and 89 above and the provisions of any order under this section or section 89 above, nothing in this Act shall require or authorise any function, duty or power to be carried out, performed or exercised in relation to the Isles of Scilly by the Agency; and references in the other provisions of this Act (apart from Part III) to England and Wales shall not include references to those Isles.

(2) The Secretary of State may, after consultation with the Council of the Isles of Scilly, by order make provision with respect to the carrying out in those Isles of functions (other than functions under or by virtue of Part III or IV of this Act) falling to be carried out in relation to other parts of England and Wales by the Agency.

(3) Without prejudice to the generality of the power conferred by subsection (2) above, an order under this section may apply any provision of this Act (other than a provision contained in Part III or IV) in relation to the Isles of Scilly with or without modifications.

(4) An order under this section may—
(a) make different provision for different cases, including different provision in relation to different persons, circumstances or localities; and
(b) contain such supplemental, consequential and transitional provision as the Secretary of State considers appropriate, including provision saving provision repealed by or under any enactment.

(5) The power of the Secretary of State to make an order under this section shall be exercisable by statutory instrument; and a statutory instrument containing such an order shall be subject to annulment in pursuance of a resolution of either House of Parliament.

DEFINITIONS
"Agency, the": s.124(1).
"functions": s.124(1).
"modifications": s.124(1).

COMMENCEMENT
February 1, 1996 (S.I. 1996 No. 186).

GENERAL NOTE
This section deals with the application of the Act to the Isles of Scilly. The general principle is that the Act does not extend to the Isles of Scilly (save for the provisions on national parks and air quality, as to which specific provision is made) but that it may be applied, with or without modifications, by order.

Application of certain other enactments to the Isles of Scilly

118.—(1) After section 10 of the Control of Pollution (Amendment) Act 1989 there shall be inserted—

"**Application to the Isles of Scilly**

10A.—(1) Subject to the provisions of any order under this section, this Act shall not apply in relation to the Isles of Scilly.

(2) The Secretary of State may, after consultation with the Council of the Isles of Scilly, by order provide for the application of any provisions of this Act to the Isles of Scilly; and any such order may provide for the

application of those provisions to those Isles with such modifications as may be specified in the order.

(3) An order under this section may—

(a) make different provision for different cases, including different provision in relation to different persons, circumstances or localities; and

(b) contain such supplemental, consequential and transitional provision as the Secretary of State considers appropriate, including provision saving provision repealed by or under any enactment.

(4) The power of the Secretary of State to make an order under this section shall be exercisable by statutory instrument; and a statutory instrument containing such an order shall be subject to annulment in pursuance of a resolution of either House of Parliament."

(2) In section 11 of that Act, subsection (3) (which provides for section 107 of the Control of Pollution Act 1974 to have effect in relation to the application and modification of that Act to the Isles of Scilly) shall cease to have effect.

(3) For section 76 of the Environmental Protection Act 1990 (which provides for Part II of that Act to have effect in its application to the Isles of Scilly with modifications specified by order) there shall be substituted—

"Application to the Isles of Scilly

76.—(1) Subject to the provisions of any order under this section, this Part shall not apply in relation to the Isles of Scilly.

(2) The Secretary of State may, after consultation with the Council of the Isles of Scilly, by order provide for the application of any provisions of this Part to the Isles of Scilly; and any such order may provide for the application of those provisions to those Isles with such modifications as may be specified in the order.

(3) An order under this section may—

(a) make different provision for different cases, including different provision in relation to different persons, circumstances or localities; and

(b) contain such supplemental, consequential and transitional provision as the Secretary of State considers appropriate, including provision saving provision repealed by or under any enactment."

(4) For section 222 of the Water Industry Act 1991 (application to Isles of Scilly) there shall be substituted—

"Application to the Isles of Scilly

222.—(1) Subject to the provisions of any order under this section, this Act shall not apply in relation to the Isles of Scilly.

(2) The Secretary of State may, after consultation with the Council of the Isles of Scilly, by order provide for the application of any provisions of this Act to the Isles of Scilly; and any such order may provide for the application of those provisions to those Isles with such modifications as may be specified in the order.

(3) An order under this section may—

(a) make different provision for different cases, including different provision in relation to different persons, circumstances or localities; and

(b) contain such supplemental, consequential and transitional provision as the Secretary of State considers appropriate, including provision saving provision repealed by or under any enactment.

(4) The power of the Secretary of State to make an order under this section shall be exercisable by statutory instrument subject to annulment in pursuance of a resolution of either House of Parliament."

(5) For section 224 of the Water Resources Act 1991 (application to Isles of Scilly) there shall be substituted—

"**Application to the Isles of Scilly**

224.—(1) Subject to the provisions of any order under this section, this Act shall not apply in relation to the Isles of Scilly.

(2) The Secretary of State may, after consultation with the Council of the Isles of Scilly, by order provide for the application of any provisions of this Act to the Isles of Scilly; and any such order may provide for the application of those provisions to those Isles with such modifications as may be specified in the order.

(3) An order under this section may—

(a) make different provision for different cases, including different provision in relation to different persons, circumstances or localities; and

(b) contain such supplemental, consequential and transitional provision as the Secretary of State considers appropriate, including provision saving provision repealed by or under any enactment.

(4) The power of the Secretary of State to make an order under this section shall be exercisable by statutory instrument subject to annulment in pursuance of a resolution of either House of Parliament."

(6) For section 75 of the Land Drainage Act 1991 (application to the Isles of Scilly) there shall be substituted—

"**Application to the Isles of Scilly**

75.—(1) Subject to the provisions of any order under this section, this Act shall not apply in relation to the Isles of Scilly.

(2) The Secretary of State may, after consultation with the Council of the Isles of Scilly, by order provide for the application of any provisions of this Act to the Isles of Scilly; and any such order may provide for the application of those provisions to those Isles with such modifications as may be specified in the order.

(3) An order under this section may—

(a) make different provision for different cases, including different provision in relation to different persons, circumstances or localities; and

(b) contain such supplemental, consequential and transitional provision as the Secretary of State considers appropriate, including provision saving provision repealed by or under any enactment.

(4) The power of the Secretary of State to make an order under this section shall be exercisable by statutory instrument subject to annulment in pursuance of a resolution of either House of Parliament."

COMMENCEMENT

Subss. (1)–(3) and (6), and (insofar as they confer power to make an order or make provision in relation to the exercise of that power) subss. (4) and (5), came into force on February 1, 1996 (S.I. 1996 No. 186); the remainder comes into force on a day to be appointed (s.125(3)).

GENERAL NOTE

Similar provision as is made in s.117 on the application of this Act to the Isles of Scilly is made in relation to the other Acts referred to in this section.

Miscellaneous and supplemental

Stamp duty

119.—(1) No transfer effected by Part I of this Act shall give rise to any liability to stamp duty.

(2) Stamp duty shall not be chargeable—

(a) on any transfer scheme; or

(b) on any instrument or agreement which is certified to the Commissioners of Inland Revenue by the Secretary of State as made in pursuance of a transfer scheme.

(3) No transfer scheme, and no instrument which is certified as mentioned in subsection (2)(b) above, shall be taken to be duly stamped unless—

(a) it has, in accordance with section 12 of the Stamp Act 1891, been stamped with a particular stamp denoting that it is not chargeable with that duty or that it is duly stamped; or

(b) it is stamped with the duty to which it would be liable, apart from this section.

(4) In this section "transfer scheme" means a scheme made or approved by the Secretary of State under section 3 or 22 above for the transfer of property, rights or liabilities to the Agency or to SEPA.

DEFINITIONS
"Agency, the": s.124(1).
"SEPA": s.124(1).
"transfer scheme": subs. (4).

COMMENCEMENT
February 1, 1996 (S.I. 1996 No. 186).

Minor and consequential amendments, transitional and transitory provisions, savings and repeals

120.—(1) The enactments mentioned in Schedule 22 to this Act shall have effect with the amendments there specified (being minor amendments and amendments consequential on provisions of this Act); and, without prejudice to any power conferred by any other provision of this Act, the Secretary of State and the Minister shall each have power by regulations to make such additional consequential amendments—

(a) of public general enactments passed before, or in the same Session as, this Act, and

(b) of subordinate legislation made before the passing of this Act,

as he considers necessary or expedient by reason of the coming into force of any provision of this Act.

(2) The transitional provisions, transitory provisions and savings contained in Schedule 23 to this Act shall have effect; but those provisions are without prejudice to sections 16 and 17 of the Interpretation Act 1978 (effect of repeals).

(3) The enactments mentioned in Schedule 24 to this Act (which include some that are spent or no longer of practical utility) are hereby repealed to the extent specified in the third column of that Schedule.

(4) The power to make regulations under subsection (1) above shall be exercisable by statutory instrument; and a statutory instrument containing any such regulations shall be subject to annulment in pursuance of a resolution of either House of Parliament.

(5) The power to make regulations under subsection (1) above includes power to make such incidental, supplemental, consequential and transitional provision as the Secretary of State or the Minister thinks necessary or expedient.

(6) In this section—

"the Minister" means the Minister of Agriculture, Fisheries and Food;

"subordinate legislation" has the same meaning as in the Interpretation Act 1978.

DEFINITIONS
"Minister, the": subs. (6).
"subordinate legislation": subs. (6).

COMMENCEMENT
Subsection (1) has been brought into force partially, to give effect to parts of Sched. 22 on July 28, 1995 and September 21, 1995 (S.I. 1995 No. 1983); October 12, 1995 (S.I. 1995 No. 2649); February 1, 1996 and April 1, 1996 (S.I. 1996 No. 183). Subs. (2) has been brought into force

partially, to give effect to parts of Sched. 23, on January 1, 1999 (S.I. 1995 No. 1983) and April 1, 1996 (S.I. 1996 No. 186). Subs (3) has been brought into force partially, to give effect to parts of Sched. 24, on September 21, 1995 and January 1, 1999 (S.I. 1995 No. 1983), November 1, 1995 (S.I. 1995 No. 2765), February 1 and April 1, 1996 (S.I. 1996 No. 186). Subsections (4)–(6) came into force on July 28, 1995 (S.I. 1995 No. 1983).

Section 125(3) makes separate provision for the commencement on July 19, 1995 of part of Sched. 22.

GENERAL NOTE

This section deals with amendments, transitional provisions and savings (in respect of which s.125(3) should be noted) and repeals. Whilst the amendments in Sched. 22 are referred to as minor and consequential, this is by no means the case with all of them: some effect significant substantive changes to existing law.

Subs. (6): "subordinate legislation"

The Interpretation Act 1978, s.21(1), defines subordinate legislation as "Orders in Council, orders, rules, regulations, schemes, warrants, byelaws and other instruments made or to be made under any Act".

Sched. 22—amendments

Many of the amendments in the Schedule are consequential, for example those inserting references to the Agency or SEPA, in place of those to the existing enforcement agencies. Some however are worthy of note:

Para. 29(15): appeals against revocation or modification notices (Scotland). A new s.39(5A)–(5C) is added to the Control of Pollution Act 1974 providing that where there is an appeal under s.39(1)(b) against such a notice on the grounds that it is unreasonable, the notice shall not take effect while the reference is pending unless this is necessary in SEPA's opinion for the purposes set out in s.39(5B). Where SEPA is of the opinion that the notice must take effect while the reference is pending, the consent holder or former consent holder may challenge the reasonableness of such a decision by application to the Secretary of State (s.39(5C)). If the Secretary of State determines that SEPA acted unreasonably the notice will not take effect until the original reference is finally determined and the applicant will also be entitled to recover compensation from SEPA for any loss suffered as a result of the notice taking effect while the original reference was still pending.

Paras. 29(22) and 162: works notices in respect of anti-pollution operations. New provisions are inserted into the Control of Pollution Act 1974 and the Water Resources Act 1991 (ss.46A–D and 161A–D respectively). These allow SEPA/the Agency, where it appears that poisonous, noxious or polluting matter or solid waste matter is likely to enter controlled waters, or to be or to have been present in such waters, to serve a "works notice" on any person who caused or knowingly permitted the matter to be present in controlled waters, or to be present at a place from which it is likely to enter such waters. The notice may require that person to carry out preventive, remedial or restorative works within specified periods. Provision is made for appeals against notices, for the granting of rights of entry necessary to comply with such notices, and offences and other remedies in relation to non-compliance. The new procedure provides a more effective remedy than existing law (s.46 of the 1974 Act and s.161 of the 1991 Act) under which the relevant authority could take clean-up action itself and then recover its reasonable costs from the polluter. Those powers are now only exercisable where it is considered necessary to act forthwith, or where after reasonable inquiry no person has been found on whom a works notice would be served (paras. 29(21)(b) and 161(3)).

Paras. 29(26) and 142: enforcement notices on discharge consents. New provisions (ss.49A and B of the Control of Pollution Act 1974 and 90B of the Water Resources Act 1991) create a new remedy in relation to breach or likely breach of consents for discharge to controlled waters. Instead of simply prosecuting for contravention of the consent conditions, the Agency/SEPA may serve a notice specifying the steps to be taken to remedy the contravention or to remedy the matters making it likely that the contravention will occur. Failure to comply with any requirement imposed by the notice is an offence, and provision is made for appeals against notices. Again, this will no doubt be a welcome power to regulators, particularly in a case where there is regular non-compliance with conditions and prosecution may not necessarily result in the necessary expenditure being made to achieve compliance.

Para. 36: road traffic regulation powers and air quality. The Road Traffic Regulation Act 1984 is amended to make it clear (if indeed it was previously in doubt) that traffic regulation orders may be made for purposes relating to air quality.

Para. 51: variation notices under Pt. I of the 1990 Act. Provision is made for an enforcing authority which has issued a notice varying the conditions of an authorisation to serve a further notice varying the variation notice (new s.10(3A)). Previously the only course would be to withdraw the first variation notice and issue a new one.

Para. 67: compensation for rights granted pursuant to waste management licence. Section 35(4) of the 1990 Act provided for the grant to the holder of a waste management licence by third parties of rights necessary in order to comply with licence conditions. The new s.35A (inserted by para. 67) confers a statutory right of compensation on such third parties.

Para. 68: waste licence applications. Express provision is made for a waste regulation authority refusing to proceed with the licence application because of the failure of the applicant to provide information reasonably required by the authority.

Para. 69: consultation before grant of waste licences. Where a waste regulation authority proposes to impose conditions under s.35(4) of the 1990 Act which would require a third party to concur in granting rights (see para. 67 above), the authority is required by new s.36A to follow a consultation procedure with the owner and occupier of affected land, and to consider representations made by them. A similar consultation procedure is applied to the variation of licence conditions (s.37A as inserted by para. 71) and to the requirements imposed where a licence is suspended (s.38(9B) as inserted by para. 72).

Para. 72: rights granted pursuant to requirements imposed on suspension of waste licence. Where a waste licence is suspended, the waste regulation authority may impose requirements pursuant to s.38(9) of the 1990 Act (subject now to the consultation procedure introduced by this paragraph: see the note to para. 69 above). As regards third parties, the new s.39(9A) inserted by para. 72 brings the position regarding such requirements into line with that regarding licence conditions (s.35(4) of the 1990 Act): any third party consent needed for such requirements to be complied with shall be granted. The new s.35A (inserted by para. 67) confers a statutory right of compensation on such third parties.

Para. 76: notice requiring compliance with waste licence conditions. Section 42 of the 1990 Act provides for the revocation or suspension of a waste licence where the holder has been required to, and has failed to, remedy non-compliance with a licence condition. Paragraph 76 amends s.42(5) so that *likely* (as opposed to actual) non-compliance may be the subject of such a requirement. Also, requirements must now take the form of a notice which, rather than merely requiring compliance, specifies the matters constituting the non-compliance and the steps to be taken.

Para. 78: waste disposal plans. Section 50 of the 1990 Act, dealing with waste disposal plans of waste regulation authorities, ceases to have effect.

Para. 79: closed landfills. Section 61 of the 1990 Act, dealing with closed landfills, ceases to have effect (never having been implemented). The provision is of course replaced by the new powers and duties relating to contaminated land introduced by Pt. II of this Act.

Paras. 88 and 95: definition of waste. Section 75 of the 1990 Act is replaced by a new definition of waste, following the definition of the EC waste framework directive 75/442/EEC as amended by 91/156/EEC: see the new Sched. 2B which is inserted into the 1990 Act for that purpose. The changes insert into primary legislation the definition contained in the Waste Management Licensing Regulations 1994. The presumption contained in s.75(3) of the 1990 Act (that anything discarded is waste unless the contrary is proved) is revoked.

Para. 91: section 143 registers. This provision, on registers of land which may be subject to contamination, ceases to have effect (never having been implemented). See, generally, the General Notes to Pt. II of this Act.

Para. 102: promotion of the efficient use of water (England and Wales). A new s.93A is inserted into the Water Industry Act 1991, imposing a duty on each water undertaker to promote the efficient use of water by its customers. The Director General of Water Services is given power to impose requirements on water undertakers in pursuance of that duty (s.93B). However, neither the duty nor any such requirements may authorise or require the imposition of any requirement on customers of the undertaker (ss.93A(3) and 93(B)(6)).

Para. 103: provision of public sewers (England and Wales). An alternative to the procedure for requisitioning public sewers is provided by the new s.101A of the Water Industry Act 1991. Water undertakers are placed under a duty to provide public sewers to serve domestic premises in certain circumstances, in particular where the lack of drainage by sewer is giving rise, or is likely to give rise, to such adverse effects on the environment or on amenity that provision is appropriate. The matters to be considered in making that decision include the number of dwellings involved, the cost of provision, and the geology of the locality.

Paras. 105–113: special category effluent (England and Wales). Some changes are made to the provisions in the Water Industry Act dealing with special category effluent. Failure by a sewerage undertaker to refer applications or agreements involving special category effluent to the Agency is made an offence (ss.120(9) and 130(7)). New powers are given to the Agency to require information for the purpose of its functions in relation to special category effluent (s.135A).

Para. 140: drought permits (England and Wales). A new section of the Water Resources Act 1991 (s.79A) provides a means whereby, in cases of serious water shortage caused by exceptional lack of rain, the Agency may issue drought permits authorising water undertakers to take water from any source specified in the permit for a limited period.

Para. 183: discharge consents (England and Wales). A new Sched. 10 is substituted in the Water Resources Act 1991 dealing with the procedure for applications for discharge consent.

An unresolved issue: the exclusivity or inclusivity of discharge consents. One matter raised but not resolved during the passage of the Act was the construction of discharge consents under the Water Resources Act 1991 (and, by implication, under the Control of Pollution Act 1974 in Scotland) and in particular whether the consent provides a defence in relation to substances not mentioned (either by way of permission or prohibition) in the consent. The legal position on this issue was thrown into doubt by the House of Lords decision in *NRA v. Yorkshire Water Services* [1995] 1 All E.R. 225 and by legal opinions obtained by the NRA. The undesirable nature of the uncertainty was referred to by the Chairman of the NRA, Lord Crickhowell, in debate (see *Hansard*, H.L. Vol. 561, col. 680). Various options for amendment of the Water Resources Act were put forward to make it clear that a consent should not be taken as authorising the discharge of substances (or at least poisonous, noxious or polluting substances) other than those referred to specifically (see for example, *Hansard*, H.L. Vol. 561, col. 680). The Government rejected such amendments on the basis that retrospective legislation was not the right way of dealing with technical problems affecting large numbers of consents (possibly the vast majority of the 110,000 estimated extant consents) granted over many years in various forms (*Hansard*, H.L. Vol. 561, cols. 681–683). On this issue see D. McGillivray, *Discharge Consents and the Unforeseen* [1995] Water Law 101.

Para. 193: spray irrigation (England and Wales). Power is given, by a new s.61F of the Water Resources Act 1991, for internal drainage boards and local authorities to operate drainage works under their control so as to manage the level of water in a watercourse for the purpose of facilitating spray irrigation.

Sched. 23—Transitional Provisions and Savings. This Schedule contains various transitional and saving provisions, ensuring the continuance in effect of any directions given to the NRA under s.15 of the Water Resources Act 1991, any statutory charging scheme, and similar matters.

Local statutory provisions: consequential amendments etc.

121.—(1) If it appears to the Secretary of State or the Minister to be appropriate to do so—

(a) for the purposes of, or in consequence of, the coming into force of any enactment contained in this Act; or

(b) in consequence of the effect or operation at any time after the transfer date of any such enactment or of anything done under any such enactment,

he may by order repeal, amend or re-enact (with or without modifications) any local statutory provision, including, in the case of an order by virtue of paragraph (b) above, a provision amended by virtue of paragraph (a) above.

(2) An order made by the Secretary of State or the Minister under subsection (1) above may—

(a) make provision applying generally in relation to local statutory provisions of a description specified in the order;

(b) make different provision for different cases, including different provision in relation to different persons, circumstances or localities;

　　(c) contain such supplemental, consequential and transitional provision as the Secretary of State or, as the case may be, the Minister considers appropriate; and

　　(d) in the case of an order made after the transfer date, require provision contained in the order to be treated as if it came into force on that date.

(3) The power under this section to repeal or amend a local statutory provision shall include power to modify the effect in relation to any local statutory provision of any provision of Schedule 23 to this Act.

(4) Nothing in any order under this section may abrogate or curtail the effect of so much of any local statutory provision as confers any right of way or confers on or preserves for the public—

　　(a) any right of enjoyment of air, exercise or recreation on land; or

　　(b) any right of access to land for the purposes of exercise or recreation.

(5) The power to make an order under subsection (1) above shall be exercisable by statutory instrument subject to annulment in pursuance of a resolution of either House of Parliament.

(6) The power to make an order under subsection (1) above shall be without prejudice to any power conferred by any other provision of this Act.

(7) In this section—

　　"local statutory provision" means—

　　　　(a) a provision of a local Act (including an Act confirming a provisional order);

　　　　(b) a provision of so much of any public general Act as has effect with respect to a particular area, with respect to particular persons or works or with respect to particular provisions falling within any paragraph of this definition;

　　　　(c) a provision of an instrument made under any provision falling within paragraph (a) or (b) above; or

　　　　(d) a provision of any other instrument which is in the nature of a local enactment;

　　"the Minister" means the Minister of Agriculture, Fisheries and Food;

　　"the transfer date" has the same meaning as in Part I of this Act.

DEFINITIONS
"local statutory provision": subs. (7).
"Minister, the": subs. (7).
"modifications": s.124(1).
"the transfer date": s.56(1).

COMMENCEMENT
This section came into force on July 28, 1995 (S.I. 1995 No. 1983).

GENERAL NOTE
This section creates a wide power for the Secretary of State to repeal, amend or re-enact any local statutes. The power is constrained by subs. (4) in that such changes may not restrict or curtail the rights of access, recreation and enjoyment referred to there.

Directions

122.—(1) Any direction given under this Act shall be in writing.

(2) Any power conferred by this Act to give a direction shall include power to vary or revoke the direction.

(3) Subsections (4) and (5) below apply to any direction given—

　　(a) to the Agency or SEPA under any provision of this Act or any other enactment, or

　　(b) to any other body or person under any provision of this Act,

being a direction to any extent so given for the purpose of implementing any obligations of the United Kingdom under the Community Treaties.

(4) A direction to which this subsection applies shall not be varied or revoked unless, notwithstanding the variation or revocation, the obligations

mentioned in subsection (3) above, as they have effect for the time being, continue to be implemented, whether by directions or any other instrument or by any enactment.

(5) Any variation or revocation of a direction to which this subsection applies shall be published in such manner as the Minister giving it considers appropriate for the purpose of bringing the matters to which it relates to the attention of persons likely to be affected by them; and—

(a) copies of the variation or revocation shall be made available to the public; and

(b) notice of the variation or revocation, and of where a copy of the variation or revocation may be obtained, shall be given—

(i) if the direction has effect in England and Wales, in the London Gazette;

(ii) if the direction has effect in Scotland, in the Edinburgh Gazette.

DEFINITIONS
    "Agency, the": s.124(1).
    "notice": s.124(1).
    "SEPA": s.124(1).

COMMENCEMENT
    This section came into force on July 28, 1995 (S.I. 1995 No. 1983).

GENERAL NOTE
    This section makes provision as to the various directions which may be given under the Act. All directions must be in writing. Restrictions apply to the variation or revocation of any direction which is given for the purpose of implementing obligations of the U.K. under EC law.

Service of documents

123.—(1) Without prejudice to paragraph 17(2)(d) of Schedule 7 to this Act, any notice required or authorised by or under this Act to be served (whether the expression "serve" or the expression "give" or "send" or any other expression is used) on any person may be served by delivering it to him, or by leaving it at his proper address, or by sending it by post to him at that address.

(2) Any such notice may—

(a) in the case of a body corporate, be served on the secretary or clerk of that body;

(b) in the case of a partnership, be served on a partner or a person having the control or management of the partnership business.

(3) For the purposes of this section and of section 7 of the Interpretation Act 1978 (service of documents by post) in its application to this section, the proper address of any person on whom any such notice is to be served shall be his last known address, except that—

(a) in the case of a body corporate or their secretary or clerk, it shall be the address of the registered or principal office of that body;

(b) in the case of a partnership or person having the control or the management of the partnership business, it shall be the principal office of the partnership;

and for the purposes of this subsection the principal office of a company registered outside the United Kingdom or of a partnership carrying on business outside the United Kingdom shall be their principal office within the United Kingdom.

(4) If the person to be served with any such notice has specified an address in the United Kingdom other than his proper address within the meaning of subsection (3) above as the one at which he or someone on his behalf will accept notices of the same description as that notice, that address shall also be treated for the purposes of this section and section 7 of the Interpretation Act 1978 as his proper address.

(5) Where under any provision of this Act any notice is required to be served on a person who is, or appears to be, in occupation of any premises then—

(a) if the name or address of such a person cannot after reasonable inquiry be ascertained, or

(b) if the premises appear to be or are unoccupied,

that notice may be served either by leaving it in the hands of a person who is or appears to be resident or employed on the premises or by leaving it conspicuously affixed to some building or object on the premises.

(6) This section shall not apply to any notice in relation to the service of which provision is made by rules of court.

(7) The preceding provisions of this section shall apply to the service of a document as they apply to the service of a notice.

(8) In this section—

"premises" includes any land, vehicle, vessel or mobile plant;

"serve" shall be construed in accordance with subsection (1) above.

DEFINITIONS

"Agency, the": s.124(1).
"notice": s.124(1).
"premises": subs. (8).
"SEPA": s.124(1).
"serve": subs. (8).

COMMENCEMENT

This section came into force on July 28, 1995 (S.I. 1995 No. 1983).

GENERAL NOTE

This section makes provision as to the service of notices under the Act. Paragraph 17(2)(d) of Sched. 7, which is referred to in subs. (1), relates only to National Park authorities, and applies ss.231–234 of the Local Government Act 1972 (service and authentication of documents). The provisions of s.123 apply to documents as well as notices (see subs. (7)).

Subss. (3)–(6): address for service

Detailed provision is made in subss. (3)–(5) as to the proper address for service of notices and other documents under the Act. It will be noted, however, that any rules of court relating to the service of such notices take precedence over subs. (3)–(5). So, for example, insofar as s.37(1)(a) authorises the Agency to take civil proceedings in the High Court, then the Rules of the Supreme Court and case law on the address for service and on proof of service under those rules will apply (for example *Berry v. Farrow* [1914] 1 K.B. 632: "address" includes both domestic and business address; *A/S Catherineholm v. Norequipment Trading Ltd* [1972] 2 Q.B. 314: proof of service by post; *Cooper v. Scott-Farnell* [1969] 1 All E.R. 178 (C.A.): defendant's temporary absence does not affect validity of service). Similar considerations apply in relation to Scotland.

The "principal" office of a body corporate or partnership (subs. (3)(a) and (b)) is where its general superintendence and management is carried out: *Davies v. British Geon* [1956] 3 All E.R. 389 (C.A.).

General interpretation

124.—(1) In this Act, except in so far as the context otherwise requires—

"the Agency" means the Environment Agency;

"financial year" means a period of twelve months ending with 31st March;

"functions" includes powers and duties;

"modifications" includes additions, alterations and omissions and cognate expressions shall be construed accordingly;

"notice" means notice in writing;

"records", without prejudice to the generality of the expression, includes computer records and any other records kept otherwise than in a document;

"SEPA" means the Scottish Environment Protection Agency.

(2) The amendment by this Act of any provision contained in subordinate legislation shall not be taken to have prejudiced any power to make further subordinate legislation amending or revoking that provision.

(3) In subsection (2) above, "subordinate legislation" has the same meaning as in the Interpretation Act 1978.

COMMENCEMENT
This section came into force on July 28, 1995 (S.I. 1995 No. 1983).

Short title, commencement, extent, etc.

125.—(1) This Act may be cited as the Environment Act 1995.

(2) Part III of this Act, except for section 78, paragraph 7(2) of Schedule 7 and Schedule 10, shall come into force at the end of the period of two months beginning with the day on which this Act is passed.

(3) Except as provided in subsection (2) above and except for this section, section 74 above and paragraphs 76(8)(a) and 135 of Schedule 22 to this Act (which come into force on the passing of this Act) and the repeal of sub-paragraph (1) of paragraph 22 of Schedule 10 to this Act (which comes into force in accordance with sub-paragraph (7) of that paragraph) this Act shall come into force on such day as the Secretary of State may specify by order made by statutory instrument; and different days may be so specified for different provisions or for different purposes of the same provision.

(4) Without prejudice to the provisions of Schedule 23 to this Act, an order under subsection (3) above may make such transitional provisions and savings as appear to the Secretary of State necessary or expedient in connection with any provision brought into force by the order.

(5) The power conferred by subsection (4) above includes power to modify any enactment contained in this or any other Act.

(6) An Order in Council under paragraph 1(1)(b) of Schedule 1 to the Northern Ireland Act 1974 (legislation for Northern Ireland in the interim period) which states that it is made only for purposes corresponding to those of section 98 of this Act—

(a) shall not be subject to paragraph 1(4) and (5) of that Schedule (affirmative resolution of both Houses of Parliament); but

(b) shall be subject to annulment in pursuance of a resolution of either House of Parliament.

(7) Except for this section and any amendment or repeal by this Act of any provision contained in—

(a) the Parliamentary Commissioner Act 1967,

(b) the Sea Fish (Conservation) Act 1967,

(c) the House of Commons Disqualification Act 1975, or

(d) the Northern Ireland Assembly Disqualification Act 1975,

this Act shall not extend to Northern Ireland.

(8) Part III of this Act, and Schedule 24 to this Act so far as relating to that Part, extends to England and Wales only.

(9) Section 106 of, and Schedule 16 to, this Act extend to Scotland only.

(10) Subject to the foregoing provisions of this section and to any express provision made by this Act to the contrary, any amendment, repeal or revocation made by this Act shall have the same extent as the enactment or instrument to which it relates.

GENERAL NOTE
With a few specified exceptions, the Act's provisions come into force on such date as the Secretary of State may specify by statutory instrument. To date there have been two such instruments: (S.I. 1995 No. 1983) and, affecting only Scotland, (S.I. 1995 No. 2649 (S.199)). See the General Note and Introduction to the Act for a table of sections in force.

The provisions on national parks (Pt. III) in general come into force two months from the passage of the Act (subs. (2)). A handful of provisions came into force immediately (subs. (3)).

Territorial extent
The Act does not (save in the cases specified) extend to Northern Ireland (see subs. (7)). The provisions on national parks (Pt. III) do not extend to Scotland (subs. (8)). Section 106 and Sched. 16 (which amend the law on water pollution in Scotland) extend to Scotland only. Further provision as to territorial extent is made by individual sections of the Act.

SCHEDULES

Section 1 SCHEDULE 1

THE ENVIRONMENT AGENCY

Membership

1.—(1) Subject to the following provisions of this paragraph, a member shall hold and vacate office in accordance with the terms of his appointment and shall, on ceasing to be a member, be eligible for re-appointment.

(2) A member may at any time resign his office by giving notice to the appropriate Minister.

(3) The appropriate Minister may remove a member from that office if he is satisfied—

(a) that the member has been absent from meetings of the Agency for a period of more than three months without the permission of the Agency;

(b) that the member has been adjudged bankrupt, that his estate has been sequestrated or that he has made a composition or arrangement with or granted a trust deed for, his creditors; or

(c) that the member is unable or unfit to carry out the functions of a member.

Chairman and deputy chairman

2. The chairman or deputy chairman of the Agency shall hold office as such unless and until—

(a) he resigns that office by giving notice to the Secretary of State, or

(b) he ceases to be a member,

and shall, on ceasing to be the chairman or deputy chairman, be eligible for further designation as such in accordance with section 1(3) of this Act at any time when he is a member.

Remuneration, pensions, etc.

3.—(1) The Agency shall pay to its members such remuneration, and such travelling and other allowances, as may be determined by the appropriate Minister.

(2) The Agency shall, if so required by the appropriate Minister,—

(a) pay such pension, allowances or gratuities as may be determined by that Minister to or in respect of a person who is or has been a member;

(b) make such payments as may be determined by that Minister towards provision for the payment of a pension, allowances or gratuities to or in respect of a person who is or has been a member; or

(c) provide and maintain such schemes (whether contributory or not) as may be determined by that Minister for the payment of pensions, allowances or gratuities to or in respect of persons who are or have been members.

(3) If, when any member ceases to hold office, the appropriate Minister determines that there are special circumstances which make it right that that member should receive compensation, the Agency shall pay to him a sum by way of compensation of such amount as may be so determined.

Staff

4.—(1) The Agency may appoint such officers and employees as it may determine.

(2) No member or other person shall be appointed by the Agency to act as chief executive of the Agency unless the Secretary of State has consented to the appointment of that person.

(3) The Agency may—

(a) pay such pensions, allowances or gratuities to or in respect of any persons who are or have been its officers or employees as it may, with the approval of the Secretary of State, determine;

(b) make such payments as it may so determine towards provision for the payment of pensions, allowances or gratuities to or in respect of any such persons;

(c) provide and maintain such schemes as it may so determine (whether contributory or not) for the payment of pensions, allowances or gratuities to or in respect of any such persons.

(4) Any reference in sub-paragraph (3) above to pensions, allowances or gratuities to or in respect of any such persons as are mentioned in that sub-paragraph includes a reference to pensions, allowances or gratuities by way of compensation to or in respect of any of the Agency's officers or employees who suffer loss of office or employment or loss or diminution of emoluments.

Proceedings of the Agency

5. Subject to the following provisions of this Schedule and to section 106 of the 1991 Act (obligation to carry out flood defence functions through committees), the Agency may regulate its own procedure (including quorum).

Delegation of powers

6. Subject to section 106 of the 1991 Act, anything authorised or required by or under any enactment to be done by the Agency may be done—

(a) by any member, officer or employee of the Agency who has been authorised for the purpose, whether generally or specially, by the Agency; or

(b) by any committee or sub-committee of the Agency which has been so authorised.

Members' interests

7.—(1) A member who is in any way directly or indirectly interested in any matter that is brought up for consideration at a meeting of the Agency shall disclose the nature of his interest to the meeting; and, where such a disclosure is made—

(a) the disclosure shall be recorded in the minutes of the meeting; and

(b) the member shall not take any part in any deliberation or decision of the Agency, or of any of its committees or sub-committees, with respect to that matter.

(2) For the purposes of sub-paragraph (1) above, a general notification given at a meeting of the Agency by a member to the effect that he—

(a) is a member of a specified company or firm, and

(b) is to be regarded as interested in any matter involving that company or firm,

shall be regarded as a sufficient disclosure of his interest in relation to any such matter.

(3) A member need not attend in person at a meeting of the Agency in order to make a disclosure which he is required to make under this paragraph if he takes reasonable steps to secure that the disclosure is made by a notice which is read and considered at the meeting.

(4) The Secretary of State may, subject to such conditions as he considers appropriate, remove any disability imposed by virtue of this paragraph in any case where the number of members of the Agency disabled by virtue of this paragraph at any one time would be so great a proportion of the whole as to impede the transaction of business.

(5) The power of the Secretary of State under sub-paragraph (4) above includes power to remove, either indefinitely or for any period, a disability which would otherwise attach to any member, or members of any description, by reason of such interests, and in respect of such matters, as may be specified or described by the Secretary of State.

(6) Nothing in this paragraph precludes any member from taking part in the consideration or discussion of, or voting on, any question whether an application should be made to the Secretary of State for the exercise of the power conferred by sub-paragraph (4) above.

(7) Any reference in this paragraph to a meeting of the Agency includes a reference to a meeting of any committee or sub-committee of the Agency.

Vacancies and defective appointments

8. The validity of any proceedings of the Agency shall not be affected by a vacancy amongst the members or by a defect in the appointment of a member.

Minutes

9.—(1) Minutes shall be kept of proceedings of the Agency, of its committees and of its sub-committees.

(2) Minutes of any such proceedings shall be evidence of those proceedings if they are signed by a person purporting to have acted as chairman of the proceedings to which the minutes relate

or of any subsequent proceedings in the course of which the minutes were approved as a correct record.

(3) Where minutes of any such proceedings have been signed as mentioned in sub-paragraph (2) above, those proceedings shall, unless the contrary is shown, be deemed to have been validly convened and constituted.

Application of seal and proof of instruments

10.—(1) The application of the seal of the Agency shall be authenticated by the signature of any member, officer or employee of the Agency who has been authorised for the purpose, whether generally or specially, by the Agency.

(2) In this paragraph the reference to the signature of a person includes a reference to a facsimile of a signature by whatever process reproduced; and, in paragraph 11 below, the word "signed" shall be construed accordingly.

Documents served etc. by or on the Agency

11.—(1) Any document which the Agency is authorised or required by or under any enactment to serve, make or issue may be signed on behalf of the Agency by any member, officer or employee of the Agency who has been authorised for the purpose, whether generally or specially, by the Agency.

(2) Every document purporting to be an instrument made or issued by or on behalf of the Agency and to be duly executed under the seal of the Agency, or to be signed or executed by a person authorised by the Agency for the purpose, shall be received in evidence and be treated, without further proof, as being so made or issued unless the contrary is shown.

(3) Any notice which is required or authorised, by or under any provision of any other Act, to be given, served or issued by, to or on the Agency shall be in writing.

Interpretation

12. In this Schedule—

"the appropriate Minister", in relation to any person who is or has been a member, means the Minister or the Secretary of State, according to whether that person was appointed as a member by the Minister or by the Secretary of State; and

"member", except where the context otherwise requires, means any member of the Agency (including the chairman and deputy chairman).

Sections 3 and 22   SCHEDULE 2

TRANSFERS OF PROPERTY ETC: SUPPLEMENTAL PROVISIONS

PART I

INTRODUCTORY

Interpretation

1. In this Schedule—

"the chief inspector"—

(a) in the application of this Schedule in relation to transfers by or under section 3 of this Act, means any of the inspectors or chief inspectors mentioned in section 2(1) of this Act;

(b) in the application of this Schedule in relation to transfers by or under section 22 of this Act, means any of the inspectors or chief inspectors mentioned in section 21(1) of this Act;

and any reference to the chief inspector for England and Wales or the chief inspector for Scotland shall be construed accordingly;

"the relevant new Agency" means—

(a) in the application of this Schedule in relation to transfers by or under section 3 of this Act, the Agency; and

(b) in the application of this Schedule in relation to transfers by or under section 22 of this Act, SEPA;

"transfer scheme" means a scheme under section 3 or 22 of this Act;

"the transferor", in relation to transfers by or under section 3 of this Act, means—

(a) in the case of any transfer by section 3(1)(a) of this Act, the National Rivers Authority or the London Waste Regulation Authority, as the case may be; or

(b) in the case of any transfer scheme, or any transfer by transfer scheme—
    (i) the Secretary of State,
    (ii) the chief inspector, or
    (iii) any waste regulation authority,
(as the case may be) from whom any property, rights or liabilities are, or are to be, transferred by that scheme;

"the transferor", in relation to transfers by or under section 22 of this Act, means—
    (a) in the case of any transfer by section 22(1)(a) of this Act, the river purification board in question; or
    (b) in the case of any transfer scheme, or any transfer by transfer scheme—
        (i) the Secretary of State;
        (ii) the chief inspector; or
        (iii) any local authority,
(as the case may be) from whom any property, rights or liabilities are or are to be, transferred by that scheme; and, as respects any such local authority which is a district or islands council, includes, in relation to any time on or after 1st April 1996, the council for any local government area named in column 1 of Schedule 1 to the Local Government etc. (Scotland) Act 1994 which is wholly or partly conterminous with the area of that council.

The property etc. which may be transferred

2.—(1) The property, rights and liabilities which are transferred by, or may be transferred by transfer scheme under, section 3 or 22 of this Act include—
    (a) property, rights and liabilities that would not otherwise be capable of being transferred or assigned by the transferor;
    (b) in the case of a transfer scheme, such property, rights and liabilities to which the transferor may become entitled or subject after the making of the scheme and before the transfer date as may be specified in the scheme;
    (c) property situated anywhere in the United Kingdom or elsewhere;
    (d) rights and liabilities under enactments;
    (e) rights and liabilities under the law of any part of the United Kingdom or of any country or territory outside the United Kingdom.

(2) The transfers authorised by paragraph (a) of sub-paragraph (1) above include transfers which, by virtue of that paragraph, are to take effect as if there were no such contravention, liability or interference with any interest or right as there would be, in the case of a transfer or assignment otherwise than by or under section 3 or 22 of this Act, by reason of any provision having effect (whether under any enactment or agreement or otherwise) in relation to the terms on which the transferor is entitled or subject to the property, right or liability in question.

(3) This paragraph is subject to paragraph 3 below.

Contracts of employment

3.—(1) The rights and liabilities that may be transferred by and in accordance with a transfer scheme include (subject to the following provisions of this paragraph) any rights or liabilities of the employer under the contract of employment of any person—
    (a) who is employed—
        (i) in the civil service of the State;
        (ii) by a body which is a waste regulation authority in England or Wales; or
        (iii) by a local authority in Scotland;
    (b) who appears to the appropriate authority to be employed for the purposes of, or otherwise in connection with, functions which are by virtue of this Act to become functions of a new Agency; and
    (c) whom the appropriate authority considers it necessary or expedient to transfer into the employment of that new Agency;
and in the following provisions of this paragraph any reference to a "qualifying employee" is a reference to such a person.

(2) A transfer scheme which provides for the transfer of rights or liabilities under the contracts of employment of qualifying employees must identify those employees—
    (a) by specifying them;
    (b) by referring to persons of a description specified in the scheme (with or without exceptions); or

(c) partly in the one way and partly in the other.

(3) A transfer scheme shall not operate to transfer rights or liabilities under so much of a contract of employment as relates to an occupational pension scheme, other than any provisions of such a pension scheme which do not relate to benefits for old age, invalidity or survivors.

(4) Where a transfer scheme provides for the transfer of rights or liabilities under the contract of employment of a qualifying employee—

(a) all the employer's rights, powers, duties and liabilities under or in connection with the contract of employment shall be transferred to the relevant new Agency on the transfer date by and in accordance with the scheme, and

(b) anything done by or in relation to the employer in respect of the qualifying employee before the transfer date shall be treated on and after that date as done by or in relation to the relevant new Agency,

except in a case where objection is made by the qualifying employee as mentioned in sub-paragraph (8)(b) below.

(5) Sub-paragraphs (6) and (7) below shall have effect in any case where rights or liabilities under the contract of employment of a qualifying employee are transferred by and in accordance with a transfer scheme.

(6) In a case falling within sub-paragraph (5) above—

(a) the transfer shall be regarded for the purposes of section 84 of the Employment Protection (Consolidation) Act 1978 (renewal of contract or re-engagement) as a renewal of the qualifying employee's contract of employment, or a re-engagement of the qualifying employee, falling within subsection (1) of that section; and

(b) the qualifying employee shall accordingly not be regarded as having been dismissed by virtue of the transfer.

(7) In a case falling within sub-paragraph (5) above, for the purposes of Schedule 13 to the Employment Protection (Consolidation) Act 1978 (ascertainment of the length of an employee's period of employment and whether that employment is continuous)—

(a) so much of the qualifying employee's period of continuous employment as ends with the day preceding the transfer date shall be treated on and after that date as a period of employment with the relevant new Agency; and

(b) the continuity of the period of employment of the qualifying employee shall be treated as not having been broken by the transfer.

(8) Sub-paragraph (9) below shall have effect in any case where—

(a) a transfer scheme contains provision for the transfer of rights or liabilities under the contract of employment of a qualifying employee, but

(b) the qualifying employee informs the appropriate authority or the relevant new Agency that he objects to becoming employed by that new Agency.

(9) In a case falling within sub-paragraph (8) above—

(a) the transfer scheme—

(i) shall not operate to transfer any rights, powers, duties or liabilities under or in connection with the contract of employment; but

(ii) shall operate so as to terminate that contract on the day preceding the transfer date; and

(b) the qualifying employee shall not, by virtue of that termination, be treated for any purpose as having been dismissed.

(10) In this paragraph—

"the appropriate authority" means—

(a) in the case of a person employed in the civil service of the State, the Secretary of State;

(b) in the case of a transfer scheme under section 3 of this Act and a person employed by a body which is a waste regulation authority, that body;

(c) in the case of a transfer scheme under section 22 of this Act and a person employed by a local authority, that authority;

"occupational pension scheme" has the meaning given by section 1 of the Pension Schemes Act 1993.

(11) This paragraph shall apply in relation to any qualifying employee as if, as respects any time before the transfer date,—

(a) any reference to a person's contract of employment included a reference to his employment in the civil service of the State or to the terms of that employment, as the case may require; and

(b) any reference to the dismissal of a person included a reference to the termination of his employment in that service.

PART II

TRANSFER SCHEMES

Description of the property etc. to be transferred by scheme

4. A transfer scheme may define the property, rights and liabilities to be transferred by the scheme—
  (a) by specifying or describing the property, rights and liabilities in question;
  (b) by referring to all (or all but so much as may be excepted) of the property, rights and liabilities comprised in a specified part of the undertaking of the transferor; or
  (c) partly in the one way and partly in the other.

Division of property etc. to be transferred by scheme: creation of new rights and interests

5.—(1) For the purpose of making any division of property, rights or liabilities which it is considered appropriate to make in connection with the transfer of property, rights and liabilities by and in accordance with a transfer scheme, any such scheme may—
  (a) create in favour of the transferor an interest in, or right over, any property transferred by the scheme;
  (b) create in favour of the relevant new Agency an interest in, or right over, any property retained by the transferor;
  (c) create new rights and liabilities as between the relevant new Agency and the transferor; or
  (d) in connection with any provision made by virtue of paragraph (a), (b) or (c) above, make incidental provision as to the interests, rights and liabilities of persons other than the transferor and the relevant new Agency with respect to the subject-matter of the transfer scheme;
and references in the other provisions of Part I of this Act to the transfer of property, rights or liabilities (so far as relating to transfers by and in accordance with transfer schemes) shall accordingly be construed as including references to the creation of any interest, right or liability by virtue of paragraph (a), (b) or (c) above or the making of provision by virtue of paragraph (d) above.

(2) The provision that may be made by virtue of paragraph (c) of sub-paragraph (1) above includes—
  (a) provision for treating any person who is entitled by virtue of a transfer scheme to possession of a document as having given another person an acknowledgement in writing of the right of that other person to the production of the document and to delivery of copies of it; and
  (b) in the case of a transfer scheme under section 3 of this Act, provision applying section 64 of the Law of Property Act 1925 (production and safe custody of documents) in relation to any case in relation to which provision falling within paragraph (a) above has effect.

Transfer schemes: incidental, supplemental and consequential provision

6.—(1) A transfer scheme may make such incidental, supplemental and consequential provision—
  (a) as the Secretary of State considers appropriate, in the case of a scheme made by him,
  (b) as a body which is a waste regulation authority considers appropriate, in the case of a scheme made by that body under section 3 of this Act, or
  (c) as a local authority considers appropriate, in the case of a scheme made by that authority under section 22 of this Act.

(2) Without prejudice to the generality of sub-paragraph (1) above, a transfer scheme may provide—
  (a) that disputes as to the effect of the scheme between the transferor and the relevant new Agency are to be referred to such arbitration as may be specified in or determined under the transfer scheme;
  (b) that determinations on such arbitrations and certificates given jointly by the transferor and the relevant new Agency as to the effect of the scheme as between them are to be conclusive for all purposes.

Modification of transfer schemes

7.—(1) If at any time after a transfer scheme has come into force the Secretary of State considers it appropriate to do so, he may by order provide that the scheme shall for all purposes be deemed to have come into force with such modifications as may be specified in the order.

(2) An order under sub-paragraph (1) above—

(a) may make, with effect from the coming into force of the transfer scheme in question, such provision as could have been made by the scheme; and

(b) in connection with giving effect to that provision from that time, may contain such supplemental, consequential or transitional provision as the Secretary of State considers appropriate.

(3) The Secretary of State shall not make an order under sub-paragraph (1) above except after consultation with—

(a) the relevant new Agency; and

(b) if the transfer scheme in question is—

(i) a scheme under section 3 of this Act which transferred property, rights or liabilities of a waste regulation authority, or

(ii) a scheme under section 22 of this Act which transferred property, rights or liabilities of a local authority,

the body which was the transferor in the case of that scheme.

(4) The power to make an order under sub-paragraph (1) above shall be exercisable by statutory instrument; and a statutory instrument containing any such order shall be subject to annulment in pursuance of a resolution of either House of Parliament.

Provision of information and assistance to the Secretary of State and the new Agencies in connection with transfer schemes

8.—(1) It shall be the duty of each of the following, that is to say—

(a) the chief inspector for England and Wales,

(b) any body which is a waste regulation authority in England or Wales, and

(c) any officer of such a body,

to provide the Secretary of State or the Agency with such information or assistance as the Secretary of State or, as the case may be, the Agency may reasonably require for the purposes of, or in connection with, the exercise of any powers of the Secretary of State or the Agency in relation to transfer schemes.

(2) It shall be the duty of each of the following, that is to say—

(a) the chief inspector for Scotland,

(b) any local authority, and

(c) any officer of a local authority,

to provide the Secretary of State or SEPA with such information or assistance as the Secretary of State or, as the case may be, SEPA may reasonably require for the purposes of, or in connection with, the exercise of any powers of the Secretary of State or SEPA in relation to transfer schemes.

PART III

GENERAL PROVISIONS WITH RESPECT TO TRANSFERS BY OR UNDER SECTION 3 OR 22

Consideration

9. No consideration shall be provided in respect of the transfer of any property, rights or liabilities by or under section 3 or 22 of this Act; but—

(a) a transfer scheme may contain provision for consideration to be provided by the relevant new Agency in respect of the creation of interests, rights or liabilities by means of the transfer scheme; and

(b) any such provision shall be enforceable in the same way as if the interests, rights or liabilities had been created, and (if the case so requires) had been capable of being created, by agreement between the parties.

Continuity

10.—(1) This paragraph applies in relation to—

(a) any transfer of property, rights or liabilities by section 3 or 22 of this Act; or

(b) subject to any provision to the contrary in the transfer scheme in question, any transfer of property, rights or liabilities by a transfer scheme.

(2) Where this paragraph applies in relation to a transfer, then, so far as may be necessary for the purposes of, or in connection with, the transfer—

(a) any agreements made, transactions effected or other things done by or in relation to the transferor shall be treated as made, effected or done by or in relation to the relevant new Agency;

(b) references (whether express or implied and, if express, however worded) to the transferor in any agreement (whether in writing or not) or in any deed, bond, instrument or other document relating to the property rights or liabilities transferred shall, as respects anything falling to be done on or after the transfer date, have effect as references to the relevant new Agency.

Remedies

11.—(1) Without prejudice to the generality of paragraph 10 above, a new Agency and any other person shall, as from the transfer date, have the same rights, powers and remedies (and, in particular, the same rights and powers as to the taking or resisting of legal proceedings or the making or resisting of applications to any authority) for ascertaining, perfecting or enforcing any right or liability transferred to that new Agency by or under this Act as that new Agency or that person would have had if that right or liability had at all times been a right or liability of that new Agency.

(2) Without prejudice to the generality of paragraph 10 above, any legal proceedings or applications to any authority pending immediately before the transfer date by or against a transferor, in so far as they relate to any property, right or liability transferred to the relevant new Agency by or under this Act or to any agreement relating to any such property, right or liability, shall be continued by or against the relevant new Agency to the exclusion of the transferor.

Perfection of vesting of foreign property, rights and liabilities

12.—(1) This paragraph applies in the case of any transfer by or under section 3 or 22 of this Act of any foreign property, rights or liabilities.

(2) It shall be the duty of the transferor and the relevant new Agency to take, as and when that new Agency considers it appropriate, all such steps as may be requisite to secure that the vesting in that new Agency by, or by transfer scheme under, section 3 or 22 of this Act of any foreign property, right or liability is effective under the relevant foreign law.

(3) Until the vesting in the relevant new Agency by, or by transfer scheme under, section 3 or 22 of this Act of any foreign property, right or liability is effective under the relevant foreign law, it shall be the duty of the transferor to hold that property or right for the benefit of, or to discharge that liability on behalf of, the relevant new Agency.

(4) Nothing in sub-paragraphs (2) and (3) above shall be taken as prejudicing the effect under the law of any part of the United Kingdom of the vesting in the relevant new Agency by, or by transfer scheme under, section 3 or 22 of this Act of any foreign property, right or liability.

(5) The transferor shall have all such powers as may be requisite for the performance of his duty under this paragraph, but it shall be the duty of the relevant new Agency to act on behalf of the transferor (so far as possible) in performing the duty imposed on the transferor by this paragraph.

(6) References in this paragraph to any foreign property, right or liability are references to any property, right or liability as respects which any issue arising in any proceedings would have been determined (in accordance with the rules of private international law) by reference to the law of a country or territory outside the United Kingdom.

(7) Duties imposed on the transferor or the relevant new Agency by this paragraph shall be enforceable in the same way as if the duties were imposed by a contract between the transferor and that new Agency.

(8) Any expenses reasonably incurred by the transferor under this paragraph shall be met by the relevant new Agency.

Section 12   SCHEDULE 3

ENVIRONMENT PROTECTION ADVISORY COMMITTEES

Introductory

1.—(1) In this Schedule, "scheme" means a scheme prepared under this Schedule.

(2) Subject to sub-paragraph (1) above, expressions used in this Schedule and in section 12 of this Act have the same meaning in this Schedule as they have in that section.

Duty of Agency to prepare and submit schemes for each region

2.—(1) It shall be the duty of the Agency, in accordance with such guidance as may be given for the purpose by the Secretary of State,—

(a) to prepare, in respect of each region, a scheme with respect to the appointment of persons as members of the advisory committee for that region; and

(b) to submit that scheme to the Secretary of State for his approval before such date as may be specified in the guidance.

(2) Every scheme shall—

(a) specify descriptions of bodies which, or persons who, appear to the Agency likely to have a significant interest in matters likely to be affected by the manner in which it carries out its functions in the region to which the scheme relates;

(b) indicate how the membership of the advisory committee is to reflect the different descriptions of bodies or persons so specified;

(c) specify or describe bodies which, and persons whom, the Agency proposes to consult in connection with appointments of persons as members of the advisory committee; and

(d) make provision with respect to such other matters as the Agency considers relevant to the membership of the advisory committee.

Approval of schemes

3.—(1) A scheme shall not come into force unless it has been approved by the Secretary of State or until such date as he may specify for the purpose in giving his approval.

(2) Where the Agency submits a scheme to the Secretary of State for his approval, it shall also submit to him—

(a) a statement of the Agency's reasons for considering that the scheme is one which it is appropriate for him to approve; and

(b) such information in support of those reasons as it considers necessary.

(3) On submitting a scheme to the Secretary of State for his approval, the Agency shall publish the scheme, in such manner as it considers appropriate for bringing it to the attention of persons likely to be interested in it, together with a notice specifying the period within which representations or objections with respect to the scheme may be made to the Secretary of State.

(4) Where a scheme has been submitted to the Secretary of State for his approval, it shall be the duty of the Secretary of State, in determining whether to—

(a) approve the scheme,

(b) reject the scheme, or

(c) approve the scheme subject to modifications,

to consider any representations or objections made to him within the period specified pursuant to sub-paragraph (3) above and not withdrawn.

(5) Where the Secretary of State approves a scheme, with or without modifications, it shall be the duty of the Agency to take such steps as it considers appropriate for bringing the scheme as so approved to the attention of persons whom it considers likely to be interested in it.

Replacement and variation of approved membership schemes

4.—(1) The Agency may from time to time, and if required to do so by the Secretary of State shall,—

(a) prepare in accordance with paragraph 2 above a fresh scheme with respect to the appointment of persons as members of the advisory committee for any particular region; and

(b) submit that scheme to the Secretary of State for his approval; and paragraph 3 above shall have effect accordingly in relation to any such scheme.

(2) An approved membership scheme may from time to time be varied by the Agency with the approval of the Secretary of State.

(3) The provisions of paragraph 3 above shall have effect in relation to any variation of an approved membership scheme as they have effect in relation to a scheme.

Appointment of members

5.—(1) Before appointing a person to be a member of an advisory committee, the Agency—

(a) shall consult such of the associates for that advisory committee as it considers appropriate in the particular case; and

(b) may, if it considers it appropriate to do so, also consult bodies or persons who are not associates for that advisory committee.

(2) In this paragraph, "associates", in the case of any advisory committee, means those bodies and persons specified or described in the approved membership scheme for that advisory committee pursuant to paragraph 2(2)(c) above.

Vacancies, defective appointments etc.

6. The validity of any proceedings of an advisory committee shall not be affected by—

(a) any vacancy amongst the members;

(b) any defect in the appointment of a member; or

(c) any temporary breach of the terms of the approved membership scheme for the advisory committee.

Remuneration and allowances

7.—(1) The Agency shall pay to the chairman of an advisory committee such remuneration, and such travelling and other allowances, as the Secretary of State may determine.

(2) The Agency shall pay to the members of an advisory committee other than the chairman such sums by way of reimbursement (whether in whole or in part) for loss of remuneration, for travelling expenses and for other out-of-pocket expenses as the Secretary of State may determine.

Section 14   SCHEDULE 4

BOUNDARIES OF REGIONAL FLOOD DEFENCE AREAS

Power to make order

1.—(1) The relevant Minister may by order made by statutory instrument—
(a) alter the boundaries of the area of any regional flood defence committee; or
(b) provide for the amalgamation of any two or more such areas.

(2) Where an order under this Schedule makes provision by reference to anything shown on a main river map, that map shall be conclusive evidence for the purposes of the order of what is shown on the map.

(3) The power to make an order under this Schedule shall include power to make such supplemental, consequential and transitional provision as the relevant Minister considers appropriate.

(4) In the case of an order under this Schedule amalgamating the areas of any two or more regional flood defence committees, the provision made by virtue of sub-paragraph (3) above may include provision determining—
(a) the total number of members of the amalgamated committee; and
(b) the total number of such members to be appointed by the constituent councils of that committee;
and subsections (7) and (8) of section 16 of this Act shall apply in relation to so much of an order under this Schedule as is made by virtue of this sub-paragraph as they apply in relation to an order under subsection (5) of that section.

(5) In this paragraph and the following paragraphs of this Schedule "the relevant Minister"—
(a) in relation to any alteration of the boundaries of an area where the whole or any part of that area is in Wales, means the Ministers;
(b) in relation to the amalgamation of any two or more areas where the whole or any part of any one of those areas is in Wales, means the Ministers; and
(c) in any other case, means the Minister.

(6) In this paragraph—
"main river" means a main river within the meaning of Part IV of the 1991 Act; and
"main river map" has, subject to section 194 of the 1991 Act, the meaning given by section 193(2) of that Act.

Consultation and notice of intention to make order

2.—(1) Before making an order under this Schedule, the relevant Minister shall—
(a) consult such persons or representative bodies as he considers it appropriate to consult at that stage;
(b) prepare a draft order;
(c) publish a notice complying with sub-paragraph (2) below in the London Gazette and in such other manner as he considers appropriate for bringing the draft order to the attention of persons likely to be affected by it if it is made.

(2) A notice for the purposes of sub-paragraph (1)(c) above with respect to a draft order shall—
(a) state the relevant Minister's intention to make the order and its general effect;
(b) specify the places where copies of the draft order and of any map to which it refers may be inspected by any person free of charge at all reasonable times during the period of twenty-eight days beginning with the date on which the notice is first published otherwise than in the London Gazette; and

(c) state that any person may within that period by notice in writing to the relevant Minister object to the making of the order.

(3) The relevant Minister shall also cause copies of the notice and of the draft order to be served on every person carrying out functions under any enactment who appears to him to be concerned.

Objections to draft order and making of order

3.—(1) Before making an order under this Schedule, the relevant Minister—

(a) shall consider any representations or objections which are duly made with respect to the draft order and are not withdrawn; and

(b) may, if he thinks fit, cause a local inquiry to be held with respect to any such representations or objections.

(2) Where notice of a draft order has been published and given in accordance with paragraph 2 above and any representations or objections considered under sub-paragraph (1) above, the relevant Minister may make the order either in the terms of the draft or in those terms as modified in such manner as he thinks fit, or may decide not to make the order.

(3) The relevant Minister shall not make a modification of a draft order in so far as the modification is such as to include in the area of any regional flood defence committee any tidal waters which, if the order had been made in the form of the draft, would have been outside the area of every regional flood defence committee.

Procedure for making of order

4.—(1) Where the relevant Minister makes an order under this Schedule, he shall serve notice of the making of the order on every person (if any) who—

(a) is a person on whom notice is required to have been served under paragraph 2(3) above; and

(b) has duly made an objection to the making of the order that has not been withdrawn.

(2) Where a notice is required to be served under sub-paragraph (1) above with respect to any order, the order shall not have effect before the end of a period of twenty-eight days from the date of service of the last notice served under that sub-paragraph.

(3) If before an order takes effect under sub-paragraph (2) above—

(a) any person who has been served with a notice under sub-paragraph (1) above with respect to that order serves notice objecting to the order on the Minister (or, in the case of an order made jointly by the Ministers, on either of them), and

(b) the objection is not withdrawn,

the order shall be subject to special parliamentary procedure.

(4) A statutory instrument containing an order under this Schedule which is not subject to special parliamentary procedure under sub-paragraph (3) above shall be subject to annulment in pursuance of a resolution of either House of Parliament.

Notice after making of order

5.—(1) Subject to sub-paragraph (2) below, after making an order under this Schedule, the relevant Minister shall publish in the London Gazette, and in such other manner as he considers appropriate for bringing the order to the attention of persons likely to be affected by it, a notice—

(a) stating that the order has been made; and

(b) naming the places where a copy of the order may be inspected at all reasonable times.

(2) In the case of an order to which sub-paragraph (2) of paragraph 4 above applies, the notice—

(a) shall not be published until the end of the period of twenty-eight days referred to in that sub-paragraph; and

(b) shall state whether or not the order is to be subject to special parliamentary procedure.

Questioning of order in courts

6.—(1) Subject to sub-paragraph (3) below, if any person desires to question the validity of an order under this Schedule on the ground—

(a) that it is not within the powers of this Schedule, or

(b) that any requirement of this Schedule has not been complied with,

he may, within six weeks after the date of the first publication of the notice required by paragraph 5 above, make an application for the purpose to the High Court.

(2) On an application under this paragraph the High Court, if satisfied—

(a) that the order is not within the powers of this Schedule, or

(b) that the interests of the applicant have been substantially prejudiced by a failure to comply with any of the requirements of this Schedule,

may quash the order either generally or in so far as it affects the applicant.

(3) Sub-paragraph (1) above—

(a) shall not apply to any order which is confirmed by Act of Parliament under section 6 of the Statutory Orders (Special Procedure) Act 1945; and

(b) shall have effect in relation to any other order which is subject to special parliamentary procedure by virtue of the provisions of this Schedule as if the reference to the date of the first publication of the notice required by paragraph 5 above were a reference to the date on which the order becomes operative under that Act of 1945.

(4) Except as provided by this paragraph the validity of an order under this Schedule shall not, either before or after the order has been made, be questioned in any legal proceedings whatsoever.

Section 19   SCHEDULE 5

Membership and proceedings of regional and local flood defence committees

Part I

Membership of flood defence committees

Terms of membership

1.—(1) Members of a flood defence committee (that is to say a regional flood defence committee or a local flood defence committee), other than those appointed by or on behalf of one or more constituent councils, shall hold and vacate office in accordance with the terms of their appointment.

(2) The first members of a local flood defence committee appointed by or on behalf of any one or more constituent councils—

(a) shall come into office on the day on which the committee comes into existence or, in the case of a member who is for any reason appointed after that day, on the day on which the appointment is made; and

(b) subject to the following provisions of this Schedule, shall hold office until the end of May in such year as may be specified for the purposes of this paragraph in the scheme establishing the committee.

(3) Any members of a flood defence committee appointed by or on behalf of any one or more constituent councils who are not members to whom sub-paragraph (2) above applies—

(a) shall come into office at the beginning of the June next following the day on which they are appointed; and

(b) subject to the following provisions of this Schedule, shall hold office for a term of four years.

(4) If for any reason any such member as is mentioned in sub-paragraph (3) above is appointed on or after the day on which he ought to have come into office, he shall—

(a) come into office on the day on which he is appointed; and

(b) subject to the following provisions of this Schedule, hold office for the remainder of the term.

(5) References in this paragraph and the following provisions of this Schedule to a member of a flood defence committee include references to the chairman of such a committee.

Membership of constituent council as qualification for membership of committee

2.—(1) Members of a flood defence committee appointed by or on behalf of any one or more constituent councils may be members of that council, or one of those councils, or other persons.

(2) Any member of a flood defence committee appointed by or on behalf of a constituent council who at the time of his appointment was a member of that council shall, if he ceases to be a member of that council, also cease to be a member of the committee with whichever is the earlier of the following—

(a) the end of the period of three months beginning with the date when he ceases to be a member of the council; and

(b) the appointment of another person in his place.

(3) For the purposes of sub-paragraph (2) above a member of a council shall not be deemed to have ceased to be a member of the council by reason of retirement if he has been re-elected a member of the council not later than the date of his retirement.

Disqualification for membership of committee

3.—(1) Subject to the following provisions of this paragraph, a person shall be disqualified for appointment as a member of a flood defence committee if he—

(a) is a paid officer of the Agency; or

(b) is a person who has been adjudged bankrupt, or whose estate has been sequestrated or who has made a composition or arrangement with, or granted a trust deed for, his creditors; or

(c) within the period of five years before the day of his appointment, has been convicted, in the United Kingdom, the Channel Islands or the Isle of Man, of any offence and has had passed on him a sentence of imprisonment (whether suspended or not) for a period of not less than three months without the option of a fine; or

(d) is disqualified for being elected or for being a member of a local authority under Part III of the Local Government Finance Act 1982 (accounts and audit) or Part III of the Representation of the People Act 1983 (legal proceedings).

(2) Where a person is disqualified under sub-paragraph (1) above by reason of having been adjudged bankrupt, the disqualification shall cease—

(a) unless the bankruptcy order made against that person is previously annulled, on his discharge from bankruptcy; and

(b) if the bankruptcy order is so annulled, on the date of the annulment.

(3) Where a person is disqualified under sub-paragraph (1) above by reason of having had his estate sequestrated, the disqualification shall cease—

(a) unless the sequestration is recalled or reduced, on the person's discharge under section 54 of the Bankruptcy (Scotland) Act 1985; and

(b) if the sequestration is recalled or reduced, on the date of the recall or reduction.

(4) Where a person is disqualified under sub-paragraph (1) above by reason of his having made a composition or arrangement with, or having granted a trust deed for, his creditors, the disqualification shall cease—

(a) if he pays his debts in full, on the date on which the payment is completed; and

(b) in any other case, at the end of five years from the date on which the terms of the deed of composition or arrangement, or of the trust deed, are fulfilled.

(5) For the purposes of sub-paragraph (1)(c) above the date of the conviction shall be taken to be—

(a) the ordinary date on which the period allowed for making an appeal or application with respect to the conviction expires; or

(b) if such an appeal or application is made, the date on which it is finally disposed of or abandoned or fails by reason of non-prosecution.

(6) Section 92 of the Local Government Act 1972 (proceedings for disqualification) shall apply in relation to disqualification under this paragraph for appointment as a member of a flood defence committee as it applies in relation to disqualification for acting as a member of a local authority.

Vacation of office by disqualifying event

4.—(1) The office of a member of a flood defence committee shall become vacant upon the fulfilment of any of the following conditions, that is to say—

(a) the person holding that office is adjudged bankrupt, is a person whose estate is sequestrated or makes a composition or arrangement with, or grants a trust deed for, his creditors;

(b) that person is convicted, in the United Kingdom, the Channel Islands or the Isle of Man, of any offence and has passed on him a sentence of imprisonment (whether suspended or not) for a period of not less than three months without the option of a fine;

(c) that person is disqualified for being elected or for being a member of a local authority under Part III of the Local Government Finance Act 1982 (accounts and audit) or Part III of the Representation of the People Act 1983 (legal proceedings); or

(d) that person has, for a period of six consecutive months been absent from meetings of the committee, otherwise than by reason of illness or some other cause approved during the period by the committee.

(2) For the purposes of sub-paragraph (1)(d) above, the attendance of a member of a flood defence committee—

(a) at a meeting of any sub-committee of the committee of which he is a member, or

(b) at any joint committee to which he has been appointed by that committee,

shall be treated as attendance at a meeting of the committee.

Resignation of office by members of regional committee

5.—(1) The chairman of a regional flood defence committee may resign his office at any time by giving notice to the chairman of the Agency and to one of the Ministers.

(2) Any other member of such a committee may resign his office at any time by giving notice to the chairman of the committee and also, if he was appointed by one of the Ministers, to that Minister.

Resignation of office by members of local committee

6.—(1) The chairman of a local flood defence committee may resign his office at any time by giving notice to the chairman of the regional flood defence committee.

(2) Any other member of a local flood defence committee may resign his office at any time by giving notice to the chairman of that local flood defence committee.

Appointments to fill casual vacancies

7.—(1) Where, for any reason whatsoever, the office of a member of a flood defence committee becomes vacant before the end of his term of office, the vacancy—

(a) shall, if the unexpired portion of the term of office of the vacating member is six months or more, be filled by the appointment of a new member; and

(b) may be so filled in any other case.

(2) A person appointed by virtue of sub-paragraph (1) above to fill a casual vacancy shall hold office for so long only as the former member would have held office.

Eligibility of previous members for re-appointment

8. Subject to the provisions of this Schedule, a member of a flood defence committee shall be eligible for reappointment.

Appointment of deputies

9.—(1) Subject to the following provisions of this paragraph, a person nominated by one or more constituent councils may act as deputy for a member of a flood defence committee appointed by or on behalf of that council or those councils and may, accordingly, attend and vote at a meeting of the committee, instead of that member.

(2) A person nominated under sub-paragraph (1) above as deputy for a member of a flood defence committee may, by virtue of that nomination, attend and vote at a meeting of a sub-committee of that committee which—

(a) has been appointed by that committee under Part II of this Schedule; and

(b) is a committee to which the member for whom he is a deputy belongs.

(3) A person acting as deputy for a member of a flood defence committee shall be treated for the purposes for which he is nominated as a member of that committee.

(4) A person shall not act as deputy for a member of a flood defence committee unless his nomination has been notified to such officer of the Agency as is appointed to receive such nominations.

(5) A nomination under this paragraph shall be in writing and may apply either to a particular meeting or to all meetings during a stated period or until the nomination is revoked.

(6) A person shall not act as deputy for more than one member of a flood defence committee.

(7) Nothing in this paragraph shall entitle a person to attend and vote at a meeting of a local flood defence committee by reason of his nomination as deputy for a member of a regional flood defence committee.

Payments to past and present chairmen and to members

10.—(1) The Agency shall pay to any person who is a chairman of a flood defence committee such remuneration and allowances as may be determined by the relevant Minister.

(2) If the relevant Minister so determines in the case of any person who is or has been chairman of a flood defence committee, the Agency shall pay or make arrangements for the payment of a pension in relation to that person in accordance with the determination.

(3) If a person ceases to be chairman of a flood defence committee and it appears to the relevant Minister that there are special circumstances which make it right that that person should receive compensation in respect of his ceasing to be chairman, the relevant Minister may require the Agency to pay to that person a sum of such amount as that Minister may determine.

(4) The Agency may pay to any person who is a member of a flood defence committee such allowances as may be determined by the relevant Minister.

(5) In this paragraph—

"pension", in relation to any person, means a pension (whether contributory or not) of any kind payable to or in respect of him, and includes an allowance, gratuity or lump sum so payable and a return of contributions with or without interest or any other addition; and

"the relevant Minister"—

(a) in relation to the regional flood defence committee for an area the whole or the greater part of which is in Wales and in relation to any local flood defence committee for any district comprised in the area of such a regional flood defence committee, means the Secretary of State; and

(b) in relation to any other flood defence committee, means the Minister.

PART II

PROCEEDINGS OF FLOOD DEFENCE COMMITTEES

Appointment of sub-committees, joint sub-committees
etc.

11.—(1) For the purpose of carrying out any functions in pursuance of arrangements under paragraph 12 below—

(a) a flood defence committee may appoint a sub-committee of the committee;

(b) two or more regional or two or more local flood defence committees may appoint a joint sub-committee of those committees;

(c) any sub-committee may appoint one or more committees of that sub-committee ("under sub-committees").

(2) The number of members of any sub-committee and their terms of office shall be fixed by the appointing committee or committees or, in the case of an under sub-committee, by the appointing sub-committee.

(3) A sub-committee appointed under this paragraph may include persons who are not members of the appointing committee or committees or, in the case of an under sub-committee, the committee or committees of whom they are an under sub-committee; but at least two thirds of the members appointed to any such sub-committee shall be members of that committee or those committees, as the case may be.

(4) A person who is disqualified for being a member of a flood defence committee shall be disqualified also for being a member of a sub-committee or under sub-committee appointed under this paragraph.

Delegation of functions to sub-committees etc.

12.—(1) Subject to section 106 of the 1991 Act and to any other express provision contained in any enactment, a flood defence committee may arrange for the carrying out of any of their functions—

(a) by a sub-committee, or an under sub-committee of the committee or an officer of the Agency; or

(b) by any other regional or, as the case may be, local flood defence committee;

and two or more regional or two or more local flood defence committees may arrange to carry out any of their functions jointly or may arrange for the carrying out of any of their functions by a joint sub-committee of theirs.

(2) Where by virtue of this paragraph any functions of a flood defence committee or of two or more such committees may be carried out by a sub-committee, then, unless the committee or committees otherwise direct, the sub-committee may arrange for the carrying out of any of those functions by an under sub-committee or by an officer of the Agency.

(3) Where by virtue of this paragraph any functions of a flood defence committee or of two or more such committees may be carried out by an under sub-committee, then, unless the committee or committees or the sub-committee otherwise direct, the under sub-committee may arrange for the carrying out of any of those functions by an officer of the Agency.

(4) Any arrangements made by a flood defence committee under this paragraph for the carrying out of any function shall not prevent the committee from discharging their functions themselves.

(5) References in the preceding provisions of this paragraph to the carrying out of any functions of a flood defence committee include references to the doing of anything which is calculated to facilitate, or is conducive or incidental to, the carrying out of any of those functions.

(6) A regional flood defence committee shall not, under this paragraph, make arrangements for the carrying out in a local flood defence district of any functions which fall to be carried out there by the local flood defence committee.

Rules of procedure

13.—(1) A flood defence committee may, with the approval of the relevant Minister, make rules for regulating the proceedings of the committee.

(2) Nothing in section 6(4) of this Act or section 105 or 106 of the 1991 Act shall entitle the Agency to make any arrangements or give any directions for regulating the proceedings of any flood defence committee.

(3) In this paragraph "the relevant Minister" has the same meaning as in paragraph 10 above.

Declarations of interest etc.

14.—(1) Subject to the following provisions of this paragraph, the provisions of sections 94 to 98 of the Local Government Act 1972 (pecuniary interests of members of local authorities) shall apply in relation to members of a flood defence committee as those provisions apply in relation to members of local authorities.

(2) In their application by virtue of this paragraph those provisions shall have effect in accordance with the following provisions—

(a) for references to meetings of the local authority there shall be substituted references to meetings of the committee;

(b) in section 94(4), for the reference to provision being made by standing orders of a local authority there shall be substituted a reference to provisions being made by directions of the committee;

(c) in section 96, for references to the proper officer of the local authority there shall be substituted a reference to an officer of the Agency appointed for the purposes of this paragraph; and

(d) section 97 shall apply as it applies to a local authority other than a parish or community council.

(3) Subject to sub-paragraph (4) below, a member of a flood defence committee shall be disqualified, for so long as he remains such a member and for twelve months after he ceases to be such a member, for appointment to any paid office by the Agency or any regional flood defence committee.

(4) Sub-paragraph (3) above shall not disqualify any person for appointment to the office of chairman of a local flood defence committee.

Authentication of documents

15.—(1) Any notice or other document which a flood defence committee are required or authorised to give, make or issue by or under any enactment may be signed on behalf of the committee by any member of the committee or any officer of the Agency who is generally or specifically authorised for that purpose by a resolution of the committee.

(2) Any document purporting to bear the signature of a person expressed to be authorised as mentioned in sub-paragraph (1) above shall be deemed, unless the contrary is shown, to be duly given, made or issued by authority of the committee.

(3) In this paragraph "signature" includes a facsimile of a signature by whatever process reproduced.

Proof and validity of proceedings

16.—(1) A minute of the proceedings of a meeting of a flood defence committee, purporting to be signed at that or the next ensuing meeting by—

(a) the chairman of the meeting to the proceedings of which the minute relates, or

(b) by the chairman of the next ensuing meeting,

shall be evidence of the proceedings and shall be received in evidence without further proof.

(2) Where a minute has been signed as mentioned in sub-paragraph (1) above in respect of a meeting of a committee or sub-committee, then, unless the contrary is shown—

(a) the meeting shall be deemed to have been duly convened and held;

(b) all the proceedings had at any such meeting shall be deemed to have been duly had; and

(c) that committee or sub-committee shall be deemed to have been duly constituted and have had power to deal with the matters referred to in the minute.

(3) The validity of any proceedings of a flood defence committee shall not be affected by any vacancy among the members of the committee or by any defect in the appointment of such a member.

Section 20   SCHEDULE 6

THE SCOTTISH ENVIRONMENT PROTECTION AGENCY

Status

1. SEPA shall be a body corporate with a common seal.

2. Subject to section 38 of this Act, SEPA shall not—

(a) be regarded as a servant or agent of the Crown;

(b) have any status, immunity or privilege of the Crown;

(c) by virtue of its connection with the Crown, be exempt from any tax, duty, rate, levy or other charge whatsoever whether general or local,

and its property shall not be regarded as property of, or held on behalf of, the Crown.

Membership

3. SEPA shall consist of not less than eight, nor more than twelve, members appointed by the Secretary of State.

4. In making appointments under paragraph 3 above, the Secretary of State shall have regard to the desirability of appointing persons who have knowledge or experience in some matter relevant to the functions of SEPA.

5. Subject to paragraphs 7 and 8 below, each member—

(a) shall hold and vacate office in accordance with the terms of his appointment;

(b) may, by giving notice to the Secretary of State, resign his office; and

(c) after ceasing to hold office shall be eligible for reappointment as a member.

6. The Secretary of State may, by order made by statutory instrument subject to annulment in pursuance of a resolution of either House of Parliament, amend paragraph 3 above so as to substitute for the numbers for the time being specified as, respectively, the minimum and maximum membership such other numbers as he thinks fit.

7. The Secretary of State may remove a member from office if he is satisfied that the member—

(a) has been absent from meetings of SEPA for a period longer than three months without the permission of SEPA; or

(b) has been adjudged bankrupt, has made an arrangement with his creditors, has had his estate sequestrated or has granted a trust deed for his creditors or a composition contract; or

(c) is unable or unfit to carry out the functions of a member.

Chairman and deputy chairman

8.—(1) The Secretary of State shall appoint one of the members of SEPA to be chairman and another of those members to be deputy chairman.

(2) The chairman and deputy chairman shall hold and vacate office in terms of their appointments.

(3) A member who is chairman or deputy chairman may resign his office by giving notice to the Secretary of State; but if the chairman or deputy chairman ceases to be a member (whether

or not on giving notice under paragraph 5(b) above) he shall cease to be chairman or, as the case may be, deputy chairman.

(4) A person who ceases to be chairman or deputy chairman shall be eligible for reappointment as such under sub-paragraph (1) above at any time when he is a member.

Remuneration, pensions, etc.

9.—(1) SEPA shall—
(a) pay to its members such remuneration and such travelling and other allowances (if any); and
(b) as regards any member or former member in whose case the Secretary of State may so determine—
    (i) pay such pension, allowance or gratuity to or in respect of him;
    (ii) make such payments towards the provision of such pension, allowance or gratuity; or
    (iii) provide and maintain such schemes (whether contributory or not) for the payment of pensions, allowances or gratuities,
as the Secretary of State may determine.

(2) If a person ceases to be a member, and it appears to the Secretary of State that there are special circumstances which make it right that he should receive compensation, the Secretary of State may require SEPA to pay to that person a sum of such amount as the Secretary of State may determine.

Staff

10.—(1) There shall be a chief officer of SEPA.

(2) The Secretary of State shall, after consultation with the chairman or person designated to be chairman (if there is a person holding or designated to hold that office), make the first appointment of chief officer on such terms and conditions as he may determine; and thereafter SEPA may, with the approval of the Secretary of State, make subsequent appointments to that office on such terms and conditions as it may with such approval determine.

11. SEPA may appoint such other employees as it thinks fit.

12.—(1) SEPA shall, in the case of such of its employees or former employees as it may, with the approval of the Secretary of State, determine—
(a) pay such pensions, allowances or gratuities to or in respect of those employees;
(b) make such payments towards provision of such pensions, allowances or gratuities; or
(c) provide and maintain such schemes (whether contributory or not) for the payment of such pensions, allowances or gratuities,
as it may, with the approval of the Secretary of State, determine.

(2) References in sub-paragraph (1) above to pensions, allowances or gratuities in respect of employees of SEPA include references to pensions allowances or gratuities by way of compensation to or in respect of any such employee who suffers loss of office or employment.

Proceedings

13.—(1) SEPA may regulate its own procedure and that of any committee established by it (including making provision in relation to the quorum for its meetings and the meetings of any such committee).

(2) The proceedings of SEPA and of any committee established by it shall not be invalidated by any vacancy amongst its members or the members of such committee or by any defect in the appointment of such member.

Committees

14.—(1) SEPA may appoint persons who are not members of it to be members of any committee established by it, but at least one member of any such committee shall be a member of SEPA.

(2) SEPA shall pay to a person so appointed such remuneration and allowances (if any) as the Secretary of State may determine.

(3) Any committee established by SEPA shall comply with any directions given to them by it.

Delegation of powers

15.—(1) Anything authorised or required by or under any enactment to be done by SEPA may be done by any of its committees which, or by any of its members or employees who, is authorised (generally or specifically) for the purpose by SEPA.

(2) Nothing in sub-paragraph (1) above shall prevent SEPA from doing anything that a committee, member or employee has been authorised or required to do. .

Regional Boards

16.—(1) Without prejudice to the generality of its power to establish committees, SEPA shall establish committees (to be known as "Regional Boards") for the purposes of discharging in relation to such areas as it may, with the approval of the Secretary of State, determine, such of its functions as it may, with such approval, determine.

(2) A Regional Board shall have a chairman who shall be a member of SEPA and appointed to that office by SEPA.

(3) It shall be the duty of SEPA to comply with such guidance as the Secretary of State may from time to time give as to—

(a) the number of persons to be appointed to a Regional Board;

(b) the qualifications and experience which persons (other than members of SEPA) should have to be eligible for appointment to a Regional Board;

(c) the descriptions of bodies which, or persons who, have a significant interest in matters likely to be affected by the discharge by a Regional Board of its functions; and

(d) how the membership of a Regional Board is to reflect the different descriptions of bodies or persons referred to in paragraph (c) above.

(4) Anything authorised or required to be done by a Regional Board by virtue of sub-paragraph (1) above may be done by any member of the Board, or by any employee of SEPA, who is authorised (generally or specifically) for the purpose by the Board.

(5) Nothing in sub-paragraph (4) above shall prevent a Regional Board doing anything that a member or employee has been authorised or required to do.

Members' interests

17.—(1) A member who is in any way directly or indirectly interested in any matter that is brought up for consideration at a meeting of SEPA shall disclose the nature of his interest to the meeting; and, where such a disclosure is made—

(a) the disclosure shall be recorded in the minutes of the meeting; and

(b) the member shall not take any part in any deliberation or decision of SEPA or of any of its committees with respect to that matter.

(2) For the purposes of sub-paragraph (1) above, a general notification given at a meeting of SEPA by a member to the effect that he—

(a) is a member of a specified company or firm, and

(b) is to be regarded as interested in any matter involving that company or firm,

shall be regarded as a sufficient disclosure of his interest in relation to any such matter.

(3) A member need not attend in person at a meeting of SEPA in order to make a disclosure which he is required to make under this paragraph if he takes reasonable steps to secure that the disclosure is made by a notice which is read and considered at the meeting.

(4) The Secretary of State may, subject to such conditions as he considers appropriate, remove any disability imposed by virtue of this paragraph in any case where the number of members of SEPA disabled by virtue of this paragraph at any one time would be so great a proportion of the whole as to impede the transaction of business.

(5) The power of the Secretary of State under sub-paragraph (4) above includes power to remove, either indefinitely or for any period, a disability which would otherwise attach to any member, or members of any description, by reason of such interests, and in respect of such matters, as may be specified or described by the Secretary of State.

(6) Nothing in this paragraph precludes any member from taking part in the consideration or discussion of, or voting on, any question whether an application should be made to the Secretary of State for the exercise of the power conferred by sub-paragraph (4) above.

(7) In this paragraph—

(a) any reference to a meeting of SEPA includes a reference to a meeting of any of SEPA's committees; and

(b) any reference to a member includes a reference to a person who is not a member of SEPA but who is a member of any such committee.

Minutes

18.—(1) Minutes shall be kept of proceedings of SEPA and of its committees.

(2) Minutes of any such proceedings shall be evidence of those proceedings if they are signed by a person purporting to have acted as chairman of the proceedings to which the minutes relate or of any subsequent proceedings in the course of which the minutes were approved as a correct record.

(3) Where minutes of any such proceedings have been signed as mentioned in sub-paragraph (2) above, those proceedings shall, unless the contrary is shown, be deemed to have been validly convened and constituted.

               SCHEDULE 7

NATIONAL PARK AUTHORITIES

Status and constitution of authorities

1.—(1) A National Park authority shall be a body corporate.

(2) A National Park authority shall consist of—

(a) such number of local authority members as may be specified in the relevant order; and

(b) such number of members to be appointed by the Secretary of State as may be so specified.

(3) In the case of a National Park authority for a National Park in England such number as may be specified in the relevant order of the number of members of the authority to be appointed by the Secretary of State shall be parish members.

(4) The number specified in the relevant order for any National Park authority as the number of members of that authority who are to be appointed by the Secretary of State shall—

(a) as respects any National Park authority for a National Park in England, be two less than the number of local authority members specified in the order; and

(b) as respects any National Park authority for a National Park in Wales, be equal to half the number of local authority members specified in the order.

(5) As respects any National Park authority for a National Park in England, the number specified in the relevant order as the number of parish members to be appointed by the Secretary of State shall be one less than one half of the total number of the members of the authority to be appointed by the Secretary of State.

(6) Accordingly—

(a) in the case of a National Park authority for a National Park in England, the effect of the relevant order shall be such that the total number of members of the authority will be an even number which is not a whole number multiple of four; and

(b) in the case of a National Park authority for a National Park in Wales, the number of local authority members specified in the relevant order shall be an even number.

Local authority members

2.—(1) The local authority members of a National Park authority shall be appointed by such of the councils for the principal areas wholly or partly comprised in the relevant Park as may be specified in or determined under the relevant order.

(2) Each of the councils who are to appoint the local authority members of a National Park authority shall be entitled to appoint such number of those members as may be so specified or determined and to make any appointment required by reason of a vacancy arising in respect of a member appointed by that council.

(3) Before making any provision by the relevant order as to—

(a) the number of members of a National Park authority who are to be local authority members,

(b) the councils by whom the local authority members of a National Park authority are to be appointed, or

(c) the number of members to be appointed by each such council,

the Secretary of State shall consult the council for every principal area the whole or any part of which is comprised in the relevant Park; and the Secretary of State may make provision for excluding the council for any such area from the councils by whom the local authority members of a National Park authority are to be appointed only at the request of that council.

(4) A person shall not be appointed as a local authority member of a National Park authority unless he is a member of a principal council the area of which is wholly or partly comprised in the relevant Park; and, in appointing local authority members of a National Park authority, a principal council shall have regard to the desirability of appointing members of the council who represent wards, or (in Wales) electoral divisions, situated wholly or partly within the relevant Park.

(5) Subject to the following provisions of this Schedule, where a person who qualifies for his appointment by virtue of his membership of any council is appointed as a local authority member of a National Park authority—

(a) he shall hold office from the time of his appointment until he ceases to be a member of that council; but

(b) his appointment may, before any such cessation, be terminated for the purposes of, and in accordance with, sections 15 to 17 of the Local Government and Housing Act 1989 (political balance).

(6) Sub-paragraph (5)(a) above shall have effect so as to terminate the term of office of a person who, on retiring from any council, immediately becomes such a member again as a newly elected councillor; but a person who so becomes a member again shall be eligible for re-appointment to the National Park authority.

(7) The appointment of any person as a local authority member of a National Park authority may provide that he is not to be treated for the purposes of sub-paragraph (5) above as qualifying for his appointment by virtue of his membership of any council other than that specified in the appointment.

(8) In paragraph 2(1) of Schedule 1 to the Local Government and Housing Act 1989 (bodies to which appointments have to be made taking account of political balance), after paragraph (b) there shall be inserted the following paragraph—

"(ba) a National Park authority;".

Parish members of English National Park authorities

3.—(1) The parish members of an English National Park authority shall be appointed by the Secretary of State.

(2) A person shall not be appointed as a parish member of an English National Park authority unless he is—

(a) a member of the parish council for a parish the whole or any part of which is comprised in the relevant Park; or

(b) the chairman of the parish meeting of a parish—

(i) which does not have a separate parish council; and

(ii) the whole or any part of which is comprised in the relevant Park.

(3) Subject to the following provisions of this Schedule, where a person who qualifies for his appointment by virtue of his membership of a parish council is appointed as a parish member of an English National Park authority, he shall hold office from the time of his appointment until he ceases to be a member of that parish council.

(4) Sub-paragraph (3) above shall have effect so as to terminate the term of office of a person who on retiring from any parish council immediately becomes such a member again as a newly elected councillor; but a person who so becomes a member again shall be eligible for re-appointment to the National Park authority.

(5) Subject to the following provisions of this Schedule, where a person who qualifies for his appointment by virtue of his being the chairman of a parish meeting is appointed as a parish member of an English National Park authority, he shall hold office from the time of his appointment until he ceases to be the chairman of that parish meeting.

(6) Sub-paragraph (5) above shall have effect so as to terminate the term of office of a person who is elected to succeed himself as chairman of any parish meeting; but a person who so becomes the chairman again shall be eligible for re-appointment to the National Park authority.

(7) Subject to the provisions of this Schedule, a parish member of an English National Park authority shall hold office in accordance with the terms of his appointment.

(8) In this paragraph, "English National Park authority" means a National Park authority for a National Park in England.

Members (other than parish members) appointed by the Secretary of State

4.—(1) Before appointing any person as a member of a National Park authority the Secretary of State shall consult, according to whether the relevant Park is in England or in Wales, either the Countryside Commission or the Countryside Council for Wales.

(2) Subject to the following provisions of this Schedule, a person appointed as a member of a National Park authority by the Secretary of State—

(a) shall hold office for such period of not less than one year nor more than three years as may be specified in the terms of his appointment; but

(b) on ceasing to hold office shall be eligible for re-appointment.

(3) The term of office of a person appointed by the Secretary of State to fill such a vacancy in the membership of a National Park authority as occurs where a person appointed by the Secretary of State ceases to be a member of the authority before the end of his term of office may be for a period of less than one year if it is made to expire with the time when the term of office of the person in respect of whom the vacancy has arisen would have expired.

(4) Subject to the provisions of this Schedule, a member of a National Park authority appointed by the Secretary of State shall hold office in accordance with the terms of his appointment.

(5) This paragraph shall not apply to persons appointed as parish members of a National Park authority for a National Park in England or to their appointment as such members.

Chairman and deputy chairman

5.—(1) The members of a National Park authority shall elect, from amongst their members, both a chairman and a deputy chairman of the authority.

(2) Subject to sub-paragraphs (3) and (4) below, the chairman and deputy chairman of a National Park authority shall be elected for a period not exceeding one year; but a person so elected shall, on ceasing to hold office at the end of his term of office as chairman or deputy chairman, be eligible for re-election.

(3) A person shall cease to hold office as chairman or deputy chairman of a National Park authority if he ceases to be a member of the authority.

(4) Where a vacancy occurs in the office of chairman or deputy chairman of a National Park authority, it shall be the duty of the members of that authority to secure that that vacancy is filled as soon as possible.

Removal of members

6.—(1) The Secretary of State may, by giving a local authority member of a National Park authority such written notice of the termination of his appointment as the Secretary of State considers appropriate, remove that member from office; but he shall do so only where he considers it appropriate to remove that member from office in consequence of the provisions of any order for varying either the area of the relevant Park or the number of local authority members of that authority.

(2) The Secretary of State may remove from office any member of a National Park authority appointed by him, other than any parish member of a National Park authority for a National Park in England, either—

(a) by giving that member three months" written notice of the termination of the appointment; or

(b) in such other manner as may be provided for in the terms of that member's appointment.

(3) The Secretary of State may remove from office any parish member of a National Park authority for a National Park in England either—

(a) by giving that member such written notice of the termination of his appointment as the Secretary of State considers appropriate; or

(b) in such other manner as may be provided for in the terms of that member's appointment;

but a parish member shall only be removed from office in the manner mentioned in paragraph (a) above where the Secretary of State considers it appropriate to do so in consequence of the provisions of any order for varying either the area of the relevant Park or the number of parish members of the National Park authority in question.

Disqualification of members

7.—(1) A person is disqualified for becoming or remaining a member of a National Park authority if he holds any paid office or employment appointments to which are or may be made or confirmed by—

(a) the authority itself or any council by whom a local authority member of the authority is appointed;

(b) any committee or sub-committee of the authority or of any such council;

(c) any joint committee on which the authority or any such council is represented;

(d) as respects a National Park authority for a National Park in England—

(i) any parish council for, or parish meeting of, a parish the whole or any part of which is comprised in the relevant Park;

(ii) any committee or sub-committee of any such parish council or any committee of any such parish meeting; or

(iii) any joint committee on which any such parish council or parish meeting is represented; or

(e) any person himself holding an office or employment which disqualifies him for becoming a member of the authority.

(2) A person is also disqualified for becoming or remaining a member of a National Park authority if he holds any employment in a company which, in accordance with Part V of the Local Government and Housing Act 1989 other than section 73, is under the control of that authority.

(3) Section 92 of the 1972 Act (proceedings for disqualification) shall have effect in relation to a person who acts or claims to be entitled to act as a member of a National Park authority as it applies in relation to a person who acts or claims to be entitled to act as a member of a local authority, but as if—

(a) references in that section to a local government elector for the area concerned were references to a local government elector for any principal area the whole or any part of which is comprised in the relevant Park; and

(b) in subsection (6)(b) of that section (failure to deliver declaration of acceptance of office), the words from "of failure" to "or by reason" were omitted.

(4) Sections 1 to 3 of the Local Government and Housing Act 1989 (disqualification of persons holding politically restricted posts) shall have effect as if a National Park authority were a local authority for the purposes of Part I of that Act.

(5) In Part III of Schedule 1 to the House of Commons Disqualification Act 1975 (other disqualifying offices), in the entry inserted by section 1 (2) of that Act of 1989 (politically restricted post), after "that Part" there shall be inserted "or a National Park authority".

Vacation of office for failure to attend meetings

8. Section 85 of the 1972 Act (failure to attend meetings) shall have effect in relation to a National Park authority as it has effect in relation to a local authority.

Code of conduct for members

9. Section 31 of the Local Government and Housing Act 1989 (code of conduct for members of local authorities) shall have effect as if a National Park authority were a local authority for the purposes of that section.

Restrictions on voting on account of interests etc.

10.—(1) Sections 94 to 98 of the 1972 Act (restrictions on voting) shall have effect in relation to meetings of a National Park authority as they have effect in relation to meetings of a local authority.

(2) Section 19 of the Local Government and Housing Act 1989 (members' interests) shall have effect as if a National Park authority were a local authority for the purposes of Part I of that Act.

Allowances and time off for members

11.—(1) A National Park authority shall be a body to which sections 174 to 176 of the 1972 Act (allowances for travelling, conferences and visits) shall apply and shall also be deemed to be a relevant authority for the purposes of section 18 of the Local Government and Housing Act 1989 (basic attendance and special responsibility allowances).

(2) For the purposes of sub-paragraph (1) above references in section 18 of that Act of 1989 to a member of an authority who is a councillor shall be deemed, in relation to a National Park authority, to include references to a member of that authority who is appointed as such a member by the Secretary of State.

(3) In section 29(1) of the Employment Protection (Consolidation) Act 1978 (time off for public duties), after paragraph (b) there shall be inserted the following paragraph—
"(ba) a National Park authority;"
but section 10 of that Act of 1989 (limit on paid leave for local authority duties) shall have effect as if a National Park authority were a relevant council for the purposes of that section.

Meetings and proceedings of the authority

12.—(1) The following provisions, that is to say—
(a) the provisions of Part VI of Schedule 12 to the 1972 Act (proceedings and meetings of local authorities) and of section 99 of that Act so far as it relates to that Part of that Schedule; and
(b) the provisions of section 100 of that Act (admission of the public and press),
shall have effect as if a National Park authority were a local authority for the purposes of those provisions.

(2) In section 100J of the 1972 Act (bodies in addition to principal councils to which provisions as to access to meetings etc. apply)—
(a) in subsection (1), after paragraph (cc) there shall be inserted the following paragraph—
"(cd) a National Park authority;"

(b) in subsection (3), after "(cc)" there shall be inserted "(cd)"; and

(c) in subsection (4)(aa)—

(i) after "Navigation Committee" there shall be inserted "or any National Park authority"; and

(ii) for "body which" there shall be substituted "person who".

(3) Section 20 of the Local Government and Housing Act 1989 (power to require adoption of certain procedural standing orders) shall have effect as if a National Park authority were a relevant authority for the purposes of that section.

(4) The validity of any proceedings of a National Park authority shall not be affected by a vacancy amongst its members, by any defect in the appointment of a member of the authority or by the want of qualification, or the disqualification, of any such member.

Committees and sub-committees and officers

13.—(1) Sections 101 to 106 of the 1972 Act (arrangements for committees and sub-committees) shall have effect as if a National Park authority were a local authority for the purposes of those sections.

(2) Accordingly, section 13 of the Local Government and Housing Act 1989 (voting rights of members of certain committees) shall have effect as if a National Park authority were a relevant authority for the purposes of that section.

(3) It shall be the duty of a National Park authority, in relation to any committee or sub-committee to which this sub-paragraph applies, to secure—

(a) that the membership of the committee or sub-committee consists of or includes both local authority members of the authority and at least one member appointed to the authority by the Secretary of State;

(b) that the division of members of the authority who are members of the committee or sub-committee between—

(i) local authority members, and

(ii) members appointed to the authority by the Secretary of State,

is (as nearly as possible using whole numbers) in the same proportions as required, by virtue of paragraph 1(2) above, in the case of the authority itself; and

(c) that the quorum of the committee or sub-committee includes at least one local authority member of the authority and at least one member appointed to the authority by the Secretary of State.

(4) Sub-paragraph (3) above applies in the case of any National Park authority to the following committees and sub-committees, except those appointed under section 102(4) or (4A) of the 1972 Act (advisory committees), that is to say—

(a) any committee or sub-committee of the authority;

(b) any joint committee on which the authority is represented; and

(c) any sub-committee of such a joint committee.

(5) The proceedings of a committee or sub-committee to which sub-paragraph (3) above applies shall not be invalidated by any failure of a National Park authority to perform its duty under that sub-paragraph.

(6) The provisions of sections 112 to 119 and 151 of the 1972 Act (staff of local authorities) and of section 30 of the Local Government (Miscellaneous Provisions) Act 1976 (power to forgo repayment of remuneration) shall have effect as if a National Park authority were a local authority for the purposes of those provisions.

(7) The following provisions of the Local Government and Housing Act 1989 shall apply in relation to a National Park authority as they apply in relation to the authorities which are relevant authorities for the purposes of those provisions, that is to say—

(a) section 4 (designation and reports of head of paid service);

(b) section 5 (designation and reports of monitoring officer); and

(c) with the omission of subsection (4)(d) (assistants for political groups), section 8 (standing orders with respect to staff);

and section 7 of that Act (staff to be appointed on merit) shall apply to any appointment to paid office or employment under a National Park authority as it applies to an appointment to paid office or employment under a body which is a local authority for the purposes of Part I of that Act.

(8) Section 12 of that Act of 1989 (conflict of interest in staff negotiations) shall have effect as if references in that section to a local authority included references to a National Park authority.

National Park Officer

14.—(1) Every National Park authority for a National Park shall secure that there is at all times an officer appointed by that authority to be responsible to the authority for the manner in which the carrying out of its different functions is co-ordinated.

(2) For the purposes of this paragraph a National Park authority may adopt—

(a) any appointment which an existing authority has made under paragraph 15 of Schedule 17 to the 1972 Act in relation to any area wholly or partly comprised in the relevant Park; or

(b) if the relevant Park is in Wales, any appointment—

(i) which was made under that paragraph in relation to any such area, and

(ii) which was adopted by a National Park planning board, as defined in section 64 of this Act, by virtue of an order under paragraph 3A of Schedule 17 to the 1972 Act or section 2(1 B) of the Town and Country Planning Act 1990.

(3) Before making or adopting an appointment under this paragraph or assigning additional responsibilities to a person holding such an appointment, a National Park authority shall consult, according to whether the Park in question is in England or in Wales, either the Countryside Commission or the Countryside Council for Wales.

(4) Sub-paragraph (3) above shall not apply in relation to the adoption of an appointment under this paragraph in relation to a National Park in Wales in any case where—

(a) the National Park authority in question is the National Park authority in relation to that National Park by virtue of an order under section 63 of this Act made by virtue of section 64(1) of this Act;

(b) the appointment in question was made or adopted by the body corporate which has so become that National Park authority, but in its capacity as the National Park planning board, as defined in section 64 of this Act, for the area of the National Park in question; and

(c) no additional responsibilities are, on the occasion of the adoption of the appointment, to be assigned to the person holding the appointment.

(5) A person who holds office with a National Park authority by virtue of an appointment made or adopted under this paragraph—

(a) may at the same time hold the office of head of that authority's paid service, the office of monitoring officer in relation to that authority or both those offices; but

(b) shall not at the same time be that authority's chief finance officer (within the meaning of section 5 of the Local Government and Housing Act 1989) or hold any office under any principal council.

(6) An officer holding office with a National Park authority by virtue of an appointment made or adopted under this paragraph shall be known as a National Park officer.

Personal liability of members and officers

15. Section 265 of the Public Health Act 1875 (personal liability of members and officers of certain authorities) shall have effect as if—

(a) a National Park authority were an authority such as is mentioned in that section;

(b) the references in that section to a member of the authority included, in relation to a National Park authority, references to any person who is not such a member but for the time being serves as a member of a committee or sub-committee of such an authority;

(c) the references in that section to the purpose of executing that Act and to the purposes of that Act were each, in relation to a National Park authority, references to the purpose of carrying out the functions of that authority by virtue of Part III of this Act; and

(d) the words "or rate" were omitted.

Liaison with parish and community councils

16. A National Park authority shall make arrangements—

(a) in the case of a National Park in England, with each parish council the area of which is comprised wholly or partly within the Park, or

(b) in the case of a National Park in Wales, with each community council the area of which is so comprised,

for the purpose of informing and consulting that council about the authority's discharge of its functions.

Documents, notices, records, byelaws etc.

17.—(1) The Local Government (Records) Act 1962 shall have effect in relation to a National Park authority as if that authority were a local authority for the purposes of that Act.

(2) Subject to sub-paragraph (3) below, the following provisions of the 1972 Act, that is to say—

(a) sections 224 and 225(1) (custody and deposit of documents with a proper officer of the local authority),

(b) sections 228 and 229 (inspection of documents and photocopies),

(c) section 230 (reports and returns),

(d) sections 231 to 234 (service and authentication of documents), and

(e) without prejudice to their application by virtue of any other provision of Part III of this Act, sections 236 to 238 (byelaws),

shall have effect as if for the purposes of those provisions a National Park authority were a local authority or, in the case of section 224, a principal council.

(3) References in section 228 of the 1972 Act to a local government elector shall have effect for the purposes of that section as applied by sub-paragraph (2) above as if, in relation to a National Park authority, they were references to a local government elector for any principal area the whole or any part of which is comprised in the relevant Park.

(4) Section 41 of the Local Government (Miscellaneous Provisions) Act 1976 (evidence of resolutions and minutes of proceedings) shall have effect as if a National Park authority were a local authority for the purposes of that Act.

(5) Where a National Park authority has made any byelaws and those byelaws have been confirmed, that authority shall send a copy of the byelaws as confirmed to every council for a principal area the whole or any part of which is comprised in the relevant Park.

Investigation in connection with maladministration etc.

18.—(1) In section 25(1) of the Local Government Act 1974 (bodies subject to investigation under Part III of that Act), after paragraph (aa) there shall be inserted the following paragraph—

"(ab) a National Park authority;".

(2) In section 26(7) of that Act (no investigation where complaint relates to all or most of the inhabitants of an area), before paragraph (a) there shall be inserted the following paragraph—

"(aa) where the complaint relates to a National Park authority, the area of the Park for which it is such an authority;".

(3) In section 34(1) of that Act (interpretation), in the definition of "member", after "the joint board" there shall be inserted "and in relation to a National Park authority, includes a member of any of the councils by whom a local authority member of the authority is appointed".

Audit by Audit Commission auditor etc.

19.—(1) In section 12(2) of the Local Government Finance Act 1982 (bodies whose accounts are subject to audit), after paragraph (ff) there shall be inserted the following paragraph—

"(fg) a National Park authority;"

and sections 1 to 7 of the Local Government Act 1992 (performance standards and further provisions relating to audit) shall have effect accordingly.

(2) Sections 19 and 20 of that Act of 1982 (unlawful payments etc.) shall have effect as if references in those sections to a local authority included references to a National Park authority.

(3) In section 36 of that Act of 1982 (interpretation), after subsection (3) there shall be inserted the following subsection—

"(3A) In the application of Part III of this Act in relation to a National Park authority, any reference to a local government elector for the area of the authority shall be construed as a reference to a local government elector for any area the whole or any part of which is comprised in the Park for which that authority is the local planning authority."

Meaning of "relevant order"

20. In this Schedule "the relevant order", in relation to a National Park authority, means—

(a) the order under section 63 of this Act establishing that authority;

(b) any order under that section relating to that authority; or

(c) any order made in relation to that authority in exercise of the power to amend an order under that section.

Section 65   SCHEDULE 8

<small>SUPPLEMENTAL AND INCIDENTAL POWERS OF NATIONAL PARK AUTHORITIES</small>

Powers in relation to land etc.

1.—(1) Subject to sub-paragraph (2) below, the following provisions, that is to say—

(a) sections 120, 122 and 123 of the 1972 Act (powers of local authorities to acquire and dispose of land), and

(b) sections 128 to 131 of that Act (general provisions in relation to land transactions), shall have effect as if, for the purposes of those provisions, a National Park authority were a principal council and the relevant Park were the authority's area.

(2) The following provisions of the Local Government (Miscellaneous Provisions) Act 1976, that is to say—

(a) section 13 (compulsory acquisition of rights over land),

(b) section 15 (survey of land for the purposes of compulsory purchase),

(c) section 16 (obtaining information about land), and

(d) section 29 (repayment of unclaimed compensation),

shall apply in relation to a National Park authority as if the authority were a local authority for the purposes of that Act.

(3) Section 33 of the Local Government (Miscellaneous Provisions) Act 1982 (enforceability by local authorities of certain covenants relating to land) shall have effect as if references to a principal council included references to a National Park authority and as if the relevant Park were that authority's area; and for the purposes of this paragraph the reference in subsection (1) of that section to section 111 of the 1972 Act shall have effect as a reference to section 65 of this Act.

(4) This paragraph shall be without prejudice to any power conferred on a National Park authority by virtue of paragraph 2 below.

2.—(1) After section 244 of the Town and Country Planning Act 1990 (powers of joint planning boards) there shall be inserted the following section—

"Powers of National Park authorities under Part IX

244A.—(1) A National Park authority shall, on being authorised to do so by the Secretary of State, have the same power to acquire land compulsorily as the local authorities to whom section 226 applies have under that section.

(2) A National Park authority shall have the same power to acquire land by agreement as the local authorities mentioned in subsection (1) of section 227 have under that subsection.

(3) Sections 226(1) and (7), 227, 229, 230, 232, 233 and 235 to 242 shall apply with the necessary modifications as if a National Park authority were a local authority to which those sections applied and as if the Park in relation to which it carries out functions were the authority's area."

(2) Every such reference in that Act to the acquisition or appropriation of land for planning purposes as falls to be construed in accordance with section 246 of that Act shall be taken (so far as it would not otherwise do so) to include a reference to an acquisition or appropriation of land under any power conferred by virtue of sub-paragraph (1) above.

(3) The following provisions of that Act, that is to say—

(a) sections 251(1), 258(1), 260(1), 261, 271, 272 and 274 (extinguishing rights of way and other rights),

(b) sections 275 and 276 (extension and modification of functions of statutory undertakers), and

(c) section 324(6) (rights of entry),

shall have effect as if a National Park authority were a local authority for the purposes of that Act.

(4) The reference to a local authority in section 66(2) of the Planning (Listed Buildings and Conservation Areas) Act 1990 (which refers to the powers of a local authority under sections 232, 233 and 235(1) of the Town and Country Planning Act 1990) shall include a reference to a National Park authority.

Miscellaneous transactions and powers

3.—(1) The following provisions of the 1972 Act shall also have effect as if a National Park authority were a principal council for the purposes of that Act and as if the relevant Park were the authority's area, that is to say—

(a) section 132 (use of premises);

(b) section 135 (contracts of local authorities);

(c) section 136 (contributions towards expenditure on concurrent functions);

(d) section 139 (acceptance of gifts of property);

(e) sections 140, 140A and 140C (insurance);

(f) section 143 (subscriptions to local government associations); and

(g) sections 222 and 223 (conduct of prosecutions and participation in other legal proceedings).

(2) Section 38 of the Local Government (Miscellaneous Provisions) Act 1976 (use of spare capacity of local authority computers) shall have effect as if a National Park authority were a local authority for the purposes of that Act.

(3) Section 41 of the Local Government (Miscellaneous Provisions) Act 1982 (lost property) shall have effect as if a National Park authority were a local authority for the purposes of that Act.

(4) Section 45 of that Act of 1982 (arrangements under the Employment and Training Act 1973) shall have effect as if a National Park authority were a local authority to which that section applies.

Transfer of securities on alteration of area

4. Section 146 of the 1972 Act (transfer of securities on alteration of area) shall have effect as if a National Park authority were a local authority for the purposes of that Act and as if the reference in subsection (1)(b) of that section to an enactment similar to a provision of the 1972 Act included a reference to any provision of Part III of this Act.

The Local Authorities (Goods and Services) Act 1970

5. The Local Authorities (Goods and Services) Act 1970 (supply of goods and services by local authorities) shall have effect as if a National Park authority were both a local authority and a public body for the purposes of that Act.

Power to execute works outside Park

6. Any power to execute works which is conferred on a National Park authority by virtue of Part III of this Act or any other enactment shall be taken, except in so far as the contrary intention appears, to include power, for the purposes of the carrying out of the authority's functions in relation to the relevant Park, to execute works of the relevant description outside, as well as inside, that Park.

Power to promote Bills

7.—(1) Section 239 of the 1972 Act (power of local authority to promote local or personal Bills) shall have effect in relation to a National Park authority as if it were a local authority for the purposes of that Act and as if the relevant Park were the authority's area.

(2) A National Park authority shall have no power by virtue of Part III of this Act to promote a Bill for—
    (a) modifying the area of any National Park or any local government area;
    (b) modifying the authority's own constitution or that of any other National Park authority; or
    (c) modifying the status or the electoral arrangements of any such local government area.

(3) In sub-paragraph (2) above—
    "electoral arrangements" means any electoral arrangements within the meaning of section 14(4) of the Local Government Act 1992 or any corresponding arrangements in relation to any area in Wales; and
    "local government area" means any local government area within the meaning of that Act or any area in Wales for which any council carries out functions of local government.

Competitive tendering etc.

8.—(1) Part III of the Local Government, Planning and Land Act 1980 (direct labour organisations) shall have effect in relation to a National Park authority as if such an authority were a local authority for the purposes of that Part.

(2) In section 1(1) of the Local Government Act 1988 (defined authorities for the purposes of the provisions of that Act relating to competition), after paragraph (a) there shall be inserted the following paragraph—

"(aa) a National Park authority;".

(3) In Schedule 2 to that Act of 1988 (bodies to which Part II of that Act applies), after the entry relating to the Broads Authority there shall be inserted—

"Any National Park authority".

(4) In section 18 of that Act of 1988 (race relations matters), after subsection (7) there shall be inserted the following subsection—

"(7A) Any reference in this section to a local authority shall be deemed to include a reference to a National Park authority."

(5) In section 33(3)(c) of that Act of 1988 (definition of "relevant public body" for the purposes of provisions relating to contracts with associated companies), after "within" there shall be inserted "paragraph (aa) or".

(6) References in sections 8 to 10 of the Local Government Act 1992 (competition) to any provisions of that Act of 1980 or of that Act of 1988 shall include references to those provisions as they have effect by virtue of this paragraph.

Restrictions on publicity

9. Part II of the Local Government Act 1986 (restrictions on publicity) shall have effect as if a National Park authority were a local authority for the purposes of that Part.

Provisions applying in relation to companies in which authorities have interests

10. In section 67(3) of the Local Government and Housing Act 1989 (local authorities for the purposes of Part V of that Act), after paragraph (m) there shall be inserted the following paragraph—

"(ma) a National Park authority;".

Provisions as to charges

11. In section 152(2) of that Act of 1989 (provisions as to charges), after paragraph (l) there shall be inserted the following paragraph—

"(ja) a National Park authority;"

and section 151 of that Act (power to amend existing provisions as to charges) shall have effect as if references to an existing provision included references to any such provision as applied by Part III of this Act.

Service agency agreements

12. Section 25 of the Local Government (Wales) Act 1994 (service agency agreements) shall have effect as if a National Park authority for any National Park in Wales were a new principal council for the purposes of that section.

Contracting out

13. Part II of the Deregulation and Contracting Out Act 1994 (contracting out) shall have effect as if a National Park authority were a local authority for the purposes of that Part.

Section 70   SCHEDULE 9

MISCELLANEOUS STATUTORY FUNCTIONS OF NATIONAL PARK AUTHORITIES

Common land etc.

1.—(1) The enactments specified in sub-paragraph (2) below shall have effect in relation to any registered common which—

(a) is within any National Park for which a National Park authority is the local planning authority, and

(b) is not owned by, or vested in, any other body which is a local authority,

as if the National Park authority were a local authority for the purposes of those enactments and as if the relevant Park were that authority's area.

(2) The enactments mentioned in sub-paragraph (1) above are—

(a) section 1 of the Commons Act 1899 (scheme for regulation);

(b) section 194(2) of the Law of Property Act 1925 (application for removal of works);

(c) section 23 of and Schedule 2 to the Caravan Sites and Control of Development Act 1960 (power of district council to prohibit caravans on commons); and

(d) section 9 of the Commons Registration Act 1965 (protection of unclaimed common land).

(3) In the Commons Act 1899 references to the council by which a scheme is made under section 1 of that Act shall be construed accordingly; and the powers conferred by sections 7 and

12 of that Act (acquisition of land and contributions to expenses) shall be exercisable by a National Park authority in relation to the relevant Park as they are exercisable by a district council in relation to their district.

(4) A National Park authority shall have the same power to make an application under section 18 of the Commons Act 1899 (modification of provisions for recreation grounds) as a local authority.

(5) References in this paragraph, in relation to an enactment specified in sub-paragraph (2) above or to any enactment contained in section 18 of the Commons Act 1899, to a local authority are references to any such local authority, within the meaning of the 1972 Act, as has functions conferred on it by or by virtue of that enactment.

(6) In this paragraph "registered common" means any land registered as common land or as a town or village green under the Commons Registration Act 1965.

Open spaces

2. The Open Spaces Act 1906 shall have effect as if references in that Act to a local authority included references to a National Park authority.

Nature reserves

3. Sections 21 and 22 of the National Parks and Access to the Countryside Act 1949 (establishment of nature reserves and application of enactments to local authority reserves) shall have effect as if the bodies on whom powers are conferred by section 21 of that Act included every National Park authority and as if the relevant Park were the authority's area; and references in those sections to a local authority and to their area shall be construed accordingly.

Caravan sites

4. In the Caravan Sites and Control of Development Act 1960—
(a) section 24 (power to provide sites for caravans), and
(b) paragraph 11 of Schedule 1 to that Act (no licence required for land occupied by a local authority),
shall have effect as if a National Park authority were a local authority for the purposes of that Act and as if the relevant Park were that authority's area.

Country Parks

5. The Countryside Act 1968 shall have effect as if a National Park authority were a local authority for the purposes of—
(a) sections 6 to 8 of that Act (country parks);
(b) section 9 of that Act (powers exercisable over or near common land); and
(c) section 41 of that Act (byelaws) in so far as it has the effect in relation to—
    (i) any country park provided under section 7 of that Act, or
    (ii) any land as respects which any powers under section 9 of that Act have been exercised,
    of conferring powers on a local authority or of applying provisions of section 92 of the National Parks and Access to the Countryside Act 1949 (wardens);
and the references to a local authority in sections 43 to 45 of that Act of 1968 (general provisions as to the powers of local authorities) shall have effect accordingly.

Provision of information and encouragement of visitors

6. Sections 142 and 144 of the 1972 Act (provision of information about local services and encouragement of visitors) shall have effect (subject to paragraph 9 of Schedule 8 to this Act) as if a National Park authority were a local authority for the purposes of that Act and as if the relevant Park were the authority's area.

Derelict land etc.

7. The provisions of section 16 of the Welsh Development Agency Act 1975 and of section 1 of the Derelict Land Act 1982 (powers for the improvement of land) shall have effect in relation to land in a National Park for which a National Park authority is the local planning authority as if references in those provisions to a local authority included references to the National Park authority and as if the relevant Park were the authority's area.

Recreational facilities

8. Section 19 of the Local Government (Miscellaneous Provisions) Act 1976 (recreational facilities) shall have effect as if the powers conferred by that section on local authorities were

also conferred, so as to be exercisable within a National Park for which a National Park authority is the local planning authority, on that authority.

Refuse Disposal

9.—(1) Subject to sub-paragraph (2) below, references to a local authority in the Refuse Disposal (Amenity) Act 1978 shall have effect in relation to land in a National Park for which a National Park authority is the local planning authority as if they included references to that authority and as if the relevant Park were the authority's area.

(2) Sub-paragraph (1) above shall not apply, in relation to any time before the coming into force of the repeal of section 1 of that Act, to any reference in that section.

Ancient Monuments and Archaeological Areas

10.—(1) Subject to sub-paragraph (2) below, Parts I and II of the Ancient Monuments and Archaeological Areas Act 1979 shall have effect as if in relation—

(a) to any monument in a National Park for which a National Park authority is the local planning authority, or

(b) to any area the whole or any part of which is comprised in such a Park,

the references in those Parts to a local authority included references to that National Park authority.

(2) Section 35 of that Act (notice of operations affecting area of archaeological importance) shall have effect in relation to land in such a National Park as is mentioned in sub-paragraph (1) above as if—

(a) any notice required to be served on a local authority under that section were required, instead, to be served on the National Park authority; and

(b) the functions conferred on a local authority by virtue of that section had been conferred instead on the National Park authority.

(3) Section 45(2) and (3) of that Act (assistance for archaeological investigations) shall have effect as if a National Park authority were a local authority for the purposes of that Act and as if the relevant Park were the authority's area.

Footpaths and bridleways

11. The following provisions of the Highways Act 1980, that is to say—

(a) sections 25 to 29 (footpaths and bridleways),

(b) section 72(2) (widening of public paths),

(c) sections 118 to 121 (stopping up and diversion of public paths), and

(d) Schedule 6 (procedure for orders),

shall have effect as if references in those sections to a local authority or council included references to a National Park authority and as if the relevant Park were the authority's area.

Litter

12. The following provisions, that is to say—

(a) section 4 of the Litter Act 1983 (consultations and proposals for the abatement of litter), and

(b) section 88 of the Environmental Protection Act 1990 (fixed penalty notices for leaving litter),

shall have effect as if a National Park authority were a litter authority for the purposes of those provisions, as if the relevant Park were the authority's area and as if the reference in that section 4 to the authority's area were a reference to any part of the relevant Park.

Listed and historic buildings

13.—(1) In the case of a building situated in a National Park for which a National Park authority is the local planning authority, that authority and no other authority shall be the appropriate authority for the purposes of sections 47 to 51 of the Planning (Listed Buildings and Conservation Areas) Act 1990 (purchase of listed buildings etc in need of repair); and the reference to a local authority in section 88(5) of that Act (rights of entry) and in section 6 of the Historic Buildings and Ancient Monuments Act 1953 (under which grants for the acquisition of buildings in Wales may be made) shall have effect accordingly.

(2) In relation to any building or land in any such National Park, the powers conferred on a county council or county borough council by section 52 of that Act of 1990 (power to acquire building and land by agreement) shall be exercisable by the National Park authority, and not (without prejudice to their powers apart from that section) by any other authority; and subsection (2) of that section shall have effect accordingly.

(3) Section 53(1) of that Act (management of listed buildings etc. acquired under the Act) shall apply in relation to the powers conferred by virtue of this paragraph on a National Park authority as it applies in relation to the powers conferred by sections 47 and 52 of that Act on a local authority.

(4) That Act shall have effect as if a National Park authority were a local authority for the purposes of—

(a) sections 54 and 55 of that Act (urgent works to preserve listed buildings etc.), and

(b) sections 57 and 58 of that Act (power of local authorities to contribute towards preservation of listed buildings etc.),

and, in relation to those provisions, as if the relevant Park were the authority's area.

(5) In relation to the powers conferred on a National Park authority by virtue of this paragraph, section 88 of that Act (powers of entry) shall have effect as if references in that section to a local authority included references to a National Park authority.

(6) References to a local authority in section 90(1) to (4) of that Act (financial provisions) shall be deemed to include references to a National Park authority.

Hazardous substances

14.—(1) For the purposes of the Planning (Hazardous Substances) Act 1990, where a National Park authority is the local planning authority for any National Park, that authority, and no other authority, shall be the hazardous substances authority for land in the relevant Park.

(2) References to a local authority in sections 12 and 38(1) to (4) of that Act (government consent to local authority activities and financial provisions) shall be deemed to include references to a National Park authority.

Local Charities

15. Sections 76 to 78 of the Charities Act 1993 (local charities) shall have effect as if the references to a council for any area included references to a National Park authority and as if the relevant Park were the authority's area.

Overseas Assistance

16. The Local Government (Overseas Assistance) Act 1993 shall have effect as if a National Park authority were a local authority for the purposes of that Act.

Section 78 SCHEDULE 10

MINOR AND CONSEQUENTIAL AMENDMENTS RELATING TO NATIONAL PARKS

The Finance Act 1931 (c. 28)

1. In Schedule 2 to the Finance Act 1931 (requirements in connection with production of instruments of transfer), in paragraph (viii), for "local authority" there shall be substituted "local planning authority".

The National Parks and Access to the Countryside Act 1949 (c. 97)

2.—(1) In section 6 of the National Parks and Access to the Countryside Act 1949 (general duties of Countryside Commission and the Countryside Council for Wales as respects the National Parks)—

(a) in subsection (3)—

(i) in paragraph (a), before "local authorities" there shall be inserted "National Park authorities and"; and

(ii) in paragraph (b), before "local authority" there shall be inserted "National Park authority";

and

(b) in subsection (6), after "means" there shall be inserted the words "a National Park authority or".

(2) In section 7 of that Act—

(a) in subsection (5) (bodies consulted about variation of the area of a National Park), after "consult with" there shall be inserted "any National Park authority for the Park in question and with"; and

(b) in subsection (6) (notices), after "as the case may be" there shall be inserted "at the offices (where the order is for the variation of an order designating a Park) of any National Park authority for the Park in question".

(3) In section 9(1) of that Act (local planning authority to consult Countryside Commission or Countryside Council for Wales about proposals for a development plan affecting a National Park), for "the local planning authority" there shall be substituted "the authority or authorities who are required to prepare the plan or, as the case may be, who are entitled to alter or add to it".

(4) In section 12(1) of that Act (provision in a National Park of facilities) for "provision in" there shall be substituted "provision for".

(5) In subsection (4) of section 51 of that Act (consultation as to proposals for a long distance route)—

(a) after the word "every", in the first place where it occurs, there shall be inserted "National Park authority,";

(b) after "whose" there shall be inserted "Park or"; and

(c) after "every such" there shall be inserted "authority,";

and in subsection (5) of that section (report to contain estimates of capital outlay by local authorities), after "local authorities" there shall be inserted "and National Park authorities".

(6) In section 52(2) of that Act (notice of determination as to any proposals on long distance routes)—

(a) after "every" there shall be inserted "National Park authority"; and

(b) after "whose" there shall be inserted "Park or".

(7) For section 88 of that Act (application to areas of outstanding natural beauty of provisions relating to National Parks) there shall be substituted—

"Functions of certain bodies in relation to areas of outstanding natural beauty

88.—(1) The following provisions of this Act, that is to say—

(a) paragraph (e) of subsection (4) of section six,

(b) section nine,

(c) subsection (1) of section sixty-two,

(d) subsection (5) of section sixty-four, and

(e) subsections (5) and (5A) of section sixty-five,

shall apply in relation to areas of outstanding natural beauty as they apply in relation to National Parks.

(2) In paragraph (e) of subsection (4) of section six of this Act as it applies by virtue of the last foregoing subsection, the expression "appropriate planning authority" means a local planning authority whose area consists of or includes the whole or any part of an area of outstanding natural beauty and includes a local authority, not being a local planning authority, by whom any powers of a local planning authority as respects an area of outstanding natural beauty are exercisable, whether under this Act or otherwise.

(3) The provisions of section 4A of this Act shall apply to the provisions mentioned in paragraphs (a) and (b) of subsection (1) of this section for the purposes of their application to areas of outstanding natural beauty as the provisions of the said section 4A apply for the purposes of Part II of this Act.

(4) A local planning authority whose area consists of or includes the whole or any part of an area of outstanding natural beauty shall have power, subject to the following provisions of this section, to take all such action as appears to them expedient for the accomplishment of the purpose of conserving and enhancing the natural beauty of the area of outstanding natural beauty or so much thereof as is included in their area.

(5) Nothing in this Act shall be construed as limiting the generality of the last foregoing subsection; but in so far as the provisions of this Act confer specific powers falling within that subsection those powers shall be exercised in accordance with those provisions and subject to any limitations expressed or implied therein.

(6) Without prejudice to the powers conferred by this Act, subsection (4) of this section shall have effect only for the purpose of removing any limitation imposed by law on the capacity of a local planning authority by virtue of its constitution, and shall not authorise any act or omission on the part of such an authority which apart from that subsection would be actionable at the suit of any person on any ground other than such a limitation."

(8) In section 114(2) of that Act (construction of references to the preservation of the natural beauty of an area) after the word "preservation"—

(a) in the first place where it occurs, there shall be inserted the words ", or the conservation,", and

(b) in the second place where it occurs, there shall be inserted the words "or, as the case may be, the conservation".

(9) In Schedule 1 to that Act (procedure for certain orders)—

(a) in paragraph 1, after sub-paragraph (3) there shall be inserted the following sub-paragraph—

"(3A) Where under this paragraph any notice is required to be given by any person in respect of any land which is already in a National Park for which a National Park authority is the local planning authority, that person shall serve a copy of that notice on that authority.";

(b) in paragraph 2(5), after "the Council" there shall be inserted "a National Park authority,";

(c) in paragraph 3(a), after "under sub-paragraph" there shall be inserted "(3A) or"; and

(d) after paragraph 3 there shall be inserted the following paragraph—

"3A. An order designating a National Park shall have effect as from such time as may be determined by the Minister and specified in the notice of the confirmation of that order."

The Landlord and Tenant Act 1954 (c. 56)

3. In section 69(1) of the Landlord and Tenant Act 1954 (interpretation), in the definition of "local authority", for the words from "has the same meaning" to "Broads Authority" there shall be substituted "means any local authority within the meaning of the Town and Country Planning Act 1990, any National Park authority, the Broads Authority or".

The Land Compensation Act 1961 (c. 33)

4.—(1) Paragraph 55(2) of Schedule 16 to the 1972 Act (which relates to the operation of section 17 of the Land Compensation Act 1961 in a National Park) shall not apply in the case of a National Park for which a National Park authority is the local planning authority.

(2) In section 39(1) of that Act of 1961 (interpretation), for the definition of "local planning authority" there shall be substituted the following definition

" "local planning authority" shall be construed in accordance with Part I of the Town and Country Planning Act 1990;".

The Trustee Investments Act 1961 (c. 62)

5. In section 11 of the Trustee Investments Act 1961 (local authority investment schemes), in subsection (4)(a), after "the Broads Authority" there shall be inserted "a National Park authority".

The Agriculture Act 1967 (c. 22)

6. In section 50(3) of the Agriculture Act 1967 (bodies transfers to whom are not subject to section 49), after paragraph (a) there shall be inserted the following paragraph—

"(aa) a National Park authority;".

The Leasehold Reform Act 1967 (c. 88)

7. In section 28 of the Leasehold Reform Act 1967 (retention or resumption of land required for public purposes), in subsection (5), after paragraph (aa) there shall be inserted the following paragraph—

"(ab) to any National Park authority; and".

The Countryside Act 1968 (c. 41)

8.—(1) In section 4(1) of the Countryside Act 1968 (experimental projects and schemes) after "local authorities" there shall be inserted "National Park authorities".

(2) In section 12(1) of that Act (provision in National Park of facilities), for "provision in" there shall be substituted "provision for".

(3) In section 13(12) of that Act (enforcement of byelaws), for "in the area of that other local authority" there shall be substituted "for an area that includes any part of the National Park in question".

The Employers Liability (Compulsory Insurance) Act 1969 (c. 57)

9. In section 3 of the Employers Liability (Compulsory Insurance) Act 1969 (employers exempted from insurance), in subsection (2), after "the Broads Authority" there shall be inserted "a National Park authority".

The 1972 Act

10.—(1) In subsection (1)(a) of section 80 of the 1972 Act (disqualification for persons holding appointments made or confirmed by a local authority or connected authority), after "joint committee" there shall be inserted "or National Park authority"; and after subsection (2) of that section there shall be inserted the following subsections—

"(2A) Subsection (2) above shall have effect as if the reference to a joint board included a reference to a National Park authority.

(2B) For the purposes of this section a local authority shall be treated as represented on a National Park authority if it is entitled to make any appointment of a local authority member of the National Park authority."

(2) In section 184 of the 1972 Act (functions under countryside legislation)—

(a) at the beginning of subsection (1) there shall be inserted the words "Subject to section 68 of the Environment Act 1995 (planning authority functions under National Parks legislation to be functions of National Park authorities in certain cases),"; and

(b) in paragraph (b) of that subsection, for the words "subsections (6) to (8) below" there shall be substituted the words "subsections (7) and (8) below".

(3) In subsection (3) of that section, for the words "sections 9 and 11" there shall be substituted the words "section 9".

The Employment Agencies Act 1973 (c. 35)

11. In section 13(7) of the Employment Agencies Act 1973 (cases in which Act does not apply), after paragraph (ff) there shall be inserted the following paragraph—

"(fg) the exercise by a National Park authority of any of its functions;".

The Health and Safety at Work etc. Act 1974 (c. 37)

12. In section 28 of the Health and Safety at Work etc. Act 1974 (restrictions on disclosure of information), for subsection (10) there shall be substituted the following subsection—

"(10) The Broads Authority and every National Park authority shall be deemed to be local authorities for the purposes of this section."

The Welsh Development Agency Act 1975 (c. 70)

13.—(1) In section 1(14) of the Welsh Development Agency Act 1975 (consultation by Agency with local authorities and other bodies), after "local authorities" there shall be inserted "National Park authorities".

(2) In subsections (1) and (2) of section 5 of that Act (assistance to the Agency from other bodies), after "local authority", in each case, there shall be inserted "a National Park authority".

(3) In section 15(1) of that Act (which refers to consultation under section 1(14)), after "local authorities" there shall be inserted "National Park authorities".

Local Land Charges Act 1975 (c. 76)

14. In sections 1 and 2 of the Local Land Charges Act 1975 (obligations that are and are not local land charges), after the words "local authority", in each place where they occur, there shall be inserted "or National Park authority".

The Race Relations Act 1976 (c. 74)

15.—(1) In section 19A of the Race Relations Act 1976 (discrimination in planning), in subsection (2)(a) (definition of "planning authority"), after "the Broads Authority" there shall be inserted "a National Park authority or".

(2) In section 71 of that Act (general statutory duty of local authorities), after "the Broads Authority" there shall be inserted "and every National Park authority".

The Development of Rural Wales Act 1976 (c. 75)

16.—(1) In section 1(4) of the Development of Rural Wales Act 1976 (consultation as to orders varying area for which the Board is responsible), after paragraph (b) there shall be inserted the following paragraph—

"(ba) every National Park authority which is the local planning authority for a National Park any part of which will be included in the area for which the Board is responsible if the order is made or which (whether the proposal is for an order under subsection (2) or for an order under subsection (3)) is included in the area for which it is responsible at the time of the proposal;".

(2) In section 4(1)(d)(i) of that Act (power to finance measures taken by local authorities), after "local authority" there shall be inserted "National Park authority".

(3) In subsections (1) and (3) of section 8 of that Act (assistance to the Board from other bodies), after "local authority", in each case, there shall be inserted "National Park authority".

(4) In paragraph 3(3) of Schedule 1 to that Act (consultation as to membership of Board), after paragraph (a) there shall be inserted the following paragraph—

"(aa) every National Park authority which is the local planning authority for a National Park any part of which is included in the area for which the Board is responsible; and".

(5) In Schedule 3 to that Act (the New Towns code), in paragraph 14 (special parliamentary procedure for compulsory purchase of local authority property), after the words "local authority", in each place where they occur, there shall be inserted "or National Park authority".

The Rent (Agriculture) Act 1976 (c.80)

17. In section 5(3) of the Rent (Agriculture) Act 1976 (no statutory tenancy where landlord's interest belongs to Crown or local authority etc.), after paragraph (bc) there shall be inserted the following paragraph—
"(bd) any National Park authority;".

The Rent Act 1977 (c.42)

18. In section 14 of the Rent Act 1977 (exemption from protection for lettings by local authorities etc.), after paragraph (bb) there shall be inserted the following paragraph—
"(bc) a National Park authority;".

The Justices of the Peace Act 1979 (c. 55)

19. In section 64 of the Justices of the Peace Act 1979 (which disqualifies in certain circumstances justices who are members of local authorities), in subsection (2A), for the words "shall be treated as a local authority" there shall be substituted "and every National Park authority shall be deemed to be local authorities."

The Local Government, Planning and Land Act 1980 (c. 65)

20.—(1) In section 103 of the Local Government, Planning and Land Act 1980—
(a) in subsection (2)(c) (consultation with local authorities as to acquisition of land by the Land Authority for Wales), the word "and" immediately preceding sub-paragraph (ii) shall be omitted and after that sub-paragraph there shall be inserted "and
(iii) any National Park authority which is the local planning authority for a National Park in which the land, or any part of the land, is situated"; and
(b) after subsection (8) there shall be inserted the following subsection—
"(8A) Subsections (6) to (8) above shall have effect as if any reference to a council included a reference to a National Park authority for a National Park in Wales and the references to the area of a council were to be construed accordingly."
(2) In paragraph 1 of Schedule 19 to that Act (public authorities who may be assisted by that Authority), after sub-paragraph (f) there shall be inserted the following sub-paragraph—
"(fa) a National Park authority;".
(3) In paragraph 4 of Schedule 20 to that Act (notice to and objections by local authorities in the case of compulsory purchase by that Authority), at the end there shall be inserted—
"For the purposes of this paragraph the references to a local authority within whose area the land is situated shall be deemed to include references to any National Park authority which is the local planning authority for a National Park in which the land is situated."
(4) In paragraph 9 of Schedule 21 to that Act (notice of planning applications) in sub-paragraph (1), after "Wales" there shall be inserted "and every National Park authority for a National Park in Wales".

The Acquisition of Land Act 1981 (c. 67)

21.—(1) In section 17(3) of the Acquisition of Land Act 1981 (special Parliamentary procedure not to apply to compulsory acquisition by certain bodies), after "subsection (4) below)" there shall be inserted ", a National Park authority".
(2) In paragraph 4(3) of Schedule 3 to that Act (which makes similar provision in relation to the acquisition of rights), after "sub-paragraph (4) below)" there shall be inserted ", a National Park authority".

The Wildlife and Countryside Act 1981 (c. 69)

22.—(1) In section 39(5)(a) of the Wildlife and Countryside Act 1981 (definition of "relevant authority"), before "in a National Park" there shall be inserted "which is not in an area for which a National Park authority is the local planning authority but is".
(2) In section 41(5A) of that Act (duties of agriculture Ministers with respect to the countryside to have effect in relation to the Broads as if the Broads were a National Park), at the end

there shall be inserted "(and, as respects land within the Broads, any reference in this section to the relevant authority is accordingly a reference to the Broads Authority)."

(3) In section 42 of that Act (notification of agricultural operations on moor and heath), for the words "local planning authority", wherever they occur, there shall be substituted "National Park authority".

(4) In section 44 of that Act (grants and loans for National Parks purposes)—

(a) in subsection (2), for "a local planning authority" there shall be substituted "the authority in question";

(b) in subsection (3), for "A local planning authority" there shall be substituted "The authority in question"; and

(c) in subsection (4), for the words from "county planning authority" onwards there shall be substituted "National Park authority and the Broads as a National Park for which it is the local planning authority".

(5) In section 51(2)(c) of that Act (definition of "relevant authority" in relation to the exercise of powers of entry for the purposes of section 42), for "local planning authority" there shall be substituted "National Park authority".

(6) In section 52(2) of that Act (construction of references to a local planning authority), after "except as respects" there shall be inserted "a National Park for which a National Park authority is the local planning authority,".

(7) Sub-paragraph (1) above shall cease to have effect with the coming into force of the repeal by this Act of section 39(5)(a) of that Act of 1981.

The County Courts Act 1984 (c.28)

23. In section 60(3) of the County Courts Act 1984 (right of audience for proper officer of local authority in certain circumstances), after "the Broads Authority" there shall be inserted "any National Park authority,".

The Housing Act 1985 (c.68)

24.—(1) In section 43 of the Housing Act 1985 (consent of the Secretary of State required for certain disposals by local authorities), after subsection (5) there shall be inserted the following subsection—

"(5A) References in this section and in section 44 to a local authority shall include references to a National Park authority."

(2) In section 45(2)(b) of that Act (definition of "public sector authority" for the purposes of provisions relating to service charges after disposal), after "a local authority" there shall be inserted—

"a National Park authority".

(3) In section 573 of that Act (definition of "public sector authority" for the purposes of assisting the owners of defective housing), after the entry relating to joint boards there shall be inserted the following entry—

"a National Park authority (or a predecessor of such an authority),".

The Landlord and Tenant Act 1985 (c. 70)

25.—(1) In sections 14(4) and 26(1) of, and in paragraph 9(1) of the Schedule to, the Landlord and Tenant Act 1985 (provisions excluding operation of certain provisions in the case of public sector housing), after "a local authority", in each case, there shall be inserted—

"a National Park authority".

(2) In section 28(6) of that Act (meaning of "qualified accountant" in the case of public sector landlords), after "local authority there shall be inserted "National Park authority".

(3) In section 31(3) of that Act (reserve powers to limit rents), in the definition of "rent", after "local authorities" there shall be inserted "National Park authorities".

The Landlord and Tenant Act 1987(c.31)

26. In section 58(1) of the Landlord and Tenant Act 1987 (exempt landlords), after paragraph (dd) there shall be inserted the following paragraph—

"(de) a National Park authority;".

The Norfolk and Suffolk Broads Act 1988 (c. 4)

27. In Schedule 3 to the Norfolk and Suffolk Broads Act 1988 (functions of the Broads authority), in paragraph 43, for the words from "as a local authority" onwards there shall be substituted "for the purposes of the Derelict Land Act 1982 as a National Park authority and the Broads as a National Park for which it is the local planning authority".

The Housing Act 1988 (c. 50)

28. In paragraph 12(2) of Schedule 1 to the Housing Act 1988 (meaning of "local authority" for the purposes of determining the tenancies to be treated as local authority tenancies), after paragraph (d) there shall be inserted the following paragraph—
"(da) a National Park authority;".

The Road Traffic Act 1988 (c. 52)

29. In section 144(2)(a)(i) of the Road Traffic Act 1988 (exemptions from requirement of third party insurance or security), after "London borough" there shall be inserted "a National Park authority".

The Electricity Act 1989 (c. 29)

30.—(1) Paragraph 2(6) of Schedule 8 to the Electricity Act 1989 (definition of "relevant planning authority" for the purposes of consents under that Act) shall be amended in accordance with the following provisions of this paragraph.
(2) In this paragraph "the 1994 amendment" means the omission of the words "and Wales" in paragraph (a) of the said paragraph 2(6) by paragraph 22 of Schedule 6 to the Local Government (Wales) Act 1994.
(3) If the 1994 amendment comes into force after this paragraph, then—
(a) in paragraph (a) of the said paragraph 2(6), for the words "England and Wales" there shall be substituted the words "land in England and Wales which is not in a National Park for which a National Park authority is the local planning authority";
(b) after that paragraph (a) there shall be inserted the following paragraph—
"(aa) in relation to land in England and Wales which is in a National Park for which a National Park authority is the local planning authority, means that National Park authority; and";
(c) the 1994 amendment shall have effect in relation to the said paragraph (a) as amended by paragraph (a) above, and on the coming into force of the 1994 amendment the words "and Wales" shall also be omitted from the paragraph (aa) inserted by paragraph (b) above.
(4) If the 1994 amendment comes into force before this paragraph, then—
(a) in paragraph (a) of the said paragraph 2(6), for the word "England" there shall be substituted the words "land in England which is not in a National Park for which a National Park authority is the local planning authority"; and
(b) after that paragraph (a) there shall be inserted the following paragraph—
"(aa) in relation to land in England which is in a National Park for which a National Park authority is the local planning authority, means that National Park authority; and".
(5) If the 1994 amendment comes into force on the same day as this paragraph, the 1994 amendment shall be deemed to have come into force immediately before this paragraph (and sub-paragraph (4) above shall have effect accordingly).
(6) The paragraph (aa) inserted by paragraph 22 of Schedule 6 to the Local Government (Wales) Act 1994 shall be re-numbered "(ab)".

The Local Government and Housing Act 1989 (c. 42)

31.—(1) In section 21(1) of the Local Government and Housing Act 1989 (interpretation of Part I) the word "and" immediately preceding paragraph (m) shall be omitted and after that paragraph there shall be added "and
(n) a joint planning board constituted for an area in Wales outside a National Park by an order under section 2(1B) of the Town and Country Planning Act 1990."
(2) In section 39(1) of that Act (application of Part IV), after paragraph (h) there shall be inserted—
"(hh) a joint planning board constituted for an area in Wales outside a National Park by an order under section 2(1 B) of the Town and Country Planning Act 1990;".
(3) In section 67(3) of that Act (local authorities for the purposes of Part V) the word "and" at the end of paragraph (o) shall be omitted and after that paragraph there shall be inserted—
"(oo) a joint planning board constituted for an area in Wales outside a National Park by an order under section 2(1 B) of the Town and Country Planning Act 1990; and".
(4) In section 152(2) of that Act (relevant authorities for the purposes of imposing certain charges) the word "and" immediately preceding paragraph (1) shall be omitted and after that paragraph there shall be added "and

(m) a joint planning board constituted for an area in Wales outside a National Park by an order under section 2(1B) of the Town and Country Planning Act 1990."

(5) In paragraph 2(1)(b) of Schedule 1 to that Act (bodies to which appointments are made taking account of political balance) for" paragraphs (k) and (m) there shall be substituted "paragraphs (k), (m) and (n)".

The Town and Country Planning Act 1990 (c. 8)

32.—(1) In paragraph (a) of section 1(5) of the Town and Country Planning Act 1990 (provisions to which subsections (1) to (4) are subject)

(a) for "sections 5 to" there shall be substituted "sections 4A to"; and
(b) at the end there shall be inserted "and".

(2) In section 2 of that Act (joint planning boards), before subsection (2) of that section there shall be inserted the following subsection—

"(1D) The areas that may be constituted as a united district for the purposes of this section shall not include the whole or any part of an area which is comprised in a National Park for which there is a National Park authority."

(3) In section 4 of that Act (National Parks), after subsection (4) there shall be inserted the following subsection—

"(5) This section shall have effect subject to section 4A below."

(4) In sections 90(1) and 101(2)(c) of that Act (development with government authorisation), after the words "local authority", in each place where they occur, there shall be inserted "or National Park authority".

(5) In sections 169 and 170(2)(b) of that Act (provisions in relation to blighted land), after "local authority" there shall be inserted "National Park authority".

(6) In section 209(5) of that Act (regulations for charging expenses of a local authority which is a local planning authority on land), after "local authority" there shall be inserted "or National Park authority".

(7) In section 252 of that Act (procedure for making certain orders)—

(a) in subsection (2) (bodies to be given notice), after paragraph (a) there shall be inserted the following paragraph—

"(aa) on any National Park authority which is the local planning authority for the area in which any highway or, as the case may be, any land to which the order relates is situated, and";

(b) in subsection (4) (objections), after "local authority" there shall be inserted "National Park authority".

(8) In section 253(2)(a) of that Act (procedure in anticipation of planning permission)—

(a) in subsections (2)(a) and (3)(a), after "local authority, in each case, there shall be inserted "National Park authority"; and

(b) in subsection (4), after "London borough" there shall be inserted "a National Park authority".

(9) In section 305(1)(a) of that Act (contribution by Ministers towards compensation paid by local authorities), after "local authority there shall be inserted "or National Park authority".

(10) In section 306 of that Act (contributions by local authorities and statutory undertakers), after subsection (5) there shall be inserted the following subsection—

"(6) This section shall have effect as if the references to a local authority included references to a National Park authority."

(11) In section 330 of that Act (power to require information as to interests in land), after subsection (5) there shall be inserted the following subsection—

"(6) This section shall have effect as if the references to a local authority included references to a National Park authority".

(12) In section 333(1) of that Act (regulations as to form of notice etc.), after "local authority" there shall be inserted "or National Park authority."

(13) In section 336(1) of that Act (interpretation), in the definition of "local authority" after "subsection (10)" there shall be inserted "below and section 71(7) of the Environment Act 1995".

(14) In Schedule 1 to that Act (distribution of planning functions)—

(a) in paragraph 4(2) (consultation with district planning authorities)—

(i) after "determined by a" there shall be inserted "National Park authority or"; and
(ii) before "the district planning authority" there shall be inserted "any authority which (but for section 4A) would be or, as the case may be, which is"; and

(b) in paragraph 13(1), for "A county planning authority" there shall be substituted "In the case of any area for which there is both a district planning authority and a county planning authority, the county planning authority";

(c) in sub-paragraph (2) of paragraph 19, after "Park" there shall be inserted "to which section 4 applies", and after that sub-paragraph there shall be inserted the following sub-paragraph—

"(2A) As respects the area of any National Park for which a National Park authority is the local planning authority those functions shall be exercised by that authority."

(d) in paragraph 20(4)—

(i) in paragraph (a), for "outside a metropolitan county" there shall be substituted "which is land in an area the local planning authority for which comprises both a county planning authority and a district planning authority"; and

(ii) in paragraph (b), for "elsewhere" there shall be substituted "other land in an area the local planning authority for which comprises both a county planning authority and a district planning authority".

(15) In paragraph 4(5)(b) of Schedule 8 to that Act (which refers to directions under section 90(1) of that Act), after "local authority" there shall be inserted "National Park authority".

(16) In Schedule 13 to that Act (blighted land), in paragraph 1(a)(i), after "local authority" there shall be inserted "National Park authority".

(17) In Schedule 14 to that Act (procedure for footpaths and bridleways orders)—

(a) after paragraph 1(2)(b)(ii) (persons on whom notice served) there shall be inserted the following sub-paragraph—

"(iia) any National Park authority for a National Park which includes any of that land; and";

(b) in paragraph 1(6) (cases where owner, occupier or lessee is local authority), after "local authority" there shall be inserted "National Park authority"; and

(c) in paragraph 3(2) (local inquiry to be held if objection by local authority), after "local authority" there shall be inserted "or a National Park authority".

(18) So much of any provision of this paragraph as amends an enactment repealed by this Act shall cease to have effect with the coming into force of the repeal.

The Planning (Listed Buildings and Conservation Areas) Act 1990 (c. 9)

33.—(1) The Planning (Listed Buildings and Conservation Areas) Act 1990 shall be amended as follows.

(2) In section 32 (purchase notice), after subsection (4) there shall be inserted the following subsection—

"(4A) This section and sections 33 to 37 shall have effect as if—

(a) the bodies on whom a listed building purchase notice may be served under this section included any National Park authority which is the local planning authority for the area in which the building and land in question are situated; and

(b) a National Park authority were a local authority for the purposes of this Act and the Park for which it is the local planning authority were its area;

and the references in these sections and in section 63(7)(a) to a council and to a local authority shall be construed accordingly."

(3) In subsection (3) of section 79 (definition of "local authority" for the purposes of town scheme agreements), after paragraph (c) there shall be inserted the following paragraph—

"(ca) in relation to any building in a National Park for which a National Park authority is the local planning authority, that authority;".

(4) In section 93(1)(a) (regulations as to form of notice etc.), after "local authority" there shall be inserted "or National Park authority".

(5) In paragraph 4 of Schedule 2, after sub-paragraph (3) (expenses of various persons and bodies with respect to listed building enforcement) there shall be inserted the following sub-paragraph—

"(4) The reference to a local authority in sub-paragraph (3) above includes a reference to any National Park authority which is the local planning authority for any area."

(6) In paragraph 2 of Schedule 4 (provision as to exercise of functions by different authorities), after "4" there shall be inserted "4A".

(7) In paragraph 3 of Schedule 4—

(a) after "determined by a" there shall be inserted "National Park authority or"; and

(b) in sub-paragraph (a), before "the district planning authority" there shall be inserted "any authority which (but for section 4A) would be or, as the case may be, which is";

(c) in sub-paragraph (b), for "the district planning" there shall be substituted "any such".

(8) In paragraph 4 of Schedule 4—

(a) in sub-paragraph (1)—

(i) in paragraph (a), after "a metropolitan county" there shall be inserted "or in any National Park for which a National Park authority is the local planning authority"; and

(ii) in paragraph (b), for "outside a metropolitan county" there shall be substituted "to which paragraph (a) above does not apply"; and
(b) in sub-paragraph (2), after "county planning authority" there shall be inserted "or National Park authority".

Water consolidation legislation

34.—(1) The references to a National Park authority in the following provisions (which impose environmental duties), that is to say—
(a) section 4 of the Water Industry Act 1991,
(b) section 17 of the Water Resources Act 1991, and
(c) section 61C of the Land Drainage Act 1991,
shall have effect, until the coming into force of the repeal by this Act of the definition for the purposes of those provisions of the expression "National Park authority", as if they included references to a National Park authority established under Part III of this Act which has become the local planning authority for the National Park in question; and thereafter those references shall have effect as if they were references to a National Park authority so established.
(2) The references to a National Park planning authority—
(a) in sections 34 and 45 of the Water Resources Act 1991 (regulations with respect to notice to be given of particulars of certain licence applications), and
(b) in any regulations under those sections,
shall have effect, until the coming into force of the repeal by this Act of subsection (5) of section 34 of that Act, as if they included references to a National Park authority established under Part III of this Act which has become the local planning authority for the National Park in question; and thereafter those references shall have effect as if they were references to a National Park authority so established.

The Local Government Finance Act 1992 (c. 14)

35. In section 35 of the Local Government Finance Act 1992 (definition of "special items") in subsection (5) (expenses of a billing authority not to be special expenses if they are expenses of meeting a levy from a National Park planning board) paragraphs (a) and (b) shall be omitted and at the end of that subsection there shall be added the words "or
(c) a National Park authority in relation to a National Park in Wales."

The Local Government (Overseas Assistance) Act 1993 (c. 25)

36. In section 1(10) of the Local Government (Overseas Assistance) Act 1993 (certain bodies on which powers are conferred by the Act), at the end there shall be added—
"(h) a joint planning board constituted for an area in Wales outside a National Park by an order under section 2(1B) of the Town and Country Planning Act 1990."

The Welsh Language Act 1993 (c. 38)

37. In section 6(1) of the Welsh Language Act 1993 (bodies which are public bodies for the purposes of the provisions of that Act about Welsh language schemes), after paragraph (c) there shall be inserted the following paragraph—
"(ca) a National Park authority;".

The Local Government (Wales) Act 1994 (c. 19)

38.—(1) In Schedule 6 to the Local Government (Wales) Act 1994 (minor and consequential amendments relating to planning) in paragraph 1, at the beginning of the subsection which that paragraph substitutes for subsection (1) of section 184 of the 1972 Act, there shall be inserted the words "Subject to section 68 of the Environment Act 1995 (planning authority functions under National Parks legislation to be functions of National Park authorities in certain cases),".
(2) In paragraph 2 of that Schedule, for the words "paragraphs 3 to 14" there shall be substituted the words "paragraphs 13 and 14".

Section 90   SCHEDULE 11

AIR QUALITY: SUPPLEMENTAL PROVISIONS

Consultation requirements

1.—(1) A local authority in carrying out its functions in relation to—
(a) any air quality review,

(b) any assessment under section 82 or 84 of this Act, or

(c) the preparation of an action plan or any revision of an action plan,

shall consult such other persons as fall within sub-paragraph (2) below.

(2) Those persons are—

(a) the Secretary of State;

(b) the appropriate new Agency;

(c) in England and Wales, the highway authority for any highway in the area to which the review or, as the case may be, the action plan or revision relates;

(d) every local authority whose area is contiguous to the authority's area;

(e) any county council in England whose area consists of or includes the whole or any part of the authority's area;

(f) any National Park authority for a National Park whose area consists of or includes the whole or any part of the authority's area;

(g) such public authorities exercising functions in, or in the vicinity of, the authority's area as the authority may consider appropriate;

(h) such bodies appearing to the authority to be representative of persons with business interests in the area to which the review or action plan in question relates as the authority may consider appropriate;

(j) such other bodies or persons as the authority considers appropriate.

(3) In this paragraph "National Park authority", subject to sub–paragraph (4) below, means a National Park authority established under section 63 of this Act which has become the local planning authority for the National Park in question.

(4) As respects any period before a National Park authority established under section 63 of this Act in relation to a National Park becomes the local planning authority for that National Park, any reference in sub-paragraph (2) above to a National Park authority shall be taken as a reference to the National Park Committee or joint or special planning board for that National Park.

Exchange of information with county councils in England

2.—(1) This paragraph applies in any case where a district in England for which there is a district council is comprised in an area for which there is a county council; and in this paragraph—

(a) any reference to the county council is a reference to the council of that area; and

(b) any reference to a district council is a reference to the council of a district comprised in that area.

(2) It shall be the duty of the county council to provide a district council with all such information as is reasonably requested by the district council for purposes connected with the carrying out of its functions under or by virtue of this Part.

(3) It shall be the duty of a district council to provide the county council with all such information as is reasonably requested by the county council for purposes connected with the carrying out of any of its functions relating to the assessment or management of the quality of air.

(4) Information provided to a district council or county council under sub-paragraph (2) or (3) above shall be provided in such form and in such manner and at such times as the district council or, as the case may be, the county council may reasonably require.

(5) A council which provides information under sub-paragraph (2) or (3) above shall be entitled to recover the reasonable cost of doing so from the council which requested the information.

(6) The information which a council may be required to provide under this paragraph shall include information which, although it is not in the possession of the council or would not otherwise come into the possession of the council, is information which it is reasonable to require the council to obtain.

Joint exercise of local authority functions

3.—(1) The appropriate authority may give directions to any two or more local authorities requiring them to exercise the powers conferred by—

(a) section 101(5) of the Local Government Act 1972 (power of two or more local authorities to discharge functions jointly), or

(b) section 56(5) of the Local Government (Scotland) Act 1973 (which makes similar provision for Scotland),

in relation to functions under or by virtue of this Part in accordance with the directions.

(2) The appropriate authority may give directions to a local authority requiring it—

(a) not to exercise those powers, or

(b) not to exercise those powers in a manner specified in the directions,

in relation to functions under or by virtue of this Part.

(3) Where two or more local authorities have exercised those powers in relation to functions under or by virtue of this Part, the appropriate authority may give them directions requiring them to revoke, or modify in accordance with the directions, the arrangements which they have made.

(4) In this paragraph, "the appropriate authority" means—

(a) in relation to England and Wales, the Secretary of State; and

(b) in relation to Scotland, SEPA acting with the approval of the Secretary of State.

Public access to information about air quality

4.—(1) It shall be the duty of every local authority—

(a) to secure that there is available at all reasonable times for inspection by the public free of charge a copy of each of the documents specified in sub-paragraph (2) below; and

(b) to afford to members of the public facilities for obtaining copies of those documents on payment of a reasonable charge.

(2) The documents mentioned in sub-paragraph (1)(a) above are—

(a) a report of the results of any air quality review which the authority has caused to be conducted;

(b) a report of the results of any assessment which the authority has caused to be made under section 82 or 84 of this Act;

(c) any order made by the authority under section 83 of this Act;

(d) any action plan prepared by the authority;

(e) any proposals or statements submitted to the authority pursuant to subsection (3) or (4) of section 86 of this Act;

(f) any directions given to the authority under this Part;

(g) in a case where section 86 of this Act applies, any directions given to the county council under this Part.

Fixed penalty offences

5.—(1) Without prejudice to the generality of paragraph (o) of subsection (2) of section 87 of this Act, regulations may, in particular, make provision—

(a) for the qualifications, appointment or authorisation of persons who are to issue fixed penalty notices;

(b) for the offences in connection with which, the cases or circumstances in which, the time or period at or within which, or the manner in which fixed penalty notices may be issued;

(c) prohibiting the institution, before the expiration of the period for paying the fixed penalty, of proceedings against a person for an offence in connection with which a fixed penalty notice has been issued;

(d) prohibiting the conviction of a person for an offence in connection with which a fixed penalty notice has been issued if the fixed penalty is paid before the expiration of the period for paying it;

(e) entitling, in prescribed cases, a person to whom a fixed penalty notice is issued to give, within a prescribed period, notice requesting a hearing in respect of the offence to which the fixed penalty notice relates;

(f) for the amount of the fixed penalty to be increased by a prescribed amount in any case where the person liable to pay the fixed penalty fails to pay it before the expiration of the period for paying it, without having given notice requesting a hearing in respect of the offence to which the fixed penalty notice relates;

(g) for or in connection with the recovery of an unpaid fixed penalty as a fine or as a civil debt or as if it were a sum payable under a county court order;

(h) for or in connection with execution or other enforcement in respect of an unpaid fixed penalty by prescribed persons;

(j) for a fixed penalty notice, and any prescribed proceedings or other prescribed steps taken by reference to the notice, to be rendered void in prescribed cases where a person makes a prescribed statutory declaration, and for the consequences of any notice, proceedings or other steps being so rendered void (including extension of any time limit for instituting criminal proceedings);

(k) for or in connection with the extension, in prescribed cases or circumstances, by a prescribed person of the period for paying a fixed penalty;

(l) for or in connection with the withdrawal, in prescribed circumstances, of a fixed penalty notice, including—

(i) repayment of any amount paid by way of fixed penalty in pursuance of a fixed penalty notice which is withdrawn; and

(ii) prohibition of the institution or continuation of proceedings for the offence in connection with which the withdrawn notice was issued;

(m) for or in connection with the disposition of sums received by way of fixed penalty;

(n) for a certificate purporting to be signed by or on behalf of a prescribed person and stating either—

(i) that payment of a fixed penalty was, or (as the case may be) was not, received on or before a date specified in the certificate, or

(ii) that an envelope containing an amount sent by post in payment of a fixed penalty was marked as posted on a date specified in the certificate,

to be received as evidence of the matters so stated and to be treated without further proof, as being so signed unless the contrary is shown;

(o) requiring a fixed penalty notice to give such reasonable particulars of the circumstances alleged to constitute the fixed penalty offence to which the notice relates as are necessary for giving reasonable information of the offence and to state—

(i) the monetary amount of the fixed penalty which may be paid;

(ii) the person to whom, and the address at which, the fixed penalty may be paid and any correspondence relating to the fixed penalty notice may be sent;

(iii) the method or methods by which payment of the fixed penalty may be made;

(iv) the period for paying the fixed penalty;

(v) the consequences of the fixed penalty not being paid before the expiration of that period;

(p) similar to any provision made by section 79 of the Road Traffic Offenders Act 1988 (statements by constables in fixed penalty cases);

(q) for presuming, in any proceedings, that any document of a prescribed description purporting to have been signed by a person to whom a fixed penalty notice has been issued has been signed by that person;

(r) requiring or authorising a fixed penalty notice to contain prescribed information relating to, or for the purpose of facilitating, the administration of the fixed penalty system;

(s) with respect to the giving of fixed penalty notices, including, in particular, provision with respect to—

(i) the methods by which,

(ii) the officers, servants or agents by, to or on whom, and

(iii) the places at which,

fixed penalty notices may be given by, or served on behalf of, a prescribed person;

(t) prescribing the method or methods by which fixed penalties may be paid;

(u) for or with respect to the issue of prescribed documents to persons to whom fixed penalty notices are or have been given;

(w) for a fixed penalty notice to be treated for prescribed purposes as if it were an information or summons or any other document of a prescribed description.

(2) The provision that may be made by regulations prescribing fixed penalty offences includes provision for an offence to be a fixed penalty offence—

(a) only if it is committed in such circumstances or manner as may be prescribed; or

(b) except if it is committed in such circumstances or manner as may be prescribed.

(3) Regulations may provide for any offence which is a fixed penalty offence to cease to be such an offence.

(4) An offence which, in consequence of regulations made by virtue of sub-paragraph (3) above, has ceased to be a fixed penalty offence shall be eligible to be prescribed as such an offence again.

(5) Regulations may make provision for such exceptions, limitations and conditions as the Secretary of State considers necessary or expedient.

(6) In this paragraph—

"fixed penalty" means a penalty of such amount as may be prescribed (whether by being specified in, or made calculable under, regulations);

"fixed penalty notice" means a notice offering a person an opportunity to discharge any liability to conviction for a fixed penalty offence by payment of a penalty of a prescribed amount;

"fixed penalty offence" means, subject to sub-paragraph (2) above, any offence (whether under or by virtue of this Part or any other enactment) which is for the time being prescribed as a fixed penalty offence;

"the fixed penalty system" means the system implementing regulations made under or by virtue of paragraph (o) of subsection (2) of section 87 of this Act;

"the period for paying", in relation to any fixed penalty, means such period as may be prescribed for the purpose;

"regulations" means regulations under or by virtue of paragraph (o) of subsection (2) of section 87 of this Act.

Section 92   SCHEDULE 12

SCHEDULE 2A TO THE ENVIRONMENTAL PROTECTION ACT 1990

Sections 44A and 44B   *"Schedule 2A*

OBJECTIVES FOR THE PURPOSES OF THE NATIONAL WASTE STRATEGY

1. Ensuring that waste is recovered or disposed of without endangering human health and without using processes or methods which could harm the environment and, in particular, without—

(a) risk to water, air, soil, plants or animals;

(b) causing nuisance through noise or odours; or

(c) adversely affecting the countryside or places of special interest.

2. Establishing an integrated and adequate network of waste disposal installations, taking account of the best available technology not involving excessive costs.

3. Ensuring that the network referred to in paragraph 2 above enables—

(a) the European Community as a whole to become self-sufficient in waste disposal, and the Member States individually to move towards that aim, taking into account geographical circumstances or the need for specialised installations for certain types of waste; and

(b) waste to be disposed of in one of the nearest appropriate installations, by means of the most appropriate methods and technologies in order to ensure a high level of protection for the environment and public health.

4. Encouraging the prevention or reduction of waste production and its harmfulness, in particular by—

(a) the development of clean technologies more sparing in their use of natural resources;

(b) the technical development and marketing of products designed so as to make no contribution or to make the smallest possible contribution, by the nature of their manufacture, use or final disposal, to increasing the amount or harmfulness of waste and pollution hazards; and

(c) the development of appropriate techniques for the final disposal of dangerous substances contained in waste destined for recovery.

5. Encouraging—

(a) the recovery of waste by means of recycling, reuse or reclamation or any other process with a view to extracting secondary raw materials; and

(b) the use of waste as a source of energy."

Section 96   SCHEDULE 13

REVIEW OF OLD MINERAL PLANNING PERMISSIONS

Interpretation

1.—(1) In this Schedule—

"dormant site" means a Phase I or Phase II site in, on or under which no minerals development has been carried out to any substantial extent at any time in the period beginning on 22nd February 1982 and ending with 6th June 1995 otherwise than by virtue of a planning permission which is not a relevant planning permission relating to the site;

"first list", in relation to a mineral planning authority, means the list prepared by them pursuant to paragraph 3 below;

"mineral planning authority"—

(a) as respects England and Wales, means a mineral planning authority within the meaning of the 1990 Act, and

(b) as respects Scotland, means a planning authority for the purposes of the 1972 Act;

"mineral site" has the meaning given by sub-paragraph (2) below;
"National Park" means an area designated as such under section 5(3) of the National Parks and Access to the Countryside Act 1949;
"old mining permission" has the meaning given—
　　(a) as respects England and Wales, by section 22(1) of the 1991 Act, and
　　(b) as respects Scotland, by section 49H(1) of the 1972 Act;
"owner", in relation to any land—
　　(a) as respects England and Wales, means any person who—
　　　　(i) is the estate owner in respect of the fee simple, or
　　　　(ii) is entitled to a tenancy granted or extended for a term of years certain of which not less than seven years remains unexpired; and
　　(b) as respects Scotland, has the meaning given by paragraph 10(1) of Schedule 10A to the 1972 Act;
"Phase I site" and "Phase II site" have the meaning given by paragraph 2 below;
"relevant planning permission" means any planning permission, other than an old mining permission or a planning permission granted by a development order, granted after 30th June 1948 for minerals development; and
"second list", in relation to a mineral planning authority, means the list prepared by them pursuant to paragraph 4 below.

(2) For the purposes of this Schedule, but subject to sub-paragraph (3) below, "mineral site" means—
　　(a) in a case where it appears to the mineral planning authority to be expedient to treat as a single site the aggregate of the land to which any two or more relevant planning permissions relate, the aggregate of the land to which those permissions relate; and
　　(b) in any other case, the land to which a relevant planning permission relates.

(3) In determining whether it appears to them to be expedient to treat as a single site the aggregate of the land to which two or more relevant planning permissions relate a mineral planning authority shall have regard to any guidance issued for the purpose by the Secretary of State.

(4) Any reference (however expressed) in this Schedule to an old mining permission or a relevant planning permission relating to a mineral site is a reference to the mineral site, or some part of it, being the land to which the permission relates; and where any such permission authorises the carrying out of development consisting of the winning and working of minerals but only in respect of any particular mineral or minerals, that permission shall not be taken, for the purposes of this Schedule, as relating to any other mineral in, on or under the land to which the permission relates.

(5) For the purposes of this Schedule, a mineral site which is a Phase I site or a Phase II site is active if it is not a dormant site.

(6) For the purposes of this Schedule, working rights are restricted in respect of a mineral site if any of—
　　(a) the size of the area which may be used for the winning and working of minerals or the depositing of mineral waste;
　　(b) the depth to which operations for the winning and working of minerals may extend;
　　(c) the height of any deposit of mineral waste;
　　(d) the rate at which any particular mineral may be extracted;
　　(e) the rate at which any particular mineral waste may be deposited;
　　(f) the period at the expiry of which any winning or working of minerals or depositing of mineral waste is to cease; or
　　(g) the total quantity of minerals which may be extracted from, or of mineral waste which may be deposited on, the site,
is restricted or reduced in respect of the mineral site in question.

(7) For the purposes of this Schedule, where an application is made under paragraph 9 below for the determination of the conditions to which the relevant planning permissions relating to the mineral site to which the application relates are to be subject, those conditions are finally determined when—
　　(a) the proceedings on the application, including any proceedings on or in consequence of an application under section 288 of the 1990 Act or, as the case may be, section 233 of the 1972 Act, have been determined, and
　　(b) any time for appealing under paragraph 11(1) below, or applying or further applying under paragraph 9 below, (where there is a right to do so) has expired.

Phase I and II sites

2.—(1) This paragraph has effect for the purposes of determining which mineral sites are Phase I sites, which are Phase II sites, and which are neither Phase I nor Phase II sites.
(2) A mineral site is neither a Phase I site nor a Phase II site where—

(a) all the relevant planning permissions which relate to the site have been granted after 21st February 1982; or

(b) some only of the relevant planning permissions which relate to the site have been granted after 21st February 1982, and the parts of the site to which those permissions relate constitute the greater part of that site.

(3) With the exception of those mineral sites which, by virtue of sub-paragraph (2) above, are neither Phase I nor Phase II sites, every mineral site is either a Phase I site or a Phase II site.

(4) Subject to sub-paragraph (2) above, where any part of a mineral site is situated within—

(a) a National Park;

(b) a site in respect of which a notification under section 28 of the Wildlife and Countryside Act 1981 (sites of special scientific interest) is in force;

(c) an area designated under section 87 of the National Parks and Access to the Countryside Act 1949 as an area of outstanding natural beauty;

(d) an area designated as a National Scenic Area under section 262C of the 1972 Act; or

(e) an area designated as a Natural Heritage Area under section 6 of the Natural Heritage (Scotland) Act 1991,

that site is a Phase I site.

(5) Subject to sub-paragraphs (2) and (4) above, where—

(a) all the relevant planning permissions which relate to a mineral site, and which were not granted after 21st February 1982, were granted after the relevant day in 1969; or

(b) the parts of a mineral site to which relate such of the relevant planning permissions relating to the site as were granted after the relevant day in 1969 but before 22nd February 1982 constitute a greater part of the site than is constituted by those parts of the site to which no such relevant planning permission relates but to which a relevant planning permission granted on or before the relevant day in 1969 does relate,

the mineral site is a Phase II site.

(6) In sub-paragraph (5) above, "the relevant day in 1969" means—

(a) as respects England and Wales, 31st March 1969; and

(b) as respects Scotland, 7th December 1969.

(7) Every other mineral site, that is to say any mineral site other than one—

(a) which is, by virtue of sub-paragraph (2) above, neither a Phase I nor a Phase II site; or

(b) which is a Phase I site by virtue of sub-paragraph (4) above; or

(c) which is a Phase II site by virtue of sub-paragraph (5) above,

is a Phase I site.

(8) In ascertaining, for the purposes of sub-paragraph (2) or (5) above, whether any parts of a mineral site constitute the greater part of that site, or whether a part of a mineral site is greater than any other part, that mineral site shall be treated as not including any part of the site—

(a) to which an old mining permission relates; or

(b) which is a part where minerals development has been (but is no longer being) carried out and which has, in the opinion of the mineral planning authority, been satisfactorily restored;

but no part of a site shall be treated, by virtue of paragraph (b) above, as being not included in the site unless the mineral planning authority are satisfied that any aftercare conditions which relate to that part have, so far as relating to that part, been complied with.

The "first list"

3.—(1) A mineral planning authority shall, in accordance with the following provisions of this paragraph, prepare a list of mineral sites in their area ("the first list").

(2) A site shall, but shall only, be included in the first list if it is a mineral site in the area of the mineral planning authority and is either—

(a) an active Phase I site;

(b) an active Phase II site; or

(c) a dormant site.

(3) In respect of each site included in the first list, the list shall indicate whether the site is an active Phase I site, an active Phase II site or a dormant site.

(4) In respect of each active Phase I site included in the first list, that list shall specify the date by which an application is to be made to the mineral planning authority under paragraph 9 below.

(5) Any date specified pursuant to sub-paragraph (4) above shall be a date—

(a) not earlier than the date upon which expires the period of 12 months from the date on which the first list is first advertised in accordance with paragraph 5 below, and

(b) not later than the date upon which expires the period of three years from the date upon which the provisions of this Schedule come into force.

(6) The preparation of the first list shall be completed before the day upon which it is first advertised in accordance with paragraph 5 below.

The "second list"

4.—(1) A mineral planning authority shall, in accordance with the following provisions of this paragraph, prepare a list of the active Phase II sites in their area ("the second list").

(2) The second list shall include each mineral site in the mineral planning authority's area which is an active Phase II site.

(3) In respect of each site included in the second list, that list shall indicate the date by which an application is to be made to the mineral planning authority under paragraph 9 below.

(4) Subject to paragraph (5) below, any date specified pursuant to sub-paragraph (3) above shall be a date—

(a) not earlier than the date upon which expires the period of 12 months from the date on which the second list is first advertised in accordance with paragraph 5 below, and

(b) not later than the date upon which expires the period of six years from the date upon which the provisions of this Schedule come into force.

(5) The Secretary of State may by order provide that sub-paragraph (4)(b) above shall have effect as if for the period of six years referred to in that paragraph there were substituted such longer period specified in the order.

(6) The power of the Secretary of State to make an order under sub-paragraph (5) above shall be exercisable by statutory instrument; and any statutory instrument containing such an order shall be subject to annulment in pursuance of a resolution of either House of Parliament.

(7) The preparation of the second list shall be completed before the day upon which it is first advertised in accordance with paragraph 5 below.

Advertisement of the first and second lists

5.—(1) This paragraph makes provision for the advertisement of the first and second lists prepared by a mineral planning authority.

(2) The mineral planning authority shall advertise each of the first and second lists by causing to be published, in each of two successive weeks, in one or more newspapers circulating in its area, notice of the list having been prepared.

(3) In respect of each of those lists, such notice shall—

(a) state that the list has been prepared by the authority; and

(b) specify one or more places within the area of the authority at which the list may be inspected, and in respect of each such place specify the times (which shall be reasonable times) during which facilities for inspection of the list will be afforded.

(4) In respect of the first list, such notice shall—

(a) be first published no later than the day upon which expires the period of three months from the date upon which the provisions of this Schedule come into force;

(b) explain the general effect of a mineral site being classified as a dormant site or, as the case may be, as an active Phase I site or an active Phase II site;

(c) explain the consequences which will occur if no application is made under paragraph 9 below in respect of an active Phase I site included in the list by the date specified in the list for that site;

(d) explain the effects for any dormant or active Phase I or II site not included in the list of its not being included in the list and—

(i) set out the right to make an application to the authority for that site to be included in the list;

(ii) set out the date by which such an application must be made; and

(iii) state that the owner of such a site has a right of appeal against any decision of the authority upon such an application; and

(e) explain that the owner of an active Phase I site has a right to apply for postponement of the date specified in the list for the making of an application under paragraph 9 below, and set out the date by which an application for such postponement must be made.

(5) In respect of the second list, such notice shall—

(a) be first published no later than the day upon which expires the period of three years, or such longer period as the Secretary of State may by order specify, from the date upon which the provisions of this Schedule come into force; and

(b) explain the consequences which will occur if no application is made under paragraph 9 below in respect of an active Phase II site included in the list by the date specified in the list for that site.

(6) The power of the Secretary of State to make an order under sub-paragraph (5) above shall be exercisable by statutory instrument; and any statutory instrument containing such an order shall be subject to annulment in pursuance of a resolution of either House of Parliament.

Applications for inclusion in the first list of sites not included in that list as originally prepared and appeals from decisions upon such applications

6.—(1) Any person who is the owner of any land, or is entitled to an interest in a mineral, may, if that land or interest is not a mineral site included in the first list and does not form part of any mineral site included in that list, apply to the mineral planning authority for that land or interest to be included in that list.

(2) An application under sub-paragraph (1) above shall be made no later than the day upon which expires the period of three months from the day when the first list was first advertised in accordance with paragraph 5 above.

(3) Where the mineral planning authority consider that—

(a) the land or interest is, or forms part of, any dormant or active Phase I or II site, they shall accede to the application; or

(b) part only of the land or interest is, or forms part of, any dormant or active Phase I or II site, they shall accede to the application so far as it relates to that part of the land or interest,

but shall otherwise refuse the application.

(4) On acceding, whether in whole or in part, to an application made under sub-paragraph (1) above, the mineral planning authority shall amend the first list as follows—

(a) where they consider that the land or interest, or any part of the land or interest, is a dormant site or an active Phase I or II site, they shall add the mineral site consisting of the land or interest or, as the case may be, that part, to the first list and shall cause the list to indicate whether the site is an active Phase I site, an active Phase II site or a dormant site;

(b) where they consider that the land or interest, or any part of the land or interest, forms part of any mineral site included in the first list, they shall amend the entry in the first list for that site accordingly.

(5) Where the mineral planning authority amend the first list in accordance with sub-paragraph (4) above, they shall also—

(a) in a case where an active Phase I site is added to the first list pursuant to paragraph (a) of that sub-paragraph, cause that list to specify, in respect of that site, the date by which an application is to be made to the mineral planning authority under paragraph 9 below;

(b) in a case where—

(i) the entry for an active Phase I site included in the first list is amended pursuant to paragraph (b) of that sub-paragraph; and

(ii) the date specified in that list in respect of that site as the date by which an application is to be made to the mineral planning authority under paragraph 9 below is a date falling less than 12 months after the date upon which the authority make their decision upon the application in question,

cause that date to be amended so as to specify instead the date upon which expires the period of 12 months from the date on which the applicant is notified under sub-paragraph (10) below of the authority's decision upon his application.

(6) Any date specified pursuant to sub-paragraph (5)(a) above shall be a date—

(a) not earlier than the date upon which expires the period of 12 months from the date on which the applicant is notified under sub-paragraph (10) below of the mineral planning authority's decision upon his application, and

(b) not later than the later of—

(i) the date upon which expires the period of three years from the date upon which the provisions of this Schedule come into force; and

(ii) the date mentioned in paragraph (a) above.

(7) On acceding, whether in whole or in part, to an application made under sub-paragraph (1) above, the mineral planning authority shall, if the second list has been first advertised in accordance with paragraph 5 above prior to the time at which they make their decision on the application, amend the second list as follows—

(a) where they consider that the land or interest, or any part of the land or interest, is an active Phase II site, they shall add the mineral site consisting of the land or interest or, as the case may be, that part, to the second list;

(b) where they consider that the land or interest, or any part of the land or interest, forms part of any active Phase II site included in the second list, they shall amend the entry in that list for that site accordingly.

(8) Where the mineral planning authority amend the second list in accordance with sub-paragraph (7) above, they shall also—

(a) in a case where an active Phase II site is added to the second list pursuant to paragraph (a) of that sub-paragraph, cause that list to specify, in respect of that site, the date by which an application is to be made to the authority under paragraph 9 below;

(b) in a case where—

(i) the entry for an active Phase II site included in the second list is amended pursuant to paragraph (b) of that sub-paragraph; and

(ii) the date specified in that list in respect of that site as the date by which an application is to be made to the authority under paragraph 9 below is a date falling less than 12 months after the date upon which the authority make their decision upon the application in question,

cause that date to be amended so as to specify instead the date upon which expires the period of 12 months from the date on which the applicant is notified under sub-paragraph (10) below of the authority's decision upon his application.

(9) Any date specified pursuant to sub-paragraph (8)(a) above shall be a date—

(a) not earlier than the date upon which expires the period of 12 months from the date on which the applicant is notified under sub-paragraph (10) below of the mineral planning authority's decision upon his application, and

(b) not later than the later of—

(i) the date upon which expires the period of six years from the date upon which the provisions of this Schedule come into force; and

(ii) the date mentioned in paragraph (a) above.

(10) When a mineral planning authority determine an application made under sub-paragraph (1) above, they shall notify the applicant in writing of their decision and, in a case where they have acceded to the application, whether in whole or in part, shall supply the applicant with details of any amendment to be made to the first or second list in accordance with sub-paragraph (4) or (8) above.

(11) Where a mineral planning authority—

(a) refuse an application made under sub-paragraph (1) above; or

(b) accede to such an application only so far as it relates to part of the land or interest in respect of which it was made,

the applicant may by notice appeal to the Secretary of State.

(12) A person who has made such an application may also appeal to the Secretary of State if the mineral planning authority have not given notice to the applicant of their decision on the application within eight weeks of their having received the application or within such extended period as may at any time be agreed upon in writing between the applicant and the authority.

(13) An appeal under sub-paragraph (11) or (12) above must be made by giving notice of appeal to the Secretary of State before the end of the period of six months beginning with—

(a) in the case of an appeal under sub-paragraph (11) above, the determination; or

(b) in the case of an appeal under sub-paragraph (12) above, the end of the period of eight weeks mentioned in that sub-paragraph or, as the case may be, the end of the extended period mentioned in that sub-paragraph.

Postponement of the date specified in the first or second list for review of the permissions relating to a Phase I or II site in cases where the existing conditions are satisfactory

7.—(1) Any person who is the owner of any land, or of any interest in any mineral, comprised in—

(a) an active Phase I site included in the first list; or

(b) an active Phase II site included in the second list,

may apply to the mineral planning authority for the postponement of the date specified in that list in respect of that site as the date by which an application is to be made to the authority under paragraph 9 below (in this paragraph referred to as "the specified date").

(2) Subject to sub-paragraph (3) below, an application under sub-paragraph (1) above shall be made no later than the day upon which expires the period of three months from the day when—

(a) in the case of an active Phase I site, the first list; or

(b) in the case of an active Phase II site, the second list,

was first advertised in accordance with paragraph 5 above.

(3) In the case of—

(a) an active Phase I site—

(i) added to the first list in accordance with paragraph 6(4)(a) above; or

(ii) in respect of which the entry in the first list was amended in accordance with paragraph 6(4)(b) above;

or

(b) an active Phase II site—

(i) added to the second list in accordance with paragraph 6(7)(a) above; or

(ii) in respect of which the entry in the second list was amended in accordance with
        paragraph 6(7)(b) above,
an application under sub-paragraph (1) above shall be made no later than the day upon which
expires the period of three months from the day on which notice was given under paragraph
6(10) above of the mineral planning authority's decision to add the site to or, as the case may be,
so to amend the list in question.

(4) An application under sub-paragraph (1) above shall be in writing and shall—
  (a) set out the conditions to which each relevant planning permission relating to the site is
      subject;
  (b) set out the applicant's reasons for considering those conditions to be satisfactory;
  (c) set out the date which the applicant wishes to be substituted for the specified date; and
  (d) be accompanied by the appropriate certificate (within the meaning of sub-paragraph (5)
      or (6) below).

(5) For the purposes of sub-paragraph (4) above, as respects England and Wales the appropriate certificate is such a certificate—
  (a) as would be required, under section 65 of the 1990 Act (notice etc. of applications for
      planning permission) and any provision of a development order made by virtue of that
      section, to accompany the application if it were an application for planning permission for
      minerals development, but
  (b) with such modifications as are required for the purposes of this paragraph,
and section 65(6) of that Act (offences) shall also have effect in relation to any certificate purporting to be the appropriate certificate.

(6) For the purposes of sub-paragraph (4) above, the appropriate certificate is, as respects
Scotland, each of the certificates which would be required, under or by virtue of sections 23 and
24 of the 1972 Act (notice etc. of applications for planning permission), to accompany the application if it were an application for planning permission for minerals development, but with such
modifications as are required for the purposes of this paragraph; and sections 23(3) and 24(5) of
that Act (offences) shall have effect in relation to any certificate purporting to be the appropriate certificate.

(7) Where the mineral planning authority receive an application made under sub-paragraph
(1) above—
  (a) if they consider the conditions referred to in sub-paragraph (4)(a) above to be satisfactory
      they shall agree to the specified date being postponed in which event they shall determine
      the date to be substituted for that date;
  (b) in any other case they shall refuse the application.

(8) Where the mineral planning authority agree to the specified date being postponed they
shall cause the first or, as the case may be, the second list to be amended accordingly.

(9) When a mineral planning authority determine an application made under sub-paragraph
(1) above, they shall notify the applicant in writing of their decision and, in a case where they
have agreed to the postponement of the specified date, shall notify the applicant of the date
which they have determined should be substituted for the specified date.

(10) Where, within three months of the mineral planning authority having received an application under sub-paragraph (1) above, or within such extended period as may at any time be
agreed upon in writing between the applicant and the authority, the authority have not given
notice, under sub-paragraph (9) above, to the applicant of their decision upon the application,
the authority shall be treated as—
  (a) having agreed to the specified date being postponed; and
  (b) having determined that the date referred to in sub-paragraph (4)(c) above be substituted
      for the specified date,
and sub-paragraph (8) above shall apply accordingly.

Service on owners etc. of notice of preparation of the first and second lists

8.—(1) The mineral planning authority shall, no later than the date upon which the first list is
first advertised in accordance with paragraph 5 above, serve notice in writing of the first list
having been prepared on each person appearing to them to be the owner of any land, or entitled
to an interest in any mineral, included within a mineral site included in the first list, but this
sub-paragraph is subject to sub-paragraph (7) below.

(2) A notice required to be served by sub-paragraph (1) above shall—
  (a) indicate whether the mineral site in question is a dormant site or an active Phase I or II
      site; and
  (b) where that site is an active Phase I site—
        (i) indicate the date specified in the first list in relation to that site as the date by
        which an application is to be made to the mineral planning authority under paragraph 9
        below;

(ii) explain the consequences which will occur if such an application is not made by the date so specified; and

(iii) explain the right to apply to have that date postponed, and indicate the date by which such an application must be made.

(3) Where, in relation to any land or mineral included in an active Phase I site, the mineral planning authority—

(a) has served notice on any person under sub-paragraph (1) above; and

(b) has received no application under paragraph 9 below from that person by the date falling eight weeks before the date specified in the first list as the date by which such applications should be made in respect of the site in question,

the authority shall serve a written reminder on that person, and such a reminder shall—

(i) indicate that the land or mineral in question is included in an active Phase I site;

(ii) comply with the requirements of sub-paragraph (2)(b)(i) and (ii) above; and

(iii) be served on that person on or before the date falling four weeks before the date specified in the first list in respect of that site as the date by which an application is to be made to the authority under paragraph 9 below.

(4) The mineral planning authority shall, no later than the date upon which the second list is first advertised in accordance with paragraph 5 above, serve notice in writing of the second list having been prepared on each person appearing to them to be the owner of any land, or entitled to an interest in any mineral, included within an active Phase II site included in the second list, but this sub-paragraph is subject to sub-paragraph (7) below.

(5) A notice required to be served by sub-paragraph (4) above shall—

(a) indicate that the mineral site in question is an active Phase II site; and

(b) indicate the date specified in the second list in relation to that site as the date by which an application is to be made to the mineral planning authority under paragraph 9 below;

(c) explain the consequences which will occur if such an application is not made by the date so specified; and

(d) explain the right to apply to have that date postponed, and indicate the date by which such an application must be made.

(6) Where, in relation to any land or mineral included in an active Phase II site, the mineral planning authority—

(a) has served notice on any person under sub-paragraph (4) above; and

(b) has received no application under paragraph 9 below from that person by the date falling eight weeks before the date specified in the second list as the date by which such applications should be made in respect of the site in question,

the authority shall serve a written reminder on that person, and such a reminder shall—

(i) comply with the requirements of sub-paragraph (5)(a) to (c) above; and

(ii) be served on that person on or before the date falling four weeks before the date specified in the second list in respect of that site as the date by which an application is to be made to the authority under paragraph 9 below.

(7) Sub-paragraph (1) or (4) above shall not require the mineral planning authority to serve notice under that sub-paragraph upon any person whose identity or address for service is not known to and cannot practicably, after reasonable inquiry, be ascertained by them, but in any such case the authority shall cause to be firmly affixed, to each of one or more conspicuous objects on the land or, as the case may be, on the surface of the land above the interest in question, a copy of the notice which they would (apart from the provisions of this sub-paragraph) have had to serve under that sub-paragraph on the owner of that land or interest.

(8) If, in a case where sub-paragraph (7) above applies, no person makes an application to the authority under paragraph 9 below in respect of the active Phase I or II site which includes the land or interest in question by the date falling eight weeks before the date specified in the first or, as the case may be, the second list as the date by which such applications should be made in respect of that site, the authority shall cause to be firmly affixed, to each of one or more conspicuous objects on the land or, as the case may be, on the surface of the land above the interest in question, a copy of the written reminder that would, in a case not falling within sub-paragraph (7) above, have been served under sub-paragraph (3) or (6) above.

(9) Where by sub-paragraph (7) or (8) above a copy of any notice is required to be affixed to an object on any land that copy shall—

(a) be displayed in such a way as to be easily visible and legible;

(b) be first displayed—

(i) in a case where the requirement arises under sub-paragraph (7) above, no later than the date upon which the first or, as the case may be, the second list is first advertised in accordance with paragraph 5 above; or

(ii) in a case where the requirement arises under sub-paragraph (8) above, no later than the date falling four weeks before the date specified in the first or, as the case may be, the second list in respect of the site in question as the date by which an application is to be made to the authority under paragraph 9 below; and

(c) be left in position for at least the period of 21 days from the date when it is first displayed, but where the notice is, without fault or intention of the authority, removed, obscured or defaced before that period has elapsed, that requirement shall be treated as having been complied with if the authority has taken reasonable steps for protection of the notice and, if need be, its replacement.

(10) In sub-paragraphs (7) and (8) above, any reference to a conspicuous object on any land includes, in a case where the person serving a notice considers that there are no or insufficient such objects on the land, a reference to a post driven into or erected upon the land by the person serving the notice for the purpose of having affixed to it the notice in question.

(11) Where the mineral planning authority, being required—

(a) by sub-paragraph (3) or (6) above to serve a written reminder on any person; or

(b) by sub-paragraph (8) above to cause a copy of such a reminder to be displayed in the manner set out in that sub-paragraph,

fail to comply with that requirement by the date specified for the purpose, they may at any later time serve or, as the case may be, cause to be displayed, such a written reminder and, in any such case, the date by which an application in relation to the mineral site in question is to be made under paragraph 9 below is the date upon which expires the period of three months from the date when the reminder was served or posted in accordance with the provisions of this sub-paragraph.

Applications for approval of conditions and appeals in cases where the conditions approved are not those proposed

9.—(1) Any person who is the owner of any land, or who is entitled to an interest in a mineral, may, if that land or mineral is or forms part of a dormant site or an active Phase I or II site, apply to the mineral planning authority to determine the conditions to which the relevant planning permissions relating to that site are to be subject.

(2) An application under this paragraph shall be in writing and shall—

(a) identify the mineral site to which the application relates;

(b) specify the land or minerals comprised in the site of which the applicant is the owner or, as the case may be, in which the applicant is entitled to an interest;

(c) identify any relevant planning permissions relating to the site;

(d) identify, and give an address for, each other person that the applicant knows or, after reasonable inquiry, has cause to believe to be an owner of any land, or entitled to any interest in any mineral, comprised in the site;

(e) set out the conditions to which the applicant proposes the permissions referred to in paragraph (c) above should be subject; and

(f) be accompanied by the appropriate certificate (within the meaning of sub-paragraph (3) or (4) below).

(3) For the purposes of sub-paragraph (2) above, as respects England and Wales the appropriate certificate is such a certificate—

(a) as would be required, under section 65 of the 1990 Act (notice etc. of applications for planning permission) and any provision of a development order made by virtue of that section, to accompany the application if it were an application for planning permission for minerals development, but

(b) with such modifications as are required for the purposes of this paragraph,

and section 65(6) of that Act (offences) shall also have effect in relation to any certificate purporting to be the appropriate certificate.

(4) For the purposes of sub-paragraph (2) above, the appropriate certificate is, as respects Scotland, each of the certificates which would be required, under or by virtue of sections 23 and 24 of the 1972 Act (notice etc. of applications for planning permission), to accompany the application if it were an application for planning permission for minerals development, but with such modifications as are required for the purposes of this paragraph; and sections 23(3) and 24(5) of that Act (offences) shall have effect in relation to any certificate purporting to be the appropriate certificate.

(5) Section 65 of the 1990 Act or, as respects Scotland, section 24 of the 1972 Act (by virtue of which a development order may provide for publicising applications for planning permission) shall have effect, with any necessary modifications, as if subsection (1) of that section also authorised a development order to provide for publicising applications under this paragraph.

(6) Where the mineral planning authority receive an application under this paragraph in relation to a dormant site or an active Phase I or II site they shall determine the conditions to which each relevant planning permission relating to the site is to be subject; and any such permission shall, from the date when the conditions to which it is to be subject are finally deter-

mined, have effect subject to the conditions which are determined under this Schedule as being the conditions to which it is to be subject.

(7) The conditions imposed by virtue of a determination under sub-paragraph (6) above—

(a) may include any conditions which may be imposed on a grant of planning permission for minerals development;

(b) may be in addition to, or in substitution for, any existing conditions to which the permission in question is subject.

(8) In determining that a relevant planning permission is to be subject to any condition relating to development for which planning permission is granted by a development order, the mineral planning authority shall have regard to any guidance issued for the purpose by the Secretary of State.

(9) Subject to sub-paragraph (10) below, where, within the period of three months from the mineral planning authority having received an application under this paragraph, or within such extended period as may at any time be agreed upon in writing between the applicant and the authority, the authority have not given notice to the applicant of their decision upon the application, the authority shall be treated as having at the end of that period or, as the case may be, that extended period, determined that the conditions to which any relevant planning permission to which the application relates is to be subject are those specified in the application as being proposed in relation to that permission; and any such permission shall, from that time, have effect subject to those conditions.

(10) Where a mineral planning authority, having received an application under this paragraph, are of the opinion that they are unable to determine the application unless further details are supplied to them, they shall within the period of one month from having received the application give notice to the applicant—

(a) stating that they are of such opinion; and

(b) specifying the further details which they require,

and where the authority so serve such a notice the period of three months referred to in sub-paragraph (9) above shall run not from the authority having received the application but from the time when the authority have received all the further details specified in the notice.

(11) Without prejudice to the generality of sub-paragraph (10) above, the further details which may be specified in a notice under that sub-paragraph include any—

(a) information, plans or drawings; or

(b) evidence verifying any particulars of details supplied to the authority in respect of the application in question,

which it is reasonable for the authority to request for the purpose of enabling them to determine the application.

Notice of determination of conditions to be accompanied by additional information in certain cases

10.—(1) This paragraph applies in a case where—

(a) on an application made to the mineral planning authority under paragraph 9 above in respect of an active Phase I or II site the authority determine under that paragraph the conditions to which the relevant planning permissions relating to the site are to be subject;

(b) those conditions differ in any respect from the proposed conditions set out in the application; and

(c) the effect of the conditions, other than any restoration or aftercare conditions, so determined by the authority, as compared with the effect of the conditions, other than any restoration or aftercare conditions, to which the relevant planning permissions in question were subject immediately prior to the authority making the determination, is to restrict working rights in respect of the site.

(2) In a case where this paragraph applies, the mineral planning authority shall, upon giving to the applicant notice of the conditions determined by the authority under paragraph 9 above, also give to the applicant notice—

(a) stating that the conditions determined by the authority differ in some respect from the proposed conditions set out in the application;

(b) stating that the effect of the conditions, other than any restoration or aftercare conditions, determined by the authority, as compared with the effect of the conditions, other than any restoration or aftercare conditions, to which the relevant planning permissions relating to the site in question were subject immediately prior to the making of the authority's determination, is to restrict working rights in respect of the site;

(c) identifying the working rights so restricted; and

(d) stating whether, in the opinion of the authority, the effect of that restriction of working rights would be such as to prejudice adversely to an unreasonable degree—

(i) the economic viability of operating the site; or

(ii) the asset value of the site.

(3) In determining whether, in their opinion, the effect of that restriction of working rights would be such as is mentioned in sub-paragraph (2)(d) above, a mineral planning authority shall have regard to any guidance issued for the purpose by the Secretary of State.

(4) In this paragraph, "the applicant" means the person who made the application in question under paragraph 9 above.

Right to appeal against mineral planning authority's determination of conditions etc.

11.—(1) Where the mineral planning authority—

(a) on an application under paragraph 9 above determine under that paragraph conditions that differ in any respect from the proposed conditions set out in the application; or

(b) give notice, under paragraph (d) of paragraph 10(2) above, stating that, in their opinion, the restriction of working rights in question would not be such as to prejudice adversely to an unreasonable degree either of the matters referred to in sub-paragraphs (i) and (ii) of the said paragraph (d),

the person who made the application may appeal to the Secretary of State.

(2) An appeal under sub-paragraph (1) above must be made by giving notice of appeal to the Secretary of State before the end of the period of six months beginning with the date on which the authority give notice to the applicant of their determination or, as the case may be, stating their opinion.

Permissions ceasing to have effect

12.—(1) Subject to paragraph 8(11) above, where no application under paragraph 9 above in respect of an active Phase I or II site has been served on the mineral planning authority by the date specified in the first or, as the case may be, the second list as the date by which applications under that paragraph in respect of that site are to be made, or by such later date as may at any time be agreed upon in writing between the applicant and the authority, each relevant planning permission relating to the site shall cease to have effect, except insofar as it imposes any restoration or aftercare condition, on the day following the last date on which such an application may be made.

(2) The reference in sub-paragraph (1) above to the date specified in the first or, as the case may be, the second list as the date by which applications under paragraph 9 above are to be made in respect of any Phase I or II site is a reference to the date specified for that purpose in respect of that site in that list as prepared by the mineral planning authority or, where that date has been varied by virtue of any provision of this Schedule, to that date as so varied.

(3) Subject to sub-paragraph (4) below, no relevant planning permission which relates to a dormant site shall have effect to authorise the carrying out of minerals development unless—

(a) an application has been made under paragraph 9 above in respect of that site; and

(b) that permission has effect in accordance with sub-paragraph (6) of that paragraph.

(4) A relevant planning permission which relates to a Phase I or II site not included in the first list shall cease to have effect, except insofar as it imposes any restoration or aftercare condition, on the day following the last date on which an application under sub-paragraph (1) of paragraph 6 above may be made in respect of that site unless an application has been made under that sub-paragraph by that date in which event, unless the site is added to that list, such a permission shall cease to have effect when the following conditions are met—

(a) the proceedings on that application, including any proceedings on or in consequence of the application under section 288 of the 1990 Act or, as the case may be, section 233 of the 1972 Act, have been determined, and

(b) any time for appealing under paragraph 6(11) or (12) above, or applying or further applying under paragraph 6(1) above, (where there is a right to do so) has expired.

Reference of applications to the Secretary of State

13.—(1) The Secretary of State may give directions requiring applications under paragraph 9 above to any mineral planning authority to be referred to him for determination instead of being dealt with by the authority.

(2) Any such direction may relate either to a particular application or to applications of a class specified in the direction.

(3) Where an application is referred to the Secretary of State in accordance with such a direction—

(a) subject to paragraph (b) below, the following provisions of this Schedule—

(i) paragraph 9(6) and (7),

(ii) paragraph 10, and

(iii) paragraph 14 so far as relating to applications under paragraph 9 above, shall apply, with any necessary modifications, as they apply to applications which fall to be determined by the mineral planning authority;

(b) before determining the application the Secretary of State must, if either the applicant or the mineral planning authority so wish, give each of them an opportunity of appearing before and being heard by a person appointed by the Secretary of State for the purpose; and

(c) the decision of the Secretary of State on the application shall be final.

Two or more applicants

14.—(1) Where a mineral planning authority has received from any person a duly made application under paragraph 7(1) or 9 above—

(a) that person may not make any further application under the paragraph in question in respect of the same site; and

(b) if the application has been determined, whether or not in the case of an application under paragraph 9 above it has been finally determined, no other person may make an application under the paragraph in question in respect of the same site.

(2) Where—

(a) a mineral planning authority has received from any person in respect of a mineral site a duly made application under paragraph 7(1) or 9 above; and

(b) the authority receives from another person a duly made application under the paragraph in question in respect of the same site,

then for the purpose of the determination of the applications and any appeal against such a determination, this Schedule shall have effect as if the applications were a single application received by the authority on the date on which the later application was received by the authority and references to the applicant shall be read as references to either or any of the applicants.

Compensation

15.—(1) This paragraph applies in a case where—

(a) an application made under paragraph 9 above in respect of an active Phase I or II site is finally determined; and

(b) the requirements of either sub-paragraph (2) or (3) below are satisfied.

(2) The requirements, referred to in sub-paragraph (1)(b) above, of this sub-paragraph are—

(a) that the conditions to which the relevant planning permissions relating to the site are to be subject were determined by the mineral planning authority;

(b) no appeal was made under paragraph 11(1)(a) above in respect of that determination or any such appeal was withdrawn or dismissed; and

(c) the authority gave notice under paragraph (d) of paragraph 10(2) above and either—

    (i) that notice stated that, in the authority's opinion, the restriction of working rights in question would be such as to prejudice adversely to an unreasonable degree either of the matters referred to in sub-paragraphs (i) and (ii) of the said paragraph (d); or

    (ii) that notice stated that, in the authority's opinion, the restriction in question would not be such as would so prejudice either of those matters but an appeal under paragraph 11(1) above in respect of the giving of the notice has been allowed.

(3) The requirements, referred to in sub-paragraph (1)(b) above, of this sub-paragraph are that the conditions to which the relevant planning permissions are to be subject were determined by the Secretary of State (whether upon an appeal under paragraph 11(1)(a) above or upon a reference under paragraph 13 above) and—

(a) in a case where those conditions were determined upon an appeal under paragraph 11(1)(a) above either—

    (i) the mineral planning authority gave notice under paragraph (d) of paragraph 10(2) above stating that, in their opinion, the restriction of working rights in question would be such as to prejudice adversely to an unreasonable degree either of the matters referred to in sub-paragraphs (i) and (ii) of the said paragraph (d), or

    (ii) the authority gave a notice under the said paragraph (d) stating that, in their opinion, the restriction in question would not be such as would so prejudice either of those matters but an appeal under paragraph 11(1)(b) above in respect of the giving of that notice has been allowed;

    or

(b) in a case where those conditions were determined upon a reference under paragraph 13 above, the Secretary of State gave notice under paragraph (d) of paragraph 10(2) above stating that, in his opinion, the restriction of working rights in question would be such as to prejudice adversely to an unreasonable degree either of the matters referred to in sub-paragraphs (i) and (ii) of the said paragraph (d).

(4) In a case to which this paragraph applies—

(a) as respects England and Wales, Parts IV and XI of the 1990 Act, or

(b) as respects Scotland, Parts VIII and XI of the 1972 Act,

shall have effect as if an order made under section 97 of the 1990 Act or, as the case may be, section 42 of the 1972 Act, had been confirmed by the Secretary of State under section 98 of the 1990 Act or, as the case may be, section 42 of the 1972 Act at the time when the application in question was finally determined and, as so confirmed, had effect to modify those permissions to the extent specified in sub-paragraph (5) below.

(5) For the purposes of sub-paragraph (4) above, the order which is treated by virtue of that sub-paragraph as having been made under section 97 of the 1990 Act or section 42 of the 1972 Act is one whose only effect adverse to the interests of any person having an interest in the land or minerals comprised in the mineral site is to restrict working rights in respect of the site to the same extent as the relevant restriction.

(6) For the purposes of section 116 of the 1990 Act and section 167A of the 1972 Act and of any regulations made under those sections, the permissions treated as being modified by the order mentioned in sub-paragraph (4) above shall be treated as if they were planning permissions for development which neither consists of nor includes any minerals development.

Appeals: general procedural provisions

16.—(1) This paragraph applies to appeals under any of the following provisions of this Schedule—

(a) paragraph 6(11) or (12) above; or

(b) paragraph 11(1) above.

(2) Notice of appeal in respect of an appeal to which this paragraph applies shall be given on a form supplied by or on behalf of the Secretary of State for use for that purpose, and giving, so far as reasonably practicable, the information required by that form.

(3) Paragraph 6 of Schedule 2 to the 1991 Act (determination of appeals) shall, as respects England and Wales, apply to an appeal to which this paragraph applies as it applies to an appeal under paragraph 5 of that Schedule.

(4) As respects England and Wales, sections 284 to 288 of the 1990 Act (validity of certain decisions and proceedings for questioning their validity) shall have effect as if the action mentioned in section 284(3) of that Act included any decision of the Secretary of State—

(a) on an appeal to which this paragraph applies; or

(b) on an application under paragraph 9 above referred to him under paragraph 13 above.

(5) Paragraph 6 of Schedule 10A to the 1972 Act (determination of appeals) shall, as respects Scotland, apply to an appeal to which this paragraph applies as it applies to appeals under paragraph 5 of that Schedule.

(6) As respects Scotland, sections 231 to 233 of the 1972 Act (validity of certain decisions and proceedings for questioning their validity) shall have effect as if the action mentioned in section 231(3) included any decision of the Secretary of State—

(a) on an appeal to which this paragraph applies; or

(b) on an application under paragraph 9 above referred to him under paragraph 13 above.

(7) As respects Scotland, Schedule 7 to the 1972 Act shall apply to appeals to which this paragraph applies.

GENERAL NOTE

Policy Background

The Planning and Compensation Act 1991 introduced new procedures for dealing with planning permissions for mineral extraction or the deposit of minerals waste granted under Interim Development Orders in the period 1943–1948. Such permissions contained few, if any, environmental protection conditions, and the provisions of the 1991 Act required that application be made to register such permissions allowing the mineral planning authority to determine a scheme of operating and restoration conditions. Mineral Planning Guidances MPG 8 and MPG 9 deal with those procedures and the type of conditions to be imposed (NPPG 4 *Land for Mineral Working* makes similar provision for Scotland). However, the issue of old mineral permissions generally, and their updating to modern standards, remained under review (DoE News Release No.181 (March 1992)). Whilst the principle that mineral permissions should be reviewed and updated, and that the industry bear some of the cost, was recognised in the Town and Country Planning (Minerals) Act 1981, the Government acknowledged that those procedures had not worked well: see H.C. Standing Committee B, Sixteenth Sitting, June 13, 1995, col. 625. The Government issued a series of proposals for reform in March 1994, *The Reform of Old Mineral Permissions 1948–81*. This was followed by bilateral meetings with the different industry sectors and with amenity and environmental groups: *Hansard*, H.L. Vol. 560, col. 1474.

Provisions as to the type of conditions required to be imposed on mineral working generally (as to duration of development, restoration and after-care) are contained in Sched. 5 of the Town and Country Planning Act 1990.

Scheme of Schedule 13

This Schedule seeks to deal with the problem of old permissions in a phased manner. The mineral planning authority must prepare a "first list" of mineral sites in their area (para. 3(1)). This list comprises three categories of site (para. 3(2)), namely (a) active Phase I sites; (b) active Phase II sites; and (c) dormant sites. All of these terms are defined in paras. 1 and 2 of the Schedule. Both Phase I and Phase II sites are those where the relevant planning permissions, or the greater part of the planning permissions by area, were granted on or before February 21, 1982 (para. 2(1)–(3)). Within this category, a site will be a Phase I site if the sensitive locational criteria of para. 2(4) apply (for example, National Parks, AONBs, SSSIs) or if the relevant permission or permissions were granted on or before March 31, 1969 (December 7, 1969 in Scotland). Dormant sites are those where no substantial minerals development has been carried out between February 22, 1982 and June 6, 1995 (para. 1(1)).

The first list of sites will only include a date for application (see below) for active Phase I sites (para. 3(4)). The second list of sites requiring action consists of active Phase II sites (para. 4(2)) and includes a date for application for them (para. 4(3)). The scheme is therefore to target first the sites with the oldest permissions and those located in the most sensitive areas, and secondly the relatively more recent permissions. The first list must be prepared and notice given of its publication within three months of the date on which the Schedule comes into force (para. 5(4)(a)). The notice of the second list must be given within three years, or such longer period as the Secretary of State may specify (para. 5(5)(a)).

Procedure for Lists

The first and second lists must be publicised by notice (para. 5). Detailed procedures also apply to require notice of the preparation of the lists to be given to the owners of land and mineral interests included (para. 8). There is also a procedure for owners of land or mineral interests to apply for inclusion in the first list so as to avoid the permission ceasing to have effect, and also for the list to be amended to include the site within the appropriate category if the mineral planning authority consider this appropriate (para. 6).

Effect of Lists

The importance of the lists is that they will specify for each active site the date by which an application has to be made under para. 9 (see paras. 3(4)–(5) and 4(3)–(4)). The application is to determine the conditions to which the relevant planning permission or permissions are to be subject (para. 9(1)). Failure to make such application by the due date will result in the permission ceasing to have effect, save in relation to any restoration or after-care conditions (para. 12(1)). Procedural safeguards are provided in para. 8 by way of written reminders and site notices, to reduce the risk of the due date being overlooked (para. 8(3), (6) and (8)).

Dormant sites are also affected, in that no planning permission relating to a dormant site shall have the effect of authorising the carrying out of minerals development unless an application has been made under para. 9 and the conditions determined by the authority (para. 12(3)).

The first list is intended to provide certainty and finality in relation to all old mineral permissions in that any permission not included on the first list will cease to have effect unless an application is made by the landowner or mineral owner under para. 6 (see above) to have it included (para. 12(4)).

Applications for Determination of Conditions

Paragraph 9 deals with applications for determination of conditions and follows a procedure broadly analogous to that for applications for planning permission. The conditions which may be imposed include any which may be imposed on a grant of planning permission for minerals development and may be in addition to, or substitution for, existing conditions (para. 9(7)). Government guidance for England and Wales on the conditions to be imposed is contained in MPG 14 (see the General Note to s.96 above, at p. 25–266). As noted above, draft guidance for Scotland is to be issued in the near future.

A right of appeal to the Secretary of State is provided by para. 11, and applications may effectively be "called in" by the Secretary of State under para. 13. Paragraph 14 deals with the situation where two or more persons make an application in respect of the same site.

Compensation

No compensation is payable where a permission ceases to have effect because no application is made. However, para. 15 provides for compensation where an application is made and determined so as to restrict the mineral working rights in question, so as to prejudice adversely to an unreasonable degree either the economic viability of operating the site, or the asset value of the site. The restriction of working rights for which compensation may be payable may take a variety of forms, including area and depth of working, period of working, rates of extraction, and total quantity of materials which may be extracted (para. 1(6)). In determining an application by imposing different conditions which have such effect, the minerals planning authority must state whether in its opinion the restriction will have that unreasonable prejudicial effect (para. 10(2)(d)). If the authority states that this will not be the effect, the applicant may appeal to the Secretary of State (para. 11(1)(b)). Compensation is payable where a statement of unreasonable effect is made, or an appeal against a statement to the opposite effect is allowed (paras. 15(1)–(3)). Compensation is payable under the Planning Acts as if an order modifying the planning permission had been made (para. 15(5)). Effectively this means that compensation can be recovered under s.107 of the Town and Country Planning Act 1990 (or, in Scotland, under s.153 of the Town and Country Planning (Scotland) Act 1972) for expenditure which is rendered abortive or for other loss or damage directly attributable to the modification. The applicable provisions on compensation are those applicable to planning permissions generally, and not as adapted for minerals development (para. 15(6)).

Whether the conditions for compensation are fulfilled will be determined on a site-by-site basis, with regard to guidance issued by the Secretary of State. In debate the example was given of a site which had no conditions controlling working hours, but had traditionally worked eighteen hours-a-day, seven days-a-week. The imposition of a limit to nine-hour working, five days-a-week, could be regarded as unreasonably prejudicing economic viability (see Standing Committee B, Sixteenth Sitting, June 13, 1995, cols. 642–643).

Section 96   SCHEDULE 14

PERIODIC REVIEW OF MINERAL PLANNING PERMISSIONS

Duty to carry out periodic reviews

1. The mineral planning authority shall, in accordance with the provisions of this Schedule, cause periodic reviews to be carried out of the mineral permissions relating to a mining site.

Interpretation

2.—(1) For the purposes of this Schedule—
   "first review date", in relation to a mining site, shall, subject to paragraph 5 below, be ascertained in accordance with paragraph 3 below;
   "mineral permission" means any planning permission, other than a planning permission granted by a development order, for minerals development;
   "mineral planning authority"—
      (a) as respects England and Wales, means a mineral planning authority within the meaning of the 1990 Act, and
      (b) as respects Scotland, means a planning authority for the purposes of the 1972 Act;
   "mining site" means—
      (a) in a case where it appears to the mineral planning authority to be expedient to treat as a single site the aggregate of the land to which any two or more mineral permissions relate, the aggregate of the land to which those permissions relate; and
      (b) in any other case, the land to which a mineral permission relates;
   "old mining permission" has the meaning given—
      (a) as respects England and Wales, by section 22(1) of the 1991 Act, and
      (b) as respects Scotland, by section 49H(1) of the 1972 Act; and
   "owner", in relation to any land—
      (a) as respects England and Wales, means any person who—
         (i) is the estate owner in respect of the fee simple, or
         (ii) is entitled to a tenancy granted or extended for a term of years certain of which not less than seven years remains unexpired; and

(b) as respects Scotland, has the meaning given by paragraph 10(1) of Schedule 10A to the 1972 Act.

(2) In determining whether it appears to them to be expedient to treat as a single site the aggregate of the land to which two or more mineral permissions relate a mineral planning authority shall have regard to any guidance issued for the purpose by the Secretary of State.

(3) Any reference (however expressed) in this Schedule to a mining site being a site to which relates—

(a) an old mining permission; or

(b) a mineral permission,

is a reference to the mining site, or some part of it, being the land to which the permission relates.

(4) For the purposes of this Schedule, an application made under paragraph 6 below is finally determined when—

(a) the proceedings on the application, including any proceedings on or in consequence of an application under section 288 of the 1990 Act or section 233 of the 1972 Act, have been determined, and

(b) any time for appealing under paragraph 9(1) below, or applying or further applying under paragraph 6 below, (where there is a right to do so) has expired.

The first review date

3.—(1) Subject to sub-paragraph (7) below, in a case where the mineral permissions relating to a mining site include an old mining permission, the first review date means—

(a) the date falling fifteen years after the date upon which, pursuant to an application made under paragraph 2 of Schedule 2 to the 1991 Act or, as the case may be, paragraph 2 of Schedule 10A to the 1972 Act, the conditions to which that old mining permission is to be subject are finally determined under that Schedule; or

(b) where there are two or more old mining permissions relating to that site and the date upon which those conditions are finally determined is not the same date for each of those permissions, the date falling fifteen years after the date upon which was made the last such final determination to be so made in respect of any of those permissions,

and paragraph 10(2) of Schedule 2 to the 1991 Act or, as the case may be, paragraph 10(2) of Schedule 10A to the 1972 Act (meaning of "finally determined") shall apply for the purposes of this sub-paragraph as it applies for the purposes of section 22 of and Schedule 2 to the 1991 Act or, as the case may be, section 49H of and Schedule 10A to the 1972 Act.

(2) Subject to sub-paragraph (7) below, in the case of a mining site which is a Phase I or II site within the meaning of Schedule 13 to this Act, the first review date means the date falling fifteen years after the date upon which, pursuant to an application made under paragraph 9 of that Schedule, there is determined under that paragraph the conditions to which the relevant planning permissions (within the meaning of that Schedule) relating to the site are to be subject.

(3) Subject to sub-paragraphs (4) and (7) below, in the case of a mining site—

(a) which is not a Phase I or II site within the meaning of Schedule 13 to this Act; and

(b) to which no old mining permission relates,

the first review date is the date falling fifteen years after the date upon which was granted the most recent mineral permission which relates to the site.

(4) Where, in the case of a mining site falling within sub-paragraph (3) above, the most recent mineral permission relating to that site relates, or the most recent such permissions (whether or not granted on the same date) between them relate, to part only of the site, and in the opinion of the mineral planning authority it is expedient, for the purpose of ascertaining, under that sub-paragraph, the first review date in respect of that site, to treat that permission or those permissions as having been granted at the same time as the last of the other mineral permissions relating to the site, the first review date for that site shall be ascertained under that sub-paragraph accordingly.

(5) A mineral planning authority shall, in deciding whether they are of such an opinion as is mentioned in sub-paragraph (4) above, have regard to any guidance issued by the Secretary of State for the purpose.

(6) Subject to sub-paragraph (7) below, in the case of a mining site—

(a) to which relates a mineral permission in respect of which an order has been made under section 97 of the 1990 Act or section 42 of the 1972 Act, or

(b) in respect of which, or any part of which, an order has been made under paragraph 1 of Schedule 9 to the 1990 Act or section 49 of the 1972 Act,

the first review date shall be the date falling fifteen years after the date upon which the order took effect or, in a case where there is more than one such order, upon which the last of those orders to take effect took effect.

(7) In the case of a mining site for which the preceding provisions of this paragraph have effect to specify two or more different dates as the first review date, the first review date shall be the latest of those dates.

Service of notice of first periodic review

4.—(1) The mineral planning authority shall, in connection with the first periodic review of the mineral permissions relating to a mining site, no later than 12 months before the first review date, serve notice upon each person appearing to them to be the owner of any land, or entitled to an interest in any mineral, included in that site.

(2) A notice required to be served under sub-paragraph (1) above shall—

(a) specify the mining site to which it relates;

(b) identify the mineral permissions relating to that site;

(c) state the first review date;

(d) state that the first review date is the date by which an application must be made for approval of the conditions to which the mineral permissions relating to the site are to be subject and explain the consequences which will occur if no such application is made by that date; and

(e) explain the right to apply for postponement of the first review date and give the date by which such an application has to be made.

(3) Where, in relation to any land or mineral included in a mining site the mineral planning authority—

(a) has served notice on any person under sub-paragraph (1) above; and

(b) has received no application under paragraph 6 below from that person by the date falling eight weeks before the first review date,

the authority shall serve a written reminder on that person.

(4) A reminder required to be served under sub-paragraph (3) above shall—

(a) indicate that the land or mineral in question is included in a mining site;

(b) comply with the requirements of sub-paragraph (2)(a) to (d) above; and

(c) be served on the person in question on or before the date falling four weeks before the first review date.

(5) Sub-paragraph (1) above shall not require the mineral planning authority to serve notice under that sub-paragraph upon any person whose identity or address for service is not known to and cannot practicably, after reasonable inquiry, be ascertained by them, but in any such case the authority shall cause to be firmly affixed, to each of one or more conspicuous objects on the land or, as the case may be, on the surface of the land above the interest in question, a copy of the notice which they would (apart from the provisions of this sub-paragraph) have had to serve under that sub-paragraph on the owner of that land or interest.

(6) If in a case where sub-paragraph (5) above applies, no person makes an application to the authority under paragraph 6 below in respect of the mining site which includes the land or interest in question by the date falling eight weeks before the first review date, the authority shall cause to be firmly affixed, to each of one or more conspicuous objects on the land or, as the case may be, on the surface of the land above the interest in question, a copy of the written reminder that would, in a case not falling within sub-paragraph (5) above, have been served under sub-paragraph (3) above.

(7) Where by sub-paragraph (5) or (6) above a copy of any notice is required to be affixed to an object on any land that copy shall—

(a) be displayed in such a way as to be easily visible and legible;

(b) be first displayed—

(i) in a case where the requirement arises under sub-paragraph (5) above, no later than 12 months before the first review date; or

(ii) in a case where the requirement arises under sub-paragraph (6) above, no later than the date falling four weeks before the first review date;

and

(c) be left in position for at least the period of 21 days from the date when it is first displayed, but where the notice is, without fault or intention of the authority, removed, obscured or defaced before that period has elapsed, that requirement shall be treated as having been complied with if the authority has taken reasonable steps for protection of the notice and, if need be, its replacement.

(8) In sub-paragraphs (5) and (6) above, any reference to a conspicuous object on any land includes, in a case where the person serving a notice considers that there are no or insufficient such objects on the land, a reference to a post driven into or erected upon the land by the person serving the notice for the purpose of having affixed to it a copy of the notice in question.

Application for postponement of the first review date

5.—(1) Any person who is the owner of any land, or of any interest in any mineral, comprised in a mining site may, no later than the day upon which expires the period of three months from the day upon which notice was served upon him under paragraph 4 above, apply under this paragraph to the mineral planning authority for the postponement of the first review date.

(2) An application under this paragraph shall be in writing and shall set out—

(a) the conditions to which each mineral permission relating to the site is subject;

(b) the applicant's reasons for considering those conditions to be satisfactory; and

(c) the date which the applicant wishes to have substituted for the first review date.

(3) Where the mineral planning authority receive an application made under this paragraph—

(a) if they consider the conditions referred to in sub-paragraph (2)(a) above to be satisfactory they shall agree to the first review date being postponed in which event they shall determine the date to be substituted for that date;

(b) in any other case they shall refuse the application.

(4) When a mineral planning authority determine an application made under this paragraph, they shall notify the applicant in writing of their decision and, in a case where they have agreed to the postponement of the first review date, shall notify the applicant of the date which they have determined should be substituted for the first review date.

(5) Where, within the period of three months of the mineral planning authority having received an application under this paragraph, or within such extended period as may at any time be agreed upon in writing between the applicant and the authority, the authority have not given notice, under sub-paragraph (4) above, to the applicant of their decision upon the application, the authority shall be treated as having, at the end of that period or, as the case may be, that extended period—

(a) agreed to the first review date being postponed; and

(b) determined that the date referred to in sub-paragraph (2)(c) above be substituted for the first review date.

Application to determine the conditions to which the mineral permissions relating to a mining site are to be subject

6.—(1) Any person who is the owner of any land, or who is entitled to an interest in a mineral, may, if that land or mineral is or forms part of a mining site, apply to the mineral planning authority to determine the conditions to which the mineral permissions relating to that site are to be subject.

(2) An application under this paragraph shall be in writing and shall—

(a) identify the mining site in respect of which the application is made and state that the application is made in connection with the first periodic review of the mineral permissions relating to that site;

(b) specify the land or minerals comprised in the site of which the applicant is the owner or, as the case may be, in which the applicant is entitled to an interest;

(c) identify the mineral permissions relating to the site;

(d) identify, and give an address for, each other person that the applicant knows or, after reasonable inquiry, has cause to believe to be an owner of any land, or entitled to any interest in any mineral, comprised in the site;

(e) set out the conditions to which the applicant proposes the permissions referred to in paragraph (c) above should be subject; and

(f) be accompanied by the appropriate certificate (within the meaning of sub-paragraph (3) or (4) below).

(3) For the purposes of sub-paragraph (2) above, as respects England and Wales the appropriate certificate is such a certificate—

(a) as would be required, under section 65 of the 1990 Act and any provision of a development order made by virtue of that section, to accompany the application if it were an application for planning permission for minerals development, but

(b) with such modifications as are required for the purposes of this paragraph,

and section 65(6) of the 1990 Act shall also have effect in relation to any certificate purporting to be the appropriate certificate.

(4) For the purposes of sub-paragraph (2) above, the appropriate certificate is, as respects Scotland, each of the certificates which would be required, under or by virtue of sections 23 and 24 of the 1972 Act (notice etc. of applications for planning permission), to accompany the application if it were an application for planning permission for minerals development, but with such modifications as are required for the purposes of this paragraph; and sections 23(3) and 24(5) of

that Act (offences) shall have effect in relation to any certificate purporting to be the appropriate certificate.

(5) Where the mineral planning authority receive an application under this paragraph in relation to a mining site they shall determine the conditions to which each mineral permission relating to the site is to be subject.

(6) The conditions imposed by virtue of a determination under sub-paragraph (5) above—

(a) may include any conditions which may be imposed on a grant of planning permission for minerals development;

(b) may be in addition to, or in substitution for, any existing conditions to which the permission in question is subject.

(7) In determining that a mineral permission is to be subject to any condition relating to development for which planning permission is granted by a development order, the mineral planning authority shall have regard to any guidance issued for the purpose by the Secretary of State.

(8) Subject to sub-paragraph (9) below, where, within the period of three months of the mineral planning authority having received an application under this paragraph, or within such extended period as may at any time be agreed upon in writing between the applicant and the authority, the authority have not given notice to the applicant of their decision upon the application, the authority shall be treated as having at the end of that period or, as the case may be, that extended period, determined that the conditions to which any mineral permission to which the application relates is to be subject are those specified in the application as being proposed in relation to that permission; and any such permission shall, from that time, have effect subject to those conditions.

(9) Where a mineral planning authority, having received an application under this paragraph, are of the opinion that they are unable to determine the application unless further details are supplied to them, they shall within the period of one month from having received the application give notice to the applicant—

(a) stating that they are of such opinion; and

(b) specifying the further details which they require,

and where the authority so serve such a notice the period of three months referred to in sub-paragraph (8) above shall run not from the authority having received the application but from the time when the authority have received all the further details specified in the notice.

(10) Without prejudice to the generality of sub-paragraph (9) above, the further details which may be specified in a notice under that sub-paragraph include any—

(a) information, plans drawings; or

(b) evidence verifying any particulars of details supplied to the authority in respect of the application in question,

which it is reasonable for the authority to request for the purpose of enabling them to determine the application.

Permissions ceasing to have effect

7. Where no application under paragraph 6 above in respect of a mining site has been served on the mineral planning authority by the first review date, or by such later date as may at any time be agreed upon in writing between the applicant and the authority, each mineral permission—

(a) relating to the site; and

(b) identified in the notice served in relation to the site under paragraph 4 above,

shall cease to have effect, except insofar as it imposes any restoration or aftercare condition, on the day following the first review date or, as the case may be, such later agreed date.

Reference of applications to the Secretary of State

8.—(1) The Secretary of State may give directions requiring applications made under paragraph 6 above to any mineral planning authority to be referred to him for determination instead of being dealt with by the authority.

(2) A direction under sub-paragraph (1) above may relate either to a particular application or to applications of a class specified in the direction.

(3) Where an application is referred to the Secretary of State in accordance with a direction under sub-paragraph (1) above—

(a) subject to paragraph (b) below, paragraph 6(5) and (6) above, and paragraph 11 below so far as relating to applications under paragraph 6 above, shall apply, with any necessary modifications, to his determination of the application as they apply to the determination of applications by the mineral planning authority;

(b) before determining the application the Secretary of State must, if either the applicant or the mineral planning authority so wish, give each of them an opportunity of appearing before and being heard by a person appointed by the Secretary of State for the purpose; and

(c) the decision of the Secretary of State on the application shall be final.

Appeals

9.—(1) Where on an application under paragraph 6 above the mineral planning authority determine conditions that differ in any respect from the proposed conditions set out in the application, the applicant may appeal to the Secretary of State.

(2) An appeal under sub-paragraph (1) above must be made by giving notice of appeal to the Secretary of State, before the end of the period of six months beginning with the determination, on a form supplied by or on behalf of the Secretary of State for use for that purpose, and giving, so far as reasonably practicable, the information required by that form.

(3) Paragraph 6 of Schedule 2 to the 1991 Act (determination of appeals) shall, as respects England and Wales, apply to appeals under sub-paragraph (1) above as it applies to appeals under paragraph 5 of that Schedule.

(4) As respects England and Wales, sections 284 to 288 of the 1990 Act shall have effect as if the action mentioned in section 284(3) of that Act included any decision of the Secretary of State—

(a) on an appeal under sub-paragraph (1) above; or

(b) on an application under paragraph 6 above referred to him under paragraph 8 above.

(5) Paragraph 6 of Schedule 10A to the 1972 Act (determination of appeals) shall, as respects Scotland, apply to appeals under sub-paragraph (1) above as it applies to appeals under paragraph 5 of that Schedule.

(6) As respects Scotland, sections 231 to 233 of the 1972 Act shall have effect as if the action mentioned in section 231(3) included any decision of the Secretary of State—

(a) on an appeal under sub-paragraph (1) above; or

(b) on an application under paragraph 6 above referred to him under paragraph 8 above.

(7) As respects Scotland, Schedule 7 to the 1972 Act shall apply to appeals under sub-paragraph (1) above.

Time from which conditions determined under this Schedule are to take effect

10.—(1) Where an application has been made under paragraph 6 above in respect of a mining site, each of the mineral permissions relating to the site shall, from the time when the application is finally determined, have effect subject to the conditions to which it is determined under this Schedule that that permission is to be subject.

(2) Sub-paragraph (1) above is without prejudice to paragraph 6(8) above.

Two or more applicants

11.—(1) Where a mineral planning authority have received from any person a duly made application under paragraph 5 or 6 above—

(a) that person may not make any further application under the paragraph in question in respect of the same site; and

(b) if the application has been determined, whether or not in the case of an application under paragraph 6 above it has been finally determined, no other person may make an application under the paragraph in question in respect of the same site.

(2) Where—

(a) a mineral planning authority have received from any person in respect of a mineral site a duly made application under paragraph 5 or 6 above; and

(b) the authority receives from another person a duly made application under the paragraph in question in respect of the same site,

then for the purpose of the determination of the applications and any appeal against such a determination, this Schedule shall have effect as if the applications were a single application received by the authority on the date on which the later application was received by the authority and references to the applicant shall be read as references to either or any of the applicants.

Second and subsequent periodic reviews

12.—(1) In this paragraph, in relation to a mining site, but subject to paragraph 5 above as applied by sub-paragraph (2) below, "review date" means—

(a) in the case of the second periodic review, the date falling fifteen years after the date upon which was finally determined an application made under paragraph 6 above in respect of the site; and

(b) in the case of subsequent periodic reviews, the date falling fifteen years after the date upon which there was last finally determined under this Schedule an application made in respect of that site under paragraph 6 above as applied by sub-paragraph (2) below.

(2) Paragraphs 4 to 11 above shall apply in respect of the second or any subsequent periodic review of the mineral permissions relating to a mining site as they apply to the first such periodic review, but as if—

   (a) any reference in those paragraphs to the "first review date" were a reference to the review date; and

   (b) the references in paragraphs 4(1) and 6(2)(a) above to the first periodic review were references to the periodic review in question.

Compensation

13.—(1) This paragraph applies where—

   (a) an application made under paragraph 6 above in respect of a mining site is finally determined; and

   (b) the conditions to which the mineral permissions relating to the site are to be subject, as determined under this Schedule, differ in any respect from the proposed conditions set out in the application; and

   (c) the effect of the new conditions, except insofar as they are restoration or aftercare conditions, as compared with the effect of the existing conditions, except insofar as they were restoration or aftercare conditions, is to restrict working rights in respect of the site.

(2) For the purposes of this paragraph—

   "the new conditions", in relation to a mining site, means the conditions, determined under this Schedule, to which the mineral permissions relating to the site are to be subject; and

   "the existing conditions", in relation to a mining site, means the conditions to which the mineral permissions relating to the site were subject immediately prior to the final determination of the application made under paragraph 6 above in respect of that site.

(3) For the purposes of this paragraph, working rights are restricted in respect of a mining site if any of—

   (a) the size of the area which may be used for the winning and working of minerals or the depositing of mineral waste;

   (b) the depth to which operations for the winning and working of minerals may extend;

   (c) the height of any deposit of mineral waste;

   (d) the rate at which any particular mineral may be extracted;

   (e) the rate at which any particular mineral waste may be deposited;

   (f) the period at the expiry of which any winning or working of minerals or depositing of mineral waste is to cease; or

   (g) the total quantity of minerals which may be extracted from, or of mineral waste which may be deposited on, the site,

is restricted or reduced in respect of the mining site in question.

(4) In a case to which this paragraph applies, but subject to sub-paragraph (6) below, as respects England and Wales, Parts IV and XI of the 1990 Act and, as respects Scotland, Parts VIII and XI of the 1972 Act, shall have effect as if an order made under section 97 of the 1990 Act or, as the case may be, section 42 of the 1972 Act—

   (a) had been confirmed by the Secretary of State under section 98 of the 1990 Act or, as the case may be, section 42 of the 1972 Act at the time when the application in question was finally determined; and

   (b) as so confirmed, had effect to modify those permissions to the extent specified in sub-paragraph (6) below.

(5) For the purposes of this paragraph, the order referred to in sub-paragraph (4) above is one whose only effect adverse to the interests of any person having an interest in the land or minerals comprised in the mineral site is to restrict working rights in respect of the site to the same extent as the relevant restriction.

(6) For the purposes of section 116 of the 1990 Act and section 167A of the 1972 Act and of any regulations made under those sections, the permissions treated as being modified by the order mentioned in sub-paragraph (4) above shall be treated as if they were planning permissions for development which neither consists of nor includes any minerals development.

GENERAL NOTE

This Schedule relates to all mineral permissions and requires minerals planning authorities to review them periodically. In this way, the problems of minerals permissions which are subject to anachronistic and inadequate conditions, and which necessitated the provisions of Sched. 13, should be avoided in the future.

The date for the first such review is ascertained under para. 3 which (at the risk of over-simplification) is based on a 15-year review period from when the conditions were last imposed or reviewed. The first periodic review is activated by the service of a notice by the mineral planning authority under para. 4, though there is a right to apply for postponement of the first review date where the landowner or mineral owner considers the existing conditions to be satisfactory (para. 5).

The effect of the notice activating review is to place the onus on the landowner or mineral owner to apply under para. 6 for the planning conditions to which the site is subject to be determined. As with applications under Sched. 13, the application procedure is similar to that for planning permission. The right of appeal against the determination by the mineral planning authority of the conditions is provided by para. 9. The consequence of failing to make application by the review date or such later date as may be agreed with the authority is serious: under para. 7 the relevant permission will cease to have effect, except insofar as it imposes restoration or after-care conditions. The notice of the first and subsequent reviews served by the authority must explain these consequences, and there are procedures for reminder notices and site notices (para. 4(2)–(8)).

Having established the first review date, successive review dates follow at fifteen-year intervals (para. 12). The same procedures and provisions apply as on first review (para. 12(2)).

As with Sched. 13 the new provisions on review may result in compensation being payable: para. 13. The criteria for compensation are in fact looser than under Sched. 13. The criteria simply require that the effect of the new conditions (except insofar as they are restoration or after-care conditions) restricts working rights in respect of the site (para. 13(1)–(3)).

Section 105   SCHEDULE 15

MINOR AND CONSEQUENTIAL AMENDMENTS RELATING TO FISHERIES

Interpretation

1. In this Schedule—

"local statutory provision" means—

(a) a provision of a local Act (including an Act confirming a provisional order);

(b) a provision of so much of any public general Act as has effect with respect to particular persons or works or with respect to particular provisions falling within any paragraph of this definition;

(c) a provision of an instrument made under any provision falling within paragraph (a) or (b) above;

(d) a provision of any other instrument which is in the nature of a local enactment;

"the Minister" means the Minister of Agriculture, Fisheries and Food;

"subordinate legislation" has the same meaning as in the Interpretation Act 1978;

"the transfer date" has the same meaning as in Part I of this Act.

General modifications of references to the National Rivers Authority

2.—(1) Subject to—

(a) the following provisions of this Schedule,

(b) the provisions of sections 102 to 104 of this Act, and

(c) any repeal made by this Act,

any provision to which this paragraph applies which contains, or falls to be construed as containing, a reference (however framed and whether or not in relation to an area) to the National Rivers Authority shall have effect on and after the transfer date as if that reference were a reference to the Agency.

(2) Sub-paragraph (1) above is subject to paragraph 1(2)(a) of Schedule 17 to the Water Act 1989 (references in certain local statutory provisions or subordinate legislation to the area of a particular water authority to have effect as references to the area which, immediately before the transfer date within the meaning of that Act, was the area of that authority for the purposes of their functions relating to fisheries).

(3) Subject as mentioned in sub-paragraph (1) above, any provision to which this paragraph applies which contains, or falls to be construed as containing, a reference (however framed) to the whole area in relation to which the National Rivers Authority carries out its functions in relation to fisheries shall have effect on and after the transfer date as if that reference were a reference to the whole area in relation to which the Agency carries out its functions relating to fisheries.

(4) The provisions to which this paragraph applies are the provisions of—

(a) the Sea Fisheries Regulation Act 1966;

(b) the Salmon and Freshwater Fisheries Act 1975; and
(c) any local statutory provision or subordinate legislation which is in force immediately before the transfer date and—
(i) relates to the carrying out by the National Rivers Authority of any function relating to fisheries; or
(ii) in the case of subordinate legislation, was made by virtue of any provision to which this paragraph applies or under the Diseases of Fish Act 1937.
(5) The modifications made by this paragraph shall be subject to any power by subordinate legislation to revoke or amend any provision to which this paragraph applies; and, accordingly, any such power, including the powers conferred by section 121 of this Act and paragraph 3 below, shall be exercisable so as to exclude the operation of this paragraph in relation to the provisions in relation to which the power is conferred.

Power to amend subordinate legislation etc.

3.—(1) If it appears to the Minister or the Secretary of State to be appropriate to do so for the purposes of, or in consequence of, the coming into force of any provision of this Schedule, he may by order revoke or amend any subordinate legislation.
(2) An order under this paragraph may—
(a) make different provision for different cases, including different provision in relation to different persons, circumstances or localities; and
(b) contain such supplemental, consequential and transitional provision as the Minister or the Secretary of State considers appropriate.
(3) The power conferred by virtue of this paragraph in relation to subordinate legislation made under any enactment shall be without prejudice to any other power to revoke or amend subordinate legislation made under that enactment, but—
(a) no requirement imposed with respect to the exercise of any such other power shall apply in relation to any revocation or amendment of that legislation by an order under this paragraph; and
(b) the power to make an order under this paragraph shall be exercisable (instead of in accordance with any such requirement) by statutory instrument subject to annulment in pursuance of a resolution of either House of Parliament.

The Diseases of Fish Act 1937

4.—(1) Subject to sub-paragraph (2) below, in the Diseases of Fish Act 1937—
(a) any reference which to any extent is, or falls to be construed as, a reference to the National Rivers Authority shall have effect, in relation to the area which by virtue of section 6(7) of this Act is the area in relation to which the Agency carries out functions under that Act, as a reference to the Agency; and
(b) references to an area (including references which fall to be construed as references to the area which by virtue of subsection (6) of section 2 of the Water Resources Act 1991 is the area in relation to which the National Rivers Authority carries out functions under the said Act of 1937), in relation to the Agency, shall have effect as references to the area described in paragraph (a) above.
(2) In section 8(3) of the said Act of 1937 (offences in relation to the Esk) for the words "National Rivers Authority" there shall be substituted the words "Environment Agency".
(3) Nothing in this paragraph or in that Act shall authorise the Agency to take legal proceedings in Scotland in respect of any offence.

The Sea Fisheries Regulation Act 1966

5.—(1) The provisions of section 1 of the Sea Fisheries Regulation Act 1966 (establishment of fisheries committees) which provide that an order under that section modifying a previous such order is to be made only on such an application and after such consultation as is mentioned in that section shall not apply to an order under that section which contains a statement that the only provision made by the order is provision which appears to the Minister making the order to be appropriate in consequence of any of the provisions of this Act.
(2) In section 2(2) of that Act (constitution of local fisheries committee) for the words "the National Rivers Authority" there shall be substituted the words "the Environment Agency".
(3) In section 18(3) of that Act (provision where a water authority or harbour authority have the powers of a local fisheries committee) for the words "National Rivers Authority)" there shall be substituted the words "Environment Agency)".

The Sea Fish (Conservation) Act 1967

6. In section 18(1) of the Sea Fish (Conservation) Act 1967 (enforcement of orders relating to salmon and migratory trout)—
    (a) for the words "subsection (6) of section 2 of the Water Resources Act 1991" there shall be substituted the words "subsection (7) of section 6 of the Environment Act 1995"; and
    (b) for the words "the National Rivers Authority" there shall be substituted the words "the Environment Agency".

The Salmon and Freshwater Fisheries Act 1975

7. In section 5 of the Salmon and Freshwater Fisheries Act 1975 (prohibition of use of explosives, poisons, electrical devices etc) in subsection (2), the words following paragraph (b) (which require Ministerial approval for the giving of permission to use noxious substances) shall be omitted.

8. In section 6(3) of that Act (definition of "unauthorised fixed engine") in paragraph (d) for the words "the National Rivers Authority" there shall be substituted the words "the Agency".

9. In section 8(2) of that Act (fishing mill dams to have attached to them fish passes of form and dimensions approved by the Minister) for the words "the Minister" there shall be inserted the words "the Agency".

10. In section 9(1) of that Act (owner or occupier of certain dams or other obstructions to make fish passes of form and dimensions approved by the Minister) for the words "the Minister" there shall be substituted the words "the Agency".

11.—(1) In section 10 of that Act, in subsection (1) (power of the National Rivers Authority, with the written consent of the Minister, to construct and maintain fish passes of form and dimensions approved by the Minister—
    (a) the words "with the written consent of the Minister," shall be omitted; and
    (b) for the words "as the Minister may approve" there shall be substituted the words "as it may determine".

(2) In subsection (2) of that section (power of the National Rivers Authority, with the consent of the Minister, to alter etc fish passes and free gaps) the words "with the written consent of the Minister," shall be omitted.

12.—(1) In section 11 of that Act (Minister's consents and approvals for fish passes) for subsection (1) there shall be substituted—

    "(1) Any approval given by the Agency to or in relation to a fish pass may, if in giving it the Agency indicates that fact, be provisional until the Agency notifies the applicant for approval that the pass is functioning to its satisfaction.

    (1A) The applicant for any such approval—
      (a) shall be liable to meet any costs incurred (whether by him or by the Agency or any other person) for the purposes of, or otherwise in connection with, the performance of the Agency's function of determining for the purposes of subsection (1) above whether or not the fish pass in question is functioning to its satisfaction; and
      (b) shall provide the Agency with such information or assistance as it may require for the purpose of performing that function."

(2) In subsection (2) of that section (Minister's power to revoke approval or consent while still provisional)—
    (a) for the words "or consent is provisional, the Minister" there shall be substituted the words "is provisional, the Agency"; and
    (b) for the words from "his intention" onwards there shall be substituted the words "its intention to do so, revoke the approval".

(3) In subsection (3) of that section (Minister's power, when revoking provisional approval, to extend period for making fish pass)—
    (a) for the words "the Minister" there shall be substituted the words "the Agency"; and
    (b) for the word "he" there shall be substituted the word "it".

(4) In subsection (4) of that section (Minister's power to approve and certify fish pass if he is of the opinion that it is efficient)—
    (a) for the words "The Minister" there shall be substituted the words "The Agency"; and
    (b) for the word "he" there shall be substituted the word "it".

(5) In subsection (5) of that section (fish passes approved by the Minister deemed to be in conformity with the Act) for the words "the Minister" there shall be substituted the words "the Agency".

13. For section 14 of that Act (gratings) there shall be substituted—

"Screens

14.—(1) This section applies in any case where—

(a) by means of any conduit or artificial channel, water is diverted from waters frequented by salmon or migratory trout; and

(b) any of the water so diverted is used for the purposes of a water or canal undertaking or for the purposes of any mill or fish farm;

and in this section "the responsible person" means the owner of the water or canal undertaking or (as the case may be) the occupier of the mill or the owner or occupier of the fish farm.

(2) Where this section applies, the responsible person shall unless an exemption from the obligation is granted by the Agency, ensure (at his own cost) that there is placed and maintained at the entrance of, or within, the conduit or channel a screen which—

(a) subject to subsection (4) below, prevents the descent of the salmon or migratory trout; and

(b) in a case where any of the water diverted is used for the purposes of a fish farm, prevents the egress of farmed fish from the fish farm by way of the conduit or channel.

(3) Where this section applies, the responsible person shall also, unless an exemption from the obligation is granted by the Agency, ensure (at his own cost) that there is placed and maintained across any outfall of the conduit or channel a screen which—

(a) prevents salmon or migratory trout from entering the outfall; and

(b) in a case where any of the water diverted is used for the purposes of a fish farm, prevents the egress of farmed fish from the fish farm by way of the outfall.

(4) Where a screen is placed within any conduit or channel pursuant to subsection (2) above, the responsible person shall ensure that a continuous by-wash is provided immediately upstream of the screen, by means of which salmon or migratory trout may return by as direct a route as practicable to the waters from which they entered the conduit or channel (and accordingly nothing in subsection (2) or (3) above applies in relation to a by-wash provided for the purposes of this subsection).

(5) Any screen placed, or by–wash provided, in pursuance of this section shall be so constructed and located as to ensure, so far as reasonably practicable, that salmon or migratory trout are not injured or damaged by it.

(6) No such screen shall be so placed as to interfere with the passage of boats on any navigable canal.

(7) Any exemption under subsection (2) or (3) above may be granted subject to conditions.

(8) If any person who is required to do so by this section fails to ensure that a screen is placed or maintained, or that a by-wash is provided, in accordance with the provisions of this section, he shall be guilty of an offence.

(9) In any proceedings for an offence under subsection (8) above, it shall, subject to subsection (10) below, be a defence for the person charged to prove that he took all reasonable precautions and exercised all due diligence to avoid the commission of the offence by himself or a person under his control.

(10) If in any case the defence provided by subsection (9) above involves the allegation that the commission of the offence was due to an act or default of another person, or to reliance on information supplied by another person, the person charged shall not, without leave of the court, be entitled to rely on that defence unless—

(a) at least seven clear days before the hearing, and

(b) where he has previously appeared before a court in connection with the alleged offence, within one month of his first such appearance,

he has served on the prosecutor a notice in writing giving such information identifying or assisting in the identification of that other person as was then in his possession.

(11) Any reference in subsection (10) above to appearing before a court includes a reference to being brought before a court.

(12) The obligations imposed by subsections (2) to (6) above, except so far as relating to farmed fish, shall not be in force during such period (if any) in each year as may be prescribed by byelaw.

(13) The obligations imposed by subsections (2) to (6) above on the occupier of a mill shall apply only where the conduit or channel was constructed on or after 18th July 1923.

(14) Any reference in this section to ensuring that a screen is placed and maintained includes, in a case where the screen takes the form of apparatus the operation of which prevents the passage of fish of the descriptions in question, a reference to ensuring that the apparatus is kept in continuous operation.

(15) In this section "by-wash" means a passage through which water flows."

14.—(1) In section 15 of that Act (power of National Rivers Authority, with the consent of the Minister, to use gratings etc. to limit movements of salmon and trout) for the word "grating" or "gratings", wherever occurring (including in the side-note), there shall be substituted respectively the word "screen" or "screens".

(2) In subsection (1) of that section (placing of gratings, deepening of channels etc.) the words "with the written consent of the Minister" shall be omitted.

(3) In subsection (3) of that section (use of such means as the Minister may approve for preventing ingress)—

(a) the words "with the written consent of the Minister" shall be omitted; and

(b) for the words "as the Minister may approve" there shall be substituted the words "as in its opinion are necessary".

(4) At the end of that section there shall be added—

"(5) In this section "open", in relation to a screen which consists of apparatus, includes the doing of anything which interrupts, or otherwise interferes with, the operation of the apparatus."

15. In section 17 of that Act (restrictions on taking salmon or trout above or below an obstruction etc) in subsection (3) (section not to be enforced, in cases where the fish pass is approved by the Minister, until compensation has been paid) for the words "approved by the Minister" there shall be substituted—

"(a) approved by the Agency, or

(b) constructed and maintained by the Agency in accordance with section 10(1) above,".

16. In section 18 of that Act (provisions supplementary to Part II) for subsection (2) (notice of application for Ministerial consent to the doing of certain acts to be given to the owner and occupier of the dam etc in question) there shall be substituted—

"(2) The Agency shall not—

(a) construct, abolish or alter any fish pass, or abolish or alter any free gap, in pursuance of section 10 above, or

(b) do any work under section 15 above,

unless reasonable notice of its intention to do so (specifying the section in question) has been served on the owner and occupier of the dam, fish pass or free gap, watercourse, mill race, cut, leat, conduit or other channel, with a plan and specification of the proposed work; and the Agency shall take into consideration any objections by the owner or occupier, before doing the proposed work."

17. In section 30 of that Act, the paragraph defining "fish farm" (which is superseded by amendments made by this Schedule) shall be omitted.

18.—(1) In section 35 of that Act (power to require production of fishing licences) in subsection (3), for the words "the National Rivers Authority" there shall be substituted the words "the Agency".

(2) For subsection (4) of that section (definition of "the appropriate office of the National Rivers Authority") there shall be substituted—

"(4) In subsection (3) above, "the appropriate office of the Agency" means—

(a) in a case where the person requiring the production of the licence or other authority specifies a particular office of the Agency for its production, that office; and

(b) in any other case, any office of the Agency;

and for the purposes of that subsection where a licence or other authority which any person has been required to produce is sent by post to an office of the Agency that licence or other authority shall be treated as produced by that person at that office."

19. After subsection (1A) of section 39 of that Act (application of Act to River Esk in Scotland) there shall be inserted—

"(1B) Sections 31 to 34 and 36(2) of this Act shall, subject to the modifications set out in subsection (1C) below, apply throughout the catchment area of the River Esk in Scotland but a water bailiff shall exercise his powers under those sections as so applied only in relation to an offence—

(a) against this Act;

(b) against section 1 of the Salmon and Freshwater Fisheries (Protection) (Scotland) Act 1951; or

(c) which is deemed to be an offence under this Act by virtue of section 211 (6) of the Water Resources Act 1991,

which he has reasonable cause to suspect has been committed in a place to which this Act applies by virtue of subsection (1)(b) above.

(1C) The modifications referred to in subsection (1B) above are—

(a) references in sections 31 to 34 of this Act to "this Act" shall be construed as including references to section 1 of the Salmon and Freshwater Fisheries (Protection) (Scotland) Act 1951 (as applied to the River Esk by section 21 of that Act); and

(b) in section 33—

(i) references to a justice of the peace shall be construed as including references to a sheriff; and

(ii) in subsection (2), the reference to an information on oath shall be construed as including a reference to evidence on oath.".

20. In section 41(1) of that Act (general definitions) the following definitions shall be inserted at the appropriate places, that is to say—

(a) " "fish farm" has the same meaning as in the Diseases of Fish Act 1937;"; and

(b) " "screen" means a grating or other device which, or any apparatus the operation of which, prevents—

(a) the passage of salmon or migratory trout, and

(b) if the screen is required in connection with a fish farm, the passage of any fish farmed at that fish farm,

or any combination of devices or apparatus which, taken together, achieve that result;"; and the definition of "grating" shall be omitted.

21. In subsection (3) of section 43 of that Act (extent of Act to Scotland), after the words "(1A)" there shall be inserted the words ", (1B), (1C)".

22. In paragraph 1 of Schedule 1 to that Act (close seasons and close times) for the words "the National Rivers Authority" there shall be substituted the words "the Agency".

The Diseases of Fish Act 1983

23. In section 9(1)(d) of the Diseases of Fish Act 1983 (disclosure of information for the purpose of enabling the National Rivers Authority to carry out any of its functions) for the words "the National Rivers Authority" there shall be substituted the words "the Environment Agency".

The Salmon Act 1986

24. In section 37(3) of the Salmon Act 1986 (byelaws requiring consent of the National Rivers Authority) for the words "the National Rivers Authority has" there shall be substituted the words "the Environment Agency has".

The Water Resources Act 1991

25. In section 115 of the Water Resources Act 1991, in subsection (1) (power by order to make provision in relation to an area defined by the order for the modification, in relation to the fisheries in that area, of the enactments specified in the paragraphs of that subsection) for paragraph (b) there shall be substituted—

"(b) of section 142 or 156 below or paragraph 6 or 7 of Schedule 25 to this Act; or"

26.—(1) In paragraph 6 of Schedule 25 to that Act (powers to make byelaws in relation to any part or parts of the area in relation to which the National Rivers Authority carries out its functions in relation to fisheries under Part V of that Act) in sub-paragraphs (1) to (5) for the words "in relation to any part or parts", in each place where they occur, there shall be substituted the words "in relation to the whole or any part or parts".

(2) In sub-paragraph (3)(c) of that paragraph (byelaws for the purpose of determining for the purposes of the Salmon and Freshwater Fisheries Act 1975 the period of the year during which gratings need not be maintained) for the word "gratings" there shall be substituted the word "screens".

Section 106   SCHEDULE 16

COMMENCEMENT

These provisions will be brought into force by a commencement order made under s.125(3) of the 1995 Act.

GENERAL NOTE

See the General Note to s.106 on p. 25–280.

POLLUTION OF RIVERS AND COASTAL WATERS IN SCOTLAND: AMENDMENT OF THE CONTROL OF POLLUTION ACT 1974

1. The Control of Pollution Act 1974, as it has effect in Scotland, shall be amended in accordance with the following paragraphs.

2. After section 30E there shall be inserted the following sections—

"Control of entry of polluting matter and effluents into water

Pollution offences

30F.—(1) A person contravenes this section if he causes or knowingly permits any poisonous, noxious or polluting matter or any solid waste matter to enter any controlled waters.

(2) A person contravenes this section if he causes or knowingly permits any matter, other than trade effluent or sewage effluent, to enter controlled waters by being discharged from a sewer or from a drain in contravention of a prohibition imposed under section 30G below.

(3) A person contravenes this section if he causes or knowingly permits any trade effluent or sewage effluent to be discharged—

　(a) into any controlled waters; or

　(b) from land in Scotland, through a pipe, into the sea outside the seaward limits of controlled waters.

(4) A person contravenes this section if he causes or knowingly permits any trade effluent or sewage effluent to be discharged, in contravention of any prohibition imposed under section 30G below, from a building or from any plant—

　(a) on to or into any land; or

　(b) into any waters of a loch or pond which are not inland waters.

(5) A person contravenes this section if he causes or knowingly permits any matter whatever to enter any inland waters so as to tend (either directly or in combination with other matter which he or another person causes or permits to enter those waters) to impede the proper flow of the waters in a manner leading, or likely to lead, to a substantial aggravation of—

　(a) pollution due to other causes; or

　(b) the consequences of such pollution.

(6) Subject to the following provisions of this Part, a person who contravenes this section shall be guilty of an offence and liable—

　(a) on summary conviction, to imprisonment for a term not exceeding three months or to a fine not exceeding £20,000 or to both;

　(b) on conviction on indictment, to imprisonment for a term not exceeding two years or to a fine or to both.

DEFINITIONS

"controlled waters": s.30A(1) of the Control of Pollution Act 1974.

"drain": s.56(1) of the Control of Pollution Act 1974; s.59(1) of the Sewerage (Scotland) Act 1968.

"effluent": s.56(1) of the Control of Pollution Act 1974.

"inland waters": s.30A(1) of the Control of Pollution Act 1974.

"sewage effluent": s.56(1) of the Control of Pollution Act 1974.

"sewer": s.56(1) of the Control of Pollution Act 1974; s.59(1) of the Sewerage (Scotland) Act 1968.

"trade effluent": s.56(1) of the Control of Pollution Act 1974.

GENERAL NOTE

This section replaces the water pollution offence provisions formerly contained in the 1974 Act, ss.31 and 32, bringing together in a single section the various offences, although it should be noted that the new provisions differ in certain ways from the previous provisions as noted below. The relevant subss. of s.31 and all of s.32 are accordingly repealed (para. 3). Subsection (1) replaces the offences previously contained in s.31(1)(a) and (c); subs. (3) those previously contained in s.32(1)(a)(i) and (ii); and subs. (5) those previously contained in s.31(1)(b). This provision together with s.30I provides the basis for the system of regulation by means of consents.

One significant difference from the previous regime is that certain discharges will no longer necessarily constitute offences in themselves (subss. (2) and (4)) unless they also contravene a prohibition notice imposed under s.30G (see also the General Note to s.30G at p. 25–382). Such discharges were previously offences under s.32(1)(a)(iii), s.32(1)(b) and s.32(1)(c) unless they were made under a consent. However, it should be noted that if a discharge takes place in terms of s.30F(2) or (4) and it contained poisonous, noxious or polluting matter which subsequently entered controlled waters, that would constitute an offence under s.30F(1) (*NRA v. Egger UK*, Newcastle Upon Tyne Crown Court, June 15–17, 1992, unreported).

Furthermore, although this section is largely based on s.85 of the 1991 Act, it differs in an important respect from that provision. Whereas s.85(6) of the 1991 Act makes it an offence to contravene the conditions of a consent (which includes a failure to comply, see s.221 of the 1991 Act) in addition to the other offences in s.85, no similar provision is found in s.30F. This may prove problematic since the contravention of certain consent conditions may not give rise to a discharge in terms of this section because they may be designed to prevent discharges, for example a condition requiring the installation of standby pumps. Although an enforcement notice could be served under the new s.49A (inserted by Sched. 22, para. 29(26)), where such a condition was contravened an appeal mechanism is available under the new s.49B which may make enforcement by such means a somewhat lengthy process even though the appeal does not suspend the operation of the notice. The provision of an offence of contravening a consent condition as provided for in the 1991 Act might have been more useful to ensure compliance in such a situation.

Causing or knowingly permitting. The courts in Scotland have indicated that Scots law on the interpretation of this phrase is the same as south of the border: see *Lockhart v. National Coal Board* 1981 S.L.T. 161. There are two distinct offences: *Mcleod v. Buchanan* [1940] 2 All E.R. 179; *Alphacell v. Woodward* [1972] A.C. 824.

Causing. A charge of causing pollution does not require proof of *mens rea* or negligence and should be given a commonsense meaning: see the *Alphacell* and *Lockhart* cases. Causing also involves an active operation or chain of operations the inevitable result of which is the polluting incident: see *Alphacell, Lockhart* and *NRA v. Yorkshire Water Services* [1994] 3 W.L.R. 1202 (H.L.). More than one person may be held to have caused the same event: *Attorney General's Reference (No. 1) of 1994* [1995] 2 All E.R. 1007. The causal chain between the person charged and the polluting incident may be broken by intervening factors: see generally the cases of *Alphacell* and *Lockhart*. Examples of intervening events include the act of a third party (*e.g.* a trespasser as in *Impress (Worcester) v. Rees* [1971] 2 All E.R. 357; and *NRA v. Wright Engineering* [1994] Env.L.R. 186), natural forces (*Southern Water Authority v. Pegrum* [1989] Crim.L.R. 442; *R. v. British Coal Corporation*, Cardiff Crown Court, December 2, 1993, unreported) or an Act of God (*Southern Water Authority v. Pegrum*). Although it is unlikely that passivity will be sufficient to found a case of causing pollution (*Price v. Cromack* [1975] 1 W.L.R. 988; *Wychavon District Council v. NRA* [1993] 1 W.L.R. 125), it should be noted that the House of Lords in *NRA v. Yorkshire Water Services* indicated *obiter* that those cases should not be regarded as having established a general principle that a positive act is required to establish causation.

Knowingly permitting. Two elements are required to establish that a person has knowingly permitted pollution: (1) knowledge of the polluting act and (2) giving leave for the polluting act or failure to take steps to prevent or terminate the pollution (*Berton v. Alliance Economic Investment Co.* [1992] 1 K.B. 742 (C.A.) at 759; see also *Carmichael v. L.A.W. Mining* [1995] Env.L.B. 9–10). Although passively standing by may not amount to causing pollution it may amount to knowingly permitting polluting: *Price v. Cromack* [1975] 1 W.L.R. 988. Where there is no evidence that a person charged with knowingly permitting pollution could have prevented the pollution, it will not be possible to establish the charge: *Schulmans Incorporated v. NRA* [1993] Env.L.R. D1.

Poisonous, noxious or polluting matter. There is no statutory definition of this phrase. However, case law indicates that *polluting* matter need only be potentially polluting or harmful: *NRA v. Egger UK* Newcastle Upon Tyne Crown Court, June 15–17, 1992, unreported; *R. v. Dovermoss* [1995] Env.L.R. 258 (C.A.).

Solid waste matter. There is no statutory definition of this phrase although it is likely to include litter. An offence is committed under s.30F(1) regardless of whether the matter is poisonous, noxious or polluting.

Subss. (2) and (4)
  Under subs. (2) a discharge of matter, other than trade effluent or sewage effluent, from a sewer or drain which enters controlled waters will now not necessarily constitute an offence unless the discharge is subject to a prohibition notice imposed under s.30G. Such matter would include rainwater run-off from a site. However, where the discharge is also poisonous, noxious or polluting an offence would be committed under s.30F(1): *NRA v. Egger UK*.
  Similarly, under subs. (4) the discharge of any trade or sewage effluent from any building or plant on to, or into, land or any waters (which are not inland waters) will now generally not constitute an offence unless a prohibition notice has been imposed under s.30G. This would include, for example, discharges to soakaways. However, where such a discharge is poisonous,

noxious or polluting and enters ground waters or surface waters which are controlled waters an offence would be committed under s.30F(1).

Prohibition of certain discharges by notice or regulations

30G.—(1) For the purposes of section 30F above a discharge of any effluent or other matter is, in relation to any person, in contravention of a prohibition imposed under this section if, subject to the following provisions of this section—

(a) SEPA has given that person notice prohibiting him from making or, as the case may be, continuing the discharge; or

(b) SEPA has given that person notice prohibiting him from making or, as the case may be, continuing the discharge unless specified conditions are observed, and those conditions are not observed.

(2) For the purposes of section 30F above a discharge of any effluent or other matter is also in contravention of a prohibition imposed under this section if the effluent or matter discharged—

(a) contains a prescribed substance or a prescribed concentration of such a substance; or

(b) derives from a prescribed process or from a process involving the use of prescribed substances or the use of such substances in quantities which exceed the prescribed amounts.

(3) Nothing in subsection (1) above shall authorise the giving of a notice for the purposes of that subsection in respect of discharges from a vessel; and nothing in any regulations made by virtue of subsection (2) above shall require any discharge from a vessel to be treated as a discharge in contravention of a prohibition imposed under this section.

(4) A notice given for the purposes of subsection (1) above shall expire at such time as may be specified in the notice.

(5) The time specified for the purposes of subsection (4) above shall not be before the end of the period of three months beginning with the day on which the notice is given, except in a case where SEPA is satisfied that there is an emergency which requires the prohibition in question to come into force at such time before the end of that period as may be so specified.

(6) Where, in the case of such a notice for the purposes of subsection (1) above as (but for this subsection) would expire at a time at or after the end of the said period of three months, an application is made before that time for a consent in pursuance of section 34 of this Act in respect of the discharge to which the notice relates, that notice shall be deemed not to expire until the result of the application becomes final—

(a) on the grant or withdrawal of the application;

(b) on the expiration, without the bringing of an appeal with respect to the decision on the application, of any period prescribed by virtue of section 39(2) below as the period within which any such appeal must be brought; or

(c) on the withdrawal or determination of any such appeal.

DEFINITIONS

"effluent": s.56(1) of the Control of Pollution Act 1974.
"notice": s.105(1) of the Control of Pollution Act 1974.
"prescribed": s.105(1) of the Control of Pollution Act 1974.
"prescribed process": s.1(5) of the Environmental Protection Act 1990.
"prescribed substance": s.1(13) and s.2(7) of the Environmental Protection Act 1990.
"regulations": s.105(1) of the Control of Pollution Act 1974.
"SEPA": s.105(1) of the Control of Pollution Act 1974.
"substance": s.56(1) of the Control of Pollution Act 1974.
"vessel": s.105(1) of the Control of Pollution Act 1974.

GENERAL NOTE

This section, which is modelled on s.86 of the 1991 Act, provides for the use of prohibition notices by SEPA in relation to discharges first, of any matter (other than trade or sewage effluent) from a sewer or drain which enter controlled waters (s.30F(2)), and secondly, of trade or sewage effluent from a building or any plant on to or into land or into any surface waters which are not controlled waters (s.30F(4)). SEPA may serve a prohibition notice to prohibit a person making a discharge or from continuing a discharge (subs. (1)(a)); or to prohibit a person making or continuing such a discharge unless specified conditions are observed (subs. (1)(b)). There is also a standing prohibition contained in subs. (2) (see below) which does not require service of a prohibition notice. A prohibition notice may also be served on a roads authority in relation to discharges from drains which it is obliged or entitled to keep open (s.30J(8)).

Although apparently designed to strengthen controls over surface water discharges, the section has a deregulatory effect since such discharges would previously have required a consent and its effects may therefore not be wholly satisfactory. For example, a person installing a septic tank with a discharge to a soakaway would fall within the ambit of these provisions (s.30F(4)(a)). Previously, such a person would have been required to apply to a river purification authority for a consent before making any discharge under s.32(1)(a)(iii). In this way unsatisfactory installations might have been dealt with prior to construction. However, unless SEPA is notified before such a discharge commences, this provision only permits SEPA to deal with such discharges after the installation of the septic tank and soakaway. This may make it much harder for SEPA to rectify defective installations where they have already been constructed. For the prohibition notice system to work effectively, SEPA will need to be informed of planned discharges by means of notification through the planning system, for example under the Town and Country Planning (General Permitted Development) (Scotland) Order 1992 (S.I. 1992 No. 223) (as amended) which currently provides for river purification authorities (and hence, SEPA) to be consulted *inter alia* where the development consists of the carrying out of building or other operations (other than, for example, the laying of sewers or building of septic tanks and cesspools for dwellings of less than 10 people) or the use of the land for the retention, treatment or disposal of sewage, trade waste or effluent.

Subs. (2)

There is a standing prohibition where the discharge contains prescribed substances or a prescribed concentration of such substance or derives from a prescribed process. Hence it will always be an offence where this subs. is contravened regardless of whether a notice has been served.

Subs. (3)

Prohibition notices under subs. (1) and the standing prohibition under subs. (2) do not apply to discharges from vessels. However, any discharge from a vessel which resulted in poisonous, noxious or polluting matter or solid waste entering controlled waters would constitute an offence under s.30F(1).

Subss. (4)–(6)

A prohibition notice will not normally take effect until the end of three months beginning with the day on which notice is given, unless SEPA is satisfied that there is an emergency in which case the notice may take effect immediately (subss. (4)–(5)). The use of the present tense, there "is" an emergency, may have the effect of restricting the use of prohibition notices in cases of anticipated discharges.

Where a person applies for a consent during the period before the notice takes effect, the notice will not take effect until the result of the application and any appeal arising out of the application becomes final (subs. (6)).

Discharges into and from sewers etc.

30H.—(1) For the purposes of section 30F above where—

(a) any sewage effluent is discharged as mentioned in subsection (3) or (4) of that section from any sewer or works—

(i) vested in a sewerage authority; or

(ii) vested in a person other than a sewerage authority and forming (or forming part of) a system provided by him such as is mentioned in section 98(1)(b) of the Local Government etc. (Scotland) Act 1994; and

(b) the authority or, as the case may be, the person did not cause or knowingly permit the discharge but was bound (either unconditionally or subject to conditions which were observed) to receive into the sewer or works matter included in the discharge,

the authority or person shall be deemed to have caused the discharge.

(2) A sewerage authority shall not be guilty of an offence under section 30F of this Act by reason only of the fact that a discharge from a sewer or works vested in the authority contravenes conditions of a consent relating to the discharge if—

(a) the contravention is attributable to a discharge which another person caused or permitted to be made into the sewer or works; and

(b) the authority either was not bound to receive the discharge into the sewer or works or was bound to receive it there subject to conditions but the conditions were not observed; and

(c) the authority could not reasonably have been expected to prevent the discharge into the sewer or works;

and a person shall not be guilty of such an offence in consequence of a discharge which he caused or permitted to be made into a sewer or works vested in a sewerage authority if the authority was bound to receive the discharge there either unconditionally or subject to conditions which were observed.

(3) A person in whom any such sewer or works as is described in subsection (1)(a)(ii) above is vested (such person being in this subsection referred to as a "relevant person")

shall not be guilty of an offence under section 30F of this Act by reason only of the fact that a discharge from the sewer or works contravenes conditions of a consent relating to the discharge if—

(a) the contravention is attributable to a discharge which another person caused or permitted to be made into the sewer or works; and

(b) the relevant person either was not bound to receive the discharge into the sewer or works or was bound to receive it there subject to conditions but the conditions were not observed; and

(c) the relevant person could not reasonably have been expected to prevent the discharge into the sewer or works;

and another person shall not be guilty of such an offence in consequence of a discharge which he caused or permitted to be made into a sewer or works vested in a relevant person if the relevant person was bound to receive the discharge there either unconditionally or subject to conditions which were observed.

DEFINITIONS

"effluent": s.56(1) of the Control of Pollution Act 1974.

"sewage effluent": s.56(1) of the Control of Pollution Act 1974.

"sewer": s.56(1) of the Control of Pollution Act 1974; s.59(1) of the Sewerage (Scotland) Act 1968.

"sewerage authority": s.56(1) of the Control of Pollution Act 1974; s.62 of the Local Government etc. (Scotland) Act 1994.

GENERAL NOTE

This section, which is modelled on s.87 of the 1991 Act, deems the sewerage authority or private sector undertaking which is working under a Build, Own, Operate (BOO) scheme (see below) to have caused the discharge for the purposes of any offence under s.30F where it has been discharged from any sewer or works vested in them; and although they did not cause or knowingly permit the discharge, they were bound to receive it (subs. (1)).

However, a defence is provided for authorities by subs. (2), and for BOO private sector undertakings by subs. (3), whereby if they contravene the conditions of their discharge consent in circumstances where the contravention (a) is attributable to a discharge into the sewer or works by another person; (b) the authority or person was not bound to receive it or was bound to receive it but the conditions to which it was subject were not observed; and (c) the authority or person could not reasonably have been expected to prevent the discharge, they will not be guilty of an offence. For the application of this defence, see *NRA v. Yorkshire Water Services* [1994] 3 W.L.R. 1202 (H.L.) which involved an unconsented discharge by an unknown party into the sewers of the defendants. The discharge could not be prevented from passing through the defendants' works and into controlled waters. Although the defendants were deemed to have caused the polluting discharge, the equivalent provision in the 1991 Act in England and Wales (s.87(2)), provided them with a defence to a charge of causing poisonous, noxious or polluting matter to enter controlled waters.

Furthermore, persons who discharge effluent into a sewer or works will not be guilty of a s.30F offence if the authority or BOO private sector undertaking was bound to receive it (subss. (2) and (3)).

Vested in a person other than a sewerage authority (subs. (1)(a)(ii))/relevant person (subs. (3)). This refers to a private sector undertaking providing water and sewerage services for one of the new Scottish water and sewerage authorities established by the Local Government etc. (Scotland) Act 1994 in return for money under a BOO scheme by virtue of the Private Finance Initiative (see *Breaking New Ground: towards a new partnership between the public and private sectors* (1993)).

Defence to principal offences in respect of authorised discharges

30I.—(1) Subject to the following provisions of this section, a person shall not be guilty of an offence under section 30F above in respect of the entry of any matter into any waters or any discharge if the entry occurs or the discharge is made under and in accordance with, or as a result of, any act or omission under and in accordance with—

(a) a consent in pursuance of section 34 of this Act or under Chapter II of Part III of the Water Resources Act 1991 (which makes corresponding provision for England and Wales);

(b) an authorisation for a prescribed process designated for central control granted under Part I of the Environmental Protection Act 1990;

(c) a waste management or disposal licence;

(d) a licence granted under Part II of the Food and Environment Protection Act 1985;

(e) section 33 of the Water (Scotland) Act 1980 (temporary discharge by authorities in connection with the construction of works);

(f) any provision of a local Act or statutory order which expressly confers power to discharge effluent into water; or

(g) any prescribed enactment.

(2) Nothing in any disposal licence shall be treated for the purposes of subsection (1) above as authorising—

(a) any such entry or discharge as is mentioned in subsections (2) to (4) of section 30F above; or

(b) any act or omission so far as it results in any such entry or discharge.

(3) In this section—

"disposal licence" means a licence issued in pursuance of section 5 of this Act;

"local Act" includes enactments in a public general Act which amend a local Act;

"statutory order" means an order, byelaw, scheme or award made under an Act of Parliament, including an order or scheme confirmed by Parliament or brought into operation in accordance with special parliamentary procedure; and

"waste management licence" means such a licence granted under Part II of the Environmental Protection Act 1990.

Definitions

"disposal licence": subs. (3); s.5 of the Control of Pollution Act 1974.

"effluent": s.56(1) of the Control of Pollution Act 1974.

"local Act": subs. (3).

"prescribed": s.105(1) of the Control of Pollution Act 1974.

"prescribed process": s.1(5) of the Environmental Protection Act 1990.

"statutory order": subs. (3).

"waste management licence": subs. (3).

General Note

This section provides for defences to the offences in s.30F where the discharge is authorised by various environmental licences or by local Act, statutory order or prescribed enactment. For an example of a waste management licence providing a defence under the equivalent English and Welsh legislation, see *NRA v. Coal Products* [1993] 227 ENDS Report at p. 45.

Other defences to principal offences

30J.—(1) A person shall not be guilty of an offence under section 30F above in respect of the entry of any matter into any waters or any discharge if—

(a) the entry is caused or permitted, or the discharge is made, in an emergency in order to avoid danger to life or health;

(b) that person takes all such steps as are reasonably practicable in the circumstances for minimising the extent of the entry or discharge and of its polluting effects; and

(c) particulars of the entry or discharge are furnished to SEPA as soon as reasonably practicable after the entry occurs.

(2) A person shall not be guilty of an offence under section 30F above by reason of his causing or permitting any discharge of trade or sewage effluent from a vessel.

(3) A person shall not be guilty of an offence under section 30F above by reason only of his permitting water from an abandoned mine or an abandoned part of a mine to enter controlled waters.

(4) Subsection (3) above shall not apply to the owner or former operator of any mine or part of a mine if the mine or part in question became abandoned after 31st December 1999.

(5) In determining for the purposes of subsection (4) above whether a mine or part of a mine became abandoned before, on or after 31st December 1999 in a case where the mine or part has become abandoned on two or more occasions, of which—

(a) at least one falls on or before that date, and

(b) at least one falls after that date,

the mine or part shall be regarded as becoming abandoned after that date (but without prejudice to the operation of subsection (3) above in relation to that mine or part at, or in relation to, any time before the first of those occasions which falls after that date).

(6) Where, immediately before a part of a mine becomes abandoned, that part is the only part of the mine not falling to be regarded as abandoned for the time being, the abandon-

ment of that part shall not be regarded for the purposes of subsection (4) or (5) above as constituting the abandonment of the mine, but only of that part of it.

(7) A person shall not, otherwise than in respect of the entry of any poisonous, noxious or polluting matter into any controlled waters, be guilty of an offence under section 30F above by reason of his depositing the solid refuse of a mine or quarry on any land so that it falls or is carried into inland waters if—

(a) he deposits the refuse on the land with the consent of SEPA;

(b) no other site for the deposit is reasonably practicable; and

(c) he takes all reasonably practicable steps to prevent the refuse from entering those inland waters.

(8) A roads authority obliged or entitled to keep open a drain by virtue of section 31 of the Roads (Scotland) Act 1984 shall not be guilty of an offence under section 30F above by reason of its causing or permitting any discharge to be made from a drain kept open by virtue of that section unless the discharge is made in contravention of a prohibition imposed under section 30G above."

3. Sections 31(1), (2), (3), (7) and (10) (offences relating to pollution of rivers and coastal waters) and 32 (control of discharges of trade and effluent etc. into rivers and coastal waters etc.) shall cease to have effect.

4. In section 31 (8) (maximum penalties) for the words "paragraphs (a) and (b) of the preceding subsection" there shall be substituted the words "section 30F(6) above".

5. In section 31B(4)(d) (nitrate sensitive areas: maximum penalties) for the words "subsection (7) of section 31 above" there shall be substituted the words "subsection (6) of section 30F above".

6. In section 34(3) (consents for discharges of trade and effluent) for the words "section 32(1)" there shall be substituted the words "section 30F(2) to (4)".

7. In section 39(1)(a) (appeals to the Secretary of State) for the words "section 31(3)" there shall be substituted the words "section 30J(4)".

8. In section 56(1) (interpretation etc. of Part II) the following definitions shall be inserted in the appropriate places—

"drain" has the same meaning as in the Sewerage (Scotland) Act 1968;"; and

"sewer" has the same meaning as in the Sewerage (Scotland) Act 1968;".

9. In section 87(3) (time-bar in relation to legal proceedings)—

(a) the words from the beginning to "offence; and" shall cease to have effect;

(b) for the words "section 23 of the Summary Jurisdiction (Scotland) Act 1954" there shall be substituted the words "section 331 of the Criminal Procedure (Scotland) Act 1975";

(c) for the words "such offence" there shall be substituted the words "offence under section 30F of this Act or regulations or byelaws made in pursuance of section 31 of this Act"; and

(d) for the words "subsection (2) of section 23 of the said Act of 1954" there shall be substituted the words "subsection (3) of section 331 of the said Act of 1975";

(e) the words "in its application to Scotland" shall cease to have effect.

DEFINITIONS

"abandoned mine": s.30Y of the Control of Pollution Act 1974.

"controlled waters": s.30A(1) of the Control of Pollution Act 1974.

"drain": s.56(1) of the Control of Pollution Act 1974; s.59(1) of the Sewerage (Scotland) Act 1968.

"effluent": s.56(1) of the Control of Pollution Act 1974.

"inland waters": s.30A(1) of the Control of Pollution Act 1974.

"mine": s.105(1) of the Control of Pollution Act 1974; s.180(1) of the Mines and Quarries Act 1954.

"quarry": s.105(1) of the Control of Pollution Act 1974; s.180(2) of the Mines and Quarries Act 1954.

"roads authority": s.105(1) of the Control of Pollution Act 1974; s.151(1) of the Roads (Scotland) Act 1984.

"SEPA": s.105(1) of the Control of Pollution Act 1974.

"sewage effluent": s.56(1) of the Control of Pollution Act 1974.

"trade effluent": s.56(1) of the Control of Pollution Act 1974.

"vessel": s.105(1) of the Control of Pollution Act 1974.

GENERAL NOTE

This section provides various other defences to the offences in s.30F. These include an emergency defence (subs. (1)), the defence to permitting water pollution from an abandoned mine or part of a mine which will be withdrawn after December 31, 1999 (see also the General Note to s.60 at p. 25–204) (subss. (3)–(6)); and a defence in specified circumstances for persons depositing the solid refuse of a mine or quarry so that it falls or is carried into inland waters (subs. (7)). A roads authority will also not be guilty of any offence in relation to a discharge made from any drain which it is obliged or entitled to keep open unless the discharge is made in contravention of a prohibition notice imposed under s.30G.

Section 107   SCHEDULE 17

STATUTORY NUISANCES: SCOTLAND

Amendments of the Environmental Protection Act 1990

1. The Environmental Protection Act 1990 shall be amended in accordance with the provisions of paragraphs 2 to 7 of this Schedule.
2. In section 79 (statutory nuisances etc.)—
(a) in subsection (1)(ga) after the word "street" there shall be inserted the words "or in Scotland, road";
(b) in subsection (7)—
　　(i) in the definition of "local authority", before the word "outside" in paragraph (b) there shall be inserted "in England and Wales", the word "and" after paragraph (b) shall cease to have effect, and after paragraph (c) there shall be inserted "and
　　　　(d) in Scotland, a district or islands council or a council constituted under section 2 of the Local Government etc (Scotland) Act 1994;";
　　(ii) in the definition of "premises" after the word "and" where it second occurs there shall be inserted the words ", in relation to England and Wales,";
　　(iii) at the appropriate place there shall be inserted—
" "road" has the same meaning as in Part IV of the New Roads and Street Works Act 1991;";
(c) in subsection (8)—
　　(i) after the words "port health district" where they first occur there shall be inserted the words "or in Scotland where by an order under section 172 of the Public Health (Scotland) Act 1897 a port local authority or a joint port local authority has been constituted for the whole or part of a port,";
　　(ii) after the words "port health authority" where they second occur there shall be inserted the words ", port local authority or joint port local authority, as the case may be";
(d) in subsection (10) after the words "or (e)" there shall be inserted "and, in relation to Scotland, paragraph (g) or (ga),";
(e) in subsection (11) after the words "subsection (12) and" there shall be inserted the words ", in relation to England and Wales,".
3. In section 80 (summary proceedings) in subsection (3) after the words "magistrate's court" there shall be inserted the words "or in Scotland, the sheriff";
4. In section 81 (supplementary provisions)—
(a) in subsection (2) after the words "magistrate's court" there shall be inserted the words "or in Scotland, the sheriff";
(b) in subsection (3) after the word "offence" there shall be inserted the words "or, in Scotland, whether or not proceedings have been taken for an offence,";
(c) in subsection (4) after the word "court" where it first occurs there shall be inserted the word "or sheriff" and after the words "court consider" there shall be inserted the words "or sheriff considers";
(d) in subsection (5) after the words "High Court" there shall be inserted the words "or, in Scotland, in any court of competent jurisdiction,".
5. In section 81A at the end, as subsection (10), and in section 81B at the end, as subsection (6), there shall be added—
"( ) This section does not apply to Scotland.".
6. In section 82 (proceedings by persons aggrieved)—
(a) in subsection (1) after the word "complaint" there shall be inserted the words "or, in Scotland, the sheriff may act under this section on a summary application,";
(b) in subsection (2)—
　　(i) after the words "magistrate's court" there shall be inserted the words "or, in Scotland, the sheriff";

(ii) after the word "street" there shall be inserted the words "or, in Scotland, road";

(iii) after the words "the court" there shall be inserted the words "or the sheriff";

(iv) in paragraph (a) after the word "defendant" there shall be inserted the words "or, in Scotland, defender";

(v) in paragraph (b) after the word "defendant" there shall be inserted the words "or defender";

(vi) after the word "and" where it third occurs there shall be inserted the words ", in England and Wales,";

(c) in subsection (3), after the words "magistrate's court" there shall be inserted the words "or the sheriff" and after the words "of the court" in both places where they occur there shall be inserted the words "or of the sheriff";

(d) in subsection (11), after the words "magistrate's court" there shall be inserted the words "or the sheriff";

(e) in subsection (12) after the word "complaint" there shall be inserted the words "or summary application", after the words "the court" in both places where they occur there shall be inserted the words "or the sheriff" and for the words "defendant (or defendants" there shall be substituted the words "defendant or defender (or defendants or defenders";

(f) in subsection (13), after the words "magistrate's court" there shall be inserted the words "or to the sheriff" and after the words "the court" in both place where they occur there shall be inserted the words "or the sheriff".

7. In Schedule 3 (statutory nuisance; supplementary provisions)—

(a) after paragraph 1 there shall be inserted—

"Appeals to Sheriff

1A.—(1) This paragraph applies in relation to appeals to the sheriff under section 80(3) against an abatement notice.

(2) An appeal to which this paragraph applies shall be by way of a summary application.

(3) The Secretary of State may make regulations as to appeals to which this paragraph applies and the regulations may in particular include or prescribe any of the matters referred to in sub-paragraphs (4)(a) to (d) of paragraph 1 above.";

(b) in paragraph 2 at the end there shall be added—

"(8) In the application of this paragraph to Scotland, a reference to a justice of the peace or to a justice includes a reference to the sheriff.";

(c) in paragraph 2A(1)(b) after the word "street" there shall be inserted the words "or, in Scotland, road";

(d) in paragraph 4 at the end there shall be added—

"(9) This paragraph does not apply to Scotland.";

(e) in paragraph 6 after the words "magistrate's court" there shall be inserted the words "or, in Scotland, the sheriff".

Amendments of the Radioactive Substances Act 1993

8. In the Radioactive Substances Act 1993, in Part II of Schedule 3—

(a) in paragraph 12, for the words "Sections 16 and 17" there shall be substituted the words "Section 16";

(b) at the end there shall be added—

"17A. Part III of the Environmental Protection Act 1990.".

GENERAL NOTE

See the General Note to s.107 on p. 25–280.

Section 108   SCHEDULE 18

SUPPLEMENTAL PROVISIONS WITH RESPECT TO POWERS OF ENTRY

Interpretation

1.—(1) In this Schedule—

"designated person" means an authorised person, within the meaning of section 108 of this Act and includes a person designated by virtue of paragraph 2 below;

"relevant power" means a power conferred by section 108 of this Act, including a power exercisable by virtue of a warrant under this Schedule.

(2) Expressions used in this Schedule and in section 108 of this Act have the same meaning in this Schedule as they have in that section.

Issue of warrants

2.—(1) If it is shown to the satisfaction of a justice of the peace or, in Scotland, the sheriff or a justice of the peace, on sworn information in writing—

(a) that there are reasonable grounds for the exercise in relation to any premises of a relevant power; and

(b) that one or more of the conditions specified in sub-paragraph (2) below is fulfilled in relation to those premises,

the justice or sheriff may by warrant authorise an enforcing authority to designate a person who shall be authorised to exercise the power in relation to those premises, in accordance with the warrant and, if need be, by force.

(2) The conditions mentioned in sub-paragraph (1)(b) above are—

(a) that the exercise of the power in relation to the premises has been refused;

(b) that such a refusal is reasonably apprehended;

(c) that the premises are unoccupied;

(d) that the occupier is temporarily absent from the premises and the case is one of urgency; or

(e) that an application for admission to the premises would defeat the object of the proposed entry.

(3) In a case where subsection (6) of section 108 of this Act applies, a justice of the peace or sheriff shall not issue a warrant under this Schedule by virtue only of being satisfied that the exercise of a power in relation to any premises has been refused, or that a refusal is reasonably apprehended, unless he is also satisfied that the notice required by that subsection has been given and that the period of that notice has expired.

(4) Every warrant under this Schedule shall continue in force until the purposes for which the warrant was issued have been fulfilled.

Manner of exercise of powers

3. A person designated as the person who may exercise a relevant power shall produce evidence of his designation and other authority before he exercises the power.

Information obtained to be admissible in evidence

4.—(1) Subject to section 108(12) of this Act, information obtained in consequence of the exercise of a relevant power, with or without the consent of any person, shall be admissible in evidence against that or any other person.

(2) Without prejudice to the generality of sub-paragraph (1) above, information obtained by means of monitoring or other apparatus installed on any premises in the exercise of a relevant power, with or without the consent of any person in occupation of the premises, shall be admissible in evidence in any proceedings against that or any other person.

Duty to secure premises

5. A person who, in the exercise of a relevant power enters on any premises which are unoccupied or whose occupier is temporarily absent shall leave the premises as effectually secured against trespassers as he found them.

Compensation

6.—(1) Where any person exercises any power conferred by section 108(4)(a) or (b) or (5) of this Act, it shall be the duty of the enforcing authority under whose authorisation he acts to make full compensation to any person who has sustained loss or damage by reason of—

(a) the exercise by the designated person of that power; or

(b) the performance of, or failure of the designated person to perform, the duty imposed by paragraph 5 above.

(2) Compensation shall not be payable by virtue of sub-paragraph (1) above in respect of any loss or damage if the loss or damage—

(a) is attributable to the default of the person who sustained it; or

(b) is loss or damage in respect of which compensation is payable by virtue of any other provision of the pollution control enactments.

(3) Any dispute as to a person's entitlement to compensation under this paragraph, or as to the amount of any such compensation, shall be referred to the arbitration of a single arbitrator or, in Scotland, arbiter appointed by agreement between the enforcing authority in question and the person who claims to have sustained the loss or damage or, in default of agreement, by the Secretary of State.

(4) A designated person shall not be liable in any civil or criminal proceedings for anything done in the purported exercise of any relevant power if the court is satisfied that the act was done in good faith and that there were reasonable grounds for doing it.

Section 112   SCHEDULE 19

OFFENCES RELATING TO FALSE OR MISLEADING STATEMENTS OR FALSE ENTRIES

The Control of Pollution Act 1974

1.—(1) The Control of Pollution Act 1974 shall be amended in accordance with the following provisions of this paragraph.

(2) For subsection (5) of section 34 (offences relating to consents for discharge of effluent etc) there shall be substituted—

"(5) A person who, in an application for consent in pursuance of this section, makes any statement which he knows to be false or misleading in a material particular or recklessly makes any statement which is false or misleading in a material particular shall be guilty of an offence and shall be liable—

(a) on summary conviction, to a fine not exceeding the statutory maximum;
(b) on conviction on indictment, to a fine or to imprisonment for a term not exceeding two years, or to both.".

(3) For subsection (3) of section 93 (offences relating to power of authorities to obtain information) there shall be substituted—

"(3) A person who—
(a) fails without reasonable excuse to comply with the requirements of a notice served on him in pursuance of this section; or
(b) in furnishing any information in compliance with such a notice, makes any statement which he knows to be false or misleading in a material particular or recklessly makes any statement which is false or misleading in a material particular,

shall be guilty of an offence.

(3A) A person guilty of an offence under this section shall be liable—
(a) on summary conviction, to a fine not exceeding the statutory maximum; or
(b) on conviction on indictment, to a fine or to imprisonment for a term not exceeding two years, or to both.".

The Water (Scotland) Act 1980

2.—(1) The Water (Scotland) Act 1980 shall be amended in accordance with the following provisions of this paragraph.

(2) In section 93 (obtaining of information as to underground water) after subsection (7) there shall be inserted—

"(8) Any person who in keeping a journal under subsection (1) or in furnishing information under subsection (2) or (3) makes any statement which he knows to be false or misleading in a material particular or recklessly makes any statement which is false or misleading in a material particular shall be guilty of an offence and shall be liable—

(a) on summary conviction, to a fine not exceeding the statutory maximum;
(b) on conviction on indictment, to a fine or to imprisonment for a term not exceeding two years, or to both.".

(3) In section 94 (false information) after the word "Act" there shall be inserted the words "(other than by or under section 93)".

The Control of Pollution (Amendment) Act 1989

3. In section 7(3)(b) of the Control of Pollution (Amendment) Act 1989 (offences of making false statements), after the word "false" in each place where it occurs there shall be inserted the words "or misleading".

The Environmental Protection Act 1990

4.—(1) For section 44 of the Environmental Protection Act 1990 (offences of making false statements) there shall be substituted—

"**Offences of making false or misleading statements or false entries**
44.—(1) A person who—
(a) in purported compliance with a requirement to furnish any information imposed by or under any provision of this Part, or
(b) for the purpose of obtaining for himself or another any grant of a licence, any modification of the conditions of a licence, any acceptance of the surrender of a licence or any transfer of a licence,
makes a statement which he knows to be false or misleading in a material particular, or recklessly makes any statement which is false or misleading in a material particular, commits an offence.
(2) A person who intentionally makes a false entry in any record required to be kept by virtue of a licence commits an offence.
(3) A person who commits an offence under this section shall be liable—
(a) on summary conviction, to a fine not exceeding the statutory maximum;
(b) on conviction on indictment, to a fine or to imprisonment for a term not exceeding two years, or to both."
(2) In section 71(3) of that Act, paragraph (b) (offence of making false or misleading statements) shall cease to have effect.

The Water Resources Act 1991

5.—(1) Section 206 of the Water Resources Act 1991 (making of false statements etc) shall be amended in accordance with the following provisions of this paragraph.
(2) For subsection (1), there shall be substituted—
"(1) If, in furnishing any information or making any application under or for the purposes of any provision of this Act, any person makes a statement which he knows to be false or misleading in a material particular, or recklessly makes any statement which is false or misleading in a material particular, he shall be guilty of an offence under this section."
(3) Subsection (2) (which is superseded by the amendment made by sub-paragraph (2) above) shall be omitted.
(4) After subsection (3) (offences relating to the use of meters in connection with licences under Chapter II of Part II) there shall be inserted—
"(3A) If a person intentionally makes a false entry in any record required to be kept by virtue of a licence under Chapter II of Part II of this Act, or a consent under Chapter II of Part III of this Act, he shall be guilty of an offence under this section."
(5) For subsections (5) to (7) (which require consent to the prosecution of certain offences and provide different penalties for different offences) there shall be substituted—
"(5) A person who is guilty of an offence under this section shall be liable—
(a) on summary conviction, to a fine not exceeding the statutory maximum;
(b) on conviction on indictment, to a fine or to imprisonment for a term not exceeding two years, or to both."

The Radioactive Substances Act 1993

6. After section 34 of the Radioactive Substances Act 1993 (offences relating to disclosure of information about trade secrets etc) there shall be inserted—

"**Offences of making false or misleading statements or false entries**
34A.—(1) Any person who—
(a) for the purpose of obtaining for himself or another any registration under section 7 or 10, any authorisation under section 13 or 14 or any variation of such an authorisation under section 17, or
(b) in purported compliance with a requirement to furnish information imposed under section 31(1)(d),
makes a statement which he knows to be false or misleading in a material particular, or recklessly makes a statement which is false or misleading in a material particular, shall be guilty of an offence.

(2) Any person who intentionally makes a false entry in any record—

(a) which is required to be kept by virtue of a registration under section 7 or 10 or an authorisation under section 13 or 14, or

(b) which is kept in purported compliance with a condition which must be complied with if a person is to have the benefit of an exemption under section 8, 11 or 15,

shall be guilty of an offence.

(3) A person guilty of an offence under this section shall be liable—

(a) on summary conviction, to a fine not exceeding the statutory maximum;

(b) on conviction on indictment, to a fine or to imprisonment for a term not exceeding two years, or to both."

Section 114   SCHEDULE 20

DELEGATION OF APPELLATE FUNCTIONS OF THE SECRETARY OF STATE

Interpretation

1. In this Schedule—

"appointed person" means a person appointed under section 114(1)(a) of this Act; and

"appointment", in the case of any appointed person, means appointment under section 114(1)(a) of this Act.

Appointments

2. An appointment under section 114(1)(a) of this Act must be in writing and—

(a) may relate to any particular appeal, matters or questions specified in the appointment or to appeals, matters or questions of a description so specified;

(b) may provide for any function to which it relates to be exercisable by the appointed person either unconditionally or subject to the fulfilment of such conditions as may be specified in the appointment; and

(c) may, by notice in writing given to the appointed person, be revoked at any time by the Secretary of State in respect of any appeal, matter or question which has not been determined by the appointed person before that time.

Powers of appointed person

3. Subject to the provisions of this Schedule, an appointed person shall, in relation to any appeal, matter or question to which his appointment relates, have the same powers and duties as the Secretary of State, other than—

(a) any function of making regulations;

(b) any function of holding an inquiry or other hearing or of causing an inquiry or other hearing to be held; or

(c) any function of appointing a person for the purpose—

(i) of enabling persons to appear before and be heard by the person so appointed; or

(ii) of referring any question or matter to that person.

Holding of local inquiries and other hearings by appointed persons

4.—(1) If either of the parties to an appeal, matter or question expresses a wish to appear before and be heard by the appointed person, the appointed person shall give both of them an opportunity of appearing and being heard.

(2) Whether or not a party to an appeal, matter or question has asked for an opportunity to appear and be heard, the appointed person—

(a) may hold a local inquiry or other hearing in connection with the appeal, matter or question, and

(b) shall, if the Secretary of State so directs, hold a local inquiry in connection with the appeal, matter or question,

but this sub-paragraph is subject to sub-paragraph (3) below.

(3) No local inquiry shall be held by virtue of this Schedule in connection with an appeal under—

(a) section 42B(5) of the Control of Pollution Act 1974,

(b) section 22(5), 66(5) or 78T(3) of the Environmental Protection Act 1990, or

(c) section 191B(5) of the Water Resources Act 1991,

(appeals against decisions that information is not commercially confidential), or any matter involved in such an appeal, and any hearing held by virtue of this Schedule in connection with any such appeal or matter must be held in private.

(4) Where an appointed person holds a local inquiry or other hearing by virtue of this Schedule, an assessor may be appointed by the Secretary of State to sit with the appointed person at the inquiry or hearing and advise him on any matters arising, notwithstanding that the appointed person is to determine the appeal, matter or question.

(5) Subject to paragraph 5 below, the costs of a local inquiry held under this Schedule shall be defrayed by the Secretary of State.

Local inquiries under this Schedule: evidence and costs

5.—(1) In relation to England and Wales, subsections (2) to (5) of section 250 of the Local Government Act 1972 (local inquiries: evidence and costs) shall apply to local inquiries or other hearings held under this Schedule by an appointed person as they apply to inquiries caused to be held under that section by a Minister, but with the following modifications, that is to say—
  (a) with the substitution in subsection (2) (evidence) for the reference to the person appointed to hold the inquiry of a reference to the appointed person;
  (b) with the substitution in subsection (4) (recovery of costs of holding the inquiry) for the references to the Minister causing the inquiry to be held of references to the Secretary of State;
  (c) taking the reference in that subsection to a local authority as including the Agency; and
  (d) with the substitution in subsection (5) (orders as to the costs of the parties) for the reference to the Minister causing the inquiry to be held of a reference to the appointed person or the Secretary of State.

(2) In relation to Scotland, subsections (3) to (8) of section 210 of the Local Government (Scotland) Act 1973 (which relate to the costs of and holding of local inquiries) shall apply to local inquiries or other hearings held under this Schedule as they apply to inquiries held under that section, but with the following modifications, that is to say—
  (a) with the substitution in subsection (3) (notice of inquiry) for the reference to the person appointed to hold the inquiry of a reference to the appointed person;
  (b) with the substitution in subsection (4) (evidence) for the reference to the person appointed to hold the inquiry and, in paragraph (b), the reference to the person holding the inquiry of references to the appointed person;
  (c) with the substitution in subsection (6) (expenses of witnesses etc.) for the references to the Minister causing the inquiry to be held of a reference to the appointed person or the Secretary of State;
  (d) with the substitution in subsection (7) (expenses) for the references to the Minister of references to the appointed person or the Secretary of State;
  (e) with the substitution in subsection (7A) (recovery of entire administrative expense)—
      (i) for the first reference to the Minister of a reference to the appointed person or the Secretary of State;
      (ii) in paragraph (a), for the reference to the Minister of a reference to the Secretary of State; and
      (iii) in paragraph (b), for the reference to the Minister holding the inquiry of a reference to the Secretary of State;
  (f) with the substitution in subsection (7B) (power to prescribe daily amount)—
      (i) for the first reference to the Minister of a reference to the Secretary of State;
      (ii) in paragraphs (a) and (c), for the references to the person appointed to hold the inquiry of references to the appointed person; and
      (iii) in paragraph (d), for the reference to the Minister of a reference to the appointed person or the Secretary of State; and
  (g) with the substitution in subsection (8) (certification of expenses) for the reference to the Minister, the reference to him and the reference to the Crown of references to the appointed person or the Secretary of State.

Revocation of appointments and making of new appointments

6.—(1) Where under paragraph 2(c) above the appointment of the appointed person is revoked in respect of any appeal, matter or question, the Secretary of State shall, unless he proposes to determine the appeal, matter or question himself, appoint another person under section 114(1)(a) of this Act to determine the appeal, matter or question instead.

(2) Where such a new appointment is made, the consideration of the appeal, matter or question, or any hearing in connection with it, shall be begun afresh.

(3) Nothing in sub-paragraph (2) above shall require any person to be given an opportunity of making fresh representations or modifying or withdrawing any representations already made.

Certain acts and omissions of appointed person to be treated as those of the Secretary of State

7.—(1) Anything done or omitted to be done by an appointed person in, or in connection with, the exercise or purported exercise of any function to which the appointment relates shall be treated for all purposes as done or omitted to be done by the Secretary of State in his capacity as such.

(2) Sub-paragraph (1) above shall not apply—

(a) for the purposes of so much of any contract made between the Secretary of State and the appointed person as relates to the exercise of the function; or

(b) for the purposes of any criminal proceedings brought in respect of anything done or omitted to be done as mentioned in that sub-paragraph.

Section 116   SCHEDULE 21

APPLICATION OF CERTAIN ENACTMENTS TO THE CROWN

PART I

ENACTMENTS RELATING TO ENGLAND AND WALES

The Water Industry Act 1991

1.—(1) For section 221 of the Water Industry Act 1991 (Crown application) there shall be substituted—

"**Crown application**

221.—(1) Subject to the provisions of this section, this Act shall bind the Crown.

(2) No contravention by the Crown of any provision made by or under this Act shall make the Crown criminally liable; but the High Court may, on the application of the Environment Agency, a water undertaker or a sewerage undertaker, declare unlawful any act or omission of the Crown which constitutes such a contravention.

(3) Notwithstanding anything in subsection (2) above, any provision made by or under this Act shall apply to persons in the public service of the Crown as it applies to other persons.

(4) If the Secretary of State certifies that it appears to him, as respects any Crown premises and any powers of entry exercisable in relation to them specified in the certificate, that it is requisite or expedient that, in the interests of national security, the powers should not be exercisable in relation to those premises, those powers shall not be exercisable in relation to those premises.

(5) Nothing in this section shall be taken as in any way affecting Her Majesty in her private capacity; and this subsection shall be construed as if section 38(3) of the Crown Proceedings Act 1947 (interpretation of references to Her Majesty in her private capacity) were contained in this Act.

(6) Subject to subsections (4) and (5) above, the powers conferred by sections 155, 159, 161(2) and 167 above shall be exercisable in relation to land in which there is a Crown or Duchy interest only with the consent of the appropriate authority.

(7) In this section—

"the appropriate authority" has the same meaning as it has in Part XIII of the Town and Country Planning Act 1990 by virtue of section 293(2) of that Act;

"Crown or Duchy interest" means an interest which belongs to Her Majesty in right of the Crown or of the Duchy of Lancaster, or to the Duchy of Cornwall, or belonging to a government department or held in trust for Her Majesty for the purposes of a government department;

"Crown premises" means premises held by or on behalf of the Crown.

(8) The provisions of subsection (3) of section 293 of the Town and Country Planning Act 1990 (questions relating to Crown application) as to the determination of questions shall apply for the purposes of this section."

The Water Resources Act 1991

2.—(1) The Water Resources Act 1991 shall be amended in accordance with the following provisions of this paragraph.

(2) In section 115 (fisheries orders) in subsection (7) (orders affecting Crown or Duchy property) in paragraph (a), after the words "an order under this section" there shall be inserted the words "making provision, by virtue of subsection (1)(b) above, for the modification of section 156 below in relation to fisheries in an area".

(3) In section 142 (orders providing for the imposition and collection of fisheries contributions), in subsection (2) (which applies, in relation to orders under that section, the provisions of subsections (2) to (9) of section 115 of that Act) for the words "(2) to (9)" there shall be substituted the words "(2) to (6)".

(4) For section 222 (Crown application) there shall be substituted—

"Crown application

222.—(1) Subject to the provisions of this section, this Act binds the Crown.

(2) No contravention by the Crown of any provision made by or under this Act shall make the Crown criminally liable; but the High Court may, on the application of the Agency, declare unlawful any act or omission of the Crown which constitutes such a contravention.

(3) Notwithstanding anything in subsection (2) above, the provisions of this Act shall apply to persons in the public service of the Crown as they apply to other persons.

(4) If the Secretary of State certifies that it appears to him, as respects any Crown premises and any powers of entry exercisable in relation to them specified in the certificate, that it is requisite or expedient that, in the interests of national security, the powers should not be exercisable in relation to those premises, those powers shall not be exercisable in relation to those premises.

(5) Subject to subsection (4) above, the powers conferred by sections 154, 156, 160, 162(3) and 168 above shall be exercisable in relation to land in which there is a Crown or Duchy interest only with the consent of the appropriate authority.

(6) Nothing in this section shall be taken as in any way affecting Her Majesty in her private capacity; and this subsection shall be construed as if section 38(3) of the Crown Proceedings Act 1947 (interpretation of references to Her Majesty in her private capacity) were contained in this Act.

(7) Nothing in this Act, as read with the other provisions of this section, shall be construed as conferring any power of levying drainage charges in respect of lands below the high-water mark of ordinary spring tides.

(8) Section 74 of the Land Drainage Act 1991 (Crown application), so far as it relates to land in which there is a Crown or Duchy interest, shall apply in relation to the flood defence provisions of this Act as it applies in relation to that Act; but nothing in this subsection shall affect any power conferred by this Act for the purposes both of the Agency's functions under those provisions and of other functions of the Agency.

(9) In this section—

> "the appropriate authority" has the same meaning as it has in Part XIII of the Town and Country Planning Act 1990 by virtue of section 293(2) of that Act;

> "Crown or Duchy interest" means an interest which belongs to Her Majesty in right of the Crown or of the Duchy of Lancaster, or to the Duchy of Cornwall, or belonging to a government department or held in trust for Her Majesty for the purposes of a government department;

> "Crown premises" means premises held by or on behalf of the Crown.

(10) The provisions of subsection (3) of section 293 of the Town and Country Planning Act 1990 (questions relating to Crown application) as to the determination of questions shall apply for the purposes of this section."

PART II

ENACTMENTS RELATING TO SCOTLAND

The Sewerage (Scotland) Act 1968

3. For section 55 of the Sewerage (Scotland) Act 1968 (Crown application) there shall be substituted—

"Application of Act to Crown

55.—(1) Subject to the provisions of this section, this Act shall bind the Crown.

(2) No contravention by the Crown of any provision made by or under this Act shall make the Crown criminally liable; but the Court of Session may, on the application of a sewerage authority, declare unlawful any act or omission of the Crown which constitutes such a contravention.

(3) Notwithstanding anything in subsection (2) above, any provision made by or under this Act shall apply to persons in the public service of the Crown as it applies to other persons.

(4) If the Secretary of State certifies that it appears to him, as respects any Crown premises and any powers of entry exercisable in relation to them specified in the certificate, that it

is requisite or expedient that, in the interests of national security, the powers should not be exercisable in relation to those premises, those powers shall not be exercisable in relation to those premises.

(5) Nothing in this section shall be taken as in any way affecting Her Majesty in her private capacity.

(6) In this section "Crown premises" means premises held by or on behalf of the Crown.".

The Control of Pollution Act 1974

4. For subsection (3) of section 105 of the Control of Pollution Act 1974 (application to Crown) as it has effect in relation to Scotland, there shall be substituted the following subsections—

"(3) Subject to subsections (3A) to (3D) below, this Act shall bind the Crown.

(3A) No contravention by the Crown of any provision made by or under this Act shall make the Crown criminally liable; but the Court of Session may, on the application of—

(a) the Scottish Environment Protection Agency; or

(b) any other public or local authority charged with enforcing that provision,

declare unlawful any act or omission of the Crown which constitutes such a contravention.

(3B) Notwithstanding anything in subsection (3A) above, any provision made by or under this Act shall apply to persons in the public service of the Crown as it applies to other persons.

(3C) If the Secretary of State certifies that it appears to him, as respects any Crown premises and any powers of entry exercisable in relation to them specified in the certificate, that it is requisite or expedient that, in the interests of national security, the powers should not be exercisable in relation to those premises, those powers shall not be exercisable in relation to those premises; and in this subsection "Crown premises" means premises held or used by or on behalf of the Crown.

(3D) Nothing in this section shall be taken as in any way affecting Her Majesty in her private capacity."

The Water (Scotland) Act 1980

5. After section 110 of the Water (Scotland) Act 1980 there shall be inserted—

"Application of Act to Crown

110A.—(1) Subject to the provisions of this section, this Act shall bind the Crown.

(2) No contravention by the Crown of any provision made by or under this Act shall make the Crown criminally liable; but the Court of Session may, on the application of a water authority, declare unlawful any act or omission of the Crown which constitutes such a contravention.

(3) Notwithstanding anything in subsection (2) above, any provision made by or under this Act shall apply to persons in the public service of the Crown as it applies to other persons.

(4) If the Secretary of State certifies that it appears to him, as respects any Crown premises and any powers of entry exercisable in relation to them specified in the certificate, that it is requisite or expedient that, in the interests of national security, the powers should not be exercisable in relation to those premises, those powers shall not be exercisable in relation to those premises.

(5) Nothing in this section shall be taken as in any way affecting Her Majesty in her private capacity.

(6) Subject to subsections (4) and (5) above, the powers conferred by sections 16 to 18 above shall be exercisable in relation to land in which there is a Crown interest only with the consent of the appropriate authority.

(7) In this section—

"the appropriate authority" has the same meaning as it has in section 253(7) of the Town and Country Planning (Scotland) Act 1972;

"Crown interest" means an interest belonging to Her Majesty in right of the Crown, or belonging to a government department or held in trust for Her Majesty for the purposes of a government department;

"Crown premises" means premises held by or on behalf of the Crown.

(8) The provisions of subsection (7) of section 253 of the Town and Country Planning (Scotland) Act 1972 (questions relating to Crown application) as to the determination of questions shall apply for the purposes of this section.".

The Local Government etc. (Scotland) Act 1994

6. After section 125 of the Local Government etc. (Scotland) Act 1994 there shall be inserted—

"Application of Part II to Crown

125A.—(1) Subject to the provisions of this section, this Part of this Act shall bind the Crown.

(2) No contravention by the Crown of any provision made by or under this Part of this Act shall make the Crown criminally liable; but the Court of Session may, on the application of a new water and sewerage authority, declare unlawful any act or omission of the Crown which constitutes such a contravention.

(3) Notwithstanding anything in subsection (2) above, any provision made by or under this Part of this Act shall apply to persons in the public service of the Crown as it applies to other persons.

(4) Nothing in this section shall be taken as in any way affecting Her Majesty in her private capacity.

(5) Subject to subsection (4) above, the powers conferred by section 99 above shall be exercisable in relation to land in which there is a Crown interest only with the consent of the appropriate authority.

(6) In this section—

"the appropriate authority" has the same meaning as it has in section 253(7) of the Town and Country Planning (Scotland) Act 1972;

"Crown interest" means an interest belonging to Her Majesty in right of the Crown, or belonging to a government department or held in trust for Her Majesty for the purposes of a government department;

"Crown premises" means premises held by or on behalf of the Crown.

(7) The provisions of subsection (7) of section 253 of the Town and Country Planning (Scotland) Act 1972 (questions relating to Crown application) as to the determination of questions shall apply for the purposes of this section.".

Section 120   SCHEDULE 22

MINOR AND CONSEQUENTIAL AMENDMENTS

The Alkali, &c., Works Regulation Act 1906

1.—(1) The Alkali, &c, Works Regulation Act 1906 shall be amended in accordance with the following provisions of this paragraph.

(2) In section 1(1) (alkali work to be carried on so as to secure that the condensation of hydrochloric acid gas, to the satisfaction of the chief inspector, falls below certain levels) for the words "the chief inspector" there shall be substituted the words "the appropriate Agency".

(3) In section 2(1) (no objection to be taken by an inspector to certain discharges) for the words "an inspector" there shall be substituted the words "the appropriate Agency".

(4) In section 9—

(a) in subsection (5) (condition of issue of certificate on first registration that the work is furnished with such appliances as appear to the chief inspector or, on appeal, the Secretary of State to be necessary for certain purposes) for the words "the chief inspector" there shall be substituted the words "the appropriate Agency";

(b) the proviso to that subsection (power of Secretary of State to dispense with certain requirements) shall cease to have effect; and

(c) in subsection (7) (notice of certain changes to be sent to the Secretary of State) for the words which are to be construed as a reference to the Secretary of State, there shall be substituted the words "the appropriate Agency".

(5) In section 22(1) (power of Secretary of State, after inquiring into a complaint, to direct proceedings to be taken by an inspector) for the words "an inspector" there shall be substituted the words "the appropriate Agency".

(6) In section 23(2) (damages not recoverable under the section from a person with a certificate of compliance from the chief inspector) for the words "the chief inspector" there shall be substituted the words "the appropriate Agency".

(7) Section 25 (basis on which the chief inspector may determine questions) shall cease to have effect.

(8) In section 27(1) (interpretation of terms)—

    (a) after the definition of the expression "alkali works" there shall be inserted—
        "The expression "the appropriate Agency" means—
            (a) in relation to England and Wales, the Environment Agency; and
            (b) in relation to Scotland, the Scottish Environment Protection Agency:"; and

    (b) the definitions of the expressions "chief inspector" and "inspector" shall be omitted.

(9) In paragraph (b) of section 28 (application to Scotland)—

    (a) the words "other than offences under subsection four of section twelve of this Act",

    (b) in sub-paragraph (ii) (prosecution not to be instituted without consent) the words from "without the consent" to "direct, nor", and

    (c) sub-paragraph (iii) (person taking proceedings presumed to be inspector),

shall cease to have effect.

The Statistics of Trade Act 1947

2. In the Statistics of Trade Act 1947, after section 9 (restrictions on disclosure of information) there shall be inserted—

"Exceptions from section 9

    9A.—(1) Nothing in section nine of this Act shall prevent or penalise the disclosure by the Secretary of State of information obtained under this Act—

    (a) to the Environment Agency or the Scottish Environment Protection Agency; or

    (b) to an officer of either of those Agencies authorised by that Agency to receive the information.

    (2) A person to whom information is disclosed in pursuance of the last foregoing subsection shall not use the information for any purpose other than the purposes of any functions of the Agency in question."

The Rivers (Prevention of Pollution) (Scotland) Act 1951

3.—(1) The Rivers (Prevention of Pollution) (Scotland) Act 1951 shall be amended in accordance with the following provisions of this paragraph.

(2) Part II (river purification boards) (so far as unrepealed) and section 17 (duties of river purification authorities) shall cease to have effect.

(3) In section 18 (provision and obtaining of information)—

    (a) in subsection (1) (power to obtain information)—
        (i) for the word "them" in each place where it occurs there shall be substituted the word "it";
        (ii) for the words "a river purification authority" there shall be substituted the words "SEPA"; and
        (iii) the words "of their area", "in their area" (where first occurring) and "in their area or any part thereof" shall cease to have effect;

    (b) in subsection (2) (Secretary of State's power to give directions) for the words "any river purification authority" and "the authority" there shall be substituted the words "SEPA", and for the word "them" there shall be substituted the word "it"; and

    (c) in subsection (3) (duty to provide reasonable facilities for inspection of records)—
        (i) for the words "Every river purification authority" and "the river purification authority" there shall be substituted the words "SEPA";
        (ii) for the word "them" there shall be substituted the word "it"; and
        (iii) the words "in their area" and the words from "whose" to "authority" where it next occurs shall cease to have effect; and

    (d) in subsection (6) (interpretation of "stream") for the words "the river purification authority's" there shall be substituted the words "SEPA's".

(4) In section 19 (power to take samples of effluents)—

    (a) in subsection (1) (power to obtain and take away samples of water from any stream or effluent)—
        (i) for the words "A river purification authority" there shall be substituted the words "SEPA"; and
        (ii) the words "in the area of the authority" shall cease to have effect; and

    (b) in subsection (3) (interpretation of "stream") for the words "the river purification authority's" there shall be substituted the words "SEPA's".

(5) In section 35 (interpretation)—

    (a) the definitions of "river purification authority", "river purification board" and "river purification board area" shall cease to have effect; and

    (b) there shall be inserted at the appropriate place—
        " "SEPA" means the Scottish Environment Protection Agency;".

The Public Records Act 1958

4. In the First Schedule to the Public Records Act 1958 (definition of public records) in Part II of the Table at the end of paragraph 3 (organisations whose records are public records) there shall be inserted at the appropriate place the entry—
"The Environment Agency.".

The Opencast Coal Act 1958

5.—(1) In section 7(8) of the Opencast Coal Act 1958 (definitions etc. for the purposes of section 7) in paragraph (i) of the definition of "statutory water undertakers" for the words "National Rivers Authority" there shall be substituted the words "Environment Agency".

(2) In section 52(3) of that Act (general application to Scotland) for the words "a river purification authority within the meaning of the Rivers (Prevention of Pollution) (Scotland) Act 1951" there shall be substituted the words "the Scottish Environment Protection Agency".

The Rivers (Prevention of Pollution) (Scotland) Act 1965

6. In section 10 of the Rivers (Prevention of Pollution) (Scotland) Act 1965 (samples of effluent)—
  (a) in subsection (2)—
    (i) for the words "A river purification authority" there shall be substituted the words "the Scottish Environment Protection Agency (in this section referred to as "SEPA")"; and
    (ii) for the words "the river purification authority's" there shall be substituted the words "SEPA's"; and
  (b) in subsections (3) to (5), for the words "the river purification authority", in each place where they occur, and "Every river purification authority" there shall be substituted the words "SEPA".

The Nuclear Installations Act 1965

7.—(1) In section 3 of the Nuclear Installations Act 1965, after subsection (1) (grant of nuclear site licences) there shall be inserted—
  "(1A) The Health and Safety Executive shall consult the appropriate Agency before granting a nuclear site licence in respect of a site in Great Britain."

(2) In subsection (3) of that section (consultation with certain bodies), in paragraph (b), the words "the National Rivers Authority," shall cease to have effect.

(3) After subsection (6) of that section (variation of nuclear site licences) there shall be inserted—
  "(6A) The Health and Safety Executive shall consult the appropriate Agency before varying a nuclear site licence in respect of a site in Great Britain, if the variation relates to or affects the creation, accumulation or disposal of radioactive waste, within the meaning of the Radioactive Substances Act 1993."

8. In section 4 of that Act (attachment of conditions to licences) after subsection (3) there shall be inserted—
  "(3A) The Health and Safety Executive shall consult the appropriate Agency—
    (a) before attaching any condition to a nuclear site licence in respect of a site in Great Britain, or
    (b) before varying or revoking any condition attached to such a nuclear site licence,
  if the condition relates to or affects the creation, accumulation or disposal of radioactive waste, within the meaning of the Radioactive Substances Act 1993."

9. In section 5 of that Act (revocation and surrender of licences) after subsection (1) there shall be inserted—
  "(1A) The Health and Safety Executive shall consult the appropriate Agency before revoking a nuclear site licence in respect of a site in Great Britain."

10. In section 26 (interpretation) in subsection (1), there shall be inserted at the appropriate place—
  " "the appropriate Agency" means—
      (a) in the case of a site in England or Wales, the Environment Agency;
      (b) in the case of a site in Scotland, the Scottish Environment Protection Agency;".

The Parliamentary Commissioner Act 1967

11. In Schedule 2 to the Parliamentary Commissioner Act 1967 (departments and authorities subject to investigation)—

(a) there shall be inserted at the appropriate places the entries—
    (i) "Environment Agency"; and
    (ii) "Scottish Environment Protection Agency";
(b) after note 1, there shall be inserted—
    "1A. The reference to the Environment Agency is a reference to that Agency in relation to all its functions other than its flood defence functions, within the meaning of the Water Resources Act 1991."; and
(c) there shall be omitted—
    (i) the entry relating to the National Rivers Authority; and
    (ii) the note 9 inserted by paragraph 11 of Schedule 1 to the Water Act 1989 (which relates to that Authority).

The Sewerage (Scotland) Act 1968

12.—(1) In section 38(3) of the Sewerage (Scotland) Act 1968 (duty of Secretary of State to consult on proposed extension of Part II to non-trade effluents)—
(a) after the word "consult" where it first occurs there shall be inserted the words "the Scottish Environment Protection Agency and"; and
(b) the words "river purification authorities," shall cease to have effect.
(2) In section 59(1) of that Act (interpretation) the definition of "river purification authority" shall cease to have effect.

The Local Authorities (Goods and Services) Act 1970

13. The Local Authorities (Goods and Services) Act 1970 (supply of goods and services by local authorities to public bodies) shall have effect as if the Agency and SEPA were each both a local authority and a public body for the purposes of that Act other than section 2(2) (accounting requirements in relation to local authority agreements entered into in pursuance of section 1).

The Agriculture Act 1970

14.—(1) The Agriculture Act 1970 shall be amended in accordance with the following provisions of this paragraph.
(2) In section 92(1) (provision of flood warning systems)—
(a) for the words from the beginning to "may" where it first occurs there shall be substituted the words "The Scottish Environment Protection Agency may";
(b) the words "for their area" and "both within (and in the case of a river purification board) outwith, that area," shall cease to have effect;
(c) in sub-paragraph (i) of the proviso—
    (i) for the words "a river purification board" there shall be substituted the words "the Scottish Environment Protection Agency";
    (ii) for the word "them" there shall be substituted the word "it"; and
    (iii) for the words "that board" there shall be substituted the words "the Agency"; and
(d) in sub-paragraph (ia) of the proviso for the words following "exercise" to "shall" there shall be substituted the words ", the Agency shall".
(3) In section 92(2)—
(a) in paragraph (a)(iii) for the words "the authority providing the system" there shall be substituted the words "the Scottish Environment Protection Agency";
(b) paragraph (c) (definition of "river purification board") shall cease to have effect.
(4) In section 94 (co-operation with other persons as regards flood warning systems)—
(a) in subsection (1) for the words following "warning system" to "may" where it first occurs there shall be substituted the words "the Scottish Environment Protection Agency may" and for the words following "belonging to the" to "for" there shall be substituted the words "Agency for";
(b) in subsection (2) for the words from the beginning to "may" and for the words following "apparatus of" there shall be substituted the words "The Agency may" and " the Agency" respectively.
(5) In section 98 (extent of Part VI)—
(a) for the words from the beginning to "England" there shall be substituted the words "The Scottish Environment Protection Agency";

(b) for the words "section 92(1)(b)" there shall be substituted the words "section 92(1)"; and
(c) for the words "the National Rivers Authority" there shall be substituted the words "the Environment Agency".

The Prevention of Oil Pollution Act 1971

15.—(1) The Prevention of Oil Pollution Act 1971 shall be amended in accordance with the following provisions of this paragraph.

(2) After section 11 (duty to report discharge of oil into waters of harbours) there shall be inserted—

> **"Certain provisions not to apply where a discharge or escape is authorised under Part I of the Environmental Protection Act 1990**
>
> 11A.—(1) The provisions of sections 2(1) and (2A), 3(1) and 11(1) of this Act shall not apply to any discharge which is made under, and the provisions of section 11(1) of this Act shall not apply to any escape which is authorised by, an authorisation granted under Part I of the Environmental Protection Act 1990.
>
> (2) This section does not extend to Northern Ireland."

(3) In section 25(1) (power to extend certain provisions of the Act to the Isle of Man etc.), after the words "other than section 3" there shall be inserted the word ", 11A".

The Town and Country Planning (Scotland) Act 1972

16. In Schedule 7 to the Town and Country Planning (Scotland) Act 1972 (determination of certain appeals by persons appointed by the Secretary of State), in paragraph 2, after sub-paragraph (f) there shall be inserted—

> "(g) in relation to appeals under paragraphs 6(11) and (12) and 11(1) of Schedule 13 and paragraph 9(1) of Schedule 14 to the Environment Act 1995, paragraph 6 of Schedule 10A to this Act.".

The Local Government Act 1972

17. In section 223 of the Local Government Act 1972 (which includes provision for authorised members or officers of the National Rivers Authority to conduct certain magistrates' court proceedings on its behalf) in subsection (2)—
(a) after the words "joint authority" there shall be inserted the word "and"; and
(b) the words "and the National Rivers Authority" shall cease to have effect.

The Local Government Act 1974

18. In section 25(1) of the Local Government Act 1974 (authorities subject to investigation by Local Commissioners), for paragraph (d) there shall be substituted—

> "(d) in relation to the flood defence functions of the Environment Agency, within the meaning of the Water Resources Act 1991, the Environment Agency and any regional flood defence committee."

The Control of Pollution Act 1974

19.—(1) Section 5 of the Control of Pollution Act 1974 (licences to dispose of waste) shall be amended in accordance with the following provisions of this paragraph.

(2) In subsection (3) (duty of recipient of application for licence where planning permission is in force)—
(a) for the words "Where a disposal authority receives an application" there shall be substituted the words "Where an application has been received"; and
(b) for the words "the authority", where first occurring, there shall be substituted the words "the appropriate Agency" and, where secondly occurring, there shall be substituted the words "that Agency".

(3) In subsection (4) (duty of disposal authority to refer to National Rivers Authority etc proposals to issue licences)—
(a) for the words "a disposal authority" there shall be substituted the words "the appropriate Agency";
(b) for the words "the authority" there shall be substituted the words "that Agency";
(c) for paragraph (a), there shall be substituted—
> "(a) to refer the proposal to any collection authority whose area includes any part of the relevant land; and";
(d) in paragraph (b), for the words "the disposal authority", in both places where they occur, there shall be substituted the words "that Agency"; and

(e) the words following paragraph (b) (reference of proposal to Secretary of State in certain cases) shall cease to have effect.

(4) Subsection (5) (separate provision for Scotland) shall cease to have effect.

20.—(1) Section 6 of that Act (provisions supplementary to section 5) shall be amended in accordance with the following provisions of this paragraph.

(2) In subsection (2) (conditions which may be included in disposal licences)—

(a) for the words "the disposal authority which issues it" there shall be substituted the words "the appropriate Agency"; and

(b) for the words "the authority" there shall be substituted the words "that Agency".

(3) In subsection (3) (offence of contravening a licence condition without reasonable excuse) for the words "the disposal authority which issued the licence" there shall be substituted the words "the Environment Agency".

(4) In subsection (4) (duty of each disposal authority to maintain registers etc)—

(a) for the words "each disposal authority" there shall be substituted the words "the Environment Agency and of SEPA";

(b) for paragraph (a) there shall be substituted—

"(a) to maintain a register containing copies of all disposal licences which are for the time being in force in respect of land in England and Wales or, as the case may be, Scotland;" and

(c) in paragraph (c), for the words "the authority" there shall be substituted the words "that Agency".

(5) In subsection (5) (applications deemed to be refused if not granted within two months of receipt)—

(a) for the words "a disposal authority receives an application duly made to it for a disposal licence" there shall be substituted the words "a duly made application for a disposal licence was received";

(b) for the words "the authority", in the first two places where they occur, there shall be substituted the words "the appropriate Agency"; and

(c) for the words "the authority", wherever else occurring, there shall be substituted the words "that Agency".

21.—(1) Section 7 of that Act (variation of conditions and revocation of licences) shall be amended in accordance with the following provisions of this paragraph.

(2) In subsection (1) (modification of conditions of disposal licences issued by disposal authorities)—

(a) the words "issued by a disposal authority" shall be omitted; and

(b) for the words "the authority", where first occurring, there shall be substituted the words "the appropriate Agency" and, wherever else occurring, there shall be substituted the words "that Agency".

(3) In subsection (2) (application of section 5(4))—

(a) the words "or, in relation to Scotland, subsection (5)" shall cease to have effect; and

(b) for paragraphs (a) and (b) there shall be substituted—

"(a) the Environment Agency or SEPA, as the case may be, may postpone the reference in pursuance of the said subsection (4) so far as it considers that by reason of an emergency it is appropriate to do so; and

(b) the Environment Agency or SEPA, as the case may be, may disregard any collection authority for the purposes of the preceding provisions of this subsection in relation to a modification which, in the opinion of that Agency, will not affect that authority."

(4) In subsection (4) (revocation of disposal licences issued by disposal authorities)—

(a) the words "issued by a disposal authority" shall be omitted;

(b) for the words "the authority", where first occurring, there shall be substituted the words "the appropriate Agency" and, in the other place where they occur, there shall be substituted the words "that Agency".

22.—(1) Section 8 of that Act (transfer and relinquishment of licences) shall be amended in accordance with the following provisions of this paragraph.

(2) In subsection (1) (transfer of licences)—

(a) for the words "the authority which issued the licence" there shall be substituted the words "the appropriate Agency"; and

(b) for the words "the authority", in both places where they occur, there shall be substituted the words "that Agency".

(3) In subsection (4) (cancellation of licences)—

(a) for the words "the authority which issued it" there shall be substituted the words "the appropriate Agency"; and

(b) for the words "the authority", in the other place where they occur, there shall be substituted the words "that Agency".

23.—(1) Section 9 of that Act (supervision of licensed activities) shall be amended in accordance with the following provisions of this paragraph.

(2) In subsection (1) (duties of the authority which issued the licence) for the words "the authority which issued the licence" there shall be substituted the words "the appropriate Agency".

(3) In subsection (2) (powers of entry of authorised officers to carry out works in an emergency)—

(a) for the words "a disposal authority" there shall be substituted the words "the Environment Agency or SEPA, as the case may be,"; and

(b) for the words "the authority", wherever occurring, there shall be substituted the words "that Agency".

(4) In subsection (3) (recovery of certain expenditure from licence holders)—

(a) for the words "a disposal authority" there shall be substituted the words "the Environment Agency or SEPA"; and

(b) for the words "the authority" there shall be substituted the word "it".

(5) In subsection (4) (breach of conditions of licences)—

(a) for the words "a disposal authority" there shall be substituted the words "the appropriate Agency";

(b) the words "issued by the authority" shall be omitted; and

(c) for the words "the authority", wherever else occurring, there shall be substituted the words "that Agency".

24.—(1) Section 10 of that Act (appeals to Secretary of State from decisions with respect to licences) shall be amended in accordance with the following provisions of this paragraph.

(2) In subsection (1) (duty of disposal authority concerned to implement Secretary of State's determination) for the words "the disposal authority concerned" there shall be substituted the words "the appropriate Agency".

(3) In subsection (3) (cases where the decision under appeal is effective pending the determination of the appeal)—

(a) for the words "to a decision of a disposal authority" there shall be substituted the words "if the decision in question is a decision";

(b) for the words "in the opinion of the authority" there shall be substituted the words "in the opinion of the body making the decision in question";

(c) for the words "the authority acted" there shall be substituted the words "that body acted"; and

(d) in paragraph (b), for the words "the authority" there shall be substituted the words "the appropriate Agency".

25. In section 11 of that Act (special provision for land occupied by disposal authorities: resolutions etc) subsections (1) to (11) shall cease to have effect.

26.—(1) Section 16 of that Act (removal of waste deposited in breach of licensing provisions) shall be amended in accordance with the following provisions of this paragraph.

(2) In subsection (1) (power of disposal or collection authority to serve notice on occupier of land in its area) for the words from "in the area" to "the authority may" there shall be substituted the words "in contravention of section 3(1) of this Act, any authority to which this section applies may".

(3) After subsection (7) there shall be added—

"(8) The authorities to which this section applies are—

(a) the appropriate Agency;

(b) any collection authority in whose area the land mentioned in subsection (1) above is situated."

27. In section 30 of that Act (interpretation of Part I) in subsection (1)—

(a) the following definition shall be inserted at the appropriate place—

" "the appropriate Agency" means—

(a) in relation to England and Wales, the Environment Agency;

(b) in relation to Scotland, SEPA;";

(b) for the definition of "waste" there shall be substituted—

" "waste" has the same meaning as it has in Part II of the Environmental Protection Act 1990 by virtue of section 75(2) of that Act;"; and

(c) the words from "and for the purposes" to the end (which provide a presumption that anything discarded is waste unless the contrary is proved) shall cease to have effect.

28. In section 62(2)(a) of that Act (exceptions to restrictions on the operation of loudspeakers in streets), as it has effect in relation to England and Wales, for the words "National Rivers Authority" there shall be substituted the words "Environment Agency".

29.—(1) The Control of Pollution Act 1974, as it has effect in relation to Scotland, shall be amended in accordance with the following provisions of this paragraph.

(2) Subject to the amendments made by the following provisions of this paragraph, for the words "a river purification authority", "the river purification authority", "river purification authority", "river purification authorities", "the river purification authorities", "each river purification authority" and "any river purification authority", in each place where they occur in the undernoted provisions, there shall be substituted the words "SEPA"—

> section 30A(2)(a) and (3);
> section 30C(1);
> section 30D;
> section 31(4)(d) and (6);
> section 31 A(2);
> section 33(1);
> sections 34 to 39;
> section 41;
> sections 46 to 51;
> section 96(3); and
> Schedule 1A.

(3) In section 30A(2)(a) (Secretary of State to deposit maps showing freshwater limits of every relevant river or watercourse) the words "in the area of that authority" shall cease to have effect.

(4) In section 30C (water quality objectives)—

(a) in subsection (1) (Secretary of State to establish water quality objectives), the words "within the area of that authority" shall cease to have effect;

(b) in subsection (3)(b) (Secretary of State to review water quality objectives) for the words "the river purification authority on which that notice has been served" there shall be substituted the words "SEPA";

(c) in subsection (4) (Secretary of State to give notice and consider representations when reviewing water quality objectives—

> (i) the words "in the area of a river purification authority" shall cease to have effect; and

> (ii) in paragraph (a) for the words "that authority" there shall be substituted the words "SEPA";

(d) in subsection (5)(b) (form of notice to be given by the Secretary of State when varying water quality objectives) for the words "the authority" there shall be substituted the words "SEPA"; and

(e) in subsection (6) (Secretary of State to serve further notice where water quality objectives remain unchanged)—

> (i) the words "in the area of a river purification authority" shall cease to have effect; and

> (ii) for the words "that authority" there shall be substituted the words "SEPA".

(5) In section 30E (consultation and collaboration)—

(a) for the word "their" there shall be substituted the word "its";

(b) for the words "river purification authorities" there shall be substituted the words "SEPA"; and

(c) for the words "National Rivers Authority" there shall be substituted the words "Environment Agency".

(6) In section 31 (control of pollution of rivers and coastal waters etc.)—

(a) in subsection (4)(b) (Secretary of State power to restrict or prohibit prescribed activities in designated areas) for the words "the river purification authority in whose area the place is situated" there shall be substituted the words "SEPA"; and

(b) in subsection (6) (power to make byelaws to prohibit or regulate prescribed activities)—

> (i) for the words "the authority" there shall be substituted the word "it"; and

> (ii) the words "in its area" shall cease to have effect.

(7) Section 31D (powers of entry in relation to agreements under section 31B) shall cease to have effect.

(8) In section 33(1) (power to make byelaws regulating or prohibiting sanitary appliances on vessels)—

(a) for the words "the authority" where they first occur there shall be substituted the word "it"; and

(b) the words "in the area of the authority" shall cease to have effect.

(9) In section 34 (consents for discharges of trade and sewage effluent etc.)—

(a) for the words "the authority" and "the authority's" in each place where they occur (other than the last reference in subsection (2)) there shall be substituted the words "SEPA" and "SEPA's" respectively;

(b) in subsection (2) (disposal of application)—
> (i) for the words "a river purification authority to which an application for consent is" there shall be substituted the words "SEPA, in relation to an application for consent";
> (ii) for the word "three" there shall be substituted the word "four"; and
> (iii) for the words "the authority shall be deemed to have refused the consent" there shall be substituted the words "the applicant may treat the consent applied for as having been refused"; and

(c) in subsection (3) (consent not to relate to discharges which occurred prior to consent) the words "in its area" shall cease to have effect.

(10) In the following provisions, for the words "an authority", "any authority", "the authority", "the authorities" and "the relevant river purification authority" in each place where they occur there shall be substituted the words "SEPA"—
> sections 35 to 39;
> section 41;
> sections 46 to 49; and
> Schedule 1A, paragraph 2.

(11) In section 36 (provisions supplementary to sections 34 and 35)—

(a) in subsection (1), after the word "shall" there shall be inserted the words ", subject to subsections (2A) and (2B) below,";

(b) after subsection (2) there shall be inserted the following subsections—

> "(2A) A person who proposes to make, or has made, an application to SEPA for consent in pursuance of section 34 of this Act may apply to the Secretary of State within a prescribed period for a certificate providing that subsection (1) above shall not apply to that application.

> (2B) If the Secretary of State is satisfied that—
> (a) it would be contrary to the interests of national security; or
> (b) it would prejudice to an unreasonable degree the commercial interests of any person,
> not to issue a certificate applied for under subsection (2A) above, he may issue the certificate and, if he does so, subsection (1) above shall not apply to the application specified in the certificate."; and

(c) in subsection (6), for the word "three" there shall be substituted the word "four".

(12) In section 37(1) (revocation of consents and alteration and imposition of conditions), for the words from the beginning to "consent" in the second place where it occurs there shall be substituted the words "SEPA may from time to time review any consent given in pursuance of section 34 of this Act".

(13) In section 38 (restriction as to variation and revocation of consent and of previous variation), in each of subsections (1) and (2), for the word "two" there shall be substituted the word "four".

(14) After section 38 there shall be inserted—

"General review of consents

38A.—(1) If it appears appropriate to the Secretary of State to do so he may at any time direct SEPA to review—
(a) the consents given under section 34 of this Act; or
(b) any description of such consents,
and the conditions (if any) to which those consents are subject.

(2) A direction given by virtue of subsection (1) above—
(a) shall specify the purpose for which; and
(b) may specify the manner in which,
the review is to be conducted.

(3) After carrying out the review, SEPA shall submit to the Secretary of State its proposals (if any) for—
(a) the modification of the conditions of any consent reviewed pursuant to the direction; or
(b) in the case of any such consent which is unconditional, subjecting the consent to conditions.

(4) Where the Secretary of State has received any proposals under subsection (3) above in relation to any consent he may, if it appears appropriate to him to do so, direct SEPA, in relation to that consent—
(a) to make modifications of the conditions of the consent; or
(b) in the case of an unconditional consent, to subject the consent to conditions.

(5) A direction given by virtue of subsection (4) above may direct SEPA to do, in relation to any such consent, only—
(a) any such thing as SEPA has proposed should be done in relation to that consent; or

(b) any such thing with such modifications as appear to the Secretary of State to be appropriate.".

(15) In section 39 (appeals to Secretary of State)—

(a) in subsection (1), in each of paragraphs (b) and (c), for the words "the preceding section" there shall be substituted the words "section 38 of this Act";

(b) in subsection (5), for the words "terms and period as are" there shall be substituted the words "period as is";

(c) after that subsection there shall be inserted the following subsections—

"(5A) Subject to subsection (5B) below, where a question is referred to the Secretary of State in pursuance of subsection (1)(b) above, the revocation of the consent or, as the case may be, the modification of the conditions of the consent or the provision that the consent (having been unconditional) shall be subject to conditions, shall not take effect while the reference is pending.

(5B) Subsection (5A) above shall not apply to a reference where the notice effecting the revocation, modification or provision in question includes a statement that in the opinion of SEPA it is necessary for the purpose of preventing or, where that is not practicable, minimising—

(a) the entry into controlled waters of any poisonous, noxious or polluting matter or any solid waste matter, or

(b) harm to human health,

that that subsection should not apply.

(5C) Where the reference falls within subsection (5B) above, if, on the application of the holder or former holder of the consent, the Secretary of State (or other person determining the question referred) determines that SEPA acted unreasonably in excluding the application of subsection (5A) above, then—

(a) if the reference is still pending at the end of the day on which that determination is made, subsection (5A) above shall apply to the reference from the end of that day; and

(b) the holder or former holder of the consent shall be entitled to recover compensation from SEPA in respect of any loss suffered by him in consequence of the exclusion of the application of that subsection;

and any dispute as to a person's entitlement to such compensation or as to the amount of it shall be determined by a single arbiter appointed, in default of agreement between the parties concerned, by the Secretary of State on the application of any of the parties."; and

(d) at the end there shall be added—

"(7) This section is subject to section 114 of the Environment Act 1995 (delegation or reference of appeals).

(8) In this section "the holder", in relation to a consent, is the person who has the consent."

(16) Section 40(4) (transitional provisions relating to consents) shall cease to have effect.

(17) In section 41(1) (maintenance of registers)—

(a) after the words "prescribed particulars of" there shall be inserted the words "or relating to";

(b) the following provisions shall cease to have effect—

(i) in paragraph (c) (information contained in registers) the words "(except section 40(4))";

(ii) in paragraph (d) (duty to maintain registers of samples of effluent), sub-paragraph (ii); and

(iii) paragraph (e) (duty to register certain notices);

(c) there shall be added at the end the following paragraphs—

"(f) enforcement notices served under section 49A of this Act;

(g) directions given by the Secretary of State in relation to SEPA's functions under this Part of this Act;

(h) convictions, for offences under this Part of this Act, of persons who have the benefit of consents under section 34 of this Act;

(j) information obtained or furnished in pursuance of conditions of such consents;

(k) works notices under section 46A of this Act;

(l) appeals under section 46C of this Act;

(m) convictions for offences under section 46D of this Act; and

(n) such other matters relating to the quality of water as may be prescribed."

(18) In section 41(2) (registers to be available for inspection by, and facilities for obtaining copies of entries to be afforded to, the public), after paragraph (b) there shall be added the words—

"and, for the purposes of this subsection, places may be prescribed at which any such registers or facilities as are mentioned in paragraph (a) or (b) above are to be available or afforded to the public in pursuance of the paragraph in question."

(19) At the end of section 41 there shall be added the following subsection—

"(3) The Secretary of State may give SEPA directions requiring the removal from any register maintained by it under this section of any specified information which is not prescribed for inclusion under subsection (1) of this section or which, by virtue of section 42A or 42B of this Act, ought to have been excluded from the registers."

(20) For section 42, there shall be substituted the following sections—

"Exclusion from registers of information affecting national security

42A.—(1) No information shall be included in a register kept or maintained by SEPA under section 41 of this Act if and so long as, in the opinion of the Secretary of State, the inclusion in such a register of that information, or information of that description, would be contrary to the interests of national security.

(2) The Secretary of State may, for the purposes of securing the exclusion from registers of information to which subsection (1) of this section applies, give SEPA directions—

    (a) specifying information, or descriptions of information, to be excluded from their registers; or

    (b) specifying descriptions of information to be referred to the Secretary of State for his determination;

and no information to be referred to the Secretary of State in pursuance of paragraph (b) of this subsection shall be included in any such register until the Secretary of State determines that it should be so included.

(3) SEPA shall notify the Secretary of State of any information it excludes from a register in pursuance of directions under subsection (2) of this section.

(4) A person may, as respects any information which appears to him to be information to which subsection (1) of this section may apply, give a notice to the Secretary of State specifying the information and indicating its apparent nature; and, if he does so—

    (a) he shall notify SEPA that he has done so; and

    (b) no information so notified to the Secretary of State shall be included in any such register until the Secretary of State has determined that it should be so included.

Exclusion from registers of certain confidential information

42B.—(1) No information relating to the affairs of any individual or business shall, without the consent of that individual or the person for the time being carrying on that business, be included in a register kept or maintained by SEPA under section 41 of this Act, if and so long as the information—

    (a) is, in relation to him, commercially confidential; and

    (b) is not required to be included in the register in pursuance of directions under subsection (7) of this section;

but information is not commercially confidential for the purposes of this section unless it is determined under this section to be so by SEPA, or, on appeal, by the Secretary of State.

(2) Where information is furnished to SEPA for the purpose of—

    (a) an application for a consent under section 34 of this Act;

    (b) complying with any condition of such a consent; or

    (c) complying with a notice under section 93 of this Act,

then, if the person furnishing it applies to SEPA to have the information excluded from any register kept or maintained by SEPA under section 41 of this Act, on the ground that it is commercially confidential (as regards himself or another person), SEPA shall determine whether the information is or is not commercially confidential.

(3) A determination under subsection (2) of this section must be made within the period of fourteen days beginning with the date of the application and if SEPA fails to make a determination within that period it shall be treated as having determined that the information is commercially confidential.

(4) Where it appears to SEPA that any information (other than information furnished in circumstances within subsection (2) of this section) which has been obtained by SEPA under or by virtue of any provision of any enactment might be commercially confidential, SEPA shall—

    (a) give to the person to whom or whose business it relates notice that that information is required to be included in a register kept or maintained by SEPA under section 41 of this Act, unless excluded under this section; and

    (b) give him a reasonable opportunity—

        (i) of objecting to the inclusion of the information on the ground that it is commercially confidential; and

        (ii) of making representations to SEPA for the purpose of justifying any such objection;

and, if any representations are made, SEPA shall, having taken the representations into account, determine whether the information is or is not commercially confidential.

    (5) Where, under subsection (2) or (4) of this section, SEPA determines that information is not commercially confidential—

    (a) the information shall not be entered on the register until the end of the period of twenty-one days beginning with the date on which the determination is notified to the person concerned; and

    (b) that person may appeal to the Secretary of State against the decision;

and, where an appeal is brought in respect of any information, the information shall not be entered on the register pending the final determination or withdrawal of the appeal.

    (6) Subsections (2), (4) and (7) of section 49B of this Act shall apply in relation to appeals under subsection (5) of this section; but

    (a) subsection (4) of that section shall have effect for the purposes of this subsection with the substitution for the words from ("which may" onwards of the words "(which must be held in private)"; and

    (b) subsection (5) of this section is subject to section 114 of the Environment Act 1995 (delegation or reference of appeals etc).

    (7) The Secretary of State may give SEPA directions as to specified information, or descriptions of information, which the public interest requires to be included in registers kept or maintained by SEPA under section 41 of this Act notwithstanding that the information may be commercially confidential.

    (8) Information excluded from a register shall be treated as ceasing to be commercially confidential for the purposes of this section at the expiry of the period of four years beginning with the date of the determination by virtue of which it was excluded; but the person who furnished it may apply to SEPA for the information to remain excluded from the register on the ground that it is still commercially confidential and SEPA shall determine whether or not that is the case.

    (9) Subsections (5) and (6) of this section shall apply in relation to a determination under subsection (8) of this section as they apply in relation to a determination under subsection (2) or (4) of this section.

    (10) The Secretary of State may prescribe the substitution (whether in all cases or in such classes or descriptions of case as may be prescribed) for the period for the time being specified in subsection (3) above of such other period as he considers appropriate.

    (11) Information is, for the purposes of any determination under this section, commercially confidential, in relation to any individual or person, if its being contained in register would prejudice to an unreasonable degree the commercial interests of that individual or person."

(21) In section 46 (operations to remedy or forestall pollution of water)—

(a) in subsection (1)—

        (i) at the beginning there shall be inserted the words "Subject to subsection (1B) below,"; and

        (ii) the words "in its area" where they first occur and "in its area or elsewhere" shall cease to have effect;

(b) after subsection (1) there shall be inserted—

    "(1A) In either case mentioned in subsection (1) of this section, SEPA shall be entitled to carry out investigations for the purpose of establishing the source of the matter and the identity of the person who has caused or knowingly permitted it to be present in controlled waters or at a place from which it was likely, in the opinion of SEPA, to enter controlled waters.

    (1B) Without prejudice to the power of SEPA to carry out investigations under subsection (1A) above, the power conferred by subsection (1) above to carry out operations shall be exercisable only in a case where—

    (a) SEPA considers it necessary to carry out forthwith any operations falling within paragraph (a) or (b) of subsection (1) above; or

    (b) it appears to SEPA, after reasonable inquiry, that no person can be found on whom to serve a works notice under section 46A of this Act.";

(c) in subsection (2) after the words "any operations" there shall be inserted the words "or investigations";

(d) in subsection (3)(b)—

(i) after the words "any operations" there shall be inserted the words "or investigations"; and

(ii) after the words "an abandoned mine" there shall be inserted the words "or an abandoned part of a mine"; and

(e) after subsection (3) there shall be inserted—

"(3A) Subsection (3)(b) of this section shall not apply to the owner or former operator of any mine or part of a mine if the mine or part in question became abandoned after 31st December 1999.

(3B) Subsections (5) and (6) of section 30J above shall apply in relation to subsections (3) and (3A) above as they apply in relation to subsections (3) and (4) of that section.".

(22) After section 46 there shall be inserted the following sections—

"Notices requiring persons to carry out anti-pollution operations

46A.—(1) Subject to the following provisions of this section, where it appears to SEPA that any poisonous, noxious or polluting matter or any solid waste matter is likely to enter, or to be or to have been present in, any controlled waters, SEPA shall be entitled to serve a works notice on any person who, as the case may be,—

(a) caused or knowingly permitted the matter in question to be present at the place from which it is likely, in the opinion of SEPA, to enter any controlled waters; or

(b) caused or knowingly permitted the matter in question to be present in any controlled waters.

(2) For the purposes of this section, a "works notice" is a notice requiring the person on whom it is served to carry out such of the following operations as may be specified in the notice, that is to say—

(a) in a case where the matter in question appears likely to enter any controlled waters, operations for the purpose of preventing it from doing so; or

(b) in a case where the matter appears to be or to have been present in any controlled waters, operations for the purpose—

(i) of removing or disposing of the matter;

(ii) of remedying or mitigating any pollution caused by its presence in the waters; or

(iii) so far as it is reasonably practicable to do so, of restoring the waters, including any flora and fauna dependent on the aquatic environment of the waters, to their state immediately before the matter became present in the waters.

(3) A works notice—

(a) must specify the periods within which the person on whom it is served is required to do each of the things specified in the notice; and

(b) is without prejudice to the powers of SEPA by virtue of section 46(1B)(a) of this Act.

(4) Before serving a works notice on any person, SEPA shall reasonably endeavour to consult that person concerning the operations which are to be specified in the notice.

(5) The Secretary of State may by regulations make provision for or in connection with—

(a) the form or content of works notices;

(b) requirements for consultation, before the service of a works notice, with persons other than the person on whom that notice is to be served;

(c) steps to be taken for the purposes of any consultation required under subsection (4) above or regulations made by virtue of paragraph (b) above; and

(d) any other steps of a procedural nature which are to be taken in connection with, or in consequence of, the service of a works notice.

(6) A works notice shall not be regarded as invalid, or as invalidly served, by reason only of any failure to comply with the requirements of subsection (4) above or of regulations made by virtue of paragraph (b) of subsection (5) above.

(7) Nothing in subsection (1) above shall entitle SEPA to require the carrying out of any operations which would impede or prevent the making of any discharge in pursuance of a consent given by SEPA by virtue of section 34 of this Act.

(8) No works notice shall be served on any person requiring him to carry out any operations in respect of water from an abandoned mine or an abandoned part of a mine which that person permitted to reach such a place as is mentioned in subsection (1)(a) above or to enter any controlled waters.

(9) Subsection (8) above shall not apply to the owner or former operator of any mine or part of a mine if the mine or part in question became abandoned after 31st December 1999.

(10) Subsections (5) and (6) of section 30J of this Act shall apply in relation to subsections (8) and (9) above as they apply in relation to subsections (3) and (4) of that section.

(11) Where SEPA—

(a) carries out any such investigations as are mentioned in section 46(1A) of this Act, and

(b) serves a works notice on a person in connection with the matter to which the investigations relate,

it shall (unless the notice is quashed or withdrawn) be entitled to recover the costs or expenses reasonably incurred in carrying out those investigations from that person.

(12) The Secretary of State may, if he thinks fit in relation to any person, give directions to SEPA as to whether or how it should exercise its powers under this section.

Grant of, and compensation for, rights of entry etc.

46B.—(1) A works notice may require a person to carry out operations in relation to any land or waters notwithstanding that he is not entitled to carry out those operations.

(2) Any person whose consent is required before any operations required by a works notice may be carried out shall grant, or join in granting, such rights in relation to any land or waters as will enable the person on whom the works notice is served to comply with any requirements imposed by the works notice.

(3) Before serving a works notice, SEPA shall reasonably endeavour to consult every person who appears to it—

(a) to be the owner or occupier of any relevant land, and

(b) to be a person who might be required by subsection (2) above to grant, or join in granting, any rights,

concerning the rights which that person may be so required to grant.

(4) A works notice shall not be regarded as invalid, or as invalidly served, by reason only of any failure to comply with the requirements of subsection (3) above.

(5) A person who grants, or joins in granting, any rights pursuant to subsection (2) above shall be entitled, on making an application within such period as may be prescribed and in such manner as may be prescribed to such person as may be prescribed, to be paid by the person on whom the works notice in question is served compensation of such amount as may be determined in such manner as may be prescribed.

(6) Without prejudice to the generality of the regulations that may be made by virtue of subsection (5) above, regulations by virtue of that subsection may make such provision in relation to compensation under this section as may be made by regulations by virtue of subsection (4) of section 35A of the Environmental Protection Act 1990 in relation to compensation under that section.

(7) In this section—

"relevant land" means—

(a) any land or waters in relation to which the works notice in question requires, or may require, operations to be carried out; or

(b) any land adjoining or adjacent to that land or those waters;

"works notice" means a works notice under section 46A of this Act.

Appeals against works notices

46C.—(1) A person on whom a works notice is served may, within the period of twenty-one days beginning with the day on which the notice is served, appeal against the notice to the Secretary of State.

(2) On any appeal under this section the Secretary of State—

(a) shall quash the notice, if he is satisfied that there is a material defect in the notice; but

(b) subject to that, may confirm the notice, with or without modification, or quash it.

(3) The Secretary of State may by regulations make provision with respect to—

(a) the grounds on which appeals under this section may be made; or

(b) the procedure on any such appeal.

(4) Regulations under subsection (3) above may (among other things)—

(a) include provisions comparable to those in section 290 of the Public Health Act 1936 (appeals against notices requiring the execution of works);

(b) prescribe the cases in which a works notice is, or is not, to be suspended until the appeal is decided, or until some other stage in the proceedings;

(c) prescribe the cases in which the decision on an appeal may in some respects be less favourable to the appellant than the works notice against which he is appealing;

(d) prescribe the cases in which the appellant may claim that a works notice should have been served on some other person and prescribe the procedure to be followed in those cases;

(e) make provision as respects—

(i) the particulars to be included in the notice of appeal;

(ii) the persons on whom notice of appeal is to be served and the particulars, if any, which are to accompany the notice; or

(iii) the abandonment of an appeal.

(5) In this section "works notice" means a works notice under section 46A of this Act.

(6) This section is subject to section 114 of the Environment Act 1995 (delegation or reference of appeals).

Consequences of not complying with a works notice

46D.—(1) If a person on whom SEPA serves a works notice fails to comply with any of the requirements of the notice, he shall be guilty of an offence.

(2) A person who commits an offence under subsection (1) above shall be liable—

(a) on summary conviction, to imprisonment for a term not exceeding three months or to a fine not exceeding £20,000 or to both;

(b) on conviction on indictment, to imprisonment for a term not exceeding two years or to a fine or to both.

(3) If a person on whom a works notice has been served fails to comply with any of the requirements of the notice, SEPA may do what that person was required to do and may recover from him any costs or expenses reasonably incurred by SEPA in doing it.

(4) If SEPA is of the opinion that proceedings for an offence under subsection (1) above would afford an ineffectual remedy against a person who has failed to comply with the requirements of a works notice, SEPA may take proceedings in any court of competent jurisdiction for the purpose of securing compliance with the notice.

(5) In this section "works notice" means a works notice under section 46A of this Act.".

(23) In section 47 (duty to deal with waste from vessels etc.)—

(a) in subsection (1) (duty), the words "in its area" shall cease to have effect; and

(b) in subsection (2) (provision of facilities), the words "in the authority's area" shall cease to have effect.

(24) In section 48(1) (power to exclude unregistered vessels from rivers etc.) the words "in its area" shall cease to have effect.

(25) In section 49 (deposit and vegetation in rivers etc.) at the end there shall be added—

"(5) This section is subject to section 114 of the Environment Act 1995 (delegation or reference of appeals)."

(26) After that section there shall be inserted—

"Enforcement notices as respects discharge consents

49A.—(1) If SEPA is of the opinion that the holder of a relevant consent is contravening any condition of the consent, or is likely to contravene any such condition, it may serve on him a notice (an "enforcement notice").

(2) An enforcement notice shall—

(a) state that SEPA is of the said opinion;

(b) specify the matters constituting the contravention or the matters making it likely that the contravention will arise;

(c) specify the steps that must be taken to remedy the contravention or, as the case may be, to remedy the matters making it likely that the contravention will arise; and

(d) specify the period within which those steps must be taken.

(3) Any person who fails to comply with any requirement imposed by an enforcement notice shall be guilty of an offence and liable—

(a) on summary conviction, to imprisonment for a term not exceeding three months or to a fine not exceeding £20,000 or to both;

(b) on conviction on indictment, to imprisonment for a term not exceeding two years or to a fine or to both.

(4) If SEPA is of the opinion that proceedings for an offence under subsection (3) above would afford an ineffectual remedy against a person who has failed to comply with the requirements of an enforcement notice, SEPA may take proceedings in any court of competent jurisdiction for the purpose of securing compliance with the notice.

(5) The Secretary of State may, if he thinks fit in relation to any person, give to SEPA directions as to whether it should exercise its powers under this section and as to the steps which must be taken.

(6) In this section—

"relevant consent" means a consent for the purposes of section 30J(7)(a), 34 or 49(1) of this Act; and

"the holder", in relation to a relevant consent, is the person who has the consent in question.

Appeals against enforcement notices

49B.—(1) A person upon whom an enforcement notice has been served under section 49A of this Act may appeal to the Secretary of State.

(2) This section is subject to section 114 of the Environment Act 1995 (delegation or reference of appeals etc.).

(3) An appeal under this section shall, if and to the extent a requirement to do so is prescribed, be advertised in the manner prescribed.

(4) If either party to the appeal so requests or the Secretary of State so decides, an appeal shall be or continue in the form of a hearing (which may, if the person hearing the appeal so decides, be held, or held to any extent, in private).

(5) On the determination of an appeal under this section, the Secretary of State may either quash or affirm the enforcement notice and, if he affirms it, may do so either in its original form or with such modifications as he may in the circumstances think fit.

(6) The bringing of an appeal under this section shall not have the effect of suspending the operation of the notice appealed against.

(7) The period within which and the manner in which appeals under this section are to be brought and the manner in which they are to be considered shall be as prescribed.".

(27) In section 50 (investigation of water pollution problems arising from closures of mines) the words "in its area" shall cease to have effect.

(28) Sections 53 (charges in respect of consents to certain discharges in Scotland), 54 (directions to the river purification authority), 55 (discharges by islands councils) and 56(4) (meaning of the area of a river purification authority) shall cease to have effect.

(29) In section 56(1) (interpretation of Part II), the following definition shall be inserted in the appropriate place in alphabetical order—

" "operations" includes works;".

(30) In section 90(3) (establishment charges etc. in relation to Scotland), for the words from "a river" to the end there shall be substituted the words "SEPA".

(31) Section 91(5)(a) (application of that section to Scotland) shall cease to have effect.

(32) In section 96(3) (local inquiries) the words from "but as if" to the end shall cease to have effect.

(33) In section 98 (interpretation of Part V), for paragraph (b) of the definition of "relevant authority" there shall be substituted—

"(b) in Scotland—

(i) as respects sections 91 and 92, a council constituted under section 2 of the Local Government etc. (Scotland) Act 1994; and

(ii) as respects this Part other than those sections, the Secretary of State, SEPA or a council constituted under section 2 of the Local Government etc. (Scotland) Act 1994.".

(34) In section 104(1) (orders and regulations) the words "59" shall cease to have effect.

(35) In section 105 (interpretation etc.—general) there shall be inserted in the appropriate place—

" "SEPA" means the Scottish Environment Protection Agency;".

The Health and Safety at Work etc. Act 1974

30.—(1) The Health and Safety at Work etc. Act 1974 (in this paragraph referred to as "the 1974 Act") shall have effect in accordance with the following provisions of this paragraph.

(2) The appropriate new Agency shall, in consequence of the transfer effected by virtue of section 2(2)(c) or, as the case may be, 21(2)(a) of this Act, be regarded for the purposes of Part I of the 1974 Act as the authority which is, by any of the relevant statutory provisions, made responsible in relation to England and Wales or, as the case may be, Scotland for the enforcement of the relevant enactments (and, accordingly, as the enforcing authority in relation to those enactments).

(3) Neither the Agency nor SEPA shall have power to appoint inspectors under section 19 of the 1974 Act.

(4) Sections 21 to 23 (improvement notices and prohibition notices) shall have effect in any case where the relevant statutory provision in question is any of the relevant enactments as if references in those sections to an inspector were references to the appropriate new Agency.

(5) Section 27 (obtaining of information by the Commission etc.) shall have effect in relation to the appropriate new Agency, in its relevant capacity, as it has effect in relation to the Health and Safety Commission (and not as it has effect in relation to an enforcing authority), except that the consent of the Secretary of State shall not be required to the service by the appropriate new Agency of a notice under subsection (1) of that section; and, accordingly, where that section has effect by virtue of this sub-paragraph—

(a) any reference in that section to the Commission shall be construed as a reference to the appropriate new Agency;

(b) any reference to an enforcing authority shall be disregarded; and

(c) in subsection (3) of that section, the words from "and also" onwards shall be disregarded.

(6) In section 28 (restrictions on disclosure of information)—

(a) in paragraph (a) of subsection (3) (exception for disclosure of information to certain bodies) after the words "the Executive," there shall be inserted the words "the Environment Agency, the Scottish Environment Protection Agency,";

(b) in paragraph (c)(ii) of that subsection (exception for disclosure to officers of certain bodies) as it applies to England and Wales—

(i) the words "of the National Rivers Authority or", and

(ii) the word "Authority," (where next occurring),

shall be omitted;

(c) for paragraph (c)(ii) of that subsection as it applies to Scotland there shall be substituted—

"(ii) an officer of a water undertaker, sewerage undertaker, sewerage authority or water authority who is authorised by that authority to receive it;";

(d) paragraph (c)(iii) of that subsection (exception for disclosure to officers of river purification boards) shall cease to have effect;

(e) in subsection (4) (references to certain bodies to include references to officers or inspectors), after the words "the Executive" (in the first place where they occur) there shall be inserted the words "the Environment Agency, the Scottish Environment Protection Agency,";

(f) in subsection (5) (information disclosed in pursuance of subsection (3) not to be used by recipient except for specified purposes)—

(i) in paragraph (a) (use for a purpose of the Executive etc.) after the words "of the Executive or" there shall be inserted the words "of the Environment Agency or of the Scottish Environment Protection Agency or";

(ii) in paragraph (b) as it applies to England and Wales (use for the purposes of certain bodies of information given to officers of those bodies), the words "the National Rivers Authority" shall be omitted;

(iii) in the said paragraph (b) as it applies to Scotland, for the words from the beginning to "in connection" there shall be substituted the words "in the case of information given to an officer of a body which is a local authority, a water undertaker, a sewerage undertaker, a sewerage authority or a water authority the purposes of the body in connection".

(7) In section 38 (restriction on institution of proceedings in England and Wales) after the words "except by an inspector or" there shall be inserted the words "the Environment Agency or".

(8) In this paragraph—

"the appropriate new Agency" means—

(a) in relation to England and Wales, the Agency; and

(b) in relation to Scotland, SEPA;

"relevant capacity", in relation to the appropriate new Agency, means its capacity as the enforcing authority, for the purposes of Part I of the 1974 Act, which is responsible in relation to England and Wales or, as the case may be, Scotland for the enforcement of the relevant enactments;

"the relevant enactments" means the Alkali, &c, Works Regulation Act 1906 and section 5 of the 1974 Act;

"the relevant statutory provisions" has the same meaning as in Part I of the 1974 Act.

The House of Commons Disqualification Act 1975 and the Northern Ireland Assembly Disqualification Act 1975

31. In Part II of Schedule I to the House of Commons Disqualification Act 1975 (bodies of which all members are disqualified for membership of the House of Commons) the following entries shall be inserted at the appropriate places—

(a) "The Environment Agency.";

(b) "The Scottish Environment Protection Agency.";

and the like insertions shall be made in Part II of Schedule 1 to the Northern Ireland Assembly Disqualification Act 1975 (bodies of which all members are disqualified for membership of the Northern Ireland Assembly).

The Local Government (Scotland) Act 1975

32.—(1) The Local Government (Scotland) Act 1975 shall be amended in accordance with the following provisions.

(2) In section 16 (borrowing and lending by local authorities and certain other bodies)—
(a) after the words "local authorities" there shall be inserted the word "and";
(b) the words "and river purification boards" shall cease to have effect.
(3) In Schedule 3 (further provision relating to borrowing and lending by local authorities and certain other bodies) in paragraph 28—
(a) in sub-paragraph (1)—
    (i) after the word "money" there shall be inserted the word "and";
    (ii) the words "or a river purification board," shall cease to have effect;
(b) in sub-paragraph (2) for sub-paragraph (a) there shall be substituted—
    "(a) a joint board; and".

The Local Government (Miscellaneous Provisions) Act 1976

33. In section 44 of the Local Government (Miscellaneous Provisions) Act 1976 (interpretation of Part I of that Act) after subsection (1A) (certain provisions of that Act, including section 16 (obtaining information about land), to have effect as if the Broads Authority were a local authority) there shall be inserted—
    "(1B) Section 16 of this Act shall have effect as if the Environment Agency were a local authority.".

The Water (Scotland) Act 1980

34.—(1) The Water (Scotland) Act 1980 shall be amended in accordance with the following provisions of this paragraph.
(2) In section 31(1) (consultation where limits of water supply adjoin any part of England) for paragraph (b) there shall be substituted—
    "(b) the Scottish Environment Protection Agency."
(3) In section 33(3)(a) (notice of temporary discharge of water into watercourses)—
(a) sub-paragraph (ii) and the preceding "and" shall cease to have effect; and
(b) at the end of the paragraph there shall be inserted—
    "and
    (ii) to the Scottish Environment Protection Agency.".
(4) In section 109(1) (interpretation) the definitions of "river purification authority" and "river purification board" shall cease to have effect.
(5) In Schedule 1—
(a) in paragraph 2(ii) for the words following "section 17(2)" to the end there shall be substituted the words "on the Scottish Environment Protection Agency";
(b) in paragraph 11(ii) the words "and any river purification authority" shall cease to have effect and at the end there shall be added the words "and on the Scottish Environment Protection Agency";
(c) in paragraph 19 for the words following "any fishery district" to the words "any public undertakers" there shall be substituted the words "any navigation authority exercising jurisdiction in relation to any watercourse from which water is proposed to be taken under the rights to be acquired, the Scottish Environment Protection Agency and any public undertakers".

The Criminal Justice (Scotland) Act 1980

35. In Schedule 1 to the Criminal Justice (Scotland) Act 1980 (sufficiency of evidence by certificate in certain routine matters) in the entry relating to the Control of Pollution Act 1974—
(a) for the words from "Section 31(1)" to "such waters etc)" there shall be substituted the words "Section 30F (pollution offences)"; and
(b) for the words "a river purification authority (within the meaning of that Act)" there shall be substituted the words "the Scottish Environment Protection Agency".

The Road Traffic Regulation Act 1984

36.—(1) In section 1 of the Road Traffic Regulation Act 1984 (traffic regulation orders outside Greater London) in subsection (1), after paragraph (f) (which allows a traffic regulation order to be made for preserving or improving the amenities of the area through which the road runs) there shall be added "or
    (g) for any of the purposes specified in paragraphs (a) to (c) of subsection (1) of section 87 of the Environment Act 1995 (air quality).".
(2) In section 6 of that Act (orders similar to traffic regulation orders in Greater London) in subsection (1)(b) (which allows orders in Greater London to be made for equivalent purposes to those in section 1(1)(a) to (f) of that Act) for the words "(a) to (f)" there shall be substituted the words "(a) to (g)".

(3) In section 122(2) of that Act (matters to which, so far as practicable, regard is to be had by local authorities in exercising their functions under the Act) after paragraph (b) there shall be inserted—

"(bb) the strategy prepared under section 80 of the Environment Act 1995 (national air quality strategy);".

The Control of Pollution (Amendment) Act 1989

37.—(1) The Control of Pollution (Amendment) Act 1989 shall be amended in accordance with the following provisions of this paragraph.

(2) In section 2 (registration of carriers)—

(a) in subsection (3), without prejudice to the power of regulation authorities to impose a charge in respect of their consideration of any such application, paragraph (e) (power to require them to impose such charges) shall cease to have effect; and

(b) after that subsection there shall be added—

"(3A) Without prejudice to the generality of paragraphs (b) and (d) of subsection (3) above—

(a) the power to prescribe a form under paragraph (b) of that subsection includes power to require an application to be made on any form of any description supplied for the purpose by the regulation authority to which the application is to be made; and

(b) the power to impose requirements with respect to information under paragraph (d) of that subsection includes power to make provision requiring an application to be accompanied by such information as may reasonably be required by the regulation authority to which it is to be made."

(3) In section 4 (appeals to the Secretary of State against refusal of registration etc.) after subsection (8) there shall be added—

"(9) This section is subject to section 114 of the Environment Act 1995 (delegation or reference of appeals etc)."

(4) In section 6 (seizure and disposal of vehicles used for illegal waste disposal) for subsection (6) there shall be substituted—

"(6) Regulations under this section shall not authorise a regulation authority to sell or destroy any property or to deposit any property at any place unless—

(a) the following conditions are satisfied, that is to say—

(i) the authority have published such notice, and taken such other steps (if any), as may be prescribed for informing persons who may be entitled to the property that it has been seized and is available to be claimed; and

(ii) the prescribed period has expired without any obligation arising under the regulations for the regulation authority to return the property to any person; or

(b) the condition of the property requires it to be disposed of without delay."

(5) In section 7 (further enforcement provisions) in subsection (1) (which applies certain provisions of the Environmental Protection Act 1990) for the words "sections 68(3), (4) and (5), 69, 70 and 71" there shall be substituted the words "section 71".

(6) Subsection (2) of that section (disclosure of information between certain authorities) shall cease to have effect.

(7) Subsection (8) of that section (which applies section 72 of the 1990 Act) shall cease to have effect.

(8) In section 9, for the definition of "regulation authority" there shall be substituted—

"regulation authority" means—

(a) in relation to England and Wales, the Environment Agency; and

(b) in relation to Scotland, the Scottish Environment Protection Agency;

and any reference to the area of a regulation authority shall accordingly be construed as a reference to any area in England and Wales or, as the case may be, in Scotland;".

The Electricity Act 1989

38.—(1) Section 3 of the Electricity Act 1989 (general duties of the Secretary of State and the Director General of Electricity Supply when exercising certain functions) shall be amended in accordance with the following provisions of this paragraph.

(2) In subsection (1)(c) (duty, subject to subsection (2), to promote competition), for the words "subsection (2)" there shall be substituted the words "subsections (2) and (2A)".

(3) After subsection (2) (duties as regards the supply of electricity in Scotland in certain cases) there shall be inserted—

"(2A) If an order under section 32(1) below requires a public electricity supplier to make, or produce evidence showing that he has made, arrangements or additional arrangements which will secure the result mentioned in subsection (2B) below, the order, so far as relating to any such requirement, may be made for the purpose of, or for purposes which include, promoting the supply to any premises of—

  (a) heat produced in association with electricity, or
  (b) steam produced from, or air or water heated by, such heat.

(2B) The result referred to in subsection (2A) above is that, for a period specified in the order, there will be available to the public electricity supplier—

  (a) from combined heat and power stations; or
  (b) from combined heat and power stations of any particular description,

an aggregate amount of generating capacity which is not less than that specified in relation to him in the order.

(2C) In subsection (2B) above, "combined heat and power station" has the meaning given by section 32(8) below.".

(4) In subsection (3) (further duties), for the words "and (2)" there shall be substituted the words ", (2) and (2A)".

39.—(1) Section 32 of that Act (electricity from non-fossil fuel sources) shall be amended in accordance with the following provisions of this paragraph.

(2) After subsection (2) (result to be secured by arrangements made pursuant to an order under subsection (1)) there shall be inserted—

  "(2A) For the purposes of this section—

  (a) combined heat and power stations generally; and
  (b) combined heat and power stations of any particular description,

are to be taken as being particular descriptions of non-fossil fuel generating stations.

(2B) A particular description of combined heat and power stations may be described by reference to, or by reference to matters which include—

  (a) the heat or, as the case may be, the steam or heated air or water to be supplied from the station to any premises;
  (b) any premises to which any such heat, steam or heated air or water is to be supplied (including, without prejudice to the generality of the foregoing, the use to which any such premises are put);
  (c) the means or method by which any such heat, steam or heated air or water is to be supplied to any premises (including, without prejudice to the generality of the fore-going, any system or network of supply or distribution); or
  (d) the arrangements (including financial or contractual arrangements) under which any such heat, steam or heated air or water is to be supplied to any premises.

(2C) Subsections (2A) and (2B) above are without prejudice to—

  (a) the generality of subsection (2)(b) above, or
  (b) section 111(2) below;

and subsection (2B) above is without prejudice to the generality of subsection (2A)(b) above.".

(3) In subsection (8) (interpretation), after the definition of "coal products" there shall be inserted—

  "combined heat and power station" means a non-fossil fuel generating station which is (or may be) operated for purposes including the supply to any premises of—

  (a) heat produced in association with electricity, or
  (b) steam produced from, or air or water heated by, such heat;".

40. In Schedule 4 to that Act (other powers etc. of licence holders) in paragraph 4(1)(b) (power for certain bodies to execute works involving alterations of electric lines or plant) for the words "National Rivers Authority" there shall be substituted the words "Environment Agency".

41. In Schedule 5 to that Act (water rights) in paragraph 8(b) for the words "river purification authority within whose area the watercourse or loch affected is situated" there shall be substituted the words "Scottish Environment Protection Agency".

The Town and Country Planning Act 1990

42. In section 2 of the Town and Country Planning Act 1990 (joint planning boards for National Parks and other areas) after subsection (6) there shall be inserted—

  "(6A) Section 241 of the Local Government Act 1972 shall be taken to authorise the application to a joint planning board, subject to any necessary modifications, of any provisions of Part III (accounts and audit) of the Local Government Finance Act 1982 (as well as of any provisions of the Local Government Act 1972) by such an order as is mentioned in subsection (6) above."

43. In Schedule 5 to that Act (conditions relating to mineral working) in paragraph 4 (consultations) after sub-paragraph (4) there shall be inserted—

"(4A) Without prejudice to the application of this paragraph in relation to consultation with the Forestry Commission, where the Minister is consulted pursuant to any provision of this paragraph—

(a) he is not required to inspect any land or to express a view on any matter or question; and

(b) he is not precluded from responding in general terms or otherwise in terms which are not specific to the land in question.".

44. In Schedule 6 to that Act (determination of certain appeals by person appointed by the Secretary of State) in paragraph 1(1) (power, in respect of appeals under certain provisions, to prescribe classes of appeals to be determined by an appointed person instead of by the Secretary of State), after "208," there shall be inserted "and paragraphs 6(11) and (12) and 11(1) of Schedule 13 and paragraph 9(1) of Schedule 14 to the Environment Act 1995,".

The Environmental Protection Act 1990

45.—(1) Section 1 of the Environmental Protection Act 1990 (interpretation of Part I) shall be amended in accordance with the following provisions of this paragraph.

(2) In subsection (7) (definition of "enforcing authority" in relation to England and Wales), for the words "the chief inspector or the local authority by whom" there shall be substituted the words "the Environment Agency or the local authority by which".

(3) For subsection (8) (definition of "enforcing authority" in relation to Scotland) there shall be substituted—

"(8) In relation to Scotland, references to the "enforcing authority" and a "local enforcing authority" are references to the Scottish Environment Protection Agency (in this Part referred to as "SEPA")."

(4) After subsection (13) there shall be added—

"(14) In this Part "the appropriate Agency" means—

(a) in relation to England and Wales, the Environment Agency; and

(b) in relation to Scotland, SEPA."

46.—(1) Section 4 of that Act (determination of authority by whom functions are exercisable) shall be amended in accordance with the following provisions of this paragraph.

(2) In subsection (2) (functions of the chief inspector etc in relation to prescribed processes designated for central control) for the words "the chief inspector appointed for England and Wales by the Secretary of State under section 16 below and, in relation to Scotland, of the chief inspector so appointed for Scotland or of the river purification authority, as determined under regulations made under section 5(1) below" there shall be substituted the words "the appropriate Agency".

(3) In subsection (3) (discharge of functions designated for local control) for paragraphs (a) and (b) there shall be substituted—

"(a) in the case of a prescribed process carried on (or to be carried on) by means of a mobile plant, where the person carrying on the process has his principal place of business—

(i) in England and Wales, the local authority in whose area that place of business is;

(ii) in Scotland, SEPA;

(b) in any other cases, where the prescribed processes are (or are to be) carried on—

(i) in England and Wales, the local authority in whose area they are (or are to be) carried on;

(ii) in Scotland, SEPA;".

(4) In subsection (4) (directions transferring functions to the chief inspector) for the words "the chief inspector" there shall be substituted the words "the Environment Agency".

(5) After that subsection there shall be inserted—

"(4A) In England and Wales, a local authority, in exercising the functions conferred or imposed on it under this Part by virtue of subsection (3) above, shall have regard to the strategy for the time being published pursuant to section 80 of the Environment Act 1995."

(6) In subsection (5) (effect of such a transfer)—

(a) for the words "the chief inspector" there shall be substituted the words "the Environment Agency"; and

(b) for the word "him" there shall be substituted the words "that Agency".

(7) In subsection (8) (giving or withdrawal of directions)—

(a) for the words "the chief inspector" in each place where they occur there shall be substituted the words "the Environment Agency"; and

(b) the words "or, as the case may be, in the Edinburgh Gazette", in each place where they occur, shall be omitted.

(8) After subsection (8) there shall be inserted—

"(8A) The requirements of sub-paragraph (ii) of paragraph (a) or, as the case may be, of paragraph (b) of subsection (8) above shall not apply in any case where, in the opinion of the Secretary of State, the publication of notice in accordance with that sub-paragraph would be contrary to the interests of national security.

(8B) Subsections (4) to (8A) above shall not apply to Scotland."

(9) For subsection (9) (which, among other things, imposed a duty on the chief inspector etc. to follow developments in technology etc and which is partly superseded by this Act) there shall be substituted—

"(9) It shall be the duty of local authorities to follow such developments in technology and techniques for preventing or reducing pollution of the environment due to releases of substances from prescribed processes as concern releases into the air of substances from prescribed processes designated for local control."

(10) In subsection (10) (duty of chief inspector etc to give effect to directions) for the words "the chief inspector, river purification authorities" there shall be substituted the words "the Environment Agency, SEPA".

(11) In subsection (11) (meaning of "local authority")—

(a) at the beginning of paragraph (b) there shall be inserted the words "in England and Wales," and

(b) paragraph (c) and the word "and" immediately preceding it shall cease to have effect.

47. Section 5 of that Act (further provision for Scotland as to discharge and scope of functions) shall cease to have effect.

48. In section 6 of that Act, in subsection (2) (fee payable on application for authorisation) after the words "shall be accompanied by" there shall be inserted—

"(a) in a case where, by virtue of section 41 of the Environment Act 1995, a charge prescribed by a charging scheme under that section is required to be paid to the appropriate Agency in respect of the application, the charge so prescribed; or

(b) in any other case,".

49.—(1) In section 7 of that Act (conditions of authorisations) in subsection (9) the words from "and, in relation to Scotland," to the end of the subsection shall be omitted.

(2) At the end of subsection (12) of that section (definition of "relevant enactments" for the purposes of subsection (2)) there shall be added "; and

(g) section 87 of the Environment Act 1995.".

50.—(1) Section 8 of that Act (fees and charges for authorisations) shall be amended in accordance with the following provisions of this paragraph.

(2) In subsection (1) (payments to be charged by, or paid to, the enforcing authority in accordance with schemes), for the words "enforcing authority" there shall be substituted the words "local enforcing authority".

(3) Subsection (4) (separate schemes for different descriptions of enforcing authority) shall cease to have effect.

(4) In subsection (7) (meaning of "relevant expenditure attributable to authorisations")—

(a) for the words "enforcing authorities" there shall be substituted the words "local enforcing authorities"; and

(b) the words from "together with the expenditure incurred by the National Rivers Authority" onwards shall be omitted.

(5) In subsection (8) (power to revoke authorisation for non-payment of charge), for the words "enforcing authority" there shall be substituted the words "local enforcing authority.

(6) Subsection (9) (payments by the Secretary of State to the National Rivers Authority) shall cease to have effect.

(7) For subsections (10) and (11) (special provision as respects Scotland) there shall be substituted—

"(10) The foregoing provisions of this section shall not apply to Scotland."

51.—(1) Section 10 of that Act (variation of authorisations by enforcing authority) shall be amended in accordance with the following provisions of this paragraph.

(2) In subsection (3) (which provides for the variation specified in a variation notice to take effect on the date so specified unless the notice is withdrawn) after the words "unless the notice is withdrawn" there shall be inserted the words "or is varied under subsection (3A) below".

(3) After that subsection there shall be inserted—

"(3A) An enforcing authority which has served a variation notice may vary that notice by serving on the holder of the authorisation in question a further notice—

(a) specifying the variations which the enforcing authority has decided to make to the variation notice; and

(b) specifying the date or dates on which the variations specified in the variation notice, as varied by the further notice, are to take effect;

and any reference in this Part to a variation notice, or to a variation notice served under subsection (2) above, includes a reference to such a notice as varied by a further notice served under this subsection."

(4) In subsection (4) of that section, for paragraph (b) (requirement to pay the fee prescribed under section 8 of that Act) there shall be substituted—

"(b) require the holder to pay, within such period as may be specified in the notice,—

(i) in a case where the enforcing authority is the Environment Agency or SEPA, the charge (if any) prescribed for the purpose by a charging scheme under section 41 of the Environment Act 1995; or

(ii) in any other case, the fee (if any) prescribed by a scheme under section 8 above."

(5) In subsection (8) of that section, in the definition of "vary", after the word " "vary" " there shall be inserted "(a)" and after the words "any of them;" there shall be added the words "and

(b) in relation to a variation notice, means adding to, or varying or rescinding the notice or any of its contents;".

52. In section 11 of that Act (application by holders of authorisations for variation of conditions etc) for subsection (9) (fees) there shall be substituted—

"(9) Any application to the enforcing authority under this section shall be accompanied—

(a) in a case where the enforcing authority is the Environment Agency or SEPA, by the charge (if any) prescribed for the purpose by a charging scheme under section 41 of the Environment Act 1995; or

(b) in any other case, by the fee (if any) prescribed by a scheme under section 8 above."

53. At the end of section 13 of that Act (enforcement notices) there shall be added—

"(4) The enforcing authority may, as respects any enforcement notice it has issued to any person, by notice in writing served on that person, withdraw the notice."

54.—(1) Section 15 of that Act (appeals against certain authorisations and notices) shall be amended in accordance with the following provisions of this paragraph.

(2) In subsection (2) (appeals against variation notices, enforcement notices or prohibition notices to the Secretary of State) after the words "to the Secretary of State" there shall be added the words "(except where the notice implements a direction of his)."

(3) For subsection (3) (reference of matters involved in appeals under that section to, and determination of such appeals by, persons appointed by the Secretary of State) there shall be substituted—

"(3) This section is subject to section 114 of the Environment Act 1995 (delegation or reference of appeals etc)."

(4) For subsection (5) (hearings) there shall be substituted—

"(5) Before determining an appeal under this section, the Secretary of State may, if he thinks fit—

(a) cause the appeal to take or continue in the form of a hearing (which may, if the person hearing the appeal so decides, be held, or held to any extent, in private); or

(b) cause a local inquiry to be held;

and the Secretary of State shall act as mentioned in paragraph (a) or (b) above if a request is made by either party to the appeal to be heard with respect to the appeal."

(5) In subsection (10) (regulations about appeals) after paragraph (b) there shall be added—

"and any such regulations may make different provision for different cases or different circumstances."

55. Sections 16 to 18 of that Act (appointment of inspectors, powers of inspectors and others and power to deal with cause of imminent danger of serious harm) shall cease to have effect.

56. In section 19 of that Act (obtaining of information from persons and authorities) in subsection (2) (power of specified authorities by notice in writing to require provision of information)—

(a) for paragraphs (c) and (d) (the chief inspector and river purification authorities) there shall be substituted—

"(c) the Environment Agency, and

(d) SEPA,"; and

(b) after the words "service of the notice" there shall be inserted the words ", or at such time,".

57.—(1) Section 20 of that Act (public registers of information) shall be amended in accordance with the following provisions of this paragraph.

(2) In subsection (2) (local registers also to contain prescribed particulars of relevance to the area which are contained in central registers) after the word "authority", where it first occurs,

there shall be inserted the words "in England and Wales" and for the words "the chief inspector or river purification authority", in each place where they occur, there shall be substituted the words "the Environment Agency".

(3) Subsection (3) (registers in Scotland) shall cease to have effect.

(4) In subsection (4) (port health authorities) after the word "authority" where it first occurs there shall be inserted the words "in England and Wales" and for the words "the chief inspector" there shall be substituted the words "the Environment Agency".

(5) In subsection (7) (registers to be available for inspection by, and facilities for obtaining copies of entries to be afforded to, the public) after paragraph (b) there shall be added the words—

"and, for the purposes of this subsection, places may be prescribed by the Secretary of State at which any such registers or facilities as are mentioned in paragraph (a) or (b) above are to be available or afforded to the public in pursuance of the paragraph in question."

(6) Subsection (9) (duty to furnish the National Rivers Authority with information for purposes of its register) shall cease to have effect.

58.—(1) Section 22 of that Act (exclusion from registers of certain confidential information) shall be amended in accordance with the following provisions of this paragraph.

(2) In subsection (5) (information not to be entered on the register until expiration of certain time limits)—

(a) in paragraph (a), for the words "on the register" there shall be substituted the words "in the register"; and

(b) in the words following paragraph (b), for the words from "on the register" onwards there shall be substituted the words "in the register until the end of the period of seven days following the day on which the appeal is finally determined or withdrawn".

(3) For subsection (6) (which applies subsections (3), (5) and (10) of section 15 in relation to appeals to the Secretary of State against decisions that information is not commercially confidential) there shall be substituted—

"(6) Subsections (5) and (10) of section 15 above shall apply in relation to an appeal under subsection (5) above as they apply in relation to an appeal under that section, but—

(a) subsection (5) of that section shall have effect for the purposes of this subsection with the substitution for the words from "(which may" onwards of the words "(which must be held in private)"; and

(b) subsection (5) above is subject to section 114 of the Environment Act 1995 (delegation or reference of appeals etc)."

59.—(1) Section 23 of that Act (offences) shall be amended in accordance with the following provisions of this paragraph.

(2) In subsection (1) (offences) paragraphs (d) to (f) and (k) shall cease to have effect.

(3) In subsection (2)(a) (which provides for a fine not exceeding £20,000 on summary conviction of any offence under section 23(1)(a), (c) or (l)) after the words "£20,000" there shall be inserted the words "or to imprisonment for a term not exceeding three months, or to both".

(4) Subsection (4) (punishment for offences under paragraph (d), (e), (f) or (k) of subsection (1)) shall cease to have effect.

(5) Subsection (5) (right of inspector to prosecute before a magistrates' court if authorised to do so by the Secretary of State) shall cease to have effect.

60.—(1) In section 27 of that Act (power of chief inspector etc to remedy harm) in subsection (1), for the words "the chief inspector or, in Scotland, a river purification authority" there shall be substituted the words "the appropriate Agency".

(2) In subsection (2) of that section (powers not to be exercised without the Secretary of State's written approval) for the words from "The chief inspector" to "their" there shall be substituted the words "The Environment Agency or SEPA, as the case may be, shall not exercise its".

61.—(1) In section 28 of that Act, in subsection (1) (which includes provision that the enforcing authority shall notify the waste regulation authority if a process involves final disposal of controlled waste by deposit in or on land) the words from "but the enforcing authority shall notify" onwards shall cease to have effect.

(2) Subsections (3) and (4) of that section (which involve liaison between the enforcing authority and the National Rivers Authority) shall cease to have effect.

62.—(1) Section 30 of that Act (authorities for purposes of Part II) shall be amended in accordance with the following provisions of this paragraph.

(2) For subsection (1) (waste regulation authorities) there shall be substituted—

"(1) Any reference in this Part to a waste regulation authority—

(a) in relation to England and Wales, is a reference to the Environment Agency; and

(b) in relation to Scotland, is a reference to the Scottish Environment Protection Agency;

and any reference in this Part to the area of a waste regulation authority shall accordingly be taken as a reference to the area over which the Environment Agency or the Scottish Environment Protection Agency, as the case may be, exercises its functions or, in the case of any particular function, the function in question."

(3) In subsection (4) of that section (construction of references to authorities constituted as particular descriptions of authority and provision for the section to be subject to orders under section 10 of the Local Government Act 1985 establishing authorities for certain purposes)—

(a) the words "or regulation", and

(b) the words from "establishing authorities" onwards,

shall cease to have effect.

(4) Subsections (6) (definition of "river purification authority"), (7) and (8) (which relate to authorities which are both waste disposal and waste regulation authorities) shall cease to have effect.

63. Section 31 of that Act (power to create regional authorities for purposes of waste regulation) shall cease to have effect.

64. In section 33 of that Act (prohibition on unauthorised or harmful deposit, treatment or disposal etc of waste) in subsection (7) (defences) for paragraph (c) there shall be substituted—

"(c) that the acts alleged to constitute the contravention were done in an emergency in order to avoid danger to human health in a case where—

(i) he took all such steps as were reasonably practicable in the circumstances for minimising pollution of the environment and harm to human health; and

(ii) particulars of the acts were furnished to the waste regulation authority as soon as reasonably practicable after they were done."

65. In section 34 of that Act (duty of care etc as respects waste), after subsection (3) (which specifies the persons who are authorised persons for the purposes of subsection (1)(c)) there shall be inserted—

"(3A) The Secretary of State may by regulations amend subsection (3) above so as to add, whether generally or in such circumstances as may be prescribed in the regulations, any person specified in the regulations, or any description of person so specified, to the persons who are authorised persons for the purposes of subsection (1)(c) above."

66.—(1) Section 35 of that Act (waste management licences: general) shall be amended in accordance with the following provisions of this paragraph.

(2) After subsection (7) there shall be inserted—

"(7A) In any case where—

(a) an entry is required under this section to be made in any record as to the observance of any condition of a licence, and

(b) the entry has not been made,

that fact shall be admissible as evidence that that condition has not been observed.

(7B) Any person who—

(a) intentionally makes a false entry in any record required to be kept under any condition of a licence, or

(b) with intent to deceive, forges or uses a licence or makes or has in his possession a document so closely resembling a licence as to be likely to deceive,

shall be guilty of an offence.

(7C) A person guilty of an offence under subsection (7B) above shall be liable—

(a) on summary conviction, to a fine not exceeding the statutory maximum;

(b) on conviction on indictment, to a fine or to imprisonment for a term not exceeding two years, or to both."

67. After section 35 of that Act there shall be inserted—

"Compensation where rights granted pursuant to section 35(4) or 38(9A)

35A.—(1) This section applies in any case where—

(a) the holder of a licence is required—

(i) by the conditions of the licence; or

(ii) by a requirement imposed under section 38(9) below,

to carry out any works or do any other thing which he is not entitled to carry out or do;

(b) a person whose consent would be required has, pursuant to the requirements of section 35(4) above or 38(9A) below, granted, or joined in granting, to the holder of the licence any rights in relation to any land; and

(c) those rights, or those rights together with other rights, are such as will enable the holder of the licence to comply with any requirements imposed on him by the licence or, as the case may be, under section 38(9) below.

(2) In a case where this section applies, any person who has granted, or joined in granting, the rights in question shall be entitled to be paid compensation under this section by the holder of the licence.

(3) The Secretary of State shall by regulations provide for the descriptions of loss and damage for which compensation is payable under this section.

(4) The Secretary of State may by regulations—

(a) provide for the basis on which any amount to be paid by way of compensation under this section is to be assessed;

(b) without prejudice to the generality of subsection (3) and paragraph (a) above, provide for compensation under this section to be payable in respect of—

(i) any effect of any rights being granted, or

(ii) any consequence of the exercise of any rights which have been granted;

(c) provide for the times at which any entitlement to compensation under this section is to arise or at which any such compensation is to become payable;

(d) provide for the persons or bodies by whom, and the manner in which, any dispute—

(i) as to whether any, and (if so) how much and when, compensation under this section is payable; or

(ii) as to the person to or by whom it shall be paid,

is to be determined;

(e) provide for when or how applications may be made for compensation under this section;

(f) without prejudice to the generality of paragraph (d) above, provide for when or how applications may be made for the determination of any such disputes as are mentioned in that paragraph;

(g) without prejudice to the generality of paragraphs (e) and (f) above, prescribe the form in which any such applications as are mentioned in those paragraphs are to be made;

(h) make provision similar to any provision made by paragraph 8 of Schedule 19 to the Water Resources Act 1991;

(j) make different provision for different cases, including different provision in relation to different persons or circumstances;

(k) include such incidental, supplemental, consequential or transitional provision as the Secretary of State considers appropriate.".

68.—(1) Section 36 of that Act (grant of licences) shall be amended in accordance with the following provisions of this paragraph.

(2) In subsection (1) (making of applications) for the words following paragraph (b) there shall be substituted—

"and shall be made on a form provided for the purpose by the waste regulation authority and accompanied by such information as that authority reasonably requires and the charge prescribed for the purpose by a charging scheme under section 41 of the Environment Act 1995.

(1A) Where an applicant for a licence fails to provide the waste regulation authority with any information required under subsection (1) above, the authority may refuse to proceed with the application, or refuse to proceed with it until the information is provided."

(3) In subsection (4) (reference of proposals to, and consideration of representations made by, other bodies)—

(a) in paragraph (a), for the words "the National Rivers Authority" there shall be substituted the words "the appropriate planning authority", and

(b) in paragraph (b), for the word "Authority" there shall be substituted the word "authority".

(4) Subsections (5) (reference by National Rivers Authority to the Secretary of State) and (6) (which makes provision for Scotland in place of subsection (4)) shall cease to have effect.

(5) After subsection (9) (application deemed to be rejected if not granted or refused within four months from being received) there shall be inserted—

"(9A) Subsection (9) above—

(a) shall not have effect in any case where, by virtue of subsection (1A) above, the waste regulation authority refuses to proceed with the application in question, and

(b) shall have effect in any case where, by virtue of subsection (1A) above, the waste regulation authority refuses to proceed with it until the required information is provided, with the substitution for the period of four months there mentioned of the period of four months beginning with the date on which the authority received the information."

(6) For subsection (10) (period of 21 days allowed for bodies to make representations) there shall be substituted—

"(10) The period allowed to the appropriate planning authority, the Health and Safety Executive or the appropriate nature conservancy body for the making of representations under subsection (4) or (7) above about a proposal is the period of twenty-eight days beginning with the day on which the proposal is received by the waste regulation authority or such longer period as the waste regulation authority, the appropriate planning authority, the Executive or the body, as the case may be, agree in writing.

(11) In this section—

"the appropriate planning authority" means—

(a) where the relevant land is situated in the area of a London borough council, that London borough council;

(b) where the relevant land is situated in the City of London the Common Council of the City of London;

(c) where the relevant land is situated in a non-metropolitan county in England, the council of that county;

(d) where the relevant land is situated in a National Park or the Broads, the National Park authority for that National Park or, as the case may be, the Broads Authority;

(e) where the relevant land is situated elsewhere in England or Wales, the council of the district or, in Wales, the county or county borough, in which the land is situated;

(f) where the relevant land is situated in Scotland, the council constituted under section 2 of the Local Government etc. (Scotland) Act 1994 for the area in which the land is situated;

"the Broads" has the same meaning as in the Norfolk and Suffolk Broads Act 1988;

"National Park authority", subject to subsection (12) below, means a National Park authority established under section 63 of the Environment Act 1995 which has become the local planning authority for the National Park in question;

"the relevant land" means—

(a) in relation to a site licence, the land to which the licence relates; and

(b) in relation to a mobile plant licence, the principal place of business of the operator of the plant to which the licence relates.

(12) As respects any period before a National Park authority established under section 63 of the Environment Act 1995 in relation to a National Park becomes the local planning authority for that National Park, any reference in this section to a National Park authority shall be taken as a reference to the National Park Committee or joint or special planning board for that National Park.

(13) The Secretary of State may by regulations amend the definition of "appropriate planning authority" in subsection (11) above.

(14) This section shall have effect subject to section 36A below."

69. After section 36 of that Act there shall be inserted—

"Consultation before the grant of certain licences

36A.—(1) This section applies where an application for a licence has been duly made to a waste regulation authority, and the authority proposes to issue a licence subject (by virtue of section 35(4) above) to any condition which might require the holder of the licence to—

(a) carry out any works, or

(b) do any other thing,

which he might not be entitled to carry out or do.

(2) Before issuing the licence, the waste regulation authority shall serve on every person appearing to the authority to be a person falling within subsection (3) below a notice which complies with the requirements set out in subsection (4) below.

(3) A person falls within this subsection if—

(a) he is the owner, lessee or occupier of any land; and

(b) that land is land in relation to which it is likely that, as a consequence of the licence being issued subject to the condition in question, rights will have to be granted by virtue of section 35(4) above to the holder of the licence.

(4) A notice served under subsection (2) above shall—

(a) set out the condition in question;

(b) indicate the nature of the works or other things which that condition might require the holder of the licence to carry out or do; and

(c) specify the date by which, and the manner in which, any representations relating to the condition or its possible effects are to be made to the waste regulation authority by the person on whom the notice is served.

(5) The date which, pursuant to subsection (4)(c) above, is specified in a notice shall be a date not earlier than the date on which expires the period—

(a) beginning with the date on which the notice is served, and

(b) of such length as may be prescribed in regulations made by the Secretary of State.

(6) Before the waste regulation authority issues the licence it must, subject to subsection (7) below, consider any representations made in relation to the condition in question, or its possible effects, by any person on whom a notice has been served under subsection (2) above.

(7) Subsection (6) above does not require the waste regulation authority to consider any representations made by a person after the date specified in the notice served on him under subsection (2) above as the date by which his representations in relation to the condition or its possible effects are to be made.

(8) In subsection (3) above—

"owner", in relation to any land in England and Wales, means the person who—

(a) is for the time being receiving the rack–rent of the land, whether on his own account or as agent or trustee for another person; or

(b) would receive the rack-rent if the land were let at a rack-rent,

but does not include a mortgagee not in possession; and

"owner", in relation to any land in Scotland, means a person (other than a creditor in a heritable security not in possession of the security subjects) for the time being entitled to receive or who would, if the land were let, be entitled to receive, the rents of the land in connection with which the word is used and includes a trustee, factor, guardian or curator and in the case of public or municipal land includes the persons to whom the management of the land is entrusted.".

70.—(1) In section 37 of that Act (variation of licences) in subsection (1)(b) (which requires an application to be accompanied by the prescribed fee) for the words "the prescribed fee payable under section 41 below," there shall be substituted the words "the charge prescribed for the purpose by a charging scheme under section 41 of the Environment Act 1995,".

(2) In subsection (5) of that section (which applies certain provisions of section 36) the words "(5), (6)," and "(8)" shall be omitted.

(3) After subsection (6) of that section (cases where an application for modification is deemed to have been rejected) there shall be added—

"(7) This section shall have effect subject to section 37A below."

71. After section 37 of that Act there shall be inserted—

"Consultation before certain variations

37A.—(1) This section applies where—

(a) a waste regulation authority proposes to modify a licence under section 37(1) or (2)(a) above; and

(b) the licence, if modified as proposed, would be subject to a relevant new condition.

(2) For the purposes of this section, a "relevant new condition" is any condition by virtue of which the holder of the licence might be required to carry out any works or do any other thing—

(a) which he might not be entitled to carry out or do, and

(b) which he could not be required to carry out or do by virtue of the conditions to which, prior to the modification, the licence is subject.

(3) Before modifying the licence, the waste regulation authority shall serve on every person appearing to the authority to be a person falling within subsection (4) below a notice which complies with the requirements set out in subsection (5) below.

(4) A person falls within this subsection if—

(a) he is the owner, lessee or occupier of any land; and

(b) that land is land in relation to which it is likely that, as a consequence of the licence being modified so as to be subject to the relevant new condition in question, rights will have to be granted by virtue of section 35(4) above to the holder of the licence.

(5) A notice served under subsection (3) above shall—

(a) set out the relevant new condition in question;

(b) indicate the nature of the works or other things which that condition might require the holder of the licence to carry out or do but which he could not be required to carry out or do by virtue of the conditions (if any) to which, prior to the modification, the licence is subject; and

(c) specify the date by which, and the manner in which any representations relating to the condition or its possible effects are to be made to the waste regulation authority by the person on whom the notice is served.

(6) The date which, pursuant to subsection (5)(c) above, is specified in a notice shall be a date not earlier than the date on which expires the period—

    (a) beginning with the date on which the notice is served, and

    (b) of such length as may be prescribed in regulations made by the Secretary of State.

(7) Before the waste regulation authority issues the licence it must, subject to subsection (8) below, consider any representations made in relation to the condition in question, or its possible effects, by any person on whom a notice has been served under subsection (3) above.

(8) Subsection (7) above does not require the waste regulation authority to consider any representations made by a person after the date specified in the notice served on him under subsection (3) above as the date by which his representations in relation to the condition or its possible effects are to be made.

(9) A waste regulation authority may postpone the service of any notice or the consideration of any representations required under the foregoing provisions of this section so far as the authority considers that by reason of an emergency it is appropriate to do so.

(10) In subsection (3) above, "owner" has the same meaning as it has in subsection (3) of section 36A above by virtue of subsection (8) of that section.".

72.—(1) In section 38 of that Act (revocation and suspension of licences) after subsection (9) (power to require certain measures to be taken where licence suspended) there shall be inserted—

    "(9A) A requirement imposed under subsection (9) above may require the holder of a licence to carry out works or do other things notwithstanding that he is not entitled to carry out the works or do the thing and any person whose consent would be required shall grant, or join in granting, the holder of the licence such rights in relation to the land as will enable the holder of the licence to comply with any requirements imposed on him under that subsection.

(9B) Subsections (2) to (8) of section 36A above shall, with the necessary modifications, apply where the authority proposes to impose a requirement under subsection (9) above which may require the holder of a licence to carry out any such works or do any such thing as is mentioned in subsection (9A) above as they apply where the authority proposes to issue a licence subject to any such condition as is mentioned in subsection (1) of that section, but as if—

    (a) the reference in subsection (3) of that section to section 35(4) above were a reference to subsection (9A) above; and

    (b) any reference in those subsections—

        (i) to the condition, or the condition in question, were a reference to the requirement; and

        (ii) to issuing a licence were a reference to serving a notice, under subsection (12) below, effecting the requirement.

(9C) The authority may postpone the service of any notice or the consideration of any representations required under section 36A above, as applied by subsection (9B) above, so far as the authority considers that by reason of an emergency it is appropriate to do so."

(2) After subsection (12) of that section (revocations and suspensions etc. to be effected by service of notice) there shall be added—

    "(13) If a waste regulation authority is of the opinion that proceedings for an offence under subsection (10) or (11) above would afford an ineffectual remedy against a person who has failed to comply with any requirement imposed under subsection (9) above, the authority may take proceedings in the High Court or, in Scotland, in any court of competent jurisdiction for the purpose of securing compliance with the requirement."

73.—(1) Section 39 of that Act (surrender of licences) shall be amended in accordance with the following provisions of this paragraph.

(2) In subsection (3) (application for surrender of a site licence) for the words from "in such form" onwards there shall be substituted the words "on a form provided by the authority for the purpose, giving such information and accompanied by such evidence as the authority reasonably requires and accompanied by the charge prescribed for the purpose by a charging scheme under section 41 of the Environment Act 1995."

(3) In subsection (7) (consideration of representations before accepting surrender of a licence)—

    (a) for the words "the National Rivers Authority" and "the Authority" there shall be substituted the words "the appropriate planning authority"; and

    (b) the words following paragraph (b) shall cease to have effect.

(4) Subsection (8) (which makes provision for Scotland in place of subsection (7)) shall cease to have effect.

(5) In subsection (11) (meaning of "the allowed period") for the words "subsections (7) and (8) above" there shall be substituted the words "subsection (7) above".

(6) After subsection (11) there shall be added—

"(12) In this section—

"the appropriate planning authority" means—

(a) where the relevant land is situated in the area of a London borough council, that London borough council;

(b) where the relevant land is situated in the City of London, the Common Council of the City of London;

(c) where the relevant land is situated in a non-metropolitan county in England, the council of that county;

(d) where the relevant land is situated in a National Park or the Broads, the National Park authority for that National Park or, as the case may be, the Broads Authority;

(e) where the relevant land is situated elsewhere in England or Wales, the council of the district or, in Wales, the county or county borough, in which the land is situated;

(f) where the relevant land is situated in Scotland, the council constituted under section 2 of the Local Government etc. (Scotland) Act 1994 for the area in which the land is situated;

"the Broads" has the same meaning as in the Norfolk and Suffolk Broads Act 1988;

"National Park authority", subject to subsection (13) below, means a National Park authority established under section 63 of the Environment Act 1995 which has become the local planning authority for the National Park in question;

"the relevant land", in the case of any site licence, means the land to which the licence relates.

(13) As respects any period before a National Park authority established under section 63 of the Environment Act 1995 in relation to a National Park becomes the local planning authority for that National Park, any reference in this section to a National Park authority shall be taken as a reference to the National Park Committee or joint or special planning board for that National Park.

(14) The Secretary of State may by regulations amend the definition of "appropriate planning authority" in subsection (12) above."

74. In section 40 of that Act (transfer of licences) in subsection (3) (mode of making application for transfer of licence) for the words from "in such form" to "section 41 below" there shall be substituted the words "on a form provided by the authority for the purpose, accompanied by such information as the authority may reasonably require, the charge prescribed for the purpose by a charging scheme under section 41 of the Environment Act 1995".

75. Section 41 of that Act (fees and charges for licences) shall cease to have effect.

76.—(1) Section 42 of that Act (supervision of licensed activities) shall be amended in accordance with the following provisions of this paragraph.

(2) Subsection (2) (consultation with the National Rivers Authority etc) shall cease to have effect.

(3) In subsection (4) (recovery of expenditure from the holder or, if it has been surrendered, the former holder of a licence) for the words "the holder of the licence or, if the licence has been surrendered, from the former holder of it" there shall be substituted the words "the holder, or (as the case may be) the former holder, of the licence".

(4) In subsection (5) (powers where it appears that a condition of a licence is not being complied with) after the words "is not being complied with" there shall be inserted the words "or is likely not to be complied with,".

(5) For paragraph (a) of that subsection there shall be substituted—

"(a) serve on the holder of the licence a notice—

(i) stating that the authority is of the opinion that a condition of the licence is not being complied with or, as the case may be, is likely not to be complied with;

(ii) specifying the matters which constitute the non-compliance or, as the case may be, which make the anticipated non-compliance likely;

(iii) specifying the steps which must be taken to remedy the non-compliance or, as the case may be, to prevent the anticipated non-compliance from occurring; and

(iv) specifying the period within which those steps must be taken; and".

(6) In paragraph (b) of that subsection (powers which become exercisable on non-compliance) for the words "has not complied with the condition within that time," there shall be substituted the words "has not taken the steps specified in the notice within the period so specified,".

(7) After subsection (6) (power to revoke or suspend a licence) there shall be inserted—

"(6A) If a waste regulation authority is of the opinion that revocation or suspension of the licence, whether entirely or to any extent, under subsection (6) above would afford an ineffectual remedy against a person who has failed to comply with any requirement imposed under subsection (5)(a) above, the authority may take proceedings in the High Court or, in Scotland, in any court of competent jurisdiction for the purpose of securing compliance with the requirement."

(8) In subsection (7) (application of certain provisions of section 38 to revocation or suspension of a licence)—

(a) for the words from "subsections (5)" to "38" there shall be substituted the words "subsections (5) and (12) or, as the case may be, subsections (8) to (12) of section 38"; and

(b) the words from "and the power" onwards shall cease to have effect.

77. In section 43 of that Act, in subsection (2), paragraphs (a) and (b) (reference of matters involved in appeals under that section to, and determination of such appeals by, persons appointed by the Secretary of State) shall cease to have effect and after that section there shall be inserted—

"(2A) This section is subject to section 114 of the Environment Act 1995 (delegation or reference of appeals etc)."

78. Section 50 of that Act (waste disposal plans of waste regulation authorities) shall cease to have effect.

79. Section 61 of that Act (duty of waste regulation authorities as respects closed landfills) shall cease to have effect.

80.—(1) Section 62 of that Act (special provision with respect to certain dangerous and intractable waste) shall be amended in accordance with the following provisions of this paragraph.

(2) In subsection (3), for paragraph (a) (regulations providing for the supervision of certain activities and the recovery of the costs from persons carrying on the activities) there shall be substituted—

"(a) for the supervision by waste regulation authorities—

(i) of activities authorised by virtue of the regulations or of activities by virtue of carrying on which persons are subject to provisions of the regulations, or

(ii) of persons who carry on activities authorised by virtue of the regulations or who are subject to provisions of the regulations,

and for the recovery from persons falling within sub-paragraph (ii) above of the costs incurred by waste regulation authorities in performing functions conferred upon those authorities by the regulations;".

(3) After that subsection (which also includes provision for regulations to provide for appeals to the Secretary of State) there shall be added—

"(3A) This section is subject to section 114 of the Environment Act 1995 (delegation or reference of appeals etc)."

81. In section 63 of that Act (waste other than controlled waste) for subsection (2) (offences relating to the deposit of waste which is not controlled waste but which, if it were such waste, would be special waste) there shall be substituted—

"(2) A person who deposits, or knowingly causes or knowingly permits the deposit of, any waste—

(a) which is not controlled waste, but

(b) which, if it were controlled waste, would be special waste,

in a case where he would be guilty of an offence under section 33 above if the waste were special waste and any waste management licence were not in force, shall, subject to subsection (3) below, be guilty of that offence and punishable as if the waste were special waste."

82.—(1) Section 64 of that Act (public registers) shall be amended in accordance with the following provisions of this paragraph.

(2) After subsection (2) there shall be inserted—

"(2A) The Secretary of State may give to a waste regulation authority directions requiring the removal from any register of its of any specified information not prescribed for inclusion under subsection (1) above or which, by virtue of section 65 or 66 below, ought to be excluded from the register."

(3) In subsection (4) (duty of waste collection authorities in England to maintain registers)—

(a) after the word "England" there shall be inserted the words "or Wales"; and

(b) the words "which is not a waste regulation authority" shall be omitted.

(4) For subsection (5) (waste regulation authorities in England to furnish information to waste collection authorities) there shall be substituted—

"(5) The waste regulation authority in relation to England and Wales shall furnish any waste collection authorities in its area with the particulars necessary to enable them to discharge their duty under subsection (4) above."

(5) In subsection (6) (registers to be available for inspection by, and facilities for obtaining copies of entries to be afforded to, the public)—

(a) after the words "waste collection authority" there shall be inserted "(a)";

(b) after the words "hours and" there shall be inserted "(b)"; and

(c) after the paragraph (b) so formed, there shall be added the words—

"and, for the purposes of this subsection, places may be prescribed by the Secretary of State at which any such registers or facilities as are mentioned in paragraph (a) or (b) above are to be available or afforded to the public in pursuance of the paragraph in question."

83.—(1) In section 66 of that Act (exclusion from registers of certain confidential information) in subsection (5) (information not to be entered on the register until expiration of certain time limits) in the words following paragraph (b), for the words from "pending" onwards there shall be substituted the words "until the end of the period of seven days following the day on which the appeal is finally determined or withdrawn".

(2) For subsection (6) (which applies section 43(2) and (8) to appeals to the Secretary of State against decisions that information is not commercially confidential) there shall be substituted—

"(6) Subsections (2) and (8) of section 43 above shall apply in relation to appeals under subsection (5) above as they apply in relation to appeals under that section; but

(a) subsection (2)(c) of that section shall have effect for the purposes of this subsection with the substitution for the words from "(which may" onwards of the words "(which must be held in private)"; and

(b) subsection (5) above is subject to section 114 of the Environment Act 1995 (delegation or reference of appeals etc)."

84. Section 67 of that Act (annual reports of waste regulation authorities) shall cease to have effect.

85. Sections 68 to 70 of that Act (functions of the Secretary of State and appointment etc of inspectors, powers of entry and power to deal with cause of imminent danger of serious pollution) shall cease to have effect.

86.—(1) In section 71 of that Act (obtaining of information from persons and authorities) subsection (1) (which is superseded by this Act) shall cease to have effect.

(2) In subsection (2) of that section (power by notice to require a person to furnish information within such period as may be specified in the notice) after the words "service of the notice" there shall be inserted the words ", or at such time,".

87. Section 72 of that Act (default powers of the Secretary of State) shall cease to have effect.

88.—(1) Section 75 of that Act (meaning of "waste" etc.) shall be amended in accordance with the following provisions of this paragraph.

(2) For subsection (2) (definition of "waste") there shall be substituted—

"(2) "Waste" means any substance or object in the categories set out in Schedule 2B to this Act which the holder discards or intends or is required to discard; and for the purposes of this definition—

"holder" means the producer of the waste or the person who is in possession of it; and

"producer" means any person whose activities produce waste or any person who carries out pre-processing, mixing or other operations resulting in a change in the nature or composition of this waste."

(3) Subsection (3) (presumption that anything discarded is waste unless the contrary is proved) shall cease to have effect.

(4) After subsection (9) there shall be added—

"(10) Schedule 2B to this Act (which reproduces Annex I to the Waste Directive) shall have effect.

(11) Subsection (2) above is substituted, and Schedule 2B to this Act is inserted, for the purpose of assigning to "waste" in this Part the meaning which it has in the Waste Directive by virtue of paragraphs (a) to (c) of Article 1 of, and Annex I to, that Directive, and those provisions shall be construed accordingly.

(12) In this section "the Waste Directive" means the directive of the Council of the European Communities, dated 15th July 1975, on waste, as amended by—

(a) the directive of that Council, dated 18th March 1991, amending directive 75/442/EEC on waste; and

(b) the directive of that Council, dated 23rd December 1991, standardising and rationalising reports on the implementation of certain Directives relating to the environment."

89.—(1) Section 79 of that Act (statutory nuisances) shall be amended in accordance with the following provisions of this paragraph.

(2) In subsection (1) (the paragraphs of which specify, subject to subsections (2) to (6A), the matters which constitute statutory nuisances) for the words "Subject to subsections (2) to (6A) below" there shall be substituted the words "Subject to subsections (1A) to (6A) below".

(3) After that subsection there shall be inserted—

"(1A) No matter shall constitute a statutory nuisance to the extent that it consists of, or is caused by, any land being in a contaminated state.

(1B) Land is in a "contaminated state" for the purposes of subsection (1A) above if, and only if, it is in such a condition, by reason of substances in, on or under the land, that—

(a) harm is being caused or there is a possibility of harm being caused; or

(b) pollution of controlled waters is being, or is likely to be, caused;

and in this subsection "harm", "pollution of controlled waters" and "substance" have the same meaning as in Part IIA of this Act.".

90. In section 141 of that Act (power to prohibit or restrict the importation or exportation of waste) subsection (5)(a)(ii) (power of Secretary of State by direction to make functions of certain authorities exercisable instead by him) shall cease to have effect.

91. Section 143 of that Act (public registers of land which may be contaminated) shall cease to have effect.

92. In section 161 of that Act (regulations and orders) in subsection (4) (which specifies the orders under that Act which are not subject to negative resolution procedure under subsection (3)) after the words "does not apply to" there shall be inserted the words "a statutory instrument—

(a) which contains an order under section 78M(4) above, or

(b) by reason only that it contains".

93.—(1) Schedule 1 to that Act (authorisations for processes: supplementary provisions) shall be amended in accordance with the following provisions of this paragraph.

(2) In Part I (grant of authorisations) in paragraph 3(3) (local inquiry or hearing to be held where request to be heard made by the applicant or the local enforcing authority) for the words "the local enforcing authority" there shall be substituted the words "the enforcing authority".

(3) In Part II (variation of authorisations) in paragraph 6, at the beginning of sub-paragraph (1) there shall be inserted the words "Except as provided by sub-paragraph (1A) below,".

(4) After that sub-paragraph there shall be inserted—

"(1A) The requirements of this paragraph shall not apply in relation to any variations of an authorisation which an enforcing authority has decided to make in consequence of representations made in accordance with this paragraph and which are specified by way of variation of a variation notice by a further notice under section 10(3A) of this Act."

(5) After paragraph 7 (applications for variation) there shall be inserted—

"Call in of applications for variation

8.—(1) The Secretary of State may give directions to the enforcing authority requiring that any particular application or any class of applications for the variation of an authorisation shall be transmitted to him for determination pending a further direction under sub-paragraph (5) below.

(2) The enforcing authority shall inform the applicant of the fact that his application is being transmitted to the Secretary of State.

(3) Where an application for the variation of an authorisation is referred to him under sub-paragraph (1) above the Secretary of State may—

(a) cause a local inquiry to be held in relation to the application; or

(b) afford the applicant and the authority concerned an opportunity of appearing before and being heard by a person appointed by the Secretary of State;

and he shall exercise one of the powers under this sub-paragraph in any case where, in the manner prescribed by regulations made by the Secretary of State, a request is made to be heard with respect to the application by the applicant or the enforcing authority concerned.

(4) Subsections (2) to (5) of section 250 of the Local Government Act 1972 (supplementary provisions about local inquiries under that section) or, in relation to Scotland, subsections (2) to (8) of section 210 of the Local Government (Scotland) Act 1973 (which make similar provision) shall without prejudice to the generality of subsection (1) of either of those sections, apply to local inquiries or other hearings in pursuance of sub-paragraph (3) above as they apply to inquiries in pursuance of either of those sections and, in relation to England and Wales, as if the reference to a local authority in subsection (4) of the said section 250 included a reference to the enforcing authority.

(5) The Secretary of State shall, on determining any application transferred to him under this paragraph, give to the enforcing authority such a direction as he thinks fit as to whether

it is to grant the application and, if so, as to the conditions that are to be attached to the authorisation by means of the variation notice.

9. The Secretary of State may give the enforcing authority a direction with respect to any particular application or any class of applications for the variation of an authorisation requiring the authority not to determine or not to proceed with the application or applications of that class until the expiry of any such period as may be specified in the direction, or until directed by the Secretary of State that they may do so, as the case may be.

10.—(1) Except in a case where an application for the variation of an authorisation has been referred to the Secretary of State under paragraph 8 above and subject to sub-paragraph (3) below, the enforcing authority shall determine an application for the variation of an authorisation within the period of four months beginning with the day on which it received the application or within such longer period as may be agreed with the applicant.

(2) If the enforcing authority fails to determine an application for the variation of an authorisation within the period allowed by or under this paragraph the application shall, if the applicant notifies the authority in writing that he treats the failure as such, be deemed to have been refused at the end of that period.

(3) The Secretary of State may, by order, substitute for the period for the time being specified in sub-paragraph (1) above such other period as he considers appropriate and different periods may be substituted for different classes of application."

94. In Schedule 2 to that Act (waste disposal authorities and companies) in paragraph 17(2) (which requires a waste regulation authority or waste disposal authority to furnish information on request to the Secretary of State) the words "a waste regulation authority or" shall cease to have effect.

95. After Schedule 2A to that Act there shall be inserted—

"Section 75   SCHEDULE 2B

CATEGORIES OF WASTE

1. Production or consumption residues not otherwise specified below.

2. Off-specification products.

3. Products whose date for appropriate use has expired.

4. Materials spilled, lost or having undergone other mishap, including any materials, equipment, etc, contaminated as a result of the mishap.

5. Materials contaminated or soiled as a result of planned actions (e.g. residues from cleaning operations, packing materials, containers, etc.).

6. Unusable parts (e.g. reject batteries, exhausted catalysts, etc.).

7. Substances which no longer perform satisfactorily (e.g. contaminated acids, contaminated solvents, exhausted tempering salts, etc.).

8. Residues of industrial processes (e.g. slags, still bottoms, etc.).

9. Residues from pollution abatement processes (e.g. scrubber sludges, baghouse dusts, spent filters, etc.).

10. Machining or finishing residues (e.g. lathe turnings, mill scales, etc.).

11. Residues from raw materials extraction and processing (e.g. mining residues, oil field slops, etc.).

12. Adulterated materials (e.g. oils contaminated with PCBs, etc.).

13. Any materials, substances or products whose use has been banned by law.

14. Products for which the holder has no further use (e.g. agricultural, household, office, commercial and shop discards, etc.).

15. Contaminated materials, substances or products resulting from remedial action with respect to land.

16. Any materials, substances or products which are not contained in the above categories."

The Natural Heritage (Scotland) Act 1991

96.—(1) The Natural Heritage (Scotland) Act 1991 shall be amended in accordance with the following provisions of this paragraph.

(2) In section 15—

(a) in subsection (2) for the words "a river purification authority, acting in pursuance of their duties under section 17(1) of the Rivers (Prevention of Pollution) (Scotland) Act 1951" there shall be substituted the words "SEPA acting in pursuance of its duties under section 34(1) of the Environment Act 1995";

(b) in subsection (3) for the words "said Act of" and "a river purification authority" where they first occur there shall be substituted the words "Rivers (Prevention of Pollution

(Scotland) Act" and "SEPA" respectively and the words "and a river purification authority of whom such a requirement is made shall make such an application" shall cease to have effect;

(c) for subsection (5) there shall be substituted—

"(5) A control area shall comprise an area or areas shown in a map or plan contained in the order."

(3) In section 17—

(a) in subsection (1) for the words "A river purification authority" there shall be substituted the words "SEPA";

(b) in subsection (3) for the words "A river purification authority", "their" in both places where it occurs, "they" and "the authority" there shall be substituted the words "SEPA", "its", "it" and "SEPA" respectively.

(4) In section 18—

(a) in subsection (1) for the words "a river purification authority" and "they" there shall be substituted the words "SEPA" and "it" respectively;

(b) in subsection (2) for the words "the river purification authority decide" there shall be substituted the words "SEPA decides";

(c) in subsection (3) for the words "a river purification authority" and "the authority" there shall be substituted the words "SEPA" and "it" respectively;

(d) in subsection (4) for the words "the river purification authority declare" there shall be substituted the words "SEPA declares";

(e) in subsection (5) for the words "A river purification authority" and "them" there shall be substituted the words "SEPA" and "it" respectively.

(5) In section 24—

(a) in subsection (1)—

(i) for the words "a river purification authority" there shall be substituted the words "SEPA"; and

(ii) in paragraph (a), after the word "on" there shall be inserted the words "SEPA or"; and

(b) in subsection (9)—

(i) for the words "a river purification authority or" there shall be substituted the words "SEPA or a"; and

(ii) in paragraph (a), after the word "by" where it second occurs there shall be inserted the words "SEPA or".

(6) After section 26 there shall be inserted—

"Meaning of SEPA

26A. In this Act "SEPA" means the Scottish Environment Protection Agency."

(7) In Schedule 5—

(a) in paragraph 1 for the words "the river purification authority concerned consider" there shall be substituted the words "SEPA considers";

(b) in paragraph 2 for the words "the river purification authority concerned" there shall be substituted the words "SEPA" and the words "in their area and" shall cease to have effect;

(c) in paragraph 3 for the words "the river purification authority" and "their" wherever they occur there shall be substituted the words "SEPA" and "its" respectively;

(d) in paragraphs 4 and 9 for the words "the river purification authority" wherever they occur there shall be substituted the words "SEPA".

(8) In Schedule 6—

(a) in paragraph 1—

(i) in sub-paragraph (1) for the words "the river purification authority" there shall be substituted the words "SEPA";

(ii) in sub-paragraph (2) for the words "A river purification authority", "them", "the authority" and "their" there shall be substituted respectively the words "SEPA", "it", "it" and "its" respectively;

(iii) in sub-paragraph (3) for the words "the river purification authority" there shall be substituted the words "SEPA";

(iv) in sub-paragraph (4) for the words "the river purification authority", "the authority fail" and "their" there shall be substituted the words "SEPA", "it fails" and "its" respectively;

(v) sub-paragraph (5) shall cease to have effect;

(vi) in sub-paragraph (6) for the words "the river purification authority to whom the application has been made" there shall be substituted the words "SEPA";

(b) in paragraph 2—

(i) in sub-paragraph (1) for the words "the river purification authority" wherever they occur there shall be substituted the words "SEPA";

    (ii) in sub-paragraphs (3) and (4) for the words "the river purification authority" wherever they occur there shall be substituted the words "SEPA";
    (iii) at the end there shall be added—

"(6) This paragraph is subject to section 114 of the Environment Act 1995 (delegation or reference of appeals etc).";

  (c) in paragraph 3—
    (i) in sub-paragraph (1) for the words "A river purification authority" there shall be substituted the words "SEPA";
    (ii) in sub-paragraph (2) for the words "A river purification authority" and "they are" there shall be substituted the words "SEPA" and "it is" respectively;
    (iii) in sub-paragraph (4) for the words "the river purification authority" there shall be substituted the words "SEPA";
    (iv) in sub-paragraph (5) for the words "the river purification authority" and "them" there shall be substituted the words "SEPA" and "it" respectively;
    (v) in sub-paragraph (6) for the words "the authority fail to intimate their" and "the river purification authority" there shall be substituted the words "SEPA fails to intimate its" and "SEPA" respectively;
  (d) in paragraph 4 for the words "A river purification authority" and "them" there shall be substituted the words "SEPA" and "it" respectively;
  (e) in paragraph 5(2) for the words "the river purification authority" there shall be substituted the words "SEPA".

(9) In Schedule 8, in paragraph 1—
  (a) for sub-paragraph (1) there shall be substituted—

"(1) Before making an application for a drought order, the applicant shall consult—
  (a) SEPA, in a case where notice of the application is required to be served on it under this paragraph; and
  (b) any district salmon fishery board on whom notice of the application is required to be served under this paragraph.";

  (b) in sub-paragraph (3), in the second column of the Table, in the fourth entry (relating to orders concerning the taking of water from a source or the discharge of water to a place), in paragraph (a) the words ", river purification authority" shall cease to have effect and at the end there shall be added—
    "(c) SEPA";
  (c) in sub-paragraph (3), in the second column of the Table, in the fifth entry (relating to orders which authorise the execution of any works) for the words "every river purification authority and" there shall be substituted the words "SEPA and every".

The Water Industry Act 1991

97. In section 3 of the Water Industry Act 1991 (general environmental and recreational duties) in subsection (4) (which imposes duties on the Director and relevant undertakers in relation to proposals relating to functions of the National Rivers Authority etc) for the words "the NRA", in each place where they occur, there shall be substituted the words "the Environment Agency".

98. In section 5 of that Act (codes of practice with respect to environmental duties) in subsection (4), in paragraph (a) (which requires consultation with the National Rivers Authority) for the words "the NRA" there shall be substituted the words "the Environment Agency".

99. In section 40 of that Act (bulk supplies of water) in subsection (5) (which requires the Director to consult the National Rivers Authority before making an order) for the words "the NRA" there shall be substituted the words "the Environment Agency".

100. In section 40A of that Act (variation and termination of bulk supply agreements) in subsection (3) (which requires the Director to consult the National Rivers authority before making an order) for the words "the NRA" there shall be substituted the words "the Environment Agency".

101.–(1) In section 71 of that Act (waste from water resources) in subsection (6) (power of court to authorise the National Rivers Authority to take steps to execute an order) for the words "the NRA" there shall be substituted—
  (a) where it first occurs, the words "the Environment Agency"; and
  (b) where it next occurs, the words "the Agency".

(2) In subsection (7) (powers of entry etc of persons designated by the National Rivers Authority) for the words "the NRA" in each place where it occurs there shall be substituted the words "the Environment Agency".

102. After section 93 of that Act (interpretation of Part III) there shall be inserted—

"Part IIIA

Promotion of the Efficient Use of Water

Duty to promote the efficient use of water

93A.—(1) It shall be the duty of every water undertaker to promote the efficient use of water by its customers.

(2) The duty of a water undertaker under this section shall be enforceable under section 18 above—

(a) by the Secretary of State; or

(b) with the consent of or in accordance with a general authorisation given by the Secretary of State, by the Director.

(3) Nothing in this Part shall have effect to authorise or require a water undertaker to impose any requirement on any of its customers or potential customers.

Power of Director to impose requirements on water undertakers

93B.—(1) The Director may require a water undertaker, in its performance of its duty under section 93A above, to—

(a) take any such action; or

(b) achieve any such overall standards of performance,

as he may specify in the document imposing the requirement.

(2) Where the Director, in the document imposing a requirement on a water undertaker under subsection (1) above, stipulates that any contravention of the requirement by the undertaker will be a breach of its duty under section 93A above, any contravention of that requirement by the undertaker shall be a breach of that duty.

(3) Without prejudice to the generality of subsection (1) above, a requirement under that subsection may—

(a) require a water undertaker to make available to its customers or potential customers such facilities as may be specified in the document imposing the requirement;

(b) require a water undertaker to provide or make available to its customers or potential customers such information as may be specified in the document imposing the requirement, and may specify the form in which, the times at which or the frequency with which any such information is to be provided or made available.

(4) In exercising his powers under this section in relation to any water undertaker the Director shall have regard to the extent to which water resources are available to that undertaker.

(5) Before imposing any requirement on a water undertaker under subsection (1) above the Director shall consult that undertaker.

(6) Nothing in this section authorises the Director to impose any requirement on a water undertaker which has or may have the effect of authorising or requiring that undertaker to impose any requirement on any of its customers or potential customers.

Publicity of requirements imposed under section 93B

93C.—(1) Where, under section 93B(1) above, the Director imposes any requirement on a water undertaker, the Director may arrange for that requirement to be publicised in any such manner as he may consider appropriate for the purpose of bringing it to the attention of that undertaker's customers.

(2) Without prejudice to the generality of subsection (1) above, the Director may arrange for such publicising of the requirement as is mentioned in that subsection by—

(a) himself publicising the requirement or causing it to be publicised; or

(b) directing the undertaker to inform or arrange to inform its customers of the requirement.

Information as to compliance with requirements under section 93B

93D.—(1) Where a water undertaker is subject to any requirement imposed under section 93B(1) above, the Director may arrange for there to be given to the customers of that undertaker at any such times or with such frequency, and in any such manner, as he may consider appropriate, such information about the level of performance achieved by the undertaker in relation to that requirement as appears to the Director to be expedient to be given to those customers.

(2) Without prejudice to the generality of subsection (1) above, the Director may arrange for such giving of information as is mentioned in that subsection by—

(a) himself disseminating the information or causing it to be disseminated; or

(b) directing the undertaker to give or arrange to give the information to its customers.

(3) At such times and in such form or manner as the Director may direct, a water undertaker shall provide the Director with such information as may be specified in the direction in connection with the undertaker's performance in relation to any requirement imposed upon the undertaker under section 93B(1) above.

(4) A water undertaker who fails without reasonable excuse to do anything required of him by virtue of subsection (3) above shall be guilty of an offence and liable on summary conviction to a fine not exceeding level 5 on the standard scale.".

103. After section 101 of that Act (which provides for the determination of certain details in relation to requisitioned sewers) there shall be inserted—

"Provision of public sewers otherwise than by requisition

Further duty to provide sewers

101A.—(1) Without prejudice to section 98 above, it shall be the duty of a sewerage undertaker to provide a public sewer to be used for the drainage for domestic sewerage purposes of premises in a particular locality in its area if the conditions specified in subsection (2) below are satisfied.

(2) The conditions mentioned in subsection (1) above are—

(a) that the premises in question, or any of those premises, are premises on which there are buildings each of which, with the exception of any shed, glasshouse or other outbuilding appurtenant to a dwelling and not designed or occupied as living accommodation, is a building erected before, or whose erection was substantially completed by, 20th June 1995;

(b) that the drains or sewers used for the drainage for domestic sewerage purposes of the premises in question do not, either directly or through an intermediate drain or sewer, connect with a public sewer; and

(c) that the drainage of any of the premises in question in respect of which the condition specified in paragraph (a) above is satisfied is giving, or is likely to give, rise to such adverse effects to the environment or amenity that it is appropriate, having regard to any guidance issued under this section by the Secretary of State and all other relevant considerations, to provide a public sewer for the drainage for domestic sewerage purposes of the premises in question.

(3) Without prejudice to the generality of subsection (2)(c) above, regard shall be had to the following considerations, so far as relevant, in determining whether it is appropriate for any sewer to be provided by virtue of this section—

(a) the geology of the locality in question or of any other locality;

(b) the number of premises, being premises on which there are buildings, which might reasonably be expected to be drained by means of that sewer;

(c) the costs of providing that sewer;

(d) the nature and extent of any adverse effects to the environment or amenity arising, or likely to arise, as a result of the premises or, as the case may be, the locality in question not being drained by means of a public sewer; and

(e) the extent to which it is practicable for those effects to be overcome otherwise than by the provision (whether by virtue of this section or otherwise) of public sewers, and the costs of so overcoming those effects.

(4) Guidance issued by the Secretary of State under this section may—

(a) relate to how regard is to be had to the considerations mentioned in paragraphs (a) to (e) of subsection (3) above;

(b) relate to any other matter which the Secretary of State considers may be a relevant consideration in any case and to how regard is to be had to any such matter;

(c) set out considerations, other than those mentioned in paragraphs (a) to (e) of subsection (3) above, to which (so far as relevant) regard shall be had in determining whether it is appropriate for any sewer to be provided by virtue of this section;

(d) relate to how regard is to be had to any such consideration as is mentioned in paragraph (c) above;

(e) without prejudice to paragraphs (a) to (d) above, relate to how a sewerage undertaker is to discharge its functions under this section.

(5) Before issuing guidance under this section the Secretary of State shall consult—

(a) the Environment Agency;

(b) the Director; and

(c) such other bodies or persons as he considers appropriate;

and the Secretary of State shall arrange for any guidance issued by him under this section to be published in such manner as he considers appropriate.

(6) Subject to the following provisions of this section, the duty of a sewerage undertaker by virtue of subsection (1) above shall be enforceable under section 18 above—

(a) by the Secretary of State: or

(b) with the consent of or in accordance with a general authorisation given by the Secretary of State, by the Director.

(7) Any dispute between a sewerage undertaker and an owner or occupier of any premises in its area as to—

(a) whether the undertaker is under a duty by virtue of subsection (1) above to provide a public sewer to be used for any such drainage of those premises as is mentioned in that subsection;

(b) the domestic sewerage purposes for which any such sewer should be provided; or

(c) the time by which any such duty of the undertaker should be performed,

shall be determined by the Environment Agency, and may be referred to the Environment Agency for determination by either of the parties to the dispute.

(8) The Environment Agency—

(a) shall notify the parties of the reasons for its decision on any dispute referred to it under subsection (7) above; and

(b) may make any such recommendations, or give any such guidance, relating to or in connection with the drainage of the premises or locality in question as it considers appropriate.

(9) The decision of the Environment Agency on any dispute referred to it under subsection (7) above shall be final.

(10) A sewerage undertaker shall only be taken to be in breach of its duty under subsection (1) above where, and to the extent that, it has accepted, or the Environment Agency has determined under this section, that it is under such a duty and where any time accepted by it, or determined by the Environment Agency under this section, as the time by which the duty is to that extent to be performed has passed.".

104. In section 110A of that Act (new connections with public sewers) in subsection (6) (which requires the Director to consult the National Rivers Authority before making an order) for the words "the NRA" there shall be substituted the words "the Environment Agency".

105.—(1) Section 120 of that Act (application for the discharge of special category effluent) shall be amended in accordance with the following provisions of this paragraph.

(2) In subsection (1) (sewerage undertakers to refer certain questions to the Secretary of State) for the words "the Secretary of State" there shall be substituted the words "the Environment Agency".

(3) In subsection (4) (undertaker not to give consent etc until Secretary of State gives notice of his determination of the questions) for the words "the Secretary of State" there shall be substituted the words "the Environment Agency".

(4) For subsections (7) and (8) (enforcement by Secretary of State) there shall be substituted—

"(9) If a sewerage undertaker fails, within the period provided by subsection (2) above, to refer to the Environment Agency any question which he is required by subsection (1) above to refer to the Agency, the undertaker shall be guilty of an offence and liable—

(a) on summary conviction, to a fine not exceeding the statutory maximum;

(b) on conviction on indictment, to a fine.

(10) If the Environment Agency becomes aware of any such failure as is mentioned in subsection (9) above, the Agency may—

(a) if a consent under this Chapter to make discharges of any special category effluent has been granted on the application in question, exercise its powers of review under section 127 or 131 below, notwithstanding anything in subsection (2) of the section in question; or

(b) in any other case, proceed as if the reference required by this section had been made."

106. In section 123 of that Act (appeals with respect to the discharge of special category effluent) for the words "the Secretary of State" or "the Secretary of State's", wherever occurring, there shall be substituted respectively the words "the Environment Agency" or "the Environment Agency's".

107. In section 127 of that Act (review by the Secretary of State of consents relating to special category effluent) for the words "the Secretary of State" or "the Secretary of State's", wherever occurring, there shall be substituted respectively the words "the Environment Agency" or "the Environment Agency's".

108.—(1) Section 130 of that Act (reference to the Secretary of State of agreements relating to special category effluent) shall be amended in accordance with the following provisions of this paragraph.

(2) For the words "the Secretary of State", wherever occurring, there shall be substituted the words "the Environment Agency".

(3) For subsections (5) and (6) (enforcement by Secretary of State) there shall be substituted—

"(7) If a sewerage undertaker fails, before giving any consent or entering into any agreement with respect to any such operations as are mentioned in paragraph (a) of subsection (1) above, to refer to the Environment Agency any question which he is required by that subsection to refer to the Agency, the undertaker shall be guilty of an offence and liable—

(a) on summary conviction, to a fine not exceeding the statutory maximum;

(b) on conviction on indictment, to a fine.

(8) If the Environment Agency becomes aware—

(a) that a sewerage undertaker and the owner or occupier of any trade premises are proposing to enter into any such agreement as is mentioned in subsection (1) above, and

(b) that the sewerage undertaker has not referred to the Agency any question which it is required to refer to the Agency by that subsection,

the Agency may proceed as if the reference required by that subsection had been made.

(9) If the Environment Agency becomes aware that any consent has been given or agreement entered into with respect to any such operations as are mentioned in paragraph (a) of subsection (1) above without the sewerage undertaker in question having referred to the Environment Agency any question which he is required by that subsection to refer to the Agency, the Agency may exercise its powers of review under section 127 above or, as the case may be, section 131 below, notwithstanding anything in subsection (2) of the section in question."

109. In section 131 of that Act (review by the Secretary of State of agreements relating to special category effluent) for the words "the Secretary of State" or "the Secretary of State's", wherever occurring, there shall be substituted respectively the words "the Environment Agency" or "the Environment Agency's".

110.–(1) Section 132 of that Act (powers and procedure on references and reviews) shall be amended in accordance with the following provisions of this paragraph.

(2) For the words "the Secretary of State", wherever occurring, there shall be substituted the words "the Environment Agency".

(3) In subsection (2)(b) of that section (duty of the Secretary of State to consider representations or objections duly made to him) for the words "him" and "he" there shall be substituted the words "the Agency".

(4) In subsection (6) of that section (section 121(1) and (2) not to restrict power to impose conditions under subsection (4)(b)) for the word "he" there shall be substituted the words "the Agency".

(5) Subsection (7) (powers of entry) shall cease to have effect.

111. In section 133 of that Act (effect of determination on reference or review) for subsection (4) (duties of sewerage undertaker to be enforceable under section 18 by the Secretary of State) there shall be substituted—

"(5) A sewerage undertaker which fails to perform its duty under subsection (1) above shall be guilty of an offence and liable—

(a) on summary conviction, to a fine not exceeding the statutory maximum;

(b) on conviction on indictment, to a fine.

(6) The Environment Agency may, for the purpose of securing compliance with the provisions of a notice under section 132 above, by serving notice on the sewerage undertaker in question and on the person specified in section 132(2)(a)(ii) above, vary or revoke—

(a) any consent given under this Chapter to make discharges of any special category effluent, or

(b) any agreement under section 129 above."

112. In section 134 of that Act (compensation in respect of determinations made for the protection of public health etc.)—

(a) for the words "the Secretary of State" or "the Secretary of State's", wherever occurring, there shall be substituted respectively the words "the Environment Agency" or "the Environment Agency's"; and

(b) in subsection (2)(b) for the word "him" there shall be substituted the words "the Agency".

113. After section 135 there shall be inserted—

"Power of the Environment Agency to acquire information for the purpose of its functions in relation to special category effluent

135A.—(1) For the purpose of the discharge of its functions under this Chapter, the Environment Agency may, by notice in writing served on any person, require that person to furnish such information specified in the notice as that Agency reasonably considers it needs, in such form and within such period following service of the notice, or at such time, as is so specified.

(2) A person who—
(a) fails, without reasonable excuse, to comply with a requirement imposed under sub-section (1) above, or
(b) in furnishing any information in compliance with such a requirement, makes any statement which he knows to be false or misleading in a material particular, or reck-lessly makes a statement which is false or misleading in a material particular,
shall be guilty of an offence.
(3) A person guilty of an offence under subsection (2) above shall be liable—
(a) on summary conviction, to a fine not exceeding the statutory maximum;
(b) on conviction on indictment, to a fine or to imprisonment for a term not exceeding two years, or to both."

114.—(1) Section 142 of that Act (powers of undertakers to charge) shall be amended in accordance with the following provisions of this paragraph.
(2) In subsection (2) (manner in which charging powers to be exercised) for the words "sub-section (3)" there shall be substituted the words "subsections (3) and (3A)".
(3) After subsection (3) (restriction on charging by agreement for trade effluent functions) there shall be inserted—
"(3A) The power of a sewerage undertaker to charge, by virtue of subsection (1) above, for any services provided in the course of carrying out its duty under section 101A(1) above shall be exercisable only by or in accordance with a charges scheme under section 143 below."

115. In section 143 of that Act (charges schemes) after subsection (3) (charges which may be imposed in certain cases) there shall be inserted—
"(3A) A sewerage undertaker is under a duty to ensure that any charges scheme made by the undertaker, so far as having effect to recover the undertaker's costs of providing a sewer by virtue of its duty under section 101A(1) above, causes those costs to be borne by the undertaker's customers generally; and a sewerage undertaker's duty under this subsection shall be enforceable under section 18 above—
(a) by the Secretary of State; or
(b) with the consent of or in accordance with a general authorisation given by the Sec-retary of State, by the Director."

116. Section 151 of that Act shall cease to have effect.

117. In section 161 of that Act (power to deal with foul water and pollution) in subsections (3) and (4) for the words "the NRA", wherever occurring, there shall be substituted the words "the Environment Agency".

118. In section 166 of that Act (consents for certain discharges under section 165) in subsec-tion (1) (which requires the consent of the National Rivers Authority to certain discharges) for the words "the NRA" there shall be substituted the words "the Environment Agency".

119. In section 184 of that Act (power of certain undertakers to alter public sewers etc) in subsection (1) for the words "NRA", in each place where it occurs there shall be substituted the words "Environment Agency".

120. In section 202 of that Act (duties of undertakers to furnish the Secretary of State with information) in subsection (6) (which defines the expression "the other consolidation Acts") for the words "the NRA" there shall be substituted the words "the Environment Agency".

121.—(1) In section 206 of that Act (restriction on disclosure of information) in subsection (2) (information furnished under section 196 or 204) the words "196 or" shall cease to have effect.
(2) In subsection (3)(a) of that section (exception for disclosure of information for purposes of functions under certain enactments)—
(a) for the words "the NRA" there shall be substituted the words "the Environment Agency, the Scottish Environment Protection Agency"; and
(b) for the words "or the Water Act 1989" there shall be substituted the words ", the Water Act 1989, Part I or IIA of the Environmental Protection Act 1990 or the Environment Act 1995".
(3) In subsection (4), in paragraph (a) (which provides that nothing in subsection (1) shall limit the matters which may be included in reports made by specified bodies under specified enactments)—
(a) for the words "the NRA" there shall be substituted the words "the Environment Agency, the Scottish Environment Protection Agency"; and
(b) for the words "or of the Water Resources Act 1991" there shall be substituted the words ", Part I or IIA of the Environmental Protection Act 1990, the Water Resources Act 1991 or the Environment Act 1995".

122. In section 209 of that Act (civil liability of undertakers for escapes of water etc) in subsec-tion (3) (exceptions for loss sustained by other public undertakers) for the words "the NRA" there shall be substituted the words "the Environment Agency".

123. In section 215 of that Act (local inquiries) in subsection (3) (application of section 250(4) of the Local Government Act 1972 in relation to the National Rivers Authority) for the words "the NRA", in each place where they occur, there shall be substituted the words "the Environment Agency".

124. In section 217 of that Act (construction of provisions conferring powers by reference to undertakers' functions) for the words "NRA", wherever occurring, there shall be substituted the words "Environment Agency".

125. In section 219 of that Act (general interpretation) in subsection (1)—
(a) the definition of "the NRA" shall be omitted; and
(b) subject to that, for the words "the NRA", wherever occurring, there shall be substituted the words "the Environment Agency".

126. In Schedule 11 to that Act (orders conferring compulsory works powers) in paragraph 1(3) (persons on whom copy notices are to be served) in paragraph (a), for the words "the NRA" there shall be substituted the words "the Environment Agency".

127. In Schedule 13 to that Act (protective provisions in respect of certain undertakers) in paragraph 1, in sub-paragraphs (2) and (5)(a), for the words "the NRA", wherever occurring, there shall be substituted the words "the Environment Agency".

The Water Resources Act 1991

128. Subject to the other provisions of this Act, in the Water Resources Act 1991, for the word "Authority" or "Authority's", wherever occurring, other than in section 119(1), there shall be substituted respectively the word "Agency" or "Agency's".

129. Sections 1 to 14 of that Act (the National Rivers Authority and committees with functions in relation to that Authority) shall cease to have effect.

130. In section 15 of that Act (general duties with respect to the water industry), in subsection (2)(a) (provisions conferring powers in the exercise of which the Ministers are to take into account the duties imposed on the Agency by subsection (1)) after the words "by virtue of" there shall be inserted the words "the 1995 Act,".

131. Sections 16 to 19 of that Act (which relate to the environmental and recreational duties of the National Rivers Authority and the general management of resources by that Authority) shall cease to have effect.

132. In section 20 of that Act (water resources management schemes) in subsection (1) of that section (duty to enter into arrangements with water undertakers for the management or operation of certain waters etc) for the words "section 19(1) above" there shall be substituted the words "section 6(2) of the 1995 Act".

133.—(1) In section 21 of that Act (minimum acceptable flows) in subsection (3), at the end of paragraph (f) (consultation with person authorised by a licence under Part I of the Electricity Act 1989 to generate electricity) there shall be added the words "who has a right to abstract water from those waters".

(2) In subsection (4)(b) of that section (which refers to certain enactments which are repealed, but whose effect is reproduced, by this Act) for the words "sections 2(2), 16 and 17 above" there shall be substituted the words "sections 6(1), 7 and 8 of the 1995 Act".

134. In section 43 of that Act (appeals to the Secretary of State from decisions with respect to licences) after subsection (1) there shall be inserted—
"(1A) This section is subject to section 114 of the 1995 Act (delegation or reference of appeals etc)."

135.—(1) In section 50 of that Act, in subsection (1) (power to make regulations, in relation to cases to which section 49 applies, for conferring succession rights to abstraction licences where a person becomes the occupier of part of the relevant land) for the words "cases to which section 49 above applies" there shall be substituted the words "cases in which the holder of a licence under this Chapter to abstract water ("the prior holder") is the occupier of the whole or part of the land specified in the licence as the land on which water abstracted in pursuance of the licence is to be used ("the relevant land")".

(2) That section shall have effect, and be taken always to have had effect, as if it had originally been enacted with the amendment made by sub-paragraph (1) above.

136. Section 58 (revocation of licence for non-payment of charges) shall cease to have effect.

137. Section 68 of that Act (power by order to establish a tribunal to which certain appeals and references shall lie) shall cease to have effect.

138. Section 69(5) of that Act (which refers to the tribunal established under section 68) shall cease to have effect.

139.—(1) Section 73 of that Act (power to make ordinary and emergency drought orders) shall be amended in accordance with the following provisions of this paragraph.

(2) In subsection (1) (power to make ordinary drought orders) for the words from the beginning to "then" there shall be substituted the words—

"(1) If the Secretary of State is satisfied that, by reason of an exceptional shortage of rain, there exists or is threatened—
(a) a serious deficiency of supplies of water in any area, or
(b) such a deficiency in the flow or level of water in any inland waters as to pose a serious threat to any of the flora or fauna which are dependent on those waters,
then,".

(3) In subsection (3) (power to make drought order not to be exercisable except where an application is made by the National Rivers Authority or a water undertaker)—
(a) for the words "except where" there shall be substituted the word "unless"; and
(b) at the beginning of paragraph (b) (water undertakers) there shall be inserted the words "except in the case of an ordinary drought order by virtue of subsection (1)(b) above,".

140. After section 79 of that Act (compensation and charges where drought order made) there shall be inserted—

"Drought permits

79A.—(1) If the Agency is satisfied that, by reason of an exceptional shortage of rain, a serious deficiency of supplies of water in any area exists or is threatened then, subject to the following provisions of this section, it may, upon the application of a water undertaker which supplies water to premises in that area, issue to that undertaker a drought permit making such provision authorised by this section as appears to the Agency to be expedient with a view to meeting the deficiency.

(2) A drought permit may contain any of the following provisions, that is to say—
(a) provision authorising the water undertaker to which it is issued to take water from any source specified in the permit subject to any conditions or restrictions so specified;
(b) provision suspending or modifying, subject to any conditions specified in the permit, any restriction or obligation to which that undertaker is subject as respects the taking of water from any source.

(3) A drought permit shall specify—
(a) the day on which it comes into force; and
(b) the period for which, subject to subsections (4) and (5) below, any authorisation given, or suspension or modification effected, by the permit is to have effect.

(4) Subject to subsection (5) below, the period for which—
(a) an authorisation given by a drought permit, or
(b) a suspension or modification effected by such a permit,
has effect shall expire before the end of the period of six months beginning with the day on which the permit comes into force.

(5) At any time before the expiration of the period for which such an authorisation, suspension or modification has effect the Agency may, by giving notice to the water undertaker to which the permit in question was issued, extend that period, but not so as to extend it beyond the end of the period of one year beginning with the day on which the permit came into force.

(6) A drought permit which—
(a) authorises the taking of water from a source from which water is supplied to an inland navigation; or
(b) suspends or modifies—
(i) a restriction as respects the taking of water from a source from which water is supplied to an inland navigation; or
(ii) an obligation to discharge compensation water into a canal or into any river or stream which forms part of, or from which water is supplied to, an inland navigation,
shall not be issued without the consent of every navigation authority exercising functions over any or all of the parts of the canal or inland navigation in question which are affected by the permit.

(7) Schedule 8 to this Act shall have effect with respect to the procedure on an application for a drought permit as it has effect with respect to the procedure on an application for a drought order, but with the following modifications, that is to say—
(a) with the substitution for any reference to a drought order of a reference to a drought permit;
(b) with the substitution for any reference to the Secretary of State of a reference to the Agency;
(c) with the omission of the reference to the Agency in the Table in paragraph 1;
(d) with the insertion, in paragraph 1(3)(c), of a requirement that the notice in question shall specify the address at which any objections are to be made to the Agency; and
(e) with the omission—
(i) of paragraph 2(1)(a) and the word "either" immediately preceding it, and

(ii) of paragraph 2(6).

(8) For the purposes of sections 125 to 129 below any water authorised by a drought permit to be abstracted from a source of supply shall be treated as if it had been authorised to be so abstracted by a licence granted under Chapter II of this Part whether the water undertaker to which the permit is issued is the holder of such a licence or not.

(9) Section 79 above and Schedule 9 to this Act shall apply in relation to drought permits and their issue as they apply in relation to ordinary drought orders and their making.

(10) A drought permit may—

(a) make different provision for different cases, including different provision in relation to different persons, circumstances or localities; and

(b) contain such supplemental, consequential and transitional provisions as the Agency considers appropriate.

(11) In this section—

"compensation water" has the same meaning as in section 77 above;

"drought permit" means a drought permit under this section;

"inland navigation" has the same meaning as in section 77 above."

141. In section 80 of that Act (offences against drought orders)—

(a) in subsection (1)(a) (taking or using water otherwise than in accordance with any condition or restriction imposed by or under a drought order) for the words "so imposed" there shall be substituted the words "imposed by or under any drought order or by any drought permit";

(b) in subsection (2)(a) (failure to construct or maintain measuring apparatus required by any drought order) after the words "by any drought order" there shall be inserted the words "or drought permit"; and

(c) in subsection (2)(b) (failure to allow person authorised by or under any such order to inspect etc apparatus or records) after the words "by or under any such order" there shall be inserted the words "or by virtue of any such permit".

142. After section 90 of that Act (offences in connection with deposits and vegetation in rivers) there shall be inserted—

"Consents for the purposes of sections 88 to 90

Applications for consent under section 89 or 90

90A.—(1) Any application for a consent for the purposes of section 89(4)(a) or 90(1) or (2) above—

(a) must be made on a form provided for the purpose by the Agency, and

(b) must be advertised in such manner as may be required by regulations made by the Secretary of State,

except that paragraph (b) above shall not have effect in the case of an application of any class or description specified in the regulations as being exempt from the requirements of that paragraph.

(2) The applicant for such a consent must, at the time when he makes his application, provide the Agency—

(a) with all such information as it reasonably requires; and

(b) with all such information as may be prescribed for the purpose by the Secretary of State.

(3) The information required by subsection (2) above must be provided either on, or together with, the form mentioned in subsection (1) above.

(4) The Agency may give the applicant notice requiring him to provide it with all such further information of any description specified in the notice as it may require for the purpose of determining the application.

(5) If the applicant fails to provide the Agency with any information required under subsection (4) above, the Agency may refuse to proceed with the application or refuse to proceed with it until the information is provided.

Enforcement notices

90B.—(1) If the Agency is of the opinion that the holder of a relevant consent is contravening any condition of the consent, or is likely to contravene any such condition, the Agency may serve on him a notice (an "enforcement notice").

(2) An enforcement notice shall—

(a) state that the Agency is of the said opinion;

(b) specify the matters constituting the contravention or the matters making it likely that the contravention will arise;

(c) specify the steps that must be taken to remedy the contravention or, as the case may be, to remedy the matters making it likely that the contravention will arise; and

(d) specify the period within which those steps must be taken.

(3) Any person who fails to comply with any requirement imposed by an enforcement notice shall be guilty of an offence and liable—

(a) on summary conviction, to imprisonment for a term not exceeding three months or to a fine not exceeding £20,000 or to both;

(b) on conviction on indictment, to imprisonment for a term not exceeding two years or to a fine or to both.

(4) If the Agency is of the opinion that proceedings for an offence under subsection (3) above would afford an ineffectual remedy against a person who has failed to comply with the requirements of an enforcement notice, the Agency may take proceedings in the High Court for the purpose of securing compliance with the notice.

(5) The Secretary of State may, if he thinks fit in relation to any person, give to the Agency directions as to whether the Agency should exercise its powers under this section and as to the steps which must be taken.

(6) In this section—

"relevant consent" means—

(a) a consent for the purposes of section 89(4)(a) or 90(1) or (2) above; or

(b) a discharge consent, within the meaning of section 91 below; and

"the holder", in relation to a relevant consent, is the person who has the consent in question."

143.—(1) In section 91 of that Act (appeals in respect of consents under Chapter II of Part III of that Act), in subsection (1) (which specifies the decisions which are subject to appeal)—

(a) in paragraph (d) (which refers to paragraph 7(1) or (2) of Schedule 10) for the words "7(1)" there shall be substituted the words "8(1)"; and

(b) at the end there shall be added—

"(g) has refused a person a variation of any such consent as is mentioned in paragraphs (a) to (f) above or, in allowing any such variation, has made the consent subject to conditions; or

(h) has served an enforcement notice on any person."

(2) In subsection (2) of that section (persons who may appeal)—

(a) after the words "who applied for the consent" there shall be inserted the words "or variation"; and

(b) after the words "would be authorised by the consent" there shall be inserted the words ", or the person on whom the enforcement notice was served,".

(3) For subsections (3) to (7) of that section there shall be substituted—

"(2A) This section is subject to section 114 of the 1995 Act (delegation or reference of appeals etc).

(2B) An appeal under this section shall, if and to the extent required by regulations under subsection (2K) below, be advertised in such manner as may be prescribed by regulations under that subsection.

(2C) If either party to the appeal so requests or the Secretary of State so decides, an appeal shall be or continue in the form of a hearing (which may, if the person hearing the appeal so decides, be held, or held to any extent, in private).

(2D) On determining an appeal brought by virtue of any of paragraphs (a) to (g) of subsection (1) above against a decision of the Agency, the Secretary of State—

(a) may affirm the decision;

(b) where the decision was a refusal to grant a consent or a variation of a consent, may direct the Agency to grant the consent or to vary the consent, as the case may be;

(c) where the decision was as to the conditions of a consent, may quash all or any of those conditions;

(d) where the decision was to revoke a consent, may quash the decision;

(e) where the decision relates to a period specified for the purposes of paragraph 8(1) or (2) of Schedule 10 to this Act, may modify any provisions specifying that period;

and where he exercises any of the powers in paragraphs (b), (c) or (d) above, he may give directions as to the conditions to which the consent is to be subject.

(2E) On the determination of an appeal brought by virtue of paragraph (h) of subsection (1) above, the Secretary of State may either quash or affirm the enforcement notice and, if he affirms it, may do so either in its original form or with such modifications as he may in the circumstances think fit.

(2F) Subject to subsection (2G) below, where an appeal is brought by virtue of subsection (1)(c) above against a decision—

(a) to revoke a discharge consent,

(b) to modify the conditions of any such consent, or

(c) to provide that any such consent which was unconditional shall be subject to conditions,

the revocation, modification or provision shall not take effect pending the final determination or the withdrawal of the appeal.

(2G) Subsection (2F) above shall not apply to a decision in the case of which the notice effecting the revocation, modification or provision in question includes a statement that in the opinion of the Agency it is necessary for the purpose of preventing or, where that is not practicable, minimising—

(a) the entry into controlled waters of any poisonous, noxious or polluting matter or any solid waste matter, or

(b) harm to human health,

that that subsection should not apply.

(2H) Where the decision under appeal is one falling within subsection (2G) above, if, on the application of the holder or former holder of the consent, the Secretary of State or other person determining the appeal determines that the Agency acted unreasonably in excluding the application of subsection (2F) above, then—

(a) if the appeal is still pending at the end of the day on which the determination is made, subsection (2F) above shall apply to the decision from the end of that day; and

(b) the holder or former holder of the consent shall be entitled to recover compensation from the Agency in respect of any loss suffered by him in consequence of the exclusion of the application of that subsection;

and any dispute as to a person's entitlement to such compensation or as to the amount of it shall be determined by arbitration.

(2J) Where an appeal is brought under this section against an enforcement notice, the bringing of the appeal shall not have the effect of suspending the operation of the notice.

(2K) Provision may be made by the Secretary of State by regulations with respect to appeals under this section and in particular—

(a) as to the period within which and the manner in which appeals are to be brought; and

(b) as to the manner in which appeals are to be considered."

(4) In subsection (8) of that section (which refers to paragraph 5 of Schedule 10) for the word "5" there shall be substituted the word "6".

144. In section 92 of that Act (requirements to take precautions against pollution) after subsection (2) (which includes provision for regulations to provide for appeals to the Secretary of State) there shall be added—

"(3) This section is subject to section 114 of the 1995 Act (delegation or reference of appeals etc)."

145. In section 96 of that Act (regulations with respect to consents required by virtue of section 93 etc, including provision with respect to appeals) after subsection (3) there shall be added—

"(4) This section is subject to section 114 of the 1995 Act (delegation or reference of appeals etc)."

146. Section 105(1) of that Act (National Rivers Authority to exercise general supervision over matters relating to flood defence) shall cease to have effect.

147.—(1) In section 110 of that Act (applications for consents and approvals under section 109) in subsection (1) (which confers power to charge an application fee of £50 or such other sum as may be specified by order made by the Ministers) for the words "specified by order made by the Ministers" there shall be substituted the word "prescribed".

(2) In subsection (4)(b) of that section (which provides for questions as to unreasonable withholding of any consent or approval to be referred to the Ministers or the Secretary of State if the parties cannot agree on an arbitrator) for the words "the Ministers" there shall be substituted the words "the Minister".

(3) After subsection (5) of that section there shall be inserted—

"(6) In subsection (1) above "prescribed" means specified in, or determined in accordance with, an order made by the Ministers; and any such order may make different provision for different cases, including different provision in relation to different persons, circumstances or localities."

148. Section 114 (general fisheries duty of the National Rivers Authority) shall cease to have effect.

149. Section 117 (general financial duties of the National Rivers Authority) shall cease to have effect.

150.—(1) Section 118 of that Act (special duties with respect to flood defence revenue) shall be amended in accordance with the following provisions of this paragraph.

(2) In subsection (1)(b) (such revenue to be disregarded in determining the amount of any surplus for the purposes of section 117(3)) for the words "section 117(3) above" there shall be substituted the words "section 44(4) of the 1995 Act".

(3) In subsection (2)(b) (flood defence revenue to include revenue raised by general drainage charges under sections 134 to 136) for the words "to 136" there shall be substituted the words "and 135".

151.—(1) In section 119 of that Act (duties with respect to certain funds raised under local enactments) for subsection (1) (duty of the National Rivers Authority, in respect of funds created for fishery purposes under local enactments, not to use those funds except for the purposes for which they could have been used if the Water Resources Act 1963 had not been passed) there shall be substituted—

"(1) Where the Agency holds any funds, or any interest in any funds, which immediately before the transfer date the National Rivers Authority, by virtue of this subsection as originally enacted, was not permitted to use except for particular purposes, those funds or that interest shall not be used except for the purposes for which they could be used by virtue of this subsection as originally enacted.

(1A) For the purposes of subsection (1) above, "the transfer date" has the same meaning as in Part I of the 1995 Act."

(2) In subsection (2) of that section (certain funds raised under local enactments to be disregarded in determining the amount of any surplus for the purposes of section 117(3)) for the words "section 117(3) above" there shall be substituted the words "section 44(3) of the 1995 Act".

152. Sections 121 to 124 of that Act (accounts of the Authority, audit and schemes imposing water resources charges) shall cease to have effect.

153. Sections 126(6) and 129(4) of that Act (each of which applies section 68) shall cease to have effect.

154. Sections 131 and 132 of that Act (schemes of charges in connection with control of pollution) shall cease to have effect.

155. Section 146 of that Act (revenue grants by the Secretary of State to the National Rivers Authority) shall cease to have effect.

156. Sections 150 to 153 of that Act (grants for national security purposes, borrowing powers of the National Rivers Authority, loans to the Authority, and Treasury guarantees of the Authority's borrowing) shall cease to have effect.

157. In section 154 of that Act (compulsory purchase etc) in subsection (6), for the words "(including section 4 above) or otherwise" there shall be substituted the words "or otherwise (including section 37 of the 1995 Act (incidental general powers of the Agency))".

158. In section 156 of that Act (acquisition of land etc for fisheries purposes) for the words "Without prejudice to section 4 above", in each place where they occur, there shall be substituted the words "Without prejudice to section 37 of the 1995 Act (incidental general powers of the Agency)".

159. In section 157 of that Act (restriction on disposals of compulsorily acquired land) for subsection (6) (meaning of "compulsorily acquired land") there shall be substituted—

"(6) In this section "compulsorily acquired land", in relation to the Agency, means any land of the Agency which—
(a) was acquired by the Agency compulsorily under the provisions of section 154 above or of an order under section 168 below;
(b) was acquired by the Agency at a time when it was authorised under those provisions to acquire the land compulsorily;
(c) being land which has been transferred to the Agency from the Authority by section 3 of the 1995 Act, was acquired by the Authority—
(i) compulsorily, under the provisions of section 154 above or of an order under section 168 below or under the provisions of section 151 of the Water Act 1989 or of an order under section 155 of that Act; or
(ii) at a time when it was authorised under those provisions to acquire the land compulsorily;
(d) being land—
(i) which has been so transferred, and
(ii) which was transferred to the Authority in accordance with a scheme under Schedule 2 to the Water Act 1989,
was acquired by a predecessor of the Authority compulsorily under so much of any enactment in force at any time before 1st September 1989 as conferred powers of compulsory acquisition; or

(e) being land transferred as mentioned in sub-paragraphs (i) and (ii) of paragraph (d) above, was acquired by such a predecessor at a time when it was authorised to acquire the land by virtue of any such powers as are mentioned in that paragraph." ·

160. In section 158 of that Act (works agreements for water resources purposes) in subsection (1) (which is expressed to be without prejudice to the generality of the powers conferred by section 4) for the words "section 4 above" there shall be substituted the words "section 37 of the 1995 Act (incidental general powers of the Agency)".

161.—(1) Section 161 of that Act (anti-pollution works and operations) shall be amended in accordance with the following provisions of this paragraph.

(2) In subsection (1) (power, subject to subsection (2), to carry out works and operations etc) for the words "Subject to subsection (2) below," there shall be substituted the words "Subject to subsections (1A) and (2) below,".

(3) After that subsection there shall be inserted—

"(1A) Without prejudice to the power of the Agency to carry out investigations under subsection (1) above, the power conferred by that subsection to carry out works and operations shall only be exercisable in a case where—

(a) the Agency considers it necessary to carry out forthwith any works or operations falling within paragraph (a) or (b) of that subsection; or

(b) it appears to the Agency, after reasonable inquiry, that no person can be found on whom to serve a works notice under section 161A below."

162. After that section there shall be inserted—

"Notices requiring persons to carry out anti-pollution works and operations

161A.—(1) Subject to the following provisions of this section, where it appears to the Agency that any poisonous, noxious or polluting matter or any solid waste matter is likely to enter, or to be or to have been present in, any controlled waters, the Agency shall be entitled to serve a works notice on any person who, as the case may be,—

(a) caused or knowingly permitted the matter in question to be present at the place from which it is likely, in the opinion of the Agency, to enter any controlled waters; or

(b) caused or knowingly permitted the matter in question to be present in any controlled waters.

(2) For the purposes of this section, a "works notice" is a notice requiring the person on whom it is served to carry out such of the following works or operations as may be specified in the notice, that is to say—

(a) in a case where the matter in question appears likely to enter any controlled waters, works or operations for the purpose of preventing it from doing so; or

(b) in a case where the matter appears to be or to have been present in any controlled waters, works or operations for the purpose—

(i) of removing or disposing of the matter;

(ii) of remedying or mitigating any pollution caused by its presence in the waters; or

(iii) so far as it is reasonably practicable to do so, of restoring the waters, including any flora and fauna dependent on the aquatic environment of the waters, to their state immediately before the matter became present in the waters.

(3) A works notice—

(a) must specify the periods within which the person on whom it is served is required to do each of the things specified in the notice; and

(b) is without prejudice to the powers of the Agency by virtue of section 161(1A)(a) above.

(4) Before serving a works notice on any person, the Agency shall reasonably endeavour to consult that person concerning the works or operations which are to be specified in the notice.

(5) The Secretary of State may by regulations make provision for or in connection with—

(a) the form or content of works notices;

(b) requirements for consultation, before the service of a works notice, with persons other than the person on whom that notice is to be served;

(c) steps to be taken for the purposes of any consultation required under subsection (4) above or regulations made by virtue of paragraph (b) above; or

(d) any other steps of a procedural nature which are to be taken in connection with, or in consequence of, the service of a works notice.

(6) A works notice shall not be regarded as invalid, or as invalidly served, by reason only of any failure to comply with the requirements of subsection (4) above or of regulations made by virtue of paragraph (b) of subsection (5) above.

(7) Nothing in subsection (1) above shall entitle the Agency to require the carrying out of any works or operations which would impede or prevent the making of any discharge in pursuance of a consent given under Chapter II of Part III of this Act.

(8) No works notice shall be served on any person requiring him to carry out any works or operations in respect of water from an abandoned mine or an abandoned part of a mine which that person permitted to reach such a place as is mentioned in subsection (1)(a) above or to enter any controlled waters.

(9) Subsection (8) above shall not apply to the owner or former operator of any mine or part of a mine if the mine or part in question became abandoned after 31st December 1999.

(10) Subsections (3B) and (3C) of section 89 above shall apply in relation to subsections (8) and (9) above as they apply in relation to subsections (3) and (3A) of that section.

(11) Where the Agency—

(a) carries out any such investigations as are mentioned in section 161(1) above, and

(b) serves a works notice on a person in connection with the matter to which the investigations relate,

it shall (unless the notice is quashed or withdrawn) be entitled to recover the costs or expenses reasonably incurred in carrying out those investigations from that person.

(12) The Secretary of State may, if he thinks fit in relation to any person, give directions to the Agency as to whether or how it should exercise its powers under this section.

(13) In this section—

"controlled waters" has the same meaning as in Part III of this Act;

"mine" has the same meaning as in the Mines and Quarries Act 1954.

Grant of, and compensation for, rights of entry etc.

161B.—(1) A works notice may require a person to carry out works or operations in relation to any land or waters notwithstanding that he is not entitled to carry out those works or operations.

(2) Any person whose consent is required before any works or operations required by a works notice may be carried out shall grant, or join in granting, such rights in relation to any land or waters as will enable the person on whom the works notice is served to comply with any requirements imposed by the works notice.

(3) Before serving a works notice, the Agency shall reasonably endeavour to consult every person who appears to it—

(a) to be the owner or occupier of any relevant land, and

(b) to be a person who might be required by subsection (2) above to grant, or join in granting, any rights,

concerning the rights which that person may be so required to grant.

(4) A works notice shall not be regarded as invalid, or as invalidly served, by reason only of any failure to comply with the requirements of subsection (3) above.

(5) A person who grants, or joins in granting, any rights pursuant to subsection (2) above shall be entitled, on making an application within such period as may be prescribed and in such manner as may be prescribed to such person as may be prescribed, to be paid by the person on whom the works notice in question is served compensation of such amount as may be determined in such manner as may be prescribed.

(6) Without prejudice to the generality of the regulations that may be made by virtue of subsection (5) above, regulations by virtue of that subsection may make such provision in relation to compensation under this section as may be made by regulations by virtue of subsection (4) of section 35A of the Environmental Protection Act 1990 in relation to compensation under that section.

(7) In this section—

"prescribed" means prescribed in regulations made by the Secretary of State;

"relevant land" means—

(a) any land or waters in relation to which the works notice in question requires, or may require, works or operations to be carried out; or

(b) any land adjoining or adjacent to that land or those waters;

"works notice" means a works notice under section 161A above.

Appeals against works notices

161C.—(1) A person on whom a works notice is served may, within the period of twenty-one days beginning with the day on which the notice is served, appeal against the notice to the Secretary of State.

(2) On any appeal under this section the Secretary of State—

(a) shall quash the notice, if he is satisfied that there is a material defect in the notice; but

(b) subject to that, may confirm the notice, with or without modification, or quash it.

(3) The Secretary of State may by regulations make provision with respect to—

(a) the grounds on which appeals under this section may be made; or

(b) the procedure on any such appeal.

(4) Regulations under subsection (3) above may (among other things)—

(a) include provisions comparable to those in section 290 of the Public Health Act 1936 (appeals against notices requiring the execution of works);

(b) prescribe the cases in which a works notice is, or is not to be suspended until the appeal is decided, or until some other stage in the proceedings;

(c) prescribe the cases in which the decision on an appeal may in some respects be less favourable to the appellant than the works notice against which he is appealing;

(d) prescribe the cases in which the appellant may claim that a works notice should have been served on some other person and prescribe the procedure to be followed in those cases;

(e) make provision as respects—

(i) the particulars to be included in the notice of appeal;

(ii) the persons on whom notice of appeal is to be served and the particulars, if any, which are to accompany the notice; or

(iii) the abandonment of an appeal.

(5) In this section "works notice" means a works notice under section 161A above.

(6) This section is subject to section 114 of the 1995 Act (delegation or reference of appeals).

Consequences of not complying with a works notice

161D.—(1) If a person on whom the Agency serves a works notice fails to comply with any of the requirements of the notice, he shall be guilty of an offence.

(2) A person who commits an offence under subsection (1) above shall be liable—

(a) on summary conviction, to imprisonment for a term not exceeding three months or to a fine not exceeding £20,000 or to both;

(b) on conviction on indictment to imprisonment for a term not exceeding two years or to a fine or to both.

(3) If a person on whom a works notice has been served fails to comply with any of the requirements of the notice, the Agency may do what that person was required to do and may recover from him any costs or expenses reasonably incurred by the Agency in doing it.

(4) If the Agency is of the opinion that proceedings for an offence under subsection (1) above would afford an ineffectual remedy against a person who has failed to comply with the requirements of a works notice, the Agency may take proceedings in the High Court for the purpose of securing compliance with the notice.

(5) In this section "works notice" means a works notice under section 161A above."

163. In section 162 of that Act (other powers to deal with foul water or pollution) in subsection (1) (which refers to section 161 of that Act) for the words "section 161" there shall be substituted the words "sections 161 to 161D".

164. In section 166 of that Act (power to carry out works for purposes of flood warning system) in subsection (1) (which is expressed to be without prejudice to the Agency's other powers by virtue of section 4) for the words "section 4 above" there shall be substituted the words "section 37 of the 1995 Act (incidental general powers of the Agency)".

165. In section 169 of that Act (powers of entry for enforcement purposes) at the beginning of subsection (3) there shall be inserted the words "Subject to subsection (4) below," and after that subsection there shall be added—

"(4) The powers conferred by this section shall not have effect for the purposes of any of the Agency's pollution control functions, within the meaning of section 108 of the 1995 Act."

166. In section 172 of that Act (powers of entry for other purposes) at the beginning of subsection (3) there shall be inserted the words "Subject to subsection (3A) below," and after that subsection there shall be added—

"(3A) The powers conferred by this section shall not have effect for the purposes of any of the Agency's pollution control functions, within the meaning of section 108 of the 1995 Act."

167. In section 174 of that Act (impersonation of persons exercising powers of entry) in subsection (1) (which creates a summary offence punishable by a fine not exceeding level 4) for the words from "liable, on summary conviction," onwards there shall be substituted the words "liable—

(a) on summary conviction, to a fine not exceeding the statutory maximum;

(b) on conviction on indictment, to a fine or to imprisonment for a term not exceeding two years, or to both."

168. Section 187 of that Act (annual report of the Authority) shall cease to have effect.

169.—(1) Section 190 of that Act (pollution control register) shall be amended in accordance with the following provisions of this paragraph.

(2) In subsection (1) (which requires a register to be kept containing prescribed particulars of the items there specified) after the words "prescribed particulars of" there shall be inserted the words "or relating to".

(3) Paragraph (d) of that subsection (which relates to certificates under paragraph 1(7) of Schedule 10) shall be omitted.

(4) Paragraph (f) of that subsection, and the word "and" immediately preceding it, shall be omitted and at the end of that subsection there shall be added—

"(g) applications made to the Agency for the variation of discharge consents;

(h) enforcement notices served under section 90B above;

(j) revocations, under paragraph 7 of Schedule 10 to this Act, of discharge consents;

(k) appeals under section 91 above;

(l) directions given by the Secretary of State in relation to the Agency's functions under the water pollution provisions of this Act;

(m) convictions, for offences under Part III of this Act, of persons who have the benefit of discharge consents;

(n) information obtained or furnished in pursuance of conditions of discharge consents;

(o) works notices under section 161A above;

(p) appeals under section 161C above;

(q) convictions for offences under section 161D above;

(r) such other matters relating to the quality of water or the pollution of water as may be prescribed by the Secretary of State.

(1A) Where information of any description is excluded from any register by virtue of section 191B below, a statement shall be entered in the register indicating the existence of information of that description."

(5) In subsection (2) (registers to be available for inspection by, and facilities for obtaining copies of entries to be afforded to, the public) after paragraph (b) there shall be added the words—

"and, for the purposes of this subsection, places may be prescribed by the Secretary of State at which any such registers or facilities as are mentioned in paragraph (a) or (b) above are to be available or afforded to the public in pursuance of the paragraph in question."

(6) After subsection (3) there shall be added—

"(4) The Secretary of State may give to the Agency directions requiring the removal from any register maintained by it under this section of any specified information which is not prescribed for inclusion under subsection (1) above or which, by virtue of section 191A or 191B below, ought to have been excluded from the register.

(5) In this section "discharge consent" has the same meaning as in section 91 above."

170. After section 191 of that Act (register for the purposes of works discharges) there shall be inserted—

"Exclusion from registers of information affecting national security

191A.—(1) No information shall be included in a register kept or maintained by the Agency under any provision of this Act if and so long as, in the opinion of the Secretary of State, the inclusion in such a register of that information, or information of that description, would be contrary to the interests of national security.

(2) The Secretary of State may, for the purpose of securing the exclusion from registers of information to which subsection (1) above applies, give to the Agency directions—

(a) specifying information, or descriptions of information, to be excluded from their registers; or

(b) specifying descriptions of information to be referred to the Secretary of State for his determination;

and no information referred to the Secretary of State in pursuance of paragraph (b) above shall be included in any such register until the Secretary of State determines that it should be so included.

(3) The Agency shall notify the Secretary of State of any information it excludes from a register in pursuance of directions under subsection (2) above.

(4) A person may, as respects any information which appears to him to be information to which subsection (1) above may apply, give a notice to the Secretary of State specifying the information and indicating its apparent nature; and, if he does so—

(a) he shall notify the Agency that he has done so; and

(b) no information so notified to the Secretary of State shall be included in any such register until the Secretary of State has determined that it should be so included.

Exclusion from registers of certain confidential information

191B.—(1) No information relating to the affairs of any individual or business shall, without the consent of that individual or the person for the time being carrying on that business, be included in a register kept or maintained by the Agency under any provision of this Act, if and so long as the information—

(a) is, in relation to him, commercially confidential; and

(b) is not required to be included in the register in pursuance of directions under subsection (7) below;

but information is not commercially confidential for the purposes of this section unless it is determined under this section to be so by the Agency or, on appeal, by the Secretary of State.

(2) Where information is furnished to the Agency for the purpose of—

(a) an application for a discharge consent or for the variation of a discharge consent,

(b) complying with any condition of a discharge consent, or

(c) complying with a notice under section 202 below,

then, if the person furnishing it applies to the Agency to have the information excluded from any register kept or maintained by the Agency under any provision of this Act, on the ground that it is commercially confidential (as regards himself or another person), the Agency shall determine whether the information is or is not commercially confidential.

(3) A determination under subsection (2) above must be made within the period of fourteen days beginning with the date of the application and if the Agency fails to make a determination within that period it shall be treated as having determined that the information is commercially confidential.

(4) Where it appears to the Agency that any information (other than information furnished in circumstances within subsection (2) above) which has been obtained by the Agency under or by virtue of any provision of any enactment might be commercially confidential, the Agency shall—

(a) give to the person to whom or whose business it relates notice that that information is required to be included in a register kept or maintained by the Agency under any provision of this Act, unless excluded under this section; and

(b) give him a reasonable opportunity—

(i) of objecting to the inclusion of the information on the ground that it is commercially confidential; and

(ii) of making representations to the Agency for the purpose of justifying any such objection;

and, if any representations are made, the Agency shall, having taken the representations into account, determine whether the information is or is not commercially confidential.

(5) Where, under subsection (2) or (4) above, the Agency determines that information is not commercially confidential—

(a) the information shall not be entered on the register until the end of the period of twenty-one days beginning with the date on which the determination is notified to the person concerned; and

(b) that person may appeal to the Secretary of State against the decision;

and, where an appeal is brought in respect of any information, the information shall not be entered on the register until the end of the period of seven days following the day on which the appeal is finally determined or withdrawn.

(6) Subsections (2A), (2C) and (2K) of section 91 above shall apply in relation to appeals under subsection (5) above; but—

(a) subsection (2C) of that section shall have effect for the purposes of this subsection with the substitution for the words from "(which may" onwards of the words "(which must be held in private)"; and

(b) subsection (5) above is subject to section 114 of the 1995 Act (delegation or reference of appeals etc).

(7) The Secretary of State may give to the Agency directions as to specified information, or descriptions of information, which the public interest requires to be included in registers kept or maintained by the Agency under any provision of this Act notwithstanding that the information may be commercially confidential.

(8) Information excluded from a register shall be treated as ceasing to be commercially confidential for the purposes of this section at the expiry of the period of four years beginning with the date of the determination by virtue of which it was excluded; but the person who furnished it may apply to the Agency for the information to remain excluded from the register on the ground that it is still commercially confidential and the Agency shall determine whether or not that is the case.

(9) Subsections (5) and (6) above shall apply in relation to a determination under subsection (8) above as they apply in relation to a determination under subsection (2) or (4) above.

(10) The Secretary of State may by regulations substitute (whether in all cases or in such classes or descriptions of case as may be specified in the regulations) for the period for the time being specified in subsection (3) above such other period as he considers appropriate.

(11) Information is, for the purposes of any determination under this section, commercially confidential, in relation to any individual or person, if its being contained in the register would prejudice to an unreasonable degree the commercial interests of that individual or person.

(12) In this section "discharge consent" has the same meaning as in section 91 above."

171. Section 196 of that Act (provision of information by the Authority to Ministers) shall cease to have effect.

172.—(1) In section 202 of that Act (information and assistance required in connection with the control of pollution) in subsection (4) (which creates a summary offence punishable by a fine not exceeding level 5 on the standard scale) for the words from "liable, on summary conviction," onwards there shall be substituted the words "liable—

(a) on summary conviction, to a fine not exceeding the statutory maximum;

(b) on conviction on indictment, to a fine or to imprisonment for a term not exceeding two years, or to both."

(2) Subsection (5) of that section (which is superseded in consequence of the amendment made by sub-paragraph (1) above) shall cease to have effect.

173.—(1) Section 204 of that Act (restriction on disclosure of information with respect to any particular business) shall be amended in accordance with the following provisions of this paragraph.

(2) In subsection (2)(a) (exception for disclosure of information for purposes of functions under certain enactments)—

(a) for the words "the Authority" there shall be substituted the words "the Agency, the Scottish Environment Protection Agency"; and

(b) for the words "or the Water Act 1989" there shall be substituted the words ", the Water Act 1989, Part I or IIA of the Environmental Protection Act 1990 or the 1995 Act".

(3) In subsection (3), in paragraph (a) (which provides that nothing in subsection (1) shall limit the matters which may be included in reports made by specified bodies under specified enactments)—

(a) after sub-paragraph (i), there shall be inserted—

"(ia) the Scottish Environment Protection Agency;"; and

(b) for the words "or that Act of 1991 " there shall be substituted the words ", Part I or IIA of the Environmental Protection Act 1990, that Act of 1991 or the 1995 Act".

(4) In paragraph (b) of that subsection, after the words "that Act" there shall be inserted the words "of 1991".

174. Sections 213 to 215 of that Act (local inquiries) shall cease to have effect.

175. Section 218 of that Act (no judicial disqualification by virtue of liability to pay charges to the Authority) shall cease to have effect.

176. In section 219 of that Act (powers to make regulations)—

(a) in subsection (2), the words "Subject to subsection (3) below,", and

(b) subsection (3) (which restricts certain powers to make regulations),

shall cease to have effect.

177.—(1) Section 221 (1) of that Act (general interpretation) shall be amended in accordance with the following provisions of this paragraph.

(2) Before the definition of "abstraction" there shall be inserted—

"the 1995 Act" means the Environment Act 1995;".

(3) After the definition of "accessories" there shall be inserted—

" "the Agency" means the Environment Agency;".

(4) The definition of "the Authority" shall be omitted.

(5) The definition of "constituent council" shall be omitted.

(6) After the definition of "enactment" there shall be inserted—

"enforcement notice" has the meaning given by section 90B above;".

(7) For the definition of "flood defence functions" there shall be substituted—

" "flood defence functions", in relation to the Agency, means—

(a) its functions with respect to flood defence and land drainage by virtue of Part IV of this Act, the Land Drainage Act 1991 and section 6 of the 1995 Act;

(b) those functions transferred to the Agency by section 2(1)(a)(iii) of the 1995 Act which were previously transferred to the Authority by virtue of section 136(8) of the Water Act 1989 and paragraph 1(3) of Schedule 15 to that Act (transfer of land drainage functions under local statutory provisions and subordinate legislation); and

(c) any other functions of the Agency under any of the flood defence provisions of this Act;".

(8) For the definition of "flood defence provisions" there shall be substituted—
"flood defence provisions", in relation to this Act, means—
    (a) any of the following provisions of this Act, that is to say—
        (i) Part IV;
        (ii) sections 133 to 141 (including Schedule 15), 143, 147 to 149, 155, 165 to 167, 180, 193, 194 and paragraph 5 of Schedule 25;
    (b) any of the following provisions of the 1995 Act, that is to say—
        (i) section 6(4) (general supervision of flood defence);
        (ii) section 53 (inquiries and other hearings); and
        (iii) Schedule 5 (membership and proceedings of regional and local flood defence committees); and
    (c) any other provision of this Act or the 1995 Act so far as it relates to a provision falling within paragraph (a) or (b) above;".

(9) For the definition of "the related water resources provisions" there shall be substituted—
" "the related water resources provisions", in relation to Chapter II of Part II of this Act, means—
    (a) the following provisions of this Act, that is to say, the provisions—
        (i) of sections 21 to 23 (including Schedule 5);
        (ii) of sections 120, 125 to 130, 158, 189, 199 to 201, 206(3), 209(3), 211(1) and 216; and
        (iii) of paragraph 1 of Schedule 25; and
    (b) the following provisions of the 1995 Act, that is to say, the provisions—
        (i) of sections 41 and 42 (charging schemes) as they have effect by virtue of subsection (1)(a) of section 41 (licences under Chapter II of Part II of this Act); and
        (ii) of subsections (1) and (2) of section 53 (inquiries and other hearings);".

(10) In the definition of "water pollution provisions"—
(a) in paragraph (b)—
    (i) after the words "161" there shall be inserted the words "to 161D"; and
    (ii) for the words "203 and 213(2) above" there shall be substituted the words "and 203"; and
(b) after paragraph (c), there shall be added the words—
"and the following provisions of the 1995 Act, that is to say, the provisions of subsections (1) and (2) of section 53."

178. Schedule 1 to that Act (the National Rivers Authority) shall cease to have effect.

179. Schedules 3 and 4 to that Act (boundaries of regional flood defence areas and membership and proceedings of regional and local flood defence committees) shall cease to have effect.

180. In Schedule 5 to that Act (procedure relating to statements on minimum acceptable flow) in paragraph 2(3)(g) (copy of notice to be served on person authorised by a licence under Part I of the Electricity Act 1989 to generate electricity) after the words "to generate electricity" there shall be added the words "who has a right to abstract water from any such waters or related inland waters".

181. In Schedule 6 to that Act (orders providing for exemption from restrictions on abstraction) in paragraph 1(4)(h) (copy of notice to be served on person authorised by a licence under Part I of the Electricity Act 1989 to generate electricity) after the words "to generate electricity" there shall be added the words "who has a right to abstract water from any such source of supply or related inland waters".

182. In Schedule 10 to that Act (discharge consents) after paragraph 7 (restriction on variation and revocation of consent and previous variation) there shall be added—

"General review of consents

8.—(1) If it appears appropriate to the Secretary of State to do so he may at any time direct the Authority to review—
(a) the consents given under paragraphs 2 and 5 above, or
(b) any description of such consents,
and the conditions (if any) to which those consents are subject.

(2) A direction given by virtue of sub-paragraph (1) above—
(a) shall specify the purpose for which, and
(b) may specify the manner in which,
the review is to be conducted.

(3) After carrying out a review pursuant to a direction given by virtue of sub-paragraph (1) above, the Authority shall submit to the Secretary of State its proposals (if any) for—

(a) the modification of the conditions of any consent reviewed pursuant to the direction, or

(b) in the case of any unconditional consent reviewed pursuant to the direction, subjecting the consent to conditions.

(4) Where the Secretary of State has received any proposals from the Authority under sub-paragraph (3) above in relation to any consent he may, if it appears appropriate to him to do so, direct the Authority to do, in relation to that consent, anything mentioned in paragraph 6(2)(b) or (c) above.

(5) A direction given by virtue of sub-paragraph (4) above may only direct the Authority to do, in relation to any consent,—

(a) any such thing as the Authority has proposed should be done in relation to that consent, or

(b) any such thing with such modifications as appear to the Secretary of State to be appropriate."

183. For that Schedule there shall be substituted—

"**Section 88** SCHEDULE 10

DISCHARGE CONSENTS

Application for consent

1.—(1) An application for a consent, for the purposes of section 88(1)(a) of this Act, for any discharges—

(a) shall be made to the Agency on a form provided for the purpose by the Agency; and

(b) must be advertised by or on behalf of the applicant in such manner as may be required by regulations made by the Secretary of State.

(2) Regulations made by the Secretary of State may make provision for enabling the Agency to direct or determine that any such advertising of an application as is required under sub-paragraph (1)(b) above may, in any case, be dispensed with if, in that case, it appears to the Agency to be appropriate for that advertising to be dispensed with.

(3) The applicant for such a consent must provide to the Agency, either on, or together with, the form mentioned in sub-paragraph (1) above—

(a) such information as the Agency may reasonably require; and

(b) such information as may be prescribed for the purpose by the Secretary of State;

but, subject to paragraph 3(3) below and without prejudice to the effect (if any) of any other contravention of the requirements of this Schedule in relation to an application under this paragraph, a failure to provide information in pursuance of this sub-paragraph shall not invalidate an application.

(4) The Agency may give the applicant notice requiring him to provide it with such further information of any description specified in the notice as it may require for the purpose of determining the application.

(5) An application made in accordance with this paragraph which relates to proposed discharges at two or more places may be treated by the Agency as separate applications for consents for discharges at each of those places.

Consultation in connection with applications

2.—(1) Subject to sub-paragraph (2) below, the Agency shall give notice of any application under paragraph 1 above, together with a copy of the application, to the persons who are prescribed or directed to be consulted under this paragraph and shall do so within the specified period for notification.

(2) The Secretary of State may, by regulations, exempt any class of application from the requirements of this paragraph or exclude any class of information contained in applications from those requirements, in all cases or as respects specified classes only of persons to be consulted.

(3) Any representations made by the persons so consulted within the period allowed shall be considered by the Agency in determining the application.

(4) For the purposes of sub-paragraph (1) above—

(a) persons are prescribed to be consulted on any description of application if they are persons specified for the purposes of applications of that description in regulations made by the Secretary of State;

(b) persons are directed to be consulted on any particular application if the Secretary of State specifies them in a direction given to the Agency;

and the "specified period for notification" is the period specified in the regulations or in the direction.

(5) Any representations made by any other persons within the period allowed shall also be considered by the Agency in determining the application.

(6) Subject to sub-paragraph (7) below, the period allowed for making representations is—

(a) in the case of persons prescribed or directed to be consulted, the period of six weeks beginning with the date on which notice of the application was given under sub-paragraph (1) above, and

(b) in the case of other persons, the period of six weeks beginning with the date on which the making of the application was advertised in pursuance of paragraph 1(1)(b) above.

(7) The Secretary of State may, by regulations, substitute for any period for the time being specified in sub-paragraph (6)(a) or (b) above, such other period as he considers appropriate.

Consideration and determination of applications

3.—(1) On an application under paragraph 1 above the Agency shall be under a duty, if the requirements—

(a) of that paragraph, and

(b) of any regulations made under paragraph 1 or 2 above or of any directions under paragraph 2 above,

are complied with, to consider whether to give the consent applied for, either unconditionally or subject to conditions, or to refuse it.

(2) Subject to the following provisions of this Schedule, on an application made in accordance with paragraph 1 above, the applicant may treat the consent applied for as having been refused if it is not given within the period of four months beginning with the day on which the application is received or within such longer period as may be agreed in writing between the Agency and the applicant.

(3) Where any person, having made an application to the Agency for a consent, has failed to comply with his obligation under paragraph 1(3) or (4) above to provide information to the Agency, the Agency may refuse to proceed with the application, or refuse to proceed with it until the information is provided.

(4) The conditions subject to which a consent may be given under this paragraph shall be such conditions as the Agency may think fit and, in particular, may include conditions—

(a) as to the places at which the discharges to which the consent relates may be made and as to the design and construction of any outlets for the discharges;

(b) as to the nature, origin, composition, temperature, volume and rate of the discharges and as to the periods during which the discharges may be made;

(c) as to the steps to be taken, in relation to the discharges or by way of subjecting any substance likely to affect the description of matter discharged to treatment or any other process, for minimising the polluting effects of the discharges on any controlled waters;

(d) as to the provision of facilities for taking samples of the matter discharged and, in particular, as to the provision, maintenance and use of manholes, inspection chambers, observation wells and boreholes in connection with the discharges;

(e) as to the provision, maintenance and testing of meters for measuring or recording the volume and rate of the discharges and apparatus for determining the nature, composition and temperature of the discharges;

(f) as to the keeping of records of the nature, origin, composition, temperature, volume and rate of the discharges and, in particular, of records of readings of meters and other recording apparatus provided in accordance with any other condition attached to the consent; and

(g) as to the making of returns and the giving of other information to the Authority about the nature, origin, composition, temperature, volume and rate of the discharges;

and it is hereby declared that a consent may be given under this paragraph subject to different conditions in respect of different periods.

(5) The Secretary of State may, by regulations, substitute for any period for the time being specified in sub-paragraph (2) above, such other period as he considers appropriate.

4. The Secretary of State may give the Agency a direction with respect to any particular application, or any description of applications, for consent under paragraph 1 above requiring the Agency not to determine or not to proceed with the application or applications of that description until the expiry of any such period as may be specified in the direction, or until directed by the Secretary of State that it may do so, as the case may be.

Reference to Secretary of State of certain applications for consent

5.—(1) The Secretary of State may, either in consequence of representations or objections made to him or otherwise, direct the Agency to transmit to him for determination such applications for consent under paragraph 1 above as are specified in the direction or are of a description so specified.

(2) Where a direction is given to the Agency under this paragraph, the Agency shall comply with the direction and inform every applicant to whose application the direction relates of the transmission of his application to the Secretary of State.

(3) Paragraphs 1(1) and 2 above shall have effect in relation to an application transmitted to the Secretary of State under this paragraph with such modifications as may be prescribed.

(4) Where an application is transmitted to the Secretary of State under this paragraph, the Secretary of State may at any time after the application is transmitted and before it is granted or refused—

(a) cause a local inquiry to be held with respect to the application; or

(b) afford the applicant and the Agency an opportunity of appearing before, and being heard by, a person appointed by the Secretary of State for the purpose.

(5) The Secretary of State shall exercise his power under sub-paragraph (4) above in any case where a request to be heard with respect to the application is made to him in the prescribed manner by the applicant or by the Agency.

(6) It shall be the duty of the Secretary of State, if the requirements of this paragraph and of any regulations made under it are complied with, to determine an application for consent transmitted to him by the Agency under this paragraph by directing the Agency to refuse its consent or to give its consent under paragraph 3 above (either unconditionally or subject to such conditions as are specified in the direction).

(7) Without prejudice to any of the preceding provisions of this paragraph, the Secretary of State may by regulations make provision for the purposes of, and in connection with, the consideration and disposal by him of applications transmitted to him under this paragraph.

Consents without applications

6.—(1) If it appears to the Agency—

(a) that a person has caused or permitted effluent or other matter to be discharged in contravention—

　(i) of the obligation imposed by virtue of section 85(3) of this Act; or

　(ii) of any prohibition imposed under section 86 of this Act; and

(b) that a similar contravention by that person is likely,

the Agency may, if it thinks fit, serve on him an instrument in writing giving its consent, subject to any conditions specified in the instrument, for discharges of a description so specified.

(2) A consent given under this paragraph shall not relate to any discharge which occurred before the instrument containing the consent was served on the recipient of the instrument.

(3) Sub-paragraph (4) of paragraph 3 above shall have effect in relation to a consent given under this paragraph as it has effect in relation to a consent given under that paragraph.

(4) Where a consent has been given under this paragraph, the Agency shall publish notice of the consent in such manner as may be prescribed by the Secretary of State and send copies of the instrument containing the consent to such bodies or persons as may be so prescribed.

(5) It shall be the duty of the Agency to consider any representations or objections with respect to a consent under this paragraph as are made to it in such manner, and within such period, as may be prescribed by the Secretary of State and have not been withdrawn.

(6) Where notice of a consent is published by the Agency under sub-paragraph (4) above the Agency shall be entitled to recover the expenses of publication from the person on whom the instrument containing the consent was served.

Revocation of consents and alteration and imposition of conditions

7.—(1) The Agency may from time to time review any consent given under paragraph 3 or 6 above and the conditions (if any) to which the consent is subject.

(2) Subject to such restrictions on the exercise of the power conferred by this sub-paragraph as are imposed under paragraph 8 below, where the Agency has reviewed a consent

under this paragraph, it may by a notice served on the person making a discharge in pursuance of the consent—

(a) revoke the consent;

(b) make modifications of the conditions of the consent; or

(c) in the case of an unconditional consent, provide that it shall be subject to such conditions as may be specified in the notice.

(3) If on a review under sub-paragraph (1) above it appears to the Agency that no discharge has been made in pursuance of the consent to which the review relates at any time during the preceding twelve months, the Agency may revoke the consent by a notice served on the holder of the consent.

(4) If it appears to the Secretary of State appropriate to do so—

(a) for the purpose of enabling Her Majesty's Government in the United Kingdom to give effect to any Community obligation or to any international agreement to which the United Kingdom is for the time being a party;

(b) for the protection of public health or of flora and fauna dependent on an aquatic environment; or

(c) in consequence of any representations or objections made to him or otherwise,

he may, subject to such restrictions on the exercise of the power conferred by virtue of paragraph (c) above as are imposed under paragraph 8 below, at any time direct the Agency, in relation to a consent given under paragraph 3 or 6 above, to do anything mentioned in sub-paragraph (2)(a) to (c) above.

(5) The Agency shall be liable to pay compensation to any person in respect of any loss or damage sustained by that person as a result of the Agency's compliance with a direction given in relation to any consent by virtue of sub-paragraph (4)(b) above if—

(a) in complying with that direction the Agency does anything which, apart from that direction, it would be precluded from doing by a restriction imposed under paragraph 8 below; and

(b) the direction is not shown to have been given in consequence of—

(i) a change of circumstances which could not reasonably have been foreseen at the beginning of the period to which the restriction relates; or

(ii) consideration by the Secretary of State of material information which was not reasonably available to the Agency at the beginning of that period.

(6) For the purposes of sub-paragraph (5) above information is material, in relation to a consent, if it relates to any discharge made or to be made by virtue of the consent, to the interaction of any such discharge with any other discharge or to the combined effect of the matter discharged and any other matter.

Restriction on variation and revocation of consent and previous variation

8.—(1) Each instrument signifying the consent of the Agency under paragraph 3 or 6 above shall specify a period during which no notice by virtue of paragraph 7(2) or (4)(c) above shall be served in respect of the consent except, in the case of a notice doing anything mentioned in paragraph 7(2)(b) or (c), with the agreement of the holder of the consent.

(2) Each notice served by the Agency by virtue of paragraph 7(2) or (4)(c) above (except a notice which only revokes a consent) shall specify a period during which a subsequent such notice which alters the effect of the first-mentioned notice shall not be served except, in the case of a notice doing anything mentioned in paragraph 7(2)(b) or (c) above, with the agreement of the holder of the consent.

(3) The period specified under sub-paragraph (1) or (2) above in relation to any consent shall not, unless the person who proposes to make or makes discharges in pursuance of the consent otherwise agrees, be less than the period of four years beginning—

(a) in the case of a period specified under sub-paragraph (1) above, with the day on which the consent takes effect; and

(b) in the case of a period specified under sub-paragraph (2) above with the day on which the notice specifying that period is served.

(4) A restriction imposed under sub-paragraph (1) or (2) above shall not prevent the service by the Agency of a notice by virtue of paragraph 7(2) or (4)(c) above in respect of a consent given under paragraph 6 above if—

(a) the notice is served not more than three months after the beginning of the period prescribed under paragraph 6(5) above for the making of representations and objections with respect to the consent; and

(b) the Agency or, as the case may be, the Secretary of State considers, in consequence of any representations or objections received by it or him within that period, that it is appropriate for the notice to be served.

(5) A restriction imposed under sub-paragraph (1) or (2) above shall not prevent the service by the Agency of a notice by virtue of paragraph 7(2)(b) or (c) or (4)(c) above in respect of a consent given under paragraph 6 above if the holder has applied for a variation under paragraph 10 below.

General review of consents

9.—(1) If it appears appropriate to the Secretary of State to do so he may at any time direct the Agency to review—

(a) the consents given under paragraph 3 or 6 above, or

(b) any description of such consents,

and the conditions (if any) to which those consents are subject.

(2) A direction given by virtue of sub-paragraph (1) above—

(a) shall specify the purpose for which, and

(b) may specify the manner in which,

the review is to be conducted.

(3) After carrying out a review pursuant to a direction given by virtue of sub-paragraph (1) above, the Agency shall submit to the Secretary of State its proposals (if any) for—

(a) the modification of the conditions of any consent reviewed pursuant to the direction, or

(b) in the case of any unconditional consent reviewed pursuant to the direction, subjecting the consent to conditions.

(4) Where the Secretary of State has received any proposals from the Agency under sub-paragraph (3) above in relation to any consent he may, if it appears appropriate to him to do so, direct the Agency to do, in relation to that consent, anything mentioned in paragraph 7(2)(b) or (c) above.

(5) A direction given by virtue of sub-paragraph (4) above may only direct the Agency to do, in relation to any consent,—

(a) any such thing as the Agency has proposed should be done in relation to that consent, or

(b) any such thing with such modifications as appear to the Secretary of State to be appropriate.

Applications for variation

10.—(1) The holder of a consent under paragraph 3 or 6 above may apply to the Agency, on a form provided for the purpose by the Agency, for the variation of the consent.

(2) The provisions of paragraphs 1 to 5 above shall apply (with the necessary modifications) to applications under sub-paragraph (1) above, and to the variation of consents in pursuance of such applications, as they apply to applications for, and the grant of, consents.

Transfer of consents

11.—(1) A consent under paragraph 3 or 6 above may be transferred by the holder to a person who proposes to carry on the discharges in place of the holder.

(2) On the death of the holder of a consent under paragraph 3 or 6 above, the consent shall, subject to sub-paragraph (4) below, be regarded as property forming part of the deceased's personal estate, whether or not it would be so regarded apart from this sub-paragraph, and shall accordingly vest in his personal representatives.

(3) If a bankruptcy order is made against the holder of a consent under paragraph 3 or 6 above, the consent shall, subject to sub-paragraph (4) below, be regarded for the purposes of any of the Second Group of Parts of the Insolvency Act 1986 (insolvency of individuals; bankruptcy), as property forming part of the bankrupt's estate, whether or not it would be so regarded apart from this sub-paragraph, and shall accordingly vest as such in the trustee in bankruptcy.

(4) Notwithstanding anything in the foregoing provisions of this paragraph, a consent under paragraph 3 or 6 above (and the obligations arising out of, or incidental to, such a consent) shall not be capable of being disclaimed.

(5) A consent under paragraph 3 or 6 above which is transferred to, or which vests in, a person under this section shall have effect on and after the date of the transfer or vesting as if it had been granted to that person under paragraph 3 or 6 above, subject to the same conditions as were attached to it immediately before that date.

(6) Where a consent under paragraph 3 or 6 above is transferred under sub-paragraph (1) above, the person from whom it is transferred shall give notice of that fact to the Agency not later than the end of the period of twenty-one days beginning with the date of the transfer.

(7) Where a consent under paragraph 3 or 6 above vests in any person as mentioned in sub-paragraph (2) or (3) above, that person shall give notice of that fact to the Agency not later than the end of the period of fifteen months beginning with the date of the vesting.

(8) If—

  (a) a consent under paragraph 3 or 6 above vests in any person as mentioned in sub-paragraph (2) or (3) above, but

  (b) that person fails to give the notice required by sub-paragraph (7) above within the period there mentioned,

the consent, to the extent that it permits the making of any discharges, shall cease to have effect.

(9) A person who fails to give a notice which he is required by sub-paragraph (6) or (7) above to give shall be guilty of an offence and liable—

  (a) on summary conviction, to a fine not exceeding the statutory maximum;

  (b) on conviction on indictment, to a fine or to imprisonment for a term not exceeding two years, or to both."

184. In Schedule 11 to that Act (water protection zone orders) in paragraph 4 (which is expressed to be without prejudice to section 213 of that Act) for the words "section 213 of this Act" there shall be substituted the words "section 53 of the 1995 Act (inquiries and other hearings)".

185. In Schedule 12 to that Act (nitrate sensitive area orders) in paragraph 6 (which is expressed to be without prejudice to section 213 of that Act) for the words "section 213 of this Act" there shall be substituted the words "section 53 of the 1995 Act (inquiries and other hearings)".

186. In Schedule 13 to that Act (transitional water pollution provisions) in paragraph 4 (discharge consents on application of undertakers etc.)—

  (a) in sub-paragraph (2), in paragraphs (a) and (b) (which contain references to paragraph 4 of Schedule 10) for the word "4", in each place where it occurs, there shall be substituted the word "5";

  (b) in sub-paragraph (3) (which contains references to various provisions of Schedule 10) for the words "paragraphs 1(4) to (6) and 2(1) or, as the case may be, paragraph 4(3)" there shall be substituted the words "paragraph 1(1), apart from paragraph (a), paragraph 2 or, as the case may be, paragraph 5(3)"; and

  (c) in sub-paragraph (4)(a) (which contains a reference to paragraph 2(5) of Schedule 10) for the words "2(5)" there shall be substituted the words "3(4)".

187.—(1) In Schedule 15 to that Act (supplemental provisions with respect to drainage charges) in paragraphs 4(3) and 9(4) (which specify the penalty for certain offences of failing, and after conviction continuing, without reasonable excuse, to comply with notices) after the words "he continues without reasonable excuse" there shall be inserted the words "to fail".

(2) In paragraph 12(2) of that Schedule (which is expressed to be without prejudice to powers by virtue of section 4 or paragraph 5 of Schedule 1) for the words "section 4 of this Act and paragraph 5 of Schedule 1 to this Act" there shall be substituted the words "section 37 of, and paragraph 6 of Schedule 1 to, the 1995 Act".

188. In Schedule 20 to that Act (supplemental provisions with respect to powers of entry) in paragraph 7 (which creates an offence of obstruction, punishable on summary conviction by a fine not exceeding level 3) for the words from "liable, on summary conviction," onwards there shall be substituted the words "liable—

  (a) on summary conviction, to a fine not exceeding the statutory maximum;

  (b) on conviction on indictment, to a fine or to imprisonment for a term not exceeding two years, or to both."

189. In Schedule 22 to that Act (protection for particular undertakings) in paragraph 5 (protection for telecommunication systems) for the words "section 4(1) of this Act)" there shall be substituted the words "section 37 of the 1995 Act)".

190. In Schedule 25 to that Act (byelaw-making powers) in paragraph 1(1) for the words "paragraphs (a), (c) and (d) of section 2(1) of this Act" there shall be substituted the words "sub-paragraphs (i), (iii) and (v) of section 2(1)(a) of the 1995 Act".

The Land Drainage Act 1991

191. In the Land Drainage Act 1991, for the words "NRA", wherever occurring, there shall be substituted the word "Agency".

192.—(1) In section 23 of that Act (prohibition on obstructions etc. in watercourses) in subsection (2) (which confers power to charge an application fee of £50 or such other sum as may be specified by order made by the Ministers) for the words "specified by order made by the Ministers" there shall be substituted the word "prescribed".

(2) After subsection (7) of that section there shall be inserted—

"(7A) In subsection (2) above "prescribed" means specified in, or determined in accordance with, an order made by the Ministers; and any such order may make different provision for different cases, including different provision in relation to different persons, circumstances or localities."

193. At the beginning of Part V of that Act (miscellaneous and supplemental provisions) there shall be inserted—

"Spray irrigation

Powers of internal drainage boards and local authorities to facilitate spray irrigation

61F.—(1) Any internal drainage board or local authority may, with the consent of the Agency, operate any drainage works under the control of the board or authority so as to manage the level of water in a watercourse for the purpose of facilitating spray irrigation.

(2) Subsection (1) above is without prejudice to—

(a) the powers of an internal drainage board or local authority in relation to drainage; or

(b) any requirement—

(i) for any other consent of the Agency or any other person; or

(ii) for any licence, approval, authorisation or other permission or registration."

194.—(1) In section 72 of that Act, in subsection (1) (general definitions) there shall be inserted at the appropriate place—

" "the Agency" means the Environment Agency;".

(2) In that subsection, the definition of "the NRA" shall be omitted.

The Clean Air Act 1993

195. In section 2 of the Clean Air Act 1993 (emission of dark smoke from industrial or trade premises) in subsection (5) (which creates a summary offence punishable with a fine not exceeding level 5 on the standard scale) for the words "level 5 on the standard scale" there shall be substituted the words "£20,000".

196.—(1) Section 19 of that Act (power to require creation of smoke control areas by local authorities) as it applies to Scotland shall be amended in accordance with the following provisions of this paragraph.

(2) In subsection (1)—

(a) for the words "Secretary of State" there shall be substituted the words "Scottish Environment Protection Agency (in this section referred to as "the Agency")"; and

(b) for the words "he", "him" and "his" there shall be substituted respectively "the Agency", "it" and "its".

(3) In subsections (2), (3), (4)(a) and (6), for the words "Secretary of State" there shall be substituted the words "Agency".

(4) In subsection (3), for the word "him" there shall be substituted the word "it".

(5) In subsection (4), before the words "the Secretary of State" in the second place where they occur there shall be inserted the words "the Agency, with the consent of".

197. In section 59 of that Act (local inquiries) in subsection (1)—

(a) for the words "a local inquiry" there shall be substituted the words "an inquiry"; and

(b) for the words "such an inquiry" there shall be substituted the words "an inquiry";

and for the side-note to that section there shall accordingly be substituted "Inquiries.".

198. In section 60(7)(b) of that Act as it applies to Scotland for the words "the Secretary of State" and "Secretary of State's" there shall be substituted the words "SEPA" and "SEPA's" respectively.

199. In section 63(1)(c) of that Act as it applies to Scotland for the words "sections 19(4) and" there shall be substituted the words "section".

The Radioactive Substances Act 1993

200. Subject to the other provisions of this Act, in the Radioactive Substances Act 1993, for the words "chief inspector" or "chief inspector's", wherever occurring, there shall be substituted respectively the words "appropriate Agency" or "appropriate Agency's".

201. Sections 4 and 5 of that Act (appointment of inspectors and chief inspectors) shall cease to have effect.

202. (1) In section 7 of that Act (registration of users of radioactive material) in subsection (1)(c) (application to be accompanied by prescribed fee), for the words "prescribed fee" there shall be substituted the words "charge prescribed for the purpose by a charging scheme under section 41 of the Environment Act 1995".

(2) In subsection (7) of that section (chief inspector to have regard exclusively to amount and character of radioactive waste), for the word "him" there shall be substituted the word "it".

203. In section 8 of that Act (exemptions from registration under section 7), in subsection (2) (power of chief inspector to impose conditions) for the word "he" there shall be substituted the word "it".

204.—(1) In section 10 of that Act (registration of mobile radioactive apparatus) in subsection (1)(c) (application to be accompanied by prescribed fee), for the words "prescribed fee" there shall be substituted the words "charge prescribed for the purpose by a charging scheme under section 41 of the Environment Act 1995".

(2) In each of subsections (3) and (5)(b) of that section (duty to supply copy of application, and to send copy of certificate, to local authority) for the word "him" there shall be substituted the words "the appropriate Agency".

205.—(1) Section 16 of that Act (authorisations) shall be amended in accordance with the following provisions of this paragraph.

(2) In subsection (2) (power to grant authorisations to be exercisable by the chief inspector) the words "Subject to subsection (3)" shall be omitted.

(3) Subsection (3) (power to grant authorisations in England, Wales and Northern Ireland) shall be omitted.

(4) In subsection (4) (application to be accompanied by prescribed fee), for the words "prescribed fee" there shall be substituted the words "charge prescribed for the purpose by a charging scheme under section 41 of the Environment Act 1995".

(5) After subsection (4) there shall be inserted—

"(4A) Without prejudice to subsection (5), on any application for an authorisation under section 13(1) in respect of the disposal of radioactive waste on or from any premises situated on a nuclear site in any part of Great Britain, the appropriate Agency—

(a) shall consult the relevant Minister and the Health and Safety Executive before deciding whether to grant an authorisation on that application and, if so, subject to what limitations or conditions, and

(b) shall consult the relevant Minister concerning the terms of the authorisation, for which purpose that Agency shall, before granting any authorisation on that application, send that Minister a copy of any authorisation which it proposes so to grant."

(6) In subsection (5) (consultation by chief inspector and, where the premises are in England, Wales or Northern Ireland, the appropriate Minister with local authorities etc.)—

(a) for the words from "and, where" to "shall each" there shall be substituted the word "shall"; and

(b) for the word "him", in each place where it occurs, there shall be substituted the words "that Agency".

(7) In subsection (7) (applications, other than those to which subsection (3) applies, deemed to be refused if not determined within prescribed period) for the words "(other than an application to which subsection (3) applies)" there shall be substituted the words "(other than an application for an authorisation under section 13(1) in respect of the disposal of radioactive waste on or from any premises situated on a nuclear site in any part of Great Britain)".

(8) In subsection (8)(b) (conditions or limitations subject to which authorisations may be granted) for the words from "or, as" to "think" there shall be substituted the word "thinks".

(9) In subsection (10) of that section (fixing of date from which authorisation is to have effect)—

(a) the words from "or, as" to "appropriate Minister" shall cease to have effect; and

(b) for the words "him or them" and "his or their" there shall be substituted respectively the words "it" and "its".

(10) After that subsection there shall be inserted—

"(11) In this section, "the relevant Minister" means—

(a) in relation to premises in England, the Minister of Agriculture, Fisheries and Food, and

(b) in relation to premises in Wales or Scotland, the Secretary of State."

206.—(1) In section 17 of that Act, after subsection (2) (variation of authorisations) there shall be inserted—

"(2A) On any proposal to vary an authorisation granted under section 13(1) in respect of the disposal of radioactive waste on or from any premises situated on a nuclear site in any part of Great Britain, the appropriate Agency—

(a) shall consult the relevant Minister and the Health and Safety Executive before deciding whether to vary the authorisation and, if so, whether by attaching, revoking or varying any limitations or conditions or by attaching further limitations or conditions, and

(b) shall consult the relevant Minister concerning the terms of any variation, for which purpose that Agency shall, before varying the authorisation, send that Minister a copy of any variations which it proposes to make."

(2) Subsection (4) of that section (adaptations for authorisations granted by the chief inspector and the appropriate Minister) shall cease to have effect.

(3) At the end of that section there shall be added—

"(5) In this section, "the relevant Minister" has the same meaning as in section 16 above."

207.—(1) In section 18 of that Act (functions of public and local authorities in relation to authorisations under section 13) in subsection (1)—

(a) the words from "(or, in a case" to "that Minister)", and

(b) the words "or the appropriate Minister, as the case may be,",

shall cease to have effect.

(2) In subsection (2)(b) of that section (special precautions taken with the approval of the chief inspector etc.) the words from "(or, where" to "that Minister)" shall cease to have effect.

208. In section 20 of that Act (retention and production of site or disposal records) subsection (3) (adaptation where powers exercisable by chief inspector and appropriate Minister) shall cease to have effect.

209.—(1) In section 21 of that Act (enforcement notices) in subsection (1) (power of chief inspector to serve such a notice) for the word "he" there shall be substituted the word "it".

(2) Subsection (3) of that section (adaptation in case of authorisations granted by the chief inspector and the appropriate Minister) shall cease to have effect.

(3) In subsection (4) of that section (copies of notices to be sent to certain public or local authorities) the words from "or, where" to "that Minister" shall cease to have effect.

210.—(1) In section 22 of that Act (prohibition notices) in subsection (1) (power of chief inspector to serve such a notice) for the word "he" there shall be substituted the word "it".

(2) Subsection (5) of that section (adaptation in case of authorisations granted by the chief inspector and the appropriate Minister) shall cease to have effect.

(3) In subsection (6) of that section (copies of notices to be sent to certain public or local authorities) the words from "or, where" to "that Minister" shall cease to have effect.

(4) In subsection (7) of that section (withdrawal of notices)—

(a) the words from "or, where" to "that Minister" shall cease to have effect; and

(b) for the word "he", in each place where it occurs, there shall be substituted the words "that Agency".

211.—(1) In section 23 of that Act (powers of Secretary of State to give directions to the chief inspector)—

(a) in subsections (1) and (3) for the word "him" there shall be substituted the word "it"; and

(b) in subsection (2) for the word "his" there shall be substituted the word "its".

(2) After subsection (4) of that section there shall be inserted—

"(4A) In the application of this section in relation to authorisations, and applications for authorisations, under section 13 in respect of premises situated on a nuclear site in England, references to the Secretary of State shall have effect as references to the Secretary of State and the Minister of Agriculture, Fisheries and Food."

212.—(1) In section 24 of that Act (power of Secretary of State to require certain applications to be determined by him) in subsections (1) and (4), for the word "him", in each place where it occurs, there shall be substituted the word "it".

(2) After subsection (4) of that section there shall be inserted—

"(4A) In the application of this section in relation to authorisations, and applications for authorisations, under section 13 in respect of premises situated on a nuclear site in England, references to the Secretary of State shall have effect as references to the Secretary of State and the Minister of Agriculture, Fisheries and Food."

213.—(1) In section 25 of that Act (power of Secretary of State to restrict knowledge of applications etc.) in subsection (1) (applications under section 7 to 10 etc.), after the words "knowledge of" there shall be inserted the words "such information as may be specified or described in the directions, being information contained in or relating to—".

(2) In subsection (2) of that section (applications under section 13 or 14 etc.)—

(a) the words from "or, in a case" to "Food," and "or their" shall cease to have effect; and

(b) after the words "knowledge of" there shall be inserted the words "such information as may be specified or described in the directions, being information contained in or relating to—".

(3) In subsection (3) of that section (copies of certain applications etc. which are the subject of a direction not to be sent to local or public authorities)—

(a) after the words "send a copy of" there shall be inserted the words "so much of"; and

(b) after the words "as the case may be" there shall be inserted the words "as contains the information specified or described in the directions—".

(4) After that subsection there shall be inserted—

"(3A) No direction under this section shall affect—

(a) any power or duty of the Agency to which it is given to consult the relevant Minister; or

(b) the information which is to be sent by that Agency to that Minister."

(5) At the end of that section there shall be added—

"(5) In this section "the relevant Minister" has the same meaning as in section 16 above."

214.—(1) Section 26 of that Act (appeals) shall be amended in accordance with the following provisions of this paragraph.

(2) Subsection (3)(a) (appeal not to lie in relation to authorisations subject to section 16(3)) shall cease to have effect.

(3) In subsection (4) (appeals in respect of enforcement or prohibition notices) the words "England, Wales or" shall be omitted.

(4) After subsection (5) there shall be inserted—

"(5A) In the application of this section in relation to authorisations, and applications for authorisations, under section 13 in respect of premises situated on a nuclear site in England, references in subsection (1) to (3) to the Secretary of State shall have effect as references to the Secretary of State and the Minister of Agriculture, Fisheries and Food."

215.—(1) Section 27 of that Act (procedure on appeals under section 26) shall be amended in accordance with the following provisions of this paragraph.

(2) In subsection (1) (power of Secretary of State to refer appeal to appointed person) after the word "26" there shall be inserted the words ", other than an appeal against any decision of, or notice served by, SEPA,".

(3) After that subsection there shall be inserted—

"(1A) As respects an appeal against any decision of, or notice served by, SEPA, this section is subject to section 114 of the Environment Act 1995 (delegation or reference of appeals)."

(4) After subsection (7) there shall be inserted—

"(7A) In the application of this section in relation to authorisations, and applications for authorisations, under section 13 in respect of premises situated on a nuclear site in England, references in subsections (1) to (6) to the Secretary of State shall have effect as references to the Secretary of State and the Minister of Agriculture, Fisheries and Food."

216. Section 28 of that Act (representations in relation to authorisations and notices where appropriate Minister is concerned) shall cease to have effect.

217.—(1) Section 30 of that Act (power of Secretary of State to dispose of radioactive waste) shall be amended in accordance with the following provisions of this paragraph.

(2) In subsection (1) (which confers the power)—

(a) for the words "the Secretary of State", in the first place where they occur, there shall be substituted the words "the appropriate Agency";

(b) for those words, wherever else occurring, there shall be substituted the words "that Agency"; and

(c) for the word "his" there shall be substituted the word "its".

(3) In subsection (3) (application of certain definitions of "owner") for the words "Secretary of State" there shall be substituted the words "Environment Agency".

(4) In subsection (4) (adaptations for Scotland) for the words "the Secretary of State" there shall be substituted the words "SEPA".

218. Section 31 of that Act (rights of entry and inspection) shall cease to have effect.

219. In section 32 of that Act (offences relating to registration or authorisation, including the offence of failure to comply with the requirements of an enforcement or prohibition notice under section 21 or 22 of the Act) after subsection (2) there shall be added—

"(3) If the appropriate Agency is of the opinion that proceedings for an offence under subsection (1)(d) would afford an ineffectual remedy against a person who has failed to comply with the requirements of a notice served on him under section 21 or 22, that Agency may take proceedings in the High Court or, in Scotland, in any court of competent jurisdiction, for the purpose of securing compliance with the notice."

220. In section 34(1) of that Act (which, with certain exceptions, makes it an offence to disclose certain trade secrets) after paragraph (b) (no offence where disclosure made in accordance with directions) there shall be inserted—

"(bb) under or by virtue of section 113 of the Environment Act 1995, or".

221. Section 35 of that Act (obstruction of inspectors or other persons) shall cease to have effect.

222. In section 38 of that Act (restriction on prosecution) in subsection (1) (provision for England and Wales) for paragraph (b) there shall be substituted—

"(b) by the Environment Agency, or".

223.—(1) In section 39 of that Act (public access to documents and records) in subsection (1) (duties of chief inspector)—

(a) for the word "him", in each place where it occurs, there shall be substituted the word "it";

(b) for the word "he" there shall be substituted the words "the appropriate Agency"; and

(c) for the words "applications or certificates" there shall be substituted the word "information".

(2) In subsection (2), the words "or, as the case may be, the appropriate Minister and the chief inspector," shall cease to have effect.

224. In section 40 of that Act (radioactivity to be disregarded for purposes of certain statutory provisions) in subsection (2)(b)(ii), after the words "imposed by the statutory provision on" there shall be inserted the words "the Environment Agency or SEPA or on".

225. Section 42(5) of that Act (which precludes, in the interests of national security, the exercise of certain powers of entry in relation to Crown premises and which is superseded by provisions of this Act) shall cease to have effect.

226. Section 43 of that Act (which relates to fees and charges and which is superseded by provisions of this Act) shall cease to have effect.

227.—(1) Subsection (1) of section 47 of that Act (general definitions) shall be amended in accordance with the following provisions of this paragraph.

(2) There shall be inserted at the appropriate place—

" "the appropriate Agency" means—

(a) in relation to England and Wales, the Environment Agency; and

(b) in relation to Scotland, SEPA;".

(3) In the definition of "the appropriate Minister", paragraphs (a) and (b) shall cease to have effect.

(4) In the definition of "the chief inspector", paragraphs (a) and (b) shall cease to have effect.

(5) In the definition of "prescribed", the words from "or, in relation to fees" onwards shall cease to have effect.

(6) In the definition of "relevant water body"—

(a) in paragraph (a), the words "the National Rivers Authority", and

(b) in paragraph (b), the words "a river purification authority within the meaning of the Rivers (Prevention of Pollution) (Scotland) Act 1951",

shall be omitted.

(7) There shall be inserted at the appropriate place—

" "SEPA" means the Scottish Environment Protection Agency;".

228. In section 48 of that Act (index of defined expressions) in the Table—

(a) the following entries shall be inserted at the appropriate place—

(i) "the appropriate Agency	section 47(1)";
(ii) "SEPA	section 47(1)";

(b) the entry relating to the chief inspector shall be omitted.

229. Schedule 2 to that Act (exercise of rights of entry and inspection) shall cease to have effect.

230.—(1) In Schedule 3 to that Act (enactments, other than local enactments, to which s.40 applies) in paragraph 9 (which specifies certain provisions in the Water Resources Act 1991) for the words "203 and 213" there shall be substituted the words "and 203".

(2) For paragraph 16 of that Schedule there shall be substituted—

"16. Sections 30A, 30B, 30D, 30F, 30G, 30H(1), 31(4), (5), (8) and (9), 31A, 34 to 42B, 46 to 46D and 56(1) to (3) of the Control of Pollution Act 1974."

The Local Government (Wales) Act 1994

231. In Schedule 9 to the Local Government (Wales) Act 1994 (which makes provision for the transfer to the new principal councils in Wales of functions in relation to public health and related matters), in paragraph 17(2) (which amends the definitions of waste regulation and disposal authorities for the purposes of Part II of the Environmental Protection Act 1990) for the words "each of subsections (1)(f) and (2)(f)" there shall be substituted the words "subsection (2)(f)"

The Local Government etc. (Scotland) Act 1994

232.—(1) In section 2(2) of the Local Government etc. (Scotland) Act 1994 (constitution of councils) after the words "this Act" there shall be inserted the words "and of the Environment Act 1995".

(2) In Schedule 13 to that Act (minor and consequential amendments) in paragraph 75(27) (which amends certain provisions of the Sewerage (Scotland) Act 1968) for the words from the beginning to "premises)" there shall be substituted the words "In section 53 (notices to be in writing)".

Subordinate legislation and local statutory provisions

233.—(1) In any subordinate legislation or local statutory provisions, for any reference (however framed) to the National Rivers Authority, and for any reference which falls to be construed as such a reference, there shall be substituted a reference to the Agency.

(2) In any subordinate legislation, for any reference (however framed) to a relevant inspector, and for any reference which falls to be construed as such a reference, there shall be substituted a reference to the appropriate Agency.

(3) The provisions of this paragraph are subject to the other provisions of this Act and to any provision made under or by virtue of this Act.

(4) In this paragraph—
"the appropriate Agency" means—
    (a) in relation to England and Wales, the Agency;
    (b) in relation to Scotland, SEPA;
"local statutory provision" means—
    (a) a provision of a local Act (including an Act confirming a provisional order);
    (b) a provision of so much of any public general Act as has effect with respect to particular persons or works or with respect to particular provisions falling within any paragraph of this definition;
    (c) a provision of an instrument made under any provision falling within paragraph (a) or (b) above;
    (d) a provision of any other instrument which is in the nature of a local enactment;
"relevant inspector" means—
    (i) the chief inspector for England and Wales constituted under section 16(3) of the Environmental Protection Act 1990;
    (ii) the chief inspector for Scotland constituted under section 16(3) of that Act;
    (iii) the chief inspector for England and Wales appointed under section 4(2)(a) of the Radioactive Substances Act 1993;
    (iv) the chief inspector for Scotland appointed under section 4(2)(b) of that Act;
    (v) the chief, or any other, inspector, within the meaning of the Alkali, &c, Works Regulation Act 1906;
    (vi) an inspector appointed under section 19 of the Health and Safety at Work etc. Act 1974 by the Secretary of State in his capacity as the enforcing authority responsible for the enforcement of the Alkali, &c, Works Regulation Act 1906 or section 5 of the said Act of 1974;
"subordinate legislation" has the same meaning as in the Interpretation Act 1978.

Section 120   SCHEDULE 23

TRANSITIONAL AND TRANSITORY PROVISIONS AND SAVINGS

PART I

GENERAL TRANSITIONAL PROVISIONS AND SAVINGS

Interpretation of Part I

1. In this Part of this Schedule, the "transfer date" has the same meaning as in Part I of this Act.

Directions

2. Any directions given to the National Rivers Authority for the purposes of section 19 of the Water Resources Act 1991 shall have effect on and after the transfer date as directions given to the Agency for the purposes of section 6(2) of this Act.

Regional and local fisheries advisory committees

3. If and so long as the Agency requires, on and after the transfer date any advisory committee established and maintained before the transfer date by the National Rivers Authority under section 8(1) of the Water Resources Act 1991 shall be treated as if—
    (a) it had been established by the Agency,

(b) the area by reference to which that committee was established had been determined by the Agency, and

(c) in the case of a regional advisory committee, the chairman of that committee had been appointed,

in accordance with section 13 of this Act.

Charging schemes

4.—(1) Without prejudice to section 55 of this Act, any charging scheme—

(a) which relates to any transferred functions,

(b) which was made before the transfer date, and

(c) which is in force immediately before that date or would (apart from this Act) have come into force at any time after that date,

shall, subject to the provisions of section 41 of this Act, have effect on and after the transfer date, with any necessary modifications, and for the remainder of the period for which the charging scheme would have been in force apart from any repeal made by this Act, as a scheme made under that section by the transferee in accordance with section 42 of this Act.

(2) Any costs or expenses incurred before the transfer date by any person in carrying out functions transferred to a new Agency by or under this Act may be treated for the purposes of subsections (3) and (4) of section 42 of this Act as costs or expenses incurred by that new Agency in carrying out those functions.

(3) In this paragraph—

"charging scheme" means a scheme specifying, or providing for the determination of, any fees or charges;

"new Agency" means the Agency or SEPA;

"transferred functions" means any functions which, by virtue of any provision made by or under this Act, become functions of a new Agency and "the transferee" means the new Agency whose functions they so become.

Preparation of reports

5.—(1) The first report prepared by the Agency under section 52 of this Act may, to the extent that it relates to functions transferred to the Agency from any other body or person include a report on the exercise and performance of those functions by the transferor during the period between the end of the last year in respect of which the transferor prepared a report and the transfer date.

(2) SEPA shall, as soon as reasonably practicable after the transfer date, prepare a report on—

(a) the exercise and performance of the functions of each river purification board during the period between the end of the last year in respect of which the board sent a report to the Secretary of State under section 16 of the Rivers (Prevention of Pollution) (Scotland) Act 1951 and the transfer date; and

(b) the exercise and performance of the functions of each waste regulation authority during the period between the end of the last financial year in respect of which the authority prepared and published a report under section 67 of the Environmental Protection Act 1990 and the transfer date.

(3) Subsections (3) and (4) of section 52 of this Act shall apply to a report prepared under sub-paragraph (2) above as they apply to a report prepared under that section.

Preparation of accounts

6. Notwithstanding the repeal by this Act of subsection (9) of section 135 of the Local Government (Scotland) Act 1973 (application to river purification board of certain provisions of that Act), the provisions applied to a river purification board by virtue of that section shall, as respects the period between the end of the last financial year in respect of which accounts have been made up by the board and the transfer date, continue to apply in relation to the board; but anything which shall or may be done or enjoyed, or any access, inspection or copying which shall or may be allowed, under or by virtue of any of those provisions or of section 118 of that Act (financial returns) by, or by an officer of, the board shall, or as the case may be may, after the transfer date, be done, enjoyed or allowed by, or by an officer of, SEPA in place of the board or of an officer of the board.

Membership of Welsh National Park authorities

7.—(1) Where a body corporate constituted as a Welsh National Park planning board becomes, or has become, the National Park authority in relation to the National Park in question by virtue of an order under section 63 of this Act made by virtue of section 64(1) of this Act, paragraph 2 of Schedule 7 to this Act shall, in its application in relation to that National Park authority at any time before 31st March 1997, have effect with the following modifications.

(2) In sub-paragraph (5)—

(a) in paragraph (a), after the word "council" there shall be inserted the words "or, if earlier, until the council which appointed him as a local authority member of that authority is excluded from the councils by whom such members of that authority are to be appointed"; and

(b) in paragraph (b), after the word "cessation" there shall be inserted the words "or exclusion".

(3) In sub-paragraph (6), after the words "Sub-paragraph (5)(a) above" there shall be inserted the words ", so far as relating to cessation of membership of a council,".

(4) In this paragraph, "Welsh National Park planning board" means a National Park planning board, as defined in section 64 of this Act, for the area of a National Park in Wales.

The Alkali, &c., Works Regulation Act 1906

8. Any dispensation which was granted under the proviso to subsection (5) of section 9 of the Alkali, &c, Works Regulation Act 1906 before the transfer date and which would, apart from this Act, have been in force on that date shall have effect on and after that date notwithstanding the repeal of that proviso by this Act.

The Public Records Act 1958

9.—(1) Such of the administrative and departmental records (in whatever form or medium) of a transferor as are transferred to and vested in the Agency by or under section 3 of this Act shall be treated for the purposes of the Public Records Act 1958 as administrative or departmental records of the Agency.

(2) In this paragraph, "transferor" means any body or person any or all of whose administrative and departmental records are transferred to and vested in the Agency by or under section 3 of this Act.

The Parliamentary Commissioner Act 1967

10.—(1) Nothing in this Act shall prevent the completion on or after the transfer date of any investigation begun before that date under the Parliamentary Commissioner Act 1967 in pursuance of a complaint made in relation to the National Rivers Authority.

(2) Nothing in this Act shall prevent the making on or after the transfer date of a complaint under that Act in respect of any action which was taken by or on behalf of the National Rivers Authority before that date.

(3) Notwithstanding the amendment of that Act by paragraph 11 of Schedule 22 to this Act, the provisions of that Act shall have effect on and after the transfer date in relation to any complaint to which sub-paragraph (1) or (2) above applies and to its investigation as they would have had effect before that date; but, in relation to any such complaint, the Agency shall on and after that date stand in the place of the National Rivers Authority for the purposes of this paragraph.

The Local Government Act 1974

11.—(1) Where for any year, a Rate Support Grant Report under section 60 of the Local Government, Planning and Land Act 1980, or a supplementary report under section 61 of that Act, has effect to determine the amount of supplementary grants to be paid under section 7 of the Local Government Act 1974 to the council of a county or county borough in Wales, and at any time—

(a) after that report or, as the case may be, that supplementary report is approved by a resolution of the House of Commons, but

(b) not later than the end of that year,

a body corporate constituted as a National Park planning board for a National Park the whole or any part of which is included in that county or county borough becomes the National Park authority for that National Park by virtue of section 64 of this Act, those supplementary grants shall, subject to the provisions of any, or any further, such supplementary report, continue to be paid for that year notwithstanding that that body corporate has ceased to be a National Park planning board.

(2) In this paragraph—

"National Park planning board" has the meaning given by section 64(9) of this Act; and

"year" means a period of 12 months beginning with 1st April.

12.—(1) Nothing in this Act shall prevent the completion on or after the transfer date by a Local Commissioner of any investigation which he began to conduct before that date and which is an investigation under Part III of the Local Government Act 1974 in pursuance of a complaint made in relation to the National Rivers Authority.

(2) Nothing in this Act shall prevent the making on or after the transfer date of a complaint under Part III of that Act in respect of any action which was taken by or on behalf of the National Rivers Authority before that date.

(3) Notwithstanding the amendment of Part III of that Act by paragraph 18 of Schedule 22 to this Act, the provisions of that Part shall have effect on and after the transfer date in relation to any complaint to which sub-paragraph (1) or (2) above applies and to its investigation as they would have had effect before that date; but, in relation to any such complaint, the Agency shall on and after that date stand in the place of the National Rivers Authority for the purposes of this paragraph.

The Control of Pollution Act 1974

13. As respects England and Wales, any resolution passed in pursuance of section 11 of the Control of Pollution Act 1974 (special provision for land occupied by disposal authorities: resolutions etc.) which is in force immediately before the day on which the repeals in that section made by this Act come into force shall have effect on and after that day as if it were a waste management licence granted by the Environment Agency under Part II of the Environmental Protection Act 1990 subject to the conditions specified in the resolution pursuant to subsection (3)(e) of that section.

The Salmon and Freshwater Fisheries Act 1975

14.—(1) Any approval or certificate given under or by virtue of section 8(2), 9(1) or 11(4) of the Salmon and Freshwater Fisheries Act 1975 by a Minister of the Crown before the transfer date shall, so far as is required for continuing its effect on and after that date, have effect as if given by the Agency.

(2) Any application for the grant of an approval or certificate by a Minister of the Crown under or by virtue of any of the provisions specified in sub-paragraph (1) above which, at the transfer date, is in the process of being determined shall on and after that date be treated as having been made to the Agency.

(3) Any notice given by a Minister of the Crown under section 11(2) of that Act before the transfer date shall, so far as is required for continuing its effect on and after that date, have effect as if given by the Agency.

(4) Any extension of a period granted by a Minister of the Crown under section 11(3) of that Act before the transfer date shall, so far as is required for continuing its effect on and after that date, have effect as if granted by the Agency.

(5) Without prejudice to section 16 or 17 of the Interpretation Act 1978, any exemption granted under subsection (1) or (2) of section 14 of the Salmon and Freshwater Fisheries Act 1975 which is in force immediately before the substitution date shall have effect on and after that date as an exemption granted by the Agency under subsection (2) or, as the case may be, subsection (3) of section 14 of that Act as substituted by paragraph 13 of Schedule 15 to this Act.

(6) Any grating constructed and placed in a manner and position approved under section 14(3) of that Act as it had effect before the substitution date (including a grating so constructed and placed at any time as a replacement for a grating so constructed and placed) shall, if—

(a) the approval was in force immediately before the substitution date, and

(b) the grating is maintained in accordance with the approval,

be taken for the purposes of section 14 of that Act, as substituted by paragraph 13 of Schedule 15 to this Act, to be a screen which complies with the requirements of subsection (2)(a) or (3)(a) of that section, according to the location of the grating, and with the requirements of subsections (4) to (6) of that section.

(7) Any notice given, or objection made, under subsection (2) of section 18 of that Act before the transfer date shall, so far as is required for continuing its effect on and after that date, have effect as a notice given under that subsection as it has effect on and after that date.

(8) In this paragraph—

"approval" includes a provisional approval;

"grating" means a device in respect of which there is in force, immediately before the substitution date, an approval given for the purposes of the definition of "grating" in section 41(1) of the Salmon and Freshwater Fisheries Act 1975 as it had effect before that date;

"the substitution date" means the date on which paragraph 13 of Schedule 15 to this Act comes into force;

"the transfer date" means the date which, by virtue of section 56(1) of this Act, is the transfer date for the purposes of Part I of this Act as it applies in relation to the Agency.

The Local Government Finance Act 1988

15.—(1) Without prejudice to the generality of subsection (4) of section 64 of this Act, where an order has been made under section 63 of this Act by virtue of section 64(1) of this Act designating a date in relation to a Welsh National Park planning board, the body corporate constituted as that board may at any time before the designated date issue a levy by virtue of section 71 of this Act for a year at or before the beginning of which that body becomes the National Park authority for the National Park in question by virtue of section 64 of this Act as if it were the National Park authority for that National Park, notwithstanding that it has not in fact become a National Park authority at the date when it issues the levy.

(2) Without prejudice to the generality of section 74 of the Local Government Finance Act 1988, where—

(a) an order is made under section 63 of this Act by virtue of section 64(1) of this Act designating a date in relation to a Welsh National Park planning board; and

(b) the designated date is a date falling after the beginning, but before the end, of a year in respect of which, at the time the order is made, that board has not issued any levy under that section 74,

that board may nonetheless issue such a levy in respect of that year as if the body corporate constituted as that board was not in fact going to become the National Park authority for the National Park in question by virtue of that order before the end of that year.

(3) Sub-paragraph (5) below applies in a case where a levy is issued in respect of any year by a Welsh National Park planning board under section 74 of the Local Government Finance Act 1988 and—

(a) that levy is issued by that board at a time when no order has been made under section 63 of this Act by virtue of section 64(1) of this Act designating a date in relation to that board; and

(b) after the levy is issued, but no later than the end of the year in respect of which it is issued, such an order is so made designating in relation to that board a date falling not later than the end of that year.

(4) Sub-paragraph (5) below also applies in a case where a levy is issued in respect of any year by a Welsh National Park planning board under section 74 of the Local Government Finance Act 1988 and—

(a) that levy is issued by that board at a time after an order has been made under section 63 of this Act by virtue of section 64(1) of this Act designating a date in relation to that board; and

(b) the designated date is a date falling after the beginning, but before the end, of that year.

(5) In a case where this sub-paragraph applies, the levy in question or any levy substituted for that levy—

(a) shall have effect or, as the case may be, continue to have effect; and

(b) in particular, but without prejudice to the generality of paragraph (a) above, shall be paid or, as the case may be, continue to be paid,

as if the body corporate constituted as that board was not to, or had not, so become the National Park authority for the National Park in question (but was to continue, or had continued, to be the National Park planning board for that Park for the whole of that year).

(6) Where a body corporate constituted as a Welsh National Park planning board has or is to become the National Park authority for the National Park in question by virtue of an order made under section 63 of this Act by virtue of section 64(1) of this Act, nothing in this paragraph authorises that body corporate to issue for any year both a levy under section 74 of the Local Government Finance Act 1988 and a levy by virtue of section 71 of this Act.

(7) In this paragraph—

"the designated date" has the same meaning as in section 64 of this Act;

"National Park planning board" has the meaning given by section 64(9) of this Act;

"Welsh National Park planning board" means a National Park planning board for the area of a National Park in Wales;

"year" means a period of 12 months beginning with 1st April;

and any reference to the issue of a levy under section 74 of the Local Government Finance Act 1988 by a Welsh National Park planning board is a reference to the issue of a levy under that section by such a board by virtue of subsection (7) of that section.

The Environmental Protection Act 1990

16.—(1) Subject to sub-paragraph (2) below, if, at the transfer date, the content of the strategy required by section 44A of the Environmental Protection Act 1990 has not been finally determined, any plan or modification under section 50 of that Act, in its application to England and Wales, whose content has been finally determined before that date shall continue in force until the contents of the strategy are finally determined, notwithstanding the repeal by this Act of that section.

(2) If the strategy required by section 44A of that Act consists, or is to consist, of more than one statement, sub-paragraph (1) above shall apply as if—

(a) references to the strategy were references to any such statement; and
(b) references to a plan or modification under section 50 of that Act were references to such plans or modifications as relate to the area covered, or to be covered, by that statement.

17. If, at the transfer date, the content of the strategy required by section 44B of that Act has not been finally determined, any plan or modification under section 50 of that Act, in its application to Scotland, whose content has been finally determined before that date shall continue in force until the contents of the strategy are finally determined, notwithstanding the repeal by this Act of that section.

18.—(1) This paragraph applies to—

(a) any resolution of a waste regulation authority under section 54 of that Act (special provision for land occupied by disposal authorities in Scotland);
(b) any resolution of a waste disposal authority having effect by virtue of subsection (16) of that section as if it were a resolution of a waste regulation authority under that section,

which is in force on the transfer date.

(2) A resolution to which this paragraph applies shall continue in force—

(a) where no application is made under section 36(1) of that Act for a waste management licence in respect of the site or mobile plant covered by the resolution, until the end of the period of 6 months commencing with the transfer date;
(b) where an application as mentioned in sub-paragraph (a) above is made, until—
    (i) the application is withdrawn;
    (ii) the application is rejected and no appeal against the rejection is timeously lodged under section 43 of that Act;
    (iii) any appeal against a rejection of the application is withdrawn or rejected; or
    (iv) the application is granted.

(3) In relation to a resolution continued in force by sub-paragraph (2) above, the said section 54 shall have effect subject to the amendments set out in the following provisions of this paragraph.

(4) In subsection (2), for paragraph (b) there shall be substituted—

"(b) specified in a resolution passed by a waste regulation authority, or by a waste disposal authority under Part I of the Control of Pollution Act 1974, before the transfer date within the meaning of section 56(1) of the Environment Act 1995".

(5) In subsection (3) for paragraph (b) there shall be substituted—

"(b) by another person, that it is on land which is the subject of a resolution, that it is with the consent of the waste disposal authority and that any conditions to which such consent is subject are within the terms of the resolution."

(6) Subsections (4) to (7) shall cease to have effect.

(7) For subsections (8) and (9) there shall be substituted—

"(8) Subject to subsection (9) below, a resolution continued in force by paragraph 18 of Schedule 23 to the Environment Act 1995 may be varied or rescinded by SEPA by a resolution passed by it.

(9) Before passing a resolution under subsection (8) above varying a resolution, SEPA shall—

(a) prepare a statement of the variation which it proposes to make;
(b) refer that statement to the Health and Safety Executive and to the waste disposal authority in whose area the site is situated or, as the case may be, which is operating the plant; and
(c) consider any representations about the variation which the Health and Safety Executive or the waste disposal authority makes to it during the allowed period.

(9A) The period allowed to the Health and Safety Executive and the waste disposal authority for the making of representations under subsection (9)(c) above is the period of 28 days beginning with that on which the statement is received by that body, or such longer period as SEPA and that body agree in writing.

(9B) SEPA may—

(a) postpone the reference under subsection (9)(b) above so far as it considers that by reason of an emergency it is appropriate to do so;

(b) disregard the Health and Safety Executive in relation to a resolution which in SEPA's opinion will not affect the Health and Safety Executive."

(8) In subsection (10)—

(a) for the words "the authority which passed the resolution" and "the waste regulation authority" there shall be substituted the words "SEPA";

(b) the words "the waste disposal authority to discontinue the activities and of" shall cease to have effect.

(9) Subsections (11) to (15) shall cease to have effect.

The Water Industry Act 1991

19.—(1) Where, before the coming into force of the repeal by this Act of section 151 of the Water Industry Act 1991 (financial contributions to rural services), the Secretary of State has received an application from a relevant undertaker for a contribution under that section, he may, notwithstanding the coming into force of that repeal—

(a) give any such undertaking for any contribution sought by that application as he could have given under that section prior to the coming into force of that repeal;

(b) make any payments provided for in an undertaking given by virtue of this sub-paragraph.

(2) Notwithstanding the coming into force of the repeal by this Act of that section—

(a) the Secretary of State may make any payments provided for in an undertaking given by him under that section prior to the coming into force of that repeal;

(b) subsection (4) of that section (withholding and reduction of contributions) shall—

(i) continue to have effect in relation to contributions which the Secretary of State, before that repeal of that section, gave an undertaking under that section to make; and

(ii) have effect in relation to contributions which the Secretary of State has, by virtue of sub-paragraph (1) above, undertaken to make.

The Water Resources Act 1991

20. Notwithstanding any provision restricting the power of the Agency to grant a licence under Chapter II of Part II of the Water Resources Act 1991 (abstracting or impounding of water), or the power of the Secretary of State to direct the Agency to grant such a licence, the Agency may grant, and the Secretary of State may direct it to grant, such licences as are necessary to ensure that water may continue to be abstracted or impounded by or on behalf of the Crown in the manner in which, and to the extent to which,—

(a) it may be so abstracted or impounded immediately before the coming into force of sub-paragraph (4) of paragraph 2 of Schedule 21 to this Act in relation to that Chapter, or

(b) it has been so abstracted or impounded at any time in the period of five years immediately preceding the coming into force of that sub-paragraph in relation to that Chapter.

21.—(1) This paragraph applies to any consent—

(a) which was given under paragraph 2 of Schedule 10 to the Water Resources Act 1991 (discharge consents), as in force before the transfer date; and

(b) which is in force immediately before that date.

(2) On and after the transfer date, a consent to which this paragraph applies—

(a) shall, for so long as it would have continued in force apart from this Act, have effect as a consent given under paragraph 3 of Schedule 10 to that Act, as substituted by this Act, subject to the same conditions as were attached to the consent immediately before the transfer date; and

(b) shall—

(i) during the period of six months beginning with the transfer date, not be limited to discharges by any particular person but extend to discharges made by any person; and

(ii) after that period, extend, but be limited, to discharges made by any person who before the end of that period gives notice to the Agency that he proposes to rely on the consent after that period.

PART II

TRANSITORY PROVISIONS IN RESPECT OF FLOOD DEFENCE

Disqualification for membership of regional flood defence committee

22. Where a person is disqualified for membership of a regional flood defence committee by virtue of having been adjudged bankrupt before the coming into force of the Insolvency Act 1986, the rules applicable apart from the repeals made by the Consequential Provisions Act or

this Act, rather than paragraph 3(2) of Schedule 5 to this Act, shall apply for determining when that disqualification shall cease.

Savings in relation to local flood defence schemes

23.—(1) In any case where—
(a) immediately before the coming into force of section 17 of this Act, any scheme or committee continues, by virtue of paragraph 14 of Schedule 2 to the Consequential Provisions Act, to be treated as a local flood defence scheme or a local flood defence committee, or
(b) immediately before the coming into force of section 18 of this Act, any person continues, by virtue of that paragraph, to hold office,

the scheme or committee shall continue to be so treated or, as the case may be, the person shall continue so to hold office, notwithstanding the provisions of section 18 of, or Schedule 5 to this Act or the repeal of any enactment by this Act.

(2) Where a person is disqualified for membership of a local flood defence committee by virtue of having been adjudged bankrupt before the coming into force of the Insolvency Act 1986, the rules applicable apart from the repeals made by the Consequential Provisions Act or this Act, rather than paragraph 3(2) of Schedule 5 to this Act, shall apply for determining when that disqualification shall cease.

Interpretation

24. In this Part of this Schedule, "the Consequential Provisions Act" means the Water Consolidation (Consequential Provisions) Act 1991.

Section 120   SCHEDULE 24

REPEALS AND REVOCATIONS

Reference	Short title or title	Extent of repeal or revocation
60 & 61 Vict. c. 38.	The Public Health (Scotland) Act 1897.	Sections 16 to 26. Sections 36 and 37.
6 Edw. 7. c. 14.	The Alkali, &c, Works Regulation Act 1906.	In section 9, the proviso to subsection (5). Section 25. In section 27(1), the definitions of the expressions "chief inspector" and "inspector". In section 28(b), the words "other than offences under subsection four of section twelve of this Act"; in sub-paragraph (ii), the words from "without the consent" to "direct, nor"; and sub-paragraph (iii).
12, 13 & 14 Geo. 6. c. 97.	The National Parks and Access to the Countryside Act 1949.	In section 6(6), the words from "or a local planning authority" to "part of a National Park". Section 11. In section 11A(6)(b), the words "district council". Section 12(2). In section 13(1), the words "and within the area of the authority". In section 111A(3)(b), the words "for the purposes of sections 64, 65 and 77". Part II.
14 & 15 Geo. 6. c. 66.	The Rivers (Prevention of Pollution) (Scotland) Act 1951.	Section 17. In section 18, in subsection (1), the words "of their area", "in their area" (where first occurring) and "in their area or any part thereof"; and in subsection (3), the words "in their area" and the words from "whose" to "authority" where next occurring; In section 19, in subsection (1), the words "in the area of the authority", subsections (2)

Reference	Short title or title	Extent of repeal or revocation
		to (2B) and, in subsection (4), the words from "any", where first occurring, to "and", where last occurring.
		In section 35, the definitions of "river purification authority", river purification board area".
2 & 3 Eliz. 2. c. 70.	The Mines and Quarries Act 1954.	Section 151(5).
8 & 9 Eliz. 2. c. 62.	The Caravan Sites and Control of Development Act 1960.	In section 24(8), the words from "and a joint planning board" to "such a National Park".
1965 c. 13.	The Rivers (Prevention of Pollution) (Scotland) Act 1965.	Section 10(6)(a).
1965 c. 57.	The Nuclear Installations Act 1965.	In section 3(3)(b), the words "the National Rivers Authority,".
1967 c. 13.	The Parliamentary Commissioner Act 1967.	In Schedule 2, the entry relating to the National Rivers Authority and the note 9 inserted by paragraph 11 of Schedule 1 to the Water Act 1989.
1967 c. 22.	The Agriculture Act 1967.	In section 50(3), paragraph (e) and the words from "and "National Parks Planning authority" means" onwards.
1968 c. 41.	The Countryside Act 1969.	In section 6(2), paragraph (c) and the word "or" immediately preceding it. Section 13(11). Section 40. In section 42(1), the words "whether or not within the area of the local planning authority". In section 47A— (a) in subsection (2), the word "18"; and (b) subsection (4).
1968 c. 47.	The Sewerage (Scotland) Act 1968.	In section 38(3), the words "river purification authorities". In section 59(1), the definition of "river purification authority".
1968 c. 59.	The Hovercraft Act 1968.	In section 1(1)(g), the words "Part III of the the Control of Pollution Act 1974 or".
1970 c. 40.	The Agriculture Act 1970.	In section 92(1), the words "for their area" and "both within (and in the case of a river purification board) outwith, that area". Section 92(2)(c).
1972 c. 52.	The Town and Country Planning (Scotland) Act 1972.	Section 251A.
1972 c. 70	The Local Government Act 1972.	Section 101(9)(h). In section 104A(2), in the definition of "local authority", the words "or reconstituted in pursuance of Schedule 17 to this Act". In section 184— (a) in subsection (2), the words "and Schedule 17 to this Act"; (b) in this subsection (4), the words "subject to Schedule 17 of this Act"; and (c) subsection (6). In section 223(2), the words "and the National Rivers Authority". In Schedule 16, paragraph 55(2). Part I of Schedule 17.

Reference	Short title or title	Extent of repeal or revocation
1972 c. v.	The Clyde River Purification Act 1972.	The whole Act.
1973 c. 65.	The Local Government (Scotland) Act 1973.	Sections 135 and 135A. Section 200. In Schedule 16, paragraphs 1 to 5 and 7 to 10. In Schedule 27, in Part II, paragraphs 30 to 32, 37 and 38.
1972 c. 7.	The Local Government Act 1974.	Section 7.
1974 c. 37.	The Health and Safety at Work etc. Act. 1974.	In section 28, in subsection (3)(c)(ii), so far as extending to England and Wales, the words "of the National Rivers Authority or" and the word "Authority" (where next occurring), subsection (3)(c)(iii) and, in subsection (5)(b), so far as extending to England and Wales, the words "the National Rivers Authority".
1974 c. 40.	The Control of Pollution Act 1974.	In section 5, in subsection (4), the words following paragraph (b), and subsection (5). In section 7, in subsections (1) and (4), the words "issued by a disposal authority" and, in subsection (2), the words "or, in relation to Scotland, subsection (5)". In section 9(4), the words "issued by the authority". In section 11, subsections (1) to (11). In section 30(1), the words from "and for the purposes" to the end. In section 30A(2)(a), the words "in the area of that authority". In section 30C, in subsection (1), the words "within the area of that authority"; and in each of subsections (4) and (6), the words "in the area of a river purification authority". In section 31, subsections (1) to (3), in subsection (6), the words "in its area" and subsections (7), and (10). Section 31D. Section 32. In section 33(1), the words "in the area of the authority". In section 34(3), the words "in its area". Section 40(4). In section 41(1), in paragraph (c), the words "(except section 40(4))" and paragraphs (d)(ii) and (e). In section 46(1), the words "in its area" where they first occur and "in its area or elsewhere". In section 47, in subsection (1), the words "in its area" and in subsection (2), the words "in the authority's area". In section 48(1), the words "in its area". In section 50, the words "in its area". Sections 53, 54, 55 and 56(4). In section 57, paragraph (a). Section 58. Section 58A. Section 58B. Section 59. Section 59A.

Reference	Short title or title	Extent of repeal or revocation
		In sections 61(9) and 65(8) the words "section 59 of this Act (in relation to Scotland) or" and the words "(in relation to England and Wales)".
		In section 69, in subsection (1), paragraph (a) and, in paragraph (c) the words "section 59(2) or", and in subsection (3) the words "section 59(6) or" and paragraph (i).
		In section 73, in subsection (1), the definition of "equipment", in the definition of "person responsible" paragraphs (b) and (c), and the definition of "road noise", and in subsection (3) the words from ";but a requirement" to the end of the subsection.
		In section 74, the words "Subject to sections 58A(8) and 59A(9) of this Act".
		In section 87(3), the words from the beginning to "offence; and" and the words "in its application to Scotland".
		Section 91(5)(a).
		In section 96(3), the words from "but as if" to the end.
		In section 104(1), the word "59".
		Section 106(2).
		In Schedule 2, paragraphs 1 to 3.
		In Schedule 3, paragraphs 12 and 13.
S.I. 1974/2170.	The Clean Air Enactments (Repeals and Modifications) Regulations 1974.	In Schedule 2, paragraph 1.
1975 c. 24.	The House of Commons Disqualification Act 1975.	In Schedule 1, in Part II, the entry relating to the National Rivers Authority.
1975 c. 25.	The Northern Ireland Assembly Disqualification Act 1975.	In Schedule 1, in Part II, the entry relating to the National Rivers Authority.
1975 c. 30.	The Local Government (Scotland) Act 1975.	In section 16, the words "and river purification boards". Section 23(1)(e). In Schedule 3, in paragraph 28(1), the words "or a river purification board".
1975 c. 51.	The Salmon and Freshwater Fisheries Act 1975.	In section 5(2), the words following paragraph (b). In section 10, in subsections (1) and (2), the words "with the written consent on the Minister" in each place where they occur. In section 15, in subsections (1) and (3), the words "with the written consent of the Minister" in each place where they occur. In section 30, the paragraph defining "fish farm". In section 41(1), the definition of "grating".
1975 c. 70.	The Welsh Development Agency Act 1975.	In section 16(9), in the definition of "local authority", paragraph (b) and the word "or" immediately preceding it.

Reference	Short title or title	Extent of repeal or revocation
1976 c. 74.	The Race Relations Act 1976.	In section 19A(2)(a), the words "a special planning board or a National Park Committee".
1980 c. 45.	The Water (Scotland) Act 1980.	In section 33(3)(a), sub-paragraph (ii) and the preceding "and".
		In section 109(1), the definitions of "river purification authority" and "river purification board".
		In Schedule 1, in paragraph 11(ii) the words "and any river purification authority".
1980 c. 65.	The Local Government Planning and Land Act 1980.	In section 52(1), paragraph (b) and the word "and" immediately preceding it.
		In section 103(2)(c), the word "and" immediately preceding sub-paragraph (ii).
		In Schedule 2, paragraph 9(2) and (3).
1980 c. 66.	The Highways Act 1980.	In section 25(2)(a) the words "or a joint planning board" to "National Park".
		In section 27(6), the words from "or any such joint planning board" onwards.
		In section 29, the words "and joint planning boards".
		In section 72(2), the words "or joint planning board".
		Section 118(7)
1981 c. 67.	The Acquisition of Land Act 1981.	In section 17, in subsection (3), the words "the Peak Park Joint or Lake District Special Planning Board" and, in subsection (4), in the definition of "a Welsh planning board", paragraph (b) and the word "or" immediately preceding it.
		In paragraph 4 of Schedule 3, in sub-paragraph (3), the words "the Peak Park Joint or Lake District Special Planning Board" and, in sub-paragraph (4), in the definition of "a Welsh planning board", paragraph (b) and the word "or" immediately preceding it.
1981 c. 69.	The Wildlife and Countryside Act 1981.	Section 39(5)(a).
		In section 44, subsection (1) and in subsection (1A), the words from the beginning to "but".
		Section 46.
		In section 52(2), paragraph (a) and, in paragraph (b), the words "in any other provision".
		Section 72(10).
1982 c. 30.	The Local Government (Miscellaneous Provisions) Act 1982.	In section 33(9), in paragraph (a), the words from "or reconstituted" to "1972" and, in paragraph (b), the words "or reconstituted".
		In section 41(13), in paragraph (b) of the definition of "local authority" the words from "or reconstituted" to "1972".
		In section 45(2)(b), the words from "or reconstituted" to "1972".
1982 c. 42.	The Derelict Land Act 1982.	In section 1(11), in the definition of "local authority", paragraph (b) and the word "or" immediately preceding it.

Reference	Short title or title	Extent of repeal or revocation
1982 c. 48.	The Criminal Justice Act 1982.	In Schedule 15, paragraphs 6 and 7.
1983 c. 35.	The Litter Act 1983.	In section 4(1)— (a) paragraph (b) and word "and" immediately preceding it; and (b) the words "the National Park Committee (if any)" in each place where they occur. In section 6(8), the words "or a Park board". In section 10, paragraph (h) of the definition of "litter authority" and the definitions of "National Park Committee" and "Park board".
1984 c. 54	The Roads (Scotland) Act 1984.	In Schedule 9, paragraph 17(3).
1985 c. 51.	The Local Government Act 1985.	In Schedule 3— (a) paragraph 4; (b) in paragraph 5, sub-paragraphs (2) to (8); (c) paragraph 6; and (d) in paragraph 7, sub-paragraph (3) and in sub-paragraph (4), the words "42" and "44".
1985 c. 68.	The Housing Act 1985.	In section 573, in subsection (1), the entries relating to the Peak Park Joint Planning Board and the Lake District Special Planning Board and, in subsection (1A), paragraph (b) and the word "or" immediately preceding it.
S.I. 1987/180.	The Control of Industrial Air Pollution (Transfer of Powers of Enforcement) Regulations 1987.	Regulations 2 and 4.
1988 c. 4.	The Norfolk and Suffolk Broads Act 1988.	In Schedule 6, paragraphs 2 and 13.
1988 c. 9.	The Local Government Act 1988.	In Schedule 2, the entries relating to the Lake District Special Planning Board, the Peak Park Joint Planning Board and a special planning board constituted under paragraph 3A of Schedule 17 to the Local Government Act 1972.
1988 c. 41.	The Local Government Finance Act 1988.	In section 74(7), paragraph (b) and the word "and" immediately preceding it.
1989 c. 14.	The Control of Pollution (Amendment) Act 1989.	Section 2(3)(e). Section 7(2) and (8). Section 11(3).
1989 c.15.	The Water Act 1989.	In Schedule 1, paragraphs 11, 12 and 13. In Schedule 17, paragraphs 3(2) and (3), 5(2), 7(9)(d) and 9(1). In Schedule 25, paragraphs 43(1) and paragraph 48(3) and (4).
1989 c. 29.	The Electricity Act 1989.	In Schedule 8, paragraph 2(6)(a)(i).
1989 c. 42.	The Local Government and Housing Act 1989.	Section 5(4)(c). Section 13(4)(d). In section 21(1), paragraph (m) and the word "and" immediately preceding it. Section 39(1)(h). Section 67(3)(o). Section 152(2)(k). In Schedule 1, in paragraph 2(1)(b), the word "(m)" and paragraph 2(1)(f).

Reference	Short title or title	Extent of repeal or revocation
1990 c. 8.	The Town and Country Planning Act 1990.	In section 1, in subsection (5)— (a) in paragraph (a), the words from "and Part I" to "National Parks)"; and (b) in paragraph (c), the words "section 4 and"; and, in subsection (6), the words "section 4(3) and". In section 2(7), the words from "and Part I" to "National Parks)". Section 4. In section 4A(1), the words "instead of section 4(1) to (4)". Section 105. In section 244(1), the words from "or a board" to "1972". In Schedule 1— (a) in paragraph 4(2), the words "or county planning authority" and the words "or, as the case may be, which is"; (b) in paragraph 6, the words from "including" to "National Park"; (c) in paragraph 13(1), paragraph (d) and the word "or" immediately preceding it; (d) in paragraph 19, sub-paragraph (2); and (e) in paragraph 20(4), paragraph (a) and, in paragraph (b), the word "other".
1990 c.9.	The Planning (Listed Buildings and Conservation Areas) Act 1990.	In section 66(3), the words from "and a board" onwards. In Schedule 4— (a) in paragraph 2, the word "4"; (b) in paragraph 3, the words "or county planning authority" and the words "or, as the case may be, which is"; and (c) in paragraph 4(1), the words "4(3) and (4).
1990 c. 10.	The Planning (Hazardous Substances) Act 1990.	In section 3— (a) in subsection (1), paragraph (a) and the words after paragraph (c); (b) subsection (2); and (c) in subsections (3) to (5A), the words "or (2)", wherever occurring.
1990 c.11.	The Planning (Consequential Provisions) Act 1990.	In Schedule 2— (a) paragraph 20; (b) paragraph 28(6); and (c) in paragraph 45, sub-paragraph (2) and in sub-paragraph (7), the words "118(7)".
1990 c. 43.	The Environmental Protection Act 1990.	In section 4, in subsection (8), the words "or, as the case may be, in the Edinburgh Gazette", in each place where they occur, and, in subsection (11), the words "and Wales" in paragraph (b) and paragraph (c) and the word "and" immediately preceding it. Section 5. In section 7(9), the words from "and, in relation to Scotland," to the end.

Reference	Short title or title	Extent of repeal or revocation
		In section 8, subsection (4) and, in subsection (7) the words from "together with" onwards and subsection (9).
		Sections 16 to 18.
		Section 20(3) and (9).
		In section 23, in subsection (1), paragraphs (d) to (f) and (k), and subsections (4) and (5).
		In section 28, in subsection (1), the words from "but" onwards and subsections (3) and (4).
		In section 30, in subsection (4), the words "or regulation authorities" and the words from "establishing authorities" onwards and subsections (6) to (8).
		Section 31.
		In section 33(1), the words "and, in relation to Scotland, section 54 below,".
		In section 36, subsections (5) and (6), in subsection (11), in the definition of "National Park authority", the words "subject to subsection (12) below" and subsection (12).
		In section 37(5), the words "(5), (6)," and "(8)".
		In section 39, in subsection (7), the words following paragraph (b), subsection (8), in subsection (12), in the definition of "National Park authority", the words "subject to subsection (13) below", and subsection (13).
		Section 41.
		In section 42, subsection (2) and, in subsection (7), the words from "and the power" onwards.
		Section 43(2)(a) and (b).
		Section 50.
		Section 54.
		Section 61.
		In section 64, subsection (1)(l) and, in subsection (4), the words "which is not a waste regulation authority".
		Sections 67 to 70.
		In section 71, subsection (1) and, in subsection (3), paragraph (b) and the word "or" immediately preceding it.
		Section 72.
		Section 75(3).
		In the heading immediately preceding section 79, the words ": England and Wales".
		In section 79, in subsection (7), in the definition of "local authority", the word "and" following paragraph (b).
		Section 83.
		In section 88, in subsection (9), paragraphs (c) and (d), and, in subsection (10), in the definition of "authorised officer", the words from "or in the case" to "on behalf of" and the definitions of "National Park Committee" and "Park board".

Reference	Short title or title	Extent of repeal or revocation
		In section 141, in subsection (5)(a), sub-paragraph (ii) and the word "and" immediately preceding it.
		Section 143.
		In Schedule 2, in paragraph 17(2), the words "a waste regulation authority or".
		In Schedule 8—
		(a) paragraph 1(13);
		(b) paragraph 3; and
		(c) in paragraph 4, the words from the beginning to "in Wales)" and".
		In Schedule 15, paragraphs 5(4) and 16 and, in paragraph 31, in sub-paragraph (2), the word "(6)," where secondly occurring, the word "(2)", where thirdly occurring, and sub-paragraphs (4)(c) and (5)(c).
1991 c. 28.	The Natural Heritage (Scotland) Act 1991.	In section 15(3) the words "and a river purification authority of whom such a requirement is made shall make such an application".
		In Schedule 2, paragraph 10(3).
		In Schedule 5, in paragraph 2 the words "in their area and".
		In Schedule 6, paragraph 1(5).
		In Schedule 8, in sub-paragraph (3) of paragraph 1, in the second column of the Table, in the fourth entry, the words ", river purification authority".
		In Schedule 10, paragraphs 1, 6, 7(2) and 9(3)(b) and (6)
1991 c. 34.	The Planning and Compensation Act 1991.	In Schedule 4, paragraph 39.
1991 c. 56.	The Water Industry Act 1991.	In section 4(6), the definition of "National Park authority" and the word "and" immediately preceding it.
		Section 132(7).
		Section 151.
		Section 171(4) and (5).
		In section 206(2), the words "196 or".
		In section 219(1), the definition of "the NRA".
1991 c. 57.	The Water Resources Act 1991.	Sections 1 to 14.
		Sections 16 to 19.
		In section 34, the word "planning", wherever it occurs, and subsection (5).
		In section 45,—
		(a) in subsection (2), the word "planning", wherever it occurs; and
		(b) in subsection (3), the words "and (5)".
		Section 58.
		Section 68.
		Section 69(5).
		In section 91, in subsection (1), the word "or" immediately preceding paragraph (f).
		Section 105(1).
		In section 113(1), in the definition of "drainage", the word "and" immediately preceding paragraph (c).
		Section 114.

Reference	Short title or title	Extent of repeal or revocation
		Section 117.
		Sections 121 to 124.
		Section 126(6).
		Section 129(4).
		Sections 131 and 132.
		Section 144.
		Section 146.
		Sections 150 to 153.
		Section 187.
		In section 190(1), paragraph (d), paragraph (f) and the word "and" immediately preceding it.
		Section 196.
		Section 202(5).
		Section 206(2)
		Section 209(1), (2) and (4).
		Sections 213 to 215.
		Section 218.
		In section 219, in subsection (2), the words "Subject to subsection (3) below," and subsection (3).
		In section 221(1), the definitions of "the Authority" and "consistent council".
		Schedule 1.
		Schedules 3 and 4.
1991 c. 59.	The Land Drainage Act 1991.	In section 61C(5), the definition of "National Park authority" and the word "and" immediately preceding it.
		In section 72(1), the definition of "the NRA".
1991 c. 60.	The Water Consolidation (Consequential Provisions) Act 1991.	In Schedule 1, paragraphs 17, 18(a), 25, 27(2) and 56(3) and (4).
1992 c. 14.	The Local Government Finance Act 1992.	Section 35(5)(a) and (b).
		In Schedule 13, paragraph 95.
1993 c. 11.	The Clean Air Act 1993.	Section 3(2)(b) and the word "or" which immediately precedes it.
		Section 17.
		Section 42(5).
		Section 51(1)(b) and the word "or" which immediately precedes it.
		In Schedule 3, paragraph 4(b).
1993 c. 12.	The Radioactive Substances Act 1993.	Section 4.
		Section 5.
		In section 16, in subsection (2), the words "Subject to subsection (3)," subsection (3) and, in subsection (10), the words from "or, as" to "appropriate Minister".
		Section 17(4).
		In section 18, in subsection (1), the words "(or, in a case" to "or that Minister)" and "or the appropriate Minister, as the case may be," and, in subsection (2)(b), the words from "(or, where" to "that Minister)".
		Section 20(3).
		In section 21, subsection (3) and, in subsection (4), the words from "or, where" to "that Minister".

Reference	Short title or title	Extent of repeal or revocation
		In section 22, subsection (5), in subsection (6), the words from "or, where" to "that Minister" and in subsection (7), the words from "or, where" to "that Minister".
		In section 25, in subsection (2), the words from "or, in a case" to "Food," and "or their".
		In section 26, subsection (3)(a) and, in sub-section (4), the words "England, Wales or".
		Section 28.
		Section 31.
		Section 35.
		In section 39, in subsection (2), the words from "or, as" to "and the chief inspector,".
		Section 42(5).
		Section 43.
		In section 47, in subsection (1), in the definition of "the appropriate Minister", paragraphs (a) and (b), in the definition of "the chief inspector", paragraphs (a) and (b), in the definition of "prescribed", the words from "or, in relation to fees" onwards and in the definition of "relevant water body", in paragraph (a), the words "the National Rivers Authority" and, in paragraph (b), the words "a river purification authority within the meaning of the Rivers (Prevention of Pollution) (Scotland) Act 1951".
		In section 48, in the Table, the entry relating to the chief inspector.
		Schedule 2.
		In Schedule 3, in Part II, in paragraph 11 the words "16, 17".
1993 c. 25.	The Local Government (Overseas Assistance) Act 1993.	Section 1(10)(g).
1993 c. 40.	The Noise and Statutory Nuisance Act 1993.	Section 6. Section 13(2). Schedule 1.
1994 c. 19.	The Local Government (Wales) Act 1994.	Section 19(2) and (3). Section 59(15). In Schedule 5, in Part III, paragraph 10. In Schedule 6, paragraphs 3 to 12, 18, 23, 24(1), 28 and 29. In Schedule 9, paragraph 17(4) and (12). In Schedule 11, paragraph 3(1) and (2). In Schedule 15, paragraph 64(b). In Scedule 16, paragraph 65(5) and (9). In Schedule 17, paragraph 13.
1994 c. 39.	The Local Government etc. (Scotland) Act 1994.	Section 37. Section 54(5). In section 165(6), the words "a river purification board". In Schedule 13, paragraphs 38(2) to (7), 85(3)(a) and (b)(i) and (4), 92(34) and (35), 93(2), 95(2), (4), (8) and (9), and 119 (54)(a)(ii) and (h)(iii) and, in paragraph 167, sub-paragraph (2), in sub-paragraph (3) the words "(1)(g),", and sub-paragraphs (4), (5), (7) and (9).

Reference	Short title or title	Extent of repeal or revocation
1995 c. 25.	The Environment Act 1995.	In section 8, in the definition of "National Park authority" in subsection (5), the words "subject to subsection (6) below" and subsection (6). In Schedule 10, paragraph 22(1) and (7) and, in paragraph 34(1), so much of paragraph (b) as precedes the word "and". In Schedule 11, in paragraph 1, in the definition of "National Park authority" in sub-paragraph (3), the words "subject to sub-paragraph (4) below" and sub-paragraph (4). In Schedule 22, paragraphs 19 to 27, 46(11)(a), 182 and 231.

INDEX

PENSIONS ACT 1995*

(1995 c. 26)

ARRANGEMENT OF SECTIONS

PART I

OCCUPATIONAL PENSIONS

---

*Annotations by Nigel Inglis-Jones, Q.C.

An Act to amend the law about pensions and for connected purposes.

[19th July 1995]

PARLIAMENTARY DEBATES
Hansard, H.L. Vol. 560, cols. 974, 1495, Vol. 561, cols. 106, 440, 511, 795, 869, 917, 993, 1036, Vol. 562, cols. 559, 637, 726, 800, 1131, 1153, Vol. 565, cols. 1683, 1729. H.C. Vol. 258, col. 525, Vol. 263, cols. 145, 390.

INTRODUCTION AND GENERAL NOTE

This Act was introduced as a result of the Maxwell scandal, which in turn prompted the setting up of the Pension Law Review Committee under the chairmanship of Professor Roy Goode. The report of this committee was presented to Parliament in September 1993. This was followed by the publication of the Government White Paper in 1994, and the introduction of the Pensions Bill in the House of Lords later that year. A large number of the recommendations of the Goode Committee were incorporated in the Bill, and are to be found in the Act.

In introducing the Act to the House of Lords the Minister of State for the Department of Social Security (Lord Mackay of Ardbrechnish) said that there were four major principles underlying the legislation, the first being to restore confidence by improving the security of occupational pension schemes: the others being to introduce the equal pension rights for men and women required by the European Court of Justice rulings, to secure a fair and sustainable state pension in the next century, and to make personal pensions attractive across a broader age range: see *Hansard*, H.L. Vol. 560, col. 975.

The Act is divided into four Parts. Part I is concerned with the provisions which amend and control certain aspects of occupational pension schemes. Part II mainly concerns the progressive equalisation of state pensions at age 65 for both sexes. Part III provides for the certification of schemes and further comprises the considerable changes which the Act makes to the conditions for contracting out of the state scheme. Part IV contains miscellaneous provisions. It deals with the extension of the scope of the right to transfer values, extends the jurisdiction of the Pensions Ombudsman, provides him with certain further powers, and provides for an annual increase in the rate of personal pensions, among other topics. It also makes provision in respect of two long-standing grievances. It provides for the court to have power to partition a pension or other benefit between spouses on divorce. It further provides pensions for certain war widows who remarried, but whose further marriages have terminated or been subject to an order for judicial separation. A grateful country deprived them of their war widows pensions—a deprivation upheld by successive governments since the war—a wrong belatedly righted.

Part I

The first main innovation under the Act is to make provision for an Occupational Pensions Regulatory Authority which is mainly concerned with overseeing the trustees of trust schemes, that is to say occupational pension schemes set up under a trust. Some of the present functions of the Occupational Pensions Board are transferred to the Authority, and the Occupational Pensions Board is abolished. The Authority is empowered to remove (and pending removal to suspend) a trustee for a serious or persistent breach of a duty under Part I of the Act or under any other part of the Act which is brought into the ambit of s.3. Consequential orders may be made.

Information may be gathered by the Authority (see s.98 onwards) by requiring a trustee, manager, professional adviser or employer connected with a scheme to produce any document, or any information, for example, stored on computer, relevant to the discharge of the Authority's functions to it by giving the appropriate notice. Inspection of premises is also provided for, together with the right of an inspector to require documents to be produced to him or information to be given to him, for the purpose of deciding whether the provisions of the Act are being, or have been, complied with. Supplementary provisions are included in the Act.

Provision is contained in the Act for the appointment of professional advisers for trust schemes, and the power of appointment is either directly or indirectly put into the hands of the trustees (see s.47 onwards). Information may flow from actuaries and auditors of such schemes to the Authority, since these persons have a duty to make a written report to the Authority if they have reasonable cause to believe that any duty imposed on the trustees, the employer, any professional adviser or any other prescribed person, whether by enactment or rule of law, is not being complied with. An actuary or accountant who fails to comply with this requirement is to be subject to a civil penalty: but if he does comply with the duty under the Act, he is to be deemed not to be in breach of any other duty, such as a duty of confidence to the trustees or the employer in question. These provisions are bound to distance actuaries and auditors from trustees and employers, and will lay on those professionals duties which, in applicable cases, will require considerable independence of attitude with respect to those whom they advise. One wonders how palatable these duties will be.

The other main innovation contained in Pt. I of the Act is the Pensions Compensation Board. This provides for compensation to be paid to the trustees of schemes instituted under a trust where the employer is insolvent, the value of the assets of the scheme has been depleted by an act or omission which constitutes a prescribed offence (so that in the case of a salary-related scheme the liabilities exceed the assets at the date of application by more than 10 per cent), and it is reasonable for the members to be assisted by the payment of compensation. The amount of compensation is to be determined in accordance with regulations to be made, but is to be restricted to 90 per cent of the shortfall, broadly to such sum as will cause the assets of the scheme to provide for 90 per cent of its liabilities. For these provisions see s.78 onwards of the Act.

Needless to say, the funds for the purposes of the Authority and the Compensation Board are to come from a levy to be imposed on occupational pension schemes generally (see s.165 of the Act).

Further provisions of the Act with regard to financial rectitude provide for minimum funding requirements for schemes which are not money purchase schemes, or otherwise excused. This is another principal innovation, which has been much debated, owing to the solvency standard which it is intended to prescribe by regulation. These are regarded as insufficient and misleading in some quarters. For these provisions see s.56 onwards of the Act.

The identity and the powers of trustees are regulated by substantial provisions within the Act. Provision is made for member-nominated trustees, unless the members and pensioners are agreeable to the existing arrangements for the appointment of trustees remaining. Provision is also made for a person who is the auditor or the actuary to the scheme not to be a trustee, and for certain persons to be disqualified from acting as trustees of occupational pension schemes, with power to the Authority to waive this requirement. For these provisions see s.16 onwards of the Act.

As to the functions of trustees of schemes, such topics as the taking of decisions by a majority of trustees, the powers of investment of the fund of a scheme, the principles to be observed in respect of investment and the delegation of these powers, the payment of surplus to employers from an ongoing scheme, a restriction on employer-related investments, and the provision of certain scheme documents for members are all covered. As noted above, there is a requirement for certain professional advisers to be appointed for a scheme by the trustees. The requirements for the functions of trustees are set out in s.32 onwards of the Act.

Other provisions of this Part of the Act provide a statutory basis for the keeping of a separate account for the receipt of scheme moneys, for the keeping of proper records and books for a scheme, and for the keeping in a separate account of moneys which the employer should pay as benefits to members of a trust scheme, but payment of which has not been made. This is in order to safeguard the moneys of a scheme where the employer pays the benefits as agent of the trustees. Legislation is put in place for arrangements to be made for the resolution of disputes, if possible, at trustee level. For these provisions see ss.49 and 50 of the Act.

Provision is contained in the Act for limited price indexation of pensions payable in respect of service after an appointed day, with supplementary provisions. The requirement of indexation of benefits payable in respect of service before the appointed day (the earlier service component) is no longer contemplated. This was to be found in s.104 of the Pension Schemes Act 1993, but was never brought into force. For this see s.51 onwards of the Act.

Other aspects of pension schemes covered by the Act include the modification of schemes, with restrictions being placed on certain powers, and certain other powers being granted to trustees. The Authority is granted the right to make or authorise yet other alterations, although its powers are more restricted than those previously available to the Occupational Pensions Board (which is now abolished). For these provisions see s.67 onwards of the Act.

The winding up of schemes is to be regulated to a considerable extent. This matter is covered by s.73 onwards of the Act.

Also covered is the equal treatment of members of schemes, so as to comply with the provisions of Art. 119 of the Treaty of Rome. Power is given to the trustees of a scheme to make the amendments necessary to comply with the requirements of equal treatment, and this power may be exercised retrospectively. This is most important, and these provisions are to be found in s.62 onwards of the Act.

It is interesting to note that the Government refused to support an amendment which in effect would have sought to codify the primary duties of trustees of occupational pension schemes and to place their enforcement on the Authority, on the grounds that these matters were better left to the courts: see *Hansard*, H.L. Vol. 561, col. 160. The amendment was lost. The Government also did not support an amendment which was intended to give the court power to make a protective order of costs where on the application of 10 per cent of the members of a scheme or of a member-nominated trustee it appeared to the court that serious or persistent breaches of trust may have been committed. Accordingly the amendment was lost: see *Hansard*, H.L. Vol. 561, col. 556.

Part II

This Part contains the provisions necessary to equalise the pensionable age for state pensions for men and women. This is dealt with in s.126: in practice this entails the progressive increase in the pensionable age for women under the state scheme in the manner readily seen by reference to the Table contained in Sched. 4 to the Act, until with effect from April 6, 2020 the pensionable age for women becomes 65. This method of equalisation was probably inevitable given the large and increasing pressure of state pensions on the resources not only of the U.K. Government, but also of the governments of the E.U. and of other affluent parts of the world. Equalisation takes place over a 10-year period commencing on April 6, 2010.

Part III

Part III concerns the new arrangements for contracting-out of the state scheme. These provisions will come into force on a day appointed under s.180 as the principal appointed day for the purpose of this Part of the Act. In respect of a period after the principal appointed day, the requirement for the provision of a guaranteed minimum pension will no longer be required. Instead schemes will have to provide benefits in respect of such a period which are broadly equivalent to, or better than, those contained in a statutory reference scheme. Very broadly, this prescribes a benefit of one-eightieth of a final pensionable salary averaged over three years, but the pension need not exceed one-half of the earnings on which it is calculated. Widow's and widower's benefits of broadly one-half the member's benefits under whom the claim is made have to be provided. A number of other amendments with regard to contracting-out are contained in this Part, not least in connection with contracted-out money purchase schemes, and appropriate personal pension schemes. Interim provisions are also made.

Part IV

This Part contains miscellaneous matters including important extensions to the powers of the Pensions Ombudsman contained in s.146 onwards of the Pension Schemes Act 1993, and these are to be found in s.156 onwards of this Act. Also included are: in s.165 the extension to the levy on prescribed occupational and personal pension schemes; in ss.166 and 167 the provisions with regard to pensions on divorce noted above; and in s.168 the extension of pensions for war widows also noted above.

PART I

OCCUPATIONAL PENSIONS

Occupational Pensions Regulatory Authority

The new authority

1.—(1) There shall be a body corporate called the Occupational Pensions Regulatory Authority (referred to in this Part as "the Authority").

(2) The Authority shall consist of not less than seven members appointed by the Secretary of State, one of whom shall be so appointed as chairman.

(3) In addition to the chairman, the Authority shall comprise—

(a) a member appointed after the Secretary of State has consulted organisations appearing to him to be representative of employers,

(b) a member appointed after the Secretary of State has consulted organisations appearing to him to be representative of employees,

(c) a member who appears to the Secretary of State to be knowledgeable about life assurance business,

(d) a member who appears to the Secretary of State to have experience of, and to have shown capacity in, the management or administration of occupational pension schemes, and

(e) two members who appear to the Secretary of State to be knowledgeable about occupational pension schemes,

and such other member or members as the Secretary of State may appoint.

(4) Neither the Authority nor any person who is a member or employee of the Authority shall be liable in damages for anything done or omitted in the discharge or purported discharge of the functions of the Authority under this Part or the Pension Schemes Act 1993, or any provisions in force in Northern Ireland corresponding to either of them, unless it is shown that the act or omission was in bad faith.

(5) Schedule 1 (constitution, procedure, etc. of the Authority) shall have effect.

(6) In this section, "life assurance business" means the issue of, or the undertaking of liability under, policies of assurance upon human life, or the granting of annuities upon human life.

DEFINITIONS
    "employee": s.124(5); the Pension Schemes Act 1993, s.181(1).
    "employer": s.124(1) and cf s.124(5); the Pension Schemes Act 1993, s.181(1).
    "occupational pension scheme": s.149.

GENERAL NOTE

Subs. (5)
    Schedule 1 contains the necessary provisions which give flesh to the functions of the Authority. From the point of view of the practitioner, the most important powers are likely to be contained in regulations made by the Secretary of State under para. 13 of this Schedule. The Authority may be given power to summon witnesses, to administer oaths to those giving evidence to the Authority, and to require persons to produce documents and to give information to the Authority in respect of a relevant scheme. These are powers which indicate that the Authority is expected to have an inquisitorial function.
    [Standing Committee D, May 2, 1995, col. 6].

Reports to Secretary of State

2.—(1) The Authority must prepare a report for the first twelve months of their existence, and a report for each succeeding period of twelve months, and must send each report to the Secretary of State as soon as practicable after the end of the period for which it is prepared.

(2) A report prepared under this section for any period must deal with the activities of the Authority in the period.

(3) The Secretary of State must lay before each House of Parliament a copy of every report received by him under this section.

DEFINITIONS
    "Authority": s.1.

GENERAL NOTE
    Section 2 prescribes that the Authority is to report at 12-month intervals, and as soon as practicable after the end of each such interval. This report must be laid before the House of Lords and the House of Commons.
    [Standing Committee D, May 9, 1995, col. 85].

Supervision by the Authority

Prohibition orders

3.—(1) The Authority may by order prohibit a person from being a trustee of a particular trust scheme in any of the following circumstances.
    (2) The circumstances are—
    (a) that the Authority are satisfied that while being a trustee of the scheme the person has been in serious or persistent breach of any of his duties under—
        (i) this Part, other than the following provisions: sections 51 to 54, 62 to 65 and 110 to 112, or
        (ii) the following provisions of the Pension Schemes Act 1993: section 6 (registration), Chapter IV of Part IV (transfer values), section 113 (information) and section 175 (levy),
    (b) that the Authority are satisfied that, while being a trustee of the scheme, this section has applied to the person by virtue of any other provision of this Part,
    (c) that the person is a company and any director of the company is prohibited under this section from being a trustee of the scheme,
    (d) that the person is a Scottish partnership and any of the partners is prohibited under this section from being a trustee of the scheme, or

(e) that the person is a director of a company which, by reason of circumstances falling within paragraph (a) or (b), is prohibited under this section from being a trustee of the scheme and the Authority are satisfied that the acts or defaults giving rise to those circumstances were committed with the consent or connivance of, or attributable to any neglect on the part of, the director;

or any other prescribed circumstances.

(3) The making of an order under subsection (1) against a person who is a trustee of the scheme in question has the effect of removing him.

(4) The Authority may, on the application of any person against whom an order under subsection (1) is in force, by order revoke the order, but a revocation made at any time cannot affect anything done before that time.

DEFINITIONS
   "Authority": s.1.
   "trust scheme": s.124(1).

GENERAL NOTE
   Section 3 contains the main power conferred on the Authority, and ss.4 and 5 are in effect subsidiary to this section, dealing with the procedures and consequences of the exercise of the power contained in this section. There is no reason to doubt that the powers contained in this section apply equally in respect of an independent trustee appointed under s.22: ss.7(2) and 8(3) make this plain. The power under s.3 only applies to a trust scheme, that is an occupational pension scheme set up under a trust, and there appear to be no cognate powers in respect of a manager of a non-trust scheme.

Subss. (1) and (2)
   Before a trustee can be removed the Authority must be satisfied of one or other of a number of requirements. The most likely requirement to bite is that the trustee is either in serious breach or in persistent breach of the duties specified in subs. (2)(a)(i) and (ii). The exceptions referred to in subs. (2)(a)(i) concern the indexation of pensions, the equal treatment requirement and the gathering of information by the Compensation Board. The duties specified in subs. (2)(a)(ii) which arise under the Pension Schemes Act 1993 are those in respect of the registration of a scheme with the Registrar of Occupational and Personal Pension Schemes (s.6), the right to a cash equivalent (ss.93 to 101, and regulations made thereunder), the requirements with regard to the provision of information to members, other beneficiaries and certain independent trade unions (s.113), and the payment of levies (s.175, as amended by s.165 of this Act). Other requirements *inter alia* pierce the corporate veil in respect of directors of corporate trustees.
   Section 3 is also expressly applied to certain sections contained in Part I Examples are to be found in ss.28(4), 31(3) and 36(8).

Subss. (3) and (4)
   Importantly, subs. (3) provides that where a prohibition order is made against either an individual trustee or a corporate trustee that trustee is removed. So far so good. The precise effect of an order against the director of a corporate trustee is not specified, but sense would be made of subs. (3) if an order against the director prohibits him from acting in the future as trustee of a particular scheme. Otherwise difficulties can be foreseen if the employer is a trustee of a scheme. Would the order have the effect of removing the director as a director of the employer for all purposes?
   Subsection (4) provides for the revocation of an order: but such revocation will not validate acts previously done by the person prohibited under subs. (1), for example, acts done by a person acting as trustee *de son tort* (but see s.6(3)).
   [Standing Committee D, May 9, 1995, col. 87].

Suspension orders

4.—(1) The Authority may by order suspend a trustee of a trust scheme—
   (a) pending consideration being given to the making of an order against him under section 3(1),
   (b) where proceedings have been instituted against him for an offence involving dishonesty or deception and have not been concluded,

(c) where a petition has been presented to the court for an order adjudging him bankrupt, or for the sequestration of his estate, and proceedings on the petition have not been concluded,

(d) where the trustee is a company, if a petition for the winding up of the company has been presented to the court and proceedings on the petition have not been concluded,

(e) where an application has been made to the court for a disqualification order against him under the Company Directors Disqualification Act 1986 and proceedings on the application have not been concluded, or

(f) where the trustee is a company or Scottish partnership and, if any director or, as the case may be, partner were a trustee, the Authority would have power to suspend him under paragraph (b), (c) or (e).

(2) An order under subsection (1)—

(a) if made by virtue of paragraph (a), has effect for an initial period not exceeding twelve months, and

(b) in any other case, has effect until the proceedings in question are concluded;

but the Authority may by order extend the initial period referred to in paragraph (a) for a further period of twelve months, and any order suspending a person under subsection (1) ceases to have effect if an order is made against that person under section 3(1).

(3) An order under subsection (1) has the effect of prohibiting the person suspended, during the period of his suspension, from exercising any functions as trustee of any trust scheme to which the order applies; and the order may apply to a particular trust scheme, a particular class of trust schemes or trust schemes in general.

(4) An order under subsection (1) may be made on one of the grounds in paragraphs (b) to (e) whether or not the proceedings were instituted, petition presented or application made (as the case may be) before or after the coming into force of that subsection.

(5) The Authority may, on the application of any person suspended under subsection (1), by order revoke the order, either generally or in relation to a particular scheme or a particular class of schemes; but a revocation made at any time cannot affect anything done before that time.

(6) An order under this section may make provision as respects the period of the trustee's suspension for matters arising out of it, and in particular for enabling any person to execute any instrument in his name or otherwise act for him and for adjusting any rules governing the proceedings of the trustees to take account of the reduction in the number capable of acting.

DEFINITIONS
"Authority": s.1.
"trust scheme": s.124(1).

GENERAL NOTE
This section provides for interim suspension of trustees pending consideration of their actions or omissions, or pending proceedings listed in subs. (1)(b) to (f), whether such proceedings were commenced before or after the coming into force of the subsection (subs. (3)). The suspension may be for 12 months or, where subs. (1)(b) to (f) applies, until the end of the proceedings in question. Any period ordered under subs. (1)(a) may be extended by a further period of 12 months (subs. (2)). Since an order under subs. (2) extends a period under subs. (1), it would appear that more than one extension may be made. The remaining provisions of this section make supplementary arrangements necessary for the administration of the scheme during the period of an interim order. Subsection (5) permits the Authority to revoke an order, but will not validate acts effected prior to such revocation. [Standing Committee D, May 9, 1995, Col. 102].

Removal of trustees: notices

5.—(1) Before the Authority make an order under section 3 against a person without his consent, the Authority must, unless he cannot be found or has no known address, give him not less than one month's notice of their proposal, inviting representations to be made to them within a time specified in the notice.

(2) Where any such notice is given, the Authority must take into consideration any representations made to them about the proposals within the time specified in the notice.

(3) Before making an order under section 3 against a person, the Authority must give notice of their intention to do so to each of the trustees of the scheme, except that person (if he is a trustee) and any trustee who cannot be found or has no known address.

(4) Where the Authority make an order under section 4 against a person, they must—
  (a) immediately give notice of that fact to that person, and
  (b) as soon as reasonably practicable, give notice of that fact to the other trustees of any trustee scheme to which the order applies, except any trustee who cannot be found or has no known address.

(5) Any notice to be given to any person under this section may be given by delivering it to him or by leaving it at his proper address or by sending it to him by post; and, for the purposes of this subsection and section 7 of the Interpretation Act 1978 in its application to this subsection, the proper address of any person is his latest address known to the Authority.

DEFINITIONS
  "Authority": s.1.
  "trust scheme": s.124(1).

GENERAL NOTE

Subs. (1)
  Under this subsection in the usual case a trustee of a trust scheme must be given one month's notice of the proposal to prohibit and remove him under s.3, and representations must be invited from him. Schedule 1, para. 13 anticipates the possibility of oral hearings at which representations may be made. No notice need be given in respect of a suspension order under s.4, but no doubt representations could be made for the revocation of an order if a prohibition order has been made unjustly, although the revocation cannot be backdated (s.4(5)).
  [Standing Committee D, May 9, 1995, col. 103].

Removal or suspension of trustees: consequences

6.—(1) A person who purports to act as trustee of a trust scheme while prohibited from being a trustee of the scheme under section 3 or suspended in relation to the scheme under section 4 is guilty of an offence and liable—
  (a) on summary conviction, to a fine not exceeding the statutory maximum, and
  (b) on conviction on indictment, to a fine or imprisonment or both.

(2) An offence under subsection (1) may be charged by reference to any day or longer period of time; and a person may be convicted of a second or subsequent offence under that subsection by reference to any period of time following the preceding conviction of the offence.

(3) Things done by a person purporting to act as trustee of a trust scheme while prohibited from being a trustee of the scheme under section 3 or suspended in relation to the scheme under section 4 are not invalid merely because of that prohibition or suspension.

(4) Nothing in section 3 or 4 or this section affects the liability of any person for things done, or omitted to be done, by him while purporting to act as trustee of a trust scheme.

DEFINITIONS
    "trust scheme": s.124(1).

GENERAL NOTE

Subs. (1)
    This provides that a person who purports to act as a trustee of a scheme while removed or suspended under s.3 or s.4 may, on summary conviction, be liable to a fine not exceeding the statutory maximum, currently £5,000; and may on conviction on indictment be liable to imprisonment for not more than two years and an unlimited fine. Fines may not be reimbursed to trustees out of trust assets: see s.31(1)(a).

Subss. (3) and (4)
    These subsections preserve the validity of acts done by a person as trustee of a scheme after he has been removed or suspended from that office, unless those acts are invalid on other grounds. The liability as *trustee de son tort* of a person so acting is also preserved.

Appointment of trustees

    7.—(1) Where a trustee of a trust scheme is removed by an order under section 3, or a trustee of such a scheme ceases to be a trustee by reason of his disqualification, the Authority may by order appoint another trustee in his place.
    (2) Where a trustee appointed under subsection (1) is appointed to replace a trustee appointed under section 23(1)(b), sections 22 to 26 shall apply to the replacement trustee as they apply to a trustee appointed under section 23(1)(b).
    (3) The Authority may also by order appoint a trustee of a trust scheme where they are satisfied that it is necessary to do so in order—
        (a) to secure that the trustees as a whole have, or exercise, the necessary knowledge and skill for the proper administration of the scheme,
        (b) to secure that the number of trustees is sufficient for the proper administration of the scheme, or
        (c) to secure the proper use or application of the assets of the scheme.
    (4) The Authority may also appoint a trustee of a trust scheme in prescribed circumstances.
    (5) The power to appoint a trustee by an order under this section includes power by such an order—
        (a) to determine the appropriate number of trustees for the proper administration of the scheme,
        (b) to require a trustee appointed by the order to be paid fees and expenses out of the scheme's resources,
        (c) to provide for the removal or replacement of such a trustee.
    (6) Regulations may make provision about the descriptions of persons who may or may not be appointed trustees under this section.

DEFINITIONS
    "Authority": s.1.
    "prescribed": s.124(1).
    "regulations": s.124(1).
    "resources": s.124(1).
    "trust scheme": s.124(1).

GENERAL NOTE
    This section contains an important power to be exercised by the Authority, namely that of appointing a trustee to a trust scheme. This may be exercised where a trustee is removed under s.3, where he is disqualified from acting as trustee, as to which see s.29. The Authority may also make an appointment to ensure that the trustees of a scheme have the appropriate skill and knowledge to administer it, to ensure that they are of a sufficient number, or to secure the proper

application of the assets of the scheme. The Authority may also make an appointment in other circumstances (if any) prescribed by regulations. These powers of appointment are wide-ranging, and may be used to protect members from incompetent as well as dishonest trustees. Subsections (2) and (5) contain consequential provisions and powers.

Appointment of trustees: consequences

8.—(1) An order under section 7 appointing a trustee may provide that an amount equal to the amount (if any) to which subsection (2) applies is to be treated for all purposes as a debt due from the employer to the trustees.

(2) This subsection applies to any amount which has been paid to the trustee so appointed out of the resources of the scheme and has not been reimbursed by the employer.

(3) Subject to subsection (4), a trustee appointed under that section shall, unless he is the independent trustee and section 22 applies in relation to the scheme, have the same powers and duties as the other trustees.

(4) Such an order may make provision—
(a) for restricting the powers or duties of a trustee so appointed, or
(b) for powers or duties to be exercisable by a trustee so appointed to the exclusion of other trustees.

DEFINITIONS
"employer": s.124(1) and *cf* s.124(5); the Pension Schemes Act 1993, s.181(1).
"independent trustee": ss.23(2) and 124(1).
"resources": s.124(1).

GENERAL NOTE

Subss. (1) and (2)
Subsections (1) and (2) in effect empower the Authority to require the employer to pay for a trustee appointed by it. This power will override any provision of the scheme, so that a situation might arise where the Authority appoints new trustees leaving former trustees to continue in that office also. The Authority might order the employer to reimburse the scheme for payments made to the trustees whom it appoints, whereas the continuing trustees might be paid from the scheme without any reimbursement being made if the trusts of the scheme so provide.

Subss. (3) and (4)
Subsection (3) makes it plain that, subject to any provision included in an order made by the Authority by virtue of subs. (4)(a), a trustee appointed by the Authority will have the same rights, powers, obligations and duties as any other trustee of the trust scheme appointed in the manner prescribed by the trusts of the scheme or appointed under statutory powers. But if he is an independent trustee and the provisions of s.22 apply to the scheme, his powers will be those appropriate to such a trustee (as to which, see s.25).

Subsection (4)(b) enables the Authority to restrict the rights of continuing trustees not appointed by it so that they are excluded from exercising their powers and duties under the scheme, leaving the same to be carried on by the trustees or trustee so appointed. This provision is wider than that contained in s.25 in respect of an independent trustee or independent trustees, because s.25(2) only refers to powers conferred on trustees, whereas this subsection encompasses duties as well as powers. Thus the Authority can take the running of a scheme out of the hands of continuing trustees while leaving them in place. This power would enable the Authority to act where the ingredients for the removal of a trustee under s.3 cannot be proved or do not exist, but one or more of the requirements set out in s.7(3) exist to an extent that it is desirable to put the running of the scheme or the care of the scheme's assets into different hands.

Removal and appointment of trustees: property

9. Where the Authority have power under this Part to appoint or remove a trustee, they may exercise the same jurisdiction and powers as are exercisable by the High Court or, in relation to a trust scheme subject to the law of

Scotland, the Court of Session for vesting any property in, or transferring any property to, trustees in consequence of the appointment or of the removal.

DEFINITIONS
  "Authority": s.1.
  "trust scheme": s.124(1).

GENERAL NOTE
  For the powers of the High Court in England and Wales, see s.44 and ss.49 to 51 of the Trustee Act 1925.

Civil penalties

10.—(1) Where the Authority are satisfied that by reason of any act or omission this section applies to any person, they may by notice in writing require him to pay, within a prescribed period, a penalty in respect of that act or omission not exceeding the maximum amount.

(2) In this section "the maximum amount" means—
  (a) £5,000 in the case of an individual and £50,000 in any other case, or
  (b) such lower amount as may be prescribed in the case of an individual or in any other case,
and the Secretary of State may by order amend paragraph (a) by substituting higher amounts for the amounts for the time being specified in that paragraph.

(3) Regulations made by virtue of this Part may provide for any person who has contravened any provision of such regulations to pay, within a prescribed period, a penalty under this section not exceeding an amount specified in the regulations; and the regulations must specify different amounts in the case of individuals from those specified in other cases and any amount so specified may not exceed the amount for the time being specified in the case of individuals or, as the case may be, others in subsection (2)(a).

(4) An order made under subsection (2) or regulations made by virtue of subsection (3) do not affect the amount of any penalty recoverable under this section by reason of an act or omission occurring before the order or, as the case may be, regulations are made.

(5) Where—
  (a) apart from this subsection, a penalty under this section is recoverable from a body corporate or Scottish partnership by reason of any act or omission of the body or partnership as a trustee of a trust scheme, and
  (b) the act or omission was done with the consent or connivance of, or is attributable to any neglect on the part of, any persons mentioned in subsection (6),
this section applies to each of those persons who consented to or connived in the act or omission or to whose neglect the act or omission was attributable.

(6) The persons referred to in subsection (5)(b)—
  (a) in relation to a body corporate, are—
      (i) any director, manager, secretary, or other similar officer of the body, or a person purporting to act in any such capacity, and
      (ii) where the affairs of a body corporate are managed by its members, any member in connection with his functions of management, and
  (b) in relation to a Scottish partnership, are the partners.

(7) Where the Authority requires any person to pay a penalty by virtue of subsection (5), they may not also require the body corporate, or Scottish partnership, in question to pay a penalty in respect of the same act or omission.

(8) A penalty under this section is recoverable by the Authority.

(9) The Authority must pay to the Secretary of State any penalty recovered under this section.

<small>DEFINITIONS</small>
"Authority": s.1.
"contravention": s.124(1).
"prescribed": s.124(1).
"regulations": s.124(1).

<small>GENERAL NOTE</small>
This section continues to provide the Authority with teeth. The amount of any penalty is set out in subs. (2). A penalty may be levied against the individuals mentioned in subs. (6) in the circumstances mentioned in subs. (5), but in such a case the relevant body corporate cannot also be required to pay a penalty. Regulations may also contain provisions for the payment of penalties, but the regulations must specify different amounts for individuals from those specified in other cases, particularly for companies. A penalty may not be reimbursed out of the trust assets to any trustee on whom it is levied: see s.31(1)(b).
[Standing Committee D, May 11, 1995, col. 111].

Powers to wind up schemes

11.—(1) Subject to the following provisions of this section, the Authority may by order direct or authorise an occupational pension scheme to be wound up if they are satisfied that—

(a) the scheme, or any part of it, ought to be replaced by a different scheme,

(b) the scheme is no longer required, or

(c) it is necessary in order to protect the interests of the generality of the members of the scheme that it be wound up.

(2) The Authority may not make an order under this section on either of the grounds referred to in subsection (1)(a) or (b) unless they are satisfied that the winding up of the scheme—

(a) cannot be achieved otherwise than by means of such an order, or

(b) can only be achieved in accordance with a procedure which—

    (i) is liable to be unduly complex or protracted, or

    (ii) involves the obtaining of consents which cannot be obtained, or can only be obtained with undue delay or difficulty,

and that it is reasonable in all the circumstances to make the order.

(3) An order made under this section on either of the grounds referred to in subsection (1)(a) or (b) may be made only on the application of—

(a) the trustees or managers of the scheme,

(b) any person other than the trustees or managers who has power to alter any of the rules of the scheme, or

(c) the employer.

(4) An order under this section authorising a scheme to be wound up must include such directions with respect to the manner and timing of the winding up as the Authority think appropriate having regard to the purposes of the order.

(5) The winding up of a scheme in pursuance of an order of the Authority under this section is as effective in law as if it had been made under powers conferred by or under the scheme.

(6) An order under this section may be made and complied with in relation to a scheme—

(a) in spite of any enactment or rule of law, or any rule of the scheme, which would otherwise operate to prevent the winding up, or

(b) except for the purpose of the Authority determining whether or not they are satisfied as mentioned in subsection (2), without regard to any such enactment, rule of law or rule of the scheme as would otherwise require, or might otherwise be taken to require, the implementation of any procedure or the obtaining of any consent, with a view to the winding up.

(7) In the case of a public service pension scheme—

(a) an order under subsection (1) directing or authorising the scheme to be wound up may only be made on the grounds referred to in paragraph (c), and

(b) such an order may, as the Authority think appropriate, adapt, amend or repeal any enactment in which the scheme is contained or under which it is made.

DEFINITIONS

"Authority": s.1.
"employer": s.124(1), and *cf* s.124(5); the Pension Schemes Act 1993, s.181(1).
"managers": s.124(1).
"member": s.124(1).
"occupational pension scheme": s.149.
"public service pension scheme": s.124(1); the Pension Schemes Act 1993, s.1.
"trustees or managers": s.124(1).

GENERAL NOTE

This section applies to all occupational pension schemes, including a public service scheme, although a public service scheme may only be wound up under this section in the circumstances set out in subs. (1)(c) (see subs. (7)(a)). The section is derived from powers contained in s.64 of the Social Security Act 1973, repealed in ss.142 and 143 of the Pension Schemes Act 1993. But the powers conferred on the Authority are wider, since the circumstances referred to in subs. (1)(c) under which the power can be exercised are new, and are applicable, where appropriate, to the generality of members, a phrase which may have to be the subject matter of judicial exposition. Substantial powers are conferred on the Authority to control the manner and timing of the winding up, in respect of which subs. (4) requires it to make orders which seem to it appropriate. Subsections (5), (6) and (7)(b) make it clear that the powers contained in this section are overriding, and may be exercised in the absence of consents which otherwise would have to be obtained.

[Standing Committee D, May 11, 1995, col. 114].

Powers to wind up public service schemes

12.—(1) The appropriate authority may by order direct a public service pension scheme to be wound up if they are satisfied that—

(a) the scheme, or any part of it, ought to be replaced by a different scheme, or

(b) the scheme is no longer required.

(2) Subsection (2) of section 11 applies for the purposes of this section as it applies for the purposes of that, but as if references to the Authority were to the appropriate authority.

(3) In this section "the appropriate authority", in relation to a scheme, means such Minister of the Crown or government department as may be designated by the Treasury as having responsibility for the particular scheme.

(4) An order under this section must include such directions with respect to the manner and timing of the winding up as that authority think appropriate.

(5) Such an order may, as that authority think appropriate, adapt, amend or repeal any enactment in which the scheme is contained or under which it is made.

DEFINITIONS

"Authority": s.1.
"public service pension scheme": s.124(1); the Pension Schemes Act 1993, s.1.

GENERAL NOTE

This section is complementary to s.11 with regard to public service pension schemes, and effectively gives like powers to the Authority in respect of such schemes as those set out in s.11(1)(a) and (b).

Injunctions and interdicts

13.—(1) If, on the application of the Authority, the court is satisfied that—

(a) there is a reasonable likelihood that a particular person will do any act which constitutes a misuse or misappropriation of assets of an occupational pension scheme, or

(b) that a particular person has done any such act and that there is a reasonable likelihood that he will continue or repeat the act in question or do a similar act,

the court may grant an injunction restraining him from doing so or, in Scotland, an interdict prohibiting him from doing so.

(2) The jurisdiction conferred by this section is exercisable by the High Court or the Court of Session.

DEFINITIONS
"Authority": s.1.
"occupational pension scheme": s.149.

GENERAL NOTE
This section empowers the authority to seek an injunction, including a *quia timet* injunction from the High Court (or the Court of Session in Scotland) to prevent, or prevent the repeat of, the misuse or misapplication of any of the assets of a scheme.

Restitution

14.—(1) If, on the application of the Authority, the court is satisfied—

(a) that a power to make a payment, or distribute any assets, to the employer, has been exercised in contravention of section 37, 76 or 77, or

(b) that any act or omission of the trustees or managers of an occupational pension scheme was in contravention of section 40,

the court may order the employer and any other person who appears to the court to have been knowingly concerned in the contravention to take such steps as the court may direct for restoring the parties to the position in which they were before the payment or distribution was made, or the act or omission occurred.

(2) The jurisdiction conferred by this section is exercisable by the High Court or the Court of Session.

DEFINITIONS
"Authority": s.1.
"contravention": s.124(1).
"employer": s.124(1), and cf s.124(5); the Pension Schemes Act 1993, s.181(1).
"trustees or managers": s.124(1).
"trust scheme": s.124(1).

GENERAL NOTE
This section enables the Authority to apply to the High Court (or the Court of Session in Scotland) for an order for restitution where there has been any contravention of the provisions of s.37 (payment of surplus to an employer from the assets of an ongoing scheme), s.40 (which, together with the regulations relating to it, controls the extent of employer-related investments), s.76 (which is relevant to the power to distribute surplus on the winding-up of a scheme) or s.77 (which relates to schemes with imperfect winding up provisions). Restitution may include the payment of interest of which the scheme has been deprived.
[Standing Committee D, May 11, 1995, col. 121].

Directions

15.—(1) The Authority may, where in the case of any trust scheme the employer fails to comply with any requirement included in regulations by virtue of section 49(5), direct the trustees to make arrangements for the payment to the members of the benefit to which the requirement relates.

(2) The Authority may—

(a) where in the case of any trust scheme an annual report is published, direct the trustees to include a statement prepared by the Authority in the report, and

(b) in the case of any trust scheme, direct the trustees to send to the members a copy of a statement prepared by the Authority.

(3) A direction under this section must be given in writing.

(4) Where a direction under this section is not complied with, sections 3 and 10 apply to any trustee who has failed to take all such steps as are reasonable to secure compliance.

DEFINITIONS

"Authority": s.1.
"employer": s.124(1), and *cf* s.124(5); the Pension Schemes Act 1993, s.181(1).
"member": s.124(1).
"regulations": s.124(1).
"trust scheme": s.124(1).

GENERAL NOTE

Subs. (1)

Section 49(5) is concerned with the situation where an employer pays scheme benefits to members of trust schemes. In such circumstances regulations must require benefit moneys not paid within a specified period to be kept in a separate account. This is to prevent the difficulty connected with impressing moneys in the general account of an employer, but which are due by way of benefit payments, with a trust for those due to receive those payments. The Authority may alter the arrangements for the payment of benefits so that it is carried out by the trustees.

Subs. (2)

This empowers the Authority to give the trustees a direction in writing for the purpose of enabling the Authority to make a statement to the members of a scheme.

Failure to comply with a direction made under subs. (1) or (2) may cause the removal or suspension of the trustee of a scheme, or the payment of a penalty by any person within the ambit of s.10.

[Standing Committee D, May 11, 1995, col. 125].

Member-nominated trustees and directors

Requirement for member-nominated trustees

16.—(1) The trustees of a trust scheme must (subject to section 17) secure—

(a) that such arrangements for persons selected by members of the scheme to be trustees of the scheme as are required by this section are made, and

(b) that those arrangements, and the appropriate rules, are implemented.

(2) Persons who become trustees under the arrangements required by subsection (1) are referred to in this Part as "member-nominated trustees".

(3) The arrangements must provide—

(a) for any person who has been nominated and selected in accordance with the appropriate rules to become a trustee by virtue of his selection, and

(b) for the removal of such a person to require the agreement of all the other trustees.

(4) Where a vacancy for a member-nominated trustee is not filled because insufficient nominations are received, the arrangements must provide for the filling of the vacancy, or for the vacancy to remain, until the expiry of the next period in which persons may be nominated and selected in accordance with the appropriate rules.

(5) The arrangements must provide for the selection of a person as a member-nominated trustee to have effect for a period of not less than three nor more than six years.

(6) The arrangements must provide for the number of member-nominated trustees to be—

(a) at least two or (if the scheme comprises less than 100 members) at least one, and

(b) at least one-third of the total number of trustees;

but the arrangements must not provide for a greater number of member-nominated trustees than that required to satisfy that minimum unless the employer has given his approval to the greater number.

(7) The arrangements must not provide for the functions of member-nominated trustees to differ from those of any other trustee but, for the purposes of this subsection—

(a) any provision made by an order under section 8(4), and

(b) section 25(2),

shall be disregarded.

(8) The arrangements must provide that, if a member-nominated trustee who was a member of the scheme when he was appointed ceases to be a member of the scheme, he ceases to be a trustee by virtue of that fact.

DEFINITIONS

"employer": s.124(1), and cf s.124(5); the Pension Schemes Act 1993, s.181(1).
"member": s.124(1).
"trust scheme": s.124(1).

GENERAL NOTE

This section prescribes that there shall be member-nominated trustees in all but excepted trust schemes. The exceptions are contained in s.17, and comprise three classes, namely schemes where the employer has proposed either the continuation of existing, or the substitution of new for existing, arrangements, and these have been approved under the statutory consultation procedure (as to which see s.21(7)); schemes where all of the members are trustees; and schemes which fall within a class prescribed for that purpose by regulations (see subs. (4)). It is most unusual for trustees, or the directors of the board of a corporate trustee, not to be members of a scheme (in the sense in which "member" is used in this Act), unless the scheme is a small insured scheme, when the employer is frequently the trustee. The normal provision is for the employer to nominate the trustees. In those cases where some of the trustees are elected by the membership or nominated by one or more trades unions, the employer usually retains control of the trustee body either by retaining the right to nominate a majority of the trustees, or by retaining the chairmanship of the trustees for one of its nominees, together with a casting vote for the chairman.

Despite the fact that the power to appoint a trustee is a fiduciary power (see *Re Skeats' Settlement* (1889) 42 Ch.D. 522 and *Re Shortridge* [1895] 1 Ch. 278), employers have found the right to nominate the trustees of a scheme a valuable power. Many of the acts of trustees of schemes are effected pursuant to a power or discretion, and the employer may well wish those who exercise such to be well aware of or sympathetic to its wishes. The courts do not exercise a close jurisdiction over the exercise of a power or discretion, in the sense that they emphasise that the exercise of a discretion is a matter for the trustees (unless the same is surrendered to the court) and they acknowledge that in many cases there is a range of possibilities for the exercise, none of which may be stigmatised as wrong: see, for the criteria adopted by the court for interference, *Stannard v. Fisons Pension Trust Ltd.* [1991] IRLR 27, and *Hastings-Bass Deceased, Re* [1975] Ch. 25. Thus a discretion exercised by a body of trustees which is wholly sympathetic to an employer may be hard to challenge.

The provisions of this section do not seek to take from the employer the right to nominate the majority of the trustees, where it has that right. They seek to ensure, however, that the views of the general membership will be heard through the member-nominated trustees, where the membership desires that this should be so; and that the membership's views will be heard at the important time, namely when a decision is taken. But it cannot be over-emphasised that member-nominated trustees are not representative trustees. Nor are employer-nominated trustees. Each trustee has a duty to all of the beneficiaries under the trust (and, no doubt, yet to be explored duties in certain respects to the employer in the case of a "balance of cost" scheme, at least) to use the powers of the trust to further its purposes.

The Government refused an amendment which would have compelled the nomination by pensioners of one of the trustees of a scheme, once the payment of pensions from it commenced, on the grounds that this would introduce unnecessary rigidity into a system of selection which needed flexibility: see *Hansard*, H.L.Vol. 561, col. 458.

For the protection against victimisation of an employee trustee, see *Hansard*, H.L. Vol. 561, col. 468.

Subs. (1)

The duty of complying with s.16 is placed on the trustees of the trust scheme. There is no corresponding provision applicable to the managers of a non-trust scheme, and such schemes are not covered by this section.

Subs. (3)

A member-nominated trustee may be removed, but only by the affirmative vote, *inter alia*, of all of the other member-nominated trustees. Any other requirement of the provisions of the scheme would have to be complied with.

Subs. (4)

This provides that the arrangements prescribed by subs. (1) must provide for the situation where there are insufficient nominations to fill a vacancy for a member-nominated trustee, and for the interregnum.

Subs. (5)

Member-nominated trustees are appointed for a minimum of three and a maximum of six years. Nothing is said about re-selection.

Subs. (6)

The usual requirement for member-nominated trustees is that they should be not less than two in number, and not less than one-third of the total number of trustees. Where the membership of the scheme is less than 100, there need only be one member-nominated trustee, but the one-third requirement still remains. The employer's consent is required for a greater number of member-nominated trustees than that needed to make up the minimum requirement.

Subss. (7) and (8)

The powers, rights and duties of a member-nominated trustee must not differ from those of other trustees (subs. (7)). A member-nominated trustee will cease to be a trustee if he ceases to be a member (subs. (8)). This latter subsection may give rise to much difficulty. Unless regulations are made under s.125(4), such a trustee will continue in his post while he is a deferred pensioner (see the definition of "member") and while he may be working for a rival concern.

[Standing Committee D, May 11, 1995, col. 126, May 15, 1995, col. 151 and col. 185].

Exceptions

17.—(1) Section 16 does not apply to a trust scheme if—

(a) a proposal has been made by the employer for the continuation of existing arrangements, or the adoption of new arrangements, for selecting the trustees of the scheme,

(b) the arrangements referred to in the proposal are for the time being approved under the statutory consultation procedure, and

(c) such other requirements as may be prescribed are satisfied.

(2) Where—

(a) by virtue of subsection (1), section 16 does not apply to a trust scheme, and

(b) the employer's proposal was for the adoption of new arrangements which, in consequence of subsection (1)(b), are adopted,

the trustees shall secure that the proposed arrangements are made and implemented.

(3) For the purposes of this section, the arrangements for selecting the trustees of a scheme include all matters relating to the continuation in office of the existing trustees, the selection or appointment of new trustees and the terms of their appointments and any special rules for decisions to be made by particular trustees.

(4) Section 16 does not apply to a trust scheme if—

(a) the trustees of the scheme consist of all the members, or

(b) it falls within a prescribed class.

(5) Section 10 applies to any employer who—

(a) makes such a proposal as is referred to in subsection (1)(a), but
(b) fails to give effect to the statutory consultation procedure.

DEFINITIONS
"employer": s.124(1), and cf s.124(5); the Pension Schemes Act 1993, s.181(1).
"member": s.124(1).
"prescribed": s.124(1).
"statutory consultation procedure": s.21(7).
"trust scheme": s.124(1).

GENERAL NOTE

Subs. (1)
Subsection (1) provides for the requirements of s.16 to be excluded (see the notes to subs. (1) of that section). The statutory consultation procedure will have to be examined to see what teeth section 16 has in practice, since it may provide an opportunity for employers, or for trades unions with entrenched positions with regard to the trusteeship of a pension scheme, to preserve the status quo by leaning on the members of the scheme.

Subs. (2)
The duty lies with the trustees to secure that new arrangements are put into effect. Since it is the employer who proposes the new arrangements, and the trustees and the employer between them usually have the power to amend a scheme, the responsibility is appropriately placed. But difficulties may occur, for instance, where an alteration to a scheme needs the affirmative vote of a substantial majority of the members, and the acceptance of the new arrangements receives only the grudging consent of many of the members.

Subs. (4)
Section 16 does not apply where the trustees comprise the whole of the membership of the scheme. This, subject to s.125(4), includes active, deferred and pensioner members. Regulations may except certain classes of scheme from the requirements of s.16.

Subs. (5)
Section 10 permits the Authority to exact a penalty.
[Standing Committee D, May 16, 1995, col. 189].

Corporate trustees: member-nominated directors

18.—(1) Where a company is a trustee of a trust scheme and the employer is connected with the company or prescribed conditions are satisfied, the company must, subject to section 19, secure—
(a) that such arrangements for persons selected by the members of the scheme to be directors of the company as are required by this section are made, and
(b) that those arrangements, and the appropriate rules, are implemented.
(2) Persons who become directors under the arrangements required by subsection (1) are referred to in this Part as "member-nominated directors".
(3) The arrangements must provide—
(a) for any person who has been nominated and selected in accordance with the appropriate rules to become a director by virtue of his selection, and
(b) for the removal of such a person to require the agreement of all the other directors.
(4) Where a vacancy for a member-nominated director is not filled because insufficient nominations are received, the arrangements must provide for the filling of the vacancy, or for the vacancy to remain, until the expiry of the next period in which persons may be nominated and selected in accordance with the appropriate rules.
(5) The arrangements must provide for the selection of a person as a member-nominated director to have effect for a period of not less than three nor more than six years.
(6) The arrangements must provide for the number of member-nominated directors to be—

(a) at least two or (if the scheme comprises less than 100 members) at least one, and

(b) at least one-third of the total number of directors;

but the arrangements must not provide for a greater number of member-nominated directors than that required to satisfy that minimum unless the employer has given his approval to the greater number.

(7) The arrangements must provide that, if a member-nominated director who was a member of the scheme when he was appointed ceases to be a member of the scheme, he ceases to be a director by virtue of that fact.

(8) Where this section applies to a company which is—

(a) a trustee of two or more trust schemes, and

(b) a wholly-owned subsidiary (within the meaning of section 736 of the Companies Act 1985) of a company which is the employer in relation to those schemes,

the following provisions apply as if those schemes were a single scheme and the members of each of the schemes were members of that scheme, that is: the preceding provisions of this section, section 20 and section 21(8).

DEFINITIONS

"employer": s.124(1), and *cf* s.124(5); the Pension Schemes Act 1993, s.181(1).
"member": s.124(1).
"trust scheme": s.124(1).

GENERAL NOTE

This section makes provision for the directors of a corporate trustee parallel to that contained in s.16 in respect of individual trustees of a scheme, as to which see the notes to that section.

Subs. (8)

This subsection is designed to provide for the situation where a wholly-owned subsidiary company of an employer is a trustee of two schemes in which that employer participates. Under these circumstances it is not required that each scheme should be treated as a separate scheme in respect of which the requirements of s.18 have to be fulfilled. The schemes are instead treated as one scheme. Otherwise, if the company were the subsidiary of more than three schemes, the requirements of s.18 would be impossible to fulfil.

[Standing Committee D, May 16, 1995, col. 202].

Corporate trustees: exceptions

19.—(1) Section 18 does not apply to a company which is a trustee of a trust scheme if—

(a) a proposal has been made by the employer for the continuation of existing arrangements, or the adoption of new arrangements, for selecting the directors of the company,

(b) the arrangements referred to in the proposal are for the time being approved under the statutory consultation procedure, and

(c) such other requirements as may be prescribed are satisfied.

(2) Where—

(a) by virtue of subsection (1), section 18 does not apply to a company which is a trustee of a trust scheme, and

(b) the employer's proposal was for the adoption of new arrangements which, in consequence of subsection (1)(b), are adopted,

the company must secure that the proposed arrangements are made and implemented.

(3) For the purposes of this section, the arrangements for selecting the directors of a company include all matters relating to the continuation in office of the existing directors, the selection or appointment of new directors and the terms of their appointments and any special rules for decisions to be made by particular directors.

(4) Section 18 does not apply to a company which is a trustee of a trust scheme if the scheme falls within a prescribed class.

(5) Section 10 applies to any employer who—
(a) makes such a proposal as is referred to in subsection (1)(a), but
(b) fails to give effect to the statutory consultation procedure.

DEFINITIONS
"employer": s.124(1), and *cf* s.124(5); the Pension Schemes Act 1993, s.181(1).
"prescribed": s.124(1).
"statutory consultation procedure": s.21(7).
"trust scheme": s.124(1).

GENERAL NOTE
This section provides exceptions to the requirements of s.18 in the way that s.17 provides
exceptions to the requirements of s.16, as to which see the notes to s.17.

Selection, and eligibility, of member-nominated trustees and directors

20.—(1) For the purposes of sections 16 to 21, the appropriate rules are
rules which—
(a) make the provision required or authorised by this section, and no
other provision, and
(b) are for the time being approved under the statutory consultation procedure or, if no rules are for the time being so approved, are prescribed
rules;
and the arrangements required by section 16 or 18 to be made must not make
any provision which is required or authorised to be made by the rules.
(2) The appropriate rules—
(a) must determine the procedure for the nomination and selection of a
person to fill a vacancy as a member-nominated trustee, and
(b) may determine, or provide for the determination of, the conditions
required of a person for filling such a vacancy.
(3) The appropriate rules must provide for a member-nominated trustee
to be eligible for re-selection at the end of his period of service.
(4) Where a vacancy for a member-nominated trustee is not filled because
insufficient nominations are received, the appropriate rules must provide for
determining the next period in which persons may be nominated and selected in accordance with the rules, being a period ending at a prescribed time.
(5) The appropriate rules must provide that, where the employer so
requires, a person who is not a member of the scheme must have the
employer's approval to qualify for selection as a member-nominated trustee.
(6) Where section 18 applies to a trust scheme, references in this section to
a member-nominated trustee include a member-nominated director.

DEFINITIONS
"member-nominated director": s.18.
"member-nominated trustee": s.16.
"prescribed": s.124(1).
"statutory consultation procedure": s.16(6).

GENERAL NOTE
This section makes general provision for the contents of the appropriate rules, and limits what
may be included in them—no doubt a necessary safeguard.

Subs. (5)
This gives the employer the power to veto the selection of a member-nominated trustee or
director who is not a member of the scheme (or of one of the schemes if section 18(8) applies).

This throws into relief the lack of power of the employer over the selection of member-nominated trustees or directors who are members, such that a deferred pensioner who is employed by a rival company, for example, might be chosen, and the employer might be powerless to prevent this, unless regulations made under s.125(4) provide otherwise.

Member-nominated trustees and directors: supplementary

21.—(1) If, in the case of a trust scheme—
(a) such arrangements as are required by section 16(1) or 17(2) to be made have not been made, or
(b) arrangements required by section 16(1) or 17(2) to be implemented, or the appropriate rules, are not being implemented,
sections 3 and 10 apply to any trustee who has failed to take all such steps as are reasonable to secure compliance.

(2) If, in the case of a company which is a trustee of a trust scheme—
(a) such arrangements as are required by section 18(1) or 19(2) to be made have not been made, or
(b) arrangements required by section 18(1) or 19(2) to be implemented, or the appropriate rules, are not being implemented,
sections 3 and 10 apply to the company.

(3) No such arrangements or rules as are required by section 16(1) or 17(2), or any corresponding provisions in force in Northern Ireland, to be made or implemented shall be treated as effecting an alteration to the scheme in question for the purposes of section 591B of the Taxes Act 1988.

(4) Regulations may make provision for determining the time by which—
(a) such arrangements (or further arrangements) as are referred to in section 16(1), 17(2), 18(1) or 19(2) are required to be made, and
(b) trustees or directors are required to be selected in pursuance of the appropriate rules.

(5) Regulations may make provision for determining when any approval under the statutory consultation procedure—
(a) of the appropriate rules, or
(b) of arrangements for selecting the trustees of a scheme, or the directors of a company, given on a proposal by the employer,
is to cease to have effect.

(6) The Secretary of State may by regulations modify sections 16 to 20 and this section in their application to prescribed cases.

(7) In sections 16 to 20 and this section, "the statutory consultation procedure" means the prescribed procedure for obtaining the views of members of schemes.

(8) For the purposes of this and those sections—
(a) approval of the appropriate rules, or of arrangements, under the statutory consultation procedure must be given by—
    (i) the active and pensioner members of the scheme, and
    (ii) if the trustees so determine, such deferred members of the scheme as the trustees may determine,
taken as a whole, and
(b) references to the approval of the appropriate rules, or of arrangements under section 17 or 19, by any persons under the statutory consultation procedure are to prescribed conditions in respect of those rules or, as the case may be, arrangements being satisfied in the case of those persons in pursuance of the procedure, and those conditions may relate to the extent to which those persons have either endorsed, or not objected to, the rules or, as the case may be, arrangements.

DEFINITIONS
"employer": s.124(1), and *cf* s.124(5); the Pension Schemes Act 1993, s.181(1).
"prescribed": s.124(1).
"regulations": s.124(1).
"Taxes Act 1988": s.124(1).

"trust scheme": s.124(1).

GENERAL NOTE

Subss. (1) and (2)
This gives teeth to ss.16 and 18. Section 3 contains the power of the Authority to remove or suspend a trustee, and section 10 contains the power of the Authority to impose a penalty.

Subs. (3)
Section 591B(2) of the Income and Corporation Taxes Act 1988 provides that an alteration to a retirement benefits scheme will cause the approval of that scheme by the Board of Inland Revenue to cease, with consequent loss of tax concessions. Section 21(3) of this Act stipulates that the adoption of arrangements under s.16 or 17 is not to trigger this.

Subss. (4), (5) and (6)
These subsections give the Secretary of State the power to make certain regulations. The most important of these are likely to be regulations which provide for rules approved for the purposes of s.14 to cease to be approved, and for the validity of arrangements proposed by an employer to cease.

Subs. (8)
This subsection provides for two important matters, namely who has to approve the appropriate rules under the statutory consultation procedure, and of what approval may consist for the purposes of the alternative arrangements under ss.17 and 19. The latter is to be prescribed by regulations yet to be made. But the provisions of subs. (8)(a) are interesting in that a distinction is made for the first time between deferred pensioners and other members. Presumably the agreement of deferred pensioners was thought to be hard to obtain. But this is subject to the contrary decision of the trustees.

Independent trustees

Circumstances in which following provisions apply

    22.—(1) This section applies in relation to a trust scheme—
  (a) if a person (referred to in this section and sections 23 to 26 as "the practitioner") begins to act as an insolvency practitioner in relation to a company which, or an individual who, is the employer in relation to the scheme, or
  (b) if the official receiver becomes—
        (i) the liquidator or provisional liquidator of a company which is the employer in relation to the scheme, or
        (ii) the receiver and the manager, or the trustee, of the estate of a bankrupt who is the employer in relation to the scheme.
    (2) Where this section applies in relation to a scheme, it ceases to do so—
  (a) if some person other than the employer mentioned in subsection (1) becomes the employer, or
  (b) if at any time neither the practitioner nor the official receiver is acting in relation to the employer;
but this subsection does not affect the application of this section in relation to the scheme on any subsequent occasion when the conditions specified in subsection (1)(a) or (b) are satisfied in relation to it.
    (3) In this section and sections 23 to 26—
    "acting as an insolvency practitioner" and "official receiver" shall be construed in accordance with sections 388 and 399 of the Insolvency Act 1986,
    "bankrupt" has the meaning given by section 381 of the Insolvency Act 1986,
    "company" means a company within the meaning given by section 735(1) of the Companies Act 1985 or a company which may be wound up under Part V of the Insolvency Act 1986 (unregistered companies), and

"interim trustee" and "permanent trustee" have the same meanings as they have in the Bankruptcy (Scotland) Act 1985.

DEFINITIONS
"employer": s.124(1), and *cf* s.124(5); the Pension Schemes Act 1993, s.181(1).
"trust scheme": s.124(1).

GENERAL NOTE
This section and ss.18 to 21 derive from s.57C *et seq* of the Social Security Pensions Act 1975 (inserted by the Social Security Act 1990), reproduced in s.119 *et seq* of the Pension Schemes Act 1993. Power to modify these sections is contained in s.107 of that Act. The Occupational Pension Schemes (Independent Trustee) Regulations 1990 came into force on November 12, 1990. Regulation 7(2) of those regulations provides that the forerunners to s.22 did not apply where an insolvency practitioner or the official receiver started to act in relation to an employer prior to that date. Regulation 6 of the regulations excludes from the operation of s.22: (i) schemes where each employee and former employee of the employer who has rights under the scheme is a trustee, (ii) money purchase schemes, (iii) schemes which provide benefits on death in service only and (iv) schemes where the benefits are secured by insurance policies specifically allocated to the provision of benefits for or in respect of particular members. The section only applies to a trust scheme.
The equivalent section under the Pension Schemes Act 1993 applied its provisions to "trustees and managers", so long as the scheme was a trust scheme. The latter requirement has now been abandoned, and was probably an oversight in any event.

Subs. (2)
Schemes frequently provide that where the principal employer goes into liquidation another employer may be substituted for it, and in such a case it is generally desirable that s.22 should cease to apply.

Requirement for independent trustee

23.—(1) While section 22 applies in relation to a scheme, the practitioner or official receiver must—
    (a) satisfy himself that at all times at least one of the trustees of the scheme is an independent person, and
    (b) if at any time he is not so satisfied, appoint under this paragraph, or secure the appointment of, an independent person as a trustee of the scheme.
(2) The duty under subsection (1)(b) must be performed as soon as reasonably practicable and, if a period is prescribed for the purposes of that subsection, within that period.
(3) For the purposes of subsection (1) a person is independent only if—
    (a) he has no interest in the assets of the employer or of the scheme, otherwise than as trustee of the scheme,
    (b) he is neither connected with, nor an associate of—
        (i) the employer,
        (ii) any person for the time being acting as an insolvency practitioner in relation to the employer, or
        (iii) the official receiver, acting in any of the capacities mentioned in section 22(1)(b) in relation to the employer, and
    (c) he satisfies any prescribed requirements;
and any reference in this Part to an independent trustee shall be construed accordingly.
(4) Where, apart from this subsection, the duties imposed by subsection (1) in relation to a scheme would fall to be discharged at the same time by two or more persons acting in different capacities, those duties shall be discharged—

  (a) if the employer is a company, by the person or persons acting as the company's liquidator, provisional liquidator or administrator, or

  (b) if the employer is an individual, by the person or persons acting as his trustee in bankruptcy or interim receiver of his property or as permanent or interim trustee in the sequestration of his estate.

  (5) References in this section to an individual include, except where the context otherwise requires, references to a partnership and to any debtor within the meaning of the Bankruptcy (Scotland) Act 1985.

DEFINITIONS
"acting as an insolvency practitioner": s.22.
"company": s.22.
"employer": s.124(1), and *cf* s.124(5); the Pension Schemes Act 1993, s.181(1).
"practitioner": s.22.
"prescribed": s.124(1).

GENERAL NOTE
For the derivation of this section and general comments, see the General Note to s.22.

Subs. (2)
This is a new requirement.

Subs. (3)
By reason of s.123 of this Act, ss.249 and 435 of the Insolvency Act 1986 apply for the purposes of subs. (3)(b) to decide whether a person is connected with or an associate of the persons listed in the subsection. Additional prescribed requirements are to be found in the Occupational Pension Schemes (Independent Trustee) Regulations 1990, reg. 2. With regard to the provision of services referred to in reg. 2(2), see *Clark v. Hicks* [1992] OPLR 185.

Members' powers to apply to court to enforce duty

  24.—(1) If—

  (a) section 22 applies in relation to a trust scheme, but

  (b) the practitioner or official receiver neglects or refuses to discharge any duty imposed on him by section 23(1) in relation to the scheme,
any member of the scheme may apply to the appropriate court for an order requiring him to discharge his duties under section 23(1).

  (2) In subsection (1) "the appropriate court" means—

  (a) if the employer in question is a company—

      (i) where a winding-up order has been made or a provisional liquidator appointed, the court which made the order or appointed the liquidator,

      (ii) in any other case, any court having jurisdiction to wind up the company, and

  (b) in any other case—

      (i) in England and Wales, the court (as defined in section 385 of the Insolvency Act 1986), or

      (ii) in Scotland, where a sequestration has been awarded or, by virtue of the proviso to section 13(1) of the Bankruptcy (Scotland) Act 1985 (petition presented by creditor or trustee acting under trust deed) an interim trustee has been appointed, the court which made the award or appointment and, if no such award or appointment has been made, any court having jurisdiction under section 9 of that Act.

DEFINITIONS
"company": s.22.
"employer": s.124(1), and *cf* s.124(5); the Pension Schemes Act 1993, s.181(1).
"interim trustee": s.22.
"member": s.124(1).
"practitioner": s.22.

"trust scheme": s.124(1).

GENERAL NOTE
For the derivation of this section and general comments, see the General Note to s.17 above.

Appointment and powers of independent trustees: further provisions

25.—(1) If, immediately before the appointment of an independent trustee under section 23(1)(b), there is no trustee of the scheme other than the employer, the employer shall cease to be a trustee upon the appointment of the independent trustee.

(2) While section 22 applies in relation to a scheme—

(a) any power vested in the trustees of the scheme and exercisable at their discretion may be exercised only by the independent trustee, and

(b) any power—

(i) which the scheme confers on the employer (otherwise than as trustee of the scheme), and

(ii) which is exercisable by him at his discretion but only as trustee of the power,

may be exercised only by the independent trustee,

but if, in either case, there is more than one independent trustee, the power may also be exercised with the consent of at least half of those trustees by any person who could exercise it apart from this subsection

(3) While section 22 applies in relation to a scheme, no independent trustee of the scheme may be removed from being a trustee by virtue only of any provision of the scheme.

(4) If a trustee appointed under section 23(1)(b) ceases to be an independent person, then—

(a) he must immediately give written notice of that fact to the practitioner or official receiver by whom the duties under that provision fall to be discharged, and

(b) subject to subsection (5), he shall cease to be a trustee of the scheme.

(5) If, in a case where subsection (4) applies, there is no other trustee of the scheme than the former independent trustee, he shall not cease by virtue of that subsection to be a trustee until such time as another trustee is appointed.

(6) A trustee appointed under section 23(1)(b) is entitled to be paid out of the scheme's resources his reasonable fees for acting in that capacity and any expenses reasonably incurred by him in doing so, and to be so paid in priority to all other claims falling to be met out of the scheme's resources.

DEFINITIONS
"employer": s.124(1), and *cf* s.124(5); the Pension Schemes Act 1993, s.181(1).
"independent trustee": s.23(3).
"practitioner": s.22.
"resources": s.124(1).

GENERAL NOTE
For the derivation of this section and general comments, see the General Note to s.17.

Subs. (2)
This subsection contains the teeth of ss.22 to 26. It removes from the trustees the power to exercise any discretionary power conferred upon them by the provisions of the scheme and transfers the exercise of the powers to the independent trustee. The most important such power in the circumstances is likely to be that which relates to the distribution of surplus on the winding up of the scheme; but where the scheme is ongoing the powers diverted to the independent trustee are likely to be many and various. The subsection also removes from an employer the right to exercise any power conferred on him as such, and of which he is a trustee. It does not remove from an employer a power conferred on him as such which he must exercise in good faith (as to which, see *Imperial Group Pension Trust v. Imperial Tobacco* [1991] 1 W.L.R. 589), but which is not a fiduciary power. For an example of a fiduciary power which usually resides in an employer as such, see *Skeats' Settlement, Re* (1889) 42 Ch.D. 522.

Insolvency practitioner or official receiver to give information to trustees

26.—(1) Notwithstanding anything in section 155 of the Insolvency Act 1986 (court orders for inspection etc.), while section 22 applies in relation to a scheme, the practitioner or official receiver must provide the trustees of the scheme, as soon as practicable after the receipt of a request, with any information which the trustees may reasonably require for the purposes of the scheme.

(2) Any expenses incurred by the practitioner or official receiver in complying with a request under subsection (1) are recoverable by him as part of the expenses incurred by him in discharge of his duties.

(3) The practitioner or official receiver is not required under subsection (1) to take any action which involves expenses that cannot be so recovered, unless the trustees of the scheme undertake to meet them.

DEFINITIONS
  "practitioner": s.17.

GENERAL NOTE
  For the derivation of this section and general comments, see the General Note to s.17.

Subs. (1)
  The trustees may need this information, since it is the fiduciary powers of trustees and employers which are removed from them, not their duties.

Subss. (2) and (3)
  These provide for the expenses of a practitioner or of the official receiver.

Trustees: general

Trustee not to be auditor or actuary of the scheme

27.—(1) A trustee of a trust scheme, and any person who is connected with, or an associate of, such a trustee, is ineligible to act as an auditor or actuary of the scheme.

(2) Subsection (1) does not make a person who is a director, partner or employee of a firm of actuaries ineligible to act as an actuary of a trust scheme merely because another director, partner or employee of the firm is a trustee of the scheme.

(3) Subsection (1) does not make a person who falls within a prescribed class or description ineligible to act as an auditor or actuary of a trust scheme.

(4) A person must not act as an auditor or actuary of a trust scheme if he is ineligible under this section to do so.

(5) In this section and section 28 references to a trustee of a trust scheme do not include—
  (a) a trustee, or
  (b) a trustee of a scheme,
falling within a prescribed class or description.

DEFINITIONS
  "actuary": s.47, s.124(1).
  "auditor": s.47, s.124(1).
  "firm": s.124(1).

"prescribed": s.124(1).
"trust scheme": s.124(1).

GENERAL NOTE

Subs. (1)
For the meaning of "connected with" and "associate", see s.123 below.

Subs. (2)
The word "firm" is defined as including a body corporate—a trap for the unwary.

Section 27: consequences

28.—(1) Any person who acts as an auditor or actuary of a trust scheme in contravention of section 27(4) is guilty of an offence and liable—

(a) on summary conviction, to a fine not exceeding the statutory maximum, and

(b) on conviction on indictment, to imprisonment or a fine, or both.

(2) An offence under subsection (1) may be charged by reference to any day or longer period of time; and a person may be convicted of a second or subsequent offence under that subsection by reference to any period of time following the preceding conviction of the offence.

(3) Acts done as an auditor or actuary of a trust scheme by a person who is ineligible under section 27 to do so are not invalid merely because of that fact.

(4) Where—

(a) a trustee of a trust scheme acts as auditor or actuary of the scheme, or

(b) a person acts as auditor or actuary of a trust scheme when he is ineligible under section 27 to do so by reason of being connected with, or an associate of, a trustee of the scheme,

section 3 applies to the trustee.

DEFINITIONS
"actuary": s.47, s.124(1).
"auditor": s.47, s.124(1).
"contravention": s.124(1).
"trust scheme": s.124(1).

GENERAL NOTE

Subs. (1)
This provides that a person who acts as an auditor or actuary of a scheme in contravention of s.27(4) may on summary conviction be liable to a fine not exceeding the statutory maximum, currently £5,000; and may on conviction on indictment be liable to imprisonment for not more than two years and an unlimited fine.

Subs. (2)
For the meaning of "connected with" and "associate", see s.123 below.

Subs. (4)
Section 3 provides for the prohibition and removal of a trustee.

Persons disqualified for being trustees

29.—(1) Subject to subsection (5), a person is disqualified for being a trustee of any trust scheme if—

(a) he has been convicted of any offence involving dishonesty or deception,

(b) he has been adjudged bankrupt or sequestration of his estate has been awarded and (in either case) he has not been discharged,

(c) where the person is a company, if any director of the company is disqualified under this section,

(d) where the person is a Scottish partnership, if any partner is disqualified under this section,

   (e) he has made a composition contract or an arrangement with, or granted a trust deed for the behoof of, his creditors and has not been discharged in respect of it, or

   (f) he is subject to a disqualification order under the Company Directors Disqualification Act 1986 or to an order made under section 429(2)(b) of the Insolvency Act 1986 (failure to pay under county court administration order).

(2) In subsection (1)—

   (a) paragraph (a) applies whether the conviction occurred before or after the coming into force of that subsection, but does not apply in relation to any conviction which is a spent conviction for the purposes of the Rehabilitation of Offenders Act 1974,

   (b) paragraph (b) applies whether the adjudication of bankruptcy or the sequestration occurred before or after the coming into force of that subsection,

   (c) paragraph (e) applies whether the composition contract or arrangement was made, or the trust deed was granted, before or after the coming into force of that subsection, and

   (d) paragraph (f) applies in relation to orders made before or after the coming into force of that subsection.

(3) Where a person—

   (a) is prohibited from being a trustee of a trust scheme by an order under section 3, or

   (b) has been removed as a trustee of a trust scheme by an order made (whether before or after the coming into force of this subsection) by the High Court or the Court of Session on the grounds of misconduct or mismanagement in the administration of the scheme for which he was responsible or to which he was privy, or which he by his conduct contributed to or facilitated,

the Authority may, if in their opinion it is not desirable for him to be a trustee of any trust scheme, by order disqualify him for being a trustee of any trust scheme.

(4) The Authority may by order disqualify a person for being a trustee of any trust scheme where—

   (a) in their opinion he is incapable of acting as such a trustee by reason of mental disorder (within the meaning of the Mental Health Act 1983 or, as respects Scotland, the Mental Health (Scotland) Act 1984), or

   (b) the person is a company which has gone into liquidation (within the meaning of section 247(2) of the Insolvency Act 1986).

(5) The Authority may, on the application of any person disqualified under this section—

   (a) give notice in writing to him waiving his disqualification,

   (b) in the case of a person disqualified under subsection (3) or (4), by order revoke the order disqualifying him,

either generally or in relation to a particular scheme or particular class of schemes.

(6) A notice given or revocation made at any time by virtue of subsection (5) cannot affect anything done before that time.

DEFINITIONS

   "Authority": s.1.

   "trust scheme": s.124(1).

GENERAL NOTE

Subs. (1)

   This section contains important disqualifications from holding the office of trustee, which by reason of subs. (1)(c) are intended to bite on the directors of corporate trustees, albeit indirectly.

Subss. (3) and (4)
These confer upon the Authority the important power to disqualify a person from acting as trustee of any trust scheme in the circumstances mentioned. The power contained in subs. (4)(b) may provide for the difficult situation which exists where an employer is the trustee of a small scheme and has gone into liquidation, leaving the liquidator in the position of having to apply to the court for directions, and thus having to spend money otherwise better spent.

Subs. (6)
Notice waiving disqualification cannot operate to validate previously invalid acts.

Persons disqualified: consequences

30.—(1) A trustee of a trust scheme who becomes disqualified under section 29 shall, while he is so disqualified, cease to be a trustee.

(2) Where—

(a) a trustee of a trust scheme becomes disqualified under section 29, or

(b) in the case of a trustee of a trust scheme who has become so disqualified, his disqualification is waived or the order disqualifying him is revoked or he otherwise ceases to be disqualified,

the Authority may exercise the same jurisdiction and powers as are exercisable by the High Court or, in relation to a trust scheme subject to the law of Scotland, the Court of Session for vesting any property in, or transferring any property to, the trustees.

(3) A person who purports to act as a trustee of a trust scheme while he is disqualified under section 29 is guilty of an offence and liable—

(a) on summary conviction to a fine not exceeding the statutory maximum, and

(b) on conviction on indictment, to a fine or imprisonment or both.

(4) An offence under subsection (3) may be charged by reference to any day or longer period of time; and a person may be convicted of a second or subsequent offence under that subsection by reference to any period of time following the preceding conviction of the offence.

(5) Things done by a person disqualified under section 29 while purporting to act as trustee of a trust scheme are not invalid merely because of that disqualification.

(6) Nothing in section 29 or this section affects the liability of any person for things done, or omitted to be done, by him while purporting to act as trustee of a trust scheme.

(7) The Authority must keep, in such manner as they think fit, a register of all persons who are disqualified under section 29(3) or (4); and the Authority must, if requested to do so, disclose whether the name of a person specified in the request is included in the register in respect of a scheme so specified.

DEFINITIONS
"Authority": s.1.
"trust scheme": s.124(1).

GENERAL NOTE

Subs. (2)
See the General Note to s.9 above.

Subss. (3), (4), (5) and (6)
See the General Note to s.6 above.

Trustees not to be indemnified for fines or civil penalties

31.—(1) No amount may be paid out of the assets of a trust scheme for the purpose of reimbursing, or providing for the reimbursement of, any trustee of the scheme in respect of—

(a) a fine imposed by way of penalty for an offence of which he is convicted, or

(b) a penalty which he is required to pay under section 10 or under section 168(4) of the Pension Schemes Act 1993.

(2) For the purposes of subsection (1), providing for the reimbursement of a trustee in respect of a fine or penalty includes (among other things) providing for the payment of premiums in respect of a policy of insurance where the risk is or includes the imposition of such a fine or the requirement to pay such a penalty.

(3) Where any amount is paid out of the assets of a trust scheme in contravention of this section, sections 3 and 10 apply to any trustee who fails to take all such steps as are reasonable to secure compliance.

(4) Where a trustee of a trust scheme—

(a) is reimbursed, out of the assets of the scheme or in consequence of provision for his reimbursement made out of those assets, in respect of any of the matters referred to in subsection (1)(a) or (b), and

(b) knows, or has reasonable grounds to believe, that he has been reimbursed as mentioned in paragraph (a),

then, unless he has taken all such steps as are reasonable to secure that he is not so reimbursed, he is guilty of an offence.

(5) A person guilty of an offence under subsection (4) is liable—

(a) on summary conviction, to a fine not exceeding the statutory maximum, and

(b) on conviction on indictment, to imprisonment, or a fine, or both.

DEFINITIONS
  "contravention": s.124(1).
  "trust scheme": s.124(1).

GENERAL NOTE

Subs. (3)
  Section 3 contains the power of the Authority to prohibit or remove a trustee, and s.10 contains the power of the Authority to impose a penalty.

Subss. (4) and (5)
  Reimbursement in the circumstances outlined is made an offence. For the extent of subs. (5), see the General Note to s.6(1) above.

Functions of trustees

Decisions by majority

32.—(1) Decisions of the trustees of a trust scheme may, unless the scheme provides otherwise, be taken by agreement of a majority of the trustees.

(2) Where decisions of the trustees of a trust scheme may be taken by agreement of a majority of the trustees—

(a) the trustees may, unless the scheme provides otherwise, by a determination under this subsection require not less than the number of trustees specified in the determination to be present when any decision is so taken, and

(b) notice of any occasions at which decisions may be so taken must, unless the occasion falls within a prescribed class or description, be given to each trustee to whom it is reasonably practicable to give such notice.

(3) Notice under subsection (2)(b) must be given in a prescribed manner and not later than the beginning of a prescribed period.

(4) This section is subject to sections 8(4)(b), 16(3)(b) and 25(2).

(5) If subsection (2)(b) is not complied with, sections 3 and 10 apply to any trustee who has failed to take all such steps as are reasonable to secure compliance.

DEFINITIONS
   "prescribed": s.124(1).
   "trust scheme": s.124(1).

GENERAL NOTE
   This section underwent much change during its passage through Parliament.

Subss. (1) and (2)
   These subsections give trustees the power to take decisions by a majority, unless the scheme provides otherwise. This must mean that there is express provision in the scheme to this effect, since the position at law is that unless a trust gives trustees the power to decide by a majority, they must be unanimous in their decisions. The usual position under a pension scheme trust deed and rules is that decisions can be taken by a majority of trustees present and voting at any meeting, and that in the case of a tie the chairman has a casting vote. Under s.32, however, the trustees referred to are all the trustees, not merely those present and voting at a meeting of trustees. Further, the trustees may require a quorum to be present when any such decision is taken, and this might be any number.
   Much attention is paid to the notice to be given to trustees of meetings, and no doubt regulations will contain some stringent requirements as to this.
   For the main thrust of the section: see *Hansard*, H.L. Vol. 561, col. 518.

Subs. (5)
   Section 3 contains the power of the Authority to remove or suspend a trustee, and s.10 contains the power of the Authority to impose a penalty.

Investment powers: duty of care

33.—(1) Liability for breach of an obligation under any rule of law to take care or exercise skill in the performance of any investment functions, where the function is exercisable—
   (a) by a trustee of a trust scheme, or
   (b) by a person to whom the function has been delegated under section 34, cannot be excluded or restricted by any instrument or agreement.

(2) In this section, references to excluding or restricting liability include—
   (a) making the liability or its enforcement subject to restrictive or onerous conditions,
   (b) excluding or restricting any right or remedy in respect of the liability, or subjecting a person to any prejudice in consequence of his pursuing any such right or remedy, or
   (c) excluding or restricting rules of evidence or procedure.

(3) This section does not apply—
   (a) to a scheme falling within any prescribed class or description, or
   (b) to any prescribed description of exclusion or restriction.

DEFINITIONS
   "prescribed": s.124(1).
   "trust scheme": s.124(1).

GENERAL NOTE

Subs. (1)
   Unless themselves authorised or exempted, the trustees of an occupational pension scheme are bound to delegate the day to day investment decisions with regard to a scheme to a person authorised or exempted for the purposes of s.191 of the Financial Services Act 1986 or to persons who, under Schedule 1 Part IV of that Act, do not require authorisation. As to the powers of the trustee to delegate such management to a person authorised under that section, see s.34 below.

Subs. (2)
For a parallel provision, see s.13 of the Unfair Contract Terms Act 1977.
[Standing Committee D, May 16, 1995, col. 211].

Power of investment and delegation

34.—(1) The trustees of a trust scheme have, subject to any restriction imposed by the scheme, the same power to make an investment of any kind as if they were absolutely entitled to the assets of the scheme.

(2) Any discretion of the trustees of a trust scheme to make any decision about investments—

(a) may be delegated by or on behalf of the trustees to a fund manager to whom subsection (3) applies to be exercised in accordance with section 36, but

(b) may not otherwise be delegated except under section 25 of the Trustee Act 1925 (delegation of trusts during absence abroad) or subsection (5) below.

(3) This subsection applies to a fund manager who, in relation to the decisions in question, falls, or is treated as falling, within any of paragraphs (a) to (c) of section 191(2) of the Financial Services Act 1986 (occupational pension schemes: exemptions where decisions taken by authorised and other persons).

(4) The trustees are not responsible for the act or default of any fund manager in the exercise of any discretion delegated to him under subsection (2)(a) if they have taken all such steps as are reasonable to satisfy themselves or the person who made the delegation on their behalf has taken all such steps as are reasonable to satisfy himself—

(a) that the fund manager has the appropriate knowledge and experience for managing the investments of the scheme, and

(b) that he is carrying out his work competently and complying with section 36.

(5) Subject to any restriction imposed by a trust scheme—

(a) the trustees may authorise two or more of their number to exercise on their behalf any discretion to make any decision about investments, and

(b) any such discretion may, where giving effect to the decision would not constitute carrying on investment business in the United Kingdom (within the meaning of the Financial Services Act 1986), be delegated by or on behalf of the trustees to a fund manager to whom subsection (3) does not apply to be exercised in accordance with section 36;

but in either case the trustees are liable for any acts or defaults in the exercise of the discretion if they would be so liable if they were the acts or defaults of the trustees as a whole.

(6) Section 33 does not prevent the exclusion or restriction of any liability of the trustees of a trust scheme for the acts or defaults of a fund manager in the exercise of a discretion delegated to him under subsection (5)(b) where the trustees have taken all such steps as are reasonable to satisfy themselves, or the person who made the delegation on their behalf has taken all such steps as are reasonable to satisfy himself—

(a) that the fund manager has the appropriate knowledge and experience for managing the investments of the scheme, and

(b) that he is carrying out his work competently and complying with section 36;

and subsection (2) of section 33 applies for the purposes of this subsection as it applies for the purposes of that section.

(7) The provisions of this section override any restriction inconsistent with the provisions imposed by any rule of law or by or under any enactment, other than an enactment contained in, or made under, this Part or the Pension Schemes Act 1993.

DEFINITIONS
    "fund manager": s.124(1).
    "trust scheme": s.124(1).

GENERAL NOTE

Subs. (1)
    Subsection (1) gives to the trustees the minimum powers which they need to invest the assets of a pension scheme properly. The section does not permit investment in funds only open to the trustees of exempt approved schemes and charities, which is also a desirable option for trustees to have. Such a power could if needed be added by amendment, assuming that powers of amendment exist.

Subs. (2)
    As noted in the General Note to s.33 above, delegation in accordance with subs. (2)(a) is almost certainly necessary for funds which are not invested with an insurance company. The powers of delegation set out in this subsection are wider than those strictly necessary for the purpose of compliance with the Financial Services Act 1986, s.191. Subsection (5) contains important additional powers of delegation, but delegation under subs. (2)(a) only carries the limited vicarious responsibility prescribed by subs. (4), whereas delegation under subs. (5) carries full vicarious responsibility.

Subs. (5)
    The important power is that set out in subs. (5)(a), but the power is limited to delegation to some two or more of the trustees, and not to outsiders. Vicarious liability for the decisions taken by those delegated to take them is unlimited. See also ss.35 and 36 which either indicate or contain obligations laid upon trustees with regard to investments.

Subs. (6)
    Subs. (5)(b) would appear to be apt to apply to an investment manager operating outside the U.K. appointed to oversee investments such as investments in the U.S.

Subs. (7)
    Section 34 is overriding, subject to stated exceptions.
    For the intended limits on the powers of delegation see *Hansard*, H.L. Vol. 561, col. 530. [Standing Committee D, May 16, 1995, col. 214].

Investment principles

35.—(1) The trustees of a trust scheme must secure that there is prepared, maintained and from time to time revised a written statement of the principles governing decisions about investments for the purposes of the scheme.
    (2) The statement must cover, among other things—
    (a) the trustees' policy for securing compliance with sections 36 and 56, and
    (b) their policy about the following matters.
    (3) Those matters are—
    (a) the kinds of investments to be held,
    (b) the balance between different kinds of investments,
    (c) risk,
    (d) the expected return on investments,
    (e) the realisation of investments, and
    (f) such other matters as may be prescribed.
    (4) Neither the trust scheme nor the statement may impose restrictions (however expressed) on any power to make investments by reference to the consent of the employer.
    (5) The trustees of a trust scheme must, before a statement under this section is prepared or revised—
    (a) obtain and consider the written advice of a person who is reasonably believed by the trustees to be qualified by his ability in and practical experience of financial matters and to have the appropriate knowledge and experience of the management of the investments of such schemes, and

(b) consult the employer.

(6) If in the case of any trust scheme—

(a) a statement under this section has not been prepared or is not being maintained, or

(b) the trustees have not obtained and considered advice in accordance with subsection (5),

sections 3 and 10 apply to any trustee who has failed to take all such steps as are reasonable to secure compliance.

(7) This section does not apply to any scheme which falls within a pre-scribed class or description.

DEFINITIONS

"employer": s.124(1), and *cf* s.124(5); the Pension Schemes Act 1993, s.181(1).
"prescribed": s.14(2), s.124(1).
"trust scheme": s.124(1).

GENERAL NOTE

Subs. (1)

This requirement is new, but accords with good practice. It applies only to the trustees of a trust scheme. There is a duty on the trustees to review the principles from time to time.

Subs. (4)

This provision is intended to prevent an employer exercising control over the investments of a scheme. Quite often the provisions struck down by this subsection will have been inserted for the good of the members of a scheme (for example, where the consent of the employer is required before investment can take place in the shares of the employer). But in other cases the control has been more sinister. All such control now falls.

Subs. (5)

Written advice must be obtained from a person who is knowledgeable with regard to the investment of pension schemes. Advice from any other investment adviser is insufficient. The requirement to consult the employer applies to a money purchase scheme as well as to a final salary "balance of cost" scheme, to which it might be thought to be more appropriate. In the latter the employer is acutely concerned with the investment performance of the assets of the scheme, since this will govern the amount which the employer is required to contribute to the scheme.

Subs. (6)

Section 3 contains the power of the Authority to remove or suspend a trustee, and s.9 contains the power of the Authority to impose a penalty.

Subs. (7)

We may suppose that very small schemes—such as those where all the members are trustees of the scheme—will be excluded.
[Standing Committee D, May 18, 1995, col. 217].

Choosing investments

36.—(1) The trustees of a trust scheme must exercise their powers of investment in accordance with subsections (2) to (4) and any fund manager to whom any discretion has been delegated under section 34 must exercise the discretion in accordance with subsection (2).

(2) The trustees or fund manager must have regard—

(a) to the need for diversification of investments, in so far as appropriate to the circumstances of the scheme, and

(b) to the suitability to the scheme of investments of the description of investment proposed and of the investment proposed as an invest-ment of that description.

(3) Before investing in any manner (other than in a manner mentioned in Part I of Schedule 1 to the Trustee Investments Act 1961) the trustees must obtain and consider proper advice on the question whether the investment is satisfactory having regard to the matters mentioned in subsection (2) and the principles contained in the statement under section 35.

(4) Trustees retaining any investment must—

(a) determine at what intervals the circumstances, and in particular the nature of the investment, make it desirable to obtain such advice as is mentioned in subsection (3), and

(b) obtain and consider such advice accordingly.

(5) The trustees, or the fund manager to whom any discretion has been delegated under section 34, must exercise their powers of investment with a view to giving effect to the principles contained in the statement under section 35, so far as reasonably practicable.

(6) For the purposes of this section "proper advice" means—

(a) where giving the advice constitutes carrying on investment business in the United Kingdom (within the meaning of the Financial Services Act 1986), advice—

(i) given by a person authorised under Chapter III of Part I of that Act,

(ii) given by a person exempted under Chapter IV of that Part who, in giving the advice, is acting in the course of the business in respect of which he is exempt,

(iii) given by a person where, by virtue of paragraph 27 of Schedule 1 to that Act, paragraph 15 of that Schedule does not apply to giving the advice, or

(iv) given by a person who, by virtue of regulation 5 of the Banking Coordination (Second Council Directive) Regulations 1992, may give the advice though not authorised as mentioned in subparagraph (i) above.

(b) in any other case, the advice of a person who is reasonably believed by the trustees to be qualified by his ability in and practical experience of financial matters and to have the appropriate knowledge and experience of the management of the investments of trust schemes.

(7) Trustees shall not be treated as having complied with subsection (3) or (4) unless the advice was given or has subsequently been confirmed in writing.

(8) If the trustees of a trust scheme do not obtain and consider advice in accordance with this section, sections 3 and 10 apply to any trustee who has failed to take all such steps as are reasonable to secure compliance.

DEFINITIONS
"fund manager": s.124(1).
"proper advice": subs. (6).
"trust scheme": s.124(1).

GENERAL NOTE

Subs. (2)
This reproduces and applies to trust schemes the provisions of the Trustee Investments Act 1961, s.6(1).

Subss. (3), (4), (6) and (7)
For similar provisions see s.6(2) to (5) of the Trustee Investments Act 1961. But note that the advice under subs. (6) must be obtained from a person with knowledge of the investment of trust schemes.

Subs. (8)
Section 3 contains the power of the Authority to remove or suspend a trustee, and s.10 contains the power of the Authority to impose a penalty.

Payment of surplus to employer

37.—(1) This section applies to a trust scheme if—

(a) apart from this section, power is conferred on any person (including the employer) to make payments to the employer out of funds which are held for the purposes of the scheme,

(b) the scheme is one to which Schedule 22 to the Taxes Act 1988 (reduction of pension fund surpluses in certain exempt approved schemes) applies, and

(c) the scheme is not being wound up.

(2) Where the power referred to in subsection (1)(a) is conferred by the scheme on a person other than the trustees, it cannot be exercised by that person but may be exercised instead by the trustees; and any restriction imposed by the scheme on the exercise of the power shall, so far as capable of doing so, apply to its exercise by the trustees.

(3) The power referred to in subsection (1)(a) cannot be exercised unless the requirements of subsection (4) and (in prescribed circumstances) (5), and any prescribed requirements, are satisfied.

(4) The requirements of this subsection are that—

(a) the power is exercised in pursuance of proposals approved under paragraph 6(1) of Schedule 22 to the Taxes Act 1988,

(b) the trustees are satisfied that it is in the interests of the members that the power be exercised in the manner so proposed,

(c) where the power is conferred by the scheme on the employer, the employer has asked for the power to be exercised, or consented to it being exercised, in the manner so proposed,

(d) the annual rates of the pensions under the scheme which commence or have commenced are increased by the appropriate percentage, and

(e) notice has been given in accordance with prescribed requirements to the members of the scheme of the proposal to exercise the power.

(5) The requirements of this subsection are that the Authority are of the opinion that—

(a) any requirements prescribed by virtue of subsection (3) are satisfied, and

(b) the requirements of subsection (4) are satisfied.

(6) In subsection (4)—

(a) "annual rate" and "appropriate percentage" have the same meaning as in section 54, and

(b) "pension" does not include—

(i) any guaranteed minimum pension (as defined in section 8(2) of the Pension Schemes Act 1993) or any increase in such a pension under section 109 of that Act, or

(ii) any money purchase benefit (as defined in section 181(1) of that Act).

(7) This section does not apply to any payment to which, by virtue of section 601(3) of the Taxes Act 1988, section 601(2) of that Act does not apply.

(8) If, where this section applies to any trust scheme, the trustees purport to exercise the power referred to in subsection (1)(a) by making a payment to which this section applies without complying with the requirements of this section, sections 3 and 10 apply to any trustee who has failed to take all such steps as are reasonable to secure compliance.

(9) If, where this section applies to any trust scheme, any person, other than the trustees, purports to exercise the power referred to in subsection (1)(a) by making a payment to which this section applies, section 10 applies to him.

(10) Regulations may provide that, in prescribed circumstances, this section does not apply to schemes falling within a prescribed class or description, or applies to them with prescribed modifications.

"member": s.124(1).
"modifications": s.124(5); the Pension Schemes Act 1993, s.181(1).
"prescribed": s.14(2), s.124(1).
"regulations": s.124(1).
"Taxes Act 1988": s.124(1).
"trust scheme": s.124(1).

GENERAL NOTE

Subs. (1)
   Section 37 applies only to an ongoing trust scheme, subject to exemptions in regulations made under subs. (10). Schedule 22 to the Income and Corporation Taxes Act 1988 withdraws tax concessions proportionately for exempt approved schemes contained in that Act where there is excess surplus in an exempt approved scheme (as measured on statutory actuarial assumptions) and no or inadequate steps are taken to reduce that surplus, contrary to the requirements of the Schedule.

Subs. (2)
   Section 37 creates no new power to make payments to an employer out of the fund of a trust scheme. If the occasion for payment to an employer arises, but there is no power to make such a payment under the trust deed and rules of the scheme, an order must be sought from the Authority under s.69 below.

Subs. (4)
   Subsection 4(b) sets the scene for the kind of bargaining between trustees and an employer foreseen at the end of the judgment of Millett J. in *Courage Group's Pension Schemes, Re* [1987] 1 All E.R. 528.

Subs. (7)
   The most common payments referred to in s.601(3) of the Income and Corporation Taxes Act 1988 are payments to the extent that if s.601 had not been enacted the employer would have been exempt or entitled to claim exemption from income tax or corporation tax in respect of the payment; and payments made before a scheme became an exempt approved scheme.

Subs. (9)
   Section 10 prescribes that the Authority may levy a civil penalty.
   [Standing Committee D, May 18, 1995, col. 251].

Power to defer winding up

   38.—(1) If, apart from this section, the rules of a trust scheme would require the scheme to be wound up, the trustees may determine that the scheme is not for the time being to be wound up but that no new members are to be admitted to the scheme.
   (2) Where the trustees make a determination under subsection (1), they may also determine—
      (a) that no further contributions are to be paid towards the scheme, or
      (b) that no new benefits are to accrue to, or in respect of, members of the scheme;
but this subsection does not authorise the trustees to determine, where there are accrued rights to any benefit, that the benefit is not to be increased.
   (3) This section does not apply to—
      (a) a money purchase scheme, or
      (b) a scheme falling within a prescribed class or description.

DEFINITIONS
   "member": s.124(1).
   "prescribed": s.14(2), s.124(1).
   "trust scheme": s.124(1).

GENERAL NOTE

Subss. (1) and (2)
   These subsections give the trustees a statutory right to run a scheme as a closed scheme instead of winding it up. This right is usually contained in a well drafted scheme document in any

event, but in fact is not often used, and if used is used for a short period only, because it provokes difficult problems for the trustees, who become, if the scheme is self-administered, their own insurers. But the power might be of assistance for a limited time if annuity rates are hard at the time when the scheme is wound up.

Subs. (3)
   Money purchase schemes are excluded from s.38.
   [Standing Committee D, June 22, 1995, col. 829].

Exercise of powers by member trustees

39. No rule of law that a trustee may not exercise the powers vested in him so as to give rise to a conflict between his personal interest and his duties to the beneficiaries shall apply to a trustee of a trust scheme, who is also a member of the scheme, exercising the powers vested in him in any manner, merely because their exercise in that manner benefits, or may benefit, him as a member of the scheme.

DEFINITIONS
   "member": s.124(1).
   "trust scheme": s.124(1).

GENERAL NOTE
   This section is intended to solve the difficulties raised as a matter of general trust law in *Manning v. Drexel Burnham Lambert Holdings Ltd* [1994] OPLR 71. No doubt it is intended that where benefits are conferred on a trustee in the exercise of a discretion in the circumstances covered by the section, he should be able to keep the benefits so conferred beneficially.
   [Standing Committee D, June 22, 1995, col. 847].

Functions of trustees or managers

Restriction on employer-related investments

40.—(1) The trustees or managers of an occupational pension scheme must secure that the scheme complies with any prescribed restrictions with respect to the proportion of its resources that may at any time be invested in, or in any description of, employer-related investments.
   (2) In this section—
      "employer-related investments" means—
            (a) shares or other securities issued by the employer or by any person who is connected with, or an associate of, the employer,
            (b) land which is occupied or used by, or subject to a lease in favour of, the employer or any such person,
            (c) property (other than land) which is used for the purposes of any business carried on by the employer or any such person,
            (d) loans to the employer or any such person, and
            (e) other prescribed investments,
      "securities" means any asset, right or interest falling within paragraph 1, 2, 4 or 5 of Schedule 1 to the Financial Services Act 1986.
   (3) To the extent (if any) that sums due and payable by a person to the trustees or managers of an occupational pension scheme remain unpaid—
      (a) they shall be regarded for the purposes of this section as loans made to that person by the trustees or managers, and
      (b) resources of the scheme shall be regarded as invested accordingly.
   (4) If in the case of a trust scheme subsection (1) is not complied with, sections 3 and 10 apply to any trustee who fails to take all such steps as are reasonable to secure compliance.
   (5) If any resources of an occupational pension scheme are invested in contravention of subsection (1), any trustee or manager who agreed in the determination to make the investment is guilty of an offence and liable—
      (a) on summary conviction, to a fine not exceeding the statutory maximum, and

(b) on conviction on indictment, to a fine or imprisonment, or both.

DEFINITIONS
"employer": s.124(1), and *cf* s.124(5); the Pension Schemes Act 1993, s.181(1).
"employer-related investments": subs. (2).
"occupational pension scheme": s.152.
"prescribed": s.14(2), s.124(1).
"resources": s.124(1).
"securities": subs. (2).
"trustees or managers": s.124(1).

GENERAL NOTE
This section is derived from s.57A of the Social Security Pensions Act 1975, repeated in s.112 of the Pension Schemes Act 1993.

Subs. (1)
For the prescribed restrictions, see the Occupational Pension Schemes (Investment of Scheme's Resources) Regulations 1992 (S.I. 1992 No. 246). The main restriction contained in these regulations is to restrict employer-related investments at any time to five per cent of the scheme's resources measured by market value.

The position of trustees under these regulations has been clarified by the decision of Millett J. in *Wright v. Ginn* [1994] O.P.L.R. 83. The judge held that the provisions of s.4 of the Trustee Act 1925 apply to both regs. 3 and 5 of the regulations. Accordingly, when the limits prescribed by the regulations are reached, an investment becomes unauthorised; but by reason of s.4, the trustees may continue to hold the investment provided that they can justify continuing to hold it. If they continue to do so without justification, or for a longer period than can be justified, they will be liable for a breach of trust. Thus trustees are given some protection against an absolute duty to sell when the limits laid down by the regulations are breached, but the protection given to trustees is limited.

Problems are anticipated in connection with cross-directorships, arising out of the definition of "employer-related investments" contained in s.112(2) of the Pension Schemes Act 1993, and thus imported into the investment regulations. Similar difficulties are anticipated in respect of the underlying holdings of unit trusts.

Subs. (2)
For the meaning of "connected with" and "associate of", see s.123 below.

Subs. (4)
Section 3 contains the power of the Authority to remove or suspend a trustee, and s.10 contains the power of the Authority to impose a penalty.

Subs. (5)
See the General Note to s.6(1) above.
[Standing Committee D, May 18, 1995, col. 267].

Provision of documents for members

41.—(1) Regulations may require the trustees or managers of an occupational pension scheme—
  (a) to obtain at prescribed times the documents mentioned in subsection (2), and
  (b) to make copies of them, and of the documents mentioned in subsection (3), available to the persons mentioned in subsection (4).

(2) The documents referred to in subsection (1)(a) are—
  (a) the accounts audited by the auditor of the scheme,
  (b) the auditor's statement about contributions under the scheme,
  (c) a valuation by the actuary of the assets and liabilities of the scheme, and a statement by the actuary concerning such aspects of the valuation as may be prescribed.

(3) The documents referred to in subsection (1)(b) are—
  (a) any valuation, or certificate, prepared under section 57 or 58 by the actuary of the scheme,
  (b) any report prepared by the trustees or managers under section 59(3).

(4) The persons referred to in subsection (1)(b) are—

(a) members and prospective members of the scheme,

(b) spouses of members and of prospective members,

(c) persons within the application of the scheme and qualifying or prospectively qualifying for its benefits,

(d) independent trade unions recognised to any extent for the purposes of collective bargaining in relation to members and prospective members of the scheme.

(5) Regulations may in the case of occupational pension schemes to which section 47 does not apply—

(a) prescribe the persons who may act as auditors or actuaries for the purposes of subsection (2), or

(b) provide that the persons who may so act shall be—

(i) persons with prescribed professional qualifications or experience, or

(ii) persons approved by the Secretary of State.

(6) Regulations shall make provision for referring to an industrial tribunal any question whether an organisation is such a trade union as is mentioned in subsection (4)(d) and may make provision as to the form and content of any such document as is referred to in subsection (2).

DEFINITIONS

"actuary": s.47, s.124(1).

"auditor": s.47, s.124(1).

"independent trade unions": s.124(5); the Pension Schemes Act 1993, s.181(1).

"member": s.124(1).

"occupational pension scheme": s.176.

"prescribed": s.14(2), s.124(1).

"regulations": s.124(1).

"trustees or managers": s.124(1).

GENERAL NOTE

This section is derived from s.56E of the Social Security Pensions Act 1975, repeated in s.114 of the Pension Schemes Act 1993, but the contents of those sections are expanded. For the regulations, see the Occupational Pension Schemes (Disclosure of Information) Regulations 1986 (S.I. 1986 No. 1046) as amended, particularly regs. 8 and 9.

[Standing Committee D, May 18, 1995, col. 271].

Employee trustees

Time off for performance of duties and for training

42.—(1) The employer in relation to a trust scheme must permit any employee of his who is a trustee of the scheme to take time off during his working hours for the purpose of—

(a) performing any of his duties as such a trustee, or

(b) undergoing training relevant to the performance of those duties.

(2) The amount of time off which an employee is to be permitted to take under this section and the purposes for which, the occasions on which and any conditions subject to which time off may be so taken are those that are reasonable in all the circumstances having regard in particular to—

(a) how much time off is required for the performance of the duties of a trustee of the scheme and the undergoing of relevant training, and how much time off is required for performing the particular duty or, as the case may be, for undergoing the particular training, and

(b) the circumstances of the employer's business and the effect of the employee's absence on the running of that business.

(3) An employee may present a complaint to an industrial tribunal that his employer has failed to permit him to take time off as required by this section.

(4) For the purposes of this section, the working hours of an employee are any time when in accordance with his contract of employment he is required to be at work.

DEFINITIONS
    "employee": s.124(1), and *cf* s.124(5); the Pension Schemes Act 1993, s.181(1).
    "employer": s.124(1), and *cf* s.124(5); the Pension Schemes Act 1993, s.181(1).
    "industrial tribunal": s.124(5); the Pension Schemes Act 1993, s.181(1).
    "trust scheme": s.124(1).

GENERAL NOTE
    For a similar provision, see s.168 of the Trade Union and Labour Relations (Consolidation) Act 1992.
    [Standing Committee D, May 18, 1995, col. 277].

Payment for time off

43.—(1) An employer who permits an employee to take time off under section 42 must pay him for the time taken off pursuant to the permission.

(2) Where the employee's remuneration for the work he would ordinarily have been doing during that time does not vary with the amount of work done, he must be paid as if he had worked at that work for the whole of that time.

(3) Where the employee's remuneration for the work he would ordinarily have been doing during that time varies with the amount of work done, he must be paid an amount calculated by reference to the average hourly earnings for that work.

(4) The average hourly earnings mentioned in subsection (3) are those of the employee concerned or, if no fair estimate can be made of those earnings, the average hourly earnings for work of that description of persons in comparable employment with the same employer or, if there are no such persons, a figure of average hourly earnings which is reasonable in the circumstances.

(5) A right to be paid an amount under this section does not affect any right of an employee in relation to remuneration under his contract of employment, but—

(a) any contractual remuneration paid to an employee in respect of a period of time off to which this section applies shall go towards discharging any liability of the employer under this section in respect of that period, and

(b) any payment under this section in respect of a period shall go towards discharging any liability of the employer to pay contractual remuneration in respect of that period.

(6) An employee may present a complaint to an industrial tribunal that his employer has failed to pay him in accordance with this section.

DEFINITIONS
    "employee": s.124(5); the Pension Schemes Act 1993, s.181(1).
    "employer": s.124(1), and *cf* s.124(5); the Pension Schemes Act 1993, s.181(1).
    "industrial tribunal": s.124(5); the Pension Schemes Act 1993, s.181(1).

Time limit for proceedings

44. An industrial tribunal must not consider a complaint under section 42 or 43 unless it is presented to the tribunal—

(a) within three months of the date when the failure occurred, or

(b) where the tribunal is satisfied that it was not reasonably practicable for the complaint to be presented within that period, within such further period as the tribunal considers reasonable.

DEFINITIONS
    "industrial tribunal": s.124(5); the Pension Schemes Act 1993, s.181(1).

GENERAL NOTE
    For a similar time limit, see s.175 of the Trade Union and Labour Relations (Consolidation) Act 1992.

Remedies

45.—(1) Where the tribunal finds a complaint under section 42 is well-founded, it must make a declaration to that effect and may make an award of compensation to be paid by the employer to the employee.

(2) The amount of the compensation shall be such as the tribunal considers just and equitable in all the circumstances having regard to the employer's default in failing to permit time off to be taken by the employee and to any loss sustained by the employee which is attributable to the matters complained of.

(3) Where on a complaint under section 43 the tribunal finds that the employer has failed to pay the employee in accordance with that section, it must order him to pay the amount which it finds to be due.

(4) The remedy of an employee for infringement of the rights conferred on him by section 42 or 43 is by way of complaint to an industrial tribunal in accordance with this Part, and not otherwise.

DEFINITIONS
   "employee": s.124(5); the Pension Schemes Act 1993, s.181(1).
   "employer": s.124(1), and *cf* s.124(5); the Pension Schemes Act 1993, s.181(1).
   "industrial tribunal": s.124(5); the Pension Schemes Act 1993, s.181(1).
   [Standing Committee D, May 23, 1995, col. 283].

Right not to suffer detriment in employment or be unfairly dismissed

46.—(1) Subject to subsection (2), an employee has the right not to be subjected to any detriment by any act, or any deliberate failure to act, by his employer done on the ground that, being a trustee of a trust scheme which relates to his employment, the employee performed (or proposed to perform) any functions as such a trustee.

(2) Subsection (1) does not apply where the detriment in question amounts to dismissal, except where an employee is dismissed in circumstances in which, by virtue of section 142 of the Employment Protection (Consolidation) Act 1978 ("the 1978 Act"), section 54 of that Act does not apply to the dismissal.

(3) Sections 22B and 22C of the 1978 Act (which relate to proceedings brought by an employee on the grounds that he has been subjected to a detriment in contravention of section 22A of that Act) shall have effect as if the reference in section 22B(1) to section 22A included a reference to subsection (1).

(4) In the following provisions of the 1978 Act—
   (a) section 129 (remedy for infringement of certain rights),
   (b) section 141(2) (employee ordinarily working outside Great Britain), and
   (c) section 150 and Schedule 12 (death of employee or employer),
any reference to Part II of that Act includes a reference to subsection (1).

(5) The dismissal of an employee by an employer shall be regarded for the purposes of Part V of the 1978 Act as unfair if the reason (or, if more than one, the principal reason) for it is that, being a trustee of a trust scheme which relates to his employment, the employee performed (or proposed to perform) any functions as such a trustee.

(6) Where the reason or the principal reason for which an employee was selected for dismissal was that he was redundant, but it is shown—
   (a) that the circumstances constituting the redundancy applied equally to one or more other employees in the same undertaking who held positions similar to that held by him and who have not been dismissed by the employer, and

(b) that the reason (or, if more than one, the principal reason) for which he was selected for dismissal was that specified in subsection (5),
then, for the purposes of Part V of the 1978 Act, the dismissal shall be regarded as unfair.

(7) Section 54 of the 1978 Act (right of employee not to be unfairly dismissed) applies to a dismissal regarded as unfair by virtue of subsection (5) or (6) regardless of the period for which the employee has been employed and of his age; and accordingly section 64(1) of that Act (which provides a qualifying period and an upper age limit) does not apply to such a dismissal.

(8) Any provision in an agreement (whether a contract of employment or not) shall be void in so far as it purports—

(a) to exclude or limit the operation of any provision of this section, or
(b) to preclude any person from presenting a complaint to an industrial tribunal by virtue of any provision of this section.

(9) Subsection (8) does not apply to an agreement to refrain from presenting or continuing with a complaint where—

(a) a conciliation officer has taken action under section 133(2) or (3) of the 1978 Act (general provisions as to conciliation) or under section 134(1), (2) or (3) (conciliation in case of unfair dismissal) of that Act, or
(b) the conditions regulating compromise agreements under the 1978 Act (as set out in section 140(3) of that Act) are satisfied in relation to the agreement.

(10) In this section, "dismissal" has the same meaning as in Part V of the 1978 Act.

(11) Section 153 of the 1978 Act (general interpretation) has effect for the purposes of this section as it has effect for the purposes of that Act.

DEFINITIONS
"employee": s.124(5); the Pension Schemes Act 1993, s.181(1).
"employer": s.124(1), and cf s.124(5); the Pension Schemes Act 1993, s.181(1).
"trust scheme": s.124(1).

GENERAL NOTE
This section provides much needed protection for employees carrying out their duties as trustees, in which position they may have to act in a way detrimental to the employer—a good reason for having pensioners as trustees. The section applies the appropriate provisions of the Employment Protection (Consolidation) Act 1978 to a trustee in the situation envisaged by the section. For commentary on this Act, see the appropriate volume of Current Law Statutes Annotated.

Advisers

Professional advisers

47.—(1) For every occupational pension scheme there shall be—

(a) an individual, or a firm, appointed by the trustees or managers as auditor (referred to in this Part, in relation to the scheme, as "the auditor"), and
(b) an individual appointed by the trustees or managers as actuary (referred to in this Part, in relation to the scheme, as "the actuary").

(2) For every occupational pension scheme the assets of which consist of or include investments (within the meaning of the Financial Services Act 1986) there shall be an individual or a firm appointed by or on behalf of the trustees or managers as fund manager.

(3) If in the case of an occupational pension scheme any person—

(a) is appointed otherwise than by the trustees or managers as legal adviser or to exercise any prescribed functions in relation to the scheme, or
(b) is appointed otherwise than by or on behalf of the trustees or managers as a fund manager,

sections 3 and 10 apply to any trustee, and section 10 applies to any manager, who in exercising any of his functions places reliance on the skill or judgment of that person.

(4) In this Part, in relation to an occupational pension scheme—

(a) the auditor, actuary and legal adviser appointed by the trustees or managers,

(b) any fund manager appointed by or on behalf of the trustees or managers, and

(c) any person appointed by the trustees or managers to exercise any of the functions referred to in subsection (3)(a),

are referred to as "professional advisers".

(5) This section does not apply to an occupational pension scheme falling within a prescribed class or description and regulations may—

(a) make exceptions to subsections (1) to (3),

(b) specify the qualifications and experience, or approval, required for appointment as a professional adviser.

(6) Regulations may make provision as to—

(a) the manner in which professional advisers may be appointed and removed,

(b) the terms on which professional advisers may be appointed (including the manner in which the professional advisers may resign).

(7) Subject to regulations made by virtue of subsection (6), professional advisers shall be appointed on such terms as the trustees or managers may determine.

(8) If in the case of an occupational pension scheme an auditor, actuary or fund manager is required under this section to be appointed but the appointment has not been made, or not been made in accordance with any requirements imposed under this section, sections 3 and 10 apply to any trustee, and section 10 applies to any manager, who has failed to take all such steps as are reasonable to secure compliance.

(9) Regulations may in the case of occupational pension schemes—

(a) impose duties on any person who is or has been the employer, and on any person who acts as auditor or actuary to such a person, to disclose information to the trustees or managers and to the scheme's professional advisers,

(b) impose duties on the trustees or managers to disclose information to, and make documents available to, the scheme's professional advisers.

(10) If in the case of an occupational pension scheme a person fails to comply with any duty imposed under subsection (9)(a), section 10 applies to him.

(11) If in the case of an occupational pension scheme any duty imposed under subsection (9)(b) is not complied with, sections 3 and 10 apply to any trustee, and section 10 applies to any manager, who has failed to take all such steps as are reasonable to secure compliance.

DEFINITIONS

"actuary": s.39, s.124(1).
"auditor": s.39, s.124(1).
"employer": s.124(1), and *cf* s.124(5); the Pension Schemes Act 1993, s.181(1).
"firm": s.124(1).
"fund manager": s.124(1).
"occupational pension scheme": s.176.
"prescribed": s.14(2), s.124(1).
"regulations": s.124(1).
"trustees or managers": s.124(1).

GENERAL NOTE

Subs. (1)

Surprisingly, subs. (1) as originally drafted only applied to a trust scheme and not to any other occupational pension scheme, but this was amended during the passage of the Bill through Parliament. An auditor and an actuary must be appointed by the trustees, subject to any exceptions contained in regulations made under subs. (5). Although this section is not made overriding (so that it nullifies any provision in a trust deed or rules to the effect that one or other of these is to be appointed by the employer), that is the practical effect of the section by reason of subss. (3) and (7). Further, for example, it is the auditor and the actuary appointed under this section who are to carry out the functions prescribed under s.41. This section will go some way towards preventing any unusually cosy relationship between the actuary and the employer, which regrettably from time to time exists.

Subs. (2)

This subsection gives statutory force to the usual position in which the trustees of a trust scheme find themselves, although it may have more of an effect in the realm of statutory schemes.

Subs. (3)

It remains to be seen what functions are prescribed. This section as presently drafted is wide enough to include members of the bar as well as solicitors. This is a highly important subsection. It has frequently been the case hitherto that the employer has appointed the legal advisers to a scheme, or that the trustees of a scheme have been content to rely on legal advice procured in respect of a scheme by the employer, with the result that they have not been given advice which looks at the problem under consideration from the point of view of the trustees and or of the beneficiaries under the scheme. Now the legal advisers will have to be appointed by the trustees, and will have to report to them. Such advice would be a normal expense of running the scheme, which the trustees would be entitled to discharge out of the assets of the scheme, whether the provisions of the scheme permit this or not.

Section 3 provides for the removal or suspension of a trustee, and s.10 for civil penalties.

Subss. (8), (10) and (11)

Section 3 provides for the removal or suspension of a trustee. Section 10 empowers the Authority to impose a penalty.

[Standing Committee D, May 23, 1995, col. 288].

"Blowing the whistle"

48.—(1) If the auditor or actuary of any occupational pension scheme has reasonable cause to believe that—

(a) any duty relevant to the administration of the scheme imposed by any enactment or rule of law on the trustees or managers, the employer, any professional adviser or any prescribed person acting in connection with the scheme has not been or is not being complied with, and

(b) the failure to comply is likely to be of material significance in the exercise by the Authority of any of their functions,

he must immediately give a written report of the matter to the Authority.

(2) The auditor or actuary of any occupational pension scheme must, in any prescribed circumstances, immediately give a written report of any prescribed matter to the Authority.

(3) No duty to which the auditor or actuary of any occupational pension scheme is subject shall be regarded as contravened merely because of any information or opinion contained in a written report under this section.

(4) If in the case of any occupational pension scheme any professional adviser (other than the auditor or actuary), any trustee or manager or any person involved in the administration of the scheme has reasonable cause to believe as mentioned in paragraphs (a) and (b) of subsection (1), he may give a report of the matter to the Authority.

(5) In the case of any such scheme, no duty to which any such adviser, trustee or manager or other person is subject shall be regarded as contravened merely because of any information or opinion contained in a report under this section; but this subsection does not apply to any information dis-

closed in such a report by the legal adviser of an occupational pension scheme if he would be entitled to refuse to produce a document containing the information in any proceedings in any court on the grounds that it was the subject of legal professional privilege or, in Scotland, that it contained a confidential communication made by or to an advocate or solicitor in that capacity.

(6) Subsections (1) to (5) apply to any occupational pension scheme to which section 47 applies.

(7) Section 10 applies to any auditor or actuary who fails to comply with subsection (1) or (2).

(8) If it appears to the Authority that an auditor or actuary has failed to comply with subsection (1) or (2), the Authority may by order disqualify him for being the auditor or, as the case may be, actuary of any occupational pension scheme specified in the order.

(9) An order under subsection (8) may specify the scheme to which the failure relates, all schemes falling within any class or description of occupational pension scheme or all occupational pension schemes.

(10) The Authority may, on the application of any person disqualified under this section who satisfies the Authority that he will in future comply with those subsections, by order revoke the order disqualifying him; but a revocation made at any time cannot affect anything done before that time.

(11) An auditor or actuary of an occupational pension scheme who becomes disqualified under this section shall, while he is so disqualified, cease to be auditor or, as the case may be, actuary of any scheme specified in the order disqualifying him.

(12) A person who, while he is disqualified under this section, purports to act as auditor or actuary of an occupational pension scheme specified in the order disqualifying him is guilty of an offence and liable—

    (a) on summary conviction, to a fine not exceeding the statutory maximum, and

    (b) on conviction on indictment, to a fine or imprisonment, or both.

(13) An offence under subsection (12) may be charged by reference to any day or longer period of time; and a person may be convicted of a second or subsequent offence under that subsection by reference to any period of time following the preceding conviction of the offence.

DEFINITIONS
    "actuary": s.47, s.124(1).
    "auditor": s.47, s.124(1).
    "Authority": s.1.
    "contravention": s.124(1).
    "occupational pension scheme": s.176.
    "prescribed": s.124(1).
    "professional adviser": s.47, s.124(1).
    "regulations": s.124(1).

GENERAL NOTE
    This is the well publicised "whistle-blowing" section. It was considerably altered during its passage through Parliament. It applies to occupational pension schemes to which s.47 apply, and it should be observed that some may be excluded by regulations made under s.47(5). It places duties on the auditor and the actuary which they might well not wish to have. It requires of them considerable knowledge of the law (statutory and otherwise) applicable to a trust scheme; and this is a considerable imposition on these professionals, since they have not hitherto professed this kind of knowledge. No doubt in cases of difficulty they will seek professional legal assistance.

    For like provisions with regard to personal pension schemes inserted into the Pension Schemes Act 1993 as a new section 33A of that Act, see s.147, below.

Subs. (1)
    An actuary or auditor is under a duty to "blow the whistle" in the circumstances set out in this subsection. He must do so if he has "reasonable cause to believe" that any duty referred to in subs. (1)(a) is not being complied with. This would appear to place an objectively judged burden

on actuaries and accountants, which will be hard to discharge given the complicated and developing branch of trust law which applies to pension schemes. It would appear that the question as to whether the failure to comply with a rule of law or any enactment is "of material significance" is also objectively judged (subs. (1)(b)). It may be foreseen that actuaries and accountants may have to take independent legal advice over matters which arise. They will have to be astute to judge when this is necessary. They should be careful to ensure that if they have to obtain legal advice, the expenses of so doing are recoverable from the scheme as part of their proper charges against it.

Subs. (3)
Other duties, such as that of confidentiality, are not infringed by carrying out the duty under subs. (1).

Subss. (4) and (5)
As to professional advisers, see s.47 above and the General Note thereto. Other professional advisers have a power, but not a duty, to make a report. The more limited cover contained in subs. (5) against breach of confidentiality, from which documents covered by legal professional privilege are excluded, is to be noted.

Subs. (7)
Section 10 gives the Authority the power to levy a penalty for failure.

Subss. (8) to (13)
The remainder of the subsections give teeth to the duties placed upon actuaries and auditors. [Standing Committee D, May 23, 1995, col. 291].

Receipts, payments and records

Other responsibilities of trustees, employers, etc.

49.—(1) The trustees of any trust scheme must, except in any prescribed circumstances, keep any money received by them in a separate account kept by them at an institution authorised under the Banking Act 1987.

(2) Regulations may require the trustees of any trust scheme to keep—

(a) records of their meetings (including meetings of any of their number), and

(b) books and records relating to any prescribed transaction.

(3) Regulations may, in the case of any trust scheme, require the employer, and any prescribed person acting in connection with the scheme, to keep books and records relating to any prescribed transaction.

(4) Regulations may require books or records kept under subsection (2) or (3) to be kept in a prescribed form and manner and for a prescribed period.

(5) Regulations must, in cases where payments of benefit to members of trust schemes are made by the employer, require the employer to make into a separate account kept by him at an institution authorised under the Banking Act 1987 any payments of benefit which have not been made to the members within any prescribed period.

(6) If in the case of any trust scheme any requirements imposed by or under subsection (1) or (2) are not complied with, sections 3 and 10 apply to any trustee who has failed to take all such steps as are reasonable to secure compliance.

(7) If in the case of any trust scheme any person fails to comply with any requirement imposed under subsection (3) or (5), section 10 applies to him.

(8) Where—

(a) on making a payment of any earnings in respect of any employment there is deducted any amount corresponding to any contribution payable on behalf of an active member of an occupational pension scheme, and

(b) the amount deducted is not, within a prescribed period, paid to the trustees or managers of the scheme and there is no reasonable excuse for the failure to do so, the employer is guilty of an offence and liable, on summary conviction, to a fine not exceeding the statutory maximum and, on conviction on indictment, to imprisonment, or a fine, or both.

DEFINITIONS
"active member": s.124(1).
"employer": s.124(1), and *cf* s.124(5); the Pension Schemes Act 1993, s.181(1).
"employment": s.124(5); the Pension Schemes Act 1993, s.181(1).
"member": s.124(1).
"occupational pension scheme": s.176.
"prescribed": s.124(1).
"regulations": s.124(1).
"trust scheme": s.124(1).
"trustees or managers": s.124(1).

GENERAL NOTE
The contents of this section only apply to trust schemes. This is intended to provide for and to safeguard the benefits payable in a case where the employer pays benefits on behalf of the scheme. It is also intended to safeguard the assets of the scheme and to ensure that they are not held in any account with any other moneys, notably those of the employer.

Subss. (2), (3) and (4)
These subsections give the Secretary of State the power to expand the requirements now contained in the Occupational Pension Schemes (Disclosure of Information) Regulations 1986 (S.I. 1986 No. 1046).

Subs. (5)
Failure to comply with this subsection gives rise to the Authority's power contained in s.15(1) (as to which, the General Note thereon).

Subss. (6) and (7)
Section 3 contains the power of the Authority to remove or suspend a trustee, and s.10 contains the power of the Authority to impose a penalty.

Subs. (8)
See the General Note to s.6(1) above.
[Standing Committee D, May 23, 1995, col. 298].

Resolution of disputes

Resolution of disputes

50.—(1) The trustees or managers of an occupational pension scheme must secure that such arrangements as are required by or under this section for the resolution of disagreements between prescribed persons about matters in relation to the scheme are made and implemented.

(2) The arrangements must—

(a) provide for a person, on the application of a complainant of a prescribed description, to give a decision on such a disagreement, and

(b) require the trustees or managers, on the application of such a complainant following a decision given in accordance with paragraph (a), to reconsider the matter in question and confirm the decision or give a new decision in its place.

(3) Regulations may make provision about—

(a) applications for decisions under such arrangements, and

(b) the procedure for reaching and giving such decisions,

including the times by which applications are to be made and decisions given.

(4) Applications and decisions under subsection (2) must be in writing.

(5) Arrangements under subsection (1) must, in the case of existing schemes, have effect as from the commencement of this section.

(6) If, in the case of any occupational pension scheme, such arrangements as are required by this section to be made have not been made, or are not being implemented, section 10 applies to any of the trustees or managers who

have failed to take all such steps as are reasonable to secure that such arrangements are made or implemented.

(7) This section does not apply to a scheme of a prescribed description and subsection (1) does not apply to prescribed matters in relation to the scheme.

DEFINITIONS
"occupational pension scheme": s.152.
"prescribed": s.124(1).
"trustees or managers": s.124(1).

GENERAL NOTE
If disagreements are not settled by the procedures set up under this section, reference to the Occupational Pensions Arbitration Service (OPAS) may be found helpful. There is power to make regulations which exempt certain schemes from this section: see subs. (7).

Subs. (6)
Section 10 provides for civil penalties to be levied.
[Standing Committee D, May 23, 1995, col. 301].

Indexation

Annual increase in rate of pension

51.—(1) Subject to subsection (6) this section applies to a pension under an occupational pension scheme if—
 (a) the scheme—
             (i) is an approved scheme, within the meaning of Chapter I of Part XIV of the Taxes Act 1988 (retirement benefit schemes approved by the Commissioners of Inland Revenue) or is a scheme for which such approval has been applied for under that Chapter and not refused, and
             (ii) is not a public service pension scheme, and
 (b) apart from this section, the annual rate of the pension would not be increased each year by at least the appropriate percentage of that rate.

(2) Subject to section 52, where a pension to which this section applies, or any part of it, is attributable to pensionable service on or after the appointed day or, in the case of money purchase benefits, to payments in respect of employment carried on on or after the appointed day—
 (a) the annual rate of the pension, or
 (b) if only part of the pension is attributable to pensionable service or, as the case may be, to payments in respect of employment carried on on or after the appointed day, so much of the annual rate as is attributable to that part,
must be increased annually by at least the appropriate percentage.

(3) Subsection (2) does not apply to a pension under an occupational pension scheme if the rules of the scheme require—
 (a) the annual rate of the pension, or
 (b) if only part of the pension is attributable to pensionable service or, as the case may be, to payments in respect of employment carried on on or after the appointed day, so much of the annual rate as is attributable to that part,
to be increased at intervals of not more than twelve months by at least the relevant percentage and the scheme complies with any prescribed requirements.

(4) For the purposes of subsection (3) the relevant percentage is—
 (a) the percentage increase in the retail prices index for the reference period, being a period determined, in relation to each periodic increase, under the rules, or
 (b) the percentage for that period which corresponds to 5 per cent per annum,

whichever is the lesser.

(5) Regulations may provide that the provisions of subsections (2) and (3) apply in relation to a pension as if so much of it as would not otherwise be attributable to pensionable service or to payments in respect of employment were attributable to pensionable service or, as the case may be, payments in respect of employment—

(a) before the appointed day,

(b) on or after that day, or

(c) partly before and partly on or after that day.

(6) This section does not apply to any pension or part of a pension which, in the opinion of the trustees or managers, is derived from the payment by any member of the scheme of voluntary contributions.

DEFINITIONS

"annual rate": s.54.

"appointed day": s.54.

"appropriate percentage": s.54.

"employment": s.124(5); the Pension Schemes Act 1993, s.181(1).

"money purchase scheme": s.124(5); the Pension Schemes Act 1993, s.181(1).

"occupational pension scheme": s.152.

"pension": s.54.

"pensionable service": s.124(1) and (3).

"prescribed": s.124(1).

"public service pension scheme": s.124(1).

"regulations": s.124(1).

"Taxes Act 1988": s.124(1).

GENERAL NOTE

Section 43 has its roots in Sched. 3A to the Social Security Pensions Act 1975 repeated in ss.102 and 103 of the Pension Schemes Act 1993. Section 104 of the 1993 Act, which contained requirements for the increase of the earlier service component (*i.e.* increases in respect of service completed before the appointed day), appear to have been abandoned without having been brought into force. The powers of the Secretary of State under subs. (5) are clearly for the purpose of providing for cases of difficulty, and are not to be used for the purpose of a wholesale change such as the reintroduction of increases for the earlier service component. As originally drafted, free-standing additional voluntary contribution schemes were excluded from this section. The present exclusion is wider, and extends to any pension which is provided by the payment of voluntary contributions by a member, thus including benefits payable under an employer's contributory scheme where the benefits are financed by members' voluntary contributions: see subs. (6).

Subs. (2)

See subs. (4) for the calculation of the appropriate percentage. The maximum percentage is five per cent.

[Standing Committee D, May 23, cols. 309 and 317].

Restriction on increase where member is under 55

52.—(1) Subject to subsection (2), no increase under section 51 is required to be paid to or for a member of a scheme whose pension is in payment but who has not attained the age of 55 at the time when the increase takes effect.

(2) Subsection (1) does not apply if the member—

(a) is permanently incapacitated by mental or physical infirmity from engaging in regular full-time employment, or

(b) has retired on account of mental or physical infirmity from the employment in respect of which, or on retirement from which, the pension is payable.

(3) The rules of a scheme may provide that if, in a case where a pension has been paid to or for a member under the age of 55 at an increased rate in consequence of subsection (2), the member—

    (a) ceases to suffer from the infirmity in question before he attains the age of 55, but

    (b) continues to be entitled to the pension,

any increases subsequently taking effect under section 51 in the annual rate of the pension shall not be paid or shall not be paid in full.

    (4) In any case where—

    (a) by virtue only of subsection (1) or (3), increases are not paid to or for a member or are not paid in full, but

    (b) the member attains the age of 55 or, in a case falling within subsection (3), again satisfies the condition set out in subsection (2)(a) or (b),

his pension shall then become payable at the annual rate at which it would have been payable apart from subsection (1) or (3).

<small>DEFINITIONS</small>
    "annual rate": s.46.
    "employment": s.124(5); the Pension Schemes Act 1993, s.181(1).
    "member": s.124(1).
    "pension": s.46.

<small>GENERAL NOTE</small>
    Section 52 is derived from para. 5 of Sched. 3A to the Social Security Pensions Act 1975, and section 106 of the Pension Schemes Act 1993. The disapplication of subs. (1) (by subs. (2)) in cases of serious ill-health reflects modern pensions practice in the private sector.
    [Standing Committee D, May 23, 1995, col. 328].

Effect of increases above the statutory requirement

    53.—(1) Where in any tax year the trustees or managers of an occupational pension scheme make an increase in a person's pension, not being an increase required by section 109 of the Pension Schemes Act 1993 or section 51 of this Act, they may deduct the amount of the increase from any increase which, but for this subsection, they would be required to make under either of those sections in the next tax year.

    (2) Where in any tax year the trustees or managers of such a scheme make an increase in a person's pension and part of the increase is not required by section 109 of the Pension Schemes Act 1993 or section 51 of this Act, they may deduct that part of the increase from any increase which, but for this subsection, they would be required to make under either of those sections in the next tax year.

    (3) Where by virtue of subsection (1) or (2) any pensions are not required to be increased in pursuance of section 109 of the Pension Schemes Act 1993 or section 51 of this Act, or not by the full amount that they otherwise would be, their amount shall be calculated for any purpose as if they had been increased in pursuance of the section in question or, as the case may be, by that full amount.

    (4) In section 110 of the Pension Schemes Act 1993 (resources for annual increase of guaranteed minimum pension)—

    (a) subsections (2) to (4) are omitted, and

    (b) in subsection (1), for "subsection (2) or (3)" there is substituted "section 53 of the Pensions Act 1995".

<small>DEFINITIONS</small>
    "guaranteed minimum pension": s.124(5); the Pension Schemes Act 1993, s.8(2).
    "occupational pension scheme": s.152.
    "tax year": s.124(5); the Pension Schemes Act 1993, s.181(1).
    "trustees or managers": s.124(1).

<small>GENERAL NOTE</small>
    This section allows a progressive set-off of any increases under scheme rules against the statutory increases required by s.1 of this Act, or s.109 of the Pension Schemes Act 1993, which prescribes certain increases to be paid from contracted out schemes for the tax year 1988–1989

and after to be curtailed under s.54 below. Increases of more than the statutory amount may be carried forward a year.

[Standing Committee D, May 23, 1995, col. 329].

Sections 51 to 53: supplementary

54.—(1) The first increase required by section 51 in the rate of a pension must take effect not later than the first anniversary of the date on which the pension is first paid; and subsequent increases must take effect at intervals of not more than twelve months.

(2) Where the first such increase is to take effect on a date when the pension has been in payment for a period of less than twelve months, the increase must be of an amount at least equal to one twelfth of the amount of the increase so required (apart from this subsection) for each complete month in that period.

(3) In sections 51 to 53 and this section—

"annual rate", in relation to a pension, means the annual rate of the pension, as previously increased under the rules of the scheme or under section 51,

"the appointed day" means the day appointed under section 180 for the commencement of section 51,

"appropriate percentage", in relation to an increase in the whole or part of the annual rate of a pension, means the revaluation percentage for the revaluation period the reference period for which ends with the last preceding 30th September before the increase is made (expressions used in this definition having the same meaning as in paragraph 2 of Schedule 3 to the Pension Schemes Act 1993 (methods of revaluing accrued pension benefits)),

"pension", in relation to a scheme, means any pension in payment under the scheme and includes an annuity.

DEFINITIONS
"occupational pension scheme": s.176.
"prescribed": s.124(1).
"public service pension scheme": s.124(1); the Pension Schemes Act 1993, s.1.
[Standing Committee D, May 23, 1995, col. 331].

Section 51: end of annual increase in GMP

55. In section 109 of the Pension Schemes Act 1993 (annual increase of guaranteed minimum pensions)—

(a) in subsection (2) (increase in rate of that part of guaranteed minimum pension attributable to earnings factors for tax year 1988–89 and subsequent tax years) for "the tax year 1988–89 and subsequent tax years" there is substituted "the tax years in the relevant period", and

(b) after subsection (3) there is inserted—

"(3A) The relevant period is the period—

(a) beginning with the tax year 1988–89, and

(b) ending with the last tax year that begins before the principal appointed day for the purposes of Part III of the Pensions Act 1995".

DEFINITIONS
"guaranteed minimum pension": s.124(5); the Pension Schemes Act 1993, s.8(2).

GENERAL NOTE
The requirement for pension schemes to pay limited increases in respect of guaranteed minimum pensions payable from the scheme was introduced by s.9 of the Social Security Act 1986

with effect from the tax year 1988–1989. Increases are limited to three per cent. This requirement is to cease when s.44 comes into force.

Minimum funding requirement

Minimum funding requirement

56.—(1) Every occupational pension scheme to which this section applies is subject to a requirement (referred to in this Part as "the minimum funding requirement") that the value of the assets of the seheme is not less than the amount of the liabilities of the scheme.

(2) This section applies to an occupational pension scheme other than—

(a) a money purchase scheme, or

(b) a scheme falling within a prescribed class or description.

(3) For the purposes of this section and sections 57 to 61, the liabilities and assets to be taken into account, and their amount or value, shall be determined, calculated and verified by a prescribed person and in the prescribed manner.

(4) In calculating the value of any liabilities for those purposes, a provision of the scheme which limits the amount of its liabilities by reference to the amount of its assets is to be disregarded.

(5) In sections 57 to 61, in relation to any occupational pension scheme to which this section applies—

(a) the amount of the liabilities referred to in subsection (1) is referred to as "the amount of the scheme liabilities",

(b) the value of the assets referred to in that subsection is referred to as "the value of the scheme assets",

(c) an "actuarial valuation" means a written valuation prepared and signed by the actuary of the scheme of the assets and liabilities referred to in subsection (1), and

(d) the "effective date" of an actuarial valuation is the date by reference to which the assets and liabilities are valued.

DEFINITIONS

"money purchase scheme": s.124(5); the Pension Schemes Act 1993, s.181(1).

"occupational pension scheme": s.152.

"prescribed": s.124(1).

GENERAL NOTE

This section applies to all schemes other than those specifically excepted by regulations and money purchase schemes, the latter needing no such underpinning. Deficiencies in the assets of a scheme on winding up are provided for to some extent under s.144 of the Pension Schemes Act 1993, which is also concerned with schemes which are not money purchase schemes. This section now introduces a minimum funding rule applicable to ongoing schemes. The name of the requirement hides the debate which has troubled the actuarial profession, because under subs. (3) the amount of a scheme's liabilities are to be calculated on a basis prescribed by regulations. This basis, it is understood, will not be calculated by the amount necessary to purchase annuity policies to satisfy those liabilities, but on other less demanding criteria: for the government refused to tie the amount of scheme liabilities to the cost of the purchase of annuities, on the grounds that this was in many cases unrealistic, on the basis that larger schemes could not get quotes: see *Hansard*, H.L. Vol. 561, col. 823. Thus an actuary may properly give a certificate that the minimum funding requirement is fulfilled in respect of a scheme, although it may be wound up the next day and be found to be in deficit because of current annuity rates in the market.

[Standing Committee D, May 23, 1995, cols. 338 and 351].

Valuation and certification of assets and liabilities

57.—(1) The trustees or managers of an occupational pension scheme to which section 56 applies must—

(a) obtain, within a prescribed period, an actuarial valuation and afterwards obtain such a valuation before the end of prescribed intervals, and

(b) on prescribed occasions or within prescribed periods, obtain a certificate prepared by the actuary of the scheme—

    (i) stating whether or not in his opinion the contributions payable towards the scheme are adequate for the purpose of securing that the minimum funding requirement will continue to be met throughout the prescribed period or, if it appears to him that it is not met, will be met by the end of that period, and

    (ii) indicating any relevant changes that have occurred since the last actuarial valuation was prepared.

(2) Subject to subsection (3), the trustees or managers must—

(a) if the actuary states in such a certificate that in his opinion the contributions payable towards the scheme are not adequate for the purpose of securing that the minimum funding requirement will continue to be met throughout the prescribed period or, if it appears to him that it is not met, will be met by the end of that period, or

(b) in prescribed circumstances,

obtain an actuarial valuation within the period required by subsection (4).

(3) In a case within subsection (2)(a), the trustees or managers are not required to obtain an actuarial valuation if—

(a) in the opinion of the actuary of the scheme, the value of the scheme assets is not less than 90 per cent of the amount of the scheme liabilities, and

(b) since the date on which the actuary signed the certificate referred to in that subsection, the schedule of contributions for the scheme has been revised under section 58(3)(b).

(4) If the trustees or managers obtain a valuation under subsection (2) they must do so—

(a) in the case of a valuation required by paragraph (a), within the period of six months beginning with the date on which the certificate was signed, and

(b) in any other case, within a prescribed period.

(5) A valuation or certificate obtained under subsection (1) or (2) must be prepared in such manner, give such information and contain such statements as may be prescribed.

(6) The trustees or managers must secure that any valuation or certificate obtained under this section is made available to the employer within seven days of their receiving it.

(7) Where, in the case of an occupational pension scheme to which section 56 applies, subsection (1), (2) or (6) is not complied with—

(a) section 3 applies to any trustee who has failed to take all such steps as are reasonable to secure compliance, and

(b) section 10 applies to any trustee or manager who has failed to take all such steps.

DEFINITIONS
"actuarial valuation": s.56.
"actuary": s.124(1).
"employer": s.124(1).
"minimum funding requirement": s.56.
"occupational pension scheme": s.176.
"prescribed": s.124(1).
"trustees or managers": s.124(1).

GENERAL NOTE
This section, together with the next three sections, lays the statutory groundwork of the nuts and bolts of the minimum solvency requirement. It is the groundwork only, since the important details will be contained in regulations for which copious provision is made throughout these sections, and to which reference must be made if the practical effect of these sections is to be arrived at. The plan of these sections is that the valuations which are prescribed by s.57(1) must be obtained. If the actuary is able to give a satisfactory certificate under subs. (1)(b), well and

good. If not, a further valuation must be obtained under subs. (2) (subject to the exceptions contained in subs. (3)) within the time limit set out in subs. (4). Before this takes place, the trustees and the employer will have to agree (or, in default of agreement, the trustees decide) under s.58 a rate of contributions to be included in the schedule of contributions prescribed by s.58, such that it may be certified by the actuary under s.58(6). This certificate can only be given where the actuary is satisfied that if subsequent rates of contributions are maintained at the same level, either the minimum solvency requirement will be met throughout the period, or, if it was not met at the beginning of the period, it will be met at the end of a period, the length of which is to be prescribed by regulations. If the minimum solvency requirement is not met at the end of the prescribed period the trustees or managers must make a report to the Authority (see s.59(3)). If the scheme is seriously underfunded (*i.e.* less than 90 per cent funded) the provisions of s.60 will apply.

It is to be noted that the rates of contributions referred to are those of the active members as well as employers. However, the practical effect of these provisions is likely to be that the remaining final salary schemes, which have a fixed rate of employer's and employee's contributions, will be turned into balance of cost schemes, since the amount of additional contributions that it may be possible to secure from members may be limited. In connection with this it may be possible to agree that, for future service, benefits will accrue at a lesser rate than hitherto, thus turning the scheme towards solvency by the end of the prescribed period. But reference to s.59 below will demonstrate how difficult any such alteration to accrued benefits would be to achieve.

Subs. (1)

The valuation will be on prescribed bases (see s.56(3)) and therefore will not necessarily be on the same actuarial and other assumptions as those normally used by the actuary for the scheme, or those prescribed for the purposes of Sched. 22 to the Income and Corporation Taxes Act 1988. The valuations will have to be obtained "within a prescribed period" and at "prescribed intervals". Thus it appears that it is the date of the valuation which is the relevant date, and not the date as at which the valuation is made, as has been usual hitherto.

Subs. (7)

Section 3 contains the power of the Authority to remove or suspend a trustee, and s.10 contains the power of the Authority to impose a penalty.

Schedules of contributions

58.—(1) The trustees or managers of an occupational pension scheme to which section 56 applies must secure that there is prepared, maintained and from time to time revised a schedule (referred to in sections 57 to 59 as a "schedule of contributions") showing—
  (a) the rates of contributions payable towards the scheme by or on behalf of the employer and the active members of the scheme, and
  (b) the dates on or before which such contributions are to be paid.
  (2) The schedule of contributions for a scheme must satisfy prescribed requirements.
  (3) The schedule of contributions for a scheme—
  (a) must be prepared before the end of a prescribed period beginning with the signing of the first actuarial valuation for the scheme,
  (b) may be revised from time to time where the revisions are previously agreed by the trustees or managers and the employer and any revision in the rates of contributions is certified by the actuary of the scheme, and
  (c) must be revised before the end of a prescribed period beginning with the signing of each subsequent actuarial valuation.
  (4) The matters shown in the schedule of contributions for a scheme—
  (a) must be matters previously agreed by the trustees or managers and the employer, or
  (b) if no such agreement has been made as to all the matters shown in the schedule, must be—

(i) rates of contributions determined by the trustees or managers, being such rates as in their opinion are adequate for the purpose of securing that the minimum funding requirement will continue to be met throughout the prescribed period or, if it appears to them that it is not met, will be met by the end of that period, and

(ii) other matters determined by the trustees or managers;

and the rates of contributions shown in the schedule must be certified by the actuary of the scheme.

(5) An agreement for the purposes of subsection (4)(a) is one which is made by the trustees or managers and the employer during the prescribed period beginning with the signing of the last preceding actuarial valuation for the scheme.

(6) The actuary may not certify the rates of contributions shown in the schedule of contributions—

(a) in a case where on the date he signs the certificate it appears to him that the minimum funding requirement is met, unless he is of the opinion that the rates are adequate for the purpose of securing that the requirement will continue to be met throughout the prescribed period, and

(b) in any other case, unless he is of the opinion that the rates are adequate for the purpose of securing that the requirement will be met by the end of that period.

(7) The Authority may in prescribed circumstances extend (or further extend) the period referred to in subsection (6).

(8) Where, in the case of any occupational pension scheme to which section 56 applies, this section is not complied with—

(a) section 3 applies to any trustee who has failed to take all such steps as are reasonable to secure compliance, and

(b) section 10 applies to any trustee or manager who has failed to take all such steps.

DEFINITIONS

"active member": s.124(1).
"actuarial valuation": s.56.
"actuary": s.124(1).
"Authority": s.1(1).
"effective date": s.56.
"employer": s.124(1).
"minimum funding requirement": s.56.
"occupational pension scheme": s.176.
"prescribed": s.124(1).
"trustees or managers": s.124(1).

GENERAL NOTE

For a general commentary on the effect of this and neighbouring sections, see the General Notes to ss.48 and 49 above.

Subs. (1)

It is to be noted that the rates of contributions include those paid by active members. Thus in cases where the actuary cannot give a satisfactory certificate with regard to the minimum solvency requirement, the members' rates of contributions are not immune from increase.

Subss. (3) and (4)

The schedule of contributions must be prepared before the end of the prescribed period following the initial actuarial valuation (presumably this valuation will be made on current rates) and then must be revised following each subsequent valuation. From subs. (4) it would appear that if the trustees and the employer cannot agree the contents of the schedule, they are for the trustees (or managers) to decide, within the limits prescribed by subs. (4)(b). Thus the trustees will be able to decide the rate of contributions in default of agreement, and will be subject to removal, suspension and a penalty if they do not do so (see subs. (8)). The rates in the schedule may be altered by agreement between the employer and the trustees in the interim.

Subs. (8)
Section 3 contains the power of the Authority to remove or suspend a trustee, and s.10 contains the power of the Authority to impose a penalty.
[Standing Committee D, June 6, 1995, col. 373].

Determination of contributions: supplementary

59.—(1) Except in prescribed circumstances, the trustees or managers of an occupational pension scheme to which section 56 applies must, where any amounts payable by or on behalf of the employer or the active members of the scheme in accordance with the schedule of contributions have not been paid on or before the due date, give notice of that fact, within the prescribed period, to the Authority and to the members of the scheme.

(2) Any such amounts which for the time being remain unpaid after that date (whether payable by the employer or not) shall, if not a debt due from the employer to the trustees or managers apart from this subsection, be treated as such a debt.

(3) If, in the case of an occupational pension scheme to which section 56 applies, it appears to the trustees or managers, at the end of any prescribed period that the minimum funding requirement is not met, they must prepare a report giving the prescribed information about the failure to meet that requirement.

(4) If in the case of any such scheme, subsection (1) or (3) is not complied with—

    (a) section 3 applies to any trustee who has failed to take all such steps as are reasonable to secure compliance, and

    (b) section 10 applies to any trustee or manager who has failed to take all such steps.

DEFINITIONS
"active members": s.124(1).
"Authority": s.1.
"employer": s.124(1), and *cf* s.124(5); the Pension Schemes Act 1993, s.181(1).
"member": s.124(1).
"minimum funding requirement": s.56.
"occupational pension scheme": s.152.
"prescribed": s.124(1).
"trustees or managers": s.124(1).

GENERAL NOTE
For a general comment on this section, see the General Notes to ss.57 and 58 above.

Subs. (1)
As a result of this subsection the members will have this information, which in the past has usually been concealed from them.

Subs. (4)
Non-compliance with subss. (1) or (3) will allow the Authority to use its powers under ss.3 and 10 above to remove or suspend one or more of the trustees, and to appoint others in their place, or simply to appoint additional trustees together with an exclusion order under s.6(4)(b).
[Standing Committee D, June 6, 1995, col. 400].

Serious underprovision

60.—(1) Subsection (2) applies where, in the case of an occupational pension scheme to which section 56 applies, an actuarial valuation shows that, on the effective date of the valuation, the value of the scheme assets is less than 90 per cent of the amount of the scheme liabilities (the difference shown in the valuation being referred to in this section as "the shortfall").

(2) The employer must—

    (a) by making an appropriate payment to the trustees or managers, or

    (b) by a prescribed method,

secure an increase in the value of the scheme assets which, taken with any contributions paid, is not less than the shortfall.

(3) The required increase in that value must be secured—

(a) before the end of a prescribed period beginning with the signing of the valuation, or

(b) if the actuarial valuation was obtained by reason of such a statement in a certificate as is referred to in section 57(2), before the end of a prescribed period beginning with the signing of the certificate.

(4) Except in prescribed circumstances, if the employer fails to secure the required increase in value before the end of the period applicable under subsection (3), the trustees or managers must, within the period of fourteen days (or such longer period as is prescribed) beginning with the end of that period, give written notice of that fact to the Authority and to the members of the scheme.

(5) If the employer fails to secure the required increase in value before the end of the period applicable under subsection (3), then so much of the shortfall as, at any subsequent time, has not been met by an increase in value under subsection (2) made—

(a) by making an appropriate payment to the trustees or managers,

(b) by a prescribed method, or

(c) by contributions made before the end of that period,

shall, if not a debt due from the employer to the trustees or managers apart from this subsection, be treated at that time as such a debt.

(6) Where an increase in value is secured by a prescribed method, the increase is to be treated for the purposes of this section as being of an amount determined in accordance with regulations.

(7) The Authority may in prescribed circumstances extend (or further extend) the period applicable under subsection (3).

(8) If subsection (4) is not complied with—

(a) section 3 applies to any trustee who has failed to take all such steps as are reasonable to secure compliance, and

(b) section 10 applies to any trustee or manager who has failed to take all such steps.

DEFINITIONS

"actuarial valuation": s.56.
"actuary": s.124(1).
"amount of the scheme's liabilities": s.56.
"Authority": s.1(1).
"effective date": s.56.
"employer": s.124(1).
"member": s.124(1).
"minimum solvency requirement": s.56.
"occupational pension scheme": s.152.
"prescribed": s.124(1).
"regulations": s.124(1).
"trustees or managers": s.124(1).
"value of the scheme's assets": s.56.

GENERAL NOTE

This General Note should be read against the background of the general comments on ss.56 to 58 above.

This section bites where the scheme is less than 90 per cent funded on the minimum solvency requirement basis. It must be remembered that this may involve the use by the actuary of different actuarial and other assumptions from that used by him otherwise in respect of the scheme. Thus it may be possible for the scheme to be less than 90 per cent funded on the latter basis, but not on the former, and vice versa.

If subs. (1) applies to the scheme then the shortfall must be made up by an appropriate payment or the adoption of a prescribed method, and within the time limits set out in subs. (3) unless these are extended by the Authority under subs. (7). This may be awkward for an employer which is in financial difficulty, particularly as the contributions may well not be ordinary annual contributions such as attract expenses relief under s.592(4) of the Income and Corporation Taxes Act 1988, but may have to be spread under s.592(6) of that Act.

Subs. (4)
The Authority may act in one or more of the ways summarised in the General Note to s.59(4) above.

Subs. (5)
This is a necessary provision, since the obligation to pay will arise under this section rather than under the trust deed and rules of the scheme. It is to be noted that it is the amount of the shortfall that has not been met which measures the debt, and that this is not measured by the appropriate payment, or that part of it not made, or by the payment due under the prescribed method.

Subs. (6)
This subsection is required for the purposes of subs. (5), where, it might be, payments in stages rather than lump sum payments are envisaged.

Subs. (8)
See the General Note to s.51(4) above.
[Standing Committee D, June 6, 1995, cols. 404 and 409].

Sections 56 to 60: supplementary

61. Regulations may modify sections 56 to 60 as they apply in prescribed circumstances.

DEFINITIONS
   "prescribed": s.124(1).
   "regulations": s.124(1).

Equal treatment

The equal treatment rule

62.—(1) An occupational pension scheme which does not contain an equal treatment rule shall be treated as including one.
   (2) An equal treatment rule is a rule which relates to the terms on which—
   (a) persons become members of the scheme, and
   (b) members of the scheme are treated.
   (3) Subject to subsection (6), an equal treatment rule has the effect that where—
   (a) a woman is employed on like work with a man in the same employment,
   (b) a woman is employed on work rated as equivalent with that of a man in the same employment, or
   (c) a woman is employed on work which, not being work in relation to which paragraph (a) or (b) applies, is, in terms of the demands made on her (for instance under such headings as effort, skill and decision) of equal value to that of a man in the same employment,
but (apart from the rule) any of the terms referred to in subsection (2) is or becomes less favourable to the woman than it is to the man, the term shall be treated as so modified as not to be less favourable.
   (4) An equal treatment rule does not operate in relation to any difference as between a woman and a man in the operation of any of the terms referred to in subsection (2) if the trustees or managers of the scheme prove that the difference is genuinely due to a material factor which—
   (a) is not the difference of sex, but
   (b) is a material difference between the woman's case and the man's case.
   (5) References in subsection (4) and sections 63 to 65 to the terms referred to in subsection (2), or the effect of any of those terms, include—

(a) a term which confers on the trustees or managers of an occupational pension scheme, or any other person, a discretion which, in a case within any of paragraphs (a) to (c) of subsection (3)—

(i) may be exercised so as to affect the way in which persons become members of the scheme, or members of the scheme are treated, and

(ii) may (apart from the equal treatment rule) be so exercised in a way less favourable to the woman than to the man, and

(b) the effect of any exercise of such a discretion;

and references to the terms on which members of the scheme are treated are to be read accordingly.

(6) In the case of a term within subsection (5)(a) the effect of an equal treatment rule is that the term shall be treated as so modified as not to permit the discretion to be exercised in a way less favourable to the woman than to the man.

DEFINITIONS

"employed": s.124(5); the Pension Schemes Act 1993, s.181(1).
"employment": s.124(5); the Pension Schemes Act 1993, s.181(1).
"member": s.124(1).
"occupational pension scheme": s.152.
"trustees or managers": s.124(1).

GENERAL NOTE

Sections 62 to 66 of the Act are designed to place on the statute book the requirements of Art. 119 of the Treaty of Rome, as explained in *Barber v. Guardian Royal Exchange Assurance Group* [1990] 2 All E.R. 660, *Ten Oever v. Stichtung Bedrijfspensioenfonds voor het Glazenwassers- en Schoonmakbedrijf* [1993] I.R.L.R. 601, and *Coloroll Pension Trustees v. Russell* [1994] I.R.L.R. 586, insofar as the Art. 119 applies to occupational pension schemes. The Article has direct application to contracts of employment in the U.K. Section 62 also implements its direct application to occupational pension schemes (as opposed to the contracts of employment), which remains doubtful even after the *Coloroll* decision. But these sections do not address the question of whether the discriminatory differences in respect of guaranteed minimum pensions, authorised by statute for contracting out, are lawful.

So far as entry into a scheme is concerned, subs. (4) will be of importance. There may be good reason to exclude a class the majority of which is predominately of one sex for reasons other than sex, and this must be examined. So far as the terms of a scheme are concerned, this will have no application to a scheme which is lawfully composed of members of one sex only. It is believed that such schemes exist.

Section 62 is somewhat curiously drafted in the context of occupational pension schemes, where the majority of existing discrimination is against men, owing to the traditional difference in the normal retirement ages of the two sexes in the private sector (a reflection of the statutory differences in their state pension ages). The fact that the section applies to discrimination against men is clarified by the reference to s.1 of the Equal Pay Act 1970 contained in s.63(4). Section 63 also contains a number of other supplementary provisions which add to or modify the general provisions contained in s.62. Section 63(6) sets out the *ratione temporis* qualification contained in the *Barber* judgment in respect of the application of Art. 119 to occupational pension schemes.

Subss. (5) and (6)

These subsections are designed to ensure that discretions are not exercised on a discriminatory basis, and were introduced late in the passage of the Act through Parliament.
[Standing Committee D, June 6, 1995, col. 422].

Equal treatment rule: supplementary

63.—(1) The reference in section 62(2) to the terms on which members of a scheme are treated includes those terms as they have effect for the benefit of dependants of members, and the reference in section 62(5) to the way in which members of a scheme are treated includes the way they are treated as it has effect for the benefit of dependants of members.

(2) Where the effect of any of the terms referred to in section 62(2) on persons of the same sex differs according to their family or marital status, the

effect of the term is to be compared for the purposes of section 62 with its effect on persons of the other sex who have the same status.

(3) An equal treatment rule has effect subject to paragraphs 5 and 6 of Schedule 5 to the Social Security Act 1989 (employment-related benefit schemes: maternity and family leave provisions).

(4) Section 62 shall be construed as one with section 1 of the Equal Pay Act 1970 (requirement of equal treatment for men and women in the same employment); and sections 2 and 2A of that Act (disputes and enforcement) shall have effect for the purposes of section 62 as if—

(a) references to an equality clause were to an equal treatment rule,
(b) references to employers and employees were to the trustees or managers of the scheme (on the one hand) and the members, or prospective members, of the scheme (on the other),
(c) for section 2(4) there were substituted—

"(4) No claim in respect of the operation of an equal treatment rule in respect of an occupational pension scheme shall be referred to an industrial tribunal otherwise than by virtue of subsection (3) above unless the woman concerned has been employed in a description or category of employment to which the scheme relates within the six months preceding the date of the reference", and

(d) references to section 1(2)(c) of the Equal Pay Act 1970 were to section 62(3)(c) of this Act.

(5) Regulations may make provision for the Equal Pay Act 1970 to have effect, in relation to an equal treatment rule, with prescribed modifications; and subsection (4) shall have effect subject to any regulations made by virtue of this subsection.

(6) Section 62, so far as it relates to the terms on which members of a scheme are treated, is to be treated as having had effect in relation to any pensionable service on or after 17th May 1990.

DEFINITIONS
"employee": s.124(5); the Pension Schemes Act 1993, s.181(1).
"employer": s.124(1), and *cf* s.124(5); the Pension Schemes Act 1993, s.181(1).
"employment": s.124(5); the Pension Schemes Act 1993, s.181(1).
"equal treatment rule": s.62.
"member": s.124(1).
"modifications": s.124(5); the Pension Schemes Act 1993, s.181(1).
"pensionable service": s.124(1).
"prescribed": s.124(1).
"regulations": s.124(1).
"trustees or managers": s.124(1).

GENERAL NOTE
See the General Note to s.62 above.

Subs. (4)
The reference to s.2 of the Equal Pay Act 1970 is important, since it ensures that claims for a breach of s.62 may be made to an industrial tribunal and imports into s.62 the time limits on such claims, for which see ss.2(4) and (5) of the Equal Pay Act 1970, as modified by this section. The European Court of Justice has held that the national rules relating to time limits may properly be applied to claims based on unlawful discrimination which fall within Art. 119, but that these must not render the exercise of the rights impossible in practice and must be similar to those limits applicable to other similar claims (see *Fissher v. Voorhuis Hengelo BV and another* [1994] OPLR 297). Whether these time limits will apply to a claim which relies directly on the statute, or to a complaint made to the Pensions Ombudsman, remains to be seen. For the considerations lying behind the time limits imposed by this subs., see *Hansard*, H.L. Vol. 561, col. 879.
[Standing Committee D, June 6, 1995, col. 456].

Equal treatment rule: exceptions

64.—(1) An equal treatment rule does not operate in relation to any variation as between a woman and a man in the effect of any of the terms referred to in section 62(2) if the variation is permitted by or under any of the provisions of this section.

(2) Where a man and a woman are eligible, in prescribed circumstances, to receive different amounts by way of pension, the variation is permitted by this subsection if, in prescribed circumstances, the differences are attributable only to differences between men and women in the benefits under sections 43 to 55 of the Social Security Contributions and Benefits Act 1992 (State retirement pensions) to which, in prescribed circumstances, they are or would be entitled.

(3) A variation is permitted by this subsection if—

(a) the variation consists of the application of actuarial factors which differ for men and women to the calculation of contributions to a scheme by employers, being factors which fall within a prescribed class or description, or

(b) the variation consists of the application of actuarial factors which differ for men and women to the determination of benefits falling within a prescribed class or description;

and in this subsection "benefits" include any payment or other benefit made to or in respect of a person as a member of the scheme.

(4) Regulations may—

(a) permit further variations, or

(b) amend or repeal subsection (2) or (3);

and regulations made by virtue of this subsection may have effect in relation to pensionable service on or after 17th May 1990 and before the date on which the regulations are made.

<small>DEFINITIONS</small>
"employer": s.124(1), and *cf* s.124(5); the Pension Schemes Act 1993, s.181(1).
"equal treatment rule": s.54.
"member": s.124(1).
"pensionable service": s.124(1).
"prescribed": s.124(1).
"regulations": s.124(1).

<small>GENERAL NOTE</small>
Subsection (3) lays the ground for the exception from the requirements of s.62 in respect of actuarial factors used in certain circumstances. In *Neath v. Hugh Steeper* [1994] 2 All E.R. 929 it was held by the European Court of Justice that Art. 119 of the Treaty of Rome had no application to matters concerning the funding of schemes and actuarial factors differing according to sex used for such a purpose, including the commutation of pensions for a lump sum.
[Standing Committee D, June 8, 1995, col. 453].

Equal treatment rule: consequential alteration of schemes

65.—(1) The trustees or managers of an occupational pension scheme may, if—

(a) they do not (apart from this section) have power to make such alterations to the scheme as may be required to secure conformity with an equal treatment rule, or

(b) they have such power but the procedure for doing so—

(i) is liable to be unduly complex or protracted, or

(ii) involves the obtaining of consents which cannot be obtained, or can only be obtained with undue delay or difficulty,

by resolution make such alterations to the scheme.

(2) The alterations may have effect in relation to a period before the alterations are made.

<small>DEFINITIONS</small>
"equal treatment rule": s.54.
"occupational pension scheme": s.152.

"trustees or managers": s.124(1).

GENERAL NOTE

This section gives trustees or managers of an occupational pension scheme the power to incorporate an equal treatment rule into a scheme retrospectively. This is important in order to ensure that direct effect is given to Art. 119 of the Treaty of Rome in relation to a scheme in circumstances in which it cannot be secured by other means. This section should be brought into force as soon as possible.

Equal treatment rule: effect on terms of employment, etc.

66.—(1) In section 6 of the Equal Pay Act 1970 (exclusions), for subsections (1A) and (2) (exclusion for terms related to death or retirement) there is substituted—

"(1B) An equality clause shall not operate in relation to terms relating to a person's membership of, or rights under, an occupational pension scheme, being terms in relation to which, by reason only of any provision made by or under sections 62 to 64 of the Pensions Act 1995 (equal treatment), an equal treatment rule would not operate if the terms were included in the scheme.

(1C) In subsection (1B), "occupational pension scheme" has the same meaning as in the Pension Schemes Act 1993 and "equal treatment rule" has the meaning given by section 62 of the Pensions Act 1995".

(2) In section 4(1) of the Sex Discrimination Act 1975 (victimisation of complainants etc.)—

(a) in paragraphs (a), (b) and (c), after "Equal Pay Act 1970" there is inserted "or sections 62 to 65 of the Pensions Act 1995", and

(b) at the end of paragraph (d) there is added "or under sections 62 to 65 of the Pensions Act 1995".

(3) In section 6 of the Sex Discrimination Act 1975 (discrimination against applicants and employees), for subsection (4) there is substituted—

"(4) Subsections 1(b) and (2) do not render it unlawful for a person to discriminate against a woman in relation to her membership of, or rights under, an occupational pension scheme in such a way that, were any term of the scheme to provide for discrimination in that way, then, by reason only of any provision made by or under sections 62 to 64 of the Pensions Act 1995 (equal treatment), an equal treatment rule would not operate in relation to that term.

(4A) In subsection (4), "occupational pension scheme" has the same meaning as in the Pension Schemes Act 1993 and "equal treatment rule" has the meaning given by section 62 of the Pensions Act 1995".

(4) Regulations may make provision—

(a) for the Equal Pay Act 1970 to have effect, in relation to terms of employment relating to membership of, or rights under, an occupational pension scheme with prescribed modifications, and

(b) for imposing requirements on employers as to the payment of contributions and otherwise in case of their failing or having failed to comply with any such terms.

(5) References in subsection (4) to terms of employment include (where the context permits)—

(a) any collective agreement or pay structure, and

(b) an agricultural wages order within section 5 of the Equal Pay Act 1970.

DEFINITIONS

"employer": s.124(1), and *cf* s.124(5); the Pension Schemes Act 1993, s.181(1).

"employment": s.124(5); the Pension Schemes Act 1993, s.181(1).

"modifications": s.124(5); the Pension Schemes Act, s.181(1).
"prescribed": s.124(1).
"regulations": s.124(1).

GENERAL NOTE

The section makes appropriate alterations to the Equal Pay Act 1970, and to the Sex Discrimination Act 1975.

Modification of schemes

Restriction on powers to alter schemes

67.—(1) This section applies to any power conferred on any person by an occupational pension scheme (other than a public service pension scheme) to modify the scheme.

(2) The power cannot be exercised on any occasion in a manner which would or might affect any entitlement, or accrued right, of any member of the scheme acquired before the power is exercised unless the requirements under subsection (3) are satisfied.

(3) Those requirements are that, in respect of the exercise of the power in that manner on that occasion—

(a) the trustees have satisfied themselves that—
   (i) the certification requirements, or
   (ii) the requirements for consent,
   are met in respect of that member, and

(b) where the power is exercised by a person other than the trustees, the trustees have approved the exercise of the power in that manner on that occasion.

(4) In subsection (3)—

(a) "the certification requirements" means prescribed requirements for the purpose of securing that no power to which this section applies is exercised in any manner which, in the opinion of an actuary, would adversely affect any member of the scheme (without his consent) in respect of his entitlement, or accrued rights, acquired before the power is exercised, and

(b) "the consent requirements" means prescribed requirements for the purpose of obtaining the consent of members of a scheme to the exercise of a power to which this section applies.

(5) Subsection (2) does not apply to the exercise of a power in a prescribed manner.

(6) Where a power to which this section applies may not (apart from this section) be exercised without the consent of any person, regulations may make provision for treating such consent as given in prescribed circumstances.

DEFINITIONS

"accrued rights": s.124(2).
"actuary": s.124(1).
"member": s.124(1).
"modifications": s.124(5); the Pension Schemes Act 1993, s.181(1).
"occupational pension scheme": s.176.
"prescribed": s.124(1).
"public service pension scheme": s.124(1).
"regulations": s.124(1).

GENERAL NOTE

This section restricts the powers of alteration contained in an occupational pension scheme other than a public service scheme. Since subss. (3), (4) and (5) all concern matters to be governed by regulations, little can be said about the ambit of this section, save that it is to be noted that there is a prohibition in subs. (2) on the alteration of an entitlement as well as an accrued right. The precise meaning of the word entitlement will no doubt be the subject of judicial clarification, but may well be used to indicate the position under a scheme where rights under it have crystallised, for instance where a pension has become payable, leaving the term "accrued rights" to be applicable to inchoate rights. These latter rights have been defined so as to be calculable on the basis that the member ceased to be an active member as at the relevant date for the calculation, a position to be compared with the two different possible positions considered by Millett J. (as he then was) in *Courage Group's Pension Schemes, Re* [1987] 1 All E.R. 528.

[Standing Committee D, June 8, 1995, col. 467].

Power of trustees to modify schemes by resolution

68.—(1) The trustees of a trust scheme may by resolution modify the scheme with a view to achieving any of the purposes specified in subsection (2).

(2) The purposes referred to in subsection (1) are—

(a) to extend the class of persons who may receive benefits under the scheme in respect of the death of a member of the scheme,

(b) to enable the scheme to conform with such arrangements as are required by section 16(1) or 17(2),

(c) to enable the scheme to comply with such terms and conditions as may be imposed by the Compensation Board in relation to any payment made by them under section 83 or 84,

(d) to enable the scheme to conform with section 37(2), 76(2), 91 or 92, and

(e) prescribed purposes.

(3) No modification may be made by virtue of subsection (2)(a) without the consent of the employer.

(4) Modifications made by virtue of subsection (2)(b) may include in particular—

(a) modification of any limit on the number of, or of any category of, trustees, or

(b) provision for the transfer or vesting of property.

(5) Nothing done by virtue of subsection (2)(d), or any corresponding provisions in force in Northern Ireland, shall be treated as effecting an alteration to the scheme in question for the purposes of section 591B (cessation of approval) of the Taxes Act 1988.

(6) Regulations may provide that this section does not apply to trust schemes falling within a prescribed class or description.

DEFINITIONS
"Compensation Board": s.70(1).
"employer": s.124(1), and *cf* s.124(5); the Pension Schemes Act 1993, s.181(1).
"member": s.124(1).
"modifications": s.124(5); the Pension Schemes Act 1993, s.181(1).
"prescribed": s.124(1).
"Taxes Act": s.124(1).
"trust scheme": s.124(1).

GENERAL NOTE

Subs. (2)
Sections 16 and 17 provide for member-nominated trustees. Sections 37 and 76 provide for the payment of surplus funds to an employer, the first from an ongoing scheme and the second on the winding-up of a scheme. Sections 91 and 92 respectively give statutory recognition to the requirement of inalienability of pension scheme rights and provide a prohibition against forfeiture save in certain circumstances controlled by statute.

Sub. (5)
Section 591B(2) of the Income and Corporation Taxes Act 1988 provides that an alteration to a retirement benefits scheme will cause the approval of that scheme by the Board of Inland Revenue to cease, with consequent loss of tax concessions. Subsection (5) ensures that the adoption of arrangements under subs. (2)(d) will not have this effect; nor will an alteration to give effect to ss.16(1) and 17(2), see s.21(3).

Subs. (6)
There is power to exclude prescribed classes of scheme from the ambit of this section by statutory instrument.
[Standing Committee D, June 8, 1995, col. 471].

Grounds for applying for modifications

69.—(1) The Authority may, on an application made to them by persons competent to do so, make an order in respect of an occupational pension scheme (other than a public service pension scheme)—

(a) authorising the modification of the scheme with a view to achieving any of the purposes mentioned in subsection (3), or

(b) modifying the scheme with a view to achieving any such purpose.

(2) Regulations may make provision about the manner of dealing with applications under this section.

(3) The purposes referred to in subsection (1) are—

(a) in the case of a scheme to which Schedule 22 to the Taxes Act 1988 (reduction of pension fund surpluses in certain exempt approved schemes) applies, to reduce or eliminate on any particular occasion any excess in accordance with any proposal submitted under paragraph 3(1) of that Schedule, where any requirements mentioned in section 37(4), and any other prescribed requirements, will be satisfied in relation to the reduction or elimination,

(b) in the case of an exempt approved scheme (within the meaning given by section 592(1) of the Taxes Act 1988) which is being wound up, to enable assets remaining after the liabilities of the scheme have been fully discharged to be distributed to the employer, where prescribed requirements in relation to the distribution are satisfied, or

(c) to enable the scheme to be so treated during a prescribed period that an employment to which the scheme applies may be contracted-out employment by reference to it.

(4) The persons competent to make an application under this section are—

(a) in the case of the purposes referred to in paragraph (a) or (b) of subsection (3), the trustees of the scheme, and

(b) in the case of the purposes referred to in paragraph (c) of that subsection—

(i) the trustees or managers of the scheme,

(ii) the employer, or

(iii) any person other than the trustees or managers who has power to alter the rules of the scheme.

(5) An order under subsection (1)(a) must be framed—

(a) if made with a view to achieving either of the purposes referred to in subsection (3)(a) or (b), so as to confer the power of modification on the trustees, and

(b) if made with a view to achieving the purposes referred to in subsection (3)(c), so as to confer the power of modification on such persons (who may include persons who were not parties to the application made to the Authority) as the Authority think appropriate.

(6) Regulations may provide that in prescribed circumstances this section does not apply to occupational pension schemes falling within a prescribed class or description or applies to them with prescribed modifications.

DEFINITIONS:
"Authority": s.1(1).
"contracted out employment": s.124(5); the Pension Schemes Act 1993, s.181(1).
"employer": s.124(1), and *cf* s.124(5); the Pension Schemes Act 1993, s.181(1).
"employment": s.124(5); the Pension Schemes Act 1993, s.181(1).
"modifications": s.124(5); the Pension Schemes Act 1993, s.181(1).
"occupational pension scheme": s.176.
"prescribed": s.124(1).
"public service pension scheme": s.124(1).

"regulations": s.124(1).
"Taxes Act": s.124(1).
"trust scheme": s.124(1).

GENERAL NOTE

This section and ss.70 and 71 are to replace the alteration powers of the Occupational Pensions Board contained in ss.136 to 140 of the Pension Schemes Act 1993 (repealed by s.161 of this Act) with the limited powers of alteration contained in this section, now conferred on the Authority. Sections 70 and 71 contain supplementary provisions with respect to the powers set out in s.69.

Subs. (3)

Note the requirements contained in s.70 in respect of the exercise by the Authority of its power, particularly that contained in s.70(3) with regard to s.69(3)(c).

[Standing Committee D, June 8, 1995, cols. 479 and 485].

Section 69: supplementary

70.—(1) The Authority may not make an order under section 69 unless they are satisfied that the purposes for which the application for the order was made—

(a) cannot be achieved otherwise than by means of such an order, or

(b) can only be achieved in accordance with a procedure which—

(i) is liable to be unduly complex or protracted, or

(ii) involves the obtaining of consents which cannot be obtained, or can only be obtained with undue delay or difficulty.

(2) The extent of the Authority's powers to make such an order is not limited, in relation to any purposes for which they are exercisable, to the minimum necessary to achieve those purposes.

(3) The Authority may not make an order under section 69 with a view to achieving the purpose referred to in subsection (3)(c) of that section unless they are satisfied that it is reasonable in all the circumstances to make it.

DEFINITIONS

"Authority": s.1(1).

Effect of orders under section 69

71.—(1) An order under paragraph (a) of subsection (1) of section 69 may enable those exercising any power conferred by the order to exercise it retrospectively (whether or not the power could otherwise be so exercised) and an order under paragraph (b) of that subsection may modify a scheme retrospectively.

(2) Any modification of a scheme made in pursuance of an order of the Authority under section 69 is as effective in law as if it had been made under powers conferred by or under the scheme.

(3) An order under section 69 may be made and complied with in relation to a scheme—

(a) in spite of any enactment or rule of law, or any rule of the scheme, which would otherwise operate to prevent the modification being made, or

(b) without regard to any such enactment, rule of law or rule of the scheme as would otherwise require, or might otherwise be taken to require, the implementation of any procedure or the obtaining of any consent, with a view to the making of the modification.

(4) In this section, "retrospectively" means with effect from a date before that on which the power is exercised or, as the case may be, the order is made.

DEFINITIONS

"Authority": s.1(1).

"modifications": s.124(5); the Pension Schemes Act 1993, s.181(1).

Modification of public service pension schemes

72.—(1) The appropriate authority may make such provision for the modification of a public service pension scheme as could be made in respect of a scheme other than a public service pension scheme by an order of the Authority under section 69(1)(b).

(2) In this section "the appropriate authority", in relation to a scheme, means such Minister of the Crown or government department as may be designated by the Treasury as having responsibility for the particular scheme.

(3) The powers of the appropriate authority under this section are exercisable by means of an order—

(a) directly modifying the scheme (without regard, in the case of a scheme contained in or made under powers conferred by an enactment, to the terms of the enactment or any of its restrictions), or

(b) modifying an enactment under which the scheme was made or by virtue of which it has effect.

(4) Any such order may adapt, amend or repeal any such enactment as is referred to in paragraph (a) or (b) of subsection (3) as that authority thinks appropriate.

DEFINITIONS
"Authority": s.1(1).
"modifications": s.124(5); the Pension Schemes Act 1993, s.181(1).
"public service pension scheme": s.124(1).

GENERAL NOTE
This section gives to appropriate authorities like powers in respect of public service pension schemes as the immediately preceding sections in respect of other occupational pension schemes.
[Standing Committee D, June 8, 1995, col. 501].

Winding up

Preferential liabilities on winding up

73.—(1) This section applies, where a salary related occupational pension scheme to which section 56 applies is being wound up, to determine the order in which the assets of the scheme are to be applied towards satisfying the liabilities in respect of pensions and other benefits (including increases in pensions).

(2) The assets of the scheme must be applied first towards satisfying the amounts of the liabilities mentioned in subsection (3) and, if the assets are insufficient to satisfy those amounts in full, then—

(a) the assets must be applied first towards satisfying the amounts of the liabilities mentioned in earlier paragraphs of subsection (3) before the amounts of the liabilities mentioned in later paragraphs, and

(b) where the amounts of the liabilities mentioned in one of those paragraphs cannot be satisfied in full, those amounts must be satisfied in the same proportions.

(3) The liabilities referred to in subsection (2) are—

(a) any liability for pensions or other benefits which, in the opinion of the trustees, are derived from the payment by any member of the scheme of voluntary contributions,

(b) where a person's entitlement to payment of pension or other benefit has arisen, liability for that pension or benefit and for any pension or other benefit which will be payable to dependants of that person on his death (but excluding increases to pensions),

(c) any liability for—

(i) pensions or other benefits which have accrued to or in respect of any members of the scheme (but excluding increases to pensions), or

(ii) (in respect of members with less than two years pensionable service) the return of contributions,

(d) any liability for increases to pensions referred to in paragraphs (b) and (c);

and, for the purposes of subsection (2), the amounts of the liabilities mentioned in paragraphs (b) to (d) are to be taken to be the amounts calculated and verified in the prescribed manner.

(4) To the extent that any liabilities, as calculated in accordance with the rules of the scheme, have not been satisfied under subsection (2), any remaining assets of the scheme must then be applied towards satisfying those liabilities (as so calculated) in the order provided for in the rules of the scheme.

(5) If the scheme confers power on any person other than the trustees or managers to apply the assets of the scheme in respect of pensions or other benefits (including increases in pensions), it cannot be exercised by that person but may be exercised instead by the trustees or managers.

(6) If this section is not complied with—

(a) section 3 applies to any trustee who has failed to take all such steps as are reasonable to secure compliance, and

(b) section 10 applies to any trustee or manager who has failed to take all such steps.

(7) Regulations may modify subsection (3).

(8) This section does not apply to an occupational pension scheme falling within a prescribed class or description.

(9) This section shall have effect with prescribed modifications in cases where part of a salary related occupational pension scheme to which section 56 applies is being wound up.

DEFINITIONS

"member": s.124(1).
"modifications": s.124(5); the Pension Schemes Act 1993, s.181(1).
"occupational pension scheme": s.176.
"pensionable service": s.124(1).
"prescribed": s.124(1).
"regulations": s.124(1).
"salary related occupational pension scheme": s.125(1).

GENERAL NOTE

This section applies only to the winding-up and to the partial winding-up (see subs. (9)) of a salary related scheme, and in respect of such a scheme sets out a statutory order of preference for the liabilities of a scheme on its being wound up. Save for the two matters mentioned below and the contents of subs. (3)(d) (which would normally attach to the main liability), this is not unlike an order which might be expected to appear in the rules of a scheme. There are two matters which call for comment. The first is that the section is contrary to the statutory requirements for a contracted out scheme, and this will presumably be the subject matter of regulations made under subs. (7). The second is that statutory provision is made for rateable reduction in respect of any class, in the event of a partial deficiency for that class. The reasoning which lies behind the statutory order contained in subss. (2) and (3), namely that it is intended to ensure that the liabilities covered by the minimum solvency requirement are secured, and thus are given priority, is to be found in *Hansard*, H.L. Vol. 561, col. 890.

Subs. (5)

This is a late addition to the Act, and would appear to be designed to deal with the situation where the main distribution of the assets of a scheme on winding-up is subject to a power in the hands of the employer—a most unusual situation, but one which may exist. Otherwise there seems to be little point in this subsection.

Subs. (6)

Section 3 contains the power of the Authority to remove or suspend a trustee, and s.10 contains the power of the Authority to impose a penalty.

[Standing Committee D, June 8, 1995, col. 506].

Discharge of liabilities by insurance, etc.

74.—(1) This section applies where a salary related occupational pension scheme to which section 56 applies, other than a scheme falling within a prescribed class or description, is being wound up.

(2) A liability to or in respect of a member of the scheme in respect of pensions or other benefits (including increases in pensions) is to be treated as discharged (to the extent that it would not be so treated apart from this section) if the trustees or managers of the scheme have, in accordance with prescribed arrangements, provided for the discharge of the liability in one or more of the ways mentioned in subsection (3).

(3) The ways referred to in subsection (2) are—

(a) by acquiring transfer credits allowed under the rules of another occupational pension scheme which satisfies prescribed requirements and the trustees or managers of which are able and willing to accept payment in respect of the member,

(b) by acquiring rights allowed under the rules of a personal pension scheme which satisfies prescribed requirements and the trustees or managers of which are able and willing to accept payment in respect of the member's accrued rights,

(c) by purchasing one or more annuities which satisfy prescribed requirements from one or more insurance companies, being companies willing to accept payment in respect of the member from the trustees or managers,

(d) by subscribing to other pension arrangements which satisfy prescribed requirements.

(4) If the assets of the scheme are insufficient to satisfy in full the liabilities, as calculated in accordance with the rules of the scheme, in respect of pensions and other benefits (including increases in pensions), the reference in subsection (2) to providing for the discharge of any liability in one or more of the ways mentioned in subsection (3) is to applying any amount available, in accordance with section 73, in one or more of those ways.

(5) Regulations may provide for this section—

(a) to have effect in relation to so much of any liability as may be determined in accordance with the regulations, or

(b) to have effect with prescribed modifications in relation to schemes falling within a prescribed class or description.

DEFINITIONS
"accrued rights": s.124(1).
"insurance company": s.124(5); the Pension Schemes Act 1993, s.181(1).
"member": s.124(1).
"modifications": s.124(5); the Pension Schemes Act 1993, s.181(1).
"occupational pension scheme": s.176.
"personal pension scheme": s.176.
"prescribed": s.124(1).
"regulations": s.124(1).
"salary related occupational pension scheme": s.125(1).
"transfer credits": s.124(1).
"trustees or managers": s.124(1).

GENERAL NOTE
This is a new statutory provision in respect of the discharge, on winding-up, of the trustees' or managers' liability for pensions or other benefits of a salary related occupational pension scheme. No startling novelty is contained in the section, but it will have a beneficial effect in the case of schemes which lack the power, for example, to pay a transfer value to another scheme on winding up. The matters contained in subs. (3) will be the subject matter of regulations yet to be published. Subsection (4) provides for a discharge where there is a partial deficiency in respect of any class, and may cover total deficiencies in respect of one or more classes.

Deficiencies in the assets

75.—(1) If, in the case of an occupational pension scheme which is not a money purchase scheme, the value at the applicable time of the assets of the scheme is less than the amount at that time of the liabilities of the scheme, an amount equal to the difference shall be treated as a debt due from the employer to the trustees or managers of the scheme.

(2) If in the case of an occupational pension scheme which is not a money purchase scheme—

(a) a relevant insolvency event occurs in relation to the employer, and

(b) a debt due from the employer under subsection (1) has not been discharged at the time that event occurs,

the debt in question shall be taken, for the purposes of the law relating to winding up, bankruptcy or sequestration as it applies in relation to the employer, to arise immediately before that time.

(3) In this section "the applicable time" means—

(a) if the scheme is being wound up before a relevant insolvency event occurs in relation to the employer, any time when it is being wound up before such an event occurs, and

(b) otherwise, immediately before the relevant insolvency event occurs.

(4) For the purposes of this section a relevant insolvency event occurs in relation to the employer—

(a) in England and Wales—

(i) where the employer is a company, when it goes into liquidation, within the meaning of section 247(2) of the Insolvency Act 1986, or

(ii) where the employer is an individual, at the commencement of his bankruptcy, within the meaning of section 278 of that Act, or

(b) in Scotland—

(i) where the employer is a company, at the commencement of its winding up, within the meaning of section 129 of that Act, or

(ii) where the employer is a debtor within the meaning of the Bankruptcy (Scotland) Act 1985, on the date of sequestration as defined in section 12(4) of that Act.

(5) For the purposes of subsection (1), the liabilities and assets to be taken into account, and their amount or value, must be determined, calculated and verified by a prescribed person and in the prescribed manner.

(6) In calculating the value of any liabilities for those purposes, a provision of the scheme which limits the amount of its liabilities by reference to the amount of its assets is to be disregarded.

(7) This section does not prejudice any other right or remedy which the trustees or managers may have in respect of a deficiency in the scheme's assets.

(8) A debt due by virtue only of this section shall not be regarded—

(a) as a preferential debt for the purposes of the Insolvency Act 1986, or

(b) as a preferred debt for the purposes of the Bankruptcy (Scotland) Act 1985.

(9) This section does not apply to an occupational pension scheme falling within a prescribed class or description.

(10) Regulations may modify this section as it applies in prescribed circumstances.

DEFINITIONS
"employer": s.124(1), and *cf* s.124(5); the Pension Schemes Act 1993, s.181(1).
"money purchase scheme": s.124(5); the Pension Schemes Act 1993, s.181(1).
"occupational pension scheme": s.176.
"prescribed": s.124(1).
"regulations": s.124(1).

"trustees or managers": s.124(1).

GENERAL NOTE
This section is derived from s.58B of the Social Security Pensions Act 1975, repeated in s.144 of the Pension Schemes Act 1993. It was activated as a result of the revelations with regard to the Maxwell and Mirror Group pension schemes. The section only applies to a scheme which is not a money purchase scheme. Regulations in force are the Occupational Pension Schemes (Deficiency on Winding up etc.) Regulations 1992 (S.I. 1992 No. 1555). Regulation 2 broadly provides for the assets and liabilities of a scheme to be valued by a method approved by an actuary, and in connection with this Guidance Note 19 of the Institute of Actuaries may be referred to. The regulations also make provision for the application of the section to centralised schemes and schemes without members in pensionable service.

Excess assets on winding up

76.—(1) This section applies to a trust scheme in any circumstances if—
  (a) it is an exempt approved scheme, within the meaning given by section 592(1) of the Taxes Act 1988,
  (b) the scheme is being wound up, and
  (c) in those circumstances power is conferred on the employer or the trustees to distribute assets to the employer on a winding up.

(2) The power referred to in subsection (1)(c) cannot be exercised unless the requirements of subsections (3) and (in prescribed circumstances) (4), and any prescribed requirements, are satisfied.

(3) The requirements of this subsection are that—
  (a) the liabilities of the scheme have been fully discharged,
  (b) where there is any power under the scheme, after the discharge of those liabilities, to distribute assets to any person other than the employer, the power has been exercised or a decision has been made not to exercise it,
  (c) the annual rates of the pensions under the scheme which commence or have commenced are increased by the appropriate percentage, and
  (d) notice has been given in accordance with prescribed requirements to the members of the scheme of the proposal to exercise the power.

(4) The requirements of this subsection are that the Authority are of the opinion that—
  (a) any requirements prescribed by virtue of subsection (2) are satisfied, and
  (b) the requirements of subsection (3) are satisfied.

(5) In subsection (3)—
  (a) "annual rate" and "appropriate percentage" have the same meaning as in section 54, and
  (b) "pension" does not include—
        (i) any guaranteed minimum pension (as defined in section 8(2) of the Pension Schemes Act 1993) or any increase in such a pension under section 109 of that Act, or
        (ii) any money purchase benefit (as defined in section 181(1) of that Act).

(6) If, where this section applies to any trust scheme, the trustees purport to exercise the power referred to in subsection (1)(c) without complying with the requirements of this section, sections 3 and 10 apply to any of them who have failed to take all such steps as are reasonable to secure compliance.

(7) If, where this section applies to any trust scheme, any person other than the trustees purports to exercise the power referred to in subsection (1)(c) without complying with the requirements of this section, section 10 applies to him.

(8) Regulations may provide that, in prescribed circumstances, this section does not apply to schemes falling within a prescribed class or description, or applies to them with prescribed modifications.

DEFINITIONS
 "Authority": s.1.
 "employer": s.124(1), and cf s.124(5); the Pension Schemes Act 1993, s.181(1).
 "member": s.124(1).
 "modifications": s.124(5); the Pension Schemes Act 1993, s.181(1).
 "prescribed": s.124(1).
 "regulations": s.124(1).
 "Taxes Act": s.124(1).
 "trust scheme": s.124(1).

GENERAL NOTE
 This section is new. It is confined to a case where there is power conferred on an employer or
 the trustees (but not on anyone else) to distribute assets to a person on the winding up of a
 scheme. It is an odd provision, since it is hard to understand why the section is not also applied to
 cases where trustees are under a duty to pay surplus to an employer. The Authority may have to
 be satisfied in prescribed circumstances.

Subs. (3)
 Increases must be given to annuitants by the "appropriate percentage" (see s.54 above), and
 the members have to be informed in accordance with prescribed requirements, before repayment can be made.

Subss. (6) and (7)
 Section 3 contains the power of the Authority to remove or suspend a trustee, and s.10 con-
 tains the power of the Authority to impose a penalty.
 [Standing Committee D, June 8, 1995, col. 514].

Excess assets remaining after winding up: power to distribute

 77.—(1) This section applies to a trust scheme in any circumstances if—
 (a) it is an exempt approved scheme, within the meaning given by section
    592(1) of the Taxes Act 1988,
 (b) the scheme is being wound up,
 (c) the liabilities of the scheme have been fully discharged,
 (d) where there is any power under the scheme, after the discharge of
    those liabilities, to distribute assets to any person other than the
    employer, the power has been exercised or a decision has been made
    not to exercise it,
 (e) any assets remain undistributed, and
 (f) the scheme prohibits the distribution of assets to the employer in those
    circumstances.
 (2) The annual rates of the pensions under the scheme which commence or
 have commenced must be increased by the appropriate percentage, so far as
 the value of the undistributed assets allows.
 (3) In subsection (2)—
 (a) "annual rate" and "appropriate percentage" have the same meaning
    as in section 54, and
 (b) "pension" does not include—
        (i) any guaranteed minimum pension (as defined in section 8(2)
     of the Pension Schemes Act 1993) or any increase in such a pension
     under section 109 of that Act, or
        (ii) any money purchase benefit (as defined in section 181(1) of
     that Act).
 (4) Where any assets remain undistributed after the discharge of the trustees' duty under subsection (2)—
 (a) the trustees must use those assets for the purpose of providing
    additional benefits or increasing the value of any benefits, but subject
    to prescribed limits, and

(b) the trustees may then distribute those assets (so far as undistributed) to the employer.

(5) If, where this section applies to a trust scheme, the requirements of this section are not complied with, section 3 applies to any trustee who has failed to take all such steps as are reasonable to secure compliance.

(6) Regulations may modify this section as it applies in prescribed circumstances.

DEFINITIONS
"employer": s.124(1), and cf s.124(5); the Pension Schemes Act 1993, s.181(1).
"regulations": s.124(1).
"Taxes Act": s.124(1).
"trust scheme": s.124(1).

GENERAL NOTE
This section is designed to fill a lacuna in trust schemes where there is no power to return surplus assets to an employer on the winding up of a scheme. So far as subs. (4)(a) is concerned, it will be interesting to see what the prescribed limits are: in schemes where the employer has negatived a resulting trust the only limits which could properly be specified, it would seem, are Inland Revenue limits.

In certain older schemes provision is made on winding up for pensions in payment to be satisfied, and for the remainder of the assets of the scheme to be divided among the membership in such proportions as the trustees decide. These schemes will not be affected by this provision, since the discharge of the liabilities of the scheme involves the distribution of the whole of its assets. But other schemes contain an absolute prohibition on the return of any part of the assets of the scheme to the employer, and do not provide, or fully provide, for the distribution of surplus assets on the winding up of the scheme. In such cases the section may be of assistance.

Subs. (5)
See the General Note to s.76(6) above.

The Pensions Compensation Board

The Compensation Board

78.—(1) There shall be a body corporate called the Pensions Compensation Board (referred to in this Part as "the Compensation Board").

(2) The Compensation Board shall consist of not less than three members appointed by the Secretary of State, one of whom shall be so appointed as chairman.

(3) In addition to the chairman, the Board shall comprise—
(a) a member appointed after the Secretary of State has consulted—
  (i) organisations appearing to him to be representative of employers, and
  (ii) the chairman,
(b) a member appointed after the Secretary of State has consulted—
  (i) organisations appearing to him to be representative of employees, and
  (ii) the chairman,
and such other member or members as the Secretary of State may appoint after consultation with the chairman.

(4) Payments made by the Compensation Board may be made on such terms (including terms requiring repayment in whole or in part) and on such conditions as the Board think appropriate.

(5) The Compensation Board may borrow from an institution authorised under the Banking Act 1987 such sums as they may from time to time require for exercising any of their functions.

(6) The aggregate amount outstanding in respect of the principal of any money borrowed by the Compensation Board under subsection (5) must not exceed the prescribed amount.

(7) Neither the Compensation Board nor any person who is a member or employee of the Compensation Board shall be liable in damages for anything done or omitted in the discharge or purported discharge of the functions of the Compensation Board under this Part, or any corresponding provisions in force in Northern Ireland, unless it is shown that the act or omission was in bad faith.

(8) Schedule 2 (constitution, procedure, etc. of the Compensation Board) shall have effect.

DEFINITIONS
"employee": s.124(5); the Pension Schemes Act 1993, s.181(1).
"employer": s.124(1), and *cf* s.124(5); the Pension Schemes Act 1993, s.181(1).
"prescribed": s.124(1).

GENERAL NOTE
The Pensions Compensation Board is a main innovation contained in the Act. In broad terms ss.78 to 86, and Sched. 2 to the Act provide for the setting up of the Compensation Board and for compensation to be paid to the trustees of schemes instituted under a trust where: the employer is insolvent; the value of the assets of the scheme have been depleted by an act or omission which there are reasonable grounds to believe constitutes a prescribed offence, so that for a salary related scheme the liabilities exceed the assets at the date of application by more than 10 per cent; and it is reasonable for the members to be assisted by the payment of compensation. The amount of compensation is to be determined in accordance with regulations to be made, but is to be restricted to 90 per cent of the shortfall, and in the case of a salary related scheme, broadly to such sum as will cause the assets of the scheme to provide for 90 per cent of its liabilities. Needless to say, the funds for the purposes of the Compensation Board are to come from a levy to be imposed on occupational pension schemes generally.

Subs. (7)
The Board, its members and its employees are only liable for acts or omissions attributable to bad faith.

Reports to Secretary of State

79.—(1) The Compensation Board must prepare a report for the first 12-months of their existence, and a report for each succeeding period of twelve months, and must send each report to the Secretary of State as soon as practicable after the end of the period for which it is prepared.

(2) A report prepared under this section for any period must deal with the activities of the Compensation Board in the period.

(3) The Secretary of State must lay before each House of Parliament a copy of every report received by him under this section.

DEFINITIONS
"Compensation Board": s.78(1).

GENERAL NOTE
Section 2 prescribes that the Authority is to report at 12-month intervals, and as soon as practicable after the end of each such interval. This report must be laid before the House of Lords and the House of Commons.

Review of decisions

80.—(1) Subject to the following provisions of this section, any determination by the Compensation Board of a question which it is within their functions to determine shall be final.

(2) The Compensation Board may on the application of a person appearing to them to be interested—

(a) at any time review any such determination of theirs as is mentioned in subsection (1) (including a determination given by them on a previous review), if they are satisfied that there has been a relevant change of circumstances since the determination was made, or that the determination was made in ignorance of a material fact or based on a mistake as to a material fact or was erroneous in point of law, and

(b) at any time within a period of three months from the date of the determination, or within such longer period as they may allow in any particular case, review such a determination on any ground.

(3) The Compensation Board's powers on a review under this section include power—

(a) to vary or revoke any determination previously made,

(b) to substitute a different determination, and

(c) generally to deal with the matters arising on the review as if they had arisen on the original determination;

and also include power to make savings and transitional provisions.

(4) Subject to subsection (5), regulations may make provision with respect to the procedure to be adopted on any application for a review under this section, or under any corresponding provision in force in Northern Ireland, and generally with respect to such applications and reviews.

(5) Nothing in subsection (4) shall be taken to prevent such a review being entered upon by the Compensation Board without an application being made.

DEFINITIONS
  "Compensation Board": s.78(1).
  "regulations": s.124(1).
  [Standing Committee D, June 13, 1995, col. 521].

The compensation provisions

Cases where compensation provisions apply

81.—(1) Subject to subsection (2), this section applies to an application for compensation under section 82 in respect of an occupational pension scheme if all the following conditions are met—

(a) the scheme is a trust scheme,

(b) the employer is insolvent,

(c) the value of the assets of the scheme has been reduced, and there are reasonable grounds for believing that the reduction was attributable to an act or omission constituting a prescribed offence,

(d) in the case of a salary related trust scheme, immediately before the date of the application the value of the assets of the scheme is less than 90 per cent of the amount of the liabilities of the scheme, and

(e) it is reasonable in all the circumstances that the members of the scheme should be assisted by the Compensation Board paying to the trustees of the scheme, out of funds for the time being held by them, an amount determined in accordance with the compensation provisions.

(2) Subsection (1) does not apply in respect of a trust scheme falling within a prescribed class or description; and paragraph (c) applies only to reductions in value since the appointed day.

(3) In this Part the "compensation provisions" means the provisions of this section and sections 82 to 85; and below in the compensation provisions as they relate to a trust scheme—

(a) "the application date" means the date of the application for compensation under section 82,

(b) "the appointed day" means the day appointed under section 180 for the commencement of this section,

(c) "the insolvency date" means the date on which the employer became insolvent,

(d) "the settlement date" means the date determined by the Compensation Board, after consulting the trustees, to be the date after which

further recoveries of value are unlikely to be obtained without disproportionate cost or within a reasonable time,

(e) "the shortfall at the application date" means the amount of the
reduction falling within subsection (1)(c) or (if there was more than
one such reduction) the aggregate of the reductions, being the amount
or aggregate immediately before the application date,

(f) "recovery of value" means any increase in the value of the assets of the
scheme, being an increase attributable to any payment received
(otherwise than from the Compensation Board) by the trustees of the
scheme in respect of any act or omission—

(i) which there are reasonable grounds for believing constituted
a prescribed offence, and

(ii) to which any reduction in value falling within subsection (1)
(c) was attributable.

(4) It is for the Compensation Board to determine whether anything
received by the trustees of the scheme is to be treated as a payment received
for any such act or omission as is referred to in subsection (3)(f); and in this
section "payment" includes any money or money's worth.

(5) Where this section applies to an application for compensation under
section 82, the trustees must obtain any recoveries of value, to the extent that
they may do so without disproportionate cost and within a reasonable time.

(6) If subsection (5) is not complied with, section 3 applies to any trustee
who has failed to take all such steps as are reasonable to secure compliance.

(7) Section 56(3) and (4) applies for the purposes of the compensation
provisions as it applies for the purposes of sections 56 to 61.

(8) Section 123 of the Pension Schemes Act 1993 (meaning of insolvency)
applies for the purposes of the compensation provisions as it applies for
the purposes of Chapter II of Part VII of that Act (unpaid scheme
contributions).

DEFINITIONS
"Compensation Board": s.78(1).
"employer": s.124(1), and *cf* s.124(5); the Pension Schemes Act 1993, s.181(1).
"member": s.124(1).
"occupational pension scheme": s.176.
"prescribed": s.124(1).
"salary related trust scheme": s.125(1).
"trust scheme": s.124(1).

GENERAL NOTE

Subs. (1)
It is to be noted that para. (c) only applies to future losses since a day has not yet been
appointed under s.180 for the commencement of s.81. Paragraph (d) is not a requirement for a
money purchase scheme, but the Board has a general discretion under para. (e), so that the
practical result of applying the requirement of para. (d) only to a salary related trust scheme may
not be very different for the two types of scheme. In principle it is hard to see why there should be
a distinction between the support given to the members of a salary related trust scheme and that
given to those of a money purchase trust scheme. The explanation may lie in the difficulty of
framing an overall requirement in respect of money purchase schemes which could be applied in
every case. In any event, the recovery which can be made by a money purchase scheme will be
governed by the provisions of s.83(3)(a).

Subs. (3)
In respect of the definition of "recovery of value" it is to be noted that only a limited class of
recovery is to be taken into account, and not general recovery on the value of any assets of the
fund such as stock and shares. In connection with this, subss. (4) and (7) are to be noted. Section
81(7) applies s.56(3) and (4) to the circumstances where the section applies. Of these subsections, the former provides for the assets and liabilities of a scheme to be determined by a prescribed person and in a prescribed manner. The latter provides that any limit on the liabilities of
a scheme by reference to its assets is to be disregarded.

Subss. (5) and (6)

The first of these subsections repeats the duty in law on the trustees to effect recoveries. It is not abrogated by the possibility of or payment of compensation. The second brings s.3 into effect in case of default.

[Standing Committee D, June 13, 1995, col. 526].

Applications for payments

82.—(1) Compensation may be paid under section 83 only on an application to which section 81 applies made within the qualifying period by a prescribed person.

(2) An application under this section must be made in the manner, and give the information, required by the Compensation Board.

(3) For the purposes of this section the "qualifying period", subject to subsection (5), is the period expiring with the period of twelve months mentioned in subsection (4).

(4) The period of twelve months referred to in subsection (3) is that beginning with the later of the following times—

    (a)   the insolvency date,

    (b)   when the auditor or actuary of the scheme, or the trustees, knew or ought reasonably to have known that a reduction of value falling within section 81(1)(c) had occurred,

being, in each case, a time after the appointed day.

(5) The Compensation Board may extend, or further extend, the qualifying period.

DEFINITIONS

    "actuary": s.39, s.124(1).
    "appointed day": s.81(3).
    "auditor": s.39, s.124(1).
    "Compensation Board": s.78(1).
    "insolvency date": s.81(3).
    "prescribed": s.124(1).

GENERAL NOTE

Subject to the overriding power to extend time limits contained in subs. (5), strict time limits are laid down in subss. (3) and (4). The insolvency of the employer is one of the prerequisites for a claim contained in s.81(1), and provision is made for the possibility that this occurs after the losses are or ought to be known.

Subs. (4)

Time clearly starts to run when the reduction in value was known or reasonably ought to have been known to either the auditor or the actuary. If either of these ought reasonably to have known, but did not know, so that an application cannot be made because of a lapse of time, and loss results, liability for the loss will probably rest on one or both of them in an action in negligence.

Amount of compensation

83.—(1) Where in the opinion of the Compensation Board section 81 applies to an application for compensation under section 82 in respect of a trust scheme, and the Board have determined the settlement date, the Board may make a payment or payments to the trustees of the scheme in accordance with this section.

(2) The amount of any payment must be determined in accordance with regulations and must take account of any payment already made under section 84, and the Compensation Board must give written notice of their determination to the person who made the application under section 82 and (if different) to the trustees.

(3) The amount of the payment or (if there is more than one) the aggregate—

    (a)   must not exceed 90 per cent of the shortfall at the application date, together with interest at the prescribed rate for the prescribed period on the shortfall or (if the shortfall comprises more than one reduction in value) on each of the reductions, and also,

(b) in the case of a salary related scheme, must not exceed the amount which, on the settlement date, is required to be paid to the trustees of the scheme in order to secure that the value on that date of the assets of the scheme is equal to 90 per cent of the amount on that date of the liabilities of the scheme.

DEFINITIONS

"Compensation Board": s.78(1).
"prescribed": s.124(1).
"regulations": s.124(1).
"salary related trust scheme": s.125(1).
"settlement date": s.81(3).
"shortfall at the application date": s.81(3).

GENERAL NOTE

Subs. (1)
The Board has the power to pay once it has determined the settlement date, but there is no mandatory requirement to do so. This is consistent with its discretion contained in s.81(1)(e).

Subs. (2)
Payments on account may be made under s.84.

Subs. (3)
To comprise a reduction in value for the purpose of this subsection, the reduction in value must be of the kind mentioned in s.81(1)(c). If there is a reduction, interest is calculated in respect of each reduction separately.
Under this subsection 90 per cent of the aggregate reductions with interest at the application date can be paid, but this amount is pegged for a salary related scheme under subs. (3)(b) by the shortfall at the settlement date. For such a scheme, it is the lesser of the sums yielded by these calculations which can be paid.
[Standing Committee D, June 13, 1995, col. 536].

Payments made in anticipation

84.—(1) The Compensation Board may, on an application for compensation under section 82, make a payment or payments to the trustees of a trust scheme where in their opinion—

(a) section 81 applies, or may apply, to the application, and
(b) the trustees would not otherwise be able to meet liabilities falling within a prescribed class,

but the Board have not determined the settlement date.

(2) Amounts payable under this section must be determined in accordance with regulations.

(3) Where any payment is made under this section, the Compensation Board may, except in prescribed circumstances—

(a) if they subsequently form the opinion that section 81 does not apply to the application for compensation in respect of the scheme, or
(b) if they subsequently form the opinion that the amount of the payment was excessive,

recover so much of the payment as they consider appropriate.

DEFINITIONS

"Compensation Board": s.78(1).
"prescribed": s.124(1).
"regulations": s.124(1).
"settlement date": s.81(3).
"trust scheme": s.124(1).

GENERAL NOTE

This section makes general provision for interim payments of compensation, consisting of amounts determined in accordance with regulations. Subsection (3) provides for the recovery of

all or part of such payments in appropriate cases.
[Standing Committee D, June 13, 1995, col. 539].

Surplus funds

85.—(1) If the Secretary of State, after consultation with the Compensation Board, considers that the funds for the time being held by the Board exceed what is reasonably required for the purpose of exercising their functions under this Part, he may by order require them to distribute any of those funds appearing to him to be surplus to their requirements among occupational pension schemes.

(2) A distribution under subsection (1) must be made in the prescribed manner and subject to the prescribed conditions.

(3) The Compensation Board may invest any funds for the time being held by them which appear to them to be surplus to their requirements—

(a) in any investment for the time being falling within Part I, Part II or Part III of Schedule 1 to the Trustee Investments Act 1961, or

(b) in any prescribed investment.

DEFINITIONS
"Compensation Board": s.78(1).
"occupational pension scheme": s.176.
"prescribed": s.124(1).
"regulations": s.124(1).
[Standing Committee D, June 13, 1995, col. 540].

Modification of compensation provisions

86. Regulations may modify the compensation provisions in their application to trust schemes falling within a prescribed class or description.

DEFINITIONS
"compensation provisions": s.81.
"prescribed": s.124(1).
"regulations": s.124(1).
"trust scheme": s.124(1).

Money purchase schemes

Schedules of payments to money purchase schemes

87.—(1) This section applies to an occupational pension scheme which is a money purchase scheme, other than one falling within a prescribed class or description.

(2) The trustees or managers of every occupational pension scheme to which this section applies must secure that there is prepared, maintained and from time to time revised a schedule (referred to in this section and section 88 as a "payment schedule") showing—

(a) the rates of contributions payable towards the scheme by or on behalf of the employer and the active members of the scheme,

(b) such other amounts payable towards the scheme as may be prescribed, and

(c) the dates on or before which payments of such contributions or other amounts are to be made (referred to in those sections as "due dates").

(3) The payment schedule for a scheme must satisfy prescribed requirements.

(4) The matters shown in the payment schedule for a scheme—

(a) to the extent that the scheme makes provision for their determination, must be so determined, and

(b) otherwise,

(i) must be matters previously agreed between the employer and the trustees or managers of the scheme, or

(ii) if no such agreement has been made as to all matters shown in the schedule (other than those for whose determination the scheme makes provision), must be matters determined by the trustees or managers of the scheme.

(5) Where in the case of a scheme this section is not complied with—

(a) section 3 applies to any trustee who has failed to take all such steps as are reasonable to secure compliance, and

(b) section 10 applies to any trustee or manager who has failed to take all such steps.

DEFINITIONS
"active member": s.124(1).
"employer": s.124(1).
"money purchase scheme": s.124(5); the Pension Schemes Act 1993, s.181(1).
"occupational pension scheme": s.176.
"prescribed": s.124(1).
"trustees or managers": s.124(1).

GENERAL NOTE
This section prescribes that a schedule of contributions should be kept for a money purchase scheme, and is the corresponding provision for such schemes to s.58, from which money purchase schemes are exempted by s.46.

Subs. (1)
It is to be noted that the rates of contributions include those paid by active members. Regulations may exempt certain classes of scheme from this section.

Subss. (3) and (4)
The schedule of contributions must be prepared in accordance with requirements to be contained in regulations. From subs. (4) it would appear that if the trustees and the employer cannot agree the contents of the schedule, and the provisions of the scheme do not make provision for the determination of them, they are for the trustees (or managers) to decide. Thus the trustees will be able to decide the rate of contributions in default of agreement, and will be subject to removal, suspension and a penalty if they do not do so (see subs. (5)).

Subs. (5)
Section 3 contains the power of the Authority to remove or suspend a trustee, and s.10 contains the power of the Authority to impose a penalty.

Schedules of payments to money purchase schemes: supplementary

88.—(1) Except in prescribed circumstances, the trustees or managers of an occupational pension scheme to which section 87 applies must, where any amounts payable in accordance with the payment schedule have not been paid on or before the due date, give notice of that fact, within the prescribed period, to the Authority and to the members of the scheme.

(2) Any such amounts which for the time being remain unpaid after that date (whether payable by the employer or not) shall, if not a debt due from the employer to the trustees or managers apart from this subsection, be treated as such a debt.

(3) Where any amounts payable in accordance with the payment schedule by or on behalf of the employer have not been paid on or before the due date, section 10 applies to the employer.

(4) If, in the case of an occupational pension scheme to which section 87 applies, subsection (1) is not complied with—

(a) section 3 applies to any trustee who has failed to take all such steps as are reasonable to secure compliance, and

(b) section 10 applies to any trustee or manager who has failed to take all such steps.

DEFINITIONS
"Authority": s.1(1).
"due dates": s.87.

"employer": s.124(1).
"member": s.124(1).
"occupational pension scheme": s.176.
"payment schedule": s.87.
"prescribed": s.124(1).
"trustees or managers": s.124(1).

GENERAL NOTE
The provisions of this section correspond with the provisions contained in s.59(1), (2) and (4), for which see the General Note to s.59 above.

Subs. (3)
This renders an employer in default liable to a civil penalty.
[Standing Committee D, June 13, 1995, col. 544].

Application of further provisions to money purchase schemes

89.—(1) In the case of money purchase schemes falling within a prescribed class or description, regulations may—
  (a) provide for any of the provisions of sections 56 to 60 to apply, or apply with prescribed modifications (in spite of anything in those sections), and
  (b) provide for any of the provisions of sections 87 and 88 to apply with prescribed modifications or not to apply,
to such extent as may be prescribed.
  (2) Regulations may provide for any of the provisions of section 75 to apply, or apply with prescribed modifications, to money purchase schemes to such extent as may be prescribed (in spite of anything in that section), and the power conferred by this subsection includes power to apply section 75 in circumstances other than those in which the scheme is being wound up or a relevant insolvency event occurs (within the meaning of that section).

DEFINITIONS
"modifications": s.124(1).
"money purchase scheme": s.124(5); the Pension Schemes Act 1993, s.181(1).
"prescribed": s.124(1).
"regulations": s.124(1).

GENERAL NOTE
This is inserted to give regulatory powers to the Secretary of State to bring the provisions applicable to money purchase schemes into line with the minimum funding requirement of the sections indicated. Section 75 provides for a deficiency in a scheme on insolvency to be a debt on the employer.

Unpaid contributions in cases of insolvency

90. In section 124 of the Pension Schemes Act 1993 (duty of Secretary of State to pay unpaid contributions to schemes), after subsection (3) there is inserted—
  "(3A) Where the scheme in question is a money purchase scheme, the sum payable under this section by virtue of subsection (3) shall be the lesser of the amounts mentioned in paragraphs (a) and (c) of that subsection",
and, accordingly, at the beginning of subsection (3) there is inserted "Subject to subsection (3A),".

GENERAL NOTE
This alteration to s.124 of the Pension Schemes Act 1993 excludes for money purchase schemes a provision which in the usual case would result in the trustees of such schemes being unable to make a claim under the section. Section 124(3)(b) of the Pension Schemes Act 1993 provides that the sum payable under that section shall not exceed such sum as is necessary to enable the scheme to meet its liabilities in respect of employees of the employer. Since the

liabilities of a money purchase scheme are usually measured by the amount of money in the scheme, or in each member's "pot", unless excluded, the subsection would have the result set out above.

[Standing Committee D, June 13, 1995, col. 548].

Assignment, forfeiture, bankruptcy etc.

Inalienability of occupational pension

91.—(1) Subject to subsection (5), where a person is entitled, or has an accrued right, to a pension under an occupational pension scheme—

(a) the entitlement or right cannot be assigned, commuted or surrendered,

(b) the entitlement or right cannot be charged or a lien exercised in respect of it, and

(c) no set-off can be exercised in respect of it,

and an agreement to effect any of those things is unenforceable.

(2) Where by virtue of this section a person's entitlement, or accrued right, to a pension under an occupational pension scheme cannot, apart from subsection (5), be assigned, no order can be made by any court the effect of which would be that he would be restrained from receiving that pension.

(3) Where a bankruptcy order is made against a person, any entitlement or right of his which by virtue of this section cannot, apart from subsection (5), be assigned is excluded from his estate for the purposes of Parts VIII to XI of the Insolvency Act 1986 or the Bankruptcy (Scotland) Act 1985.

(4) Subsection (2) does not prevent the making of—

(a) an attachment of earnings order under the Attachment of Earnings Act 1971, or

(b) an income payments order under the Insolvency Act 1986.

(5) In the case of a person ("the person in question") who is entitled, or has an accrued right, to a pension under an occupational pension scheme, subsection (1) does not apply to any of the following, or any agreement to effect any of the following—

(a) an assignment in favour of the person in question's widow, widower or dependant,

(b) a surrender, at the option of the person in question, for the purpose of—

(i) providing benefits for that person's widow, widower or dependant, or

(ii) acquiring for the person in question entitlement to further benefits under the scheme,

(c) a commutation—

(i) of the person in question's benefit on or after retirement or in exceptional circumstances of serious ill health,

(ii) in prescribed circumstances, of any benefit for that person's widow, widower or dependant, or

(iii) in other prescribed circumstances,

(d) subject to subsection (6), a charge or lien on, or set-off against, the person in question's entitlement, or accrued right, to pension (except to the extent that it includes transfer credits other than prescribed transfer credits) for the purpose of enabling the employer to obtain the discharge by him of some monetary obligation due to the employer and arising out of a criminal, negligent or fraudulent act or omission by him,

(e) subject to subsection (6), except in prescribed circumstances a charge or lien on, or set-off against, the person in question's entitlement, or accrued right, to pension, for the purpose of discharging some monetary obligation due from the person in question to the scheme and—

(i) arising out of a criminal, negligent or fraudulent act or omission by him, or

(ii) in the case of a trust scheme of which the person in question is a trustee, arising out of a breach of trust by him.

(6) Where a charge, lien or set-off is exercisable by virtue of subsection (5)(d) or (e)—

(a) its amount must not exceed the amount of the monetary obligation in question, or (if less) the value (determined in the prescribed manner) of the person in question's entitlement or accrued right, and

(b) the person in question must be given a certificate showing the amount of the charge, lien or set-off and its effect on his benefits under the scheme,

and where there is a dispute as to its amount, the charge, lien or set-off must not be exercised unless the obligation in question has become enforceable under an order of a competent court or in consequence of an award of an arbitrator or, in Scotland, an arbiter to be appointed (failing agreement between the parties) by the sheriff.

(7) This section is subject to section 159 of the Pension Schemes Act 1993 (inalienability of guaranteed minimum pension and protected rights payments).

DEFINITIONS
"accrued right": s.124(1).
"assign": s.94 (Scotland).
"employer": s.124(1).
"normal pension age": s.124(1).
"occupational pension scheme": s.176.
"pension": s.94.
"prescribed": s.124(1).
"transfer credits": s.124(1).

GENERAL NOTE
Sections 91 to 94 have their statutory origins in Sched. 16 to the Social Security Act 1973, repeated in ss.77 to 80 of the Pension Schemes Act 1993. Those provisions only applied to short service benefits. However, it has long been the practice of the Board of Inland Revenue to require a provision to be inserted in an exempt approved scheme which provides for forfeiture of benefits on their alienation or attempted alienation, and this is usually combined with a power given to trustees to make the forfeited payments for the benefit of the relevant member or his dependants, provided that no payment should be made to or for the benefit of an assignee or purported assignee. This is now subject to two exceptions, both new. In the first place, subs. (4) provides that an attachment of earnings order under the Attachment of Earnings Act 1971, or an income payments order under the Insolvency Act 1986 may be made. Secondly, subs. (5)(e) introduces a new right available to the public at large (as opposed to the employer whose rights have long been in existence, and are preserved under subs. (5)(d)), in respect of monetary obligations arising out of criminal, negligent or fraudulent acts. Also new is the charge which may arise on a pension payable from a trust scheme, in respect of a breach of trust by a trustee of that scheme.

These sections now re-enact and enact the above requirements. It is to be noted that s.94 contains a definition of the word "pension" in relation to an occupational pension scheme which is applicable only to ss.91 to 93. Elsewhere in the Act it will bear its usual meaning.

Subs. (7)
Guaranteed minimum pensions are well protected under s.159 of the Pension Schemes Act 1993.
[Standing Committee D, June 13, 1995, col. 557].

Forfeiture, etc.

92.—(1) Subject to the provisions of this section and section 93, an entitlement, or accrued right, to a pension under an occupational pension scheme cannot be forfeited.

(2) Subsection (1) does not prevent forfeiture by reference to—

(a) a transaction or purported transaction which under section 91 is of no effect, or

(b) the bankruptcy of the person entitled to the pension or whose right to it has accrued, whether or not that event occurred before or after the pension became payable.

(3) Where such forfeiture as is mentioned in subsection (2) occurs, any pension which was, or would but for the forfeiture have become, payable may, if the trustees or managers of the scheme so determine, be paid to all or any of the following—

(a) the member of the scheme to or in respect of whom the pension was, or would have become, payable,

(b) the spouse, widow or widower of the member,

(c) any dependant of the member, and

(d) any other person falling within a prescribed class.

(4) Subsection (1) does not prevent forfeiture by reference to the person entitled to the pension, or whose right to it has accrued, having been convicted of one or more offences—

(a) which are committed before the pension becomes payable, and

(b) which are—

(i) offences of treason,

(ii) offences under the Official Secrets Acts 1911 to 1989 for which the person has been sentenced on the same occasion to a term of imprisonment of, or to two or more consecutive terms amounting in the aggregate to, at least 10 years, or

(iii) prescribed offences.

(5) Subsection (1) does not prevent forfeiture by reference to a failure by any person to make a claim for pension—

(a) where the forfeiture is in reliance on any enactment relating to the limitation of actions, or

(b) where the claim is not made within six years of the date on which the pension becomes due.

(6) Subsection (1) does not prevent forfeiture in prescribed circumstances.

(7) In this section and section 93, references to forfeiture include any manner of deprivation or suspension.

DEFINITIONS
"accrued right": s.124(1).
"assign": s.94 (Scotland).
"member": s.124(1).
"occupational pension scheme": s.176.
"pension": s.94.
"prescribed": s.124(1).
"trustees or managers": s.124(1).

GENERAL NOTE
See the General Note to s.82 above.

Forfeiture by reference to obligation to employer

93.—(1) Subject to subsection (2), section 92(1) does not prevent forfeiture of a person's entitlement, or accrued right, to a pension under an occupational pension scheme by reference to the person having incurred some monetary obligation due to the employer and arising out of a criminal, negligent or fraudulent act or omission by the person.

(2) A person's entitlement or accrued right to a pension may be forfeited by reason of subsection (1) to the extent only that it does not exceed the amount of the monetary obligation in question, or (if less) the value (determined in the prescribed manner) of the person's entitlement or accrued right to a pension under the scheme.

(3) Such forfeiture as is mentioned in subsection (1) must not take effect where there is a dispute as to the amount of the monetary obligation in question, unless the obligation has become enforceable under an order of a competent court or in consequence of an award of an arbitrator or, in Scotland, an

arbiter to be appointed (failing agreement between the parties) by the sheriff.

(4) Where a person's entitlement or accrued right to a pension is forfeited by reason of subsection (1), the person must be given a certificate showing the amount forfeited and the effect of the forfeiture on his benefits under the scheme.

(5) Where such forfeiture as is mentioned in subsection (1) occurs, an amount not exceeding the amount forfeited may, if the trustees or managers of the scheme so determine, be paid to the employer.

DEFINITIONS
   "accrued right": s.124(1).
   "employer": s.124(1).
   "member": s.124(1).
   "occupational pension scheme": s.176.
   "pension": s.94.
   "trustees or managers": s.124(1).

GENERAL NOTE
   This section provides in respect of forfeiture the same exceptions against the provisions of the Act which prohibit the alienation of a pension or of pension rights as s.91(5)(b) and (6) provides in respect of assignment, as to which see the General Note to s.91.

Sections 91 to 93: supplementary

94.—(1) Regulations may—
(a) modify sections 91 to 93 in their application to public service pension schemes or to other schemes falling within a prescribed class or description, or
(b) provide that those sections do not apply in relation to schemes falling within a prescribed class or description.

(2) In those sections, "pension" in relation to an occupational pension scheme, includes any benefit under the scheme and any part of a pension and any payment by way of pension.

(3) In the application of sections 91 and 92 to Scotland—
(a) references to a charge are to be read as references to a right in security or a diligence and "charged" is to be interpreted accordingly,
(b) references to assignment are to be read as references to assignation and "assign" is to be interpreted accordingly,
(c) the reference to a person's bankruptcy is to be read as a reference to the sequestration of his estate or the appointment on his estate of a judicial factor under section 41 of the Solicitors (Scotland) Act 1980,
(d) the reference to an income payments order under the Insolvency Act 1986 is to be read as a reference to an order under section 32(2) of the Bankruptcy (Scotland) Act 1985, and
(e) the reference to the making of a bankruptcy order is to be read as a reference to the award of sequestration or the making of the appointment of such a judicial factor.

DEFINITIONS
   "modification": s.124(5); the Pension Schemes Act 1993, s.181(1).
   "prescribed": s.124(1).
   "public service pension scheme": s.124(1).
   "regulations": s.124(1).

GENERAL NOTE
   See the General Note to s.91 above.

Pension rights of individuals adjudged bankrupt etc.

95.—(1) After section 342 of the Insolvency Act 1986 (adjustment of certain transactions entered into by individuals subsequently adjudged bankrupt), there is inserted—

"Recovery of excessive pension contributions

342A.—(1) Where an individual is adjudged bankrupt and—

(a) he has during the relevant period made contributions as a member of an occupational pension scheme, or

(b) contributions have during the relevant period been made to such a scheme on his behalf,

the trustee of the bankrupt's estate may apply to the court for an order under this section.

(2) If, on an application for an order under this section, the court is satisfied that the making of any of the contributions ("the excessive contributions") has unfairly prejudiced the individual's creditors, the court may make such order as it thinks fit for restoring the position to what it would have been if the excessive contributions had not been made.

(3) The court shall, in determining whether it is satisfied under subsection (2), consider in particular—

(a) whether any of the contributions were made by or on behalf of the individual for the purpose of putting assets beyond the reach of his creditors or any of them,

(b) whether the total amount of contributions made by or on behalf of the individual (including contributions made to any other occupational pension scheme) during the relevant period was excessive in view of the individual's circumstances at the time when they were made, and

(c) whether the level of benefits under the scheme, together with benefits under any other occupational pension scheme, to which the individual is entitled, or is likely to become entitled, is excessive in all the circumstances of the case.

Orders under section 342A

342B.—(1) Without prejudice to the generality of section 342A(2), an order under that section may include provision—

(a) requiring the trustees or managers of the scheme to pay an amount to the individual's trustee in bankruptcy,

(b) reducing the amount of any benefit to which the individual (or his spouse, widow, widower or dependant) is entitled, or to which he has an accrued right, under the scheme,

(c) reducing the amount of any benefit to which, by virtue of any assignment, commutation or surrender of the individual's entitlement (or that of his spouse, widow, widower or dependant) or accrued right under the scheme, another person is entitled or has an accrued right,

(d) otherwise adjusting the liabilities of the scheme in respect of any such person as is mentioned in paragraph (b) or (c).

(2) The maximum amount by which an order under section 342A may require the assets of an occupational pension scheme to be reduced is the lesser of—

(a) the amount of the excessive contributions, and

(b) the value (determined in the prescribed manner) of the assets of the scheme which represent contributions made by or on behalf of the individual.

(3) Subject to subsections (4) and (5), an order under section 342A must reduce the amount of the liabilities of the scheme by an amount equal to the amount of the reduction made in the value of the assets of the scheme.

(4) Subsection (3) does not apply where the individual's entitlement or accrued right to benefits under the scheme which he acquired by virtue of the excessive contributions (his "excessive entitlement") has been forfeited.

(5) Where part of the individual's excessive entitlement has been forfeited, the amount of the reduction in the liabilities of the scheme required by subsection (3) is the value of the remaining part of his excessive entitlement.

(6) An order under section 342A in respect of an occupational pension scheme shall be binding on the trustees or managers of the scheme.

Orders under section 342A: supplementary

342C.—(1) Nothing in—

(a) any provision of section 159 of the Pension Schemes Act 1993 or section 91 of the Pensions Act 1995 (which prevent assignment, or orders being made restraining a person from receiving anything which he is prevented from assigning, and make provision in relation to a person's pension on bankruptcy),

(b) any provision of any enactment (whether passed or made before or after the passing of the Pensions Act 1995) corresponding to any of the provisions mentioned in paragraph (a), or

(c) any provision of the scheme in question corresponding to any of those provisions,

applies to a court exercising its powers under section 342A.

(2) Where any sum is required by an order under section 342A to be paid to the trustee in bankruptcy, that sum shall be comprised in the bankrupt's estate.

(3) Where contributions have been made during the relevant period to any occupational pension scheme and the entitlement or accrued right to benefits acquired thereby has been transferred to a second or subsequent occupational pension scheme ("the transferee scheme"), sections 342A and 342B and this section shall apply as though the contributions had been made to the transferee scheme.

(4) For the purposes of this section and sections 342A and 342B—

(a) contributions are made during the relevant period if—

(i) they are made by or on behalf of the individual at any time during the period of 5 years ending with the day of presentation of the bankruptcy petition on which the individual is adjudged bankrupt, or

(ii) they are made on behalf of the individual at any time during the period between the presentation of the petition and the commencement of the bankruptcy,

and

(b) the accrued rights of an individual under an occupational pension scheme at any time are the rights which have accrued to or in respect of him at that time to future benefits under the scheme.

(5) In this section and sections 342A and 342B—

"occupational pension scheme" has the meaning given by section 1 of the Pension Schemes Act 1993, and

"trustees or managers", in relation to an occupational pension scheme, means—

(a) in the case of a scheme established under a trust, the trustees of the scheme, and

(b) in any other case, the managers of the scheme."

(2) After section 36 of the Bankruptcy (Scotland) Act 1985 there is inserted—

"Recovery of excessive pension contributions

36A.—(1) Where a debtor's estate has been sequestrated and—

(a) he has during the relevant period made contributions as a member of an occupational pension scheme; or

(b) contributions have during the relevant period been made to such a scheme on his behalf;

the permanent trustee may apply to the court for an order under this section.

(2) If, on an application for an order under this section, the court is satisfied that the making of any of the contributions ("the excessive contributions") has unfairly prejudiced the debtor's creditors, the court may make such order as it thinks fit for restoring the position to what it would have been if the excessive contributions had not been made.

(3) The court shall, in determining whether it is satisfied under subsection (2) above, consider in particular—

(a) whether any of the contributions were made by or on behalf of the debtor for the purpose of putting assets beyond the reach of his creditors or any of them;

(b) whether the total amount of contributions made by or on behalf of the debtor (including contributions made to any other occupational pension scheme) during the relevant period was excessive in view of the debtor's circumstances at the time when they were made; and

(c) whether the level of benefits under the scheme, together with benefits under any other occupational pension scheme, to which the debtor is entitled, or is likely to become entitled, is excessive in all the circumstances of the case.

Orders under section 36A

36B.—(1) Without prejudice to the generality of subsection (2) of section 36A of this Act, an order under that section may include provision—

(a) requiring the trustees or managers of the scheme to pay an amount to the permanent trustee;

(b) reducing the amount of any benefit to which the debtor (or his spouse, widow, widower or dependant) is entitled, or to which he has an accrued right, under the scheme;

(c) reducing the amount of any benefit to which, by virtue of any assignation, commutation or surrender of the debtor's entitlement (or that of his spouse, widow, widower or dependant) or accrued right under the scheme, another person is entitled or has an accrued right;

(d) otherwise adjusting the liabilities of the scheme in respect of any such person as is mentioned in paragraph (b) or (c) above.

(2) The maximum amount by which an order under section 36A of this Act may require the assets of an occupational pension scheme to be reduced is the lesser of—

(a) the amount of the excessive contributions; and

(b) the value (determined in the prescribed manner) of the assets of the scheme which represent contributions made by or on behalf of the debtor.

(3) Subject to subsections (4) and (5) below, an order under section 36A of this Act must reduce the amount of the liabilities of the scheme by an amount equal to the amount of the reduction made in the value of the assets of the scheme.

(4) Subsection (3) above does not apply where the debtor's entitlement or accrued right to benefits under the scheme which he acquired by virtue of the excessive contributions (his "excessive entitlement") has been forfeited.

(5) Where part of the debtor's excessive entitlement has been forfeited, the amount of the reduction in the liabilities of the scheme required by subsection (3) above is the value of the remaining part of his excessive entitlement.

(6) An order under section 36A of this Act in respect of an occupational pension scheme shall be binding on the trustees or managers of the scheme.

(7) The court may, on the application of any person having an interest, review, rescind or vary an order under section 36A of this Act.

Orders under section 36A: supplementary

36C.—(1) Nothing in—

(a) any provision of section 159 of the Pension Schemes Act 1993 or 91 of the Pensions Act 1995 (which prevent assignation, or orders being made restraining a person from receiving anything which he is prevented from assigning, and make provision in relation to a person's pension on sequestration);

(b) any provision of any enactment (whether passed or made before or after the passing of the Pensions Act 1995) corresponding to any of the provisions mentioned in paragraph (a) above; or

(c) any provision of the scheme in question corresponding to any of those provisions,

applies to a court exercising its powers under section 36A of this Act.

(2) Where any sum is required by an order under section 36A of this Act to be paid to the permanent trustee, that sum shall be comprised in the debtor's estate.

(3) Where contributions have been made during the relevant period to any occupational pension scheme and the entitlement or accrued right to benefits acquired thereby has been transferred to a second or subsequent occupational pension scheme ("the transferee scheme"), sections 36A and 36B of this Act and this section shall apply as though the contributions had been made to the transferee scheme.

(4) For the purposes of this section and sections 36A and 36B of this Act—

(a) contributions are made during the relevant period if they are made at any time during the period of 5 years ending with the date of sequestration; and

(b) the accrued rights of a debtor under an occupational pension scheme at any time are the rights which have accrued to or in respect of him at that time to future benefits under the scheme.

(5) In this section and sections 36A and 36B of this Act—

"occupational pension scheme" has the meaning given by section 1 of the Pension Schemes Act 1993; and

"trustees or managers", in relation to an occupational pension scheme, means—

(a) in the case of a scheme established under a trust, the trustees of the scheme; and

(b) in any other case, the managers of the scheme."

GENERAL NOTE

This is a new section. It inserts new provisions into the Insolvency Act 1986 and the Bankruptcy (Scotland) Act 1985, which are designed to provide for the repayment to a trustee in bankruptcy where an individual has made excessive contributions to an occupational pension scheme during the relevant period. The matters particularly to be taken into consideration by the court are those set out in the new s.342A(3). The court may make orders directly against the trustees or managers of a scheme, and is confined to reducing the assets of a scheme by whichever is the less of the amount of the excessive contributions and "the value of the assets of the scheme which represent the contributions made by or on behalf of the individual"—words which are designed to cater for the situation where the scheme is in deficit.

The contributions caught by this provision are not only those made by the member (presumably with voluntary contributions in mind—ordinary members' contributions are usually fixed by the rules of the scheme), but also contributions paid on behalf of the member. Contributions paid in respect of him are not caught.

[Standing Committee D, June 22, 1995, col. 850].

Questioning the decisions of the Authority

Review of decisions

96.—(1) Subject to the following provisions of this section and to section 97, any determination by the Authority of a question which it is within their functions to determine shall be final.

(2) The Authority must, on the application of any person ("the applicant") at any time within the prescribed period, review any determination of theirs—

(a) to make an order against the applicant under section 3,

(b) to require the applicant to pay a penalty under section 10 of this Act or section 168(4) of the Pension Schemes Act 1993, or

(c) to disqualify the applicant from being a trustee of any trust scheme under section 29(3) or (4).

(3) The Authority may on the application of a person appearing to them to be interested—

(a) at any time review any other such determination of theirs as is mentioned in subsection (1) (including a determination given by them on a previous review), if they are satisfied that there has been a relevant change of circumstances since the determination was made, or that the determination was made in ignorance of a material fact or based on a mistake as to a material fact or was erroneous in point of law,

(b) at any time within a period of six months from the date of the determination, or within such longer period as they may allow in any particular case, review such a determination on any ground.

(4) The Authority's powers on a review under subsection (2) or (3) include power—

(a) to vary or revoke any determination or order previously made,

(b) to substitute a different determination or order, and

(c) generally to deal with the matters arising on the review as if they had arisen on the original determination;

and also include power to make savings and transitional provisions.

(5) Subject to subsection (6), regulations may make provision with respect to the procedure to be adopted on any application for a review under subsection (2) or (3) or under any corresponding provision in force in Northern Ireland and generally with respect to such applications and reviews.

(6) Nothing in subsection (5) shall be taken to prevent such a review being entered upon by the Authority without an application being made.

DEFINITIONS

"Authority": s.1(1).
"prescribed": s.124(1).
"regulations": s.124(1).
"trust scheme": s.124(1).

GENERAL NOTE

This section gives the power to the Authority to review its decisions, and is similar to that given to appeal tribunals under the social security legislation. The review may be self-generated by the Authority (see subs. (6)), or may be upon appropriate application.

References and appeals from the Authority

97.—(1) Any question of law arising in connection with—

(a) any matter arising under this Part for determination, or

(b) any matter arising on an application to the Authority for a review of a determination, or on a review by them entered upon without an application,

may, if the Authority think fit, be referred for decision to the court.

(2) If the Authority determine in accordance with subsection (1) to refer any question of law to the court, they must give notice in writing of their intention to do so—

(a) in a case where the question arises on an application made to the Authority, to the applicant, and

(b) in any case to such persons as appear to them to be concerned with the question.

(3) Any person who is aggrieved—

(a) by a determination of the Authority given on a review under section 96, or

(b) by the refusal of the Authority to review a determination,

where the determination involves a question of law and that question is not referred by the Authority to the court under subsection (1), may on that question appeal from the determination to the court.

(4) The Authority is entitled to appear and be heard on any reference or appeal under this section.

(5) The rules of court must include provision for regulating references and appeals to the court under this section and for limiting the time within which such appeals may be brought.

(6) The decision of the court on a reference or appeal under this section is final, and this subsection overrides any other enactment.

(7) On any such reference or appeal the court may order the Authority to pay the costs or, in Scotland, the expenses of any other person, whether or not the decision is in that other person's favour and whether or not the Authority appear on the reference or appeal.

(8) In this section "the court" means the High Court or the Court of Session.

DEFINITIONS
"Authority": s.1(1).

GENERAL NOTE

Subs. (3)
An appeal lies on a point of law only to the High Court. This appeal finds a parallel in appeals from the decisions of the Pensions Ombudsman under s.151 of the Pension Schemes Act 1993.
[Standing Committee D, June 13, 1995, col. 566].

Gathering information: the Authority

Provision of information

98.—(1) In the case of any occupational pension scheme—

(a) a trustee, manager, professional adviser or employer, and

(b) any other person appearing to the Authority to be a person who holds, or is likely to hold, information relevant to the discharge of the Authority's functions,

must, if required to do so by them by notice in writing, produce any document relevant to the discharge of those functions.

(2) To comply with subsection (1) the document must be produced in such a manner, at such a place and within such a period as may be specified in the notice.

(3) In this section and sections 99 to 101, "document" includes information recorded in any form, and any reference to production of a document, in relation to information recorded otherwise than in legible form, is to producing a copy of the information in legible form.

DEFINITIONS
"Authority": s.1(1).
"employer": s.124(1).
"occupational pension scheme": s.152.
"professional adviser": s.47.
"trustees or managers": s.124(1).

GENERAL NOTE
The duties under this section are subject to the provisions of s.102, which principally gives protection against self-incrimination and preserves legal professional privilege.

Subs. (3)
This is clearly aimed at and includes information stored on computer.
[Standing Committee D, June 13, 1995, col. 570].

Inspection of premises

99.—(1) An inspector may, for the purposes of investigating whether, in the case of any occupational pension scheme, the regulatory provisions are being, or have been, complied with, at any reasonable time enter premises liable to inspection and, while there—
  (a) may make such examination and inquiry as may be necessary for such purposes,
  (b) may require any person on the premises to produce, or secure the production of, any document relevant to compliance with those provisions for his inspection, and
  (c) may, as to any matter relevant to compliance with those provisions, examine, or require to be examined, either alone or in the presence of another person, any person on the premises whom he has reasonable cause to believe to be able to give information relevant to that matter.
(2) In subsection (1), "the regulatory provisions" means provisions made by or under—
  (a) the provisions of this Part, other than the following provisions: sections 51 to 54, 62 to 65 and 110 to 112,
  (b) the following provisions of the Pension Schemes Act 1993: section 6 (registration), Chapter IV of Part IV (transfer values), section 113 (information) or section 175 (levy), or
  (c) any corresponding provisions in force in Northern Ireland.
(3) Premises are liable to inspection for the purposes of this section if the inspector has reasonable grounds to believe that—
  (a) members of the scheme are employed there,
  (b) documents relevant to the administration of the scheme are being kept there, or
  (c) the administration of the scheme, or work connected with the administration of the scheme, is being carried out there,
unless the premises are a private dwelling-house not used by, or by permission of, the occupier for the purposes of a trade or business.
(4) An inspector applying for admission to any premises for the purposes of this section must, if so required, produce his certificate of appointment.
(5) In this Part "inspector" means a person appointed by the Authority as an inspector.

DEFINITIONS
"Authority": s.1(1).
"document": s.98.

"employed": s.124(5); the Pension Schemes Act 1993, s.181.
"member": s.124(1).
"occupational pension scheme": s.176.

GENERAL NOTE
   The duties under this section are subject to the provisions of s.102, which gives protection against self-incrimination and preserves legal professional privilege. Sections 51 to 54 provide for the indexation of pensions; ss.62 to 65 provide for equal treatment and ss.110 to 112 make provision for the Compensation Board to gather information. The general right of entry of the Authority's inspectors does not extend to the investigation of these matters. Otherwise the section is self-explanatory.
   [Standing Committee D, June 13, 1995, col. 573].

Warrants

   100.—(1) A justice of the peace may issue a warrant under this section if satisfied on information on oath given by or on behalf of the Authority that there are reasonable grounds for believing—
   (a) that there are on any premises documents whose production has been required under section 98(1) or 99(1)(b), or any corresponding provisions in force in Northern Ireland, and which have not been produced in compliance with the requirement,
   (b) that there are on any premises documents whose production could be so required and that if their production were so required the documents would not be produced but would be removed from the premises, hidden, tampered with or destroyed, or
   (c) that—
      (i) an offence has been committed under this Act or the Pension Schemes Act 1993, or any enactment in force in Northern Ireland corresponding to either of them,
      (ii) a person will do any act which constitutes a misuse or misappropriation of the assets of an occupational pension scheme,
      (iii) a person is liable to pay a penalty under section 10 of this Act or section 168(4) of the Pension Schemes Act 1993, or any enactment in force in Northern Ireland corresponding to either of them, or
      (iv) a person is liable to be prohibited from being a trustee of a trust scheme under section 3,
   and that there are on any premises documents which relate to whether the offence has been committed, whether the act will be done, or whether the person is so liable, and whose production could be required under section 98(1) or 99(1)(b) or any corresponding provisions in force in Northern Ireland.
   (2) A warrant under this section shall authorise an inspector—
   (a) to enter the premises specified in the information, using such force as is reasonably necessary for the purpose,
   (b) to search the premises and take possession of any documents appearing to be such documents as are mentioned in subsection (1) or to take in relation to such documents any other steps which appear necessary for preserving them or preventing interference with them,
   (c) to take copies of any such documents, or
   (d) to require any person named in the warrant to provide an explanation of them or to state where they may be found.
   (3) A warrant under this section shall continue in force until the end of the period of one month beginning with the day on which it is issued.
   (4) Any documents of which possession is taken by virtue of a warrant under this section may be retained—
   (a) for a period of six months, or
   (b) if within that period proceedings to which the documents are relevant are commenced against any person for any offence under this Act or

the Pension Schemes Act 1993, or any enactment in force in Northern Ireland corresponding to either of them, until the conclusion of those proceedings.

(5) In the application of this section in Scotland—

(a) the reference to a justice of the peace is to be read as a reference to a justice within the meaning of the Criminal Procedure (Scotland) Act 1975, and

(b) the references to information are to be read as references to evidence.

DEFINITIONS
  "Authority": s.1(1).
  "document": s.98.
  "inspector": s.99.

GENERAL NOTE
  This section is subject to the exceptions in s.102.

Subs. (1)
  See ss.168 and 169 of the Pension Schemes Act 1993 for offences under that Act. A warrant may be issued to prevent the misuse or misappropriation of scheme funds under subs. (1)(c)(ii). Subsection (1)(c)(iv) is draconian, covering a multitude of possible situations.

Information and inspection: penalties

101.—(1) A person who, without reasonable excuse, neglects or refuses to produce a document when required to do so under section 98 is guilty of an offence.

(2) A person who without reasonable excuse—

(a) intentionally delays or obstructs an inspector exercising any power under section 99,

(b) neglects or refuses to produce, or secure the production of, any document when required to do so under that section, or

(c) neglects or refuses to answer a question or to provide information when so required,

is guilty of an offence.

(3) A person guilty of an offence under subsection (1) or (2) is liable on summary conviction to a fine not exceeding level 5 on the standard scale.

(4) An offence under subsection (1) or (2)(b) or (c) may be charged by reference to any day or longer period of time; and a person may be convicted of a second or subsequent offence by reference to any period of time following the preceding conviction of the offence.

(5) Any person who knowingly or recklessly provides the Authority with information which is false or misleading in a material particular is guilty of an offence if the information—

(a) is provided in purported compliance with a requirement under section 99, or

(b) is provided otherwise than as mentioned in paragraph (a) above but in circumstances in which the person providing the information intends, or could reasonably be expected to know, that it would be used by the Authority for the purpose of discharging their functions under this Act.

(6) Any person who intentionally and without reasonable excuse alters, suppresses, conceals or destroys any document which he is or is liable to be required under section 98 or 99 to produce to the Authority is guilty of an offence.

(7) Any person guilty of an offence under subsection (5) or (6) is liable—
(a) on summary conviction, to a fine not exceeding the statutory maximum,
(b) on conviction on indictment, to imprisonment or a fine, or both.

DEFINITIONS
    "Authority": s.1(1).
    "document": s.98.
    "inspector": s.99.

GENERAL NOTE
    This section is subject to the exceptions in s.102.

Subs. (3)
    The maximum fine at present is £5,000.

Subs. (7)
    This provides that a person guilty of an offence under subss. (5) or (6) may on summary conviction be liable to a fine not exceeding the statutory maximum, currently £5,000; and may on conviction on indictment be liable to imprisonment for not more than two years and an unlimited fine.
    [Standing Committee D, June 13, 1995, col. 575].

Savings for certain privileges etc.

102.—(1) Nothing in sections 98 to 101 requires a person to answer any question or give any information if to do so would incriminate that person or that person's spouse.

(2) Nothing in those sections requires any person to produce any document to the Authority, or to any person acting on their behalf, if he would be entitled to refuse to produce the document in any proceedings in any court on the grounds that it was the subject of legal professional privilege or, in Scotland, that it contained a confidential communication made by or to an advocate or solicitor in that capacity.

(3) Where a person claims a lien on a document, its production under section 98 or 99 shall be without prejudice to the lien.

DEFINITIONS
    "Authority": s.1(1).
    "document": s.98.

GENERAL NOTE
    This section negatives any obligation of self-incrimination, or incrimination of a person's spouse. It preserves the right of legal professional privilege on the assumed basis that proceedings are taking place , as to which see the notes to R.S.C., Ord. 24, r. 5 contained in the Supreme Court Practice ("the White Book"). It also preserves a lien on documents where such applies.
    [Standing Committee D, June 13, 1995, col. 575].

Publishing reports

103.—(1) The Authority may, if they consider it appropriate to do so in any particular case, publish in such form and manner as they think fit a report of any investigation under this Part and of the result of that investigation.

(2) For the purposes of the law of defamation, the publication of any matter by the Authority shall be absolutely privileged.

DEFINITIONS
    "Authority": s.1(1).

GENERAL NOTE
    Compare s.113 below, which gives power and protection to the Compensation Board parallel to this.

Disclosure of information: the Authority

Restricted information

104.—(1) Except as provided by sections 106 to 108, restricted information must not be disclosed by the Authority or by any person who receives the information directly or indirectly from them, except with the consent of the person to whom it relates and (if different) the person from whom the Authority obtained it.

(2) For the purposes of this section and sections 105 to 108, "restricted information" means any information obtained by the Authority in the exercise of their functions which relates to the business or other affairs of any person, except for information—

(a) which at the time of the disclosure is or has already been made available to the public from other sources, or

(b) which is in the form of a summary or collection of information so framed as not to enable information relating to any particular person to be ascertained from it.

(3) Any person who discloses information in contravention of this section is guilty of an offence and liable—

(a) on summary conviction, to a fine not exceeding the statutory maximum, and

(b) on conviction on indictment, to a fine or imprisonment, or both.

DEFINITIONS
"Authority": s.1(1).
"restricted information": ss.104 and 105.

GENERAL NOTE
For an extension of the meaning of "restricted information" see s.105(1).

Subs. (3)
This provides that a person guilty of the offence of disclosure may on summary conviction be liable to a fine not exceeding the statutory maximum, currently £5,000; and may on conviction on indictment be liable to imprisonment for not more than two years and an unlimited fine.

Information supplied to the Authority by corresponding overseas authorities

105.—(1) Subject to subsection (2), for the purposes of section 104, "restricted information" includes information which has been supplied to the Authority for the purposes of their functions by an authority which exercises functions corresponding to the functions of the Authority in a country or territory outside the United Kingdom.

(2) Sections 106 to 108 do not apply to such information as is mentioned in subsection (1), and such information must not be disclosed except—

(a) as provided in section 104,

(b) for the purpose of enabling or assisting the Authority to discharge their functions, or

(c) with a view to the institution of, or otherwise for the purposes of, criminal proceedings, whether under this Act or otherwise.

DEFINITIONS
"Authority": s.1(1).
"restricted information": ss.104 and 105.

GENERAL NOTE
It is to be noted that ss.106 to 108 do not apply to information referred to in subs. (1). General provisions for disclosure of information by the Authority are contained in those sections.
[Standing Committee D, June 13, 1995, col. 575].

Disclosure for facilitating discharge of functions by the Authority

106.—(1) Section 104 does not preclude the disclosure of restricted information in any case in which disclosure is for the purpose of enabling or assisting the Authority to discharge their functions.

(2) If, in order to enable or assist the Authority properly to discharge any of their functions, the Authority consider it necessary to seek advice from any qualified person on any matter of law, accountancy, valuation or other matter requiring the exercise of professional skill, section 104 does not preclude the disclosure by the Authority to that person of such information as appears to the Authority to be necessary to ensure that he is properly informed with respect to the matters on which his advice is sought.

DEFINITIONS
"Authority": s.1(1).
"restricted information": ss.104 and 105.

GENERAL NOTE
For restrictions on the width of this section see s.105(2) above and s.109(4) below.
[Standing Committee D, June 13, 1995, col. 577].

Disclosure for facilitating discharge of functions by other supervisory authorities

107.—(1) Section 104 does not preclude the disclosure by the Authority of restricted information to any person specified in the first column of the following Table if the Authority consider that the disclosure would enable or assist that person to discharge the functions specified in relation to him in the second column of that Table.

TABLE

Persons	*Functions*
The Secretary of State.	Functions under the Insurance Companies Act 1982, Part XIV of the Companies Act 1985, the Insolvency Act 1986, the Financial Services Act 1986, Part III of the Companies Act 1989 or Part III of the Pension Schemes Act 1993.
The Treasury.	Functions under the Financial Services Act 1986.
The Bank of England.	Functions under the Banking Act 1987 or any other functions.
The Charity Commissioners.	Functions under the Charities Act 1993.
The Lord Advocate.	Functions under Part I of the Law Reform (Miscellaneous Provisions) (Scotland) Act 1990.
The Pensions Ombudsman and the Registrar of Occupational and Personal Pension Schemes.	Functions under the Pension Schemes Act 1993 or the Pension Schemes (Northern Ireland) Act 1993.
The Compensation Board.	Functions under this Act or any corresponding enactment in force in Northern Ireland.
The Policyholders Protection Board.	Functions under the Policyholders Protection Act 1975.
The Deposit Protection Board.	Functions under the Banking Act 1987.
The Investor Protection Board.	Functions under the Building Societies Act 1986.
The Friendly Societies Commission.	Functions under the enactments relating to friendly societies.
The Building Societies Commission.	Functions under the Building Societies Act 1986.
The Commissioners of Inland Revenue or their officers.	Functions under the Taxes Act 1988 or the Taxation of Chargeable Gains Act 1992.
The Official Receiver, or, in Northern Ireland, the Official Receiver for Northern Ireland.	Functions under the enactments relating to insolvency.

Persons	*Functions*
An inspector appointed by the Secretary of State.	Functions under Part XIV of the Companies Act 1985 or section 94 or 177 of the Financial Services Act 1986.
A person authorised to exercise powers under section 43A or 44 of the Insurance Companies Act 1982, section 447 of the Companies Act 1985, section 106 of the Financial Services Act 1986, Article 440 of the Companies (Northern Ireland) Order 1986, or section 84 of the Companies Act 1989.	Functions under those sections or that Article.
A designated agency or transferee body or the competent authority (within the meaning of the Financial Services Act 1986).	Functions under the Financial Services Act 1986.
A recognised self-regulating organisation, recognised professional body, recognised investment exchange or recognised clearing house (within the meaning of the Financial Services Act 1986).	Functions in its capacity as an organisation, body, exchange or clearing house recognised under the Financial Services Act 1986.
A person administering a scheme for compensating investors under section 54 of the Financial Services Act 1986.	Functions under that section.
A recognised professional body (within the meaning of section 391 of the Insolvency Act 1986).	Functions in its capacity as such a body under that Act.
The Department of Economic Development in Northern Ireland.	Functions under Part XV of the Companies (Northern Ireland) Order 1986, the Insolvency (Northern Ireland) Order 1989 or Part II of the Companies (No. 2) (Northern Ireland) Order 1990.
The Department of Health and Social Services for Northern Ireland.	Functions under Part III of the Pension Schemes (Northern Ireland) Act 1993.
An inspector appointed by the Department of Economic Development in Northern Ireland.	Functions under Part XV of the Companies (Northern Ireland) Order 1986.
A recognised professional body within the meaning of Article 350 of the Insolvency (Northern Ireland) Order 1989.	Functions in its capacity as such a body under that Order.

(2) The Secretary of State may after consultation with the Authority—
 (a) by order amend the Table in subsection (1) by—
  (i) adding any person exercising regulatory functions and specifying functions in relation to that person,
  (ii) removing any person for the time being specified in the Table, or
  (iii) altering the functions for the time being specified in the Table in relation to any person, or
 (b) by order restrict the circumstances in which, or impose conditions subject to which, disclosure may be made to any person for the time being specified in the Table.

DEFINITIONS
 "Authority": s.1(1).
 "Compensation Board": s.78.
 "restricted information": ss.104 and 105.

GENERAL NOTE
 For restrictions on the width of this section see s.105(2) above and s.109(4) below.
 [Standing Committee D, June 13, 1995, col. 577].

Other permitted disclosures

108.—(1) Section 104 does not preclude the disclosure by the Authority of restricted information to—
  (a) the Secretary of State, or
  (b) the Department of Health and Social Services for Northern Ireland,
if the disclosure appears to the Authority to be desirable or expedient in the interests of members of occupational pension schemes or in the public interest.
  (2) Section 104 does not preclude the disclosure of restricted information—
  (a) with a view to the institution of, or otherwise for the purposes of, criminal proceedings, whether under this Act or otherwise,
  (b) in connection with any other proceedings arising out of—
      (i) this Act, or
      (ii) the Pension Schemes Act 1993,
    or any corresponding enactment in force in Northern Ireland or any proceedings for breach of trust in relation to an occupational pension scheme,
  (c) with a view to the institution of, or otherwise for the purposes of, proceedings under section 7 or 8 of the Company Directors Disqualification Act 1986 or Article 10 or 11 of the Companies (Northern Ireland) Order 1989,
  (d) in connection with any proceedings under the Insolvency Act 1986 or the Insolvency (Northern Ireland) Order 1989 which the Authority have instituted or in which they have a right to be heard,
  (e) with a view to the institution of, or otherwise for the purposes of, any disciplinary proceedings relating to the exercise of his professional duties by a solicitor, an actuary or an accountant,
  (f) with a view to the institution of, or otherwise for the purposes of, any disciplinary proceedings relating to the discharge by a public servant of his duties,
  (g) for the purpose of enabling or assisting an authority in a country outside the United Kingdom to exercise functions corresponding to those of the Authority under this Act, or
  (h) in pursuance of a Community obligation.
  (3) Section 104 does not preclude the disclosure by the Authority of information to the Director of Public Prosecutions, the Director of Public Prosecutions for Northern Ireland, the Lord Advocate, a procurator fiscal or a constable.
  (4) Section 104 does not preclude the disclosure by any person mentioned in subsection (1) or (3) of information obtained by the person by virtue of that subsection, if the disclosure is made with the consent of the Authority.
  (5) Section 104 does not preclude the disclosure by any person specified in the first column of the Table in section 107 of information obtained by the person by virtue of that subsection, if the disclosure is made—
  (a) with the consent of the Authority, and
  (b) for the purpose of enabling or assisting the person to discharge any functions specified in relation to him in the second column of the Table.
  (6) The Authority must, before deciding whether to give their consent to such a disclosure as is mentioned in subsection (4) or (5), take account of any representations made to them by the person seeking to make the disclosure as to the desirability of the disclosure or the necessity for it.
  (7) In subsection (2), "public servant" means an officer or servant of the Crown or of any prescribed authority.

Definitions
    "actuary": s.39.
    "Authority": s.1(1).
    "member": s.124(1).
    "occupational pension scheme": s.152.
    "restricted information": ss.104 and 105.
    "trust scheme": s.124(1).

General Note
    For a restriction on the width of this section see s.105(4) above and 109(4) below. [*Hansard*, H.L. Vol. 263, col. 451].

Disclosure of information by the Inland Revenue

109.—(1) This section applies to information held by any person in the exercise of tax functions about any matter relevant, for the purposes of those functions, to tax or duty in the case of an identifiable person (in this section referred to as "tax information").

(2) No obligation as to secrecy imposed by section 182 of the Finance Act 1989 or otherwise shall prevent the disclosure of tax information to the Authority for the purpose of enabling or assisting the Authority to discharge their functions.

(3) Where tax information is disclosed to the Authority by virtue of subsection (2), it shall, subject to subsection (4), be treated for the purposes of section 104 as restricted information.

(4) Sections 106 to 108 do not apply to tax information and such information must not be disclosed except—

    (a) to, or in accordance with authority duly given by, the Commissioners of Inland Revenue or the Commissioners of Customs and Excise, or

    (b) with a view to the institution of, or otherwise for the purposes of, criminal proceedings under this Act or the Pension Schemes Act 1993, or any enactment in force in Northern Ireland corresponding to either of them.

(5) In this section "tax functions" has the same meaning as in section 182 of the Finance Act 1989.

Definitions
    "Authority": s.1(1).
    "restricted information": ss.104 and 105.

General Note
    This section applies to tax information held in pursuance of a tax function, and concerns information held by or on behalf of the Commissioners of Inland Revenue, or the Commissioners of Customs and Excise.
    [Standing Committee D, June 13, 1995, col. 578].

Gathering information: the Compensation Board

Provision of information

110.—(1) In the case of any trust scheme—

    (a) a trustee, professional adviser or employer, and

    (b) any other person appearing to the Compensation Board to be a person who holds, or is likely to hold, information relevant to the discharge of the Board's functions,

must, if required to do so by the Board by notice in writing, produce any document relevant to the discharge of those functions.

(2) To comply with subsection (1) the document must be produced in such a manner, at such a place and within such a period as may be specified in the notice.

(3) In this section and section 111, "document" includes information recorded in any form, and any reference to production of a document, in

relation to information recorded otherwise than in legible form, is to producing a copy of the information in legible form.

DEFINITIONS
"Compensation Board": s.78(1).
"professional adviser": s.47.
"trust scheme": s.124(1).

GENERAL NOTE
This section provides the Board with the power to gather information necessary to fulfil its role. For the powers of the Authority (which are more extensive), see ss.98 to 103 above.

Subs. (1)
"Any other person" no doubt would include an insurance company.

Subs. (3)
This is clearly aimed at, and covers, information stored on a computer.

Information: penalties

111.—(1) A person who without reasonable excuse neglects or refuses to produce a document when required to do so under section 110 is guilty of an offence.

(2) A person guilty of an offence under subsection (1) is liable on summary conviction to a fine not exceeding level 5 on the standard scale.

(3) An offence under subsection (1) may be charged by reference to any day or longer period of time; and a person may be convicted of a second or subsequent offence by reference to any period of time following the preceding conviction of the offence.

(4) Any person who knowingly or recklessly provides the Compensation Board with information which is false or misleading in a material particular is guilty of an offence if the information is provided in circumstances in which the person providing the information intends, or could reasonably be expected to know, that it would be used by the Board for the purpose of discharging their functions under this Act or any corresponding enactment in force in Northern Ireland.

(5) Any person who intentionally and without reasonable excuse alters, suppresses, conceals or destroys any document which he is or is liable to be required under section 110 to produce to the Compensation Board is guilty of an offence.

(6) Any person guilty of an offence under subsection (4) or (5) is liable—
(a) on summary conviction, to a fine not exceeding the statutory maximum,
(b) on conviction on indictment, to imprisonment or a fine, or both.

DEFINITIONS
"Compensation Board": s.78(1).
"document": s.99.

GENERAL NOTE

Subs. (2)
The maximum fine at present is £5,000.

Subs. (4)
For "knowingly or recklessly" compare *City Equitable Fire Insurance Company, Re* [1925] Ch. 407.

Subs. (6)
This provides that a person guilty of an offence under subss. (4) or (5) may on summary conviction be liable to fine not exceeding the statutory maximum, currently £5,000; and may on

conviction on indictment be liable to imprisonment for not more than two years and an unlimited fine.

Savings for certain privileges

112. Nothing in section 110 or 111 requires a person—

(a) to answer any question or give any information if to do so would incriminate that person or that person's spouse, or

(b) to produce any document if he would be entitled to refuse to produce the document in any proceedings in any court on the grounds that it was the subject of legal professional privilege or, in Scotland, that it contained a confidential communication made by or to an advocate or solicitor in that capacity.

DEFINITIONS
"document": s.110.

GENERAL NOTE
This section preserves the right against self-incrimination, which extends to the spouse of the relevant person. It also preserves the right to legal professional privilege for documents on the assumed basis that proceedings are taking place, as to which see the notes to R.S.C., Ord. 24, r. 5 contained in the Supreme Court Practice ("the White Book").

Publishing reports

113.—(1) The Compensation Board may, if they consider it appropriate to do so in any particular case, publish in such form and manner as they think fit a report of any investigation under this Part and of the result of that investigation.

(2) For the purposes of the law of defamation, the publication of any matter by the Compensation Board shall be absolutely privileged.

DEFINITIONS
"Compensation Board": s.78(1).

GENERAL NOTE
This is a parallel provision to that contained in s.103 with regard to the Authority.

Disclosure of information

114.—(1) A person to whom this section applies may disclose to the Compensation Board any information received by him under or for the purposes of any enactment if the disclosure is made by him for the purpose of enabling or assisting the Board to discharge any of their functions.

(2) In the case of information which a person holds or has held in the exercise of functions—

(a) of the Commissioners of Inland Revenue or their officers, and

(b) relating to any tax within the general responsibility of the Commissioners,

subsection (1) does not authorise any disclosure unless made in accordance with an authorisation given by the Commissioners.

(3) Subject to subsection (4), the Compensation Board may disclose to a person to whom this section applies any information received by them under or for the purposes of any enactment, where the disclosure is made by the Board—

(a) for any purpose connected with the discharge of their functions, or

(b) for the purpose of enabling or assisting that person to discharge any of his functions.

(4) Where any information disclosed to the Compensation Board under this section is so disclosed subject to any express restriction on the disclosure of the information by the Board, the Board's power of disclosure under sub-

section (3) is, in relation to the information, exercisable by them subject to any such restriction.

(5) In the case of any such information as is mentioned in subsection (2), subsection (3) does not authorise any disclosure of that information by the Compensation Board unless made—

  (a) to, or in accordance with authority duly given by, the Commissioners of Inland Revenue or the Commissioners of Customs and Excise, or

  (b) with a view to the institution of, or otherwise for the purposes of, criminal proceedings under this Act or the Pension Schemes Act 1993, or any enactment in force in Northern Ireland corresponding to either of them.

(6) Nothing in this section shall be construed as affecting any power of disclosure exercisable apart from this section.

(7) This section applies to the following (and, accordingly, in this section "person" shall be construed as including any of them)—

  (a) any department of the Government (including the government of Northern Ireland),

  (b) the Director of Public Prosecutions,

  (c) the Director of Public Prosecutions for Northern Ireland,

  (d) the Lord Advocate,

  (e) any constable,

  (f) any designated agency or recognised self-regulating organisation (within the meaning of the Financial Services Act 1986),

  (g) a recognised professional body (within the meaning of section 391 of the Insolvency Act 1986),

  (h) the Pensions Ombudsman,

  (j) the Policyholders Protection Board,

  (k) the Authority,

  (l) the Registrar of Occupational and Personal Pension Schemes,

  (m) the Official Receiver, or, in Northern Ireland, the Official Receiver for Northern Ireland, and

  (n) such other persons as may be prescribed.

DEFINITIONS
  "Authority": s.1(1).
  "Compensation Board": s.78(1).
  "prescribed": s.124(1).

GENERAL NOTE
  This section provides for the exchange of information between the Board and the bodies and persons named in subs. (7). For the power of the Authority to disclose restricted information to the Board see s.107, but in this connection note the limitations contained in s.105(2) and 109(4).
  [Standing Committee D, June 13, 1995, col. 579].

General

Offences by bodies corporate and partnerships

115.—(1) Where an offence under this Part committed by a body corporate is proved to have been committed with the consent or connivance of, or to be attributable to any neglect on the part of, a director, manager, secretary or other similar officer of the body, or a person purporting to act in any such capacity, he as well as the body corporate is guilty of the offence and liable to be proceeded against and punished accordingly.

(2) Where the affairs of a body corporate are managed by its members, subsection (1) applies in relation to the acts and defaults of a member in connection with his functions of management as to a director of a body corporate.

(3) Where an offence under this Part committed by a Scottish partnership is proved to have been committed with the consent or connivance of, or to be

attributable to any neglect on the part of, a partner, he as well as the partner-ship is guilty of the offence and liable to be proceeded against and punished accordingly.

GENERAL NOTE

This section is designed to pierce the corporate and other veils in respect of criminal offences. For the piercing of the corporate veil in respect of corporate trustees, see *French Protestant Hospital, Re* [1951] Ch. 567.

Breach of regulations

116.—(1) Regulations made by virtue of any provision of this Part may provide for the contravention of any provision contained in any such regulations to be an offence under this Part and for the recovery on summary conviction for any such offence of a fine not exceeding level 5 on the standard scale.

(2) An offence under any provision of the regulations may be charged by reference to any day or longer period of time; and a person may be convicted of a second or subsequent offence under such a provision by reference to any period of time following the preceding conviction of the offence.

(3) Where by reason of the contravention of any provision contained in regulations made by virtue of this Part—

(a) a person is convicted of an offence under this Part, or

(b) a person pays a penalty under section 10,

then, in respect of that contravention, he shall not, in a case within paragraph (a), be liable to pay such a penalty or, in a case within paragraph (b), be convicted of such an offence.

DEFINITIONS

"regulations": s.124(1).

GENERAL NOTE

Subs. (1)

The maximum fine at present is £5,000.

Subs. (3)

This prevents double punishment.

Overriding requirements

117.—(1) Where any provision mentioned in subsection (2) conflicts with the provisions of an occupational pension scheme—

(a) the provision mentioned in subsection (2), to the extent that it con-flicts, overrides the provisions of the scheme, and

(b) the scheme has effect with such modifications as may be required in consequence of paragraph (a).

(2) The provisions referred to in subsection (1) are those of—

(a) this Part,

(b) any subordinate legislation made or having effect as if made under this Part, or

(c) any arrangements under section 16(1) or 17(2).

DEFINITIONS

"modifications": s.124(5); the Pension Schemes Act 1993, s.181(1).

"occupational pension scheme": s.176.

GENERAL NOTE

This important section prescribes that the provisions of Part I of the Act (*i.e.* ss.1 to 125 inclus-ive) and the regulations (for which there is extensive provision) made under it should be over-riding. This provision renders some of the powers of trustees under s.68(2) to modify schemes purely cosmetic.

Powers to modify this Part

118.—(1) Regulations may modify any provisions of this Part, in their application—
  (a) to a trust scheme which applies to earners in employments under different employers,
  (b) to a trust scheme of which there are no members who are in pensionable service under the scheme, or
  (c) to any case where a partnership is the employer, or one of the employers, in relation to a trust scheme.

(2) Regulations may provide for sections 22 to 26, and section 117 (so far as it applies to those sections), not to apply in relation to a trust scheme falling within a prescribed class or description.

DEFINITIONS
  "earner": s.124(5); the Pension Schemes Act 1993, s.181(1).
  "employer": s.124(1).
  "employment": s.124(5); the Pension Schemes Act 1993, s.181(1).
  "member": s.124(1).
  "modifications": s.124(5); the Pension Schemes Act 1993, s.181(1).
  "pensionable service": s.124(1).
  "regulations": s.124(1).
  "trust scheme": s.124(1).

GENERAL NOTE
  By far the most useful powers of modification contained in this section are those in relation to centralised schemes (in subs. (1)(a)) and those relating to schemes with no active members (in subs. (1)(b)).

Calculations etc. under regulations: sub-delegation

119. Regulations made by virtue of section 56(3), 73(3) or 75 may provide for the values of the assets and the amounts of the liabilities there mentioned to be calculated and verified in accordance with guidance—
  (a) prepared and from time to time revised by a prescribed body, and
  (b) approved by the Secretary of State.

DEFINITIONS
  "prescribed": s.124(1).
  "regulations": s.124(1).

GENERAL NOTE
  This section lays the foundation for actuarial guidance notes issued by the Institute of Actuaries and the Faculty of Actuaries in Scotland to have statutory effect.

Consultations about regulations

120.—(1) Before the Secretary of State makes any regulations by virtue of this Part, he must consult such persons as he considers appropriate.

(2) Subsection (1) does not apply—
  (a) to regulations made for the purpose only of consolidating other regulations revoked by them,
  (b) to regulations in the case of which the Secretary of State considers consultation inexpedient because of urgency,
  (c) to regulations made before the end of the period of six months beginning with the coming into force of the provision of this Part by virtue of which the regulations are made, or
  (d) to regulations which—
        (i) state that they are consequential upon a specified enactment, and
        (ii) are made before the end of the period of six months beginning with the coming into force of that enactment.

DEFINITIONS
"regulations": s.124(1).

GENERAL NOTE
This makes statutory provision for what has become a happy feature of pension scheme law, namely wide consultation by the Department of Social Security and the Pension Schemes Office particularly in respect of subordinate legislation. Legislation has greatly benefited thereby.

Crown application

121.—(1) This Part applies to an occupational pension scheme managed by or on behalf of the Crown as it applies to other occupational pension schemes; and, accordingly, references in this Part to a person in his capacity as a trustee or manager of an occupational pension scheme include the Crown, or a person acting on behalf of the Crown, in that capacity.

(2) References in this Part to a person in his capacity as employer in relation to an occupational pension scheme include the Crown, or a person acting on behalf of the Crown, in that capacity.

(3) This section does not apply to any provision made by or under this Part under which a person may be prosecuted for an offence; but such a provision applies to persons in the public service of the Crown as it applies to other persons.

(4) This section does not apply to sections 42 to 46.

(5) Nothing in this Part applies to Her Majesty in Her private capacity (within the meaning of the Crown Proceedings Act 1947).

DEFINITIONS
"employer": s.124(1).
"occupational pension scheme": s.176.
"trustees or managers": s.124(1).

GENERAL NOTE
This applies Part I of the Act to the Crown, subject to subs. (3).

Subs. (4)
Sections 42 to 46 concern employee trustees.

Consequential amendments

122. Schedule 3 (amendments consequential on this Part) shall have effect.

"Connected" and "associated" persons

123.—(1) Sections 249 and 435 of the Insolvency Act 1986 (connected and associated persons) shall apply for the purposes of the provisions of this Act listed in subsection (3) as they apply for the purposes of that Act.

(2) Section 74 of the Bankruptcy (Scotland) Act 1985 (associated persons) shall apply for the purposes of the provisions so listed as it applies for the purposes of that Act.

(3) The provisions referred to in subsections (1) and (2) are—
(a) section 23(3)(b),
(b) sections 27 and 28,
(c) section 40,
but in the case of section 40 the provisions mentioned in subsections (1) and (2) shall apply for those purposes with any prescribed modifications.

DEFINITIONS
"modifications": s.124(5); the Pension Schemes Act 1993, s.181(1).
"prescribed": s.124(1).

GENERAL NOTE
Section 23(3)(b) concerns independent trustees; ss.27 and 28 concern the appointment of auditors and actuaries; and s.40 concerns employer-related investments.

Interpretation of Part I

124.—(1) In this Part—

"active member", in relation to an occupational pension scheme, means a person who is in pensionable service under the scheme,

"the actuary" and "the auditor", in relation to an occupational pension scheme, have the meanings given by section 47,

"the Authority" has the meaning given by section 1(1),

"the Compensation Board" has the meaning given by section 78(1),

"the compensation provisions" has the meaning given by section 81(3),

"contravention" includes failure to comply,

"deferred member", in relation to an occupational pension scheme, means a person (other than an active or pensioner member) who has accrued rights under the scheme,

"employer", in relation to an occupational pension scheme, means the employer of persons in the description or category of employment to which the scheme in question relates (but see section 125(3)),

"equal treatment rule" has the meaning given by section 62,

"firm" means a body corporate or a partnership,

"fund manager", in relation to an occupational pension scheme, means a person who manages the investments held for the purposes of the scheme,

"independent trustee" has the meaning given by section 23(3),

"managers", in relation to an occupational pension scheme other than a trust scheme, means the persons responsible for the management of the scheme,

"member", in relation to an occupational pension scheme, means any active, deferred or pensioner member (but see section 125(4)),

"member-nominated director" has the meaning given by section 18(2),

"member-nominated trustee" has the meaning given by section 16(2),

"the minimum funding requirement" has the meaning given by section 56,

"normal pension age" has the meaning given by section 180 of the Pension Schemes Act 1993,

"payment schedule" has the meaning given by section 87(2),

"pensionable service", in relation to a member of an occupational pension scheme, means service in any description or category of employment to which the scheme relates which qualifies the member (on the assumption that it continues for the appropriate period) for pension or other benefits under the scheme,

"pensioner member", in relation to an occupational pension scheme, means a person who in respect of his pensionable service under the scheme or by reason of transfer credits, is entitled to the present payment of pension or other benefits,

"prescribed" means prescribed by regulations,

"professional adviser", in relation to a scheme, has the meaning given by section 47,

"public service pension scheme" has the meaning given by section 1 of the Pension Schemes Act 1993,

"regulations" means regulations made by the Secretary of State,

"resources", in relation to an occupational pension scheme, means the funds out of which the benefits provided by the scheme are payable from time to time, including the proceeds of any policy of insurance taken out, or annuity contract entered into, for the purposes of the scheme,

"Scottish partnership" means a partnership constituted under the law of Scotland, "the Taxes Act 1988" means the Income and Corporation Taxes Act 1988,

"transfer credits" means rights allowed to a member under the rules of an occupational pension scheme by reference to a transfer to that scheme of his accrued rights from another scheme (including any transfer credits allowed by that scheme),

"trustees or managers", in relation to an occupational pension scheme, means—

(a) in the case of a trust scheme, the trustees of the scheme, and

(b) in any other case, the managers of the scheme,

"trust scheme" means an occupational pension scheme established under a trust.

(2) For the purposes of this Part—

(a) the accrued rights of a member of an occupational pension scheme at any time are the rights which have accrued to or in respect of him at that time to future benefits under the scheme, and

(b) at any time when the pensionable service of a member of an occupational pension scheme is continuing, his accrued rights are to be determined as if he had opted, immediately before that time, to terminate that service;

and references to accrued pension or accrued benefits are to be interpreted accordingly.

(3) In determining what is "pensionable service" for the purposes of this Part—

(a) service notionally attributable for any purpose of the scheme is to be disregarded, and

(b) no account is to be taken of any rules of the scheme by which a period of service can be treated for any purpose as being longer or shorter than it actually is.

(4) In the application of this Part to Scotland, in relation to conviction on indictment, references to imprisonment are to be read as references to imprisonment for a term not exceeding two years.

(5) Subject to the provisions of this Act, expressions used in this Act and in the Pension Schemes Act 1993 have the same meaning in this Act as in that.

GENERAL NOTE

For the definition of "salary related trust scheme" and extensions or restrictions to the meaning of "employer" and "member" see s.125 below.

[Standing Committee D, June 13, 1995, col. 582].

Section 124: supplementary

125.—(1) For the purposes of this Part, an occupational pension scheme is salary related if—

(a) the scheme is not a money purchase scheme, and

(b) the scheme does not fall within a prescribed class or description,

and "salary related trust scheme" is to be read accordingly.

(2) Regulations may apply this Part with prescribed modifications to occupational pension schemes—

(a) which are not money purchase schemes, but

(b) where some of the benefits that may be provided are money purchase benefits.

(3) Regulations may, in relation to occupational pension schemes, extend for the purposes of this Part the meaning of "employer" to include persons who have been the employer in relation to the scheme.

(4) For any of the purposes of this Part, regulations may in relation to occupational pension schemes—

(a) extend or restrict the meaning of "member",

(b) determine who is to be treated as a prospective member, and

(c) determine the times at which a person is to be treated as becoming, or as ceasing to be, a member or prospective member.

DEFINITIONS
"employer": s.124(1).
"member": s.124(1).
"modifications": s.124(5); the Pension Schemes Act 1993, s.181(1).
"money purchase scheme": s.124(5); the Pension Schemes Act 1993, s.181(1).
"occupational pension scheme": s.152.
"prescribed": s.124(1).
"regulations": s.124(1).

PART II

STATE PENSIONS

Equalisation of pensionable age and of entitlement to certain benefits

126. Schedule 4 to this Act, of which—
  (a) Part I has effect to equalise pensionable age for men and women progressively over a period of ten years beginning with 6th April 2010,
  (b) Part II makes provision for bringing equality for men and women to certain pension and other benefits, and
  (c) Part III makes consequential amendments of enactments,
shall have effect.

DEFINITIONS
"pensionable age": s.124(5); the Pension Schemes Act 1993, s.181(1).

GENERAL NOTE
Part I of Sched. 4 makes provision for the pensionable age of women to be increased to age 65. A woman born before April 6, 1950 will reach pensionable age when she attains age 60; and a woman born after April 5, 1955 will reach that age only when she reaches age 65. The Table in Part I of the Schedule provides a sliding scale for those born between the above dates.

Part II of the Schedule makes a number of changes to the Social Security Contributions and Benefits Act 1992 ("the 1992 Act"). Paragraph 2 of Part II of the Schedule substitutes unisex increase provisions for pension and invalidity benefit where one spouse is living with or contributing to the maintenance of the other, replacing the provisions previously contained in ss.83 and 84 of the 1992 Act, which were applicable to those entitled to Category A and Category C retirement pensions. Paragraph 3 of Part II of the Schedule substitutes unisex rights as set out in the new ss.48A, 48B and 48C inserted into the 1992 Act by this paragraph in place of the Category B retirement and death benefits for women in light of their husbands' contributions. Men do not get the rights under the new section 48A to retirement pension by reason of their wives' contributions where the wife was born before April 6, 1950. They get no right to death benefit if they attain pensionable age before April 6, 2010. Where a man attains pensionable age after April 5, 2010, he is not entitled to rights under s.51 of the 1992 Act. The remainder of Part II to the Schedule contains more minor amendments.

Part II of this Act (*i.e.* ss.126 to 134 inclusive) comes into force on the date on which the Act is passed, subject to the provisions contained in Sched. 4 to the Act.
[Standing Committee D, June 13, 1995, col. 598].

Enhancement of additional pension, etc. where family credit or disability working allowance paid

127.—(1) After section 45 of the Social Security Contributions and Benefits Act 1992 (additional pension in a Category A retirement pension) there is inserted—

  "Effect of family credit and disability working allowance on earnings factor
    45A.—(1) For the purpose of calculating additional pension under sections 44 and 45 above where, in the case of any relevant year, family credit is paid in respect of any employed earner, or disability working

allowance is paid to any employed earner, section 44(6)(a)(i) above shall have effect as if—

(a) where that person had earnings of not less than the qualifying earnings factor for that year, being earnings upon which primary Class 1 contributions were paid or treated as paid ('qualifying earnings') in respect of that year, the amount of those qualifying earnings were increased by the aggregate amount (call it 'AG') of family credit or, as the case may be, disability working allowance paid in respect of that year, and

(b) in any other case, that person had qualifying earnings in respect of that year and the amount of those qualifying earnings were equal to AG plus the qualifying earnings factor for that year.

(2) The reference in subsection (1) above to the person in respect of whom family credit is paid—

(a) where it is paid to one of a married or unmarried couple, is a reference to the prescribed member of the couple, and

(b) in any other case, is a reference to the person to whom it is paid.

(3) A person's qualifying earnings in respect of any year cannot be treated by virtue of subsection (1) above as exceeding the upper earnings limit for that year multiplied by fifty-three.

(4) Subsection (1) above does not apply to any woman who has made, or is treated as having made, an election under regulations under section 19(4) above, which has not been revoked, that her liability in respect of primary Class 1 contributions shall be at a reduced rate.

(5) In this section—

'married couple' and 'unmarried couple' (defined in section 137 below) have the same meaning as in Part VII, and

'relevant year' has the same meaning as in section 44 above."

(2) Accordingly, in the following provisions of the Social Security Contributions and Benefits Act 1992, for "sections 44 and 45" there is substituted "sections 44 to 45A": sections 39(1) to (3), 50(3) to (5) and 51(2) and (3).

(3) Subject to subsections (4) and (5) below, this section applies to a person ("the pensioner") who attains pensionable age after 5th April 1999 and, in relation to such persons, has effect for 1995–96 and subsequent tax years.

(4) Where the pensioner is a woman, this section has effect in the case of additional pension falling to be calculated under sections 44 and 45 of the Social Security Contributions and Benefits Act 1992 by virtue of section 39 of that Act (widowed mother's allowance and widow's pension), including Category B retirement pension payable under section 48B(4), if her husband—

(a) dies after 5th April 1999, and

(b) has not attained pensionable age on or before that date.

(5) This section has effect where additional pension falls to be calculated under sections 44 and 45 of the Social Security Contributions and Benefits Act 1992 as applied by sections 48A or 48B(2) of that Act (other Category B retirement pension) if—

(a) the pensioner attains pensionable age after 5th April 1999, and

(b) the pensioner's spouse has not attained pensionable age on or before that date.

DEFINITIONS

"pensionable age": s.124(5); the Pension Schemes Act 1993, s.181(1).

GENERAL NOTE

This section has effect in relation to the calculation of additional pension under ss.44 and 45 of the Social Security Contributions and Benefits Act 1992. It brings into account family credit and disability working allowance. Subsection (3) provides that this will apply to persons who attain pensionable age after April 5, 1999, and in relation to such persons has effect for the 1995–1996 tax year and subsequent tax years. Subsections (4) and (5) make supplementary provisions in the first case where the pensioner is a woman, and in the second where the pensioner attains pen-

sionable age after April 5, 1999 and his or her spouse has not attained pensionable age on or before that date.
[Standing Committee D, June 15, 1995, col. 621].

Additional pension: calculation of surpluses

128.—(1) In section 44 of the Social Security Contributions and Benefits Act 1992 (Category A retirement pension), for subsection (5) (surplus on which additional pension is calculated) there is substituted—

"(5A) For the purposes of this section and section 45 below—

(a) there is a surplus in the pensioner's earnings factor for a relevant year if that factor exceeds the qualifying earnings factor for that year, and

(b) the amount of the surplus is the amount of that excess, as increased by the last order under section 148 of the Administration Act to come into force before the end of the final relevant year".

(2) In subsection (6) of that section (calculation of earnings factors), for paragraphs (a)(ii) and (b) there is substituted—

"(ii) his earnings factors derived from Class 2 and Class 3 contributions actually paid in respect of that year, or, if less, the qualifying earnings factor for that year; and

(b) where the relevant year is an earlier tax year, to the aggregate of—

(i) his earnings factors derived from Class 1 contributions actually paid by him in respect of that year, and

(ii) his earnings factors derived from Class 2 and Class 3 contributions actually paid by him in respect of that year, or, if less, the qualifying earnings factor for that year."

(3) Section 148 of the Social Security Administration Act 1992 (revaluation of earnings factors) shall have effect in relation to surpluses in a person's earnings factors under section 44(5A) of the Social Security Contributions and Benefits Act 1992 as it has effect in relation to earnings factors.

(4) Subject to subsections (5) and (6) below, this section has effect in relation to a person ("the pensioner") who attains pensionable age after 5th April 2000.

(5) Where the pensioner is a woman, this section has effect in the case of additional pension falling to be calculated under sections 44 and 45 of the Social Security Contributions and Benefits Act 1992 by virtue of section 39 of that Act (widowed mother's allowance and widow's pension), including Category B retirement pension payable under section 48B(4), if her husband—

(a) dies after 5th April 2000, and

(b) has not attained pensionable age on or before that date.

(6) This section has effect where additional pension falls to be calculated under sections 44 and 45 of the Social Security Contributions and Benefits Act 1992 as applied by section 48A or 48B(2) of that Act (other Category B retirement pension) if—

(a) the pensioner attains pensionable age after 5th April 2000, and

(b) the pensioner's spouse has not attained pensionable age on or before that date.

DEFINITIONS
"pensionable age": s.124(5); the Pension Schemes Act 1993, s.181(1).

GENERAL NOTE
    This section amends s.44 of the Social Security Contributions and Benefits Act 1992. It changes the way in which surpluses are calculated for the purpose of the calculation of additional pension under ss.44(3)(b) and 45(2) of that Act. Subject to s.128(5) and (6), these changes have effect only in relation to a pensioner who attains pensionable age after April 5, 2000. In the case of a woman, where additional pension has to be calculated by virtue of s.39 of the 1992 Act, these changes have effect only where the husband dies after April 5, 2000 and has not attained pen-

sionable age by that date (subs. (5)). Subsection (6) makes provision for the case where a pensioner attains pensionable age after April 5, 2000, but his or her spouse has not attained that age before April 6, 2000. On this, compare s.127(4) and (5) above.

[Standing Committee D, June 15, 1995, cols. 645 and 657].

Contribution conditions

129. In Schedule 3 to the Social Security Contributions and Benefits Act 1992 (contribution conditions), in paragraph 5(3)(a) (conditions for widowed mother's allowance, widow's pension and Category A and Category B retirement pension), after "class" there is inserted "or been credited (in the case of 1987–88 or any subsequent year) with earnings".

Up-rating of pensions increased under section 52 of the Social Security Contributions and Benefits Act

130.—(1) For section 156 of the Social Security Administration Act 1992 there is substituted—

"**Up-rating under section 150 above of pensions increased under section 52(3) of the Contributions and Benefits Act**

156.—(1) This section applies in any case where a person is entitled to a Category A retirement pension with an increase, under section 52(3) of the Contributions and Benefits Act, in the additional pension on account of the contributions of a spouse who has died.

(2) Where in the case of any up-rating order under section 150 above—

(a) the spouse's final relevant year is the tax year preceding the tax year in which the up-rating order comes into force, but

(b) the person's final relevant year was an earlier tax year,

then the up-rating order shall not have effect in relation to that part of the additional pension which is attributable to the spouse's contributions.

(3) Where in the case of any up-rating order under section 150 above—

(a) the person's final relevant year is the tax year preceding the tax year in which the up-rating order comes into force, but

(b) the spouse's final relevant year was an earlier tax year,

then the up-rating order shall not have effect in relation to that part of the additional pension which is attributable to the person's contributions."

(2) In section 151(1) of that Act (effect of up-rating orders on additional pensions), after "and shall apply" there is inserted "subject to section 156 and".

GENERAL NOTE

This amends s.156 of the Social Security Administration Act 1992 so that the withdrawal of uprating is altered and now bites on the two special cases mentioned in the new section where the person is entitled to an additional pension in respect of the additional contributions of a spouse who has died.

[Standing Committee D, June 22, 1995, col. 825].

Graduated retirement benefit

131.—(1) In section 62(1) of the Social Security Contributions and Benefits Act 1992 (graduated retirement benefit), after paragraph (a) there is inserted—

"(aa) for amending section 36(7) of that Act (persons to be treated as receiving nominal retirement pension) so that where a person has claimed a Category A or Category B retirement pension but—

(i) because of an election under section 54(1) above, or

(ii) because he has withdrawn his claim for the pension,

he is not entitled to such a pension, he is not to be treated for the purposes of the preceding provisions of that section as receiving such a pension at a nominal weekly rate;".

(2) In section 150(11) of the Social Security Administration Act 1992 (application of up-rating provisions to graduated retirement benefit) for the words following "provisions of this section" there is substituted—

"(a) to the amount of graduated retirement benefit payable for each unit of graduated contributions,

(b) to increases of such benefit under any provisions made by virtue of section 24(1)(b) of the Social Security Pensions Act 1975 or section 62(1)(a) of the Contributions and Benefits Act, and

(c) to any addition under section 37(1) of the National Insurance Act 1965 (addition to weekly rate of retirement pension for widows and widowers) to the amount of such benefit."

(3) In section 155(7) of that Act (effect of alteration of rates of graduated retirement benefit) for the words following "provisions of this section" there is substituted—

"(a) to the amount of graduated retirement benefit payable for each unit of graduated contributions,

(b) to increases of such benefit under any provisions made by virtue of section 24(1)(b) of the Social Security Pensions Act 1975 or section 62(1)(a) of the Contributions and Benefits Act, and

(c) to any addition under section 37(1) of the National Insurance Act 1965 (addition to weekly rate of retirement pension for widows and widowers) to the amount of such benefit".

GENERAL NOTE

This section provides additional powers to regulate graduated retirement benefit payable under ss.36 and 37 of the National Insurance Act 1965, an Act which continued the system first put into force under the National Insurance Act 1959. This was the system in force which preceded the graduated benefits under the Social Security Pensions Act 1975. There was an interregnum between the ending of the accumulation of benefits under the 1965 Act, and the coming into force (on April 5, 1978) of the 1975 Act.

[Standing Committee D, June 22, 1995, col. 837].

Extension of Christmas bonus for pensioners

132.—(1) Section 150 of the Social Security Contributions and Benefits Act 1992 (Christmas bonus: interpretation) is amended as follows.

(2) In subsection (1), after paragraph (k) there is inserted—

"(l) a mobility supplement".

(3) In subsection (2)—

(a) after the definition of "attendance allowance" there is inserted—

" "mobility supplement" means a supplement awarded in respect of disablement which affects a person's ability to walk and for which the person is in receipt of war disablement pension;",

(b) in the definition of "retirement pension", "if paid periodically" is omitted,

(c) in paragraph (b) of the definition of "unemployability supplement or allowance", after sub-paragraph (iv) there is inserted "or

(v) under the Pensions (Navy, Army, Air Force and Mercantile Marine) Act 1939."

and accordingly, the "or" immediately following sub-paragraph (iii) is omitted.

GENERAL NOTE

This section widens the entitlement to Christmas Bonus, payable under s.148 of the Social Security Contributions and Benefits Act by the addition of the persons entitled to the classes of benefit mentioned in the amendments to s.150 of that Act.

Contributions paid in error

133. After section 61 of the Social Security Contributions and Benefits Act 1992 there is inserted—

"**Contributions paid in error**

61A.—(1) This section applies in the case of any individual if—

(a) the individual has paid amounts by way of primary Class 1 contributions which, because the individual was not an employed earner, were paid in error, and

(b) prescribed conditions are satisfied.

(2) Regulations may, where—

(a) this section applies in the case of any individual, and

(b) the Secretary of State is of the opinion that it is appropriate for the regulations to apply to the individual,

provide for entitlement to, and the amount of, additional pension to be determined as if the individual had been an employed earner and, accordingly, those contributions had been properly paid.

(3) The reference in subsection (2) above to additional pension is to additional pension for the individual or the individual's spouse falling to be calculated under section 45 above for the purposes of—

(a) Category A retirement pension,

(b) Category B retirement pension for widows or widowers,

(c) widowed mother's allowance and widow's pension, and

(d) incapacity benefit (except in transitional cases).

(4) Regulations may, where—

(a) this section applies in the case of any individual, and

(b) the Secretary of State is of the opinion that it is appropriate for regulations made by virtue of section 4(8) of the Social Security (Incapacity for Work) Act 1994 (provision during transition from invalidity benefit to incapacity benefit for incapacity benefit to include the additional pension element of invalidity pension) to have the following effect in the case of the individual,

provide for the regulations made by virtue of that section to have effect as if, in relation to the provisions in force before the commencement of that section with respect to that additional pension element, the individual had been an employed earner and, accordingly, the contributions had been properly paid.

(5) Where such provision made by regulations as is mentioned in subsection (2) or (4) above applies in respect of any individual, regulations under paragraph 8(1)(m) of Schedule 1 to this Act may not require the amounts paid by way of primary Class 1 contributions to be repaid.

(6) Regulations may provide, where—

(a) such provision made by regulations as is mentioned in subsection (2) or (4) above applies in respect of any individual,

(b) prescribed conditions are satisfied, and

(c) any amount calculated by reference to the contributions in question has been paid in respect of that individual by way of minimum contributions under section 43 of the Pension Schemes Act 1993 (contributions to personal pension schemes),

for that individual to be treated for the purposes of that Act as if that individual had been an employed earner and, accordingly, the amount had been properly paid".

GENERAL NOTE

This section will, subject to prescribed conditions, permit pensions to be paid in respect of Class 1 contributions paid in error.

[Standing Committee D, June 22, 1995, col. 844].

Minor amendments

134.—(1) In section 23(1) of the Social Security Contributions and Benefits Act 1992 (contribution conditions: supplemental), for "22(1)(a)" there is substituted "22(1)".

(2) Section 54(4) of that Act (effect on advance claims for retirement pension of deferral of entitlement) is omitted.

(3) For section 55 of that Act (deferred entitlement) there is substituted—

"Increase of retirement pension where entitlement is deferred

55.—(1) Where a person's entitlement to a Category A or Category B retirement pension is deferred, Schedule 5 to this Act shall have effect for increasing the rate of pension.

(2) For the purposes of this Act a person's entitlement to a Category A or Category B retirement pension is deferred if and so long as that person—

(a) does not become entitled to that pension by reason only—

(i) of not satisfying the conditions of section 1 of the Administration Act (entitlement to benefit dependent on claim), or

(ii) in the case of a Category B retirement pension payable by virtue of a spouse's contributions, of the spouse not satisfying those conditions with respect to his Category A retirement pension; or

(b) in consequence of an election under section 54(1) above, falls to be treated as not having become entitled to that pension;

and, in relation to any such pension, 'period of deferment' shall be construed accordingly".

(4) In section 122(1) of that Act (interpretation of Parts I to VI), after the definition of "week" there is inserted—

" 'working life' has the meaning given by paragraph 5(8) of Schedule 3 to this Act".

(5) In paragraph 5(8) of Schedule 3 to that Act (contribution conditions: meaning of "working life") for "this paragraph" there is substituted "Parts I to VI of this Act".

GENERAL NOTE

This section makes minor adjustments to the Social Security Contributions and Benefits Act 1992.

Subs. (3)

This subsection now brings those who elect deferment of their pension under s.54 of that Act into the same regime as those whose pension is classed as deferred under s.55 of that Act.

PART III

CERTIFICATION OF PENSION SCHEMES AND EFFECTS ON MEMBERS STATE SCHEME RIGHTS AND DUTIES

Introductory

The "principal appointed day" for Part III

135. An order under section 180 of this Act appointing a day for the coming into force of any provisions of this Part, being 6th April in any year, may designate that day as the principal appointed day for the purposes of this Part.

GENERAL NOTE
This section contains the usual powers permitting different provisions of the Act to come into force on different days as the Secretary of State appoints by statutory instrument.

New certification requirements applying as from the principal appointed day

New requirements for contracted-out schemes

136.—(1) In section 7 of the Pension Schemes Act 1993 (issue of contracting-out etc. certificates), after subsection (2) there is inserted—

"(2A) The regulations may provide, in the case of contracting-out certificates issued before the principal appointed day, for their cancellation by virtue of the regulations—

(a) at the end of a prescribed period beginning with that day, or

(b) if prescribed conditions are not satisfied at any time in that period,

but for them to continue to have effect until so cancelled; and the regulations may provide that a certificate having effect on and after that day by virtue of this subsection is to have effect, in relation to any earner's service on or after that day, as if issued on or after that day.

(2B) In this Part, 'the principal appointed day' means the day designated by an order under section 180 of the Pensions Act 1995 as the principal appointed day for the purposes of Part III of that Act".

(2) In section 8 of that Act (definition of terms), for subsection (1)(a)(i) there is substituted—

"(i) his service in the employment is for the time being service which qualifies him for a pension provided by an occupational pension scheme contracted out by virtue of satisfying section 9(2) (in this Act referred to as 'a salary related contracted-out scheme')".

(3) In section 9 of that Act (requirements for certification of schemes: general), for subsection (2) (requirement for guaranteed minimum pension) there is substituted—

"(2) An occupational pension scheme satisfies this subsection only if—

(a) in relation to any earner's service before the principal appointed day, it satisfies the conditions of subsection (2A), and

(b) in relation to any earner's service on or after that day, it satisfies the conditions of subsection (2B).

(2A) The conditions of this subsection are that—

(a) the scheme complies in all respects with sections 13 to 23 or, in such cases or classes of case as may be prescribed, with those sections as modified by regulations, and

(b) the rules of the scheme applying to guaranteed minimum pensions are framed so as to comply with the relevant requirements.

(2B) The conditions of this subsection are that the Secretary of State is satisfied that—

(a) the scheme complies with section 12A,

(b) restrictions imposed under section 40 of the Pensions Act 1995 (restriction on employer-related investments) apply to the scheme and the scheme complies with those restrictions,

(c) the scheme satisfies such other requirements as may be prescribed (which—

(i) must include requirements as to the amount of the resources of the scheme, and

(ii) may include a requirement that, if the only members of the scheme were those falling within any prescribed class or description, the scheme would comply with section 12A); and

(d) the scheme does not fall within a prescribed class or description, and is satisfied that the rules of the scheme are framed so as to comply with the relevant requirements.

(2C) Regulations may modify subsection (2B)(a) and (b) in their application to occupational pension schemes falling within a prescribed class or description."

(4) In subsection (3) of that section (requirement for protected rights, etc.) after "case" in paragraph (a) there is inserted—

"(aa) the Secretary of State is satisfied that the scheme does not fall within a prescribed class or description".

(5) After section 12 of that Act there is inserted—

"Requirements for certification of occupational pension schemes applying from the principal appointed day of the Pensions Act 1995

The statutory standard

12A.—(1) Subject to the provisions of this Part, the scheme must, in relation to the provision of pensions for earners in employed earner's employment, and for their widows or widowers, satisfy the statutory standard.

(2) Subject to regulations made by virtue of section 9(2B)(c)(ii), in applying this section regard must only be had to—

(a) earners in employed earner's employment, or

(b) their widows or widowers,

collectively, and the pensions to be provided for persons falling within paragraph (a) or (b) must be considered as a whole.

(3) For the purposes of this section, a scheme satisfies the statutory standard if the pensions to be provided for such persons are broadly equivalent to, or better than, the pensions which would be provided for such persons under a reference scheme.

(4) Regulations may provide for the manner of, and criteria for, determining whether the pensions to be provided for such persons under a scheme are broadly equivalent to, or better than, the pensions which would be provided for such persons under a reference scheme.

(5) Regulations made by virtue of subsection (4) may provide for the determination to be made in accordance with guidance prepared from time to time by a prescribed body and approved by the Secretary of State.

(6) The pensions to be provided for such persons under a scheme are to be treated as broadly equivalent to or better than the pensions which would be provided for such persons under a reference scheme if and only if an actuary (who, except in prescribed circumstances, must be the actuary appointed for the scheme in pursuance of section 47 of the Pensions Act 1995) so certifies.

Reference scheme

12B.—(1) This section applies for the purposes of section 12A.

(2) A reference scheme is an occupational pension scheme which—

(a) complies with each of subsections (3) and (4), and

(b) complies with any prescribed requirements.

(3) In relation to earners employed in employed earner's employment, a reference scheme is one which provides—

(a) for them to be entitled to a pension under the scheme commencing at a normal pension age of 65 and continuing for life, and

(b) for the annual rate of the pension at that age to be—

(i) 1/80th of average qualifying earnings in the last three tax years preceding the end of service,

multiplied by

(ii) the number of years' service, not exceeding such number as would produce an annual rate equal to half the earnings on which it is calculated.

(4) In relation to widows or widowers, a reference scheme is one which provides—

(a) for the widows or widowers of earners employed in employed earner's employment (whether the earners die before or after attaining the age of 65) to be entitled, except in prescribed circumstances, to pensions under the scheme, and

(b) except in prescribed circumstances, for the annual rate of the pensions, at the time when the widows or widowers first become entitled to them, to be—

(i) in the case of widows or widowers of persons whose age when they died was, or was greater than, normal pension age, 50 per cent. of the annual rate which a reference scheme is required to provide for persons of that age, and

(ii) in the case of widows or widowers of other persons, 50 per cent. of the annual rate which a reference scheme would have been required to provide in respect of the persons' actual periods of service if those persons had attained that age.

(5) For the purposes of this section, an earner's qualifying earnings in any tax year are 90 per cent. of the amount by which the earner's earnings—

(a) exceed the qualifying earnings factor for that year, and

(b) do not exceed the upper earnings limit for that year multiplied by fifty-three.

(6) Regulations may modify subsections (2) to (5).

(7) In this section—

'normal pension age', in relation to a scheme, means the age specified in the scheme as the earliest age at which pension becomes payable under the scheme (apart from any special provision as to early retirement on grounds of ill-health or otherwise),

'qualifying earnings factor', in relation to a tax year, has the meaning given by section 122(1) of the Social Security Contributions and Benefits Act 1992, and

'upper earnings limit', in relation to a tax year, means the amount specified for that year by regulations made by virtue of section 5(3) of that Act as the upper earnings limit for Class 1 contributions.

Transfer, commutation, etc.

12C.—(1) Regulations may prohibit or restrict—

(a) the transfer of any liability—

(i) for the payment of pensions under a relevant scheme, or

(ii) in respect of accrued rights to such pensions,

(b) the discharge of any liability to provide pensions under a relevant scheme, or

(c) the payment of a lump sum instead of a pension payable under a relevant scheme,

except in prescribed circumstances or on prescribed conditions.

(2) In this section 'relevant scheme' means a scheme contracted out by virtue of section 9(2B) of this Act and references to pensions and accrued rights under the scheme are to such pensions and rights so far as attributable to an earner's service on or after the principal appointed day.

(3) Regulations under subsection (1) may provide that any provision of this Part shall have effect subject to such modifications as may be specified in the regulations.

Entitlement to benefit

12D. In the case of a scheme contracted out by virtue of section 9(2B) of this Act, regulations may make provision as to the ages by reference to which benefits under the scheme are to be paid".

GENERAL NOTE

This section inserts new provisions into the Pension Schemes Act 1993, which provide for new certificates, and for new criteria to be fulfilled for the purpose of obtaining those certificates, in respect of the contracting out of schemes under that Act.

Subs. (1)

Subsection (1) inserts a new s.7(2A) into the Pension Schemes Act 1993, which enables regulations to be made for the cancellation of certificates already given before an appointed day. But the regulations may provide for such certificates to continue in force for what is in effect a change-over period.

Subss. (3), (4) and (5)

These subsections make changes in the certification requirements. To be contracted out after the principal appointed day appointed under s.9 of the 1993 Act a scheme will have to comply with the present requirements for contracting out (as set out in ss.13 to 24 of the 1993 Act) in respect of any period before that day. In respect of any period after the principal appointed day, the scheme will have to comply with the requirements of s.12A, as expanded by s.12B of the 1993 Act and any regulations made under s.12C of that Act, with the requirements of that Act regarding employer-related investments, and with any other requirements which are prescribed by regulations.

Subsection (5) inserts into the Pension Schemes Act 1993 new ss.12A to 12D. The first two of these contain the new contracting out requirements in force after the principal appointed day. The requirement for a guaranteed minimum pension is abandoned, and instead there is required a minimum rate of pension highly reminiscent of the minimum level which was required (together with the guaranteed minimum pension) under s.34 of the Social Security Pensions Act 1975, as originally enacted. In order to qualify, the scheme has to provide a pension at normal pension age for earners and their widows or widowers pensions broadly equivalent to or better than pensions prescribed by a "reference scheme".

A reference scheme is one which provides that the annual rate of pension for an earner is to be 1/80th of average "qualifying earnings" in the last three tax years of service for each year of service which is necessary to provide a pension equal to one half of the earnings on which it is calculated. These are the average qualifying earnings. Qualifying earnings in any tax year are 90 per cent of the amount by which the earner's earnings exceed the qualifying earnings factor for that year, subject to an upper limit of 53 times the upper earnings limit for that year. This factor is to be found in the definition contained in s.122(1) of the Social Security Contributions and Benefits Act 1992, and is 52 times the lower earnings limit for the tax year in question. The lower earnings limit is to be found in s.5 of that Act. Normal pension age is the earliest age at which a pension is payable under the scheme except under special provisions as to early retirement.

Widows and widowers pensions of one-half of the above amount has to be provided, save that for death in service before normal pension age the earner's pension on which the one-half is calculated is based on actual years of service.

[Standing Committee D, June 15, 1995, col. 664].

Reduction in State scheme contributions, payment of rebates and reduction in State scheme benefits

State scheme contributions and rebates

137.—(1) In section 40 of the Pension Schemes Act 1993 (scope of Chapter II of Part III), in paragraph (b), after "members of" there is inserted "money purchase contracted-out schemes and members of".

(2) For section 41(1) of that Act (reduced rates of Class 1 contributions for earners in contracted-out employment), including the sidenote and the preceding heading, there is substituted—

"Reduced rates of contributions for members of salary related contracted-out schemes

Reduced rates of Class 1 contributions

41.—(1) Where—

(a) the earnings paid to or for the benefit of an earner in any tax week are in respect of an employment which is contracted-out employment at the time of the payment, and

(b) the earner's service in the employment is service which qualifies him for a pension provided by a salary related contracted-out scheme,

the amount of a Class 1 contribution in respect of so much of the earnings paid in that week as exceeds the current lower earnings limit but not the current upper earnings limit for that week (or the prescribed equivalents if he is paid otherwise than weekly) shall be reduced by the following amount.

(1A) The amount is—

(a) in the case of a primary Class 1 contribution, an amount equal to 1.8 per cent. of that part of those earnings, and

(b) in the case of a secondary Class 1 contribution, an amount equal to 3 per cent. of that part of those earnings".

(3) In section 42 of that Act (review and alteration of rates of contributions applicable under section 41), for subsection (1)(a) there is substituted—

"(a) a report by the Government Actuary or the Deputy Government Actuary on—

(i) the percentages for the time being applying under section 41(1A)(a) and (b), and

(ii) any changes since the preparation of the last report under this paragraph in the factors in his opinion affecting the cost of providing benefits of an actuarial value equivalent to that of the benefits which, under section 48A, are foregone by or in respect of members of salary related contracted-out schemes".

(4) In relation to the first report under section 42(1)(a) of that Act laid after the passing of this Act, that section shall have effect as if—

(a) in subsection (1)(a), sub-paragraph (i) and, in sub-paragraph (ii), "any changes since the preparation of the last report under this paragraph in" were omitted,

(b) for subsection (1)(b) there were substituted—

"(b) a report by the Secretary of State stating what, in view of the report under paragraph (a), he considers the percentages under section 41(1A)(a) should be",

(c) for subsections (3) and (4) there were substituted—

"(3) The Secretary of State shall prepare and lay before each House of Parliament with the report the draft of an order specifying the percentages; and if the draft is approved by resolution of each House the Secretary of State shall make the order in the form of the draft.

(4) An order under subsection (3) shall have effect from the beginning of the tax year which begins with the principal appointed day, not being a tax year earlier than the second after that in which the order is made",

(d) in subsection (5), for "alteration" there were substituted "determination", and

(e) in subsection (6), for "an order making alterations in either or both of those percentages" there were substituted "such an order".

(5) After that section there is inserted—

"Reduced rates of contributions, and rebates, for members of money purchase contracted-out schemes

Reduced rates of Class 1 contributions, and rebates

42A.—(1) Subsections (2) and (3) apply where—

    (a) the earnings paid to or for the benefit of an earner in any tax week are in respect of an employment which is contracted-out employment at the time of the payment, and

    (b) the earner's service in the employment is service which qualifies him for a pension provided by a money purchase contracted-out scheme.

(2) The amount of a Class 1 contribution in respect of so much of the earnings paid in that week in respect of that employment as exceeds the current lower earnings limit but not the current upper earnings limit for that week (or the prescribed equivalents if he is paid otherwise than weekly) shall be reduced by an amount equal to the appropriate flat-rate percentage of that part of those earnings.

(3) The Secretary of State shall except in prescribed circumstances or in respect of prescribed periods pay in respect of that earner and that tax week to the trustees or managers of the scheme or, in prescribed circumstances, to a prescribed person the amount by which—

    (a) the appropriate age-related percentage of that part of those earnings,

exceeds

    (b) the appropriate flat-rate percentage of that part of those earnings.

(4) Regulations may make provision—

    (a) as to the manner in which and time at which or period within which payments under subsection (3) are to be made,

    (b) for the adjustment of the amount which would otherwise be payable under that subsection so as to avoid the payment of trivial or fractional amounts,

    (c) for earnings to be calculated or estimated in such manner and on such basis as may be prescribed for the purpose of determining whether any, and if so what, payments under subsection (3) are to be made.

(5) If the Secretary of State pays an amount under subsection (3) which he is not required to pay or is not required to pay to the person to whom, or in respect of whom, he pays it, he may recover it from any person to whom, or in respect of whom, he paid it.

(6) Where—

    (a) an earner has ceased to be employed in an employment, and

    (b) earnings are paid to him or for his benefit within the period of six weeks, or such other period as may be prescribed, from the day on which he so ceased,

that employment shall be treated for the purposes of this section as contracted-out employment at the time when the earnings are paid if it was contracted-out employment in relation to the earner when he was last employed in it.

(7) Subsection (3) of section 41 applies for the purposes of this section as it applies for the purposes of that.

**Determination and alteration of rates of contributions, and rebates,
applicable under section 42A**

42B.—(1) The Secretary of State shall at intervals of not more than
five years lay before each House of Parliament—

(a) a report by the Government Actuary or the Deputy Government
Actuary on the percentages which, in his opinion, are required to
be specified in an order under this section so as to reflect the cost
of providing benefits of an actuarial value equivalent to that of the
benefits which, under section 48A, are foregone by or in respect
of members of money purchase contracted-out schemes,

(b) a report by the Secretary of State stating what, in view of the
report under paragraph (a), he considers those percentages
should be, and

(c) a draft of an order under subsection (2).

(2) An order under this subsection shall have effect in relation to a
period of tax years (not exceeding five) and may—

(a) specify different percentages for primary and secondary Class 1
contributions, and

(b) for each of the tax years for which it has effect—

(i) specify a percentage in respect of all earners which is 'the
appropriate flat-rate percentage' for the purposes of section
42A, and

(ii) specify different percentages (not being less than the
percentage specified by virtue of sub-paragraph (i)) in respect
of earners by reference to their ages on the last day of the preceding year (the percentage for each group of earners being
'the appropriate age-related percentage' in respect of earners
in that group for the purposes of section 42A).

(3) If the draft of an order under subsection (2) is approved by resolution of each House of Parliament, the Secretary of State shall make the
order in the form of the draft.

(4) An order under subsection (2) shall have effect from the beginning
of such tax year as may be specified in the order, not being a tax year
earlier than the second after that in which the order is made.

(5) Subsection (2) is without prejudice to the generality of section
182".

(6) In Schedule 4 to that Act (priority in bankruptcy, etc.), in paragraph
2(3)—

(a) in paragraph (a), for "4.8 per cent." there is substituted "the percentage for non-contributing earners",

(b) in paragraph (b), for "3 per cent." there is substituted "the percentage
for contributing earners".

(7) In paragraph 2(5) of that Schedule—

(a) before the definition of "employer" there is inserted—
" 'appropriate flat-rate percentage' has the same meaning as in section 42A", and

(b) after the definition there is inserted—
" 'the percentage for contributing earners' means—

(a) in relation to a salary related contracted-out scheme, 3
per cent, and

(b) in relation to a money purchase contracted-out scheme,
the percentage which is the appropriate flat-rate percentage
for secondary Class 1 contributions,

'the percentage for non-contributing earners' means—

(a) in relation to a salary related contracted-out scheme, 4.8
per cent, and

(b) in relation to a money purchase contracted-out scheme,
a percentage equal to the sum of the appropriate flat-rate percentages for primary and secondary Class 1 contributions".

This section continues the alterations to the contracting-out arrangements contained in the Pension Schemes Act 1993. It provides for payments to be made by the Secretary of State in respect of members of money purchase contracted-out schemes, as well as in respect of members of appropriate personal pension schemes, which is the case at present. This is done by splitting the provisions which prescribe reduced rates of Class 1 contributions to the state scheme in respect of members of contracted-out money purchase schemes, from those applicable to contracted-out salary related schemes. The Secretary of State is to make contributions only in respect of members of the former type of schemes. Provision is made for a separate report by the Government Actuary in respect of each type of contracted-out scheme mentioned above, and for periodic revision of the Class 1 contributions to be paid to the state scheme by members of each type of scheme.

Contributions of the Secretary of State to contracted-out money purchase schemes will be age related (see new 42B(2)(b)) as are those under s.45 for appropriate personal pension schemes.

Minimum contributions towards appropriate personal pension schemes

138.—(1) Section 45 of the Pension Schemes Act 1993 (minimum contributions to personal pension schemes) is amended as follows.

(2) For subsection (1) there is substituted—

"(1) In relation to any tax week falling within a period for which the Secretary of State is required to pay minimum contributions in respect of an earner, the amount of those contributions shall be an amount equal to the appropriate age-related percentage of so much of the earnings paid in that week (other than earnings in respect of contracted-out employment) as exceeds the current lower earnings limit but not the current upper earnings limit for that week (or the prescribed equivalents if he is paid otherwise than weekly)".

(3) Subsection (2) is omitted.

(4) In subsection (3)(e), the words following "prescribed period" are omitted.

(5) After that section there is inserted—

"**Determination and alteration of rates of minimum contributions under section 45**

45A.—(1) The Secretary of State shall at intervals of not more than five years lay before each House of Parliament—

(a) a report by the Government Actuary or the Deputy Government Actuary on the percentages which, in his opinion, are required to be specified in an order under this section so as to reflect the cost of providing benefits of an actuarial value equivalent to that of the benefits which, under section 48A, are foregone by or in respect of members of appropriate personal pension schemes,

(b) a report by the Secretary of State stating what, in view of the report under paragraph (a), he considers those percentages should be, and

(c) a draft of an order under subsection (2).

(2) An order under this subsection—

(a) shall have effect in relation to a period of tax years (not exceeding five), and

(b) may, for each of the tax years for which it has effect, specify different percentages in respect of earners by reference to their ages on the last day of the preceding year (the percentage for each group of earners being 'the appropriate age-related percentage' in respect of earners in that group for the purposes of section 45).

(3) If the draft of an order under subsection (2) is approved by resolution of each House of Parliament, the Secretary of State shall make the order in the form of the draft.

(4) An order under subsection (2) shall have effect from the beginning of such tax year as may be specified in the order, not being a tax year earlier than the second after that in which the order is made.

(5) Subsection (2) is without prejudice to the generality of section 182".

DEFINITIONS
"personal pension scheme": s.176.

GENERAL NOTE
This section is another which alters and inserts new sections into the Pension Schemes Act 1993, making changes to s.45 of that Act. Prior to these alterations, s.45 prescribed the amount of minimum contributions which the Secretary of State had to pay to an appropriate personal pension scheme. This consisted of a non-age related amount equal to the difference between the Class 1 contributions which would have been payable if the earner was not contracted-out and those in fact paid. Added to this was a flat one per cent of so much of the earnings of the earner as respects which the reductions in Class 1 contributions fall to be made. A new provision is made for payment of the appropriate age-related percentage of the earnings of the earner as fall between the current lower and upper earnings limits.

The new s.45A provides for quinquennial reports by the Government Actuary, and for an order to be laid which contains the appropriate age-related percentages for earners of differing ages.

[Standing Committee D, June 20, 1995, col. 691].

Money purchase and personal pension schemes: verification of ages

139. After section 45A of the Pension Schemes Act 1993 (inserted by section 138) there is inserted—

> **"Money purchase and personal pension schemes: verification of ages**
>
> 45B.—(1) Regulations may make provision for the manner in which an earner's age is to be verified in determining the appropriate age-related percentages for the purposes of sections 42A and 45(1).
>
> (2) Information held by the Secretary of State as to the age of any individual may, whether or not it was obtained in pursuance of regulations under subsection (1), be disclosed by the Secretary of State—
>
>> (a) to the trustees or managers of a money purchase contracted-out scheme or an appropriate personal pension scheme, and
>>
>> (b) to such other persons as may be prescribed,
>
> in connection with the making of payments under section 42A(3) or the payment of minimum contributions."

GENERAL NOTE
This section inserts a new s.45B into the Pension Schemes Act 1993, whereby regulations may be made for the verification of the ages of earners. This is essential for the Secretary of State and the trustees of relevant schemes to know, for the purposes of the new ss.42A, 42B and 45 of the 1993 Act.

[Standing Committee D, June 20, 1995, col. 715].

Reduction in benefits for members of certified schemes

140.—(1) After section 48 of the Pension Schemes Act 1993 there is inserted—

> *"Effect of reduced contributions and rebates on social security benefits*
>
> **Additional pension and other benefits**
>
> 48A.—(1) In relation to any tax week where—
>
>> (a) the amount of a Class 1 contribution in respect of the earnings paid to or for the benefit of an earner in that week is reduced under section 41 or 42A, or
>>
>> (b) an amount is paid under section 45(1) in respect of the earnings paid to or for the benefit of an earner,
>
> section 44(6) of the Social Security Contributions and Benefits Act 1992 (earnings factors for additional pension) shall have effect, except in pre-

scribed circumstances, as if no primary Class 1 contributions had been paid or treated as paid upon those earnings for that week and section 45A of that Act did not apply (where it would, apart from this subsection, apply).

(2) Where the whole or part of a contributions equivalent premium has been paid or treated as paid in respect of the earner, the Secretary of State may make a determination reducing or eliminating the application of subsection (1).

(3) Subsection (1) is subject to regulations under paragraph 5(3A) to (3E) of Schedule 2.

(4) Regulations may, so far as is required for the purpose of providing entitlement to additional pension (such as is mentioned in section 44(3)(b) of the Social Security Contributions and Benefits Act 1992) but to the extent only that the amount of additional pension is attributable to provision made by regulations under section 45(5) of that Act, disapply subsection (1).

(5) In relation to earners where, by virtue of subsection (1), section 44(6) of the Social Security Contributions and Benefits Act 1992 has effect, in any tax year, as mentioned in that subsection in relation to some but not all of their earnings, regulations may modify the application of section 44(5) of that Act."

(2) In section 48 of the Pension Schemes Act 1993 (effect of membership of money purchase contracted-out scheme or appropriate scheme on payment of social security benefits) in subsection (2), paragraph (b) is omitted and, in paragraph (c), "if the earner dies before reaching pensionable age" is omitted.

(3) Section 48 of that Act shall cease to have effect in relation to minimum payments made, or minimum contributions paid, on or after the principal appointed day.

GENERAL NOTE

This section adds a new s.48A to the Pension Schemes Act 1993. It gives effect within the state scheme to the contracting-out of an earner in that it deprives him of the earnings factors for the additional pension to which he would otherwise be entitled if he were not contracted out, and applies this to members of salary-related and money purchase contracted-out schemes, and to earners with appropriate personal pension schemes.

Provision is made in s.48A(2) for buy back, and s.48A(4) allows regulations to be made to provide for borderline cases.

[Standing Committee D, June 20, 1995, col. 718].

Premiums and return to State scheme

State scheme etc. premiums and buyback into State scheme

141.—(1) In section 55 of the Pension Schemes Act 1993 (payment of state scheme premiums on termination of certified status), for subsection (2) there is substituted—

"(2) Where—

(a) an earner is serving in employment which is contracted-out employment by reference to an occupational pension scheme (other than a money purchase contracted-out scheme),

(b) paragraph (a) ceases to apply, by reason of any of the following circumstances, before the earner attains the scheme's normal pension age or (if earlier) the end of the tax year preceding that in which the earner attains pensionable age, and

(c) the earner has served for less than two years in the employment, the prescribed person may elect to pay a premium under this subsection (referred to in this Act as a 'contributions equivalent premium').

(2A) The circumstances referred to in subsection (2) are that—

(a) the earner's service in the employment ceases otherwise than on the earner's death,

(b) the earner ceases to be a member of the scheme otherwise than on the earner's death,

(c) the earner's service in the employment ceases on the earner's death and the earner dies leaving a widow or widower,

(d) the scheme is wound up,

(e) the scheme ceases to be a contracted-out occupational pension scheme;

but paragraph (a), (b), (d) or (e) does not apply if the earner has an accrued right to short service benefit".

(2) In Schedule 2 to that Act, in paragraph 5 (state scheme premiums)—

(a) in sub-paragraph (3)—

(i) "in relation to state scheme premiums" is omitted,

(ii) paragraph (b) is omitted, and

(iii) at the end there is added—

"and in this sub-paragraph and the following provisions of this paragraph 'premium' means a contributions equivalent premium",

(b) after sub-paragraph (3) there is inserted—

"(3A) Sub-paragraph (3B) applies in relation to a member of a contracted-out occupational pension scheme which is being wound up if, in the opinion of the Secretary of State—

(a) the resources of the scheme are insufficient to meet the whole of the liability for the cash equivalent of the member's rights under the scheme, and

(b) if the resources of the scheme are sufficient to meet a part of that liability, that part is less than the amount required for restoring his State scheme rights.

(3B) Where this sub-paragraph applies—

(a) regulations may provide for treating the member as if sections 46 to 48 or, as the case may be, section 48A(1) did not apply, or applied only to such extent as is determined in accordance with the regulations, and

(b) the amount required for restoring the member's State scheme rights, or a prescribed part of that amount, shall be a debt due from the trustees or managers of the scheme to the Secretary of State.

(3C) Regulations may make provision—

(a) for determining the cash equivalent of a member's rights under a scheme and the extent (if any) to which the resources of the scheme are insufficient to meet the liability for that cash equivalent,

(b) for the recovery of any debt due under sub-paragraph (3B)(b), and

(c) for determining the amount required for restoring a member's State scheme rights including provision requiring the Secretary of State to apply whichever prescribed actuarial table in force at the appropriate time is applicable.

(3D) Section 155 shall apply as if sub-paragraphs (3A) and (3B)(a), and regulations made by virtue of this sub-paragraph and sub-paragraph (3B)(b), were included among the provisions there referred to.

(3E) In sub-paragraphs (3A) and (3B), 'State scheme rights', in relation to a member of a scheme, are the rights for which, if the scheme had not been a contracted-out scheme, the member would have been eligible by virtue of section 44(6) of the Social Security Contributions and Benefits Act 1992 (earnings factors for additional pension).", and

(c) sub-paragraph (5) is omitted.

"state scheme premiums": s.124(5); the Pension Schemes Act 1993, s.181(1).

GENERAL NOTE
This section principally inserts new provisions into s.55 of the Pension Schemes Act 1993 which alter the conditions for the payment of a contributions equivalent premium. The new conditions are contained in subs. (2A) of the s.55.

The section also makes additions to Schedule 2 to the 1993 Act. These provide for the treatment of earners as though they had not been contracted out where a scheme in relation to which an earner is contracted out is wound up and the resources of the scheme are insufficient to provide the cash equivalent of the members' rights under the scheme.

[Standing Committee D, June 20, 1995, col. 725].

Protected rights

Interim arrangements for giving effect to protected rights

142.—(1) Section 28 of the Pension Schemes Act 1993 (ways of giving effect to protected rights) is amended as follows.

(2) In subsection (1), after paragraph (a) there is inserted—

"(aa) in any case where subsection (1A) so requires, by the making of such payments as are mentioned in that subsection,".

(3) After that subsection there is inserted—

"(1A) In the case of a personal pension scheme, where the member so elects, effect shall be given to his protected rights—

(a) during the interim period, by the making of payments under an interim arrangement which—

(i) complies with section 28A,

(ii) satisfies such conditions as may be prescribed, and

(b) at the end of the interim period, in such of the ways permitted by the following subsections as the rules of the scheme may specify."

(4) In subsection (3)—

(a) in paragraph (b), after "the member" there is inserted "or, where section 28A(2) applies, the member's widow or widower", and

(b) in the words following that paragraph, after "subsection" there is inserted "(1A)(a) or".

(5) In subsection (4)(a), for the words from "65" to the end there is substituted—

"65 or such later date as has been agreed by him, or

(ii) in the case of a personal pension scheme, where the member has elected to receive payments under an interim arrangement, the date by reference to which the member elects to terminate that arrangement, and otherwise such date as has been agreed by him and is not earlier than his 60th birthday nor later than his 75th birthday."

(6) In subsection (5), after "subsection" there is inserted "(1A)".

(7) After subsection (7) there is added—

"(8) In this section and sections 28A, 28B and 29—

'the interim period' means the period beginning with the starting date in relation to the member in question and ending with the termination date;

'the starting date' means the date, which must not be earlier than the member's 60th birthday, by reference to which the member elects to begin to receive payments under the interim arrangement;

'the termination date' means the date by reference to which the member (or, where section 28A(2) applies, the member's widow or widower) elects to terminate the interim arrangement, and that date must be not later than—

(i) the member's 75th birthday, or

(ii) where section 28A(2) applies, the earlier of the member's widow or widower's 75th birthday and the 75th anniversary of the member's birth."

DEFINITIONS
"protected rights": s.112(5); the Pension Schemes Act 1993, s.181(1).

GENERAL NOTE
There has been much difficulty caused in respect of pension arrangements, both in respect of the winding-up of salary-related schemes and in respect of money purchase schemes and personal pension schemes, by the hard annuity rates which have recently been a feature of the insurance market. This has been the subject of a concession in respect of small self-administered schemes, where the period for the purchase of an annuity on retirement has been extended to age 75 (see PSO Memorandum No. 119). This concession is now being extended to protected rights by alterations made by this section to s.28 of the Pension Schemes Act 1993. The annuity may be purchased at any date between the 60th and 75th birthdays of the member.

Provision is also made allowing interim payments to be made from the fund by way of annuity payments, to the member and to the widow or widower of the member (see the new s.28A of the Pension Schemes Act 1993). The new s.28B of the 1993 Act provides for information regarding interim payments to be given by the trustees of the scheme to the Secretary of State if required to do so (see s.143 below).
[Standing Committee D, June 20, 1995, col. 729].

Requirements for interim arrangements

143. After section 28 of the Pension Schemes Act 1993 there is inserted—

"Requirements for interim arrangements

28A.—(1) An interim arrangement must provide for payments to be made to the member, and, where subsection (2) applies, to the member's widow or widower, throughout the interim period, at intervals not exceeding twelve months.

(2) This subsection applies where the member dies during the interim period and is survived by a widow or widower who at the date of the member's death has not yet attained the age of 75 years.

(3) The aggregate amount of payments made to a person under an interim arrangement in each successive period of twelve months must not be—

(a) greater than the annual amount of the annuity which would have been purchasable by him on the relevant reference date, or

(b) less than the prescribed percentage of that amount.

(4) The percentage prescribed under subsection (3)(b) may be zero.

(5) For the purposes of this section—

(a) the annual amount of the annuity which would have been purchasable by a person on any date shall be calculated in the prescribed manner by reference to—

(i) the value on that date, determined by or on behalf of the trustees or managers of the scheme, of the person's protected rights, and

(ii) the current published tables of rates of annuities prepared in the prescribed manner by the Government Actuary for the purposes of this section, and

(b) the relevant reference date is—

(i) in relation to payments made to the member during the three years beginning with the member's starting date, that date, and in relation to such payments made during each succeeding period of three years, the first day of the period of three years in question, or

(ii) where subsection (2) applies, in relation to payments made to the member's widow or widower during the three years beginning with the date of the member's death, that date, and in relation to such payments made during each succeeding period of three years, the first day of the period of three years in question.

Information about interim arrangements

28B.—(1) The trustees or managers of a personal BL pension scheme must, if required to do so by the Secretary of State, produce any document relevant to—

(a) the level of payments made under any interim arrangement, or

(b) the value of protected rights to which such an arrangement gives effect,

or otherwise connected with the making of payments under such an arrangement.

(2) In this section, "document" includes information recorded in any form, and the reference to the production of a document, in relation to information recorded otherwise than in legible form, is a reference to producing a copy of the information in legible form."

GENERAL NOTE

For comment on this section see the General Note to s.142 above.

Interim arrangements: supplementary

144.—(1) Section 29 of the Pension Schemes Act 1993 (the pension and annuity requirements) is amended as follows.

(2) In subsection (1) for paragraph (a) there is substituted—

"(a) in the case of an occupational pension scheme it commences on a date—

(i) not earlier than the member's 60th birthday, and

(ii) not later than his 65th birthday,

or on such later date as has been agreed by him, and continues until the date of his death, or

(aa) in the case of a personal pension scheme—

(i) where the member has elected under section 28(1A) to receive payments under an interim arrangement, it commences on the termination date, and continues until the date of the member's death or, where section 28A(2) applies, until the death of the member's widow or widower, or

(ii) otherwise, it commences on such a date as has been agreed by the member and is not earlier than his 60th birthday nor later than his 75th birthday, and continues until the date of his death;".

(3) In subsection (3)(b)(iii), after "member" there is inserted "or, where section 28A(2) applies, the member's widow or widower".

(4) In subsection (4), after "member" there is inserted "(or a member's widow or widower)".

GENERAL NOTE

This section makes alterations to s.29 of the Pension Schemes Act 1993 consequent upon the alterations to that Act contained in ss.142 and 143 above, as to which see the General Note to s.142.

Extension of interim arrangements to occupational pension schemes

145. Regulations made by the Secretary of State may provide that sections 141 to 143 shall have effect, subject to prescribed modifications, in relation to protected rights under an occupational pension scheme as they have effect in relation to protected rights under a personal pension scheme.

DEFINITIONS

"modifications": s.124(5); the Pension Schemes Act 1993, s.181.

"occupational pension scheme": s.176.

"personal pension scheme": s.176.

"prescribed": s.124(5); the Pension Schemes Act 1993, s.181.
"protected rights": s.124(5); the Pension Schemes Act 1993, s.181.
"regulations": s.124(5); the Pension Schemes Act 1993, s.181.

GENERAL NOTE
One can only regret that such an important matter should prospectively be the subject of secondary legislation. The cross references contained in this section of the Act are wrong. They should be ss.142 to 144, and not ss.141 to 143.

Discharge of protected rights on winding up: insurance policies

146.—(1) After section 32 of the Pension Schemes Act 1993 there is inserted—

"Discharge of protected rights on winding up: insurance policies

32A.—(1) Where an occupational pension scheme is being wound up and such conditions as may be prescribed are satisfied, effect may be given to the protected rights of a member of the scheme (in spite of section 28) by—

(a) taking out an appropriate policy of insurance, or a number of such policies, under which the member is the beneficiary, or

(b) assuring the benefits of a policy of insurance, or a number of such policies, to the member, where the policy assured is an appropriate policy.

(2) A policy of insurance is appropriate for the purposes of this section if—

(a) the insurance company with which it is or was taken out or entered into—

(i) is, or was at the time when the policy was taken out or (as the case may be) the benefit of it was assured, carrying on ordinary long-term insurance business (within the meaning of the Insurance Companies Act 1982) in the United Kingdom or any other Member State, and

(ii) satisfies, or at that time satisfied, prescribed requirements, and

(b) it may not be assigned or surrendered except on conditions which satisfy such requirements as may be prescribed, and

(c) it contains or is endorsed with terms whose effect is that the amount secured by it may not be commuted except on conditions which satisfy such requirements as may be prescribed, and

(d) it satisfies such other requirements as may be prescribed".

(2) At the end of section 28 of that Act, as amended by this Act, (ways of giving effect to protected rights) there is inserted—

"(9) This section is subject to section 32A".

GENERAL NOTE
This section, inserting a new s.32A into the Pension Schemes Act 1993, provides for the discharge of protected rights on the winding up of an occupational pension scheme by the purchase of insurance policies. It is no doubt a necessary and useful addition.
[Standing Committee D, June 22, 1995, col. 833].

Miscellaneous

Monitoring personal pension schemes

147. After section 33 of the Pension Schemes Act 1993 there is inserted—

"Appropriate schemes: "Blowing the whistle"

33A.—(1) If any person acting as an auditor or actuary of an appropriate scheme has reasonable cause to believe that—

(a) any requirement which, in the case of the scheme, is required by section 9(5)(a) to be satisfied is not satisfied, and

(b) the failure to satisfy the requirement is likely to be of material significance in the exercise by the Secretary of State of any of his functions relating to appropriate schemes,

that person must immediately give a written report of the matter to the Secretary of State.

(2) No duty to which a person acting as auditor or actuary of an appropriate scheme is subject shall be regarded as contravened merely because of any information or opinion contained in a written report under this section."

GENERAL NOTE

This section brings a reduced concept of "whistle-blowing" into the Pension Schemes Act 1993. For the main provisions applying to occupational pension schemes, see s.48 above. Section 9(5)(a) of the Pension Schemes Act 1993 refers to the requirements to be fulfilled by a personal pension scheme for certification as an appropriate scheme for the purposes of contracting out.

[Standing Committee D, June 20, 1995, col. 732].

Earner employed in more than one employment

148.—(1) Paragraph 1 of Schedule 1 to the Social Security Contributions and Benefits Act 1992 (Class 1 contributions where earner in more than one employment) is amended as follows.

(2) For sub-paragraph (3) there is substituted—

"(3) The amount of the primary Class 1 contribution shall be the aggregate of the amounts determined under the following paragraphs (applying earlier paragraphs before later ones)—

(a) if the aggregated earnings are paid to or for the benefit of an earner in respect of whom minimum contributions are payable under section 43(1) of the Pension Schemes Act 1993 (contributions to personal pension schemes), the amount obtained by applying the rate of primary Class 1 contributions that would apply if all the aggregated earnings were attributable to employments which are not contracted-out to such part of the aggregated earnings so attributable as does not exceed the current upper earnings limit (referred to in this paragraph as "the APPS earnings"),

(b) if some of the aggregated earnings are attributable to COMPS service, the amount obtained by applying the rate of primary Class 1 contributions that would apply if all the aggregated earnings were attributable to COMPS service—

(i) to such part of the aggregated earnings attributable to COMPS service as does not exceed the current upper earnings limit, or

(ii) if paragraph (a) applies, to such part of the earnings attributable to COMPS service as, when added to the APPS earnings, does not exceed the current upper earnings limit,

(c) if some of the aggregated earnings are attributable to COSRS service, the amount obtained by applying the rate of primary Class 1 contributions that would apply if all the aggregated earnings were attributable to COSRS service—

(i) to such part of the aggregated earnings attributable to COSRS service as does not exceed the current upper earnings limit, or

(ii) if paragraph (a) or (b) applies, to such part of the earnings attributable to COSRS service as, when added to the APPS earnings or the part attributable to COMPS service (or both), does not exceed the current upper earnings limit,

(d) the amount obtained by applying the rate of primary Class 1 contributions that would apply if all the aggregated earnings were attributable to employments which are not contracted-out to such part of the aggregated earnings as, when added to the part or parts attributable to COMPS or COSRS service, does not exceed the current upper earnings limit".

(3) For sub-paragraph (6) there is substituted—

"(6) The amount of the secondary Class 1 contribution shall be the aggregate of the amounts determined under the following paragraphs (applying earlier paragraphs before later ones)—

(a) if the aggregated earnings are paid to or for the benefit of an earner in respect of whom minimum contributions are payable under section 43(1) of the Pension Schemes Act 1993, the amount obtained by applying the rate of secondary Class 1 contributions that would apply if all the aggregated earnings were attributable to employments which are not contracted-out to the APPS earnings,

(b) if some of the aggregated earnings are attributable to COMPS service, the amount obtained by applying the rate of secondary Class 1 contributions that would apply if all the aggregated earnings were attributable to COMPS service to the part of the aggregated earnings attributable to such service,

(c) if some of the aggregated earnings are attributable to COSRS service, the amount obtained by applying the rate of secondary Class 1 contributions that would apply if all the aggregated earnings were attributable to COSRS service to the part of the aggregated earnings attributable to such service,

(d) the amount obtained by applying the rate of secondary Class 1 contributions that would apply if all the aggregated earnings were attributable to employments which are not contracted-out to the remainder of the aggregated earnings".

(4) At the end of that paragraph there is added—

"(9) In this paragraph—

"COMPS service" means service in employment in respect of which minimum payments are made to a money purchase contracted-out scheme,

"COSRS service" means service in employment which qualifies the earner for a pension provided by a salary related contracted-out scheme".

(5) Until the principal appointed day, that paragraph, as amended by this section, shall have effect as if—

(a) for sub-paragraph (3)(b) there were substituted—

"(b) if some of the aggregated earnings are attributable to service in contracted-out employment, the amount obtained by applying the rate of primary Class 1 contributions that would apply if all the aggregated earnings were attributable to such service—

(i) to such part of the aggregated earnings attributable to such service as does not exceed the current upper earnings limit, or

(ii) if paragraph (a) applies, to such part of the earnings attributable to such service as, when added to the APPS earnings, does not exceed the current upper earnings limit",

(b) sub-paragraph (3)(c) were omitted,

(c) in sub-paragraph (3)(d), for "COMPS or COSRS service" there were substituted "service in contracted-out employment",

(d) for sub-paragraph (6)(b) there were substituted—

"(b) if some of the aggregated earnings are attributable to service in contracted-out employment, the amount obtained by applying the rate of secondary Class 1 contributions that would apply if all the aggregated earnings were attributable to such service to the part of the aggregated earnings attributable to such service",

(e) sub-paragraph (6)(c) were omitted, and

(f) in sub-paragraph (9) the definitions of "COMPS service" and "COSRS service" were omitted.

GENERAL NOTE

This section makes a complicated alteration to the rate payable by way of Class 1 contributions where an earner is in more than one employment. This is to allow for the fact that he may be in a combination of employments, one of which might require the Secretary of State to make minimum payments to a personal pension scheme in respect of the earner under s.43 of the Pension Schemes Act 1993. The same person might be in a contracted-out salary-related pension scheme, or a contracted-out money purchase pension scheme. Finally such a person, or another person, might have employment in respect of which he was not contracted out. In the substituted section the earlier paragraphs are applied before the later.

[Standing Committee D, June 22, 1995, col. 841].

Hybrid occupational pension schemes

149.—(1) In spite of anything in sections 9 and 12 of the Pension Schemes Act 1993 (requirements for certification and determination of basis on which scheme is contracted-out), the Secretary of State may by regulations provide, where the pensions provided by an occupational pension scheme include both—

(a) such pensions that, if the scheme provided only those pensions, it would satisfy section 9(2) of that Act, and

(b) such other pensions that, if the scheme provided only those other pensions, it would satisfy section 9(3) of that Act,

for Part III of that Act to have effect as if the scheme were two separate schemes providing, respectively, the pensions referred to in paragraphs (a) and (b).

(2) Regulations made by the Secretary of State may, in connection with any provision made by virtue of subsection (1), make such modifications of the following Acts, and the instruments made or having effect as if made under them, as appear to the Secretary of State desirable: the Social Security Contributions and Benefits Act 1992, the Pension Schemes Act 1993 and Part I of this Act.

DEFINITIONS

"modifications": s.124(5); the Pension Schemes Act 1993, s.181.

"occupational pension scheme": s.176.

"protected rights": s.124(5); the Pension Schemes Act 1993, s.181.

"regulations": s.124(5); the Pension Schemes Act 1993, s.181.

GENERAL NOTE

This section provides for regulations to be made permitting hybrid occupational pension schemes, namely those with protected rights and with guaranteed minimum pensions, to be contracted out. [*Hansard*, H.L. Vol. 263, Col. 146].

Dissolution of Occupational Pensions Board

150.—(1) The Occupational Pensions Board (referred to in this section as "the Board") is hereby dissolved.

(2) An order under section 180 appointing the day on which subsection (1) is to come into force may provide—

(a) for all property, rights and liabilities to which the Board is entitled or subject immediately before that day to become property, rights and liabilities of the Authority or the Secretary of State, and

(b) for any function of the Board falling to be exercised on or after that day, or which fell to be exercised before that day but has not been exercised, to be exercised by the Authority, the Secretary of State or the Department of Health and Social Services for Northern Ireland.

DEFINITIONS
"Authority": s.1(1).

GENERAL NOTE
This section abolishes the Occupational Pensions Board. This is consequent upon the new approach to contracting out contained in this Act.
[Standing Committee D, June 20, 1995, col. 735].

Minor and consequential amendments

Minor and consequential amendments related to sections 136 to 150

151. Schedule 5 (which makes amendments related to sections 136 to 150) shall have effect.

PART IV

MISCELLANEOUS AND GENERAL

Transfer values

Extension of scope of right to cash equivalent

152.—(1) Section 93 of the Pension Schemes Act 1993 (scope of provisions relating to transfer values) is amended as follows.
(2) For subsection (1)(a) there is substituted—
"(a) to any member of an occupational pension scheme—
(i) whose pensionable service has terminated at least one year before normal pension age, and
(ii) who on the date on which his pensionable service terminated had accrued rights to benefit under the scheme,
except a member of a salary related occupational pension scheme whose pensionable service terminated before 1st January 1986 and in respect of whom prescribed requirements are satisfied".
(3) After subsection (1) there is inserted—
"(1A) For the purposes of this section and the following provisions of this Chapter, an occupational pension scheme is salary related if—
(a) the scheme is not a money purchase scheme, and
(b) the scheme does not fall within a prescribed class.
(1B) Regulations may—
(a) provide for this Chapter not to apply in relation to a person of a prescribed description, or
(b) apply this Chapter with prescribed modifications to occupational pension schemes—
(i) which are not money purchase schemes, but
(ii) where some of the benefits that may be provided are money purchase benefits."

GENERAL NOTE
This section extends rights to cash equivalents under Chapter IV of the Pension Schemes Act 1993. It does so by limiting the exclusion from the right of those whose pensionable service terminated before January 1, 1986 to persons in salary-related pension schemes. Thus those in money purchase pension schemes whose pensionable service terminated before January 1, 1986 are now given the right to a cash equivalent, as are those in schemes of a prescribed class. Moreover, salary-related schemes will have to comply with prescribed requirements if the right is to be excluded.
Government thinking with regard to the right to transfer values and the timing of their payment is to be found in *Hansard*, H.L. Vol. 561, col. 1090.
[Standing Committee D, June 20, 1995, col. 735].

Right to guaranteed cash equivalent

153. After section 93 of the Pension Schemes Act 1993 there is inserted—

"Salary related schemes: right to statement of entitlement

93A.—(1) The trustees or managers of a salary related to occupational pension scheme must, on the application of any member, provide the member with a written statement (in this Chapter referred to as a "statement of entitlement") of the amount of the cash equivalent at the guarantee date of any benefits which have accrued to or in respect of him under the applicable rules.

(2) In this section—

"the applicable rules" has the same meaning as in section 94;

"the guarantee date" means the date by reference to which the value of the cash equivalent is calculated, and must be—

(a) within the prescribed period beginning with the date of the application, and

(b) within the prescribed period ending with the date on which the statement of entitlement is provided to the member.

(3) Regulations may make provision in relation to applications for a statement of entitlement, including, in particular, provision as to the period which must elapse after the making of such an application before a member may make a further such application.

(4) If, in the case of any scheme, a statement of entitlement has not been provided under this section, section 10 of the Pensions Act 1995 (power of the Regulatory Authority to impose civil penalties) applies to any trustee or manager who has failed to take all such steps as are reasonable to secure compliance with this section."

General Note

This section inserts a new s.93A into the Pension Schemes Act 1993, whereby a member is entitled on application to a statement of entitlement showing him the amount of his cash equivalent. Regulations will control the date at which a statement has to be made and other matters concerning the application, including the frequency with which applications can be made. Failure to give the statement may incur a penalty under s.10 of this Act.

[Standing Committee D, June 20, 1995, col. 744].

Right to guaranteed cash equivalent: supplementary

154.—(1) In paragraph (a) of section 94(1) of the Pension Schemes Act 1993—

(a) after "occupational pension scheme" there is inserted "other than a salary related scheme", and

(b) after "terminates" there is inserted "(whether before or after 1st January 1986)".

(2) After that paragraph there is inserted—

"(aa) a member of a salary related occupational pension scheme who has received a statement of entitlement and has made a relevant application within three months beginning with the guarantee date in respect of that statement acquires a right to his guaranteed cash equivalent".

(3) After that subsection there is inserted—

"(1A) For the purposes of subsection (1)(aa), a person's "guaranteed cash equivalent" is the amount stated in the statement of entitlement mentioned in that subsection."

(4) In subsection (2) of that section, after the definition of "the applicable rules" there is inserted—

"the guarantee date" has the same meaning as in section 93A(2)".
(5) After that subsection there is inserted—
"(3) Regulations may provide that, in prescribed circumstances, subsection (1)(aa) does not apply to members of salary related occupational pension schemes or applies to them with prescribed modifications."

GENERAL NOTE
This section amends the Pension Schemes Act 1993 in a number of respects consequent upon the amendments to it contained in s.153 above, the most important of which is to give the member the right to a cash equivalent of the amount contained in the statement of entitlement if an application is made within three months of it being supplied.
[Standing Committee D, June 20, 1995, col. 746].

Penalties

Breach of regulations under the Pension Schemes Act 1993

155.—(1) For section 168 of the Pension Schemes Act 1993 (penalties for breach of regulations) there is substituted—

"Breach of regulations
168.—(1) Regulations under any provision of this Act (other than Chapter II of Part VII) may make such provision as is referred to in subsection (2) or (4) for the contravention of any provision contained in regulations made or having effect as if made under any provision of this Act.
(2) The regulations may provide for the contravention to be an offence under this Act and for the recovery on summary conviction of a fine not exceeding level 5 on the standard scale.
(3) An offence under any provision of the regulations may be charged by reference to any day or longer period of time; and a person may be convicted of a second or subsequent offence under such a provision by reference to any period of time following the preceding conviction of the offence.
(4) The regulations may provide for a person who has contravened the provision to pay to the Regulatory Authority, within a prescribed period, a penalty not exceeding an amount specified in the regulations; and the regulations must specify different amounts in the case of individuals from those specified in other cases and any amount so specified may not exceed the amount for the time being specified in the case of individuals or, as the case may be, others in section 10(2)(a) of the Pensions Act 1995.
(5) Regulations made by virtue of subsection (4) do not affect the amount of any penalty recoverable under that subsection by reason of an act or omission occurring before the regulations are made.
(6) Where—
(a) apart from this subsection, a penalty under subsection (4) is recoverable from a body corporate or Scottish partnership by reason of any act or omission of the body or partnership as a trustee of a trust scheme, and
(b) the act or omission was done with the consent or connivance of, or is attributable to any neglect on the part of, any persons mentioned in subsection (7),
such a penalty is recoverable from each of those persons who consented to or connived in the act or omission or to whose neglect the act or omission was attributable.

(7) The persons referred to in subsection (6)(b)—
(a) in relation to a body corporate, are—
    (i) any director, manager, secretary, or other similar officer of the body, or a person purporting to act in any such capacity, and
    (ii) where the affairs of a body corporate are managed by its members, any member in connection with his functions of management, and
(b) in relation to a Scottish partnership, are the partners.

(8) Where the Regulatory Authority requires any person to pay a penalty by virtue of subsection (6), they may not also require the body corporate, or Scottish partnership, in question to pay a penalty in respect of the same act or omission.

(9) A penalty under subsection (4) is recoverable by the Authority and any such penalty recovered by the Authority must be paid to the Secretary of State.

(10) Where by reason of the contravention of any provision contained in regulations made, or having effect as if made, under this Act—
(a) a person is convicted of an offence under this Act, or
(b) a person pays a penalty under subsection (4),
then, in respect of that contravention, he shall not, in a case within paragraph (a), be liable to pay such a penalty or, in a case within paragraph (b), be convicted of such an offence.

(11) In this section "contravention" includes failure to comply, and "Scottish partnership" means a partnership constituted under the law of Scotland.

Offence in connection with the Registrar

168A.—(1) Any person who knowingly or recklessly provides the Registrar with information which is false or misleading in a material particular is guilty of an offence if the information—
(a) is provided in purported compliance with a requirement under section 6, or
(b) is provided otherwise than as mentioned in paragraph (a) above but in circumstances in which the person providing the information intends, or could reasonably be expected to know, that it would be used by the Registrar for the purpose of discharging his functions under this Act.

(2) Any Person guilty of an offence under subsection (1) is liable—
(a) on summary conviction, to a fine not exceeding the statutory maximum,
(b) on conviction on indictment, to imprisonment or a fine, or both".

(2) In section 186 of that Act (Parliamentary control of orders and regulations), in subsection (3), after paragraph (c) there is inserted "or
(d) regulations made by virtue of section 168(2)".

GENERAL NOTE

This section amends s.168 of the Pension Schemes Act 1993, substituting new provisions for fines on summary conviction for offences under regulations made under that Act; and providing for a penalty to be levied at the instance of the Authority in certain circumstances. This penalty may pierce the corporate veil, under s.168(6) and (7). Double recovery is prevented under s.168(8) and (10).

A new offence is also created of knowingly or recklessly providing the Registrar with false or misleading information, and provision made for fines or imprisonment after conviction. For commentary see the General Note to ss.111(4) and (6) above.

Pensions Ombudsman

Employment of staff by the Pensions Ombudsman

156. For section 145(4) of the Pension Schemes Act 1993 (staff of the Pensions Ombudsman), there is substituted—

"(4A) The Pensions Ombudsman may (with the approval of the Secretary of State as to numbers) appoint such persons to be employees of his as he thinks fit, on such terms and conditions as to remuneration and other matters as the Pensions Ombudsman may with the approval of the Secretary of State determine.

(4B) The Secretary of State may, on such terms as to payment by the Pensions Ombudsman as the Secretary of State thinks fit, make available to the Pensions Ombudsman such additional staff and such other facilities as he thinks fit.

(4C) Any function of the Pensions Ombudsman, other than the determination of complaints made and disputes referred under this Part, may be performed by any—

(a) employee appointed by the Pensions Ombudsman under subsection (4A), or

(b) member of staff made available to him by the Secretary of State under subsection (4B),

who is authorised for that purpose by the Pensions Ombudsman."

GENERAL NOTE

For the creation of the office of Pensions Ombudsman, see s.145 of the Pension Schemes Act 1993.

Jurisdiction of Pensions Ombudsman

157.—(1) Sections 146 to 151 of the Pension Schemes Act 1993 are amended as shown in subsections (2) to (11).

(2) In section 146 (investigations concerning the trustees or managers of schemes), for subsections (1) to (4) there is substituted—

"(1) The Pensions-Ombudsman may investigate and determine the following complaints and disputes—

(a) a complaint made to him by or on behalf of an actual or potential beneficiary of an occupational or personal pension scheme who alleges that he has sustained injustice in consequence of maladministration in connection with any act or omission of a person responsible for the management of the scheme,

(b) a complaint made to him—

(i) by or on behalf of a person responsible for the management of an occupational pension scheme who in connection with any act or omission of another person responsible for the management of the scheme, alleges maladministration of the scheme, or

(ii) by or on behalf of the trustees or managers of an occupational pension scheme who in connection with any act or omission of any trustee or manager of another such scheme, allege maladministration of the other scheme,

and in any case falling within sub-paragraph (ii) references in this Part to the scheme to which the complaint relates is to the other scheme referred to in that paragraph,

(c) any dispute of fact or law which arises in relation to an occupational or personal pension scheme between—

(i) a person responsible for the management of the scheme, and

(ii) an actual or potential beneficiary,

and which is referred to him by or on behalf of the actual or potential beneficiary, and

(d) any dispute of fact or law which arises between the trustees or managers of an occupational pension scheme and—

(i) another person responsible for the management of the scheme, or

(ii) any trustee or manager of another such scheme,

and which is referred to him by or on behalf of the person referred to in sub-paragraph (i) or (ii); and in any case falling within sub-paragraph (ii) references in this Part to the scheme to which the reference relates is to the scheme first mentioned in that paragraph.

(2) Complaints and references made to the Pensions Ombudsman must be made to him in writing.

(3) For the purposes of this Part, the following persons (subject to subsection (4)) are responsible for the management of an occupational pension scheme—

(a) the trustees or managers, and

(b) the employer;

but, in relation to a person falling within one of those paragraphs, references in this Part to another person responsible for the management of the same scheme are to a person falling within the other paragraph.

(3A) For the purposes of this Part, a person is responsible for the management of a personal pension scheme if he is a trustee or manager of the scheme.

(4) Regulations may provide that, subject to any prescribed modifications or exceptions, this Part shall apply in the case of an occupational or personal pension scheme in relation to any prescribed person or body of persons where the person or body—

(a) is not a trustee or manager or employer, but

(b) is concerned with the financing or administration of, or the provision of benefits under, the scheme,

as if for the purposes of this Part he were a person responsible for the management of the scheme".

(3) In subsection (7) of that section, for "authorised complainants" there is substituted "actual or potential beneficiaries".

(4) In section 147 (death, insolvency etc.), in subsections (1) and (2), for "authorised complainant" there is substituted "actual or potential beneficiary" and for "the authorised complainant's" there is substituted "his".

(5) In subsection (3) of that section, for "an authorised complainant" there is substituted "a person by whom, or on whose behalf, a complaint or reference has been made under this Part".

(6) In section 148 (staying court proceedings), in subsection (5), for paragraphs (a) and (b) there is substituted—

"(a) the person by whom, or on whose behalf, the complaint or reference has been made,

(b) any person responsible for the management of the scheme to which the complaint or reference relates".

(7) In section 149 (procedure on investigation), in subsection (1)(a), for "the trustees and managers of the scheme concerned" there is substituted "any person (other than the person by whom, or on whose behalf, the complaint or reference was made) responsible for the management of the scheme to which the complaint or reference relates".

(8) In section 150 (investigations: further provisions), in subsection (1)(a), for "any trustee or manager of the scheme concerned" there is substituted

"any person responsible for the management of the scheme to which the complaint or reference relates".

(9) In section 151 (determinations of Pensions Ombudsman), for subsection (1)(a) and (b) there is substituted—

"(a) to the person by whom, or on whose behalf, the complaint or reference was made, and

(b) to any person (if different) responsible for the management of the scheme to which the complaint or reference relates".

(10) In subsection (2) of that section, for "the trustees or managers of the scheme concerned" there is substituted "any person responsible for the management of the scheme to which the complaint or reference relates".

(11) In subsection (3) of that section, for paragraphs (a) to (c) there is substituted—

"(a) the person by whom, or on whose behalf, the complaint or reference was made,

(b) any person (if different) responsible for the management of the scheme to which the complaint or reference relates, and

(c) any person claiming under a person falling within paragraph (a) or (b)".

(12) In Part I of Schedule 1 to the Tribunals and Inquiries Act 1992 (tribunals under the direct supervision of the Council on Tribunals), in paragraph 35(e), for "section 146(2)" there is substituted "section 146(1)(c) and (d)".

GENERAL NOTE

This section contains important amendments to the powers of the Pensions Ombudsman as set out in s.146 of the Pension Schemes Act 1993. The scope of complainant is widened to include actual and potential beneficiaries of a scheme, rather than being confined to members. It also widens the scope of complaint to include complaints made by one trustee against another, by trustees of one scheme against the trustees of another scheme, and by employers against trustees. Regulations may widen the ambit of complaints to insurers of schemes. But the nature of the complaint is still the same, namely "maladministration", and this will restrict the ambit of the Ombudsman's enquiries.

Amongst other consequential alterations the parties to a proceeding are widened for the purposes of s.148 of the Pension Schemes Act 1993, so that the ambit of those entitled to apply for a stay of legal proceedings commenced after the Pensions Ombudsman has started his investigation is widened.

[Standing Committee D, June 20, 1995, col. 749].

Costs and expenses

158. In section 149 of the Pension Schemes Act 1993—

(a) after subsection (3)(b) there is inserted "and

(c) for the payment by the Ombudsman of such travelling and other allowances (including compensation for loss of remunerative time) as the Secretary of State may determine, to—

(i) actual or potential beneficiaries of a scheme to which a complaint or reference relates, or

(ii) persons appearing and being heard on behalf of such actual or potential beneficiaries,

who attend at the request of the Ombudsman any oral hearing held in connection with an investigation into the complaint or dispute.", and

(b) at the end of subsection (3)(a), "and" is omitted.

GENERAL NOTE

This provision, inserted into s.149 of the Pension Schemes Act 1993, will enable the Secretary of State to make regulations to entitle the Pensions Ombudsman to make an award of travelling

expenses out of his own funds to those who appear at oral hearings before him.
[Standing Committee D, June 20, 1995, col. 758].

Disclosing information

159.—(1) In section 149 of the Pension Schemes Act 1993, after subsection (4) there is added—

"(5) The Pensions Ombudsman may disclose any information which he obtains for the purposes of an investigation under this Part to any person to whom subsection (6) applies, if the Ombudsman considers that the disclosure would enable or assist that person to discharge any of his functions.

(6) This subsection applies to the following—
　(a) the Regulatory Authority,
　(b) the Pensions Compensation Board,
　(c) the Registrar,
　(d) any department of the Government (including the government of Northern Ireland),
　(e) the Bank of England,
　(f) the Friendly Societies Commission,
　(g) the Building Societies Commission,
　(h) an inspector appointed by the Secretary of State under Part XIV of the Companies Act 1985 or section 94 or 177 of the Financial Services Act 1986,
　(j) an inspector appointed by the Department of Economic Development in Northern Ireland under Part XV of the Companies (Northern Ireland) Order 1986,
　(k) a person authorised under section 106 of the Financial Services Act 1986 to exercise powers conferred by section 105 of that Act,
　(l) a designated agency or transferee body or the competent authority within the meaning of that Act, and
　(m) a recognised self-regulating organisation, recognised professional body, recognised investment exchange or recognised clearing house, within the meaning of that Act.

(7) The Secretary of State may by order—
　(a) amend subsection (6) by adding any person or removing any person for the time being specified in that subsection, or
　(b) restrict the circumstances in which, or impose conditions subject to which, disclosure may be made to any person for the time being specified in that subsection."

(2) In section 151 of that Act, in subsection (7)(a), after "this section" there is inserted—

"(aa) in disclosing any information under section 149(5)".

GENERAL NOTE

This section inserts into the Pension Schemes Act 1993 a power for the Pensions Ombudsman to disclose information to the persons specified in the new s.149(6) of that Act.
[Standing Committee D, June 20, 1995, col. 759].

Interest on late payment of benefit

160. After section 151 of the Pension Schemes Act 1993 there is inserted—

"Interest on late payment of benefit
151A. Where under this Part the Pensions Ombudsman directs a person responsible for the management of an occupational or personal pen-

sion scheme to make any payment in respect of benefit under the scheme which, in his opinion, ought to have been paid earlier, his direction may also require the payment of interest at the prescribed rate".

GENERAL NOTE
This section may well be unnecessary, because one would have thought that the power to order trustees to pay interest was subsumed in the steps which the Pensions Ombudsman could order the trustees or managers of a scheme to take under s.151(2) of the Pension Schemes Act 1993. This is particularly so because interest and dividends are the life blood of the funding of pension schemes, and therefore should be reflected in the late payment of benefits as a matter of course. This amendment puts the matter beyond doubt however.

Modification and winding up of schemes

Repeal of sections 136 to 143 of the Pension Schemes Act 1993

161. Sections 136 to 141 (modification) and 142 and 143 (winding up) of the Pension Schemes Act 1993 are repealed.

GENERAL NOTE
For the powers conferred on trustees and the Authority to modify occupational pension schemes see ss.67 to 71 above. The powers conferred in these sections are less wide than those previously conferred on the Occupational Pensions Board under the sections now repealed, and the power of the Occupational Pensions Board to wind up schemes has not been replaced, for reasons which have not been explained.

Personal pensions

Annual increase in rate of personal pension

162.—(1) This section applies to any pension provided to give effect to protected rights of a member of a personal pension scheme if—
  (a) there is in force, or was in force at any time after the appointed day, an appropriate scheme certificate issued in accordance with Chapter I of Part III (certification) of the Pension Schemes Act 1993, and
  (b) apart from this section, the annual rate of the pension would not be increased each year by at least the appropriate percentage of that rate.
(2) Where a pension to which this section applies, or any part of it, is attributable to contributions in respect of employment carried on or after the appointed day—
  (a) the annual rate of the pension, or
  (b) if only part of the pension is attributable to contributions in respect of employment carried on or after the appointed day, so much of the annual rate as is attributable to that part,
must be increased annually by at least the appropriate percentage.

DEFINITIONS
  "annual rate": s.163.
  "appointed day": s.163.
  "appropriate percentage": s.163.
  "pension": s.163.
  "personal pension scheme": s.176.
  "protected rights": s.163.

GENERAL NOTE
This section provides for protected rights under personal pension schemes to be increased annually by the appropriate percentage. Presumably the money to pay for this will have to come from within the scheme, since no other source is provided. Since the personal pension scheme more often than not comprises a personal pot of money the point of this provision is not clear.
[Standing Committee D, June 20, 1995, col. 762].

Section 162: supplementary

163.—(1) The first increase required by section 162 in the rate of a pension must take effect not later than the first anniversary of the date on which the pension is first paid; and subsequent increases must take effect at intervals of not more than twelve months.

(2) Where the first such increase is to take effect on a date when the pension has been in payment for a period of less than 12 months, the increase must be of an amount at least equal to one twelfth of the amount of the increase so required (apart from this subsection) for each complete month in that period.

(3) In section 162 and this section—
"annual rate", in relation to a pension, means the annual rate of the pension, as previously increased under the rules of the scheme or under section 162,
"the appointed day" means the day appointed under section 180 for the commencement of section 162,
"appropriate percentage", in relation to an increase in the whole or part of the annual rate of a pension, means the revaluation percentage for the revaluation period the reference period for which ends with the last preceding 30th September before the increase is made (expressions used in this definition having the same meaning as in paragraph 2 of Schedule 3 to the Pension Schemes Act 1993 (methods of revaluing accrued pension benefits)),
"pension", in relation to a scheme, means any pension in payment under the scheme and includes an annuity,
"protected rights" has the meaning given by section 10 of the Pension Schemes Act 1993 (money purchase benefits).

Power to reject notice choosing appropriate personal pension scheme

164. In section 44 of the Pension Schemes Act 1993 (earner's chosen scheme)—
(a) in subsection (1), after paragraph (b) there is inserted—
"then, unless the Secretary of State rejects the notice on either or both of the grounds mentioned in subsection (1A)", and
(b) after that subsection there is inserted—
"(1A) The grounds referred to in subsection (1) are that the Secretary of State is of the opinion—
(a) that section 31(5) is not being complied with in respect of any members of the scheme,
(b) that, having regard to any other provisions of sections 26 to 32 and 43 to 45, it is inexpedient to allow the scheme to be the chosen scheme of any further earners".

GENERAL NOTE
These amendments to s.44 of the Pension Schemes Act 1993 enable the Secretary of State to veto a choice of personal pension scheme on specified grounds. Failure to comply with invest-

ment requirements is singled out as a particular ground on which he may do so, by the particular reference to s.31(5) of that Act.
[Standing Committee D, June 20, 1995, col. 766].

Levy

Levy

165. For section 175 of the Pension Schemes Act 1993 (levies towards meeting certain costs and grants) there is substituted—

"**Levies towards certain expenditure**
175.—(1) For the purpose of meeting expenditure—
   (a) under section 6,
   (b) under Part X and section 174, or
   (c) of the Regulatory Authority (including the establishment of the authority and, if the authority are appointed as Registrar under section 6 of this Act, their expenditure as Registrar),
regulations may make provision for imposing levies in respect of prescribed occupational or prescribed personal pension schemes.
   (2) Any levy imposed under subsection (1) is payable to the Secretary of State by or on behalf of—
   (a) the administrators of any prescribed public service pension scheme,
   (b) the trustees or managers of any other prescribed occupational or prescribed personal pension scheme, or
   (c) any other prescribed person,
at prescribed rates and at prescribed times.
   (3) Regulations made by virtue of subsection (1)—
   (a) in determining the amount of any levy in respect of the Regulatory Authority, must take account (among other things) of any amounts paid to the Secretary of State under section 168(4) of this Act or section 10 of the Pensions Act 1995, and
   (b) in determining the amount of expenditure in respect of which any levy is to be imposed, may take one year with another and, accordingly, may have regard to expenditure estimated to be incurred in current or future periods and to actual expenditure incurred in previous periods (including periods ending before the coming into force of this subsection).
   (4) Regulations may make provision for imposing a levy in respect of prescribed occupational pension schemes for the purpose of meeting expenditure of the Pensions Compensation Board (including the establishment of the Board).
   (5) Any levy imposed under subsection (4) is payable to the Board by or on behalf of—
   (a) the trustees of any prescribed occupational pension scheme, or
   (b) any other prescribed person,
at prescribed times and at a rate, not exceeding the prescribed rate, determined by the Board.
   (6) In determining the amount of expenditure in respect of which any levy under subsection (4) is to be imposed, the Board, and regulations made by virtue of subsection (5), may take one year with another and, accordingly, may have regard to expenditure estimated to be incurred in current or future periods and to actual expenditure incurred in previous periods (including periods ending before the coming into force of this subsection).
   (7) Notice of the rates determined by the Board under subsection (5) must be given to prescribed persons in the prescribed manner.

(8) An amount payable by a person on account of a levy imposed under this section shall be a debt due from him to the appropriate person, that is—

(a) if the levy is imposed under subsection (1), the Secretary of State, and

(b) if the levy is imposed under subsection (4), the Board,

and an amount so payable shall be recoverable by the appropriate person accordingly or, if the appropriate person so determines, be recoverable by the Registrar on behalf of the appropriate person.

(9) Without prejudice to the generality of subsections (1) and (4), regulations under this section may include provision relating to—

(a) the collection and recovery of amounts payable by way of levy under this section, or

(b) the circumstances in which any such amount may be waived."

GENERAL NOTE

Subs. (1)

No one supposed that government money would be made available to pay for the Authority or the Compensation Board, or even for setting either of them up. The amendments made to s.175 of the Pension Schemes Act 1993 by this section is the fulfilment of those expectations. It is clear that the whole of the costs of the former of these two bodies is to be paid for by levies under s.175, and we may confidently expect that regulations will be put in place to provide for a levy in respect of the Compensation Board also.

For Government reasons for not meeting the cost of the Authority from the Treasury: see *Hansard*, H.L. Vol. 561, col. 144.

[Standing Committee D, June 20, 1995, col. 768].

Pensions on divorce, etc.

Pensions on divorce etc.

166.—(1) In the Matrimonial Causes Act 1973, after section 25A there is inserted—

"Pensions

25B.—(1) The matters to which the court is to have regard under section 25(2) above include—

(a) in the case of paragraph (a), any benefits under a pension scheme which a party to the marriage has or is likely to have, and

(b) in the case of paragraph (h), any benefits under a pension scheme which, by reason of the dissolution or annulment of the marriage, a party to the marriage will lose the chance of acquiring,

and, accordingly, in relation to benefits under a pension scheme, section 25(2)(a) above shall have effect as if "in the foreseeable future" were omitted.

(2) In any proceedings for a financial provision order under section 23 above in a case where a party to the marriage has, or is likely to have, any benefit under a pension scheme, the court shall, in addition to considering any other matter which it is required to consider apart from this subsection, consider—

(a) whether, having regard to any matter to which it is required to have regard in the proceedings by virtue of subsection (1) above, such an order (whether deferred or not) should be made, and

(b) where the court determines to make such an order, how the terms of the order should be affected, having regard to any such matter.

(3) The following provisions apply where, having regard to any benefits under a pension scheme, the court determines to make an order under section 23 above.

(4) To the extent to which the order is made having regard to any benefits under a pension scheme, the order may require the trustees or managers of the pension scheme in question, if at any time any payment

in respect of any benefits under the scheme becomes due to the party with pension rights, to make a payment for the benefit of the other party.

(5) The amount of any payment which, by virtue of subsection (4) above, the trustees or managers are required to make under the order at any time shall not exceed the amount of the payment which is due at that time to the party with pension rights.

(6) Any such payment by the trustees or managers—

(a) shall discharge so much of the trustees or managers liability to the party with pension rights as corresponds to the amount of the payment, and

(b) shall be treated for all purposes as a payment made by the party with pension rights in or towards the discharge of his liability under the order.

(7) Where the party with pension rights may require any benefits which he has or is likely to have under the scheme to be commuted, the order may require him to commute the whole or part of those benefits; and this section applies to the payment of any amount commuted in pursuance of the order as it applies to other payments in respect of benefits under the scheme.

Pensions: lump sums

25C.—(1) The power of the court under section 23 above to order a party to a marriage to pay a lump sum to the other party includes, where the benefits which the party with pension rights has or is likely to have under a pension scheme include any lump sum payable in respect of his death, power to make any of the following provision by the order.

(2) The court may—

(a) if the trustees or managers of the pension scheme in question have power to determine the person to whom the sum, or any part of it, is to be paid, require them to pay the whole or part of that sum, when it becomes due, to the other party,

(b) if the party with pension rights has power to nominate the person to whom the sum, or any part of it, is to be paid, require the party with pension rights to nominate the other party in respect of the whole or part of that sum,

(c) in any other case, require the trustees or managers of the pension scheme in question to pay the whole or part of that sum, when it becomes due, for the benefit of the other party instead of to the person to whom, apart from the order, it would be paid.

(3) Any payment by the trustees or managers under an order made under section 23 above by virtue of this section shall discharge so much of the trustees, or managers, liability in respect of the party with pension rights as corresponds to the amount of the payment.

Pensions: supplementary

25D.—(1) Where—

(a) an order made under section 23 above by virtue of section 25B or 25C above imposes any requirement on the trustees or managers of a pension scheme ("the first scheme") and the party with pension rights acquires transfer credits under another pension scheme ("the new scheme") which are derived (directly or indirectly) from a transfer from the first scheme of all his accrued rights under that scheme (including transfer credits allowed by that scheme), and

(b) the trustees or managers of the new scheme have been given notice in accordance with regulations,

the order shall have effect as if it has been made instead in respect of the trustees or managers of the new scheme; and in this subsection "transfer credits" has the same meaning as in the Pension Schemes Act 1993.

(2) Regulations may—

(a) in relation to any provision of sections 25B or 25C above which authorises the court making an order under section 23 above to require the trustees or managers of a pension scheme to make a payment for the benefit of the other party, make provision as to the person to whom, and the terms on which, the payment is to be made,

(b) require notices to be given in respect of changes of circumstances relevant to such orders which include provision made by virtue of sections 25B and 25C above,

(c) make provision for the trustees or managers of any pension scheme to provide, for the purposes of orders under section 23 above, information as to the value of any benefits under the scheme,

(d) make provision for the recovery of the administrative expenses of—

(i) complying with such orders, so far as they include provision made by virtue of sections 25B and 25C above, and

(ii) providing such information,

from the party with pension rights or the other party,

(e) make provision for the value of any benefits under a pension scheme to be calculated and verified, for the purposes of orders under section 23 above, in a prescribed manner,

and regulations made by virtue of paragraph (e) above may provide for that value to be calculated and verified in accordance with guidance which is prepared and from time to time revised by a prescribed person and approved by the Secretary of State.

(3) In this section and sections 25B and 25C above—

(a) references to a pension scheme include—

(i) a retirement annuity contract, or

(ii) an annuity, or insurance policy, purchased or transferred for the purpose of giving effect to rights under a pension scheme,

(b) in relation to such a contract or annuity, references to the trustees or managers shall be read as references to the provider of the annuity,

(c) in relation to such a policy, references to the trustees or managers shall be read as references to the insurer, and in section 25B(1) and (2) above, references to benefits under a pension scheme include any benefits by way of pension, whether under a pension scheme or not.

(4) In this section and sections 25B and 25C above—

"the party with pension rights" means the party to the marriage who has or is likely to have benefits under a pension scheme and "the other party" means the other party to the marriage,

"pension scheme" means an occupational pension scheme or a personal pension scheme (applying the definitions in section 1 of the Pension Schemes Act 1993, but as if the reference to employed earners in the definition of "personal pension scheme" were to any earners),

"prescribed" means prescribed by regulations, and

"regulations" means regulations made by the Lord Chancellor;

and the power to make regulations under this section shall be exercisable by statutory instrument, which shall be subject to annulment in pursuance of a resolution of either House of Parliament."

(2) In section 25(2)(h) of that Act (loss of chance to acquire benefits) "(for example, a pension)" is omitted.

(3) In section 31 of that Act (variation, discharge, etc. of orders)—

(a) in subsection (2), after paragraph (d) there is inserted—
"(dd) any deferred order made by virtue of section 23(1)(c) (lump sums) which includes provision made by virtue of—
(i) section 25B(4), or
(ii) section 25C,
(provision in respect of pension rights)", and
(b) after subsection (2A) there is inserted—
"(2B) Where the court has made an order referred to in subsection (2)(dd)(ii) above, this section shall cease to apply to the order on the death of either of the parties to the marriage".

(4) Nothing in the provisions mentioned in subsection (5) applies to a court exercising its powers under section 23 of the Matrimonial Causes Act 1973 (financial provision in connection with divorce proceedings, etc.) in respect of any benefits under a pension scheme (within the meaning of section 25B(1) of the Matrimonial Causes Act 1973) which a party to the marriage has or is likely to have.

(5) The provisions referred to in subsection (4) are—
(a) section 203(1) and (2) of the Army Act 1955, 203(1) and (2) of the Air Force Act 1955, 128G(1) and (2) of the Naval Discipline Act 1957 or 159(4) and (4A) of the Pension Schemes Act 1993 (which prevent assignment, or orders being made restraining a person from receiving anything which he is prevented from assigning),
(b) section 91 of this Act,
(c) any provision of any enactment (whether passed or made before or after this Act is passed) corresponding to any of the enactments mentioned in paragraphs (a) and (b), and
(d) any provision of the scheme in question corresponding to any of those enactments.

(6) Subsections (3) to (7) of section 25B, and section 25C of the Matrimonial Causes Act 1973, as inserted by this section, do not affect the powers of the court under section 31 of that Act (variation, discharge, etc.) in relation to any order made before the commencement of this section.

GENERAL NOTE

This deceptively simple section puts to rest an argument which has troubled family lawyers for many years, and divorce lawyers before them. One of the chief assets which a spouse may have is his (and now her) pension rights. After the family home this is likely to be the most valuable asset which the couple has between them. The court has always wished to divide the assets of husband and wife fairly on divorce, but successive governments have refrained from introducing the necessary legislation, largely owing to the objections of the actuarial profession, in that it was felt that to make orders against a scheme would upset the actuarial calculations which lie behind the benefits payable under it. This has been largely avoided as will be seen later. A new s.25B is inserted into the Matrimonial Causes Act 1973. Subsection (1) of the new section provides for benefits which either spouse has or is likely to have under a pension scheme to be taken into account by the court, which is also to take into account any benefits which a party to the marriage is likely to lose under a scheme. A pension scheme is defined in s.25D(4) as meaning an occupational or personal pension scheme, applying the definition in s.1 of the Pension Schemes Act 1993 with a minor modification.

The new s.25B(2) requires the court to consider whether to make an order in respect of the pension benefits. If it does so, the order may be made under subs. (4) directly against the trustees or managers of the scheme and may require that where any payment is due at any time under the scheme to one party to a marriage it shall be paid to the other party. This overcomes the objections to an order being made in that the rights of the receiving spouse are contingent on the subsistence of the right of the yielding spouse (unless an order had been made, where the whole of the benefit is ordered to be payable to the receiving spouse). This maintains the actuarial value of the benefit vis-à-vis the scheme, since the life contingent on which it is paid is not altered.

The new s.25B(5) limits the amount which the trustees or managers of a scheme can be ordered to pay by reference to the payment otherwise due to the yielding spouse.

The new s.25B(6) provides for the trustees or managers to be *pro tanto* discharged on the making of a payment which they are ordered to make. Section 25B(7) provides that a yielding party may be ordered to commute the whole or any part of his pension if he has the right to do so.

The new s.25C empowers the court to order trustees or managers of a scheme who have a discretion in respect of a lump sum to exercise it in favour of the receiving party. They may order trustees who have no discretion to make a similar payment. They may order a yielding party with the power to nominate a beneficiary of a lump sum to nominate the receiving party. One or other of these types of order would be expected to be made in respect of a lump sum payable on the death of the yielding party during active membership of a scheme, or on the death of that party within five years of the pension commencing, if the payment of pension is guaranteed for that time.

The new s.25D provides for a miscellany of matters, including the knotty matter of the transfer of pension rights. Here, for the order to bite, the new trustees will have to be given notice in accordance with regulations yet to be made.

[Standing Committee D, June 22, 1995, cols. 777, 815].

Pensions on divorce, etc.: Scotland

167.—(1) In section 8(1) (orders for financial provision) of the Family Law (Scotland) Act 1985 ("the 1985 Act"), after paragraph (b) there is inserted—

"(ba) an order under section 12A(2) or (3) of this Act;".

(2) In section 10 of the 1985 Act (sharing of value of matrimonial property)—

(a) in subsection (5)—

(i) after "party" there is inserted "(a)"; and

(ii) for "or occupational pension scheme or similar arrangement" there is substituted—

"or similar arrangement; and

(b) in any benefits under a pension scheme which either party has or may have (including such benefits payable in respect of the death of either party),

which is"; and

(b) after subsection (7) there is inserted—

"(8) The Secretary of State may by regulations make provision—

(a) for the value of any benefits under a pension scheme to be calculated and verified, for the purposes of this Act, in a prescribed manner;

(b) for the trustees or managers of any pension scheme to provide, for the purposes of this Act, information as to that value, and for the recovery of the administrative expenses of providing such information from either party,

and regulations made by virtue of paragraph (a) above may provide for that value to be calculated and verified in accordance with guidance which is prepared and from time to time revised by a prescribed body and approved by the Secretary of State.

(9) Regulations under subsection (8) above shall be made by statutory instrument which shall be subject to annulment in pursuance of a resolution of either House of Parliament.

(10) In this section—

"benefits under a pension scheme" includes any benefits by way of pension, whether under a pension scheme or not;

"pension scheme" means—

(a) an occupational pension scheme or a personal pension scheme (applying the definitions in section 1 of the Pension Schemes Act 1993, but as if the reference to employed earners in the definition of "personal pension scheme" were to any earners);

(b) a retirement annuity contract; or

(c) an annuity, or insurance policy, purchased or transferred for the purpose of giving effect to rights under a pension scheme falling within paragraph (a) above; and

"prescribed" means prescribed by regulations.

(11) In this section, references to the trustees or managers of a pension scheme—

(a) in relation to a contract or annuity referred to in paragraph (b) or (c) of the definition of "pension scheme" in subsection (10) above, shall be read as references to the provider of the annuity;

(b) in relation to an insurance policy referred to in paragraph (c) of that definition, shall be read as a reference to the insurer".

(3) After section 12 of the 1985 Act there is inserted—

"Orders for payment of capital sum: pensions lump sums

12A.—(1) This section applies where the court makes an order under section 8(2) of this Act for payment of a capital sum (a "capital sum order") by a party to the marriage ("the liable party") in circumstances where—

(a) the matrimonial property within the meaning of section 10 of this Act includes any rights or interests in benefits under a pension scheme which the liable party has or may have (whether such benefits are payable to him or in respect of his death); and

(b) those benefits include a lump sum payable to him or in respect of his death.

(2) Where the benefits referred to in subsection (1) above include a lump sum payable to the liable party, the court, on making the capital sum order, may make an order requiring the trustees or managers of the pension scheme in question to pay the whole or part of that sum, when it becomes due, to the other party to the marriage ("the other party").

(3) Where the benefits referred to in subsection (1) above include a lump sum payable in respect of the death of the liable party, the court, on making the capital sum order, may make an order—

(a) if the trustees or managers of the pension scheme in question have power to determine the person to whom the sum, or any part of it, is to be paid, requiring them to pay the whole or part of that sum, when it becomes due, to the other party;

(b) if the liable party has power to nominate the person to whom the sum, or any part of it, is to be paid, requiring the liable party to nominate the other party in respect of the whole or part of that sum;

(c) in any other case, requiring the trustees or managers of the pension scheme in question to pay the whole or part of that sum, when it becomes due, to the other party instead of to the person to whom, apart from the order, it would be paid.

(4) Any payment by the trustees or managers under an order under subsection (2) or (3) above—

(a) shall discharge so much of the trustees' or managers' liability to or in respect of the liable party as corresponds to the amount of the payment; and

(b) shall be treated for all purposes as a payment made by the liable party in or towards the discharge of his liability under the capital sum order.

(5) Where the liability of the liable party under the capital sum order has been discharged in whole or in part, other than by a payment by the trustees or managers under an order under subsection (2) or (3) above, the court may, on an application by any person having an interest, recall any order under either of those subsections or vary the amount specified in such an order, as appears to the court appropriate in the circumstances.

(6) Where—

(a) an order under subsection (2) or (3) above imposes any requirement on the trustees or managers of a pension scheme ("the first scheme") and the liable party acquires transfer credits under another scheme ("the new scheme") which are derived (directly or indirectly) from a transfer from the first scheme of all his accrued rights under that scheme; and

(b) the trustees or managers of the new scheme have been given notice in accordance with regulations under subsection (8) below,

the order shall have effect as if it had been made instead in respect of the trustees or managers of the new scheme; and in this subsection "transfer credits" has the same meaning as in the Pension Schemes Act 1993.

(7) Without prejudice to subsection (6) above, the court may, on an application by any person having an interest, vary an order under subsection (2) or (3) above by substituting for the trustees or managers specified in the order the trustees or managers of any other pension scheme under which any lump sum referred to in subsection (1) above is payable to the liable party or in respect of his death.

(8) The Secretary of State may by regulations—

(a) require notices to be given in respect of changes of circumstances relevant to orders under subsection (2) or (3) above;

(b) make provision for the recovery of the administrative expenses of complying with such orders from the liable party or the other party.

(9) Regulations under subsection (8) above shall be made by statutory instrument which shall be subject to annulment in pursuance of a resolution of either House of Parliament.

(10) Subsection (10) (other than the definition of "benefits under a pension scheme") and subsection (11) of section 10 of this Act shall apply for the purposes of this section as those subsections apply for the purposes of that section.".

(4) Nothing in the provisions mentioned in section 166(5) above applies to a court exercising its powers under section 8 (orders for financial provision on divorce, etc.) or 12A (orders for payment of capital sum: pensions lump sums) of the 1985 Act in respect of any benefits under a pension scheme which fall within subsection (5)(b) of section 10 of that Act ("pension scheme" having the meaning given in subsection (10) of that section).

GENERAL NOTE

This appears to make similar provision for Scotland to that made for England and Wales by s.166. The General Note to this may be consulted. [*Hansard*, H.L. Vol. 263, Col. 163].

War pensions for widows: effect of remarriage

168.—(1) In determining whether a pension is payable to a person as a widow under any of the enactments mentioned in subsection (3) in respect of any period beginning on or after the commencement of this section, no account may be taken of the fact that the widow has married another if, before the beginning of that period, the marriage has been terminated or the parties have been judicially separated.

(2) For the purposes of this section—

(a) the reference to the termination of a marriage is to the termination of the marriage by death, dissolution or annulment, and

(b) the reference to judicial separation includes any legal separation obtained in a country or territory outside the British Islands and recognised in the United Kingdom;

and for those purposes a divorce, annulment or legal separation obtained in a country or territory outside the British Islands must, if the Secretary of State so determines, be treated as recognised in the United Kingdom even though no declaration as to its validity has been made by any court in the United Kingdom.

(3) The enactments referred to in subsection (1) are—

(a) The Naval, Military and Air Forces Etc. (Disablement and Death) Service Pensions Order 1983, and any order re-enacting the provisions of that order,
(b) The Personal Injuries (Civilians) Scheme 1983, and any subsequent scheme made under the Personal Injuries (Emergency Provisions) Act 1939,
(c) any scheme made under the Pensions (Navy, Army, Air Force and Mercantile Marine) Act 1939 or the Polish Resettlement Act 1947 applying the provisions of any such order as is referred to in paragraph (a),
(d) the order made under section 1(5) of the Ulster Defence Regiment Act 1969 concerning pensions and other grants in respect of disablement or death due to service in the Ulster Defence Regiment.

GENERAL NOTE

Subs. (1)
   This section partially rights a long-standing wrong, which successive governments have refused to right, until the matter was raised in the House of Lords by Lord Freyberg during the debate on the second reading of the Bill (*Hansard*, H.L. Vol. 560, col. 987). The section comes into force on the passing of the Act. It restores from that date the widow's pension to war widows who have remarried but whose further marriage has terminated by death or otherwise, or in respect of which a decree of judicial separation has been made.

Subs. (2)
   This subsection contains supplementary provisions to those contained in subs. (1).
   [Standing Committee D, June 13, 1995, col. 583].

Extensions of Pensions Appeal Tribunals Act 1943

169.—(1) The Pensions Appeal Tribunals Act 1943 is amended as follows.
   (2) In section 1 (appeals against rejection of war pension claims made in respect of members of armed forces)—
   (a) in subsection (1), after "administered by the Minister" there is inserted "or under a scheme made under section 1 of the Polish Resettlement Act 1947", and
   (b) in subsections (3) and (3A), for "or Order of His Majesty" there is substituted ", Order of Her Majesty or scheme".
   (3) In section 7 (application of Act to past decisions and assessments)—
   (a) in subsection (2), at the beginning there is inserted "Subject to subsection (2A) of this section,", and
   (b) after that subsection, there is inserted—
      "(2A) Subsection (2) of this section shall not apply in relation to any decision given by the Minister before the passing of this Act which corresponds, apart from any difference of the kind referred to in that subsection, with such a decision as is referred to in section 1 of this Act in respect of claims made under the scheme referred to in that section."
   (4) In section 10 (power to modify sections 1 to 4 by Order in Council), in subsections (1) and (2), for "or Order of His Majesty" there is substituted ", Order of Her Majesty or scheme".
   (5) In section 12 (interpretation), in the definition of "relevant service"—
   (a) for "or Order of His Majesty" there is substituted ", Order of Her Majesty or scheme", and
   (b) for "or Order" there is substituted ", Order or scheme".
   (6) In the Schedule (constitution, jurisdiction and procedure of Pensions Appeal Tribunals), in paragraph 3(2), after paragraph (b) there is inserted—
      "(ba) if the claim was made under the scheme referred to in section 1 of this Act in respect of a person who is treated under the scheme as an officer, shall be a retired or demobilised officer of Her Majesty's naval, military or air forces;

(bb) if the claim was made under the aforesaid scheme in respect of a person who is treated under the scheme as a soldier, shall be a discharged or demobilised member of any of the said forces who was not at the time of his discharge or demobilisation an officer;".

Official and public service pensions

Pensions for dependants of the Prime Minister etc.

170.—(1) Section 27 of the Parliamentary and Other Pensions Act 1972 (application of certain provisions with modifications in relation to the Prime Minister and the Speaker) is amended as follows.

(2) For subsection (1)(b) (amount by reference to which dependant's pension calculated) there is substituted—

"(b) for the purposes of that scheme, that person's basic or prospective pension were of an amount equal to his section 26 entitlement".

(3) After subsection (1) there is inserted—

"(1A) For the purposes of subsection (1)(b), the amount of a person's section 26 entitlement—

(a) where at the time of his death he was entitled to receive a pension under section 26 of this Act (whether or not, by virtue of subsection (2) of that section, the pension was payable), is the annual amount of the pension to which he was entitled under that section at the time when he ceased to hold that office or (if later) on 28th February 1991, and

(b) where at the time of his death he held office as Prime Minister and First Lord of the Treasury or as Speaker of the House of Commons, is the annual amount of the pension to which he would have been entitled under that section if he had ceased to hold office immediately before his death,

but in either case, any provision which deems such a pension to have begun on a day earlier than the day referred to in section 8(2) of the Pensions (Increase) Act 1971 shall be disregarded."

(4) For the purposes of the Pensions (Increase) Act 1971, a pension payable under section 27 of the Parliamentary and Other Pensions Act 1972 in respect of a person who ceased to hold the office of Prime Minister and First Lord of the Treasury or Speaker of the House of Commons before 28th February 1991 shall be deemed to have begun on that date.

(5) Where a person—

(a) is entitled to receive a pension under that section by reason of the death of a person who, at any time before the commencement of this section, held the office of Prime Minister and First Lord of the Treasury or Speaker of the House of Commons, and

(b) the amount of that pension determined in accordance with subsection (6) is greater than the amount of the pension determined in accordance with subsections (1) to (4),

it shall be determined in accordance with subsection (6).

(6) The annual amount of the pension shall be determined as if—

(a) subsections (1) to (3) had not been enacted, and

(b) for the purposes of the Pensions (Increase) Act 1971, the pension had begun on the day following the date of the death.

(7) This section has effect, and shall be treated as having had effect, in relation to any person who becomes entitled to a pension payable under section 27 of the Parliamentary and Other Pensions Act 1972 on or after 15th December 1994.

This section makes amendments to the Parliamentary and Other Pensions Act 1972, in order to clarify the calculation of pensions payable to dependants of the Prime Minister, former prime ministers, the Speaker of the House of Commons and former speakers, after the death of any of these. This is effected by alterations made to s.27 of that Act. For the pensions payable to the former holders of the offices just mentioned, see s.26 of that Act.

This section comes into force on the passing of this Act (see s.180).

Equal treatment in relation to official pensions

171.—(1) Section 3 of the Pensions (Increase) Act 1971 (qualifying conditions for pensions increase) is amended as follows.

(2) In subsection (2)(c), "is a woman who" is omitted.

(3) In subsection (10)—

(a) for "woman is in receipt of a pension" there is substituted "person is in receipt of a pension the whole or any part of", and

(b) for "woman and that pension" there is substituted "person and that pension or part".

(4) In subsection (11)—

(a) for "woman's" there is substituted "person's", and

(b) for "woman" there is substituted "person",

and accordingly for "she" there is substituted "he".

(5) This section shall have effect, and shall be deemed to have had effect, in relation to pensions commencing after 17th May 1990, and in relation to so much of any such pension as is referable to service on or after that date.

This provides for equal treatment in respect of the qualifying conditions for increases in official pensions prescribed by the Pensions (Increase) Act 1971. The effect of these changes reflects the *ratione temporis* relief granted by the European Court of Justice in *Barber v. Guardian Royal Exchange Assurance Group* [1990] 2 All E.R. 660.

Information about public service schemes

172.—(1) In prescribed circumstances, the Secretary of State may provide information to any prescribed person in connection with the following questions—

(a) whether an individual who during any period—

  (i) has been eligible to be an active member of an occupational pension scheme under the Superannuation Act 1972, but

  (ii) has instead made contributions to a personal pension scheme, has suffered loss as a result of a contravention which is actionable under section 62 of the Financial Services Act 1986 (actions for damages in respect of contravention of rules etc. made under the Act), and

(b) if so, what payment would need to be made to the occupational scheme in respect of the individual to restore the position to what it would have been if the individual had been an active member of the occupational scheme throughout the period in question,

and may impose on that person reasonable fees in respect of administrative expenses incurred in providing that information.

(2) Where—

(a) such an individual as is mentioned in subsection (1) is admitted or readmitted as an active member of an occupational pension scheme under the Superannuation Act 1972, or

(b) a payment is made to the Secretary of State in respect of such an individual for the purpose mentioned in paragraph (b) of that subsection, the Secretary of State may impose on any prescribed person reasonable fees in respect of administrative expenses incurred in connection with the admission, readmission or payment.

(3) In the case of an occupational pension scheme under section 1 of the Superannuation Act 1972 (superannuation of civil servants), the references

in subsections (1) and (2) to the Secretary of State shall be read as references to the Minister for the Civil Service, or such person as may be prescribed.

(4) In the case of an occupational pension scheme under section 7 of the Superannuation Act 1972 (superannuation of persons employed in local government etc.), the references in subsections (1) and (2) to the Secretary of State shall be read as references to a prescribed person.

(5) In this section—

"prescribed" means—

(i) in the case of a scheme made under section 1 of the Superannuation Act 1972, prescribed by a scheme made by the Minister for the Civil Service, or

(ii) in any other case, prescribed by regulations made by the Secretary of State, and

"active member", in relation to an occupational pension scheme, has the same meaning as in Part I.

GENERAL NOTE

This section permits the Secretary of State to give information to persons who have opted for personal pensions rather than becoming a member of a public service pension scheme under the Superannuation Act 1972, where that member has suffered loss actionable under s.62 of the Financial Services Act 1986. It further makes supplementary provision for the payment of expenses by a person prescribed by regulations where a person is admitted or readmitted to such a public service pension scheme.

[Standing Committee D, June 22, 1995, col. 823].

General minor and consequential amendments

General minor and consequential amendments

173. Schedule 6, which makes general minor and consequential amendments, shall have effect.

GENERAL NOTE

Schedule 6 contains a number of amendments to the provisions of the Pension Schemes Act 1993 appertaining to cash equivalents. The time limits for the payment of these are altered by the amendment to s.99 of that Act contained in para. 5 of the Schedule.

Subordinate legislation etc.

Orders and regulations (general provisions)

174.—(1) Any power under this Act to make regulations or orders (except a power of the court or the Authority to make orders) shall be exercisable by statutory instrument.

(2) Except in so far as this Act provides otherwise, any power conferred by it to make regulations or an order may be exercised—

(a) either in relation to all cases to which the power extends, or in relation to those cases subject to specified exceptions, or in relation to any specified cases or classes of case,

(b) so as to make, as respects the cases in relation to which it is exercised—

(i) the full provision to which the power extends or any less provision (whether by way of exception or otherwise),

(ii) the same provision for all cases in relation to which the power is exercised, or different provision for different cases or different classes of case or different provision as respects the same case or class of case for different purposes of this Act, or

(iii) any such provision either unconditionally or subject to any specified condition,

and where such a power is expressed to be exercisable for alternative purposes it may be exercised in relation to the same case for any or all of those purposes; and any power to make regulations or an order for the purposes of any one provision of this Act shall be without prejudice to any power to make regulations or an order for the purposes of any other provision.

(3) Any power conferred by this Act to make regulations or an order includes power to make such incidental, supplementary, consequential or transitional provision as appears to the authority making the regulations or order to be expedient for the purposes of the regulations or order.

(4) Regulations made by the Secretary of State may, for the purposes of or in connection with the coming into force of any provisions of this Act, make any such provision as could be made, by virtue of subsection (4)(a) of section 180, by an order bringing those provisions into force.

GENERAL NOTE
    This section desirably widens the powers of those authorised by this Act to make regulations or orders.

Parliamentary control of orders, and regulations

175.—(1) Subject to subsections (2) and (3), a statutory instrument which contains any regulations or order made under this Act shall be subject to annulment in pursuance of a resolution of either House of Parliament.

(2) A statutory instrument which contains any regulations made by virtue of—
    (a) section 64(4),
    (b) section 78(6),
    (c) section 116(1), or
    (d) section 149
or order under section 10(2) must not be made unless a draft of the instrument has been laid before and approved by a resolution of each House of Parliament.

(3) Subsection (1) does not apply to an order under section 180.

GENERAL NOTE
    Regulations made under this Act are for the most part only subject to annulment by either House of Parliament. This does not apply to regulations to vary requirements in respect of equal treatment under s.64(4) of the Act or to regulations to increase the borrowing power of the Compensation Board under s.78(6).

General

Interpretation

176. In this Act—
    "enactment" includes an enactment comprised in subordinate legislation (within the meaning of the Interpretation Act 1978),
    "occupational pension scheme" and "personal pension scheme" have the meaning given by section 1 of the Pension Schemes Act 1993,
and the definition of "enactment" shall apply for the purposes of section 114 as if "Act" in section 21(1) of the Interpretation Act 1978 included any enactment.

Repeals

177. The enactments shown in Schedule 7 are repealed to the extent specified in the third column.

Extent

178.—(1) Subject to the following provisions, this Act does not extend to Northern Ireland.

(2) Sections 1, 2, 21(3), 68(5), 78, 79, 80(4), 150, 168, 170(4) to (7), 172 and 179 extend to Northern Ireland.

(3) The amendment by this Act of an enactment which extends to Northern Ireland extends also to Northern Ireland.

Northern Ireland

179. An Order in Council under paragraph 1(1)(b) of Schedule 1 to the Northern Ireland Act 1974 (legislation for Northern Ireland in the interim period) which states that it is made only for purposes corresponding to those of this Act—

(a) shall not be subject to paragraph 1(4) and (5) of that Schedule (affirmative resolution of both Houses of Parliament), but
(b) shall be subject to annulment in pursuance of a resolution of either House.

Commencement

180.—(1) Subject to the following provisions, this Act shall come into force on such day as the Secretary of State may by order made by statutory instrument appoint and different days may be appointed for different purposes.

(2) The following provisions shall come into force on the day this Act is passed—

(a) subject to the provisions of Schedule 4, Part II,
(b) section 168,
(c) sections 170 and 171,
(d) section 179,
and any repeal in Schedule 7 for which there is a note shall come into force in accordance with that note.

(3) Section 166 shall come into force on such day as the Lord Chancellor may by order made by statutory instrument appoint and different days may be appointed for different purposes.

(4) Without prejudice to section 174(3), the power to make an order under this section includes power—

(a) to make transitional adaptations or modifications—
    (i) of the provisions brought into force by the order, or
    (ii) in connection with those provisions, of any provisions of this Act, or the Pension Schemes Act 1993, then in force, or
(b) to save the effect of any of the repealed provisions of that Act, or those provisions as adapted or modified by the order,
as it appears to the Secretary of State expedient, including different adaptations or modifications for different periods.

GENERAL NOTE
    Under this section the provisions of the Act are to come into force on one or more appointed days, save for the provisions specified in subs. (2), which come into force on the passing of the

Act. The most notable of these are the amendments to the Social Security Contributions and Benefits Act 1992 contained in Part II of Sched. 4.

Short title

181. This Act may be cited as the Pensions Act 1995.

SCHEDULES

SCHEDULE 1

OCCUPATIONAL PENSIONS REGULATORY AUTHORITY

General

1. The Authority shall not be regarded as the servant or agent of the Crown, or as enjoying any status, privilege or immunity of the Crown, and its property shall not be regarded as property of, or property held on behalf of, the Crown.

2. The Authority may do anything (except borrow money) which is calculated to facilitate the discharge of their functions, or is incidental or conducive to their discharge.

Tenure of members

3. Subject to the following provisions, a person shall hold and vacate office as chairman or other member of the Authority in accordance with the terms of the instrument appointing him.

4. If a member of the Authority becomes or ceases to be chairman, the Secretary of State may vary the terms of the instrument appointing him to be a member so as to alter the date on which he is to vacate office.

5. A person may at any time resign office as chairman or other member of the Authority by giving written notice of his resignation signed by him to the Secretary of State.

6.—(1) The chairman of the Authority may at any time be removed from office by notice in writing given to him by the Secretary of State.

(2) If a person ceases to be chairman by virtue of sub-paragraph (1), he shall cease to be a member of the Authority.

7.—(1) If the Secretary of State is satisfied that a member of the Authority other than the chairman—

(a) has been absent from meetings of the Authority for a period longer than three consecutive months without the Authority's permission,

(b) has become bankrupt or made an arrangement with his creditors, or

(c) is unable or unfit to discharge the functions of a member,

the Secretary of State may remove that member by notice in writing.

(2) In the application of sub-paragraph (1) to Scotland—

(a) the reference to a member's having become bankrupt shall be read as a reference to sequestration of the member's estate having been awarded, and

(b) the reference to a member having made an arrangement with his creditors shall be read as a reference to his having made a trust deed for the behoof of his creditors or a composition contract.

Expenses, remuneration, etc.

8.—(1) The Secretary of State may pay the Authority such sums as he thinks fit towards their expenses.

(2) The Authority may pay, or make provision for paying, to or in respect of the chairman or any other member such salaries or other remuneration, and such pensions, allowances, fees, expenses or gratuities, as the Secretary of State may determine.

(3) Where a person ceases to be a member of the Authority otherwise than on the expiration of his term of office and it appears to the Secretary of State that there are circumstances which make it right for that person to receive compensation, the Authority may make to that person a payment of such amount as the Secretary of State may determine.

Parliamentary disqualification

9. In Part II of Schedule 1 to the House of Commons Disqualification Act 1975, and in Part II of Schedule 1 to the Northern Ireland Assembly Disqualification Act 1975 (bodies all members of which are disqualified), there is inserted at the appropriate place—

"The Occupational Pensions Regulatory Authority".

The Ombudsman

10. In the Parliamentary Commissioner Act 1967, in Schedule 2 (departments and authorities subject to investigation), there is inserted at the appropriate place—
"The Occupational Pensions Regulatory Authority".

Staff

11.—(1) There shall be a chief executive and, with the approval of the Secretary of State as to numbers, other employees of the Authority.

(2) The first chief executive shall be appointed by the Secretary of State on such terms and conditions as to remuneration and other matters as the Secretary of State may determine.

(3) Any reappointment of the first chief executive, and the appointment of the second and any subsequent chief executive, shall be made by the Authority, with the approval of the Secretary of State, on such terms and conditions as to remuneration and other matters as the Authority may, with the approval of the Secretary of State, determine.

(4) The other employees shall be appointed by the Authority on such terms and conditions as to remuneration and other matters as the Authority may, with the approval of the Secretary of State, determine.

(5) The Secretary of State may, on such terms as to payment by the Authority as he thinks fit, make available to the Authority such additional staff and such other facilities as he thinks fit.

The Superannuation Act 1972 (c. 11)

12.—(1) Employment with the Authority shall be included among the kinds of employment to which a scheme under section 1 of the Superannuation Act 1972 can apply, and accordingly in Schedule 1 to that Act (in which those kinds of employment are listed), at the end of the list of Other Bodies there is inserted—
"The Occupational Pensions Regulatory Authority".

(2) The Authority must pay to the Treasury, at such times as the Treasury may direct, such sums as the Treasury may determine in respect of the increase attributable to this paragraph in the sums payable out of money provided by Parliament under the Superannuation Act 1972.

Proceedings

13.—(1) The Secretary of State may make regulations generally as to the procedure to be followed by the Authority in the exercise of their functions and the manner in which their functions are to be exercised.

(2) Such regulations may in particular make provision—
(a) as to the hearing of parties, the taking of evidence and the circumstances (if any) in which a document of any prescribed description is to be treated, for the purposes of any proceedings before the Authority, as evidence, or conclusive evidence, of any prescribed matter,
(b) as to the time to be allowed for making any application or renewed application to the Authority (whether for an order or determination of the Authority or for the review of a determination, or otherwise),
(c) as to the manner in which parties to any proceedings before the Authority may or are to be represented for the purposes of the proceedings.

(3) Regulations under sub-paragraph (1) may provide for enabling the Authority to summon persons—
(a) to attend before them and give evidence (including evidence on oath) for any purposes of proceedings in connection with an occupational pension scheme,
(b) to produce any documents required by the Authority for those purposes, or
(c) to furnish any information which the Authority may require relating to any such scheme which is the subject matter of proceedings pending before them.

14.—(1) The Authority may establish a committee for any purpose.

(2) The quorum of the Authority shall be such as they may determine, and the Authority may regulate their own procedure and that of any of their committees.

(3) The Authority may authorise the chairman or any other member, the chief executive or any committee established by the Authority to exercise such of the Authority's functions as they may determine.

(4) This paragraph is subject to regulations made by virtue of paragraph 13 and to section 96(5).

Validity

15. The validity of any proceedings of the Authority, or of any of their committees, shall not be affected by any vacancy among the members or by any defect in the appointment of any member.

Accounts

16.—(1) It shall be the duty of the Authority—
(a) to keep proper accounts and proper records in relation to the accounts,
(b) to prepare in respect of each financial year of the Authority a statement of accounts, and
(c) to send copies of the statement to the Secretary of State and to the Comptroller and Auditor General before the end of the month of August next following the financial year to which the statement relates.

(2) The statement of accounts shall comply with any directions given by the Secretary of State with the approval of the Treasury as to—
(a) the information to be contained in it,
(b) the manner in which the information contained in it is to be presented, or
(c) the methods and principles according to which the statement is to be prepared,
and shall contain such additional information as the Secretary of State may with the approval of the Treasury require to be provided for the information of Parliament.

(3) The Comptroller and Auditor General shall examine, certify and report on each statement received by him in pursuance of this paragraph and shall lay copies of each statement and of his report before each House of Parliament.

(4) In this paragraph, "financial year" means the period beginning with the date on which the Authority is established and ending with the next following 31st March, and each successive period of twelve months.

Other expenses

17. The Authority may—
(a) pay to persons attending meetings of the Authority at the request of the Authority such travelling and other allowances (including compensation for loss of remunerative time) as the Secretary of State may determine, and
(b) pay to persons from whom the Authority may decide to seek advice, as being persons considered by the Authority to be specially qualified to advise them on particular matters, such fees as the Secretary of State may determine.

Fees

18. Regulations made by the Secretary of State may authorise the Authority to charge fees for their services in respect of the modification of an occupational pension scheme on an application made under section 69, or under any corresponding provision in force in Northern Ireland, including services in connection with the drawing up of any order of the Authority made on application.

Application of seal and proof of instruments

19.—(1) The fixing of the common seal of the Authority shall be authenticated by the signature of the secretary of the Authority or some other person authorised by them to act for that purpose.

(2) Sub-paragraph (1) does not apply in relation to any document which is or is to be signed in accordance with the law of Scotland.

20. A document purporting to be duly executed under the seal of the Authority shall be received in evidence and shall, unless the contrary is proved, be deemed to be so executed.

Section 78   SCHEDULE 2

PENSIONS COMPENSATION BOARD

General

1. The Compensation Board shall not be regarded as the servant or agent of the Crown, or as enjoying any status, privilege or immunity of the Crown; and their property shall not be regarded as property of, or property held on behalf of, the Crown.

2. The Compensation Board may do anything which is calculated to facilitate the discharge of their functions, or is incidental or conducive to their discharge, including in particular—

(a) giving guarantees or indemnities in favour of any person, or
(b) making any other agreement or arrangement with or for the benefit of any person.

Tenure of members

3. Subject to the following provisions, a person shall hold and vacate office as chairman or other member of the Compensation Board in accordance with the terms of the instrument appointing him.

4. If a member of the Compensation Board becomes or ceases to be chairman, the Secretary of State may vary the terms of the instrument appointing him to be a member so as to alter the date on which he is to vacate office.

5. A person may at any time resign office as chairman or other member of the Compensation Board by giving written notice of his resignation signed by him to the Secretary of State.

6. The chairman or any other member of the Compensation Board may at any time be removed from office by notice in writing given to him by the Secretary of State.

Expenses, remuneration, etc.

7.—(1) The Compensation Board may pay, or make provision for paying, to or in respect of the chairman or any other member such salaries or other remuneration, and such pensions, allowances, fees, expenses or gratuities, as the Secretary of State may determine.

(2) Where a person ceases to be a member of the Compensation Board otherwise than on the expiration of his term of office and it appears to the Secretary of State that there are circumstances which make it right for that person to receive compensation, the Compensation Board may make to that person a payment of such amount as the Secretary of State may determine.

Parliamentary disqualification

8. In Part II of Schedule 1 to the House of Commons Disqualification Act 1975, and in Part II of Schedule 1 to the Northern Ireland Assembly Disqualification Act 1975 (bodies all members of which are disqualified), there is inserted at the appropriate place—
"The Pensions Compensation Board".

The Ombudsman

9. In the Parliamentary Commissioner Act 1967, in Schedule 2 (departments and authorities subject to investigation), there is inserted at the appropriate place—
"The Pensions Compensation Board".

Staff

10.—(1) The Compensation Board may (with the approval of the Secretary of State as to numbers) appoint such persons to be employees of theirs as the Board think fit, on such terms and conditions as to remuneration and other matters as the Board may with the approval of the Secretary of State determine.

(2) The Secretary of State may, on such terms as to payment by the Compensation Board as he thinks fit, make available to the Compensation Board such additional staff and such other facilities as he thinks fit.

(3) The Pensions Ombudsman may, on such terms as to payment by the Compensation Board as he thinks fit, make available to the Compensation Board such of his employees as he thinks fit.

The Superannuation Act 1972 (c. 11)

11.—(1) Employment with the Compensation Board shall be included among the kinds of employment to which a scheme under section 1 of the Superannuation Act 1972 can apply, and accordingly in Schedule 1 to that Act (in which those kinds of employment are listed), at the end of the list of Other Bodies there is inserted—
"The Pensions Compensation Board".

(2) The Compensation Board must pay to the Treasury, at such times as the Treasury may direct, such sums as the Treasury may determine in respect of the increase attributable to this paragraph in the sums payable out of money provided by Parliament under the Superannuation Act 1972.

Proceedings

12. The Secretary of State may make regulations generally as to the procedure to be followed by the Compensation Board in the exercise of their functions and the manner in which their functions are to be exercised.

13. The Compensation Board must meet at least once in the first twelve months of their existence, and at least once in each succeeding period of twelve months.

14.—(1) The Compensation Board may (subject to sub-paragraph (2)) authorise any of their members to exercise such of the Compensation Board's functions as the Board may determine.

(2) The Compensation Board may not authorise any of their members to—

(a) determine whether section 81 applies to an application for compensation under section 82 in respect of any occupational pension scheme,

(b) determine the amount of any payment under section 83,

(c) determine whether any payment should be made under section 84 or the amount of any such payment, or

(d) exercise such functions of the Compensation Board as may be prescribed.

(3) The quorum of the Compensation Board shall be such as they may determine, and the Board may regulate their own procedure.

(4) The decisions of the Compensation Board must be taken by agreement of a majority of the members of the Compensation Board who are present at the meeting where the decision is taken.

(5) This paragraph is subject to regulations made by virtue of paragraph 12.

15.—(1) Where the Compensation Board notify any person of a decision on any matter dealt with by them by means of a formal hearing, or on review, they shall furnish a written statement of the reasons for the decision.

(2) Any statement by the Compensation Board of their reasons for a decision, whether the statement is given by them in pursuance of this paragraph or otherwise, shall be taken to form part of the decision, and accordingly to be incorporated in the record.

Validity

16. The validity of any proceedings of the Compensation Board shall not be affected by any vacancy among the members or by any defect in the appointment of any member.

Accounts

17.—(1) The Compensation Board must—

(a) keep proper accounts and proper records in relation to the accounts,

(b) prepare in respect of each financial year of the Compensation Board a statement of accounts, and

(c) send copies of the statement to the Secretary of State and to the Comptroller and Auditor General before the end of the month of August next following the financial year to which the statement relates.

(2) The statement of accounts must comply with any directions given by the Secretary of State with the approval of the Treasury as to—

(a) the information to be contained in it,

(b) the manner in which the information contained in it is to be presented, or

(c) the methods and principles according to which the statement is to be prepared,

and must contain such additional information as the Secretary of State may with the approval of the Treasury require to be provided for the information of Parliament.

(3) The Comptroller and Auditor General must examine, certify and report on each statement received by him in pursuance of this paragraph and must lay copies of each statement and of his report before each House of Parliament.

(4) In this paragraph, "financial year" means the period beginning with the date on which the Board is established and ending with the next following 5th April, and each successive period of twelve months.

Other expenses

18.—(1) The Compensation Board may—

(a) pay to persons attending meetings of the Compensation Board at the request of the Board such travelling and other allowances (including compensation for loss of remunerative time) as the Board may determine, and

(b) pay to persons from whom the Compensation Board may decide to seek advice, as being persons considered by the Board to be specially qualified to advise them on particular matters, such fees as the Board may determine.

Pensions Act 1995

(2) A determination under sub-paragraph (1) requires the approval of the Secretary of State.

Application of seal and proof of instruments

19.—(1) The fixing of the common seal of the Compensation Board shall be authenticated by the signature of the chairman of the Compensation Board or some other person authorised by them to act for that purpose.

(2) Sub-paragraph (1) above does not apply in relation to any document which is or is to be signed in accordance with the law of Scotland.

20. A document purporting to be duly executed under the seal of the Compensation Board shall be received in evidence and shall, unless the contrary is proved, be deemed to be so executed.

Section 122   SCHEDULE 3

AMENDMENTS CONSEQUENTIAL ON PART I

The Employment Protection (Consolidation) Act 1978 (c. 44)

1. The Employment Protection (Consolidation) Act 1978 is amended as follows.

2. In section 60A(4) (dismissal on grounds of assertion of statutory right), after paragraph (c) there is added—
   "(d) the rights conferred by sections 42, 43 and 46 of the Pensions Act 1995.".

3. In section 71(2B) (compensation award for failure to comply with section 69 not to be made), at the end there is added "of this Act or section 46 of the Pensions Act 1995.".

4. In section 72(2) (special award), at the end there is added "of this Act or section 46 of the Pensions Act 1995.".

5. In section 73(6B) (calculation of basic award), at the end there is added "of this Act or section 46 of the Pensions Act 1995.".

6. In section 77(1) (interim relief), after "57A(1)(a) and (b)" there is inserted "of this Act or section 46 of the Pensions Act 1995.".

7. In section 77A(1) (procedure on application for interim relief), after "57A(1)(a) and (b)" there is inserted "of this Act or section 46 of the Pensions Act 1995.".

8. In section 133(1) (conciliation officers), after paragraph (e) there is added—
   "or
      (ea) arising out of a contravention, or alleged contravention, of section 42, 43 or 46 of the Pensions Act 1995.".

9. In section 136(1) (appeals to Employment Appeal Tribunal), after paragraph (f) there is added—
   "(g) the Pensions Act 1995;".

10. In section 138 (application of Act to Crown employment), in subsection (1), after "and section 53" there is inserted "of this Act and sections 42 to 46 of the Pensions Act 1995;".

The Insurance Companies Act 1982 (c. 50)

11.—(1) In the Table in sub-paragraph (1) of paragraph 3 of Schedule 2B to the Insurance Companies Act 1982, after the entry relating to the Building Societies Commission there is inserted—

"The Occupational Pensions Regulatory Authority.	Functions under the Pension Schemes Act 1993 or the Pensions Act 1995, or any enactment in force in Northern Ireland corresponding to either of them.".

(2) In sub-paragraph (9) of that paragraph, after paragraph (b) there is added—
   "or
      (c) persons involved in the operation of occupational pension schemes (within the meaning of the Pension Schemes Act 1993 or in Northern Ireland, the Pension Schemes (Northern Ireland) Act 1993)",
and accordingly the "or" after paragraph (a) is omitted.

The Companies Act 1985 (c. 6)

12. In section 449(1) of the Companies Act 1985, after paragraph (df) there is inserted—
   "(dg) for the purpose of enabling or assisting the Occupational Pensions Regulatory Authority to discharge their functions under the Pension Schemes Act 1993 or the Pensions Act 1995 or any enactment in force in Northern Ireland corresponding to either of them,".

The Bankruptcy (Scotland) Act 1985 (c. 66)

13. In section 31(1) of the Bankruptcy (Scotland) Act 1985 (vesting in permanent trustee of debtor's estate on sequestration), after "Act" there is inserted "and section 91(3) of the Pensions Act 1995".

14. In section 32 of that Act (vesting of estate, and dealings of debtor, after sequestration), after subsection (2) there is inserted—

"(2A) The amount allowed for the purposes specified in paragraphs (a) and (b) of subsection (2) above shall not be less than the total amount of any income received by the debtor—

(a) by way of guaranteed minimum pension; and

(b) in respect of his protected rights as a member of a pension scheme,

"guaranteed minimum pension" and "protected rights" having the same meanings as in the Pension Schemes Act 1993.".

The Insolvency Act 1986 (c. 45)

15. In section 310 of the Insolvency Act 1986 (income payments orders)—

(a) in subsection (2), after "income of the bankrupt" there is inserted "when taken together with any payments to which subsection (8) applies", and

(b) at the end of subsection (7), there is added—

"and any payment under a pension scheme but excluding any payment to which subsection (8) applies.

(8) This subsection applies to—

(a) payments by way of guaranteed minimum pension; and

(b) payments giving effect to the bankrupt's protected rights as a member of a pension scheme.

(9) In this section, "guaranteed minimum pension" and "protected rights" have the same meaning as in the Pension Schemes Act 1993.".

The Building Societies Act 1986 (c. 53)

16. In section 53(15) of the Building Societies Act 1986, after paragraph (b) there is added—
"or

(c) persons involved in the operation of occupational pension schemes (within the meaning of the Pension Schemes Act 1993 or, in Northern Ireland, the Pension Schemes (Northern Ireland) Act 1993)",

and accordingly the "or" after paragraph (a) is omitted.

The Financial Services Act 1986 (c. 60)

17. In section 180(1) of the Financial Services Act 1986, after paragraph (m) there is inserted—

"(mm) for the purpose of enabling or assisting the Occupational Pensions Regulatory Authority or the Pensions Compensation Board to discharge their functions under the Pension Schemes Act 1993 or the Pensions Act 1995 or any enactment in force in Northern Ireland corresponding to either of them;".

The Banking Act 1987 (c. 22)

18.—(1) In the Table in subsection (1) of section 84 of the Banking Act 1987, at the end there is added—

"20. The Occupational Pensions Regulatory Authority.	Functions under the Pension Schemes Act 1993 or the Pensions Act 1995 or any enactment in force in Northern Ireland corresponding to either of them.".

(2) In subsection (10) of that section, after paragraph (b) there is added—

"or

(c) persons involved in the operation of occupational pension schemes (within the meaning of the Pension Schemes Act 1993 or, in Northern Ireland, the Pension Schemes (Northern Ireland) Act 1993)",

and accordingly the "or" after paragraph (a) is omitted.

The Companies Act 1989 (c. 40)

19. In the Table in section 87(4) of the Companies Act 1989, after the entry relating to the Building Societies Commission there is inserted—

"The Occupational Pensions Regulatory Authority.	Functions under the Pension Schemes Act 1993 or the Pensions Act 1995 or any enactment in force in Northern Ireland corresponding to either of them.".

The Friendly Societies Act 1992 (c. 40)

20. In the Table in section 64(5) of the Friendly Societies Act 1992, after the entry relating to the Building Societies Commission there is inserted—

"The Occupational Pensions Regulatory Authority.	Functions under the Pension Schemes Act 1993 or the Pensions Act 1995 or any enactment in force in Northern Ireland corresponding to either of them.".

The Tribunals and Inquiries Act 1992 (c. 53)

21. The Tribunals and Inquiries Act 1992 is amended as follows—
(a) in section 7(2) (concurrence required for removal of tribunal members), after "(e)" there is inserted "(g) or (h)",
(b) in section 10 (reasons to be given on request), at the end of subsection (5) there is added—
"(ba) to decisions of the Pensions Compensation Board referred to in paragraph 35(h) of Schedule 1",
(c) in section 14 (restricted application of the Act in relation to certain tribunals), after subsection (1) there is inserted—
"(1A) In this Act—
(a) references to the working of the Occupational Pensions Regulatory Authority referred to in paragraph 35(g) of Schedule 1 are references to their working so far as relating to matters dealt with by them by means of a formal hearing or on review, and
(b) references to procedural rules for the Authority are references to regulations under—
(i) section 96(5) of the Pensions Act 1995 (procedure to be adopted with respect to reviews), or
(ii) paragraph 13 of Schedule 1 to that Act (procedure of the Authority), so far as the regulations relate to procedure on any formal hearing by the Authority.", and
(d) in paragraph 35 of Schedule 1 (tribunals under the direct supervision of the Council on Tribunals: pensions), after paragraph (f) there is inserted—
"(g) the Occupational Pensions Regulatory Authority established by section 1 of the Pensions Act 1995;
(h) the Pensions Compensation Board established by section 78 of that Act".

The Pension Schemes Act 1993 (c. 48)

22. The Pension Schemes Act 1993 is amended as follows.
23. In section 6 (registration)—
(a) after subsection (5) there is inserted—
"(5A) The regulations may make provision for information obtained by or furnished to the Registrar under or for the purposes of this Act to be disclosed to the Regulatory Authority or the Pensions Compensation Board", and

(b) in subsection (7), for "(5)" there is substituted "(5A)".

24. Sections 77 to 80 (assignment, forfeiture etc. of short service benefit) are repealed.

25. Sections 102 to 108 (annual increase in pensions in payment) are repealed.

26. Section 112 (restriction on investment in employer-related assets) is repealed.

27. Section 114 (documents for members etc.) is repealed.

28. Section 116 (regulations as to auditors) is repealed.

29. Section 118 (equal access) is repealed.

30. Sections 119 to 122 (independent trustees) are repealed.

31. In section 129 (overriding requirements)—

(a) in subsection (1), "Chapter I of Part V", "sections 119 to 122", "under Chapter I of Part V or" and "or sections 119 to 122" are omitted,

(b) in subsection (2), for the words from "Chapter III" to "section 108)" there is substituted "and Chapter III of that Part", and

(c) subsection (3)(a) is omitted.

32. In section 132 (conformity of schemes with requirements), "the equal access requirements" is omitted.

33. In section 133(1) (advice of the Board), "the equal access requirements" is omitted.

34. In section 134 (determination of questions)—

(a) in subsection (3), "the equal access requirements", and

(b) in subsection (4), "or the equal access requirements" and "or, as the case may be, section 118(1)",

are omitted.

35. In section 136(2)(e)(iv) (applications to modify schemes), "or the equal access requirements" is omitted.

36. In section 139(2) (functions of the Board), "the equal access requirements" is omitted.

37. In section 140(4) (effect of orders), paragraph (c) and the "and" immediately preceding it are omitted.

38. Section 144 (deficiencies in assets on winding up) is repealed.

39. In section 153 (power to modify Act)—

(a) in subsection (1), the words from "and Chapter I" to "section 108)" are omitted,

(b) subsections (3) and (4) are omitted,

(c) in subsection (5), "Chapter I of Part VII" is omitted, at the end of paragraph (b) there is inserted "or", and paragraph (d) and the preceding "or" are omitted, and

(d) subsections (6) and (7) are omitted.

40. In section 154(1) (application of provisions to personal pension schemes), after "provision of this Act" there is inserted "or of sections 22 to 26 and 40 of the Pensions Act 1995".

41. In section 159 (inalienability of certain pensions), after subsection (4) there is inserted—

"(4A) Where a person—

(a) is entitled or prospectively entitled as is mentioned in subsection (1), or

(b) is entitled to such rights or to such a payment as is mentioned in subsection (4),

no order shall be made by any court the effect of which would be that he would be restrained from receiving anything the assignment of which is or would be made void by either of those subsections.

(4B) Subsection (4A) does not prevent the making of an attachment of earnings order under the Attachment of Earnings Act 1971.".

42. In section 170 (determination of questions by Secretary of State), subsections (5) and (6) are omitted.

43. In section 178 (meaning of "trustee" and "manager") in paragraph (a), after "Administration Act 1992" there is inserted "or of sections 22 to 26 of the Pensions Act 1995", and the "or" after "Social Security Acts 1975 to 1991" is omitted.

44. In section 181 (general interpretation)—

(a) in subsection (1)—

(i) the definition of "equal access requirements" is omitted, and

(ii) after the definition of "regulations" there is inserted—

" 'the Regulatory Authority' means the Occupational Pensions Regulatory Authority;", and

(b) in subsection (2), for the words from "160" to "requirements" there is substituted "and 160".

45. In section 183 (sub-delegation), in subsection (3)—

(a) for "97(1), 104(8) and 144(5)" there is substituted "and 97(1)",

(b) the words from "or, in the case of" to "determined" are omitted, and

(c) the words following paragraph (b) are omitted.

46. In section 185(1) (consultation about regulations), "I or" is omitted.

47. In Schedule 7 (re-enactment or amendment of certain provisions not in force), paragraphs 1 and 3 are omitted.

Section 126　　　　　　　　SCHEDULE 4

EQUALISATION

PART I

PENSIONABLE AGES FOR MEN AND WOMEN

Rules for determining pensionable age

1. The following rules apply for the purposes of the enactments relating to social security, that is, the following Acts and the instruments made, or having effect as if made, under them: the Social Security Contributions and Benefits Act 1992, the Social Security Administration Act 1992 and the Pension Schemes Act 1993.

Rules

(1) A man attains pensionable age when he attains the age of 65 years.

(2) A woman born before 6th April 1950 attains pensionable age when she attains the age of 60.

(3) A woman born on any day in a period mentioned in column 1 of the following table attains pensionable age at the commencement of the day shown against that period in column 2.

(4) A woman born after 5th April 1955 attains pensionable age when she attains the age of 65.

TABLE

(1) *Period within which woman's birthday falls*	*(2)* *Day pensionable age attained*
6th April 1950 to 5th May 1950	6th May 2010
6th May 1950 to 5th June 1950	6th July 2010
6th June 1950 to 5th July 1950	6th September 2010
6th July 1950 to 5th August 1950	6th November 2010
6th August 1950 to 5th September 1950	6th January 2011
6th September 1950 to 5th October 1950	6th March 2011
6th October 1950 to 5th November 1950	6th May 2011
6th November 1950 to 5th December 1950	6th July 2011
6th December 1950 to 5th January 1951	6th September 2011
6th January 1951 to 5th February 1951	6th November 2011
6th February 1951 to 5th March 1951	6th January 2012
6th March 1951 to 5th April 1951	6th March 2012
6th April 1951 to 5th May 1951	6th May 2012
6th May 1951 to 5th June 1951	6th July 2012
6th June 1951 to 5th July 1951	6th September 2012
6th July 1951 to 5th August 1951	6th November 2012
6th August 1951 to 5th September 1951	6th January 2013
6th September 195! to 5th October 1951	6th March 2013
6th October 1951 to 5th November 1951	6th May 2013
6th November 1951 to 5th December 1951	6th July 2013
6th December 1951 to 5th January 1952	6th September 2013
6th January 1952 to 5th February 1952	6th November 2013
6th February 1952 to 5th March 1952	6th January 2014
6th March 1952 to 5th April 1952	6th March 2014
6th April 1952 to 5th May 1952	6th May 2014
6th May 1952 to 5th June 1952	6th July 2014
6th June 1952 to 5th July 1952	6th September 2014
6th July 1952 to 5th August 1952	6th November 2014
6th August 1952 to 5th September 1952	6th January 2015
6th September 1952 to 5th October 1952	6th March 2015
6th October 1952 to 5th November 1952	6th May 2015
6th November 1952 to 5th December 1952	6th July 2015

(1) *Period within which woman's birthday falls*	(2) *Day pensionable age attained*
6th December 1952 to 5th January 1953	6th September 2015
6th January 1953 to 5th February 1953	6th November 2015
6th February 1953 to 5th March 1953	6th January 2016
6th March 1953 to 5th April 1953	6th March 2016
6th April 1953 to 5th May 1953	6th May 2016
6th May 1953 to 5th June 1953	6th July 2016
6th June 1953 to 5th July 1953	6th September 2016
6th July 1953 to 5th August 1953	6th November 2016
6th August 1953 to 5th September 1953	6th January 2017
6th September 1953 to 5th October 1953	6th March 2017
6th October 1953 to 5th November 1953	6th May 2017
6th November 1953 to 5th December 1953	6th July 2017
6th December 1953 to 5th January 1954	6th September 2017
6th January 1954 to 5th February 1954	6th November 2017
6th February 1954 to 5th March 1954	6th January 2018
6th March 1954 to 5th April 1954	6th March 2018
6th April 1954 to 5th May 1954	6th May 2018
6th May 1954 to 5th June 1954	6th July 2018
6th June 1954 to 5th July 1954	6th September 2018
6th July 1954 to 5th August 1954	6th November 2018
6th August 1954 to 5th September 1954	6th January 2019
6th September 1954 to 5th October 1954	6th March 2019
6th October 1954 to 5th November 1954	6th May 2019
6th November 1954 to 5th December 1954	6th July 2019
6th December 1954 to 5th January 1955	6th September 2019
6th January 1955 to 5th February 1955	6th November 2019
6th February 1955 to 5th March 1955	6th January 2020
6th March 1955 to 5th April 1955	6th March 2020

PART II

ENTITLEMENT TO CERTAIN PENSION AND OTHER BENEFITS

Pension increases for dependent spouses

2.—(1) For sections 83 and 84 of the Social Security Contributions and Benefits Act 1992 (pension increases for dependent wife or husband) there is substituted—

"Pension increase for spouse

83A.—(1) Subject to subsection (3) below, the weekly rate of a Category A or Category C retirement pension payable to a married pensioner shall, for any period mentioned in subsection (2) below, be increased by the amount specified in relation to the pension in Schedule 4, Part IV, column (3).

(2) The periods referred to in subsection (1) above are—

(a) any period during which the pensioner is residing with the spouse, and

(b) any period during which the pensioner is contributing to the maintenance of the spouse at a weekly rate not less than the amount so specified, and the spouse does not have weekly earnings which exceed that amount.

(3) Regulations may provide that for any period during which the pensioner is residing with the spouse and the spouse has earnings there shall be no increase of pension under this section".

(2) This paragraph shall have effect on or after 6th April 2010.

Category B retirement pensions

3.—(1) For sections 49 and 50 of the Social Security Contributions and Benefits Act 1992 (Category B retirement pensions for women) there is substituted—

"Category B retirement pension for married person

48A.—(1) A person who—

(a) has attained pensionable age, and

(b) on attaining that age was a married person or marries after attaining that age,

shall be entitled to a Category B retirement pension by virtue of the contributions of the other party to the marriage ("the spouse") if the following requirement is met.

(2) The requirement is that the spouse—

(a) has attained pensionable age and become entitled to a Category A retirement pension, and

(b) satisfies the conditions specified in Schedule 3, Part 1, paragraph 5.

(3) During any period when the spouse is alive, a Category B retirement pension payable by virtue of this section shall be payable at the weekly rate specified in Schedule 4, Part I, paragraph 5.

(4) During any period after the spouse is dead, a Category B retirement pension payable by virtue of this section shall be payable at a weekly rate corresponding to—

(a) the weekly rate of the basic pension, plus

(b) half of the weekly rate of the additional pension,

determined in accordance with the provisions of sections 44 to 45A above as they apply in relation to a Category A retirement pension, but subject to section 46(2) above and the modification in section 48C(4) below.

(5) A person's Category B retirement pension payable by virtue of this section shall not be payable for any period falling before the day on which the spouse's entitlement is to be regarded as beginning for that purpose by virtue of section 5(1)(k) of the Administration Act.

"Category B retirement pension for widows and widowers

48B.—(1) A person ('the pensioner') whose spouse died—

(a) while they were married, and

(b) after the pensioner attained pensionable age,

shall be entitled to a Category B retirement pension by virtue of the contributions of the spouse if the spouse satisfied the conditions specified in Schedule 3, Part 1, paragraph 5.

(2) A Category B retirement pension payable by virtue of subsection (1) above shall be payable at a weekly rate corresponding to—

(a) the weekly rate of the basic pension, plus

(b) half of the weekly rate of the additional pension,

determined in accordance with the provisions of sections 44 to 45A above as they apply in relation to a Category A retirement pension, but subject to section 46(2) above and the modifications in subsection (3) below and section 48C(4) below.

(3) Where the spouse died under pensionable age, references in the provisions of sections 44 to 45A above as applied by subsection (2) above to the tax year in which the pensioner attained pensionable age shall be taken as references to the tax year in which the spouse died.

(4) A person who has attained pensionable age ('the pensioner') whose spouse died before the pensioner attained that age shall be entitled to a Category B retirement pension by virtue of the contributions of the spouse if—

(a) where the pensioner is a woman, the following condition is satisfied, and

(b) where the pensioner is a man, the following condition would have been satisfied on the assumption mentioned in subsection (7) below.

(5) The condition is that the pensioner—

(a) is entitled (or is treated by regulations as entitled) to a widow's pension by virtue of section 38 above, and

(b) became entitled to that pension in consequence of the spouse's death.

(6) A Category B retirement pension payable by virtue of subsection (4) above shall be payable—

(a) where the pensioner is a woman, at the same weekly rate as her widow's pension, and

(b) where the pensioner is a man, at the same weekly rate as that of the pension to which he would have been entitled by virtue of section 38 above on the assumption mentioned in subsection (7) below.

(7) The assumption referred to in subsections (4) and (6) above is that a man is entitled to a pension by virtue of section 38 above on the same terms and conditions, and at the same rate, as a woman.

Category B retirement pension: general

48C.—(1) Subject to the provisions of this Act, a person's entitlement to a Category B retirement pension shall begin on the day on which the conditions of entitlement become satisfied and shall continue for life.

(2) In any case where—

(a) a person would, apart from section 43(1) above, be entitled both to a Category A and to a Category B retirement pension, and

(b) section 47(1) above would apply for the increase of the Category A retirement pension, section 47(1) above shall be taken as applying also for the increase of the Category B retirement pension, subject to reduction or extinguishment of the increase by the application of section 47(2) above or section 46(5) of the Pensions Act.

(3) In the case of a pensioner whose spouse died on or before 5th April 2000, sections 48A(4)(b) and 48B(2)(b) above shall have effect with the omission of the words 'half of'.

(4) In the application of the provisions of sections 44 to 45A above by virtue of sections 48A(4) or 48B(2) above, references in those provisions to the pensioner shall be taken as references to the spouse".

(2) Section 48A of that Act (as inserted by this paragraph) does not confer a right to a Category B retirement pension on a man by reason of his marriage to a woman who was born before 6th April 1950.

(3) Section 48B of that Act (as inserted by this paragraph) does not confer a right to a Category B retirement pension on a man who attains pensionable age before 6th April 2010; and section 51 of that Act does not confer a right to a Category B retirement pension on a man who attains pensionable age on or after that date.

Home responsibilities protection

4.—(1) In paragraph 5 of Schedule 3 to the Social Security Contributions and Benefits Act 1992 (contribution conditions for entitlement to retirement pension), in sub-paragraph (7)(a) (condition that contributor must have paid or been credited with contributions of the relevant class for not less than the requisite number of years modified in the case of those precluded from regular employment by responsibilities at home), "(or at least 20 of them, if that is less than half)" is omitted.

(2) This paragraph shall have effect in relation to any person attaining pensionable age on or after 6th April 2010.

Additional pension

5. In section 46(2) of the Social Security Contributions and Benefits Act 1992 (benefits calculated by reference to Category A retirement pension), for the words following "45(4)(b) above-" there is substituted—

" 'N' =
  (a) the number of tax years which begin after 5th April 1978 and end before the date when the entitlement to the additional pension commences, or
  (b) the number of tax years in the period—
      (i) beginning with the tax year in which the deceased spouse ('S') attained the age of 16 or if later 1978–79, and
      (ii) ending immediately before the tax year in which S would have attained pensionable age if S had not died earlier,
whichever is the smaller number".

Increments

6.—(1) In section 54(1) of the Social Security Contributions and Benefits Act 1992 (election to defer right to pension), in paragraph (a), the words from "but" to "70" are omitted.

(2) In Schedule 5 to that Act—
  (a) in paragraph 2(2), the definition of "period of enhancement" (and the preceding "and") are omitted, and
  (b) for "period of enhancement" (in every other place in paragraphs 2 and 3 where it appears) there is substituted "period of deferment".

(3) In paragraph 2(3) of that Schedule, for "1/7th per cent." there is substituted "1/5th per cent.".

(4) In paragraph 8 of that Schedule, sub-paragraphs (1) and (2) are omitted.

(5) Sub-paragraph (1) above shall come into force on 6th April 2010; and sub-paragraphs (2) to (4) above shall have effect in relation to incremental periods beginning on or after that date.

Graduated retirement benefit

7. In section 62(1) of the Social Security Contributions and Benefits Act 1992 (graduated retirement benefit continued in force by regulations)—
  (a) in paragraph (a), for "replacing section 36(4) of the National Insurance Act 1965" there is substituted "amending section 36(2) of the National Insurance Act 1965 (value of unit of graduated contributions) so that the value is the same for women as it is for men and for replacing section 36(4) of that Act", and
  (b) at the end of paragraph (b) there is added "and for that section (except subsection (5)) so to apply as it applies to women and their late husbands".

Christmas bonus for pensioners

8. In section 149(4) of that Act (Christmas bonus: supplementary), for "70 in the case of a man or 65 in the case of a woman" there is substituted "65".

PART III

CONSEQUENTIAL AMENDMENTS

Pensionable age

9. In section 50 of the London Regional Transport Act 1984 (travel concessions), for subsection (7)(a) there is substituted—
"(a) persons who have attained pensionable age (within the meaning given by the rules in paragraph 1 of Schedule 4 to the Pensions Act 1995)".

10. In section 93 of the Transport Act 1985 (travel concessions), for subsection (7)(a) there is substituted—
"(a) persons who have attained pensionable age (within the meaning given by the rules in paragraph 1 of Schedule 4 to the Pensions Act 1995)".

11. In section 73B(2)(b)(ii) of the Housing (Scotland) Act 1987 (rent loan scheme), for "of the Social Security Act 1975" there is substituted "given by the rules in paragraph 1 of Schedule 4 to the Pensions Act 1995)".

12. In the Income and Corporation Taxes Act 1988—
(a) in section 187(2) (interpretation), the definition of "pensionable age" is omitted,
(b) in the words following paragraph (d) of paragraph 2 of Schedule 10 (retention of shares in connection with profit sharing schemes), for "to pensionable age" there is substituted "in the case of a man, to the age of 65, and in the case of a woman, to the age of 60".
(c) in sub-paragraph (2) of paragraph 3A of that Schedule, for "pensionable age" there is substituted—
"(a) in the case of a man, 65, and
(b) in the case of a woman, 60.", and
(d) in sub-paragraph (4) of that paragraph, for "pensionable age" there is substituted "in the case of a man, 65, and in the case of a woman, 60.".

13. In the Social Security Contributions and Benefits Act 1992—
(a) in section 122(1) (interpretation of Parts I to VI), for the definition of "pensionable age" there is substituted—
" 'pensionable age' has the meaning given by the rules in paragraph 1 of Schedule 4 to the Pensions Act 1995", and
(b) in section 150(2) (interpretation of Part X), for the definition of "pensionable age" there is substituted—
" 'pensionable age' has the meaning given by the rules in paragraph 1 of Schedule 4 to the Pensions Act 1995".

14. In section 191 of the Social Security Administration Act 1992 (interpretation), for the definition of "pensionable age" there is substituted—
" 'pensionable age' has the meaning given by the rules in paragraph 1 of Schedule 4 to the Pensions Act 1995".

15. In section 58 of the Trade Union and Labour Relations (Consolidation) Act 1992 (exemption from requirement for election), in subsection (3)(b), for the words following "pensionable age" there is substituted "(within the meaning given by the rules in paragraph 1 of Schedule 4 to the Pensions Act 1995)".

16. For section 49 of the Pension Schemes Act 1993 (married women and widows), including the cross heading preceding it, there is substituted—

"Women, married women and widows
49. The Secretary of State may make regulations modifying, in such manner as he thinks proper—
(a) this Chapter in its application to women born on or after 6th April 1950, and
(b) sections 41, 42, 46(1), 47(2) and (5) and 48, in their application to women who are or have been married".

17. In section 181(1) of that Act (interpretation), for the definition of "pensionable age" there is substituted—

" 'pensionable age'—

    (a) so far as any provisions (other than sections 46 to 48) relate to guaranteed minimum pensions, means the age of 65 in the case of a man and the age of 60 in the case of a woman, and

    (b) in any other case, has the meaning given by the rules in paragraph 1 of Schedule 4 to the Pensions Act 1995".

Pension increases for dependent spouses

18. In the Social Security Contributions and Benefits Act 1992—

(a) in section 25(6)(c) (unemployment benefit), for "83" there is substituted "83A",

(b) in section 30B(3) (incapacity benefit: rate, inserted by the Social Security (Incapacity for Work) Act 1994), for "83" there is substituted "83A",

(c) in section 78(4)(d) (benefits for the aged), for "83" there is substituted "83A",

(d) in section 85(4) (pension increase: care of children), for "83(3)" there is substituted "83A(3)",

(e) in section 88 (pension increase: supplementary), for "83" there is substituted "83A",

(f) in section 114(4) (persons maintaining dependants, etc.), for "84" there is substituted "83A", and

(g) in section 149(3)(b) (Christmas bonus), for "83(2) or (3)" there is substituted "83A(2) or (3)".

19. In the Social Security (Incapacity for Work) Act 1994, in Schedule 1, paragraphs 20 and 21 are omitted.

20. Paragraphs 18 and 19 shall have effect on or after 6th April 2010.

Category B retirement pensions

21.—(1) In section 20(1)(f) of the Social Security Contributions and Benefits Act 1992 (general description of benefits), for sub-paragraph (ii) there is substituted—

    "(ii) Category B, payable to a person by virtue of the contributions of a spouse (with increase for child dependants)".

(2) In section 25(6) of that Act, in paragraph (b), for "(for married women) under section 53(2)" there is substituted "(for married people) under section 51A(2)".

(3) In section 30B of that Act (incapacity benefit), in paragraph (a) of the proviso to subsection (3), for "(for married women) under section 53(2)" there is substituted "(for married people) under section 51A(2)".

(4) In section 41(5)(a) of that Act (long-term incapacity benefit for widowers), for "section 51 below" there is substituted "the contributions of his wife".

(5) In section 46(2) of that Act (calculation of additional pension in certain benefits), for "50(3)" there is substituted "48A(4) or 48B(2)".

(6) After section 51 of that Act there is inserted—

"Special provision for married people

51A.—(1) This section has effect where, apart from section 43(1) above, a married person would be entitled both—

    (a) to a Category A retirement pension, and

    (b) to a Category B retirement pension by virtue of the contributions of the other party to the marriage.

(2) If by reason of a deficiency of contributions the basic pension in the Category A retirement pension falls short of the weekly rate specified in Schedule 4, Part I, paragraph 5, that basic pension shall be increased by the lesser of—

    (a) the amount of the shortfall, or

    (b) the amount of the weekly rate of the Category B retirement pension.

(3) This section does not apply in any case where both parties to the marriage attained pensionable age before 6th April 1979",

and section 53 of that Act (special provision for married women) is omitted.

(7) In section 52 of that Act (special provision for surviving spouses), for subsection (1)(b) there is substituted—

    "(b) to a Category B retirement pension by virtue of the contributions of a spouse who has died".

(8) In section 54 of that Act (supplemental provisions), for subsection (3) there is substituted—

    "(3) Where both parties to a marriage (call them 'P' and 'S') have become entitled to retirement pensions and—

    (a) P's pension is Category A, and

    (b) S's pension is—

(i) Category B by virtue of P's contributions, or

(ii) Category A with an increase under section 51A(2) above by virtue of P's contributions,

P shall not be entitled to make an election in accordance with regulations made under subsection (1) above without S's consent, unless that consent is unreasonably withheld".

(9) In section 60 of that Act (complete or partial failure to såtisfy contribution conditions)—

(a) in subsection (2), for "him" (in paragraph (b)) there is substituted "the employed earner" and for "his widow's entitlement" there is substituted "the entitlement of the employed earner's widow or widower", and

(b) for subsection (3)(d) there is substituted—

"(d) a Category B retirement pension payable by virtue of section 48B above".

(10) In section 85 of that Act (pension increase for person with care of children), in subsection (3), for "man whose wife" there is substituted "person whose spouse".

(11) In Schedule 4 to that Act (rates of benefit, etc.), in paragraph 5 of Part I, for "section 50(1)(a)(i)" there is substituted "section 48A(3)".

(12) In Schedule 5 to that Act (increased pension where entitlement deferred), in paragraph 2(5)(a), for "5 or 6" there is substituted "5, 5A or 6".

(13) In paragraph 4 of that Schedule, for sub-paragraphs (1) and (2) there is substituted—

"(1) Subject to sub-paragraph (3) below, where—

(a) a widow or widower (call that person 'W') is entitled to a Category A or Category B retirement pension and was married to the other party to the marriage (call that person 'S') when S died, and

(b) S either—

(i) was entitled to a Category A or Category B retirement pension with an increase under this Schedule, or

(ii) would have been so entitled if S's period of deferment had ended on the day before S's death,

the rate of W's pension shall be increased by an amount equal to the increase to which S was or would have been entitled under this Schedule apart from paragraphs 5 to 6".

(14) Paragraph 4(1) of that Schedule (as inserted by sub-paragraph (13) above) shall have effect where W is a man who attains pensionable age before 6th April 2010 as if paragraph (a) also required him to have been over pensionable age when S died.

(15) For paragraphs 5 and 6 of that Schedule there is substituted—

"5.—(1) Where—

(a) a widow or widower (call that person 'W') is entitled to a Category A or Category B retirement pension and was married to the other party to the marriage (call that person 'S') when S died, and

(b) S either—

(i) was entitled to a guaranteed minimum pension with an increase under section 15(1) of the Pensions Act, or

(ii) would have been so entitled if S had retired on the date of S's death,

the rate of W's pension shall be increased by the following amount.

(2) The amount is—

(a) where W is a widow, an amount equal to the sum of the amounts set out in paragraph 5A(2) or (3) below (as the case may be), and

(b) where W is a widower, an amount equal to the sum of the amounts set out in paragraph 6(2), (3) or (4) below (as the case may be).

5A.—(1) This paragraph applies where W (referred to in paragraph 5 above) is a widow.

(2) Where the husband dies before 6th April 2000, the amounts referred to in paragraph 5(2)(a) above are the following—

(a) an amount equal to one-half of the increase mentioned in paragraph 5(1)(b) above,

(b) the appropriate amount, and

(c) an amount equal to any increase to which the husband had been entitled under paragraph 5 above.

(3) Where the husband dies after 5th April 2000, the amounts referred to in paragraph 5(2)(a) above are the following—

(a) one-half of the appropriate amount after it has been reduced by the amount of any increases under section 109 of the Pensions Act, and

(b) one-half of any increase to which the husband had been entitled under paragraph 5 above.

6.—(1) This paragraph applies where W (referred to in paragraph 5 above) is a widower.

(2) Where the wife dies before 6th April 1989, the amounts referred to in paragraph 5(2)(b) above are the following—

(a) an amount equal to the increase mentioned in paragraph 5(1)(b) above,

(b) the appropriate amount, and

(c) an amount equal to any increase to which the wife had been entitled under paragraph 5 above.

(3) Where the wife dies after 5th April 1989 but before 6th April 2000, the amounts referred to in paragraph 5(2)(b) above are the following—

(a) the increase mentioned in paragraph 5(1)(b) above, so far as attributable to employment before 6th April 1988,

(b) one-half of that increase, so far as attributable to employment after 5th April 1988,

(c) the appropriate amount reduced by the amount of any increases under section 109 of the Pensions Act, and

(d) any increase to which the wife had been entitled under paragraph 5 above.

(4) Where the wife dies after 5th April 2000, the amounts referred to in paragraph 5(2)(b) above are the following—

(a) one-half of the increase mentioned in paragraph 5(1)(b) above, so far as attributable to employment before 6th April 1988,

(b) one-half of the appropriate amount after it has been reduced by the amount of any increases under section 109 of the Pensions Act, and

(c) one-half of any increase to which the wife had been entitled under paragraph 5 above".

(16) Paragraph 5(1) of that Schedule (inserted by sub-paragraph (15) above) shall have effect, where W is a man who attained pensionable age before 6th April 2010, as if paragraph (a) also required him to have been over pensionable age when S died.

(17) In paragraph 7 of that Schedule—

(a) in sub-paragraph (1), for "paragraphs 5 and 6" there is substituted "paragraphs 5 to 6", and

(b) in sub-paragraph (2), for "paragraph 5 or 6" there is substituted "paragraph 5, 5A or 6".

(18) In paragraph 8 of that Schedule, for sub-paragraphs (3) and (4) there is substituted—

"(3) In the case of the following pensions (where 'P' is a married person and 'S' is the other party to the marriage), that is—

(a) a Category B retirement pension to which P is entitled by virtue of the contributions of S, or

(b) P's Category A retirement pension with an increase under section 51A(2) above attributable to the contributions of S,

the reference in paragraph 2(3) above to the pension to which a person would have been entitled if that person's entitlement had not been deferred shall be construed as a reference to the pension to which P would have been entitled if neither P's nor S's entitlement to a retirement pension had been deferred.

(4) Paragraph 4(1)(b) above shall not apply to a Category B retirement pension to which S was or would have been entitled by virtue of 'W's contributions ('W' and 'S' having the same meaning as in paragraph 4(1)); and where the Category A retirement pension to which S was or would have been entitled includes an increase under section 51A(2) above attributable to W's contributions, the increase to which W is entitled under that paragraph shall be calculated as if there had been no increase under that section".

22. In section 46 of the Pension Schemes Act 1993 (effect of entitlement to guaranteed minimum pension on payment of benefits), in subsection (6)(b)(iii), for "section 49" there is substituted "section 48A or 48B".

Section 151   SCHEDULE 5

AMENDMENTS RELATING TO PART III

The Public Records Act 1958 (c. 51)

1. In Schedule 1 to the Public Records Act 1958 (definition of "Public Record"), in the Table—

(a) in Part I, the entry relating to the Occupational Pensions Board is omitted, and

(b) in Part II—

(i) after the entry relating to the Nature Conservancy Council for England, there is inserted—

"Occupational Pensions Regulatory Authority.", and

(ii) after the entry relating to the Office of the Director General of Fair Trading, there is inserted—
"Pensions Compensation Board."

The Administration of Justice Act 1970 (c. 31)

2. In Schedule 4 to the Administration of Justice Act 1970 (taxes, social insurance contributions, etc. subject to special enforcement provisions), in paragraph 3, for "State scheme premiums" there is substituted "Contributions equivalent premiums".

The Attachment of Earnings Act 1971 (c. 31)

3. In Schedule 2 to the Attachment of Earnings Act 1971 (taxes, social security contributions, etc. relevant for purposes of section 3(6)), in paragraph 3, for "State scheme premiums" there is substituted "Contributions equivalent premiums".

The House of Commons Disqualification Act 1975 (c. 24)

4. In Part II of Schedule 1 to the House of Commons Disqualification Act 1975 (bodies of which all members are disqualified), the entry relating to the Occupational Pensions Board is omitted.

The Northern Ireland Assembly Disqualification Act 1975 (c. 25)

5. In Part II of Schedule 1 to the Northern Ireland Assembly Disqualification Act 1975 (bodies of which all members are disqualified), the entry relating to the Occupational Pensions Board is omitted.

The Social Security Pensions Act 1975 (c. 60)

6.—(1) In section 61 of the Social Security Pensions Act 1975 (consultation about regulations) for the words from "refer the proposals" in subsection (2) to the end of subsection (3) there is substituted "consult such persons as he may consider appropriate".
(2) In section 61B(1) of that Act (orders and regulations: general provisions), "except any power of the Occupational Pensions Board to make orders" is omitted.
(3) In section 64(3) of that Act (expenses and receipts), for "state scheme premium" there is substituted "contributions equivalent premium".

The European Parliament (Pay and Pensions) Act 1979 (c. 50)

7. In section 6(4) of the European Parliament (Pay and Pensions) Act 1979 (provision for payment of block transfer value into another pension scheme), "and the Occupational Pensions Board" is omitted.

The Justices of the Peace Act 1979 (c. 55)

8. In section 55(6)(b)(ii) of the Justices of the Peace Act 1979 (duties of local authorities), for "state scheme premiums" there is substituted "contributions equivalent premiums".

The Judicial Pensions Act 1981 (c. 20)

9. In section 14A(2) of the Judicial Pensions Act 1981 (modifications of that Act in relation to personal pensions), in the definition of "personal pension scheme", for the words from "by" to the end there is substituted "in accordance with section 7 of the Pension Schemes Act 1993;".

The Insurance Companies Act 1982 (c. 50)

10. In the Table in paragraph 3(1) of Schedule 2B to the Insurance Companies Act 1982 (restriction on disclosure of information), the entry relating to the Occupational Pensions Board is omitted.

The Companies Act 1985 (c. 6)

11. In Schedule 2 to the Companies Act 1985 (interpretation of references to "beneficial interest"), in paragraphs 3(2)(b) and 7(2)(b), for "state scheme premium" there is substituted "contributions equivalent premium".

The Income and Corporation Taxes Act 1988 (c. 1)

12.—(1) In section 649 of the Income and Corporation Taxes Act 1988 (minimum contributions towards approved personal pension schemes), in subsection (2), for the definition of "the employee's share" there is substituted—

" 'the employee's share' of minimum contributions is the amount that would be the minimum contributions if, for the reference in section 45(1) of the Pension Schemes Act 1993 to the appropriate age-related percentage, there were substituted a reference to the percentage mentioned in section 41(1A)(a) of that Act".

(2) This paragraph does not extend to Northern Ireland.

The Social Security Act 1989 (c. 24)

13.—(1) Section 29(7) of the Social Security Act 1989 (regulations and orders) is omitted.

(2) In Schedule 5 to that Act (equal treatment in employment related schemes for pensions etc.), paragraph 4 is omitted.

The Social Security Contributions and Benefits Act 1992 (c. 4)

14. In Schedule 1 to the Social Security Contributions and Benefits Act 1992 (supplementary provisions), in paragraph 8(1)(g), for "state scheme premium" there is substituted "contributions equivalent premium".

The Social Security Administration Act 1992 (c. 5)

15.—(1) The Social Security Administration Act 1992 is amended as follows.

(2) In section 110 (appointment and powers of inspectors)—

(a) in subsections (2)(c)(ii) and (6)(a)(ii), for "state scheme premium" there is substituted "contributions equivalent premium", and

(b) in subsection (7)(e)(i), for "state scheme premiums" there is substituted "contributions equivalent premiums".

(3) In section 120 (proof of previous offences), in subsections (3) and (4), for "state scheme premiums" there is substituted "contributions equivalent premiums".

(4) In Schedule 4 (persons employed in social security administration etc.), the entries in Part I relating to the Occupational Pensions Board are omitted.

The Tribunals and Inquiries Act 1992 (c. 53)

16.—(1) The Tribunals and Inquiries Act 1992 is amended as follows.

(2) In section 7(2) (concurrence needed for removal of members of certain tribunals), "(d) or" is omitted.

(3) In section 10(5) (reasons to be given for decisions of tribunals and Ministers), paragraph (c) is omitted.

(4) In section 13(5)(a) (power to amend), "and (d)" is omitted.

(5) In section 14 (restricted application of Act in relation to certain tribunals), subsection (2) is omitted.

(6) In Schedule 1 (Tribunals under the direct supervision of the Council on Tribunals), paragraph 35(d) is omitted.

The Judicial Pensions and Retirement Act 1993 (c. 8)

17. In section 13(9) of the Judicial Pensions and Retirement Act 1993 (election for personal pension), in the definition of "personal pension scheme", "by the Occupational Pensions Board" is omitted.

The Pension Schemes Act 1993 (c. 48)

18. The Pension Schemes Act 1993 is amended as follows.

19. Sections 2 to 5 (constitution, membership etc. of the Board) are repealed.

20. For section 6(8) (Board may be appointed as Registrar), there is substituted—

"(8) Nothing in this Act or the Pensions Act 1995 shall be taken to imply that the Regulatory Authority may not be appointed as the Registrar."

21. In the provisions listed in the first column of the table—

(a) in each place where the word appears, for "Board" there is substituted "Secretary of State", and

(b) the additional amendments listed in the second column of the table in relation to those provisions shall have effect.

TABLE

Provision	Additional amendments
Section 8 (meaning of terms).	—
Section 9 (requirements for certification).	In subsection (4), for "they think" there is substituted "he thinks".
Section 11 (employer's right to elect as to contracting-out).	In subsection (4), for "consider" and "they" there is substituted, respectively, "considers" and "he". In subsection (5)(d), for "they are" there is substituted "he is".
Section 30 (protected rights).	—
Section 34 (cancellation etc. of certificates).	In subsection (2)(a), for "they have" there is substituted "he has". In subsections (4) and (5), for "they consider" (in both places) and "they" (in both places) there is substituted, respectively, "he considers" and "he".
Section 50 (schemes ceasing to be certified).	In subsection (2), for "have" (in both places) and "their" there is substituted, respectively, "has" and "his". In subsection (3), for "they subsequently approve" there is substituted "he subsequently approves". In subsection (4), for the first "have" there is substituted "has".
Section 57 (contribution equivalent premiums).	In subsection (4) for "consider" and "they" there is substituted, respectively, "considers" and "he".
Section 163 (rule against perpetuities).	In subsection (6), for "consider" there is substituted "considers".

22. In section 7—
(a) in subsections (1) and (6), for "Board" there is substituted "Secretary of State", and
(b) in subsection (4), "by the Board" is omitted.
23. In section 8 (definition of terms)—
(a) in subsection (2), for the words following the definition of "minimum payment" there is substituted—
"and for the purposes of this subsection "rebate percentage" means the appropriate flat rate percentage for the purposes of section 42A(2)", and
(b) subsection (5) is omitted.
24. In section 9 (requirements for certification), in subsection (3) "22 and" is omitted.
25. In section 10 (protected rights), in subsection (2)(a), after "minimum payments" there is inserted "and payments under section 42A(3)".
26. In section 13 (minimum pensions for earners), in subsection (2)(a), the words from "and does" to the end are omitted.
27. In section 14 (earner's guaranteed minimum)—
(a) subsection (3) is omitted,
(b) in subsection (8) after "1978–79" there is inserted "or later than the tax year ending immediately before the principal appointed day".
28. In section 16 (revaluation of earnings factors)—
(a) in subsection (3), for the words following "at least" there is substituted "the prescribed percentage for each relevant year after the last service tax year; and the provisions included by virtue of this subsection may also conform with such additional requirements as may be prescribed", and
(b) for the definition of "final relevant year" in subsection (5) there is substituted—
" 'final relevant year' means the last tax year in the earner's working life".
29. In section 17 (minimum pensions for widows and widowers), at the end of subsection (7) there is added "or widows".
30. Section 22 (financing of benefits) is repealed.
31. In section 23 (securing of benefits)—
(a) subsections (1) and (5) are omitted,

(b) in subsection (4), for "(1) to (3)" there is substituted "(2) and (3)";
and subsections (2) and (3) of that section do not apply where the winding up is begun on or after the principal appointed day.

32. Section 24 (sufficiency of resources) is repealed.

33. In section 25 (conditions as to investments, etc.)—
(a) subsections (1) and (3) are repealed, and
(b) for subsection (2) there is substituted—
"(2) A salary related contracted-out scheme must, in relation to any earner's service before the principal appointed day, comply with any requirements prescribed for the purpose of securing that—
(a) the Secretary of State is kept informed about any matters affecting the security of the minimum pensions guaranteed under the scheme, and
(b) the resources of the scheme are brought to and are maintained at a level satisfactory to the Secretary of State".

34. In section 28 (ways of giving effect to protected rights)—
(a) in subsection (4)(d), for "a manner satisfactory to the Board" there is substituted "the prescribed manner", and
(b) subsection (7) is omitted.

35. In section 29 (the pension and annuity requirements), in subsection (1)(b)(ii), for "a manner satisfactory to the Board" there is substituted "the prescribed manner".

36. In section 31 (investment and resources of schemes)—
(a) subsection (1) is omitted,
(b) in subsection (3)(a), after "minimum payments" there is inserted "and payments under section 42A(3)", and
(c) at the end of that section there is added—
"(5) Any minimum contributions required by reason of this section to be applied so as to provide money purchase benefits for or in respect of a member of a scheme must be so applied in the prescribed manner and within the prescribed period".

37. In section 34 (cancellation, etc. of certificates)—
(a) in subsection (1), for paragraph (a) there is substituted—
"(a) in the case of a contracting-out certificate—
(i) on any change of circumstances affecting the treatment of an employment as contracted-out employment, or
(ii) where the scheme is a salary related contracted-out scheme and the certificate was issued on or after the principal appointed day, if any employer of persons in the description or category of employment to which the scheme in question relates, or the actuary of the scheme, fails to provide the Secretary of State, at prescribed intervals, with such documents as may be prescribed for the purpose of verifying that the conditions of section 9(2B) are satisfied",
(b) subsection (6) is omitted, and
(c) for subsection (7) there is substituted—
"(7) Without prejudice to the previous provisions of this section, failure of a scheme to comply with any requirements prescribed by virtue of section 25(2) shall be a ground on which the Secretary of State may, in respect of any employment to which the scheme relates, cancel a contracting-out certificate".

38. Sections 35 (surrender, etc. issue of further certificates) and 36 (surrender etc. cancellation of further certificates) are repealed.

39. For section 37 (alteration of rules of contracted-out schemes) there is substituted—

"Alteration of rules of contracted-out schemes

37.—(1) Except in prescribed circumstances, the rules of a contracted-out scheme cannot be altered unless the alteration is of a prescribed description.

(2) Regulations made by virtue of subsection (1) may operate so as to validate with retrospective effect any alteration of the rules which would otherwise be void under this section.

(3) References in this section to a contracted-out scheme include a scheme which has ceased to be contracted-out so long as any person is entitled to receive, or has accrued rights to, any benefits under the scheme attributable to a period when the scheme was contracted-out.

(4) The reference in subsection (3) to a person entitled to receive benefits under a scheme includes a person so entitled by virtue of being the widower of an earner only in such cases as may be prescribed.".

40. In section 38 (alteration of rules of appropriate schemes)—
(a) in subsection (1), the words from "unless" to the end are omitted,

(b) in subsection (3), the words from "if" to the end are omitted,

(c) in subsection (4), for the words from the beginning to "direct" there is substituted "Regulations made by virtue of subsection (2) may", and

(d) subsection (7) is omitted.

41. In section 42 (review of reduced rates of contributions), in subsection (3), for "41(1)(a)" there is substituted "41(1A)(a)".

42. In section 43 (payment of minimum contributions), in subsection (1), after "circumstances" there is inserted "or in respect of such periods".

43. In section 45 (minimum contributions towards personal pension schemes), subsection (3)(d) is omitted.

44. In section 46(1) (effect of entitlement to guaranteed minimum pensions on payment of social security benefits), for sub-paragraph (i) there is substituted—

"(i) to that part of its additional pension which is attributable to earnings factors for any tax years ending before the principal appointed day".

45. In section 50 (powers to approve arrangements for scheme ceasing to be certified)—

(a) in subsection (1)(a)—

(i) at the end of sub-paragraph (i) there is inserted "or accrued rights to pensions under the scheme attributable to their service on or after the principal appointed day", and

(ii) in sub-paragraph (ii), for "guaranteed minimum pensions under the scheme" there is substituted "such pensions",

(b) after subsection (1) there is inserted—

"(1A) The power of the Secretary of State to approve arrangements under this section—

(a) includes power to approve arrangements subject to conditions, and

(b) may be exercised either generally or in relation to a particular scheme.

(1B) Arrangements may not be approved under this section unless any prescribed conditions are met", and

(c) subsection (7) is omitted.

46. In section 51 (calculation of GMPs preserved under approved arrangements), in subsection (1)(a), for "are subject to approved arrangements" there is substituted "satisfy prescribed conditions".

47. In section 52 (supervision of schemes which have ceased to be certified)—

(a) in subsection (2), for paragraphs (a) and (b) there is substituted—

"(a) the scheme has ceased to be a contracted-out scheme, and

(b) any persons remain who fall within any of the following categories.

(2A) Those categories are—

(a) any persons entitled to receive, or having accrued rights to—

(i) guaranteed minimum pensions, or

(ii) pensions under the scheme attributable to service on or after the principal appointed day but before the scheme ceased to be contracted-out,

(b) any persons who have protected rights under the scheme or are entitled to any benefit giving effect to protected rights under it",

(b) in subsection (3), for paragraphs (a) and (b) there is substituted—

"(a) the scheme has ceased to be an appropriate scheme, and

(b) any persons remain who have protected rights under the scheme or are entitled to any benefit giving effect to protected rights under it", and

(c) subsections (4) to (6) are omitted.

48. In section 53 (supervision: former contracted-out schemes)—

(a) for subsection (1) there is substituted—

"(1) The Secretary of State may direct the trustees or managers of the scheme, or the employer, to take or refrain from taking such steps as the Secretary of State may specify in writing; and such a direction shall be final and binding on the person directed and any person claiming under him.

(1A) An appeal on a point of law shall lie to the High Court or, in Scotland, the Court of Session from a direction under subsection (1) at the instance of the trustees or managers or the employer, or any person claiming under them.

(1B) A direction under subsection (1) shall be enforceable—

(a) in England and Wales, in a county court as if it were an order of that court, and

(b) in Scotland, by the sheriff, as if it were an order of the sheriff and whether or not the sheriff could himself have given such an order",

(b) subsection (2) is omitted,

(c) for subsection (3) there is substituted—

"(3) If a certificate has been issued under subsection (2) of section 50 and has not been cancelled under subsection (3) of that section, any liabilities in respect of such entitlement or rights as are referred to in section 52(2A)(a) or (b) must, except in prescribed circumstances, be discharged (subject to any directions under subsection (1)) in a prescribed manner and within a prescribed period or such longer period as the Secretary of State may allow", and

(d) subsections (4) and (5) are omitted.

49. In section 54 (supervision: former appropriate personal pension schemes)—

(a) for subsections (1) and (2) there is substituted—

"(1) The Secretary of State may direct the trustees or managers of the scheme to take or refrain from taking such steps as the Secretary of State may specify in writing; and such a direction shall be final and binding on the person directed and any person claiming under him.

(1A) An appeal on a point of law shall lie to the High Court or, in Scotland, the Court of Session from a direction under subsection (1) at the instance of the trustees or managers or the employer, or any person claiming under them.

(1B) A direction under subsection (1) shall be enforceable—

(a) in England and Wales, in a county court as if it were an order of that court, and

(b) in Scotland, by the sheriff, as if it were an order of the sheriff and whether or riot the sheriff could himself have given such an order.

(2) If a certificate has been issued under subsection (2) of section 50 and has not been cancelled under subsection (3) of that section, any liabilities in respect of such entitlement or rights as are referred to in section 52(3)(b) must, except in prescribed circumstances, be discharged (subject to any directions under subsection (1)) in a prescribed manner and within a prescribed period or such longer period as the Secretary of State may allow", and

(b) subsection (3) is omitted.

50. In section 55 (state scheme premiums), subsections (1) and (3) to (6) are omitted.

51. In section 56 (provisions supplementary to section 55)—

(a) subsection (1), in subsection (2) the words following "the prescribed period" and subsection (3) are omitted, and

(b) for subsections (5) and (6) there is substituted—

"(5) The references in section 55(2A) to an accrued right to short service benefit include an accrued right to any provision which, under the preservation requirements, is permitted as an alternative to short service benefit (other than provision for return of contributions or for benefit in the form of a lump sum).

(6) Subject to regulations under paragraph 1 of Schedule 2, service in any employment which ceases with the death of the employer shall be treated for the purposes of section 55(2A) as ceasing immediately before the death".

52. In section 58 (amount of premiums under section 55), subsections (1) to (3), (5) and (6) are omitted.

53. Section 59 (alternative basis for revaluation) is repealed.

54. In section 60 (effect of payment of premiums on rights)—

(a) subsections (1) to (3) are omitted,

(b) in subsection (4)—

(i) for "55(2)(i)" there is substituted "55(2A)(a) and (b), (d) and (e)", and

(ii) at the end there is added "or (in relation to service on or after the principal appointed day) rights to pensions under the scheme so far as attributable to the amount of the premium", and

(c) in subsection (5), for "55(2)(ii)" there is substituted "55(2A)(c)", and after "widow" there is added "or widower", and

(d) subsections (6) to (10) are omitted.

55. In section 61 (deduction of contributions equivalent premium from refund of scheme contributions)—

(a) in subsection (1), for paragraph (a) there is substituted—

"(a) an earner's service in contracted-out employment ceases or his employment ceases to be contracted-out employment, and",

(b) in subsection (8)—

(i) for paragraph (a) there is substituted—

"(a) an earner's service in contracted-out employment ceases or his employment ceases to be contracted-out employment", and

(ii) for "termination" there is substituted "cessation", and

(c) in subsection (9), for "termination" (in both places) there is substituted "cessation".

56. In section 62 (no recovery of premiums from earners)—

(a) in subsection (1), for "state scheme" there is substituted "contributions equivalent", and

(b) subsection (2) is omitted.

57. In section 63 (further provisions concerning calculations relating to premiums)—
(a) in subsection (1)—
    (i) paragraph (a) is omitted,
    (ii) in paragraph (b), for "that section" there is substituted "section 58", and
    (iii) paragraph (c) is omitted,
(b) subsection (2) is omitted,
(c) in subsection (3)—
    (i) paragraph (a) is omitted,
    (ii) in paragraph (b), for "subsection (4) of that section" there is substituted "section 58(4)", and
    (iii) the words following sub-paragraph (ii) are omitted, and
(d) subsection (4) is omitted.
58. Section 64 (actuarial tables) is repealed.
59. Section 65 (former and future earners) is repealed.
60. Section 66 (widowers) is repealed.
61. In sections 67 and 68 (non-payment of state scheme premiums), for "state scheme premium" (in each place) there is substituted "contributions equivalent premium".
62. In section 84(5), paragraph (b) and the preceding "or" are omitted.
63. In section 96 (right to cash equivalent: exercise of options)—
(a) in subsection (2)(a), after "guaranteed minimum pensions" there is inserted "his accrued rights so far as attributable to service in contracted-out employment on or after the principal appointed day", and
(b) in subsection (3)(a), for "guaranteed minimum pensions" there is substituted "pensions, being guaranteed minimum pensions or pensions so far as attributable to service in contracted-out employment on or after the principal appointed day".
64. Sections 133 to 135 (advice and determinations as to conformity of schemes with requirements) are repealed.
65. In section 155 (requirement to give information to the Secretary of State or the Board)—
(a) "or the Board" is omitted,
(b) for "or they require" there is substituted "requires", and
(c) for the words from "sections 7" to "premiums" there is substituted "Part III".
66. In section 158 (disclosure of information between government departments)—
(a) subsections (2) and (3) are omitted,
(b) in subsection (6), "(2) or (3)", paragraph (d) and the "or" immediately preceding it are omitted,
(c) in subsection (7)—
    (i) for "the Inland Revenue and the Board", there is substituted "and the Inland Revenue",
    (ii) after paragraph (a), there is inserted "or", and
    (iii) paragraph (c) and the "or" immediately preceding it are omitted, and
(d) subsection (8) is omitted.
67. In section 164(1)(b)(i) (Crown employment), "2 to 5", "172, 173" and "and Schedule 1" are omitted.
68. In section 165 (application of certain provisions to case with foreign element), in subsection (2)(a), for the words from "sections 7" to "premiums)" there is substituted "Part III".
69. In section 166(5) (reciprocity with other countries), "sections 2 to 5", "172, 173" and "and Schedule 1" are omitted.
70. In section 170 (determinations by the Secretary of State)—
(a) in subsection (1)—
    (i) in paragraph (b) for "state scheme premium" (in both places) there is substituted "contributions equivalent premium",
    (ii) the "and" at the end of paragraph (c) is omitted, and
    (iii) for the words following paragraph (d) there is substituted "and
        (e) any question whether an employment is, or is to be treated, for the purposes of the Pension Schemes Act 1993 as contracted-out employment or as to the persons in relation to whom, or the period for which, an employment is, or is to be treated, for the purposes of that Act as such employment",
(b) subsections (3) and (4) are omitted, and
(c) at the end of that section there is added—
    "(7) Sections 18 and 19 of the Social Security Administration Act 1992 (appeals and reviews) shall have effect as if the questions mentioned in subsection (1) of section 17 of that Act included—
    (a) any question arising in connection with the issue, cancellation or variation of contracting-out certificates or appropriate scheme certificates, not being a question mentioned in subsection (1)(e) above, and

(b) any other question arising under this Act which falls to be determined by the Secretary of State, not being a question mentioned in that subsection.

(8) Regulations may make provision with respect to the procedure to be adopted on any application for a review made under section 19 of that Act by virtue of subsection (7) above and generally with respect to such applications and reviews, but may not prevent such a review being entered upon without an application being made".

71. In section 171 (questions arising in proceedings), in subsection (1)(b), for "state scheme premium" there is substituted "contributions equivalent premium".

72. Sections 172 and 173 (reviews and appeals) are repealed.

73. In section 174 (grants), for "Board" (in both places) there is substituted "Regulatory Authority".

74. In section 176 (fees), for "either by the Secretary of State or by the Board on his behalf" there is substituted "by the Secretary of State".

75. In section 177 (general financial arrangements)—

(a) in subsection (3)(b)—

(i) in sub-paragraph (i), "sections 2 to 5", "172, 173" and "and Schedule 1" are omitted, and

(ii) in sub-paragraph (ii), the words from "sections 55" to "premiums)" are omitted, and

(b) subsection (7)(b) is omitted.

76. In section 178(b) (meaning of "trustee" and "manager"), "sections 2 to 5", "172, 173" and "and Schedule 1" are omitted.

77. In section 181 (general interpretation)—

(a) in subsection (1)—

(i) the definitions of "accrued rights premium", "the Board", "contracted-out protected rights premium", "limited revaluation premium", "pensioner's rights premium", "personal pension protected rights premium", "state scheme premium" and "transfer premium" are omitted, and

(ii) in the definition of "contributions equivalent premium", for "section 55(6)(e)" there is substituted "section 55(2)",

(b) in subsection (3), for "sections 2 to" there is substituted "section", and "172, 173" and "and Schedule 1" are omitted, and

(c) in subsection (7), "and Schedule 1" is omitted.

78. In section 182(1) (orders and regulations), "the Board or" is omitted.

79. In section 183 (sub-delegation), in subsection (1), "sections 2 to 5", "172, 173" and "or Schedule 1", and subsection (2) are omitted.

80. In section 185 (consultation about regulations)—

(a) in subsection (1), for the words from the beginning to "make" there is substituted "Subject to subsection (2), before the Secretary of State makes", and for the words from "refer the proposals" to the end there is substituted "consult such persons as he may consider appropriate",

(b) in subsection (2), at the end of paragraph (c) there is added—

"(d) regulations in the case of which the Secretary of State considers consultation inexpedient because of urgency, or

(e) regulations which—

(i) state that they are consequential upon a specified enactment, and

(ii) are made before the end of the period of six months beginning with the coming into force of that enactment,"

(c) subsections (3) and (4) are omitted,

(d) in subsection (5), for "subsections (1) to (4)" there is substituted "subsection (1)",

(e) subsection (6) is omitted, and

(f) in subsection (8), for "172(4)" there is substituted "170(8)".

81. In section 186(5) (Parliamentary control of regulations and orders), "or section 185(4)" is omitted.

82. In section 192(2) (extent), for "sections 1 to 5" there is substituted "section 1" and "section 172(4) and (5)" is omitted.

83. Schedule 1 (the Occupational Pensions Board) is repealed.

84. In Schedule 2 (certification regulations)—

(a) in paragraph 2(1), for "the Board" there is substituted "the Secretary of State",

(b) in paragraph 4(3), for the words from "does not cease" to the end there is substituted "which, apart from the regulations, would not be contracted-out employment is treated as contracted-out employment where any benefits provided under the scheme are attributable to a period when the scheme was contracted-out",

(c) in paragraph 5(1)—
   (i) "or the Board" and "or, as the case may be, the Board" are omitted, and
   (ii) for "65" there is substituted "63",
(d) in paragraph 5(2), "to 65" is omitted, and
(e) in paragraph 9, for sub-paragraphs (3) to (5) there is substituted—
   "(2A) Sub-paragraphs (3) and (4) shall be omitted".
85. In Schedule 4 (priority in bankruptcy), in paragraph 3(1), for "state scheme premium" there is substituted "contributions equivalent premium".
86. In Schedule 6 (transitional provisions and savings), paragraph 11 is omitted.

Section 177   SCHEDULE 6

GENERAL MINOR AND CONSEQUENTIAL AMENDMENTS

The Public Records Act 1958 (c. 51)

1. In Schedule 1 to the Public Records Act 1958 (definition of "Public Record"), in Part II of the Table, there is inserted at the appropriate place—
   "Pensions Ombudsman."

The Pension Schemes Act 1993 (c. 48)

2. The Pension Schemes Act 1993 is amended as follows.
3. In section 95(1) (ways of taking right to cash equivalent), for "this Chapter" there is substituted "paragraph (a), (aa) or (b) of section 94(1)".
4. In section 97 (calculation of cash equivalents)—
(a) in subsection (2)(a) after "cash equivalents" there is inserted "except guaranteed cash equivalents",
(b) in subsection (3)(b), for the words from "the date" to the end there is substituted "the appropriate date", and
(c) after that subsection there is inserted—
   "(3A) For the purposes of subsection (3), the 'appropriate date'—
   (a) in the case of a salary related occupational pension scheme, is the guarantee date (within the meaning of section 93A), and
   (b) in any other case, is the date on which the trustees receive an application from the member under section 95."
5. In section 98 (variation and loss of rights to cash equivalents)—
(a) in subsection (1), after "occupational pension scheme" there is inserted "other than a salary related scheme",
(b) after that subsection there is inserted—
   "(1A) Regulations may provide that a member of a salary related occupational pension scheme who continues in employment to which the scheme applies after his pensionable service in that employment terminates—
   (a) acquires a right to only part of his guaranteed cash equivalent, or
   (b) acquires no right to his guaranteed cash equivalent.",
(c) in subsection (2), after "(1)" there is inserted "or (1A)", and
(d) in subsection (3)—
   (i) in paragraph (a), after "occupational pension scheme" there is inserted "other than a salary related scheme", and
   (ii) for paragraph (b) and the "and" immediately preceding it there is substituted—
"or
   (aa) by virtue of regulations under subsection (1A) or (2), a member of a salary related occupational pension scheme does not, on such a termination, acquire a right to the whole or any part of his guaranteed cash equivalent,
and his employment terminates at least one year before normal pension age".
6. In section 99 (trustee's duties after exercise of an option under section 95)—
(a) in subsection (2), for paragraphs (a) and (b) there is substituted—
   "(a) in the case of a member of a salary related occupational pension scheme, within 6 months of the guarantee date, or (if earlier) by the date on which the member attains normal pension age,
   (b) in the case of a member of any other occupational pension scheme, within 6 months of the date on which they receive the application, or (if earlier) by the date on which the member attains normal pension age, or

    (c) in the case of a member of a personal pension scheme, within 6 months of the date on which they receive the application.",

(b) after subsection (3) there is inserted—

"(3A) In this section, 'guarantee date' has the same meaning as in section 93A.",

(c) for subsections (4) and (5) there is substituted—

"(4) The Regulatory Authority may, in prescribed circumstances, grant an extension of the period within which the trustees or managers of the scheme are obliged to do what is needed to carry out what a member of the scheme requires.

(4A) Regulations may make provision in relation to applications for extensions under subsection (4).",

(d) in subsection (6), for "Board" there is substituted "Regulatory Authority", and

(e) after that subsection there is added—

"(7) Where the trustees or managers of an occupational pension scheme have not done what is needed to carry out what a member of the scheme requires within six months of the date mentioned in paragraph (a) or (b) of subsection (2)—

    (a) they must, except in prescribed cases, notify the Regulatory Authority of that fact within the prescribed period, and

    (b) section 10 of the Pensions Act 1995 (power of the Regulatory Authority to impose civil penalties) shall apply to any trustee or manager who has failed to take all such steps as are reasonable to ensure that it was so done.

(8) Regulations may provide that in prescribed circumstances subsection (7) shall not apply in relation to an occupational pension scheme."

7. In section 145 (Pensions Ombudsman), in subsection (5) "with the approval of the Treasury" is omitted.

8. In section 151(5)(b) (enforcement in Scotland of Pensions Ombudsman's determinations), for the words from "Scotland," to the end there is substituted "in like manner as an extract registered decree arbitral bearing warrant for execution issued by the sheriff court of any sheriffdom in Scotland.".

9. After section 158 there is inserted—

"Other disclosures by the Secretary of State

158A.—(1) The Secretary of State may, in spite of any obligation as to secrecy or confidentiality imposed by statute or otherwise on him or on persons employed in the Department of Social Security, disclose any information received by him in connection with his functions under this Act or the Pensions Act 1995 to any person specified in the first column of the following Table if he considers that the disclosure would enable or assist the person to discharge the functions specified in relation to the person in the second column of the Table.

TABLE

Persons	Functions
The Treasury.	Functions under the Financial Services Act 1986.
The Bank of England.	Functions under the Banking Act 1987 or any other functions.
The Regulatory Authority.	Functions under this Act or the Pensions Act 1995, or any enactment in force in Northern Ireland corresponding to either of them.
The Pensions Compensation Board.	Functions under the Pensions Act 1995 or any corresponding enactment in force in Northern Ireland.
The Friendly Societies Commission.	Functions under the enactments relating to friendly societies.
The Building Societies Commission.	Functions under the Building Societies Act 1986.
An inspector appointed by the Secretary of State.	Functions under section 94 or 177 of the Financial Services Act 1986.
A person authorised to exercise powers under section 106 of the Financial Services Act 1986.	Functions under that section.
A designated agency or transferee body or the competent authority (within the meaning of the Financial Services Act 1986).	Functions under the Financial Services Act 1986.
A recognised self-regulating organisation, recognised professional body, recognised investment exchange or recognised clearing house (within the meaning of the Financial Services Act 1986).	Functions in its capacity as an organisation, body, exchange or clearing house recognised under the Financial Services Act 1986.

(2) The Secretary of State may by order—
    (a) amend the Table in subsection (1) by—
          (i) adding any person exercising regulatory functions and specifying functions in relation to that person,
          (ii) removing any person for the time being specified in the Table, or
          (iii) altering the functions for the time being specified in the Table in relation to any person, or
    (b) restrict the circumstances in which, or impose conditions subject to which, disclosure may be made to any person for the time being specified in the Table".

10. In section 164(1)(b)(i) (Crown employment), the words from "136" to "143" are omitted.

11. In section 166(5) (reciprocity with other countries), the words from "136" to "143" are omitted.

12. In section 177 (general financial arrangements), in subsection (3)(b)(i), the words from "136" to "143" are omitted.

13. In section 178 (meaning of "trustee" and "manager"), in paragraph (b), the words from "136" to "143" are omitted.

14. In section 181 (general interpretation), in subsection (3), the words from "136" to "143" are omitted.

15. In section 183 (sub-delegation)—
(a) in subsection (1), the words from "136" to "143" are omitted, and
(b) in subsection (3)(b), after "prepared" there is inserted "and from time to time revised".

16.—(1) Schedule 9 (transitory modifications) is amended as follows.
(2) In paragraph 1—
(a) in sub-paragraph (1), sub-paragraphs (ii) to (v) are omitted,
(b) in sub-paragraph (3)(a)(i), for "provisions mentioned in paragraphs (i) to (v)" there is substituted "provision mentioned in paragraph (i)", and
(c) sub-paragraph (5) is omitted.
(3) Paragraphs 3 and 4 are omitted.

SCHEDULE 7

REPEALS

PART I

OCCUPATIONAL PENSIONS

Chapter	Short title	Extent of repeal
1982 c. 50.	The Insurance Companies Act 1982.	In Schedule 2B, in paragraph 3(9), the "or" after paragraph (a).
1986 c. 53.	The Building Societies Act 1986.	In section 53(15), the "or" after paragraph (a).
1987 c. 22.	The Banking Act 1987.	In section 84(10), the "or" after paragraph (a).
1989 c. 24.	The Social Security Act 1989.	In Schedule 5, paragraph 14.
1993 c. 48.	The Pension Schemes Act 1993.	Sections 77 to 80. Sections 102 to 108. In section 110, subsections (2) to (4). Section 112. Section 114. Section 116. Section 118. Sections 119 to 122. In section 129, in subsection (1), "Chapter I of Part V", "sections 119 to 122", "under Chapter I of Part V or" and "or sections 119 to 122", and subsection (3)(a). In section 132, "the equal access requirements". In section 133(1), "the equal access requirements". In section 134, in subsection (3), "the equal access requirements" and, in subsection (4), "or the equal access requirements" and "or, as the case may be, section 118(1)". In section 136(2)(e)(iv), "or the equal access requirements". In section 139(2), "the equal access requirements". In section 140(4), paragraph (c) and the "and" immediately preceding it. Section 144. In section 153, in subsection (1), the words from "and Chapter I" to "section 108)", subsections (3) and (4), in subsection (5), "Chapter I of Part VII", paragraph (d) and the preceding "or", and subsections (6) and (7). In section 170, subsections (5) and (6). In section 178, in paragraph (a), the second "or". In section 181(1), the definition of "equal access requirements". In section 183, in subsection (3), the words from "or, in the case of" to "determined" and the words following paragraph (b).

Chapter	Short title	Extent of repeal
		In section 185, in subsection (1), "I or". In Schedule 7, paragraphs 1 and 3. In Schedule 8, paragraph 3.

PART II

STATE PENSIONS

Chapter	Short title	Extent of repeal
1988 c. 1.	The Income and Corporation Taxes Act 1988.	In section 187, in subsection (2), the definition of "pensionable age".
1992 c. 4.	The Social Security Contributions and Benefits Act 1992.	Section 53. In section 54, in subsection (1)(a), the words from "but" to "70", and subsection (4). In Schedule 3, in paragraph 5(7)(a), "(or at least 20 of them, if that is less than half". In Schedule 5, in paragraph 2(2), the definition of "period of enhancement" and the previous "and", and in paragraph 8, sub-paragraphs (1) and (2).
1994 c. 18.	The Social Security (Incapacity for Work) Act 1994.	In Schedule 1, paragraphs 20 and 21.

These repeals have effect in accordance with Schedule 4 to this Act.

PART III

CERTIFICATION OF PENSION SCHEME ETC.

Chapter	Short title	Extent of repeal
1958 c. 51.	The Public Records Act 1958.	In Schedule 1, in the Table, the entry relating to the Occupational Pensions Board.
1975 c. 24.	The House of Commons Disqualification Act 1975.	In Part II of Schedule 1, the entry relating to the Occupational Pensions Board.
1975 c. 25.	The Northern Ireland Assembly Disqualification Act 1975.	In Part II of Schedule 1, the entry relating to the Occupational Pensions Board.
1975 c. 60.	The Social Security Pensions Act 1975.	In section 61B(1), "except any power of the Occupational Pensions Board to make orders".
1979 c. 50.	The European Parliament (Pay and Pensions) Act 1979.	In section 6(4), "and the Occupational Pensions Board".
1982 c. 50.	The Insurance Companies Act 1982.	In Schedule 2B, in paragraph 3(1), in the Table, the entry relating to the Occupational Pensions Board.
1989 c. 24.	The Social Security Act 1989.	Section 29(7). In Schedule 5, paragraph 4.
1992 c. 5.	TheSocial Security Administration Act 1992.	In Schedule 4, the entries in Part I relating to the Occupational Pensions Board.
1992 c. 53.	The Tribunals and Inquiries Act 1992.	In section 7(2), "(d) or". In section 10(5), paragraph (c). In section 13(5)(a), "and (d)". In section 14, subsection (2). In Schedule 1, paragraph 35(d).
1993 c. 8.	The Judicial Pensions and Retirement Act 1993.	In section 13(9), in the definition of "personal pension scheme", "by the Occupational Pensions Board".

Chapter	Short title	Extent of repeal
1993 c. 48.	The Pension Schemes Act 1993.	Sections 2 to 5. In section 7(4), "by the Board". Section 8(5). In section 9(3), "22 and". In section 13(2)(a), the words from "and does" to the end. In section 14, subsection (3). Section 22. In section 23, subsections (1) and (5). Section 24. In section 25, subsections (1) and (3). Section 28(7). Section 31(1). Section 34(6). Section 35 and 36. In section 38, in subsection (1), the words from "unless" to the end, in subsection (3), the words from "if" to the end, and subsection (7). In section 45, subsection (2) and, in subsection (3), paragraph (d) and, in paragraph (e), the words following "prescribed period". In section 48(2), paragraph (b) and, in paragraph (c), "if the earner dies before reaching pensionable age". Section 50(7). In section 52, subsections (4) to (6). In section 53, subsections (2), (4) and (5). Section 54(3). In section 55, subsection (1) and subsections (3) to (6). In section 56, subsection (1), in subsection (2), the words following "the prescribed period", and subsection (3). In section 58, subsections (1) to (3), (5) and (6). Section 59. In section 60, subsections (1) to (3) and (6) to (10). In section 62, subsection (2). In section 63, in subsection (1), paragraphs (a) and (c), subsection (2), in subsection (3), paragraph (a) and the words following sub-paragraph (ii), and subsection (4). Sections 64 to 66. In section 84, in subsection (5), paragraph (b) and the preceding "or". Sections 133 to 135. In section 155, "or the Board". In section 158, subsections (2) and (3), in subsection (6), "(2) or (3)", paragraph (d) (and the "or" immediately preceding it), in subsection (7), paragraph (c) (and the "or" immediately preceding it) and subsection (8). In section 164(1)(b)(i), "2 to 5", "172, 173" and "and Schedule 1". In section 166(5), "sections 2 to 5", "172, 173" and "and Schedule 1". In section 170, in subsection (1), the "and" at the end of paragraph (c) and subsections (3) and (4).

Chapter	Short title	Extent of repeal
		Sections 172 and 173. In section 177, in subsection 3(b)(i), "sections 2 to 5", "172, 173" and "and Schedule 1" in subsection (3)(b)(ii), the words from "sections 55" to "premiums)", and in subsection (7), paragraph (b). In section 178, in paragraph (b), "sections 2 to 5", "172, 173" and "and Schedule 1". In section 181, in subsection (1), the definitions of "accrued rights premium,", "the Board", "contracted-out protected rights premium", "limited revaluation premium", "pensioner's rights premium", "personal pension protected rights premium", "state scheme premium" and "transfer premium", in subsection (3) "172, 173" and "and Schedule 1", and in subsection (7) "and Schedule 1". In section 182(1), "the Board or". In section 183, in subsection (1), "sections 2 to 5", "172, 173", and "or Schedule 1" and subsection (2). In section 185, subsections (3), (4) and (6). In section 186(5), "or section 185(4)". In section 192(2), "section 172(4) and (5)". Schedule 1. In Schedule 2, in paragraph 5, in sub-paragraph (1), "or the Board" and "or, as the case may be, the Board", in sub-paragraph (2), "to 65", in sub-paragraph (3), "in relation to state scheme premiums" and paragraph (b), and sub-paragraph (5). In Schedule 6, paragraph 11. In Schedule 8, paragraph 44(a) and (b)(i) and the "and" immediately following it.

PART IV

MISCELLANEOUS AND GENERAL

Chapter	Short title	Extent of repeal
1971 c. 56.	The Pensions (Increase) Act 1971.	In section 3, in subsection (2)(c), "is a woman who".
1993 c. 48.	The Pension Schemes Act 1993.	Sections 136 to 143. In section 145, "with the approval of the Treasury". In section 149, in subsection (3), at the end of paragraph (a), "and". In section 164(1)(b)(i), the words from "136" to "143". In section 166(5), the words from "136" to "143". Section 172(1)(b). In section 177, in subsection (3)(b)(i), the words from "136" to "143".

Chapter	Short title	Extent of repeal
		In section 178, in paragraph (b), the words from "136" to "143".
		In section 181, in subsection (3), the words from "136" to "143".
		In section 183, in subsection (1), the words from "136" to "143".
		In Schedule 9, in paragraph 1, in sub-paragraph (1), sub-paragraphs (ii) to (v), and sub-paragraph (5), and paragraphs 3 and 4.

The repeal in the Pensions (Increase) Act 1971 shall come into force on the day this Act is passed.

INDEX

References are to sections and Schedules

Other than in the entries under STATE PENSIONS, PERSONAL PENSION SCHEMES and GENERAL MATTERS, all entries refer to Occupational pensions